关于增值服务的说明

为答谢本版《税则》的新老用户，我们为您花重金统一购买了易通网(www.i-tong.com)通关查询服务及权威专家归类、关务咨询服务等等增值服务。

增值服务内容包括：

1. 提供包括申报要素填写实例、反倾销反补贴税、检验检疫类别、报检查询、3C 认证、危险化学品目录等增值查询服务；

2. 网站提供特惠、普通、最惠国、出口退税、检验检疫类别、监管条件等信息的实时维护更新，保证您查询的税率的准确性；

3. 免费提供三次权威专家线上归类咨询和关务咨询服务；

4. 提供与海关计算结果一致的模拟计税服务；

5. 提供通关状态查询。

增值服务的使用方法：

1. 刮开封面上的防伪标涂层，可以得到两个数字(第一行是登录账号，第二行是密码)；

2. 激活账号，登录 www.i-tong.com，在网站的左上角注册页面找到激活按钮，点击激活，按照提示填写相关信息，完成后提交；

3. 提交激活信息后，系统会给您的注册邮箱中发送一封邮件，打开后点击激活，完成激活程序；

4. 在登录页面输入账号和密码，即可登录使用。

特别申明：

凡是图书上未贴增值服务防伪标的一律为盗版图书。

提　示：

此二维码为易通网微信公众服务号，您只需要添加关注，并将防伪标上的账号进行绑定，即可使用微信端进行查询使用。(此账号必须先在网站上激活后才能正常使用)

本书特别提示新增部分内容：

1. 税则部分

税则号列	货品名称	最惠(%)	普通	增值税率	出口退税	计量单位	监管条件	Article Description
9013.2000 99	其他激光器(但激光二极管除外)	6	11	17	17	个		Other laser (except laser diode)
9401.8090 91	儿童用汽车安全座椅	0	100	17	15	个/千克		Child safety seat in the car

2. 关区代码表

关区代码 Code	关区名称 Name of International Trade Port (Customs Establishment)	关区代码 Code	关区代码 Code	关区名称 Name of International Trade Port (Customs Establishment)	关区代码 Code
2379	苏州海关驻相城办事处	苏相城办	2380	太仓港综合保税区	太仓综保
4381	滨州保税物流中心	滨州物流	4619	河南德众保税物流中心	德众物流
4720	黄石棋盘洲保税物流中心	黄石物流			

中华人民共和国
海关进出口税则

十位编码·监管条件·申报目录·出口退税·政策法规·海关代征税一览表

2015年中英文对照版　附光盘

中华人民共和国海关进出口税则 编委会　编

Customs Import and Export Tariff of the People's Republic of China

Decade Coding of HS, Customs Control Conditions, Declare Contents, Export Drawback, Regulations Detailed Customs Duties Levied on Commission Basis

Compiled by the Editorial Department of the Customs Import and Export Tariff of the People's Republic of China

经济日报出版社
Economic Daily Press

图书在版编目(CIP)数据

中华人民共和国海关进出口税则：2015年：汉英对照/《中华人民共和国海关进出口税则》编委会编. —北京：经济日报出版社，2015.1

ISBN 978-7-80257-746-6

Ⅰ. ①中… Ⅱ. ①中… Ⅲ. ①海关税则—中国—2015—汉、英 Ⅳ. ①F752.50

中国版本图书馆CIP数据核字(2014)第291935号

中华人民共和国海关进出口税则(2015年中英文版)

编　　者：中华人民共和国海关进出口税则　编委会　编
责任编辑：郑　玮　颜贺华　徐晓燕
责任校对：送天明
出版发行：经济日报出版社
地　　址：北京市西城区右安门内大街65号（邮政编码：100054）
电　　话：010-85849108（总编室）　010-51393396（发行部）
网　　址：www.edpbook.com.cn
E-mail：edpbook@126.com
经　　销：全国新华书店
印　　刷：北京富达印务有限公司
开　　本：850×1168mm　1/16
印　　张：74
字　　数：1500千字
版　　次：2015年1月第一版
印　　次：2015年1月第一次印刷
书　　号：ISBN 978-7-80257-746-6
定　　价：280.00元

《中华人民共和国海关进出口税则》
光盘安装使用说明

系统运行环境

硬件：486/Pentium、32M 以上内存、CD－ROM 驱动器、VGA/SVGA 显示器。

系统：简体中文版 2000/ XP / NT、中文版 Acrobat Reader。

光盘安装与使用

安装：

1. 将光盘插入光驱，光盘将自动安装浏览器、数据库及字体文件。
2. 若您的电脑中没有安装 Acrobat Reader，系统会自动提示安装 Acrobat Reader 5．05 浏览器，然后根据提示继续完成安装。

运行：

系统安装完毕，在左下角“开始→程序→相应的程序名”中调用相应的光盘名；也可在“我的电脑”中双击光盘图标直接打开阅读。

《Customs Import and Export Tariff of the People's Republic of China》
The instruction for installment of compact disc

The system operational setting

Hardware：486/Pentium、Above 32 M memory、CD-ROM Drive、VGA/SVGA Display

System：Chinese edition Windows2000/XP/NT、Chinese edition Acrobat Reader

Installment and use

Installment：

1. Insert the compact disc into the CD-ROM，the disk will automatically install the browser，data base and fout file.
2. If your computer already has installed Acrobat Reader 3.0，please uninstall it. The system will automatically remind you to install Acrobat Reader5.05 . Please then complete the installment according to the prompt.
3. If the operational system is Windows2000/NT，please restart the computer after the installment so that the font will display dffectively. Computers with operational system WinXP need not be restarted.

Operational：

1. After finishing the installment of operational system，please find the correspondent disc name through “start-program-correspondent program's name”，or double-click the icon of compact disc in “my computer”，and reda it directly.
2. If there are any other questions，please call 010-85997935，and then transfer to technology department.

重 要 提 示

2015年版《中华人民共和国海关进出口商品规范申报目录》

一、2015年版《中华人民共和国海关进出口商品规范申报目录》使用说明

进出口货物收货人或其代理人在填报海关进出口货物报关单的“商品名称、规格型号”栏目时，应按照本《申报目录》中所列申报要素的内容填报。为方便《申报目录》的使用，特作说明如下：

一、《申报目录》采用了与《中华人民共和国海关进出口税则》（以下简称《税则》）一致的结构，所列商品按照类、章层次排列。除了《税则》中已有的类注释、章注释外，为了准确理解对商品规范申报的要求，在相关章前对该章的共性问题用“注解”加以说明。在使用《申报目录》时，首先应阅读各章的注解，再查阅具体商品对应的规范申报内容。

二、《申报目录》正文由“税则号列”、“商品名称”、“申报要素及说明举例”栏组成。

三、《申报目录》的“税则号列”栏所列的全部编码与《税则》中“税则号列”栏所列全部编码保持一致；《申报目录》的“商品名称”与《税则》中“货品名称”内容相同。

四、《申报目录》对不同商品设置了特定的申报要素内容。报关单中的“商品名称、规格型号”栏应当按照《申报目录》中相应商品所列“申报要素及说明举例”的各项内容填写。

五、《申报目录》属于结构性目录，其中所列商品按照不同位数编码所代表的层次进行排列，当某一层次编码商品所要求的申报要素与上一层次编码商品的申报要素相同时，则该商品的“税则号列”就不列示在书中，但表示该层次“税则号列”对应的商品使用上一层次编码商品所列的“申报要素”。

二、“出口退税”数据说明

因为出口退税率数据变化次数频繁，本《税则》出版时出口退税数据为最新数据，但国家税务总局退税率文库数据变更新时间较晚，本年度新变化的税则号列对应的退税率暂无数据，在本《税则》出版后退税率数据再次变化的本《税则》中无法修正，请按最新公布的数据执行。如企业对本《税则》中退税率数据有疑问的请登录“易通网”查询。如一个商品的“出口退税”栏中出现2个或2个以上退税率，是此商品有2个或2个以上增值税征税率，则此商品的退税率亦有相应不同税率。

三、“税则号列”排列格式说明

本《税则》中“税则号列”排列是以国际通用的《商品名称及编码协调制度公约》（以下简称《协调制度》）商品分类目录体系为基础，根据海关征税和海关统计工作的需要，我国在《协调制度》的基础上增设了本国子目（三级和四级子目），“税则号列”的编排是有一定规律的，以“13.02”章举例说明如下：

具体列名的商品都会有其对应的“税则号列”，若没有具体列名的商品都归为“货品名称”是“其他”的“税则号列”。

-植物液汁及浸膏：（一级子目）

1302.1100 --鸦片
1302.1200 --甘草
1302.1300 --啤酒花的
（二级子目）均是归属于“-植物液汁及浸膏”项下的商品

--其他： （注：“--其他：”全部货品名称为：其他植物液汁及浸膏）

1302.1910 ---生漆
1302.1920 ---印楝素
1302.1930 ---除虫菊的或含鱼藤酮植物根茎的
1302.1990 ---其他
（三级子目）均是归属于“--其他：”项下的货品

与我们联系：

如有任何疑问或需要订购经贸类、海关类等图书请按以下方式与发行部联系。

发行部电话：010－51393396 传真：010－85843117 邮箱：jinhaiguantong@126. com

税率适用说明

一、进口税则

进口税则商品分类目录采用《商品名称及编码协调制度》。进口税则税目税率设置税则号列、货品中文名称、最惠国税率、普通税率、增值税税率、出口退税率、计量单位、监管条件、货品英文名称等栏目。

（一）正文税率使用说明

1. 最惠国税率

根据《条例》规定，原产于共同适用最惠国待遇条款的世界贸易组织成员的进口货物，原产于与中华人民共和国签订含有互给予最惠国待遇条款的双边贸易协定的国家或者地区的进口货物，以及原产于中华人民共和国境内的进口货物，适用最惠国税率。

（1）“税则号列”栏目中的右上角标有“暂”字的税号所对应的“最惠国税率”栏目的税率为“进口暂定税率”，根据海关征收关税采用“从低征收”的原则，适用最惠国税率的进口货物有暂定税率的，应当适用暂定税率。税则号前标注“ex”的，表示适用暂定税率的应税进口货物以货品名称栏中的描述为准。

（2）税率栏目中标有“T2”的表示此商品实行从量、复合税，具体税率参见附表2。

2. 暂定税率

根据《条例》规定，适用最惠国税率、协定税率、特惠税率、关税配额税率的进口货物在一定期限内可以实行暂定税率。

本书“税则号列”上标注有“暂”字的商品，对应“最惠国”税率列明的是进口暂定税率。

适用最惠国税率、协定税率、特惠税率的进口货物有暂定税率的，应当从低适用税率；适用关税配额税率的进口货物有暂定税率的，应当适用暂定税率。适用普通税率的进口货物，不适用暂定税率。

3. 普通税率

根据《条例》规定，原产于除适用最惠国税率、协定税率、特惠税率国家或地区以外的国家或者地区的进口货物，以及原产地不明的进口货物，适用普通税率。

4. 增值税税率

海关代征的进口货物法定增值税税率，栏目空白时为免征，其他分为13%和17%两种。

5. 出口退税税率

国家为鼓励出口对出口商品已征收的国内税部分或全部退还给出口企业的税率。本书收录截止2015年1月1日前实施的退税率因出口税率在年度内调整频繁，所以本书所列出口退税率仅供企业参考，若年度内出口税率有调整，请参照最新出台的税率政策。其中部分税号项下存在同一税号退税率不一致的情况，退税率一栏会出现一个或以上退税率，按商品不同情况分别退税。

（二）附件税率使用说明

1. 协定税率（参见附表1）

根据我国与有关国家或地区签署的贸易或关税优惠协定，对有关国家或地区实施协定税率。

（1）对原产于韩国、印度、斯里兰卡、孟加拉和老挝的1891个税目商品实施亚太贸易协定税率；

（2）对原产于文莱、印度尼西亚、马来西亚、新加坡、泰国、菲律宾、越南、缅甸、老挝和柬埔寨的部分税目商品实施中国－东盟自由贸易协定税率；

（3）对原产于智利的7347个税目商品实施中国－智利自由贸易协定税率；

（4）对原产于巴基斯坦的6546个税目商品实施中国－巴基斯坦自由贸易协定税率；

（5）对原产于新西兰的7358个税目商品实施中国－新西兰自由贸易协定税率；

（6）对原产于新加坡的2794个税目商品实施中国－新加坡自由贸易协定税率；

（7）对原产于秘鲁的7124个税目商品实施中国－秘鲁自由贸易协定税率；

（8）对原产于哥斯达黎加的7320个税目商品实施中国－哥斯达黎加自由贸易协定税率；

（9）对原产于瑞士的7110个税目商品实施中国－瑞士自由贸易协定税率；

（10）对原产于冰岛的7248个税目商品实施中国－冰岛自由贸易协定税率；

（11）对原产于香港特别行政区且已制定优惠原产地标准的1812个税目商品实施零关税；

（12）对原产于澳门特别行政区且已制定优惠原产地标准的1315个税目商品实施零关税；

（13）对原产于台湾地区的622个税目商品实施海峡两岸经济合作框架协议货物贸易早期收获计划协定税

率

2. 特惠税率（参见附表1）

根据我国与有关国家或地区签署的贸易或关税优惠协定，双边换文情况，以及国务院有关决定，对以下国家实施优惠税率：

根据我国与有关国家或地区签署的贸易或关税优惠协定、双边换文情况以及国务院有关决定，对原产于孟加拉国和老挝的部分商品实施亚太贸易协定项下特惠税率；对原产于埃塞俄比亚、布隆迪、赤道几内亚、刚果（金）、吉布提、几内亚、几内亚比绍、莱索托、马达加斯加、马拉维、马里、莫桑比克、南苏丹、塞拉利昂、塞内加尔、苏丹、索马里、坦桑尼亚、乌干达、乍得、中非、阿富汗、也门和瓦努阿图共24个国家的部分商品实施97%税目零关税特惠税率；对原产于安哥拉、贝宁、多哥、厄立特里亚、科摩罗、利比里亚、卢旺达、尼日尔、赞比亚、东帝汶、柬埔寨、缅甸、尼泊尔和萨摩亚共14个国家的部分商品实施95%税目零关税特惠税率；对原产于毛里塔尼亚和孟加拉国的部分商品实施60%税目零关税特惠税。

3. 配额税率

根据《条例》规定，按照国家规定实行关税配额管理的进口货物，关税配额内的，适用关税配额税率。见附表3。

4. 非全税目税率

该税目的部分商品凭信息产业部出具的用于信息技术产品的证明，可按附件4的税率计征税款，具体税率参见附表4。

二、出口税则

出口税则的商品分类目录与进口税则相同。出口税则设置税则号列、货品中文名称、出口税率、出口暂定税率、货品英文名称等栏目。税同号前标注“ex”，表示适用该税率的应税出口货物以货品名称栏中的描述为准。

根据《条例》规定，对出口货物在一定期限内可以实行暂定税率；适用出口税率的出口货物有暂定税率的，应当适用暂定税率。

三、关税减免

特定地区、特定企业或者特定用途的进出口货物减征或者免征关税的，以及其他依法减征或者免征关税的，按照国务院的有关规定执行。

编者按

为方便海关等有关管理部门、从事进出口的企业、报关企业、预录入企业和其他单位及个人了解最新的进出口税则税率、进口环节代征税税率和海关监管条件，准确地将外贸单证中的英文商品名称翻译成规范的中文名称，及时办理报关手续，我们编写了2015版《中华人民共和国海关进出口税则》（中英文对照版），（以下简称《税则》）。

2015版《税则》内容根据国务院关税税则委员会2015年最新调整的进出口关税税率编制而成。根据对外贸易形势的需要，2015年1月1日起，我国将继续按照加入世界贸易组织的关税减让承诺，根据海关监管的需要，2015年进出口商品监管证件进行了大范围的调整，因此本《税则》内涉及的“监管条件”内容也相应进行了较大的调整。

为配合海关总署出台的进出口商品申报最新规定，2015版《税则》内“进出口商品规范申报目录”附件（以下简称“申报说明”）内容也相应作出了最新调整，为企业填制报关单、加工手册等报关单证提供了规范依据。“进出口商品规范申报目录”对不同商品设置了特定的申报要素内容。报关单中的“商品名称、规格型号”栏应当按照“进出口商品规范申报目录”中相应商品所列申报要素各项内容填写。

为便于使用本书，现将《中英文税则》说明如下：

第一部分为《进口关税税则》：

第1列为“税则号列”，其8位数与国务院关税税则委员会所调整编制的税目税率数据完全一致，并在此基础上增加了海关申报所需的10位数编码。税则号列未增列9位，10位时，请自动用“00”补齐10位；

第2列为“货品的中文名称”；

第3列为“最惠国税率”，适用原产于世贸组织成员或与我国签有互惠双边贸易协定的国家或地区进口的货物（如有对应的进口暂定税率，则此列列示进口暂定税率）；

第4列为“普通税率”适用原产于除适用最惠国税率、协定税率、特惠税率以外国家或地区进口的货物；

第5列为“增值税率”，栏目空白时为免征，其他分为13%和17%两种；

第6列为“出口退税”，栏内数字表示相应退税税率；

第7列为“计量单位”，为海关统计使用的法定计量单位；

第8列为“监管条件”，相应的代码表示在一般贸易进口或出口时应向海关提交的监管证件代码（监管证件代码表在本书P821页）；

第9列为“货品的英文名称”。

随后加列了从量税和复合税税率表、进口商品协定税率表、进口商品关税配额税率表、非全税目信息技术产品税率表、进口商品消费税税率表、特惠税目税率表等。

第二部分为《出口关税税则》。

第三部分为“报关自动化系统常用代码表及说明”。

第四部分为“进出口关税税款计算方法”。

第五部分为“进出口商品规范申报目录”。

由于作者水平的限制和时间仓促，本书不足之处在所难免，恳请社会各界和广大读者批评指正。其中不准确和不全面之处敬请以发布的规范性文件为准！

Editor' s Note

Aiming at assisting Customs and other governing bodies, enterprises participating import and export, Customs brokers, other trading partners and persons to query up-to-date tariff rates, other rates related to import and Custom supervision conditions, translate English commodity names in trade documents into standard Chinese names and go through declaring procedures to Customs, this Press compiles this Customs Import and Export Tariff of the People's Republic of China (Chinese-English Version , referred to as Chinese-English Tariff later)

2015 Tariff Regulations are compiled according to the latest adjustments of Import and Export Tariff rate made by StateCouncil Tariff Regulation Committee. according to the demand of foreign trade circumstances, from Jan. lst in 2015, China will continue to carry on its commitment of tariff concession as a member of WTO. After the adjustment, according to the demand of Customs supervision, an extesive adjustment will have been made to Supervision Certificate of Customs Import and Export Good. Therefore, 2015 Tariff Regulations will make readjustment to the Supervision Conditions.

To go with the newly issued regulations by Custom of P. R. C. on the import and export goods, the accessories Instruction on Import and Export Commodities Standard content (hereafter referred to as Declaration Instruction), of 2015 Tariff Regulation will make latest adjustments in accordance. Providing standards for enterprises to prepare customs declaration documents. Declaration Instruction sets key declaration factors for different commodities. The columns as to the description of goods and specification of goods should be filled in according to the dey factors listed in Declaration Statement.

In order to acquaint enterprises with what inspection and quarantion are necessary for import and export commodities when they declare them, this book adds "legal inspection codes", i. e. "legal inspection and quarantine class codes" to represent different commodity inspection and quarantine names by different codes so that enterprises can learn about classes of legal inspection of import and export commoditics and handle inspection and quarantine business rapidly and clear the Customs quickly.

For ease of using this bood, the Chinese-English Tariff is explained as follow:

The first part is about "Import Tariff Regulations":

Column 1 is Serial Number, the eight digits of which are in accordance with the data of tax items and rates adjusted and compiled by the State Council of Finance Tariff Regulation committee, onto which the code of ten digits required in customs declaration is added;

Column 2 is Commodity Chinese name;

Column 3 is Most-Favored-Nation rate, applicable to the goods originally produced in the members of WTO or in countries and regions that have bilateral trade agreement with China (If there is provisional duty rates of import, this column shown provision duty rates of import).

Column4 is average rate, The general tariff rates shall apply to the import goods with undetermind origins and originating in the countries and regions that are ont applicable to the MFN tariff rate, agreement tariff rates, or special preferential tariff rates.

Column 5 is VAT Rate, it will be exempted when this column is empty, and in other conditions the VAT rate is either 13% or 17%;

Column 6 is Export Drawback Rate, the numbers is this Column represents export drawback rates. the number is this Column represents export drawback rates.

Column 7 is Measurement Unit which is the official measurement units applied by Customs;

Column 8 is Supervision Conditions, respective codes represent the licenses or other documents that should be submitted to Customs at import or export in general trade pattern. For specific names, please refer to List of License names and their codes attached in this bood.

Column 9 is Commodity English name.

In the following ranks, table of Interim Duty rate on Agreemene, tables of specific duty and compound duty , table of duty quota and rate on imported and exported goods, table of excise on imported goods, table of Special Preferential Duty Rate, table of duty Items and Duty Rates for Tainwan Fruits and vegetables in zero-Tariff Measure

The second part is about "Export Tariff Regulations":

The third part is about "Code list to Supporting Documents Subject to Customs":

The fourth Part is about "Calculation Methods for Import and Export Tax":

The fifth part is about "Norm Declares Explanation for the Customs Import and Export Goods":

Due to limits of time and the knowledge of the author, some weaknesses in this book should be inevitable. Here I am open to readers' corrections and comments with great sincerity. If there is any inaccuracy and inadequacy, the official documents prevail.

总目录

Table of Contents

1. 中华人民共和国海关进口税则（2015） ······ 1
（进口关税税率附表详见第三部分）
Customs Import Tariff of the People's Republic of China（2015） ······ 1
（Import tariff attached table details as per third part）
2. 中华人民共和国海关进出口货物报关单填报规范和报关自动化系统常用代码表及说明 ······ 737
Standards for Filling Import/Export Goods Declaration Form and Code list to Supporting Documents subject to Customs of the People' s Republic of China ······ 737
（1）中华人民共和国海关进出口货物报关单填制规范 ······ 739
（1）Standards for Filling Import/Export Goods Declaration Form ······ 739
（2）海关总署关于优惠贸易协定项下进口货物的报关单填制规范公告 ······ 751
（2）General Administration of Customs P. R. C. Announcement for Standards of Filling Declaration for Import Goods Stipulated Under Preferential Trading Agreements ······ 751
（3）报关自动化系统常用代码表说明 ······ 753
（3）Explantlons. about table of codes often used in customs clearance system ······ 753
（4）报关自动化系统常用代码表 ······ 802
（4）Common Codes for Automated Customs Declartion System（EDI） ······ 802
监管方式代码表 ······ 802
Codes for Customs Procedures（Modes of International Trade） ······ 802
征免性质代码表 ······ 805
Codes for the Nature of Levy, Reduction and Exemption of Customs Duties and Taxes ······ 805
征减免税方式代码表 ······ 806
Codes For Type of Levy, Reduction and Exemption of Customs Duties and Taxes ······ 806
运输方式代码表 ······ 806
Codes for Modes of Transport ······ 806
关区代码表 ······ 806
Codes for International Trade Ports（Customs Establishment） ······ 806
国内地区代码表 ······ 814
Codes for Sub-entity of the P. R. C. ······ 814
★监管证件名称代码表 ······ 821
Code list of Supporting Documents Subject to Customs Control of the People's Republic of China ······ 821
结汇方式代码表 ······ 822
Codes for Modes of Bank's Exchange Settlement ······ 822
用途代码表 ······ 823
Codes for Use of Imported Goods ······ 823
货币代码表 ······ 823
Codes for the Representation of Currencies ······ 823
计量单位代码表 ······ 823
Codes for Units of Measure Used in International Trade ······ 823
成交方式代码表 ······ 824
Codes for Trade Terms ······ 824
国别（地区）代码表 ······ 824
Codes for the Representation of Names of Countries and Regions ······ 824
地区性质代码表 ······ 827
Codes for the Nature of Designated Areas ······ 827
企业性质代码表 ······ 827
Codes for Class of Enterprises ······ 827

3. 中华人民共和国海关进口关税税率附表（2015） ………… 829
Import tariff attached table（2015） ………… 829
附 表 1 2015年进口商品协定、特惠税目、税率表 ………… 831
Attached table 1 Conventional，special Preferential Duty Item and Duty Rates for Import（2015） ………… 831
附 表 2 2015年进口商品从量税、复合税税目、税率表 ………… 993
Attached table 2 Specific、Compound Scale Dutits（2015） ………… 993
附 表 3 2015年关税配额商品税目、税率表 ………… 995
Attached table 3 In-Quota Interim Duty Rate on Imported Goods（2015） ………… 995
附 表 4 2015年非全税目信息技术产品税率表 ………… 997
Attached table 4 Duty Rate on Imported IT Goods（Incomplete）（2015） ………… 997
附 表 5 2015年进口商品消费税税率表 ………… 998
Attached table 5 Consumption tax on Imported Goods（2015） ………… 998
附 表 6 中华人民共和国进境物品进口税率表 ………… 1004
Attached table 6 Duty Rate on Inward Articles of the People's Republic of China， ………… 1004
4. 中华人民共和国海关出口税则（2015） ………… 1005
Customs Export Tariff of the People's Republic of China（2015） ………… 1005
5。中华人民共和国进出口关税税款计算方法 ………… 1015
Calculation Methods for Import and Export Tax of the People's Republic of China ………… 1015
表1 进口关税与进口环节代征税（消费税及增值税）计税常数表 ………… 1017
Table of import tariff and import tax（Consumption tax and value added tax） ………… 1017
表2 进口关税与进口环节代征税（增值税）计税常数表 ………… 1018
Table of Import Tariff and Import Tax（Value added Tax） ………… 1018
计量单位换算表 ………… 1019
Conversion Table ………… 1019
6. 2015版中华人民共和国进出口商品规范申报目录 ………… 1021
Norm Declares contents for the Customs Import and Export Goods of the People' s Republic of China ………… 1021
7. 欲知更全面，更详细的中英文对照法规，请登录网址：www. i－tong. cn。
Please log on to www. i－tong. cn. for more detailed and complete version of laws and regulations with both Chinese and English translation Facilities used for medical treatment，surgery，dentistry or veterinary

1

中华人民共和国海关进口税则

（2015 年 1 月 1 日起实施）

Customs Import Tariff of the People's Republic of China

(Enforced from January 1, 2015)

1

中华人民共和国海关进口税则

（2015 年 1 月 1 日起实施）

Customs Import Tariff of the People's Republic of China

（Enforced from January 1, 2015）

目　录

归类总规则 ………………………………（11）

第一类　活动物；动物产品

第　一　章　活动物 ……………………（13）

第　二　章　肉及食用杂碎 ……………（18）

第　三　章　鱼、甲壳动物、软体动物及其他水生无脊椎动物 ………（23）

第　四　章　乳品；蛋品；天然蜂蜜；其他食用动物产品 …………（41）

第　五　章　其他动物产品 ……………（44）

第二类　植物产品

第　六　章　活树及其他活植物；鳞茎、根及类似品；插花及装饰用簇叶 ………………（48）

第　七　章　食用蔬菜、根及块茎 ……（51）

第　八　章　食用水果及坚果；柑桔属水果或甜瓜的果皮 ………（57）

第　九　章　咖啡、茶、马黛茶及调味香料…（62）

第　十　章　谷物 ……………………（64）

第十一章　制粉工业产品；麦芽；淀粉；菊粉；面筋 …………（67）

第十二章　含油子仁及果实；杂项子仁及果实；工业用或药用植物；稻草、秸秆及饲料 …………（70）

第十三章　虫胶；树胶、树脂及其他植物液、汁 ………………（76）

第十四章　编结用植物材料；其他植物产品 …………………（78）

第三类　动、植物油、脂及其分解产品；精制的食用油脂；动、植物蜡

第十五章　动、植物油、脂及其分解产品；精制的食用油脂；动、植物蜡 ………………（79）

INDEX

GENERAL RULES FOR THE INTERPRETATION OF THE HARMONIZED SYSTEM …………………… (11)

SECTION Ⅰ　LIVE ANIMALS; ANIMAL PRODUCTS

Chapter 1　Live animals ………………………… (13)

Chapter 2　Meat and edible meat offal ………………… (18)

Chapter 3　Fish and crustaceans, molluscs and other aquatic invertebrates ………………………… (23)

Chapter 4　Dairy produce; birds eggs; natural honey; edible products of animal origin, not elsewhere specified or included …………… (41)

Chapter 5　Products of animal origin, not elsewhere specified or included …………………… (44)

SECTION Ⅱ　VEGETABLE PRODUCTS

Chapter 6　Live trees and other plants; bulbs, roots and the like; cut flowers and ornamental foliage ………………………… (48)

Chapter 7　Edible vegetables and certain roots and tubers ………………………… (51)

Chapter 8　Edible fruit and nuts; peel of citrus fruit or melons ………………………… (57)

Chapter 9　Coffee, tea, mate and spices ………… (62)

Chapter 10　Cereals ………………………… (64)

Chapter 11　Products of the milling industry; malt; starches; inulin; wheat gluten …………… (67)

Chapter 12　Oil seeds and oleaginous fruits; miscellaneous grains, seeds and fruit; industrial or medicinal plants; straw and fodder …… (70)

Chapter 13　Lac; gums, resins and other vegetable saps and extracts ………………………… (76)

Chapter 14　Vegetable plaiting materials; vegetable products not elsewhere specified or included ……… (78)

SECTION Ⅲ　ANIMAL OR VEGETABLE FATS AND OILS AND THEIR CLEAVAGE PRODUCTS; PREPARED EDIBLE FATS; ANIMAL OR VEGETABLE WAXES

Chapter 15　Animal or vegetable fats and oils and their cleavage products; prepared edible fats; animal or vegetable waxes ………………… (79)

第四类 食品;饮料、酒及醋;烟草、烟草及烟草代用品的制品

第十六章 肉、鱼、甲壳动物、软体动物及其他水生无脊椎动物的制品 …………… (83)
第十七章 糖及糖食 …………… (88)
第十八章 可可及可可制品 …………… (90)
第十九章 谷物、粮食粉、淀粉或乳的制品;糕饼点心 …………… (91)
第二十章 蔬菜、水果、坚果或植物其他部分的制品 …………… (93)
第二十一章 杂项食品 …………… (98)
第二十二章 饮料、酒及醋 …………… (100)
第二十三章 食品工业的残渣及废料;配制的动物饲料 …………… (103)
第二十四章 烟草及烟草代用品的制品 …………… (105)

第五类 矿产品

第二十五章 盐;硫磺;泥土及石料;石膏料、石灰及水泥 …………… (106)
第二十六章 矿砂、矿渣及矿灰 …………… (112)
第二十七章 矿物燃料、矿物油及其蒸馏产品;沥青物质;矿物蜡 …………… (116)

第六类 化学工业及其相关工业的产品

第二十八章 无机化学品;贵金属、稀土金属、放射性元素及其同位素的有机及无机化合物 …………… (121)
第二十九章 有机化学品 …………… (138)
第三十章 药品 …………… (184)
第三十一章 肥料 …………… (196)
第三十二章 鞣料浸膏及染料浸膏;鞣酸及其衍生物;染料、颜料及其他着色料;油漆及清漆;油灰及其他类似胶粘剂;墨水、油墨 … (199)
第三十三章 精油及香膏;芳香料制品及化妆盥洗品 …………… (203)
第三十四章 肥皂、有机表面活性剂、洗涤剂、润滑剂、人造蜡、调制蜡、光洁剂、蜡烛及类似品、塑型用膏、“牙科用蜡”及牙科用熟石膏制剂 …………… (206)

SECTION Ⅳ PREPARED FOODSTUFFS; BEVERAGES, SPIRITS AND VINEGAR; TOBACCO AND MANUFACTURED TOBACCO SUBSTITUTES

Chapter 16 Preparations of meat, of fish or of crustaceans, molluscs or other aquatic invertebrates …………… (83)
Chapter 17 Sugars and sugar confectionery …………… (88)
Chapter 18 Cocoa and cocoa preparations …………… (90)
Chapter 19 Preparations of cereals, flour, starch or milk, pastrycooks' products …………… (91)
Chapter 20 Preparations of vegetables, fruit, nuts or other parts of plants …………… (93)
Chapter 21 Miscellaneous edible preparations …………… (98)
Chapter 22 Beverages, spirits and vinegar …………… (100)
Chapter 23 Residues and waste from the food industries; prepared animal fodder …………… (103)
Chapter 24 Tobacco and manufactured tobacco substitutes …………… (105)

SECTION Ⅴ MINERAL PRODUCTS

Chapter 25 Salt; sulphur; earths and stone; plastering materials, lime and cement …………… (106)
Chapter 26 Ores, slag and ash …………… (112)
Chapter 27 Mineral fuels, mineral oils and products of their distillation; bituminous substances; mineral waxes …………… (116)

SECTION Ⅵ PRODUCTS OF THE CHEMICAL OR ALLIED INDUSTRIES

Chapter 28 Inorganic chemicals; organic or inorganic compounds of precious metals, of rare-earth metals of radioactive elements or of isotopes …………… (121)
Chapter 29 Organic chemicals …………… (138)
Chapter 30 Pharmaceutical products …………… (184)
Chapter 31 Fertilizers …………… (196)
Chapter 32 Tanning or dyeing extracts; tannins and their derivatives; dyes, pigments and other colouring matter; paints and varnishes; putty and other mastics; inks …………… (199)
Chapter 33 Essential oils and resinoids; perfumery, cosmetic or toilet preparations …………… (203)
Chapter 34 Soap, organic surface-active agents, washing preparations, lubricating preparations, artificial waxes, prepared waxes, polishing or scouring preparations, candles and similar articles, modelling pastes, “dental waxes” and dental preparations with a basis of plaster …………… (206)

第三十五章 蛋白类物质;改性淀粉;胶;酶 ……………………… (209)
第三十六章 炸药;烟火制品;火柴;引火合金;易燃材料制品 …………………… (211)
第三十七章 照相及电影用品 ……… (213)
第三十八章 杂项化学产品 ………… (216)

Chapter 35 Albuminoidal substances; modified starches; glues; enzymes ……… (209)
Chapter 36 Explosives; pyrotechnic products; matches; pyrophoric alloys; certain combustible preparations ……………… (211)
Chapter 37 Photographic or cinematographic goods … (213)
Chapter 38 Miscellaneous chemical products ………… (216)

第七类 塑料及其制品;橡胶及其制品

SECTION Ⅶ PLASTICS AND ARTICLES THEREOF; RUBBER AND ARTICLES THEREOF

第三十九章 塑料及其制品 ………… (226)
第 四 十 章 橡胶及其制品 ………… (238)

Chapter 39 Plastics and articles thereof ……………… (226)
Chapter 40 Rubber and articles thereof ……………… (238)

第八类 生皮、皮革、毛皮及其制品;鞍具及挽具;旅行用品、手提包及类似容器;动物肠线(蚕胶丝除外)制品

SECTION Ⅷ RAW HIDES AND SKINS, LEATHER, FURSKINS AND ARTICLES THEREOF; SADDLERY AND HARNESS; TRAVEL GOODS, HANDBAGS AND SIMILAR CONTAINERS; ARTICLES OF ANIMAL GUT (OTHER THAN SILK-WORM GUT)

第四十一章 生皮(毛皮除外)及皮革 ………………………… (246)
第四十二章 皮革制品;鞍具及挽具;旅行用品、手提包及类似容器;动物肠线(蚕胶丝除外)制品 ……………… (254)
第四十三章 毛皮、人造毛皮及其制品 ………………………… (258)

Chapter 41 Raw hides and skins (other than furskins) and leather ……………………………… (246)
Chapter 42 Articles of leather; saddlery and harness; travel goods, handbags and similar containers; articles of animal gut (other than silk-worm gut) ……………………… (254)
Chapter 43 Furskins and artificial fur; manufactures thereof ………………………………… (258)

第九类 木及木制品;木炭;软木及软木制品;稻草、秸秆、针茅或其他编结材料制品;篮筐及柳条编结品

SECTION Ⅸ WOOD AND ARTICLES OF WOOD; WOOD CHARCOAL; CORK AND ARTICLES OF CORK; MANUFACTURES OF STRAW, OF ESPARTO OR OF OTHER PLAITING MATERIALS; BASKETWARE AND WICKERWORK

第四十四章 木及木制品;木炭 ……… (261)
第四十五章 软木及软木制品 ……… (281)
第四十六章 稻草、秸秆、针茅或其他编结材料制品;篮筐及柳条编结品 ……………… (282)

Chapter 44 Wood and articles of wood; wood charcoal ……………………………… (261)
Chapter 45 Cork and articles of cork ……………… (281)
Chapter 46 Manufactures of straw, of esparto or of other plaiting materials; basketware and wickerwork ……………………… (282)

第十类 木浆及其他纤维状纤维素浆;回收(废碎)纸或纸板;纸、纸板及其制品

SECTION Ⅹ PULP OF WOOD OR OF OTHER FIBROUS CELLULOSIC MATERIAL; RECOVERED (WASTE AND SCRAP) PAPER OR PAPERBOARD; PAPER AND PAPERBOARD AND ARTICLES THEREOF

第四十七章 木浆及其他纤维状纤维素浆;回收(废碎)纸或纸板 ……………………… (284)

Chapter 47 Pulp of wood or of other fibrous cellulosic material; recovered (waste and scrap) paper or paperboard ……………………… (284)

第四十八章	纸及纸板；纸浆；纸或纸板制品	（287）	Chapter 48	Paper and paperboard; articles of paper pulp, of paper or of paperboard	(287)
第四十九章	书籍、报纸、印刷图画及其他印刷品；手稿、打字稿及设计图纸	（299）	Chapter 49	Printed books, newspapers, pictures and other products of the printing industry; manuscripts, typescripts and plans	(299)
第十一类	**纺织原料及纺织制品**		**SECTION XI**	**TEXTILES AND TEXTILE ARTICLES**	
第 五 十 章	蚕丝	（308）	Chapter 50	Silk	(308)
第五十一章	羊毛、动物细毛或粗毛；马毛纱线及其机织物	（311）	Chapter 51	Wool, fine or coarse animal hair; horsehair yarn and woven fabric	(311)
第五十二章	棉花	（317）	Chapter 52	Cotton	(317)
第五十三章	其他植物纺织纤维；纸纱线及其机织物	（344）	Chapter 53	Other vegetable textile fibres; paper yarn and woven fabrics of paper yarn	(344)
第五十四章	化学纤维长丝	（352）	Chapter 54	Man-made filaments; strip and the like of man made textile materials	(352)
第五十五章	化学纤维短纤	（365）	Chapter 55	Man-made staple fibres	(365)
第五十六章	絮胎、毡呢及无纺织物；特种纱线；线、绳、索、缆及其制品	（389）	Chapter 56	Wadding, felt and nonwovens; special yarns; twine, cordage, ropes and cables and articles thereof	(389)
第五十七章	地毯及纺织材料的其他铺地制品	（394）	Chapter 57	Carpets and other textile floor coverings	(394)
第五十八章	特种机织物；簇绒织物；花边；装饰毯；装饰带；刺绣品	（395）	Chapter 58	Special woven fabrics; tufted textile fabrics; lace; tapestries; trimmings; embroidery	(395)
第五十九章	浸渍、涂布、包覆或层压的纺织物；工业用纺织制品	（401）	Chapter 59	Impregnated, coated, covered or laminated textile fabrics; textile articles of a kind suitable for industrial use	(401)
第 六 十 章	针织物及钩编织物	（411）	Chapter 60	Knitted or crocheted fabrics	(411)
第六十一章	针织或钩编的服装及衣着附件	（415）	Chapter 61	Articles of apparel and clothing accessories, knitted or crocheted	(415)
第六十二章	非针织或非钩编的服装及衣着附件	（447）	Chapter 62	Articles of apparel and clothing accessories, not knitted or crocheted	(447)
第六十三章	其他纺织制成品；成套物品；旧衣着及旧纺织品；碎织物	（481）	Chapter 63	Other made up textile articles; sets; worn clothing and worn textile articles; rags	(481)
第十二类	**鞋、帽、伞、杖、鞭及其零件；已加工的羽毛及其制品；人造花；人发制品**		**SECTION XII**	**FOOTWEAR, HEADGEAR, UMBRELLAS, SUN UMBRELLAS, WALKING-STICKS, SEAT-STICKS, WHIPS, RIDING-CROPS AND PARTS THEREOF; PREPARED FEATHERS AND ARTICLES MADE THEREWITH; ARTIFICIAL FLOWERS; ARTICLES OF HUMAN HAIR**	
第六十四章	鞋靴、护腿和类似品及其零件	（491）	Chapter 64	Footwear, gaiters and the like; parts of such articles	(491)
第六十五章	帽类及其零件	（496）	Chapter 65	Headgear and parts thereof	(496)
第六十六章	雨伞、阳伞、手杖、鞭子、马鞭及其零件	（498）	Chapter 66	Umbrellas, sun umbrellas, walking-sticks, seat-sticks, whips, riding-crops and parts thereof	(498)

第六十七章　已加工羽毛、羽绒及其制品；人造花；人发制品 ……… (499)
Chapter 67　Prepared feathers and down and articles made of feathers or of down; artificial flowers; articles of human hair ………… (499)

第十三类　石料、石膏、水泥、石棉、云母及类似材料的制品；陶瓷产品；玻璃及其制品
SECTION XIII　ARTICLES OF STONE, PLASTER, CEMENT, ASBESTOS, MICA OR SIMILAR MATERIALS; CERAMIC PRODUCTS; GLASS AND GLASSWARE

第六十八章　石料、石膏、水泥、石棉、云母及类似材料的制品 … (501)
Chapter 68　Articles of stone, plaster, cement, asbestos, mica or similar materials ………………… (501)
第六十九章　陶瓷产品 ………………… (506)
Chapter 69　Ceramic products ………………………… (506)
第七十章　玻璃及其制品 ………… (509)
Chapter 70　Glass and glassware ……………………… (509)

第十四类　天然或养殖珍珠、宝石或半宝石、贵金属、包贵金属及其制品；仿首饰；硬币
SECTION XIV　NATURAL OR CULTURED PEARLS, PRECIOUS OR SEMI-PRECIOUS STONES, PRECIOUS METALS, METALS CLAD WITH PRECIOUS METAL AND ARTICLES THEREOF; IMITATION JEWELLERY; COIN

第七十一章　天然或养殖珍珠、宝石或半宝石、贵金属、包贵金属及其制品；仿首饰；硬币 …………………… (516)
Chapter 71　Natural or cultured pearls, precious or semi-precious stones, precious metals, metals clad with precious metal and articles thereof, imitation jewellery; coin ……… (516)

第十五类　贱金属及其制品
SECTION XV　BASE METALS AND ARTICLES OF BASE METAL

第七十二章　钢铁 …………………… (525)
Chapter 72　Iron and steel …………………………… (525)
第七十三章　钢铁制品 ……………… (538)
Chapter 73　Articles of iron or steel ………………… (538)
第七十四章　铜及其制品 …………… (546)
Chapter 74　Copper and articles thereof …………… (546)
第七十五章　镍及其制品 …………… (553)
Chapter 75　Nickel and articles thereof …………… (553)
第七十六章　铝及其制品 …………… (556)
Chapter 76　Aluminium and articles thereof ………… (556)
第七十七章　（保留为税则将来所用）
Chapter 77　(Reserved for possible future use in the Tariff)
第七十八章　铅及其制品 …………… (562)
Chapter 78　Lead and articles thereof ……………… (562)
第七十九章　锌及其制品 …………… (564)
Chapter 79　Zinc and articles thereof ……………… (564)
第八十章　锡及其制品 …………… (566)
Chapter 80　Tin and articles thereof ……………… (566)
第八十一章　其他贱金属、金属陶瓷及其制品 …………… (568)
Chapter 81　Other base metals; cermets; artiles thereof …………………………………… (568)
第八十二章　贱金属工具、器具、利口器、餐匙、餐叉及其零件 … (573)
Chapter 82　Tools, implements, cutlery, spoons and forks, parts thereof of base metal ……… (573)
第八十三章　贱金属杂项制品 ……… (578)
Chapter 83　Miscellaneous articles of base metal …… (578)

第十六类　机器、机械器具、电气设备及其零件；录音机及放声机、电视图像、声音的录制和重放设备及其零件、附件
SECTION XVI　MACHINERY AND MECHANICAL APPLIANCES; ELECTRICAL EQUIPMENT; PARTS THEREOF; SOUND RECORDERS AND REPRODUCERS, TELEVISION IMAGE AND SOUND RECORDERS AND REPRODUCERS, AND PARTS AND ACCESSORIES OF SUCH ARTICLES

第八十四章 核反应堆、锅炉、机器、机械器具及其零件 ……… (582) | Chapter 84 Nuclear reactors, boilers, machinery and mechanical appliances; parts thereof ……… (582)

第八十五章 电机、电气设备及其零件;录音机及放声机、电视图像、声音的录制和重放设备及其零件、附件 ……… (638) | Chapter 85 Electrical machinery and equipment and parts thereof; sound recorders and reproducers, television image and sound recorders and reproducers, and parts and accessories of such articles ……… (638)

第十七类 车辆、航空器、船舶及有关运输设备 | SECTION XVII VEHICLES, AIRCRAFT, VESSELS AND ASSOCIATED TRANSPORT EQUIPMENT

第八十六章 铁道及电车道机车、车辆及其零件;铁道及电车道轨道固定装置及其零件、附件;各种机械(包括电动机械)交通信号设备 ……… (667) | Chapter 86 Railway or tramway locomotives, rolling-stock and parts thereof; railway or tramway track fixtures and fittings and parts thereof; mechanical (including electro-mechanical) traffic signalling equipment of all kinds ……… (667)

第八十七章 车辆及其零件、附件,但铁道及电车道车辆除外 … (670) | Chapter 87 Vehicles other than railway or tramway rolling-stock, and parts and accessories thereof ……… (670)

第八十八章 航空器、航天器及其零件 ……… (689) | Chapter 88 Aircraft, spacecraft and parts thereof ……… (689)

第八十九章 船舶及浮动结构体 …… (691) | Chapter 89 Ships, boats and floating structures …… (691)

第十八类 光学、照相、电影、计量、检验、医疗或外科用仪器及设备、精密仪器及设备;钟表;乐器;上述物品的零件、附件 | SECTION XVIII OPTICAL, PHOTOGRAPHIC, CINEMATOGRAPHIC MEASURING, CHECKING, PRECISION MEDICAL OR SURGICAL INSTRUMENTS AND APPARATUS; CLOCKS AND WATCHES; MUSICAL INSTRUMENTS; PARTS AND ACCESSORIES THEREOF

第九十章 光学、照相、电影、计量、检验、医疗或外科用仪器及设备、精密仪器及设备;上述物品的零件、附件 ……… (693) | Chapter 90 Optical, photographic, cinematographic, measuring, checking, precision, medical or surgical instruments and apparatus; parts and accessories thereof ……… (693)

第九十一章 钟表及其零件 ……… (710) | Chapter 91 Clocks and watches and parts thereof …… (710)

第九十二章 乐器及其零件、附件 …… (714) | Chapter 92 Musical instruments; parts and accessories of such articles ……… (714)

第十九类 武器、弹药及其零件、附件 | SECTION XIX ARMS AND AMMUNITION; PARTS AND ACCESSORIES THEREOF

第九十三章 武器、弹药及其零件、附件 ……… (716) | Chapter 93 Arms and ammunition; parts and accessories thereof ……… (716)

第二十类 杂项制品 | SECTION XX MISCELLANEOUS MANUFACTURED ARTICLES

第九十四章　家具；寝具、褥垫、弹簧床垫、软座垫及类似的填充制品；未列名灯具及照明装置；发光标志、发光铭牌及类似品；活动房屋 ……………………………… (718)
第九十五章　玩具、游戏品、运动用品及其零件、附件 …………… (723)
第九十六章　杂项制品 ……………… (727)

第二十一类　艺术品、收藏品及古物

第九十七章　艺术品、收藏品及古物 … (733)

第二十二类　特殊交易品及未分类商品

第九十八章　特殊交易品及未分类商品 ………………………… (735)

Chapter 94　Furniture; bedding, mattresses, mattress supports, cushions and similar stuffed furnishings; lamps and lighting fittings, not elsewhere specified or included; illuminated signs, illuminated name-plates and the like; prefabricated buildings …… (718)
Chapter 95　Toys, games and sports requisites; parts and accessories thereof ………………… (723)
Chapter 96　Miscellaneous manufactured articles …… (727)

SECTION XXI　WORKS OF ART, COLLECTORS' PIECES AND ANTIQUES

Chapter 97　Works of art, collectors' pieces and antiques ……………………………………………… (733)

SECTION XXII　ARTICLES OF SPECIAL TRADE AND GOOD UNCLASSIFIED

Chapter 98　Articles of Special Trade and Good Unclassified ……………………………………………… (735)

归类总规则

货品在本税则目录上的归类,应遵循以下原则:

规则一 类、章及分章的标题,仅为查找方便而设;具有法律效力的归类,应按税目条文和有关类注或章注确定,如税目、类注或章注无其他规定,按以下规则确定。

规则二 (一)税目所列货品,应视为包括该项货品的不完整品或未制成品,只要在进口或出口时该项不完整品或未制成品具有完整品或制成品的基本特征;还应视为包括该项货品的完整品或制成品(或按本款可作为完整品或制成品归类的货品)在进口或出口时的未组装件或拆散件。

(二)税目中所列材料或物质,应视为包括该种材料或物质与其他材料或物质混合或组合的物品。税目所列某种材料或物质构成的货品,应视为包括全部或部分由该种材料或物质构成的货品。由一种以上材料或物质构成的货品,应按规则三归类。

规则三 当货品按规则二(二)或由于其他原因看起来可归入两个或两个以上税目时,应按以下规则归类:

(一)列名比较具体的税目,优先于列名一般的税目。但是,如果两个或两个以上税目都仅述及混合或组合货品所含的某部分材料或物质,或零售的成套货品中的某些货品,即使其中某个税目对该货品描述得更为全面、详细,这些货品在有关税目的列名应视为同样具体。

(二)混合物、不同材料构成或不同部件组成的组合物以及零售的成套货品,如果不能按照规则三(一)归类时,在本款可适用的条件下,应按构成货品基本特征的材料或部件归类。

(三)货品不能按照规则三(一)或(二)归类时,应按号列顺序归入其可归入的最末一个税目。

GENERAL RULES FOR THE INTERPRETATION OF THE HARMONIZED SYSTEM

Classification of goods in the Nomenclature shall be governed by the following Ruks:

1. The titles of Sections, Chapters and sub-Chapters are provided for ease of reference only; for legal purposes, classification shall be determined according to the terms of the headings and any relative Section or Chapter Notes and provided such headings or Notes do not otherwise require, according to the following provisions.

2. (a) Any reference in a heading to an article shall be taken to include a reference to that article incomplete or unfinished, provided that, as presented, the incomplete or unfinished article has the essential character of the complete or finished article. It shall also be taken to include a reference to that article complete or finished (or falling to be classified as complete or finished by virtue of this Rule), presented unassembled or disassembled.

   (b) Any reference in a heading to a material or substance shall be taken toinclude a reference to mixtures or combinations of that material or substance with other materials or substances. Any reference to goods of a given material or substance shall be taken to include a reference to goods consisting wholly or partly of such material or substance. The classification of goods consisting of more than one material or substance shall be according to the principles of Rule 3.

3. When by application of Rule 2(b) or for any other reason, goods are, *prima facie*, classifiable under two or more headings, classification shall be effected as follows:

   (a) The heading which provides the most specific description shall be preferred to headings providing a more general description. However, when two or more headings each refer to part only of the materials or substances contained in mixed or composite goods or to part only of the items in a set put up for retail sale, those headings are to be regarded as equally specific in relation to those goods, even if one of them gives a more complete or precise description of the goods.

   (b) Mixtures, composite goods consisting of different materials or made up of different components, and goods put up in sets for retail sale, which cannot be classified by reference to Rule 3 (a), shall be classified as they consisted of the material or component which gives them their essential character, insofar as this criterion is applicable.

   (c) When goods cannot be classified by reference to Rule 3(a) or Rule 3(b), they shall be classified under the heading which occurs last in numerical order among those which equally merit consideration.

规则四　根据上述规则无法归类的货品，应归入与其最相类似的货品的税目。	4. Goods which cannot be classified in accordance with the above Rules shall be classified under the heading appropriate to the goods to which they are most akin.
规则五　除上述规则外，本规则适用于下列货品的归类： （一）制成特殊形状，适用于盛装某个或某套物品并适合长期使用的照像机套、乐器盒、枪套、绘图仪器盒、项链盒及类似容器，如果与所装物品同时进口或出口，并通常与所装物品一同出售的，应与所装物品一并归类。但本款不适用于本身构成整个货品基本特征的容器。 （二）除规则五（一）规定的以外，与所装货品同时进口或出口的包装材料或包装容器，如果通常是用来包装这类货品的，应与所装货品一并归类。但明显可重复使用的包装材料和包装容器可不受本款限制。	5. In addition to the foregoing Rules, the following Rules shall apply in respect of the goods referred to therein: (a) Camera cases, musical instrument cases, gun cases, drawing instrument cases, necklace cases and similar containers, specially shaped or fitted to contain a specific article or set of articles, suitable for long-term use and presented with the articles for which they are intended, shall be classified with such articles when of a kind normally sold therewith. This Rule does not, however, apply to containers which give the whole its essential character; (b) Subject to the provisions of Rule 5(a) above, packing materials and packing containers presented with the goods therein shall be classified with the goods if they are of a kind normally used for packing such goods. However, this provision is not binding when such packing materials or packing containers are clearly suitable for repetitive use.
规则六　货品在某一税目项下各子目的法定归类，应按子目条文或有关的子目注释以及以上各条规则来确定，但子目的比较只能在同一数级上进行。除本税则目录条文另有规定的以外，有关的类注、章注也适用于本规则。	6. For legal purposes, the classification of goods in the subheadings of aheading shall be determined according to the terms of those subheadings and any related Subheading Notes and, *mutatis mutandis*, to the above Rules, on the understanding that only subheadings at the same level are comparable. For the purposes of this Rule the relative Section and Chapter Notes also apply, unless the context otherwise requires.

第一类
活动物;动物产品

SECTION Ⅰ
LIVE ANIMALS;ANIMAL PRODUCTS

注释:

一、本类所称的各属种动物,除条文另有规定的以外,均包括其幼仔在内。

二、除条文另有规定的以外,本协调制度所称干的产品,均包括经脱水、蒸发或冷冻干燥的产品。

Notes:

1. Any reference in this Section to a particular genus or species of an animal, except where the context otherwise requires, includes a reference to the young of that genus or species.
2. Except where the context otherwise requires, throughout the Nomenclature any reference to "dried" products also covers products which have been dehydrated, evaporated or freeze-dried.

第一章
活 动 物

Chapter 1
Live animals

注释:

本章包括所有活动物,但下列各项除外:

一、税目 03.01、03.06、03.07 或 03.08 的鱼、甲壳动物、软体动物及其他水生无脊椎动物;

二、税目 30.02 的培养微生物及其他产品;

三、税目 95.08 的动物。

Notes:

This Chapter covers all live animals except:

1. Fish and crustaceans, molluscs and other aquatic invertebrates, of heading No. 03.01,03.06,03.07 or 03.08
2. Cultures of micro-organisms and other products of heading No. 30.02;
3. Animals of heading No. 95.08.

税则号列	货品名称	最惠(%)	普通	增值税率	出口退税	计量单位	监管条件	Article Description
01.01	马、驴、骡:							**Live horses, asses, mules and hinnies:**
	-马:							-Horses:
0101.2100	--改良种用	0	0	13		千克/头		--Pure-bred breeding
0101.2100 10	改良种用的濒危野马	0	0	13		千克/头	ABEF	Endangered wild horses, pure - bred breeding
0101.2100 90	其他改良种用马	0	0	13	5	千克/头	AB	Other horses, pure-bred breeding
0101.2900	--其他	10	30	13		千克/头		--Other
0101.2900 10	非改良种用濒危野马	10	30	13		千克/头	ABEF	Endangered wild horses, not for breeding
0101.2900 90	非改良种用其他马	10	30	13	5	千克/头	AB	Other horses, not for breeding
	-驴:							-Asses:
0101.3010	---改良种用	0	0	13		千克/头		---Pure-bred breeding
0101.3010 10	改良种用的濒危野驴	0	0	13		千克/头	ABEF	Endangered wild asses, pure-bred breeding
0101.3010 90	改良种用的其他驴	0	0	13	5	千克/头	AB	Other asses, pure-bred breeding
0101.3090	---其他	10	30	13		千克/头		---Other
0101.3090 10	非改良种用濒危野驴	10	30	13		千克/头	ABEF	Endangered wild asses, not for breeding
0101.3090 90	非改良种用其他驴	10	30	13	5	千克/头	AB	Other asses, not for breeding
0101.9000	-其他	10	30	13	5	千克/头	AB	-Other
01.02	牛:							**Live bovine animals:**
	-家牛:							-Cattle:
0102.2100	--改良种用	0	0	13	5	千克/头	AB	--Pure-bred breeding
0102.2900	--其他	10	30	13	5	千克/头	4xAB	--Other
	-水牛:							-Buffalo:
0102.3100	--改良种用	0	0	13		千克/头		--Pure-bred breeding
0102.3100 10	改良种用濒危水牛	0	0	13		千克/头	ABEF	Endangered buffalo, pure - bred breeding
0102.3100 90	改良种用其他水牛	0	0	13	5	千克/头	AB	Other buffalo, prue - bred breeding
0102.3900	--其他	10	30	13		千克/头		--Other
0102.3900 10	非改良种用濒危水牛	10	30	13		千克/头	4ABEFx	Endangered buffalo, not for breeding
0102.3900 90	非改良种用其他水牛	10	30	13	5	千克/头	4ABx	Other buffalo, not for breeding
	-其他:							-Other:
0102.9010	---改良种用	0	0	13		千克/头		---Pure-bred breeding
0102.9010 10	改良种用濒危野牛	0	0	13		千克/头	ABEF	Endangered wild bovine, pure-bred breeding
0102.9010 90	其他改良种用牛	0	0	13	5	千克/头	AB	Other bovine pure-bred breeding
0102.9090	---其他	10	30	13		千克/头		---Other
0102.9090 10	非改良种用濒危野牛	10	30	13		千克/头	4ABEFx	Endangered wild bovine, not for breeding
0102.9090 90	非改良种用其他牛	10	30	13	5	千克/头	4ABx	Other bovine not for breeding
01.03	猪:							**Live swine:**

税则号列	货品名称	最惠(%)	普通	增值税率	出口退税	计量单位	监管条件	Article Description
0103.1000	-改良种用	0	0	13	5	千克/头		-Pure-bred breeding
0103.1000 10	改良种用的鹿豚、姬猪	0	0	13	5	千克/头	AFEB	Pig-deer (*Babyrousa*)、pygmy pig (*Porcula*), pure-bred breeding
0103.1000 90	其他改良种用的猪	0	0	13	5	千克/头	AB	Other swine, pure-bred breeding
	-其他:							-Other:
	--重量在50千克以下:							--Weighing less than 50kg:
0103.9110	---重量在10千克以下	10	50	13	5	千克/头		---Weighing less than 10kg
0103.9110 10	重量在10千克以下的其他野猪(改良种用的除外)	10	50	13	5	千克/头	4xABFE	Other wild swine, W < 10kg (other than pure-bred breeding)
0103.9110 90	重量在10千克以下的其他猪(改良种用的除外)	10	50	13	5	千克/头	4xAB	Other swine, W < 10kg (other than pure-bred breeding)
0103.9120	---重量在10千克及以上,但在50千克以下	10	50	13	5	千克/头		---Weighing 10kg or more, but less than 50kg
0103.9120 10	10千克≤重量<50千克的其他野猪(改良种用的除外)	10	50	13	5	千克/头	4xABFE	Other wild swine, 10kg≤W<50kg (other than pure-bred breeding)
0103.9120 90	10千克≤重量<50千克的其他猪(改良种用的除外)	10	50	13	5	千克/头	4xAB	Other swine, 10kg≤W<50kg (other than pure-bred breeding)
0103.9200	--重量在50千克及以上	10	50	13	5	千克/头		--Weighing 50kg or more
0103.9200 10	重量在50千克及以上的其他野猪(改良种用的除外)	10	50	13	5	千克/头	4xABFE	Other wild swine, W≥50kg (other than pure-bred breeding)
0103.9200 90	重量在50千克及以上的其他猪(改良种用的除外)	10	50	13	5	千克/头	4xAB	Other swine, W≥50kg (other than pure-bred breeding)
01.04	**绵羊、山羊:**							**Live sheep and goats:**
	-绵羊:							-Sheep:
0104.1010	---改良种用	0	0	13	5	千克/头	AB	---Pure-bred breeding
0104.1090	---其他	10	50	13	5	千克/头	AB	---Other
	-山羊:							-Goats:
0104.2010	---改良种用	0	0	13	5	千克/头	AB	---Pure-bred breeding
0104.2090	---其他	10	50	13	5	千克/头	AB	---Other
01.05	**家禽,即鸡、鸭、鹅、火鸡及珍珠鸡:**							**Live poultry, that is to say, fowls of the species *Gallus domesticus*, ducks, geese, turkeys and guinea fowls:**
	-重量不超过185克:							-Weighing not more than 185g:
	--鸡:							--Fowls of the species *Gallus domesticus*:
0105.1110	---改良种用	0	0	13	5	千克/只	AB	---Pure-bred breeding
0105.1190	---其他	10	50	13	5	千克/只	AB	---Other
	--火鸡:							--Turkeys:
0105.1210	---改良种用	0	0	13	5	千克/只	AB	---Pure-bred breeding
0105.1290	---其他	10	50	13	5	千克/只	AB	---Other
	--鸭:							--Ducks:
0105.1310	---改良种用	0	0	13	5	千克/只	AB	---Pure-bred breeding
0105.1390	---其他	10	50	13	5	千克/只	AB	---Other
	--鹅:							--Geese:
0105.1410	---改良种用	0	0	13	5	千克/只	AB	---Pure-bred breeding
0105.1490	---其他	10	50	13	5	千克/只	AB	---Other
	--珍珠鸡:							--Guinea fowls:
0105.1510	---改良种用	0	0	13	5	千克/只	AB	---Pure-bred breeding
0105.1590	---其他	10	50	13	5	千克/只	AB	---Other
	-其他:							-Other:
	--鸡:							--Fowls of the species *Gallus domesticus*:
0105.9410	---改良种用	0	0	13	5	千克/只	4xAB	---Pure-bred breeding
0105.9490	---其他	10	50	13	5	千克/只	4xAB	---Other
	--其他:							--Other:
0105.9910	---改良种用	0	0	13	5	千克/只	AB	---Pure-bred breeding
	---其他:							---Other:
0105.9991	----鸭	10	50	13	5	千克/只	AB	----Ducks

税则号列	货品名称	最惠(%)	普通	增值税率	出口退税	计量单位	监管条件	Article Description
0105.9992	----鹅	10	50	13	5	千克/只	AB	----Geese
0105.9993	----珍珠鸡	10	50	13	5	千克/只	4xAB	----Guinea fowls
0105.9994	----火鸡	10	50	13	5	千克/只	AB	----Turkeys
01.06	**其他活动物：**							**Other live animals:**
	-哺乳动物：							-Mammals:
	--灵长目：							--Primates:
0106.1110	---改良种用	0	0	13	5	千克/只	AFEB	---pure-bred breeding
0106.1190	---其他	10	50	13	5	千克/只	AFEB	---Other
	--鲸、海豚及鼠海豚（鲸目哺乳动物）；海牛及儒艮（海牛目哺乳动物）；海豹、海狮及海象（鳍足亚目哺乳动物）：							--Whales, dolphins and porpoises (mammals of the order Cetacea); manatees and dugongs (mammals of the order Sirenia); seal、sea lion and walrus (Pinnipedia mammal):
	---鲸、海豚及鼠海豚（鲸目哺乳动物）；海牛及儒艮（海牛目哺乳动物）：							---Whales, dolphins and porpoises (mammals of the order Cetacea); manatees and dugongs (mammals of the order Sirenia):
0106.1211[暂]	----改良种用	0	50	13	5	千克/只	ABEF	----Pure-bred breeding
0106.1219	----其他	10	50	13	5	千克/只	ABEF	----Other
	---海豹、海狮及海象（鳍足亚目哺乳动物）：							---Seal、sea lion and walrus (mammals of the suborder Pinnipedia):
0106.1221	----改良种用	0	0	13	5	千克/只	ABEF	----Pure-bred breeding
0106.1229	----其他	10	50	13	5	千克/只	ABEF	----Other
	--骆驼及其他骆驼科动物：							--Camel and other camelids (camelidae)
0106.1310	---改良种用	0	0	13		千克/只		---Pure-bred breeding
0106.1310 10	改良种用濒危骆驼及其他濒危骆驼科动物（包括人工驯养、繁殖的）	0	0	13		千克/只	ABFE	Endangered camel and other endangered camel familia animals, pure-bred breeding (including domesticated and artificially bred)
0106.1310 90	其他改良种用骆驼及其他骆驼科动物	0	0	13	5	千克/只	AB	Other camel and other camel familia animals, pure-bred brdding
0106.1390	---其他	10	50	13		千克/只		---Other
0106.1390 10	其他濒危骆驼及其他濒危骆驼科动物（包括人工驯养、繁殖的）	10	50	13		千克/只	AFEB	Endangered camel and other endangered camel familia animals (including domesticated and artificially bred)
0106.1390 90	其他骆驼及其他骆驼科动物	10	50	13	5	千克/只	AB	Other camel and other camel familia animals
	--家兔及野兔：							--Rabbits and hares:
0106.1410	---改良种用	0	0	13		千克/只		---Pure-bred breeding
0106.1410 10	改良种用濒危野兔（包括人工驯养、繁殖的）	0	0	13		千克/只	ABEF	Endangered hares, pure - bred breeding (including donesticatd and artificiauy bred)
0106.1410 90	改良种用家兔及其他改良种用野兔	0	0	13	5	千克/只	AB	Rabbits and Other hares, pure-bred breeding
0106.1490	---其他	10	50	13		千克/只		---Other
0106.1490 10	其他濒危野兔（包括人工驯养、繁殖的）	10	50	13		千克/只	ABEF	Other endangered hares (including domes ticatedandan tificiauy bred)
0106.1490 90	其他家兔及野兔	10	50	13	5	千克/只	AB	Other rabbits and hares
	--其他：							--Other:
0106.1910	---改良种用	0	0	13		千克/只		---pure-bred breeding
0106.1910 10	其他改良种用濒危哺乳动物（包括人工驯养、繁殖的）	0	0	13		千克/只	ABFE	Other endangered mammals, pure-bred breeding (including domesticated and artificially bred)
0106.1910 90	其他改良种用哺乳动物	0	0	13	5	千克/只	AB	Other mammals, pure-bred breeding
0106.1990	---其他	10	50	13		千克/只		---Other
0106.1990 10	其他濒危哺乳动物（包括人工驯养、繁殖的）	10	50	13		千克/只	AFEB	Other endangered mammals, including domesticated and artificially bred
0106.1990 90	其他哺乳动物	10	50	13	5	千克/只	AB	Other mammals
	-爬行动物（包括蛇及龟鳖）：							-Reptiles (including snakes and turtles):
	---改良种用：							---pure-bred breeding:
0106.2011	----鳄鱼苗	0	0	13	5	千克/只	AFEB	----Crocodiles for cultivation
0106.2019	----其他	0	0	13	5	千克/只	FEAB	----Other
0106.2020	---食用	10	50	13	5	千克/只		---For human consumption

税则号列	货品名称	最惠(%)	普通	增值税率	出口退税	计量单位	监管条件	Article Description
0106.2020 10	食用蛇(包括人工驯养、繁殖的)	10	50	13	5	千克/只	AFEB	Snakes, for human consumption(including domesticated and artificially bred)
0106.2020 20	食用龟鳖(包括人工驯养、繁殖的)	10	50	13	5	千克/只	ABFE	Turtles, for human consumption(including domesticated and artificially bred)
0106.2020 90	其他食用爬行动物(包括人工驯养、繁殖的)	10	50	13	5	千克/只	FEAB	Other reptiles, for human consumption(including domesticated and artificially bred)
0106.2090	---其他	10	50	13	5	千克/只	FEAB	---Other
	-鸟:							-Birds:
	--猛禽:							--Birds of prey:
0106.3110	---改良种用	0	0	13	5	千克/只	AFEB	---pure-bred breeding
0106.3190	---其他	10	50	13	5	千克/只	ABFE	---Other
	--鹦形目(包括普通鹦鹉、长尾鹦鹉、金刚鹦鹉及美冠鹦鹉):							--Psittaciformes (including parrots, parakeets, macaws and cockatoos):
0106.3210	---改良种用	0	0	13	5	千克/只		---Pure-bred breeding
0106.3210 10	改良种用虎皮鹦鹉	0	0	13	5	千克/只	AB	Budgerigar, pure-bred breeding
0106.3210 20	改良种用鸡尾鹦鹉	0	0	13	5	千克/只	AB	Cockatiel (*Nymphicus hollandicus*), pure-bred breeding
0106.3210 90	改良种用其他鹦形目的鸟(包括人工驯养、繁殖的)	0	0	13	5	千克/只	ABFE	Other birds of psittaciformes, pure-bred breeding(including domesticated and artificially bred)
0106.3290	---其他	10	50	13	5	千克/只		---Other
0106.3290 10	非改良种用虎皮鹦鹉	10	50	13	5	千克/只	AB	Budgerigar, other than pure-bred breeding
0106.3290 20	非改良种用鸡尾鹦鹉	10	50	13	5	千克/只	AB	Cockatiel (*Nymphicus hollandicus*), other than pure-bred breeding
0106.3290 90	非改良种用其他鹦形目的鸟(包括人工驯养、繁殖的)	10	50	13	5	千克/只	ABFE	Other birds of psittaciformes (including domesticated and artificially bred) other than pure-bred breeding
	--鸵鸟;鸸鹋:							--Ostriches; emus:
0106.3310	---改良种用	0	0	13		千克/只		---Pure-bred breeding
0106.3310 10	改良种用濒危鸵鸟(包括人工驯养、繁殖的)	0	0	13		千克/只	ABFE	Endangered ostriches, pure-bred breeding (including domesticated and artificially bred)
0106.3310 90	其他改良种用鸵鸟和改良种用鸸鹋	0	0	13	5	千克/只	AB	Other ostriches and emus, pure-bred breeding
0106.3390	---其他	10	50	13		千克/只		---Other
0106.3390 10	其他濒危鸵鸟(包括人工驯养、繁殖的)	10	50	13		千克/只	ABFE	Other endangered ostriches (including domesticated and artificially bred)
0106.3390 90	其他鸵鸟、鸸鹋	10	50	13	5	千克/只	AB	Other ostriches and emus
	-其他:							-Other:
0106.3910	---改良种用	0	0	13		千克/只		---pure-bred breeding
0106.3910 10	其他濒危改良种用的鸟(包括人工驯养、繁殖的)	0	0	13		千克/只	ABFE	Other endangered birds, pure-bred breeding (including domesticated and artificially bred)
0106.3910 90	其他改良种用的鸟	0	0	13	5	千克/只	AB	Other birds, pure-bred breeding
	---食用:							---For human consumption:
0106.3921	----乳鸽	10	50	13	5	千克/只	AB	----Squabs
0106.3923	----野鸭	10	50	13	5	千克/只	FEAB	----Teals
0106.3929	----其他	10	50	13		千克/只		----Other
0106.3929 10	其他食用濒危鸟(包括人工驯养、繁殖的)	10	50	13		千克/只	ABFE	Other endangered birds, for human consumption(including domesticated and artificially bred)
0106.3929 90	其他食用鸟	10	50	13	5	千克/只	AB	Other birds for human consumption
0106.3990	---其他	10	50	13		千克/只		---Other
0106.3990 10	其他濒危鸟(包括人工驯养、繁殖的)	10	50	13		千克/只	ABFE	Other endangered bird, including domesticated and artificially bred
0106.3990 90	其他鸟	10	50	13	5	千克/只	AB	Other birds
	-昆虫:							-Insects:
	--蜂:							--Bees:
0106.4110	---改良种用	0	0	13	5	千克/只	AB	---Pure-bred breeding
0106.4190	---其他		50	13	5	千克/只		---Other
0106.4190[暂] 01	赤眼蜂	0	50	13	5	千克/只	ABS	Trichogramma
0106.4190 90	其他蜂	10	50	13	5	千克/只	AB	Other bees

税则号列	货品名称	最惠(%)	普通	增值税率	出口退税	计量单位	监管条件	Article Description
	--其他：							--Other：
0106.4910	---改良种用	0	0	13		千克/只		---Pure-bred breeding
0106.4910 10	其他改良种用濒危昆虫（包括人工驯养、繁殖的）	0	0	13		千克/只	ABFE	Other endangered insects, pure - bred breeding (including domesticated and artificially bred)
0106.4910 90	其他改良种用非濒危昆虫	0	0	13	5	千克/只	AB	Other insects, pure-bred breeding
0106.4990	---其他		50	13		千克/只		---Other
0106.4990暂 01	捕食螨	0	50	13	5	千克/只	ABS	Predatory mites
0106.4990 10	其他濒危昆虫（包括人工驯养、繁殖的）	10	50	13		千克/只	ABFE	Other endangered insects (including domesticated and artificially bred)
0106.4990 90	其他非濒危昆虫	10	50	13	5	千克/只	AB	Other insects
	-其他：							-Other：
	---改良种用：							---Pure-bred breeding：
0106.9011	----蛙苗	0	0	13		千克/只		----Tadpole and young frogs
0106.9011 10	改良种用濒危蛙苗	0	0	13		千克/只	ABFE	Endangered tadpole and young frogs, pure-bred breeding
0106.9011 90	其他改良种用蛙苗	0	0	13	5	千克/只	AB	Other tadpole and young frogs, pure-bred breeding
0106.9019	----其他	0	0	13		千克/只		----Other
0106.9019 10	其他改良种用濒危动物（包括人工驯养、繁殖的）	0	0	13		千克/只	ABFE	Other endangered animals, pure-bred breeding (including domesticated and artificially bred)
0106.9019 90	其他改良种用动物	0	0	13	5	千克/只	AB	Other animals, pure-bred breeding
0106.9090	---其他		50	13		千克/只		---Other
0106.9090 10	其他濒危动物（包括人工驯养、繁殖的）	10	50	13		千克/只	ABFE	Other endangered animals, purebred breeding (including domesticated and artificially bred)
0106.9090 90	其他动物	10	50	13	5	千克/只	AB	Other animals

第二章
肉及食用杂碎

Chapter 2
Meat and edible meat offal

注释：

本章不包括：

一、税目02.01至02.08或02.10的不适合供人食用的产品；

二、动物的肠、膀胱、胃（税目05.04）或动物血（税目05.11、30.02）；

三、税目02.09所列产品以外的动物脂肪（第十五章）。

Notes:

This Chapter does not cover:

1. Products of the kinds described in headings No. 02.01 to 02.08 or 02.10, unfit or unsuitable for human consumption;
2. Guts, bladders or stomachs of animals (heading No. 05.04) or animal blood (heading No. 05.11 or 30.02);
3. Animal fat, other than products of heading No. 02.09 (Chapter15).

税则号列	货品名称	最惠(%)	普通	增值税率	出口退税	计量单位	监管条件	Article Description
02.01	**鲜、冷牛肉：**							**Meat of bovine animals, fresh or chilled:**
0201.1000	-整头及半头	20	70	13	5	千克		-Carcasses and half-carcasses
0201.1000 10	整头及半头鲜或冷藏的野牛肉	20	70	13	5	千克	4xABFE	Meat of wild bovine animals, carcasses and half-carcasses, fresh or chilled
0201.1000 90	其他整头及半头鲜或冷藏的牛肉	20	70	13	5	千克	4xAB	Other meat of bovine animals, carcasses and half-carcasses, fresh or chilled
0201.2000	-带骨肉	12	70	13	5	千克		-Other cuts with bone in
0201.2000 10	鲜或冷藏的带骨野牛肉	12	70	13	5	千克	47ABEFx	Meat of wild bovine animals, with bone in, fresh or chilled
0201.2000 90	其他鲜或冷藏的带骨牛肉	12	70	13	5	千克	47xAB	Other meat of bovine animals, with bone in, fresh or chilled
0201.3000	-去骨肉	12	70	13		千克		-Boneless
0201.3000 10	鲜或冷藏的去骨野牛肉	12	70	13	5	千克	47xABFE	Meat of wild bovine animals, boneless, fresh or chilled
0201.3000 90	其他鲜或冷藏的去骨牛肉	12	70	13	13	千克	47xAB	Other meat of bovine animals, boneless, fresh or chilled
02.02	**冻牛肉：**							**Meat of bovine animals, frozen:**
0202.1000	-整头及半头	25	70	13	5	千克		-Carcasses and half-carcasses
0202.1000 10	冻藏的整头及半头野牛肉	25	70	13	5	千克	4xABFE	Meat of wild bovine animals, carcasses and half-carcasses, frozen
0202.1000 90	其他冻藏的整头及半头牛肉	25	70	13	5	千克	4xAB	Other meat of bovine animals, carcasses and half-carcasses, frozen
0202.2000	-带骨肉	12	70	13	5	千克		-Other cuts with bone in
0202.2000 10	冻藏的带骨野牛肉	12	70	13	5	千克	47xABFE	Meat of wild bovine animals, with bone in, frozen
0202.2000 90	其他冻藏的带骨牛肉	12	70	13	5	千克	47xAB	Other meat of bovine animals, with bone in, frozen
0202.3000	-去骨肉	12	70	13	5	千克		-Boneless
0202.3000 10	冻藏的去骨野牛肉	12	70	13	5	千克	47xABFE	Meat of wild bovine animals, boneless, frozen
0202.3000 90	其他冻藏的去骨牛肉	12	70	13	13	千克	47xAB	Other meat of bovine animals, boneless, frozen
02.03	**鲜、冷、冻猪肉：**							**Meat of swine, fresh, chilled or frozen:**
	-鲜或冷的：							-Fresh or chilled:
	--整头及半头：							--Carcasses and half-carcasses:
0203.1110	---乳猪	20	70	13	5	千克		---Sucking pig
0203.1110 10	鲜或冷藏的整头及半头野乳猪肉	20	70	13	5	千克	4ABEFx	Meat of wild sucking pig, carcasses and half-carcasses, fresh or chilled
0203.1110 90	其他鲜或冷藏的整头及半头乳猪肉	20	70	13	5	千克	4ABx	Meat of other sucking pig, carcasses and half-carcasses, fresh or chilled
0203.1190	---其他	20	70	13	5	千克		---Other
0203.1190 10	其他鲜或冷藏的整头及半头野猪肉	20	70	13	5	千克	4ABEFx	Other meat of wild swine, carcasses and half-carcasses, fresh or chilled
0203.1190 90	其他鲜或冷藏的整头及半头猪肉	20	70	13	5	千克	4ABx	Other meat of swine, carcasses and half-carcasses, fresh or chilled
0203.1200	--带骨的前腿、后腿及其肉块	20	70	13	5	千克		--Hams, shoulders and cuts thereof, with bone in
0203.1200 10	鲜或冷的带骨野猪前腿、后腿及肉块	20	70	13	5	千克	47ABEFx	Hams, shoulders and cuts thereof, with bone in, of wild swine, fresh or chilled

税则号列	货品名称	最惠(%)	普通	增值税率	出口退税	计量单位	监管条件	Article Description
0203.1200 90	鲜或冷的带骨猪前腿、后腿及其肉块	20	70	13	5	千克	47ABx	Hams, shoulders and cuts thereof, with bone in, of swine, fresh or chilled
0203.1900	--其他	20	70	13	5	千克		--Other
0203.1900 10	其他鲜或冷藏的野猪肉	20	70	13	5	千克	47ABEFx	Other meat of wild swine, fresh or chilled
0203.1900 90	其他鲜或冷藏的猪肉	20	70	13	5	千克	47ABx	Other meat of swine, fresh or chilled
	-冻的:							-Frozen:
	--整头及半头:							--Carcasses and half-carcasses:
0203.2110	---乳猪	12	70	13	5	千克		---Sucking pig
0203.2110 10	冻整头及半头野乳猪肉	12	70	13	5	千克	4ABEFx	Meat of wild sucking pig, carcasses and half-carcasses, frozen
0203.2110 90	冻整头及半头乳猪肉	12	70	13	5	千克	4ABx	Meat of sucking pig, carcasses and half-carcasses, frozen
0203.2190	---其他	12	70	13	5	千克		---Other
0203.2190 10	其他冻整头及半头野猪肉	12	70	13	5	千克	47ABEFx	Other meat of wild swine, carcasses and half-carcasses, frozen
0203.2190 90	其他冻整头及半头猪肉	12	70	13	5	千克	47ABx	Other meat of swine, carcasses and half-carcasses, frozen
0203.2200	--带骨的前腿、后腿及其肉块	12	70	13	5	千克		--Hams, shoulders and cuts thereof, with bone in
0203.2200 10	冻带骨野猪前腿、后腿及肉	12	70	13	5	千克	47ABEFx	Hams, shoulders and cuts thereof, with bone in, of wild swine, frozen
0203.2200 90	冻藏的带骨猪前腿、后腿及其肉块	12	70	13	5	千克	47ABx	Hams, shoulders and cuts thereof, with bone in, of swine, frozen
0203.2900	--其他	12	70	13		千克		--Other
0203.2900 10	冻藏野猪其他肉	12	70	13	5,13	千克	47ABEFx	Other meat of wild swine, frozen
0203.2900 90	其他冻藏猪肉	12	70	13	5,13	千克	47ABx	Other meat of swine, frozen
02.04	**鲜、冷、冻绵羊肉或山羊肉:**							**Meat of sheep or goats, fresh, chilled or frozen:**
0204.1000	-鲜或冷的整头及半头羔羊	15	70	13	5	千克	7AB	-Carcasses and half-carcasses of lamb, fresh or chilled
	-其他鲜或冷的绵羊肉:							-Other meat of sheep, fresh or chilled:
0204.2100	--整头及半头	23	70	13	5	千克	7AB	--Carcasses and half-carcasses
0204.2200	--带骨肉	15	70	13	5	千克	7AB	--Other cuts with bone in
0204.2300	--去骨肉	15	70	13	5	千克	7AB	--Boneless
0204.3000	-冻的整头及半头羔羊	15	70	13	5	千克	7AB	-Carcasses and half-carcasses of lamb, frozen
	-其他冻的绵羊肉:							-Other meat of sheep, frozen:
0204.4100	--整头及半头	23	70	13	5	千克	7AB	--Carcasses and half-carcasses
0204.4200	--带骨肉	12	70	13	5	千克	7AB	--Other cuts with bone in
0204.4300	--去骨肉	15	70	13	13	千克	7AB	--Boneless
0204.5000	-山羊肉	20	70	13	13	千克	7AB	-Meat of goats
02.05	**鲜、冷、冻马、驴、骡肉:**							**Meat of horses, asses, mules or hinnies, fresh, chilled or frozen:**
0205.0000	鲜、冷、冻马、驴、骡肉	20	70	13		千克		Meat of horses, asses, mules or hinnies, fresh, chilled or frozen
0205.0000 10	鲜、冷或冻的濒危野马、野驴肉	20	70	13		千克	ABFE	Meat of endangered wild horses and asses, fresh, chilled or frozen
0205.0000 90	鲜、冷或冻的马、驴、骡肉	20	70	13	5	千克	AB	Other meat of horses, asses, mules or hinnies, fresh, chilled or frozen
02.06	**鲜、冷、冻牛、猪、绵羊、山羊、马、驴、骡的食用杂碎:**							**Edible offal of bovine animals, swine, sheep, goats, horses, asses, mules or hinnies, fresh, chilled or frozen:**
0206.1000	-鲜、冷牛杂碎	12	70	13	5	千克	4xAB	-Of bovine animals, fresh or chilled
	-冻牛杂碎:							-Of bovine animals, frozen:
0206.2100	--舌	12	70	13	5	千克	47xAB	--Tongues
0206.2200	--肝	12	70	13	5	千克	47xAB	--Livers
0206.2900	--其他	12	70	13	5	千克	47xAB	--Other
0206.3000	-鲜、冷猪杂碎	20	70	13	5	千克	4ABx	-Of swine, fresh or chilled
	-冻猪杂碎:							-Of swine, frozen:

税则号列	货品名称	最惠(%)	普通	增值税率	出口退税	计量单位	监管条件	Article Description
0206.4100	--肝	20	70	13	5	千克	47ABx	--Livers
0206.4900	--其他	12	70	13	5	千克	47ABx	--Other
0206.8000	-其他鲜或冷杂碎	20	70	13	5	千克		-Other, fresh or chilled
0206.8000 10	鲜或冷的羊杂碎	20	70	13	5	千克	AB	Edible offal of sheep or goats, fresh or chilled
0206.8000 90	鲜或冷的马、驴、骡杂碎	20	70	13	5	千克	AB	Edible offal of horses, asses, mules or hinnies, fresh or chilled
0206.9000	-其他冻杂碎	18	70	13	5	千克		-Other, frozen
0206.9000 10	冻藏的羊杂碎	18	70	13	5	千克	7AB	Edible offal of sheep or goats, frozen
0206.9000 90	冻藏的马、驴、骡杂碎	18	70	13	5	千克	AB	Edible offal of horses, asses, mules or hinnies, frozen
02.07	**税目01.05所列家禽的鲜、冷、冻肉及食用杂碎:**							**Meat and edible offal, of the poultry of heading No. 01.05, fresh, chilled or frozen:**
	-鸡:							-Of fowls of the species *Gallus domesticus*:
0207.1100	--整只,鲜或冷的	20	70	13	5	千克	4ABx	--Not cut in pieces, fresh or chilled
0207.1200	--整只,冻的	T2	T2	13	5	千克	4x7AB	--Not cut in pieces, frozen
	--块及杂碎,鲜或冷的:							--Chicken cuts and offal, fresh or chiued
	---块:							---Cuts:
0207.1311	----带骨的	20	70	13	13	千克	4xAB	----With bone
0207.1319	----其他	20	70	13	13	千克	4xAB	----Other
	---杂碎:							---Offal:
0207.1321	----翼(不包括翼尖)	20	70	13	13	千克	4xAB	----Midjoint wing
0207.1329	----其他	20	70	13	5	千克	AB4x	----Other
	--块及杂碎,冻的:							--Cuts and offal, frozen:
	---块:							---Cuts:
0207.1411	----带骨的	T2	T2	13	13	千克	7AB4x	----With bone
0207.1419	----其他	T2	T2	13	13	千克	7AB4x	----Other
	---杂碎:							---Offal:
0207.1421	----翼(不包括翼尖)	T2	T2	13	13	千克	7AB4x	----Midjoint wing
0207.1422	----鸡爪	T2	T2	13	5	千克	7AB4x	----Chicken claw
0207.1429	----其他	T2	T2	13	5	千克	7AB4x	----Other
	-火鸡:							-Of turkeys:
0207.2400	--整只,鲜或冷的	20	70	13	5	千克	AB	--Not cut in pieces, fresh or chilled
0207.2500	--整只,冻的	20	70	13	5	千克	AB	--Not cut in pieces, frozen
0207.2600	--块及杂碎,鲜或冷的	20	70	13	5,13	千克	AB	--Cuts and offal, fresh or chilled
0207.2700	--块及杂碎,冻的	10	70	13	5,13	千克	AB	--Cuts and offal, frozen
	-鸭:							-Ducks:
0207.4100	--整只,鲜或冷的	20	70	13	5	千克	AB	--Not cut in pieces, fresh or chilled
0207.4200	--整只,冻的	20	70	13	5	千克	AB	--Not cut in pieces, frozen
0207.4300	--肥肝,鲜或冷的	20	70	13	5	千克	AB	--Fatty livers(foie gras), fresh chilled
0207.4400	--其他,鲜或冷的	20	70	13	5,13	千克	AB	--Other, fresh or chilled
0207.4500	--其他,冻的	20	70	13	5,13	千克	AB	--Other, frozen
	-鹅:							-Geeses:
0207.5100	--整只,鲜或冷的	20	70	13	5	千克	AB	--Not cut in pieces, fresh or chilled
0207.5200	--整只,冻的	20	70	13	5	千克	AB	--Not cut in pieces, frozen
0207.5300	--肥肝,鲜或冷的	20	70	13	5	千克	AB	--Fatty livers(foie gras), fresh or chilled
0207.5400	--其他,鲜或冷的	20	70	13	5,13	千克	AB	--Other, fresh or chilled
0207.5500	--其他,冻的	20	70	13	5,13	千克	AB	--Other, frozen
0207.6000	-珍珠鸡	20	70	13	5,13	千克	AB	-Guinea fowls
02.08	**其他鲜、冷、冻肉及食用杂碎:**							**Other meat and edible meat offal, fresh, chilled or frozen:**
	-家兔或野兔的:							-Of rabbits or hares:
0208.1010	---鲜、冷家兔肉,兔头除外	20	70	13	5,13	千克	AB	---Meat of rabbits, fresh or chilled, other than head
0208.1020	---冻家兔肉,兔头除外	20	70	13	5,13	千克	AB	---Meat of rabbits, frozen, other than head
0208.1090	---其他	20	70	13		千克		---Other
0208.1090 10	鲜、冷或冻濒危野兔肉及其食用杂碎(不包括兔头)	20	70	13		千克	ABFE	Meat and offal, of endangered wild hares (other than head), fresh, chilled or frozen
0208.1090 90	鲜、冷或冻家兔食用杂碎	20	70	13	5	千克	AB	Edible offal of rabbits, fresh、chilled or frozen

税则号列	货品名称	最惠(%)	普通	增值税率	出口退税	计量单位	监管条件	Article Description
0208.3000	-灵长目的	23	70	13	5	千克	ABFE	-Of primates
0208.4000	--鲸、海豚及鼠海豚(鲸目哺乳动物)的;海牛及儒艮(海牛目哺乳动物)的;海豹、海狮及海象(鳍足亚目哺乳动物)的	23	70	13	5	千克	ABEF	--Of whales, dolphins and porpoises (mammals of the order Cetacea); manatees and dugongs (mammals of the order Sirenia); seal、sea lion and walrus (mammals of the suborder Pinnipedia)
0208.5000	-爬行动物(包括蛇及龟鳖)的	23	70	13	5	千克	ABFE	-Of reptiles (including snakes and turtles)
0208.6000	-骆驼及其他骆驼科动物的	23	70	13		千克		-Of camel and other camelids (camelidae):
0208.6000 10	鲜、冷或冻的濒危野生骆驼及其他濒危野生骆驼科动物的肉及食用杂碎	23	70	13		千克	ABFE	Meat and offal of endangered wild camel and other endangered camel familia animals, fresh, chilled or frozen
0208.6000 90	其他鲜、冷或冻骆驼及其他骆驼科动物的肉及食用杂碎	23	70	13	5	千克	AB	Meat and offal of other camel and other camel familia animals, fresh, chilled or frozen
	-其他:							-Other:
0208.9010	---乳鸽的	20	70	13	5	千克	AB	---Of squabs
0208.9090	---其他	23	70	13		千克		---Other
0208.9090 10	其他鲜、冷或冻的濒危野生动物肉	23	70	13		千克	ABFE	Other meat of endangered wild animals, fresh, chilled or frozen
0208.9090 90	其他鲜、冷或冻肉及食用杂碎	23	70	13	5	千克	AB	Other meat and edible offal, fresh、chilled or frozen
02.09	**未炼制或用其他方法提取的不带瘦肉的肥猪肉、猪脂肪及家禽脂肪,鲜、冷、冻、干、熏、盐腌或盐渍的:**							**Pig fat free of lean meat and poultry fat not rendered or otherwise extracted, fresh, chilled, frozen, salted, in brine, dried or smoked:**
0209.1000	-猪的	20	70	13	5	千克	AB	-Of swine
0209.9000	-其他	20	70	13	5	千克	AB	-Other
02.10	**肉及食用杂碎,干、熏、盐腌或盐渍的;可供食用的肉或杂碎的细粉、粗粉:**							**Meat and edible meat offal, salted, in brine, dried or smoked; edible flours and meals of meat or meat offal:**
	-猪肉:							-Meat of swine:
	--带骨的前腿、后腿及其肉块:							--Hams, shoulders and cuts thereof, with bone in:
0210.1110	---带骨的腿	25	80	13	5	千克		---Hams and shoulders, with bone in
0210.1110 10	干、熏、盐制的带骨鹿豚、姬猪腿	25	80	13	5	千克	ABFE	Hams and shoulders of pig-deer (*Babyrousa*)、pygmy pig (*Porcula*), with bone in, salted, in brine, dried or smoked
0210.1110 90	其他干、熏、盐制的带骨猪腿	25	80	13	5	千克	AB	Other hams and shoulders of swine, with bone in, salted, in brine, dried or smoked
0210.1190	---其他	25	80	13	5	千克		---Other
0210.1190 10	干、熏、盐制的带骨鹿豚、姬猪腿肉块	25	80	13	5	千克	ABFE	Cuts of pig-deer (*Babyrousa*)、pygmy pig (*Porcula*), with bone in, salted, in brine, dried or smoked
0210.1190 90	其他干、熏、盐制的带骨猪腿肉	25	80	13	5	千克	AB	Other meat of hams and shoulders, with bone in, salted, in brine, dried or smoked
0210.1200	--腹肉(五花肉)	25	80	13	5	千克		--Bellies (streaky) and cuts thereof
0210.1200 10	干、熏、盐制的鹿豚、姬猪腹肉(指五花肉)	25	80	13	5	千克	ABFE	Bellies (streaky) and cuts thereof, of pig-deer (*Babyrousa*)、pygmy pig (*Porcula*), salted, in brine, dried or smoked
0210.1200 90	其他干、熏、盐制的猪腹肉(指五花肉)	25	80	13	5	千克	AB	Other bellies (streaky) and cuts thereof of swine, salted, in brine, dried or smoked
0210.1900	--其他	25	80	13	5	千克		--Other
0210.1900 10	干、熏、盐制的鹿豚、姬猪其他肉	25	80	13	5	千克	ABFE	Other meat of pig-deer (*Babyrousa*)、pygmy pig (*porcula*), salted, in brine, dried or smoked
0210.1900 90	其他干、熏、盐制的其他猪肉	25	80	13	5	千克	AB	Other meat of swine, salted, in brine, dried or smoked
0210.2000	-牛肉	25	80	13		千克		-Meat of bovine animals
0210.2000 10	干、熏、盐制的濒危野牛肉	25	80	13		千克	ABFE	Meat of endangered wild bovine animals, salted, in brine, dried or smoked
0210.2000 90	干、熏、盐制的其他牛肉	25	80	13	5	千克	AB	Other meat of bovine animals, salted, in brine, dried or smoked

税则号列	货品名称	最惠(%)	普通	增值税率	出口退税	计量单位	监管条件	Article Description
	-其他,包括可供食用的肉或杂碎的细粉、粗粉:							-Other, including edible flours and meals of meat and meat offal:
0210.9100	--灵长目的	25	80	13	5	千克	ABFE	--Of primates
0210.9200	--鲸、海豚及鼠海豚(鲸目哺乳动物)的;海牛及儒艮(海牛目哺乳动物)的;海豹、海狮及海象(鳍足亚目哺乳动物)的	25	80	13	5	千克	ABEF	--Of whales, dolphins and porpoises (mammals of the order Cetacea); manatees and dugongs (mammals of the order Sirenia); seal、sea lion and walrus (mammals of the suborder Pinnipedia)
0210.9300	--爬行动物(包括蛇及龟鳖)的	25	80	13	5	千克	ABFE	--Of reptiles (including snakes and turtles)
0210.9900	--其他	25	80	13		千克		--Other
0210.9900 10	干、熏、盐制其他濒危动物肉及杂碎(包括可供食用的肉或杂碎的细粉、粗粉)	25	80	13		千克	ABFE	Meat and edible offal of other endangered wild animals (including edible flours and meals of meat and meat offal), salted, in brine, dried or smoked
0210.9900 90	干、熏、盐制的其他肉及食用杂碎(包括可供食用的肉或杂碎的细粉、粗粉)	25	80	13	5	千克	AB	Other meat and edible offal (including edible flours and meals of meat and meat offal), salted, in brine, dried or smoked

第三章
鱼、甲壳动物，软体动物及其他水生无脊椎动物

注释：

一、本章不包括：

（一）税目 01.06 的哺乳动物

（二）税目 01.06 的哺乳动物的肉（税目 02.08 或 02.10）

（三）因品种或鲜度不适合供人食用的死鱼（包括鱼肝及鱼卵）、死甲壳动物、死软体动物及其他死水生无脊椎动物（第五章）；不适合供人食用的鱼、甲壳动物、软体动物、其他水生无脊椎动物的粉、粒（税目 23.01）；或

（四）鲟鱼子酱及用鱼卵制成的鲟鱼子酱代用品（税目 16.04）。

二、本章所称"团粒"，是指直接挤压或加入少量粘合剂制成的粒状产品。

Chapter 3
Fish and crustaceans, molluscs and other aquatic invertebrates

Notes:

1. This Chapter does not cover:

(a) Mammals of heading No. 01.06;

(b) Meat of mammals of heading No. 01.06 (heading No. 02.08 or 02.10)

(c) Fish (including livers and roes thereof) or crustaceans, molluscs or other aquatic invertebrates, dead and unfit or unsuitable for human consumption by reason of either their species or their condition (Chapter 5); flours, meals or pellets of fish or of crustaceans, molluscs or other aquatic invertebrates, unfit for human consumption (heading No. 23.01); or

(d) Caviar or caviar substitutes prepared from fish eggs (heading No. 16.04).

2. In this Chapter the term "pellets" means products which have been agglomerated either directly by compression or by the addition of a small quantity of binder.

税则号列	货品名称	最惠(%)	普通	增值税率	出口退税	计量单位	监管条件	Article Description
03.01	活鱼：							**Live fish:**
	-观赏鱼：							-Ornamental fish:
0301.1100	--淡水鱼	17.5	80	13		千克		--Freshwater fish
0301.1100 10	观赏用濒危淡水鱼	17.5	80	13		千克	ABEF	Ornamental endangered freshwater fish
0301.1100 90	观赏用其他淡水鱼	17.5	80	13	5	千克	AB	Ornamental other freshwater fish
0301.1900	--其他	17.5	80	13		千克		--Other
0301.1900 10	观赏用濒危非淡水鱼	17.5	80	13		千克	ABFE	Ornamental endangered not freshwater fish
0301.1900 90	其他观赏用非淡水鱼	17.5	80	13	5	千克	AB	Ornamental other not freshwater fish
	-其他活鱼：							-Other live fish:
	--鳟鱼（河鳟、虹鳟、克拉克大麻哈鱼、阿瓜大麻哈鱼、吉鱼大麻哈鱼、亚利桑那大麻哈鱼、金腹大麻哈鱼）：							--Trout (*Salmo trutta*, *Oncorhynchus my kiss*, *Oncorhynchus clarki*, *Oncorhynchus aguabonita*, *Oncorhynchus gilae*, *Oncorhynchus apache* and *Oncorhynchus chrysogaster*):
0301.9110	---鱼苗	0	0	13	5	千克	AB	---Fry
0301.9190	---其他	10.5	40	13	5	千克	AB	---Other
	--鳗鱼（鳗鲡属）：							--Eels (*Anguilla spp.*):
0301.9210	---鱼苗	0	0	13		千克		---Fry
0301.9210 10	花鳗鲡鱼苗	0	0	13		千克	ABE	Fry of marbled eels (*Anguilla marmorata*)
0301.9210 20	欧洲鳗鲡鱼苗	0	0	13		千克	ABEF	Fry eruopean eels
0301.9210 90	其他鳗鱼（鳗鲡属）苗	0	0	13		千克	AB	Other fry of eels (*Anguilla marmorata*)
0301.9290	---其他	10	40	13	5	千克		---Other
0301.9290 10	花鳗鲡	10	40	13	5	千克	ABE	Marbled eels (*Anguilla marmorata*)
0301.9290 20	欧洲鳗鲡	10	40	13	5	千克	ABEF	European eels
0301.9290 90	其他活鳗鱼（鳗鲡属）	10	40	13	5	千克	AB	Other live eels (*Anguilla marmorata*)
	--鲤科鱼（西鲤、黑鲫、草鱼、鲢属、鲮属、青鱼）：							--Cyprinus carpio, Carassius carassius, Ctenopharyngodon idellus, Hypophthalmichthys spp., Cirrhinus spp., Mylopharyngodon piceus:
0301.9310	---鱼苗	0	0	13	5	千克	AB	---Fry
0301.9390	---其他	10.5	40	13	5	千克	AB	---Other
	--大西洋及太平洋蓝鳍金枪鱼：							--Atlantic and pacific bluefin tunas (Thunnus thynnus, Thunnus orientalis):
0301.9410	---鱼苗	0	0	13	5	千克	AB	---Fry
	---其他：							---Other:
0301.9491	----大西洋蓝鳍金枪鱼	10.5	40	13	5	千克	AB	----Atlantic bluefin tunas
0301.9492	----太平洋蓝鳍金枪鱼	10.5	40	13	5	千克	AB	----Pacific bluefin tunas
	--南方蓝鳍金枪鱼：							--Southern bluefin tunas (*thunnus maccoyii*):

税则号列	货品名称	最惠(%)	普通	增值税率	出口退税	计量单位	监管条件	Article Description
0301.9510	---鱼苗	0	0	13	5	千克	AB	---Fry
0301.9590	---其他	10.5	40	13	5	千克	AB	---Other
	--其他:							--Other:
	---鱼苗:							---Fry:
0301.9911	----鲈鱼	0	0	13	5	千克	AB	----Of perches
0301.9912	----鲟鱼	0	0	13	5	千克	ABFE	----Of sturgeon
0301.9919	----其他	0	0	13		千克		----Other
0301.9919 10	其他濒危鱼苗	0	0	13		千克	ABFE	Other endangered fry
0301.9919 90	其他鱼苗	0	0	13	5	千克	AB	Other fry
	---其他:							---Other:
0301.9991	----罗非鱼	10.5	40	13	5	千克	AB	----Tilapia
0301.9992	----鲀	10.5	40	13	5	千克	AB	----Puffer fish
0301.9993	----其他鲤科鱼	10.5	40	13		千克		----Other cyprinidae fish
0301.9993 10	活的濒危鲤科鱼	10.5	40	13		千克	ABFE	Other endangered live carp
0301.9993 90	活的其他鲤科鱼[鲤科鱼(西鲤、黑鲫、草鱼、鲢属、鲮属、青鱼)除外]	10.5	40	13	5	千克	AB	Other live carp(Cyprinus carpio, Carassius carassius, Ctenopharyngodon idellus, Hypophthalmichthys spp., Cirrhinus spp., Mylopharyngodon piceus)
0301.9999	----其他	10.5	40	13		千克		----Other
0301.9999 10	其他濒危活鱼	10.5	40	13		千克	ABFE	Other endangered live fish
0301.9999 90	其他活鱼	10.5	40	13	5	千克	AB	Other live fish
03.02	**鲜、冷鱼,但税目03.04的鱼片及其他鱼肉除外:**							**Fish, fresh or chilled, excluding fish fillets and other fish meat of heading No. 03.04:**
	-鲑科鱼,但鱼肝及鱼卵除外:							-Salmonidae, excluding livers and roes:
0302.1100	--鳟鱼(河鳟、虹鳟、克拉克大麻哈鱼、阿瓜大麻哈鱼、吉鱼大麻哈鱼、亚利桑那大麻哈鱼、金腹大麻哈鱼)	12	40	13	5	千克	AB	--Trout (*Salmo trutta*, *Oncorhynchus my-kiss*, *Oncorhynchus clarki*, *Oncorhynchus aguabonita*, *Oncorhynchus gilae*, *Oncorhynchus apache* and *Oncorhynchus chrysogaster*)
0302.1300	--大麻哈鱼[红大麻哈鱼、细鳞大麻哈鱼、大麻哈鱼(种)、大鳞大麻哈鱼、银大麻哈鱼、马苏大麻哈鱼、玫瑰大麻哈鱼]	10	40	13	5	千克	ABU	--Pacific salmon(Oncorhynchus nerka, Oncorhynchus gorbuscha, Oncorhynchus keta, Oncorhynchus tschawytscha, Oncorhynchus kisutch, Oncorhynchus masou and Oncorhynchus rhodurus)
	--大西洋鲑鱼及多瑙哲罗鱼:							--Atlantic salmon (salmo salar) and Danube salmon (Hucho hucho):
0302.1410	---大西洋鲑鱼	10	40	13	5	千克	AB	---Atlantic salmon
0302.1420	---多瑙哲罗鱼	10	40	13	5	千克	AB	---Danube salmon
0302.1900	--其他	12	40	13	5	千克		--Other
0302.1900 10	鲜或冷川陕哲罗鲑(鱼肝及鱼卵除外)	12	40	13	5	千克	ABE	Chuan-shan taimen (*Hucho taimen*) (excluding livers and roes), fresh or chilled
0302.1900 20	鲜或冷秦岭细鳞鲑(鱼肝及鱼卵除外)	12	40	13	5	千克	ABE	Qinling mountains sweetlips salmon (excluding livers and roes)
0302.1900 90	其他鲜或冷鲑科鱼(鱼肝及鱼卵除外)	12	40	13	5	千克	AB	Other salmonidae, (excluding livers and roes), fresh or chilled
	-比目鱼,但鱼肝及鱼卵除外:							-Flat fish (*Pleuronectidae*, *Bothidae*, *Cynoglossidae*, *Soleidae*, *Scophthalmidae and Citharidae*), excluding livers and roes:
0302.2100	--庸鲽鱼	12	40	13	5	千克		--Halibut (*Reinhardtius hippoglossoides*, *Hippoglossus hippoglossus*, *Hippoglossus stenolepis*)
0302.2100 10	鲜或冷大西洋庸鲽(庸鲽)(鱼肝及鱼卵除外)	12	40	13	5	千克	ABU	Atlantic halibut(halibut), fresh or chilled, excluding livers and roes
0302.2100 20	鲜或冷马舌鲽(鱼肝及鱼卵除外)	12	40	13	5	千克	ABU	Reinhardtius, fresh or chilled, excluding livers and roes
0302.2100 90	其他鲜或冷庸鲽鱼(鱼肝及鱼卵除外)	12	40	13	5	千克	AB	Other halibut, fresh or chilled, excluding livers and roes
0302.2200	--鲽鱼	12	40	13	5	千克	AB	--Plaice (*Pleuronectes platessa*)
0302.2300	--鳎鱼	12	40	13	5	千克	AB	--Sole (*Solea spp.*)
0302.2400	--大菱鲆(瘤棘鲆)	12	40	13	5	千克	AB	--Turbot(Psetta maxima)
0302.2900	--其他	12	40	13	5	千克		--Other

税则号列	货品名称	最惠(%)	普通	增值税率	出口退税	计量单位	监管条件	Article Description
0302.2900 10	鲜或冷的亚洲箭齿鲽(鱼肝及鱼卵除外)	12	40	13	5	千克	ABU	Arrowtooth halibut, fresh or chilled, excluding livers and roes
0302.2900 90	其他鲜或冷比目鱼(鱼肝及鱼卵除外)	12	40	13	5	千克	AB	Other flat fish , fresh or chilled, excluding livers and roes
	-金枪鱼(金枪鱼属)、鲣鱼或狐鲣(鲣),但鱼肝及鱼卵除外:							-Tuna(tuna genus)、bonito or belted bonito(bonito), excluding livers and roes:
0302.3100	--长鳍金枪鱼	12	40	13	5	千克	AB	--Albacore or longfinned tunas (*Thunnus alalunga*)
0302.3200	--黄鳍金枪鱼	12	40	13	5	千克	AB	--Yellowfin tunas (*Thunnus albacares*)
0302.3300	--鲣鱼或狐鲣	12	40	13	5	千克	AB	--Skipjack or stripe-bellied bonito
0302.3400	--大眼金枪鱼	12	40	13	5	千克	AB	--Bigeye tunas (*Thunnus obesus*)
	--大西洋及太平洋蓝鳍金枪鱼:							--Atlantic and pacific bluefin tunas:
0302.3510	---大西洋蓝鳍金枪鱼	12	40	13	5	千克	ABU	---Atlantic bluefin tunas
0302.3520	---太平洋蓝鳍金枪鱼	12	40	13	5	千克	AB	---Pacific bluefin tunas
0302.3600	--南方蓝鳍金枪鱼	12	40	13	5	千克	AB	--Southern bluefin tunas(Thunnus maccoyii)
0302.3900	--其他	12	40	13	5	千克	AB	--Other
	-鲱鱼(大西洋鲱鱼、太平洋鲱鱼)、鳀鱼(属)、沙丁鱼(沙丁鱼、沙瑙鱼属)、小沙丁鱼属、黍鲱或西鲱、鲭鱼[大西洋鲭、澳洲鲭(鲐)、日本鲭(鲐)]、对称竹荚鱼、新西兰竹荚鱼及竹荚鱼(竹荚鱼属)、军曹鱼及剑鱼,但鱼肝及鱼卵除外:							-Herrings(Clupea harengus, Clupea pallasii), anchovies(Engraulis spp.), sardines(Sardina pilchardus, Sardinops spp.), sardinella(Sardinella spp.), brisling or sprats(Sprattus sprattus), mackerel(Scomber scombrus, Scomber australasicus, Scomber japonicus), jack and horse mackerel(Trachurus spp.), cobia(Rachycentron canadum) and swordfish(Xiphias gladius), excluding livers and roes:
0302.4100	--鲱鱼(大西洋鲱鱼、太平洋鲱鱼)	12	40	13	5	千克		--Herring(Clupea harengus, clupea pallasii)
0302.4100 10	鲜或冷太平洋鲱鱼(鱼肝及鱼卵除外)	12	40	13	5	千克	ABU	Clupea pallasii, fresh or chilled, excluding livers and roes
0302.4100 90	鲜或冷鲱鱼(大西洋鲱鱼)(鱼肝及鱼卵除外)	12	40	13	5	千克	AB	Herrings(Clupea harengus), fresh or chilled, excluding livers and roes
0302.4200	--鳀鱼(鳀属)	12	40	13	5	千克	AB	--anchovies(Engraulis spp.)
0302.4300	--沙丁鱼(沙丁鱼、沙瑙鱼属)、小沙丁鱼属、黍鲱或西鲱	12	40	13	5	千克	AB	--sardines (Sardina pilchardus, Sardinops spp.), sardinella (Sardinella spp.), brisling or sprats (Sprattus sprattus)
0302.4400	--鲭鱼[大西洋鲭、澳洲鲭(鲐)、日本鲭(鲐)]	12	40	13	5	千克	AB	--mackerel (Scomber scombrus, Scomber australasicus, Scomber japonicus)
0302.4500	--对称竹荚鱼、新西兰竹荚鱼及竹荚鱼(竹荚鱼属)	12	40	13	5	千克	AB	--jack and horse mackerel (Trachurus spp.), cobia (Rachycentron canadum)
0302.4600	--军曹鱼	12	40	13	5	千克	AB	--Cobia(Rachycentron canadum)
0302.4700	--剑鱼	12	40	13	5	千克	ABU	--Swordfish(Xiphias gladius)
	-犀鳕科、多丝真鳕科、鳕科、长尾鳕科、黑鳕科、无须鳕科、深海鳕科及南极鳕科鱼,但鱼肝及鱼卵除外:							-Fish of the families bregmacerotidae、euclichthyidae、gadidae、macrouridae、melanonidae、merlucciidae、moridae and muraenolepididae, excluding livers and roes:
0302.5100	--鳕鱼(大西洋鳕鱼、格陵兰鳕鱼、太平洋鳕鱼)	12	40	13	5	千克	AB	--Cod(Gadus morhua, Gadus ogac, Gadus macrocephalus)
0302.5200	--黑线鳕鱼(黑线鳕)	12	40	13	5	千克	AB	--Haddock(Melanogrammus aeglefinus)
0302.5300	--绿青鳕鱼	12	40	13	5	千克	AB	--Coalfish(Pollachius virens)
0302.5400	--狗鳕鱼(无须鳕属、长鳍鳕属)	12	40	13	5	千克	AB	--Hake(Merluccius spp., Urophycis spp.)
0302.5500	--狭鳕鱼	12	40	13	5	千克	ABU	--Alaska Pollack(Theragra chalcogramma)
0302.5600	--蓝鳕鱼(小鳍鳕、南蓝鳕)	12	40	13	5	千克	AB	--Blue whitings(Micromesistius poutassou, Micromesistius australis)
0302.5900	--其他	12	40	13	5	千克	AB	--Other

税则号列	货品名称	最惠(%)	普通	增值税率	出口退税	计量单位	监管条件	Article Description
	-罗非鱼(口孵非鲫属)、鲶鱼(鲑鲶属、鲶属、胡鲶属、真鮰属)、鲤科鱼(西鲤、黑鲫、草鱼、鲢属、鲮属、青鱼)、鳗鱼(鳗鲡属)、尼罗河鲈(尼罗尖吻鲈)及黑鱼(鳢属),但鱼肝及鱼卵除外:							-Tilapias (Oreochromis spp.), catfish (Pangasius spp., Silurus spp., Clarias spp., Ictalurus spp.), carp(Cyprinus carpio, Carassius carassius, Ctenopharyngodon idellus, Hypophthalmichthys spp., Cirrhinus spp., Mylopharyngodon piceus), eels (Anguilla spp.), Nile perch (Lates niloticus) and snakeheads (Channa spp.), excluding livers and roes:
0302.7100	--罗非鱼(口孵非鲫属)	12	40	13	5	千克	AB	--Tilapia(oreochromis spp.)
0302.7200	--鲶鱼(鲑鲶属、鲶属、胡鲶属、真鮰属)	12	40	13	5	千克	AB	--catfish(Pangasius spp., Silurus spp., Clarias spp., Ictalurus spp.)
0302.7300	--鲤科鱼(西鲤、黑鲫、草鱼、鲢属、鲮属、青鱼)	12	40	13	5	千克	AB	--carp (Cyprinus carpio, Carassius carassius, Ctenopharyngodon idellus, Hypophthalmichthys spp., Cirrhinus spp., Mylopharyngodon piceus)
0302.7400	--鳗鱼(鳗鲡属)	12	40	13	5	千克		--Eel(anguilla spp.)
0302.7400 10	鲜或冷花鳗鲡(鱼肝及鱼卵除外)	12	40	13	5	千克	ABE	Marbled eels, fresh or chilled (excluding livers and roes)
0302.7400 20	鲜或冷的欧洲鳗鲡(鱼肝及鱼卵除外)	12	40	13	5	千克	ABEF	European eels, fresh or chilled (excluding livers and roes)
0302.7400 90	其他鲜或冷鳗鱼(鳗鲡属)(鱼肝及鱼卵除外)	12	40	13	5	千克	AB	Other eels(anguilla spp.), fresh or chilled(excluding livers and roes)
0302.7900	--其他	12	40	13	5	千克		--Other
0302.7900 01	鲜或冷尼罗河鲈鱼(尼罗尖吻鲈)(鱼肝及鱼卵除外)	12	40	13	5	千克	AB	Nile perch(Lates niloticus), fresh or chilled(excluding livers and roes)
0302.7900 90	鲜或冷的黑鱼(鳢属)(鱼肝及鱼卵除外)	12	40	13	5	千克	AB	Snakeheads(Channa spp.), fresh or chilled(excluding livers and roes)
	-其他鱼,但鱼肝及鱼卵除外:							-Other fish, excluding livers and roes:
0302.8100	--角鲨及其他鲨鱼	12	40	13	5	千克		--Dogfish and other sharks
0302.8100 10	鲜或冷濒危鲨鱼(鱼肝及鱼卵除外)	12	40	13	0	千克	ABEF	Whale shark(rhincodon), man-eating shark(Carcharodon), basking shark(Cetorhinus), (excluding livers and roes), fresh or chilled)
0302.8100 90	鲜或冷其他鲨鱼(鱼肝及鱼卵除外)	12	40	13	5	千克	AB	Other dogfish and other sharks(excluding livers and roes), fresh or chilled)
0302.8200	--魟鱼及鳐鱼(鳐科)	12	40	13	5	千克	AB	--Rays and skates(Rajidae)
0302.8300	--南极犬牙鱼(南极犬牙鱼属)	12	40	13	5	千克	ABU	--Toothfish(dissostichus spp)
0302.8400	--尖吻鲈鱼(舌齿鲈属)	12	40	13	5	千克	AB	--Seabass(Dicentrarchus spp.)
0302.8500	--菱羊鲷(鲷科)	12	40	13	5	千克	AB	--Seabream(Sparidae)
	--其他:							--Other:
0302.8910	---带鱼	12	40	13	5	千克	AB	---Scabber fish(Trichurius)
0302.8920	---黄鱼	12	40	13	5	千克	AB	---Yellow croaker(Pseudosicaena)
0302.8930	---鲳鱼	12	40	13	5	千克	AB	---Tilapia
0302.8940	---鲀	12	40	13	5	千克	AB	---Puffer fish
0302.8990	---其他	12	40	13		千克		---Other
0302.8990 01	鲜或冷的其他鲈鱼(鱼肝及鱼卵除外)	12	40	13	5	千克	AB	Other perch, fresh or chilled (excluding livers and roes)
0302.8990 10	其他未列名濒危鲜或冷鱼(鱼肝及鱼卵除外)	12	40	13		千克	ABFE	Other endangered fish, fresh or chilled(excluding livers and roes)
0302.8990 20	鲜或冷的平鲉属(鱼肝及鱼卵除外)	12	40	13	0	千克	ABU	Fresh and cold flat scorpionfish genera(excluding livers and roes)
0302.8990 30	鲜或冷的鲪鲉属(叶鳍鲉属)(鱼肝及鱼卵除外)	12	40	13	0	千克	ABU	Fresh and cold Jun scorpionfish genera (leaf scorpionfish fins)(excluding livers and roes)
0302.8990 90	其他鲜或冷鱼(鱼肝及鱼卵除外)	12	40	13	5	千克	AB	Other fish, fresh or chilled
0302.9000	-鱼肝及鱼卵	12	50	13		千克		-Livers and roes
0302.9000 10	鲜或冷濒危鱼种的肝及鱼卵	12	50	13		千克	ABEF	Livers and roes of endangered fish, fresh or chilled
0302.9000 90	其他鲜或冷鱼肝及鱼卵	12	50	13	5	千克	AB	Other livers and roes, fresh or chilled
03.03	冻鱼,但税目03.04的鱼片及其他鱼肉除外:							**Fish, frozen, excluding fish fillets and other fish meat of heading No. 03.04:**
	-鲑科鱼,但鱼肝及鱼卵除外:							--Salmonidae, excluding livers and roes:
0303.1100	--红大麻哈鱼	10	40	13	13	千克	AB	--Sockeye salmon(red salmon)(*Oncorhynchus nerka*)

税则号列	货品名称	最惠(%)	普通	增值税率	出口退税	计量单位	监管条件	Article Description
0303.1200	--其他大麻哈鱼[细鳞大麻哈鱼、大麻哈鱼(种)、大鳞大麻哈鱼、银大麻哈鱼、马苏大麻哈鱼、玫瑰大麻哈鱼]	10	40	13	13	千克	ABU	--Other Pacific salmon(Oncorhynchus gorbuscha, Oncorhynchus keta, Oncorhynchus tschawytscha, Oncorhynchus kisutch, Oncorhynchus masou and Oncorhynchus rhodurus)
0303.1300	--大西洋鲑鱼及多瑙哲罗鱼	10	40	13	13	千克	AB	--Atlantic salmon(Salmo salar) and Danube salmon (Hucho hucho)
0303.1400	--鳟鱼(河鳟、虹鳟、克拉克大麻哈鱼、阿瓜大麻哈鱼、吉雨大麻哈鱼、亚利桑那大麻哈鱼、金腹大麻哈鱼)	12	40	13	13	千克	AB	--Trout (Salmo trutta, Oncorhynchus mykiss, Oncorhynchus clarki, Oncorhynchus aguabonita, Oncorhynchus gilae, Oncorhynchus apache and Oncorhynchus chrysogaster)
0303.1900	--其他	10	40	13	13	千克		--Other
0303.1900 10	冻川陕哲罗鲑(鱼肝及鱼卵除外)	10	40	13	13	千克	ABE	Chuan-shan taimen(hucho taimen)(excluding liver and roes)frozen
0303.1900 20	冻秦岭细鳞鲑(鱼肝及鱼卵除外)	10	40	13	13	千克	ABE	Qinling lenok(brachymystax lenok)(excluding liver and roes)frozen
0303.1900 90	其他冻鲑科鱼(鱼肝及鱼卵除外)	10	40	13	13	千克	AB	Other salmonidae(excluding liver and roes) frozen (excluding livers and roes)
	-罗非鱼(口孵非鲫鱼属)、鲶鱼(鲑鲶属、鲶属、胡鲶属、真鮰属)、鲤科鱼(西鲤、黑鲫、草鱼、鲢属、鲮属、青鱼)、鳗鱼(鳗鲡属)、尼罗河鲈鱼(尼罗尖吻鲈)及黑鱼(鳢属),但鱼肝及鱼卵除外:							-Tilapias (Oreochromis spp.), catfish (Pangasius spp., Silurus spp., Clarias spp., Ictalurus spp.), carp(Cyprinus carpio, Carassius carassius, Ctenopharyngodon idellus, Hypophthalmichthys spp., Cirrhinus spp., Mylopharyngodon piceus), eels(Anguilla spp.), Nile perch(Lates niloticus) and snakeheads (Channa spp.), excluding livers and roes:
0303.2300	--罗非鱼(口孵非鲫属)	10	40	13	13	千克	AB	--Tilapia(oreochromis spp.)
0303.2400	--鲶鱼(鲑鲶属、鲶属、胡鲶属、真鮰属)	10	40	13	13	千克	AB	--Catfish(Pangasius spp., Silurus spp., Clarias spp., Ictalurus spp.)
0303.2500	--鲤科鱼(西鲤、黑鲫、草鱼、鲢属、鲮属、青鱼)	10	40	13	13	千克	AB	--Carp(Cyprinus carpio, Carassius carassius, Ctenopharyngodon idellus, Hypophthalmichthys spp., Cirrhinus spp., Mylopharyngodon piceus)
0303.2600	--鳗鱼(鳗鲡属)	12	40	13	13	千克		--Eel(anguilla spp.)
0303.2600 10	冻花鳗鲡(鱼肝及鱼卵除外)	12	40	13	13	千克	ABE	Marbled eels, frozen (excluding livers and roes)
0303.2600 20	冻欧洲鳗鲡(鱼肝及鱼卵除外)	12	40	13	13	千克	ABEF	European eels, frozen (excluding livers and roes)
0303.2600 90	其他冻鳗鱼(鳗鲡属)(鱼肝及鱼卵除外)	12	40	13	13	千克	AB	Other eels (anguilla spp.), frozen (excluding livers and roes)
0303.2900	--其他	10	40	13	13	千克		--Other
0303.2900 01	冻尼罗河鲈鱼(尼罗尖吻鲈)(鱼肝及鱼卵除外)	10	40	13	13	千克	AB	Nile perch(Lates niloticus), frozen(excluding livers and roes)
0303.2900 90	冻黑鱼(鳢属)(鱼肝及鱼卵除外)	10	40	13	13	千克	AB	Snakeheads(Channa spp.), frozen(excluding livers and roes)
	-比目鱼(鲽科、鲆科、舌鳎科、鳎科、菱鲆科、刺鲆科),但鱼肝及鱼卵除外:							-Flatfish (*Pleuronectidae*, *Bothidae*, *Cynoglossidae*, *Soleidae*, *Scophthalmidae and Citharidae*), excluding livers and roes:
	--庸鲽鱼:							--Halibut (*Reinhardtius hippoglossoides*, *Hippoglossus hippoglossus*, *Hippoglossus stenolepis*):
0303.3110暂	---格陵兰庸鲽鱼	5	40	13	13	千克	AB	---Greenland halibut
0303.3190	---其他	10	40	13	13	千克		---Other
0303.3190 10	冻大西洋庸鲽(庸鲽)(鱼肝及鱼卵除外,冻格陵兰庸鲽鱼除外)	10	40	13	13	千克	ABU	Frozen Atlantic agent sole (commonplace sole)
0303.3190 20	冻马舌鲽(鱼肝及鱼卵除外,冻格陵兰庸鲽鱼除外)	10	40	13	13	千克	ABU	Frozen horse tongue sole
0303.3190 90	其他冻庸鲽鱼(鱼肝及鱼卵除外,冻格陵兰庸鲽鱼除外)	10	40	13	13	千克	AB	Other frozen agent flatfish
0303.3200暂	--鲽鱼	2	40	13	13	千克	AB	--Plaice (*Pleuronectes platessa*)
0303.3300	--鳎鱼	12	40	13	13	千克	AB	--Sole (*Solea spp.*)
0303.3400	--大菱鲆(瘤棘鲆)	10	40	13	13	千克	AB	--Turbots(Psetta maxima)
0303.3900	--其他	10	40	13	13	千克		--Other
0303.3900 10	冻亚洲箭齿鲽(鱼肝及鱼卵除外)	10	40	13	13	千克	ABU	Frozen arrow tooth sole in Asia

税则号列	货　品　名　称	最惠(%)	普通	增值税率	出口退税	计量单位	监管条件	Article Description
0303.3900 90	其他冻比目鱼(鲽科、鲆科、舌鳎科、鳎科、菱鲆科、刺鲆科)	10	40	13	13	千克	AB	Other flatfish(Pleuronectidae, Bothidae, Cynoglossidae, Soleidae, Scophthalmidae and Citharidae) frozen
	-金枪鱼(金枪属)、鲣鱼或狐鲣(鲣),但鱼肝及鱼卵除外:							-Tunas (*of the genus Thunnus*) (tuna genus), skipjack or stripe-bellied bonito (*Euthynnus* (*Katsuwonus*) *pelamis*) or belteol bonito(oceanic bonito), excluding livers and roes:
0303.4100	--长鳍金枪鱼	12	40	13	13	千克	AB	--Albacore or longfinned tunas (*Thunnus alalunga*)
0303.4200	--黄鳍金枪鱼	12	40	13	13	千克	AB	--Yellowfin tunas (*Thunnus albacares*)
0303.4300	--鲣鱼或狐鲣	12	40	13	13	千克	AB	--Skipjack or belted bonito
0303.4400	--大眼金枪鱼	12	40	13	13	千克	ABU	--Bigeye tunas(*Thunnus obesus*)
	--大西洋及太平洋蓝鳍金枪鱼:							--Atlantic and pacific bluefin tunas (Thunnus thynnus, Thunnus orientalis):
0303.4510	---大西洋蓝鳍金枪鱼	12	40	13	13	千克	ABU	--Atlantic bluefin tunas:
0303.4520	---太平洋蓝鳍金枪鱼	12	40	13	13	千克	AB	--pacific bluefin tunas:
0303.4600	--南方蓝鳍金枪鱼	12	40	13	13	千克	AB	--Southern bluefin tunas(*Thunnus maccoyii*)
0303.4900	--其他	12	40	13	13	千克	AB	--Other
	-鲱鱼(大西洋鲱鱼、太平洋鲱鱼),沙丁鱼(沙丁鱼、沙瑙鱼属)、小沙丁鱼属、黍鲱或西鲱、鲭鱼[大西洋鲭、澳洲鲭(鲐)、日本鲭(鲐)],对称竹荚鱼、新西兰竹荚鱼及竹荚鱼(竹荚鱼属)、军曹鱼及剑鱼,但鱼肝及鱼卵除外:							-Herrings (Clupea harengus, Clupea pallasii), sardines (Sardina pilchardus, Sardinops spp.), sardinella (Sardinella spp.), brisling or sprats (Sprattus sprattus), mackerel (Scomber scombrus, Scomber australasicus, Scomber japonicus), jack and horse mackerel (Trachurus spp.), cobia (Rachycentron canadum) and swordfish (Xiphias gladius), excluding livers and roes:
0303.5100[暂]	--鲱鱼(大西洋鲱鱼、太平洋鲱鱼)	2	40	13	13	千克		--Herrings(Clupea harengus, Clupea pallosii)
0303.5100[暂] 10	冻太平洋鲱鱼(鱼肝及鱼卵除外)	2	40	13	13	千克	ABU	Frozen Pacific herring(excluding livers and roes)
0303.5100[暂] 90	冻鲱鱼(大西洋鲱鱼)(鱼肝及鱼卵除外)	2	40	13	13	千克	AB	Herrings(Clupea harengus) Frozen(excluding livers and roes)
0303.5300	--沙丁鱼(沙丁鱼、沙瑙鱼属)、小沙丁鱼属、黍鲱或西鲱	12	40	13	13	千克	AB	--Sardines (Sardina pilchardus, Sardinops spp.), sardinella (Sardinella spp.), brisling or sprats (Sprattus sprattus)
0303.5400	--鲭鱼[大西洋鲭、澳洲鲭(鲐)、日本鲭(鲐)]	10	40	13	13	千克	AB	--Mackerel (Scomber scombrus, Scomber australasicus, Scomber japonicus)
0303.5500	--对称竹荚鱼、新西兰竹荚鱼及竹荚鱼(竹荚鱼属)	10	40	13	13	千克	AB	-Jack and horse mackerel(Trachurus spp.)
0303.5600	--军曹鱼	10	40	13	13	千克	AB	--Cobia(Rachycentron canadum)
0303.5700	--剑鱼	10	40	13	13	千克	ABU	--Swordfish(Xiphias gladius)
	-犀鳕科、多丝真鳕科、鳕科、长尾鳕科、黑鳕科、无须鳕科、深海鳕科及南极鳕科鱼,但鱼肝及鱼卵除外:							-Fish of the families bregmacerotidae、euclichthyidae、gadidae、macrouridae、melanonidae、merluccidae、moridae and muraenolepididae, excluding livers and roes:
0303.6300[暂]	--鳕鱼(大西洋鳕鱼、格陵兰鳕鱼、太平洋鳕鱼)	2	40	13	13	千克	AB	--Cod (Gadus morhua, Gadus ogac, Gadus macrocephalus)
0303.6400	--黑线鳕鱼(黑线鳕)	12	40	13	13	千克	AB	--Haddock(melanogrammus aeglefinus)
0303.6500	--绿青鳕鱼	12	40	13	13	千克	AB	--Coalfish(Pollachius virens)
0303.6600	--狗鳕鱼(无须鳕属、长鳍鳕属)	12	40	13	13	千克	AB	--Hake(Merluccius spp., urophycis spp.)
0303.6700	--狭鳕鱼	10	40	13	13	千克	ABU	--Alaska pollack(Theragra chalcogramma)
0303.6800	--蓝鳕鱼(小鳍鳕、南蓝鳕)	10	40	13	13	千克	AB	--Blue whitings (Micromesistius poutassou, Micromesistius australis)
0303.6900	--其他	10	40	13	13	千克	AB	--Other
	-其他鱼,但鱼肝及鱼卵除外:							-Other fish, excluding livers and roes:
0303.8100	--角鲨及其他鲨鱼	12	40	13	13	千克		--Dogfish and other sharks
0303.8100 10	冻濒危鲨鱼(鱼肝及鱼卵除外)	12	40	13	0	千克	ABEF	Whale shark(Rhincodon), man-eating shark(Ccharodon), basking shark(Cetorhinus) (excluding livers and roes), frozen
0303.8100 90	冻其他鲨鱼(鱼肝及鱼卵除外)	12	40	13	13	千克	AB	Other dogfish and other sharks (excluding livers and roes), frozen
0303.8200	--魟鱼及鳐鱼(鳐科)	10	40	13	13	千克	AB	--Rays and skates(Rajidae)

税则号列	货　品　名　称	最惠(%)	普通	增值税率	出口退税	计量单位	监管条件	Article Description
0303.8300	--南极犬牙鱼(南极犬牙鱼属)	10	40	13	13	千克	ABU	--Toothfish(Dissostichus spp.)
0303.8400	--尖吻鲈鱼(舌齿鲈属)	12	40	13	13	千克	AB	--Seabass(Dicentrarchus spp.)
	--其他:							--Other:
0303.8910	---带鱼	10	40	13	13	千克	AB	---Scabber fish(Trichurius)
0303.8920	---黄鱼	10	40	13	13	千克	AB	---Yellow croaker(Pseudosicaena)
0303.8930	---鲳鱼	10	40	13	13	千克	AB	---Tilapia
0303.8990	---其他	10	40	13		千克		---Other
0303.8990 01	其他冻鲈鱼(鱼肝及鱼卵除外)	10	40	13	13	千克	AB	Other perch,frozen(excluding livers and roes)
0303.8990 10	其他未列名濒危冻鱼(鱼肝及鱼卵除外)	10	40	13		千克	ABFE	Other endangered fish, frozen (excluding livers and roes)
0303.8990 20	冻平鲉属(鱼肝及鱼卵除外)	10	40	13	0	千克	ABU	Frozen flat scorpionfish genera (excluding livers and roes)
0303.8990 30	冻鲳鲉属(叶鳍鲉属)(鱼肝及鱼卵除外)	10	40	13	0	千克	ABU	Frozen Jun scorpionfish belongs to fin (leaf scorpionfish)
0303.8990 90	其他未列名冻鱼(鱼肝及鱼卵除外)	10	40	13	13	千克	AB	Other fish,frozen(excluding livers and roes)
0303.9000	-鱼肝及鱼卵	10	50	13		千克		-Livers and roes
0303.9000 10	冻濒危鱼种的肝及鱼卵	10	50	13		千克	ABEF	Livers and roes of endangered fish,frozen
0303.9000 90	其他冻鱼肝及鱼卵	10	50	13	13	千克	AB	Other livers and roes,frozen
03.04	**鲜、冷、冻鱼片及其他鱼肉(不论是否绞碎):**							**Fish fillets and other fish meat (whether or not minced), fresh, chilled or frozen:**
	-鲜或冷的罗非鱼(口孵非鲫属)、鲶鱼(鲑鲶属、鲶属、胡鲶属、真鮰属)、鲤科鱼(西鲤、黑鲫、草鱼、鲢属、鳙属、青鱼)、鳗鱼(鳗鲡属)、尼罗河鲈鱼(尼罗尖吻鲈)及黑鱼(鳢属)的鱼片:							-Fresh or chilled fillets of tilapias (Oreochromis spp.),catfish(Pangasius spp., Silurus spp., Clarias spp., Ictalurus spp.), carp(Cyprinus carpio, Carassius carassius, Ctenopharyngodon idellus, Hypophthalmichthys spp., Cirrhinus spp., Mylopharyngodon piceus), eels (Anguilla spp.), Nile perch (Lates niloticus) and snakeheads(Channa spp.):
0304.3100	--罗非鱼(口孵非鲫属)	12	70	13	5	千克	AB	--Tilapia(oreochromis spp.)
0304.3200	--鲶鱼(鲑鲶属、鲶属、胡鲶属、真鮰属)	12	70	13	5	千克	AB	--Catfish(pangasius spp.、silurus spp.、clarias spp.、ictalurus spp.)
0304.3300	--尼罗河鲈鱼(尼罗尖吻鲈)	12	70	13	5	千克	AB	--Nile perch(lates niloticus)
0304.3900	--其他	12	70	13	5	千克		--Other
0304.3900 10	鲜或冷的花鳗鲡鱼片	12	70	13	5	千克	ABE	Fresh or chilled fillets of marbled eels
0304.3900 20	鲜或冷的欧洲鳗鲡鱼片	12	70	13	5	千克	ABEF	Fresh or chilled fillets of european eels
0304.3900 90	鲜或冷的鲤科鱼(西鲤、黑鲫、草鱼、鲢属、鳙属、青鱼),其他鳗鱼(鳗鲡属)及黑鱼(鳢属)的鱼片	12	70	13	5	千克	AB	Fresh or chilled fillets of carp(Cyprinus carpio, Carassius carassius, Ctenopharyngodon idellus, Hypophthalmichthys spp., Cirrhinus spp., Mylopharyngodon piceus), other eels (Anguilla spp.) and snakeheads (Channa spp.)
	-鲜或冷的其他鱼片:							-Other fish fillets,fresh and chilled:
0304.4100	--大麻哈鱼[红大麻哈鱼、细鳞大麻哈鱼、大麻哈鱼(种)、大鳞大麻哈鱼、银大麻哈鱼、马苏大麻哈鱼、玫瑰大麻哈鱼]、大西洋鲑鱼及多瑙哲罗鱼	12	70	13	5	千克	AB	--Pacific salmon(Oncorhynchus nerka, Oncorhynchus gorbuscha, Oncorhynchus keta, Oncorhynchus tschawytscha, Oncorhynchus kisutch, Oncorhynchus masou and Oncorhynchus rhodurus), Atlantic salmon (Salmo salar) and Danube salmon(Hucho hucho)
0304.4200	--鳟鱼(河鳟、虹鳟、克拉克大麻哈鱼、阿瓜大麻哈鱼、吉雨大麻哈鱼、亚利桑那大麻哈鱼、金腹大麻哈鱼)	12	70	13	5	千克	AB	--Trout (Salmo trutta, Oncorhynchus mykiss, Oncorhynchus clarki, Oncorhynchus aguabonita, Oncorhynchus gilae, Oncorhynchus apache and Oncorhynchus chrysogaster)
0304.4300	--比目鱼(鲽科、鲆科、舌鳎科、鳎科、菱鲆科、刺鲆科)	12	70	13	5	千克	AB	--Flat fish (Pleuronectidae, Bothidae, Cynoglossidae, Soleidae, Scophthalmidae and Citharidae)
0304.4400	--犀鳕科、多丝真鳕科、鳕科、长尾鳕科、黑鳕科、无须鳕科、深海鳕科及南极鳕科鱼	12	70	13	5	千克	AB	-Fish of the families Bregmacerotidae, Euclichthyidae, Gadidae, Macrouridae, Melanonidae, Merlucciidae, Moridae and Muraenolepididae
0304.4500	--剑鱼	12	70	13	5	千克	ABU	--Swordfish(Xiphias gladius)
0304.4600	--南极犬牙鱼(南极犬牙鱼属)	12	70	13	5	千克	ABU	--Toothfish(Dissostichus spp)
0304.4900	--其他	12	70	13		千克		--Other

税则号列	货品名称	最惠(%)	普通	增值税率	出口退税	计量单位	监管条件	Article Description
0304.4900 10	鲜或冷的其他濒危鱼鱼片	12	70	13		千克	ABFE	Fresh or chilled fillets of Other endangered fish
0304.4900 90	鲜或冷的其他鱼鱼片	12	70	13	5	千克	AB	Fresh or chilled fillets of fish
	-其他,鲜或冷的:							--Other, fresh and chilled:
0304.5100	--罗非鱼(口孵非鲫属)、鲶鱼(鲑鲶属、鲶属、胡鲶属、真鮰属)、鲤科鱼(西鲤、黑鲫、草鱼、鲢属、鲮属、青鱼)、鳗鱼(鳗鲡属)、尼罗河鲈鱼(尼罗尖吻鲈)及黑鱼(鳢属)	12	70	13	5	千克		-Tilapias (Oreochromis spp.), catfish (Pangasius spp., Silurus spp., Clarias spp., Ictalurus spp.), carp (Cyprinus carpio, Carassius carassius, Ctenopharyngodon idellus, Hypophthalmichthys spp., Cirrhinus spp., Mylopharyngodon piceus), eels (Anguilla spp.), Nile perch (Lates niloticus) and snakeheads (Channa spp.)
0304.5100 10	鲜或冷的花鳗鲡的鱼肉(不论是否绞碎)	12	70	13	5	千克	ABE	Marbled eels, fresh or chilled (whether or not minced)
0304.5100 20	鲜或冷的欧洲鳗鲡的鱼肉(不论是否绞碎)	12	70	13	5	千克	ABEF	Meat of european eels, fresh or chilled (whether or not minced)
0304.5100 90	鲜或冷的罗非鱼(口孵非鲫属)、鲶鱼(鲑鲶属、鲶属、胡鲶属、真鮰属)、鲤科鱼(西鲤、黑鲫、草鱼、鲢属、鲮属、青鱼)、其他鳗鱼(鳗鲡属)、尼罗河鲈鱼(尼罗尖吻鲈)及黑鱼(醴属)的鱼肉(不论是否绞碎)	12	70	13	5	千克	AB	Tilapia (oreochromis spp.), catfish (Pangasius spp., Silurus spp., Clarias spp., Ictalurus spp.), carp (Cyprinus carpio, Carassius carassius, Ctenopharyngodon idellus, Hypophthalmichthys spp., Cirrhinus spp., Mylopharyngodon piceus), eels (Aguilla spp.), nile perch (Lates niloticus) and snakeheads (Channa spp.), fresh or chilled (whether or not minced)
0304.5200	--鲑科鱼	12	70	13	5	千克	AB	--Salmonoids
0304.5300	--犀鳕科、多丝真鳕科、鳕科、长尾鳕科、黑鳕科、无须鳕科、深海鳕科及南极鳕科鱼	12	70	13	5	千克	AB	-Fish of the families bregmacerotidae、euclichthyidae、gadidae、macrouridae、melanonidae、merluccidae、moridae and Muraenolepididae
0304.5400	--剑鱼	12	70	13	5	千克	ABU	--Swordfish (Xiphias gladius)
0304.5500	--南极犬牙鱼(南极犬牙鱼属)	12	70	13	5	千克	ABU	--Toothfish (Dissostichus spp)
0304.5900	--其他	12	70	13		千克		--Other
0304.5900 10	鲜或冷的其他濒危鱼鱼肉(不论是否绞碎)	12	70	13		千克	ABEF	Other endangered fish meat, fresh or chilled (whether or not minced)
0304.5900 90	鲜或冷的其他鱼鱼肉(不论是否绞碎)	12	70	13	5	千克	AB	Other fish meat, fresh or chilled (whether or not minced)
	-冻的罗非鱼(口孵非鲫属)、鲶鱼(鲑鲶属、鲶属、胡鲶属、真鮰属)、鲤科鱼(西鲤、黑鲫、草鱼、鲢属、鲮属、青鱼)、鳗鱼(鳗鲡属)、尼罗河鲈鱼(尼罗尖吻鲈)及黑鱼(鳢属)的鱼片:							-Frozen fillets of tilapias (Oreochromis spp.), catfish (Pangasius spp., Silurus spp., Clarias spp., Ictalurus spp.), carp (Cyprinus carpio, Carassius carassius, Ctenopharyngodon idellus, Hypophthalmichthys spp., Cirrhinus spp., Mylopharyngodon piceus), eels (Anguilla spp.), Nile perch (Lates niloticus) and snakeheads (Channa spp.)
0304.6100	--罗非鱼(口孵非鲫属)	10	70	13	13	千克	AB	--Tilapia (oreochromis spp.)
	--鲶鱼(鲑鲶属、鲶属、胡鲶属、真鮰属):							--catfish (Pangasius spp., Silurus spp., Clarias spp., Ictalurus spp.):
	---叉尾鮰鱼(真鮰属):							---Of Ictalurus:
0304.6211	----斑点叉尾鮰鱼	10	70	13	13	千克	AB	----Channel catfish (ictaluru punctatus)
0304.6219	----其他	10	70	13	13	千克	AB	----Other
0304.6290	---其他	10	70	13	13	千克	AB	---Other
0304.6300	--尼罗河鲈鱼(尼罗尖吻鲈)	10	70	13	13	千克	AB	--Nile perch (Lates niloticus)
0304.6900	--其他	10	70	13	13	千克		--Other
0304.6900 10	冻的花鳗鲡鱼片	10	70	13	13	千克	ABE	Frozen fillets of marbled eels
0304.6900 20	冻的欧洲鳗鲡鱼片	10	70	13	13	千克	ABEF	Frozen fillets of european eels
0304.6900 90	冻的鲤科鱼(西鲤、黑鲫、草鱼、鲢属、鲮属、青鱼)、其他鳗鱼(鳗鲡属)及黑鱼(鳢属)的鱼片	10	70	13	13	千克	AB	Frozen fillets of carp (Cyprinus carpio, Carassius carassius, Ctenopharyngodon idellus, Hypophthalmichthys spp., Cirrhinus spp., Mylopharyngodon piceus), eels (Aguilla spp.), nile perch (Lates niloticus) and snakeheads (Channa spp.)

税则号列	货品名称	最惠(%)	普通	增值税率	出口退税	计量单位	监管条件	Article Description
	-冻的犀鳕科、多丝真鳕科、鳕科、长尾鳕科、黑鳕科、无须鳕科、深海鳕科及南极鳕科鱼的鱼片：							-Frozen fillets of fish of the families Bregmacerotidae, Euclichthyidae, Gadidae, Macrouridae, Melanonidae, Merlucciidae, Moridae and Muraenolepididae
0304.7100	--鳕鱼（大西洋鳕鱼、格陵兰鳕鱼、太平洋鳕鱼）	10	70	13	13	千克	AB	--Cod(Gadus morhua, Gadus ogac, Gadus macrocephalus)
0304.7200	--黑线鳕鱼（黑线鳕）	10	70	13	13	千克	AB	--Haddock(Melanogrammus aeglefinus)
0304.7300	--绿青鳕鱼	10	70	13	13	千克	AB	--Coalfish(Pollachius virens)
0304.7400	--狗鳕鱼（无须鳕属、长鳍鳕属）	10	70	13	13	千克	AB	--Hake(Merluccius spp. Urophycis spp.)
0304.7500	--狭鳕鱼	10	70	13	13	千克	AB	--Alaska pollack(Theragra chalcogramma)
0304.7900	--其他	10	70	13	13	千克	AB	--Other
	-其他冻鱼片：							-Other fish fillets, frozen:
0304.8100	--大麻哈鱼［红大麻哈鱼、细鳞大麻哈鱼、大麻哈鱼（种）、大鳞大麻哈鱼、银大麻哈鱼、马苏大麻哈鱼、玫瑰大麻哈鱼］、大西洋鲑鱼及多瑙哲罗鱼	10	70	13	13	千克	AB	--Pacific salmon(Oncorhynchus nerka, Oncorhynchus gorbuscha, Oncorhynchus keta, Oncorhynchus tschawytscha, Oncorhynchus kisutch, Oncorhynchus masou and Oncorhynchus rhodurus), Atlantic salmon(Salmo salar) and Danube salmon(Hucho hucho)
0304.8200	--鳟鱼（河鳟、虹鳟、克拉克大麻哈鱼、阿瓜大麻哈鱼、吉雨大麻哈鱼、亚利桑那大麻哈鱼、金腹大麻哈鱼）	10	70	13	13	千克	AB	--Trout (Salmo trutta, Oncorhynchus mykiss, Oncorhynchus clarki, Oncorhynchus aguabonita, Oncorhynchus gilae, Oncorhynchus apache and Oncorhynchus chrysogaster)
0304.8300	--比目鱼（鲽科、鲆科、舌鳎科、鳎科、菱鲆科、刺鲆科）	10	70	13	13	千克	AB	--Flat fish (Pleuronectidae, Bothidae, Cynoglossidae, Soleidae, Scophthalmidae and Citharidae)
0304.8400	--剑鱼	10	70	13	13	千克	ABU	--Swordfish(Xiphias gladius)
0304.8500	--南极犬牙鱼（南极犬牙鱼属）	10	70	13	13	千克	ABU	--Toothfish(Dissostichus spp)
0304.8600	--鲱鱼（大西洋鲱鱼、太平洋鲱鱼）	10	70	13	13	千克	AB	--Herring(Clupea harengus, clupea pallasii)
0304.8700	--金枪鱼（金枪鱼属）、鲣鱼或狐鲣（鲣）	10	70	13	13	千克	AB	--Tunas(of the genus Thunnus), skipjack or stripe-bel-lied bonito(Euthynnus[Katsuwonus)pelamis]
0304.8900	--其他	10	70	13		千克		--Other
0304.8900 10	冻的其他濒危鱼片	10	70	13		千克	ABEF	Other endangered fish fillets
0304.8900 90	冻的其他鱼片	10	70	13	13	千克	AB	Other fish fillets
	-其他，冻的：							-Other, frozen:
0304.9100	--剑鱼	10	70	13	13	千克	ABU	--Swordfish(Xiphias gladius)
0304.9200	--南极犬牙鱼（南极犬牙鱼属）	10	70	13	13	千克	ABU	--Toothfish(Dissostichus spp.)
0304.9300	--罗非鱼（口孵非鲫属）、鲶鱼（鲑鲶属、鲶属、胡鲶属、真鮰属）、鲤科鱼（西鲤、黑鲫、草鱼、鲢属、鲮属、青鱼）、鳗鱼（鳗鲡属）、尼罗河鲈鱼（尼罗尖吻鲈）及黑鱼（鳢属）	10	70	13	13	千克		-Tilapias (Oreochromis spp.), catfish (Pangasius spp., Silurus spp., Clarias spp., Ictalurus spp.), carp(Cyprinus carpio, Carassius carassius, Ctenopharyngodon idellus, Hypophthalmichthys spp., Cirrhinus spp., Mylopharyngodon piceus), eels(Anguilla spp.), Nile perch(Lates niloticus) and snakeheads (Channa spp.)
0304.9300 10	冻的花鳗鲡鱼肉（不论是否绞碎）	10	70	13	13	千克	ABE	Frozen meat of marbled eels(whether or not minced)
0304.9300 20	冻的欧洲鳗鲡鱼肉（不论是否绞碎）	10	70	13	13	千克	ABEF	Frozen meat of european eels(whether or not minced)
0304.9300 90	冻的罗非鱼（口孵非鲫属）、鲶鱼（鲑鲶属、鲶属、胡鲶属、真鮰属）、鲤科鱼（西鲤、黑鲫、草鱼、鲢属、鲮属、青鱼）、其他鳗鱼（鳗鲡属）、尼罗河鲈鱼（尼罗尖吻鲈）及黑鱼（鳢属）鱼肉（不论是否绞碎）	10	70	13	13	千克	AB	Frozen meat tilapia(oreochromis spp.), catfish(Pangasius spp., Silurus spp., Clarias spp., Ictalurus spp.), carp (Cyprinus carpio, Carassius carassius, Ctenopharyngodon idellus, Hypophthalmichthys spp., Cirrhinus spp., Mylopharyngodon piceus), eels(Aguilla spp.), nile perch(Lates niloticus) and snakeheads(Channa spp.), (whether or not minced)
0304.9400	--狭鳕鱼	10	70	13	13	千克	AB	--Alaska Pollack(Theragra chalcogramma)
0304.9500	--犀鳕科、多丝真鳕科、鳕科、长尾鳕科、黑鳕科、无须鳕科、深海鳕科及南极鳕科鱼，狭鳕鱼除外	10	70	13	13	千克	AB	--Fish of the families Bregmacerotidae, Euclichthyidae, Gadidae, Macrouridae, Melanonidae, Merlucciidae, Moridae and Muraenolepididae, other than Alaska Pollack(Theragra chalcogramma)
0304.9900	--其他	10	70	13		千克		--Other

税则号列	货品名称	最惠(%)	普通	增值税率	出口退税	计量单位	监管条件	Article Description
0304.9900 10	其他冻濒危鱼类鱼肉(不论是否绞碎)	10	70	13		千克	ABFE	Other meat of endangered fish (whether or not minced) frozen
0304.9900 90	其他冻鱼肉(不论是否绞碎)	10	70	13	13	千克	AB	Other fish meat (whether or not minced) frozen
03.05	干、盐腌或盐渍的鱼;熏鱼,不论在熏制前或熏制过程中是否烹煮;适合供人食用的鱼的细粉、粗粉及团粒:							**Fish, dried, salted or in brine; smoked fish, whether or not cooked before or during the smoking process; flours, meals and pellets of fish, fit for human consumption:**
0305.1000	-适合供人食用的鱼的细粉、粗粉及团粒	10	80	13	13,15	千克	AB	-Flours, meals and pellets of fish, fit for human consumption
0305.2000	-干、熏、盐腌或盐渍的鱼肝及鱼卵	10	80	13		千克		-Livers and roes, dried, smoked, salted or in brine
0305.2000 10	干、熏、盐制的濒危鱼种肝、卵	10	80	13		千克	ABFE	Livers and roes of endangered fish, dried, smoked, salted or in brine
0305.2000 90	其他干、熏、盐制的鱼肝及鱼卵	10	80	13	13,15	千克	AB	Other livers and roes of fish, dried, smoked, salted or in brine
	-干、盐腌或盐渍的鱼片,但熏制的除外:							-Fish fillets, dried, salted or in brine, but not smoked:
0305.3100	--罗非鱼(口孵非鲫属)、鲶鱼(𩷶鲶属、鲶属、胡鲶属、真鮰属)、鲤科鱼(西鲤、黑鲫、草鱼、鲢属、鲮属、青鱼)、鳗鱼(鳗鲡属)、尼罗河鲈鱼(尼罗尖吻鲈)及黑鱼(鳢属)	10	80	13	13,15	千克		-Tilapias (Oreochromis spp.), catfish (Pangasius spp., Silurus spp., Clarias spp., Ictalurus spp.), carp (Cyprinus carpio, Carassius carassius, Ctenopharyngodon idellus, Hypophthalmichthys spp., Cirrhinus spp., Mylopharyngodon piceus), eels (Anguilla spp.), Nile perch (Lates niloticus) and snakeheads (Channa spp.)
0305.3100 10	干、盐腌或盐渍的花鳗鲡鱼片(熏制的除外)	10	80	13	13,15	千克	ABE	Fish fillets of marbled eels, dried, salted or in brine, but not smoked
0305.3100 20	干、盐腌或盐渍的欧洲鳗鲡鱼片(熏制的除外)	10	80	13	13,15	千克	ABEF	Fish fillets of european eels, dried, salted or in brine, but not smoked
0305.3100 90	干、盐腌或盐渍的罗非鱼(口孵非鲫属)、鲶鱼(𩷶鲶属、鲶属、胡鲶属、真鮰属)、鲤科鱼(西鲤、黑鲫、草鱼、鲢属、鲮属、青鱼)、其他鳗鱼(鳗鲡属)、尼罗河鲈鱼(尼罗尖吻鲈)及黑鱼(鳢属)的鱼片(熏制的除外)	10	80	13	13,15	千克	AB	Fish fillets of tilapia (oreochromis spp.), catfish (Pangasius spp., Silurus spp., Clarias spp., Ictalurus spp.), carp (Cyprinus carpio, Carassius carassius, Ctenopharyngodon idellus, Hypophthalmichthys spp., Cirrhinus spp., Mylopharyngodon piceus), eels (Aguilla spp.), nile perch (Lates niloticus) and snakeheads (Channa spp.), dried, salted or in brine, but not smoked
0305.3200	--犀鳕科、多丝真鳕科、鳕科、长尾鳕科、黑鳕科、无须鳕科、深海鳕科及南极鳕科鱼	10	80	13	13,15	千克	AB	--Fish of the families Bregmacerotidae, Euclichthyidae, Gadidae, Macrouridae, Melanonidae, Merlucciidae, Moridae and Muraenolepididae
0305.3900	--其他	10	80	13		千克		--Other
0305.3900 10	干、盐腌或盐渍的濒危鱼类的鱼片(熏制的除外)	10	80	13		千克	FEAB	Endangered fish fillets, dried, salted or in brine (other than smoked)
0305.3900 90	其他干、盐腌或盐渍的鱼片(熏制的除外)	10	80	13	13,15	千克	AB	Other fish fillets, dried, salted or in brine (other than smoked)
	-熏鱼,包括鱼片,但食用杂碎除外:							-Smoked fish, including fillets, but excluding offal for human consumption:
	--大麻哈鱼[红大麻哈鱼、细鳞大麻哈鱼、大麻哈鱼(种)、大鳞大麻哈鱼、银大麻哈鱼、马苏大麻哈鱼、玫瑰大麻哈鱼]、大西洋鲑鱼及多瑙哲罗鱼:							----Pacific salmon (Oncorhynchus nerka, Oncorhynchus gorbuscha, Oncorhynchus keta, Oncorhynchus tschawytscha, Oncorhynchus kisutch, Oncorhynchus masou and Oncorhynchus rhodurus), Altantic salmon (salmo salar) and Danube salmon (hucho hucho):
0305.4110	---大西洋鲑鱼	14	80	13	13	千克	AB	---Atlantic salmon
0305.4120	---大马哈鱼及多瑙哲罗鱼	14	80	13	13	千克	AB	---Pacific salmon and Danube salmon
0305.4200	--鲱鱼(大西洋鲱鱼、太平洋鲱鱼)	16	80	13	13	千克	AB	--Herrings (Atlantic herring, Pacific herring)

税则号列	货品名称	最惠(%)	普通	增值税率	出口退税	计量单位	监管条件	Article Description
0305.4300	--鳟鱼(河鳟、虹鳟、克拉克大麻哈鱼、阿瓜大麻哈鱼、吉雨大麻哈鱼、亚利桑那大麻哈鱼、金腹大麻哈鱼)	14	80	13	13	千克	AB	--Trout (Salmo trutta, Oncorhynchus mykiss, Oncorhynchus clarki, Oncorhynchus aguabonita, Oncorhynchus gilae, Oncorhynchus apache and Oncorhynchus chrysogaster)
0305.4400	--罗非鱼(口孵非鲫属)、鲶鱼(鲑鲶属、鲶属、胡鲶属、真鮰属)、鲤科鱼(西鲤、黑鲫、草鱼、鲢属、鲮属、青鱼)、鳗鱼(鳗鲡属)、尼罗河鲈鱼(尼罗尖吻鲈)及黑鱼(鳢属)	14	80	13	13	千克		-Tilapias (Oreochromis spp.), catfish (Pangasius spp., Silurus spp., Clarias spp., Ictalurus spp.), carp(Cyprinus carpio, Carassius carassius, Ctenopharyngodon idellus, Hypophthalmichthys spp., Cirrhinus spp., Mylopharyngodon piceus), eels (Anguilla spp.), Nile perch (Lates niloticus) and snakeheads (Channa spp.)
0305.4400 10	熏制花鳗鲡及鱼片(食用杂碎除外)	14	80	13	13	千克	ABE	Marbled eels and fillets, smoked(other than edible for human consumption)
0305.4400 20	熏制欧洲鳗鲡及鱼片(食用杂碎除外)	14	80	13	13	千克	ABEF	European eels and fillets, smoked (other than edible for human consumption)
0305.4400 90	熏制罗非鱼(口孵非鲫属)、鲶鱼(鲑鲶属、鲶属、胡鲶属、真鮰属)、鲤科鱼(西鲤、黑鲫、草鱼、鲢属、鲮属、青鱼)、其他鳗鱼(鳗鲡属)、尼罗河鲈鱼(尼罗尖吻鲈)及黑鱼(鳢属)及鱼片(食用杂碎除外)	14	80	13	13	千克	AB	Tilapia(oreochromis spp.), catfish(Pangasius spp., Silurus spp., Clarias spp., Ictalurus spp.), carp (Cyprinus carpio, Carassius carassius, Ctenopharyngodon idellus, Hypophthalmichthys spp., Cirrhinus spp., Mylopharyngodon piceus), eels(Aguilla spp.), nile perch(Lates niloticus) and snakeheads(Channa spp.) and fillets, (other than edible for human consumption)
0305.4900	--其他	14	80	13		千克		--Other
0305.4900 20	熏制其他濒危鱼及鱼片(食用杂碎除外)	14	80	13		千克	ABEF	Other endangered fish and its fillets, smoked
0305.4900 90	其他熏鱼及鱼片(食用杂碎除外)	14	80	13	13	千克	AB	Other fish and their fillets, smoked
	-干鱼(不包括食用杂碎),不论是否盐腌,但熏制的除外:							-Dried fish, other than edible fish offal, whether or not salted but not smoked:
0305.5100	--鳕鱼(大西洋鳕鱼、格陵兰鳕鱼、太平洋鳕鱼)	16	80	13	13	千克	AB	--Cod(Gadus morhua, Gadus ogac, Gadus macrocephalus)
	--其他:							--Other:
0305.5910	---海龙、海马	2	20	13	13	千克	FEAB	---Pipefish and hippocampi
0305.5990	---其他	16	80	13		千克		---Other
0305.5990 10	其他濒危干鱼,食用杂碎除外(不论是否盐腌,但熏制的除外)	16	80	13		千克	AFEB	Other endangered fish other than edible for human consumption, dried (whether or not salted but not smoked)
0305.5990 90	其他干鱼,食用杂碎除外(不论是否盐腌,但熏制的除外)	16	80	13	13	千克	AB	Other fish other than edible for human consumption, dried (whether or not salted but not smoked)
	-盐腌及盐渍的鱼(不包括食用杂碎),但干或熏制的除外:							-Fish(excluding offal for human consumptior), salted but not dried nor smoked and fish in brine
0305.6100	--鲱鱼(大西洋鲱鱼、太平洋鲱鱼)	16	80	13	13	千克	AB	--Herrings (Atlantic herring, pacific herring)
0305.6200	--鳕鱼(大西洋鳕鱼、格陵兰鳕鱼、太平洋鳕鱼)	16	80	13	13	千克	AB	--Cod(Atlantic cod、Pacific cod、Greenland cod)
0305.6300	--鳀鱼	16	80	13	13	千克	AB	--Anchovies (*Engraulis spp.*)
0305.6400	--罗非鱼(口孵非鲫属)、鲶鱼(鲑鲶属、鲶属、胡鲶属、真鮰属)、鲤科鱼(西鲤、黑鲫、草鱼、鲢属、鲮属、青鱼)、鳗鱼(鳗鲡属)、尼罗河鲈鱼(尼罗尖吻鲈)及黑鱼(鳢属)	16	80	13	13	千克		-Tilapias (Oreochromis spp.), catfish (Pangasius spp., Silurus spp., Clarias spp., Ictalurus spp.), carp(Cyprinus carpio, Carassius carassius, Ctenopharyngodon idellus, Hypophthalmichthys spp., Cirrhinus spp., Mylopharyngodon piceus), eels (Anguilla spp.), Nile perch (Lates niloticus) and snakeheads (Channa spp.)
0305.6400 10	盐腌及盐渍的花鳗鲡,食用杂碎除外(干或熏制的除外)	16	80	13	13	千克	ABE	Marbled eels, dried, salted or in brine, other than deible for human consumption, but not smoked
0305.6400 20	盐腌及盐渍的欧洲鳗鲡,食用杂碎除外(干或熏制的除外)	16	80	13	13	千克	ABEF	European eels, dried, salted or in brine, other than deible for human consumption, but not smoked

税则号列	货 品 名 称	最惠(%)	普通	增值税率	出口退税	计量单位	监管条件	Article Description
0305. 6400 90	盐腌及盐渍的罗非鱼(口孵非鲫属)、鲶鱼(鲇鲶属、鲶属、胡鲶属、真鮰属)、鲤科鱼(西鲤、黑鲫、草鱼、鲢属、鲮属、青鱼)、其他鳗鱼(鳗鲡属)、尼罗河鲈鱼(尼罗尖吻鲈)及黑鱼(鳢属),食用杂碎除外(干或熏制的除外)	16	80	13	13	千克	AB	Tilapia(oreochromis spp.), catfish(Pangasius spp., Silurus spp., Clarias spp., Ictalurus spp.), carp (Cyprinus carpio, Carassius carassius, Ctenopharyngodon idellus, Hypophthalmichthys spp., Cirrhinus spp., Mylopharyngodon piceus), eels(Aguilla spp.), nile perch(Lates niloticus) and snakeheads(Channa spp.), other than edible for human consumption, but not smoked
	--其他:							--Other:
0305. 6910	---带鱼	16	80	13	13	千克	AB	---Scabber fish (*Trichurius*)
0305. 6920	---黄鱼	16	80	13	13	千克	AB	---Yellow croaker (*Pseudosicaena*)
0305. 6930	---鲳鱼	16	80	13	13	千克	AB	---Butterfish (*Pampus*)
0305. 6990	---其他	16	80	13		千克		---Other
0305. 6990 10	盐腌及盐渍的其他濒危鱼,食用杂碎除外(干或熏制的除外)	16	80	13		千克	ABFE	Other endangered fish, other than edible for human consuption, salted or in brine (not dried nor smoked)
0305. 6990 90	盐腌及盐渍的其他鱼,食用杂碎除外(干或熏制的除外)	16	80	13	13	千克	AB	Other fish, other than edible for human consuption salted or in brine (not dried nor smoked)
	-鱼鳍、鱼头、鱼尾、鱼鳔及其他可食用杂碎:							-Fish head、tail、maws and other edible fish offal, for human consumption:
0305. 7100	--鲨鱼翅	15	80	13	13	千克		--Shark fin
0305. 7100 10	濒危鲸鲨鱼翅(不论是否干制、盐腌、盐渍和熏制)	15	80	13	0	千克	ABEF	Sharks fins of whale(Rhincodon), man-eating shark (Cacharodon), basking shark(Cetorhinus), whether or not dried, salted, in brine and smoked
0305. 7100 90	其他的鲨鱼翅(不论是否干制、盐腌、盐渍和熏制)	15	80	13	13	千克	AB	Other sharks fins, whether or not dried, salted, in brine and smoked, whether or not dried, salted, in brine and smoked
0305. 7200	--鱼头、鱼尾、鱼鳔	16	80	13		千克		--Fish head、tail and maws
0305. 7200 10	濒危鱼的鱼头、鱼尾、鱼鳔(不论是否干制、盐腌、盐渍和熏制)	16	80	13		千克	ABEF	Endangered fish of fish head, tail and maws, whether or not dried, salted, in brine and smoked
0305. 7200 90	其他鱼的鱼头、鱼尾、鱼鳔(不论是否干制、盐腌、盐渍和熏制)	16	80	13	13	千克	AB	Other fish of fish head, tail and maws, whether or not dried, salted, in brine and smoked
0305. 7900	--其他	16	80	13		千克		--Other
0305. 7900 10	其他濒危可食用鱼杂碎(不论是否干制、盐腌、盐渍和熏制)	16	80	13		千克	ABEF	Other endangered fish edible for human consumption, whether or not dried, salted, in brine and smoked
0305. 7900 90	其他可食用鱼杂碎(不论是否干制、盐腌、盐渍和熏制)	16	80	13	13	千克	AB	Other fish edible for human consumption, whether or not dried, salted, in brine and smoked
03. 06	**带壳或去壳的甲壳动物,活、鲜、冷、冻、干、盐腌或盐渍的;熏制的带壳或去壳甲壳动物,不论是在熏制前或熏制过程中是否烹煮;蒸过或用水煮过的带壳甲壳动物,不论是否冷、冻、干、盐腌或盐渍的;适合供人食用的甲壳动物的细粉、粗粉及团粒:**							**Crustaceans, whether in shell or not, live, fresh, chilled, frozen, dried, salted or in brine; smoked crustaceans, whether or not cooked before or during the smoking process; crustaceans, in shell, cooked by steaming or by boiling in water, whether or not chilled, frozen, dried, salted or in brine; flours, meals and pellets of crustaceans, fit for human consumption**
	-冻的:							-Frozen:
0306. 1100	--岩礁虾和其他龙虾(真龙虾属、龙虾属、岩龙虾属)	10	70	13	13	千克	AB	– – Reef shrimp and shrimp(Palinurus、Lobster genus、Rock lobster genus)
0306. 1200	––鳌龙虾(鳌龙虾属)	10	70	13	13	千克	AB	--Ao lobster(Ao lobster genus)
	--蟹:							--Crabs:
0306. 1410	---梭子蟹	10	70	13	13	千克	AB	---Swimming crab
0306. 1490	---其他	10	70	13	13	千克		---Other
0306. 1490 10	冻的毛蟹、金霸王蟹(帝王蟹)、仿石蟹(仿岩蟹)、堪察加拟石蟹、短足拟石蟹、扁足拟石蟹、雪蟹、日本雪蟹	10	70	13	13	千克	ABU	Frozen hairy crab, duracell crab, king crab, imitation stone crab (imitation rock crab), Kamchatka king, short foot king, flat feet to stone crab, snow crab, snow crab, Japan

税则号列	货 品 名 称	最惠(%)	普通	增值税率	出口退税	计量单位	监管条件	Article Description
0306.1490 90	其他冻蟹	10	70	13	13	千克	AB	Other crab, frozen
0306.1500	--挪威海鳌虾	16	70	13	13	千克	AB	--Norway Lobsters(Nehrops norvegicus)
	--冷水小虾及对虾(长额虾属、褐虾):							--Cold-water shrimp and prawns (pandalus、spp., Crangon crangon):
	---冷水小虾:							---Cold-water shrimp:
0306.1611	----虾仁	8	70	13	13	千克	AB	----Shelled
0306.1612	----其他,北方长额虾	5	70	13	13	千克	AB	----Other, pandaius borealis
0306.1619	----其他	5	70	13	13	千克	AB	----Other
	---冷水对虾:							---Cold-water prawns:
0306.1621	----虾仁	8	70	13	13	千克	AB	----Shelled
0306.1629	----其他	5	70	13	13	千克	AB	----Other
	--其他小虾及对虾:							--Other shrimps and prawns:
	---小虾:							---Shrimps:
0306.1711	----虾仁	8	70	13	13	千克	AB	----Shelled
0306.1719	----其他	5	70	13	13	千克	AB	----Other
	---对虾:							---Prawns:
0306.1721	----虾仁	8	70	13	13	千克	AB	----Shelled
0306.1729	----其他	5	70	13	13	千克	AB	----Other
	--其他,包括适合供人食用的甲壳动物的细粉、粗粉及团粒:							--Other, including flours, meals and pellets of crustaceans, fit for human consumption:
	---淡水小龙虾:							---Freshwater crawfish:
0306.1911	----虾仁	16	70	13	13	千克	AB	----Shelled
0306.1919	----其他	16	70	13	13	千克	AB	----Other
0306.1990	---其他	16	70	13	13	千克	AB	---Other
	-未冻的:							-Not frozen:
	--岩礁虾和其他龙虾(真龙虾属、龙虾属、岩龙虾属):							--Reef shrimp and shrimp (Palinurus、Lobster genus、Rock lobster: genus):
0306.2110	---种苗	0	0	13	13	千克	AB	---For cultivation
0306.2190	---其他	15	70	13	13	千克	AB	---Other
	--螯龙虾(螯龙虾属):							--Ao lobster(Ao lobster genus):
0306.2210	---种苗	0	0	13	13	千克	AB	---For cultivation
0306.2290	---其他	15	70	13	13	千克	AB	---Other
	--蟹:							--Crabs:
0306.2410	---种苗	0	0	13	13	千克	AB	---For cultivation
	---其他:							---Other:
0306.2491	----中华绒螯蟹	14	70	13	13	千克	AB	----Freshwater crabs, live
0306.2492	----梭子蟹	14	70	13	13	千克	AB	----Swimming crab
0306.2499	----其他	14	70	13	13	千克		----Other
0306.2499 10	其他活、鲜、冷、干、盐腌或盐渍的带壳或去壳蟹(包括熏制的带壳或去壳的,不论在熏制前或熏制过程中是否烹煮;蒸过或用水煮过的带壳的)	14	70	13	13	千克	ABU	Other crabs, whether in shell or not, live, dried, salted or in brine(other crabs, in shell, cooked by steaming or boiling in water, whether or not chilled, frozen, dried, salted or in brine)
0306.2499 90	其他活、鲜、冷、干、盐腌或盐渍的带壳或去壳蟹(包括熏制的带壳或去壳的,不论在熏制前或熏制过程中是否烹煮;蒸过或用水煮过的带壳的)	14	70	13	13	千克	AB	The other live, fresh, cold, dry, salted or pickled crab shell or shell (other crabs, in shell, cooked by steaming or boiling in water, whether or not chilled, frozen, dried, salted or in brine)
	--挪威海螯虾:							--Norway lobsters(Nephrops norvegicus):
0306.2510	---种苗	0	0	13	13	千克	AB	---For cultivation
0306.2590	---其他	14	70	13	13,15	千克	AB	---Other
	--冷水小虾及对虾(长额虾属、褐虾):							--Cold-water shrimp and prawns (pandalus spp., Crangon crangon):
0306.2610	---种苗	0	0	13	13	千克	AB	---For cultivation
0306.2620	---鲜、冷对虾	15	70	13	13	千克	AB	---Prawns, fresh or chilled
0306.2690	---其他	12	70	13	13	千克		---Other
0306.2690 01	鲜、冷的冷水小虾	12	70	13	13	千克	AB	Cold-water shrimp, fresh or chilled

税则号列	货品名称	最惠(%)	普通	增值税率	出口退税	计量单位	监管条件	Article Description
0306.2690 90	其他活、干、盐腌或盐渍的带壳或去壳冷水对虾、冷水小虾(包括熏制的带壳或去壳的,不论在熏制前或熏制过程中是否烹煮;蒸过或用水煮过的带壳的)	12	70	13	13	千克	AB	Cold-water prawns and shrimp, whether in shell or not, live, dried, salted or in brine (including smoked, whether in shell or not, whether or not cooked before or during the smoking process; in shell, cooked by steaming or by boiling in water)
	--其他小虾及对虾:							--Other shrimps and prawns:
0306.2710	---种苗	0	0	13	13	千克	AB	---For cultivation
0306.2720	---鲜、冷对虾	15	70	13	13	千克	AB	---Prawns, fresh or chilled
0306.2790	---其他	12	70	13	13	千克		---Other
0306.2790 01	其他鲜、冷小虾	12	70	13	13	千克	AB	Other shrimp, fresh or chilled
0306.2790 90	其他活、干、盐腌或盐渍的带壳或去壳小虾及对虾(包括熏制的带壳或去壳的,不论在熏制前或熏制过程中是否烹煮;蒸过或用水煮过的带壳的)	12	70	13	13	千克	AB	Other prawns and shrimp, whether in shell or not, live, dried, salted or in brine (including smoked, whether or not cooked before or during the smoking process; in shell, cooked by steaming or by boiling in water)
	--其他,包括适合供人食用的甲壳动物的细粉、粗粉及团粒:							--Other, including flours, meals and pellets of crustaceans, fit for human consumption:
0306.2910	---种苗	0	0	13	13	千克	AB	---For cultivation
0306.2990	---其他	14	70	13	13,15	千克	AB	---Other
03.07	**带壳或去壳的软体动物,活、鲜、冷、冻、干、盐腌或盐渍的;熏制的带壳或去壳软体动物,不论在熏制前或熏制过程中是否烹煮;适合供人食用的软体动物的细粉、粗粉及团粒:**							**molluscs, whether in shell or not, live, fresh, chilled, frozen, dried, salted or in brine; smoked molluscs, whether in shell or not, whether or not cooked before or during the smoking pracess; flours, meals and pellets of mollusks, fit for human consumption:**
	-牡蛎(蚝):							-Oysters:
	--活、鲜或冷的:							--Live, fresh or chilled:
0307.1110	---种苗	0	0	13	5	千克	AB	---For cultivation
0307.1190	---其他	14	70	13	5	千克	AB	---Other
0307.1900	--其他	14	70	13	5	千克	AB	--Other
	-扇贝,包括海扇:							-Scallops, including queen scallops, of the genera *Pecten*, *Chlamys or Placopecten*:
	--活、鲜或冷的:							--Live, fresh or chilled:
0307.2110	---种苗	0	0	13	5	千克		---For cultivation
0307.2110 10	大珠母贝种苗	0	0	13	5	千克	ABE	Pearloyster (*Pinctada maxima*), for cultivation
0307.2110 90	其他扇贝种苗(包括海扇种苗)	0	0	13	5	千克	AB	Other scallops (including queen scallops) for cultivation)
0307.2190	---其他	14	70	13	5	千克		---Other
0307.2190 10	其他活、鲜、冷大珠母贝	14	70	13	5	千克	ABE	Other pearloyster (*Pinctada maxima*), live, fresh or chilled
0307.2190 90	其他活、鲜、冷扇贝(包括海扇,种苗除外)	14	70	13	5	千克	AB	Other scallops (including queen scallops, excluding for cultivation) live, fresh or chilled
0307.2900	--其他	14	80	13	13	千克		--Other
0307.2900 10	其他冻、干、盐腌或盐渍的大珠母贝(包括熏制的带壳或去壳的,不论在熏制前或熏制过程中是否烹煮)	14	80	13	13	千克	ABE	Other pearloyster (pinctada maxima), frozen, dried, salted or in brine (including smoked, in whether in shell or not, whether or not cooked before or during the smoking process)
0307.2900 90	其他冻、干、盐腌或盐渍的扇贝(包括海扇;包括熏制的带壳或去壳的,不论在熏制前或熏制过程中是否烹煮)	14	80	13	13	千克	AB	Other scallops (including queen scallops), frozen, dried, salted or in brine (including smoked, in whether in shell or not, whether or not cooked before or during the smoking process)
	-贻贝:							-Mussels (*Mytilus spp.*, *Perna spp.*):
	--活、鲜或冷的:							--Live, fresh or chilled:
0307.3110	---种苗	0	0	13	5	千克	AB	---For cultivation
0307.3190	---其他	14	70	13	5	千克		---Other
0307.3190 01	鲜、冷贻贝	14	70	13	5	千克	AB	Mussels, fresh or chilled
0307.3190 90	其他活贻贝	14	70	13	5	千克	AB	Other mussels, live

税则号列	货品名称	最惠(%)	普通	增值税率	出口退税	计量单位	监管条件	Article Description
0307.3900	--其他	14	70	13	13	千克		--Other
0307.3900 01	冻贻贝	14	70	13	13	千克	AB	Mussels, frozen
0307.3900 90	其他干、盐腌或盐渍的贻贝(包括熏制的带壳或去壳的,不论在熏制前或熏制过程中是否烹煮)	14	70	13	13	千克	AB	Other mussels, dried, salted or in brine (including smoked, in whether in shell or not, whether or not cooked before or during the smoking process)
	-墨鱼及鱿鱼:							-Cuttle fish (*Sepia officinalis*, *Rossia macrosoma*, *Sepiola spp.*) and squid (*Ommastrephes spp.*, *Loligo spp.*, *Nototodarus spp.*, *Sepioteuthis spp.*):
	--活、鲜或冷的:							--Live, fresh or chilled:
0307.4110	---种苗	0	0	13	5	千克	AB	---For cultivation
0307.4190	---其他	12	70	13	5	千克	AB	---Other
0307.4900	--其他	12	70	13	13	千克	AB	--Other
	-章鱼:							-Octopus (*Octopus spp.*):
0307.5100	--活、鲜或冷的	17	70	13	5	千克	AB	--Live, fresh or chilled
0307.5900	--其他	17	70	13	13	千克	AB	--Other
	-蜗牛及螺,海螺除外:							-Snails, other than sea snails:
0307.6010	---种苗	0	0	13		千克		---For cultivation
0307.6010 10	濒危蜗牛及螺种苗,海螺除外	0	0	13		千克	ABFE	Endangered snails, other than sea snails, for cultivation
0307.6010 90	其他蜗牛及螺种苗,海螺除外	0	0	13	5	千克	AB	Other snails, other than sea snails, for cultivation
0307.6090	---其他	14	70	13		千克		---Other
0307.6090 10	其他濒危蜗牛及螺,海螺除外	14	70	13		千克	ABFE	Other endangered snails, other than sea snails
0307.6090 90	其他活、鲜、冷、冻、干、盐腌或盐渍的蜗牛及螺,海螺除外(包括熏制的带壳或去壳的,不论在熏制前或熏制过程中是否烹煮)	14	70	13	5	千克	AB	Other snails, other than sea snails, live, fresh, chilled, frozen, dried, salted or in brine (including smoked, in whether in shell or not, whether or not cooked before or during the smoking process)
	-蛤、鸟蛤及舟贝(蚶科、北极蛤科、鸟蛤科、斧蛤科、缝栖蛤科、蛤蜊科、中带蛤科、海螂科、双带蛤科、截蛏科、竹蛏科、砗磲科、帘蛤科):							-Clam、cockle and ark shell (families arcidae、arcticidae、cardiidae、donacidae、hiatellidae、mactridae、mesodesmatidae、myidae、semelidae、solecurtidae、solenidae、tridacnidae、veneridae):
	--活、鲜或冷的:							--Live, fresh or chilled:
0307.7110	---种苗	0	0	13	5	千克		---For cultivation
0307.7110 10	活、鲜、冷砗磲的种苗	0	0	13	5	千克	ABEF	Tridacna stone, live, fresh or chilled, for cultivation -
0307.7110 90	活、鲜、冷蛤、鸟蛤及舟贝(蚶科、北极蛤科、鸟蛤科、斧蛤科、缝栖蛤科、蛤蜊科中带蛤科、海螂科、双带蛤科、截蛏科、竹蛏科、帘蛤科)的种苗	0	0	13	5	千克	AB	Clam、cockle and ark shell (arcidae、arcticidae、cardiidae、donacidae、hiatellidae、mactridae、mesodesmatidae、myidae、mesodesmatidae、solecurtidae、solenidae、tridacnidae、veneridae), live, fresh or chilled, for cultivation
	---其他:							---Other:
0307.7191	----蛤	14	70	13	5	千克	AB	----Clam
0307.7199	----其他	14	70	13	5	千克		----Other
0307.7199 10	活、鲜、冷砗磲	14	70	13	5	千克	ABEF	Tridacna stone, live, fresh or chilled
0307.7199 20	活、鲜、冷的粗饰蚶	14	70	13		千克	ABU	Live, fresh, cold coarse act the role of cockle
0307.7199 90	活、鲜、冷鸟蛤及舟贝(蚶科、北极蛤科、鸟蛤科、斧蛤科、缝栖蛤科、蛤蜊科中带蛤科、海螂科、双带蛤科、截蛏科、竹蛏科、帘蛤科)	14	70	13	5	千克	AB	Clam、cockle and ark shell (arcidae、arcticidae、cardiidae、donacidae、hiatellidae、mactridae、mesodesmatidae、myidae、mesodesmatidae、solecurtidae、solenidae、tridacnidae、veneridae), live, fresh or chilled
	--其他:							--Other:
0307.7910	---蛤	10	70	13	13	千克	AB	---Ceam
0307.7990	---其他	10	70	13	13,15	千克	AB	---Other
0307.7990 10	冻、干、盐制砗磲(包括熏制的带壳或去壳的,不论在熏制前或熏制过程中是否烹煮)	10	70	13	13,15	千克	ABEF	Tridacna stone, frozen, dried, salted (including smoked, in whether in shell or not, whether or not cooked before or during the smoking process)
0307.7990 20	冻、干、盐制的粗饰蚶(包括熏制的带壳或去壳的,不论在熏制前或熏制过程中是否烹煮)	10	70	13	13.15	千克	ABU	Cold, dry, coarse salt system ACTS the role of cockle (including smoked, in whether in shell or not, whether or not cooked before or during the smoking process)

税则号列	货 品 名 称	最惠(%)	普通	增值税率	出口退税	计量单位	监管条件	Article Description
0307.7990 90	冻、干、盐制鸟蛤及舟贝(蚶科、北极蛤科、鸟蛤科、斧蛤科、缝栖蛤科、蛤蜊科中带蛤科、海螂科、双带蛤科、截蛏科、竹蛏科、帘蛤科)(包括熏制的带壳或去壳的,不论在熏制前或熏制过程中是否烹煮)	10	70	13	13,15	千克	AB	Clam、cockle and ark shell(arcidae、arcticidae、cardiidae、donacidae、hiatellidae、mactridae、mesodesmatidae、myidae、mesodesmatidae、solecurtidae、solenidae、tridacnidae、veneridae), frozen, dried, salted (including smoked , in whether in shell or not, whether or not cooked before or during the smoking process)
	-鲍鱼(鲍属):							-Abalone(ormer):
	--活、鲜或冷的:							--Live, fresh or chilled:
0307.8110	---种苗	0	0	13	5	千克	AB	---For cultivation
0307.8190	---其他	14	80	13	5	千克	AB	---Other
0307.8900	--其他	10	80	13	13	千克	AB	--Other
	-其他,包括适合供人食用的的细粉、粗粉及团粒:							-Other, including flours, meals and pellets, fit for human consumption:
	--活、鲜或冷的:							--Live, fresh or chilled:
0307.9110	---种苗	0	0	13		千克		---For cultivation
0307.9110 10	活、鲜、冷的濒危软体动物的种苗	0	0	13		千克	AFEB	Endangered molluscs, live, fresh, chilled, for cultivation
0307.9110 90	其他活、鲜、冷的软体动物的种苗	0	0	13	5	千克	AB	Other molluscs, live, fresh, chilled, for cultivation
0307.9190	---其他	14	70	13		千克		---Other
0307.9190 10	其他活、鲜、冷的濒危软体动物	14	70	13		千克	ABEF	Other endangered molluscs, live, fresh, chilled
0307.9190 20	活、鲜、冷蚬属	14	70	13		千克	ABU	Live, fresh, cold clam
0307.9190 90	其他活、鲜、冷的软体动物	14	70	13	5	千克	AB	Other molluscs, live, fresh, chilled
0307.9900	--其他	10	70	13		千克		--Other
0307.9900 10	其他冻、干、盐腌或盐渍的濒危软体动物(包括供人食用的软体动物粉、团粒,甲壳动物除外;包括熏制的带壳或去壳的,不论在熏制前或熏制过程中是否烹煮)	10	70	13		千克	ABEF	Other endangered molluscs, frozen, dried, salted or in brine, including flours, meals and pellets of mollusks, fit for human consumption, excluding crustaceans, (including smoked, whether in shell or not, whether or not cooked ebfore or during the smoking proccess)
0307.9900 20	冻、干、盐腌或盐渍蚬属(包括供人食用的软体动物粉、团粒,甲壳动物除外;包括熏制的带壳或去壳的,不论在熏制前或熏制过程中是否烹煮)	10	70	13	0	千克	ABU	Frozen, dried, salted or pickled clam (including smoked, whether in shell or not, whether or not cooked ebfore or during the smoking proccess)
0307.9900 90	其他冻、干、盐腌或盐渍软体动物(包括供人食用的软体动物粉、团粒,甲壳动物除外;包括熏制的带壳或去壳的,不论在熏制前或熏制过程中是否烹煮)	10	70	13	13,15	千克	AB	Other molluscs, frozen, dried, salted or in brine, including flours, meals and pellets of mollusks, fit for human consumption, excluding crustaceans, (including smoked, whether in shell or not, whether or not cooked ebfore or during the smoking proccess)
03.08	**不属于甲壳动物及软体动物的水生无脊柱动物,活、鲜、冷、冻、干、盐腌或盐渍的;熏制的不属于甲壳动物及软体动物的水生无脊柱动物,不论在熏制前或熏制过程中是否烹煮;适合供人食用的不属于甲壳动物及软体动物的水生无脊柱动物的细粉、粗粉及团粒:**							**Aquatic invertebrates other than crustaceans and molluscs, live, fresh, chilled, frozen, dried, salted or in brine; smoked aquatic invertebrates other than crustaceans and molluscs, whether or not cooked before or during the smoking process; flours, meals and pellets of aquatic invertebrates other than crustaceans and molluscs, fit for human consumption:**
	-海参(仿刺参、海参纲):							-Sea cucumbers (Stichopus japonicus、holothurioidea):
	--活、鲜或冷的:							--Live, fresh and chilled:
0308.1110	---种苗	0	0	13	5	千克		---For cultivation
0308.1110 10	活、鲜或冷的暗色刺参的种苗	0	0	13	5	千克	ABEF	Isostichopus fuscus, live, fresh or chilled, for cultivation
0308.1110 90	活、鲜或冷的其他海参(仿刺参、海参纲)的种苗	0	0	13	5	千克	AB	Other sea cucumbers (Stichopus japonicus, holothurioidea), live, fresh or chilled, for cultivation
0308.1190	---其他	14	70	13	5	千克		---Other

税则号列	货品名称	最惠(%)	普通	增值税率	出口退税	计量单位	监管条件	Article Description
0308.1190 10	活、鲜或冷的暗色刺参	14	70	13	5	千克	ABEF	Isostichopus fuscus, live, fresh or chilled
0308.1190 20	活、鲜或冷的刺参(暗色刺参除外)	14	70	13	5	千克	ABU	Live, fresh trepang or cold(exceptisostichopus fuscus)
0308.1190 90	活、鲜或冷的其他海参(仿刺参、海参纲)	14	70	13	5	千克	AB	Other sea cucumbers (Stichopus japonicus, holothurioidea), live, fresh or chilled
0308.1900	--其他	10	80	13	13	千克		
0308.1900 10	其他冻、干、盐腌或盐渍暗色刺参(包括熏制的,不论在熏制前或熏制过程中是否烹煮;适合供人食用的细粉、粗粉及团粒)	10	80	13	13	千克	ABEF	Other isostichopus fuscus, frozen, dried, salted or in brine (including smoked, whether in shell or not, whether or not cooked ebfore or during the smoking proccess; fit for human consumption)
0308.1900 20	冻、干、盐腌或盐渍的刺参,暗色刺参除外(包括熏制的,不论在熏制前或熏制过程中是否烹煮;适合供人食用的细粉、粗粉及团粒)	10	80	13	13	千克	ABEFU	Frozen, dried, salted or pickled trepang, except the dark trepang (including smoked, whether in shell or not, whether or not cooked ebfore or during the smoking proccess; fit for human consumption)
0308.1900 90	其他冻、干、盐腌或盐渍的海参(仿刺参、海参纲)(包括熏制的,不论在熏制前或熏制过程中是否烹煮;适合供人食用的细粉、粗粉及团粒)	10	80	13	13	千克	AB	Other sea cucumbers (Stichopus japonicus, holothurioidea), frozen, dried, salted or in brine (including smoked, whether in shell or not, whether or not cooked ebfore or during the smoking proccess; fitfor human consumption)
	-海胆(球海胆属、拟球海胆、智利海胆、食用正海胆):							-Sea urchin (strongylocentrotus spp., paracentrotus lividus, Loxechinus albus, Echichinus esculentus):
	--活、鲜或冷的:							--Live, fresh or chilled:
0308.2110	---种苗	0	0	13	5	千克	AB	---For cultivation
0308.2190	---其他	14	70	13	5	千克		----Other
0308.2190 10	活、鲜或冷的食用海胆纲	14	70	13	5	千克	ABU	Live, fresh and cold edible echinoidea
0308.2190 90	其他活、鲜或冷的海胆(球海胆属、拟球海胆、智利海胆、食用正海胆)	14	70	13	5	千克	AB	OtherSea urchins, live, fresh, chilled, not for cultivation
0308.2900	--其他	10	70	13	13,15	千克	AB	--Other
0308.2900 10	冻、干、盐制食用海胆纲(包括熏制的,不论在熏制前或熏制过程中是否烹煮;适合供人食用的细粉、粗粉及团粒)	10	70	13		千克	ABU	Frozen, dried, salted or pickled echinoidea (including smoked, whether in shell or not, wherther or not cooked abfore or during the smoking proccess; fit for human consumption)
0308.2900 90	其他冻、干、盐制海胆(包括熏制的,不论在熏制前或熏制过程中是否烹煮;适合供人食用的细粉、粗粉及团粒)	10	70	13		千克	AB	Frozen, dried, salted or pickled other sea urchin (including smoked, whether in shell or not, wherther or not cooked abfore or during the smoking proccess; fit for human consumption)
	-海蜇(海蜇属):							-Jellyfish (Rhopilema spp.)
	---活、鲜或冷的:							---Live, fresh or chilled:
0308.3011	----种苗	0	0	13	5	千克	AB	----For cultivation
0308.3019	----其他	14	70	13	5	千克	AB	----Other
0308.3090	---其他	10	70	13	13,15	千克	AB	---Other
	-其他:							-Other:
	---活、鲜或冷的:							---Live, fresh or chilled:
0308.9011	----种苗	0	0	13		千克		----For cultivation
0308.9011 10	活、鲜或冷的其他濒危水生无脊椎动物的种苗(甲壳动物及软体动物除外)	0	0	13		千克	ABFE	Other endangered aquatic invertebrates, live, fresh or chilled, for cultivation (other than crustaceans and molluscs)
0308.9011 90	活、鲜或冷的其他水生无脊椎动物的种苗(甲壳动物及软体动物除外)	0	0	13	5	千克	AB	Other aquatic invertebrates, live, fresh or chilled, for cultivation (other than crustaceans and molluscs)
0308.9012	----沙蚕,种苗除外	14	70	13	5	千克	AB	----Clamworm, other than for cultivation
0308.9019	----其他	14	70	13		千克		----Other
0308.9019 10	活、鲜或冷的其他濒危水生无脊椎动物(甲壳动物及软体动物除外)	14	70	13		千克	ABFE	Other endangered aquatic invertebrates, live, fresh or chilled (other than crustaceans and molluscs)
0308.9019 90	活、鲜或冷的其他水生无脊椎动物(甲壳动物及软体动物除外)	14	70	13	5	千克	AB	Other aquatic invertebrates, live, fresh or chilled (other than crustaceans and molluscs)
0308.9090	---其他	10	70	13		千克		---Other

税则号列	货品名称	最惠(%)	普通	增值税率	出口退税	计量单位	监管条件	Article Description
0308.9090 10	其他冻、干、盐制濒危水生无脊椎动物,包括供人食用的水生无脊椎动物粉、团粒(甲壳动物及软体动物除外;包括熏制的,不论在熏制前或熏制过程中是否烹煮;适合供人食用的细粉、粗粉及团粒)	10	70	13		千克	ABFE	Other endangered aquatic invertebrates, frozen, dried, salted, including flours, meals and pellets of aquatic invertebrates, fit for human consumption (other than crustaceans and molluscs, including smoked, whether in shell or not, whether or not cooked ebfore or during the smoking proccess; flours, meals and pellets fit for human consumption)
0308.9090 90	其他冻、干、盐制水生无脊椎动物,包括供人食用的水生无脊椎动物粉、团粒(甲壳动物及软体动物除外;包括熏制的,不论在熏制前或熏制过程中是否烹煮;适合供人食用的细粉、粗粉及团粒)	10	70	13	13,15	千克	AB	Other aquatic invertebrates, frozen, dried, salted, including flours, meals and pellets of aquatic invertebrates, fit for human consumption (other than crustaceans and molluscs, including smoked, whether in shell or not, whether or not cooked ebfore or during the smoking proccess; flours, meals and pellets fit for human consumption)

第四章
乳品;蛋品;天然蜂蜜;其他食用动物产品

Chapter 4
Dairy produce; birds eggs; natural honey; edible products of animal origin, not elsewhere specified or included

注释:

一、所称"乳",是指全脂乳及半脱脂或全脱脂的乳。

二、税目04.05所称:

(一)"黄油",仅指从乳中提取的天然黄油、乳清黄油及调制黄油(淡的、加盐或酸败的,包括罐装黄油),按重量计乳脂含量在80%及以上,但不超过95%,乳的无脂固形物最大含量不超过2%,以及水的最大含量不超过16%。黄油中不含添加的乳化剂,但可含有氯化钠、食用色素、中和盐及无害乳酸菌的培养物。

(二)"乳酱"是一种油包水型可涂抹的乳状物,乳脂是该制品所含的唯一脂肪,按重量计其含量在39%及以上,但小于80%。

三、乳清经浓缩并加入乳或乳脂制成的产品,若同时具有下列三种特性,则视为乳酪归入税目04.06:

(一)按干重计乳脂含量在5%及以上的;

(二)按重量计干质成分至少为70%,但不超过85%的;

(三)已成形或可以成形的。

四、本章不包括:

(一)按重量计乳糖含量(以干燥无水乳糖计)超过95%的乳清制品(税目17.02);

(二)白蛋白(包括按重量计干质成分的乳清蛋白含量超过80%的两种或两种以上的乳清蛋白浓缩物)(税目35.02)及球蛋白(税目35.04)。

Notes:

1. The expression "milk" means full cream milk or partially or completely skimmed milk.
2. For the purposes of heading No. 04.05:
   (a) The term "butter" means natural butter, whey butter or recombined butter (fresh, salted or rancid, including canned butter) derived exclusively from milk, with a milkfat content of 80% or more but not more than 95% by weight, a maximum milk solids-not-fvat content of 2% by weight and a maximum water content of 16% by weight. Butter does not contain added emulsifiers, but may contain sodium chloride, food colours, neutralising salts and cultures of harmless lactic-acid-producing bacteria.
   (b) The expression "dairy spreads" means a spreadable emulsion of the water-in-oil type, containing milkfat as the only fat in the product, with a milkfat content of 39% or more but less than 80% by weight.
3. Products obtained by the concentration of whey and with the addition of milk or milkfat are to be classified as cheese in heading No. 04.06. Provided that they have the three following characteristics:
   (a) A milkfat content, by weight of the dry matter, of 5% or more;
   (b) A dry matter content, by weight, of at least 70% but not exceeding 85%; and
   (c) They are moulded or capable of being moulded.
4. This Chapter does not cover:
   (a) Products obtained from whey, containing by weight more than 95% lactose, expressed as anhydrous lactose calculated on the dry matter (heading No. 17.02); or
   (b) Albumins (including concentrates of two or more whey proteins, containing by weight more than 80% whey proteins, calculated on the dry matter) (heading No. 35.02) or globulins (heading No. 35.04)

子目注释:

一、子目号0404.10所称"改性乳清",是指由乳清成分构成的制品,即全部或部分去除乳糖、蛋白或矿物质的乳清、加入天然乳清成分的乳清及由混入天然乳清成分制成的产品。

二、子目0405.10所称"黄油",不包括脱水黄油及印度酥油(子目号0405.90)。

Subheading Notes:

1. For the purpose of subheading No. 0404.10, the expression "modified whey" means products consisting of whey constituents, that is, whey from which all or part of the lactose, proteins or minerals have been removed, whey to which natural whey constituents have been added and products obtained by mixing natural whey constituents.
2. For the purposes of subheading No. 0405.10 the term "butter" does not include dehydrated butter or ghee (subheading No. 0405.90).

税则号列	货品名称	最惠(%)	普通	增值税率	出口退税	计量单位	监管条件	Article Description
04.01	未浓缩及未加糖或其他甜物质的乳及奶油:							**Milk and cream, not concentrated nor containing added sugar or other sweetening matter:**
0401.1000	-按重量计脂肪含量不超过1%	15	40	17	5,15	千克	7AB	-Of a fat content, by weight, not exceeding 1%
0401.2000	-按重量计脂肪含量超过1%,但不超过6%	15	40	17	5,15	千克	7AB	-Of a fat content, by weight, exceeding 1% but not exceeding 6%
0401.4000	-按重量计脂肪含量超过6%,但不超过10%	15	40	17	5,15	千克	7AB	-Of a fat content, by weight, exceeding 6%, but not exceeding 10%
0401.5000	-按重量计脂肪含量超过10%	15	40	17	5,15	千克	7AB	-Of a fat content, by weight, exceeding 10%
04.02	浓缩、加糖或其他甜物质的乳及奶油:							**Milk and cream, concentrated or containing added sugar or other sweetening matter:**

税则号列	货品名称	最惠(%)	普通	增值税率	出口退税	计量单位	监管条件	Article Description
0402.1000	-粉状、粒状或其他固体形状,按重量计脂肪含量不超过1.5%	10	40	17	15	千克	7AB	-In powder, granules or other solid forms, of a fat content, by weight, not exceeding 1.5%
	-粉状、粒状或其他固体形状,按重量计脂肪含量超过1.5%:							-In powder, granules or other solid forms, of a fat content, by weight, exceeding 1.5%:
0402.2100	--未加糖或其他甜物质	10	40	17	15	千克	7AB	--Not containing added sugar or other sweetening matter
0402.2900	--其他	10	40	17	15	千克	7AB	--Other
	-其他:							-Other:
0402.9100	--未加糖或其他甜物质	10	90	17	5,15	千克	AB	--Not containing added sugar or other sweetening matter
0402.9900	--其他	10	90	17	5,15	千克	AB	--Other
04.03	**酪乳、结块的乳及奶油、酸乳、酸乳酒及其他发酵或酸化的乳和奶油,不论是否浓缩、加糖、加其他甜物质、加香料、加水果、加坚果或加可可:**							**Buttermilk, curdled milk and cream, yogurt, kephir and other fermented or acidified milk and cream, whether or not concentrated or containing added sugar or other sweetening matter or flavoured or containing added fruit, nuts or cocoa:**
0403.1000	-酸乳	10	90	17	15	千克	AB	-Yogurt
0403.9000	-其他	20	90	17	15	千克	AB	-Other
04.04	**乳清,不论是否浓缩、加糖或其他甜物质;其他税目未列名的含天然乳的产品,不论是否加糖或其他甜物质:**							**Whey, whether or not concentrated or containing added sugar or other sweetening matter; products consisting of natural milk constituents, whether or not containing added sugar or other sweetening matter, not elsewhere specified or included:**
0404.1000暂	-乳清及改性乳清,不论是否浓缩、加糖或其他甜物质	2	30	17	15	千克	AB	-Whey and modified whey, whether or not concentrated or containing added sugar or other sweetening matter
0404.9000	-其他	20	90	17	15	千克	AB	-Other
04.05	**黄油及其他从乳中提取的脂和油;乳酱:**							**Butter and other fats and oils derived from milk; dairy spreads:**
0405.1000	-黄油	10	90	17	15	千克	AB	-Butter
0405.2000	-乳酱	10	90	17	15	千克	AB	-Dairy spreads
0405.9000	-其他	10	90	17	15	千克	AB	-Other
04.06	**乳酪及凝乳:**							**Cheese and curd:**
0406.1000	-鲜乳酪(未熟化或未固化的),包括乳清乳酪;凝乳	12	90	17	15	千克	AB	-Fresh (unripened or uncured) cheese, including whey cheese, and curd
0406.2000	-各种磨碎或粉化的乳酪	12	90	17	15	千克	AB	-Grated or powdered cheese, of all kinds
0406.3000	-经加工的乳酪,但磨碎或粉化的除外	12	90	17	15	千克	AB	-Processed cheese, not grated or powdered
0406.4000	-蓝纹乳酪和娄地青霉生产的带有纹理的其他乳酪	15	90	17	15	千克	AB	-Blue-veined cheese and other cheese containing veins produced by *Penicillium roqueforti*
0406.9000	-其他乳酪	12	90	17	15	千克	AB	-Other cheese
04.07	**带壳禽蛋,鲜、腌制或煮过的:**							**Birds' eggs, in shell, fresh, preserved or cooked:**
	-孵化用受精禽蛋:							-Fertilised eggs for incubation:
0407.1100	--鸡的	0	0	13		千克/个		--Of fowls of the species Gallus domesticus
0407.1100 10	孵化用受精的濒危鸡的蛋	0	0	13		千克/个	AFEB	Of endangered hen's fertilised eggs for incubation
0407.1100 90	孵化用受精的其他鸡的蛋	0	0	13	5	千克/个	AB	Of hen's fertilised eggs for incubation
0407.1900	--其他	0	0	13		千克/个		--Other
0407.1900 10	其他孵化用受精濒危禽蛋	0	0	13		千克/个	AFEB	Other fertilised endangered eggs for incubation
0407.1900 90	其他孵化用受精禽蛋	0	0	13	5	千克/个	AB	Other fertilised eggs for incubation
	-其他鲜蛋:							-Other eggs, fresh:
0407.2100	--鸡的	20	80	13	5	千克/个	AB	--Of fowls of the species Gallus domesticus
0407.2900	--其他	20	80	13		千克/个		--Other
0407.2900 10	其他鲜的带壳濒危禽蛋	20	80	13		千克/个	ABFE	Other endangered birds' eggs, in shell, fresh
0407.2900 90	其他鲜的带壳禽蛋	20	80	13	5	千克/个	AB	Other birds' eggs, in shell, fresh
	-其他:							-Other:
0407.9010	---咸蛋	20	90	13	5	千克/个	AB	---Salted eggs
0407.9020	---皮蛋	20	90	13	5	千克/个	AB	---Lime-preserved eggs

税则号列	货　品　名　称	最惠(%)	普通	增值税率	出口退税	计量单位	监管条件	Article Description
0407.9090	---其他	20	90	13		千克/个		---Other
0407.9090 10	其他腌制或煮过的带壳濒危野鸟蛋	20	90	13		千克/个	ABFE	Other endangered wild birds' eggs, in shell, preserved or cooked
0407.9090 90	其他腌制或煮过的带壳禽蛋	20	90	13	5,15	千克/个	AB	Other birds' eggs, in shell, preserved or cooked
04.08	**去壳禽蛋及蛋黄，鲜、干、冻、蒸过或水煮、制成型或用其他方法保藏的，不论是否加糖或其他甜物质：**							**Birds' eggs, not in shell, and egg yolks, fresh, dried, cooked by steaming or by boiling in water, moulded, frozen or otherwise preserved, whether or not containing added sugar or other sweetening matter:**
	-蛋黄：							-Egg yolks:
0408.1100	--干的	20	90	13	5,15	千克	AB	--Dried
0408.1900	--其他	20	90	13	5	千克	AB	--Other
	-其他：							-Other:
0408.9100	--干的	20	90	13	5,15	千克	AB	--Dried
0408.9900	--其他	20	90	13	5,15	千克	AB	--Other
04.09	**天然蜂蜜：**							**Natural honey:**
0409.0000	天然蜂蜜	15	80	13	5	千克	AB	Natural honey
04.10	**其他税目未列名的食用动物产品：**							**Edible products of animal origin, not elsewhere specified or included:**
0410.0010	---燕窝	25	80	17	5	千克	AB	---Salanganes' nests
	---蜂产品：							---Bee products:
0410.0041	----鲜蜂王浆	15	70	13	5	千克	AB	----Pure royal jelley
0410.0042	----鲜蜂王浆粉	15	70	17	5	千克	AB	----Pure royal jelley, in powder
0410.0043	----蜂花粉	20	70	17	5	千克	AB	----Bee pollen
0410.0049	----其他	20	70	17	5	千克	AB	----Other
0410.0090	---其他	20	70	17		千克		---Other
0410.0090 10	其他编号未列名濒危野生动物产品（食用）	20	70	17		千克	ABFE	Other edible products of endangered wild animals origin, not elsewhere specified or included
0410.0090 90	其他编号未列名的食用动物产品	20	70	17	5	千克	AB	Other edible products of animals origin, not elsewhere specified or included

第五章
其他动物产品

Chapter 5
Products of animal origin, not elsewhere specified or included

注释：

一、本章不包括：

（一）食用产品（整个或切块的动物肠、膀胱和胃以及液态或干制的动物血除外）；

（二）生皮或毛皮（第四十一章、第四十三章），但税目 05.05 的货品及税目 05.11 的生皮或毛皮的边角废料仍归入本章；

（三）马毛及废马毛以外的动物纺织原料（第十一类）；

（四）供制帚、制刷用的成束、成簇的材料（税目 96.03）。

二、仅按长度而未按发根和发梢整理的人发，视为未加工品，归入税目 05.01。

三、本目录所称"兽牙"，是指象、河马、海象、一角鲸和野猪的长牙、犀角及其他动物的牙齿。

四、本目录所称"马毛"，是指马科、牛科动物的鬃毛和尾毛。

Notes:

1. This Chapter does not cover:
(a) Edible products (other than guts, bladders and stomachs of animals, whole and pieces thereof, and animal blood, liquid or dried);
(b) Hides or skins (including furskins) other than goods of heading No. 05.05 and parings and similar waste of raw hides or skins of heading No. 05.11 (Chapter 41 or 43)
(c) Animal textile materials, other than horsehair and horsehair waste (Section XI); or
(d) Prepared knots or tufts for broom or brush making (heading No. 96.03).
2. For the purposes of heading No. 05.01, the sorting of human hair by length (provided the root ends and tip ends respectively are not arranged together) shall be deemed not to constitute working.
3. Throughout the Nomenclature, elephant, hippopotamus, walrus, narwhal and wild boar tusks, rhinoceros horns and the teeth of all animals are regarded as "ivory".
4. Throughout the Nomenclature, the expression "horsehair" means hair of the manes or tails of equine or bovine animals.

税则号列	货品名称	最惠(%)	普通	增值税率	出口退税	计量单位	监管条件	Article Description
05.01	未经加工的人发，不论是否洗涤；废人发：							**Human hair, unworked, whether or not washed or scoured; waste of human hair:**
0501.0000	未经加工的人发；废人发（不论是否洗涤）	15	90	17	15	千克	B9	Human hair, unworked, whether or not washed or scoured; waste of human hair
05.02	猪鬃、猪毛；獾毛及其他制刷用兽毛；上述鬃毛的废料：							**Pigs', hogs', or boars', bristles and hair; badger hair and other brush making hair; waste of such bristles or hair:**
	-猪鬃、猪毛及其废料：							-Pigs', hogs', or boars', bristles and hair and waste thereof:
0502.1010	---猪鬃	20	90	13	5,15	千克	AB	---Bristles
0502.1020	---猪毛	20	90	13	5,15	千克	AB	---Hair
0502.1030	---废料	20	90	13	5	千克	B9	---Waste
	-其他：							-Other:
	---獾毛及其他制刷用兽毛：							---Badger hair and other brush making hair:
0502.9011	----山羊毛	20	90	13	5,15	千克	AB	----Goat hair
0502.9012	----黄鼠狼尾毛	20	90	13	5,15	千克	ABEF	----Weasel tail hair
0502.9019	----其他	20	90	13		千克		----Other
0502.9019 10	濒危獾毛及其他制刷用濒危兽毛	20	90	13		千克	ABFE	Endangered badger hair and other brush making hair of endangered animals
0502.9019 90	其他獾毛及其他制刷用兽毛	20	90	13	5,15	千克	AB	Other badger hair and other brush making hair of other animal
0502.9020	---废料	20	90	13		千克		---Waste
0502.9020 10	濒危獾毛及其他制刷濒危兽毛废料	20	90	13		千克	BEF	Waste of endangered badger hair and other brush making hair of endangered animals
0502.9020 90	其他獾毛及其他制刷用兽毛的废料	20	90	13	5	千克	9B	Waste of badger hair and other brush making hair of other animals
05.04	整个或切块的动物（鱼除外）的肠、膀胱及胃，鲜、冷、冻、干、熏、盐腌或盐渍的：							**Guts, bladders and stomachs of animals (other than fish), whole and pieces thereof, fresh, chilled, frozen, salted, in brine, dried or smoked:**
	---肠衣：							---Casings:

税则号列	货品名称	最惠(%)	普通	增值税率	出口退税	计量单位	监管条件	Article Description
0504.0011	----盐渍猪肠衣(猪大肠头除外)	20	90	13	13	千克	AB	----Hog casings, salted(excluding hog fat - ends)
0504.0012	----盐渍绵羊肠衣	18	90	13	13	千克	AB	----Sheep casings, salted
0504.0013	----盐渍山羊肠衣	18	90	13	13	千克	AB	----Goat casings, salted
0504.0014	----盐渍猪大肠头	20	90	13	13	千克	AB	----Hog fat-ends, salted
0504.0019	----其他	18	90	13	13	千克	AB	----Other
	---胃:							---Gizzard:
0504.0021	----冷、冻的鸡胗	T2	T2	13	5	千克	7AB	----Cold, frozen gizzard
0504.0029	----其他	20	90	13	5	千克	AB	----Other
0504.0090	---其他	20	80	13	5	千克	AB	---Other
05.05	**带有羽毛或羽绒的鸟皮及鸟体其他部分;羽毛及不完整羽毛(不论是否修边)、羽绒,仅经洗涤、消毒或为了保藏而作过处理,但未经进一步加工;羽毛或不完整羽毛的粉末及废料:**							**Skins and other parts of birds, with their feathers or down; feathers and parts of feathers (whether or not with trimmed edges) and down, not further worked than cleaned, disinfected or treated for preservation; powder and waste of feathers or parts of feathers:**
0505.1000暂	-填充用羽毛;羽绒	5	100	13		千克		-Feathers of a kind used for stuffing; down
0505.1000暂 10	填充用濒危野生禽类羽毛、羽绒(仅经洗涤、消毒等处理,未进一步加工)	5	100	13		千克	ABFE	Feathers of endangered wild birds, of a kind used for stuffing; down(not further worked than cleaned, disinfected or treated for preservation)
0505.1000暂 90	其他填充用羽毛;羽绒(仅经洗涤、消毒等处理,未进一步加工)	5	100	13	5,15	千克	AB	Feathers of other birds, of a kind used for stuffing; down(not further worked than cleaned, disinfected or treated for preservation)
	-其他:							-Other:
0505.9010	---羽毛或不完整羽毛的粉末及废料	10	35	13	5	千克	9AB	---Powder and waste of feathers or parts of feathers
0505.9090	---其他	10	90	13		千克		---Other
0505.9090 10	其他濒危野生禽类羽毛、羽绒(包括带有羽毛或羽绒的鸟皮及鸟体的其他部分)	10	90	13		千克	AFEB	Feathers and down of endangered wild birds (including skins and other parts of birds, with their feathers or down)
0505.9090 90	其他羽毛、羽绒(包括带有羽毛或羽绒的鸟皮及鸟体的其他部分)	10	90	13	5,15	千克	AB	Feathers and down of other birds (including skins and other parts of birds, with their feathers or down)
05.06	**骨及角柱,未经加工或经脱脂、简单整理(但未切割成形)、酸处理或脱胶;上述产品的粉末及废料:**							**Bones and horn-cores, unworked, defatted, simply prepared (but not cut to shape), treated with acid or degelatinized; powder and waste of these products:**
0506.1000	-经酸处理的骨胶原及骨	12	50	17		千克	AB	-Ossein and bones treated with acid
	-其他:							-Other:
	---骨粉、骨废料:							---Powder and waste of bones:
0506.9011	----含牛羊成分的	12	35	17		千克		----Of bovine and sheep
0506.9011 10	含牛羊成分的骨废料(未经加工或仅经脱脂等加工的)	12	35	17		千克	9AB	Waste of bones, containing bovine composition or sheep and goats composition(unworked, defatted, simply prepared)
0506.9011 90	含牛羊成分的骨粉(未经加工或仅经脱脂等加工的)	12	35	17		千克	AB	Powder of bones, containing bovine composition or sheep and goats composition (unworked, defatted, simply prepared)
0506.9019	----其他	12	35	17		千克		----Other
0506.9019 10	其他骨废料(未经加工或仅经脱脂等加工的)	12	35	17		千克	9AB	Other waste of bones (unworked, defatted, simply prepared)
0506.9019 90	其他骨粉(未经加工或仅经脱脂等加工的)	12	35	17		千克	AB	Other powder of bones(unworked, defatted, simply prepared)
0506.9090	---其他	12	50	13		千克		---Other
0506.9090 11	已脱胶的虎骨(指未经加工或经脱脂等加工的)	12	50	13		千克	89	Tiger-bone (*as tigris*), degelatinized(unworked, defatted, simply prepared)
0506.9090 19	未脱胶的虎骨(指未经加工或经脱脂等加工的)	12	50	13		千克	89	Tiger-bone (*as tigirs*), not degelatinized(unworked, defatted, simply prepared)
0506.9090 21	已脱胶的豹骨(指未经加工或经脱脂等加工的)	12	50	13		千克	ABFE	Leopard-bone, degelatinized (unworked, defatted, simply prepared)
0506.9090 29	未脱胶的豹骨(指未经加工或经脱脂等加工的)	12	50	13		千克	ABFE	Leopard-bone, not degelatinized (unworked, defatted, simply prepared)

税则号列	货品名称	最惠(%)	普通	增值税率	出口退税	计量单位	监管条件	Article Description
0506.9090 31	已脱胶的濒危野生动物的骨及角柱(不包括虎骨、豹骨,指未经加工或经脱脂等加工的)	12	50	13		千克	AFEB	Bones and horn-cores of endangered wild animals, degelatinized (other than tiger-bone, leopard-bone, unworked, defatted, simply prepared)
0506.9090 39	未脱胶的濒危野生动物的骨及角柱(不包括虎骨、豹骨,指未经加工或经脱脂等加工的)	12	50	13		千克	AFEB	Bones and horn-cores of endangered wild animals, not degelatinized (other than tiger-bone, leopard-bone, unworked, defatted, simply prepared)
0506.9090 91	已脱胶的其他骨及角柱(不包括虎骨、豹骨,指未经加工或经脱脂等加工的)	12	50	13		千克	AB	Bones and horn-cores of other animals, degelatinized (other than tiger-bone, leopard-bone, unworked, defatted, simply prepared)
0506.9090 99	未脱胶的其他骨及角柱(不包括虎骨、豹骨,指未经加工或经脱脂等加工的)	12	50	13		千克	AB	Bones and horn-cores of other animals, not degelatinized (other than tiger-bone, leopard-bone, unworked, defatted, simply prepared)
05.07	兽牙、龟壳、鲸须、鲸须毛、角、鹿角、蹄、甲、爪及喙,未经加工或仅简单整理但未切割成形;上述产品的粉末及废料:							**Ivory, tortoise-shell, whalebone and whalebone hair, horns, antlers, hooves, nails, claws and beaks, unworked or simply prepared but not cut to shape; powder and waste of these products:**
0507.1000	-兽牙;兽牙粉末及废料	10	30	13		千克		-Ivory; ivory powder and waste
0507.1000 10	犀牛角	10	30	13	5	千克	89	Rhinocerus horn (*cornu rhinocerotis*)
0507.1000 20	其他濒危野生兽牙、兽牙粉末及废料	10	30	13		千克	AFEB	Ivory, ivory powder and waste thereof of other endangered wild animals
0507.1000 30	其他兽牙	10	30	13	5	千克	AB	Other ivory
0507.1000 90	其他兽牙粉末及废料	10	30	13	5	千克	9AB	Other ivory powedr and waste thereof
	-其他:							-Other:
0507.9010	---羚羊角及其粉末和废料	3	14	13	5	千克	ABFE	---Antelope horns and powder or waste thereof
0507.9020	---鹿茸及其粉末	11	30	13	5	千克	ABFE	---Pilose antlers and powder thereof
0507.9090	---其他	10	50	13	5	千克	AFEB	---Other
05.08	珊瑚及类似品,未经加工或仅简单整理但未经进一步加工;软体动物壳、甲壳动物壳、棘皮动物壳、墨鱼骨,未经加工或仅简单整理但未切割成形,上述壳、骨的粉末及废料:							**Coral and similar materials, unworked or simply prepared but not otherwise worked; shells of molluscs, crustaceans or echinoderms and cuttle-bone, unworked or simply prepared but not cut to shape, powder and waste thereof:**
0508.0010	---粉末及废料	12	35	13		千克		---Powder and waste
0508.0010 10	珊瑚及濒危水产品的粉末、废料(包括介、贝、棘皮动物壳,不包括墨鱼骨的粉末及废料)	12	35	13		千克	AFEB	Powder and waste of endangered aquatic product (including shells of molluscs, crustaceans or echinoderms and cuttle-bone)
0508.0010 90	其他水产品壳、骨的粉末及废料(包括介、贝、棘皮动物壳、墨鱼骨的粉末及废料)	12	35	13	5	千克	AB	Powder and waste of other aquatic products (including shells of molluscs, crustaceans or echinoderms and cuttle-bone)
0508.0090	---其他	12	50	13		千克		---Other
0508.0090 10	珊瑚及濒危水产品的壳、骨(包括介、贝、棘皮动物的壳,不包括墨鱼骨)	12	50	13		千克	AFEB	Shells ,bone of endangered coral and endangered aquatic products (including shells of molluscs, crustaceans or echinoderms and cuttle-bone)
0508.0090 90	其他水产品的壳、骨(包括介、贝、棘皮动物的壳、不包括墨鱼骨)	12	50	13	5	千克	AB	Shells and bone of other aquatic products (including shells of molluscs, crustaceans or echinoderms and cuttle-bone)
05.10	龙涎香、海狸香、灵猫香及麝香;斑蝥;胆汁,不论是否干制;供配制药用的腺体及其他动物产品,鲜、冷、冻或用其他方法暂时保藏的:							**Ambergris, castoreum, civet and musk; cantharides; bile, whether of not dried; glands and other animal products used in the preparation of pharmaceutical products, fresh, chilled, frozen or otherwise provisionally preserved:**
0510.0010	---黄药	3	14	13	5	千克		---Bezoar
0510.0010 10	牛黄	3	14	13	5	千克	8A	Calculus bovis
0510.0010 20	猴枣	3	14	13	5	千克	QAFEB	Calculus macaca mulatta
0510.0010 90	其他黄药(不包括牛黄)	3	14	13	5	千克	AFEB	Other bezoar (excluding calculus bovis)
0510.0020	---龙涎香、海狸香、灵猫香	7	50	13	5	千克	AFEB	---Ambergris, castoreum and civet
0510.0020 10	海狸香、灵猫香	7	50	13	5	千克	ABEF	castoreum and civet

税则号列	货品名称	最惠(%)	普通	增值税率	出口退税	计量单位	监管条件	Article Description
0510.0020 20	龙涎香	7	50	13	5	千克	AB	Ambergris
0510.0030	---麝香	7	20	13		千克	8AF	---Musk
0510.0040	---斑蝥	7	50	13	5	千克	QAB	---Cantharides
0510.0090	---其他	6	20	13		千克		---Other
0510.0090 10	其他濒危野生动物胆汁及其他产品(不论是否干制;鲜、冷、冻或用其他方法暂时保藏的)	6	20	13		千克	AFEB	Bile and other products of other endangered wild animals(whether or not dried, fresh, chilled, frozen or otherwise provisionally preserved)
0510.0090 90	胆汁,配药用腺体及其他动物产品(不论是否干制;鲜、冷、冻或用其他方法暂时保藏的)	6	20	13	5	千克	AB	Bile, glands and other animal products used in the preparation of pharmaceutical products (whether or not dried, fresh, chilled, frozen or otherwise provisionally preserved)
05.11	**其他税目未列名的动物产品;不适合供人食用的第一章或第三章的死动物:**							**Animal products not elsewhere specified or included; dead animals of Chapter 1 or 3, unfit for human consumption:**
0511.1000	-牛的精液	0	0	13		千克		-Bovine semen
0511.1000 10	濒危野生牛的精液	0	0	13		千克	ABFE	Semen of endangered wild bovine
0511.1000 90	其他牛的精液	0	0	13	5	千克	AB	Other bovine semen
	-其他:							-Other:
	--鱼、甲壳动物、软体动物、其他水生无脊椎动物的产品;第三章的死动物:							--Products of fish or crustaceans, molluscs or other aquatic invertebrates; dead animals of Chapter 3:
	---鱼的:							---Fish:
0511.9111暂	----受精鱼卵	0	35	13		千克		----Fertilized fish eggs
0511.9111暂 10	濒危鱼的受精卵	0	35	13		千克	ABFE	Fertilized eggs of endangered fish
0511.9111暂 90	其他受精鱼卵	0	35	13	5	千克	AB	Other fertilized fish eggs
0511.9119	----其他	12	35	13		千克		----Other
0511.9119 10	濒危鱼的非食用产品(包括鱼肚)	12	35	13		千克	ABFE	Products of endangered fish(including fish maw) unfit for human consumption
0511.9119 90	其他鱼的非食用产品(包括鱼肚)	12	35	13	5	千克	AB	Products of other fish (including fish maw) unfit for human consumption
0511.9190	---其他	12	35	13		千克		---Other
0511.9190 10	濒危水生无脊椎动物产品(包括甲壳动物、软体动物、第三章死动物)	12	35	13		千克	ABFE	Products of endangererd crustaceans molluscs or other aquatic invertebrates; dead animals of Chapter 3
0511.9190 90	其他水生无脊椎动物产品(包括甲壳动物、软体动物、第三章死动物)	12	35	13	5	千克	AB	Other products of crustaceans, molluscs or other aquatic invertebrates; dead animals of Chapter 3
	--其他:							--Other:
0511.9910	---动物精液(牛的精液除外)	0	0	13		千克		---Animal semen, other than bovine semen
0511.9910 10	濒危野生动物精液(牛的精液除外)	0	0	13		千克	AFEB	Semen of endangered wild animals(other than bovine semen)
0511.9910 90	其他动物精液(牛的精液除外)	0	0	13	5	千克	AB	Semen of other animals (other than bovine semen)
0511.9920	---动物胚胎	0	0	13		千克		---Animal embryo
0511.9920 10	濒危野生动物胚胎	0	0	13		千克	AFEB	Embryo of endangered wild animals
0511.9920 90	其他动物胚胎	0	0	13	5	千克	AB	Embryo of other animals
0511.9930	---蚕种	0	0	13	5	千克	AB	---Silkworm graine
0511.9940	---马毛及废马毛,不论是否制成有或无衬垫的毛片	15	90	13	5,15	千克		---Horsehair and horsehair waster, whether or not put up as a layer with or without supporting material
0511.9940 10	废马毛(不论是否制成有或无衬垫的毛片)	15	90	13	5,15	千克	9B	Horsehair waster (whether or not put up as a lalyer with or without supporting material)
0511.9940 90	其他马毛(不论是否制成有或无衬垫的毛片)	15	90	13	5,15	千克	AB	Other horsehair (whether or not put up as a lalyer with or without supporting material)
0511.9990	---其他	12	35	13		千克		---Other
0511.9990 10	其他编号未列名濒危野生动物产品(包括不适合供人食用的第一章的死动物)	12	35	13		千克	AFEB	Products of endangered wild animals, not elsewhere specified or included (including dead animals of Chapter 1, unfit for human consumption)
0511.9990 90	其他编号未列名的动物产品(包括不适合供人食用的第一章的死动物)	12	35	13	5	千克	AB	Animal products not elsewhere specified or included(including dead animals of Chapter 1, unfit for human consumption)

第二类 植物产品

SECTION Ⅱ VEGETABLE PRODUCTS

注释：

本类所称"团粒"，是指直接挤压或加入按重量计比例不超过3%的黏合剂制成的粒状产品。

Notes:

In this Section the term "pellets" means products which have been agglomerated either directly by compression or by the addition of a binder in a proportion not exceeding 3% by weight.

第六章 活树及其他活植物；鳞茎、根及类似品；插花及装饰用簇叶

Chapter 6 Live trees and other plants; bulbs, roots and the like; cut flowers and ornamental foliage

注释：

一、除税号06.01的菊苣植物及其根以外，本章包括通常由苗圃或花店供应为种植或装饰用的活树及其他货品（包括植物秧苗）；但不包括马铃薯、洋葱、青葱、大蒜及其他第七章的产品。

二、税号06.03、06.04的各种货品，包括全部或部分用这些货品制成的花束、花篮、花圈及类似品，不论是否有其他材料制成的附件。但这些货品不包括税号97.01的拼贴画或类似的装饰板。

Notes:

1. Subject to the second part of heading No. 06.01 this Chapter covers only live trees and goods (including seeding vegetables) of a kind commonly supplied by nursery gardeners or florists for planting or for ornamental use; nevertheless it does not include potatoes, onions, shallots, garlic or other products of Chapter 7.

2. Any reference in heading No. 06.03 or 06.04 to goods of any kind shall be construed as including a reference to bouquets, floral baskets, wreaths and similar articles made wholly or partly of goods of that kind, account not being taken of accessories of other materials. However, these headings do not include collages or similar decorative plaques of heading No. 97.01.

税则号列	货品名称	最惠(%)	普通	增值税率	出口退税	计量单位	监管条件	Article Description
06.01	**鳞茎、块茎、块根、球茎、根颈及根茎，休眠、生长或开花的；菊苣植物及其根，但税目12.12的根除外：**							**Bulbs, tubers, tuberous roots, corms, crowns and rhizomes, dormant, in growth or in flower; chicory plants and roots other than roots of heading No. 12.12:**
	-休眠的鳞茎、块茎、块根、球茎、根颈及根茎：							-Bulbs, tubers, tuberous roots, corms, crowns and rhizomes, dormant:
0601.1010	---番红花球茎	4	14	13	5	个/千克	AB	---Stigma croci corms
	---百合球茎：							---lily corms
0601.1021	----种用	0	0	13		个/千克	AB	---Seed
0601.1029	----其他	5	40	13		个/千克	AB	---Other
	---其他：							---Other:
0601.1091	----种用	0	0	13		个/千克		----Seed
0601.1091 10	种用休眠的兰花块茎（包括球茎、根颈及根茎）	0	0	13	5	个/千克	AFEB	Orchid tubers, dormant, seed (including corms, crowns and rhizomes)
0601.1091 91	种用休眠其他濒危植物鳞茎等（包括球茎、根颈、根茎、鳞茎、块茎、块根）	0	0	13		个/千克	ABFE	Bulbs, tubers, tuberous roots, dormant, seed (including corms, crowns and rhizomes) of endaergered plants
0601.1091 99	种用休眠的其他鳞茎、块茎、块根（包括球茎、根颈及根茎）	0	0	13	5	个/千克	AB	Other bulbs, tubers, tuberous roots, dormant, seed (including corms, crowns and rhizomes)
0601.1099	----其他	5	40	13		个/千克		----Other
0601.1099 10	其他休眠的兰花块茎（包括球茎、根颈及根茎）	5	40	13	5	个/千克	AFEB	Other orchid tubers, dormant (including corms, crowns and rhizomes)
0601.1099 91	其他休眠濒危植物鳞茎等（包括球茎、根颈、根茎、鳞茎、块茎、块根）	5	40	13		个/千克	AFEB	Other endangered plants bulbs (including corms, crowns, rhizomes, bulbs, tuber, tuberous roots, dormant)
0601.1099 99	其他休眠的其他鳞茎、块茎、块根（包括球茎、根颈及根茎）	5	40	13	5	个/千克	AB	Other bulbs, tubers, tuberous roots, dormant, seed (including corms, crowns and rhizomes), dormant

税则号列	货　品　名　称	最惠(%)	普通	增值税率	出口退税	计量单位	监管条件	Article Description
0601.2000	-生长或开花的鳞茎、块茎、块根、球茎、根颈及根茎；菊苣植物及其根	15	80	13		个/千克		-Bulbs, tubers, tuberous roots, corms, crowns and rhizomes, in growth or in flower; chicory plants and roots
0601.2000 10	生长或开花的兰花块茎(包括球茎、根颈及根茎)	15	80	13	5	个/千克	AFEB	Orchid tubers, in growth or in flower (in-cluding corms, crowns and rhizomes)
0601.2000 20	生长或开花的仙客来鳞茎	15	80	13	5	个/千克	AFEB	Cyclamen tubers, in growth or in flower
0601.2000 91	生长或开花的其他濒危植物鳞茎等(包括球茎、根颈、根茎、鳞茎、块茎、块根、菊苣植物)	15	80	13		个/千克	AFEB	Other endangered plants bulbs (including corms, crowns, rhizomes, bulbs, tubers, tuberous roots, chicory plants) in growth or in flower
0601.2000 99	生长或开花的其他鳞茎及菊苣植物(包括块茎、块根、球茎、根颈及根茎，编号1212根除外)	15	80	13	5	个/千克	AB	Other bulbs and chicory plants (including tubers, tuberous roots, corms, crowns and rhizomes, other than roots of heading No. 1212) in growth or in flower
06.02	**其他活植物(包括其根)、插枝及接穗；蘑菇菌丝：**							**Other live plants (including their roots) cuttings and slips; mushroom spawn:**
0602.1000	-无根插枝及接穗	0	0	13		株/千克		-Unrooted cuttings and slips
0602.1000 10	濒危植物的无根插枝及接穗	0	0	13		株/千克	ABFE	Unrooted cuttings and slips of endangered pl-ants
0602.1000 90	其他无根插枝及接穗	0	0	13	5	株/千克	AB	Other unrooted cuttings and slips
	-食用水果或食用坚果的树、灌木，不论是否嫁接：							-Trees, shrubs and bushes, grafted or not, of kinds which bear edible fruit or nuts:
0602.2010	---种用苗木	0	0	13		株/千克	AB	---Seedlings
0602.2090	---其他	10	80	13	5	株/千克	AB	---Other
	-杜鹃，不论是否嫁接：							-Rhododendrons and azaleas, grafted or not:
0602.3010	---种用	0	0	13	5	株/千克	AB	---Seedlings
0602.3090	---其他	15	80	13	5	株/千克	AB	---Other
	-玫瑰，不论是否嫁接：							-Roses, grafted or not:
0602.4010	---种用	0	0	13	5	株/千克	AB	---Seedlings
0602.4090	---其他	15	80	13	5	株/千克	AB	---Other
	-其他：							-Other:
0602.9010	---蘑菇菌丝	0	0	13	5	千克	AB	---Mushroom spawn
	---其他：							---Other:
0602.9091	----种用苗木	0	0	13		株/千克		----Seedlings
0602.9091 10	种用兰花	0	0	13		株/千克	AFEB	Orchid, seedlings
0602.9091 20	种用红豆杉苗木	0	0	13		株/千克	AFEB	Chinese yew, seeding
0602.9091 91	其他濒危植物种用苗木	0	0	13		株/千克	AFEB	Other seedlings of endangered plants
0602.9091 99	其他种用苗木	0	0	13		株/千克	AB	Other nursery stock, seedlings
0602.9092	----兰花	10	80	13	5	株/千克	ABFE	----Orchid
0602.9093	----菊花	10	80	13	0,5	株/千克	AB	----Chrysathemum
0602.9094	----百合	10	80	13	5	株/千克		----Lily
0602.9094 10	芦荟(种用除外)	10	80	13	5	株/千克	ABFEQ	Aloe(other than seedlings)
0602.9094 90	其他百合(种用除外)	10	80	13		株/千克	AB	Other lily(other than seedling)
0602.9095	----康乃馨	10	80	13	5	株/千克	AB	----Carnation
0602.9099	----其他	10	80	13		株/千克		----Other
0602.9099 10	苏铁(铁树)类	10	80	13	5	株/千克	ABFE	Sago cycas (*Cycas revoluta*)
0602.9099 20	仙人掌(包括仙人球、仙人柱、仙人指)	10	80	13	5	株/千克	ABFE	Cactus (including ball cactus, column cactus, finger cactus)
06029099 30	红豆杉(种用除外)	10	80	13		株/千克	ABFE	"Chinese yew(other than seeding)
0602.9099 91	其他濒危活植物(种用除外)	10	80	13		株/千克	AFEB	Other live endangered plants(other than seedlings)
0602.9099 99	其他活植物(种用除外)	10	80	13	5	株/千克	AB	Other live plants (other than seedlings)
06.03	**制花束或装饰用的插花及花蕾，鲜、干、染色、漂白、浸渍或用其他方法处理的：**							**Cut flowers and flower buds of a kind suitable for bouquets or for ornamental purposes, fresh, dried, dyed, bleached, impregnated or otherwise prepared:**
	-鲜的：							-Fresh:
0603.1100	--玫瑰	10	100	13	5	千克/枝	AB	--Roses
0603.1200	--康乃馨	10	100	13	5	千克/枝	AB	--Carnations
0603.1300	--兰花	10	100	13	5	千克/枝	ABEF	--Orchids
0603.1400	--菊花	10	100	13	5	千克/枝	AB	--Chrysanthemums

税则号列	货　品　名　称	最惠(%)	普通	增值税率	出口退税	计量单位	监管条件	Article Description
0603.1500	--百合花(百合属)	10	100	13	5	千克/枝	AB	--Lily(Lilium spp.)
0603.1900	--其他	10	100	13		千克/枝		--Other
0603.1900 10	鲜的濒危植物插花及花蕾(制花束或装饰用的)	10	100	13		千克/枝	ABFE	Cut flowers and flower buds of endangered plants(of a kind suitable for bouquets or for ornamental purposes)fresh
0603.1900 90	其他鲜的插花及花蕾(制花束或装饰用的)	10	100	13	5	千克/枝	AB	Other cut flower and flower buds(of a kind suitable for bouquets or for ornamental purposes)fresh
0603.9000	-其他	23	100	17		千克/枝		-Other
0603.9000 10	干或染色等加工濒危植物的插花及花蕾(制花束或装饰用的,鲜的除外)	23	100	17		千克/枝	ABFE	Cut flowers and flower buds of endangered plants(of a kind suitable for bouquets or for ornamental purposes), other than fresh dried, dyed or otherwise prepared, other than fresh
0603.9000 90	其他干或染色等加工的插花及花蕾(制花束或装饰用的,鲜的除外)	23	100	17	5	千克/枝	AB	Other cut flowers and flower buds(of a kind suitable for bouquets or for ornamental purposes) dried, dyed or otherwise prepared, other than fresh
06.04	**制花束或装饰用的不带花及花蕾的植物枝、叶或其他部分,草、苔藓及地衣,鲜、干、染色、漂白、浸渍或用其他方法处理的:**							**Foliage, branches and other parts of plants, without flowers or flower -buds, and grasses, mosses and lichens, being goods of a kind suitable for bouquets or for ornamental purposes, fresh, dried, dyed, bleached, impregnated or otherwise prepared:**
	-鲜的:							-Fresh:
0604.2010	-苔藓及地衣	23	100	13	5	千克	AB	-Mosses and lichens
0604.2090	-其他	10	100	13		千克		-Other
0604.2090 10	其他鲜濒危植物枝、叶或其他部分,草(枝、叶或其他部分是指制花束或装饰用并且不带花及花蕾)	10	100	13		千克	ABFE	Other foliage, branches and other parts of endangered plants, fresh, and grasses, without flowers or flower buds(being goods of a kind suitable for bouquets or for ornamental purposes)
0604.2090 90	其他鲜植物枝、叶或其他部分,草(枝、叶或其他部分是指制花束或装饰用并且不带花及花蕾)	10	100	13	5	千克	AB	Other foliage, branches or other parts of plants, fresh, and grasses, without flowers or flower buds (being good of a kind suitable for bouquets or for ornamental prposes)
	-其他:							-Other:
0604.9010	--苔藓及地衣	23	100	13	5	千克	AB	--Mosses and hiehens:
0604.9090	--其他	10	100	17		千克		--Other
0604.9090 10	其他染色或经加工濒危植物枝、叶、草等(枝、叶或其他部分是指制花束或装饰用并且不带花及花蕾)	10	100	17		千克	ABFE	Other foliage, branches and other parts of endangered plants, and grasses without flowers or flower buds, (being goods of a kind suitable for bouquets or for ornamental purposes)
0604.9090 90	其他染色或加工的植物枝、叶、草等(枝、叶或其他部分是指制花束或装饰用并且不带花及花蕾)	10	100	17	5	千克	AB	Other foliage, branches and other parts of plants, and grasses without flowers or flower buds, (being goods of a kind sitable for banquets or for ornamental purposes)

第七章
食用蔬菜、根及块茎

Chapter 7
Edible vegetables and certain roots and tubers

注释：

一、本章不包括税号12.14的草料。

二、税号07.09、07.10、07.11及07.12所称"蔬菜"，包括食用的蘑菇、块菌、油橄榄、刺山柑、菜葫芦、南瓜、茄子、甜玉米、辣椒、茴香菜、欧芹、细叶芹、龙蒿、水芹、甜茉乔栾那。

三、税号07.12包括干制的归入税号07.01至07.11的各种蔬菜，但下列各项除外：

（一）作蔬菜用的脱荚干豆（税号07.13）；

（二）税目11.02至11.04所列形状的甜玉米；

（三）马铃薯细粉、粗粉、粉末、粉片、颗粒及团粒（税号11.05）；

（四）用税目07.13的干豆制成的细粉、粗粉及粉末（税目11.06）。

四、本章不包括辣椒干及辣椒粉（税目09.04）。

Notes:

1. This Chapter does not cover forage products of heading 12.14.
2. In headings No. 07.09, 07.10, 07.11 and 07.12 the word "vegetables" includes edible mushrooms, truffles, olives, capers, marrows, pumpkins, aubergines, sweet corn (*Zea maysvar. saccharata*), fruits of the genus *Capsicum* or of the genus *Pimenta*, fennel, parsley, chervil, tarragon, cress and sweet marjoram (*Majorana hortensis or Origanum majorana*).
3. Heading No. 07.12 covers all dried vegetables of the kinds falling in headings No. 07.01 to 07.11, other than:
   (a) dried leguminous vegetables, shelled (heading No. 07.13);
   (b) sweet corn in the forms specified in headings No. 11.02 to 11.04;
   (c) flour, meal, powder, flakes, granules and pellets of potatoes (heading No. 11.05);
   (d) flour, meal and powder of the dried leguminous vegetables of heading No. 07.13 (heading No. 11.06).
4. However, dried or crushed or ground fruits of the genus *Capsicum* or of the genus *Pimenta* are excluded from this Chapter (heading No. 09.04).

税则号列	货品名称	最惠(%)	普通	增值税率	出口退税	计量单位	监管条件	Article Description
07.01	鲜或冷藏的马铃薯：							**Potatoes, fresh or chilled:**
0701.1000	-种用	13	70	13		千克	AB	-Seeds
0701.9000	-其他	13	70	13		千克	AB	-Other
07.02	鲜或冷藏的番茄：							**Tomatoes, fresh or chilled:**
0702.0000	鲜或冷藏的番茄	13	70	13		千克	AB	Tomatoes, fresh or chilled
07.03	鲜或冷藏的洋葱、青葱、大蒜、韭葱及其他葱属蔬菜：							**Onions, shallots, garlic, leeks and other alliaceous vegetables, fresh or chilled:**
	-洋葱及青葱：							-Onions and shallots:
0703.1010	---洋葱	13	70	13		千克	AB	---Onions
0703.1020	---青葱	13	70	13		千克	AB	---Shallots
	-大蒜：							-Garlic:
0703.2010	---蒜头	13	70	13		千克	AB	---Garlic bulbs
0703.2020	---蒜苔及蒜苗（青蒜）	13	70	13		千克	AB	---Garlic stems, garlic seedlings
0703.2090	---其他	13	70	13		千克	AB	---Other
	-韭葱及其他葱属蔬菜：							-Leeks and other alliaceous vegetables:
0703.9010	---韭葱	13	70	13		千克	AB	---Leeks
0703.9020	---大葱	13	70	13		千克	AB	---Scallion
0703.9090	---其他	13	70	13		千克	AB	---Other
07.04	鲜或冷藏的卷心菜、菜花、球茎甘蓝、羽衣甘蓝及类似的食用芥菜类蔬菜：							**Cabbages, cauliflowers, kohlrabi, kale and similar edible brassicas, fresh or chilled:**
0704.1000	-菜花及硬花甘蓝	10	70	13		千克		-Cauliflowers and headed broccoli
0704.1000 01	鲜、冷硬花甘蓝	10	70	13		千克	AB	Headed broccoli, fresh or chilled
0704.1000 02	鲜、冷花椰菜（花椰菜也叫菜花）	10	70	13		千克	AB	Cauliflowers, fresh or chilled
0704.2000	-抱子甘蓝	13	70	13		千克	AB	-Brussels sprouts
	-其他：							-Other:
0704.9010	---卷心菜	13	70	13		千克	AB	---Cabbage (Brassica oleracea var. capitata)
0704.9020	---西兰花	13	70	13		千克	AB	---Broccolis (Brassica oleracea var italica)
0704.9090	---其他	13	70	13		千克		---Other
0704.9090 01	鲜、冷其他甘蓝	13	70	13		千克	AB	Other Cabbage, fresh or chilled
0704.9090 90	鲜或冷藏的其他食用芥菜类蔬菜	13	70	13		千克	AB	Other edible brassicas, fresh or chilled
07.05	鲜或冷藏的莴苣及菊苣：							**Lettuce (*lactuca sativa*) and chicory (*Cichorium spp.*), fresh or chilled:**
	-莴苣：							-Lettuce:
0705.1100	--结球莴苣（包心生菜）	10	70	13		千克	AB	--Cabbage lettuce (head lettuce)

税则号列	货品名称	最惠(%)	普通	增值税率	出口退税	计量单位	监管条件	Article Description
0705.1900	--其他	10	70	13		千克	AB	--Other
	-菊苣							-Chicory:
0705.2100	--维特罗夫菊苣	13	70	13		千克	AB	--Witloof chicory (*Cichoriym intybus var. foliosum*)
0705.2900	--其他	13	70	13		千克	AB	--Other
07.06	鲜或冷藏的胡萝卜、萝卜、色拉甜菜根、婆罗门参、块根芹、小萝卜及类似的食用根茎:							**Carrots, turnips, salad beetroot, salsify, celeriac, radishes and similar edible roots, fresh or chilled:**
0706.1000	-胡萝卜及萝卜	13	70	13		千克		-Carrots and turnips
0706.1000 01	鲜、冷胡萝卜	13	70	13		千克	AB	Carrots, fresh or chilled
0706.1000 90	鲜或冷藏的萝卜	13	70	13		千克	AB	Turnips, fresh or chilled
0706.9000	-其他	13	70	13		千克	AB	-Other
07.07	鲜或冷藏的黄瓜及小黄瓜:							**Cucumbers and gherkins, fresh or chilled:**
0707.0000	鲜或冷藏的黄瓜及小黄瓜	13	70	13		千克	AB	Cucumbers and gherkins, fresh or chilled
07.08	鲜或冷藏的豆类蔬菜,不论是否脱荚:							**Leguminous vegetables, shelled or unshelled, fresh or chilled:**
0708.1000	-豌豆	13	70	13		千克	AB	-Peas (*Pisum sativum*)
0708.2000	-豇豆及菜豆	13	70	13		千克	AB	-Beans (*Vigna spp.*, *Phaseolus spp.*)
0708.9000	-其他豆类蔬菜	13	70	13		千克	AB	-Other leguminous vegetables
07.09	鲜或冷藏的其他蔬菜:							**Other vegetables, fresh or chilled:**
0709.2000	-芦笋	13	70	13		千克	AB	-Asparagus
0709.3000	-茄子	13	70	13		千克	AB	-Aubergines (egg-plants)
0709.4000	-芹菜,但块根芹除外	10	70	13		千克	AB	-Celery, other than celeriac
	-蘑菇及块菌:							-Mushrooms and truffles:
0709.5100	--伞菌属蘑菇	13	90	13		千克	AB	--Mushrooms of the genus *Agaricus*
	--其他:							--Other:
0709.5910	---松茸	13	90	13		千克	ABE	---Sungmo
0709.5920	---香菇	13	90	13		千克	AB	---shiitake
0709.5930	---金针菇	13	90	13		千克	AB	---Winter mushroom
0709.5940	---草菇	13	90	13		千克	AB	---Paddy straw mushroom
0709.5950	---口蘑	13	90	13		千克	AB	---Tricholoma mongolicum Imai
0709.5960	---块菌	13	90	13	5	千克	AB	---Truffle
0709.5990	---其他	13	90	13		千克	AB	---Other
0709.6000	-辣椒,包括甜椒	13	70	13		千克	AB	-Fruits of the genus *Capsicum* or of the genus *Pimenta*
0709.7000	-菠菜	13	70	13		千克	AB	-Spinach, New Zealand spinach and orache spinach (garden spinach)
	--其他:							--Other:
0709.9100	--洋蓟	13	70	13	5	千克	AB	--Globe artichokes
0709.9200	--油橄榄	13	70	13	5	千克	AB	--Olives
0709.9300	--南瓜、笋瓜及瓠瓜(南瓜属)	13	70	13		千克	AB	--Pumpkin、squash and gourd(cucurbita spp.)
	--其他:							--Other:
0709.9910	---竹笋	13	70	13		千克		---Bamboo shoots
0709.9910 10	鲜或冷藏的酸竹笋	13	70	13		千克	ABE	Acidosasa shoots, fresh or chilled
0709.9910 90	鲜或冷藏的其他竹笋	13	70	13		千克	AB	Other bamboo shoots, fresh or chilled
0709.9990	---其他	13	70	13		千克		---Other
0709.9990 01	鲜或冷藏的丝瓜	13	70	13		千克	AB	Loofah, fresh or chilled
0709.9990 02	鲜或冷藏的青江菜	13	70	13		千克	AB	Bok choy, fresh or chilled
0709.9990 03	鲜或冷藏的小白菜	13	70	13		千克	AB	Pakchoi, fresh or chilled
0709.9990 04	鲜或冷藏的苦瓜	13	70	13		千克	AB	Balsum pear, fresh or chilled
0709.9990 05	鲜或冷藏的山葵	13	70	13		千克	AB	Horseradish, fresh or chilled
0709.9990 10	鲜或冷藏的莼菜	13	70	13		千克	ABE	Water shield, fresh or chilled
0709.9990 90	鲜或冷藏的其他蔬菜	13	70	13		千克	AB	Other vegetables, fresh or chilled
07.10	冷冻蔬菜(不论是否蒸煮):							**Vegetables (uncooked or cooked by steaming or boiling in water), frozen:**
0710.1000	-马铃薯	13	70	13	0,5	千克	AB	-Potatoes
	-豆类、蔬菜,不论是否脱荚:							-Leguminous vegetables, shelled or unshelled:

税则号列	货　品　名　称	最惠(%)	普通	增值税率	出口退税	计量单位	监管条件	Article Description
0710.2100	--豌豆	13	70	13	0,5	千克	AB	--Peas (*Pisum sativum*)
	--豇豆及菜豆:							--Beans (*Vigna spp.*, *Phaseolus spp.*):
0710.2210	---红小豆(赤豆)	13	70	13	0,5	千克	AB	---Small red (Adzuki) beans (*Phaseolus* or *Vigna angularis*)
0710.2290	---其他	13	70	13	0,5	千克	AB	---Other
0710.2900	--其他	13	70	13	0,5	千克	AB	--Other
0710.3000	-菠菜	13	70	13	0,5	千克	AB	-Spinach, New Zealand spinach and orache spinach (garden spinach)
0710.4000	-甜玉米	10	70	13	0,5	千克	AB	-Sweet corn
	-其他蔬菜:							-Other vegetables:
0710.8010	---松茸	13	70	13	0,5	千克	ABE	---Sungmo
0710.8020	---蒜苔及蒜苗(青蒜)	13	70	13	0,5	千克	AB	---Garlic stems, garlic seedlings
0710.8030	---蒜头	13	70	13	0,5	千克	AB	---Garlic bulbs
0710.8040	---牛肝菌	13	70	13	0.5	千克	AB	---Boletus
0710.8090	---其他	13	70	13	0,5	千克		---Other
0710.8090 10	冷冻的大蒜瓣(不论是否蒸煮)	13	70	13	0,5	千克	AB	Garlic cloves, frozen (uncooked or cooked by steaming or boiling in water)
0710.8090 20	冷冻的香菇(不论是否蒸煮)	13	70	13	0,5	千克	AB	Shiitake, frozen (uncooked or cooked by steaming or boiling in water)
0710.8090 30	冷冻莼菜(不论是否蒸煮)	13	70	13	0,5	千克	ABE	Water shield, frozen (uncooked or cooked by steaming or boiling in water)
0710.8090 90	冷冻的未列名蔬菜(不论是否蒸煮)	13	70	13	0,5	千克	AB	Vegetables, frozen, not elsewhere specified or included (uncooked or cooked by steaming or boiling in water)
0710.9000	-什锦蔬菜	10	70	13	0,5	千克	AB	-Mixtures of vegetables
07.11	**暂时保藏(例如,使用二氧化硫气体、盐水、亚硫酸水或其他防腐液)的蔬菜,但不适于直接食用的:**							**Vegetables provisionally preserved (for example, by sulphur dioxide gas, in brine, in suphur water or in other preservative solutions), but unsuitable in that state for immediate consumption:**
0711.2000	-油橄榄	13	70	13	5	千克	AB	-Olives
0711.4000	-黄瓜及小黄瓜	13	70	13	5	千克	AB	-Cucumbers and gherkins
	-蘑菇及块菌:							-Mushrooms and truffles:
	--伞菌属蘑菇:							--Mushrooms of the genus *Agaricus*:
	---盐水的:							---In brine:
0711.5112	----小白蘑菇	13	90	13	5	千克	AB	----White mushroom
0711.5119	----其他	13	90	13	5	千克	AB	----Other
0711.5190	---其他	13	90	13	5	千克	AB	---Other
	--其他:							--Other:
	---盐水的:							---In brine:
0711.5911	----松茸	13	90	13	5	千克	EAB	----Sungmo
0711.5919	----其他	13	90	13	5	千克		----Other
0711.5919 10	盐水的香菇(不适于直接食用的)	13	90	13	5	千克	AB	Shiitake, in brine (unsuitable in that state for immediate consumption)
0711.5919 90	盐水的其他非伞菌属蘑菇及块菌(不适于直接食用的)	13	90	13	5	千克	AB	Other mushroom except the genus *Agaricus* and truffles, in brine, (unsuitable in that state for immediate consumption)
0711.5990	---其他	13	90	13	5	千克		---Other
0711.5990 10	暂时保藏的香菇(用二氧化硫气体等物质处理,但不适于直接食用的)	13	90	13	5	千克	AB	Shiitake, provisionally preserved (by sulphur dioxide gas, or other wise prepared, but unsuitable in that state for immediate consumption)
0711.5990 90	暂时保藏的蘑菇及块菌(用二氧化硫气体等物质处理,但不适于直接食用的)	13	90	13	5	千克	AB	Mushrooms and truffles (by sulphur dioxide gas or other wise prepared, but unsuitable in that state for immediate consumption)
	-其他蔬菜;什锦蔬菜:							-Other vegetables; mixtures of vegetables:
	---盐水的:							---In brine:
0711.9031	----竹笋	13	70	13	5	千克		----Bamboo shoots
0711.9031 10	盐水酸竹笋(不适于直接食用的)	13	70	13	5	千克	ABE	Acidosasa chinensis shoots, in brine (unsuitable in that state for immediate consumption)

税则号列	货品名称	最惠(%)	普通	增值税率	出口退税	计量单位	监管条件	Article Description
0711.9031 90	其他盐水竹笋(不适于直接食用的)	13	70	13	5	千克	AB	Other bamboo shoots, in brine(unsuitable in that state for immediate consumption)
0711.9034	----大蒜	13	70	13	5	千克		----Garlic
0711.9034 10	盐水简单腌制的大蒜头、大蒜瓣(无论是否去皮,但不适于直接食用)	13	70	13	5	千克	AB	Garlic bulbs and garlic cloves, in brine(but unsuitable in that state for immediate consumption, whether skinned or not)
0711.9034 90	盐水简单腌制的其他大蒜(不含蒜头、蒜瓣,无论是否去皮,但不适于直接食用)	13	70	13	5	千克	AB	Other garlic in brine (other than garlic bulbs, garlic cloves, whether or not skinned, but unsuitable in that state for immediate consumption)
0711.9039	----其他	13	70	13	5	千克	AB	----Other
0711.9090	---其他	13	90	13	5	千克	AB	---Other
07.12	**干蔬菜,整个、切块、切片、破碎或制成粉状,但未经进一步加工的:**							**Dried vegetables, whole, cut, sliced, broken or in powder, but not further prepared:**
0712.2000	-洋葱	13	80	13	0,5	千克	AB	-Onions
	-蘑菇、木耳、银耳及块菌:							-Mushrooms, wood ears(*Auricularia spp.*), jelly fungi (*Tremella spp.*) and truffles:
0712.3100	--伞菌属蘑菇	13	80	13	0,5	千克	AB	--Mushrooms of the genus *Agaricus*
0712.3200	--木耳	13	100	13	0,5,15	千克	AB	--Wood ears(*Auricularia spp.*)
0712.3300	--银耳	13	90	13	0,5,15	千克	AB	--Jelly fungi (*Tremella spp.*)
	--其他:							--Other:
0712.3910	---香菇	13	100	13	5,15	千克	AB	---Shiitake
0712.3920	---金针菇	13	100	13	0,5	千克	AB	---Winter mushroom
0712.3930	---草菇	13	100	13	0,5	千克	AB	---Paddy straw mushroom
0712.3940	---口蘑	13	100	13	0,5	千克	AB	---Tricholoma mongolicum lmai
0712.3950	---牛肝菌	13	100	13	0,5	千克	AB	---Boletus
0712.3990	---其他	13	100	13	0,5	千克		---Other
0712.3990 10	干制松茸(整个、切块、切片、破碎或制成粉状,但未经进一步加工的)	13	100	13	0,5	千克	ABE	Dried sungmo(whole, cut, sliced, broken or in powder, but not further prepared)
0712.3990 90	其他干制蘑菇及块菌(整个、切块、切片、破碎或制成粉状,但未经进一步加工的)	13	100	13	0,5	千克	AB	Other dried mushrooms and truffles (whole, cut, sliced, broken or in powder, but not further prepared)
	-其他蔬菜;什锦蔬菜:							-Other vegetables; mixtures of vegetables:
0712.9010	---笋干丝	13	80	13		千克		---Bamboo shoots
0712.9010 10	酸竹笋干丝	13	80	13		千克	ABE	Dried acidosasa chinensis shoots
0712.9010 90	其他笋干丝	13	80	13		千克	AB	Other bamboo shoots
0712.9020	---紫萁(薇菜干)	13	80	13	0,5	千克	AB	---Osmund
0712.9030	---金针菜(黄花菜)	13	80	13	0,5	千克	AB	---Day lily flowers
0712.9040	---蕨菜	13	80	13	0,5	千克	AB	---Wild brake
0712.9050	---大蒜	13	80	17		千克		---Garlic
0712.9050 10	干燥或脱水的大蒜头、大蒜瓣(无论是否去皮)	13	80	17		千克	AB	Dried or dewatered garlic bulbs or garlic cloves (whether or not skinned)
0712.9050 90	干燥或脱水的其他大蒜(不含蒜头、蒜瓣,无论是否去皮)	13	80	17	5,15	千克	AB	Other dried or dewatered garlic (other than garlic bulbs garlic cloves, whether or not skinned)
	---其他:							---Other:
0712.9091	----辣根	13	80	13	0,5	千克	AB	---Cochlearia
0712.9099	----其他	13	80	13	0,5	千克		----Other
0712.9099 10	干莼菜(整个、切块、切片、破碎或制成粉状,但未经进一步加工的)	13	80	13	0,5	千克	ABE	Dried water shield(whole, cut, sliced, broken or in powder, but not further prepared)
0712.9099 90	干制的其他蔬菜及什锦蔬菜(整个、切块、切片、破碎或制成粉状,但未经进一步加工的)	13	80	13	0,5	千克	AB	Other dried vegetable and mixtures of vegetables (whole, cut, sliced, broken or in powder, but not further prepared)
07.13	脱荚的干豆,不论是否去皮或分瓣:							**Dried leguminous vegetables, shelled, whether or not skinned or split:**
	-豌豆:							-Peas (*Pisum sativum*):
0713.1010	---种用	0	0	13		千克	AB	---Seed
0713.1090	---其他	5	20	13		千克	AB	---Other

税则号列	货品名称	最惠(%)	普通	增值税率	出口退税	计量单位	监管条件	Article Description
	-鹰嘴豆:							-Chickpeas (garbanzos):
0713.2010	---种用	0	0	13	5	千克	AB	---Seed
0713.2090	---其他	7	20	13	5	千克	AB	---Other
	-豇豆属及菜豆属:							-Vigna and lunatus:
	--绿豆:							--Beans of the species *Vigna mungo* (*L.*) *Hepper or Vigna radiata* (*L.*) *Wilczek*:
0713.3110	---种用	0	0	13	5	千克	AB	---Seed
0713.3190	---其他	3	11	13	5	千克	AB	---Other
	--红小豆(赤豆):							--Small red (Adzuki) beans (*Phaseolus* or *Vigna angularis*):
0713.3210	---种用	0	0	13	5	千克	AB	---Seed
0713.3290	---其他	3	14	13	5	千克	AB	---Other
	--芸豆:							--Kidney beans, including white pea-beans (*Phaseolus vulgaris*):
0713.3310	---种用	0	0	13		千克	AB	---Seed
0713.3390	---其他	7.5	20	13		千克	AB	---Other
0713.3400	--巴姆巴拉豆	7	20	13	5	千克	AB	--Bambara beans (Vigna subterranea or Voandzeia subterranea)
0713.3500	--牛豆(豇豆)	7	20	13	5	千克	AB	--Cow peas(Vigna unguiculata)
0713.3900	--其他	7	20	13		千克	AB	--Other
	-扁豆:							-Lentils:
0713.4010	---种用	0	0	13		千克	AB	---Seed
0713.4090	---其他	7	20	13		千克	AB	---Other
	-蚕豆:							-Broad beans (*Vicia faba var. Major*) and horse beans (*Vicia faba var. equina*, *Vicia faba var. minor*):
0713.5010	---种用	0	0	13	5	千克	AB	---Seed
0713.5090	---其他	7	20	13	5	千克	AB	---Other
	-木豆(木豆属):							-Pigeon peas(Cajanus cajan)
0713.6010	---种用	0	0	13	5	千克	AB	---For cultivation
0713.6090	---其他	7	20	13	5	千克	AB	---Other
	-其他:							-Other:
0713.9010	---种用干豆	0	0	13		千克	AB	---Seed
0713.9090	---其他	7	20	13		千克	AB	---Other
07.14	**鲜、冷、冻或干的木薯、竹芋、兰科植物块茎、菊芋、甘薯及含有高淀粉或菊粉的类似根茎,不论是否切片或制成团粒;西谷茎髓:**							**Manioc, arrowroot, salep, Jerusalem artichokes, sweet potatoes and similar roots and tubers with high starch or inulin content, fresh, chilled, frozen or dried, whether or not sliced or in the form of pellets; sago pith:**
	-木薯:							-Manioc(cassava):
0714.1010	---鲜的	10	30	13	5	千克	AB	---Fresh
0714.1020	---干的	5	30	13	5	千克	AB	---Dried
0714.1030	---冷或冻的	10	80	13	5	千克	AB	---Chilled or frozen
	-甘薯:							-Sweet potatoes:
	---鲜的:							---Fresh:
0714.2011	----种用	0	50	13		千克	AB	----For Cultivation
0714.2019	----其他	13	50	13		千克	AB	----Other
0714.2020	---干的	13	50	13		千克	AB	---Dried
0714.2030	---冷或冻的	13	80	13		千克	AB	---Chilled or frozen
0714.3000	-山药	13	50	13		千克	AB	-Yams(dioscoreae spp.)
0714.4000	-芋头(芋属)	13	50	13		千克		-Taros(colocasia spp.)
0714.4000 01	鲜、冷的芋头(芋属)(不论是否切片或制成团粒;芋头又称芋艿,为天南星科芋属植物,分旱芋、水芋)	13	50	13		千克	AB	Fresh, chilled taros(colocasia spp.)(whether or not sliced or made granule; taros are also called yunai belong to Spath hyttum of the Araceae vegetables, classified into ground taros and river taros)

税则号列	货 品 名 称	最惠(%)	普通	增值税率	出口退税	计量单位	监管条件	Article Description
0714.4000 90	冻、干的芋头(芋属)(不论是否切片或制成团粒;芋头又称芋艿,为天南星科芋属植物,分旱芋、水芋)	13	50	13		千克	AB	Frozen, dried taros (colocasia spp.) (whether or not sliced or made granule; taros are also called yunai belong to Spath hyttum of the Araceae vegetables, classified into ground taros and river taros)
0714.5000	-箭叶黄体芋(黄肉芋属)	13	50	13	5	千克	AB	-Yautia (Xanthosoma spp.)
	-其他:							-Other:
0714.9010	---荸荠	13	50	13		千克	AB	---Water chestnut
	---藕:							---Lotus (*Nelumbo nucifera*) rootstock:
0714.9021	----种用	0	0	13		千克	AB	----For cultivation
0714.9029	----其他	13	50	13		千克	AB	----Other
0714.9090	---其他	13	50	13		千克		---Other
0714.9090 10	鲜、冷、冻、干的兰科植物块茎	13	50	13		千克	ABFE	Tubers of orchid family, fresh, chilled, frozen or dried
0714.9090 91	含高淀粉或菊粉其他濒危类似根茎(包括西谷茎髓,不论是否切片或制成团粒,鲜、冷、冻或干的)	13	50	13		千克	ABFE	Other endangered similar roots and tubers with high starch or inulin content (including sago pith, whether or not sliced or made gramule, fresh, chilled, frozen, dried)
0714.9090 99	含有高淀粉或菊粉的其他类似根茎(包括西谷茎髓,不论是否切片或制成团粒,鲜、冷、冻或干的)	13	50	13		千克	AB	Other similar roots and tubers with high starch or inulin content (including sago pith whether or not sliced or in the form of pellets fresh, chilled, frozen, dried)

第八章
食用水果及坚果；柑桔属水果或甜瓜的果皮

Chapter 8
Edible fruit and nuts; peel of citrus fruit or melons

注释：

一、本章不包括非供食用的坚果或水果。

二、冷藏的水果和坚果应按相应的鲜果税目归类。

三、本章的干果可以部分复水或为下列目的进行其他处理：

（一）为保藏或保持其稳定性（例如，经适度热处理或硫化处理、添加山梨酸或山梨酸钾）；

（二）为改进或保持其外观（例如，添加植物油或少量葡萄糖浆）。

但必须保持干果的特征。

Notes:

1. This Chapter does not cover inedible nuts or fruits.
2. Chilled fruits and nuts are to be classified in the same headings as the corresponding fresh fruits and nuts.
3. Dried fruit or dried nuts of this Chapter may be partially rehydrated, or treated for the following purposes:

(a) For additional preservation or stabilization (for example, by moderate heat treatment, sulphuring, the addition of sorbic acid or potassium sorbate).

(b) To improve or maintain their appearance (for example., by the addition of vegetable oil or small quantities of glucose syrup),

provided that they retain the character of dried fruit or dried nuts.

税则号列	货品名称	最惠(%)	普通	增值税率	出口退税	计量单位	监管条件	Article Description
08.01	**鲜或干的椰子、巴西果及腰果，不论是否去壳或去皮：**							**Coconuts, Brazil nuts and cashew- nuts, fresh or dried, whether or not shelled or peeled:**
	-椰子：							-Coconuts:
0801.1100	--干的	12	80	13	5	千克	AB	--Desiccated
0801.1200	--未去内壳（内果皮）	12	80	13	5	千克	AB	-In the inner shell(endocarp)
	--其他：							--Other:
0801.1910	---种用	0	0	13	5	千克	AB	---Seedlings
0801.1990	---其他	12	80	13	5	千克	AB	---Other
	-巴西果：							-Brazil nuts:
0801.2100	--未去壳	10	80	13	5	千克	AB	--In shell
0801.2200	--去壳	10	80	13	5	千克	AB	--Shelled
	-腰果：							-Cashew nuts:
0801.3100[暂]	--未去壳	10	70	13	5	千克	AB	--In shell
0801.3200	--去壳	10	70	13	5	千克	AB	--Shelled
08.02	**鲜或干的其他坚果，不论是否去壳或去皮：**							**Other nuts, fresh or dried, whether or not shelled or peeled:**
	-扁桃仁：							-semen amygdalae:
0802.1100[暂]	--未去壳	10	70	13	5	千克	AB	--In shell
0802.1200	--去壳	10	70	13	5	千克	AB	--Shelled
	-榛子：							-Hazelnuts or filberts (*Corylus spp.*):
0802.2100	--未去壳	25	70	13	5	千克	AB	--In shell
0802.2200	--去壳	10	70	13	5	千克	AB	--Shelled
	-核桃：							-Walnuts:
0802.3100	--未去壳	25	70	13	5	千克	AB	--In shell
0802.3200	--去壳	20	70	13	5	千克	AB	--Shelled
	-栗子：							-Chestnuts (*Castanea spp.*):
	--未去壳：							-In shell:
0802.4110	---板栗	25	70	13	5	千克	AB	---Chinese chestnuts
0802.4190[暂]	---其他	20	70	13	5	千克	AB	---Other
	--去壳：							--Shelled
0802.4210	---板栗	25	70	13	5	千克	AB	---Chinese chestnuts
0802.4290[暂]	---其他	20	70	13	5	千克	AB	---Other
	-阿月浑子果（开心果）：							-Pistachios:
0802.5100[暂]	--未去壳	5	70	13	5	千克	AB	--In shell
0802.5200[暂]	--去壳	5	70	13	5	千克	AB	--Shelled
	-马卡达姆坚果（夏威夷果）：							-Macadamia nuts:
	--未去壳：							--In shell:
0802.6110	---种用	0	70	13	5	千克	AB	---Seedlings
0802.6190[暂]	---其他	19	70	13	5	千克	AB	---Other

税则号列	货品名称	最惠(%)	普通	增值税率	出口退税	计量单位	监管条件	Article Description
0802.6200暂	--去壳	19	70	13	5	千克	AB	--Shelled
0802.7000	-可乐果(可乐果属)	24	70	13	5	千克	AB	-Cola nut(Cola spp.)
0802.8000	-槟榔果	10	30	13	5	千克		-Areca nut
0802.8000 01	鲜的槟榔果(不论是否去壳或去皮)	10	30	13	5	千克	AB	Areca nuts,fresh(whether or not shelled or peeled)
0802.8000 90	干的槟榔果(不论是否去壳或去皮)	10	30	13	5	千克	AB	Areca nuts,dried(whether or not shelled or peeled)
	-其他:							-Other:
0802.9020暂	---白果	20	70	13	5	千克	ABE	---Gingko nuts
0802.9030	---松子仁	25	70	13		千克		---Pine-nuts, shelled
0802.9030 10	鲜或干的红松子仁	25	70	13		千克	ABE	Korean pine-nuts, shelled, fresh or dried
0802.9030 20	鲜或干的其他濒危松子仁	25	70	13		千克	ABEF	Other endangered pine-nuts, shelled, fresh or dried
0802.9030 90	鲜或干的其他松子仁	25	70	13	5	千克	AB	Other pine-nuts,shelled,fresh or dried
0802.9090	---其他	10	70	13		千克		---Other
0802.9090 10	鲜或干的榧子、红松子(不论是否去壳或去皮)	24	70	13	5	千克	ABE	semen torreyae or korean pine, fresh or dried(whether or not shelled or peeled)
0802.9090 20	鲜或干的其他濒危松子(不论是否去壳或去皮)	24	70	13		千克	ABEF	Endangered pine nut, fresh or dried(whether or not shelled or peeled)
0802.9090 30	鲜或干的巨籽棕(海椰子)果仁	24	70	13	5	千克	ABEF	Lodoicea maldivica nut,fresh or dried
0802.9090暂 40	鲜或干的碧根果(不论是否去壳或去皮)	10	70	13	5	千克	AB	Pecan fresh or dried (whether or not shelled or peeled)
0802.9090 90	鲜或干的其他坚果(不论是否去壳或去皮)	24	70	13	5	千克	AB	Other nuts, fresh or dried(whether or not shelled or peeled)
08.03	**鲜或干的香蕉,包括芭蕉:**							**Bananas, including plantains, fresh or dried:**
0803.1000	-芭蕉	10	40	13	5	千克	AB	-Plantains
0803.9000	-其他	10	40	13	5	千克	AB	-Other
08.04	**鲜或干的椰枣、无花果、菠萝、鳄梨、番石榴、芒果及山竹果:**							**Dates, figs, pineapples, avocados, guavas, mangoes and mangosteens, fresh or dried:**
0804.1000	-椰枣	15	40	13	5	千克	AB	-Dates
0804.2000	-无花果	30	70	13	5	千克	AB	-Figs
0804.3000	-菠萝	12	80	13	5	千克		-Pineapples
0804.3000 01	鲜菠萝	12	80	13	5	千克	AB	Pineapples, fresh
0804.3000 90	干菠萝	12	80	13	5	千克	AB	Pineapples, dried
0804.4000	-鳄梨	25	80	13	5	千克	AB	-Avocados
	-番石榴、芒果及山竹果:							-Guavas, mangoes and mangosteens:
0804.5010	---番石榴	15	80	13	5	千克		---Guavas
0804.5010 01	鲜番石榴	15	80	13	5	千克	AB	Guavas, fresh
0804.5010 90	干番石榴	15	80	13	5	千克	AB	Guavas, dried
0804.5020	---芒果	15	80	13	5	千克		---Mangoes
0804.5020 01	鲜芒果	15	80	13	5	千克	AB	Mangoes, fresh
0804.5020 90	干芒果	15	80	13	5	千克	AB	Mangoes, dried
0804.5030	---山竹果	15	80	13	5	千克	AB	---Mangosteens
08.05	**鲜或干的柑橘属水果:**							**Citrus fruit, fresh or dried:**
0805.1000	-橙	11	100	13	5	千克	AB	-Oranges
	-柑橘;杂交柑橘:							-Mandarins (including tangerines and satsumas); clementines, wilkings and similar citrus hybrids:
0805.2010	---蕉柑	12	100	13	5	千克	AB	---Chiao-Kan
0805.2020	---阔叶柑橘	12	100	13	5	千克	AB	---Latifolia Citrus
0805.2090	---其他	12	100	13	5	千克	AB	---Other
0805.4000	-葡萄柚,包括柚	12	100	13	5	千克		-Grapefruit,including pomelos
0805.4000 01	鲜葡萄柚,包括鲜柚	12	100	13	5	千克	AB	Grapefruit fresh,including pomelos
0805.4000 90	干葡萄柚,包括干柚	12	100	13	5	千克	AB	Grapefruit dried,including pomelos
0805.5000	-柠檬及酸橙	11	100	13	5	千克	AB	-Lemons (*Citrus limon*, *Citrus limonum*) and limes (*Citrus aurantifolia*)
0805.9000	-其他	30	100	13	5	千克	AB	-Other
08.06	**鲜或干的葡萄:**							**Grapes, fresh or dried:**
0806.1000	-鲜的	13	80	13	5	千克	AB	-Fresh
0806.2000	-干的	10	80	13	5	千克	AB	-Dried

税则号列	货品名称	最惠(%)	普通	增值税率	出口退税	计量单位	监管条件	Article Description
08.07	鲜的甜瓜(包括西瓜)及木瓜:							**Melons (including watermelons) and papaws (papayas), fresh:**
	-甜瓜,包括西瓜:							-Melons (including watermelons):
0807.1100	--西瓜	25	70	13	5	千克	AB	--Watermelons
	--其他:							--Other:
0807.1910	---哈蜜瓜	12	70	13	5	千克	AB	---Hami melons
0807.1920	---罗马甜瓜及加勒比甜瓜	12	70	13	5	千克	AB	---Cantaloupe and Galia melons
0807.1990	---其他	12	70	13	5	千克	AB	---Other
0807.2000	-木瓜	25	70	13	5	千克	AB	-Papaws(papayas)
08.08	**鲜的苹果、梨及榅桲:**							**Apples, pears and quinces, fresh:**
0808.1000	-苹果	10	100	13	5	千克	AB	-Apples
	-梨:							-Pears:
0808.3010	---鸭梨及雪梨	12	100	13	5	千克	AB	---Ya pears and snowy pearwhite
0808.3020	---香梨	12	100	13	5	千克	AB	---Fragrant pear
0808.3090	---其他	10	100	13	5	千克	AB	---Other
0808.4000	-榅桲	16	100	13	5	千克	AB	-Quinces
08.09	**鲜的杏、樱桃、桃(包括油桃)、梅及李:**							**Apricots, cherries, peaches (including nectarines), plums and sloes, fresh:**
0809.1000	-杏	25	70	13	5	千克	AB	-Apricots
	-樱桃:							-Cherries:
0809.2100	--欧洲酸樱桃	10	70	13	5	千克	AB	--Sour cherries(Prunus cerasus)
0809.2900	--其他	10	70	13	5	千克	AB	--Other
0809.3000	-桃,包括油桃	10	70	13	5	千克	AB	-Peaches, including nectarines
0809.4000	-梅及李	10	70	13	5	千克		-Plums and sloes
0809.4000 01	鲜梅	10	70	13	5	千克	AB	Plums,fresh
0809.4000 90	鲜李子	10	70	13	5	千克	AB	Sloes,fresh
08.10	**其他鲜果:**							**Other fruit, fresh:**
0810.1000	-草莓	14	80	13	5	千克	AB	-Strawberries
0810.2000	-木莓、黑莓、桑葚及罗甘莓	25	80	13	5	千克	AB	-Raspberries, blackberries, mulberries and loganberries
0810.3000	-黑、白或红的穗醋栗(加仑子)及醋栗	25	80	13	5	千克	AB	-Black,white or red currant and gooseberries
0810.4000	-蔓越橘及越橘	30	80	13	5	千克	AB	-Cranberries, bilberries and other fruits of the genus *Vaccinium*
0810.5000	-猕猴桃	20	80	13	5	千克	AB	-Kiwifruit
0810.6000	-榴莲	20	80	13	5	千克	AB	-Durian
0810.7000	-柿子	20	80	13	5	千克	AB	-Persimmons
	-其他:							-Other:
0810.9010	---荔枝	30	80	13	5	千克	AB	---Lychee
0810.9030	---龙眼	12	80	13	5	千克	AB	---Longan
0810.9040	---红毛丹	20	80	13	5	千克	AB	---Rambutan
0810.9050	---蕃荔枝	20	80	13	5	千克	AB	---Sugar apple
0810.9060	---杨桃	20	80	13	5	千克	AB	---Carambola
0810.9070	---莲雾	20	80	13	5	千克	AB	---Wax apple
0810.9080	---火龙果	20	80	13	5	千克	AB	---Dragon fruit
0810.9090	---其他	20	80	13	5	千克		---Other
0810.9090 01	鲜枣	20	80	13	5	千克	AB	Chinese date,fresh
0810.9090 02	鲜枇杷	20	80	13	5	千克	AB	Loquat,fresh
0810.9090 10	鲜的翅果油树果	20	80	13	5	千克	ABE	Fruit of elaeagnus mollis diels
0810.9090 90	其他鲜果	20	80	13	5	千克	AB	Other fruit, fresh
08.11	冷冻水果及坚果,不论是否蒸煮、加糖或其他甜物质:							**Fruit and nuts, uncooked or cooked by steaming or boiling in water, frozen, whether or not containing added sugar or other sweetening matter:**
0811.1000	-草莓	30	80	13	5	千克	AB	-Strawberries
0811.2000	-木莓、黑莓、桑葚、罗甘莓、黑、白或红的醋栗(加仑子)及鹅莓	30	80	13	5	千克	AB	-Raspberries, blackberries, mulberries, loganberries, black, white or red currants and gooseberries
	-其他:							-Other:
0811.9010	---栗子,未去壳	30	80	13	5	千克	AB	---Chestnuts, in shell

税则号列	货品名称	最惠(%)	普通	增值税率	出口退税	计量单位	监管条件	Article Description
0811.9090	---其他	30	80	13		千克		---Other
0811.9090 10	冷冻的白果	30	80	13	5	千克	ABE	Ginkgo, frozen
0811.9090 21	冷冻的红松子(不论是否去壳或去皮)	30	80	13	5	千克	ABE	Korean pine-nuts, shelled, frozen (whethe or not shelled or peeled)
0811.9090 22	冷冻的其他濒危松子(不论是否去壳或去皮)	30	80	13		千克	ABEF	Other endangered pine-nuts, shelled (whethe or not shelled or peeled)
0811.9090 30	冷冻的榧子	30	80	13	5	千克	ABE	Semen torreyae, frozen
0811.9090 40	冷冻的翅果油树果	30	80	13	5	千克	ABE	Fruit of wingfruit elaeagus (Elaeagus mollis Diels), frozen
0811.9090 50	冷冻的巨籽棕(海椰子)果仁	30	80	13	5	千克	ABEF	Lodoicea maldivica nut, frozen
0811.9090 90	其他未列名冷冻水果及坚果	30	80	13	5	千克	AB	Other fruit and nuts, frozen, not elsewhere specified or included
08.12	**暂时保藏(例如,使用二氧化硫气体、盐水、亚硫酸水或其他防腐液)的水果及坚果,但不适于直接食用的:**							**Fruit and nuts, provisionally preserved (for example, by sulphur dioxide gas, in brine, in sulphur water or in other preservative solutions), but unsuitable in that state for immediate consumption:**
0812.1000	-樱桃	30	80	13	5	千克	AB	-Cherries
0812.9000	-其他	25	80	13		千克		-Other
0812.9000 10	暂时保存的白果(用二氧化硫气体、盐水等物质处理,但不适于直接食用的)	25	80	13	5	千克	ABE	Ginkgo, provisionally preserved (by sulphur dioxide gas, in brine or in other preservative solutions but unsuitable in that state for immediate consumption)
0812.9000 21	暂时保存的红松子(用二氧化硫气体、盐水等物质处理,但不适于直接食用的)	25	80	13	5	千克	ABE	Korean pine-nuts, provisionally preserved (by sulphur dioxide gas, in brine or in other wise prepared, but unsuitable in that state for immediate consumption)
0812.9000 22	暂时保存的其他濒危松子(用二氧化硫气体,盐水等物质处理,但不适于直接食用的)	25	80	13		千克	ABFE	Other endangered pine-nuts, provisionally preserved (by sulphur dioxide gas, in brine or in otherwise prepared, but unsuitable in that state for immediate consumption)
0812.9000 30	暂时保存的榧子(用二氧化硫气体、盐水等物质处理,但不适于直接食用的)	25	80	13	5	千克	ABE	Semen torreyae provisionally preserved (by sulphur dioxide gas, in brine or in otherwise prepared, but unsuitable in that state for immediate consumption)
0812.9000 40	暂时保存的翅果油树果(用二氧化硫气体、盐水等物质处理,但不适于直接食用的)	25	80	13	5	千克	ABE	Fruit of elaeagnus mollis diels (*Elaeagus mollis Diels*) provisionally preserved (by sulphur dioxide gas, in brine or in otherwise prepared, but unsuitable in that state for immediate consumption)
0812.9000 50	暂时保存的巨籽棕(海椰子)果仁(用二氧化硫气体、盐水等物质处理,但不适于直接食用的)	25	80	13	5	千克	ABEF	Lodoicea maldivica nut, provisionally preserved (by sulphur dioxide gas, in brine or in other preservative solutions, but unsuitable in that state for immediate consumoption)
0812.9000 90	暂时保存的其他水果及坚果(用二氧化硫气体,盐水等物质处理,但不适于直接食用的)	25	80	13	5	千克	AB	Other fruit and nuts, provisionally preserved (by sulphur dioxide gas, in brine or in otherwise prepared, but unsuitable in that state for immediate consumption)
08.13	**税目08.01至08.06以外的干果;本章的什锦坚果或干果:**							**Fruit, dried, other than that of headings No. 08.01 to 08.06; mixtures of nuts or dried fruits of this Chapter:**
0813.1000	-杏	25	70	13	5	千克	AB	-Apricots
0813.2000	-梅及李	25	70	13	5	千克	AB	-Prunes
0813.3000	-苹果	25	70	13	5	千克	AB	-Apples
	-其他:							-Other:
0813.4010	---龙眼干、肉	20	70	13	5	千克	AB	---Longans and longan pulps
0813.4020	---柿饼	25	70	13	5	千克	AB	---Persimmons
0813.4030	---红枣	25	70	13	5	千克	AB	---Red jujubes
0813.4040	---荔枝干	25	70	13	5	千克	AB	---Preserved litchi
0813.4090	---其他	25	70	13	5	千克		---Other

税则号列	货品名称	最惠(%)	普通	增值税率	出口退税	计量单位	监管条件	Article Description
0813.4090 10	翅果油树干果	25	70	13	5	千克	ABE	Fruit of wingfruit elaeagus (*Elaeagus mollis Diels*), dried
0813.4090 90	其他干果(税号0801至0806的干果除外)	25	70	13	5	千克	AB	Other fruit, dried (other than that of headings No. 08.01 to 08.06)
0813.5000	本章的什锦坚果或干果	18	70	13	5	千克	AB	-Mixtures of nuts or dried fruits of this Chapter
08.14	**柑橘属水果或甜瓜(包括西瓜)的果皮,鲜、冻、干或用盐水、亚硫酸水或其他防腐液暂时保藏的:**							**Peel of citrus fruit or melons (including water-melons), fresh, frozen, dried or provisionally preserved in brine, in sulphur water or in other preservative solutions:**
0814.0000	柑橘属水果或甜瓜(包括西瓜)的果皮鲜、冻、干或用盐水、亚硫酸水或其他防腐液暂时保藏的	25	70	13	5	千克	AB	Peel of citrus fruit or melons (including watermelons), fresh, frozen, dried or provisionally preserved in brine, in sulphur water or in other preservative solutions

第九章
咖啡、茶、马黛茶及调味香料

Chapter 9
Coffee, tea, mate and spices

注释：

一、税目 09.04 至 09.10 所列产品的混合物，应按下列规定归类：

（一）同一税目的两种或两种以上产品的混合物仍应归入该税目；

（二）不同税目的两种或两种以上产品的混合物应归入税目 09.10。

税目 09.04 至 09.10 的产品［或上述（一）或（二）项的混合物］如添加了其他物质，只要所得的混合物保持了原产品的基本特性，其归类应不受影响。基本特性已经改变的，则不应归入本章；构成混合调味品的，应归入税目 21.03。

二、本章不包括荜澄茄椒或税目 12.11 的其他产品。

Notes:

1. Mixtures of the products of headings No. 09.04 to 09.10 are to be classified as follows:

(a) Mixtures of two or more of the products of the same heading are to be classified in that heading;

(b) Mixtures of two or more of the products of different headings are to be classified in heading No. 09.10.

The addition of other substances to the products of headings No. 09.04 to 09.10 (or to the mixtures referred to in paragraph (a) or (b) above) shall not affect their classification provided the resulting mixtures retain the essential character of the goods of those headings. Otherwise such mixtures are not classified in this Chapter; those constituting mixed condiments or mixed seasonings are classified in heading No. 21.03.

2. This Chapter does not cover Cubeb pepper (*Piper cubeba*) or other products of heading No. 12.11.

税则号列	货品名称	最惠(%)	普通	增值税率	出口退税	计量单位	监管条件	Article Description
09.01	**咖啡，不论是否焙炒或浸除咖啡碱；咖啡豆荚及咖啡豆皮；含咖啡的咖啡代用品：**							**Coffee, whether or not roasted or decaffeinated; coffee husks and skins; coffee substitutes containing coffee in any proportion:**
	-未焙炒的咖啡：							-Coffee, not roasted:
0901.1100	--未浸除咖啡碱	8	50	17	5	千克	AB	--Not decaffeinated
0901.1200	--已浸除咖啡碱	8	50	17	5	千克	AB	--Decaffeinated
	-已焙炒的咖啡：							-Coffee, roasted:
0901.2100	--未浸除咖啡碱	15	80	17	15	千克	AB	--Not decaffeinated
0901.2200	--已浸除咖啡碱	15	80	17	15	千克	AB	--Decaffeinated
	-其他：							-Other:
0901.9010	---咖啡豆荚及咖啡豆皮	10	30	17	5	千克	AB	---Coffee husks and skins
0901.9020	---含咖啡的咖啡代用品	30	80	17	15	千克	AB	---Coffee substitutes containing coffee
09.02	**茶，不论是否加香料：**							**Tea, whether or not flavoured:**
	-绿茶（未发酵），内包装每件净重不超过3千克：							-Green tea (not fermented) in immediate packings of a content not exceeding 3kg:
0902.1010	---花茶	15	100	13	5,15	千克	AB	---Flavoured
0902.1090	---其他	15	100	13	5,15	千克	AB	---Other
	-其他绿茶（未发酵）：							-Other green tea (not fermented):
0902.2010	---花茶	15	100	13	5,15	千克	AB	---Flavoured
0902.2090	---其他	15	100	13	5,15	千克	AB	---Other
	-红茶（已发酵）及半发酵茶，内包装每件净重不超过3千克：							-Black tea (fermented) and partly fermented tea, in immediate packings of a content not exceeding 3 kg:
0902.3010	---乌龙茶	15	100	13	5,15	千克	AB	---Oolong tea
0902.3020	---普洱茶	15	100	13	5,15	千克	AB	---Pu-er tea
0902.3090	---其他	15	100	13	5,15	千克	AB	---Other
	-其他红茶（已发酵）及半发酵茶：							-Other black tea (fermented) and other partly fermented tea:
0902.4010	---乌龙茶	15	100	13	5,15	千克	AB	---Oolong tea
0902.4020	---普洱茶	15	100	13	5,15	千克	AB	---Pu-er tea
0902.4090	---其他	15	100	13	5,15	千克	AB	---Other
09.03	**马黛茶：**							**Mate:**
0903.0000	马黛茶	10	100	13	15	千克	AB	Mate
09.04	**胡椒；辣椒干及辣椒粉：**							**Pepper of the genus Piper; dried or crushed or ground fruits of the genus Capsicum or of the genus Pimenta:**
	-胡椒：							-Pepper:
0904.1100	--未磨	20	70	13	5	千克		--Neither crushed nor ground
0904.1100 10	毕拨	20	70	13	5	千克	QAB	Piper longum
0904.1100 90	未磨胡椒（毕拨除外）	20	70	13	5	千克	AB	Pepper of the genus *Piper*, neither crushed nor ground (other than piper longum)

税则号列	货品名称	最惠(%)	普通	增值税率	出口退税	计量单位	监管条件	Article Description
0904.1200	--已磨	20	70	13	15	千克	AB	--Crushed or ground
	-辣椒:							– Chili:
0904.2100	--干,未磨	20	70	13		千克	AB	--Dried, neither crushed nor ground
0904.2200	--已磨	20	70	13	15	千克	AB	--Crushed or ground
09.05	香子兰豆:							**Vanilla:**
0905.1000	-未磨	15	50	13	5	千克	AB	-Neither crushed nor ground
0905.2000	-已磨	15	50	13	5	千克	AB	-Crushed or ground
09.06	肉桂及肉桂花:							**Cinnamon and cinnamon-tree flowers:**
	-未磨:							-Neither crushed nor ground:
0906.1100	--锡兰肉桂	5	50	13	5	千克	AB	--Cinnamon(*Cinnamomum zeylan-icum blume*)
0906.1900	--其他	5	50	13	5	千克	AB	--Other
0906.2000	-已磨	15	50	13	15	千克	QAB	-Crushed or ground
09.07	丁香(母丁香、公丁香及丁香梗):							**Cloves (whole fruit, cloves and stems):**
0907.1000	-未磨	3	14	13	5	千克	QAB	-Neither crushed nor ground
0907.2000	-已磨	3	14	13	5	千克	QAB	-Crushed or ground
09.08	肉豆蔻、肉豆蔻衣及豆蔻:							**Nutmeg, mace and cardamoms:**
	-肉豆蔻:							-Nutmeg:
0908.1100	-未磨	8	30	13	5	千克	QABE	-Neither crushed nor ground
0908.1200	-已磨	8	30	13	5	千克	QABE	-Crushed or ground
	-肉豆蔻衣:							-Mace:
0908.2100	-未磨	8	30	13	5	千克	ABE	-Neither crushed nor ground
0908.2200	-已磨	8	30	13	5	千克	ABE	-Crushed or ground
	-豆蔻:							-Cardamoms:
0908.3100	-未磨	3	14	13	5	千克	QABE	-Neither crushed nor ground
0908.3200	-已磨	3	14	13	15	千克	QABE	-Crushed or ground
09.09	茴芹子、八角茴香、小茴香子、芫荽子、枯茗子及黄蒿子;杜松果:							**Seeds of anise, star anise, fennel, coriander, cumin or caraway; juniper berries:**
	-芫荽子:							-Seeds of coriander:
0909.2100	-未磨	15	50	13	5	千克	AB	-Neither crushed nor ground
0909.2200	-已磨	15	50	13	15	千克	AB	-Crushed or ground
	-枯茗子:							-Seeds of cumin:
0909.3100	-未磨	15	50	13	5	千克	AB	-Neither crushed nor ground
0909.3200	-已磨	15	50	13	15	千克	AB	-Crushed nor ground
	-茴芹子或八角茴香、贲蒿子或小茴香子;杜松果:							-Seeds of pimpinella or star anise、seeds of caraway or seeds of fennel; juniper berries:
	--未磨:							--Neither crushed nor ground:
0909.6110	---八角茴香	20	90	13	5	千克	QAB	---Star anises
0909.6190	---其他	15	50	13	5	千克	QAB	---Other
0909.6190 10	未磨的小茴香子;未磨的杜松果	15	50	13	5	千克	QAB	Seed of fennel, seed of juniper berries, neither crushed nor ground
0909.6190 90	未磨的茴芹子;未磨的贲蒿子	15	50	13	5	千克	AB	Seed of pimpinella, seed of caraway, neither crushed nor ground
	--已磨:							--Crushed nor ground:
0909.6210	---八角茴香	20	90	13	15	千克	QAB	---Star anises
0909.6290	---其他	15	50	13	15	千克	QAB	---Other
0909.6290 10	已磨的小茴香子;已磨的杜松果	15	50	13	15	千克	QAB	Seed of fennel, seed of juniper berries, crushed or ground
0909.6290 90	已磨的茴芹子;已磨的贲蒿子	15	50	13	15	千克	AB	Seed of pimpinella, seed of caraway, crushed or ground
09.10	姜、番红花、姜黄、麝香草、月桂叶、咖喱及其他调味香料:							**Ginger, saffron, turmeric (curcuma), thyme, bay leaves, curry and other spices:**
	-姜:							-Ginger:
0910.1100	--未磨	15	50	13		千克	AB	--Neither crushed nor ground
0910.1200	--已磨	15	50	13	5	千克	AB	--Crushed or ground
0910.2000	-番红花	2	14	13	5,15	千克	QAB	-Saffron
0910.3000	-姜黄	15	50	13	5	千克	QAB	-Turmeric (curcuma)
	-其他调味香料:							-Other spices:
0910.9100	--本章注释一(二)所述的混合物	15	50	17	15	千克	AB	--Mixtures referred to in Note 1(b) to this Chapter
0910.9900	--其他	15	50	17	5,15	千克	AB	--Other

第十章 谷　物

Chapter 10 Cereals

注释：

一、(一)本章各税目所列产品必须带有谷粒，不论是否成穗或带杆。

(二)本章不包括已去壳或经其他加工的谷物。但去壳、碾磨、磨光、上光、半熟或破碎的稻米仍应归入税目10.06。

二、税目10.05不包括甜玉米(第七章)。

子目注释：

所称"硬粒小麦"，是指硬粒小麦属的小麦及以该属具有相同染色体数目(28)的小麦种间杂交所得的小麦。

Notes:

1. (a) The products specified in the headings of this Chapter are to be classified in those headings only if grains are present, whether or not in the ear or on the stalk.

   (b) The Chapter does not cover grains which have been hulled or otherwise worked. However, rice, husked, milled, polished, glazed, parboiled or broken remains classified in heading No. 10.06

2. Heading No. 10.05 does not cover sweet corn (Chapter 7).

Subheading Note:

The term "durum wheat" means wheat of the *Triticum durum* species and the hybrids derived from the inter-specific crossing of *Triticum durum* which have the same number (28) of chromosomes as that species.

税则号列	货品名称	最惠(%)	普通	增值税率	出口退税	计量单位	监管条件	Article Description
10.01	**小麦及混合麦：**							**Wheat and maslin:**
	-硬粒小麦：							-Durum wheat:
1001.1100	--种用		180	13		千克		--Seed
1001.1100 01	种用硬粒小麦(配额内)	1	180	13		千克	4xABty	Durum wheat, seed(in-quota)
1001.1100 90	种用硬粒小麦(配额外)	65	180	13		千克	4xABy	Durum wheat, seed(out-quota)
1001.1900	--其他		180	13		千克		--Other
1001.1900 01	其他硬粒小麦(配额内)	1	180	13		千克	4xABty	Other durum wheat(in-quota)
1001.1900 90	其他硬粒小麦(配额外)	65	180	13		千克	4xABy	Other durum wheat(out-quota)
	-其他：							-Other:
1001.9100	---种用		180	13		千克		---Seed
1001.9100 01	其他种用小麦及混合麦(配额内)	1	180	13		千克	4xABty	Other wheat, seed and maslin(in-quota)
1001.9100 90	其他种用小麦及混合麦(配额外)	65	180	13		千克	4xABy	Other wheat, seed and maslin(out-quota)
1001.9900	---其他			13		千克		---Other
1001.9900 01	其他小麦及混合麦(配额内)	1	180	13		千克	4xABty	Other wheat and maslin (in-quota)
1001.9900 90	其他小麦及混合麦(配额外)	65	180	13		千克	4xABy	Other wheat and maslin (out-quota)
10.02	**黑麦：**							**Rye:**
1002.1000	---种用	0	0	13		千克	AB	---Seed
1002.9000	---其他	3	8	13		千克	AB	---Other
10.03	**大麦：**							**Barley:**
1003.1000	---种用	0	160	13		千克	AB	---Seed
1003.9000	---其他	3	160	13		千克	AB	---Other
10.04	**燕麦：**							**Oats:**
1004.1000	---种用	0	0	13		千克	AB	---Seed
1004.9000	---其他	2	8	13		千克	AB	---Other
10.05	**玉米：**							**Maize (corn):**
1005.1000	-种用		180	13		千克		-Seed
1005.1000 01	种用玉米(配额内)	1	180	13		千克	4xAByt	Maize (corn) seed (in-quota)
1005.1000 90	种用玉米(配额外)	20	180	13		千克	4xABy	Maize (corn) seed (out-quota)
1005.9000	-其他			13		千克		-Other
1005.9000 01	其他玉米(配额内)	1	180	13		千克	4xAByt	Other maize (corn) (in-quota)
1005.9000 90	其他玉米(配额外)	65	180	13		千克	4xABy	Other maize (corn) (out-quota)
10.06	**稻谷、大米：**							**Rice:**
	-稻谷：							-Rice in husk (paddy or rough):
	---种用：							---Seed:
1006.1011	----籼米		180	13		千克		----Long grain
1006.1011 01	种用籼米稻谷(配额内)	1	180	13		千克	4xAByt	Rice in husk (paddy or rough), shien rice (*long-grained nonglutinous rice*), seed (in-quota)
1006.1011 90	种用籼米稻谷(配额外)	65	180	13		千克	4xABy	Rice in husk (paddy or rough), shien rice (*long-grained nonglutinous rice*), seed (out-quota)
1006.1019	----其他		180	13		千克		----Other

税则号列	货品名称	最惠(%)	普通	增值税率	出口退税	计量单位	监管条件	Article Description
1006.1019 01	其他种用稻谷(配额内)	1	180	13		千克	4xAByt	Other rice in husk (paddy or rough), seed (in-quota)
1006.1019 90	其他种用稻谷(配额外)	65	180	13		千克	4xABy	Other rice in husk (paddy or rough), seed (out-quota)
	---其他:							---Other:
1006.1091	----籼米		180	13		千克		----Long grain
1006.1091 01	其他籼米稻谷(配额内)	1	180	13		千克	4xAByt	Other rice in husk (paddy or rough), long grain (*long-grained nonglutinous rice*) (in-quota)
1006.1091 90	其他籼米稻谷(配额外)	65	180	13		千克	4xABy	Other rice in husk (paddy or rough), long grain (*long-grained nonglutinous rice*) (out-quota)
1006.1099	----其他		180	13		千克		----Other
1006.1099 01	其他稻谷(配额内)	1	180	13		千克	4xAByt	Other rice in husk (paddy or rough) (in-quota)
1006.1099 90	其他稻谷(配额外)	65	180	13		千克	4xABy	Other rice in husk (paddy or rough) (out-quota)
	-糙米:							-Husked (brown) rice:
1006.2010	---籼米		180	13		千克		---Shien rice
1006.2010 01	籼米糙米(配额内)	1	180	13		千克	4xAByt	Husked (brown) rice, long grain(*long-grained nonglutinous rice*) (in-quota)
1006.2010 90	籼米糙米(配额外)	65	180	13		千克	4xABy	Husked (brown) rice, long grain(*long-grained nonglutinous rice*) (out-quota)
1006.2090	---其他		180	13		千克		---Other
1006.2090 01	其他糙米(配额内)	1	180	13		千克	4xAByt	Other husked(brown) rice (in-quota)
1006.2090 90	其他糙米(配额外)	65	180	13		千克	4xABy	Other husked (brown) rice, (out-quota)
	-精米,不论是否磨光或上光:							-Semi-milled or wholly missed rice, whether or not polished or glazed:
1006.3010	---籼米		180	13		千克		---long grain
1006.3010 01	籼米精米[不论是否磨光或上光(配额内)]	1	180	13		千克	4xAByt	Semi-milled or wholly milled rice, long grain(*long-grained nonglutinous rice*), whether or not polished or glazed (in-quota)
1006.3010 90	籼米精米[不论是否磨光或上光(配额外)]	65	180	13		千克	4xABy	Semi-milled or wholly milled rice, long grain(*long-grained nonglutinous rice*)[whether or not polished or glazed (out-quota)]
1006.3090	---其他		180	13		千克		---Other
1006.3090 01	其他精米[不论是否磨光或上光(配额内)]	1	180	13		千克	4xAByt	Other semi-milled or wholly milled rice[whether or not polished or glazed (in-quota)]
1006.3090 90	其他精米[不论是否磨光或上光(配额外)]	65	180	13		千克	4xABy	Other semi-milled or wholly milled rice[whether or not polished or glazed (out-quota)]
	-碎米:							-Broken rice:
1006.4010	---籼米		180	13		千克		---long grain
1006.4010 01	籼米碎米(配额内)	1	180	13		千克	4xAByt	Broken rice, long grain (*long-grained nonglutinous rice*) (in-quota)
1006.4010 90	籼米碎米(配额外)	65	180	13		千克	4xABy	Broken rice, long grain (*long-grained nonglutinous rice*) (out-quota)
1006.4090	---其他		180	13		千克		---Other
1006.4090 01	其他碎米(配额内)	1	180	13		千克	4xAByt	Other broken rice (in-quota)
1006.4090 90	其他碎米(配额外)	65	180	13		千克	4xABy	Other broken rice (out-quota)
10.07	**食用高粱:**							**Grain sorghum:**
1007.1000	---种用	0	0	13		千克	AB	---Seed
1007.9000	---其他	2	8	13		千克	AB	---Other
10.08	**荞麦、谷子及加那利草子;其他谷物:**							**Buckwheat, millet and canary seed; other cereals:**
1008.1000	-荞麦	2	8	13		千克	AB	-Buckwheat
	-谷子:							-Millet:
1008.2100	--种用	2	8	13		千克	AB	--Seed
1008.2900	--其他	2	8	13		千克	AB	--Other
1008.3000	-加那利草子	2	8	13	5	千克	AB	-Canary seed
	-直长马唐(马唐属):							-Fonio(Digitaria spp.):
1008.4010	---种用	0	0	13		千克	AB	---Seed

税则号列	货品名称	最惠(%)	普通	增值税率	出口退税	计量单位	监管条件	Article Description
1008.4090	---其他	3	8	13		千克	AB	---Other
	-昆诺阿藜：							-Quinoa(Chenopodium quinoa):
1008.5010	---种用	0	0	13		千克	AB	---Seed
1008.5090	---其他	3	8	13		千克	AB	---Other
	-黑小麦：							-Triticale:
1008.6010	---种用	0	0	13		千克	AB	---Seed
1008.6090	---其他	3	80	13		千克	AB	---Other
	-其他谷物：							-Other cereals:
1008.9010	---种用	0	0	13		千克	AB	---Seed
1008.9090	---其他	3	8	13		千克	AB	---Other

第十一章
制粉工业产品;麦芽;淀粉;菊粉;面筋

注释:

一、本章不包括:

(一)作为咖啡代用品的焙制麦芽(税目 09.01 或 21.01);

(二)税目 19.01 的经制作的细粉、粗粒、粗粉或淀粉;

(三)税目 19.04 的玉米片及其他产品;

(四)税目 20.01、20.04 或 20.05 的经加工或保藏的蔬菜;

(五)药品(第三十章);

(六)具有芳香料制品或化妆盥洗品性质的淀粉(第三十三章)。

二、(一)下表所列谷物碾磨产品按干制品重量计如果同时符合以下两个条件,应归入本章;但是,整粒、滚压、制片或磨碎的谷物胚芽均应归入税目 11.04:

1. 淀粉含量(按修订的尤艾斯旋光法测定)超过表列第(2)栏的比例;以及

2. 灰分含量(除去任何添加的矿物质)不超过表列第(3)栏的比例。

否则,应归入税目 23.02。

(二)符合上述规定归入本章的产品,如果用表列第(4)或第(5)栏规定孔径的金属丝网筛过筛,其通过率按重量计不低于表列比例的,应归入税目 11.01 或 11.02。

否则,应归入税目 11.03 或 11.04。

谷　物 (1)	淀粉含量 (2)	灰分含量 (3)	通过下列孔径筛子的比率	
			315 微米 (4)	500 微米 (5)
小麦及黑麦	45%	2.5%	80%	—
大　麦	45%	3%	80%	—
燕　麦	45%	5%	80%	—
玉米及高粱	45%	2%	—	90%
大　米	45%	1.6%	80%	—
荞　麦	45%	4%	80%	—

三、税目 11.03 所称"粗粒"及"粗粉",是指谷物经碾碎所得的下列产品:

(一)玉米产品,用 2 毫米孔径的金属丝网筛过筛后通过率按重量计不低于95%的;

(二)其他谷物产品,用 1.25 毫米孔径的金属丝网筛过筛,通过率按重量计不低于95%的。

Chapter 11
Products of the milling industry; malt; starches; inulin; wheat gluten

chorpterr Notes:

1. This Chapter does not cover:

(a) Roasted malt put up as coffee substitutes (heading No. 09.01 or 21.01);

(b) Prepared flours, groats, meals or starches of heading No. 19.01;

(c) Corn flakes or other products of heading No. 19.04;

(d) Vegetables, prepared or preserved, of heading No. 20.01, 20.04 or 20.05;

(e) Pharmaceutical products (Chapter 30);

(f) Starches having the character of perfumery, cosmetic or toilet preparations (Chapter 33).

2. (A) Products from the milling of the cereals listed in the table below fall in this Chapter if they have, by weight on the dry product. However, germ of cereals, whole, rolled, flaked or ground is always classified in heading No. 11.04.

(ⅰ) a starch content (determined by the modified Ewers polarimetric method) exceeding that indicated in Column (2); and

(ⅱ) an ash content (after deduction of any added minerals) not exceeding that indicated in Column (3).

Otherwise, they fall in heading No. 23.02

(B) Products falling in this Chapter under the above provisions shall be classified in heading No. 11.01 or 11.02 if the percentage passing through a woven metal wire cloth sieve with the aperture indicated in Column (4) or (5) is not less, by weight, than that shown against the cereal concerned.

Otherwise, they fall in heading No. 11.03 or 11.04.

Cereal (1)	Starch content (2)	Ash content (3)	Rate of passage through a sieve with an aperture of	
			315 micrometres (microns) (4)	500 micrometres (microns) (5)
Wheat and rye	45%	2.5%	80%	-
Barley	45%	3%	80%	-
Oats	45%	5%	80%	-
Maize (corn) and grain Sorghum	45%	2%	-	90%
Rice	45%	1.6%	80%	-
Buckwheat	45%	4%	80%	-

3. For the purposes of heading No. 11.03, the terms "groats" and "meal" mean products obtained by the fragmentation of cereal grains, of which:

(a) in the case of maize (corn) products, at least 95% by weight passes through a woven metal wire cloth sieve with an aperture of 2mm.

(b) in the case of other cereal products, at least 95% by weight passes through a woven metal wire cloth sieve with an aperture of 1.25mm.

税则号列	货品名称	最惠(%)	普通	增值税率	出口退税	计量单位	监管条件	Article Description
11.01	**小麦或混合麦的细粉:**							**Wheat or maslin flour:**
1101.0000	小麦或混合麦的细粉		130	13		千克		Wheat or maslin flour
1101.0000 01	小麦或混合麦的细粉(配额内)	6	130	13		千克	4ABtxy	Wheat or maslin flour (in-quota)
1101.0000 90	小麦或混合麦的细粉(配额外)	65	130	13		千克	4ABxy	Wheat or maslin flour (out-quota)
11.02	**其他谷物细粉,但小麦或混合麦的细粉除外:**							**Cereal flours other than of wheat or maslin:**
1102.2000	-玉米细粉		130	13		千克		-Maize (corn) flour
1102.2000 01	玉米细粉(配额内)	9	130	13		千克	4ABtxy	Maize (corn) flour (in-quota)
1102.2000 90	玉米细粉(配额外)	40	130	13		千克	4ABxy	Maize(corn)flour(out-quota)
	-其他:							-Other:
	---大米细粉:							---Rice flour:
1102.9011	----籼米的		130	13		千克		----Of long grain
1102.9011 01	籼米大米细粉(配额内)	9	130	13		千克	4ABtxy	long grain (long-grained nonglutinous rice flourc in-quota)
1102.9011 90	籼米大米细粉(配额外)	40	130	13		千克	4ABxy	long grain (long-grained noglutinous rice flour out-quota)
1102.9019	----其他		130	13		千克		----Other
1102.9019 01	其他大米细粉(配额内)	9	130	13		千克	4ABtxy	Other rice flour (in-quota)
1102.9019 90	其他大米细粉(配额外)	40	130	13		千克	4ABxy	Other rice flour (out-quota)
1102.9090	---其他	5	14	13		千克	AB	---Other
11.03	**谷物的粗粒、粗粉及团粒:**							**Cereal groats, meal and pellets:**
	-粗粒及粗粉:							-Groats and meal:
1103.1100	--小麦的		130	13		千克		--Of wheat
1103.1100 01	小麦粗粒及粗粉(配额内)	9	130	13		千克	4ABtxy	Wheat groats and meal (in-quota)
1103.1100 90	小麦粗粒及粗粉(配额外)	65	130	13		千克	4ABxy	Wheat groats and meal (out-quota)
1103.1300	--玉米的		130	13		千克		--Of maize (corn)
1103.1300 01	玉米粗粒及粗粉(配额内)	9	130	13		千克	4ABtxy	Maize(corn) groats and meal (in-quota)
1103.1300 90	玉米粗粒及粗粉(配额外)	65	130	13		千克	4ABxy	Maize (corn) groats and meal (out-quota)
	--其他:							--Other:
1103.1910	---燕麦的	5	14	13		千克	AB	---Of oats
	---大米的:							---Of rice:
1103.1921	----籼米的		70	13		千克		----Of long grain
1103.1921 01	籼米大米粗粒及粗粉(配额内)	9	70	13		千克	4ABtxy	long grain groats and meal (in-quota)
1103.1921 90	籼米大米粗粒及粗粉(配额外)	10	70	13		千克	4ABxy	long grain groats and meal (out-quota)
1103.1929	----其他		70	13		千克		----Other
1103.1929 01	其他大米粗粒及粗粉(配额内)	9	70	13		千克	4ABtxy	Other rice groats and meal (in-quota)
1103.1929 90	其他大米粗粒及粗粉(配额外)	10	70	13		千克	4ABxy	Other rice groats and meal (out-quota)
1103.1990	---其他	5	14	13		千克	AB	---Other
	-团粒:							-Pellets:
1103.2010	---小麦的		180	13		千克		---Of wheat
1103.2010 01	小麦团粒(配额内)	10	180	13		千克	4ABtxy	Wheat pellets (in-quota)
1103.2010 90	小麦团粒(配额外)	65	180	13		千克	4ABxy	Wheat pellets (out-quota)
1103.2090	---其他	20	50	13		千克	AB	---Of other cereals
11.04	**经其他加工的谷物(例如,去壳、滚压、制片、制成粒状、切片或粗磨),但税目10.06的稻谷、大米除外;谷物胚芽,整粒、滚压、制片或磨碎的:**							**Cereal grains otherwise worked (for example, hulled, rolled, flaked, pearled, sliced or kibbled), except rice of heading No. 10.06; germ of cereals, whole, rolled, flaked or ground:**
	-滚压或制片的谷物:							-Rolled or flaked grains:
1104.1200	--燕麦的	20	50	17		千克	AB	--Of oats
	--其他:							--Other:
1104.1910	---大麦的	20	50	17		千克	AB	---Of barley
1104.1990	---其他	20	50	17		千克		---Other
1104.1990 10	滚压或制片的玉米	20	50	17		千克	4ABxy	Rolled or flaked maize
1104.1990 90	滚压或制片的其他谷物	20	50	17		千克	AB	Rolled or flaked other corns
	-经其他加工的谷物(例如,去壳、制成粒状、切片或粗磨):							-Other worked grains (for example, hulled, pearled, sliced or kibbled):

税则号列	货品名称	最惠(%)	普通	增值税率	出口退税	计量单位	监管条件	Article Description
1104.2200	--燕麦的	20	50	17		千克	AB	--Of oats
1104.2300	--玉米的		180	13		千克		--Of maize (corn)
1104.2300 01	经其他加工的玉米(配额内)	10	180	13		千克	4xAByt	Maize (corn) otherwise worked (in-quota)
1104.2300 90	经其他加工的玉米(配额外)	65	180	13		千克	4xABy	Maize (corn) otherwise worked (out-quota)
	--其他:							--Other:
1104.2910	---大麦的	65	114	13		千克	AB	---Of barley
1104.2990	---其他	20	50	13		千克	AB	---Other
1104.3000	-谷物胚芽,整粒、滚压、制片或磨碎的	20	50	17		千克	AB	-Germ of cereals, whole, rolled, flaked or ground
11.05	**马铃薯的细粉、粗粉、粉末、粉片、颗粒及团粒:**							**Flour, meal, powder, flakes, granules and pellets of potatoes:**
1105.1000	-细粉、粗粉及粉末	15	50	17	15	千克	AB	-Flour, meal and powder
1105.2000	-粉片、颗粒及团粒	15	50	17	15	千克	AB	-Flakes, granules and pellets
11.06	**用税目07.13的干豆或税目07.14的西谷茎髓及植物根茎、块茎制成的细粉、粗粉及粉末;用第八章的产品制成的细粉、粗粉及粉末:**							**Flour, meal and powder of the dried leguminous vegetables of heading No. 07.13, of sago or of roots or tubers of heading No. 07.14; or of the products of Chapter 8:**
1106.1000	-用税目07.13的干豆制成的	10	30	17	15	千克	AB	-Of the dried leguminous vegetables of heading No. 07.13
1106.2000	-用税目07.14的西谷茎髓及植物根茎、块茎制成的	20	50	17	15	千克	AB	-Of sago or of roots or tubers of heading No. 07.14
1106.3000	-用第八章的产品制成的	20	80	17	5,15	千克	AB	-Of the products of Chapter 8
11.07	**麦芽,不论是否焙制:**							**Malt, whether or not roasted:**
1107.1000	-未焙制	10	50	17	15	千克	AB	-Not roasted
1107.2000	-已焙制	10	50	17	15	千克	AB	-Roasted
11.08	**淀粉;菊粉:**							**Starches; inulin:**
	-淀粉:							-Starches:
1108.1100	--小麦淀粉	20	50	17		千克	AB	--Wheat starch
1108.1200	--玉米淀粉	20	50	17		千克	AB	--Maize (corn) starch
1108.1300	--马铃薯淀粉	15	50	17	15	千克	AB	--Potato starch
1108.1400	--木薯淀粉	10	50	17	15	千克	AB	--Manioc (cassava) starch
1108.1900	--其他	20	50	17	15	千克	AB	--Other starches
1108.2000	-菊粉	20	50	17	15	千克	AB	-Inulin
11.09	**面筋,不论是否干制:**							**Wheat gluten, whether or not dried:**
1109.0000	面筋,不论是否干制	18	80	17	15	千克	AB	Wheat gluten, whether or not dried

第十二章
含油子仁及果实;杂项子仁及果实;工业用或药用植物;稻草、秸杆及饲料

Chapter 12
Oil seeds and oleaginous fruits; miscellaneous grains, seeds and fruit; industrial or medicinal plants; straw and fodder

注释:

一、税目12.07主要包括油棕果及油棕仁、棉子、蓖麻子、芝麻、芥子、红花子、罂粟子、牛油树果。但不包括税目08.01或08.02的产品及油橄榄(第七章或第二十章)。

二、税目12.08不仅包括未脱脂的细粉和粗粉,而且包括部分或全部脱脂以及用其本身的油料全部或部分复脂的细粉和粗粉。但不包括税目23.04至23.06的残渣。

三、甜菜子、草子及其他草本植物种子、观赏用花的种子、蔬菜种子、林木种子、果树种子、巢菜子(蚕豆除外)、羽扇豆属植物种子,可一律视为种植用种子,归入税目12.09。

但下列各项即使用作种子用,也不归入税目12.09:

(一)第七章作蔬菜用的豆类或甜玉米;
(二)第九章的调味香料及其他产品;
(三)第十章的谷物;
(四)税目12.01至12.07或12.11的产品。

四、税目12.11主要包括下列植物或这些植物的某部分:

罗勒、琉璃苣、人参、海索草、甘草、薄荷、迷迭香、芸香、鼠尾草及苦艾。

但税目12.11不包括:

(一)第三十章的药品;
(二)第三十三章的芳香料制品及化妆盥洗品;
(三)税目38.08的杀虫剂、杀菌剂、除草剂、消毒剂及类似产品。

五、税目12.12的"海草及其他藻类"不包括:

(一)税目21.02的已死的单细胞微生物;
(二)税目30.02的培养微生物;
(三)税目31.01或31.05的肥料。

子目注释:

子目1205.10所称"低芥子酸油菜籽",是指所获取的固定油中芥子酸含量按重量计低于2%,以及所得的固体成份每克葡萄糖苷酸(酯)含量低于30微摩尔的油菜籽。

Notes:

1. Heading No. 12.07 applies, *inter alia*, to palm nuts and kernels, cotton seeds, castor oil seeds, sesamum seeds, mustard seeds, safflower seeds, poppy seeds and shea nuts (karite nuts). It does not apply to products of heading No. 08.01 or 08.02 or to olives (Chapter 7 or Chapter 20).
2. Heading No. 12.08 applies not only to non-defatted flours and meals but also to flours and meals which have been partially defatted or defatted and wholly or partially refatted with their original oils. It does not, however, apply to residues of headings No. 23.04 to 23.06
3. For the purposes of heading No. 12.09, beet seeds, grass and other herbage seeds, seeds of ornamental flowers, vegetable seeds, seeds of forest trees, seeds of fruit trees, seeds of vetches (other than those of the species *Vicia faba*) or of lupines are to be regarded as "seeds of a kind used for sowing".

   Heading No. 12.09 does not, however, apply to the following even if for sowing:

   (a) Laguminous vegetables or sweet corn (Chapter 7);
   (b) Spices or other products of Chapter 9;
   (c) Cereals (Chapter 10); or
   (d) Products of headings No. 12.01 to 12.07 or 12.11
4. Heading No. 12.11 applies, *inter alia*, to the following plants or parts thereof:

   Basil, borage, ginseng, hyssop, liquorice, all species of mint, rosemary, rue, sage and wormwood.

   Heading No. 12.11 does not, however, apply to:

   (a) Medicaments of Chapter 30;
   (b) Perfumery, cosmetic or toilet preparations of Chapter 33;
   (c) Insecticides, fungicides, herbicides, disinfectants or similar products of heading No. 38.08.
5. For the purposes of heading No. 12.12, the term "seaweeds and other algae" does not include:

   (a) Dead single-cell micro-organisms of heading No. 21.02;
   (b) Cultures of micro-organisms of heading No. 30.02;
   (c) Fertillizers of heading No. 31.01 or 31.05.

Subheading Notes:

For the purposes of subheading No. 1205.10, the expression "low erucic acid rape or colza seeds" means rape or colza seeds yielding a fixed oil which has an erucic acid content of less than 2% by weight and yielding a solid component which contains less than 30 micromoles of glucosinolates per gram.

税则号列	货品名称	最惠(%)	普通	增值税率	出口退税	计量单位	监管条件	Article Description
12.01	大豆,不论是否破碎:							**Soya beans, whether or not broken:**
1201.1000	---种用	0	180	13		千克	7AB	---Seed
	-其他:							-Other:
1201.9010	----黄大豆	3	180	13		千克	7AB	----Yellow soya beans
1201.9020	----黑大豆	3	180	13		千克	7AB	----Black soya beans
1201.9030	----青大豆	3	180	13		千克	7AB	----Green soya beans
1201.9090	----其他	3	180	13		千克	7AB	----Other
12.02	未焙炒或未烹煮的花生,不论是否去壳或破碎:							**Ground-nuts, not roasted or otherwise cooked, whether or not shelled or broken:**
1202.3000	-种用	0	0	13		千克	AB	-Seed

税则号列	货品名称	最惠(%)	普通	增值税率	出口退税	计量单位	监管条件	Article Description
	-其他:							-Other:
1202.4100	--未去壳	15	70	13		千克	AB	--In shell
1202.4200	--去壳,不论是否破碎	15	70	13		千克	AB	--Shell, whether or not broken
12.03	**干椰子肉:**							**Copra:**
1203.0000	干椰子肉	15	30	13	5	千克	AB	Copra
12.04	**亚麻子,不论是否破碎:**							**Linseed, whether or not broken:**
1204.0000	亚麻子,不论是否破碎	15	70	13	5	千克	AB	Linseed, whether or not broken
12.05	**油菜子,不论是否破碎:**							**Rape or colza seeds, whether or not broken:**
	-低芥子酸油菜籽:							-Low erucic acid rape or colza seeds:
1205.1010	---种用	0	80	13		千克	7AB	---Seed
1205.1090	---其他	9	80	13	5	千克	7AB	---Other
	-其他:							-Other:
1205.9010	---种用	0	80	13		千克	7AB	---Seed
1205.9090	---其他	9	80	13	5	千克	7AB	---Other
12.06	**葵花子,不论是否破碎:**							**Sunflower seeds, whether or not broken:**
1206.0010	---种用	0	0	13	5	千克	AB	---Seed
1206.0090	---其他	15	70	13	5	千克	AB	---Other
12.07	**其他含油子仁及果实,不论是否破碎:**							**Other oil seeds and oleaginous fruits, whether or not broken:**
	-棕榈果及棕榈仁:							-Palm fruit and palm nut:
1207.1010	---种用	0	0	13		千克	AB	---Seed
1207.1010 10	种用濒危棕榈果及棕榈仁	0	0	13		千克	ABEF	Endangered palm fruit and palm nut, seed
1207.1010 90	其他种用棕榈果及棕榈仁	0	0	13	5	千克	AB	Other palm fruit and palm nut, seed
1207.1090	---其他	10	70	13		千克	AB	---Other
1207.1090 10	其他濒危棕榈果及棕榈仁(不论是否破碎)	10	70	13		千克	ABEF	Other endangered palm fruit and palm nut(whether or not broken)
1207.1090 90	其他棕榈果及棕榈仁(不论是否破碎)	10	70	13	5	千克	AB	Other palm fruit and palm nut (whether or not broken)
	-棉子:							-Cotton seeds:
1207.2100	---种用	0	0	13	5	千克	AB	---Seeds
1207.2900	---其他	15	70	13	5	千克	AB	---Other
	-蓖麻子:							-Castor oil seeds:
1207.3010	---种用	0	0	13	5	千克	AB	---Seed
1207.3090	---其他	15	70	13	5	千克	AB	---Other
	-芝麻:							-Sesamum seeds:
1207.4010	---种用	0	0	13	5	千克	AB	---Seeds for cultivation
1207.4090	---其他	10	70	13	5	千克	AB	---Other
	-芥子:							-Mustard seeds:
1207.5010	---种用	0	0	13	5	千克	AB	---Seeds for cultivation
1207.5090	---其他	15	70	13	5	千克	AB	---Other
	-红花子:							-Safflower seeds:
1207.6010	---种用	0	0	13	5	千克	AB	---Seed
1207.6090	---其他	20	70	13	5	千克	AB	---Other
	-甜瓜的子:							-Melon seeds:
1207.7010	---种用	0	0	13		千克	AB	---Seed
	---其他:							---Other:
1207.7091	----黑瓜子	20	80	13	5	千克	AB	----Black melon seeds
1207.7092	----红瓜子	20	80	13	5	千克	AB	----Red melon seeds
1207.7099	----其他	30	70	13	5	千克	AB	----Other
	-其他:							-Other:
1207.9100	--罂粟子	20	70	13	5	千克	AB	--Poppy seeds
	--其他:							--Other:
1207.9910	---种用	0	0	13	5	千克	AB	---Seed
	---其他:							---Other:
1207.9991	----牛油树果	20	70	13	5	千克	AB	----Shea nuts(*karite nuts*)
1207.9999	----其他	10	70	13	5	千克	AB	----Other

税则号列	货品名称	最惠(%)	普通	增值税率	出口退税	计量单位	监管条件	Article Description
12.08	**含油子仁或果实的细粉及粗粉，但芥子粉除外：**							**Flours and meals of oil seeds or oleaginous fruits, other than those of mustard:**
1208.1000	-大豆粉	9	70	17		千克	AB	-Of soya beans
1208.9000	-其他	15	80	17	15	千克	AB	-Other
12.09	**种植用的种子、果实及孢子：**							**Seeds, fruit and spores, of a kind used for sowing:**
1209.1000	-糖甜菜籽	0	0	13	5	千克	AB	-Sugar beet seed
	-饲料植物种子：							-Seeds of forage plants:
1209.2100	--紫苜蓿子	0	0	13		千克	AB	--Lucerne (alfalfa) seed
1209.2200	--三叶草子	0	0	13		千克	AB	--Clover (*Trifolium spp.*) seed
1209.2300	--羊茅子	0	0	13		千克	AB	--Fescue seed
1209.2400	--草地早熟禾子	0	0	13		千克	AB	--Kentucky blue grass (*Poa-pratensis L.*) seed
1209.2500	--黑麦草种子	0	0	13		千克	AB	--Rye grass (*Lolium multiflorum Lam.*, *Lolium perenne L.*) seed
	--其他：							--Other:
1209.2910	---甜菜籽，糖甜菜籽除外	0	0	13	5	千克	AB	---Beet seed, excluding sugar beet seed
1209.2990	---其他	0	0	13		千克	AB	---Other
1209.3000	-草本花卉植物种子	0	0	13		千克		-Seeds of herbaceous plants cultivated principally for their flowers
1209.3000 10	濒危草本花卉植物种子	0	0	13		千克	ABFE	Seeds of endangered herbaceous plants cultivated principally for their flowers
1209.3000 90	其他草本花卉植物种子	0	0	13		千克	AB	Other seeds of herbaceous plants cultivated principally for their flowers
	-其他：							-Other:
1209.9100	--蔬菜种子	0	0	13		千克	AB	--Vegetable seeds
1209.9900	--其他	0	0	13		千克		--Other
1209.9900 10	其他种植用濒危种子、果实及孢子	0	0	13		千克	AFEB	Other endangered seeds, fruit and spores, of a kind used for sowing
1209.9900 90	其他种植用的种子、果实及孢子	0	0	13		千克	AB	Other seeds, fruit and spores, of a kind used for sowing
12.10	**鲜或干的啤酒花，不论是否研磨或制成团粒；蛇麻腺：**							**Hop cones, fresh or dried, whethr or not ground, powdered or in the form of pellets; lupulin:**
1210.1000	-啤酒花，未经研磨也未制成团粒	20	50	17	15	千克	AB	-Hop cones, neither ground nor powdered nor in the form of pellets
1210.2000	-啤酒花，经研磨或制成团粒；蛇麻腺	10	50	17	15	千克	AB	-Hop cones, ground, powdered or in the form of pellets; lupulin
12.11	**主要用作香料、药料、杀虫、杀菌或类似用途的植物或这些植物的某部分（包括子仁及果实），鲜或干的，不论是否切割、压碎或研磨成粉：**							**Plants and parts of plants (including seeds and fruits), of a kind used primarily in perfumery, in pharmacy or for insecticidal, fungicidal or similar purposes, fresh or dried, whether or not cut, crushed or powdered:**
	-人参：							-Ginseng roots:
1211.2010	---西洋参	7.5	70	13	5	千克	AQBFE	---American ginseng
1211.2020	---野山参（西洋参除外）	20	90	13	5	千克	ABFE	---Wild ginseng (other than American ginseng)
	---其他：							---Other:
1211.2091	----鲜的	20	50	13	5	千克	AB	----Fresh
1211.2099	----其他	20	50	13	5	千克	ABQ	----Other
1211.3000	-古柯叶	9	50	13	5	千克		-Coca leaf
1211.3000 10	药用古柯叶（不论是否切割、压碎或研磨成粉）	9	50	13	5	千克	ABW	Coca leaf of a kind used primarily in pharmacy (whether or not cut, crushed or powdered)
1211.3000 20	做香料用古柯叶（不论是否切割、压碎或研磨成粉）	9	50	13	5	千克	AB	Coca leaf of a kind used primarily in perfumery (whether or not cut, crushed or powdered)
1211.3000 90	杀虫杀菌用古柯叶（不论是否切割、压碎或研磨成粉）	9	50	13	5	千克	AB	Coca leaf of a kind used for insecticidal (fungicidal, whether or not cut, crushed or powdered)
1211.4000	-罂粟杆	9	50	13	5	千克		-Poppy straw

税则号列	货　品　名　称	最惠(%)	普通	增值税率	出口退税	计量单位	监管条件	Article Description
1211.4000 10	药用罂粟杆(不论是否切割、压碎或研磨成粉)	9	50	13	5	千克	AB	Poppy straw of a kind used primarily in pharmacy (whether or not cut, crushed or powdered)
1211.4000 20	做香料用罂粟杆(不论是否切割、压碎或研磨成粉)	9	50	13	5	千克	AB	Poppy straw of a kind used primarily in perfumery (whether or not cut, crushed or powdered)
1211.4000 90	杀虫杀菌用罂粟杆(不论是否切割、压碎或研磨成粉)	9	50	13	5	千克	AB	Poppy straw of a kind used for insecticidal, fungicidal (whether or not cut, crushed or powdered)
	-其他:							-Other:
	---主要用作药料的植物及其某部分:							---Of a kind used primarily in pharmacy:
1211.9011	----当归	6	30	13	5	千克	AQB	----Radix angelicae sinensis
1211.9012	----三七(田七)	6	20	13	5	千克	AQB	----Radix pseudoginseng
1211.9013	----党参	6	20	13	5	千克	AQB	----Radix codonopsitis
1211.9014	----黄连	6	20	13	5	千克	AQB	----Rhizoma coptidis
1211.9015	----菊花	6	20	13	0,5	千克	AQB	----Flos chrysanthemi
1211.9016	----冬虫夏草	6	20	13	5	千克	AQBE	----Cordyceps sinensis
1211.9017	----贝母	6	20	13	5	千克	AQB	----Bulbs fritillariae thunbergii
1211.9018	----川芎	6	20	13	5	千克	AQB	----Rhizoma ligustici
1211.9019	----半夏	6	20	13	5	千克	AQB	----Rhizoma pinelliae
1211.9021	----白芍	6	20	13	5	千克	AQB	----Radix paeoniae lactiflorae
1211.9022	----天麻	6	20	13	5	千克	AQBFE	----Rhizoma gastrodiae
1211.9023	----黄芪	6	30	13	5	千克	AQB	----Radix astragali
1211.9024	----大黄、籽黄	6	20	13	5	千克	AQB	----Rhubarb
1211.9025	----白术	6	20	13	5	千克	AQB	----Rhizoma atractylodis macrocephalae
1211.9026	----地黄	6	20	13	5	千克	AQB	----Radix rehmanniae
1211.9027	----槐米	6	20	13	5	千克	AQB	----Flos sophorae
1211.9028	----杜仲	6	20	13	5	千克	AQB	----Cortex eucommiae
1211.9029	----茯苓	6	20	13	5	千克	AQB	----Poria
1211.9031	----枸杞	6	30	13	5	千克	AQB	----Fructus lycii
1211.9032	----大海子	6	20	13	5	千克	AQB	----Bantaroi seeds
1211.9033	----沉香	3	20	13	5	千克	AQFEB	----Aloes wood
1211.9034	----沙参	6	20	13	5	千克	AQB	----Adenophora axilliflora
1211.9035	----青蒿	6	20	13		千克	AB	----Southernwood
1211.9036[新]	----甘草	0	30	13	5	千克	AQB4xy	----Liquorice roots
1211.9037	----黄芩	6	20	13	5	千克	ABQ	----scutellaria root
1211.9038	----椴(欧椴)花及叶子	6	30	13	5	千克		----Flower and leaves of linden tree (lindens)
1211.9038 10	海南椴、紫椴(籽椴)花及叶(不论是否切割、压碎或研磨成粉)	6	30	13	5	千克	ABEQ	Flower and leaves of hainan linden, amur linden (whether or not cut, crushed or powdered)
1211.9038 90	其他椴树(欧椴)花及叶	6	30	13	5	千克	ABQ	Flower and leaves of other linden tree(lindens)
1211.9039	----其他	6	20	13		千克		----Other
1211.9039 10	药料用麻黄草粉	6	20	13	5	千克	23AQB	Chinese ephedra (Ephedrasinica) powder, of a kind used primarily in pharmacy
1211.9039 20	药料用麻黄草	6	20	13	5	千克	8AQ	Chinese ephedra (Ephedrasinica), of a kind used in primarily pharmacy
1211.9039 30	大麻	6	20	13	5	千克	AWB	Hemp
1211.9039 40	罂粟壳	6	20	13	5	千克	AWB	Poppy pod
1211.9039 50	鲜或干的木香(不论是否切割、压碎或研磨成粉)	6	20	13	5	千克	ABFE	Banksia rose, fresh or dried (whether or not cut, crushed or powdered)
1211.9039 60	鲜或干的黄草及枫斗(石斛)(不论是否切割、压碎或研磨成粉)	6	20	13	5	千克	ABFE	Herba dendrobii (in straight form or in earring form), fresh or dried (whether or not cut, crushed or powdered)
1211.9039 70	鲜或干的苁蓉(不论是否切割、压碎或研磨成粉)	6	20	13	5	千克	ABFE	Cistanche deserticola, fresh or dried (whether or not cut, crushed or powdered)
1211.9039 80	鲜或干的红豆杉皮、枝叶等(不论是否切割、压碎或研磨成粉)	6	20	13	5	千克	ABFE	Bark, banch and leaf of taxusl, fresh or dried (wheth-er or not cut, crushed or powdered)
1211.9039 91	其他主要用作药料鲜或干濒危植物(包括其某部分,不论是否切割、压碎或研磨成粉)	6	20	13		千克	ABFE	Other endangered plants, of a kind used primarily in pharmacy, fresh or dried (whether or not cut, crushed or powdered)

税则号列	货品名称	最惠(%)	普通	增值税率	出口退税	计量单位	监管条件	Article Description
1211.9039 92	加纳籽、车前子壳粉、育亨宾皮(包括其某部分,不论是否切割、压碎或研磨成粉)	6	20	13	5	千克	AB	Carbon Ghana seeds, plantago shell powder, yohimbe bark (including part of its, whether or not cut, crushed or ground to powder)
1211.9039 93	恰特草(包括其某部分,不论是否切割、压碎或研磨成粉)	6	20	13	5	千克	ABI	Khat(including part of its, whether or not cutccrushed or powdered)
1211.9039 99	其他主要用作药料的鲜或干的植物(包括其某部分,不论是否切割、压碎或研磨成粉)	6	20	13	5	千克	ABQ	Other plants, of a kind used primarily in pharmacy, fresh or dried (including parts of its, whether or not cut, crushed or powdered)
1211.9050	---主要用作香料的植物及其某部分	8	50	13		千克		---Of a kind used primarily in perfumery
1211.9050 10	香料用麻黄草粉	8	50	13	5	千克	23AB	Chinese ephedra (Ephedrasinica) powder, of a kind used primarily in perfumery
1211.9050 20	香料用麻黄草	8	50	13	5	千克	8A	Chinese ephedra (Ephedrasinica), of a kind used primarily in perfumery
1211.9050 30	香料用沉香木及拟沉香木(包括其某部分,不论是否切割、压碎或研磨成粉)	8	50	13		千克	ABFE	Spices (including part of its, whether or not cutc-crushed or powdered)
1211.9050 91	其他主要用作香料的濒危植物(包括其某部分,不论是否切割、压碎或研磨成粉)	8	50	13		千克	ABFE	Other endangered plants, of a kind used primarily in perfumery(including parts of its, whether or not cut, crushed or powdered)
1211.9050 99	其他主要用作香料的植物(包括其某部分,不论是否切割、压碎或研磨成粉)	8	50	13	5	千克	AB	Other plants, of a kind used primarily in perfumery (including parts of its, whether or not cut, crushed or powdered)
	---其他:							---Other:
1211.9091	----鱼藤根、除虫菊	3	11	13	5	千克	ABS	----Derris roots and pyrethrum
1211.9099	----其他	9	30	13		千克		----Other
1211.9099 10	其他用麻黄草粉	9	30	13	5	千克	23AB	Other chinese ephedra (*Ephedra sinica*) powder
1211.9099 20	其他用麻黄草	9	30	13	5	千克	8A	Other Chinese ephedra (Ephedrasinica)
1211.9099 91	其他鲜或干杀虫、杀菌用濒危植物(不论是否切割、压碎或研磨成粉)	9	30	13		千克	ABFE	Other endangered plants, of a kind used for insecticidal, fungicidal, fresh or dried (whether or not cut, crushed or powdered)
1211.9099 99	其他鲜或干的杀虫、杀菌用植物(不论是否切割、压碎或研磨成粉)	9	30	13	5	千克	AB	Other plants, of a kind used for insecticidal, fungicidal, fresh or dried (whether or not cut, crushed or powdered)
12.12	**鲜、冷、冻或干的刺槐豆、海草及其他藻类、甜菜及甘蔗,不论是否碾磨;主要供人食用的其他税目未列名的果核、果仁及植物产品(包括未焙制的菊苣根):**							**Locust beans, seaweeds and other algae, sugar beet and sugar cane, fresh, chilled, frozen or dried, whether or not ground; fruit stones and kernels and other vegetable products (including unroasted chicory roots of the variety *Cichorium intybus sativum*) of a kind used primarily for human consumption, not elsewhere specified or included:**
	-海草及其他藻类:							-Seaweeds and other algae:
	--适合供人食用的:							--Fit for human consumption:
1212.2110	---海带	20	70	13		千克	AB	---Sea tangle
1212.2120	---发菜	20	70	13	5	千克	8A	---Black moss
	---裙带菜:							---Pinnatifida:
1212.2131	----干的	15	70	13	5	千克	AB	----Dried
1212.2132	----鲜的	15	70	13	5	千克	AB	----Fresh
1212.2139	----其他	15	70	13	5	千克	AB	----Other
	---紫菜:							---Laver:
1212.2141	----干的	15	70	13		千克	AB	----Dried
1212.2142	----鲜的	15	70	13		千克	AB	----Fresh
1212.2149	----其他	15	70	13		千克	AB	----Other
	---麒麟菜:							---Eucheuma:
1212.2161	----干的	15	70	13	5	千克	AB	----Dried
1212.2169	----其他	15	70	13	5	千克	AB	----Other

税则号列	货品名称	最惠(%)	普通	增值税率	出口退税	计量单位	监管条件	Article Description
	---江蓠：							----Garcilaria：
1212.2171	----干的	15	70	13	5	千克	AB	----Dried
1212.2179	----其他	15	70	13	5	千克	AB	----Other
1212.2190暂	---其他	2	70	13	5	千克	AB	---Other
	--其他：							-Other：
1212.2910暂	---马尾藻	2	70	13	5	千克	AB	---Sargass
1212.2990暂	---其他	2	70	13	5	千克	AB	---Other
	-其他：							-Other：
1212.9100	--甜菜	20	70	13	5	千克	AB	--Sugar beet
1212.9200	--刺槐豆	20	70	13	5	千克	AB	--Locust beans
1212.9300	--甘蔗	20	70	13	5	千克	AB	--Sugar cane
1212.9400	--菊苣根	20	70	13	5	千克	AB	--Chicory roots
	--其他：							--Other：
	---杏、桃(包括油桃)、梅或李的核及核仁：							---Apricot, peach (including nectarine) or plum stones and kernels：
1212.9911	----苦杏仁	20	80	13	5	千克	QAB	----Bitter apricot kernels
1212.9912	----甜杏仁	20	80	13	5	千克	AB	----Sweet apricot kernels
1212.9919	----其他	20	80	13	5	千克	AB	----Other
	---其他：							---Other：
1212.9993	----白瓜子	20	80	13	5	千克	AB	----Pumpkin seeds
1212.9994	----莲子	20	80	13	5	千克	AB	----Lotus seeds(*Semen Nelumbinis*)
1212.9996	----甜叶菊叶	30	70	13	5	千克	AB	----leaf of steviol
1212.9999	----其他	30	70	13		千克		----Other
1212.9999 10	其他供人食用濒危植物产品(包括未焙制的菊苣根,包括果核、仁等)	30	70	13		千克	ABFE	Other endangered vegetable products (including unroasted chicory roots of the variety *Cichorium intybus sativum*) of a kind used primarily for human consumption
1212.9999 90	其他供人食用果核、仁及植物产品(包括未焙制的菊苣根)	30	70	13	5	千克	AB	Other fruit stones and kernels and vegetable products (including unroasted chicory roots of the variety *Cichorium intybus sativum*) of a kind used primarily for human consumption
12.13	**未经处理的谷类植物的茎、秆及谷壳,不论是否切碎、碾磨、挤压或制成团粒：**							**Cereal straw and husks, unprepared, whether or not chopped, ground, pressed or in the form of pellets：**
1213.0010	---未经处理的稻草的茎、秆	12	35	13	5	千克	AB	---Cereal straw unprepared
1213.0090	---其他	12	35	13	5	千克	AB	---Other
12.14	**芜菁甘蓝、饲料甜菜、饲料用根、干草、紫苜蓿、三叶草、驴喜豆、饲料羽衣甘蓝、羽扇豆、巢菜及类似饲料,不论是否制成团粒：**							**Swedes, mangolds, fodder roots, hay, lucerne (alfalfa), clover, sainfoin, forage kale, lupines, vetches and similar forage products, whether or not in the form of pellets：**
1214.1000	-紫苜蓿粗粉及团粒	5	35	13		千克	AB	-Lucerne (alfalfa) meal and pellets
1214.9000	-其他		35	13		千克		-Other
1214.9000暂 01	其他紫苜蓿(粗粉及团粒除外)	7	35	13		千克	AB	Other lucerne(other than meal and pellets)
1214.9000暂 02	以除紫苜蓿外的禾本科和豆科为主的多种混合天然饲草	4	35	13		千克	AB	In addition to alfalfa variety of graminaceous and leguminous based mixed natural forage grass
1214.9000 90	芜菁甘蓝、饲料甜菜、其他植物饲料(包括饲料用根、干草、三叶草、驴喜豆等,不论是否制成团粒)	9	35	13		千克	AB	Swedes, mangolds, other vegetable fodder (including fodder roots, hay, clover, sainfoin, whether or not in the form of pellets)

第十三章
虫胶;树胶、树脂及其他植物液、汁

注释:

税目 13.02 主要包括甘草、除虫菊、啤酒花、芦荟的浸膏及鸦片,但不包括:

一、按重量计蔗糖含量在 10% 以上或制成糖食的甘草浸膏(税目 17.04);

二、麦芽膏(税目 19.01);

三、咖啡精、茶精、马黛茶精(税目 21.01);

四、构成含酒精饮料的植物汁、液(第二十二章);

五、樟脑、甘草甜及税目 29.14 或 29.38 的其他产品;

六、按重量计生物碱含量不低于 50% 的罂粟杆的浓缩物(税目 29.39);

七、税目 30.03 或 30.04 的药品及税目 30.06 的血型试剂;

八、鞣料或染料的浸膏(税目 32.01 或 32.03);

九、精油、浸膏、净油、香膏提取的油树脂或精油的水质馏出液或其水溶液;饮料制造业用的以芳香物质为基料的制剂(第三十三章);

十、天然橡胶、巴拉塔胶、古塔波胶、银胶菊胶、糖胶树胶或类似的天然树胶(税目 40.01)。

本国注释:

子目 1302.1100 的鸦片,我国禁止进口。

Chapter 13
Lac; gums, resins and other vegetable saps and extracts

Notes:

Heading No. 13.02 applies, *inter alia*, to liquorice extract and extract of pyrethrum, extract of hops, extract of aloes and opium. The heading does not apply to:

(1) Liquorice extract containing more than 10% by weight of sucrose or put up as confectionery (heading No. 17.04);

(2) Malt extract (heading No. 19.01);

(3) Extracts of coffee, tea or mate (heading No. 21.01);

(4) Vegetable saps or extracts constituting alcoholic beverages (Chapter 22);

(5) Camphor, glycyrrhizin or other products of heading No. 29.14 or 29.38;

(6) Concentrates of poppy straw containing not less than 50% by weight of alkaloids (heading No. 29.39);

(7) Medicaments of heading No. 30.03 or 30.04 or bloodgrouping reagents (heading No. 30.06);

(8) Tanning or dyeing extracts (heading No. 32.01 or 32.03);

(9) Essential oils, concretes, absolutes, resinoids, extracted oleoresins, aqueous distillates or aqueous solutions of essential oils or preparations based on odoriferous substances of a kind used for the manufacture of beverages (Chapter 33);

(10) Natural rubber, balata, gutta-percha, guayule, chicle or similar natural gums (heading No. 40.01).

National note:

Opium of Subheading No. 1302.1100 is subject to import ban.

税则号列	货品名称	最惠(%)	普通	增值税率	出口退税	计量单位	监管条件	Article Description
13.01	虫胶;天然树胶、树脂、树胶脂及油树脂(例如,香树脂):							**Lac; natural gums, resins, gum-resins and oleoresins (for example, balsams):**
1301.2000	-阿拉伯胶	15	40	13	5	千克	AB	-Gum Arabic
	-其他:							-Other:
1301.9010	---胶黄耆树胶(卡喇杆胶)	15	40	13	5	千克	AB	---Gum tragacanth
1301.9020	---乳香、没药及血竭	3	17	13	5	千克	ABQ	---Olibanum, myrrh and dragon's blood
1301.9030	---阿魏	3	17	13	5	千克	AB	---Asafoetida
1301.9040	---松脂	15	45	13		千克		---Pine-resin
1301.9040 10	濒危松科植物的松脂	15	45	13		千克	ABE	Pine-resin of endangered plants of pine family
1301.9040 90	其他松脂	15	45	13	5	千克	AB	Other pine-resin
1301.9090	---其他	15	45	13		千克		---Other
1301.9090 10	龙血树脂、大戟脂、愈疮树脂	15	45	13	5	千克	ABFE	Resin of daemonorops draco, resin of euphorbia, resin of lignum vitae
1301.9090 20	大麻脂	15	45	13	5	千克	ABW	Charas, churrus
1301.9090 91	其他濒危植物的天然树胶、树脂[包括天然树胶、树脂及其他油树脂(例如:香树脂)]	15	45	13		千克	ABFE	Other natural gums, resins, gum-resins and oleoresins (for example, balsams) of endangered plants
1301.9090 99	其他天然树胶、树脂[包括天然树胶、树脂及其他油树脂(例如:香树脂)]	15	45	13	5	千克	AB	Other natural gums, resins, gum-resins and oleoresins (for example, balsams)
13.02	植物液汁及浸膏;果胶、果胶酸盐及果胶酸酯;从植物产品制得的琼脂、其他胶液及增稠剂,不论是否改性:							**Vegetable saps and extracts; pectic substances, pectinates and pectates; agar-agar and other mucilages and thickeners, whether or not modified, derived from vegetable products:**
	-植物液汁及浸膏:							-Vegetable saps and extracts:
1302.1100	--鸦片	0	0	0	15	千克	WB9	--Opium

税则号列	货品名称	最惠(%)	普通	增值税率	出口退税	计量单位	监管条件	Article Description
1302.1200暂	--甘草的	0	20	17	15	千克	4xABy	--Of liquorice
1302.1300	--啤酒花的	10	80	17	15	千克	AB	--Of hops
	--其他:							--Other:
1302.1910	---生漆	20	90	17	5	千克	AB	---Crude lacquer
1302.1920	---印楝素	3	11	17	5	千克	ABS	---Azadirachtin
1302.1930	---除虫菊的或含鱼藤酮植物根茎的	3	11	17	15	千克	ABS	---Of pyrethrum or of the roots of plants containing rotenone
1302.1940	----银杏的	20	80	17	15	千克	ABE	----Gingko
1302.1990	---其他		80	17		千克		---Other
1302.1990暂 01	苦参碱	3	80	17	15	千克	ABS	Matrine
1302.1990 11	供制农药用麻黄浸膏粉	20	80	17	15	千克	23AB	Chinese ephedra extract powder used primarily in pesticide
1302.1990 12	供制农药用麻黄浸膏	20	80	17	15	千克	23AB	Chinese ephedra extract used primarily in pesticide
1302.1990 13	供制农药用的濒危植物液汁及浸膏	20	80	17		千克	ABFE	Endangered vegetable saps and extracts for used primarily in pesticide
1302.1990 19	供制农药用的其他植物液汁及浸膏	20	80	17	15	千克	AB	Other vegetable saps and extracts used primarily in pharmacy
1302.1990 91	供制医药用麻黄浸膏粉	20	80	17	15	千克	Q23AB	Chinese ephedra extract powder used primarily in pharmacy
1302.1990 92	供制医药用麻黄浸膏	20	80	17	15	千克	Q23AB	Chinese ephedra extract used in pharmacy
1302.1990 93	其他麻黄浸膏粉	20	80	17	15	千克	23AB	Other chinese ephedra extract powder
1302.1990 94	其他麻黄浸膏	20	80	17	15	千克	23AB	Other chinese ephedra extract
1302.1990 95	红豆杉液汁及浸膏	20	80	17	15	千克	ABFE	Saps and extracts of taxusl
1302.1990 96	黄草汁液及浸膏	20	80	17	15	千克	ABFE	Saps and extracts of herba dendroii
1302.1990 97	其他濒危植物液汁及浸膏	20	80	17		千克	ABFE	Saps and extracts of other endangered vegetable
1302.1990 99	其他植物液汁及浸膏	20	80	17	15	千克	AB	Other vegetable saps and extracts
1302.2000	-果胶、果胶酸盐及果胶酸酯	20	80	17	15	千克	AB	-Pectic substances, pectinates and pectates
	-从植物产品制得的胶液及增稠剂,不论是否改性:							-Mucilages and thickeners, whether or not modified, derived from vegetable products:
1302.3100	--琼脂	10	80	17	15	千克	AB	--Agar-agar
1302.3200	--从刺槐豆、刺槐豆子或瓜尔豆制得的胶液及增稠剂,不论是否改性	15	80	17	15	千克	AB	--Mucilages and thickeners, whether or not modified, derived from locust beans, locust bean seeds or guar seeds
	--其他:							--Other:
	---海草及其他藻类制品:							---Preparations of seaweeds and other algae:
1302.3911	----卡拉胶	15	80	17	15	千克	AB	----Carrageenan
1302.3912	----褐藻胶	15	80	17	15	千克	AB	----Algin
1302.3919	----其他	15	80	17	15	千克	AB	----Other
1302.3990	---其他	15	80	17		千克		---Other
1302.3990 10	未列名濒危植物胶液及增稠剂	15	80	17		千克	ABFE	Mucilages and thickeners, derived from endangered vegetable products, not elsewhere specified or included
1302.3990 90	其他未列名植物胶液及增稠剂	15	80	17	15	千克	AB	Other mucilages and thickeners, derived from vegetable products, not elsewhere specified or included

第十四章
编结用植物材料；
其他植物产品

Chapter 14
Vegetable plaiting materials; vegetable products not elsewhere specified or included

注释：

一、本章不包括归入第十一类的下列产品：

主要供纺织用的植物材料或植物纤维，不论其加工程度如何；或经过处理使其只能作为纺织原料用的其他植物材料。

二、税目14.01主要包括竹（不论是否劈开、纵锯、切段、圆端、漂白、磨光、染色或进行不燃处理）、劈开的柳条、芦苇及类似品和藤心、藤丝、藤片。但不包括木片条（税目44.04）。

三、税目14.04不包括木丝（税目44.05）及供制帚、制刷用成束、成簇的材料（税目96.03）。

Notes:

1. This Chapter does not cover the following products which are to be classified in Section XI:

Vegetable materials or fibres of vegetable materials of a kind used primarily in the manufacture of textiles, however prepared, or other vegetable materials which have undergone treatment so as to render them suitable for use only as textile materials.

2. Heading No. 14.01 applies, *inter alia*, to bamboos (whether or not split, sawn lengthwise, cut to length, rounded at the ends, bleached, rendered non-inflammable, polished or dyed), split osier, reeds and the like, to rattan cores and to drawn or split rattans. The heading does not apply to chipwood (heading No. 44.04).

3. Heading No. 14.04 does not apply to wood wool (heading No. 44.05) and prepared knots or tufts for broom or brush making (heading No. 96.03).

税则号列	货品名称	最惠(%)	普通	增值税率	出口退税	计量单位	监管条件	Article Description
14.01	主要作编结用的植物材料（例如，竹、藤、芦苇、灯芯草、柳条、酒椰叶，已净、漂白或染色的谷类植物的茎秆，椴树皮）：							**Vegetable materials of a kind used primarily for plaiting (for example, bamboos, rattans, reeds, rushes, osier, raffia, cleaned, bleached or dyed cereal straw, and lime bark):**
1401.1000	-竹	10	70	13	5	千克		-Bamboos
1401.1000 10	酸竹	10	70	13	5	千克	ABE	Acidosasa chinensis(*Raphia vinifera*)
1401.1000 90	其他竹	10	70	13	5	千克	AB	Other bamboos
1401.2000	-藤	10	35	13		千克		-Rattans
1401.2000 10	濒危藤	10	35	13		千克	ABFE	Endangered rattans
1401.2000 90	其他藤	10	35	13	5	千克	AB	Other rattans
	-其他：							-Other:
1401.9010	---谷类植物的茎秆（麦秸除外）	10	70	13	5	千克	AB	---Cereal straw (other than wheat straw)
1401.9020	---芦苇	10	70	13	5	千克	AB	---Reeds
	---灯芯草属：							---Rushes:
1401.9031	----蔺草	10	70	13	5	千克	AB4xy	----Mat rush
1401.9039	----其他	10	70	13	5	千克	AB	----Other
1401.9090	---其他	10	70	13	5	千克	AB	---Other
14.04	其他税目未列名的植物产品：							**Vegetable products not elsewhere specified or included:**
1404.2000	-棉短绒	4	30	13	5	千克	AB	-Cotton linters
	-其他：							-Other:
1404.9010	---主要供染料、鞣料用的植物原料	5	45	13	5	千克	AB	---Raw vegetable materials of a kind used primarily in dyeing or tanning
1404.9090	---其他	15	70	13	5	千克	AB	---Other

第三类

动、植物油、脂及其分解产品；精制的食用油脂；动、植物蜡

第十五章

动、植物油、脂及其分解产品；精制的食用油脂；动、植物蜡

注释：

一、本章不包括：

（一）税目 02.09 的猪脂肪及家禽脂肪；

（二）可可脂、可可油（税目 18.04）；

（三）按重量计税目 04.05 所列产品的含量超过 15%的食品（通常归入第二十一章）；

（四）税目 23.01 的油渣或税目 23.04 至 23.06 的残渣；

（五）第六类的脂肪酸、精制蜡、药品、油漆、清漆、肥皂、芳香料制品、化妆品、盥洗品、磺化油及其他货品；

（六）从油类提取的油膏（税目 40.02）。

二、税目 15.09 不包括用溶剂提取的橄榄油（税目 15.10）。

三、税目 15.18 不包括变性的油、脂及其分离品，这些货品应归入其相应的未变性油、脂及其分离品的税目。

四、皂料、油脚、硬脂沥青、甘油沥青及羊毛脂残渣，归入税目 15.22。

子目注释：

子目 1514.11 及 1514.19 所称"低芥子酸菜籽油"，是指按重量计芥子酸含量低于 2%的固定油。

SECTION Ⅲ

ANIMAL OR VEGETABLE FATS AND OILS AND THEIR CLEAVAGE PRODUCTS; PREPARED EDIBLE FATS; ANIMAL OR VEGETABLE WAXES

Chapter 15

Animal or vegetable fats and oils and their cleavage products; prepared edible fats; animal or vegetable waxes

Notes:

1. This Chapter does not cover:

(a) Pig fat or poultry fat of heading No. 02.09;

(b) Cocoa butter, fat or oil (heading No. 18.04);

(c) Edible preparations containing by weight more than 15% of the products of heading No. 04.05 (generally Chapter 21);

(d) Greaves (heading No. 23.01) or residues of headings No. 23.04 to 23.06;

(e) Fatty acids, prepared waxes, medicaments, paints, varnishes, soap, perfumery, cosmetic or toilet preparations, sulphonated oils or other goods of Section Ⅵ;

(f) Factice derived from oils (heading No. 40.02).

2. Heading No. 15.09 does not apply to oils obtained from olives by solvent extraction (heading No. 15.10).

3. Heading No. 15.18 does not cover fats or oils or their fractions, merely denatured, which are to be classified in the heading appropriate to the corresponding undenatured fats and oils and their fractions.

4. Soap-stocks, oil foots and dregs, stearin pitch, glycerol pitch and wool grease residues fall in heading No. 15.22.

Subheading Note:

For the purposes of subheadings No. 1514.11 and 1514.19, the expression "low erucic acid rape or colza oil" means the fixed oil which has an erucic acid content of less than 2% by weight.

税则号列	货品名称	最惠(%)	普通	增值税率	出口退税	计量单位	监管条件	Article Description
15.01	**猪脂肪(包括已炼制的猪油)及家禽脂肪，但税目 02.09 及 15.03 的货品除外：**							**Pig fat (including lard) and poultry fat, other than that of heading No. 02.09 or 15.03:**
1501.1000	-猪油	10	35	17	15	千克	AB	-Lard
1501.2000	-其他猪脂肪	10	35	17	15	千克	AB	-Other pig fat
1501.9000	-其他	10	35	17	15	千克	AB	-Other
15.02	**牛、羊脂肪，但税目 15.03 的货品除外：**							**Fats of bovine animals, sheep or goats, other than those of heading No. 15.03:**
1502.1000[暂]	---牛、羊油脂	4	30	17	15	千克	AB	---Tallow
1502.9000[暂]	---其他	4	70	17	5	千克	AB	---Other
15.03	**猪油硬脂、液体猪油、油硬脂、食用或非食用脂油，未经乳化、混合或其他方法制作：**							**Lard stearin, lard oil, oleostearin, oleooil and tallow oil, not emulsified or mixed or otherwise prepared:**
1503.0000	猪油硬脂、液体猪油、油硬脂、食用或非食用脂油，未经乳化、混合或其他方法制作	10	30	17	15	千克	AB	Lard stearin, lard oil, oleostearin, oleooil and tallow oil, not emulsified or mixed or otherwise prepared
15.04	**鱼或海生哺乳动物的油、脂及其分离品，不论是否精制，但未经化学改性：**							**Fats and oils and their fractions, of fish or marine mammals, whether or not refined, but not chemically modified:**
1504.1000	-鱼肝油及其分离品	12	30	17	15	千克	AB	-Fish-liver oils and their fractions
1504.1000 10	濒危鱼鱼肝油及其分离品	12	30	17	15	千克	ABEF	Endangered species of fish cod - liver oil and its fractions
1504.1000 90	其他鱼鱼肝油及其分离品	12	30	17	15	千克	AB	Other fish cod - liver oil and its fractions

税则号列	货品名称	最惠(%)	普通	增值税率	出口退税	计量单位	监管条件	Article Description
1504.2000	-除鱼肝油以外的鱼油、脂及其分离品	12	50	17	15	千克	AB	-Fats and oils and their fractions, of fish, other than liver oils
1504.2000 10	濒危鱼其他鱼油、脂及其分离品(鱼肝油除外)	12	50	17	15	千克	ABEF	Other endangered fish, fish oil, fat and its fractions (cod - liver oil except)
1504.2000 90	其他鱼油、脂及其分离品(鱼肝油除外)	12	50	17	15	千克	AB	Other fish oil, fat and its fractions (cod - liver oil except)
1504.3000	-海生哺乳动物的油、脂及其分离品	14.4	50	17		千克		-Fats and oils and their fractions, of marine mammals
1504.3000 10	濒危哺乳动物的油、脂及其分离品(仅指海生)	14.4	50	17		千克	ABFE	Fats and oils and their fractions, of endangered marine mammals
1504.3000 90	其他海生哺乳动物油、脂及其分离品	14.4	50	17	15	千克	AB	Other fats and oils and their fractions of marine mammals
15.05	**羊毛脂及从羊毛脂制得的脂肪物质(包括纯净的羊毛脂):**							**Wool grease and fatty substances derived therefrom (including lanolin):**
1505.0000	羊毛脂及羊毛脂肪物质(包括纯净的羊毛脂)	20	70	17	15	千克	AB	Wool grease and fatty substances derived therefrom (including lanolin)
15.06	**其他动物油、脂及其分离品,不论是否精制,但未经化学改性:**							**Other animal fats and oils and their fractions, whether or not refined, but not chemically modified:**
1506.0000	其他动物油、脂及其分离品,不论是否精制,但未经化学改性	20	70	17		千克		Other animal fats and oils and their fractions, whether or not refined, but not chemically modified
1506.0000 10	其他濒危动物为原料制取的脂肪(包括河马、熊、野兔、海龟为原料的及海龟蛋油)	20	70	17		千克	ABFE	Fats made of materials of endangered wild animals (including hippo, bear, hare, green turtle and green turtle egg)
1506.0000 90	其他动物油、脂及其分离品(不论是否精制,但未经化学改性)	20	70	17	15	千克	AB	Fats and oils and their fractions, of other animals (whether or not refined, but not chemically modified)
15.07	**豆油及其分离品,不论是否精制,但未经化学改性:**							**Soya-bean oil and its fractions, whether or not refined, but not chemically modified:**
1507.1000	-初榨的,不论是否脱胶	9	190	13		千克	7AB	-Crude oil whether or not degummed
1507.9000	-其他	9	190	13		千克	7AB	-Other
15.08	**花生油及其分离品,不论是否精制,但未经化学改性:**							**Ground-nut oil and its fractions, whether or not refined, but not chemically modified:**
1508.1000	-初榨的	10	100	13		千克	AB	-Crude oil
1508.9000	-其他	10	100	13		千克	AB	-Other
15.09	**油橄榄油及其分离品,不论是否精制,但未经化学改性:**							**Olive oil and its fractions, whether or not refined, but not chemically modified:**
1509.1000	-初榨的	10	30	13		千克	7AB	-Crude oil
1509.9000	-其他	10	30	17		千克	7AB	-Other
15.10	**其他橄榄油及其分离品,不论是否精制,但未经化学改性,包括掺有税目15.09的油或分离品的混合物:**							**Other oils and their fractions, obtained solely from olives, whether or not refined, but not chemically modified, including blends of these oils or fractions with oils or fractions of heading No. 15.09:**
1510.0000	其他橄榄油及其分离品,不论是否精制,但未经化学改性,包括掺有税目15.09的油或分离品的混合物	10	30	17		千克	7AB	Other oils and their fractions, obtained solely from olives, whether or not refined, but not chemically modified, including blends of these oils or fractions with oils or fractions of heading No. 15.09
15.11	**棕榈油及其分离品,不论是否精制,但未经化学改性:**							**Palm oil and its fractions, whether or not refined, but not chemically modified:**
1511.1000	-初榨的	9	60	13		千克	7AB	-Crude oil
	-其他:							-Other:
1511.9010	---棕榈液油(熔点19~24度)	9	60	13		千克	7AB	---Palm olein(cmelting point 19℃ ~24℃)
1511.9020	---棕榈硬脂(熔点44~56度)		60	13		千克		---Palm stearin(cmelting point 44℃ ~56℃)
1511.9020[暂] 01	固态棕榈硬脂(50度≤熔点≤56度)(未经化学改性)	2	60	13		千克	7AB	Solid plam stearin(cmelting point 50℃ ~56℃, not chemically modified)
1511.9020 90	棕榈硬脂(44度≤熔点<50度,未经化学改性)	8	60	13		千克	AB	Palm Stearin(melting point 44℃ ~50℃, not chemically modified)
1511.9090	---其他	9	60	17		千克	7AB	---Other

税则号列	货品名称	最惠(%)	普通	增值税率	出口退税	计量单位	监管条件	Article Description
15.12	**葵花油、红花油或棉子油及其分离品,不论是否精制,但未经化学改性:**							**Sunflower-seed, safflower or cotton-seed oil and fractions thereof, whether or not refined, but not chemically modified:**
	-葵花油或红花油及其分离品:							-Sunflower-seed or safflower oil and fractions thereof:
1512.1100	--初榨的	9	160	13		千克	AB	--Crude oil
1512.1900	--其他	9	160	17		千克	AB	--Other
	-棉子油及其分离品:							-Cotton-seed oil and its fractions:
1512.2100	--初榨的,不论是否去除棉子酚	10	70	13		千克	AB	--Crude oil, whether or not gossypol has been removed
1512.2900	--其他	10	70	17		千克	AB	--Other
15.13	**椰子油、棕榈仁油或巴巴苏棕榈果油及其分离品,不论是否精制,但未经化学改性:**							**Coconut (copra), palm kernel or babassu oil and fractions thereof, whether or not refined, but not chemically modified:**
	-椰子油及其分离品:							-Coconut (copra) oil and its fractions:
1513.1100	--初榨的	9	40	13		千克	AB	--Crude oil
1513.1900	--其他	9	40	13		千克	AB	--Other
	-棕榈仁油或巴巴苏棕榈果油及其分离品:							-Palm kernel or babassu oil and fractions thereof:
1513.2100	--初榨的	9	40	13		千克	AB	--Crude oil
1513.2900	--其他	9	40	17		千克	AB	--Other
15.14	**菜子油或芥子油及其分离品,不论是否精制,但未经化学改性:**							**Rape, colza or mustard oil and fractions thereof, whether or not refined, but not chemically modified:**
	-低芥子酸菜籽油及其分离品:							-Low erucic acid rape of colza oil and its fractions:
1514.1100	--初榨的	9	170	13		千克	7AB	--Crude oil
1514.1900	--其他	9	170	13		千克	7AB	--Other
	-其他:							-Other:
	--初榨的:							--Crude oil:
1514.9110	---菜籽油	9	170	13		千克	7AB	---Rape oil
1514.9190	---芥子油	9	170	13		千克	7AB	---Mustard oil
1514.9900	--其他	9	170	17		千克	7AB	--Other
15.15	**其他固定植物油、脂(包括希蒙得木油)及其分离品,不论是否精制,但未经化学改性:**							**Other fixed vegetable fats and oils (including jojoba oil) and fractions thereof, whether or not refined, but not chemically modified:**
	-亚麻子油及其分离品:							-Linseed oil and its fractions:
1515.1100	--初榨的	15	30	13		千克	AB	--Crude oil
1515.1900	--其他	15	30	17		千克	AB	--Other
	-玉米油及其分离品:							-Maize (corn) oil and its fractions:
1515.2100	--初榨的	10	160	13		千克	AB	--Crude oil
1515.2900	--其他	10	160	17		千克	AB	--Other
1515.3000	-蓖麻油及其分离品	10	70	17	5	千克	AB	-Castor oil and its fractions
1515.5000	-芝麻油及其分离品	12	20	13		千克	AB	-Sesame oil and its fractions
	-其他:							-Other:
1515.9010	---希蒙得木油(霍霍巴油)及其分离品	20	70	17	5	千克	AB	---Jojoba oil and its fractions
1515.9020	---印楝油及其分离品	20	70	17	5	千克	ABS	---Neem oil and its fractions
1515.9030	---桐油及其分离品	20	70	17	5	千克	AB	---Tung oil and its fractions
1515.9090	---其他	20	70	17		千克		---Other
1515.9090 10	红松子油(不论是否精制,但未经化学改性)	20	70	17		千克	ABE	Korean pine seed oil (whether or not refined, but not chemical modified)
1515.9090 90	其他固定植物油、脂及其分离品(不论是否精制,但未经化学改性)	20	70	17		千克	AB	Other fixed vegetable fats and oils and fraction thereof oil (whether or not refined, but not chemically modified)
15.16	**动、植物油、脂及其分离品,全部或部分氢化、相互酯化、再酯化或反油酸化,不论是否精制,但未经进一步加工:**							**Animal or vegetable fats and oil and fractions thereof, partly or wholly hydrogenated, inter-esterified, reesterified or elaidinized, whether or not refined, but not further prepared:**

税则号列	货 品 名 称	最惠(%)	普通	增值税率	出口退税	计量单位	监管条件	Article Description
1516.1000	-动物油、脂及其分离品	5	70	17	15	千克	AB	-Animal fats and oils and fractions thereof
1516.2000	-植物油、脂及其分离品	25	70	17		千克	AB	-Vegetable fats and oils and fractions thereof
15.17	**人造黄油;本章各种动、植物油、脂及其分离品混合制成的食用油、脂或制品,但税目15.16的食用油、脂及其分离品除外:**							**Margarine; edible mixtures or preparations of animal or vegetable fats or oils or of fractions of different fats or oils of this Chapter, other than edible fats or oils or their fractions of heading No. 15.16:**
1517.1000	-人造黄油,但不包括液态的	30	80	17		千克	AB	-Margarine, excluding liquid margarine
	-其他:							-Other:
1517.9010	---起酥油	25	70	17		千克		---Shortening
1517.9010 01	动物油脂制造的起酥油(税号1516的食用油、脂及其分离品除外)	25	70	17	15	千克	AB	Shortening made of animal grease (other than edible fats or oils or their fractions of heading No. 1516)
1517.9010 90	植物油脂制造的起酥油(税号1516的食用油、脂及其分离品除外)	25	70	13		千克	AB	Shortening made of plant oil (other than edible fats or oils or their fractions of heading No. 1516)
1517.9090	---其他	25	70	17		千克		---Other
1517.9090 01	其他混合制成的动物质食用油脂或制品(税号1516的食用油、脂及其分离品除外)	25	70	17	15	千克	AB	Edible mixtures or preparations of animal fats or oil or of fractions (Other than edible fats or oil or their fractions of heading No. 15.16)
1517.9090 90	其他混合制成的植物质食用油脂或制品(品目1516的食用油、脂及其分离品除外)	25	70	13		千克	AB	Edible mixtures or preparations of vegetable fats or oil or of fractions (Other than edible fats or oil or their fractions of heading No. 15.16)
15.18	**动、植物油、脂及其分离品,经过熟炼、氧化、脱水、硫化、吹制或在真空、惰性气体中加热聚合及用其他化学方法改性的,但税目15.16的产品除外;本章各种油、脂及其分离品混合制成的其他税目未列名的非食用油、脂或制品:**							**Animal or vegetable fats and oils and fractions thereof, boiled, oxidized, dehydrated, sulphurized, blown, polymerized by heat in vacuum or in inert gas or otherwise chemically modified, excluding those of heading No. 15.16; inedible mixtures or preparations of animal or vegetable fats or oils or of fractions of different fats or oils of this Chapter, not elsewhere specified or included:**
1518.0000	动、植物油、脂及其分离品,经过熟炼、氧化、脱水、硫化、吹制或在真空、惰性气体中加热聚合及用其他化学方法改性的,但税目15.16的产品除外;本章各种油、脂及其分离品混合制成的其他税目未列名的非食用油、脂或制品	10	70	17	15	千克	AB	Animal or vegetable fats and oils and fractions thereof, boiled, oxidized, dehydrated, sulphurized, blown, polymerized by heat in vacuum or in inert gas or otherwise chemically modified, excluding those of heading No. 15.16; inedible mixtures or preparations of animal or vegetable fats or oils or of fractions of different fats or oils of this Chapter, not elsewhere specified or included
15.20	**粗甘油;甘油水及甘油碱液:**							**Glycerol, crude; glycerol waters and glycerol lyes:**
1520.0000[暂]	粗甘油,甘油水及甘油碱液	6	50	17	15	千克	AB	Glycerol, crude; glycerol waters and glycerol lyes
15.21	**植物蜡(甘油三酯除外)、蜂蜡、其他虫蜡及鲸蜡,不论是否精制或着色:**							**Vegetable waxes (other than triglycerides), beeswax, other insect waxes and spermaceti, whether or not refined or coloured:**
1521.1000	-植物蜡	20	80	17	15	千克		-Vegetable waxes
1521.1000 10	小烛树蜡	20	80	17	15	千克	ABEF	Candelilla waxes
1521.1000 90	其他植物蜡	20	80	17	15	千克	AB	Other vegetable waxes
	-其他:							-Other:
1521.9010	---蜂蜡	20	80	17	15	千克	AB	---Beeswax
1521.9090	---其他	20	80	17	15	千克		---Other
1521.9090 10	鲸蜡(不论是否精制或着色)	20	80	17	15	千克	AFEB	Spermaceti (whether or not refined or coloured)
1521.9090 90	其他虫蜡(不论是否精制或着色)	20	80	17	15	千克	AB	Other insect waxes (whether or not refined or coloured)
15.22	**油鞣回收脂;加工处理油脂物质及动、植物蜡所剩的残渣:**							**Degras; residues resulting from the treatment of fatty substances of animal or vegetable waxes:**
1522.0000	油鞣回收脂;加工处理油脂物质及动、植物蜡所剩的残渣	20	50	17	15	千克	9	Degras; residues resulting from the treatment of fatty substances of animal or vegetable waxes

第四类
食品；饮料、酒及醋；烟草、烟草及烟草代用品的制品

注释：

本类所称"团粒"，是指直接挤压或加入按重量计比例不超过3%的粘合剂制成的粒状产品。

SECTION Ⅳ
PREPARED FOODSTUFFS; BEVERAGES, SPIRITS AND VINEGAR, TOBACCO AND MANUFACTURED TOBACCO SUBSTITUTES

Note:

In this Section the term "pellets" means products which have been agglomerated either directly by compression or by the addition of a binder in a proportion not exceeding 3% by weight.

第十六章
肉、鱼、甲壳动物，软体动物及其他水生无脊椎动物的制品

注释：

一、本章不包括用第二章、第三章及税目05.04所列方法制作或保藏的肉、食用杂碎、鱼、甲壳动物、软体动物或其他水生无脊椎动物。

二、本章的食品按重量计必须含有20%以上的香肠、肉、食用杂碎、动物血、鱼、甲壳动物、软体动物或其他水生无脊椎动物及其混合物。对于含有两种或两种以上前述产品的食品，则应按其中重量最大的产品归入第十六章的相应税目。但本条规定不适用于税目19.02的包馅食品和税目21.03及21.04的食品。

子目注释：

一、子目1602.10的"均化食品"，是指用肉、食用杂碎或动物血经精细均化制成供婴幼儿食用或营养用的零售包装食品（每件净重不超过250克）。为了调味、保藏或其他目的，均化食品中可以加入少量其他配料，还可以含有少量可见的肉粒或食用杂碎粒。归类时该子目优先于税目16.02的其他子目。

二、税目16.04或16.05项下各子目所列的是鱼、甲壳动物、软体动物及其他水生无脊柱动物的俗名，它们与第三章中相同名称的鱼、甲壳动物、软体动物及其水生无脊柱动物种类范围相同。

Chapter 16
Preparations of meat, of fish or of crustaceans, molluscs or other aquatic invertebrates

Notes:

1. This Chapter does not cover meat, meat offal, fish, crustaceans, molluscs or other aquatic invertebrates, prepared or preserved by the processes specified in Chapter 2 or 3 or heading No. 05.04.
2. Food preparations fall in this Chapter provided that they contain more than 20% by weight of sausage, meat, meat offal, blood, fish or crustaceans, molluscs or other aquatic invertebrates, or any combination thereof. In cases where the preparation contains two or more of the products mentioned above, it is classified in the heading of Chapter 16 corresponding to the component or components which predominate by weight. These provisions do not apply to the stuffed products of heading No. 19.02 or to the preparations of heading No. 21.03 or 21.04.

Subheading Notes:

1. For the purposes of subheading No. 1602.10, the expression "homogenized preparations" means preparations of meat, meat offal or blood, finely homogenized, put up for retail sale as infant food or for dietetic purposes, in containers of a net weight content not exceeding 250g. For the application of this definition no account is to be taken of small quantities of any ingredients which may have been added to the preparation for seasoning, preservation or other purposes. These preparations may contain a small quantity of visible pieces of meat or meat offal. This subheading takes precedence over all other subheadings of heading No. 16.02.
2. Ther fish、crustaceans、Molluscs and other aquatic invertebrates specified in the subheadings of heading No. 16.04 or 16.05 under their common names only, are of the same species as those mentionde in Chpapter 3 under the same name.

税则号列	货品名称	最惠(%)	普通	增值税率	出口退税	计量单位	监管条件	Article Description
16.01	肉、食用杂碎或动物血制成的香肠及类似产品；用香肠制成的食品：							**Sausages and similar products, of meat, meat offal or blood; food preparations based on these products:**
1601.0010	---用天然肠衣做外包装的香肠及类似产品	15	90	17		千克		---Sausages and similar products, with a natural casing
1601.0010 10	濒危野生动物肉、杂碎，血制天然肠衣香肠（含编号0208的野生动物，包括类似品）	15	90	17		千克	ABFE	Sausages packed with natural casing of meat, meat offal or blood of endangered wild animals (including wild animals of heading No. 0208 and similar products)
1601.0010 90	其他动物肉，杂碎及血制天然肠衣香肠（包括类似品）	15	90	17	15	千克	AB	Sausages packed with natural casing of meat, meat offal or blood of other aminals (including similar products)
1601.0020	---其他香肠及类似产品	15	90	17		千克		---Other sausages and similar products
1601.0020 10	濒危野生动物肉，杂碎，血制其他肠衣香肠（含编号0208的野生动物，包括类似品）	15	90	17		千克	ABFE	Sausages packed with other casing of meat, meal offal or blood of endangered wild animals (including wild animals of heading No. 0208 and similar products)

税则号列	货品名称	最惠(%)	普通	增值税率	出口退税	计量单位	监管条件	Article Description
1601.0020 90	其他动物肉、杂碎及血制其他肠衣香肠(包括类似品)	15	90	17	15	千克	AB	Sauages packed with other cosing of meat, meat offal or blood of other animals(including simiple products)
1601.0030	---用香肠制成的食品	15	90	17		千克		---Food preparations basd on sausages food products
1601.0030 10	用含濒危野生动物成分的香肠制的食品(含编号0208的野生动物)	15	90	17		千克	ABFE	Food preparations based on sauages, containing compositions of endangered wild animals (including endangered wild animals of heading No. 0208)
1601.0030 90	用含其他动物成分的香肠制的食品	15	90	17	5,15	千克	AB	Food preparation based on other sauages, containing compositions of other animals
16.02	其他方法制作或保藏的肉、食用杂碎或动物血:							**Other Prepared or preserved meat, meat offal or blood:**
1602.1000	-均化食品	15	90	17		千克		-Homogenized preparations
1602.1000 10	含濒危野生动物成分的均化食品(指用肉、食用杂碎或动物血经精细均化制成,零售包装)	15	90	17		千克	ABFE	Homogenized preparations, with containing compositions of endangered wild animals(prepared or preserved meat, meat offal or blood, put up for retail sale)
1602.1000 90	其他动物肉或食用杂碎的均化食品(指用肉、食用杂碎或动物血经精细均化制成,零售包装)	15	90	17	15	千克	AB	Homogenized preparations, with containing compositions of other animals (prepared or preserved meat, meat offal or blood, put up for retail sale)
1602.2000	-动物肝	15	90	17		千克		-Of liver of any animal
1602.2000 10	制作或保藏的濒危动物肝(第2、3章所列方法制作或保藏的除外)	15	90	17		千克	ABFE	Liver of endangered animal, prepared or preserved (other than prepared or preserved of Chapter 2 and 3)
1602.2000 90	制作或保藏的其他动物肝(第2、3章所列方法制作或保藏的除外)	15	90	17	15	千克	AB	eiver of other animals, prepared or preserved (other than prepared or preserved of Chapter 2 and 3)
	-税目01.05的家禽的:							-Of poultry of heading No. 01.05:
1602.3100	--火鸡的	15	90	17	15	千克	AB	--Of turkeys
	--鸡的:							--Of fowls of the species *Gallus domesticus*:
1602.3210	---罐头	15	90	17	15	千克	AB	---In airtight containers
	---其他:							---Other:
1602.3291	----鸡胸肉	15	90	17	15	千克	AB	----Chicken breast filets
1602.3292	----鸡腿肉	15	90	17	15	千克	AB	----Chicken leg meat
1602.3299	----其他	15	90	17	15	千克	AB	----Other
	--其他:							--Other:
1602.3910	---罐头	15	90	17	15	千克	AB	---In airtight containers
	---其他:							---Other:
1602.3991	----鸭的	15	90	17	5,15	千克	AB	----Of duck
1602.3999	----其他	15	90	17	15	千克	AB	----Other
	-猪的:							-Of swine:
1602.4100	--后腿及其肉块	15	90	17	15	千克		--Hams and cuts thereof
1602.4100 10	制作或保藏的鹿豚、姬猪后腿及肉块	15	90	17	15	千克	ABFE	Prepared or preserved hams and cuts of pig-deer (*Babyrousa*)、pygmy pig (*Porcula*)
1602.4100 90	制作或保藏的猪后腿及其肉块	15	90	17	15	千克	AB	Prepared or preserved hams and cuts of swine
1602.4200	--前腿及其肉块	15	90	17	15	千克		--Shoulders and cuts thereof
1602.4200 10	制作或保藏的鹿豚,姬猪前腿及其肉块	15	90	17	15	千克	ABFE	Prepared or preserved shoulders and cuts of pig-deer (*Babyrousa*)、pygmy pig (*Porcula*)
1602.4200 90	制作或保藏的猪前腿及其肉块	15	90	17	15	千克	AB	Prepared or preserved shoulders and cuts of swine
	--其他,包括混合的肉:							--Other, including mixtures:
1602.4910	---罐头	15	90	17	15	千克		---In airtight containers
1602.4910 10	其他含鹿豚、姬猪肉及杂碎的罐头	15	90	17	15	千克	ABFE	Other meat, meat offal of pig-deer (*Babyrousa*)、pygmy pig (*Porcula*), tinned
1602.4910 90	其他猪肉及杂碎的罐头	15	90	17	15	千克	AB	Other meat, meat offal of swine, tinned
1602.4990	---其他	15	90	17	15	千克		---Other
1602.4990 10	制作或保藏的其他鹿豚、姬猪肉、杂碎(包括血等)	15	90	17	15	千克	ABFE	Prepared or preserved meat, meat offal or blood of pig-deer (*Babyrousa*)、pygmy pig (*Porcula*)
1602.4990 90	制作或保藏的其他猪肉、杂碎、血	15	90	17	15	千克	AB	Prepared or preserved meat, meat offal or blood of swine
	-牛的:							-Of bovine animals:
1602.5010	---罐头	12	90	17		千克		---In airtight containers
1602.5010 10	含濒危野牛肉的罐头	12	90	17		千克	ABFE	Meat of endangered wild bovine animals, tinned

税则号列	货品名称	最惠(%)	普通	增值税率	出口退税	计量单位	监管条件	Article Description
1602.5010 90	其他牛肉及牛杂碎罐头(含野牛肉的除外)	12	90	17	15	千克	AB	Other meat, meat offal of bovine animals, tinned (other than meat of wild bovine animals)
1602.5090	---其他	12	90	17		千克		---Other
1602.5090 10	其他制作或保藏濒危野牛肉、杂碎(包括血等)	12	90	17		千克	ABFE	Other prepared or preserved meat, meat offal or blood of endangered wild bovine animals
1602.5090 90	其他制作或保藏的牛肉、杂碎、血	12	90	17	15	千克	AB	Other prepared or preserved meat, meat offal or blood of bovine animals
	-其他,包括动物血的食品:							-Other, including preparations of blood of any animal:
1602.9010	---罐头	15	90	17		千克		---In airtight containers
1602.9010 10	其他濒危野生动物肉及杂碎罐头	15	90	17		千克	ABFE	Other meat, meat offal of endangered wild animals, tinned
1602.9010 90	其他肉及杂碎罐头	15	90	17	15	千克	AB	Other meat, meat offal of other animals, tinned
1602.9090	---其他	15	90	17		千克		---Other
1602.9090 10	制作或保藏其他濒危野生动物肉(包括杂碎、血)	15	90	17		千克	ABFE	Other prepared or preserved meat, meat offal or blood of endangered wild animals
1602.9090 90	经制作或保藏的其他肉、杂碎及血	15	90	17	15	千克	AB	Other prepared or preserved meat, meat offal or blood of other animals
16.03	**肉、鱼、甲壳动物、软体动物或其他水生无脊椎动物的精及汁:**							**Extracts and juices of meat, fish or crustaceans, molluscs or other aquatic invertebrates:**
1603.0000	肉、鱼、甲壳动物、软体动物或其他水生无脊椎动物的精及汁	23	90	17		千克		Extracts and juices of meat, fish or crustaceans, molluscs or other aquatic invertebrates
1603.0000 10	含濒危野生动物及鱼类成分的肉(指编号0208及子目030192野生动物及鱼类)	23	90	17		千克	ABFE	Meat containing compositions of endangered wild animals and fish of heading No. 0208 or of subheading No. 030192
1603.0000 90	肉及水产品的精、汁(水产品指鱼、甲壳动物、软体动物或其他水生无脊椎动物)	23	90	17	15	千克	AB	Extracts and juices of meat, fish or crustaceans, molluscs or other aquatic invertebrates
16.04	**制作或保藏的鱼;鲟鱼子酱及鱼卵制的鲟鱼子酱代用品:**							**Prepared or preserved fish; caviar and caviar substitutes prepared from fish eggs:**
	-鱼,整条或切块,但未绞碎:							-Fish, whole or in pieces, but not minced:
	--鲑鱼:							--Salmon:
1604.1110	---大西洋鲑鱼	12	90	17	15	千克	AB	---Atlantic Salmon
1604.1190	---其他	12	90	17	15	千克		---Other
1604.1190 10	制作或保藏的川陕哲罗鲑鱼(整条或切块,但未绞碎)	12	90	17	15	千克	AEB	Prepared or preserved sichuan tamen (*Hucho taimen*) (whole or in pieces, but not minced)
1604.1190 20	制作或保藏的秦岭细鳞鲑鱼(整条或切块,但未绞碎)	12	90	17	15	千克	AEB	Prepared or preserved Qinling lenok (*Brachymystax lenok*) (whole or in pieces, but not minced)
1604.1190 90	制作或保藏的其他鲑鱼	12	90	17	15	千克	AB	Prepared or preserved other salmon
1604.1200	--鲱鱼	12	90	17	15	千克	AB	--Herrings
1604.1300	--沙丁鱼、小沙丁鱼属、黍鲱或西鲱	5	90	17	15	千克	AB	--sardines, sardinella, brisling or sprats
1604.1400	--金枪鱼、鲣鱼及狐鲣(狐鲣属)	5	90	17	15	千克	AB	--Tuna、bonito or belted bonito (bonito)
1604.1500	--鲭鱼	12	90	17	15	千克	AB	--Mackerel
1604.1600	--鳀鱼	12	90	17	15	千克	AB	--Anchovies
1604.1700	--鳗鱼	12	90	17	15	千克		--Eels
1604.1700 10	制作或保藏的花鳗鲡(整条或切块,但未绞碎)	12	90	17	15	千克	ABE	Preared or preserved marbled eels (whole or in pieces, but not minced)
1604.1700 20	制作或保藏的欧洲鳗鲡(整条或切块,但未绞碎)	12	90	17	15	千克	ABEF	Preared or preserved europea eels (whole or in pieces, but not minced)
1604.1700 90	其他制作或保藏的鳗鱼(整条或切块,但未绞碎)	12	90	17	15	千克	AB	Preared or preserved other eels (whole or in pieces, but not minced)
	--其他:							--Other:
1604.1920	---罗非鱼	12	90	17	15	千克	AB	---Tilapia
	---叉尾鮰鱼:							---Ictalurus:
1604.1931	----斑点叉尾鮰鱼	12	90	17	15	千克	AB	----Channel catfish (*Ictalurus punctatus*)
1604.1939	----其他	12	90	17	15	千克	AB	----Other
1604.1990	---其他	12	90	17		千克		---Other

税则号列	货品名称	最惠(%)	普通	增值税率	出口退税	计量单位	监管条件	Article Description
1604.1990 10	制作或保藏的濒危鱼类(整条或切块,但未绞碎)	12	90	17		千克	AFEB	Prepared or preserved endangered fish (whole or in pieces, but not minced)
1604.1990 90	制作或保藏的其他鱼(整条或切块,但未绞碎)	12	90	17	15	千克	AB	Prepared or preserved other fish (whole or in pieces, but not minced)
	-其他制作或保藏的鱼:							-Other prepared or preserved fish:
	---罐头:							---In airtight containers:
1604.2011	----鱼翅	12	90	17		千克		----Shark's fin
1604.2011 10	濒危鲨鱼鱼翅罐头	12	90	17		千克	ABFE	Shark's fins of endangered shark (Cetorhinus) in airtight containers
1604.2011 90	其他鲨鱼鱼翅罐头	12	90	17	15	千克	AB	Other shark's of shark fins in airtight containers
1604.2019	----其他	12	90	17		千克		----Other
1604.2019 10	非整条或切块的濒危鱼罐头(鱼翅除外)	12	90	17		千克	ABFE	Endangered fish in airtight containers, other than whole or in pieces (other than shark's fins)
1604.2019 90	非整条或切块的其他鱼罐头(鱼翅除外)	12	90	17	15	千克	AB	Other fish in airtight containers, other than whole or in pieces (other than shark's fins)
	---其他:							---Other:
1604.2091	----鱼翅	12	90	17		千克		----Shark's fin
1604.2091 10	制作或保藏的濒危鲨鱼鱼翅(非整条、非切块、非罐头)	12	90	17		千克	ABFE	Prepared or preserved shark's fins of endangered shark (Cetorhinus) (other than whole or in pieces, not in airtight containers)
1604.2091 90	制作或保藏其他鱼翅(非整条、非切块、非罐头)	12	90	17	15	千克	AB	Prepared or preserved other shark's fins (other than whole or in pieces, not in airtight containers)
1604.2099	----其他	12	90	17		千克		----Other
1604.2099 10	其他制作或保藏的濒危鱼(非整条、非切块、非罐头,鱼翅除外)	12	90	17		千克	ABFE	Prepared or preserved engdangered fish (other than whole or in pieces, not in airtight containers, other than shark's fins)
1604.2099 90	其他制作或保藏的鱼(非整条、非切块、非罐头,鱼翅除外)	12	90	17	15	千克	AB	Other prepared or preserved fish (other than whole or in pieces, not in airtight containers, other than shark's fins)
	-鲟鱼子酱及鲟鱼子酱代用品:							-Caviar and caviar substitutes:
1604.3100	--鲟鱼子酱	12	90	17	15	千克	ABFE	--Caviar
1604.3200	--鲟鱼子酱代用品	12	90	17	15	千克	AB	--Caviar substiutes
16.05	**制作或保藏的甲壳动物、软体动物及其他水生无脊椎动物:**							**Crustaceans, molluscs and other aquatic invertebrates, prepared or preserved:**
1605.1000	-蟹	5	90	17	15	千克	AB	-Crab
	-小虾及对虾:							-Shrimps and prawns:
1605.2100	--非密封包装	5	90	17	15	千克	AB	--Not in airtight container
1605.2900	--其他	5	90	17	15	千克	AB	--Other
1605.3000	-龙虾	5	90	17	15	千克	AB	-Lobster
	-其他甲壳动物:							-Other crustaceans:
	---淡水小龙虾:							---Freshwater crawfish:
1605.4011	----虾仁	5	90	17	15	千克	AB	----Shelled
1605.4019	----其他	5	90	17	15	千克	AB	----Other
1605.4090	---其他	5	90	17	15	千克	AB	---Other
	-软体动物:							-Molluscs:
1605.5100	--牡蛎(蚝)	5	90	17	15	千克	AB	--Oysters
1605.5200	--扇贝,包括海扇	5	90	17	15	千克	AB	--Scallops, including queen scallops
1605.5200 10	制作或保藏的大珠母贝	5	90	17	15	千克	ABE	Pinctada maxima, prepared or preserved
1605.5200 90	其他制作或保藏的扇贝,包括海扇	5	90	17	15	千克	AB	Other scallops, including queen scallops, prepared or preserved
1605.5300	--贻贝	5	90	17	15	千克	AB	--Mussels
1605.5400	--墨鱼及鱿鱼	5	90	17	15	千克	AB	--Cuttle fish and squid
1605.5500	--章鱼	5	90	17	15	千克	AB	--Octopus
	--蛤、鸟蛤及舟贝:							--Clams, cockles and arkshells:
1605.5610	---蛤	5	90	17	5,15	千克	AB	---Clam

税则号列	货品名称	最惠(%)	普通	增值税率	出口退税	计量单位	监管条件	Article Description
1605.5620	---鸟蛤及舟贝	5	90	17	15	千克		---Cockles and ark shells
1605.5620 10	制作或保藏的砗磲	5	90	17	15	千克	ABEF	Tridacna stone, prepared or preserved
1605.5620 90	其他制作或保藏的鸟蛤及舟贝	5	90	17	15	千克	AB	Other cockles and ark shells, prepared or preserved
1605.5700	--鲍鱼	5	90	17	15	千克	AB	--Abalone
1605.5800	--蜗牛及螺,海螺除外	5	90	17		千克		--Snails, other than sea snails
1605.5800 10	制作或保藏的濒危蜗牛及螺,海螺除外	5	90	17		千克	ABFE	Endangered snails, other than sea snails, prepared or preserved
1605.5800 90	其他制作或保藏的蜗牛及螺,海螺除外	5	90	17	15	千克	AB	Other snails, other than sea snails, prepared or preserved
1605.5900	--其他	5	90	17		千克		--Other
1605.5900 10	其他制作或保藏的濒危软体动物	5	90	17		千克	ABFE	Endangered molluscs, prepared or preserved
1605.5900 90	其他制作或保藏的软体动物	5	90	17	15	千克	AB	Other molluscs, prepared or preserved
	-其他水生无脊柱动物:							-Other aquatic invertebrates:
1605.6100	--海参	5	90	17	15	千克		--Sea cucumbers
1605.6100 10	制作或保藏的暗色刺参	5	90	17	15	千克	ABFE	Isostichopus fuscus, prepared or preserved
1605.6100 90	其他制作或保藏的海参	5	90	17	15	千克	AB	Other sea cucumbers, prepared or preserved
1605.6200	--海胆	5	90	17	15	千克	AB	--Sea urchin
1605.6300	--海蜇	15	90	17	5,15	千克	AB	--Jellyfish
1605.6900	--其他	5	90	17		千克		--Other
1605.6900 10	其他制作或保藏的濒危水生无脊椎动物	5	90	17		千克	ABFE	Endangered aquatic invertebrates, prepared or preserved
1605.6900 90	其他制作或保藏的水生无脊椎动物	5	90	17	15	千克	AB	Other aquatic invertebrates, prepared or preserved

第十七章
糖及糖食

Chapter 17
Sugars and sugar confectionery

注释：

本章不包括：

一、含有可可的糖食（税目 18.06）；

二、税目 29.40 的化学纯糖（蔗糖、乳糖、麦芽糖、葡萄糖及果糖除外）及其他产品；

三、第三十章的药品及其他产品。

子目注释：

一、子目号 1701.12、1701.13 及 1701.14 所称"原糖"，是指按重量计干燥状态的蔗糖含量对应的旋光读数低于 99.5°的糖。

二、子目 1701.13 仅包括非离心甘蔗糖，其按重量计干燥状态的蔗糖含量对应的旋光读数不低于 69°但低于 93°。该产品仅含肉眼不可见的不规则形状天然他形微晶，外被糖蜜残余及其他甘蔗成分。

Note:

This Chapter does not cover:

(1) Sugar confectionery containing cocoa (heading No. 18.06);

(2) Chemically pure sugars (other than sucrose, lactose, maltose, glucose and fructose) or other products of heading No. 29.40;

(3) Medicaments or other products of Chapter 30.

Subheading Note:

1. For the purposes of subheadings No. 1701.12、1701.13 及 1701.14, "raw sugar" means sugar whose content of sucrose by weight, in the dry state, corresponds to a polarimeter reading of less than 99.5°.
2. Subheading 1701.13 covers only cane sugar obtained without centrifugation, whose content of sucrose by weight, in the dry state, corresponds to a polarimeter reading of 69° or more but less than 93°. The product contains only natural anhedral microcrystals, of irregular shape, not visible to the naked eye, which are surrouded by residues of molasses and other constituents of sugar cane

税则号列	货品名称	最惠(%)	普通	增值税率	出口退税	计量单位	监管条件	Article Description
17.01	固体甘蔗糖、甜菜糖及化学纯蔗糖：							**Cane or beet sugar and chemically pure sucrose, in solid form:**
	-未加香料或着色剂的原糖：							-Raw sugar not containing added flavouring or colouring matter:
1701.1200	--甜菜糖		125	17	15	千克		--Beet sugar
1701.1200 01	未加香料或着色剂的甜菜原糖［按重量计干燥状态的糖含量低于旋光读数 99.5 度(配额内)］	15	125	17	15	千克	ABt	Raw beet sugar not containing added flavouring or colouring matter[sugar whose content of sucrose by weight, in the dry state, corresponds to a polarimeter reading of less than 99.5°(in-quota)]
1701.1200 90	未加香料或着色剂的甜菜原糖［按重量计干燥状态的糖含量低于旋光读数 99.5 度(配额外)］	50	125	17	15	千克	7AB	Raw beet sugar not containing added flavouring or colouring matter[sugar whose content of sucroseby weight, in the dry state, corresponds to a polarimeter reading of less than 99.5°(out-quota)]
1701.1300	--本章子目注释二所述的甘蔗糖		125	17	15	千克		--Cane sugar in subheading Note 2 to this chapter
1701.1300 01	未加香料或着色剂的本章子目注释二所述的甘蔗原糖［按重量计干燥状态的蔗糖含量对应的旋光读数不低于 69 度，但低于 93 度(配额内)］	15	125	17	15	千克	ABt	Of cane sugar in subheading Note 2 to this chapter not containing added flavouring or colouring matter [whose content of sucrose by weight, in the dry state, corresponds to a polarimeter reading of 69° or more but less 93°(in－quota)]
1701.1300 90	未加香料或着色剂的本章子目注释二所述的甘蔗原糖［按重量计干燥状态的蔗糖含量对应的旋光读数不低于 69 度，但低于 93 度(配额外)］	50	125	17	15	千克	7AB	Of cane sugar in subheading Note 2 to this chapter not containing added flavouring or colouring matter [whose content of sucrose by weight, in the dry state, corresponds to a polarimeter reading of 69° or more but less 93°(out－quota)]
1701.1400	--其他甘蔗糖		125	17	15	千克		--Other cane sugar
1701.1400 01	未加香料或着色剂其他甘蔗原糖［按重量计干燥状态的糖含量低于旋光读数 99.5 度(配额内)］	15	125	17	15	千克	ABt	Other cane sugar not containing added flavouring or colouring matter[sugar whose content of sucrose by weight, in the dry state, corresponds to a polarimeter reading of less than 99.5°(in－quota)]
1701.1400 90	未加香料或着色剂其他甘蔗原糖［按重量计干燥状态的糖含量低于旋光读数 99.5 度(配额外)］	50	125	17	15	千克	7AB	Other cane sugar not containing added flavouring or colouring matter[sugar whose content of sucrose by weight, in the dry state, corresponds to a polarimeter reading of less than 99.5°(out－quota)]
	-其他：							-Other:
1701.9100	--加有香料或着色剂		125	17	15	千克		--Containing added flavouring or colouring matter

税则号列	货品名称	最惠(%)	普通	增值税率	出口退税	计量单位	监管条件	Article Description
1701.9100 01	加有香料或着色剂的糖[指甘蔗糖、甜菜糖及化学纯蔗糖(配额内)]	15	125	17	15	千克	ABt	Cane or beet sugar and chemically pure sucrose, containing added flavouring or colouring matter (in-quota)
1701.9100 90	加有香料或着色剂的糖[指甘蔗糖、甜菜糖及化学纯蔗糖(配额外)]	50	125	17	15	千克	7AB	Cane or beet sugar and chemically pure sucrose, containing added flavouring or colouring matter (out-quota)
	--其他:							--Other:
1701.9910	---砂糖		125	17	15	千克		---Granulated sugar
1701.9910 10	砂糖(配额内)	15	125	17	15	千克	ABt	Granulated sugar (in-quota)
1701.9910 90	砂糖(配额外)	50	125	17	15	千克	7AB	Granulated sugar (out-quota)
1701.9920	---绵白糖		125	17	15	千克		---Superfine sugar
1701.9920 01	绵白糖(配额内)	15	125	17	15	千克	BAt	Superfine sugar (in-quota)
1701.9920 90	绵白糖(配额外)	50	125	17	15	千克	7BA	Superfine sugar (out-quota)
1701.9990	---其他		125	17	15	千克		---Other
1701.9990 01	其他精制糖(配额内)	15	125	17	15	千克	ABt	Other refined sugar (in-quota)
1701.9990 90	其他精制糖(配额外)	50	125	17	15	千克	7AB	Other refined sugar (out-quota)
17.02	**其他固体糖,包括化学纯乳糖、麦芽糖、葡萄糖及果糖;未加香料或着色剂的糖浆;人造蜜,不论是否掺有天然蜂蜜;焦糖:**							**Other sugars, including chemically pure lactose, maltose, glucose and fructose, in solid form; sugar syrups not containing added flavouring or colouring matter; artificial honey, whether or not mixed with natural honey; caramel:**
	-乳糖及乳糖浆:							-Lactose and lactose syrup:
1702.1100	--按重量计干燥无水乳糖含量在99%及以上	10	80	17	15	千克	AB	--Containing by weight 99% or more lactose, expressed as anhydrous lactose, calculated on the dry matter
1702.1900	--其他	10	80	17	15	千克	AB	--Other
1702.2000	-槭糖及槭糖浆	30	80	17	15	千克	AB	-Maple sugar and maple syrup
1702.3000	-葡萄糖及葡萄糖浆,不含果糖或按重量计干燥状态的果糖含量在20%以下	30	80	17	15	千克	BA	-Glucose and glucose syrup, not containing fructose or containing in the dry state less than 20% by weight of fructose
1702.4000	-葡萄糖及葡萄糖浆,按重量计干燥状态的果糖含量在20%及以上,但在50%以下	30	80	17	15	千克	BA	-Glucose and glucose syrup, containing in the dry state at least 20% but less than 50% by weight of fructose
1702.5000	-化学纯果糖	30	80	17	15	千克	AB	-Chemically pure fructose
1702.6000	-其他果糖及果糖浆,按重量计干燥状态的果糖含量在50%以上	30	80	17	15	千克	BA	-Other fructose and fructose syrup, containing in the dry state more than 50% by weight of fructose
1702.9000	-其他,包括转化糖	30	80	17	15	千克		-Other, including invert sugar
1702.9000 10	人造蜜	30	80	17	15	千克	AB	Artificial honey
1702.9000 90	其他固体糖、焦糖(包括转化糖及按重量计干燥状态果糖含量为50%的糖、糖浆)	30	80	17	15	千克	AB	Other sugars, caramel (including invert sugar, in the dry state 50% by weight of fructose)
17.03	**制糖后所剩的糖蜜:**							**Molasses resulting from the extraction or refining or sugar:**
1703.1000	-甘蔗糖蜜	8	50	17	15	千克	ABP	-Cane molasses
1703.9000	-其他	8	50	17	15	千克	ABP	-Other
17.04	**不含可可的糖食(包括白巧克力):**							**Sugar confectionery (including white chocolate), not containing cocoa:**
1704.1000	-口香糖,不论是否裹糖	12	50	17	15	千克	AB	-Chewing gum, whether or not sugarcoated
1704.9000	-其他	10	50	17	15	千克	AB	-Other

第十八章
可可及可可制品

Chapter 18
Cocoa and cocoa preparations

注释：

一、本章不包括税目 04.03、19.01、19.04、19.05、21.05、22.02、22.08、30.03、30.04 的制品。

二、税目 18.06 包括含有可可的糖食及注释一以外的其他含可可的食品。

Notes:

1. This Chapter does not cover the preparations of heading No. 04.03, 19.01, 19.04, 19.05, 21.05, 22.02, 22.08, 30.03, or 30.04.
2. Heading No. 18.06 includes sugar confectionery containing cocoa and, subject to Note 1 to this Chapter, other food preparations containing cocoa.

税则号列	货 品 名 称	最惠(%)	普通	增值税率	出口退税	计量单位	监管条件	Article Description
18.01	**整颗或破碎的可可豆，生的或焙炒的：**							**Cocoa beans, whole or broken, raw or roasted:**
1801.0000[暂]	整颗或破碎的可可豆，生的或焙炒的	2	30	17	5,15	千克	AB	Cocoa beans, whole or broken, raw or roasted
18.02	**可可荚、壳、皮及废料：**							**Cocoa shells, husks, skins and other cocoa waste:**
1802.0000	可可荚、壳、皮及废料	10	30	17	5	千克	AB	Cocoa shells, husks, skins and other cocoa waste
18.03	**可可膏，不论是否脱脂：**							**Cocoa paste, whether or not defatted:**
1803.1000	-未脱脂	10	30	17	15	千克	AB	-Not defatted
1803.2000	-全脱脂或部分脱脂	10	30	17	15	千克	AB	-Wholly or partly defatted
18.04	**可可脂、可可油：**							**Cocoa butter, fat and oil:**
1804.0000	可可脂、可可油	22	70	17	15	千克		Cocoa butter, fat and oil
1804.0000 10	可可脂	22	70	17	15	千克	AB	Cocoa fat
1804.0000 90	可可油	22	70	17	15	千克	AB	Cocoa oil
18.05	**未加糖或其他甜物质的可可粉：**							**Cocoa powder, not containing added sugar or other sweetening matter:**
1805.0000	未加糖或其他甜物质的可可粉	15	40	17	15	千克	AB	Cocoa powder, not containing added sugar or other sweetening matter
18.06	**巧克力及其他含可可的食品：**							**Chocolate and other food preparations containing cocoa:**
1806.1000	-加糖或其他甜物质的可可粉	10	50	17	15	千克	AB	-Cocoa powder, containing added sugar or other sweetening matter
1806.2000	-其他重量超过2千克的块状或条状含可可食品，或液状、膏状、粉状、粒状或其他散装形状的含可可食品，容器包装或内包装每件净重超过2千克的	10	50	17	15	千克	AB	-Other preparations in blocks, slabs or bars weighing more than 2kg or in liquid, paste, powder, granular or other bulk form in containers or immediate packings, of a content exceeding 2kg
	-其他块状或条状的含可可食品：							-Other, in blocks, slabs or bars:
1806.3100	--夹心	8	50	17	15	千克	AB	--Filled
1806.3200	--不夹心	10	50	17	15	千克	AB	--Not filled
1806.9000	-其他	8	50	17	15	千克	AB	-Other

第十九章
谷物、粮食粉、淀粉或乳的制品；糕饼点心

注释：

一、本章不包括：

（一）按重量计含香肠、肉、食用杂碎、动物血、鱼、甲壳动物，软体动物、其他水生无脊椎动物及其混合物超过20%的食品（第十六章），但税目19.02的包馅食品除外；

（二）用粮食粉或淀粉制的专作动物饲料用的饼干及其他制品（税目23.09）；

（三）第三十章的药品及其他产品。

二、税目19.01所称：

（一）"粗粒"是指第十一章谷物的粗粒；

（二）"细粉"及"粗粉"，是指：

1. 第十一章谷物的细粉及粗粉；

2. 其他章植物的细粉、粗粉及粉末，但不包括干蔬菜、马铃薯和干豆类的细粉、粗粉及粉末（应分别归入税目07.12、11.05和11.06）。

三、税目19.04不包括按重量计全脱脂可可含量超过6%或用巧克力完全包裹的食品以及税目18.06的其他含可可食品（税目18.06）。

四、税目19.04所称"其他方法制作的"，是指制作或加工程度超过第十章或第十一章各税目或注释所规定范围的。

Chapter 19
Preparations of cereals, flour, starch or milk; pastrycooks' products

Notes:

1. This Chapter does not cover:

(a) Except in the case of stuffed products of heading No. 19.02, food preparations containing more than 20% by weight of sausage, meat, meat offal, blood, fish or crustaceans, molluscs or other aquatic invertebrates, or any combination thereof (Chapter 16);

(b) Biscuits or other articles made from flour or from starch, specially prepared for use in animal feeding (heading No. 23.09);

(c) Medicaments or other products of Chapter 30.

2. For the purposes of heading No. 19.01:

(a) The term "groats" means cereal groats of Chapter 11;

(b) The terms "flour" and "meal" mean:

(1) Cereal flour and meal of Chapter 11, and

(2) Flour, meal and powder of vegetable origin of any Chapter, other than flour, meal or powder of driedvegetables (heading No. 07.12), of potatoes(heading No. 11.05) or of dried leguminous vegetables (heading No. 11.06).

3. Heading No. 19.04 does not cover preparations containing more than 6% by weight of cocoa calculated on a totally defatted basis or completely coated with chocolate or other food preparations containing cocoa of heading 18.06 (heading No. 18.06).

4. For the purposes of heading No. 19.04, the expression "otherwise prepared" means preparedor or processed to an extent beyond that provided for in the headings of or Notes to Chapter 10 or 11.

税则号列	货品名称	最惠(%)	普通	增值税率	出口退税	计量单位	监管条件	Article Description
19.01	**麦精；细粉、粗粒、粗粉、淀粉或麦精制的其他税目未列名的食品，不含可可或按重量计全脱脂可可含量低于40%；税目04.01至04.04所列货品制的其他税目未列名的食品，不含可可或按重量计全脱脂可可含量低于5%：**							**Malt extract; food preparations of flour, groats, meal, starch or malt extract, not containing cocoa or containing less than 40% by weight of cocoa calculated on a totally defatted basis, not elsewhere specified or included; food preparations of goods of headings No. 04.01 to 04.04, not containing cocoa or containing less than 5%by weight of cocoa calculated on a totally defatted basis, not elsewhere specified or included:**
	-供婴幼儿食用的零售包装食品							-Preparations for infant use, put up for retail sale
1901.1010暂	配方奶粉	5	40	17	15	千克	7AB	Powdered formulas
1901.1090暂	其他	5	40	17	15	千克	AB	Other
1901.2000	-供烘焙税目19.05所列面包糕饼用的调制品及面团	25	80	17	5,15	千克	AB	-Mixes and doughs for the preparation of bakers' wares of heading No. 19.05
1901.9000暂	-其他	5	80	17	15	千克	AB	-Other
19.02	**面食，不论是否煮熟、包馅（肉馅或其他馅）或其他方法制作，例如，通心粉、面条、汤团、馄饨、饺子、奶油面卷；古斯古斯面食，不论是否制作：**							**Pasta, whether or not cooked or stuffed (with meat or other substances) or otherwise prepared, such as spaghetti, macaroni, noodles, lasagne, gnocchi, ravioli, cannelloni; couscous, whether or not prepared:**
	-生的面食，未包馅或未经其他方法制作：							-Uncooked pasta, not stuffed or otherwise prepared:
1902.1100	--含蛋	15	80	17	5	千克	AB	--Containing eggs
1902.1900	--其他	15	80	17	5,15	千克	AB	--Other
1902.2000	-包馅面食，不论是否烹煮或经其他方法制作	15	80	17	5,15	千克	AB	-Stuffed pasta, whether or not cooked or otherwise prepared
	-其他面食：							-Other pasta:
1902.3010	---米粉干	15	80	17	5	千克	AB	---Rice vermicelli, cooked

税则号列	货品名称	最惠(%)	普通	增值税率	出口退税	计量单位	监管条件	Article Description
1902.3020	---粉丝	15	80	17	15	千克	AB	---Bean vermicelli, cooked
1902.3030	---即食或快熟面条	15	80	17	5,15	千克	AB	---Instant noodle
1902.3090	---其他	15	80	17	5,15	千克	AB	---Other
1902.4000	-古斯古斯面食	25	80	17	5,15	千克	AB	-Couscous
19.03	珍粉及淀粉制成的珍粉代用品,片、粒、珠、粉或类似形状的:							**Tapioca and substitutes therefor prepared from starch, in the form of flakes, grains, pearls, siftings or in similar forms:**
1903.0000	珍粉及淀粉制成的珍粉代用品,片、粒、珠、粉或类似形状的	15	80	17	15	千克	AB	Tapioca and substitutes therefor prepared from starch, in the form of flakes, grains, pearls, siftings or in similar forms
19.04	谷物或谷物产品经膨化或烘炒制成的食品(例如,玉米片);其他税目未列名的预煮或经其他方法制作的谷粒(玉米除外),谷物片或经其他加工的谷粒(细粉粗粒及粗粉除外):							**Prepared foods obtained by the swelling or roasting of cereals or cereal products (for example, corn flakes); cereals (other than maize (corn)) in grain form or in the form of flakes or other worked grains (except flour, groats and meal), precooked or otherwise prepared, not elsewhere specified or included:**
1904.1000	-谷物或谷物产品经膨化或烘炒制成的食品	25	80	17	15	千克	AB	-Prepared foods obtained by the swelling or roasting of cereals or cereal products
1904.2000	-未烘炒谷物片制成的食品及未烘炒的谷物片与烘炒的谷物片或膨化的谷物混合制成的食品	30	80	17	15	千克	AB	-Prepared foods obtained from unroasted cereal flakes or from mixtures of unroasted cereal flakes and roasted cereal flakes or swelled cereals
1904.3000	-碾碎的干小麦	30	80	17	15	千克	AB	-Bulgur wheat
1904.9000	-其他	30	80	17	15	千克	AB	-Other
19.05	面包、糕点、饼干及其他烘焙糕饼,不论是否含可可;圣餐饼、装药空囊、封缄、糯米纸及类似制品:							**Bread, pastry, cakes, biscuits and other bakers' wares, whether or not containing cocoa; communion wafers, empty cachets of a kind suitable for pharmaceutical use, sealing wafers, rice paper and similar products:**
1905.1000	-黑麦脆面包片	20	80	17	15	千克	AB	-Crispbread
1905.2000	-姜饼及类似品	20	80	17	15	千克	AB	-Gingerbread and the like
	-甜饼干;华夫饼干及圣餐饼:							-Sweet biscuits; waffles and wafers:
1905.3100	--甜饼干	15	80	17	15	千克	AB	--Sweet biscuits
1905.3200	--华夫饼干及圣餐饼	15	80	17	15	千克	AB	--Waffles and wafers
1905.4000	-面包干、吐司及类似的烤面包	20	80	17	15	千克	AB	-Rusks, toasted bread and similar toasted products
1905.9000	-其他	20	80	17	15	千克	AB	-Other

第二十章
蔬菜、水果、坚果或植物其他部分的制品

注释：

一、本章不包括：

（一）用第七章、第八章或第十一章所列方法制作或保藏的蔬菜、水果或坚果；

（二）按重量计含香肠、肉、食用杂碎、动物血、鱼、甲壳动物、软体动物、其他水生无脊椎动物及其混合物超过20%的食品（第十六章）；

（三）税目19.05的烘焙糕饼及其他制品；

（四）税目21.04的均化混合食品。

二、税目20.07及20.08不包括制成糖食的果冻、果膏、糖衣杏仁或类似品（税目17.04）及巧克力糖食（税目18.06）。

三、税目20.01、20.04及20.05仅分别包括用本章注释一（一）以外的方法制作或保藏的第七章或税目11.05、11.06的产品（第八章产品的细粉、粗粉除外）。

四、干重量在7%及以上的番茄汁归入税目20.02。

五、税目20.07所称“烹煮的”是指，在常压或减压下，通过减少水份或其他方法增加产品粘稠度的热处理。

六、税目20.09所称“未发酵及未加酒精的水果汁”，是指按容量计酒精浓度（标准见第二十二章注释二）不超过0.5%的水果汁。

子目注释：

一、子目号2005.10所称“均化蔬菜”，是指蔬菜经精细均化制成供婴幼儿食用或营养用的零售包装食品（每件净重不超过250克）。为了调味、保藏或其他目的，均化蔬菜中可以加入少量其他配料，还可以含有少量可见的蔬菜粒。归类时，子目号2005.10优先于税目20.05的其他子目。

二、子目号2007.10所称“均化食品”，是指果实经精细均化制成供婴幼儿食用或营养用的零售包装食品（每件净重不超过250克）。为了调味、保藏或其他目的，均化食品中可以加入少量其他配料，还可以含有少量可见的果粒。归类时，子目号2007.10优先于税目20.07的其他子目。

三、子目2009.12、2009.21、2009.31、2009.41、2009.61及2009.71所称“白利糖度值”，是指直接从白利糖度计读取的度数或在20℃时从折射计读取的以蔗糖百分比含量计的折射率，在其他温度下读取的数值应折算为20℃时的折射率。

Chapter 20
Preparations of vegetables, fruit, nuts or other parts of plants

Notes:

1. This Chapter does not cover:

(a) Vegetables, fruit or nuts, prepared or preserved by the processes specified in Chapter 7,8 or 11;

(b) Food preparations containing more than 20% by weight of sausage, meat, meat offal, blood, fish or crustaceans, molluscs or other aquatic invertebrates, or any combination thereof (Chapter 16)

(c) Bakers' wares and other products of heading No. 19.05;

(d) Homogenized composite food preparations of heading No. 21.04.

2. Headings No. 20.07 and 20.08 do not apply to fruit jellies, fruit pastes, sugar-coated almonds or the like in the form of sugar confectionery (heading No. 17.04) or chocolate confectionery (heading No. 18.06).

3. Headings No. 20.01, 20.04 and 20.05 cover, as the case may be, only those products of Chapter 7 or of heading No. 11.05 or 11.06 (other than flour, meal and powder of the products of Chapter 8) which have been prepared or preserved by processes other than those referred to in Note 1 (a).

4. Tomato juice the dry weight content of which is 7% or more, is to be classified in heading No. 20.02.

5. For the purposes of heading No. 20.07, the expression "obtained by cooking" means obtained by heat treatment at atmospheric pressure or under reduced pressure to increase the viscosity of a product through reduction of water content or other means.

6. For the purposes of heading No. 20.09, the expression "juices, unfermented and not containing added spirit" means juices of an alcoholic strength by volume (see Note 2 to Chapter 22) not exceeding 0.5% vol.

Subheading Notes:

1. For the purposes of subheading No. 2005.10, the expression "homogenized vegetables" means preparations of vegetables, finely homogenized, put up for retail sale as infant food or for dietetic purposes, in containers of a net weight content not exceeding 250g. For the application of this definition no account is to be taken of small quantities of any ingredients which may have been added to the preparation for seasoning, preparation or other purposes. These preparations may contain a small quantity of visible pieces of vegetables. Subheading No. 2005.10 takes precedence over all other subheadings of heading No. 20.05.

2. For the purposes of subheading No. 2007.10, the expression "homogenized preparations" means preparations of fruit, finely homogenized, put up for retail sale as infant food or for dietetic purposes, in containers of a net weight content not exceeding 250g. For the application of this definition no account is to be taken of small quantities of any ingredients which may have been added to the preparation for seasoning, preservation or other purposes. These preparations may contain a small quantity of visible pieces of fruit. Subheading No. 2007.10 takes precedence over all other subheadings of heading No. 20.07.

3. For the purposes of subheadings No. 2009.12, 2009.21, 2009.31, 2009.41, 2009.61 and 2009.71, the expression "Brix value" means the direct reading of degrees Brix obtained from a Brix hydrometer or of refractive index expressed in terms of percentage sucrose content obtained from a refractometer, at a temperature of 20℃ or corrected for 20℃ if the reading is made at a different temperature.

税则号列	货品名称	最惠(%)	普通	增值税率	出口退税	计量单位	监管条件	Article Description
20.01	蔬菜、水果、坚果及植物的其他食用部分，用醋或醋酸制作或保藏的：							**Vegetagbles, fruit, nuts and other edible parts of plants, prepared or preserved by vinegar or acetic acid:**
2001.1000	-黄瓜及小黄瓜	25	70	17	5,15	千克	AB	-Cucumbers and gherkins
	-其他：							-Other:
2001.9010	---大蒜	25	70	17	5,15	千克		---Garlic
2001.9010 10	用醋或醋酸腌制的大蒜头、大蒜瓣（无论是否加糖或去皮）	25	70	17	5,15	千克	AB	Garlic bulbs, garlic cloves, prepared by vinegar or acetic acid(whether or not added sugars or skinned)
2001.9010 90	用醋或醋酸腌制的其他大蒜（不含蒜头、蒜瓣，无论是否加糖或去皮）	25	70	17	5,15	千克	AB	Other garlic prepared by vinegar or acetic acid (whether or not added sugars or skinned other than garlic bulbs, galic cloves)
2001.9090	---其他	25	70	17		千克		---Other
2001.9090 10	用醋或醋酸制作或保藏的松茸	25	70	17	5	千克	ABE	Matsutske, prepared or preserved by vinegar or acetic acid
2001.9090 20	用醋或醋酸制作或保藏的酸竹笋	25	70	17	5	千克	ABE	Acidosasa chinensis shoots, prepared or preserved by vinegar or acetic acid
2001.9090 30	用醋或醋酸制作或保藏的芦荟	25	70	17	5	千克	ABFE	Aloe, prepared or preserved by vinegar or acetic acid
2001.9090 40	用醋或醋酸制作或保藏的仙人掌植物	25	70	17	5	千克	ABFE	Cactus, prepared or preserved by vinegar or acetic acid
2001.9090 50	用醋或醋酸制作或保藏的莼菜	25	70	17	5	千克	ABE	Water shield, prepared or preserved by vinegar or acetic acid
2001.9090 90	用醋制作的其他果、菜及食用植物（包括用醋酸制作或保藏的）	25	70	17	5,15	千克	AB	Vegetagbles, fruit, nuts and other edible parts of plants, prepared or preserved by vinegar or acetic acid
20.02	番茄，用醋或醋酸以外的其他方法制作或保藏的：							**Tomatoes prepared or preserved otherwise than by vinegar or acetic acid:**
	-番茄，整个或切片：							-Tomatoes, whole or in pieces:
2002.1010	---罐头	19	80	17	15	千克	AB	---In airtight containers
2002.1090	---其他	25	70	17	5,15	千克	AB	---Other
	-其他：							-Other:
	---番茄酱罐头：							---Tomato paste, in airtight containers:
2002.9011	----重量不超过5千克的	20	80	17	15	千克	AB	---Weighing not more than 5kg
2002.9019	----重量超过5千克的	20	80	17	15	千克	AB	---Weighing more than 5kg
2002.9090	---其他	18	70	17	5,15	千克	AB	---Other
20.03	蘑菇及块菌，用醋或醋酸以外的其他方法制作或保藏的：							**Mushrooms and truffles, prepared or preserved otherwise than by vinegar or acetic acid:**
	-伞菌属蘑菇：							Mushrooms
	---罐头：							---In airtight containers:
2003.1011	----小白蘑菇	25	90	17	15	千克	AB	----Small white agaric
2003.1019	----其他	25	90	17	15	千克	AB	----Other
2003.1090	---其他	25	90	17	5,15	千克	AB	---Other
	-其他：							-Other:
2003.9010	---罐头	25	90	17	15	千克		---In airtight containers
2003.9010 10	非用醋制作的香菇罐头［用醋或醋酸以外其他方法制作或保藏的（非伞菌属蘑菇）］	25	90	17	15	千克	AB	Shiitake in airtight containiers, not prepared by vinegar [prepared or preserved otherwise than by vinegar or acetic(not mushrooms of the genera agaricus)]
2003.9010 20	非用醋制作的松茸罐头（用醋或醋酸以外其他方法制作或保藏的）	25	90	17	15	千克	ABE	Matsutske in airtight containiers, not prepared by vinegar [prepared or preserved otherwise than by vinegar or acetic(not mushrooms of the genera agaricus)]
2003.9010 90	非用醋制作的其他蘑菇罐头［用醋或醋酸以外其他方法制作或保藏的（非伞菌属蘑菇）］	25	90	17	15	千克	AB	Other mushrooms in airtight containiers, not prepared by vinegar [prepared or preserved otherwise than by vinegar or acetic (not mushrooms of the genera agaricus)]
2003.9090	---其他	25	90	17	5,15	千克		---Other
2003.9090 10	非用醋制作的其他香菇［用醋或醋酸以外其他方法制作或保藏的（非伞菌属蘑菇）］	25	90	17	5,15	千克	AB	Other Matsutske mushroom, prepared or preserved otherwise than by vinegar (not mushrooms of the genera agaricus)

税则号列	货品名称	最惠(%)	普通	增值税率	出口退税	计量单位	监管条件	Article Description
2003.9090 20	非用醋制作的其他松茸(用醋或醋酸以外其他方法制作或保藏的)	25	90	17	5,15	千克	ABE	Other sungmo, not prepared by vinegar(prepared or preserved otherwise than by vinegar or acetic)
2003.9090 90	非用醋制作的其他蘑菇[用醋或醋酸以外其他方法制作或保藏的(非伞菌属蘑菇)]	25	90	17	5,15	千克	AB	Other mushrooms, not prepared by vinegar or [prepared or preserved otherwise than by vinegar or acetic(not mushrooms of the genera agaricus)]
20.04	**其他冷冻蔬菜,用醋或醋酸以外的其他方法制作或保藏的,但税目20.06的产品除外:**							**Other vegetables prepared or preserved otherwise than by vinegar or acetic acid, other than products of heading No. 20.06:**
2004.1000	-马铃薯	13	70	17	5,15	千克	AB	-Potatoes
2004.9000	-其他蔬菜及什锦蔬菜	25	70	17	5,15	千克		-Other vegetables and mixtures of vegetables
2004.9000 10	非用醋制作的冷冻松茸	25	70	17	5,15	千克	ABE	Sungmo, not prepared by vinegar or acetic acid, frozen
2004.9000 20	非用醋制作的冷冻酸竹笋	25	70	17	5,15	千克	ABE	Acidosasa chinensis shoots, frozen, not prepared by vinegar
2004.9000 30	非用醋制作的冷冻芦荟	25	70	17	5,15	千克	ABFE	Aloe, frozen, not prepared by vinegar
2004.9000 40	非用醋制作的冷冻仙人掌植物	25	70	17	5,15	千克	ABFE	Cactus, frozen, not prepared by vinegar
2004.9000 90	非用醋制作的其他冷冻蔬菜(编号2006的货品除外)	25	70	17	5,15	千克	AB	Other vegetables, not prepared by vinegar(other than products of heading No. 2006)
20.05	**其他未冷冻蔬菜,用醋或醋酸以外的其他方法制作或保藏的,但税目20.06的产品除外:**							**Other vegetables prepared or preserved otherwise than by vinegar or acetic acid, not frozen, other than products of heading No. 20.06:**
2005.1000	-均化蔬菜	25	70	17	15	千克	AB	-Homogenized vegetables
2005.2000	-马铃薯	15	70	17	5,15	千克	AB	-Potatoes
2005.4000	-豌豆	25	70	17	5,15	千克	AB	-Peas (*Pisum sativum*)
	-豇豆及菜豆:							-Beans (*Vigna spp.*, *Phaseolus spp.*):
	--脱荚的:							--Beans, shelled:
	---罐头:							---In airtight containers:
2005.5111	----赤豆馅	25	80	17	15	千克	AB	----Red bean paste
2005.5119	----其他	25	80	17	15	千克	AB	----Other
	---其他:							---Other:
2005.5191	----赤豆馅	25	70	17	15	千克	AB	----Red bean paste
2005.5199	----其他	25	70	17	5,15	千克	AB	----Other
	--其他:							--Other:
2005.5910	---罐头:	25	80	17	15	千克	AB	---In airtight containers
2005.5990	---其他	25	70	17	5,15	千克	AB	---Other
	-芦笋:							-Asparagus:
2005.6010	---罐头	25	80	17	15	千克	AB	---In airtight containers
2005.6090	---其他	25	70	17	5,15	千克	AB	---Other
2005.7000	-油橄榄	10	70	17	5,15	千克	AB	-Olives
2005.8000	-甜玉米	10	80	17	5,15	千克	AB	-Sweet corn (*Zea mays var. saccharata*)
	-其他蔬菜及什锦蔬菜:							-Other vegetables and mixtures of vegetables:
	--竹笋:							--Bamboo shoots:
2005.9110	---竹笋罐头	25	80	17	15	千克		---Bamboo shoots in airtight containers
2005.9110 10	非用醋制作的酸竹笋罐头	25	80	17	15	千克	ABE	Acidosasa chinensis shoots in airtight containers, not preserved by vinegar
2005.9110 90	非用醋制作的其他竹笋罐头	25	80	17	15	千克	AB	Other bamboo shoots in airtight containers, not preserved by vinegar
2005.9190	---其他	25	70	17	5,15	千克		---Other
2005.9190 10	非用醋制作的酸竹笋	25	70	17	5,15	千克	ABE	Acidosasa chinensis shoots, not preserved by vinegar
2005.9190 90	非用醋制作的其他竹笋	25	70	17	5,15	千克	AB	Other bamboo shoots, not prepared or preserved by vinegar
	--其他:							--Other:
2005.9920	---蚕豆罐头	25	80	17	15	千克	AB	---Broad beans, in airtight containers
2005.9940	---榨菜	25	70	17	5,15	千克	AB	---Hot pickled mustard tubers
2005.9950	---咸蕨菜	25	70	17	5,15	千克	AB	---Chueh tsai (fiddle-head), salted
2005.9960	---咸藠头	25	70	17	5,15	千克	AB	---Scallion, salted
	---其他:							---Other:
2005.9991	----罐头	25	70	17	15	千克	AB	----In airtight containers
2005.9999	----其他	25	70	17	5,15	千克		----Other
2005.9999 10	非用醋制作的仙人掌	25	70	17	5,15	千克	ABFE	Cactus, not preserved by vinegar
2005.9999 20	非用醋制作的芦荟	25	70	17	5,15	千克	ABFE	Aloe, not preserved by vinegar

税则号列	货品名称	最惠(%)	普通	增值税率	出口退税	计量单位	监管条件	Article Description
2005.9999 90	非用醋制作的其他蔬菜及什锦蔬菜	25	70	17	5,15	千克	AB	Other vegetables and mixtures of vegetables, not preserved by vinegar
20.06	糖渍蔬菜、水果、坚果、果皮及植物的其他部分(沥干、糖渍或裹糖的):							**Vegetables, fruit, nuts, fruit-peel and other parts of plants, preserved by sugar (drained, glac or crystallized):**
2006.0010	---蜜枣	30	90	17	15	千克	AB	---Preserved jujubes
2006.0020	---橄榄	30	90	17	15	千克	AB	---Preserved olives
2006.0090	---其他	30	90	17	15	千克		---Other
2006.0090 10	糖渍制松茸	30	90	17	15	千克	ABE	Matsutske, preserved by sugar
2006.0090 90	其他糖渍蔬菜、水果、坚果、果皮(包括糖渍植物的其他部分)	30	90	17	15	千克	AB	Other vegetables, fruit, nuts, fruit-peel (including other parts of plants) preserved by sugar
20.07	烹煮的果酱、果冻、柑桔酱、果泥及果膏,不论是否加糖或其他甜物质:							**Jams, fruit jellies, marmalades, fruit or nut pure and fruit or nut pastes, being cooked preparations, whether or not containing added sugar or other sweetening matter:**
2007.1000	-均化食品	30	80	17	15	千克	AB	-Homogenized preparations
	-其他:							-Other:
2007.9100	--柑橘属水果的	30	80	17	15	千克	AB	--Citrus fruit
	--其他:							--Other:
2007.9910	---罐头	5	80	17	15	千克	AB	---In airtight containers
2007.9990	---其他	5	80	17	15	千克	AB	---Other
20.08	用其他方法制作或保藏的其他品目未列名水果、坚果及植物的其他食用部分,不论是否加酒、加糖或其他甜物质:							**Fruit, nuts and other edible parts of plants, otherwise prepared or preserved, whether or not containing added sugar or other sweetening matter or spirit, not elsewhere specified or included:**
	-坚果、花生及其他子仁,不论是否混合:							-Nuts, groundnuts and other seeds, whether or not mixed together:
	--花生:							--Ground-nuts:
2008.1110	---花生米罐头	30	90	17	15	千克	AB	---Ground-nuts kernels, in airtight containers
2008.1120	---烘焙花生	30	80	17	15	千克	AB	---Roasted ground-nuts
2008.1130	---花生酱	30	90	17	15	千克	AB	---Ground-nut butter
2008.1190	---其他	30	80	17	5,15	千克	AB	---Other
	--其他,包括什锦坚果及其他子仁:							--Other, including mixtures:
2008.1910	---核桃仁罐头	20	90	17	15	千克	AB	---Walnut meats, in airtight containers
2008.1920	---其他果仁罐头	13	90	17	15	千克	AB	---Other nuts, in airtight containers
	---其他:							---Other:
2008.1991	----栗仁	10	80	17	5,15	千克	AB	----Chestnut seed
2008.1992	----芝麻	10	80	17	5,15	千克	AB	----Sesame
2008.1999	----其他	10	80	17		千克		----Other
2008.1999 10	其他方法制作保藏的红松子仁(用醋或醋酸以外其他方法制作或保藏的)	10	80	17		千克	ABE	Korean pine-nuts, shelled, (not prepared or preserved by vinegar or acetic acid)
2008.1999 90	未列名制作或保藏坚果及其他子仁(用醋或醋酸以外其他方法制作或保藏的)	10	80	17	5,15	千克	AB	Nuts and other seeds, (not prepared or preserved by vinegar or acetic acid) not elsewhere specified or included
	-菠萝:							-Pineapples:
2008.2010	---罐头	15	90	17	15	千克	AB	---In airtight containers
2008.2090	---其他	15	80	17	5,15	千克	AB	---Other
	-柑橘属水果:							-Citrus fruit:
2008.3010	---罐头	20	90	17	15	千克	AB	---In airtight containers
2008.3090	---其他	20	80	17	5,15	千克	AB	---Other
	-梨:							-Pears:
2008.4010	---罐头	20	90	17	15	千克	AB	---In airtight containers
2008.4090	---其他	20	80	17	5,15	千克	AB	---Other
2008.5000	-杏	20	90	17	5,15	千克	AB	-Apricots
	-樱桃:							-Cherries:
2008.6010	---罐头	20	90	17	15	千克	AB	---In airtight containers
2008.6090	---其他	20	90	17	5,15	千克	AB	---Other
	-桃,包括油桃:							-Peaches:
2008.7010	---罐头	10	90	17	15	千克	AB	---In airtight containers
2008.7090	---其他	20	80	17	5,15	千克	AB	---Other

税则号列	货品名称	最惠(%)	普通	增值税率	出口退税	计量单位	监管条件	Article Description
2008.8000	-草莓	15	90	17	5,15	千克	AB	-Strawberries
	-其他,包括子目号 2008.19 以外的什锦果实:							-Other, including mixtures other than those of subheading No. 2008.19:
2008.9100	--棕榈芯	5	80	17	5,15	千克	AB	--Palm hearts
2008.9300	--蔓越橘(大果蔓越橘,小果蔓越橘、越橘)	15	80	17	5,15	千克	AB	--Cranberry(Vaccinium macrocarpon vaccinium oxycoccos, vaccinium vitis-idaea.)
2008.9700	--什锦果实	10	80	17	5,15	千克	AB	--Mixtures
	--其他:							--Other:
2008.9910	---荔枝罐头	20	90	17	15	千克	AB	---Lychee can
2008.9920	---龙眼罐头	15	80	17	15	千克	AB	---Longan can
	---海草及其他藻类制品:							---Preparations of seaweeds and other alga:
2008.9931	----调味紫菜	15	90	17	15	千克	AB	----Seasoned laver
2008.9932	----盐腌海带	15	80	17	5,15	千克	AB	----Salted, sea tangle
2008.9933	----盐腌裙带菜	15	80	17	5,15	千克	AB	----Pinnatifida, salted
2008.9939	----其他	15	80	17	5,15	千克	AB	----Other
2008.9940	---清水荸荠(马蹄)罐头	25	80	17	15	千克	AB	---Water chestnut, in airtight containers
2008.9990	---其他	15	80	17	5,15	千克	AB	---Other
20.09	**未发酵及未加酒精的水果汁(包括酿酒葡萄汁)、蔬菜汁,不论是否加糖或其他甜物质:**							**Fruit juices (including grape must) and vegetable juices, unfermented and not containing added spirit, whether or not containing added sugar or other sweetening matter:**
	-橙汁:							-Orange juice:
2009.1100	--冷冻的	7.5	90	17	15	千克	AB	--Frozen
2009.1200	--非冷冻的,白利糖度值不超过 20 的	30	90	17	15	千克	AB	--Not frozen, of a Brix value not exceeding 20
2009.1900	--其他	30	90	17	15	千克	AB	--Other
	-葡萄柚(包括柚)汁:							-Grapefruit (including pomelo) juice:
2009.2100	--白利糖度值不超过 20 的	15	90	17	15	千克	AB	--Of a Brix value not exceeding 20
2009.2900	--其他	15	90	17	15	千克	AB	--Other
	-其他未混合的柑橘属水果汁:							-Juice of any other single citrus fruit:
	--白利糖度值不超过 20 的:							--Of a Brix value not exceeding 20:
2009.3110	---柠檬汁	18	90	17	15	千克	AB	---Lemon Juice
2009.3190	---其他	18	90	17	15	千克	AB	---Other
	--其他:							--Other:
2009.3910	---柠檬汁	18	90	17	15	千克	AB	---Lemon juice
2009.3990	---其他	18	90	17	15	千克	AB	---Other
	-菠萝汁:							-Pineapple juice:
2009.4100	--白利糖度值不超过 20 的	10	90	17	15	千克	AB	--Of a Brix value not exceeding 20
2009.4900	--其他	10	90	17	15	千克	AB	--Other
2009.5000	-番茄汁	30	80	17	15	千克	AB	-Tomato juice
	-葡萄汁,包括酿酒葡萄汁:							-Grape juice(including grape must):
2009.6100	--白利糖度值不超过 30 的	20	90	17	15	千克	AB	--Of a Brix value not exceeding 30
2009.6900	--其他	20	90	17	15	千克	AB	--Other
	-苹果汁:							-Apple juice:
2009.7100	--白利糖度值不超过 20 的	20	90	17	15	千克	AB	--Of a Brix value not exceeding 20
2009.7900	--其他	20	90	17	15	千克	AB	--Other
	-其他未混合的水果汁或蔬菜汁:							-Juice of any other single fruit or vegetable:
2009.8100	--蔓越橘汁(大果蔓越橘,小果蔓越橘、越橘)	20	90	17	15	千克	AB	--Cranberry juice
	--其他:							--Other:
	---水果汁:							---Fruit juice:
2009.8912	----芒果汁	20	90	17	15	千克	AB	----Mango juice
2009.8913	----西番莲果汁	20	90	17	15	千克	AB	----Passion-fruit juice
2009.8914	----番石榴果汁	20	90	17	15	千克	AB	----Guva juice
2009.8915	----梨汁	20	90	17	15	千克	AB	----Pear Juice
2009.8919	----其他	20	90	17	15	千克	AB	----Other
2009.8920	---蔬菜汁	20	80	17	15	千克	AB	---Vegetable juice
	-混合汁:							-Mixtures of juices:
2009.9010	---水果汁	20	90	17	15	千克	AB	---Of fruit juices
2009.9090	---其他	20	80	17	15	千克	AB	---Other

第二十一章
杂项食品

Chapter 21
Miscellaneous edible preparations

注释：

一、本章不包括：

(一)税目07.12的什锦蔬菜；

(二)含咖啡的焙炒咖啡代用品(税目09.01)；

(三)加香料的茶(税目09.02)；

(四)税目09.04至09.10的调味香料或其他产品；

(五)按重量计含香肠、肉、食用杂碎、动物血、鱼、甲壳动物、软体动物、其他水生无脊椎动物及其混合物超过20%的食品(第十六章)，但税目21.03或21.04的产品除外；

(六)税目30.03或30.04的药用酵母及其他产品；

(七)税目35.07的酶制品。

二、上述注释一(二)所述咖啡代用品的精汁归入税目21.01。

三、税目21.04所称“均化混合食品”，是指两种或两种以上的基本配料，例如，肉、鱼、蔬菜或果实等，经精细均化制成供婴幼儿食用或营养用的零售包装食品(每件净重不超过250克)。为了调味、保藏或其他目的，可以加入少量其他配料，还可以含有少量可见的小块配料。

Notes:

1. This Chapter does not cover:

(a) Mixed vegetables of heading No. 07.12;

(b) Roasted coffee substitutes containing coffee in any proportion (heading No. 09.01);

(c) Flavoured tea (heading No. 09.02);

(d) Spices or other products of headings No. 09.04 to 09.10;

(e) Food preparations, other than the products described in heading No. 21.03 or 21.04, containing more than 20% by weight of sausage, meat, meat offal, blood, fish or crustaceans, molluscs or other aquatic invertebrates, or any combination thereof (Chapter 16);

(f) Yeast put up as a medicament or other products of heading No. 30.03 or 30.04; or

(g) Prepared enzymes of heading No. 35.07.

2. Extracts of the substitutes referred to in Note 1(b) above are to be classified in heading No. 21.01.

3. For the purposes of heading No. 21.04, the expression "homogenized composite food preparations" means preparations consisting of a finely homogenized mixture of two or more basic ingredients such as meat, fish, vegetables or fruit, put up for retail sale as infant food or for dietetic purposes, in containers of a net weight content not exceeding 250g. For the application of this definition, no account is to betaken of small quantities of any ingredients which may be added to the mixture for seasoning, preservation or other purposes. Such preparations may contain a small quantity of visible pieces of ingredients.

税则号列	货品名称	最惠(%)	普通	增值税率	出口退税	计量单位	监管条件	Article Description
21.01	**咖啡、茶、马黛茶的浓缩精汁及以其为基本成分或以咖啡、茶、马黛茶为基本成分的制品；烘焙菊苣和其他烘焙咖啡代用品及其浓缩精汁：**							**Extracts, essences and concentrates, of coffee, tea or maté and preparations with a basis of these products or with a basis of coffee, tea or maté; roasted chicory and other roasted coffee substitutes, and extracts, essences and concentrates thereof:**
	-咖啡浓缩精汁及以其为基本成分或以咖啡为基本成分的制品：							-Extracts, essences and concentrates of coffee, and preparations with a basis of these extracts, essences or concentrates or with a basis of coffee:
2101.1100	--浓缩精汁	17	130	17	15	千克	AB	--Extracts, essences and concentrates
2101.1200	--以浓缩精汁或咖啡为基本成分的制品	30	130	17	15	千克	AB	--Preparations with a basis of extracts, essences or concentrates or with a basis of coffee
2101.2000	-茶、马黛茶浓缩精汁及以其为基本成分或以茶、马黛茶为基本成分的制品	32	130	17	15	千克	AB	-Extracts, essences and concentrates, of tea or maté, and preparations with a basis of these extracts, essences or concentrates or with a basis of tea or mate
2101.3000	-烘焙菊苣和其他烘焙咖啡代用品及其浓缩精汁	32	130	17	15	千克	AB	-Roasted chicory and other roasted coffee substitutes, and extracts, essences and concentrates thereof
21.02	**酵母(活性或非活性)；已死的其他单细胞微生物(不包括税目30.02的疫苗)；发酵粉：**							**Yeasts (active or inactive); other singlecell micro-organisms, dead (but not including vaccines of heading No. 30.02); prepared baking powders:**
2102.1000	-活性酵母	25	80	17	15	千克	AB	-Active yeasts
2102.2000	-非活性酵母；已死的其他单细胞微生物	25	70	13	15	千克	AB	-Inactive yeasts; other single-cell microorganisms, dead

税则号列	货品名称	最惠(%)	普通	增值税率	出口退税	计量单位	监管条件	Article Description
2102.3000	-发酵粉	25	70	17	15	千克	AB	-Prepared baking powders
21.03	**调味汁及其制品；混合调味品；芥子粉及其调制品：**							**Sauces and preparations therefor; mixed condiments and mixes seasonings; mustard flour and meal and prepared mustard:**
2103.1000[暂]	-酱油	15	90	17	15	千克	AB	-Soya sauce
2103.2000	-番茄沙司及其他番茄调味汁	15	90	17	15	千克	AB	-Tomato ketchup and other tomato sauces
2103.3000	-芥子粉及其调制品	15	70	17	15	千克	AB	-Mustard flour and meal and prepared mustard
	-其他：							-Other:
2103.9010	---味精	21	130	17		千克	AB	---Gourmet powder
2103.9020	---别特酒(Aromatic bitters)，按体积计酒精含量44.2%～49.2%，按重量计含1.5%～6%的香料、各种配料以及4%～10%的糖	21	90	17	15	千克	AB	---Aromatic bitters, 44.2% -49.2% of which is alcoholic strength by volume, 1.5% -6% of which is spiles and various ingredients by weight and 4%～10% of which is sugar by weight
2103.9090	---其他	21	90	17	5,15	千克	AB	---Other
21.04	**汤料及其制品；均化混合食品：**							**Soups and broths and preparations therefor; homogenized composite food preparations:**
2104.1000	-汤料及其制品	15	90	17	15	千克	AB	-Soups and broths and preparations therefor
2104.2000	-均化混合食品	32	90	17	15	千克	AB	-Homogenized composite food preparations
21.05	**冰淇淋及其他冰制食品，不论是否含可可：**							**Ice cream and other edible ice, whether or not containing cocoa:**
2105.0000	冰淇淋及其他冰制食品，不论是否含可可	19	90	17	15	千克	AB	Ice cream and other edible ice, whether or not containing cocoa
21.06	**其他税目未列名的食品：**							**Food preparations not elsewhere specified or included:**
2106.1000	-浓缩蛋白质及人造蛋白物质	10	90	17	15	千克	AB	-Protein concentrates and textured protein substances
	-其他：							-Other:
2106.9010	---制造碳酸饮料的浓缩物	35	100	17	15	千克	AB	---Beverage bases
2106.9020	---制造饮料用的复合酒精制品	20	180	17	15	千克	AB	---Compound alcoholic preparations of a kind used for the manufacture of beverages
2106.9030	---蜂王浆制剂	3	80	17		千克		---Royal jelly, put up as tonic essences
2106.9030 10	含濒危植物成分的蜂王浆制剂	3	80	17		千克	ABFE	Royal jelly, put up as tonic essences containing composition of endangered plants
2106.9030 90	其他蜂王浆制剂	3	80	17	15	千克	AB	Other royal jelly, put up as tonic essences
2106.9040	---椰子汁	10	90	17	15	千克	AB	---Coconut juice
2106.9050	---海豹油胶囊	20	90	17		千克		---Seal oil capsules
2106.9050 10	濒危海豹油胶囊	20	90	17		千克	ABEF	Endangered seal oil capsules
2106.9050 90	其他海豹油胶囊	20	90	17	15	千克	AB	Other seal oil capsules
2106.9090	---其他		90	17		千克		---Other
2106.9090[暂] 01	乳蛋白部分水解配方，乳蛋白深度水解配方、氨基酸配方、无乳糖配方特殊婴幼儿奶粉	5	90	17	15	千克	AB	Milk protein partial hydrolysate formula, milk protein hydrolysis amino acid formula special depth formula, infant milk powder
2106.9090 11	含濒危鱼软骨素胶囊	20	90	17		千克	ABEF	Endangered species of fish cartilage capsules
2106.9090 19	含濒危动植物成分的其他编号未列名食品	20	90	17		千克	ABEF	Other food preparations containing composition of endangered plants, not eleswhere specified or included
2106.9090 90	其他编号未列名的食品	20	90	17	5,15	千克	AB	Other food preparations, not eleswhere specified or included

第二十二章
饮料、酒及醋

注释：

一、本章不包括：

(一)本章的产品(税目22.09的货品除外)经配制后，用于烹饪而不适于作为饮料的制品(通常归入税目21.03)；

(二)海水(税目25.01)；

(三)蒸馏水、导电水及类似的纯净水(税目28.53)；

(四)按重量计浓度超过10%的醋酸(税目29.15)；

(五)税目30.03或30.04的药品；

(六)芳香料制品及盥洗品(第三十三章)。

二、本章及第二十章和第二十一章所称"按容量计酒精浓度"，应是温度在20℃时测得的浓度。

三、税目号22.02所称"无酒精饮料"，是指按容量计酒精浓度不超过0.5%的饮料。含酒精饮料应分别归入税目22.03至22.06或税目22.08。

子目注释：

子目号2204.10所称"汽酒"，是指温度在20℃时装在密封容器中超过大气压力3巴及以上的酒。

Chapter 22
Beverages, spirits and vinegar

Notes:

1. This Chapter does not cover:

(a) Products of this Chapter (other than those of heading No. 22.09) prepared for culinary purposes and thereby rendered unsuitable for consumption as beverages (generally heading No. 21.03);

(b) Sea water (heading No. 25.01);

(c) Distilled or conductivity water or water of similar purity (heading No. 28.53);

(d) Acetic acid of a concentration exceeding 10% by weight of acetic acid (heading No. 29.15);

(e) Medicaments of heading No. 30.03 or 30.04; or

(f) Perfumery or toilet preparations (Chapter 33).

2. For the purposes of this Chapter and of Chapter 20 and 21, the "alcoholic strength by volume" shall be determined at a temperature of 20℃.

3. For the purposes of heading No. 22.02, the term "non-alcoholic beverages" means beverages of an alcoholic strength by volume not exceeding 0.5% vol. Alcoholic beverages are classified in headings No. 22.03 to 22.06 or heading No. 22.08 as appropriate.

Subheading Note:

For the purposes of subheading No. 2204.10, the expression "sparkling wine" means wine which, when kept at a temperature of 20℃ in closed containers, has an excess pressure of not less than 3 bars.

税则号列	货品名称	最惠(%)	普通	增值税率	出口退税	计量单位	监管条件	Article Description
22.01	未加糖或其他甜物质及未加味的水，包括天然或人造矿泉水及汽水；冰及雪：							**Waters, including natural or artificial mineral waters and aerated waters, not containing added sugar or other sweetening matter or flavoured; ice and snow:**
	-矿泉水及汽水：							-Mineral waters and aerated waters:
2201.1010	---矿泉水	20	90	17		升/千克	AB	---Mineral waters
2201.1020	---汽水	20	90	17	15	升/千克	AB	---Aerated waters
	-其他：							-Other:
2201.9010	---天然水	10	30	17		千升/千克	AB	---Natural waters
2201.9090	---其他	10	30	17		千升/千克	AB	---Other
22.02	加味、加糖或其他甜物质的水，包括矿泉水及汽水，其他无酒精饮料，但不包括税目20.09的水果汁或蔬菜汁：							**Waters, including mineral waters and aerated waters, containing added sugar or other sweetening matter or flavoured, and other non-alcoholic beverages, not including fruit or vegetable juices of heading No. 20.09:**
2202.1000	-加味、加糖或其他甜物质的水，包括矿泉水及汽水	20	100	17		升/千克		-Waters, including mineral waters and aerated waters, containing added sugar or other sweetening matter or flavoured
2202.1000 10	含濒危动植物成分的加味、加糖或其他甜物质的水(包括矿泉水及汽水)	20	100	17		升/千克	ABEF	Waters, containing added sugar or other sweetening matter or flavoured of endangered animals and plant (including mineral waters and aerated water)
2202.1000 90	其他加味、加糖或其他甜物质的水(包括矿泉水及汽水)	20	100	17	15	升/千克	AB	Other waters, containing added sugan or other sweetening matter or flavoured (including mineral waters and aerated waters)
2202.9000	-其他	35	100	17		升/千克		-Other
2202.9000 11	含濒危动植物成分散装无酒精饮料(不包括编号2009的水果汁或蔬菜汁)	35	100	17		升/千克	ABEF	Non-alcoholic beverages, in bulk, containing endangered animals and plants componsitions (Other than fruit juices and vegetable juices of heading No. 2009)

税则号列	货品名称	最惠(%)	普通	增值税率	出口退税	计量单位	监管条件	Article Description
2202.9000 19	其他散装无酒精饮料(不包括编号2009的水果汁或蔬菜汁)	35	100	17	15	升/千克	AB	Other non-alcoholic beverages, in bluk (Other than fruit juices and vegetable juices of heading No. 2009)
2202.9000 91	含濒危动植物成分的其他包装无酒精饮料(不包括编号2009的水果汁或蔬菜汁)	35	100	17		升/千克	ABEF	Non-alcoholic beverages, with other packing containing compositions of endangered animals and plants (Other than fruit juices and vegetable juices of heading No. 2009)
2202.9000 99	其他包装无酒精饮料(不包括编号2009的水果汁或蔬菜汁)	35	100	17	15	升/千克	AB	Non-alcoholic beverages, with other packing (other than fruit juices and vegetable juices of heading No. 2009)
22.03	**麦芽酿造的啤酒:**							**Beer made from malt:**
2203.0000	麦芽酿造的啤酒	T2	T2	17	15	升/千克	AB	Beer made from malt
22.04	**鲜葡萄酿造的酒,包括加酒精的;税目20.09以外的酿酒葡萄汁:**							**Wine of fresh grapes, including fortified wines; grape must other than that of heading No. 20.09:**
2204.1000	-汽酒	14	180	17	15	升/千克	AB	-Sparkling wine
	-其他酒;加酒精抑制发酵的酿酒葡萄汁:							-Other wine; grape must with fermentation prevented or arrested by the addition of alcohol:
2204.2100	--装入2升及以下容器的	14	180	17	15	升/千克	AB	--In containers holding 2L or less
2204.2900	--其他	20	180	17	15	升/千克	AB	--Other
2204.3000	-其他酿酒葡萄汁	30	90	17	15	升/千克	AB	-Other grape must
22.05	**味美思酒及其他加植物或香料的用鲜葡萄酿造的酒:**							**Vermouth and other wine of fresh grapes flavoured with plants or aromatic substances:**
2205.1000	-装入2升及以下容器的	65	180	17	15	升/千克	AB	-In containers holding 2L or less
2205.9000	-其他	65	180	17	15	升/千克	AB	-Other
22.06	**其他发酵饮料(例如,苹果酒、梨酒、蜂蜜酒);其他税目未列名的发酵饮料的混合物及发酵饮料与无酒精饮料的混合物:**							**Other fermented beverages (for example, cider, perry, mead); mixtures of fermented beverages and mixtures of fermented beverages and non-alcoholic beverages, not elsewhere specified or included:**
2206.0010	---黄酒	40	180	17	15	升/千克	AB	--Yellow rice wine
2206.0090	---其他	40	180	17	15	升/千克	AB	---Other
22.07	**未改性乙醇,按容量计酒精浓度在80%及以上;任何浓度的改性乙醇及其他酒精:**							**Undenatured ethyl alcohol of an alcoholic strength by volume of 80% vol or higher; ethyl alcohol and other spirits, denatured, of any strength:**
2207.1000	-未改性乙醇,按容量计酒精浓度在80%及以上	40	100	17		升/千克	ABG	-Undenatured ethyl alcohol of an alcoholic strength by volume of 80% vol or higher
2207.2000暂	-任何浓度的改性乙醇及其他酒精	5	80	17		升/千克		-Ethyl alcohol and other spirits, denatured, of any strength
2207.2000暂 10	任何浓度的改性乙醇	5	80	17		升/千克	ABG	Ethyl alcohol, denatured of any strength
2207.2000暂 90	任何浓度的其他酒精	5	80	17		升/千克	ABG	Other spirits, of any strength
22.08	**未改性乙醇,按容量计酒精浓度在80%以下;蒸馏酒、利口酒及其他酒精饮料:**							**Undenatured ethyl alcohol of an alcoholic strength by volume of less than 80% vol; spirits, liqueurs and other spirituous beverages:**
2208.2000	-蒸馏葡萄酒制得的烈性酒	10	180	17	15	升/千克	AB	-Spirits obtained by distilling grape wine or grape marc
2208.2000 10	装入200升及以上容器的蒸馏葡萄酒制得的烈性酒	10	180	17		升/千克	AB	In more than 200 litres and containers of alcohol distillation wine
2208.2000 90	其他蒸馏葡萄酒制得的烈性酒	10	180	17		升/千克	AB	Other wine of liquor distillation
2208.3000	-威士忌酒	10	180	17	15	升/千克	AB	-Whiskies
2208.4000	-朗姆酒及蒸馏已发酵甘蔗产品制得的其他烈性酒	10	180	17	15	升/千克	AB	-Rum and other spirit obtained by distilling fermented sugarcane products
2208.5000	-杜松子酒	10	180	17	15	升/千克	AB	-Gin and geneva
2208.6000	-伏特加酒	10	180	17	15	升/千克	AB	-Vodka
2208.7000	-利口酒及柯迪尔酒	10	180	17	15	升/千克	AB	-Liqueurs and cordials
	-其他:							-Other:
2208.9010	---龙舌兰酒	10	180	17	15	升/千克		---Tequila, Mezcal

税则号列	货品名称	最惠(%)	普通	增值税率	出口退税	计量单位	监管条件	Article Description
2208.9010 10	濒危龙舌兰酒	10	180	17	0	升/千克	ABFE	Endangered Tequila
2208.9010 90	其他龙兰舌酒	10	180	17	15	升/千克	AB	Other Tequila
2208.9020	---白酒	10	180	17	15	升/千克	AB	---Chinese distilled spirits
2208.9090	---其他	10	180	17		升/千克		---Other
2208.9090 01	酒精浓度在80%以下的未改性乙醇	10	180	17	15	升/千克	AB	Undenatured ethyl alcohol of an alcoholic strength by volume of less than 80% vol
2208.9090 21	含濒危野生动植物成分的薯类蒸馏酒	10	180	17		升/千克	ABEF	Potato spirits, endangered wild animals and plants
2208.9090 29	其他薯类蒸馏酒	10	180	17	15	升/千克	AB	Other spirits by distilling potatoes
2208.9090 91	含濒危野生动植物成分的其他蒸馏酒及酒精饮料	10	180	17		升/千克	ABEF	Spirits and spirituous beverages, containins endangered wild animals and plants
2208.9090 99	其他蒸馏酒及酒精饮料	10	180	17	15	升/千克	AB	Other spirits and spirituous beverages
22.09	醋及用醋酸制得的醋代用品：							**Vinegar and substitutes for vinegar obtained from acetic acid:**
2209.0000[暂]	醋及用醋酸制得的醋代用品	15	70	17	15	升/千克	AB	Vinegar and substitutes for vinegar obtained from acetic acid

第二十三章
食品工业的残渣及废料；配制的动物饲料

注释：

税目23.09包括其他税目未列号的配制动物饲料，这些饲料是由动、植物原料加工而成的，并且已改变了原料的基本特性，但加工过程中的植物废料、植物残渣及副产品除外。

子目注释：

子目2306.41所称“低芥子酸油菜籽”，是指第十二章子目注释一所定义的油菜籽。

Chapter 23
Residues and waste from the food industries; prepared animal fodder

Note:

Heading No. 23.09 includes products of a kind used in animal feeding, not elsewhere specified or included, obtained by processing vegetable or animal materials to such an extent that they have lost the essential characteristics of the original material, other than vegetable waste, vegetable residues and by-products of such processing.

Subheading Note:

For the purposes of subheading No. 2306.41, the expression “low erucic acid rape or colza seeds” means seeds as defined in Subheading Note 1 to Chapter 12.

税则号列	货品名称	最惠(%)	普通	增值税率	出口退税	计量单位	监管条件	Article Description
23.01	不适于供人食用的肉、杂碎、鱼、甲壳动物、软体动物或其他水生无脊椎动物的渣粉及团粒；油渣：							**Flours, meals and pellets, of meat or meat offal, of fish or of crustaceans, molluscs or other aquatic invertebrates, unfit for human consumption; greaves:**
	-肉、杂碎的渣粉及团粒；油渣：							-Flours, meals and pellets, of meat or meat offal; greaves:
	---肉骨粉：							---Flours and meals, of meat bones:
2301.1011	----含牛羊成分的	2	11	13	15	千克	AB	----Of bovine and sheep
2301.1019	----其他	2	11	13	15	千克	AB	----Other
2301.1020	---油渣	5	50	13		千克	AB	---Greaves
2301.1090	---其他	5	30	13		千克	AB	---Other
	-鱼、甲壳动物、软体动物或其他水生无脊椎动物的渣粉及团粒：							-Flours, meals and pellets, of fish or of crustaceans, molluscs or other aquatic invertebrates:
2301.2010	---饲料用鱼粉	2	11	13		千克	AB	---Flours and meals of fish, of a kind used in animal feeding
2301.2090	---其他	5	30	13		千克	AB	---Other
23.02	谷物或豆类植物在筛、碾或其他加工过程中所产生的糠、麸及其他残渣，不论是否制成团粒：							**Bran, sharps and other residues, whether or not in the form of pellets, derived from the sifting, milling or other working of cereals or of leguminous plants:**
2302.1000	-玉米的	5	30	13		千克	AB	-Of maize (corn)
2302.3000	-小麦的	3	30	13		千克	AB	-Of wheat
2302.4000	-其他谷物的	5	30	13		千克	AB	-Of other cereals
2302.5000	-豆类植物的	5	30	13		千克	AB	-Of leguminous plants
23.03	制造淀粉过程中的残渣及类似的残渣，甜菜渣、甘蔗渣及制糖过程中的其他残渣，酿造及蒸馏过程中的糟粕及残渣，不论是否制成团粒：							**Residues of starch manufacture and similar residues, beet-pulp, bagasses and other waste of sugar manufacture, brewing or distilling dregs and waste, whether or not in the form of pellets:**
2303.1000	-制造淀粉过程中的残渣及类似的残渣	5	30	13		千克	AB	-Residues of starch manufacture and similar residues
2303.2000	-甜菜渣、甘蔗渣及制糖过程中的其他残渣	5	30	13	5,0	千克	AB	-Beet-pulp, bagasses and other waste of sugar manufacture
2303.3000	-酿造及蒸馏过程中的糟粕及残渣	5	30	13		千克	AB	-Brewing or distilling dregs and waste
2303.3000 10	玉米酒糟	5	30	13		千克	AB	Distiller's grains with or without Solubles
2303.3000 90	其他酿造及蒸馏过程中的糟粕及残渣	5	30	13		千克	AB	Other brewing or distilling dregs and waste
23.04	提炼豆油所得的油渣饼及其他固体残渣，不论是否碾磨或制成团粒：							**Oil-cake and other solid residues, whether or not ground or in the form of pellets, resulting from the extraction of soyabean oil:**
2304.0010	---油渣饼	5	30	13	13	千克	7AB	---Oil-cake
2304.0090	---其他	5	30	13	13	千克	7AB	---Other

税则号列	货品名称	最惠(%)	普通	增值税率	出口退税	计量单位	监管条件	Article Description
23.05	**提炼花生油所得的油渣饼及其他固体残渣,不论是否碾磨或制成团粒:**							**Oil-cake and other solid residues, whether or not ground or in the form of pellets, resulting from the extraction of groundnut oil:**
2305.0000	提炼花生油所得的油渣饼及其他固体残渣,不论是否碾磨或制成团粒	5	30	13		千克	AB	Oil-cake and other solid residues, whether or not ground or in the form of pellets, resulting from the extraction of groundnut oil
23.06	**税目 23.04 或 23.05 以外的提炼植物油脂所得的油渣饼及其他固体残渣,不论是否碾磨或制成团粒:**							**Oil-Cake and other solid residues, whether or not ground or in the form of pellets, resulting from the extraction of vegetable fats or oils, other than those of heading No. 23.04 or 23.05:**
2306.1000	-棉子的	5	30	13	13	千克	AB	-Of cotton seeds
2306.2000	-亚麻子的	5	30	13	13	千克	AB	-Of linseed
2306.3000	-葵花子的	5	30	13	13	千克	AB	-Of sunflower seeds
	-油菜籽的:							-Of rape or colza seeds:
2306.4100	--低芥子酸的	5	30	13	13	千克	AB	--Of low erucic acid rape or colza seeds
2306.4900	--其他	5	30	13	13	千克	AB	--Other
2306.5000	-椰子或干椰肉的	5	30	13	13	千克	AB	-Of coconut or copra
2306.6000	-油棕果或油棕仁的	5	30	13		千克		-Of palm nuts or kernels
2306.6000 10	濒危棕榈果或濒危棕榈仁油渣饼及固体残渣(品目 2304 或 2305 以外提炼植物油脂所得的)	5	30	13		千克	ABEF	Endangered oil-cake and other solid residues of palm nuts or dernels (other than those of heading No. 23.04 or 23.05)
2306.6000 90	其他棕榈果或其他棕榈仁油渣饼及固体残渣(品目 2304 或 2305 以外提炼植物油脂所得的)	5	30	13	13	千克	AB	Other oil-cake and other solid residues of palm nuts or dernels (other than those of heading No. 23.04 or 23.05)
2306.9000	-其他	5	30	13	0,13,15	千克	AB	-Other
23.07	**葡萄酒渣;粗酒石:**							**Wine lees; argol:**
2307.0000	葡萄酒渣;粗酒石	5	30	13		千克	AB	Wine lees; argol
23.08	**动物饲料用的其他税目未列名的植物原料、废料、残渣及副产品,不论是否制成团粒:**							**Vegetable materials and vegetable waste, vegetable residues and by-products, whether or not in the form of pellets, of a kind used in animal feeding, not elsewhere specified or included:**
2308.0000	动物饲料用的其他税目未列名的植物原料、废料、残渣及副产品,不论是否制成团粒	5	35	13	0,15,5	千克	AB	Vegetable materials and vegetable waste, vegetable residues and by-products, whether or not in the form of pellets, of a kind used in animal feeding, not elsewhere specified or included
23.09	**配制的动物饲料:**							**Preparations of a kind used in animal feeding:**
	-零售包装的狗食或猫食:							-Dog or cat food, put up for retail sale:
2309.1010	---罐头	15	90	13	13	千克	AB	---In airtight containers
2309.1090	---其他	15	90	13	13	千克	AB	---Other
	-其他:							-Other:
2309.9010	---制成的饲料添加剂	5	14	17	13,15	千克	AB	---Preparations for use in making the complete feeds or supplementary feeds
2309.9090暂	---其他	4	14	13	0,13,15	千克	AB	---Other

第二十四章 烟草及烟草代用品的制品

Chapter 24 Tobacco and manufactured tobacco substitutes

注释：

本章不包括药用卷烟(第三十章)。

Note：

This Chapter does not cover medicinal cigarettes (Chapter 30).

子目注释：

子目 2403.11 所称"水烟料"，是指由烟草和甘油混合而成用水烟筒吸用的烟草，不论是否含有芳香油及提取物、糖蜜或糖，也不论是否用水果调味，但供在水烟筒中吸用的非烟草产品除外。

Subheading Note：

For the purposes of Subheading 2403.11, the expression "water pipe tobacco" means tobacco intended for smoking in a water pipe and which consists of a mixture of tobacco and glycerol, whether or not containing aromatic oils and extracts, molasses or sugar, and whether or not flavoured with fruit. However, tobacco-free products intended for smoking in a water pipe are excluded from this Subheading

税则号列	货品名称	最惠(%)	普通	增值税率	出口退税	计量单位	监管条件	Article Description
24.01	烟草；烟草废料：							**Unmanufactured tobacco; tobacco refuse:**
	-未去梗的烟草：							-Tobacco, not stemmed/stripped:
2401.1010	---烤烟	10	70	17	5,15	千克	7AB	---Flue-cured
2401.1090	---其他	10	70	17	5	千克	7AB	---Other
	-部分或全部去梗的烟草：							-Tobacco, partly or wholly stemmed/stripped:
2401.2010	---烤烟	10	70	17	5,15	千克	7AB	---Flue-cured
2401.2090	---其他	10	70	17	15	千克	7AB	---Other
2401.3000	-烟草废料	10	70	17	5,15	千克	AB7	-Tobacco refuse
24.02	烟草或烟草代用品制成的雪茄烟及卷烟：							**Cigars, cheroots, cigarillos and cigarettes, of tobacco or of tobacco substitutes:**
2402.1000	-烟草制的雪茄烟	25	180	17		千克/千支	7AB	-Cigars, cheroots and cigarillos, containing tobacco
2402.2000	-烟草制的卷烟	25	180	17		千克/千支	7AB	-Cigarettes containing tobacco
2402.9000	-其他	25	180	17		千克/千支		-Other
2402.9000 01	烟草代用品制的卷烟	25	180	17		千克/千支	7AB	Cigarettes containing tobacco substitutes
2402.9000 09	烟草代用品制的雪茄烟	25	180	17		千克/千支	7AB	Cigars, cheroots and cigarillos, containing tobacco substitutes
24.03	其他烟草及烟草代用品的制品；"均化"或"再造"烟草；烟草精汁：							**Other manufactured tobacco and manufactured tobacco substitutes; "homogenized" or "reconstituted" tobacco; tobacco extracts and essences:**
	-供吸用的烟草，不论是否含有任何比例的烟草代用品：							-Smoking tobacco, whether or not containing tobacco substitutes in any proportion:
2403.1100	--本章子目注释所述的水烟料	57	180	17	15	千克	7AB	--Water pipe tobacco specified in Subheading Note 1 to this Chapter
2403.1900	--其他	57	180	17	15	千克	7AB	--Other
	-其他：							-Other:
2403.9100	--"均化"或"再造"烟草		180	17	15	千克		--"Homogenized" or "reconstituted" tobacco
2403.9100暂 10	再造烟草	40	180	17	15	千克	AB7	Reconstituted tobacco
2403.9100 90	均化烟草	57	180	17	15	千克	AB7	Homogenized tobacco
2403.9900	--其他	57	180	17	15	千克		--Other
2403.9900 10	烟草精汁	57	180	17	15	千克	7AB	Tobacco extracts and essences
2403.9900 90	其他烟草及烟草代用品的制品	57	180	17	15	千克	AB	Other manufactured tobacco and manufactured tobacco substitutes

第五类
矿　产　品

SECTION V
MINERAL PRODUCTS

第二十五章
盐;硫磺;泥土及石料;石膏料、石灰及水泥

Chapter 25
Salt; sulphur; earths and stone; plastering materials, lime and cement

注释:

一、除条文及注释四另有规定的以外,本章各税目只包括原产状态的矿产品,或只经过洗涤(包括用化学物质清除杂质而未改变产品结构的)、破碎、磨碎、研粉、淘洗、筛分以及用浮选、磁选和其他机械物理方法(不包括结晶法)精选过的货品,但不得经过焙烧、煅烧、混合或超过税目所列的加工范围。

本章产品可含有添加的抗尘剂,但所加剂料并不使原产品改变其一般用途而适合于某些特殊用途。

二、本章不包括:

(一)升华硫磺、沉淀硫磺及胶态硫磺(税目28.02);

(二)土色料,按重量计三氧化二铁含量在70%及以上(税目28.21);

(三)第三十章的药品及其他产品;

(四)芳香料制品及化妆盥洗品(第三十三章);

(五)长方砌石、路缘石、扁平石(税目68.01)、镶嵌石或类似石料(税目68.02)及铺屋顶、饰墙面或防潮用的板石(税目68.03);

(六)宝石或半宝石(税目71.02或71.03);

(七)每颗重量不低于2.5克的氯化钠或氧化镁培养晶体(光学元件除外)(税目38.24);氯化钠或氧化镁制的光学元件(税目90.01);

(八)台球用粉块(税目95.04);或

(九)书写或绘画用粉笔及裁缝划粉(税目96.09)。

三、既可归入税目25.17又可归入本章其他税目的产品,应归入税目25.17。

四、税目25.30主要包括:未膨胀的蛭石、珍珠岩及绿泥石;不论是否煅烧或混合的土色料;天然云母氧化铁;海泡石(不论是否磨光成块);琥珀;模制后未经进一步加工的片、条、杆或类似形状的粘聚海泡石及粘聚琥珀;黑玉;菱锶矿(不论是否煅烧),但不包括氧化锶;破碎陶器;砖或混凝土的碎块。

Notes:

1. Except where their context or Note 4 to this Chapter otherwise requires, the headings of this Chapter cover only products which are in the crude state or which have been washed (even with chemical substances eliminating the impurities without changing the structure of the product), crushed, ground, powdered, levigated, sifted, screened, concentrated by flotation, magnetic separation or other mechanical or physical processes (except crystallization), but not products which have been roasted, calcined, obtained by mixing or subjected to processing beyond that mentioned in each heading.

   The products of this Chapter may contain an added antidusting agent, provided that such addition does not render the product particularly suitable for specific use rather than for general use.

2. This Chapter does not cover:

   (a) Sublimed sulphur, precipitated sulphur or colloidal sulphur (heading No. 28.02);

   (b) Earth colours containing 70% or more by weight of combined iron evaluated as Fe_2O_3 (heading No. 28.21);

   (c) Medicaments or other products of Chapter 30;

   (d) Perfumery, cosmetic or toilet preparations (Chapter 33);

   (e) Setts, curbstones or flagstones (heading No. 68.01); mosaic cubes or the like (heading No. 68.02); roofing, facing or damp course slates (heading No. 68.03);

   (f) Precious or semi-precious stones (heading No. 71.02 or 71.03);

   (g) Cultured crystals (other than optical elements) weighing not less than 2.5g each, of sodium chloride or of magnesium oxide, of heading No. 38.24; optical elements of sodium chloride or of magnesium oxide (heading No. 90.01);

   (h) Billiard chalks (heading No. 95.04); or

   (i) Writing or drawing chalks or tailors' chalks (heading No. 96.09).

3. Any products classifiable in heading No. 25.17 and any other heading of this Chapter are to be classified in heading No. 25.17.

4. Heading No. 25.30 applies, *inter alia*, to: vermiculite, perlite and chlorites, unexpanded; earth colours, whether or not calcined or mixed together; natural micaceous iron oxides; meerschaum (whether or not in polished pieces); amber; agglomerated meerschaum and agglomerated amber, in plates, rods, sticks or similar forms, not worked after moulding; jet; strontianite (whether or not calcined), other than strontium oxide; broken pieces of pottery, brick or concrete.

税则号列	货品名称	最惠(%)	普通	增值税率	出口退税	计量单位	监管条件	Article Description
25.01	盐(包括精制盐及变性盐)及纯氯化钠,不论是否为水溶液,也不论是否添加抗结块剂或松散剂;海水:							**Salt (including table salt and denatured salt) and pure sodium chloride, whether or not in aqueous solution or containing added anticaking or free-flowing agents; sea water:**
	---盐:							---Salt:
2501.0011	----食用盐	0	0	13	13	千克	AB	----Edible salt
2501.0019	----其他	0	0	17	13	千克	AB	----Other
2501.0020	---纯氯化钠	3	35	17	13	千克		---Pure sodium chloride

税则号列	货品名称	最惠(%)	普通	增值税率	出口退税	计量单位	监管条件	Article Description
2501.0030	---海水	0	0	17		千克		---Sea water
25.02	未焙烧的黄铁矿:							**Unroasted iron pyrites:**
2502.0000暂	未焙烧的黄铁矿	1	20	17		千克		Unroasted iron pyrite
25.03	**各种硫磺,但升华硫磺、沉淀硫磺及胶态硫磺除外:**							**Sulphur of all kinds, other than sublimed sulphur, precipitated sulphur and colloidal sulphur:**
2503.0000暂	各种硫磺,但升华硫磺、沉淀硫磺及胶态硫磺除外	1	17	17		千克	AB	Sulphur of all kinds, other than sublimed sulphur, precipitated sulphur and colloidal sulphur
25.04	**天然石墨:**							**Natural graphite:**
	-粉末或粉片:							-In powder or in flakes:
2504.1010暂	---鳞片	1	30	17		千克		---In flakes
	---其他:							---Other:
2504.1091	----球化石墨	3	30	17	13	千克		----Spheroidized graphite
2504.1099	----其他	3	30	17		千克		----Other
2504.9000	-其他	3	30	17		千克		-Other
25.05	**各种天然砂,不论是否着色,但第二十六章的含金属矿砂除外:**							**Natural sands of all kinds, whether or not coloured, other than metal-bearing sands of Chapter 26:**
2505.1000暂	-硅砂及石英砂	1	40	17		千克	48xy	-Silica sands and quartz sands
2505.9000暂	-其他	1	40	17		千克		-Other
2505.9000暂 10	标准砂(不论是否着色,第二十六章的金属矿砂除外)	1	40	17		千克	4xy	Standard sands(whether or not coloured, other than metal-bearing sands of Chapter 26)
2505.9000暂 90	其他天然砂(不论是否着色,第二十六章的金属矿砂除外)	1	40	17		千克	48xy	Other natural sands of all kinds(whether or not coloured, other than metal-bearing sands of Chapter 26)
25.06	**石英(天然砂除外);石英岩,不论是否粗加修整或仅用锯或其他方法切割成矩形(包括正方形)的板、块:**							**Quartz (other than natural sands); quartzite, whether or not roughly trimed or merely cut, by sawing or otherwise, intoblocks or slabs of a rectangular (including square) shape:**
2506.1000暂	-石英	1	40	17		千克		-Quartz
2506.2000暂	-石英岩	1	40	17		千克		-Quartzite
25.07	**高岭土及类似土,不论是否煅烧:**							**Kaolin and other kaolinic clays, whether or not calcined:**
	高岭土及类似土,不论是否煅烧:							Kaolin and other kaolinic clays, whether or not calcined:
2507.0010暂	---高岭土	1	50	17		千克		---Kaolin
2507.0090暂	---其他	1	50	17		千克		---Other
25.08	**其他粘土(不包括税目68.06的膨胀粘土)、红柱石、蓝晶石及硅线石,不论是否煅烧;富铝红柱石;火泥及第纳斯土:**							**Other clays (not including expanded clays of heading No. 68.06), andalusite, kyanite and sillimanite, whether or not calcined; mullite; chamotte or dinas earths:**
2508.1000	-膨润土	3	50	17		千克		-Bentonite
2508.3000暂	-耐火粘土	1	20	17		千克	4xy	-Fire-clay
2508.4000	-其他粘土	3	50	17		千克		-Other clays
2508.5000	-红柱石、蓝晶石及硅线石	3	40	17		千克		-Andalusite, kyanite and sillimanite
2508.6000	-富铝红柱石	3	40	17		千克		-Mullite
2508.7000	-火泥及第纳斯土	3	20	17		千克		-Chamotte or dinas earths
2508.7000 10	火泥	3	20	17		千克		Chamotte
2508.7000 90	第纳斯土	3	20	17		千克		Dinas earths
25.09	**白垩:**							**Chalk:**
2509.0000	白垩	3	45	17		千克		Chalk
25.10	**天然磷酸钙、天然磷酸铝钙及磷酸盐白垩:**							**Natural calcium phosphates, natural aluminium calcium phosphates and phosphatic chalk:**
	-未碾磨:							-Unground:
2510.1010暂	---磷灰石	0	11	17		千克	4xy	---Apatite
2510.1090	---其他	3	20	17		千克	4xy	---Other
	-已碾磨:							-Ground:

税则号列	货品名称	最惠(%)	普通	增值税率	出口退税	计量单位	监管条件	Article Description
2510.2010暂	---磷灰石	0	11	17		千克	4xy	---Apatite
2510.2090	---其他	3	20	17		千克	4xy	---Other
25.11	**天然硫酸钡(重晶石);天然碳酸钡(毒重石),不论是否煅烧,但税目28.16的氧化钡除外:**							**Natural barium sulphate (barytes); natural barium carbonate (witherite), whether or not calcined, other than barium oxide of heading No. 28.16:**
2511.1000暂	-天然硫酸钡(重晶石)	1	45	17		千克		-Natural barium sulphate (barytes)
2511.2000	-天然碳酸钡(毒重石)	3	45	17		千克		-Natural barium carbonate (witherite)
25.12	**硅质化石粗粉(例如各种硅藻土)及类似的硅质土,不论是否煅烧,其表观比重不超过1:**							**Siliceous fossil meals (for example, kieselguhr, tripolite and diatomite) and similar siliceous earths, whether or not calcined, of an apparent specific gravity of 1 or less:**
2512.0010	---硅藻土	3	40	17		千克	AB	---Kieselguhr
2512.0090	---其他	3	40	17		千克		---Other
25.13	**浮石;刚玉岩;天然刚玉砂;天然石榴石及其他天然磨料,不论是否热处理:**							**Pumice stone; emery; natural corundum, natural garnet and other natural abrasives, whether or not heat-treated:**
2513.1000	-浮石	3	35	17		千克		-Pumice stone
2513.2000	-刚玉岩、天然刚玉砂、天然石榴石及其他天然磨料	3	17	17		千克		-Emery, natural corundum, narural garnet and other natural abrasives
25.14	**板岩,不论是否粗加修整或仅用锯或其他方法切割成矩形(包括正方形)的板、块:**							**Slate, whether or not roughly trimmed or merely cut, by sawing or otherwise, into blocks or slabs of a rectangular (including square) shape:**
2514.0000	板岩,不论是否粗加修整或仅用锯或其他方法切割成矩形(包括正方形)的板、块	3	50	17		千克		Slate, whether or not roughly trimmed or merely cut, by sawing or otherwise, into blocks or slabs of a rectangular (including square) shape
25.15	**大理石、石灰华及其他石灰质碑用或建筑用石,表观比重为2.5及以上,蜡石,不论是否粗加修整或仅用锯或其他方法切割成矩形(包括正方形)的板、块:**							**Marble, travertine, ecaussine and other calcareous monumental or building stone of an apparent specific gravity of 2.5 or more, and alabaster, whether or not roughly trimmed or merely cut, by sawing or otherwise, into blocks or slabs of a rectangular (including square) shape:**
	-大理石及石灰华:							-Marble and travertine:
2515.1100暂	--原状或粗加修整	0	80	17		千克		--Crude or roughly trimmed Marble crude or roughly trimmed
2515.1200暂	--用锯或其他方法切割成矩形,包括正方形	0	80	17		千克		--Merely cut, by sawing or otherwise, into blocks or slabs of a rectangular (including square) shape
2515.2000暂	-其他石灰质碑用或建筑用石,蜡石	0	50	17		千克		-Ecaussine and other calcareous monumental or building stone; alabaster
25.16	**花岗石、斑岩、玄武岩、砂岩以及其他碑用或建筑用石,不论是否粗加修整或仅用锯或其他方法切割成矩形(包括正方形)的板、块:**							**Granite, porphyry, basalt, sandstone and other monumental or building stone, whether or not building stone whether or not roughly trimmed or merely cut, by sawing or otherwise, into blocks or slabs of a rectangular (including square) shape:**
	-花岗岩:							-Granite:
2516.1100暂	--原状或粗加修整	0	50	17		千克	A	--Crude or roughly trimmed
2516.1200暂	--仅用锯或其他方法切割成矩形,包括正方形	0	50	17		千克	A	--Merely cut, by sawing or otherwise, into blocks or slabs of a rectangular (including square) shape
2516.2000暂	-砂岩	0	50	17		千克		-Sandstone
2516.2000暂 01	原状或粗加修整砂岩	0	50	17		千克	A	Crude or roughly trimmed sandstone
2516.2000暂 90	矩形(包括正方形)砂岩(用锯或其他方法切割成矩形的板、块)	0	50	17		千克		Rectangular (including square) sandstone (cut, by sawing or otherwise, into blocks or slabs of a rectangular)
2516.9000暂	-其他碑用或建筑用石	0	50	17		千克		-Other monumental or building stone

税则号列	货品名称	最惠(%)	普通	增值税率	出口退税	计量单位	监管条件	Article Description
25.17	**通常作混凝土粒料、铺路、铁道路基或其他路基用的卵石、砾石及碎石,圆石子及燧石,不论是否热处理;矿渣、浮渣及类似的工业残渣,不论是否混有本税目第一部分所列的材料;沥青碎石;税目25.15、25.16所列各种石料的碎粒、碎屑及粉末,不论是否热处理:**							**Pebbles, gravel, broken or crushed stone, of a kind commonly used for concrete aggregates, for road metalling or for railway or other ballast, shingle and flint, whether or not heat-treated; macadam of slag, dross or similar industrial waste, whether or not incorporating the materials cited in the first part of the heading; tarred macadam; granules, chippings and powder, of stones of heading No. 25.15 or 25.16, whether or not heat-treated:**
2517.1000	-通常作混凝土粒料、铺路、铁道路基或其他路基用的卵石、砾石及碎石,圆石子及燧石,不论是否热处理	4	50	17		千克		-Pebbles, gravel, broken or crushed stone, of a kind commonly used for concrete aggregates, for road metalling or for railway or other ballast, shingle and flint, whether or not heat-treated
2517.2000	-矿渣、浮渣及类似的工业残渣,不论是否混有子目号2517.10所列的材料	3	50	17		千克	9	-Macadam of slag, dross or similar industrial waste, whether or not incorporating the materials cited in subheading No. 2517.10
2517.3000	-沥青碎石	3	50	17		千克	9	-Tarred macadam
	-税目25.15及25.16所列各种石料的碎粒、碎屑及粉末,不论是否热处理:							-Granules, chippings and powder, stones of heading No. 25.15 or 25.16, whether or not heat-treated:
2517.4100	--大理石的	3	50	17		千克		--Of marble
2517.4900	--其他	3	50	17		千克		--Other
25.18	**白云石,不论是否煅烧或烧结、粗加修整或仅用锯或其他方法切割成矩形(包括正方形)的板、块;夯混白云石:**							**Dolomite, whether or not calcined, including dolomite roughly trimmed or merely cut, by sawing or otherwise, into blocks or slabs of a rectangular (including square) shape; dolomite ramming mix:**
2518.1000[暂]	-未煅烧或烧结的白云石	0	40	17		千克		-Dolomite, not calcined or sintered
2518.2000[暂]	-已煅烧或烧结的白云石	0	40	17		千克		-Calcined or sintered dolomite
2518.3000[暂]	-夯混白云石	0	40	17		千克		-Dolomite ramming mix
25.19	**天然碳酸镁(菱镁矿);熔凝镁氧矿;烧结镁氧矿,不论烧结前是否加入少量其他氧化物;其他氧化镁,不论是否纯净:**							**Natural magnesium carbonate (magnesite); fused magnesia; dead-burned (sintered) magnesia, whether or not containing small quantities of other oxides added before sintering; other magnesium oxide, whether or not pure:**
2519.1000[暂]	-天然碳酸镁(菱镁矿)	1	40	17		千克	y4x	-Natural magnesium carbonate (magnesite)
	-其他:							-Other:
2519.9010[暂]	---熔凝镁氧矿	1	40	17		千克	y4x	---Fused magnesia
2519.9020[暂]	---烧结镁氧矿(重烧镁)	1	40	17		千克	y4x	---Dead-burned (sintered) magnesia
2519.9030[暂]	---碱烧镁(轻烧镁)	1	40	17		千克	y4x	---Light-burned magnesia
	---其他:							---Other:
2519.9091	----化学纯氧化镁	3	35	17		千克	AB	----Magnesium oxide, chemically pure
2519.9099	----其他		40	17		千克		----Other
2519.9099[暂] 10	其他氧化镁含量在70%及以上的矿产品	1	40	17		千克	4xy	Other mineral products containing ≥70% by weight of magnesium oxide
2519.9099 90	其他氧化镁	3	40	17		千克		Other magnesium oxide
25.20	**生石膏;硬石膏;熟石膏(由煅烧的生石膏或硫酸钙构成),不论是否着色,也不论是否带有少量促凝剂或缓凝剂:**							**Gypsum; anhydrite; plasters (consisting of calcined gypsum or calcium sulphate) whether or not coloured, with or without small quantities of accelerators or retarders:**
2520.1000	-生石膏;硬石膏	5	80	17		千克		-Gypsum; anhydrite
	-熟石膏:							-Plasters:
2520.2010	---牙科用	5	40	17		千克		---For dental use
2520.2090	---其他	5	80	17		千克		---Other

税则号列	货品名称	最惠(%)	普通	增值税率	出口退税	计量单位	监管条件	Article Description
25.21	**石灰石助熔剂；通常用于制造石灰或水泥的石灰石及其他钙质石：**							**Limestone flux; limestone and other calcareous stone, of a kind used for the manufacture of lime or cement:**
2521.0000	石灰石助熔剂；通常用于制造石灰或水泥的石灰石及其他钙质石	5	50	17		千克		Limestone flux; limestone and other calcareous stone, of a kind used for the manufacture of lime or cement
25.22	**生石灰、熟石灰及水硬石灰，但税目 28.25 的氧化钙及氢氧化钙除外：**							**Quicklime, slaked lime and hydraulic lime, other than calcium oxide and hydroxide of heading No. 28.25:**
2522.1000	-生石灰	5	80	17		千克		-Quicklime
2522.2000	-熟石灰	5	80	17		千克		-Slaked lime
2522.3000	-水硬石灰	5	80	17		千克		-Hydraulic lime
25.23	**硅酸盐水泥、矾土水泥、矿渣水泥、富硫酸盐水泥及类似的水凝水泥，不论是否着色，包括水泥熟料：**							**Portland cement, aluminous cement, slag cement, supersulphate cement and similar hydraulic cements, whether or not coloured or in the form of clinkers:**
2523.1000	-水泥熟料	8	30	17		千克		-Cement clinkers
	-硅酸盐水泥：							-Portland cement:
2523.2100	--白水泥，不论是否人工着色	6	30	17		千克		--White cement, whether or not artificially coloured
2523.2900	--其他	8	30	17		千克	A	--Other
2523.3000	-矾土水泥	6	30	17		千克		-Aluminous cement
2523.9000	-其他水凝水泥	8	30	17		千克	A	-Other hydraulic cements
25.24	**石棉：**							**Asbestos:**
2524.1000	-青石棉	5	30	17		千克	89	-Grocidlite
	-其他：							-Other:
2524.9010	---长纤维石棉	5	30	17		千克		---Of long staple
2524.9010 10	长纤维阳起石石棉（包括长纤维铁石棉、透闪石石棉及直闪石石棉）	5	30	17		千克	89	Actinolite asbestas of long fibre (including amosite asbestos、tremolite asbestos or anthopylite asbestos)
2524.9010 90	其他长纤维石棉	5	30	17		千克		Other asbestos of long fibre
2524.9090	---其他	5	35	17		千克		---Other
2524.9090 10	其他阳起石石棉（包括其他铁石棉、透闪石石棉及直闪石石棉）	5	35	17		千克	89	Other actinolite asbestas (including other amosa asbestos、tremolite asbestos or anthopylite asbestos)
2524.9090 90	其他石棉	5	35	17		千克		Other asbestos
25.25	**云母，包括云母片；云母废料：**							**Mica, including splittings; mica waste:**
2525.1000暂	-原状云母及劈开的云母片	1	30	17		千克		-Crude mica and mica rifted into sheets or splittings
2525.2000	-云母粉	5	30	17		千克		-Mica powder
2525.3000	-云母废料	5	30	17		千克	AP	-Mica waste
25.26	**天然冻石，不论是否粗加修整或仅用锯或其他方法切割成矩形（包括正方形）的板、块；滑石：**							**Natural steatite, whether or not roughly trimmed or merely cut, by sawing or otherwise, into blocks or slabs or a rectangular (including square) shape; talc:**
	-未破碎及未研粉：							-Not crushed, not powdered:
2526.1010	---冻石	3	50	17		千克		---Natural steatite
2526.1020暂	---滑石	1	50	17		千克	y4x	---Talc
	-已破碎或已研粉：							-Crushed or powdered:
2526.2010	---冻石	3	50	17		千克		---Natural steatite
2526.2020暂	---滑石	1	50	17		千克		---Talc
2526.2020暂 01	滑石粉（体积百分比90%及以上的产品颗粒度小于等于18微米的）	1	50	17		千克	4ABxy	Talc Powder (volume percent ≥90%, granularity≤18 micron)
2526.2020暂 90	已破碎或已研粉的其他天然滑石	1	50	17		千克	4xy	Other natural talc, crushed or powdered
25.28	**天然硼酸盐及其精矿（不论是否煅烧），但不包括从天然盐水析离的硼酸盐；天然粗硼酸，含硼酸干重不超过85%：**							**Natural borates and concentrates thereof (whether or not calcined), but not including borates separated from natural brine; natural boric acid containing not more than 85% of H_3BO_3 calulated on the dry weight:**

税则号列	货 品 名 称	最惠(%)	普通	增值税率	出口退税	计量单位	监管条件	Article Description
2528.0010暂	-天然硼砂及其精矿(不论是否煅烧)	0	30	17		千克	A	-Natural borates and concentrates thereof (whether or not calcined)
2528.0090暂	-其他	0	30	17		千克		-Other
25.29	**长石:白榴石;霞石及霞石正长岩;萤石(氟石):**							**Feldspar; leucite; nepheline and nepheline syenite; fluorspar:**
2529.1000暂	-长石	1	50	17		千克		-Feldspar
	-萤石:							-Fluorspar:
2529.2100	--按重量计氟化钙含量在97%及以下	3	50	17		千克	4xy	--Containing by weight 97% or less of calcium fluoride
2529.2200	--按重量计氟化钙含量在97%以上	3	50	17		千克	4xy	--Containing by weight more than 97% of calcium fluoride
2529.3000	-白榴石;霞石及霞石正长岩	5	50	17		千克		-Leucite; nepheline and nepheline syenite
25.30	**其他税目未列名的矿产品:**							**Mineral substances not elsewhere specified or included:**
	-未膨胀的蛭石、珍珠岩及绿泥石:							-Vermiculite, perlite and chlorites, unexpanded:
2530.1010	---绿泥石	5	30	17		千克		---Chlorites
2530.1020	---未膨胀的蛭石和珍珠岩	5	30	17		千克		---Vermiculite, perlite unexpanded
2530.2000	-硫镁矾矿及泻盐矿(天然硫酸镁)	3	30	17		千克		-Kieserite, epsomite (natural magnesium sulphates)
	-其他:							-Other:
2530.9010	---矿物性药材	3	30	17		千克		---Mineral medicinal substances
2530.9020	---稀土金属矿	0	0	17		千克		---Ores of rare earth metals
2530.9020 10	按重量计中重稀土总含量≥30%的稀土金属矿	0	0	17		千克	4Bxy	Containing by weight ≥30% heavy rare - earth, ores of rare earth metals
2530.9020 90	其他稀土金属矿	0	0	17		千克	4Bxy	Other ores of rate earth metals
	---其他:							---Other:
2530.9091	----硅灰石	3	50	17		千克		----Wollastonite
2530.9099	----其他		50	17		千克		----Other
2530.9099暂 01	天青石	1	50	17		千克		Celestite
2530.9099暂 02	锂辉石矿	0	50	17		千克		Spodumene
2530.9099暂 10	废镁砖	1	50	17		千克	49xy	Bricks of magnesia waste
2530.9099 20	叶蜡石	3	50	17		千克		Pyrophyllite
2530.9099暂 30	未锻烧的水镁石	1	50	17		千克	4xy	Brucite
2530.9099 92	其他品目未列名氧化镁含量在70%及以上的矿产品	3	50	17		千克		Mianeral products with 70% or more of magnesia which are not listed in other items
2530.9099 99	其他矿产品	3	50	17		千克		Other mineral products

第二十六章
矿砂、矿渣及矿灰

注释：

一、本章不包括：

(一)铺路用的矿渣及类似的工业废渣(税目25.17)；

(二)天然碳酸镁(菱镁矿)，不论是否煅烧(税目25.19)；

(三)主要含有石油的石油储罐的淤渣(品目27.10)

(四)第三十一章的碱性熔渣；

(五)矿物棉(税目68.06)；

(六)贵金属或包贵金属的废碎料；主要用于回收贵金属的含贵金属或贵金属化合物的其他废碎料(税目71.12)；

(七)通过熔炼所产生的铜锍、镍锍或钴锍(第十五类)。

二、税目26.01至26.17所称"矿砂"，是指冶金工业中提炼汞，税目28.44的金属以及第十四类、第十五类金属的矿物，即使这些矿物不用于冶金工业，也包括在内。但税目26.01至26.17不包括不是以冶金工业正常加工方法处理的各种矿物。

三、税目26.20只适用于：

(一)在工业上提炼金属或作为生产金属化合物基本原料的矿渣、矿灰及残渣，但焚化城市垃圾所产生的灰、渣除外(税目26.21)；

(二)含有砷的矿渣、矿灰及残渣，不论其是否含有金属，用于提取、生产砷、金属及其化合物。

子目注释：

一、子目2620.21所称"含铅汽油的淤渣及含铅抗震化合物的淤渣"，是指含铅汽油及含铅抗震化合物(例如，四乙基铅)储罐的淤渣，主要含有铅、铅化合物以及铁的氧化物。

二、含有砷、汞、铊及其混合物的矿渣，矿灰及残渣，用于提取或生产砷、汞、铊及其化合物，归入子目2620.60。

Chapter 26
Ores, slag and ash

Notes:

1. This Chapter does not cover:

(a) Slag or similar industrial waste prepared as macadam (heading No. 25.17);

(b) Natural magnesium carbonate (magnesite), whether or not calcined (heading No. 25.19);

(c) Sludges from the storage tanks of petroleum oils, consisting mainly of such oils (heading No. 27.10);

(d) Basic slag of Chapter 31;

(e) Slag wool, rock wool or similar mineral wools (heading No. 68.06);

(f) Waste or scrap of precious metal or of metal clad with precious metal; other waste or scrap containing precious metal or precious metal compounds, of a kind used principally for the recovery of precious metal (heading No. 71.12);

(g) Copper, nickel or cobalt mattes produced by any process of smelting (Section XV).

2. For the purposes of headings No. 26.01 to 26.17, the term "ores" means minerals of mineralogical species actually used in the metallurgical industry for the extraction of mercury, of the metals of heading No. 28.44 or of the metals of Section XIV or XV, even if they are intended for non-metallurgical purposes. Headings No. 26.01 to 26.17 do not, however, include minerals which have been submitted to processes not normal to the metallurgical industry.

3. Heading No. 26.20 applies only to:

(a) Slag, ash and residues of a kind used in industry either for the extraction of metals or as a basis for the manufacture of chemical compounds of metals, excluding ash and residues from the incineration of municipal waste (heading No. 26.21);

(b) Slag, ash and residues containing arsenic, whether or not containing metals, of a kind used either for the extraction of arsenic or matals or for the manufacture of their chemical compounds.

Subheading Notes:

1. For the purposes of subheading No. 2620.21, "leaded gasoline sludges and leaded anti-knock compound sludges" mean slud-ges obtained from storage tanks of leaded gasoline and leaded anti-knock compounds (for example, tetraethyl lead), and consisting essentially of lead, lead compounds and iron oxide.

2. Slag ash and residues containing arsenic, mercury, thallium or their mixtures, of a kind used for the extraction of arsenic or those metals or for the manufacture of their chemical compounds, are to be classified in subheading No. 2620.60.

税则号列	货品名称	最惠(%)	普通	增值税率	出口退税	计量单位	监管条件	Article Description
26.01	铁矿砂及其精矿，包括焙烧黄铁矿：							**Iron ores and concentrates, including roasted iron pyrites:**
	-铁矿砂及其精矿，但焙烧黄铁矿除外：							-Iron ores and concentrates, other than roasted iron pyrites:
	--未烧结：							--Non-agglomerated:
2601.1110	---平均粒度小于0.8毫米的	0	0	17		千克	7A	---The average grain size less than 0.8mm
2601.1120	---平均粒度不小于0.8毫米，但不大于6.3毫米的	0	0	17		千克	7A	---The average grain size not less than 0.8mm, but not more than 6.3 mm
2601.1190	---其他	0	0	17		千克	7A	---Other
2601.1200	--已烧结	0	0	17		千克	7A	--Agglomerated
2601.2000	-焙烧黄铁矿	0	0	17		千克	7A	-Roasted iron pyrites

税则号列	货品名称	最惠(%)	普通	增值税率	出口退税	计量单位	监管条件	Article Description
26.02	**锰矿砂及其精矿,包括以干重计含锰量在20%及以上的锰铁矿及其精矿:**							**Manganese ores and concentrates, including ferruginous manganese ores and concentrates with a manganese content of 20% or more, calculated on the dry weight:**
2602.0000	锰矿砂及其精矿,包括以干重计含锰量在20%及以上的锰铁矿及其精矿	0	0	17		千克	A	Manganese ores and concentrates, including ferruginous manganese ores and concentrates with a manganese content of 20% or more, calculated on the dry weight
26.03	**铜矿砂及其精矿:**							**Copper ores and concentrates:**
2603.0000	铜矿砂及其精矿	0	0				千克	Copper ores and concentrates
2603.0000 10	铜矿砂及其精矿(黄金价值部分)	0	0	0		千克	7A	Copper ores and concentrates (part of gold value)
2603.0000 90	铜矿砂及其精矿(非黄金价值部分)	0	0	17		千克	7A	Copper ores and concentrates (part of non-gold value)
26.04	**镍矿砂及其精矿:**							**Nickel ores and concentrates:**
2604.0000	镍矿砂及其精矿	0	0			千克		Nickel ores and concentrates
2604.0000 01	镍矿砂及其精矿(黄金价值部分)	0	0	0		千克		Niclcel ores and concentrates(Part gold value part)
2604.0000 90	镍矿砂及其精矿(非黄金价值部分)	0	0	17		千克		Nickel ores and concen trates(Part of non – gold Value)
26.05	**钴矿砂及其精矿:**							**Cobalt ores and concentrates:**
2605.0000	钴矿砂及其精矿	0	0			千克		Cobalt ores and concentrates
2605.0000 01	钴矿砂及其精矿(黄金价值部分)	0	0	0		千克		Cobalt ores and concentrates(Part gold value part)
2605.0000 90	钴矿砂及其精矿(非黄金价值部分)	0	0	17		千克		Cobalt ores and concen trates(Part of non – gold value)
26.06	**铝矿砂及其精矿:**							**Aluminium ores and concentrate:**
2606.0000	铝矿砂及其精矿	0	0	17		千克	47xy	Aluminium ores and concentrate
26.07	**铅矿砂及其精矿:**							**Lead ores and concentrates:**
2607.0000	铅矿砂及其精矿	0	0			千克		Lead ores and concentrates
2607.0000 01	铅矿砂及其精矿(黄金价值部分)	0	0	0		千克	A	Lead ores and concentrates(Gold value part)
2607.0000 90	铅矿砂及其精矿(非黄金价值部分)	0	0	17		千克	A	Lead ores and con centrates(Non – gold value part)
26.08	**锌矿砂及其精矿:**							**Zinc ores and concentrates:**
2608.0000	锌矿砂及其精矿	0	0	17		千克		Zinc ores and concentrates
2608.0000 01	灰色饲料氧化锌(氧化锌 ZnO 含量大于80%)	0	0	17		千克	A	Grey feed grade zinc oxide (containing > 80% by weight of ZnO)
2608.0000 90	其他锌矿砂及其精矿	0	0	17		千克	A	Other zinc ores and concentrates
26.09	**锡矿砂及其精矿:**							**Tin ores and concentrates:**
2609.0000	锡矿砂及其精矿	0	0	17		千克	4xy	Tin ores and concentrates
26.10	**铬矿砂及其精矿:**							**Chromium ores and concentrates:**
2610.0000	铬矿砂及其精矿	0	0	17		千克	A	Chromium ores and concentrates
26.11	**钨矿砂及其精矿:**							**Tungsten ores and concentrates:**
2611.0000	钨矿砂及其精矿	0	0	17		千克	4xy	Tungsten ores and concentrates
26.12	**铀或钍矿砂及其精矿:**							**Uranium or thorium ores and concentrates:**
2612.1000	-铀矿砂及其精矿	0	0	17		千克		-Uranium ores and concentrates
2612.2000	-钍矿砂及其精矿	0	0	17		千克	4xy	-Thorium ores and concentrates
26.13	**钼矿砂及其精矿:**							**Molybdenum ores and concentrates:**
2613.1000	-已焙烧	0	0	17		千克	4xy	-Roasted
2613.9000	-其他	0	0	17		千克	4xy	-Other
26.14	**钛矿砂及其精矿:**							**Titanium ores and concentrates:**
2614.0000	钛矿砂及其精矿	0	0	17		千克		Titanium ores and concentrates
26.15	**铌、钽、钒或锆矿砂及其精矿:**							**Niobium, tantalum, vanadium or zirconium ores and concentrates:**
2615.1000	-锆矿砂及其精矿	0	0	17		千克		-Zirconium ores and concentrates
	-其他:							-Other:
2615.9010	---水合钽铌原料(钽铌矿富集物)	0	0	17		千克		---Hydrated Tantalum-Niobium materials or enriched materials from Tantalum/Niobium ores
2615.9090	---其他	0	0	17		千克		---Other
2615.9090 10	铌,钽精矿及其矿砂	0	0	17		千克		Tantalum and niobium concentrates and ores thereof
2615.9090 90	钒矿砂;钒精矿	0	0	17		千克		Vanadium ores and concentrates
26.16	**贵金属矿砂及其精矿:**							**Precious metal ores and concentrates:**

税则号列	货品名称	最惠(%)	普通	增值税率	出口退税	计量单位	监管条件	Article Description
2616.1000	-银矿砂及其精矿	0	0	17		千克		-Silver ores and concentrates
2616.9000	-其他	0	0			千克		-Other
2616.9000 01	黄金矿砂	0	0	0		千克		Gold ores and concentrates
2616.9000 09	其他贵金属矿砂及其精矿	0	0	17		千克		Other precious metal ores and concentrates
26.17	**其他矿砂及其精矿：**							**Other ores and concentrates:**
	-锑矿砂及其精矿：							-Antimony ores and concentrates:
2617.1010	---生锑(锑精矿,选矿产品)	0	0	17		千克	4xy	---Crude antimony(Antimony concentrates which are mineral products)
2617.1090	---其他	0	0			千克		---Other
2617.1090 01	其他锑矿砂及其精矿(黄金价值部分)	0	0	0		千克	4xy	Other antimony ores and concentrates(parts of gold value)
2617.1090 90	其他锑矿砂及其精矿(非黄金价值部分)	0	0	17		千克	4xy	Other antimony ores and concentrates(parts of non-gold value)
	-其他：							-Other:
2617.9010	---朱砂(辰砂)	3	14	17		千克	X	---Cinnabar
2617.9090	---其他	0	0	17		千克		---Other
26.18	**冶炼钢铁所产生的粒状熔渣(熔渣砂)：**							**Granulated slag (slag sand) from the manufacture of iron or steel:**
2618.0010	---主要含锰		35	17		千克		---Containing mainly Manganese
2618.0010[暂] 01	冶炼钢铁产生的锰渣,含锰量大于25%(包括熔渣砂)	1	35	17		千克	AP	Manganese slag from the manufacture of iron or steel,more than 25% of manganese(including slag sand)
2618.0010 90	其他主要含锰的冶炼钢铁产生的粒状熔渣(包括熔渣砂)	4	35	17		千克	9A	Other granulated slag(slag sand)from the manufacture of iron or steel,containing mainly Manganese
2618.0090	---其他	4	35	17		千克	9A	---Other
26.19	**冶炼钢铁所产生的熔渣、浮渣(粒状熔渣除外)、氧化皮及其他废料：**							**Slag, dross (other than granulated slag), scalings and other waste from the manufacture of iron or steel:**
2619.0000	冶炼钢铁所产生的熔渣、浮渣(粒状熔渣除外)、氧化皮及其他废料		35	17		千克		Slag, dross (other than granulated slag), scalings and other waste from the manufacture of iron or steel
2619.0000 10	轧钢产生的氧化皮	4	35	17		千克	AP	Scalings from the manufacture of steel
2619.0000[暂] 21	冶炼钢铁所产生的含钒浮渣、熔渣,五氧化二钒含量>20%(冶炼钢铁所产生的粒状熔渣除外)	1	35	17		千克	AP	Slag,drog,scalings and other waste from the manufacture of iron or steel, more than 20% vanadium pentoxide(other than granulated slag)
2619.0000 29	其他冶炼钢铁所产生的含钒浮渣、熔渣(冶炼钢铁所产生的粒状熔渣除外)	4	35	17		千克	AP	Slap,dross from the manufaceure of iron or steel, containing vanadium(Other than granulated slag)
2619.0000 30	含铁大于80%的冶炼钢铁产生的渣钢铁	4	35	17		千克	AP	Steel slag with more than 80% of steel form the manufaceure of steel and iron
2619.0000 90	冶炼钢铁产生的其他熔渣、浮渣及其他废料(冶炼钢铁所产生的粒状熔渣除外)	4	35	17		千克	9A	Slap,dross and other waster from the manufacture of iron or steel(Other than granulated slag)
26.20	**含有金属、砷及其化合物的矿渣、矿灰及残渣(冶炼钢铁所产生的灰、渣除外)：**							**Slag, ash and residues (other than from the manufacture of iron or steel), containing metals arsenic, or their compounds:**
	-主要含锌：							-Containing mainly zinc:
2620.1100	--含硬锌	4	35	17		千克	9	--Hard zinc spelter
2620.1900	--其他	4	35	17		千克	9	--Other
	-主要含铅：							-Containing mainly lead:
2620.2100	--含铅汽油的淤渣及含铅抗震化合物的淤渣	4	35	17		千克	9	--Leaded gasoline sludges and leaded anti-knock compound sludges
2620.2900	--其他	4	35	17		千克	9	--Other
2620.3000	-主要含铜	4	35	17		千克	9	-Containing mainly copper
2620.4000	-主要含铝	4	35	17		千克	9	-Containing mainly aluminium
2620.6000	-含砷、汞、铊及其混合物,用于提取或生产砷、汞、铊及其化合物	4	35	17		千克	9	-Containing arsenic, mercury, thallium or their mixtures, of a kind used for the extraction of arsenic or those metals or for the manufacture of their chemical compounds

税则号列	货品名称	最惠(%)	普通	增值税率	出口退税	计量单位	监管条件	Article Description
	-其他:							-Other:
2620.9100	--含锑、铍、镉、铬及其混合物	4	35	17		千克	9	--Containing antimony, beryllium, cadmium, chromium or their mixtures
	--其他:							--Other:
2620.9910	---主要含钨	4	35	17		千克	y4x9	---Containing mainly tungsten
2620.9990	---其他		35	17		千克		---Other
2620.9990暂 11	含其他金属及其化合物的矿渣、矿灰及残渣,五氧化二钒 > 20%(冶炼钢铁所产生的除外)	1	35	17		千克	AP	Slag, ash and residues, containing other metals or their compounds, more than 20% vanadium pentoxide (other than from the manufacture of iron or steel)
2620.9990 19	含其他金属及其化合物的矿渣、矿灰及残渣,10% < 五氧化二钒≤20%的(冶炼钢铁所产生的及含钒废催化剂除外)	4	35	17		千克	AP	Slag, ash and residues, containing other metals or their compounds, 10% < containing vanadium pentoxide≤20% (other than from the manufacture of iron or steel and including vanadium spent catalyst)
2620.9990 20	含铜大于10%的铜冶炼转炉渣及火法精炼渣,其他铜冶炼渣	4	35	17		千克	9	Copper converter slag fire refining slag from copper smelter, containing copper > 10%
2620.9990 90	含其他金属及其化合物的矿渣、矿灰及残渣(冶炼钢铁所产生灰、渣的除外)	4	35	17		千克	9	Slag, ash and residues, containing other metals or their compounds (other than from the manufacture of iron or steel)
26.21	**其他矿渣及矿灰,包括海藻灰(海草灰);焚化城市垃圾所产生的灰、渣:**							**Other slag and ash, including seaweed ash (kelp); ash and residues from the incineration of municipal waste:**
2621.1000	-焚化城市垃圾所产生的灰、渣	4	35	17		千克	9	-Ash and residues from the incineration of municipal waste
2621.9000	-其他	4	35	17		千克		-Other
2621.9000 10	海藻灰及其他植物灰(包括稻壳灰)	4	35	17		千克	9	Algae ash and other plant ash (including rice husk ash)
2621.9000 90	其他矿渣及矿灰	4	35	17		千克	9	Other ore slag and ore ash

第二十七章
矿物燃料、矿物油及其蒸馏产品;沥青物质;矿物蜡

注释:

一、本章不包括:

(一)单独的已有化学定义的有机化合物,但纯甲烷及纯丙烷应归入税目27.11;

(二)税目30.03及30.04的药品;或

(三)税目33.01、33.02及38.05的不饱和烃混合物。

二、税目27.10所称"石油及从沥青矿物提取的油类",不仅包括石油、从沥青矿物提取的油及类似油,还包括那些用任何方法提取的主要含有不饱和烃混合物的油,但其非芳族成份的重量必须超过芳族成份。然而,它不包括温度在300℃时,压力转为1013毫巴后减压蒸馏出的以体积计小于60%的液体合成聚烯烃(第三十九章)。

三、税目27.10所称"废油",是指主要含石油及从沥青矿物提取的油类(参见本章注释二)的废油,不论其是否与水混合。它们包括:

(一)不再适于作为原产品使用的废油(例如,用过的润滑油、液压油及变压器油);

(二)石油储罐的淤渣油,主要含有废油及高浓度的在生产原产品时使用的添加剂(例如,化学品);

(三)水乳浊液状或与水混合的废油,例如,浮油、清洗油罐所得的油或机械加工中已用过的切削油。

子目注释:

一、子目号2701.11所称"无烟煤",是指含挥发物(以干燥、无矿物质计)不超过14%的煤。

二、子目号2701.12所称"烟煤",是指含挥发物(以干燥、无矿物质计)超过14%,并且热值(以潮湿、无矿物质计)等于或大于5833大卡/公斤的煤。

三、子目号2707.10、2707.20、2707.30及2707.40所称"粗苯"、"粗甲苯"、"粗二甲苯"、"萘",是分别指按重量计苯、甲苯、二甲苯、萘的含量在50%以上的产品。

四、子目号2710.12所称"轻油及其制品",是指温度在210℃时以体积计馏出量(包括损耗)在90%及以上的产品(美国标准试验法D86为准)。

五、税目27.10的子目所称"生物柴油",是指从动物植物油脂(不论是否使用过)得到的用作燃料的脂肪酸单烷基酯。

Chapter 27
Mineral fuels, mineral oils and products of their distillation; bituminous substances; mineral waxes

Notes:

1. This Chapter does not cover:

(a) Separate chemically defined organic compounds, other than pure methane and propane which are to be classified in heading No. 27.11;

(b) Medicaments of heading No. 30.03 or 30.04; or

(c) Mixed unsaturated hydrocarbons of heading No. 33.01, 33.02 or 38.05.

2. References in heading No. 27.10 to "petroleum oils and oils obtained from bituminous minerals" include not only petroleum oils and oils obtained from bituminous minerals but also similar oils, as well as those consisting mainly of mixed unsaturated hydrocarbons, obtained by any process, provided that the weight of the non-aromatic constituents exceeds that of the aromatic constituents. However, the references do not include liquid synthetic polyolefins of which less than 60% by volume distils at 300℃, after conversion to 1,013 millibars when a reduced-pressure distillation method is used (Chapter 39).

3. For the purposes of heading No. 27.10, "waste oils" means waste containing mainly petroleum oils and oils obtained from bituminous minerals (as described in Note 2 to this Chapter), whether or not mixed with water. These include:

(a) Such oils no longer fit for use as primary products (for example, used lubricating oils, used hydraulic oils and used transformer oils);

(b) Sludge oils from the storage tanks of petroleum oils, mainly containing such oils and a high concentration of additives (for example, chemicals) used in the manufacture of the primary products; and

(c) Such oils in the form of emulsions in water or mixtures with water, such as those resulting from oil spills or storage tank washings, or from the use of cutting oils for machining operations.

Subheading Notes:

1. For the purposes of subheading No. 2701.11, "anthracite" means coal having a volatile matter limit (on a dry, mineral-matter-free basis) not exceeding 14%.

2. For the purposes of subheading No. 2701.12, "bituminous coal" means coal having a volatile matter limit (on a dry, mineral-matter-free basis) exceeding 14% and a calorific value limit (on a moist, mineral-matter-free basis) equal to or greater than 5,833kcal/kg.

3. For the purposes of subheadings. 2707.10, 2707.20, 2707.30 and 2707.40, the terms "benzole"(benzene), "toluole"(toluene), "xylole"(xylenes) and "naphthalene" apply to products which contain more than 50% by weight of benzene, toluene, xylene, or naphthalene, respectively.

4. For the purposes of subheading No. 2710.11, "light oils and preparations" are those of which 90% or more by volume (including losses) distil at 210℃ (ASTM D86 method).

5. For the purposes of the Subheadings of heading 27.10, the term "biodiesel" means mono-alkyl esters of fatty acids of a kind used as a fuel, derived from animal or vegetable fats and oils whether or not used

税则号列	货品名称	最惠(%)	普通	增值税率	出口退税	计量单位	监管条件	Article Description
27.01	**煤;煤砖、煤球及用煤制成的类似固体燃料:**							**Coal; briquettes, ovoids and similar solid fuels manufactured from coal:**
	-煤,不论是否粉化,但未制成型:							-Coal, whether or not pulverized, but not agglomerated:
2701.1100[暂]	--无烟煤	0	20	17		千克		--Anthracite
2701.1100[暂] 10	无烟煤(不论是否粉化,但未制成型)	0	20	17		千克	47Axy	Anthracite(whether or not pulverized, but not agglomerated)
2701.1100[暂] 90	无烟煤滤料	0	20	17		千克	7A	Anthracite filter medium
	--烟煤:							--Bituminous coal:
2701.1210[暂]	---炼焦煤	0	20	17		千克	47Axy	---Coking coal
2701.1290[暂]	---其他	0	20	17		千克	47Axy	---Other
2701.1900[暂]	--其他煤	0	20	17		千克	47Axy	--Other coal
2701.2000[暂]	-煤砖、煤球及用煤制成的类似固体燃料	0	50	17		千克		-Briquettes, ovoids and similar solid fuels manufactured from coal
27.02	**褐煤,不论是否制成型,但不包括黑玉:**							**Lignite, whether or not agglomerated, excluding jet:**
2702.1000	-褐煤,不论是否粉化,但未制成型	3	20	17		千克	A4xy	-Lignite, whether or not pulverized, but not agglomerated
2702.2000	-制成型的褐煤	3	20	17		千克	A	-Agglomerated lignite
27.03	**泥煤(包括肥料用泥煤),不论是否制成型:**							**Peat (including peat litter), whether or not agglomerated:**
2703.0000	泥煤(包括肥料用泥煤),不论是否制成型	5	20	17		千克		Peat (including peat litter), whether or not agglomerated
2703.0000 10	泥炭(草炭)[沼泽(湿地)中,地上植物枯死、腐烂堆积而成的有机矿体(不论干湿)]	5	20	17		千克	8AB	In peat and swamp (wetland), organic ore bodies formed by dried and rotten plants on the ground (whether dry or wet)
2703.0000 90	泥煤(包括肥料用泥煤)(不论是否制成型)	5	20	17		千克	AB	Peat (including peat used as fertilizer), whether shaped or not
27.04	**煤、褐煤或泥煤制成的焦炭及半焦炭,不论是否制成型;甑炭:**							**Coke and semi-coke of coal, of lignite or of peat, whether or not agglomerated; retort carbon:**
2704.0010[暂]	---焦炭及半焦炭	0	11	17		千克	4xy	---Coke and semi-coke
2704.0090[暂]	---其他	0	11	17		千克		---Other
27.05	**煤气、水煤气、炉煤气及类似气体,但石油气及其他烃类气除外:**							**Coal gas, water gas, producer gas and similar gases, other than petroleum gases and other gaseous hydrocarbons:**
2705.0000[暂]	煤气、水煤气、炉煤气及类似气体(但石油气及其他烃类气除外)	1	20	13		千克		Coal gas, water gas, producer gas and similar gases, other than petroleum gases and other gaseous hydrocarbons
2705.0000[暂] 10	煤气	1	20	13		千克	AB	Coal gas
2705.0000[暂] 90	水煤气、炉煤气及类似气体(石油气及其他烃类气除外)	1	20	13		千克		Water gas, producer gas and similar gases, other than petroleum gases and other gaseous hydrocarbons
27.06	**从煤、褐煤或泥煤蒸馏所得的焦油及其他矿物焦油,不论是否脱水或部分蒸馏,包括再造焦油:**							**Tar distilled from coal, from lignite or from peat, and other mineral tars, whether or not dehydrated or partially distilled, including reconstituted tars:**
2706.0000[暂]	从煤、褐煤或泥煤蒸馏所得的焦油及其他矿物焦油,不论是否脱水或部分蒸馏,包括再造焦油	1	30	17		千克		Tar distilled from coal, from lignite or from peat, and other mineral tars, whether or not dehydrated or partially distilled, including reconstituted tars
2706.0000[暂] 01	含蒽油≥50%及沥青≥40%的"炭黑油"	1	30	17		千克		Containing anthracene oil ≥ 50% and asphalt ≥ 40%, carbon"black oil"
2706.0000[暂] 90	其他从煤、褐煤或泥煤蒸馏所得的焦油及矿物焦油(不论是否脱水或部分蒸馏,包括再造焦油)	1	30	17	0	千克	AB	

税则号列	货品名称	最惠(%)	普通	增值税率	出口退税	计量单位	监管条件	Article Description
27.07	蒸馏高温煤焦油所得的油类及其他产品；芳族成份重量超过非芳族成份的类似产品：							**Oils and other products of the distillation of high temperature coal tar; similar products in which the weight of the aromatic constituents exceeds that of the non-aromatic constituents:**
2707.1000	-粗苯	6	20	17		千克	AB	-Benzole
2707.2000	-粗甲苯	6	30	17		千克		-Toluole
2707.3000[暂]	-粗二甲苯	2	20	17		千克		-Xylole
2707.4000	-萘	7	30	17		千克		-Naphthalene
2707.5000	-其他芳烃混合物，温度在250℃时蒸馏出芳烃含量以体积计（包括损耗）在65%及以上（以美国标准试验法D86为准）	7	30	17		千克		-Other aromatic hydrocarbon mixtures of which 65% or more by volume (including losses) distils at 250℃ by the ASTM D86 method
	-其他：							-Other:
2707.9100	--杂酚油	7	30	17		千克		--Creosote oils
	--其他：							--Other:
2707.9910	---酚	7	30	17		千克		---Phenols
2707.9990	---其他	7	30	17		千克		---Other
27.08	从煤焦油或其他矿物焦油所得的沥青及沥青焦：							**Pitch and pitch coke, obtained from coal tar or from other mineral tars:**
2708.1000	-沥青	7	35	17		千克		-Pitch
2708.2000	-沥青焦		11	17		千克		-Pitch coke
2708.2000[暂] 01	针状沥青焦	3	11	17		千克		Needle－shaped pitch coke
2708.2000 90	其他沥青焦	6	11	17		千克		Other Needle-shaped pitch coke
27.09	石油原油及从沥青矿物提取的原油：							**Petroleum oils and oils obtained from bituminous minerals, crude:**
2709.0000	石油原油及从沥青矿物提取的原油	T2	T2	17		千克	4x7AByv	Petroleum oils and oils obtained from bituminous minerals, crude
27.10	石油及从沥青矿物提取的油类，但原油除外；以上述油为基本成份（按重量计不低于70%）的其他税目未列名制品；废油：							**Petroleum oils and oils obtained from bituminous minerals, other than crude; preparations not elsewhere specified or included, containing by weight 70% or more of petroleum oils or of oils obtained from bituminous minerals, these oils being the basic constituents of the preparations; waste oils:**
	-石油及从沥青矿物提取的油类（但原油除外）；以及以上述油为基本成份（按重量计不低于70%）的其他税目未列名制品；不含有生物柴油，但废油除外：							-Petroleum oils and oils obtained from bituminous minerals (other than crude) and preparations not elsewhere specified or included, containing by weight 70% or more of petroleum oils or of oils obtained from bituminous minerals, these oils being the basic constituents of the preparations; excluding biodiesel, other than waste oils:
	--轻油及其制品：							--Light oils and preparations:
2710.1210[暂]	---车用汽油及航空汽油	1	14	17		千克/升		---Motor gasoline, aviation gasoline
2710.1210[暂] 01	车用汽油及航空汽油，不含生物柴油（铅含量每升不超过0.013克）	1	14	17		千克/升	47ABvy	Motor gasoline, aviation gasoline, excluding biodiesel (containing lead≤0.013 L/g)
2710.1210[暂] 02	车用汽油及航空汽油，不含生物柴油（铅含量每升超过0.013克）	1	14	17		千克/升	47ABvy	Motor gasoline, aviation gasoline, excluding biodiesel (containing lead＞0.013 L/g)
2710.1220[暂]	---石脑油	0	20	17		千克/升	47ABvy	---Naphtha
2710.1230	---橡胶溶剂油、油漆溶剂油、抽提溶剂油	6	30	17		千克/升		---Rubber solvent, paint solvent, extractive solvent
	---其他：							---Other:
2710.1291	----壬烯		20	17		千克		----Nonene
2710.1291[暂] 01	壬烯，不含生物柴油（碳九异构体混合物含量高于90%）	4	20	17		千克	4Ay	Nonene, excluding biodiesel, excluding biodiesel (Carbon 9 isomer mixtures containing ＞90%)
2710.1291 90	其他壬烯，不含生物柴油	9	20	17		千克	4Ay	Other nonene exctuding biodiesel
2710.1299	----其他		20	17		千克		----Other
2710.1299[暂] 10	异戊烯同分异构体混合物，不含生物柴油	5	20	17		千克	4Ay	Mixture of isomers of isoamylene, excluding biodiesel

税则号列	货　品　名　称	最惠(%)	普通	增值税率	出口退税	计量单位	监管条件	Article Description
2710.1299 90	其他轻油及制品,不含生物柴油(包括按重量计含油≥70%的制品)	9	20	17		千克	4Ay	Other light oils and preparations, excluding biodiesel (containing≥70% by weight of oils)
	--其他:							--Other:
	---煤油馏分:							---Kerosene distillages:
2710.1911[暂]	----航空煤油	0	14	17		千克/升	47ABvy	----Aviation kerosene
2710.1912	----灯用煤油	9	14	17		千克/升	47ABvy	----Lamp-kerosene
2710.1919	----其他		20	17		千克/升		----Other
2710.1919[暂] 10	正构烷烃(C_9 ~ C_{13}),不含生物柴油	2	20	17		千克/升	4y	Normal paraffin hydrocarbon (C_9 ~ C_{13}), excluding biodiesel
2710.1919 90	其他煤油馏分的油及制品,不含生物柴油	6	20	17		千克/升	4yAB	Other kerosene distillages oils and preparations, excluding biodiesel
	---柴油及其他燃料油:							---Diesel oils and other fuel oils:
2710.1922[暂]	----5 ~ 7 号燃料油	1	20	17		千克/升	7ABv	----Fuel oils No. 5 ~ No. 7
2710.1923[暂]	----柴油	1	11	17		千克/升	47ABvy	----Diesel engine
2710.1929	----其他		20	17		千克/升		----Other
2710.1929[暂] 10	蜡油,不含生物柴油(350℃以下馏出物体积<20%,550℃以下馏出物体积>80%)	0	20	17		千克/升	7ABv	Paraffin oils excluding biodiesel (which < 20% by volume distil <350℃, which >80% by volume distil <550℃)
2710.1929 90	其他燃料油,不含生物柴油	6	20	17		千克/升	7ABv	Other fuel oils, excluding biodiesel
	---润滑油、润滑脂及其他重油:							---Lubricating oils, lubricating greases and other heavy oils:
2710.1991	----润滑油	6	17	17		千克/升	4Ayx	----Lubricating grease
2710.1992	----润滑脂	6	17	17		千克/升	4Ayx	----Lubricating oils
2710.1993	----润滑油基础油	6	17	17		千克/升	4yx	----Basic oils for lubricating oils
2710.1994	----液体石蜡和重质液体石蜡	6	20	17		千克	AB	----Liquid paraffin and heavy liquid paraffin
2710.1999	----其他	6	20	17		千克/升	B	----Other
2710.2000	-石油及从沥青矿物提取的油类(但原油除外)以及以上述油为基本成分(按重量计不低于70%)的其他税目未列名制品,含生物柴油<30%,废油除外	6	20	17		千克/升	4Ay	-Petroleum oils and oils obtained from bituminous minerals, other than crude; preparations not elsewhere specified or included, containing by weight 70% or more of petroleum oils or of oils obtained from bituminous minerals, these oils being the basic constituents of thepreparations; containing biodiesel <30%, other than waste oils
	-废油:							-Waste oils:
2710.9100	--含多氯联苯(PCBs)、多氯三联苯(PCTs)或多溴联苯(PBBs)的	6	20	17		千克	9	--Containing polychlorinated biphenyls (PCBs), polychlorinated terphenyls (PCTs) or polybrominated biphenyls (PBBs)
2710.9900	--其他	6	20	17		千克	9	--Other
27.11	**石油气及其他烃类气:**							**Petroleum gases and other gaseous hydrocarbons:**
	-液化的:							-Liquefied:
2711.1100	--天然气	0	20	13		千克	4ABy	--Natural gas
2711.1200[暂]	--丙烷	1	20	13		千克	AB	--Propane
	--丁烷:							--Butanes:
2711.1310	---直接灌注香烟打火机及类似打火器用,其包装容器的容积超过300立方厘米	11	80	17		千克		---Liquid or liquefied-gas fuels in containers of a kind used for filling or refilling cigarette or similar lighters and of a capacity exceeding $300cm^3$
2711.1390[暂]	---其他	1	20	13		千克		---Other
2711.1400	--乙烯、丙烯、丁烯及丁二烯	5	20	17		千克		--Ethylene, propylene, butylene and butadiene
2711.1400 10	液化的乙烯	5	20	17		千克	AB	Liquefied ethylene,
2711.1400 90	液化的丙烯、丁烯及丁二烯	5	20	17		千克		Liquefied propylene, butylene and butadiene,
	--其他:							--Other:

税则号列	货品名称	最惠(%)	普通	增值税率	出口退税	计量单位	监管条件	Article Description
2711.1910	---直接灌注香烟打火机及类似打火器用的燃料,其包装容器的容积超过300立方厘米	10	80	17		千克		---Liquid or liquefied-gas fuels in containers of a kind used for filling or refilling cigarette or similar lighters and of a capacity exceeding 300cm^3
2711.1990	---其他	3	20	13		千克		---Other
2711.1990 10	其他液化石油气	3	20	13		千克	AB	Other liquefied petroleum gases
2711.1990 90	其他液化烃类气	3	20	13		千克		Other liquefied gaseous hydrocar
	-气态的:							-In gaseous state:
2711.2100	--天然气	0	20	13		千克	AB	--Natural gas
2711.2900	--其他	6	20	13		千克		--Other
2711.2900 10	其他气态石油气	6	20	13		千克	AB	Other petroleum gases, in gaseous state
2711.2900 90	其他气态烃类气	6	20	13		千克		Other gaseous hydrocar, in gaseous state
27.12	**凡士林;石蜡、微晶石蜡、疏松石蜡、地蜡、褐煤蜡、泥煤蜡、其他矿物蜡及用合成或其他方法制得的类似产品,不论是否着色:**							**Petroleum jelly; paraffin wax, microcrystalline petroleum wax, slack wax, ozokerite, lignite wax, peat wax, other mineral waxes, and similar products obtained by synthesis or by other processes, whether or not coloured:**
2712.1000	-凡士林	8	45	17		千克	AB	-Petroleum jelly
2712.2000	-石蜡,按重量计含油量小于0.75%	8	45	17		千克	4ABx	-Paraffin wax containing by weight less than 0.75% of oil
	-其他:							-Other:
2712.9010	---微晶石蜡	8	45	17		千克	4ABx	---Microcrystalline petroleum wax
2712.9090	---其他	8	45	17		千克		---Other
27.13	**石油焦、石油沥青及其他石油或从沥青矿物提取的油类的残渣:**							**Petroleum coke, petroleum bitumen and other residues of petroleum oils or of oils obtained from bituminous minerals:**
	-石油焦:							-Petroleum coke:
	--未煅烧:							--Not calcined:
2713.1110	---硫的重量百分比小于3%的	3	11	17		千克		---Containing by weight less than 3% of Sulphur
2713.1190	---其他	3	11	17		千克		---Other
	--已煅烧:							--Calcined:
2713.1210	---硫的重量百分比小于0.8%的	3	11	17		千克		---Containing by weight less than 0.8% of Sulphur
2713.1290	---其他	3	11	17		千克		---Other
2713.2000	-石油沥青	8	35	17		千克		-Petroleum bitumen
2713.9000	-其他石油或从沥青矿物提取的油类的残渣	6	35	17		千克	9	-Other residues of petroleum oils or of oils obtained from bituminous minerals
27.14	**天然沥青(地沥青)、沥青页岩、油页岩及焦油砂;沥青岩:**							**Bitumen and asphalt, natural; bituminous or oil shale and tar sands; asphaltites and asphaltic rocks:**
2714.1000	-沥青页岩、油页岩及焦油砂	6	20	17		千克		-Bituminous or oil shale and tar sands
	-其他:							-Other:
2714.9010[暂]	---天然沥青(地沥青)	8	35	17		千克		---Natural bitumen and asphalt
2714.9020	---乳化沥青	0	20	17		千克		---Emulsified bitumen and asphalt
2714.9090	---其他	3	20	17		千克		---Other
27.15	**以天然沥青(地沥青)、石油沥青、矿物焦油或矿物焦油沥青为基本成份的沥青混合物(例如,沥青胶粘剂、稀释沥青):**							**Bituminous mixtures based on natural asphalt, on natural bitumen, on petroleum bitumen, on mineral tar or on mineral tar pitch (for example, bituminous mastics, cut-backs):**
2715.0000	以天然沥青(地沥青)、石油沥青、矿物焦油或矿物焦油沥青为基本成分的沥青混合物(例如,沥青胶粘剂、稀释沥青)	8	35	17		千克		Bituminous mixtures based on natural asphalt, on natural bitumen, on petroleum bitumen, on mineral tar or on mineral tar pitch (for example, bituminous mastics, cut-backs)
27.16	**电力:**							**Electrical energy:**
2716.0000	电力	0	8	17	13	千瓦时		Electrical energy

第六类

化学工业及其相关工业的产品

注释：

一、（一）凡符合税目28.44或28.45规定的货品（放射性矿砂除外），应分别归入这两个税目而不归入其他税目。

（二）除上述（一）款另有规定的以外，凡符合税目28.43、28.46或28.52规定的货品，应分别归入这两个税目而不归入本类的其他税目。

二、除上述注释一另有规定的以外，凡由于按一定剂量或作为零售包装而可归入税目30.04、30.05、30.06、32.12、33.03、33.04、33.05、33.06、33.07、35.06、37.07或38.08的货品，应分别归入以上税目，而不归入本目录的其他税目。

三、由两种或两种以上单独成分配套的货品，其部分或全部成分属于本类范围以内，混合后则构成第六类或第七类的货品，应按混合后产品归入相应的税目，但其组成成分必须同时符合下列条件：

（一）其包装形式足以表明这些成分不需经过改装就可一起使用的；

（二）一起进口或出口的；

（三）这些成分的属性及相互比例足以表明是相互配用的。

SECTION Ⅵ
PRODUCTS OF THE CHEMICAL OR ALLIED INDUSTRIES

Notes:

1. (a) Goods (other than radioactive ores) answering to a description in heading No. 28.44 or 28.45 are to be classified in those headings and in no other heading of the Nomenclature.
   (b) Subject to paragraph (a) above, goods answering to a description in heading No. 28.43、28.46 or 28.52 are to be classified in those headings and in no other heading of this Seciton.
2. Subject to Note 1 above, goods classifiable in heading No. 30.04, 30.05, 30.06, 32.12, 33.03, 33.04, 33.05, 33.06, 33.07, 35.06, 37.07, or 38.08 by reason of being put up in measured doses or for retail sale are to be classified in those headings and in no other headings of the Nomenclature.
3. Goods put up in sets consisting of two or more separate constituents, some or all of which fall in this Section and are intended to be mixed together to obtain a product of Section Ⅵ or Ⅶ, are to be classified in the heading appropriate to that product, provided that the constituents are:
   (a) having regard to the manner in which they are put up, clearly identifiable as being intended to be used together without first being repacked;
   (b) presented together; and
   (c) identifiable, whether by their nature or by the relative proportions in which they are present, as being complementary one to another.

第二十八章

无机化学品；贵金属、稀土金属、放射性元素及其同位素的有机及无机化合物

注释：

一、除条文另有规定的以外，本章各税目只适用于：

（一）单独的化学元素及单独的已有化学定义的化合物，不论是否含有杂质；

（二）上述（一）款产品的水溶液；

（三）溶于其他溶剂的上述（一）款产品，但该产品处于溶液状态只是为了安全或运输所采取的正常必要方法，其所用溶剂并不使该产品改变其一般用途而适合于某些特殊用途；

（四）为了保存或运输需要，加入稳定剂（包括抗结块剂）的上述（一）、（二）、（三）款产品；

（五）为了便于识别或安全起见，加入抗尘剂或着色剂的上述（一）、（二）、（三）、（四）款产品，但所加剂料并不使原产品改变其一般用途而适合于某些特殊用途。

Chapter 28

Inorganic chemicals; organic or inorganic compounds of precious metals, of rare-earth metals of radioactive elements or of isotopes

Notes:

1. Except where the context otherwise requires, the headings of this Chapter apply only to:
   (a) Separate chemical elements and separate chemically defined compounds, whether or not containing impurities;
   (b) The products mentioned in (a) above dissolved in water;
   (c) The products mentioned in (a) above dissolved in other solvents, provided that the solution constitutes a normal and necessary method of putting up these products adopted solely for reasons of safety or for transport, and that the solvent does not render the product particularly suitable for specific use rather than for general use;
   (d) The products mentioned in (a), (b) or (c) above with an added stabilizer (including an anti-caking agent) necessary for their preservation or transport;
   (e) The products mentioned in (a), (b), (c) or (d) above with an added antidusting agent or a colouring substance added to facilitate their identification or for safety reasons, provided that the additions do not render the product particularly suitable for specific use rather than for general use.

二、除以有机物质稳定的连二亚硫酸盐及次硫酸盐(税目28.31),无机碱的碳酸盐及过碳酸盐(税目28.36),无机碱的氰化物、氧氰化物及氰络合物(税目28.37),无机碱的雷酸盐、氰酸盐及硫氰酸盐(税目28.42),税目28.43至28.46及28.52的有机产品,以及碳化物(税目28.49)之外,本章仅包括下列碳化合物:

(一)碳的氧化物,氰化氢及雷酸、异氰酸、硫氰酸及其他简单或络合氰酸(税目28.11);

(二)碳的卤氧化物(税目28.12);

(三)二硫化碳(税目28.13);

(四)硫代碳酸盐、硒代碳酸盐、碲代碳酸盐、硒代氰酸盐、碲代氰酸盐、四氰硫基二氨基络酸盐及其他无机碱络合氰酸盐(税目28.42);

(五)用尿素固化的过氧化氢(税目28.47)、氧硫化碳、硫代羰基卤化物、氰、卤化氰、氨基氰及其金属衍生物(税目28.53),不论是否纯净,但氰氨化钙除外(第三十一章)。

三、除第六类注释一另有规定的以外,本章不包括:

(一)氯化钠或氧化镁(不论是否纯净)及第五类的其他产品;

(二)上述注释二所述以外的有机——无机化合物;

(三)第三十一章注释二、三、四或五所述的产品;

(四)税目32.06的用作发光剂的无机产品;税目32.07的搪瓷玻璃料及其他玻璃,呈粉、粒或粉片状的;

(五)人造石墨(税目38.01);税目38.13的灭火器的装配药及已装药的灭火弹;税目38.24的零售包装的除墨剂;税目38.24的每颗重量不少于2.5克的碱金属或碱土金属卤化物的培养晶体(光学元件除外);

(六)宝石或半宝石(天然、合成或再造)及这些宝石、半宝石的粉末(税目71.02至71.05),第七十一章的贵金属及贵金属合金;

(七)第十五类的金属(不论是否纯净)、金属合金或金属陶瓷,包括硬质合金(与金属烧结的金属碳化物);

(八)光学元件,例如用碱金属或碱土金属卤化物制成的(税目90.01)。

四、由本章第二分章的非金属酸和第四分章的金属酸所构成的已有化学定义的络酸,应归入税目28.11。

五、税目28.26至28.42只适用于金属盐、铵盐及过氧酸盐。除条文另有规定的以外,复盐及络盐应归入税目28.42。

六、税目28.44只适用于:

(一)锝(原子序数43)、钷(原子序数61)、钋(原子序数84)及原子序数大于84的所有化学元素;

(二)天然或人造放射性同位素(包括第十四类及第十五类的贵金属和贱金属的放射性同位素),不论是否混合;

2. In addition to dithionites and sulphoxylates, stabilized with organic substances (heading No. 28.31), carbonates and peroxocarbonates of inorganic bases (heading No. 28.36), cyanides, cyanide oxides and complex cyanides of inorganic bases (heading No. 28.37), fulminates, cyanates and thiocyanates, of inorganic bases (heading No. 28.42), organic products included in headings No. 28.43 to 28.46 and 28.52 and carbides (heading No. 28.49), only the following compounds of carbon are to the classified in this Chapter:

(a) Oxides of carbon, hydrogen cyanide and fulminic, isocyanic, thiocyanic and other simple or complex cyanogen acids (heading No. 28.11);

(b) Halide oxides of carbon (heading No. 28.12);

(c) Carbon disulphide (heading No. 28.13);

(d) Thiocarbonates, selenocarbonates, tellurocarbonates, selenocyanates, tellurocyanates, tetrathiocyanatodiamminochromates (reineckates) and other complex cyanates, of inorganic bases (heading No. 28.42);

(e) Hydrogen peroxide, solidified with urea (heading No. 28.47), carbon oxysulphide, thiocarbonyl halides, cyanogen, cyanogen halides and cyanamide and its metal derivatives (heading No. 28.53) other than calcium cyanamide, whether or not pure (Chapter 31).

3. Subject to the provisions of Note 1 to Section Ⅵ, this Chapter does not cover:

(a) Sodium chloride or magnesium oxide, whether or not pure, or other products of Section Ⅴ;

(b) Organo-inorganic compounds other than those mentioned in Note 2 above;

(c) Products mentioned in Note 2,3,4 or 5 to Chapter 31;

(d) Inorganic products of a kind used as luminophores, of heading No. 32.06; glass frit and other glass in the form of powder, granules of flakes, of heading No. 32.07;

(e) Artificial graphite (heading No. 38.01); products put up as charges for fire-extinguishers or put up in fire-extinguishing grenades, of heading No. 38.13; ink removers put up in packings for retail sale, of heading No. 38.24, cultured crystals (other than optical elements) weighing not less than 2.5g each, of the halides of the alkali or alkaline-earth metals, of heading No. 38.24;

(f) Precious or semi-precious stones (natural, synthetic or reconstructed) or dust or powder of such stones (headings Nos. 71.02 to 71.05), or precious metals or precious metal alloys of Chapter 71;

(g) The metals, whether or not pure, metal alloys or cermets, including sintered metal carbides (metal carbides sintered with a metal), of Section ⅩⅤ; or

(h) Optical elements, for example, of the halides of the alkali or alkaline-earth metals (heading No. 90.01).

4. Chemically defined complex acids consisting of a nonmetal acid of sub-Chapter Ⅱ and a metal acid of sub-Chapter Ⅳ are to be classified in heading No. 28.11.

5. Headings Nos. 28.26 to 28.42 apply only to metal or ammonium salts or peroxysalts. Except where the context otherwise requires, double or complex salts are to be classified in heading No. 28.42.

6. Heading No. 28.44 applies only to:

(a) Technetium (atomic No. 43), promethium (atomic No. 61), polonium (atomic No. 84) and all elements with an atomic number greater than 84;

(b) Natural or artificial radioactive isotopes (including those of the precious metals or of the base metals of Sections ⅩⅣ and ⅩⅤ), whether or not mixed together;

（三）上述元素或同位素的无机或有机化合物，不论是否已有化学定义或是否混合；

（四）含有上述元素或同位素及其无机或有机化合物并且具有某种放射性强度超过 74 贝克勒尔/克(0.002 微居里/克)的合金、分散体(包括金属陶瓷)、陶瓷产品及混合物；

（五）核反应堆已耗尽(已辐照)的燃料元件(释热元件)；

（六）放射性的残渣，不论是否有用。

税目 28.44、28.45 及本注释所称"同位素"，是指：

1. 单独的核素，但不包括自然界中以单一同位素状态存在的核素；
2. 同一元素的同位素混合物，其中一种或几种同位素已被浓缩，即人工地改变了该元素同位素的自然构成。

七、税目 28.48 包括按重量计含磷量超过 15% 的磷化铜(磷铜)。

八、经掺杂用于电子工业的化学元素(例如，硅、硒)，如果拉制后未经加工或呈圆筒形、棒形，应归入本章；如果已切成圆片、薄片或类似形状，则归入税目 38.18。

子目注释：

子目 2812.10 所称"已有化学定义"是指符合第二十八章注释一(一)至(五)或第二十九章注释一(一)至(八)规定的汞的无机或有化合物。

(c) Compounds, inorganic or organic, of these elements or isotopes, whether or not chemically defined, whether or not mixed together;

(d) Alloys, dispersions (including cermets), ceramic products and mixtures containing these elements or isotopes or inorganic or organic compounds thereof and having a specific radioactivity exceeding 74 Bq/g (0.002μ Ci/g);

(e) Spent (irradiated) fuel elements (cartridges) of nuclear reactors;

(f) Radioactive residues whether or not usable.

The term "isotopes", for the purposes of this Note and of the wording of headings No. 28.44 and 28.45, refers to:

(1) individual nuclides, excluding, however, those existing in nature in the monoisotopic state;

(2) mixtures of isotopes of one and the same element, enriched in one or several of the said isotopes, that is, elements of which the natural isotopic composition has been artificially modified.

7. Heading No. 28.48 includes copper phosphide (phosphor copper) containing more than 15% by weight of phosphorus.

8. Chemical elements (for example, silicon and selenium) doped for use in electronics are to be classified in this Chapter, provided that they are in forms unworked as drawn, or in the form of cylinders or rods. When cut in the form of discs, wafers or similar forms, they fall in heading No. 38.18.

Subheading Note:

For the purposes of Subheading 2852.10, the expression "chemically defined" means all organic or inorganic compounds of mercury meeting the requirements of paragraphs (a) to (e) of Note 1 to Chapter 28 or paragraphs (a) to (h) of Note 1 to Chapter 29

税则号列	货品名称	最惠(%)	普通	增值税率	出口退税	计量单位	监管条件	Article Description
	第一分章 化学元素							I.-CHEMICAL ELEMENTS
28.01	氟、氯、溴及碘：							**Fluorine, chlorine, bromine and iodine:**
2801.1000	-氯	5.5	80	17		千克	AB	-Chlorine
2801.2000	-碘	5.5	30	17		千克	G	-Iodine
	-氟；溴：							-Fluorine; bromine:
2801.3010	---氟	5.5	30	17		千克	AB	---Fluorine
2801.3020[暂]	---溴	1	30	17		千克	AB	---Bromine
28.02	升华硫磺、沉淀硫磺；胶态硫磺：							**Sulphur, sublimed or precipitated; colloidal sulphur:**
2802.0000[暂]	升华硫磺、沉淀硫磺；胶态硫磺	1	17	17		千克	AB	Sulphur, sublimed or precipitated; colloidal sulphur
28.03	碳(碳黑及其他税目未列名的其他形态的碳)：							**Carbon (carbon blacks and other forms of carbon not elsewhere specified or included):**
2803.0000	碳(包括碳黑及其他税号未列名的其他形态的碳)	5.5	35	17		千克		Carbon (carbon blacks and other forms of carbon not elsewhere specified or included)
28.04	氢、稀有气体及其他非金属：							**Hydrogen, rare gases and other non-metals:**
2804.1000	-氢	5.5	30	17		千克/立方米	AB	-Hydrogen
	-稀有气体：							-Rare gases:
2804.2100	--氩	5.5	30	17		千克/立方米	AB	--Argon
2804.2900	--其他	5.5	30	17		千克/立方米		--Other
2804.3000	-氮	5.5	30	17		千克/立方米	AB	-Nitrogen
2804.4000	-氧	5.5	80	17		千克/立方米	AB	-Oxygen
2804.5000	-硼；碲		17	17		千克		-Boron; tellurium
2804.5000[暂] 01	碲	0	17	17		千克		tellurium
2804.5000 10	颗粒＜500μm 的硼及其合金(含量≥97%，不论球形、椭球体、雾化、片状、研碎金属燃料)	5.5	17	17		千克	3	Boron and its alloys, granularity ＜500μm (containing boron ≥97%, whether in the form of spheroid, ellipsoid, flakes, atomized or pulverized metallic fuel)

税则号列	货 品 名 称	最惠(%)	普通	增值税率	出口退税	计量单位	监管条件	Article Description
2804.5000 20	能量密度>40MJ/kg的硼浆(硼溶于溶剂形成的硼浆)	5.5	17	17		千克	3	Boron paste, energy density > 4 Mega J/kg, boron dissolved in solvent
2804.5000 90	其他硼	5.5	17	17		千克		Other boron
	-硅:							-Silicon:
	--按重量计含硅量不少于99.99%:							--Containing by weight not less than 99.99% of silicon:
	---经掺杂用于电子工业的直径在7.5厘米及以上的单晶硅棒:							---Monocrystals doped for use in electronics, in the form of cylinders or rods, 7.5cm or more in diameter:
2804.6117	----直径在30厘米及以上的	4	11	17	17	千克		----30cm or more in diameter
2804.6119	----其他	4	11	17		千克		----Other
2804.6120	---经掺杂用于电子工业的其他单晶硅棒	4	17	17		千克		---Other monocrystals doped for use in electronics, in the form of cylinders or rods
2804.6190	---其他		30	17		千克		---Other
2804.6190 11	含硅量≥99.9999999%的多晶硅废碎料(太阳能级多晶硅除外)	1	30	17		千克	AP	Waste and scrape of polycrystalline silicon, containing by weight not less than 99.9999999% (excluding solar - grade polysilicon)
2804.6190 12	含硅量≥99.9999999%的太阳能级多晶硅	4	30	17		千克		Solar grade polysilicon silicon content ≥ 99.9999999%
2804.6190 13	含硅量≥99.9999999%的太阳能级多晶硅废碎料	4	30	17		千克	AP	Solar grade polysilicon silicon content ≥ 99.9999999% of waste and scrap
2804.6190 19	其他含硅量≥99.9999999%的多晶硅(太阳能极多晶硅除外)	4	30	17		千克		Other polycrystalline silicon, containing by weight not less than 99.9999999% (excluding solay - grade poly silicon)
2804.6190 91	其他含硅量≥99.99%的硅废碎料(太阳能级多晶硅除外)	4	30	17		千克	AP	Waste and scrape of silicon, containing by weight not less than 99.99% (excluding solar - grade polysilicon)
2804.6190 92	含硅量≥99.99%的太阳能级多晶硅	4	30	17		千克		Solar grade polysilicon silicon content ≥ 99.99%
2804.6190 93	含硅量≥99.99%的太阳能级多晶硅废碎料	4	30	17		千克	AP	Solar grade polysilicon silicon content ≥ 99.99% of waste and scrap
2804.6190 99	其他含硅量≥99.99%的硅(太阳能级多晶硅除外)	4	30	17		千克		Other silicon, containing by weight not less than 99.99% (excluding solar - grade polysilicon)
2804.6900	--其他	4	30	17		千克		--Other
	-磷:							-Phosphorus:
2804.7010	---黄磷(白磷)	5.5	30	17		千克	AB	---Yellow phosphorus (white phosphorus)
2804.7090	---其他	5.5	30	17		千克		---Other
2804.7090 10	红磷	5.5	30	17		千克	ABG	Red phosphorus
2804.7090 90	其他磷	5.5	30	17		千克		Other phosphorus
2804.8000	-砷	5.5	30	17		千克	X	-Arsenic
	-硒:							-Selenium:
2804.9010	---经掺杂用于电子工业的硒晶体棒	4	17	17		千克		---Crystals doped for use in electronics, in the form of cylinders or rods
2804.9090暂	---其他	0	30	17		千克		---Other
28.05	**碱金属、碱土金属;稀土金属、钪及钇,不论是否相互混合或相互熔合;汞:**							**Alkali or alkaline-earth metals; rare-earth metals, scandium and yttrium, whether or not intermixed or interalloyed; mercury:**
	-碱金属及碱土金属:							-Alkali metals or alkaline-earth metals:
2805.1100	--钠	5.5	30	17		千克	AB	--Sodium
2805.1200暂	--钙	1	30	17		千克		--Calcium
2805.1200暂 10	高纯度钙[金属杂质(除镁外)含量<1‰,硼含量小于十万分之一]	1	30	17		千克	3A	Calcium, with a high purity, metallic impurity (other than Magnesium) < 1‰, containing boron < 1/10[5]
2805.1200暂 90	其他钙	1	30	17		千克		Other Calcium
2805.1900暂	--其他	1	30	17		千克		--Other
	-稀土金属、钪及钇,不论是否相互混合或相互熔合:							-Rare-earth metals, scandium and yttrium, whether or not intermixed or interalloyed:

税则号列	货品名称	最惠(%)	普通	增值税率	出口退税	计量单位	监管条件	Article Description
	---稀土金属、钪及钇,未相互混合或相互熔合:							---Not intermixed or interalloyed:
2805.3011[暂]	----钕	0	30	17		千克	4Bxy	----Neodymium
2805.3012[暂]	----镝	0	30	17		千克	4Bxy	----Dysprosium
2805.3013[暂]	----铽	0	30	17		千克	4Bxy	----Terbium
2805.3014[暂]	----镧	0	30	17		千克	4Bxy	----Lanthanum
2805.3015[暂]	----铈	0	30	17		千克		----Cerium
2805.3015[暂] 10	颗粒 < 500μm 的铈及其合金(含量≥97%,不论球形,椭球体,雾化,片状,研碎金属燃料;未相互混合或相互熔合)	0	30	17		千克	3B	Cerium and its alloys, granularity < 500μm, containing cerium≥97%, whether in the form of spheroid, ellipsoid, flakes, atomized or pulverized metallic fuel
2805.3015[暂] 90	其他金属铈(未相互混合或相互熔合)	0	30	17		千克	4Bxy	Other metalic cerium, not intermixed or interalloyed
2805.3016[暂]	----镨	0	30	17		千克	4Bxy	----Praseodymium
2805.3017[暂]	----钇	0	30	17		千克	4Bxy	----Yttrium
2805.3019[暂]	----其他	0	30	17		千克		----Other
2805.3019[暂] 13	金属钐(未相互混合或相互熔合)	0	30	17		千克	4Bxy	Metallic samarium(not intermixed or interalloyed)
2805.3019[暂] 14	金属铕(未相互混合或相互熔合)	0	30	17		千克	4Bxy	Metallic europium(not intermixed or interalloyed)
2805.3019[暂] 15	金属钪(未相互混合或相互熔合)	0	30	17		千克	4Bxy	Metallic scandium(not intermixed or interalloyed)
2805.3019[暂] 90	其他稀土金属(未相互混合或相互熔合)	0	30	17		千克	4Bxy	Other rare-earth metals, not intermixed or interalloyed
	---稀土金属、钪及钇,相互混合或相互熔合:							---intermixed or interalloyed:
2805.3021[暂]	----电池级	0	30	17		千克	4Bxy	----Battery grade
2805.3021[暂] 10	按重量计中重稀土总含量≥30%电池级的稀土金属、钪及钇(已相互混合或相互熔合)	0	30	17		千克	4Bxy	Containing by weight more than 30% of middle heavy rare-earth, battery grade rare-earth metals, scandium and yttrium
2805.3021[暂] 90	其他电池级的稀土金属、钪及钇(已相互混合或相互熔合)	0	30	17		千克	4Bxy	Other battery grade rare-earth metals, scandium and yttrium
2805.3029[暂]	----其他	0	30	17		千克	4Bxy	----Other
2805.3029[暂] 10	按重量计中重稀土总含量≥30%的其他稀土金属、钪及钇(已相互混合或相互熔合)	0	30	17		千克	4Bxy	Containing by wehgt more than 30% of middle heavy rare-earth, battery grade rare – earth metals, scandium and yttrium
2805.3029[暂] 90	其他稀土金属、钪及钇(已相互混合或相互熔合)	0	30	17		千克	4Bxy	Other rare-earth metals, scandium, yttrium
2805.4000	-汞	5.5	17	17		千克	X	-Mercury
	第二分章　无机酸及非金属无机氧化物							Ⅱ. INORGANIC ACIDS AND INORGANIC OXYGEN COMPOUNDS OF NON-METALS
28.06	**氯化氢(盐酸);氯磺酸:**							**Hydrogen chloride (hydrochloric acid); chlorosulphuric acid:**
2806.1000	-氯化氢(盐酸)	5.5	80	17		千克	23AB	-Hydrogen chloride (hydrochloric acid)
2806.2000	-氯磺酸	5.5	40	17		千克	AB	-Chlorosulphuric acid
28.07	**硫酸;发烟硫酸:**							**Sulphuric acid; oleum:**
2807.0000[暂]	硫酸;发烟硫酸	1	35	17		千克		Sulphuric acid; oleum
2807.0000[暂] 10	硫酸	1	35	17		千克	32	Sulphuric acid
2807.0000[暂] 90	发烟硫酸	1	35	17		千克	AB	Oleum
28.08	**硝酸;磺硝酸:**							**Nitric acid; sulphonitric acids:**
2808.0000	硝酸;磺硝酸	5.5	40	17		千克		Nitric acid; sulphonitric acids
2808.0000 10	红发烟硝酸	5.5	40	17		千克	3A	Red fuming nitric acid
2808.0000 90	磺硝酸及其他硝酸	5.5	40	17		千克		Sulphonitric acids, other nitric acids
28.09	**五氧化二磷;磷酸;多磷酸,不论是否已有化学定义:**							**Diphosphorus pentaoxide; phosphoric acid; polyphosphoric acids, whether or not chemically defined:**
2809.1000	-五氧化二磷	1	8	17		千克	AB	-Diphosphorus pentaoxide
	-磷酸及多磷酸:							-Phosphoric acid and polyphosphoric acids:
	---磷酸及偏磷酸、焦磷酸:							---Phosphoric acid, metaphosphoric acid and pyrophosphoric acid:
2809.2011	----食品级磷酸	1	8	17		千克	AB	----Phosphoric acid, food grade

税则号列	货 品 名 称	最惠(%)	普通	增值税率	出口退税	计量单位	监管条件	Article Description
2809.2019	----其他	1	8	17		千克	B	----Other
2809.2090	---其他	5.5	35	17		千克		---Other
28.10	**硼的氧化物;硼酸:**							**Oxides of boron; boric acids:**
2810.0010	---硼的氧化物	5.5	30	17		千克		---Oxides of boron
2810.0020	---硼酸	5.5	30	17		千克	A	---Boric acids
28.11	**其他无机酸及非金属无机氧化物:**							**Other inorganic acids and other inorganic oxygen compounds of non-metals:**
	-其他无机酸:							-Other inorganic acids:
2811.1100	--氟化氢(氢氟酸)	5.5	35	17		千克	3A	--Hydrofluoric acid
	--其他:							--Other:
2811.1910	---氢氰酸	5.5	35	17		千克	23	---Hydrocyanic acid
2811.1920	---硒化氢	5.5	35	17		千克	AB	---Hydrogen selenide
2811.1990	---其他	5.5	35	17		千克		---Other
2811.1990 10	氢碘酸	5.5	35	17		千克	ABG	Hydroiodic acid
2811.1990 20	砷酸、焦砷酸、偏砷酸	5.5	35	17		千克	X	Arsenic acid, pyroarsenic acid, metaardsenic acid
2811.1990 90	其他无机酸	5.5	35	17		千克	AB	Other inorganic acids
	-其他非金属无机氧化物:							-Other inorganic oxygen compounds of non-metals:
2811.2100	--二氧化碳	5.5	30	17		千克	AB	--Carbon dioxide
	--二氧化硅:							--Silicon dioxide:
2811.2210	---硅胶	5.5	30	17	9	千克	AB	---Silica gel
2811.2290	---其他	5.5	30	17	9	千克	AB	---Other
2811.2900	--其他	5.5	30	17		千克		--Other
2811.2900 10	三氧化二砷、五氧化二砷[亚砷(酸)酐、砒霜、白砒、氧化亚砷、砷(酸)酐、三氧化砷]	5.5	30	17		千克	X	Arsenous oxide (*arsenic trioxide*), arsenic pentoxide (including arsenic trioxide, arsenous anhydride, arsenic white)
2811.2900 20	四氧化二氮	5.5	30	17		千克	3A	Dinitrogen tetroxide
2811.2900 90	其他非金属无机氧化物	5.5	30	17		千克		Other inorganic oxygen compounds of non-metals
	第三分章 非金属卤化物及硫化物							Ⅲ. HALOGEN OR SULPHUR COMPOUNDS OF NON-METALS
28.12	**非金属卤化物及卤氧化物:**							**Halides and halide oxides of non-metals:**
	-氯化物及氯氧化物:							-Chlorides and chloride oxides:
2812.1010[暂]	---氯化亚砜	2	30	17		千克	23	---Sulphoxide chloride
2812.1020	---氧氯化磷(磷酰氯;三氯氧磷)	5.5	30	17		千克	23	---Phosphorus oxychloride (phosphoryl monochloride, phosphorus oxytrichloride)
2812.1030	---碳酰二氯(光气)	5.5	30	17		千克	23	---Carbonyl dichloride (phosgene)
	---非金属氯化物:							---Other chlorides of non-metals:
2812.1041	----一氯化硫(氯化硫)	5.5	30	17		千克	23	----Sulfur monochloride
2812.1042	----二氯化硫	5.5	30	17		千克	23	----Sulfur dichloride
2812.1043	----三氯化磷	5.5	30	17		千克	23	----Phosphorus trichloride
2812.1044	----三氯化砷	5.5	30	17		千克	23	----Arsenic trichloride
2812.1045	----五氯化磷	5.5	30	17		千克	23	----Phosphorus pentachloride
2812.1049	----其他	5.5	30	17		千克		----Other
2812.1090	---其他	5.5	30	17		千克		---Other
	-其他:							-Other:
	---氟化物及氟氧化物:							---Fluoride and oxyfluoride:
2812.9011	----三氟化氮	5.5	30	17		千克	AB	----Nitrogen trifluoride
2812.9019	----其他	5.5	30	17		千克		----Other
2812.9019 10	三氟化氯	5.5	30	17		千克	3A	Chlorine trifluoride
2812.9019 20	三氟化砷(氟化亚砷)	5.5	30	17		千克	X	Arsenic trifluoride
2812.9019 30	硫酰氟	5.5	30	17		千克	S	Sulphurylfluoride
2812.9019 90	其他氟化物及氟氧化物	5.5	30	17		千克		Other fluoride and oxyfluoride
2812.9090	---其他	5.5	30	17		千克		---Other
2812.9090 10	三溴化砷,三碘化砷(溴化亚砷,碘化亚砷)	5.5	30	17		千克	X	Arsenic tribromide, arsenic triiodide
2812.9090 90	其他非金属卤化物及卤氧化物	5.5	30	17		千克		Other halides and halide oxides of non – metals
28.13	**非金属硫化物;商品三硫化二磷:**							**Sulphides of non-metals; commercial phosphorus trisulphides:**
2813.1000	-二硫化碳	5.5	30	17		千克	X	-Carbon disulphide
2813.9000	-其他	5.5	30	17		千克		-Other
2813.9000 10	五硫化二磷	5.5	30	17		千克	23	Phosphorus pentasulfide

税则号列	货品名称	最惠(%)	普通	增值税率	出口退税	计量单位	监管条件	Article Description
2813.9000 20	三硫化二磷	5.5	30	17		千克	AB	Phosphorus trisulfide
2813.9000 90	其他非金属硫化物	5.5	30	17		千克		Other sulphides of non-metals
	第四分章　无机碱和金属氧化物、氢氧化物及过氧化物							Ⅳ .-INORGANIC BASES AND OXIDES, HYDROXIDES AND PEROXIDES OF METALS
28.14	**氨及氨水：**							**Ammonia, anhydrous or in aqueous solution:**
2814.1000暂	-氨	0	35	17		千克	AB	-Anhydrous ammonia
2814.2000暂	-氨水	0	35	17		千克		-Ammonia in aqueous solution
2814.2000暂 10	氨水(含量≥10%)	0	35	17		千克	AB	Ammonia in aqueous solution
2814.2000暂 90	其他氨水	0	35	17		千克		Other ammonia in aqueous solution
28.15	**氢氧化钠(烧碱)；氢氧化钾(苛性钾)；过氧化钠及过氧化钾：**							**Sodium hydroxide (caustic soda); potassium hydroxide (caustic potash); peroxides or sodium or potassium:**
	-氢氧化钠(烧碱)：							-Sodium hydroxide (caustic soda):
2815.1100	--固体	10	35	17		千克	ABG	--Solid
2815.1200	--水溶液(氢氧化钠浓溶液及液体烧碱)	8	35	17		千克	ABG	--In aqueous solution (soda lye or liquid soda)
2815.2000	-氢氧化钾(苛性钾)	5.5	30	17	13	千克	AB	-Potassium hydroxide (caustic potash)
2815.3000	-过氧化钠及过氧化钾	5.5	30	17		千克	AB	-Peroxides of sodium or potassium
28.16	**氢氧化镁及过氧化镁；锶或钡的氧化物、氢氧化物及过氧化物：**							**Hydroxide and peroxide of magnesium; oxides, hydroxides and peroxides, of strontium or barium:**
2816.1000	-氢氧化镁及过氧化镁	5.5	30	17		千克		-Hydroxide and peroxide of magnesium
2816.1000 10	过氧化镁	5.5	30	17		千克	AB	Peroxide of magnesium
2816.1000 90	氢氧化镁	5.5	30	17		千克		Hydroxide
2816.4000暂	-锶或钡的氧化物、氢氧化物及过氧化物	2	30	17		千克		-Oxides, hydroxides and peroxides, of strontium or barium
28.17	**氧化锌及过氧化锌：**							**Zinc oxide; Zinc peroxide:**
2817.0010	---氧化锌	5.5	40	17		千克	AB	---Zinc oxide
2817.0090	---过氧化锌	5.5	30	17		千克	AB	---Zinc peroxide
28.18	**人造刚玉，不论是否已有化学定义；氧化铝；氢氧化铝：**							**Artificial corundum, whether or not chemically defined; aluminium oxide; aluminium hydroxide:**
	-人造刚玉，不论是否已有化学定义：							-Artificial corundum, whether or not chemically defined:
2818.1010	---棕刚玉	5.5	20	17		千克		---Brown fused alumina
2818.1090	---其他	5.5	20	17		千克		---Other
2818.2000暂	-氧化铝，但人造刚玉除外	0	30	17		千克	7	-Aluminium oxide, other than artificial corundum
2818.3000	-氢氧化铝	5.5	30	17		千克		-Aluminium hydroxide
28.19	**铬的氧化物及氢氧化物：**							**Chromium oxides and hydroxides:**
2819.1000	-三氧化铬	5.5	20	17		千克	AB	-Chromium trioxide
2819.9000	-其他	5.5	30	17		千克		-Other
28.20	**锰的氧化物：**							**Manganese oxide:**
2820.1000	-二氧化锰	5.5	40	17		千克		-Manganese dioxide
2820.9000	-其他	5.5	30	17		千克		-Other
28.21	**铁的氧化物及氢氧化物；土色料，按重量计三氧化二铁含量在70%及以上：**							**Iron oxides and hydroxides; earth colours containing 70% or more by weight of combined iron evaluated as Fe_2O_3:**
2821.1000	-铁的氧化物及氢氧化物	5.5	30	17		千克		-Iron oxides and hydroxides
2821.2000	-土色料	5.5	45	17		千克		-Earth colours
28.22	**钴的氧化物及氢氧化物；商品氧化钴：**							**Cobalt oxides and hydroxides; commercial cobalt oxides:**
	钴的氧化物及氢氧化物；商品氧化钴：							Cobalt oxides and hydroxides; commercial cobalt oxides:
2822.0010暂	---四氧化三钴	2	30	17	13	千克	4xy	---Cobalt tetroxide
2822.0090暂	---其他	2	30	17		千克	4xy	---Other
28.23	**钛的氧化物：**							**Titanium oxides:**

税则号列	货　品　名　称	最惠(%)	普通	增值税率	出口退税	计量单位	监管条件	Article Description
2823.0000	钛的氧化物	5.5	30	17		千克		Titanium oxides
28.24	铅的氧化物；铅丹及铅橙：							**Lead oxides; red lead and orange lead:**
2824.1000	-一氧化铅（铅黄、黄丹）	5.5	30	17		千克	X	-Lead monoxide (litharge, massicot)
	-其他：							-Other:
2824.9010	---铅丹及铅橙	5.5	45	17		千克	X	---Red lead and orange lead
2824.9090	---其他	5.5	30	17		千克		---Other
28.25	肼（联氨）、胲（羟胺）及其无机盐；其他无机碱；其他金属氧化物、氢氧化物及过氧化物：							**Hydrazine and hydroxylamine and their inorganic salts; other inorganic bases; other metal oxides, hydroxides and peroxides:**
	-肼（联氨）、胲（羟胺）及其无机盐：							-Hydrazine and hydroxylamine and their inorganic salts:
2825.1010	---水合肼	5.5	30	17		千克		---Hydrazine hydrate
2825.1010 10	纯度70%及以上的水合肼	5.5	30	17		千克	3A	Hydrazine hydrate, purity≥70%
2825.1010 90	纯度70%以下的水合肼	5.5	30	17		千克	AB	Hydrazine hydrate, purity<70%
2825.1020	---硫酸羟胺	5.5	30	17		千克	AB	---Hydroxylamine sulphate
2825.1090	---其他	5.5	30	17		千克		---Other
	-锂的氧化物及氢氧化物：							-Lithium oxide and hydroxide:
2825.2010	---氢氧化锂	5.5	30	17		千克	AB	---Lithium hydroxide
2825.2090	---其他	5.5	30	17		千克		---Other
	-钒的氧化物及氢氧化物：							-Vanadium oxides and hydroxides:
2825.3010	---五氧化二钒	5.5	30	17		千克	4ABxy	---Divanadium pentaoxide
2825.3090	---其他	5.5	30	17		千克	4xy	---Other
2825.4000[暂]	-镍的氧化物及氢氧化物	2	30	17		千克		-Nickel oxides and hydroxides
2825.5000	-铜的氧化物及氢氧化物	5.5	30	17		千克		-Copper oxides and hydroxides
2825.6000	-锗的氧化物及二氧化锆	5.5	30	17		千克		-Germanium oxides and zirconium dioxide
2825.6000 01	锗的氧化物	5.5	30	17		千克	4xy	Cermaniurn oxides
2825.6000 90	二氧化锆	5.5	30	17		千克	3	Zirconium dioxide
2825.7000	-钼的氧化物及氢氧化物	5.5	30	17		千克	4xy	-Molybdenum oxides and hydroxides
2825.8000	-锑的氧化物	5.5	30	17		千克	4xBy	-Antimony oxides
	-其他：							-Other:
	---钨的氧化物及氢氧化物：							---Tungsten oxides and hydroxides:
2825.9011	----钨酸	5.5	30	17		千克	4xy	----Tungstic acid
2825.9012	----三氧化钨	5.5	30	17		千克	4xy	----Tungstic oxide
2825.9019	----其他	5.5	30	17		千克		---Other
2825.9019 10	蓝色氧化钨	5.5	30	17		千克	4xy	Blue tungsten oxides
2825.9019 90	其他钨的氧化物及氢氧化物	5.5	30	17		千克		Other tungsten oxides and hydroxides
	---铋的氧化物及氢氧化物：							---Bismuth oxdes and hydroxides:
2825.9021	----三氧化二铋	5.5	30	17		千克	4xyAB	----Bismuth trioxide
2825.9029	----其他	5.5	30	17		千克	4xyAB	----Other
	---锡的氧化物及氢氧化物					千克		---Tin oxides and hydroxides:
2825.9031	----二氧化锡	5.5	30	17		千克	4xyAB	----Tin dioxide
2825.9039	----其他	5.5	30	17		千克	4xyAB	----Other
	---铌的氧化物及氢氧化物：							---Niobium oxdes and hydroxides:
2825.9041	----一氧化铌	5.5	30	17		千克	A	----Columbium monoxide
2825.9049	----其他	5.5	30	17		千克	AB	----Other
2825.9090	---其他	5.5	30	17		千克	AB	---Other
	第五分章　无机酸盐、无机过氧酸盐及金属酸盐、金属过氧酸盐							V.-SALTS AND PEROXYSALTS, OF INORGANIC ACIDS AND METALS
28.26	氟化物；氟硅酸盐、氟铝酸盐及其他氟络盐：							**Fluorides; fluorosilicates, fluoroaluminates and other complex fluorine salts:**
	-氟化物：							-Fluorides:
	--氟化铝：							--Of aluminium:
2826.1210	---无水氟化铝	5.5	30	17		千克	AB	---Anhydrous aluminium chloride
2826.1290	---其他	5.5	30	17		千克	AB	---Other
	--其他：							--Other:
2826.1910	---铵的氟化物	5.5	30	17		千克		---Of ammonium
2826.1910 10	氟化氢铵	5.5	30	17		千克	3A	Ammonium hydrogen fluoride
2826.1910 90	其他铵的氟化物	5.5	30	17		千克		Other ammonium fluorid

税则号列	货　品　名　称	最惠(%)	普通	增值税率	出口退税	计量单位	监管条件	Article Description
2826.1920	---钠的氟化物	5.5	30	17		千克		---Of sodium
2826.1920 10	氟化钠	5.5	30	17		千克	3AB	Sodium fluoride
2826.1920 20	氟化氢钠	5.5	30	17		千克	3A	Sodium hydrogen fluoride
2826.1920 90	其他钠的氟化物	5.5	30	17		千克		Other sodium fluorid
2826.1990	---其他	5.5	30	17		千克		---Other
2826.1990 10	氟化钾	5.5	30	17		千克	3A	Potassium fluoride
2826.1990 20	氟化氢钾	5.5	30	17		千克	3A	Potassium hydrogen fluoride
2826.1990 30	氟化铅,四氟化铅,氟化镉	5.5	30	17		千克	X	Lead fluoride, lead tetrafluoried , cadmium fluoride
2826.1990 90	其他氟化物	5.5	30	17		千克		Other fluorides
2826.3000	-六氟铝酸钠(人造冰晶石)	5.5	30	17	13	千克		-Sodium hexafluoroaluminate (synthetic cryolite)
	-其他:							-Other:
2826.9010	---氟硅酸盐	5.5	30	17		千克		---Fluorosilicates
2926.9020	---六氟磷酸锂	5.5	30	17		千克		---Lithium Hexafluoroarsenate
2826.9090	---其他	5.5	30	17		千克		---Other
2826.9090 10	氟钽酸钾	5.5	30	17		千克		Potassium tantalifluoride
2826.9090 30	氟硼酸铅,氟硼酸镉	5.5	30	17		千克	X	lead fluoboriate, cadmium fluoboriate
2826.9090 90	氟铝酸盐及其他氟络盐	5.5	30	17		千克		Fluoroaluminates and other complex fluorine salts
28.27	**氯化物、氯氧化物及氢氧基氯化物;溴化物及溴氧化物;碘化物及碘氧化物:**							**Chlorides, chloride oxides and chloride hydroxides; bromides and bromide oxides; iodides and iodide oxides:**
	-氯化铵:							-Ammonium chloride:
2827.1010	---肥料用	4	11	17		千克	G	---For use as fertilizer
2827.1090	---其他	5.5	30	17		千克	G	---Other
2827.2000	-氯化钙	5.5	50	17	9	千克	AB	-Calcium chloride
	-其他氯化物:							-Other chlorides:
2827.3100	--氯化镁	5.5	30	17		千克	AB	--Of magnesium
2827.3200	--氯化铝	5.5	30	17		千克		--Of aluminium
2827.3500	--氯化镍	5.5	30	17		千克		--Of nickel
	--其他:							--Other:
2827.3910	---氯化锂	5.5	30	17		千克		---Lithium chloride
2827.3920	---氯化钡	5.5	30	17		千克	AB	---Barium chleride
2827.3930	---氯化钴	5.5	30	17		千克	4ABxy	---Cobalt chleride
2827.3990	---其他	5.5	30	17		千克	AB	---Other
	-氯氧化物及氢氧基氯化物:							-Chloride oxides and chloride hydroxides:
2827.4100	--铜的氯氧化物及氢氧基氯化物	5.5	30	17		千克		--of copper
	--其他:							--Other:
2827.4910	---锆的氯氧化物及氢氧基氯化物	5.5	30	17		千克		---of zirconium
2827.4990	---其他	5.5	30	17		千克		---Other
	-溴化物及溴氧化物:							-Bromides and bromide oxides:
2827.5100	--溴化钠及溴化钾	5.5	30	17		千克		--Bromides of sodium or of potassium
2827.5900	--其他	5.5	30	17		千克		--Other
2827.6000	-碘化物及碘氧化物	5.5	30	17		千克	AB	-Iodides and iodide oxides
28.28	**次氯酸盐;商品次氯酸钙;亚氯酸盐;次溴酸盐:**							**Hypochlorites; commercial calcium hypochlorite; chlorites; hypobromites:**
2828.1000	-商品次氯酸钙及其他钙的次氯酸盐	12	80	17	5	千克		-Commercial calcium hypochlorite and other calcium hypochlorites
2828.9000	-其他	5.5	30	17		千克	AB	-Other
28.29	**氯酸盐及高氯酸盐;溴酸盐及过溴酸盐;碘酸盐及高碘酸盐:**							**Chlorates and perchlorates; bromates and perbromates; iodates and periodates:**
	-氯酸盐:							-Chlorates:
2829.1100	--氯酸钠	12	30	17		千克	AB	--Of sodium
	--其他:							--Other:
2829.1910	---氯酸钾(洋硝)	5.5	20	17		千克	9B	---Potassium chlorate
2829.1990	---其他	5.5	30	17		千克		---Other
2829.9000	-其他	5.5	30	17		千克		-Other

税则号列	货品名称	最惠(%)	普通	增值税率	出口退税	计量单位	监管条件	Article Description
2829.9000 10	颗粒<500μm的球形高氯酸铵	5.5	30	17		千克	3A	Ammonium perchlorate, spheroids. Granularity < 500μm
2829.9000 90	其他高氯酸盐、溴酸盐等(包括过溴酸盐、碘酸盐及高碘酸盐)	5.5	30	17		千克		Other perchlorates, bromates (Including perbromates iodates and periodates)
28.30	**硫化物;多硫化物,不论是否已有化学定义:**							**Sulphides; polysulphides, whether or not chemically defined:**
	-钠的硫化物:							-Sodium sulphides:
2830.1010	---硫化钠	5.5	40	17		千克	3A	---Sodium sulphide
2830.1090	---其他	5.5	30	17		千克		---Other
	-其他:							-Other:
2830.9020	---硫化锑	5.5	45	17		千克	B	---Antimony sulphide
2830.9030	---硫化钴	5.5	30	17		千克		---Cobalt sulphide
2830.9090	---其他	5.5	30	17		千克		---Other
28.31	**连二亚硫酸盐及次硫酸盐:**							**Dithionites and sulphoxylates:**
	-钠的连二亚硫酸盐及次硫酸盐:							-of sodium:
2831.1010	---钠的连二亚硫酸盐	5.5	30	17		千克	AB	---Sodium Dithionites
2831.1020	---钠的次硫酸盐	5.5	30	17		千克		---Sodium Sulphoxylates
2831.9000	-其他	5.5	30	17		千克		-Other
28.32	**亚硫酸盐;硫代硫酸盐:**							**Sulphites; thiosulphates:**
2832.1000	-钠的亚硫酸盐	5.5	30	17		千克		-Sodium sulphites
2832.2000	-其他亚硫酸盐	5.5	30	17		千克	AB	-Other sulphites
2832.3000	-硫代硫酸盐	5.5	30	17		千克		-Thiosulphates
28.33	**硫酸盐;矾;过硫酸盐:**							**Sulphates; alums; peroxosulphates (persulphates):**
	-钠的硫酸盐:							-Sodium sulphates:
2833.1100	--硫酸钠	5.5	40	17		千克	4xy	--Disodium sulphate
2833.1900	--其他	5.5	30	17		千克		--Other
	-其他硫酸盐:							-Other sulphates:
2833.2100	--硫酸镁	5.5	30	17		千克	AB	--Of magnesium
2833.2200	--硫酸铝	5.5	30	17		千克		--Of aluminium
2833.2400	--镍的硫酸盐	5.5	30	17		千克		--Of nickel
2833.2500	--铜的硫酸盐	5.5	30	17		千克		--Of copper
2833.2700	--硫酸钡	5.5	30	17		千克	G	--Of barium
	--其他:							--Other:
2833.2910	---硫酸亚铁	5.5	45	17		千克	AB	---Ferrous sulphate
2833.2920	---铬的硫酸盐	5.5	30	17		千克		---Chromium sulphate
2833.2930	---硫酸锌	5.5	30	17	5	千克	AB	--- Zinc sulphates
2833.2990	---其他	5.5	30	17		千克		---Other
2833.2990 10	硫酸钴	5.5	30	17		千克	4ABxy	Cobalt sulphate
2833.2990 90	其他硫酸盐	5.5	30	17		千克	AB	Other sulphates
	-矾:							-Alums:
2833.3010	---钾铝矾	5.5	45	17		千克		---Potassium aluminum sulfate
2833.3090	---其他	5.5	30	17		千克		---Other
2833.4000	-过硫酸盐	5.5	30	17		千克		-Peroxosulphates (persulphates)
28.34	**亚硝酸盐;硝酸盐:**							**Nitrites; nitrates:**
2834.1000	-亚硝酸盐	5.5	30	17		千克	AB	-Nitrites
	-硝酸盐:							-Nitrates:
	--硝酸钾:							--Of potassium:
2834.2110[暂]	---肥料用	1	11	17		千克	AB	---For use as fertilizer
2834.2190	---其他	5.5	30	17		千克	AB	---Other
	--其他:							--Other:
2834.2910	---硝酸钴	5.5	30	17		千克	AB	---Of cobalt
2834.2990	---其他		30	17		千克		---Other
2834.2990[暂] 01	硝酸钡	2	30	17		千克	AB	Barium nitrate
2834.2990 90	其他硝酸盐	5.5	30	17		千克		Other nitrates

税则号列	货品名称	最惠(%)	普通	增值税率	出口退税	计量单位	监管条件	Article Description
28.35	次磷酸盐、亚磷酸盐、磷酸盐及多磷酸盐，无论是否已有化学定义：							**Phosphinates (hypophosphites), phosphonates (phosphites), phosphates and polyphosphates, whether or not chemically defined:**
2835.1000	-次磷酸盐及亚磷酸盐	5.5	20	17		千克		-Phosphinates (hypophosphites) and phosphonates (phosphites)
	-磷酸盐：							-Phosphates:
2835.2200	--磷酸一钠及磷酸二钠	5.5	20	17		千克		--Of mono- or disodium
2835.2400	--钾的磷酸盐	5.5	20	17		千克		--Of potassium
	--正磷酸氢钙(磷酸二钙)：							--Calcium hydrogenorthophosphate (dicalcium phosphate):
2835.2510	---饲料级的	5.5	20	17		千克	AB	---Feed grade
2835.2520	---食品级的	5.5	20	17	5	千克	AB	---Food grade
2835.2590	---其他	5.5	20	17		千克		---Other
2835.2600	--其他磷酸钙	5.5	20	17		千克		--Other phosphates of calcium
	--其他：							--Other:
2835.2910	---磷酸三钠	5.5	20	17		千克	AB	---Trisodium phosphate
2835.2990	---其他	5.5	20	17		千克	A	---Other
	-多磷酸盐：							-Polyphosphates:
	--三磷酸钠(三聚磷酸钠)：							--Sodium triphosphate (sodium tripolyphosphate):
2835.3110	---食品级的	5.5	20	17		千克	AB	---Food grade
2835.3190	---其他	5.5	20	17		千克		---Other
	--其他：							--Other:
	---六偏磷酸钠：							---Sodium hexametaphosphate
2835.3911	----食品级的	5.5	20	17	5	千克	AB	----Food grade
2835.3919	----其他	5.5	20	17		千克		----Other
2835.3990	---其他	5.5	20	17		千克		---Other
28.36	碳酸盐；过碳酸盐；含氨基甲酸铵的商品碳酸铵：							**Carbonates; peroxocarbonates (percarbonates); commercial ammonium carbonate containing ammonium carbamate:**
2836.2000	-碳酸钠(纯碱)	5.5	35	17	9	千克	AG	-Disodium carbonate
2836.3000	-碳酸氢钠(小苏打)	5.5	45	17	9	千克	ABG	-Sodium hydrogencarbonate (sodium bicarbonate)
2836.4000	-钾的碳酸盐	5.5	30	17		千克		-Potassium carbonates
2836.5000	-碳酸钙	5.5	45	17		千克	AB	-Calcium carbonate
2836.6000[暂]	-碳酸钡	1	40	17		千克		-Barium carbonate
	-其他：							-Other:
2836.9100[暂]	--锂的碳酸盐	2	30	17		千克		--Lithium carbonates
2836.9200[暂]	--锶的碳酸盐	2	30	17		千克		--Strontium carbonate
	--其他：							--Other:
2836.9910	---碳酸镁	5.5	45	17		千克	AB	---Magnesium carbonate
2836.9930[暂]	---碳酸钴	2	30	17		千克	4xy	---Cobalt carbonate
2836.9940	---商品碳酸铵及其他铵的碳酸盐	5.5	30	17		千克		---Commericial ammonium carbonate and other ammonium carbonates
2836.9950	---碳酸锆	5.5	30	17		千克	AB	---Zirconium carbonate
2836.9990	---其他	5.5	30	17	13	千克	A	---Other
28.37	氰化物、氧氰化物及氰络合物：							**Cyanides, cyanide oxides and complex cyanides:**
	-氰化物及氧氰化物：							-Cyanides and cyanide oxides:
	--氰化钠及氧氰化钠：							--Of sodium:
2837.1110	---氰化钠	5.5	20	17		千克	X23	---Sodium cyanide
2837.1120	---氧氰化钠	5.5	30	17		千克		---Sodium cyanide oxide
	--其他：							--Other:
2837.1910	---氰化钾	5.5	20	17		千克	23X	---Potassium cyanide
2837.1990	---其他	5.5	30	17		千克		---Other
2837.1990 11	氰化锌、氰化亚铜、氰化铜(氰化高铜)	5.5	30	17		千克	X	Znic cyanide, cuprous cyanide, copper cyanide (cupric cyanide)

税则号列	货品名称	最惠(%)	普通	增值税率	出口退税	计量单位	监管条件	Article Description
2837.1990 12	氰化镍、氰化钙(氰化亚镍)	5.5	30	17		千克	X	Nickel cyanide, calcium cyanide (Nickelous cygnide)
2837.1990 13	氰化钡、氰化镉、氰化铅	5.5	30	17		千克	X	Barium cyanide, cadmium cyanide, lead cyanide
2837.1990 14	氰化钴[氰化钴(Ⅱ)、氰化钴(Ⅲ)]	5.5	30	17		千克	X	Cobalt cyanide [Cobalt cyanide (Co(CN)3), Cobalt cyanide (Co(CN)2)]
2837.1990 90	其他氰化物及氧氰化物	5.5	30	17		千克		Other cyanides and cyanide oxides
2837.2000	-氰络合物	5.5	30	17		千克		-Complex cyanides
2837.2000 11	氰化镍钾、氰化钠铜锌(氰化钾镍、镍氰化钾、铜盐)	5.5	30	17		千克	X	Potassium nickel cyanide, sodium coopper-zinc cyanide (nickel potassium cyanide, nantokite)
2837.2000 12	氰化亚铜(三)钠、氰化亚铜(三)钾(紫铜盐、紫铜矾、氰化铜钠、氰化亚铜钾、亚铜氰化钾)	5.5	30	17		千克	X	Cuprous cyanide (c) sodium, cuprous cyanide (c) potassium (copper salt, copper alum, sodium cyanide copper, cuprous potassium cyanide, cuprous potassium cyanide)
2837.2000 90	其他氰络合物	5.5	30	17		千克		Other complex cyanide
28.39	**硅酸盐;商品碱金属硅酸盐:**							**Silicates; commercial alkali metal silicates:**
	-钠盐:							-Of sodium:
2839.1100	--偏硅酸钠	5.5	40	17		千克		--Sodium metasilicates
	--其他:							--Other:
2839.1910	---硅酸钠	5.5	30	17		千克	A	---Sodium silicate
2839.1990	---其他钠盐	5.5	30	17		千克		---Other Sodium salts
2839.9000	-其他		30	17		千克		-Other
2839.9000暂 01	锆的硅酸盐	2	30	17		千克		Zirconium silicate
2839.9000 10	硅酸铅	5.5	30	17		千克	X	lead silicate
2839.9000 90	其他硅酸盐;商品碱金属硅酸盐	5.5	30	17		千克		Other silicate, commercial alkali metal silicates
28.40	**硼酸盐及过硼酸盐:**							**Borates; peroxoborates (perborates):**
	-四硼酸钠(精炼硼砂):							-Disodium tetraborate (refined borax):
2840.1100暂	--无水四硼酸钠	2	20	17		千克		--Anhydrous
2840.1900暂	--其他	2	20	17		千克		--Other
2840.2000	-其他硼酸盐	5.5	30	17		千克		-Other borates
2840.2000 10	硼酸锌	5.5	30	17		千克	S	zinc borate
2840.2000 90	其他硼酸盐	5.5	30	17		千克		Other borate
2840.3000	-过硼酸盐	5.5	30	17		千克		-Peroxoborates (perborates)
28.41	**金属酸盐及过金属酸盐:**							**Salts of oxometallic or peroxometallic acids:**
2841.3000	-重铬酸钠	5.5	20	17		千克	AB	-Sodium dichromate
2841.5000	-其他铬酸盐及重铬酸盐;过铬酸盐	5.5	30	17		千克		-Other chromates and dichromates; peroxochromates
	-亚锰酸盐、锰酸盐及高锰酸盐:							-Manganites, manganates and permanganates:
2841.6100	--高锰酸钾	5.5	30	17		千克	23AB	--Potassium permanganate
	--其他:							--Other:
2841.6910	---锰酸锂	5.5	30	17		千克		---Lithium manganate
2841.6990	---其他	5.5	30	17		千克		---Other
	-钼酸盐:							-Molybdates:
2841.7010	---钼酸铵	5.5	30	17		千克	4xy	---Ammonium molybdates
2841.7090	---其他	5.5	30	17		千克	4xy	---Other
	-钨酸盐:							-Tungstates (wolframates):
2841.8010	---仲钨酸铵	5.5	30	17		千克	4xy	---Ammonium paratungstate
2841.8020	---钨酸钠	5.5	30	17		千克	4xy	---Sodium tungstate
2841.8030	---钨酸钙	5.5	30	17		千克	4xy	---Calcium wolframate
2841.8040	---偏钨酸铵	5.5	30	17		千克	4xy	---Ammonium metatungstate
2841.8090	---其他	5.5	30	17		千克		---Other
2841.9000	-其他		30	17		千克		-Other
2841.9000暂 10	钴酸锂	2	30	17	13	千克		Lithium cobaltate
2841.9000暂 20	铼酸盐	0	30	17		千克		Rhenate
2841.9000 90	其他金属酸盐及过金属酸盐	5.5	30	17		千克		Other salts of oxometallic or peroxometallic acids
28.42	**其他无机酸盐及过氧酸盐(包括不论是否已有化学定义的硅铝酸盐),但迭氮化物除外:**							**Other salts of inorganic acids or peroxoacids (including aluminosilicates whether or not chemically defined), other than azides:**

税则号列	货品名称	最惠(%)	普通	增值税率	出口退税	计量单位	监管条件	Article Description
2842.1000	-硅酸复盐及硅酸络盐(包括不论是否已有化学定义的硅铝酸盐)	5.5	30	17		千克	AB	-Double or complex silicates, including aluminosilicates whether or not chemically defined
	-其他:							-Other:
	---雷酸盐、氰酸盐及硫氰酸盐:							---Fulminates, cyanates and thiocyanates:
2842.9011	----硫氰酸钠	5.5	30	17		千克	A	----Sodium sulfocyanate
2842.9019	----其他	5.5	30	17		千克		----Other
2842.9019 10	其他硫氰酸盐	5.5	30	17		千克	AB	Other thiocyanates
2842.9019 90	雷酸盐及氰酸盐	5.5	30	17		千克		Fulminates and cyanates
2842.9020	---碲化镉	5.5	30	17		千克	X	---Cadmium telluride
2842.9030	---锂镍钴锰氧化物	5.5	30	17		千克	AB	---Lithium nickel cobalt manganese oxides
2842.9040	---磷酸铁锂	5.5	30	17		千克	A	---Lithium iron phosphate
2842.9050	---硒酸盐及亚硒酸盐	5.5	30	17		千克	AB	---Colloidal selenium and selenite
2842.9090	---其他	5.5	30	17		千克		---Other
2842.9090 13	亚砷酸钠、亚砷酸钾、亚砷酸钙(偏亚砷酸钠)	5.5	30	17		千克	X	Sodium arsenite, potassium arsenite, calcium arsenite
2842.9090 14	亚砷酸锶、亚砷酸钡、亚砷酸铁	5.5	30	17		千克	X	Strontium arsenite, barium arsenite, Arsenous acid
2842.9090 15	亚砷酸铜、亚砷酸锌、亚砷酸铅(亚砷酸氢铜)	5.5	30	17		千克	X	Copper arsonate, arsenen ous acrd, lead arsenite
2842.9090 16	亚砷酸锑、砷酸铵、砷酸氢二铵	5.5	30	17		千克	X	Antimony arsenite, ammonium arsenate, diammonium hydrogen arsenate
2842.9090 17	砷酸钠、砷酸氢二钠、砷酸二氢钠(砷酸三钠)	5.5	30	17		千克	X	Sodium arsenate, sodium arsenate dibasic, sodium arsenate monobasic
2842.9090 18	砷酸钾、砷酸二氢钾、砷酸镁	5.5	30	17		千克	X	Potassium arsenate, potassium dihyrogwn arsenate, magnesium arsenate
2842.9090 19	砷酸钙、砷酸钡、砷酸铁(砷酸三钙)	5.5	30	17		千克	X	Calcium arsenate, barium arsenate, ferric arsenate (tricalcium arsenate)
2842.9090 21	砷酸亚铁、砷酸铜、砷酸锌	5.5	30	17		千克	X	Ferrous arsenate, cupric arsenate, zinc arsenate
2842.9090 22	砷酸铅、砷酸锑、偏砷酸钠	5.5	30	17		千克	X	Lead arsenate, antimony arsenate, sodium metaarsenate
2842.9090 23	硒化铅、硒化镉	5.5	30	17		千克	X	Lead selenide, cadmium selenide
2842.9090 90	其他无机酸盐及过氧酸盐(迭氮化物除外)	5.5	30	17		千克	AB	Other salts of inorganic acids or peroxoacids
	第六分章　杂项产品							Ⅵ. -MISCELLANEOUS
28.43	**胶态贵金属;贵金属的无机或有机化合物,不论是否已有化学定义;贵金属汞齐:**							**Colloidal precious metals; inorganic or organic compounds of precious metals, whether or not chemically defined; amalgams of precious metals:**
2843.1000	-胶态贵金属	5.5	30	17		克		-Colloidal precious metals
	-银化合物:							-Silver compounds:
2843.2100	--硝酸银	5.5	30	17		克	AB	--Silver nitrate
2843.2900	--其他	5.5	30	17		克		--Other
2843.2900 10	氰化银、氰化银钾、亚砷酸银(银氰化钾、砷酸银)	5.5	30	17		克	X	Silver cyanide, potassium arsentocyanide, silverarsenite (potassium silver(I) cyanide, slilver arsenate)
2843.2900 90	其他银化合物(不论是否已有化学定义)	5.5	30	17		克		Other silver compounds (whether or not chemically defined)
2843.3000	-金化合物	5.5	30	17		克		-Gold compounds
2843.3000 10	氰化金、氰化金钾(含金40%)等(包括氰化亚金(Ⅰ)钾(含金68.3%)、氰化亚金(Ⅲ)钾(含金57%))	5.5	30	17		克	JX	Gold cyanide, potassium cyanide gold (gold content 40%) (containing 40% of gold) (including subcyanide gold (Ⅰ) (gold content 68.3%) postassium subcyanide gold (Ⅲ) (gold content 57%))
2843.3000 90	其他金化合物(不论是否已有化学定义)	5.5	30	17		克	J	Other gold compounds (whether or not chemically defined)
2843.9000	-其他贵金属化合物;贵金属汞齐	5.5	30	17		克		-Other compounds; amalgams
2843.9000 10	氯化钯	5.5	30	17		克	G	Palladium chloride
2843.9000 20	氯化铂	5.5	30	17		克	4xy	Platinum chloride
2843.9000 30	其他铂化合物	5.5	30	17		克	4xy	Other platinum compounds
2843.9000 90	其他贵金属化合物,贵金属汞齐(不论是否已有化学定义)	5.5	30	17		克	4xy	Other precious metal compounds or precious amalgam (whether chemical definition exists or not)

税则号列	货品名称	最惠(%)	普通	增值税率	出口退税	计量单位	监管条件	Article Description
28.44	**放射性化学元素及放射性同位素(包括可裂变或可转换的化学元素及同位素)及其化合物;含上述产品的混合物及残渣:**							**Radioactive chemical elements and radioactive isotopes (including the fissile or fertile chemical elements and isotopes) and their compounds; mixtures and residues containing these products:**
2844.1000	-天然铀及其化合物;含天然铀或天然铀化合物的合金、分散体(包括金属陶瓷)、陶瓷产品及混合物	5.5	30	17		克/百万贝可	23	-Natural uranium and its compounds; alloys, dispersions (including cermets), ceramic products and mixtures containing natural uranium or natural uranium compounds
2844.2000	-U235浓缩铀及其化合物;钚及其化合物;含U235浓缩铀、钚或它们的化合物的合金、分散体(包括金属陶瓷)、陶瓷产品及混合物	5.5	30	17		克/百万贝可	23	-Uranium enriched in U235 and its compounds; plutonium and its compounds; alloys dispersion (including cermets), ceramic products and mixtures containing uranium enriched in U235, plutonium or compounds of these products
2844.3000	-U235贫化铀及其化合物;钍及其化合物;含U235贫化铀、钍或它们的化合物的合金、分散体(包括金属陶瓷)、陶瓷产品及混合物	5.5	30	17		克/百万贝可	23	-Uranium depleted in U235and its compounds; thorium and its compounds; alloys, dispersions (including cermets), ceramic products and mixtures containing uranium depleted in U235, thorium or compounds of these products
	-除子目2844.10、2844.20及2844.30以外的放射性元素、同位素及其化合物;含这些元素、同位素及其化合物的合金、分散体(包括金属陶瓷)、陶瓷产品及混合物:							-Radioactive elements and isotopes and compounds other than those of subheading No. 2844.10,2844.20 or 2844.30; alloys, dispersions (including cermets), ceramic products and mixtures containing these elements, isotopes or compounds; radioactive residues:
2844.4010	---镭及镭盐	4	14	17		克/百万贝可		---Radium and its salts
2844.4010 10	镭-226及其化合物、混合物(两用物项管制商品)	4	14	17		克/百万贝可	23	Radium-226 and its compounds
2844.4010 90	其他镭及镭盐	4	14	17		克/百万贝可	2	Other radium and its salts
2844.4020	---钴及钴盐	4	14	17		克/百万贝可	2	---Cobalt and its salts
2844.4090	---其他	5.5	30	17		克/百万贝可		---Other
2844.4090 10	铀-233及其化合物(包括呈金属、合金、化合物或浓缩物形态的各种材料)	5.5	30	17		克/百万贝可	23	Uranium-233 and its compounds (including metallic material, alloys, compounds or enriched materials)
2844.4090 20	氚、氚化物和氚的混合物,以及含有上述任何一种物质的产品(氚-氢原子比超过千分之一的,不包括含氚(任何形态)量小于1.48×10^3GBq的产品)	5.5	30	17		克/百万贝可	23	"Tritium, tritiated compound , tritium mixture and Containing any of the foregoing a material product"
2844.4090 30	氦-3(3He)、含有氦-3的混合物(不包括氦-3的含量<1g的产品)	5.5	30	17		克/百万贝可	3	"3He, containing 3He mixture"
2844.4090 40	发射α粒子,其α半衰期为10天或更长但小于200年的放射性核素(1. 单质;2. 含有α总活度为37GBq/kg或更大的任何这类放射性核素的化合物;3. 含有α总活度为37GBq/kg或更大的任何这类放射性核素的混合物;4. 含有任何上述物质的产品,不包括所含α活度小于3.7GBq的产品)	5.5	30	17		克/百万贝可	23	Emission of alpha particles, the alpha half - life of 10 days or more but less than 200 years of radionuclides(1. single matter; 2. Containing a total activity of 37GBq / kg or greater in any of these types of radioactive compounds; 3. Containing a total activity of 37GBq / kg or greater in any of these types of radioactive mixture; 4. Containing any of the above substances in products, not including the alpha activity less than 3.7GBq products)
2844.4090 90	其他放射性元素、同位素及其化合物(编号284410,284420,284430以外的放射性元素、同位素)	5.5	30	17		克/百万贝可	2	Other radioactive elements and isotopes and their compounds (radioactive elements and isotopes other than those of subheading No. 2844.10, 2844.20 or 2844.30)
2844.5000	-核反应堆已耗尽(已辐照)的燃料元件(释热元件)	5.5	30	17		克		-Spent (irradiated) fuel elements (cartridges) of nuclear reactors
28.45	**税目28.44以外的同位素;这些同位素的无机或有机化合物,不论是否已有化学定义:**							**Isotopes other than those of heading No. 28.44; compounds, inorganic or organic, of such isotopes, whether or not chemically defined:**
2845.1000	-重水(氧化氘)	5.5	30	17		克	3	-Heavy water (deuterium oxide)

税则号列	货品名称	最惠(%)	普通	增值税率	出口退税	计量单位	监管条件	Article Description
2845.9000	-其他	5.5	30	17		克		-Other
2845.9000 10	除重水外的氘及氘化物	5.5	30	17		克	3	Deuterium and deuterides, other than heavy water
2845.9000 20	硼-10同位素及其化合物、混合物(硼-10同位素占硼总量>20%的硼及其化合物、混合物)	5.5	30	17		克	3	Boron-10 and its compounds (boron and its compounds and mixtures with a containing of boron-10 > 20% of the total boron content)
2845.9000 30	富集锂-6同位素及其化合物,混合物[富集锂-6同位素指锂-6同位素富集度>7.5%(按原子数计)]	5.5	30	17		克	3	Lithium enriched in lithium-6 and its compounds and mixtures (lithium enriched in lithium-6 refers to enrichment of lithium-6 isotope > 7.5% (atomicity))
2845.9000 90	其他同位素及其他化合物(编号2844以外的同位素)	5.5	30	17		克		Other isotopes and other compounds (other than isotopes of heading No. 28.44)
28.46	**稀土金属、钇、钪及其混合物的无机或有机化合物:**							**Compounds, inorganic or organic, of rareearth metals, of yttrium or of scandium or of mixtures of these metals:**
	-铈的化合物:							-Ceric compounds:
2846.1010[暂]	---氧化铈	0	30	17		千克	4Bxy	---Cerium oxide
2846.1020[暂]	---氢氧化铈	0	30	17		千克	4Bxy	---Cerium hydroxide
2846.1030[暂]	---碳酸铈	0	30	17		千克	4Bxy	---Cerium carbonate
2846.1090[暂]	---其他	0	30	17		千克		---Other
2846.1090[暂] 10	氰化铈	0	30	17		千克	4BXxy	Cerium cyanide
2846.1090[暂] 90	铈的其他化合物	0	30	17		千克	4Bxy	Other cerium compounds with
	-其他:							-Other:
	---氧化稀土(氧化铈除外):							---Rare-earth oxides (other than cerium oxide):
2846.9011[暂]	----氧化钇	0	30	17		千克	4xBy	----Yttrium oxide
2846.9012[暂]	----氧化镧	0	30	17		千克	4Bxy	----Lanthanum oxide
2846.9013[暂]	----氧化钕	0	30	17		千克	4Bxy	----Neodymium oxide
2846.9014[暂]	----氧化铕	0	30	17		千克	4Bxy	----Europium oxide
2846.9015[暂]	----氧化镝	0	30	17		千克	4Bxy	----Dysprosium oxide
2846.9016[暂]	----氧化铽	0	30	17		千克	4Bxy	----Terbium oxide
2846.9017[暂]	----氧化镨	0	30	17		千克	4Bxy	----Praseodymium oxide
2846.9019[暂]	----其他	0	30	17		千克		----Other
2846.9019[暂] 20	氧化铒	0	30	17		千克	4Bxy	Erbium oxide
2846.9019[暂] 30	氧化钆	0	30	17		千克	4Bxy	Gadolinium oxide
2846.9019[暂] 40	氧化钐	0	30	17		千克	4Bxy	Samarium oxide
2846.9019[暂] 70	氧化镱	0	30	17		千克	4Bxy	Ytterbium oxide
2846.9019[暂] 80	氧化钪	0	30	17		千克	4Bxy	Scandium oxide
2846.9019[暂] 91	灯用红粉	0	30	17		千克	4Bxy	Red powder for lumination
2846.9019[暂] 92	按重量计中重稀土总含量≥30%的其他氧化稀土(灯用红粉、氧化铈除外)	0	30	17		千克	4Bxy	Other rare-earth oxide, containing by weihgt ≥30% of middle heavy rare-earth (other than red powder for lumination, cerium cyanide)
2846.9019[暂] 99	其他氧化稀土(灯用红粉、氧化铈除外)	0	30	17		千克	4Bxy	Other rare - earth oxide (other than red powder for lumination, cerium cyanide)
	---氯化稀土:							---Rare-earth chlorides:
2846.9021[暂]	----氯化铽	0	30	17		千克	4Bxy	----Terbium chlorinates
2846.9022[暂]	----氯化镝	0	30	17		千克	4Bxy	----Dysprosium chlorinates
2846.9023[暂]	----氯化镧	0	30	17		千克	4Bxy	----Lan thanum chloride
2846.9024[暂]	----氯化钕	0	30	17		千克	4Bxy	----Neodymium chlorinates
2846.9025[暂]	----氯化镨	0	30	17		千克	4Bxy	----Praseodymium chlorinates
2846.9026[暂]	----氯化钇	0	30	17		千克	4Bxy	----Yttrium chlorinates
2846.9028[暂]	----混合氯化稀土	0	30	17		千克		----Mixture of rareearth chlorides
2846.9028[暂] 10	按重量计中重稀土总含量≥30%的混合氯化稀土	0	30	17		千克	4Bxy	Other mixed rare - earth chlorides, containing by weihgt ≥30% of middle heavy rare - earth,
2846.9028[暂] 90	其他混合氯化稀土	0	30	17		千克	4Bxy	Other rare-earth chlorides
2846.9029[暂]	----其他	0	30	17		千克	4Bxy	----Other
	---氟化稀土:							---Rare-earth fluorides:
2846.9031[暂]	----氟化铽	0	30	17		千克	4Bxy	----Terbium fluoride
2846.9032[暂]	----氟化镝	0	30	17		千克	4Bxy	----Dysprosium fluoride
2846.9033[暂]	----氟化镧	0	30	17		千克	4Bxy	----Lanthanum fluoride
2846.9034[暂]	----氟化钕	0	30	17		千克	4Bxy	----Neodymium fluoride
2846.9035[暂]	----氟化镨	0	30	17		千克	4Bxy	----Praseodymium fluoride
2846.9036[暂]	----氟化钇	0	30	17		千克	4Bxy	----Yttrium fluoride

税则号列	货品名称	最惠(%)	普通	增值税率	出口退税	计量单位	监管条件	Article Description
2846.9039[暂]	----其他	0	30	17		千克	4Bxy	----Other
	---氟化稀土:							---Rare-earth carbonate:
2846.9041[暂]	----碳酸镧	0	30	17		千克	4Bxy	----Lanthanum carbonates
2846.9042[暂]	----碳酸铽	0	30	17		千克	4Bxy	----Terbium carbonates
2846.9043[暂]	----碳酸镝	0	30	17		千克	4Bxy	----Dysprosium carbonates
2846.9044[暂]	----碳酸钕	0	30	17		千克	4Bxy	----Neodymium carbonates
2846.9045[暂]	----碳酸镨	0	30	17		千克	4Bxy	----Praseodymium carbonates
2846.9046[暂]	----碳酸钇	0	30	17		千克	4Bxy	----Yttrium carbonates
2846.9048[暂]	----混合碳酸稀土	0	30	17		千克		----Mixture of rare earth carbonate
2846.9048[暂] 10	按重量计中重稀土总含量≥30%的混合碳酸稀土	0	30	17		千克	4Bxy	Other mixed rare - earth carbonates, containing by weihgt ≥30% of middle heavy rare - earth,
2846.9048[暂] 90	其他混合碳酸稀土	0	30	17		千克	4Bxy	Other mixed rare - earth carbonates
2846.9049[暂]	----其他	0	30	17		千克	4Bxy	----Other
	---其他							---Other:
2846.9091[暂]	----镧的其他化合物	0	30	17		千克	4Bxy	----Other compounds ,of lanthanum
2846.9092[暂]	----钕的其他化合物	0	30	17		千克	4Bxy	----Other compounds ,of lanthanum
2846.9093[暂]	----铽的其他化合物	0	30	17		千克	4Bxy	----Other compounds ,of neodymium
2846.9094[暂]	----镝的其他化合物	0	30	17		千克	4Bxy	----Other compounds ,of dysprosium
2846.9095[暂]	----镨的其他化合物	0	30	17		千克	4Bxy	----Other compounds ,of praseodymium
2846.9096[暂]	----钇的其他化合物	0	30	17		千克	4Bxy	----Other compounds ,of yttrium
2846.9096[暂] 01	LED用荧光粉(成分含钇的其他化合物)	0	30	17		千克	B	LED phosphor (Other compounds containing yttrium)
2846.9096[暂] 90	钇的其他化合物	0	30	17		千克	4Bxy	Other compounds containing yttrium
2846.9099[暂]	----其他	0	30	17		千克		----Other
2846.9099 01	LED用荧光粉(成分含稀土金属、钪的其他化合物,铈的化合物除外)	5.5	30	17		千克	B	LED phosphor (other compounds containing rare earth metals, scandium, except for cerium compounds)
2846.9099[暂] 10	按重量计中重稀土总含量≥30%的稀土金属、钪的其他化合物(铈的化合物除外)	0	30	17		千克	4Bxy	Other rare-earth metals, other compounds of scandium ,containing by weihgt ≥30% of middle heavy rare-earth,
2846.9099[暂] 90	其他稀土金属、钪的其他化合物(铈的化合物除外)	0	30	17		千克	4Bxy	Other rare-earth metals, compounds of scandium
28.47	**过氧化氢,不论是否用尿素固化:**							**Hydrogen peroxide, whether or not solidified with urea:**
2847.0000	过氧化氢,不论是否用尿素固化	5.5	30	17		千克	AB	Hydrogen peroxide, whether or not solidified with urea
28.48	**磷化物,不论是否已有化学定义,但不包括磷铁:**							**Phosphides, whether or not chemically defined, excluding ferrophosphorus:**
2848.0000	磷化物,不论是否已有化学定义,但不包括磷铁	5.5	20	17		千克		Phosphides, whether or not chemically defined, excluding ferrophophorus
2848.0000 10	磷化铝,磷化锌	5.5	20	17		千克	S	Aluminum phosphide, zinc phosphide
2848.0000 90	其他磷化物(不论是否已有化学定义,但不包括磷铁)	5.5	20	17		千克		Other phosphides (whether or not chemically defined, excluding ferrophosphorus)
28.49	**碳化物,不论是否已有化学定义:**							**Carbides, whether or not chemically defined:**
2849.1000	-碳化钙	5.5	45	17		千克	AB	-Of calcium
2849.2000	-碳化硅	5.5	30	17		千克	4xy	-Of silicon
	-其他:							-Other:
2849.9010	---碳化硼	5.5	30	17		千克		---Of boron
2849.9020	---碳化钨	5.5	30	17		千克	4xy	---Of tungsten
2849.9090	---其他	5.5	30	17		千克		---Other
28.50	**氢化物、氮化物、叠氮化物、硅化物及硼化物,不论是否已有化学定义,但可归入税目28.49的碳化物除外:**							**Hydrides, nitrides, azides, silicides and borides, whether or not chemically defined, other than compounds which are also carbides of heading No. 28.49:**
	---氮化物:							---Nitride:
2850.0011	----氮化锰	5.5	30	17		千克		----Manganese nitride
2850.0012	----氮化硼	5.5	30	17		千克		----Boron Nitride
2850.0019	----其他	5.5	30	17		千克		----Other
2850.0090	---其他	5.5	30	17		千克		---Other
2850.0090 10	砷化氢(砷烷、砷化三氢、胂)	5.5	30	17		千克	X	Arsenic hydride(arsine, hydride; arsine)

税则号列	货品名称	最惠(%)	普通	增值税率	出口退税	计量单位	监管条件	Article Description
2850.0090 90	其他氢化物、硅化物等(包括硼化物、可归入编号2849的碳化物除外)	5.5	30	17		千克		Other hydrides, silicides (including borides, other than compounds which qre also carbides of heading No. 28.49)
28.52	**汞的无机或有机化合物,不论是否已有化学定义,汞齐除外:**							**Compounds, inorganic or organic, of mercury, whether or not chemically defined, excluding amalgams:**
2852.1000	-已有化学定义的	5.5	30	17		千克	X	-Chemically defined
2852.9000	-其他	5.5	30	17		千克	X	-Other
28.53	**其他无机化合物(包括蒸馏水、导电水及类似的纯净水);液态空气(不论是否除去稀有气体);压缩空气;汞齐,但贵金属汞齐除外:**							**Other inorganic compounds (including distilled or conductivity water and water of similar purity); liquid air (whether or not rare gases have been removed); compressed air; amalgams, other than amalgams of precious metals:**
2853.0010	---饮用蒸馏水	5.5	70	17		千克	AB	---Distilled water for human consumption
2853.0020	---氯化氰	5.5	30	17		千克	23	---Chlorocyanogen, cyanogen chloride
2853.0030	---镍钴锰氢氧化物	6.5	30	17		千克		---Nickel cobalt manganese composite hydroxide
2853.0090	---其他	5.5	30	17		千克		---Other
2853.0090 10	饮用纯净水	5.5	30	17		千克	AB	Purified water for human consumption
2853.0090 21	氰、氰化碘、氰化溴、铅汞齐等(包括氰气、碘化氰、溴化氰)	5.5	30	17		千克	X	Cyanogen, cyanogen iodide, bromine cyanide, lead amalgam (including cyanogen dicyanogen, iodine cyanide, bromine cyanide)
2853.0090 22	砷化锌,砷化镓	5.5	30	17		千克	X	Zinc arsenide, gallium arsenide
2853.0090 30	单氰胺	5.5	30	17		千克		monocyanamide
2853.0090 90	其他无机化合物、压缩空气等(包括导电水、液态空气、汞齐等,贵金属汞齐除外)	5.5	30	17		千克		Other inorganic compounds, compressed air (including conductivity water, liquid air, amalgams, other than amalgams of precious metals)

第二十九章
有机化学品

注释：

一、除条文另有规定的以外，本章各税目只适用于：

（一）单独的已有化学定义的有机化合物，不论是否含有杂质；

（二）同一有机化合物的两种或两种以上异构体的混合物（不论是否含有杂质），但无环烃异构体的混合物（立体异构体除外），不论是否饱和，应归入第二十七章；

（三）税目29.36至29.39的产品，税目29.40的糖醚、糖缩醛、糖酯及其盐类和税目29.41的产品，不论是否已有化学定义；

（四）上述（一）、（二）、（三）款产品的水溶液；

（五）溶于其他溶剂的上述（一）、（二）、（三）款的产品，但该产品处于溶液状态只是为了安全或运输所采取的正常必要方法，其所用溶剂并不使该产品改变其一般用途而适合于某些特殊用途；

（六）为了保存或运输的需要，加入稳定剂（包括抗结块剂）的上述（一）、（二）、（三）、（四）、（五）各款产品；

（七）为了便于识别或安全起见，加入抗尘剂、着色剂或气味剂的上述（一）、（二）、（三）、（四）、（五）、（六）各款产品，但所加剂料并不使原产品改变其一般用途而适合于某些特殊用途；

（八）为生产偶氮染料而稀释至标准浓度的下列产品：重氮盐，用于重氮盐、可重氮化的胺及其盐类的耦合剂。

二、本章不包括：

（一）税目15.04的货品及税目15.20的粗甘油；

（二）乙醇（税目22.07或22.08）；

（三）甲烷及丙烷（税目27.11）；

（四）第二十八章注释二所述的碳化合物；

（五）税目30.02的免疫制品。

（六）尿素（税目31.02或31.05）；

（七）植物性或动物性着色料（税目32.03）、合成有机着色料、用作萤光增白剂或发光体的合成有机产品（税目32.04）及零售包装的染料或其他着色料（税目32.12）；

（八）酶（税目35.07）；

（九）聚乙醛、环六亚甲基四胺（乌洛托品）及类似物质，制成片、条或类似形状作为燃料用的，以及包装容器的容积不超过300立方厘米的直接灌注香烟打火机及类似打火器用的液体燃料或液化气体燃料（税目36.06）；

（十）灭火器的装配药及已装药的灭火弹（税目38.13）；零售包装的除墨剂（税目38.24）；

（十一）光学元件，例如用酒石酸乙二胺制成的（税目90.01）。

三、可以归入本章两个或两个以上税目的货品，应归入有关税目中的最后一个税目。

Chapter 29
Organic chemicals

Notes:

1. Except where the context otherwise requires, the headings of this Chapter apply only to:

(a) Separate chemically defined organic compounds, whether or not containing impurities;

(b) Mixtures of two or more isomers of the same organic compound (whether or not containing impurities), except mixtures of acyclic hydrocarbon isomers (other than stereoisomers), whether or not saturated (Chapter 27);

(c) The products of headings No 29.36 to 29.39 or the sugar ethers, sugar acetals and sugar esters, and their salts, of heading No. 29.40, or the products of heading No. 29.41, whether or not chemically defined;

(d) The products mentioned in (a), (b) or (c) above dissolved in water;

(e) The products mentioned in (a), (b) or (c) above dissolved in other slovents provided that the solution constitutes a normal and necessary method of putting up these products adopted solely for reasons of safety or for transport and that the solvent does not render the product particularly suitable for specific use rather than for general use;

(f) The products mentioned in (a), (b), (c), (d) or (e) above with an added stabilizer (including an anti-caking agent) necessary for their preservation or transport;

(g) The products mentioned in (a), (b), (c), (d), (e) or (f) above with an added anti-dusting agent or a colouring or odoriferous substance added to facilitate their identification or for safety reasons, provided that the additions do not render the product particularly suitable for specific use rather than for general use;

(h) The following products, diluted to standard strengths, for the production of azo dyes: diazonium salts, couplers used for these salts and diazotisable amines and their salts.

2. This Chapter does not cover:

(a) Goods of heading No. 15.04 or crude glycerol of heading No. 15.20;

(b) Ethyl alcohol (heading No. 22.07 or 22.08);

(c) Methane or propane (headng No. 27.11);

(d) The compounds of carbon mentioned in Note 2 to Chapter 28;

(e) Immunological products of heading No. 30.02

(f) Urea (heading No. 31.02 or 31.05);

(g) Colouring matter of vegetable or animal origin (heading No. 32.03), synthetic organic colouring matter, synthetic organic products of a kind used as fluorescent brightening agents or as luminophores (heading No. 32.04) or dyes or other colouring matter put up in forms or packings for retail sale (heading No. 32.12);

(h) Enzymes (heading No. 35.07);

(i) Metaldehyde, hexamethylenetetramine or similar substances, put up in forms (for example, tablets, sticks or similar forms) for use as fuels, or liquid or liquefied-gas fuels in containers of a kind used for filling or refilling cigarette or similar lighters and of a capacity not exceeding 300 cm^3 (heading No. 36.06);

(j) Products put up as charges for fire-extinguishers or put up in fire-extinguishing grenades, of heading No. 38.13; ink removers put up in packings for retail sale, of heading No. 38.24; or

(k) Optical elements, for example, of ethylenediamine tartrate (heading No. 90.01)

3. Goods which could be included in two or more of the headings of this Chapter are to be classified in that one of those headings which occurs last in numerical order.

四、税目 29.04 至 29.06、29.08 至 29.11 及 29.13 至 29.20 的卤化、磺化、硝化或亚硝化衍生物均包括复合衍生物，例如，卤磺化、卤硝化、磺硝化及卤磺硝化衍生物。

硝基及亚硝基不作为税目 29.29 的含氮基官能团。

税目 29.11、29.12、29.14、29.18 及 29.22 所称"含氧基"，仅限于税目 29.05 至 29.20 的各种含氧基（其特征为有机含氧基）。

五、（一）本章第一分章至第七分章的酸基有机化合物与这些分章的有机化合物构成的酯，应归入有关税号中的最后一个税号。

（二）乙醇与本章第一分章至第七分章的酸基有机化合物所构成的酯，应按有关酸基化合物归类。

（三）除第六类注释一及第二十八章注释二另有规定的以外。

1. 第一分章至第十分章及税目 29.42 的有机化合物的无机盐，例如，含酸基、酚基或烯醇基的化合物及有机碱的无机盐，应归入相应的有机化合物的税目；

2. 第一分章至第十分章及税目 29.42 的有机化合物之间生成的盐，应按生成该盐的碱或酸（包括酚基或烯醇基化合物）归入本章有关税目中的最后一个税目；

3. 除第十一分章或税目 29.41 的产品外，配位化合物应按该化合物所有金属键（金属-碳键除外）"断开"所形成的片段归入第二十九章有关税目中的最后一个税目。

（四）除乙醇外，金属醇化物应按相应的醇归类（税目 29.05）。

（五）羧酸酰卤化物应按相应的酸归类。

六、税目 29.30 及 29.31 的化合物是指有机化合物，其分子中除含氢、氧或氮原子外，还含有与碳原子直接连接的其他非金属或金属原子（例如，硫、砷或铅）。

税目 29.30（有机硫化合物）及税目 29.31（其他有机-无机化合物）不包括某些磺化或卤化衍生物（含复合衍生物）。这些衍生物分子中除氢、氧、氮之外，只有具有磺化或卤化衍生物（或复合衍生物）性质的硫原子或卤素原子与碳原子直接连接。

七、税目 29.32、29.33 及 29.34 不包括三节环环氧化物、过氧化酮、醛或硫醛的环聚合物、多元羧酸酐、多元醇或酚与多元酸构成的环酯及多元酸酰亚胺。

本条规定只适用于由本条所列环化功能形成环内杂原子的化合物。

八、税目 29.37 所称：

（一）"激素"包括激素释放因子、激素刺激和释放因子、激素抑制剂以及激素抗体；

（二）"主要起激素作用的"，不仅适用于激素衍生物以及主要起激素作用的结构类似物，也适用于在本税目所列产品合成过程中主要用作中间体的激素衍生物及结构类似物。

4. In headings No. 29.04 to 29.06, 29.08 to 29.11 and 29.13 to 29.20, any reference to halogenated, sulphonated, nitrated or nitrosated derivatives includes a reference to compound derivatives, such as sulphohalogenated, nitrohalogenated, nitrosulphonated or nitrosulphohalogenated derivatives.

Nitro or nitroso groups are not to be taken a "nitrogen-functions" for the purpose of heading No. 29.29.

For the purposes of headings No. 29.11, 29.12, 29.14, 29.18 and 29.22, "oxygen-function" is to be restricted to the functions (the characteristic organic oxygen-containing groups) referred to in headings No. 29.05 to 29.20.

5. (a) The esters of acid-function organic compounds of sub-Chapters Ⅰ to Ⅶ with organic compounds of these sub-Chapters are to be classified with that compound which is classified in the heading which occurs last in numerical order in these sub-Chapters.

(b) Esters of ethyl alcohol with acid-function organic compounds of sub-Chapters Ⅰ to Ⅶ are to be classified in the same heading as the corresponding acid-function compounds.

(c) Subject to Note 1 to Section Ⅵ and Note 2 to Chapter 28:

(1) Inorganic salts of organic compounds such as acid, phenol or enol-function compounds or organic bases, of sub-Chapters Ⅰ to Ⅹ or heading No. 29.42, are to be classified in the heading appropriate to the organic compound;

(2) Salts formed between organic compounds of sub-Chapters Ⅰ to Ⅹ or heading No. 29.42 are to be classified in the heading appropriate to the base or to the acid (including phenol or enol-function compounds) from which they are formed, whichever occurs last in numerical order in the Chapter;

(3) Co-ordination compounds, other than products classifiable in sub-Chapter Ⅺ or heading 29.41, are to be classified in the heading which occurs last in numberical order in chapter 29. among those appropriate to the fragments formed by "cleaving" of all metal bonds, other than metal carbon bonds.

(d) Metal alcoholates are to be classified in the same heading as the corresponding alcohols except in the case of ethanol (heading No. 29.05).

(e) Halides of carboxylic acids are to be classified in the same heading as the corresponding acids.

6. The compounds of headings No. 29.30 and 29.31 are organic compounds the molecules of which contain, in addition to atoms of hydrogen, oxygen or nitrogen, atoms of other non-metals or of metals (such assulphur, arsenic or lead) directly linked to carbon atoms.

Heading No. 29.30 (organo-sulphur compounds) and heading No. 29.31 (other organo-inorganic compounds) do not include sulphonated or halogenated derivatives (including compound derivatives) which, apart from hydrogen, oxygen and nitrogen, only have directly linked to carbon the atoms of sulphur or of a halogen which give them their nature of sulphonated or halogenated derivatives (or compound derivatives).

7. Headings No. 29.32, 29.33 and 29.34 do not include epoxides with a three-membered ring, ketone peroxides, cyclic polymers of aldehydes or of thioaldehydes, anhydrides of polybasic carboxylic acids, cyclic esters of polyhydric alcohols or phenols with polybasic acids, or imides of polybasic acids.

These provisions apply only when the ring-position hetero-atoms are those resulting solely form the cyclising function or functions here listed.

8. For the purposes of heading No. 29.37:

(a) the term "hormones" includes hormone-releasing or hormone-stimulating factors, hormone inhibitors and hormone antagonists (anti-hormones);

(b) the expression "used primarily as hormones" applies not only to hormone derivatives and structural analogues used primarily for their hormonal effect, but also to those derivatives and structural analogues used primarily as intermediates in the synthesis of products of this heading.

子目注释：

一、属于本章任一税目项下的一种（组）化合物的衍生物，如果该税目其他子目未明确将其包括在内，而且有关的子目中又无列名为“其他”的子目，则应与该种（组）化合物归入同一子目。

二、第二十九章注释三不适用于本章的子目。

Subheading Notes：

1. Within any one heading of this Chapter, derivatives of a chemical compound (or group of chemical compounds) are to be classified in the same subheading as that compound (or group of compounds) provided that they are not more specifically covered by any other subheading and that there is no residual subheading named "other" in the series of subheadings concerned.
2. Note 3 of Chapter 29 does not apply to the subheading of this Chapter.

税则号列	货品名称	最惠(%)	普通	增值税率	出口退税	计量单位	监管条件	Article Description
	第一分章　烃类及其卤化、磺化、硝化或亚硝化衍生物							Ⅰ.-HYDROCARBONS AND THEIR HALOGENATED, SULPHONATED, NITRATED OR NITROSATED DERIVATIVES
29.01	无环烃：							**Acyclic hydrocarbons：**
2901.1000	-饱和	2	30	17	9	千克		-Saturated
	-不饱和：							-Unsaturated：
2901.2100暂	--乙烯	1	20	17	9	千克	AB	--Ethylene
2901.2200暂	--丙烯	1	20	17	9	千克	AB	--Propene (propylene)
	--丁烯及其异构体：							--Butene (butylene) and isomers thereof：
2901.2310	---1-丁烯	2	20	17	9	千克	AB	---1-butene
2901.2320	---2-丁烯	2	20	17	9	千克	AB	---2-butene
2901.2330	---2-甲基丙烯	2	20	17	9	千克		---2-methyl-propene
	--1,3-丁二烯及异戊二烯：							--Buta-1, 3-diene and isoprene：
2901.2410	---1.3-丁二烯	2	20	17	9	千克	AB	---Buta-1,3-diene
2901.2420	---异戊二烯	2	20	17	9	千克		---Isoprene
	--其他：							--Other：
2901.2910	---异戊烯	2	30	17	9	千克	AB	---Isopentene
2901.2920	---乙炔	2	45	17	9	千克	AB	---Acetylene
2901.2990	---其他	2	30	17	9	千克		---Other
2901.2990 10	诱虫烯	2	30	17	9	千克	S	Muscalure
2901.2990 90	其他不饱和无环烃	2	30	17	9	千克		Other unsaturated acyclic hydrocarbon
29.02	环烃：							**Cyclic hydrocarbons：**
	-环烷烃、环烯及环萜烯：							-Cyclanes, cyclenes and cycloterpenes：
2902.1100	--环己烷	2	30	17	9	千克	AB	--Cyclohexane
	--其他：							--Other：
2902.1910	---蒎烯	2	30	17	9	千克		---Pinene
2902.1920	---4-烷基-4'-烷基双环已烷	2	30	17	9	千克		---4-alkyl-4'-alkyl-bicyclohexane
2902.1990	---其他	2	30	17	9	千克		---Other
2902.1990 11	1－甲基环丙烯	2	30	17	9	千克	S	1-methyl cyclopropene
2902.1990 12	d－柠檬烯	2	30	17	9	千克		D-limonene
2902.1990 90	其他环烷烃、环烯及环萜稀	2	30	17	9	千克		Other cyclanes, cyclenes and cycloterpenes
2902.2000	-苯	2	20	17		千克	AB	-Benzene
2902.3000	-甲苯	2	30	17	13	千克	23	-Toluene
	-二甲苯：							-Xylenes：
2902.4100	--邻二甲苯	2	20	17	9	千克		--*o*-Xylene
2902.4200	--间二甲苯	2	20	17	9	千克		--*m*-Xylene
2902.4300	--对二甲苯	2	20	17	13	千克		--*p*-Xylene
2902.4400	--混合二甲苯异构体	2	20	17	13	千克		--Mixed xylene isomers
2902.5000	-苯乙烯	2	30	17	9	千克	AB	-Styrene
2902.6000	-乙苯	2	30	17	9	千克	AB	-Ethylbenzene
2902.7000	-异丙基苯	2	30	17	9	千克	AB	-Cumene
	-其他：							-Other：
2902.9010	---四氢萘	2	11	17	9	千克		---Tetrahydronaphthalene (tetralin)
2902.9020	---精萘	2	35	17	9	千克	AB	---Naphthalene
2902.9030	---十二烷基苯	2	30	17	9	千克		---Dodecylbenzene
2902.9040	---4-(4'-烷基环已基)环已基乙烯	2	30	17	13	千克		---4－(4′－alkyl cyclohexyl) cyclohexyl ethylene

税则号列	货　品　名　称	最惠(%)	普通	增值税率	出口退税	计量单位	监管条件	Article Description
2902.9090	---其他	2	30	17	9	千克		---Other
2902.9090 10	联苯	2	30	17	9	千克		Biphenyl
2902.9090 90	其他芳香烃	2	30	17	9	千克		Other aromatic hydrocarbons
29.03	烃的卤化衍生物:							**Halogenated derivatives of hydrocarbons:**
	-无环烃的饱和氯化衍生物:							-Saturated chlorinated derivatives of acyclic hydrocarbons:
2903.1100	--一氯甲烷及氯乙烷	5.5	30	17	9	千克		--Chloromethane (methyl chloride) and chloroethane (ethyl chloride)
2903.1200	--二氯甲烷	8	30	17	9	千克		--Dichloromethane (methylene chloride)
2903.1200 01	纯度在99%及以上的二氯甲烷	8	30	17	9	千克	X	Dichloromethane (methylene chloride) (purity ≥ 99%)
2903.1200 90	其他二氯甲烷	8	30	17	9	千克	X	Other dichloromethane (methylene chloride)
2903.1300	--氯仿(三氯甲烷)	10	30	17	9	千克	23X	--Chloroform (trichloromethane)
2903.1400	--四氯化碳	8	30	17	9	千克		--Carbon tetrachloride
2903.1400 10	非用于清洗剂的四氯化碳	8	30	17	9	千克	49Bxy	Carbon tetrachloride, other than for cleaner preparation
2903.1400 90	用于清洗剂的四氯化碳	8	30	17	9	千克	89	Carbon tetrachloride, for cleaner preparation
2903.1500[暂]	--1,2-二氯乙烷(ISO)	1	30	17		千克	ABX	--1,2-Dichloroethane (ISO)(ethylene dichloride)
	--其他:							--Other:
2903.1910	---1,1,1-三氯乙烷(甲基氯仿)	8	30	17	9	千克		---1,1,1-Trichloroethane (methylchloro form)
2903.1910 10	1,1,1-三氯乙烷(甲基氯仿)(用于清洗剂的除外)	8	30	17	9	千克	ABy14x	1,1,1-Trichloroethane (methylchloro form) (other than for cleaner preparation)
2903.1910 90	1,1,1-三氯乙烷(甲基氯仿)(用于清洗剂的)	8	30	17	9	千克	18A	1,1,1-Trichloroethane (methylchloro form) (for cleaner preparation)
2903.1990	---其他	5.5	30	17	9	千克		---Other
	-无环烃的不饱和氯化衍生物:							-Unsaturated chlorinated derivatives of acyclic hydrocarbons:
2903.2100[暂]	--氯乙烯	1	30	17	9	千克	AB	--Vinyl chloride (chloroethylene)
2903.2200	--三氯乙烯	8	30	17	9	千克	X	--Trichloroethylene
2903.2300	--四氯乙烯(全氯乙烯)	5.5	30	17	9	千克	X	--Tetrachloroethylene (perchloroethylene)
	--其他:							--Other:
2903.2910	---3-氯-1-丙烯(氯丙烯)	5.5	30	17	9	千克		---3-Chloro-1-propene (chloropropene)
2903.2990	---其他	5.5	30	17	9	千克		---Other
2903.2990 10	1,1-二氯乙烯	5.5	30	17	9	千克	X	1,1-dichloroethylene
2903.2990 90	其他无环烃的不饱和氯化衍生物	5.5	30	17	9	千克		Other unsaturated chlorinated derivatives of acyclic hydrocarbons
	-无环烃的氟化、溴化或碘化衍生物:							-Fluorinated, brominated or iodinated derivatives of acyclic hydrocarbons:
2903.3100	--1,2-二溴乙烷(ISO)	5.5	30	17		千克	89	--Ethylene dibromide (ISO)
	--其他:							--Other:
2903.3910	---1,1,3,3,3-五氟-2-三氟甲基-1-丙烯(全氟异丁烯;八氟异丁烯)	5.5	30	17	9	千克	23	---1,1,3,3,3-Pentafluro-2-trifluromethyl-1-propene (Perfluorolisobutylene, isobutylene octafluoride)
2903.3990	---其他	5.5	30	17		千克		---Other
2903.3990 10	二溴甲烷	5.5	30	17	9	千克	AB	Dibromomethane
2903.3990 20	溴甲烷(别名甲基溴)	5.5	30	17		千克	AB14xy	Methyl bromide
2903.3990 30	碘甲烷	5.5	30	17	13	千克	AB	Methyl iodide
2903.3990 90	其他无环烃的氟化、溴化或碘化衍生物	5.5	30	17	13	千克		Other fluorinated, brominated or iodinated derivatives of acyclic hydrocarbons
	-含有两种或两种以上不同卤素的无环烃卤化衍生物:							-Halogenated derivatives of acyclic hydrocarbons containing two or more different halogens:
2903.7100	--一氯二氟甲烷	5.5	30	17	13	千克	AB14xy	--Chlorodifluoromethane
2903.7200	--二氯三氟乙烷	5.5	30	17	9	千克	14xy	--Dichlorotrifluoroethane
2903.7300	--二氯一氟乙烷	5.5	30	17	9	千克	14xy	--Dichlorofluoroethane
2903.7400	--一氯二氟乙烷	5.5	30	17	9	千克	14xy	--Chlorodifluoroethane
2903.7500	--二氯五氟丙烷	5.5	30	17	9	千克	14xy	--Dichloropentafluoropropane
2903.7500 10	1,1,1,2,2-五氟-3,3-二氯丙烷	5.5	30	17	9	千克	14xy	1,1,1,2,2-Pentafluoro-3,3-dichloropropane

税则号列	货品名称	最惠(%)	普通	增值税率	出口退税	计量单位	监管条件	Article Description
2903.7500 20	1,1,2,2,3-五氟-1,3-二氯丙烷	5.5	30	17	9	千克	14xy	1,1,1,2,2-Pentafluoro-1,3-dichloropropane
2903.7500 90	其他二氯五氟丙烷	5.5	30	17	9	千克	14xy	Other Dichloropentafluoropropane
2903.7600	--溴氯二氟甲烷、溴三氟甲烷及二溴四氟乙烷	5.5	30	17	9	千克		--Bromochlorodifluoromethane、bromotrifluoromethane、dibromotetrafluoroethane
2903.7600 10	溴氯二氟甲烷(Halon－1211)	5.5	30	17	9	千克	14ABxy	Bromochlorodifluoromethane(Halon-1211)
2903.7600 20	溴三氟甲烷(Halon－1301)	5.5	30	17	9	千克	14ABxy	Bromotrifluoromethane(Halon-1301)
2903.7600 30	二溴四氟乙烷	5.5	30	17	9	千克		Dibromotetrafluoroethane
	--其他,仅含氟和氯的全卤化物:							--Other,perhalogenated,only with fluorine and chlorine:
2903.7710	---三氯氟甲烷	5.5	30	17	9	千克	AB14xy	---Trichlorofluoromethane
2903.7720	---其他仅含氟和氯的甲烷、乙烷及丙烷的全卤化物	5.5	30	17	9	千克		--Other, methane, ethane and propane halogenide, only with fluorine and chlorine
2903.7720 11	二氯二氟甲烷(CFC－12)	5.5	30	17	9	千克	14ABxy	Dichlorodifluoromethane(CFC－12)
2903.7720 12	三氯三氟乙烷,用于清洗剂除外(CFC－113)	5.5	30	17	9	千克	14xy	Trichlorotrifluoroethanes, other than for cleaner preparation (CFC－113)
2903.7720 13	三氯三氟乙烷,用于清洗剂(CFC－113)	5.5	30	17	9	千克	89	Trichlorotrifluoroethanes, for cleaner preparation (CFC－113)
2903.7720 14	二氯四氟乙烷(CFC－114)	5.5	30	17	9	千克	14ABxy	Dichlorotetrafluoroethane(CFC－114)
2903.7720 15	一氯五氟乙烷(CFC－115)	5.5	30	17	9	千克	14ABxy	Chloropentafluoroethane(CFC－115)
2903.7720 16	一氯三氟甲烷(CFC－13)	5.5	30	17	9	千克	14ABxy	Chlorotrifluoromethane(CFC－13)
2903.7720 17	五氯一氟乙烷	5.5	30	17	9	千克		Chloropentafluoroethane
2903.7720 18	四氯二氟乙烷	5.5	30	17	9	千克		Difluorotetrachloroethane
2903.7720 19	七氯一氟丙烷	5.5	30	17	9	千克		Heptachlorofluoropropane
2903.7720 21	六氯二氟丙烷	5.5	30	17	9	千克		Hexachlorodifluoropropane
2903.7720 22	五氯三氟丙烷	5.5	30	17	9	千克		Pentachlorotrifluoropropane
2903.7720 23	四氯四氟丙烷	5.5	30	17	9	千克		Tetrachlorodifluoroethane
2903.7720 24	三氯五氟丙烷	5.5	30	17	9	千克		Trichloropentafluoropropane
2903.7720 25	二氯六氟丙烷	5.5	30	17	9	千克		Dichlorohexafluoropropane
2903.7720 26	一氯七氟丙烷	5.5	30	17	9	千克		Chloroheptafluoropropane
2903.7790	---其他	5.5	30	17	13	千克		---Other
2903.7800	--其他全卤化衍生物	5.5	30	17	9	千克		--Other perhalogenated derivatives
	--其他:							--Other:
2903.7910	---其他仅含氟和氯的甲烷、乙烷及丙烷的全卤化衍生物	5.5	30	17	9	千克		---Other methane, ethane and propane halogenated derivatives only with fluorine and chlorine
2903.7910 11	一氟二氯甲烷	5.5	30	17	9	千克	14xy	Dichlorofluoromethane
2903.7910 12	1,1,1,2-四氟-2-氯乙烷	5.5	30	17	9	千克	14xy	1,1,1,2-Tetrafluoro-2,2-dichloroethane
2903.7910 13	三氟一氯乙烷	5.5	30	17	9	千克	14ABxy	Trifluoromonochloroethane
2903.7910 14	1-氟-1,1-二氯乙烷	5.5	30	17	9	千克	14xy	1,1-dichloro-1-fluoroethane
2903.7910 15	1,1-二氟-1-氯乙烷	5.5	30	17	9	千克	14xy	1,1-Difluoro--1-chloroethane
2903.7910 90	其他仅含氟和氯的甲烷、乙烷及丙烷的卤化衍生物	5.5	30	17	9	千克	14xy	Other methane, ethane and propane halogenated derivatives with fluorine and chlorine
2903.7990	---其他	5.5	30	17	9	千克		---Other
2903.7990 10	二溴氯丙烷(1,2-二溴-3-氯丙烷)	5.5	30	17	9	千克	89	Dibromochloropropane (1, 2 － dibromo － 3chloropropane)
2903.7990 21	其他仅含溴、氟的甲烷、乙烷和丙烷	5.5	30	17	9	千克	14xy	Other methane, ethane and propane only with fluorine and bromine
2903.7990 29	其他仅含氟和溴的甲烷等卤化物(包括其他仅含氟和溴的乙烷及丙烷的卤化衍生物)	5.5	30	17	9	千克		Other methane halogenated derivatives only with fluorine and bromine(including other ethane, propane halogenated derivatives only fluorine and bromine)
2903.7990 90	其他无环烃卤化衍生物(含二种或二种以上不同卤素)	5.5	30	17	9	千克		Other halogenated derivatives of acyclic hydrocarbons containing two or more different halogens
	-环烷烃、环烯烃或环萜烯烃的卤化衍生物:							-Halogenated derivatives of cyclanic, cyclenic or cycloterpenic hydrocarbons:
2903.8100	--1,2,3,4,5,6-六氯环己烷[六六六(ISO)],包括林丹(ISO,INN)	5.5	30	17		千克		--1,2,3,4,5,6-Hexachlorocyclohexane clohexane [HCH(ISO)], including lindane(ISO,INN)
2903.8100 10	林丹(ISO,INN)	5.5	30	17		千克	S	Lindan(ISO,INN)
2903.8100 20	α－六氯环己烷、β－六氯环己烷	5.5	30	17		千克	89	α－hexachlorocyclohexane, β－hexachlorocyclohexane

税则号列	货品名称	最惠(%)	普通	增值税率	出口退税	计量单位	监管条件	Article Description
2903.8100 90	1,2,3,4,5,6-六氯环己烷{六六六(ISO)}(混合异构体)	5.5	30	17		千克	X	1,2,3,4,5,6-hexachlorocyclohexane
2903.8200	--艾氏剂(ISO)、氯丹(ISO)及七氯(ISO)	5.5	30	17		千克	89	--Aldrin (ISO) chlordane (ISO) and heptachlor (ISO)
2903.8200 10	艾氏剂(ISO)及七氯(ISO)	5.5	30	17		千克	89	Aldrin(ISO), haptachlor(ISO)
2903.8200 90	氯丹(ISO)(别名八氯化甲桥茚)	5.5	30	17		千克	89	Chlordane(ISO)
2903.8900	--其他	5.5	30	17		千克		--Other
2903.8900 10	毒杀芬	5.5	30	17		千克	89	Camphechlor
2903.8900 30	灭蚁灵	5.5	30	17		千克	89	Mirex(ESA)
2903.8900 90	其他环烷烃、环烯烃或环萜烯烃的卤化衍生物	5.5	30	17	13	千克		Other halogenatives of acycanlic, cyclenic or cycloterpenic hydrocarbons
	-芳烃卤化衍生物:							-Halogenated derivatives of aromatic hydrocarbons:
	--氯苯、邻二氯苯及对二氯苯:							--Chlorobenzene, o-dichlorobenzene and p-dichlorobenzene:
2903.9110	---邻二氯苯	5.5	30	17	9	千克		---o-Dichlorobenzene
2903.9190	---其他	5.5	30	17	9	千克		---Other
2903.9190 10	1,4-二氯苯(对二氯苯)	5.5	30	17	9	千克	S	1,4-dichlorobenzene
2903.9190 90	氯苯	5.5	30	17	9	千克	AB	Cldorobenzene
2903.9200	--六氯苯(ISO)及滴滴涕(ISO,INN)[1,1,1-三氯-2,2-双(4-氯苯基)乙烷]	5.5	30	17		千克	89	--Hexachlorobenzene(ISO) and DDT(ISO) clofenotane(INN) [1,1,1-trichloro-2,2-bis (p-chlorophenyl) ethane]
	--其他:							--Other:
2903.9910	---对氯甲苯	5.5	30	17	9	千克	AB	---p-Chlorotoluene
2903.9920	---3,4-二氯三氟甲苯	5.5	30	17	9	千克		---3,4-Dichlorotrifluoride toluene
2903.9930	---4-(4'-烷基苯基)-1-(4'-烷基苯基)-2-氟苯	5.5	30	17	13	千克		---4-(4'-alkyl phenyl)-1-(4'-alkyl phenyl)-2-fluorobenzene
2903.9990	---其他	5.5	30	17		千克		---Other
2903.9990 10	多氯联苯,多溴联苯	5.5	30	17	9	千克	89	Polychlorinated biphenyls, polybromobiphenyl
2903.9990 30	多氯三联苯(PCT)	5.5	30	17	9	千克	X	Polychlorinated terphenyl(pct)
2903.9990 40	稗草烯	5.5	30	17		千克	S	Tavron
2903.9990 50	五氯苯	5.5	30	17		千克	89	Pentachlorobenzene
2903.9990 90	其他芳烃卤化衍生物	5.5	30	17	9	千克		Other halogen derivatives of aromatic hydrocarbons
29.04	**烃的磺化、硝化或亚硝化衍生物,不论是否卤化:**							**Sulphonated, nitrated or nitrosated derivatives of hydrocarbons, whether or not halogenated:**
2904.1000	-仅含磺基的衍生物及其盐和乙酯	5.5	30	17	9	千克		-Derivatives containing only sulpho groups, their salts and ethyl esters
	-仅含硝基或亚硝基的衍生物:							-Derivatives containing only nitro or only nitroso groups:
2904.2010	---硝基苯	5.5	20	17	9	千克	AB	---Nitrobenzene
2904.2020	---硝基甲苯	5.5	30	17	9	千克		---Nitrotoluene and nitrochlorobenzene
2904.2030	---二硝基甲苯	5.5	20	17	9	千克	AB	---Dinitrotoluene and dinitrochlorobenzene
2904.2040	---三硝基甲苯(TNT)	5.5	40	17	9	千克	AB	---Trinitrotoluene(TNT)
2904.2090	---其他	5.5	30	17	9	千克		---Other
2904.2090 10	六硝基芪	5.5	30	17	9	千克	3	Hexanitrostilbene
2904.2090 20	4－硝基联苯	5.5	30	17	9	千克	X	4－Nitrobiphenyl
2904.2090 90	其他仅含硝基或亚硝基衍生物	5.5	30	17	9	千克		Other derivatives containing only nitro or only nitroso groups
	-其他:							-Other:
	---硝基氯化苯:							---Nitrochlorobenzene:
2904.9011	----邻硝基氯化苯	5.5	30	17	9	千克		----o-Nitrochlorobenzene
2904.9012	----间硝基氯化苯	5.5	30	17	9	千克		----m-Nitrochlorobenzene
2904.9013	----对硝基氯化苯	5.5	30	17	9	千克		----p-Nitrochlorobenzene
2904.9020	---二硝基氯化苯	5.5	20	17	9	千克		---Dinitrochlorobenzene
2904.9030	---三氯硝基甲烷(氯化苦;硝基氯仿)	5.5	30	17		千克、	23S	---Trichloronitromethane (chloropicrin, nitrochloroform)
2904.9090	---其他	5.5	30	17		千克		---Other
2904.9090 11	氯硝丙烷	5.5	30	17		千克	S	Saltpetre chlorine propane
2904.9090 12	四氯硝基苯	5.5	30	17		千克	S	Tecnazene

税则号列	货品名称	最惠(%)	普通	增值税率	出口退税	计量单位	监管条件	Article Description
2904.9090 13	五氯硝基苯	5.5	30	17		千克	S	Quintozene
2904.9090 14	全氟辛基磺酸、全氟辛基磺酸钾、全氟辛基磺酸锂、全氟辛基磺酸铵、全氟辛基磺酰氟	5.5	30	17	9	千克	X	Perfluorooctanesulfonic acid, perfluorooctanesulfonic acid potassium, perfluorooctanesulfonic acid lithium, perfluorooctanesulfonic acid ammonium, Perfluoro-1-octanesulfonylfluoride
2904.9090 90	其他烃的磺化、硝化、亚硝化衍生物(不论是否卤化)	5.5	30	17	9	千克		Other sulphonated, nitrated or nitrosated derivatives of hydrocarbons(whether or not halogenated)
	第二分章　醇类及其卤化、磺化、硝化或亚硝化衍生物							Ⅱ.-ALCOHOLS AND THEIR HALO-GENATED, SULPHONATED, NITRATED OR NITROSATED DERIVATIVES
29.05	**无环醇及其卤化、磺化、硝化或亚硝化衍生物:**							**Acyclic alcohols and their halogenated, sulphonated, nitrated or nitrosated derivatives:**
	-饱和一元醇:							-Saturated monohydric alcohols:
2905.1100	--甲醇	5.5	30	17	13	千克	AB	--Methanol (methyl alcohol)
	--丙醇及异丙醇:							--Propan-1-ol (propyl alcohol) and propan-2-ol (isopropyl alcohol):
2905.1210暂	---正丙醇	3	30	17	9	千克	AB	---Propan-1-ol (propyl alcohol)
2905.1220	---异丙醇	5.5	30	17	9	千克	ABG	---Propan-2-ol (isopropyl alcohol)
2905.1300	--正丁醇	5.5	30	17	13	千克	AB	--Butan-1-ol (*n*-butyl alcohol)
	--其他丁醇:							--Other butanols:
2905.1410	---异丁醇	5.5	30	17	9	千克		---iso-Butyl alcohol
2905.1420	---仲丁醇	5.5	30	17	9	千克		---sec-Butyl alcohol
2905.1430	---叔丁醇	5.5	30	17	9	千克		---tert-Butgl alcohol
	--辛醇及其异构体:							--Octanol (octyl alcohol) and isomors thereof:
2905.1610	---正辛醇	5.5	30	17	13	千克		---n-Octanol
2905.1690	---其他	5.5	30	17	9	千克		---Other
2905.1700	--十二醇、十六醇及十八醇	7	30	17	9	千克		--Dodecan-1-ol (lauryl alcohol), hexadecan-1-ol (cetyl alcohol) and octadecan-1-ol (stearyl alcohol)
	--其他:							--Other:
2905.1910	---3,3-二甲基丁-2-醇(频哪基醇)	5.5	30	17	9	千克	23	---3,3-Dimethyl-2-butanol (pinacolyl alcohol)
2905.1990	---其他	5.5	30	17	13	千克		---Other
2905.1990 10	三十烷醇	5.5	30	17	13	千克	S	Triacontanol
2905.1990 90	其他饱和一元醇	5.5	30	17	13	千克		Other saturated monohydric alcohols
	-不饱和一元醇:							-Unsaturated monohydric alcohols:
	--无环萜烯醇:							--Acyclic terpene alcohols:
2905.2210	---香叶醇、橙花醇(3,7-二甲基-2,6-辛二烯-1-醇)	5.5	30	17	9	千克		---Geraniol, nerol (cis-3,7-Dimethyl-2,6-octadien-1-ol)
2905.2220	---香茅醇(3,7-二甲基-6辛烯-1-醇)	5.5	30	17	9	千克		---Citronellol (3,7-Dimethyl-6-octen-1-ol)
2905.2230	---芳樟醇	5.5	30	17	13	千克	AB	---Linalool
2905.2290	---其他	5.5	30	17	9	千克		---Other
2905.2900	--其他	5.5	30	17	9	千克		--Other
	-二元醇:							-Diols:
2905.3100	--1,2-乙二醇	5.5	30	17	9	千克		--Ethylene glycol (ethanediol)
2905.3200暂	--1,2-丙二醇	3	30	17	9	千克		--Propylene glycol (propane-1,2-diol)
	--其他:							--Other:
2905.3910	---2,5-二甲基己二醇	4	11	17	9	千克		---2,5-dimethyl hexandiol
2905.3990	---其他		30	17	9	千克		---Other
2905.3990暂 01	1,3-丙二醇	3	30	17	9	千克	AB	1,3-Propanediol
2905.3990 02	1,4-丁二醇	5.5	30	17	9	千克	AB	1,4-Butanediol
2905.3990 10	驱蚊醇	5.5	30	17	9	千克	S	Ethohexadiol
2905.3990 90	其他二元醇	5.5	30	17	9	千克	AB	Other diatomic alcohols
	-其他多元醇:							-Other polyhydric alcohols:
2905.4100	--2-乙基-2-(羟甲基)丙烷-1,3-二醇(三羟甲基丙烷)	5.5	30	17	9	千克		--2-Ethyl-2-(hydroxymethyl) propane-1,3-diol (trimethylolpropane)
2905.4200	--季戊四醇	5.5	30	17	9	千克		--Pentaerythritol
2905.4300	--甘露糖醇	8	30	17	9	千克	AB	--Mannitol
2905.4400	--山梨醇	14	40	17	9	千克		--D-glucitol (sorbitol)
2905.4500暂	--丙三醇(甘油)	3	50	17	9	千克	AB	--Glycerol
	--其他:							--Other:
2905.4910	---木糖醇	5.5	30	17	9	千克	AB	---Xylitol

税则号列	货品名称	最惠(%)	普通	增值税率	出口退税	计量单位	监管条件	Article Description
2905.4990	---其他	5.5	30	17	9	千克		---Other
	-无环醇的卤化、磺化、硝化或亚硝化衍生物：							-Halogenated, sulphonated, nitrated or nitrosated derivatives of acyclic alcohols:
2905.5100	--乙氯维诺(INN)	5.5	30	17	9	千克	I	--Ethchlorvynol (INN)
2905.5900	--其他	5.5	30	17	9	千克		--Other
2905.5900 10	乙氯维诺的盐	5.5	30	17	9	千克	I	Salts of Ethchlorvynol (INN)
2905.5900 20	2-氯乙醇	5.5	30	17	9	千克	3A	2-Chloroethanol
2905.5900 30	溴硝醇	5.5	30	17	9	千克		Bronopol
2905.5900 40	鼠甘伏	5.5	30	17	9	千克	S	Geiftor
2905.5900 90	其他无环醇的卤化、磺化等衍生物	5.5	30	17	9	千克		Other halogenated, sulphonated derivatives, of acyclic alcohol
29.06	**环醇及其卤化、磺化、硝化或亚硝化衍生物：**							**Cyclic alcohols and their halogenated, sulphonated, nitrated or nitrosated derivatives:**
	-环烷醇、环烯醇及环萜烯醇：							-Cyclanic, cyclenic or cycloterpenic:
2906.1100	--薄荷醇	5	70	17	13	千克		--Menthol
2906.1200	--环已醇、甲基环已醇及二甲基环已醇	5.5	30	17	9	千克		--Cyclohexanol, methylcyclohexanols and dimethylcyclohexanols
2906.1200 10	甲基环己醇	5.5	30	17	9	千克	AB	Methylcyclohexanol
2906.1200 90	环己醇,二甲基环己醇	5.5	30	17	9	千克		Cyclohexanol, Dimethylcyclohexanol
	--固醇及肌醇：							--Sterols and inositols:
2906.1310[暂]	---固醇	3	30	17	9	千克		---Sterol
2906.1320	---肌醇	5.5	30	17	9	千克	AB	---Inositol
	--其他：							--Other:
2906.1910	---萜品醇	5.5	30	17	9	千克		---Terpineols
2906.1990	---其他	5.5	30	17	13	千克		---Other
2906.1990 11	5α－雄烷－3α，17α－二醇(阿法雄烷二醇)(包括5α－雄烷－3β，17β－二醇(倍他雄烷二醇))	5.5	30	17	13	千克	L	5 α － androstane －3 α, 17 α － diol (including 5 α － androstane －3 β, 17 β － estradiol
2906.1990 12	雄甾－4－烯－3α，17α－二醇{包括雄甾－4－烯－3α，17β－二醇[4－雄烯二醇(3α,17β)]}	5.5	30	17	13	千克	L	Androst －4－ allyl －3 α, 17 α － diol {including androst －4－ allyl －3 α, 17 β － estrad [4－androstendione(3α,17β)]}
2906.1990 13	雄甾－5－烯－3α，17α－二醇[5－雄烯二醇(3α,17α)]{包括雄甾－5－烯－3α，17β－二醇}	5.5	30	17	13	千克	L	Androst －5－ allyl －3α,17α－diol [5－androstendione(3α,17α)]{including androst －5 －allyl －3α, 17β－estra}
2906.1990 90	其他环烷醇,环烯醇及环萜烯醇	5.5	30	17	13	千克		Other cyclanic, cyclenic or cycloterpenic
	-芳香醇：							-Aromatic:
2906.2100	--苄醇	5	30	17	9	千克		--Benzyl alcohol
	--其他：							--Other:
2906.2910	---2-苯基乙醇	5.5	30	17	9	千克		---2-Phenyl alcohol
2906.2990	---其他	5.5	30	17	9	千克		---Other
2906.2990 10	三氯杀螨醇、杀螨醇	5.5	30	17	9	千克	S	Dicofol, chlorfenethol
2906.2990 90	其他芳香醇	5.5	30	17	9	千克		Other aromatic alcohols
	第三分章　酚、酚醇及其卤化、磺化、硝化或亚硝化衍生物							Ⅲ. PHENOLS, PHENOLALCOHOLS, AND THEIR HALOGENATED, SULPHONATED, NITRATED OR NITROSATED DERIVATIVES
29.07	**酚;酚醇：**							**Phenols; phenol-alcohols:**
	-一元酚：							-Monophenols:
	--苯酚及其盐：							--Phenol (hydroxybenzene) and its salts:
2907.1110	---苯酚	5.5	30	17	13	千克	AB	---Phenol
2907.1190	---其他	5.5	30	17	9	千克		---Other
	--甲酚及其盐：							--Cresol and its salts:
	---甲酚：							---Cresol:
2907.1211[暂]	----间甲酚	3	30	17	9	千克		----m-Cresol
2907.1212[暂]	----邻甲酚	3	30	17	9	千克		----o-Cresol
2907.1219	----其他	5.5	30	17	9	千克	AB	----Other

税则号列	货品名称	最惠(%)	普通	增值税率	出口退税	计量单位	监管条件	Article Description
2907.1290	---其他	5.5	30	17	9	千克		---Other
	--辛基酚、壬基酚及其异构体以及它们的盐:							--Octylphenol, nonylphenol and their isomers; salts thereof:
2907.1310	---壬基酚	5.5	30	17	9	千克	X	---Nonylphenol
2907.1390	---其他	5.5	30	17	9	千克		---Other
	--萘酚及其盐:							--Naphthols and their salts:
2907.1510	---2-萘酚(β-萘酚)	5.5	30	17	9	千克		---2-Naphthols (β-naphthol)
2907.1590	---其他	5.5	30	17	9	千克	AB	---Other
	--其他:							--Other:
2907.1910暂	---邻仲丁基酚、邻异丙基酚	2	11	17	9	千克		---*o*-Sec-butyl phenol, *o*-isopropyl phenol
2907.1910暂 10	邻异丙基(苯)酚	2	11	17	9	千克	AB	o – Iisopropylphenol
2907.1910暂 90	邻仲丁基酚	2	11	17	9	千克		Ortho secondary phenol
2907.1990	---其他	5.5	30	17		千克		---Other
2907.1990 11	邻苯基苯酚及其盐	5.5	30	17		千克		o-Phenylphenol and its salt
2907.1990 12	邻烯丙基苯酚及盐	5.5	30	17		千克	S	o-Allylphenol and its salt
2907.1990 90	其他一元酚	5.5	30	17	9	千克		Other monophenols
	-多元酚;酚醇:							-Polyphenols; phenol-alcohols:
2907.2100	--间苯二酚及其盐	5.5	30	17	9	千克		--*m*-Dihydroxybenzene (resorcinol) and its salts
2907.2100 01	间苯二酚	5.5	30	17	9	千克		m – Dihydroxybenzene
2907.2100 90	间苯二酚盐	5.5	30	17	9	千克		m – Dihydroxybenzene salts
	--对苯二酚及其盐:							--*p*-Dihydroxybenzene (hydroquinone) and its salts:
2907.2210	---对苯二酚	5.5	30	17	9	千克		---Hydroquinone
2907.2290	---其他	5.5	30	17	9	千克		---Other
2907.2300	--4,4'-异亚丙基联苯酚(双酚A,二苯基酚丙烷)及其盐	5.5	30	17	9	千克		--4,4'-Isopropylidenediphenol (bisphenol A, diphenylolpropane) and its salts
2907.2300 01	双酚A(4,4-异亚丙基联苯酚)	5.5	30	17	9	千克		Bisphenol-A(4,4'-Isopropylidenediphenol)
2907.2300 90	双酚A的盐(4,4-异亚丙基联苯酚的盐)	5.5	30	17	9	千克		Salts of bisphenol-A (salts of 4,4'-Isopropylidenediphenol)
	--其他:							--Other:
2907.2910	---邻苯二酚	4	11	17	9	千克		---*o*-Dihydroxybenzene (catechol, pyrocatechol)
2907.2990	---其他	5.5	30	17		千克		---Other
2907.2990 01	特丁基对苯二酚	5.5	30	17		千克	AB	tert – Butylhydroquinone
2907.2990 10	毒菌酚	5.5	30	17		千克	S	Hexachlorophene
2907.2990 90	其他多元酚;酚醇	5.5	30	17	9	千克	AB	Other polyphenols, phenol – alcohol
29.08	酚及酚醇的卤化、磺化、硝化或亚硝化衍生物:							**Halogenated, sulphonated, nitrated or nitrosated derivatives of phenols or phenolalcohols:**
	-仅含卤素取代基的衍生物及其盐:							-Derivatives containing only halogen substituents and their salts:
2908.1100	--五氯苯酚(ISO)	5.5	30	17		千克	X	--Pentachlorophenol(ISO)
	--其他:							--Other:
2908.1910	---对氯苯酚	4	11	17	9	千克		---*p*-Chlorophenol
2908.1990	---其他	5.5	30	17		千克		---Other
2908.1990 21	格螨酯	5.5	30	17		千克	S	Genit
2908.1990 22	双氯酚	5.5	30	17		千克	S	Dichlorophen
2908.1990 23	五氯酚钠	5.5	30	17		千克	S	Sodium pentachlorophenate
2908.1990 90	其他仅含卤素取代基的衍生物及盐	5.5	30	17	9	千克		Other derivatives containing only halogen substituents and their salts
	-其他:							-Other:
2908.9100	--地乐酚(ISO)及其盐	5.5	30	17		千克	89	--Dinoseb(ISO) and its salts
2908.9200	--4,6-二硝基邻甲酚[二硝酚(ISO)]及其盐	5.5	30	17	9	千克	89	--4,6-Dinitro-o-cresol [DNOC(ISO)] and its salts
	--其他:							--Other:
2908.9910	---对硝基酚、对硝基酚钠	5.5	30	17		千克		---*p*-Nitrophenol, sodium *p*-nitro-phenolate

税则号列	货　品　名　称	最惠(%)	普通	增值税率	出口退税	计量单位	监管条件	Article Description
2908.9910 10	4-硝基苯酚(对硝基苯酚)	5.5	30	17	9	千克	X	4 – Nitrophenol(P – nitrophenol)
2908.9910 90	对硝基苯酚钠	5.5	30	17		千克	S	Sodium P – nitro – phenolate
2908.9990	---其他	5.5	30	17		千克		---Other
2908.9990 21	芬螨酯	5.5	30	17		千克	S	Fenson
2908.9990 22	消螨酚	5.5	30	17		千克	S	Dinex
2908.9990 23	戊硝酚	5.5	30	17		千克	S	Dinosam
2908.9990 24	特乐酚	5.5	30	17		千克	S	Dinoterb
2908.9990 90	其他酚及酚醇的卤化等衍生物(包括其磺化、硝化或亚硝化衍生物)	5.5	30	17	9	千克		Other halogenated, sulphonated, nitrated or nitrosated derivatives of hpenols or phenolalcohols
	第四分章　醚、过氧化醇、过氧化醚、过氧化酮、三节环环氧化物、缩醛及半缩醛及其卤化、磺化、硝化或亚硝化衍生物							Ⅳ. -ETHERS, ALCOHOL PEROXIDES, ETHER PEROXIDES, KETONE PEROXIDES, EPOXIDES WITH A THREE-MEMBERED RING, ACETALS AND HEMIACETALS, AND THEIR HALOGENATED, SULPHONATED, NITRATED OR NITROSATED DERIVATIVES
29.09	**醚、醚醇、醚酚、醚醇酚、过氧化醇、过氧化醚、过氧化酮(不论是否已有化学定义)及其卤化、磺化、硝化或亚硝化衍生物:**							**Ethers, ether-alcohols, ether-phenols, ether-alcohol-phenols, alcohol peroxides, ether peroxides, ketone peroxides (whether or not chemically defined), and their halogenated, sulphonated, nitrated or nitrosated derivatives:**
	-无环醚及其卤化、磺化、硝化或亚硝化衍生物:							-Acyclic ethers and their halogenated, sulphonated, nitrated or nitrosated derivatives:
2909.1100	--乙醚	5.5	30	17	9	千克	23	--Diethyl ether
	--其他:							--Other
2909.1910	---甲醚	5.5	30	17	13	千克		---Methyl ether
2909.1990	---其他	5.5	30	17	13,15	千克		---Other
2909.1990 11	八氯二丙醚	5.5	30	17	13,15	千克	S	Octachlorodipropyl ether
2909.1990 12	二氯异丙醚	5.5	30	17	13,15	千克	S	Nemamort(DCIP)
2909.1990 90	其他无环醚及其卤化等衍生物(包括其磺化、硝化或亚硝化衍生物)	5.5	30	17	13,15	千克		Other acyclic ethers and their halogenated(including sulphonated, nitrated or nitrosated derivatives and their halogenated)
2909.2000	-环烷醚、环烯醚或环萜烯醚及其卤化、磺化、硝化或亚硝化衍生物	5.5	30	17	9	千克		-Cyclanic, cyclenic or cycloterpenic ethers and their halogenated, sulphonated, nitrated or nitrosated derivatives
	-芳香醚及其卤化、磺化、硝化或亚硝化衍生物:							-Aromatic ethers and their halogenated, sulphonated, nitrated or nitrosated derivatives:
2909.3010	---1-烷氧基-4-(4-乙烯基环已基)-2,3-二氟苯	5.5	30	17	9	千克		---1-alkoxylate-4-(4-vingl cyclohexyl)-2, 3-difluoro benzene
2909.3090	---其他	5.5	30	17		千克		---Other
2909.3090 11	甲氧滴滴涕、除草醚	5.5	30	17		千克	S	Methoxychlor, nitrofen
2909.3090 12	醚菊酯、苄螨醚、三氟醚	5.5	30	17	9	千克	S	Ethofenprox, halfenprox, trifluoro
2909.3090 13	氯苯甲醚、甲氧除草醚	5.5	30	17	9	千克	S	Chloroanisole, chlomethoxyfen
2909.3090 14	三氟硝草醚、草枯醚	5.5	30	17	9	千克	S	Fluorodifen, chlomitrofen
2909.3090 15	氟除草醚、乙氧氟草醚	5.5	30	17	9	千克	S	Fluoronitrofen, oxyfluorfen
2909.3090 16	四溴二苯醚、五溴二苯醚、六溴二苯醚、七溴二苯醚	5.5	30	17	9	千克	89	Tetrabromodiphenyl ether, Pentabromodiphenyl ether, Hexabromodiphenyl ether, Heptabromodiphenyl ether
2909.3090 90	其他芳香醚及其卤化、磺化、硝化衍生物(包括其亚硝化衍生物)	5.5	30	17	9	千克		Other aromatic ethers and its halogenated, sulphonated, nitrated or nitrosated derivatives
	-醚醇及其卤化、磺化、硝化或亚硝化衍生物:							-Ether-alcohols and their halogenated, sulphonated, nitrated or nitrosated derivatives:
2909.4100暂	--2,2′-氧联二乙醇(二甘醇)	3	30	17	9	千克		--2,2′-Oxydiethanol (diethylene glycol, digol)
2909.4300	--乙二醇或二甘醇的单丁醚	5.5	30	17	9	千克		--Monobutyl ethers of ethylene glycol or of diethylene glycol

税则号列	货品名称	最惠(%)	普通	增值税率	出口退税	计量单位	监管条件	Article Description
2909.4400	--乙二醇或二甘醇的其他单烷基醚	5.5	30	17	9	千克		--Other monoalkylethers of ethylene glycol or of diethylene glycol
	--其他:							--Other:
2909.4910	---间苯氧基苄醇	4	11	17	9	千克		---*m*-Phenoxy benzalcohol
2909.4990	---其他	5.5	30	17	9	千克		---Other
2909.5000	-醚酚、醚醇酚及其卤化、磺化、硝化或亚硝化衍生物	5.5	30	17	9	千克		-Ether-phenols, ether-alcohol-phenols and their halogenated, sulphonated, nitrated or nitrosated derivatives
2909.6000	-过氧化醇、过氧化醚、过氧化酮及其卤化、磺化、硝化或亚硝化衍生物	5.5	30	17	9	千克		-Alcohol peroxides, ether peroxides, ketone peroxides and their halogenated, sulphonated, nitrated or nitrosated derivatives
29.10	三节环环氧化物、环氧醇、环氧酚、环氧醚及其卤化、磺化、硝化或亚硝化衍生物:							**Epoxides, epoxyalcohols, epoxyphenols and epoxyethers, with a three-membered ring, and their halogenated, sulphonated, nitrated or nitrosated derivatives:**
2910.1000	-环氧乙烷(氧化乙烯)	5.5	30	17	13	千克	X	-Oxirane (ethylene oxide)
2910.2000	-甲基环氧乙烷(氧化丙烯)	5.5	30	17		千克		-Methyloxirane (propylene oxide)
2910.3000	-1-氯-2,3-环氧丙烷(表氯醇)	5.5	30	17		千克		-1-Chloro-2,3-epoxypropane (epichlorohydrin)
2910.4000	-狄氏剂(ISO,INN)	5.5	30	17		千克	89	-Dieldrin(ISO,INN)
2910.9000	-其他	5.5	30	17		千克		-Other
2910.9000 10	异狄氏剂	5.5	30	17		千克	89	Endrine
2910.9000 20	灭草环	5.5	30	17	13	千克	S	Tridiphane
2910.9000 90	三节环环氧化物、环氧醇(酚、醚)(包括其卤化、磺化、硝化或亚硝化的衍生物)	5.5	30	17	13	千克		Three－ring epoxide, epoxy alcohol (phenols, ether) (including their halogenated, sulphonated, nitration or nitrosated derivatives)
29.11	缩醛及半缩醛,不论是否含有其他含氧基,及其卤化、磺化、硝化或亚硝化衍生物:							**Acetals and hemiacetals, whether or not with other oxygen function, and their halogenated, sulphonated, nitrated or nitrosated derivatives:**
2911.0000	缩醛及半缩醛,不论是否含有其他含氧基,及其卤化、磺化、硝化或亚硝化衍生物	5.5	30	17	9	千克		Acetals and hemiacetals, whether or not with other oxygen function, and their halogenated, sulphonated, nitrated or nitrosated derivatives
	第五分章　醛基化合物							Ⅴ. -ALDEHYDE-FUNCTION COMPOUNDS
29.12	醛,不论是否含有其他含氧基;环聚醛;多聚甲醛:							**Aldehydes, whether or not with other oxygen function; cyclic polymers of aldehydes; paraformaldehyde:**
	-不含其他含氧基的无环醛:							-Acyclic aldehydes without other oxygen function:
2912.1100	--甲醛	5.5	30	17	9	千克	AB	--Methanal (formaldehyde)
2912.1200	--乙醛	5.5	30	17	9	千克	X	--Ethanal (acetaldehyde)
2912.1900	--其他		30	17	9	千克		--Other
2912.1900[暂] 01	乙二醛	3	30	17	9	千克		Glyoxal (ethanedial)
2912.1900 30	丙烯醛	5.5	30	17	9	千克	X	Acrolein
2912.1900 90	其他无环醛(指不含其他含氧基)	5.5	30	17	9	千克		Other acyclic aldehydes(without other oxygen function)
	-不含其他含氧基的环醛:							-Cyclic aldehydes without other oxygen function:
2912.2100	--苯甲醛	5.5	30	17	9	千克		--Benzaldehyde
	--其他:							--Other:
2912.2910	---铃兰醛(对叔丁基-α-甲基-氧化肉桂醛)	5.5	30	17	9	千克		---Lilial (p-tert-butyl-α-methyl-oxocinn amaldehyde)
2912.2990	---其他	5.5	30	17	13	千克		---Other
	-醛醇、醛酚及含其他含氧基的醛:							-Aldehyde-alcohols, aldehyde-phenols and aldehydes with other oxygen function:
2912.4100	--香草醛(3-甲氧基-4-羟基苯甲醛)	5.5	30	17	13	千克		--Vanillin (4-hydroxy-3-methoxybenzaldehyde)
2912.4200	--乙基香草醛(3-乙氧基-4-羟基苯甲醛)	5.5	30	17	13	千克		--Ethylvanillin (3-ethoxy-4-hydroxybenzaldehyde)
	--其他:							--Other:
2912.4910	---醛醇	5.5	30	17	13	千克		---Aldehyde-alcohols

税则号列	货品名称	最惠(%)	普通	增值税率	出口退税	计量单位	监管条件	Article Description
2912.4990	---其他	5.5	30	17	9	千克		---Other
2912.5000	-环聚醛	5.5	30	17	9	千克		-Cyclic polymers of aldehydes
2912.5000 10	四聚乙醛	5.5	30	17	9	千克	S	Metaldehyde
2912.5000 90	其他环聚醛	5.5	30	17	9	千克		Other cyclic polymers of aldehydes
2912.6000	-多聚甲醛	5.5	30	17	9	千克	AB	-Paraformaldehyde
29.13	**税目 29.12 所列产品的卤化、磺化、硝化或亚硝化衍生物:**							**Halogenated, sulphonated, nitrated or nitrosated derivatives of products of heading No. 29.12:**
2913.0000	税目 29.12 所列产品的卤化、磺化、硝化或亚硝化衍生物	5.5	30	17	9	千克		Halogenated, sulphonated, nitrated or nitrosated derivatives of products of heading No. 29.12
2913.0000 10	三氯乙醛	5.5	30	17	9	千克	ABG	Chloral
2913.0000 90	税号 2912 所列产品的其他衍生物(指卤化、磺化、硝化或亚硝化的衍生物)	5.5	30	17	9	千克		Halogenated, sulphonated, nitrated or nitrosated derivatives of products of heading No. 2912
	第六分章　酮基化合物及醌基化合物							Ⅵ. -KETONE-FUNCTION COMPOUNDS AND QUINONE-FUNCTION COMPOUNDS
29.14	**酮及醌,不论是否含有其他含氧基,及其卤化、磺化、硝化或亚硝化衍生物:**							**Ketones and quinones, whether or not with other oxygen function, and their halogenated, sulphonated, nitrated or nitrosated derivatives:**
	-不含其他含氧基的无环酮:							-Acyclic ketones without other oxygen function:
2914.1100	--丙酮	5.5	20	17	13	千克	23	--Acetone
2914.1200	--丁酮[甲基乙基(甲)酮]	5.5	30	17	9	千克	23	--Butanone (methyl ethyl ketone)
2914.1300	--4-甲基-2-戊酮[甲基异丁基(甲)酮]	5.5	30	17	9	千克		--4-Methyl-2-pentanone (isobutyl methyl ketone)
2914.1900	--其他	5.5	30	17	9	千克		--Other
2914.1900 10	频哪酮	5.5	30	17	9	千克	23	Pinacolone
2914.1900 90	其他不含其他含氧基的无环酮	5.5	30	17	9	千克		Other acyclic ketones, without other oxygen function
	-不含其他含氧基的环烷酮、环烯酮或环萜烯酮:							-Cyclanic, cyclenic or cycloterpenic ketones without other oxygen function:
2914.2200	--环已酮及甲基环乙酮	5.5	30	17	9	千克	AB	--Cyclohexanone and methylcyclohexanone
2914.2300	--芷香酮及甲基芷香酮	5.5	30	17	9	千克		--Ionones and methylionones
	--其他:							--Other:
2914.2910	---樟脑	5.5	40	17	9	千克	B	---Camphor
2914.2990	---其他	5.5	30	17	13	千克		---Other
	-不含其他含氧基的芳香酮:							-Aromatic ketones without other oxygen function:
2914.3100	--苯丙酮(苯基丙-2-酮)	5.5	30	17	9	千克	23	--Propiophenone (phenylpropan-2-one)
	--其他:							--Other:
2914.3910	---苯乙酮	4	11	17	9	千克		---Acetophenone
2914.3990	---其他	5.5	30	17		千克		---Other
2914.3990 11	杀鼠酮	5.5	30	17	9	千克	S	Duocide
2914.3990 12	鼠完	5.5	30	17		千克	S	Pindone
2914.3990 13	敌鼠	5.5	30	17	9	千克	S	Diphacinone
2914.3990 14	邻氯苯基环戊酮	5.5	30	17	9	千克	23	O_Chlorophenyl Cyclopentyl Ketone
2914.3990 90	其他不含其他含氧基的芳香酮	5.5	30	17	13	千克		Other aromatic ketones without other oxygen function
2914.4000	-酮醇及酮醛	5.5	30	17		千克		-Ketone-alcohols and ketone-aldehydes
2914.4000 10	敌鼠钠	5.5	30	17		千克	S	Natrium diphacinone
2914.4000 20	雄酮(3β-羟基-5α-雄烷-17-酮)、表睾酮	5.5	30	17	9	千克	L	androsterone(3β-Hydroxy-5α-androstane-17-ketone), epitestosterone
2914.4000 90	其他酮醇及酮醛	5.5	30	17	9	千克		Other ketone-alcohols and ketone-aldehydes
	-酮酚及含有其他含氧基的酮:							-Ketone-phenols and ketones with other oxygen function:
	---酮酚:							---Ketone-phenols:
2914.5011	----覆盆子酮	5.5	30	17	9	千克		----Raspberry ketone
2914.5019	----其他	5.5	30	17	9	千克		----Other
2914.5020	---2-羟基-4-甲氧基二苯甲酮	5.5	30	17	9	千克		---2-Hydroxy-4-methoxybenzophenone
2914.5090	---其他	5.5	30	17	9	千克		---Other
2914.5090 11	肟草酮,双炔酰菌胺	5.5	30	17	9	千克	S	Tralkoxydim, mandipropamid
2914.5090 12	甲氧虫酰肼	5.5	30	17	9	千克	S	Methoxyfenoxide
2914.5090 90	含其他含氧基的酮	5.5	30	17	9	千克		Other ketone with other oxygen function

税则号列	货品名称	最惠(%)	普通	增值税率	出口退税	计量单位	监管条件	Article Description
	-醌:							-Quinones:
2914.6100	--蒽醌	5.5	30	17	9	千克		--Anthraquinone
	--其他:							--Other:
2914.6910	---辅酶 QIO	5.5	30	17	9	千克		--Coenzyme Q10
2914.6990	---其他	5.5	30	17	9	千克		--Other
2914.6990 10	大黄素甲醚	5.5	30	17	9	千克	S	Physcione
2914.6990 90	其他醌	5.5	30	17	9	千克		Other quinones
2914.7000	-卤化、磺化、硝化或亚硝化衍生物	5.5	30	17		千克		-Halogenated, sulphonated, nitrated or nitrosated derivatives
2914.7000 11	氯鼠酮,表苯草酮、茚草酮	5.5	30	17		千克	S	Chlorophacinone, indanofan
2914.7000 12	二氯萘醌	5.5	30	17		千克	S	Dichlone
2914.7000 13	四氯对醌	5.5	30	17		千克	S	Chloranil
2914.7000 14	六氯丙酮	5.5	30	17		千克	S	Hexachloroacetone
2914.7000 15	氯敌鼠钠盐	5.5	30	17	9	千克	S	Chlorophacinone
2914.7000 16	1－苯基－2－溴－1－丙酮	5.5	30	17		千克	23	1 – Bromo – 1 – phenyl – 2 – propanone
2914.7000 17	十氯酮	5.5	30	17		千克	89	Chlordecone
2914.7000 90	其他酮及醌的卤化、磺化衍生物(包括硝化或亚硝化衍生物)	5.5	30	17	9	千克		Other halogenated and sulphurated, nitrated or nitrosated derivatives of ketones and quinones
	第七分章　羧酸及其酸酐、酰卤化物、过氧化物和过氧酸以及它们的卤化、磺化、硝化或亚硝化衍生物							Ⅶ. -CARBOXYLIC ACIDS AND THEIR ANHYDRIDES, HALIDES, PEROXIDES AND PEROXYACIDS AND THEIR HALOGENATED, SULPHONATED, NITRATED OR NITROSATED DERIVATIVES
29.15	**饱和无环一元羧酸及其酸酐、酰卤化物、过氧化物和过氧酸以及它们的卤化、磺化、硝化或亚硝化衍生物:**							**Saturated acyclic monocarboxylic acids and their anhydrides, halides, peroxides and peroxyacids; their halogenated, sulphonated, nitrated or nitrosated derivatives:**
	-甲酸及其盐和酯:							-Formic acid, its salts and esters:
2915.1100	--甲酸	5.5	40	17	9	千克	AB	--Formic acid
2915.1200	--甲酸盐	5.5	30	17	9	千克		--Salts of formic acid
2915.1300	--甲酸酯	5.5	30	17	9	千克		--Esters of formic acid
	-乙酸及其盐;乙酸酐:							-Acetic acid and its salts; acetic anhydride:
	--乙酸:							--Acetic acid:
	---冰乙酸:							---Acetic acid, glacial:
2915.2111	----食品级的	5.5	30	17	9	千克	ABG	----food-grade
2915.2119	----其他	5.5	30	17	9	千克	G	----Other
2915.2190	---其他	5.5	50	17	9	千克		---Other
2915.2190 10	乙酸溶液,80≥含量>10%	5.5	50	17	9	千克	ABG	Acetic acid solution, 80%≥content>10%
2915.2190 20	乙酸,含量>80%	5.5	50	17	9	千克	ABG	Acetic acid, content>80%
2915.2190 90	其他乙酸	5.5	50	17	9	千克	ABG	Other acetic acid
2915.2400	--乙酸酐	5.5	50	17	9	千克	23	--Acetic anhydride
	--其他:							--Other:
2915.2910	---乙酸钠	5.5	50	17	9	千克	ABG	---Sodium acetate
2915.2990	---其他	5.5	50	17	9	千克		---Other
2915.2990 11	乙酸铜	5.5	50	17	9	千克		Copper acetate
2915.2990 23	乙酸铅(醋酸铅)	5.5	50	17	9	千克	X	Lead acetate
2915.2990 90	其他乙酸盐	5.5	50	17	9	千克	AB	Other Salts of acetate acid
	-乙酸酯:							-Esters of acetic acid:
2915.3100	--乙酸乙酯	5.5	30	17	9	千克	ABG	--Ethyl acetate
2915.3200	--乙酸乙烯酯	5.5	30	17	9	千克	AB	--Vinyl acetate
2915.3300	--乙酸(正)丁酯	5.5	30	17	9	千克	AB	--*n*-Butyl acetate
2915.3600	--地乐酚(ISO)乙酸酯	5.5	30	17		千克	S	--Dinoseb (ISO) acetate acid
2915.3900	--其他	5.5	30	17		千克		--Other
2915.3900 11	三氯杀虫酯	5.5	30	17	13	千克	S	Acetofenate
2915.3900 13	特乐酯	5.5	30	17	13	千克	S	Dinoterb acetate
2915.3900 14	灭螨醌	5.5	30	17		千克	S	Acequinocy

税则号列	货品名称	最惠(%)	普通	增值税率	出口退税	计量单位	监管条件	Article Description
2915.3900 15	红铃虫性诱素	5.5	30	17	13	千克	S	11 – Hexadecadien – l – yl acetate
2915.3900 16	种衣酯	5.5	30	17	13	千克	S	Fenitropan
2915.3900 90	其他乙酸酯	5.5	30	17	13	千克	AB	Other esters of acetic acid
2915.4000	-一氯代乙酸、二氯乙酸或三氯乙酸及其盐和酯	5.5	30	17		千克		-Mono-, di- or trichloroacetic acids, their salts and esters
2915.4000 10	一氯醋酸钠	5.5	30	17		千克		Sodium monochloracetate
2915.4000 90	其他一氯代乙酸的盐和酯(包括二氯乙酸或三氯乙酸的盐和酯)	5.5	30	17	9	千克		Other mono-, di-or trichloroacetic acids, their salts and esters
	-丙酸及其盐和酯:							-Propionic acid, its salts and esters:
2915.5010[暂]	---丙酸	3	30	17	9	千克	AB	---Propionic acid
2915.5090	---其他	5.5	30	17	9	千克	AB	---Other
2915.6000	-丁酸、戊酸及其盐和酯	5.5	30	17	9	千克		-Butanoic acids, pentanoic acids, their salts and esters
	-棕榈酸、硬脂酸及其盐和酯:							-Palmitic acid, stearic acid, their salts and esters:
2915.7010	---硬脂酸	7	50	17	9	千克	AB	---Stearic acid
2915.7090	---其他	5.5	30	17	9	千克		---Other
2915.9000	-其他	5.5	30	17		千克		-Other
2915.9000 11	茅草枯	5.5	30	17		千克	S	Dalapon
2915.9000 12	抑草蓬	5.5	30	17		千克	S	Erbon
2915.9000 13	四氟丙酸	5.5	30	17	9	千克	S	Flupropanate
2915.9000 20	氟乙酸钠	5.5	30	17	9	千克	89	Sodium fluoroacetate
2915.9000 90	其他饱和无环一元羧酸及其酸酐[(酰卤、过氧)化物,过氧酸及其卤化、硝化、磺化、亚硝化衍生物]	5.5	30	17	9	千克	AB	Other saturaed acyclic monocarboxylic acids and their anhydrides, halides, peroxides and peroxyacids; their halogenated, sulphonated, nitrated or nitrosated derivatives
29.16	不饱和无环一元羧酸、环一元羧酸及其酸酐、酰卤化物、过氧化物和过氧酸以及它们的卤化、磺化、硝化或亚硝化衍生物:							**Unsaturated acyclic monocarboxylic acids, cyclic monocarboxylic acids, their anhydrides, halides, peroxides and peroxyacids; their halogenated, sulphonated, nitrated or nitrosated derivatives:**
	-不饱和无环一元羧酸及其酸酐、酰卤化物、过氧化物和过氧酸以及它们的衍生物:							-Unsaturated acyclic monocarboxylic acids, their anhydrides, halides, peroxides, peroxyacids and their derivatives:
2916.1100	--丙烯酸及其盐	6.5	30	17	9	千克		--Acrylic acid and its salts
	--丙烯酸酯:							--Esters of acrylic acid:
2916.1210	---丙烯酸甲酯	6.5	30	17	9	千克	AB	--Methacylate
2916.1220	---丙烯酸乙酯	6.5	30	17	9	千克	AB	---Ethyl acrylate
2916.1230	---丙烯酸丁酯	6.5	30	17	9	千克		---Butyl achylate
2916.1230 01	丙烯酸正丁酯	6.5	30	17	9	千克	AB	N-butyl acrylate
2916.1230 90	丙烯酸异丁酯	6.5	30	17	9	千克	AB	Isobutyl acrylate
2916.1240	---丙烯酸异辛酯	6.5	30	17	9	千克		---Isooctyl acrylate
2916.1290	---其他	6.5	30	17	9	千克		---Other
2916.1300	--甲基丙烯酸及其盐	6.5	80	17	13	千克		--Methacrylic acid and its salts
2916.1300 10	甲基丙烯酸	6.5	80	17	13	千克	AB	Methacrylic acid
2916.1300 90	甲基丙烯酸盐	6.5	80	17	13	千克		Salts of methacrylic acid
2916.1400	--甲基丙烯酸酯	6.5	80	17	13	千克		--Esters of methacrylic acid
2916.1500	--油酸、亚油酸或亚麻酸及其盐和酯	6.5	30	17	9	千克		--Oleic, linoleic or linolenic acids, their salts and esters
2916.1600	--乐杀螨(ISO)	6.5	30	17		千克	S	--Binapacryl(ISO)
2916.1900	--其他	6.5	30	17	9	千克		--Other
2916.1900 11	烯虫乙酯	6.5	30	17	9	千克	S	Hydroprene
2916.1900 12	烯虫炔酯	6.5	30	17	9	千克	S	Kinoprene
2916.1900 13	消螨普	6.5	30	17	9	千克	S	Dinocap
2916.1900 90	其他不饱和无环一元羧酸(包括其酸酐、酰卤化物、过氧化物和过氧酸及它们的衍生物)	6.5	30	17	9	千克	AB	Other unsaturated acyclic monocarboxylic acids, their anhydrides, halides, peroxides, peroxyacids and their derivatives

税则号列	货品名称	最惠(%)	普通	增值税率	出口退税	计量单位	监管条件	Article Description
	-环烷一元羧酸、环烯一元羧酸或环萜烯一元羧酸及其酸酐、酰卤化物、过氧化物和过氧酸以及它们的衍生物：							-Cyclanic, cyclenic or cycloterpenic monocarboxylic acids, their anhydrides, halides, peroxides, peroxyacids and their derivatives:
2916.2010	---二溴菊酸、DV菊酸甲酯	4	11	17	9	千克		---Dibromochrysanthemicacid, DV chrysanthemimono carboxylate
2916.2090	---其他	6.5	30	17	9	千克		---Other
2916.2090 21	苄菊酯、苯醚菊酯(包括右旋苯醚菊酯、富右旋反式苯醚菊酯)	6.5	30	17	9	千克	S	Dimethirn, Phenothrin (including d-phenothrin, rich-d-trans-phenothrin)
2916.2090 22	苄烯菊酯、氯菊酯(包括生物氯菊酯)	6.5	30	17	9	千克	S	Butethrin, Permethrin (including biopermethrin)
2916.2090 23	氯烯炔菊酯、联苯菊酯	6.5	30	17	9	千克	S	Chlorempenthrin, Bifenthrin
2916.2090 24	七氟菊酯、四氟苯菊酯、五氟苯菊酯、七氟甲醚菊酯(包括甲氧苄菊酯、氯氟醚菊酯)	6.5	30	17	9	千克	S	Tefluthrin, transfluthrin, fenfluthrin, methothrin heptafluoride (including matofluthrin)
2916.2090 25	戊菊酯、环螨酯	6.5	30	17	9	千克	S	Valerate, cyclopropate
2916.2090 26	四氟甲醚菊酯、烯炔菊酯四氟醚菊酯(包括右旋烯炔菊酯、富右旋反式烯炔菊酯)	6.5	30	17	9	千克	S	Dimefluthrin, empenthrin Four fluorine ethofenprox (including d-empenthrin, rich-d-empenthrin)
2916.2090 27	炔丙菊酯(包括右旋炔丙菊酯、富右旋反式炔丙菊酯)	6.5	30	17	9	千克	S	Prallethrin (including d-prallethrin、rich-d-t-prallethrin)
2916.2090 28	氯丙炔菊酯(包括右旋反式氯丙炔菊酯)	6.5	30	17	9	千克	S	Chlorpromazine acetylene permethrin (including d-trans-permethrin chlorpromazine acetylene)
2916.2090 90	其他(环烷、环烯、环萜烯)一元羧酸(包括酸酐、酰卤化物、过氧化物和过氧酸及该编号的衍生物)	6.5	30	17	9	千克	AB	Other cyclanic, cyclenic or cycloterpenic monocarboxylic acids, their anhydrides, halides, peroxides, peroxyacids and their derivatives
	-芳香一元羧酸及其酸酐、酰卤化物、过氧化物和过氧酸以及它们的衍生物：							-Aromatic monocarboxylic acids, their anhydrides, halides, peroxides, peroxyacids and their derivatives:
2916.3100	--苯甲酸及其盐和酯	6.5	30	17		千克		--Benzoic acid, its salts and esters
2916.3100 20	2-(乙酰氧基)苯甲酸	6.5	30	17		千克	S	2-(Acetoxy)benzoic acid
2916.3100 90	其他苯甲酸及其盐和酯	6.5	30	17	9	千克	AB	Other benzoic acid and salt and ester
2916.3200	--过氧化苯甲酰及苯甲酰氯	6.5	30	17	9	千克	AB	--Benzoyl peroxide and benzoyl chloride
2916.3400	--苯乙酸及其盐	6.5	30	17	9	千克		--Phenylacetic acid and its salts
2916.3400 10	苯乙酸	6.5	30	17	9	千克	23	Phenylacetic acid
2916.3400 90	苯乙酸盐	6.5	30	17	9	千克		Salts of phenylacetic acid
	--其他：							--Other:
2916.3910	---邻甲基苯甲酸	6.5	30	17	9	千克		---*M*-methylbenzoic acid
2916.3920	---布洛芬	6.5	30	17	9	千克		---Brufen (Ibuprofen)
2916.3990	---其他	6.5	30	17		千克		---Other
2916.3990 12	草芽畏、燕麦酯	6.5	30	17	9	千克	S	2,3,6-TAB, methachlorphenprop
2916.3990 13	5-硝基邻甲氧基苯酸钠	6.5	30	17		千克	S	5-Sodium nitro-o-methoxy-benzene
2916.3990 14	对氯苯氧乙酸及其盐	6.5	30	17	9	千克	S	p-Chlorophenoxyacetic acid and its salt
2916.3990 15	三碘苯甲酸	6.5	30	17		千克	S	Triiodobenzoic acid
2916.3990 16	萘乙酸	6.5	30	17	9	千克	S	Naphthylacetic acid
2916.3990 17	伐草克	6.5	30	17	9	千克	S	Chlorfenac
2916.3990 18	α-萘乙酸及其盐	6.5	30	17	9	千克	S	α-Naphthylacetic acid and its salt
2916.3990 90	其他芳香一元羧酸	6.5	30	17	9	千克		Other aromatic monocarboxylic acids
29.17	多元羧酸及其酸酐、酰卤化物、过氧化物和过氧酸以及它们的卤化、磺化、硝化或亚硝化衍生物：							**Polycarboxylic acids, their anhydrides, halides, peroxides and peroxyacids; their halogenated, sulphonated, nitrated or nitrosated derivatives:**
	-无环多元羧酸及其酸酐、酰卤化物、过氧化物和过氧酸以及它们的衍生物：							-Acyclic polycarboxylic acids, their anhydrides, halides, peroxides, peroxyacids and their derivatives:
	--草酸及其盐和酯：							--Oxalic acid, its salts and esters:
2917.1110	---草酸	6.5	40	17	9	千克		---Oxalic acid
2917.1120	---草酸钴	9	30	17	9	千克	4xy	---Cobalt oxalate
2917.1190	---其他	6.5	30	17	9	千克		---Other
2917.1200	--已二酸及其盐和酯	6.5	30	17	13	千克	AB	--Adipic acid, its salts and esters
2917.1200 01	已二酸	6.5	30	17	13	千克	AB	Adipic acid

税则号列	货品名称	最惠(%)	普通	增值税率	出口退税	计量单位	监管条件	Article Description
2917.1200 90	己二酸盐和酯	6.5	30	17	13	千克	AB	Adipic acid, its salts and esters
	--壬二酸、癸二酸及其盐和酯：							--Azelaic acid, sebacic acid, their salts and esters:
2917.1310	---癸二酸及其盐和酯	6.5	30	17	9	千克		---Sebacic acid, its salts and esters
2917.1390	---其他	6.5	30	17	9	千克		---Other
2917.1400	--马来酐	6.5	30	17	9	千克		--Maleic anhydride
2917.1900	--其他	6.5	30	17		千克		--Other
2917.1900 10	驱虫特、硝苯菌酯	6.5	30	17		千克	S	Dibutyl succinate, nifedipinestrobin
2917.1900 90	其他无环多元羧酸	6.5	30	17	9	千克		Other acyclic pohycarboxylic acid
	-环烷多元羧酸、环烯多元羧酸、环萜烯多元羧酸及其酸酐、酰卤化物、过氧化物和过氧酸以及它们的衍生物：							-Cyclanic, cyclenic or cycloterpenic polycarboxylic acids, their anhydrides, halides, peroxides, peroxyacids and their derivatives:
2917.2010	---四氢苯酐	4	11	17	9	千克		---Tetrahydro benzoic anhydride
2917.2090	---其他	6.5	30	17		千克		---Other
2917.2090 10	驱蚊灵	6.5	30	17		千克	S	Dimethyl carbate
2917.2090 90	其他(环烷、环烯、环萜烯)多元羧酸	6.5	30	17	9	千克	AB	Other cyclanic, cyclenic or cycloterpenic) polycarboxylic acids
	-芳香多元羧酸及其酸酐、酰卤化物、过氧化物和过氧酸以及它们的衍生物：							-Aromatic polycarboxylic acids, their anhydrides, halides, peroxides, peroxyacids and their derivatives:
2917.3200	--邻苯二甲酸二辛酯	6.5	30	17	9	千克		--Dioctyl orthophthalates
2917.3300	--邻苯二甲酸二壬酯及邻苯二甲酸二癸酯)	6.5	30	17	9	千克		--Dinonyl or didecyl orthophthalates
	--其他邻苯二甲酸酯：							--Other esters of orthaphthalic acid:
2917.3410	---邻苯二甲酸二丁酯	6.5	30	17		千克		---Dibutyl orthophthalates
2917.3410 10	驱蚊叮	6.5	30	17		千克	S	Dinbutyl phthalate
2917.3410 90	其他邻苯二甲酸二丁酯	6.5	30	17	9	千克		Other phthalic acid dibutyl ester
2917.3490	---其他	6.5	30	17	9	千克		---Other
2917.3500	--邻苯二甲酸酐	6.5	30	17	9	千克	AB	--Phthalic anhydride
	--对苯二甲酸及其盐：							--Terephthalic acid and its salts:
	---对苯二甲酸：							---Tere phthalic acid:
2917.3611	----精对苯二甲酸	6.5	30	17	13	千克		----Purified terephthalic acid
2917.3619	----其他	6.5	30	17	9	千克		----Other
2917.3690	---其他	6.5	30	17	9	千克		---Other
2917.3700	--对苯二甲酸二甲酯	6.5	30	17	9	千克		--Dimethyl terephthalate
	--其他：							--Other:
2917.3910	---间苯二甲酸	6.5	30	17	9	千克		---Isophthalic acid
2917.3990	---其他	6.5	30	17	9	千克		---Other
2917.3990 11	酞菌酯	6.5	30	17	9	千克	S	Nitrotalisopropyl
2917.3990 12	氯酞酸甲酯	6.5	30	17	9	千克	S	Chlorthal - dimethyl
2917.3990 13	氯酞酸	6.5	30	17	9	千克	S	Chlorthal
2917.3990 90	其他芳香多元羧酸	6.5	30	17	9	千克		Other aromatic polycarboxylic acid
29.18	含附加含氧基的羧酸及其酸酐、酰卤化物、过氧化物和过氧酸以及它们的卤化、磺化、硝化或亚硝化衍生物：							**Carboxylic acids with additional oxygen function and their anhydrides, halides, peroxides and peroxyacids; their halogenated, sulphonated, nitrated or nitrosated derivatives:**
	-含醇基但不含其他含氧基的羧酸及其酸酐、酰卤化物、过氧化物和过氧酸以及它们的衍生物：							-Carboxylic acids with alcohol function but without other oxygen function, their anhydrides, halides, peroxides, peroxyacids and their derivatives:
2918.1100	--乳酸及其盐和酯	6.5	30	17	9	千克	AB	--Lactic acid, its salts and esters
2918.1200	--酒石酸	6.5	35	17	9	千克	AB	--Tartaric acid
2918.1300	--酒石酸盐及酒石酸酯	6.5	30	17	9	千克	AB	--Salts and esters of tartaric acid
2918.1400	--柠檬酸	6.5	35	17	13	千克	4ABxy	--Citric acid
2918.1500	--柠檬酸盐及柠檬酸酯	6.5	30	17	13	千克	4ABxy	--Salts and esters of citric acid
2918.1600	--葡糖酸及其盐和酯	6.5	30	17	9	千克		--Gluconic acid, its salts and esters
2918.1800	--乙酯杀螨醇(ISO)	6.5	30	17		千克	S	--Chlorobenzilate(ISO)
	--其他：							--Other:

税则号列	货品名称	最惠(%)	普通	增值税率	出口退税	计量单位	监管条件	Article Description
2918.1910	---2,2-二苯基-2-羟基乙酸(二苯羟乙酸;二苯乙醇酸)	6.5	30	17	9	千克	23	---2,2-Diphenyl-2-hydroxyacetic acid (a-hydroxydiphenylacetic acid, benzilic acid)
2918.1990	---其他	6.5	30	17		千克		---Other
2918.1990 10	二苯乙醇酸甲酯(包括其酸酐、酰卤化物、过氧化物和过氧酸及其衍生物)	6.5	30	17	9	千克	23	Methyl benzilate and their anhydrides, halides, peroxides, peroxyacids and their derivatives
2918.1990 30	γ-羟基丁酸及其盐	6.5	30	17	9	千克	I	γ-Hydroxybutyric acid and its salts
2918.1990 41	丙酯杀螨醇	6.5	30	17		千克	S	Chlorobenzilate
2918.1990 42	溴螨酯	6.5	30	17	9	千克	S	Bromopropylate
2918.1990 43	劳丁酯	6.5	30	17	9	千克	S	Flurenol
2918.1990 44	整形醇	6.5	30	17	9	千克	S	Chlorflurenol
2918.1990 90	其他含醇基但不含其他含氧基羧酸(包括其酸酐、酰卤化物、过氧化物和过氧酸及其衍生物)	6.5	30	17	9	千克		Other Carboxylic acids with phenol function but without other oxygen function, including their anhydrides, halides, peroxides, peroxyacids and their derivatives
	-含酚基但不含其他含氧基的羧酸及其酸酐、酰卤化物、过氧化物和过氧酸以及它们的衍生物:							-Carboxylic acids with phenol function but without other oxygen function, their anhydrides, halides, peroxides, peroxyacids and their derivatives:
	--水杨酸及其盐:							--Salicylic acid and its salts:
2918.2110	---水杨酸、水杨酸钠	6.5	20	17	9	千克		---Salicylic acid and sodium salicylate
2918.2190	---其他	6.5	30	17	9	千克		---Other
	--邻乙酰水杨酸及其盐和酯:							--o-Acetylsalicylic acid, its salts and esters:
2918.2210	---邻乙酰水杨酸(阿司匹林)	6	20	17	9	千克		---Acetylsalicylic acid
2918.2290	---其他	6.5	30	17	9	千克		---Other
2918.2300	--水杨酸的其他酯及其盐	6.5	30	17	9	千克		--Other esters of salicylic acid and their salts
2918.2900	--其他	6.5	30	17	9	千克	AB	--Other
2918.3000	-含醛基或酮基但不含其他含氧基的羧酸及其酸酐、酰卤化物、过氧化物和过氧酸以及它们的衍生物	6.5	30	17	9	千克		-Carboxylic acids with aldehyde or ketone function but without other oxygen function, their anhydrides, halides, peroxides, peroxyacids and their derivatives
2918.3000 11	除虫菊素Ⅰ、除虫菊素Ⅱ	6.5	30	17	9	千克	S	Pyrethrum Ⅰ, Pyrethrum Ⅱ.
2918.3000 12	瓜叶菊素Ⅰ、瓜叶菊素Ⅱ	6.5	30	17	9	千克	S	Cinerin Ⅰ, cinerin Ⅱ
2918.3000 13	茉酮菊素Ⅰ、茉酮菊素Ⅱ	6.5	30	17	9	千克	S	Jasmplin Ⅰ, Jasmolin Ⅱ
2918.3000 14	环戊烯丙菊酯	6.5	30	17	9	千克	S	Terallethrin
2918.3000 15	调环酸、抗倒酯、环虫菊酯	6.5	30	17	9	千克	S	Prohexadione, trinexapac - ethyl, cyclethrin
2918.3000 16	烯丙菊酯等(包括右旋烯丙菊酯、富右旋反式烯丙菊酯,右旋反式烯丙菊酯)	6.5	30	17	9	千克	S	Allethrin (including d-allethrin、rich-d-t-allethrin、d-t-allethrin)
2918.3000 17	Es-生物烯丙菊酯、生物烯丙菊酯等(包括S-生物烯丙菊酯)	6.5	30	17	9	千克	S	Es-bioallethrin, bioallethrin (including S - bioallethrin)
2918.3000 18	乙酰氟菊酯	6.5	30	17	9	千克	S	acetyl - fluthrinate
2918.3000 90	其他含醛基或酮基不含其他含氧基羧酸(包括酸酐、酰卤化物、过氧化物和过氧酸及其衍生物)	6.5	30	17	9	千克		Other carboxylic acid with aldehyde or ketone function but without other oxygen function, their anhydrides, halides, peroxides, peroxyacids and their derivatives
	-其他:							-Other:
2918.9100	--2,4,5-涕(ISO)(2,4,5-三氯苯氧乙酸)及其盐或酯	6.5	30	17		千克	89	--2,4,5-T(ISO) (2,4,5-trichlorophenoxy acetic acid), ist salts and esters
2918.9900	--其他	6.5	30	17	9	千克		--Other
2918.9900 21	2,4-滴,2,4-滴丙酸,2,4-滴丁酸等(包括精2,4-滴丙酸、苯醚菌酯)	6.5	30	17	9	千克	S	2,4 - d, 2,4 - dichlorprop - p, 2,4 - embutox (including J - 2,4 - ichlorprop - p)
2918.9900 22	2甲4氯、2甲4氯丙酸等(包括精2甲4氯丙酸)	6.5	30	17	9	千克	S	MCPA, Mecoprop (including mecoprop-P)
2918.9900 23	2甲4氯丁酸	6.5	30	17	9	千克	S	MCPA butyric acid
2918.9900 24	麦草畏、杀草畏	6.5	30	17	9	千克	S	Dicamba, tricamba
2918.9900 25	禾草灵、乳氟禾草灵	6.5	30	17	9	千克	S	Diclofop, lactofen
2918.9900 26	氟萘禾草灵、甲羧除草醚	6.5	30	17	9	千克	S	Fluoro - naphthalene diclofop, bifenox
2918.9900 27	三氟羧草醚、乙羧氟草醚	6.5	30	17	9	千克	S	Acifluorfen, benzofluorfen

税则号列	货 品 名 称	最惠(%)	普通	增值税率	出口退税	计量单位	监管条件	Article Description
2918.9900 28	氟乳醚、调果酸、座果酸	6.5	30	17	9	千克	S	Ethoxycarbofen, cloprop, cloxyfonac
2918.9900 29	增糖酯、S-诱抗素、氯氟草醚乙酯(包括烯虫酯)	6.5	30	17	9	千克	S	Dlcamba - methyl - ester, abscisic acid, ethoxyfen - ethyl(including methoprene)
2918.9900 30	调磺酸钙	6.5	30	17	9	千克	S	Adjustable calcium sulfonate
2918.9900 41	2 甲 4 氯异辛酯	6.5	30	17	9	千克	S	2 a 4 chloride isooctyl
2918.9900 90	其他含其他附加含氧基羧酸(包括其酸酐、酰卤化物、过氧化物和过氧酸及其衍生物)	6.5	30	17	9	千克		Other carboxylic acids with other additional oxygen function and their anhydrides, halides, peroxides and peroxyacids; their derivatives
	第八分章　非金属无机酸酯及其盐以及它们的卤化、磺化、硝化或亚硝化衍生物							Ⅷ. -ESTERS OF INORGANIC ACIDS OF NON-METALS AND THEIR SALTS, AND THEIR HALOGENATED, SULPHONATED, NITRATED OR NITROSATED DERIVATIVES
29.19	**磷酸酯及其盐,包括乳磷酸盐,以及它们的卤化、磺化、硝化或亚硝化衍生物:**							**Phosphoric esters and their salts, including lactophosphates; their halogenated, sulphonated, nitrated or nitrosated derivatives:**
2919.1000	-三(2,3-二溴丙基)磷酸酯	6.5	30	17	9	千克	89	-Tris(2,3-dibromopropyl) phosphate
2919.9000	-其他	6.5	30	17		千克		-Other
2919.9000 20	磷酸三丁酯	6.5	30	17	9	千克	3	Tributyl phosphate
2919.9000 31	敌敌钙,敌敌畏	6.5	30	17	9	千克	S	Calvinphos, dichlorvos
2919.9000 32	速灭磷、二溴磷	6.5	30	17	9	千克	S	Mevinphos, dibron
2919.9000 33	巴毒磷、杀虫畏	6.5	30	17		千克	S	Crotoxyphos, tetrachlorvinphos
2919.9000 34	毒虫畏、甲基毒虫畏	6.5	30	17		千克	S	Chlorfenvinphos, dimethylvinphos
2919.9000 35	庚烯磷、特普	6.5	30	17		千克	S	Heptenophos, tepp
2919.9000 36	三乙膦酸铝、乙膦酸	6.5	30	17	9	千克	S	Fosetyl-aluminium, phosphonoacetic acid
2919.9000 37	氯瘟磷、伐草磷	6.5	30	17		千克	S	Phosdiphen, grass-killing phosphate
2919.9000 90	其他磷酸酯及其盐(包括乳磷酸盐)(包括它们的卤化、磺化、硝化或亚硝化衍生物)	6.5	30	17	9	千克	AB	Other phosphoric esters and their salts, including lactophosphates; their halogenated, sulphonated, nitrated or nitrosated derivatives
29.20	**其他非金属无机酸酯(不包括卤化氢的酯)及其盐以及它们的卤化、磺化、硝化或亚硝化衍生物:**							**Esters of other inorganic acids of non-metals (excluding esters of hydrogen halides) and their salts; their halogenated, sulphonated, nitrated or nitrosated derivatives:**
	-硫代磷酸酯及其盐以及它们的卤化、磺化、硝化或亚硝化衍生物:							-Thiophosphoric esters (phosphorothioates) and their salts; their halogenated, sulphonated, nitrated or nitrosated derivatives:
2920.1100	--对硫磷(ISO)及甲基对硫磷(ISO)	6.5	30	17		千克	X	--Parathion(ISO) and parathion-metlyl(ISO) (methyl-parathion)
2920.1900	--其他	6.5	30	17		千克		--Other
2920.1900 12	氯氧磷、虫螨畏	6.5	30	17		千克	S	Chlorethoxyfos, methacrifos
2920.1900 13	杀螟硫磷、除线磷	6.5	30	17	9	千克	S	Fenitrothion, dichlofention
2920.1900 14	异氯磷、皮蝇磷	6.5	30	17	9	千克	S	Isochlorthion, fenchlorphos
2920.1900 15	溴硫磷、乙基溴硫磷、硝虫硫磷	6.5	30	17	9	千克	S	Bromophos, bromofos - ethyl, xiaochongthion
2920.1900 16	甲基增效磷、增效磷	6.5	30	17	9	千克		Methyl piperonyl phosphorus, piperonyl phosphorus
2920.1900 17	碘硫磷、苯稻瘟净	6.5	30	17		千克	S	Lodofenphos, inezin 2920. 1900 171 Lodofenphos,
2920.1900 18	甲基立枯磷、克菌磷	6.5	30	17	9	千克	S	Tolclofos - methyl, pyrazophos
2920.1900 19	速杀硫磷、丰丙磷	6.5	30	17	9	千克	S	Heterophos, apidan
2920.1900 90	其他硫代磷酸酯及其盐(包括它们的卤化、磺化、硝化或亚硝化衍生物)	6.5	30	17	9	千克		Other thiophosphoric esters (phosphorothioates) and their salts; their halogenated, sulphonated, nitrated or nitrosated derivatives
	-其他:							-Other:
	---亚磷酸酯:							---Phosphites:
2920.9011	----亚磷酸三甲酯	6.5	30	17	9	千克	23	----Trimethyl phosphite
2920.9012	----亚磷酸三乙酯	6.5	30	17	9	千克	23	----Triethyl phosphite
2920.9013	----亚磷酸二甲酯	6.5	30	17	9	千克	23	----Dimethyl phosphite
2920.9014	----亚磷酸二乙酯	6.5	30	17	9	千克	23	----Diethyl phosphite

税则号列	货 品 名 称	最惠(%)	普通	增值税率	出口退税	计量单位	监管条件	Article Description
2920.9019	----其他	6.5	30	17	9	千克		----Other
2920.9090	---其他		30	17		千克		---Other
2920.9090暂 01	碳酸二苯酯	2	30	17	9	千克		Diphenyl carbonate
2920.9090 11	硫丹	6.5	30	17		千克	S	Endosulfan
2920.9090 12	治螟磷	6.5	30	17		千克	S	Sulfotep
2920.9090 13	消螨通	6.5	30	17		千克	S	Dinobuton
2920.9090 14	炔螨特	6.5	30	17	9	千克	S	Propargite
2920.9090 15	浸种磷	6.5	30	17		千克	S	Izopamfos
2920.9090 16	赛松	6.5	30	17		千克	S	Sesone
2920.9090 20	三乙基砷酸酯	6.5	30	17	9	千克	X	Thiethyl arsenate
2920.9090 90	其他无机酸酯(不包括卤化氢的酯)(包括其盐以及它们的卤化、磺化、硝化或亚硝化衍生物)	6.5	30	17	9	千克		Other esters of other inorganic acids (excluding esters of hydrogen halides) and their salts; their halogenated, sulphonated, nitrated or nitrosated derivatives.
	第九分章　含氮基化合物							IX. -NITROGEN-FUNCTION COMPOUNDS
29.21	氨基化合物:							**Amine-function compounds:**
	-无环单胺及其衍生物以及它们的盐:							-Acyclic monoamines and their derivatives; salts thereof:
2921.1100	--甲胺、二甲胺或三甲胺及其盐	6.5	30	17	9	千克		--Methylamine, di- or trimethylamine and their salts
2921.1100 10	二甲胺	6.5	30	17	9	千克	23	Dimethylamine
2921.1100 20	二甲胺盐酸盐	6.5	30	17	9	千克	23	Dimethylamine hydrochloride
2921.1100 30	甲胺盐	6.5	30	17	9	千克		Salts of methylamine
2921.1100 90	甲胺、三甲胺及其盐	6.5	30	17	9	千克	AB	Methylamine, trimethylamine and their salts
	--其他:							--Other:
2921.1910	---二正丙胺	4	11	17	9	千克	AB	---Di-*n*-propylamine
2921.1920暂	---异丙胺	2	30	17	9	千克		---Isopropyl amine
2921.1930	---N,N-二(2-氯乙基)乙胺	6.5	30	17	9	千克	32	---N,N-Bis(2-chloroethyl) ethylamine
2921.1940	---N,N-二(2-氯乙基)甲胺	6.5	30	17	9	千克	32	---N,N-Bis(2-chloroethyl) methylamine
2921.1950	---三(2-氯乙基)胺	6.5	30	17	9	千克	32	---Tri-(2-chloroethyl) amine
2921.1960	---二烷(甲、乙、正丙或异丙)氨基乙基-2-氯及其质子化盐	6.5	30	17	9	千克	23	---N,N-Dialkyl (Me, Et, n-Pr or i-Pr) aminoethyl-2-chlorides and corresponking protonated salts
2921.1990	---其他	6.5	30	17		千克		---Other
2921.1990 11	三乙胺(单一成分,用做点火剂)	6.5	30	17	9	千克	3A	Triethylamine (Single component, used for igniter)
2921.1990 20	二异丙胺	6.5	30	17	9	千克	3	Diisopropylamine
2921.1990 31	2-氨基丁烷	6.5	30	17		千克	S	2-Amidobutane
2921.1990 33	胺鲜酯	6.5	30	17	9	千克	S	Diethyl aminoethyl hexanoate
2921.1990 90	其他无环单胺及其衍生物及其盐	6.5	30	17	9	千克		Other acyclic monoamines and their derivatives; salts thereof
	-无环多胺及其衍生物以及它们的盐:							-Acyclic polyamines and their derivatives; salts thereof:
	--乙二胺及其盐:							--Ethylenediamine and its salts:
2921.2110	---乙二胺	6.5	30	17	9	千克		---Ethylenediamine
2921.2190	---其他	6.5	30	17	9	千克		---Other
	--六亚甲基二胺及其盐:							--Hexamethylenediamine and its salts:
2921.2210	---己二酸己二胺盐(尼龙-6,6盐)	6.5	20	17	9	千克		---Hexamethylene adipamide (nylon-6,6 salt)
2921.2290	---其他	6.5	30	17	9	千克		---Other
2921.2900	--其他	6.5	30	17	9	千克		--Other
2921.2900 10	辛菌胺	6.5	30	17	9	千克	S	2921290010
2921.2900 90	其他无环多胺及其衍生物(包括它们的盐)	6.5	30	17	9	千克		2921290090
2921.3000	-环烷单胺或多胺、环烯单胺或多胺、环萜烯单胺或多胺及其衍生物以及它们的盐	6.5	30	17	9	千克		-Cyclanic, cyclenic or cycloterpenic monoor polyamines, and their derivatives; salts thereof
2921.3000 10	丙己君及其盐	6.5	30	17	9	千克	I	Propylhexedrine and its salts
2921.3000 30	氨基羧酸环丙烷	6.5	30	17	9	千克	S	1-Aminocy-clopropane-1-carboxylic acid (ACC)
2921.3000 40	乙撑亚胺	6.5	30	17	9	千克	AB	Ethylenimine

税则号列	货品名称	最惠(%)	普通	增值税率	出口退税	计量单位	监管条件	Article Description
2921.3000 90	其他环(烷、烯、萜烯)单胺或多胺(包括其衍生物及它们的盐)	6.5	30	17	9	千克		Other cyclanic, cyclenic or cycloterpenic monoor polyamines, and their derivatives; salts thereof
	-芳香单胺及其衍生物以及它们的盐:							-Aromatic monoamines and their derivatives; salts thereof:
	--苯胺及其盐:							--Aniline and its salts:
2921.4110	---苯胺	6.5	20	17	9	千克	X	---Aniline
2921.4190	---其他	6.5	30	17	9	千克		---Other
2921.4200	--苯胺衍生物及其盐	6.5	30	17	9	千克		--Aniline derivatives and their salts
2921.4200 12	敌锈钠	6.5	30	17	9	千克	S	Sodium – p – aminbenzene sulfonate
2921.4200 13	苯草醚	6.5	30	17	9	千克	S	Dicloran
2921.4200 90	其他苯胺衍生物及其盐	6.5	30	17	9	千克		Other aniline derivatives and their salts
2921.4300	--甲苯胺及其衍生物以及它们的盐	6.5	30	17		千克		--Toluidines and their derivatives; salts thereof
2921.4300 01	间甲苯胺或对甲苯胺	6.5	30	17	9	千克		M – toluidine or p – toluidine
2921.4300 10	氟乐灵	6.5	30	17	9	千克	S	Trifluralin (TC)
2921.4300 20	邻甲苯胺	6.5	30	17	9	千克		*O*-Toluidine
2921.4300 31	溴鼠胺	6.5	30	17		千克	S	Bromethalin
2921.4300 32	乙丁氟灵	6.5	30	17	9	千克	S	Benfluralin
2921.4300 33	氯乙氟灵	6.5	30	17	9	千克	S	Fluchloraline
2921.4300 34	环丙氟灵	6.5	30	17	9	千克	S	Profluralin
2921.4300 35	乙丁烯氟灵	6.5	30	17	9	千克	S	Ethalfluralin
2921.4300 36	地乐灵	6.5	30	17	9	千克	S	Dipropalin
2921.4300 37	氯乙灵	6.5	30	17	9	千克	S	Chlornidine
2921.4300 38	氟节胺	6.5	30	17	9	千克	S	Flumetralin
2921.4300 90	甲苯胺盐、甲苯胺衍生物及其盐	6.5	30	17	9	千克		Toluidines, toluidine derivatives and salts thereof
2921.4400	--二苯胺及其衍生物以及它们的盐	6.5	30	17	17	千克		--Diphenylamine and its derivatives; salts thereof
2921.4500	--1-萘胺(α-萘胺)、2-萘胺(β-萘胺)及其衍生物以及它们的盐	6.5	30	17	9	千克		--1-Naphthylamine (α-naphthylamine), 2-naphthylamine (β-naphthylamine) and their derivatives; salts thereof
2921.4500 10	2–萘胺	6.5	30	17	9	千克	X	2-Naphthylamine
2921.4500 90	1–萘胺和2–萘胺的衍生物及盐(包括1–萘胺)	6.5	30	17	9	千克		1-Naphthylamine and 2-Naphthylamine and its derivatires salis thereof
2921.4600	--安非他明(INN)、苄非他明(INN)、右苯丙胺(INN)、乙非他明、芬坎法明(INN)、利非他明、左苯丙胺(INN)、美芬雷司(INN)、苯丁胺(INN)以及它们的盐	6.5	30	17	9	千克		--Amfetamine(INN), benzfetamine(INN), dexamfetamine(INN), etilamfetamine(INN), fencamfamin(INN), lefetamine(INN), levamfetamine(INN), mefenorex(INN) and phentermine(INN); salts thereof
2921.4600 11	安非他明、苄非他明、右苯丙胺(包括它们的盐)	6.5	30	17	9	千克	I	Amfetamine(INN), benzfetamine(INN), dexamfetamine(INN)(salts thereof)
2921.4600 12	乙非他明、芬坎法明、利非他明(包括它们的盐)	6.5	30	17	9	千克	I	Etilamfetamine(INN), fencamfamin(INN), lefetamine(INN)(salts thereof)
2921.4600 13	左苯丙胺、美芬雷司、芬特明(包括它们的盐)	6.5	30	17	9	千克	I	levamfetamine(INN), mefenorex(INN) and phentermine(INN)(salts thereof)
	--其他:							--Other:
2921.4910	---对异丙基苯胺	4	11	17	9	千克		---*p*-Isopropyl-aniline
2921.4920	---二甲基苯胺	6.5	20	17	9	千克		---Dimethylanilines
2921.4930	---2,6-甲基乙基苯胺	4	11	17	9	千克		---2,6-Methyl ethyl aniline
2921.4940	---2,6-二乙基苯胺	6.5	20	17	9	千克		---2,6-Diethylaniline
2921.4990	---其他	6.5	30	17	9	千克		---Other
2921.4990 11	异丙乐灵	6.5	30	17	9	千克	S	Isopropalin
2921.4990 12	仲丁灵	6.5	30	17	9	千克	S	Butralin
2921.4990 13	二甲戊灵	6.5	30	17	9	千克	S	Pendimethalin
2921.4990 20	4–氨基联苯	6.5	30	17	9	千克	X	4 – Aminobiphenyl
2921.4990 31	乙环利定,二甲基安非他明(以及它们的盐)	6.5	30	17	9	千克	I	Eticyclidine, dimethylamphetamine (and their salt)
2921.4990 32	芬氟拉明、右旋芬氟拉明(以及它们的盐)	6.5	30	17	9	千克	I	Fenfluramine, d – fenfluramine (and their salt)

税则号列	货品名称	最惠(%)	普通	增值税率	出口退税	计量单位	监管条件	Article Description
2921.4990 90	其他芳香单胺及衍生物及它们的盐	6.5	30	17	9	千克		Other aromatic monoamine and derivants and their salt
	-芳香多胺及其衍生物以及它们的盐:							-Aromatic polyamines and their derivatives; salts thereof:
	--邻-、间-、对-苯二胺、二氨基甲苯及其衍生物以及它们的盐:							--*O*-, *m*-, *p*-Phenylenediamine, diaminotoluenes, and their derivatives; salts thereof:
2921.5110	---邻苯二胺	4	11	17	9	千克		---*o*-Phenylenediamine
2921.5190	---其他	6.5	30	17		千克		---Other
2921.5190 11	氨氟灵	6.5	30	17	9	千克	S	Dinitamine
2921.5190 12	氨氟乐灵	6.5	30	17	9	千克	S	Prodiamine
2921.5190 20	2,4-二氨基甲苯	6.5	30	17	17	千克	X	2,4-Diaminotoluene
2921.5190 90	间-、对-苯二胺、二氨基甲苯等(包括衍生物及它们的盐)	6.5	30	17	17	千克		O-, m-, p-Phenylene diamine, diaminotoluene (including and their derivatives; salts thereof)
2921.5900	--其他	6.5	30	17		千克		--Other
2921.5900 10	三氨基三硝基苯	6.5	30	17	9	千克	3	Triamino trinitrobenzene
2921.5900 20	联苯胺(4,4'-二氨基联苯)	6.5	30	17	9	千克	89	Benzidine(4,4′-diaminobiphenyl)
2921.5900 31	4,4'-二氨基-3,3'-二氯二苯基甲烷	6.5	30	17	9	千克	X	4,4′-Diamino-3,3′-dicophane
2921.5900 32	3,3'-二氯联苯胺	6.5	30	17	9	千克	X	3,3′-Dichlorobenzidine
2921.5900 33	4,4'-二氨基二苯基甲烷	6.5	30	17	13	千克	X	4,4′-Methylenedianiline
2921.5900 90	其他芳香多胺及衍生物及它们的盐	6.5	30	17	13	千克		Other aromatic polyamines and their derivatives; salts thereof
29.22	**含氧基氨基化合物:**							**Oxygen-function amino-compounds:**
	-氨基醇(但含有一种以上含氧基的除外)及其醚和酯,以及它们的盐:							-Amino-alcohols, other than those containing more than one kind of oxygen function, their ethers and esters; salts thereof:
2922.1100	--单乙醇胺及其盐	6.5	30	17	9	千克		--Monoethanolamine and its salts
2922.1100 01	单乙醇胺	6.5	30	17	9	千克	AB	Monoethanolamine
2922.1100 90	单乙醇胺盐	6.5	30	17	9	千克		Salts of monoethanolamine
2922.1200	--二乙醇胺及其盐	6.5	30	17	9	千克		--Diethanolamine and its salts
2922.1200 01	二乙醇胺	6.5	30	17	9	千克		Diethanolamine
2922.1200 10	全氟辛基磺酸二乙醇胺	6.5	30	17	9	千克	X	Perfluorooctylsulfonyl diethanolamine
2922.1200 90	二乙醇胺盐	6.5	30	17	9	千克		Salts of diethanolamine
	--三乙醇胺及其盐:							--Triethanolamine and its salts:
2922.1310	---三乙醇胺	6.5	30	17	9	千克	23AB	---Triethanolamine
2922.1320	---三乙醇胺盐	6.5	30	17	9	千克		---Salts of triethanolamine
2922.1320 20	三乙醇胺盐酸盐	6.5	30	17	9	千克	23	Triethanolamine hydrochloride
2922.1320 90	其他三乙醇胺的盐	6.5	30	17	9	千克		Other salts of triethanolamine
2922.1400	--右丙氧吩(INN)及其盐	6.5	30	17	9	千克	W	--Dextropropoxyphene (INN) and its salts
	--其他:							--Other:
2922.1910	---乙胺丁醇	6.5	30	17	9	千克		---Ethylamino butanol (Ethambutol)
	---二烷(甲、乙、正丙或异丙)氨基乙-2-醇及其质子化盐:							---N, N-Dialkyl-(Me, Et, n-Pr or i-Pr) aminoethane-2-ols and corresponding protonated salts:
2922.1921	----二甲氨基乙醇及其质子化盐	6.5	30	17	9	千克		----N, N-Dimethylaminoethanol and corresponding protonated salts
2922.1922	----二乙氨基乙醇及其质子化盐	6.5	30	17	9	千克		----N, N-Diethylaminoethanol and corresponding protonated salts
2922.1922 10	2-二乙氨基乙醇(或称N,N-二乙基乙醇胺)	6.5	30	17	9	千克	3	2-Diethylaminoethanol (N,N-Diethylethanolamine)
2922.1922 90	二乙氨基乙醇的质子化盐	6.5	30	17	9	千克		Protonated salts of 2-Diethylaminoethanol
2922.1929	----其他	6.5	30	17	9	千克	23	----Other
2922.1930	---乙基二乙醇胺	6.5	30	17	9	千克	23	---Ethyldiethanolamine
2922.1940	---甲基二乙醇胺	6.5	30	17	9	千克	23	---Methyldiethanolamine
2922.1950	---本芴醇	6.5	30	17	9	千克		---Benflumelol

税则号列	货品名称	最惠(%)	普通	增值税率	出口退税	计量单位	监管条件	Article Description
2922.1990	---其他	6.5	30	17	9	千克		---Other
2922.1990 10	增产胺	6.5	30	17	9	千克	S	Ethanamine
2922.1990 20	克仑特罗	6.5	30	17	9	千克	L	Clenbuterol
2922.1990 31	醋美沙朵、阿醋美沙朵、阿法美沙朵(以及它们的盐)	6.5	30	17	9	千克	W	Acetylmethadol, alphacetylmethadol, alphamethadol (and its salts)
2922.1990 32	倍醋美沙多、倍他美沙朵(以及它们的盐)	6.5	30	17	9	千克	W	Betacetylmethadol, betamethadol (and their salt)
2922.1990 33	地美沙多、地美庚醇、诺美沙朵(以及它们的盐)	6.5	30	17	9	千克	W	Dimenoxadol, dimepheptanol, noracymethadol (and their salt)
2922.1990 90	其他氨基醇及其醚、酯和它们的盐(但含有一种以上含氧基的除外)	6.5	30	17	9	千克		Other alkamine and their ethers, esters and their salt (other than those containing more than one kind of Oxygen function)
	-氨基萘酚和其他氨基酚(但含有一种以上含氧基的除外)及其醚和酯,以及它们的盐:							-Amino-naphthols and amino-phenols, other than those containing more than one kind of oxygen function, their ethers and esters; salts thereof:
2922.2100	--氨基羟基萘磺酸及其盐	6.5	30	17	13	千克		--Aminohydroxynaphthal-ene-sulphonic acid and their salts
	--其他:							--Other:
2922.2910	---茴香胺、二茴香胺、氨基苯乙醚及其盐	6.5	30	17	9	千克		---Anisidine, dianisidine, phenetidine and their salts
2922.2990	---其他	6.5	30	17	9	千克		---Other
2922.2990 11	布苯丙胺、二甲氧基乙基安非他明(以及它们的盐)	6.5	30	17	9	千克	I	Brolamfetamine, dimethoxy-4 – ethyl, amphetamine (and their salt)
2922.2990 12	二甲氧基安非他明、副甲氧基安非他明(以及它们的盐)	6.5	30	17	9	千克	I	12,5 – Dimethoxyamfetamine, paramethoxyamfetamine (and their salt)
2922.2990 13	二甲氧基甲苯异丙胺、三甲氧基安非他明(以及它们的盐)	6.5	30	17	9	千克	I	Domdimethoxy – methyl – amphetamine, trimethoxyamfetamine (and their salt)
2922.2990 14	2,5-二甲氧基 – 4 – 溴苯乙胺、地佐辛(以及它们的盐)	6.5	30	17	9	千克	I	4-bromo – 2,5 – dimethoxyphenethylamine, dezocine (and their salt)
2922.2990 15	他喷他多(CAS 号:175591 – 23 – 8)	6.5	30	17	9	千克	I	Tapentadol(CAS:175591 – 23 – 8)
2922.2990 16	2,5 – 二甲氧基 – 4 – 碘苯乙胺(CAS 号:69587 – 11 – 7)	6.5	30	17	9	千克	I	2,5 – Dimethoxy – 4 – iodophenethylamine (CAS:69587 – 11 – 7)
2922.2990 17	2,5 – 二甲氧基苯乙胺(CAS 号:3600 – 86 – 0)	6.5	30	17	9	千克	I	2,5 – Dimethoxy – phenethylamine(CAS:3600 – 86 – 0)
2922.2990 90	其他氨基(萘酚、酚)及醚、酯(包括它们的盐,但含有一种以上含氧基的除外)	6.5	30	17	9	千克		Other amino (naphthol, hydroxybenzene) and aether, ester (including their salt, but with the exception of those containing one or more oxygen containing groups
	-氨基醛、氨基酮和氨基醌,但含有一种以上含氧基的除外,以及它们的盐:							-Amino-aldehydes, amino-ketones and amino-quinones, other than those containing more than one kind of oxygen function; salts thereof:
2922.3100	--安非拉酮、美沙酮和去甲美沙酮以及它们的盐	6.5	30	17	9	千克		--Amfepramone (INN), methadone (INN) and normethadone(INN); salts thereof
2922.3100 10	安非拉酮及其盐	6.5	30	17	9	千克	I	Amfepramone(INN) and salts thereof
2922.3100 20	美沙酮、去甲美沙酮及它们的盐	6.5	30	17	9	千克	W	Methadone (INN), normethadone (INN) and salts thereof
	--其他:							--Other:
2922.3910	---4-甲基甲卡西酮	6.5	30	17	9	千克	I	---4-Methcathinone
2922.3990	---其他	6.5	30	17	9	千克		---Other
2922.3990 10	氯胺酮及其盐	6.5	30	17	9	千克	I	Ketamine and salts thereof
2922.3990 20	灭藻醌	6.5	30	17	9	千克	S	Quinoclamine
2922.3990 30	异美沙酮及其盐	6.5	30	17	9	千克	W	Isomethadone and salts thereof
2922.3990 40	甲卡西酮及其盐	6.5	30	17	9	千克	I	Methcathinone and salts thereof
2922.3990 50	4 – 甲基乙卡西酮(4 – MEC)(CAS 号:1225617 – 18 – 4)	6.5	30	17	9	千克	I	4 – Methylethcathinone(CAS:1225617 – 18 – 4)

税则号列	货品名称	最惠(%)	普通	增值税率	出口退税	计量单位	监管条件	Article Description
2922.3990 90	其他氨基醛、氨基酮及其盐(包括氨基醌及其盐,但含有一种以上含氧基除外)	6.5	30	17	9	千克		Other amino - aldehydes, amino - ketones and amino - quinones, other than those containing more than one kind of oxygen function and salts thereof
	-氨基酸及其酯但含有一种以上含氧基的除外以及它们的盐:							-Amino-acids, other than those containing more than one kind of oxygen function, and their esters, salts thereof:
	--赖氨酸及其酯,以及它们的盐:							--Lysine and its esters; salts thereof:
2922.4110	---赖氨酸	5	20	17	9	千克	AB	---Lysine
2922.4190	---其他	6	30	17	9	千克	AB	---Other
	--谷氨酸及其盐:							--Glutamic acid and its salts:
2922.4210暂	---谷氨酸	5	90	17	9	千克	AB	---Glutamic acid
2922.4220	---谷氨酸钠	10	130	17		千克	AB	---Sodium glutamate
2922.4290	---其他	6.5	30	17	9	千克	AB	---Other
	--邻氨基苯甲酸(氨茴酸)及其盐:							--Anthranilic acid and its salts:
2922.4310	---邻氨基苯甲酸(氨茴酸)	6.5	20	17	9	千克	23	---Anthranilic acids
2922.4390	---其他	6.5	30	17	9	千克		---Other
2922.4400	--替利定(INN)及其盐	6.5	30	17	9	千克	W	--Tilidine(INN) and its salts
	--其他:							--Other:
	---其他氨基酸:							---Amino acids:
2922.4911	----氨甲环酸	6.5	20	17	13	千克	AB	----Tranexamic acid
2922.4919	----其他	6.5	20	17	13	千克		----Other
2922.4919 10	安咪奈丁	6.5	20	17	13	千克	I	Amineptine
2922.4919 90	其他氨基酸	6.5	20	17	13	千克	AB	Other amino acids
	---其他:							---Other:
2922.4991	----普鲁卡因	6	20	17	9	千克		----Procaine
2922.4999	----其他	6.5	30	17		千克		----Other
2922.4999 11	草灭畏	6.5	30	17	9	千克	ABS	Chloramben
2922.4999 12	灭杀威、灭除威、混灭威等(害扑威、速灭威、残杀威、猛杀威)	6.5	30	17	9	千克	ABS	Meobal, XMC, dimethacarb (etrofol, metolcarb, propoxur, promecarb)
2922.4999 13	兹克威、除害威	6.5	30	17		千克	ABS	Mexacarbate, allyxycarb
2922.4999 14	异丙威	6.5	30	17	9	千克	ABS	Isoprocarb
2922.4999 15	仲丁威、畜虫威、合杀威	6.5	30	17	9	千克	ABS	Fenobucarb, butacarb, bufencarb
2922.4999 16	甲萘威、地麦威、蜱虱威	6.5	30	17	9	千克	ABS	Carbaryl, dimetan, promacyl
2922.4999 17	除线威	6.5	30	17	9	千克	ABS	cloethocarb
2922.4999 18	氨酰丙酸(盐酸盐)	6.5	30	17	9	千克	ABS	Hydrochlorate
2922.4999 19	安咪奈丁的盐	6.5	20	17	13	千克	I	Salts of amineptine
2922.4999 90	其他氨基酸及其酯及它们的盐(含有一种以上含氧基的除外)	6.5	30	17	9	千克	AB	Other amino - acids and their esters; their salt(Other than those containing more than one kind of oxygen function)
	-氨基醇酚、氨基酸酚及其他含氧基氨基化合物:							-Amino-alcohol-phenols, amino-acid-phenols and other amino-compounds with oxygen function
2922.5010	---对羟基苯甘氨酸及其邓钾盐	6.5	30	17		千克	AB	---D-p-hydroxyphenylglycine and deng sylvite
2922.5020	---莱克多巴胺和盐酸莱克多巴胺	6.5	30	17	9	千克	89	---Ractopamine and ractopamine hydrochloride
2922.5090	---其他	6.5	30	17		千克		---Other
2922.5090 10	曲马多	6.5	30	17		千克	I	Tramadol
2922.5090 90	其他氨基醇酚、氨基酸酚(包括其他含氧基氨基化合物)	6.5	30	17		千克	AB	Other amino - alcohol - phenols, amino - acid phenols(including other amino - compounds with oxygen function)
29.23	**季铵盐及季铵碱;卵磷脂及其他磷氨基类脂,不论是否已有化学定义:**							**Quaternary ammonium salts and hydroxides; lecithins and other phosphoaminolipids, whether or not chemically defined:**
2923.1000	-胆碱及其盐	6.5	30	17	9	千克	AB	-Choline and its salts
2923.2000	-卵磷脂及其他磷氨基类脂	6.5	30	17	9	千克	AB	-Lecithins and other phosphoaminolipids
2923.9000	-其他	6.5	30	17	9	千克		-Other
2923.9000 11	矮壮素	6.5	30	17	9	千克	S	Chlorocholine chloride
2923.9000 12	菊胺酯	6.5	30	17	9	千克	S	Tetramethrin

税则号列	货品名称	最惠(%)	普通	增值税率	出口退税	计量单位	监管条件	Article Description
2923.9000 13	全氟辛基磺酸四乙胺、全氟辛基磺酸双癸基二甲基铵	6.5	30	17	9	千克	X	Perfluorooctanesulfonic acid four triethylamine, perfluorooctanesulfonic acid bis decyl two methyl ammonium
2923.9000 90	其他季铵盐及季铵碱	6.5	30	17	9	千克		Other quaternary ammonium salts and hydroxides
29.24	**羧基酰胺基化合物;碳酸酰胺基化合物:**							**Carboxyamide-function compounds; amide-function compounds of carbonic acid:**
	-无环酰胺(包括无环氨基甲酸酯)及其衍生物以及它们的盐:							-Acyclic amides (including acyclic carbamates) and their derivatives; salts thereof:
2924.1100	--甲丙氨酯(INN)	6.5	30	17	9	千克	I	--Meprobamate(INN)
2924.1200	--氟乙酰胺(ISO)久效磷(ISO)及磷胺(ISO)	6.5	30	17		千克		--Fluoroacetamide(ISO), monocrotophos(ISO). and phophamidon(ISO)
2924.1200 10	氟乙酰胺(ISO)(氟乙酰胺别名敌蚜胺)	6.5	30	17		千克	89	Fluoroacetamide(ISO)
2924.1200 90	久效磷(ISO)及磷胺(ISO)	6.5	30	17		千克	X	Monocrotophos(ISO), phosphamidor(ISO)
	--其他(INN):							--Other:
2924.1910	---二甲基甲酰胺	6.5	30	17	9	千克		---N,N-dimethylformamide
2924.1990	---其他	6.5	30	17		千克		---Other
2924.1990 12	百治磷	6.5	30	17		千克	S	Dicrotophos
2924.1990 13	溴乙酰胺	6.5	30	17		千克	S	Bromoacetamide
2924.1990 14	霜霉威	6.5	30	17	9	千克	S	Propamocarb
2924.1990 15	叶枯炔	6.5	30	17		千克	S	Cellocidin
2924.1990 16	二丙烯草胺	6.5	30	17	9	千克	S	Allidochlor
2924.1990 17	解草烯	6.5	30	17	9	千克		Solution humulene
2924.1990 18	驱蚊酯	6.5	30	17	9	千克	S	Dimethyl phthalate
2924.1990 30	甲丙氨酯的盐	6.5	30	17	9	千克	I	Salts of meprobamate (INN)
2924.1990 40	丙烯酰胺	6.5	30	17	9	千克	X	Acrylamide
2924.1990 90	其他无环酰胺(包括无环氨基甲酸酯)(包括其衍生物及其盐)	6.5	30	17	13	千克		Other acyclic amides (including acyclic carbamates) (and their derivatives; salts thereof)
	-环酰胺(包括环氨基甲酸酯)及其衍生物以及它们的盐:							-Cyclic amides (including cyclic carbamates) and their derivatives; salts thereof:
2924.2100	--酰脲及其衍生物以及它们的盐	6.5	30	17	9	千克		--Ureides and their derivatives; salts thereof
2924.2100 10	氟环脲	6.5	30	17	9	千克	S	Flucycloxuron
2924.2100 20	绿麦隆	6.5	30	17	9	千克	S	chlortoluron
2924.2100 90	其他酰脲及其衍生物以及它们的盐	6.5	30	17	9	千克		Other ureides and its derivants and their salt
2924.2300	--2-乙酰氨基苯甲酸(N-乙酰邻氨基苯甲酸)及其盐	6.5	30	17	9	千克		--2-Acetamidobenzoic acid (N-Acetylanthranilic acid) and its salts
2924.2300 10	2-乙酰氨基苯甲酸、N-乙酰邻氨基苯酸(包括N-乙酰邻氨基苯甲酸)	6.5	30	17	9	千克	23	2-Acetamidobenzoic acid; N - acetylanthranilicacid (including N-acetamidobenzoic acid)
2924.2300 90	2-乙酰氨基苯甲酸的盐	6.5	30	17	9	千克		Salts of 2-acetamidobenzoic acid
2924.2400	--炔己蚁胺(INN)	6.5	30	17	9	千克	I	--Ethinamate(INN)
	--其他:							--Other:
2924.2910	---对乙酰氨基苯乙醚(非那西丁)	6	30	17	9	千克	Q	---Phenacetin
2924.2920	---对乙酰氨基酚(扑热息痛)	6	30	17	9	千克	Q	---*p*-Acetaminophenol (paracetanol)
2924.2930	---阿斯巴甜	6.5	30	17	9	千克		---Aspartame
2924.2990	---其他	6.5	30	17	9	千克		---Other
2924.2990 11	避蚊胺、灭锈胺、叶枯酞、水杨菌胺、氟丁酰草胺(包括苯酰菌胺)	6.5	30	17	9	千克	S	Deet, mepronil, tecloftalam, trichlamide, buflubutamid(including zoxamide)
2924.2990 12	萘草胺、新燕灵、非草隆、氯炔灵、苄草隆	6.5	30	17	9	千克	S	Naptalam, benzoylprop-ethyl , fenuron , chlorbufam chlorbufam
2924.2990 13	燕麦灵、苄胺灵、特草灵、特胺灵、环丙酰亚胺	6.5	30	17	9	千克	S	Barban dichlormate, terbutol , karbutilate
2924.2990 14	毒草胺、丁烯草胺、二氯己酰草胺	6.5	30	17	9	千克	S	Propachlor, butenachlor, dichloro acetyl thenylchlor
2924.2990 15	萘丙胺、牧草胺、溴丁酰草胺	6.5	30	17	9	千克	S	Naproanilide, tebutam, bromobutide
2924.2990 16	氯甲酰草胺、麦草伏M、麦草伏	6.5	30	17	9	千克	S	Clomeprop, flamprop M, flamprop
2924.2990 17	氯虫酰肼、异丙甲草胺、苯肽胺酸等(包括精异丙甲草胺、缬霉威)	6.5	30	17	9	千克	S	Halofenozide, metolachlor, phthalanillic (including s-metolachlor, iprovalicarb)

税则号列	货品名称	最惠(%)	普通	增值税率	出口退税	计量单位	监管条件	Article Description
2924.2990 18	灭害威	6.5	30	17	9	千克	S	aminocarb ;
2924.2990 19	苯氧威	6.5	30	17	9	千克	S	fenoxycarb
2924.2990 20	氟酰脲、环丙酰草胺、烯草胺	6.5	30	17	9	千克	S	Fluoylureas, cyclanilide, pethoxamid
2924.2990 31	苯胺灵、苯霜灵、丙草胺、敌稗等(包括丙炔草胺、草不隆、草完隆、除虫脲、除幼脲)	6.5	30	17	9	千克	S	Propham, benalaxyl, pretilachlor, propanil (including prynachlor、neburon, noruron diful Benzuron, penfluron, dichlorbenzuron)
2924.2990 32	敌草胺、敌草隆、二甲苯草胺等(包括丁草胺、丁酰草胺、二甲草胺、氟苯脲、氟草隆)	6.5	30	17	9	千克	S	Napropamide, diuron, xylachlor (including Butachlor, chloranocryl dimethachlor , teflubenzuron, fluometuron)
2924.2990 33	庚酰草胺、环丙草胺、环酰草胺、氟虫隆等(包括氟虫脲、氟铃脲、氟酰胺、氟蚁灵、氟幼脲)	6.5	30	17	9	千克	S	Monalide, cyclanilide, cypromid, flufenoxuron (including fluorobenzamide, hexaflumuron, flutolanil nifluridide, penfluron)
2924.2990 34	甲氯酰草胺、甲霜灵、环草隆等(包括环莠隆、甲草胺、甲氧隆、克草胺、枯草隆)	6.5	30	17	9	千克	S	Pentanochlor metalaxyl, siduron (including cycluron, alachlor, metoxuron, kecaoan, chloroxuron)
2924.2990 35	甲基杀草隆、枯莠隆、邻酰胺等(包括绿麦隆、氯苯胺灵、麦草氟甲酯、麦草氟异丙酯)	6.5	30	17	9	千克	S	Methyldymron, difenoxuron, mebenil (including chlortoluron, chlorpropham, flamprop – methyl, flamprop – isopropyl)
2924.2990 36	灭草隆、灭幼脲、炔苯酰草胺等(包括麦锈灵、棉胺宁、灭草灵、炔草隆、杀草胺)	6.5	30	17	9	千克	S	Monuron, chlorbenzuron, propyzamide (including benodanil, phenisopham , swep, buturon, ethaprochlor)
2924.2990 37	虱螨脲、双苯酰草胺、双酰草胺等(包括杀草隆、杀铃脲、杀螺胺、莎稗磷)	6.5	30	17	9	千克	S	Lufenuron diphenamide, carbetamide (includaimuron, triflumuron, niclosamide, anilofos, dichlormide)
2924.2990 38	甜菜安、特丁草胺、乙氧苯草胺等(包括甜菜宁、戊菌隆、酰草隆、乙草胺、乙霉威)	6.5	30	17	9	千克	S	Desmedipham, terbuchlor, ethobenzanid (including Phenmedipham, Pencycuron, Acetochlor, Polystyrene resin)
2924.2990 39	乙酰甲草胺、异丙隆、异草完隆等(包括异丙草胺、异丁草胺)	6.5	30	17	9	千克	S	Diethatyl, isoproturon, isonoruron (including propisochlor, delachlor)
2924.2990 40	炔己蚁胺的盐	6.5	30	17	9	千克	I	Salts of ethinamate(INN)
2924.2990 50	地恩丙胺及其盐	6.5	30	17	9	千克	W	Diampromide and its salts
2924.2990 90	其他环酰胺(包括环氨基甲酸酯)(包括其衍生物以及它们的盐)	6.5	30	17	9	千克		Other cyclic amides (including cyclic carbamates and their derivatives; salts thereof)
29.25	**羧基酰亚胺化合物(包括糖精及其盐)及亚胺基化合物:**							**Carboxyimide-function compounds (including saccharin and its salts) and imine-function compounds:**
	-酰亚胺及其衍生物以及它们的盐:							-Imides and their derivatives; salts thereof:
2925.1100	--糖精及其盐	9	90	17	9	千克	AB	--Saccharin and its salts
2925.1200	--格鲁米特(INN)	6.5	30	17	9	千克	I	--Glutethimide(INN)
2925.1900	--其他	6.5	30	17	9	千克		--Other
2925.1900 10	格鲁米特的盐	6.5	30	17	9	千克	I	Salts of glutethimide (INN)
2925.1900 21	腐霉利	6.5	30	17	9	千克	S	Procymidone
2925.1900 22	菌核净、菌核利、甲菌利、乙菌利	6.5	30	17	9	千克	S	Dimetachlone, dichlozoline, myclozolin, chlozolinate
2925.1900 23	氟烯草酸	6.5	30	17	9	千克	S	Flumiclorac – pentyl
2925.1900 24	胺菊酯(包括右旋胺菊酯、右旋反式胺菊酯、富右旋反式胺菊酯)	6.5	30	17	9	千克	S	Tetramethrin (including d-tetramethrin, d-t-tetramethrin, rich-d-t-tetramethrin
2925.1900 90	其他酰亚胺及其衍生物、盐	6.5	30	17	9	千克		Other imides and their derivatives; salts thereof
	-亚胺及其衍生物以及它们的盐:							-Imines and their derivatives; salts thereof:
2925.2100	--杀虫脒(ISO)	6.5	30	17		千克	89	--Chlordimeform(ISO)
2925.2900	--其他	6.5	30	17	9	千克		--Other
2925.2900 11	杀螨特、杀螨脒	6.5	30	17	9	千克	S	Aramite, semiamitraz
2925.2900 12	单甲脒、伐虫脒、丙烷脒	6.5	30	17	9	千克	S	Semiamitraz, formetanate, propamidine
2925.2900 13	烯肟菌胺、烯肟菌酯、醚菌酯	6.5	30	17	9	千克	S	Trichlamide, enostroburin, kresoxim-methyl
2925.2900 14	双胍辛胺、多果啶、双胍辛胺乙酸盐等(包括双胍三辛烷基苯磺酸盐)	6.5	30	17	9	千克	S	Iminoctadine, dodine, iminoctadine triacetate (including iminoctadinris)
2925.2900 15	禾草灭、氟草醚、增产肟	6.5	30	17	9	千克	S	Alloxydim-sodium, ethoxyfen-ethyl, heptopargil
2925.2900 16	氯代水杨胺、双胍辛乙酸盐、顺己烯醇	6.5	30	17	9	千克	S	LDS, Iminoctadine triacetate, cis – hexenyl
2925.2900 20	羟亚胺及其盐	6.5	30	17	9	千克	23	Oxyamino and its salts

税则号列	货　品　名　称	最惠(%)	普通	增值税率	出口退税	计量单位	监管条件	Article Description
2925.2900 30	双甲脒	6.5	30	17	9	千克	S	Amitraz
2925.2900 90	其他亚胺及其衍生物以及它们的盐	6.5	30	17	9	千克		Other imines and their derivatives; salts thereof
29.26	腈基化合物：							**Nitrile-function compounds:**
2926.1000暂	-丙烯腈	3	30	17	13	千克	X	-Acrylonitrile
2926.2000	-1-氰基胍(双氰胺)	6.5	30	17	13	千克		-1-Cyanoguanidine (dicyandiamide)
2926.3000	-芬普雷司(INN)及其盐;美沙酮中间体(4-氰基-2-二甲氨基-4,4-二苯基丁烷)	6.5	30	17	9	千克		-Fenproporex(INN) and its salts; methadone(INN) intermediate (4-cyano-2-dimethylamino-4, 4-diphenylbutane)
2926.3000 10	美沙酮中间体(4-氰基-2-二甲氨基-4,4-二苯基丁烷)	6.5	30	17	9	千克	W	Methadone (INN) intermediate (4-cyano-2-dimethylamino-4, 4-diphenylbutane)
2926.3000 20	芬普雷司及其盐	6.5	30	17	9	千克	I	Fenproporex (INN) and salts thereof
	-其他：							-Other:
2926.9010	---对氯氰苄	4	11	17	9	千克		---*p*-Chlorobenzyl cyanide
2926.9020	---间苯二甲腈	6.5	30	17	9	千克		---*m*-Phthalonitrile
2926.9090	---其他		30	17	9	千克		---Other
2926.9090 10	甲氰菊酯、S-氰戊菊酯、氯氟氰菊酯(包括氰氟虫腙)	6.5	30	17	9	千克	S	Fenpropathrin, s – fenvalerate, cyhalothrin
2926.9090暂 20	己二腈	1	30	17	9	千克		Hexanedinitrile
2926.9090 30	杀灭菊酯乳剂(含量>25%)	6.5	30	17	9	千克	AB	Fenvalerate emulsion
2926.9090 31	氯氰菊酯、氟氯氰菊酯等(包括高效氯氰菊酯、高效反式氯氰菊酯、高效氟氯氰菊酯)	6.5	30	17	9	千克	S	Cypermethrin, cynuthrin (including beta – cypermethrin, theta-cypermethrin, beta – cyfluthrin)
2926.9090 32	杀螟腈、甲基辛硫磷等(包括敌草腈、碘苯腈、辛酰碘苯腈、溴苯腈、辛酰溴苯腈)	6.5	30	17	9	千克	S	Cyanophos Phoxim – methyl (including dichlobenil, ioxynil, ioxynil octanoate, bromooxynil, bromoxynil octanoate)
2926.9090 33	氯辛硫磷、戊氰威、苯醚氰菊酯等(包括稻瘟酰胺、丙螨氰、右旋苯醚氰菊酯)	6.5	30	17	9	千克	S	Chlorphoxim, nitrilacarb, cyphenothrin (including fenoxanil, malonoben, d – cyphenothrin)
2926.9090 34	戊烯氰氯菊酯、溴氯氰菊酯(包括高效氯氟氰菊酯、精高效氯氟氰菊酯)	6.5	30	17	9	千克	S	Pentmethrin, tralocythrin (including lambda-cyhalothrin, gamma- cyhalothrin)
2926.9090 35	溴氰菊酯、四溴菊酯、氟丙菊酯	6.5	30	17	9	千克	S	Deltamethrin, tralomerhrin, acrinathrin
2926.9090 36	氟氯苯菊酯、氰戊菊酯、乙氰菊酯	6.5	30	17	9	千克	S	Flumethrin, fenvalerate, cycloprothrin
2926.9090 37	氟氰戊菊酯、溴氟菊酯、溴灭菊酯	6.5	30	17	9	千克	S	Flucythrinate, brofluthrinate, brofenvalerate
2926.9090 38	氰菌胺、百菌清、霜脲氰、溴菌腈	6.5	30	17	9	千克	S	Fenoxanil, chlorothalonil, cymoxanil, bromothalonil
2926.9090 39	氟胺氰菊酯、氰氟草酯、苯氰菊酯(包括富右旋反式苯氰菊酯)	6.5	30	17	9	千克	S	Tau – fluralinate cyhalofop-butyl, cyphenothrin (including rich-d-t-cyphenothrin)
2926.9090 41	氰烯菌酯	6.5	30	17	9	千克	S	js399 – 19
2926.9090 50	辛硫磷	6.5	30	17	9	千克	S	Phoxim
2926.9090 60	丁氟螨酯	6.5	30	17	9	千克	S	Cyflumetofen
2926.9090 70	3－氧－2－苯基丁腈	6.5	30	17	9	千克	23	3 – Methyl – 2 – phenylbutyronitrile
2926.9090 90	其他腈基化合物	6.5	30	17	9	千克		Other nitrile-function compounds
29.27	重氮化合物、偶氮化合物及氧化偶氮化合物：							**Diazo-, azo-. or azoxy-compounds:**
2927.0000	重氮化合物、偶氮化合物及氧化偶氮化合物	6.5	30	17	9	千克		Diazo-, azo-. or azoxy-compounds
2927.0000 10	敌磺钠(包括氧化偶氮化合物)	6.5	30	17	9	千克	S	Dexon (including azoxy-compounds)
2927.0000 20	4-二丙基氨基苯重氮氯化锌盐	6.5	30	17	9	千克	AB	4-Dipropylaminobenzenediazoniumzinc chloride
2927.0000 90	其他重氮化合物、偶氮化合物等(包括氧化偶氮化合物)	6.5	30	17	9	千克		Other diazo-azo-compounds (including azoxy compounds)
29.28	肼(联氨)及胲(羟胺)的有机衍生物：							**Organic derivatives of hydrazine or of hydroxylamine:**
2928.0000	肼(联氨)及胲(羟胺)的有机衍生物	6.5	20	17	9	千克		Organic derivatives of hydrazine or of hydroxylamine
2928.0000 10	偏二甲肼	6.5	20	17	9	千克	3	Dimethylhydrazine
2928.0000 20	甲基肼	6.5	20	17	9	千克	3A	Methylhydrazine
2928.0000 31	抑食肼、虫酰肼、丁酰肼、联苯肼酯(包括肟菌酯,苯氧菌胺)	6.5	20	17	9	千克	S	RH – 5849, tebufenozide, daminozide, bifenazate (including, trifloxystrobin, metomiuostrobin)
2928.0000 32	绿谷隆、溴谷隆、利谷隆、氯溴隆	6.5	20	17	9	千克	S	Monolinuron, metobromuron, linuron, chlorbromuron

税则号列	货品名称	最惠(%)	普通	增值税率	出口退税	计量单位	监管条件	Article Description
2928.0000 33	溴酚肟、乙二肟	6.5	20	17	9	千克	S	Bromofenoxim, glyoxime
2928.0000 34	苯螨特	6.5	20	17	9	千克	S	Benzoximate
2928.0000 35	醌肟腙	6.5	20	17	9	千克	S	Benquinox
2928.0000 36	三甲苯草酮	6.5	20	17	9	千克	S	Tralkoxydim
2928.0000 37	解草胺腈	6.5	20	17	9	千克		Cyometrinil
2928.0000 90	其他肼(联氨)及胲(羟胺)的有机衍生物	6.5	20	17	9	千克		Organic derivatives of hydrazine or of hydroxylamine
29.29	**其他含氮基化合物:**							**Compounds with other nitrogen function:**
	-异氰酸酯:							-Isocyanates:
2929.1010	---2,4-和2,6-甲苯二异氰酸酯混合物(甲苯二异氰酸酯 TDI)	6.5	30	17	9	千克		---Toluene diisocyanate
2929.1020	---二甲苯二异氰酸酯(TODI)	6.5	30	17	9	千克		---o-Xylene diisocyanate
2929.1030	---二苯基甲烷二异氰酸酯(纯 MDI)	6.5	30	17	13	千克		---Diphenylmethane diisocyanate
2929.1040	---六亚基甲二异氰酸酯	6.5	30	17	9	千克		---Hexamethylene diisocyanate
2929.1090	---其他	6.5	30	17	13	千克		---Other
	-其他:							-Other:
2929.9010	---环已基氨基磺酸钠(甜蜜素)	9	90	17	9	千克	AB	---Sodium cyclamate
2929.9020	---二烷(甲、乙、正丙或异丙)氨基膦酰二卤	6.5	30	17	9	千克	23	---N, N-Dialkyl (Me, Et, n-Pr or i-Pr) phosphoramidic dihalides
2929.9030	---二烷(甲、乙、正丙或异丙)氨基膦酸二烷(甲、乙、正丙或异丙)酯	6.5	30	17	9	千克	23	---Dialkyl (Me, Et, n-Pr or i-Pr) N, N-dialkyl (Me, Et, n-Pr or i-Pr)-phosphoramidates
2929.9040	---乙酰甲胺磷	6.5	30	17	9	千克	S	---Acephate
2929.9090	---其他	6.5	30	17		千克		---Other
2929.9090 11	胺丙畏、胺草磷、抑草磷,丁苯草酮等(包括甲基胺草磷)	6.5	30	17	9	千克	S	Propetamaphos, amiprophos, butamifos (including amiprophos-methl)
2929.9090 12	异柳磷、甲基异柳磷、丙胺氟磷等	6.5	30	17		千克	S	Isofenphos, isofenphos-methy, mipafox
2929.9090 13	八甲磷、育畜磷、甘氨硫磷等(包括甲氟磷、毒鼠磷、水胺硫磷)	6.5	30	17	9	千克	S	Schradan, crufomate, phosglycin (including dimefox, phosazetim, isocarbophos)
2929.9090 90	其他含氮基化合物	6.5	30	17	9	千克		Compounds with other nitrogen function
	第十分章　有机—无机化合物、杂环化合物、核酸及其盐以及磺(酰)胺							X. -ORGANO-INORGANIC COMPOUNDS, HETEROCYCLIC COMPOUNDS, NUCLEIC ACIDS AND THEIR SALTS, AND SULPHONAMIDES
29.30	**有机硫化合物:**							**Organo-sulphur compounds:**
2930.2000	-硫代氨基甲酸盐(或酯)及二硫代氨基甲酸盐	6.5	30	17	9	千克		-Thiocarbamates and dithiocarbamates
2930.2000 11	禾草丹、杀螟丹	6.5	30	17	9	千克	S	Thiobencarb, cartap
2930.2000 12	威百亩、代森钠、丙森锌、福美铁等(包括福美锌、代森福美锌、安百亩)	6.5	30	17	9	千克	S	Metam-sodium, nabam, propineb, ferbam (including ziram, polycarbamate, meta-ammonium
2930.2000 13	燕麦敌、野麦畏、硫草敌	6.5	30	17	9	千克	S	Diallate, triallate, ethiolate
2930.2000 14	苄草丹、戊草丹、坪草丹、仲草丹	6.5	30	17	9	千克	S	Prosulfocarb, esprocarb, orbencarb, tiocarbazil
2930.2000 15	丁草敌、克草敌、茵草敌、灭草敌等(包括环草敌)	6.5	30	17	9	千克	S	Butylate, pebulate, eradicane, vernolate (including cycloate)
2930.2000 16	硫菌威、菜草畏	6.5	30	17	9	千克	S	Prothiocarb, sulfallate
2930.2000 90	其他硫代氨基甲酸盐(或酯)(包括二硫代氨基甲酸盐)	6.5	30	17	9	千克		Other thiocarbamates and dithiocarbamates
2930.3000	-一硫化二烃氨基硫羰、二硫化二烃氨基硫羰及四硫化二烃氨基硫羰	6.5	30	17	9	千克		-Thiuram mono-, di or tetrasulphide
2930.3000 10	福美双	6.5	30	17	9	千克	S	Thiram
2930.3000 90	其他一硫化二烃氨基硫羰等(包括二硫化二烃氨基硫羰及四硫化二烃氨基硫羰)	6.5	30	17	9	千克		Other thiuram mono -, including dihydrocarbon - sulfur vulcanization carbonylation and thiuram tetrasulphides)
2930.4000	-甲硫氨酸(蛋氨酸)	6.5	30	17	13	千克	AB	-Methionine
2930.5000	-敌菌丹(ISO)及甲胺磷(ISO)	6.5	30	17		千克		-Captafol(ISO) and methan Midophos(ISO)
2930.5000 10	甲胺磷(ISO)	6.5	30	17		千克	X	Methamidophos(ISO)
2930.5000 20	敌菌丹(ISO)	6.5	30	17		千克	S	Coptafol(ISO)
	-其他:							-Other:
2930.9010	---双巯丙氨酸(胱氨酸)	6.5	30	17	9	千克	AB	---Cystine

税则号列	货品名称	最惠(%)	普通	增值税率	出口退税	计量单位	监管条件	Article Description
2930.9020	---二硫代碳酸酯(或盐)[黄原酸酯(或盐)]	6.5	30	17	9	千克		---Dithiocarbonates (Xanth – ates)
2930.9090	---其他		30	17		千克		---Other
2930.9090 11	烯禾啶、双环磺草酮、氟虫酰胺、氟虫双酰胺	6.5	30	17	9	千克	S	Sethoxydinm, benzobicylon, flubendiamide
2930.9090 13	2-氯乙基氯甲基硫醚	6.5	30	17	9	千克	32	2-chloroethyl chloromethyl sulfide
2930.9090 14	二(2-氯乙基)硫醚(即芥子气)	6.5	30	17	9	千克	32	Bis (2-chloroethyl) sulfide
2930.9090 15	二(2-氯乙硫基)甲烷	6.5	30	17	9	千克	32	Bis (2-chloroethyl sulfide) methane
2930.9090 16	1,2-二(2-氯乙硫基)乙烷(倍半芥气)	6.5	30	17	9	千克	32	1,2-Bis(2-chloroethyl sulfide) ethane
2930.9090 17	1,3-二(2-氯乙硫基)正丙烷	6.5	30	17	9	千克	32	1,3-Bis(2-chloroethyl sulfide) propane
2930.9090 18	1,4-二(2-氯乙硫基)正丁烷	6.5	30	17	9	千克	32	1,4-Bis(2-chloroethyl sulfide) butane
2930.9090 19	1,5-二(2-氯乙硫基)正戊烷	6.5	30	17	9	千克	32	1,5-Bis(2-chloroethyl sulfide) pentane
2930.9090 21	二(2-氯乙硫基甲基)醚	6.5	30	17	9	千克	32	Bis (2-chloroethyl sulfide methyl) ester
2930.9090 22	二(2-氯乙硫基乙基)醚(氧芥气)	6.5	30	17	9	千克	32	Bis (2-chloroethyl sulfide ethyl) ester
2930.9090 23	胺吸膦(硫代磷酸二乙基-S-2-二乙氨基乙酯及烷基化或质子化盐)	6.5	30	17	9	千克	23	Amiton O, O-Diethyl S-2-(diethy lamino) ethyl phosphorothilolate and corresponding alkylated or protonated salts
2930.9090 24	烷基氨基乙-2-硫醇及相应质子盐	6.5	30	17	9	千克	23	N,N-dialkyl aminoethane-2-thiols and corresponding protonated salts
2930.9090 25	硫二甘醇[二(2-羟乙基)硫醚,硫代双乙醇]	6.5	30	17	9	千克	23	Thiodiglycol: Bis (2-hydroxyethyl) sulfide; thiodiethanol
2930.9090 26	烷基硫代膦酸烷S-2-二烷氨基乙酯(包括相应烷基化盐、质子化盐,烷基指甲、乙、正丙、异丙基)	6.5	30	17	9	千克	23	Alkyl alkane thiophosphate-S-2-aminoethyl, including cyclo alkane-S-2-dialkane (Me, Et, n-Pr or i-Pr) aminoethyl and corresponding alkylated or protonated salts
2930.9090 27	含一磷原子与甲、乙、丙基结合化合物(不包括地虫磷)	6.5	30	17	9	千克	23	Chemicals, containing a phosphorus atom to which is boned one methyl, ethyl or propyl group
2930.9090 28	内吸磷	6.5	30	17	9	千克	X	Demeton
2930.9090 31	4－甲基硫基安非他明	6.5	30	17	9	千克	I	4 – methylthioamfetamine
2930.9090 32	莫达非尼	6.5	30	17	9	千克	I	Modafinil
2930.9090 40	DL-羟基蛋氨酸	6.5	30	17	9	千克	AB	DL-Methionine hydroxy analogue
2930.9090 51	甲基硫菌灵、硫菌灵、苯螨醚等(包括乙蒜素、敌灭生、丁酮威、丁酮砜威、棉铃威)	6.5	30	17	9	千克	S	Thiophanate – methyl, thiophanate, phenproxide. (including ethylicin, dimexano , butocarboxim, butoxycarboxim, alanycarb)
2930.9090 52	灭多威、涕灭威、乙硫苯威等(包括杀线威、甲硫威、多杀威、涕灭砜威、硫双威)	6.5	30	17		千克	S	Methomyl, aldicarb, ethiofencarb, (including oxamyl, methiocarb, toxisamate, aldoxycarb, thiodicarb)
2930.9090 53	丁醚脲、久效威、苯硫威等(包括敌螨特、2甲4氯乙硫酯)	6.5	30	17	9	千克	S	Diafenthiuron, thiofanox, fenothiocarb (including chlorfensulphide, MCPA-thioethyl)
2930.9090 54	杀虫双、杀虫单、灭虫脲等(包括避虫醇、烯虫硫酯、三氯杀螨砜、杀螨醚、杀螨酯)	6.5	30	17	9	千克	S	Disosultap, monosultap, chloromethiuron (including (octylthio) ethanol, triprene, tetradifon, chlorbenside, chlorfenson)
2930.9090 55	代森锌、代森锰、代森锰锌等(包括福美胂、福美甲胂、代森铵、代森联)	6.5	30	17	9	千克	S	Zineb, maneb, mancozeb, (including asomate , urbacide(JMAP) , amobam, metiram)
2930.9090 56	烯草酮、磺草酮、嗪草酸甲酯、硝磺草酮等(包括苯氟磺胺、甲磺乐灵、氯硫酰草胺、脱叶磷)	6.5	30	17	9	千克	S	Clethodim, sulcotrione, fluthiacet – methyl mesotrione(including dichlofluanid, nitralin, chlorthiamide, tribuphons)
2930.9090 57	灭菌丹、克菌丹、杀螨硫醚等(包括氟杀螨、硫肟醚、莠不生)	6.5	30	17	9	千克	S	Folpet, captan, tetrasul (including fluorbenside, sulfoxime, EXD)
2930.9090 58	稻瘟净、异稻瘟净、稻丰散等(包括敌瘟磷)	6.5	30	17	9	千克	S	Kitazine, iprobenfos phenthoate (including edifenphos)
2930.9090 59	安妥、灭鼠特、二硫氰基甲烷等(包括灭鼠肼、氟硫隆)	6.5	30	17	9	千克	S	Antu, thiosemicarbazide, dithiocyano-methane(including promurit, flurothiuron)
2930.9090 61	马拉硫磷、苏硫磷、赛硫磷等(包括丙虫磷、双硫磷、亚砜磷、异亚砜磷)	6.5	30	17	9	千克	S	Malathion, sophamide, amidithion (including propaphos, temephos, oxydemeton – methyl, oxydeprofos)
2930.9090 62	丙溴磷、田乐磷、特丁硫磷等(包括硫丙磷、地虫硫膦、乙硫磷、丙硫磷、甲基乙拌磷)	6.5	30	17	9	千克	S	Profenofos, demephion, terbufos (including sulprofos, fonofos, ethion, prothiofos, thiometon)

税则号列	货品名称	最惠(%)	普通	增值税率	出口退税	计量单位	监管条件	Article Description
2930.9090 63	乐果、益硫磷、氧乐果等(包括甲拌磷、乙拌磷、虫螨磷、果虫磷)	6.5	30	17	9	千克	S	Dimethoate, ethoate - methyl, omethoate (including phorate, disulfoton, chlorthiophos, cyanthoate)
2930.9090 64	氯胺磷、家蝇磷、灭蚜磷等(包括安硫磷、四甲磷、丁苯硫磷、苯线磷、蚜灭磷)	6.5	30	17	9	千克	S	Chloramine phosphorus, acethion mecarbam (including formothion, mecarphon, fosmethilan, fenamiphos, vamidothion)
2930.9090 65	硫线磷、氯甲硫磷、杀虫磺等(包括砜吸磷、砜拌磷、异拌磷、三硫磷、芬硫磷)	6.5	30	17	9	千克	S	Cadusafos, chlormephos, bensultap (including oxydemetonmethyl, oxydisulfoton, isothioate, carbophenothion, phenkapton)
2930.9090 66	倍硫磷、甲基内吸磷、乙酯磷等(包括丰索磷、内吸磷、发硫磷)	6.5	30	17	9	千克	S	Fenthion, demeton - s - methyl, acetophos (including fensulfothion, demeton , prothoate, methylacetophos)
2930.9090 67	灭线磷	6.5	30	17	9	千克	S	Ethoprophos
2930.9090 91	DL-羟基蛋氨酸	6.5	30	17	13	千克	AB	DL - hydroxy methionine
2930.9090 99	其他有机硫化合物	6.5	30	17	13	千克		Other organic sulfur compounds
29.31	**其他有机—无机化合物:**							**Other organo-inorganic compounds:**
2931.1000	-四甲基铅及四乙基铅	6.5	30	17	9	千克	X	-Tetramethyl lead and tetraethyl lead
2931.2000	-三丁基锡化合物	6.5	30	17		千克	X	-Tributyltin compounds
	-其他:							-Other:
	---含有磷原子的:							---Containing phosphorus atom
2931.9011	----双甘膦	6.5	30	17		千克	AB	----N-Phosphonomethyl aminodiacetic acid
2931.9019	----其他	6.5	30	17		千克		----Other
2931.9019 11	烷基亚膦酰烷基-2-二烷氨基乙酯(包括相应烷基化盐或质子化盐)	6.5	30	17	9	千克	23	2 - Chlorovinyl dichloroarsine
2931.9019 12	氯沙林、氯梭曼(氯沙林即甲基氯膦酸异丙酯,氯梭曼即甲基氯膦酸频那酯)	6.5	30	17	9	千克	23	2 - Proyl - methylphosphonochloridate, chlorine soman
2931.9019 13	烷基氟膦酸烷酯,10碳原子以下(烷基指甲,乙,正丙,异丙基,例如沙林,梭曼)	6.5	30	17	9	千克	23	Alkyl(Me, Et, n - Pr or i - Pr) alkane fluorophosphate esters, < 10carboatons, for example, sarin; methyl isopropyl fluorophosphate, soman; methyl pinacolyl fluorophosphate
2931.9019 14	二烷氨基氰膦酸烷酯10碳原子以下(烷基指甲,乙,正丙,异丙基,例如塔崩)	6.5	30	17	9	千克	23	Dialkyl(Me, Et, n - Pr or i - Pr) cyanamide alkane phospate esters, <10carboatoms, for example tabun, dimethylamino ethyl cyanophosphorate
2931.9019 15	烷基膦酰二氟(烷基指甲,乙,正丙,异丙基,例如,DF:甲基膦酰二氟)	6.5	30	17	9	千克	23	Alkyl(Me, Et, n - Pr or i - Pr) phosphoryl difluoride, for example , DF, methyl phosphoryl difloride
2931.9019 16	草甘膦	6.5	30	17		千克	S	Glyphosate
2931.9019 17	草铵膦,草硫膦,杀木膦等(包括双丙氨膦,双丙氨酰膦,增甘膦及其盐)	6.5	30	17	9	千克	S	Glufosinate - ammonium, sulphosate, fosamine - ammonium (including bialaphos - sodium, glyphosine and its salt)
2931.9019 18	三丁氯苄鏻	6.5	30	17	9	千克	S	Chlorphonium
2931.9019 19	乙烯利	6.5	30	17	9	千克	S	Ethephon
2931.9019 21	敌百虫,氟硅菊酯,毒壤膦等(包括苯硫膦,溴苯膦,苯腈膦,丁酯膦)	6.5	30	17	9	千克	S	Trichlorfon, salifluofen, trichloronant (including EPN, leptophos, cyanofenphos, butonate)
2931.9019 22	甲基膦酰二氯、甲基膦酸二甲酯、丙基膦酸、甲基膦酸、乙基膦酸二乙酯、甲基膦酸二聚乙二醇酯(CAS号:294675-51-7){包括甲基膦酸甲基,5-(5-乙基-2-甲基-2-氧代-1,3,2-二氧磷杂环己基)甲基酯(CAS号:41203-81-0);甲基膦酸二[5-(5-乙基-2-甲基-2-氧代-1,3,2-二氧磷杂环己基)甲基]酯(CAS号:42595-45-9),地虫磷除外}	6.5	30	17	9	千克	23	Methyl phosphonic acid, two chlorine methyl phosphonic acid two methyl ester, propyl phosphonic acid, methyl phosphonic acid, ethyl phosphonic acid ethyl ester two, methyl phosphonic acid polyethylene glycol two (CAS: 294675 - 51 - 7) {including methyl phosphonic acid, methyl 5 - (5 - ethyl - 2 - methyl - 2 - oxo - 1,3,2 - two oxygen phosphorus heterocyclic methyl ester (2 - ethylhexyl) CAS number: 41203 - 81 - 0); methyl phosphonic acid (two 5 - (5 - ethyl - 2 - methyl - 2 - oxo - 1,3,2 - two oxygen phosphorus heterocyclic hexyl) methyl] ester (CAS number: 42595 - 45 - 9), except the Fonofos}
2931.9019 90	其他含磷原子的有机-无机化合物	6.5	30	17	9	千克	AB	Other organo - inorganic compound, containning phosphours atom
2931.9090	---其他	6.5	30	17		千克		---Other

税则号列	货品名称	最惠(%)	普通	增值税率	出口退税	计量单位	监管条件	Article Description
2931.9090 01	六甲基环三硅氧烷(包括八甲基环四硅氧烷,十甲基环五硅氧烷,十二甲基环六硅氧烷)	6.5	30	17	9	千克		Hexamethylcyclotrixane(including o-ctamethylcyclotetrasiloxane, decamethylcyclopentasiloxane, dodecamethylcyclohexasiloxane
2931.9090 11	2-氯乙烯基二氯胂	6.5	30	17		千克	23	2-Chlorovinyl dichloroarsine
2931.9090 12	二(2-氯乙烯基)氯胂	6.5	30	17		千克	23	Bis(2-chlorovinyl) chloro-arsine
2931.9090 13	三(2-氯乙烯基)胂	6.5	30	17		千克	23	Tri(2-chlorovinyl)-arsine
2931.9090 14	锆试剂、二甲胂酸等(包括4-二甲基偶氮苯-4′-胂酸、卡可基酸、二甲基胂酸钠)	6.5	30	17		千克	X	Zirconin, silvisar(including 4-dimethyl amino-azobenzene-4-arsenic acid, cacodylic acid, sodium eacodylate)
2931.9090 15	4-氨基苯胂酸钠、二氯化苯胂(对氨基苯胂酸钠、二氯苯胂、苯胂化二氯)	6.5	30	17		千克	X	Arsanilic acid phenyldichlorarsine (sodium arsamilate, dichlorophenarsine, phenylarsine dichloride)
2931.9090 16	蒽醌-1-胂酸、三环锡(普特丹)等(包括月桂酸三丁基锡、醋酸三丁基锡)	6.5	30	17		千克	X	Anthraquinone-1-arsonic acid, cyhexatin; (plictran) [including tributyl (lauroyloxy) stannane, tributyltin acetate]
2931.9090 17	硫酸三乙基锡、二丁基氧化锡等(包括氧化二丁基锡、乙酸三乙基锡、三乙基酸锡)	6.5	30	17	9	千克	X	Triethyltin sulphate, dibutyltin, oxide (including dibutyltin oxide, acetoxytriethyl stannare, triethyltin acetate)
2931.9090 18	四乙基锡、乙酸三甲基锡(四乙锡、醋酸三甲基锡)	6.5	30	17	9	千克	X	Tetraethyltin, trimethyltin acetate (tetraethyltin, acetoxy trimethyl)
2931.9090 19	毒菌锡[三苯基羟基锡(含量>20%)]	6.5	30	17	9	千克	X	Triphenyltin hydroxide [trimethyltin aceate (proportion >20%)]
2931.9090 21	乙酰亚砷酸铜、二苯(基)胺氯胂(祖母绿;翡翠绿;醋酸亚砷酸铜、吩吡嗪化氯;亚当氏气)	6.5	30	17		千克	X	Copper acetoarsenite, phenarsazinechloride
2931.9090 22	3-硝基-4羟基苯胂酸(4-羟基-3-硝基苯胂酸)	6.5	30	17		千克	X	3-nitryl-4-carboxyl benzene arsine acid
2931.9090 23	乙基二氯胂、二苯(基)氯胂(包括二氯化乙基胂、氯化二苯胂)	6.5	30	17		千克	X	Ethyldichloroarsine, diphenylchloroarsine (including dichloroethylarsine, diphenychlorarsine)
2931.9090 24	甲(基)胂酸、丙(基)胂酸、二碘化苯胂(苯基二碘胂)	6.5	30	17		千克	X	Methylarsonic acid, propylarsonic acid, phenyldiiodoarsine (phenylarsinediiondide)
2931.9090 25	苯胂酸、2-硝基苯胂酸等(包括邻硝基苯胂酸、3-硝基苯胂酸、间硝基苯胂酸等)	6.5	30	17		千克	X	Phenylarsonic acid, 2-nitrophenylarsonic acid (including o-nitrophenyl arsonic acid, 3-nitrophenylarsonic acid, m-nitrophenol arsonic acid)
2931.9090 26	4-硝基苯胂酸、2-氨基苯胂酸(对硝基苯胂酸、邻氨基苯胂酸)	6.5	30	17		千克	X	4-Nitrophenylarsonic acid, 2-aminophenylarsonic acid (para-nitrotoluene arsonic acid, o-phenetidine arsonic acid)
2931.9090 27	3-氨基苯胂酸、4-氨基苯胂酸(间氨基苯胂酸、对氨基苯胂酸)	6.5	30	17		千克	X	3-Aminophenylarsonic acid, 4-aminophenylarsonic acid (m-aminophenylarsonic acid, p-aminophenylarsonic acid)
2931.9090 28	三苯锡,三苯基乙酸锡等,包括三苯基氯化锡,三苯基氢氧化锡,苯丁锡,三唑锡	65	30	17	9	千克	S	Fentin, fentin acetate (including fentin chloride, fentin chloride, fentin hydroxide, fenbutatin Oxide, azocyclotin
2931.9090 29	田安	65	30	17	13	千克	S	Arsonate
2931.9090 31	乙烯硅	6.5	30	17	9	千克	S	Etacelasil
2931.9090 90	其他有机-无机化合物	6.5	30	17	13	千克	AB	Other organo-inorganic compound
29.32	仅含有氧杂原子的杂环化合物:							**Heterocyclic compounds with oxygen hetero-atom(s) only:**
	-结构上含有一个非稠合呋喃环(不论是否氢化)的化合物:							-Compounds containing an unfused furan ring (whether or not hydrogenated) in the structure:
2932.1100	--四氢呋喃	6	20	17	9	千克	AB	--Tetrahydrofuran
2932.1200	--2-糠醛	6	20	17	9	千克	B	--2-Furaldehyde (furfuraldehyde)
2932.1300	--糠醇及四氢糠醇	6	20	17	9	千克		--Furfuryl alcohol and tetrahydrofurfuryl alcohol

税则号列	货 品 名 称	最惠(%)	普通	增值税率	出口退税	计量单位	监管条件	Article Description
2932.1900	--其他	6.5	20	17	9	千克		--Other
2932.1900 11	喃烯菊酯、炔呋菊酯等(包括甲呋炔菊酯、溴苄呋菊酯、右旋炔呋菊酯)	6.5	20	17	9	千克	S	Japothrins, furamethrin (JMAF) (including proparthrin, bromethrin, d-furamethrin)
2932.1900 12	呋菌胺、酯菌胺、抑霉胺等(包括环菌胺、甲呋酰胺、二甲呋酰胺)	6.5	20	17	9	千克	S	Metomedan, cyprofuram, vangard (including cyprodinil, fenfuram, furcarbanil)
2932.1900 13	呋氧草醚、环庚草醚、呋草酮等(包括茵多酸)	6.5	20	17	9	千克	S	Furyloxyfen, cinmethylin, flurtamone (including endothal)
2932.1900 14	楝素、呋霜灵等(包括呋菌隆、螺螨酯)	6.5	20	17	9	千克	S	Toosendanin, furalaxyl (including furophanat, spirodiclofen
2932.1900 15	苄呋菊酯(包括右旋苄呋菊酯、生物苄呋菊酯)	6.5	20	17	9	千克	S	Resmethrin (including d-resmethrin, bioresmethrin)
2932.1900 16	呋虫胺	6.5	20	17	9	千克	S	Dinotefuran;
2932.1900 20	呋芬雷司	6.5	20	17	9	千克	I	Furfennorex
2932.1900 90	其他结构上有非稠合呋喃环化合物	6.5	20	17	9	千克		Other compounds containing an unfused furaning in the structure
	-内酯:							-Lactones:
2932.2010	--香豆素、甲基香豆素及乙基香豆素	6.5	20	17	13	千克		--Coumarin, methylcoumarins and ethyl-coumarins
2932.2090	--其他内酯	6.5	20	17		千克		--Other lactones
2932.2090 11	杀鼠灵、克鼠灵、敌鼠灵、溴鼠灵等(包括氯灭鼠灵、氟鼠灵、鼠得克、杀鼠醚)	6.5	20	17		千克	S	warfarin, coumafuryl, melitoxin, brodifacoum (including coumachlor, flocoumafen, difenacoum, coumatetralyl)
2932.2090 12	赤霉酸	6.5	20	17	13	千克	S	Gibberellic acid
2932.2090 13	蝇毒磷、茴蒿素、溴敌隆、呋酰胺等(包括四氯苯酞,畜虫磷)	6.5	20	17		千克	S	Coumaphos, saneonin, bromadiolone, ofurace (including phthalide, coumithoate)
2932.2090 14	丁香菌酯	6.5	20	17	13	千克	S	Coumoxystrobin
2932.2090 15	甲氨基阿维菌素苯甲酸盐	6.5	20	17	13	千克	S	Emamectin benzoate
2932.2090 16	阿维菌素	6.5	20	17	13	千克	S	Avermectin
2932.2090 90	其他内酯	6.5	20	17	13	千克		Other lactones
	-其他:							-Other:
2932.9100	--4-丙烯基-1,2-亚甲二氧基苯(即异黄樟脑)	6.5	20	17	9	千克	23	--2 – methoxy – 4 – (1 – propenyl) – pheno benzoate (Isosafrole)
2932.9200	--1-(1,3-苯并二噁茂-5基)丙烷-2酮	6.5	20	17	9	千克	23	--1-(1,3-Benzodioxol-5-yl) propan-2-one
2932.9300	--3,4-亚甲二氧基苯甲醛(胡椒醛)	6.5	20	17	13	千克	23	--Piperonal
2932.9400	--4-烯丙基-1,2-亚甲二氧基苯(黄樟脑)	6.5	20	17	13	千克	23	--Safrole
2932.9500	--四氢大麻酚(所有异构体)	6.5	20	17	9	千克	I	--Tetrahydrocannabinols (all is omers)
	--其他:							--Other:
2932.9910	---7-羟基苯并呋喃(呋喃酚)	4	11	17	9	千克		---Furan phenol
2932.9920	---2,2′-双甲氧羰基-4,4′-双甲氧基-5,6,5′,6′-双亚甲二氧基联苯(联苯双酯)	6.5	20	17	9	千克		---Bifendate
2932.9930	---蒿甲醚	6.5	20	17	13	千克		---Artemether
2932.9990	---其他	6.5	20	17		千克		---Other
2932.9990 11	克百威	6.5	20	17	13	千克	S	Carbofuran
2932.9990 12	二氧威、恶虫威、丙硫克百威等(包括丁硫克百威、呋线威)	6.5	20	17	13	千克	S	Dioxocarb, bendiocarb, benfuracarb (including carbosulfan, furathiocarb)
2932.9990 13	因毒磷、敌恶磷、碳氯灵	6.5	20	17	13	千克	S	Endothion, dioxathion, isobenzan
2932.9990 14	增效特、增效砜、增效醚、增效酯等(包括增效环、增效散)	6.5	20	17	13	千克		Bucarpolate, sufoxide, piperonyl butoxide, propylisorne (including piperonyl cyclonene, sesamex)
2932.9990 15	吡喃灵、吡喃隆、乙氧呋草黄等(包括呋草黄、氟草肟)	6.5	20	17	13	千克	S	Pyracarbolin, metobenzuron, ethofumesate (including benfuresate, fluxofenim)
2932.9990 16	避蚊酮、苯虫醚、鱼藤酮	6.5	20	17	13	千克	S	Butopyronoxyl, difenolan, rotenone
2932.9990 17	调呋酸、芸苔素内酯	6.5	20	17	13	千克	S	Dikegulac, brassinolide
2932.9990 21	紫杉醇	6.5	20	17		千克	QFE	Taxinol
2932.9990 22	三尖杉宁碱	6.5	20	17	13	千克	FE	Cephalomanine
2932.9990 23	十去乙酰基巴卡丁三(红豆杉提取物10-DAB)	6.5	20	17	13	千克	FE	10-Deacetyl – baccatin Ⅲ (Extracts of taxus chinensis 10 – DAB)

税则号列	货品名称	最惠(%)	普通	增值税率	出口退税	计量单位	监管条件	Article Description
2932.9990 24	十去乙酰基紫杉醇(红豆杉提取物 10-DAT)	6.5	20	17		千克	FE	10-Deacetyl – paclitaxel(Extracts of taxus chinensis 10 – DAB)
2932.9990 25	巴卡丁三	6.5	20	17	13	千克	FE	Baccatin Ⅲ
2932.9990 26	7-表紫杉醇	6.5	20	17		千克	FE	7-Epitaxinol
2932.9990 27	10-去乙酰 7-表紫杉醇	6.5	20	17		千克	FE	10-Deacetyl-7-epi – taxinol
2932.9990 28	7,10 – 双(三氯乙酰基)-10-去乙酰基巴卡丁三类似物	6.5	20	17	13	千克	EF	Analogues of 7,10 – double(3 – trichloroacetyl) – 10 – deacetyl Baccatin
2932.9990 29	多烯紫杉醇	6.5	20	17		千克	EF	Docetaxel
2932.9990 31	7,10-双(三氯乙酰基)-多西他赛	6.5	20	17	13	千克	EF	7,10-double(3-trichloroacetyl)-taxotere
2932.9990 40	替苯丙胺及其盐	6.5	20	17	13	千克	I	Tenamfetamine and its salts
2932.9990 51	(1,2 – 二甲基庚基)羟基四氢甲基二苯吡喃(包括六氢大麻酚)	6.5	20	17	13	千克	I	(1,2 – Dimetol) hydroxytetrahydrobiopterin (including parahexyl)
2932.9990 52	甲羟芬胺,乙芬胺,羟芬胺	6.5	20	17	13	千克	I	MMDA, N – ethyl MDA, N – hydroxy MDA.
2932.9990 53	二亚甲基双氧安非他明及其盐(IMDMA)	6.5	20	17	13	千克	I	2-methylenedioxy – n – methylamphetamine and its salts
2932.9990 54	3,4 – 亚甲二氧基甲卡西酮(CAS 号: 186028 – 79 – 5)	6.5	20	17	13	千克	I	3,4 – methylenedioxy – N – methylcathinone(CAS: 186028 – 79 – 5)
2932.9990 60	二噁英,呋喃(多氯二苯并对二噁英,多氯二苯并呋喃)	6.5	20	17	13	千克	89	Dioxin, Furan (Polychrorinate. dibenzo-p-dioxins, polychlorinated dibenzofurans)
2932.9990 70	1,4-二噁烷	6.5	20	17	13	千克	X	1,4-Diaxane
2932.9990 80	二氢黄樟素	6.5	20	17	13	千克	G	Dihydrosafrol
2932.9990 91	其他濒危植物提取的仅含氧杂原子的杂环化合物	6.5	20	17		千克	EF	Other heterocyclic compounds with oxygen hetero-atom only, distilled from endangered plants
2932.9990 99	其他仅含氧杂原子的杂环化合物	6.5	20	17	13	千克		Other heterocyclic compounds with oxygen hetero-atom(s) only
29.33	**仅含有氮杂原子的杂环化合物:**							**Heterocyclic compounds with nitrogen hetero-atom(s) only:**
	-结构上含有一个非稠合吡唑环(不论是否氢化)的化合物:							-Compounds containing an unfused pyrazole ring (whether or not hydrogenated) in the structure:
2933.1100	--二甲基苯基吡唑酮(安替比林)及其衍生物	6.5	20	17	9	千克		--Phenazone (antipyrin) and its derivatives
	--其他:							--Other:
2933.1920	---安乃近	6	20	17	9	千克	Q	---Analgin
2933.1990	---其他	6.5	20	17	9	千克		---Other
2933.1990 11	吡硫磷、吡唑硫磷、敌蝇威、乙虫腈等(包括异索威、吡唑威)	6.5	20	17	9	千克	S	Pyrazothion, pyraclofos, dimetilan (includins isolan, pyrolan)
2933.1990 12	氟虫腈、唑螨酯、吡螨胺等(包括吡唑醚菌酯)	6.5	20	17	9	千克	S	Fipronil, fenpyroximate, tebufenpyrad (including pyraclost)
2933.1990 13	吡草醚、吡唑草胺、氟氯草胺等(包括野燕枯、苄草唑、吡唑特、吡草酮)	6.5	20	17	9	千克	S	Pyraflufen – ethyl, metazachlor, nipyralo fen (indnding difenzoquat, pyrazoxyfen, pyrazolate, benzofenap)
2933.1990 14	吡唑萘菌胺(包括氟唑菌胺、乙唑螨腈、异丙吡草酯、唑虫酰胺)	6.5	20	17	9	千克	S	Isopyrazam(penflufen, fluazolate, tolfenpyrad)
2933.1990 15	苯并烯氟菌唑	6.5	20	17	9	千克	S	Benzene and olefin triflumizole
2933.1990 90	其他结构上有非稠合吡唑环化合物	6.5	20	17	9	千克		Other compounds containing an unfused pyrazole ring in the structure
	-结构上含有一个非稠合咪唑环(不论是否氢化)的化合物:							-Compounds containing an unfused imidazole ring (whether or not hydrogenated) in the structure:
2933.2100	--乙内酰脲及其衍生物	6.5	30	17	9	千克		--Hydantoin and its derivatives
2933.2900	--其他	6.5	20	17	9	千克		--Other
2933.2900 11	异菌脲	6.5	20	17	9	千克	S	Iprodine
2933.2900 12	抑霉唑、咪菌腈、咪菌酮、咪鲜胺等(包括克霉唑、咪鲜胺锰盐)	6.5	20	17	9	千克	S	Imazalil, fenapanil, climbazole, prochloraz (including clotrimazole prochloraz-manganese)
2933.2900 13	咪草酸、丁咪酰胺	6.5	20	17	9	千克	S	Imazamethabenz – methyl, isocarbamide
2933.2900 14	果绿啶	6.5	20	17	9	千克	S	Glyodin
2933.2900 15	氟菌唑	6.5	20	17	9	千克	S	Triflumizole

税则号列	货品名称	最惠(%)	普通	增值税率	出口退税	计量单位	监管条件	Article Description
2933.2900 90	其他结构上有非稠合咪唑环化合物	6.5	20	17	9	千克		Other compounds containing an unfused imidazole ring in the structure
	-结构上含有一个非稠合吡啶环(不论是否氢化)的化合物:							-Compounds containing an unfused pyridine ring (whether or not hydrogenated) in the structure:
2933.3100	--吡啶及其盐	6	20	17	9	千克		--Pyridine and its salts
2933.3100 10	吡啶	6	20	17	9	千克	AB	Pyridine
2933.3100 90	吡啶盐	6	20	17	9	千克		Pyridine salt
	--六氢吡啶(哌啶)及其盐:							--Piperidine and its salts:
2933.3210	---六氢吡啶(哌啶)	4	11	17	9	千克	23	---Hexahydropyridine (piperidine)
2933.3220	---六氢吡啶(哌啶)盐	6.5	20	17	9	千克		---Isoniazidum
2933.3300	--阿芬太尼(INN),阿尼利定(INN),苯氰米特(INN),溴西泮(INN),地芬诺新(INN),地芬诺酯(INN),地匹哌酮(INN),芬太尼(INN),凯托米酮(INN),哌醋甲酯(INN),喷他左辛(INN),哌替啶(INN),哌替啶中间体A(INN),苯环利定(INN),苯哌利定(INN),哌苯甲醇(INN),哌氰米特(INN),哌丙吡胺(INN)和三甲利定(INN)以及它们的盐	6.5	20	17	9	千克		--Alfentanil (INN), anileridine (INN), bezitramide (INN), bromazepam (INN), difenoxin (INN), diphenoxylate (INN), dipipanone (INN), fentanyl (INN), ketobemidone (INN), methylphenidate (INN), pentazocine (INN), pethidine (INN), pethidine (INN) intermediate A, phencyclidine (INN) (PCP), phenoperidine (INN), pipradrol (INN), piritramide (INN), propiram (INN) and trimeperidine (INN); salts thereof
2933.3300 11	阿芬太尼、芬太尼(以及它们的盐)	6.5	20	17	9	千克	W	Alfentanil (INN), fentanyl (INN); salts thereof
2933.3300 12	哌替啶、地芬诺酯(以及它们的盐)	6.5	20	17	9	千克	W	Pethidine (INN), diphenoxylate (INN); salts thereof
2933.3300 13	哌腈(氰)米特,丙吡兰(哌丙吡胺)(以及它们的盐)	6.5	20	17	9	千克	W	Bezitramide (INN), propiram (INN); salts thereof
2933.3300 21	哌醋甲酯、喷他左辛、溴西泮(以及它们的盐)	6.5	20	17	9	千克	I	Methylphenidate (INN), pentazocine (INN), bromazepam (INN); salts thereof
2933.3300 22	苯环利定、哌苯甲醇(以及它们的盐)	6.5	20	17	9	千克	I	Phencyclidine (INN) (PCP), pipradrol (INN), salts thereof
2933.3300 31	地匹哌酮、凯托米酮、地芬诺新(以及它们的盐)	6.5	20	17	9	千克	W	Dipipanone (INN), ketobemidone (INN), difenoxin (INN); salts thereof
2933.3300 32	哌替啶中间体A、苯哌利定、三甲利定(以及它们的盐)	6.5	20	17	9	千克	W	Pethidine (INN), phenoperidine (INN); trimeperidine (iNN); salts thereof
2933.3300 33	阿尼利定、苯氰米特(以及它们的盐)	6.5	20	17	9	千克	W	Anileridine (INN), piritramide (INN), salts thereof
	--其他:							--Other:
2933.3910	---二苯乙醇酸-3-奎宁环酯	6.5	20	17	9	千克	23	---Benzilic acid-3-quinuclidinate
2933.3920	---奎宁环-3-醇	6.5	20	17	9	千克	23	---Quinuclidine-3-ol
2933.3990	---其他	6.5	20	17	9	千克		---Other
2933.3990 10	甲基吡啶、氰基吡啶、吡啶硫铜锌(包括三甲基吡啶)	6.5	20	17	9	千克		Methyl - pyridine, cyanopyridine, zinc - pyrithione (including 3 - methylpyridine)
2933.3990 21	精吡氟禾草灵、毒死蜱、二氯氨基吡啶羧酸(包括二氟吡隆、三氟甲吡醚,氯虫苯甲酰胺)	6.5	20	17	9	千克	S	Fluazifop - p - butyl, chlorpyrifos, dichloro - aminoacetophen - one - carboxylic acid (including diflufenzopyr, pyridalyl, chlorantraniliprole)
2933.3990 22	百草枯、啶虫脒	6.5	20	17	9	千克	S	Paraquat, acetamiprid
2933.3990 23	精喹禾灵	6.5	20	17	9	千克	S	Quizalofop-p-ethyl
2933.3990 24	喹禾灵、氟吡禾灵、吡氟禾草灵等(包括炔禾灵、氟吡乙禾灵、氟吡胺、卤草啶)	6.5	20	17	9	千克	S	Quizalofop-ethyl, heptenophos, fluazifop, (including chloroazifop-propyny, haloxyfop-methyl picolinafen, haloxydin)
2933.3990 25	高效氟吡甲禾灵、氟吡甲禾灵等(包括鼠特灵、灭鼠优、灭鼠安、氟鼠啶)	6.5	20	17	9	千克	S	Haloxyfop-P-methyl , haloxyfop-methyl (including norbormide, pyrinuron, flupropadine)
2933.3990 26	甲基毒死蜱、吡虫啉等(包括吡氯氰菊酯、啶蜱脲、氟啶脲、哒幼酮、吡丙醚)	6.5	20	17	9	千克	S	Chlorpyrifos - methyl, imidacloprid (including fenpyrithrin, fluazuron, chlorfluazuron, pyridaben, pyriproxyfen)
2933.3990 27	驱蝇啶、烯啶虫胺	6.5	20	17	9	千克	S	Dipropyl pyridine, nitenpyram
2933.3990 28	咪唑烟酸、甲咪唑烟酸、咪唑乙烟酸等(包括氨氯吡啶酸、三氯吡氧乙酸、氯氟吡氧乙酸、二氯吡啶酸)	6.5	20	17	9	千克	S	Imazapyr, imazameth, imazethapyr (including picloram, fluroxypyr, clopyralid)

税则号列	货品名称	最惠(%)	普通	增值税率	出口退税	计量单位	监管条件	Article Description
2933.3990 29	炔草酸、哌草磷、哌草丹、稗草丹等(包括吡氟酰草胺、氟啶草酮、氟硫草啶、甲氧咪草烟)	6.5	20	17	9	千克	S	Clodinafop-propargyl, piperophos, dimepiperate, pyributicarb(including diflufenican, fluridon, dithiopyr, imazamox)
2933.3990 30	3-羟基-1-甲基哌啶	6.5	20	17	9	千克	23	3-hydroxy-1-methyl piperidine
2933.3990 40	3-奎宁环酮	6.5	20	17	9	千克	23	3-Quinuclidone
2933.3990 51	甲哌翁、抗倒胺、氯吡脲、吡啶醇	6.5	20	17	9	千克	S	Mepiquate chloride, inabenfide, forchlorfenuron, pyripropanol
2933.3990 52	啶菌噁唑、苯锈啶、啶斑肟等(包括啶菌腈)	6.5	20	17	9	千克	S	SYP – Z048, fenpropidin, pyrifenox (includins pyridintril)
2933.3990 53	氟啶胺、氟啶虫酰胺、三氯甲基吡啶	6.5	20	17	9	千克	S	Fluazinam, flonicamid, nitrapyrin
2933.3990 54	咪唑嗪、丁硫啶、氯苯吡啶、哌丙灵	6.5	20	17	9	千克	S	Triazoxide, buthiobate, parinol, piperlin
2933.3990 55	氟吡菌酰胺	6.5	20	17	9	千克	S	Fluopyram
2933.3990 56	氯啶菌酯	6.5	20	17	9	千克	S	Carbamate
2933.3990 57	氯氨吡啶酸	6.5	20	17	9	千克	S	Picloram
2933.3990 58	哌壮素	6.5	20	17	9	千克	S	Pai Zhuang Su
2933.3990 60	啶氧菌酯(包括氟啶虫胺腈、环啶菌胺、四氯虫酰胺、溴氰虫酰胺、玉雄杀、氟吡菌胺)	6.5	20	17	9	千克	S	Picoxystrobin
2933.3990 71	乙酰阿法甲基芬太尼、烯丙罗定、阿法美罗定(以及它们的盐)	6.5	20	17	9	千克	W	Acetyl – alpha – methylfentanyl, allylprodine, alphameprodine (and their salt)
2933.3990 72	阿法甲基芬太尼、阿法罗定、苄替啶(以及它们的盐)	6.5	20	17	9	千克	W	Alpha – methylfentanyl, alphaprodine, benzethidine
2933.3990 73	倍他羟基芬太尼、倍他羟基 – 3 – 甲基芬太尼、倍他美罗定(以及它们的盐)	6.5	20	17	9	千克	W	Betahydroxyfentanyl, betahydroxy – 3 – methylfentanyl, betameprodine (and their salt)
2933.3990 74	倍他罗啶、依托利啶、羟哌替定、美他佐辛(以及它们的盐)	6.5	20	17	9	千克	W	Betaprodine, etoxeridine, hydroxypethidine, metazocine (and their salt)
2933.3990 75	3 – 甲基芬太尼、1 – 甲基 4 – 苯基 – 4 – 哌啶丙酸酯、诺匹哌酮(以及它们的盐)	6.5	20	17	9	千克	W	3 – methylfentanyl, 1 – methyl – 4 – phenyl – 4 – piperidine propionate, norpipanone (and their salt)
2933.3990 76	对氟芬太尼、1 – 苯乙基 – 4 – 苯基 – 4 – 哌啶乙酸酯(以及它们的盐)	6.5	20	17	9	千克	W	Parafluorofentanyl, 1 – phenylethyl – 4 – phenyl – 4 – piperidine acetate (and their salt)
2933.3990 77	哌替啶中间体 B、哌替啶中间体 C(以及它们的盐)	6.5	20	17	9	千克	W	Pethidine intermediate B, pethidine intermediate C (and their salt)
2933.3990 78	非那丙胺、非那佐辛、匹米诺定、丙哌利定(以及它们的盐)	6.5	20	17	9	千克	W	Phenampromide, phenazocine, piminodine, porperidine (and their salt)
2933.3990 80	瑞太尼及其盐	6.5	20	17	9	千克	W	Ramifentanil and salts thereof
2933.3990 90	其他结构上有非稠合吡啶环化合物	6.5	20	17	9	千克		Other compounds containing an unfused pyridine ring in the structure
	-结构上含有一个喹啉或异喹啉环系(不论是否氢化)的化合物,但未经进一步稠合的:							-Compounds containing a quinoline or isoquinoline ringsystem (whether or not hydrogenated), not further fused:
2933.4100	--左非诺(INN)及其盐	6.5	20	17	9	千克	W	--Levorpharol(INN) and its salts
2933.4900	--其他	6.5	20	17	9	千克		--Other
2933.4900 11	丙烯酸喹啉酯,苯氧喹啉	6.5	20	17	9	千克	S	Halacrinate, quinoxyfen
2933.4900 12	咯喹酮	6.5	20	17	9	千克	S	Pyroquilon
2933.4900 13	氯甲喹啉酸、喹草酸、乙氧喹啉	6.5	20	17	9	千克	S	Quinmerac, quinmerac, ethoxyquin
2933.4900 14	二氯喹啉酸	6.5	20	17	9	千克	S	Quinclorac
2933.4900 15	FG – 4592(CAS 号:808118 – 40 – 3)(一种缺氧诱导因子—脯氨酸羟化酶抑制剂)	6.5	20	17	9	千克	L	FG – 4592 (CAS: 808118 – 40 – 3) (a kind of hypoxia inducible factor – prolinehydroxylase inhibitor)
2933.4900 21	羟蒂巴酚、左美沙芬、左芬啡烷	6.5	20	17	9	千克	W	Drotebanol, levomethorphan, levophenacylmorphan.
2933.4900 22	去甲左啡诺、非诺啡烷、消旋甲啡烷、消旋啡烷	6.5	20	17	9	千克	W	Norlevorphanol, phenomorphan, racemethorphan, racemorphan
2933.4900 30	布托啡诺	6.5	20	17	9	千克	I	Butorphanol
2933.4900 90	其他含喹啉或异喹啉环系的化合物(但未进一步稠合的)	6.5	20	17	9	千克		Other compounds containingan quinoline or isoquinoline ringsysterm(not further fused)

税则号列	货品名称	最惠(%)	普通	增值税率	出口退税	计量单位	监管条件	Article Description
	-结构上含有一个嘧啶环(不论是否氢化)或哌嗪环的化合物:							-Compounds containing a pyrimidine ring (whether or not hydrogenated) or piperazine ring in the structure:
2933.5200	--丙二酰脲(巴比妥酸)及其盐	6.5	20	17	9	千克		--Malonylurea (barbituric acid) and its salts
2933.5300	--阿洛巴比妥(INN),异戊巴比妥(INN),巴比妥(INN),布他比妥(INN),正丁巴比妥(INN),环己巴比妥(INN),甲苯巴比妥(INN),戊巴比妥(INN),苯巴比妥(INN),仲丁巴比妥(INN),司可巴比妥(INN),和乙烯比妥(INN)以及它们的盐	6.5	20	17	9	千克		--Allobarbital (INN), amobarbital (INN), barbital (INN), butalbital (INN), butobarbital (INN), cyclobarbital (INN), methylphenobarbital (INN), pentobarbital (INN), phenobarbital (INN), secbutabarbital (INN), secobarbital (INN) and vinylbital (INN); salts thereof
2933.5300 11	阿洛巴比妥、仲丁巴比妥(以及它们的盐)	6.5	20	17	9	千克	I	Allobarbital (INN), secbutabarbital (INN); salts thereof
2933.5300 12	乙烯比妥、布他比妥、丁巴比妥(以及它们的盐)	6.5	20	17	9	千克	I	Vinylbital (INN), butalbital (INN), butobarbital (INN); salts thereof
2933.5300 13	环已巴比妥、甲苯巴比妥(以及它们的盐)	6.5	20	17	9	千克	I	Cyclobarbital (INN), methylphenobarbital (INN); salts thereof
2933.5300 14	司可巴比妥、异戊巴比妥(以及它们的盐)	6.5	20	17	9	千克	I	Secobarbital (INN), amobarbital (INN), salts thereof
2933.5300 15	戊巴比妥、苯巴比妥、巴比妥(以及它们的盐)	6.5	20	17	9	千克	I	Pentobarbital (INN), phenobarbital (INN), barbital (INN); salts thereof
2933.5400	--其他丙二酰脲(巴比妥酸)的衍生物以及它们的盐	6.5	20	17	9	千克		--Other derivatives of malonylurea (barbituric acid); salts thereof
2933.5500	--氯普唑仑(INN),甲氯喹酮(INN),甲喹酮(INN)和齐培丙醇(INN)以及它们的盐	6.5	20	17	9	千克		--Loprazolam (INN), mecloqualone (INN), methaqualone (INN) and zipeprol (INN); salts thereof
2933.5500 11	甲氯喹酮、甲喹酮(以及它们的盐)	6.5	20	17	9	千克	I	Mecloqualone (INN), methaqualone (INN); salts thereof
2933.5500 12	氯普唑仑、齐培丙醇(以及它们的盐)	6.5	20	17	9	千克	I	Loprazolam (INN), zipeprol (INN); salts thereof
	--其他:							--Other:
2933.5910	---胞嘧啶	6.5	20	17	9	千克		---Cytosine
2933.5920	---环丙氟哌酸	6.5	20	17	9	千克		---Ciprofloxacin
2933.5990	---其他	6.5	20	17	9	千克		---Other
2933.5990 11	嘧啶磷、甲基嘧啶磷、二嗪磷、双苯嘧草酮等(包括嘧啶氧磷、乙嘧硫磷)	6.5	20	17	9	千克	S	Pyrimithate, pirimiphos - methyl, diazinon (including midinyangrin, etrimfos)
2933.5990 12	烯腺嘌呤、苄腺嘌呤、丁基嘧啶磷、嘧啶肟草醚等(包括苄氨基嘌呤、羟烯腺嘌呤)	6.5	20	17	9	千克	S	Enadenine, 6-benzylaminopurine tebupirimfos, pyribenzonxim (including benzolaminopurine, oxyenadenine)
2933.5990 13	嘧草醚、双草醚、除草啶、环草啶等(包括异草啶、异丙酯草醚、嘧草硫醚、特草啶)	6.5	20	17	9	千克	S	Pyriminobac-methl, bispyribac-sodium, bromacil, lenacil (including isocil, pyribambenz isoprop pyrithiobac-sodium, terbacil)
2933.5990 14	吡菌磷、嘧霉胺、嘧菌胺、嘧菌酯等(包括嘧菌环胺、嘧菌腙)	6.5	20	17	9	千克	S	Pyrazophos, pyrimethanil, mepampyrim, azoxystrobin (including cyprodinil, ferimzone)
2933.5990 15	嘧啶威、抗蚜威、环虫腈、嘧螨醚等(包括嘧螨酯)	6.5	20	17	9	千克	S	Pyramat, pirimicarb, dicyclanil, pyrimidifen (including fluacrypyrim)
2933.5990 16	氯苯嘧啶醇、环丙嘧啶醇、呋嘧醇等(包括氟苯嘧啶醇)	6.5	20	17	9	千克	S	Fenarimol, ancymidol, flurprimidol (including nuarimol)
2933.5990 17	氟蚁腙、鼠立死	6.5	20	17	9	千克	S	Hydramethylnon, crimidine
2933.5990 18	二甲嘧酚、乙嘧酚、乙嘧酚磺酸酯	6.5	20	17	9	千克	S	Dimethirimol, ethirmol, bupirimate
2933.5990 19	嗪氨灵、咪唑喹啉酸、丙酯草醚	6.5	20	17	9	千克	S	Triforin, imazquin, pyribambenz - propyl
2933.5990 20	氟丙嘧草酯、氯丙嘧啶酸	6.5	20	17	9	千克	S	Butafenacil
2933.5990 30	溴嘧草醚	6.5	20	17	9	千克	S	Bromide-pyriminobac-methyl
2933.5990 40	唑嘧菌胺	6.5	20	17	9	千克	S	Mepanipyrim
2933.5990 51	依他喹酮(CAS号:7432-25-9)	6.5	20	17	9	千克	I	Etaqualone (CAS:7432-25-9)
2933.5990 52	苄基哌嗪(CAS号:2759-28-6)	6.5	20	17	9	千克	I	Benzylpiperazine (CAS号:2759-28-6)
2933.5990 90	其他结构上有嘧啶环等的化合物(包括其他结构上有哌嗪环的化合物)	6.5	20	17	9	千克		Other compounds containing pyrimidine rings in the structure (including other compounds containing piperazine rings in the strcture)
	-结构上含有一个非稠合三嗪环(不论是否氢化)的化合物:							-Compounds containing an unfused triazine ring (whether or not hydrogenated) in the structure:
2933.6100	--三聚氰胺(蜜胺)	6.5	20	17	9	千克	A	--Melamine

税则号列	货品名称	最惠(%)	普通	增值税率	出口退税	计量单位	监管条件	Article Description
	--其他:							--Other:
2933.6910	---三聚氰氯	6	20	17	9	千克		---Cyanuric chloride
	---异氰脲酸氯化衍生物:							---Chloroisocyanurate:
2933.6921	----二氯异氰脲酸	6.5	20	17	9	千克	AB	----Dichloroisocyanurate acid
2933.6922	----三氯异氰脲酸	6.5	20	17	9	千克	AB	----Trichloroisooyanurate acid
2933.6929	----其他	6.5	20	17	9	千克		----Other
2933.6929 10	二氯异氰尿酸钠	6.5	20	17	9	千克	AB	Sodium dichloro isocyanurate
2933.6929 90	其他异氰脲酸氯化衍生物	6.5	20	17	9	千克		Other chloroisocyanuric acid derivatives
2933.6990	---其他	6.5	20	17	9	千克		---Other
2933.6990 11	西玛津、莠去津、扑灭津、草达津等(包括特丁津、氰草津、环丙津、甘扑津、甘草津)	6.5	20	17	9	千克	S	Simazine, atrazine, propazine, trietazine (including terbuthylazine , cyanazine, cyprazine, proglinazine, eglinazine)
2933.6990 12	西草净、扑草净、敌草净、莠灭净等(包括特丁净、异丙净、异戊乙净、氰草净、氟草净、甲氧丙净)	6.5	20	17	9	千克	S	Simetryn, prometryn, desmetryn, ametryn (including terbutryn, dipropetryn, dimethametryn, cyanatryn, SSH-108, methoprotryne)
2933.6990 13	扑灭通、仲丁通	6.5	20	17	9	千克	S	Prometon, secbumeton
2933.6990 14	丁嗪草酮、环嗪酮、嗪草酮等(包括苯嗪草酮、乙嗪草酮)	6.5	20	17	9	千克	S	Isomethiozin, hexazinone, metribuzin (including metamitron , ethiozin)
2933.6990 15	灭蚜硫磷、灭蝇胺、吡蚜酮等(包括敌菌灵)	6.5	20	17	9	千克	S	Memazon, cyromazine, pymetrozime (including anilazine)
2933.6990 16	三嗪氟草胺	6.5	20	17	9	千克	S	Triaziflam
2933.6990 90	其他结构上含非稠合三嗪环化合物	6.5	20	17	9	千克		Other compounds cortainins an unfused triazing ring in the structur
	-内酰胺:							-Lactams:
2933.7100	--6-己内酰胺	9	35	17	9	千克	A	--6-Hexanolactam (epsilon-caprolactam)
2933.7200	--氯巴占(INN)和甲乙哌酮(INN)	9	15	17	9	千克	I	--Clobazam(INN) and methyprylon(INN)
2933.7900	--其他内酰胺	9	20	17	9	千克		--Other lactams
2933.7900 10	氯巴占和甲乙哌酮的盐	9	20	17	9	千克	I	Salts of clobazam(INN) and methyprylon(INN)
2933.7900 20	灭菌磷、螺虫乙酯	9	20	17	9	千克	S	Ditalimfos, spirotetramat
2933.7900 30	佐匹克隆(CAS 号:43200－80－2)	9	20	17		千克	I	Zopiclone(CAS:43200－80－2)
2933.7900 90	其他内酰胺	9	20	17	9	千克		Other lactams
	-其他:							-Other:
2933.9100	--阿普唑仑(INN),卡马西泮(INN),氯氮卓(INN),氯硝西泮(INN),氯拉卓酸,地洛西泮(INN),地西泮(INN),艾司唑仑(INN),氯氟卓乙酯(INN),氟地西泮(INN),氟硝西泮(INN),氟西泮(INN),哈拉西泮(INN),劳拉西泮(INN),氯甲西泮(INN),马吲哚(INN),美达西泮(INN),咪达唑仑(INN),硝甲西泮(INN),去甲西泮(INN),奥沙西泮(INN),匹那西泮(INN),普拉西泮(INN),吡咯戊酮(INN),替马西泮(INN),四氢西泮(INN)和三唑仑(INN)以及它们的盐	6.5	20	17	9	千克		--Alprazolam (INN), camazepam (INN), chlordiazepoxide(INN), clonazepam(INN), clorazepate, delorazepam (INN), diazepam (INN), estazolam (INN), ethyl loflazepate(INN), fludiazepam(INN), flunitrazepam(INN), flurazepam(INN), halazepam (INN), lorazepam (INN), lormetazepam (INN), mazindol (INN), medazepam (INN), midazolam (INN), nimetazepam (INN), nitrazepam (INN), nordazepam (INN), oxazepam (INN), pinazepam (INN), prazepam (INN), pyrovalerone (INN), temazepam(INN), tetrazepam(INN) and triazolam (INN); salts thereof
2933.9100 11	阿普唑仑、卡马西泮、氯氮卓(以及它们的盐)	6.5	20	17	9	千克	I	Alprazolam(INN), camazepam(INN), chlordiazepoxide(INN); salts thereof
2933.9100 12	氯硝西泮、氯拉卓酸、地洛西泮(以及它们的盐)	6.5	20	17	9	千克	I	Clonazepam (INN), clorazepate, delorazepam (INN); salts thereof
2933.9100 13	地西泮、艾司唑仑、氯氟卓乙酯(以及它们的盐)	6.5	20	17	9	千克	I	Diazepam(INN), estazolam(INN), ethyl loflazepate(INN); salts thereof
2933.9100 14	氟地西泮、氟硝西泮、氟西泮(以及它们的盐)	6.5	20	17	9	千克	I	Fludiazepam(INN), flunitrazepam (INN), flurazepam (INN); salts thereof

税则号列	货品名称	最惠(%)	普通	增值税率	出口退税	计量单位	监管条件	Article Description
2933.9100 15	哈拉西泮、劳拉西泮、氯甲西泮(以及它们的盐)	6.5	20	17	9	千克	I	Halazepam(INN), lorazepam(INN), lormetazepam(INN); salts thereof
2933.9100 16	马吲哚、咪达唑仑、硝西泮(以及它们的盐)	6.5	20	17	9	千克	I	Mazindol(INN), midazolam(INN), nimetazepam(INN); salts thereof
2933.9100 17	奥沙西泮、匹那西泮、普拉西泮(以及它们的盐)	6.5	20	17	9	千克	I	Oxazepam(INN), pinazepam(INN), prazepam(INN); salts thereof
2933.9100 18	去甲西泮、三唑仑(以及它们的盐)	6.5	20	17	9	千克	I	Nordazepam(INN), triazolam(INN); salts thereof
2933.9100 21	硝甲西泮、美达西泮(以及它们的盐)	6.5	20	17	9	千克	I	Nimetazepam(INN), medazepam(INN);salts thereof
2933.9100 22	吡咯戊酮、替马西泮、四氢西泮(以及它们的盐)	6.5	20	17	9	千克	I	Pyrovalerone(INN), temazepam(INN), tetrazepam(INN); salts thereof
2933.9900	--其他	6.5	20	17	9	千克		--Other
2933.9900 11	抑芽丹、三唑磷、虫线磷、喹硫磷、哒嗪草酮等(包括哒嗪硫磷、亚胺硫磷、氯亚胺硫磷、保棉磷、益棉磷、威菌磷)	6.5	20	17	9	千克	S	Maleic hydrazide, triazophos, thionazin, quinalphos, azafenidin (including pyridaphenthione (JMAF), phosmet, dialifos, azinphos - methyl, azinphos - ethyl, triamiphos)
2933.9900 12	氯唑磷、炔咪菊酯、吲哚酮草酯等(包括呋喃虫酰肼、唑蚜威、不育胺、虫螨腈、抗螨唑、四螨嗪)	6.5	20	17	9	千克	S	Isazofos, imiprothrin, cinidon - ethyl(including furan - tebufenozide triaamate, metepa, fenazaflor, clofentezine, chlorfenapyr)
2933.9900 13	多菌灵、苯菌灵、氰菌灵、麦穗宁、氟哒嗪草酯等(包括咪菌威、丙硫多菌灵、氟氯菌核利、哒菌酮、拌种咯、杀草强)	6.5	20	17	9	千克	S	Carbendazim, benomyl, cypendazole, fuberidazole (including debacarb, albendazole TOP, fluoromide (JMAF), pyridinitril, amitrole)
2933.9900 14	三唑酮、醚草敏、三唑醇、唑草酮等(包括四氯喹恶啉、己唑醇、腈苯唑、亚胺唑、四氟醚唑、氟环唑)	6.5	20	17	9	千克	S	Triadimefo, credazine, triadimeno, carfentrazone - ethyl (including 4 - chloroquinoxaline, hexaconazole, fenbuconazole, imbenconazole, tetraconazole, epoxiconazole)
2933.9900 15	苄氯三唑醇、戊菌唑、粉唑醇等(包括联苯三唑醇、腈菌唑、环丙唑醇、烯唑醇、戊唑醇、氟硅唑)	6.5	20	17	9	千克	S	Diclobutrazol, penconzole, flutriafol (including bitertanol, myclobutanil, cyproconazole, diniconazole, tebuconazole, flusilazole)
2933.9900 16	环菌唑、叶菌唑、灭菌唑、种菌唑等(包括申嗪霉素、氟喹唑、哒螨灵、喹螨醚、氟草敏、氟咯草酮)	6.5	20	17	9	千克	S	Cyproconazole, metconazole, triticonazole, ipconazole (including shenqinmycin, fluquinconazole, pyridaben, fenazaquin, norflurazon, fluorochloridone)
2933.9900 17	唑草酯、四环唑、恶草酸等(包括喹禾糠酯、哒草特、咯草隆、禾草敌、唑草胺、敌草快、氯草敏)	6.5	20	17	9	千克	S	Carfentrazone - ethyl, tetcyclacis, propaquizafop(including quizalofop-P - tefuryl, pyridate, cisanilide, molinate, cafenstrole, diquat, chloridazon)
2933.9900 18	氟胺草唑、酰胺磺隆、三氟苯唑等(包括吲哚丁酸、溴莠敏、哌壮素、吲熟酯、三唑磺、四唑酰草胺)	6.5	20	17	9	千克	S	Flupoxam, foramsulfuron, fluotrimazole(including indole - butytic - acid), brompyrazon, piproctanly, ethychlozate(JMAF), fentrazamide)
2933.9900 19	多效唑、烯效唑、抑芽唑等(包括异麦赛津、叶枯净、叶锈特、吡喃草酮、吲哚乙酸)	6.5	20	17	9	千克	S	Paclobutrazol, uniconazole, triapenthenol, bifenthrin (including phenazineoxide, butrizol, tepraloxydim, heteroauxin)
2933.9900 21	氯尼他秦	6.5	20	17	9	千克	W	Clonitazene
2933.9900 22	依托尼秦	6.5	20	17	9	千克	W	Etonitazene
2933.9900 23	普罗庚嗪,布桂嗪	6.5	20	17	9	千克	W	Proheptazine, bucinnazine
2933.9900 30	扎莱普隆、唑吡坦(以及它们的盐)	6.5	20	17	9	千克	I	Zaleplon zolpidem(salts thereof)
2933.9900 40	齐帕特罗	6.5	20	17	9	千克	L	zilpaterol
2933.9900 51	二甲基色胺、二乙基色胺	6.5	20	17	9	千克	I	dimethyltryptamine, diethyltryptamine
2933.9900 52	乙色胺,咯环利定	6.5	20	17	9	千克	I	Etryptamine, rolicyclidine
2933.9900 53	[1 - (5 - 氟戊基) - 1H - 吲哚 - 3 - 基](2 - 碘苯基)甲酮(CAS 号:335161 - 03 - 0)	6.5	20	17	9	千克	I	1 - [(5 - Fluoropentyl) - 1H - indol - 3 - yl] - (2 - iodophenyl) methanone(CAS:335161 - 03 - 0)
2933.9900 54	1 - (5 - 氟戊基) - 3 - (1 - 萘甲酰基) - 1H - 吲哚(CAS 号:335161 - 24 - 5)	6.5	20	17	9	千克	I	1 - (5 - Fluoropentyl) - 3 - (1 - naphthoyl) indole (CAS:335161 - 24 - 5)

税则号列	货品名称	最惠(%)	普通	增值税率	出口退税	计量单位	监管条件	Article Description
2933.9900 55	1－戊基－3－(1－萘甲酰基)吲哚(CAS号:209414－07－3)	6.5	20	17	9	千克	I	1－Pentyl－3－(1－naphthoyl)indole(CAS:209414－07－3)
2933.9900 56	1－丁基－3－(1－萘甲酰基)吲哚(CAS号:208987－48－8)	6.5	20	17	9	千克	I	1－Butyl－3－(1－naphthoyl)indole(CAS:208987－48－8)
2933.9900 57	2－(2－甲氧基苯基)－1－(1－戊基－1H－吲哚－3－基)乙酮(CAS号:864445－43－2)	6.5	20	17	9	千克	I	2－(2－Methoxyphenyl)－1－(1－pentyl－1H－indol－3－yl)ethanone(CAS:864445－43－2)
2933.9900 60	(环)四亚甲基四硝胺(俗名奥托金HMX)	6.5	20	17	9	千克	3	Cyclotetramethylene tetranitramine(octogen)
2933.9900 70	(环)三亚甲基三硝基胺(俗名黑索金RDX)	6.5	20	17	9	千克	3	Cycltrimethylene－trinitramine(hexogen)
2933.9900 80	丁羟咯酮(包括杀雄啉、杀雄嗪酸、双唑草腈、唑酮草酯)	6.5	20	17	9	千克	S	Tepraloxydim(including sintofen, clofencet, pyraclonil, carfentrazone－ethyl)
2933.9900暂 91	阿托伐他汀钙	4	20	17	9	千克		Atorvastatin calcium
2933.9900 99	其他仅含氮杂原子的杂环化合物	6.5	20	17	9	千克		Nitrogen containing heterocyclic compounds other atoms
29.34	**核酸及其盐;无论是否已有化学定义;其他杂环化合物:**							**Nucleic acids and their salts, whether or not chemically defined; other heterocyclic compounds:**
2934.1000	-结构上含有一个非稠合噻唑环(不论是否氢化)的化合物	6.5	20	17	9	千克		-Compounds containing an unfused thiazole ring (whether or not hydrogenated) in the structure
2934.1000 11	噻螨酮	6.5	20	17	9	千克	S	Hexythiazox
2934.1000 12	噻唑膦、噻唑硫磷	6.5	20	17	9	千克	S	Fosthiazate, colophonate
2934.1000 13	噻唑烟酸、噻唑菌胺	6.5	20	17	9	千克	S	Thiazopyr, ethaboxam
2934.1000 14	氯噻啉、氟螨噻	6.5	20	17	9	千克	S	Imidaclothiz, flubenzimine
2934.1000 15	噻菌灵、噻菌胺、噻丙腈	6.5	20	17	9	千克	S	Thiabendazole, metsulfovax, thiapronil
2934.1000 16	噻呋酰胺、噻虫胺、噻虫嗪、噻虫啉	6.5	20	17	9	千克	S	Thiabendazole, metsulfovax, thiapronil, thiacloprid
2934.1000 17	辛噻酮、拌种灵	6.5	20	17	9	千克	S	Octhilinone, seedavay
2934.1000 18	稻瘟灵	6.5	20	17	9	千克	S	Isoprothiolane
2934.1000 19	甲噻诱胺	6.5	20	17	9	千克	S	A thiazide induced amine
2934.1000 90	结构上含有非稠合噻唑环的化合物(非稠合噻唑环不论是否氢化)	6.5	20	17	9	千克		Compounds containing an unfused thiazole ring (whether or not hydrogenated) in the structure
2934.2000	-结构上含有一个苯并噻唑环系(不论是否氢化)的化合物,但未经进一步稠合的	6.5	20	17		千克		-Compounds containing in the structure a benzothiazole ring-system (whether or not hydrogenated), not further fused
2934.2000 11	噻螨威,噻霉酮	6.5	20	17	9	千克	S	Tazimcarb, benziothiazolinone
2934.2000 12	苯噻硫氰	6.5	20	17	9	千克	S	Benthiozole
2934.2000 13	烯丙苯噻唑	6.5	20	17	9	千克	S	Probenazole
2934.2000 14	草除灵	6.5	20	17	9	千克	S	Benazolin ethyl
2934.2000 15	噻唑禾草灵	6.5	20	17	9	千克	S	Fenthiaprop-ethyl
2934.2000 16	苯噻隆	6.5	20	17	9	千克	S	Benzthiazuron
2934.2000 17	甲基苯噻隆	6.5	20	17	9	千克	S	Methabenzthiazuron
2934.2000 18	苯噻酰草胺	6.5	20	17	9	千克	S	Mefenacet
2934.2000 19	苯噻菌酯	6.5	20	17	13	千克	S	Benzothiostrobin
2934.2000 90	其他含一个苯并噻唑环系的化合物	6.5	20	17	13	千克		Other compounds containing in the structure a benzothiazole ring-system
2934.3000	-结构上含有一个吩噻嗪环系(不论是否氢化)的化合物,但未经进一步稠合的	6.5	20	17	9	千克		-Compounds containing in the structure a phenothiazine ring-system (whether or not hydrogenated), not further fused
	-其他:							-Other:

税则号列	货品名称	最惠(%)	普通	增值税率	出口退税	计量单位	监管条件	Article Description
2934.9100	--阿米雷司(INN),溴替唑仑(INN),氯噻西泮(INN),氯恶唑仑(INN),右吗拉胺(INN),卤恶唑仑(INN),凯他唑仑(INN),美索卡(INN),恶唑仑(INN),匹莫林(INN),苯甲曲嗪(INN),芬美曲嗪(INN)和舒芬太尼(INN)及它们的盐	6.5	20	17	9	千克		--Aminorex(INN), brotizolam(INN), clotiazepam(INN), cloxazolam(INN), dextromoramide(INN), haloxazolam(INN), ketazolam(INN), mesocarb(INN), oxazolam(INN), pemoline(INN), phendimetrazine(INN), phenmetrazine(INN) and sufentanil(INN); salts thereof
2934.9100 11	阿米雷司、溴替唑仑、氯噻西泮(以及它们的盐)	6.5	20	17	9	千克	I	Aminorex(INN), brotizolam(INN), clotiazepam(INN)(salts thereof)
2934.9100 12	氯恶唑仑、卤沙(恶)唑仑(以及它们的盐)	6.5	20	17	9	千克	I	Cloxazolam(INN), haloxazolam(INN); (salts thereof)
2934.9100 13	凯他唑仑、美索卡、奥沙(恶)唑仑(以及它们的盐)	6.5	20	17	9	千克	I	Ketazolam(INN), mesocarb(INN), oxazolam(INN)(salts thereof)
2934.9100 14	匹莫林、苯甲曲嗪、芬美曲嗪(以及它们的盐)	6.5	20	17	9	千克	I	Pemoline(INN), phendimetrazine(INN), phenmetrazine(INN)(salts thereof)
2934.9100 20	右吗拉胺、舒芬太尼(以及它们的盐)	6.5	20	17	9	千克	W	Dextromoramide(INN), sufentanil(INN)(salts thereof)
	--其他:							--Other:
2934.9910	---磺内酯及磺内酰胺	6.5	30	17	9	千克		---Sultones and sultams
2934.9920	---呋喃唑酮	6	20	17	9	千克	A	---Furazolidone
2934.9930	---核酸及其盐	6.5	35	17	9	千克		---Nucleic acids and their salts
2934.9940	---奈韦拉平,依发韦仑,利托那韦及它们的盐	6.5	20	17	13	千克		---Nevirapine, Efavirenz, Ritonavir and their salts
2934.9950	---克拉维酸及其盐	6.5	20	17	13	千克		---Clavulante acid and its salt
2934.9960	---7-苯乙酰氨基-3-氯甲基-4-头孢烷酸对甲氧基苄酯、7-氨基头孢烷酸、7-氨基脱乙酰氧基头孢烷酸	6	20	17	9,15	千克		"---7-phenylacetamido-3-chloromethylcephem-4-carbonicacidp-methoxybenzylester; 2, 0) oct-2-ene-2-carboxylicacid, 7-Aminocephalosporanic acid, 7-amido acetoxy eicosanoic acid removal"
2934.9990	---其他	6.5	20	17	9	千克		---Other
2934.9990 01	核苷酸类食品添加剂	6.5	20	17	9	千克	AB	Nucleotides food additives, hgslmof
2934.9990 10	恶草酮、氟噻草胺、活化酯、高效二甲吩草胺(包括吡噻菌胺)	6.5	20	17	9	千克	S	Oxadiazon, flufenacet, acibenzolar, dimethenamid (including penthiopyrad)
2934.9990 21	恶唑磷、蔬果磷、茂硫磷、除害磷等(包括甲基吡恶磷、丁硫环磷、硫环磷、杀扑磷、伏杀硫磷、地胺磷)	6.5	20	17	9	千克	S	Isoxathion, salithion dioxabenzofos, morphothion, (including azamethiphos, fosthietan, phosfolan, methidathion, phosalone, mephosfolan)
2934.9990 22	环线威、杀虫环、杀虫钉、多噻烷等(包括甲基硫环磷、噻嗯菊酯、噻嗪酮、恶虫酮、茚虫威)	6.5	20	17	9	千克	S	Tirpate, thiocyclam, trithialan, polythialan(including phosfolan - methyl, kadethrin, buprofezin, metoxadiazone, indoxacarb)
2934.9990 23	恶唑禾草灵、毒鼠硅、噻鼠灵等(包括福拉比、噻节因、糠菌唑、精恶唑禾草灵)	6.5	20	17	9	千克	S	Fenoxaprop-ethyl, silatrane, difethialone (including furametpyr, dimethipin, bromuconazole, fenoxaprop-p-ethyl)
2934.9990 24	代森硫、代森环、福吗啉、咯菌腈等(包括稻瘟酯、烯酰吗啉、噻菌腈、土菌灵、恶霜灵、恶霉灵)	6.5	20	17	9	千克	S	Etem(BSI), milmeb(BSI), flumorph fludioxonil (including pefurazoate, dimethomoph, thicyofen, etridiazole, oxadixyl, hymexazol)
2934.9990 25	噻霉酮、丙环唑、乙环唑等(包括恶唑菌酮、金核霉素、呋菌唑、叶枯唑、呋醚唑、苯醚甲环唑)	6.5	20	17	9	千克	S	Benziothiazolinone, propiconazole, etaconazole (including famoxadone, aureonuclemycin, furconazole bismerthiazol, furconazole - cis, difenoconazole)
2934.9990 26	嗪草酸、噻氟隆、丁噻隆、异恶隆等(包括噻苯隆、磺噻隆、恶唑隆、异恶草醚、噻吩草胺、二甲吩草胺)	6.5	20	17	9	千克	S	Fluthiacet thiazfluron, tebuthiuron, isoproturon (including thidiazuron, ethidimuron, dimefuron, isoxapyrifop, thenychlor, dimethachlor)
2934.9990 27	苯草灭、灭草松、灭草唑等(包括异恶草松、恶嗪草酮、环苯草酮、丙炔氟草胺)	6.5	20	17	9	千克	S	Bentranil, bentazone, methazole (including, clomazone, oxaziclomefone, cloproxydim, flumioxazin)
2934.9990 28	氟噻乙草酯、丙炔恶草酮、噻草酮等(包括糖氨基嘌呤、苯螨噻、异恶酰草胺、异恶唑草酮)	6.5	20	17	9	千克	S	Fulthiacet-methyl, oxakiargyl, cycloxydim (including kinetin, triarathene, ixoxaben, isoxaflutole)

税则号列	货 品 名 称	最惠(%)	普通	增值税率	出口退税	计量单位	监管条件	Article Description
2934.9990 29	炔丙恶唑草、韩乐宁、噻唑锌等(包括噻菌茂、硅丰环)	6.5	20	17	9	千克	S	Oxadiargyl, ethaboxam, zinc thiazole (including Saijunmao, silatrane)
2934.9990 31	多抗霉素、灰瘟素	6.5	20	17	9	千克	S	Polyoxin, blasticidin
2934.9990 32	三环唑、氧环唑	6.5	20	17	9	千克	S	Tricyclazole, azaconazole
2934.9990 33	灭螨猛、克杀螨、螨蜱胺	6.5	20	17	9	千克	S	Chinomethionate, thioquino, tifatol
2934.9990 34	二氰蒽醌、吗菌威	6.5	20	17	9	千克	S	Dithianon, carbamorph
2934.9990 35	十二环吗啉、十三吗啉	6.5	20	17	9	千克	S	Dodemorph, tridemorph
2934.9990 36	杀螺吗啉、丁苯吗啉	6.5	20	17	9	千克	S	Trifenmorph, fenpropimorph
2934.9990 37	喹菌酮、肼菌酮	6.5	20	17	9	千克	S	Oxolinic acid, drazoxolon
2934.9990 38	萎锈灵、氧化萎锈灵	6.5	20	17	9	千克	S	Carboxin, oxycarboxin
2934.9990 39	棉隆、乙烯菌核利	6.5	20	17	9	千克	S	Dazomet, vinclozolin
2934.9990 41	环酯草醚	6.5	20	17	9	千克	S	Pyriftalid
2934.9990 42	噻菌铜	6.5	20	17	9	千克	S	Thiodiazole - copper
2934.9990 43	苯唑草酮	6.5	20	17	9	千克	S	Carfentrazone - ethyl
2934.9990 44	丁吡吗啉	6.5	20	17	9	千克	S	Pyrimorph
2934.9990 50	恶唑酰草胺(包括环氧虫啶、噻恩菊酯、双苯恶唑酸、乙螨唑、异恶氯草酮、唑啉草酯)	6.5	20	17	9	千克	S	Metamifop (including kadethrin, isoxadifen ethyletoxazole, clomazone, pinoxaden)
2934.9990 61	甲米雷司及其盐	6.5	20	17	9	千克	I	4 - methylaminorex and its salt
2934.9990 62	替诺环定及其盐	6.5	20	17	9	千克	I	Tenocyclidine and its salt
2934.9990 71	硫代芬太尼、阿法甲基硫代芬太尼(以及它们的盐)	6.5	20	17	9	千克	W	Thiofentanyl, alpha - methylthiofentanyl (and their salt)
2934.9990 72	二乙噻丁、二甲噻丁、吗苯丁酯、乙甲噻丁(以及它们的盐)	6.5	20	17	9	千克	W	Diethylthiambutene, dimethylthiambutene, dioxaphetylbutyrate, ethyl - methylthiambutene (and their salts)
2934.9990 73	呋替啶、左吗拉胺、3 - 甲基硫代芬太尼(以及它们的盐)	6.5	20	17	9	千克	W	Furethidine, levomoramide, 3 - methylthiofentanyl (and their salts)
2934.9990 74	吗拉胺中间体、吗哌利定、苯吗庚酮、消旋吗拉胺(以及它们的盐)	6.5	20	17	9	千克	W	Moramide intermediate, morpheridine, benmaliangtong, racemoramide (and their salts)
2934.9990 75	亚甲基二氧吡咯戊酮(CAS 号:687603 - 66 - 3)	6.5	20	17	9	千克	I	Methylenedioxypyrovalerone (CAS:687603 - 66 - 3)
2934.9990 90	其他杂环化合物	6.5	20	17	9	千克		Other heterocyclic compounds
29.35	**磺(酰)胺:**							**Sulphonamides:**
2935.0010	---磺胺嘧啶	6.5	35	17	9	千克		---Sulphadiazine
2935.0020	---磺胺双甲基嘧啶	6.5	35	17	9	千克	A	---Sulfadimidine
2935.0030	---磺胺甲噁唑	6.5	35	17	9	千克		---Sulfamethoxazole
2935.0090	---其他	6.5	35	17	9	千克		---Other
2935.0090 11	氟唑磺隆、氟吡磺隆、磺酰磺隆、氯酯磺草胺等(包括甲酰氨基嘧磺隆、乙氧磺隆、氯磺隆、甲磺隆、苯磺隆、胺苯磺隆)	6.5	35	17	9	千克	S	Flucarbazone, flucetosulfuron, sulfosulfuron, cloransulam - methyl (including ormyl amino sulfometuron methyl, ethoxysulfuron, chlorsulfuron, metsulfuron-methyl, tribenuron-methyl, ethametsulfuron)
2935.0090 12	醚苯磺隆、噻吩磺隆、醚磺隆、氟啶嘧磺隆等(包括氟胺磺隆、氟磺隆、甲嘧磺隆、氯嘧磺隆、氟嘧磺隆)	6.5	35	17	9	千克	S	Triasulfuron, thifensulfuron-methyl, cinosulfuron, flupyrsulfuron - methyl - sodium (including triflusulfuron-methyl, prosulfuron, sulfometuron-methyl, chlorimuron-ethyl, primisulfuron-methyl)
2935.0090 13	苄嘧磺隆、吡嘧磺隆、烟嘧磺隆、双氟磺草胺等(包括啶嘧磺隆、砜嘧磺隆、唑嘧磺隆)	6.5	35	17	9	千克	S	Bensulfuron-methyl, pyrazosulfuron-ethyl, nicosulfuron, diclosulam (including flazasulfuron, rimsulfuron, imazosulfuron)
2935.0090 14	四唑嘧磺隆、唑吡嘧磺隆、三氟甲磺隆等(包括氯吡嘧磺隆、酰嘧磺隆、环丙嘧磺隆、甲基二磺隆)	6.5	35	17	9	千克	S	Imazosulfuron, azimsulfuron, tritosulfuron (including halosulfuron-methyl, amidosulfuron, cyclosulfamuron, mesosulfuron)
2935.0090 15	氟磺酰草胺、甲磺草胺、嘧苯胺磺隆等(包括唑嘧磺草胺、双氟磺草胺、五氟磺草胺)	6.5	35	17	9	千克	S	Mefluidide, sulfentrazone, orthosulfamuron (including flumetsulam, florasulam, penoxsuam)

税则号列	货品名称	最惠(%)	普通	增值税率	出口退税	计量单位	监管条件	Article Description
2935.0090 16	氟磺胺草醚、磺草灵、吲唑磺菌胺等(包括单嘧磺酯、磺草唑胺、三氟啶磺隆钠)	6.5	35	17	9	千克	S	Fomesafen, asulam, amisulbrom (including monosulfuron ester, metosulam)
2935.0090 17	磺草膦、氨磺乐灵、三氟啶磺隆、啶磺草胺等(包括甲基碘磺隆钠盐)	6.5	35	17	9	千克	S	LS 830556, oryzalin, trifloxysulfuron, pyroxsulam (including odosulfuron methyl sodium)
2935.0090 18	磺菌胺、增糖胺等(包括甲苯氟磺胺、氟虫胺)	6.5	35	17	9	千克	S	Flusulfamide, fluoridamid (including tolyfluanid, sulfluramid)
2935.0090 19	畜蜱磷、伐灭磷、地散磷等(包括磺菌威、氰霜唑)	6.5	35	17	9	千克	S	Cythioate , famphur (ESA), bensulide (including methasulfocarb, cyazofamid)
2935.0090 20	环氧嘧磺隆	6.5	35	17	9	千克	S	Oxasulfuron
2935.0090 31	苯嘧磺草胺	6.5	35	17	9	千克	S	Saflufenacil
2935.0090 32	噻酮磺隆	6.5	35	17	9	千克	S	Chlorthalidone chlorsulfuron
2935.0090 33	N－乙基全氟辛基磺酰胺、N－甲基全氟辛基磺酰胺、N－乙基－N－(2－羟乙基)全氟辛基磺酰胺、N－(2－羟乙基)－N－甲基全氟辛基磺酰胺	6.5	35	17	9	千克	X	N－ethyl perfluorooctane sulfonamide, N－methyl perfluorooctyl sulfonamide, N－ethyl －N－(2－hydroxyethyl) perfluorooctanesulfonamide, N－(2－hydroxyethyl) －N－ methyl perfluorooctyl sulfonamide
2935.0090 90	其他磺(酰)胺	6.5	35	17	9	千克		Other sulphonamides
	第十一分章　维生素原、维生素及激素							XI. -PROVITAMINS, VITAMINS AND HORMONES
29.36	**天然或合成再制的维生素原和维生素(包括天然浓缩物)及其主要用作维生素的衍生物,上述产品的混合物,不论是否溶于溶剂:**							**Provitamins and vitamins, natural or reproduced by synthesis (including natural concentrates), derivatives thereof used primarily as vitamins, and intermixtures of the foregoing, whether or not in any solvent:**
	-未混合的维生素及其衍生物:							-Vitamins and their derivatives, unmixed:
2936.2100	--维生素A及其衍生物	4	20	17	17	千克	AB	--Vitamins A and their derivatives
2936.2200	--维生素B_1及其衍生物	4	20	17	13	千克	AB	--Vitamin B_1 and its derivatives
2936.2300	--维生素B_2及其衍生物	4	20	17	13	千克	AB	--Vitamin B_2 and its derivatives
2936.2400	--D或DL-泛酸(维生素B_3或维生素B_5)及其衍生物	4	20	17	13	千克	AB	--D-or DL-Pantothenic acid (Vitamin B_3 or Vitamin B_5) and its derivatives
2936.2500	--维生素B_6及其衍生物	4	20	17	13	千克	AB	--Vitamin B_6 and its derivatives
2936.2600	--维生素B_{12}及其衍生物	4	20	17	13	千克	AB	--Vitamin B_{12} and its derivatives
2936.2700	--维生素C及其衍生物	4	20	17	13	千克		--Vitamin C and its derivatives
2936.2700 10	未混合的维生素C原粉(不论是否溶于溶剂)	4	20	17	13	千克	4ABxy	Not mixed vitamin C of original powder
2936.2700 20	未混合的维生素C钙、维生素C钠(不论是否溶于溶剂)	4	20	17	13	千克	4ABxy	Not mixed Calcium ascorbate, odiumascorbate (whether or not in orny solvent)
2936.2700 30	颗粒或包衣维生素C(不论是否溶于溶剂)	4	20	17	13	千克	4ABxy	Particles or coated vitamin C
2936.2700 90	维生素C酯类及其他(不论是否溶于溶剂)	4	20	17	13	千克	4ABxy	vitamin c of ester and other
2936.2800	--维生素E及其衍生物	4	20	17	17	千克	AB	--Vitamin E and its derivatives
2936.2900	--其他	4	20	17	17	千克		--Other
2936.2900 10	胆钙化醇(不论是否溶于溶剂)	4	20	17	17	千克	ABS	Cholecalciferol (whether or not in any solvent)
2936.2900 90	其他未混合的维生素及其衍生物(不论是否溶于溶剂)	4	20	17	17	千克	AB	Other vitamins and their derivatives, unmixed (whether or not in any solvent)
2936.9000	-其他,包括天然浓缩物	4	20	17	13	千克	AB	-Other, including natural concentrates
29.37	**天然或合成再制的激素、前列腺素、血栓烷、白细胞三烯及其衍生物和结构类似物,包括主要用作激素的改性链多肽:**							**Hormones, prostaglandins, thromboxanes and leukotrienes, natural or reproduced by synthesis; derivatives and structural analogues thereof, including chain modified polypeptides, used primarily as hormones:**
	-多肽激素、蛋白激素、糖蛋白激素及其衍生物和结构类似物:							-Polypeptide hormones, protein hormones and glycoprotein hormones, their derivatives and structural analogues:
2937.1100	--生长激素及其衍生物和结构类似物	4	20	17	9	千克		--Somatotropin, its derivatives and structural analogues

税则号列	货品名称	最惠(%)	普通	增值税率	出口退税	计量单位	监管条件	Article Description
2937.1100 10	生长激素(GH)	4	20	17	9	千克	L	Growth hormone(GH)
2937.1100 90	生长激素的衍生物和结构类似物	4	20	17	9	千克		Growth hormone derivatives and structural analogues
	--胰岛素及其盐:							--Insulin and its salts:
2937.1210	---重组人胰岛素及其盐	4	20	17	15	千克	L	---Recombinant human insulin and its salts
2937.1290	---其他	4	20	17	15	千克	L	---Other
2937.1900	--其他	4	20	17	9	千克		--Other
2937.1900 13	绒促性素及促黄体生成素[包括生长激素释放肽类(GHRPs)、普拉莫瑞林(生长激素释放肽-2)、CJC-1295(CAS号863288-34-0)、生长激素释放肽-6、生长激素释放激素及其类似物、生长激素促分泌剂]	4	20	17	9	千克	L	HCG and luteinizing hormone[Including growth hormone releasing peptide (GHRPs), Plummer Relin (growth hormone releasing peptide -2), CJC-1295 (CAS No. 863288-34-0), growth hormone releasing peptide -6, growth hormone releasing hormone and its analogues, growth hormone secretagogue]
2937.1900 15	促皮质素类[包括艾瑞莫瑞林、阿那瑞林、布舍瑞林、可的瑞林、海沙瑞林、伊莫瑞林、舍莫瑞林、替莫瑞林、戈那瑞林、曲普瑞林、葛瑞林(脑肠肽)及其模拟物类]	4	20	17	9	千克	L	Adrenocoticotropin [including Ai Rui, A Bernard Relin, Bushrui Lin, Mo Ruilin corticorelin, sea Sha Ruilin, Iraq, Mo Ruilin, Mo Ruilin, Gore Bernard Relin, for Mo Ruilin Ge Ruilin (triptorelin, brain gut peptide) and its analogue]
2937.1900 90	其他多肽激素及衍生物和结构类似物(包括蛋白激素、糖蛋白激素及其衍生物和结构类似物)	4	20	17	9	千克	Q	Other polypeptide hormones, including protein hormones 、glycoprotein hormones , their derivatives and structural analogues
	-甾族激素及其衍生物和结构类似物:							-Steroidal hormones, their derivatives and structural analogues:
2937.2100	--可的松、氢化可的松、脱氢可的松及脱氢皮质醇	4	20	17	9	千克	Q	--Cortisone, hydrocortisone, prednisone (dehydrocortisone) and prednisolone (dehydrohydrocortisone)
	--皮质甾类激素的卤化衍生物:							--Halogenated derivatives of corticosteroidal hormones:
2937.2210	---地塞米松	4	30	17	9	千克	Q	---Dexamethasone
2937.2290	---其他	4	30	17	9	千克	Q	---Other
	--雌(甾)激素和孕激素:							--Oestrogens and progestogens:
	---动物源的:							---Animal source:
2937.2311	----孕马结合雌激素	4	30	17	9	千克	Q	----Pregnant mare conjugated estrogens
2937.2319	----其他	4	30	17	9	千克	Q	----Other
2937.2390	---其他	4	30	17	9	千克		---Other
2937.2390 10	泽仑诺;孕三烯酮;替勃龙(包括四氢孕三烯酮)	4	30	17	9	千克	L	Zearalanol, gestrinone, tibolone (including tetrahydrogestrinone)
2937.2390 90	其他雌(甾)激素及孕激素	4	30	17	9	千克	Q	Other oestrogens and progestogens
2937.2900	--其他	4	30	17	9	千克		--Other
2937.2900 11	1-雄烯二醇;1-雄烯二酮(包括雄甾-4-烯-3β, 17α-二醇;雄甾-5-烯-3β, 17α-二醇)	4	30	17	9	千克	L	1- androstenediol; 1- androstene two ketone (including androst -4- allyl -3 β, 17 α - glycol; androst -5- allyl -3 β, 17 α - gly
2937.2900 12	4-雄烯二醇;5-雄烯二酮(包括5α-雄烷-3α, 17β-二醇;5α-雄烷-3β, 17α-二醇;勃拉睾酮)	4	30	17	9	千克	L	Including 5 α - androstane -3 α, 17 β - estradiol; 5 α - androstane -3 β, 17 α - glycol; bolas
2937.2900 13	勃地酮;卡芦睾酮(包括勃二酮;氯司替勃)	4	30	17	9	千克	L	Boldenone; calusterone (including clostebol) Boldenone, calusterone (including 1,4-amdrostodiene-3;17-dione;clostebol)
2937.2900 14	达那唑;脱氢氯甲睾酮(包括普拉睾酮;去氧甲睾酮)	4	30	17	9	千克	L	Danazol; dehydrochloromethy (including prasterone; desoxymethyl - testosterone)
2937.2900 15	双氢睾酮;屈他雄酮(包括表双氢睾酮;乙雌烯醇;氟甲睾酮;甲酰勃龙)	4	30	17	9	千克	L	Dihydrotestosterone; drostanolone (including epi-dihydrotestosterone ; ethylestrenol ; fluoxymesterone , formebolone)
2937.2900 16	夫拉扎勃(包括4-羟基睾酮;3α-羟基-5α-雄烷-17-酮)	4	30	17	9	千克	L	Furazabol(including 4-hydroxy - testosterone ;4-hydroxy-nandrolone; 3α-hydroxy-5α-androstan-17-ketone)

税则号列	货品名称	最惠(%)	普通	增值税率	出口退税	计量单位	监管条件	Article Description
2937.2900 17	美雄诺龙;美睾酮;美雄酮(包括甲基屈他雄酮)	4	30	17	9	千克	L	Mestanolone; mesterolone; methandienone (including methyl drostanolone)
2937.2900 18	甲基-1-睾酮;甲睾酮;甲诺睾酮(包括甲二烯诺龙;去甲雄酮)	4	30	17	9	千克	L	Methyl-1-testosterone, methyltestosterone; Kanok testosterone(including diene nandrolone; 19-norandrosterone)
2937.2900 19	美替诺龙;美雄醇(包括美曲勃龙)	4	30	17	9	千克	L	Methenolone; methandriol(including methyltrienolone)
2937.2900 21	米勃酮;诺龙;诺勃酮;诺司替勃(包括19-去甲雄烯二醇;诺乙雄龙)	4	30	17	9	千克	L	Mibolerone; nandrolone; norbolethone; norclostebol (including 19-norandrostenediol, norethandrolone)
2937.2900 22	19-去甲胆烷醇酮(包括羟勃龙;氧雄龙)	4	30	17	9	千克	L	19-noretiocholanolone (including oxandrolone; oxymesterone)
2937.2900 23	羟甲睾酮;羟甲烯龙(包括前列他唑)	4	30	17	9	千克	L	Oxymesterone, oxymetholone(including prostanozol)
2937.2900 24	奎勃龙;司坦唑醇;司腾勃龙(包括1-睾酮;睾酮;群勃龙)	4	30	17	9	千克	L	Quinbolone, stanozolol, stenbolone(including 1-testosterone, testosterone, trenbolone)
2937.2900 25	7α-羟基-普拉睾酮	4	30	17	9	千克	L	7α-Hydroxy-DHEA
2937.2900 26	7β-羟基-普拉睾酮	4	30	17	9	千克	L	7β-Hydroxy-DHEA
2937.2900 27	7-羰基-普拉睾酮	4	30	17	9	千克	L	7-Keto-prasterone
2937.2900 28	胆烷醇酮	4	30	17	9	千克	L	Androstane
2937.2900 31	雄甾-5-烯-3β,17β-二醇	4	30	17	9	千克	L	Androst-5-allyl-3β, 17β-estradi
2937.2900 32	雄甾-4-烯-3,17-二酮	4	30	17	9	千克	L	Androst-4-allyl-3,17-two ketone
2937.2900 33	勃雄二醇	4	30	17	9	千克	L	Bolandiol
2937.2900 90	其他甾类激素及其衍生物和结构类似物	4	30	17	9	千克	Q	Other somatotropin its derivatives and structural analogues
2937.5000	-前列腺素、血栓烷和白细胞三烯及其衍生物和结构类似物	4	30	17	9	千克		-Prostaglandins, thromboxanes and leukotrienes, their derivatives and structural analogues
2937.9000	-其他	4	30	17	9	千克		-Other
2937.9000 10	氨基酸衍生物	4	30	17	9	千克	ABQ	Amino-acid dervatives
2937.9000 90	其他激素及其衍生物和结构类似物	4	30	17	9	千克	Q	Other hormone its derivatives and structural analogues
	第十二分章　天然或合成再制的苷(配糖物)、植物碱及其盐、醚、酯和其他衍生物							Ⅻ. GLYCOSIDES AND VEGETABLE ALKALOIDS, NATURAL OR REPRODUCED BY SYNTHESIS, AND THEIR SALTS, ETHERS, ESTERS AND OTHER DERIVATIVES
29.38	**天然或合成再制的苷(配糖物)及其盐、醚、酯和其他衍生物:**							**Glycosides, natural or reproduced by synthesis, and their salts, ethers, esters and other derivatives:**
2938.1000	-芸香苷及其衍生物	6.5	20	17	9	千克	Q	-Rutoside (rutin) and its derivatives
	-其他:							-Other:
2938.9010	---齐多夫定、拉米夫定、司他夫定、地达诺新及它们的盐	6.5	20	17	13	千克		---Zidovudine, lamivudine, Stavudine, didanosine and their salts
2938.9090	---其他	6.5	20	17	9	千克		---Other
2938.9090 10	甘草酸粉	6.5	20	17	9	千克	y4x	Glycyrrhizic acid powder
2938.9090 20	甘草酸盐类	6.5	20	17	9	千克	4ABxy	Salts of glycyrrhizic acid
2938.9090 30	甘草次酸及其衍生物	6.5	20	17	9	千克	y4x	Glycyrrhetic acid and its derivatives
2938.9090 90	其他天然或合成再制的苷及其盐等(包括醚、酯和其他衍生物)	6.5	20	17	9	千克		Other glycosides, natural or reproduced by synthesis, and their salts, ethers, esters and other derivatives
29.39	**天然或合成再制的生物碱及其盐、醚、酯和其他衍生物:**							**Vegetable alkaloids, natural or reproduced by synthesis, and their salts, ethers, esters and other derivatives:**
	-鸦片碱及其衍生物以及它们的盐:							-Alkaloids of opium and their derivatives; salts thereof:

税则号列	货品名称	最惠(%)	普通	增值税率	出口退税	计量单位	监管条件	Article Description
2939.1100	--罂粟杆浓缩物、丁丙诺啡(INN)、可待因、双氢可待因(INN)、乙基吗啡、埃托啡(INN)、海洛因、氢可酮(INN)、氢吗啡酮(INN)、吗啡、尼可吗啡(INN)、羟考酮(INN)、羟吗啡酮(INN)、福尔可定(INN)、醋氢可酮(INN)和蒂巴因,以及它们的盐	4	50	17	9	千克		--Concentrates of poppy straw; buprenorphine (INN), codeine, dihydrocodeine (INN), ethylmorphine, etorphine (INN), heroin, hydrocodone (INN), hydromorphone (INN), morphine, nicomorphine (INN), oxycodone (INN), oxymorphone (INN), pholcodine (INN), thebacon (INN) and thebaine; salts thereof
2939.1100 11	罂粟杆浓缩物	4	50	17	9	千克	W	Concentrates of poppy straw
2939.1100 12	可待因、双氢可待因、乙基吗啡(以及它们的盐)	4	50	17	9	千克	W	Codeine, dihydrocodeine (INN), ethylmorphine (salts thereof)
2939.1100 13	埃托啡、海洛因、氢可酮(以及它们的盐)	4	50	17	9	千克	W	Etorphine (INN), heroin, hydrocodone (INN) (salts thereof)
2939.1100 14	氢吗啡酮、吗啡、尼可吗啡(以及它们的盐)	4	50	17	9	千克	W	Hydromorphone (INN), morphine, nicomorphine (INN) (salts thereof)
2939.1100 15	羟考酮、羟吗啡酮、福尔可定(以及它们的盐)	4	50	17	9	千克	W	Oxycodone (INN), oxymorphone (INN), pholcodine (INN) (salts thereof)
2939.1100 16	醋氢可酮、蒂巴因(以及它们的盐)	4	50	17	9	千克	W	Thebacon (INN) and thebaine (salts thereof)
2939.1100 20	丁丙诺啡及其盐	4	50	17	9	千克	I	Buprenorphine and salts thereof
2939.1900	--其他	4	50	17	9	千克		--Other
2939.1900 10	二氢埃托啡及其盐	4	50	17	9	千克	W	Dihydroetorphine and its salts
2939.1900 21	苄吗啡、可多克辛、地索吗啡、酯托啡(以及它们的盐)	4	50	17	9	千克	W	Benzylmorphine, codoxime, desomorphine, acteorphinp (and their salt)
2939.1900 22	双氢吗啡、氢吗啡醇、甲地索啡、甲二氢吗啡(以及它们的盐)	4	50	17	9	千克	W	Dihydromorphine, hydromorphinol, methyldesorphine, methyldihydromorphine (and their salt)
2939.1900 23	美托酮、吗啡-N-氧化物、麦罗啡、去甲吗啡(以及它们的盐)	4	50	17	9	千克	W	Metopon, morphine - N - oxide, myrophine, normorphine (and their salt)
2939.1900 24	醋氢可待因、尼可待因、尼二氢可待因、去甲可待因(以及它们的盐)	4	50	17	9	千克	W	Acetyldihydrocodeine, nicocodine, nicomorphine, norcodeine (and their salt)
2939.1900 25	吗啡甲溴化物及其盐	4	50	17	9	千克	W	Morphine methobromide and its salt
2939.1900 30	纳布啡及其盐	4	50	17	9	千克	I	Nalbuphine and its salt
2939.1900 40	奥列巴文(CAS号:467-04-9)	4	50	17	9	千克	W	Oripavine (CAS:467-04-9)
2939.1900 90	其他鸦片碱及其衍生物及它们的盐	4	50	17	9	千克	Q	Other alkaloids of opium and their derivatives; salts thereof
2939.2000	-金鸡纳生物碱及其衍生物以及它们的盐	4	20	17	9	千克	Q	-Alkaloids of cinchona and their derivatives; salts thereof
2939.3000	-咖啡因及其盐	4	20	17	9	千克		-Caffeine and its salts
2939.3000 10	咖啡因	4	20	17	9	千克	ABI	Caffeine
2939.3000 90	咖啡因的盐	4	20	17	9	千克	ABI	Salts of caffeine
	-麻黄碱类及其盐:							-Ephedrines and their salts:
2939.4100	--麻黄碱及其盐	4	20	17	9	千克		--Ephedrine and its salts
2939.4100 10	麻黄碱(麻黄素,盐酸麻黄碱)	4	20	17	9	千克	23Q	Ephedrine (ephedrine, ephedrine - hydrochloride)
2939.4100 20	硫酸麻黄碱	4	20	17	9	千克	23Q	Ephedrine sulfate
2939.4100 30	消旋盐酸麻黄碱	4	20	17	9	千克	23Q	Racephedrine hydrochloride
2939.4100 40	草酸麻黄碱	4	20	17	9	千克	23Q	Ephedrine oxalate
2939.4100 90	麻黄碱盐	4	20	17	9	千克	Q	Salts of ephedrine
2939.4200	--假麻黄碱及其盐	4	20	17	9	千克		--Pseudoephedrine (INN) and its salts
2939.4200 10	伪麻黄碱(伪麻黄素、盐酸伪麻黄碱)	4	20	17	9	千克	23Q	Pseudoephedrine (pseudoephedrine, pseudoephedrine hydrochloride)
2939.4200 20	硫酸伪麻黄碱	4	20	17	9	千克	23Q	Pseudoephedrine sulfate
2939.4200 90	假麻黄碱盐(D-2-甲胺基-1-苯基丙醇)	4	20	17	9	千克	Q	Salts of pseudoephedrine (D - 2 - methylamino - 1 - phenylethyl carbinol)
2939.4300	--d-去甲假麻黄碱(INN)及其盐	4	20	17	9	千克	I	--d-Norpseudoephedrine and its salts
2939.4400	--去甲麻黄碱及其盐	4	20	17	9	千克	23	--Norephedrine and its salts
2939.4900	--其他	4	20	17	9	千克		--Other
2939.4900 10	盐酸甲基麻黄碱	4	20	17	9	千克	Q23	Methylephedrine hydrochloride
2939.4900 20	消旋盐酸甲基麻黄碱	4	20	17	9	千克	Q23	DL - methylephedrine hydrochloride

税则号列	货品名称	最惠(%)	普通	增值税率	出口退税	计量单位	监管条件	Article Description
2939.4900 90	其他麻黄碱及其盐	4	20	17	9	千克	Q	Other ephedrines and their salts
	-茶碱和氨茶碱及其衍生物以及它们的盐:							-Theophylline and aminophylline (theophylline-ethylenediamine) and their derivatives; salts thereof:
2939.5100	--芬乙茶碱(INN)及其盐	4	20	17	9	千克	I	--Fenetylline(INN) and its salts
2939.5900	--其他	4	20	17	9	千克	Q	--Other
	-麦角生物碱及其衍生物以及它们的盐:							-Alkaloids of rye ergot and their derivatives; salts thereof:
2939.6100	--麦角新碱及其盐	4	20	17	9	千克		--Ergometrine (INN) and its salts
2939.6100 10	麦角新碱	4	20	17	9	千克	3Q2	Ergometrine (INN)
2939.6100 90	麦角新碱盐	4	20	17	9	千克	Q	Salt of ergometrine (INN)
2939.6200	--麦角胺及其盐	4	20	17	9	千克		--Ergotamine (INN) and its salts
2939.6200 10	麦角胺	4	20	17	9	千克	3Q2	Ergotamine (INN)
2939.6200 90	麦角胺盐	4	20	17	9	千克	Q	Salts of ergotamine (INN)
2939.6300	--麦角酸及其盐	4	20	17	9	千克		--Lysergic acid and its salts
2939.6300 10	麦角酸	4	20	17	9	千克	3Q2	Lysergic acid
2939.6300 90	麦角酸盐	4	20	17	9	千克	Q	Salts of lysergic acid
2939.6900	--其他	4	20	17	9	千克		--Other
2939.6900 10	麦角二乙胺及其盐	4	20	17	9	千克	I	Lysergide and its salts
2939.6900 90	其他麦角生物碱及其衍生物(包括它们的盐)	4	20	17	9	千克	Q	Other alkaloids of rye ergot and their derivatives (salts thereof)
	-其他:							-Other:
	--可卡因、芽子碱、左甲苯丙胺、去氧麻黄碱(INN)、去氧麻黄碱外消旋体,它们的盐、酯及其他衍生物:							--Cocaine, ecgonine, levometamfetamine, metamfetamine (INN), metamfetamine racemate; salts, esters and other derivatives thereof:
2939.9110	---可卡因及其盐	4	20	17	9	千克	W	---Cocaine and its salts
2939.9190	---其他	4	20	17	9	千克		---Other
2939.9190 11	左甲苯丙胺(以及它们的盐、酯及其他衍生物)	4	20	17	9	千克	I	Levometamfetamine(and their salts, esters and other derivatives)
2939.9190 12	去氧麻黄碱(以及它们的盐、酯及其他衍生物)	4	20	17	9	千克	I	Metamfetamine(INN) (and their salts, esters and other derivatives)
2939.9190 13	去氧麻黄碱外消旋体(以及它们的盐、酯及其他衍生物)	4	20	17	9	千克	I	Metamfetamine racemate(and their salts, esters and other derivatives)
2939.9190 20	芽子碱及其盐	4	20	17	9	千克	W	Ecgonine and their salts
	--其他:							--Other:
2939.9910	---烟碱及其盐	4	20	17	9	千克		---Nicotine and its salts
2939.9910 10	烟碱	4	20	17	9	千克	ABQ	Nicotine
2939.9910 90	烟碱盐	4	20	17	9	千克	Q	Nicotine salts
2939.9920	---番木鳖碱(士的年)及其盐	4	17	17	9	千克		---Strychnine and its salts
2939.9920 10	番木鳖碱	4	17	17	9	千克	ABQ	Strychnine
2939.9920 90	番木鳖碱盐	4	17	17	9	千克	Q	Strychnine salts
2939.9990	---其他	4	20	17	9	千克		---Other
2939.9990 11	卡西酮、麦司卡林(以及它们的盐)	4	20	17	9	千克	I	Cathinone mescaline and their salts
2939.9990 12	赛洛新、赛洛西宾(以及它们的盐)	4	20	17	9	千克	I	Psilocine ,psilocybine and their salts
2939.9990 90	其他生物碱及其衍生物(包括生物碱的盐、酯及其他衍生物)	4	20	17	9	千克	ABQ	Other rye ergot and their derivatives; salts thereof
	第十三分章　其他有机化合物							XIII. -OTHER ORGANIC COMPOUNDS
29.40	**化学纯糖,但蔗糖、乳糖、麦芽糖、葡萄糖及果糖除外;糖醚、糖缩醛、糖酯及其盐,但不包括税目29.37、29.38及29.39的产品:**							**Sugars, chemically pure, other than sucrose, lactose, maltose, glucose and fructose, sugar ethers, sugar acetals and sugar esters, and their salts, other than products of heading No. 29.37, 29.38 or 29.39:**
	化学纯糖,但蔗糖、乳糖、麦芽糖、葡萄糖及果糖除外;糖醚、糖缩醛、糖酯及其盐,但不包括税目29.37、29.38及29.39的产品:							Sugars, chemically pure, other than sucrose, lactose, maltose, glucose and fructose; sugar ethers and sugar esters, and their salts, other than products of heading No. 29.37, 29.38 or 29.39:
2940.0010	---木糖	6	30	17	9	千克	ABQ	---Xylose
2940.0090	---其他	6	30	17	9	千克	ABQ	---Other
29.41	**抗菌素:**							**Antibiotics:**

税则号列	货品名称	最惠(%)	普通	增值税率	出口退税	计量单位	监管条件	Article Description
	-青霉素和具有青霉烷酸结构的青霉素衍生物及其盐:							-Penicillins and their derivatives with a penicillanic acid structure; salts thereof:
	---氨苄青霉素及其盐:							---Ampicillin and its salts:
2941.1011	----氨苄青霉素	6	20	17	13	千克	Q	----Ampicillin
2941.1012	----氨苄青霉素三水酸	6	20	17	13	千克	Q	----Ampicillin trihydrate
2941.1019	----其他	6	20	17	13	千克	Q	----Other
	---其他:							---Other:
2941.1091	----羟氨苄青霉素	4	20	17	13	千克	Q	----Amoxycillin
2941.1092	----羟氨苄青霉素三水酸	4	20	17	13	千克	Q	----Amoxycillin trihydrate
2941.1093	----6 氨基青霉烷酸(6APA)	4	20	17	13	千克		----6-Aminopenicillanic acid
2941.1094	----青霉素 V	4	20	17	13	千克	Q	----Penicillin V
2941.1095	----磺苄青霉素	4	20	17	13	千克	Q	----Sulfobenzylpenicillin
2941.1096	----邻氯青霉素	4	20	17	13	千克	Q	----Cloxacillin
2941.1099	----其他	4	20	17	13	千克	4Qxy	----Other
2941.2000	-链霉素及其衍生物以及它们的盐	4	20	17	13	千克	Q	-Streptomycins and their derivatives; salts thereof
2941.2000 11	硫酸链霉素	4	20	17	13	千克	QS	Streptomycin sulfate
2941.2000 90	其他链霉素及其衍生物、盐	4	20	17	13	千克	Q	Other streptomycin and its derivatives, salt
	-四环素及其衍生物以及它们的盐:							-Tetracyclines and their derivatives; salts thereof:
	---四环素及其盐:							---Tetracyclines and their salts:
2941.3011	----四环素	4	20	17	13	千克	Q	----Tetracyclines
2941.3012	----四环素盐	4	20	17	13	千克	Q	----Salts of tetracyclines
2941.3020	---四环素衍生物及其盐	4	20	17	13	千克	Q	---Tetracyclines derivatives and their salts:
2941.4000	-氯霉素及其衍生物以及它们的盐	4	20	17	13	千克	Q	-Chloramphenicol and its derivatives; salts thereof
2941.5000	-红霉素及其衍生物以及它们的盐	4	20	17	13	千克	Q	-Erythromycin and its derivatives; salts thereof
	-其他:							-Other:
2941.9010	---庆大霉素及其衍生物以及它们的盐	4	20	17	13	千克	Q	---Gentamycin and its derivatives; salts thereof
2941.9020	---卡那霉素及其衍生物以及它们的盐	4	20	17	13	千克	Q	---Kanamycin and its derivatives; salts thereof
2941.9030	---利福平及其衍生物以及它们的盐	4	20	17	13	千克	Q	---Rifampicin (RFP); salts thereof
2941.9040	---林可霉素及其衍生物以及它们的盐	4	20	17	13	千克	Q	---Lincomycin and its derivatives; salts thereof
	---头孢菌素及其衍生物以及它们的盐:							---Cephamycin and its derivatives; salts thereof:
2941.9052	----头孢氨苄及其盐	6	20	17	13	千克	Q	----Cefalexin and its salts
2941.9053	----头孢唑啉及其盐	6	20	17	13	千克	Q	----Cefazolin and its salts
2941.9054	----头孢拉啶及其盐	6	20	17	13	千克	Q	----Cefradine and its salts
2941.9055	----头孢三嗪(头孢曲松)及其盐	6	20	17	13	千克	Q	----Ceftriaxone and its salts
2941.9056	----头孢哌酮及其盐	6	20	17	13	千克	Q	----Cefoperazone and its salts
2941.9057	----头孢噻肟及其盐	6	20	17	13	千克	Q	----Cefotaxime and its salts
2941.9058	----头孢克罗及其盐	6	20	17	13	千克	Q	----Cefaclor and its salts
2941.9059	----其他	6	20	17	13	千克		----Other
2941.9059 10	放线菌酮	6	20	17	13	千克	QS	Actidione
2941.9059 90	其他头孢菌素及其衍生物(包括它们的盐)	6	20	17	13	千克	Q	Other cephamycin and its derivaatives; salts thereof
2941.9060	---麦迪霉素及其衍生物以及它们的盐	6	20	17	13	千克	Q	---Midecamycin and its derivatives; salts thereof
2941.9070	---乙酰螺旋霉素及其衍生物以及它们的盐	4	20	17	13	千克	Q	---Acetyl-spiramycin and its derivatives; salts thereof
2941.9090	---其他	6	20	17	15	千克	Q	---Other
2941.9090 11	中生菌素	6	20	17	13	千克	QS	Zhongshengmycin
2941.9090 12	春雷霉素	6	20	17	13	千克	QS	Kasugamycin
2941.9090 90	其他抗菌素	6	20	17	13	千克	Q	Other antibiotics
29.42	**其他有机化合物:**							**Other organic compounds:**
2942.0000	其他有机化合物	6.5	30	17	9	千克		Other organic compounds

第三十章
药　品

Chapter 30
Pharmaceutical products

注释：

一、本章不包括：

（一）食品及饮料（例如，营养品、糖尿病食品、强化食品、保健食品、滋补饮料及矿泉水）第四类，但不包括供静脉摄入用的滋养品；

（二）用于帮助吸烟者戒烟的制剂，例如，片剂、咀嚼胶或透皮贴片（税目21.06或38.24）；

（三）经特殊煅烧或精细研磨的牙科用熟石膏（税目25.20）；

（四）适合医药用的精油水馏液及水溶液（税目33.01）；

（五）税目33.03至33.07的制品，不论是否具有治疗及预防疾病的作用；

（六）加有药料的肥皂及税目34.01的其他产品；

（七）以熟石膏为基本成分的牙科用制品（税目34.07）；或

（八）不作治疗及预防疾病用的血清蛋白（税目35.02）。

二、税目30.02所称的"免疫制品"是指直接参与免疫过程调节的多肽及蛋白质（税目29.37的货品除外），例如，单克隆抗体（MAB）、抗体片段、抗体偶联物及抗体片段偶联物、白介素、干扰素（IFN）、趋化因子及特定的肿瘤坏死因子（TNF）、生长因子（GF）、促红细胞生成素及集落刺激因子（CSF）。

三、税目30.03及30.04以及本章注释四（四）所述的非混合产品及混合产品，按下列规定处理：

（一）非混合产品：

1. 溶于水的非混合产品；
2. 第二十八章及第二十九章的所有货品；以及
3. 税目13.02的单一植物浸膏，只经标定或溶于溶剂的。

（二）混合产品：

1. 胶体溶液及悬浮液（胶态硫磺除外）；
2. 从植物性混合物加工所得的植物浸膏；
3. 蒸发天然矿质水所得的盐及浓缩物。

四、税目30.06仅适用于下列物品（这些物品只能归入税目30.06而不得归入本目录其他税目）：

（一）无菌外科肠线、类似的无菌缝合材料（包括外科或牙科用无菌可吸收缝线）及外伤创口闭合用的无菌粘合胶布；

（二）无菌昆布及无菌昆布塞条；

（三）外科或牙科用无菌吸收性止血材料；外科或牙科用无菌抗粘连阻隔材料，不论是否可吸收；

（四）用于病人的X光检查造影剂及其他诊断试剂，这些药剂是由单一产品配定剂量或由两种以上成分混合而成的；

（五）血型试剂；

（六）牙科粘固剂及其他牙科填料；骨骼粘固剂；

Notes:

1. This Chapter does not cover:

(a) Foods or beverages (such as dietetic, diabetic or fortified foods, food supplements, tonic beverages and mineral waters), other than nutritional preparations for intraverwas administration (Section Ⅳ);

(b) Preparations, such as tablets, chewing gum or patches (transdermal systems), intended to assist smokers to stop smoking (heading 21.06 or 38.24);

(c) Plasters specially calcined or finely ground for use in dentistry (heading No. 25.20);

(d) Aqueous distillates or aqueous solutions of essential oils, suitable for medicinal uses (heading No. 33.01);

(e) Preparations of headings No. 33.03 to 33.07, even if they have therapeutic or prophylactic properties;

(f) Soap or other products of heading No. 34.01 containing added medicaments;

(g) Preparations with a basis of plaster for use in dentistry (heading No. 34.07); or

(h) Blood albumin not prepared for therapeutic or prophylactic uses (heading No. 35.02).

2. For the purposes of heading 30.02, the expression "immunological products" applies to peptides and proteins (other than goods of heading 29.37) which are directly involved in the regulation of immunological processes, such as monoclonal antibodies (MAB), antibody fragments, antibody conjugates and antibody fragment conjugates, interleukins, interferons (IFN), chemodines and certain tumor necrosis factors (TNF), growth factors (GF), hematopoietins and colony stimulating factors (CSF)

3. For the purposes of headings No. 30.03 and 30.04 and of Note 4 (d) to this Chapter, the following are to be treated:

(a) As unmixed products:

(1) Unmixed products dissolved in water;

(2) All goods of Chapter 28 or 29;

(3) Simple vegetable extracts of heading No. 13.02, merely standardised or dissolved in any solvent;

(b) As products which have been mixed:

(1) Colloidal solutions and suspensions (other than colloidal sulphur);

(2) Vegetable extracts obtained by the treatment of mixtures of vegetable materials;

(3) Salts and concentrates obtained by evaporating natural mineral waters.

4. Heading No. 30.06 applies only to the following, which are to be classified in that heading and in no other heading of the Nomenclature:

(a) Sterile surgical catgut, similar sterile suture materials (including sterile absorbable surgical or denfal yams) and sterile tissue adhesives for surgical wound closure;

(b) Sterile laminaria and sterile laminaria tents;

(c) Sterile absorbable surgical or dental haemostatics; sterile surgical or dental adhesion barriers, whether or not absorbable

(d) Opacifying preparations for X-ray examinations and diagnostic reagents designed to be administered to the patient, being unmixed products put up in measured doses or products consisting of two or more ingredients which have been mixed together for such uses;

(e) Blood-grouping reagents;

(f) Dental cements and other dental fillings; bone reconstruction cements;

（七）急救药箱、药包；

（八）以激素、税目29.37的其他产品或杀精子剂为基本成分的化学避孕药物；

（九）专用于人类或作兽药用的凝胶制品，作为外科手术或体检时躯体部位的润滑剂，或者作为躯体和医疗器械之间的耦合剂；

（十）废药物，即那些因超过有效保存期等原因而不适于作原用途的药品；

（十一）可确定用于造口术的用具，即裁切成型的结肠造口术，回肠造口术、尿道造口术用袋及其具有粘性的片或底盘。

(g) First-aid boxes and kits;

(h) Chemical contraceptive preparations based on hormones, on other products of heading No. 29.37 or on spermicides;

(i) Gel preparations designed to be used in human or veterinary medicine as a lubricant for parts of the body for surgical operations or physical examinations or as a coupling agent between the body and medical instruments;

(j) Waste pharmaceuticals, that is, pharmaceutical products which are unfit for their original intended purpose due to, for example, expiry of shelf life;

(k) Appliances identifiable for ostomy use, that is, cdostomy, ileostomy and utosto my pouches cut to shape and their adhesive wafers or faceplates.

税则号列	货品名称	最惠(%)	普通	增值税率	出口退税	计量单位	监管条件	Article Description
30.01	**已干燥的器官疗法用腺体及其他器官，不论是否制成粉末；器官疗法用腺体、其他器官及其分泌物的提取物；肝素及其盐；其他供治疗或预防疾病用的其他税目未列名的人体或动物制品：**							**Glands and other organs for organo-therapeutic uses, dried, whether or not powdered; extracts of glands or other organs or of their secretions for organo-therapeutic uses; heparin and its salts; other human or animal substances prepared for therapeutic or prophylactic uses, not elsewhere specified or included:**
3001.2000	-腺体、其他器官及其分泌物的提取物	3	30	17		千克		-Extracts of glands or other organs or of their secretions
3001.2000 10	其他濒危野生动物腺体、器官（包括分泌物）	3	30	17		千克	AQFEB	Extracts of glands or other organs or of their secretions of endangered wild animals
3001.2000 20	人类的腺体、器官及其分泌物提取物	3	30	17	15	千克	AQB	Human extracts of glands of organs or of their secretions
3001.2000 90	其他腺体、器官及其分泌物提取物	3	30	17	15	千克	AQB	Other extracts of glands of other organs or of their secretions
	-其他：							-Other:
3001.9010	---肝素及其盐	3	30	17	15	千克	Q	---Heparin and its salts
3001.9090	---其他	3	30	17		千克		---Other
3001.9090 10	蛇毒制品（供治疗或预防疾病用）	3	30	17	15	千克	AQFEB	Venom substances prepared (for therapeutic or prophylactic uses)
3001.9090 91	其他濒危动物制品（供治疗或预防疾病用）	3	30	17		千克	ABFEQ	Other substances of endangered animals for therapeutic or prophylactic uses
3001.9090 99	其他未列名的人体或动物制品（供治疗或预防疾病用）	3	30	17	13,15	千克	ABQ	Other human or animal substances prepared (for therapeutic or prophylactic uses) not elsewhere specified or included
30.02	**人血；治病、防病或诊断用的动物血制品；抗血清、其他血份及免疫制品，不论是否修饰或通过生物工艺加工制得；疫苗、毒素、培养微生物（不包括酵母）及类似产品：**							**Human blood; animal blood prepared for therapeutic, prophylactic or diagnostic uses; antisera, other blood fractions and immunological products, whether or not modified or obtained by means of biotechnological processes; vaccines, toxins, cultures of micro-organisms (other than yeasts) and similar products:**
3002.1000暂	-抗血清、其他血份及免疫制品，不论是否修饰或通过生物工艺加工制得	0	20	17	15	千克		-Antisera and other blood fractions and immunological products, whether or not modified or obtained by means of biotechnological processes
3002.1000暂 11	促红素（EPO）类［包括培促红素β、培尼沙肽、达促红素、缺氧诱导因子（HIF）稳定剂类、ARA-290（一种促红素衍生肽）、唾液酸促红素、氨甲酰促红素、CNTO530（一种EPO-lg4-FC融合蛋白）、EPO-FC融合蛋白、促红素模拟肽类、缺氧诱导因子（HIF）激活剂类］	0	20	17	15	千克	ABL	Erythropoietin (EPO) class (including training of erythropoietin beta, Penny Shah, erythropoietin, hypoxia inducible factor (HIF) stabilizer, ARA-290 (a kind of erythropoietin derived peptide), sialic acid of erythropoietin, carbamylated erythropoietin, CNTO530 (a EPO-lg4-FC fusion protein), EPO-FC fusion protein, erythropoietin hormone analog peptides, hypoxia inducible factor (HIF) activators)

税则号列	货品名称	最惠(%)	普通	增值税率	出口退税	计量单位	监管条件	Article Description
3002.1000暂 12	胰岛素样生长因子1(IGF－1)及其类似物	0	20	17	15	千克	ABL	Insulin－like growth factors－1 and similar products
3002.1000暂 13	机械生长因子类	0	20	17	15	千克	ABL	Mechano growth factor
3002.1000暂 14	成纤维细胞生长因子类(FGFs)	0	20	17	15	千克	ABL	Fibroblast growth factor
3002.1000暂 15	肝细胞生长因子(HGF)	0	20	17	15	千克	ABL	Hepatocyte growth factor
3002.1000暂 16	血小板衍生生长因子(PDGF)	0	20	17	15	千克	ABL	Platelet－derived growth factor
3002.1000暂 17	血管内皮生长因子(VEGF)	0	20	17	15	千克	ABL	Vascular endothelial growth factor
3002.1000暂 90	其他抗血清、其他血份及免疫制品(不论是否通过修饰或生物工艺加工制得)	0	20	17	15	千克	AB	Other antisera, other blood fractions and modified immunological products(whether or not obtained by means of biotechnological processes or modified)
3002.2000暂	-人用疫苗	0	20	17	15	千克	QAB	-Vaccines for human medicine
3002.3000	-兽用疫苗	3	20	17	15	千克	R	-Vaccines for veterinary medicine
	-其他:							-Other:
3002.9010	---石房蛤毒素	3	20	17	15	千克	23Q	---Saxitoxin
3002.9020	---蓖麻毒素	3	20	17	15	千克	23Q	---Ricitoxin
3002.9030	---细菌及病毒	3	20	17	15	千克		---Bacteria and virus
3002.9030 10	两用物项管制细菌及病毒	3	20	17	15	千克	3AB	Bacteria and virus under sensitive items control
3002.9030 20	苏云金杆菌	3	20	17	13,15	千克	ABS	Bacillus thurinsiensis
3002.9030 30	枯草芽孢杆菌	3	20	17	15	千克	ABS	Bacillus subtilis
3002.9030 90	其他细菌及病毒	3	20	17	15	千克	AB	Other bacteria and virus
3002.9040暂	---遗传物质和基因修饰生物体	0	20	17	15	千克		---Genetics material and gene-modified or ganism
3002.9040暂 10	两用物项管制遗传物质和基因修饰生物体	0	20	17	15	千克	3AB	Genetics material and gene-modified or ganism under sensitive items control
3002.9040暂 90	其他遗传物质和基因修饰生物体	0	20	17	15	千克	AB	Other genetics material and gene－modified or ganism
3002.9090暂	---其他	0	20	17		千克		---Other
3002.9090暂 11	濒危动物血制品	0	20	17		千克	ABQFE	Blood preparations of endangered animals
3002.9090暂 19	其他人血制品、动物血制品	0	20	17	15	千克	ABQ	Other human or animal blood preparations
3002.9090暂 21	噬菌核霉	0	20	17	15	千克	ABS	Sclerotinia Rot mildew bite
3002.9090暂 22	淡紫拟青霉	0	20	17	15	千克	ABS	Paecilomyces lilacinus
3002.9090暂 23	哈茨木霉菌	0	20	17	15	千克	ABS	Trichoderma harzianum
3002.9090暂 24	寡雄腐霉	0	20	17	15	千克	ABS	Pythium oligandrum
3002.9090暂 91	两用物项管制毒素	0	20	17	15	千克	3AB	Toxin under sensitive items control
3002.9090暂 99	人血、其他毒素等[包括培养微生物(不包括酵母)及类似产品]	0	20	17	15	千克	AB	Other human blood, other toxins, [including cultures of micro-organisms (excluding yeasts) and similar products]
30.03	**两种或两种以上成分混合而成的治病或防病用药品(不包括税目30.02、30.05或30.06的货品),未配定剂量或制成零售包装:**							**Medicaments (excluding goods of heading No. 30.02, 30.05 or 30.06) consisting of two or more constituents which have been mixed together for therapeutic or prophylactic uses, not put up in measured doses or in forms or packings for retail sale:**
	-含有青霉素及具有青霉烷酸结构的青霉素衍生物或链霉素及其衍生物:							-Containing penicillins or derivatives thereof, with a penicillanic acid structure, or streptomycins or their derivatives:
	---青霉素:							---Containing penicillins:
3003.1011	----氨苄青霉素	6	30	17	15	千克	Q	----Ampicillin
3003.1012	----羟氨苄青霉素	6	30	17	15	千克	Q	----Amoxycillin

税则号列	货品名称	最惠(%)	普通	增值税率	出口退税	计量单位	监管条件	Article Description
3003.1013	----青霉素 V	6	30	17	15	千克	Q	----Penicillin V
3003.1019	----其他	6	30	17	15	千克	Q	----Other
3003.1090	---其他	6	30	17	15	千克	Q	---Other
	-含有其他抗菌素:							-Containing other antibiotics:
	---头孢菌素:							---Containing cephamycins:
3003.2011	----头孢噻肟	6	30	17	15	千克	Q	----Cefotaxime
3003.2012	----头孢他啶	6	30	17	15	千克	Q	----Ceftazidime
3003.2013	----头孢西丁	6	30	17	15	千克	Q	----Cefoxitin
3003.2014	----头孢替唑	6	30	17	15	千克	Q	----Ceftezole
3003.2015	----头孢克罗	6	30	17	15	千克	Q	----Cefaclor
3003.2016	----头孢呋辛	6	30	17	15	千克	Q	----Cefuroxime
3003.2017	----头孢三嗪(头孢曲松)	6	30	17	15	千克	Q	----Ceftriaxone
3003.2018	----头孢哌酮	6	30	17	15	千克	Q	----Cefoperazone
3003.2019	----其他	6	30	17	15	千克	Q	----Other
3003.2090	---其他	6	30	17	15	千克	Q	---Other
	-含有激素或税目 29.37 的其他产品,但不含抗菌素:							-Containing hormones or other products of heading 29.37 but not containing antibiotics:
3003.3100	--含有胰岛素	5	30	17	15	千克	Q	--Containing insulin
3003.3900	--其他	6	30	17	15	千克	Q	--Other
	-含有生物碱及其衍生物,但不含抗菌素及税目 29.37 的激素或其他产品:							-Containing alkaloids or derivatives thereof but not containing hormones or other products of heading 29.37 or antibiotics:
3003.4010	---含有奎宁或其盐	5	35	17	15	千克	Q	---Containing quinine or its salts
3003.4090	---其他	5	30	17	15	千克	Q	---Other
	-其他:							-Other:
3003.9010	---含有磺胺类	6	40	17	15	千克	Q	---Containing sulfa drugs
3003.9020	---含有青蒿素及其衍生物	5	30	17	15	千克	Q	---Containing artemisinins and their derivatives
3003.9090	---其他	5	30	17		千克		---Other
3003.9090 10	含紫杉醇的混合药品(未配定剂量或非零售包装,混合指含两种或两种以上成分)	5	30	17		千克	EFQ	Medicaments, containing paclitaxec (not put up in measured doses or in forms of packing for retail sale, containing of two or more constituents)
3003.9090 20	含其他未列名濒危动植物混合药品(未配定剂量或非零售包装,混合指含两种或两种以上成分)	5	30	17		千克	QFE	Medicaments, containing other constituents endangered of animals, not elsewhere specified or included (not put up in measured doses or in forms of packing for retail sale, consisting of two or more constituents)
3003.9090 90	含其他未列名成分混合药品(未配定剂量或非零售包装,混合指含两种或两种以上成分)	5	30	17	15	千克	Q	Medicaments, not elsewhere specified or included (not put up in measured doses or in forms or packing for retail sale, consisting of two or more constituents)
30.04	**由混合或非混合产品构成的治病或防病用药品(不包括税目 30.02、30.05 或 30.06 的货品),已配定剂量或(包括制成皮肤摄入形式的)或制成零售包装:**							**Medicaments (excluding goods of heading No. 30.02, 30.05 or 30.06) consisting of mixed or unmixed products for therapeutic or prophylactic uses, put up in measured doses (including those in the form of transdermal administration systems) or in forms or packings for retail sale:**
	-含有青霉素及具有青霉烷酸结构的青霉素衍生物或链霉素及其衍生物:							-Containing penicillins or derivatives thereof, with a penicillanic acid structure, or streptomycins or their derivatives:
	---青霉素:							---Containing penicillins:
3004.1011	----氨苄青霉素制剂	6	30	17	15	千克		----Ampicillin
3004.1011 10	兽用普鲁卡因青霉素、奈夫西林钠制剂(包括制成零售包装)	6	30	17	15	千克	R	Procaine benzylpenicillin, nafcillin sodium for veterinary purposes (including in forms or packing for retail sale)
3004.1011 90	氨苄青霉素制剂(包括制成零售包装)	6	30	17	15	千克	Q	Ampicillin (including in forms or packings for retail sale)
3004.1012	----羟氨苄青霉素制剂	6	30	17	15	千克	Q	----Amoxycillin
3004.1013	----青霉素 V 制剂	6	30	17	15	千克	Q	----Penicillin V

税则号列	货品名称	最惠(%)	普通	增值税率	出口退税	计量单位	监管条件	Article Description
3004.1019	----其他	6	30	17	15	千克	Q	----Other
3004.1090	---其他	6	30	17	15	千克	Q	---Other
	-含有其他抗菌素:							-Containing other antibiotics:
	---头孢菌素:							---Containing cephamycins:
3004.2011	----头孢噻肟制剂	6	30	17	15	千克	Q	----Cefotaxime
3004.2012	----头孢他啶制剂	6	30	17	15	千克	Q	----Ceftazidime
3004.2013	----头孢西丁制剂	6	30	17	15	千克	Q	----Cefoxitin
3004.2014	----头孢替唑制剂	6	30	17	15	千克	Q	----Ceftezole
3004.2015	----头孢克罗制剂	6	30	17	15	千克	Q	----Cefaclor
3004.2016	----头孢呋辛制剂	6	30	17	15	千克	Q	----Cefuroxime
3004.2017	----头孢三嗪(头孢曲松)制剂	6	30	17	15	千克	Q	----Ceftriaxone
3004.2018	----头孢哌酮制剂	6	30	17	15	千克	Q	----Cefoperazone
3004.2019	----其他	6	30	17	15	千克		----Other
3004.2019 11	兽用已配剂量的头孢氨苄,头孢噻呋钠制剂(包括零售包装的制成品)	6	30	17	15	千克	R	Cefalexin, ceftiofur sodium, for veterinary purposes, put up in measured doses (including in forms or packings for retail sale)
3004.2019 12	兽用已配剂量的头孢噻呋晶体,硫酸头孢喹肟制剂(包括零售包装的制成品)	6	30	17	15	千克	R	Cefliofur crystalline, cefquinome sulfate, for veterinary purposes, put up in measured doses (including in forms of packing for retail sale)
3004.2019 90	其他已配剂量头孢菌素制剂(包括零售包装的制成品)	6	30	17	15	千克	Q	Other cephalosporin preparations, put up in measured doses (including in forms of packing for retail sale)
3004.2090	---其他	6	30	17	15	千克		---Other
3004.2090 11	兽用已配剂量的土霉素,延胡索酸泰妙菌素,泰拉霉素制剂(包括制成零售包装)	6	30	17	15	千克	R	Teramycin, tiamulin fumarate, tulathromycin for veterinarypurposes, put up in measured doses (including in forms or packing for retail sale)
3004.2090 12	兽用已配剂量的氟苯尼考,多拉菌素,硫酸庆大霉素制剂(包括制成零售包装)	6	30	17	15	千克	R	Florfenicol, doramectin, gentamycin sulfate for veterinary purposes, put up in measured dose (including in forms or packing for retail sale)
3004.2090 13	兽用已配剂量的硫酸双羟链霉素制剂(包括制成零售包装)	6	30	17	15	千克	R	Streptomycin sulfate for veterinary purposes, put up in measured dose (including in forms or packing for retail sale)
3004.2090 90	已配剂量含有其他抗菌素的药品(包括制成零售包装)	6	30	17	15	千克	Q	Containing other antibiotics of drugs, put up in measured dose (including in forms or packing for retail sale)
	-含有激素或税目29.37的其他产品,但不含抗菌素:							-Containing hormones or other products of heading No. 29.37 but not containing antibiotics:
	--含有胰岛素:							--Containing insulin:
3004.3110	---含有重组人胰岛素的	5	30	17	15	千克		---Containing recombinant human insulin
3004.3110 10	已配剂量含重组人胰岛素的单方制剂(包括零售包装)	5	30	17	15	千克	L	Simple preparation with recombinant human insulin, put up in measured doses (including in forms or packing for retail sale)
3004.3110 90	已配剂量含重组人胰岛素的其他药品(不含抗菌素,包括零售包装)	5	30	17	15	千克	Q	Containing recombinant human insulin of other drugs, put up in measured doses (excluding antibiotics, including in forms or packing for retail sale)
3004.3190	---其他	5	30	17	15	千克		---Other
3004.3190 10	其他已配剂量含胰岛素的单方制剂(包括零售包装)	5	30	17	15	千克	L	Other single preparations, containing insulin, put up in measured dose (including in forms or packing for retail sale)
3004.3190 90	其他已配剂量含胰岛素的其他药品(不含抗菌素,包括零售包装)	5	30	17	15	千克	Q	Other medicaments, containing insulin, put up in measured doses (excluding antibiotics, including in forms or packing for retail sale)
3004.3200	--含有皮质甾类激素及其衍生物或结构类似物	5	30	17	15	千克		--Containing corticosteroid hormones, their derivatives and structural analogues

税则号列	货　品　名　称	最惠(%)	普通	增值税率	出口退税	计量单位	监管条件	Article Description
3004.3200 11	已配剂量含1－雄烯二醇或1－雄烯二酮的单方制剂(包括其衍生物及结构类似物,包括零售包装)	5	30	17	15	千克	L	Single preparations, containing androstenediol or androstenedione, put up in measured doses (including in forms or packing for retail sale)
3004.3200 12	已配剂量含甲酰勃龙的单方制剂(包括其衍生物及结构类似物,包括零售包装)	5	30	17	15	千克	L	Single preparations, containing formebolone, put up in measured dose (including their derivatives and structural analogues, in forms or packing for retail sale)
3004.3200 13	已配剂量含雄甾－4－烯－3β,17α－二醇[4－雄烯二醇(3β,17α)]的单方制剂(包括其衍生物及结构类似物,包括零售包装)	5	30	17	15	千克	L	Single preparations, containing androst－4－ene－3β, 17α－diol [4－androstenediol (3β,17α)], put up in measured dose (including their derivatives and structural analogues, in forms or packing for retail sale)
3004.3200 14	已配剂量含雄甾－5－烯－3β,17α－二醇[5－雄烯二醇(3β,17α)]的单方制剂(包括其衍生物及结构类似物,包括零售包装)	5	30	17	15	千克	L	Single peparations, containing androst－5－ene－3β, 17α－diol [5－androstenediol (3β,17α)], put up in measured dose (including their derivatives and structural analogues, in forms or packing for retail sale)
3004.3200 15	已配剂量含4－雄烯二醇或乙雌烯醇的单方制剂(包括其衍生物及结构类似物,包括零售包装)	5	30	17	15	千克	L	Single preparations, containing 4－androstenediol or ethylestrenol, put up in measured dose (including their derivatives and structural analogues, in froms or packing for retail sale)
3004.3200 16	已配剂量含5－雄烯二酮的单方制剂(包括其衍生物及结构类似物,包括零售包装)	5	30	17	15	千克	L	Single preparations, containing androstenedione isomer, put up in measured doses (including their derivatives and structural analogues, in forms or packing for retail sale)
3004.3200 17	已配剂量含5α－雄烷－3α,17β－二醇[雄烷二醇(3α,17β)]或5β－雄烷－3α,17β－二醇[5β－雄烷二醇(3α,17β)]的单方制剂(包括其衍生物及结构类似物,包括零售包装)	5	30	17	15	千克	L	Single preparations, containing 5α－androstane－3α,17β－estrad[dihydroandrosterone(3β,17α)] or 5β－androstane－3α,17β－glycol[5β－dihydroandrosterone(3α,17β)], put up in measured doses (including their derivatives and structural analogues, in forms or packing for retail sale)
3004.3200 18	已配剂量含5α－雄烷－3β,17α－二醇[雄烷二醇(3β,17α)]的单方制剂(包括其衍生物及结构类似物,包括零售包装)	5	30	17	15	千克	L	Single preparations, containing 5α－androstane－3α,17β－estrad[dihydroandrosterone(3β,17α)], put up in measured doses (including their derivatives and structural analogues, in forms or packing for retail sale)
3004.3200 19	已配剂量含勃拉睾酮的单方制剂(包括其衍生物及结构类似物,包括零售包装)	5	30	17	15	千克	L	Single preparations, containing bolasterone, put up in measured doses (including their derivatives and structural analogues, in forms or packing for retail sale)
3004.3200 21	已配剂量含勃地酮的单方制剂(包括其衍生物及结构类似物,包括零售包装)	5	30	17	15	千克	L	Single preparations, containing boldenone, put up in measured doses (including their derivatives and structural analogues, in forms or packing for retail sale)
3004.3200 22	已配剂量含勃二酮的单方制剂(包括其衍生物及结构类似物,包括零售包装)	5	30	17	15	千克	L	Single preparations, containing androstadien－3,17－dione, put up in measured doses (including their derivatives and structural analogues, in forms or packing for retail sale)
3004.3200 23	已配剂量含卡芦睾酮或达那唑的单方制剂(包括其衍生物及结构类似物,包括零售包装)	5	30	17	15	千克	L	Single preparations, containing calusterone or danazol, put up in measured doses (including their derivatives and structural analogues, in forms or packing for retail sale)
3004.3200 24	已配剂量含氯司替勃的单方制剂(包括其衍生物及结构类似物,包括零售包装)	5	30	17	15	千克	L	Single preparations, containing clostebol, put up in measured doses (including their derivatives and structural analogues, in forms or packing for retail sale)
3004.3200 25	已配剂量含脱氢氯甲睾酮的单方制剂(包括其衍生物及结构类似物,包括零售包装)	5	30	17	15	千克	L	Single preparations, containing dehydrochloro－methyltestosterone, put up in measured doses (including their derivatives and structural analogues, in forms or packing for retail sale)

税则号列	货品名称	最惠(%)	普通	增值税率	出口退税	计量单位	监管条件	Article Description
3004.3200 28	已配剂量含普拉睾酮或屈他雄酮的单方制剂(包括其衍生物及结构类似物,包括零售包装)	5	30	17	15	千克	L	Single preparations, containing prasterone or dormostanolone, put up in measured doses (including their derivatives and structural analogues, in forms or packing for retail sale)
3004.3200 29	已配剂量含去氧甲睾酮或双氢睾酮的单方制剂(包括其衍生物及结构类似物,包括零售包装)	5	30	17	15	千克	L	Single preparations, containing deoxymethyltestosterone or dihydrotestosterone, put up in measured doses (including their derivatives and structural analogues, in forms or packing for retail sale)
3004.3200 31	已配剂量含表双氢睾酮或氟甲睾酮的单方制剂(包括其衍生物及结构类似物,包括零售包装)	5	30	17	15	千克	L	Single preparations, containing epi – dihydrotestosterone or fluoxymesterone, put up in measured doses (including their derivatives and structural analogues, in forms or packing for retail sale)
3004.3200 32	已配剂量含夫拉扎勃的单方制剂(包括其衍生物及结构类似物,包括零售包装)	5	30	17	15	千克	L	Single preparations, containing furazabol, put up in measured doses (including their derivatives and structural analogues, in forms or packing for retail sale)
3004.3200 33	已配剂量含孕三烯酮或4－羟基睾酮的单方制剂(包括其衍生物及结构类似物,包括零售包装)	5	30	17	15	千克	L	Single preparations, containing gestrinone or 4 – hydroxyltestosterone, put up in measured doses (including their derivatives and structural analogues, in forms or packing for retail sale)
3004.3200 34	含3α-羟基-5α-雄烷-17-酮的单方制剂(包括其衍生物及结构类似物,已配剂量或制成零售包装)	5	30	17	15	千克	L	Single preparations, containing 3α – hydroxide – 5α – androstane – 17 – ketone, put up in measured doses (including their derivatives and structural analogues, in forms or packing for retail sale)
3004.3200 35	已配剂量含美睾酮或美雄酮的单方制剂(包括其衍生物及结构类似物,包括零售包装)	5	30	17	15	千克	L	Single preparations, containing mesterolone or methandienone, put up in measured doses (including their derivatives and structural analogues, in forms or packing for retail sale)
3004.3200 36	已配剂量含甲基屈他雄酮的单方制剂(包括其衍生物及结构类似物,包括零售包装)	5	30	17	15	千克	L	Single preparations, containing 2α, 17α – dimethyl – 5α – androstane – 3 – ketone – 17β – alcohol, put up in measured doses (including their derivatives and structural analogues, in forms or packing for retail sale)
3004.3200 37	已配剂量含甲二烯诺龙的单方制剂(包括其衍生物及结构类似物,包括零售包装)	5	30	17	15	千克	L	Single preparations, containing 17α – methyl – 17β – hydroxy – estr – 4, 9(10) – di – 3 – ketone, put up in measured doses (including their derivatives and structural analogues, in forms or packing for retail sale)
3004.3200 38	已配剂量含甲基－1－睾酮或甲睾酮的单方制剂(包括其衍生物及结构类似物,包括零售包装)	5	30	17	15	千克	L	Single preparations, containing Methyl – 1 – testosterone or methylnortestosterone, put up in measured doses (including their derivatives and structural analogues, in forms or packing for retail sale)
3004.3200 39	已配剂量含美曲勃龙的单方制剂(包括其衍生物及结构类似物,包括零售包装)	5	30	17	15	千克	L	Single preparations, containing 17α – methyl – 17β – hydroxy – estr – 4, 9, 11triene – 3 – ketone, put up in measured doses (including their derivatives and structural analogues, in forms or packing for retail sale)
3004.3200 41	已配剂量含美雄诺龙或美替诺龙的单方制剂(包括其衍生物及结构类似物,包括零售包装)	5	30	17	15	千克	L	Single preparations, containing mestanolone or methenolone, put up in measured doses (including their derivatives and structural analogues, in forms or packing for retail sale)
3004.3200 42	已配剂量含美雄醇或甲睾酮或米勃酮的单方制剂(包括其衍生物及结构类似物,包括零售包装)	5	30	17	15	千克	L	Single preparations, containing methandriol or methyltestosterone or mibolerone, put up in measured doses (including their derivatives and structural analogues, in forms or packing for retail sale)

税则号列	货 品 名 称	最惠(%)	普通	增值税率	出口退税	计量单位	监管条件	Article Description
3004.3200 43	已配剂量含诺龙或诺勃酮或诺司替勃的单方制剂(包括其衍生物及结构类似物,包括零售包装)	5	30	17	15	千克	L	Single preparations, containing nandrolone or norboletone or norclostebol, put up in measured doses (including their derivatives and structural analogues, in forms or packing for retail sale)
3004.3200 44	已配剂量含19-去甲雄烯二酮的单方制剂(包括其衍生物及结构类似物,包括零售包装)	5	30	17	15	千克	L	Single preparations, containing 19 - norandrostenedion or 19 - norandrostenedione, put up in measured doses (including their derivatives and structural analogues, in forms or packing for retail sale)
3004.3200 45	已配剂量含去甲雄酮或诺乙雄龙的单方制剂(包括其衍生物及结构类似物,包括零售包装)	5	30	17	15	千克	L	Single preparations, containing norandrosterone or norethandrolone, put up in measured doses (including their derivatives and structural analogues, in forms or packing for retailsale)
3004.3200 46	已配剂量含19-去甲胆烷醇酮的单方制剂(包括其衍生物及结构类似物,包括零售包装)	5	30	17	15	千克	L	Single preparations, containing 19 - noretiocholanolone, put up in measured doses (including their derivatives and structural analogues, in forms or packing for retail sale)
3004.3200 47	已配剂量含羟勃龙或氧雄龙的单方制剂(包括其衍生物及结构类似物,已配剂量或制成零售包装)	5	30	17	15	千克	L	Single preparations, containing oxabolone or oxandrolone, put up in measured doses (including their derivatives and structural analogues, in forms or packing for retail sale)
3004.3200 48	已配剂量含羟甲睾酮或羟甲烯龙的单方制剂(包括其衍生物及结构类似物,包括零售包装)	5	30	17	15	千克	L	Single preparations, containing Oxymesterone or oxymetholone, put up in measured doses (including their derivatives and structural analogues, in forms or packing for retailsale)
3004.3200 49	已配剂量含前列他唑的单方制剂(包括其衍生物及结构类似物,包括零售包装)	5	30	17	15	千克	L	Single preparations, containing 17β-hydroxy-5α-androstane[3,2-c] pyrazole, put up in measured doses (including their derivatives and structural analogues, in forms or packing for retail sale)
3004.3200 51	含奎勃龙或替勃龙或群勃龙的单方制剂(包括其衍生物及结构类似物,已配剂量或制成零售包装)	5	30	17	15	千克	L	Single preparations, containing quinbolone or tibolone or trenbolone, put up in measured doses (including their derivatives andstructural analogues, in forms or packing for retail sale)
3004.3200 52	已配剂量含司坦唑醇或司腾勃龙的单方制剂(包括其衍生物及结构类似物,包括零售包装)	5	30	17	15	千克	L	Single preparations, containing stanozolol or stenbolone, put up in measured doses (including their derivatives and structural analogues, in forms or packing for retail sale)
3004.3200 53	已配剂量含1-睾酮或睾酮的单方制剂(包括其衍生物及结构类似物,包括零售包装)	5	30	17	15	千克	L	Single preparations, containing 1 - testosterone or testosterone, put up in measured doses (including their derivatives and structural analogues, in forms or packing for retail sale)
3004.3200 54	已配剂量含四氢孕三烯酮或泽仑诺的单方制剂(包括其衍生物及结构类似物,包括零售包装)	5	30	17	15	千克	L	Single preparations, containing tetrahydrogestrinone or zeranol, put up in measured doses (including their derivatives and structural analogues, in forms or packing for retail sale)
3004.3200 60	兽用已配剂量倍他米松戊酸酯制剂(包括其衍生物及结构类似物,包括零售包装)	5	30	17	15	千克	R	Betamethasone valerate for veterinary, put up in measured doses (including their derivatives and Structural analogues, in forms or packing for retail sale)
3004.3200 71	已配剂量含雄甾-5-烯-3β,17β-二醇[5-雄烯二醇(3β,17β)]的单方制剂(包括其衍生物及结构类似物,不含抗菌素,包括零售包装)	5	30	17	15	千克	L	Single preparartions, 5 - Androstenediol (3β, 17β) [5 - androstene - glycol (3β, 17β)], put up in measured doses (including their derivatives and structural analogues, in forms or packing for retailsale)
3004.3200 72	已配剂量含雄甾-4-烯-3,17-二酮(4-雄烯二酮)的单方制剂(包括其衍生物及结构类似物,不含抗菌素,包括零售包装)	5	30	17	15	千克	L	Single preparartions, androstenedione (4 - androstene - glycol), put up in measured doses (including their derivatives and strutural analogues, in forms or packing for retailsale)

税则号列	货品名称	最惠(%)	普通	增值税率	出口退税	计量单位	监管条件	Article Description
3004.3200 73	已配剂量含勃雄二醇的单方制剂(包括其衍生物及结构类似物,不含抗菌素,包括零售包装)	5	30	17	15	千克	L	Single preparartions, bolandiol (put up in measured doses and in forms or packing for retail sale)
3004.3200 74	已配剂量含7α-羟基-普拉睾酮的单方制剂(包括其衍生物及结构类似物,不含抗菌素,包括零售包装)	5	30	17	15	千克	L	]Single preparartions, 7α - hydroxy - DHEA, put up in measured doses (including their derivatives and strutural analogues, in forms or packing for retail-sale)
3004.3200 75	已配剂量含7β-羟基-普拉睾酮的单方制剂(包括其衍生物及结构类似物,不含抗菌素,包括零售包装)	5	30	17	15	千克	L	Single preparartions, 7β - hydroxy - DHEA, put up in measured doses (including their derivatives and strutural analogues, in forms or packing for retail-sale)
3004.3200 76	已配剂量含7-羰基-普拉睾酮的单方制剂(包括其衍生物及结构类似物,不含抗菌素,包括零售包装)	5	30	17	15	千克	L	Single preparartions, 7 - carbonyl Prasterone (put up in measured doses and in forms or packing for retail sale)
3004.3200 77	已配剂量含胆烷醇酮的单方制剂(包括其衍生物及结构类似物,不含抗菌素,包括零售包装)	5	30	17	15	千克	L	Single preparartions, Androstane, put up in measured doses (including their derivatives and strutural analogues, in forms or packing for retailsale)
3004.3200 90	已配剂量含其他皮质甾类激素的药品(包括其衍生物及结构类似物,不含抗菌素,包括零售包装)	5	30	17	15	千克	Q	Drugs containing corticosteroed hormone, put up in-measured doses (excluding antibiotics, including their derivatives and structural analogues, in forms or packing for retail sale)
3004.3900	--其他	5	30	17	15	千克		--Other
3004.3900 11	已配剂量含克仑特罗的单方制剂(包括零售包装)	5	30	17	15	千克	L	Single preparations, containting clenbuterol, put up in measured doses (including packing for retail sale)
3004.3900 22	已配剂量含生长激素(GH)的单方制剂(包括零售包装)	5	30	17	15	千克	L	Single preparartions, Growth hormone put up in measured doses (including packing for retail sale)
3004.3900 25	已配剂量含绒促性素及促黄体生成素的单方制剂[包括含生长激素释放肽类(GHRPs)、普拉莫瑞林(生长激素释放肽-2)、CJC-1295(CAS号863288-34-0)、生长激素释放肽-6、生长激素释放激素及其类似物、生长激素促分泌剂,包括零售包装]	5	30	17	15	千克	L	Single preparartions, HCG and luteinizing hormone put up in measured doses [including Growth hormone releasing peptide (GHRPs), Plummer Relin (growth hormone releasing peptide -2), CJC - 1295 (CAS No. 863288 - 34 - 0), growth hormone releasing peptide -6, growth hormone releasing hormone and its analogues, growth Ji Sucu secretion agent, packing for retail sale]
3004.3900 26	已配剂量含促皮质素类等肽类激素的单方制剂[包括零售包装,以及已配剂量或零售包装的艾瑞莫瑞林、阿那瑞林、布舍瑞林、可的瑞林、海沙瑞林、伊莫瑞林、舍莫瑞林、替莫瑞林、戈那瑞林、曲普瑞林、葛瑞林(脑肠肽)及其模拟物类的单方制剂]	5	30	17	15	千克	L	Single preparations, peptide hormones[including retail packaging, and have dosage or retail packaging Ai Rui Mo Ruilin, A Bernard Relin, Bushrui Lin, Sha Ruilin, sea corticorelin, Iraq Mo Ruilin, Mo Ruilin, Mo Ruilin, Gore Bernard Relin, on behalf of triptorelin, Ge Ruilin (brain gut peptide) and its preparations) analogue.]
3004.3900 30	兽用血促性素、绒促性素制剂(包括零售包装)	5	30	17	15	千克	R	Sera gonadotrophin, chorionic gonadotrophin for veterinary purposes (including in forms or packing for retail sale)
3004.3900 90	其他已配剂量含激素或税号2937产品的药品(不含抗菌素,包括零售包装)	5	30	17	15	千克	Q	Other drugs containing hormones or products of heading No. 29.37, put up in measured doses (excluding antibiotics, including in forms or packing for retail sale)
	-含有生物碱及其衍生物,但不含抗菌素及税目29.37的激素或其他产品:							-Containing alkaloids or derivatives thereof but not containing hormones, other products of heading No. 29.37 or antibiotics:
3004.4010	---含有奎宁或其盐	5	35	17	15	千克	Q	---Containing quinine or its salts
3004.4090	---其他	5	30	17	15	千克		---Other
3004.4090 10	麻黄碱盐类单方制剂[指盐酸(伪)麻黄碱片、盐酸麻黄碱注射剂、硫酸麻黄碱片]	5	30	17	15	千克	23Q	Single preparations, containing salts of ephedrine (ephedrine hydrochloride tablets, ephedrine hydrochloride injection, ephedrine sulphuric tablets)

税则号列	货品名称	最惠(%)	普通	增值税率	出口退税	计量单位	监管条件	Article Description
3004.4090 20	含可待因及衍生物及盐的复方制剂(已配定剂量或制成零售包装)	5	30	17	15	千克	I	Compound preparations, containing condeine, its derivatives and salts(put up in measured doses and in forms or packing for retail sale)
3004.4090 31	丁丙诺啡透皮贴剂(包括其衍生物,已配定剂量或制成零售包装)	5	30	17	15	千克	I	Buprenorphine Transdermal Patch(put up in measured doses and in forms or packing for retail sale)
3004.4090 39	其他含生物碱类精神药品的单方制剂(包括其衍生物,已配定剂量或制成零售包装)	5	30	17	15	千克	I	Other Single preparations, containing alkaloids spirit drug and its derivatives (put up in measured doses and in forms or packing for retail sale)
3004.4090 40	含生物碱类麻醉药品的单方制剂(包括其衍生物,已配定剂量或制成零售包装)	5	30	17	15	千克	W	Single preparations, containing Alkaloids narcotic drug and its derivatives (put up in measured doses and in forms or packing for retail sale)
3004.4090 50	吗啡阿托品注射液	5	30	17	15	千克	W	Morphine and atropinesulfate injection
3004.4090 61	含有氨酚氢可酮片或其盐	5	30	17	15	千克	I	Containing paracetamol and hydrocodone bitartrate tablets or its salt
3004.4090 62	含有麦角胺咖啡因片/安钠咖或其盐	5	30	17	15	千克	I	Containing ergotamine and caffeine tablets or caffeine and sodium benzoate or its salt
3004.4090 63	阿桔片、复方甘草片(含阿片粉,已配定剂量或制成零售包装)	5	30	17	15	千克	I	Compound platycodon tablets, compound liquorice tablets(including powdered opium, put up in measured doses, in forms or packing for retail sale)
3004.4090 70	氨酚双氢可待因片	5	30	17	15	千克	I	Paracetamol and Dihydrocodeine Tartrate Tablets
3004.4090 90	已配剂量含有其他生物碱等的药品(不含抗菌素及编号2937的激素或其他产品,包括零售包装)	5	30	17	15	千克	Q	Drug containing other alkaloids, put up in measured doses (excluding antibiotics and hormones or other products of heading No 29.37, including in forms or packing for retail sale)
3004.5000	-含有维生素或税目29.36所列产品的其他药品	6	40	17	15	千克	Q	-Other medicaments containing vitamins or other products of heading No. 29.36
	-其他:							-Other:
3004.9010	---含有磺胺类	6	40	17	15	千克	Q	---Containing sulfa drugs
3004.9020	---含有联苯双酯	4	30	17	15	千克	Q	---Containing biphenyl dicarbxybte
	---中式成药:							---Medicaments of Chinese type:
3004.9051	----中药酒	3	30	17		千克		----Medicated liquors or wines
3004.9051 10	含濒危动植物成分的中药酒(已配定剂量或零售包装)	3	30	17		千克	FE	Medicated liquors or wines, containing composition of endangered animals or plants, (put up in measured doses or in forms or packings for retail sale)
3004.9051 90	含其他成分的中药酒(已配定剂量或零售包装)	3	30	17	15	千克		Medicated liquors or wines, containing other composition (put up in measured doses or in forms or packings for retail sale)
3004.9052	----片仔癀	3	30	17	15	千克	QFE	----Pien Tzu Huang
3004.9053	----白药	3	30	17	15	千克		----Bai Yao
3004.9053 10	含天然麝香的白药(已配定剂量或零售包装)	3	30	17	15	千克	FEQ	Bai Yao, containing natural musk (put up in measured doses or in form or packing for retail sale)
3004.9053 90	含人工麝香的白药(已配定剂量或零售包装)	3	30	17	15	千克	Q	Bai Yao, containing artificial musk(put up in measured doses or in form or packing for retail sale)
3004.9054	----清凉油	3	30	17	15	千克	Q	----Essential balm
3004.9055	----安宫牛黄丸	3	30	17		千克		----Angong niuhuang pills
3004.9055 10	含天然麝香的安宫牛黄丸(已配定剂量或零售包装)	3	30	17		千克	QFE	Angongniuhuang pills, containing natural musk (put up in measured doses or in form or packings for retail sale)
3004.9055 90	其他安宫牛黄丸(已配定剂量或零售包装)	3	30	17	15	千克	Q	Other angongniuhuang pills, (put up in measured doses or in form or packings for retail sale)
3004.9059	----其他	3	30	17		千克		----Other

税则号列	货　品　名　称	最惠(%)	普通	增值税率	出口退税	计量单位	监管条件	Article Description
3004.9059 10	含濒危动植物成分的中式成药(已配定剂量或零售包装)	3	30	17		千克	QFE	Medicaments of Chinese style, containing composition of endangered animals or plants (put up in measured doses or in forms or packings for retail sale)
3004.9059 90	含其他成分的中式成药(已配定剂量或零售包装)	3	30	17	15	千克	Q	Medicaments of Chinese style, containing other composition (put up in measured doses or in forms or packings for retail sale)
3004.9060	---含有青蒿素及其衍生物	4	30	17	17	千克	Q	---Containing artemisinins and their derivatives
3004.9090	---其他	4	30	17		千克		---Other
3004.9090 10	含濒危野生动植物成分的药品(已配定剂量或零售包装,不含紫杉醇)	4	30	17		千克	FEQ	Medicaments containing composition of endangered animals or plants (not containing taxinol, put up in measured doses or in forms or packings for retail sale)
3004.9090 20	含紫杉醇成分的药品(已配定剂量或制成零售包装)	4	30	17		千克	EFQ	Medicaments containing taxinol (put up in measured doses or in forms or packings for retail sale)
3004.9090 30	其他含第29章麻醉药品的单方制剂(已配定剂量或制成零售包装)	4	30	17	15	千克	W	Other single preparations containing narcotic drngs of Chapter 29 (put up in measured doses or in forms or packings for retail sale)
3004.9090 41	地芬诺酯复方制剂(已配定剂量或制成零售包装)	4	30	17	15	千克	I	Compound preparations, containing diphenoxylate (put up in measured doses and in forms or packing for retail sale)
3004.9090 49	其他含第29章精神药品的单方制剂(已配定剂量或制成零售包装)	4	30	17	15	千克	I	Other single preparations , containing psychotropic substances of Chapter 29 (put up in measured doses and in forms or packing for retail sale)
3004.9090 50	含右丙氧芬及其盐的复方制剂(已配定剂量或制成零售包装)	4	30	17	15	千克	I	Compound preparations, containing propoxyphene and its salts (put up in measured doses or in forms or packings for retail sale)
3004.9090 60	复方樟脑酊(含阿片酊、樟脑、苯甲酸、八角茴香油等,包括零售包装)	4	30	17	15	千克	W	Compound camphor tincture (containing opium tincture, camphor benzoic acid, star - anise oil, including in forms or packing for retail sale)
3004.9090 71	已配剂量含雄甾-4-烯-3α,17β-二醇[4-雄烯二醇(3α,17β)]的单方制剂(包括零售包装)	4	30	17	15	千克	L	Single preparartions, androst - 4 - allyl - 3α, 17β - estradi[4 - androstene - glycol (3α, 17β)], put up in measured doses (including in forms or packing for retail sale)
3004.9090 72	已配剂量含雄甾-5-烯-3α,17α-二醇[5-雄烯二醇(3α,17α)]的单方制剂(包括零售包装)	4	30	17	15	千克	L	Single preparartions, androst - 5 - allyl - 3α, 17α - estradi[5 - androstene - glycol (3α, 17α)], put up in measured doses (including in forms or packing for retail sale)
3004.9090 73	已配剂量含雄甾-5-烯-3α,17β-二醇[5-雄烯二醇(3α,17β)]的单方制剂(包括零售包装)	4	30	17	15	千克	L	Single preparartions, androst - 5 - allyl - 3α, 17β - estradi[5 - androstene - glycol (3α, 17β)], put up in measured doses (including in forms or packing for retail sale)
3004.9090 74	已配剂量含5α-雄烷-3α,17α-二醇(阿法雄烷二醇)或雄甾-4-烯-3α,17α-二醇[4-雄烯二醇(3α,17α)]的单方制剂(包括零售包装)	4	30	17	15	千克	L	Single preparations, containting 5α - androstane - 3α, 17α - diol or androst - 4 - allyl - 3α, 17α - estradi[4 - androstene - glycol (3α, 17α)], put up in measured doses (including in forms or packing for retail sale)
3004.9090 75	已配剂量含5α-雄烷-3β,17β-二醇(倍他雄烷二醇)的单方制剂(包括零售包装)	4	30	17	15	千克	L	Single preparations, containting 5α - androstan - 3β, 17β - estradi, put up in measured doses (including in forms or packing for retail sale)
3004.9090 77	含雄酮(3β-羟基-5α-雄烷-17-酮)的单方制剂(已配剂量或制成零售包装)	4	30	17	15	千克	L	Single preparations, containting androsterone (3β - hydroxy - 5α - androstane - 17 - ketone), put up in measured doses (including in forms or packing for retail sale)
3004.9090 78	已配剂量含齐帕特罗的单方制剂(包括零售包装)	4	30	17	15	千克	L	Single preparations, containting zilpaterol, put up in measured doses (including in forms or packing for retail sale)

税则号列	货品名称	最惠(%)	普通	增值税率	出口退税	计量单位	监管条件	Article Description
3004.9090 79	已配剂量含表睾酮的单方制剂(包括零售包装)	4	30	17	15	千克	L	Single preparations, containting epitestosterone, put up in measured doses(including in forms or packing for retail sale)
3004.9090 81	兽用已配剂量含右旋糖苷铁、替泊沙林、布他磷制剂(包括零售包装)	4	30	17	15	千克	R	Preparations containting iron dextran, tepoxalin, butafosfan for veterinary purposes, put up in measured doses(including in forms or packing for retail sale)
3004.9090 82	兽用已配剂量含硝碘酚腈、氟尼辛葡甲胺、美洛昔康制剂(包括零售包装)	4	30	17	15	千克	R	Preparations containting nitroxinil, flunixin meglumine, meloxicam for veterinary purposes, put up in measured doses(including in forms or packingfor retail sale)
3004.9090 91	含FG-4592(CAS号808118-40-3,一种缺氧诱导因子-脯氨酸羟化酶抑制剂)的已配定剂量的制剂(包括零售包装)	4	30	17	15	千克	Q	With FG-4592 (CAS 808118-40-3, a kind of hypoxia inducible factor - prolinehydroxylase inhibitors) have been preparations dosage (including retail wrapping)
3004.9090 99	其他已配定剂量的药品(包括零售包装)	4	30	17	15	千克	Q	Other equipped with fixed dose drug (including retail wrapping)
30.05	**软填料、纱布、绷带及类似物品(例如,敷料、橡皮膏、泥罨剂),经过药物浸涂或制成零售包装供医疗、外科、牙科或兽医用:**							**Wadding, gauze, bandages and similar articles (for example, dressings, adhesive plasters, poultices), impregnated or coated with pharmaceutical substances or put up in forms or packings for retail sale for medical, surgical, dental or veterinary purposes:**
	-胶粘敷料及有胶粘涂层的其他物品:							-Adhesive dressings and other articles having an adhesive layer:
3005.1010	---橡皮膏	5	70	17	15	千克		---Adhesive plasters
3005.1090	---其他	5	35	17	15	千克		---Other
	-其他:							-Other:
3005.9010	---药棉、纱布、绷带	5	70	17	15	千克		---Absorbent cotton, gauze, bandages
3005.9090	---其他	5	35	17	15	千克		---Other
30.06	本章注释四所规定的医药用品:							**Pharmaceutical goods specified in Note 4 to this Chapter:**
3006.1000	-无菌外科肠线、类似的无菌缝合材料(包括外科或牙科用无菌可吸收缝线)及外伤创口闭合用的无菌粘合胶布;无菌昆布及无菌昆布塞条;外科或牙科用无菌吸收性止血材料;外科或牙科用无菌抗粘连阻隔材料,不论是否可吸收	5	30	17	15	千克		-Sterile surgical catgut, similar sterile suture materials(including sterile absorbable surgical or donfal yams) and sterile tissue adhesives for surgical wound closure; sterile laminaria and sterile laminaria tents; sterile absorbable surgical or dental haemostatics; sterile surgical or dontal adhesion borriers, whether or not absorbable
3006.2000	-血型试剂	3	20	17	15	千克	AB	-Blood-grouping reagents
3006.3000	-X光检查造影剂;用于病人的诊断试剂	4	30	17	15	千克	ABQ	-Opacifying preparations for X-ray examinations; diagnostic reagents designed to be administered to the patient
3006.4000	-牙科粘固剂及其他牙科填料;骨骼粘固剂	5	30	17	15	千克		-Dental cements and other dental fillings; bone reconstruction cements
3006.5000	-急救药箱、药包	5	30	17	15	千克		-First-aid boxes and kits
	-以激素,税目29.37的其他产品或杀精子剂为基本成分的化学避孕药物:							-Chemical contraceptive preparations based on hormones on other products of heading No. 29.37 or on spermicides:
3006.6010	---以激素为基本成分的避孕药	0	0			千克	Q	---Contraceptive preparations based on hormones
3006.6090	---其他	0	0			千克	Q	---Other
3006.7000	-专用于人类或作兽药用的凝胶制品,作为外科手术或体检时躯体部位的润滑剂,或者作为躯体和医疗器械之间的耦合剂	6.5	30	17	15	千克		-Gel preparations designed to be used in human or veterinary medicine as a lubricant for parts of the body for surgical operations or physical examinations or as a coupling agent between the body and medical instruments
	-其他:							-Other:
3006.9100	--可确定用于造口术的用具	10	80	17	15	千克		--Appliamces identifiable for ostomy use
3006.9200	--废药物	5	30	17	15	千克	9	--Waste pharmaceuticals

第三十一章
肥　　料

注释：

一、本章不包括：

(一)税目05.11的动物血；

(二)单独的已有化学定义的化合物(符合下列注释二(一)、三(一)、四(一)或五所规定的化合物除外)；

(三)税目38.24的每颗重量不低于2.5克的氯化钾培养晶体(光学元件除外)；氯化钾光学元件(税目90.01)。

二、税目31.02只适用于下列货品，但未制成税目31.05所述形状或包装：

(一)符合下列任何一条规定的货品：

1. 硝酸钠，不论是否纯净；
2. 硝酸铵，不论是否纯净；
3. 硫酸铵及硝酸铵的复盐，不论是否纯净；
4. 硫酸铵，不论是否纯净；
5. 硝酸钙及硝酸铵的复盐(不论是否纯净)或硝酸钙及硝酸铵的混合物；
6. 硝酸钙及硝酸镁的复盐(不论是否纯净)或硝酸钙及硝酸镁的混合物；
7. 氰氨化钙，不论是否纯净或用油处理；
8. 尿素，不论是否纯净。

(二)由上述(一)款任何货品相互混合的肥料。

(三)由氯化铵或上述(一)或(二)款任何货品与白垩、石膏或其他无肥效无机物混合而成的肥料。

(四)由上述(一)2或8项的货品或其混合物溶于水或液氨的液体肥料。

三、税目31.03只适用于下列货品，但未制成税目31.05所述形状或包装：

(一)符合下列任何一条规定的货品：

1. 碱性熔渣；
2. 税目25.10的天然磷酸盐，已焙烧或经过超出清除杂质范围的热处理；
3. 过磷酸钙(一过磷酸钙、二过磷酸钙或三过磷酸钙)；
4. 磷酸氢钙，按干燥无水产品重量计含氟量不低于0.2%。

(二)由上述(一)款的任何货品互相混合的肥料，不论含氟量多少。

(三)由上述(一)或(二)款的任何货品与白垩、石膏或其他无肥效无机物混合而成的肥料，不论含氟量多少。

四、税目31.04只适用于下列货品，但未制成税目31.05所述形状或包装：

(一)符合下列任何一条规定的货品：

1. 天然粗钾盐(例如，光卤石、钾盐镁矾及钾盐)；
2. 氯化钾，不论是否纯净，但上述注释一(三)所述的产品除外；

Chapter 31
Fertilizers

Notes:

1. This Chapter does not cover:

(a) Animal blood of heading No. 05.11;

(b) Separate chemically defined compounds (other than those answering to the descriptions in Note 2(a), 3(a), 4(a) or 5 below); or

(c) Cultured potassium chloride crystals (other than optical elements) weighing not less than 2.5g each, of heading No. 38.24; optical elements of potassium chloride (heading No. 90.01).

2. Heading No. 31.02 applies only to the following goods, provided that they are not put up in the forms or packages described in heading No. 31.05:

(a) Goods which answer to one or other of the descriptions given below:

(1) Sodium nitrate, whether or not pure;

(2) Ammonium nitrate, whether or not pure;

(3) Double salts, whether or not pure, of ammonium sulphate and ammonium nitrate;

(4) Ammonium sulphate, whether or not pure;

(5) Double salts (whether or not pure) or mixtures of calcium nitrate and ammonium nitrate;

(6) Double salts (whether or not pure) or mixtures of calcium nitrate and magnesium nitrate;

(7) Calcium cyanamide, whether or not pure or treated with oil;

(8) Urea, whether or not pure.

(b) Fertilizers consisting of any of the goods described in (a) above mixed together.

(c) Fertilizers consisting of ammonium chloride or of any of the goods described in (a) or (b) above mixed with chalk, gypsum or other inorganic nonfertilizing substances.

(d) Liquid fertilizers consisting of the goods of subparagraph (a) (ii) or (viii) above, or of mixtures of those goods, in an aqueous or ammoniacal solution.

3. Heading No. 31.03 applies only to the following goods, provided that they are not put up in the forms or packages described in heading No. 31.05:

(a) Goods which answer to one or other of the descriptions given below:

(i) Basic slag;

(ii) Natural phosphates of heading No. 25.10, calcined or further heat-treated than for the removal of impurities;

(iii) Superphosphates (single, double or triple);

(iv) Calcium hydrogenorthophosphate containing not less than 0.2% by weight of flourine calculated on the dry anhydrous product.

(b) Fertilizers consisting of any of the goods described in (a) above mixed together, but with no account being taken of the fluorine content limit.

(c) Fertilizers consisting of any of the goods described in (a) or (b) above, but with no account being taken of the fluorine content limit, mixed with chalk, gypsum or other inorganic non-fertilizing substances.

4. Heading No. 31.04 applies only to the following goods, provided that they are not put up in the forms or packages described in heading No. 31.05:

(a) Goods which answer to one or other of the descriptions given below:

(i) Crude natural potassium salts (for example, carnallite, kainite and sylvite);

(ii) Potassium chloride, whether or not pure, except as provided in Note 1(c) above;

3. 硫酸钾,不论是否纯净;

4. 硫酸镁钾,不论是否纯净。

(二)由上述(一)款任何货品相互混合的肥料。

(iii) Potassium sulphate, whether or not pure;

(iv) Magnesium potassium sulphate, whether or not pure.

(b) Fertilizers consisting of any of the goods described in (a) above mixed together.

五、磷酸二氢铵及磷酸氢二铵(不论是否纯净)及其相互之间的混合物应归入税目31.05。

5. Ammonium dihydrogenorthophosphate (monoammonium phosphate) and diammonium hydrogenorthophosphate (diammonium phosphate), whether or not pure, and intermixtures thereof, are to be classified in heading No. 31.05.

六、税目31.05所称"其他肥料",仅适用于其基本成分至少含有氮、磷、钾中一种肥效元素的肥料用产品。

6. For the purposes of heading No. 31.05, the term "other fertilizers" applies only to products of a kind used as fertilizers and containing, as an essential constituent, at least one of the fertilizing elements nitrogen, phosphorus or potassium.

税则号列	货品名称	最惠(%)	普通	增值税率	出口退税	计量单位	监管条件	Article Description
31.01	**动物或植物肥料,不论是否相互混合或经化学处理;动植物产品经混合或化学处理制成的肥料:**							**Animal or vegetable fertilizers, whether or not mixed together or chemically treated; fertilizers produced by the mixing or chemical treatment of animal or vegetable products:**
	---未经化学处理:							---Not chemically treated:
3101.0011	----鸟粪	3	11	13		千克	AB	----Guano
3101.0019	----其他	6.5	30	13		千克		----Other
3101.0019 10	未经化学处理的森林凋落物(包括腐叶、腐根、树皮、树叶、树根等森林腐殖质)	6.5	30	13		千克	8AB	Forest litter, not chemically treated (including rotten leaves, rotten roots, bark, leaves, roots and other forest humus)
3101.0019 90	未经化学处理的其他动植物肥料	6.5	30	13		千克	AB	Other animal and vegetable fertilizer not chemically treated
3101.0090	---其他	4	11	13		千克		---Other
3101.0090 10	经化学处理含动物源性成分(如粪、羽毛等)动植物肥料	4	11	13		千克	AB	Animals or vegetable fertilizer, chemically treated, containing, compositions of animals' natural character
3101.0090 20	经化学处理的森林凋落物(包括腐叶、腐根、树皮、树叶、树根等森林腐殖质)	4	11	13		千克	8AB	Forest litter, chemically treated (including rotten leaves, rotten roots, bark, leaves, roots and other forest humus)
3101.0090 90	经化学处理的其他动植物肥料	4	11	13		千克	AB	Other vegetable fertilizere, chemical treated
31.02	矿物氮肥及化学氮肥:							**Mineral or chemical fertilizers, nitrogenous:**
3102.1000	-尿素,不论是否水溶液			13		千克		-Urea, whether or not in aqueous solution
3102.1000 10	尿素(配额内,不论是否水溶液)	4	150	13		千克	tA	Urea (whether or not in aqueous solution, in-quota)
3102.1000 90	尿素(配额外,不论是否水溶液)	50	150	13		千克	A	Urea (whether or not in aqueous solution, out-quota)
	-硫酸铵,硫酸铵和硝酸铵的复盐及混合物:							-Ammonium sulphate; double salts and mixtures of ammonium sulphate and ammonium nitrate:
3102.2100	--硫酸铵	4	11	13		千克	7AB	--Ammonium sulphate
3102.2900	--其他	4	11	13		千克	7	--Other
3102.3000	-硝酸铵,不论是否水溶液	4	11	13		千克	9	-Ammonium nitrate, whether or not in aqueous solution
3102.4000	-硝酸铵与碳酸钙或其他无肥效无机物的混合物	4	11	13		千克	7	-Mixtures of ammonium nitrate with calcium carbonate or other inorganic nonfertilizing substances
3102.5000	-硝酸钠	4	11	13		千克	7AB	-Sodium nitrate
3102.6000	-硝酸钙和硝酸铵的复盐及混合物	4	11	13		千克	7	-Double salts and mixtures of calcium nitrate and ammonium nitrate
3102.8000	-尿素及硝酸铵混合物的水溶液或氨水溶液	4	11	13		千克	7	-Mixtures of urea and ammonium ni-trate in aqueous or ammoniacal solution
	-其他,包括上述子目未列名的混合物:							-Other, including mixtures not specified in the foregoing subheadings:
3102.9010	---氰氨化钙	4	11	13		千克	7AB	---Calcium cyanamide
3102.9090	---其他	4	11	13		千克	7	---Other
31.03	矿物磷肥及化学磷肥:							**Mineral or chemical fertilizers, phosphatic:**
	-过磷酸钙:							-Superphosphates:
3103.1010[暂]	---重过磷酸钙	1	11	13		千克	7A	---Triple superphosphates

税则号列	货 品 名 称	最惠(%)	普通	增值税率	出口退税	计量单位	监管条件	Article Description
3103. 1090暂	---其他	1	11	13		千克	7A	---Other
3103. 9000暂	-其他	1	11	13		千克	7	-Other
31. 04	**矿物钾肥及化学钾肥：**							**Mineral or chemical fertilizers, potassic:**
	-氯化钾：							-Potassium chloride:
3104. 2020	---纯氯化钾（按重量计氯化钾含量≥99. 5%）	3	11	13		千克	7A	---Pure potassium chloride (Potassium chloride≥99. 5% by weigh)
3104. 2090暂	---其他	1	11	13		千克	7AB	---Other
3104. 3000暂	-硫酸钾	1	11	13		千克	7A	-Potassium sulphate
	-其他：							-Other:
3104. 9010暂	---光卤石、钾盐及其他天然粗钾盐	1	11	13		千克	7	---Carnallite, sylvite and other crude natural potassium salts
3104. 9090暂	---其他	1	11	13		千克	7	---Other
31. 05	**含氮、磷、钾中两种或三种肥效元素的矿物肥料或化学肥料；其他肥料；制成片及类似形状或每包毛重不超过10千克的本章各项货品：**							**Mineral or chemical fertilizers containing two or three of the fertilizing elements nitrogen, phosphorus and potassium; other fertilizers; goods of this Chapter in tablets or similar forms or in packages of a gross weight not exceeding 10kg:**
3105. 1000暂	-制成片及类似形状或每包毛重不超过10千克的本章各项货品	1	11	13		千克		-Goods of this Chapter in tablets or similar forms or in packages of a gross weight not exceeding 10kg
3105. 1000暂 10	制成片状及类似形状或零售包装的硝酸铵（零售包装每包毛重不超过10千克）	1	11	13		千克	9	Ammonium nitrate, goods of this in tablets or similar in forms or packages of a gross weight≤10kg
3105. 1000暂 90	制成片状及类似形状或零售包装的第31章其他货品（零售包装每包毛重不超过10千克）	1	11	13		千克	7	Other goods of the chapter 31, in tablets or similar in forms or packages of a gross weight≤10kg
3105. 2000	-含氮、磷、钾三种肥效元素的矿物肥料或化学肥料			13		千克		-Mineral or chemical fertilizers containing the three fertilizing elements nitrogen, phosphorus and potassium
3105. 2000 10	化学肥料或矿物肥料（配额内，含氮、磷、钾三种肥效元素）	4	150	13		千克	At	Mineral or chemical fertilizers containing the three fertilizing elemtnts nitrogen, phosphorus and potassium, in-quota
3105. 2000 90	化学肥料或矿物肥料（配额外，含氮、磷、钾三种肥效元素）	50	150	13		千克	A	Mineral or chemical fertilizers (containing the three fertilizing elements nitrogen, phosphorus and potassium, out -quota)
3105. 3000	-磷酸氢二铵			13		千克		-Diammonium hydrogenorthophosphate (diammonium phosphate)
3105. 3000 10	磷酸氢二铵（配额内）	4	150	13		千克	ABt	Diammonium hydrogenorthophosphate (diammonium phosphate), in-quota
3105. 3000 90	磷酸氢二铵（配额外）	50	150	13		千克	AB	Diammonium hydrogenorthophosphate (diammonium phosphate), out -quota
3105. 4000暂	-磷酸二氢铵及磷酸二氢铵与磷酸氢二铵的混合物	1	11	13		千克	7A	-Ammonium dihydrogenorthophosphate (monoammonium phosphate) and mixtures thereof with diammonium hydrogenorthophosphate (diammonium phosphate)
	-其他含氮、磷两种肥效元素的矿物肥料或化学肥料：							-Other mineral or chemical fertilizers containing the two fertilizing elements nitrogen and phosphorus:
3105. 5100暂	--含有硝酸盐及磷酸盐	1	11	13		千克	7A	--Containing nitrates and phosphates
3105. 5900暂	--其他	1	11	13		千克	7A	--Other
3105. 6000暂	-含磷、钾两种肥效元素的矿物肥料或化学肥料	1	11	13		千克	7A	-Mineral or chemical fertilizers containing the two fertilizing elements phosphorus and potassium
3105. 9000暂	-其他	1	11	13		千克	7A	-Other

第三十二章
鞣料浸膏及染料浸膏；鞣酸及其衍生物；染料、颜料及其他着色料；油漆及清漆；油灰及其他类似胶粘剂；墨水、油墨

Chapter 32
Tanning or dyeing extracts; tannins and their derivatives; dyes, pigments and other colouring matter; paints and varnishes; putty and other mastics; inks

注释：

一、本章不包括：

（一）单独的已有化学定义的化学元素及化合物（税目32.03及32.04的货品、税目32.06的用作发光体的无机产品、税目32.07所述形状的熔融石英或其他熔融硅石制成的玻璃及税目32.12的零售形状或零售包装的染料及其他着色料除外）；

（二）税目29.36至29.39、29.41及35.01至35.04的鞣酸盐及其他鞣酸衍生物；

（三）沥青胶粘剂（税目27.15）。

二、税目32.04包括生产偶氮染料用的稳定重氮盐与偶合物的混合物。

三、税目32.03、32.04、32.05及32.06也包括以着色料为基本成分的制品（例如，税目32.06包括以税目25.30或第二十八章的颜料，金属粉片及金属粉末为基本成分的制品）。该制品是用作原材料着色剂的拼料。但以上税目不包括分散在非水介质中呈液状或浆状的制漆用颜料，例如，税目32.12的瓷漆及税目32.07、32.08、32.09、32.10、32.12、32.13及32.15的其他制品。

四、税目32.08包括由税目39.01至39.13所列产品溶于挥发性有机溶剂的溶液（胶棉除外），但溶剂重量必须超过溶液重量的50%。

五、本章所称"着色料"，不包括作为油漆填料的产品，不论这些产品能否用于水浆涂料的着色。

六、税目32.12所称"压印箔"，只包括用以压印诸如书本封面或帽带之类的薄片，这些薄片由以下材料构成：

（一）金属粉（包括贵金属粉）或颜料经胶水、明胶及其他粘合剂凝结而成的；或

（二）金属（包括贵金属）或颜料沉积于任何材料衬片上的。

Notes:

1. This Chapter does not cover:

(a) Separate chemically defined elements or compounds (except those of heading No. 32.03 or 32.04, inorganic products of a kind used as luminophores (heading No. 32.06), glass obtained from fused quartz or other fused silica in the forms provided for in heading No. 32.07, and also dyes and other colouring matter put up in forms or packings for retail sale, of heading No. 32.12);

(b) Tannates or other tannin derivatives of products of headings No. 29.36 to 29.39, 29.41 or 35.01 to 35.04;

(c) Mastics of asphalt or other bituminous mastics (heading No. 27.15)

2. Heading No. 32.04 includes mixtures of stabilized diazonium salts and couplers for the production of azo dyes.

3. Headings No. 32.03, 32.04, 32.05 and 32.06 apply also to preparations based on colouring matter (including, in the case of heading No. 32.06, colouring pigments of heading No. 25.30 or Chapter 28, metal flakes and metal powders), of a kind used for colouring any material or used as ingredi-ents in the manufacture of colouring preparations. The headings do not apply, however, to pigments dispersed in nonaqueous media, in liquid or paste form, of a kind used in the manufacture of paints, including enamels (heading No. 32.12), or to other preparations of heading No. 32.07, 32.08, 32.09, 32.10, 32.12, 32.13 or 32.15.

4. Heading No. 32.08 includes solutions (other than collodions) consisting of any of the products specified in headings No. 39.01 to 39.13 in volatile organic solvents when the weight of the solvent exceeds 50% of the weight of the solution.

5. The expression "colouring matter" in this Chapter does not include products of a kind used as extenders in oil paints, whether or not they are also suitable for colouring distempers.

6. The expression "stamping foils" in heading No. 32.12 applies only to thin sheets of a kind used for printing, for example, book covers or hat bands, and consisting of:

(a) Metallic powder (including powder of precious metal) or pigment, agglomerated with glue, gelatin or other binder; or

(b) Metal (including precious metal) or pigment, deposited on a supporting sheet of any material.

税则号列	货 品 名 称	最惠(%)	普通	增值税率	出口退税	计量单位	监管条件	Article Description
32.01	植物鞣料浸膏；鞣酸及其盐、醚、酯和其他衍生物：							Tanning extracts of vegetable origin; tannins and their salts, ethers, esters and other derivatives:
3201.1000	-坚木浸膏	5	35	17		千克		-Quebracho extract
3201.2000	-荆树皮浸膏	6.5	35	17		千克		-Wattle extract
	-其他：							-Other:
3201.9010	---其他鞣料浸膏	6.5	40	17		千克		---Other tanning extracts
3201.9010 10	其他濒危植物鞣料浸膏	6.5	40	17		千克	FE	Other tanning extracts of endangered vegetable origin
3201.9010 90	其他植物鞣料浸膏	6.5	40	17		千克		Other tanning extracts of vegetable origin
3201.9090	---其他	6.5	35	17		千克		---Other

税则号列	货品名称	最惠(%)	普通	增值税率	出口退税	计量单位	监管条件	Article Description
32.02	有机合成鞣料;无机鞣料;鞣料制剂,不论是否含有天然鞣料;预鞣用酶制剂:							**Synthetic organic tanning substances; inorganic tanning substances; tanning preparations, whether or not containing natural tanning substances; enzymatic preparations for pre-tanning:**
3202.1000	-有机合成鞣料	6.5	35	17		千克		-Synthetic organic tanning substances
3202.9000	-其他	6.5	35	17		千克		-Other
32.03	动植物质着色料(包括染料浸膏,但动物炭黑除外),不论是否已有化学定义;本章注释三所述的以动植物质着色料为基本成分的制品:							**Colouring matter of vegetable or animal origin (including dyeing extracts but excluding animal black), whether or not chemically defined; preparations as specified in Note 3 to this Chapter based on colouring matter of vegetable or animal origin:**
	---植物质着色料及以其为基本成分的制品:							---Colouring matter of vegetable origin and preparations based thereon:
3203.0011	----天然靛蓝及以其为基本成分的制品	6.5	80	17		千克	AB	----Natural indigo and preparations based thereon
3203.0019	----其他	6.5	45	17		千克		----Other
3203.0019 10	濒危植物质着色料及制品(制品是指以植物质着色料为基本成分的)	6.5	45	17		千克	ABEF	Colouring matter and preparations based thereon of endangered vegetable origin
3203.0019 90	其他植物质着色料及制品(制品是指以植物质着色料为基本成分的)	6.5	45	17		千克	AB	Other colouring matter of vegetable origin based thereon of vegetable origin
3203.0020	---动物质着色料及以其为基本成分的制品	6.5	50	17	13	千克	A	---Colouring matter of animal origin and preparations based thereon
32.04	有机合成着色料,不论是否已有化学定义;本章注释三所述的以有机合成着色料为基本成分的制品;用作荧光增白剂或发光体的有机合成产品,不论是否已有化学定义:							**Synthetic organic colouring matter, whether or not chemically defined; preparations as specified in Note 3 to this Chapter based on synthetic organic colouring matter; synthetic organic products of a kind used as fluorescent brightening agents or as luminophores, whether or not chemically defined:**
	-有机合成着色料及本章注释三所述的以有机合成着色料为基本成分的制品:							-Synthetic organic colouring matter and preparations based thereon as specified in Note 3 to this Chapter:
3204.1100	--分散染料及以其为基本成分的制品	6.5	35	17		千克	AB	--Disperse dyes and preparations based thereon
3204.1200	--酸性染料(不论是否与金属络合)及以其为基本成分的制品;媒染染料及以其为基本成分的制品	6.5	35	17		千克	AB	--Acid dyes, whether or not premetallized, and preparations based thereon; mordant dyes and preparations based thereon
3204.1300	--碱性染料及以其为基本成分的制品	6.5	35	17		千克	AB	--Basic dyes and preparations based thereon
3204.1400	--直接染料及以其为基本成分的制品	6.5	35	17		千克	AB	--Direct dyes and preparations based thereon
	--瓮染料(包括颜料用的)及以其为基本成分的制品:							--Vat dyes (including those usable in that state as pigments) and preparations based thereon:
3204.1510	---合成靛蓝(还原靛蓝)	6.5	35	17		千克	AB	---Synthetic indigo (reductive indigo)
3204.1590	---其他	6.5	35	17		千克		---Other
3204.1600	--活性染料及以其为基本成分的制品	6.5	35	17		千克		--Reactive dyes and preparations based thereon
3204.1700	--颜料及以其为基本成分的制品	6.5	35	17		千克		--Pigments and preparations based thereon
	--其他,包括由子目号3204.11至3204.19中两个或多个子目所列着色料组成的混合物:							--Other, including mixtures of colouring matter of two or more of the subheadings No. 3204.11 to 3204.19:
	---硫化染料及以其为基本成分的制品:							---Sulphur dyes and preparations based thereon:
3204.1911	----硫化黑(硫化青)及以其为基本成分的制品	6.5	35	17		千克		----Sulphur black and preparations based thereon
3204.1919	----其他	6.5	35	17		千克		----Other
3204.1990	---其他	6.5	35	17		千克	AB	---Other
3204.2000	-用作荧光增白剂的有机合成产品	6.5	40	17		千克	A	-Synthetic organic products of a kind used as flourescent brightening agents
	-其他:							-Other:
3204.9010	---生物染色剂及染料指示剂	6.5	20	17		千克		---Biological stains and dye indicators
3204.9090	---其他	6.5	40	17		千克		---Other
32.05	色淀;本章注释三所述的以色淀为基本成分的制品:							**Colour lakes; preparations as specified in Note 3 to this Chapter based on colour lakes:**
3205.0000	色淀;本章注释三所述的以色淀为基本成分的制品	6.5	35	17		千克	AB	Colour lakes; preparations as specified in Note 3 to this Chapter based on colour lakes

税则号列	货品名称	最惠(%)	普通	增值税率	出口退税	计量单位	监管条件	Article Description
32.06	**其他着色料；本章注释三所述的制品，但税目32.03、32.04及32.05的货品除外；用作发光体的无机产品，不论是否已有化学定义：**							**Other colouring matter; preparations as specified in Note 3 to this Chapter, other than those of heading No. 32.03, 32.04 or 32.05; inorganic products of a kind used as luminophores, whether or not chemically defined:**
	-以二氧化钛为基本成分的颜料及制品：							-Pigments and preparations based on titanium dioxide:
	--以干物质计二氧化钛含量在80%及以上的：							--Containing 80% or more by weight of titanium dioxide calculated on the dry matter:
3206.1110	---钛白粉	6.5	30	17		千克	4xy	---Titanium White
3206.1190	---其他	6.5	30	17		千克		---Other
3206.1900	--其他	10	30	17		千克		--Other
3206.2000	-以铬化合物为基本成分的颜料及制品	6.5	35	17		千克		-Pigments and preparations based on chromium compounds
	-其他着色料及其他制品：							-Other colouring matter and other preparations:
3206.4100	--群青及以其为基本成分的制品	6.5	35	17		千克		--Ultramarine and preparations based thereon
	--锌钡白及以硫化锌为基本成分的其他颜料和制品：							--Lithopone and other pigments and preparations based on zinc sulphide:
3206.4210	---锌钡白	6.5	30	17		千克		---Lithopone
3206.4290	---其他	6.5	30	17		千克		---Other
	--其他：							--Other:
	---以铋化合物为基本成分的颜料及制品：							---Pigmenlts and preparations based on bismuth compound:
3206.4911	---以钒酸铋为基本成基本成分的颜料及制品	6.5	35	17		千克		---Pigmenlts and preparations based on pucherite
3206.4919	---其他	6.5	35	17		千克		---Other
3206.4990	--其他	6.5	35	17		千克		---Other
3206.5000	-用作发光体的无机产品	6.5	35	17		千克		-Inorganic products of a kind used as luminophores
32.07	**陶瓷、搪瓷及玻璃工业用的调制颜料、遮光剂、着色剂、珐琅和釉料、釉底料（泥釉）、光瓷釉以及类似产品；搪瓷玻璃料及其他玻璃，呈粉、粒或粉片状的：**							**Prepared pigments, prepared opacifiers and prepared colours, vitrifiable enamels and glazes, engobes (slips), liquid lustres and similar preparations, of a kind used in the ceramic, enamelling or glass industry; glass frit and other glass, in the form of powder, granules or flakes:**
3207.1000	-调制颜料、遮光剂、着色剂及类似制品	5	50	17		千克		-Prepared pigments, prepared opacifiers, prepared colours and similar preparations
3207.2000	-珐琅和釉料、釉底料（泥釉）及类似制品	5	50	17		千克		-Vitrifiable enamels and glazes, engobes (slips) and similar preparations
3207.3000	-光瓷釉及类似制品	5	50	17		千克		-Liquid lustres and similar preparations
3207.4000	-搪瓷玻璃料及其他玻璃，呈粉、粒或粉片状的	5	50	17		千克		-Glass frit and other glass, in the form of powder, granules or flakes
32.08	**以合成聚合物或化学改性天然聚合物为基本成分的油漆及清漆（包括瓷漆及大漆），分散于或溶于非水介质的；本章注释四所述的溶液：**							**Paints and varnishes (including enamels and lacquers) based on synthetic polymers or chemically modified natural polymers, dispersed or dissolved in a nonaqueous medium; solutions as defined in Note 4 to this Chapter:**
3208.1000	-以聚酯为基本成分	10	50	17		千克	A	-Based on polyesters
	-以丙烯酸聚合物或乙烯聚合物为基本成分：							-Based on acrylic or vinyl polymers:
3208.2010	---以丙烯酸聚合物为基本成分		50	17		千克		---Based on acrylic polymers
3208.2010暂 01	分散于或溶于非水介质的光导纤维用涂料（主要成分为聚胺酯丙烯酸脂类化合物，以丙烯酸聚合物为基本成分）	6	50	17		千克	A	Paints for optial fibers, dispersed or disolved in a nonaqueous medium (based on acrylic or vinyl poly mers)
3208.2010 90	其他聚丙烯酸油漆、清漆等（溶于非水质的以丙烯酸聚合物为基本成分，包括瓷漆大漆）	10	50	17		千克	A	Other paints and varnishes (including enamels and lacquers), based on acrylic polymers, dissolved in a nonaqueous medium
3208.2020	---以乙烯聚合物为基本成分	10	50	17		千克	A	---Based on vinyl polymers
	-其他：							-Other:
3208.9010	---以聚胺酯类化合物为基本成分		50	17		千克		---Based on polyurethane polymers

税则号列	货品名称	最惠(%)	普通	增值税率	出口退税	计量单位	监管条件	Article Description
3208.9010暂 01	分散于或溶于非水介质的光导纤维用涂料(主要成分为聚胺酯丙烯酸酯类化合物,以聚胺酯类化合物为基本成分)	6	50	17		千克	A	Paints for optial fibers, dispersed or disolved in a nonaqueous medium consisting chiefly of acrylic polymrs, based on polyesters.
3208.9010 90	其他聚胺酯油漆清漆等(溶于非水介质以聚胺酯类化合物为基本成分,含瓷漆大漆)	10	50	17		千克	A	Other paints and varnishes (including enamels and lacquers, based on polyurethane polymers, dissolved in a nonaqueous medium)
3208.9090	---其他	10	50	17		千克	A	---Other
32.09	**以合成聚合物或化学改性天然聚合物为基本成分的油漆及清漆(包括瓷漆及大漆),分散于或溶于水介质的:**							**Paints and varnishes (including enamels and lacquers) based on synthetic polymers or chemically modified natural polymers, dispersed or dissolved in an aqueous medium:**
3209.1000	-以丙烯酸聚合物或乙烯聚合物为基本成分	10	50	17		千克	A	-Based on acrylic or vinyl polymers
	-其他:							-Other:
3209.9010	---以环氧树脂为基本成分	10	50	17		千克	A	---Based on epoxy resin
3209.9020	---以氟树脂为基本成分	10	50	17		千克	A	---Based on fluororesin
3209.9090	---其他	10	50	17		千克	A	---Other
32.10	**其他油漆及清漆(包括瓷漆、大漆及水浆涂料);加工皮革用的水性颜料:**							**Other paints and varnishes (including enamels, lacquers and distempers); prepared water pigments of a kind used for finishing leather:**
3210.0000	其他油漆及清漆(包括瓷漆、大漆及水浆涂料);加工皮革用的水性颜料		50	17		千克		Other paints and varnishes (including enamels, lacquers and distempers); prepared water pigments of a kind used for finishing leather
3210.0000暂 01	其他光导纤维用涂料	6	50	17		千克		Other paint of a kind used for Optical fiber
3210.0000 90	其他油漆及清漆,皮革用水性颜料(包括非聚合物为基料的瓷漆,大漆及水浆涂料)	10	50	17		千克		Other paints and varnishes ,water - based pigment for leather(including enamels,lacquers and distempers)
32.11	**配制的催干剂:**							**Prepared driers:**
3211.0000	配制的催干剂	10	50	17		千克		Prepared driers
32.12	**制造油漆(含瓷漆)用的颜料(包括金属粉末或金属粉片),分散于非水介质中呈液状或浆状的;压印箔;零售形状及零售包装的染料或其他着色料:**							**Pigments (including metallic powders and flakes) dispersed in non-aqueous media, in liquid or paste form, of a kind used in the manufacture of paints (including enamels); stamping foils; dyes and other colouring matter put up in forms or packings for retail sale:**
3212.1000	-压印箔	15	80	17		千克		-Stamping foils
3212.9000	-其他	10	50	17		千克		-Other
32.13	**艺术家、学生和广告美工用的颜料、调色料、文娱颜料及类似品,片状、管装、罐装、瓶装、扁盒装以及类似形状或包装的:**							**Artists', students' or signboard painters' colours, modifying tints, amusement colours and the like, in tablets, tubes, jars, bottles, pans or in similar forms or packings:**
3213.1000	-成套的颜料	10	70	17	13	千克		-Colours in sets
3213.9000	-其他	10	70	17	13	千克		-Other
32.14	**安装玻璃用油灰、接缝用油灰、树脂胶泥、嵌缝胶及其他类似胶粘剂;漆工用填料;非耐火涂面制剂,涂门面、内墙、地板、天花板等用:**							**Glaziers' putty, graftig putty, resin cements, caulking compounds and other mastics; painters' fillings; non-refractory surfacing preparations for facades, indoor walls, floors, ceilings or the like:**
	-安装玻璃用油灰、接缝用油灰、树脂胶泥、嵌缝胶及其他类似胶粘剂;漆工用填料:							-Glaziers' putty, grafting putty, resin cements, caulking compounds and other mastics; painters' fillings:
3214.1010	---半导体器件封装材料	9	70	17		千克		---Encpackaging materials for semiconductor device
3214.1090	---其他	9	70	17		千克		---Other
3214.9000	-其他	9	70	17		千克		-Other
32.15	**印刷油墨、书写或绘图墨水及其他墨类,不论是否固体或浓缩:**							**Printing ink, writing or drawing ink and other inks, whether or not concentrated or solid:**
	-印刷油墨:							-Printing ink:
3215.1100	--黑色	6.5	45	17		千克	AB	--Black
3215.1900	--其他	6.5	45	17		千克		--Other
	-其他:							-Other:
3215.9010	---书写墨水	6.5	70	17	13	千克		---Writing or drawing inks
3215.9020	---水性喷墨墨水	10	70	17	13	千克		---Aqueous ink jet ink
3215.9090	---其他	10	70	17	13	千克		---Other

第三十三章
精油及香膏；芳香料制品及化妆盥洗品

Chapter 33
Essential oils and resinoids; perfumery, cosmetic or toilet preparations

注释：

一、本章不包括：

（一）税目 13.01 及 13.02 的天然油树脂及植物浸膏；

（二）税目 34.01 的肥皂及其他产品；

（三）税目 38.05 的脂松节油、木松节油和硫酸盐松节油及其他产品。

二、税目 33.02 所称"香料"仅指税目 33.01 所列的物质，从这些物质离析出来的香料组分以及合成芳香剂。

三、税目 33.03 至 33.07 主要包括适合作这些税目所列用途的零售包装产品，不论其是否混合（精油水馏液及水溶液除外）。

四、税目 33.07 所称"芳香料制品及化妆盥洗品"，主要适用于下列产品：香袋；通过燃烧散发香气的制品；香纸及用化妆品浸渍或涂布的纸；隐形眼镜片或假眼用的溶液；用香水或化妆品浸渍、涂布、包覆的絮胎、毡呢及无纺织物；动物用盥洗品。

Notes:

1. This Chapter does not cover:
   (a) Natural oleoresins or vegetable extracts of heading No. 13.01 or 13.02;
   (b) Soap or other products of heading No. 34.01; or
   (c) Gum, wood or sulphate turpentine or other products of heading No. 38.05.
2. The expression "odoriferous substances" in heading No. 33.02 refers only to the substances of heading No. 33.01, to odoriferous constituents isolated from those substances or to synthetic aromatics.
3. Headings No. 33.03 to 33.07 apply, *inter alia*, to products, whether or not mixed (other than aqueous distillates and aqueous solutions of essential oils), suitable for use as goods of these headings and put up in packings of a kind sold by retail for such use.
4. The expression "perfumery, cosmetic or toilet preparations" in heading No. 33.07 applies, *inter alia*, to the following products: scented sachets; odoriferous preparations which operate by burning; perfumed papers and papers impregnated or coated with cosmetics; contact lens or artificial eye solutions; wadding, felt and nonwovens, impregnated, coated or covered with perfume or cosmetics; animal toilet preparations.

税则号列	货品名称	最惠(%)	普通	增值税率	出口退税	计量单位	监管条件	Article Description
33.01	精油（无萜或含萜），包括浸膏及净油；香膏；提取的油树脂；用花香吸取法或浸渍法制成的含浓缩精油的脂肪、固定油、蜡及类似品；精油脱萜时所得的萜烯副产品；精油水馏液及水溶液：							**Essential oils (terpeneless or not), including concretes and absolutes; resinoids; extracted oleoresins; concentrates of essential oils in fats, in fixed oils, in waxes or the like, obtained by enfleurage or maceration; terpenic byproducts of the deterpenation of essential oils; aqueous distillates and aqueous solutions of essential oils:**
	-柑桔属果实的精油：							-Essential oils of citrus fruit:
3301.1200	--橙油	20	80	17	9	千克	A	--Of orange
3301.1300	--柠檬油	20	80	17	9	千克	A	--Of lemon
	--其他：							--Other:
3301.1910	---白柠檬油（酸橙油）	20	80	17	9	千克	A	---Of lime
3301.1990	---其他	20	80	17	9	千克	A	---Other
	-非柑橘属果实的精油：							-Essential oils other than those of citrus fruit:
3301.2400	--胡椒薄荷油	20	90	17	9	千克	A	--Of peppermint (Mentha piperita)
3301.2500暂	--其他薄荷油	5	90	17	13	千克	A	--Of other mints
	--其他：							--Other:
3301.2910	---樟脑油	20	90	17	9	千克	ABE	---Of camphor
3301.2920	---香茅油	15	70	17	9	千克	A	---Of citronella
3301.2930	---茴香油	20	80	17	9	千克	A	---Of aniseed
3301.2940	---桂油	20	80	17	9	千克	A	---Of cassia
3301.2950	---山苍子油	20	80	17	9	千克	A	---Of litsea cubeba
3301.2960	---桉叶油	20	80	17	9	千克	AB	---Of eucalyptus
	---其他：							---Other:
3301.2991	----老鹳草油（香叶油）	20	80	17	9	千克	A	----Of geranium
3301.2999	----其他		80	17		千克		----Other
3301.2999暂 10	黄樟油	7	80	17	9	千克	23A	Oil of sassafras
3301.2999 91	其他濒危植物精油（柑桔属果实除外）（包括浸膏及净油）	15	80	17		千克	AFE	Other endangered essential (other than citrus fruit) (including concretes and absolutes)

税则号列	货品名称	最惠(%)	普通	增值税率	出口退税	计量单位	监管条件	Article Description
3301.2999 99	其他非柑橘属果实的精油(包括浸膏及净油)	15	80	17	9	千克	A	Other essential oils other than those of citrus fruit (including concretes and absolutes)
	-香膏:							-Resinoids:
3301.3010暂	---鸢尾凝脂	10	80	17	13	千克		---Balsam of irises
3301.3090	---其他	20	80	17		千克		---Other
3301.3090 10	其他濒危植物香膏	20	80	17		千克	FE	Other resinoids of endangered vegetable
3301.3090 90	其他香膏	20	80	17	9	千克		Other resinoids
	-其他:							-Other:
3301.9010	---提取的油树脂	20	80	17		千克		---Extracted oleoresins
3301.9010 10	濒危植物提取的油树脂	20	80	17		千克	FE	Extracted oleoresins of endangered vegetable
3301.9010 90	其他提取的油树脂	20	80	17	9	千克		Other extracted oleoresins
3301.9020	---柑橘属果实的精油脱萜的萜烯副产品	20	80	17	9	千克		---Terpenic byproducts of the deterpenation of essential oils of citrus fruit
3301.9090	---其他	20	80	17	9	千克		---Other
33.02	**工业原料用的混合香料以及以一种或多种香料为基本成分的混合物(包括酒精溶液);生产饮料用的以香料为基本成分的其他制品:**							**Mixtures of odoriferous substances and mixtures (including alcoholic solutions) with a basis of one or more of these substances, of a kind used as raw materials in industry; other preparations based on odoriferous substances, of a kind used for the manufacture of beverages:**
	-食品或饮料工业用:							-Of a kind used in the food or drink industry:
3302.1010	---生产饮料用的以香料为基本成分的制品,按容量计酒精浓度不超过0.5%的	15	90	17	13	千克	AB	---Preparations based on odoriferous substances, of a kind used for the manufacture of beverages, alcoholic strength by volume not ≤0.5% vol.
3302.1090	---其他	15	130	17	13	千克		---Other
3302.1090 01	生产食品、饮料用混合香料及制品(含以香料为基本成分的混合物,按容量计酒精浓度>0.5%)	15	130	17	13	千克	A	Mixtures of odoriferous substances and products, alcoholic strength by vol >0.5%, of a kind used in the food or drink industry
3302.1090 90	其他生产食品用混合香料及制品(含以香料为基本成分的混合物)	15	130	17	13	千克	A	Other mistures of odoriferous substances and preparations, based on oboriferous substances, of a kind used in the food industry
3302.9000	-其他	10	130	17	13	千克		-Other
33.03	**香水及花露水:**							**Perfumes and toilet waters:**
3303.0000	香水及花露水	10	150	17	13	千克/件	AB	Perfumes and toilet waters
33.04	**美容品或化妆品及护肤品(药品除外),包括防晒油或晒黑油;指(趾)甲化妆品:**							**Beauty or make-up preparations and preparations for the care of the skin (other than medicaments), including sunscreen or suntan preparations; manicure or pedicure preparations:**
3304.1000	-唇用化妆品	10	150	17		千克/件		-Lip make-up preparations
3304.1000 10	含濒危植物成分唇用化妆品	10	150	17		千克/件	ABEF	Lip make-up preparations, containing composition of endangered vegetable
3304.1000 90	其他唇用化妆品	10	150	17	13	千克/件	AB	Other lip make-up preparations
3304.2000	-眼用化妆品	10	150	17		千克/件		-Eye make-up preparations
3304.2000 10	含濒危植物成分眼用化妆品	10	150	17		千克/件	ABEF	Eye make-up preparations, containing composition of endangered vegetable
3304.2000 90	其他眼用化妆品	10	150	17	13	千克/件	AB	Other eye make-up preparations
3304.3000暂	-指(趾)甲化妆品	10	150	17	13	千克/件	AB	-Manicure or pedicure preparations
	-其他:							-Other:
3304.9100	--香粉,不论是否压紧	10	150	17	13	千克/件		--Powders, whether or not compressed
3304.9100 01	痱子粉、爽身粉	10	150	17	13	千克/件	AB	Bath powder, talcum powder
3304.9100 90	香粉,不论是否压紧	10	150	17	13	千克/件	AB	Powders, whether or not compressed
3304.9900	--其他		150	17		千克/件		--Other
3304.9900暂 10	护肤品(包括防晒油或晒黑油,但药品除外)	5	150	17	13	千克/件	AB	Preparations for the care of the skin, (including sunscreen or sun tan preparations other than medicaments)

税则号列	货　品　名　称	最惠(%)	普通	增值税率	出口退税	计量单位	监管条件	Article Description
3304.9900 91	其他含濒危植物成分美容品或化妆品	6.5	150	17		千克/件	ABFE	Beauty or make-up preparations, containing composition of endangered vegetable
3304.9900 99	其他美容品或化妆品	6.5	150	17	13	千克/件	AB	Other beauty or make-up preparations
33.05	**护发品:**							**Preparations for use on the hair:**
3305.1000	-洗发剂(香波)	6.5	150	17		千克		-Shampoos
3305.1000 10	含濒危植物成分的洗发剂	6.5	150	17		千克	ABFE	Shampoos containing composition of endangered vegetable
3305.1000 90	其他洗发剂(香波)	6.5	150	17	13	千克	AB	Other shampoos
3305.2000暂	-烫发剂	10	150	17	13	千克	AB	-Preparations for permanent waving or straightening
3305.3000暂	-定型剂	10	150	17	13	千克	AB	-Hair lacquers
3305.9000	-其他	10	150	17	13	千克	AB	-Other
33.06	**口腔及牙齿清洁剂,包括假牙模膏及粉;清洁牙缝用的纱线(牙线),单独零售包装的:**							**Preparations for oral or dental hygiene, including denture fixative pastes and powders; yarn used to clean between the teeth (dental floss), in individual retail package:**
	-洁齿品:							-Dentifrices:
3306.1010	---牙膏	10	150	17		千克		---Toothpastes
3306.1010 10	含濒危植物成分牙膏	10	150	17		千克	ABEF	Toothpastes containing composition of endangered vegetable
3306.1010 90	其他牙膏	10	150	17	13	千克	AB	Other toothpastes
3306.1090	---其他	10	150	17	9	千克		---Other
3306.2000	-清洁牙缝用的纱线(牙线)	10	70	17	9	千克		-Yarn used to clean between the teeth (dental floss)
3306.9000	-其他	10	70	17	9	千克	AB	-Other
33.07	**剃须用制剂、人体除臭剂、沐浴用制剂、脱毛剂和其他税目未列名的芳香料制品及化妆盥洗品;室内除臭剂,不论是否加香水或消毒剂:**							**Pre-shave, shaving or after-shave preparations, personal deodorants, bath preparations, depilatories and other perfumery, cosmetic or toilet preparations, not elsewhere specified or included; prepared room deodorizers, whether or not perfumed or having disinfectant properties:**
3307.1000	-剃须用制剂	10	150	17	13	千克	AB	-Pre-shave, shaving or after-shave preparations
3307.2000	-人体除臭剂及止汗剂	10	150	17	13	千克	AB	-Personal deodorants and antiperspirants
3307.3000	-香浴盐及其他沐浴用制剂	10	150	17	13	千克	AB	-Perfumed bath salts and other bath preparations
	-室内散香或除臭制品,包括宗教仪式用的香:							-Preparations for perfuming or deodorizing rooms, including odoriferous preparations used during religious rites:
3307.4100	--神香及其他通过燃烧散发香气的制品	10	150	17	9	千克		--Agarbatti and other odoriferous preparations which operate by burning
3307.4900	--其他	10	150	17	9	千克		--Other
3307.9000	-其他	9	150	17	13	千克		-Other

第三十四章
肥皂、有机表面活性剂、洗涤剂、润滑剂、人造蜡、调制蜡、光洁剂、蜡烛及类似品、塑型用膏、“牙科用蜡”及牙科用熟石膏制剂

注释：

一、本章不包括：

（一）用作脱模剂的食用动植物油、脂混合物或制品（税目 15.17）；

（二）单独的已有化学定义的化合物；

（三）含肥皂或其他有机表面活性剂的洗发剂、洁齿品、剃须膏及沐浴用制剂（税目 33.05、33.06 及 33.07）。

二、税目 34.01 所称“肥皂”，只适用于水溶性肥皂。税目 34.01 的肥皂及其他产品可以含有添加料（例如，消毒剂、磨料粉、填料或药料）。含磨料粉的产品，只有条状、块状或模制形状可以归入税目 34.01。其他形状的应作为“去污粉及类似品”归入 税目 34.05。

三、税目 34.02 所称“有机表面活性剂”，是指温度在 20℃时与水混合配成 0.5%浓度的 水溶液，并在同样温度下搁置一小时后与下列规定相符的产品：

（一）成为透明或半透明的液体或稳定的乳浊液而未离析出不溶解物质；

（二）将水的表面张力减低到每厘米 45 达因及以下。

四、税目 34.03 所称“石油及从沥青矿物提取的油类”，适用于第二十七章注释二所规定的产品。

五、税目 34.04 所称“人造蜡及调制蜡”，仅适用于：

applies only to:

(a) Chemically produced organic products of a waxy character, whether or not water-soluble;

(b) Products obtained by mixing different waxes;

(c) Products of a waxy character with a basis of one or more waxes and containing fats, resins, mineral substances or other materials.

The heading does not apply to:

(a) Products of heading No. 15.16, 34.02 or 38.23, even if having a waxy character;

(b) Unmixed animal waxes or unmixed vegetable waxes, whether or not refined or coloured, of heading No. 15.21;

(c) Mineral waxes or similar products of heading No. 27.12, whether or not intermixed or merely coloured;

(d) Waxes mixed with, dispersed in or dissolved in a liquid medium (headings No. 34.05, 38.09, etc.).

Chapter 34
Soap, organic surface-active agents, washing preparations, lubricating preparations, artificial waxes, prepared waxes, polishing or scouring preparations, candles and similar articles, modelling pastes, "dental waxes" and dental preparations with a basis of plaster

Notes:

1. This Chapter does not cover:

(a) Edible mixtures or preparations of animal or vegetable fats or oils of a kind used as mould release preparations (heading No. 15.17);

(b) Separate chemically defined compounds; or

(c) Shampoos, dentifrices, shaving creams and foams, or bath preparations, containing soap or other organic surface-active agents (heading No. 33.05, 33.06 or 33.07).

2. For the purposes of heading No. 34.01, the expression "soap" applies only to soap soluble in water. Soap and the other products of heading No. 34.01 may contain added substances (for example, disinfectants, abrasive powders, fillers or medicaments). Products containing abrasive powders remain classified in heading No. 34.01 only if in the form of bars, cakes or moulded pieces or shapes. In other forms they are to be classified in heading No. 34.05 as "scouring powders and similar preparations".

3. For the purposes of heading No. 34.02, "organic surface-active agents" are products which when mixed with water at a concentration of 0.5% at 20℃ and left to stand for one hour at the same temperature:

(a) give a transparent or translucent liquid or stable emulsion without separation of insoluble matter; and

(b) reduce the surface tension of water to 4.5×10^{-2} N/m (45 dyen/cm) or less.

4. In heading No. 34.03 the expression "petroleum oils and oils obtained from bituminous minerals" applies to the products defined in Note 2 to Chapter 27.

5. In heading No. 34.04, subject to the exclusions provided below, the expression "artificial waxes and prepared waxes"

（一）用化学方法生产的具有蜡质特性的有机产品，不论是否为水溶性的；

（二）各种蜡混合制成的产品；

（三）以一种或几种蜡为基本原料并含有油脂、树脂、矿物质或其他原料的具有蜡质特性的产品。

本税目不包括：

（一）税目 15.16、34.02 或 38.23 的产品，不论是否具有蜡质特性；

（二）税目 15.21 的未混合的动物蜡或未混合的植物蜡，不论是否精制或着色；

（三）税目 27.12 的矿物蜡或类似产品，不论是否相互混合或仅经着色；

（四）混合、分散或溶解于液体溶剂的蜡（税目 34.05、38.09 等）。

税则号列	货品名称	最惠(%)	普通	增值税率	出口退税	计量单位	监管条件	Article Description
34.01	**肥皂;作肥皂用的有机表面活性产品及制品,条状、块状或模制形状的,不论是否含有肥皂;洁肤用的有机表面活性产品及制品,液状或膏状并制成零售包装的,不论是否含有肥皂;用肥皂或洗涤剂浸渍、涂面或包覆的纸、絮胎、毡呢及无纺织物:**							**Soap; organic surface-active products and preparations for use as soap, in the form of bars, cakes, moulded pieces or shapes, whether or not containing soap; organic surface-active products and preparations for washing the skin, in the form of liquid or cream and put up for retail sale, whether or not containing soap; paper, wadding, felt and nonwovens, impregnated, coated or covered with soap or detergent:**
	-肥皂及有机表面活性产品及制品,条状、块状或模制形状的,以及用肥皂或洗涤剂浸渍、涂面或包覆的纸、絮胎、毡呢及无纺织物:							-Soap and organic surface-active products and preparations, in the form of bars, cakes, moulded pieces or shapes, and paper, wadding, felt and nonwovens, impregnated, coated or covered with soap or detergent:
3401.1100	--盥洗用(包括含有药物的产品)	10	130	17	13	千克	AB	--For toilet use (including medicated products)
	--其他:							--Other:
3401.1910	---洗衣皂	10	80	17	13	千克		---Laundry soap
3401.1990暂	---其他	10	130	17	13	千克		---Other
3401.2000暂	-其他形状的肥皂	10	130	17	13	千克		-Soap in other forms
3401.3000	-洁肤用的有机表面活性产品及制品,液状或膏状并制成零售包装的,不论是否含有肥皂	10	130	17	13	千克	AB	-Organic surface-active products and preparations for washing the skin, in the form of liquid or cream and put up for retail sale, whether or not containing soap
34.02	**有机表面活性剂(肥皂除外);表面活性剂制品、洗涤剂(包括助洗剂)及清洁剂,不论是否含有肥皂,但税号34.01的产品除外:**							**Organic surface-active agents (other than soap); surface-active preparations, washing preparations (including auxiliary washing preparations) and cleaning preparations, whether or not containing soap, other than those of heading No. 34.01:**
	-有机表面活性剂,不论是否零售包装:							-Organic surface-active agents, whether or not put up for retail sale:
3402.1100	--阴离子型	6.5	30	17	13	千克		--Anionic
3402.1200	--阳离子型	6.5	30	17	13	千克		--Cationic
3402.1300	--非离子型	6.5	30	17	13	千克		--Non-ionic
3402.1300 10	含有壬基酚聚氧乙烯醚的有机表面活性剂(不论是否零售包装,肥皂除外)	6.5	30	17	13	千克	X	Organic surface – active agents, containing polyoxy ethrlene nonyl phinyl ether (whether or not put up for retail sale, other than soap)
3402.1300 90	其他非离子型有机表面活性剂(不论是否零售包装,肥皂除外)	6.5	30	17	13	千克		Other organic surface – active agents (whether or not put up for retail sale, other than soap)
3402.1900	--其他	6.5	30	17	13	千克		--Other
	-零售包装的制品:							-Preparations put up for retail sale:
3402.2010	---合成洗涤粉	10	80	17	13	千克		---Synthetic detergents in powder form
3402.2090	---其他	10	80	17	13	千克		---Other
3402.9000	-其他		80	17	13	千克		-Other
3402.9000暂 01	十二烷基苯磺酸钙甲醇溶液(非零售包装,十二烷基苯磺酸钙含量高于70%)	7	80	17	13	千克		Calcium dodecyl benzen sulfonate methanol solution (containing more than 70% of calcium dodecyl benzosulfonate, not put up for retail sale)
3402.9000 90	非零售包装有机表面活性剂制品(包括洗涤剂及清洁剂,不论是否含有肥皂)	9	80	17	13	千克		Organic surface-active agents, including washing preparations and cleaning preparations, whether or not containing soap, not in forms or packing for retail sale

税则号列	货品名称	最惠(%)	普通	增值税率	出口退税	计量单位	监管条件	Article Description
34.03	**润滑剂(包括以润滑剂为基本成分的切削油制剂、螺栓或螺母松开剂、防锈或防腐蚀制剂及脱模剂)及用于纺织材料、皮革、毛皮或其他材料油脂处理的制剂,但不包括以石油或从沥青矿物提取的油类为基本成分(按重量计不低于70%)的制剂:**							**Lubricating preparations (including cutting-oil preparations, bolt or nut release preparations, anti-rust or anticorrosion preparations and mould release preparations, based on lubricants) and preparations of a kind used for the oil or grease treatment of textile materials, leather, furskins or other materials, but excluding preparations containing, as basic constituents, 70% or more by weight of petroleum oils or of oils obtained from bituminous minerals:**
	-含有石油或从沥青矿物提取的油类:							-Containing petroleum oils or oils obtained from bituminous minerals:
3403.1100暂	--处理纺织材料、皮革、毛皮或其他材料的制剂	8	50	17	9	千克		--Preparations for the treatment of textile materials, leather, furskins or other materials
3403.1900暂	--其他	8	50	17	9	千克		--Other
	-其他:							-Other:
3403.9100暂	--处理纺织材料、皮革、毛皮或其他材料的制剂	8	50	17	9	千克		--Preparations for the treatment of textile materials, leather, furskins or other materials
3403.9900	--其他	10	50	17	9	千克		--Other
34.04	**人造蜡及调制蜡:**							**Artificial waxes and prepared waxes:**
3404.2000	-聚氧乙烯(聚乙二醇)蜡	10	70	17	9	千克		-Of poly(oxyethylene)(polyethylene glycol)
3404.9000	-其他	10	70	17		千克		-Other
34.05	**鞋靴、家具、地板、车身、玻璃或金属用的光洁剂、擦洗膏、去污粉及类似制品(包括用这类制剂浸渍、涂面或包覆的纸、絮胎、毡呢、无纺织物、泡沫塑料或海绵橡胶),但不包括税目34.04的蜡:**							**Polishes and creams, for footwear, furniture, floors, coachwork, glass or metal, scouring pastes and powders and similar preparations (whether or not in the form of paper, wadding, felt, nonwovens, cellular plastics or cellular rubber, impregnated, coated or covered with such preparations), excluding waxes of heading No. 34.04:**
3405.1000	-鞋靴或皮革用的上光剂及类似制品	10	80	17	9	千克		-Polishes, creams and similar preparations for footwear or leather
3405.2000	-保养木制家具、地板或其他木制品用的上光剂及类似制品	10	80	17	9	千克		-Polishes, creams and similar preparations for the maintenance of wooden furniture, floors or other woodwork
3405.3000	-车身用的上光剂及类似制品,但金属用的光洁剂除外	10	80	17	9	千克		-Polishes and similar preparations for coachwork, other than metal polishes
3405.4000	-擦洗膏、去污粉及类似制品	10	80	17	9	千克		-Scouring pastes and powders and other scouring preparations
3405.9000	-其他	10	80	17	9	千克		-Other
34.06	**各种蜡烛及类似品:**							**Candles, tapers and the like:**
3406.0000	各种蜡烛及类似品	10	130	17		千克		Candles, tapers and the like
3406.0000 10	含濒危动物成分的蜡烛及类似品	10	130	17		千克	EF	Candle and gimilar products made from on endangered animals
3406.0000 90	其他各种蜡烛及类似品	10	130	17	13	千克		Other candles, tapers and the like
34.07	**塑型用膏,包括供儿童娱乐用的在内;通称为"牙科用蜡"或"牙科造形膏"的制品,成套、零售包装或制成片状、马蹄形、条状及类似形状的;以熟石膏(煅烧石膏或硫酸钙)为基本成分的牙科用其他制品:**							**Modelling pastes, including those put up for children's amusement; preparations known as "dental wax" or as "dental impression compounds", put up in sets, in packings for retail sale or in plates, horseshoe shapes, sticks or similar forms; other preparations for use in dentistry, with a basis of plaster (of calcined gypsum or calcium sulphate):**
3407.0010	---牙科用蜡及造型膏	6.5	30	17	9	千克		---Preparations of a kind known as "dental wax" or as "dental impression compounds"
3407.0020	---以熟石膏为基本成分的牙科用其他制品	6.5	40	17	9	千克		---Other preparations for use in dentistry, with a basis of plaster
3407.0090	---其他	10	100	17	9	千克		---Other

第三十五章
蛋白类物质;改性淀粉;胶;酶

Chapter 35
Albuminoidal substances; modified starches; glues; enzymes

注释:

一、本章不包括:

(一)酵母(税目 21.02);

(二)第三十章的血份(非治病、防病用的血清白蛋白除外)、药品及其他产品;

(三)预鞣用酶制剂(税目 32.02);

(四)第三十四章的加酶的浸透剂、洗涤剂及其他产品;

(五)硬化蛋白(税目 39.13);

(六)印刷工业用的明胶产品(第四十九章)。

二、税目 35.05 所称"糊精",是指淀粉的降解产品,其还原糖含量以右旋糖的干重量计不超过 10%。

如果还原糖含量超过 10%,应归入税目 17.02。

Notes:

1. This Chapter does not cover:

(a) Yeasts (heading No. 21.02);

(b) Blood fractions (other than blood albumin not prepared for therapeutic or prophylactic uses), medicaments or other products of Chapter 30;

(c) Enzymatic preparations for pre-tanning (heading No. 32.02);

(d) Enzymatic soaking or washing preparations or other products of Chapter 34;

(e) Hardened proteins (heading No. 39.13); or

(f) Gelatin products of the printing industry (Chapter 49).

2. For the purposes of heading No. 35.05, the term "dextrins" means starch degradation products with a reducing sugar content, expressed as dextrose on the dry substance, not exceeding 10%.

Such products with a reducing sugar content exceeding 10% fall in heading No. 17.02.

税则号列	货品名称	最惠(%)	普通	增值税率	出口退税	计量单位	监管条件	Article Description
35.01	**酪蛋白、酪蛋白酸盐及其他酪蛋白衍生物;酪蛋白胶:**							**Casein, caseinates and other casein derivatives; casein glues:**
3501.1000	-酪蛋白	10	35	17	13	千克	AB	-Casein
3501.9000	-其他	10	35	17	13	千克	AB	-Other
35.02	**白蛋白(包括按重量计干质成分的乳清蛋白含量超过 80%的两种或两种以上的乳清蛋白浓缩物)、白蛋白盐及其他白蛋白衍生物:**							**Albumins (including concentrates of two or more whey proteins, containing by weight more than 80% whey proteins, calculated on the dry matter), albuminates and other albumin derivatives:**
	-卵清蛋白:							-Egg albumin:
3502.1100	--干的	10	80	17	13	千克	AB	--Dried
3502.1900	--其他	10	80	17	13	千克	AB	--Other
3502.2000	-乳白蛋白(包括两种或两种以上的乳清蛋白浓缩物)	10	35	17	13	千克	AB	-Milk albumin, including concentrates of two or more whey proteins
3502.9000	-其他	10	35	17	13	千克	AB	-Other
35.03	**明胶(包括长方形、正方形明胶薄片,不论是否表面加工或着色)及其衍生物;鱼鳔胶;其他动物胶,但不包括税目 35.01 的酪蛋白胶:**							**Gelatin (including gelatin in rectangular (including square) sheets, whether or not surface-worked or coloured) and gelatin derivatives; isinglass; other glues of animal origin, excluding casein glues of heading No. 35.01:**
3503.0010	---明胶及其衍生物		35	17	13	千克		---Gelatin and gelatin derivatives
3503.0010暂 01	明胶	5	35	17	13	千克	AB	Gelatin
3503.0010 90	明胶的衍生物(包括长方形、正方形明胶薄片,不论是否表面加工或着色)	12	35	17	13	千克	AB	Gelatin derivatives (including gelatin in rectangular, square sheets, whether or not surface-worked or coloured)
3503.0090	---其他	12	50	17	13	千克	AB	---Other
35.04	**蛋白胨及其衍生物;其他税目未列名的蛋白质及其衍生物;皮粉,不论是否加入铬矾:**							**Peptones and their derivatives; other protein substances and their derivatives, not elsewhere specified or included; hide powder, whether or not chromed:**
3504.0010	---蛋白胨	3	11	17	13	千克	AB	---Peptones
3504.0090	---其他	8	35	17	13	千克	AB	---Other
35.05	**糊精及其他改性淀粉(例如,预凝化淀粉或酯化淀粉);以淀粉、糊精或其他改性淀粉为基本成分的胶:**							**Dextrins and other modified starches (for example, pregelatinized or esterified starches); glues based on starches, or on dextrins or other modified starches:**

税则号列	货 品 名 称	最惠(%)	普通	增值税率	出口退税	计量单位	监管条件	Article Description
3505.1000暂	-糊精及其他改性淀粉	6	50	17	13	千克	A	-Dextrins and other modified starches
3505.2000	-胶	20	50	17	13	千克	A	-Glues
35.06	**其他税目未列名的调制胶及其他调制粘合剂;适于作胶或粘合剂用的产品,零售包装每件净重不超过1千克:**							**Prepared glues and other prepared adhesives, not elsewhere specified or included; products suitable for use as glues or adhesives, put up for retail sale as glues or adhesives, not exceeding a net weight of 1 kg:**
3506.1000	-适于作胶或粘合剂用的产品,零售包装每件净重不超过1千克	10	90	17	13	千克		-Products suitable for use as glues or adhesives, put up for retail sale as glues or adhesives, not exceeding a net weight of 1kg
3506.1000 10	硅酮结构密封胶(零售包装每件净重不超过1千克)	10	90	17	13	千克	A	Structure silicone sealant (in forms or packing for retail sale as glues or adhesives, not exceeding a net weight of 1kg)
3506.1000 90	其他适于作胶或粘合剂的零售产品(零售包装每件净重不超过1千克)	10	90	17	13	千克		Other-products suitable for use as glues or adhesives, in forms or packing for retail sale as glues or adhesives, not exceeding a net weight of 1kg
	-其他:							-Other:
	--以橡胶或税目39.01至39.13的聚合物为基本成分的粘合剂:							--Adhesives based on polymers of headings Nos. 39.01 to 39.13 or on rubber:
3506.9110	---以聚酰胺为基本成分的	10	90	17	13	千克		---Based on polyamide
3506.9120	---以环氧树脂为基本成分的	10	90	17	13	千克		---Based on epoxy resin
3506.9190	---其他	10	90	17	13	千克		---Other
3506.9190 10	非零售,硅酮结构密封胶	10	90	17	13	千克	A	Structure silicone sealant, not in forms or packing for retail sale
3506.9190 90	其他橡胶或塑料为基本成分粘合剂[包括以人造树脂(环氧树脂除外)为基本成分的]	10	90	17	13	千克		Other adhesives based on rubber or plastic including [artificial resin (other than epoxy resin)]
3506.9900	--其他	10	90	17	13	千克		--Other
35.07	**酶;其他税目未列名的酶制品:**							**Enzymes; prepared enzymes not elsewhere specified or included:**
3507.1000	-粗制凝乳酶及其浓缩物	6	30	17	13	千克	AB	-Rennet and concentrates thereof
	-其他:							-Other:
3507.9010	---碱性蛋白酶	6	30	17	13	千克	AB	---Basic proteinase
3507.9020	---碱性脂肪酶	6	30	17	13	千克	AB	---Basic lipase
3507.9090	---其他	6	30	17	13	千克	AB	---Other

第三十六章
炸药;烟火制品;火柴;引火合金;易燃材料制品

Chapter 36
Explosives; pyrotechnic products; matches; pyrophoric alloys; certain combustible preparations

注释:

一、本章不包括单独的已有化学定义的化合物,但下列注释二(一)、(二)所述物品除外。

二、税目36.06所称"易燃材料制品",只适用于:

(一)聚乙醛、六甲撑四胺及类似物质,已制成片、棒或类似形状作燃料用的;以酒精为基本成分的固体或半固体燃料及类似的配制燃料;

(二)直接灌注香烟打火机及类似打火器用的液体燃料或液化气体燃料,其包装容器的容积不超过300立方厘米;

(三)树脂火炬、引火物及类似品。

Notes:

1. This Chapter does not cover separate chemically defined compounds other than those described in Note 2 (a) or (b) below.
2. The expression "articles of combustible materials" in heading No. 36.06 applies only to:

(a) Metaldehyde, hexamethylenetetramine and similar substances, put up in forms (for example, tablets, sticks or similar forms) for use as fuels; fuels with a basis of alcohol, and similar prepared fuels, in solid or semi-solid form;

(b) Liquid or liquefied-gas fuels in containers of a kind used for filling or refilling cigarette or similar lighters and of a capacity not exceeding 300 cm^3;

(c) Resin torches, firelighters and the like.

税则号列	货品名称	最惠(%)	普通	增值税率	出口退税	计量单位	监管条件	Article Description
36.01	**发射药:**							**Propellent powders:**
3601.0000	发射药	9	50	17		千克		Propellent powders
3601.0000 10	模压的胶质推进剂	9	50	17		千克	3	Colloidal propellant, molded
3601.0000 20	含硝化粘接剂及铝粉>5%的推进剂	9	50	17		千克	3	Propellant, containing cementing agent and aluminum powder >5%
3601.0000 90	其他发射药	9	50	17		千克		Other propellent powders
36.02	**配制炸药,但发射药除外:**							**Prepared explosives, other than propellent powders:**
3602.0010	---硝铵炸药	9	50	17		千克		---Based on ammonals nitrate
3602.0010 10	符合特定标准的硝胺炸药(硝胺类物质超过2%,或密度>1.8g/cm^3、爆速>8000m/s)	9	50	17		千克	3	Meet specific standared of ammonium nitrate exploseives(containing of ammonium nitrate >2%,density >1.8g/cm^3,explodingvelocity >8000m/s)
3602.0010 90	其他硝铵炸药,但发射药除外	9	50	17		千克		Other ammonium nitrate explosives, other than propellent powders
3602.0090	---其他	9	50	17		千克		---Other
3602.0090 10	符合特定标准的其他配制炸药(含六硝基芪>2%,或密度>1.8g/cm^3、爆速>8000m/s)	9	50	17		千克	3	Meet specific standared of explosives (containing hexanitrostilbene >2%, density >1.8g/cm^3, exploding velocity >8000m/s)
3602.0090 90	其他配制炸药,但发射药除外	9	50	17		千克		Other prepared explosives, other than propellent powders
36.03	**安全导火索;导爆索;火帽或雷管;引爆器;电雷管:**							**Safety fuses; detonating fuses; percussion or detonating caps; igniters; electric detonators:**
3603.0000	安全导火索;导爆索;火帽或雷管;引爆器;电雷管	9	50	17		千克		Safety fuses; detonating fuses; percussion or detonating caps; igniters; electric detonators
3603.0000 10	爆炸桥	9	50	17		千克	3	Detonating bridge
3603.0000 20	爆炸桥丝	9	50	17		千克	3	Detonating bridge filaments
3603.0000 30	冲击片	9	50	17		千克	3	Percussion cap
3603.0000 40	爆炸箔起爆器	9	50	17		千克	3	Detonating foil igniter
3603.0000 50	使用单个或多个雷管的装置(由单一点火信号同时起爆,不包括仅使用起药的雷管)	9	50	17		千克	3	Devices with one or more detonator (detonated by one electric firing signal at the same time, other than those used detonating powder only)

税则号列	货品名称	最惠(%)	普通	增值税率	出口退税	计量单位	监管条件	Article Description
3603.0000 60	炸药雷管点火装置(用于引爆上述税目3603各子目列名的爆炸配件的雷管)	9	50	17		千克	3	Explosive detonator ignition (for igniting detonators assembled with parts of subheadings of heading NO. 3603)
3603.0000 90	其他安全导火索导爆索等引爆器件(包括火帽或雷管、引爆器、电雷管)	9	50	17		千克		Other safety fuses; detonating fuses; percussion or detonating caps; igniters; electric detonators
36.04	**烟花、爆竹、信号弹、降雨火箭、浓雾信号弹及其他烟火制品:**							**Fireworks, signalling flares, rain rockets, fog signals and other pyrotechnic articles:**
3604.1000	-烟花、爆竹	6	130	17	13	千克	AB	-Fireworks
3604.9000	-其他	6	100	17	13	千克		-Other
36.05	**火柴,但税目36.04的烟火制品除外:**							**Matches, other than pyrotechnic articles of heading No. 36.04:**
3605.0000	火柴,但税目36.04的烟火制品除外	6	100	17		千克	AB	Matches, other than pyrotechnic articles of heading No. 36.04
36.06	**各种形状的铈铁及其他引火合金;本章注释二所述的易燃材料制品:**							**Ferro-cerium and other pyrophoric alloys in all forms; articles of combustible materials as specified in Note 2 to this Chapter:**
3606.1000	-直接灌注香烟打火机及类似打火器用的液体燃料或液化气体燃料,其包装容器的容积不超过300立方厘米	10	80	17		千克		-Liquid or liquefied-gas fuels in containers of a kind used for filling or refilling cigarette or similar lighters and of a capacity not exceeding 300 cm^3
	--其他:							--Other:
	---铈铁及其他引火合金:							---Ferro-cerium and other pyrophoric alloys:
3606.9011	----已切成形可直接使用	9	80	17		千克		----Cut to shape, for immediate use
3606.9019	----其他	9	50	17		千克		----Other
3606.9090	---其他	9	80	17		千克		---Other

第三十七章
照相及电影用品

Chapter 37
Photographic or cinematographic goods

注释：

一、本章不包括废碎料。

二、本章所称"摄影"，是指光或其他射线作用于感光面上直接或间接形成可见影像的过程。

Chapter Notes:

1. This Chapter does not cover waste or scrap.
2. In this Chapter the word "photographic" relates to the process by which visible images are formed, directly or indirectly, by the action of light or other forms of radiation on photosensitive surfaces.

税则号列	货品名称	最惠(%)	普通	增值税率	出口退税	计量单位	监管条件	Article Description
37.01	**未曝光的摄影感光硬片及平面软片，用纸、纸板及纺织物以外任何材料制成；未曝光的一次成像感光平片，不论是否分装：**							**Photographic plates and film in the flat, sensitized, unexposed, of any material other than paper, paperboard or textiles; instant print film in the flat, sensitized, unexposed, whether or not in packs:**
3701.1000暂	-X 光用	10	40	17	13	千克/平方米		-For X-ray
3701.2000	-一次成像平片	5	40	17	13	千克		-Instant print film
	-其他硬片及软片，任何一边超过 255 毫米：							-Other plates and film, with any side exceeding 255 mm:
	---照相制版用：							---For preparing printing plates or cylinders:
3701.3021	----激光照排片	10	50	17	13	千克/平方米		----Laser phototypesetting film
3701.3022	----PS 版	10	50	17	13	千克/平方米		----Precoated sensitized plate
3701.3024	----CTP 版	10	50	17	13	千克/平方米		----CTP plate
3701.3025暂	----柔性印刷板	5	50	17	13	千克/平方米		----Flexible printed board
3701.3025暂 10	柔性印刷版（厚度<3 毫米的）（任何一边>255 毫米）	5	50	17		千克/平方米		Flexible printing plate (thickness <3 mm) (any side of > 255 mm)
3701.3025 90	其他柔性印刷版（任何一边>255 毫米）	10	50	17		千克/平方米		Other flexible printed version (either side of > 255 mm)
3701.3029	----其他	10	50	17	13	千克/平方米		----Other
3701.3090	---其他	20	70	17	13	千克/平方米		---Other
	-其他：							-Other:
3701.9100	--彩色摄影用	22	70	17	13	千克		--For colour photography (polychrome)
	--其他：							--Other:
3701.9920	---照相制版用		40	17	13	千克/平方米		---For preparing printing plates or cylinders
3701.9920暂 01	石英玻璃基质的未曝光感光硬片	5	40	17	13	千克/平方米		Quartz glass matrix of photographic film, unexposed
3701.9920 10	超微粒干版	10	40	17	13	千克/平方米		Ultrtafine-grain plate
3701.9920 90	照相制版用其他未曝光软片及硬片（非彩色摄影用，边长≤255mm）	10	40	17	13	千克/平方米		Other photographic plates and film in the flat sensitized for preparing printing plates or cylinders, with any side ≤ 255mm, (other than ultrtafine-grain plate, other than for colour photography)
3701.9990	---其他	25	70	17	13	千克/平方米		---Other
37.02	**成卷的未曝光摄影感光胶片，用纸、纸板及纺织物以外任何材料制成；未曝光的一次成像感光卷片：**							**Photographic film in rolls, sensitized, unexposed, of any material other than paper, paperboard or textiles; instant print film in rolls, sensitized, unexposed:**
3702.1000	-X 光用	10	40	17	13	千克/平方米		-For X-ray
	-无齿孔的其他胶片，宽度不超过 105 毫米：							-Other film, without perforations, of a width not exceeding 105 mm:
	--彩色摄影用：							--For colour photography (polychrome):
3702.3110	---一次成像卷片	5	40	17	13	个/平方米		---Instant print film
3702.3190	---其他	T3	T3	17	13	个/平方米		---Other
	--其他涂卤化银乳液的：							--Other, with silver halide emulsion:
3702.3210	---一次成像卷片	5	40	17	13	千克/平方米		---Instant print film
3702.3220	---照相制版用	T2	T2	17	13	千克/平方米		---For preparing printing plates or cylinders
3702.3290	---其他	T2	T2	17	13	千克/平方米		---Other
	--其他：							--Other:
3702.3920	---照相制版用	T2	T2	17	13	千克/平方米		---For preparing printing plates or cylinders
3702.3990	---其他	T2	T2	17	13	千克/平方米		---Other
	-无齿孔的其他胶片，宽度超过 105 毫米：							-Other film, without perforations, of a width exceeding 105 mm:
3702.4100	--彩色摄影用，宽度超过 610 毫米，长度超过 200 米	T3	T3	17	13	千克/平方米		--Of a width exceeding 610 mm and of a length exceeding 200 m, for colour photography (polychrome)

税则号列	货品名称	最惠(%)	普通	增值税率	出口退税	计量单位	监管条件	Article Description
	--非彩色摄影用,宽度超过610毫米,长度超过200米:							--Of a width exceeding 610 mm and of a length exceeding 200 m, other than for colour photography:
	---照相制版用:							---For preparing printing plates or cylinders:
3702.4221	----印刷电路板制造用光致抗蚀干膜	T2	T2	17	13	千克/平方米		----Wide anticorrosive photographic plate for printed circuit processing
3702.4229	----其他	T2	T2	17	13	千克/平方米		----Other
	---其他:							---Other:
3702.4292	----红色或红外激光胶片		T2	17	13	千克/平方米		----Red or infra-red laser film
3702.4292暂 01	未曝光红色或红外激光胶片(宽长胶卷指宽度>800mm,长度>1000m)	①	T2	17	13	千克/平方米		Red or infra－red laser film, unexposed, of a width >800mm, of a length >1000m,
3702.4292 90	其他未曝光红色或红外激光胶片(610mm<宽度≤800mm,200m<长度≤1000m)	T2	T2	17	13	千克/平方米		Other red or infra－red laser film, unexposed, 610mm< width≤800mm, 200m<length≤1001m,
3702.4299	----其他	T2	T2	17	13	千克/平方米		----Other
	--宽度超过610毫米,长度不超过200米:							--Of a width exceeding 610 mm and of a length not exceeding 200 m:
	---照相制版用:							---For preparing printing plates or cylinders:
3702.4321	----激光照排片	T2	T2	17	13	千克/平方米		----Laser phototypesetting film
3702.4329	----其他	T2	T2	17	13	千克/平方米		----Other
3702.4390	---其他	T2	T2	17	13	千克/平方米		---Other
	--宽度超过105毫米,但不超过610毫米:							--Of a width exceeding 105 mm but not exceeding 610 mm:
	---照相制版用:							---For preparing printing plates or cylinders:
3702.4421	----激光照排片	T2	T2	17	13	千克/平方米		----Laser phototypesetting film
3702.4422	----印刷电路板制造用光致抗蚀干膜	T2	T2	17	13	千克/平方米		----Narrow anticorrosive photographic plate for printed circuit processing
3702.4429	----其他	T2	T2	17	13	千克/平方米		----Other
3702.4490	---其他	T2	T2	17	13	千克/平方米		---Other
	-彩色摄影用的其他胶片:							-Other film, for colour photography (polychrome):
3702.5200	--宽度不超过16毫米,长度超过14m	T2	T2	17	13	米/平方米		--Of a width not exceeding 16 mm, and of lengh exceeding 14mm
3702.5300	--幻灯片用,宽度超过16毫米,但不超过35毫米,长度不超过30米	T2	T2	17	13	米/平方米		--Of a width exceeding 16 mm but not exceeding 35 mm and of a length not exceeding 30 m, for slides
	--非幻灯片用,宽度超过16毫米,但不超过35毫米,长度不超过30米:							--Of a width exceeding 16 mm but not exceeding 35 mm and of a length not exceeding 30 m, other than for slides:
3702.5410	---宽度为35毫米,长度不超过2米	T2	T2	17	13	米/平方米		---Of a width 35 mm and of a length not exceeding 2 m
3702.5490	---其他	T2	T2	17	13	米/平方米		---Other
	--宽度超过16毫米,但不超过35毫米,长度超过30米:							--Of a width exceeding 16 mm but not exceeding 35 mm and of a length exceeding 30 m:
3702.5520	---电影胶片	②	T2	17	13	米/平方米		---Cinematographic film
3702.5590	---其他	T2	T2	17	13	米/平方米		---Other
	--宽度超过35毫米:							--Of a width exceeding 35 mm:
3702.5620	---电影胶片	T2	T2	17	13	米/平方米		---Cinematographic film
3702.5690	---其他	T2	T2	17	13	米/平方米		---Other
	-其他:							-Other:
3702.9600	--宽度不超过35毫米,长度不超过30米	T2	T2	17	13	米/平方米		--Of a width not exceeding 35 mm and of a length not exceeding 30 mm
3702.9700	--宽度不超过35毫米,长度超过30米	T2	T2	17	13	米/平方米		--Of a width not exceeding 35 mm and of a length exceeding 30 mm
3702.9800	--宽度超过35毫米	T2	T2	17	13	米/平方米		--Of a width exceeding 35 mm
37.03	未曝光的摄影感光纸、纸板及纺织物:							**Photographic paper, paperboard and textiles, sensitized, unexposed:**
	-成卷,宽度超过610毫米:							-In rolls of a width exceeding 610 mm:
3703.1010	---感光纸及纸板	18	100	17	13	千克		---Photographic paper and paperboard

① 3702.4292 01 暂定税率为:1.05元/平方米。

② 3702.5520 暂定税率为:9元/平方米。

税则号列	货　品　名　称	最惠(%)	普通	增值税率	出口退税	计量单位	监管条件	Article Description
3703.1090	---其他	18	70	17	13	千克		---Other
	-其他，彩色摄影用：							-Other, for colour photography (polychrome):
3703.2010	---感光纸及纸板	35	100	17	13	千克		---Photographic paper and paperboard
3703.2090	---其他	18	70	17	13	千克		---Other
	-其他：							-Other:
3703.9010	---感光纸及纸板	35	100	17	13	千克		---Photographic paper and paperboard
3703.9090	---其他	18	70	17	13	千克		---Other
37.04	**已曝光未冲洗的摄影硬片、软片、纸、纸板及纺织物：**							**Photographic plates, film, paper, paperboard and textiles, exposed but not developed:**
3704.0010	---电影胶片	6.5	30	17	13	千克	Z	---Cinematographic film
3704.0090	---其他	18	70	17	13	千克		---Other
37.05	**已曝光已冲洗的摄影硬片及软片，但电影胶片除外：**							**Photographic plates and film, exposed and developed, other than cinematographic film:**
3705.1000	-供复制胶版用	18	70	17	13	千克		-For offset reproduction
	-其他：							-Other:
3705.9010	---教学专用幻灯片	0	0	17	13	千克		---Lantern slides, for educational use only
	---缩微胶片：							---Mictofilms:
3705.9021	----书籍、报刊的	0	0	17	13	千克		----For printed books and newspapers
3705.9029	----其他	4	14	17	13	千克		----Other
3705.9090	---其他	18	70	17	13	千克		---Other
37.06	**已曝光已冲洗的电影胶片，不论是否配有声道或仅有声道：**							**Cinematographic film, exposed and developed, whether or not incorporating sound track or consisting only of sound track:**
	-宽度在35毫米及以上：							-Of a width of 35 mm or more:
3706.1010	---教学专用	0	0	17	13	千克/米	Z	---For educational use only
3706.1090	---其他	5	14	17	13	千克/米	Z	---Other
	-其他：							-Other:
3706.9010	---教学专用	0	0	17	13	千克/米	Z	---For educational use only
3706.9090	---其他	4	14	17	13	千克/米	Z	---Other
37.07	**摄影用化学制剂（不包括上光漆、胶水、粘合剂及类似制剂）；摄影用未混合产品；定量包装或零售包装可立即使用的：**							**Chemical preparations for photographic uses (other than varnishes, glues, adhesives and similar preparations); unmixed products for photographic uses, put up in measured portions or put up for retail sale in a form ready for use:**
3707.1000	-感光乳液		35	17	13	千克		-Sensitizing emulsions
3707.1000暂 01	不含银的感光乳液剂	4	35	17	13	千克		Sensitizing emulsions agent, not containing silver
3707.1000 90	其他感光乳液	8	35	17	13	千克		Other sensitizing emulsions
	-其他：							-Other:
3707.9010	---冲洗照相胶卷及相片用	16	100	17	13	千克		---For use in developing photographic film and photographs
3707.9020暂	---复印机用	8	45	17	13	千克		---For use in photo-copying apparatus
3707.9090	---其他	8	35	17	13	千克		---Other

第三十八章
杂项化学产品

注释：

一、本章不包括：

（一）单独的已有化学定义的元素及化合物，但下列各项除外：

1. 人造石墨(税目 38.01)；
2. 制成税目 38.08 所述的形状或包装的杀虫剂、杀鼠剂、杀菌剂、除草剂、抗萌剂、植物生长调节剂、消毒剂及类似产品；
3. 灭火器的装配药及已装药的灭火弹(税目 38.13)；
4. 下列注释二所规定的检定参照物；
5. 下列注释三(一)及三(三)所规定的产品。

（二）配制食品用的与食物或其他营养物质混合的化学品，一般归入税目 21.06)。

（三）符合第二十六章注释三(一)或三(二)的规定，含有金属，砷及其混合物的矿渣、矿灰及残渣(包括淤渣，但下水道淤泥除外)(税目 26.20)；

（四）药品(税目 30.03 及 30.04)。

（五）用于提取贱金属或生产贱金属化合物的废催化剂(税目 26.20)，主要用于回收贵金属的废催化剂(税目 71.12)，或某种形状(例如，精细粉末或纱网状)的金属或金属合金催化剂(第十四类或第十五类)。

二、（一）税目 38.22 所称的“检定参照物”，是指附有证书的参照物，该证书标明了参照物属性的指标、确定这些指标的方法以及与每一指标相关的确定度，这些参照物适用于分析、校准和比较。

（二）除第二十八章和二十九章的产品外，检定参照物在本目录中应优先归入税目 38.22。

三、税目 38.24 包括不归入本协调制度其他品目的下列货品：

（一）每颗重量不小于 2.5 克的氧化镁、碱金属或碱土金属卤化物制成的培养晶体(光学元件除外)；

（二）杂醇油；骨焦油；

（三）零售包装的除墨剂；

（四）零售包装的蜡纸改正液、其他改正液及改正带(税目 96.12 的产品除外)；

（五）可熔性陶瓷测温器(例如，塞格测温锥)。

四、本目录所称“城市垃圾”，是指一种从家庭、宾馆、餐馆、医院、商店、办公室等收集来的废物、马路和人行道的垃圾以及建筑垃圾或废墟废物。城市垃圾通常含有大量各种各样的材料，例如，塑料、橡胶、木材、纸张、纺织品、玻璃、金属、食物、破碎家具和其他已损坏或被丢弃的物品，但不包括：

Chapter 38
Miscellaneous chemical products

Notes:

1. This Chapter does not cover:

(a) Separate chemically defined elements or compounds with the exception of the following:

(1) Artificial graphite (heading No. 38.01);

(2) Insecticides, rodenticides, fungicides, herbicides, anti-sprouting products and plant-growth regulators, disinfectants and similar products, put up as described in heading No. 38.08;

(3) Products put up as charges for fire-extinguishers or put up in fire-extinguishing grenades (heading No. 38.13);

(4) Certified reference materials specified in Note 2 below;

(5) Products specified in Note 3(a) or 3(c) below.

(b) Mixtures of chemicals with foodstuffs or other substances with nutritive value, of a kind used in the preparations of human foodstuffs (generally heading No. 21.06).

(c) Slag, ash and residues (including sludges, other than sewage sludge), containing metals, arsenic or their mixtures and meeting the requirements of Note 3(a) or (b) to Chapter 26 (heading No. 26.20).

(d) Medicaments (heading No. 30.03 or 30.04). or

(e) Spent catalysts of a kind used for the extraction of base metals or for the manufacture of chemical compounds of base metals (heading No. 26.20), spent catalysts of a kind used principally for the recovery of precious metal (heading No. 71.12) or catalysts consisting of metals or metal alloys in the form of, for example, finely divided powder or woven gauze (Section XIV or XV).

2. (a) For the purpose of heading No. 38.22, the expression “certified reference materials” means reference materials which are accompanied by a certificate which indicates the values of the certified properties, the methods used to detemine these values and the degree of certainty associated with each value and which are suitable for analytical, calibrating or referencing purposes.

(b) With the exception of the products of Chapter 28 or 29, for the classification of certified reference materials, heading No. 38.22 shall take precedence over any other heading in the Nomenclature.

3. Heading No. 38.24 includes the following goods which are not to be classified in any other heading of the Nomenclature:

(a) Cultured crystals (other than optical elements) weighing not less than 2.5 g each, of magnesium oxide or of the halides of the alkali or alkaline-earth metals;

(b) Fusel oil; Dippel's oil;

(c) Ink removers put up in packings for retail sale;

(d) Stencil correctors, other correcting fluids and correction tape, put up in packings for retail sale (other than those of heading, 96.12);

(e) Ceramic firing testers, fusible (for example, Seger cones).

4. Throughout the Nomenclature, “municipal waste” means waste of a kind collected from households, hotels, restaurants, hospitals, shops, offices, etc., road and pavement sweepings, as well as construction and demolition waste. Municipal waste generally contains a large variety of materials such as plastics, rubber, wood, paper, textiles, glass, metals, food materials, broken furniture and other damaged or discarded articles. The term “municipal waste”, however, does not cover:

（一）已从垃圾中分拣出来的单独的材料或物品，例如，塑料、橡胶、木材、纸张、纺织品、玻璃、金属的废品及用尽的电池，这些材料或物品应归入本目录中适当税目；

（二）工业废物；

（三）在第三十章注释四（十）所规定的废药物；

（四）本章注释六（一）所规定的医疗废物。

五、税目 38.25 所称"下水道淤泥"，是指城市污水处理厂产生的淤渣，包括预处理的废物、洗涤污垢和性质不稳定的淤泥。但适合作为肥料用的性质稳定的淤泥除外（第三十一章）。

六、税目 38.25 所称"其他废物"适用于：

（一）医疗废物，即医学研究、诊断、治疗以及其他内科、外科、牙科或兽医治疗所产生的被污染的废物，通常含有病菌和药物，需作专门处理（例如，脏的敷料、用过的手套及注射器）；

（二）废有机溶剂；

（三）废的金属酸洗液、液压油、制动油及防冻液；

（四）其他化学工业及相关工业的废物。

但不包括主要含有石油及从沥青矿物提取的油类的废油（税目 27.10）。

七、税目 38.26 所称的"生物柴油"是指从动植物油脂（不论是否使用过）得到的用作燃料的脂肪酸单烷基酯。

子目注释：

一、子目 3808.50 仅包括税目 38.08 的货品，含有一种或多种下列物质：艾氏剂（ISO）；乐杀螨（ISO）；毒杀芬（ISO）；敌菌丹（ISO）；氯丹（ISO）；杀虫脒（ISO）；乙酯杀螨醇（ISO）；滴滴涕（ISO，INN）[1，1，1－三氯－2，2－双（4 氯苯基）乙烷]；狄氏剂（ISO，INN）；4，6-二硝基邻甲酚[二硝酚（ISO）]及其盐；地乐酚（ISO）及其盐或酯；1，2－二溴乙烷（ISO）；1，2－二氯乙烷（ISO）；氯乙酰胺（ISO）；七氯（ISO）；六氯苯（ISO）；1，2，3，4，5，6－六氯环己烷[六六六（ISO）]，包括林丹（ISO，INN）；汞化合物；甲胺磷（ISO）；久效磷（ISO）；环氧乙烷（氧化乙烯）；对硫磷（ISO）；甲基对硫磷（ISO）；五氯苯酚（ISO）及其盐或酯；磷胺（ISO）；2，4，5－涕（ISO）（2，4，5－三氯苯氧基乙酸）及其盐或酯汀三丁基锡化合物。

子目 3808.50 还包括含有苯菌录（ISO）、克百威（ISO）及福美双（ISO）混合物的粉状制剂。

二、子目 3825.41 和 3825.49 所称"废有机溶剂"，是指主要含有机溶剂的废物，不适合再作原产品使用，不论其是否用于回收溶剂。

(a) Individual materials or articles segregated from the waste, such as wastes of plastics, rubber, wood, paper, textiles, glass or metals and spent batteries which fall in their appropriate headings of the Nomenclature;

(b) Industrial waste;

(c) Waste pharmaceuticals, as defined in Note 4(k) to Chapter 30; or

(d) Clinical waste, as defined in Note 6 (a) below.

5. For the purposes of heading 38.25, "sewage sludge" means sludge arising from urban effluent treatment plant and includes pretreatment waste, scourings and unstabilised sludge. Stabilised sludge when suitable for use as fertiliser is excluded (Chapter 31).

6. For the purposes of heading No. 38.25, the expression "other wastes" applies to:

(a) Clinical waste, that is, contaminated waste arising from medical research, diagnosis, treatment or other medical, surgical, dental or veterinary procedures, which often contain pathogens and pharmaceutical substances and require special disposal procedures (for example, soiled dressings, used gloves and used syringes);

(b) Waste organic solvents;

(c) Wastes of metal pickling liquors, hydraulic fluids, brake fluids and anti-freezing fluids; and

(d) Other wastes from chemical or allied industries.

The expression "other wastes" does not, however, cover wastes which contain mainly petroleum oils or oils obtained from bituminous minerals (heading No. 27.10).

7. For the purposes of heading 38.26, the term "biodiesel" means mono－alkyl esters of fatty acids of a kind used ao a fuel, derived from animal or vegetable fats and oils whether or not used

Subheading Note:

1. Subheading No. 3808.50 covers only goods of heading No. 38.08, containing one or more of the following substances: aldrin (ISO); binapacryl (ISO); camphechlor (ISO) (toxaphene); captafol (ISO); chlordane (ISO); chlordimeform (ISO); chlorobenzilate (ISO); DDT (ISO) (clofenotane (INN), 1,1,1－trichloro－2,2－bis (pchlorophenyl) ethane); dieldrin (ISO, INN); 4,6-Dinitro-o-cresol [acetochlor (ISO)] and its salts and its esters; dinoseb (ISO), its salts or its esters; ethylene dibromide (ISO) (1,2－dibromoethane); ethylene dichloride (ISO) (1,2－dichloroethane); fluoroacetamide (ISO); heptachlor (ISO); hexachlorobenzene (ISO); 1,2,3,4,5,6－hexachlorocyclohexane (HCH (ISO)), including lindane (ISO, INN); mercury compounds; methamidophos (ISO); monocrotophos (ISO); oxirane (ethylene oxide) parathion (ISO); parathion－methyl (ISO) (methylparathion) and its salts and its essters; pentachlorophenol (ISO); phosphamidon (ISO); 2,4,5－T (ISO) (2,4,5-trichlorophenoxyaceticacid), its salts or its esters; Tributyl stannane compounds.

Subheading 3808.50 also covers dustable powder formulations containing a mixture of benomyl (ISO), carbofuran (ISO) and thiram (ISO)

2. For the purposes of subheadings No. 3825.41 and 3825.49, "waste organic solvents" are wastes containing mainly organic solvents, not fit for further use as presented as primary products, whether or not intended for recovery of the solvents.

税则号列	货品名称	最惠(%)	普通	增值税率	出口退税	计量单位	监管条件	Article Description
38.01	人造石墨；胶态或半胶态石墨；以石墨或其他碳为基本成分的糊状、块状、板状制品或半制品：							**Artificial graphite; colloidal or semi-colloidal graphite; preparations based on graphite or other carbon in the form of pastes, blocks, plates or other semi-manufactures:**
3801.1000暂	-人造石墨	3	30	17		千克		-Artificial graphite
3801.1000暂 10	核级石墨(纯度高于百万分之五硼当量，密度大于1.50g/cm³)	3	30	17		千克	3	Nuclear graphite (purity > 5/million boron equivalent, density > 1.50g/cm³)
3801.1000暂 20	人造细晶粒整体石墨(20℃下的密度、拉伸断裂应变、热膨胀系数符合特殊要求)	3	30	17		千克	3	Artificial fine - grainedgraphite (density, temsile fracture strain, coefficient of thermal expansion in line with specific requirements at 20℃ or below)
3801.1000暂 90	其他人造石墨	3	30	17		千克	3	Other artificial graphite
3801.2000	-胶态或半胶态石墨	6.5	30	17		千克		-Colloidal or semi-colloidal graphite
3801.3000	-电极用碳糊及炉衬用的类似糊	6.5	35	17		千克		-Carbonaceous pastes for electrodes and similar pastes for furnace linings
	-其他:							-Other:
3801.9010	---表面处理的球化石墨	6.5	35	17		千克	3	---Surface treatment of spherical graphite
3801.9090	---其他	6.5	35	17		千克	3	---Other
38.02	**活性碳；活性天然矿产品；动物炭黑，包括废动物炭黑：**							**Activated carbon; activated natural mineral products; animal black, including spent animal black:**
	-活性碳:							-Activated carbon:
3802.1010	---木质的	6.5	20	17		千克	G	---Of wood.
3802.1090	---其他	6.5	20	17		千克	ABG	---Other
3802.9000	-其他	10	45	17		千克		-Other
3802.9000 10	濒危动物炭黑(包括废动物炭黑)	10	45	17		千克	FE	Endangered animals black (including spent animal black)
3802.9000 90	活性天然矿产品；其他动物炭黑(包括废动物炭黑)	10	45	17		千克		Activated natural mineral products; other animal black (including spent animal black)
38.03	**妥尔油，不论是否精炼：**							**Tall oil, whether or not refined:**
3803.0000	妥尔油，不论是否精炼	6.5	35	17		千克		Tall oil, whether or not refined
38.04	**木浆残余碱液，不论是否浓缩、脱糖或经化学处理，包括木素磺酸盐，但不包括税号38.03的妥尔油：**							**Residual lyes from the manufacture of wood pulp, whether or not concentrated, desugared or chemically treated, including lignin sulphonates, but excluding tall oil of heading No. 38.03:**
3804.0000	木浆残余碱液，不论是否浓缩、脱糖或经化学处理，包括木素磺酸盐，但不包括税目38.03的妥尔油	6.5	35	17		千克		Residual lyes from the manufacture of wood pulp, whether or not concentrated, desugared or chemically treated, including lignin sulphonates, but excluding tall oil of heading No. 38.03
3804.0000 10	未经浓缩、脱糖或经过化学处理的木浆残余碱液(妥尔油除外)	6.5	35	17		千克	9	Residual lyes from the manufactare of wood pulp, non-concentrated, non-desugared or non-chemically treated (exincluding tall oil)
3804.0000 90	经浓缩、脱糖或经过化学处理的木浆残余碱液，包括木素磺酸盐(妥尔油除外)	6.5	35	17		千克		Residual lyes from the manufacture of wood pulp, concentrated, desugared or chemically treated, including lignin Sulp-honates (excluding tall oil)
38.05	**脂松节油、木松节油和硫酸盐松节油及其他萜烯油，用蒸馏或其他方法从针叶木制得；粗制二聚戊烯；亚硫酸盐松节油及其他粗制对异丙基苯甲烷；以α萜品醇为基本成分的松油：**							**Gum, wood or sulphate turpentine and other terpenic oils produced by the distillation or other treatment of coniferous woods; crude dipentene; sulphite turpentine and other crude paracymene; pine oil containing alpha-terpineol as the main constituent:**
3805.1000	-脂松节油、木松节油和硫酸盐松节油	6.5	50	17		千克	AB	-Gum, wood or sulphate turpentine oils
	-其他:							-Other:
3805.9010	---松油	6.5	50	17		千克	AB	---Pine oil
3805.9090	---其他	6.5	50	17		千克		---Other
38.06	**松香和树脂酸及其衍生物；松香精及松香油；再熔胶：**							**Rosin and resin acids, and derivatives thereof; rosin spirit and rosin oils; run gums:**
	-松香及树脂酸:							-Rosin and resin acids:
3806.1010	---松香	10	70	17		千克		---Rosin
3806.1020	---树脂酸	10	70	17		千克		---Resin acides

税则号列	货品名称	最惠(%)	普通	增值税率	出口退税	计量单位	监管条件	Article Description
	-松香盐、树脂酸盐及松香或树脂酸衍生物的盐,但松香加合物的盐除外:							-Salts of rosin, of resin acids or of derivatives of rosin or resin acids, other than salts of rosin adducts:
3806.2010	---松香盐及树脂酸盐	6.5	40	17	13	千克		---Salts of rosin, of resin acids
3806.2090	---其他	6.5	40	17	13	千克		---Other
3806.3000	-酯胶	6.5	50	17		千克	AB	-Ester gums
3806.9000	-其他	6.5	40	17		千克		-Other
3806.9000 10	歧化松香及松香衍生物	6.5	40	17		千克		Disproportionated rosin and its derivatives
3806.9000 90	其他松香及树脂酸衍生物(包括松香精及松香油;再熔胶)	6.5	40	17		千克		Other rosin and resin acids, and derivatives thereof; (ircluding rosin spirit and rosin oils; run gums)
38.07	**木焦油;精制木焦油;木杂酚油;粗木精;植物沥青;以松香、树脂酸或植物沥青为基本成分的啤酒桶沥青及类似制品:**							**Wood tar; wood tar oils; wood creosote; wood naphtha; vegetable pitch; brewers pitch and similar preparations based on rosin, resin acids or on vegetable pitch:**
3807.0000	木焦油;精制木焦油;木杂酚油;粗木精;植物沥青;以松香、树脂酸或植物沥青为基本成分的啤酒桶沥青及类似制品	6.5	35	17		千克		Wood tar; wood tar oils; wood creosote; wood naphtha; vegetable pitch; brewers' pitch and similar preparations based on rosin, resin acids or on vegetable pitch
38.08	**杀虫剂、杀鼠剂、杀菌剂、除草剂、抗萌剂、植物生长调节剂、消毒剂及类似产品,零售形状、零售包装或制成制剂及成品(例如,经硫磺处理的带子、杀虫灯芯、蜡烛及捕蝇纸):**							**Insecticides, rodenticides, fungicides, herbicides, anti-sprouting products and plantgrowth regulators, disinfectants and similar products, put up in forms or packings for retail sale or as preparations or articles (for example, sulphur-treated bands, wicks and candies, and fly-papers):**
	-本章子目注释一所规定的货品:							-Goods specified in subheading Note 1 to this Chapter:
3808.5010	---零售包装	9	35	13	5	千克		---Put up for retail sale
3808.5010 10	零售包装的含有一种第38章子目注释一所列物质的货品	9	35	13	5	千克	S	Including a kind of the substances specified of subsatances specified in subheading note 1 to Chapter 38, put up for retail sale
3808.5010 90	零售包装含有多种第38章子目注释一所列物质的货品	9	35	13	5	千克	X	Including all kind of the substances specified of subsatances specified in subheading note 1 to Chapter 38, put up for retail sale
3808.5090	---其他	5	11	13	5	千克		---Other
3808.5090 10	非零售包装的含有一种第38章子目注释一所列物质的货品	5	11	13	5	千克	S	Including a kind of the substances specified of subsatances specified in subheading note 1 to Chapter 38, not put up for retail sale
3808.5090 90	非零售包装含有多种第38章子目注释一所列物质的货品	5	11	13	5	千克	X	Including all kind of the substances specified of subsatances specified in subheading note 1 to Chapter 38, not put up for retail sale
	-其他:							-Other:
	--杀虫剂:							--Insecticides:
	---零售包装:							---Put up for retail sale:
3808.9111	----蚊香	10	80	17	5	千克	AS	----Mosquito smudges
3808.9112	----生物杀虫剂	10	35	17	5	千克	AS	----Biotic insecticide
3808.9119	----其他	10	35	13	5	千克	AS	----Other
3808.9190	---其他	6	11	13	5	千克	AS	---Other
	--杀菌剂:							--Fungicides:
3808.9210	---零售包装	9	35	17	5	千克	S	---Put up for retail sale
3808.9290	---其他	6	11	17	5	千克		---Other
3808.9290 10	非零售包装的医用杀菌剂	6	11	17	5	千克		Medical fungicides, not in forms or packing for retail sale

税则号列	货品名称	最惠(%)	普通	增值税率	出口退税	计量单位	监管条件	Article Description
3808.9290 21	经农药杀菌剂浸渍的纸质水果套袋	6	11	17	5	千克	S	Paper bags for fruit protecion, agricultural fungicides scaked
3808.9290 29	非零售包装的其他农用杀菌剂成药	6	11	13	5	千克	S	Other agricultural fungicides medicine, not in forms or packing for retail sale
3808.9290 90	非零售包装的非农用杀菌剂成药(包括非医用杀菌剂)	6	11	13	5	千克		Non-agricultural fungicides medicine and non-medical fungicides, not in forms packing for retail sale
	--除草剂、抗萌剂及植物生长调节剂:							--Herbicides anti-sprouting products and plant-growth regulators:
	---除草剂:							---Herbicides:
3808.9311	----零售包装	9	35	13	5	千克	AS	----Put up for retail sale
3808.9319	----其他	5	11	13	5	千克		----Other
3808.9319 10	非零售包装百草枯母液	5	11	13	5	千克	AS	Paraquat liquor, not put up for retail sale
3808.9319 90	其他非零售包装的除草剂成药	5	11	13	5	千克	AS	Other herbicides Patent medicine, not put up for retail sale
	---其他:							---Other:
3808.9391	----零售包装	9	35	13	5	千克	S	----Put up for retail sale
3808.9399	----其他	6	14	13	5	千克	S	----Other
3808.9400	--消毒剂	9	35	17	5	千克		--Disinfectants
3808.9400 10	医用消毒剂	9	35	17	5	千克		Medical disinfectants
3808.9400 20	兽用已配剂量含戊二醛,癸甲溴铵消毒剂等(包括复方煤焦油酸溶液消毒防腐药)	9	35	13	5	千克	R	Disinfectant of glutaraldehyde, disinfectant of deciquan solution, for veterinary purposes (including disinfectant and antiseptics for compound coal tar acid solution)
3808.9400 90	其他非医用消毒剂	9	35	13	5	千克		Non-medical disinfectants
	--其他:							--Other:
3808.9910	---零售包装	9	35	13	5	千克	S	---Put up for retail sale
3808.9990	---其他	9	14	13	5	千克	S	---Other
38.09	纺织、造纸、制革及类似工业用的其他税目未列名的整理剂、染料加速着色或固色助剂及其他产品和制剂(例如,修整剂及媒染剂):							**Finishing agents, dye carriers to accelerate the dyeing or fixing of dye-stuffs and other products and preparations (for example, dressings and mordants), of a kind used in the textile, paper, leather or like industries, not elsewhere specified or included:**
3809.1000	-以淀粉物质为基本成分	10	35	17		千克		-With a basis of amylaceous substances
	-其他:							-Other:
3809.9100	--纺织工业及类似工业用	6.5	35	17		千克		--Of a kind used in the textile or like industries
3809.9200	--造纸工业及类似工业用	6.5	35	17		千克		--Of a kind used in the paper or like industries
3809.9300	--制革工业及类似工业用	6.5	35	17		千克		--Of a kind used in the leather or like industries
38.10	金属表面酸洗剂;焊接用的焊剂及其他辅助剂;金属及其他材料制成的焊粉或焊膏;作焊条芯子或焊条涂料用的制品:							**Pickling preparations for metal surfaces; fluxes and other auxiliary preparations for soldering, brazing or welding; soldering, brazing or welding powders and pastes consisting of metal and other materials; preparations of a kind used as cores or coatings for welding electrodes or rods:**
3810.1000	-金属表面酸洗剂;金属及其他材料制成的焊粉或焊膏	6.5	35	17	13	千克		-Pickling preparations for metal surfaces; soldering, brazing or welding powders and pastes consisting of metal and other materials
3810.9000	-其他	6.5	35	17		千克		-Other
38.11	抗震剂、抗氧剂、防胶剂、粘度改良剂、防腐蚀制剂及其他配制添加剂,用于矿物油(包括汽油)或与矿物油同样用途的其他液体:							**Anti-knock preparations, oxidation inhibitors, gum inhibitors, viscosity improvers, anti-corrosive preparations and other prepared additives, for mineral oils (including gasoline) or for other liquids used for the same purposes as mineral oils:**
	-抗震剂:							-Anti-knock preparations:
3811.1100	--以铅化合物为基本成分	6.5	35	17		千克	X	--Based on lead compounds
3811.1900	--其他	6.5	35	17		千克		--Other

税则号列	货品名称	最惠(%)	普通	增值税率	出口退税	计量单位	监管条件	Article Description
	-润滑油添加剂:							-Additives for lubricating oils:
3811.2100	--含有石油或从沥青矿物提取的油类	6.5	35	17		千克		--Containing petroleum oils or oils obtained from bituminous minerals
3811.2900	--其他	6.5	35	17		千克		--Other
3811.9000	-其他	6.5	35	17		千克		-Other
38.12	**配制的橡胶促进剂;其他税目未列名的橡胶或塑料用复合增塑剂;橡胶或塑料用抗氧制剂及其他复合稳定剂:**							**Prepared rubber accelerators; compounds plasticizers for rubber or plastics, not elsewhere specified or included; anti-oxidizing preparations and other compound stabilizers for rubber or plastics:**
3812.1000	-配制的橡胶促进剂	6	20	17	13	千克		-Prepared rubber accelerators
3812.2000	-橡胶或塑料用复合增塑剂	6.5	35	17	5	千克		-Compound plasticizers for rubber or plastics
	-橡胶或塑料用抗氧制剂及其他复合稳定剂:							-Anti-oxidizing preparations and other compound stabilizers for rubber or plastics:
3812.3010	---橡胶防老剂	6	20	17	5	千克		---Rubber antioxidants
3812.3090	---其他	6.5	35	17	5	千克		---Other
38.13	**灭火器的装配药;已装药的灭火弹:**							**Preparations and charges for fire-extinguishers; charged fire-extinguishing grenades:**
3813.0010	---灭火器的装配药	6.5	35	17		千克		---Preparations and charges for fire-extinguishers
3813.0020	---已装药的灭火弹	10	70	17		千克		---Charged fire-extinguishing grenades
38.14	**其他税目未列名的有机复合溶剂及稀释剂;除漆剂:**							**Organic composite solvents and thinners, not elsewhere specified or included; prepared paint or varnish removers:**
3814.0000	其他税目未列名的有机复合溶剂及稀释剂;除漆剂	10	50	17		千克		Organic composite solvents and thinners, not elsewhere specified or included; prepared paint or varnish removers
38.15	**其他税目未列名的反应引发剂、反应促进剂、催化剂:**							**Reaction initiators, reaction accelerators and catalytic preparations, not elsewhere specified or included:**
	-载体催化剂:							-Supported catalysts:
3815.1100	--以镍及其化合物为活性物的	6.5	35	17		千克		--With nickel or nickel compounds as the active substance
3815.1200[暂]	--以贵金属及其化合物为活性物的	4	35	17		千克		--With precious metal or precious metal compounds as the active substance
3815.1200[暂] 10	载铂催化剂(为了从重水中回收氚或为了生产重水而专门设计或制备,用于加速氢和水之间的氢同位素交换反应)	4	35	17		千克	3	Platinum supported catalyst(in order to reclaim tritium from heavy water or design or prepare for production of heavy water for accelerate exchange reaction of hydrogen isotope between hydrogen and water)
3815.1200[暂] 90	其他以贵金属为活性物的载体催化剂	4	35	17		千克		Other supported catalysts with precious metal compounds as the active substance
3815.1900	--其他	6.5	35	17		千克		--Other
3815.9000	-其他	6.5	35	17		千克		-Other
38.16	**耐火的水泥、灰泥、混凝土及类似耐火混合制品,但税目38.01的产品除外:**							**Refractory cements, mortars, concretes and similar compositions, other than products of heading No. 38.01:**
3816.0000	耐火的水泥、灰泥、混凝土及类似耐火混合制品,但税目38.01的产品除外	6.5	35	17		千克		Refractory cements, mortars, concretes and similar compositions, other than products of heading No. 38.01
38.17	**混合烷基苯及混合烷基萘,但税目27.07及29.02的货品除外:**							**Mixed alkylbenzenes and mixed alkylnaphthalenes, other than those of heading No. 27.07 or 29.02:**
3817.0000	混合烷基苯及混合烷基萘	6.5	35	17		千克		Mixed alkylbenzenes and alkylnaphthalenes
38.18	**经掺杂用于电子工业的化学元素,已切成圆片、薄片或类似形状;经掺杂用于电子工业的化合物:**							**Chemical elements doped for use in electronics, in the form of discs, wafers or similar forms; chemical compouds doped for use in electronics:**
	---直径在7.5厘米及以上的单晶硅切片:							---Monocrystalline sillicon, in the form of discs, wafers or similar form, 7.5 cm or more in diameter:

税则号列	货品名称	最惠(%)	普通	增值税率	出口退税	计量单位	监管条件	Article Description
3818.0011	----直径在15.24厘米及以下的	0	11	17	13	千克/片		----Diameter not exceeding 15.24cm
3818.0019	----其他	0	11	17	13	千克/片		----Other
3818.0090	---其他	0	17	17	13	千克		---Other
38.19	**闸用液压油及其他液压传动用液体,不含石油或从沥青矿物提取的油类,或者按重量计石油或从沥青矿物提取的油类含量低于70%:**							**Hydraulic brake fluids and other prepared liquids for hydraulic transmission, not containing or containing less than 70% by weight of petroleum oils or oils obtained from bituminous minerals:**
3819.0000	闸用液压油及其他液压传动用液体,不含石油或从沥青矿物提取的油类,或者按重量计石油或从沥青矿物提取的油类含量低于70%	6.5	35	17		千克		Hydraulic brake fluids and other prepared liquids for hydraulic transmission, not containing or containing less than 70% by weight of petroleum oils or oils obtaines from bituminous minerals
38.20	**防冻剂及解冻剂:**							**Anti-freezing preparations and prepared de-icing fluids:**
3820.0000	防冻剂及解冻剂	10	35	17		千克		Anti-freezing preparations and prepared de-icing fluids
38.21	**制成的供微生物(包括病毒及类似品)或植物、人体、动物细胞生长或维持用的培养基:**							**Prepared culture media for the development or maintenance of micro-organisms (including virus and the like) or of plant, human or animal cells:**
3821.0000	制成的供微生物(包括病毒及类似品)或植物,人体,动物细胞生长或维持用的培养基	3	11	17		千克		Prepared culture media for the development or maintenance of micro-organisms (including viruses and the like) or of plant, human or animal cells:
38.22	**附于衬背上的诊断或实验用试剂及不论是否附于衬背上的诊断或实验用配制试剂,但税目30.02及30.06的货品除外;检定参照物:**							**Diagnostic or laboratory reagents on a backing and prepared diagnostic or laboratory reagents whether or not on a backing, other than those of heading No. 30.02 or 30.06; certified reference materials:**
3822.0010	---附于衬背上的	4	35	17		千克	AB	---On a backing
3822.0090	---其他	5	35	17		千克	AB	---Other
38.23	**工业用单羧脂肪酸;精炼所得的酸性油;工业用脂肪醇:**							**Industrial monocarboxylic fatty acids; acid oils from refining; industrial fatty alcohols:**
	-工业用单羧脂肪酸;精炼所得的酸性油:							-Industrial monocarboxylic fatty acids; acid oils from refining:
3823.1100	--硬脂酸	16	50	17	13	千克		--Stearic acid
3823.1200暂	--油酸	8	50	17		千克	AB	--Oleic acid
3823.1300	--妥尔油脂肪酸	16	50	17		千克		--Tall oil fatty acids
3823.1900	--其他		50	17		千克		--Other
3823.1900暂 01	植物酸性油(酸性油仅指精炼所得的)	5	50	17		千克		Acid oils of plant(acid oils from refining)
3823.1900 90	其他工业用单羧脂肪酸、酸性油(酸性油仅指精炼所得的)	16	50	17		千克		Other industrial monocarboxylic fatty acids, acid oils (acid oils from refining)
3823.7000暂	-工业用脂肪醇	9	50	17		千克		-Industrial fatty alcohols
38.24	**铸模及铸芯用粘合剂;其他税目未列名的化学工业及其相关工业的化学产品及配制品(包括由天然产品混合组成的):**							**Prepared binders for foundry moulds or cores; chemical products and preparations of the chemical or allied industries (including those consisting of mixtures of natural products), not elsewhere specified or included:**
3824.1000	-铸模及铸芯用粘合剂	6.5	35	17	5	千克		-Prepared binders for foundry moulds or cores
3824.3000	-自身混合或与金属粘合剂混合的未烧结金属碳化物	6.5	35	17		千克		-Non-agglomerated metal carbides mixed together or with metallic binders
3824.3000 10	混合的未烧结金属碳化钨(包括自身混合或与金属粘合剂混合的)	6.5	35	17		千克	4xy	Non – agglomerated metal carbonizded tungsten (containing mixed together or with metallic binders)
3824.3000 90	其他混合的未烧结金属碳化物(包括自身混合或与金属粘合剂混合的)	6.5	35	17		千克		Other non – agglomerated metal carbides(containing mixed together or with metallic binders)

税则号列	货　品　名　称	最惠(%)	普通	增值税率	出口退税	计量单位	监管条件	Article Description
	-水泥、灰泥及混凝土用添加剂：							-Prepared additives for cements, mortars or concretes:
3824.4010	---高效减水剂	6.5	35	17	13	千克		---High efficiency water reducing agent
3824.4090	---其他	6.5	35	17		千克		---Other
3824.5000	-非耐火的灰泥及混凝土	6.5	35	17		千克		-Non-refraciory mortars and concretes
3824.6000	-子目号2905.44以外的山梨醇	14	40	17		千克		-Sorbitol other than that of subheading No. 2905.44
	-含有甲烷、乙烷或丙烷的卤化衍生物的混合物：							-Mixtures containing halogenated dervatives of methane, ethane or propane:
3824.7100	--含全氯氟烃(CFCs)的,不论是否含氢氯氟烃(HCFCs)、全氟烃(PFCs)或氢氟烃(HFCs)	6.5	35	17		千克		--Containing chorofluorocarbons(CFCs), whether or not containing hydrochlorofluorocarbons(HCFCs) perfluorocarbons(PFCs) orhydrofluorocarbons(HFCs)
3824.7100 11	二氯二氟甲烷和二氟乙烷的混合物(R-500)	6.5	35	17		千克	AB14xy	Mixture of dichlorodifluoromethane and difluoroethane(R－500)
3824.7100 12	一氯二氟甲烷和二氯二氟甲烷的混合物(R-501)	6.5	35	17		千克	14xy	Mixture of difluorochloromethane and dichlorodifluoromethane(R－501)
3824.7100 13	一氯二氟甲烷和一氯五氟乙烷的混合物(R-502)	6.5	35	17		千克	AB14xy	Mixture of difluorochloromethane and Chloropentafluoroethane(R－502)
3824.7100 14	三氟甲烷和一氯三氟甲烷的混合物(R-503)	6.5	35	17		千克	AB14xy	Mixture of trifluoromethane and monochlorotrifluoromethane (R－503)
3824.7100 15	二氟甲烷和一氯五氟乙烷的混合物(R-504)	6.5	35	17		千克	14xy	Mixture of difluoromethane and Chloropentafluoroethane (R－504)
3824.7100 16	二氯二氟甲烷和一氟一氯甲烷的混合物(R-505)	6.5	35	17		千克	14xy	Mixture of dichlorodifluoromethane and fluouochlouomethane (R－505)
3824.7100 17	一氟一氯甲烷和二氯四氟乙烷的混合物(R-506)	6.5	35	17		千克	14xy	Mixture offluouochlouomethane and difluorotetrachloroethane (R－506)
3824.7100 18	二氯二氟甲烷和二氯四氟乙烷的混合物(R-400)	6.5	35	17		千克	14xy	Mixture of dichlorodifluoromethane and difluorotetrachloroethane (R－400)
3824.7100 90	其他含甲烷、乙烷或丙烷的全氯氟烃(CFCs)的混合物[不论是否含甲烷、乙烷或丙烷的氢氯氟烃(HCFCs)、全氟烃(PFCs)或氢氟烃(HFCs)]	6.5	35	17		千克		Other mixtures containing chlorojluorocarbons of methane, ethane or propane. (whether or not containing) hydrochlorofluorocarbons, chorofluoro carbons or orhydrofluorocarbons of methane, ethane or propane
3824.7200	--含溴氯二氟甲烷、溴三氟甲烷或二溴四氟乙烷的混合物	6.5	35	17		千克		--Containing bromochlorodifluoromethane, bromotrifluoromethane or dibromotetrafluoroethanes
3824.7300	--含氢溴氟烃(HBFCs)的	6.5	35	17		千克		--Containing hydrobromofluocarbons(HBFCs)
3824.7400	--含氢氯氟烃(HCFCs)的,不论是否含全氟烃(PFCs)或氢氟烃(HFCs)但不含全氯氟烃(CFCs)	6.5	35	17		千克		--Containing hydrochlorofluorocarbons (HCFCs), whether or not containing perfluorocarbons (PFCs) or hydrofluorocarbons(HFCs), but not containing chlorofluorocarbons(CFCs)
3824.7400 11	二氟一氯甲烷、二氟乙烷和一氯四氟乙烷的混合物(R－401)	6.5	35	17		千克	14xy	Mixture of Monochlorodifluoromethane, difluoroethane and chlorotetrafluoroethane (R－401)
3824.7400 12	五氟乙烷、丙烷和二氟一氯甲烷的混合物(R402)	6.5	35	17		千克	14xy	Mixture of pentafluoroethane, propane and chlorodifluoromethane (R－402)
3824.7400 13	丙烷、二氟一氯甲烷和八氟丙烷的混合物(R403)	6.5	35	17		千克	14xy	Mixture of propane, chlorotetrafluoroethane and octafluoropropane (R－403)
3824.7400 14	二氟一氯甲烷、二氟乙烷、一氯二氟乙烷和八氟环丁烷的混合物(R405)	6.5	35	17		千克	14xy	Mixture of chlorotetrafluoroethane, difluoroethane, chlordifluoroethane and octafluorocyclobutane (R－405)
3824.7400 15	二氟一氯甲烷、2－甲基丙烷(异丁烷)和一氯二氟乙烷的混合物(R406)	6.5	35	17		千克	14xy	Mixture of Chlorotetrafluoroethane, 2 － methylpropane and chlordifluoroethane (R－406)
3824.7400 16	五氟乙烷、三氟乙烷和二氟一氯甲烷的混合物(R408)	6.5	35	17		千克	14xy	Mixture of pentafluoroethane, trifluoroethane and chlorodifluoromethane (R－408)
3824.7400 17	二氟一氯甲烷、一氯四氟乙烷和一氯二氟乙烷的混合物(R409)	6.5	35	17		千克	14xy	Mixture of chlorodifluoromethane, chlorotetrafluoroethane and difluoromonochloroethane (R－409)
3824.7400 18	丙烯、二氟一氯甲烷和二氟乙烷的混合物(R411)	6.5	35	17		千克	14xy	Mixture of propene, chlorodifluoromethane and difluoroethane (R－411)
3824.7400 19	二氟一氯甲烷、八氟丙烷和一氯二氟乙烷的混合物(R412)	6.5	35	17		千克	14xy	Mixture of chlorodifluoromethane, octafluoropropane and difluoromonochloroethane (R－412)

税则号列	货品名称	最惠(%)	普通	增值税率	出口退税	计量单位	监管条件	Article Description
3824.7400 21	二氟一氯甲烷、一氯四氟乙烷、一氯二氟乙烷和2－甲基丙烷的混合物(R414)	6.5	35	17		千克	14xy	Mixture of chlorodifluoromethane, chlorotetrafluoroethane, difluoromonochloroethane and 2－methylpropane (R－414)
3824.7400 22	二氟一氯甲烷和二氟乙烷的混合物(R415)	6.5	35	17		千克	14xy	Mixture of chlorodifluoromethane, difluoroethane (R-415)
3824.7400 23	四氟乙烷、一氯四氟乙烷和丁烷的混合物(R416)	6.5	35	17		千克	14xy	Mixture of tetrafluoroethane, Chlorotetrafluoroethane and butane (R－416)
3824.7400 24	丙烷、二氟一氯甲烷和二氟乙烷的混合物(R418)	6.5	35	17		千克	14xy	Mixture of propane, chlorodifluoromethane difluoroethane (R－418)
3824.7400 25	二氟一氯甲烷和八氟丙烷的混合物(R509)	6.5	35	17		千克	14xy	Mixture of chlorodifluoromethane and octafluoropropane (R－509)
3824.7400 26	二氟一氯甲烷和一氯二氟乙烷的混合物	6.5	35	17		千克	14xy	Mixture of chlorodifluoromethane and difluoromonochloroethane
3824.7400 90	其他含甲烷、乙烷或丙烷的氢氯氟烃混合物(不论是否含甲烷、乙烷或丙烷的全氟烃或氢氟烃,但不含全氯氟烃)	6.5	35	17		千克	14xy	Other mixtures containing chorofluorocarbons of methane, ethane or propane (whether or not containing hydrofluorocarbons or perfluorocarbons, but not containing chlorofluorocarbons)
3824.7500	--含四氯化碳的	6.5	35	17		千克		--Containing Carbon tetrachloride
3824.7600	--含1,1,1－三氯乙烷(甲基氯仿)的	6.5	35	17		千克		--Containing 1,1,1-trichloroethane (methyl chloroform)
3824.7700	--含溴化甲烷(甲基溴)或溴氯甲烷的	6.5	35	17		千克		--Containing bromomethane (methyl bromide) or bromochloromethane
3824.7800	--含全氟烃(PFCs)或氢氟烃(HFCs)的,但不含全氯氟烃(CFCs)或氢氯氟烃(HCFCs)的	6.5	35	17	13	千克		--Containing perfluorocarbons (PFCs) or hydrofluorocarbons (HFCs), but not containing chlorofluorocarbons (CFCs) or hydrochlorofluorocarbons (HCFCs)
3824.7900	--其他	6.5	35	17		千克		--Other
	-含环氧乙烷(氧化乙烯)、多溴联苯(PBBs)、多氯联苯(PCBs)、多氯三联苯(PCTs)或三(2,3一二溴丙基)磷酸酯的混合物及制品:							-Mixtures and preparations containing oxirane (ethylene oxide), polybrominated biphenyls (PBBs), polychlorna ted biphenyls (PCBs), polychlorinated terphenyls (PCTs) or tris (2,3-dibromopropyl) phosphate:
3824.8100	--含环氧乙烷(氧化乙烯)的	6.5	35	17		千克		--Containing oxirane (ethylene oxide)
3824.8200	--含多氯联苯(PCB_S)、多氯三联苯(PCT_S)或多溴联苯(PBB_S)的	6.5	35	17		千克	X	--Containing polychlorinated biphenyls (PCBs), polychlorinoted terphenyls (PCTs) or polybrominated biphenyls (PBBs)
3824.8300	--含三(2,3-二溴丙基)磷酸酯的	6.5	35	17		千克		--Contaning tris (2,3-dibromopopyl) phosphate
	-其他:							-Other:
3824.9010	---杂醇油	6.5	40	17		千克		---Fusel oil
3824.9020	---除墨剂、蜡纸改正液及类似品	9	80	17		千克		---Ink-removers, stencil correctors and the like
3824.9030	---增炭剂	6.5	35	17		千克		---Carburetant
	---其他:							---Other:
3824.9091	----按重量计含滑石50%以上的混合物	6.5	35	17		千克	4xy	----Mixtures containing 50% more than to by weight of talc
3824.9092	----按重量计含氧化镁70%以上的混合物	6.5	35	17		千克	4xy	---Mixtures of containing 70% or more than by weight of magnesium oxide
3824.9093	----表层包覆钴化合物的氢氧化镍(掺杂碳)	6.5	35	17	5	千克		----Surface covering cobalt compounds of nickel hydroxide
3824.9099	----其他		35	17		千克		----Other
3824.9099暂 01	高钛渣(二氧化钛质量百分含量＞70%的)	0	35	17		千克		Titanium Slag (proportion of titania ＞70%)
3824.9099 04	水解物或水解料、DMC(六甲基环三硅氧烷,八甲基环四硅氧烷,十甲基环五硅氧烷,十二甲基环六硅氧烷中任何2种,3种或4种组成的混合物)	6.5	35	17	13	千克		Hydrolyzate or hydrolysis materials, DMC (the mixtures, composed of any 2,3 or 4 kinds of Hexamethylcyclotrisiloxane, Octamethylcyclotetrasiloxane, Decamethylcyclopentasiloxane, dodecamethylcyclohexasiloxane)
3824.9099 05	核苷酸类食品添加剂	6.5	35	17	5	千克	AB	Nucleotides food additives

税则号列	货品名称	最惠(%)	普通	增值税率	出口退税	计量单位	监管条件	Article Description
3824.9099[暂] 06	按重量计氧化锌含量在50%及以上的混合物	3	35	17		千克		Mixtures containing 50% more than to by weigh of zinc oxide
3824.9099 10	粗制碳化硅[其中碳化硅含量大于15%(按重量计)]	6.5	35	17		千克	y4x	Silicon carbide, rough (silicon carbide > 15% by weight)
3824.9099 20	混胺(二甲胺和三乙胺混合物的水溶液)	6.5	35	17		千克	3	Mixed amine (the solution of mixture of dimethylamine and triethylamine)
3824.9099 30	氰化物的混合物	6.5	35	17		千克	X	Mixed amin of cyanide
3824.9099 40	膨胀石墨	6.5	35	17		千克	3	Expandable graphite
3824.9099 51	甲基膦酸的混合物(CAS号:170836-68-7){由甲基膦酸甲基、5-(5-乙基-2-甲基-2-氧代-1,3,2-二氧磷杂环己基)甲基酯(CAS号:41203-81-0)和甲基膦酸二[5-(5-乙基-2-甲基-2-氧代-1,3,2-二氧磷杂环己基)甲基]酯(CAS号:42595-45-9)混合而成}	6.5	35	17		千克	23	A mixture of methyl phosphonic acid (CAS: 170836-68-7) {by methyl phosphonic acid, methyl 5-(5-ethyl-2-methyl-2-oxo-1,3,2-two oxygen phosphorusheterocyclic hexyl) methyl ester (CAS: 41203-81-0) and methyl phosphonic acidtwo (5-(5-ethyl-2-methyl-2-oxo-1,3,2-two oxygen phosphorus heterocyclichexyl) methyl) ester (CAS number: 42595-45-9) and mixed}
3824.9099 90	其他编号未列名的化工产品	6.5	35	17	5	千克		Other chemical products, not elsewhere specified or included
38.25	**其他税目未列名的化学工业及其相关工业的副产品;城市垃圾;下水道淤泥;本章注释六所规定的其他废物:**							**Residual products of the chemical or allied industries, not elsewhere specified or included; municipal waste; sewage sludge; other wastes specified in Note 6 to this Chapter:**
3825.1000	-城市垃圾	6.5	35	17		千克	9	-Municipal waste
3825.2000	-下水道淤泥	6.5	35	17		千克	9	-Sewage sludge
3825.3000	-医疗废物	6.5	35	17		千克	9	-Clinical waste
	-废有机溶剂:							-Waste organic solvents:
3825.4100	--卤化物的	6.5	35	17		千克	9	--Halogenated
3825.4900	--其他	6.5	35	17		千克	9	--Other
3825.5000	-废的金属酸洗液、液压油、制动油及防冻液	6.5	35	17		千克	9	-Wastes of metal pickling liquors, hydraulic fluids, brake fluids and anti-freeze fluids
	-其他化学工业及相关工业的废物:							-Other wastes from chemical or allied industries:
3825.6100	--主要含有有机成分的	6.5	35	17		千克	9	--Mainly containing organic constituents
3825.6900	--其他	6.5	35	17		千克	9	--Other
3825.9000	-其他	6.5	35	17		千克		-Other
3825.9000 10	浓缩糖蜜发酵液	6.5	35	17		千克	AB	Condensed molasses fermented solubles
3825.9000 90	其他商品编号未列名化工副产品及废物	6.5	35	17		千克	9	Other chemical by-product or waste, not elsewhere specified or included
38.26	**生物柴油及其混合物,不含或含有按重量计低于70%的石油或从沥青矿物提取的油类:**							**-Biodiesel and mixture thereof, not containing or containing less than 70% by weight of petroleum oils or oils obtaines from bituminous minerals:**
3826.0000	生物柴油及其混合物,不含或含有按重量计低于70%的石油或从沥青矿物提取的油类	6.5	35	17		千克/升		-Biodiesel and mixture thereof, not containing or containingless than 70% by weight of petroleum oils or oils obtained from bituminous minerals
3826.0000 01	纯生物柴油	6.5	35	17		千克/升		Pure biodiesel
3826.0000 90	其他生物柴油及其混合物	6.5	35	17		千克/升		Other biodiesel and mixture thereof

第七类

塑料及其制品;橡胶及其制品

注释:

一、由两种或两种以上单独成分配套的货品,其部分或全部成分属于本类范围以内,混合后则构成第六类或第七类的货品,应按混合后产品归入相应的税目,但其组成成分必须同时符合下列条件:

(一)其包装形式足以表明这些成分不需经过改装就可以一起使用的;

(二)一起进口或出口的;

(三)这些成分的属性及相互比例足以表明是相互配用的。

二、除税目 39.18 或 39.19 的货品外,印有花纹、文字、图画的塑料、橡胶及其制品,如果所印花纹、字画作为其主要用途,应归入第四十九章。

SECTION Ⅶ

PLASTICS AND ARTICLES THEREOF; RUBBER AND ARTICLES THEREOF

Notes:

1. Goods put up in sets consisting of two or more separate constituents, some or all of which fall in this Section and are intended to be mixed together to obtain a product of Section Ⅵ or Ⅶ, are to be classified in the heading appropriate to that product, provided that the constituents are:
   (a) having regard to the manner in which they are put up, clearly identifiable as being intended to be used together without first being repacked;
   (b) presented together;
   (c) identifiable, whether by their nature or by the relative proportions in which they are present, as being complementary one to another.
2. Except for the goods of heading No. 39. 18 or 39. 19, plastics, rubber, and articles thereof, printed with motifs, characters or pictorial representations, which are not merely incidental to the primary use of the goods, fall in Chapter 49.

第三十九章
塑料及其制品

注释:

一、本目录所称"塑料",是指税目 39.01 至 39.14 的材料,这些材料能够在聚合时或聚合后在外力(一般是热力和压力,必要时加入溶剂或增塑剂)作用下通过模制、浇铸、挤压、滚轧或其他工序制成一定的形状,成形后除去外力,其形状仍保持不变。

本目录所称"塑料",还应包括钢纸,但不包括第十一类的纺织材料。

二、本章不包括:

(一)税目 27.10 或 34.03 的润滑油;

(二)税目 27.12 或 34.04 的蜡;

(三)单独的已有化学定义的有机化合物(第二十九章);

(四)肝素及其盐(税目 30.01);

(五)税目 39.01 至 39.13 所列的任何产品溶于挥发性有机溶剂的溶液(火胶棉除外),但溶剂的重量必须超过溶液重量的 50%(税目 32.08);税目 32.12 的压印箔;

(六)有机表面活性剂或税目 34.02 的制剂;

(七)再熔胶及酯胶(税目 38.06);

(八)配制的添加剂,用于矿物油(包括汽油)或与矿物油同样用途的其他液体(税目 38.11);

(九)以第三十九章的聚乙二醇、聚硅氧烷或其他聚合物为基本成分的液压用液体;(税目 38.19)

(十)有塑料衬背的诊断或实验用试剂(税号 38.22);

(十一)第四十章规定的合成橡胶及其制品;

Chapter 39
Plastics and articles thereof

Notes:

1. Throughout the Nomenclature the expression "plastics" means those materials of headings No. 39. 01 to 39. 14 which are or have been capable, either at the moment of polymerization or at some subsequent stage, of being formed under external influence (usually heat and pressure, if necessary with a solvent or plasticizer) by moulding, casting, extruding, rolling or other process into shapes which are retained on the removal of the external influence.

   Throughout the Nomenclature any reference to "plastics" also includes vulcanized fibre. The expression, however, does not apply to materials regarded as textile materials of Section Ⅺ.
2. This Chapter does not cover:
   (a) Lubricating preparations of heading No. 27. 10 or 34. 03.
   (b) Waxes of heading No. 27. 12 or 34. 04;
   (c) Separate chemically defined organic compounds (Chapter 29);
   (d) Heparin or its salts (heading No. 30. 01);
   (e) Solutions (other than collodions) consisting of any of the products specified in headings No. 39. 01 to 39. 13 in volatile organic solvents when the weight of the solvent exceeds 50% of the weight of the solution (heading No. 32. 08); stamping foils of heading No. 32. 12;
   (f) Organic surface-active agents or preparations of heading No. 34. 02;
   (g) Run gums or ester gums (heading No. 38. 06);
   (h) Prepared additives for mineral oils (including gasoline) or for other liquids used for the same purposes as mineral oils (heading No. 38. 11)
   (i) Prepared hydronlic fluids based on polyglycols silianes or other polymers of chapter 39 (heading No. 38. 19);
   (j) Diagnostic or laboratory reagents on a backing of plastics (heading No. 38. 22);
   (k) Synthetic rubber, as defined for the purposes of Chapter 40, or articles thereof;

（十二）鞍具及挽具（税号42.01）；税号42.02的衣箱、提箱、手提包及其他容器；
（十三）第四十六章的缏条、编结品及其他制品；
（十四）税号48.14的壁纸；
（十五）第十一类的货品（纺织原料及纺织制品）；
（十六）第十二类的物品（例如，鞋靴、帽类、雨伞、阳伞、手杖、鞭子、马鞭及其零件）；
（十七）税号71.17的仿首饰；
（十八）第十六类的物品（机器、机械器具或电气器具）；
（十九）第十七类的航空器零件及车辆零件；
（二十）第九十章的物品（例如，光学元件、眼镜架及绘图仪器）；
（二十一）第九十一章的物品（例如，钟壳及表壳）；
（二十二）第九十二章的物品（例如，乐器及其零件）；
（二十三）第九十四章的物品（例如，家具、灯具、照明装置、灯箱及活动房屋）；
（二十四）第九十五章的物品（例如，玩具、游戏品及运动用品）；
（二十五）第九十六章的物品（例如，刷子、钮扣、拉链、梳子、烟斗的嘴及柄、香烟嘴及类似品、保温瓶的零件及类似品、钢笔、活动铅笔）。

三、税目39.01至39.11仅适用于化学合成的下列货品：
（一）温度在300℃时，压力转为1013毫巴后减压蒸馏出的以体积计小于60%的液体合成聚烯烃（税目39.01及39.02）；
（二）非高度聚合的苯并呋喃－茚式树脂（税目39.11）；
（三）平均至少有五个单体单元的其他合成聚合物；
（四）聚硅氧烷（税目39.10）；
（五）甲阶酚醛树脂（税目39.09）及其他预聚物。

四、所称“共聚物”，包括在整个聚合物中按重量计没有一种单体单元的含量在95%及以上的各种聚合物。

在本章中，除条文另有规定以外，共聚物（包括共缩聚物、共加聚物、嵌段共聚物及接枝共聚物）及聚合物混合体应按聚合物中重量最大的那种共聚单体单元所构成的聚合物归入相应税目。在本注释中，归入同一税目的聚合物的共聚单体单元应作为一种单体单元对待。

如果没有任何一种共聚单体单元重量为最大，共聚物或聚合物混合体应按号列顺序归入其可归入的最末一个税目。

五、化学改性聚合物，即聚合物主链上的支链通过化学反应发生了变化的聚合物，应按未改性的聚合物的相应税目归类。本规定不适用于接枝共聚物。

六、税目39.01至39.14所称“初级形状”，只限于下列各种形状：
（一）液状及糊状，包括分散体（乳浊液及悬浮液）及溶液；

(l) Saddlery or harness (heading No. 42.01) or trunks, suitcases, handbags or other containers of heading No. 42.02;
(m) Plaits, wickerwork or other articles of Chapter 46;
(n) Wall coverings of heading No. 48.14;
(o) Goods of Section XI (textiles and textile articles);
(p) Articles of Section XII (for example, footwear, headgear, umbrellas, sun umbrellas, walking-sticks, whips, riding-crops or parts thereof);
(q) Imitation jewellery of heading No. 71.17;
(r) Articles of Section XVI (machines and mechanical or electrical appliances);
(s) Parts of aircraft or vehicles of Section XVII;
(t) Articles of Chapter 90 (for example, optical elements, spectacle frames, drawing instruments);
(u) Articles of Chapter 91 (for example, clock or watch cases);
(v) Articles of Chapter 92 (for example, musical instruments or parts thereof);
(w) Articles of Chapter 94 (for example, furniture, lamps and lighting fittings. illuminated signs, prefabricated buildings);
(x) Articles of Chapter 95 (for example, toys, games, sports requisites); or
(y) Articles of Chapter 96 (for example, brushes, buttons, slide fasteners, combs, mouthpieces or stems for smoking pipes, cigaretteholders or the like, parts of vacuum flasks or the like, pens, propelling pencils).

3. Headings No. 39.01 to 39.11 apply only to goods of a kind produced by chemical synthesis, falling in the following categories:
(a) Liquid synthetic polyolefins of which less than 60% by volume distils at 300℃, after conversion to 1,013 millibars when a reduced-pressure distillation method is used (headings No. 39.01 and 39.02);
(b) Resins, not highly polymerized, of the coumarone-indene type (heading No. 39.11);
(c) Other synthetic polymers with an average of at least 5 monomer units;
(d) Silicones (heading No. 39.10);
(e) Resols (heading No. 39.09) and other prepolymers.

4. The expression "copolymers" covers all polymers in which no single monomer unit contributes 95% or more by weight to the total polymer content.

For the purposes of this Chapter, except where the context otherwise requires, copolymers (including copolycondensates, co-polyaddition products, block copolymers and graft copolymers) and polymer blends are to be classified in the heading covering polymers of that comonomer unit which predominates by weight over every other single comonomer unit. For the purposes of this Note, constituent comonomer units of polymers falling in the same heading shall be taken together.

If no single comonomer unit predominates, copolymers or polymer blends, as the case may be, are to be classified in the heading which occurs last in numerical order among those which equally merit consideration.

5. Chemically modified polymers, that is those in which only appendages to the main polymer chain have been changed by chemical reaction, are to be classified in the heading appropriate to the unmodified polymer. This provision does not apply to graft copolymers.

6. In headings No. 39.01 to 39.14, the expression "primary forms" applies only to the following forms:
(a) Liquids and pastes, including dispersions (emulsions and suspensions) and solutions;

(二)不规则形状的块,团、粉(包括压型粉)、颗粒、粉片及类似的散装形状。

七、税目39.15不适用于已制成初级形状的单一的热塑材料废碎料及下脚料(税目39.01至39.14)。

八、税目39.17所称"管子",是指通常用于输送或供给气体或液体的空心制品或半制品(例如,肋纹浇花软管、多孔管),还包括香肠用肠衣及其他扁平管。除肠衣及扁平管外,内截面如果不呈圆形、椭圆形、矩形(其长度不超过宽度的1.5倍)或正几何形,则不能视为管子,而应作为异型材。

九、税目39.18所称"塑料糊墙品",适用于墙壁或天花板装饰用的宽度不小于45厘米的成卷产品,这类产品是将塑料牢固地附着在除纸张以外任何材料的衬背上,并且在塑料面起纹、压花、着色、印制图案或用其他方法装饰。

十、税目39.20及39.21所称"板、片、膜、箔、扁条",只适用于未切割或仅切割成矩形(包括正方形)(含切割后即可供使用的),但未经进一步加工的板、片、膜、箔、扁条(第五十四章的物品除外)及正几何形块,不论是否经过印制或其他表面加工。

十一、税目39.25只适用于第二分章以前各税目未包括的下列物品:

(一)容积超过300升的囤、柜(包括化粪池)、罐、桶及类似容器;

(二)用于地板、墙壁、隔墙、天花板或屋顶等方面的结构件;

(三)槽管及其附件;

(四)门、窗及其框架和门槛;

(五)阳台、栏杆、栅栏、栅门及类似品;

(六)窗板、百叶窗(包括威尼斯式百叶窗)或类似品及其零件、附件;

(七)商店、工棚、仓库等用的拼装式固定大型货架;

(八)建筑用的特色(例如,凹槽、圆顶及鸽棚式)装饰件;

(九)固定装于门窗、楼梯、墙壁或建筑物其他部位的附件及架座,例如,球形把手、拉手、挂钩、托架、毛巾架、开关板及其他护板。

子目注释:

一、属于本章任一税号项下的聚合物(包括共聚物)及化学改性聚合物应按下列规则归类:

(一)在同级子目中有一个"其他"子目的:

1. 子目所列聚合物名称冠有"聚(多)"的(例如,聚乙烯及聚酰胺-6,6),是指列名的该种聚合物单体单元一种或多种总量在整个聚合物中按重量计必须占95%及以上。

2. 子目3901.30、3903.20、3903.30及3904.30所列的共聚物,如果其共聚单体单元在整个聚合物中按重量计占95%及以上,即应归入上述子目。

(b) Blocks of irregular shape, lumps, powders (including moulding powders), granules, flakes and similar bulk forms.

7. Heading No. 39.15 does not apply to waste, parings and scrap of a single thermoplastic material, transformed into primary forms (headings No. 39.01 to 39.14).

8. For the purposes of heading No. 39.17, the expression "tubes, pipes and hoses" means hollow products, whether semi-manufactures or finished products, of a kind generally used for conveying, conducting or distributing gases or liquids (for example, ribbed garden hose, perforated tubes) This expression also includes sausage casings and other layflat tubing. However, except for the last-mentioned, those having an internal cross-section other than round, oval, rectangular (in which the length does not exceed 1.5 times the width) or in the shape of a regular polygon are not to be regarded as tubes, pipes and hoses but as profile shapes.

9. For the purposes of heading No. 39.18, the expression "wall or ceiling coverings of plastics" applies to products in rolls, of a width not less than 45 cm, suitable for wall or ceiling decoration, consisting of plastics fixed permanently on a backing of any material other than paper, the layer of plastics (on the face side) being grained, embossed, coloured, design-printed or otherwise decorated.

10. In headings No. 39.20 and 39.21, the expression "plates, sheets, film, foil and strip" applies only to plates, sheets, film, foil and strip (other than those of Chapter 54) and to blocks of regular geometric shape, whether or not printed or otherwise surface-woked, uncut or cut into rectangles (including squares) but not further worked (even if when so cut they become articles ready for use).

11. Heading No. 39.25 applies only to the following articles, not being products covered by any of the earlier headings of sub-Chapter Ⅱ:

(a) Reservoirs, tanks (including septic tanks), vats and similar containers, of a capacity exceeding 300 L;

(b) Structural elements used, for example, in floors, walls or partitions, ceilings or roofs;

(c) Gutters and fittings therefor;

(d) Doors, windows and their frames and thresholds for doors;

(e) Balconies, balustrades, fencing, gates and similar barriers;

(f) Shutters, blinds (including Venetian blinds) and similar articles and parts and fittings thereof;

(g) Large-scale shelving for assembly and permanent installation, for example, in shops, workshops, warehouses;

(h) Ornamental architectural features, for example, flutings, cupolas, dovecotes; and

(i) Fittings and mountings intended for permanent installation in or on doors, windows, staircases, walls or other parts of buildings, for example, knobs, handles, hooks, brackets, towel rails, switch-plates and other protective plates.

Subheading Notes:

Within any one heading of this Chapter, polymers (including copolymers) and chemically modified polymers are to be classified according to the following provisions:

1. Where there is a subheading named "Other" in the same series:

(a) The designation in a subheading of a polymer by the prefix "poly" (forexample, polyethylene and polyamide-6,6) means that the constituent monomer unit or monomer units of the named polymer taken together must contribute 95% or more by weight of the total polymer content.

(b) The copolymers named in subheadings Nos. 3901.30, 3903.20, 3903.30 and 3904.30 are to be classified in those subheadings, provided that the comonomer units of the named copolymers contribute 95% or more by weight of the total polymer content.

3. 化学改性聚合物如未在其他子目具体列名,应归入列明为"其他"的子目内。

4. 不符合上述 1.2.3. 款规定的聚合物,应按聚合物中重量最大的那种单体单元(与其他各种单一的共聚单体单元相比)所构成的聚合物归入该级其他相应子目。为此,归入同一子目的聚合物单体单元应作为一种单体单元对待。只有在同级子目中的聚合物共聚单体单元才可以进行比较。

(二)在同级子目中没有"其他"子目的:

1. 聚合物应按聚合物中重量最大的那种单体单元(与其他各种单一的共聚单体单元相比)所构成的聚合物归入该级相应子目。为此,归入同一子目的聚合物单体单元应作为一种单体单元对待。只有在同一组子目中的聚合物共聚单体单元才可以进行比较。

2. 化学改性聚合物应按相应的未改性聚合物的子目归类。聚合物混合体应按单体单元比例相等、种类相同的聚合物归入相应子目。

二、子目 3920.43 所称"增塑剂",包括"次级增塑剂"。

(c) Chemically modified polymers are to be classified in the subheading named "Other", provided that the chemically modified polymers are not more specifically covered by another subheading.

(d) Polymers not meeting (1), (2) or (3) above, are to be classified in the subheading, among the remaining subheadings in the series, covering polymers of that monomer unit which predominates by weight over every other single comonomer unit. For this purpose, constituent monomer units of polymers falling in the same subheading shall be taken together. Only the constituent comonomer units of the polymers in the series of subheadings under consideration are to be compared.

2. Where there is no subheading named "Other" in the same series:

(a) Polymers are to be classified in the subheading covering polymers of that monomer unit which predominates by weight over every other single comonomer unit. For this purpose, constituent monomer units of polymers falling in the same subheading shall be taken together. Only the constituent comonomer units of the polymers in the series under consideration are to be compared.

(b) Chemically modified polymers are to be classified in the subheading appropriate to the unmodified polymer.
Polymer blends are to be classified in the same subheading as polymers of the same monomer units in the same proportions.

3. For the purposes of subheading No. 3920.43, the term "plasticisers" includes "secondary plasticisers."

税则号列	货品名称	最惠(%)	普通	增值税率	出口退税	计量单位	监管条件	Article Description
	第一分章　初级形状							1. -PRIMARY FORMS
39.01	初级形状的乙烯聚合物:							**Polymers of ethylene, in primary forms:**
3901.1000	-聚乙烯,比重小于0.94		45	17	13	千克		-Polyethylene having a specific gravity of less than 0.94
3901.1000暂 01	初级形状比重<0.94 的聚乙烯(进口 CIF 价高于 3800 美元/吨)	3	45	17	13	千克		Polyethylene having a sopecific gravity of less than 0.94, in primary forms(CIF > USD3800/ton)
3901.1000 90	初级形状比重<0.94 的聚乙烯	6.5	45	17	13	千克		Polyethylene having a specific gravity of less than 0.94, in primary forms
3901.2000	-聚乙烯,比重在0.94 及以上		45	17	13	千克		-Polyethylene having a specific gravity of 0.94 or more
3901.2000暂 01	初级形状比重≥0.94 的聚乙烯(进口 CIF 价高于 3800 美元/吨)	3	45	17	13	千克		Polyethylene having a specific gravity of 0.94 or more in primary forms(CIF > USD3800/ton)
3901.2000 90	初级形状比重≥0.94 的聚乙烯	6.5	45	17	13	千克		Polyethylene having aspecific gravity of 0.94 or more, in primary forms
3901.3000	-乙烯-乙酸乙烯酯共聚物	6.5	45	17	5	千克		-Ethylene-vinyl acetate copolymers
	-其他:							-Other:
3901.9010	---乙烯-丙烯共聚物(乙丙橡胶)	6.5	45	17	5	千克		---Ethylene-propylene copolymers
3901.9020	---线型低密度聚乙烯	6.5	45	17	13	千克		---Linearity low-density polyethylene
3901.9090	---其他	6.5	45	17	13	千克		---Other
39.02	初级形状的丙烯或其他烯烃聚合物:							**Polymers of propylene or of other olefins, in primary forms:**
3902.1000	-聚丙烯		45	17	13	千克		-Polypropylene
3902.1000暂 10	电工级初级形状聚丙烯树脂(灰分含量不大于30ppm)	3	45	17	13	千克		Polypropylene resin, in primary forms, electrical grade (ash content≤30ppm)
3902.1000 90	其他初级形状的聚丙烯	6.5	45	17	13	千克		Other polypropylene, in primary forms
3902.2000	-聚异丁烯	6.5	45	17	5	千克	AB	-Polyisobutylene
	-丙烯共聚物:							-Propylene copolymers:
3902.3010	---乙烯-丙烯共聚物(乙丙橡胶)	6.5	45	17	5	千克		---Ethylene-propylene copolymers
3902.3090	---其他	6.5	45	17	5	千克		---Other
3902.9000	-其他	6.5	45	17	5	千克		-Other

税则号列	货品名称	最惠(%)	普通	增值税率	出口退税	计量单位	监管条件	Article Description
3902.9000 10	端羧基聚丁二烯,CTPB(作粘接剂或燃料)	6.5	45	17	5	千克	3	Carboxyl-terminal polybutadiene, CTPB (used as adhesive or fuel)
3902.9000 20	端羟基聚丁二烯,HTPB(作粘接剂或燃料)	6.5	45	17	5	千克	3	Hydroxyl-terminal polybutadiene, HTPB (used as adhesive or fuel)
3902.9000 90	其他初级形状的烯烃聚合物	6.5	45	17	5	千克		Other polymers of olefins, in primary forms
39.03	**初级形状的苯乙烯聚合物:**							**Polymers of styrene, in primary forms:**
	-聚苯乙烯:							-Polystyrene:
3903.1100	--可发性的	6.5	45	17	5	千克	AB	--Expansible
	--其他:							--Other:
3903.1910	---改性的	6.5	45	17	13	千克		---Modified
3903.1990	---其他	6.5	45	17	5	千克		---Other
3903.2000	-苯乙烯-丙烯腈(SAN)共聚物	12	45	17	5	千克		-Styrene-acrylonitrile (SAN) copolymers
	-丙烯腈-丁二烯-苯乙烯(ABS)共聚物:							-Acrylonitrile-butadiene-styrene (ABS) copolymers:
3903.3010	---改性的	6.5	45	17	13	千克		---Modified
3903.3090	---其他	6.5	45	17	5	千克		---Other
3903.9000	-其他	6.5	45	17	5	千克		-Other
39.04	**初级形状的氯乙烯或其他卤化烯烃聚合物:**							**Polymers of vinyl chloride or of other halogenated olefins, in primary forms:**
	-聚氯乙烯,未掺其他物质:							-Poly (vinyl chloride), not mixed with any other substances:
3904.1010	---糊树脂	6.5	45	17	13	千克		---Paste resins
3904.1090	---其他	6.5	45	17	13	千克		---Other
3904.1090 01	聚氯乙烯纯粉(纯指未掺其他物质)	6.5	45	17	13	千克		Poly (vinyl chloride) (not mixed with any other substances) in powder
3904.1090 90	其他初级形状的纯聚氯乙烯(纯指未掺其他物质)	6.5	45	17	13	千克		Other poly (vinyl chloride) (not mixed with any other substances)
	-其他聚氯乙烯:							-Other poly(vinyl chloride):
3904.2100	--未塑化	6.5	45	17	13	千克		--Non-plasticized
3904.2200	--已塑化	6.5	45	17	13	千克		--Plasticized
3904.3000	-氯乙烯-乙酸乙烯酯共聚物	9	45	17	5	千克		-Vinyl chloride-vinyl acetate copolymers
3904.4000	-其他氯乙烯共聚物	12	45	17	5	千克		-Other vinyl chloride copolymers
3904.5000	-偏二氯乙烯聚合物	6.5	45	17	5	千克		-Vinylidene chloride polymers
	-氟聚合物:							-Fluoro-polymers:
3904.6100	--聚四氟乙烯	10	45	17	13	千克		--Polytetrafluoroethylene
3904.6900	--其他	6.5	45	17	13	千克		--Other
3904.9000	-其他	10	45	17	5	千克		-Other
39.05	**初级形状的乙酸乙烯酯或其他乙烯酯聚合物;初级形状的其他乙烯基聚合物:**							**Polymers of vinyl acetate or of other vinyl esters, in primary forms; other vinyl polymers in primary forms:**
	-聚乙酸乙烯酯:							-Poly(vinyl acetate):
3905.1200	--水分散体	10	45	17	5	千克		--In aqueous dispersion
3905.1900	--其他	10	45	17	5	千克		--Other
	-乙酸乙烯酯共聚物:							-Vinyl acetate copolymers:
3905.2100	--水分散体	10	45	17	5	千克		--In aqueous dispersion
3905.2900	--其他	10	45	17	5	千克		--Other
3905.3000	-聚乙烯醇,不论是否含有未水解的乙酸酯基	14	45	17	5	千克	AB	-Poly(vinyl alcohol), whether or not containing unhydrolyzed acetate groups
	-其他:							-Other:
3905.9100	--共聚物	10	45	17	5	千克		--Copolymers
3905.9900	--其他	10	45	17	5	千克		--Other
39.06	**初级形状的丙烯酸聚合物:**							**Acrylic polymers in primary forms:**
3906.1000	-聚甲基丙烯酸甲酯	6.5	45	17	13	千克		-Poly(methyl methacrylate)
	-其他:							-Other:
3906.9010	---聚丙烯酰胺	6.5	45	17	5	千克	AB	---Polyacrylamide
3906.9090	---其他		45	17		千克		---Other
3906.9090[暂] 10	丙烯酸钠聚合物	3	45	17	13	千克		Sodium acrylate polymer

税则号列	货品名称	最惠(%)	普通	增值税率	出口退税	计量单位	监管条件	Article Description
3906.9090 90	其他初级形状的丙烯酸聚合物	6.5	45	17	13	千克		Other pure polyvinychlorid, in primary forms
39.07	初级形状的聚缩醛、其他聚醚及环氧树脂;初级形状的聚碳酸酯、醇酸树脂、聚烯丙基酯及其他聚酯:							**Polyacetals, other polyethers and epoxide resins, in primary forms; polycarbonates, alkyd resins, polyallyl esters and other polyesters, in primary forms:**
	-聚缩醛:							-Polyacetals:
3907.1010	---聚甲醛	6.5	45	17	13	千克		---Polyoxymethylene(POM)
3907.1090	---其他	6.5	45	17	5	千克		---Other
	-其他聚醚:							-Other polyethers:
3907.2010暂	---聚四亚甲基醚二醇	3	45	17	5	千克		---Polytetramethylene ether glycol
3907.2090	---其他	6.5	45	17	13	千克		---Other
3907.3000	-环氧树脂		45	17	5	千克		-Epoxide resins
3907.3000暂 01	初级形状溴质量≥18%或进口 CIF 价>3800 美元/吨的环氧树脂(如溶于溶剂,以纯环氧树脂折算溴百分比含量)	4	45	17	5	千克	A	Epoxide resins, in primary forms, containing ≥18% by weight of bromine, or import CIF price >3800 USD/ton (If dissolved into solutions, convert the content percentage of bromine by pure epoxy resin)
3907.3000 90	初级形状的环氧树脂(溴重量百分比含量在18%以下)	6.5	45	17	5	千克	AB	Epoxide resins, in primary forms, containing <18% by weight of bromine
3907.4000暂	-聚碳酸酯	3	45	17	13	千克		-Polycarbonates
3907.5000	-醇酸树脂	10	45	17	5	千克	AB	-Alkyd resins
	-聚对苯二甲酸乙二酯:							-Poly(ethylene terephthalate):
	---切片:							---In the form of slices or chips:
3907.6011	----高粘度	6.5	45	17	13	千克		----High viscosity
3907.6019	----其他	6.5	45	17	13	千克		----Other
3907.6090	---其他	6.5	45	17	13	千克		---Other
3907.7000暂	-聚乳酸	3	45	17	5	千克		-Poly(lactic acid)
	-其他聚酯:							-Other polyesters:
3907.9100	--不饱和	6.5	45	17	5	千克		--Unsaturated
	--其他:							--Other:
3907.9910	---聚对苯二甲酸丁二酯	6.5	45	17	13	千克		---Poly butylene terephthalate
3907.9910 01	未经增强或改性的初级形状 PBT 树脂	6.5	45	17	13	千克		Not reinforced or modified PBT resins, in primary forms
3907.9910 90	其他聚对苯二甲酸丁二酯	6.5	45	17	13	千克		Other Poly butylene terephthalate
	---其他:							---Other:
3907.9991	----聚对苯二甲酸-己二醇-丁二醇酯	6.5	45	17	5	千克	AB	----Poly terephthalic acid hexylene glycol - butanediol ester
3907.9999	----其他	6.5	45	17	5	千克	AB	----Other
39.08	初级形状的聚酰胺:							**Polyamides in primary forms:**
	-聚酰胺-6、-11、-12、-6,6、-6,9、-6,10 或 -6,12:							-Polyamide-6, -11, -12, -6,6, -6,9, -6,10 or -6,12:
	---切片:							---In the form of slices or chips:
3908.1011	----聚酰胺-6,6 切片	6.5	45	17	13	千克		----Of polyamide-6,6
3908.1011 01	聚酰胺-6,6 切片	6.5	45	17	13	千克		Polyamide -6,6 slice
3908.1011 90	改性聚酰胺-6,6 切片(经螺杆二次混炼加入玻璃纤维、矿物质、增韧剂、阻燃剂的改性聚酰胺-6,6切片)	6.5	45	17	13	千克		Modification polyamide -6,6 slice(screw secondary mixing, adding glass fiber, minerals, plasticizer, flame retardant)
3908.1012	----聚酰胺-6 切片	6.5	45	17	13	千克		----Of polyamide-6
3908.1019	----其他	6.5	45	17	13	千克		----Other
3908.1019 10	尼龙 11、尼龙 12 切片(即聚酰胺-11;-12 切片)	6.5	45	17	13	千克		Nylon 11, Nylon 12, in the form of slices or chips (polyamide-11;-12)
3908.1019 99	聚酰胺-6,9 切片等(包括聚酰胺-6,9;-6,10;-6,12)	6.5	45	17	13	千克		Polyamide -6,9 slice(including Polyamide -6,9; -6,10; -6,12)
3908.1090	---其他	6.5	45	17	5	千克		---Other
3908.9000	-其他	10	45	17	5	千克		-Other
39.09	初级形状的氨基树脂、酚醛树脂及聚氨酯类:							**Amino-resins, phenolic resins and polyurethanes, in primary forms:**
3909.1000	-尿素树脂;硫尿树脂	6.5	45	17	5	千克		-Urea resins; thiourea resins

税则号列	货品名称	最惠(%)	普通	增值税率	出口退税	计量单位	监管条件	Article Description
3909.2000	-蜜胺树脂:	6.5	45	17	5	千克		-Melamine resins
	-其他氨基树脂:							-Other amino-resins:
3909.3010	---聚(亚甲基苯基异氰酸酯)(聚合 MDI 或粗 MDI)	6.5	35	17	13	千克		---Poly (methylene phenyl isocyanate)
3909.3090	---其他	6.5	45	17	5	千克	AB	---Other
3909.4000	-酚醛树脂	6.5	45	17	5	千克	AB	-Phenolic resins
3909.5000	-聚氨基甲酸酯	6.5	45	17	13	千克	AB	-Polyurethanes
39.10	**初级形状的聚硅氧烷:**							**Silicones in primary forms:**
3910.0000	初级形状的聚硅氧烷	6.5	45	17	13	千克		Silicones in primary forms
39.11	**初级形状的石油树脂、苯并呋喃－茚树脂、多萜树脂、多硫化物、聚砜及本章注释三所规定的其他税目未列名产品:**							**Petroleum resins, coumarone-indene resins, polyterpenes, polysulphides, polysulphones and other products specified in Note 3 to this Chapter, not elsewhere specified or included, in primary forms:**
3911.1000	-石油树脂、苯并呋喃树脂、茚树脂、苯并呋喃－茚树脂及多萜树脂	6.5	45	17	5	千克		-Petroleum resins, coumarone, indene or coumarone-indene resins and polyterpenes
3911.9000	-其他		45	17		千克		-Other
3911.9000暂 01	芳基酸与芳基胺预缩聚物	3	45	17	5	千克		Precondensed polymer of aromatic acid and aromatic amide
3911.9000暂 03	改性三羟乙基脲酸酯类预缩聚物	3	45	17	5	千克		Precondensed polymer of modified trihydroxy acetate
3911.9000 04	聚苯硫醚	6.5	45	17	13	千克		Polyphenylene sulfide
3911.9000暂 05	偏苯三酸酐和异氰酸预缩聚物	3	45	17	5	千克		Precondensed polymer of trimelltic anhydride and isocyanic acid
3911.9000 90	其他初级形状的多硫化物、聚砜等(包括本章注释三所规定的其他编号未列名产品)	6.5	45	17	13	千克		Other polysulphides, polysulphones (including other products specified in Note 3 to this Chapter, not elsewhere specified or included) in primary forms
39.12	**初级形状的其他税目未列名的纤维素及其化学衍生物:**							**Cellulose and its chemical derivatives, not elsewhere specified or included, in primary forms:**
	-乙酸纤维素:							-Cellulose acetates:
3912.1100	--未塑化	6.5	40	17	0	千克		--Non-plasticized
3912.1200	--已塑化	6.5	40	17		千克		--Plasticized
3912.2000	-硝酸纤维素(包括胶棉)	6.5	45	17		千克		-Cellulose nitrates (including collodions)
	-纤维素醚:							-Cellulose ethers:
3912.3100	--羧甲基纤维素及其盐	6.5	45	17		千克		--Carboxymethylcellulose and its salts
3912.3900	--其他	6.5	45	17		千克		--Other
3912.9000	-其他	6.5	45	17		千克		-Other
39.13	**初级形状的其他税目未列名的天然聚合物(例如藻酸)及改性天然聚合物(例如,硬化蛋白、天然橡胶的化学衍生物):**							**Natural polymers (for example, alginic acid) and modified natural polymers (for example, hardened proteins, chemical derivatives of natural rubber), not elsewhere specified or included, in primary forms:**
3913.1000	-藻酸及其盐和酯	10	45	17		千克	AB	-Alginic acid, its salts and esters
3913.9000	-其他	6.5	50	17	13	千克		-Other
3913.9000 11	香菇多糖	6.5	50	17	13	千克	S	Mushrooms polysaccharide
3913.9000 90	其他初级形状的未列名天然聚合物[包括改性天然聚合物(如硬化蛋白)]	6.5	50	17	13	千克		Other primary NES (including natural polymer modified natural polymer (such ashardening protein))
39.14	**初级形状的离子交换剂,以税目 39.01 至 39.13 的聚合物为基本成分的:**							**Ion-exchangers based on polymers of headings No. 39.01 to 39.13, in primary forms:**
3914.0000	初级形状的离子交换剂,以税目 39.01 至 39.13 的聚合物为基本成分的	6.5	45	17	5	千克		Ion-exchangers based on polymers of headings Nos. 39.01 to 39.13, in primary forms
	第二分章　废碎料及下脚料;半制品;制成品							Ⅱ-WASTE, PARINGS AND SCRAP; SEMI-MANUFACTURES; ARTICLES
39.15	**塑料的废碎料及下脚料:**							**Waste, parings and scrap, of plastics:**
3915.1000	-乙烯聚合物的	6.5	50	17		千克	AP	-Of polymers of ethylene
3915.2000	-苯乙烯聚合物的	6.5	50	17		千克	AP	-Of polymers of styrene
3915.3000	-氯乙烯聚合物的	6.5	50	17		千克	AP	-Of polymers of vinyl chloride
	-其他塑料的:							-Of other plastics:

税则号列	货品名称	最惠(%)	普通	增值税率	出口退税	计量单位	监管条件	Article Description
3915.9010	---聚对苯二甲酸乙二酯的	6.5	50	17		千克	AP	---Of pdyethylene glycol terephthalate
3915.9090	---其他	6.5	50	17		千克	AP	---Other
39.16	**塑料制的单丝(截面直径超过1毫米)、条、杆、型材及异型材,不论是否经表面加工,但未经其他加工:**							**Monofilament of which any cross-sectional dimension exceeds 1 mm, rods, sticks and profile shapes, whether or not surface-worked but not otherwise worked, of plastics:**
3916.1000	-乙烯聚合物制	10	45	17	13	千克		-Of polymers of ethylene
	-氯乙烯聚合物制:							-Of polymers of vinyl chloride:
3916.2010	---异型材	10	45	17	13	千克		---Profile shapes
3916.2090	---单丝、条、杆及型材	10	45	17	13	千克		---Monofilament, rods, sticks and profile
	-其他塑料制:							-Of other plastics:
3916.9010	---聚酰胺制	10	45	17	13	千克		---Of polyamides
3916.9090	---其他	10	45	17	13	千克		---Other
39.17	**塑料制的管子及其附件(例如,接头、肘管、法兰):**							**Tubes, pipes and hoses, and fittings therefor (for example, joints, elbows, flanges), of plastics:**
3917.1000	-硬化蛋白或纤维素材料制的人造肠衣(香肠用肠衣)	10	50	17	13	千克	A	-Artificial guts (sausage casings) of hardened protein or of cellulosic materials
	-硬管:							-Tubes, pipes and hoses, rigid:
3917.2100	--乙烯聚合物制	10	45	17	13	千克		--Of polymers of ethylene
3917.2200	--丙烯聚合物制	10	45	17	13	千克		--Of polymers of propylene
3917.2300	--氯乙烯聚合物制	10	45	17	13	千克		--Of polymers of vinyl chloride
3917.2900	--其他塑料制	10	45	17	13	千克		--Of other plastics
	-其他管:							-Other tubes, pipes and hoses:
3917.3100	--软管,最小爆破压力为27.6兆帕斯卡	10	45	17	13	千克		--Flexible tubes, pipes and hoses, having a minimum burst pressure of 27.6 MPa
3917.3200	--其他未装有附件的塑料制管子,未经加强也未与其他材料合制	6.5	45	17	13	千克		--Other, not reinforced or otherwise combined with other materials, without fittings
3917.3300	--其他装有附件的管子,未经加强也未与其他材料合制	6.5	45	17	13	千克		--Other, not reinforced or otherwise combined with other materials, with fittings
3917.3900	--其他	6.5	45	17	13	千克		--Other
3917.4000	-管子附件	10	45	17	13	千克		-Fittings
39.18	**块状或成卷的塑料铺地制品,不论是否胶粘;本章注释九所规定的塑料糊墙品:**							**Floor coverings of plastics, whether or not self-adhesive, in rolls or in the form of tiles; wall or ceiling coverings of plastics, as defined in Note 9 to this Chapter:**
	-氯乙烯聚合物制:							-Of polymers of vinyl chloride:
3918.1010	---糊墙品	10	45	17	13	千克		---Wall or ceiling coverings
3918.1090	---其他	10	45	17	13	千克		---Other
	-其他塑料制:							-Of other plastics:
3918.9010	---糊墙品	10	45	17	13	千克		---Wall or ceiling coverings
3918.9090	---其他	10	45	17	13	千克		---Other
39.19	**自粘的塑料板、片、膜、箔、带、扁条及其他扁平形状材料,不论是否成卷:**							**Self-adhesive plates, sheets, film, foil, tape, strip and other flat shapes, of plastics, whether or not in rolls:**
	-成卷,宽度不超过20厘米:							-In rolls of a width not exceeding 20 cm:
3919.1010	---丙烯酸树脂类为基本成分	6.5	45	17	13	千克		---Based on acrylic resin
	---其他:							---Other:
3919.1091	----胶囊型反光膜	6.5	45	17	13	千克		----Encapsulant reflective film
3919.1099	----其他	6.5	45	17	13	千克		----Other
	-其他:							-Other:
3919.9010	---胶囊型反光膜	6.5	45	17	13	千克		---Encapsulant reflective film
3919.9090	---其他	6.5	45	17	13	千克		---Other
39.20	**其他非泡沫塑料的板、片、膜、箔及扁条,未用其他材料强化、层压、支撑或用类似方法合制:**							**Other plates, sheets, film, foil and strip, of plastics, non-cellular and not reinforced, laminated, supported or similarly combined with other materials:**

税则号列	货品名称	最惠(%)	普通	增值税率	出口退税	计量单位	监管条件	Article Description
	-乙烯聚合物制:							-Of polymers of ethylene:
3920.1010[暂]	---乙烯聚合物制电池隔膜	3	45	17	13	千克		---Battery separator, of polymers of ethylene
3920.1090	---其他	6.5	45			千克		---Other
3920.1090 10	农用非泡沫聚乙烯薄膜(未用其他材料强化、层压、支撑或用类似方法合制)	6.5	45	13		千克		Agricultural PE film, non-cellular (not reinforced, laminated, supported or similarly combined with other materials)
3920.1090 90	其他非泡沫乙烯聚合物板、片、膜、箔及扁条(未用其他材料强化、层压、支撑或用类似方法合制,非农用)	6.5	45	17	13	千克		Plates, sheets, film, foil and strip, of PE film, non-cellular (not reinforced, laminated, supported or similarly combined with other materials, non-agricultural)
	-丙烯聚合物制:							-Of polymers of propylene:
3920.2010	---丙烯聚合物制电池隔膜	6.5	45	17	13	千克		---Battery separator, of polymers of propylene
3920.2090	---其他	6.5	45			千克		---Other
3920.2090 10	农用非泡沫聚丙烯薄膜(未用其他材料强化、层压、支撑或用类似方法合制)	6.5	45	13		千克		Agricultural PP film, non-cellular (not reinforced, laminated, supported or similarly combined with other materials)
3920.2090 90	非泡沫丙烯聚合物板、片、膜、箔及扁条(未用其他材料强化、层压、支撑或用类似方法合制,非农用)	6.5	45	17	5	千克		Plates, sheets, film, foil and strip, of PP film, non-cellular (not reinforced, laminated, supported or similarly combined with other materials, non-agricultural)
3920.3000	-苯乙烯聚合物制	6.5	45	17	13	千克		-Of polymers of styrene
	-氯乙烯聚合物制:							-Of polymers of vinyl chloride:
3920.4300	--按重量计增塑剂含量不小于6%	6.5	45			千克		--Containing by weight not less than 6% of plasticisers
3920.4300 10	农用软质聚氯乙烯薄膜(增塑剂含量≥6%,未用其他材料强化、层压、支撑)	6.5	45	13		千克		Agricultural PVC-P film (containing by weight not less than 6% of plasticisers, not reinforced, laminated, supported or similarly combined with other materials)
3920.4300 90	氯乙烯聚合物板、片、膜、箔及扁条(增塑剂含量≥6%,未用其他材料强化、层压、支撑)	6.5	45	17	5	千克		Plates, sheets, film (foil and strip, of PVC film containing by weight not less than 6% of plasticisers, not reinforced, laminated, supported or similarly combined with other materials)
3920.4900	--其他	6.5	45	13		千克		--Other
3920.4900 10	其他农用软质聚氯乙烯薄膜(非泡沫料的,未用其他材料强化、层压、支撑)	6.5	45	13		千克		Other agricultural PVC-P film (non-cellular, not reinforced, laminated, supported or similarly combined with other materials)
3920.4900 90	其他氯乙烯聚合物板、片、膜、箔及扁条(非泡沫料的,未用其他材料强化、层压、支撑,非农用)	6.5	45	17	5	千克		Other plates, sheets, film, foil and strip, of PVC (non-cellular, not reinforced, laminated, supported or similarly combined with other materials, non-agricultural)
	-丙烯酸聚合物制:							-Of acrylic polymers:
3920.5100	--聚甲基丙烯酸甲酯制	6.5	45	17	13	千克		--Of poly(methyl methacrylate)
3920.5900	--其他	6.5	45	17	13	千克		--Other
	-聚碳酸酯、醇酸树脂、聚烯丙酯或其他聚酯制:							-Of polycarbonates, alkyd resins, polyallyl esters or other polyesters:
3920.6100	--聚碳酸酯制	6.5	45	17	13	千克		--Of polycarbonates
3920.6200	--聚对苯二甲酸乙二酯制	6.5	45	17	13	千克		--Of poly(ethylene terephthalate)
3920.6200 01	9微米≤厚度≤15.9微米聚酯薄膜(聚对苯二甲酸乙二酯制,型号XA10AUDIO)	6.5	45	17	13	千克		PE film, thickness 9 ~ 15.9μ (ethylens terephthalate, Type: XA10AUDIO)
3920.6200 02	5微米≤厚度≤8.9微米聚酯薄膜(聚对苯二甲酸乙二酯制,型号XL07AUTEN)	6.5	45	17	13	千克		PE film, thickness 5 ~ 8.9μ (ethylens terephthalate, Type: XL07AUTEN)
3920.6200 03	16微米≤厚度≤29.9微米聚酯薄膜[聚对苯二甲酸乙二酯制,型号XB30CAB(N)]	6.5	45	17	13	千克		PE film, thickness16 ~ 29.9μ (ethylens terephthalate, Type: XB30CAB(N))
3920.6200 04	50微米≤厚度≤99.9微米聚酯薄膜[聚对苯二甲酸乙二酯制,型号XB30CAB(M)]	6.5	45	17	13	千克		PE film, thickness50 ~ 99.9μ (ethylens terephthalate, Type: XB30CAB(M))

税则号列	货品名称	最惠(%)	普通	增值税率	出口退税	计量单位	监管条件	Article Description
3920. 6200 09	其他聚对苯二甲酸乙二酯板片膜等(包括箔及扁条,非泡沫料,未用其他材料强化、层压、支撑)	6. 5	45	17	13	千克		Other plates, sheets, film, foil and strip, of poly (ethylene terephthalate), non-cellular, not reinforced, laminated, supported or similarly combined with other materials
3920. 6300	--不饱和聚酯制	10	45	17	13	千克		--Of unsaturated polyesters
3920. 6900	--其他聚酯制	10	45	17	13	千克		--Of other polyesters
	-纤维素及其化学衍生物制:							-Of cellulose or its chemical derivatives:
3920. 7100	--再生纤维素制	6. 5	45	17	13	千克		--Of regenerated cellulose
3920. 7300	--醋酸纤维素制	6. 5	45	17	13	千克		--Of cellulose acetate
3920. 7900	--其他纤维素衍生物制	10	45	17	13	千克		--Of other cellulose derivatives
	-其他塑料制:							-Of other plastics:
3920. 9100	--聚乙烯醇缩丁醛制		45	17	13	千克		--Of poly(vinyl butyral)
3920. 9100暂 01	聚乙烯醇缩丁醛膜(厚度不超过3毫米)(非泡沫料的,未用其他材料强化、层压、支撑)	3	45	17	13	千克		Film of poly vinyl butyral. (thieck ness ≤ 3mm) (non-cellular, not reinforced, laminated, supported or similarly combined with other materials)
3920. 9100 90	聚乙烯醇缩丁醛板、片、箔、扁条及厚度超过3毫米的膜(非泡沫料的,未用其他材料强化、层压、支撑)	6. 5	45	17	13	千克		Plates, sheets, foil and strip, of poly vinyl butyral. (thickness ≤ 3mm) (non-cellular, not reinforced, laminated, supported or similarly combined with other materials)
3920. 9200	--聚酰胺制	10	45	17	13	千克		--Of polyamides
3920. 9300	--氨基树脂制	6. 5	45	17	13	千克		--Of amino-resins
3920. 9400	--酚醛树脂制	10	45	17	13	千克		--Of phenolic resins
	--其他塑料制:							--Of other plastics:
3920. 9910	---聚四氟乙烯制	6. 5	45	17	13	千克		---Of polytetrafluoroethylene
3920. 9990	---其他塑料制		45	17	13	千克		---Of other plastics
3920. 9990暂 01	聚酰亚胺膜,厚度不超过0. 03mm(未用其他材料强化、层压、支撑)	3	45	17	13	千克		Polyimide(PI) film, thickness ≤ 0. 03mm (not reinforced, laminated, supported or similarly combined with other materials)
3920. 9990 90	其他非泡沫塑料板、片、膜、箔、扁条(未用其他材料强化、层压、支撑)	6. 5	45	17	13	千克		Other plates, sheets, foil and strip, non-cellular (not reinforced, laminated, supported or similarly combined with other materials)
39. 21	**其他塑料板、片、膜、箔、扁条:**							**Other plates, sheets, film, foil and strip, of plastics:**
	-泡沫塑料的:							-Cellular:
3921. 1100	--苯乙烯聚合物制	10	45	17	13	千克		--Of polymers of styrene
	--氯乙烯聚合物制:							--Of polymers of vinyl chloride:
3921. 1210	---人造革及合成革	9	70	17	13	千克/米		---Combined with textile fabrics
3921. 1290	---其他	6. 5	45	17	13	千克		---Other
	--氨酯聚合物制:							--Of polyurethanes:
3921. 1310	---人造革及合成革	9	70	17	13	千克/米		---Combined with textile fabrics
3921. 1390	---其他	6. 5	45	17	13	千克		---Other
3921. 1400	--再生纤维素制	10	45	17	13	千克		--Of regenerated cellulose
	--其他塑料制:							--Of other plastics:
3921. 1910	---人造革及合成革	9	45	17	13	千克/米		---Combined with textile fabrics
3921. 1990	---其他	6. 5	45	17	13	千克		---Other
	-其他:							-Other:
3921. 9020	---聚乙烯嵌有玻璃纤维的板,片	6. 5	45	17	13	千克		---Plates, sheets of polyethylene with glass fibres
3921. 9030	---聚异丁烯为基本成分的附有人造毛毡的板,片,卷材	6. 5	45	17	13	千克		---Plates, sheets, coils of polyisobutylene with man-made felt
3921. 9090	---其他		45	17	13	千克		---Other
3921. 9090暂 01	离子交换膜	5	45	17	13	千克		Ion exchange membrane

税则号列	货品名称	最惠(%)	普通	增值税率	出口退税	计量单位	监管条件	Article Description
3921.9090 10	两用物项管制结构复合材料的层压板(用纤维和丝材增强而制成的各种预浸件和预成形件,其中增强材料的比拉伸强度大于 7.62×10^4m 和比模量大于 3.18×10^6m)	6.5	45	17	13	千克	3	Laminated structural board made of composite materials under sensitive items control (various per-soaked and fabricated parts reinforced by fibers and threads, therein the specific tensile strength of reinforcing materials is greater than 7.62×10^4m and specific modulus greater than 3.18×10^6m)
3921.9090 90	未列名塑料板、片、膜、箔、扁条(离子交换膜,两用物项管制结构复合材料的层压板除外)	6.5	45	17	13	千克		Other plates, sheets, film, foil fiol and strip of plastic not elsewhere specified or in cluded (other than ion exchanging membrane and laminated structural board made of composite materials under sensitive product control)
39.22	**塑料浴缸、淋浴盘、洗涤槽、盥洗盆、坐浴盆、便盆、马桶座圈及盖、抽水箱及类似卫生洁具:**							**Baths, shower-baths, sinks, wash-basins, bidets, lavatory pans, seats and covers, flushing cisterns and similar sanitary ware, of plastics:**
3922.1000	-浴缸、淋浴盘、洗涤槽及盥洗盆	10	80	17	13	千克		-Baths, shower-baths, sinks and wash-basins
3922.2000	-马桶座圈及盖	10	80	17		千克		-Lavatory seats and covers
3922.2000 10	含濒危动物成分的塑料马桶座圈及盖	10	80	17		千克	EF	Lavatory seats and covers, of plastics, containing compositions of endangered animds
3922.2000 90	其他塑料马桶座圈及盖	10	80	17	13	千克		Other laratory seats and covers, of plastics
3922.9000	-其他	10	80	17	13	千克		-Other
39.23	**供运输或包装货物用的塑料制品;塑料制的塞子、盖子及类似品:**							**Articles for the conveyance or packing of goods, of plastics; stoppers, lids, caps and other closures, of plastics:**
3923.1000	-盒、箱(包括板条箱)及类似品	10	80	17	13	千克		-Boxes, cases, crates and similar articles
	-袋及包(包括锥形的):							-Sacks and bags (including cones):
3923.2100	--乙烯聚合物制	10	80	17	13	千克		--Of polymers of ethylene
3923.2900	--其他塑料制	10	80	17	13	千克		--Of other plastics
3923.3000	-坛、瓶及类似品	6.5	80	17	13	千克		-Carboys, bottles, flasks and similar articles
3923.4000	-卷轴、纡子、筒管及类似品	10	35	17	13	千克		-Spools, cops, bobbins and similar supports
3923.5000	-塞子、盖子及类似品	10	80	17	13	千克		-Stoppers, lids, caps and other closures
3923.9000	-其他	10	80	17	13	千克		-Other
39.24	**塑料制的餐具、厨房用具、其他家庭用具及卫生或盥洗用具:**							**Tableware, kitchenware, other household articles and hygienic or toilet articles, of plastics:**
3924.1000	-餐具及厨房用具	10	80	17	13	千克	A	-Tableware and kitchenware
3924.9000	-其他	10	80	17	13	千克	A	-Other
39.25	**其他税目未列名的建筑用塑料制品:**							**Builders' ware of plastics, not elsewhere specified or included:**
3925.1000	-囤、柜、罐、桶及类似容器,容积超过300升	10	80	17	13	千克		-Reservoirs, tanks, vats and similar containers, of a capacity exceeding 300L
3925.2000	-门、窗及其框架、门槛	10	80	17	13	千克		-Doors, windows and their frames and thresholds for doors
3925.3000	-窗板、百叶窗(包括威尼斯式百叶窗)或类似制品及其零件	10	80	17	13	千克		-Shutters, blinds (including Venetian blinds) and similar articles and parts thereof
3925.9000	-其他	10	80	17	13	千克		-Other
39.26	**其他塑料制品及税号39.01至39.14所列其他材料的制品:**							**Other articles of plastics and articles of other materials of headings Nos. 39.01 to 39.14:**
3926.1000	-办公室或学校用品	10	80	17	13	千克		-Offices or school supplies
	-衣服及衣着附件(包括分指手套、连指手套及露指手套):							-Articles of apparel and clothing accessories (including gloves, mittens and mitts):
	---手套(包括分指手套、连指手套及露指手套):							---Gloves (including gloves, mittens and mitts):
3926.2011	----聚氯乙烯制	10	90	17	13	千克/双		----Of poly (vinyl chrlrride)
3926.2019	----其他	10	90	17	13	千克/双		----Other
3926.2090	---其他	10	90	17	13	千克		---Other
3926.3000	-家具、车厢或类似品的附件	10	80	17	13	千克		-Fittings for furniture, coachwork or the like
3926.4000	-小雕塑品及其他装饰品	10	100	17	13	千克		-Statuettes and other ornamental articles

税则号列	货 品 名 称	最惠(%)	普通	增值税率	出口退税	计量单位	监管条件	Article Description
	-其他:							-Other:
3926.9010	---机器及仪器用零件	10	35	17	13	千克		---Of a kind for used in machines or instruments
3926.9090	---其他	10	80	17	13	千克		---Other
3926.9090 10	两用物项管制结构复合材料的预成形件和制品(用纤维和丝材增强而制成的各种预浸件和预成形件,其中增强材料的比拉伸强度大于 7.62×10^4m 和比模量大于 3.18×10^6m)	10	80	17	13	千克	3	Laminated structural board made of composite materials under sensitive items control (various per-soaked and fabricated parts reinforced by fibers and threads, therein the specific tensile strength of reinforcing materials is greater than 7.62×10^4m and specific modulus greater than 3.18×10^6m)
3926.9090 90	其他塑料制品(包括编号3901至3914所列材料的制品)	10	80	17	13	千克		Other articles of plastics (including articles of other materials of heading 39.01 to 39.14)

第四十章
橡胶及其制品

注释：

一、除条文另有规定的以外，本目录所称"橡胶"，是指不论是否硫化或硬化的下列产品：天然橡胶、巴拉塔胶、古塔波胶、银胶菊胶、糖胶树胶及类似的天然树胶、合成橡胶、从油类中提取的油膏以及上述物品的再生品。

二、本章不包括：

（一）第十一类的货品（纺织原料及纺织制品）；

（二）第六十四章的鞋靴及其零件；

（三）第六十五章的帽类及其零件（包括游泳帽）；

（四）第十六类的硬质橡胶制的机械器具、电气器具及其零件（包括各种电气用品）；

（五）第九十章、第九十二章、第九十四章或第九十六章的物品；

（六）第九十五章的物品（运动用分指手套、连指手套、露指手套及税目 40.11 至 40.13 的制品除外）。

三、税目 40.01 至 40.03 及 40.05 所称"初级形状"，只限于下列形状：

（一）液状及糊状，包括胶乳（不论是否预硫化）及其他分散体和溶液；

（二）不规则形状的块，团、包、粉、粒、碎屑及类似的散装形状。

四、本章注释一和税目 40.02 所称"合成橡胶"，适用于：

（一）不饱和合成物质，即用硫磺硫化能使其不可逆地变为非热塑物质，这种物质能在温度 18℃至 29℃之间被拉长到其原长度的三倍而不致断裂，拉长到原长度的两倍时，在五分钟内能回复到不超过原长度的一倍半。为了进行上述试验，可以加入交联所需的硫化活化剂或促进剂；也允许含有注释五（二）2 及 3 所述的物质。但不能加入非交联所需的物质，例如，增量剂、增塑剂及填料；

（二）聚硫橡胶（TM）；

（三）与塑料接枝共聚或混合而改性的天然橡胶、解聚天然橡胶以及不饱和合成物质与饱和合成高聚物的混合物，但这些产品必须符合以上（一）款关于硫化、延伸及回复的要求。

五、（一）税目 40.01 及 40.02 不适用于任何凝结前或凝结后与下列物质相混合的橡胶或橡胶混合物：

1. 硫化剂、促进剂、防焦剂或活性剂（为制造预硫胶乳所加入的除外）；

2. 颜料或其他着色料，但仅为易于识别而加入的除外；

3. 增塑剂或增量剂（用油增量的橡胶中所加的矿物油除外）、填料、增强剂、有机溶剂或其他物质，但以下（二）款所述的除外；

Chapter 40
Rubber and articles thereof

Notes:

1. Except where the context otherwise requires, throughout the Nomenclature the expression "rubber" means the following products, whether or not vulcanized or hard: natural rubber, balata, gutta-percha, guayule, chicle and similar natural gums, synthetic rubber, factice derived from oils, and such substances reclaimed.

2. This Chapter does not cover:

(a) Goods of Section XI (texitils and textile articles);

(b) Footwear or parts thereof of Chapter 64;

(c) Headgear or parts thereof (including bathing caps) of Chapter 65;

(d) Mechanical or electrical appliances or parts thereof of Section XVI (including electrical goods of all kinds), of hard rubber;

(e) Articles of Chapter 90, 92, 94 or 96;

(f) Articles of Chapter 95 (other than sports gloves, mittens and mitts and articles of headings No. 40.11 to 40.13).

3. In headings No. 40.01 to 40.03 and 40.05, the expression "primary forms" applies only to the following forms:

(a) Liquids and pastes (including latex, whether or not pre-vulcanized, and other dispersions and solutions);

(b) Blocks of irregular shape, lumps, bales, powders, granules, crumbs and similar bulk forms.

4. In Note I to this Chapter and in heading No. 40.02, the expression "synthetic rubber" applies to:

(a) Unsaturated synthetic substances which can be irreversibly transformed by vulcanization with sulphur into non-thermoplastic substances which, at a temperature between 18℃ and 29℃, will not break on being extended to three times their original length and will return, after being extended to twice their original length, within a period of five minutes, to a length not greater than one and a half times their original length. For the purposes of this test, substances necessary for the cross-linking, such as vulcanisng activators or accelerators, may be added; the presence of substances as provided for by Note 5 (b) (ii) and (iii) is also permitted. However, the presence of any substances not necessary for the cross-linking, such as extenders, plasticizers and fillers, is not permitted;

(b) Thioplasts (TM); and

(c) Natural rubber modified by grafting or mixing with plastics, depolymerized natural rubber, mixtures of unsaturated synthetic substances with saturated synthetic high polymers provided that all the above-mentioned products comply with the requirements concerning vulcanization, elongation and recovery in (a) above.

5. (a) Headings No. 40.01 and 40.02 do not apply to any rubber or mixture of rubbers which has been compounded, before or after coagulation, with:

(i) vulcanizing agents, accelerators, retarders or activators (other than those added for the preparation of pre-vulcanized rubber latex);

(ii) pigments or other colouring matter, other than those added solely for the purpose of identification;

(iii) plasticizers or extenders (except mineral oil in the case of oil-extended rubber), fillers, reinforcing agents, organic solvents or any other substances, except those permitted under (b);

（二）含有下列物质的橡胶或橡胶混合物，只要仍具有原料的基本特性，应归入税目 40.01 或 40.02：

1. 乳化剂或防粘剂；
2. 少量的乳化剂分解产品；
3. 微量的下列物质：热敏剂（一般为制造热敏胶乳用）、阳离子表面活性剂（一般为制造阳性胶乳用）、抗氧剂、凝固剂、碎裂剂、抗冻剂、胶溶剂、保存剂、稳定剂、粘度控制剂或类似的特殊用途添加剂。

六、税目 40.04 所称“废碎料及下脚料”，是指在橡胶或橡胶制品生产或加工过程中由于切割、磨损或其他原因所造成没有使用价值的废橡胶及下脚料。

七、全部用硫化橡胶制成的线，其任一截面的尺寸超过 5 毫米的，应作为带、杆或型材及异型材归入税目 40.08。

八、税目 40.10 包括用橡胶浸渍、涂布、包覆或层压的织物制成的或用橡胶浸渍、涂布、包覆或套裹的纱线或绳制成的传动带、输送带。

九、税目 40.01、40.02、40.03、40.05 及 40.08 所称“板”、“片”、“带”，仅指未切割或只简单切割成矩形（包括正方形）的板、片、带及正几何形块，不论是否具有成品的特征，也不论是否经过印制或其他表面加工，但未切割成其他形状或进一步加工。税目 40.08 所称“杆”或“型材及异型材”，仅指不论是否切割成一定长度或表面加工，但未经进一步加工的该类产品。

(b) The presence of the following substances in any rubber or mixture of rubbers shall not affect its classification in heading No. 40.01 or 40.02, as the case may be, provided that such rubber or mixture of rubbers retains its essential character as a raw material:

(1) emulsifiers or anti-tack agents;
(2) small amounts of breakdown products of emulsifiers;
(3) very small amounts of the following: heat-sensitive agents (generally for obtaining thermosensitive rubber latexes), cationic surface-active agents (generally for obtaining electro-positive rubber latexes), antioxidants, coagulants, crumbling agents, freeze-resisting agents, peptizers, preservatives, stabilizers, viscosity-control agents, or similar special-purpose additives.

6. For the purposes of heading No. 40.04, the expression “waste, parings and scrap” means rubber waste, parings and scrap from the manufacture or working of rubber and rubber goods definitely not usable as such because of cutting-up, wear or other reasons.

7. Thread wholly of vulcanized rubber, of which any cross-sectional dimension exceeds 5 mm, is to be classified as strip, rods or profile shapes, of heading No. 40.08.

8. Heading No. 40.10 includes conveyor or transmission belts or belting of textile fabric impregnated, coated, covered or laminated with rubber or made from textile yarn or cord impregnated, coated, covered or sheathed with rubber.

9. In headings No. 40.01, 40.02, 40.03, 40.05, and 40.08, the expressions “plates”, “sheets” and “strip” apply only to plates, sheets and strip and to blocks of regular geometric shape, uncut or simply cut to rectangular (including square) shape, whether or not having the character of articles and whether or not printed or otherwise surface-worked, but not otherwise cut to shape or further worked.

In heading No. 40.08 the expressions “rods” and “profile shapes” apply only to such products, whether or not cut to length or surface-worked but not otherwise worked.

税则号列	货品名称	最惠(%)	普通	增值税率	出口退税	计量单位	监管条件	Article Description
40.01	天然橡胶、巴拉塔胶、古塔波胶、银胶菊胶、糖胶树胶及类似的天然树胶，初级形状或板、片、带：							**Natural rubber, balata, gutta-percha, guayule, chicle and similar natural gums, in primary forms or in plates, sheets or strip:**
4001.1000[暂]	-天然胶乳，不论是否预硫化	①	40	17	5	千克	AB	-Natural rubber latex, whether or not prevulcanized
	-其他形状的天然橡胶：							-Natural rubber in other forms:
4001.2100[暂]	--烟胶片	②	40	17	5	千克	AB	--Smoked sheets
4001.2200[暂]	--技术分类天然橡胶(TSNR)	③	40	17	5	千克		--Technically specified natural rubber (TSNR)
4001.2900	--其他	20	40	17	5	千克		--Other
4001.3000	-巴拉塔胶、古塔波胶、银胶菊胶、糖胶树胶及类似的天然树胶	20	40	17	5	千克		-Balata, gutta-percha, guayule, chicle and similar natural gums
40.02	合成橡胶及从油类提取的油膏，初级形状或板、片、带；税号 **40.01** 所列产品与本税号所列产品的混合物，初级形状或板、片、带：							**Synthetic rubber and factice derived from oils, in primary forms or in plates, sheets or strip; mixtures of any products of heading No. 40.01 with any product of this heading, in primary forms or in plates, sheets or strip:**
	-丁苯橡胶(SBR)；羧基丁苯橡胶(XSBR)：							-Styrene-butadiene rubber (SBR); carboxylated styrene-butadiene rubber (XSBR):
	--胶乳：							--Latex:

① 4001.1000 暂定税率为：10% 或 900 元/吨，两者从低。
② 4001.2100 暂定税率为：20% 或 1500 元/吨，两者从低。
③ 4001.2200 暂定税率为：20% 或 1500 元/吨，两者从低。

税则号列	货 品 名 称	最惠(%)	普通	增值税率	出口退税	计量单位	监管条件	Article Description
4002.1110	---羧基丁苯橡胶	7.5	14	17	5	千克		---Carboxylated styrene-butadiene rubber (XSBR)
4002.1190	---其他	7.5	14	17	5	千克		---Other
	--其他:							--Other:
	---初级形状的:							---In primary forms:
4002.1911	----未经任何加工的丁苯橡胶(溶聚的除外)	7.5	14	17	13	千克		----SBR, not worked(except solution polymerized)
4002.1912	----充油丁苯橡胶(溶聚的除外)	7.5	14	17	5	千克		----SBR, oil-filled(except solution polymerized)
4002.1913	----热塑丁苯橡胶	7.5	14	17	5	千克		----SBR, thermo-plasticated
4002.1914	----充油热塑丁苯橡胶(溶聚的除外)	7.5	14	17	5	千克		----SBR, oil-filled and thermo-plasticated
4002.1915	----未经任何加工的溶聚丁苯橡胶	7.5	14	17	5	千克		----SBR, Solution polymerized ,not worked
4002.1916	----充油溶聚丁苯橡胶	7.5	14	17	5	千克		----SBR, Solution polymerized ,oil-filled
4002.1919	----其他	7.5	14	17	5	千克		----Other
4002.1990	---其他	7.5	35	17		千克		---Other
4002.1990 01	简单处理的丁苯橡胶,热塑或充油热塑丁苯橡胶除外(指为便于运输,对初级形状进行压缩、挤压等简单成型处理)	7.5	35	17	5	千克		Except simple treatment of styrene - butadiene rubber or styrene - butadiene - styrene block copolymer (referring to compression, extrusion in order to facilitate transportation)
4002.1990 90	其他丁苯橡胶及羧基丁苯橡胶板,片,带(4002199010 项下的除外)	7.5	35	17		千克		Other styrene - butadiene rubber and carboxy lated styrene - butadiene rubber, plates, sheets or strip (except those under item 4002199010)
	-丁二烯橡胶(BR):							-Butadiene rubber (BR):
4002.2010	---初级形状的	7.5	14	17	5	千克		---In primary forms
4002.2090	---其他	7.5	35	17		千克		---Other
	-异丁烯-异戊二烯(丁基)橡胶(IIR);卤代丁基橡胶(CIIR 或 BIIR):							-Isobutene-isoprene (butyl) rubber (IIR); halo-isobutene-isoprene rubber (CIIR or BIIR):
	--异丁烯-异戊二烯(丁基)橡胶(IIR):							--Isobutene-isoprene (butyl) rubber (IIR):
4002.3110	---初级形状的	6	14	17	5	千克		---In primary forms
4002.3190	---其他	7.5	35	17		千克		---Other
	--其他:							--Other:
4002.3910	---初级形状的	7.5	14	17	5	千克		---In pimary forms
4002.3990	---其他	7.5	35	17		千克		---Other
	-氯丁二烯(氯丁)橡胶(CR):							-Chloroprene (ehlorobutadiene) rubber(CR):
4002.4100	--胶乳	7.5	14	17	5	千克		--Latex
	--其他:							--Other:
4002.4910	---初级形状的	7.5	14	17	5	千克		---In primary forms
4002.4990	---其他	7.5	35	17		千克		---Other
	-丁腈橡胶(NBR):							-Acrylonitrile-butadient rubber(NBR):
4002.5100	--胶乳	7.5	14	17	5	千克		--Latex
	--其他:							--Other:
4002.5910	---初级形状的	7.5	14	17	5	千克		---In primary forms
4002.5990	---其他	7.5	35	17		千克		---Other
	-异戊二烯橡胶(IR):							-Isoprene rubber (IR):
4002.6010	---初级形状的	3	14	17	5	千克		---In primary forms
4002.6090	---其他	5	35	17		千克		---Other
	-乙丙非共轭二烯橡胶(EPDM):							-Ethylene-propylene-non-conjugated diene rubber (EPDM):
4002.7010	---初级形状的	7.5	14	17	5	千克		---In primary forms
4002.7090	---其他	7.5	35	17		千克		---Other
4002.8000	-税目 40.01 所列产品与本税目所列产品的混合物	7.5	35	17		千克		-Mixtures of any product of heading No. 40.01 with any product of this heading
	-其他:							-Other:
4002.9100	--胶乳	7.5	14	17		千克		--Latex
	--其他:							--Other:
	---其他合成橡胶:							---Other synthetic rubber:
4002.9911	----初级形状的	7.5	14	17	13	千克		----In primary forms
4002.9919	----其他	7.5	35	17		千克		----Other
4002.9990	---其他	4	14	17		千克		---Other

税则号列	货品名称	最惠(%)	普通	增值税率	出口退税	计量单位	监管条件	Article Description
40.03	**再生橡胶,初级形状或板、片、带:**							**Reclaimed rubber in primary forms or in plates, sheets or strip:**
4003.0000	再生橡胶,初级形状或板、片、带	8	30	17	13	千克		Reclaimed rubber in primary forms or in plates, sheets or strip
40.04	**橡胶(硬质橡胶的除外)的废碎料、下脚料及其粉、粒:**							**Waste, parings and scrap of rubber (other than hard rubber) and powders and granules obtained therefrom:**
4004.0000	橡胶(硬质橡胶的除外)的废碎料、下脚料及其粉、粒	8	30	17		千克		Waste, parings and scrap of rubber (other than hard rubber) and powders and granules obtained therefrom
4004.0000 10	废轮胎及其切块	8	30	17		千克	9	Waste rubber tyres and their cuts
4004.0000 20	硫化橡胶废碎料、下脚料及其粉、粒(硬质橡胶的除外)	8	30	17		千克	9	Waste, parings and scrap of vulcanized rubber (other than hard rubber) and powders and granules obtained therefrom
4004.0000 90	未硫化橡胶废碎料、下脚料及其粉、粒	8	30	17		千克	AP	Other waste, parings and scrap of rubber (other than hard rubber) and powders and granules obtained therefrom
40.05	**未硫化的复合橡胶,初级形状或板、片、带:**							**Compounded rubber, unvulcanized, in primary forms or in plates, sheets or strip:**
4005.1000	-与炭黑或硅石混合	8	35	17		千克		-Compounded with carbon black or silica
4005.2000	-溶液;子目号4005.10以外的分散体	8	35	17		千克		-Solutions; dispersions other than those of subheading No. 4005.10
	-其他:							-Other:
4005.9100	--板、片、带	8	35	17		千克		--Plates, sheets and strip
4005.9900	--其他	8	35	17		千克		--Other
40.06	**其他形状(例如,杆、管或型材及异型材)的未硫化橡胶及未硫化橡胶制品(例如,盘、环):**							**Other forms (for example, rods, tubes and profile shapes) and articles (for example, discs and rings), or unvulcanized rubber:**
4006.1000	-轮胎翻新用胎面补料胎条	8	35	17		千克/立方米		-"Camel-back" strips for retreading rubber tyres
	-其他:							-Other:
4006.9010	---其他形状的未硫化橡胶	8	35	17		千克		---Other forms of unvulcanized rubber
4006.9020	---未硫化橡胶制品	14	80	17		千克		---Articles of unvulcanized rubber
40.07	**硫化橡胶线及绳:**							**Vulcanized rubber thread and cord:**
4007.0000	硫化橡胶线及绳	14	80	17	9	千克		Vulcanized rubber thread and cord
40.08	**硫化橡胶(硬质橡胶除外)制的板、片、带、杆或型材及异型材:**							**Plates, sheets, strip, rods and profile shapes, of vulcanized rubber other than hard rubber:**
	-海绵橡胶制:							-Of cellular rubber:
4008.1100	--板、片、带	8	35	17	9	千克		--Plates, sheets and strip
4008.1900	--其他	8	35	17	9	千克		--Other
	-非海绵橡胶制:							-Of non-cellular rubber:
4008.2100	--板、片、带	8	35	17	9	千克		--Plates, sheets and strip
4008.2900	--其他	8	35	17	9	千克		--Other
40.09	**硫化橡胶(硬质橡胶除外)制的管子,不论是否装有附件(例如,接头、肘管、法兰):**							**Tubes, pipes and hoses, of vulcanized rubber other than hard rubber, with or without their fittings (for example, joints, elbows, flanges):**
	-未经加强或未与其他材料合制:							-Not reinforced or otherwise combined with other materials:
4009.1100	--未装有附件	10.5	40	17	9	千克		--Without fittings
4009.1200	--装有附件	10	40	17	9	千克		--With fittings
	-用金属加强或只与金属合制:							-Reinforced or otherwise combined only with metal:
4009.2100	--未装有附件	10.5	40	17	9	千克		--Without fittings
4009.2200	--装有附件	10	40	17	9	千克		--With fittings
	-用纺织材料加强或只与纺织材料合制:							-Reinforced or otherwise combined only with textile materials:
4009.3100	--未装有附件	10.5	40	17	9	千克		--Without fittings

税则号列	货品名称	最惠(%)	普通	增值税率	出口退税	计量单位	监管条件	Article Description
4009.3200	--装有附件	10	40	17	9	千克		--With fittings
	-用其他材料加强或与其他材料合制：							-Reinforced or otherwise combined with other materials:
4009.4100	--未装有附件	10.5	40	17	9	千克		--Without fittings
4009.4200	--装有附件	10	40	17	9	千克		--With fittings
40.10	硫化橡胶制的传动带或输送带及带料：							**Conveyor or transmission belts or belting, of vulcanized rubber:**
	-输送带及带料：							-Conveyor belts or belting:
4010.1100	--仅用金属加强的	10	35	17	9	千克		--Reinforced only with metal
4010.1200	--仅用纺织材料加强的	10	35	17	9	千克		--Reinforced only with textile materials
4010.1900	--其他	10	35	17	9	千克		--Other
	-传动带及带料：							-Transmission belts or belting:
4010.3100	--梯形截面的环形传动带(三角带)，V形肋状的，外周长超过60厘米，但不超过180厘米	8	35	17	9	千克		--Endless transmission belts of trapezoidal cross-section (V-belts), whether or not groved of a circumference exceeding 60cm but not exceeding 180cm
4010.3200	--梯形截面的环形传动带(三角带)，外周长超过60厘米，但不超过180厘米，V形肋状的除外	8	35	17	9	千克		--Endless transmission belts of trapezoidal cross-section (V-belts), V-ribbed, of an outside circumference exceeding 60cm but not exceeding 180cm
4010.3300	--梯形截面的环形传动带(三角带)，V形肋状的，外周长超过180厘米，但不超过240厘米	8	35	17	9	千克		--Endless transmission belts of trapezoidal cross-section (V-belts), other than V-ribbed, of an outside circumference exceeding 180cm but not exceeding 240cm
4010.3400	--梯形截面的环形传动带(三角带)，外周长超过180厘米，但不超过240厘米，V形肋状的除外	8	35	17	9	千克		--Endless transmission belts of trapezoidal cross-section (V-belts), V-ribbed, of an outside circumference exceeding 180cm but not exceeding 240cm
4010.3500	--环形同步带，外周长超过60厘米，但不超过150厘米	10	35	17	9	千克		--Endless transmission belts, of trapezodal crosselltionl (V-belts) other tlan V-ibbed, of an outside circumference exceeding 60cm but not exceeding 150cm
4010.3600	--环形同步带，外周长超过150厘米，但不超过198厘米	10	35	17	9	千克		--Endless synchronous belts, of an outside circumference exceeding 150cm but not exceeding 198cm
4010.3900	--其他	8	35	17	9	千克		--Other
40.11	新的充气橡胶轮胎：							**New pneumatic tyres, of rubber:**
4011.1000	-机动小客车(包括旅行小客车及赛车)用	10	50	17	9	千克/条	A	-Of a kind used on motor cars (including station wagons and racing cars)
4011.2000	-客运机动车辆或货运机动车辆用		50	17	9	千克/条		-Of a kind used on buses or lorries
4011.2000暂 10	断面宽≥30英寸客或货车用新充气橡胶轮胎(指机动车辆用橡胶轮胎，断面宽度≥30英寸)	3	50	17	9	千克/条	A	The section width is greater than or equal to 30 inches off or a truck with new rubber tyres (of a motor vehicle with rubber tires, section width is more than or equal to 30 inches)
4011.2000 90	其他客或货车用新充气橡胶轮胎(指机动车辆用橡胶轮胎)	10	50	17	9	千克/条	A	Other passengers or freight cars with new rubber tyres (refers to the rubber tirefor motor vehicles)
4011.3000	-航空器用	1	11	17	9	千克/条		-Of a kind used on aircraft
4011.4000	-摩托车用	15	80	17	9	千克/条	A	-Of a kind used on motorcycles
4011.5000	-自行车用	20	80	17	13	千克/条		-Of a kind used on bicycles
	-其他，人字型胎面或类似胎面的：							-Other, having a "herring-bone" or similar tread:
4011.6100	--农业或林业车辆及机器用		50	17	9	千克/条		--Of a kind used on agricultural or forestry vehicles and machines
4011.6100暂 10	断面宽≥24英寸人字形轮胎(新充气橡胶轮胎，含胎面类似人字形的，农林车辆机械用)	6	50	17	9	千克/条	A	The section width is greater than or equal to 24 inches herringbone tire (new rubber tyres, containing similar herringbone tread, forestry vehicles machinery)
4011.6100 90	其他人字形胎面轮胎(新充气橡胶轮胎，含胎面类似人字形的，农林车辆机械用)	17.5	50	17	9	千克/条	A	Other herringbone tread for tyre (new rubber tyres, containing tread herringbone like agriculture and forestry machinery, vehicles with)
4011.6200	--建筑业或工业搬运车辆及机器用，辋圈尺寸不超过61厘米	17.5	50	17	9	千克/条		--Of a kind used on construction or industrial handling vehicles and machines and having a rim size not exceeding 61cm

税则号列	货品名称	最惠(%)	普通	增值税率	出口退税	计量单位	监管条件	Article Description
4011.6200　10	断面宽≥24 英寸人字形轮胎(建筑业、工业用,辋圈≤61 厘米,新充气橡胶轮胎,含类似人字形)	17.5	50	17	9	千克/条	A	The section width is greater than or equal to 24 inches (herringbone tire building industry, industrial use, the rim is less than or equal to 61 cm, new pneumatic tyres of rubber, containing similar herringbone)
4011.6200　90	其他人字形胎面轮胎(建筑业、工业用,辋圈≤61 厘米,新充气橡胶轮胎,含类似人字形)	17.5	50	17	9	千克/条	A	Other herringbone tread for tyre (construction industry, industrial use, the rim is less than or equal to 61 cm, new pneumatic tyres of rubber, containing similarher-ringbone)
4011.6300	--建筑业或工业搬运车辆及机器用,辋圈尺寸超过 61 厘米		50	17	9	千克/条		--Of a kind used on construction or industrial handling vehicles and machines and having a rim size exceeding >61cm
4011.6300[暂]　10	断面宽≥24 英寸人字形子轮胎(建筑业、工业用,辋圈>61 厘米,新充气橡胶胎,含类似人字形)	8	50	17	9	千克/条	A	The section width is greater than or equal to 24 inches (herringbone sub tirebuilding industry, industrial, bead > 61 cm, new pneumatic tyres of rubber, containing similar herringbone)
4011.6300　90	其他人字形胎面轮胎(建筑业、工业用,辋圈>61 厘米,新充气橡胶胎,含类似人字形)	17.5	50	17	9	千克/条	A	Other herringbone tread for tyre (construction industry, industrial, bead > 61 cm, new pneumatic tyres of rubber, containing similar herringbone)
4011.6900	--其他		50	17	9	千克/条		--Other
4011.6900[暂]　10	断面宽≥30 英寸人字形轮胎(其他用途,新充气橡胶轮胎,含胎面类似人字形的)	6	50	17	9	千克/条	A	The section width is greater than or equal to 30 inches herringbone tire (other uses, the new pneumatic rubber tire tread, containing similar herringbone)
4011.6900　90	其他人字形胎面轮胎(其他用途,新充气橡胶轮胎,含胎面类似人字形的)	17.5	50	17	9	千克/条	A	Other herringbone tread for tyre (other uses, the new pneumatic rubber tiretread, containing similar herring-bone)
	-其他:							-Other:
4011.9200	--农业或林业车辆及机器用	25	50	17	9	千克/条		--Of a kind used on agricultural or forestry vehicles and machines
4011.9300	--建筑业或工业搬运车辆及机器用,辋圈尺寸不超过 61 厘米	25	50	17	9	千克/条		--Of a kind used on construction or industrial handling vehicles and machines and having a rim size not exceeding 61cm
4011.9300　10	其他断面宽度≥24 英寸轮胎(建筑业、工业用,辋圈≤61 厘米,新充气橡胶轮胎,非人字形胎面)	25	50	17	9	千克/条		The other section width is greater than or equal to 24 inch tires (construction industry, industrial use, the rim is less than or equal to 61 cm, new pneumatic tyres of rubber, nonhuman shaped tread)
4011.9300　90	其他新的充气橡胶轮胎(建筑业、工业用,辋圈≤61 厘米,新充气橡胶轮胎,非人字形胎面)	25	50	17	9	千克/条		Other new pneumatic tyres of rubber (construction industry, industrial use, the rim is less than or equal to 61 cm, new pneumatic tyres of rubber, nonhumanshaped tread)
4011.9400	--建筑业或工业搬运车辆及机器用,辋圈尺寸超过 61 厘米		50	17	9	千克/条		--Of a kind used on construction or industrial handling vehicles and machines and having a rim size exceeding >61cm
4011.9400[暂]　10	其他断面宽度≥24 英寸轮胎(建筑业、工业用,辋圈>61 厘米,新充气橡胶胎,非人字形胎面)	8	50	17	9	千克/条		The other section width is greater than or equal to 24 inch tires (construction industry, for industry, the bead > 61 cm, new pneumatic tyres of rubber, nonhuman shaped tread)
4011.9400　90	其他新的充气橡胶轮胎(建筑业、工业用,辋圈>61 厘米,新充气橡胶胎,非人字形胎面)	25	50	17	9	千克/条		Other new pneumatic tyres of rubber (construction industry, industrial, bead > 61cm, new pneumatic tyres of rubber, nonhuman shaped tread)
4011.9900	--其他		50	17	9	千克/条		--Other
4011.9900[暂]　10	其他断面宽度≥30 英寸轮胎(其他用途,新充气橡胶轮胎,非人字形胎面)	5	50	17	9	千克/条		The other section width is greater than or equal to 30 inch tires (other uses, new rubber tyres, nonhuman shaped tread)
4011.9900　90	其他新的充气橡胶轮胎(其他用途,新充气橡胶轮胎,非人字形胎面)	25	50	17	9	千克/条		Other new pneumatic tyres of rubber (other uses, new rubber tyres, nonhumanshaped tread)

税则号列	货品名称	最惠(%)	普通	增值税率	出口退税	计量单位	监管条件	Article Description
40.12	翻新的或旧的充气橡胶轮胎;实心或半实心橡胶轮胎、橡胶胎面及橡胶轮胎衬带:							**Retreaded or used pneumatic tyres of rubber; solid or cushion tyres, tyre treads and tyre flaps, of rubber:**
	-翻新轮胎:							-Retreaded tyres:
4012.1100	--机动小客车(包括旅行小客车及赛车)用	20	50	17	9	千克/条	A	--Of a kind used on motor cars (including station wagons and racing cars)
4012.1200	--机动大客车或货运机动车辆用	20	50	17	9	千克/条	A	--Of a kind used on buses or lorries
4012.1300暂	--航空器用	8	50	17	9	千克/条		--Of a kind used on aircraft
4012.1900	--其他	20	50	17	9	千克/条		--Other
	-旧的充气轮胎:							-Used pneumatic tyres:
4012.2010	---汽车用	25	50	17	9	千克/条	A	---Of a kind used on motor cars, buses or lorries
4012.2090	---其他	25	80	17	9	千克/条		---Other
	-其他:							-Other:
4012.9010暂	---航空器用	1	11	17	9	千克		---Of a kind used on aircraft
4012.9020	---汽车用	22	50	17	9	千克	A	---Of a kind used on motor cars, buses or lorries
4012.9090	---其他	22	50	17	9	千克		---Other
40.13	橡胶内胎:							**Inner tubes, of rubber:**
4013.1000	-机动小客车(包括旅行小客车及赛车)、客运机动车辆或货运机动车辆用	15	50	17	9	千克/条	A	-Of a kind used on motor cars (including station wagons and racing cars), buses or lorries
4013.2000	-自行车用	15	80	17	13	千克/条		-Of a kind used on bicycles
	-其他:							-Other:
4013.9010暂	---航空器用	1	11	17	9	千克/条		---Of a kind used on aircraft
4013.9090	---其他	15	50	17	9	千克/条		---Other
40.14	硫化橡胶(硬质橡胶除外)制的卫生及医疗用品(包括奶嘴),不论是否装有硬质橡胶制的附件:							**Hygienic or pharmaceutical articles (including teats), of vulcanized rubber other than hard rubber, with or without fittings of hard rubber:**
4014.1000	-避孕套	0	0			千克		-Sheath contraceptives
4014.9000	-其他	17.5	50	17	9	千克	A	-Other
40.15	硫化橡胶(硬质橡胶除外)制的衣着用品及附件(包括手套):							**Articles of apparel and clothing accessories (including gloves), for all purposes, of vulcanized rubber other than hard rubber:**
	-分指手套、连指手套及露指手套:							-Gloves, mitens and mias:
4015.1100	--外科用	8	30	17	13	千克/双		--Surgical
4015.1900	--其他	18	80	17	13	千克/双		--Other
	-其他:							-Other:
4015.9010	---医疗用	8	30	17	9	千克		---For medical purpose
4015.9090	---其他	15	90	17	9	千克		---Other
40.16	硫化橡胶(硬质橡胶除外)的其他制品:							**Other articles of vulcanized rubber other than hard rubber:**
	-海绵橡胶制:							-Of cellular rubber:
4016.1010	---机器及仪器用零件	8	30	17	9	千克		---of a kind used in machines or instruments
4016.1090	---其他	15	80	17	9	千克		---Other
	-其他:							-Other:
4016.9100	--铺地制品及门垫	18	80	17	9	千克		--Floor coverings and mats
4016.9200	--橡皮擦	18	80	17	9	千克		--Erasers
	--垫片、垫圈及其他密封垫:							--Gaskets, washers and other seals:
4016.9310	---机器及仪器用	8	30	17	9	千克		---Of a kind used in machines or instruments
4016.9390	---其他	15	80	17	9	千克		---Other
4016.9400	--船舶或码头的碰垫,不论是否可充气	18	80	17	9	千克		--Boat or dock fenders, whether or not inflatable
4016.9500	--其他可充气制品		80	17	9	千克		--Other inflatable articles
4016.9500暂 01	硫化橡胶制液压隔离式蓄能器用胶囊	9	80	17	9	千克		Of a kind used on Hydraulic separator accumulator, capsule
4016.9500 90	硫化橡胶制其他可充气制品	18	80	17	9	千克		Other inflatable articles, of vulcanized rubber
	--其他:							--Other:
4016.9910	---机器及仪器用零件		30	17	9	千克		---Of a kind used in machines or instruments

税则号列	货　品　名　称	最惠(%)	普通	增值税率	出口退税	计量单位	监管条件	Article Description
4016.9910暂 01	奶衬(硬质橡胶除外)	4	30	17	9	千克		Milk lining (other than hard rubber)
4016.9910 90	硫化橡胶制机器及仪器其他零件(硬质橡胶除外)	8	30	17	9	千克		Other machines or instruments of vulcanized rubbtrother than hard and its articles
4016.9990	---其他		80	17	9	千克		---Other
4016.9990暂 01	动车组用胶囊、外风挡板,硬质橡胶除外	5	80	17	9	千克		Of a kind used on motor train set, capsule and External wind baffle
4016.9990 90	其他未列名硫化橡胶制品(硬质橡胶除外)	10	80	17	9	千克		Other articles of vulcanized rubber other than hard rubber
40.17	**各种形状的硬质橡胶(例如纯硬质胶),包括废碎料;硬质橡胶制品:**							**Hard rubber (for example, ebonite) in all forms, including waste and scrap; articles of hard rubber:**
4017.0010	---各种形状的硬质橡胶,包括废碎料	8	35	17	9	千克		---Hard rubber in all forms, including waste and scrap
4017.0010 10	各种形状的硬质橡胶废碎料	8	35	17	9	千克	9	Waster and scrap of hard rubber in all forms
4017.0010 90	各种形状的硬质橡胶	8	35	17	9	千克		Hard rubber in all forms
4017.0020	---硬质橡胶制品	15	90	17	9	千克		---Articles of hard rubber

第八类

生皮、皮革、毛皮及其制品；鞍具及挽具；旅行用品、手提包及类似容器；动物肠线（蚕胶丝除外）制品

第四十一章
生皮（毛皮除外）及皮革

注释：

一、本章不包括：

（一）生皮的边角废料（税目05.11）；

（二）税目05.05或67.01的带羽毛或羽绒的整张或部分鸟皮；

（三）带毛生皮或已鞣的带毛皮张（第四十三章）；但下列动物的带毛生皮应归入第四十一章：牛（包括水牛）、马、绵羊及羔羊（不包括阿斯特拉罕、喀拉科尔、波斯羔羊或类似羔羊、印度、中国或蒙古羔羊）、山羊或小山羊（不包括也门或蒙古山羊及小山羊）、猪（包括西貒）、小羚羊、瞪羚、骆驼（包括单峰骆驼）、驯鹿、麋、鹿、狍或狗。

二、（一）税目41.04至41.06不包括经退鞣（包括预鞣）加工的皮（酌情归入税目41.01至41.03）；

（二）税目41.04至41.06所称"坯革"，包括在干燥前经复鞣、染色或加油（加脂）的皮。

三、本目录所称"再生皮革"，仅指税目41.15的皮革。

SECTION Ⅷ

RAW HIDES AND SKINS, LEATHER, FURSKINS AND ARTICLES THEREOF; SADDLERY AND HARNESS; TRAVEL GOODS, HANDBAGS AND SIMILAR CONTAINERS; ARTICLES OF ANIMAL GUT (OTHER THAN SILK-WORM GUT)

Chapter 41
Raw hides and skins (other than furskins) and leather

Notes:

1. This Chapter does not cover:

(a) Parings or similar waste, of raw hides or skins (heading No. 05.11);

(b) Birdskins or parts of birdskins, with their feathers or down, of heading No. 05.05 or 67.01; or

(c) Hides or skins, with the hair or wool on, raw, tanned or dressed (Chapter 43); the following are, however, to be classified in Chapter 41, namely, raw hides and skins with the hair or wool on, of bovine animals (including buffalo), of equine animals, of sheep or lambs (except Astrakhan, Broadtail, Caracul, Persian or similar lambs, Indian, Chinese, Mongolian or Tibetan lambs), of goats or kids (except Yemen, Mongolian or Tibetan goats and kids), of swine (including peccary), of chamois, of gazelle, of camels (including dromedaries) of reindeer, of elk, of deer, of roebucks or of dogs.

2. (a) Headings No. 41.04 to 41.06 do not cover hides and skins which have undergone a tanning (including pre-tanning) process which is reversible (headings No. 41.01 to 41.03, as the case may be).

(b) For the purposes of headings No. 41.04 to 41.06, the term "crust" includes hides and skins that have been retanned, coloured or fat-liquored (stuffed) prior to drying.

3. Throughout the Nomenclature the expression "composition leather" means only substances of the kind referred to in heading No. 41.15.

税则号列	货品名称	最惠(%)	普通	增值税率	出口退税	计量单位	监管条件	Article Description
41.01	生牛皮（包括水牛皮）、生马皮（鲜的、盐腌的、干的、石灰浸渍的、浸酸的或以其他方法保藏，但未鞣制、未经羊皮纸化处理或进一步加工的），不论是否去毛或剖层：							**Raw hides and skins of bovine (including buffalo) or equine animals (fresh, or salted, dried, limed, pickled or otherwise preserved, but not tanned, parchment-dressed or further prepared), whether or not dehaired or split:**
	-未剖层的整张皮，简单干燥的每张重量不超过8千克，干盐腌的不超过10千克，鲜的、湿盐腌的或以其他方法保藏的不超过16千克：							-Not split Whole hides and skins, unsplit, of a weight per skin not exceeding 8 kg when simply dried, 10 kg when dry-salted, or 16 kg when fresh, wet-salted or otherwise preserved:
	---牛皮：							---Of bovine animals:
4101.2011	----经退鞣处理的	8	17	13		千克/张		----Have undergone a reversible tanning process

税则号列	货　品　名　称	最惠(%)	普通	增值税率	出口退税	计量单位	监管条件	Article Description
4101.2011 10	规定重量退鞣未剖层整张濒危生野牛皮(指每张,简单干燥≤8kg,干盐渍≤10kg,鲜或湿盐≤16kg)	8	17	13		千克/张	ABFE	Whole raw hides and skins of endangered wild bovine animals, not split, have undergone a reversible tanning, w≤8kg when simply dried, w≤10kg when dry-salted, w≤16kg when fresh, wet-salted
4101.2011 90	规定重量未剖层退鞣处理整张生牛皮(包括水牛皮)(指每张,简单干燥≤8kg,干盐渍≤10kg,鲜或湿盐≤16kg)	8	17	13		千克/张	AB	Whole raw hides and skins of bovine animals, not split, have undergone a reversible tanning, w≤8kg when simply dried, w≤10kg when dry-salted, w≤16kg when fresh, wet-salted(including buffalo hides)
4101.2019	----其他	5	17	13		千克/张		----Other
4101.2019 10	规定重量非退鞣未剖层整张濒危生野牛皮(指每张,简单干燥≤8kg,干盐渍≤10kg,鲜或湿盐≤16kg)	5	17	13		千克/张	ABFE	Whole raw hides and skins of endangered wild bovine animals, not split, not have undergone a reversible tanning, not split, w≤8kg when simply dried, w≤10kg when dry-salted, w≤16kg when fresh, wet-salted
4101.2019 90	规定重量非退鞣未剖层处理整张生牛皮(包括水牛皮)(指每张,简单干燥≤8kg,干盐渍≤10kg,鲜或湿盐≤16kg)	5	17	13		千克/张	AB	Whole raw hides and skins of bovine animals, not split, not have undergone a reversible tanning, w≤8kg when simply dried, w≤10kg when dry-salted, w≤16kg when fresh, wet-salted(including buffalo hides)
4101.2020	---马皮	5	30	13		千克/张		---Of equine animals
4101.2020 10	规定重量未剖层整张濒危生野马皮(指每张,简单干燥≤8kg,干盐渍≤10kg,鲜或湿盐≤16kg)	5	30	13		千克/张	ABFE	Whole raw hides and skins of endangered wild equine animals, not split w≤8kg when simply dried, w≤10kg when dry-salted, w≤16kg when fresh, wet-salted
4101.2020 90	规定重量未剖层整张生马皮(指每张,简单干燥≤8kg,干盐渍≤10kg,鲜或湿盐≤16kg)	5	30	13		千克/张	AB	Whole raw hides and skins of equine animals, w≤8kg when simply dried, w≤10kg when dry-salted, w≤16kg when fresh, wet-salted
	-整张皮,重量超过16千克:							-Whole hides and skins, of a weight exceeding 16 kg:
	---牛皮:							---Of bovine animals:
4101.5011	----经退鞣处理的	8.4	17	13		千克/张		----Have undergone a reversible tanning process
4101.5011 10	重>16千克退鞣整张濒危生野牛皮	8.4	17	13		千克/张	ABFE	Whole raw hides and skins of endangered wild equine animals, have undergone a reversible tanning, W>16kg
4101.5011 90	重>16千克退鞣处理整张生牛皮(包括水牛皮)	8.4	17	13		千克/张	AB	Whole raw hides and skins of equine animals, have undergone a tanning which is reversible, W>16kg
4101.5019	----其他	5	17	13		千克/张		----Other
4101.5019 10	重>16千克非退鞣整张濒危生野牛皮	5	17	13		千克/张	ABFE	Whole raw hides and skins of endangered wild equine animals, not have undergone a reversible tanning, W>16kg
4101.5019 90	重>16千克非退鞣处理整张生牛皮(包括水牛皮)	5	17	13		千克/张	AB	Whole raw hides and skins of equine animals, not have undergone a reversible tanning, W>16kg(including buffalo hioles)
4101.5020	---马皮	5	30	13		千克/张		---Of equine animals
4101.5020 10	重>16千克整张濒危生野马皮	5	30	13		千克/张	ABFE	Whole raw hides and skins of endangered wild equine animals, W>16kg
4101.5020 90	重>16千克整张生马皮	5	30	13		千克/张	AB	Whole raw hides and skins of equine animals, W>16kg
	-其他,包括整张或半张的背皮及腹皮:							-Other, including butts, bends and bellies:
	---牛皮:							---Of bovine animals:
4101.9011	----经退鞣处理的	8.4	17	13		千克		----Have undergone a reversible tanning process
4101.9011 10	其他退鞣处理濒危生野牛皮(包括整张或半张的背皮及腹皮)	8.4	17	13		千克	FEAB	Other whole raw hides and skins (including butts, bends and bellies), of endangered wild bovine animals, have undergone a reversible tanning
4101.9011 90	其他退鞣处理生牛皮(包括整张或半张的背皮及腹皮)	8.4	17	13		千克	AB	Other whole raw hides and skins (including butts, bends and bellies), of bovine animals, have undergone a reversible tanning
4101.9019	----其他	5	17	13		千克		----Other

税则号列	货品名称	最惠(%)	普通	增值税率	出口退税	计量单位	监管条件	Article Description
4101.9019 10	其他濒危生野牛皮(包括整张或半张的背皮及腹皮)	5	17	17		千克	FEAB	Other whole raw hides and skins (including butts, bends and bellies), of endangered wild bovine animals
4101.9019 90	其他生牛皮(包括整张或半张的背皮及腹皮)	5	17	13		千克	AB	Other whole raw hides and skins (including butts, bends and bellies), of bovine animals
4101.9020	---马皮	5	30	13		千克		---of equine animals
4101.9020 10	其他濒危生野马皮(包括整张或半张的背皮及腹皮)	5	30	13		千克	FEAB	Other whole raw hides and skins (including butts, bends and bellies), of endangered wild equine animals
4101.9020 90	其他生马皮(包括整张或半张的背皮及腹皮)	5	30	13		千克	AB	Other whole raw hides and skins (including butts, bends and bellies), of equine animals
41.02	绵羊或羔羊生皮(鲜的、盐腌的、干的、石灰浸渍的、浸酸的或经其他方法保藏,但未鞣制、未经羊皮纸化处理或进一步加工的),不论是否带毛或剖层,但本章注释一(三)所述不包括的生皮除外:							**Raw skins of sheep or lambs (fresh, or salted, dried, limed, pickled or otherwise preseved, but not tanned, parchment-dressed or further prepared), whether or not with wool on or split, other than those excluded by Note 1 (c) to this Chapter:**
4102.1000	-带毛	7	30	13		千克/张	AB	-With wool on
	-不带毛:							-Without wool on:
	--浸酸的:							--Pickled:
4102.2110	---经退鞣处理的	14	30	13		千克/张	AB	---Have undergone a reversible tanning process
4102.2190	---其他	9	30	13		千克/张	AB	---Other
	--其他:							--Other:
4102.2910	---经退鞣处理的	14	30	13		千克/张	AB	---Have undergone a reversible tanning process
4102.2990	---其他	7	30	13		千克/张	AB	---Other
41.03	其他生皮(鲜的、盐渍的、干的、石灰浸渍的、浸酸的或以其他方法保藏,但未鞣制、未经羊皮纸化处理或进一步加工的),不论是否去毛或剖层,但本章注释一(二)或(三)所述不包括的生皮除外:							**Other raw hides and skins (fresh, or salted, dried, limed, pickled or otherwise preserved, but not tanned, parchment-dressed or further prepared), whether or not dehaired or split, other than those excluded by Note 1 (b) or 1 (c) to this Chapter:**
4103.2000	-爬行动物皮	9	30	13		千克/张	ABFE	-Of reptiles
4103.3000	-猪皮	9	30	13		千克/张		-Of swine
4103.3000 10	生鹿豚、姬猪皮	9	30	13		千克/张	ABFE	Raw hides and skins of pig-deer (*Babyrousa*)、pygmy pig (*Porcula*)
4103.3000 90	生猪皮	9	30	13		千克/张	AB	Raw hides and skins of swine
	-其他:							-Other:
	---山羊板皮:							---Of goats:
4103.9011	----经退鞣处理的	14	35	13		千克/张	AB	----Have undergone a reversible tanning process
4103.9019	-----其他	9	35	13		千克/张	AB	-----Other
	---其他山羊或小山羊皮:							---Other of goats or kids:
4103.9021	----经退鞣处理的	14	30	13		千克/张	AB	----Have undergone a reversible tanning process
4103.9029	----其他	9	30	13		千克/张	AB	----Other
4103.9090	---其他	9	30	13		千克/张		---Other
4103.9090 10	其他濒危野生动物生皮[本章注释一(二)或(三)所述不包括的生皮除外]	9	30	13		千克/张	ABEF	Other raw hides and skins of endangered wild animals, other than those excluded by Note 1(b) or 1 (c) to this Chapter
4103.9090 90	其他生皮[本章注释一(二)或(三)所述不包括的生皮除外]	9	30	13		千克/张	AB	Other raw hides and skins of animals, other than those excluded by Note 1 (b) or (c) to this Chapter
41.04	经鞣制的不带毛牛皮(包括水牛皮)、马皮及其坯革,不论是否剖层,但未经进一步加工:							**Tanned or crust hides and skins of bovine (including buffalo) or equine animals, without hair on, whether or not split, but not further prepared:**
	-湿革(包括蓝湿皮):							-In the wet state (including wet-blue)
	--全粒面未剖层革;粒面剖层革:							--Full grains, unsplit; grain splits:
	---牛皮:							---Of bovine animals:
4104.1111暂	----蓝湿的	3	17	17		千克		----Wet-blue

税则号列	货品名称	最惠(%)	普通	增值税率	出口退税	计量单位	监管条件	Article Description
4104.1111暂 10	蓝湿濒危野牛皮(全粒面未剖或粒面剖层,经鞣制不带毛)	3	17	17		千克	ABFE	Tanned or crust hides and skins of endangered wild bovine animals, without hair on, in the wet-blue state, full grains, unsplit or grain splits
4104.1111暂 90	全粒面未剖层或粒面剖层蓝湿牛皮(经鞣制不带毛)	3	17	17		千克	AB	Tanned or crust hides and skins of bovine animals, without hair on, in the wet-blue state, full grains, unsplit, grain splits
4104.1119	----其他	8	35	17		千克		----Other
4104.1119 10	湿濒危野牛皮(全粒面未剖或粒面剖层,经鞣制不带毛)	8	35	17		千克	FE	Tanned or crust hides and skins of endangered wild bovine animals, without hair on, full grains, unsplit or grain splits, in the wet state
4104.1119 90	全粒面未剖层或粒面剖层湿牛皮(经鞣制不带毛)	8	35	17		千克		Tanned or crust hides and skins of bovine animals, without hair on, full grains, unsplit or grain splits, in the wet state
4104.1120	---马皮	5	35	17		千克		---Of equine animals
4104.1120 10	湿濒危野马皮(全粒面未剖或粒面剖层,经鞣制不带毛)	5	35	17		千克	FE	Tanned or crust hides and skins of endangered wild equine animals, without hair on, full grains, unsplit or grain splits, in the wet state
4104.1120 90	全粒面未剖层或粒面剖层湿马皮(经鞣制不带毛)	5	35	17		千克		Tanned or crust hides and skins of equine animals, without hair on, full grains, unsplit or grain splits, in the wet state
	--其他:							--Other:
	---牛皮:							---Of bovine animals:
4104.1911暂	----蓝湿的	3	17	17		千克		----Wet-blue
4104.1911暂 10	其他蓝湿濒危野牛皮(经鞣制不带毛)	3	17	17		千克	ABFE	Other tanned or crust hides and skins of endangered wild bovine animals, without hair on, in the wet-blue state
4104.1911暂 90	其他蓝湿牛皮(经鞣制不带毛)	3	17	17		千克	AB	Other tanned or crust hides and skins, of bovine animals, without hair on, in the wet-blue state
4104.1919	----其他	7	35	17		千克		----Other
4104.1919 10	其他湿濒危野牛皮(经鞣制不带毛)	7	35	17		千克	FE	Other tanned or crust hides and skins of endangered wild bovine animals, without hair on, in the wet state
4104.1919 90	其他湿牛皮(经鞣制不带毛)	7	35	17		千克		Other tanned or crust hides and skins of bovine animals, without hair on, in the wet state
4104.1920暂	---马皮	5	35	17		千克		---Of equine animals
4104.1920暂 10	其他湿濒危野马皮(经鞣制不带毛)	5	35	17		千克	FE	Other tanned or crust hides and skins of endangered wild equine animals, without hair on, in the wet state
4104.1920暂 90	其他湿马皮(经鞣制不带毛)	5	35	17		千克		Other tanned or crust hides and skins of equine animals, without hair on, in the wet state
	-干革(坯革):							-In the dry state(crust):
4104.4100暂	--全粒面未剖层或粒面剖层革的	3	35	17		千克		--Full grain, unsplit; grain splits
4104.4100暂 10	濒危野牛马干革(全粒面未剖或粒面剖层,经鞣制不带毛)	3	35	17		千克	FE	Tanned or crust hides and skins of endangered wild bovine or equine animals, without hair on, full grains, unsplit or grain splits, in the dry state (crust)
4104.4100暂 90	全粒面未剖层或粒面剖层干革(经鞣制不带毛)	3	35	17		千克		Tanned or crust hides and skins, without hair on, full grains, unsplit; grain splits, in the dry state (crust)
	--其他:							--Other:
4104.4910	---机器带用牛、马皮革	5	20	17		千克		---For machinery belting
4104.4910 10	其他机器带用濒危野牛马皮革(经鞣制不带毛)	5	20	17		千克	FE	Tanned or crust hides and skins of endangered wild bovine or equine animals, without hair on, for machinery belting
4104.4910 90	其他机器带用牛马皮革(经鞣制不带毛)	5	20	17		千克		Tanned or crust hides and skins of bovine, equine animals, without hair on, for machinery belting
4104.4990	---其他	7	35	17		千克		---Other
4104.4990 10	其他濒危野牛马皮革(经鞣制不带毛)	7	35	17		千克	FE	Other tanned or crust hides and skins of endangered wild bovine or equine animals, without hair on

税则号列	货品名称	最惠(%)	普通	增值税率	出口退税	计量单位	监管条件	Article Description
4104.4990 90	其他牛马皮革(经鞣制不带毛)	7	35	17		千克		Other tanned or crust hides and skins of bovine, equine animals, without hair on
41.05	**经鞣制的不带毛绵羊或者羔羊皮及其坯革,不论是否剖层,但未经进一步加工:**							**Tanned or crust skins of sheep or lambs, without wool on, whether or not split, but not further prepared:**
	-湿革(包括蓝湿皮):							-In the wet state(including wet-blue):
4105.1010暂	---蓝湿的	10	50	17		千克	AB	---Wet-blue
4105.1090	---其他	10	50	17		千克		---Other
4105.3000	-干革(坯革)	8	50	17		千克		-In the dry state(crust)
41.06	**经鞣制的其他不带毛动物皮及其坯革,不论是否剖层,但未经进一步加工:**							**Tanned or crust hides and skins of other animals, without wool or hair on, whether or not split, but not further prepared:**
	-山羊或小山羊的:							-Of goats or kids:
4106.2100	--湿革(包括蓝湿皮)		50	17		千克		--In the wet state (including wet – blue)
4106.2100暂 01	蓝湿山羊皮(经鞣制不带毛)	10	50	17		千克		Tannde or crust hides and skins of goats in wet – blue, without hair on, in the wet state
4106.2100 90	其他山羊或小山羊湿革(经鞣制不带毛)	14	50	17		千克		Other tanned or crust skins of goats or kids, in the dry state, without hair on, in the wet state
4106.2200	--干革(坯革)	14	50	17		千克		--In the dry state(crust)
	-猪的:							-Of swine:
	--湿革(包括蓝湿皮):							--In the wet state(including wet-blue):
4106.3110暂	---蓝湿的	10	50	17		千克		---Wet-blue
4106.3110暂 10	蓝湿鹿豚、姬猪皮(经鞣制不带毛)	10	50	17		千克	FEAB	Tanned or crust hides and skins of pig-deer (*Babyrousa*)、pygmy pig (*Porcula*), without hair on, in the wet-blue state
4106.3110暂 90	其他蓝湿猪皮(经鞣制不带毛)	10	50	17		千克	AB	Other tanned or crust hides and skins of swine, without hair on, in the wet-blue state
4106.3190	---其他	14	50	17		千克		---Other
4106.3190 10	鹿豚、姬猪湿革(经鞣制不带毛)	14	50	17		千克	FE	Tanned or crust hides and skins of pig-deer (*Babyrousa*)、pygmy pig (*Porcula*), without hair on, in the wet state
4106.3190 90	其他猪湿革(经鞣制不带毛)	14	50	17		千克		Other tanned or crust hides and skins of swine, without hair on, in the wet state
4106.3200	--干革(坯革)	14	50	17		千克		--In the dry state(crust)
4106.3200 10	鹿豚、姬猪干革(经鞣制不带毛,坯革)	14	50	17		千克	FE	Tanned or crust hides and skins of pig-deer (*Babyrousa*)、pygmy pig (*Porcula*), without hair on, in the dry state
4106.3200 90	其他猪干革(经鞣制不带毛,坯革)	14	50	17		千克		Other tanned or crust hides and skins of swine, without hair on, in the dry state
4106.4000	-爬行动物的	14	50	17		千克	FE	-Of reptiles
	-其他:							-Other:
4106.9100	--湿革(包括蓝湿皮)	14	50	17		千克		--In the wet state(including wet-blue)
4106.9100 10	其他濒危野生动物湿革(经鞣制不带毛)	14	50	17		千克	FE	Tanned or crust hides and skins of other endangered wild animals, without wool or hair on, in the wet state
4106.9100 90	其他动物湿革(经鞣制不带毛)	14	50	17		千克		Tanned or crust hides and skins of other animals, without wool or hair on, in the wet state
4106.9200	--干革(坯革)	14	50	17		千克		--In the dry state(crust)
4106.9200 10	濒危其他野生动物干革(经鞣制不带毛)	14	50	17		千克	FE	Tanned or crust hides and skins of other endangered wild animals, without wool or hair on, in the dry state
4106.9200 90	其他动物干革(经鞣制不带毛)	14	50	17		千克		Tanned or crust hides and skins of other animals, without wool or hair on, in the dry state

税则号列	货品名称	最惠(%)	普通	增值税率	出口退税	计量单位	监管条件	Article Description
41.07	经鞣制或半硝处理后进一步加工的不带毛的牛皮革(包括水牛皮革)及马皮革,包括羊皮纸化处理的皮革,不论是否剖层,但税目**41.14**的皮革除外:							**Leather further prepared after tanning or crusting, including parchment-dressed leather, of bovine (including buffalo) or equine animals, without hair on, whether or not split, other than leather of heading 41.14:**
	-整张的:							-Whole hides and skins:
	--全粒面未剖层革:							--Full grains, unsplit:
4107.1110	---牛皮	8	50	17		千克/张		---Of bovine animals
4107.1110 10	全粒面未剖层整张濒危野牛皮(经鞣制或半硝后进一步加工,羊皮纸化处理)	8	50	17		千克/张	FE	Leather further prepared after tanning or crusting, including parchment-dressed leather, of endangered wild bovine animals, whole hides and skins, full grains, unsplit
4107.1110 90	全粒面未剖层整张牛皮(经鞣制或半硝后进一步加工,羊皮纸化处理)	8	50	17		千克/张		Leather further prepared after tanning or crusting, including parchment-dressed leather, of bovine animals, whole hides and skins, full grains, unsplit
4107.1120	---马皮	5	50	17		千克/张		---Of equine animals
4107.1120 10	全粒面未剖层整张濒危野马皮(经鞣制或半硝后进一步加工,羊皮纸化处理)	5	50	17		千克/张	FE	Leather further prepared after tanning or crusting, including parchment-dressed leather, of endangered wild equine animals, whole hides and skins, full grains, unsplit
4107.1120 90	全粒面未剖层整张马皮(经鞣制或半硝后进一步加工,羊皮纸化处理)	5	50	17		千克/张		Leather further prepared after tanning or crusting, including parchment-dressed leather, of equine animals, whole hides and skins, full grains, unsplit
	--粒面剖层革:							--Grain splits:
4107.1210暂	---牛皮	6	50	17		千克/张		---Of bovine animals
4107.1210暂 10	粒面剖层整张濒危野牛皮(经鞣制或半硝后进一步加工,羊皮纸化处理)	6	50	17		千克/张	FE	Leather further prepared after tanning or crusting, including parchment-dressed leather, of endangered wild bovine animals, whole hides and skins, grain splits
4107.1210暂 90	粒面剖层整张牛皮(经鞣制或半硝后进一步加工,羊皮纸化处理)	6	50	17		千克/张		Leather further prepared after tanning or crusting, including parchment-dressed leather, of bovine animals, whole hides and skins, grain splits
4107.1220	---马皮	5	50	17		千克/张		---Of equine animals
4107.1220 10	粒面剖层整张濒危野马皮(经鞣制或半硝后进一步加工,羊皮纸化处理)	5	50	17		千克/张	FE	Leather further prepared after tanning or crusting, including parchment-dressed leather, of endangered wild equine animals, whole hides and skins, grain splits
4107.1220 90	粒面剖层整张马皮(经鞣制或半硝后进一步加工,羊皮纸化处理)	5	50	17		千克/张		Leather further prepared after tanning or crusting, including parchment-dressed leather, of equine animals, whole hides and skins, grain splits
	--其他:							--Other:
4107.1910	---机器带用	5	50	17		千克/张		---For machinery belting
4107.1910 10	其他机器带用整张濒危野牛马皮革(经鞣制或半硝后进一步加工,羊皮纸化处理)	5	50	17		千克/张	FE	Leather further prepared after tanning or crusting, including parchment-dressed leather, of endangered wild bovine or wild equine amimals, whole hides and skins, for machinery belting
4107.1910 90	其他机器带用整张牛马皮革(经鞣制或半硝后进一步加工,羊皮纸化处理)	5	50	17		千克/张		Leather further prepared after tanning or crusting, including parchment-dressed leather, of bevine or equine animals, whole hides and skins, for machinery belting
4107.1990	---其他	7	50	17		千克/张		---Other
4107.1990 10	其他整张濒危野牛马皮革(经鞣制或半硝后进一步加工,羊皮纸化处理)	7	50	17		千克/张	FE	Other leather further prepared after tanning or crusting, including parchment-dressed leather of endangered wild bovine or wild equine amimals, whole hides and skins

税则号列	货品名称	最惠(%)	普通	增值税率	出口退税	计量单位	监管条件	Article Description
4107.1990 90	其他整张牛马皮革(经鞣制或半硝后进一步加工,羊皮纸化处理)	7	50	17		千克/张		Other leather further prepared after tanning or crusting, including parchment - dressed leather of bovine or equine animals, whole hides and skins
	-其他,包括半张的:							-Other, including sides:
4107.9100	--全粒面未剖层革	5	50	17		千克		--Full grains, unsplit
4107.9100 10	全粒面未剖层非整张濒危野牛马皮(经鞣制或半硝后进一步加工,羊皮纸化处理)	5	50	17		千克	FE	Leather further prepared after tanning or crusting, including parchment-dressed leather of endangered wild bovine or wild equine animals, other than whole hides and skins, full grains, unsplit
4107.9100 90	全粒面未剖层非整张革(经鞣制或半硝后进一步加工,羊皮纸化处理)	5	50	17		千克		Leather further prepared after tanning or crusting, including parchment-dressed leather, other than whole hides and skins, full grains, unsplit
4107.9200	--粒面剖层革	5	50	17		千克		--Grain splits
4107.9200 10	粒面剖层非整张濒危野牛马皮革(经鞣制或半硝后进一步加工,羊皮纸化处理)	5	50	17		千克	FE	Leather further prepared after tanning or crusting, including parchment-dressed leather, of endangered wild bovine or wild equine animals, other than whole hides and skins, grain, splits
4107.9200 90	粒面剖层非整张革(经鞣制或半硝后进一步加工,羊皮纸化处理)	5	50	17		千克		Leather further prepared after tanning or crusting, including parchment-dressed leather, other than whole hides and skins, grain, splits
	--其他:							--Other:
4107.9910	---机器带用	5	50	17		千克		---For machinery belting
4107.9910 10	其他机器带用非整张濒危野牛马皮(经鞣制或半硝后进一步加工,羊皮纸化处理)	5	50	17		千克	FE	Leather further prepared after tanning or crusting, including parchment-dressed leather of endangered wild bovine or wild equine animals, other than whole hides and skins, for machinery belting
4107.9910 90	其他机器带用非整张牛马皮革(经鞣制或半硝后进一步加工,羊皮纸化处理)	5	50	17		千克		Leather further prepared after tanning or crusting, including parchment-dressed leather, of bovine or equine animals, other than whole hides and skins, for machinery belting
4107.9990	---其他	7	50	17		千克		---Other
4107.9990 10	其他非整张濒危野牛马皮革(经鞣制或半硝后进一步加工,羊皮纸化处理)	7	50	17		千克	FE	Other leather further prepared after tanning or crusting, including parchment-dressed leather, of endangered wild bovine or wild equine animals, other than whole hides and skins
4107.9990 90	其他非整张牛马皮革(经鞣制或半硝后进一步加工,羊皮纸化处理)	7	50	17		千克		Other leather further prepared after tanning or crusting, (including parchment-dressed leather, of bovine or equine animals, other than whole hides and skins)
41.12	**经鞣制或半硝处理后进一步加工的不带毛的绵羊或羔羊皮革,包括羊皮纸化处理的,不论是否剖层,但税目41.14的皮革除外:**							**Leather further prepared after tanning or crusting, including parchment-dressed leather, of sheep or lamb, without wool on, whether or not split, other than leather of heading No. 41.14:**
4112.0000	经鞣制或半硝处理后进一步加工的不带毛的绵羊或羔羊皮革,包括羊皮纸化处理的,不论是否剖层,但税目41.14的皮革除外	8	50	17		千克		Leather further prepared after tanning or crusting, including parchment-dressed leather, of sheep or lamb, without wool on, whether or not split, other than leather of heading No. 41.14
41.13	**经鞣制或半硝处理后进一步加工的不带毛的其他动物皮革,包括羊皮纸化处理的,不论是否剖层,但税目41.14的皮革除外:**							**Leather further prepared after tanning or crusting, including parchment-dressed leather, of other animals, without wool or hair on, whether or not split, other than leather of heading No. 41.14:**
4113.1000	-山羊或小山羊皮的	14	50	17		千克		-Of goats or kids
4113.2000	-猪皮的	14	50	17		千克		-Of swine

税则号列	货 品 名 称	最惠(%)	普通	增值税率	出口退税	计量单位	监管条件	Article Description
4113.2000 10	加工的鹿豚、姬猪皮革(经鞣制或半硝后进一步加工,不带毛,羊皮纸化处理)	14	50	17		千克	FE	Leather further prepared after tanning or crusting, including parchment-dressed leather, of pig-deer (*Babyrousa*)、pygmy pig (*Porcula*), without hair on
4113.2000 90	加工的猪皮革(经鞣制或半硝后进一步加工,不带毛,羊皮纸化处理)	14	50	17		千克		Leather further prepared after tanning or crusting, including parchment-dressed leather, of swine, without hair on
4113.3000	-爬行动物皮的	14	50	17		千克	FE	-Of reptiles
4113.9000	-其他	14	50	17		千克		-Other
4113.9000 10	加工的其他濒危野生动物皮革(经鞣制或半硝后进一步加工,不带毛,羊皮纸化处理)	14	50	17		千克	FE	Leather further prepared after tanning or crusting, including parchment-dressed leather, of endangered wild animals, without wool or hair on
4113.9000 90	加工的其他动物皮革(经鞣制或半硝后进一步加工,不带毛,羊皮纸化处理)	14	50	17		千克		Leather further prepared after tanning or crusting, including parchment-dressed leather, of other animals, without wool or hair on
41.14	**油鞣皮革(包括结合鞣制的油鞣皮革);漆皮及层压漆皮;镀金属皮革:**							**Chamois(including combination chamois) leather; patent leather and patent laminated leather; metallised leather:**
4114.1000	-油鞣皮革(包括结合鞣制的油鞣皮革)	14	50	17		千克		-Chamois(including combination chamois) leather
4114.1000 10	油鞣其他濒危野生动物皮革(包括结合鞣制的油鞣皮革)	14	50	17		千克	FE	Chamois (including combination chamois) leather of endangered wild animals
4114.1000 90	油鞣其他动物皮革(包括结合鞣制的油鞣皮革;野生动物皮革除外)	14	50	17		千克		Chamois (including combination chamois) leather of other animals
4114.2000	-漆皮及层压漆皮;镀金属皮革	10	50	17		千克		-Patent leather and patent laminated leather; metallised leather
41.15	**以皮革或皮革纤维为基本成分的再生皮革,成块、成张或成条的,不论是否成卷;皮革或再生皮革的边角废料,不适宜作皮革制品用;皮革粉末:**							**Composition leather with a basis of leather or leather fibre, in slabs, sheets or strip, whether or not in rolls; parings and other waste of leather or of composition leather, not suitable for the manufacture of leather articles; leather dust, powder and flour:**
4115.1000	-以皮革或皮革纤维为基本成分的再生皮革,成块、成张或成条,不论是否成卷	14	50	17		千克		-Composition leather with a basis of leather or leather fibre, in slabs, sheets or strip, whether or not in rolls
4115.2000	-皮革或再生皮革的边角废料,不适宜作皮革制品用;皮革粉末	14	50	17		千克		-Parings and other waste of leather or of composition leather, not suitable for the manufacture of leather articles; leather dust, powder and flour
4115.2000 10	皮革废渣、灰渣、淤渣及粉末	14	50	17		千克	9	Waste residue, dust, powder and flour of leather or of composition leather
4115.2000 90	成品皮革、皮革制品或再生皮革的边角料(经过筛选的,面积≥200 平方厘米的皮革边角料,用于手套、配饰、玩具等的加工)	14	50	17		千克	AP	The leftover bits and pieces of finished leather, leather or recycled leather products (after screening, area is larger than 200 square centimeters of leather scrap, used for processing gloves, accessories, toys, etc.)

第四十二章
皮革制品;鞍具及挽具;旅行用品、手提包及类似容器;动物肠线(蚕胶丝除外)制品

注释:

一、本章所称的“皮革”包括油鞣皮革(含结合鞣制的油鞣皮革)、漆皮、层压漆皮和镀金属皮革。

二、本章不包括:

(一)外科用无菌肠线或类似的无菌缝合材料(税目30.06);

(二)以毛皮或人造毛皮衬里或作面(仅饰边的除外)的衣服及衣着附件(分指手套、连指手套及露指手套除外)(税目43.03或43.04);

(三)网线袋及类似品(税目56.08);

(四)第六十四章的物品;

(五)第六十五章的帽类及其零件;

(六)税目66.02的鞭子、马鞭或其他物品;

(七)袖扣、手镯或其他仿首饰(税目71.17);

(八)单独进口或出口的挽具附件或装饰物,例如,马镫、马嚼子、马铃铛及类似品、带扣(一般归入第十五类);

(九)弦线、鼓面皮或类似品及其他乐器零件(税目92.09);

(十)第九十四章的物品(例如,家具、灯具及照明装置);

(十一)第九十五章的物品(例如,玩具、游戏品及运动用品);

(十二)税目96.06的钮扣、揿扣、钮扣芯或这些物品的其他零件、钮扣坯。

三、(一)除上述注释二所规定的以外,税目42.02也不包括:

1. 非供长期使用的带把手塑料薄膜袋,不论是否印制(税目39.23);

2. 编结材料制品(税目46.02)。

(二)税目42.02、42.03的制品,如果装有用贵金属、包贵金属、天然或养殖珍珠、宝石或半宝石(天然、合成或再造)制的零件,即使这些零件不是仅作为小配件或小饰物的,只要其未构成物品的基本特征,仍应归入上述税号。但如果这些零件已构成物品的基本特征,则应归入第七十一章。

四、税目42.03所称“衣服及衣着附件”,主要包括分指手套、连指手套及露指手套(包括运动及防护手套)、围裙及其他防护用衣着、裤吊带、腰带、子弹带及腕带,但不包括表带(税目91.13)。

Chapter 42
Articles of leather; saddlery and harness; travel goods, handbags and similar containers; articles of animal gut (other than silk-worm gut)

Notes:

1. For the purposes of this Chapter, the term “leather” includes chamois (including combination chamois) leather, patent leather, patent laminated leather and metallised leather

2. This Chapter does not cover:

(a) Sterile surgical catgut or similar sterile suture materials (heading No. 30.06);

(b) Articles of apparel or clothing accessories (except gloves, mittens and mitts), lined with furskin or artificial fur or to which furskin or artificial fur is attached on the outside except as mere trimming (heading No. 43.03 or 43.04);

(c) Made up articles of netting (heading No. 56.08);

(d) Articles of Chapter 64;

(e) Headgear or parts thereof of Chapter 65;

(f) Whips, riding-crops or other articles of heading No. 66.02;

(g) Cuff-links, bracelets or other imitation jewellery (heading No. 71.17);

(h) Fittings or trimmings for harness, such as stirrups, bits, horse brasses and buckles, separately presented (generally Section XV);

(i) Strings, skins for drums or the like, or other parts of musical instruments (heading No. 92.09);

(j) Articles of Chapter 94 (for example, furniture, lamps and lighting fittings);

(k) Articles of Chapter 95 (for example, toys, games, sports requisites);

(l) Buttons, press-fasteners, snap-fasteners, pres-sstuds, button moulds or other parts of these articles, button blanks, of heading No. 96.06.

3. (a) In addition to the provisions of Note 2 above, heading No. 42.02 does not cover:

(1) Bags made of sheeting of plastics, whether or not printed, with handles, not designed for prolonged use (heading No. 39.23);

(2) Articles of plaiting materials (heading No. 46.02).

(b) Articles of headings No. 42.02 and 42.03 which have parts of precious metal or metal clad with precious metal, of natural or cultured pearls, of precious or semi-precious stones (natural, synthetic or reconstructed) remain classified in those headings even if such parts constitute more than minor fittings or minor ornamentation, provided that these parts do not give the articles their essential character. If, on the other hand, the parts give the articles their essential character, the articles are to be classified in Chapter 71.

4. For the purpose of heading No. 42.03, the expression “articles of apparel and clothing accessories” applies, *inter alia*, to gloves, mittens and mitts (including those for sport or for protection), aprons and other protective clothing, braces, belts, bandoliers and wrist straps, but excluding watch straps (heading No. 91.13).

税则号列	货　品　名　称	最惠(%)	普通	增值税率	出口退税	计量单位	监管条件	Article Description
42.01	各种材料制成的鞍具及挽具(包括缰绳、挽绳、护膝垫、口套、鞍褥、马褡裢、狗外套及类似品),适合各种动物用:							**Saddlery and harness for any animal (including traces, leads, knee pads, muzzles, saddle cloths, saddle bags, dog coats and the like), of any material:**
4201.0000	各种材料制成的鞍具及挽具(包括缰绳、挽绳、护膝垫、口套、鞍褥、马褡裢、狗外套及类似品),适合各种动物用	20	100	17		千克		Saddlery and harness for any animal (including traces, leads, knee pads, muzzles, saddle cloths, saddle bags, dog coats and the like), of any material
4201.0000 10	濒危野生动物材料制的鞍具及挽具(适合各种动物用)	20	100	17		千克	FE	Saddlery and harness for any animal of material of endangered wild animals
4201.0000 90	各种材料制成的鞍具及挽具(野生动物材料制的除外;适合各种动物用)	20	100	17	13	千克		Saddlery and harness for any animal, of any material, other than the material of wild animals
42.02	衣箱、提箱、小手袋、公文箱、公文包、书包、眼镜盒、望远镜盒、照相机套、乐器盒、枪套及类似容器;旅行包、食品或饮料保温包、化妆包、帆布包、手提包、购物袋、钱夹、钱包、地图盒、烟盒、烟袋、工具包、运动包、瓶盒、首饰盒、粉盒、刀叉餐具盒及类似容器,用皮革或再生皮革、塑料片、纺织材料、钢纸或纸板制成,或者全部或主要用上述材料或纸包覆制成:							**Trunks, suit-cases, vanity-cases, executive-cases, brief-cases, school satchels, spectacle cases, binocular cases, camera cases, musical instrument cases, gun cases, holsters and similar containers; travelling-bags, insulated food or beverages bags, toilet bags, rucksacks, handbags, shopping-bags, wallets, purses, map-cases, cigarett-cases, tobacco-pouches, tool bags, sports bags, bottle-cases, jewellery boxes, powder-boxes, cutlery cases and similar containers, of leather or of composition leather, of sheeting of plastics, of textile materials, of vulcanized fibre or of paperboard, or wholly or mainly covered with such materials or with paper:**
	-衣箱、提箱、小手袋、公文箱、公文包、书包及类似容器:							-Trunks, suit-cases, vanity-cases, executive-cases, brief-cases, school satchels and similar containers:
	--以皮革或再生皮革作面:							--With outer surface of leather or of composition leather:
4202.1110	---衣箱	15	100	17		千克/个		---Trunks and suit-cases
4202.1110 10	以含濒危野生动物皮革或再生皮革作面的衣箱	15	100	17		千克/个	FE	Trunks with outer surface of leather, of composition leather or of patent leather, of endangered wild animals
4202.1110 90	其他以皮革或再生皮革作面的衣箱	15	100	17	15	千克/个		Trunks with outer surface of leather, of composition leather, other than of wild animals
4202.1190	---其他	10	100	17		千克/个		---Other
4202.1190 10	以濒危野生动物皮革或再生皮革作面的箱包(包括提箱、小手袋、公文包、书包及类似容器,但不包括衣箱)	10	100	17		千克/个	FE	Cases with outer surface of leather, of composition leather, of wild animals, in imminent dangers (including trunks, suit - cases, vanity - cases, executive - cases, brief - cases, school satchels and similar containers)
4202.1190 90	其他以皮革或再生皮革作面的箱包(包括提箱、小手袋、公文包、书包及类似容器,但不包括衣箱)	10	100	17	15	千克/个		Cases (suit - cases, brief - cases, school satchels and similar containers, other than trunks) with outer surface of leather, of composition leather
	--以塑料或纺织材料作面:							--With outer surface of plastics or of textile materials:
4202.1210	---衣箱	20	100	17	15	千克/个		---Trunks and suit-cases
4202.1290	---其他	20	100	17	15	千克/个		---Other
4202.1900	--其他	20	100	17	15	千克/个		--Other
	-手提包,不论是否有背带,包括无把手的:							-Handbags, whether or not with shoulder strap, including those without handle:
4202.2100	--以皮革或再生皮革作面	10	100	17		千克/个		--With outer surface of leather or of composition leather
4202.2100 10	以濒危野生动物皮革或再生皮革作面的手提包(不论是否有背带,包括无把手的)	10	100	17		千克/个	FE	Handbags with outer surface of leather, of composition leather, of endangered wild animals (whether or not with shoulder strap, including those without handle)
4202.2100 90	其他以皮革或再生皮革作面手提包(不论是否有背带,包括无把手的)	10	100	17	15	千克/个		Handbags, whether or not with shoulder strap, including those without handle, with outer surface of leather, of composition leather

税则号列	货 品 名 称	最惠(%)	普通	增值税率	出口退税	计量单位	监管条件	Article Description
4202.2200	--以塑料片或纺织材料作面	10	100	17	15	千克/个		--With outer surface of plastic sheeting or of textile materials
4202.2900	--其他	20	100	17	15	千克/个		--Other
	-通常置于口袋或手提包内的物品:							-Articles of a kind normally carried in the pocket or in the handbag:
4202.3100	--以皮革或再生皮革或作面	10	100	17		千克/个		--With outer surface of leather or of composition leather
4202.3100 10	以濒危野生动物皮革或再生皮革作面的钱包等物品(指通常置于口袋或手提包内的物品)	10	100	17		千克/个	FE	Wallets or purses, with outer surface of leather, of composition leather of endangered wild animals
4202.3100 90	以皮革或再生皮革作面的钱包等物品(指通常置于口袋或手提包内的物品)	10	100	17	15	千克/个		Wallets or purses, with outer surface of leather, of composition leather
4202.3200	--以塑料片或纺织材料作面	20	100	17	15	千克/个		--With outer surface of plastic sheeting or of textile materials
4202.3900	--其他	20	100	17	15	千克/个		--Other
	-其他:							-Other:
4202.9100	--以皮革或再生皮革或作面	10	100	17		千克/个		--With outer surface of leather or of composition leather
4202.9100 10	濒危野生动物皮革或再生革作面的其他容器	10	100	17		千克/个	FE	Other containers with outer surface of leather, of composition leather, of endangered wild animals
4202.9100 90	其他皮革或再生皮革作面其他容器	10	100	17	15	千克/个		Other containers with outer surface of leather, of composition leather
4202.9200	--以塑料片或纺织材料作面	10	100	17	15	千克/个		--With outer surface of plastic sheeting or of textile materials
4202.9900	--其他	20	100	17	15	千克/个		--Other
42.03	**皮革或再生皮革制的衣服及衣着附件:**							**Articles of apparel and clothing accessories, of leather or of composition leather:**
4203.1000	-衣服	10	100	17		千克/件		-Articles of apparel
4203.1000 10	濒危野生动物皮革制的衣服(包括再生野生动物皮革制作的)	10	100	17		千克/件	FE	Articles of apparel of leather or of composition leather, of endangered wild animals
4203.1000 90	皮革或再生皮革制的衣服(野生动物皮革制作的除外)	10	100	17	13	千克/件		Articles of apparel of leather or of composition leather (other than leather of wild animals)
	-手套,包括连指或露指的:							-Gloves, mittens and mitts:
4203.2100	--专供运动用	20	100	17		千克/双		--Specially designed for use in sports
4203.2100 10	濒危野生动物皮革制的运动手套(包括再生野生动物皮革制作的)	20	100	17		千克/双	FE	Gloves, specially designed for use in sports, of leather or of composition leather, of endangered wild animals
4203.2100 90	皮革或再生皮革制专供运动用手套(包括连指或露指的,野生动物皮革制作的除外)	20	100	17	13	千克/双		Gloves, mittens and mitts, specially designed for use in sports, of leather or of composition leather, other than leather of wild animals
	--其他:							--Other:
4203.2910	---劳保手套	20	100	17		千克/双		---Working gloves
4203.2910 10	濒危野生动物皮革制的劳保手套(包括再生野生动物皮革制作的)	20	100	17		千克/双	FE	Working gloves, of leather or of composition leather, of endangered wild animals
4203.2910 90	皮革或再生皮革制的劳保手套(野生动物皮革制作的除外)	20	100	17	13	千克/双		Working gloves, of leather or of composition leather, other than leather of wild animals
4203.2990	---其他	20	100	17		千克/双		---Other
4203.2990 10	濒危野生动物皮革制的其他手套(包括再生野生动物皮革制作的)	20	100	17		千克/双	FE	Other gloves, mittens and mitts, of leather or of composition leather of endangered wild animals
4203.2990 90	皮革或再生皮革制的其他手套(包括连指或露指的)	20	100	17	13	千克/双		Other gloves, mittens and mitts, of leather or of composition leather
	-腰带及子弹带:							-Belts and bandoliers:
4203.3010	---腰带	10	100	17		千克		---Belts
4203.3010 10	濒危野生动物皮革制的腰带(包括再生野生动物皮革制作的)	10	100	17		千克	FE	Belts of leather or of composition leather of endangered wild animals
4203.3010 90	其他动物皮革制的腰带(包括再生动物皮革制作的)	10	100	17	13	千克		Belts of leather or of composition leather, of other animals
4203.3020	---子弹带	10	100	17		千克		---Bandoliers

税则号列	货品名称	最惠(%)	普通	增值税率	出口退税	计量单位	监管条件	Article Description
4203.3020 10	濒危野生动物皮革制的子弹带(包括再生野生动物皮革制作的)	10	100	17		千克	FE	Bandoliers of leather or of composition leather of endangered wild animals
4203.3020 90	其他动物皮革制的子弹带(包括再生动物皮革制作的)	10	100	17	13	千克		Bandoliers of leather or of composition leather of other animals
4203.4000	-其他衣着附件	20	100	17		千克		-Other clothing accessories
4203.4000 10	濒危野生动物皮革制的衣着附件(包括再生野生动物皮革制作的)	20	100	17		千克	FE	Clothing accessories of leather or of composition leather, of endangered wild animals
4203.4000 90	皮革或再生皮革制的其他衣着附件	20	100	17	13	千克		Other clothing accessories, of leather or of composition leather
42.05	**皮革或再生皮革的其他制品:**							**Other articles of leather or of composition leather:**
	-皮革或再生皮革的其他制品:							-Other articles of leather or of composition leather:
4205.0010	---坐具套	12	100	17		千克		---Cover of seat
4205.0010 10	濒危野生动物皮革制的坐具套(包括再生野生动物皮革制作的)	12	100	17		千克	FE	Covering of seats, of leather or of composition leather, of endangered wild animals
4205.0010 90	其他动物皮革制的坐具套(包括再生皮革制作的)	12	100	17	13	千克		Covering of seats, of leather or of composition leather, of other animals
4205.0020	---机器、机械器具或其他专门技术用途的	8	35	17		千克		---Of a kind used in machinery or mechanical apilances or for other technical uses
4205.0020 10	濒危野生动物皮革制工业用皮革或再生皮革制品(工业用指机器,机械器具或其他专门技术用途的)	8	35	17		千克	FE	Articles of leather or of composition leather of endangered animals, of a kind used in machinery or mechanial appilances or for other technical uses
4205.0020 90	其他工业用皮革或再生皮革制品(工业用指机器,机械器具或其他专门技术用途的)	8	35	17	13	千克		Other articles of leather or of composition leather, of a kind used in machinery or mechanial appilances or for other technical uses
4205.0090	---其他	12	100	17		千克		---Other
4205.0090 10	濒危野生动物皮革的其他制品(包括再生野生动物皮革制作的)	12	100	17		千克	FE	Other articles, of leather or of composition leather, of endangered wild animals
4205.0090 20	皮革或再生皮革制宠物用品	12	100	17	13	千克	AB	Articles for pets, of leather or of compostition leather
4205.0090 90	皮革或再生皮革的其他制品	12	100	17	13	千克		Other articles of leather or of composition leather
42.06	**肠线(蚕胶丝除外)、肠膜、膀胱或筋腱制品:**							**Articles of gut (other than silk-worm gut), of goldbeater's skin, of bladders or of tendons:**
4206.0000	肠线(蚕胶丝除外)、肠膜、膀胱或筋腱制品(不包括外科用无菌肠线或制成乐器弦的肠线,蚕胶丝除外)	20	90	17	5	千克		Articles of gut (other than silk-worm gut), of goldbeater's skin, of bladders or of tendons

第四十三章
毛皮、人造毛皮及其制品

Chapter 43
Furskins and artificial fur; manufactures thereof

注释:

一、本目录所称"毛皮",是指已鞣的各种动物的带毛毛皮,但不包括税目 43.01 的生毛皮。

二、本章不包括:

(一)带羽毛或羽绒的整张或部分鸟皮(税目 05.05 或 67.01);

(二)第四十一章的带毛生皮[见该章注释一(三)];

(三)用皮革与毛皮或用皮革与人造毛皮制成的分指手套、连指手套及露指手套(税目 42.03);

(四)第六十四章的物品;

(五)第六十五章的帽类及其零件;

(六)第九十五章的物品(例如,玩具、游戏品及运动用品)。

三、税目 43.03 包括加有其他材料缝合的毛皮和毛皮部分品,以及缝合成衣服、衣服部分品、衣着附件或其他制品的毛皮和毛皮部分品。

四、以毛皮或人造毛皮衬里或作面(仅饰边的除外)的衣服及衣着附件(不包括注释二所述的货品),应分别归入税目 43.03 或 43.04,但毛皮或人造毛皮仅作为装饰的除外。

五、本目录所称"人造毛皮",是指以毛、发或其他纤维粘附或缝合于皮革、织物或其他材料之上而构成的仿毛皮,但不包括以机织或针织方法制得的仿毛皮(一般应归入税目 58.01 或 60.01)。

Notes:

1. Throughout the Nomenclature references to "furskins", other than to raw furskins of heading No. 43.01, apply to hides or skins of all animals which have been tanned or dressed with the hair or wool on.

2. This Chapter does not cover:

(a) Birdskins or parts of birdskins, with their feathers or down (heading No. 05.05 or 67.01);

(b) Raw hides or skins, with the hair or wool on, of Chapter 41 (see Note 1 (c) to that Chapter);

(c) Gloves, mittens and mitts, consisting of leather and furskin or of leather and artificial fur (heading No. 42.03);

(d) Articles of Chapter 64;

(e) Headgear or parts thereof of Chapter 65;

(f) Articles of Chapter 95 (for example, toys, games, sports requisites).

3. Heading No. 43.03 includes furskins and parts thereof, assembled with the addition of other materials, and furskins and parts thereof, sewn together in the form of garments or parts or accessories of garments or in the form of other articles.

4. Articles of apparel and clothing accessories (except those excluded by Note 2) lined with furskin or artificial fur or to which furskin or artificial fur is attached on the outside except as mere trimming are to be classified in heading No. 43.03 or 43.04 as the case may be.

5. Throughout the Nomenclature the expression "artificial fur" means any imitation of furskin consisting of wool, hair or other fibres gummed or sewn on to leather, woven fabric or other materials, but does not include imitation furskins obtained by weaving or knitting (generally, heading No. 58.01 or 60.01).

税则号列	货品名称	最惠(%)	普通	增值税率	出口退税	计量单位	监管条件	Article Description
43.01	**生毛皮(包括适合加工皮货用的头、尾、爪及其他块、片),但税目 41.01、41.02 或 41.03 的生皮除外:**							**Raw furskins (including heads, tails, paws and other pieces or cuttings, suitable for furriers' use), other than raw hides and skins of heading No. 41.01, 41.02 or 41.03:**
4301.1000暂	-整张水貂皮,不论是否带头、尾或爪	10	100	13		千克	AB	-Of mink, whole, with or without head, tail or paws
4301.3000	-下列羔羊的整张毛皮,不论是否带头、尾或爪:阿斯特拉罕、喀拉科尔、波斯羔羊及类似羔羊、印度、中国或蒙古羔羊	20	90	13		千克	AB	-Of lamb, the following: Astrakhan, Broadtail, Caracul, Persian and similar lamb, Indian, Chinese, Mongolian or Tibetan lamb, whole, with or without head, tail or paws
4301.6000暂	--整张狐皮,不论是否带头、尾或爪	15	100	13		千克/张		-Of fox, whole, with or without head, tail or paws
4301.6000暂 10	整张濒危生狐皮(不论是否带头、尾或爪)	15	100	13		千克/张	AFEB	Raw furskins of endangered fox, whole, with or without head, tail or paws
4301.6000暂 90	其他整张生狐皮(不论是否带头、尾或爪)	15	100	13		千克/张	AB	Other raw furskins of fox, whole, with or without head, tail or paws
	-整张的其他毛皮,不论是否带头、尾或爪:							-Other furskins, whole, with or without head, tail or paws:
4301.8010	---整张兔皮,不论是否带头,尾或爪	20	90	13		千克/张		---Of rabbit or hare, whole, with or without head, tail or paws
4301.8010 10	整张生濒危野兔皮(不论是否带头,尾或爪)	20	90	13		千克/张	AFEB	Raw furskins of endangered wild rabbit or hare, whole, with or without head tail or paws
4301.8010 90	整张生兔皮(不论是否带头,尾或爪)	20	90	13		千克/张	AB	Raw furskins of rabbit or hare, whole, with or without head tail or paws

税则号列	货品名称	最惠(%)	普通	增值税率	出口退税	计量单位	监管条件	Article Description
4301.8090	---其他	20	90	13		千克/张		---Other
4301.8090 10	整张的其他生濒危野生动物毛皮(不论是否带头,尾或爪,包括整张濒危生海豹皮)	20	90	13		千克/张	ABEF	Raw furskins of other endangered wild animals, whole, with or without head tail or paws including endangered raw sealskin
4301.8090 90	整张的其他生毛皮(不论是否带头,尾或爪,包括整张生海豹皮)	20	90	13		千克/张	AB	Raw furskins of other animals, whole, with or without head tail or paws including raw sealskin
	-适合加工皮货用的头、尾、爪及其他块、片:							-Heads, tails, paws and other pieces or cuttings, suitable for furriers' use:
4301.9010	---黄鼠狼尾	20	50	13		千克	EABF	---Weasel tails
4301.9090	---其他	20	90	13		千克		---Other
4301.9090 10	其他濒危野生动物未鞣头尾(加工皮货用,包括爪及其他块、片)	20	90	13		千克	ABFE	Heads, tails, paws and other pieces or cuttings, of endangered wild animals, not tanned or dressed, suitable for furriers' use
4301.9090 90	适合加工皮货用的其他未鞣头、尾(包括爪及其他块、片)	20	90	13		千克	AB	Other heads, tails, paws and other pieces or cuttings of animals, not tanned or dressed, suitable for furriers' use
43.02	**未缝制或已缝制(不加其他材料)的已鞣毛皮(包括头、尾、爪及其他块、片),但税目43.03的货品除外:**							**Tanned or dressed furskins (including heads, tails, paws and other pieces or cuttings), unassembled, or assembled (without the addition of other materials) other than those of heading No. 43.03:**
	-未缝制的整张毛皮,不论是否带头、尾或爪:							-Whole skins, with or without head, tail or paws, not assembled:
4302.1100	--水貂皮	12	130	17	5	千克/张		--Of mink
	--其他:							--Other:
4302.1910	---灰鼠皮、白鼬皮、其他貂皮、狐皮、水獭皮、旱獭皮及猞猁皮	10	130	17		千克/张		---Of grey squirrel, ermine, other marten, fox, otter, marmot and lynx
4302.1910 10	已鞣未缝制的濒危狐皮(兰狐皮、银狐皮除外)	10	130	17		千克/张	FE	Tanned or dressed furskins of endangered fox, unassembled(other than furskins of blue fox or silver fox)
4302.1910 20	已鞣未缝制的兰狐皮、银狐皮	10	130	17	5	千克/张		Tanned or dressed furskins of blue fox, silver fox, unassembled
4302.1910 90	已鞣未缝制的其他贵重濒危动物毛皮(灰鼠皮、白鼬皮、其他貂皮、水獭皮、旱獭皮、猞猁皮)	10	130	17		千克/张	FE	Tanned or dressed furskins precious furskins of endangered animals(grey squirrel, ermine, other marten, fox, otter, marmot and lynx) unassembled
4302.1920	---兔皮	10	100	17		千克/张		---Of rabbit or hare
4302.1920 10	已鞣未缝制的整张濒危野兔皮(不论是否带头、尾或爪)	10	100	17		千克/张	FE	Tanned or dressed furskins of endangered rabbit or hare, endangered whole, with or without head tail or paws, unassembled
4302.1920 90	已鞣未缝制的整张兔皮(不论是否带头、尾或爪)	10	100	17	5	千克/张		Tanned or dressed furskins of rabbit or hare, whole, with or without head tail or paws, unassembled
4302.1930	---下列羔羊皮:阿斯特拉罕、喀拉科尔、波斯羔羊及类似羔羊、印度、中国或蒙古羔羊	20	100	17	5	千克/张		---Of lamb, the following: Astrakhan, Broadtail, Caracul, Persian and similar lamb, Indian, Chinese Mongolian or Tibetan lamb
4302.1990	---其他	10	100	17		千克/张		---Other
4302.1990 10	已鞣未缝制的其他濒危野生动物毛皮	10	100	17		千克/张	FE	Tanned or dressed furskins of other endangered wild animals, unassembled
4302.1990 90	已鞣未缝制的其他毛皮	10	100	17	5	千克/张		Other tanned or dressed furskins of other animals, unassembled
4302.2000	-未缝制的头、尾、爪及其他块、片	20	100	17		千克		-Heads, tails, paws and other pieces or cuttings, not assembled
4302.2000 10	已鞣未缝濒危野生动物头、尾、爪等(包括块、片)	20	100	17		千克	FE	Tanned or dressed heads, tails, paws and other pieces or cuttings, of endangered wild animals, unassembled
4302.2000 90	已鞣未缝制的头、尾、爪及其他块片	20	100	17	5	千克		Tanned or dressed heads, tails, paws and other pieces or cuttings of other animals, unassembled
	-已缝制的整张毛皮及其块、片:							-Whole skins and pieces or cuttings thereof, assembled:

税则号列	货品名称	最惠(%)	普通	增值税率	出口退税	计量单位	监管条件	Article Description
4302.3010	---灰鼠、白鼬、貂、狐、水獭、旱獭及猞猁的整张毛皮及其块、片	20	130	17		千克		---Of grey squirrel, ermine, other marten, fox, otter, marmot and lynx
4302.3010 10	已鞣已缝制貂皮、狐皮及其块、片(兰狐银狐、水貂、艾虎的整张毛皮及块、片除外)	20	130	17	5	千克	FE	Tanned or dressed whole skins and pieces or cuttings thereof, of marten, fox, other than whole skins and pieces or cuttings of blue fox, silver fox, mink, perwitsky (ferret-polecat), assembled
4302.3010 90	已鞣已缝制的贵重濒危动物毛皮及其块、片(灰鼠皮、白鼬皮、其他貂皮、水獭皮、旱獭皮、猞猁皮及块、片)	20	130	17		千克	FE	Tanned or dressed whole skins and pieces or cuttings thereof, of grey squirrel, ermine, other marten, fox, otter, marmot and lynx, endangered, assembled
4302.3090	---其他	20	100	17		千克		---Other
4302.3090 10	已鞣缝的其他整张濒危野生毛皮(包括块、片)	20	100	17		千克	FE	Tanned or dressed whole skins and pieces or cuttings thereof, of other endangered wild animals, assembled
4302.3090 90	已鞣已缝制的其他整张毛皮及块片	20	100	17	5	千克		Tanned or dressed whole skins and pieces or cuttings thereof, of other animals, assembled
43.03	**毛皮制的衣服、衣着附件及其他物品:**							**Articles of apparel, clothing accessories and other articles of furskin:**
	-衣服及衣着附件:							-Articles of apparel and clothing accessories:
4303.1010	---毛皮衣服	23	150	17		千克/件		---Articles of apparel
4303.1010 10	濒危野生动物毛皮衣服	23	150	17		千克/件	EF	Articles of apparel of endangered wild animals
4303.1010 90	其他毛皮衣服	23	150	17	13	千克/件		Articles of apparel of other animals
4303.1020	---毛皮衣着附件	18	150	17		千克		---Clothing accessories
4303.1020 10	濒危野生动物毛皮衣着附件	18	150	17		千克	EF	Clothing accessories of endangered wild animals
4303.1020 90	其他毛皮衣着附件	18	150	17	13	千克		Clothing accessories of other animals
4303.9000	-其他	18	150	17		千克		-Other
4303.9000 10	濒危野生动物毛皮制其他物品	18	150	17		千克	EF	Other articles of furskin, of endangered wild animals
4303.9000 90	其他毛皮制物品	18	150	17	13	千克		Other articles of furskin, of other animals
43.04	**人造毛皮及其制品:**							**Artificial fur and articles thereof:**
4304.0010	---人造毛皮	18	130	17	13	千克		---Artificial fur
4304.0020	---人造毛皮制品	18	150	17	13	千克		---Articles of artificial fur

第九类
木及木制品;木炭;软木及软木制品;稻草、秸秆、针茅或其他编结材料制品;篮筐及柳条编结品

SECTION IX
WOOD AND ARTICLES OF WOOD; WOOD CHARCOAL; CORK AND ARTICLES OF CORK; MANUFACTURES OF STRAW, OF ESPARTO OR OF OTHER PLAITING MATERIALS; BASKETWARE AND WICKERWORK

第四十四章
木及木制品;木炭

注释:

一、本章不包括:

(一)主要作香料、药料、杀虫、杀菌或类似用途的木片、刨花、碎木、木粒或木粉(品目12.11);

(二)竹或主要作编织用的其他木质材料呈原木状,不论是否经劈开,纵锯或切段(品目14.01);

(三)主要作染料或鞣料用的木片、刨花、木粒或木粉(品目14.04);

(四)活性炭(品目38.02);

(五)品目42.02的物品;

(六)第四十六章的货品;

(七)第六十四章的鞋靴及其零件;

(八)第六十六章的货品(例如,伞、手杖及其零件);

(九)税目68.08的货品;

(十)税目71.17的仿首饰;

(十一)第十六类或第十七类的货品(例如,机器零件,机器及器具的箱、罩、壳,车辆部件);

(十二)第十八类的货品(例如,钟壳、乐器及其零件);

(十三)火器的零件(税目93.05);

(十四)第九十四章的物品(例如,家具、灯具及照明器具、活动房屋);

(十五)第九十五章的物品(例如,玩具、游戏品及运动用品);

(十六)第九十六章的物品(例如,烟斗及其零件、钮扣、铅笔),但税目96.03所列物品的木身及木柄除外;

(十七)第九十七章的物品(例如,艺术品)。

二、本章所称"强化木",是指经过化学或物理方法处理(对于多层粘合木材,其处理应超出一般粘合需要),从而增加了密度或硬度并改善了机械强度、抗化学或抗电性能的木材。

Chapter 44
Wood and articles of wood; wood charcoal

Notes:

1. This Chapter does not cover:

(a) Wood, in chips, in shavings, crushed, ground or powdered, of a kind used primarily in perfumery, in pharmacy, or for insecticidal, fungicidal or similar purposes (heading No. 12. 11);

(b) Bamboos or other materials of a woody nature of a kind used primarily for plaiting, in the rough, whether or not split, sawn lengthwise or cut to length (heading No. 14. 01);

(c) Wood, in chips, in shavings, ground or powdered, of a kind used primarily in dyeing or in tanning (heading No. 14. 04);

(d) Activated charcoal (heading No. 38. 02);

(e) Articles of heading No. 42. 02;

(f) Goods of Chapter 46;

(g) Footwear or parts thereof of Chapter 64;

(h) Goods of Chapter 66 (for example, umbrellas and walking-sticks and parts thereof);

(i) Goods of heading No. 68. 08;

(j) Imitation jewellery of heading No. 71. 17;

(k) Goods of Section XVI or Section XVII (for example, machine parts, cases, covers, cabinets for machines and apparatus and wheel wrights' wares);

(l) Goods of Section XVIII (for example, clock cases and musical instruments and parts thereof);

(m) Parts of firearms (heading No. 93. 05);

(n) Articles of Chapter 94 (for example, furniture, lamps and lighting fittings, prefabricated buildings);

(o) Articles of Chapter 95 (for example, toys, games, sports requisites);

(p) Articles of Chapter 96 (for example, smoking pipes and parts thereof, buttons, pencils) excluding bodies and handles, of wood, for articles of heading No. 96. 03;

(q) Articles, of Chapter 97 (for example, works of art).

2. In this Chapter, the expression "densified wood" means wood which has been subjected to chemical or physical treatment (being, in the case of layers bonded together, treatment in excess of that needed to ensure a good bond), and which has thereby acquired increased density or hardness together with improved mechanical strength or resistance to chemical or electrical agencies.

三、税目44.14至44.21适用于木质碎料板或类似木质材料板、纤维板、层压板或强化木的制品。

四、税目44.10、44.11或44.12的产品,可以加工成税目44.09所述的各种形状,也可以加工成弯曲、瓦楞、多孔或其他形状(正方形或矩形除外),以及经其他任何加工,但未具有其他税目所列制品的特性。

五、税目44.17不包括装有第八十二章注释一所述材料制成的刀片、工作刃、工作面或其他工作部件的工具。

六、除上述注释一及其他条文另有规定的以外,本章税目中所称"木",也包括竹及其他木质材料。

子目注释:

一、子目4401.31所称"木屑棒"是指由木材加工工业、家具制造业及其他木材加工活动中产生的副产品(例如,刨花、锯末及碎木片)直接压制而成或加入按重量计不超过3%的粘合剂后粘聚而成的产品。此类产品呈圆柱状,其直径不超过25毫米,长度不超过100毫米。

二、子目号4403.41至4403.49,4407.21至4407.29,4408.31至4408.39及4412.31至4417.99所称"热带木",是指下列木材:

大叶帽柱木、非洲桃花心木、西非红豆木、箭毒木、阿兰木、圭亚那苦油楝木、非洲甘比山榄木、杜楝木、非洲栎柞木、婆罗双木、美洲轻木、白驼峰楝木、黑驼峰楝木、卡蒂沃木、雪松木、西非褐红椴木、深红色红柳桉木、非洲核桃楝木、阿夫苏木、象牙海岸榄仁木、破布木、吉贝木、丝棉木、乔状黄牛木、安哥拉丛花木、巴西胡桃木、皮蚁木、伊罗科木、拟爱神木、夹竹桃木、巴西红木、绒根木、龙脑香木、开姆帕斯木、羯布罗香木、康多非洲楝木、象牙海岸褐红椴木、象牙海岸翼梧桐木、浅红色红柳桉木、非洲榄仁木、南美樟木、圭亚那铁线子木、西印度桃花心木、猴子果木、肖民夸利亚木、曼孙梧桐木、马来蝴蝶木、巴梼红柳桉木、粗轴坡垒木、印茄木、斯温漆木、异翅香木、非洲梨木、非洲银叶木、胶木、非洲白梧桐木、加蓬榄木、蓖麻木、爱里古夷苏木、奥文科尔木、中非蜡烛木、紫檀木、人面子木、危地马拉黑黄檀木、印度黑黄檀木、巴西黑黄檀木、巴西柚、巴西花梨木、白坚木、鸡骨常山木、印马四出香木、大沃契希亚木、东西亚棱柱木、萨撇列木、萌生木棉木、苏帕楠木、西波木、苏古皮拉木、红椿木、圭亚那考拉玉蕊木、柚木、安哥拉香桃花心木、非洲阿勃木、南美肉豆蔻木、白柳桉木、白色红柳桉木、白色柳桉木、黄色红柳桉木。

3. Headings No. 44.14 to 44.21 apply to articles of the respective descriptions of particle board or similar board, fibreboard, laminated wood or densified wood as they apply to such articles of wood.

4. Products of heading No. 44.10, 44.11 or 44,12 may be worked to form the shapes provided for in respect of the goods of heading No. 44.09, curved, corrugated, perforated, cut or formed to shapes other than square or rectangular or submitted to any other operation provided it does not give them the character of articles of other headings.

5. Heading No. 44.17 does not apply to tools in which the blade, working edge, working surface or other working part is formed by any of the materials specified in Note 1 to Chapter 82.

6. Subject to Note 1 above and except where the context otherwise requires, any reference to "wood" in a heading of this Chapter applies also to bamboos and other materials of a woody nature.

Subheading Note:

1. For the purposes of Subheading 4401.31, the expression "wood pellets" means by – products such as cutter shavings, sawdust or chips, of the mechanical wood processing industry, furnitrue – mading industry or other wood transformation activities, which have been agglomerated either directly by compression or by the addition of a binder in a proportion not exceeding 3% by weight. Such pellets are cylindrical, with a diameter not exceeding 25mm and a length not exceeding 100mm

2. For the purposes of subheadings No. 4403.41 to 4403.49, 4407.21 to 4407.29, 4408.12 to 4408.39 and 4412.31, the expression "tropical wood" means one of the following types of wood:

Abura, Acajou d'Afrique, Afrormosia, Ako, Alan, Andiroba, Aningré, Avodiré, Azobé, Balau, Balsa, Bossé clair, Bossé- foncé, Cativo, Cedro, Dabema, Dark Red Meranti, Dibétou, Doussié, Framiré, Freijo, Fromager, Fuma, Geronggang, Ilomba, Imbuia, Ipé, Iroko, Jaboty, Jelutong, Jequitiba, Jongkong, Kapur, Kempas, Keruing, Kosipo, Kotib, Koto, Light Red Meranti, Limba, Louroé, Macaranduba, Mahogany, Makore, Mandioqueira, Mansonia, Mengkulang, Meranti Bakau, Merawan, Merbau, Merpauh, Mersawa, Moabi, Niangon, Nyatoh, Obeche, Okoum, Onzabili, Orey, Ovengkol, Ozigo, Padauk, Paldao, Palissandre de Guatemala, Palissandre de Para, Palissandre de Rio, Palissandre de Rose, Pau Amarelo, Pau Marfim, Pulai, Punah, Quaruba, Ramin, Sapelli, Saqui-Saqui, Sepetir, Sipo, Sucupira, Suren, Tauari Teak, Tiama, Tola, Virola, White Lauan, White Meranti, White Seraya, Yellow Meranti.

税则号列	货品名称	最惠(%)	普通	增值税率	出口退税	计量单位	监管条件	Article Description
44.01	**薪柴(圆木段、块、枝、成捆或类似形状);木片或木粒;锯末、木废料及碎片,不论是否粘结成圆木段、块、片或类似形状:**							**Fuel wood, in logs, in billets, in twigs, in faggots or in similar forms; wood in chips or particles; sawdust and wood waste and scrap, whether or not agglomerated in logs, briquettes, pellets or similar forms:**
4401.1000	-薪柴(圆木段、块、枝、成捆或类似形状)	0	70	17		千克	AB	-Fuel wood, in logs, in billets, in twigs, in faggots or in similar forms
	-木片或木粒:							-Wood in chips or particles:
4401.2100	--针叶木	0	8	17		千克		--Coniferous
4401.2100 10	濒危针叶木木片或木粒	0	8	17		千克	ABFE	Chips or particles of endangered coniferous wood
4401.2100 90	其他针叶木木片或木粒	0	8	17		千克	AB	Chips or particles of other coniferous wood
4401.2200	--非针叶木	0	8	17		千克		--Non-coniferous
4401.2200 10	濒危非针叶木木片或木粒	0	8	17		千克	ABFE	Chips or particles of endangered non-coniferous wood
4401.2200 90	其他非针叶木木片或木粒	0	8	17		千克	AB	Chips or particles of other non-coniferous wood

税则号列	货 品 名 称	最惠(%)	普通	增值税率	出口退税	计量单位	监管条件	Article Description
	-锯末、木废料及碎片,不论是否粘结成圆木段、块、片或类似形状:							-Sawdust and wood waste and scrap, whether or not agglomerated in logs, briquettes, pellets or similar forms:
4401.3100	--木屑棒	0	8	17		千克	ABP	--Wood pellets
4401.3900	--其他	0	8	17		千克	ABP	--Other
44.02	**木炭(包括果壳炭及果核炭),不论是否结块:**							**Wood charcoal (including shell or nut charcoal), whether or not agglomerated:**
4402.1000	-竹炭的	10.5	70	17		千克		-Of bamboo
4402.9000	-其他	10.5	70	17		千克		-Other
4402.9000 10	以木材为原料直接烧制的木炭	10.5	70	17		千克	8	Wood charcoal, obtained by burning wood
4402.9000 90	其他木炭(包括果壳炭及果核炭,不论是否结块)	10.5	70	17		千克		Other wood charcoal (including shell or nut charcoal, whether or not agglomerated)
44.03	**原木,不论是否去皮、去边材或粗锯成方:**							**Wood in the rough, whether or not stripped of bark or sapwood, or roughly squared:**
4403.1000	-用油漆,着色剂,杂酚油或其他防腐剂处理	0	8	13		千克/立方米		-Treated with paint, stains, creosote or other preservatives (treated with paint, stains, creosote or other preservatives)
4403.1000 10	油漆,着色剂等处理的红豆杉原木(包括用杂酚油或其他防腐剂处理)	0	8	13		千克/立方米	8AF	Other taxaceae wood in the rough (treated with paint, stains, creosote or other preservatives)
4403.1000 20	油漆,着色剂等处理的其他濒危树种原木(包括用杂酚油或其他防腐剂处理)	0	8	13		千克/立方米	8AF	Other endangered coniferous wood in the rough (treated with paint, stains, creoso te or other presevatives)
4403.1000 90	其他油漆,着色剂等处理的原木(包括用杂酚油或其他防腐剂处理)	0	8	13		千克/立方米	8A	Other wood in the rough, treated with paint, stains, creosote or other preservatives
	-其他针叶木:							-Other coniferous:
4403.2010	---红松和樟子松	0	8	13		千克/立方米		---Korean pine and Mongolian scotch pine
4403.2010 10	其他红松原木(用油漆着色剂、杂酚油或其他防腐剂处理的除外)	0	8	13		千克/立方米	8AEF	Other korean pine wood in the rough (other than the wood treated with paint, stains, creosote or other preservatives)
4403.2010 90	其他樟子松原木(用油漆着色剂、杂酚油或其他防腐剂处理的除外)	0	8	13		千克/立方米	8A	Other mongolian scotch pine in the rough (other than the wood treated with paint, stains, creosote or other preservatives)
4403.2020	---白松(云杉和冷杉)	0	8	13		千克/立方米	8AF	---White pine (spruce and fir)
4403.2020 10	濒危白松、云杉和冷杉原木	0	8	13		千克/立方米	8AF	Endangered white pine, spruce and fir, wood in the rough
4403.2020 90	其他白松、云杉和冷杉原木	0	8	13		千克/立方米	8A	Other white pine, spruce and fir, wood in the rough
4403.2030	---辐射松	0	8	13		千克/立方米	8A	---Radiata pine
4403.2040	---落叶松	0	8	13		千克/立方米	8A	---Larch
4403.2050	---花旗松	0	8	13		千克/立方米	8A	---Douglas fir
4403.2090	---其他	0	8	13		千克/立方米		---Other
4403.2090 10	其他红豆杉原木	0	8	13		千克/立方米	8AF	Other Endangered coniferous wood in the rough
4403.2090 20	其他濒危针叶木原木	0	8	13		千克/立方米	8AF	Other eandangered coniferous in the rough
4403.2090 90	其他针叶木原木	0	8	13		千克/立方米	8A	Other coniferous wood in the rough
	-其他,本章子目注释二所列的热带木:							-Other, of tropical wood specified in Subheading Note 2 to this Chapter:
4403.4100	--深红色红柳安木、浅红色红柳安木及巴栲红柳安木	0	8	13		千克/立方米	8A	--Dark Red Meranti, Light Red Meranti and Meranti Bakau
	--其他:							--Other (of tropical non-contiferous wood specified in subheading note 1 to this chapter):
4403.4910	---柚木	0	35	13		千克/立方米	8A	---Teak
4403.4920	---奥克曼(奥克榄)	0	35	13		千克/立方米	8A	---*Okoume*(Au koumed)
4403.4930	---龙脑香木(克隆)	0	35	13		千克/立方米	8A	---*Dipterocarpus spp.* Keruing
4403.4940	---山樟(香木)	0	35	13		千克/立方米	8A	---Kapur (*Dryobalanops spp.*)
4403.4950	---印加木(波罗格)	0	35	13		千克/立方米	8A	---*Intsia spp.* (Mengaris)
4403.4960	---大干巴豆(门格里斯或康派斯)	0	35	13		千克/立方米	8A	---Koompassia spp. (Mengaris or Kempas)
4403.4970	---异翅香木	0	35	13		千克/立方米	8A	---Anisopter spp.
4403.4990	---其他	0	8	13		千克/立方米		---Other

税则号列	货品名称	最惠(%)	普通	增值税率	出口退税	计量单位	监管条件	Article Description
4403.4990 10	其他本章子目注释二濒危热带原木(用油漆、着色剂、杂酚油或其他防腐剂处理的除外)	0	8	13		千克/立方米	8AF	Endangered tropical wood in the rough, specified in Subheading Note 2 to this Chapter (other than the wood treated with paint, stains, creosote or other preservatives)
4403.4990 90	其他本章子目注释二所列热带原木(用油漆、着色剂、杂酚油或其他防腐剂处理的除外)	0	8	13		千克/立方米	8A	Tropical wood in the rough, specified in Subheading Note 2 to this Chapter (other than the wood treated with paint, stains, creosote or other preservatives)
	-其他:							-Other:
4403.9100	--栎木(橡木)	0	8	13		千克/立方米	8A	--Of oak (*Quercus spp.*)
4403.9100 10	蒙古栎原木(用油漆、着色剂、杂酚油或其他防腐剂处理的除外)	0	8	13		千克/立方米	8AEF	Mongolia oak logs (paint, colorant, creosote or other preservative treatmentexcept)
4403.9100 90	其他栎木(橡木)原木(用油漆、着色剂、杂酚油或其他防腐剂处理的除外)	0	8	13		千克/立方米	8A	Other oak (oak) log (paint, colorant, creosote or other preservative treatmentexcept)
4403.9200	--山毛榉木	0	8	13		千克/立方米	8A	--Of beech (*Fagus spp.*)
	--其他:							--Other:
4403.9910	---楠木	0	35	13		千克/立方米	8A	---Of nan mu (*Phoebe*)
4403.9920	---樟木	0	35	13		千克/立方米	8A	---Of camphor wood
4403.9930	---红木	0	35	13		千克/立方米	8AF	---Of rosewood
4403.9940	---泡桐木	0	8	13		千克/立方米	8A	---Of Kiri (*Paulownia*)
4403.9950	---水曲柳	0	8	13		千克/立方米	8AF	---Ash
4403.9960	---北美硬阔叶木(包括樱桃木、黑胡桃木、枫木)	0	8	13		千克/立方米	8A	---North American hard wood (including cherry, walnut and maple)
4403.9980	---其他未列名的温带非针叶木	0	8	13		千克/立方米		---Other, temperate non-coniferous, not specified
4403.9980 10	其他未列名温带濒危非针叶木原木(用油漆、着色剂、杂酚油或其他防腐剂处理的除外)	0	8	13		千克/立方米	8AF	Other temperate zone endangered non-coniferous wood (other than the wood treated with paint, stains, creosote or other preservatives) not elsewhere specified or included
4403.9980 90	其他未列名温带非针叶木原木(用油漆、着色剂、杂酚油或其他防腐剂处理的除外)	0	8	13		千克/立方米	8A	Other temperate zone non-coniferous wood (other than the wood treated with paint, stains, creosote or other preservatives) not elsewhere specified or included
4403.9990	---其他	0	8	13		千克/立方米		---Other
4403.9990 11	南美蒺藜木(玉檀木)原木(用油漆,着色剂,杂酚油或其他防腐剂处理的除外)	0	8	13		千克/立方米	8AEF	Puncture vine wood in the rough of South America (other than the wood treated with paint, stains, creosote or other preservatives)
4403.9990 12	沉香木及拟沉香木原木(用油漆,着色剂,杂酚油或其他防腐剂处理的除外)	0	8	13		千克/立方米	8AEF	"Chinese eaglewood and similar chinese eaglewood (other than the wood treated with paint, stains, creosote or other preservatives)"
4403.9990 19	其他未列名濒危非针叶原木(用油漆、着色剂、杂酚油或其他防腐剂处理的除外)	0	8	13		千克/立方米	8AEF	Other endangered non – coniferous wood in the rough (other than the wood treated with paint, stains, creosote or other preservatives)
4403.9990 90	其他未列名非针叶原木(用油漆、着色剂、杂酚油或其他防腐剂处理的除外)	0	8	13		千克/立方米	8A	Other non-coniferous wood in the rough (other than the wood treated with paint, stains, creosote or other preservatives) not elsewhere specified or included
44.04	箍木;木劈条;已削尖但未经纵锯的木桩;粗加修整但未经车圆、弯曲或其他方式加工的木棒,适合制手杖、伞柄、工具把柄及类似品;木片条及类似品:							**Hoopwood; split poles; piles, pickets and stakes of wood, pointed but not sawn lengthwise; wooden sticks, roughly trimmed but not turned, bent or otherwise worked, suitable for the manufacture of walking-sticks, umbrellas, tool handles or the like; chipwood and the like:**
4404.1000	-针叶木的	8	50	17		千克		-Coniferous
4404.1000 10	濒危针叶木的箍木等及类似品(包括木劈条、棒及类似品)	8	50	17		千克	ABFE	Hoopwood; split poles; wooden sticks or the like; of endangered coniferous wood
4404.1000 90	其他针叶木的箍木等及类似品(包括木劈条、棒及类似品)	8	50	17		千克	AB	Other hoopwood; split poles; wooden sticks or the like; of coniferous wood
4404.2000	-非针叶木的	8	50	17		千克		-Non-coniferous
4404.2000 10	濒危非针叶木箍木等(包括木劈条、棒及类似品)	8	50	17		千克	ABFE	Hoopwood; split poles, wooden sticks or the like, of endangered non-coniferous wood

税则号列	货品名称	最惠(%)	普通	增值税率	出口退税	计量单位	监管条件	Article Description
4404.2000 90	其他非针叶木箍木等(包括木劈条、棒及类似品)	8	50	17		千克	AB	Other hoopwood; split poles, wooden sticks or the like, of non-coniferous wood
44.05	**木丝;木粉:**							**Wood wool; wood flour:**
4405.0000	木丝;木粉	8	40	17		千克	AB	Wood wool; wood flour
44.06	**铁道及电车道枕木:**							**Railway or tramway sleepers (cross-ties) of wood:**
4406.1000	-未浸渍	0	14	17		千克/立方米	4ABxy	-Not impregnated
4406.9000	-其他	0	14	17		千克/立方米		-Other
4406.9000 10	濒危木已浸渍铁道及电车道枕木	0	14	17		千克/立方米	FE	Railway or tramway sleepers (crossties) of endangered wood, impregnated
4406.9000 90	其他已浸渍的铁道及电车道枕木	0	14	17		千克/立方米		Other railway or tramway sleepers (crossties) of wood, impregnated
44.07	**经纵锯、纵切、刨切或旋切的木材,不论是否刨平、砂光或指榫接合,厚度超过6毫米:**							**Wood sawn or chipped lengthwise, sliced or peeled, whether or not planed, sanded or finger-jointed, of a thickness exceeding 6 mm:**
	-针叶木:							-Coniferous:
4407.1010	---红松和樟子松	0	14	17		千克/立方米		---Korean pine and Mongolian scotch pine
4407.1010 11	端部接合的红松厚板材(经纵锯、纵切、刨切或旋切的,厚度超过6mm)	0	14	17		千克/立方米	ABEF	Korean pine wood sawn or chipped lengthwise, sliced or peeled, end-jointed, thickness >6mm
4407.1010 19	端部接合的樟子松厚板材(经纵锯、纵切、刨切或旋切的,厚度超过6mm)	0	14	17		千克/立方米	AB	Mongolian scotch pine wood sawn or chipped lengthwise, sliced or peeled, end-jointed, thickness >6mm
4407.1010 91	非端部接合的红松厚板材(经纵锯、纵切、刨切或旋切的,厚度超过6mm)	0	14	17		千克/立方米	4ABEFxy	Wood sawn or chipped lengthwise, sliced or peeled, of Korean pine ,not end - jointed, thickness >6mm
4407.1010 99	非端部接合的樟子松厚板材(经纵锯、纵切、刨切或旋切的,厚度超过6mm)	0	14	17		千克/立方米	4ABxy	Wood sawn or chipped lengthwise, sliced or peeled, of Mongolian scotch pine , not end - jointed, thickness >6mm
4407.1020	---白松(云杉和冷杉)	0	14	17		千克/立方米		---White pine (spruce and fir)
4407.1020 11	端部接合的濒危白松(云杉,冷杉)厚板材(经纵锯、纵切、刨切或旋切的,厚度超过6mm)	0	14	17		千克/立方米	ABEF	Wood sawn or chipped lengthwise, sliced or peeled, of endangered white pine (spruce and fir), end - jointed, thickness >6mm
4407.1020 19	端部接合的其他白松(云杉,冷杉)厚板材(经纵锯、纵切、刨切或旋切的,厚度超过6mm)	0	14	17		千克/立方米	AB	Wood sawn or chipped lengthwise, sliced or peeled, of other white pine (spruce and fir), end - jointed, thickness >6mm
4407.1020 91	非端部接合濒危白松(云杉,冷杉)厚板材(经纵锯、纵切、刨切或旋切的,厚度超过6mm)	0	14	17		千克/立方米	4ABEFxy	Wood sawn or chipped lengthwise, sliced or peeled, of endangered white pine (spruce and fir), not end - jointed, thickness >6mm
4407.1020 99	非端部接合其他白松(云杉,冷杉)厚板材(经纵锯、纵切、刨切或旋切的,厚度超过6mm)	0	14	17		千克/立方米	4ABxy	Wood sawn or chipped lengthwise, sliced or peeled, of other white pine (spruce and fir), not end - jointed, thickness >6mm
4407.1030	---辐射松	0	14	17		千克/立方米		---Rediata pine
4407.1030 10	端部接合的辐射松厚板材(经纵锯、纵切、刨切或旋切的,厚度超过6mm)	0	14	17		千克/立方米	AB	Wood sawn or chipped lengthwise, sliced or peeled, of rediata pine, end-jointed, thickness >6mm
4407.1030 90	非端部接合的辐射松厚板材(经纵锯、纵切、刨切或旋切的,厚度超过6mm)	0	14	17		千克/立方米	4ABxy	Wood sawn or chipped lengthwise, sliced or peeled, of rediata pine, not end-jointed, thickness >6mm
4407.1040	---花旗松	0	14	17		千克/立方米		---Douglas fir
4407.1040 10	端部接合的花旗松厚板材(经纵锯、纵切、刨切或旋切的,厚度超过6mm)	0	14	17		千克/立方米	AB	Wood sawn or chipped lengthwise, sliced or peeled, of douglas fir (Pseudotsuga menziesii), end-jointed, thickness >6mm
4407.1040 90	非端部接合的花旗松厚板材(经纵锯、纵切、刨切或旋切的,厚度超过6mm)	0	14	17		千克/立方米	4ABxy	Wood sawn or chipped lengthwise, sliced or peeled, of douglas fir (Pseudotsuga menziesii) not end-jointed, thickness >6mm
4407.1090	---其他	0	14	17		千克/立方米		---Other
4407.1090 11	端部接合其他濒危针叶木厚板材(经纵锯、纵切、刨切或旋切的,厚度超过6mm)	0	14	17		千克/立方米	FEAB	Other endangered coniferous wood sawn or chipped lengthwise, sliced or peeled, end-jointed, thickness >6mm

税则号列	货品名称	最惠(%)	普通	增值税率	出口退税	计量单位	监管条件	Article Description
4407.1090 19	端部接合其他针叶木厚板材(经纵锯、纵切、刨切或旋切的,厚度超过6mm)	0	14	17		千克/立方米	AB	Other coniferous wood sawn or chipped lengthwise, sliced or peeled, end-jointed, thickness >6mm
4407.1090 91	非端部接合其他濒危针叶木厚板材(经纵锯、纵切、刨切或旋切的,厚度超过6mm)	0	14	17		千克/立方米	FEAB4xy	Other endangered coniferous wood sawn or chipped lensthwise, sliced or peeled, not end-jointed, thick ness >6mm
4407.1090 99	非端部接合的其他针叶木厚板材(经纵锯、纵切、刨切或旋切的,厚度超过6mm)	0	14	17		千克/立方米	AB4xy	Other coniferous wood sawn or chipped lensthwise, sliced or peeled, not end-jointed, thickness >6mm
	-本章子目注释二所列的热带木:							-Of tropical wood specified in Subheading Note 2 to this chapter:
4407.2100	--美洲桃花心木	0	14	17		千克/立方米		--Mahogany (Swietenia spp.)
4407.2100 10	端部接合美洲桃花心木(经纵锯、纵切、刨切或旋切的,厚度超过6mm)	0	14	17		千克/立方米	FEAB	Wood sawn or chipped lengthwise, sliced or peeled, of mashogany (swietenia spp.), end-jointed, thickness >6mm
4407.2100 90	非端部接合美洲桃花心木(经纵锯、纵切、刨切或旋切的,厚度超过6mm)	0	14	17		千克/立方米	4ABEFxy	Wood sawn or chipped lengthwise, sliced or peeled, of mashogany (swietenia spp.), not - end-jointed, thickness >6mm
4407.2200	--苏里南肉豆蔻木、美洲桃花心木、巴西胡桃木及美洲轻木	0	14	17		千克/立方米		--Virola, Imbuia and Balsa
4407.2200 10	端部接合的苏里南肉豆蔻木、巴西胡桃木及美洲轻木(经纵锯、纵切、刨切或旋切的,厚度超过6mm)	0	14	17		千克/立方米	AB	Wood sawn or chipped lengthwise sliced or peeled, of virola, imbuia and balsa, end-jointed, thickness >6mm
4407.2200 90	非端部接合的苏里南肉豆蔻木、巴西胡桃木及美洲轻木(经纵锯、纵切、刨切或旋切的,厚度超过6mm)	0	14	17		千克/立方米	4ABxy	Wood sawn or chipped lengthwise, slicec or peeled, of virola imbuia, and balsa, not end-joined, thickness >6mm
4407.2500	--深红色红柳桉木、浅红色红柳桉木及巴栲红柳桉木	0	14	17		千克/立方米		--Dark Red Meranti, Light Red Meranti and Meranti Bakau
4407.2500 10	端部接合的红柳桉木板材(指深红色、浅红色及巴栲红柳桉木,厚度超过6mm)	0	14	17		千克/立方米	AB	Wood sawn or chipped lengthwise, sliced or peeled, of Dark Red Meranti, Light Red Meranti and Meranti Bakau, end-jointed, thickness >6mm
4407.2500 90	非端部接合的红柳桉木板材(指深红色、浅红色及巴栲红柳桉木,经纵锯、纵切、刨切或旋切的,厚度超过6mm)	0	14	17		千克/立方米	y4xAB	Wood sawn or chipped lengthwise, sliced or peeled, of Dark Red Meranti, Light Red Meranti and Meranti Bakau, not end-jointed, thickness >6mm
4407.2600	--白柳桉木、白色红柳桉木、白色柳桉木、黄色红柳桉木及阿兰木	0	14	17		千克/立方米		--White Lauan, White Meranti, White Seraya, Yellow Meranti and Alan
4407.2600 10	端部接合的白柳桉,其他柳桉木和阿兰木板材(经纵锯、纵切、刨切或旋切的,厚度超过6mm)	0	14	17		千克/立方米	AB	Wood sawn or chipped lengthwise, sliced or peeled, of White Lauan, White Meranti, White Seraya, Yellow Meranti and Alan, end-jointed, thickness >6mm
4407.2600 90	非端部接合的白柳桉,其他柳桉木和阿兰木板材(经纵锯、纵切、刨切或旋切的,厚度超过6mm)	0	14	17		千克/立方米	y4xAB	Wood sawn or chipped lengthwise, sliced or peeled, of White Lauan, White Meranti, White Seraya, Yellow Meranti and Alan, not end-jointed, thickness >6mm
4407.2700	--沙比利	0	40	17		千克/立方米		--Sapelli
4407.2700 10	端部接合的沙比利木板材(经纵锯、纵切、刨切或旋切的,厚度超过6mm)	0	40	17		千克/立方米	AB	Wood sawn or chipped lengihwise, sliced or peeled, of sapelli, end-jointed, thinkness >6mm
4407.2700 90	非端部接合的沙比利木板材(经纵锯、纵切、刨切或旋切的,厚度超过60mm)	0	40	17		千克/立方米	4ABxy	Wood sawn or chipped lengthwise, sliced or peeled, of sapelli, not end-jointed, thinkness >6mm
4407.2800	---伊罗科木	0	14	17		千克/立方米		---Iroko
4407.2800 10	端部接合的伊罗科木板材(经纵锯、纵切、刨切或旋切的,厚度超过6mm)	0	14	17		千克/立方米	AB	Wood sawn or chipped lengthwise, sliced or peeled, of Iroko, end - jointed, thickness >6mm
4407.2800 90	非端部接合的伊罗科木板材(经纵锯、纵切、刨切或旋切的,厚度超过6mm)	0	14	17		千克/立方米	4ABxy	Wood sawn or chipped lengthwise, sliced or peeled, of Iroko, not end - jointed, thickness >6mm
	--其他:							--Other:
4407.2910	---柚木	0	40	17		千克/立方米		---Teak
4407.2910 10	端部接合的柚木板材(经纵锯、纵切、刨切或旋切的,厚度超过6mm)	0	40	17		千克/立方米	AB	Wood sawn or chipped lengthwise, sliced or peeled, of teak, end-jointed, thickness >6mm

税则号列	货品名称	最惠(%)	普通	增值税率	出口退税	计量单位	监管条件	Article Description
4407.2910 90	非端部接合的柚木板材(经纵锯、纵切、刨切或旋切的,厚度超过6mm)	0	40	17		千克/立方米	y4xAB	Wood sawn or chipped lengthwise, sliced or peeled, of teak, not end-jointed, thickness >6mm
4407.2920	---非洲桃花心木	0	40	17		千克/立方米		---Acajou
4407.2920 10	端部接合的非洲桃花心木板材(经纵锯、纵切、刨切或旋切的,厚度超过6mm)	0	40	17		千克/立方米	AB	Wood sawn or chipped lengthwise, sliced or peeled, of acajou, end-jointed, thickness >6mm
4407.2920 90	非端部接合的非洲桃花心木板材(经纵锯、纵切、刨切或旋切的,厚度超过6mm)	0	40	17		千克/立方米	AB	Wood sawn or chipped lengthwise, sliced or peeled, of acajou, not end-jointed, thickness >6mm
4407.2930	---波罗格	0	40	17		千克/立方米		---Merban
4407.2930 10	端部接合的波罗格Merban板材(经纵锯、纵切、刨切或旋切的,厚度超过6mm)	0	40	17		千克/立方米	AB	Wood sawn or chipped lengthwise, sliced or peeled, of merban, end-jointed, thickness >6mm
4407.2930 90	非端部接合的波罗格 Merban 板材(经纵锯、纵切、刨切或旋切的,厚度超过6mm)	0	40	17		千克/立方米	AB	Wood sawn or chipped lengthwise, sliced or peeled, of merban, not end-jointed, thickness >6mm
4407.2990	---其他	0	14	17		千克/立方米		---Other
4407.2990 11	端部接合拉敏木厚板材(经纵锯、纵切、刨切或旋切的,厚度超过6mm)	0	14	17		千克/立方米	FEAB	Wood sawn or chipped lengthwise, sliced or peeled, of Ramin wood, end-jointed, thickness >6mm
4407.2990 12	端部接合其他未列名本章子目注释二濒危热带木厚板材(经纵锯、纵切、刨切或旋切的,厚度超过6mm)	0	14	17		千克/立方米	FEAB	Other endangered tropical wood, not elsewhere specified or included in subheading Note. 2 to this Chapter, sawn or chipped lengthwise, sliced or peeled, end-jointed, thickness >6mm
4407.2990 19	端部接合其他未列名本章子目注释二热带木厚板材(经纵锯、纵切、刨切或旋切的,厚度超过6mm)	0	14	17		千克/立方米	AB	Wood sawn or chipped lengthwise, sliced or peeled, of other tropical wood not elsewhere specified or included in subheading Note. 2 to this Chapter, end-jointed, thickness >6mm
4407.2990 91	非端部接合其他未列名本章子目注释二濒危热带木板材(经纵锯、纵切、刨切或旋切的,厚度超过6mm)	0	14	17		千克/立方米	y4xAFEB	Other tropical endangered wood, not elsewhere specified or included in subheading Note. 2 to this Chapter, sawn or chipped lengthwise, sliced or peeled, not end-jointed, thickness >6mm
4407.2990 99	非端部接合其他未列名本章子目注释二热带木板材(经纵锯、纵切、刨切或旋切的,厚度超过6mm)	0	14	17		千克/立方米	y4xAB	Other tropical wood, not elsewhere specified or included in subheading Note. 2 to this Chapter, sawn or chipped lensthwise, shiced or peeled, not end-jointed, thickness >6mm
	-其他:							-Other:
4407.9100	--栎木(橡木)	0	14	17		千克/立方米		--Of oak (*Quercus spp.*)
4407.9100 11	端部接合的蒙古栎厚板材(经纵锯、纵切、刨切或旋切的,厚度>6毫米)	0	14	17	0	千克/立方米	ABEF	Mongolia oak planks end joining (sawn or chipped lengthwise, sliced or peeled, the thickness of >6 mm)
4407.9100 19	端部接合的栎木(橡木)厚板材(经纵锯、纵切、刨切或旋切的,厚度超过6mm)	0	14	17		千克/立方米	AB	Wood sawn or chipped lengthwise, sliced or peeled, of oak (*Quercus spp.*), end-jointed, thickness >6mm
4407.9100 91	非端部接合的蒙古栎厚板材(经纵锯、纵切、刨切或旋切的,厚度>6毫米)	0	14	17	0	千克/立方米	4ABEFxy	Mongolia oak planks - end joining (sawn or chipped lengthwise, sliced or peeled, the thickness of >6 mm)
4407.9100 99	非端部接合的栎木(橡木)厚板材(经纵锯、纵切、刨切或旋切的,厚度超过6mm)	0	14	17		千克/立方米	y4xAB	Wood sawn or chipped lengthwise, sliced or peeled, of oak (*Quercus spp.*), not end-jointed, thickness >6mm
4407.9200	--山毛榉木	0	14	17		千克/立方米		--Of beech (*Fagus spp.*)
4407.9200 10	端部接合的山毛榉木厚板材(经纵锯、纵切、刨切或旋切的,厚度超过6mm)	0	14	17		千克/立方米	ABE	Wood sawn or chipped lengthwise, sliced or peeled, of beech (*Fagus spp.*), end-jointed, thickness >6mm
4407.9200 90	非端部接合的山毛榉木厚板材(经纵锯、纵切、刨切或旋切的,厚度超过6mm)	0	14	17		千克/立方米	4ABExy	Wood sawn or chipped lengthwise, sliced or peeled, of beech (*Fagus spp.*), not end-jointed, thickness >6mm
4407.9300	--枫木	0	14	17		千克/立方米		--Of maple(Acer spp.)
4407.9300 10	端部接合的枫木厚板材(经纵锯、纵切、刨切或旋切的,厚度超过6mm)	0	14	17		千克/立方米	AB	Wood sawn or chipped lengthwise, sliced or peeled, of maple, end-jointed, thickness >6mm

税则号列	货品名称	最惠(%)	普通	增值税率	出口退税	计量单位	监管条件	Article Description
4407.9300 90	非端部接合的枫木厚板材(经纵锯、纵切、刨切或旋切的,厚度超过6mm)	0	14	17		千克/立方米	4ABxy	Wood sawn or chipped lengthwise, sliced or peeled, of maple, not end-jointed, thickness >6mm
4407.9400	--樱桃木	0	14	17		千克/立方米		--Of cherry (Prunus spp.)
4407.9400 10	端部接合的樱桃木厚板材(经纵锯、纵切、刨切或旋切的,厚度超过6mm)	0	14	17		千克/立方米	AB	Wood sawn or chipped lengthwise, sliced or peeled, of cherry, end-jointed, thickness >6mm
4407.9400 90	非端部接合的樱桃木厚板材(经纵锯、纵切、刨切或旋切的,厚度超过6mm)	0	14	17		千克/立方米	4ABxy	Wood sawn or chipped lengthwise, sliced or peeled, of cherry, not end-jointed, thickness >6mm
4407.9500	--白蜡木	0	14	17		千克/立方米		--Of ash (Fraxinus, spp)
4407.9500 11	端部接合的水曲柳厚板材(经纵锯、纵切、刨切或旋切的,厚度>6毫米)	0	14	17	0	千克/立方米	ABEF	Fraxinus mandshurica thick plate end joining (sawn or chipped lengthwise, sliced or peeled, the thickness of >6 mm)
4407.9500 19	端部接合的白蜡木厚板材(经纵锯、纵切、刨切或旋切的,厚度超过6mm)	0	14	17		千克/立方米	AB	Wood sawn or chipped lengthwise, sliced or peeled, of ash, end-jointed, thickness >6mm
4407.9500 91	非端部接合的水曲柳厚板材(经纵锯、纵切、刨切或旋切的,厚度>6毫米)	0	14	17	0	千克/立方米	4ABEFxy	Fraxinus mandshurica thick plate non end joining (sawn or chipped lengthwise, sliced or peeled, the thickness of >6 mm)
4407.9500 99	非端部接合的白蜡木厚板材(经纵锯、纵切、刨切或旋切的,厚度超过6mm)	0	14	17		千克/立方米	4ABxy	Wood sawn or chipped lengthwise, sliced or peeled, of ash, not end-jointed, thickness >6mm
	--其他:							--Other:
4407.9910	---樟木、楠木、红木	0	40	17		千克/立方米		---Of camphor-wood, nanmu or rosewood
4407.9910 10	端部接合樟木/楠木/红木厚板材(经纵锯、纵切、刨切或旋切的,厚度超过6mm)	0	40	17		千克/立方米	AFEB	Wood sawn or chipped lengthwise, sliced or peeled, of camphor-wood, nanmu or rosewood, end-jointed, thickness >6mm
4407.9910 90	非端部接合樟木/楠木/红木厚板材(经纵锯、纵切、刨切或旋切的,厚度超过6mm)	0	40	17		千克/立方米	y4xAFEB	Wood sawn or chipped lengthwise, sliced or peeled, of camphor-wood, nanmu or rosewood, not end-jointed, thickness >6mm
4407.9920	---泡桐木	0	14	17	13	千克/立方米		---Of paulownia
4407.9920 10	端部接合的泡桐木厚板材(经纵锯、纵切、刨切或旋切的,厚度超过6mm)	0	14	17	13	千克/立方米	AB	Wood sawn or chipped lengthwise, sliced or peeled, of paulownia, end-jointed, thickness >6mm
4407.9920 90	非端部接合的泡桐木厚板材(经纵锯、纵切、刨切或旋切的,厚度超过6mm)	0	14	17	13	千克/立方米	AB	Wood sawn or chipped lengthwise, sliced or peeled, of paulownia, not end-jointed, thickness >6mm
4407.9930	---北美硬阔叶材(含黑胡桃木)	0	14	17		千克/立方米		---North American hardwood (including walnut)
4407.9930 10	端部接合的北美硬阔叶材厚板材(含黑胡桃木,经纵锯、纵切、刨切或旋切,厚度超过6mm)	0	14	17		千克/立方米	AB	Wood sawn or chipped lengthwise, sliced or peeled, of North American broadleaf hardwood (including walnut), end-jointed, thickness >6mm
4407.9930 90	非端部接合的北美硬阔叶材厚板材(含黑胡桃木,经纵锯、纵切、刨切或旋切,厚度超过6mm)	0	14	17		千克/立方米	AB	Wood sawn or chipped lengthwise, sliced or peeled, of North American broadleaf hardwood (including walnut), not end-jointed, thickness >6mm
4407.9980	---其他温带非针叶木	0	14	17		千克/立方米		---Other temperate, non-coniferous wood
4407.9980 11	端部接合其他温带濒危非针叶板材(经纵锯、纵切、刨切或旋切的,厚度超过6mm)	0	14	17		千克/立方米	FEAB	Wood sawn or chipped lengthwise, sliced or peeled, endangered non-coniferous wood, of temperate, end-jointed, thickness >6mm
4407.9980 19	端部接合的其他温带非针叶厚板材(纵锯、纵切、刨切或旋切的,厚度超过6mm)	0	14	17		千克/立方米	AB	Wood sawn or chipped lengthwise, sliced or peeled, of temperate zone, non-coniferous wood, end-jointed, thick-ness >6mm
4407.9980 91	非端部接合其他温带濒危非针叶厚板材(经纵锯、纵切、刨切或旋切的,厚度超过6mm)	0	14	17		千克/立方米	4ABEFxy	Wood sawn or chipped lengthwise, sliced or peeled, endangered non-coniferous wood of temperate, not end-jointed, thickness >6mm
4407.9980 99	非端部接合的其他温带非针叶厚板材(经纵锯、纵切、刨切或旋切的,厚度超过6mm)	0	14	17		千克/立方米	4ABxy	Wood sawn or chipped lengthwise, sliced or peeled, of temperate zone, non-coniferous wood, not end-jointed, thickness >6mm
4407.9990	---其他	0	14	17		千克/立方米		---Other
4407.9990 11	端部接合的南美蒺藜木(玉檀木)厚板材(经纵锯、纵切、刨切或旋切的,厚度超过6mm)	0	14	17		千克/立方米	AFEB	Wood sawn or chipped lengthwise, sliced or peeled, of Puncture vine wood of South America, end-jointed, thickness >6mm

税则号列	货品名称	最惠(%)	普通	增值税率	出口退税	计量单位	监管条件	Article Description
4407.9990 12	端部接合的沉香木及拟沉香木厚板材(经纵锯、纵切、刨切或旋切的,厚度超过6mm)	0	14	17		千克/立方米	AFEB	Wood sawn or chipped lengthwise, sliced or peeled, of Chinese eaglewood and similar chinese eaglewood, end-jointed, thickness >6mm
4407.9990 15	端部接合的其他濒危木厚板材(经纵锯、纵切、刨切或旋切的,厚度超过6mm)	0	14	17		千克/立方米	AFEB	Wood sawn or chipped lengthwise, sliced or peeled, of other endangered wood , end - jointed, thickness >6mm
4407.9990 19	端部接合的其他木厚板材(经纵锯、纵切、刨切或旋切的,厚度超过6mm)	0	14	17		千克/立方米	AB	Other wood sawn or chipped lengthwise, sliced or peeled, end-jointed thickness >6mm
4407.9990 91	非端部接合的南美蒺藜木(玉檀木)厚板材(经纵锯、纵切、刨切或旋切的,厚度超过6mm)	0	14	17		千克/立方米	y4xAFEB	Wood sawn or chipped lengthwise, sliced or peeled, of Puncture vine wood of South America ,not end - jointed, thickness >6mm
4407.9990 92	非端部接合的沉香木及拟沉香木厚板材(经纵锯、纵切、刨切或旋切的,厚度超过6mm)	0	14	17		千克/立方米	y4xAFEB	Wood sawn or chipped lengthwise, sliced or peeled, of Chinese eaglewood and similar chinese eaglewood , not end - jointed, thickness >6mm
4407.9990 95	非端部接合的其他濒危木厚板材(经纵锯、纵切、刨切或旋切的,厚度超过6mm)	0	14	17		千克/立方米	y4xAFEB	Wood sawn or chipped lengthwise, sliced or peeled, of other endangered wood , not end - jointed, thickness >6mm
4407.9990 99	非端部接合的其他木厚板材(经纵锯、纵切、刨切或旋切的,厚度超过6mm)	0	14	17		千克/立方米	y4xAB	Other wood sawn or chipped lengthwise, sliced or peeled, not end-jointed, thickness >6mm
44.08	**饰面用单板(包括刨切积层木获得的单板)、制胶合板或类似多层板用单板以及其他经纵锯、刨切或旋切的木材,不论是否刨平、砂光、拼接或端部结合,厚度不超过6毫米:**							**Sheets for veneering (including those obtained by slicing laminated wood), for plywood or for other similar laminated wood and other wood, sawn lengthwise, sliced or peeled, whether or not planed, sanded, spliced or end-jointed, of a thickness not exceeding 6mm:**
	-针叶木:							-Coniferous:
	---饰面用单板:							---Veneer sheets:
4408.1011	----用胶合板等多层板制的	8	40	17		千克		----Of laminated plywood
4408.1011 10	胶合板等多层板制濒危针叶木单板(厚度≤6mm,饰面用)	8	40	17		千克	ABFE	Veneer sheets of endangered coniferous wood, of laminated wood of plywood, thickness≤6mm
4408.1011 90	其他胶合板等多层板制针叶木单板(厚度≤6mm,饰面用)	8	40	17		千克	AB	Other veneer sheets of coniferous wood, of laminated wood of plywood, thickness≤6mm
4408.1019	----其他	4	40	17		千克		----Other
4408.1019 10	其他饰面濒危针叶木单板(厚度≤6mm)	4	40	17		千克	ABFE	Other veneer sheets of endangered coniferous wood, thickness≤6mm
4408.1019 90	其他饰面针叶木单板(厚度≤6mm)	4	40	17		千克	AB	Other veneer sheets of coniferous wood, thickness≤6mm
4408.1020	---制胶合板用单板	4	17	17		千克		---Sheets for plywood
4408.1020 10	制胶合板用濒危针叶木单板(厚度≤6mm)	4	17	17		千克	ABFE	Sheets for plywood of coniferous endangered wood, thickness≤6mm
4408.1020 90	其他制胶合板用针叶木单板(厚度≤6mm)	4	17	17		千克	AB	Other sheets for plywood of coniferous wood, thickness≤6mm
4408.1090	---其他	4	30	17		千克		---Other
4408.1090 10	其他濒危针叶木单板材(经纵锯,刨切或旋切的,厚度≤6mm)	4	30	17		千克	ABFE	Sheets for plywood of endangered coniferous wood, wood sawn or chipped lengthwise, sliced or peeled, thickness≤6mm
4408.1090 90	其他针叶木单板材(经纵锯,刨切或旋切的,厚度≤6mm)	4	30	17		千克	AB	Sheets for plywood of coniferous wood, wood sawn or chipped lengthwise, sliced or peeled, thickness≤6mm
	-本章子目注释二所列的热带木:							-Of tropical wood specified in Subheading Note. 2 to this Chapter:
	--深红色红柳安木、浅红色红柳安木及巴栲红柳安木:							--Dark Red Meranti, Light Red Meranti and Meranti Bakau:
	---饰面用单板:							---Veneer sheets:
4408.3111	----用胶合板等多层板制的	10	40	17		千克	AB	----Of laminated plywood
4408.3119	----其他	4	40	17		千克	AB	----Other

税则号列	货品名称	最惠(%)	普通	增值税率	出口退税	计量单位	监管条件	Article Description
4408.3120	---制胶合板用单板	4	17	17		千克	AB	---Sheets for plywood
4408.3190	---其他	4	30	17		千克	AB	---Other
	--其他：							--Other:
	---饰面用单板：							---Veneer sheets:
4408.3911	----用胶合板等多层板制的	10	40	17		千克		----Of laminated plywood
4408.3911 10	胶合板多层板制饰面桃花心木单板（厚度≤6mm）	10	40	17		千克	ABFE	Veneer sheets, of acajou d'afrique, of laminated wood of plywood, thickness≤6mm
4408.3911 20	胶合板多层板制饰面拉敏木单板（厚度≤6mm）	10	40	17		千克	ABFE	Sheets for veneering, of Ramin wood, of laminated wood of plywood, thickness≤6mm
4408.3911 30	胶合板多层板制饰面濒危木单板（本章子目注释二所列其他热带木，厚度≤6mm）	10	40	17		千克	ABFE	Veneer sheets, of other tropical endangered wood, specified in Subheading Note 2 to this Chapter, of laminated wood of plywood, thickness≤6mm
4408.3911 90	胶合板多层板制饰面热带木单板（本章子目注释二所列其他热带木，厚度≤6mm）	10	40	17		千克	AB	Veneer sheets, of tropical wood, specified in Subheading Note 2 to this Chapter, of laminated wood of plywood, thickness≤6mm
4408.3919	----其他	4	40	17		千克		----Other
4408.3919 10	其他饰面用桃花心木单板（厚度≤6mm）	4	40	17		千克	ABFE	Other veneer sheets, of acajou d'afri-que, thickness ≤6mm
4408.3919 20	其他饰面用拉敏木单板（厚度≤6mm）	4	40	17		千克	ABFE	Other veneer sheets, of Ramin wood, thickness ≤ 6mm
4408.3919 30	其他饰面用濒危热带木制饰面用单板（本章子目注释二所列其他热带木，厚度≤6mm）	4	40	17		千克	ABFE	Other veneer sheets, of endangered tropical wood, specified in Subheading Note 2 to this Chapter, thickness≤6mm
4408.3919 90	厚度≤6mm 其他饰面用单板（本章子目注释二所列其他热带木）	4	40	17		千克	AB	Other veneer sheets, of tropical wood, specified in subheading Note 2 to this chapter, thickness >6mm
4408.3920	---制胶合板用单板	4	17	17		千克		---Sheets for plywood
4408.3920 10	其他桃花心木制的胶合板用单板（厚度≤6mm）	4	17	17		千克	ABFE	Other sheets for plywood, of acajou d'afrique, thick-ness≤6mm
4408.3920 20	其他拉敏木制的胶合板用单板（厚度≤6mm）	4	17	17		千克	ABFE	Other sheets for plywood, of ramin wood, thickness ≤6mm
4408.3920 30	其他濒危热带木制的胶合板用单板（本章子目注释二所列其他热带木，厚度≤6mm）	4	17	17		千克	ABFE	Other Sheets for plywood, of endangered tropical wood specified in Subheading Note 2 to this Chap-ter, thickness≤6mm
4408.3920 90	其他列名热带木制的胶合板用单板（本章子目注释二所列其他热带木，厚度≤6mm）	4	17	17		千克	AB	Other sheets for plywood, of tropical wood specified in Subheading Note 1 to this Chapter, thickness≤ 6mm
4408.3990	---其他	4	30	17		千克		---Other
4408.3990 10	其他桃花心木制的其他单板（本章子目注释二所列其他热带木，厚度≤6mm）	4	30	17		千克	ABFE	Other sheets of acajou d'afrique, of tropical wood specified in Subheading Note 2 to this Chapter, thickness≤6mm
4408.3990 20	其他拉敏木制的其他单板（本章子目注释二所列其他热带木，厚度≤6mm）	4	30	17		千克	ABFE	Other sheets of ramin wood, of tropical plood speci-fied in Subheading Note 2 to this Chapter, thickness ≤6mm
4408.3990 30	其他列名濒危热带木制的其他单板（本章子目注释二所列其他热带木，厚度≤6mm）	4	30	17		千克	ABFE	Other of endangered tropical wood of tropical wood specified in Subheading Note 2 to this Chapter, thickness≤6mm
4408.3990 90	其他列名的热带木制的其他单板（本章子目注释二所列其他热带木，厚度≤6mm）	4	30	17		千克	AB	Other sheets of tropical wood specified in Sub-heading Note 2 to this Chapter, thickness≤6mm
	-其他：							-Other:
	---饰面用单板：							---Veneer sheets:
4408.9011	----用胶合板等多层板制的	4	40	17		千克		----Of laminated plywood
4408.9011 10	胶合板多层板制饰面濒危木单板（厚度≤6mm）	4	40	17		千克	ABFE	Veneer sheets, of wood, of laminatedr plywood of endangered wood , thickness≤6mm
4408.9011 90	胶合板多层板制饰面其他木单板（厚度≤6mm，针叶木、热带木除外）	4	40	17		千克	AB	Veneer sheets, of other wood, other than tropical coniferous wood, of laminated ply wood of plywood, thickness≤6mm

税则号列	货品名称	最惠(%)	普通	增值税率	出口退税	计量单位	监管条件	Article Description
4408.9012暂	----温带非针叶木制	1	40	17			千克	----Of temperate non-coniferous wood
4408.9012暂 10	温带濒危非针叶木制饰面用木单板(厚度≤6mm,针叶木、热带木除外)	1	40	17		千克	ABFE	Venner sheets, of temperate zone non-coniferous endangered wood, other than tropical coniferous wood, thickness≤6mm
4408.9012暂 90	其他温带非针叶木制饰面用木单板(厚度≤6mm,针叶木、热带木除外)	1	40	17		千克	AB	Venner sheets of temperate zone non-coniferous wood(other than tropical coniferous wood, thickness ≤6mm)
4408.9013	----竹制	4	40	17		千克		----Of bamboo
4408.9013 10	濒危竹制饰面用单板(厚度≤6mm)	4	40	17		千克	ABE	Veneer sheets of endangered bamboo (thickness ≤ 6mm)
4408.9013 90	其他竹制饰面用单板(厚度≤6mm)	4	40	17		千克	AB	Veneer sheets of other bamboo(thickness≤6mm)
4408.9019	----其他		40	17		千克		----Other
4408.9019暂 11	家具饰面用濒危木单板(厚度≤6mm)	1	40	17		千克	ABFE	Venner sheets of endangered wood (thickness ≤ 6mm)
4408.9019暂 19	其他家具饰面用单板(厚度≤6mm)	1	40	17		千克	AB	Other venner sheets of wood (thickness≤6mm)
4408.9019 91	其他饰面用濒危木单板(厚度≤6mm)	3	40	17		千克	ABFE	Other venner sheets of endangered wood (thickness ≤6mm)
4408.9019 99	其他饰面用单板(厚度≤6mm)	3	40	17		千克	AB	Other veneer sheets(thickness≤6mm)
	---胶合板用单板:							---Sheets for plywood:
4408.9021	----温带非针叶木制	3	17	17		千克		----Of temperate non-coniferous wood
4408.9021 10	温带濒危非针叶木制胶合板用单板(厚度≤6mm)	3	17	17		千克	ABFE	Sheets for plywood of temperate zone non-coniferous endangered wood (thickness≤6mm)
4408.9021 90	其他温带非针叶木制胶合板用单板(厚度≤6mm)	3	17	17		千克	AB	Other sheets for plywood of temperate zone non-coniferous wood(thickness ≤6mm)
4408.9029	----其他		17	17		千克		----Other
4408.9029暂 11	其他濒危木制胶合板用旋切单板(厚度≤6mm)	1	17	17		千克	ABFE	Other sheets for plywood of endangered wood, peeled sheets(thickness≤6mm)
4408.9029 19	其他濒危木制胶合板用其他单板(厚度≤6mm,旋切单板除外)	3	17	17		千克	ABFE	Other sheets for plywood of endangered wood (thinckness≤6mm, other than peeled sheets)
4408.9029暂 91	其他木制胶合板用旋切单板(厚度≤6mm)	1	17	17		千克	AB	Other sheets for plywood of wood, peeled sheets (thickness≤6mm)
4408.9029 99	其他木制胶合板用其他单板(厚度≤6mm,旋切单板除外)	3	17	17		千克	AB	Other sheets for plywood of wood (thiekness≤6mm, other than peeled sheets)
	---其他:							---Other:
4408.9091	----温带非针叶木制	3	30	17		千克		----Of temperate non-coniferous wood
4408.9091 10	温带濒危非针叶木制其他单板材(经纵锯、刨切或旋切的,厚度≤6mm)	3	30	17		千克	ABFE	Sheets of temperate zone endangered non-coniferous wood(sawn or chipped lengthwise, sliced or peeled, thickness ≤6mm)
4408.9091 90	温带非针叶木制其他单板材(经纵锯、刨切或旋切的,厚度≤6mm)	3	30	17		千克	AB	Other sheets of temperate zone non-coniferous wood (sawn or chipped lengthwise, sliced or peeled, thickness ≤6mm)
4408.9099	----其他	3	30	17		千克		----Other
4408.9099 10	其他濒危木制的其他单板材(经纵锯、刨切或旋切的,厚度≤6mm)	3	30	17		千克	ABFE	Other sheets of endangered wood(sawn or chipped lengthwise, sliced or peeled, thickness≤6mm)
4408.9099 90	其他木材,但针叶木热带木除外(经纵锯、刨切或旋切的,厚度≤6mm)	3	30	17		千克	AB	Other wood, other than tropical coniferous wood (sawn or chipped lengthwise, sliced or peeled, thickness≤6mm)
44.09	**任何一边端或面制成连续形状(舌榫、槽榫、半槽榫、斜角、V形接头、珠榫、缘饰、刨圆及类似形状)的木材(包括未装拼的拼花地板用板条及缘板),不论是否刨平、砂光或端部结合:**							**Wood (including strips and friezes for parquet flooring, not assembled) continuously shaped (tongues, grooved, rebated, chamfered, V-jointed, beaded, moulded, rounded or the like) along any of its "edges, ends or faces, whether or not planed, sanded or end-jointed":**
	-针叶木:							-Coniferous:
4409.1010	---地板条(块)	7.5	50	17		千克		---Floor board strips

税则号列	货品名称	最惠(%)	普通	增值税率	出口退税	计量单位	监管条件	Article Description
4409.1010 10	一边或面制成连续形状的濒危针叶木制地板条、块(包括未装拼的拼花地板用板条及缘板)	7.5	50	17		千克	ABFE	Endangered coniferous wood (including strips and friezes for parquet flooring, not assembled) continuously shaped along any of its edges or faces
4409.1010 90	一边或面制成连续形状的其他针叶木地板条,块(包括未装拼的拼花地板用板条及缘板)	7.5	50	17		千克	AB	Other coniferous wood (including strips and friezes for parquet flooring, not assembled) continuously shaped along any of its edges or faces
4409.1090	---其他	7.5	50	17		千克		---Other
4409.1090 10	一边或面制成连续形状濒危针叶木材	7.5	50	17		千克	ABFE	Endangered coniferous wood, continuously shaped along any of its edges or faces
4409.1090 90	其他一边或面制成连续形状的针叶木材	7.5	50	17		千克	AB	Coniferous wood, continuously shaped along any of its edges or faces
	-非针叶木:							-Non-coniferous:
	--竹的:							--Of bamboo:
4409.2110	---地板条(块)	4	50	17		千克		---Floor board strips
4409.2110 10	一边或面制成连续形状的濒危竹地板条(块)(包括未装拼的拼花竹地板用板条及缘板)	4	50	17		千克	ABE	Endangered bamboo (including strips and friezes for parquet flooring, not assembled) continuously shaped along any of its edges or faces
4409.2110 90	一边或面制成连续形状的竹地板条(块)(包括未装拼的拼花竹地板用板条及缘板)	4	50	17	13	千克	AB	Bamboo (including strips and friezes for parquet flooring, not assembled) continuously shaped along any of its edges or faces
4409.2190	---其他	4	50	17		千克		---Other
4409.2190 10	一边或面制成连续形状的其他濒危竹材	4	50	17		千克	ABE	Other endangered bamboo, continuously shaped along any of its edges or faces
4409.2190 90	一边或面制成连续形状的其他竹材	4	50	17	13	千克	AB	Other bamboo, continuously shaped along any of its edges or faces
	--其他:							--Other:
4409.2910	---地板条(块)	4	50	17		千克		---Floor board strips
4409.2910 10	一边或面制成连续形状的拉敏木地板条、块(包括未装拼的拉敏木拼花地板用板条及缘板)	4	50	17		千克	ABFE	Ramin wood (including strips and friezes for parquet flooring, not assembled) continuously shaped along any of its edges or faces
4409.2910 20	一边或面制成连续形状的桃花心木地板条、块(包括未装拼的桃花心木拼花地板用板条及缘板)	4	50	17		千克	ABFE	Acajou wood (including strips and friezes for parquet flooring, not assembled) continuously shaped along any of its edges or faces)
4409.2910 30	一边或面制成连续形状的其他濒危木地板条、块(包括未装拼的其他濒危木拼花地板用板条及缘板)	4	50	17		千克	ABFE	Other endangered wood (including strips and friezes for parquet flooring, not assembled) continuously shaped along any of its edges or faces
4409.2910 90	一边或面制成连续形状的其他非针叶木地板条、块(包括未装拼的其他非针叶木拼花地板用板条及缘板)	4	50	17		千克	AB	Other non-coniferous wood (including strips and friezes for parquet flooring, not assembled) continuously shaped along anyof its edges or faces
4409.2990	---其他	4	50	17		千克		---Other
4409.2990 10	一边或面制成连续形状的拉敏木	4	50	17		千克	ABFE	Ramin wood, continuously shaped along any of its edges or faces
4409.2990 20	一边或面制成连续形状的桃花心木	4	50	17		千克	ABFE	Acajou d'afrique wood, continuously shaped along any of its edges or faces
4409.2990 30	一边或面制成连续形状的其他濒危木	4	50	17		千克	ABFE	Other endangered wood , continuously shaped along any of its edges or faces
4409.2990 90	一边或面制成连续形状的其他非针叶木材	4	50	17		千克	AB	Other non-coniferous wood, continuously sh-aped along any of its edges or faces
44.10	**碎料板,定向刨花板(OSB)及类似板(例如,华夫板),木或其他木质材料制,不论是否用树脂或其他有机黏合剂粘合:**							**Particle board and similar board of wood or other ligneous materials (for example, oriented strand board and waferboabd) where or not agglomerated with resins or other organlc binging, substancec**
	-木制:							-Of wood:
4410.1100	--碎料板	4	40	17	9	千克	AB	--Particle board

税则号列	货品名称	最惠(%)	普通	增值税率	出口退税	计量单位	监管条件	Article Description
4410.1200	--定向刨花板	4	40	17	9	千克	AB	--Oriented standard board (OSB)
4410.1900	--其他	4	40	17	9	千克	AB	--Other
	-其他:							-Other:
	---碎料板:							---Particle board:
4410.9011	----麦稻秸秆制	7.5	40	17	9	千克	AB	----Of wheat and rice straw
4410.9019	----其他	7.5	40	17	9	千克	AB	----Other
4410.9090	---其他	7.5	40	17	9	千克	AB	---Other
44.11	**木纤维板或其他木质材料纤维板,不论是否用树脂或其他有机粘合剂粘合:**							**Fibreboard of wood or other ligneous materials, whether or not bonded with resins or other organic substances:**
	-中密度纤维板(MDF):							-Medium density fibreboard (MDF):
	--厚度不超过5毫米:							--Of a thickness not exceeding 5mm:
	---密度超过每立方厘米0.8克:							---Of a density exceeding 0.8/cm^3:
4411.1211	----未经机械加工或盖面的	4	40	17	9	千克	AB	----Not mechanically worked or surface covered
4411.1219	----其他	7.5	40	17	9	千克	AB	----Other
	---密度超过每立方厘米0.5克,但未超过每立方厘米0.8克:							---Of a density exceeding 0.5 g/cm^3 but not exceeding 0.8 g/cm^3:
4411.1221	---辐射松制的	4	40	17	9	千克	AB	---Of radiata pine
4411.1229	---其他	4	40	17	9	千克	AB	---Other
	---其他:							---Other:
4411.1291	----未经机械加工或盖面的	7.5	40	17	9	千克	AB	----Not mechanically worked or surface covered
4411.1299	----其他	4	40	17	9	千克	AB	----Other
	--厚度超过5毫米但未超过9毫米:							--Of a thickness exceeding 5mm but not exceeding 9mm:
	---密度超过每立方厘米0.8克:							---Of a density exceeding 0.8g/cm^3:
4411.1311	----未经机械加工或盖面的	4	40	17	9	千克	AB	----Not mechanically worked or surface covered
4411.1319	----其他	7.5	40	17	9	千克	AB	----Other
	---密度超过每立方厘米0.5克,但未超过每立方厘米0.8克:							---Of a density exceeding 0.5g/cm^3 but not exceeding 0.8g/cm^3:
4411.1321	---辐射松制的	4	40	17	9	千克	AB	---Of radiata pine
4411.1329	---其他	4	40	17	9	千克	AB	---Other
	---其他:							---Other:
4411.1391	----未经机械加工或盖面的	7.5	40	17	9	千克	AB	----Not mechanically worked or surface covered
4411.1399	----其他	4	40	17	9	千克	AB	----Other
	--厚度超过9毫米:							--Of a thickness exceeding 9mm:
	---密度超过每立方厘米0.8克:							---Of a density exceeding 0.8g/cm^3:
4411.1411	----未经机械加工或盖面的	4	40	17	9	千克	AB	----Not mechanically worked or surface covered
4411.1419	----其他	7.5	40	17	9	千克	AB	----Other
	---密度超过每立方厘米0.5克,但未超过每立方厘米0.8克:							---Of a density exceeding 0.5g/cm^3 but not exceeding 0.8g/cm^3:
4411.1421	---辐射松制的	4	40	17	9	千克	AB	---Of radiata pine
4411.1429	---其他	4	40	17	9	千克	AB	---Other
	---其他:							---Other:
4411.1491	----未经机械加工或盖面的	7.5	40	17	9	千克	AB	----Not mechanically worked or surface covered
4411.1499	----其他	4	40	17	9	千克		AB Other
	-其他:							-Other:
	--密度超过每立方厘米0.8克:							--Of a density exceeding 0.8g/cm^3:
4411.9210	---未经机械加工或盖面的	4	40	17	9	千克	AB	---Not mechanically worked or surface covered
4411.9290	---其他	7.5	40	17	9	千克	AB	---Other
	--密度超过每立方厘米0.5克,但未超过每立方厘米0.8克:							--Of a density exceeding 0.5g/cm^3 but not exceeding 0.8g/cm^3:
4411.9310	---辐射松制的	4	40	17	9	千克	AB	---Of radiata pine
4411.9390	---其他	4	40	17	9	千克	AB	---Other
	--密度未超过每立方厘米0.5克:							--Of a density not exceeding 0.5g/cm^3:
4411.9410	---密度超过每立方厘米0.35克,但未超过每立方厘米0.5克	7.5	40	17	9	千克	AB	---Of a density exceeding 0.35g/cm^3 but not exceeding 0.5g/cm^3

税则号列	货品名称	最惠(%)	普通	增值税率	出口退税	计量单位	监管条件	Article Description
	---密度未超过每立方厘米0.35克:							---Of a density not exceeding 0.35g/cm³:
4411.9421	----未经机械加工或盖面的	7.5	40	17	9	千克	AB	----Not mechanically worked or suface covered
4411.9429	----其他	4	40	17	9	千克	AB	----Other
44.12	胶合板、单板饰面板及类似的多层板:							**Plywood, veneered panels and similar laminated wood:**
	-竹制的:							-Of bamboo:
	---仅由薄板制的胶合板,每层厚度不超过6毫米:							---Plywood consisting solely of sheets of wood, each ply not exceeding 6 mm thickness
4412.1011	----至少有一表层是本章子目注释二所列的热带木	12	30	17		千克/立方米		----With at least one outer ply of tropical wood specified in Subheading Note. 2 to this Chapter
4412.1011 11	至少有一表层为濒危热带木薄板制濒危竹胶合板(每层厚度≤6mm)	12	30	17		千克/立方米	ABFE	Plywood consisting solely of sheets of endangered bamboo, with at least one outer ply of endangered tropical wood, each ply thickness≤6mm
4412.1011 19	至少有一表层为濒危热带木薄板制其他竹胶合板(每层厚度≤6mm 热带木指本章子目注释二所列木材)	12	30	17		千克/立方米	ABFE	Plywood consisting solely of sheets of bamboo with at least one outer ply of endangered tropical wood specified in subheading Note 2 to this Chapter, each ply thickness≤6mm
4412.1011 91	至少有一表层是其他热带木薄板制濒危竹胶合板(每层厚度≤6mm,热带木指本章子目注释二所列木材)	12	30	17		千克/立方米	ABEF	Plywood consisting solely of sheets of endangered bamboo, with at least one outer ply of other tropical wood specified in subheading Note 2 to this Chapter, each ply thickness≤6mm
4412.1011 99	至少有一表层是其他热带木薄板制其他竹胶合板(每层厚度≤6mm,热带木指本章子目注释二所列木材)	12	30	17	9	千克/立方米	AB	Plywood consisting solely of sheets of bamboo, with at least one outer ply of non-coniferous other tropical wood specified in subheading Note 2 to this Chapter, each ply thickness≤6mm
4412.1019	----其他	4	30	17		千克/立方米		-----Other
4412.1019 11	至少有一表层为濒危非针叶木薄板胶合板(至少有一表层为温带非针叶木制,每层厚度≤6mm)	4	30	17		千克/立方米	ABFE	Plywood consisting solely of sheets of wood, with at least one outer ply of endangered non-coniferous wood, each ply thickness≤6mm
4412.1019 19	其他至少有一表层为非针叶木薄板胶合板(至少有一表层为温带非针叶木制,每层厚度≤6mm)	4	30	17	9	千克/立方米	AB	Plywood consisting solely of sheets of wood, with at least one outer ply of non-coniferous wood each ply thickness≤6mm
4412.1019 21	濒危竹地板层叠胶合而成的多层板(每层厚度≤6mm)	4	30	17		千克/立方米	ABE	Plywood with two or more plies of endangered bamboo, each ply thickness≤6mm
4412.1019 29	其他竹地板层叠胶合而成的多层板(每层厚度≤6mm)	4	30	17	13	千克/立方米	AB	Plywood with two or more plies of bamboo, each ply thickness≤6mm .
4412.1019 91	其他濒危竹胶合板(每层厚度≤6mm)	4	30	17		千克/立方米	ABE	Plywood consisting solely of sheets of endangered bamboo, each ply thickness≤6mm
4412.1019 99	其他竹胶合板(每层厚度≤6mm)	4	30	17	13	千克/立方米	AB	Other plywood consisting solely of sheets of other bamboo, each ply thickness≤6mm
4412.1020	---其他,至少有一表层是非针叶木	10	30	17		千克/立方米		---Other, with at least one outer ply of non-coniferous wood
4412.1020 11	至少有一表层是濒危非针叶木的濒危竹制多层板(每层厚度≤6mm)	10	30	17		千克/立方米	ABFE	Laminated wood of endangered bamboo, with at least one outer ply of endangered non-coniferous wood, each ply thickness≤6mm
4412.1020 19	至少有一表层是其他非针叶木的其他濒危竹制多层板(每层厚度≤6mm)	10	30	17		千克/立方米	ABEF	Laminated wood of endangered bamboo, with at least one outer ply of non-coniferous wood, each ply thickness≤6mm
4412.1020 91	至少有一表层是濒危非针叶木的其他竹制多层板(每层厚度≤6mm)	10	30	17		千克/立方米	ABEF	Laminated wood of bamboo, with at least one outer ply of endangered non-coniferous wood in imminent dangers, each ply thickness≤6mm
4412.1020 99	至少有一表层是其他非针叶木的其他竹制多层板(每层厚度≤6mm)	10	30	17	9	千克/立方米	AB	Laminated wood of bamboo, with at least one outer ply of non-coniferous wood, each ply thickness≤6mm
	---其他:							---Other:

税则号列	货 品 名 称	最惠(%)	普通	增值税率	出口退税	计量单位	监管条件	Article Description
4412.1091	----至少有一表层是本章子目注释二所列的热带木	8	30	17		千克/立方米		----With at least one ply of tropical wood specified in Subheading Note 2 to this Chapter
4412.1091 10	至少有一层是热带木的濒危竹制多层板(热带木指本章子目注释二所列木材)	8	30	17		千克/立方米	ABEF	Laminated wood of endangered bamboo, with at least one outer ply of tropical wood, each ply thickness≤6mm
4412.1091 90	至少有一层是热带木的其他竹制多层板(热带木指本章子目注释二所列木材)	8	30	17	9	千克/立方米	AB	Laminated wood of bamboo, with at least one outer ply of tropical wood, each ply thickness≤6mm
4412.1092	----至少含有一层木碎料板	10	30	17		千克/立方米		----Containing at least one layer of particle board
4412.1092 10	至少含有一层木碎料板的濒危竹制多层板	10	30	17		千克/立方米	ABEF	Laminated wood, at least one outer ply of endangered bamboo, containing at least one layer of particle board
4412.1092 90	至少含有一层木碎料板的其他竹制多层板	10	30	17	9	千克/立方米	AB	Laminated wood, at least one outer ply of other bamboo, containing at least one layer of particle board
4412.1099	----其他	4	30	17		千克/立方米		----Other
4412.1099 10	其他濒危竹制多层板	4	30	17		千克/立方米	ABE	Other laminated wood of endangered bamboo
4412.1099 90	其他竹制多层板	4	30	17	13	千克/立方米	AB	Other laminated of bamboo
	-其他仅由薄木板制的胶合板(竹制除外),每层厚度不超过6毫米:							-Other plywood consisting solely of sheets of wood (other than bamboo), each ply exceeding 6mm thickness:
4412.3100	--至少有一表层是本章子目注释二所列的热带木	12	30	17		千克/立方米		--With at least one outer ply of tropical wood specified in subheading Note 2 to this Chapter
4412.3100 10	至少有一表层为桃花心木薄板制胶合板(每层厚度≤6mm)	12	30	17	5	千克/立方米	ABFE	Plywood, with at least one outer ply of Acajou d' afrique, each ply thickness≤6mm
4412.3100 20	至少有一表层为拉敏木薄板制胶合板(每层厚度≤6mm)	12	30	17	5	千克/立方米	ABFE	Plywood, with at least one outer ply of Ramin wood, each ply thickness≤6mm
4412.3100 30	一表层为濒危热带木薄板制胶合板(每层厚度≤6mm 热带木指本章子目注释二所列木材)	12	30	17		千克/立方米	ABFE	Plywood, with at least one outer ply of endangered tropical wood specified in subheading Note 2 to this capter, each ply thickness≤6mm
4412.3100 90	至少有一表层是其他热带木制的胶合板(每层厚度≤6mm,竹制除外,热带木指本章子目注释二所列木材)	12	30	17	9	千克/立方米	AB	Plywood, with at least one outer ply of tropical wood, specified in subheading Note 2 to this Chapter, each ply thickness≤6mm
	--其他,至少有一表层是非针叶木:							--Other, with at least one outer ply of non-coniferons wood:
4412.3210	---至少有一表层是温带非针叶木	4	30	17		千克/立方米		---With at least one outer ply of temperate nonconiferous wood
4412.3210 10	至少有一表层是濒危温带非针叶木薄板制胶合板(每层厚度≤6mm,竹制除外)	4	30	17		千克/立方米	ABFE	Plywood, with at least one outer ply of temperate zone endangered non-coniferous wood (other than bamboo, each ply thickness≤6mm)
4412.3210 90	至少有一表层是其他温带非针叶木薄板制胶合板(每层厚度≤6mm,竹制除外)	4	30	17	9	千克/立方米	AB	Plywood, with at least one outer ply of other temperate non-conifeous wood (other than bamboo, each ply thickness≤6mm)
4412.3290	---其他	4	30	17		千克/立方米		---Other
4412.3290 10	至少有一表层是濒危其他非针叶胶合板(每层厚度≤6mm,竹制除外)	4	30	17		千克/立方米	ABEF	Plywood, with at least one outer ply of other endangered non-conifeous wood (other than bamboo, each ply thichness≤6mm)
4412.3290 90	至少有一表层是其他非针叶胶合板(每层厚度≤6mm,竹制除外)	4	30	17	9	千克/立方米	AB	Plywood, with one outer ply of other non-coniferous wood, other than bamboo (other than bamboo, each ply thickness≤6mm)
4412.3900	--其他	4	30	17		千克/立方米		--Other
4412.3900 10	其他濒危薄板制胶合板(每层厚度≤6mm,竹制除外)	4	30	17		千克/立方米	ABFE	Plywood, consisting solely of sheets of endangered wood (other than bamboo, each ply thickness≤6mm)
4412.3900 90	其他薄板制胶合板(每层厚度≤6mm,竹制除外)	4	30	17	9	千克/立方米	AB	Plywood, consisting solely of sheets of wood (other than bamboo, each ply thickness≤6mm)
	-其他:							-Other:

税则号列	货品名称	最惠(%)	普通	增值税率	出口退税	计量单位	监管条件	Article Description
	--木块芯胶合板,侧板条芯胶合板及板条芯胶合板:							--Blockboard, laminboard and battenboard:
4412.9410	---至少有一表层是非针叶木	10	30	17		千克/立方米		---With at least one outer ply of non－coniferous wood
4412.9410 10	至少有一表层是桃花心木的木块芯胶合板等(还包括侧板条芯胶合板及板条芯胶合板)	10	30	17	5	千克/立方米	ABFE	Blockboard (including laminboard and battenboard) with at least one outer ply of acajou board
4412.9410 20	至少有一表层是拉敏木的木块芯胶合板等(还包括侧板条芯胶合板及板条芯胶合板)	10	30	17	5	千克/立方米	ABFE	Blockboard (including laminboard and battenboard) with at least one outer ply of Ramin board
4412.9410 30	至少有一表层是濒危热带木的木块芯胶合板等(还包括侧板条芯胶合板及板条芯胶合板)	10	30	17		千克/立方米	ABFE	Blockboard (including laminboard and battenboard) with at least one outer ply of endangered tropical wood
4412.9410 40	至少有一表层是濒危非针叶木的木块芯胶合板等(还包括侧板条芯胶合板及板条芯胶合板)	10	30	17		千克/立方米	ABFE	Blockboard (including laminboard and battenboard) with at least one outer ply of endangered non－coniferous wood
4412.9410 90	至少有一表层是非针叶木的木块芯胶合板等(还包括侧板条芯胶合板及板条芯胶合板)	10	30	17	9	千克/立方米	AB	Boockboard (including laminboard and battenboard) with at least one outer ply of non－coniferous wood
	---其他:							---Other:
4412.9491	----至少有一层是本章子目注释二所列的热带木	8	30	17		千克/立方米		----With at least one ply of tropical wood specified in Subheading Note 2 to this Chapter
4412.9491 10	至少有一层是濒危热带木的针叶木面木块芯胶合板等(还包括侧板条芯胶合板及板条芯胶合板,热带木指本章子目注释二所列木材)	8	30	17		千克/立方米	ABFE	Blockboard (including laminboard and battenboard) with at least one surface layer of endangered tropical coniferous wood specified in Subheading Note 2 to this Chapter
4412.9491 90	至少有一层是热带木的针叶木面木块芯胶合板等(还包括侧板条芯胶合板及板条芯胶合板,热带木指本章子目注释二所列木材)	8	30	17	9	千克/立方米	AB	Blockboard (including laminboard and battenboard) with at least one surface layer of tropical coniferous wood specified in Subheading Note 2 to this Chapter
4412.9492	----其他,至少含有一层木碎料板	10	30	17		千克/立方米		----Other, containing at least one layer of particle board
4412.9492 10	至少含有一层木碎料板的濒危针叶木面木块芯胶合板等(还包括侧板条芯胶合板及板条芯胶合板)	10	30	17		千克/立方米	ABFE	Blockboard (including laminboard and battenboard), with at least one layer of particle board, surface layer of endangered coniferous wood
4412.9492 90	至少含有一层木碎料板的针叶木面木块芯胶合板等(还包括侧板条芯胶合板及板条芯胶合板)	10	30	17	9	千克/立方米	AB	Blockboard (including laminboard and battenboard), with at least one layer of particle board, surface layer of coniferous wood
4412.9499	----其他	4	30	17		千克/立方米		----Other
4412.9499 10	其他濒危针叶木面木块芯胶合板等(还包括侧板条芯胶合板及板条芯胶合板)	4	30	17		千克/立方米	ABEF	Other laminated wood, containing an least one layer of particle board, surface layer of endangered coniferous wood
4412.9499 90	其他针叶木面木块芯胶合板等(还包括侧板条芯胶合板及板条芯胶合板)	4	30	17	9	千克/立方米	AB	Other laminated wood, containing an least one layer of particle board, surface layer of coniferous wood
	--其他:							--Other:
4412.9910	---至少有一表层是非针叶木	10	30	17		千克/立方米		---With at least one outer ply of non-coniferous wood
4412.9910 10	至少有一表层是桃花心木的多层板	10	30	17	0,5	千克/立方米	ABFE	Laminated wood with at least one outer ply of Acajou d'afrique
4412.9910 20	至少有一表层是拉敏木的多层板	10	30	17	0,5	千克/立方米	ABFE	Laminated wood with a least one outer ply of Ramin wood
4412.9910 30	至少有一表层是濒危热带木的多层板	10	30	17		千克/立方米	ABFE	Laminated wood with at least one outer ply of endangered tropical wood
4412.9910 40	其他至少有一表层是濒危非针叶木的多层板	10	30	17		千克/立方米	ABFE	Laminated wood with at least one outer ply of endangered non－coniferous wood
4412.9910 90	其他至少有一表层是非针叶木的多层板	10	30	17	9	千克/立方米	AB	Laminated wood with at least one outer ply of non－coniferous wood

税则号列	货品名称	最惠(%)	普通	增值税率	出口退税	计量单位	监管条件	Article Description
	---其他:							---Other:
4412.9991	----至少有一层是本章子目注释二所列的热带木	8	30	17		千克/立方米		----With at least one ply of tropical wood specified in Suheading Note 2 to this chapter
4412.9991 10	其他至少有一层是濒危热带木的针叶木面多层板(热带木指本章子目注释二所列木材)	8	30	17		千克/立方米	ABFE	Laminated wood, with at least one surface layer of tropical endangered coniferous board specified in Subheading Note 2 to this Chapter
4412.9991 90	其他至少有一层是热带木的针叶木面多层板(热带木指本章子目注释二所列木材)	8	30	17	9	千克/立方米	AB	Laminated wood, with at least one surface layer of tropical coniferous board specified in Subheading Note 1 to this Chapter
4412.9992	----其他,至少含有一层木碎料板	10	30	17		千克/立方米		----Other, containing at least one layer of particle board
4412.9992 10	其他至少含有一层木碎料板的濒危针叶木面多层板	10	30	17		千克/立方米	ABFE	Other laminated wood, containing at least one layer of particle bodrd, surface layer of endangered conirterus wood
4412.9992 90	其他至少含有一层木碎料板的针叶木面多层板	10	30	17	9	千克/立方米	AB	Other laminated wood, containing at least one layer of particle board, surface layer of conirerous wood
4412.9999	----其他	4	30	17		千克/立方米		----Other
4412.9999 10	其他濒危针叶木面多层板	4	30	17		千克/立方米	ABFE	The endangered coniferous board veneer particle board
4412.9999 90	其他针叶木面多层板	4	30	17	9	千克/立方米	AB	The coniferous board veneer particle board
44.13	**强化木,成块、板、条或异型的:**							**Densified wood, in blocks, plates, strips or profile shapes:**
4413.0000	强化木(成块、板、条或异型的)	6	20	17	9	千克	AB	Densified wood, in blocks, plates, strips or profile shapes
44.14	**木制的画框、相框、镜框及类似品:**							**Wooden frames for paintings, photographs, mirrors or similar objects:**
	木制的画框、相框、镜框及类似品:							Wooden frames for paintings, photographs, mirrors or similar objects:
4414.0010	---辐射松制的	20	100	17	5	千克	AB	---Of radiata pine
4414.0090	---其他	20	100	17		千克		---Other
4414.0090 10	拉敏木制画框、相框、镜框及类似品	20	100	17	5	千克	ABFE	Frames for paintings, photographs, mirrors or similar objects, of Ramin wood
4414.0090 20	濒危木制画框、相框、镜框及类似品	20	100	17		千克	ABFE	Frames for paintings, photographs, mirrors or similar objects, of endangered wood
4414.0090 90	其他木制的画框、相框、镜框及类似品	20	100	17	13	千克	AB	Frames for paintings, photographs, mirrors or similar objects, of wood
44.15	**包装木箱、木盒、板条箱、圆桶及类似的包装容器;木制电缆卷筒;木托板、箱形托盘及其他装载用木板;木制的托盘护框:**							**Packing cases, boxes, crates, drums and similar packings, of wood; cable-drums of wood; pallets, box pallets and other load boards, of wood; pallet collars of wood:**
4415.1000	-箱、盒、板条箱、圆桶及类似的包装容器;电缆卷筒	7.5	80	17		千克/件		-Cases, boxes, crates, drums and similar packing; cabledrums
4415.1000 10	拉敏木制木箱及类似包装容器(电缆卷筒)	7.5	80	17	5	千克/件	ABFE	Cases and similar packing; cable-drums, of Ramin wood (*gonystylus. spp.*)
4415.1000 20	濒危木制木箱及类似包装容器(电缆卷筒)	7.5	80	17		千克/件	ABFE	Cases and similar packing; cable-drums, of endangered wood
4415.1000 90	木箱及类似的包装容器、电缆卷筒	7.5	80	17	9	千克/件	AB	Cases and similar packing; cable-drums, of wood
	-木托板、箱形托盘及其他装载用木板;木制的托盘护框:							-Pallets, box pallets and other load boards; pallet collars:
4415.2010	---辐射松制的	7.5	80	17	5	千克/件	AB	---Of radiatat pine
4415.2090	---其他	7.5	80	17		千克/件		---Other
4415.2090 10	拉敏木托板、箱形托盘及装载木板(包括拉敏木制托盘护框)	7.5	80	17	5	千克/件	ABFE	Pallets, box pallets and other load boards; pallet collars, of Ramin wood (*gonystylus. spp.*)
4415.2090 20	濒危木托板、箱形托盘及装载木板(包括濒危木制托盘护框)	7.5	80	17		千克/件	ABFE	Pallets, box pallets and other load boards; pallet collars, of endangered wood

税则号列	货 品 名 称	最惠(%)	普通	增值税率	出口退税	计量单位	监管条件	Article Description
4415.2090 90	其他木制托板、箱形托盘及其他装载木板(包括其他木制托盘护框)	7.5	80	17	9	千克/件	AB	Pallets, box pallets and other load boards; pallet collars, of wood
44.16	**木制大桶、琵琶桶、盆和其他木制箍桶及其零件,包括桶板:**							**Casks, barrels, vats, tubs and other coopers' products and parts thereof, of wood, including staves:**
4416.0010	---辐射松制的	16	80	17		千克	AB	---Of radiata pine
4416.0090	---其他	16	80	17		千克		---Other
4416.0090 10	拉敏木制大桶、琵琶桶、盆和其他箍桶及其零件(包括拉敏木制桶板)	16	80	17		千克	ABFE	Coopers' products and parts thereof (including staves), of Ramin wood (*gonystylus. spp.*)
4416.0090 20	濒危木制大桶、琵琶桶、盆和其他箍桶及其零件(包括濒危木制桶板)	16	80	17		千克	ABFE	Coopers' products and parts thereof (including staves), of endangered wood
4416.0090 90	其他木制大桶、琵琶桶、盆和其他箍桶及其零件(包括其他木制桶板)	16	80	17		千克	AB	Coopers' products and parts thereof (including staves), of other wood
44.17	**木制的工具、工具支架、工具柄、扫帚及刷子的身及柄;木制鞋靴楦及楦头:**							**Tools, tool bodies, tool handles, broom or brush bodies and handles, of wood; boot or shoe lasts and trees, of wood:**
4417.0010	---辐射松制的	16	80	17		千克	AB	---Of radiata pine
4417.0090	---其他	16	80	17		千克		---Other
4417.0090 10	拉敏木制工具、工具支架、工具柄、扫帚及刷子的身及柄(包括拉敏木制鞋靴楦及楦头)	16	80	17		千克	ABFE	Tools, tool bodies, tool handles, broom or brush bodies and handles, of ramin wood (including boot or shoe lasts and trees, of ramin wood)
4417.0090 20	濒危木制工具、工具支架、工具柄、扫帚及刷子的身及柄(包括濒危木制鞋靴楦及楦头)	16	80	17		千克	ABFE	Tools, tool bodies, tool handles, broom or brush bodies and handles, of endangered wood (including boot or shoe lasts and trees, of endangered wood)
4417.0090 90	其他木制工具、工具支架、工具柄、扫帚及刷子的身及柄(包括其他木制鞋靴楦及楦头)	16	80	17		千克	AB	Tools, tool bodies, tool handles, broom or brush bodies and handles, of wood (including boot or shoe lasts and trees, of wood)
44.18	**建筑用木工制品,包括蜂窝结构木镶板、已装拼的拼花地板、木瓦及盖屋板:**							**Builders' joinery and carpentry of wood, including cellular wood panels, assembled flooring parquet panels, shingles and shakes:**
	-窗、法兰西式(落地)窗及其框架:							-Windows, French-windows and their frames:
4418.1010	---辐射松制的	4	70	17	5	千克	AB	---Of radiata pine
4418.1090	---其他	4	70	17		千克		---Other
4418.1090 10	拉敏木制木窗、落地窗及其框架	4	70	17	5	千克	ABFE	Windows, French-windows and their frames of Ramin wood (*gonystylus. spp.*)
4418.1090 20	濒危木制木窗、落地窗及其框架	4	70	17		千克	ABFE	Windows, French-windows and their frames of endangered wood
4418.1090 90	其他木制木窗、落地窗及其框架	4	70	17	9	千克	AB	Windows, French-windows and their frames of other wood
4418.2000	-门及其框架和门槛	4	70	17		千克		-Doors and their frames and thresholds
4418.2000 10	拉敏木制的木门及其框架和门槛	4	70	17	5	千克	ABFE	Doors and their frames and thresholds of Ramin wood (*gonystylus. spp.*)
4418.2000 20	濒危木制的木门及其框架和门槛	4	70	17		千克	ABFE	Doors and their frames and thresholds of endangered wood
4418.2000 90	木门及其框架和门槛	4	70	17	9	千克	AB	Doors and their frames and thresholds of other wood
4418.4000	-水泥构件的木模板	4	70	17	9	千克	AB	-Shuttering for concrete constructional work
4418.5000	-木瓦及盖屋板	7.5	70	17	9	千克	AB	-Shingles and shakes
4418.6000	-柱和梁	4	70	17		千克		-Poles and beams
4418.6000 10	濒危木制柱和梁	4	70	17		千克	FEAB	Endangered wood made poles and girder
4418.6000 90	其他木制柱和梁	4	70	17	9	千克	AB	Other wood made poles and girder
	-已装拼的地板:							-Assembled flooring panels:
4418.7100	--马赛克地板用	4	70	17		千克		--For mosaic floors
4418.7100 10	已装拼的拉敏木制马赛克地板	4	70	17		千克	ABFE	Assembled mosaic floors of ramin wood
4418.7100 20	已装拼的其他濒危木制马赛克地板	4	70	17		千克	ABFE	Assembled mosaic floors of other endangered wood
4418.7100 90	已装拼的其他木制马赛克地板	4	70	17		千克	AB	Assembled mosaic floors of other wood
	--其他,多层的:							--Other, multilayer:
4418.7210	---竹制	4	70	17	13	千克	AB	---Of bomboo

税则号列	货品名称	最惠(%)	普通	增值税率	出口退税	计量单位	监管条件	Article Description
4418.7290	---其他	4	70	17		千克		---Other
4418.7290 10	已装拼的拉敏木制多层地板	4	70	17		千克	ABFE	Assembled mosaie floors of ramin wood
4418.7290 20	已装拼的其他濒危木制多层地板	4	70	17		千克	ABFE	Assembled mosaic floors of other endangered wood
4418.7290 90	已装拼的其他木制多层地板	4	70	17		千克	AB	Assembled mosaic floors of other wood
	--其他：							--Other:
4418.7910	---竹制	4	70	17	13	千克	AB	---Of bomboo
4418.7990	---其他	4	70	17		千克		---Other
4418.7990 10	已装拼的拉敏木制其他地板	4	70	17		千克	ABFE	Assembled mosaic floors of ramin wood
4418.7990 20	已装拼的其他濒危木制地板	4	70	17		千克	ABFE	Assembled mosaic floors of other endangered wood
4418.7990 90	已装拼的木制其他地板	4	70	17		千克	AB	Assembled mosaic floors of other wood
	-其他：							-Other:
4418.9010	---竹制	4	70	17		千克		---Of bamboo
4418.9010 10	濒危竹制其他建筑用木工制品（包括蜂窝结构的木镶板）	4	70	17		千克	ABE	Builders´ joinery and carpentry (including cellular wood panels, of endangered bamboo)
4418.9010 90	其他竹制其他建筑用木工制品（包括蜂窝结构的木镶板）	4	70	17	9	千克	AB	Builders´ joinery and carpentry (including cellular wood panels, of other bamboo)
4418.9090	---其他	4	70	17		千克		---Other
4418.9090 10	拉敏木制其他建筑用木工制品（包括蜂窝结构的木镶板）	4	70	17	5	千克	FEAB	Builders´ joinery and carpentry (including cellular wood panels), of Ramin wood)
4418.9090 20	濒危木制其他建筑用木工制品（包括蜂窝结构的木镶板）	4	70	17		千克	FEAB	Builders´ joinery and carpentry (including cellular wood panels), of endangered wood)
4418.9090 90	其他建筑用木工制品（包括蜂窝结构的木镶板）	4	70	17	9	千克	AB	Builders´ joinery and carpentry (including cellular wood panels), of other wood)
44.19	木制餐具及厨房用具：							**Tableware and kitchenware, of wood:**
	---一次性筷子：							---One-time chopsticks:
4419.0031	----木制	0	100	17		千克	AB	----Of wood
4419.0032	----竹制	0	100	17		千克		----Of bamboo
4419.0032 10	酸竹制一次性筷子	0	100	17		千克	ABE	One-time chopsticks, of acidosasa chinensis
4419.0032 90	其他竹制一次性筷子	0	100	17	13	千克	AB	Other one-time chopsticks, of bamboo
	---其他：							---Other:
4419.0091	----竹制	0	100	17	13	千克	AB	---Of abmboo
4419.0099	----其他	0	100	17		千克		---Other
4419.0099 10	拉敏木制的餐具及厨房用具	0	100	17	5	千克	FEAB	Tableware and kitchenware of Ramin wood
4419.0099 20	濒危木制的餐具及厨房用具	0	100	17		千克	FEAB	Tableware and kitchenware of endangered wood
4419.0099 90	其他木制餐具及厨房用具	0	100	17	9	千克	AB	Tableware and kitchenware, of other wood
44.20	镶嵌木（包括细工镶嵌木）；装珠宝或刀具用的木制盒子和小匣子及类似品；木制小雕像及其他装饰品；第九十四章以外的木制家具：							**Wood marquetry and inlaid wood; caskets and cases for jewellery or cutlery, and similar articles, of wood; statuettes and other ornaments, of wood; wooden articles or furniture not falling in Chapter 94:**
	-木制小雕像及其他装饰品：							-Statuettes and other ornaments, of wood:
	---木刻及竹刻							---Wood or bamboo carvings
4420.1011	----木刻	0	100	17		千克		---wood carving
4420.1011 10	拉敏木制的木刻	0	100	17	5	千克	FEAB	Wood carving of Ramin wood
4420.1011 20	濒危木制的木刻	0	100	17		千克	FEAB	Wood carving of endangered wood
4420.1011 90	其他木刻	0	100	17	9	千克	AB	Other wood carving
4420.1012	----竹刻	0	100	17	9	千克	AB	----Bamboo carving
4420.1020	---木扇	0	100	17		千克		---Wooden fans
4420.1020 10	拉敏木制的木扇	0	100	17	5	千克	FEAB	Wooden fans of Ramin wood
4420.1020 20	濒危木制的木扇	0	100	17		千克	FEAB	Wooden fans of endangered wood
4420.1020 90	木扇	0	100	17	9	千克	AB	Wooden fans
4420.1090	---其他	0	100	17		千克		---Other
4420.1090 10	拉敏木制其他小雕像及其他装饰品	0	100	17	5	千克	FEAB	Statuettes and other ornaments of Ramin wood
4420.1090 30	沉香木及拟沉香木制其他小雕像及其他装饰品	0	100	17		千克	FEAB	Statuettes and other ornaments of chinese eaglewood and quasi chinese eaglewood
4420.1090 40	其他濒危木制其他小雕像及其他装饰品	0	100	17		千克	FEAB	Statuettes and other ornaments of endangered wood

税则号列	货 品 名 称	最惠(%)	普通	增值税率	出口退税	计量单位	监管条件	Article Description
4420.1090 90	其他木制小雕像及其他装饰品	0	100	17	13	千克	AB	Statuettes and other ornaments of other wood
	-其他:							-Other:
4420.9010	---镶嵌木	0	45	17		千克		---Wood marquetry and inlaid wood
4420.9010 10	拉敏木制的镶嵌木	0	45	17	5	千克	FEAB	Wood marquetry and inlaid wood of Ramin wood
4420.9010 20	濒危木制的镶嵌木	0	45	17		千克	FEAB	Wood marquetry and inlaid wood of endangered wood
4420.9010 90	镶嵌木	0	45	17	13	千克	AB	Wood marquetry and inlaid wood
4420.9090	---其他	0	100	17		千克		---Other
4420.9090 10	拉敏木盒及类似品,非落地木家具(前者用于装珠宝或家具;后者不包括第九十四章的家具)	0	100	17	5	千克	FEAB	Caskets and similar articles non – floor type furniture not falling, of Ramin wood (the former used for jewelry or furniture, the latter not including furniture falling in Chapter 94)
4420.9090 20	濒危木盒及类似品,非落地木家具(前者用于装珠宝或家具;后者不包括第九十四章的家具)	0	100	17		千克	FEAB	Caskets and similar articles or non – floor type furniture of endangered wood in(the former used for jewelry or furniture, the latter not including furniture falling in Chapter 94)
4420.9090 90	木盒子及类似品;非落地式木家具(前者用于装珠宝或家具;后者不包括第九十四章的家具)	0	100	17	9	千克	AB	Caskets and similar articles or furniture not falling, of wood (the former used for jewelry or furniture, the latter not including furniture falling in Chapter 94)
44.21	**其他木制品:**							**Other articles of wood:**
4421.1000	-衣架	0	90	17		千克		-Clothes hangers
4421.1000 10	拉敏木制木衣架	0	90	17	5	千克	FEAB	Clothes hangers of Ramin wood
4421.1000 20	濒危木制木衣架	0	90	17		千克	FEAB	Clothes hangers of endangered wood
4421.1000 90	木衣架	0	90	17	9	千克	AB	Clothes hangers of wood
	-其他:							-Other:
4421.9010	---卷轴、纡子、筒管、缝纫用线轴及类似品	0	35	17		千克		---Spools, cops, bobbins, sewing thread reels and the like
4421.9010 10	拉敏木纡子、筒管、卷轴、线轴及类似品	0	35	17	5	千克	FEAB	Spools cops, bobbins, sewing thread reels and the like, of Ramin wood
4421.9010 20	濒危木纡子、筒管、卷轴、线轴及类似品	0	35	17		千克	FEAB	Spools, cops, bobbins, sewing thread reels and the like, of endangered wood
4421.9010 90	木卷轴、纡子、筒管、线轴及类似品	0	35	17	9	千克	AB	Spools, cops, bobbins, sewing thread reels and the like, of wood
	---圆签、圆棒、冰果棒、压舌片及类似一次性制品:							---Circle sticks, cirde bars, popside sticks, spatala and the like
4421.9021	----木制	0	35	17		千克		----Of wood
4421.9021 10	一次性拉敏木制圆签、圆棒、冰果棒、压舌片(包括类似的一次性制品)	0	35	17		千克	FEAB	Round toobtpick, round stick, ice fruit stick tongue-pressing plate and similar one-time of Ramin wood
4421.9021 20	一次性濒危木制圆签、圆棒、冰果棒、压舌片(包括类似的一次性制品)	0	35	17		千克	FEAB	Round toobtpick, round stick, ice fruit stick tongue-pressing plate and similar one-time of endangered wood
4421.9021 90	一次性其他木制圆签、圆棒、冰果棒、压舌片(包括类似的一次性制品)	0	35	17		千克	AB	Round toobtpick, round stick, ice fruit stick tongue-pressing plate and similar one-time of other wood
4421.9022	----竹制	0	35	17		千克		----of bamboo
4421.9022 10	一次性酸竹制圆签、圆棒、冰果棒、压舌片(包括类似的一次性制品)	0	35	17		千克	ABE	round toothpick, round stick, ice fruit stick, tongue – pressing plate and similar one – off products of acidosasa chinensis
4421.9022 90	一次性其他竹制圆签、圆棒、冰果棒、压舌片(包括类似的一次性制品)	0	35	17	13	千克	AB	round toothpick, round stick, ice fruit stick, tongue – pressing plate and similar one – off products of bamboo
4421.9090	---其他	0	90	17		千克		---Other
4421.9090 10	拉敏木制的未列名的木制品	0	90	17	5	千克	FEAB	Articles of Ramin wood, not elsewhere specified or included
4421.9090 20	濒危木制的未列名的木制品	0	90	17		千克	FEAB	Articles of endangered wood, not elsewhere specified or included
4421.9090 90	未列名的木制品	0	90	17	13	千克	AB	Articles of wood, not elsewhere specified or included

第四十五章
软木及软木制品

Chapter 45
Cork and articles of cork

注释：

本章不包括：

一、第六十四章的鞋靴及其零件；

二、第六十五章的帽类及其零件；

三、第九十五章的物品（例如，玩具、游戏品及运动用品）。

Notes:

This Chapter does not cover:

(a) Footwear or parts of footwear of Chapter 64;

(b) Headgear or parts of headgear of Chapter 65;

(c) Articles of Chapter 95 (for example, toys, games, sports requisites).

税则号列	货品名称	最惠(%)	普通	增值税率	出口退税	计量单位	监管条件	Article Description
45.01	未加工或简单加工的天然软木；软木废料；碎的、粒状的或粉状的软木：							**Natural cork, raw or simply prepared; waste cork; crushed, granulated or ground cork:**
4501.1000[暂]	-未加工或简单加工的天然软木	1	17	17		千克	AB	-Natrual cork, raw or simply prepared
	-其他：							-Other:
4501.9010	---软木废料	0	17	17		千克	AB	---Waste cork
4501.9020	---碎的、粉粒状的或粉状的软木（软木碎，软木粒或软木粉）	0	17	17		千克	AB	---Crushed, granulated or ground cork (Cork wood is broken, the cork wood granule or cork wood turns to powder)
45.02	天然软木，除去表皮或粗切成方形，或成长方块、正方块、板、片或条状（包括作塞子用的方块坯料）：							**Natural cork, debarked or roughly squared, or in rectangular (including square) blocks, plates, sheets or strip, (including sharp-edged blanks for corks or stoppers):**
4502.0000	天然软木，除去表皮或粗切成方形，或成长方块、正方块、板、片或条状（包括作塞子用的方块坯料）	8	30	17		千克	AB	Natural cork, debarked or roughly squared, or in rectangular (including square) blocks, plates, sheets or strip, (including sharp-edged blanks for corks or stoppers)
45.03	天然软木制品：							**Articles of natural cork:**
4503.1000	-塞子	8	50	17		千克	AB	-Corks and stoppers
4503.9000	-其他	10.5	50	17		千克	AB	-Other
45.04	压制软木（不论是否使用粘合剂压成）及其制品：							**Agglomerated cork (with or without a binding substance) and articles of agglomerated cork:**
4504.1000	块、板、片及条状压制软木（包括任何形状的压制软木的砖，瓦，实心圆柱体，圆片）	8.4	30	17		千克	AB	-Blocks, plates, sheets and strip; tiles of any shape; solid cylinders, including discs
4504.9000	-其他	0	50	17		千克	AB	-Other

第四十六章
稻草、秸秆、针茅或其他编结材料制品;篮筐及柳条编结品

Chapter 46
Manufactures of straw, of esparto or of other plaiting materials; basketware and wickerwork

注释:

一、本章所称“编结材料”,是指其状态或形状适于编结、交织或类似加工的材料,包括稻草、秸秆、柳条、竹、藤灯芯草、芦苇、木片条、其他植物材料扁条(例如,树皮条、狭叶、酒椰叶纤维或其他从阔叶获取的条)、未纺的天然纺织纤维、塑料单丝及扁条、纸带,但不包括皮革、再生皮革、毡呢或无纺织物的扁条、人发、马毛、纺织粗纱或纱线以及第五十四章的单丝和扁条。

二、本章不包括:

(一)税目48.14的壁纸;

(二)不论是否编结而成的线、绳、索、缆(税目56.07);

(三)第六十四章和第六十五章的鞋靴、帽类及其零件;

(四)编结而成的车辆或车身(第八十七章);

(五)第九十四章的物品(例如,家具、灯及灯具)。

三、税目46.01所称“平行连结的成片编结材料、缏条或类似的编结材料产品”,是指编结材料、缏条及类似的编结材料产品平行排列连结成片的制品,其连结材料不论是否为纺制的纺织材料。

Notes:

1. In this Chapter the expression “plaiting materials” means materials in a state or form suitable for plaiting, interlacing or similar processes; it includes straw, osier or willow, bamboos, rattans rushes, reeds, strips of wood, strips of other vegetable material (for example, strips of bark, narrow leaves and raffia or other strips obtained from broad leaves), unspun natural textile fibres, monofilament and strip and the like of plastics and strips of paper, but not strips of leather or composition leather or of felt or nonwovens, human hair, horsehair, textile rovings or yarns, or monofilament and strip and the like of Chapter 54.
2. This Chapter does not cover:
(a) Wall coverings of heading No. 48.14;
(b) Twine, cordage, ropes or cables, plaited or not (heading No. 56.07);
(c) Footwear or headgear or parts thereof of Chapter 64 or 65;
(d) Vehicles or bodies for vehicles of basketware (Chapter 87);
(e) Articles of Chapter 94 (for example, furniture, lamps).
3. For the purposes of heading No. 46.01, the expression “plaiting materials, plaits and similar products of plaiting materials, bound together in parallel strands” means plaiting materials, plaits and similar products of plaiting materials, placed side by side and bound together, in the form of sheets, whether or not the binding materials are of spun textile materials.

税则号列	货品名称	最惠(%)	普通	增值税率	出口退税	计量单位	监管条件	Article Description
46.01	用编结材料编成的缏条及类似产品,不论是否缝合成宽条;平行连结或编结的成片材料、缏条或类似的编结材料产品,不论是否制成品(例如,席子、席料、帘子):							**Plaits and similar products of plaiting materials, whether or not assembled into strips; plaiting materials, plaits and similar products of plaiting materials, bound together in parallel strands or woven, in sheet form, whether or not being finished articles (for example, mats, matting, screens):**
	-植物材料制的席子、席料及帘子:							-Mats, matting and screens of vegetable materials:
4601.2100	--竹制的	9	90	17	13	千克/张	AB	--Of bamboo
4601.2200	--藤制的	9	100	17	13	千克/张	AB	--Of rattan
	--其他:							--Other:
	---草制的:							---Of grass or straw:
4601.2911	----灯心草属材料制的	9	90	17	13	千克/张		----Of rushes
4601.2911 11	蔺草制的提花席、双苜席、垫子(单位面积$>1m^2$,不论是否包边)	9	90	17	13	千克/张	AB	Juncaceae mats, pairs of clover mats, mat (ubit area $>1m^2$, whether or not edged)
4601.2911 12	蔺草制的其他席子(单位面积$>1m^2$,不论是否包边)	9	90	17	13	千克/张	AB	Other mats, matting and screens, of Juncaceae, area $>1m^2$, whether or not edged
4601.2911 19	蔺草制的其他席子、席料及帘子(单位面积$\leq 1m^2$,不论是否包边)	9	90	17	13	千克/张	AB	Jacquard mats, clover mats and cushion, of rush, of per unit area exceeding $1m^2$, whether or not deged
4601.2911 90	其他灯芯草属材料制的席子等(包括席子、席料、帘子、垫子)	9	90	17	13	千克/张	AB	Other mats, matting, of rushes (including mat, matting screens)
4601.2919	----其他	9	90	17	13	千克/张	AB	----Other
	---芦苇制的:							---Of reeds:
4601.2921	----苇帘	9	90	17	13	千克/张	AB	----Screens of reeds
4601.2929	----其他	9	90	17	13	千克/张	AB	----Other
4601.2990	---其他	9	90	17	13	千克/张	AB	---Other
	-其他:							-Other:

税则号列	货品名称	最惠(%)	普通	增值税率	出口退税	计量单位	监管条件	Article Description
	--竹制的:							--Of bamboo:
4601.9210	---缏条及类似产品,不论是否缝合成宽条	9	100	17	13	千克	AB	---Plaits and similar products of plaiting materials, whether or not assembled into strips
4601.9290	---其他	9	90	17	13	千克	AB	---Other:
	--藤制的:							--Of rattan:
4601.9310	---缏条及类似产品,不论是否缝合成宽条	9	100	17	13	千克	AB	---Plaits and similar products of plaiting materials, whether or not assembled into strips
4601.9390	---其他	9	90	17	13	千克	AB	---Other
	--其他植物材料制的:							--Of other vegetable materials:
	---稻草制的:							---Of straw:
4601.9411	----缏条(绳)	10	90	17	13	千克	AB	----Plaits
4601.9419	----其他	10	90	17	13	千克	AB	----Other
	---其他:							---Other:
4601.9491	----缏条及类似产品,不论是否缝合成宽条	9	100	17	13	千克	AB	----Plaits and similar products of plaiting materials, whether or not assembled into strips
4601.9499	----其他	9	90	17	13	千克	AB	----Other
	--其他:							--Other:
4601.9910	---缏条及类似产品,不论是否缝合成宽条	9	90	17	13	千克		--Plaits and similar products of plaiting materials, whether or not assembled into strips
4601.9990	---其他	9	90	17	13	千克		---Other
46.02	**用编结材料直接编成或用税目46.01所列货品制成的篮筐、柳条编结品及其他制品;丝瓜络制品:**							**Basketwork, wickerwork and other articles, made directly to shape from plaiting materials or made up from goods of heading No. 46.01; articles of loofah:**
	-植物材料制:							-Of vegetable materials:
4602.1100	--竹制的	9	100	17	13	千克	AB	--Of bamboo
4602.1200	--藤制的	9	100	17	13	千克	AB	--Of rattan
	--其他:							--Other:
4602.1910	---草制的	9	100	17	13	千克	AB	---Of grass or straw
4602.1920	---玉米皮制的	9	100	17	13	千克	AB	---Of maize - shuck
4602.1930	---柳条制的	9	100	17	13	千克	AB	---Of osier
4602.1990	---其他	9	100	17	13	千克	AB	---Other
4602.9000	-其他	9	100	17	13	千克		-Other

第十类
木浆及其他纤维状纤维素浆；回收(废碎)纸或纸板；纸、纸板及其制品

SECTION X
PULP OF WOOD OR OF OTHER FIBROUS CELLULOSIC MATERIAL; ZRCOVERED (WASTE AND SCRAP) PAPER OR PAPERBOARD; PAPER AND PAPERBOARD AND ARTICLES THEREOF

第四十七章
木浆及其他纤维状纤维素浆；回收(废碎)纸或纸板

Chapter 47
Pulp of wood or of other fibrous cellulosic material; recovered (waste and scrap) paper or paperboard

注释：

税目47.02所称"化学木浆,溶解级",是指温度在20℃时浸入含18%氢氧化钠的苛性碱溶液内,一小时后,按重量计含有92%及以上的不溶级分的碱木浆或硫酸盐木浆,或者含有88%及以上的不溶级分的亚硫酸盐木浆。对于亚硫酸盐木浆,按重量计灰分含量不得超过0.15%。

Notes:

For the purposes of heading No. 47.02, the expression "chemical wood pulp, dissolving grades" means chemical wood pulp having by weight an insoluble fraction of 92% or more for soda or sulphate wood pulp or of 88% or more for sulphite wood pulp after one hour in a caustic soda solution containing 18% sodium bydroxide (NaOH) at 20℃, and for sulphite wood pulp an ash content that does not exceed 0.15% by weight.

税则号列	货品名称	最惠(%)	普通	增值税率	出口退税	计量单位	监管条件	Article Description
47.01	机械木浆:							**Mechanical wood pulp:**
4701.0000	机械木浆	0	8	17		千克		Mechanical wood pulp
47.02	化学木浆,溶解级:							**Chemical wood pulp, dissolving grades:**
4702.0000	化学木浆,溶解级	0	8	17		千克		Chemical wood pulp, dissolving grades
4702.0000 01	用于生产粘胶等化学纤维(不含醋酸纤维)的化学木浆,溶解级(浆粕的粘度≧3.7dl/g,且<6.4dl/g,或者≧350ml/g,且<700ml/g,α 纤维素含量(R18,硫酸盐法)≧88%,且<95.5%,或者α纤维素含量(R18,亚硫酸盐法)≧87%,且<94%,灰分≦0.15%)	0	8	17		千克		For the production of viscose chemical fiber (not containing cellulose acetate) of chemical wood pulp, dissolving (content of alpha cellulose pulp viscosity is greater than or equal to 3.7dl/g, and <6.4dl/g, and ⩾ 350ml/g, and (< 700ml/g, R18, sulfate) ⩾ 88%, and <95.5%, or the content of alpha cellulose (R18, sulfite) ⩾ 87%, and <94%, ash ⩽ 0.15%)
4702.0000 90	其他化学木浆,溶解级	0	8	17		千克		Other chemical wood pulp, dissolving grades
47.03	碱木浆或硫酸盐木浆,但溶解级的除外:							**Chemical wood pulp, soda or sulphate, other than dissolving grades:**
	-未漂白:							-Unbleached:
4703.1100	--针叶木的	0	8	17		千克		--Coniferous
4703.1900	--非针叶木的	0	8	17		千克		--Non-coniferous
	-半漂白或漂白:							-Semi-bleached or bleached:
4703.2100	--针叶木的	0	8	17		千克		--Coniferous
4703.2100 01	用于生产粘胶等化学纤维(不含醋酸纤维)的漂白针叶木碱木浆或硫酸盐木浆(包括半漂白的,溶解级的除外)(浆粕的粘度≧3.7dl/g,且<6.4dl/g,或者≧350ml/g,且<700ml/g,α 纤维素含量(R18,硫酸盐法)≧88%,且<95.5%,灰分≦0.15%)	0	8	17		千克		For the production of viscose chemical fiber (not containing cellulose acetate) of bleached softwood pulp of wood or kraft pulp (including semi bleached, dissolving except) (content of alpha cellulose pulp viscosity is greater than or equal to 3.7dl/g, and <6.4dl/g, and ⩾ 350ml/g, and < 700ml/g, (R18, sulfur acid salt) ⩾ 88%, and < 95.5%, ash ⩽ 0.15%)
4703.2100 90	其他漂白针叶木碱木浆或硫酸盐木浆(包括半漂白的,溶解级的除外)	0	8	17		千克		Other chemical wood pulp, soda or sulhate (including semi - bleached or bleached, other than dissolving grades)
4703.2900	--非针叶木的	0	8	17		千克		--Non-coniferous

税则号列	货品名称	最惠(%)	普通	增值税率	出口退税	计量单位	监管条件	Article Description
47.04	亚硫酸盐木浆,但溶解级的除外:							**Chemical wood pulp, sulphite, other than dissolving grades:**
	-未漂白:							-Unbleached:
4704.1100	--针叶木的	0	8	17		千克		--Coniferous
4704.1900	--非针叶木的	0	8	17		千克		--Non-coniferous
	-半漂白或漂白:							-Semi-bleached or bleached:
4704.2100	--针叶木的	0	8	17		千克		--Coniferous
4704.2900	--非针叶木的	0	8	17		千克		--Non-coniferous
47.05	**用机械与化学联合制浆法制得的木浆:**							**Wood pulp obtained by a combination of mechanical and chemical pulping processes:**
4705.0000	用机械与化学联合制浆法制得的木浆	0	8	17		千克		Wood pulp obtained by a combination of mechanical and chemical pulping processes
47.06	**从回收(废碎)纸或纸板提取的纤维浆或其他纤维状纤维素浆:**							**Pulps of fibres derived from recovered (waste and scrap) paper or paperboard or of other fibrous cellulosic material:**
4706.1000	-棉短绒纸浆	0	8	17	13	千克		-Cotton linters pulp
4706.1000 01	用于生产粘胶等化学纤维(不含醋酸纤维)的棉短绒浆粕(浆粕的粘度≧3.7dl/g,且＜6.4dl/g,或者≧350ml/g,且＜700ml/g,α纤维素含量(R18,硫酸盐法)≧88%,且＜95.5%,或者α纤维素含量(R18,亚硫酸盐法)≧87%,且＜94%,灰分≦0.15%)	0	8	17	13	千克		For the production of viscose chemical fiber (not containing cellulose acetate) of cotton linter pulp (content of alpha cellulose pulp viscosity is greater than or equal to 3.7dl/g, and ＜6.4dl/g, and ≥350ml/g, and (＜700ml/g, R18, sulfate) ≥88%, and ＜95.5%, or the content of alpha cellulose (R18, sulfurous acid salt) ≥87%, and ＜94%, ash ≤0.15%)
4706.1000 90	其他棉短绒纸浆	0	8	17	13	千克		Other cotton linters pulp
4706.2000	-从回收(废碎)纸或纸板提取的纤维浆	0	8	17		千克		-Pulps of fibres derived from recovered (waste and scrap) paper or paperboard
4706.3000	-其他,竹浆	0	8	17		千克		-Other, of bamboo
4706.3000 01	-用于生产粘胶等化学纤维(不含醋酸纤维)的其他纤维状纤维素竹浆(包括机械浆、化学浆、半化学浆)(浆粕的粘度≧3.7dl/g,且＜6.4dl/g,或者≧350ml/g,且＜700ml/g,α纤维素含量(R18,硫酸盐法)≧88%,且＜95.5%,或者α纤维素含量(R18,亚硫酸盐法)≧87%,且＜94%,灰分≦0.15%)	0	8	17		千克		-For the production of viscose chemical fiber (not containing cellulose acetate) of cellulose pulp (including mechanical pulp, chemical pulp, semi chemical pulp) (content of alpha cellulose pulp viscosity is greater than or equal to 3.7dl/g, and ＜6.4dl/g, and ≥350ml/g, and (＜700ml/g, R18, sulfate) ≥88%, and ＜95.5%, or alpha the content of cellulose (R18, sulfite) ≥87%, and ＜94%, ash ≤0.15%)
4706.3000 90	其他纤维状纤维素竹浆(包括机械浆、化学浆、半化学浆)	0	8	17		千克		Other fibrous cellulosic material(including mechanical wood pulp, chemical pulp, semi－chemical)
	-其他:							-Other:
4706.9100	--机械浆	0	8	17		千克		--Mechanical
4706.9200	--化学浆	0	8	17		千克		--Chemical
4706.9300	--用机械和化学联合法制得的浆	0	8	17		千克		--Pulp obtained by a combination of mechanical and chemical pulping processes
47.07	**回收(废碎)纸或纸板:**							**Recovered (waste and scrap) paper or paperboard:**
4707.1000	-未漂白的牛皮纸或纸板及瓦楞纸或纸板	0	8	17		千克	ABP	-Unbleached kraft paper or paperboard or of corrugated paper or paperboard
4707.2000	-主要由漂白化学木浆制成未经本体染色的其他纸和纸板	0	8	17		千克	ABP	-Other paper or paperboard made mainly of bleached chemical pulp, not coloured in the mass
4707.3000	-主要由机械浆制成的纸或纸板(例如,报纸、杂志及类似印刷品)	0	8	17		千克	ABP	-Paper or paperboard made mainly of mechanical pulp (for example, newspapers, journals and similar printed matter)
4707.9000	-其他,包括未分选的废碎品	0	8	17		千克		-Other, including unsorted waste and scrap

税则号列	货品名称	最惠(%)	普通	增值税率	出口退税	计量单位	监管条件	Article Description
4707.9000 10	回收(废碎)墙(壁)纸、涂蜡纸、浸蜡纸、复写纸(包括未分选的废碎品)	0	8	17		千克	AB9	Recoverd(waste and scrap) wallpaper, mimeograph or waxed paper and carbon paper(including unsorted waste and scrap)
4707.9000 90	其他回收纸或纸板(包括未分选的废碎品)	0	8	17		千克	ABP	Other recovered paper or paperboard(including unsorted waste and scrap)

第四十八章
纸及纸板;纸浆、纸或纸板制品

注释:

一、除条文另有规定的以外,本章所称"纸"包括"纸板"(不论其厚度或每平方米重量如何)。

二、本章不包括:
(一)第三十章的物品;
(二)税目32.12的压印箔;
(三)香纸及用化妆品浸渍或涂布的纸(第三十三章);
(四)用肥皂或洗涤剂浸渍、覆盖或涂布的纸或纤维素絮纸(税号34.01)和用光洁剂、擦光膏及类似制剂浸渍、覆盖或涂布的纸或纤维素絮纸(税目34.05);
(五)税目37.01至37.04的感光纸或感光纸板;
(六)用诊断或实验用试剂浸渍的纸(税目38.22);
(七)第三十九章的用纸强化的层压塑料板,用塑料覆盖或涂布的单层纸或纸板(塑料部分占总厚度的一半以上),以及上述材料的制品,但税目48.14的壁纸除外;
(八)税目42.02的物品(例如旅行用品);
(九)第四十六章的物品(编结材料制品);
(十)纸纱线或纸纱线纺织物(第十一类);
(十一)第六十四章或第六十五章的物品;
(十二)税目68.05的砂纸或税目68.14的用纸或纸板衬底的云母(但涂布云母粉的纸及纸板归入本章);
(十三)用纸或纸板衬底的金属箔(通常为第十四类或第十五类);
(十四)税目92.09的制品;
(十五)第九十五章的物品(例如,玩具、游戏品及运动用品;
(十六)(十六)第九十六章的物品[例如,钮扣、卫生巾(护垫)及止血塞、婴儿尿布及尿布衬里]。

三、除注释七另有规定的以外,税目48.01至48.05包括经研光、高度研光、釉光或类似处理、仿水印、表面施胶的纸及纸板;同时还包括用各种方法本体着色或染成斑纹的纸、纸板、纤维素絮纸及纤维素纤维网纸。除税目48.03另有规定的以外,上述税目不适用于经过其他方法加工的纸、纸板、纤维素絮纸或纤维素纤维网纸。

四、本章所称"新闻纸",是指所含用机械或化学——机械方法制得的木纤维不少于全部纤维重量的50%的未经涂布的报刊用纸,未施胶或微施胶,每面的粗糙度[帕克印刷表面粗糙度(1兆帕)]超过2.5微米,每平方米重量不小于40克,但不超过65克。

Chapter 48
Paper and paperboard; articles of paper pulp, of paper or of paperboard

Notes:

1. For the purposes of this Chapter, except where the context otherwise requires, a reference to "paper" includes references to paperboard (irrespective of thickness or weight per m^2).
2. This Chapter does not cover:
(a) Articles of Chapter 30;
(b) Stamping foils of heading No. 32.12;
(c) Perfumed papers or papers impregnated or coated with cosmetics (Chapter 33);
(d) Paper or cellulose wadding impregnated, coated or covered with soap or detergent (heading No. 34.01), or with polishes, creams or similar preparations (heading No. 34.05);
(e) Sensitized paper or paperboard of headings No. 37.01 to 37.04;
(f) Paper impregnated with diagnostic or laboratory reagents (heading No. 38.22);
(g) Paper-reinforced stratified sheeting of plastics, or one layer of paper or paperboard coated or covered with a layer of plastics, the latter constituting more than half the total thickness, or articles of such materials, other than wall coverings of heading No. 48.14 (Chapter 39);
(h) Articles of heading No. 42.02 (for example, travel goods);
(i) Articles of Chapter 46 (manufactures of plaiting material);
(j) Paper yarn or textile articles of paper yarn (Section XI);
(k) Articles of Chapter 64 or Chapter 65;
(l) Abrasive paper or paperboard (heading No. 68.05) or paper backed or paperboard-backed mica (heading No. 68.14) (paper and paperboard coated with mica powder are, however, to be classified in this Chapter);
(m) Metal foil backed with paper or paperboard (generally to be classified in Section XIV or XV);
(n) Articles of heading No. 92.09;
(o) Articles of Chapter 95 (for example, toys, games, sports requisites)
(p) Chapter96 (for example buttons、sanitary (sanitary napkin) and hemostatic plug、napkins and napkin liners for babies
3. Subject to the provisions of Note 7, headings Nos. 48.01 to 48.05 include paper and paperboard which have been subjected to calendering, supercalendering, glazing or similar finishing, false watermarking or surface sizing, and also paper, paperboard, cellulose wading and webs of cellulose fibres, coloured or marbled throughout the mass by any method. Except where heading No. 48.03 otherwise requires, these headings do not apply to paper, paperboard, cellulose wadding or webs of cellulose fibres which have been otherwise processed.
4. In this Chapter the expression "newsprint" means uncoated paper of a kind used for the printing of newspapers, of which not less than 50% by weight of the total fibre content consists of wood fibres obtained by a mechanical or chemi-mechanical process, unsized or very lightly sized, having a surface roughness Parker Print Surf (1 MPa) on each side exceeding 2.5 micrometres (microns), weighing not less than 40 g/m^2 and not more than 65 g/m^2.

五、税目48.02所称"书写、印刷或类似用途的纸及纸板"及"未打孔的穿孔卡片纸及穿孔纸带纸",是指主要用漂白纸浆或用机械或化学—机械方法制得的纸浆制成的纸及纸板,并且符合下列任一标准:

每平方米重量不超过150克的纸或纸板:

(一)用机械或化学—机械方法制得的纤维含量在10%及以上,并且

1. 每平方米重量不超过80克;

2. 本体着色;

(二)灰分含量在8%以上,并且

1. 每平方米重量不超过80克;

2. 本体着色;

(三)灰分含量在3%以上,亮度在60%及以上;

(四)灰分含量在3%以上,但不超过8%,亮度低于60%,耐破指数等于或小于2.5千帕斯卡·平方米/克;

(五)灰分含量在3%及以下,亮度在60%及以上,耐破指数等于或小于2.5千帕斯卡·平方米/克。

每平方米重量超过150克的纸或纸板:

(一)本体着色;或

(二)亮度在60%及以上,并且

1. 厚度在225微米及以下;或

2. 厚度在225微米以上,但不超过508微米,灰分含量在3%以上;

(三)亮度低于60%,厚度不超过254微米,灰分含量在8%以上。

税目48.02不包括滤纸及纸板(含茶袋纸)或毡纸及纸板。

六、本章所称"牛皮纸及纸板",是指所含用硫酸盐法或烧碱法制得的纤维不少于全部纤维重量的80%的纸及纸板。

七、除税目条文另有规定的以外,符合税目48.01至48.11中两个或两个以上税目所规定的纸、纸板、纤维素絮纸及纤维素纤维网纸,应按号列顺序归入有关税目中的最末一个税目。

八、税目48.01及48.03至48.09仅适用于下列规格的纸、纸板、纤维素絮纸及纤维素纤维网纸:

(一)成条或成卷,宽度超过36厘米;

(二)成张矩形(包括正方形),一边超过36厘米,另一边超过15厘米(以未折叠计)。

九、税目48.14所称"壁纸及类似品",仅限于:

(一)适合作墙壁或天花板装饰用的成卷纸张,宽度不小于45厘米,但不超过160厘米:

1. 起纹、压花、染面、印有图案或经其他装饰的(例如起绒),不论是否用透明的防护塑料涂布或覆盖;

2. 表面饰有木粒或草粒而凹凸不平的;

3. 表面用塑料涂布或覆盖并起纹、压花、染面、印有图案或经其他装饰的;

5. For the purposes of heading No. 48.02, the expressions "paper and paperboard, of a kind used for writing, printing or other graphic purposes" and "non perforated punch-cards and punch tape paper" mean paper and paperboard made mainly from bleached pulp or from pulp obtained by a mechanical or chemi-mechanical process and satisfying any of the following criteria:

For paper or paperboard weighing not more than $150g/m^2$:

(a) containing 10% or more of fibres obtained by a mechanical or chemi-mechanical process, and

①weighing not more than 80 g/m^2,

②coloured throughout the mass; or

(b) containing more than 8% ash, and

①weighing not more than 80 g/m^2,

②coloured throughout the mass; or

(c) containing more than 3% ash and having a brightness of 60% or more;

(d) containing more than 3% but not more than 8% ash, having a brightness less than 60%, and a burst index equal to or less than 2.5 $kPa/m^2/g$;

(e) containing 3% ash or less, having a brightness of 60% or more and a burst index equal to or less than 2.5 $kPa \cdot m^2/g$.

For paper or paperboard weighing more than 150 g/m^2:

(a) coloured throughout the mass; or

(b) having a brightness of 60% or more, and

①a caliper of 225 micrometres (microns) or less, or

②a caliper more than 225 micrometres (microns) but not more than 508 micrometres (microns) and an ash content more than 3%; or

(c) having a brightness of less than 60%, a caliper of 254 micrometres (microns) or less and an ash content of more than 8%.

Heading No. 48.02 does not, however, cover filter paper and paperboard (including tea-bag paper) or felt paper or paperboard.

6. In this Chapter "kraft paper and paperboard" means paper and paperhoard of which not less than 80% by weight of the total fibre content consists of fibres obtained by the chemical sulphate or soda processes.

7. Except where the terms of the headings otherwise require, paper, paperboard, cellulose wadding and webs of cellulose fibres answering to a description in two or more of the headings No. 48.01 to 48.11 are to be classified under that one of such headings which occurs last in numerical order in the Nomenclature.

8. Headings No. 48.01 and 48.03to 48.09 apply only to paper, paperboard, cellulose wadding and webs of cellulose fibres:

(A) in strips or rolls of a width exceeding 36 cm;

(B) in rectangular (including square) sheets with one side exceeding 36 cm and the other side exceeding 15 cm in the unfolded state.

9. For the purposes of heading No. 48.14, the expression "wallpaper and similar wall coverings" applies only to:

(a) Paper in rolls, of a width of not less than 45 cm and not more than 160 cm, suitable for wall or ceiling decoration:

①Grained, embossed, surface-coloured, designprinted or otherwise surface-decorated (for exanple, with textile flock), whether or not coated or covered with transparent protective plastics;

②With an uneven surface resulting from the incorporation of particles of wood, straw, etc.;

③Coated or covered on the face side with plastics, the layer of plastics being grained, embossed, coloured, design-printed or otherwise decorated;

4. 表面用不论是否平行连结或编织的编结材料覆盖的；

（二）适于装饰墙壁或天花板用的经上述加工的纸边及纸条，不论是否成卷；

（三）由几幅拼成的壁纸，成卷或成张，贴到墙上可组成印制的风景或图案。

既可作铺地制品，也可作壁纸的以纸或纸板为底的产品，应归入税目 48.23。

十、税目 48.20 不包括切成一定尺寸的活页纸张或卡片，不论是否印制、压花、打孔。

十一、税目 48.23 主要适用于提花机或类似机器用的穿孔纸或卡片，以及纸花边。

十二、除税目 48.14 及 48.21 的货品外，印有图案、文字或图画的纸、纸板、纤维素絮纸及其制品，如果所印图案、文字或图画作为其主要用途，应归入第四十九章。

子目注释：

一、子目号 4804.11 及 4804.19 所称"牛皮挂面纸"，是指所含用硫酸盐法或烧碱法制得的木纤维不少于全部纤维重量的 80% 的成卷机器上光或研光纸及纸板，每平方米重量超过 115 克，并且最低缪伦耐破度符合下表所示（其他重量的耐破度可参照下表换算）：

重　量 克/平方米	最低耐破度 千帕斯卡
115	393
125	417
200	637
300	824
400	961

二、子目号 4804.21 及 4804.29 所称"袋用牛皮纸"，是指所含用硫酸盐法或烧碱法制得的木纤维不少于全部纤维重量的 80% 的成卷机器上光纸，每平方米重量不小于 60 克，但不超过 115 克，并且符合下列一种规格：

（一）缪伦耐破指数不小于 3.7 千帕斯卡·平方米/克，并且横向伸长率大于 4.5%，纵向伸长率大于 2%；

（二）至少能达到下表所示的最小撕裂度和抗张强度（其他重量的可参照下表换算）：

重　量	最小撕裂度 毫牛顿		最小抗张强度 千牛顿/米	
克/平方米	纵　向	纵向 加横向	横　向	纵向 加横向
60	700	1510	1.9	6
70	830	1790	2.3	7.2
80	965	2070	2.8	8.3
100	1230	2635	3.7	10.6
115	1425	3060	4.4	12.3

④Covered on the face side with plaiting material, whether or not bound together in parallel strands or woven;

(b) Borders and friezes, of paper, treated as above, whether or not in rolls, suitable for wall or ceiling decoration;

(c) Wall coverings of paper made up of several panels, in rolls or sheets, printed so as to make up a scene, design or motif when applied to a wall.

Products on a base of paper or paperboard, suitable for use both as floor coverings and as wall coverings, are to be classified in heading No. 48.23.

10. Heading No. 48.20 does not cover loose sheets or cards, cut to size, whether or not printed, embossed or perforated.

11. Heading No. 48.23 applies, *inter alia*, to perforated paper or paperboard cards for Jacquard or similar machines and paper lace.

12. Except for the goods of heading No. 48.14 or 48.21, paper, paperboard, cellulose wadding and articles thereof, printed with motifs, characters or pictorial representations, which are not merely incidental to the primary use of the goods, fall in Chapter 49.

Subheading Notes:

1. For the purposes of subheadings No. 4804.11 and 4804.19. "kraftliner" means machine-finished or machine-glazed paper and paperboard, of which not less than 80% by weight of the total fibre content consists of wood fibres obtained by the chemical sulphate or soda processes, in rolls, weighing more than 115 g/m^2 and having a minimum Mullen bursting strength as indicated in the following table or the linearly interpolated or extrapolated equivalent for any other weight.

Weight **g/m^2**	**Minimum Mullen bursting strength** **kPa**
115	393
125	417
200	637
300	834
400	961

2. For the puposes of subheadings Nos. 4804.21 and 4804.29, "sack kraft paper" means machine-finished paper, of which not less than 80% by weight of the total fibre content consists of fibres obtained by the chemical sulphate or soda processes, in rolls, weighing not less than 60 g/m^2 but not more than 115 g/m^2 and meeting one of the following sets of specifications:

(a) Having a Mullen burst index of not less than 3.7 kPa · m^2/g and a stretch factor of more than 4.5% in the cross direction and of more than 2% in the machine direction.

(b) Having minima for tear and tensile as indicated in the following table or the linearly interpolated equivalent for any other weight:

Weight **g/m^2**	**Minimum tear** **mN**		**Minimum tensile** **kN/m**	
	Machine direction	**Machine direction plus cross direction**	**Cross direction**	**Machine direction plus cross direction**
60	700	1,510	1.9	6
70	830	1,790	2.3	7.2
80	2965	2070	2.8	8.3
100	1230	2635	3.7	10.6
115	1425	3060	4.4	12.3

三、子目号 4805.11 所称"半化学的瓦楞纸"，是指所含用机械和化学联合法制得的未漂白硬木纤维不少于全部纤维重量的65%的成卷纸张，并且在温度为23℃和相对湿度为50%时，经过30分钟的瓦楞芯纸平压强度测定(CMT30)，抗压强度超过1.8牛顿/克/平方米。

四、子目4805.12包括主要用机械和化学联合法制得的草浆制成的成卷纸张，每平方米重量在130克及以上，并且在温度为23℃和相对湿度为50%时，经过30分钟的瓦楞芯纸平压强度测定(CMT30)，抗压强度超过1.4牛顿/克/平方米。

五、子目4805.24及4805.25包括全部或主要用回收(废碎)纸及纸板制得的纸浆制成的纸及纸板。强韧箱纸板也可以有一面用染色纸或由漂白或未漂白的非再生浆制得的纸做表层。这些产品缪伦耐破指数不小于2千帕斯卡·平方米/克。

六、子目号4805.30所称"亚硫酸盐包装纸"，是指所含用亚硫酸盐法制得的木纤维超过全部纤维重量的40%的机器研光纸，灰分含量不超过8%，并且缪伦耐破指数不小于1.47千帕斯卡·平方米/克。

七、子目号4810.22所称"轻质涂布纸"，是指双面涂布纸，其每平方米总重量不超过72克，每面每平方米的涂层重量不超过15克，原纸中所含用机械方法制得的木纤维不少于全部纤维重量的50%。

3. For the purposes of subheading No. 4805.11, "semi-chemical fluting paper" means paper, in rolls, of which not less than 65% by weight of the total fibre content consists of unbleached hardwood fibres obtained by a combination of mechanical and chemical pulping processes, and having a CMT 30 (Corrugated Medium Test with 30 minutes of conditioning) crush resistance exceeding 1.8 N/g/m^2 at 50% relative humidity, at 23℃.
4. Subheading No. 4805.12 covers paper, in rolls, made mainly of straw pulp obtained by a combination of mechanical and chemical process, weighing 130 g/m^2 or more, and having a CMT 30 (Corrugated Medium Test with 30 minutes of conditioning) crush resistance exceeding 1.4 newtons/g/m^2 at 50% relative humidity, at 23℃.
5. Subheadings 4805.24 and 4805.25 cover paper and paperboard made wholly or mainly of pulp of recovered (waste and scrap) paper or paperboard. Testliner may also have a surface layer of dyed paper or of paper made of bleached or unbleached non-recovered pulp. These products have a Mullen burst index of not less than 2 kPa · m^2/g.
6. For the purposes of subheading No. 4805.30, "sulphite wrapping paper" means machine-glazed paper, of which more than 40% by weight of the total fibre content consists of wood fibres obtained by the chemical sulpohite process, having an ash content not exceeding 8% and having a Mullen burst index of not less than 1.47 kPa · m^2/g.
7. For the purposes of subheading No. 4810.22, "lightweight coated paper" means paper, coated on both sides, of a total weight not exceeding 72 g/m^2, with a coating weight not exceeding 15 g/m^2 per side, on a base of which not less than 50% by weight of the total fibre content consists of wood fibres obtained by a mechanical process.

税则号列	货品名称	最惠(%)	普通	增值税率	出口退税	计量单位	监管条件	Article Description
48.01	成卷或成张的新闻纸：							**Newsprint, in rolls or sheets:**
4801.0000	成卷或成张的新闻纸	5	30	17		千克		Newsprint, in rolls or sheets
48.02	书写、印刷或类似用途的未经涂布的纸及纸板、未打孔的穿孔卡片纸及穿孔纸带纸，成卷或成张矩形(包括正方形)，任何尺寸，但税目48.01或48.03的纸除外；手工制纸及纸板：							**Uncoated paper and paperboard, of a kind used for writing, printing or other graphic purposes, and non perforated punchcards and punch tape paper, in rolls or rectangular (including square) sheets, of any size, other than paper of heading No. 48.01 or 48.03; hand-made paper and paperboard:**
	-手工制纸及纸板：							-Hand-made paper and paperboard:
4802.1010	---宣纸	7.5	70	17	13	千克		---Rice paper
4802.1090	---其他	7.5	70	17	13	千克		---Other
	-光敏、热敏、电敏纸及纸板的原纸和原纸板：							-Paper and paperboard of a kind used as a base for photo-sensitive, heat-sensitive or electro-sensitive paper or paperboard:
4802.2010暂	---照相原纸	5	40	17		千克		---Photo paper base
4802.2090	---其他	7.5	40	17		千克		---Other
4802.4000	-壁纸原纸	7.5	40	17		千克		-Wallpaper base
	-其他纸及纸板，不含用机械或化学—机械方法制得的纤维或所含前述纤维不超过全部纤维重量的10%：							-Other paper and paperboard, not containing fibres obtained by a mechanical or chemi-mechanical process or of which not more than 10% by weight of the total fibre content consists of such fibres:
4802.5400	--每平方米重量小于40克	7.5	30	17		千克		--Weighing less than 40 g/m^2
4802.5500	--每平方米重量在40克及以上，但不超过150克，成卷	5	30	17		千克		--Weighing 40 g/m^2 or more but not more than 150 g/m^2, in rolls
4802.5500 10	40g＜每平方米重≤150g的胶版纸(成卷，机械或化学－机械法制得的纤维含量≤10%)	5	30	17		千克		Offset paper, in rolls, 40g/m^2 < w ≤ 150g/m^2, containing fibres ≤ 10%, obtained by a mechanical or chemi-mechanical process

税则号列	货品名称	最惠(%)	普通	增值税率	出口退税	计量单位	监管条件	Article Description
4802.5500 90	40g＜每平方米重≤150g 未涂布中厚纸(书写印刷用,成卷,含机械或化学－机械法制纤维含量≤10%)	5	30	17		千克		Paper, of a kind used for writing, printing or other graphic purposes, in rolls, $40g/m^2 < w \leq 150g/m^2$, containing fibres≤10%, obtained by a mechanical or chemi-mechanical process
4802.5600	--每平方米重量在 40 克及以上,但不超过 150 克,一边不超过 435 毫米,另一边不超过 297 毫米(以未折叠计),成张的	5	30	17		千克		--Weighing 40 g/m^2 or more but not more than 150 g/m^2, in sheets with one side not exceeding 435 mm and the other side not exceeding 297 mm in the unfolded state
4802.5600 10	成张 40g＜每平方米重≤150g 胶版纸(长≤435mm,宽≤297mm 含机械或化学－机械法制纤维≤10%)	5	30	17		千克		Offset paper, in sheets, $40g/m^2 < w \leq 150g/m^2$ (length≤435mm, width≤297mm, containing fibres≤10%, obtained by a mechanical or chemi-mechanical process)
4802.5600 90	40g＜每平方米重≤150g 未涂布纸,成张(书写印刷,长≤435mm,宽≤297mm 含机械或半化学浆≤10%)	5	30	17		千克		Uncoated paper, $40g/m^2 < w \leq 150g/m^2$ (of a kind used for writing, printing or other graphic purposes, in sheets, length≤435mm, width≤297mm, containing fibres≤10%, obtained by a mechanical or chemi-mechanical process)
4802.5700	--其他,每平方米重量在 40 克及以上,但不超过 150 克	5	30	17		千克		--Other, weighing 40 g/m^2 or more but not more than 150 g/m^2
4802.5700 10	其他 40g＜每平方米重≤150g 的胶版纸(机械或化学－机械法制得的纤维含量≤10%)	5	30	17		千克		Other offset paper, $40g/m^2 < w \leq 150g/m^2$, containing fibres≤10%, obtained by a mechanical or chemi-mechanical process
4802.5700 90	其他 40g＜每平方米重≤150g 未涂中厚纸(书写印刷用,含机械或化学－机械法制纤维≤10%)	5	30	17		千克		Other uncoated paper, $40g/m^2 < w \leq 150g/m^2$, of a kind used for writing, printing or other graphic purposes, containing fibres≤10%, obtained by a mechanical or chemi-mechanical process
4802.5800	--每平方米重量超过 150 克	5	30	17		千克		--Weighing more than 150 g/m^2
	-其他纸及纸板,所含用机械或化学—机械方法制得的纤维超过全部纤维重量的 10%:							-Other paper and paperboard, of which more than 10% by weight of the total fibre content consists of fibres obtained by a mechanical or chemi-mechanical process:
	--成卷的:							--In rolls:
4802.6110	---新闻纸	7.5	30	17		千克		---Newsprint
4802.6190	---其他	5	30	17		千克		---Other
4802.6200	--成张的,一边不超过 435 毫米,另一边不超过 297 毫米(以未折叠计)	5	30	17		千克		--In sheets with one side not exceeding 435 mm and the other side not exceeding 297 mm in the unfolded state
	--其他:							--Other:
4802.6910	---新闻纸	7.5	30	17		千克		---Newsprint
4802.6990	---其他	5	30	17		千克		---Other
48.03	**卫生纸、面巾纸、餐巾纸以及家庭或卫生用的类似纸、纤维素絮纸和纤维素纤维网纸,不论是否起纹、压花、打孔、染面、饰面或印花,成卷或成张的:**							**Toilet or facial tissue stock, towel or napkin stock and similar paper of a kind used for household or sanitary purposes, cellulose wadding and webs of cellulose fibres, whether or not creped, crinkled, embossed, perforated, surface-coloured, surface-decorated or printed, in rolls or sheets:**
4803.0000	卫生纸、面巾纸、餐巾纸以及家庭或卫生用的类似纸、纤维素絮纸和纤维素纤维网纸,不论是否起纹、压花、打孔、染面、饰面或印花,成卷或成张的	7.5	40	17		千克	A	Toilet or facial tissue stock, towel or napkin stock and similar paper of a kind used for household or sanitary purposes, cellulose wadding and webs of cellulose fibres, whether or not creped, crinkled, embossed, perforated, surface-coloured, surface-decorated or printed, in rolls or sheets
48.04	**成卷或成张的未经涂布的牛皮纸及纸板,但不包括税目 48.02 或 48.03 的货品:**							**Uncoated kraft paper and paperboard, in rolls or sheets, other than that of heading No. 48.02 or 48.03:**

税则号列	货 品 名 称	最惠(%)	普通	增值税率	出口退税	计量单位	监管条件	Article Description
	-牛皮挂面纸：							-Krafliner:
4804.1100	--未漂白	5	30	17		千克		--Unbleached
4804.1100 10	每平方米重115－360克未漂白、成卷或成张未涂布牛皮挂面纸（紧度不小于0.68g/cm³，耐破指数不小于2.6kPa·m²/g，横向环压指数不小于7.5N/m·m²/g，横向耐折度不小于60次，饱和牛皮纸除外）	5	30	17		千克		Uncoated krafliner paper and paperboard, in rolls or sheets, 115g/m² ≤ weight ≤ 360g/m² (not tighter than 0.68g/cm³, bursting index not smller than 2.6kPa·m²/g, cross direction ring crush index not smaller than 7.5N/m·m²/g, cross direction fold endurance not less than 60 times, excluding saturated kraft paper)
4804.1100 90	其他未漂白的牛皮挂面纸（成卷或成张的及未经涂布的）	5	30	17		千克		Other uncoated krafliner paper, unbleached, in rolls or sheets (uncoated kraft paper and paperboard, in rolls or sheets)
4804.1900	--其他	5	30	17		千克		--Other
	-袋用牛皮纸：							-Sack kraft paper:
4804.2100	--未漂白	5	30	17		千克		--Unbleached
4804.2900	--其他	5	30	17		千克		--Other
	-其他牛皮纸及纸板，每平方米重量不超过150克：							-Other kraft paper and paperboard weighing 150 g/m² or less:
4804.3100	--未漂白	2	30	17		千克		--Unbleached
4804.3100 10	每平米重115－150克未漂白、成卷或成张未涂布其他牛皮纸（紧度不小于0.68g/cm³，耐破指数不小于2.6kPa·m²/g，横向环压指数不小于7.5N/m·m²/g，横向耐折度不小于60次，饱和牛皮纸除外）	2	30	17		千克		Uncoated krafliner paper and paperboard, in rolls or sheets, 115g/m² ≤ weight ≤ 150g/m² (not tighter than 0.68g/cm³, bursting index not smaller than 2.6kPa·m²/g, cross-direction ring crush index not samller than 7.5N/m·m²/g, cross-direction fold endurance not less than 60 times, excluding saturated kraft paper)
4804.3100 90	其他未漂白的其他薄牛皮纸及纸板（薄纸指每平方米重≤150克，成卷或成张未经涂布的）	2	30	17		千克		Other uncoated kraft paper and paperboard, unbleached (w≤150g/m², in rolls or sheets)
4804.3900	--其他	2	30	17		千克		--Other
	-其他牛皮纸及纸板，每平方米重量超过150克，但小于225克：							-Other kraft paper and paperboard weighing more than 150 g/m² but less than 225g/m²:
4804.4100	--未漂白	2	30	17		千克		--Unbleached
4804.4100 10	150克＜每平米重＜225克未漂白、成卷或成张未涂布其他牛皮纸（紧度不小于0.68g/cm³，耐破指数不小于2.6kPa·m²/g，横向环压指数不小于7.5N/m·m²/g，横向耐折度不小于60次，饱和牛皮纸除外）	2	30	17		千克		Uncoated kraft paper and paperboard, unbleached, 150g/m² < 225g/m² in rolls or sheets (not tighter than 0.68g/cm³, bursting index not smaller than 2.6kPa·m²/g, cross－direction ring crush index not samller than 7.5N/m·m²/g, cross direction fold endurance not less than 60 times, excluding saturated kraft paper)
4804.4100 90	其他未漂白的其他中厚牛皮纸及纸板（中厚指150克＜每平米重＜225克，成卷或成张未涂布的）	2	30	17		千克		Other Uncoated kraft paper and paperboard, unbleached (150g/m² < w < 225g/m², in rolls or sheets)
4804.4200	--本体均匀漂白，所含用化学方法制得的木纤维超过全部纤维重量的95%	5	30	17		千克		--Bleached uniformly throughout the mass and of which more than 95% by weight of the total fibre content consists of wood fibres obtained by a chemical process
4804.4900	--其他	2	30	17		千克		--Other
	-其他牛皮纸及纸板，每平方米重量在225克及以上：							-Other kraft paper and paperboard weighing 225 g/m² or more:

税则号列	货品名称	最惠(%)	普通	增值税率	出口退税	计量单位	监管条件	Article Description
4804.5100	--未漂白	2	30	17		千克		--Unbleached
4804.5100 10	每平米重225－360克未漂白、成卷或成张未涂布其他牛皮纸（紧度不小于0.68g/cm³，耐破指数不小于2.6kPa·m²/g，横向环压指数不小于7.5N/m·m²/g，横向耐折度不小于60次，饱和牛皮纸除外）	2	30	17		千克		Uncoated kraft paper and paperboard, unbleached, 225g/m² < 360g/ m² in rolls or sheets (not tighter than 0.68g/cm³, bursting index not smaller than 2.6kPa · m²/g, cross – direction ring crush index not samller than 7.5N/m · m²/g, cross direction fold endurance not less than 60 times, excluding saturated kraft paper)
4804.5100 90	其他未漂白的其他厚牛皮纸及纸板（厚纸指每平米重量≥225克，成卷或成张未经涂布的）	2	30	17		千克		Other Uncoated kraft paper and paperboard, unbleached (w≥225g/m², in rolls or sheets)
4804.5200	--本体均匀漂白，所含用化学方法制得的木纤维超过全部纤维重量的95%	5	30	17		千克		--Bleached uniformly throughout the mass and of which more than 95% by weight of the total fibre content consists of wood fibres obtained by a chemical process
4804.5900	--其他	2	30	17		千克		--Other
48.05	**成卷或成张的其他未经涂布的纸及纸板，加工程度不超过本章注释三所列范围：**							**Other uncoated paper and paperboard, in rolls or sheets, not further worked or processed than as specified in Note 3 to this Chapter:**
	-瓦楞原纸：							-Fluting paper:
4805.1100	--半化学的瓦楞原纸	7.5	30	17		千克		--Semi-chemical fluting paper
4805.1200	--草浆瓦楞原纸	7.5	30	17		千克		--Straw fluting paper
4805.1900	--其他	7.5	30	17		千克		--Other
	-强韧箱纸板（再生挂面纸板）：							-Testliner (recycled liner board):
4805.2400	--每平方米重量在150克及以下	7.5	30	17		千克		--Weighing 150 g/m² or less
4805.2500	--每平方米重量超过150克	7.5	30	17		千克		--Weighing more than 150 g/m²
4805.3000	-亚硫酸盐包装纸	7.5	30	17		千克		-Sulphite wrapping paper
4805.4000	-滤纸及纸板	7.5	30	17		千克		-Filter paper and paperboard
4805.5000	-毡纸及纸板	7.5	30	17		千克		-Felt paper and paperboard
	-其他：							-Other:
	--每平方米重量在150克及以下：							--Weighing 150 g/m² or less:
4805.9110	---电解电容器原纸	7.5	30	17		千克		---Paper for electrolytic capacitor
4805.9190	---其他	7.5	30	17		千克		---Other
4805.9200	--每平方米重量超过150克以上，但小于225克	7.5	30	17		千克		--Weighing more than 150 g/m² but less than 225 g/m²
4805.9300	--每平方米重量在225克及以上	7.5	30	17		千克		--Weighing 225 g/m² or more
48.06	**成卷或成张的植物羊皮纸、防油纸、描图纸、半透明纸及其他高光泽透明或半透明纸：**							**Vegetable parchment, greaseproof papers, tracing papers and glassine and other glazed transparent or translucent papers, in rolls or sheets:**
4806.1000	-植物羊皮纸	7.5	40	17		千克		-Vegetable parchment
4806.2000	-防油纸	7.5	40	17		千克		-Greaseproof papers
4806.3000	-描图纸	7.5	30	17		千克		-Tracing papers
4806.4000暂	-高光泽透明或半透明纸	5	40	17		千克		-Glassine and other glazed transparent or translucent papers
48.07	**成卷或成张的复合纸及纸板（用粘合剂粘合各层纸或纸板制成），未经表面涂布或未浸渍，不论内层是否有加强材料：**							**Composite paper and paperboard (made by sticking flat layers of paper or paperboard together with an adhesive), not surface-coated or impregnated, whether or not internally reinforced, in rolls or sheets:**
4807.0000暂	成卷或成张的复合纸及纸板（用粘合剂粘合各层纸或纸板制成），未经表面涂布或未浸渍，不论内层是否有加强材料	5	40	17		千克		Composite paper and paperboard (made by sticking flat layers of paper or paperboard together with an adhesive), not surface-coated or impregnated, whether or not internally reinforced, in rolls or sheets

税则号列	货品名称	最惠(%)	普通	增值税率	出口退税	计量单位	监管条件	Article Description
48.08	成卷或成张的瓦楞纸及纸板(不论是否与平面纸胶合)、皱纹纸及纸板、压纹纸及纸板、穿孔纸及纸板,但税目48.03的纸除外:							**Paper and paperboard, corrugated (with or without glued flat surface sheets), creped, crinkled, embossed or perforated, in rolls or sheets, other than paper of the kind described in heading No. 48.03:**
4808.1000	-瓦楞纸及纸板,不论是否穿孔	7.5	30	17		千克		-Corrugated paper and paperboard, whether or not perforated
4808.4000	-皱纹牛皮纸,不论是否压花或穿孔	7.5	40	17		千克		-Kraft paper, creped or crinkled, whether or not embossed or perforated
4808.9000	-其他	7.5	40	17		千克		-Other
48.09	复写纸、自印复写纸及其他拷贝或转印纸(包括涂布或浸渍的油印蜡纸或胶印版纸),不论是否印制,成卷或成张的:							**Carbon paper, self-copy paper and other copying or transfer papers (including coated or impregnated paper for duplicator stencils or offset plates), whether or not printed, in rolls or sheets:**
4809.2000	-自印复写纸	7.5	40	17		千克		-Self-copy paper
4809.9000	-其他	7.5	40	17		千克		-Other
48.10	成卷或成张矩形(包括正方形)的任何尺寸的单面或双面涂布高岭土或其他无机物质(不论是否加粘合剂)的纸及纸板,未涂布其他涂料,不论是否染面、饰面或印花:							**Paper and paperboard, coated on one or both sides with kaolin (China clay) or other inorganic substances, with or without a binder, and with no other coating, whether or not surface-coloured, surface-decorated or printed, in rolls or rectangular (including square) sheets, of any size:**
	-书写、印刷或类似用途的纸及纸板,不含用机械或化学—机械方法制得的纤维或所含前述纤维不超过全部纤维重量的10%:							-Paper and paperboard of a kind used for writing, printing or other graphic purposes, not containing fibres obtained by a mechanical or chemi-mechanical process or of which not more than 10% by weight of the total fibre content consists of such fibres:
4810.1300	--成卷的	5	40	17		千克		--In rolls
4810.1300 01	成卷的铜版纸(所含用机械或化学-机械法制得的纤维≤10%)	5	40	17		千克		Art paper, in rolls (containing fibres ≤ 10%, obtained by a mechanical or chemi-mechanical process)
4810.1300 90	涂无机物的其他书写/印刷或类似用途纸/纸板(成卷的,所含用机械或化学-机械法制得的纤维≤10%)	5	40	17		千克		Other paper and paperboard, coated with inorganic substances, of a kind used for writing, printing or other graphic purposes (containing fibres ≤ 10%, obtained by a mechanical or chemi-mechanical process, in rolls)
4810.1400	--成张的,一边不超过435毫米,另一边不超过297毫米(以未折叠计)	5	40	17		千克		--In sheets with one side not exceeding 435 mm and the other side not exceeding 297 mm in the unfolded state
4810.1400 01	成张的铜版纸(一边≤435mm,另一边≤297mm,机械或化学-机械纤维≤10%)	5	40	17		千克		Art paper, in sheets (one side ≤ 435mm, other side ≤ 297mm, containing fibres ≤ 10%, obtained by a mechanical or chemi-mechanical process)
4810.1400 90	涂无机物的其他成张的书写、印刷的纸及纸板(一边≤435mm,另一边≤297mm,机械或化学-机械纤维≤10%)	5	40	17		千克		Other paper and paperboard, coated with inorganic substances of a kind used for writing, printing or other graphic purposes, in sheet (one side ≤ 435mm other side ≤ 297mm, containing fibres ≤ 10%, obtained by a mechanical or chemi-mechanical process)
4810.1900	--其他	5	40	17		千克		--Other
4810.1900 01	其他铜版纸(所含用机械或化学-机械法制得的纤维≤10%)	5	40	17		千克		Other art paper (containing fibres ≤ 10%, obtained by a mechanical or chemi-mechanical process)

税则号列	货品名称	最惠(%)	普通	增值税率	出口退税	计量单位	监管条件	Article Description
4810.1900 90	涂无机物的其他书写、印刷用途的纸及纸板(所含用机械或化学－机械法制得的纤维≤10%)	5	40	17		千克		Other paper and paperboard, coated with inorganic substances of a kind used for writing, printing or other graphic purposes (containing fibres ≤10%, obtained by a mechanical or chemi-mechanical process)
	-书写、印刷或类似用途的纸及纸板,所含用机械或化学—机械方法制得的纤维超过全部纤维重量的10%:							-Paper and paperboard of a kind used for writing, printing or other graphic purposes, of which more than 10% by weight of the total fibre content consists of fibres obtained by a mechanical or chemi-mechanical process:
4810.2200	--轻质涂布纸	5	40	17		千克		--Light-weight coated paper
4810.2900	--其他	5	40	17		千克		--Other
	-牛皮纸及纸板,但书写、印刷或类似用途的除外:							-Kraft paper and paperboard, other than that of a kind used for writing, printing or other graphic purposes:
4810.3100	--本体均匀漂白,所含用化学方法制得的木纤维超过全部纤维重量的95%,每平方米重量不超过150克	5	40	17		千克		--Bleached uniformly throughout the mass and of which more than 95% by weight of the total fibre content consists of wood fibres obtained by a chemical process, and weighing 150 g/m^2 or less
4810.3100 10	涂无机物的白板纸、白卡纸(薄纸指每平方米重≤150g,含用化学方法制得木纤维)	5	40	17		千克		White board and ivory board, bleached, coated with inarganic substances ($w \leq 150g/m^2$, consisting of wood fibres obtained by a chemical process)
4810.3100 90	涂无机物的薄漂白牛皮纸及纸板(薄纸指每平方米重量≤150克,含用化学方法制得的木纤维)	5	40	17		千克		White kraft paper and paperboard, bleached, coated with inorganic substances, ($w \leq 150g/m^2$, consisting of wood fibres obtained by a chemical process)
4810.3200	--本体均匀漂白,所含用化学方法制得的木纤维超过全部纤维重量的95%,每平方米重量超过150克	5	40	17		千克		--Bleached uniformly throughout the mass and of which more than 95% by weight of the total fibre content consists of wood fibres obtained by a chemical process, and weighing more than $150g/m^2$
4810.3200 10	涂无机物的白板纸、白卡纸(厚纸指每平方米重量>150克,含用化学方法制得的木纤维)	5	40	17		千克		White board and ivory board, bleached, coated with inorganic substances ($w > 150g/m^2$ consisting of wood fibres obtained by a chemical process)
4810.3200 90	涂无机物的厚漂白牛皮纸及纸板(厚纸指每平方米重量>150g,含用化学方法制得的木纤维)	5	40	17		千克		White kraft paper and paperboard, bleached, coated with inorganic substances($w > 150g/m^2$, consisting of wood fibres obtained by a chemical process)
4810.3900	--其他	5	40	17		千克		--Other
	-其他纸及纸板:							-Other paper and paperboard:
4810.9200	--多层的	5	40	17		千克		--Multiply
4810.9900	--其他	7.5	40	17		千克		--Other
48.11	**成卷或成张矩形(包括正方形)的任何尺寸的经涂布、浸渍、覆盖、染面、饰面或印花的纸、纸板、纤维素絮纸及纤维素纤维网纸,但税目48.03、48.09或48.10的货品除外:**							**Paper, paperboard, cellulose wadding and webs of cellulose fibres, coated, impregnated, covered, surface-coloured, surface-decorated or printed, in rolls or rectangular (including square) sheets, of any size, other than goods of the kind described in heading No. 48.03, 48.09or 48.10:**
4811.1000	-焦油纸及纸板、沥青纸及纸板	7.5	40	17		千克		-Tarred, bituminised or asphalted paper and paperboard
	-胶粘纸及纸板:							-Gummed or adhesive paper and paperboard:
4811.4100	--自粘的	7.5	40	17		千克		--Self-adhesive
4811.4900	--其他	7.5	40	17		千克		--Other
	-用塑料(不包括粘合剂)涂布、浸渍或覆盖的纸及纸板:							-Paper and paperboard coated, impregnated or covered with plastics (excluding adhesives):
	--漂白的,每平方米重量超过150克:							--Bleached, weighing more than $150g/m^2$:
4811.5110[暂]	---彩色相纸用双面涂塑厚纸	1	40	17		千克		---Paper coated on both sides with plastics for colour photography

税则号列	货品名称	最惠(%)	普通	增值税率	出口退税	计量单位	监管条件	Article Description
	---其他:							---Other:
4811.5191	----纸塑铝复合材料	7.5	40	17		千克		----Paper-plastic compound material
4811.5199	----其他	7.5	40	17		千克		----Other
	--其他:							--Other:
4811.5910	---绝缘纸及纸板	7.5	30	17		千克		---Insulating paper and paperboard
	---其他:							---Other:
4811.5991	----镀铝的	7.5	40	17		千克		----Aluminium plated
4811.5999	----其他	7.5	40	17		千克		----Other
	-用蜡、石蜡、硬脂精、油或甘油涂布、浸渍、覆盖的纸及纸板:							-Paper and paperboard, coated, impregnated or covered with wax, paraffin wax, stearin, oil or glycerol:
4811.6010	---绝缘纸及纸板	7.5	30	17		千克		---Insulating paper and paperboard
4811.6090	---其他	7.5	40	17		千克		---Other
4811.9000	-其他纸、纸板、纤维素絮纸及纤维素纤维网纸	7.5	40	17		千克		-Other paper, paperboard, cellulose wadding and webs of cellulose fibres
48.12	**纸浆制的滤块、滤板及滤片:**							**Filter blocks, slabs and plates, of paper pulp:**
4812.0000	纸浆制的滤块、滤板及滤片	7.5	40	17		千克		Filter blocks, slabs and plates, of paper pulp
48.13	**卷烟纸,不论是否切成一定尺寸、成小本或管状:**							**Cigarette paper, whether or not cut to size or in the form of booklets or tubes:**
4813.1000	-成小本或管状	7.5	100	17		千克	7	-In the form of booklets or tubes
4813.2000	-宽度不超过5厘米成卷的	7.5	100	17		千克	7	-In rolls of a width not exceeding 5 cm
4813.9000	-其他	7.5	100	17		千克	7	-Other
48.14	**壁纸及类似品;窗用透明纸:**							**Wallpaper and similar wall coverings; window transparencies of paper:**
4814.2000	-用塑料涂面或盖面的壁纸及类似品,起纹、压花、着色、印刷图案或经其他装饰	7.5	50	17	13	千克		-Wallpaper and similar wall coverings, consisting of paper coated or covered, on the face side, with a grained, embossed, coloured, design-printed or otherwise decorated layer of plastics
4814.9000	-其他	7.5	50	17		千克		-Other
4814.9000 10	用木粒或草粒等饰面的壁纸	7.5	50	17		千克	A	"Ingrain" paper
4814.9000 90	其他壁纸及类似品,窗用透明纸	7.5	50	17		千克		Other wallpaper and similar wall coverings, window transparencies of paper
48.16	**复写纸、自印复写纸及其他拷贝或转印纸(不包括税目48.09的纸)、油印蜡纸或胶印版纸,不论是否盒装:**							**Carbon paper, self-copy paper and other copying or transfer papers (other than those of heading No. 48.09), duplicator stencils and offset plates, of paper, whether or not put up in boxes:**
4816.2000	-自印复写纸	7.5	70	17		千克		-Self-copy paper
	-其他:							-Other:
4816.9010	---热敏转印纸	7.5	40	17		千克		---Heat transfer paper
4816.9090	---其他	7.5	70	17		千克		---Other
48.17	**纸或纸板制的信封、封缄信片、素色明信片及通信卡片;纸或纸板制的盒子、袋子及夹子,内装各种纸制文具:**							**Envelopes, letter cards, plain postcards and correspondence cards, of paper or paperboard; boxes, pouches, wallets and writing compendiums, of paper or paperboard, containing an assortment of paper stationery:**
4817.1000	-信封	7.5	80	17	13	千克		-Envelopes
4817.2000	-封缄信片、素色明信片及通信卡片	7.5	80	17	13	千克		-Letter cards, plain postcards and correspondence cards
4817.3000	-纸或纸板制的盒子、袋子及夹子,内装各种纸制文具	7.5	80	17	13	千克		-Boxes, pouches, wallets and writing compendiums, of paper or paperboard, containing an assortment of paper stationery

税则号列	货品名称	最惠(%)	普通	增值税率	出口退税	计量单位	监管条件	Article Description
48.18	卫生纸及类似纸，家庭或卫生用纤维素絮纸及纤维素纤维网纸，成卷宽度不超过36厘米或切成一定尺寸或形状的；纸浆、纸、纤维素絮纸或纤维素纤维网纸制的手帕、面巾、台布、餐巾、床单及类似的家庭、卫生或医院用品、衣服及衣着附件：							**Toilet paper and similar paper, cellulose wadding or webs of cellulose fibres, of a kind used for household or sanitary purposes, in rolls of a width not exceeding 36 cm, or cut to size or shape; handkerchiefs, cleansing tissues, towels, tablecloths, serviettes, bed sheets and similar household, sanitary or hospital articles, articles of apparel and clothing accessories, of paper pulp, paper, cellulose wadding or webs of cellulose fibres:**
4818.1000	-卫生纸	7.5	80	17	5	千克	A	-Toilet paper
4818.2000	-纸手帕及纸面巾	7.5	90	17	5	千克	A	-Handkerchiefs, cleansing or facial tissues and towels
4818.3000	-纸台布及纸餐巾	7.5	90	17	5	千克	A	-Tablecloths and serviettes
4818.5000	-衣服及衣着附件	7.5	90	17	13	千克	A	-Articles of apparel and clothing accessories
4818.9000	-其他	7.5	90	17	13	千克	A	-Other
48.19	纸、纸板、纤维素絮纸或纤维素纤维网纸制的箱、盒、匣、袋及其他包装容器；纸或纸板制的卷宗盒、信件盘及类似品，供办公室、商店及类似场所使用的：							**Cartons, boxes, cases, bags and other packing containers, of paper, paperboard, cellulose wadding or webs of cellulose fibres; box files, letter trays and similar articles, of paper or paperboard of a kind used in offices, shops or the like:**
4819.1000	-瓦楞纸或纸板制的箱、盒、匣	5	80	17	13	千克		-Cartons, boxes and cases, of corrugated paper or paperboard
4819.2000	-非瓦楞纸或纸板制的可折叠箱、盒、匣	5	80	17	13	千克		-Folding cartons, boxes and cases, of noncorrugated paper or paperboard
4819.3000	-底宽40厘米及以上的纸袋	7.5	80	17	13	千克		-Sacks and bags, having a base of a width of 40 cm or more
4819.4000	-其他纸袋，包括锥形袋	7.5	80	17	13	千克		-Other sacks and bags, including cones
4819.5000	-其他包装容器，包括唱片套	7.5	80	17	13	千克	A	-Other packing containers, including record sleeves
4819.6000	-办公室、商店及类似场所使用的卷宗盒、信件盘、存储盒及类似品	7.5	80	17	13	千克		-Box files, letter trays, storage boxes and similar articles, of a kind used in offices, shops or the like
48.20	纸或纸板制的登记本、账本、笔记本、定货本、收据本、信笺本、记事本、日记本及类似品、练习本、吸墨纸本、活动封面（活页及非活页）、文件夹、卷宗皮、多联商业表格纸、页间夹有复写纸的本及其他文具用品；纸或纸板制的样品簿、粘贴簿及书籍封面：							**Registers, account books, note books, order books, receipt books, letter pads, memorandum pads, diaries and similar articles, exercise books, blotting-pads, binders (loose-leaf or other), folders, file covers, manifold business forms, interleaved carbon sets and other articles of stationery, of paper or paperboard; albums for samples or for collections and book covers, of paper or paperboard:**
4820.1000	-登记本、账本、笔记本、订货本、收据本、信笺本、记事本、日记本及类似品	7.5	80	17	13	千克		-Registers, account books, note books, order books, receipt books, letter pads, memorandum pads, diaries and similar articles
4820.2000	-练习本	7.5	80	17	13	千克		-Exercise books
4820.3000	-活动封面（书籍封面除外）、文件夹及卷宗皮	7.5	80	17	13	千克		-Binders (other than book covers), folders and file covers
4820.4000	-多联商业表格纸、本页间夹有复写纸的本	7.5	80	17	13	千克		-Manifold business forms and interleaved carbon sets
4820.5000	-样品簿及粘贴簿	7.5	80	17	13	千克		-Albums for samples or for collections
4820.9000	-其他	7.5	80	17	13	千克		-Other
48.21	纸或纸板制的各种标签，不论是否印制：							**Paper or paperboard labels of all kinds, whether or not printed:**
4821.1000	-印制	7.5	50	17	13	千克		-Printed
4821.9000	-其他	7.5	50	17	13	千克		-Other

税则号列	货品名称	最惠(%)	普通	增值税率	出口退税	计量单位	监管条件	Article Description
48.22	纸浆、纸或纸板(不论是否穿孔或硬化)制的筒管、卷轴、纡子及类似品:							**Bobbins, spools, cops and similar supports of paper pulp, paper or paperboard (whether or not perforated or hardened):**
4822.1000	-纺织纱线用	7.5	35	17	13	千克		-Of a kind used for winding textile yarn
4822.9000	-其他	7.5	70	17	13	千克		-Other
48.23	**切成一定尺寸或形状的其他纸、纸板、纤维素絮纸及纤维素纤维网纸;纸浆、纸、纸板、纤维素絮纸及纤维素纤维网纸制的其他物品:**							**Other paper, paperboard, cellulose wadding and webs of cellulose fibres, cut to size or shape; other articles of paper pulp, paper, paperboard, cellulose wadding or webs of cellulose fibres:**
4823.2000	-滤纸及纸板	7.5	30	17	13	千克		-Filter paper and paperboard
4823.4000	-已印制的自动记录器用打印纸卷、纸张及纸盘	7.5	30	17	13	千克		-Rolls, sheets and dials, printed for sel-frecording apparatus
	-纸或纸板制的盘、碟、盆、杯及类似品:							-Trays, dishes, plates, cups and the like, of paper or paperboard:
4823.6100	--竹浆纸制	7.5	90	17	13	千克	A	--Of bamboo
	--其他:							--Other:
4823.6910	---非木植物浆制	7.5	90	17	13	千克	A	---Non woody plant pulp
4823.6990	---其他	7.5	90	17	13	千克	A	---Other
4823.7000	-压制或模制纸浆制品	7.5	90	17	13	千克		-Moulded or pressed articles of paper pulp
	-其他:							-Other:
4823.9010	---以纸或纸板为底制的铺地制品	7.5	90	17		千克		---Floor coverings on a base of paper or of paperboard whether or not cut to size
4823.9020	---神纸及类似用品	7.5	180	17	13	千克		---Joss paper and the like
4823.9030	---纸扇	7.5	90	17	13	千克		---Paper fans
4823.9090	---其他	7.5	90	17	13	千克		---Other

第四十九章
书籍、报纸、印刷图画及其他印刷品；手稿、打字稿及设计图纸

注释：

一、本章不包括：

（一）透明基的照相负片或正片（第三十七章）；

（二）立体地图、设计图表或地球仪、天体仪，不论是否印刷（税目 90.23）；

（三）第九十五章的扑克牌或其他物品；

（四）雕版画、印刷画、石印画的原本（税目 97.02），税目 97.04 的邮票、印花税票、纪念封、首日封、邮政信笺及类似品，以及第九十七章的超过一百年的古物或其他物品。

二、第四十九章所称"印刷"，也包括用胶版复印机、油印机印制，在自动数据处理设备控制下打印绘制，压印、冲印、感光复印、热敏复印或打字。

三、用纸以外材料装订成册的报纸、杂志和期刊，以及一期以上装订在同一封面里的成套报纸、杂志和期刊，应归入税目 49.01，不论是否有广告材料。

四、税目 49.01 还包括：

（一）附有说明文字，每页编有号数以便装订成一册或几册的整集印刷复制品，例如，美术作品、绘画；

（二）随同成册书籍的图画附刊；

（三）供装订书籍或小册子用的散页、集页或书帖形式的印刷品，已构成一部作品的全部或部分。

但没有说明文字的印刷图画或图解，不论是否散页或书帖形式，应归入税目49.11。

五、除本章注释三另有规定的以外，税目 49.01 不包括主要作广告用的出版物（例如，小册子、散页印刷品、商业目录、同业公会出版的年鉴、旅游宣传品），这类出版物应归入税目49.11。

六、税目 49.03 所称"儿童图画书"，是指以图画为主、文字为辅，供儿童阅览的书籍。

Chapter 49
Printed books, newspapers, pictures and other products of the printing industry; manuscripts, typescripts and plans

Notes:

1. This Chapter does not cover:

(a) Photographic negatives or positives on transparent bases (Chapter 37);

(b) Maps, plans or globes, in relief, whether or not printed (heading No. 90.23);

(c) Playing cards or other goods of Chapter 95;

(d) Original engravings, prints or lithographs (heading No. 97.02), postage or revenue stamps, stamp-postmarks, first-day covers, postal stationery or the like of heading No. 97.04, antiques of an age exceeding one hundred years or other articles of Chapter 97.

2. For the purposes of Chapter 49, the term "printed" also means reproduced by means of a duplicating machine, produced under the control of an automatic data processing machine, embossed, photographed, photocopied, thermocopied or typewritten.

3. Newspapers, journals and periodicals which are bound otherwise than in paper, and sets of newspapers, journals or periodicals comprising more than one number under a single cover are to be classified in heading No. 49.01, whether or not containing advertising material.

4. Heading No. 49.01 also covers:

(a) A collection of printed reproductions of, for example, works of art or drawings, with a relative text, put up with numbered pages in a form suitable for binding into one or more volumes;

(b) A pictorial supplement accompanying, and subsidiary to, a bound volume;

(c) Printed parts of books or booklets, in the form of assembled or separate sheets or signatures, constituting the whole or a part of a complete work and designed for binding.

However, printed pictures or illustrations not bearing a text, whether in the form of signatures or separate sheets, fall in heading No. 49.11.

5. Subject to Note 3 to this Chapter, heading No. 49.01 does not cover publications which are essentially devoted to advertising (for example, brochures, pamphlets, leaflets, trade catalogues, year books published by trade associations, tourist propaganda). Such publications are to be classified in heading No. 49.11.

6. For the purposes of heading No. 49.03, the expression "children's picture books" means books for children in which the pictures form the principal interest and the text is subsidiary

税则号列	货品名称	最惠(%)	普通	增值税率	出口退税	计量单位	监管条件	Article Description
49.01	书籍、小册子、散页印刷品及类似印刷品，不论是否单张：							**Printed books, brochures, leaflets and similar printed matter, whether or not in single sheets:**
4901.1000	-单张的，不论是否折叠	0	0	13	0,13	千克		-In single sheets, whether or not folded
	-其他：							-Other:
4901.9100	--字典或百科全书及其连续出版的分册	0	0	13	0,13	千克		--Dictionaries and encyclopaedias, and serial instalments thereof
4901.9900	--其他	0	0	13	0,13	千克		--Other
49.02	报纸、杂志及期刊，不论有无插图或广告材料：							**Newspapers, journals and periodicals, whether or not illustrated or containing advertising material:**
4902.1000	-每周至少出版四次	0	0	13	13	千克		-Appearing at least four times a week
4902.9000	-其他	0	0	13	13	千克		-Other

税则号列	货品名称	最惠(%)	普通	增值税率	出口退税	计量单位	监管条件	Article Description
49.03	儿童图画书、绘画或涂色书:							**Children's picture, drawing or colouring books:**
4903.0000	儿童图画书、绘画或涂色书	0	0	13	0,13	千克		Children's picture, drawing or colouring books
49.04	乐谱原稿或印本,不论是否装订或印有插图:							**Music, printed or in manuscript, whether or not bound or illustrated:**
4904.0000	乐谱原稿或印本,不论是否装订或印有插图	0	0	13	0,13	千克		Music, printed or in manuscript, whether or not bound or illustrated
49.05	各种印刷的地图、水道图及类似图表,包括地图册、挂图、地形图及地球仪、天体仪:							**Maps and hydrographic or similar charts of all kinds, including atlases, wall maps, topographical plans and globes, printed:**
4905.1000	-地球仪、天体仪	0	0	17	13	千克		-Globes
	-其他:							-Other:
4905.9100	--成册的	0	0	17	0,13	千克		--In book form
4905.9900	--其他	0	0	17	0,13	千克		--Other
49.06	手绘的建筑、工程、工业、商业、地形或类似用途的设计图纸原稿;手稿;用感光纸照相复印或用复写纸誊写的上述物品复制件:							**Plans and drawings for architectural, engineering, industrial, commercial, topographical or similar purposes, being originals drawn by hand; hand-written text; photographic reproductions on sensitized paper and carbon copies of the foregoing:**
4906.0000	手绘的建筑、工程、工业、商业、地形或类似用途的设计图纸原稿;手稿;用感光纸照相复印或用复写纸誊写的上述物品复制件	0	0	17	13	千克		Plans and drawings for architectural, engineering, industrial, commercial, topographical or similar purposes, being originals drawn by hand; hand-written text; photographic reproductions on sensitized paper and carbon copies of the foregoing
49.07	在承认或将承认其面值的国家流通或新发行并且未经使用的邮票、印花税票及类似票证;印有邮票或印花税票的纸品;钞票;空白支票;股票、债券及类似所有权凭证:							**Unused postage, revenue or similar stamps of current or new issue in the country in which they have, or will have, a recognised face value; stamp-impressed paper; banknotes; cheque forms; stock, share or bond certificates and similar documents of title:**
4907.0010	---邮票	7.5	50	17	13	千克		---Postage
4907.0020	---钞票	0	50	17	13	千克		---Banknotes
4907.0030	---证券凭证	0	50	17	13	千克		---Documents of title
4907.0090	---其他		50	17	13	千克		---Other
4907.0090暂 01	特许权使用凭证(包括软件升级许可证、软件用户许可证等,但游戏软件升级许可证、游戏软件用户许可证除外)	0	50	17	13	千克		Concession using credential licence(including software upgrading license, software user license, Unless the game software upgrade license, game software license)
4907.0090 90	其他印有邮票等的其他纸品(包括印有印花税票的纸品,特许权使用凭证除外)	7.5	50	17	13	千克		Other stamp-impressed raper (including revenue stamps, other than concession using credential)
49.08	转印贴花纸(移画印花法用图案纸):							**Transfers (decalcomanias):**
4908.1000	-釉转印贴花纸(移画印花法用图案纸)	7.5	50	17	13	千克		-Transfers (decalcomanias), vitrifiable
4908.9000	-其他	7.5	50	17	13	千克		-Other
49.09	印刷或有图画的明信片;印有个人问候、祝贺、通告的卡片,不论是否有图画、带信封或饰边:							**Printed or illustrated postcards; printed cards bearing personal greetings, messages or announcements, whether or not illustrated, with or without envelopes or trimmings:**
4909.0010	---印刷或有图画的明信片	7.5	50	17	13	千克		---Printed or illustrated postcards
4909.0090	---其他	7.5	50	17	13	千克		---Other
49.10	印刷的各种日历,包括日历芯:							**Calendars of any kind, printed, including calendar blocks:**
4910.0000	印刷的各种日历(包括日历芯)	7.5	50	17	13	千克		Calendars of any kind, printed, including calendar blocks
49.11	其他印刷品,包括印刷的图片及照片:							**Other printed matter, including printed pictures and photographs:**
	-商业广告品、商品目录及类似印刷品:							-Trade advertising material, commercial catalogues and the like:

税则号列	货品名称	最惠(%)	普通	增值税率	出口退税	计量单位	监管条件	Article Description
4911.1010	---无商业价值的	0	0	17	13	千克		---No commercial value
4911.1090	---其他	7.5	50	17	13	千克		---Other
	-其他：							-Other:
4911.9100	--图片、设计图样及照片	7.5	50	17	13	千克		--Pictures, designs and photographs
	--其他：							--Other:
4911.9910	---纸质的		50	17	13	千克		---Of paper
4911.9910暂 01	印有自动数据处理设备用程序的纸张	0	50	17	13	千克		Papers printed with programs for automatic data processing equipment
4911.9910 90	其他纸质的印刷品，不包括纸质的图片，设计图样及照片（印有自动数据处理设备用程序的纸张除外）	7.5	50	17	13	千克		Other printed matter of papers, excluding pictures, designs and photographs of papers (other than papers printed with programs for automatic data processing equipment)
4911.9990	---其他	7.5	50	17	13	千克		---Other

第十一类

纺织原料及纺织制品

注释：

一、本类不包括：

（一）制刷用的动物鬃、毛（税目05.02）；马毛及废马毛（税目05.11）；

（二）人发及人发制品（税目05.01、67.03或67.04），但通常用于榨油机或类似机器的滤布除外（税目59.11）；

（三）第十四章的棉短绒或其他植物材料；

（四）税目25.24的石棉、税目68.12或68.13的石棉制品或其他产品；

（五）税目30.05或30.06的物品；税号33.06的用于清洁牙缝的纱线（牙线），单独零售包装的；

（六）税目37.01至37.04的感光布；

（七）截面尺寸超过1毫米的塑料单丝和表面宽度超过5毫米的塑料扁条及类似品（例如，人造草）（第三十九章），以及上述单丝或扁条的缏条、织物、篮筐或柳条编结品（第四十六章）；

（八）第三十九章的用塑料浸渍、涂布、包覆或层压的机织物、针织物或钩编织物、毡呢或无纺织物及其制品；

（九）第四十章的用橡胶浸渍、涂布、包覆或层压的机织物、针织物或钩编织物、毡呢或无纺织物及其制品；

（十）带毛皮张（第四十一章或第四十三章）、税目43.03或43.04的毛皮制品、人造毛皮及其制品；

（十一）税目42.01或42.02的用纺织材料制成的物品；

（十二）第四十八章的产品或物品（例如纤维素絮纸）；

（十三）第六十四章的鞋靴及其零件、护腿、裹腿及类似品；

（十四）第六十五章的发网、其他帽类及其零件；

（十五）第六十七章的货品；

（十六）涂有研磨料的纺织材料（税目68.05）以及税目68.15的碳纤维及其制品；

（十七）玻璃纤维及其制品，但可见底布的玻璃线刺绣品除外（第七十章）；

（十八）第九十四章的物品（例如，家具、寝具、灯具及照明装置）；

（十九）第九十五章的物品（例如，玩具、游戏品、运动用品及网具）；

（二十）第九十六章的物品（例如：刷子、旅行用成套缝纫用具、拉链及打字机色带、卫生巾（护垫）及止血塞、婴儿尿布及尿布衬里；

（二十一）第九十七章的物品。

SECTION XI

TEXTILES AND TEXTILE ARTICLES

Notes:

1. This Section does not cover:

(a) Animal brush making bristles or hair (heading No. 05.02); horsehair or horsehair waste (heading No. 05.11);

(b) Human hair or articles of human hair (heading No. 05.01, 67.03 or 67.04), except straining cloth of a kind commonly used in oil presses or the like (heading No. 59.11);

(c) Cotton linters or other vegetable materials of Chapter 14;

(d) Asbestos of heading No. 25.24 or articles of asbestos or other products of heading No. 68.12 or 68.13;

(e) Articles of heading No. 30.05 or 30.06; yarn used to clean between the teeth, in individual, retail packages dental floss, of heading No. 33.06;

(f) Sensitized textiles of headings No. 37.01 to 37.04;

(g) Monofilament of which any cross-sectional dimension exceeds 1mm or strip or the like (for example, artificial straw) of an apparent width exceeding 5mm, of plastics (Chapter 39), or plaits or fabrics or other basketware or wickerwork of such monofilament or strip (Chapter 46);

(h) Woven, knitted or crocheted fabrics, felt or nonwovens, impregnated, coated, covered or laminated with plastics, or articles thereof, of Chapter 39;

(i) Woven, knitted or crocheted fabrics, felt or nonwovens, impregnated, coated, covered or laminated with rubber, or articles thereof, of Chapter 40;

(j) Hides or skins with their hair or wool on (Chapter 41 or 43) or articles of furskin, artificial fur or articles thereof, of heading No. 43.03 or 43.04;

(k) Articles of textile materials of heading No. 42.01 or 42.02;

(l) Products or articles of Chapter 48 (for example, cellulose wadding);

(m) Footwear or parts of footwear, gaiters or leggings or similar articles of Chapter 64;

(n) Hair-nets or other headgear or parts thereof of Chapter 65;

(o) Goods of Chapter 67;

(p) Abrasive-coated textile material (Heading No. 68.05) and also carbon fibres or articles of carbon fibres of heading No. 68.15;

(q) Glass fibres or articles of glass fibres, other than embroidery with glass thread on a visible ground of fabric (Chapter 70);

(r) Articles of Chapter 94 (for example, furniture, bedding, lamps and lighting fittings);

(s) Articles of Chapter 95 (for example, toys, games, sports requisites and nets);

(t) Articles of Chapter 96 (for example, brushes, travel sets for sewing, slide fasteners and typewriter ribbons, Sanitary towels (pads) and napkin liners for babies);

(u) Articles of Chapter 97.

二、(一)可归入第五十章至第五十五章及税目 58.09 或 59.02 的由两种或两种以上纺织材料混合制成的货品,应按其中重量最大的那种纺织材料归类。

当没有一种纺织材料的重量较大时,应按可归入的有关税目中最后一个税目所列的纺织材料归类。

(二)应用上述规定时:

1. 马毛粗松螺旋花线(税目 51.10)和含金属纱线(税目 56.05)均应作为一种单一的纺织材料,其重量应为它们在纱线中的合计重量;在机织物的归类中,金属线应作为一种纺织材料;

2. 在选择合适的税目时,应首先确定章,然后再确定该章的有关税目,至于不归入该章的其他材料可不予考虑;

3. 当归入第五十四章及第五十五章的货品与其他章的货品进行比较时,应将这两章作为一个单一的章对待;

4. 同一章或同一税目所列各种不同的纺织材料应作为单一的纺织材料对待。

(三)上述(一)、(二)两款规定亦适用于以下注释三、四、五或六所述纱线。

三、(一)本类的纱线(单纱、多股纱线或缆线)除下列(二)款另有规定的以外,凡符合以下规格的应作为"线、绳、索、缆":

1. 丝或绢丝纱线,细度在20000 分特以上;
2. 化学纤维纱线(包括第五十四章的用两根及以上单丝纺成的纱线),细度在 10000 分特以上;
3. 大麻或亚麻纱线:
   (1)加光或上光的,细度在 1429 分特及以上;
   (2)未加光或上光的,细度在 20000 分特以上;
4. 三股或三股以上的椰壳纤维纱线;
5. 其他植物纤维纱线,细度在 20000 分特以上;
6. 用金属线加强的纱线。

(二)下列各项不按上述(一)款规定办理:

1. 羊毛或其他动物毛纱线及纸纱线,但用金属线加强的纱线除外;
2. 第五十五章的化学纤维长丝丝束以及第五十四章的未加捻或捻度每米少于 5 转的复丝纱线;
3. 税目 50.06 的蚕胶丝及第五十四章的单丝;
4. 税目 56.05 的含金属纱线;但用金属线加强的纱线按上述(一)款 6 项规定办理;
5. 税目 56.06 的绳绒线、粗松螺旋花线及纵行起圈纱线。

四、(一)除下列(二)款另有规定的以外,第五十章、第五十一章、第五十二章、第五十四章和第五十五章所称"供零售用"纱线,是指以下列方式包装的纱线(单纱、股纱线或缆线):

2. (A) Goods classifiable in Chapters 50 to 55 or of heading No. 58.09 or 59.02 and of a mixture of two or more textile materials are to be classified as if consisting wholly of that one textile material which predominates by weight over any other single textile material.

When no one textile material predominates by weight, the goods are to be classified as if consisting wholly of that one textile material which is covered by the heading which occurs last in numerical order among those which equally merit consideration.

(B) For the purposes of the above rule:

(a) Gimped horsehair yarn (heading No. 51.10) and metallized yarn (heading No. 56.05) are to be treated as a single textile material the weight of which is to be taken as the aggregate of the weights of its components; for the classification of woven fabrics, metal thread is to be regarded as a textile material;

(b) The choice of appropriate heading shall be effected by determining first the Chapter and then the applicable heading within that Chapter, disregarding any materials not classified in that Chapter;

(c) When both Chapters 54 and 55 are involved with any other Chapter, Chapters 54 and 55 are to be treated as a single Chapter;

(d) Where a Chapter or a heading refers to goods of different textile materials, such materials are to be treated as a single textile material.

(C) The provisions of paragraphs (A) and (B) above apply also to the yarns referred to in Notes 3,4,5 or 6 below.

3. (A) For the purposes of this Section, and subject to the exceptions in paragraph (B) below, yarns (single, multiple (folded) or cabled) of the following descriptions are to be treated as "twine, cordage, ropes and cables":

(a) Of silk or waste silk, measuring more than 20,000 decitex;
(b) Of man-made fibres (including yarn of two or more monofilaments of Chapter 54), measuring more than 10,000 decitex;
(c) Of true hemp or flax:
   (Ⅰ) Polished or glazed, measuring 1,429 decitex or more;
   (Ⅱ) Not polished or glazed, measuring more than 20,000 decitex;
(d) Of coir, consisting of three or more plies;
(e) Of other vegetable fibres, measuring more than 20,000 decitex;
(f) Reinforced with metal thread.

(B) Exceptions:

(a) Yarn of wool or other animal hair and paper yarn, other than yarn reinforced with metal thread;
(b) Man-made filament tow of Chapter 55 and multifilament yarn without twist or with a twist of less than 5 turns per metre of Chapter 54;
(c) Silk worm gut of heading No. 50.06, and monofilaments of Chapter 54;
(d) Metallized yarn of Heading No. 56.05; yarn reinforced with metal thread is subject to paragraph (A) (f) above; and
(e) Chenille yarn, gimped yarn and loop wale-yarn of heading 56.06.

4. (A) For the purposes of Chapters 50,51,52,54 and 55, the expression "put up for retail sale" in relation to yarn means, subject to the exceptions in paragraph (B) below, yarn (single, multiple (folded) or cabled) put up:

1. 绕于纸板、线轴、纱管或类似芯子上，其重量(含线芯)符合下列规定：

(1)丝、绢丝或化学纤维长丝纱线，不超过85克；

(2)其他纱线，不超过125克。

2. 绕成团、绞或束，其重量符合下列规定：

(1) 细度在3000分特以下的化学纤维长丝纱线，丝或绢丝纱线，不超过85克；

(2)细度在2000分特以下的任何其他纱线，不超过125克；

(3)其他纱线，不超过500克。

3. 绕成绞或束，每绞或每束中有若干用线分开的小绞或小束，每小绞或小束的重量相等，并且符合下列规定：

(1)丝、绢丝或化学纤维长丝纱线，不超过85克；

(2)其他纱线，不超过125克。

(二)下列各项不按上述(一)款规定办理：

1. 各种纺织材料制的单纱，但下列两种除外：

(1)未漂白的羊毛或动物细毛单纱；

(2)漂白、染色或印色的羊毛或动物细毛单纱，细度在5000分特以上。

2. 未漂白的多股纱线或缆线：

(1)丝或绢丝制的，不论何种包装；

(2)除羊毛或动物细毛外其他纺织材料制，成绞或成束的。

3. 漂白、染色或印色丝或绢丝制的多股纱线或缆线，细度在133分特及以下；

4. 任何纺织材料制的单纱、多股纱线或缆线：

(1)交叉绕成绞或束的；

(2)绕于纱芯上或以其他方式卷绕，明显用于纺织工业的(例如，绕于纱管、加捻管、纬纱管、锥形筒管或锭子上的或者绕成蚕茧状以供绣花机使用的纱线)。

五、税目52.04、54.01及55.08所称"缝纫线"，是指下列多股纱线或缆线：

(一)绕于芯子(例如，线轴、纱管)上，重量(包括纱芯)不超过1000克；

(二)作为缝纫线上过浆的；

(三)终捻为反手(Z)捻的。

六、本类所称"高强力纱"，是指断裂强度大于下列标准的纱线：

尼龙、其他聚酰胺或聚酯制的单纱—60厘牛顿/特克斯；
尼龙、其他聚酰胺或聚酯制的多股纱线或缆线—53厘牛顿/特克斯；
粘胶纤维制的单纱、多股纱线或缆线—27厘牛顿/特克斯。

七、本类所称"制成的"，是指：

(一)裁剪成除正方形或长方形以外的其他形状的；

(二)呈制成状态，无需缝纫或其他进一步加工(或仅需剪断分隔联线)即可使用的(例如，某些抹布、毛巾、台布、方披巾、毯子)；

(三)裁剪成一定尺寸，至少有一边为带有可见的锥形或压平形的热封边，其余各边经本注释其他各项所述加工，但不包括为防止剪边脱纱而用热切法或其他简单方法处理的织物。

(a) On cards, reels, tubes or similar supports, of a weight (including support) not exceeding:

(Ⅰ) 85g in the case of silk, waste silk or man-made filaments; or

(Ⅱ) 125g in other cases;

(b) In balls, hanks or skeins of a weight not exceeding:

(Ⅰ) 85g in the case of man-made filament yarn of less than 3,000 decitex, silk or silk waste;

(Ⅱ) 125g in the case of all other yarns of less than 2,000 decitex; or

(Ⅲ) 500g in other cases;

(c) In hanks or skeins comprising several smaller hanks or skeins separated by dividing threads which render them independent one of the other, each of uniform weight not exceeding:

(Ⅰ) 85g in the case of silk, waste silk or man-made filament yarn; or

(Ⅱ) 125g in other cases.

(B) Exceptions:

(a) Single yarn of any textile material, except:

(Ⅰ) Single yarn of wool or fine animal hair, unbleached; and

(Ⅱ) Single yarn of wool or fine animal hair, bleached, dyed or printed, measuring more than 5,000 decitex;

(b) Multiple (folded) or cabled yarn, unbleached:

(Ⅰ) Of silk or waste silk, however put up;

(Ⅱ) Of other textile material except wool or fine animal hair, in hanks or skeins;

(c) Multiple (folded) or cabled yarn of silk or waste silk, bleached, dyed or printed, measuring 133 decitex or less; and

(d) Single, multiple (folded) or cabled yarn of any textile material:

(Ⅰ) In cross-reeled hanks or skeins;

(Ⅱ) Put up on supports or in some other manner indicating its use in the textile industry (for example, on cops, twisting mill tubes, pirns, conical bobbins or spindles, or reeled in the form of cocoons for embroidery looms).

5. For the purposes of headings No. 52.04, 54.01 and 55.08 the expression "sewing thread" means multiple (folded) or cabled yarn:

(a) Put up on supports (for example, reels, tubes) of a weight (including support) not exceeding 1,000g;

(b) Dressed for use as sewing thread;

(c) With a final "Z" twist.

6. For the purposes of this Section, the expression "high tenacity yarn" means yarn having a tenacity, expressed in cN/tex (centinewton per tex), greater than the following:

Single yarn of nylon or other polyamides, or of polyesters 60 cN/tex
Multiple (folded) or cabled yarn of nylon or other polyamides, or of polyesters 53 cN/tex
Single, multiple (folded) or cabled yarn of viscose rayon 27 cN/tex

7. For the purposes of this Section, the expression "made up" means:

(a) Cut otherwise than into squares or rectangles;

(b) Produced in the finished state, ready for use (or merely needing separation by cutting dividing threads) without sewing or other working (for example, certain dusters, towels, table cloths, scarf squares, blankets);

(c) Cut to size and with at least one heatsealed edge with a visibly tapered or compressed border and the other edges treated as described in any other subparagraph of this Note, but excluding fabrics the cut edges of which have been prevented from unravelling by hot cutting or by other simple means;

（四）已缝边或滚边，或者在任一边带有结制的流苏，但不包括为防止剪边脱纱而锁边或用其他简单方法处理的织物；

（五）裁剪成一定尺寸并经抽纱加工的；

（六）缝合、胶合或用其他方法拼合而成的（将两段或两段以上同样料子的织物首尾连接而成的匹头，以及由两层或两层以上的织物，不论中间有无胎料，层迭而成的匹头除外）；

（七）针织或钩编成一定形状，不论进口或出口时是单件还是以若干件相连成幅的。

八、对于第五十章至第六十章：

（一）第五十章至第五十五章和第六十章，以及除条文另有规定以外的第五十六章至第五十九章，不适用于上述注释七所规定的制成货品；

（二）第五十章至第五十五章及第六十章不包括第五十六章至第五十九章的货品。

九、第五十章至第五十五章的机织物包括由若干层平行纱线以锐角或直角相互层迭，在纱线交叉点用粘合剂或以热粘合法粘合而成的织物。

十、用纺织材料和橡胶线制成的弹性产品归入本类。

十一、本类所称“浸渍”，包括“浸泡”。

十二、本类所称“聚酰胺”，包括“芳族聚酰胺”。

十三、本类及本目录所称“弹性纱线”是指合成纤维纺织材料制成的长丝纱线（包括单丝变形纱线除外）。这些纱线可拉伸至原长的三倍而不断裂，并可在拉伸至原长两倍后五分钟内回复到不超过原长度的一倍半。

十四、除条文另有规定的以外，各种服装即使成套包装供零售用，也应按各自税目分别归类。本注释所称“纺织服装”，是指税目 61.01 至 61.14 及税目 62.01 至 62.11 所列的各种服装。

子目注释：

一、本类及本目录所用有关名词解释如下：

（一）未漂白纱线

1. 带有纤维自然色泽并且未经漂染（不论是否整体染色）或印色的纱线；

2. 从回收纤维制得，色泽未定的纱线（本色纱）。

这种纱线可用无色浆料或易褪色染料（可轻易地用肥皂洗去）处理，如果是化学纤维纱线，则整体用消光剂（例如二氧化钛）进行处理。

（二）漂白纱线

1. 经漂白加工、用漂白纤维制得或经染白（除条文另有规定的以外）（不论是否整体染色）及用白浆料处理的纱线；

2. 用未漂白纤维和漂白纤维混纺制得的纱线；

3. 用未漂白纱和漂白纱纺成多股纱线或缆线。

（三）着色（染色或印色）纱线

(d) Hemmed or with rolled edges, or with a knotted fringe at any of the edges, but excluding fabrics the cut edges of which have been prevented from unravelling by whipping or by other simple means;

(e) Cut to size and having undergone a process of drawn thread work;

(f) Assembled by sewing, gumming or otherwise (other than piece goods consisting of two or more lengths of identical material joined end to end and piece goods composed of two or more textiles assembled in layers, whether or not padded);

(g) Knitted or crocheted to shape, whether presented as separate items or in the form of a number of items in the length.

8. For the purposes of Chapters 50 to 60:

(a) Chapters 50 to 55 and 60 and, except where the context otherwise requires, Chapters 56 to 59 do not apply to goods made up within the meaning of Note 7 above; and

(b) Chapters 50 to 55 and 60 do not apply to goods of Chapters 56 to 59.

9. The woven fabrics of Chapters 50 to 55 include fabrics consisting of layers of parallel textile yarns superimposed on each other at acute or right angles. These layers are bonded at the intersections of the yarns by an adhesive or by thermal bonding.

10. Elastic products consisting of textile materials combined with rubber threads are classified in this Section.

11. For the purposes of this Section, the expression “impregnated” includes “dipped”.

12. For the purposes of this Section, the expression “polyamides” includes “aramides”.

13. For the purposes of this section and where applicaple throughout the nomeclature the expression “elastomencyarn” means Filament yarn, including monofilament, of synthetic textile material, other than textured yarn, which does not break on being extended to three times its original length and which returns, after being extended to twice its original length, within a period of five minutes, to a length not greater than one and a half times its original length.

14. Unless the context otherwise requires, textile garments of different headings are to be classified in their own headings even if put up in sets for retail sale. For the purposes of this Note, the expression “textile garments” means garments of headings No. 61.01 to 61.14 and headings No. 62.01 to 62.11.

Subheading Notes:

1. In the Section and, where applicable, throughout the Nomenclature, the following expressions have the meanings hereby assigned to them:

(a) Unbleached yarn Yarn which:

(Ⅰ) has the natural colour of its constituent fibres and has not been bleached, dyed (whether or not in the mass) or printed;

(Ⅱ) is of indeterminate colour (“grey yarn”), manufactured from garnetted stock.

Such yarn may have been treated with a colourless dressing or fugitive dye (which disappears after simple washing with soap) and, in the case of man-made fibres, treated in the mass with delustring agent (for example, titanium dioxide).

(b) Bleached yarn Yarn which:

(Ⅰ) has undergone a bleaching process, is made of bleached fibres or, unless the context otherwise requires, has been dyed white (whether or not in the mass) or treated with a white dressing;

(Ⅱ) consists of a mixture of unbleached and bleached fibres;

(Ⅲ) is multiple (folded) or cabled and consists of unbleached and bleached yarns.

(c) Coloured (dyed or printed) yarn Yarn which:

1. 染成彩色(不论是否整体染色,但白色或易褪色除外)或印色的纱线,以及用染色或印色纤维纺制的纱线;

2. 用各色染色纤维混合纺制或用未漂白或漂白纤维与着色纤维混合制得的纱线(夹色纱或混色纱),以及用一种或几种颜色间隔印色而获得点纹印迹的纱线;

3. 用已经印色的纱条或粗纱纺制的纱线;

4. 用未漂白纱和漂白纱与着色纱纺成的多股纱线或缆线。

上述定义作相应调整后适用于第五十四章的单丝、扁条或类似产品。

(四)未漂白机织物

用未漂白纱线织成后未经漂白、染色或印花的机织物。这类织物可用无色浆料或易褪色染料处理。

(五)漂白机织物

1. 经漂白、染白或用白浆料处理(除条文另有规定的以外)的成匹机织物;

2. 用漂白纱线织成的机织物;

3. 用未漂白纱线和漂白纱线织成的机织物;

(六)染色机织物

1. 除条文另有规定的以外,染成白色以外的其他单一颜色或用白色以外的其他有色整理剂处理的成匹机织物;

2. 以单一颜色的着色纱线织成的机织物。

(七)色织机织物

除印花机织物以外的下列机织物:

1. 用各种不同颜色纱线或同一颜色不同深浅(纤维的自然色彩除外)纱线织成的机织物;

2. 用未漂白或漂白与着色纱线织成的机织物;

3. 用夹色纱线或混色纱线织成的机织物。

不论何种情况,布边或布头的纱线均可忽略不计。

(八)印花机织物

成匹印花的机织物,不论是否用各色纱线织成。

用刷子或喷枪,经转印纸转印、植绒或蜡防印花等方法印成花纹图案的机织物亦可视为印花机织物。

上述各类纱线或织物如经丝光工艺处理并不影响其归类。

上述(四)至(八)的定义在作必要修改后适用于针织或钩编织物。

(九)平纹织物

每根纬纱在并排的经纱间上下交错而过,而每根经纱也在并排的纬纱间上下交错而过的织物组织。

二、(一)含有两种或两种以上纺织材料的第五十六章至第六十三章的产品,应根据本类注释二对第五十章至第五十五章或税目58.09的此类纺织材料产品归类的规定来确定归类。

(二)运用本条规定时:

(Ⅰ) is dyed (whether or not in the mass) other than white or in a fugitive colour, or printed, or made from dyed or printed fibres;

(Ⅱ) consists of a mixture of dyed fibres of different colours or of a mixture of unbleached or bleached fibres with coloured fibres (marl or mixture yarns), or is printed in one or more colours at intervals to give the impression of dots;

(Ⅲ) is obtained from slivers or rovings which have been printed; or

(Ⅳ) is multiple (folded) or cabled and consists of unbleached or bleached yarn and coloured yarn.

The above definitions also apply, *mutatis mutandis*, to monofilament and to strip or the like of Chapter 54.

(d) Unbleached woven fabric

Woven fabric made from unbleached yarn and which has not been bleached, dyed or printed. Such fabric may have treated with a colourless dressing or a fugitive dye.

(e) Bleached woven fabric woven fabric which:

(Ⅰ) has been bleached or, unless the context otherwise requires, dyed white or treated with a white dressing, in the piece;

(Ⅱ) consists of bleached yarn; or

(Ⅲ) consists of unbleached and bleached yarn.

(f) Dyed woven fabric woven fabric which:

(Ⅰ) is dyed a single uniform colour other than white (unless the context otherwise requires) or has been treated with a coloured finish other than white (unless the context otherwise requires), in the piece; or

(Ⅱ) consists of coloured yarn of a single uniform colour.

(g) Woven fabric of yarns of different colours

Woven fabric (other than printed woven fabric) which:

(Ⅰ) consists of yarns of different colours or yarns of different shades of the same colour (other than the natural colour of the constituent fibres);

(Ⅱ) consists of unbleached or bleached yarn and coloured yarn; or

(Ⅲ) consists of marl or mixture yarns.

(In all cases, the yarn used in selvedges and piece ends is not taken into consideration.)

(h) Printed woven fabric

Woven fabric which has been printed in the piece, whether or not made from yarns of differenent colours. (The following are also regarded as printed woven fabrics: woven fabrics bearing designs made, for example, with a brush or spray gun, by means of transfer paper, by flocking or by the batik process.)

The process of mercerization does not affect the classification of yarns or fabrics within the above categories.

The definitions at (d) to (h) above apply, *mutatis mutandis*, to knitted or crocheted fabrics.

(i) Plain weave

A fabric construction in which each yarn of the weft passes alternately over and under successive yarns of the warp and each yarn of the warp passes alternately over and under successive yarns of the weft.

2. (A) Products of Chapters 56 to 63 containing two or more textile materials are to be regarded as consisting wholly of that textile material which would be selected under Note 2 to this Section for the classification of the product of Chapters 50 to 55 or of heading No. 58.09 consisting of the same textile materials.

(B) For the application of this rule:

1. 应酌情考虑按归类总规则第三条来确定归类
2. 对由底布和绒面或毛圈面构成的纺织品，在归类时可不考虑底布的属性
3. 对税目58.10的刺绣品及其制品，归类时应只考虑底布的属性，但不见底布的刺绣品及其制品应根据绣线的属性确定归类。

(a) where appropriate, only the part which determines the classification under interpretative Rule 3 shall be taken into account;

(b) in the case of textile products consisting of a ground fabric and a pile or looped surface, no account shall be taken of the ground fabric;

(c) in the case of embroidery of heading No. 58.10 and goods thereof, only the ground fabric shall be taken into account. However, embroidery without visible ground, and goods thereof, shall be classified with reference to the embroidering threads alone.

第五十章 蚕 丝

Chapter 50 Silk

税则号列	货品名称	最惠(%)	普通	增值税率	出口退税	计量单位	监管条件	Article Description
50.01	**适于缫丝的蚕茧：**							**Silk-worm cocoons suitable for reeling:**
5001.0010	---适于缫丝的桑蚕茧	6	70	17	5	千克	AB	---Bombyx mori cocoons (Mulberry feeding silk-worm cocoons)
5001.0090	---其他	6	70	17	5	千克	AB	---Other
50.02	**生丝(未加捻)：**							**Raw silk (not thrown):**
	---桑蚕丝：							---Steam filature silk:
5002.0011	----厂丝	9	80	17	15	千克	AB	----Plant reeled (filature silk)
5002.0012	----土丝	9	80	17	15	千克	AB	----Home reeled
5002.0013	----双宫丝	9	80	17	15	千克	AB	----Doupion
5002.0019	----其他	9	80	17	15	千克	AB	----Other
5002.0020	---柞蚕丝	9	80	17	15	千克	AB	---Tussah silk
5002.0090	---其他	9	80	17	15	千克	AB	---Other
50.03	**废丝(包括不适于缫丝的蚕茧、废纱及回收纤维)：**							**Silk waste (including cocoons unsuitable for reeling, yarn waste and garnetted stock):**
	---未梳：							---Not carded or combed:
5003.0011	----下茧、茧衣、长吐、滞头	9	70	17	13	千克	AB	---Spoiled cocoon, cocoon outer floss, frison, frigon
5003.0012	----回收纤维	9	70	17	13	千克	AB	----Garnetted stock
5003.0019	----其他	9	70	17	13	千克	AB	----Other
	---其他：							---Other:
5003.0091	----绵球	9	70	17	13	千克	AB	---silk top
5003.0099	----其他	9	70	17	13	千克	AB	----Other
50.04	**丝纱线(绢纺纱线除外)，非供零售用：**							**Silk yarn (other than yarn spun from spun silk waste) not put up for retail sale:**
5004.0000	丝纱线(绢纺纱线除外)，非供零售用	6	90	17	16	千克		Silk yarn (other than yarn spun from spun silk waste) not put up for retail sale
50.05	**绢纺纱线，非供零售用：**							**Yarn spun from silk spum waste, not put up for retail sale:**
5005.0010	---䌷丝纱线	6	90	17	16	千克		---Spun from noil
5005.0010 10	非供零售用䌷丝纱线(䌷丝为主，含丝及绢丝85%及以上纱线)	6	90	17	16	千克		Spun from noil, not in forms or packing for retail sale, containing ≥85% by weight of silk or spun silk
5005.0010 90	非供零售用䌷丝纱线(䌷丝为主，含丝及绢丝85%以下纱线)	6	90	17	16	千克		Spun from noil, not in forms or packing for retail sale, containing < 85% by weight of silk or spun silk
5005.0090	---其他	6	90	17	16	千克		---Other
5005.0090 10	非供零售用其他绢纺纱线(含丝及绢丝85%及以上纱线)	6	90	17	16	千克		Other yarn spun from spun silk, not in forms or packing for retail sale(containing ≥85% by weight of silk or spun silk)
5005.0090 20	非供零售用其他绢纺纱线(含丝及绢丝85%以下纱线)	6	90	17	16	千克		Other yarn spun from spun silk, not in forms or packing for retail sale(containing < 85% by weight of silk or spun silk)
50.06	**丝纱线及绢纺纱线，供零售用；蚕胶丝：**							**Silk yarn and yarn spun from silk waste, put up for retail sale; silk-worm gut:**
5006.0000	丝纱线及绢纺纱线，供零售用；蚕胶丝	6	100	17	16	千克		Silk yarn and yarn spun from spun silk, put up for retail sale; silk-worm gut
5006.0000 10	零售用丝纱线，绢纺纱线；蚕胶丝(含丝及绢丝85%及以上纱线)	6	100	17	16	千克		Silk yarn , yarn spun from spun silk and silk-worm gut, put up for retail sale (containing ≥ 85% by weight of silk or spun silk)
5006.0000 20	零售用丝纱线，绢纺纱线；蚕胶丝(含丝及绢丝85%以下纱线)	6	100	17	16	千克		Silk yarn, yarn spun from spun silk and silk-worm gut, put up for retail sale(containing <85% by weight of silk or spun silk)
50.07	**丝或绢丝机织物：**							**Woven fabrics of silk or of spun silk:**

税则号列	货　品　名　称	最惠(%)	普通	增值税率	出口退税	计量单位	监管条件	Article Description
	-细丝机织物:							-Fabrics of noil silk:
5007.1010	---未漂白(包括未练白或练白)或漂白	10	130	17	16	米/千克		---Unbleaded (unscoured or scoured) or bleached
5007.1010 10	未漂白或漂白的细丝机织物(包括未练白或练白的,含细丝85%及以上)	10	130	17	16	米/千克		Fabrics of noil silk, unbleached (unscoured or scoured) or bleached, containing ≥85% by weight of noil silk
5007.1010 20	未漂白或漂白的细丝机织物(包括未练白或练白的,含细丝85%以下,棉或化纤限内)	10	130	17	16	米/千克		Fabrics of noil silk, unbleached (unscoured or scoured) or bleached, containing <85% by weight of noil silk, cotton or man-made fibres within limitations
5007.1010 31	未漂白或漂白的细丝机织物(含未练白或练白,细丝<85%与精梳羊毛或动物细毛混纺,羊毛限内)	10	130	17	16	米/千克		Fabrics of noil silk, unbleached (unscoured or scoured) or bleached, containing <85% by weight of noil silk, mixed with combed wool or combed fine animal hair, wool within limitations
5007.1010 39	未漂白或漂白的细丝机织物(未练白或练白的,含细丝85%以下,与其他混纺,羊毛限内)	10	130	17	16	米/千克		Fabrics of noil silk, unbleached (unscoured or scoured) or bleached, containing <85% by weight of noil silk, mixed with other fibres, wool within limitations
5007.1010 91	未漂白或漂白的细丝机织物(未练白或练白的,含细丝<85%与精梳羊毛或动物细毛混纺)	10	130	17	16	米/千克		Fabrics of noil silk, unbleached (unscoured or scoured) or bleached, containing <85% by weight of noil silk, mixed with combed wool or combed fine animal hair
5007.1010 99	未漂白或漂白的细丝机织物(包括未练白或练白的,含细丝85%以下,与其他混纺)	10	130	17	16	米/千克		Fabrics of noil silk, unbleached (unscoured or scoured) or bleached, containing <85% by weight of noil silk, mixed with other fibres
5007.1090	---其他	10	130	17	16	米/千克		---Other
5007.1090 10	其他细丝机织物(含油丝85%及以上)	10	130	17	16	米/千克		Other fabrics of noil silk, containing ≥85% by weight of noil silk
5007.1090 21	其他色织细丝机织物(含细丝85%以下,棉或化纤限内)	10	130	17	16	米/千克		Other fabrics of noil silk, containing <85% by weight of noil silk, coloured, cotton or man-made fibres within limitations
5007.1090 29	其他非色织细丝机织物(含细丝85%以下,棉或化纤限内)	10	130	17	16	米/千克		Other fabrics of noil silk, containing <85% by weight of noil silk, not coloured, cotton or man-made fibres within limitations
5007.1090 31	其他细丝机织物(含细丝85%以下,与精梳羊毛或动物细毛混纺,羊毛限内)	10	130	17	16	米/千克		Other fabrics of noil silk, containing <85% by weight of noil silk, mixed with combed wool or combed fine animal hair, wool within limitations
5007.1090 39	其他细丝机织物(含细丝85%以下,与其他混纺,羊毛限内)	10	130	17	16	米/千克		Other fabrics of noil silk, containing <85% by weight of noil silk, mixed with other fibres, wool within limitations
5007.1090 91	其他细丝机织物(含细丝85%以下,与精梳羊毛或动物细毛混纺)	10	130	17	16	米/千克		Other fabrics of noil silk, containing <85% by weight of noil silk, mixed with combed wool or combed fine animal hair
5007.1090 99	其他细丝机织物(含细丝85%以下,与其他混纺)	10	130	17	16	米/千克		Other fabrics of noil silk, containing <85% by weight of noil silk, mixed with other fibres
	-其他机织物,按重量计丝或绢丝(细丝除外)含量在85%及以上:							-Other fabrics, containing 85% or more by weight of silk or of spun silk other than noil silk:
	---桑蚕丝机织物:							---Of Bombyx mori silk:
5007.2011	----未漂白(包括未练白或练白)或漂白	10	130	17	16	米/千克		----Unbleached (unscoured or scoured) or bleached
5007.2019	----其他	10	130	17	16	米/千克		----Other
	---柞蚕丝机织物:							---Of tussah silk:
5007.2021	----未漂白(包括未练白或练白)或漂白	10	130	17	16	米/千克		----Unbleached (unscoured or scoured) or bleached
5007.2029	----其他	10	130	17	16	米/千克		----Other
	---绢丝机织物:							---Of spun silk other than noil silk:
5007.2031	----未漂白(包括未练白或练白)或漂白	10	130	17	16	米/千克		----Unbleached (unscoured or scoured) or bleached
5007.2039	----其他	10	130	17	16	米/千克		----Other
5007.2090	---其他	10	130	17	16	米/千克		---Other

税则号列	货品名称	最惠(%)	普通	增值税率	出口退税	计量单位	监管条件	Article Description
5007.2090 10	未漂白或漂白其他丝机织物(包括未练白或练白,按重量计丝或绢丝含量在85%及以上)	10	130	17	16	米/千克		Other woven fabrics of silk, unbleached (unscoured or scoured) or bleached, containing ≥ 85% by weight of silk and spun silk
5007.2090 90	其他丝机织物(按重量计丝或绢丝含量在85%及以上)	10	130	17	16	米/千克		Other woven fabrics of silk, containing≥85% by weight of silk and spun silk
	-其他机织物:							-Other fabrics:
5007.9010	---未漂白(包括未练白或练白)或漂白	10	130	17	16	米/千克		---Unbleached (unscoured or scoured) or bleached
5007.9010 10	未漂白或漂白其他丝机织物(包括未练白或练白,含丝及绢丝85%及以上)	10	130	17	16	米/千克		Other woven fabrics of silk, unbleached (unscoured or scoured) or bleached, containing ≥ 85% by weight of silk and spun silk
5007.9010 20	未漂白或漂白其他丝机织物(包括未练白或练白,含丝及绢丝85%以下与其他混纺,棉或化纤限内)	10	130	17	16	米/千克		Other woven fabrics of silk, unbleached (unscoured or scoured) or bleached, containing <85% by weight of silk and spun silk, mixed, with other fibres cotton or man-made fibres within limitations
5007.9010 31	未漂白或漂白其他丝机织物(未练白或练白,含丝及绢丝85%以下,与精梳羊毛或动物细毛混纺,羊毛限内)	10	130	17	16	米/千克		Other woven fabrics of silk, unbleached (unscoured or scoured) or bleached, containing < 85% by weight of silk and spun silk, mixed with combed wool or combed fine animals hair, wool within limitations
5007.9010 39	未漂白或漂白其他丝机织物(未练白或练白,含丝及绢丝85%以下,与其他混纺,羊毛限内)	10	130	17	16	米/千克		Other woven fabrics of silk, unbleached (unscoured or scoured) or bleached, containing < 85% by weight of silk and spun silk, mixed, with other fibres, wool within limitations
5007.9010 91	未漂白或漂白其他丝机织物(未练白或练白,含丝及绢丝85%以下,与精梳羊毛或动物细毛混纺)	10	130	17	16	米/千克		Other woven fabrics of silk, unbleached (unscoured or scoured) or bleached, containing <85% by weight of silk and spun silk, mixed with combed wool or combed fine animals hair
5007.9010 99	未漂白或漂白其他丝机织物(未练白或练白,含丝及绢丝85%以下,与其他混纺)	10	130	17	16	米/千克		Other woven fabrics of silk, unbleached (unscoured or scoured) or bleached, containing <85% by weight of silk and spun silk, mixed with other fibres
5007.9090	---其他	10	130	17	16	米/千克		---Other
5007.9090 10	其他丝机织物(含丝及绢丝85%及以上)	10	130	17	16	米/千克		Other woven fabrics of silk, containing ≥ 85% by weight of silk and spun silk
5007.9090 21	其他色织丝机织物(含丝及绢丝85%以下,与其他混纺,棉或化学纤维限内)	10	130	17	16	米/千克		Other woven fabrics of silk, containing < 85% by weight of silk and spun silk, coloured, mixed with other fibres, cotton or man-made fibres within limitations
5007.9090 29	其他非色织丝机织物(含丝及绢丝85%以下,与其他混纺,棉或化学纤维限内)	10	130	17	16	米/千克		Other woven fabrics of silk, containing < 85% by weight of silk and spun silk, not coloured, mixed with other fibres, cotton or man-made within limitations
5007.9090 31	其他丝机织物(含丝及绢丝85%以下,与精梳羊毛或动物细毛混纺,羊毛限内)	10	130	17	16	米/千克		Other woven fabrics of silk, containing < 85% by weight of silk and spun silk, mixed with combed wool or combed fine animal hair, wool within limitations
5007.9090 39	其他丝机织物(含丝及绢丝85%以下,与其他混纺,羊毛限内)	10	130	17	16	米/千克		Other woven fabrics of silk, containing < 85% by weight of silk and spun silk, mixed with other fibres wool within limitations
5007.9090 91	其他丝机织物(含丝及绢丝85%以下,与精梳羊毛或动物细毛混纺)	10	130	17	16	米/千克		Other woven fabrics of silk, containing < 85% by weight of silk and spun silk, mixed with combed, wool or combed fine animal hair
5007.9090 99	其他丝机织物(含丝及绢丝85%以下,与其他混纺)	10	130	17	16	米/千克		Other woven fabrics of silk, containing < 85% by weight of silk and spun silk, mixed with other fibres

第五十一章
羊毛、动物细毛或粗毛；马毛纱线及其机织物

Chapter 51
Wool, fine or coarse animal hair; horsehair yarn and woven fabric

注释：

本目录所称：

一、"羊毛"，是指绵羊或羔羊身上长的天然纤维；

二、"动物细毛"，是指下列动物的毛：羊驼、美洲驼、驼马、骆驼(包括单峰骆驼)、牦牛、安哥拉山羊、西藏山羊、喀什米尔山羊及类似山羊(普通山羊除外)、家兔(包括安哥拉兔)、野兔、海狸、河狸鼠或麝鼠；

三、"动物粗毛"，是指以上未提及的其他动物的毛，但不包括制刷用鬃、毛(税目05.02)以及马毛(税目05.11)。

Notes:

1. Throughout the Nomenclature:
   1. "Wool" means the natural fibre grown by sheep or lambs;
   2. "Fine animal hair" means the hair of alpaca, llama, vicuna, camel, (including dromedary) yak, Angora, Tibetan, Kashmir or similar goats (but not common goats), rabbit (including Angora rabbit), hare, beaver, nutria or muskrat;
   3. "Coarse animal hair" means the hair of animals not mentioned above, excluding brush-making hair and bristles (heading No. 05.02) and horsehair (heading No. 05.11).

税则号列	货品名称	最惠(%)	普通	增值税率	出口退税	计量单位	监管条件	Article Description
51.01	未梳的羊毛：							**Wool, not carded or combed:**
	-含脂羊毛,包括剪前水洗毛：							-Greasy, including fleece-washed wool:
5101.1100	--剪羊毛		50	13	5	千克		--Shorn wool
5101.1100 01	未梳的含脂剪羊毛(配额内)	1	50	13	5	千克	tAB	Greasy shorn wool, not carded or combeb, in-quota
5101.1100 90	未梳的含脂剪羊毛(配额外)	38	50	13	5	千克	AB	Greasy shorn wool, not carded or combeb, out-quota
5101.1900	--其他		50	13	5	千克		--Other
5101.1900 01	未梳的其他含脂羊毛(配额内)	1	50	13	5	千克	tAB	Other greasy wool, not carded or combed, in-quota
5101.1900 90	未梳的其他含脂羊毛(配额外)	38	50	13	5	千克	AB	Other greasy wool, not carded or combed, out-quota
	-脱脂羊毛,未碳化：							-Degreased, not carbonized:
5101.2100	--剪羊毛		50	17	13	千克		--Shorn wool
5101.2100 01	未梳的脱脂剪羊毛(未碳化)(配额内)	1	50	17	13	千克	tAB	Degreased shorn wool, not carded or combed, not carbonized, in-quota
5101.2100 90	未梳的脱脂剪羊毛(未碳化)(配额外)	38	50	17	13	千克	AB	Degreased shorn wool, not carded or combed, not carbonized, out-quota
5101.2900	--其他		50	17	13	千克		--Other
5101.2900 01	未梳的其他脱脂羊毛(未碳化)(配额内)	1	50	17	13	千克	tAB	Other degreased wool, not carded or combeb, not carbonized, in-quota
5101.2900 90	未梳的其他脱脂羊毛(未碳化)(配额外)	38	50	17	13	千克	AB	Other degreased wool, not carded or combeb, not carbonized, out-quota
5101.3000	-碳化羊毛		50	17	13	千克		-Carbonized
5101.3000 01	未梳碳化羊毛(配额内)	1	50	17	13	千克	tAB	Carbonized wool, not carded or combed, in-quota
5101.3000 90	未梳碳化羊毛(配额外)	38	50	17	13	千克	AB	Carbonized wool, not carded or combed, out-quota
51.02	未梳的动物细毛或粗毛：							**Fine or coarse animal hair, not carded or combed:**
	-细毛：							-Fine animal hair:
5102.1100	--喀什米尔山羊的	9	45	17		千克	AB	--Of Kashmir(cashmere) goats
	--其他：							--Other:
5102.1910	---兔毛	9	50	17		千克		---Of rabbit and hare
5102.1910 10	未梳濒危兔毛	9	50	17		千克	ABFE	Hair of endangered rabbit and hare, not carded or combed
5102.1910 90	其他未梳兔毛	9	50	17	5	千克	AB	Other hair of rabbit and hare, not carded or combed
5102.1920	---其他山羊绒	9	45	17		千克	AB	---Of other goats
5102.1930	---骆驼毛、骆驼绒	9	45	17		千克		---Of camel
5102.1930 10	未梳濒危野生骆驼科动物毛、绒	9	45	17		千克	FEAB	Hair and down of endangered wild camel, not carded or combed
5102.1930 90	其他未梳骆驼毛、绒	9	45	17	5	千克	AB	Other hair and down of camel, not carded or combed
5102.1990	---其他	9	45	17		千克		---Other
5102.1990 10	未梳的其他濒危野生动物细毛	9	45	17		千克	FEAB	Fine hair of other endangered wild animals dangers, not carded or combed
5102.1990 90	未梳的其他动物细毛	9	45	17	5	千克	AB	Fine hair of other animals, not carded or combed
5102.2000	-粗毛	9	50	17		千克		-Coarse animal hair

税则号列	货品名称	最惠(%)	普通	增值税率	出口退税	计量单位	监管条件	Article Description
5102.2000 10	未梳的濒危野生动物粗毛	9	50	17		千克	FEAB	Coarse hair of endangered wild animals not carded or combed
5102.2000 90	未梳的其他动物粗毛	9	50	17	5	千克	AB	Coarse hair of other animals, not carded or combed
51.03	羊毛或动物细毛或粗毛的废料,包括废纱线,但不包括回收纤维:							**Waste of wool or of fine or coarse animal hair, including yarn waste but excluding garnetted stock:**
	-羊毛及动物细毛的落毛:							-Noils of wool or of fine animal hair:
5103.1010	---羊毛落毛		50	17	5	千克		---Of wool
5103.1010 01	羊毛落毛(配额内)	1	50	17	5	千克	tAB	Noils of wool(in-quota)
5103.1010 90	羊毛落毛(配额外)	38	50	17	5	千克	AB	Noils of wool(out-quota)
5103.1090	---其他	9	50	17		千克		---Other
5103.1090 10	其他濒危野生动物细毛的落毛	9	50	17		千克	FEAB	Other noils of fine hair of endangered wild animal
5103.1090 90	其他动物细毛的落毛	9	50	17	5	千克	ABP	Other noils of fine hair of animal
	-羊毛或动物细毛的其他废料:							-Other waste of wool or of fine animal hair:
5103.2010	---羊毛废料	13.5	20	17	5	千克	AB	---Of wool
5103.2090	---其他	9	50	17		千克		---Other
5103.2090 10	其他濒危野生动物细毛废料(包括废纱线,不包括回收纤维)	9	50	17		千克	FEAB	Other waste of fine hair of endangered wild animal (including yarn waste, but excluding garnetted stock)
5103.2090 90	其他动物细毛废料(包括废纱线,不包括回收纤维)	9	50	17	5	千克	ABP	Other waste of fine hair of other animals (including yarn waste, but excluding garnetted stock)
5103.3000	-动物粗毛废料	9	50	17		千克		-Waste of coarse animal hair
5103.3000 10	濒危野生动物粗毛废料(包括废纱线,不包括回收纤维)	9	50	17		千克	FEAB	Waste of coarse hair of endangered wild animal (including yarn waste but excluding garnetted stock)
5103.3000 90	其他动物粗毛废料(包括废纱线,不包括回收纤维)	9	50	17	5	千克	ABP	Other waste of coarse hair of animals (including yarn waste but excluding garnetted stock)
51.04	羊毛或动物细毛或粗毛的回收纤维:							**Garnetted stock of wool or of fine or coarse animal hair:**
5104.0010	---羊毛的回收纤维	15	20	17	5	千克	AB	---Of wool
5104.0090	---其他	5	50	17		千克		---Other
5104.0090 10	其他濒危野生动物细毛(包括粗毛回收纤维)	5	50	17		千克	FEAB	Garnetted stock of other fine or coarse hair of endangered wild animal
5104.0090 90	其他动物细毛或粗毛的回收纤维	5	50	17	13	千克	ABP	Garnetted stock of other of fine or coarse animal hair
51.05	已梳的羊毛及动物细毛或粗毛(包括精梳片毛):							**Wool and fine or coarse animal hair, carded or combed (including combed wool in fragments):**
5105.1000	-粗梳羊毛			17	13	千克		-Carded wool
5105.1000 01	粗梳羊毛(配额内)	3	50	17	13	千克	tAB	Carded wool(in-quota)
5105.1000 90	粗梳羊毛(配额外)	38	50	17	13	千克	AB	Carded wool(out-quota)
	-羊毛条及其他精梳羊毛:							-Wool tops and other combed wool:
5105.2100	--精梳片毛			17	13	千克		--Combed wool in fragments
5105.2100 01	精梳羊毛片毛(配额内)	3	50	17	13	千克	tAB	Combed wool in fragments(in-quota)
5105.2100 90	精梳羊毛片毛(配额外)	38	50	17	13	千克	AB	Combed wool in fragments(out-quota)
5105.2900	--其他			17	13	千克		--Other
5105.2900 01	羊毛条及其他精梳羊毛(配额内)	3	50	17	13	千克	tAB	Wool tops and other combed wool(in-quota)
5105.2900 90	羊毛条及其他精梳羊毛(配额外)	38	50	17	13	千克	AB	Wool tops and other combed wool(out-quota)
	-已梳动物细毛:							-Fine animal hair, Carded or combed:
5105.3100	--喀什米尔山羊的	5	50	17		千克	AB	--Of Kashmir(cashmere) goats
	--其他:							--Other:
5105.3910	---兔毛	5	70	17		千克		---Of rabbit or hare
5105.3910 10	已梳濒危兔毛	5	70	17		千克	ABFE	Fine hair of endangered rabbit and hare, carded or combed
5105.3910 90	其他已梳兔毛	5	70	17	13	千克	AB	Other fine hair of rabbit and hare, carded or combed
	---其他山羊绒:							---Of other goats:
5105.3921	----无毛山羊绒	5	50	17		千克	AB	----Dehaired goats wool
5105.3929	----其他	5	50	17		千克	AB	----Other
5105.3990	---其他	5	50	17	13	千克		---Other

税则号列	货品名称	最惠(%)	普通	增值税率	出口退税	计量单位	监管条件	Article Description
5105.3990 10	其他已梳野生动物细毛	5	50	17	13	千克	ABEF	Other fine hair of wild animals, carded or combed
5105.3990 90	其他已梳动物细毛	5	50	17	13	千克	AB	Other fine hair of animals, carded or combed
5105.4000	-已梳动物粗毛	5	50	17		千克		-Coarse animal hair, carded or combed
5105.4000 10	其他已梳濒危野生动物粗毛	5	50	17		千克	FEAB	Other coarse hair of endangered wild animals, carded or combed
5105.4000 90	其他已梳动物粗毛	5	50	17	13	千克	AB	Other coarse hair of animals, carded or combed
51.06	**粗梳羊毛纱线,非供零售用:**							**Yarn of carded wool, not put up for retailsale:**
5106.1000	-按重量计羊毛含量在85%及以上	5	70	17	16	千克		-Containing 85% or more by weight of wool
5106.2000	-按重量计羊毛含量在85%以下	5	70	17	16	千克		-Containing less than 85% by weight of wool
51.07	**精梳羊毛纱线,非供零售用:**							**Yarn of combed wool, not put up for retail sale:**
5107.1000	-按重量计羊毛含量在85%及以上	5	70	17	16	千克		-Containing 85% or more by weight of wool
5107.2000	-按重量计羊毛含量在85%以下	5	70	17	16	千克		-Containing less than 85% by weight of wool
51.08	**动物细毛(粗梳或精梳)纱线,非供零售用:**							**Yarn of fine animal hair (carded or combed), not put up for retailsale:**
	-粗梳:							-Carded:
	---按重量计动物细毛含量在85%及以上的							---Containing 85% or more by weight of fine animal hair
5108.1011	----山羊绒的	5	70	17	16	千克		----Of goats
5108.1019	----其他	5	70	17		千克		----Other
5108.1019 10	非供零售用粗梳其他濒危动物细毛纱线(按重量计其他动物细毛含量≥85%)	5	70	17		千克	FE	Yarn of fine hair of endangered animals, carded, not in forms or packing for retail sale(containing≥85% by weight of other animals hair)
5108.1019 90	非供零售用粗梳其他动物细毛纱线(按重量计其他动物细毛含量≥85%)	5	70	17	16	千克		Yarn of fine hair of animals, carded, not in forms or packing for retailsale(containing≥85% by weight of other fine animals hair)
5108.1090	---其他	5	70	17		千克		---Other
5108.1090 10	非供零售用粗梳其他濒危动物细毛纱线(按重量计其他粗梳动物细毛含量<85%)	5	70	17		千克	FE	Yarn of fine hair of endangered animals, carded, not in forms or packingfor retail sale(containing <85% by weight of other fine animals hair)
5108.1090 90	非供零售用粗梳其他动物细毛纱线(按重量计其他粗梳动物细毛含量<85%)	5	70	17	16	千克		Yarn of fine hair of animals, carded, not in forms or packing for retail sale(containing <85% by weight of other fine animals hair)
	-精梳:							-Combed:
	---按重量计动物细毛含量在85%及以上的:							---Containing 85% or more by weight of fine animal hair:
5108.2011	----山羊绒的	5	70	17	16	千克		----Of goats
5108.2019	----其他	5	70	17		千克		----Other
5108.2019 10	非供零售用精梳其他濒危动物细毛纱线(按重量计其他动物细毛含量≥85%)	5	70	17		千克	FE	Yarn of fine hair of endangered animals, combed, not in formsorpacking for retail sale (containing ≥ 85% by weight of other fine animals hair)
5108.2019 90	非供零售用精梳其他动物细毛纱线(按重量计其他动物细毛含量≥85%)	5	70	17	16	千克		Yarn of fine hair of other animals, combed, not put up for retail sale (containing ≥85% by weight of other fine animals hair)
5108.2090	---其他	5	70	17		千克		---Other
5108.2090 10	非供零售用精梳其他濒危动物细毛纱线(按重量计其他精梳动物细毛含量<85%)	5	70	17		千克	FE	Yarn of fine hair of endangered animal, combed, not in forms or packing for retail sale (containing < 85% by weight of other fine animals hair)
5108.2090 90	非供零售用精梳其他动物细毛纱线(按重量计其他精梳动物细毛含量<85%)	5	70	17	16	千克		Yarn of fine hair of animal; combed, not in forms or packing for retail sale(containing <85% by weight of other animals, hair)
51.09	**羊毛或动物细毛的纱线,供零售用:**							**Yarn of wool or of fine animal hair, put up for retail sale:**
	-按重量计羊毛或动物细毛含量在85%及以上:							-Containing 85% or more by weight of wool or of fine animal hair:
	---动物细毛:							---Of fine animal hair:
5109.1011	----山羊绒的	6	80	17	16	千克		----Of goats

税则号列	货品名称	最惠(%)	普通	增值税率	出口退税	计量单位	监管条件	Article Description
5109.1019	----其他	6	80	17	16	千克		----Other
5109.1090	---其他	6	80	17	16	千克		---Other
	-其他：							-Other:
	---动物细毛：							---Of fine animal hair:
5109.9011	----山羊绒的	6	80	17	16	千克		----Of goats
5109.9019	----其他	6	80	17	16	千克		----Other
5109.9090	---其他	6	80	17	16	千克		---Other
51.10	**动物粗毛或马毛的纱线(包括马毛粗松螺旋花线),不论是否供零售用：**							**Yarn of coarse animal hair or of horsehair (including gimped horsehair yarn), whether or not put up for retail sale:**
5110.0000	动物粗毛或马毛的纱线(包括马毛粗松螺旋花线),不论是否供零售用	6	70	17		千克		Yarn of coarse animal hair or of horsehair (including gimped horsehair yarn), whether or not put up for retail sale
5110.0000 10	濒危动物粗毛的纱线(包括马毛粗松螺旋花线,不论是否供零售用)	6	70	17		千克	FE	Yarn of coarse hair of endangered animals hair (including gimped horsehair yarn, whether or not in forms or packing for retail sale)
5110.0000 90	其他动物粗毛或马毛的纱线(包括马毛粗松螺旋花线,不论是否供零售用)	6	70	17	16	千克		Other yarn of coarse hair of animal or horsehair (including gimped horsehair yarn, whether or not put up for retail sale)
51.11	**粗梳羊毛或粗梳动物细毛的机织物：**							**Woven fabrics of carded wool or of carded fine animal hair:**
	-按重量计羊毛或动物细毛含量在85%及以上：							-Containing 85% or more by weight of wool or of fine animal hair:
	--每平方米重量不超过300克：							--Of a weight not exceeding 300 g/m^2:
	---动物细毛的：							---Of fine animal hair:
5111.1111	----山羊绒的	10	130	17	16	米/千克		----Of goats
5111.1119	----其他	10	130	17	16	米/千克		----Other
5111.1190	---其他	10	130	17	16	米/千克		---Other
	--其他：							--Other:
	---动物细毛的：							---Of fine animal hair:
5111.1911	----山羊绒的	10	130	17	16	米/千克		----Of goats
5111.1919	----其他	10	130	17	16	米/千克		----Other
5111.1990	---其他	10	130	17	16	米/千克		---Other
5111.2000	-其他,主要或仅与化学纤维长丝混纺	10	130	17	16	米/千克		-Other, mixed mainly or solely with manmade filaments
5111.2000 10	与化纤长丝混纺提花/装饰家具布(每平方米重量≤140克或>300克/平米,羊毛或动物细毛含量<85%)	10	130	17	16	米/千克		Jacquard/decorative, w≤140g/m^2, or w>300g/m^2, mixed with man-made filaments, containing<85% by weight of wool and fine animal hair
5111.2000 90	与化纤长丝混纺其他粗梳毛机织物(羊毛或动物细毛含量<85%)	10	130	17	16	米/千克		Other woven fabrics of carded wool or of carded animal hair, mixed with man-made filaments, containing<85% by weight of wool and fine animal hair
5111.3000	-其他,主要或仅与化学纤维短纤混纺	10	130	17	16	米/千克		-Other, mixed mainly or solely with man-made staple fibres
5111.3000 10	与化纤短纤混纺提花/装饰家具布(每平方米重量≤140g或>300g,羊毛或动物细毛含量<85%)	10	130	17	16	米/千克		Jacquard/decorative, mixed with man-made staple fibres, (w≤140g/m^2 or w>300g/m^2, mixed with containing<85% by weight of wool and fine animal hair)
5111.3000 90	与化纤短纤混纺其他粗梳毛机织物(羊毛或动物细毛含量<85%)	10	130	17	16	米/千克		Other woven fabrics of carded wool or of carded fine animal hair, mixed with man-made staple fibres (containing<85% by weight of wool and fine animal hair)
5111.9000	-其他	10	130	17	16	米/千克		-Other
5111.9000 11	其他丝与粗梳羊毛或动物细毛混纺(丝及绢丝≥30%,粗梳羊毛或动物细毛含量<85%,价值>$33/kg)	10	130	17	16	米/千克		Mixed with other silk and carded wool or of fine animal hair (containing≥30% by weight of silk and spun silk, containing<85% by weight of carded wool or of carded fine animal hair, value>USD 33/kg)

税则号列	货品名称	最惠(%)	普通	增值税率	出口退税	计量单位	监管条件	Article Description
5111.9000 19	其他丝混纺机织物(丝及绢丝≥30%,粗梳羊毛或动物细毛含量<85%,价值>$33/kg)	10	130	17	16	米/千克		Other woven fabrics, mixed with silk (containing ≥30% by weight of silk and spun silk, containing <85% by weight of carded wool or of fine animal hair, value > USD 33/kg)
5111.9000 21	其他毛混纺提花/装饰家具布(粗梳羊毛或动物细毛<85%,重量≤140克/平方米或>300克/平方米)	10	130	17	16	米/千克		Jacquard/decorative, mixed with wool or animals hair (w ≤ 140g/m² or w > 300g/m², containing < 85% by weight of carded wool or of fine animal hair)
5111.9000 29	其他毛混纺提花/装饰家具布(粗梳羊毛/动物细毛含量<85%,重量≤140克/平方米或>300克/平方米)	10	130	17	16	米/千克		Other jacquard/decorative, mixed with wool or animal hair (containing <85% by weight of carded wool or of fine animal hair, w ≤ 140g/m² or w > 300g/m²)
5111.9000 91	其他机织物(与粗梳羊毛或动物细毛混纺,粗梳羊毛或动物细毛含量<85%)	10	130	17	16	米/千克		Other woven fabrics (mixed with carded wool or fine animal hair, containing <85% by weight of carded wool or of fine animal hair)
5111.9000 99	其他机织物(与其他混纺,粗梳羊毛或动物细毛含量<85%)	10	130	17	16	米/千克		Other woven fabrics (mixed, containing < 85% by weight of carded wool or of fine animal hair)
51.12	**精梳羊毛或精梳动物细毛的机织物:**							**Woven fabrics of combed wool or of combed fine animal hair:**
	-按重量计羊毛或动物细毛含量在85%及以上:							-Containing 85% or more by weight of wool or of fine animal hair:
5112.1100	--每平方米重量不超过200克	10	130	17	16	米/千克		--Of a weight not exceeding 200 g/m²
5112.1100 10	每平方米重≤140g的毛提花/装饰家具布(精梳羊毛或动物细毛含量≥85%)	10	130	17	16	米/千克		Jacquard/decorative, w ≤ 140g/m² (containing ≥ 85% by weight of combed wool or of fine animal hair)
5112.1100 90	其他每平方米重量≤200g毛制机织物(精梳羊毛或动物细毛含量≥85%)	10	130	17	16	米/千克		Other wool woven fabrics, w≤200g/m² (containing ≥85% by weight of combed wool or of fine animal hair)
5112.1900	--其他	10	130	17	16	米/千克		--Other
5112.1900 10	每平方米重>200g的毛提花/装饰家具布(精梳羊毛或动物细毛含量≥85%)	10	130	17	16	米/千克		Jacquard/decorative, w > 200g/m², containing ≥ 85% by weight of combed wool or of fine animal hair
5112.1900 90	每平方米重量>200g的其他毛制机织物(精梳羊毛或动物细毛含量≥85%)	10	130	17	16	米/千克		Other wool woven fabrics, w >200g/m² (containing ≥85% by weight of combed wool or of fine animal hair)
5112.2000	-其他,主要或仅与化学纤维长丝混纺	10	130	17	16	米/千克		-Other, mixed mainly or solely with manmade filaments
5112.2000 10	与化纤长丝混纺毛制提花/家具布(精梳羊毛或动物细毛含量<85%,每平方米重≤140g或每平方米>300g)	10	130	17	16	米/千克		Jacquard/decorative, mixed with man-made filaments, (w≤140g/m² or w >300g/m², containing < 85% by weight of combed wool or of fine animal hair)
5112.2000 90	与化纤长丝混纺其他毛制机织物(精梳羊毛或动物细毛含量<85%)	10	130	17	16	米/千克		Other wool woven fabrics, mixed with man-made filaments (containing <85% by weight of combed wool or of fine animal hair)
5112.3000	-其他,主要或仅与化学纤维短纤混纺	10	130	17	16	米/千克		-Other, mixed mainly or solely with man-made staple fibres
5112.3000 10	与化纤短纤混纺毛制提花/家具布(精梳羊毛或动物细毛含量<85%,重≤140克/平方米或>300克/平方米)	10	130	17	16	米/千克		Jacquard/decorative, mixed with man-made staple fibres (containing <85% by weight of combed wool or of fine animal hair, w≤140g/m² or w >300 g/m²)
5112.3000 90	与化纤短纤混纺其他毛制机织物(精梳羊毛或动物细毛含量<85%)	10	130	17	16	米/千克		Other wool woven fabrics, mixed with man-made staple fibres (containing <85% by weight of combed wool or of fine animals, hair)
5112.9000	-其他	10	130	17	16	米/千克		-Other

税则号列	货品名称	最惠(%)	普通	增值税率	出口退税	计量单位	监管条件	Article Description
5112.9000 10	其他丝与毛混纺机织物(精梳羊毛或动物细毛含量<85%,丝及绢丝≥30%,价值>＄33/kg)	10	130	17	16	米/千克		Other woven fabrics, mixed with silk and wool or animal hair(containing <85% by weight of combed wool or of fine animal hair, containing ≥30% by weight of silk and spun silk, value >USD 33/Kg)
5112.9000 20	其他精梳毛制提花/装饰家具布(含羊毛或动物细毛<85%,每平方米重量≤140g或>300g)	10	130	17	16	米/千克		Other jacquard/decorative of combed hair(containing <85% by weight of wool or fine animal hair, w ≤140g/m² or w >300g/m²)
5112.9000 90	其他机织物(精梳羊毛或动物细毛<85%)	10	130	17	16	米/千克		Other woven fabrics(containing <85% by weight of combed wool or of fine animal hair)
51.13	**动物粗毛或马毛的机织物:**							**Woven fabrics of coarse animal hair or of horsehair:**
5113.0000	动物粗毛或马毛的机织物	10	130	17	16	米/千克		Woven fabrics of coarse animal hair or of horsehair

第五十二章
棉　　花

Chapter 52
Cotton

子目注释：

子目号5209.42及5211.42所称"粗斜纹布(劳动布)"，是指用不同颜色的纱线织成的三线或四线斜纹织物，包括破斜纹组织的织物，这种织物以经纱为面，经纱染成一种相同的颜色，纬纱未漂白或经漂白、染成灰色或比经纱稍浅的颜色。

Subheading Note:

For the purposes of subheadings Nos. 5209.42 and 5211.42, the expression "denim" means fabrics of yarns of different colours, of 3-thread or 4-thread twill, including broken twill, warp faced, the warp yarns of which are of one and the same colour and the weft yarns of which are unbleached, bleached, dyed grey or coloured a lighter shade of the colour of the warp yarns.

税则号列	货品名称	最惠(%)	普通	增值税率	出口退税	计量单位	监管条件	Article Description
52.01	**未梳的棉花:**							**Cotton, not carded or combed:**
5201.0000	未梳的棉花			13	13	千克		Cotton, not carded or combed
5201.0000 01	未梳的棉花[包括脱脂棉花(配额内)]	1	125	13	13	千克	t4xAB	Cotton, not carded or combed[including absorbent cotton(in-quota)]
5201.0000 80	未梳的棉花[包括脱脂棉花(关税配额外暂定)]	0	0	13	13	千克	4ABex	Cotton, not carded or combed[including absorben cotton (custom,out - guota,interim)]
5201.0000 90	未梳的棉花[包括脱脂棉花(配额外)]	40	125	13	13	千克	4xAB	Cotton, not carded or combed[including absorbent cotton(out-quota)]
52.02	**废棉(包括废棉纱线及回收纤维):**							**Cotton waste (including yarn waste and garnetted stock):**
5202.1000	-废棉纱线(包括废棉线)	10	30	17	13	千克	AP	-Yarn waste (including thread waste)
	-其他:							-Other:
5202.9100	--回收纤维	10	30	17	13	千克	ABP	--Garnetted stock
5202.9900	--其他	10	30	17	13	千克	ABP	--Other
52.03	**已梳的棉花:**							**Cotton, carded or combed:**
5203.0000	已梳的棉花		125	17	13	千克		Cotton, carded or combed
5203.0000 01	已梳的棉花(配额内)	1	125	17	13	千克	t4xAB	Cotton, carded or combed(in-quota)
5203.0000 90	已梳的棉花(配额外)	40	125	17	13	千克	4xAB	Cotton, carded or combed(out-quota)
52.04	**棉制缝纫线,不论是否供零售用:**							**Cotton sewing thread, whether or not put up for retail sale:**
	-非供零售用:							-Not put up for retail sale:
5204.1100	--按重量计含棉量在85%及以上	5	40	17	16	千克		--Containing 85% or more by weight of cotton
5204.1900	--其他	5	40	17	16	千克		--Other
5204.2000	-供零售用	5	50	17	16	千克		-Put up for retail sale
52.05	**棉纱线(缝纫线除外),按重量计含棉量在85%及以上,非供零售用:**							**Cotton yarn (other than sewing thread), containing 85% or more by weight of cotton, not put up for retail sale:**
	-未精梳纤维纺制的单纱:							-Single yarn, of uncombed fibres:
5205.1100	--细度在714.29分特及以上(不超过14公支)	5	40	17	16	千克		--Measuring 714.29 decitex or more (not exceeding 14 metric number)
5205.1200	--细度在714.29分特以下,但不细于232.56分特(超过14公支,但不超过43公支)	5	40	17	16	千克		--Measuring less than 714.29 decitex but not less than 232.56 decitex (exceeding 14 metric number but not exceeding 43 metric number)
5205.1300	--细度在232.56分特以下,但不细于192.31分特(超过43公支,但不超过52公支)	5	40	17	16	千克		--Measuring less than 232.56 decitex but not less than 192.31 decitex (exceeding 43 metric number but not exceeding 52 metric number)
5205.1400	--细度在192.31分特以下,但不细于125分特(超过52公支,但不超过80公支)	5	40	17	16	千克		--Measuring less than 192.31 decitex but not less than 125 decitex (exceeding 52 metric number but not exceeding 80 metric number)
5205.1500	--细度在125分特以下(超过80公支)	5	40	17	16	千克		--Measuring less than 125 decitex (exceeding 80 metric number)
	-精梳纤维纺制的单纱:							-Single yarn, of combed fibres:
5205.2100	--细度在714.29分特及以上(不超过14公支)	5	40	17	16	千克		--Measuring 714.29 decitex or more (not exceeding 14 metric number)

税则号列	货品名称	最惠(%)	普通	增值税率	出口退税	计量单位	监管条件	Article Description
5205.2200	--细度在714.29分特以下,但不细于232.56分特(超过14公支,但不超过43公支)	5	40	17	16	千克		--Measuring less than 714.29 decitex but not less than 232.56 decitex (exceeding 14 metric number but not exceeding 43 metric number)
5205.2300	--细度在232.56分特以下,但不细于192.31分特(超过43公支,但不超过52公支)	5	40	17	16	千克		--Measuring less than 232.56 decitex but not less than 192.31 decitex (exceeding 43 metric number but not exceeding 52 metric number)
5205.2400	--细度在192.31分特以下,但不细于125分特(超过52公支,但不超过80公支)	5	40	17	16	千克		--Measuring less than 192.31 decitex but not less than 125 decitex (exceeding 52 metric number but not exceeding 80 metric number)
5205.2600	--细度在125分特以下,但不细于106.38分特(超过80公支,但不超过94公支)	5	40	17	16	千克		--Measuring less than 125 decitex but not less than 106.38 decitex (exceeding 80 metric number but not exceeding 94 metric number)
5205.2700	--细度在106.38分特以下,但不细于83.33分特(超过94公支,但不超过120公支)	5	40	17	16	千克		--Measuring less than 106.38 decitex but not less than 83.33 decitex (exceeding 94 metric number but not exceeding 120 metric number)
5205.2800	--细度在83.33分特以下(超过120公支)	5	40	17	16	千克		--Measuring less than 83.33 decitex (exceeding 120 metric number)
	-未精梳纤维纺制的多股纱线或缆线:							-Multiple (folded) or cabled yarn, of uncombed fibres:
5205.3100	--每根单纱细度在714.29分特及以上(每根单纱不超过14公支)	5	40	17	16	千克		--Measuring per single yarn 714.29 decitex or more (not exceeding 14 metric number per single yarn)
5205.3200	--每根单纱细度在714.29分特以下,但不细于232.56分特(每根单纱超过14公支,但不超过43公支)	5	40	17	16	千克		--Measuring per single yarn less than 714.29 decitex but not less than 232.56 decitex (exceeding 14 metric number but not exceeding 43 metric number per single yarn)
5205.3300	--每根单纱细度在232.56分特以下,但不细于192.31分特(每根单纱超过43公支,但不超过52公支)	5	40	17	16	千克		--Measuring per single yarn less than 232.56 decitex but not less than 192.31 decitex (exceeding 43 metric number but not exceeding 52 metric number per single yarn)
5205.3400	--每根单纱细度在192.31分特以下,但不细于125分特(每根单纱超过52公支,但不超过80公支)	5	40	17	16	千克		--Measuring per single yarn less than 192.31 decitex but not less than 125 decitex (exceeding 52 metric number but not exceeding 80 metric number per single yarn)
5205.3500	--每根单纱细度在125分特以下(每根单纱超过80公支)	5	40	17	16	千克		--Measuring per single yarn less than 125 decitex (exceeding 80 metric number per single yarn)
	-精梳纤维纺制的多股纱线或缆线:							-Multiple (folded) or cabled yarn, of combed fibres:
5205.4100	--每根单纱细度在714.29分特及以上(每根单纱不超过14公支)	5	40	17	16	千克		--Measuring per single yarn 714.29 decitex or more (not exceeding 14 metric number per single yarn)
5205.4200	--每根单纱细度在714.29分特以下,但不细于232.56分特(每根单纱超过14公支,但不超过43公支)	5	40	17	16	千克		--Measuring per single yarn less than 714.29 decitex but not less than 232.56 decitex (exceeding 14 metric number but not exceeding 43 metric number per single yarn)
5205.4300	--每根单纱细度在232.56分特以下,但不细于192.31分特(每根单纱超过43公支,但不超过52公支)	5	40	17	16	千克		--Measuring per single yarn less than 232.56 decitex but not less than 192.31 decitex (exceeding 43 metric number but not exceeding 52 metric number per single yarn)
5205.4400	--每根单纱细度在192.31分特以下,但不细于125分特(每根单纱超过52公支,但不超过80公支)	5	40	17	16	千克		--Measuring per single yarn less than 192.31 decitex but not less than 125 decitex (exceeding 52 metric number but not exceeding 80 metric number per single yarn)
5205.4600	--每根单纱细度在125分特以下,但不细于106.38分特(每根单纱超过80公支,但不超过94公支)	5	40	17	16	千克		--Measuring per single yarn less than 125 decitex but not less than 106.38 decitex (exceeding 80 metric number but not exceeding 94 metric number per single yarn)

税则号列	货品名称	最惠(%)	普通	增值税率	出口退税	计量单位	监管条件	Article Description
5205.4700	--每根单纱细度在106.38分特以下,但不细于83.33分特(每根单纱超过94公支,但不超过120公支)	5	40	17	16	千克		--Measuring per single yarn less than 106.38 decitex but not less than 83.33 decitex (exceeding 94 metric number but not exceeding 120 metric number per single yarn)
5205.4800	--每根单纱细度83.33分特以下(每根单纱超过120公支)	5	40	17	16	千克		--Measuring per single yarn less than 83.33 decitex (exceeding 120 metric number per single yarn)
52.06	**棉纱线(缝纫线除外),按重量计含棉量在85%以下,非供零售用:**							**Cotton yarn (other than sewing thread), containing less than 85% by weight of cotton, not put up for retail sale:**
	-未精梳纤维纺制的单纱:							-Single yarn, of uncombed fibres:
5206.1100	--细度在714.29分特及以上(不超过14公支)	5	40	17	16	千克		--Measuring 714.29 decitex or more (not exceeding 14 metric number)
5206.1200	--细度在714.29分特以下,但不细于232.56分特(超过14公支,但不超过43公支)	5	40	17	16	千克		--Measuring less than 714.29 decitex but not less than 232.56 decitex (exceeding 14 metric number but not exceeding 43 metric number)
5206.1300	--细度在232.56分特以下,但不细于192.31分特(超过43公支,但不超过52公支)	5	40	17	16	千克		--Measuring less than 232.56 decitex but not less than 192.31 decitex (exceeding 43 metric number but not exceeding 52 metric number)
5206.1400	--细度在192.31分特以下,但不细于125分特(超过52公支,但不超过80公支)	5	40	17	16	千克		--Measuring less than 192.31 decitex but not less than 125 decitex (exceeding 52 metric number but not exceeding 80 metric number)
5206.1500	--细度在125分特以下(超过80公支)	5	40	17	16	千克		--Measuring less than 125 decitex (exceeding 80 metric number)
	-精梳纤维纺制的单纱:							-Single yarn, of combed fibres:
5206.2100	--细度在714.29分特及以上(不超过14公支)	5	40	17	16	千克		--Measuring 714.29 decitex or more (not exceeding 14 metric number)
5206.2200	--细度在714.29分特以下,但不细于232.56分特(超过14公支,但不超过43公支)	5	40	17	16	千克		--Measuring less than 714.29 decitex but not less than 232.56 decitex (exceeding 14 metric number but not exceeding 43 metric number)
5206.2300	--细度在232.56分特以下,但不细于192.31分特(超过43公支,但不超过52公支)	5	40	17	16	千克		--Measuring less than 232.56 decitex but not less than 192.31 decitex (exceeding 43 metric number but not exceeding 52 metric number)
5206.2400	--细度在192.31分特以下,但不细于125分特(超过52公支,但不超过80公支)	5	40	17	16	千克		--Measuring less than 192.31 decitex but not less than 125 decitex (exceeding 52 metric number but not exceeding 80 metric number)
5206.2500	--细度在125分特以下(超过80公支)	5	40	17	16	千克		--Measuring less than 125 decitex (exceeding 80 metric number)
	-未精梳纤维纺制的多股纱线或缆线:							-Multiple (folded) or cabled yarn, of uncombed fibres:
5206.3100	--每根单纱细度在714.29分特及以上(每根单纱不超过14公支)	5	40	17	16	千克		--Measuring per single yarn 714.29 decitex or more (not exceeding 14 metric number per single yarn)
5206.3200	--每根单纱细度在714.29分特以下,但不细于232.56分特(每根单纱超过14公支,但不超过43公支)	5	40	17	16	千克		--Measuring per single yarn less than 714.29 decitex but not less than 232.56 decitex (exceeding 14 metric number but not exceeding 43 metric number per single yarn)
5206.3300	--每根单纱细度在232.56分特以下,但不细于192.31分特(每根单纱超过43公支,但不超过52公支)	5	40	17	16	千克		--Measuring per single yarn less than 232.56 decitex but not less than 192.31 decitex (exceeding 43 metric number but not exceeding 52 metric number per single yarn)
5206.3400	--每根单纱细度在192.31分特以下,但不细于125分特(每根单纱超过52公支,但不超过80公支)	5	40	17	16	千克		--Measuring per single yarn less than 192.31 decitex but not less than 125 decitex (exceeding 52 metric number but not exceeding 80 metric number per single yarn)
5206.3500	--每根单纱细度在125分特以下(每根单纱超过80公支)	5	40	17	16	千克		--Measuring per single yarn less than 125 decitex (exceeding 80 metric number per single yarn)

税则号列	货品名称	最惠(%)	普通	增值税率	出口退税	计量单位	监管条件	Article Description
	-精梳纤维纺制的多股纱线或缆线:							-Multiple (folded) or cabled yarn, of combed fibres:
5206.4100	--每根单纱细度在714.29分特及以上(每根单纱不超过14公支)	5	40	17	16	千克		--Measuring per single yarn 714.29 decitex or more (not exceeding 14 metric number per single yarn)
5206.4200	--每根单纱细度在714.29分特以下,但不细于232.56分特(每根单纱超过14公支,但不超过43公支)	5	40	17	16	千克		--Measuring per single yarn less than 714.29 decitex but not less than 232.56 decitex (exceeding 14 metric number but not exceeding 43 metric number per single yarn)
5206.4300	--每根单纱细度在232.56分特以下,但不细于192.31分特(每根单纱超过43公支,但不超过52公支)	5	40	17	16	千克		--Measuring per single yarn less than 232.56 decitex but not less then 192.31 decitex (exceeding 43 metric number but not exceeding 52 metric number per single yarn)
5206.4400	--每根单纱细度在192.31分特以下,但不细于125分特(每根单纱超过52公支,但不超过80公支)	5	40	17	16	千克		--Measuring per single yarn less than 192.31 decitex but not less than 125 decitex (exceeding 52 metric number but not exceeding 80 metric number per single yarn)
5206.4500	--每根单纱细度在125分特以下(每根单纱超过80公支)	5	40	17	16	千克		--Measuring per single yarn less than 125 decitex (exceeding 80 metric number per single yarn)
52.07	**棉纱线(缝纫线除外),供零售用:**							**Cotton yarn (other than sewing thread) put up for retail sale:**
5207.1000	-按重量计含棉量在85%及以上	6	50	17	16	千克		-Containing 85% or more by weight of cotton
5207.9000	-其他	6	50	17	16	千克		-Other
52.08	**棉机织物,按重量计含棉量在85%及以上,每平方米重量不超过200克:**							**Woven fabrics of cotton, containing 85% or more by weight of cotton, weighing not more than 200 g/m²:**
	-未漂白:							-Unbleached:
5208.1100	--平纹机织物,每平方米重量不超过100克	10	70	17	16	米/千克		--Plain weave, weighing not more than 100 g/m²
5208.1100 10	未漂白全棉平纹府绸及细平布(每平方米重量≤100g,含棉85%及以上)	10	70	17	16	米/千克		Poplin and muslin of cotton, w≤100g/m², containing≥85% by weight of cotton, unbleached
5208.1100 20	未漂白全棉平纹机织平布(每平方米重≤100g,68号及以下)	10	70	17	16	米/千克		Plain cloth of cotton (w≤100g/m², unbleached, ≤No. 68)
5208.1100 30	未漂白全棉平纹奶酪布(每平方米重≤100g,含棉量≥85%)	10	70	17	16	米/千克		Cheese cloth, plain weave, w≤100g/m², containing≥85% by weight of cotton, unbleached
5208.1100 40	未漂白全棉平纹印染用布(每平方米重≤100g,43-68号)	10	70	17	16	米/千克		Cloth for printing and dying of cotton, plain weave, No. 43 ~ No. 68, w≤100g/m², unbleached
5208.1100 50	未漂白全棉平纹巴里纱及薄细布(每平方米重≤100g,69号及以上)	10	70	17	16	米/千克		Voiles and fine thin cloth of cotton, plain weave, w≤100g/m², unbleached, ≥No. 69
5208.1100 60	未漂白全棉平纹机织打字布(每平方米重≤100g,含棉量≥85%)	10	70	17	16	米/千克		Typewriter ribbon of cotton, plain weave, w≤100g/m², containing ≥85% by weight of cotton, unbleached
5208.1100 70	未漂白全棉医用纱布(每平方米重≤100g,含棉量85%及以上)	10	70	17	16	米/千克		Medical gauze of cotton, w≤100g/m², containing ≥85% by weight of cotton, unbleached
5208.1200	--平纹机织物,每平方米重量超过100克	10	70	17	16	米/千克		--Plain weave, weighing more than 100 g/m²
5208.1200 10	未漂白全棉平纹府绸及细平布(100g<每平方米重≤200g,含棉量≥85%)	10	70	17	16	米/千克		Poplin and fine plain cloth of cotton, 100g/m² < w ≤200g/m², containing≥85% by weight of cotton, unbleached
5208.1200 20	未漂白全棉平纹机织平布(100g<每平方米重量≤200g,68号及以下)	10	70	17	16	米/千克		Plain cloth of cotton, 100g/m² < w≤200g/m², ≤ No. 68, unbleached
5208.1200 30	未漂白全棉平纹奶酪布(100g<每平方米重≤200g,含棉量≥85%)	10	70	17	16	米/千克		Cheese cloth of cotton, plain weave, 100g/m² < w≤200g/m², containing≥85% by weight of cotton, unbleached
5208.1200 40	未漂白全棉平纹印染用布(100g<每平方米重≤200g,43-68号)	10	70	17	16	米/千克		Cloth for printing and dying of cotton, plain weave, No. 43 ~ No. 68, 100g/m² < w ≤ 200g/m², unbleached

税则号列	货　品　名　称	最惠(%)	普通	增值税率	出口退税	计量单位	监管条件	Article Description
5208.1200 50	未漂白全棉平纹巴里纱及薄细布(100g＜每平方米重≤200g,69号及以上)	10	70	17	16	米/千克		Voiles and swiss muslin of cotton, plain weave, 100g/m^2 < w≤200g/m^2, ≥No. 69, unbleached
5208.1300	--三线或四线斜纹机织物,包括双面斜纹机织物	10	70	17	16	米/千克		--3-thread or 4-thread twill, including cross twill
5208.1900	--其他机织物	10	70	17	16	米/千克		--Other fabrics
5208.1900 10	未漂白其他全棉机织缎布(每平方米重量不超过200克,含棉85%及以上)	10	70	17	16	米/千克		Woven fabrics of cotton, satin weave, w ≤ 200g/m^2, containing ≥ 85% by weight of cotton, unbleached
5208.1900 20	未漂白其他全棉机织斜纹布(每平方米重≤200g,含棉量≥85%)	10	70	17	16	米/千克		Woven fabrics of cotton, twill weave, w≤200g/m^2, containing≥85% by weight of cotton, unbleached
5208.1900 30	未漂白其他全棉机织牛津布(每平方米重≤200g,含棉量≥85%)	10	70	17	16	米/千克		Woven fabrics of cotton oxford weave, w ≤ 200g/m^2, containing ≥ 85% by weight of cotton, unbleached
5208.1900 90	未漂白的其他全棉机织物(每平方米重≤200g,含棉量≥85%)	10	70	17	16	米/千克		Other woven fabrics of cotton, w≤200g/m^2, containing≥85% by weight of cotton, unbleached
	-漂白:							-Bleached:
5208.2100	--平纹机织物,每平方米重量不超过100克	10	70	17	16	米/千克		--Plain weave, weighing not more than 100 g/m^2
5208.2100 10	漂白全棉平纹府绸及细平布(每平方米重≤100g,含棉量≥85%)	10	70	17	16	米/千克	A	Poplin and fine plain cloth of cotton, w≤100g/m^2, containing≥85% by weight of cotton, bleached
5208.2100 20	漂白全棉平纹机织平布(每平方米重≤100g,68号及以下)	10	70	17	16	米/千克	A	Woven fabrics of cotton, plain weave, ≤No. 68, w≤100g/m^2, bleached
5208.2100 30	漂白全棉平纹奶酪布(每平方米重≤100g,含棉量≥85%)	10	70	17	16	米/千克	A	Cheese cloth of cotton, plain weave, w≤100g/m^2, containing≥85% by weight of cotton, bleached
5208.2100 40	漂白全棉平纹印染用布(每平方米重≤100g,43-68号)	10	70	17	16	米/千克	A	Cloth for printing and dying of cotton, plain weave, No. 43 ~ No. 68, w≤100g/m^2, bleached
5208.2100 50	漂白全棉平纹巴里纱及薄细布(每平方米重量≤100g,69号及以上)	10	70	17	16	米/千克	A	Voiles and swiss muslim of cotton, plain weave, w≤100g/m^2, containing≥85% by weight of cotton, ≥No. 69, bleached
5208.2100 60	漂白全棉医用纱布(每平方米重≤100g,含棉量≥85%)	10	70	17	16	米/千克	A	Medical gauze of cotton, w≤100g/m^2, containing ≥85% by weight of cotton, bleached
5208.2200	--平纹机织物,每平方米重量超过100克	10	70	17	16	米/千克		--Plain weave, weighing more than 100 g/m^2
5208.2200 10	漂白全棉平纹府绸及细平布(100g＜每平方米重量≤200g,含棉量≥85%)	10	70	17	16	米/千克	A	Poplin and fine plain cloth of cotton, plain weave, 100g/m^2 < w ≤ 200g/m^2, containing ≥ 85% by weight of cotton, bleached
5208.2200 20	漂白全棉平纹机织平布(100g＜每平方米重≤200g,68号及以下)	10	70	17	16	米/千克	A	Plain cloth of cotton, plain weave, 100g/m^2 < w≤200g/m^2, ≤No. 68, bleached
5208.2200 30	漂白全棉平纹奶酪布(100g＜每平方米重≤200g,含棉量≥85%)	10	70	17	16	米/千克	A	Cheese cloth of cotton, plain weave, 100g/m^2 < w≤200g/m^2, containing≥85% by weight of cotton, bleached
5208.2200 40	漂白全棉平纹印染用布(100g＜每平方米重≤200g,43-68号)	10	70	17	16	米/千克	A	Cloth for printing and dying, of cotton, plain weave, No. 43 ~ No. 68, 100g/m^2 < w≤200g/m^2, bleached
5208.2200 50	漂白全棉巴里纱及薄细布(100g＜每平方米重≤200g,69号及以上)	10	70	17	16	米/千克	A	Voiles and swiss muslin of cotton, 100g/m^2 < w≤200g/m^2, ≥No. 69, bleached
5208.2300	--三线或四线斜纹机织物,包括双面斜纹机织物	12	70	17	16	米/千克	A	--3-thread or 4-thread twill, including cross twill
5208.2900	--其他机织物	10	70	17	16	米/千克		--Other fabrics
5208.2900 10	漂白其他全棉机织缎布(每平方米重≤200g,含棉量≥85%)	10	70	17	16	米/千克	A	Woven fabrics of cotton, satin weave, w ≤ 200 g/m^2, containing ≥ 85% by weight of cotton, bleached
5208.2900 20	漂白其他全棉机织斜纹布(每平方米重≤200g,含棉量≥85%)	10	70	17	16	米/千克	A	Woven fabrics of cotton, twill weave, w ≤ 200 g/m^2, containing ≥ 85% by weight of cotton, bleached

税则号列	货品名称	最惠(%)	普通	增值税率	出口退税	计量单位	监管条件	Article Description
5208.2900 30	漂白其他全棉机织牛津布(每平方米重≤200g,含棉量≥85%)	10	70	17	16	米/千克	A	Woven fabrics of cotton, oxford weave, w ≤ 200 g/m^2, containing ≥ 85% by weight of cotton, bleached
5208.2900 90	漂白其他全棉机织物(每平方米重≤200g,含棉量≥85%)	10	70	17	16	米/千克	A	Other woven fabrics of cotton, w≤200g/m^2, containing≥85% by weight of cotton, bleached
	-染色:							-Dyed:
5208.3100	--平纹机织物,每平方米重量不超过100克	10	70	17	16	米/千克		--Plain weave, weighing not more than 100 g/m^2
5208.3100 10	染色全棉手工织布(每平方米重≤100g,含棉量≥85%)	10	70	17	16	米/千克	A	Handwoven plain cloth of cotton, w ≤ 100g/m^2, containing≥85% by weight of cotton, dyed
5208.3100 91	染色全棉平纹府绸及细平布(每平方米重≤100g,含棉量≥85%)	10	70	17	16	米/千克	A	Popin and fine plain cloth of cotton, w≤100g/m^2, containing≥85% by weight of cotton, dyed
5208.3100 92	染色全棉平纹机织平布(每平方米重≤100g,68号及以下)	10	70	17	16	米/千克	A	Plain cloth of cotton, w≤100g/m^2, ≤No. 68, dyed
5208.3100 93	染色全棉平纹奶酪布(每平方米重≤100g,含棉量≥85%)	10	70	17	16	米/千克	A	Cheese cloth of cotton, w≤100 g/m^2, containing≥85% by weight of cotton, dyed
5208.3100 94	染色全棉平纹印染用布(每平方米重≤100g,43-68号)	10	70	17	16	米/千克	A	Cloth for printing and dying, of cotton, plain weave, No. 43 ~ No. 68, w≤100g/m^2, dyed
5208.3100 95	染色全棉巴里纱及薄细布(每平方米重≤100g,69号及以上)	10	70	17	16	米/千克	A	Voiles and fine thin cloth of cotton, w≤100g/m^2, ≥No. 69, dyed
5208.3200	--平纹机织物,每平方米重量超过100克	10	70	17	16	米/千克		--Plain weave, weighing more than 100 g/m^2
5208.3200 10	染色全棉手工织布(100g<每平方米重≤200g,含棉量≥85%)	10	70	17	16	米/千克	A	Handwoven plain cloth of cotton, 100g/m^2 < w ≤ 200g/m^2, containing ≥ 85% by weight of cotton, dyed
5208.3200 91	染色全棉平纹府绸及细平布(100g<每平方米重≤200g,含棉量≥85%)	10	70	17	16	米/千克	A	Poplin and fine plain cloth of cotton, 100g/m^2 < w ≤200g/m^2, containing≥85% by weight of cotton, dyed
5208.3200 92	染色全棉平纹机织平布(100g<每平方米重≤200g,68号及以下)	10	70	17	16	米/千克	A	Plain cloth of cotton, 100g/m^2 < w≤200g/m^2, ≤ No. 68, dyed
5208.3200 93	染色全棉平纹奶酪布(100g<每平方米重≤200g,含棉量≥85%)	10	70	17	16	米/千克	A	Cheese cloth of cotton, plain weave, 100g/m^2 < w ≤200g/m^2, containing≥85% by weight of cotton, dyed
5208.3200 94	染色全棉平纹印染用布(100g<每平方米重≤200g,43-68号)	10	70	17	16	米/千克	A	Cloth for printing and dying of cotton, plain weave, No. 43 ~ No. 68, 100g/m^2 < w≤200g/m^2, dyed
5208.3200 95	染色全棉巴里纱及薄细布(100g<每平方米重≤200g,69号及以上)	10	70	17	16	米/千克	A	Voiles and swiss muslin of cotton, 100g/m^2 < w ≤ 200g/m^2, ≥No. 69, dyed
5208.3300	--三线或四线斜纹机织物,包括双面斜纹机织物	10	70	17	16	米/千克	A	--3-thread or 4-thread twill, including cross twill
5208.3900	--其他机织物	10	70	17	16	米/千克		--Other fabrics
5208.3900 10	染色其他全棉机织缎布(每平方米重≤200g,含棉量≥85%)	10	70	17	16	米/千克	A	Woven fabrics of cotton, satin weave, w≤200 g/m^2, containing≥85% by weight of cotton, dyed
5208.3900 20	染色其他全棉机织斜纹布(每平方米重≤200g,含棉量≥85%)	10	70	17	16	米/千克	A	Woven fabrics of cotton, twill weave, w≤200 g/m^2, containing≥85% by weight of cotton, dyed
5208.3900 30	染色其他全棉机织牛津布(每平方米重≤200g,含棉量≥85%)	10	70	17	16	米/千克	A	Woven fabrics of cotton, oxford weave, w ≤ 200 g/m^2, containing≥85% by weight of cotton, dyed
5208.3900 90	染色其他全棉机织物(每平方米重≤200g,含棉量≥85%)	10	70	17	16	米/千克	A	Other woven fabrics of cotton, w≤200g/m^2, containing≥85% by weight of cotton, dyed
	-色织:							-Of yarns of different colours:
5208.4100	--平纹机织物,每平方米重量不超过100克	10	70	17	16	米/千克		--Plain weave, weighing not more than 100 g/m^2
5208.4100 10	色织的全棉手工织布(每平方米重≤100g,含棉量≥85%)	10	70	17	16	米/千克	A	Handwoven cloth of cotton, w≤100g/m^2, containing≥85% by weight of cotton, of yarns of different colours
5208.4100 90	色织的全棉平纹机织物(每平方米重≤100g,含棉量≥85%)	10	70	17	16	米/千克	A	Woven fabrics of cotton, plain weave, w ≤ 100 g/m^2, containing ≥ 85% by weight of cotton, of yarns of different colours
5208.4200	--平纹机织物,每平方米重100克	10	70	17	16	米/千克		--Plain weave, weighing more than 100 g/m^2

税则号列	货品名称	最惠(%)	普通	增值税率	出口退税	计量单位	监管条件	Article Description
5208.4200 10	色织的全棉手工织布(100g<每平方米重≤200g,含棉量≥85%)	10	70	17	16	米/千克	A	Handwoven cloth of cotton, 100g/m² < w ≤ 200 g/m², containing ≥ 85% by weight of cotton, of yarns of different colours
5208.4200 90	色织的全棉平纹机织物(100克<每平方米重≤200g,含棉量≥85%)	10	70	17	16	米/千克	A	Woven fabrics of cotton, plain weave, 100g/m² < w ≤200g/m², containing≥85% by weight of cotton, of yarns of different colours
5208.4300	--三线或四线斜纹机织物,包括双面斜纹机织物	10	70	17	16	米/千克	A	--3-thread or 4-thread twill, including cross twill
5208.4900	--其他机织物	10	70	17	16	米/千克		--Other fabrics
5208.4900 10	色织的其他全棉提花机织物(每平方米重≤200g,含棉量≥85%)	10	70	17	16	米/千克	A	Other woven fabrics of cotton, jacquard weave, w≤200g/m², containing≥85% by weight of cotton, of yarns of different colours
5208.4900 90	色织的其他全棉机织物(每平方米重≤200g,含棉量≥85%)	10	70	17	16	米/千克	A	Other woven fabrics of cotton, w≤200g/m², containing≥85% by weight of cotton, of yarns of different colours
	-印花:							-Printed:
5208.5100	--平纹机织物,每平方米重量不超过100克	10	70	17	16	米/千克		--Plain weave, weighing not more than 100 g/m²
5208.5100 10	印花全棉手工织布(每平方米重≤100g,含棉量≥85%)	10	70	17	16	米/千克	A	Handwoven cloth of cotton, w≤100g/m², containing≥85% by weight of cotton, printed
5208.5100 91	印花全棉平纹府绸及细平布(每平方米重≤100g,含棉量≥85%)	10	70	17	16	米/千克	A	Poplin and fine plain cloth of cotton, w≤100g/m², containing≥85% by weight of cotton, printed
5208.5100 92	印花全棉平纹机织平布(每平方米重≤100g,68号及以下)	10	70	17	16	米/千克	A	Plain cloth of cotton, plain weave, w≤100g/m², ≤No. 68, printed
5208.5100 93	印花全棉平纹奶酪布(每平方米重≤100g,含棉量≥85%)	10	70	17	16	米/千克	A	Cheese cloth of cotton, plain weave, w≤100 g/m², containing≥85% by weight of cotton, printed
5208.5100 94	印花全棉平纹印染用布(每平方米重≤100g,43-68号)	10	70	17	16	米/千克	A	Cloth for printing and dying of cotton, plain weave, w≤100g/m², No. 43 ~ No. 68, printed
5208.5100 95	印花全棉平纹巴里纱及薄细布(每平方米重≤100g,69号及以上)	10	70	17	16	米/千克	A	Voiles and swiss muslin of cotton, w≤100g/m², ≥No. 69, printed
5208.5200	--平纹机织物,每平方米重量超过100g	10	70	17	16	米/千克		--Plain weave, weighing more than 100 g/m²
5208.5200 10	印花的全棉手工织布(100g<每平方米重≤200g,含棉量≥85%)	10	70	17	16	米/千克	A	Handwoven cloth of cotton, 100g/m² <w≤200 g/m², containing≥85% by weight of cotton, printed
5208.5200 91	印花的全棉平纹府绸及细平布(100g<每平方米重≤200g,含棉量≥85%)	10	70	17	16	米/千克	A	Poplin and fine plain cloth of cotton, 100g/m² < w ≤200g/m², containing≥85% by weight of cotton, printed
5208.5200 92	印花的全棉平纹机织平布(100g<每平方米重≤200g,68号及以下)	10	70	17	16	米/千克	A	Plain cloth of cotton, 100g/m² < w ≤ 200g/m², ≤No. 68 printed
5208.5200 93	印花的全棉平纹奶酪布(100g<每平方米重量≤200g,含棉量≥85%)	10	70	17	16	米/千克	A	Cheese cloth of cotton, plain weave, 100g/m² < w≤200g/m², containing ≥ 85% by weight of cotton, printed
5208.5200 94	印花的全棉平纹印染用布(100g<每平方米重≤200g,43-68号)	10	70	17	16	米/千克	A	Cloth for printing and dying of cotton, plain weave, 100g/m² < w≤200g/m², No. 43 ~ No. 68, printed
5208.5200 95	印花的全棉巴里纱及薄细布(100g<每平方米重≤200g,69号及以上)	10	70	17	16	米/千克	A	Voiles and swiss muslin of cotton 100g/m² < w ≤ 200g/m², ≥No. 69, printed
	--其他机织物:							--Other fabrics:
5208.5910	---三线或四线斜纹机织物,包括双面斜纹机织物	10	70	17	16	米/千克	A	---3-thread or 4-thread twill, including cross twill
5208.5990	---其他	10	70	17	16	米/千克		---Other
5208.5990 10	印花其他全棉机织缎布(每平方米重≤200g,含棉量≥85%)	10	70	17	16	米/千克	A	Woven fabrics of cotton, satin weave, w≤200g/m² containing≥85% by weight of cotton, printed
5208.5990 20	印花其他全棉机织斜纹布(每平方米重≤200g,含棉量≥85%)	10	70	17	16	米/千克	A	Woven fabrics of cotton, twill weave, w≤200 g/m², containing≥85% by weight of cotton, printed
5208.5990 30	印花其他全棉机织牛津布(每平方米重≤200g,含棉量≥85%)	10	70	17	16	米/千克	A	Woven fabrics of cotton, oxford weave w ≤ 200 g/m², containing≥85% by weight of cotton, printed

税则号列	货品名称	最惠(%)	普通	增值税率	出口退税	计量单位	监管条件	Article Description
5208.5990 90	印花其他全棉机织物(每平方米重≤200g,含棉量≥85%)	10	70	17	16	米/千克	A	Other woven fabrics of cotton, w≤200g/m², containing≥85% by weight of cotton, printed
52.09	**棉机织物,按重量计含棉量在85%及以上,每平方米重量超过200克:**							**Woven fabrics of cotton, containing 85% or more by weight of cotton, weighing more than 200 g/m²:**
	-未漂白:							-Unbleached:
5209.1100	--平纹机织物	10	70	17	16	米/千克		--Plain weave
5209.1100 10	未漂白全棉平纹府绸及细平布(指每平方米重>200克,含棉量≥85%)	10	70	17	16	米/千克		Poplin and fine plain cloth of cotton, w>200g/m², containing≥85% by weight of cotton, unbleached
5209.1100 20	未漂白的全棉平纹机织平布(指每平方米重>200克,含棉量≥85%)	10	70	17	16	米/千克		Plain cloth of cotton, w>200g/m², containing≥85% by weight of cotton, unbleached
5209.1100 30	未漂白的全棉平纹机织帆布(指每平方米重>200克,含棉量≥85%)	10	70	17	16	米/千克		Canvas of cotton, plain weave, w>200g/m², containing≥85% by weight of cotton, unbleached
5209.1200	--三线或四线斜纹机织物,包括双面斜纹机织物	10	70	17	16	米/千克		--3-thread or 4-thread twill, including cross twill
5209.1900	--其他机织物	10	70	17	16	米/千克		--Other fabrics
5209.1900 10	未漂白的其他全棉机织缎布(指每平方米重>200克,含棉量≥85%)	10	70	17	16	米/千克		Other woven fabrics of cotton, satin weave, w>200g/m², containing≥85% by weight of cotton, unbleached
5209.1900 20	未漂白的其他全棉机织斜纹布(指每平方米重>200克,含棉量≥85%)	10	70	17	16	米/千克		Other woven fabrics of cotton, twill weave, w>200g/m², containing≥85% by weight of cotton, unbleached
5209.1900 30	未漂白的其他全棉机织帆布(指每平方米重>200克,含棉量≥85%)	10	70	17	16	米/千克		Other woven canvas of cotton, w>200g/m², containing≥85% by weight of cotton, unbleached
5209.1900 90	未漂白的其他全棉机织物(指每平方米重>200克,含棉量≥85%)	10	70	17	16	米/千克		Other woven fabrics of cotton, w>200g/m², containing≥85% by weight of cotton, unbleached
	-漂白:							-Bleached:
5209.2100	--平纹机织物	12	70	17	16	米/千克		--Plain weave
5209.2100 10	漂白的全棉平纹府绸及细平布(指每平方米重>200克,含棉量≥85%)	12	70	17	16	米/千克		Poplin and fine plain cloth of cotton, w>200g/m², containing≥85% by weight of cotton, bleached
5209.2100 20	漂白的全棉平纹机织平布(指每平方米重>200克,含棉量≥85%)	12	70	17	16	米/千克		Plain cloth of cotton, w>200g/m², containing≥85% by weight of cotton, bleached
5209.2100 30	漂白的全棉平纹机织帆布(指每平方米重>200克,含棉量≥85%)	12	70	17	16	米/千克		Woren canvas of cotton, plain weave, w>200 g/m², containing≥85% by weight of cotton, bleached
5209.2200	--三线或四线斜纹机织物,包括双面斜纹机织物	12	70	17	16	米/千克		--3-thread or 4-thread twill, including cross twill
5209.2900	--其他机织物	12	70	17	16	米/千克		--Other fabrics
5209.2900 10	漂白的其他全棉机织缎布(指每平方米重>200克,含棉量≥85%)	12	70	17	16	米/千克		Other woven fabrics of cotton, satin weave, w>200g/m², containing≥85% by weight of cotton, bleached
5209.2900 30	漂白的其他全棉机织帆布(指每平方米重>200克,含棉量≥85%)	12	70	17	16	米/千克		Other woren canvas of cotton, w>200g/m², containing≥85% by weight of cotton, bleached
5209.2900 90	漂白的其他全棉机织物(指每平方米重>200克,含棉量≥85%)	12	70	17	16	米/千克		Other woven fabrics of cotton, w>200g/m², containing≥85% by weight of cotton, bleached
	-染色:							-Dyed:
5209.3100	--平纹机织物	10	70	17	16	米/千克		--Plain weave
5209.3100 10	染色全棉手工织布(指每平方米重>200克,含棉量≥85%)	10	70	17	16	米/千克	A	Handwoven cloth of cotton, w>200g/m², containing≥85% by weight of cotton, dyed
5209.3100 91	染色全棉平纹府绸及细平布(指每平方米重>200克,含棉量≥85%)	10	70	17	16	米/千克	A	Poplin and fine plain cloth of cotton, w>200g/m², containing≥85% by weight of cotton, dyed
5209.3100 92	染色的全棉平纹机织平布(指每平方米重>200克,含棉量≥85%)	10	70	17	16	米/千克	A	Plain cloth of cotton, w>200g/m², containing≥85% by weight of cotton, dyed
5209.3100 93	染色的全棉平纹机织帆布(指每平方米重>200克,含棉量≥85%)	10	70	17	16	米/千克	A	Woven canvas of cotton, plain weave, w>200 g/m², containing≥85% by weight of cotton, dyed

税则号列	货品名称	最惠(%)	普通	增值税率	出口退税	计量单位	监管条件	Article Description
5209.3200	--三线或四线斜纹机织物,包括双面斜纹机织物	10	70	17	16	米/千克	A	--3-thread or 4-thread twill, including cross twill
5209.3900	--其他机织物	10	70	17	16	米/千克		--Other fabrics
5209.3900 10	染色的其他全棉机织缎布(指每平方米重>200克,含棉量≥85%)	10	70	17	16	米/千克	A	Other woven fabrics of cotton, satin weave, w>200 g/m², containing≥85% by weight of cotton, dyed
5209.3900 20	染色的其他全棉机织斜纹布(指每平方米重>200克,含棉量≥85%)	10	70	17	16	米/千克	A	Other woven fabrics of cotton, twill weave, w>200 g/m², containing≥85% by weight of cotton, dyed
5209.3900 30	染色的其他全棉机织帆布(指每平方米重量>200克,含棉量≥85%)	10	70	17	16	米/千克	A	Other woren canvas of cotton, w>200g/m², containing≥85% by weight of cotton, dyed
5209.3900 90	染色的其他全棉机织物(指每平方米重量>200克,含棉量≥85%)	10	70	17	16	米/千克	A	Other woven fabrics of cotton, w>200g/m², containing≥85% by weight of cotton, dyed
	-色织:							-Of yarns of different colours:
5209.4100	--平纹机织物	10	70	17	16	米/千克		--Plain weave
5209.4100 10	色织的全棉手工织布(指每平方米重>200克,含棉量≥85%)	10	70	17	16	米/千克	A	Handwoven cloth of cotton, w>200g/m² containing≥85% by weight of cotton, of yarns of different colours
5209.4100 90	色织的全棉平纹机织物(指每平方米重>200克,含棉量≥85%)	10	70	17	16	米/千克	A	Woven fabrics of cotton, plain weave, w>200g/m², containing≥85% by weight of cotton, of yarns of different colours
5209.4200	--粗斜纹布(劳动布)	10	70	17	16	米/千克		--Denim
5209.4200 10	色织全棉蓝粗斜纹布(劳动布)(指每平方米重>200克,含棉量≥85%)	10	70	17	16	米/千克	A	Blue denim of cotton, w>200g/m², containing≥85% by weight of cotton, of yarns of different colours
5209.4200 90	色织其他全棉粗斜纹布(劳动布)(指每平方米重>200克,含棉量≥85%)	10	70	17	16	米/千克	A	Other denim of cotton, w>200g/m², containing≥85% by weight of cotton, of yarns of different colours
5209.4300	--其他三线或四线斜纹机织物,包括双面斜纹机织物	10	70	17	16	米/千克	A	--Other fabrics of 3-thread or 4-thread twill, including cross twill
5209.4900	--其他机织物	10	70	17	16	米/千克		--Other fabrics
5209.4900 10	色织的其他全棉提花机织物(指每平米重>200克,含棉量≥85%)	10	70	17	16	米/千克	A	Other woven fabrics of cotton, jacquad weave, w>200g/m², containing≥85% by weight of cotton, of yarns of different colours
5209.4900 90	色织的其他全棉机织物(指每平米重>200克,含棉量≥85%)	10	70	17	16	米/千克	A	Other woven fabrics of cotton, w>200g/m², containing≥85% by weight of cotton, of yarns of different colours
	-印花:							-Printed:
5209.5100	--平纹机织物	10	70	17	16	米/千克		--Plain weave
5209.5100 10	印花全棉手工织布(指每平方米重>200克,含棉量≥85%)	10	70	17	16	米/千克	A	Handwoven cloth of cotton, w>200g/m², containing≥85% by weight of cotton, printed
5209.5100 91	印花全棉平纹府绸及细平布(指每平方米重>200克,含棉量≥85%)	10	70	17	16	米/千克	A	Poplin and fine plain cloth of cotton, w>200g/m², containing≥85% by weight of cotton, printed
5209.5100 92	印花全棉平纹机织平布(指每平方米重>200克,含棉量≥85%)	10	70	17	16	米/千克	A	Plain cloth of cotton, w>200g/m², containing≥85% by weight of cotton, printed
5209.5100 93	印花全棉平纹机织帆布(指每平方米重>200克,含棉量≥85%)	10	70	17	16	米/千克	A	Woven canvas of cotton, plain weave, w>200g/m², containing≥85% by weight of cotton, printed
5209.5200	--三线或四线斜纹机织物,包括双面斜纹机织物	10	70	17	16	米/千克	A	--3-thread or 4-thread twill, including cross twill
5209.5900	--其他机织物	10	70	17	16	米/千克		--Other fabrics
5209.5900 10	印花的其他全棉机织缎布(指每平方米重>200克,含棉量≥85%)	10	70	17	16	米/千克	A	Other woven fabrics of cotton, satin weave, w>200g/m², containing≥85% by weight of cotton, printed
5209.5900 20	印花的其他全棉机织斜纹布(指每平方米重>200克,含棉量≥85%)	10	70	17	16	米/千克	A	Other woven fabrics of cotton, twill weave, w>200 g/m², containing≥85% by weight of cotton, printed
5209.5900 30	印花的其他全棉机织帆布(指每平方米重>200克,含棉量≥85%)	10	70	17	16	米/千克	A	Otver canvas of cotton, w>200g/m², containing≥85% by weight of cotton, printed
5209.5900 90	印花的其他全棉机织物(指每平方米重>200克,含棉量≥85%)	10	70	17	16	米/千克	A	Other woven fabrics of cotton, w>200g/m², containing≥85% by weight of cotton, printed

税则号列	货品名称	最惠(%)	普通	增值税率	出口退税	计量单位	监管条件	Article Description
52.10	**棉机织物,按重量计含棉量在85%以下,主要或仅与化学纤维混纺,每平方米重量不超过200克:**							**Woven fabrics of cotton, containing less than 85% by weight of cotton, mixed mainly or solely with man-made fibres, weighing not more than 200 g/m^2:**
	-未漂白:							-Unbleached:
5210.1100[暂]	--平纹机织物	6	90	17	16	米/千克		--Plain weave
5210.1100[暂] 11	未漂白与聚酯短纤混纺的棉制府绸(指每平方米重≤200克,含棉量<85%,含平细布)	6	90	17	16	米/千克		Poplin and fine plain cloth of cotton, mixed with polyester staple fibres, w≤200g/m^2, containing <85% by weight of cotton, unbleached
5210.1100[暂] 12	未漂白与聚酯短纤混纺棉机织平布(指每平方米重≤200克,68号及以下,含棉量<85%)	6	90	17	16	米/千克		Plain cloth of cotton, mixed with polyester staple fibres, w≤200g/m^2, ≤No. 68, containing <85% by weight of cotton, unbleached
5210.1100[暂] 13	未漂白与聚酯短纤混纺棉奶酪布(指每平方米重≤200克,含棉量<85%)	6	90	17	16	米/千克		Cheese cloth of cotton, plain weave, mixed with polyester staple fibres, w≤200g/m^2, containing <85% by weight of cotton, unbleached
5210.1100[暂] 14	未漂白与聚酯短纤混纺棉印染用布(指每平方米重≤200克,43-68号,含棉量<85%)	6	90	17	16	米/千克		Cloth for printing and dying of cotton, plain weave, mixed with polyester staple fibres, w≤200g/m^2, No. 43 ~ No. 68, containing <85% by weight of cotton, unbleached
5210.1100[暂] 15	未漂白与聚酯短纤混纺棉巴里纱(指每平方米重≤200克,69号及以上,含棉量<85%,含薄细布)	6	90	17	16	米/千克		Voiles and swiss muslin of cotton, plain weave, mixed with polyester staple fibres, w≤200g/m^2, containing <85% by weight of cotton, unbleached
5210.1100[暂] 91	未漂白与其他化纤混纺棉府绸(指每平方米重≤200克,含棉量<85%,含细平布)	6	90	17	16	米/千克		Poplin and fine plain cloth of cotton, mixed with other man-made fibres, w≤200g/m^2, containing <85% by weight of cotton, unbleached
5210.1100[暂] 92	未漂白与其他化纤混纺棉机织平布(指每平方米重≤200克,≤68号,含棉量<85%)	6	90	17	16	米/千克		Plain cloth of cotton, mixed with other man-made fibres, w≤200g/m^2, ≤No. 68, containing <85% by weight of cotton, unbleached
5210.1100[暂] 93	未漂白与其他化纤混纺棉奶酪布(指每平方米重≤200克,含棉量<85%)	6	90	17	16	米/千克		Cheese cloth of cotton, plain weave, mixed with other man-made fibres, w≤200g/m^2, containing <85% by weight of cotton, unbleached
5210.1100[暂] 94	未漂白与其他化纤混纺棉印染用布(指每平方米重≤200克,43-68号,含棉量<85%)	6	90	17	16	米/千克		Cloth for printing and dying of cotton, plain weave, mixed with other man-made fibres, w≤200g/m^2, No. 43 ~ No. 68, containing <85% by weight of cotton, unbleached
5210.1100[暂] 95	未漂白与其他化纤混纺棉巴里纱(指每平方米重≤200克,69号及以上,含棉量<85%,含薄细布)	6	90	17	16	米/千克		Voiles and swiss muslin of cotton, mixed with man-made fibres, w≤200g/m^2, containing <85% by weight of cotton, ≥No. 69, unbleached
	--其他机织物:							--Other fabrics:
5210.1910	---三线或四线斜纹机织物,包括双面斜纹机织物	12	90	17	16	米/千克		---3-thread or 4-thread twill, including cross twill
5210.1910 10	未漂白与聚酯短纤混纺三、四线或双面棉斜纹布(每平方米重≤200克,含棉量<85%)	12	90	17	16	米/千克		Woven fabrics of cotton, twill weave, mixed with polyester staple fibres(3 or 4-thread), w≤200g/m^2, containing <85% by weight of cotton, unbleached
5210.1910 90	未漂白与其他化纤混纺三、四线或双面棉斜纹布(每平方米重≤200克,含棉量<85%)	12	90	17	16	米/千克		Woven fabrics of cotton, twill weave, mixed with other man-made fibres(3 or 4-thread), w≤200g/m^2, containing <85% by weight of cotton, unbleached)
5210.1990[暂]	---其他	6	90	17	16	米/千克		---Other
5210.1990[暂] 11	其他未漂白与聚酯短纤混纺的缎布(每平方米重≤200克,含棉量<85%)	6	90	17	16	米/千克		Other woven fabrics of cotton, satin weave, mixed with polyester staple fibres, w≤200g/m^2, containing <85% by weight of cotton, unbleached
5210.1990[暂] 12	其他未漂白与聚酯短纤混纺斜纹布(每平方米重≤200克,含棉量<85%)	6	90	17	16	米/千克		Other woven fabrics of cotton, twill weave, mixed with polyester staple fibres, w≤200g/m^2, containing <85% by weight of cotton, unbleached

税则号列	货品名称	最惠(%)	普通	增值税率	出口退税	计量单位	监管条件	Article Description
5210.1990暂 13	其他未漂白与聚酯短纤混纺牛津布(每平方米重≤200克,含棉量<85%)	6	90	17	16	米/千克		Other woven fabrics of cotton, oxford weave, mixed with polyester staple fibres, w≤200g/m^2, containing <85% by weight of cotton, unbleached
5210.1990暂 19	其他未漂白与聚酯短纤混纺棉布(每平方米重≤200克,含棉量<85%)	6	90	17	16	米/千克		Other woven fabrics of cotton, mixed with polyester staple fibres, w ≤ 200g/m^2, containing < 85% by weight of cotton, unbleached
5210.1990暂 91	其他未漂白与其他化纤混纺缎布(每平方米重≤200克,含棉量<85%)	6	90	17	16	米/千克		Other woven of cotton, stain weave, mixed with other man-made fibres, w ≤ 200g/m^2, containing < 85% by weight of cotton, unbleached
5210.1990暂 92	其他未漂白与其他化纤混纺斜纹布(每平方米重≤200克,含棉量<85%)	6	90	17	16	米/千克		Other woven fabrics of cotton, twill weave, mixed with other man-made fibres, w≤200 g/m^2, containing <85% by weight of cotton, unbleached
5210.1990暂 93	其他未漂白与其他化纤混纺的牛津布(每平方米重≤200克,含棉量<85%)	6	90	17	16	米/千克		Other woven fabrics of cotton, oxford weave, mixed with other man-made fibres, w≤200g/m^2, by weight of cotton, unbleached
5210.1990暂 99	其他未漂白与其他化纤混纺棉布(每平米重≤200克,含棉量<85%)	6	90	17	16	米/千克		Other woven fabrics of cotton, mixed with other man-made fibres. w ≤ 200g/m^2, containing < 85% by weight of cotton, unbleached
	-漂白:							-Bleached:
5210.2100	--平纹机织物	14	90	17	16	米/千克		--Plain weave
5210.2100 11	漂白与聚酯短纤混纺棉府绸(每平方米重≤200克,含棉量<85%,含细平布)	14	90	17	16	米/千克		Poplin and fine plain cloth of cotton, mixed with polyester staple fibres w ≤ 200g/m^2, containing < 85% by weight of cotton, bleached
5210.2100 12	漂白与聚酯短纤混纺棉机织平布(每平方米重≤200克,68号及以下,含棉量<85%)	14	90	17	16	米/千克		Plain cloth of cotton, mixed with polyester staple fibres w≤200g/m^2, containing <85% by weight of cotton, bleached, ≤No. 68
5210.2100 13	漂白与聚酯短纤混纺棉奶酪布(每平方米重≤200克,含棉量<85%)	14	90	17	16	米/千克		Cheese cloth of cotton, plain weave, mixed with polyester staple fibres, w≤200g/m^2, containing < 85% by weight of cotton, bleached
5210.2100 14	漂白与聚酯短纤混纺棉印染布(每平方米重≤200克,43-68号,含棉量<85%)	14	90	17	16	米/千克		Cloth for printing and dying of cotton, mixed with polyester staple fibres, w ≤ 200g/m^2 containing < 85% by weight of cotton, No. 43 ~ 68, bleached
5210.2100 15	漂白与聚酯短纤混纺棉巴里纱(每平方米重≤200克,69号及以上,含棉量<85%,含薄细布)	14	90	17	16	米/千克		Poplin and swiss muslin of cotton, plain weave, mixed with polyester staple fibres w ≤ 200g/m^2, containing < 85% by weight of cotton, ≥ No. 69, bleached
5210.2100 21	漂白与化纤长丝混纺棉府绸(每平方米重≤200克,含棉量<85%,含细平布)	14	90	17	16	米/千克		Poplin and fine plain cloth of cotton, plain weave, mixed with man-made filaments w≤200g/m^2, containing <85% by weight of cotton, bleached
5210.2100 22	漂白与化纤长丝混纺棉机织平布(每平方米重≤200克,68号及以下,含棉量<85%)	14	90	17	16	米/千克		Plain cloth of cotton, mixed with man-made filaments, w≤200g/m^2, containing <85% by weight of cotton, ≤No. 68, bleached
5210.2100 23	漂白与化纤长丝混纺棉奶酪布(每平方米重≤200克,含棉量<85%)	14	90	17	16	米/千克		Cheese cloth of cotton, plain weave, mixed with man-made filaments, w ≤ 200g/m^2, containing < 85% by weight of cotton, bleached
5210.2100 24	漂白与化纤长丝混纺棉印染布(每平方米重≤200克,43-68号,含棉量<85%)	14	90	17	16	米/千克		Cloth for printing and dying of cotton, plain weave, mixed with man-made filaments, w≤200g/m^2, containing < 85% by weight of cotton, No. 43 ~ 68, bleached
5210.2100 25	漂白与化纤长丝混纺棉巴里纱(每平方米重≤200克,69号及以上,含棉量<85%,含薄细布)	14	90	17	16	米/千克		Voiles and swiss muslin of cotton, plain weave, mixed with man-made filaments w≤200g/m^2, containing < 85% by weight of cotton, ≥ No. 69, bleached
5210.2100 91	漂白与其他化纤混纺棉府绸(每平方米重≤200克,含棉量<85%,含细平布)	14	90	17	16	米/千克		Poplin and fine plain cloth of cotton, mixed with other man-mad fibres w ≤ 200g/m^2, containing < 85% by weight of cotton, bleached

税则号列	货品名称	最惠(%)	普通	增值税率	出口退税	计量单位	监管条件	Article Description
5210.2100 92	漂白与其他化纤混纺棉机织平布(每平方米重≤200克,68号及以下,含棉量<85%)	14	90	17	16	米/千克		Plain cloth of cotton, plain weave, mixed with other man-made fibres w≤200g/m², containing <85% by weight of cotton, ≤No. 68, bleached
5210.2100 93	漂白与其他化纤混纺棉奶酪布(每平方米重≤200克,含棉量<85%)	14	90	17	16	米/千克		Cheese cloth of cotton, plain weave, mixed with other man-made fibres, w≤200g/m², containing <85% by weight of cotton, bleached
5210.2100 94	漂白与其他化纤混纺棉印染布(每平方米重≤200克,43-68号,含棉量<85%)	14	90	17	16	米/千克		Cloth for printing and dying of cotton, plain weave, mixed with other man-made fibres w≤200g/m², containing <85% by weight of cotton, No. 43~68, bleached
5210.2100 95	漂白与其他化纤混纺棉巴里纱(每平方米重≤200克,69号及以上,含棉量<85%,含薄细布)	14	90	17	16	米/千克		Voiles and swiss muslin of cotton, plain weave, mixed with other man-made fibres, w≤200g/m², containing <85% by weight of cotton, ≥No. 69, bleached
	--其他机织物:							--Other fabrics:
5210.2910	---三线或四线斜纹机织物,包括双面斜纹机织物	14	90	17	16	米/千克		---3-thread or 4-thread twill, including cross twill
5210.2910 10	漂白与聚酯短纤混纺三、四线或双面棉斜纹布(每平方米重≤200克,含棉量<85%)	14	90	17	16	米/千克		Woven fabrics of cotton, twill weave, 3 or 4-thread twill, mixed with polyester staple fibres, w≤200g/m², containing <85% by weight of cotton
5210.2910 20	漂白与化纤长丝混纺三、四线或双面棉斜纹布(每平方米重≤200克,含棉量<85%)	14	90	17	16	米/千克		Wove fabrics of cotton, twill weave, 3 or 4-thread, mixed with man-made fila-ments, w≤200g/m², con-taining <85% by weight of cotton, bleached
5210.2910 90	漂白与其他化纤混纺三、四线或双面棉斜纹布(每平方米重≤200克,含棉量<85%)	14	90	17	16	米/千克		Woren fabrics of cotton, twill weave, 3 or 4-thread twill, mixed with man-made fibres, w≤200g/m², containing <85% by weight of cotton, bleached
5210.2990	---其他	14	90	17	16	米/千克		---Other
5210.2990 11	其他漂白与聚酯短纤混纺缎布(每平方米重≤200克,含棉量<85%)	14	90	17	16	米/千克		Other woven fabrics, satin weave, mixed with polyester staple fibres, w≤200g/m², containing <85% by weight of cotton, bleached
5210.2990 12	其他漂白与聚酯短纤混纺斜纹布(每平方米重≤200克,含棉量<85%)	14	90	17	16	米/千克		Other woven fabrics, twill weave, mixed with polyester staple fibres, w≤200g/m², containing <85% by weight of cotton, bleached
5210.2990 13	其他漂白与聚酯短纤混纺牛津布(每平方米重≤200克,含棉量<85%)	14	90	17	16	米/千克		Other woven fabrics, oxford weave, mixed with polyester staple fibres, w≤200g/m², containing <85% by weight of cotton, bleached
5210.2990 19	其他漂白与聚酯短纤混纺棉布(每平方米重≤200克,含棉量<85%)	14	90	17	16	米/千克		Other woven fabrics of cotton, mixed with polyester staple fibres, w≤200g/m², containing <85% by weight of cotton, bleached
5210.2990 21	其他漂白与化纤长丝混纺缎布(每平方米重≤200克,含棉量<85%)	14	90	17	16	米/千克		Other woven fabrics, satin weave, mixed with man-made filaments, w≤200g/m², containing <85% by weight of cotton, bleached
5210.2990 22	其他漂白与化纤长丝混纺斜纹布(每平方米重≤200克,含棉量<85%)	14	90	17	16	米/千克		Other woven fabrics, twill weave, mixed with man-made filaments, w≤200g/m², containing <85% by weight of cotton, bleached
5210.2990 23	其他漂白与化纤长丝混纺牛津布(每平方米重≤200克,含棉量<85%)	14	90	17	16	米/千克		Other woven fabrics, oxford weave, mixed with man-made filaments, w≤200g/m², containing <85% by weight of cotton, bleached
5210.2990 29	其他漂白与化纤长丝混纺棉布(每平方米重≤200克,含棉量<85%)	14	90	17	16	米/千克		Other woven fabrics of cotton, mixed with man-made filaments, w≤200g/m², containing <85% by weight of cotton, bleached
5210.2990 91	其他漂白与其他化纤混纺的缎布(每平方米重≤200克,含棉量<85%)	14	90	17	16	米/千克		Other woven fabrics, satin weave, mixed with other man-made fibres, w≤200g/m², containing <85% by weight of cotton, bleached
5210.2990 92	其他漂白与其他化纤混纺斜纹布(每平方米重≤200克,含棉量<85%)	14	90	17	16	米/千克		Other woven fabrics, twill weave, mixed with other man-made fibres, w≤200g/m², containing <85% by weight of cotton, bleached

税则号列	货品名称	最惠(%)	普通	增值税率	出口退税	计量单位	监管条件	Article Description
5210.2990 93	其他漂白与其他化纤混纺牛津布(每平方米重≤200克,含棉量<85%)	14	90	17	16	米/千克		Other woven fabrics, oxford weave, mixed with other man-made fibres, w≤200g/m², containing <85% by weight of cotton, bleached
5210.2990 99	其他漂白与其他化纤混纺棉布(每平方米重≤200克,含棉量<85%)	14	90	17	16	米/千克		Other woven fabrics of cotton, mixed with other man-made fibres, w≤200g/m², containing <85% by weight of cotton, bleached
	-染色:							-Dyed:
5210.3100	--平纹机织物	10	90	17	16	米/千克		--Plain weave
5210.3100 11	染色与聚酯短纤混纺棉府绸(每平方米重≤200克,含棉量<85%,含细平布)	10	90	17	16	米/千克		Poplin and fine plain cloth of cotton, mixed with polyester staple fibres, w≤200g/m², containing <85% by weight of cotton, dyed
5210.3100 12	染色与聚酯短纤混纺棉机织平布(每平方米重≤200克,68号及以下,含棉量<85%)	10	90	17	16	米/千克		Plain cloth of cotton, mixed with polyester staple fibres, w≤200g/m², containing <85% by weight of cotton, ≤No. 68, dyed
5210.3100 13	染色与聚酯短纤混纺棉奶酪布(每平方米重≤200克,含棉量<85%)	10	90	17	16	米/千克		Cheese cloth of cotton, plain weave, mixed with polyester staple fibres, w≤200g/m², containing <85% by weight of cotton, dyed
5210.3100 14	染色与聚酯短纤混纺棉印染布(每平方米重≤200克,43-68号,含棉量<85%)	10	90	17	16	米/千克		Cloth for printing and dying of cotton, plain weave, mixed with polyester staple fibres w≤200 g/m², containing <85% by weight of cotton, No. 43 ~ 68, dyed
5210.3100 15	染色与聚酯短纤混纺棉巴里纱(每平方米重≤200克,69号及以上,含棉量<85%,含薄细布)	10	90	17	16	米/千克		Voiles and swiss muslin of cotton, mixed with polyester staple fibres, w≤200g/m², containing <85% by weight of cotton, ≥No. 69, dyed
5210.3100 21	染色与化纤长丝混纺棉府绸(每平方米重≤200克,含棉量<85%,含细平布)	10	90	17	16	米/千克		Poplin and fine plain cloth of cotton, mixed with man-made filaments, w≤200g/m², containing <85% by weight of cotton, dyed
5210.3100 22	染色与化纤长丝混纺棉机织平布(每平方米重≤200克,含棉量<85%)	10	90	17	16	米/千克		Plain cloth of cotton, mixed with man-made filaments, w≤200g/m², containing <85% by weight of cotton, dyed
5210.3100 23	染色与化纤长丝混纺棉奶酪布(每平方米重≤200克,含棉量<85%)	10	90	17	16	米/千克		Cheese cloth of cotton, plain weave, mixed with man-made filaments, w≤200g/m², containing <85% by weight of cotton, dyed
5210.3100 24	染色与化纤长丝混纺棉印染布(每平方米重≤200克,43-68号,含棉量<85%)	10	90	17	16	米/千克		Cloth for printing and dying of cotton, plain weave, mixed with man-made filaments, w≤200g/m², containing <85% by weight of cotton, No. 43 ~ 68, dyed
5210.3100 25	染色与化纤长丝混纺棉巴里纱(每平方米重≤200克,69号及以上,含棉量<85%,含薄细布)	10	90	17	16	米/千克		Voiles and swiss muslin of cotton, plain weave, mixed with man-made filaments, w≤200g/m², containing <85% by weight of cotton, ≥No. 69, dyed
5210.3100 91	染色与其他化纤混纺棉府绸(每平方米重≤200克,含棉量<85%,含细平布)	10	90	17	16	米/千克		Poplin and fine plain cloth of cotton, mixed with other man-made fibres, w≤200g/m², containing <85% by weight of cotton, dyed
5210.3100 92	染色与其他化纤混纺棉机织平布(每平方米重≤200克,68号及以下,含棉量<85%)	10	90	17	16	米/千克		Plain cloth of cotton, mixed with other man-made fibres, w≤200g/m², containing <85% by weight of cotton, ≤No. 68, dyed
5210.3100 93	染色与其他化纤混纺棉奶酪布(每平方米重≤200克,含棉量<85%)	10	90	17	16	米/千克		Cheese cloth of cotton, plain weave, mixed with other man-made fibres, w≤200g/m², containing <85% by weight of cotton, dyed
5210.3100 94	染色与其他化纤混纺棉印染布(每平方米重≤200克,43-68号,含棉量<85%)	10	90	17	16	米/千克		Cloth for printing and dying of cotton, plain weave, mixed with other man-made fibres, w≤200g/m², containing <85% by weight of cotton, No. 43 ~ 68, dyed
5210.3100 95	染色与其他化纤混纺棉巴里纱(每平方米重≤200克,69号及以上,含棉量<85%,含薄细布)	10	90	17	16	米/千克		Voiles and swiss muslin of cotton, plain weave, mixed with other man-made fibres, w≤200g/m², containing <85% by weight of cotton, ≥No. 69, dyed

税则号列	货品名称	最惠(%)	普通	增值税率	出口退税	计量单位	监管条件	Article Description
5210.3200	--三线或四线斜纹机织物,包括双面斜纹机织物	10	90	17	16	米/千克		--3-thread or 4-thread twill, including cross twill
5210.3200 10	染色与聚酯短纤混纺的三、四线斜纹棉布(每平方米重≤200克,含棉量<85%,含双面斜纹布)	10	90	17	16	米/千克		Woven fabrics of cotton, twill weave, 3 or 4-thread, including cross twill, mixed with polyester staple fibres, w≤200g/m², containing <85% by weight of cotton, dyed
5210.3200 20	染色与化纤长丝混纺的三、四线斜纹棉布(每平方米重≤200克,含棉量<85%,含双面斜纹布)	10	90	17	16	米/千克		Woven fabrics of cotton, twill weave, 3 or 4-thread, including cross twill, mixed with man-made filaments, w≤200g/m², containing <85% by weight of cotton, dyed
5210.3200 90	染色与其他化纤混纺的三、四线斜纹棉布(每平方米重≤200克,含棉量<85%,含双面斜纹布)	10	90	17	16	米/千克		Woven fabrics of cotton, twill weave, 3 or 4-thread, including cross twill, mixed with other man-made fibres, w≤200g/m², containing <85% by weight of cotton, dyed
5210.3900	--其他机织物	10	90	17	16	米/千克		--Other fabrics
5210.3900 11	其他染色与聚酯短纤混纺缎布(每平方米重≤200克,含棉量<85%)	10	90	17	16	米/千克		Other woven fabrics of cotton, satin weave, mixed with polyester staple fibres, w≤200g/m², containing <85% by weight of cotton, dyed
5210.3900 12	其他染色与聚酯短纤混纺斜纹布(每平方米重≤200克,含棉量<85%)	10	90	17	16	米/千克		Other woven fabrics of cotton, twill weave, mixed with polyester staple fibres, w≤200g/m², containing <85% by weight of cotton, dyed
5210.3900 13	其他染色与聚酯短纤混纺牛津布(每平方米重≤200克,含棉量<85%)	10	90	17	16	米/千克		Other woven fabrics of cotton, oxford weave, mixed with polyester staple fibres, w≤200g/m², containing <85% by weight of cotton, dyed
5210.3900 19	其他染色与聚酯短纤混纺棉布(每平方米重≤200克,含棉量<85%)	10	90	17	16	米/千克		Other woven fabrics of cotton, mixed with polyester staple fibres, w≤200g/m², containing <85% by weight of cotton, dyed
5210.3900 21	其他染色与化纤长丝混纺缎布(每平方米重≤200克,含棉量<85%)	10	90	17	16	米/千克		Other woven fabrics of cotton, satin weave, mixed with man-made filaments, w≤200g/m², containing <85% by weight of cotton, dyed
5210.3900 22	其他染色与化纤长丝混纺斜纹布(每平方米重≤200克,含棉量<85%)	10	90	17	16	米/千克		Other woven fabrics of cotton, twill weave, mixed with man-made filaments, w≤200g/m², containing <85% by weight of cotton, dyed
5210.3900 23	其他染色与化纤长丝混纺牛津布(每平方米重≤200克,含棉量<85%)	10	90	17	16	米/千克		Other woven fabrics of cotton, oxford weave, mixed with man-made filaments, w≤200g/m², containing <85% by weight of cotton, dyed
5210.3900 29	其他染色与化纤长丝混纺棉布(每平方米重≤200克,含棉量<85%)	10	90	17	16	米/千克		Other woven fabrics of cotton, mixed with man-made filaments, w ≤ 200g/m², containing < 85% by weight of cotton, dyed
5210.3900 91	其他染色与其他化纤混纺缎布(每平方米重≤200克,含棉量<85%)	10	90	17	16	米/千克		Other woven fabrics of cotton, satin weave, mixed with other man-made fibres, w≤200g/m², containing <85% by weight of cotton, dyed
5210.3900 92	其他染色与其他化纤混纺斜纹布(每平方米重≤200克,含棉量<85%)	10	90	17	16	米/千克		Other woven fabrics of cotton, twill weave, mixed with other man-made fibres, w≤200g/m², containing <85% by weight of cotton, dyed
5210.3900 93	其他染色与其他化纤混纺牛津布(每平方米重≤200克,含棉量<85%)	10	90	17	16	米/千克		Other woven fabrics of cotton, oxford weave, mixed with other man-made fibres, w≤200g/m², containing <85% by weight of cotton, dyed
5210.3900 99	其他染色与其他化纤混纺棉布(每平方米重≤200克,含棉量<85%)	10	90	17	16	米/千克		Other woven fabrics of cotton, mixed with other man-made fibres, w≤200g/m², containing <85% by weight of cotton, dyed
	-色织:							-Of yarns of different colours:
5210.4100	--平纹机织物	10	90	17	16	米/千克		--Plain weave
5210.4100 10	色织与聚酯短纤混纺棉平纹布(每平方米重≤200克,含棉量<85%)	10	90	17	16	米/千克		Plain cloth of cotton, mixed with polyester staple fibres, w≤200g/m², containing <85% by weight of cotton, of yarns of different colours

税则号列	货品名称	最惠(%)	普通	增值税率	出口退税	计量单位	监管条件	Article Description
5210.4100 20	色织与化纤长丝混纺棉平纹布(每平方米重≤200克,含棉量<85%)	10	90	17	16	米/千克		Plain cloth of cotton, mixed with man-made filaments, w≤200g/m², containing <85% by weight of cotton, of yarns of different colours
5210.4100 90	色织与其他化纤混纺棉平纹布(每平方米重≤200克,含棉量<85%)	10	90	17	16	米/千克		Plain cloth of cotton, mixed with other man-made fibres, w≤200g/m², containing <85% by weight of cotton, of yarns of different colours
	--其他机织物:							--Other fabrics:
5210.4910	---三线或四线斜纹机织物,包括双面斜纹机织物	10	90	17	16	米/千克		---3-thread or 4-thread twill, including cross twill, including double twill
5210.4910 10	色织与聚酯短纤混纺三、四斜纹棉布(每平方米重≤200克,含棉量<85%,含双面斜纹布)	10	90	17	16	米/千克		Woven fabrics of cotton, twill weave(3 or 4-thread, cross twill), mixed with polyester staple fibres, w≤200g/m², containing <85% by weight of cotton, of yarns of different colours
5210.4910 20	色织与化纤长丝混纺三、四斜纹棉布(每平方米重≤200克,含棉量<85%,含双面斜纹布)	10	90	17	16	米/千克		Woven fabrics of cotton, twill weave(including 3 or 4-thread, cross twill), mixed with other man-made fibres, w≤200g/m², containing <85% by weight of cotton, of yarns of different colours
5210.4910 90	色织其他化纤混纺三、四斜纹棉布(每平方米重≤200克,含棉量<85%,含双面斜纹布)	10	90	17	16	米/千克		Woven fabrics of cotton, twill weave(including 3 or 4-thread, cross twill), mixed with other man-made fibres, w≤200g/m², containing <85% by weight of cotton, of yarns of different colours
5210.4990	---其他	10	90	17	16	米/千克		---Other
5210.4990 11	色织与聚酯短纤混纺提花布(每平方米重≤200克,含棉量<85%)	10	90	17	16	米/千克		Other woven fabrics of cotton, jacquard weave, mixed with polyester staple fibres, w≤200g/m², containing <85% by weight of cotton, of yarns of different colours
5210.4990 19	色织与聚酯短纤混纺其他棉布(每平方米重量≤200克,含棉量<85%)	10	90	17	16	米/千克		Other woven fabrics of cotton, mixed with polyester staple fibres, w≤200g/m², containing <85% by weight of cotton, of yarns of different colours
5210.4990 20	色织与化纤长丝混纺棉布(每平米重不超过200克,含棉85%以下)	10	90	17	16	米/千克		Woven fabrics of cotton, mixed with man - made filaments, w≤200g/m², containing <85% by weight of cotton, of yarn of different colours
5210.4990 90	色织与其他化纤混纺棉布(每平米重不超过200克,含棉85%以下)	10	90	17	16	米/千克		Woven fabrics of cotton, mixed with other man - made fibres, w≤200g/m², containing <85% by weight of cotton, of yarn of different colours
5210.5100	--平纹机织物	10	90	17	16	米/千克		--Plain weave
5210.5100 11	印花与聚酯短纤混纺的棉府绸(每平方米重≤200克,含棉量<85%,含细平布)	10	90	17	16	米/千克		Poplin and fine plain cloth of cotton, mixed with polyester staple fibres, w≤200g/m², containing <85% by weight of cotton printed
5210.5100 12	印花与聚酯短纤混纺棉机织平布(每平方米重≤200克,68号及以下,含棉量<85%)	10	90	17	16	米/千克		Plain cloth of cotton, mixed with polyester staple fibres, w≤200g/m², containing <85% by weight of cotton, ≤No. 68, printed
5210.5100 13	印花与聚酯短纤混纺的棉奶酪布(每平方米重≤200克,含棉量<85%)	10	90	17	16	米/千克		Cheese cloth of cotton, plain weave, mixed with polyester staple fibres, w≤200g/m², containing <85% by weight of cotton, printed
5210.5100 14	印花与聚酯短纤混纺棉印染布(每平方米重≤200克,43-68号,含棉量<85%)	10	90	17	16	米/千克		Cloth for printing and dying of cotton, plain weave, mixed with polyester staple fibres, w≤200g/m², containing <85% by weight of cotton, No. 43~68, printed
5210.5100 15	印花与聚酯短纤混纺棉巴里纱(每平方米重≤200克,69号及以上,含棉量<85%,含薄细布)	10	90	17	16	米/千克		Voiles and swiss muslin of cotton, mixed with polyester staple fibres, w≤200g/m², containing <85% by weight of cotton, ≥No. 69, printed
5210.5100 21	印花与化纤长丝混纺的棉府绸(每平方米重≤200克,含棉量<85%,含细平布)	10	90	17	16	米/千克		Poplin and fine plain cloth of cotton, mixed with man-made filaments, w≤200g/m², containing <85% by weight of cotton, printed

税则号列	货品名称	最惠(%)	普通	增值税率	出口退税	计量单位	监管条件	Article Description
5210.5100 22	印花与化纤长丝混纺棉机织平布(每平方米重≤200克,68号及以下,含棉量<85%)	10	90	17	16	米/千克		Plain cloth of cotton, mixed with man-made filaments, w≤200g/m^2, containing <85% by weight of cotton, ≤No. 68, printed
5210.5100 23	印花与化纤长丝混纺棉奶酪布(每平方米重≤200克,含棉量<85%)	10	90	17	16	米/千克		Cheese cloth of cotton, plain weave, mixed with man-made filaments, w≤200g/m^2, containing <85% by weight of cotton, printed
5210.5100 24	印花与化纤长丝混纺棉印染布(每平方米重≤200克,43-68号,含棉量<85%)	10	90	17	16	米/千克		Cloth for printing and dying of cotton, plain weave, mixed with man-made filaments, w≤200g/m^2, containing <85% by weight of cotton, No. 43 ~ 68, printed
5210.5100 25	印花与化纤长丝混纺棉巴里纱(每平方米重≤200克,69号及以上,含棉量<85%,含薄细布)	10	90	17	16	米/千克		Voiles and swiss muslin of cotton, mixed with man-made filaments, w≤200g/m^2, containing <85% by weight of cotton, ≥No. 69, printed
5210.5100 91	印花与其他化纤混纺的棉府绸(每平方米重≤200克,含棉量<85%,含细平布)	10	90	17	16	米/千克		Poplin and fine plain cloth of cotton, mixed with other man-made fibres, w≤200g/m^2, containing <85% by weight of cotton, printed
5210.5100 92	印花与其他化纤混纺棉机织平布(每平方米重≤200克,68号及以下,含棉量<85%)	10	90	17	16	米/千克		Plain cloth of cotton, mixed with other man-made fibres, w≤200g/m^2, containing <85% by weight of cotton, ≤No. 68, printed
5210.5100 93	印花与其他化纤混纺的棉奶酪布(每平方米重≤200克,含棉量<85%)	10	90	17	16	米/千克		Cheese cloth of cotton, plain weave mixed with other man-made fibres, w≤200g/m^2, containing <85% by weight of cotton, printed
5210.5100 94	印花与其他化纤混纺棉印染布(每平方米重≤200克,43-68号,含棉量<85%)	10	90	17	16	米/千克		Cloth for printing and dying of cotton, plain meave, mixed with other man-made fibres, w≤200g/m^2, containing <85% by weight of cotton, No. 43 ~ 68, printed
5210.5100 95	印花与其他化纤混纺棉巴里纱(每平方米重≤200克,65号及以上,含棉量<85%,含薄细布)	10	90	17	16	米/千克		Voiles and swiss muslin of cotton, mixed with other man-made fibres, w≤200g/m^2, containing <85% by weight of cotton, ≥No. 65, printed
	--其他机织物:							--Other fabrics:
5210.5910	---三线或四线斜纹机织物,包括双面斜纹机织物	10	90	17	16	米/千克		---3-thread or 4-thread twill, including cross twill
5210.5910 10	印花聚酯短纤混纺三、四线斜纹棉布(每平方米重≤200克,含棉量<85%,含双面斜纹布)	10	90	17	16	米/千克		Woven fabrics of cotton, twill weave(3 or 4-thread, cross twill), mixed with polyester staple fibres, w≤200g/m^2, containing <85% by weight of cotton, printed
5210.5910 20	印花化纤长丝混纺三、四线斜纹棉布(每平方米重≤200克,含棉量<85%,含双面斜纹布)	10	90	17	16	米/千克		Woven fabrics of cotton, twill weave(3 or 4-thread, cross twill), mixed with man-made filaments, w≤200g/m^2, con-taining <85% by weight of cotton, printed
5210.5910 90	印花其他化纤混纺三、四线斜纹棉布(每平方米重≤200克,含棉量<85%,含双面斜纹布)	10	90	17	16	米/千克		Woven fabrics of cotton, twill weave(3 or 4-thread, cross twill), mixed with other man-made fibres, w≤200g/m^2, containing <85% by weight of cotton, printed
5210.5990	---其他	10	90	17	16	米/千克		---Other
5210.5990 11	其他印花与聚酯短纤混纺缎布(每平方米重≤200克,含棉量<85%)	10	90	17	16	米/千克		Other woven fabrics of cotton, satin weave, mixed with polyester staple fibres, w≤200g/m^2, containing <85% by weight of cotton, printed
5210.5990 12	其他印花与聚酯短纤混纺斜纹布(每平方米重≤200克,含棉量<85%)	10	90	17	16	米/千克		Other woven fabrics of cotton, twill weave, mixed with polyester staple fibres, w≤200g/m^2, containing <85% by weight of cotton, printed
5210.5990 13	其他印花与聚酯短纤混纺牛津布(每平方米重≤200克,含棉量<85%)	10	90	17	16	米/千克		Other woven fabrics of cotton, oxford weave, mixed with man-made filaments, w≤200g/m^2, containing <85% by weight of cotton, printed
5210.5990 19	其他印花与聚酯短纤混纺棉布(每平方米重≤200克,含棉量<85%)	10	90	17	16	米/千克		Other woven fabrics of cotton, mixed with polyester staple fibres, w≤200g/m^2, containing <85% by weight of cotton, printed

税则号列	货　品　名　称	最惠(%)	普通	增值税率	出口退税	计量单位	监管条件	Article Description
5210.5990 21	其他印花与化纤长丝混纺缎布(每平方米重≤200克,含棉量<85%)	10	90	17	16	米/千克		Other woven fabrics of cotton, satin weave, mixed with man-made filaments, w≤200g/m², containing <85% by weight of cotton, printed
5210.5990 22	其他印花与化纤长丝混纺斜纹布(每平方米重≤200克,含棉量<85%)	10	90	17	16	米/千克		Other woven fabrics of cotton, twill weave, mixed with man-made filaments, w≤200g/m², containing <85% by weight of cotton, printed
5210.5990 23	其他印花与化纤长丝混纺牛津布(每平方米重≤200克,含棉量<85%)	10	90	17	16	米/千克		Other woven fabrics of cotton, oxford weave, mixed with man-made filaments, w≤200g/m², containing <85% by weight of cotton, printed
5210.5990 29	其他印花与化纤长丝混纺棉布(每平方米重≤200克,含量<85%)	10	90	17	16	米/千克		Other woven fabrics of cotton, mixed with man-made filaments, w≤200g/m², containing <85% by weight of cotton, printed
5210.5990 91	其他印花与其他化纤混纺缎布(每平方米重≤200克,含棉量<85%)	10	90	17	16	米/千克		Other woven fabrics of cotton, satin weave, mixed with other man-made fibres, w≤200g/m², containing <85% by weight of cotton, printed
5210.5990 92	其他印花与其他化纤混纺斜纹布(每平方米重≤200克,含棉量<85%)	10	90	17	16	米/千克		Other woven fabrics of cotton, twill weave, mixed with other man-made fibres, w≤200g/m², containing <85% by weight of cotton, printed
5210.5990 93	其他印花与其他化纤混纺牛津布(每平方米重≤200克,含棉量<85%)	10	90	17	16	米/千克		Other woven fabrics of cotton, oxford weave, mixed with other man-made fibres, w≤200g/m², containing <85% by weight of cotton, printed
5210.5990 99	其他印花与其他化纤混纺棉布(每平方米重≤200克,含棉量<85%)	10	90	17	16	米/千克		Other woven fabrics of cotton, mixed with other man-made fibres, w≤200g/m², containing <85% by weight of cotton, printed
52.11	**棉机织物,按重量计含棉量在85%以下,主要或仅与化学纤维混纺,每平方米重量超过200克:**							**Woven fabrics of cotton, containing less than 85% by weight of cotton, mixed mainly or solely with man-made fibres, weighing more than 200 g/m²:**
	-未漂白:							-Unbleached:
5211.1100暂	--平纹机织物	6	90	17	16	米/千克		--Plain weave
5211.1100暂 11	未漂白与聚酯短纤混纺棉府绸(每平方米重>200克,含棉量<85%,含细平布)	6	90	17	16	米/千克		Poplin and fine plain cloth of cotton, mixed with polyester staple fibres, w>200g/m², containing <85% by weight of cotton, unbleached
5211.1100暂 12	未漂白与聚酯短纤混纺棉机织平布(每平方米重>200克,含棉量<85%)	6	90	17	16	米/千克		Plain cloth of cotton, mixed with polyester staple fibres, w>200g/m², containing <85% by weight of cotton, unbleached
5211.1100暂 19	未漂白与聚酯短纤混纺棉平纹帆布(每平方米重>200克,含棉量<85%)	6	90	17	16	米/千克		Canvas of cotton, mixed with polyester staple fibres, plain weave, w>200g/m², containing <85% by weight of cotton, unbleached
5211.1100暂 91	未漂白与其他化纤混纺棉府绸(每平方米重>200克,含棉量<85%,含细平布)	6	90	17	16	米/千克		Poplin and fine plain cloth of cotton, mixed with other man-made fibres, w>200g/m², containing <85% by weight of cotton, unbleached
5211.1100暂 92	未漂白与其他化纤混纺棉机织平布(每平方米重>200克,含棉量<85%)	6	90	17	16	米/千克		Plain cloth of cotton, mixed with other man-made fibres, w>200g/m², containing <85% by weight of cotton, unbleached
5211.1100暂 99	未漂白与其他化纤混纺棉平纹帆布(每平方米重>200克,含棉量<85%)	6	90	17	16	米/千克		Canvas of cotton, mixed with other man-made fibres, plain weave, w>200g/m², containing <85% by weight of cotton, unbleached
5211.1200暂	--三线或四线斜纹机织物,包括双面斜纹机织物	6	90	17	16	米/千克		--3-thread or 4-thread twill, including cross twill
5211.1200暂 10	未漂白聚酯短纤混纺斜纹棉布(每平方米重>200克,含棉量<85%,三、四线斜纹布,双面斜纹布)	6	90	17	16	米/千克		Woven fabrics of cotton, twill weave (3-or 4-thread), mixed with polyester staple fibres, w>200 g/m², containing <85% by weight of cotton, unbleached

税则号列	货品名称	最惠(%)	普通	增值税率	出口退税	计量单位	监管条件	Article Description
5211.1200暂 90	未漂白其他化纤混纺斜纹棉布(每平方米重>200克,含棉量<85%,三、四线斜纹布,双面斜纹布)	6	90	17	16	米/千克		Woven fabrics of cotton, twill weave (3-or 4-thread), mixed with other man-made fibres, w>200g/m², containing <85% by weight of cotton, unbleached
5211.1900	--其他机织物	12	90	17	16	米/千克		--Other fabrics
5211.1900 11	未漂白与聚酯短纤混纺其他棉缎布(每平方米重>200克,含棉量<85%)	12	90	17	16	米/千克		Other woven fabrics of cotton, satin weave, mixed with polyester staple fibres, w>200g/m², containing <85% by weight of cotton, unbleached
5211.1900 12	未漂白与聚酯短纤混纺其他棉斜纹布(每平方米重>200克,含棉量<85%)	12	90	17	16	米/千克		Other woven fabrics of cotton, twill weave, mixed with polyester staple fibres, w>200g/m², containing <85% by weight of cotton, unbleached
5211.1900 13	未漂白与聚酯短纤混纺其他棉帆布(每平方米重>200克,含棉量<85%)	12	90	17	16	米/千克		Other canvas of cotton, mixed with polyester staple fibres, w>200g/m², containing <85% by weight of cotton, unbleached
5211.1900 19	未漂白与聚酯短纤混纺其他棉布(每平方米重>200克,含棉量<85%)	12	90	17	16	米/千克		Other woven fabrics of cotton, mixed with polyester staple fibres, w>200g/m², containing <85% by weight of cotton, unbleached
5211.1900 91	未漂白与其他化纤混纺其他棉缎布(每平方米重>200克,含棉量<85%)	12	90	17	16	米/千克		Other woven fabrics of cotton, satin weave, mixed with other man-made fibres, w>200g/m², containing <85% by weight of cotton, unbleached
5211.1900 92	未漂白与其他化纤混纺其他棉斜纹布(每平方米重>200克,含棉量<85%)	12	90	17	16	米/千克		Other woven fabrics of cotton, twill weave, mixed with other man-made fibres, w>200g/m², containing <85% by weight of cotton, unbleached
5211.1900 93	未漂白与其他化纤混纺其他棉帆布(每平方米重>200克,含棉量<85%)	12	90	17	16	米/千克		Other canvas of cotton, mixed with other man-made fibres, w>200g/m², containing <85% by weight of cotton, unbleached
5211.1900 99	未漂白与其他化纤混纺其他棉布(每平方米重>200克,含棉量<85%)	12	90	17	16	米/千克		Other woven fabrics of cotton, mixed with other man-made fibres, w>200g/m², containing <85% by weight of cotton, unbleached
5211.2000	-漂白	14	90	17	16	米/千克		-Bleached
	-染色:							-Dyed:
5211.3100	--平纹机织物	10	90	17	16	米/千克		--Plain weave
5211.3100 11	染色与聚酯短纤混纺棉府绸(每平方米重>200克,含棉量<85%,含细平布)	10	90	17	16	米/千克		Poplin and fine plain cloth of cotton, mixed with polyester staple fibres, w>200g/m², containing <85% by weight of cotton, dyed
5211.3100 12	染色与聚酯短纤混纺机织平布(每平方米重>200克,含棉量<85%)	10	90	17	16	米/千克		Plain cloth of cotton, mixed with polyester staple fibres, w>200g/m², containing <85% by weight of cotton, dyed
5211.3100 13	染色与聚酯短纤混纺平纹帆布(每平方米重>200克,含棉量<85%)	10	90	17	16	米/千克		Canvas of cotton, plain weave, mixed with polyester staple fibres, w>200g/m², containing <85% by weight of cotton, dyed
5211.3100 21	染色与化纤长丝混纺棉府绸(每平方米重>200克,含棉量<85%,含细平布)	10	90	17	16	米/千克		Poplin and fine plain cloth of cotton, mixed with man-made filaments, w>200g/m², containing <85% by weight of cotton, dyed
5211.3100 22	染色与化纤长丝混纺机织平布(每平方米重>200克,含棉量<85%)	10	90	17	16	米/千克		Plain cloth of cotton, mixed with man-made filaments, w>200g/m², containing <85% by weight of cotton, dyed
5211.3100 23	染色与化纤长丝混纺平纹帆布(每平方米重>200克,含棉量<85%)	10	90	17	16	米/千克		Canvas of cotton, mixed with man-made filaments, w>200g/m², containing <85% by weight of cotton, dyed
5211.3100 91	染色与其他化纤混纺棉府绸(每平方米重>200克,含棉量<85%,含细平布)	10	90	17	16	米/千克		Poplin and fine plain cloth of cotton, mixed with other man-made fibres, w>200g/m², containing <85% by weight of cotton, dyed
5211.3100 92	染色与其他化纤混纺机织平布(每平方米重>200克,含棉量<85%)	10	90	17	16	米/千克		Plain cloth of cotton, mixed with other man-made fibres, w>200g/m², containing <85% by weight of cotton, dyed

税则号列	货 品 名 称	最惠(%)	普通	增值税率	出口退税	计量单位	监管条件	Article Description
5211.3100 93	染色与其他化纤混纺平纹帆布(每平方米重>200克,含棉量<85%)	10	90	17	16	米/千克		Canvas of cotton, plain weave, mixed with other man-made fibres, w>200g/m², containing <85% by weight of cotton, dyed
5211.3200	--三线或四线斜纹机织物,包括双面斜纹机织物	10	90	17	16	米/千克		--3-thread or 4-thread twill, including cross twill
5211.3200 10	染色与聚酯短纤混纺3/4线斜纹棉布(每平方米重>200克,含棉量<85%,含双面斜纹布)	10	90	17	16	米/千克		Woven fabrics of cotton, twill weave (3 or 4-thread, cross twill), mixed with polyester staple fibres, w>200g/m², containing<85% by weight of cotton, dyed
5211.3200 20	染色与化纤长丝混纺3/4线斜纹棉布(每平方米重>200克,含棉量<85%,含双面斜纹布)	10	90	17	16	米/千克		Woven fabrics of cotton, twill weave (3 or 4-thread, cross twill), mixed with man-made filaments, w>200g/m², containing<85% by weight of cotton, dyed
5211.3200 90	染色其他化纤混纺3/4线斜纹棉布(每平方米重>200克,含棉量<85%,含双面斜纹布)	10	90	17	16	米/千克		Woven fabrics of cotton, twill weave (3 or 4-thread, cross twill), mixed with other man-made fibres, w>200g/m², containing<85% by weight of cotton, dyed
5211.3900	--其他机织物	10	90	17	16	米/千克		--Other fabrics
5211.3900 11	染色与聚酯短纤混纺的棉缎布(每平方米重>200克,含棉量<85%)	10	90	17	16	米/千克		Woven fabrics of cotton, satin weave, mixed with polyester staple fibres, w>200g/m², containing<85% by weight of cotton, dyed
5211.3900 12	染色与聚酯短纤混纺的棉斜纹布(每平方米重>200克,含棉量<85%)	10	90	17	16	米/千克		Woven fabrics of cotton, twill weave, mixed with polyester staple fibres, w>200g/m², containing<85% by weight of cotton, dyed
5211.3900 13	染色与聚酯短纤混纺的棉帆布(每平方米重>200克,含棉量<85%)	10	90	17	16	米/千克		Canvas of cotton, mixed with polyester staple fibres, w>200g/m², containing<85% by weight of cotton, dyed
5211.3900 19	染色与聚酯短纤混纺其他棉布(每平方米重>200克,含棉量<85%)	10	90	17	16	米/千克		Other woven fabrics of cotton, mixed with polyester staple fibres, w>200g/m², containing <85% by weight of cotton, dyed
5211.3900 21	染色与化纤长丝混纺的棉缎布(每平方米重>200克,含棉量<85%)	10	90	17	16	米/千克		Woven fabrics of cotton, satin weave, mixed with man-made filaments, w>200g/m², containing<85% by weight of cotton, dyed
5211.3900 22	染色与化纤长丝混纺的棉斜纹布(每平方米重>200克,含棉量<85%)	10	90	17	16	米/千克		Woven fabrics of cotton, twill weave, mixed with man-made filaments, w>200g/m², containing<85% by weight of cotton, dyed
5211.3900 23	染色与化纤长丝混纺的棉帆布(每平方米重>200克,含棉量<85%)	10	90	17	16	米/千克		Canvas of cotton, mixed with man-made filaments, w>200g/m², containing<85% by weight of cotton, dyed
5211.3900 29	染色与化纤长丝混纺的其他棉布(每平方米重>200克,含棉量<85%)	10	90	17	16	米/千克		Woven fabrics of cotton, mixed with man-made filaments, w>200g/m², containing<85% by weight of cotton, dyed
5211.3900 91	染色与其他化纤混纺的棉缎布(每平方米重>200克,含棉量<85%)	10	90	17	16	米/千克		Woven fabrics of cotton, satin weave, mixed with other man-made fibres, w>200g/m², containing<85% by weight of cotton, dyed
5211.3900 92	染色与其他化纤混纺的棉斜纹布(每平方米重>200克,含棉量<85%)	10	90	17	16	米/千克		Woven fabrics of cotton, twill weave, mixed with other man-made fibres w>200g/m², containing<85% by weight of cotton, dyed
5211.3900 93	染色与其他化纤混纺的棉帆布(每平方米重>200克,含棉量<85%)	10	90	17	16	米/千克		Canvas of cotton, mixed with other man-made fibres, w>200g/m², containing<85% by weight of cotton, dyed
5211.3900 99	染色与其他化纤混纺其他棉布(每平方米重>200克,含棉量<85%)	10	90	17	16	米/千克		Other woven fabrics of cotton, mixed with other man-made fibres, w>200g/m², containing <85% by weight of cotton, dyed
	-色织:							-Of yarns of different colours:
5211.4100	--平纹机织物	10	90	17	16	米/千克		--Plain weave

税则号列	货品名称	最惠(%)	普通	增值税率	出口退税	计量单位	监管条件	Article Description
5211.4100 10	色织与聚酯短纤混纺平纹棉布(每平方米重超过200克,含棉量<85%)	10	90	17	16	米/千克		Woven fabrics of cotton, plain weave, mixed with polyester staple fibres, w > 200g/m², containing < 85% by weight of cotton, of yarns of different colours
5211.4100 20	色织与化纤长丝混纺平纹棉布(每平方米重超过200克,含棉量<85%)	10	90	17	16	米/千克		Woven fabrics of cotton, plain weave, mixed with man-made filaments, w > 200g/m², containing < 85% by weight of cotton, of yarns of different colours
5211.4100 90	色织与其他化纤混纺平纹棉布(每平方米重超过200克,含棉量<85%)	10	90	17	16	米/千克		Woven fabrics of cotton, plain weave, mixed with other man-made fibres, w > 200g/m², containing < 85% by weight of cotton, of yarns of different colours
5211.4200	--粗斜纹布(劳动布)	10	90	17	16	米/千克		--Denim
5211.4200 10	色织与化纤混纺蓝色粗斜纹棉布(每平方米重超过200克,含棉量<85%)	10	90	17	16	米/千克		Blue denim of cotton, mixed with other man-made fibres, w > 200g/m², containing < 85% by weight of cotton, of yarns of different colours
5211.4200 90	色织与化纤混纺非蓝色粗斜纹棉布(每平方米重超过200克,含棉量<85%)	10	90	17	16	米/千克		Denim of cotton, other than blue, w > 200g/m², containing < 85% by weight of cotton, of yarns of different colours
5211.4300	--其他三线或四线斜纹机织物,包括双面斜纹机织物	10	90	17	16	米/千克		--Other fabrics of 3-thread or 4-thread twill, including cross twill
5211.4300 10	其他色织与聚酯短纤混纺3/4线斜纹棉布(每平方米重超过200克,含棉量<85%,含双面斜纹布)	10	90	17	16	米/千克		Woven fabrics of cotton, twill weave (3 or 4-thread, cross twill), mixed with polyester staple fibres, w > 200g/m², containing < 85% by weight of cotton, of yarns of different colours
5211.4300 20	其他色织与化纤长丝混纺3/4线斜纹棉布(每平方米重超过200克,含棉量<85%,含双面斜纹布)	10	90	17	16	米/千克		Woven fabrics of cotton, twill weave (3 or 4-thread, cross twill), mixed with man-made filaments, w > 200g/m², containing < 85% by weight of cotton, of yarns of different colours
5211.4300 90	其他色织与其他化纤混纺3/4线斜纹棉布(每平方米重超过200克,含棉量<85%,含双面斜纹布)	10	90	17	16	米/千克		Woven fabrics of cotton twill weave (3 or 4-thread, cross twill), mixed with other man-made fibres, w > 200g/m², containing < 85% by weight of cotton, of yarns of different colours
5211.4900	--其他机织物	10	90	17	16	米/千克		--Other fabrics
5211.4900 11	色织与聚酯短纤混纺的提花布(每平方米重超过200克,含棉量<85%)	10	90	17	16	米/千克		Woven fabrics, jacquard weave, mixed with polyester staple fibres, w > 200g/m², containing < 85% by weight of cotton, of yarns of different colours
5211.4900 19	色织与聚酯短纤混纺其他棉布(每平方米重超过200克,含棉量<85%)	10	90	17	16	米/千克		Other woven fabrics of cotton, mixed with polyester staple fibres, w > 200g/m², containing <85% by weight of cotton, of yarns of different colours
5211.4900 21	色织与化纤长丝混纺的提花布(每平方米重超过200克,含棉量<85%)	10	90	17	16	米/千克		Woven fabrics, jacquard weave, mixed with man-made filaments, w > 200g/m², containing <85% by weight of cotton, of yarns of different colours
5211.4900 29	色织与化纤长丝混纺其他棉布(每平方米重超过200克,含棉量<85%)	10	90	17	16	米/千克		Other woven fabrics of cotton, mixed with man-made filaments, w > 200g/m², containing <85% by weight of cotton, of yarns of different colours
5211.4900 91	色织与其他化纤混纺的提花布(每平方米重超过200克,含棉量<85%)	10	90	17	16	米/千克		Woven fabrics, jacquard weave, mixed with other man-made fibres, w > 200g/m², containing <85% by weight of cotton, of yarns of different colours
5211.4900 99	色织与其他化纤混纺其他棉布(每平方米重超过200克,含棉量<85%)	10	90	17	16	米/千克		Other woven fabrics of cotton, mixed with other man-made fibres, w > 200g/m², containing <85% by weight of cotton, of yarns of different colours
	-印花:							-Printed:
5211.5100	--平纹机织物	10	90	17	16	米/千克		--Plain weave

税则号列	货品名称	最惠(%)	普通	增值税率	出口退税	计量单位	监管条件	Article Description
5211.5100 11	印花与聚酯短纤混纺棉府绸(每平方米重超过200克,含棉量<85%,含细平布)	10	90	17	16	米/千克		Poplin and fine plain cloth of cotton, mixed with polyester staple fibres, w > 200g/m², containing < 85% by weight of cotton, printed
5211.5100 12	印花与聚酯短纤混纺的机织平布(每平方米重超过200克,含棉量<85%)	10	90	17	16	米/千克		Plain cloth, mixed with polyester staple fibres, w > 200g/m², containing < 85% by weight of cotton, printed
5211.5100 13	印花与聚酯短纤混纺的平纹帆布(每平方米重超过200克,含棉量<85%)	10	90	17	16	米/千克		Canvas, plain weave, mixed with polyester staple fibres, w > 200g/m², containing < 85% by weight of cotton, printed
5211.5100 21	印花与化纤长丝混纺棉府绸(每平方米重超过200克,含棉量<85%,含细平布)	10	90	17	16	米/千克		Poplin and fine plain cloth of cotton, mixed with man-made filaments, w > 200g/m², containing < 85% by weight of cotton, printed
5211.5100 22	印花与化纤长丝混纺机织平布(每平方米重超过200克,含棉量<85%)	10	90	17	16	米/千克		Plain cloth, mixed with man-made filaments, w > 200g/m², containing < 85% by weight of cotton, printed
5211.5100 23	印花与化纤长丝混纺平纹帆布(每平方米重超过200克,含棉量<85%)	10	90	17	16	米/千克		Canvas, plain weave, mixed with man-made filaments, w > 200g/m², containing < 85% by weight of cotton, printed
5211.5100 91	印花与其他化纤混纺棉府绸(每平方米重超过200克,含棉量<85%,含细平布)	10	90	17	16	米/千克		Poplin and fine plain cloth of cotton, mixed with man-made filaments, w > 200g/m², containing < 85% by weight of cotton, printed
5211.5100 92	印花与其他化纤混纺的机织平布(每平方米重超过200克,含棉量<85%)	10	90	17	16	米/千克		Plain cloth, mixed with man-made filaments, w > 200g/m², containing < 85% by weight of cotton, printed
5211.5100 93	印花与其他化纤混纺的平纹帆布(每平方米重超过200克,含棉量<85%)	10	90	17	16	米/千克		Canvas, plain weave, mixed with man-made filaments, w > 200g/m², containing < 85% by weight of cotton, printed
5211.5200	--三线或四线斜纹机织物,包括双面斜纹机织物	10	90	17	16	米/千克		--3-thread or 4-thread twill, including cross twill, including double twill
5211.5200 10	印花与聚酯短纤混纺3/4线斜纹棉布(每平方米重超过200克,含棉量<85%,含双面斜纹布)	10	90	17	16	米/千克		Woven fabrics of cotton, twill weave (3 or 4-thread, cross twill), mixed with polyester staple fibres, w > 200 g/m², containing < 85% by weight of cotton, printed
5211.5200 20	印花与化纤长丝混纺3/4线斜纹棉布(每平方米重超过200克,含棉量<85%,含双面斜纹布)	10	90	17	16	米/千克		Woven fabrics of cotton, twill weave (3 or 4-thread, cross twill), mixed with man-made filaments, w > 200g/m², containing < 85% by weight of cotton, printed
5211.5200 90	印花与其他化纤混纺3/4线斜纹棉布(每平方米重超过200克,含棉量<85%,含双面斜纹布)	10	90	17	16	米/千克		Woven fabrics of cotton, twill weave (3 or 4-thread, cross twill), mixed with other man-made fibres, w > 200 g/m², containing < 85% by weight of cotton, printed
5211.5900	--其他机织物	10	90	17	16	米/千克		--Other fabrics
5211.5900 11	印花与聚酯短纤混纺棉缎布(每平方米重超过200克,含棉量<85%)	10	90	17	16	米/千克		Other woven fabrics of cotton, satin weave, mixed with polyester staple fibres, w > 200g/m², containing < 85% by weight of cotton, printed
5211.5900 12	印花与聚酯短纤混纺斜纹棉布(每平方米重超过200克,含棉量<85%)	10	90	17	16	米/千克		Other woven fabrics of cotton, twill weave, mixed with polyester staple fibres, w > 200g/m², containing < 85% by weight of cotton, printed
5211.5900 13	印花与聚酯短纤混纺棉帆布(每平方米重超过200克,含棉量<85%)	10	90	17	16	米/千克		Other canvas of cotton, mixed with polyester staple fibres, w > 200g/m², containing < 85% by weight of cotton, printed
5211.5900 19	印花与聚酯短纤混纺其他棉布(每平方米重超过200克,含棉量<85%)	10	90	17	16	米/千克		Other woven fabrics of cotton, mixed with polyester staple fibres, w > 200g/m², containing < 85% by weight of cotton, printed
5211.5900 21	印花与化纤长丝混纺棉缎布(每平方米重超过200克,含棉量<85%)	10	90	17	16	米/千克		Other woven fabrics of cotton, satin weave, mixed with man-made filaments, w > 200g/m², containing < 85% by weight of cotton, printed

税则号列	货品名称	最惠(%)	普通	增值税率	出口退税	计量单位	监管条件	Article Description
5211.5900 22	印花与化纤长丝混纺斜纹棉布(每平方米重超过200克,含棉量<85%)	10	90	17	16	米/千克		Other woven fabrics of cotton, twill weave, mixed with man-made filaments, w>200g/m², containing<85% by weight of cotton, printed
5211.5900 23	印花与化纤长丝混纺棉帆布(每平方米重超过200克,含棉量<85%)	10	90	17	16	米/千克		Other canvas of cotton, mixed with man-made filaments, w>200g/m², containing<85% by weight of cotton, printed
5211.5900 29	印花与化纤长丝混纺其他棉布(每平方米重超过200克,含棉量<85%)	10	90	17	16	米/千克		Other woven fabrics of cotton, mixed with man-made filaments, w>200g/m², containing<85% by weight of cotton, printed
5211.5900 91	印花与其他化纤混纺棉缎布(每平方米重超过200克,含棉量<85%)	10	90	17	16	米/千克		Other woven fabrics of cotton, satin weave, mixed with other man-made fibres, w>200g/m², containing<85% by weight of cotton, printed
5211.5900 92	印花与其他化纤混纺斜纹棉布(每平方米重超过200克,含棉量<85%)	10	90	17	16	米/千克		Other woven fabrics of cotton, twill weave, mixed with other man-made fibres, w>200g/m², containing<85% by weight of cotton, printed
5211.5900 93	印花与其他化纤混纺棉帆布(每平方米重超过200克,含棉量<85%)	10	90	17	16	米/千克		Other canvas of cotton, mixed with other man-made fibres, w>200g/m², containing<85% by weight of cotton, printed
5211.5900 99	印花与其他化纤混纺其他棉布(每平方米重超过200克,含棉量<85%)	10	90	17	16	米/千克		Other woven fabrics of cotton, mixed with other man-made fibres, w>200g/m², containing<85% by weight of cotton, printed
52.12	**其他棉机织物:**							**Other woven fabrics of cotton:**
	-每平方米重量不超过200克:							-Weighing not more than 200 g/m²:
5212.1100	--未漂白	12	80	17	16	米/千克		--Unbleached
5212.1100 11	未漂白的其他混纺棉布(每平方米重≤200克,与36%及以上精梳羊毛或动物细毛混纺)	12	80	17	16	米/千克		Other woven fabrics of cotton, mixed, containing≥36% by weight of combed wool or fine animal hair, w≤200g/m², unbleached
5212.1100 19	未漂白的其他混纺棉布(每平方米重≤200克,与36%以下精梳羊毛或动物细毛混纺)	12	80	17	16	米/千克		Other woven fabrics of cotton, mixed, containing<36% by weight of combed wool or fine animal hair, w≤200g/m², unbleached
5212.1100 21	未漂白的其他混纺棉布(每平方米重≤200克,与36%及以上其他羊毛或动物细毛混纺)	12	80	17	16	米/千克		Other woven fabrics of cotton, mixed, containing≥36% by weight other wool or fine animal hair, w≤200g/m², unbleached
5212.1100 29	未漂白的其他混纺棉布(每平方米重≤200克,与其他羊毛或动物细毛混纺)	12	80	17	16	米/千克		Other woven fabrics of cotton, mixed with other wool or fine animal hair, w≤200g/m², unbleached
5212.1100 30	未漂白的其他混纺府绸及细平布(每平米重≤200克,与化纤、羊毛/动物细毛以外其他纤维混纺)	12	80	17	16	米/千克		Other poplin and fine plain cloth, mixed with other fibres, other than man-made fibres, wool or fine animals hair, w≤200g/m², unbleached
5212.1100 40	未漂白的其他混纺棉机织平布(每平米重≤200克,与化纤、羊毛/动物细毛以外其他纤维混纺)	12	80	17	16	米/千克		Other plain cloth of cotton, mixed with other fibres, other than man-made fibres, wool or fine animals hair, w≤200g/m², unbleached
5212.1100 50	未漂白的其他混纺棉印染布(每平米重≤200克,与化纤、羊毛/动物细毛以外其他纤维混纺)	12	80	17	16	米/千克		Other cloth for printing and dying of cotton, mixed with other fibres, other than man-made fibres, wool or fine animals hair, w≤200g/m², unbleached
5212.1100 60	未漂白其他混纺棉奶酪布、薄细布、巴里纱(每平米重≤200克,与化纤、羊毛/动物细毛以外其他纤维混纺)	12	80	17	16	米/千克		Other cheese cloth and fine thin cloth of cotton, mixed with other fibres, other than man-made fibres、wool or fine animals hair w≤200g/m², unbleached
5212.1100 70	未漂白的其他混纺棉缎布(每平米重≤200克,与化纤、羊毛/动物细毛以外其他纤维混纺)	12	80	17	16	米/千克		Other woven fabrics of cotton, satin weave, mixed with other fibres, other than man-made fibres, wool or fine animals hair, w≤200g/m², unbleached
5212.1100 81	未漂白的其他混纺斜纹棉布(每平米重≤200克,与化纤、羊毛/动物细毛以外其他纤维混纺)	12	80	17	16	米/千克		Other woven fabrics of cotton, twill weave, mixed with other fibres, other than man-made fibres, wool or fine animals hair, w≤200g/m², unbleached

税则号列	货品名称	最惠(%)	普通	增值税率	出口退税	计量单位	监管条件	Article Description
5212.1100 89	未漂白的其他混纺棉牛津布(每平米重≤200克,与化纤、羊毛/动物细毛以外其他纤维混纺)	12	80	17	16	米/千克		Other woven fabrics of cotton, oxford weave, mixed with other fibres, other than man-made fibres、wool or fine animals hair, w≤200g/m², unbleached
5212.1100 90	未漂白的其他混纺棉布(每平米重≤200克,与化纤、羊毛/细毛以外其他纤维混纺)	12	80	17	16	米/千克		Other woven fabrics of cotton, mixed with other fibres, other than man-made fibres, wool or fine animals hair, w≤200g/m², unbleached
5212.1200	--漂白	14	80	17	16	米/千克		--Bleached
5212.1200 11	漂白的其他混纺棉布(每平米重≤200克,与36%及以上精梳羊毛或动物细毛混纺)	14	80	17	16	米/千克		Other woven fabrics of cotton, w ≤ 200g/m², mixed, containing≥36% by weight of combed wool or fine animal hair, bleached
5212.1200 19	漂白的其他混纺棉布(每平米重≤200克,与36%以下精梳羊毛或动物细毛混纺)	14	80	17	16	米/千克		Other woven fabrics of cotton, w ≤ 200g/m², mixed, containing<36% by weight of combed wool or fine animal hair, bleached
5212.1200 20	漂白的其他混纺棉布(每平米重≤200克,与其他羊毛或动物细毛混纺)	14	80	17	16	米/千克		Other woven fabrics of cotton(w≤200g/m², mixed, of wool ro fine animal hair, bleached)
5212.1200 50	漂白的其他混纺棉印染布(每平米重≤200克,与化纤/羊毛/动物细毛以外其他纤维混纺)	14	80	17	16	米/千克		Cloth for printing and dying, mixed with other fibres (other than man-made fibres, wool or fine animal hair, w≤200g/m², bleached)
5212.1200 60	漂白其他混纺棉奶酪布/薄细布/纱(每平米重≤200克,与除化纤/羊毛/动物细毛以外其他纤维混纺)	14	80	17	16	米/千克		Cheese cloth/swiss muslin/yarn, mixed with other fibres(other than man-made fibres, wool or fine animal hair, w≤200g/m², bleached)
5212.1200 71	漂白的其他混纺棉缎布(每平米重≤200克,与化纤/羊毛/动物细毛以外其他纤维混纺)	14	80	17	16	米/千克		Woven fabrics of cotton, satin weave, mixed with other fibres, other than man-made fibres、wool or fine animal hair, w≤200g/m², bleached
5212.1200 72	漂白的其他混纺斜纹棉布(每平米重≤200克,与化纤/羊毛/动物细毛以外其他纤维混纺)	14	80	17	16	米/千克		Woven fabrics of cotton, twill weave, mixed with other fibres, other than man-made fibres、wool or fine animal hair, w≤200g/m², bleached
5212.1200 79	漂白的其他混纺棉牛津布(每平米重≤200克,与化纤/羊毛/动物细毛以外其他纤维混纺)	14	80	17	16	米/千克		Woven fabrics of cotton, oxford weave, mixed with other fibres, other than man-made fibres, wool or fine animal hair, w≤200g/m², bleached
5212.1200 90	漂白的其他混纺棉机织物(每平米重≤200克,与化纤/羊毛/动物细毛以外其他纤维混纺)	14	80	17	16	米/千克		Other woven fabrics of cotton, mixed with other fibres, other than man-made fibres、wool or fine animal hair, w≤200g/m², bleached
5212.1300	--染色	10	80	17	16	米/千克		--Dyed
5212.1300 11	染色其他混纺棉布(每平方米重≤200克,与36%及以上精梳羊毛/动物细毛混纺)	10	80	17	16	米/千克		Other woven fabrics of cotton, w≤200g/m², mixed, containing≥36% by weight of combed wool or fine animal hair, dyed
5212.1300 19	染色其他混纺棉布(每平方米重≤200克,与36%及以下精梳羊毛/动物细毛混纺)	10	80	17	16	米/千克		Other woven fabrics of cotton, w ≤ 200g/m², mixed, containing < 36% by weight, of combed wool or fine animal hair, dyed
5212.1300 21	染色其他混纺棉布(每平米重≤200克,与36%及以上其他羊毛/动物细毛混纺)	10	80	17	16	米/千克		Other woven fabrics of cotton, w ≤ 200g/m², mixed, containing≥36% by weight of wool or fine animal hair, dyed
5212.1300 29	染色其他混纺棉布(每平米重≤200克,与36%及以下其他羊毛/动物细毛混纺)	10	80	17	16	米/千克		Other woven fabrics of cotton, w ≤ 200g/m², mixed, containing<36% by weight of wool or fine animal hair, dyed
5212.1300 30	染色其他混纺府绸及平细布(每平米重≤200克,与化纤以外其他纤维混纺)	10	80	17	16	米/千克		Poplin and fine plain cloth, mixed with other fibres, other than man-made fibres, w≤200g/m², dyed
5212.1300 60	染色其他混纺奶酪布,薄细布,巴里纱(每平米重≤200克,与化纤以外其他纤维混纺)	10	80	17	16	米/千克		Cheese cloth, voiles and swiss muslin, mixed with other fibres, other than man-made fibres, w≤200g/m², dyed
5212.1300 71	染色其他混纺棉缎布(每平米重≤200克,与化纤以外其他纤维混纺)	10	80	17	16	米/千克		Other woven fabrics of cotton, satin weave, mixed with other fibres, other than man-made fibres, w≤200g/m², dyed

税则号列	货品名称	最惠(%)	普通	增值税率	出口退税	计量单位	监管条件	Article Description
5212.1300 72	染色其他混纺斜纹棉布(每平米重≤200克,与化纤以外其他纤维混纺)	10	80	17	16	米/千克		Other woven fabrics of cotton, twill weave, mixed with other fibres, other than man-made fibres, w≤200g/m², dyed
5212.1300 79	染色其他混纺棉牛津布(每平米重≤200克,与化纤以外其他纤维混纺)	10	80	17	16	米/千克		Other woven fabrics of cotton, oxford weave, mixed with other fibres, other than man-made fibres, w≤200g/m², dyed
5212.1300 90	染色其他混纺棉布(每平米重≤200克,与化纤以外其他纤维混纺)	10	80	17	16	米/千克		Other woven fabrics of cotton, mixed with other fibres, other than man-made fibres, w≤200g/m², dyed
5212.1400	--色织	10	80	17	16	米/千克		--Of yarns of different colours
5212.1400 11	色织其他混纺棉布(每平米重≤200克,与36%及以上精梳羊毛/动物细毛混纺)	10	80	17	16	米/千克		Other woven fabrics of cotton, w≤200g/m², mixed, containing≥36% by weight of combed wool or fine animal hair, of yarns of different colours
5212.1400 19	色织其他混纺棉布(每平米重≤200克,与36%及以下精梳羊毛/动物细毛混纺)	10	80	17	16	米/千克		Other woven fabrics of cotton, w≤200g/m² mixed, containing<36% by weight of combed wool or fine animal hair, of yarns of different colours
5212.1400 21	色织其他混纺棉布(每平米重≤200克,与36%及以上其他羊毛/动物细毛混纺)	10	80	17	16	米/千克		Other woven fabrics of cotton, w≤200g/m², mixed, containing≥36% by weight of wool or fine animal hair, of yarns of different colours
5212.1400 29	色织其他混纺棉布(每平米重≤200克,与36%及以下其他羊毛/动物细毛混纺)	10	80	17	16	米/千克		Other woven fabrics of cotton, mixed, containing<36% by weight of wool or fine animal hair, w≤200g/m², of yarns of different colours
5212.1400 30	色织其他混纺棉提花布(每平米重≤200克,与化纤以外其他纤维混纺)	10	80	17	16	米/千克		Other woven fabrics of cotton, jacquard weave, mixed with other fibres, other than man-made fibres, w≤200g/m², of yarns of different colours
5212.1400 90	色织其他混纺棉布(每平米重≤200克,与化纤以外其他纤维混纺)	10	80	17	16	米/千克		Other woven fabrics of cotton, mixed with other fibres other than man-made fibres w≤200g/m², of yarns of different colours
5212.1500	--印花	10	80	17	16	米/千克		--Printed
5212.1500 11	印花其他混纺棉布(每平米重≤200克,与36%及以上精梳羊毛/动物细毛混纺)	10	80	17	16	米/千克		Other woven fabrics of cotton, mixed, containing≥36% by weight of combed wool or fine animal hair, w≤200g/m², printed
5212.1500 19	印花其他混纺棉布(每平米重≤200克,与36%及以下精梳羊毛/动物细毛混纺)	10	80	17	16	米/千克		Other woven fabrics of cotton, mixed, containing<36% by weight of combed wool or fine animal hair, w≤200g/m², printed
5212.1500 21	印花其他混纺棉布(每平米重≤200克,与36%及以上其他羊毛/动物细毛混纺)	10	80	17	16	米/千克		Other woven fabrics of cotton, mixed, containing≥36% by weight of wool or fine animal hair, w≤200g/m², printed
5212.1500 29	印花其他混纺棉布(每平米重≤200克,与36%及以下其他羊毛/动物细毛混纺)	10	80	17	16	米/千克		Other woven fabrics of cotton, mixed, containing<36% by weight of wool or fine animal hair, w≤200g/m², printed
5212.1500 40	印花其他混纺棉机织平布(每平米重≤200克,与化纤/羊毛/细毛以外其他纤维混纺)	10	80	17	16	米/千克		Plain cloth, mixed with other fibres, other than man-made fibres, wool or fine animals hair, w≤200g/m², printed
5212.1500 50	印花其他混纺棉印染布(每平米重≤200克,与化纤/羊毛/细毛以外其他纤维混纺)	10	80	17	16	米/千克		Cloth for printing and dying of cotton, mixed with other fibres, other than man-made fibres, wool or fine animals hair, w≤200g/m², printed
5212.1500 60	印花其他混纺棉奶酪布,薄细布,巴里纱(每平米重≤200克,与化纤/羊毛/细毛以外其他纤维混纺)	10	80	17	16	米/千克		Cheese cloth, voiles and swiss muslin, mixed with other fibres, other than man-made fibres, wool or fine animals hair, w≤200g/m², printed
5212.1500 71	印花其他混纺棉缎布(每平米重≤200克,与化纤/羊毛/细毛以外其他纤维混纺)	10	80	17	16	米/千克		Other woven fabrics of cotton, satin weave, mixed with other fibres, other than man-made fibres, wool or fine animals hair, w≤200g/m², printed
5212.1500 72	印花其他混纺斜纹棉布(每平米重≤200克,与化纤/羊毛/细毛以外其他纤维混纺)	10	80	17	16	米/千克		Other woven fabrics of cotton, twill weave, mixed with other fibres, other than man-made fibres, wool or fine animals hair, w≤200g/m², printed

税则号列	货品名称	最惠(%)	普通	增值税率	出口退税	计量单位	监管条件	Article Description
5212.1500 79	印花其他混纺棉牛津布(每平米重≤200克,与化纤/羊毛/细毛以外其他纤维混纺)	10	80	17	16	米/千克		Other woven fabrics of cotton, oxford weave, mixed with other fibres, other than man-made fibres, wool or fine animals hair, w≤200g/m^2, printed
5212.1500 90	印花其他混纺棉布(每平米重≤200克,与化纤/羊毛/细毛以外其他纤维混纺)	10	80	17	16	米/千克		Other woven fabrics of cotton, mixed with other fibres, other than man-made fibres, wool or fine animals hair, w≤200g/m^2, printed
	-每平方米重量超过200克:							-Weighing more than 200 g/m^2:
5212.2100暂	--未漂白	6	80	17	16	米/千克		--Unbleached
5212.2100暂 11	未漂白其他混纺棉布(每平米重>200克,与36%及以上精梳羊毛/动物细毛混纺)	6	80	17	16	米/千克		Other woven fabrics of cotton, mixed, containing≥36% by weight of combed wool or fine animal hair, w>200g/m^2, unbleached
5212.2100暂 19	未漂白其他混纺棉布(每平米重>200克,与36%及以下精梳羊毛/动物细毛混纺)	6	80	17	16	米/千克		Other woven fabrics of cotton, mixed, containing<36% by weight of combed wool or fine animal hair, w>200g/m^2, unbleached
5212.2100暂 21	未漂白其他混纺棉布(每平米重>200克,与36%及以上其他羊毛/动物细毛混纺)	6	80	17	16	米/千克		Other woven fabrics of cotton, mixed, containing≥36% by weight of wool or fine animal hair, w>200g/m^2, unbleached
5212.2100暂 29	未漂白其他混纺棉布(每平米重>200克,与36%及以下其他羊毛/动物细毛混纺)	6	80	17	16	米/千克		Other woven fabrics of cotton, mixed, containing<36% by weight of wool or fine animal hair, w>200g/m^2, unbleached
5212.2100暂 30	未漂白其他混纺府绸及平细布(每平米重>200克,与化纤以外其他纤维混纺)	6	80	17	16	米/千克		Poplin and fine plain cloth, mixed with other fibres, other than man-made fibres, w>200g/m^2, unbleached
5212.2100暂 40	未漂白其他混纺棉机织平布(每平米重>200克,与化纤以外其他纤维混纺)	6	80	17	16	米/千克		Plain cloth of cotton, mixed with other fibres, other than man-made fibres, w>200g/m^2, unbleached
5212.2100暂 50	未漂白其他混纺棉帆布(每平米重>200克,与化纤以外其他纤维混纺)	6	80	17	16	米/千克		Canvas of cotton, mixed with other fibres, other than man-made fibres, w>200g/m^2, unbleached
5212.2100暂 60	未漂白其他混纺棉缎布(每平方米重>200克,与化纤以外其他纤维混纺)	6	80	17	16	米/千克		Other woven fabrics of cotton, satin weave, mixed with other fibres, other than man-made fibres, w>200g/m^2, unbleached
5212.2100暂 70	未漂白其他混纺斜纹棉布(每平方米重>200克,与化纤以外其他纤维混纺)	6	80	17	16	米/千克		Other woven fabrics of cotton, twill weave, mixed with other fibres, other than man-made fibres, w>200g/m^2, unbleached
5212.2100暂 90	未漂白其他混纺棉布(每平方米重>200克,与化纤以外其他纤维混纺)	6	80	17	16	米/千克		Other woven fabrics of cotton, mixed with other fibres, other than man-made fibres, w>200g/m^2, unbleached
5212.2200	--漂白	14	80	17	16	米/千克		--Bleached
5212.2200 11	漂白的其他混纺棉布(每平方米重>200克,与36%及以上精梳羊毛/动物细毛混纺)	14	80	17	16	米/千克		Other woven fabrics of cotton, mixed, containing≥36% by weight of combed wool or fine animal hair, w>200g/m^2, bleached
5212.2200 19	漂白的其他混纺棉布(每平方米重>200克,与36%及以下精梳羊毛/动物细毛混纺)	14	80	17	16	米/千克		Other woven fabrics of cotton, mixed, containing<36% by weight of combed wool or fine animal hair, w>200g/m^2, bleached
5212.2200 21	漂白的其他混纺棉布(每平方米重>200克,与36%及以上其他羊毛/动物细毛混纺)	14	80	17	16	米/千克		Other woven fabrics of cotton, mixed, containing≥36% by weight of wool or fine animal hair, w>200g/m^2, bleached
5212.2200 29	漂白的其他混纺棉布(每平方米重>200克,与36%及以下其他羊毛/动物细毛混纺)	14	80	17	16	米/千克		Other woven fabrics of cotton, mixed, containing<36% by weight of wool or fine animal hair, w>200 g/m^2, bleached
5212.2200 30	漂白的其他混纺府绸及细平布(每平方米重>200克,与化纤/羊毛/动物细毛以外其他纤维混纺)	14	80	17	16	米/千克		Poplin and fine plain cloth, mixed with other fibres, other than man-made fibres, wool or fine animals hair, w>200g/m^2, bleached
5212.2200 40	漂白的其他混纺棉机织平布(每平方米重>200克,与化纤/羊毛/动物细毛以外其他纤维混纺)	14	80	17	16	米/千克		Plain cloth of cotton, mixed with other fibres, other than man-made fibres, wool or fine animals hair, w>200g/m^2, bleached

税则号列	货品名称	最惠(%)	普通	增值税率	出口退税	计量单位	监管条件	Article Description
5212.2200 50	漂白的其他混纺棉帆布(每平方米重>200克,与化纤/羊毛/动物细毛以外其他纤维混纺)	14	80	17	16	米/千克		Canvas of cotton, mixed with other fibres, other than man-made fibres, wool or fine animals hair, w >200g/m^2, bleached
5212.2200 60	漂白的其他混纺棉缎布(每平方米重>200克,与化纤/羊毛/动物细毛以外其他纤维混纺)	14	80	17	16	米/千克		Woven fabrics of cotton, satin weave, mixed with other fibres, other than man-made fibres, wool or fine animals hair, w >200g/m^2, bleached
5212.2200 70	漂白的其他混纺棉斜纹布(每平方米重>200克,与化纤/羊毛/动物细毛以外其他纤维混纺)	14	80	17	16	米/千克		Woven fabrics of cotton, twill weave, mixed with other fibres, other than man-made fibres, wool or fine animals hair, w >200g/m^2, bleached
5212.2200 90	漂白的其他混纺棉布(每平方米重>200克,与化纤/羊毛/动物细毛以外其他纤维混纺)	14	80	17	16	米/千克		Woven fabrics of cotton, mixed with other fibres, other than man-made fibres, wool or fine animals hair, w >200g/m^2, bleached
5212.2300	--染色	10	80	17	16	米/千克		--Dyed
5212.2300 11	染色的其他混纺棉布(每平米重>200克,与36%及以上精梳羊毛/动物细毛混纺)	10	80	17	16	米/千克		Other woven fabrics of cotton, mixed, containing≥36% by weight of combed wool or fine animal hair, w >200g/m^2, dyed
5212.2300 19	染色的其他混纺棉布(每平米重>200克,与36%及以下精梳羊毛/动物细毛混纺)	10	80	17	16	米/千克		Other woven fabrics of cotton, mixed, containing < 36% by weight of combed wool or fine animal hair, w >200g/m^2, dyed
5212.2300 21	染色的其他混纺棉布(每平米重>200克,与36%及以上其他羊毛/动物细毛混纺)	10	80	17	16	米/千克		Other woven fabrics of cotton, mixed, containing≥36% by weight of wool or fine animal hair, w >200 g/m^2, dyed
5212.2300 29	染色的其他混纺棉布(每平米重>200克,与36%及以下其他羊毛/动物细毛混纺)	10	80	17	16	米/千克		Other woven fabrics of cotton, mixed, containing < 36% by weight of wool or fine animal hair, w >200 g/m^2, dyed
5212.2300 30	染色的其他混纺府绸及细平布(每平米重>200克,与化纤/羊毛/动物细毛以外其他纤维混纺)	10	80	17	16	米/千克		Poplin and fine plain cloth, mixed with other fibres, other than man-made fibres, wool or fine animals hair, w >200g/m^2, dyed
5212.2300 40	染色的其他混纺棉机织平布(每平米重>200克,与化纤/羊毛/动物细毛以外其他纤维混纺)	10	80	17	16	米/千克		Plain cloth of cotton, mixed with other fibres, other than man-made fibres, wool or fine animals hair, w >200g/m^2, dyed
5212.2300 50	染色的其他混纺棉帆布(每平米重>200克,与化纤/羊毛/动物细毛以外其他纤维混纺)	10	80	17	16	米/千克		Canvas of cotton, mixed with other fibres except man-made fibres, wool or fine animals hair, w >200 g/m^2, dyed
5212.2300 60	染色的其他混纺棉缎布(每平米重>200克,与化纤/羊毛/动物细毛以外其他纤维混纺)	10	80	17	16	米/千克		Other woven fabrics of cotton, satin weave, mixed with other fibres, other than man-made fibres, wool or fine animals hair, w >200g/m^2, dyed
5212.2300 70	染色的其他混纺棉斜纹布(每平米重>200克,与化纤/羊毛/动物细毛以外其他纤维混纺)	10	80	17	16	米/千克		Other woven fabrics of cotton, twill weave, mixed with other fibres, other than man-made fibres, wool or fine animals hair, w >200g/m^2, dyed
5212.2300 90	染色的其他混纺棉布(每平米重>200克,与化纤/羊毛/动物细毛以外其他纤维混纺)	10	80	17	16	米/千克		Other woven fabrics of cotton, mixed with other fibres, other than man-made fibres, wool or fine animals hair, w >200g/m^2, dyed
5212.2400	--色织	10	80	17	16	米/千克		--Of yarns of different colours
5212.2400 11	色织的其他混纺棉布(每平米重>200克,与36%及以上精梳羊毛/动物细毛混纺)	10	80	17	16	米/千克		Other woven fabrics of cotton, mixed, containing≥36% by weight of combed wool or fine animal hair, w >200g/m^2, of yarns of different colours
5212.2400 19	色织的其他混纺棉布(每平米重>200克,与36%及以下精梳羊毛/动物细毛混纺)	10	80	17	16	米/千克		Other woven fabrics of cotton, mixed, containing < 36% by weight of combed wool or fine animal hair, w >200g/m^2, of yarns of different colours
5212.2400 21	色织的其他混纺棉布(每平米重>200克,与36%及以上其他羊毛/动物细毛混纺)	10	80	17	16	米/千克		Other woven fabrics of cotton, mixed, containing≥36% by weight of wool or fine animal hair, w >200 g/m^2, of yarns of different colours
5212.2400 29	色织的其他混纺棉布(每平方米重>200克,与36%及以下其他羊毛/动物细毛混纺)	10	80	17	16	米/千克		Other woven fabrics of cotton, mixed, containing≤36% by weight of wool or fine animal hair, w >200 g/m^2, of yarns of different colours

税则号列	货品名称	最惠(%)	普通	增值税率	出口退税	计量单位	监管条件	Article Description
5212.2400 30	色织的其他混纺蓝色粗斜纹布(每平方米重>200克,与化纤/羊毛/动物细毛以外其他纤维混纺)	10	80	17	16	米/千克		Other blue denim of cotton, mixed with other fibres, other than man-made fibres, wool or fine animals hair, w>200g/m², of yarns of different colours
5212.2400 40	色织的其他混纺提花布(每平方米重>200克,与化纤/羊毛/动物细毛以外其他纤维混纺)	10	80	17	16	米/千克		Other woven fabrics of cotton, jacquard weave, mixed with other fibres, other than man-made fibres、wool or fine animals hair, w>200g/m², of yarns of different colours
5212.2400 90	色织的其他混纺棉布(每平方米重>200克,与化纤/羊毛/动物细毛以外其他纤维混纺)	10	80	17	16	米/千克		Other woven fabrics of cotton, mixed with other fibres, other than man-made fibres、wool or fine animals hair, w>200g/m², of yarns of different colours
5212.2500	--印花	10	80	17	16	米/千克		--Printed
5212.2500 11	印花的其他混纺棉布(每平方米重>200克,与36%及以上精梳羊毛/动物细毛混纺)	10	80	17	16	米/千克		Other woven fabrics of cotton, mixed, containing≥36% by weight of combed wool or fine animal hair, w>200g/m², printed
5212.2500 19	印花的其他混纺棉布(每平方米重>200克,与36%及以下精梳羊毛/动物细毛混纺)	10	80	17	16	米/千克		Other woven fabrics of cotton, mixed, containing<36% by weight of combed wool or fine animal hair, w>200g/m², printed
5212.2500 21	印花的其他混纺棉布(每平方米重>200克,与36%及以上其他羊毛/动物细毛混纺)	10	80	17	16	米/千克		Other woven fabrics of cotton, mixed, containing≥36% by weight of wool or fine animal hair, w>200g/m², printed
5212.2500 29	印花的其他混纺棉布(每平方米重>200克,与36%及以下其他羊毛/动物细毛混纺)	10	80	17	16	米/千克		Other woven fabrics of cotton, mixed, containing<36% by weight of wool or fine animal hair, w>200g/m², printed
5212.2500 30	印花的其他混纺府绸及细平布(每平方米重>200克,与化纤/羊毛/动物细毛以外其他纤维混纺)	10	80	17	16	米/千克		Poplin and fine plain cloth, mixed with other fibres, other than man-made fibres, wool or fine animals hair, w>200g/m², printed
5212.2500 40	印花的其他混纺棉机织平布(每平方米重>200克,与化纤/羊毛/动物细毛以外其他纤维混纺)	10	80	17	16	米/千克		Plain cloth of cotton, mixed with other fibres, other than man-made fibres,wool or fine animals hair, w>200g/m², printed
5212.2500 50	印花的其他混纺棉帆布(每平方米重>200克,与化纤/羊毛/动物细毛以外其他纤维混纺)	10	80	17	16	米/千克		Canvas of cotton, mixed with other fibres, other than man-made fibres,wool or fine animals hair, w>200g/m², printed
5212.2500 60	印花的其他混纺棉缎布(每平方米重>200克,与化纤/羊毛/动物细毛以外其他纤维混纺)	10	80	17	16	米/千克		Other woven fabrics of cotton, satin weave, mixed with other fibres, other than man-made fibres,wool or fine animals hair, w>200g/m², printed
5212.2500 70	印花的其他混纺棉斜纹布(每平方米重>200克,与化纤/羊毛/动物细毛以外其他纤维混纺)	10	80	17	16	米/千克		Other woven fabrics of cotton, twill weave, mixed with other fibres, other than man-made fibres,wool or fine animals hair, w>200g/m², printed
5212.2500 90	印花的其他混纺棉布(每平米重>200克,与化纤/羊毛/动物细毛以外其他纤维混纺)	10	80	17	16	米/千克		Other woven fabrics of cotton other, mixed with other fibres, other than man-made fibres, wool or fine animals hair, w>200g/m², printed

第五十三章
其他植物纺织纤维；纸纱线及其机织物

Chapter 53
Other vegetable textile fibres; paper yarn and woven fabrics of paper yarn

税则号列	货品名称	最惠(%)	普通	增值税率	出口退税	计量单位	监管条件	Article Description
53.01	亚麻,生的或经加工但未纺制的;亚麻短纤及废麻(包括废麻纱线及回收纤维):							**Flax, raw or processed but not spun; flax tow and waste (including yarn waste and garnetted stock):**
5301.1000	-生的或沤制的亚麻	6	30	17	5	千克	AB	-Flax, raw or retted
	-破开、打成、栉梳或经其他加工但未纺制的亚麻:							-Flax, broken, scutched, hackled or otherwise processed, but not spun:
5301.2100[暂]	--破开的或打成的	1	30	17	5	千克	AB	--Broken or scutched
5301.2900	--其他	6	30	17	5	千克	AB	--Other
5301.3000[暂]	-亚麻短纤及废麻	1	30	17	5	千克	AB	-Flax tow and waste
53.02	大麻,生的或经加工但未纺制的;大麻短纤及废麻(包括废麻纱线及回收纤维):							**True hemp (*Cannabis sativa L*), raw or processed but not spun; tow and waste of true hemp (including yarn waste and garnetted stock):**
5302.1000	-生的或经沤制的大麻	6	30	17	5	千克	AB	-True hemp, raw or retted
5302.9000	-其他	6	30	17	5	千克	AB	-Other
53.03	黄麻及其他纺织用韧皮纤维(不包括亚麻、大麻及苎麻),生的或经加工但未纺制的;上述纤维的短纤及废麻(包括废纱线及回收纤维):							**Jute and other textile bast fibres (excluding flax, true hemp and ramie), raw or processed but not spun; tow and waste of these fibres (including yarn waste and garnetted stock):**
5303.1000	-生的或经沤制的黄麻及其他纺织用韧皮纤维	5	20	13	5	千克	AB	-Jute and other textile bast fibres, raw or retted
5303.9000	-其他	5	30	17	5	千克	AB	-Other
53.05	椰壳纤维、蕉麻(马尼拉麻)、苎麻及其他税目未列名的纺织用植物纤维,生的或经加工但未纺制的;上述纤维的短纤、落麻及废料(包括废纱线及回收纤维):							**Coconut, abaca (Manila hemp or *Musatextilis Nee*), ramie and other vegetable textile fibres, not elsewhere specified or included, raw or processed but not spun; tow, noils and waste of these fibres (including yarn waste and garnetted stock):**
	---苎麻:							---Ramie:
5305.0011	----生的	5	30	17	5	千克	AB	----Raw
5305.0012	----经加工但未纺制的	5	30	17	5	千克	AB	----Processed but not spun
5305.0013	----短纤及废麻	5	30	17	5	千克	AB	----Tow and waste
5305.0019	----其他	5	20	17	5	千克	AB	----Other
5305.0020	---蕉麻	3	20	17	5	千克	AB	---Of Abaca
	---其他							---Other:
5305.0091	----西沙尔麻及其他纺织用龙舌兰纤维	5	30	17	5	千克	AB	----Sisal and other textile fabircs of the genus Agave
5305.0092	----椰壳纤维	5	30	17	5	千克	AB	----of Coconut(coir)
5305.0099	----其他	5	30	17	5	千克	AB	----Other
53.06	亚麻纱线:							**Flax yarn:**
5306.1000	-单纱	6	50	17	16	千克		-Single
5306.2000[暂]	-多股纱线或缆线	5	50	17	16	千克		-Multiple (folded) or cabled
53.07	黄麻纱线或税号53.03的其他纺织用韧皮纤维纱线:							**Yarn of jute or of other textile bast fibres of heading No. 53.03:**
5307.1000	-单纱	6	35	17	16	千克		-Single
5307.2000	-多股纱线或缆线	6	35	17	16	千克		-Multiple (folded) or cabled
53.08	其他植物纺织纤维纱线;纸纱线:							**Yarn of other vegetable textile fibres; paper yarn:**
5308.1000	-椰壳纤维纱线	6	45	17	16	千克		-Coir yarn
5308.2000	-大麻纱线	6	45	17	16	千克		-True hemp yarn
	-其他:							-Other:
	---苎麻纱线:							---Ramie yarn:
5308.9011	----按重量计苎麻含量在85%及以上的未漂白或漂白纱线	6	50	17	16	千克		----Containing 85% or more by weight of ramie, unbleached or bleached yarn

税则号列	货品名称	最惠(%)	普通	增值税率	出口退税	计量单位	监管条件	Article Description
5308.9012	----按重量计苎麻含量在85%及以上的色纱线	6	50	17	16	千克		----Containing 85% or more by weight of ramie, coloured yarn
5308.9013	----按重量计苎麻含量在85%以下的未漂白或漂白纱线	6	50	17	16	千克		----Containing less than 85% by weight of ramie, unbleached or bleached yarn
5308.9014	----按重量计苎麻含量在85%以下的色纱线	6	50	17	16	千克		----Containing less than 85% by weight of coloured yarn
	---其他:							---Other:
5308.9091	----纸纱线	6	70	17	16	千克		----Paper yarn
5308.9099	----其他	6	45	17	16	千克		----Other
53.09	亚麻机织物:							**Woven fabrics of flax:**
	-按重量计亚麻含量在85%及以上:							-Containing 85% or more by weight of flax:
	--未漂白或漂白:							--Unbleached or bleached:
5309.1110	---未漂白	10	80	17	16	米/千克		---Unbleached
5309.1120	---漂白	10	80	17	16	米/千克		---Bleached
5309.1900	--其他	10	80	17	16	米/千克		--Other
	-按重量计亚麻含量在85%以下:							-Containing less than 85% by weight of flax:
	--未漂白或漂白:							--Unbleached or bleached:
5309.2110	---未漂白	10	80	17	16	米/千克		---Unbleached
5309.2110 11	未漂白与精梳毛混纺的亚麻机织物(亚麻含量在85%以下,含17%以上羊毛或动物细毛)	10	80	17	16	米/千克		Woven fabrics of flax, mixed, containing ≥17% by weight of combed wool or fine animal hair, containing <85% by weight of flax, unbleached
5309.2110 19	未漂白的其他混纺亚麻机织物(亚麻含量在85%以下,含17%以上羊毛或动物细毛)	10	80	17	16	米/千克		Woven fabrics of flax, mixed, containing ≥17% by weight of wool or fine animal hair, containing <85% by weight of flax, unbleached
5309.2110 21	未漂白的混纺亚麻府绸及细平布(亚麻含量在85%以下,与棉及化纤混纺,棉限内)	10	80	17	16	米/千克		Poplin and fine plain cloth, mixedwith cotton and man-made fibres, containing <85% by weightof flax, unbleached, cotton within limitations
5309.2110 22	未漂白的混纺亚麻机织平布(亚麻含量在85%以下,与棉及化纤混纺,棉限内)	10	80	17	16	米/千克		Plain cloth, mixed with cotton and man-made fibres, containing <85% by weight of flax, unbleached, cotton within limitations
5309.2110 23	未漂白的混纺亚麻机织印染用布(亚麻含量在85%以下,与棉及化纤混纺,棉限内)	10	80	17	16	米/千克		Woven fabrics of flax for printing and dying, mixed with cotton and man-made fibres, containing <85% by weight of flax, unbleached, cotton within limitations
5309.2110 24	未漂白的混纺亚麻其他机织物(亚麻含量在85%以下,与棉及化纤混纺,棉限内)	10	80	17	16	米/千克		Other woven fabrics of flax, mixed with cotton and man-made fibres, containing < 85% by weight of flax, unbleached, cotton within limitations
5309.2110 25	未漂白的混纺亚麻府绸及细平布(亚麻含量在85%以下,与棉及化纤混纺,化纤限内)	10	80	17	16	米/千克		Poplin and fine plain cloth, mixed with cotton and man-made fibres, containing < 85% by weight of flax, unbleached, man-made fibres within limitations
5309.2110 26	未漂白的混纺亚麻机织平布(亚麻含量在85%以下,与棉及化纤混纺,化纤限内)	10	80	17	16	米/千克		Plain cloth, mixed with cotton and man-made fibres, containing < 85% by weight of flax, unbleached, man-made fibres within limitations
5309.2110 27	未漂白的混纺亚麻机织印染用布(亚麻含量在85%以下,与棉及化纤混纺,化纤限内)	10	80	17	16	米/千克		Woven fabrics of flax for printing and dying, mixed with cotton and man-made fibres, containing < 85% by weight of flax, unbleached, man-made fibres within limitations
5309.2110 28	未漂白的混纺亚麻其他机织物(亚麻含量在85%以下,与棉及化纤混纺,化纤限内)	10	80	17	16	米/千克		Other woven fabrics of flax, mixed with cotton and man-made fibres, containing < 85% by weight of flax, unbleached, man-made fibres within limitations
5309.2110 29	未漂白的混纺亚麻其他机织物(亚麻含量在85%以下,与棉及化纤混纺)	10	80	17	16	米/千克		Other woven fabrics of flax, mixed with cotton and man-made fibres, containing < 85% by weight of flax, unbleached
5309.2110 91	未漂白的混纺亚麻其他机织物(亚麻含量<85%,主要或仅与精梳羊毛或动物细毛混纺)	10	80	17	16	米/千克		Other woven fabrics of flax, mixed mainly or solely with combed wool or fine animal hair, containing < 85% by weight of flax, unbleached

税则号列	货品名称	最惠(%)	普通	增值税率	出口退税	计量单位	监管条件	Article Description
5309.2110 99	未漂白的混纺亚麻其他机织物(亚麻含量在85%以下)	10	80	17	16	米/千克		Other woven fabrics of flax, mixed, containing < 85% by weight of flax, unbleached
5309.2120	---漂白	10	80	17	16	米/千克		---Bleached
5309.2120 11	漂白与精梳毛混纺的亚麻机织物(亚麻含量在85%以下,含17%以上羊毛或动物细毛)	10	80	17	16	米/千克		Woven fabrics of flax, mixed, containing ≥17% by weight of combed wool or fine animal hair, containing < 85% by weight of flax, bleached
5309.2120 19	漂白的其他混纺亚麻机织物(亚麻含量在85%以下,含17%以上羊毛或动物细毛)	10	80	17	16	米/千克		Other woven fabrics of flax, mixed, containing ≥17% by weight of wool or fine animal hair, containing < 85% by weight of flax, bleached
5309.2120 21	漂白的混纺亚麻府绸及细平布(亚麻含量在85%以下,与棉及化纤混纺,棉限内)	10	80	17	16	米/千克		Poplin and fine plain cloth, mixed with cotton and man-made fibres, containing < 85% by weight of flax, bleached, cotton within limitations
5309.2120 22	漂白的混纺亚麻机织平布(亚麻含量在85%以下,与棉及化纤混纺,棉限内)	10	80	17	16	米/千克		Plain cloth, mixed with cotton and man-made fibres, containing < 85% by weight of flax, bleached, cotton within limitations
5309.2120 23	漂白的混纺亚麻机织印染用布(亚麻含量在85%以下,与棉及化纤混纺,棉限内)	10	80	17	16	米/千克		Woven fabrics of flax for printing and dying, mixed with cotton and man-made fibres, containing < 85% by weight of flax, bleached, cotton within limitations
5309.2120 24	漂白的混纺亚麻其他机织物(亚麻含量在85%以下,与棉及化纤混纺,棉限内)	10	80	17	16	米/千克		Other woven fabrics of flax, mixed with cotton and man-made fibres, containing < 85% by weight of flax, bleached, cotton within limitations
5309.2120 25	漂白的混纺亚麻府绸及细平布(亚麻含量在85%以下,与棉及化纤混纺,化纤限内)	10	80	17	16	米/千克		Poplin and fine plain cloth, mixed with cotton and man-made fibres, containing < 85% by weight of flax, bleached, man-made fibres within limitations
5309.2120 26	漂白的混纺亚麻机织平布(亚麻含量在85%以下,与棉及化纤混纺,化纤限内)	10	80	17	16	米/千克		Plain cloth, mixed with cotton and man-made fibres, containing < 85% by weight of flax, bleached, man-made fibres within limitations
5309.2120 27	漂白的混纺亚麻机织印染用布(亚麻含量在85%以下,与棉及化纤混纺,化纤限内)	10	80	17	16	米/千克		Woven fabrics of flax for printing and dying, mixed with cotton and man-made fibres, containing < 85% by weight of flax, bleached, man-made fibres within limitations
5309.2120 28	漂白的混纺亚麻其他机织物(亚麻含量在85%以下,与棉及化纤混纺,化纤限内)	10	80	17	16	米/千克		Other woven fabrics of flax, mixed with cotton and man-made fibres, containing < 85% by weight of flax, bleached, man-made fibres within limitations
5309.2120 29	漂白的混纺亚麻其他机织物(亚麻含量在85%以下,与棉及化纤混纺)	10	80	17	16	米/千克		Other woven fabrics of flax, mixed with cotton and man-made fibres, containing < 85% by weight of flax, bleached
5309.2120 91	漂白的混纺亚麻其他机织物(亚麻含量<85%,主要或仅与精梳羊毛或动物细毛混纺)	10	80	17	16	米/千克		Other woven fabrics of flax, mixed mainly or solely with combed wool or fine animal hair, containing < 85% by weight of flax, bleached
5309.2120 99	漂白的混纺亚麻其他机织物(亚麻含量在85%以下)	10	80	17	16	米/千克		Other woven fabrics of flax, mixed, containing < 85% by weight of flax, bleached
5309.2900	--其他	10	80	17	16	米/千克		--Other
5309.2900 11	其他与精梳毛混纺的亚麻机织物(亚麻含量在85%以下,含17%以上羊毛或动物细毛)	10	80	17	16	米/千克		Other woven fabrics of flax, mixed, containing ≥17% by weight of combed wool or fine animal hair, containing < 85% by weight of flax
5309.2900 19	其他混纺亚麻机织物(亚麻含量在85%以下,含17%以上羊毛或动物细毛)	10	80	17	16	米/千克		Other woven fabrics of flax, mixed, containing ≥17% by weight of wool or fine animal hair, containing < 85% by weight of flax
5309.2900 21	其他混纺亚麻府绸及细平布(亚麻含量在85%以下,与棉及化纤混纺,棉限内)	10	80	17	16	米/千克		Other poplin and fine plain cloth of flax, mixed with cotton and man-made fibres, containing < 85% by weight of flax, cotton within limitations
5309.2900 22	其他混纺亚麻机织平布(亚麻含量在85%以下,与棉及化纤混纺,棉限内)	10	80	17	16	米/千克		Other plain cloth of flax, mixed with cotton and man-made fibres, containing < 85% by weightof flax, cotton within limitations

税则号列	货品名称	最惠(%)	普通	增值税率	出口退税	计量单位	监管条件	Article Description
5309.2900 23	其他混纺亚麻机织印染用布(亚麻含量在85%以下,与棉及化纤混纺,棉限内)	10	80	17	16	米/千克		Other woven fabrics of flax for printing and dying, mixed with cotton and man-made fibres, containing < 85% by weight of flax, cotton within limitations
5309.2900 24	其他混纺亚麻其他机织物(亚麻含量在85%以下,与棉及化纤混纺,棉限内)	10	80	17	16	米/千克		Other woven fabrics of flax, mixed with cotton and man-made fibres, containing < 85% by weight of flax, cotton within limitations
5309.2900 25	其他混纺亚麻府绸及细平布(亚麻含量在85%以下,与棉及化纤混纺,化纤限内)	10	80	17	16	米/千克		Poplin and fine plain cloth of flax, mixed with cotton and man-made fibres, containing < 85% by weight of flax, man-made fibres within limitations
5309.2900 26	其他混纺亚麻机织平布(亚麻含量在85%以下,与棉及化纤混纺,化纤限内)	10	80	17	16	米/千克		Plain cloth of flax, mixed with cotton and man-made fibres, containing < 85% by weight of flax, man-made fibres within limitations
5309.2900 27	其他混纺亚麻机织印染用布(亚麻含量在85%以下,与棉及化纤混纺,化纤限内)	10	80	17	16	米/千克		Other woven fabrics of flax for printing and dying, mixed with cotton and man-made fibres, containing < 85% by weight of flax, man-made fibres within limitations
5309.2900 28	其他混纺亚麻其他机织物(亚麻含量在85%以下,与棉及化纤混纺,化纤限内)	10	80	17	16	米/千克		Other woven fabrics of flax, mixed with cotton and man-made fibres, containing < 85% by weight of flax, man-made fibres within limitations
5309.2900 29	其他混纺亚麻其他机织物(亚麻含量在85%以下,与棉及化纤混纺)	10	80	17	16	米/千克		Other woven fabrics of flax, mixed with cotton and man-made fibres, containing < 85% by weight of flax
5309.2900 91	其他混纺亚麻其他机织物(亚麻含量<85%以下,主要或仅与精梳羊毛或动物细毛混纺)	10	80	17	16	米/千克		Other woven fabrics of flax, mixed mainly or solely with combed wool or fine animal hair, containing < 85% by weight of flax
5309.2900 99	其他混纺亚麻机织物(亚麻含量在85%以下)	10	80	17	16	米/千克		Other woven fabrics of flax, mixed, containing < 85% by weight of flax
53.10	黄麻或税目53.03的其他纺织用韧皮纤维机织物:							**Woven fabrics of jute or of other textilebast fibres of heading No. 53.03:**
5310.1000	-未漂白	10	40	17	16	米/千克		-Unbleached
5310.1000 11	未漂白黄麻或其他韧皮纤维机织物(宽度不超过150厘米,与精梳羊毛或动物细毛混纺)	10	40	17	16	米/千克		Woven fabrics of jute or of other textilebast fibres, width≤150cm, mixed with combed wool or fine animal hair, unbleached
5310.1000 19	未漂白黄麻或其他韧皮纤维机织物(宽度不超过150厘米,与其他纤维混纺)	10	40	17	16	米/千克		Woven fabrics of jute or of other textilebast fibres, width ≤150cm, mixed with other fibres, unbleached
5310.1000 91	未漂白黄麻或其他韧皮纤维机织物(宽度超过150厘米,与精梳羊毛或动物细毛混纺)	10	40	17	16	米/千克		Woven fabrics of jute or of other textilebast fibres, width > 150cm, mixed with combed wool or fine animal hair, unbleached
5310.1000 99	未漂白黄麻或其他韧皮纤维机织物(宽度超过150厘米,与其他纤维混纺)	10	40	17	16	米/千克		Woven fabrics of jute or of other textilebast fibres, width > 150cm, mixed with other fibres, unbleached
5310.9000	-其他	10	40	17	16	米/千克		-Other
5310.9000 11	其他黄麻机织物,宽度≤150厘米(含税号5303其他纺织用韧皮纤维布与精梳羊毛或动物细毛混纺)	10	40	17	16	米/千克		Other woven fabrics of jute or of other textilebast fibres of heading No. 53.03, width ≤ 150cm, mixed with combed wool or fine animal hair
5310.9000 19	其他黄麻机织物,宽度≤150厘米(含税号5303的其他纺织用韧皮纤维布,与其他纤维混纺)	10	40	17	16	米/千克		Other woven fabrics of jute or of other textilebast fibres of heading No. 53.03, width ≤ 150cm, mixed with other fibres
5310.9000 91	其他黄麻机织物,宽度>150厘米(含税号5303其他纺织用韧皮纤维布与精梳羊毛或动物细毛混纺)	10	40	17	16	米/千克		Other woven fabrics of jute or of other textilebast fibres of heading No. 53.03, width > 150cm, mixed with combed wool or fine animal hair
5310.9000 99	其他黄麻机织物,宽度>150厘米(含税号5303的其他纺织用韧皮纤维布,与其他纤维混纺)	10	40	17	16	米/千克		Other woven fabrics of jute or of other textilebast fibres of heading No. 53.03, width > 150cm, mixed with other fibres
53.11	其他纺织用植物纤维机织物;纸纱线机织物:							**Woven fabrics of other vegetable textile fibres; woven fabrics of paper yarn:**
	---苎麻的:							---Of ramie:

税则号列	货品名称	最惠(%)	普通	增值税率	出口退税	计量单位	监管条件	Article Description
5311.0012	----按重量计苎麻含量在85%及以上的未漂白机织物	10	80	17	16	米/千克		----Containing 85% or more by weight of ramie, unbleached woven fabrics
5311.0012 11	未漂白与精梳毛混纺的苎麻机织物(苎麻含量在85%及以上,含17%以上羊毛或动物细毛)	10	80	17	16	米/千克		Woven fabrics of ramie, mixed, containing≥17% by weight of combed wool or fine animal hair, containing≥85% by weight of ramie, unbleached
5311.0012 19	未漂白苎麻机织物(苎麻含量在85%及以上,含17%以上羊毛或动物细毛)	10	80	17	16	米/千克		Woven fabrics of ramie, mixed, containing ≥ 17% by weight of wool or fine animal hair, containing≥85% by weight of ramie, unbleached
5311.0012 21	未漂白的苎麻府绸及细平布(苎麻含量在85%及以上,与棉及化纤混纺,棉限内)	10	80	17	16	米/千克		Poplin and fine plain cloth of ramie, mixed withcotton and man-made fibres, containing ≥85% by weight of ramie, unbleached, cotton within limitations
5311.0012 22	未漂白的苎麻机织平布(苎麻含量在85%及以上,与棉及化纤混纺,棉限内)	10	80	17	16	米/千克		Plain cloth of ramie, mixed with cotton and man-made fibres, containing ≥85% by weight of ramie, unbleached, cotton within limitations
5311.0012 23	未漂白的苎麻机织印染用布(苎麻含量在85%及以上,与棉及化纤混纺,棉限内)	10	80	17	16	米/千克		Woven fabrics of ramie for printing and dying, mixed with cotton and man-made fibres, containing ≥85% by weight of ramie, unbleached, cotton within limitations
5311.0012 29	未漂白的苎麻其他机织物(苎麻含量在85%及以上,与棉及化纤混纺,棉限内)	10	80	17	16	米/千克		Other woven fabrics of ramie, mixed with cotton and man-made fibres, containing ≥ 85% by weight of ramie, unbleached, cotton within limitations
5311.0012 31	未漂白的苎麻府绸及细平布(苎麻含量在85%及以上,与棉及化纤混纺,化纤限内)	10	80	17	16	米/千克		Poplin and fine plain cloth of ramie, mixed with cotton and man-made fibres, containing ≥ 85% by weight of ramie unbleached, man-made fibres within limitations
5311.0012 32	未漂白的苎麻机织平布(苎麻含量在85%及以上,与棉及化纤混纺,化纤限内)	10	80	17	16	米/千克		Plain cloth of ramie, mixed with cotton and man-made fibres, containing≥85% by weight of ramie, unbleached, man-made fibres within limitations
5311.0012 33	未漂白的苎麻机织印染用布(苎麻含量在85%及以上,与棉及化纤混纺,化纤限内)	10	80	17	16	米/千克		Woven fabrics of ramie for printing and dying, mixed with cotton and man-made fibres, containing≥85% by weight of ramie unbleached, man-made fibres within limitations
5311.0012 39	未漂白的苎麻其他机织物(苎麻含量在85%及以上,与棉及化纤混纺,化纤限内)	10	80	17	16	米/千克		Other woven fabrics of ramie, mixed with cotton and man-made fibres, containing ≥ 85% by weight of ramie, unbleached, man-made fibres within limitations
5311.0012 40	未漂白的苎麻其他机织物(苎麻含量在85%及以上,与棉及化纤混纺)	10	80	17	16	米/千克		Other woven fabrics of ramie, mixed with cotton and man-made fibres, containing ≥ 85% by weight of ramie, unbleached
5311.0012 91	未漂白的苎麻其他机织物(苎麻含量在85%及以上,主要或仅与精梳羊毛/细毛混纺)	10	80	17	16	米/千克		Other woven fabrics of ramie, mixed mainly or solely with combed wool or fine animal hair, containing ≥ 85% by weight of ramie, unbleached
5311.0012 99	未漂白的苎麻其他机织物(苎麻含量在85%及以上)	10	80	17	16	米/千克		Other woven fabrics of ramie, containing ≥ 85% by weight of ramie, unbleached
5311.0013	----按重量计苎麻含量在85%及以上的其他机织物	12	80	17	16	米/千克		----Containing 85% or more by weight of ramie, other woven fabrics
5311.0013 11	与精梳毛混纺的苎麻其他机织物(苎麻含量≥85%,含17%以上羊毛或动物细毛)	12	80	17	16	米/千克		Other woven fabrics of ramie, mixed, containing ≥ 17% by weight of combedwool or fine animal hair, containing≥85% by weight of ramie
5311.0013 19	苎麻其他机织物(苎麻含量≥85%,羊毛/细毛>17%)	12	80	17	16	米/千克		Other woven fabrics of ramie, mixed, containing < 17% by weight of wool or fine animal hair, containing≥85% by weight of ramie
5311.0013 21	苎麻府绸及细平布(苎麻含量≥85%,与棉及化纤混纺,棉限内)	12	80	17	16	米/千克		Poplin and fine plain cloth of ramie, mixed with cotton and man-made fibres, containing ≥ 85% by weight of ramie, cotton within limitations

税则号列	货　品　名　称	最惠(%)	普通	增值税率	出口退税	计量单位	监管条件	Article Description
5311.0013 22	苎麻机织平布(苎麻含量≥85%,与棉及化纤混纺,棉限内)	12	80	17	16	米/千克		Plain cloth of ramie,mixed with cotton andman-made fibres, containing ≥85% by weight of ramie, cotton within limitations
5311.0013 23	苎麻机织印染布(苎麻含量≥85%,与棉及化纤混纺,棉限内)	12	80	17	16	米/千克		Woven fabrics of ramie for printing and dying,mixed with cotton and man-made fibres, containing ≥85% by weight of ramie,cotton within limitations
5311.0013 29	苎麻其他机织物(苎麻含量≥85%,与棉及化纤混纺,棉限内)	12	80	17	16	米/千克		Woven fabrics of ramie, mixed with cotton and man-made fibres, containing ≥85% by weight of ramie, cotton within limitations
5311.0013 31	苎麻府绸及细平布(苎麻含量≥85%,与棉及化纤混纺,化纤限内)	12	80	17	16	米/千克		Poplin and fine plain cloth of ramie,mixed with cotton and man-made fibres, containing ≥ 85% by weight of ramie,man-made fibres within limitations
5311.0013 32	苎麻机织平布(苎麻含量≥85%,与棉及化纤混纺,化纤限内)	12	80	17	16	米/千克		Plain cloth of ramie, mixed with cotton and man-made fibres, containing ≥85% by weight of ramie, man-made fibres within limitations
5311.0013 33	苎麻机织印染布(苎麻含量≥85%,与棉及化纤混纺,化纤限内)	12	80	17	16	米/千克		Woven fabrics of ramie for printing and dying, mixed with cotton and man-made fibres, containing ≥85% by weight of ramie, man-made fibres within limitations
5311.0013 39	苎麻其他机织物(苎麻含量≥85%,与棉及化纤混纺,化纤限内)	12	80	17	16	米/千克		Other woven fabrics of ramie mixed with cotton and man-made fibres, containing≥85% by weight of ramie, man-made fibres within limitations
5311.0013 40	苎麻其他机织物(苎麻含量≥85%,与棉及化纤混纺)	12	80	17	16	米/千克		Other woven fabrics of ramie mixed, with cotton and man-made fibres, containing≥85% by weight of ramie
5311.0013 91	苎麻其他机织物(苎麻含量≥85%,主要/仅与精梳羊毛/细毛混纺)	12	80	17	16	米/千克		Other woven fabrics of ramie, mixed mainly or solely with combed wool or fine animal hair, containing ≥ 85% by weight of ramie
5311.0013 99	苎麻其他机织物(苎麻含量≥85%)	12	80	17	16	米/千克		Other woven fabrics of ramie, containing ≥85% by weight of ramie
5311.0014	----按重量计苎麻含量在85%以下的未漂白机织物	10	80	17	16	米/千克		----Containing less than 85% by weight of ramie, unbleached woven fabrics
5311.0014 11	未漂白与精梳羊毛混纺苎麻机织物(苎麻含量<85%,含17%以上羊毛/细毛)	10	80	17	16	米/千克		Other woven fabrics of ramie, mixed, containing < 85% by weight of ramie, containing ≥ 17% by weight of combed wool or fine animal hair, unbleached
5311.0014 19	未漂白苎麻机织物(苎麻含量<85%,含17%以上羊毛/细毛)	10	80	17	16	米/千克		Other woven fabrics of ramie, containing ≥17% by weight of wool or fine animal hair, containing < 85% by weight of ramie, unbleached
5311.0014 21	未漂白的苎麻府绸及细平布(苎麻含量<85%,与棉及化纤混纺,棉限内)	10	80	17	16	米/千克		Poplin and fine plain cloth of ramie, mixed with cotton and man-made fibres, containing < 85% by weight of ramie, unbleached, cotton within limitations
5311.0014 22	未漂白的苎麻机织平布(苎麻含量<85%,与棉及化纤混纺,棉限内)	10	80	17	16	米/千克		Plain cloth of ramie, mixed with cotton and man-made fibres, containing < 85% by weight of ramie, unbleached, cotton within limitations
5311.0014 23	未漂白的苎麻机织印染用布(苎麻含量<85%,与棉及化纤混纺,棉限内)	10	80	17	16	米/千克		Woven fabrics of ramie for printing and dying, mixed with cotton and man-made fibres, containing < 85% by weight of ramie, unbleached, cotton within limitations
5311.0014 29	未漂白的苎麻其他机织物(苎麻含量<85%,与棉及化纤混纺,棉限内)	10	80	17	16	米/千克		Other woven fabrics of ramie, mixed with cotton and man-made fibres, containing < 85% by weight of ramie, unbleached, cotton within limitations
5311.0014 31	未漂白的苎麻府绸及细平布(苎麻含量<85%,与棉及化纤混纺,化纤限内)	10	80	17	16	米/千克		Poplin and fine plain cloth of ramie, mixed with cotton and man-made fibres, containing < 85% by weight of ramie, unbleached, man-made fibres within limitations
5311.0014 32	未漂白的苎麻机织平布(苎麻含量<85%,与棉及化纤混纺,化纤限内)	10	80	17	16	米/千克		Plain cloth of ramie, mixed with cotton and man-made fibres, containing < 85% by weight of ramie, unbleached, man-made fibres within limitations

税则号列	货品名称	最惠(%)	普通	增值税率	出口退税	计量单位	监管条件	Article Description
5311.0014 33	未漂白的苎麻机织印染用布(苎麻含量<85%,与棉及化纤混纺,化纤限内)	10	80	17	16	米/千克		Woven fabrics of ramie for printing and dying, mixed with cotton and man-made fibres, containing < 85% by weight of ramie, unbleached, man-made fibres within limitations
5311.0014 39	未漂白的苎麻其他机织物(苎麻含量<85%,与棉及化纤混纺,化纤限内)	10	80	17	16	米/千克		Other woven fabrics of ramie, mixed with cotton and man-made fibres, containing <85% by weight of ramie, unbleached, man-made fibres within limitations
5311.0014 40	未漂白的苎麻其他机织物(苎麻含量<85%,与棉及化纤混纺)	10	80	17	16	米/千克		Other woven fabrics of ramie, mixed with cotton and man-made fibres, containing < 85% by weight of ramie, unbleached
5311.0014 91	未漂白的苎麻其他机织物(苎麻含量<85%,主要或仅与精梳羊毛或动物细毛混纺)	10	80	17	16	米/千克		Other woven fabrics of ramie, mixed mainly or solely with combed wool or fine animal hair, containing < 85% by weight of ramie, unbleached
5311.0014 99	未漂白的苎麻其他机织物(苎麻含量<85%)	10	80	17	16	米/千克		Other woven fabrics of ramie, containing < 85% by weight of ramie, unbleached
5311.0015	----按重量计苎麻含量在85%以下的其他机织物	12	80	17	16	米/千克		----Containing less than 85% by weight of ramie, other woven fabrics
5311.0015 11	其他苎麻机织物,含量<85%(毛重>17%,主要或仅与精梳羊毛或动物细毛混纺)	12	80	17	16	米/千克		Other woven fabrics of ramie, mixed mainly or solely with combed wool or of fine animal hair, containing < 85% by weight of ramie, containing > 17% by weight of combed wool or fine animal hair
5311.0015 19	其他苎麻机织物(苎麻含量<85%,含>17%羊毛或动物细毛)	12	80	17	16	米/千克		Other woven fabrics of ramie, mixed, containing > 17% by weight of wool or fine animal hair, containing < 85% by weight of ramie
5311.0015 21	苎麻府绸及细平布(苎麻含量<85%,与棉及化纤混纺,棉限内)	12	80	17	16	米/千克		Poplin and fine plain cloth of ramie, mixed with cotton and man-made fibres, containing < 85% by weight of ramie, cotton within limitations
5311.0015 22	苎麻机织平布(苎麻含量<85%,与棉及化纤混纺,棉限内)	12	80	17	16	米/千克		Plain cloth of ramie, mixed with cotton and man-made fibres, containing < 85% by weight of ramie, cotton within limitations
5311.0015 29	其他苎麻机织物(苎麻含量<85%,与棉及化纤混纺,棉限内)	12	80	17	16	米/千克		Other woven fabrics of ramie, mixed with cotton and man-made fibres, containing < 85% by weight of ramie, cotton within limitations
5311.0015 31	苎麻府绸及细平布(苎麻含量<85%,与棉及化纤混纺,化纤限内)	12	80	17	16	米/千克		Poplin and fine plain cloth of ramie, mixed with cotton and man-made fibres, containing < 85% by weight of ramie, man-made fibres within limitations
5311.0015 32	苎麻机织平布(苎麻含量<85%,与棉及化纤混纺,化纤限内)	12	80	17	16	米/千克		Plain cloth of ramie, mixed with cotton and man-made fibres, containing < 85% by weight of ramie, man-made fibres within limitations
5311.0015 33	苎麻机织印染用布(苎麻含量<85%,与棉及化纤混纺,化纤限内)	12	80	17	16	米/千克		Woven fabrics of ramie for printing and dying, mixed with cotton and man-made fibres, containing <85% by weight of ramie, man-made fibres within limitations
5311.0015 39	其他苎麻机织物(苎麻含量<85%,与棉及化纤混纺,化纤限内)	12	80	17	16	米/千克		Other woven fabrics of ramie, mixed with cotton and man-made fibres, containing <85% by weight of ramie, man-made fibres within limitations
5311.0015 91	其他苎麻机织物(苎麻含量<85%,主要或仅与精梳羊毛或动物细毛混纺)	12	80	17	16	米/千克		Other woven fabrics of ramie, mixed mainly or solely with combed wool or fine animal hair, containing < 85% by weight of ramie
5311.0015 99	其他苎麻机织物(指按重量计苎麻含量<85%)	12	80	17	16	米/千克		Other woven fabrics of ramie, containing < 85% by weight of ramie
5311.0020	---纸纱线的	10	90	17	16	米/千克		---Of paper yarn
5311.0020 10	纸纱线机织物(主要或仅与精梳羊毛或动物细毛混纺)	10	90	17	16	米/千克		Woven fabrics of paper yarn, mixed mainly or solely with combed wool or combed fine animal hair
5311.0020 90	纸纱线机织物	10	90	17	16	米/千克		Woven fabrics of paper yarn
5311.0030	---大麻的	10	50	17	16	米/千克		---Of true hemp
5311.0090	---其他	10	50	17	16	米/千克		---Other

税则号列	货　品　名　称	最惠(%)	普通	增值税率	出口退税	计量单位	监管条件	Article Description
5311.0090 10	其他纺织用植物纤维机织物(含17%以上羊毛或动物细毛)	10	50	17	16	米/千克		Other woven fabrics of vegetable textile fibres(containing > 17% by weight of combed wool or of combed fine animal hair)
5311.0090 21	其他纺织用植物纤维府绸及细平布(与棉及化纤混纺,棉限内)	10	50	17	16	米/千克		Poplin and fine plain cloth of other vegetable textile fibres, mixed with cotton and man-made fibres, cotton within limitations
5311.0090 22	其他纺织用植物纤维机织平布(与棉及化纤混纺,棉限内)	10	50	17	16	米/千克		Plain cloth of other vegetable textilefibres,mixed with cotton and man-made fibres,cotton within limitations
5311.0090 29	其他纺织用植物纤维机织物(与棉及化纤混纺,棉限内)	10	50	17	16	米/千克		Other woven fabrics of other vegetable textile fibres, mixed with cotton and man-made fibres, cotton within limitations
5311.0090 32	其他纺织用植物纤维机织平布(与棉及化纤混纺,化纤限内)	10	50	17	16	米/千克		Plain cloth of other vegetable textile fibres, mixed with cotton and man-made fibres, man-made fibres within limitations
5311.0090 33	其他纺织用植物纤维机织印染用布(与棉及化纤混纺,化纤限内)	10	50	17	16	米/千克		Other woven fabrics of other vegetable textile fibres for printing and dying, mixed with cotton and man-made fibres, man-made fibres within limitations
5311.0090 39	其他纺织用植物纤维其他机织物(与棉及化纤混纺,化纤限内)	10	50	17	16	米/千克		Other woven fabrics of other vegetable textile fibres, mixed with cotton and man-made fibres, man-made fibres within limitations
5311.0090 40	其他纺织用植物纤维其他机织物(与棉及化纤混纺)	10	50	17	16	米/千克		Other woven fabrics of other vegetable textile fibres, mixed with cotton and man-made fibres
5311.0090 90	其他纺织用植物纤维其他机织物	10	50	17	16	米/千克		Other woven fabrics of other vegetable texile fibres

第五十四章
化学纤维长丝，化学纤维纺织材料制扁条及类似品

Chapter 54
Man-made filaments; strip and the like of man made textile materials

注释：

一、本协调制度所称"化学纤维"，是指通过下列任一方法加工制得的有机聚合物的短纤或长丝：

(一)将有机单体物质加以聚合而制成聚合物，例如，聚酰胺、聚酯、聚烯烃、聚氨基甲酸酯；或通过上述加工将聚合物经化学改性制得(例如，聚乙酸乙烯酯水解得的聚乙烯醇)；

(二)将天然有机聚合物(例如，纤维素)溶解或化学处理制成聚合物，例如，铜铵纤维或粘胶纤维；或将天然有机聚合物(例如，纤维素、酪蛋白及其他蛋白质、或藻酸)经化学改性制成聚合物，例如，醋酸纤维素纤维或藻酸盐纤维。

对于化学纤维，所称"合成"，是指(一)款所述的纤维；所称"人造"，是指(二)款所述的纤维。税目54.04或54.05的扁条及类似品不视作化学纤维。

对于纺织材料，所称"化学纤维""合成纤维"及"人造纤维"，其含义应与上述解释相同。

二、税目54.02及54.03不适用于第五十五章的合成纤维或人造纤维的长丝丝束。

Notes:

1. Throughout the Nomenclature, the term "man-made fibres" means stapl fibres and filaments of organic polymers produced by manufacruring processes, either:

(a) By polymerization of organic monomers to prduce polymers such as polyamides, polyesters, polyolefins or polyurethanes, or by chemical modification of polymers plrduced by this process (for example, poly (vinyl alcohol) prepared by the hydrolysis of poly (vinyl acetate);

(b) By dissolution or chemical treatment of natural organic polymers (for example, cellulose) to produce polymers such as cuprammonium rayon (cupro) or viscose rayon, or by chemical modification of narural organic polymers (for example, cellulose, casein and other proteins, or alginic acid), to produce polymers such as cellulose acetate or alginates.

The terms "synthetic" and "artificial", used in relation to fibres, mean: synthetic: fibres as defined at (a); artificial: fibres as defined at (b). Strip and the like of heading 50.04 or 54.05are not considered to be man made fibres.

The tems "man-made", "synthetic" and "artificial" shall have the same meanings when used in relation to "textile materials".

2. Headings 54.02 and 54.03 do not apply to synthetic or artificial filament tow of chapter 55.

税则号列	货品名称	最惠(%)	普通	增值税率	出口退税	计量单位	监管条件	Article Description
54.01	**化学纤维长丝纺制的缝纫线，不论是否供零售用：**							**Sewing thread of man-made filaments, whether or not put up for retail sale:**
	-合成纤维长丝纺制：							-Of synthetic filaments:
5401.1010	---非供零售用	5	70	17	16	千克		---Not put up for retail sale
5401.1020	---供零售用	5	90	17	16	千克		---Put up for retail sale
	-人造纤维长丝纺制：							-Of artificial filaments:
5401.2010	---非供零售用	5	35	17	16	千克		---Not put up for retail sale
5401.2020	---供零售用	5	90	17	16	千克		---Put up for retail sale
54.02	**合成纤维长丝纱线(缝纫线除外)，非供零售用，包括细度在67分特以下的合成纤维单丝：**							**Synthetic filament yarn (other than sewing thread), not put up for retail sale, including synthetic monofilament of less than 67 decitex:**
	-尼龙或其他聚酰胺纺制的高强力纱：							-High tenacity yarn of nylon or other polyamides:
	--芳香族聚酰胺纺制：							--Of aramides:
5402.1110	---聚间苯二甲酰间苯二胺纺制	5	70	17	16	千克	A	---Of poly-isophthaloyl metaphenylene diamide
5402.1120	---聚对苯二甲酰对苯二胺纺制	5	70	17	16	千克	A	---Of poly-p-phenylene terephthalamide
5402.1190	---其他	5	70	17	16	千克	A	---Other
	--其他：							--Other:
5402.1910	---聚酰胺-6(尼龙-6)纺制的	5	70	17	16	千克	A	---Of nylon-6
5402.1920	---聚酰胺-6,6(尼龙-6,6)纺制的	5	70	17	16	千克	A	---Of nylon-6,6
5402.1990	---其他	5	70	17	16	千克	A	---Other
5402.2000	-聚酯高强力纱	5	70	17	16	千克		-High tenacity yarn of polyesters
5402.2000 10	非零售聚酯高强力纱(单丝/未捻或捻度<5转/米复丝单纱)	5	70	17	16	千克	A	High tenacity yarn of polyesters, single yarn, untwisted or twist < 5 turns/m multiple (folded), not put up for retail sale
5402.2000 20	非零售聚酯高强力纱(捻度≥5转/米复丝单纱)	5	70	17	16	千克	A	High tenacity yarn of polyesters single yarn, twist≥5 turns/m multiple (folded), not put up for retail sale
5402.2000 90	非零售聚酯高强力多股纱	5	70	17	16	千克	A	High tenacity yarn of polyesters, multiple (folded), not put up for retail sale
	-变形纱线：							-Textured yarn:

税则号列	货品名称	最惠(%)	普通	增值税率	出口退税	计量单位	监管条件	Article Description
	--尼龙或其他聚酰胺纺制,每根单纱细度不超过50特:							--Of nylon or other polyamides, measuring per single yarn not more than 50 tex:
	---弹力丝:							---Elastic filament:
5402.3111	----聚酰胺-6(尼龙-6)纺制的	5	80	17	16	千克	A	----Of nylon-6
5402.3112	----聚酰胺-6,6(尼龙-6,6)纺制	5	80	17	16	千克	A	----Of nylon-6,6
5402.3113	----芳香族聚酰胺纺制	5	80	17	16	千克	A	----Of aramides
5402.3119	----其他	5	80	17	16	千克	A	----Other
5402.3190	---其他	5	70	17	16	千克	A	---Other
	--尼龙或其他聚酰胺纺制,每根单纱细度超过50特:							--Of nylon or other polyamides, measuring per single yarn more than 50tex:
	---弹力丝:							---Elastic filament:
5402.3211	----聚酰胺-6(尼龙-6)纺制	5	80	17	16	千克		----Of nylon-6
5402.3212	----聚酰胺-6,6(尼龙-6,6)纺制	5	80	17	16	千克		----Of nylon-6,6
5402.3213	----芳香族聚酰胺纺制	5	80	17	16	千克		----Of aramides
5402.3219	----其他	5	80	17	16	千克		----Other
5402.3290	---其他	5	70	17	16	千克		---Other
	--聚酯纺制:							--Of polyesters:
5402.3310	---弹力丝	5	90	17	16	千克	A	---Elastic filament
5402.3390	---其他	5	70	17	16	千克	A	---Other
5402.3400	--聚丙烯纺制	5	70	17	16	千克		--Of polypropylene
5402.3900	--其他	5	70	17	16	千克		--Other
	-其他单纱,未加捻或捻度每米不超过50转:							-Other yarn, single, untwisted or with a twist not exceeding 50 turns per metre:
	--弹性纱线:							--Elastomeric:
5402.4410	---氨纶纺制单纱	5	70	17	16	千克		---Of polyurethane
5402.4490	---其他	5	70	17	16	千克	A	---Other
	---其他,尼龙或其他聚酰胺纱线:							---Other, of nylon or other polyamides:
5402.4510	---聚酰胺-6(尼龙-6)仿制的	5	70	17	16	千克		---Of nylon-6
5402.4520	---聚酰胺-6,6(尼龙-6,6)制的	5	70	17	16	千克		---Of nylon-6,6
5402.4530	---芳香族聚酰胺制的	5	70	17	16	千克		---Of aramides
5402.4590	---其他	5	70	17	16	千克		---Other
5402.4600	--其他,部分定向聚酯纱线	5	70	17	16	千克	A	--Other, of polyesters, partially oriented
5402.4700	--其他,聚酯纱线	5	70	17	16	千克	A	--Other, of polyesters
5402.4800	--其他,聚丙烯纱线	5	70	17	16	千克		--Other, Of polypropylene
	--其他:							--Other:
5402.4910	---聚乙烯长丝纱线(单纱)	5	70	17	16	千克		---Polyethylene filament yarn (yarn)
5402.4990	---其他	5	70	17	16	千克		---Other
5402.4990 01	非弹性氨纶单纱(非供零售用,未加捻或捻度每米不超过50转,缝纫线除外)	5	70	17	16	千克		Single yarn of polyurethane [untwisted or twist < 50turns/m multiple(folded), not in forms or packing for retail sale]
5402.4990 90	其他合成纤维长丝单纱(非供零售用,未加捻或捻度每米不超过50转,缝纫线除外)	5	70	17	16	千克		Other single yarn of synthetic filaments [untwisted or twist < 50turns/m multiple (folded), not in forms or packing for retail sale]
	-其他单纱,捻度每米超过50转:							-Other yarn, single, with a twist exceeding 50 turns per metre:
	--尼龙或其他聚酰胺纱线:							--Of nylon or other polyamides:
5402.5110	---聚酰胺-6(尼龙-6)制	5	70	17	16	千克		---Of nylon-6
5402.5120	---聚酰胺-6,6(尼龙-6,6)制	5	70	17	16	千克		---Of nylon-6,6
5402.5130	---芳香族聚酰胺纺制	5	70	17	16	千克		---Of aramides
5402.5190	---其他	5	70	17	16	千克		---Other
5402.5200	--聚酯纱线	5	70	17	16	千克		--Of polyesters
	--其他:							--Other:
5402.5910	---聚丙烯纱线	5	70	17	16	千克		---Of polypropylene
5402.5920	---聚乙烯长丝纱线(单纱)	5	70	17	16	千克		---Polyethylene filament yarn (yarn)
5402.5990	---其他	5	70	17	16	千克		---Other
	-其他纱线(多股纱线或缆线):							-Other yarn, multiple (folded) or cabled:

税则号列	货品名称	最惠(%)	普通	增值税率	出口退税	计量单位	监管条件	Article Description
	--尼龙或其他聚酰胺纺制:							--Of nylon or other polyamides:
5402.6110	---聚酰胺-6(尼龙-6)制	5	70	17	16	千克		---Of nylon-6
5402.6120	---聚酰胺-6,6(尼龙-6,6)制	5	70	17	16	千克		---Of nylon-6,6
5402.6130	---芳香族聚酰胺纺制	5	70	17	16	千克		---Of aramides
5402.6190	---其他	5	70	17	16	千克		---Other
5402.6200	--聚酯纺制	5	70	17	16	千克		--Of polyesters
	--其他:							--Other:
5402.6910	---聚丙烯纱线	5	70	17	16	千克		---Of polypropylene
5402.6920	---氨纶纱线	5	70	17	16	千克		---Of polyurethane
5402.6990	---其他	5	70	17	16	千克		---Other
54.03	**人造纤维长丝纱线(缝纫线除外),非供零售用,包括细度在67分特以下的人造纤维单丝:**							**Artificial filament yarn (other than sewing thread), not put up for retail sale, including artificial monofilament of less than 67 decitex:**
5403.1000	-粘胶纤维纺制的高强力纱	5	35	17	16	千克		-High tenacity yarn of viscose rayon
5403.1000 10	非零售粘胶纤维高强力纱(单丝/未捻或捻度5转/米以下的复丝单纱,非供零售用)	5	35	17	16	千克		High tenacity yarn of viscose rayon, single yarn, untwisted or twist < 5 turns/m, multiple (folded), not put up for retail sale
5403.1000 20	非零售粘胶纤维高强力纱(捻度5转/米及以上的复丝单纱)	5	35	17	16	千克		High tenacity yarn of viscose rayon, single yarn, twist > 5 turns/m, multiple (folded), not put up for retail sale
5403.1000 90	非零售粘胶纤维高强力多股纱	5	35	17	16	千克		High tenacity yarn of viscose rayon, multiple (folded), not put up for retail sale
	-其他单纱:							-Other yarn, single:
	--粘胶纤维纺制,未加捻或捻度每米不超过120转:							--Of viscose rayon, untwisted or with a twist not exceeding 120 turns per metre:
5403.3110	---竹制	5	35	17	16	千克		---Of bamboo
5403.3190	---其他	5	35	17	16	千克		---Other
	--粘胶纤维纺制,捻度每米超过120转:							--Of viscose rayon, with a twist exceeding 120 turns per metre:
5403.3210	---竹制	5	35	17	16	千克		---Of bomboo
5403.3290	---其他	5	35	17	16	千克		---Other
	--醋酸纤维纺制:							--Of cellulose acetate:
5403.3310	---二醋酸纤维纺制	5	40	17	16	千克		---Of cellulose diacetate
5403.3310 10	非零售二醋酸纤维单纱(单丝/未捻或捻度5转/米以下的复丝单纱,包括变形纱线)	5	40	17	16	千克	A	Single yarn of cellulose diacetate, untwisted or twist < 5 turns/m multiple (folded), not in forms or packing for retail sale, including textured yarn
5403.3310 20	非零售二醋酸纤维单纱(捻度5转/米及以上不超过250转,包括变形纱线)	5	40	17	16	千克	A	Single yarn of cellulose diacetate, 5 turns/m ≤ twist ≤250 turns/m, not put up for retail sale, including Deformation yarn
5403.3310 90	非零售二醋酸纤维单纱(捻度超过250转/米)	5	40	17	16	千克	A	Single yarn of cellulose diacetate, twist > 250 turns/m, not put up for retail sale
5403.3390	---其他	5	35	17	16	千克		---Other
5403.3390 10	非零售其他醋酸纤维单纱(单丝/未捻或捻度5转/米以下的复丝单纱,非供零售用,包括变形纱线)	5	35	17	16	千克		Other single yarn of cellulose acetate, untwisted or twist < 5 turns/m multiple (folded), not in forms or packing for retail sale, including textured yarn
5403.3390 20	非零售其他醋酸纤维单纱(捻度5转/米及以上不超过250转/米,包括变形纱线)	5	35	17	16	千克		Other single yarn of cellulose acetate, 5 turns/m ≤ twist≤250 turns/m, not put up for retail sale, including textured yarn
5403.3390 90	非零售其他醋酸纤维单纱(捻度超过250转/米,包括变形纱线)	5	35	17	16	千克		Other single yarn of cellulose acetate, twist > 250 turns/m, not put up for retail sale, including textured yarn
5403.3900	--其他	5	35	17	16	千克		--Other
5403.3900 10	非零售其他人纤长丝单纱(单丝/未捻或捻度5转/米以下的复丝单纱,非供零售用,包括变形纱线)	5	35	17	16	千克		Other single yarn of artificial filaments, untwisted or twist < 5 turns/m multiple (folded), not in forms or packing for retail sale, including textured yarn

税则号列	货品名称	最惠(%)	普通	增值税率	出口退税	计量单位	监管条件	Article Description
5403.3900 90	非零售其他人纤长丝单纱(捻度5转/米及以上,包括变形纱线)	5	35	17	16	千克		Other single yarn of artificial filaments, twist ≥ 5 turns/m, not in forms or packing for retail sale including textured yarn
	-其他纱线(多股纱线或缆线):							-Other yarn, multiple (folded) or cabled:
5403.4100	--粘胶纤维纺制	5	35	17	16	千克		--Of viscose rayon
5403.4200	--醋酸纤维纺制	5	35	17	16	千克		--Of cellulose acetate
5403.4900	--其他	5	35	17	16	千克		--Other
54.04	**截面尺寸不超过1毫米,细度在67分特及以上的合成纤维单丝;表观宽度不超过5毫米的合成纤维纺织材料制扁条及类似品(例如人造草):**							**Synthetic monofilament of 67 decitex or more and of which no cross-sectional dimension exceeds 1 mm; strip and the like (for example, artificial straw) of synthetic textile materials of an apparent width not exceeing 5 mm:**
	-单丝							-Monofilament:
5404.1100	--弹性	5	80	17	16	千克		--Elastomeric
5404.1100 10	细度≥67分特的涤纶纤维弹性单丝(截面尺寸≤1mm,细度<67分特的合纤单丝归入编号5402)	5	80	17	16	千克		Elastomeric monofilament of polyester, fineness ≥ 67 decitex (cross-sectional dimension ≤ 1mm, fineness < 67 decitex, should be classified under No. 5402)
5404.1100 90	细度≥67分特的其他合成纤维弹性单丝(截面尺寸≤1mm,细度<67分特的合纤单丝归入编号5402)	5	80	17	16	千克		Other synthetic elastomeric monofilament, fineness ≥ 67 decitex (cross-sectional dimension ≤ 1mm, fineness < 67 decitex, should be classified under No. 5402)
5404.1200	--其他,聚丙烯制	5	80	17	16	千克		--Other, of polypropylene
5404.1900	--其他	5	80	17	16	千克		--Other
5404.1900 10	细度≥67分特的涤纶纤维单丝(截面尺寸≤1mm,细度<67分特的合纤单丝归入编号5402)	5	80	17	16	千克		Monofilament of polyester, fineness ≥ 67 decitex (cross – sectional dimension ≤ 1mm, fineness < 67 decitex, should be classified under No. 5402)
5404.1900 90	细度≥67分特的其他合成纤维单丝(截面尺寸≤1mm,细度<67分特的合纤单丝归入编号5402)	5	80	17	16	千克		Other synthetic monofilament, fineness ≥ 67 decitex (cross – sectional dimension ≤ 1mm, fineness < 67 decitex, should be classified under No. 5402)
5404.9000	-其他	5	80	17	16	千克		-Other
54.05	**截面尺寸不超过1毫米,细度在67分特及以上的人造纤维单丝;表观宽度不超过5毫米的人造纤维纺织材料制扁条及类似品(例如人造草):**							**Artificial monofilament of 67 decitex or more and of which no cross-sectional dimension exceeds 1 mm; strip and the like (for example, artificial straw) of artificial textile materials of an apparent width not exceeding 5 mm:**
5405.0000	截面尺寸不超过1毫米,细度在67分特及以上的人造纤维单丝;表观宽度不超过5毫米的人造纤维纺织材料制扁条及类似品(例如人造草)	5	80	17	16	千克		Artificial monofilament of 67 decitex or more of whichno cross-sectional dimension exceeds 1 mm; strip and the like (for example, artificial straw) of artificial textile materials of an apparent width not exceeding 5 mm
54.06	**化学纤维长丝纱线(缝纫线除外),供零售用:**							**Man-made filament yarn (other than sewing thread), put up for retail sale:**
5406.0010	--合成纤维长丝纱线	5	90	17	16	千克		--Synthetic filament yarn
5406.0020	--人造纤维长丝纱线	5	90	17	16	千克		--Artificial filament yarn
54.07	**合成纤维长丝纱线的机织物,包括税目54.04所列材料的机织物:**							**Woven fabrics of synthetic filamentyarn, including woven fabrics obtained from materials of heading 54.04:**
	-尼龙或其他聚酰胺高强力纱、聚酯高强力纱纺制的机织物:							-Woven fabrics obtained from high tenacity yarn of nylon or other polyamides or of polyesters:
5407.1010	---尼龙或其他聚酰胺高强力纱纺制	10	130	17	16	米/千克	A	---Of nylon or other polyamides
5407.1020	---聚酯高强力纱纺制	10	130	17	16	米/千克		---Of polyesters
5407.1020 10	聚酯高强力纱纺制机织物(重量≤170克/平方米)	10	130	17	16	米/千克	A	Woven fabrics of high tenacity yarn of polyesters, weight ≤ $170g/m^2$
5407.1020 90	聚酯高强力纱纺制机织物(重量>170克/平方米)	10	130	17	16	米/千克	A	Woven fabrics of high tenacity yarn of polyesters, weight > $170g/m^2$
5407.2000	-扁条及类似品的机织物	10	130	17	16	米/千克		-Woven fabrics obtained from strip or the like

税则号列	货品名称	最惠(%)	普通	增值税率	出口退税	计量单位	监管条件	Article Description
5407.2000 10	聚乙烯聚丙烯扁条或类似机织物(宽度3米以下)	10	130	17	16	米/千克		Woven fabrics of strip or the like, of polyethylene or of polypropylene, width < 3m
5407.2000 90	其他合成纤维扁条及类似品机织物	10	130	17	16	米/千克		Other woven fabrics of strip or the like of synthetic fibre
5407.3000	-第十一类注释九所列的机织物	10	130	17	16	米/千克		-Fabrics specified in Note 9 to Section Ⅺ
5407.3000 10	平行纱线相互层叠并粘合织物(第十一类注释九所列的机织物,含塑料>60%)	10	130	17	16	米/千克		Woven fabrics consisting of layers of parallel textile yarn superimposed on each other, the layers are bounded at the intersections of the yarns, specified in Note 9 to Section Ⅺ, containing >60% by weight of plastics
5407.3000 20	平行纱线相互层叠并粘合织物(第十一类注释九所列的机织物,含塑料≤60%)	10	130	17	16	米/千克		Woven fabrics consisting of layers of parallel textile yarn superimposed on each other, the layers are bounded at the intersections of the yarns, specified in Note 9 to Section Ⅺ, containing ≤60% by weight of plastics
	-其他机织物,按重量计尼龙或其他聚酰胺长丝含量在85%及以上:							-Other woven fabrics, containing 85% or more by weight of filaments of nylon or other polyamides:
5407.4100	--未漂白或漂白	10	130	17	16	米/千克		--Unbleached or bleached
5407.4100 10	未漂白或漂白的打字机带用机织物(尼龙或其他聚酰胺长丝含量≥85%)	10	130	17	16	米/千克		Woven fabrics for typewriter ribbon, containing ≥85% by weight of filaments of nylon or of other polyamides, unbleached or bleached
5407.4100 20	未漂白纯尼龙机织物(含尼龙量≥85%)	10	130	17	16	米/千克		Woven fabrics of nylon, containing ≥85% by weight of filaments of nylon, unbleached
5407.4100 90	未漂白的或漂白的其他机织物(其他聚酰胺长丝含量≥85%)	10	130	17	16	米/千克		Other woven fabrics, containing ≥85% by weight of nylon-6 filaments, unbleached or bleached
5407.4200	--染色	10	130	17	16	米/千克		--Dyed
5407.4300	--色织	10	130	17	16	米/千克		--Of yarns of different colours
5407.4400	--印花	10	130	17	16	米/千克		--Printed
	-其他机织物,按重量计聚酯变形长丝含量在85%及以上:							-Other woven fabrics, containing 85% or more by weight of textured polyester filaments:
5407.5100	--未漂白或漂白	10	130	17	16	米/千克		--Unbleached or bleached
5407.5100 10	未漂白或漂白纯聚酯变形长丝布(聚酯变形长丝含量≥85%,重量≤170克/平米)	10	130	17	16	米/千克		Woven fabrics, containing ≥85% by weight of textured polyester filaments, weight ≤ 170g/m^2, unbleached or bleached
5407.5100 20	未漂白或漂白纯聚酯变形长丝机织物(聚酯变形长丝含量≥85%,重量大于170克/平米)	10	130	17	16	米/千克		Woven fabrics, containing ≥85% by weight of textured polyester filaments, weight > 170g/m^2, unbleached or bleached
5407.5200	--染色	10	130	17	16	米/千克		--Dyed
5407.5200 10	染色的聚酯变形长丝布,含量≥85%(宽<77厘米,每厘米经纱密70-142根,纬密32-71根)	10	130	17	16	米/千克		Woven fabrics, containing ≥85% by weight of textured polyester filaments, of width <77cm, warp yarn 70~142/cm, weft yarn 32~71/cm, dyed
5407.5200 91	染色的其他聚酯变形长丝机织物(聚酯变形长丝含量≥85%,重量≤170克/平米)	10	130	17	16	米/千克		Other woven fabrics, containing ≥85% by weight of textured polyester filaments, weight ≤170g/m^2, dyed
5407.5200 92	染色的其他聚酯变形长丝机织物(聚酯变形长丝含量≥85%,重量>170克/平米)	10	130	17	16	米/千克		Other woven fabrics, containing ≥85% by weight of textured polyester filaments, weight >170g/m^2, dyed
5407.5300	--色织	10	130	17	16	米/千克		--Of yarns of different colours
5407.5300 10	色织的聚酯变形长丝布,含量≥85%(宽<77厘米,每厘米经纱密70-142根,纬密32-71根)	10	130	17	16	米/千克		Woven fabrics, containing ≥85% by weight of textured polyester filaments, width <77cm, warp yarn 70~142/cm, weft yarn 32~71/cm, of different colours
5407.5300 91	色织的聚酯变形长丝机织物(聚酯变形长丝含量≥85%,重量≤170克/平米)	10	130	17	16	米/千克		Woven fabrics, containing ≥85% by weight of textured polyester filaments, weight ≤170g/m^2, of different colours
5407.5300 92	色织的聚酯变形长丝机织物(聚酯变形长丝含量≥85%,重量>170克/平米)	10	130	17	16	米/千克		Woven fabrics, containing ≥85% by weight of textured polyester filaments, weight >170g/m^2, of different colours
5407.5400	--印花	10	130	17	16	米/千克		--Printed

税则号列	货品名称	最惠(%)	普通	增值税率	出口退税	计量单位	监管条件	Article Description
5407.5400 10	印花的聚酯变形长丝机织物(聚酯变形长丝含量≥85%,重量≤170克/平米)	10	130	17	16	米/千克		Woven fabrics, containing ≥85% by weight of textured polyester filaments, weight ≤170g/m², printed
5407.5400 20	印花的聚酯变形长丝机织物(聚酯变形长丝含量≥85%,重量>170克/平米)	10	130	17	16	米/千克		Woven fabrics, containing ≥85% by weight of textured polyester filaments, weight >170g/m², printed
	-其他机织物,按重量计聚酯长丝含量在85%及以上:							-Other woven fabrics, containing 85% or more by weight of polyester filaments:
5407.6100	--按重量计聚酯非变形长丝含量在85%及以上	10	130	17	16	米/千克		--Containing 85% or more by weight of non-textured polyester filaments
5407.6100 11	染色聚酯非变形长丝布,含量≥85%(宽<77厘米,每厘米经纱密70-142根,纬密32-71根)	10	130	17	16	米/千克		Woven fabrics, containing ≥85% by weight of non-textured polyester filaments, dyed, width < 77cm, warp yarn 70 ~ 142/cm, weft yarn 32 ~ 71/cm
5407.6100 12	色织聚酯非变形长丝布,含量≥85%(宽<77厘米,每厘米经纱密70-142根,纬密32-71根)	10	130	17	16	米/千克		Woven fabrics, containing ≥85% by weight of non-textured polyester filaments, of yarns of different colours, width < 77cm warp yarn 70 ~ 142/cm, weft yarn 31 ~ 71/cm
5407.6100 20	全聚酯其他非变形长丝机织物(单纱含27根丝,细75-80分特,捻度900转及以上)	10	130	17	16	米/千克		Woven fabrics of non-textured polyester filaments, a single yarn twisted with 27 threads, 75-80 decitex, twist >900turns/m
5407.6100 31	未漂白或漂白的聚酯非变形长丝机织物(聚酯非变形长丝含量≥85%,重量>170克/平米)	10	130	17	16	米/千克		Woven fabrics, containing ≥85% by weight of non-textured polyester filaments, weight > 170g/m², unbleached or bleached
5407.6100 32	未漂白或漂白的聚酯非变形长丝机织物(聚酯非变形长丝含量≥85%,重量≤170克/平米)	10	130	17	16	米/千克		Woven fabrics, containing ≥85% by weight of non-textured polyester filaments, weight ≤170g/m², unbleached or bleached
5407.6100 41	染色其他聚酯非变形长丝布(聚酯非变形长丝含量≥85%,重量>170克/平米)	10	130	17	16	米/千克		Other woven fabrics, containing ≥85% by weight of non-textured polyester filaments of weight > 170g/m², dyed
5407.6100 42	染色其他纯聚酯非变形长丝布(聚酯非变形长丝含量≥85%,重量≤170克/平米)	10	130	17	16	米/千克		Other woven fabrics, containing ≥85% by weight of non-textured polyester filaments, weight ≤170g/m², dyed
5407.6100 51	色织其他聚酯非变形长丝布(聚酯非变形长丝含量≥85%,重量>170克/平米)	10	130	17	16	米/千克		Other woven fabrics, containing ≥85% by weight of non-textured polyester filaments, weight >170g/m², of different colours
5407.6100 52	色织其他聚酯非变形长丝布(聚酯非变形长丝含量≥85%,重量≤170克/平米)	10	130	17	16	米/千克		Other woven fabrics, containing ≥85% by weight of non-textured polyester filaments of weight ≤ 170g/m², of different colours
5407.6100 61	印花其他聚酯非变形长丝布(聚酯非变形长丝含量≥85%,重量>170克/平米)	10	130	17	16	米/千克		Other woven fabrics, containing ≥85% by weight of non-textured polyester filaments, weight >170g/m², printed
5407.6100 62	印花其他聚酯非变形长丝布(聚酯非变形长丝含量≥85%,重量≤170克/平米)	10	130	17	16	米/千克		Other woven fabrics, containing ≥85% by weight of non-textured polyester filaments, weight ≤170g/m², printed
5407.6900	--其他	10	130	17	16	米/千克		--Other
5407.6900 11	未漂白或漂白其他聚酯长丝布(聚酯长丝含量≥85%,重量>170克/平米)	10	130	17	16	米/千克		Other woven fabrics, containing ≥85% by weight of polyester filaments, weight >170g/m², unbleached or bleached
5407.6900 12	未漂白或漂白其他聚酯长丝布(聚酯长丝含量≥85%,重量≤170克/平方米)	10	130	17	16	米/千克		Other woven fabrics, containing ≥85% by weight of polyester filaments, weight ≤170g/m², unbleached or bleached
5407.6900 21	染色其他聚酯长丝布(聚酯长丝含量≥85%,重量>170克/平方米)	10	130	17	16	米/千克		Other woven fabrics, containing ≥85% by weight of polyester filaments, weight >170g/m², dyed
5407.6900 22	染色其他聚酯长丝布(聚酯长丝含量≥85%,重量≤170克/平方米)	10	130	17	16	米/千克		Other woven fabrics, containing ≥85% by weight of polyester filaments, weight ≤170g/m², dyed
5407.6900 31	色织其他聚酯长丝布,含量≥85%(每厘米经纱密70-142根,纬密32-71根)	10	130	17	16	米/千克		Other woven fabrics, containing ≥85% by weight of polyester filaments, warp yarn 70 ~ 142/cm, weft yarn 32 ~ 71/cm, of different colours

税则号列	货品名称	最惠(%)	普通	增值税率	出口退税	计量单位	监管条件	Article Description
5407.6900 32	色织其他聚酯长丝布(聚酯长丝含量≥85%,重量>170克/平方米)	10	130	17	16	米/千克		Other woven fabrics, containing≥85% by weight of polyester filaments, of weight>170g/m², of yarns of different colours
5407.6900 33	色织其他聚酯长丝布(聚酯长丝含量≥85%,重量≤170克/平方米)	10	130	17	16	米/千克		Other woven fabrics, containing≥85% by weight of polyester filaments, of weight≤170g/m², of yarns of different colours
5407.6900 41	印花其他聚酯长丝布(聚酯长丝含量≥85%,重量>170克/平方米)	10	130	17	16	米/千克		Other woven fabrics, containing≥85% by weight of polyester filaments, of weight>170g/m², printed
5407.6900 42	印花其他聚酯长丝布(聚酯长丝含量≥85%,重量≤170克/平方米)	10	130	17	16	米/千克		Other woven fabrics, containing≥85% by weight of polyester filaments, of weight ≤ 170g/m², printed
	-其他机织物,按重量计其他合成纤维长丝含量在85%及以上:							-Other woven fabrics, containing 85% or more by weight of synthetic filaments:
5407.7100	--未漂白或漂白	10	130	17	16	米/千克		--Unbleached or bleached
5407.7200	--染色	10	130	17	16	米/千克		--Dyed
5407.7300	--色织	10	130	17	16	米/千克		--Of yarns of different colours
5407.7400	--印花	10	130	17	16	米/千克		--Printed
	-其他机织物,按重量计其他合成纤维长丝含量在85%以下,主要或仅与棉混纺:							-Other woven fabrics, containing less than 85% by weight of synthetic filaments, mixed mainly or solely with cotton:
5407.8100	--未漂白或漂白	10	130	17	16	米/千克		--Unbleached or bleached
5407.8100 10	未漂白或漂白与棉混纺府绸及细平布(其他合成纤维长丝含量<85%)	10	130	17	16	米/千克		Poplin and fine plain cloth, mixed with cotton, containing<85% by weight of synthetic filaments, unbleached orbleached
5407.8100 20	未漂白或漂白的与棉混纺平布(其他合成纤维长丝含量<85%)	10	130	17	16	米/千克		Plain cloth, mixed with cotton, containing<85% by weight of synthetic filaments, unbleached or bleached
5407.8100 30	未漂白或漂白的与棉混纺印染用布(混纺合纤布指按重量计其他合成纤维长丝含量<85%)	10	130	17	16	米/千克		Woven fabrics for printing and dying, mixed with cotton, containing<85% by weight of synthetic filaments, unbleached or bleached
5407.8100 40	未漂白或漂白与棉混纺缎纹或斜纹布(混纺合纤布指按重量计其他合成纤维长丝含量<85%)	10	130	17	16	米/千克		Woven fabrics, satin weave or twill weave mixed with cotton, containing<85% by weight of synthetic filaments, unbleached or bleached
5407.8100 90	未漂白或漂白与棉混纺其他合纤布(混纺合纤布指按重量计其他合成纤维长丝含量<85%)	10	130	17	16	米/千克		Other woven fabrics, mixed with cotton containing<85% by weight of synthetic filaments, unbleached or bleached
5407.8200	--染色	10	130	17	16	米/千克		--Dyed
5407.8200 10	染色的与棉混纺府绸及细平布(混纺合纤布指按重量计其他合成纤维长丝含量<85%)	10	130	17	16	米/千克		Poplin and fine plain cloth, mixed with cotton, containing<85% by weight of synthetic filaments, dyed
5407.8200 20	染色的与棉混纺平布(混纺合纤布指按重量计其他合成纤维长丝含量<85%)	10	130	17	16	米/千克		Plain cloth, mixed with cotton, containing<85% by weight of synthetic filaments, dyed
5407.8200 30	染色的与棉混纺印染用布(混纺合纤布指按重量计其他合成纤维长丝含量<85%)	10	130	17	16	米/千克		Woven fabrics for printing and dying mixed with cotton, containing < 85% by weight of synthetic filaments, dyed
5407.8200 40	染色的与棉混纺缎纹或斜纹布(混纺合纤布指按重量计其他合成纤维长丝含量<85%)	10	130	17	16	米/千克		Woven fabrics, satin weave or twill weave, mixed withcotton, containing<85% by weight of synthetic filaments, dyed
5407.8200 90	染色的与棉混纺其他合成纤维布(混纺合纤布指按重量计其他合成纤维长丝含量<85%)	10	130	17	16	米/千克		Other woven fabrics, mixed with cotton, containing<85% by weight of synthetic filaments, dyed
5407.8300	--色织	10	130	17	16	米/千克		--Of yarns of different colours
5407.8300 10	色织的与棉混纺府绸及细平布(混纺合纤布指按重量计其他合成纤维长丝含量<85%)	10	130	17	16	米/千克		Poplin and fine plain cloth, mixed with cotton, containing < 85% by weight of synthetic filaments, of yarns of different colours
5407.8300 20	色织的与棉混纺平布(混纺合纤布指按重量计其他合成纤维长丝含量<85%)	10	130	17	16	米/千克		Plain cloth, mixed with cotton, containing<85% by weight of synthetic filaments, of yarns of different colours

税则号列	货品名称	最惠(%)	普通	增值税率	出口退税	计量单位	监管条件	Article Description
5407.8300 30	色织的与棉混纺印染用布(混纺合纤布指按重量计其他合成纤维长丝含量<85%)	10	130	17	16	米/千克		Woven fabrics for printing and dying, mixed with cotton, containing <85% by weight of synthetic filaments, of yarns of different colours
5407.8300 40	色织的与棉混纺缎纹或斜纹布(混纺合纤布指按重量计其他合成纤维长丝含量<85%)	10	130	17	16	米/千克		Woven fabrics, satin weave or twill weave, mixed with cotton, containing <85% by weight of synthetic filaments, of yarnsof different colours
5407.8300 90	色织的与棉混纺其他合成纤维布(混纺合纤布指按重量计其他合成纤维长丝含量<85%)	10	130	17	16	米/千克		Other woven fabrics, mixed with cotton, containing <85% by weight of synthetic filaments, of yarns of different colours
5407.8400	--印花	10	130	17	16	米/千克		--Printed
5407.8400 10	印花的与棉混纺府绸及细平布(混纺合纤布指按重量计其他合成纤维长丝含量<85%)	10	130	17	16	米/千克		Poplin and fine plain cloth, mixed with cotton, containing <85% by weight of synthetic filaments, printed
5407.8400 30	印花的与棉混纺印染用布(混纺合纤布指按重量计其他合成纤维长丝含量<85%)	10	130	17	16	米/千克		Woven fabrics for printing and dying, mixed with cotton, containing <85% by weight of synthetic filaments, printed
5407.8400 90	印花的与棉混纺其他合成纤维布(混纺合纤布指按重量计其他合成纤维长丝含量<85%)	10	130	17	16	米/千克		Other woven fabrics, mixed with cotton, containing <85% by weight of synthetic filaments, printed
	-其他机织物:							-Other woven fabrics:
5407.9100	--未漂白或漂白	10	130	17	16	米/千克		--Unbleached or bleached
5407.9100 11	未漂白或漂白的其他混纺合成纤维布(与精梳羊毛或动物细毛≥36%混纺,合纤<85%)	10	130	17	16	米/千克		Other woven fabrics, mixed, containing ≥36% by weight of combed wool or fine animal hair, containing <85% by weight of synthetic fibres, unbleached or bleached
5407.9100 19	未漂白或漂白的其他混纺合成纤维布(合纤含量<85%,与36%及以上其他羊毛或动物细毛混纺)	10	130	17	16	米/千克		Other woven fabrics, mixed, containing ≥36% by weight of wool or fine animal hair, containing <85% by weight of synthetic fibres, unbleached or bleached
5407.9100 21	未漂白或漂白的其他混纺合成纤维布(与36%以下精梳羊毛或动物细毛混纺、合纤含量<85%)	10	130	17	16	米/千克		Other woven fabrics, mixed, containing <36% by weight of combed wool or fine animal hair, containing <85% by weight of synthetic filaments, unbleached or bleached
5407.9100 29	未漂白或漂白的其他混纺合成纤维布(与36%以下其他羊毛或动物细毛混纺,合纤<85%)	10	130	17	16	米/千克		Other woven fabrics, mixed, containing <36% by weight of other wool or fine animal hair, containing <85% by weight of synthetic fibres, unbleached or bleached
5407.9100 30	未漂白或漂白的其他混纺合成纤维布(与人造纤维长丝混纺,合纤含量<85%)	10	130	17	16	米/千克		Other woven fabrics, other, mixed with artificial filaments, containing <85% by weight of synthetic fibres, unbleached or bleached
5407.9100 91	未漂白或漂白其他混纺府绸及细平布(合成纤维长丝含量<85%,与其他纤维混纺)	10	130	17	16	米/千克		Poplin and fine plain cloth, mixed with other fibres, containing <85% by weight of synthetic filaments, unbleached or bleached
5407.9100 92	未漂白或漂白的其他混纺平布(合成纤维长丝含量<85%,与其他纤维混纺)	10	130	17	16	米/千克		Plain cloth, mixed with other fibres, containing <85% by weight of synthetic filaments, unbleached or bleached
5407.9100 93	未漂白或漂白的其他混纺印染用布(合成纤维长丝含量<85%,与其他纤维混纺)	10	130	17	16	米/千克		Other woven fabrics for printing and dying, mixed with other fibres, containing <85% by weight of synthetic filaments, unbleached or bleached
5407.9100 94	未漂白或漂白其他混纺缎纹或斜纹布(合成纤维长丝含量<85%,与其他纤维混纺)	10	130	17	16	米/千克		Other woven fabrics, satin weave or twill weave, mixed with other fibres, containing <85% by weight of synthetic filaments, unbleached or bleached
5407.9100 99	未漂白或漂白的其他混纺合成纤维布(合成纤维长丝含量<85%,与其他纤维混纺)	10	130	17	16	米/千克		Other woven fabrics, mixed with other fibres, containing <85% by weight of synthetic filaments, unbleached or bleached
5407.9200	--染色	10	130	17	16	米/千克		--Dyed

税则号列	货品名称	最惠(%)	普通	增值税率	出口退税	计量单位	监管条件	Article Description
5407.9200 11	染色的其他混纺合成纤维布(与36%及以上精梳羊毛或动物细毛混纺,合纤<85%)	10	130	17	16	米/千克		Other woven fabrics, mixed, containing ≥36% by weight of combed wool or fine animal hair, containing<85% by weight, of synthetic fibres, dyed
5407.9200 19	染色的其他混纺合成纤维布(与36%及以上其他羊毛或动物细毛混纺,合纤<85%)	10	130	17	16	米/千克		Other woven fabrics, mixed, containing ≥36% by weight of wool or fine animal hair, containing<85% by weight of synthetic fibres, dyed
5407.9200 21	染色的其他混纺合成纤维布(与<36%精梳羊毛或动物细毛混纺,合纤<85%)	10	130	17	16	米/千克		Other woven fabrics, mixed, containing <36% by weight of combed wool or fine animal hair, containing<85% by weight, of synthetic fibres, dyed
5407.9200 29	染色的其他混纺合成纤维布(与<36%其他羊毛或动物细毛混纺,合纤<85%)	10	130	17	16	米/千克		Other woven fabrics, mixed, containing <36% by weight of wool or fine animal hair, containing<85% by weight, of synthetic fibres, dyed
5407.9200 30	染色的其他混纺合成纤维布(与人造纤维长丝或含金属纱线混纺,合纤含量<85%)	10	130	17	16	米/千克		Other woven fabrics, mixed with artificial filaments or metallized yarn, containing <85% by weight of synthetic fibres, dyed
5407.9200 91	染色的其他混纺府绸及细平布(合成纤维长丝含量<85%,与其他纤维混纺)	10	130	17	16	米/千克		Poplin and fine plain cloth, mixed with other fibres, containing<85% by weight of synthetic filaments, dyed
5407.9200 92	染色的其他混纺平布(合成纤维长丝含量<85%,与其他纤维混纺)	10	130	17	16	米/千克		Plain cloth, mixed with other fibres, containing <85% by weight of synthetic filaments, dyed
5407.9200 93	染色的其他混纺印染用布(合成纤维长丝含量<85%,与其他纤维混纺)	10	130	17	16	米/千克		Other woven fabrics for printing and dying, mixed with other fibres, containing<85% by weight of synthetic filaments, dyed
5407.9200 94	染色的其他混纺缎纹或斜纹布(合成纤维长丝含量<85%,与其他纤维混纺)	10	130	17	16	米/千克		Other woven fabrics, satin weave or twill weave, mixed with other fibres, containing<85% by weight of synthetic filaments, dyed
5407.9200 99	染色的其他混纺合成纤维布(合成纤维长丝含量<85%,与其他纤维混纺)	10	130	17	16	米/千克		Other woven fabrics, mixed with other fibres, containing<85% by weight of synthetic filaments, dyed
5407.9300	--色织	10	130	17	16	米/千克		--Of yarns of different colours
5407.9300 11	色织的其他混纺合成纤维布(与≥36%精梳羊毛或动物细毛混纺,合纤<85%)	10	130	17	16	米/千克		Other woven fabrics, mixed, containing ≥36% by weight of combed wool or fine animal hair, containing<85% by weight of synthetic fibres, of yarns of different colours
5407.9300 19	色织的其他混纺合成纤维布(与≥36%其他羊毛或动物细毛混纺,合纤<85%)	10	130	17	16	米/千克		Other woven fabrics, mixed, containing ≥36% by weight of wool or fine animal hair, containing<85% by weight of synthetic fibres, of yarns of different colours
5407.9300 21	色织的其他混纺合成纤维布(与<36%精梳羊毛或动物细毛混纺,合纤<85%)	10	130	17	16	米/千克		Other woven fabrics, mixed containing<36% by weight of combed wool or fine animal hair, containing<85% by weight of synthetic fibres, of yarns of different colours
5407.9300 29	色织的其他混纺合成纤维布(与<36%其他羊毛或动物细毛混纺,合纤<85%)	10	130	17	16	米/千克		Other woven fabrics, mixed, containing <36% by weight of wool or fine animal hair, containing<85% by weight of synthetic fibres, of yarns of different colours
5407.9300 30	色织其他混纺合纤布,合纤<85%(含化纤长丝≥85%,每厘米经密70-142根,纬密32-71根)	10	130	17	16	米/千克		Other woven fabrics, mixed containing <85% by weight of chemical filaments (containing ≥85% by weight of sychemical fibres, warp yarn 70—142/cm, weft yarn 32~71/cm) of yarns of different colours
5407.9300 40	色织的其他混纺合成纤维布(与人造纤维长丝或含金属纱线混纺,合纤长丝含量<85%)	10	130	17	16	米/千克		Other woven fabrics, mixed with artificial filaments or metallized yarn, containing <85% by weight of synthetic filaments, of yarns of different colours
5407.9300 91	色织的其他混纺府绸及细平布(合成纤维长丝含量<85%,与其他纤维混纺)	10	130	17	16	米/千克		Poplin and fine plain cloth, mixed with other fibres, containing<85% by weight of synthetic filaments, of yarns of different colours
5407.9300 92	色织的其他混纺平布(合成纤维长丝含量<85%,与其他纤维混纺)	10	130	17	16	米/千克		Plain cloth, mixed with other fibres, containing <85% by weight of synthetic filaments, of yarns of different colours

税则号列	货品名称	最惠(%)	普通	增值税率	出口退税	计量单位	监管条件	Article Description
5407.9300 93	色织的其他混纺印染用布(合成纤维长丝含量<85%,与其他纤维混纺)	10	130	17	16	米/千克		Other woven fabrics for printing and dying, mixed with other fibres, containing <85% by weight of synthetic filaments, of yarns of different colours
5407.9300 94	色织的其他混纺缎纹或斜纹布(合成纤维长丝含量<85%,与其他纤维混纺)	10	130	17	16	米/千克		Other woven fabrics, satin weave or twill weave, mixed with other fibres, containing <85% by weight of synthetic filaments, of yarns of different colours
5407.9300 99	色织的其他混纺合成纤维布(合成纤维长丝含量<85%,与其他纤维混纺)	10	130	17	16	米/千克		Other woven fabrics, mixed with other fibres, containing <85% by weight of synthetic filaments, of yarn of different colours
5407.9400	--印花	10	130	17	16	米/千克		--Printed
5407.9400 10	印花的其他混纺合成纤维布(与羊毛或动物细毛≥36%混纺,合纤<85%)	10	130	17	16	米/千克		Other woven fabrics, mixed, containing ≥ 36% by weight of combed wool or fine animal hair, containing <85% by weight of synthetic fibres, printed
5407.9400 20	印花的其他混纺合成纤维布(与羊毛或动物细毛<36%混纺,合纤<85%)	10	130	17	16	米/千克		Other woven fabrics, mixed, containing < 36% by weight of combed wool or fine animal hair, containing <85% by weight of synthetic fibres, printed
5407.9400 30	印花的其他混纺合成纤维布(与人造纤维长丝或含金属纱线混纺,合纤含量<85%)	10	130	17	16	米/千克		Other woven fabrics, mixed with artificial filaments or metallized yarn, containing < 85% by weight of synthetic fibres, printed
5407.9400 91	印花的其他混纺府绸及细平布(合成纤维长丝含量<85%,与其他纤维混纺)	10	130	17	16	米/千克		Poplin and fine plain cloth, mixed with other fibres, containing < 85% by weight of synthetic filaments, printed
5407.9400 92	印花的其他混纺平布(合成纤维长丝含量<85%,与其他纤维混纺)	10	130	17	16	米/千克		Plain cloth, mixed with other fibres, containing < 85% by weight of synthetic filaments, printed
5407.9400 93	印花的其他混纺印染用布(合成纤维长丝含量<85%,与其他纤维混纺)	10	130	17	16	米/千克		Other woven fabrics for printing and dying, mixed with other fibres, containing <85% by weight of synthetic filaments, printed
5407.9400 94	印花的其他混纺缎纹或斜纹布(合成纤维长丝含量<85%,与其他纤维混纺)	10	130	17	16	米/千克		Other woven fabrics, satin weave or twill weave, mixed with other fibres, containing <85% by weight of synthetic filaments, printed
5407.9400 99	印花的其他混纺合成纤维布(合成纤维长丝含量<85%,与其他纤维混纺)	10	130	17	16	米/千克		Other woven fabrics, mixed with other fibres, containing <85% by weight of synthetic filaments, printed
54.08	**人造纤维长丝纱线的机织物,包括品目54.05所列材料的机织物:**							**Woven fabrics of artificial filament yarn, including woven fabrics obtained from materials of heading No. 54.05:**
5408.1000	-粘胶纤维高强力纱的机织物	10	130	17	16	米/千克		-Woven fabrics obtained from high tenacity yarn of viscose rayon
	-其他机织物,按重量计人造纤维长丝、扁条或类似品含量在85%及以上:							-Other woven fabrics, containing 85% or more by weight of artificial filament or strip or the like:
	--未漂白或漂白:							--Unbleached or bleached:
5408.2110	---粘胶纤维制	12	130	17	16	米/千克		---Of yarns of viscose rayon
5408.2120	---醋酸纤维制	12	130	17	16	米/千克		---Of yarns of cellulose acetate
5408.2190	---其他	12	130	17	16	米/千克		---Other
	--染色:							--Dyed:
5408.2210	---粘胶纤维制	10	130	17	16	米/千克		---Of yarns of viscose rayon
5408.2220	---醋酸纤维制	10	130	17	16	米/千克		---Of yarns of cellulose acetate
5408.2290	---其他	10	130	17	16	米/千克		---Other
	--色织:							--Of yarns of different colours:
5408.2310	---粘胶纤维制	10	130	17	16	米/千克		---Of yarns of viscose rayon
5408.2320	---醋酸纤维制	10	130	17	16	米/千克		---Of yarns of cellulose acetate
5408.2390	---其他	10	130	17	16	米/千克		---Other
	--印花:							--Printed:
5408.2410	---粘胶纤维制	10	130	17	16	米/千克		---Of yarns of viscose rayon
5408.2420	---醋酸纤维制	10	130	17	16	米/千克		---Of yarns of cellulose acetate

税则号列	货品名称	最惠(%)	普通	增值税率	出口退税	计量单位	监管条件	Article Description
5408.2490	---其他	10	130	17	16	米/千克		---Other
	-其他机织物:							-Other woven fabrics:
5408.3100	--未漂白或漂白	10	130	17	16	米/千克		--Unbleached or bleached
5408.3100 11	未漂白或漂白人纤长丝机织物(与精梳羊毛或动物细毛≥36%混纺,人纤<85%)	10	130	17	16	米/千克		Woven fabrics of artificial filaments, mixed, containing≥36% by weight of combed wool or fine animal hair, containing <85% by weight of artificial fibres, unbleached or bleached
5408.3100 19	未漂白或漂白人纤长丝机织物(与其他羊毛或动物细毛≥36%混纺,人纤<85%)	10	130	17	16	米/千克		Woven fabrics of artificial filaments, mixed, containing≥36% by weight of wool or fine animal hair, containing <85% by weight of artificial fibres, unbleached or bleached
5408.3100 21	未漂白或漂白人纤长丝机织物(与精梳羊毛或动物细毛<36%混纺,人纤<85%)	10	130	17	16	米/千克		Woven fabrics of artificial filaments, mixed, containing <36% by weight of combed wool or fine animal hair, containing <85% by weight of artificial fibres, unbleached or bleached
5408.3100 29	未漂白或漂白人纤长丝机织物(与其他羊毛或动物细毛<36%混纺,人纤<85%)	10	130	17	16	米/千克		Woven fabrics of artificial filaments, mixed, containing <36% by weight of wool or fine animal hair, containing <85% by weight of artificial fibres, unbleached or bleached
5408.3100 30	未漂白或漂白人纤长丝机织物(与人纤长丝混纺,人纤长丝含量<85%)	10	130	17	16	米/千克		Woven fabrics, mixed with artificial filament, containing < 85% by weight of artificial filaments, unbleached or bleached
5408.3100 91	未漂白或漂白人纤长丝府绸及细平布(混纺布指按重量计人纤长丝,扁条或类似品含量<85%)	10	130	17	16	米/千克		Poplin and fine plain cloth, mixed, containing <85% by weight of filament or strip or the like of artificial fibres, unbleached or bleached
5408.3100 92	未漂白或漂白人纤长丝平布(混纺布指按重量计人纤长丝,扁条或类似品含量<85%)	10	130	17	16	米/千克		Plain cloth, mixed, containing < 85% by weight of filament or strip or the like of artificial fibres, unbleached or bleached
5408.3100 93	未漂白或漂白人纤长丝印染用布(混纺布指按重量计人纤长丝,扁条或类似品含量<85%)	10	130	17	16	米/千克		Woven fabrics for printing and dying, mixed, containing <85% by weight of filament or strip or the like of artificial fibres, unbleached or bleached
5408.3100 94	未漂白或漂白人纤长丝缎纹或斜纹布(混纺布指按重量计人纤长丝,扁条或类似品含量<85%)	10	130	17	16	米/千克		Woven fabrics, satin weave or twill weave, mixed, containing < 85% by weight of filament or strip or the like of artificial fibres, unbleached or bleached
5408.3100 99	未漂白或漂白人纤长丝其他混纺布(混纺布指按重量计人纤长丝,扁条或类似品含量<85%)	10	130	17	16	米/千克		Other woven fabrics, mixed, containing < 85% by weight of filament or strip or the like of artificial fibres, unbleached or bleached
5408.3200	--染色	10	130	17	16	米/千克		--Dyed
5408.3200 11	染色的人纤长丝机织物(与精梳羊毛或动物细毛≥36%混纺,人纤<85%)	10	130	17	16	米/千克		Woven fabrics, mixed, containing ≥36% by weight of combed wool or fine animal hair, containing < 85% by weight of artificial fibres, dyed
5408.3200 19	染色的人纤长丝机织物(与其他羊毛或动物细毛≥36%混纺,人纤<85%)	10	130	17	16	米/千克		Woven fabrics, mixed, containing ≥36% by weight of wool or fine animal hair, containing < 85% by weight of artificial fibres, dyed
5408.3200 21	染色的人纤长丝机织物(与精梳羊毛或动物细毛<36%混纺,人纤<85%)	10	130	17	16	米/千克		Woven fabrics, mixed, containing < 36% by weight of combed wool or fine animal hair, containing < 85% by weight of artificial fibres, dyed
5408.3200 29	染色的人纤长丝机织物(与其他羊毛或动物细毛<36%混纺,人纤<85%)	10	130	17	16	米/千克		Woven fabrics, mixed, containing < 36% by weight of wool or fine animal hair, containing < 85% by weight of artificial fibres, dyed
5408.3200 30	染色的人纤长丝机织物(丝及绢丝含量30%及以上,每千克价值超过$33,人纤<85%)	10	130	17	16	米/千克		Woven fabrics, containing ≥30% by weight of silk and spun silk, value > $33/kg, containing < 85% by weight of artificial fibres, dyed
5408.3200 40	染色的人纤长丝机织物(与合纤长丝混纺,人纤长丝、扁条或类似品含量<85%)	10	130	17	16	米/千克		Woven fabrics, mixed with synthetic filament, containing <85% by weight of filament or strip or the like of artificial fibres, dyed

税则号列	货品名称	最惠(%)	普通	增值税率	出口退税	计量单位	监管条件	Article Description
5408.3200 91	染色的人纤长丝府绸或细平布(混纺布指按重量计人纤长丝、扁条或类似品含量<85%)	10	130	17	16	米/千克		Poplin and fine plain cloth, mixed, containing <85% by weight of filament or strip or the like, of artificial fibres, dyed
5408.3200 92	染色的人纤长丝平布(混纺布指按重量计人纤长丝、扁条或类似品含量<85%)	10	130	17	16	米/千克		Plain cloth, mixed, containing < 85% by weight of filament or strip or the like of artificial fibres, dyed
5408.3200 93	染色的人纤长丝印染用布(混纺布指按重量计人纤长丝、扁条或类似品含量<85%)	10	130	17	16	米/千克		Woven fabrics for printing and dying, mixed, containing <85% by weight of filament or strip or the like of artificial fibres, dyed
5408.3200 99	染色的人纤长丝其他机织物(混纺布指按重量计人纤长丝、扁条或类似品含量<85%)	10	130	17	16	米/千克		Other woven fabrics, mixed, containing < 85% by weight of filament or strip or the like of artificial fibres, dyed
5408.3300	--色织	10	130	17	16	米/千克		--Of yarns of different colours
5408.3300 11	色织的人纤长丝机织物(与精梳羊毛或动物细毛≥36%混纺,人纤<85%)	10	130	17	16	米/千克		Woven fabrics of artificial filaments, mixed, containing≥36% by weight of combed wool or fine animal hair, containing <85% by weight of artificial fibres, of yarns of different colours
5408.3300 19	色织的人纤长丝机织物(与其他羊毛或动物细毛≥36%混纺,人纤<85%)	10	130	17	16	米/千克		Woven fabrics of artificial filaments, mixed, containing≥36% by weight of wool or fine animal hair, containing < 85% by weight of artificial fibres, of yarns of different colours
5408.3300 21	色织的人纤长丝机织物(与精梳羊毛或动物细毛<36%混纺,人纤<85%)	10	130	17	16	米/千克		Woven fabrics of artificial filaments, mixed, containing < 36% by weight of combed wool or fine animal hair, containing <85% by weightof artificial fibres, of yarns of different colours
5408.3300 29	色织的人纤长丝机织物(与其他羊毛或动物细毛<36%混纺,人纤<85%)	10	130	17	16	米/千克		Woven fabrics of artificial filaments, mixed, containing <36% by weight of wool or fine animal hair, containing < 85% by weight of artificial fibres, of yarns of different colours
5408.3300 30	色织的人纤长丝机织物,人纤<85%(含化纤长丝≥85%,每厘米经密70-142根,纬密32-71根)	10	130	17	16	米/千克		Woven fabrics of artificial filaments, containing ≥ 85% by weight of chemical filaments, containing < 85% by weight of artificial fibres, warp yarn70 ~ 142/cm, weft yarn 32 ~ 71/cm, of yarns of different colours
5408.3300 40	色织的人纤长丝机织物(丝及绢丝含量30%及以上,每千克价值超过$33,人纤<85%)	10	130	17	16	米/千克		Woven fabrics, containing ≥30% by weight of silk and spun silk, value > $33/kg, containing < 85% by weight of filament or strip or the like of artificial fibres, of yarns of different colours
5408.3300 50	色织的人纤长丝机织物(与合纤长丝混纺,人纤长丝、扁条或类似品含量<85%)	10	130	17	16	米/千克		Woven fabrics, mixed with synthetic filament, containing <85% by weight of artificial filament or strip or the like, of yarns of different colours
5408.3300 92	色织的人纤长丝平布(混纺布指按重量计人纤长丝、扁条或类似品含量<85%)	10	130	17	16	米/千克		Plain cloth, containing <85% by weight of artificial filament or strip or the like, of yarns of different colours
5408.3300 94	色织的人纤长丝缎纹或斜纹布(混纺布指按重量计人纤长丝、扁条或类似品含量<85%)	10	130	17	16	米/千克		Woven fabrics, satin weave or twill weave, containing <85% by weight of artificial filament or strip or the like, of yarns of different colours
5408.3300 99	色织的人纤长丝其他机织物(混纺布指按重量计人纤长丝、扁条或类似品含量<85%)	10	130	17	16	米/千克		Other woven fabrics of artificial filaments, containing <85% by weight of artificial filament or strip or the like, of yarns of different colours
5408.3400	--印花	10	130	17	16	米/千克		--Printed
5408.3400 10	印花的人纤长丝机织物(与羊毛或动物细毛≥36%混纺,人纤<85%)							Woven fabrics of artificial filaments, mixed, containing≥36% by weight of combed wool or fine animal hair, containing≤85% by weight of ateificial fibres, printed

税则号列	货品名称	最惠(%)	普通	增值税率	出口退税	计量单位	监管条件	Article Description
5408.3400 20	印花的人纤长丝机织物(与羊毛或动物细毛<36%混纺,人纤<85%)							Woven fabrics of artificial filaments, mixed, containing <36% by weight of combed wool or fine animal hair, containing≤85% by weight of ateificial fibres, printed
5408.3400 30	印花的人纤长丝机织物(含丝及绢丝含量30%及以上,每千克超过$33,人纤<85%)	10	130	17	16	米/千克		Woven fabrics of artificial filaments, containing ≥ 30% by weight of silk and spun silk, value > $33/kg, containing < 85% by weight of artificial fibres, printed
5408.3400 40	印花的人纤长丝机织物(与合纤长丝混纺,人纤长丝、扁条或类似品含量<85%)	10	130	17	16	米/千克		Woven fabrics, mixed with synthetic filament, containing <85% by weight of filaments or strip or the like of artificial fibres, printed
5408.3400 91	印花的人纤长丝府绸或细平布(混纺布指按重量计人纤长丝、扁条或类似品含量<85%)	10	130	17	16	米/千克		Poplin and fine plain cloth, mixed, containing <85% by weight of artificial filaments or strip or the like of artificial fibres, printed
5408.3400 92	印花的人纤长丝平布(混纺布指按重量计人纤长丝、扁条或类似品含量<85%)	10	130	17	16	米/千克		Plain cloth, mixed, containing <85% by weight of filaments or strip or the like of artificial fibres, printed
5408.3400 93	印花的人纤长丝印染用布(混纺布指按重量计人纤长丝、扁条或类似品含量<85%)	10	130	17	16	米/千克		Woven fabrics for printing and dying, mixed, containing <85% by weight of filaments or strip or the like of artificial fibres, printed
5408.3400 94	印花的人纤长丝缎纹或斜纹布(混纺布指按重量计人纤长丝、扁条或类似品含量<85%)	10	130	17	16	米/千克		Woven fabrics, satin weave or twill weave, mixed, containing <85% by weight of filaments or strip or the like of artificial fibres, printed
5408.3400 99	印花的人纤长丝其他机织物(混纺布指按重量计人纤长丝、扁条或类似品含量<85%)	10	130	17	16	米/千克		Other woven fabrics, containing <85% by weight of artificial filaments or strip or the like of artificial fibres, printed

第五十五章
化学纤维短纤

Chapter 55
Man-made staple fibres

注释：

税目55.01和55.02仅适用于每根与丝束长度相等的平行化学纤维长丝丝束。前述丝束应同时符合下列规格：

一、丝束长度超过2米；

二、捻度每米少于5转；

三、每根长丝细度在67分特以下；

四、合成纤维长丝丝束，须经拉伸处理，即本身不能被拉伸至超过本身长度的一倍；

五、丝束总细度大于20000分特。

丝束长度不超过2米的归入税目55.03或55.04。

Notes:

Headings 55.01 and 55.02 apply only to man-made filament tow, consisting of parallel filaments of a uniform length equal to the length of the tow, meeting the following specifications:

1. Length of tow exceeding 2 m;
2. Twist less than 5 turns per metre;
3. Measuring per filament less than 67 decitex;
4. Synthetic filament tow only: the tow must be drawn, that is to say, be incapable of being stretched by more than 100% of its length;
5. Total measurement of tow more than 20,000 decitex.

Tow of a length not exceeding 2 m is to be classified in heading No. 55.03 or 55.04.

税则号列	货品名称	最惠(%)	普通	增值税率	出口退税	计量单位	监管条件	Article Description
55.01	**合成纤维长丝丝束：**							**Synthetic filament tow:**
5501.1000	-尼龙或其他聚酰胺制	5	70	17	16	千克		-Of nylon or other polyamides
5501.2000	-聚酯制	5	70	17	16	千克		-Of polyesters
5501.3000	-聚丙烯腈或变性聚丙烯腈制	5	35	17	16	千克		-Acrylic or modacrylic
5501.4000	-聚丙烯制	5	70	17	16	千克		-Of polypropylene
5501.9000	-其他	5	70	17	16	千克		-Other
55.02	**人造纤维长丝丝束：**							**Artificial filament tow:**
5502.0010	---二醋酸纤维丝束	3	40	17	16	千克	7	---Cellulose diacetate filament tow
5502.0090	---其他	5	35	17	16	千克		---Other
55.03	**合成纤维短纤，未梳或未经其他纺前加工：**							**Synthetic staple fibres, not carded, combed or otherwise processed for spinning:**
	-尼龙或其他聚酰胺制：							-Of nylon or other polyamides:
	--芳族聚酰胺纺制：							--Of aramides:
5503.1110	---聚间苯二甲酰间苯二胺纺制	5	70	17	16	千克		---Of poly-isophthaloyl metaphenylene diamine
5503.1120	---聚对苯二甲酰对苯二胺纺制	5	70	17	16	千克		---Of poly-p-phenylene terephthalamide
5503.1190	---其他	5	70	17	16	千克		---Other
5503.1900	--其他	5	70	17	16	千克		--Other
5503.2000	-聚酯制	5	70	17	16	千克		-Of polyesters
5503.3000	-聚丙烯腈或变性聚丙烯腈制	5	35	17	16	千克		-Acrylic or modacrylic
5503.4000	-聚丙烯制	5	70	17	16	千克		-Of polypropylene
	-其他：							-Other:
5503.9010	---聚苯硫醚短纤	5	70	17	16	千克		---Polyphe – nylenesu staple fibres
5503.9090	---其他合成纤维短纤	5	70	17	16	千克		---Other synthetic staple fibres
55.04	**人造纤维短纤，未梳或未经其他纺前加工：**							**Artificial staple fibres, not carded, combed or otherwise processed for spinning:**
	-粘胶纤维制：							-Of viscose rayon:
5504.1010	---竹制	5	35	17	16	千克		---Of bamboo
	---木制：							---of wood:
5504.1021	----阻燃的	5	35	17	16	千克		----Flame retardancy
5504.1029	----其他	5	35	17	16	千克		----Other
5504.1029 10	高湿模量未梳木制非阻燃粘胶纤维（湿强≥2.0cn/dtex，干强≥3.0cn/dtex，干伸>14%，湿伸>18%，纤度0.89～2.67dtex）	5	35	17	16	千克		High wet modulus viscose of wood, not carded, not flame retardancy (wet strength ≥ 2.0cn/dtex, dry strength≥3.0cn/dtex, dry elongation > 14%, wet elongation > 18%, fibrousness 0.89 ~ 2.67dtex)
5504.1029 90	其他未梳的木制非阻燃粘胶短纤（包括未经其他纺前加工的）	5	35	17	16	千克		Other viscose of wood, not carded, not flame retardancy(including otherwise processed for spinning)
5504.1090	---其他	5	35	17	16	千克		---Other
5504.9000	-其他	5	35	17	16	千克		-Other
55.05	**化学纤维废料（包括落棉、废纱及回收纤维）：**							**Waste (including noils, yarn waste and garnetted stock) of man-made fibres:**

税则号列	货品名称	最惠(%)	普通	增值税率	出口退税	计量单位	监管条件	Article Description
5505.1000	-合成纤维的	5	70	17	16	千克	AP	-Of synthetic fibres
5505.2000	-人造纤维的	5	70	17	16	千克	AP	-Of artificial fibres
55.06	**合成纤维短纤,已梳或经其他纺前加工:**							**Synthetic staple fibres, carded, combed or otherwise processed for spinning:**
	-尼龙或其他聚酰胺制:							-Of nylon or other polyamides:
	---芳族聚酰胺纺制:							---Of aramides
5506.1011	----聚间苯二甲酰间苯二胺纺制	5	70	17	16	千克		----Of poly isophthaloy polpamides: l metaphenylene diamine
5506.1012	----聚对苯二甲酰对苯二胺纺制	5	70	17	16	千克		----Of poly-p-phenylene terephthalamide
5506.1019	----其他	5	70	17	16	千克		----Other
5506.1090	---其他	5	70	17	16	千克		---Other
5506.2000	-聚酯制	5	70	17	16	千克		-Of polyesters
5506.3000	-聚丙烯腈或变性聚丙烯腈制	5	35	17	16	千克		-Acrylic or modacrylic
	-其他:							-Other:
5506.9010	---聚苯硫醚短纤	5	70	17	16	千克		Polyphe-nylenesu staple fibres
5506.9090	---其他合成纤维短纤	5	70	17	16	千克		Other synthetic staple fibres
55.07	**人造纤维短纤,已梳或经其他纺前加工:**							**Artificial staple fibres, carded, combed or otherwise processed for spinning:**
5507.0000	人造纤维短纤,已梳或经其他纺前加工	5	35	17	16	千克		Artificial staple fibres, carded, combed or otherwise processed for spinning
55.08	**化学纤维短纤纺制的缝纫线,不论是否供零售用:**							**Sewingthread of man-made staple fibres, whether or not put up for retail sale:**
5508.1000	-合成纤维短纤纺制	5	90	17	16	千克		-Of synthetic staple fibres
5508.1000 11	非零售用聚丙烯腈短纤缝纫线	5	90	17	16	千克		Sewing thread of acrylic staple fibres, not put up for retail sale
5508.1000 19	非零售用其他合纤短纤缝纫线	5	90	17	16	千克		Sewing thread of synthetic staple fibres, not put up for retail sale
5508.1000 90	零售用合成纤维短纤缝纫线	5	90	17	16	千克		Sewing thread of synthetic staple fibres, put up for retail sale
5508.2000	-人造纤维短纤纺制	5	70	17	16	千克		-Of artificial staple fibres
5508.2000 10	非零售用人造纤维短纤缝纫线	5	70	17	16	千克		Sewing thread of artificial staple fibres, not put up for retail sale
5508.2000 90	零售用人造纤维短纤缝纫线	5	70	17	16	千克		Sewing thread of artificial staple fibres, put up for retail sale
55.09	**合成纤维短纤纺制的纱线(缝纫线除外),非供零售用:**							**Yarn (other than sewing thread) of synthetic staple fibres, not put up for retail sale:**
	-按重量计尼龙或其他聚酰胺短纤含量在85%及以上:							-Containing 85% or more by weight of staple fibres of nylon or other polyamides:
5509.1100	--单纱	5	90	17	16	千克		--Single yarn
5509.1200	--多股纱线或缆线	5	90	17	16	千克		--Multiple (folded) or cabled yarn
	-按重量计聚酯短纤含量在85%及以上:							-Containing 85% or more by weight of polyester staple fibres:
5509.2100	--单纱	5	90	17	16	千克		--Single yarn
5509.2200	--多股纱线或缆线	5	90	17	16	千克		--Multiple (folded) or cabled yarn
5509.2200 10	非零售聚酯短纤多股纱线或缆线(终捻为Z捻,聚酯短纤含量≥85%,缝纫线除外)	5	90	17	16	千克		Multiple (folded) or cabled yarn, with a final "Z" twist, containing≥85% by weight of polyester staple fibres, not put up for retail sale, other than sewing thread
5509.2200 90	非零售其他聚酯短纤多股纱线缆线(聚酯短纤含量≥85%,缝纫线除外)	5	90	17	16	千克		Other multiple (folded) or cabled yarn, containing ≥85% by weight of polyester staple fibres, not put up for retail sale, other than sewing thread
	-按重量计聚丙烯腈或变性聚丙烯腈短纤含量在85%及以上:							-Containing 85% or more by weight of acrylic or modacrylic staple fibres:
5509.3100	--单纱	5	90	17	16	千克		--Single yarn
5509.3200	--多股纱线或缆线	5	90	17	16	千克		--Multiple (folded) or cabled yarn

税则号列	货品名称	最惠(%)	普通	增值税率	出口退税	计量单位	监管条件	Article Description
	-其他纱线,按重量计合成纤维短纤含量在85%及以上:							-Other yarn, containing 85% or more by weight of synthetic staple fibres:
5509.4100	--单纱	5	90	17	16	千克		--Single yarn
5509.4200	--多股纱线或缆线	5	90	17	16	千克		--Multiple (folded) or cabled yarn
	-其他聚酯短纤纺制的纱线:							-Other yarn, of polyester staple fibres:
5509.5100	--主要或仅与人造纤维短纤混纺	5	90	17	16	千克		--Mixed mainly or solely with artificial staple fibres
5509.5200	--主要或仅与羊毛或动物细毛混纺	5	90	17	16	千克		--Mixed mainly or solely with wool or fine animal hair
5509.5300	--主要或仅与棉混纺	5	90	17	16	千克		--Mixed mainly or solely with cotton
5509.5900	--其他	5	90	17	16	千克		--Other
	-其他聚丙烯腈或变性聚丙烯腈短纤纺制的纱线:							-Other yarn, of acrylic or modacrylic staple fibres:
5509.6100	--主要或仅与羊毛或动物细毛混纺	5	90	17	16	千克		--Mixed mainly or solely with wool or fine animal hair
5509.6200	--主要或仅与棉混纺	5	90	17	16	千克		--Mixed mainly or solely with cotton
5509.6900	--其他	5	90	17	16	千克		--Other
	-其他纱线:							-Other yarn:
5509.9100	--主要或仅与羊毛或动物细毛混纺	5	90	17	16	千克		--Mixed mainly or solely with wool or fine animal hair
5509.9200	--主要或仅与棉混纺	5	90	17	16	千克		--Mixed mainly or solely with cotton
5509.9900	--其他	5	90	17	16	千克		--Other
55.10	**人造纤维短纤纺制的纱线(缝纫线除外),非供零售用:**							**Yarn (other than sewing thread) of artificial staple fibres, not put up for retail sale:**
	-按重量计人造纤维短纤含量在85%及以上:							-Containing 85% or more by weight of artificial staple fibres:
5510.1100	--单纱	5	70	17	16	千克		--Single yarn
5510.1200	--多股纱线或缆线	5	70	17	16	千克		--Multiple (folded) or cabled yarn
5510.2000	-其他纱线,主要或仅与羊毛或动物细毛混纺	5	70	17	16	千克		-Other yarn, mixed mainly or solely with wool or fine animal hair
5510.3000	-其他纱线,主要或仅与棉混纺	5	70	17	16	千克		-Other yarn, mixed mainly or solely with cotton
5510.9000	-其他	5	70	17	16	千克		-Other yarn
55.11	**化学纤维短纤纺制的纱线(缝纫线除外),供零售用:**							**Yarn (other than sewing thread) of man-made staple fibres, put up for retail sale:**
5511.1000	-按重量计合成纤维短纤含量在85%及以上	5	90	17	16	千克		-Of synthetic staple fibres, containing 85% or more by weight of such fibres
5511.2000	-按重量计合成纤维短纤含量在85%以下	5	90	17	16	千克		-Of synthetic staple fibres, containing less than 85% by weight of such fibres
5511.3000	-人造纤维短纤纺制	5	90	17	16	千克		-Of artificial staple fibres
55.12	**合成纤维短纤纺制的机织物,按重量计合成纤维短纤含量在85%及以上:**							**Woven fabrics of synthetic staple fibres, containing 85% or more by weight of synthetic staple fibres:**
	-按重量计聚酯短纤含量在85%及以上:							-Containing 85% or more by weight of polyester staple fibres:
5512.1100	--未漂白或漂白	15	130	17	16	米/千克		--Unbleached or bleached
5512.1100 10	未漂或漂白聚酯短纤机织府绸(聚酯短纤含量≥85%,包括细平布)	15	130	17	16	米/千克		Poplin and fine plain cloth, containing ≥85% by weight of polyester staple fibres, unbleached or bleached
5512.1100 20	未漂或漂白聚酯短纤机织平布(聚酯短纤含量≥85%)	15	130	17	16	米/千克		Plain cloth, containing≥85% by weight of polyester staple fibres, unbleached or bleached
5512.1100 30	未漂或漂白聚酯短纤印染用布(纯聚酯布指按重量计聚酯短纤含量≥85%)	15	130	17	16	米/千克		Woven fabrics for printing and dying, containing ≥ 85% by weight of polyester staple fibres, unbleached or bleached
5512.1100 40	未漂或漂白聚酯短纤平纹奶酪布(聚酯短纤含量85%及以上,含薄细布,巴里纱)	15	130	17	16	米/千克		Cheese cloth, plain weave, including fine thin cloth, voiles, containing≥85% by weight of polyester staple fibres, unbleached or bleached

税则号列	货品名称	最惠(%)	普通	增值税率	出口退税	计量单位	监管条件	Article Description
5512.1100 50	未漂或漂白聚酯短纤机织帆布(纯聚酯布指按重量计聚脂短纤含量≥85%)	15	130	17	16	米/千克		Canvas, containing≥85% by weight of polyester staple fibres, unbleached or bleached
5512.1100 60	未漂或漂白聚酯短纤其他斜纹机织物(聚酯短纤含量≥85%,含缎纹)	15	130	17	16	米/千克		Woven fabrics, twill weave, satin weave, containing ≥85% by weight of polyester staple fibres, unbleached or bleached
5512.1100 70	未漂或漂白聚酯短纤牛津布(纯聚酯布指按重量计聚酯短纤含量≥85%)	15	130	17	16	米/千克		Woven fabrics, oxford weave, containing ≥ 85% by weight of polyester staple fibres, unbleached or bleached
5512.1100 90	未漂或漂白聚酯短纤其他机织物(纯聚酯布指按重量计聚酯短纤含量≥85%)	15	130	17	16	米/千克		Other woven fabrics, containing≥85% by weight of polyester staple fibres, unbleached or bleached
5512.1900	--其他	10	130	17	16	米/千克		--Other
5512.1900 10	聚酯短纤色织机织物(聚酯短纤含量≥85%,蓝粗斜纹布及提花织物除外)	10	130	17	16	米/千克		Woven fabrics, other than blue denim and jacquard weave, containing≥85% by weight of polyester staple fibres, of yarns of different colours
5512.1900 20	聚酯短纤蓝粗斜纹布(纯聚酯布指按重量计聚酯短纤含量≥85%)	10	130	17	16	米/千克		Blue denim, containing≥85% by weight of polyester staple fibres
5512.1900 31	聚酯短纤其他机织府绸或细平布(纯聚酯布指按重量计聚酯短纤含量≥85%)	10	130	17	16	米/千克		Other poplin and fine plain cloth, containing≥85% by weight of polyester staple fibres
5512.1900 32	聚酯短纤其他机织平布(纯聚酯布指按重量计聚酯短纤含量≥85%)	10	130	17	16	米/千克		Other plain cloth, containing ≥ 85% by weight of polyester staple fibres
5512.1900 33	聚酯短纤其他机织印染用布(纯聚酯布指按重量计聚酯短纤含量≥85%)	10	130	17	16	米/千克		Other woven fabrics for printing and dying, containing≥85% by weight of polyester staple fibres
5512.1900 34	聚酯短纤其他平纹奶酪布等(聚酯短纤含量≥85%,含薄细布,巴里纱)	10	130	17	16	米/千克		Other cheese cloth, including voiles and swiss muslin, containing ≥ 85% by weight of polyester staple fibres
5512.1900 35	聚酯短纤其他机织帆布(纯聚酯布指按重量计聚酯短纤含量≥85%)	10	130	17	16	米/千克		Other canvas, containing≥85% by weight of polyester staple fibres
5512.1900 36	聚酯短纤其他缎纹或斜纹机织物(纯聚酯布指按重量计聚酯短纤含量≥85%)	10	130	17	16	米/千克		Other woven fabrics, satin weave or twill weave, containing≥85% by weight of polyester staple fibres
5512.1900 37	聚酯短纤其他牛津布(纯聚酯布指按重量计聚酯短纤含量≥85%)	10	130	17	16	米/千克		Other woven fabrics, oxford weave, containing≥85% by weight of polyester staple fibres
5512.1900 90	聚酯短纤其他机织物(纯聚酯布指按重量计聚酯短纤含量≥85%)	10	130	17	16	米/千克		Other woven fabrics, containing≥85% by weight of polyester staple fibres
	-按重量计聚丙烯腈或变性聚丙烯腈短纤含量在85%及以上:							-Containing 85% or more by weight of acrylic or modacrylic staple fibres:
5512.2100	--未漂白或漂白	13	130	17	16	米/千克		--Unbleached or bleached
5512.2100 10	未漂或漂白的腈纶短纤机织府绸细平布(纯腈纶布指按重量计腈纶短纤含量≥85%)	13	130	17	16	米/千克		Poplin and fine plain cloth, containing ≥ 85% by weight of acrylic or modacrylic staple fibres, unbleached or bleached
5512.2100 20	未漂或漂白的腈纶短纤机织平布(纯腈纶布指按重量计腈纶短纤含量≥85%)	13	130	17	16	米/千克		Plain cloth, containing≥85% by weight of acrylic or modacrylic staple fibres, unbleached or bleached
5512.2100 30	未漂或漂白的腈纶短纤机织印染用布(纯腈纶布指按重量计腈纶短纤含量≥85%)	13	130	17	16	米/千克		Woven fabrics for printing and dying, containing ≥ 85% by weight of acrylic or modacrylic staple fibres, unbleached or bleached
5512.2100 40	未漂或漂白的腈纶短纤平纹奶酪布等(腈纶短纤含量≥85%,含薄细布,巴里纱)	13	130	17	16	米/千克		Cheese cloth, including voiles and fine thin cloth, containing≥85% by weight of acrylic or modacrylic staple fibres, unbleached or bleached
5512.2100 50	未漂或漂白腈纶短纤机织帆布(纯腈纶布指按重量计腈纶短纤含量≥85%)	13	130	17	16	米/千克		Canvas, containing ≥ 85% by weight of acrylic or modacrylic staple fibres, unbleached or bleached
5512.2100 60	未漂或漂白的腈纶短纤其他斜纹机织物(腈纶短纤含量≥85%,含缎纹机织物)	13	130	17	16	米/千克		Woven fabrics, twill weave, satin weave, containing ≥85% by weight of acrylic or modacrylic staple fibres, unbleached or bleached
5512.2100 70	未漂或漂白的腈纶短纤牛津布(纯腈纶布指按重量计腈纶短纤含量≥85%)	13	130	17	16	米/千克		Woven fabrics, oxford weave, containing ≥ 85% by weight of acrylic or modacrylic staple fibres, unbleached or bleached

税则号列	货品名称	最惠(%)	普通	增值税率	出口退税	计量单位	监管条件	Article Description
5512.2100 90	未漂或漂白的腈纶短纤其他机织物(纯腈纶布指按重量计腈纶短纤含量≥85%)	13	130	17	16	米/千克		Other woven fabrics, containing≥85% by weight of acrylic or modacrylic staple fibres, unbleached or bleached
5512.2900	--其他	10	130	17	16	米/千克		--Other
5512.2900 10	腈纶短纤色织机织物(腈纶短纤含量≥85%,蓝粗斜纹布及提花织物除外)	10	130	17	16	米/千克		Woven fabrics, other than blue denim and jacquard weave, containing≥85% by weight of acrylic or modacrylic staple fibres, of yarns of different colours
5512.2900 20	腈纶短纤蓝粗斜纹布(纯腈纶布指按重量计腈纶短纤含量≥85%)	10	130	17	16	米/千克		Blue denim, containing≥85% by weight of acrylic or modacrylic staple fibres
5512.2900 31	腈纶短纤其他机织府绸或细平布(纯腈纶布指按重量计腈纶短纤含量≥85%)	10	130	17	16	米/千克		Poplin and fine plain cloth, containing ≥85% by weight of acrylic or modacrylic staple fibres
5512.2900 32	腈纶短纤其他机织平布(纯腈纶布指按重量计腈纶短纤含量≥85%)	10	130	17	16	米/千克		Plain cloth, containing≥85% by weight of acrylic or modacrylic staple fibres
5512.2900 33	腈纶短纤其他机织印染用布(纯腈纶布指按重量计腈纶短纤含量≥85%)	10	130	17	16	米/千克		Woven fabrics for printing and dying, containing ≥85% by weight of acrylic or modacrylic staple fibres
5512.2900 34	腈纶短纤其他平纹奶酪布等(腈纶短纤含量≥85%,含薄细布,巴里纱)	10	130	17	16	米/千克		Cheese cloth, plain weave, including voiles and swiss muslin, containing ≥ 85% by weight of acrylic or. modacrylic staple fibres
5512.2900 35	腈纶短纤其他机织帆布(纯腈纶布指按重量计腈纶短纤含量≥85%)	10	130	17	16	米/千克		Other canvas, containing≥85% by weight of acrylic or modacrylic staple fibres
5512.2900 36	腈纶短纤其他缎纹或斜纹机织物(纯腈纶布指按重量计腈纶短纤含量≥85%)	10	130	17	16	米/千克		Woven fabrics, satin weave or twill weave, containing≥85% by weight of acrylic or modacrylic staple fibres
5512.2900 37	腈纶短纤其他牛津布(纯腈纶布指按重量计腈纶短纤含量≥85%)	10	130	17	16	米/千克		Woven fabrics, oxford weave, containing ≥85% by weight of acrylic or modacrylic staple fibres
5512.2900 90	腈纶短纤其他机织物(纯腈纶布指按重量计腈纶短纤含量≥85%)	10	130	17	16	米/千克		Other woven fabrics, containing≥85% by weight of acrylic or modacrylic staple fibres
	-其他:							-Other:
5512.9100	--未漂白或漂白	18	130	17	16	米/千克		--Unbleached or bleached
5512.9100 10	未漂白或漂白的其他合纤短纤机织府绸(其他合纤短纤含量≥85%,含细平布)	18	130	17	16	米/千克		Poplin, including fine plain cloth, containing≥85% by weight of synthetic staple fibres, unbleached or bleached
5512.9100 20	未漂白或漂白的其他合纤短纤机织平布(其他纯合纤布指按重量计其他合纤短纤含量≥85%)	18	130	17	16	米/千克		Plain cloth, containing≥85% by weight of synthetic staple fibres, unbleached or bleached
5512.9100 30	未漂白或漂白的其他合纤短纤印染用布(其他纯合纤布指按重量计其他合纤短纤含量≥85%)	18	130	17	16	米/千克		Woven fabrics for printing and dying, containing ≥85% by weight of synthetic staple fibres, unbleached or bleached
5512.9100 40	未漂白或漂白的其他合纤短纤平纹奶酪布(其他合纤短纤含量≥85%,含薄细布,巴里纱)	18	130	17	16	米/千克		Cheese cloth, including voiles and swiss muslin, containing≥85% by weight of synthetic staple fibres, unbleached or bleached
5512.9100 50	未漂白或漂白的其他合纤短纤机织帆布(其他纯合纤布指按重量计其他合纤短纤含量≥85%)	18	130	17	16	米/千克		Canvas, containing≥85% by weight of synthetic staple fibres, unbleached or bleached
5512.9100 60	未漂白或漂白的其他合纤短纤斜纹机织物(其他合纤短纤含量≥85%,含缎纹机织物)	18	130	17	16	米/千克		Woven fabrics, twill weave or satin weave, containing ≥85% by weight of synthetic staple fibres, unbleached or bleached
5512.9100 70	未漂白或漂白的其他合纤短纤牛津布(其他纯合纤布指按重量计其他合纤短纤含量≥85%)	18	130	17	16	米/千克		Woven fabrics, oxford weave, containing ≥85% by weight of synthetic staple fibres, unbleached or bleached
5512.9100 90	未漂白或漂白的其他合纤短纤其他机织物(其他纯合纤布指按重量计其他合纤短纤含量≥85%)	18	130	17	16	米/千克		Other woven fabrics, containing≥85% by weight of synthetic staple fibres, unbleached or bleached
5512.9900	--其他	10	130	17	16	米/千克		--Other
5512.9900 10	其他合纤短纤色织机织物(其他合纤短纤含量≥85%,蓝粗斜纹布及提花织物除外)	10	130	17	16	米/千克		Other woven fabrics, other than blue denim and jacquard weave, containing≥85% by weight of synthetic staple fibres, of yarns of different colours

税则号列	货品名称	最惠(%)	普通	增值税率	出口退税	计量单位	监管条件	Article Description
5512.9900 20	其他合纤短纤蓝粗斜纹布(其他纯合纤布指按重量计其他合纤短纤含量≥85%)	10	130	17	16	米/千克		Other blue denim, containing ≥85% by weight of synthetic staple fibres
5512.9900 31	其他合纤短纤机织府绸或细平布(其他纯合纤布指按重量计其他合纤短纤含量≥85%)	10	130	17	16	米/千克		Other poplin and fine plain cloth, containing ≥85% by weight of synthetic staple fibres
5512.9900 32	其他合纤短纤其他机织平布(其他纯合纤布指按重量计其他合纤短纤含量≥85%)	10	130	17	16	米/千克		Other plain cloth, containing ≥85% by weight of synthetic staple fibres
5512.9900 33	其他合纤短纤其他机织印染用布(其他纯合纤布指按重量计其他合纤短纤含量≥85%)	10	130	17	16	米/千克		Other woven fabrics for printing and dying, containing≥85% by weight of synthetic staple fibres
5512.9900 34	其他合纤短纤平纹奶酪布等(其他合纤短纤≥85%,含薄细布,巴里纱)	10	130	17	16	米/千克		Other cheese cloth, including voiles and swiss muslin, containing ≥85% by weight of synthetic staple fibres
5512.9900 35	其他合纤短纤其他机织帆布(其他纯合纤布指按重量计其他合纤短纤含量≥85%)	10	130	17	16	米/千克		Other canvas, containing ≥85% by weight of synthetic staple fibres
5512.9900 36	其他合纤短纤缎纹或斜纹机织物(其他纯合纤布指按重量计其他合纤短纤含量≥85%)	10	130	17	16	米/千克		Other woven fabrics, satin weave or twill weave, containing≥85% by weight of synthetic staple fibres
5512.9900 39	其他合纤短纤其他牛津布(其他纯合纤布指按重量计其他合纤短纤含量≥85%)	10	130	17	16	米/千克		Other woven fabrics, oxford weave, containing≥85% by weight of synthetic staple fibres
5512.9900 90	其他合纤短纤其他机织物(其他纯合纤布指按重量计其他合纤短纤含量≥85%)	10	130	17	16	米/千克		Other woven fabrics, containing≥85% by weight of synthetic staple fibres
55.13	**合成纤维短纤纺制的机织物,按重量计合成纤维短纤含量在85%以下,主要或仅与棉混纺,每平方米重量不超过170克:**							**Woven fabrics of synthetic staple fibres, containing less than 85% by weight of such fibres, mixed mainly or solely with cotton, of a weight not exceeding 170 g/m²:**
	-未漂白或漂白:							-Unbleached or bleached:
	--聚酯短纤纺制的平纹机织物:							--Of polyester staple fibres, plain weave:
5513.1110	---未漂白	16	130	17	16	米/千克		---Unbleached
5513.1110 10	与棉混纺未漂白聚酯短纤平纹府绸(聚酯短纤85%以下,每平方米重量≤170克,含细平布)	16	130	17	16	米/千克		Poplin, including fine plain cloth, mixed with cotton, containing < 85% by weight of polyester staple fibres, weight≤170g/m², unbleached
5513.1110 20	与棉混纺未漂白聚酯短纤机织平布(混纺为含聚酯短纤85%以下,轻质指每平方米重量≤170克)	16	130	17	16	米/千克		Plain cloth, mixed with cotton, containing < 85% by weight of polyester staple fibres, weight≤170g/m², unbleached
5513.1110 30	与棉混纺未漂白聚酯短纤平纹印染用布(混纺为含聚酯短纤85%以下,轻质指每平方米重≤170克)	16	130	17	16	米/千克		Woven fabrics for printing and dying, plain weave, mixed with cotton, containing < 85% by weight of polyester staple fibres, weight ≤ 170 g/m², unbleached
5513.1110 40	与棉混纺未漂白聚酯短纤平纹奶酪布(聚酯短纤<85%,轻质指每平方米重≤170克,含薄细布、巴里纱)	16	130	17	16	米/千克		Cheese cloth, plain weave, including voiles and swiss muslin, mixed with cotton, containing < 85% by weight of polyester staple fibres, weight≤170g/m², unbleached
5513.1120	---漂白	15	130	17	16	米/千克		---Bleached
5513.1120 10	与棉混纺漂白聚酯短纤平纹府绸(聚酯短纤85%以下,每平方米重≤170克,含细平布)	15	130	17	16	米/千克	A	Poplin, plain weave, including fine plain cloth, mixed with cotton, containing <85% by weight of polyester staple fibres, weight≤170g/m², bleached
5513.1120 20	与棉混纺漂白聚酯短纤机织平布(混纺为含聚酯短纤85%以下,轻质指每平方米重≤170克)	15	130	17	16	米/千克	A	Plain cloth, mixed with cotton, containing < 85% by weight of polye ster staple fibres, weight≤170g/m², bleached
5513.1120 30	与棉混纺漂白聚酯平纹印染用布(混纺为含聚酯短纤85%以下,轻质指每平方米重≤170克)	15	130	17	16	米/千克	A	Woven fabrics for printing and dying, plain weave, mixed with cotton, containing < 85% by weight of polyesterstaple fibres, weight≤170g/m², bleached

税则号列	货品名称	最惠(%)	普通	增值税率	出口退税	计量单位	监管条件	Article Description
5513.1120 40	与棉混纺漂白聚酯短纤平纹奶酪布等(聚酯短纤<85%,每平方米重≤170克,含薄细布、巴里纱)	15	130	17	16	米/千克	A	Cheese cloth, plain weave, including voiles and fine thin cloth, mixed with cotton, containing < 85% by weight of polyester staple fibres, weight≤170g/m², bleached
	--聚酯短纤纺制的三线或四线斜纹机织物,包括双面斜纹机织物:							--3-thread or 4-thread twill, including cross twill, of polyester staple fibres:
5513.1210	---未漂白	16	130	17	16	米/千克		---Unbleached
5513.1220	---漂白	18	130	17	16	米/千克		---Bleached
	--其他聚酯短纤纺制的机织物:							--Other woven fabrics of polyester staple fibres:
5513.1310	---未漂白	16	130	17	16	米/千克		---Unbleached
5513.1310 10	与棉混纺未漂聚酯短纤斜纹机织物(聚酯短纤<85%,轻质指每平方米重≤170克,含缎纹布)	16	130	17	16	米/千克		Woven fabrics, twill weave, satin weave, mixed with cotton, containing < 85% by weight of polyester staple fibres, weight≤170g/m², unbleached
5513.1310 20	与棉混纺未漂聚酯短纤牛津布(混纺为含聚酯短纤85%以下,轻质指每平方米重≤170克)	16	130	17	16	米/千克		Woven fabrics, oxford weave, mixed with cotton, containing < 85% by weight of polyester staple fibres, weight≤170g/m², unbleached
5513.1310 90	与棉混纺未漂白聚酯短纤其他机织物(混纺为含聚酯短纤85%以下,轻质指每平方米重≤170克)	16	130	17	16	米/千克		Other woven fabrics, mixed with cotton containing < 85% by weight of polyester staple fibres, weight ≤ 170g/m², unbleached
5513.1320	---漂白	18	130	17	16	米/千克		---Bleached
5513.1320 10	与棉混纺漂白聚酯短纤斜纹机织物(含聚酯短纤85%以下,轻质指每平方米重≤170克,含缎纹)	18	130	17	16	米/千克		Woven fabrics, twill weave, satin weave, mixed with cotton, containing < 85% by weight of polyester staple fibres, weight≤170g/m², bleached
5513.1320 20	与棉混纺漂白聚酯短纤牛津布(混纺为含聚酯短纤85%以下,轻质指每平方米重≤170克)	18	130	17	16	米/千克		Woven fabrics, oxford weave, mixed with cotton, containing < 85% by weight of polyester staple fibres, weight≤170g/m², bleached
5513.1320 90	与棉混纺漂白聚酯短纤其他机织物(混纺为含聚酯短纤85%以下,轻质指每平方米重≤170克)	18	130	17	16	米/千克		Other woven fabrics, mixed with cotton, containing < 85% by weight of polyester staple fibres, weight ≤ 170g/m², bleached
5513.1900	--其他机织物	18	130	17	16	米/千克		--Other woven fabrics
5513.1900 10	与棉混纺未漂白或漂白其他合纤短纤布(其他合短纤<85%,每平方米重≤170克,专指府绸或细平布)	18	130	17	16	米/千克		Poplin and fine plain cloth, mixed with cotton, containing < 85% by weight of synthetic staple fibres, weight≤170g/m², unbleached or bleached
5513.1900 20	与棉混纺未漂白或漂白其他合纤短纤布(其他合短纤<85%,每平方米重≤170克,专指机织平布)	18	130	17	16	米/千克		Plain cloth, mixed with cotton, containing < 85% by weight of synthetic staple fibres, weight≤170g/m², unbleached or bleached
5513.1900 30	与棉混纺未漂白或漂白其他合纤短纤布(其他合短纤<85%,每平方米重≤170克,专指平纹印染用布)	18	130	17	16	米/千克		Other woven fabrics for printing and dying, mixed with cotton, containing < 85% by weight of synthetic staple fibres, weight ≤ 170g/m², unbleached or bleached
5513.1900 40	与棉混纺未漂白或漂白其他合纤短纤布(合短纤<85%,每平方米重≤170克,指奶酪布、薄细布、巴里纱)	18	130	17	16	米/千克		Cheese cloth, voiles and swiss muslin, mixed with cotton, containing < 85% by weight of synthetic staple fibres, weight ≤ 170g/m², unbleached or bleached
5513.1900 50	与棉混纺未漂白或漂白其他合纤短纤布(其他合短纤<85%,每平方米重≤170克,专指缎纹或斜纹布)	18	130	17	16	米/千克		Other woven fabrics, satin weave, twill weave, mixed with cotton, containing < 85% by weight of synthetic staple fibres, weight ≤ 170g/m², unbleached or bleached
5513.1900 60	与棉混纺未漂白或漂白其他合纤短纤布(其他合短纤<85%,每平方米重≤170克,专指牛津布)	18	130	17	16	米/千克		Other woven fabrics, oxford weave, mixed with cotton, containing < 85% by weight of synthetic staple fibres, weight≤170g/m², unbleached or bleached
5513.1900 90	与棉混纺未漂白或漂白其他合纤短纤布(其他合短纤<85%,每平方米重≤170克,特指其他机织物)	18	130	17	16	米/千克		Other woven fabrics, mixed with cotton, containing < 85% by weight of synthetic staple fibres, weight ≤ 170g/m², unbleached or bleached
	-染色:							-Dyed:
5513.2100	--聚酯短纤纺制的平纹机织物	10	130	17	16	米/千克		--Of polyester staple fibres, plain weave

税则号列	货品名称	最惠(%)	普通	增值税率	出口退税	计量单位	监管条件	Article Description
5513.2100 10	与棉混纺染色聚酯短纤平纹府绸(聚酯短纤85%以下,每平方米重≤170克,含细平布)	10	130	17	16	米/千克		Poplin,plain weave,including fine plain cloth,mixed with cotton containing <85% by weight of polyester staple fibres,weight≤170g/m²,dyed
5513.2100 20	与棉混纺染色聚酯短纤机织平布(混纺为含聚酯短纤85%以下,轻质指每平方米重≤170克)	10	130	17	16	米/千克		Plain cloth,mixed with cotton,containing <85% by weight of polyester staple fibres,weight≤170g/m²,dyed
5513.2100 30	与棉混纺染色聚酯短纤平纹印染用布(混纺为含聚酯短纤85%以下,轻质指每平方米重≤170克)	10	130	17	16	米/千克		Woven fabrics for printing and dying, mixed with cotton,containing <85% by weight of polyester staple fibres,weight≤170g/m²,dyed
5513.2100 40	与棉混纺染色聚酯短纤平纹奶酪布等(聚酯短纤85%以下,每平方米重≤170克,含薄细布、巴里纱)	10	130	17	16	米/千克		Cheese cloth,plain weave,including voiles and swiss muslin, mixed with cotton, containing < 85% by weight of polyester staple fibres,weight≤170g/m²,dyed
	--其他聚酯短纤纺制的机织物:							--Other woven fabrics of polyester staple fibres:
5513.2310	---聚酯短纤纺制的三线或四线斜纹机织物,包括双面斜纹机织物	10	130	17	16	米/千克		---3-thread or 4-thread twill,including cross twill,of polyester staple fibres
5513.2390	---其他	10	130	17	16	米/千克		---Other
5513.2900	--其他机织物	10	130	17	16	米/千克		--Other woven fabrics
5513.2900 10	与棉混纺染色其他合纤短纤府绸(其他合短纤<85%,每平方米重≤170克,含细平布)	10	130	17	16	米/千克		Poplin,including fine plain cloth,mixed with cotton,containing <85% by weight of synthetic staple fibres,weight≤170g/m²,dyed
5513.2900 20	与棉混纺染色其他合纤短纤平布(混纺为含其他合短纤<85%,轻质指每平方米重≤170克)	10	130	17	16	米/千克		Plain cloth,mixed with cotton,containing <85% by weight of synthetic staple fibres,weight≤170g/m²,dyed
5513.2900 30	与棉混纺染色其他合纤短纤平纹布(印染用,其他合短纤<85%,指每平方米重≤170克)	10	130	17	16	米/千克		Plain weave for printing and dying,mixed with cotton,containing <85% by weight of synthetic staple fibres,weight≤170g/m²,dyed
5513.2900 40	与棉混染色其他合纤短纤平纹布(合短纤<85%,每平方米重≤170克,指奶酪布、薄细布、巴里纱)	10	130	17	16	米/千克		Cheese cloth, voiles and swiss muslin, mixed with cotton,containing <85% by weight of synthetic staple fibres,weight≤170g/m²,dyed
5513.2900 50	与棉混纺染色其他合纤短纤斜纹布(其他合短纤<85%,每平方米重≤170克,含缎纹布)	10	130	17	16	米/千克		Woven fabrics, twill weave, including satin weave, mixed with cotton, containing <85% by weight of synthetic staple fibres,weight≤170g/m²,dyed
5513.2900 60	与棉混纺染色其他合纤短纤牛津布(混纺为含其他合短纤<85%,轻质指每平方米重≤170克)	10	130	17	16	米/千克		Woven fabrice,oxford weave,mixed with cotton,containing <85% by weight of synthetic staple fibres,weight≤170g/m²,dyed
5513.2900 90	与棉混纺染色其他合纤短纤其他布(混纺为含其他合短纤<85%,轻质指每平方米重≤170克)	10	130	17	16	米/千克		Other woven fabric,mixed with cotton,containing <85% by weight of synthetic staple fibres,weight≤170g/m²,dyed
	-色织:							-Of yarns of different colours:
5513.3100	--聚酯短纤纺制的平纹机织物	10	130	17	16	米/千克		--Of polyester staple fibres,plain weave
	--其他机织物:							--Other woven fabrics:
5513.3910	---聚酯短纤纺制的三线或四线斜 纹机织物,包括双面斜纹机织物	10	130	17	16	米/千克		---3-thread or 4-thread twill,including cross twill,of polyester staple fibres
5513.3920	---其他聚酯短纤纺制的机织物	10	130	17	16	米/千克		---Other woven fabrics of polyester staple fibres
5513.3990	---其他机织物	10	130	17	16	米/千克		---Other woven fabrics
	-印花:							-Printed:
5513.4100	--聚酯短纤纺制的平纹机织物	10	130	17	16	米/千克		--Of polyester staple fibres,plain weave
5513.4100 10	与棉混纺印花聚酯短纤平纹府绸(聚酯短纤85%以下,每平方米重≤170克,含细平布)	10	130	17	16	米/千克		Poplin,plain weave,including fine plain cloth,mixed with cotton,containing <85% by weight of polyester staple fibres,weight≤170g/m²,printed
5513.4100 20	与棉混纺印花聚酯短纤机织平布(混纺为含聚酯短纤85%以下,轻质指每平方米重≤170克)	10	130	17	16	米/千克		Plain cloth,mixed with cotton containing <85% by weight of polyester staple fibres,weight≤170g/m²,printed

税则号列	货品名称	最惠(%)	普通	增值税率	出口退税	计量单位	监管条件	Article Description
5513.4100 30	与棉混纺的印花聚酯短纤平纹印染用布(混纺为含聚酯短纤85%以下,轻质指每平方米重≤170克)	10	130	17	16	米/千克		Woven fabrics for printing and dying, mixed with cotton, containing < 85% by weight of polyester staple fibres, weight≤170g/m², printed
5513.4100 40	与棉混印花聚酯短纤平纹奶酪布等(聚酯短纤<85%,每平方米重≤170克,含薄细布、巴里纱)	10	130	17	16	米/千克		Cheese cloth, including voiles and swiss muslin, mixed with cotton, containing < 85% by weight of polyester staple fibres, weight≤170g/m², printed
	--其他机织物:							--Other woven fabrics:
5513.4910	---聚酯短纤纺制的三线或四线斜纹机织物,包括双面斜纹机织物	10	130	17	16	米/千克		---3-thread or 4-thread twill, including cross twill, of polyeste staple fibres
5513.4920	---其他聚酯短纤纺制的机织物	10	130	17	16	米/千克		---Other woven fabrics of polyester staple fibres
5513.4990	---其他	10	130	17	16	米/千克		---Other
55.14	**合成纤维短纤纺制的机织物,按重量计合成纤维短纤含量在85%以下,主要或仅与棉混纺,每平方米重量超过170克:**							**Woven fabrics of synthetic staple fibres, containing less than 85% by weight of such fibres, mixed mainly or solely with cotton, of a weight exceeding 170 g/m²:**
	-未漂白或漂白:							-Unbleached or bleached:
	--聚酯短纤纺制的平纹机织物:							--Of polyester staple fibres, plain weave:
5514.1110	---未漂白	16	130	17	16	米/千克		---Unbleached
5514.1110 10	与棉混纺未漂白聚酯短纤平纹府绸(聚酯短纤85%以下,每平方米重>170克,含细平布)	16	130	17	16	米/千克		Poplin, including fine plain cloth, mixed with cotton, containing < 85% by weight of polyester staple fibres, weight > 170g/m², unbleached
5514.1110 20	与棉混纺未漂白聚酯短纤机织平布(混纺为含聚酯短纤85%以下,重质指每平方米重>170克)	16	130	17	16	米/千克		Plain cloth, mixed with cotton, containing < 85% by weight of polyester staple fibres, weight > 170g/m², unbleached
5514.1110 30	与棉混纺未漂白聚酯短纤平纹帆布(混纺为含聚酯短纤85%以下,重质指每平方米重>170克)	16	130	17	16	米/千克		Canvas, plain weave, mixed with cotton, containing < 85% by weight of polyester staple fibres, weight > 170g/m², unbleached
5514.1120	---漂白	18	130	17	16	米/千克		---Bleached
5514.1120 10	与棉混纺漂白聚酯短纤平纹府绸(聚酯短纤85%以下,每平方米重>170克,含细平布)	18	130	17	16	米/千克		Poplin, including fine plain cloth, mixed with cotton, containing < 85% by weight of polyester staple fibres, weight > 170g/m², bleached
5514.1120 20	与棉混纺漂白聚酯短纤机织平布(混纺为含聚酯短纤85%以下,重质指每平方米重>170克)	18	130	17	16	米/千克		Plain cloth, mixed with cotton, containing < 85% by weight of polyester staple fibres, weight > 170g/m², bleached
5514.1120 30	与棉混纺漂白聚脂短纤平纹帆布(混纺为含聚酯短纤85%以下,重质指每平方米重>170克)	18	130	17	16	米/千克		Canvas, mixed with cotton, containing < 85% by weight of polyester staple fibres, weight > 170 g/m², bleached
	--聚酯短纤纺制的三线或四线斜纹机织物,包括双面斜纹机织物:							--3-thread or 4-thread twill, including cross twill, of polyester staple fibres:
5514.1210	---未漂白	16	130	17	16	米/千克		---Unbleached
5514.1220	---漂白	18	130	17	16	米/千克		---Bleached
	--其他机织物:							--Other woven fabrics:
	---聚酯短纤纺制的机织物:							---Other woven fabrics of polyester staple fibres:
5514.1911	----未漂白	16	130	17	16	米/千克		----Unbleached
5514.1912	----漂白	18	130	17	16	米/千克		----Bleached
5514.1990	---其他	16	130	17	16	米/千克		---Other
	-染色:							-Dyed:
5514.2100	--聚酯短纤纺制的平纹机织物	10	130	17	16	米/千克		--Of polyester staple fibres, plain weave
5514.2100 10	与棉混纺染色聚酯短纤平纹府绸(含细平布,聚酯短纤85%以下,重质指每平方米重>170克)	10	130	17	16	米/千克		Poplin, plain weave, including fine plain cloth, mixed with cotton, containing < 85% by weight of polyester staple fibres, weight > 170g/m², dyed
5514.2100 20	与棉混纺染色聚酯短纤机织平布(混纺为含聚酯短纤85%以下,重质指每平方米重>170克)	10	130	17	16	米/千克		Plain cloth, plain weave, mixed with cotton, containing < 85% by weight of polyester staple fibres, weight > 170g/m², dyed

税则号列	货品名称	最惠(%)	普通	增值税率	出口退税	计量单位	监管条件	Article Description
5514.2100 30	与棉混纺染色聚酯短纤平纹帆布(混纺为含聚酯短纤85%以下,重质指每平方米重>170克)	10	130	17	16	米/千克		Canvas, mixed with cotton, containing < 85% by weight of polyester staple fibres, weight > 170g/m², dyed
5514.2200	--聚酯短纤纺制的三线或四线斜纹机织物,包括双面斜纹机织物	10	130	17	16	米/千克		--3-thread or 4-thread twill, including cross twill, of polyester staple fibres
5514.2300	--其他聚酯短纤纺制的机织物	10	130	17	16	米/千克		--Other woven fabrics of polyester staple fibres
5514.2300 10	与棉混纺染色聚酯短纤其他斜纹布(聚酯短纤85%以下,每平米重>170克,含缎纹布)	10	130	17	16	米/千克		Woven fabrics, twill weave, including satin weave, mixed with cotton, containing < 85% by weight of polyester staple fibres, weight > 170g/m², dyed
5514.2300 20	与棉混纺染色聚酯短纤其他帆布(混纺为含聚酯短纤85%以下,重质指每平方米重>170克)	10	130	17	16	米/千克		Other canvas, mixed with cotton, containing < 85% by weight of polyester staple fibres, weight > 170 g/m², dyed
5514.2300 90	与棉混纺染色聚酯短纤其他机织物(混纺为含聚酯短纤85%以下,重质指每平方米重>170克)	10	130	17	16	米/千克		Other woven fabrics, mixed with cotton, containing < 85% by weight of polyester staple fibres, weight > 170g/m², dyed
5514.2900	--其他机织物	10	130	17	16	米/千克		--Other woven fabrics
5514.2900 10	与棉混纺染色其他合纤短纤府绸(含细平布,其他合短纤<85%,重质指每平方米重>170克)	10	130	17	16	米/千克		Poplin, including fine plain cloth, mixed with cotton, containing < 85% by weight of synthetic staple fibres, weight > 170g/m², dyed
5514.2900 20	与棉混纺染色其他合纤短纤平布(混纺为含其他合短纤<85%,重质指每平方米重>170克)	10	130	17	16	米/千克		Plain cloth, mixed with cotton, containing < 85% by weight of synthetic staple fibres, weight > 170g/m², dyed
5514.2900 30	与棉混纺染色其他合纤短纤帆布(混纺为含其他合短纤<85%,重质指每平方米重>170克)	10	130	17	16	米/千克		Other canvas, mixed with cotton, containing < 85% by weight of synthetic staple fibres, weight > 170g/m², dyed
5514.2900 40	与棉混纺染色其他合纤短纤斜纹布(含缎纹布,其他合短纤<85%,重质指每平方米重>170克)	10	130	17	16	米/千克		Other woven fabrics twill weave, including satin weave, mixed with cotton, containing < 85% by weight of synthetic staple fibres, weight > 170g/m², dyed
5514.2900 90	与棉混纺染色其他合纤短纤其他布(混纺为含其他合短纤<85%,重质指每平方米重>170克)	10	130	17	16	米/千克		Other woven fabrics, mixed with cotton, containing < 85% by weight of synthetic staple fibres, weight > 170g/m², dyed
	-色织:							-Of yarns of different colours:
5514.3010	---聚酯短纤纺制的平纹机织物	10	130	17	16	米/千克		---Of polyester staple fibres, plain weave
5514.3020	---聚酯短纤纺制的三线或四线斜纹机织物,包括双面斜纹机织物	10	130	17	16	米/千克		---3-thread or 4-thread twill, including cross twill, of polyester staple fibres
5514.3030	---其他聚酯短纤纺制的机织物	10	130	17	16	米/千克		---Other woven fabrics of polyester staple fibres
5514.3090	---其他机织物	10	130	17	16	米/千克		---Other woven fabrics
	-印花:							-Printed:
5514.4100	--聚酯短纤纺制的平纹机织物	10	130	17	16	米/千克		--Of polyester staple fibres, plain weave
5514.4100 10	与棉混纺印花聚酯短纤平纹府绸(聚酯短纤85%以下,每平方米重>170克,含细平布)	10	130	17	16	米/千克		Poplin, including fine plain cloth, mixed with cotton, containing < 85% by weight of polyester staple fibres, weight > 170g/m², printed
5514.4100 20	与棉混纺印花聚酯短纤机织平布(混纺为含聚酯短纤85%以下,重质指每平方米重>170克)	10	130	17	16	米/千克		Plain cloth, mixed with cotton, containing < 85% by weight of polyester staple fibres, weight > 170g/m², printed
5514.4100 30	与棉混纺印花聚酯短纤平纹帆布(混纺为含聚酯短纤85%以下,重质指每平方米重>170克)	10	130	17	16	米/千克		Canvas, mixed with cotton, containing < 85% by weight of polyester staple fibres, weight > 170g/m², printed
5514.4200	--聚酯短纤纺制的三线或四线斜纹机织物,包括双面斜纹机织物	10	130	17	16	米/千克		--3-thread or 4-thread twill, including cross twill, of polyester staple fibres
5514.4300	--其他聚酯短纤纺制的机织物	10	130	17	16	米/千克		--Other woven fabrics of polyester staple fibres
5514.4300 10	与棉混纺印花聚酯短纤其他斜纹布(含缎纹布,聚酯短纤85%以下,重质指每平方米重>170克)	10	130	17	16	米/千克		Other woven fabrics, twill weave, including satin weave, mixed with cotton, containing < 85% by weight of polyesterstaple fibres, weight > 170g/m², printed

税则号列	货品名称	最惠(%)	普通	增值税率	出口退税	计量单位	监管条件	Article Description
5514.4300 20	与棉混纺印花聚酯短纤其他帆布(混纺为含聚酯短纤85%以下,重质指每平方米重>170克)	10	130	17	16	米/千克		Other canvas, mixed with cotton, containing < 85% by weight of polyester staple fibres, weight > 170g/m², printed
5514.4300 90	与棉混纺印花聚酯短纤其他机织物(混纺为含聚酯短纤85%以下,重质指每平方米重>170克)	10	130	17	16	米/千克		Other woven fabrics, mixed with cotton, containing < 85% by weight of polyester staple fibres, weight > 170g/m², printed
5514.4900	--其他机织物	10	130	17	16	米/千克		--Other woven fabrics
5514.4900 10	与棉混纺印花其他合纤短纤府绸(含细平布,其他合短纤<85%,重质指每平方米重>170克)	10	130	17	16	米/千克		Other poplin, including fine plain cloth, mixed with cotton, containing < 85% by weight of synthetic staple fibres, weight > 170g/m², printed
5514.4900 20	与棉混纺印花其他合纤短纤平布(混纺为含其他合短纤<85%,重质指每平方米重>170克)	10	130	17	16	米/千克		Other plain cloth, mixed with cotton, containing < 85% by weight of synthetic staple fibres, weight > 170g/m², printed
5514.4900 30	与棉混纺印花其他合纤短纤帆布(混纺为含其他合短纤<85%,重质指每平方米重>170克)	10	130	17	16	米/千克		Canvas, mixed with cotton, containing < 85% by weight of synthetic staple fibres, weight > 170g/m², printed
5514.4900 40	与棉混纺印花其他合纤短纤斜纹布(含缎纹布,其他合短纤<85%,重质指每平方米重>170克)	10	130	17	16	米/千克		Woven fabrics twill weave, including satin weave, mixed with cotton, containing < 85% by weight of synthetic staple fibres, weight > 170g/m², printed
5514.4900 90	与棉混纺印花其他合纤短纤其他布(混纺为含其他合短纤<85%,重质指每平方米重>170克)	10	130	17	16	米/千克		Other woven fabrics, mixed with cotton, containing < 85% by weight of synthetic staple fibres, weight > 170g/m², printed
55.15	**合成纤维短纤纺制的其他机织物:**							**Other woven fabrics of synthetic staple fibres:**
	-聚酯短纤纺制:							-Of polyester staple fibres:
5515.1100	--主要或仅与粘胶纤维短纤混纺	10	130	17	16	米/千克		--Mixed mainly or solely with viscose rayon staple fibres
5515.1100 11	聚酯短纤蓝粗斜纹布(与粘胶纤维短纤混纺,聚酯短纤含量<85%)	10	130	17	16	米/千克		Blue denim, mixed with viscose rayon staple fibres, containing < 85% by weight of polyester staple fibres
5515.1100 19	聚酯短纤其他色织布(短纤含量<85%,提花织物除外,与粘胶纤维短纤混纺)	10	130	17	16	米/千克		Woven fabrics, other than jacquard weave, mixed with viscose rayon staple fibres, containing < 85% by weight of polyester staple fibres, of yarns of different colours
5515.1100 21	未漂白或漂白聚酯短纤府绸或细平布(聚酯短纤含量<85%,主要或仅与粘胶纤维短纤混纺)	10	130	17	16	米/千克		Poplin and fine plain cloth, containing < 85% by weight of polyester staple fibres, mixed mainly or solely with viscose rayon staple fibres, unbleached or bleached
5515.1100 22	未漂白或漂白聚酯短纤其他机织平布(聚酯短纤含量<85%,主要或仅与粘胶纤维短纤混纺)	10	130	17	16	米/千克		Plain cloth, containing < 85% by weight of polyester staple fibres, mixed mainly or solely with viscose rayon staple fibres, unbleached or bleached
5515.1100 23	未漂白或漂白聚酯短纤其他印染用布(聚酯短纤含量<85%,主要或仅与粘胶纤维短纤混纺)	10	130	17	16	米/千克		Woven fabrics for printing and dying containing < 85% by weight of polyester staple fibres, mixed mainly or solely with viscose rayon staple fibres, unbleached or bleached
5515.1100 24	未漂白或漂白聚酯短纤奶酪布等(短纤含量<85%,含薄细布、巴里纱,与粘胶纤维短纤混纺)	10	130	17	16	米/千克		Cheese cloth, including voiles and fine thin cloth, containing < 85% by weight of polyester staple fibres, mixed with viscose rayon staple fibres, unbleached or bleached
5515.1100 25	未漂白或漂白聚酯短纤机织帆布(聚酯短纤含量<85%,主要或仅与粘胶纤维短纤混纺)	10	130	17	16	米/千克		Canvas, containing < 85% by weight of polyester staple fibres, mixed mainly or solely with viscose rayon staple fibres, unbleached or bleached
5515.1100 26	未漂白或漂白聚酯短纤缎纹或斜纹布(聚酯短纤含量<85%,主要或仅与粘胶纤维短纤混纺)	10	130	17	16	米/千克		Other woven fabrics, satin weave or twill weave, unbleached or bleached, containing < 85% by weight of polyester staple fibres, mixed mainly or solely with viscose rayon staple fibres

税则号列	货品名称	最惠(%)	普通	增值税率	出口退税	计量单位	监管条件	Article Description
5515.1100 27	未漂白或漂白聚酯短纤牛津布(聚酯短纤含量<85%,主要或仅与粘胶纤维短纤混纺)	10	130	17	16	米/千克		Other woven fabrics, oxford weave, containing <85% by weight of polyester staple fibres, mixed mainly or solely with viscose rayon staple fibres, unbleached or bleached
5515.1100 29	未漂白或漂白聚酯短纤其他机织物(聚酯短纤含量<85%,主要或仅与粘胶纤维短纤混纺)	10	130	17	16	米/千克		Other woven fabrics, containing <85% by weight of polyester staple fibres, mixed mainly or solely with viscose rayon staple fibres, unbleached or bleached
5515.1100 31	其他聚酯短纤府绸或细平布(聚酯短纤含量<85%,主要或仅与粘胶纤维短纤混纺)	10	130	17	16	米/千克		Other poplin and fine plain cloth, containing <85% by weight of polyester staple fibres, mixed mainly or solely with viscose rayon staple fibres
5515.1100 32	其他聚酯短纤机织平布(聚酯短纤含量<85%,主要或仅与粘胶纤维短纤混纺)	10	130	17	16	米/千克		Other plain cloth, containing <85% by weight of polyester staple fibres, mixed mainly or solely with viscose rayon staple fibres
5515.1100 33	其他聚酯短纤机织印染用布(聚酯短纤含量<85%,主要或仅与粘胶纤维短纤混纺)	10	130	17	16	米/千克		Other woven fabrics for printing and dying, containing <85% by weight of polyester staple fibres, mixed mainly or solely with viscose rayon staple fibres
5515.1100 34	其他聚酯短纤奶酪布等(短纤含量<85%,含薄细布、巴里纱,与粘胶纤维短纤混纺)	10	130	17	16	米/千克		Other cheese cloth, including voiles and fine thin cloth, containing <85% by weight of polyester staple fibres, mixed mainly or solely with viscose rayon staple fibres
5515.1100 35	其他聚酯短纤机织帆布(聚酯短纤含量<85%,主要或仅与粘胶纤维短纤混纺)	10	130	17	16	米/千克		Other canvas, containing <85% by weight of polyester staple fibres, mixed mainly or solely with viscose rayon staple fibres
5515.1100 36	其他聚酯短纤缎纹或斜纹机织物(聚酯短纤含量<85%,主要或仅与粘胶纤维短纤混纺)	10	130	17	16	米/千克		Other woven fabrics, twill weave or satin weave, containing <85% by weight of polyester staple fibres, mixed mainly or solely with viscose rayon staple fibres
5515.1100 37	其他聚酯短纤牛津布(聚酯短纤含量<85%,主要或仅与粘胶纤维短纤混纺)	10	130	17	16	米/千克		Other woven fabrics oxford weave, containing <85% by weight of polyester staple fibres, mixed mainly or solely with viscose rayon staple fibres
5515.1100 39	其他聚酯短纤其他机织物(聚酯短纤含量<85%,主要或仅与粘胶纤维短纤混纺)	10	130	17	16	米/千克		Other woven fabrics, containing <85% by weight of polyester staple fibres, mixed mainly or solely with viscose rayon staple fibres
5515.1200	--主要或仅与化学纤维长丝混纺	10	130	17	16	米/千克		--Mixed mainly or solely with man-made filaments
5515.1200 11	未漂白或漂白聚酯短纤府绸或细平布(聚酯短纤含量<85%,与化纤长丝混纺)	10	130	17	16	米/千克		Poplin and fine plain cloth, containing <85% by weight of polyester staple fibres, mixed mainly or solely with man-made filaments, unbleached or bleached
5515.1200 12	未漂白或漂白的聚酯短纤平布(聚酯短纤含量<85%,与化纤长丝混纺)	10	130	17	16	米/千克		Plain cloth, containing <85% by weight of polyester staple fibres, mixed mainly or solely with man-made filaments, unbleached or bleached
5515.1200 13	未漂白或漂白的聚酯短纤印染用布(聚酯短纤含量<85%,与化纤长丝混纺)	10	130	17	16	米/千克		Woven fabrics for printing and dying, containing <85% by weight of polyester staple fibres, mixed mainly or solely with man-made filaments, unbleached or bleahed
5515.1200 14	未漂白或漂白的聚酯短纤缎纹或斜纹布(聚酯短纤含量<85%,与化纤长丝混纺)	10	130	17	16	米/千克		Woven fabrics, satin weave or twill weave, containing <85% by weight of polyester staple fibres, mixed mainly or solely with man-made filaments, unbleached or bleached
5515.1200 19	未漂或漂白的聚酯短纤其他机织物(聚酯短纤含量<85%,与化纤长丝混纺)	10	130	17	16	米/千克		Woven fabrics, containing <85% by weight of polyester staple fibres, mixed mainly or solely with man-made filaments, unbleached or bleached
5515.1200 21	其他聚酯短纤府绸或细平布(聚酯短纤含量<85%,与化纤长丝混纺)	10	130	17	16	米/千克		Other poplin and fine plain cloth, containing <85% by weight of polyester staple fibres, mixed mainly or solely with man-made filaments

税则号列	货品名称	最惠(%)	普通	增值税率	出口退税	计量单位	监管条件	Article Description
5515.1200 22	其他聚酯短纤平布(聚酯短纤含量<85%,与化纤长丝混纺)	10	130	17	16	米/千克		Other plain cloth, containing <85% by weight of polyester staple fibres, mixed mainly or solely with man-made filaments
5515.1200 23	其他聚酯短纤印染用布(聚酯短纤含量<85%,与化纤长丝混纺)	10	130	17	16	米/千克		Other woven fabrics for printing and dying, containing < 85% by weight of polyester staple fibres, mixed mainly or solely with man-made filaments
5515.1200 24	其他聚酯短纤缎纹或斜纹机织物(聚酯短纤含量<85%,与化纤长丝混纺)	10	130	17	16	米/千克		Other woven fabrics, satin weave or twill weave, containing < 85% by weight of polyester staple fibres, mixed mainly or solely with man-made filaments, containing < 85% by weight of polyester staple fibres
5515.1200 29	其他聚酯短纤其他机织物(聚酯短纤含量<85%,与化纤长丝混纺)	10	130	17	16	米/千克		Other woven fabrics, containing < 85% by weight of polyester staple fibres, mixed mainly or solely with man-made filaments
5515.1300	--主要或仅与羊毛或动物细毛混纺	10	130	17	16	米/千克		--Mixed mainly or solely with wool or fine animal hair
5515.1300 11	未漂白或漂白聚酯短纤与精梳毛混纺布(含羊毛或动物细毛36%及以上,聚酯短纤含量<85%)	10	130	17	16	米/千克		Woven fabrics, mixed, containing ≥36% by weight of combed wool or fine animal hair, containing < 85% by weight of polyester staple fibres, unbleached or bleached
5515.1300 12	未漂白或漂白聚酯短纤与粗梳毛混纺布(含羊毛或动物细毛36%及以上,聚酯短纤含量在85%以下)	10	130	17	16	米/千克		Woven fabrics, mixed, containing ≥36% by weight carded wool or of fine animal hair, containing < 85% by weight of polyester staple fibres, unbleached or bleached
5515.1300 13	未漂白或漂白聚酯短纤与精梳毛混纺布(含羊毛或动物细毛36%以下,聚酯短纤含量在85%以下)	10	130	17	16	米/千克		Woven fabrics, mixed, containing < 36% by weight of combed wool or fine animal hair, containing < 85% by weight of polyester staple fibres, unbleached or bleached
5515.1300 19	未漂白或漂白聚酯短纤与粗梳毛混纺布(含羊毛或动物细毛<36%,聚酯短纤含量在85%以下)	10	130	17	16	米/千克		Woven fabrics, mixed, containing < 36% by weight of carded wool or of fine animal hair, containing < 85% by weight of polyester staple fibres, unbleached or bleached
5515.1300 21	其他聚酯短纤与精梳毛混纺机织物(含羊毛或动物细毛36%及以上,聚酯短纤含量在85%以下)	10	130	17	16	米/千克		Other woven fabrics, mixed, containing ≥ 36% by weight of combed wool or fine animal hair, containing < 85% by weight of polyester staple fibres
5515.1300 22	其他聚酯短纤与粗梳毛混纺机织物(含羊毛或动物细毛36%及以上,聚酯短纤含量在85%以下)	10	130	17	16	米/千克		Other woven fabrics, mixed, containing ≥ 36% by weight carded wool or fine animal hair, containing < 85% by weight of polyester staple fibres
5515.1300 23	其他聚酯短纤与精梳毛混纺机织物(含羊毛或动物细毛<36%,聚酯短纤含量在85%以下)	10	130	17	16	米/千克		Other woven fabrics, mixed, containing < 36% by weight of combed wool or fine animal hair, containing < 85% by weight of polyester staple fibres
5515.1300 29	其他聚酯短纤与粗梳毛混纺机织物(含羊毛或动物细毛<36%,聚酯短纤含量在85%以下)	10	130	17	16	米/千克		Other woven fabrics, mixed, containing < 36% by weight of carded wool or fine animal hair, containing < 85% by weight of polyester staple fibres
5515.1900	--其他	10	130	17	16	米/千克		--Other
5515.1900 11	聚酯短纤与其他纤维混蓝粗斜纹布(混纺为以聚酯短纤为主,但聚酯短纤含量在85%以下)	10	130	17	16	米/千克		Blue denim, twill weave, mixed with other fibres, mixed mainly with polyester staple fibres, containing < 85% by weight of polyester staple fibres
5515.1900 19	聚酯短纤其他色织机织物(聚酯短纤<85%,提花织物除外,与其他纤维混纺)	10	130	17	16	米/千克		Woven fabrics, other than jacquard weave, mixed with other fibres, containing < 85% by weight of polyester staple fibres
5515.1900 21	未漂白或漂白聚酯短纤其他府绸(聚酯短纤含量在85%以下,与其他纤维混纺,含细平布)	10	130	17	16	米/千克		Poplin and fine plain cloth, mixed with other fibres, containing < 85% by weight of polyester staple fibres, unbleached or bleached
5515.1900 22	未漂白或漂白聚酯短纤其他机织平布(聚酯短纤含量在85%以下,与其他纤维混纺)	10	130	17	16	米/千克		Plain cloth, containing < 85% by weight of polyester staple fibres, mixed with other fibres, unbleached or bleached

税则号列	货品名称	最惠(%)	普通	增值税率	出口退税	计量单位	监管条件	Article Description
5515.1900 23	未漂白或漂白聚酯短纤其他机织印染布(聚酯短纤含量在85%以下,与其他纤维混纺)	10	130	17	16	米/千克		Woven fabrics for printing and dying, containing < 85% by weight of polyester staple fibres, mixed with other fibres, unbleached or bleached
5515.1900 24	未漂白或漂白聚酯短纤奶酪布等(短纤含量<85%,与其他纤维混纺,含薄细布、巴里纱)	10	130	17	16	米/千克		Cheese cloth, voiles and fine thin cloth, containing < 85% by weight of polyester staple fibres, mixed with other fibres, unbleached or bleached
5515.1900 25	未漂白或漂白聚酯短纤机织帆布(聚酯短纤含量在85%以下,与其他纤维混纺)	10	130	17	16	米/千克		Canvas, containing < 85% by weight of polyester staple fibres, mixed with other fibres, unbleached or bleached
5515.1900 26	未漂白或漂白聚酯短纤缎纹或斜纹布(聚酯短纤含量在85%以下,与其他纤维混纺)	10	130	17	16	米/千克		Other woven fabrics, satin weave or twill weave, containing < 85% by weightof polyester staple fibres, mixed with other fibres, unbleached or bleached
5515.1900 27	未漂白或漂白聚酯短纤牛津布(聚酯短纤含量在85%以下,与其他纤维混纺)	10	130	17	16	米/千克		Other woven fabrics, oxford weave, containing < 85% by weight of polyester staple fibres, mixed with other fibres, unbleached or bleached
5515.1900 29	未漂白或漂白聚酯短纤其他机织物(聚酯短纤含量在85%以下,与其他纤维混纺)	10	130	17	16	米/千克		Other woven fabrics, containing < 85% by weight of polyester staple fibres, mixed with other fibres, unbleached or bleached
5515.1900 31	其他聚酯短纤府绸或细平布(聚酯短纤含量在85%以下,与其他纤维混纺)	10	130	17	16	米/千克		Other poplin and fine plain cloth, containing < 85% by weight of polyester staple fibres, mixed with other fibres
5515.1900 32	其他聚酯短纤机织平布(聚酯短纤含量在85%以下,与其他纤维混纺)	10	130	17	16	米/千克		Other plain cloth, containing < 85% by weight of polyester staple fibres, mixed with other fibres
5515.1900 33	其他聚酯短纤机织印染用布(聚酯短纤含量在85%以下,与其他纤维混纺)	10	130	17	16	米/千克		Other woven fabrics for printing and dying, containing < 85% by weight of polyester staple fibres, mixed with other fibres
5515.1900 34	其他聚酯短纤奶酪布等(短纤含量<85%,与其他纤维混纺,含薄细布、巴里纱)	10	130	17	16	米/千克		Other cheese cloth, voiles and fine thin cloth, containing < 85% by weight of polyester staple fibres, mixed with other fibres
5515.1900 35	其他聚酯短纤机织帆布(聚酯短纤含量在85%以下,与其他纤维混纺)	10	130	17	16	米/千克		Other canvas, containing < 85% by weight of polyester staple fibres, mixed with other fibres
5515.1900 36	其他聚酯短纤缎纹或斜纹机织物(聚酯短纤含量在85%以下,与其他纤维混纺)	10	130	17	16	米/千克		Other woven fabrics, satin weave or twill weave, containing < 85% by weight of polyester staple fibres, mixed with other fibres
5515.1900 37	其他聚酯短纤牛津布(聚酯短纤含量在85%以下,与其他纤维混纺)	10	130	17	16	米/千克		Other woven fabrics, oxford weave, containing < 85% by weight of polyester staple fibres, mixed with other fibres
5515.1900 39	其他聚酯短纤其他机织物(聚酯短纤含量在85%以下,与其他纤维混纺)	10	130	17	16	米/千克		Other woven fabrics, containing < 85% by weight of polyester staple fibres, mixed with other fibres
	-聚丙烯腈或变性聚丙烯腈短纤纺制:							-Of acrylic or modacrylic staple fibres:
5515.2100	--主要或仅与化学纤维长丝混纺	10	130	17	16	米/千克		--Mixed mainly or solely with man-made filaments
5515.2100 11	未漂白或漂白腈纶短纤府绸或细平布(腈短纤含量在85%以下,主要或仅与化纤长丝混纺)	10	130	17	16	米/千克		Poplin and fine plain cloth, unbleached or bleached, containing < 85% by weight of acrylic or modacrylic staple fibres, mixed mainly or solely with man-made filaments
5515.2100 12	未漂白或漂白腈纶短纤平布(腈短纤含量在85%以下,主要或仅与化纤长丝混纺)	10	130	17	16	米/千克		Plain cloth, unbleached or bleached, containing < 85% by weight of acrylic or modacrylic staple fibres, mixed mainly or solely with man-made filaments
5515.2100 13	未漂白或漂白腈纶短纤印染用布(腈短纤含量在85%以下,主要或仅与化纤长丝混纺)	10	130	17	16	米/千克		Woven fabrics for printing and dying, unbleached or bleached, containing < 85% by weight of acrylic or modacrylic staple fibres, mixed mainly or solely with man – made filaments

税则号列	货　品　名　称	最惠(%)	普通	增值税率	出口退税	计量单位	监管条件	Article Description
5515.2100 14	未漂白或漂白腈纶短纤缎纹或斜纹布(腈短纤含量在85%以下,主要或仅与化纤长丝混纺)	10	130	17	16	米/千克		Woven fabrics, satin weave or twill weave, unbleached or bleached, containing <85% by weight of acrylic or modacrylic staple fibres, mixed mainly or solely with man-made filaments
5515.2100 19	未漂白或漂白腈纶短纤其他机织物(腈短纤含量在85%以下,主要或仅与化纤长丝混纺)	10	130	17	16	米/千克		Other woven fabrics unbleached or bleached, containing <85% by weight of acrylic staple fibres, mixed mainly or solely with man-made filaments
5515.2100 21	其他腈纶短纤混纺府绸或细平布(腈短纤含量在85%以下,主要或仅与化纤长丝混纺)	10	130	17	16	米/千克		Other poplin and fine plain cloth, containing <85% by weight of acrylic staple fibres, mixed mainly or solely with man-made filaments
5515.2100 22	其他腈纶短纤平布(腈短纤含量在85%以下,主要或仅与化纤长丝混纺)	10	130	17	16	米/千克		Other plain cloth, containing <85% by weight of acrylic staple fibres, mixed mainly or solely with man-made filaments
5515.2100 23	其他腈纶短纤印染用布(腈短纤含量在85%以下,主要或仅与化纤长丝混纺)	10	130	17	16	米/千克		Other woven fabrics for printing and dying, containing <85% by weight of acrylic staple fibres, mixed mainly or solely with man-made filaments
5515.2100 24	其他腈纶短纤混纺缎纹或斜纹布(腈短纤含量在85%以下,主要或仅与化纤长丝混纺)	10	130	17	16	米/千克		Other woven fabrics, satin weave or twill weave, containing < 85% by weight of acrylic staple fibres, mixed mainly or solely with man – made filaments
5515.2100 29	其他腈纶短纤混纺其他机织物(腈短纤含量在85%以下,主要或仅与化纤长丝混纺)	10	130	17	16	米/千克		Other woven fabrics, containing <85% by weight of acrylic staple fibres, mixed mainly or solely with man-made filaments
5515.2200	--主要或仅与羊毛或动物细毛混纺	12	130	17	16	米/千克		--Mixed mainly or solely with wool or fine animal hair
5515.2200 11	未漂白或漂白腈纶短纤与精梳毛混纺布(腈短纤含量<85%,含羊毛或动物细毛36%及以上)	12	130	17	16	米/千克		Woven fabrics, mixed, containing ≥36% by weight of combed wool or fine animal hair, containing <85% by weight of acrylic staple fibres, unbleached or bleached
5515.2200 12	未漂白或漂白腈纶短纤与粗梳毛混纺布(腈短纤含量<85%,含羊毛或动物细毛36%及以上)	12	130	17	16	米/千克		Woven fabrics, mixed, containing ≥36% by weight carded wool or fine animal hair, containing <85% by weight of acrylic staple fibres, unbleached or bleached
5515.2200 13	未漂白或漂白腈纶短纤与精梳毛混纺布(腈短纤含量<85%,含羊毛或动物细毛<36%)	12	130	17	16	米/千克		Woven fabrics, mixed, containing <36% by weight of combed wool or fine animal hair, containing <85% by weight of acrylic staple fibres, unbleached or bleached
5515.2200 19	未漂白或漂白腈纶短纤与粗梳毛混纺布(腈短纤含量<85%,含羊毛或动物细毛<36%)	12	130	17	16	米/千克		Woven fabrics, mixed, containing <36% by weight of carded wool or fine animal hair, containing <85% by weight of acrylic staple fibres, unbleached or bleached
5515.2200 21	其他腈纶短纤与精梳毛混纺机织物(腈短纤含量<85%,含羊毛或动物细毛36%及以上)	12	130	17	16	米/千克		Other woven fabrics, mixed, containing ≥36% by weight of combed wool or fine animal hair, containing <85% by weight of acrylic staple fibres
5515.2200 22	其他腈纶短纤与粗梳毛混纺机织物(腈短纤含量<85%,含羊毛或动物细毛36%及以上)	12	130	17	16	米/千克		Other woven fabrics, mixed, containing ≥36% by weight carded wool or of fine animal hair, containing <85% by weight of acrylic staple fibres
5515.2200 23	其他腈纶短纤与精梳毛混纺机织物(腈短纤含量<85%,含羊毛或动物细毛<36%)	12	130	17	16	米/千克		Other woven fabrics, mixed, containing <36% by weight of combed wool or fine animal hair, containing <85% by weight of acrylic staple fibres
5515.2200 29	其他腈纶短纤与粗梳毛混纺机织物(腈短纤含量<85%,含羊毛或动物细毛<36%)	12	130	17	16	米/千克		Other woven fabrics, mixed, containing <36% by weight of carded wool or fine animal hair, containing <85% by weight of acrylic staple fibres
5515.2900	--其他	10	130	17	16	米/千克		--Other
5515.2900 11	腈纶短纤与其他纤维混蓝粗斜纹布(混纺以聚丙烯腈短纤为主,腈短纤含量在85%以下)	10	130	17	16	米/千克		Blue denim, twill weave, mixed, mainly with acrylic staple fibres, containing <85% by weight of acrylic staple fibres

税则号列	货品名称	最惠(%)	普通	增值税率	出口退税	计量单位	监管条件	Article Description
5515.2900 19	其他腈纶短纤色织机织布(腈短纤含量<85%,提花织物除外,与其他纤维混纺)	10	130	17	16	米/千克		Other woven fabrics, mixed, other than jacquard weave, containing <85% by weight of acrylic staple fibres, of different colours
5515.2900 21	其他未漂白或漂白腈纶短纤府绸(腈短纤含量在85%以下,与其他纤维混纺,含细平布)	10	130	17	16	米/千克		Other poplin and fine plain cloth, containing <85% by weight of acrylic staple fibres, mixed with other fibres, unbleached or bleached
5515.2900 22	其他未漂白或漂白腈纶短纤平布(腈短纤含量在85%以下,与其他纤维混纺)	10	130	17	16	米/千克		Other plain cloth, containing <85% by weight of acrylic staple fibres, mixed with other fibres, unbleached or bleached
5515.2900 23	其他未漂白或漂白腈纶短纤印染用布(腈短纤含量在85%以下,与其他纤维混纺)	10	130	17	16	米/千克		Other woven fabrics for printing and dying, containing <85% by weight of acrylic staple fibres, mixed with other fibres, unbleached or bleached
5515.2900 24	其他未漂白或漂白腈纶短纤奶酪布等(腈短纤含量<85%,与其他纤维混纺,含薄细布、巴里纱)	10	130	17	16	米/千克		Other cheese cloth, voiles and swiss muslin, containing <85% by weight of acrylic staple fibres, mixed with other fibres, unbleached or bleached
5515.2900 25	其他未漂白或漂白腈纶短纤机织帆布(腈短纤含量在85%以下,与其他纤维混纺)	10	130	17	16	米/千克		Other canvas, containing <85% by weight of acrylic staple fibres, mixed with other fibres, unbleached or bleached
5515.2900 26	其他未漂白或漂白腈纶短纤缎纹布(含斜纹机织物,腈短纤含量<85%,与其他纤维混纺)	10	130	17	16	米/千克		Other woven fabrics, satin weave or twill weave, containing <85% by weightof acrylic staple fibres, mixed with other fibres, unbleached or bleached
5515.2900 27	其他未漂白或漂白腈纶短纤牛津布(腈短纤含量在85%以下,与其他纤维混纺)	10	130	17	16	米/千克		Other woven fabrics, oxford weave, containing <85% by weight of acrylic staple fibres, mixed with other fibres, unbleached or bleached
5515.2900 29	其他未漂白或漂白腈纶短纤其他机织物(腈短纤含量在85%以下,与其他纤维混纺)	10	130	17	16	米/千克		Other woven fabrics, containing <85% by weight of acrylic staple fibres, mixed with other fibres, unbleached or bleached
5515.2900 31	其他腈纶短纤府绸或细平布(腈短纤含量在85%以下,与其他纤维混纺)	10	130	17	16	米/千克		Other poplin and fine plain cloth, containing <85% by weight of acrylic staple fibres, mixed with other fibres
5515.2900 32	其他腈纶短纤机织平布(腈短纤含量在85%以下,与其他纤维混纺)	10	130	17	16	米/千克		Other plain cloth, containing <85% by weight of acrylic staple fibres, mixed with other fibres
5515.2900 33	其他腈纶短纤机织印染用布(腈短纤含量在85%以下,与其他纤维混纺)	10	130	17	16	米/千克		Other woven fabrics for printing and dying, containing <85% by weight of acrylic staple fibres, mixed with other fibres
5515.2900 34	其他腈纶短纤奶酪布等(腈短纤含量<85%,与其他纤维混纺,含薄细布、巴里纱)	10	130	17	16	米/千克		Other cheese cloth, voiles and fine thin cloth, containing <85% by weight of acrylic staple fibres, mixed with other fibres
5515.2900 35	其他腈纶短纤机织帆布(腈短纤含量在85%以下,与其他纤维混纺)	10	130	17	16	米/千克		Other canvas, containing <85% by weight of acrylic staple fibres, mixed with other fibres
5515.2900 36	其他腈纶短纤与其他纤维混纺牛津布(腈短纤含量在85%以下,与其他纤维混纺)	10	130	17	16	米/千克		Other woven fabrics, oxford weave, containing <85% by weight of acrylic staple fibres, mixed with other fibres
5515.2900 37	其他腈纶短纤缎纹或斜纹机织物(腈短纤含量在85%以下,与其他纤维混纺)	10	130	17	16	米/千克		Other woven fabrics, satin weave or twill weave, containing <85% by weight of acrylic staple fibres, mixed with other fibres
5515.2900 39	其他腈纶短纤与其他纤维混机织物(混纺为以聚丙烯腈短纤为主,腈短纤含量在85%以下)	10	130	17	16	米/千克		Other woven fabrics, containing <85% by weight of acrylic staple fibres, mixed with other fibres
	-其他机织物:							-Other woven fabrics:
5515.9100	--主要或仅与化学纤维长丝混纺	10	130	17	16	米/千克		--Mixed mainly or solely with man-made filaments
5515.9100 11	未漂白或漂白其他合纤短府绸(与化纤长丝混纺,合成纤维短纤含量<85%,含细平布)	10	130	17	16	米/千克		Poplin and fine plain cloth, containing <85% by weight of synthetic staple fibres, mixed mainly or solely with man-made filaments

税则号列	货品名称	最惠(%)	普通	增值税率	出口退税	计量单位	监管条件	Article Description
5515.9100 12	未漂白或漂白其他合纤短纤平布(与化纤长丝混纺,合成纤维短纤含量在85%以下)	10	130	17	16	米/千克		Plain cloth, containing <85% by weight of synthetic staple fibres, mixed mainly or solely with man-made filaments, unbleached or bleached
5515.9100 13	未漂白或漂白其他合纤短纤混印染用布(与化纤长丝混纺,合成纤维短纤含量在85%以下)	10	130	17	16	米/千克		Other woven fabrics for printing and dying, containing < 85% by weight of synthetic staple fibres, mixed mainly or solely with man-made filaments, unbleached or bleached
5515.9100 14	未漂白或漂白其他合纤短纤缎纹布等(与化纤长丝混纺,合成纤维短纤含量<85%,含斜纹机织物)	10	130	17	16	米/千克		Other woven fabrics, satin weave, twill weave, containing < 85% by weight of synthetic staple fibres, mixed mainly or solely with man-made filaments, unbleached or bleached
5515.9100 19	未漂白或漂白其他合纤短纤其他机织物(与化纤长丝混纺,合成纤维短纤含量在85%以下)	10	130	17	16	米/千克		Other woven fabrics, containing <85% by weight of synthetic staple fibres, mixed mainly or solely with man-made filaments, unbleached or bleached
5515.9100 21	其他合纤短纤府绸或细平布(与化纤长丝混纺,合成纤维短纤含量在85%以下)	10	130	17	16	米/千克		Other poplin and fine plain cloth, containing <85% by weight of synthetic staple fibres, mixed mainly or solely with man-made filaments
5515.9100 22	其他合纤短纤平布(与化纤长丝混纺,合成纤维短纤含量在85%以下)	10	130	17	16	米/千克		Other plain cloth, containing < 85% by weight of synthetic staple fibres, mixed mainly or solely with man-made filaments
5515.9100 23	其他合纤短纤印染用布(与化纤长丝混纺,合成纤维短纤含量在85%以下)	10	130	17	16	米/千克		Other woven fabrics for printing and dying, containing < 85% by weight of synthetic staple fibres, mixed mainly or solely with man-made filaments
5515.9100 24	其他合纤短纤缎纹或斜纹机织物(与化纤长丝混纺,合成纤维短纤含量在85%以下)	10	130	17	16	米/千克		Other woven fabrics, satin weave or twill weave, containing <85% by weightof synthetic staple fibres, mixed mainly or solely with man-made filaments
5515.9100 29	其他合纤短纤其他机织物(与化纤长丝混纺,合成纤维短纤含量在85%以下)	10	130	17	16	米/千克		Other woven fabrics, containing <85% by weight of synthetic staple fibres, mixed mainly or solely with man-made filaments
5515.9900	--其他	10	130	17	16	米/千克		--Other
5515.9900 11	其他合纤短纤蓝粗斜纹布(合成纤维短纤含量在85%以下,与其他纤维混纺)	10	130	17	16	米/千克		Other blue denim, twill weave, containing <85% by weight of synthetic staple fibres, mixed with other fibres
5515.9900 19	其他合纤短纤其他色织机织物(合成纤维短纤含量<85%,与其他纤维混纺,提花织物除外)	10	130	17	16	米/千克		Other woven fabrics, of yarns of different colours other than jacquard weave, containing <85% by weight of synthetic staple fibres, mixed with other fibres
5515.9900 21	未漂白或漂白其他合纤短纤府绸(合成纤维短纤含量在85%以下,与其他纤维混纺,含细平布)	10	130	17	16	米/千克		Other poplin and fine plain cloth, containing <85% by weight of synthetic staple fibres, unbleached or bleached, mixed with other fibres
5515.9900 22	未漂白或漂白其他合纤短纤其他平布(合成纤维短纤含量在85%以下,与其他纤维混纺)	10	130	17	16	米/千克		Other plain cloth, containing < 85% by weight of synthetic staple fibres, unbleached or bleached, mixed with other fibres
5515.9900 23	未漂白或漂白其他合纤短纤印染用布(合成纤维短纤含量在85%以下,与其他纤维混纺)	10	130	17	16	米/千克		Other woven fabrics for printing and dying, containing <85% by weight of synthetic staple fibres, unbleached or bleached, mixed with other fibres
5515.9900 24	未漂白或漂白其他合纤短纤奶酪布等(合纤短纤含量<85%,与其他纤维混纺,含薄细布、巴里纱)	10	130	17	16	米/千克		Other cheese cloth, voiles and swiss muslin, containing <85% by weight of synthetic staple fibres, unbleached or bleached, mixed with other fibres
5515.9900 25	未漂白或漂白其他合纤短纤帆布(合成纤维短纤含量在85%以下,与其他纤维混纺)	10	130	17	16	米/千克		Other canvas, containing < 85% by weight of synthetic staple fibres, unbleached or bleached, mixed with other fibres
5515.9900 26	未漂白或漂白其他合纤短纤混纺缎纹布(合成纤维短纤含量<85%,与其他纤维混纺,含斜纹机织物)	10	130	17	16	米/千克		Other woven fabrics, satin weave or twill weave, containing < 85% by weight of synthetic staple fibres, unbleached or bleached, mixed with other fibres

税则号列	货品名称	最惠(%)	普通	增值税率	出口退税	计量单位	监管条件	Article Description
5515.9900 27	未漂白或漂白其他合纤短纤牛津布(合成纤维短纤含量在85%以下,与其他纤维混纺)	10	130	17	16	米/千克		Other woven fabrics, oxford weave, containing <85% by weight of synthetic staple fibres, unbleached or bleached, mixed with other fibres
5515.9900 29	未漂白或漂白其他合纤短纤其他机织物(合成纤维短纤含量在85%以下,与其他纤维混纺)	10	130	17	16	米/千克		Other woven fabrics, containing <85% by weight of synthetic staple fibres, unbleached or bleached, mixed with other fibres
5515.9900 31	其他合纤短纤府绸或细平布(合成纤维短纤含量在85%以下,与其他纤维混纺)	10	130	17	16	米/千克		Other poplin and fine plain cloth, containing <85% by weight of synthetic staple fibres, mixed with other fibres
5515.9900 32	其他合纤短纤其他机织平布(合成纤维短纤含量在85%以下,与其他纤维混纺)	10	130	17	16	米/千克		Other plain cloth, containing < 85% by weight of synthetic staple fibres, mixed with other fibres
5515.9900 33	其他合纤短纤机织印染用布(合成纤维短纤含量在85%以下,与其他纤维混纺)	10	130	17	16	米/千克		Other woven fabrics for printing and dying, containing < 85% by weight of synthetic staple fibres, mixed with other fibres
5515.9900 34	其他合纤短纤奶酪布等(合纤短纤含量<85%,与其他纤维混纺,含薄细布、巴里纱)	10	130	17	16	米/千克		Other cheese cloth, voiles and suiss muslin, containing < 85% by weight of synthetic staple fibres, mixed with other fibres
5515.9900 35	其他合纤短纤机织帆布(合成纤维短纤含量在85%以下,与其他纤维混纺)	10	130	17	16	米/千克		Other canvas, containing < 85% by weight of synthetic staple fibres, mixed with other fibres
5515.9900 36	其他合纤短纤缎纹或斜纹机织物(合成纤维短纤含量在85%以下,与其他纤维混纺)	10	130	17	16	米/千克		Other woven fabrics, satin weave or twill weave, containing < 85% by weight of synthetic staple fibres, mixed with other fibres
5515.9900 37	其他合纤短纤其他纤维混纺牛津布(合成纤维短纤含量在85%以下,与其他纤维混纺)	10	130	17	16	米/千克		Other woven fabrics, oxford weave, containing <85% by weight of synthetic staple fibres, mixed with other fibres
5515.9900 39	其他合纤短纤其他机织物(合成纤维短纤含量在85%以下,与其他纤维混纺)	10	130	17	16	米/千克		Other woven fabrics, containing <85% by weight of synthetic staple fibres, mixed with other fibres
55.16	人造纤维短纤纺制的机织物:							**Woven fabrics of artificial staple fibres:**
	-按重量计人造纤维短纤含量在85%及以上:							-Containing 85% or more by weight of artificial staple fibres:
5516.1100	--未漂白或漂白	12	130	17	16	米/千克		--Unbleached or bleached
5516.1200	--染色	10	130	17	16	米/千克		--Dyed
5516.1300	--色织	10	130	17	16	米/千克		--Of yarns of different colours
5516.1400	--印花	10	130	17	16	米/千克		--Printed
	-按重量计人造纤维短纤含量在85%以下,主要或仅与化学纤维长丝混纺:							-Containing less than 85% by weight of artificial staple fibres, mixed mainly or solely with man-made filaments:
5516.2100	--未漂白或漂白	12	130	17	16	米/千克		--Unbleached or bleached
5516.2100 10	未漂白或漂白人纤短纤府绸或细平布(人造纤维短纤含量在85%以下,与化纤长丝混纺)	12	130	17	16	米/千克		Poplin and fine plain cloth, containing <85% by weight of artificial staple fibres, mixed mainly or solely with man-made filaments, unbleached or blea-ched
5516.2100 20	未漂白或漂白人纤短纤平布(人造纤维短纤含量在85%以下,与化纤长丝混纺)	12	130	17	16	米/千克		Plain cloth, containing <85% by weight of artificial staple fibres, mixed mainly or solely with man-made filaments, unbleached or bleached
5516.2100 30	未漂白或漂白人纤短纤印染用布(人造纤维短纤含量在85%以下,与化纤长丝混纺)	12	130	17	16	米/千克		Woven fabrics for printing and dying, containing < 85% by weight of artificial staple fibres, mixed mainly or solely with man-made filaments, unbleached or bleached
5516.2100 40	未漂白或漂白人纤短纤缎纹或斜纹布(人造纤维短纤含量在85%以下,与化纤长丝混纺)	12	130	17	16	米/千克		Woren fabrics, satin weave or twill weave, containing < 85% by weight of artificial staple fibres, mixed mainly or solely with man-made filaments, unbleached or blea-ched
5516.2100 90	未漂白或漂白人纤短纤其他机织物(人造纤维短纤含量在85%以下,与化纤长丝混纺)	12	130	17	16	米/千克		Other woven fabrics, containing <85% by weight of artificial staple fibres, mixed mainly or solely with man-made filaments, unbleached or bleached
5516.2200	--染色	10	130	17	16	米/千克		--Dyed

税则号列	货品名称	最惠(%)	普通	增值税率	出口退税	计量单位	监管条件	Article Description
5516.2200 10	染色人纤短纤府绸或细平布(人造纤维短纤含量在85%以下,与化纤长丝混纺)	10	130	17	16	米/千克		Poplin and fine plain cloth, containing < 85% by weight of artificial staple fibres, mixed mainly or solely with man-made filaments, dyed
5516.2200 20	染色人纤短纤平布(人造纤维短纤含量在85%以下,与化纤长丝混纺)	10	130	17	16	米/千克		Plain cloth, containing < 85% by weight of artificial staple fibres, mixed mainly or solely with man-made filaments, dyed
5516.2200 30	染色人纤短纤印染用布(人造纤维短纤含量在85%以下,与化纤长丝混纺)	10	130	17	16	米/千克		Woven fabrics for printing and dying, containing < 85% by weight of artificial staple fibres, mixed mainly or solely with man-made filaments, dyed
5516.2200 40	染色人纤短纤缎纹或斜纹机织物(人造纤维短纤含量在85%以下,与化纤长丝混纺)	10	130	17	16	米/千克		Woven fabrics satin weave or twill weave, containing < 85% by weight of artificial staple fibres, mixed mainly or solely with man-made filaments, dyed
5516.2200 90	染色人纤短纤其他机织物(人造纤维短纤含量在85%以下,与化纤长丝混纺)	10	130	17	16	米/千克		Other woven fabrics, containing < 85% by weight of artificial staple fibres, mixed mainly or solely with man-made filaments, dyed
5516.2300	--色织	10	130	17	16	米/千克		--Of yarns of different colours
5516.2300 10	色织人纤短纤府绸和细平布(人造纤维短纤含量在85%以下,与化纤长丝混纺)	10	130	17	16	米/千克		Poplin and fine plain cloth, containing < 85% by weight of artificial staple fibres, mixed mainly or solely with man-made filaments, of different colours
5516.2300 20	色织人纤短纤平布(人造纤维短纤含量在85%以下,与化纤长丝混纺)	10	130	17	16	米/千克		Plain cloth, containing < 85% by weight of artificial staple fibres, mixed mainly or solely with man-made filaments, of different colours
5516.2300 30	色织人纤短纤印染用布(人造纤维短纤含量在85%以下,与化纤长丝混纺)	10	130	17	16	米/千克		Woven fabrics for printing and dying, containing < 85% by weight of artificialstaple fibres, mixed mainly or solely with man-made filaments, of different colours
5516.2300 40	色织人纤短纤缎纹或斜纹机织物(人造纤维短纤含量在85%以下,与化纤长丝混纺)	10	130	17	16	米/千克		Woven fabrics, satin weave or twill weave, containing < 85% by weight of artificial staple fibres, mixed mainly or solely with man-made filaments, of different colours
5516.2300 90	色织人纤短纤其他机织物(人造纤维短纤含量在85%以下,与化纤长丝混纺)	10	130	17	16	米/千克		Other woven fabrics, containing < 85% by weight of artificial staple fibres, mixed mainly or solely with man-made filaments, of different colours
5516.2400	--印花	10	130	17	16	米/千克		--Printed
5516.2400 10	印花人纤短纤府绸或细平布(人造纤维短纤含量在85%以下,与化纤长丝混纺)	10	130	17	16	米/千克		Poplin and fine plain cloth, containing < 85% by weight of artificial staple fibres, mixed mainly or solely with man-made filaments, printed
5516.2400 20	印花人纤短纤平布(人造纤维短纤含量在85%以下,与化纤长丝混纺)	10	130	17	16	米/千克		Plain cloth, containing < 85% by weight of artificial staple fibres, mixed mainly or solely with man-made filaments, printed
5516.2400 30	印花人纤短纤印染用布(人造纤维短纤含量在85%以下,与化纤长丝混纺)	10	130	17	16	米/千克		Woven fabrics for printing and dying, containing < 85% by weight of artificial staple fibres, mixed mainly or solely with man-made filaments, printed
5516.2400 40	印花人纤短纤缎纹或斜纹机织物(人造纤维短纤含量在85%以下,与化纤长丝混纺)	10	130	17	16	米/千克		Woven fabrics, satin weave or twill weave, containing < 85% by weight of artificial staple fibres, mixed mainly orsolely with man-made filaments, printed
5516.2400 90	印花人纤短纤其他布(人造纤维短纤含量在85%以下,与化纤长丝混纺)	10	130	17	16	米/千克		Other woven fabrics, containing < 85% by weight of artificial staple fibres, mixed mainly or solely with man-made filaments, printed
	-按重量计人造纤维短纤含量在85%以下,主要或仅与羊毛或动物细毛混纺:							-Containing less than 85% by weight of artficial staple fibres, mixed mainly or solely with wool or fine animal hair:
5516.3100	--未漂白或漂白	12	130	17	16	米/千克		--Unbleached or bleached
5516.3100 11	未漂白或漂白人纤短纤与精梳毛混纺布(人造纤维短纤含量<85%,羊毛或动物细毛36%及以上)	12	130	17	16	米/千克		Woven fabrics, mixed, containing ≥36% by weight of combed wool or fine animal hair, containing < 85% by weight of artificial staple fibres, unbleached or bleached

税则号列	货 品 名 称	最惠(%)	普通	增值税率	出口退税	计量单位	监管条件	Article Description
5516.3100 19	未漂白或漂白人纤短纤与粗梳毛混纺布(人造纤维短纤含量<85%,羊毛或动物细毛36%及以上)	12	130	17	16	米/千克		Woven fabrics, mixed, containing ≥36% by weight of carded wool or fine animal hair, containing <85% by weight of artificial staple fibres, unbleached or bleached
5516.3100 21	未漂白或漂白人纤短纤与精梳毛混纺布(人造纤维短纤含量<85%,羊毛或动物细毛<36%)	12	130	17	16	米/千克		Woven fabrics, mixed, containing <36% by weight of combed wool or fine animal hair, containing <85% by weight of artificial staple fibres, unbleached or bleached
5516.3100 29	未漂白或漂白人纤短纤与粗梳毛混纺布(人造纤维短纤含量<85%,羊毛或动物细毛<36%)	12	130	17	16	米/千克		Woven fabrics, mixed, containing <36% by weight of carded wool or fine animal hair, containing <85% by weight of artificial staple fibres, unbleached or bleached
5516.3200	--染色	10	130	17	16	米/千克		--Dyed
5516.3200 11	染色人纤短纤与精梳毛混纺机织物(人造纤维短纤含量<85%,羊毛或动物细毛36%及以上)	10	130	17	16	米/千克		Woven fabrics, mixed, containing ≥36% by weight of combed wool or fine animal hair, containing <85% by weight of artificial staple fibres, dyed
5516.3200 19	染色人纤短纤与粗梳毛混纺机织物(人造纤维短纤含量<85%,羊毛或动物细毛36%及以上)	10	130	17	16	米/千克		Woven fabrics, mixed, containing ≥36% by weight carded of wool or fine animal hair, containing <85% by weight of artificial staple fibres, dyed
5516.3200 21	染色人纤短纤与精梳毛混纺机织物(人造纤维短纤含量<85%,羊毛或动物细毛<36%)	10	130	17	16	米/千克		Woven fabrics, mixed, containing <36% by weight of combed wool or fine animal hair, containing <85% by weight of artificial staple fibres, dyed
5516.3200 29	染色人纤短纤与粗梳毛混纺机织物(人造纤维短纤含量<85%,羊毛或动物细毛<36%)	10	130	17	16	米/千克		Woven fabrics, mixed, containing <36% by weight of carded wool or fine animal hair, containing <85% by weight of artificial staple fibres, dyed
5516.3300	--色织	10	130	17	16	米/千克		--Of yarns of different colours
5516.3300 11	色织人纤短纤与精梳毛混纺机织物(人造纤维短纤含量<85%,羊毛或动物细毛36%及以上)	10	130	17	16	米/千克		Woven fabrics, mixed, containing ≥36% by weight of combed wool or of combed fine animal hair, containing <85% by weight of artificial staple fibres, of different colours
5516.3300 19	色织人纤短纤与粗梳毛混纺机织物(人造纤维短纤含量<85%,羊毛或动物细毛36%及以上)	10	130	17	16	米/千克		Woven fabrics, mixed, containing ≥36% by weight of carded wool or fine animal hair, containing <85% by weight of artificial staple fibres, of different colours
5516.3300 21	色织人纤短纤与精梳毛混纺机织物(人造纤维短纤含量<85%,羊毛或动物细毛<36%)	10	130	17	16	米/千克		Woven fabrics, mixed, containing <36% by weight of combed wool or of combed fine animal hair, containing <85% by weight of artificial staple fibres, of different colours
5516.3300 29	色织人纤短纤与粗梳毛混纺机织物(人造纤维短纤含量<85%,羊毛或动物细毛<36%)	10	130	17	16	米/千克		Woven fabrics, mixed, containing <36% by weight of carded wool or fine animal hair, containing <85% by weight of artificial staple fibres, of different colours
5516.3400	--印花	10	130	17	16	米/千克		--Printed
5516.3400 11	印花人纤短纤与精梳毛混纺机织物(人造纤维短纤含量<85%,羊毛或动物细毛36%及以上)	10	130	17	16	米/千克		Woven fabrics, mixed, containing ≥36% by weight of combed wool or of combed fine animal hair, containing <85% by weight of artificial staple fibres, printed
5516.3400 19	印花人纤短纤与粗梳毛混纺机织物(人造纤维短纤含量<85%,羊毛或动物细毛36%及以上)	10	130	17	16	米/千克		Woven fabrics, mixed, containing ≥36% by weight of carded wool or fine animal hair, containing <85% by weight of artificial staple fibres, printed
5516.3400 21	印花人纤短纤与精梳毛混纺机织物(人造纤维短纤含量<85%,羊毛或动物细毛<36%)	10	130	17	16	米/千克		Woven fabrics, mixed, containing <36% by weight of combed wool or of combed fine animal hair, containing <85% by weight of artificial staple fibres, printed
5516.3400 29	印花人纤短纤与粗梳毛混纺机织物(人造纤维短纤含量<85%,羊毛或动物细毛<36%)	10	130	17	16	米/千克		Woven fabrics, mixed, containing <36% by weight of carded wool or fine animal hair, containing <85% by weight of artificial staple fibres, printed

税则号列	货品名称	最惠(%)	普通	增值税率	出口退税	计量单位	监管条件	Article Description
	-按重量计人造纤维短纤含量在85%以下,主要或仅与棉混纺:							-Containing less than 85% by weight of artificial staple fibres, mixed mainly or solely with cotton:
5516.4100	--未漂白或漂白	12	130	17	16	米/千克		--Unbleached or bleached
5516.4100 10	未漂白或漂白人纤短纤府绸或细平布(人造纤维短纤含量在85%以下,与棉混纺)	12	130	17	16	米/千克		Poplin and fine plain cloth, mixed with cotton, containing < 85% by weight of artificial staple fibres, unbleached or bleached
5516.4100 20	未漂白或漂白人纤短纤与棉混纺平布(混纺以人纤短纤为主,但人造纤维短纤含量在85%以下)	12	130	17	16	米/千克		Plain cloth, mixed with cotton, mixed maihly with artificial staple fibres, containing < 85% by weight of artificial staple fibres, unbleached or bleached
5516.4100 30	与棉混纺未漂白或漂白人纤短纤印染用布(混纺以人纤短纤为主,但人造纤维短纤含量在85%以下)	12	130	17	16	米/千克		Woven fabrics for printing and dying, mixed with cotton, containing < 85% by weight of artificial staple fibres, unbleached or bleached
5516.4100 40	未漂白或漂白人纤短纤与棉混纺的奶酪布等(人造纤维短纤含量在85%以下,含薄细布、巴里纱)	12	130	17	16	米/千克		Cheese cloth, voiles and swiss muslin, mixed with cotton, containing < 85% by weight of artificial staple fibres, unbleached or bleached
5516.4100 50	与棉混纺未漂白或漂白人纤短纤机织帆布(混纺以人纤短纤为主,但人造纤维短纤含量在85%以下)	12	130	17	16	米/千克		Canvas, mixed with cotton, containing < 85% by weight of artificial staple fibres, unbleached or bleached
5516.4100 60	与棉混纺的未漂白或漂白人纤短纤缎纹布等(含斜纹布,人造纤维短纤含量在85%以下)	12	130	17	16	米/千克		Woven fabrics, satin weave or twill weave, mixed with cotton, containing < 85% by weight of artificial staple fibres, unbleached or bleached
5516.4100 70	与棉混纺的未漂白或漂白人纤短纤牛津布(混纺以人纤短纤为主,但人造纤维短纤含量在85%以下)	12	130	17	16	米/千克		Woven fabrics, oxford weave, mixed with cotton, containing < 85% by weight of artificial staple fibres, unbleached or bleached
5516.4100 90	与棉混纺的未漂白或漂白人纤短纤其他布(混纺以人纤短纤为主,但人造纤维短纤含量在85%以下)	12	130	17	16	米/千克		Other woven fabrics, mixed with cotton, containing < 85% by weight of artificial staple fibres, unbleached or bleached
5516.4200	--染色	12	130	17	16	米/千克		--Dyed
5516.4200 10	与棉混纺的染色人纤短纤府绸或细平布(混纺以人纤短纤为主,但人造纤维短纤含量在85%以下)	12	130	17	16	米/千克		Poplin and fine plain cloth, mixed with cotton, containing < 85% by weight of artificial staple fibres, dyed
5516.4200 20	与棉混纺的染色人纤短纤平布(混纺以人纤短纤为主,但人造纤维短纤含量在85%以下)	12	130	17	16	米/千克		Plain cloth, mixed with cotton, containing < 85% by weight of artificial staple fibres, dyed
5516.4200 30	与棉混纺的染色人纤短纤印染用布(混纺以人纤短纤为主,但人造纤维短纤含量在85%以下)	12	130	17	16	米/千克		Woven fabrics for printing and dying, mixed with cotton, containing < 85% by weight of artificial staple fibres, dyed
5516.4200 40	与棉混纺的染色人纤短纤奶酪布等(含薄细布,巴里纱,人造纤维短纤含量在85%以下)	12	130	17	16	米/千克		Cheese cloth, voiles and fine thin cloth, mixed with cotton, containing < 85% by weight of artificial staple fibres, dyed
5516.4200 50	与棉混纺的染色人纤短纤机织帆布(混纺以人纤短纤为主,但人造纤维短纤含量在85%以下)	12	130	17	16	米/千克		Canvas, mixed with cotton, containing < 85% by weight of artificial staple fibres, dyed
5516.4200 60	与棉混纺的染色人纤短纤缎纹或斜纹布(混纺以人纤短纤为主,但人造纤维短纤含量在85%以下)	12	130	17	16	米/千克		Woven fabrics, satin weave or twill weave, mixed with cotton, containing < 85% by weight of artificial staple fibres, dyed
5516.4200 70	与棉混纺的染色人纤短纤牛津布(混纺以人纤短纤为主,但人造纤维短纤含量在85%以下)	12	130	17	16	米/千克		Woven fabrics, oxford weave, mixed with cotton, containing < 85% by weight of artificial staple fibres, dyed
5516.4200 90	与棉混纺染色人纤短纤其他机织物(混纺以人纤短纤为主,但人造纤维短纤含量在85%以下)	12	130	17	16	米/千克		Woven fabrics, mixed with cotton, containing < 85% by weight of artificial staple fibres, dyed
5516.4300	--色织	10	130	17	16	米/千克		--Of yarns of different colours
5516.4300 10	与棉混纺的人纤短纤色织蓝色粗斜纹布(混纺以人纤短纤为主,但人造纤维短纤含量在85%以下)	10	130	17	16	米/千克		Blue denim, twill weave, mixed with cotton, containing < 85% by weight of artificial staple fibres, of different colours

税则号列	货品名称	最惠(%)	普通	增值税率	出口退税	计量单位	监管条件	Article Description
5516.4300 20	与棉混纺人纤短纤色织提花机织物(混纺以人纤短纤为主,但人造纤维短纤含量在85%以下)	10	130	17	16	米/千克		Woven fabrics, jacquard weave, mixed with cotton, containing < 85% by weight of artificial staple fibres, of different colours
5516.4300 90	与棉混纺人纤短纤其他色织机织物(混纺以人纤短纤为主,但人造纤维短纤含量在85%以下)	10	130	17	16	米/千克		Woven fabrics, mixed with cotton, containing < 85% by weight of artificial staple fibres, of different colours
5516.4400	--印花	10	130	17	16	米/千克		--Printed
5516.4400 10	与棉混纺的印花人纤短纤府绸或细平布(混纺以人纤短纤为主,但人造纤维短纤含量在85%以下)	10	130	17	16	米/千克		Poplin and fine plain cloth, mixed with cotton, containing < 85% by weight of artificial staple fibres, printed
5516.4400 20	与棉混纺的印花人纤短纤平布(混纺以人纤短纤为主,但人造纤维短纤含量在85%以下)	10	130	17	16	米/千克		Plain cloth, mixed with cotton, containing < 85% by weight of artificial staple fibres, printed
5516.4400 30	与棉混纺的印花人纤短纤印染用布(混纺以人纤短纤为主,但人造纤维短纤含量在85%以下)	10	130	17	16	米/千克		Woven fabrics for printing and dying, mixed with cotton, containing < 85% by weight of artificial staple fibres, printed
5516.4400 40	与棉混纺的印花人纤短纤奶酪布等(含薄细布、巴里纱、人造纤维短纤含量在85%以下)	10	130	17	16	米/千克		Cheese cloth, voiles and fine thin cloth, mixed with cotton, containing < 85% by weight of artificial staple fibres, printed
5516.4400 50	与棉混纺的印花人纤短纤机织帆布(混纺以人纤短纤为主,但人造纤维短纤含量在85%以下)	10	130	17	16	米/千克		Canvas, mixed with cotton, containing < 85% by weight of artificial staple fibres, printed
5516.4400 60	印花人纤短纤缎纹或斜纹机织物(与棉混纺,人造纤维短纤含量在85%以下)	10	130	17	16	米/千克		Woven fabrics, satin weave or twill weave, mixed with cotton, containing < 85% by weight of artificial staple fibres, printed
5516.4400 70	与棉混纺印花人纤短纤牛津布(混纺以人纤短纤为主,但人造纤维短纤含量在85%以下)	10	130	17	16	米/千克		Woven fabrics, oxford weave, mixed with cotton, containing < 85% by weight of artificial staple fibres, printed
5516.4400 90	与棉混纺的印花人纤短纤其他机织物(混纺以人纤短纤为主,但人造纤维短纤含量在85%以下)	10	130	17	16	米/千克		Other woven fabrics, mixed with cotton, containing < 85% by weight of artificial staple fibres, printed
	-其他:							-Other:
5516.9100	--未漂白或漂白	12	130	17	16	米/千克		--Unbleached or bleached
5516.9100 10	未漂白或漂白人纤短纤府绸或细平布(与其他纤维混纺,人造纤维短纤含量在85%以下)	12	130	17	16	米/千克		Poplin and fine plain cloth, mixed with other fibres, containing < 85% by weight of artificial staple fibres, unbleached or bleached
5516.9100 20	未漂白或漂白人纤短纤机织平布(与其他纤维混纺,人造纤维短纤含量在85%以下)	12	130	17	16	米/千克		Plain cloth, mixed with other fibres, containing < 85% by weight of artificial staple fibres, unbleached or bleached
5516.9100 30	未漂白或漂白人纤短纤印染用布(与其他纤维混纺,人造纤维短纤含量在85%以下)	12	130	17	16	米/千克		Woven fabrics for printing and dying, mixed with other fibres, containing < 85% by weight of artificial staple fibres, unbleached or bleached
5516.9100 40	未漂白或漂白人纤短纤奶酪布等(与其他纤维混纺,人纤短纤含量<85%,含薄细布,巴里纱)	12	130	17	16	米/千克		Cheese cloth, voiles and fine thin cloth, mixed with other fibres, containing < 85% by weight of artificial staple fibres, unbleached or bleached
5516.9100 50	未漂白或漂白人纤短纤机织帆布(与其他纤维混纺,人造纤维短纤含量在85%以下)	12	130	17	16	米/千克		Canvas, mixed with other fibres, containing < 85% by weight of artificial staple fibres, unbleached or bleached
5516.9100 60	未漂白或漂白人纤短纤缎纹或斜纹布(与其他纤维混纺,人造纤维短纤含量在85%以下)	12	130	17	16	米/千克		Woven fabrics, satin weave or twill weave, mixed with other fibres, containing < 85% by weight of artificial staple fibres, unbleached or bleached
5516.9100 70	未漂白或漂白人纤短纤牛津布(与其他纤维混纺,人造纤维短纤含量在85%以下)	12	130	17	16	米/千克		Woven fabrics, oxford weave, mixed with other fibres, containing < 85% by weight of artificial staple fibres, unbleached or bleached

税则号列	货　品　名　称	最惠(%)	普通	增值税率	出口退税	计量单位	监管条件	Article Description
5516.9100 90	未漂白或漂白人纤短纤其他机织物(与其他纤维混纺,人造纤维短纤含量在85%以下)	12	130	17	16	米/千克		Other woven fabrics,mixed with other fibres,containing < 85% by weight of artificial staple fibres, unbleached or bleached
5516.9200	--染色	10	130	17	16	米/千克		--Dyed
5516.9200 10	染色人纤短纤府绸或细平布(与其他纤维混纺,人造纤维短纤含量在85%以下)	10	130	17	16	米/千克		Poplin and fine plain cloth,mixed with other fibres, containing < 85% by weight of artificial staple fibres,dyed
5516.9200 20	染色人纤短纤机织平布(与其他纤维混纺,人造纤维短纤含量在85%以下)	10	130	17	16	米/千克		Plain cloth, mixed with other fibres, containing < 85% by weight of artificial staple fibres,dyed
5516.9200 30	染色人纤短纤印染用布(与其他纤维混纺,人造纤维短纤含量在85%以下)	10	130	17	16	米/千克		Woven fabrics for printing and dying, mixed with other fibres,containing < 85% by weight of artificial staple fibres,dyed
5516.9200 40	染色人纤短纤奶酪布等(与其他纤维混纺,人纤短纤含量 < 85%,含薄细布、巴里纱)	10	130	17	16	米/千克		Cheese cloth, voiles and fine thin cloth, mixed with other fibres,containing < 85% by weight of artificial staple fibres,dyed
5516.9200 50	染色人纤短纤机织帆布(与其他纤维混纺,人造纤维短纤含量在85%以下)	10	130	17	16	米/千克		Canvas, mixed with other fibres, containing < 85% by weight of artificial staple fibres,dyed
5516.9200 60	染色人纤短纤缎纹或斜纹机织物(与其他纤维混纺,人造纤维短纤含量在85%以下)	10	130	17	16	米/千克		Woven fabrics, satin weave or twill weave, mixed with other fibres,containing < 85% by weight of artificial staple fibres,dyed
5516.9200 70	染色人纤短纤牛津布(与其他纤维混纺,人造纤维短纤含量在85%以下)	10	130	17	16	米/千克		Woven fabrics, oxford weave, mixed with other fibres, containing < 85% by weight of artificial staple fibres, dyed
5516.9200 90	染色人纤短纤其他机织物(与其他纤维混纺,人造纤维短纤含量在85%以下)	10	130	17	16	米/千克		Other woven fabrics,mixed with other fibres,containing < 85% by weight of artificial staple fibres,dyed
5516.9300	--色织	10	130	17	16	米/千克		--Of yarns of different colours
5516.9300 10	人纤短纤色织蓝粗斜纹布(与其他纤维混纺,人造纤维短纤含量在85%以下)	10	130	17	16	米/千克		Blue denim, twill weave, mixed with other fibres, containing < 85% by weight of artificial staple fibres,of different colours
5516.9300 20	色织人纤短纤提花机织物(与其他纤维混纺,人造纤维短纤含量在85%以下)	10	130	17	16	米/千克		Woven fabrics,jacquard weave,mixed with other fibres,containing < 85% by weight of artificial staple fibres,of different colours
5516.9300 90	色织人纤短纤其他机织物(与其他纤维混纺,人造纤维短纤含量在85%以下)	10	130	17	16	米/千克		Other woven fabrics,mixed with other fibres,containing < 85% by weight of artificial staple fibres, of different colours
5516.9400	--印花	10	130	17	16	米/千克		--Printed
5516.9400 10	印花人造纤维短纤府绸或细平布(与其他纤维混纺,按重量计人造纤维短纤含量在85%以下)	10	130	17	16	米/千克		Poplin and fine plain cloth,mixed with other fibres, containing < 85% by weight of artificial staple fibres,printed
5516.9400 20	印花人造纤维短纤机织平布(与其他纤维混纺,按重量计人造纤维短纤含量在85%以下)	10	130	17	16	米/千克		Plain cloth, mixed with other fibres, containing < 85% by weight of artificial staple fibres,printed
5516.9400 30	印花人造纤维短纤印染用布(与其他纤维混纺,按重量计人造纤维短纤含量在85%以下)	10	130	17	16	米/千克		Woven fabrics for printing and dying, mixed with other fibres,containing < 85% by weight of artificial staple fibres,printed
5516.9400 40	印花人造纤维短纤奶酪布等(含薄细布、巴里纱,与其他纤维混纺,含人纤短纤含量 < 85%)	10	130	17	16	米/千克		Cheese cloth, voiles and fine thin cloth, mixed with other fibres,containing < 85% by weight of artificial staple fibres,printed
5516.9400 50	印花人造纤维短纤机织帆布(与其他纤维混纺,按重量计人造纤维短纤含量在85%以下)	10	130	17	16	米/千克		Canvas, mixed with other fibres, containing < 85% by weight of artificial staple fibres,printed
5516.9400 60	印花人纤短纤缎纹或斜纹机织物(与其他纤维混纺,按重量计人造纤维短纤含量在85%以下)	10	130	17	16	米/千克		Woven fabrics, satin weave or twill weave, mixed with other fibres,containing < 85% by weight of artificial staple fibres,printed

税则号列	货品名称	最惠(%)	普通	增值税率	出口退税	计量单位	监管条件	Article Description
5516.9400 70	印花人造纤维短纤牛津布(与其他纤维混纺,按重量计人造纤维短纤含量在85%以下)	10	130	17	16	米/千克		Woven fabrics, oxford weave, mixed with other fibres, containing < 85% by weight of artificial staple fibres, printed
5516.9400 90	印花人造纤维短纤其他机织物(与其他纤维混纺,按重量计人造纤维短纤含量在85%以下)	10	130	17	16	米/千克		Other woven fabrics, mixed with other fibres, containing < 85% by weight of artificial staple fibres, printed

第五十六章
絮胎、毡呢及无纺织物；特种纱线；线、绳、索、缆及其制品

注释：

一、本章不包括：

（一）用各种物质或制剂（例如，第三十三章的香水或化妆品、税目34.01的肥皂或洗涤剂、税目34.05的光洁剂及类似制剂、税目38.09的织物柔软剂）浸渍、涂布、包覆的絮胎、毡呢或无纺织物，其中的纺织材料仅作为承载介质；

（二）税目58.11的纺织产品；

（三）以毡呢或无纺织物为底的砂布及类似品（税目68.05）；

（四）以毡呢或无纺织物为底的粘聚或复制云母（税目68.14）；

（五）以毡呢或无纺织物为底的金属箔（通常归入第十四类或第十五类）。

（六）税目96.19的卫生巾（护垫）及止血塞、婴儿尿布及尿布衬里和类似品。

二、所称"毡呢"，包括针刺机制毡呢以及纤维本身通过缝编工序增强了抱合力的纺织纤维网状织物。

三、税目56.02及56.03分别包括用各种性质（紧密结构或泡沫状）的塑料或橡胶浸渍、涂布、包覆或层压的毡呢及无纺织物。

税目56.03还包括用塑料或橡胶作粘合材料的无纺织物。

但税目56.02及56.03不包括：

（一）用塑料或橡胶浸渍、涂布、包覆或层压，按重量计纺织材料含量在50%及以下的毡呢或者完全嵌入塑料或橡胶之内的毡呢（第三十九章或第四十章）；

（二）完全嵌入塑料或橡胶之内的无纺织物，以及用肉眼可辨别出两面都用塑料或橡胶涂布、包覆的无纺织物，涂布或包覆所引起的颜色变化可不予考虑（第三十九章或第四十章）；

（三）与毡呢或无纺织物混制的泡沫塑料或海绵橡胶板、片或扁条，纺织材料仅在其中起增强作用（第三十九章或第四十章）。

四、税目56.04不包括用肉眼无法辨别出是否经过浸渍、涂布或包覆的纺织纱线或税目54.04或54.05的扁条及类似品（通常归入第五十章至第五十五章）；运用本条规定，可不考虑浸渍、涂布或包覆所引起的颜色变化。

Chapter 56
Wadding, felt and nonwovens; special yarns; twine, cordage, ropes and cables and articles thereof

Notes:

1. This Chapter does not cover:

(a) Wadding, felt or nonwovens, impregnated, coated or covered with substances or preparations (for example, pefumes or cosmetics of Chapter 33, soaps or detergents of heading No. 34.01, polishes, creams or similar preparations of heading No. 34.05, fabric softeners of heading No. 38.09) where the textile material is present merely as a carrying medium;

(b) Textile products of heading No. 58.11;

(c) Natural or artificial abrasive powder or grain, on a backing of felt or nonwovens (heading No. 68.05);

(d) Agglomerated or reconstituted mica, on a backing of felt or nonwovens (heading No. 68.14);

(e) Metal foil on a backing of felt or nonwovens (Generelly section XIV or section XV).

(f) Sanitary towels (pads) and tampons, napkins and napkin liners for babies and similar articles of heading 96.19

2. The term "felt" includes needleloom felt and fabrics consisting of a web of textile fibres the cohesion of which has been enhanced by a stitch-bonding process using fibres from the web itself.

3. Headings No. 56.02 and 56.03 cover respectively felt and nonwovens, impregnated, coated, covered or laminated with plastics or rubber whatever the nature of these materials (compact or cellular).

Heading No. 56.03 also includes nonwovens in which plastics or rubber forms the bonding substance.

Headings No. 56.02 and 56.03 do not, however, cover:

(a) Felt impregnated, coated, covered or laminated with plastics or rubber, containing 50% or less by weight of textile material or felt completely embedded in plastics or rubber (Chapter 39 or 40);

(b) Nonwovens, either completely embedded in plastics or rubber, or entirely coated or covered on both sides with such materials, provided that such coating or covering can be seen with the naked eye with no account being taken of any resulting change of colour (Chapter 39 or 40); or

(c) Plates, sheets or strips of cellular plastics or cellular rubber combined with felt or nonwovens, where the textile material is present merely for reinforcing purposes (Chapter 39 or 40).

4. Heading No. 56.04 does not cover textile yarn, or strip or the like of heading No. 54.04 or 54.05, in which the impregnation, coating or covering cannot be seen with the naked eye (usually Chapters 50 to 55); for the purpose of this provision, no account should be taken of any resulting change of colour.

税则号列	货品名称	最惠(%)	普通	增值税率	出口退税	计量单位	监管条件	Article Description
56.01	**纺织材料絮胎及其制品；长度不超过5毫米的纺织纤维（纤维屑）、纤维粉末及球结：**							**Wadding of textile materials and articles thereof; textile fibres, not exceeding 5 mm in length (flock), textile dust and mill neps:**
	-絮胎；其他絮胎制品：							-Wadding; other articles of wadding:
5601.2100	--棉制	10	50	17	16	千克		--Of cotton
5601.2100 10	棉制的成匹絮胎	10	50	17	16	千克		Wadding of cotton, in the piece
5601.2100 90	其他棉制的絮胎及絮胎制品	10	50	17	16	千克		Other wadding and articles of wadding, of cotton
	--化学纤维制：							--Of man-made fibres:

税则号列	货品名称	最惠(%)	普通	增值税率	出口退税	计量单位	监管条件	Article Description
5601.2210	---卷烟滤嘴	12	100	17	16	千克	7	---Cigarette filter tips
5601.2290	---其他	12	100	17	16	千克		---Other
5601.2290 10	化学纤维制的成匹絮胎	12	100	17	16	千克		Wadding of man-made fibres in the piece
5601.2290 90	化学纤维制的其他絮胎及絮胎制品	12	100	17	16	千克		Other wadding and articles of wadding of man-made fibres
5601.2900	--其他	10	90	17	16	千克		--Other
5601.2900 10	羊毛或动物细毛制絮胎及制品	10	90	17	16	千克		Wadding and articles of wadding, of wool or fine animal hair
5601.2900 90	其他纺织材料制絮胎及制品	10	90	17	16	千克		Wadding and articles of wadding, of other textile materials
5601.3000	-纤维屑、纤维粉末及球结		100	17	16	千克		-Textile flock and dust and mill neps
5601.3000[暂] 10	由两种或以上有机聚合物纺制的纤维(横截面为皮芯结构或并列结构或海岛结构,长度不超过5mm)	5	100	17	16	千克		Textile fibres of two or more organic polymers (skin/core, side-by-side or island-in-the-sea type cross-section, length ≤5mm)
5601.3000 90	纺织纤维屑,纤维粉末及球结(纺织纤维长度不超过5mm)	10	100	17	16	千克		Textile flock and dust and mill neps, length≤5mm
56.02	毡呢,不论是否浸渍、涂布、包覆或层压:							**Felt, whether or not impregnated, coated, covered or laminated:**
5602.1000	-针刺机制毡呢及纤维缝编织物	10	100	17	16	千克		-Needleloom felt and stitch-bonded fibre fabrics
5602.1000 10	毛制针刺机制毡呢及纤维缝编织(不论是否浸渍,涂布,包覆或层压)	10	100	17	16	千克		Needleloom felt and stitch-bonded fibre fabrics, of wool or other animal hair (whether or not impregnated, coat covered, laminated)
5602.1000 90	其他纺织料制针刺机制毡呢等(含缝编织物,不论是否浸渍、涂布、包覆或层压)	10	100	17	16	千克		Needleloom felt and stitch-bonded fibre fabrics, of other textile materials (whether or not impregnated, coat covered, laminated)
	-其他毡呢,未浸渍、涂布、包覆或层压:							-Other felt, not impregnated, coated, covered or laminated:
5602.2100	--羊毛或动物细毛制	10	100	17	16	千克		--Of wool or fine animal hair
5602.2900	--其他纺织材料制	10	100	17	16	千克		--Of other textile materials
5602.9000	-其他	10	100	17	16	千克		-Other
5602.9000 10	其他纺织材料制其他毡呢(层压)	10	100	17	16	千克		Other felt, of other textile materials, laminated
5602.9000 91	化学纤维制其他毡呢(浸渍、涂布、包覆)	10	100	17	16	千克		Other felt, of man-made fibres impregnated, coated, covered
5602.9000 99	其他纺织材料制其他毡呢(浸渍、涂布、包覆)	10	100	17	16	千克		Other felt of other textile mateerials (impregnated, coated, covered)
56.03	无纺织物,不论是否浸渍、涂布、包覆或层压:							**Nonwovens, whether or not impregnated, coated, covered or laminated:**
	-化学纤维长丝制:							-Of man-made filaments:
	--每平方米重量不超过25克:							--Weighing not more than 25 g/m²
5603.1110	---经浸渍、涂布、包覆或层压	10	70	17	16	千克		---Impregnated, coated, covered or laminated
5603.1190	---其他	10	130	17	16	千克		---Other
	--每平方米重量超过25克,但不超过70克:							--Weighing more than 25 g/m² but not more than 70 g/m²:
5603.1210	---经浸渍、涂布、包覆或层压	10	70	17	16	千克		---Impregnated, coated, covered or laminated
5603.1290	---其他	10	130	17	16	千克		---Other
	--每平方米重量超过70克,但不超过150克:							--Weighing more than 70 g/m² but not more than 150 g/m²:
5603.1310	---经浸渍、涂布、包覆或层压	10	70	17	16	千克		---Impregnated, coated, covered or laminated
5603.1390	---其他	10	130	17	16	千克		---Other
	--每平方米重量超过150克:							--Weighing more than 150 g/m²:
5603.1410	---经浸渍、涂布、包覆或层压	10	70	17	16	千克		---Impregnated, coated, covered or laminated
5603.1490	---其他	10	130	17	16	千克		---Other
	-其他:							-Other:
	--每平方米重量不超过25克:							--Weighing not more than 25 g/m²:
5603.9110	---经浸渍、涂布、包覆或层压	5	70	17	16	千克		---Impregnated, coated, covered or laminated
5603.9110[暂] 10	每平方米重量≤25克经浸渍的乙烯聚合物制电池隔膜基布(浸渍包括涂布、包覆或层压)	5	70	17	17	千克		The weight per square meter is less than or equal to 25 grams of the impregnated polymers of ethylene (including battery diaphragm base fabricimpregnated, coated or laminated coating)

税则号列	货品名称	最惠(%)	普通	增值税率	出口退税	计量单位	监管条件	Article Description
5603.9110 90	每平方米重量≤25克经浸渍其他无纺布(浸渍包括涂布、包覆或层压)	10	70	17	16	千克		The weight per square meter is less than or equal to 25 grams of impregnatedother non – woven (impregnated, coated or laminated including coating)
5603.9190	---其他	10	85	17	16	千克		---Other
	--每平方米重量超过25克,但不超过70克:							--Weighing more than 25 g/m^2 but not more than 70 g/m^2:
5603.9210	---经浸渍、涂布、包覆或层压	10	70	17	16	千克		---Impregnated, coated, covered or laminated
5603.9210暂 10	25克<每平方米重量≤70克浸渍的乙烯聚合物制电池隔膜基布(浸渍包括涂布、包覆或层压)	5	70	17		千克		25 g < the weight per square meter is less than or equal to 70 grams ofimpregnated polymers of ethylene (including battery diaphragm base fabricimpregnated, coated or laminated coating)
5603.9210 90	25克<每平方米重量≤70克经浸渍其他无纺布(浸渍包括涂布、包覆或层压)	10	70	17		千克		25 g < the weight per square meter is less than or equal to 70 grams ofimpregnated other non – woven (impregnated, coated or laminated including coating)
5603.9290	---其他	10	85	17	16	千克		---Other
	--每平方米重量超过70克,但不超过150克:							--Weighing more than 70 g/m^2 but not more than 150 g/m^2:
5603.9310	---经浸渍、涂布、包覆或层压	10	70	17	16	千克		---Impregnated, coated, covered or laminated
5603.9390	---其他	10	85	17	16	千克		---Other
	--每平方米重量超过150克:							--Weighing more than 150 g/m^2:
5603.9410	---经浸渍、涂布、包覆或层压	10	70	17	16	千克		---Impregnated, coated, covered or laminated
5603.9410 11	毛制铺地品衬底用物纺织物(浸渍、涂布、包覆或压层,每平米重>150克)	10	70	17	16	千克		Nonwovens floor coverings, on a backing of wool or animal hair (impregnated, coated, covered or laminated, w > 150g/m²)
5603.9410 19	其他材料制铺地品衬底用无纺织物(浸渍、涂布、包覆或压层,每平米重>150克)	10	70	17	16	千克		Nonwovens floor coverings, on a backing of other materials (impregnated, coated, covered or laminated w > 150g/m²)
5603.9410 90	其他材料制无纺织物(浸渍、涂布、包覆或压层,每平米重>150克)	10	70	17	16	千克		Nonwovens of other materials (impregnated, coated, covered or laminated w > 150g/m²)
5603.9490	---其他	10	85	17	16	千克		---Other
5603.9490 11	毛制铺地品衬底用无纺织物(每平米重>150克)	10	85	17	16	千克		Nonwovens floor coverings, on a backing of woolor animal hair (w > 150g/m²)
5603.9490 19	其他材料制铺地品衬底用无纺织物(每平米重>150克)	10	85	17	16	千克		Nonwovens floor coverings, on a backing of other materials (w > 150g/m²)
5603.9490 90	其他材料制无纺织物(每平米重>150克)	10	85	17	16	千克		Nonwovens of other materials (w > 150g/m²)
56.04	**用纺织材料包覆的橡胶线及绳;用橡胶或塑料浸渍、涂布、包覆或套裹的纺织纱线及税目54.04或54.05的扁条及类似品:**							**Rubber thread and cord, textile covered; textile yarn, and strip and the like of heading No. 54.04 or 54.05, impregnated, coated, covered or sheathed with rubber or plastics:**
5604.1000	-用纺织材料包覆的橡胶线及绳	5	80	17	16	千克		-Rubber thread and cord, textile covered
5604.9000	-其他	5	80	17	16	千克		-Other
5604.9000 10	棉制纱线(用橡胶或塑料浸渍、涂布、包覆、套裹)	5	80	17	16	千克		Cotton yarn (impregnated, coated, covered or sheathed, with rubber or plastics)
5604.9000 20	品目5404的合成纤维单丝、扁条(用橡胶或塑料浸渍、涂布、包覆、套裹)	5	80	17	16	千克		Synthetic monofilament or strip of heading 5404 (impregnated or coated covered or sheathed, with rubber or plastics)
5604.9000 30	品目5404的人造纤维单丝、扁条(用橡胶或塑料浸渍、涂布、包覆、套裹)	5	80	17	16	千克		Artificial monofilament or strip of heading 5404 (impregnated, coated, covered or sheathed, with rubber or plastics)
5604.9000 90	其他纺织纱线(用橡胶或塑料浸渍、涂布、包覆、套裹)	5	80	17	16	千克		Other textile yarn (impregnated, coated, covered or sheathed, with rubber or plastics)

税则号列	货品名称	最惠(%)	普通	增值税率	出口退税	计量单位	监管条件	Article Description
56.05	**含金属纱线,不论是否螺旋花线,由纺织纱线或税号 54.04 或 54.05 的扁条及类似品与金属线、扁条或粉末混合制得或用金属包覆制得:**							**Metallized yarn, whether or not gimped, being textile yarn, or strip or the like of heading No. 54.04 or 54.05, combined with metal in the form of thread, strip or powder or covered with metal:**
5605.0000	含金属纱线,不论是否螺旋花线,由纺织纱线或税号 54.04 或 54.05 的扁条及类似品与金属线、扁条或粉末混合制得或用金属包覆制得	5	70	17	16	千克		Metallzied yarn, whether or not gimped, being textile yarn, or strip or the like of heading No. 54.04 or 54.05, combined with metal in the form of thread, strip or powder or covered with metal
5605.0000 10	金属涂层或层压化纤长丝等(扁条及类似品、非螺旋、未加捻或捻度每米低于5转)	5	70	17	16	千克		Chemical filament fibres, coated or laminated with metal (strip or the like, not gimped, not twisted or twist < 5turns/m)
5605.0000 90	其他含金属纱线,可含螺旋花边(与金属线、扁条或粉末混合制的或用金属包覆制)	5	70	17	16	千克		Other metallized yarn, gimped, combined with metal in the form of thread, strip or powder or covered with metal
56.06	**粗松螺旋花线,税号 54.04 或 54.05 的扁条及类似品制的螺旋花线(税号 56.05 的货品及马毛粗松螺旋花线除外);绳绒线(包括植绒绳绒线);纵行起圈纱线:**							**Gimped yarn, and strip and the like of heading No. 54.04 or 54.05, gimped (other than those of heading No. 56,05 and gimped horsehair yarn); chenille yarn (including flock chenille yarn); loop wale -yarn:**
5606.0000	粗松螺旋花线,税目 54.04 或 54.05 的扁条及类似品制的螺旋花线(税目 56.05 的货品及马毛粗松螺旋花线除外);绳绒线(包括植绒绳绒线);纵行起圈纱线	5	70	17	16	千克		Gimped yarn, and strip and the like of heading No. 54.04 or 54.05, gimped (other than those of heading No. 56.05 and gimped horsehair yarn); chenille yarn (including flock chenille yarn); loop-wale-yarn
56.07	**线、绳、索、缆,不论是否编织或编结而成,也不论是否用橡胶或塑料浸渍、涂布、包覆或套裹:**							**Twine, cordage, ropes and cables, whether or not plaited or braided and whether or not impregnated, coated, covered or sheathed with rubber or plastics:**
	-西沙尔麻或其他纺织用龙舌兰类纤维纺制:							-Of sisal or other textile fibres of the genus Agave:
5607.2100	--包扎用绳	5	50	17	16	千克		--Binder or baler twine
5607.2100 10	剑麻或其他龙舌兰纤维制包扎用绳(农机用,可编织或编结,可用橡胶或塑料浸涂包套)	5	50	17	16	千克		Binder or baler twine of sisal or other textile fibres of the genus agave (for agricultural machinery, plaited or braided, impregnated or coated covered or sheathed with rubber or plastics)
5607.2100 90	剑麻或龙舌兰纤维制其他包扎用绳(农机用,可编织或编结,可用橡胶或塑料浸涂包套)	5	50	17	16	千克		Other binder or baler twine of sisal or other textile fibres of the genus agave (for agricultural use, plaited or braided, impregnated or coated covered or sheathed with rubber or plastics)
5607.2900	--其他	5	50	17	16	千克		--Other
	-聚乙烯或聚丙烯纺制:							-Of polyethylene or polypropylene:
5607.4100	--包扎用绳	5	100	17	16	千克		--Binder or baler twine
5607.4100 10	宽的非裂膜扁条聚乙烯包扎用绳(可编织或编结,可用橡胶或塑料浸渍、涂布,包覆,套裹)	5	100	17	16	千克		Binder or baler twine of polyethylene, wide strip of non-split film fibre (plaited or braided, impregnated or coated, covered or sheathed, with rubber or plastics)
5607.4100 90	其他聚乙烯或聚丙烯制包扎用绳(可编织或编结,可用橡胶或塑料浸渍、涂布,包覆,套裹)	5	100	17	16	千克		Other binder or baler twine of polyethylene or polypropylene (plaited or braided impregnated or coated, covered or sheathed with rubber or plastics)
5607.4900	--其他	5	100	17	16	千克		--Other
5607.4900 10	宽非裂膜扁条聚乙烯其他线绳索缆(可编织或编结用橡胶或塑料浸涂包套,含聚丙烯制)	5	100	17	16	千克		Other twine, cordage, ropes and cables, of polyethylene or polypropylene, wide strip of non-split film fibre (plaited or braided, impregnated or coated, covered or sheathed, with rubber or plastics)
5607.4900 20	其他聚乙烯或聚丙烯制线绳索缆(未经编织或编结,可用橡胶或塑料浸渍、涂布,包覆、套裹)	5	100	17	16	千克		Other twine, cordage, ropes and cables of polyethylene or polypropylene (not plaited or braided, impregnated, or coated covered or sheathed, with rubber or plastics)

税则号列	货品名称	最惠(%)	普通	增值税率	出口退税	计量单位	监管条件	Article Description
5607.4900 90	其他聚乙烯或聚丙烯制线绳索缆(已编织或编结,可用橡胶或塑料浸渍、涂布,包覆,套裹)	5	100	17	16	千克		Other twine, cordage, ropes and cables of polyethylene or polypropylene (plaited or braided, impregnated or coated, covered or sheathed, with rubber or plastics)
5607.5000	-其他合成纤维纺制	5	100	17	16	千克		-Of other synthetic fibres
5607.5000 10	其他合纤制未编织或编织线绳索缆(可用橡胶或塑料浸渍、涂布,包覆,套裹)	5	100	17	16	千克		Twine, cordage, ropes and cables of other synthetic fibres (not plaited or braided, impregnated or coated, covered or sheathed with rubber or plastics)
5607.5000 90	其他合纤制已编织或编织线绳索缆(可用橡胶或塑料浸渍、涂布,包覆,套裹)	5	100	17	16	千克		Twine, cordage, ropes and cables of other synthetic fibres (plaited or braided, impregnated or coated, covered or sheathed, with rubber or plastics)
	-其他:							-Other:
5607.9010	---蕉麻(马尼拉麻)或其他硬质(叶)纤维纺制	5	50	17	16	千克		---Of abaca (Manila hemp or *Musa textilis Nee*) or other hard (leaf) fibres
5607.9090	---其他	5	100	17	16	千克		---Other
5607.9090 10	大麻制线,绳,索,缆(可编织或编结,可用橡胶或塑料浸渍、涂布,包覆,套裹)	5	100	17	16	千克		Twine, cordage, ropes and cables of hemp (plaited or braided, impregnated or coated, covered or sheathed, with rubber or plastics)
5607.9090 90	其他纺织材料制线,绳,索,缆(可编织或编结,可用橡胶或塑料浸渍、涂布,包覆,套裹)	5	100	17	16	千克		Twine, cordage, ropes and cables of other textile materials (plaited or braided, impregnated or coated, covered or sheathed, with rubber or plastics)
56.08	**线、绳或索结制的网料;纺织材料制成的渔网及其他网:**							**Knotted netting of twine, cordage or rope; made up fishing nets and other made up nets, of textile materials:**
	-化学纤维材料制:							-Of man-made textile materials:
5608.1100	--制成的渔网	10	50	17	16	千克		--Made up fishing nets
5608.1100 10	化纤材料制成手撒线拉的渔网	10	50	17	16	千克		Casting made up fishing nets of man-made textile materials
5608.1100 90	化纤材料制成其他渔网	10	50	17	16	千克		Other made up fishing nets of man-made textile materials
5608.1900	--其他	12	100	17	16	千克		--Other
5608.1900 10	化纤材料制用拉线收口的诱饵包(罗网及篓状网除外)	12	100	17	16	千克		Bait bag with a drawstring (other than toils or basket-shaped nets, of man-made textile materials)
5608.1900 90	化纤材料制成的网料和其他网(包括化纤线、绳、索结制的网料,罗网及篓状网除外)	12	100	17	16	千克		Other knotted netting of twine, cordage or rope; made up fishing nets and other made up nets, of man-made textile materials (other than toils or basket-shaped nets)
5608.9000	-其他	10	100	17	16	千克		-Other
5608.9000 11	毛、棉制的渔网	10	100	17	16	千克		Other made up fishing nets of wool of animal or of cotton
5608.9000 19	其他纺织纤维制的渔网	10	100	17	16	千克		Other made up fishing nets of other textile materials
5608.9000 91	棉制的其他网及网料(吊床,罗网及篓状网除外)	10	100	17	16	千克		Other made up fishing nets of cotton (other than nammock, toils or basket-shaped nets)
5608.9000 92	毛制的其他网及网料(包括棉制的网式吊床,罗网及篓状网除外)	10	100	17	16	千克		Other made up nets and knotted netting of wool or animal hair (including nammock of cotton, other than toils or basket-shaped nets)
5608.9000 99	其他纺织纤维制成的其他网及网料(罗网及篓状网除外)	10	100	17	16	千克		Other made up nets and knotted netting of other textile materials (other than toils or basket-shaped nets)
56.09	**用纱线、税目 54.04 或 54.05 的扁条及类似品或线、绳、索、缆制成的其他税目未列名物品:**							**Articles of yarn, strip or the like of heading No. 54.04 or 54.05, twine, cordage, rope or cables, not elsewhere specified or included:**
5609.0000	用纱线、税目 54.04 或 54.05 的扁条及类似品或线、绳、索、缆制成的其他税目未列名物品	10	100	17	16	千克		Articles of yarn, strip or the like of heading No. 54.04 or 54.05, twine, cordage, rope or cables, not elsewhere specified or included

第五十七章
地毯及纺织材料的其他铺地制品

Chapter 57
Carpets and other textile floor coverings

注释：

一、本章所称"地毯及纺织材料的其他铺地制品"，是指使用时以纺织材料作面的铺地制品，也包括具有纺织材料铺地制品特征但作其他用途的物品。

二、本章不包括铺地制品衬垫。

Notes:

1. For the purposes of this Chapter, the term "carpets and other textilefloor coverings" means floor coverings in which textile materials serve as the exposed surface of the article when in use and includes articles having the characteristics of textile floor coverings but intended for use for other purposes.
2. This Chapter does not cover floor covering underlays.

税则号列	货品名称	最惠(%)	普通	增值税率	出口退税	计量单位	监管条件	Article Description
57.01	结织栽绒地毯及纺织材料的其他结织栽绒铺地制品，不论是否制成的：							**Carpets and other textile floor coverings, knotted, whether or not made up:**
5701.1000	-羊毛或动物细毛制	14	130	17	16	千克/平方米		-Of wool or fine animal hair
	-其他纺织材料制：							-Of other textile materials:
5701.9010	---化学纤维制	16	130	17	16	千克/平方米		---Of man-made textile materials
5701.9020	---丝制	14	100	17	16	千克/平方米		---Of silk
5701.9090	---其他	14	100	17	16	千克/平方米		---Other
57.02	机织地毯及纺织材料的其他机织铺地制品，未簇绒或未植绒，不论是否制成的，包括"开来姆"、"苏麦克"、"卡拉马尼"及类似的手织地毯：							**Carpets and other textile floor coverings, woven, not tufted or flocked, whether or not made up, including "Kelem", "Schumacks", "Karamanie" and similar handwoven rugs:**
5702.1000	-"开来姆"、"苏麦克"、"卡拉马尼"及类似的手织地毯	14	130	17	16	千克/平方米		-"Kelem", "Schumacks", "Karamanie" and similar handwoven rugs
5702.2000	-椰壳纤维制的铺地制品	14	100	17	16	千克/平方米		-Floor coverings of coconut fibres (coir)
	-其他起绒结构的铺地制品，未制成的：							-Other, of pile construction, not made up:
5702.3100	--羊毛或动物细毛制	10	130	17	16	千克/平方米		--Of wool or fine animal hair
5702.3200	--化学纤维制	16	130	17	16	千克/平方米		--Of man-made textile materials
5702.3900	--其他纺织材料制	14	100	17	16	千克/平方米		--Of other textile materials
	-其他起绒结构的铺地制品，制成的：							-Other, of pile construction, made up:
5702.4100	--羊毛或动物细毛制	10	130	17	16	千克/平方米		--Of wool or fine animal hair
5702.4200	--化学纤维制	10	130	17	16	千克/平方米		--Of man-made textile materials
5702.4900	--其他纺织材料制	14	100	17	16	千克/平方米		--Of other textile materials
	-其他非起绒结构的铺地制品，未制成的：							-Other, not of pile construction, not made up:
5702.5010	---羊毛或动物细毛制	14	130	17	16	千克/平方米		---Of wool or fine animal hair
5702.5020	---化学纤维制	16	130	17	16	千克/平方米		---Of man made textile materials
5702.5090	---其他纺织材料制	14	100	17	16	千克/平方米		---Of other textile materials
	-其他非起绒结构的铺地制品，制成的：							-Other, not of pile construction, made up:
5702.9100	--羊毛或动物细毛制	14	130	17	16	千克/平方米		--Of wool or fine animal hair
5702.9200	--化学纤维制	16	130	17	16	千克/平方米		--Of man-made textile materials
5702.9900	--其他纺织材料制	14	100	17	16	千克/平方米		--Of other textile materials
57.03	簇绒地毯及纺织材料的其他簇绒铺地制品，不论是否制成的：							**Carpets and other textile floor coverings, tufted, whether or not made up:**
5703.1000	-羊毛或动物细毛制	14	130	17	16	千克/平方米		-Of wool or fine animal hair
5703.2000	-尼龙或其他聚酰胺制	10	130	17	16	千克/平方米		-Of nylon or other polyamides
5703.3000	-其他化学纤维制	10	130	17	16	千克/平方米		-Of other man-made textile materials
5703.9000	-其他纺织材料制	14	100	17	16	千克/平方米		-Of other textile materials
57.04	毡呢地毯及纺织材料的其他毡呢铺地制品，未簇绒或未植绒，不论是否制成的：							**Carpets and other textile floor coverings, of felt, not tufted or flocked, whether or not made up:**
5704.1000	-最大表面面积不超过0.3平方米	14	130	17	16	千克/平方米		-Tiles, having a maximum surface area of 0.3 m^2
5704.9000	-其他	10	130	17	16	千克/平方米		-Other
57.05	其他地毯及纺织材料的其他铺地制品，不论是否制成的：							**Other carpets and other textile floor coverings, whether or not made up:**
5705.0010	---羊毛或动物细毛制	14	130	17	16	千克/平方米		---Of wool or fine animal hair
5705.0020	---化学纤维制	10	130	17	16	千克/平方米		---Of man-made textile materials
5705.0090	---其他纺织材料制	14	100	17	16	千克/平方米		---Of other textile materialar

第五十八章
特种机织物;簇绒织物;花边;装饰毯;装饰带;刺绣品

注释:

一、本章不适用于经浸渍、涂布、包覆或层压的第五十九章注释一所述的纺织物或第五十九章的其他货品。

二、税目 58.01 也包括因未将浮纱割断而使表面无竖绒的纬起绒织物。

三、税目 58.03 所称"纱罗",是指经线全部或部分由地经纱和绞经纱构成的织物,其中绞经纱绕地经纱半圈、一圈或几圈而形成圈状,纬纱从圈中穿过。

四、税目 58.04 不适用于税目 56.08 的线、绳、索结制的网状织物。

五、税目 58.06 所称"狭幅机织物",是指:

(一)幅宽不超过30厘米的机织物,不论是否织成或从宽幅料剪成,但两侧必须有织成的、胶粘的或用其他方法制成的布边;

(二)压平宽度不超过30厘米的圆筒机织物;

(三)折边的斜裁滚条布,其未折边时的宽度不超过30厘米。

流苏状的狭幅织物归入税目 58.08。

六、税目 58.10 所称"刺绣品",除了一般纺织材料绣线绣制的刺绣品外,还包括在可见底布上用金属线或玻璃线刺绣的刺绣品,也包括用珠片、饰珠或纺织材料或其他材料制的装饰用花纹图案所缝绣的贴花织物。但不包括手工针绣嵌花装饰毯(税目 58.05)。

七、除税目号 58.09 的产品外,本章还包括金属线制的用于衣着、装饰及类似用途的物品。

Chapter 58
Special woven fabrics; tufted textile fabrics; lace; tapestries; trimmings; embroidery

Notes:

1. This Chapter does not apply to textile fabrics referred to in Note 1 to Chapter 59, impregnated, coated, covered or laminated, or to other goods of Chapter 59.
2. Heading No. 58.01 also includes woven weft pile fabrics which have not yet had the floats cut, at which stage they have no pile standing up.
3. For the purpose of heading No. 58.03, "gauze" means a fabric with a warp composed wholly or in part of standing or ground threads and crossing or doup threads which cross the standing or ground threads making a half turn, a complete turn or more to form loops through which weft threads pass.
4. Heading No. 58.04 does not apply to knotted net fabrics of twine, cordage or rope, of heading No. 56.08.
5. For the purposes of heading No. 58.06, the expression "narrow woven fabrics" means:
   (a) Woven fabrics of a width not exceeding 30 cm, whether woven as such or cut from wider pieces, provided with selvedges (woven, gummed or otherwise made) on both edges;
   (b) Tubular woven fabrics of a flattened width not exceeding 30 cm;
   (c) Bias binding with folded edges, of a width when unfolded not exceeding 30 cm.

   Narrow woven fabrics with woven fringes are to be classified in heading No. 58.08.
6. In heading No. 58.10, the expression "embroidery" means, *inter alia*, embroidery with metal or glass thread on a visible ground of textile fabric, and sewn appliquè work of sequins, beads or ornamental motifs of textile or other materials. The heading does not apply to needlework tapestry (heading No. 58.05).
7. In addition to the products of heading No. 58.09, this Chapter also includes articles made of metal thread and of a kind used in apparel, as furnishing fabrics or for similar purposes.

税则号列	货 品 名 称	最惠(%)	普通	增值税率	出口退税	计量单位	监管条件	Article Description
58.01	**起绒机织物及绳绒织物,但税号 58.02 或 58.06 的织物除外:**							**Woven pile fabrics and chenille fabrics, other than fabrics of heading No. 58.02 or 58.06:**
5801.1000	-羊毛或动物细毛制	10	130	17	16	米/千克		-Of wool or fine animal hair
	-棉制:							-Of cotton:
5801.2100	--不割绒的纬起绒织物	12	70	17	16	米/千克		--Uncut weft pile fabrics
5801.2100 10	未漂白不割绒的棉制纬起绒织物(品目5802或5806的织物除外)	12	70	17	16	米/千克		Woven weft pile fabrics of cotton, uncut (other than fabrics of heading No. 58.02 or 58.06) unbleached
5801.2100 90	其他不割绒的棉制纬起绒织物(品目5802或5806的织物除外)	12	70	17	16	米/千克		Other woven weft pile fabrics of cotton (uncut, other than fabrics of heading No. 58.02 or 58.06) unbleached
5801.2200	--割绒的灯芯绒	10	70	17	16	米/千克		--Cut corduroy
5801.2300	--其他纬起绒织物	10	70	17	16	米/千克		--Other weft pile fabrics
5801.2300 10	未漂白其他棉制纬起绒织物(品目5802或5806的织物除外)	10	70	17	16	米/千克		Other woven weft pile fabrics of cotton (other than fabrics of heading No. 58.02 or 58.06) unbleached
5801.2300 90	其他棉制纬起绒织物(品目5802或5806的织物除外)	10	70	17	16	米/千克		Other woven weft pile fabrics of cotton (other than fabrics of heading No. 58.02 or 58.06)
5801.2600	--绳绒织物	10	70	17	16	米/千克		--Chenille fabrics
5801.2600 10	未漂白棉制绳绒织物(品目5802或5806的织物除外)	10	70	17	16	米/千克		Woven chenille fabrics of cotton (other than fabrics of heading No. 58.02 or 58.06) unbleached

税则号列	货品名称	最惠(%)	普通	增值税率	出口退税	计量单位	监管条件	Article Description
5801.2600 90	其他棉制绳绒织物(品目5802或5806的织物除外)	10	70	17	16	米/千克		Other woven chenille fabrics of cotton (other than fabrics of heading No. 58.02 or 58.06)
	--经起绒织物:							--Warp pile fabrics:
5801.2710	---不割绒的(棱纹绸)	10	70	17	16	米/千克		---Warp pile fabrics(epingle)(nucut)
5801.2720	---割绒的	10	70	17	16	米/千克		---Warp pile fabrics(epingle)(cut)
	-化学纤维制:							-Of man-made fibres:
5801.3100	--不割绒的纬起绒织物	10	130	17	16	米/千克		--Uncut weft pile fabrics
5801.3200	--割绒的灯芯绒	10	130	17	16	米/千克		--Cut corduroy
5801.3300	--其他纬起绒织物	10	130	17	16	米/千克		--Other weft pile fabrics
5801.3600	--绳绒织物	10	130	17	16	米/千克		--Chenille fabrics
	--经起绒织物:							--Warp pile fabrics:
5801.3710	---不割绒的(棱纹绸)	10	130	17	16	米/千克		---Warp pile fabrics(epingle)(nucut)
5801.3720	---割绒的	10	130	17	16	米/千克		---Warp pile fabrics(epingle)(cut)
	-其他纺织材料制:							-Of other textile materials:
5801.9010	---丝及绢丝制	10	130	17	16	米/千克		---Of silk or spun silk
5801.9090	---其他	10	80	17	16	米/千克		---Other
5801.9090 10	亚麻和苎麻起绒机织物及绳绒织物(品目5802或5806的织物除外)	10	80	17	16	米/千克		Woven chenille fabrics and pile fabrics, of flax and ramie (other than fabrics of heading No. 58.02 or 58.06)
5801.9090 90	其他材料制起绒机织物及绳绒织物(品目5802或5806的织物除外)	10	80	17	16	米/千克		Woven chenille fabrics and pile fabrics, of other materials (other than fabrics of heading No. 58.02 or 58.06)
58.02	**毛巾织物及类似的毛圈机织物,但税号58.06的狭幅织物除外;簇绒织物,但税号57.03的产品除外:**							**Terry towelling and similar woven terry fabrics, other than narrow fabricsof heading No. 58.06; tufted textile fabrics, other than products of heading No. 57.03:**
	-棉制毛巾织物及类似毛圈机织物:							-Terry towelling and similar woven terry fabrics, of cotton:
5802.1100	--未漂白	12	70	17	16	米/千克		--Unbleached
5802.1900	--其他	10	70	17	16	米/千克		--Other
	-其他纺织材料制的毛巾织物及类似的毛圈机织物:							-Terry towelling and similar woven terry fabrics, of other textile materials:
5802.2010	---丝及绢丝制	12	130	17	16	米/千克		---Of silk or spun silk
5802.2010 10	丝及绢丝毛巾织物及类似毛圈织物(品目5806的狭幅织物除外,含丝85%及以上)	12	130	17	16	米/千克		Terry towelling and similar woven terry fabrics of silk or spun silk (other than narrow fabrics of heading No. 58.06, containing≥85% by weight)
5802.2010 90	丝及绢丝毛巾织物及类似毛圈织物(品目5806的狭幅织物除外,含丝85%以下)	12	130	17	16	米/千克		Terry towelling and similar woven terry fabrics of silk or spun silk (other than narrow fabrics of heading No. 58.06, containing <85% by weight)
5802.2020	---羊毛或动物细毛制	12	130	17	16	米/千克		---Of wool or fine animal hair
5802.2030	---化学纤维制	14	130	17	16	米/千克		---Of man-made fibres
5802.2090	---其他	12	80	17	16	米/千克		---Other
	-簇绒织物:							-Tufted textile fabrics:
5802.3010	---丝及绢丝制	10	130	17	16	米/千克		---Of silk or spun silk
5802.3010 10	丝及绢丝制簇绒织物(品目5703的产品除外,含丝85%及以上)	10	130	17	16	米/千克		Woven tufted textile fabrics of silk or spun silk (other than products of heading No. 5703, containing≥85% by weight of silk or silk waste)
5802.3010 90	其他丝及绢丝制簇绒织物(品目5703的产品除外,含丝85%以下)	10	130	17	16	米/千克		Other woven tufted textile fabrics of silk or spun silk (other than products of heading No. 5703, containing <85% by weight of silk or silk waste)
5802.3020	---羊毛或动物细毛制	10	130	17	16	米/千克		---Of wool or fine animal hair
5802.3030	---棉或麻制	10	70	17	16	米/千克		---Of cotton or bast fibres
5802.3030 10	麻制簇绒织物(品目5703的产品除外)	10	70	17	16	米/千克		Woven tufted textile fabrics of bast fibres (other than products of heading No. 5703)
5802.3030 90	棉制簇绒织物(品目5703的产品除外)	10	70	17	16	米/千克		Woven tufted textile fabrics of cotton (other than products of heading No. 5703)
5802.3040	---化学纤维制	10	130	17	16	米/千克		---Of man-made fibres
5802.3090	---其他纺织材料制	10	80	17	16	米/千克		---Of other textile materials

税则号列	货品名称	最惠(%)	普通	增值税率	出口退税	计量单位	监管条件	Article Description
58.03	纱罗,但税目58.06的狭幅织物除外:							**Gauze, other than narrow fabrics of heading No. 58.06:**
5803.0010	---棉制	10	70	17	16	米/千克		---Of cotton
5803.0020	---丝及绢丝制	10	130	17	16	米/千克		---Of silk or spun silk
5803.0030	---化学纤维制	10	130	17	16	米/千克		---Of man-made fibres
5803.0090	---其他纺织材料制	10	80	17	16	米/千克		---Of other textile materials
58.04	网眼薄纱及其他网眼织物,但不包括机织物、针织物或钩编织物;成卷、成条或成小块图案的花边,但税号60.02的织物除外:							**Tulles and other net fabrics, not including woven, knitted or crocheted fabrics; lace in the piece, in strips or in motifs, other than fabrics of headings No. 60.02:**
	-网眼薄纱及其他网眼织物:							-Tulles and other net fabrics:
5804.1010	---丝及绢丝制	10	130	17	16	千克		---Of silk or spun silk
5804.1010 10	丝及绢丝网眼薄纱及其他网眼织物(含丝85%及以上,不包括机织物,针织物或钩编织物)	10	130	17	16	千克		Tulles and other net fabrics, other than woven, knitted or crocheted fabrics, containing≥85% by weight of silk or spun silk
5804.1010 90	丝及绢丝网眼薄纱及其他网眼织物(含丝85%以下,不包括机织物,针织物或钩编织物)	10	130	17	16	千克		Tulles and other net fabrics, other than woven, knitted or crocheted fabrics, containing <85% by weight of silk or spun silk
5804.1020	---棉制	10	70	17	16	千克		---Of cotton
5804.1030	---化学纤维制	12	130	17	16	千克		---Of man-made fibres
5804.1090	---其他纺织材料制	10	90	17	16	千克		---Of other textile materials
	-机制花边:							-Mechanically made lace:
5804.2100	--化学纤维制	10	130	17	16	千克		--Of man-made fibres
	--其他纺织材料制:							--Of other textile materials:
5804.2910	---丝及绢丝制	10	130	17	16	千克		---Of silk or spun silk
5804.2910 10	丝及绢丝含量85%及以上机制花边(成卷成条或成小块图案的,但品目6002的织物除外)	10	130	17	16	千克		Mechanically made lace, in the piece, in strips or in motifs, other than fabrics of headings No. 60.02, containing≥85% by weight of silk or spun silk
5804.2910 90	丝及绢丝含量85%以下机制花边(成卷成条或成小块图案的,但品目6002的织物除外)	10	130	17	16	千克		Mechanically made lace (in the piece, in strips or in motifs, other than fabrics of headings No. 60.02) containing <85% by weight of silk or spun silk
5804.2920	---棉制	10	70	17	16	千克		---Of cotton
5804.2990	---其他	10	90	17	16	千克		---Other
5804.3000	-手工制花边	10	100	17	16	千克		-Hand-made lace
5804.3000 11	丝含量达85%及以上制手工制花边(成卷成条或成小块图案的,但品目6002的织物除外)	10	100	17	16	千克		Hand-made lace (in the piece, in strips or in motifs, other than fabrics of headings No. 60.02) containing ≥85% by weight of silk or spun silk
5804.3000 19	丝含量达85%以下制手工制花边(成卷成条或成小块图案的,但品目6002的织物除外)	10	100	17	16	千克		Hand-made lace (in the piece, in strips or in motifs, other than fabrics of headings No. 60.02), containing <85% by weight of silk or spun silk
5804.3000 20	棉或化纤制手工制花边(成卷成条或成小块图案的,但品目6002的织物除外)	10	100	17	16	千克		Hand-made lace, of cotton or of man-made fibres (in the piece, in strips or in motifs, other than fabrics of headings No. 60.02)
5804.3000 90	其他纺织材料制手工制其他花边(成卷成条或成小块图案的,但品目6002的织物除外)	10	100	17	16	千克		Other hand-made lace of other textile materials (in the piece, in strips or in motifs, other than fabrics of headings No. 60.02)
58.05	"哥白林"、"弗朗德"、"奥步生"、"波威"及类似式样的手织装饰毯,以及手工针绣嵌花装饰毯(例如,小针脚或十字绣),不论是否制成的:							**Hand-woven tapestries of the type Gobelins, Flanders, Aubusson, Beauvais and the like, and needle-worked tapestries (for example, petit point, cross stitch), whether or not made up:**
5805.0010	---手工针绣嵌花装饰毯	12	130	17	16	平方米/千克		---Needle-worked tapestries
5805.0010 10	毛制非民间工艺针绣嵌花其他装饰毯(不论是否制成的)	12	130	17	16	平方米/千克		Needle-worked tapestries of wool or fine animal hair, non-craftsmanship, whether or not made up
5805.0010 20	棉制手工针绣嵌花其他装饰毯(不论是否制成的)	12	130	17	16	平方米/千克		Needle-worked tapestries of cotton (whether or not made up)

税则号列	货品名称	最惠(%)	普通	增值税率	出口退税	计量单位	监管条件	Article Description
5805.0010 30	化纤制手工针绣嵌花其他装饰毯(不论是否制成的)	12	130	17	16	平方米/千克		Needle-worked tapestries of man-made fibres(whether or not made up)
5805.0010 90	其他纺织料制手工针绣嵌花装饰毯(不论是否制成的)	12	130	17	16	平方米/千克		Needle-worked tapestries of other textile materials (whether or not made up)
5805.0090	---其他	12	130	17	16	千克/平方米		---Other
5805.0090 10	毛制非民间工艺的手织装饰毯(包括"哥白林","弗朗德","奥步生","波威"及类似式样的)	12	130	17	16	平方米/千克		Hand-woven tapestries of the type gobelins, flanders, aubusson, beauvais and the like, of wool or fine animal hair, non-craftsmanship
5805.0090 20	棉制"哥白林"等手织装饰毯(包括"弗朗德","奥步生","波威"及类似式样的手织装饰毯)	12	130	17	16	平方米/千克		Hand-woven tapestries of the type gobelins, flanders, aubusson, beauvais and the like, of cotton
5805.0090 30	化纤制"哥白林"等手织装饰毯(包括"弗朗德","奥步生","波威"及类似式样的手织装饰毯)	12	130	17	16	平方米/千克		Hand-woven tapestries of the type gobelins (including flanders, aubusson, beauvais and the like) of man-made fibres
5805.0090 90	其他纺织料制"哥白林"等手织装饰毯(包括"弗朗德","奥步生","波威"及类似式样的手织装饰毯)	12	130	17	16	平方米/千克		Hand-woven tapestries of the type gobelins (including flanders, aubusson, beauvais and the like) of other textile materials
58.06	**狭幅机织物,但税号58.07的货品除外;用粘合剂粘合制成的有经纱而无纬纱的狭幅织物(包扎匹头用带):**							**Narrow woven fabrics, other than goods of heading No. 58.07; narrow fabrics consisting of warp without weft assembled by means of an adhesive (bolducs):**
	-起绒机织物(包括毛巾织物及类似的毛圈织物)及绳绒织物:							-Woven pile fabrics (including terry towelling and similar terry fabris) and chenille fabrics:
5806.1010	---棉或麻制	10	70	17	16	千克		---Of cotton or bast fibres
5806.1010 10	棉制狭幅起绒机织物及绳绒织物(包括狭幅毛巾织物及类似毛圈织物,品目5807的货品除外)	10	70	17	16	千克		Narrow woven pile fabrics and chenille fabrics of cotton (including terry towelling and similar terry fabris, other than goods of heading No. 5807)
5806.1010 90	麻制狭幅起绒机织物及绳绒织物(包括狭幅毛巾织物及类似毛圈织物,品目5807的货品除外)	10	70	17	16	千克		Narrow woven pile fabrics and chenille fabrics of bast fibres (including terry towelling and similar terry fabris, other than goods of heading No. 5807)
5806.1090	---其他纺织材料制	10	80	17	16	千克		---Of other textile materials
5806.1090 10	含丝≥85%狭幅起绒及绳绒等织物(包括狭幅毛巾织物及类似毛圈织物,品目5807的货品除外)	10	80	17	16	千克		Narrow woven pile fabrics and chenille fabrics (including terry towelling and similar terry fabris, other than goods of heading No. 5807), containing ≥85% by weight of silk
5806.1090 20	毛制狭幅起绒织物及绳绒织物(包括狭幅毛巾织物及类似毛圈织物,品目5807的货品除外)	10	80	17	16	千克		Narrow woven pile fabrics and chenille fabrics of wool or fine animal hair (including terry towelling and similar terry fabris, other than goods of heading No. 5807)
5806.1090 30	化纤制狭幅起绒织物及绳绒织物(包括狭幅毛巾织物及类似毛圈织物,品目5807的货品除外)	10	80	17	16	千克		Narrow woven pile fabrics and chenille fabrics of man-made fibres (including terry towellingand similar terry fabris, other than goods of heading No. 58.07)
5806.1090 90	其他材料狭幅起绒织物及绳绒织物(包括狭幅毛巾织物及类似毛圈织物,品目5807的货品除外)	10	80	17	16	千克		Narrow woven pile fabrics and chenille fabrics of other textile materials (including terry towelling and similar terry fabris, other than goods of heading No. 5807)
5806.2000	-按重量计弹性纱线或橡胶线含量在5%及以上的其他机织物	10	100	17	16	千克		-Other woven fabrics, containing by weight 5% or more of elastomeric yarn or rubber thread
	-其他机织物:							-Other woven fabrics:
5806.3100	--棉制	10	70	17	16	千克		--Of cotton
5806.3200	--化学纤维制	10	130	17	16	千克		--Of man-made fibres
5806.3200 10	化纤制用于打字机色带狭幅机织物(品目5807的货品除外)	10	130	17	16	千克		Narrow woven fabrics, typewriter ribbon, of man-made fibres(other than goods of heading No. 5807)
5806.3200 90	化纤制其他狭幅机织物(品目5807的货品除外)	10	130	17	16	千克		Other narrow woven fabrics of man-made fibres(other than goods of heading No. 5807)
	--其他纺织材料制:							--Of other textile materials:
5806.3910	---丝及绢丝制	10	130	17	16	千克		---Of silk or spun silk

税则号列	货品名称	最惠(%)	普通	增值税率	出口退税	计量单位	监管条件	Article Description
5806.3920	---羊毛或动物细毛制	10	130	17	16	千克		---Of wool or fine animal hair
5806.3990	---其他	10	80	17	16	千克		---Other
5806.3990 10	含金属纱线制其他狭幅机织物(品目5807的货品除外)	10	80	17	16	千克		Other narrow woven fabrics of metallized yarn(other than goods of heading No. 5807)
5806.3990 90	其他材料制其他狭幅机织物(品目5807的货品除外)	10	80	17	16	千克		Other narrow woven fabrics of other textile materials (other than goods of heading No. 5807)
	-用粘合剂粘合制成的有经纱而无纬纱的织物(包扎匹头用带):							-Fabrics consisting of warp without weft assembled by means of an adhesive (bolducs):
5806.4010	---棉或麻制	10	70	17	16	千克		---Of cotton or bast fibres
5806.4090	---其他纺织材料制	10	80	17	16	千克		---Of other textile materials
58.07	**非绣制的纺织材料制标签、徽章及类似品,成匹、成条或裁成一定形状或尺寸:**							**Labels,badges and similar articles of textile materials,in the piece,in strips or cut to shape or size,not embroidered:**
5807.1000	-机织	10	100	17	16	千克		-Woven
5807.1000 10	棉制机织非绣制标签(成匹、成条或裁成一定形状或尺寸)	10	100	17	16	千克		Woven labels of cotton(in the piece,in strips or cut to shape or size)onot embroidered
5807.1000 20	化纤制机织非绣制标签(成匹、成条或裁成一定形状或尺寸)	10	100	17	16	千克		Woven labels of man-made fibres(in the piece,in strips or cut to shape or size)not embroidered
5807.1000 90	其他纺织材料制机织非绣制标签等(包括徽章及类似品,成匹、成条或裁成一定形状或尺寸)	10	100	17	16	千克		Woven labels(includind badges and similar articles, in the piece,in strips or cut to shape or size)not embroidered,of other textile materials
5807.9000	-其他	10	100	17	16	千克		-Other
5807.9000 10	棉制非绣制的标签(成匹、成条或裁成一定形状或尺寸)	10	100	17	16	千克		Labels of cotton(in the piece, in strips or cut to shape or size),not embroidered
5807.9000 20	化纤制非绣制的标签(成匹、成条或裁成一定形状或尺寸)	10	100	17	16	千克		Labels of man-made fibres(in the piece,in strips or cut to shape or size)not embroidered
5807.9000 90	其他纺织材料制非绣制的标签等(包括徽章及类似品,成匹、成条或裁成一定形状或尺寸)	10	100	17	16	千克		Labels,of other textile materials(including badges similar articles, in the piece, in strips or cut to shape or size)not embroidered
58.08	**成匹的编带;非绣制的成匹装饰带,但针织或钩编的除外;流苏、绒球及类似品:**							**Braids in the piece; ornamental trimmings in the piece,without embroidery,other than knitted or crocheted; tassels,pompons and similar articles:**
5808.1000	-成匹的编带	10	100	17	16	千克		-Braids in the piece
5808.1000 10	棉或化纤制成匹的编带	10	100	17	16	千克		Braids in the piece,of cotton or of man-made fibres
5808.1000 20	蕉麻或苎麻制成匹的编带(适合制造或装饰帽类用)	10	100	17	16	千克	A	Braids in the piece,of abaca or ramie (suitable for manufacturing or decoration of head gear)
5808.1000 90	其他纺织材料制成匹的编带	10	100	17	16	千克		Braids in the piece,of other textile materials
5808.9000	-其他	10	100	17	16	千克		-Other
5808.9000 10	棉或化纤制非绣制成匹装饰带(针织或钩编的除外)	10	100	17	16	千克		Ornamental trimmings in the piece, of cotton or of man-made fibres,other than knitted or crocheted
5808.9000 90	其他非绣制成匹装饰带,流苏等(含绒球及类似品,针织或钩编的除外)	10	100	17	16	千克		Other ornamental trimmings in the piece, tassels, pompons and similar articles without embroidery, other than knitted or crocheted
58.09	**其他税目未列名的金属线机织物及税目56.05所列含金属纱线的机织物,用于衣着、装饰及类似用途:**							**Woven fabrics of metal thread and woven fabrics of metallized yarn of heading No. 56.05, of a kind used in apparel,as furnishing fabrics or for similar purposes, not elsewhere specified or included:**
5809.0010	---与棉混制	10	90	17	16	米/千克		---Combined with cotton
5809.0020	---与化学纤维混制	10	130	17	16	米/千克		---Combined with man-made fibres
5809.0090	---其他	10	100	17	16	米/千克		---Other
58.10	**成匹、成条或成小块图案的刺绣品:**							**Embroidery in the piece,in strips or in motifs:**
5810.1000	-不见底布的刺绣品	10	130	17	16	千克		-Embroidery without visible ground
	-其他刺绣品:							-Other embroidery:
5810.9100	--棉制	10	130	17	16	千克		--Of cotton
5810.9200	--化学纤维制	10	130	17	16	千克		--Of man-made fibres

税则号列	货品名称	最惠(%)	普通	增值税率	出口退税	计量单位	监管条件	Article Description
5810.9200 10	化学纤维制见底布刺绣标签(成匹,成条或成小块图案)	10	130	17	16	千克		Embroidered labels, without visible ground, in the piece, in strips or in motifs, of man-made fibres
5810.9200 90	其他化学纤维制见底布刺绣品(成匹,成条或成小块图案)	10	130	17	16	千克		Other embroidery visible ground, in the piece, in strips or in motifs, of man-made fibres
5810.9900	--其他纺织材料制	10	130	17	16	千克		--Of other textile materials
5810.9900 10	羊毛或动物细毛制见底布刺绣品(成匹,成条或成小块图案)	10	130	17	16	千克		Embroidery visible ground, in the piece, in strips or in motifs, of wool or fine animal hair
5810.9900 90	其他纺织材料制见底布刺绣品(成匹,成条或成小块图案)	10	130	17	16	千克		Embroidery visible ground, in the piece, in strips or in motifs, of other textile materials
58.11	**用一层或几层纺织材料与胎料经绗缝或其他方法组合制成的被褥状纺织品,但税目58.10的刺绣品除外:**							**Quilted textile products in the piece, composed of one or more layers of textile materials assembled with padding by stitching or otherwise, other than embroidery of heading No. 58.10:**
5811.0010	---丝及绢丝制	10	130	17	16	千克		---Of silk or spun silk
5811.0020	---羊毛或动物细毛制	10	130	17	16	千克		---Of wool or fine animal hair
5811.0030	---棉制	10	80	17	16	千克		---Of cotton
5811.0030 10	未漂白或漂白棉制被褥状纺织品(经绗缝等法用一或几层织物与胎料组合不含品目5810刺绣品)	10	80	17	16	千克		Quilted textile products in the piece, composed of one or more layers of textile materials assembled with padding by stitching or otherwise, other than embroidery of heading No. 58.10, of cotton, unbleached or bleached
5811.0030 90	其他棉制被褥状纺织品(经绗缝等法用一或几层织物与胎料组合不含品目5810刺绣品)	10	80	17	16	千克		Other quilted textile products in the piece, composed of one or more layers of textile materials assembled with padding by stitching or otherwise, other than embroidery of heading No. 58.10, of cotton
5811.0040	---化学纤维制	12	130	17	16	千克		---Of man-made fibres
5811.0090	---其他纺织材料制	10	90	17	16	千克		---Of other textile materials

第五十九章
浸渍、涂布、包覆或层压的纺织物；工业用纺织制品

注释：

一、除条文另有规定的以外，本章所称“纺织物”，仅适用于第五十章至第五十五章、税目58.03及58.06的机织物、税目58.08的成匹编带和装饰带及税目60.02至60.06的针织物或钩编织物。

二、税目59.03适用于：

(一)用塑料浸渍、涂布、包覆或层压的纺织物，不论每平方米重量多少以及塑料的性质如何(紧密结构或泡沫状的)，但下列各项除外：

1. 用肉眼无法辨别出是否经过浸渍、涂布、包覆或层压的织物(通常归入第五十章至第五十五章、第五十八章或第六十章)；但由于浸渍、涂布、包覆或层压所引起的颜色变化可不予考虑；

2. 温度在15℃至30℃时，用手工将其绕于直径7毫米的圆柱体上会发生断裂的产品(通常归入第三十九章)；

3. 纺织物完全嵌入塑料内或在其两面均用塑料完全包覆或涂布，而这种包覆或涂布用肉眼是能够辨别出的产品(但由于包覆或涂布所引起的颜色变化可不予考虑)(第三十九章)；

4. 用塑料部分涂布或包覆并由此而形成图案的织物(通常归入第五十章至第五十五章、第五十八章或第六十章)；

5. 与纺织物混制而其中纺织物仅起增强作用的泡沫塑料板、片或带(第三十九章)；

6. 税目58.11的纺织品；

(二)由税目56.04的用塑料浸渍、涂布、包覆或套裹的纱线、扁条或类似品制成的织物。

三、税目59.05所称“糊墙织物”，是指以纺织材料作面，固定在一衬背上或在背面进行处理(浸渍或涂布以便于裱糊)，适于装饰墙壁或天花板，且宽度不小于45厘米的成卷产品。

但本税目不适用于以纺织纤维屑或粉末直接粘于纸上(税目48.14)或布底上(通常归入税目59.07)的糊墙物品。

四、税目59.06所称“用橡胶处理的纺织物”是指：

(一)用橡胶浸渍、涂布、包覆或层压的纺织物：

1. 每平方米重量不超过1 500克；

2. 每平方米重量超过1 500克，按重量计纺织材料含量在50%以上。

(二)由税目56.04的用橡胶浸渍、涂布、包覆或套裹的纱线、扁条或类似品制成的织物；以及

(三)平行纺织纱线经橡胶粘合的织物，不论每平方米重量多少。

Chapter 59
Impregnated, coated, covered or laminated textile fabrics; textile articles of a kind suitable for industrial use

Notes:

1. Except where the context otherwise requires, for the purposes of this Chapter the expression "textile fabrics" applies only to the woven fabrics of Chapters 50 to 55 and headings No. 58.03 and 58.06, the braids and ornamental trimmings in the piece of heading No. 58.08 and the knitted or crocheted fabrics of headings No. 60.02 to 60.06.

2. Heading No. 59.03 applies to:

(a) Textile fabrics, impregnated, coated, covered or laminated with plastics, whatever the weight per square metre and whatever the nature of the plastic material (compact or cellular), other than:

(1) Fabrics in which the impregnation, coating, or covering cannot be seen with the naked eye (usually Chapters 50 to 55, 58 or 60); for the purpose of this provision, no account should be taken of any resulting change of colour;

(2) Products which cannot, without fracturing, be bent manually around a cylinder of a diameter of 7 mm, at a temperature between 15℃ and 30℃ (usually Chapter 39);

(3) Products in which the textile fabric is either completely embedded in plastics or entirely coated or covered on both sides with such material, provided that such coating or covering can be seen with the naked eye with no account being taken of any resulting change of colour (Chapter 39);

(4) Fabrics partially coated or partially covered with plastics and bearing designs resulting from these treatments (usually Chapters 50 to 55, 58 or 60);

(5) Plates, sheets or strip of cellular plastics, combined with textile fabric, where the textile fabric is present merely for reinforcing purposes (Chapter 39);

(6) Textile products of heading No. 58.11;

(b) Fabrics made from yarn, strip or the like, impregnated, coated, covered or sheathed with plastics, of heading No. 56.04.

3. For the purposes of heading No. 59.05, the expression "textile wall coverings" applies to products in rolls, of a width of not less than 45 cm, suitable for wall or ceiling decoration, consisting of a textile surface which has been fixed on a backing or has been treated on the back (impregnated or coated to permit pasting).

This heading does not, however, apply to wall coverings consisting of textile flock or dust fixed directly on a backing of paper (heading No. 48.14) or on a textile backing (generally heading No. 59.07).

4. For the purposes of heading No. 59.06, the expression "rubberized textile fabrics" means:

(a) Textile fabrics impregnated, coated, covered or laminated with rubber:

(Ⅰ) Weighing not more than 1,500 g/m²; or

(Ⅱ) Weighing more than 1,500 g/m² and containing more than 50% by weight of textile material。

(b) Fabrics made from yarn, strip or the like, impregnated, coated, covered or sheathed with rubber, of heading No. 56.04; and

(c) Fabrics composed of parallel textile yarns agglomerated with rubber, irrespective of their weight per square metre.

但本税目不包括与纺织物混制而其中纺织物仅起增强作用的海绵橡胶板、片或带(第四十章),也不包括税目58.11的纺织品。

This heading does not, however, apply to plates, sheets or strip of cellular rubber, combined with textile fabric, where the textile fabric is present merely for reinforcing purposes (Chapter 40), or textile products of heading No. 58.11.

五、税目59.07不适用于:

(一)用肉眼无法辨别出是否经过浸渍、涂布或包覆的织物(通常归入第五十章至第五十五章、第五十八章或第六十章),但由于浸渍、涂布或包覆所引起的颜色变化可不予考虑;

(二)绘有图画的织物(作为舞台、摄影布景或类似品的已绘制的画布除外);

(三)用短绒、粉末、软木粉或类似品部分覆面并由此而形成图案的织物,但仿绒织物仍归入本税目;

(四)以淀粉或类似物质为基本成分的普通浆料上浆整理的织物;

(五)以纺织物为底的木饰面板(税目44.08);

(六)以纺织物为底的砂布及类似品(税号68.05);

(七)以纺织物为底的粘聚或复制云母片(税号68.14);

(八)以纺织物为底的金属箔(通常为第十四类或第十五类)。

5. Heading No. 59.07 does not apply to:

(a) Fabrics in which the impregnation, coating or covering cannot be seen with the naked eye (usually Chapters 50 to 55, 58 or 60); for the purpose of this provision, no account should be taken of any resulting change of colour;

(b) Fabrics painted with designs (other than painted canvas being theatrical scenery, studio back-cloths or the like);

(c) Fabrics partially covered with flock, dust, powdered cork or the like and bearing designs resulting from these treatments; however, imitation pile fabrics remain classified in this heading;

(d) Fabrics finished with normal dressings having a basis of amylaceous or similar substances;

(e) Wood veneered on a backing of textile fabrics (heading No. 44.08);

(f) Natural or artificial abrasive powder or grain, on a backing of textile fabrics (heading No. 68.05);

(g) Agglomerated or reconstituted mica, on a backing of textile fabrics (heading No. 68.14); or

(h) Metal foil on a backing of textile fabrics (Generauy section XIV or XV).

六、税目59.10不适用于:

(一)厚度小于3毫米的纺织材料制传动带或输送带;

(二)用橡胶浸渍、涂布、包覆或层压的织物制成的或用橡胶浸渍、涂布、包覆或套裹的纱线或绳制成的传动带及运输带(税目40.10)。

6. Heading No. 59.10 does not apply to:

(a) Transmission or conveyor belting, of textile material, of a thickness of less than 3 mm; or

(b) Transmission or conveyor belts or belting of textile fabric impregnated, coated, covered or laminated with rubber or made from textile yarn or cord impregnated, coated, covered or sheathed with rubber (heading No. 40.10).

七、税目59.11适用于下列不能归入第十一类其他税目的货品:

(一)下列成匹的、裁成一定长度或仅裁成矩形(包括正方形)的纺织产品(具有税目59.08至59.10所列产品特征的产品除外):

1. 用橡胶、皮革或其他材料涂布、包覆或层压的作针布用的纺织物、毡呢及毡呢衬里机织物,以及其他专门技术用途的类似织物,包括用橡胶浸渍的用于包覆纺缍(织轴)的狭幅丝绒织物。

2. 筛布;

3. 用于榨油机器或类似机器的纺织材料制或人发制滤布;

4. 用多股经纱或纬纱平织而成的纺织物,不论是否毡化、浸渍或涂布,通常用于机械或其他专门技术用途;

5. 专门技术用途的增强纺织物;

6. 工业上作填塞或润滑材料的线绳、编带及类似品,不论是否涂布、浸渍或用金属加强。

(二)专门技术用途的纺织制品(税目59.08至59.10的货品除外),例如,造纸机器或类似机器(如制浆机或制石棉水泥的机器)用的环状或装有连接装置的纺织物或毡呢、密封垫、垫圈、抛光盘及其他机器零件。

7. Heading No. 59.11 applies to the following goods, which do not fall in any other heading of Section XI:

(a) Textile products in the piece, cut to length or simply cut to rectangular (including square) shape (other than those having the character of the products of headings No. 59.08 to 59.10), the following only:

(Ⅰ) Textile fabrics, felt and felt-lined woven fabrics, coated, covered or laminated with rubber, leather or other material, of a kind used for card clothing, and similar fabrics of a kind used for other technical purposes, including narrow fabrics made of velvet impregnated with rubber, for covering weaving spindles (weaving beams);

(Ⅱ) Bolting cloth;

(Ⅲ) Straining cloth of a kind used in oil presses or the like, of textile material or of human hair;

(Ⅳ) Flat woven textile fabrics with multiple warp or weft, whether or not felted, impregnated or coated, of a kind used in machinery or for other technical purposes;

(Ⅴ) Textile fabrics reinforced with metal, of a kind used for technical purposes;

(Ⅵ) Cords, braids and the like, whether or not coated, impregnated or reinforced with metal, of a kind used in industry as packing or lubricating materials;

(b) Textile articles (other than those of headings No. 59.08 to 59.10) of a kind used for technical purposes, for example, textile fabrics and felts, endless or fitted with linking devicse, of a kind used in paper-making or similar machines (for example, for pulp or asbestos-cement), gaskets, washers, polishing discs and other machinery parts.

税则号列	货品名称	最惠(%)	普通	增值税率	出口退税	计量单位	监管条件	Article Description
59.01	用胶或淀粉物质涂布的纺织物,作书籍封面及类似用途的;描图布;制成的油画布;作帽里的硬衬布及类似硬挺纺织物:							**Textile fabrics coated with gum or amylaceous substances, of a kind used for the outer covers of books or the like; tracing cloth; prepared painting canvas; buckram and similar stiffened textile fabrics of a kind used for hat foundations:**
	-用胶或淀粉物质涂布的纺织物,作书籍封面及类似用途的:							-Textile fabrics coated with gum or amylaceous substances, of a kind used for the outer covers of books or the like:
5901.1010	---棉或麻制	10	80	17	16	千克		---Of cotton or bast fibres
5901.1010 10	胶或淀粉涂布的棉纺织物(作书籍封面,棉织物重≥50%,经漂染印花)	10	80	17	16	千克		Textile fabrics coated with gum or amylaceous substances, of a kind used for the outer covers of books or the like, containing ≥50% by weight of cotton, bleached, dyed, printed
5901.1010 90	胶或淀粉涂布的麻及其他棉纺织(作书籍封面及类似用途的)	10	80	17	16	千克		Textile fabrics coated with gum or amylaceous substances, of a kind used for the outer covers of books or the like, of bast fibres and other cotton
5901.1020	---化学纤维制	10	130	17	16	千克		---Of man-made fibres
5901.1020 10	胶或淀粉涂布的涤棉短纤混纺织品(书籍封面及类似用途,聚酯短纤棉混纺漂染织物重>50%)	10	130	17	16	千克		Textile fabrics coated with gum or amylaceous substances, of a kind used for the outer covers of books or the like, containing≥50% by weight of polyester staple fibres and cotton, bleached, dyed
5901.1020 90	胶或淀粉涂布的其他化纤纺织物(作书籍封面及类似用途的)	10	130	17	16	千克		Other man-made textile fabrics coated with gum or amylaceous substances, of a kind used for the outer covers of books or the like, of other textile fabrics
5901.1090	---其他	10	100	17	16	千克		---Other
5901.1090 10	用胶或淀粉涂布的精梳毛纺织物(书籍封面及类似用途,精梳羊毛或动物细毛织物重≥50%)	10	100	17	16	千克		Woollen textile fabrics coated with gum or amylaceous substances, of a kind used for the outer covers of books or the like, containing≥50% by weight of combed wool or fine animal hair
5901.1090 90	用胶或淀粉涂布的其他纺织物(作书籍封面及类似用途的)	10	100	17	16	千克		Other textile fabrics coated with gum or amylaceous substances, of a kind used for the outer covers of books or the like, of other textile fabrics
	-其他:							-Other:
5901.9010	---制成的油画布	10	50	17	16	千克		---Prepared painting canvas
5901.9010 10	精梳毛织物制油画布(精梳羊毛或动物细毛织物重≥50%)	10	50	17	16	千克		Prepared painting canvas, containing ≥ 50% by weight of combed wool or fine animal hair
5901.9010 20	棉制油画布(棉织物重≥50%,经漂白染色印花等加工)	10	50	17	16	千克		Prepared painting canvas, containing ≥ 50% by weight of cotton, bleached, dyed or printed
5901.9010 30	聚酯短纤与棉混纺织物制油画(织物重≥50%经漂白染色印花等加工)	10	50	17	16	千克		Prepared painting canvas, mixed, containing≥50% by weight of polyester staple fibres and cotton
5901.9010 90	其他纺织物制成的油画布	10	50	17	16	千克		Prepared painting canvas of other textile fabrics
	---其他:							---Other:
5901.9091	----棉或麻制	10	80	17	16	千克		----Of cotton or bast fibres
5901.9091 10	棉制描图布、帽里硬衬布等(包括类似硬挺纺织物,棉织物≥50%经漂染印花)	10	80	17	16	千克		Tracing cloth, buckram and similar stiffened textile fabrics, of a kind used for hat foundations, of cotton, containing≥50% by weight of cotton, bleached dyed printed
5901.9091 90	麻及其他棉制描图布、帽里硬衬布(包括类似硬挺纺织物)	10	80	17	16	千克		Tracing cloth, buckram and similar stiffened textile fabrics, of a kind used for hat foundations, of bast fibres and other cotton
5901.9092	----化学纤维制	10	130	17	16	千克		----Of man-made fibres
5901.9092 10	聚酯短纤与棉混纺织物制描图布(含帽里硬衬类似硬挺纺织物,织物重≥50%,经漂染印)	10	130	17	16	千克		Tracing cloth, buckram and similar stiffened textile fabrics, of a kind used for hat foundations, mixed, containing≥50% by weight of polyester staple fibres and cotton, bleached, dyed, printed

税则号列	货品名称	最惠(%)	普通	增值税率	出口退税	计量单位	监管条件	Article Description
5901.9092 90	其他化纤制描图布,帽里硬衬布等(包括类似硬挺纺织物)	10	130	17	16	千克		Tracing cloth, buckram and similar stiffened textile fabrics, of a kind used for hat foundations, of other man-made fibres
5901.9099	----其他	10	100	17	16	千克		----Other
5901.9099 10	精梳毛纺织物制描图布,帽里硬衬(包括类似硬挺纺织物,精梳羊毛或动物细毛织物重≥50%)	10	100	17	16	千克		Tracing cloth, buckram and similar stiffened textile fabrics, of a kind used for hat foundations, containing ≥50% by weight, of combed wool or combed fine animals hair
5901.9099 90	其他纺织物制描图布,帽里硬衬布(包括类似硬挺纺织物)	10	100	17	16	千克		Tracing cloth, buckram and similar stiffened textile fabrics, of a kind used for hat foundations, of other textile fabrics
59.02	**尼龙或其他聚酰胺,聚酯或粘胶纤维高强力纱制的帘子布:**							**Tyre cord fabric of high tenacity yarn of nylon or other polyamides, polyesters or viscose rayon:**
	-尼龙或其他聚酰胺制:							-Of nylon or other polyamides:
5902.1010	---聚酰胺-6(尼龙-6)制	10	40	17	16	千克		---Of polyamides(nylon-6)
5902.1020	---聚酰胺-6,6(尼龙-6,6)制	10	40	17	16	千克		---Of polyamides(nylon-6,6)
5902.1090	---其他	10	40	17	16	千克		---Other
5902.2000	-聚酯制	10	40	17	16	千克		-Of polyesters
5902.9000	-其他	10	40	17	16	千克		-Other
59.03	**用塑料浸渍、涂布、包覆或层压的纺织物,但税目59.02的货品除外:**							**Textile fabrics impregnated, coated, covered or laminated with plastics, other than those of heading No. 59.02:**
	-用聚氯乙烯浸渍、涂布、包覆或层压的:							-With poly(vinyl chloride):
5903.1010	---绝缘布或带	10	40	17	16	千克		---Insulating cloth or tape
5903.1010 10	若干平行化纤纱线粘合绝缘布或带(聚氯乙烯浸渍、涂布、包覆或层压,塑料占60%及以下)	10	40	17	16	千克		Insulating cloth or tape of man-made fibres, impregnated, coated, covered or laminated with poly (vinyl chloride), of fabrics consisting of layers of parallel textile yarns, bonded, containing≤60% by weight of plastics
5903.1010 20	聚氯乙烯浸渍涤棉混纺绝缘布或带(聚氯乙烯涂布、包覆、漂染聚酯短纤棉混纺,塑或胶<50%)	10	40	17	16	千克		Insulating cloth or tape of mixed with polyester staple fibres and cotton, impregnated, coated, covered or laminated with poly (vinyl chloride), containing <50% by weight of plastics or glue
5903.1010 30	聚氯乙烯浸渍其他化纤绝缘布或带(用聚氯乙烯涂布、包覆或层压,塑或胶≤70%)	10	40	17	16	千克		Insulating cloth or tape of man-made fibres, impregnated, coated, covered or laminated with poly (vinyl chloride), containing≤70% by weight of plastics or glue
5903.1010 90	用聚氯乙烯浸渍的其他绝缘布或带(包括用聚氯乙烯涂布,包覆或层压的)	10	40	17	16	千克		Other insulating cloth or tape, impregnated, coated, covered or laminated with poly (vinyl chloride)
5903.1020	---人造革	10	70	17	16	千克/米		---Imitation leather
5903.1020 10	若干层平行纱线粘合的化纤人造革(用聚氯乙烯浸渍,涂布、包覆、层压,塑料占60%及以下)	10	70	17	16	千克/米		Imitation leather of man-made fibres, impregnated, coated, covered or laminated with poly (vinyl chloride) of fabrics consisting of layers of parallel textile yarns, bonded, containing≤60% by weight of plastics
5903.1020 20	用聚氯乙烯浸渍的涤棉织物人造革(聚氯乙烯涂布、漂印、染,聚酯短纤棉混纺,塑或胶<50%)	10	70	17	16	千克/米		Imitation leather of mixed with polyester staple fibres and cotton, impregnated, coated, covered or laminated with poly (vinyl chloride), containing <50% by weight of plastics or glue
5903.1020 30	用聚氯乙烯浸渍的其他化纤人造革(包括用聚氯乙烯涂布、包覆或层压,塑或胶≤70%)	10	70	17	16	千克/米		Imitation leather of man-made fibres, impregnated, coated, covered or laminated with poly (vinyl chloride), containing≤70% by weight of plastics or glue
5903.1020 40	用聚氯乙烯浸渍的棉织物人造革(聚氯乙烯涂布,包覆或层压漂染,印花织物≥50%)	10	70	17	16	千克/米		Imitation leather of cotton, impregnated, coated, covered or laminated with poly (vinyl chloride), containing≥50% by weight of cotton, bleached, dyed or printed

税则号列	货品名称	最惠(%)	普通	增值税率	出口退税	计量单位	监管条件	Article Description
5903.1020 90	用聚氯乙烯浸渍的其他人造革(包括用聚氯乙烯涂布、包覆或层压的)	10	70	17	16	千克/米		Other imitation leather, impregnated, coated, covered or laminated with poly (vinyl chloride)
5903.1090	---其他	10	90	17	16	千克		---Other
5903.1090 10	若干层平行纱线粘合化纤其他织物(聚氯乙烯浸渍涂布、包覆层压,塑料重≤60%)	10	90	17	16	千克		Other textile fabrics of man-made fibres, impregnated, coated, covered or laminated with poly (vinyl chloride), of fabrics consisting of layers of parallel textile yarns, bonded, containing≤60% by weight of plastics
5903.1090 21	聚氯乙烯浸渍的其他涤棉混纺织物(聚氯乙烯涂布漂印染,聚酯短纤棉混纺,塑或胶<50%)	10	90	17	16	千克		Other textile fabrics of mixed with polyester staple fibres and cotton, impregnated, coated, covered or laminated with poly (vinyl chloride), containing <50% by weight of plastics or glue
5903.1090 29	聚氯乙烯浸渍的其他化纤织物(包括用聚氯乙烯涂布包覆、层压,塑或胶≤70%)	10	90	17	16	千克		Other textile fabrics of man-made fibres, impregnated, coated, covered or laminated with poly (vinyl chloride), containing≤70% by weight of plastics or glue
5903.1090 30	聚氯乙烯浸渍的棉织物(聚氯乙烯涂布包覆层压、漂染、印花织物≥50%)	10	90	17	16	千克		Other textile fabrics of cotton, impregnated, coated, covered or laminated with poly (vinyl chloride), containing ≥ 50% by weight of fabrics of cotton, bleached, dyed or printed
5903.1090 40	用聚氯乙烯浸渍的精梳毛织物(聚氯乙烯涂布、包覆或层压,精梳羊毛或动物细毛≥50%)	10	90	17	16	千克		Other woollen textile fabrics, impregnated, coated, covered or laminated with poly (vinyl chloride), containing≥50% by weight of combed wool or fine animal hair
5903.1090 90	聚氯乙烯浸渍的其他纺织物(包括用聚氯乙烯涂布,包覆或层压的)	10	90	17	16	千克		Other textile fabrics, impregnated, coated, covered or laminated with poly (vinyl chloride)
	-用聚氨基甲酸酯浸渍、涂布、包覆或层压的:							-With polyurethane:
5903.2010	---绝缘布或带	10	40	17	16	千克		---Insulating cloth or tape
5903.2010 10	若干平行纱线粘合化纤绝缘布或带(聚氨基甲酸酯浸渍、涂布、包覆或层压,塑料≤60%)	10	40	17	16	千克		Insulating cloth or tape of man-made fibres, impregnated, coated, covered or laminated with polyurethane of fabrics consisting of layers of parallel textile yarns, bonded, containing ≤ 60% by weight of plastics
5903.2010 20	聚氨基甲酸酯浸渍涤棉绝缘布或带(聚氨基甲酸酯浸涂漂染,聚酯短纤棉混纺,塑或胶<50%)	10	40	17	16	千克		Insulating cloth or tape of mixed with polyester staple fibres and cotton, impregnated, coated, covered or laminated with polyurethane, containing <50% by weight of plastics or glue
5903.2010 30	聚氨基甲酸酯浸渍其他化纤绝缘布(包括用聚氨基甲酸酯涂布,包覆、层压,塑或胶≤70%)	10	40	17	16	千克		Other insulating cloth or tape of man-made fibres, impregnated, coated, covered or laminated with polyurethane containing≤70% by weight of plastics or glue
5903.2010 90	聚氨基甲酸酯浸渍其他绝缘布或带(包括用聚氨基甲酸酯涂布,包覆或层压的)	10	40	17	16	千克		Other insulating cloth or tape, impregnated, coated, covered or laminated with polyurethane
5903.2020	---人造革	10	70	17	16	千克/米		---Imitation leather
5903.2020 10	若干层平行纱线粘合化纤人造革(聚氨基甲酸酯浸渍、涂布,包覆、层压,塑料≤60%)	10	70	17	16	千克/米		Imitation leather of man-made fibres, impregnated, coated, covered or laminated with polyurethane, of fabrics consisting of layers of parallel textile yarns, bonded, containing≤60% by weight of plastics
5903.2020 20	用聚氨基甲酸酯浸渍的涤棉人造革(聚氨基甲酸酯涂布漂染,聚酯短纤棉混纺,塑或胶<50%)	10	70	17	16	千克/米		Imitation leather of mixed with polyester staple fibres and cotton, impregnated, coated, covered or laminated with polyurethane, containing <50% by weight of plastics or glue
5903.2020 30	聚氨基甲酸酯浸渍其他化纤人造革(包括用聚氨基甲酸酯涂布,包覆,层压,塑或胶≤70%)	10	70	17	16	千克/米		Imitation leather of man-made fibres, impregnated, coated, covered or laminated with polyurethane, other, containing≤70% by weight of plastics or glue

税则号列	货品名称	最惠(%)	普通	增值税率	出口退税	计量单位	监管条件	Article Description
5903.2020 40	聚氨基甲酸酯浸渍的棉织物人造革(聚氨基甲酸酯涂布,包覆、层压,漂染印织物≥50%)	10	70	17	16	千克/米		Imitation leather of cotton, impregnated, coated, covered or laminated with polyurethane, containing ≥50% by weight of fabrics of cotton, bleached dyed or printed
5903.2020 90	用聚氨基甲酸酯浸渍的其他人造革(包括用聚氨基甲酸酯涂布,包覆或层压的)	10	70	17	16	千克/米		Other imitation leather, impregnated, coated, covered or laminated with polyurethane
5903.2090	---其他	10	90	17	16	千克		---Other
5903.2090 10	若干层平行纱线粘合化纤其他织物(聚氨基甲酸酯浸渍涂布,包覆层压,塑料≤60%)	10	90	17	16	千克		Other textile fabrics of man-made fibres, impregnated, coated, covered or laminated with polyurethane, of fabrics consisting of layers of parallel textile yarns, bonded, containing≤60% by weight of plastics
5903.2090 21	聚氨基甲酸酯浸渍其他涤棉织物(聚氨基甲酸酯涂布漂染聚酯短纤棉混纺,塑或胶<50%)	10	90	17	16	千克		Other textile fabrics of mixed with polyester staple fibres and cotton, impregnated, coated, covered or laminated with polyurethane, containing < 50% by weight of plastics or glue
5903.2090 29	聚氨基甲酸酯浸渍其他化纤织物(含聚氨基甲酸酯涂布,包覆或层压,塑或胶≤70%)	10	90	17	16	千克		Other textile fabrics of man-made fibres, impregnated, coated, covered or laminated with polyurethane, containing≤70% by weight of plastics or glue
5903.2090 30	用聚氨基甲酸酯浸渍的棉织物(聚氨基甲酸酯涂布、包覆、层压,漂染印织物≥50%)	10	90	17	16	千克		Other textile fabrics of cotton, impregnated, coated, covered or laminated with polyurethane, containing ≥50% by weight of fabrics of cotton, bleached dyed printed
5903.2090 41	用聚氨基甲酸酯浸渍的精梳毛织物(聚氨基甲酸酯涂布包覆层压,精梳羊毛或动物细毛≥50%)	10	90	17	16	千克		Other woollen textile fabrics, impregnated, coated, covered or laminated with polyurethane, containing ≥50% by weight of combed wool or fine animal hair
5903.2090 49	用聚氨基甲酸酯浸渍的其他毛织物(聚氨基甲酸酯涂布包覆或层压,精梳毛织物除外)	10	90	17	16	千克		Other woollen textile fabrics, impregnated, coated, covered or laminated with polyurethane, other than woven fabrics of combed wool or fine animal hair
5903.2090 90	用聚氨基甲酸酯浸渍的其他纺织物(包括用聚氨基甲酸酯涂布,包覆或层压的)	10	90	17	16	千克		Other textile fabrics impregnated, coated, covered or laminated with polyurethane
	-其他:							-Other:
5903.9010	---绝缘布或带	10	40	17	16	千克		---Insulating cloth or tape
5903.9010 10	若干平行化纤纱线粘合绝缘布或带(其他塑料浸渍、涂布,包覆或层压、塑料重≤60%)	10	40	17	16	千克		Insulating cloth or tape, impregnated, coated, covered or laminated with plastics, of fabrics consisting of layers of parallel textile yarns, bonded, containing ≤60% by weight of plastics
5903.9010 20	其他塑料浸渍涤棉混纺绝缘布或带(塑料浸涂包的漂染聚酯短纤棉混纺,塑料橡胶<50%)	10	40	17	16	千克		Insulating cloth or tape of mixed with polyester staple fibres and cotton, impregnated, coated, covered or laminated with plastics, containing < 50% by weight of plastics or glue
5903.9010 30	其他塑料浸渍其他化纤绝缘布或带(包括用其他塑料涂布、包覆或层压,塑料或橡胶≤70%)	10	40	17	16	千克		Insulating cloth or tape, impregnated, coated, covered or laminated with plastics, other, containing ≤70% by weight of plastics or glue
5903.9010 90	用其他塑料浸渍的其他绝缘布或带(包括用其他塑料涂布、包覆或层压的)	10	40	17	16	千克		Other insulating cloth or tape, impregnated, coated, covered or laminated with plastics
5903.9020	---人造革	10	70	17	16	千克/米		---Imitation leather
5903.9020 10	由若干层平行纱线粘合化纤人造革(用其他塑料涂布、包覆或层压,塑料重≤60%)	10	70	17	16	千克/米		Imitation leather of man-made fibres, impregnated, coated, covered or laminated, with plastics of fabrics consisting of layers of parallel textile yarns, bonded, containing≤60% by weight of plastics
5903.9020 20	用其他塑料浸渍的涤棉织物人造革(其他塑料涂布、包覆、漂染,印花聚酯短纤棉混纺,塑料或橡胶<50%)	10	70	17	16	千克/米		Imitation leather of mixed with polyester staple fibres and cotton, impregnated, coated, covered or laminated with plastics, containing<50% by weight of plastics or glue

税则号列	货品名称	最惠(%)	普通	增值税率	出口退税	计量单位	监管条件	Article Description
5903.9020 30	用其他塑料浸渍的其他化纤人造革(包括用其他塑料涂布,包覆的,塑料或橡胶≤70%)	10	70	17	16	千克/米		Imitation leather of man-made fibres, impregnated, coated, covered or laminated with other plastics, containing≤70% by weight of plastics or glue
5903.9020 40	用其他塑料浸渍的棉织物人造革(用其他塑料涂布,包覆或层压,漂染印花织物≥50%)	10	70	17	16	千克/米		Imitation leather of cotton, impregnated, coated, covered or laminated with plastics, containing≥50% by weight of fabrics of cotton, bleached, dyed or printed
5903.9020 90	用其他塑料浸渍的其他人造革(包括用其他塑料涂布,包覆或层压的)	10	70	17	16	千克/米		Mmitation leather, impregnated, coated, covered or laminated with other plastics
5903.9090	---其他	10	90	17	16	千克		---Other
5903.9090 10	若干层化纤平行纱线粘合其他织物(用其他塑料浸渍涂布、包覆或层压.塑料重≤60%)	10	90	17	16	千克		Other textile fabrics, impregnated, coated, covered or laminated with plastics, of fabrics consisting of layers of parallel textile yarns, bonded, containing ≤ 60% by weight of plastics
5903.9090 21	其他塑料浸渍的其他涤棉混纺织物(其他塑料涂布、漂印染花,聚酯短纤棉混纺,塑料或橡胶<50%)	10	90	17	16	千克		Other textile fabrics of mixed with polyester staple fibres and cotton, impregnated, coated, covered or laminated with plastics, containing < 50% by weight of plastics or glue
5903.9090 29	用其他塑料浸渍的其他化纤织物(包括用其他塑料涂布、包覆或层压的,塑料或橡胶≤70%)	10	90	17	16	千克		Other textile fabrics of man-made fibres, impregnated, coated, covered or laminated with other plastics, containing≤70% by weight of plastics or glue
5903.9090 30	用其他塑料浸渍的棉织物(用其他塑料涂布、包覆或层压的,漂染印花织物≥50%)	10	90	17	16	千克		Other textile fabrics, of cotton, impregnated, coated, covered or laminated with other plastics, containing ≥50% by weight of fabrics of cotton, bleached, dyed or printed
5903.9090 41	用其他塑料浸渍的精梳毛织物(用其他塑料涂布、包覆或层压的,精梳羊毛或动物细毛≥50%)	10	90	17	16	千克		Other woollen textile fabrics, impregnated, coated, covered or laminated with plastics, containing≥50% by weight of combed wool or fine animal hair
5903.9090 49	用其他塑料浸渍的其他毛织物(用其他塑料涂布、包覆或层压的,精梳毛织物除外)	10	90	17	16	千克		Other woollen textile fabrics, impregnated, coated, covered or laminated with plastics, other than woven fabric of combed wool or fine animal hair
5903.9090 90	用其他塑料浸渍的其他纺织物(包括用其他塑料涂布,包覆或层压的)	10	90	17	16	千克		Other textile fabrics, impregnated, coated, covered or laminated with other plastics
59.04	**列诺伦(亚麻油地毡),不论是否剪切成形;以织物为底布经涂布或覆面的铺地制品,不论是否剪切成形:**							**Linoleum, whether or not cut to shape; floor coverings consisting of a coating or covering applied on a textile backing, whether or not cut to shape:**
5904.1000	-列诺伦(亚麻油地毡)	14	90	17	16	千克/平方米		-Linoleum
5904.9000	-其他	14	90	17	16	千克/平方米		-Other
59.05	**糊墙织物:**							**Textile wall coverings:**
5905.0000	糊墙织物	10	80	17	16	千克/平方米		Textile wall coverings
5905.0000 11	以纸衬背的合成短纤制糊墙织物	10	80	17	16	千克/平方米		Textile wall coverings of synthetic staple fibres, fixed on backing of paper
5905.0000 19	以纸衬背的人造短纤制糊墙织物	10	80	17	16	千克/平方米		Textile wall coverings of artificial staple fibres, fixed on backing of paper
5905.0000 20	平行纱线固定的糊墙织物(固定在任何其他衬背上的)	10	80	17	16	千克/平方米		Textile wall coverings of fabrics consisting of layers of parallel textile yarns, fixed on backing
5905.0000 31	其他合成短纤制糊墙织物	10	80	17	16	千克/平方米		Other textile wall coverings of other synthetic fibres
5905.0000 39	其他人造短纤制糊墙织物	10	80	17	16	千克/平方米		Other textile wall coverings of other artificial fibres
5905.0000 90	其他纺织糊墙织物	10	80	17	16	千克/平方米		Other textile wall coverings of other fabrics
59.06	**用橡胶处理的纺织物,但税目59.02的货品除外:**							**Rubberized textile fabrics, other than those of heading No. 59.02:**
	-宽度不超过20厘米的胶粘带:							-Adhesive tape of a width not exceeding 20 cm:
5906.1010	---绝缘带	10	40	17	16	千克		---Insulating tape
5906.1090	---其他	10	100	17	16	千克		---Other
	-其他:							-Other:
5906.9100	--针织或钩编的	10	130	17	16	千克		--Knitted or crocheted

税则号列	货品名称	最惠(%)	普通	增值税率	出口退税	计量单位	监管条件	Article Description
5906.9100 10	用橡胶处理的针织或钩编化纤纺织物(按重量计塑料或橡胶不超过70%,宽>20cm)	10	130	17	16	千克		Rubberized textile fabrics, knitted or crocheted, width>20cm, containing≤70% by weight of plastics or rubber
5906.9100 90	用橡胶处理的针织或钩编其他纺织物(宽>20cm)	10	130	17	16	千克		Other rubberized textile fabrics, knitted or crocheted, width>20cm
	--其他:							--Other:
5906.9910	---绝缘布或带	10	40	17	16	千克		---Insulating cloth or tape
5906.9910 10	用橡胶处理的精梳毛纺绝缘布或带(非针织或钩编、精梳羊毛或动物细毛≥50%,宽>20cm)	10	40	17	16	千克		Rubberized woollen insulating cloth or tape, containing≥50% by weight of combed wool or fine animal hair, width>20cm, other than knitted or crocheted
5906.9910 20	用橡胶处理的棉织物绝缘布或带(非针织或钩编,漂染印花棉织物≥50%,宽>20cm)	10	40	17	16	千克		Rubberized insulating cloth or tape of cotton, containing ≥50% by weight of cotton, bleached, dyed or printed, width>20cm, other than knitted or crocheted
5906.9910 31	用橡胶处理聚酯短纤棉混纺绝缘布带(非针织或钩编,漂染印花混纺布≥50%,宽>20cm)	10	40	17	16	千克		Rubberized insulating cloth or tape, mixed, containing≥50% by weight of polyester staple fibres and cotton, width>20cm, other than knitted or crocheted
5906.9910 39	用橡胶处理的其他化纤绝缘布或带(非针织或钩编,宽>20cm,塑料或橡胶≤70%)	10	40	17	16	千克		Rubberized insulating cloth or tape of other man-made fibres, containing≤70% by weight of plastics or glue, width>20cm, other than knitted or crocheted
5906.9910 90	用橡胶处理宽>20cm 的其他绝缘布或带(非针织或钩编的,宽>20cm)	10	40	17	16	千克		Other rubberized insulating cloth or tape, width>20cm, other than knitted or crocheted
5906.9990	---其他	10	100	17	16	千克		---Other
5906.9990 10	用橡胶处理的精梳毛纺织物(精梳羊毛或动物细毛≥50%,非针织或钩编的,宽>20cm)	10	100	17	16	千克		Rubberized woollen textile fabrics, containing≥50% by weight of combed wool or fine animal hair, width>20cm, other than knitted or crochet-ed
5906.9990 20	用橡胶处理的其他棉纺织物(非针织或钩编,宽>20cm,漂染印花棉织物≥50%)	10	100	17	16	千克		Rubberized textile fabrics of cotton, containing ≥50% by weight of cotton, bleached, dyed or printed, width>20cm, other than knitted or crochet-ed
5906.9990 31	用橡胶处理的聚酯短纤棉混纺织物(非针织或钩编,宽>20cm,漂染印花聚酯混纺布≥50%)	10	100	17	16	千克		Rubberized textile fabrics mixed, containing≥50% by weight of polyester staple fibres and cotton, bleached, dyed or printed, width>20cm, other than knitted or crocheted
5906.9990 39	用橡胶处理的其他化纤纺织物(非针织或钩编,宽>20cm,塑料或橡胶≤70%)	10	100	17	16	千克		Rubberized textile fabrics of other man-made fibres, containing≤70% by weight of plastics or glue, width>20cm, other than knitted or crocheted
5906.9990 90	用橡胶处理的其他纺织物(非针织或钩编,宽>20cm)	10	100	17	16	千克		Other rubberized textile fabrics, width>20cm, other than knitted or crocheted
59.07	用其他材料浸渍、涂布或包覆的纺织物;作舞台、摄影布景或类似用途的已绘制画布:							**Textile fabrics otherwise impregnated, coated or covered; painted canvas being theatrical scenery, studio back-cloths or the like:**
5907.0010	---绝缘布或带	10	40	17	16	千克		---Insulating cloth or tape
5907.0010 10	其他材料浸渍涂布植物纤维绝缘布或带(用橡胶,塑料,浆料以外材料浸渍涂布或包覆,棉除外)	10	40	17	16	千克		Insulating cloth or tape of vegetable fibres (other than cotton), impregnated, coated or covered with materials other than rubber, plastic, gum or amylaceous substances
5907.0010 20	其他材料浸涂的棉制绝缘布或带(用橡胶,塑料,浆料以外材料浸涂或包覆,漂染棉织物≥50%)	10	40	17	16	千克		Insulating cloth or tape of cotton, containing≥50% by weight of fabrics of cotton, bleached, dyed or printed, impregnated, coated or covered with materials other than rubber, plastic, gum or amylaceous substances
5907.0010 30	其他材料浸涂涤短纤棉混纺绝缘布(用橡胶,塑料,浆料以外材料浸涂或包覆,漂染涤棉织物≥50%)	10	40	17	16	千克		Insulating cloth or tape, mixed, containing≥50% by weight of fabrics of polyester staple fibres and cotton, bleached, dyed or printed, impregnated, coated or covered with materials other than rubber, plastic, gum or amylaceous substances

税则号列	货品名称	最惠(%)	普通	增值税率	出口退税	计量单位	监管条件	Article Description
5907.0010 90	其他材料浸涂其他纺织绝缘布或带(用橡胶,塑料,浆料以外材料浸渍,涂布或包覆)	10	40	17	16	千克		Insulating cloth or tape, impregnated, coated or covered with materials other than rubber, plastic, gum or amylaceous substances
5907.0020	---已绘制画布	10	50	17	16	千克		---Painted canvas
5907.0020 10	其他材料浸涂植物纤维已绘制画布(用橡胶,塑料,浆料以外材料浸渍,涂布或包覆,棉除外)	10	50	17	16	千克		Painted canvas of vegetable fibres (other than cotton), impregnated, coated or covered with materials other than rubber, plastic, gum or amylaceous substances
5907.0020 20	其他材料浸涂精梳毛已绘制画布(用橡胶、塑料、浆料以外材料浸涂或包覆,精梳羊/动物细毛≥50%)	10	50	17	16	千克		Painted woollen canvas, containing≥50% by weight of combed wool or combed fine animal hair, impregnated, coated or covered with materials other than rubber, plastic, gum or amylaceous substances
5907.0020 30	用其他材料浸涂的棉制已绘制画布(用橡胶、塑料、浆料以外材料浸涂或包覆,漂染棉织物≥50%)	10	50	17	16	千克		Painted canvas of cotton, containing ≥ 50% by weight of fabrics of cotton, bleached, dyed or printed, impregnated, coated or covered with materials other than rubber, plastic, gum or amylaceous substances
5907.0020 40	其他材料浸涂涤短纤棉混已绘画布(用橡胶、塑料、浆料以外材料浸涂或包覆,漂染涤短棉织物≥50%)	10	50	17	16	千克		Painted canvas mixed, containing≥50% by weight of fabrics of polyester staple fibres and cotton, bleached, dyed or printed, impregnated, coated or covered with materials other than rubber, plastic, gum or amylaceous substances
5907.0020 90	其他材料浸涂其他织物已绘制画布(用橡胶、塑料、浆料以外材料浸渍,涂布或包覆)	10	50	17	16	千克		Painted canvas, impregnated, coated or covered with materials other than rubber, plastic, gum or amylaceous substances
5907.0090	---其他	10	100	17	16	千克		---Other
5907.0090 10	用其他材料浸涂的植物纤维纺织物(用橡胶、塑料、浆料以外材料浸渍,涂布或包覆,棉除外)	10	100	17	16	千克		Textile fabrics of vegetable fibres (other than cotton) impregnated, coated or covered with materials other than rubber, plastic, gum or amylaceous substances
5907.0090 20	用其他材料浸涂的精梳毛纺织物(用橡胶、塑料、浆料以外材料浸涂或包覆,精梳羊/动物细毛≥50%)	10	100	17	16	千克		Woollen textile fabrics, containing≥50% by weight of combed wool or combed fine animal hair impregnated, coated or covered with materials other than rubber, plastic, gum or amylaceous substances
5907.0090 30	用其他材料浸涂的棉制纺织物(用橡胶、塑料、浆料以外材料浸涂或包覆,漂染棉织物≥50%)	10	100	17	16	千克		Textile fabrics of cotton, containing≥50% by weight of fabrics of cotton, bleached, dyed or printed, impregnated, coated or covered with materials other than rubber, plastic, gum or amylaceous substances
5907.0090 40	用其他材料浸涂的涤短纤棉混纺织物(用橡胶、塑料、浆料以外材料浸涂或包覆,漂染涤棉织物≥50%)	10	100	17	16	千克		Textile fabrics, mixed, containing≥50% by weight of fabrics of polyester staple fibres and cotton impregnated, coated or covered with materials other than rubber, plastic, gum or amylaceous substances
5907.0090 90	用其他材料浸涂的其他纺织物(用橡胶、塑料、浆料以外材料浸渍,涂布或包覆)	10	100	17	16	千克		Other textile fabrics, impregnated, coated or covered with materials other than rubber, plastic, gum or amylaceous substances
59.08	**用纺织材料机织、编结或针织而成的灯芯、炉芯、打火机芯、烛芯或类似品;煤气灯纱筒及纱罩,不论是否浸渍:**							**Textile wicks, woven, plaited or knitted, for lamps, stoves, lighters, candles or the like; incandescent gas mantles and tubular knitted gas mantle fabric therefor, whether or not impregnated:**
5908.0000	用纺织材料机织、编结或针织而成的灯芯、炉芯、打火机芯、烛芯或类似品;煤气灯纱筒及纱罩,不论是否浸渍	10	70	17	16	千克		Textile wicks, woven, plaited or knitted, for lamps, stoves, lighters, candles or the like; incandescent gas mantles and tubular knitted gas mantle fabric therefor, whether or not impregnated
59.09	**纺织材料制的水龙软管及类似的管子,不论有无其他材料作衬里、护套或附件:**							**Textile hosepiping and similar textile tubing, with or without lining, armour or accessories of other materials:**

税则号列	货品名称	最惠(%)	普通	增值税率	出口退税	计量单位	监管条件	Article Description
5909.0000	纺织材料制的水龙软管及类似的管子,不论有无其他材料作衬里、护套或附件	8	35	17	16	千克		Textile hosepiping and similar textile tubing, with or without lining, armour or accessories of other materials
59.10	**纺织材料制的传动带或输送带及带料,不论是否用塑料浸渍、涂布、包覆或压层,也不论是否用金属或其他材料加强:**							**Transmission or conveyor belts or belting, of textile material, whether or not impregnated, coated, covered or laminated with plastics, or reinforced with metal or other material:**
5910.0000	纺织材料制的传动带或输送带及带料,不论是否用塑料浸渍、涂布、包覆或压层,也不论是否用金属或其他材料加强	8	35	17	16	千克		Transmission or conveyor belts or belting, of textile material, whether or not impregnated, coated, covered or laminated with plastics, or reinforced with metal or other material
59.11	**本章注释七所规定的作专门技术用途的纺织产品及制品:**							**Textile products and articles, for technical uses, specified in Note 7 to this Chapter:**
	-用橡胶、皮革或其他材料涂布、包覆或层压的作针布用的纺织物、毡呢及毡呢衬里机织物,以及作专门技术用途的类似织物,包括用橡胶浸渍的、用于包覆纺锤(织轴)的狭幅丝绒织物:							-Textile fabrics, felt and felt-lined woven fabrics, coated, covered or laminated with rubber, leather or other material, of a kind used for card clothing, and similar fabrics of a kind used for other technical purposes, including narrow fabrics made of velvet impregnated with rubber, for covering weaving spindles (weaving beams):
5911.1010	---用橡胶浸渍的、用于包覆纺锤(织轴)的狭幅丝绒织物	8	75	17	16	千克		---Narrow fabrics made of velvet impregnated with rubber, for covering weaving spindles (weaving beams)
5911.1090	---其他	8	35	17	16	千克		---Other
5911.2000	-筛布,不论是否制成的	8	35	17	16	千克		-Bolting cloth, whether or not made up
5911.2000 10	丝制筛布(不论是否制成的)	8	35	17	16	千克		Bolting cloth of silk, whether or not made up
5911.2000 90	其他纺织材料制筛布(不论是否制成的,刻版筛网印布除外)	8	35	17	16	千克		Bolting cloth of other textile materials, whether or not made up, other than stencil screen
	-环状或装有联接装置的纺织物及毡呢,用于造纸机器或类似机器(例如,制浆机或制石棉水泥的机器):							-Textile fabrics and felts, endless or fitted with linking devices, of a kind used in paper-making or similar machines (for example, for pulp or asbestos-cement):
5911.3100	--每平方米重量在650克以下	8	35	17	16	千克		--Weighing less than 650 g/m^2
5911.3200	--每平方米重量在650克及以上	8	35	17	16	千克		--Weighing 650 g/m^2 or more
5911.4000	-用于榨油机器或类似机器的滤布,包括人发制滤布	8	35	17	16	千克		-Straining cloth of a kind used in oil presses or the like, including that of human hair
5911.9000	-其他	8	35	17	16	千克		-Other

第六十章
针织物及钩编织物

Chapter 60
Knitted or crocheted fabrics

注释：

一、本章不包括：

（一）税目58.04的钩编花边；

（二）税目58.07的针织或钩编的标签、徽章及类似品；或

（三）第五十九章的经浸渍、涂布、包覆或层压的针织物及钩编织物。但经浸渍、涂布、包覆或层压的起绒针织物及起绒钩编织物仍归入税目60.01。

二、本章还包括用金属线制的用于衣着、装饰或类似用途的织物。

三、本协调制度所称"针织物"，包括由纺织纱线用链式针法构成的缝编织物。

Notes:

1. This Chapter does not cover:

(a) Crochet lace of heading No. 58.04;

(b) Labels, badges or similar articles, knitted or crocheted, of heading No. 58.07; or

(c) Knitted or crocheted fabrics, impregnated, coated, covered or laminated, of Chapter 59. However, knitted or crocheted pile fabrics, impregnated, coated, covered or laminated, remain classified in heading No. 60.01.

2. This Chapter also includes fabrics made of metal thread and of a kind used in apparel, as furnishing fabrics or for similar purposes.

3. Throughout the Nomenclature any reference to "knitted" goods includes a reference to stitch-bonded goods in which the chain stitches are formed of textile yarn.

税则号列	货品名称	最惠(%)	普通	增值税率	出口退税	计量单位	监管条件	Article Description
60.01	**针织或钩编的起绒织物，包括"长毛绒"织物及毛圈织物：**							**Pile fabrics, including "long pile" fabrics and terry fabrics, knitted or crocheted:**
6001.1000	-"长毛绒"织物	10	130	17	16	米/千克		-"Long pile" fabrics
6001.1000 10	毛制针织或钩编的长毛绒织物（羊毛及动物细毛制）	10	130	17	16	米/千克		"Long pile" fabrics, knitted or crocheted, of wool and fine animal hair
6001.1000 20	棉制针织或钩编的长毛绒织物	10	130	17	16	米/千克		"Long pile" fabrics, knitted or crocheted, of cotton
6001.1000 30	化纤制针织或钩编的长毛绒织物	10	130	17	16	米/千克		"Long pile" fabrics, knitted or crocheted, of man-made fibres
6001.1000 90	其他纺织材料制针织或钩编长毛绒织物	10	130	17	16	米/千克		Other "long pile" fabrics, knitted or crocheted, of other textile materials
	-毛圈绒头织物：							-Looped pile fabrics:
6001.2100	--棉制	10	70	17	16	米/千克		--Of cotton
6001.2200	--化学纤维制	10	130	17	16	米/千克		--Of man-made fibres
6001.2900	--其他纺织材料制	12	130	17	16	米/千克		--Of other textile materials
6001.2900 10	毛制针织或钩编毛圈绒头织物（羊毛及动物细毛制）	12	130	17	16	米/千克		Looped pile fabrics, knitted or crocheted, of wool and fine animal hair
6001.2900 90	其他材料制针织或钩编毛圈绒头布	12	130	17	16	米/千克		Looped pile fabrics, knitted or crocheted, of other textile materials
	-其他：							-Other:
6001.9100	--棉制	10	70	17	16	米/千克		--Of cotton
6001.9200	--化学纤维制	10	130	17	16	米/千克		--Of man-made fibres
6001.9900	--其他纺织材料制	12	130	17	16	米/千克		--Of other textile materials
6001.9900 10	丝制针织或钩编其他起绒织物（按重量计含丝及绢丝85%及以上）	12	130	17	16	米/千克		Other pile fabrics, knitted or crocheted, containing ≥85% by weight of silk or spun silk
6001.9900 20	毛制针织或钩编其他起绒织物（羊毛及动物细毛制）	12	130	17	16	米/千克		Other pile fabrics, knitted or crocheted, of wool and fine animal hair
6001.9900 90	其他纺织材料制针织或钩编起绒织物	12	130	17	16	米/千克		Pile fabrics, knitted or crocheted, of other textile materials
60.02	**宽度不超过30厘米，按重量计弹性纱线或橡胶线含量在5%及以上的针织物或钩编织物，但税目60.01的货品除外：**							**Knitted or crocheted fabrics of a width not exceeding 30 cm, containing by weight 5% or more of elastomeric yarn or rubber thread, other than those of heading No. 60.01:**
	-按重量计弹性纱线含量在5%及以上，但不含橡胶线：							-Containing by weight 5% or more of elastomeric yarn but not containing rubber thread:
6002.4010	---棉制	10	70	17	16	米/千克		---Of cotton
6002.4020	---丝及绢丝制	10	130	17	16	米/千克		---Of silk or spun silk
6002.4030	---合成纤维制	10	130	17	16	米/千克		---Of synthetic fibres
6002.4040	---人造纤维制	10	130	17	16	米/千克		---Of artificial fibres

税则号列	货品名称	最惠(%)	普通	增值税率	出口退税	计量单位	监管条件	Article Description
6002.4090	---其他	10	130	17	16	米/千克		---Other
	-其他:							-Other:
6002.9010	---棉制	10	70	17	16	米/千克		---Of cotton
6002.9020	---丝及绢丝制	10	130	17	16	米/千克		---Of silk or spun silk
6002.9030	---合成纤维制	10	130	17	16	米/千克		---Of synthetic fibres
6002.9040	---人造纤维制	10	130	17	16	米/千克		---Of artificial fibres
6002.9090	---其他	10	130	17	16	米/千克		---Other
60.03	**宽度不超过30厘米的针织或钩编织物,但税目60.01或60.02的货品除外:**							**Knitted or crocheted fabrics of a width not exceeding 30 cm, other than those of heading No. 60.01 or 60.02:**
6003.1000	-羊毛或动物细毛制	10	130	17	16	米/千克		-Of wool or fine animal hair
6003.2000	-棉制	10	70	17	16	米/千克		-Of cotton
6003.2000 10	棉制宽≤30cm经编织物(按重量计弹性纱线或橡胶线含量<5%)	10	70	17	16	米/千克		Warp knit fabric of cotton, width≥30cm(containing by weight < 5% of elastomeric yarn or rubber thread)
6003.2000 90	棉制宽≤30cm非经编针织或钩编织物(按重量计弹性纱线或橡胶线含量<5%)	10	70	17	16	米/千克		Not warp knit or crochete fabrics, of cotton, width ≤ 30cm, containing by weight < 5% of elastomeric yarn or rubber thread
6003.3000	-合成纤维制	10	130	17	16	米/千克		-Of synthetic fibres
6003.3000 10	合纤制宽小于等于30厘米经编织物(按重量计弹性纱线或橡胶线含量<5%)	10	130	17	16	米/千克		Warp knit fabric of synthetic fiber, width≥30cm (containing by weight < 5% of elastomeric yarn or rubber thread)
6003.3000 90	合纤制宽小于等于30厘米非经编针织或钩编织物(按重量计弹性纱线或橡胶线含量<5%)	10	130	17	16	米/千克		Not warp knit or knitted or crochetedfabrics of synthetic fiber, width≥30cm(containing by weight < 5% of elastomeric yarn or rubber thread)
6003.4000	-人造纤维制	10	130	17	16	米/千克		-Of artificial fibres
6003.4000 10	人纤制宽小于等于30厘米经编织物(按重量计弹性纱线或橡胶线含量<5%)	10	130	17	16	米/千克		Warp knit fabrics of artificial fibrics, width ≤30cm (containing by weight < 5% of elastomeric yarn or rubber thread)
6003.4000 90	人纤制宽小于等于30厘米非经编织物(按重量计弹性纱线或橡胶线含量<5%)	10	130	17	16	米/千克		Not warp knit fabrics of artifical fibres, width ≤ 30cm(containing by weight < 5% of elastomeric yarn or rubber thread)
6003.9000	-其他	10	130	17	16	米/千克		-Other
60.04	**宽度超过30厘米,按重量计弹性纱线或橡胶线含量在5%及以上的针织物或钩编织物,但税目60.01的货品除外:**							**Knitted or crocheted fabrics of a width exceeding 30 cm, containing by weight 5% or more of elastomeric yarn or rubber thread, other than those of heading No. 60.01:**
	-按重量计弹性纱线含量在5%及以上,但不含橡胶线							-Containing by weight 5% or more of elastomeric yarn but not containing rubber thread:
6004.1010	---棉制	10	70	17	16	米/千克		---Of cotton
6004.1020	---丝及绢丝制	10	130	17	16	米/千克		---Of silk or spun silk
6004.1030	---合成纤维制	10	130	17	16	米/千克		---Of synthetic fibres
6004.1040	---人造纤维制	10	130	17	16	米/千克		---Of artificial fibres
6004.1090	---其他	10	130	17	16	米/千克		---Other
	-其他:							-Other:
6004.9010	---棉制	10	70	17	16	米/千克		---Of cotton
6004.9020	---丝及绢丝制	10	130	17	16	米/千克		---Of silk or spun silk
6004.9030	---合成纤维制	10	130	17	16	米/千克		---Of synthetic fibres
6004.9040	---人造纤维制	10	130	17	16	米/千克		---Of artificial fibres
6004.9090	---其他	10	130	17	16	米/千克		---Other
60.05	**经编织物(包括由花边针织机织成的),但税目60.01至60.04的货品除外:**							**Warp knit fabrics (including those made on galloon knitting machines), other than those of headings Nos. 60.01 to 60.04:**
	-棉制:							-Of cotton:
6005.2100	--未漂白或漂白	10	70	17	16	米/千克		--Unbleached or bleached
6005.2200	--染色	10	70	17	16	米/千克		--Dyed

税则号列	货　品　名　称	最惠(%)	普通	增值税率	出口退税	计量单位	监管条件	Article Description
6005.2300	--色织	10	70	17	16	米/千克		--Of yarns of different colours
6005.2400	--印花	10	70	17	16	米/千克		--Printed
	-合成纤维制：							-Of synthetic fibres:
6005.3100	--未漂白或漂白	10	130	17	16	米/千克		--Unbleached or bleached
6005.3100 10	漂白或未漂白合成纤维制经编透孔织物(包括由花边针织机织成的经编织物)	10	130	17	16	米/千克		Warp knit openwork fabrics of synthetic fibers, bleached or unbleached (includng those made on gallon knitting machines)
6005.3100 90	漂白或未漂白合成纤维制经编非透孔织物(包括由花边针织机织成的经编织物)	10	130	17	16	米/千克		Warp knit not openwork fabrics of synthetic fibers, bleached or unbleached (includng those made on gallon knitting machines)
6005.3200	--染色	10	130	17	16	米/千克		--Dyed
6005.3200 10	染色合成纤维制经编透孔织物(包括由花边针织机织成的经编织物)	10	130	17	16	米/千克		Warp knit openwork fabrics of synthetic fibers, dyed (includng those made on gallon knitting machines)
6005.3200 90	染色合成纤维制经编非透孔织物(包括由花边针织机织成的经编织物)	10	130	17	16	米/千克		Warp knit not openwork fabrics of synthetic fibers, dyed (includng those made on gallon knitting machines)
6005.3300	--色织	10	130	17	16	米/千克		--Of yarns of different colours
6005.3300 10	色织合成纤维制经编透孔织物(包括由花边针织机织成的经编织物)	10	130	17	16	米/千克		Warp knit openwork fabrics of synthetic fibers, of yarns of different colours (includng those made on gallon knitting machines)
6005.3300 90	色织合成纤维制经编非透孔织物(包括由花边针织机织成的经编织物)	10	130	17	16	米/千克		Warp knit not openwork fabrics of synthetic fibers, of yarns of different colours (includng those made on gallon knitting machines)
6005.3400	--印花	10	130	17	16	米/千克		--Printed
6005.3400 10	印花合成纤维制经编透孔织物(包括由花边针织机织成的经编织物)	10	130	17	16	米/千克		Warp knit openwork fabrics of synthetic fibers, printed (includng those made on gallon knitting machines)
6005.3400 90	印花合成纤维制经编非透孔织物(包括由花边针织机织成的经编织物)	10	130	17	16	米/千克		Warp knit not openwork fabrics of synthetic fibers, printed (includng those made on gallon knitting machines)
	-人造纤维制：							-Of artificial fibres:
6005.4100	--未漂白或漂白	10	130	17	16	米/千克		--Unbleached or bleached
6005.4100 10	漂白或未漂白人造纤维制经编透孔织物(包括由花边针织机织成的经编织物)	10	130	17	16	米/千克		Warp knit openwork fabrics of artificial fibers, bleached or unbleached (includng those made on gallon knitting machines)
6005.4100 90	漂白或未漂白人造纤维制经编非透孔织物(包括由花边针织机织成的经编织物)	10	130	17	16	米/千克		Warp knit not openwork fabrics of artificial fibers, bleached or unbleached (includng those made on gallon knitting machines)
6005.4200	--染色	10	130	17	16	米/千克		--Dyed
6005.4200 10	染色人造纤维制经编透孔织物(包括由花边针织机织成的经编织物)	10	130	17	16	米/千克		Warp knit openwork fabrics of artificial fibers, dyed (includng those made on gallon knitting machines)
6005.4200 90	染色人造纤维制经编非透孔织物(包括由花边针织机织成的经编织物)	10	130	17	16	米/千克		Warp knit not openwork fabrics of artificial fibers, dyed (includng those made on gallon knitting machines)
6005.4300	--色织	10	130	17	16	米/千克		--Of yarns of different colours
6005.4300 10	色织人造纤维制经编透孔织物(包括由花边针织机织成的经编织物)	10	130	17	16	米/千克		Warp knit openwork fabrics of artificial fibers, of yarns of different colours (includng those made on gallon knitting machines)
6005.4300 90	色织人造纤维制经编非透孔织物(包括由花边针织机织成的经编织物)	10	130	17	16	米/千克		Warp knit not openwork fabrics of artificial fibers, of yarns of different colours (includng those made on gallon knitting machines)
6005.4400	--印花	10	130	17	16	米/千克		--Printed
6005.4400 10	印花人造纤维制经编透孔织物(包括由花边针织机织成的经编织物)	10	130	17	16	米/千克		Warp knit openwork fabrics of artificial fibers, printed (includng those made on gallon knitting machines)

税则号列	货品名称	最惠(%)	普通	增值税率	出口退税	计量单位	监管条件	Article Description
6005. 4400 90	印花人造纤维制经编非透孔织物（包括由花边针织机织成的经编织物）	10	130	17	16	米/千克		Warp knit not openwork fabrics of artificial fibers, printed（includng those made on gallonknitting machines）
	-其他：							-Other：
6005. 9010	---羊毛或动物细毛制	12	130	17	16	米/千克		---Of wool or fine animal hair
6005. 9090	---其他	12	130	17	16	米/千克		---Other
60. 06	**其他针织或钩编织物：**							**Other knitted or crocheted fabrics：**
6006. 1000	-羊毛或动物细毛制	12	130	17	16	米/千克		-Of wool or fine animal hair
	-棉制：							-Of cotton：
6006. 2100	--未漂白或漂白	10	70	17	16	米/千克		--Unbleached or bleached
6006. 2200	--染色	10	70	17	16	米/千克		--Dyed
6006. 2300	--色织	10	70	17	16	米/千克		--Of yarns of different colours
6006. 2400	--印花	10	70	17	16	米/千克		--Printed
	-合成纤维制：							-Of synthetic fibres：
6006. 3100	--未漂白或漂白	10	130	17	16	米/千克		--Unbleached or bleached
6006. 3200	--染色	10	130	17	16	米/千克		--Dyed
6006. 3300	--色织	10	130	17	16	米/千克		--Of yarns of different colours
6006. 3400	--印花	10	130	17	16	米/千克		--Printed
	-人造纤维制：							-Of artificial fibres：
6006. 4100	--未漂白或漂白	10	130	17	16	米/千克		--Unbleached or bleached
6006. 4200	--染色	10	130	17	16	米/千克		--Dyed
6006. 4300	--色织	10	130	17	16	米/千克		--Of yarns of different colours
6006. 4400	--印花	10	130	17	16	米/千克		--Printed
6006. 9000	-其他	12	130	17	16	米/千克		-Other
6006. 9000 10	丝及绢丝制其他针织或钩编织物（按重量计含丝及绢丝85%及以上）	12	130	17	16	米/千克		Other knitted or crocheted fabrics of silk or spun silk, containing≥85% by weight of silk or spun silk
6006. 9000 90	其他纺织材料制其他针织或钩编织物	12	130	17	16	米/千克		Other knitted or crocheted fabrics of other textile materials

第六十一章
针织或钩编的服装及衣着附件

注释：

一、本章仅适用于制成的针织品或钩编织品。

二、本章不包括：

（一）税目 62.12 的货品；

（二）税目 63.09 的旧衣着或其他旧物品；

（三）矫形器具、外科手术带、疝气带及类似品（税目 90.21）。

三、税目 61.03 及 61.04 所称：

（一）“西服套装”，是指面料用相同的织物制成的两件套或三件套的下列成套服装：

一件人体上半身穿着的外套或短上衣，除袖子外，其面料数为四片或四片以上；也可附带一件马甲（西服背心），这件马甲（西服背心）的前片面料应与套装其他各件的面料相同，后片面料则应与外套或短上衣的衬里料相同；

以及一件人体下半身穿着的服装，即不带背带或护胸的长裤、马裤、短裤（游泳裤除外）、裙子或裙裤。

西服套装各件面料质地、颜色及构成必须相同，其款式也必须相同，尺寸大小还须相互般配，但可以用不同织物滚边（缝口上缝入长条织物）。

如果数件人体下半身穿着的服装同时报验或出口（例如，两条长裤、长裤与短裤、裙子或裙裤与长裤），构成西服套装下装的应是一条长裤，而对于女式西服套装，则应是一条裙子或裙裤，其他服装应分别归类。

所称“西服套装”，包括不论是否完全符合上述条件的下列配套服装：

1. 常礼服，由一件后襟下垂并下端开圆弧形叉的素色短上衣和一条条纹长裤组成；
2. 晚礼服（燕尾服），一般用黑色织物制成，上衣前襟较短且不闭合，背后有燕尾；
3. 无燕尾套装夜礼服，其中上衣款式与普通上衣相似（可以更为显露衬衣前胸），但有光滑丝质或仿丝质的翻领。

（二）“便服套装”，是指面料相同并作零售包装的下列成套服装（西服套装及税目 61.07、61.08 或 61.09 的物品除外）：

一件人体上半身穿着的服装，但套衫及背心除外，因为套衫可在两件套服装中作为内衣，背心也可作为内衣；以及一件或两件不同的人体下半身穿着的服装，即长裤、护胸背带工装裤、马裤、短裤（游泳裤除外）、裙子或裙裤。

便服套装各件面料质地、款式、颜色及构成必须相同；尺寸大小也须相互般配。所称“便服套装”，不包括税目 61.12 的运动服及滑雪服。

Chapter 61
Articles of apparel and clothing accessories, knitted or crocheted6

Notes:

1. This Chapter applies only to made up knitted or crocheted articles.
2. This Chapter does not cover:

(a) Goods of heading No. 62.12;

(b) Worn clothing or other worn articles of heading No. 63.09; or

(c) Orthopaedic appliances, surgical belts, trusses or the like (heaing No. 90.21).

3. For the purposes of headings Nos. 61.03 and 61.04:

(a) The term "suit" means a set of garments composed of two or three pieces made up, in respect of their outer surface, in identical fabric and comprising:

-One suit coat or jacket the outer shell of which, exclusive of sleeves, consists of four or more panels, designed to cover the upper part of the body, possibly with a tailored waistcoat in addition whose front is made from the same fabric as the outer sulrace of the other components of the set and whose back is made from the same fabric as the lining of the suit coat or jacket, and

one garment designed to cover the lower part of the body and consisting of trousers, breeches or shorts (other than swimwear), a skirt or a divided skirt, having neither braces nor bibs.

All of the components of a suit must be of the same fabric construction, style, colour and composition; they must also be of corresponding or compatible size. However, these components may have bindings of different fabric (the narrow fabric stitched to finish raw edges).

If several separate components to cover the lower part of the body are presented together (for example, trousers and shorts, or a skirt or divided skirt and trousers), the constituent lower part shall be one pair of trousers, or, in the case of women's or girls' suits, the skirt or divided skirt, the other garments being considered separately.

The term "suit" includes the following sets of garments, whether or not they fulfill all the above conditions:

-morning dress, comprising a plain jacket (cutaway) with rounded tails hanging well down at the back and striped trousers;

-evening dress (tailcoat), generally made of black fabric, the jacket of which is relatively short at the front, does not close and has narrow skirts cut in at the hips and hanging down behind;

-dinner jacket suits, in which the jacket is similar in style to an ordinary jacket (though perhaps revealing more of the shirt front), but has shiny silk or imitation silk lapels.

(b) The term "ensemble" means a set of garments (other than suits and articles of heading No. 61.07, 61.08 or 61.09), composed of several pieces made up in identical fabric, put up for retail sale, and comprising:

-One garment designed to cover the upper part of the body, with the exception of pullovers which may form a second upper garment in the sole context of twin sets, and of waistcoats which may also form a second upper garment, and

One or two different garments, designed to cover the lower part of the body and consisting of trousers, bib and brace overalls, breeches, shorts (other than swimwear), a skirt or a divided skirt.

All of the components of an ensemble must be of the same fabric construction, style, colour and composition; they also must be of corresponding or compatible size. The term "ensemble" does not apply to track suits or ski suits, of heading No. 61.12.

四、税目61.05及61.06不包括在腰围以下有口袋的服装、带有罗纹腰带及以其他方式收紧下摆的服装或其织物至少在10厘米×10厘米的面积内沿各方向的直线长度上平均每厘米少于10针的服装。税目61.05不包括无袖服装。

五、税目61.09不包括带有束带、罗纹腰带或其他方式收紧下摆的服装。

六、对于税目61.11:

(一)所称"婴儿服装及衣着附件",是指用于身高不超过86厘米幼儿的服装;

(二)既可归入税目61.11,也可归入本章其他税目的物品,应归入税目61.11。

七、税目61.12所称"滑雪服",是指从整个外观和织物质地来看,主要在滑雪(速度滑雪或高山滑雪)时穿着的下列服装或成套服装:

(一)"滑雪连身服",即上下身连在一起的单件服装;除袖子和领子外,滑雪连身服可有口袋或脚带;或

(二)"滑雪套装",即由两件或三件构成一套并作零售包装的下列服装:

一件用一条拉链扣合的带风帽的厚夹克、防风衣、防风短上衣或类似的服装,可以附带一件背心;以及一条不论是否过腰的长裤、一条马裤或一条护胸背带工装裤。

"滑雪套装"也可由一件类似以上(一)款所述的连身服和一件可套在连身服外面的有胎料背心组成。

"滑雪套装"各件颜色可以不同,但面料质地、款式及构成必须相同;尺寸大小也须相互般配。

八、既可归入税目61.13,也可归入本章其他税号的服装,除税目61.11所列的仍归入该税号外,其余的应一律归入税目61.13。

九、本章的服装,凡门襟为左压右的,应视为男式;右压左的,应视为女式。但本规定不适用于其式样已明显为男式或女式的服装。无法区别是男式还是女式的服装,应按女式服装归入有关税目。

十、本章物品可用金属线制成。

4. Headings Nos. 61.05 and 61.06 do not cover garments with pockets below the waist, with a ribbed waistband or other means of tightening at the bottom of the garment, or garments having an average of less than 10 stitches per linear centimetre in each direction counted on an area measuring at least 10cm × 10cm. Heading No. 61.05 does not cover sleeveless garments.

5. Heading No. 61.09 does not cover garments with a drawstring, a ribbed waistband or other means of tightening at the bottom of the garment.

6. For the purposes of heading No. 61.11:

(a) The expression "babies' garments and clothing accessories" means articles for young children of a body height not exceeding 86cm;

(b) Articles which are, *prima facie*, classifiable both in heading No. 61.11 and in other headings of this Chapter are to be classified in heading No. 61.11.

7. For the purposes of heading No. 61.12, "ski suits" means garments or sets of garments which, by their general appearance and texture, are identifiable as intended to be worn principally for skiing (cross-country or alpine). They consist either of:

(a) a "ski overall", that is, a one-piece garment designed to cover the upper and the lower parts of the body; in addition to sleeves and a collar the ski overall may have pockets or footstraps; or

(b) a "ski ensemble", that is, a set of garments composed of two or three pieces, put up for retail sale and comprising:

-one garment such as an anorak, wind-cheater, windjacket or similar article, closed by a slide fastener (zipper), possibly with a waistcoat in addition, and-one pair of trousers whether or not extending above waist-level, one pair of breeches or one bib and brace overall.

The "ski ensemble" may also consist of an overall similar to the one mentioned in paragraph (a) above and a type of padded, sleeveless jacket worn over the overall.

All the components of a "ski ensemble" must be made up in a fabric of the same texture, style and composition whether or not of the same colour; they also must be of corresponding or compatible size.

8. Garments which are, *prima facie*, classifiable both in heading No. 61.13 and in other headings of this Chapter, excluding heading No. 61.11, are to be classified in heading No. 61.13.

9. Garments of this Chapter desinged for left over right closure at the front shall be regarded as men's or boys' garments, and those designed for right over left closure at the front as women's or girls' garments. These provisions do not apply where the cut of the garment clearly indicates that it is designed for one or other of the sexes. Garments which cannot be identified as either men's or boys' garments or as women's or girls' garments are to be classified in the headings covering women's or girls' garments.

10. Articles of this Chapter may be made of metal thread.

税则号列	货品名称	最惠(%)	普通	增值税率	出口退税	计量单位	监管条件	Article Description
61.01	针织或钩编的男式大衣、短大衣、斗篷、短斗篷、带风帽的防寒短上衣(包括滑雪短上衣)、防风衣、防风短上衣及类似品,但税目61.03的货品除外:							**Men's or boys' overcoats, car-coats, capes, cloaks, anoraks (including ski-jackets), wind-cheaters, wind-jackets and similar articles, knitted or crocheted, other than those of heading No. 61.03:**
6101.2000	-棉制	17.5	90	17	16	件/千克		-Of cotton
6101.2000 10	棉制针织或钩编男式大衣(包括短大衣、斗篷、短斗篷及类似品,雨衣除外)	17.5	90	17	16	件/千克		Men's or boys' overcoats, car-coats, capes, cloak and similar articles, other than raincoats, knitted or crocheted, of cotton

税则号列	货 品 名 称	最惠(%)	普通	增值税率	出口退税	计量单位	监管条件	Article Description
6101.2000 21	棉制针织或钩编手工制男式防风衣(包括防寒短上衣、防风短上衣及类似品)	17.5	90	17	16	件/千克		Men's or boys' wind-cheaters, anoraks, wind-jackets and similar articles, hand-worked, knitted or crocheted, of cotton
6101.2000 29	棉制针织或钩编男式防风衣(包括防寒短上衣、防风短上衣及类似品)	17.5	90	17	16	件/千克		Men's or boys' wind-cheaters, anoraks, wind-jackets and similar articles, knitted or crocheted, of cotton
6101.2000 30	棉制针织或钩编男式雨衣	17.5	90	17	16	件/千克		Men's or boys' raincoats of cotton, knitted or crocheted
6101.3000	-化学纤维制	17.5	130	17	16	件/千克		-Of man-made fibres
6101.3000 11	化纤制针织或钩编男式大衣等(含毛≥23%,包括短上衣、斗篷、短斗篷及类似品,雨衣除外)	17.5	130	17	16	件/千克		Men's or boys' overcoats, car-coats, capes, cloak and similar articles, other than raincoats, containing ≥23% by weight of wool or fine animal hair, knitted or crocheted, of man-made fibres
6101.3000 19	其他化纤制针织或钩编男式大衣等(包括短大衣、斗篷、短斗篷及类似品,雨衣除外)	17.5	130	17	16	件/千克		Other men's or boys' overcoats, car-coats, capes, cloak and similar articles, other than raincoats, knitted or crocheted, of man-made fibres
6101.3000 21	化纤制针织或钩编手工男式防风衣(含毛≥23%,包括防寒短上衣、防风短上衣及类似品)	17.5	130	17	16	件/千克		Men's or boys' wind-cheaters, anoraks, wind-jackets and similar articles, hand-worked, containing≥23% by weight of wool or fine animal hair, knitted or crocheted, of man-made fibres
6101.3000 22	化纤制针织或钩编男式防风衣(含毛≥23%,包括防寒短上衣、防风短上衣及类似品)	17.5	130	17	16	件/千克		Men's or boys' wind-cheaters, anoraks, wind-jackets and similar articles, containing≥23% by weight of wool or fine animal hair, knitted or crocheted, of man-made fibres
6101.3000 23	其他化纤针织钩编手工男式防风衣(包括防寒短上衣、防风短上衣及类似品)	17.5	130	17	16	件/千克		Men's or boys' wind-cheaters, anoraks, wind-jackets and similar articles, hand-worked, knitted or crocheted, of man-made fibres
6101.3000 29	其他化纤制其他男式防风衣(包括防寒短上衣、防风短上衣及类似品)	17.5	130	17	16	件/千克		Other men's or boys' wind-cheaters, anoraks, wind-jackets and similar articles, knitted or crocheted, of man-made fibres
6101.3000 31	化纤制针织或钩编男式雨衣(按重量计含羊毛或动物细毛≥23%)	17.5	130	17	16	件/千克		Men's or boys' raincoats, containing≥23% by weight of wool or fine animal hair, knitted or crocheted, of man-made fibres
6101.3000 39	化纤制针织或钩编男式雨衣	17.5	130	17	16	件/千克		Other men's or boys' raincoats, knitted or crocheted, of man-made fibres
	-其他纺织材料制:							-Of other textile materials:
6101.9010	---羊毛或动物细毛制	25	130	17	16	件/千克		---Of wool or fine animal hair
6101.9010 10	毛制针织或钩编非手工制男式防风衣(包括防寒短上衣、防风短上衣及类似品)	25	130	17	16	件/千克		Men's or boys' wind - cheaters, anoraks, wind - jackets and similar articles, not hand - worked, knitted or crocheted, of wool or fine animal hair
6101.9010 90	毛制针织或钩编其他男大衣、斗篷、防风衣等(包括防寒短上衣,防风短上衣、短大衣,短斗篷及类似品)	25	130	17	16	件/千克		Men's or boys' overcoats, capes, wind - cheaters, anoraks, wind - jackets, car - coats, cloak and similar articles, knitted or crocheted, of wool or fine animal hair
6101.9090	---其他纺织材料制	17.5	130	17	16	件/千克		---Of other textile materials
61.02	**针织或钩编的女式大衣、短大衣、斗篷、短斗篷、带风帽的防寒短上衣(包括滑雪短上衣)、防风衣、防风短上衣及类似品,但税目61.04的货品除外:**							**Women's or girls' overcoats, car-coats, capes, cloaks, anoraks (including ski-jackets), wind-cheaters, wind-jackets and similar articles, knitted or crocheted, other than those of heading No. 61.04:**
6102.1000	-羊毛或动物细毛制	25	130	17	16	件/千克		-Of wool or fine animal hair
6102.1000 10	毛制针织或钩编女式大衣等(包括短大衣、斗篷、短斗篷及类似品,雨衣除外)	25	130	17	16	件/千克		Women's or girls' overcoats, car-coats, capes, cloak and similar articles, other than raincoats, knitted or crocheted, of wool or fine animal hair
6102.1000 21	毛制针织或钩编手工制女式防风衣(包括防寒短上衣、防风短上衣及类似品)	25	130	17	16	件/千克		Women's or girls' wind-cheaters, anoraks, wind-jackets and similar articles, hand-worked, knitted or crocheted, of wool or fine animal hair

税则号列	货品名称	最惠(%)	普通	增值税率	出口退税	计量单位	监管条件	Article Description
6102.1000 29	毛制针织或钩编女式防风衣(包括防寒短上衣,防风短上衣及类似品)	25	130	17	16	件/千克		Other women's or girls' wind-cheaters, anoraks, wind-jackets and similar articles, knitted or crocheted, of wool or fine animal hair
6102.1000 30	毛制针织或钩编女式雨衣	25	130	17	16	件/千克		Women's or girls' raincoats, knitted or crocheted, of wool or fine animal hair
6102.2000	-棉制	17.5	90	17	16	件/千克		-Of cotton
6102.2000 10	棉制针织或钩编女式大衣(包括短大衣、斗篷、短斗篷及类似品,雨衣除外)	17.5	90	17	16	件/千克		Women's or girls' overcoats, car-coats, capes, cloak and similar articles, other than raincoats, knitted or crocheted, of cotton
6102.2000 21	棉制针织或钩编手工女式防风衣(包括防风短上衣、防寒短上衣及类似品)	17.5	90	17	16	件/千克		Women's or girls' wind-cheaters, anoraks, wind-jackets and similar articles, hand-worked, knitted or crocheted, of cotton
6102.2000 29	棉制针织或钩编女式防风衣(包括防风短上衣,防寒短上衣及类似品)	17.5	90	17	16	件/千克		Other women's or girls' wind-cheaters, anoraks, wind-jackets and similar articles, knitted or crocheted, of cotton
6102.2000 30	棉制针织或钩编女式雨衣	17.5	90	17	16	件/千克		Women's or girls' raincoats, knitted or crocheted, of cotton
6102.3000	-化学纤维制	17.5	130	17	16	件/千克		-Of man-made fibres
6102.3000 11	化纤制针织或钩编女式大衣等(含毛≥23%,含短大衣、斗篷、短斗篷及类似品,雨衣除外)	17.5	130	17	16	件/千克		Women's or girls' overcoats, car-coats, capes, cloak and similar articles, other than raincoats, containing ≥23% by weight of wool or fine animal hair, knitted or crocheted, of man-made fibres
6102.3000 19	其他化纤制针织或钩编女式大衣(含短大衣、斗篷、短斗篷及类似品,雨衣除外)	17.5	130	17	16	件/千克		Other women's or girls' overcoats, car-coats, capes, cloak and similar articles, other than raincoats, knitted or crocheted, of man-made fibres
6102.3000 21	化纤制针织或钩编手工女式防风衣(含毛≥23%,包括防寒短上衣,防风短上衣及类似品)	17.5	130	17	16	件/千克		Women's or girls' wind-cheaters, anoraks, wind-jackets and similar articles, hand-worked, containing ≥23% by weight of wool or fine animal hair, knitted or crocheted, of man-made fibres
6102.3000 22	化纤制针织或钩编女式防风衣(含毛≥23%,包括防寒短上衣,防风短上衣及类似品)	17.5	130	17	16	件/千克		Women's or girls' wind-cheaters, anoraks, wind-jackets and similar articles, containing≥23% by weight of wool or fine animal hair, knitted or crocheted, of man-made fibres
6102.3000 23	其他化纤制针织钩编手工女防风衣(包括防寒短上衣、防风短上衣及类似品)	17.5	130	17	16	件/千克		Women's or girls' wind-cheaters, anoraks, wind-jackets and similar articles, hand-worked, knitted or crocheted, of man-made fibres
6102.3000 29	其他化纤制针织钩编其他女防风衣(包括防寒短上衣、防风短上衣及类似品)	17.5	130	17	16	件/千克		Other women's or girls' wind-cheaters, anoraks, wind-jackets and similar articles, knitted or crocheted, of man-made fibres
6102.3000 31	化纤针织或钩编女式雨衣(按重量计羊毛及动物细毛≥23%)	17.5	130	17	16	件/千克		Women's or girls' raincoats, containing ≥ 23% by weight of wool or fine animal hair, knitted or crocheted, of man-made fibres
6102.3000 39	化纤针织或钩编女式雨衣	17.5	130	17	16	件/千克		Women's or girls' raincoats, knitted or crocheted, of man-made fibres
6102.9000	-其他纺织材料制	20	130	17	16	件/千克		-Of other textile materials
6102.9000 11	丝及绢丝制针织或钩编女式大衣等(含丝≥70%包括短大衣、斗篷、短斗篷及类似品,雨衣除外)	20	130	17	16	件/千克		Women's or girls' overcoats, car-coats, capes, cloak and similar articles, other than raincoats, containing ≥70% by weight of silk or spun silk knitted or crocheted
6102.9000 14	丝及绢丝制针织或钩编女式防风衣(含丝≥70%,包括防寒短上衣,防风短上衣及类似品)	20	130	17	16	件/千克		Women's or girls' wind-cheaters, anoraks, wind-jackets and similar articles, containing≥70% by weight of silk or spun silk knitted or crocheted
6102.9000 15	丝及绢丝制针织或钩编女式雨衣(含丝≥70%)	20	130	17	16	件/千克		Women's or girls' raincoats, containing ≥ 70% by weight of silk or spun silk knitted or crocheted

税则号列	货品名称	最惠(%)	普通	增值税率	出口退税	计量单位	监管条件	Article Description
6102.9000 21	其他纺织材料制针织或钩编女大衣(包括短大衣、斗篷、短斗篷及类似品,雨衣除外,棉限内)	20	130	17	16	件/千克		Women's or girls' overcoats, car-coats, capes, cloak and similar articles, other than raincoats, knitted or crocheted, of other textile materials, cotton within limitations
6102.9000 22	其他纺织材料制针织或钩编女大衣(包括短大衣、斗篷、短斗篷及类似品,雨衣除外,羊毛限内)	20	130	17	16	件/千克		Women's or girls' overcoats, car-coats, capes, cloak and similar articles, other than raincoats, knitted or crocheted, of other textile materials, wool within limitations
6102.9000 23	其他纺织材料制针织或钩编女大衣(包括短大衣、斗篷、短斗篷及类似品,雨衣除外,化纤限内)	20	130	17	16	件/千克		Women's or girls' overcoats, car-coats, capes, cloak and similar articles, other than raincoats, knitted or crocheted, of other textile materials, man-made fibres within limitations
6102.9000 29	其他纺织材料制针织或钩编女大衣(包括短大衣、斗篷、短斗篷及类似品,雨衣除外)	20	130	17	16	件/千克		Women's or girls' overcoats, car-coats, capes, cloak and similar articles, other than raincoats, knitted or crocheted, of other textile materials
6102.9000 31	其他纺织材料制针织或钩编女式防风衣(包括防寒短上衣、防风短上衣及类似品,棉限内)	20	130	17	16	件/千克		Women's or girls' wind-cheaters, anoraks, wind-jackets and similar articles, knitted or crocheted, of other textile materials, cotton within limitations
6102.9000 32	其他纺织材料制针织或钩编女式防风衣(包括防寒短上衣、防风短上衣及类似品,羊毛限内)	20	130	17	16	件/千克		Women's or girls' wind-cheaters, anoraks, wind-jackets and similar articles, knitted or crocheted, of other textile materials, wool within limitations
6102.9000 33	其他纺织材料针织或钩编女式防风衣(包括防寒短上衣、防风短上衣及类似品,化纤限内)	20	130	17	16	件/千克		Women's or girls' wind-cheaters, anoraks, wind-jackets and similar articles, knitted or crocheted, of other textile materials, man-made fibres within limitations
6102.9000 39	其他纺织材料针织或钩编女式防风衣(包括防寒短上衣、防风短上衣及类似品)	20	130	17	16	件/千克		Other women's or girls' wind-cheaters, anoraks, wind-jackets and similar articles, knitted or crocheted, of other textile materials
6102.9000 41	其他纺织材料制针织或钩编女式雨衣(棉限内)	20	130	17	16	件/千克		Women's or girls' raincoats, knitted or crocheted, of other textile materials, cotton within limitations
6102.9000 42	其他纺织材料制针织或钩编女式雨衣(羊毛限内)	20	130	17	16	件/千克		Women's or girls' raincoats, knitted or crocheted, of other textile materials, wool within limitations
6102.9000 43	其他纺织材料制针织或钩编女式雨衣(化纤限内)	20	130	17	16	件/千克		Women's or girls' raincoats, knitted or crocheted, of other textile materials, man-made fibres within limitations
6102.9000 49	其他纺织材料制针织或钩编女式雨衣	20	130	17	16	件/千克		Other women's or girls' raincoats, knitted or crocheted, of other textile materials
61.03	**针织或钩编的男式西服套装、便服套装、上衣、长裤、护胸背带工装裤、马裤及短裤(游泳裤除外):**							**Men's or boys' suits, ensembles, jackets, blazers, trousers, bib and brace overalls, breeches and shorts (other than swimwear), knitted or crocheted:**
	-西服套装:							-Suits:
6103.1010	---羊毛或动物细毛制	25	130	17	16	套/千克		---Of wool or fine animal hair
6103.1020	---合成纤维制	25	130	17	16	套/千克		---Of synthetic fibres
6103.1020 10	合成纤维制针织或钩编男式西服套装(含羊毛或动物细毛23%及以上)	25	130	17	16	套/千克		Men's or boys' suits, knitted or crocheted, of synthetic fibres, containing≥23% by weight of wool or fine animal hair
6103.1020 90	其他合成纤维制针织或钩编男式西服套装	25	130	17	16	套/千克		Men's or boys' suits, knitted or crocheted, of synthetic fibres
6103.1090	---其他纺织材料制	17.5	130	17	16	套/千克		---Of other textile materials
6103.1090 11	人造纤维针织或钩编男式西服套装(含羊毛或动物细毛23%及以上)	17.5	130	17	16	套/千克		Men's or boys' suits, knitted or crocheted, of artificial fibres, containing ≥23% by weight of wool or fine animal hair
6103.1090 19	其他人纤针织或钩编男式西服套装	17.5	130	17	16	套/千克		Men's or boys' suits, knitted or crocheted, of other artificial fibres
6103.1090 20	棉制针织或钩编男式西服套装	17.5	130	17	16	套/千克		Men's or boys' suits, knitted or crocheted, of cotton

税则号列	货品名称	最惠(%)	普通	增值税率	出口退税	计量单位	监管条件	Article Description
6103.1090 30	丝及绢丝制针织或钩编男西服套装	17.5	130	17	16	套/千克		Men's or boys' suits, knitted or crocheted, of silk and silk waste
6103.1090 41	其他纺织材料制针织或钩编男西服套装（棉限内）	17.5	130	17	16	套/千克		Men's or boys' suits, knitted or crocheted, of other textile materials, cotton within limitations
6103.1090 42	其他纺织材料制针织或钩编男西服套装（羊毛限内）	17.5	130	17	16	套/千克		Men's or boys' suits, knitted or crocheted, of other textile materials, wool within limitations
6103.1090 43	其他纺织材料制针织或钩编男西服套装（化纤限内）	17.5	130	17	16	套/千克		Men's or boys' suits, knitted or crocheted, of other textile materials, man-made fibres within limitations
6103.1090 49	其他纺织材料制针织或钩编男西服套装	17.5	130	17	16	套/千克		Men's or boys' suits, knitted or crocheted, of other textile materials
	-便服套装:							-Ensembles:
6103.2200	--棉制	20	90	17	16	套/千克		--Of cotton
6103.2300	--合成纤维制	25	130	17	16	套/千克		--Of synthetic fibres
6103.2300 10	合成纤维制针织或钩编男便服套装（含羊毛或动物细毛23%及以上）	25	130	17	16	套/千克		Men's or boys' ensembles of synthetic fibres, knitted or crocheted, containing≥23% by weight of wool or fine animal hair
6103.2300 91	其他合纤制针织或钩编含毛衫或针织衬衫或裤子的男便服套装	25	130	17	16	套/千克		Men's or boys' ensembles, knitted or crocheted, of synthetic fibres, including hair shirt or knitted shirt or trousers
6103.2300 99	其他合纤制针织或钩编其他男便服套装	25	130	17	16	套/千克		Men's or boys' ensembles, knitted or crocheted, of synthetic fibres
	--其他纺织材料制:							--Of other textile materials:
6103.2910	---羊毛或动物细毛制	25	130	17	16	套/千克		---Of wool or fine animal hair
6103.2990	---其他纺织材料制	25	130	17	16	套/千克		---Of other textile materials
6103.2990 10	丝或绢丝制针织或钩编男便服套装（含丝或绢丝70%及以上）	25	130	17	16	套/千克		Men's or boys' ensembles, knitted or crocheted containing≥70% by weight of silk and spun silk
6103.2990 20	人造纤维制针织或钩编男便服套装	25	130	17	16	套/千克		Men's or boys' ensembles, knitted or crocheted, of artificial fibres
6103.2990 31	其他纺织材料制针织或钩编男便服套装（上装为毛衫，棉限内）	25	130	17	16	套/千克		Men's or boys' ensembles, knitted or crocheted, of other textile materials, the upper garment is a sweater, cotton within limitations
6103.2990 32	其他纺织材料制针织或钩编男便服套装（上装为毛衫，羊毛限内）	25	130	17	16	套/千克		Men's or boys' ensembles, knitted or crocheted, of other textile materials, the upper garment is a sweater, wool within limitations
6103.2990 33	其他纺织材料制针织或钩编男便服套装（上装为毛衫，化纤限内）	25	130	17	16	套/千克		Men's or boys' ensembles, knitted or crocheted, of other textile materials, the upper garment is a sweater, man-made fibres within limitations
6103.2990 34	其他纺织材料制针织或钩编男便服套装（上装为毛衫）	25	130	17	16	套/千克		Men's or boys' ensembles, knitted or crocheted, of other textile materials, the upper garment is a sweater
6103.2990 35	其他纺织材料制针织或钩编男便服套装	25	130	17	16	套/千克		Men's or boys' ensembles, knitted or crocheted, of other textile materials
	-上衣:							-Jackets and blazers:
6103.3100	--羊毛或动物细毛制	16	130	17	16	件/千克		--Of wool or fine animal hair
6103.3200	--棉制	16	90	17	16	件/千克		--Of cotton
6103.3300	--合成纤维制	19	130	17	16	件/千克		--Of synthetic fibres
6103.3300 10	合成纤维制针织或钩编男式上衣（含羊毛或动物细毛23%及以上）	19	130	17	16	件/千克		Men's or boys' jackets and blazers, knitted or crocheted, of synthetic fibres, containing≥23% by weight of wool or fine animal hair
6103.3300 90	其他合纤制针织或钩编男式上衣	19	130	17	16	件/千克		Other men's or boys' jackets and blazers, knitted or crocheted, of synthetic fibres
6103.3900	--其他纺织材料制	16	130	17	16	件/千克		--Of other textile materials
6103.3900 10	人造纤维制针织或钩编男式上衣	16	130	17	16	件/千克		Men's or boys' jackets and blazers, knitted or crocheted, of artificial fibres
6103.3900 20	丝制针织或钩编男式上衣（含丝及绢丝70%及以上）	16	130	17	16	件/千克		Men's or boys' jackets and blazers, knitted or crocheted, containing≥70% by weight of silk or spun silk

税则号列	货品名称	最惠(%)	普通	增值税率	出口退税	计量单位	监管条件	Article Description
6103.3900 31	其他纺织材料制针织或钩编男式上衣(棉限内)	16	130	17	16	件/千克		Men's or boys' jackets and blazers, knitted or crocheted, of other textile materials, cotton within limitations
6103.3900 32	其他纺织材料制针织或钩编男式上衣(羊毛限内)	16	130	17	16	件/千克		Men's or boys' jackets and blazers, knitted or crocheted, of other textile materials, wool within limitations
6103.3900 33	其他纺织材料制针织或钩编男式上衣(化纤限内)	16	130	17	16	件/千克		Men's or boys' jackets and blazers, knitted or crocheted, of other textile materials, man-made fibres within limitations
6103.3900 39	其他纺织材料制针织或钩编男式上衣	16	130	17	16	件/千克		Men's or boys' jackets and blazers, knitted or crocheted, of other textile materials
	-长裤、护胸背带工装裤、马裤及短裤:							-Trousers, bib and brace overalls, breeches and shorts:
6103.4100	--羊毛或动物细毛制	16	130	17	16	条/千克		--Of wool or fine animal hair
6103.4100 10	毛制针织或钩编护胸背带男工装裤(羊毛或动物细毛制)	16	130	17	16	条/千克		Bib and brace overalls, knitted or crocheted, of wool or fine animal hair
6103.4100 20	毛制针织或钩编男长裤(羊毛或动物细毛制,包括8-18号男童长裤)	16	130	17	16	条/千克		Men's trousers or boys' trousers, including boy's No. 8 ~ No. 18, knitted or crocheted, of wool or fine animal hair
6103.4100 90	毛制针织或钩编其他男裤(羊毛或动物细毛制,包括马裤、短裤及其他长裤)	16	130	17	16	条/千克		Other men's trousers or boys' trousers, breeches and short, knitted or crocheted, of wool or fine animal hair
6103.4200	--棉制	16	90	17	16	条/千克		--Of cotton
6103.4200 11	棉制针织或钩编护胸背带男工装裤(保暖)	16	90	17	16	条/千克		Men's or boys' bib and brace overalls (keep warm), knitted or crocheted, of cotton
6103.4200 12	棉制针织钩编男童非保暖背带工装裤(2-7号男童护胸背带工装裤)	16	90	17	16	条/千克	A	Boys' bib and brace overalls (not keep warm), No. 2 ~ No. 7, knitted or crocheted, of cotton
6103.4200 19	棉制针织钩编男式非保暖背带工装裤(护胸背带工装裤,2-7号男童的除外)	16	90	17	16	条/千克		Men's or boys' bib and brace overalls, other than boys' No. 2 ~ No. 7, knitted or crocheted, of cotton
6103.4200 21	棉制针织或钩编男童游戏套装长裤(指男童8-18号)	16	90	17	16	条/千克	A	Boys' playsuit trousers No. 8 ~ No. 18, knitted or crocheted, of cotton
6103.4200 29	棉制针织或钩编其他男童游戏套装裤(包括长裤、马裤、短裤)	16	90	17	16	条/千克	A	Other boys' playsuit, including trousers, breeches and shorts, knitted or crocheted, of cotton
6103.4200 30	棉制针织或钩编男长裤(包括8-18号男童长裤)	16	90	17	16	条/千克		Men's trousers or boys' trousers including boy's No. 8 ~ No. 18, knitted or crocheted, of cotton
6103.4200 90	棉制针织或钩编其他男裤等(包括马裤、短裤及其他长裤)	16	90	17	16	条/千克		Other men's or boys' trousers, breeches and shorts, knitted or crocheted, of cotton
6103.4300	--合成纤维制	17.5	130	17	16	条/千克		--Of synthetic fibres
6103.4300 10	合纤针织或钩编护胸背带男工装裤(含羊毛或动物细毛23%及以上)	17.5	130	17	16	条/千克		Men's or boys' bib and brace overalls, containing ≥23% by weight of wool or fine animal hair, knitted or crocheted, of synthetic fibres
6103.4300 21	合成纤维制针织或钩编男长裤(含羊毛或动物细毛23%及以上,包括8-18号男童长裤)	17.5	130	17	16	条/千克		Men's trousers or boys' trousers, including boy's No. 8 ~ No. 18, containing ≥23% by weight of wool or fine animal hair, knitted or crocheted, of synthetic fibres
6103.4300 29	合成纤维制针织或钩编其他男裤(含毛23%及以上,包括马裤、短裤及其他长裤)	17.5	130	17	16	条/千克		Other men's or boys' trousers, breeches and shorts, containing ≥23% by weight of wool or fine animal hair, knitted or crocheted, of synthetic fibres
6103.4300 91	其他合纤制护胸背带男工装裤(针织或钩编)	17.5	130	17	16	条/千克		Other men's or boys' bib and brace overalls, knitted or crocheted, of synthetic fibres
6103.4300 92	其他合纤制男童游戏套装长裤(针织或钩编,指男童8-18号)	17.5	130	17	16	条/千克	A	Other boys' playsuit trousers No. 8 ~ No. 18, knitted or crocheted, of synthetic fibres
6103.4300 93	其他合纤制男童游戏套装长裤(针织或钩编,包括马裤、短裤及其他长裤)	17.5	130	17	16	条/千克	A	Other boys' playsuit trousers, including breeches, shorts and other trousers, knitted or crocheted, of synthetic fibres
6103.4300 94	其他合纤制针织或钩编男长裤(包括8-18号男童长裤)	17.5	130	17	16	条/千克		Other men's or boys' trousers, including boy's No. 8 ~ No. 18, knitted or crocheted, of synthetic fibres
6103.4300 99	其他合纤制针织或钩编其他男裤(包括马裤、短裤及其他长裤)	17.5	130	17	16	条/千克		Other men's or boys' trousers, breeches and shorts, knitted or crocheted, of synthetic fibres

税则号列	货品名称	最惠(%)	普通	增值税率	出口退税	计量单位	监管条件	Article Description
6103.4900	--其他纺织材料制	16	130	17	16	条/千克		--Of other textile materials
6103.4900 11	丝制男式护胸背带工装裤(针织或钩编,丝及绢丝含量在70%及以上	16	130	17	16	条/千克		Men's or boy's bib and brace overalls, containing ≥ 70% by weight of silk or spun silk, knitted or crocheted
6103.4900 12	丝制针织或钩编男成人长裤、马裤(含8-18号男童长裤及马裤,丝及绢丝含量在70%以上)	16	130	17	16	条/千克		Men's trousers and breeches and boys' No. 8 ~ No. 17, containing ≥ 70% by weight of silk or spun silk, knitted or crocheted
6103.4900 13	丝制针织或钩编其他男童长裤、马裤(丝及绢丝含量在70%及以上)	16	130	17	16	条/千克	A	Boys' trousers and breeches, containing ≥ 70% by weight of silk or spun silk knitted or crocheted
6103.4900 14	丝制针织或钩编其他男式短裤(丝及绢丝含量在70%及以上)	16	130	17	16	条/千克		Other men's or boys' shorts, containing ≥ 70% by weight of silk or spun silk, knitted or crocheted
6103.4900 21	人造纤维制男式护胸背带工装裤(针织或钩编)	16	130	17	16	条/千克		Men's or boys' bib and brace overalls of artificial fibres, knitted or crocheted
6103.4900 22	人纤制针织或钩编男式长裤、马裤(含8-18号男童长裤及马裤,含毛23%及以上)	16	130	17	16	条/千克		Men's or boy's trousers, breeches, including boys' No. 8 ~ No. 18, of artificial fibres, containing ≥ 23% by weight of wool or fine animal hair, knitted or crocheted
6103.4900 23	人纤制针织或钩编其他男童长裤、马裤(含毛23%及以上)	16	130	17	16	条/千克	A	Other boys' trousers, breeches, of artificial fibres, containing ≥ 23% by weight of wool or fine animal hair, knitted or crocheted
6103.4900 24	人纤制针织或钩编男式短裤(含毛23%及以上)	16	130	17	16	条/千克		Men's or boys' shorts of artificial fibres, containing ≥ 23% by weight of wool or fine animal hair, knitted or crocheted
6103.4900 25	其他人纤制针织或钩编男长裤、马裤(含8-18号男童长裤及马裤)	16	130	17	16	条/千克		Other men's or boy's trousers, breeches, including boys' No. 8 ~ No. 18, of artificial fibres, knitted or crocheted
6103.4900 26	其他人纤制针织或钩编其他男童长裤(包括马裤)	16	130	17	16	条/千克	A	Other boys' trousers and breeches, of artificial fibres, knitted or crocheted
6103.4900 27	其他人纤制针织或钩编其他男短裤	16	130	17	16	条/千克		Other men's or boys' shorts of artificial fibres, knitted or crocheted
6103.4900 31	其他纺材制男式护胸背带工装裤(针织或钩编,棉限内)	16	130	17	16	条/千克		Men's or boys' bib and brace overalls, cotton within limitations, knitted or crocheted, of other textile materials
6103.4900 32	其他纺材制男式护胸背带工装裤(针织或钩编,羊毛限内)	16	130	17	16	条/千克		Men's or boys' bib and brace overalls, wool within limitations, knitted or crocheted, of other textile materials
6103.4900 33	其他纺材制男式护胸背带工装裤(针织或钩编,化纤限内)	16	130	17	16	条/千克		Men's boys' bib and brace overalls, man-made fibres within limitations, knitted or crocheted, of other textile materials
6103.4900 39	其他纺材制男式护胸背带工装裤(针织或钩编)	16	130	17	16	条/千克		Other men's or boys' bib and brace overalls, knitted or crocheted, of other textile materials
6103.4900 41	其他纺材制针织或钩编男长裤、马裤(包括8-18号男童长裤、马裤,棉限内)	16	130	17	16	条/千克		Men's or boy's trousers, breeches, including boys' No. 8 ~ No. 18, knitted or crocheted, of other textile materials, cotton within limitations
6103.4900 42	其他纺材制针织或钩编男长裤、马裤(包括8-18号男童长裤、马裤,羊毛限内)	16	130	17	16	条/千克		Men's or boy's trousers, breeches, including boys' No. 8 ~ No. 18, knitted or crocheted, of other textile materials, wool within limitations
6103.4900 43	其他纺材制针织或钩编男长裤、马裤(包括8-18号男童长裤、马裤,化纤限内)	16	130	17	16	条/千克		Men's or boy's trousers, breeches, including boys' No. 8 ~ No. 18, knitted or crocheted, of other textile materials, man-made fibres within limitations
6103.4900 49	其他纺材制针织或钩编男长裤、马裤(包括8-18号男童长裤、马裤)	16	130	17	16	条/千克		Men's or boy's trousers and breeches, including boys' No. 8 ~ No. 18, knitted or crocheted, of other textile materials
6103.4900 51	其他纺织材料制其他男童长裤、马裤(针织或钩编,棉限内)	16	130	17	16	条/千克	A	Other boys' trousers and breeches, cotton within limitations, knitted or crocheted, of other textile materials
6103.4900 52	其他纺织材料制其他男童长裤、马裤(针织或钩编,羊毛限内)	16	130	17	16	条/千克	A	Other boys' trousers and breeches, wool within limitations, knitted or crocheted, of other textile materials

税则号列	货品名称	最惠(%)	普通	增值税率	出口退税	计量单位	监管条件	Article Description
6103.4900 53	其他纺织材料制其他男童长裤、马裤(针织或钩编,化纤限内)	16	130	17	16	条/千克	A	Other boys' trousers and breeches, man-made fibres within limitations, knitted or crocheted, of other textile materials
6103.4900 59	其他纺织材料制其他男童长裤、马裤(针织或钩编)	16	130	17	16	条/千克	A	Other boys' trousers and breeches, knitted or crocheted, of other textile materials
6103.4900 61	其他纺材制针织或钩编男式短裤(棉限内)	16	130	17	16	条/千克		Other men's or boys' shorts, knitted or crocheted, of other textile materials, cotton within limitations
6103.4900 62	其他纺材制针织或钩编男式短裤(羊毛限内)	16	130	17	16	条/千克		Other men's or boys' shorts, knitted or crocheted, of other textile materials, wool within limitations
6103.4900 63	其他纺材制针织或钩编男式短裤(化纤限内)	16	130	17	16	条/千克		Other men's or boys' shorts, knitted or crocheted, of other textile materials, man-made fibres within limitations
6103.4900 69	其他纺材制针织或钩编男式短裤	16	130	17	16	条/千克		Other men's or boys' shorts, knitted or crocheted, of other textile materials
61.04	**针织或钩编的女式西服套装、便服套装、上衣、连衣裙、裙子、裙裤、长裤、护胸背带工装裤、马裤及短裤(游泳服除外):**							**Women's or girls' suits, ensembles, jackets, blazers, dresses, skirts, divided skirts, trousers, bib and brace overalls, breeches and shorts (otherthan swimwear), knitted or crocheted:**
	-西服套装:							-Suits:
6104.1300	--合成纤维制	25	130	17	16	套/千克		--Of synthetic fibres
6104.1300 10	合成纤维制针织或钩编女西服套装(含羊毛或动物细毛23%及以上)	25	130	17	16	套/千克		Women's or girls' suits, knitted or crocheted, containing≥23% by weight of wool or fine animal hair, of synthetic fibres
6104.1300 90	其他合成纤维制针织或钩编女西服套装	25	130	17	16	套/千克		Women's or girls' suits, knitted or crocheted, of synthetic fibres
	--其他纺织材料制:							--Of other textile materials:
6104.1910	---羊毛或动物细毛制	17.5	130	17	16	套/千克		---Of wool or fine animal hair
6104.1920	---棉制	17.5	90	17	16	套/千克		---Of cotton
6104.1920 10	含裤子的棉针织或钩编女西服套装	17.5	90	17	16	套/千克		Women's or girls' suits, knitted or crocheted, of cotton, including trousers
6104.1920 90	不含裤子的棉针织或钩编女西服套装	17.5	90	17	16	套/千克		Women's or girls' suits, knitted or crocheted, of cotton, excluding trousers
6104.1990	---其他	17.5	130	17	16	套/千克		---Other
6104.1990 10	含裤子的其他纺材制针织或钩编女西服套装(棉限内)	17.5	130	17	16	套/千克		Other women's or girls' suits, knitted or crocheted, of other textile materials, cotton within limitations, including trousers
6104.1990 90	其他纺织材料制针织或钩编女式西服套装(除合成纤维、羊毛或动物细毛、棉以外的其他纺织材料)	17.5	130	17	16	套/千克		Women's or girls' suits, knitted or crocheted, of other textile matrials, other than synthetic fibres, wool or fine animal hair, cotton materials
	-便服套装:							-Ensembles:
6104.2200	--棉制	17.5	90	17	16	套/千克		--Of cotton
6104.2200 10	含针织衬衫或毛衫或裤子棉制针织或钩编女便服套装	17.5	90	17	16	套/千克		Women's or girls' suits, knitted or crocheted, of cotton, including knitted shirt or hair shirt or trousers
6104.2200 90	其他棉针织或钩编女便服套装	17.5	90	17	16	套/千克		Other women's or girls' ensembles, knitted or crocheted, of cotton
6104.2300	--合成纤维制	25	130	17	16	套/千克		--Of synthetic fibres
6104.2300 10	合纤制针织或钩编女便服套装(含羊毛23%及以上)	25	130	17	16	套/千克		Women's or girls' ensembles, knitted or crocheted, containing≥23% by weight of wool, of synthetic fibres
6104.2300 91	含针织衬衫或毛衫或裤子的其他合纤针织或钩编女便服套装(含毛23%以下)	25	130	17	16	套/千克		Women's or girls' suits, knitted or crocheted, of other synthetic fibres, including knitted shirt or hair shirt or trousers, containing < 23% by weight of wool or fine animal hair
6104.2300 99	其他合纤针织或钩编其他女便服套装(含毛23%以下)	25	130	17	16	套/千克		Other women's or girls' suits, knitted or crocheted, of synthetic fibres, containing < 23% by weight of
	--其他纺织材料制:							--Of other textile materials:

税则号列	货品名称	最惠(%)	普通	增值税率	出口退税	计量单位	监管条件	Article Description
6104.2910	---羊毛或动物细毛制	17.5	130	17	16	套/千克		---Of wool or fine animal hair
6104.2990	---其他	15	130	17	16	套/千克		---Other
6104.2990 21	含针织衬衫或毛衫或裤子的人纤制其他女便服套装(针织或编织)	15	130	17	16	套/千克		Other women's or girls' suits, knitted or crocheted, of artificial fibres, including knitted shirt or hair shirt or trousers
6104.2990 29	人纤制其他女便服套装(针织或编织)	15	130	17	16	套/千克		Women's or girls'ensembles, of artifcial fibrts
6104.2990 31	含针织衬衫或毛衫或裤子的其他纺材针织或钩编女便服套装(棉限内)	15	130	17	16	套/千克		Women's or girls' suits, knitted or crocheted, of other textile materials, including knitted shirt or hair shirt or trousers, cotton within limitations
6104.2990 32	其他纺材针织或钩编女式便服套装(羊毛限内)	15	130	17	16	套/千克		Women's or girls'ensembles, knitted or crocheted, of other textile materials, wool within limitations
6104.2990 33	含针织衬衫或毛衫或裤子的其他纺材针织或钩编女便服套装(化纤限内)	15	130	17	16	套/千克		Women's or girls' suits, knitted or crocheted, of other textile materials, including knitted shirt or hair shirt or trousers, man – made fibres within limitations
6104.2990 34	含裤子的其他纺材针织或钩编女式便服套装	15	130	17	16	套/千克		Women's or girls'ensembles, knitted or crocheted, of other textile materials, including trousers
6104.2990 39	其他纺织材料针织或钩编其他女式便服套装	15	130	17	16	套/千克		Other women's or girls' ensembles, knitted or crocheted, of other texlile materials
	-上衣:							-Jackets and blazers:
6104.3100	--羊毛或动物细毛制	16	130	17	16	件/千克		--Of wool or fine animal hair
6104.3100 10	毛制钩编女式上衣	16	130	17	16	件/千克		Women's or girls' jackets and blazers of wool or fine animal hair, crocheted
6104.3100 90	毛制针织女式上衣	16	130	17	16	件/千克		Women's or girls' jackets and blazers of wool or fine animal hair, knitted
6104.3200	--棉制	16	90	17	16	件/千克		--Of cotton
6104.3200 10	棉制钩编女式上衣	16	90	17	16	件/千克		Women's or girls' jackets and blazers of cotton, crocheted
6104.3200 90	棉制针织女式上衣	16	90	17	16	件/千克		Women's or girls' jackets and blazers of cotton, knitted
6104.3300	--合成纤维制	19	130	17	16	件/千克		--Of synthetic fibres
6104.3300 11	合成纤维制钩编女上衣(含羊毛或动物细毛23%及以上)	19	130	17	16	件/千克		Women's or girls' jackets and blazers of synthetic fibres, crocheted, containing≥23% by weight of wool or fine animal hair
6104.3300 19	其他合成纤维制钩编女上衣	19	130	17	16	件/千克		Other women's or girls' jackets and blazers of synthetic fibres, crocheted
6104.3300 91	合成纤维制针织女上衣(含羊毛或动物细毛23%及以上)	19	130	17	16	件/千克		Women's or girls' jackets and blazers of synthetic fibres, knitted, containing≥23% by weight of wool or fine animal hair
6104.3300 99	其他合成纤维制针织女上衣	19	130	17	16	件/千克		Other women's or girls' jackets and blazers of synthetic fibres, knitted
6104.3900	--其他纺织材料制	16	130	17	16	件/千克		--Of other textile materials
6104.3900 11	丝及绢丝制钩编女上衣(含丝70%及以上)	16	130	17	16	件/千克		Women's or girls' jackets and blazers, crocheted, containing≥70% by weight of silk or spun silk
6104.3900 19	丝及绢丝制针织女上衣(含丝70%及以上)	16	130	17	16	件/千克		Women's or girls' jackets and blazers, knitted, containing≥70% by weight of silk or spun silk
6104.3900 21	人造纤维制钩编女上衣	16	130	17	16	件/千克		Women's or girls' jackets and blazers, crocheted, of artificial fibres
6104.3900 29	人造纤维制针织女上衣	16	130	17	16	件/千克		Women's or girls' jackets and blazers, knitted, of artificial fibres
6104.3900 31	其他纺织材料制钩编女上衣(棉限内)	16	130	17	16	件/千克		Women's or girls' jackets and blazers, of other textile materials, crocheted, cotton within limitations
6104.3900 32	其他纺织材料制钩编女上衣(羊毛限内)	16	130	17	16	件/千克		Women's or girls' jackets and blazers, crocheted, wool within limitations
6104.3900 33	其他纺织材料制钩编女上衣(化纤限内)	16	130	17	16	件/千克		Women's or girls' jackets and blazers, crocheted, man-made fibres within limitations
6104.3900 39	其他纺织材料制钩编女上衣	16	130	17	16	件/千克		Women's or girls' jackets and blazers, crocheted, of other textile materials

税则号列	货品名称	最惠(%)	普通	增值税率	出口退税	计量单位	监管条件	Article Description
6104.3900 41	其他纺织材料制针织女上衣(棉限内)	16	130	17	16	件/千克		Women's or girls' jackets and blazers, knitted, of other textile materials, cotton within limitations
6104.3900 42	其他纺织材料制针织女上衣(羊毛限内)	16	130	17	16	件/千克		Women's or girls' jackets and blazers, knitted, of other textile materials, wool within limitations
6104.3900 43	其他纺织材料制针织女上衣(化纤限内)	16	130	17	16	件/千克		Women's or girls' jackets and blazers, knitted, of other textile materials, man-made fibres within limitations
6104.3900 49	其他纺织材料制针织女上衣	16	130	17	16	件/千克		Women's or girls' jackets and blazers, knitted, of other textile materials
	-连衣裙:							-Dresses:
6104.4100	--羊毛或动物细毛制	16	130	17	16	件/千克		--Of wool or fine animal hair
6104.4200	--棉制	16	90	17	16	件/千克		--Of cotton
6104.4300	--合成纤维制	17.5	130	17	16	件/千克		--Of synthetic fibres
6104.4300 10	合成纤维制针织或钩编连衣裙(含羊毛或动物细毛23%及以上)	17.5	130	17	16	件/千克		Dresses, knitted or crocheted, containing ≥23% by weight of wool or fine animal hair, of synthetic fibres
6104.4300 90	其他合纤制针织或钩编连衣裙	17.5	130	17	16	件/千克		Other dresses knitted or crocheted of synthetic fibres
6104.4400	--人造纤维制	16	130	17	16	件/千克		--Of artificial fibres
6104.4400 10	人纤制针织或钩编连衣裙(含羊毛或动物细毛23%及以上)	16	130	17	16	件/千克		Dresses, knitted or crocheted, containing ≥23% by weight of wool or fine animal hair, of artificial fibres
6104.4400 90	其他人纤制针织或钩编连衣裙	16	130	17	16	件/千克		Other dresses, knitted or crocheted of artificial fibres
6104.4900	--其他纺织材料制	16	130	17	16	件/千克		--Of other textile materials
6104.4900 10	丝及绢丝制针织或钩编连衣裙(含丝70%及以上)	16	130	17	16	件/千克		Dresses, knitted or crocheted, containing ≥70% by weight of silk or spun silk
6104.4900 91	其他纺织材料制针织或钩编连衣裙(棉限内)	16	130	17	16	件/千克		Dresses, knitted or crocheted, cotton within limitations, of other textile materials
6104.4900 92	其他纺织材料制针织或钩编连衣裙(羊毛限内)	16	130	17	16	件/千克		Dresses, knitted or crocheted, wool within limitations, of other textile materials
6104.4900 93	其他纺织材料制针织或钩编连衣裙(化纤限内)	16	130	17	16	件/千克		Dresses, knitted or crocheted, man-made fibres within limitations, of other textile materials
6104.4900 99	其他纺织材料制针织或钩编连衣裙	16	130	17	16	件/千克		Dresses, knitted or crocheted, of other textile materials
	-裙子及裙裤:							-Skirts and divided skirts:
6104.5100	--羊毛或动物细毛制	14	130	17	16	件/千克		--Of wool or fine animal hair
6104.5200	--棉制	14	90	17	16	件/千克		--Of cotton
6104.5300	--合成纤维制	16	130	17	16	件/千克		--Of synthetic fibres
6104.5300 10	合纤制针织或钩编裙子及裙裤(含羊毛或动物细毛23%及以上)	16	130	17	16	件/千克		Skirts and divided skirts, knitted or crocheted, containing≥23% by weight of wool or fine animal hair
6104.5300 90	其他合纤制针织或钩编裙子及裙裤	16	130	17	16	件/千克		Other skirts and divided skirts, knitted or crocheted, of synthetic fibres
6104.5900	--其他纺织材料制	14	130	17	16	件/千克		--Of other textile materials
6104.5900 10	丝及绢丝制针织或钩编裙子及裙裤(含丝70%及以上)	14	130	17	16	件/千克		Skirts and divided skirts, knitted or crocheted, containing≥70% by weight of silk or spun silk
6104.5900 21	人纤制针织或钩编裙子及裙裤(含羊毛或动物细毛23%及以上)	14	130	17	16	件/千克		Skirts and divided skirts, knitted or crocheted, of artificial fibres, containing≥23% by weight of wool or fine animal hair
6104.5900 29	其他人纤制针织或钩编裙子及裙裤	14	130	17	16	件/千克		Skirts and divided skirts, knitted or crocheted other, of artificial fibres
6104.5900 91	其他纺材制针织或钩编裙子及裙裤(棉限内)	14	130	17	16	件/千克		Skirts and divided skirts, knitted or crocheted, of other textile materials, cotton within limitations
6104.5900 92	其他纺材制针织或钩编裙子及裙裤(羊毛限内)	14	130	17	16	件/千克		Skirts and divided skirts, knitted or crocheted, of other textile materials, wool within limitations
6104.5900 93	其他纺材制针织或钩编裙子及裙裤(化纤限内)	14	130	17	16	件/千克		Skirts and divided skirts, knitted or crocheted, of other textile materials, man-made fibres within limitations
6104.5900 99	其他纺材制针织或钩编裙子及裙裤	14	130	17	16	件/千克		Skirts and divided skirts, knitted or crocheted, of other textile materials
	-长裤、护胸背带工装裤、马裤及短裤:							-Trousers, bib and brace overalls, breeches and shorts:
6104.6100	--羊毛或动物细毛制	16	130	17	16	条/千克		--Of wool or fine animal hair

税则号列	货品名称	最惠(%)	普通	增值税率	出口退税	计量单位	监管条件	Article Description
6104.6100 10	毛制针织或钩编女护胸背带工装裤	16	130	17	16	条/千克		Women's or girl's bib and brace overalls, knitted or crocheted, of wool or fine animal hair
6104.6100 20	毛制针织或钩编女长裤、马裤(包括女童7-16号)	16	130	17	16	条/千克		Women's trousers, breeches and girls' No. 7 ~ No. 16, knitted or crocheted, of wool or fine animal hair
6104.6100 90	毛制针织或钩编其他女裤(包括短裤及其他女童裤)	16	130	17	16	条/千克		Other women's trousers, including shorts and other girls' trousers, knitted or crocheted, of wool or fine animal hair
6104.6200	--棉制	16	90	17	16	条/千克		--Of cotton
6104.6200 10	棉制针织或钩编护胸背带女工装裤(保暖护胸背带工装裤)	16	90	17	16	条/千克		Women's or girls' bib and brace overalls (keep warm) knitted or crocheted, of cotton
6104.6200 20	棉针织或钩编非保暖女成人工装裤(护胸背带工装裤)	16	90	17	16	条/千克		Women's bib and brace overalls (not keep warm), knitted or crocheted, of cotton
6104.6200 30	棉制针织或钩编女童游戏套装长裤(指女童7-16号,包括马裤)	16	90	17	16	条/千克	A	Girls' playsuit trousers No. 7 ~ No. 16, including breeches, knitted or crocheted, of cotton
6104.6200 40	棉针织或钩编其他女童游戏套装裤(包括马裤、短裤、非保暖护胸背带工装裤及其他长裤)	16	90	17	16	条/千克	A	Other girls' playsuit, including breeches, shorts, bib and brace overalls and other trousers, knitted or crocheted, of cotton
6104.6200 50	棉制针织或钩编女长裤、马裤(包括女童7-16号)	16	90	17	16	条/千克		Women' trousers, breeches and girls' No. 7 ~ No. 16, knitted or crocheted, of cotton
6104.6200 90	棉制针织或钩编其他女裤(包括短裤及其他女童裤)	16	90	17	16	条/千克		Other women's trousers, including shorts and girls' trousers, knitted or crocheted, of cotton
6104.6300	--合成纤维制	17.5	130	17	16	条/千克		--Of synthetic fibres
6104.6300 10	合成纤维制护胸背带女工装裤(针织或钩编,包括女童护胸背带工装裤)	17.5	130	17	16	条/千克		Women's or girls' bib and brace overalls, knitted or crocheted, of synthetic fibres
6104.6300 21	合成纤维制针织或钩编女长裤(含毛或动物细毛23%及以上,包括女童7-16号)	17.5	130	17	16	条/千克		Women's trousers and girls' No. 7 ~ No. 16, containing≥23% by weight of wool or fine animal hair, knitted or crocheted, of synthetic fibres
6104.6300 29	合成纤维制针织或钩编其他女裤(含毛或动物细毛23%及以上,包括长裤、短裤)	17.5	130	17	16	条/千克		Other women's or girls' trousers and shorts, containing≥23% by weight of wool or fine animal hair, knitted or crocheted, of synthetic fibres
6104.6300 91	其他合纤制女童游戏套装长裤、马裤(针织或钩编,指女童7-16号)	17.5	130	17	16	条/千克	A	Girls' playsuit trousers or breeches No. 7 ~ No. 16, knitted or crocheted, of synthetic fibres
6104.6300 92	其他合成纤维制女童游戏套装裤(针织或钩编,包括短裤及其他长裤)	17.5	130	17	16	条/千克	A	Other girls' playsuit, shorts and other trousers, knitted or crocheted, of synthetic fibres
6104.6300 99	其他合成纤维制针织或钩编女裤(包括长裤、马裤、短裤)	17.5	130	17	16	条/千克		Other women's or girls' trousers, breeches, shorts, knitted or crocheted, of synthetic fibres
6104.6900	--其他纺织材料制	16	130	17	16	条/千克		--Of other textile materials
6104.6900 11	丝及绢丝制针织或钩编女工装裤(含丝70%及以上)	16	130	17	16	条/千克		Women's or girls' bib and brace overalls, containing ≥70% by weight of silk or spun silk, knitted or crocheted
6104.6900 12	丝及绢丝制针织或钩编女长裤、马裤(含丝70%及以上,包括女童7-16号)	16	130	17	16	条/千克		Women's trousers, breeches and girls' No. 7 ~ No. 16, containing≥70% by weight of silk or spun silk, knitted or crocheted
6104.6900 13	丝及绢丝制针织或钩编女短裤(含丝70%及以上,包括女童7-16号)	16	130	17	16	条/千克		Women's shorts, including girls' No. 7 ~ No. 16, knitted or crocheted, containing≥70% by weight of silk or spun silk
6104.6900 19	丝及绢丝制针织或钩编其他女长裤(含丝70%及以上)	16	130	17	16	条/千克		Other women's or girls' trousers, containing ≥70% by weight of silk or spun silk, knitted or crocheted
6104.6900 21	人造纤维制护胸背带女工装裤(针织或钩编)	16	130	17	16	条/千克		Women's or girls' bib and brace overalls, of artificial fibres, knitted or crocheted
6104.6900 22	人造纤维制针织或钩编女长裤、马裤(含毛或动物细毛23%及以上,包括女童7-16号)	16	130	17	16	条/千克		Women's trousers, breeches and girls' No. 7 ~ No. 16, of artificial fibres, containing≥23% by weight of wool or fine animal hair, knitted or crocheted
6104.6900 23	人造纤维制针织或钩编其他女裤(含毛或动物细毛23%及以上,包括长裤、短裤)	16	130	17	16	条/千克		Other women's or girls' trousers, shorts of artificial fibres, containing≥23% by weight of wool or fine animal hair, knitted or crocheted

税则号列	货　品　名　称	最惠(%)	普通	增值税率	出口退税	计量单位	监管条件	Article Description
6104.6900 24	其他人造纤维制女长裤(针织或钩编,包括女童7-16号)	16	130	17	16	条/千克		Women's trousers and girls' No.7 ~ No.16, of artificial fibres, knitted or crocheted
6104.6900 29	其他人纤制针织或钩编其他女裤(包括长裤、马裤)	16	130	17	16	条/千克		Other women's or girls' trousers, breeches, knitted or crocheted, of artificial fibres
6104.6900 31	其他纺材制针织或钩编女工装裤(棉限内)	16	130	17	16	条/千克		Women's or girls' bib and brace overalls, cotton within limitations, of other textile materials
6104.6900 32	其他纺材制针织或钩编女工装裤(羊毛限内)	16	130	17	16	条/千克		Women's or girls' bib and brace overalls, wool within limitations, knitted or crocheted, of other textile materials
6104.6900 33	其他纺材制针织或钩编女工装裤(化纤限内)	16	130	17	16	条/千克		Women's or girls' bib and brace overalls, man-made fibres within limitations, knitted or crocheted, of other textile materials
6104.6900 39	其他纺材制针织或钩编女工装裤	16	130	17	16	条/千克		Women's or girls' bib and brace overalls, knitted or crocheted, of other textile materials
6104.6900 41	其他纺织材料制针织或钩编女长裤(棉限内,包括女童7-16号,包括马裤)	16	130	17	16	条/千克		Women's trousers and breeches girls' No. 7 ~ No. 16, cotton within limitations, knitted or crocheted, of other textile materials
6104.6900 42	其他纺织材料制针织或钩编女长裤(羊毛限内,包括女童7-16号,包括马裤)	16	130	17	16	条/千克		Women's trousers breeches and girls' No. 7 ~ No. 16, wool within limitations, knitted or crocheted, of other textile materials
6104.6900 43	其他纺织材料制针织或钩编女长裤(化纤限内,包括女童7-16号,包括马裤)	16	130	17	16	条/千克		Women's trousers breeches, girls' No. 7 ~ No. 16, man-made fibres within limitations, knitted or crocheted, of other textile materials
6104.6900 49	其他纺织材料制针织或钩编女长裤(包括女童7-16号,包括马裤)	16	130	17	16	条/千克		Women's trousers breeches, including girls' No. 7 ~ No. 16, knitted or crocheted of other textile materials
6104.6900 51	其他纺织材料制针织钩编其他女长裤(棉限内)	16	130	17	16	条/千克		Other women's or girls' trousers, of other textile materials, cotton within limitations
6104.6900 52	其他纺织材料制针织钩编其他女长裤(羊毛限内)	16	130	17	16	条/千克		Other women's or girls' trousers, knitted or crocheted, of other textile materials, wool within limitations
6104.6900 53	其他纺织材料制针织钩编其他女长裤(化纤限内)	16	130	17	16	条/千克		Other women's or girls' trousers, knitted or crocheted, of other textile materials, man-made fibres within limitations
6104.6900 59	其他纺织材料制针织或钩编其他女长裤	16	130	17	16	条/千克		Other women's or girls' trousers, knitted or crocheted, of other textile materials
6104.6900 61	其他纺织材料制针织或钩编女短裤(棉限内)	16	130	17	16	条/千克		Other women's or girls' shorts, knitted or crocheted, of other textile materials, cotton within limitations
6104.6900 62	其他纺织材料制针织或钩编女短裤(羊毛限内)	16	130	17	16	条/千克		Other women's or girls' shorts, knitted or crocheted, of other textile materials, wool within limitations
6104.6900 63	其他纺织材料制针织或钩编女短裤(化纤限内)	16	130	17	16	条/千克		Other women's or girls' shorts, knitted or crocheted of other textile materials, man-made fibres within limitations
6104.6900 69	其他纺织材料制针织或钩编女短裤	16	130	17	16	条/千克		Other women's or girls' shorts, knitted or crocheted, of other textile materials
61.05	针织或钩编的男衬衫:							**Men's or boys' shirts, knitted or crocheted:**
6105.1000	-棉制	16	90	17	16	件/千克		-Of cotton
6105.1000 11	棉制针织或钩编男童游戏套装衬衫(不带缝制领,指男童8-18号)	16	90	17	16	件/千克	A	Boys' playsuit shirts No. 8 ~ No. 18, having no made-to-order collar, knitted or crocheted, of cotton
6105.1000 19	棉制其他男童游戏套装衬衫(针织或钩编)	16	90	17	16	件/千克	A	Other boys' playsuit shirts, knitted or crocheted, of cotton
6105.1000 91	其他棉制针织或钩编男衬衫(不带缝制领,包括男童8-18号)	16	90	17	16	件/千克		Other men's shirts having no made-to-order collar, including boys' No. 8 ~ No. 18, knitted or crocheted, of cotton
6105.1000 99	其他棉制针织或钩编其他男衬衫	16	90	17	16	件/千克		Other men's or boys' shirts, knitted or crocheted, of cotton
6105.2000	-化学纤维制	17.5	130	17	16	件/千克		-Of man-made fibres

税则号列	货品名称	最惠(%)	普通	增值税率	出口退税	计量单位	监管条件	Article Description
6105.2000 11	化纤制针织或钩编男衬衫(含羊毛23%及以上,不带缝制领,包括男童8-18号)	17.5	130	17	16	件/千克		Men's shirts, containing≥23% by weight of wool or fine animal hair, having no made-to-order collar, including boys' No. 8 ~ No. 18, knitted or crocheted, of man-made fibres
6105.2000 19	化纤制针织或钩编其他男衬衫(含羊毛23%及以上)	17.5	130	17	16	件/千克		Other men's or boys' shirts, containing ≥23% by weight of wool or fine animal hair, knitted or crocheted, of man-made fibres
6105.2000 21	化纤制针织或钩编男童游戏套装衬衫(不带缝制领,指男童8-18号)	17.5	130	17	16	件/千克	A	Boys' playsuit shirts No. 8 ~ No. 18, having no made-to-order collar, knitted or crocheted, of man-made fibres
6105.2000 29	化纤制其他男童游戏套装衬衫(针织或钩编)	17.5	130	17	16	件/千克	A	Other boys' playsuit shirts, knitted or crocheted, of man-made fibres
6105.2000 91	其他化纤制针织或钩编男衬衫(不带缝制领,包括男童8-18号)	17.5	130	17	16	件/千克		Other men's shirts having no made-to-order collar, including boys' No. 8 ~ No. 18, knitted or crocheted, of man-made fibres
6105.2000 99	其他化纤制针织或钩编其他男衬衫	17.5	130	17	16	件/千克		Other men's or boys' shirts, knitted or crocheted, of man-made fibres
6105.9000	-其他纺织材料制	16	130	17	16	件/千克		-Of other textile materials
6105.9000 11	丝及绢丝制针织或钩编男衬衫(含丝70%及以上,不带特制领,包括男童8-18号)	16	130	17	16	件/千克		Men's shirts containing≥70% by weight of silk or spun silk waste, having no made-to-order collar, including boys' No. 8 ~ No. 18, knitted or crocheted
6105.9000 19	丝及绢丝制针织或钩编其他男衬衫(含丝70%及以上)	16	130	17	16	件/千克		Other men's or boys' shirts containing ≥70% by weight of silk or spun silk, knitted or crocheted
6105.9000 21	羊毛或动物细毛制男衬衫(针织或钩编,不带缝制领,包括男童8-18号)	16	130	17	16	件/千克		Men's shirts of wool or fine animal hair, having no made-to-order collar, including boys' No. 8 ~ No. 18, knitted or crocheted
6105.9000 29	羊毛或动物细毛制其他男衬衫(针织或钩编)	16	130	17	16	件/千克		Other men's or boys' shirts of wool or fine animal hair, knitted or crocheted, of other textile materials
6105.9000 31	其他纺织材料制针织或钩编男衬衫(棉限内,不带特制领,包括男童8-18号)	16	130	17	16	件/千克		Other men's shirts, having no made-to-order collar, including boys' No. 8 ~ No. 18, knitted or crocheted of other textile materials, cotton within limitations
6105.9000 32	其他纺织材料制针织或钩编男衬衫(羊毛限内,不带特制领,包括男童8-18号)	16	130	17	16	件/千克		Men's shirts, having no made-to-order collar, including boys' No. 8 ~ No. 18, knitted or crocheted of other textile materials, wool within limitations
6105.9000 33	其他纺织材料制针织或钩编男衬衫(化纤限内,不带特制领,包括男童8-18号)	16	130	17	16	件/千克		Men's shirts, having no made-to-order collar, including boys' No. 8 ~ No. 18, knitted or crocheted, of other textile materials, man-made fibres within limitations
6105.9000 39	其他纺织材料制针织或钩编男衬衫(不带特制领,包括男童8-18号)	16	130	17	16	件/千克		Men's or boys' shirts, having no made-to-order collar, including boys' No. 8 ~ No. 18, knitted or crocheted, of other textile materials
6105.9000 41	其他纺织材料制针织或钩编男衬衫(棉限内)	16	130	17	16	件/千克		Men's or boys' shirts, knitted or crocheted, of other textile materials, cotton within limitations
6105.9000 42	其他纺织材料制针织或钩编男衬衫(羊毛限内)	16	130	17	16	件/千克		Men's or boys' shirts, knitted or crocheted, of other textile materials, wool within limitations
6105.9000 43	其他纺织材料制针织或钩编男衬衫(化纤限内)	16	130	17	16	件/千克		Men's or boys' shirts, knitted or crocheted, of other textile materials, man-made fibres within limitations
6105.9000 49	其他纺材制针织或钩编其他男衬衫	16	130	17	16	件/千克		Other men's or boys' shirts, knitted or crocheted, of other textile materials
61.06	针织或钩编的女衬衫:							**Women's or girls' blouses, shirts and shirt-blouses, knitted or crocheted:**
6106.1000	-棉制	16	90	17	16	件/千克		-Of cotton
6106.1000 10	棉制针织或钩编女童游戏套装衬衫	16	90	17	16	件/千克	A	Girls'playsuit shirts, knittedor crocheted, knitted or crocheted, of cotton
6106.1000 90	棉制针织或钩编其他女衬衫	16	90	17	16	件/千克		Other women's or girls' shirts, knitted or crocheted, of cotton

税则号列	货　品　名　称	最惠(%)	普通	增值税率	出口退税	计量单位	监管条件	Article Description
6106.2000	-化学纤维制	17.5	130	17	16	件/千克		-Of man-made fibres
6106.2000 10	化纤制针织或钩编女衬衫(含羊毛23%及以上)	17.5	130	17	16	件/千克		Women's or girls' shirts, knitted or crocheted, containing≥23% by weight of wool or fine animal hair, of man-made fibres
6106.2000 20	其他化纤制女童游戏套装衬衫(针织或钩编)	17.5	130	17	16	件/千克	A	Girls' playsuit shirts, knitted or crocheted, of man-made fibres
6106.2000 90	其他化纤制针织或钩编未列名女衬衫(针织或钩编)	17.5	130	17	16	件/千克		Other women's or girls' shirts, knitted or crocheted, not elsewhere specified or included, of man-made fibres
6106.9000	-其他纺织材料制	16	130	17	16	件/千克		-Of other textile materials
6106.9000 10	丝及绢丝制针织或钩编女衬衫(含丝70%及以上)	16	130	17	16	件/千克		Women's or girls' shirts, knitted or crocheted, containing≥70% by weight of silk or spun silk
6106.9000 20	羊毛或动物细毛针织或钩编女衬衫	16	130	17	16	件/千克		Women's or girls' shirts, knitted or crocheted, of wool or fine animal hair
6106.9000 31	其他纺织材料制针织或钩编女衬衫(棉限内)	16	130	17	16	件/千克		Women's or girls' shirts, knitted or crocheted, of other textile materials, cotton within limitations
6106.9000 32	其他纺织材料制针织或钩编女衬衫(羊毛限内)	16	130	17	16	件/千克		Women's or girls' shirts, knitted or crocheted, of other textile materials, wool within limitations
6106.9000 33	其他纺织材料制针织或钩编女衬衫(化纤限内)	16	130	17	16	件/千克		Women's or girls' shirts, knitted or crocheted, of other textile materials, man-made fibres within limitations
6106.9000 39	其他纺织材料制针织或钩编女衬衫	16	130	17	16	件/千克		Women's or girls' shirts, knitted or crocheted, of other textile materials
61.07	**针织或钩编的男式内裤、三角裤、长睡衣、睡衣裤、浴衣、晨衣及类似品:**							**Men's or boys' underpants, briefs, nightshirts, pyjamas, bathrobes, dressing gowns and similar articles, knitted or crocheted:**
	-内裤及三角裤:							-Underpants and briefs:
6107.1100	--棉制	14	90	17	16	件/千克	A	--Of cotton
6107.1200	--化学纤维制	16	130	17	16	件/千克	A	--Of man-made fibres
	--其他纺织材料制:							--Of other textile materials:
6107.1910	---丝及绢丝制	14	130	17	16	件/千克		---Of silk or spun silk
6107.1910 10	丝及绢丝制男内裤及三角裤(含丝70%及以上,针织或钩编)	14	130	17	16	件/千克	A	Men's or boys' underpants and briefs, knitted or crocheted, containing≥70% by weight of silk or spun silk
6107.1910 90	其他丝及绢丝制男内裤及三角裤(含丝70%以下,针织或钩编)	14	130	17	16	件/千克	A	Men's or boys' underpants and briefs, knitted or crocheted, other, containing < 70% by weight of silk or spun silk
6107.1990	---其他	14	130	17	16	件/千克		---Other
6107.1990 10	羊毛或动物细毛制男内裤及三角裤(针织或钩编)	14	130	17	16	件/千克	A	Men's or boys' underpants and briefs, knitted or crocheted, of wool or fine animal hair
6107.1990 90	其他纺织材料制男内裤及三角裤(针织或钩编)	14	130	17	16	件/千克	A	Men's or boys' underpants and briefs, knitted or crocheted, of other textile fibres
	-长睡衣及睡衣裤:							-Nightshirts and pyjamas:
6107.2100	--棉制	14	90	17	16	件/千克	A	--Of cotton
6107.2200	--化学纤维制	16	130	17	16	件/千克	A	--Of man-made fibres
	--其他纺织材料制:							--Of other textile materials:
6107.2910	---丝及绢丝制	14	130	17	16	件/千克		---Of silk or spun silk
6107.2910 10	丝及绢丝制针织或钩编男睡衣裤(含丝70%及以上,包括长睡衣)	14	130	17	16	件/千克	A	Men's or boys' nightshirts, pyjamas, knitted or crocheted, containing≥70% by weight of silk or spun silk
6107.2910 90	其他丝及绢丝制针织或钩编男睡衣裤(含丝70%以下,包括长睡衣)	14	130	17	16	件/千克	A	Men's or boys' nightshirts, pyjamas, knitted or crocheted, containing < 70% by weight of silk or spun silk
6107.2990	---其他	14	130	17	16	件/千克	A	---Other
	-其他:							-Other:
6107.9100	--棉制	14	90	17	16	件/千克		--Of cotton
6107.9100 10	棉制针织或钩编其他睡衣裤	14	90	17	16	件/千克	A	Other men's or boys' pyjamas, knitted or crocheted, of cotton
6107.9100 90	棉制针织或钩编男浴衣、晨衣等(包括类似品)	14	90	17	16	件/千克	A	Men's or boys' bathrobes, dressing gowns and similar articles, knitted or crocheted, of cotton

税则号列	货品名称	最惠(%)	普通	增值税率	出口退税	计量单位	监管条件	Article Description
	--其他纺织材料制：							--Of other textile materials：
6107.9910	---化学纤维制	16	130	17	16	件/千克	A	---Of man-made fibres
6107.9990	---其他	14	130	17	16	件/千克	A	---Of other
61.08	针织或钩编的女式长衬裙、衬裙、三角裤、短衬裤、睡衣、睡衣裤、浴衣、晨衣及类似品：							**Women's or girls' slips, petticoats, briefs, panties, nightdresses, pyjamas, nègligès, bathrobes, dressing gowns and similar articles, knitted or crocheted：**
	-长衬裙及衬裙：							-Slips and petticoats：
6108.1100	--化学纤维制	16	130	17	16	件/千克		--Of man-made fibres
	--其他纺织材料制：							--Of other textile materials：
6108.1910	---棉制	14	90	17	16	件/千克		---Of cotton
6108.1920	---丝及绢丝制	14	130	17	16	件/千克		---Of silk or silk waste
6108.1920 10	丝及绢丝制女式长衬裙及衬裙(针织或钩编,含丝70%及以上)	14	130	17	16	件/千克		Women's or girls' slips and petticoats, containing ≥70% by weight of silk or spun silk, knitted or crocheted
6108.1920 90	其他丝及绢丝制女式长衬裙及衬裙(针织或钩编,含丝70%以下)	14	130	17	16	件/千克		Women's or girls' slips and petticoats, other, containing <70% by weight of silk or spun silk, knitted or crocheted
6108.1990	---其他	14	130	17	16	件/千克		---Other
	-三角裤及短衬裤：							-Briefs and panties：
6108.2100	--棉制	14	90	17	16	件/千克	A	--Of cotton
6108.2200	--化学纤维制	16	130	17	16	件/千克		--Of man-made fibres
6108.2200 10	化纤制一次性女三角裤及短衬裤(针织或钩编)	16	130	17	16	件/千克	A	Women's or girls' briefs and panties, knitted or crocheted, throw away, of man-made fibres
6108.2200 90	化纤制其他女三角裤及短衬裤(针织或钩编)	16	130	17	16	件/千克	A	Other women's or girls' briefs and panties, knitted or crocheted, of man-made fibres
	--其他纺织材料制：							--Of other textile materials：
6108.2910	---丝及绢丝制	14	130	17	16	件/千克		---Of silk or silk waste
6108.2910 10	丝及绢丝制女三角裤及短衬裤(针织或钩编,含丝70%及以上)	14	130	17	16	件/千克	A	Women's or girls' briefs and panties, knitted or crocheted containing ≥70% by weight of silk or spun silk
6108.2910 90	其他丝及绢丝制女三角裤及短衬裤(针织或钩编,含丝70%以下)	14	130	17	16	件/千克	A	Other women's or girls' briefs and panties, knitted or crocheted, containing < 70% by weight of silk or spun silk
6108.2990	---其他	14	130	17	16	件/千克		---Other
6108.2990 10	羊毛制女三角裤及短衬裤(针织或钩编)	14	130	17	16	件/千克	A	Women's or girls' briefs and panties, knitted or crocheted, of wool
6108.2990 90	其他纺织材料制女三角裤及短衬裤(针织或钩编)	14	130	17	16	件/千克	A	Women's or girls' briefs and panties, knitted or crocheted, of other textile materials
	-睡衣及睡衣裤：							-Nightdresses and pyjamas：
6108.3100	--棉制	14	90	17	16	件/千克	A	--Of cotton
6108.3200	--化学纤维制	16	130	17	16	件/千克	A	--Of man-made fibres
	--其他纺织材料制：							--Of other textile materials：
6108.3910	---丝及绢丝制	14	130	17	16	件/千克		---Of silk or spun silk
6108.3910 10	丝及绢丝制女睡衣及睡衣裤(针织或钩编,含丝70%及以上)	14	130	17	16	件/千克	A	Women's or girls' nightshirts and pyjamas, knitted or crocheted, containing ≥ 70% by weight of silk or spun silk
6108.3910 90	其他丝及绢丝制女睡衣及睡衣裤(针织或钩编,含丝70%以下)	14	130	17	16	件/千克	A	Other women's or girls' nightshirts and pyjamas, knitted or crocheted, containing <70% by weight of silk or spun silk
6108.3990	---其他	14	130	17	16	件/千克		---Other
6108.3990 10	羊毛或动物细毛制女睡衣及睡衣裤(针织或钩编)	14	130	17	16	件/千克	A	Women's or girls' nightshirts and pyjamas, knitted or crocheted, of wool or fine animal hair
6108.3990 90	其他纺织材料制女睡衣及睡衣裤(针织或钩编)	14	130	17	16	件/千克	A	Women's or girls' nightshirts and pyjamas, knitted or crocheted, of other textile materials

税则号列	货品名称	最惠(%)	普通	增值税率	出口退税	计量单位	监管条件	Article Description
	-其他：							-Other：
6108.9100	--棉制	14	90	17	16	件/千克		--Of cotton
6108.9100 10	棉制针织或钩编女内裤，内衣	14	90	17	16	件/千克	A	Women's or girls' briefs, panties and underwear, knitted or crocheted, of cotton
6108.9100 90	其他棉制针织或钩编女浴衣、晨衣等(包括类似品)	14	90	17	16	件/千克	A	Women's or girls' bathrobes, dressing gowns and similar articles, knitted or crocheted, of cotton
6108.9200	--化学纤维制	16	130	17	16	件/千克		--Of man-made fibres
6108.9200 10	化纤制针织或钩编女内裤，内衣	16	130	17	16	件/千克	A	Women's or girls' briefs, panties and underwear, of man-made fibres
6108.9200 90	其他化纤针织或钩编女浴衣、晨衣等(包括类似品)	16	130	17	16	件/千克	A	Women's or girls' bathrobes, dressing gowns and similar articles, knitted or crocheted, of man-made fibres
6108.9900	--其他纺织材料制	14	130	17	16	件/千克		--Of other textile materials
6108.9900 10	丝及绢丝制女浴衣、晨衣等(针织或钩编，包括类似品，含丝70%及以上)	14	130	17	16	件/千克	A	Women's or girls' bathrobes, dressing gowns and similar articles, containing ≥70% by weight of silk or spun silk, knitted or crocheted
6108.9900 20	羊毛或动物细毛制女浴衣、晨衣等(针织或钩编，包括类似品)	14	130	17	16	件/千克	A	Women's or girls' bathrobes, dressing gowns and similar articles, of wool or fine animal hair, knitted or crocheted
6108.9900 90	其他纺织材料制女浴衣、晨衣等(针织或钩编，包括类似品)	14	130	17	16	件/千克	A	Women's or girls' bathrobes, dressing gowns and similar articles, of other textile materials, knitted or crocheted
61.09	**针织或钩编的T恤衫、汗衫及其他背心：**							**T-shirts, singlets and other vests, knitted or crocheted：**
6109.1000	-棉制	14	90	17	16	件/千克		-Of cotton
6109.1000 10	棉制针织或钩编T恤衫、汗衫等(内衣式，包括其他背心)	14	90	17	16	件/千克	A	T-shirts, singlets, underwear style, including other vests, of cotton, knitted or crocheted
6109.1000 21	其他棉制针织或钩编男式T恤衫(内衣除外)	14	90	17	16	件/千克	A	Other men's or boys' T-shirts, other than underwear, of cotton, knitted or crocheted
6109.1000 22	其他棉制针织或钩编女式T恤衫(内衣除外)	14	90	17	16	件/千克	A	Other women's or girls' T-shirts other than underwear, of cotton, knitted or crocheted
6109.1000 91	其他棉制男式汗衫及其他背心(针织或钩编，内衣除外，包括男童8－18号)	14	90	17	16	件/千克	A	Other men's singlets and other vests, including boys' No. 8 ~ No. 18, other than underwear, of cotton, knitted or crocheted
6109.1000 92	其他棉制男式汗衫及其他背心(针织或钩编，内衣除外)	14	90	17	16	件/千克	A	Other men's or boys' singlets and other vests, other than underwear, of cotton, knitted or crocheted
6109.1000 99	其他棉制女式汗衫及其他背心(针织或钩编，内衣除外)	14	90	17	16	件/千克	A	Other women's or girls' singlets and other vests, other than underwear, of cotton, knitted or crocheted
	-其他纺织材料制：							-Of other textile materials：
6109.9010	---丝及绢丝制	14	130	17	16	件/千克		---Of silk or spun silk
6109.9010 11	丝及绢丝针织钩编T恤衫、汗衫、背心(内衣式，含丝≥70%)	14	130	17	16	件/千克	A	T-shirts, singlets and other vests, underwear, containing≥70% by weightof silk or spun silk, knitted or crocheted
6109.9010 19	其他丝及绢丝针织钩编T恤衫、背心(包括汗衫，内衣式，含丝70%以下)	14	130	17	16	件/千克	A	Other T-shirts, singlets and other vests, underwear, containing < 70% by weight of silk or spun silk, knitted or crocheted
6109.9010 21	丝及绢丝针织钩编汗衫、背心(内衣除外，含丝≥70%，男童8－18号，女童7－16号)	14	130	17	16	件/千克	A	Singlets, vests, including boys' No. 8 ~ No. 18, girls' No. 7 ~ No. 16, other than underwear, containing≥70% by weightof silk or spun silk, knitted or crocheted
6109.9010 29	其他丝及绢丝针织或钩编汗衫、背心(内衣除外，含丝<70%，男童8－18号，女童7－16号)	14	130	17	16	件/千克	A	Other singlets, vests, including boys' No. 8 ~ No. 18, girls' No. 7 ~ No. 16, other than underwear, containing < 70% by weight of silk or spun silk, knitted or crocheted
6109.9010 91	其他丝及绢丝针织或钩编T恤衫、汗衫(含丝≥70%，包括其他背心)	14	130	17	16	件/千克	A	Other T-shirts, singlets and other vests, including other vests, containing ≥70% by weight of silk or spun silk, knitted or crocheted

税则号列	货品名称	最惠(%)	普通	增值税率	出口退税	计量单位	监管条件	Article Description
6109.9010 99	其他丝及绢丝针织或钩编T恤衫、汗衫(含丝<70%,包括其他背心)	14	130	17	16	件/千克	A	Other of other textile materials, including other vests, containing < 70% by weight of silk or spun silk, knitted or crocheted
6109.9090	---其他	14	130	17	16	件/千克		---Other
6109.9090 11	毛制针织或钩编T恤衫、汗衫等(内衣式,长袖衫)	14	130	17	16	件/千克	A	T-shirts, singlets and other vests, underwear style, long sleeve, of wool or fine animal hair, knitted or crocheted
6109.9090 12	毛制针织或钩编男式T恤衫、汗衫(内衣式,长袖衫除外)	14	130	17	16	件/千克	A	Men's or boys' T-shirts, singlets, underwear style, other than long sleeve, of wool or fine animal hair, knitted or crocheted
6109.9090 13	毛制针织或钩编女式T恤衫、汗衫(内衣式,长袖衫除外)	14	130	17	16	件/千克	A	Women's or grils' T-shirts, singlets, underwear style, other than long sleeve, of wool or fine animal hair, knitted or crocheted
6109.9090 21	毛制针织或钩编男式其他T恤衫(内衣除外)	14	130	17	16	件/千克	A	Men's or boys' T-shirts, other than underwear, of wool or fine animal hair, knitted or crocheted
6109.9090 22	毛制针织或钩编女式其他T恤衫(内衣除外)	14	130	17	16	件/千克	A	Women's or girls' T-shirts, other than underwear, of wool or fine animal hair, knitted or crocheted
6109.9090 31	毛制男式汗衫及其他背心(针织或钩编,内衣除外,含男童8-18号)	14	130	17	16	件/千克	A	Men's singlets, vests, and boys' No. 8 ~ No. 18, other than underwear, knitted or crocheted, of wool or fine animal hair
6109.9090 32	其他毛制男式汗衫及其他背心(针织或钩编,内衣除外)	14	130	17	16	件/千克	A	Men's or boys' singlets, vests, other than underwear, of wool or fine animal hair, knitted or crocheted
6109.9090 33	其他毛制女式汗衫及其他背心(针织或钩编,内衣除外)	14	130	17	16	件/千克	A	Women's or girls singlets vests, other than underwear, of wool or fine animal hair, knitted or crocheted
6109.9090 40	化纤制针织或钩编内衣	14	130	17	16	件/千克	A	Underwear, of man - made fibres, knitted or crocheted
6109.9090 50	化纤制针织或钩编T恤衫	14	130	17	16	件/千克	A	T - shirts, of man - made fibres, knitted or crocheted
6109.9090 60	化纤针织或钩编汗衫及其他背心	14	130	17	16	件/千克	A	Other singlets, vests, of man - made fibres, knitted or crocheted
6109.9090 91	其他纺织材料制T恤衫.汗衫等(针织或钩编,内衣式,包括其他背心)	14	130	17	16	件/千克	A	Other T-shirts, singlets and other vests underwear style, of other textile materials, knitted or crocheted
6109.9090 92	其他纺材针织钩编汗衫及其他背心(内衣除外,包括男童8-18号,女童7-16号)	14	130	17	16	件/千克	A	Other singlets, and other vests, other than underwear, of other textile materials, including boys' No. 8 ~ No. 18 or girls' No. 7 ~ No. 16, knitted or crocheted
6109.9090 93	其他纺材制针织钩编T恤衫、汗衫(内衣除外,包括其他背心)	14	130	17	16	件/千克	A	Other T-shirts, singlets and other vests, other than underwear, of other textile materials, knitted or crocheted
61.10	针织或钩编的套头衫、开襟衫、背心及类似品:							**Jerseys, pullovers, cardigans, waistcoats and similar articles, knitted or crocheted:**
	-羊毛或动物细毛制:							-Of wool or fine animal hair:
6110.1100	--羊毛制	14	130	17	16	件/千克		--Of wool
6110.1100 11	羊毛制手工针织或钩编起绒外穿背心	14	130	17	16	件/千克		Waistcoats, piled, hand-worked, knitted or crocheted, of wool
6110.1100 19	羊毛制针织或钩编起绒外穿背心	14	130	17	16	件/千克		Waistcoats, piled, knitted or crocheted, of wool
6110.1100 21	羊毛制手工制起绒男毛衫(针织或钩编)	14	130	17	16	件/千克		Men's or boys' sweater, piled, hand-worked, knitted or crocheted, of wool
6110.1100 29	羊毛制针织或钩编起绒男毛衫	14	130	17	16	件/千克		Men's or boys' sweater, piled, knitted or crocheted, of wool
6110.1100 31	羊毛制手工制起绒女毛衫(针织或钩编)	14	130	17	16	件/千克		Women's or girls' sweater, hand-worked, piled, knitted or crocheted, of wool
6110.1100 39	羊毛制针织或钩编起绒女毛衫	14	130	17	16	件/千克		Women's or girls' sweater, piled, knitted or crocheted, of wool
6110.1100 41	羊毛手工制起绒套头衫等(包括开襟衫、背心及类似品,针织或钩编)	14	130	17	16	件/千克		Pullovers, cardigans, waistcoats and similar articles, knitted or crocheted, of wool, hand-worked, piled
6110.1100 49	羊毛针织或钩编起绒套头衫等(包括开襟衫、背心及类似品)	14	130	17	16	件/千克		Pullovers, cardigans, waistcoats and similar articles, knitted or crocheted, of wool, piled

税则号列	货品名称	最惠(%)	普通	增值税率	出口退税	计量单位	监管条件	Article Description
6110.1100 51	羊毛手工制非起绒外穿背心(针织或钩编)	14	130	17	16	件/千克		Waistcoats, hand-worked, not piled, knitted or crocheted, of wool
6110.1100 59	羊毛针织或钩编非起绒外穿背心	14	130	17	16	件/千克		Waistcoats, not piled, knitted or crocheted, of wool
6110.1100 61	其他羊毛手工制非起绒男毛衫(针织或钩编)	14	130	17	16	件/千克		Other men's or boys' sweater, hand-worked, not piled, knitted or crocheted, of wool
6110.1100 69	其他羊毛针织或钩编非起绒男毛衫	14	130	17	16	件/千克		Other men's or boys' sweater, not piled, knitted or crocheted of wool
6110.1100 71	其他羊毛制手工制非起绒女毛衫(针织或钩编)	14	130	17	16	件/千克		Other women's or girls' sweater, hand-worked, not piled, knitted or crocheted, of wool
6110.1100 79	其他羊毛针织或钩编非起绒女毛衫	14	130	17	16	件/千克		Other women's or girls' sweater, not piled, knitted or crocheted, of wool
6110.1100 91	其他羊毛制手工制非起绒套头衫等(针织或钩编,包括开襟衫、背心及类似品)	14	130	17	16	件/千克		Pullovers, cardigans, waistcoats and similar articles, knitted or crocheted, of wool other, hand-worked, not piled
6110.1100 99	其他羊毛制非起绒套头衫等(针织或钩编,包括开襟衫、背心及类似品)	14	130	17	16	件/千克		Pullovers, cardigans, waistcoats and similar articles, knitted or crocheted, of wool other, not piled
6110.1200	--喀什米尔山羊细毛制	14	130	17	16	件/千克		--Of Kashmir(cashmere) goats
6110.1200 11	喀什米尔山羊细毛手工起绒男套头衫(针织或钩编,包括开襟衫、外穿背心及类似品)	14	130	17	16	件/千克		Men's or boys' pullovers, cardigans, waistcoats and similar articles, of fine hair of Kashmir (cashmere) goats, knitted or crocheted, piled, hand-worked
6110.1200 19	喀什米尔山羊细毛制起绒男套头衫(针织或钩编,包括开襟衫、外穿背心及类似品)	14	130	17	16	件/千克		Men's or boys' pullovers, cardigans, waistcoats and similar articles of fine hair of Kashmir (cashmere) goats, knitted or crocheted, piled
6110.1200 21	喀什米尔山羊细毛手工起绒女套头衫(针织或钩编,包括开襟衫、外穿背心及类似品)	14	130	17	16	件/千克		Women's or girls' pullovers, cardigans, waistcoats and similar articles, of fine hair of Kashmir (cashmere) goats, knitted or crocheted, piled, hand-worked
6110.1200 29	喀什米尔山羊细毛制起绒女套头衫(针织或钩编,包括开襟衫、外穿背心及类似品)	14	130	17	16	件/千克		Women's or girls' pullovers, cardigans, waistcoats and similar articles, of fine hair of Kashmir (cashmere) goats, knitted or crocheted, piled
6110.1200 31	喀什米尔山羊细毛手工非起绒男套头衫(针织或钩编,包括开襟衫、外穿背心及类似品)	14	130	17	16	件/千克		Men's or boys' pullovers, cardigans, waistcoats and similar articles, of fine hair of Kashmir (cashmere) goats, knitted or crocheted, not piled, hand-worked
6110.1200 39	喀什米尔山羊细毛非起绒男套头衫(针织或钩编,包括开襟衫、外穿背心及类似品)	14	130	17	16	件/千克		Men's or boys' pullovers, cardigans, waistcoats and similar articles, of fine hair of Kashmir (cashmere) goats, knitted or crocheted, not piled
6110.1200 41	喀什米尔山羊细毛手工非起绒女套头衫(针织或钩编,包括开襟衫、外穿背心及类似品)	14	130	17	16	件/千克		Women's or girls' pullovers, cardigans, waistcoats and similar articles, of fine hair of Kashmir (cashmere) goats, knitted or crocheted, not piled, hand-worked
6110.1200 49	喀什米尔山羊细毛非起绒女套头衫(针织或钩编,包括开襟衫、外穿背心及类似品)	14	130	17	16	件/千克		Women's or girls' pullovers, cardigans, waistcoats and similar articles, of fine hair of Kashmir (cashmere) goats, knitted or crocheted, not piled
	--其他:							--Other:
6110.1910	---其他山羊细毛制	14	130	17	16	件/千克		---Of other goats
6110.1910 11	其他山羊细毛手工起绒男套头衫(针织或钩编,包括开襟衫、背心及类似品)	14	130	17	16	件/千克		Other men's or boys' pullovers, cardigans, waistcoats and similar articles, of fine hair or wool of other goats, knitted or crocheted, piled, hand-worked
6110.1910 19	其他山羊细毛制起绒男套头衫(针织或钩编,包括开襟衫、背心及类似品)	14	130	17	16	件/千克		Other men's or boys' pullovers, cardigans, waistcoats and similar articles, of fine hair or wool of other goats, knitted or crocheted, piled
6110.1910 21	其他山羊细毛手工起绒女套头衫(针织或钩编,包括开襟衫、背心及类似品)	14	130	17	16	件/千克		Other women's or girls' pullovers, cardigans, waistcoats and similar articles, of fine hair or wool of other goats, knitted or crocheted, piled, hand-worked

税则号列	货品名称	最惠(%)	普通	增值税率	出口退税	计量单位	监管条件	Article Description
6110.1910 29	其他山羊细毛制起绒女套头衫(针织或钩编,包括开襟衫、背心及类似品)	14	130	17	16	件/千克		Other women's or girls' pullovers, cardigans, waistcoats and similar articles, of fine hair or wool of other goats, knitted or crocheted, piled
6110.1910 31	其他山羊细毛手工非起绒男套头衫(针织或钩编,包括开襟衫、背心及类似品)	14	130	17	16	件/千克		Other men's or boys' pullovers, cardigans, waistcoats and similar articles, of fine hair or wool of other goats, knitted or crocheted, not piled hand-worked
6110.1910 39	其他山羊细毛非起绒男套头衫(针织或钩编,包括开襟衫、背心及类似品)	14	130	17	16	件/千克		Other men's or boys' pullovers, cardigans, waistcoats and similar articles, of fine hair or wool of other goats, knitted or crocheted, not piled
6110.1910 41	其他山羊细毛手工非起绒女套头衫(针织或钩编,包括开襟衫、背心及类似品)	14	130	17	16	件/千克		Other women's or girls' pullovers, cardigans, waistcoats and similar articles of fine hair or wool of other goats, knitted or crocheted, not piled, hand-worked
6110.1910 49	其他山羊细毛非起绒女套头衫(针织或钩编,包括开襟衫、背心及类似品)	14	130	17	16	件/千克		Other women's or girls' pullovers, cardigans, waistcoats and similar articles, of fine hair or wool of other goats, knitted or crocheted, not piled
6110.1920	---兔毛制	14	130	17	16	件/千克		---Of rabbit and hare
6110.1920 11	兔毛制手工针织或钩编起绒马甲	14	130	17	16	件/千克		Waistcoats, piled, hand-worked, knitted or crocheted, of rabbit' or hare' fine hair
6110.1920 19	兔毛制针织或钩编起绒马甲	14	130	17	16	件/千克		Waistcoats, piled, knitted or crocheted, of rabbit' or hare' fine hair
6110.1920 21	兔毛制手工针织或钩编起绒男毛衫	14	130	17	16	件/千克		Men's or boys' sweater, piled, hand-worked, knitted or crocheted, of rabbit' or hare' fine hair
6110.1920 29	兔毛制针织或钩编起绒男毛衫	14	130	17	16	件/千克		Men's or boys' sweater, piled, knitted or crocheted, of rabbit' or hare' fine hair
6110.1920 31	兔毛制手工针织或钩编起绒女毛衫	14	130	17	16	件/千克		Women's or girls' sweater, piled, hand-worked, knitted or crocheted, of rabbit' or hare' fine hair
6110.1920 39	兔毛制针织或钩编起绒女毛衫	14	130	17	16	件/千克		Women's or girls' sweater, piled, knitted or crocheted, of rabbit' or hare' fine hair
6110.1920 41	其他兔毛制手工制起绒套头衫等(针织或钩编,包括开襟衫、背心及类似品)	14	130	17	16	件/千克		Pullovers, cardigans, waistcoats and similar articles, knitted or crocheted, piled, of rabbit' or hare' fine hair, hand-worked
6110.1920 49	其他兔毛制起绒套头衫等(针织或钩编,包括开襟衫、背心及类似品)	14	130	17	16	件/千克		Pullovers, cardigans, waistcoats and similar articles, knitted or crocheted, piled, of rabbit' or hare' fine hair
6110.1920 51	兔毛制手工制非起绒马甲(针织或钩编)	14	130	17	16	件/千克		Waistcoats, hand-worked, not piled, knitted or crocheted, of rabbit' or hare' fine hair
6110.1920 59	兔毛制针织或钩编非起绒马甲	14	130	17	16	件/千克		Waistcoats, not piled, knitted or crocheted, of rabbit' or hare' fine hair
6110.1920 61	兔毛制手工制非起绒男毛衫(针织或钩编)	14	130	17	16	件/千克		Men's or boys' sweater, hand-worked, not piled, knitted or crocheted, of rabbit' or hare' fine hair
6110.1920 69	兔毛制针织或钩编非起绒男毛衫	14	130	17	16	件/千克		Men's or boys' sweater, not piled, knitted or crocheted, of rabbit' or hare' fine hair
6110.1920 71	兔毛制手工制非起绒女毛衫(针织或钩编)	14	130	17	16	件/千克		Women's or girls' sweater, hand-worked, not piled, knitted or crocheted, of rabbit' or hare' fine hair
6110.1920 79	兔毛制针织或钩编非起绒女毛衫	14	130	17	16	件/千克		Women's or girls' sweater, not piled, knitted or crocheted, of rabbit' or hare' fine hair
6110.1920 91	其他兔毛制手工制非起绒套头衫等(针织或钩编,包括开襟衫、背心及类似品)	14	130	17	16	件/千克		Other pullovers, cardigans, waistcoats and similar articles, knitted or crocheted, not piled, of rabbit' or hare' fine hair hand-worked
6110.1920 99	其他兔毛制非起绒套头衫等(针织或钩编,包括开襟衫、背心及类似品)	14	130	17	16	件/千克		Other pullovers, cardigans, waistcoats and similar articles, knitted or crocheted, not piled, of rabbit' or hare' fine hair
6110.1990	---其他	14	130	17	16	件/千克		---Other
6110.1990 11	其他动物细毛制手工起绒马甲(针织或钩编)	14	130	17	16	件/千克		Waistcoats, piled, hand-worked, of other fine animal hair, knitted or crocheted
6110.1990 19	其他动物细毛制起绒马甲(针织或钩编)	14	130	17	16	件/千克		Waistcoats, piled, of other fine animal hair, knitted or crocheted

税则号列	货品名称	最惠(%)	普通	增值税率	出口退税	计量单位	监管条件	Article Description
6110. 1990 21	其他动物细毛制手工起绒男毛衫(针织或钩编)	14	130	17	16	件/千克		Men's or boys' sweater, piled, hand-worked, of other fine animal hair, knitted or crocheted
6110. 1990 29	其他动物细毛制起绒男毛衫(针织或钩编)	14	130	17	16	件/千克		Men's or boys' sweater, piled, of other fine animal hair, knitted or crocheted
6110. 1990 31	其他动物细毛制手工起绒女毛衫(针织或钩编)	14	130	17	16	件/千克		Women's or girls' sweater, piled, hand-worked, of other fine animal hair, knitted or crocheted
6110. 1990 39	其他动物细毛制起绒女毛衫(针织或钩编)	14	130	17	16	件/千克		Women's or girls' sweater, piled, of other fine animal hair, knitted or crocheted
6110. 1990 41	其他动物细毛制手工起绒套头衫(针织或钩编,包括开襟衫、背心及类似品)	14	130	17	16	件/千克		Pullovers, cardigans, waistcoats and similar articles, knitted or crocheted, piled, of other fine animal hair, hand-worked
6110. 1990 49	其他动物细毛制起绒套头衫(针织或钩编,包括开襟衫、背心及类似品)	14	130	17	16	件/千克		Pullovers, cardigans, waistcoats and similar articles, knitted or crocheted, piled, of other fine animal hair
6110. 1990 51	其他动物细毛制手工非起绒马甲(针织或钩编)	14	130	17	16	件/千克		Waistcoats, hand-worked, not piled, knitted or crocheted, of other fine animal hair
6110. 1990 59	其他动物细毛制非起绒马甲(针织或钩编)	14	130	17	16	件/千克		Waistcoats, hand-worked, knitted or crocheted, not piled, of other fine animal hair
6110. 1990 61	其他动物细毛制手工非起绒男毛衫(针织或钩编)	14	130	17	16	件/千克		Men's or boys' sweater, hand-worked, not piled, knitted or crocheted, of other fine animal hair
6110. 1990 69	其他动物细毛制非起绒男毛衫(针织或钩编)	14	130	17	16	件/千克		Men's or boys' sweater, knitted or crocheted, not piled, of other fine animal hair
6110. 1990 71	其他动物细毛制手工非起绒女毛衫(针织或钩编)	14	130	17	16	件/千克		Women's or girls' sweater, not piled, hand-worked, knitted or crocheted, of other fine animal hair
6110. 1990 79	其他动物细毛制非起绒女毛衫(针织或钩编)	14	130	17	16	件/千克		Women's or girls' sweater, not piled, knitted or crocheted, of other fine animal hair
6110. 1990 91	其他动物细毛制手工非起绒套头衫(针织或钩编,包括开襟衫、背心及类似品)	14	130	17	16	件/千克		Pullovers, cardigans, waistcoats and similar articles, knitted or crocheted, not piled, of other fine animal hair, hand-worked
6110. 1990 99	其他动物细毛制非起绒套头衫(针织或钩编,包括开襟衫、背心及类似品)	14	130	17	16	件/千克		Pullovers, cardigans, waistcoats and similar articles, knitted or crocheted, not piled, of other fine animal hair
6110. 2000	-棉制	14	90	17	16	件/千克		-Of cotton
6110. 2000 11	棉制儿童游戏套装紧身衫及套头衫(针织起绒,轻薄细针翻领、开领、高领,含亚麻36%以下)	14	90	17	16	件/千克	A	Boys' or girls' playsuit, jerseys, pullovers, tricolette turn-down collar, open-necked collar, high-necked collar, containing <36% by weight of flax, of cotton knitted, piled
6110. 2000 12	棉制其他起绒儿童游戏套头衫等(针织或钩编,包括开襟衫、背心及类似品,含亚麻36%以下)	14	90	17	16	件/千克	A	Other boys' or girls' playsuit, pullovers, cardigans, waistcoats and similar articles, containing <36% by weight of flax, of cotton, knitted or crocheted
6110. 2000 20	棉制针织或钩编起绒马甲(毛衫、背心除外)	14	90	17	16	件/千克		Waistcoats, piled, other than sweater, of cotton, knitted or crocheted
6110. 2000 31	棉制针织起绒紧身及套头毛衫(轻薄细针翻领、开领、高领)	14	90	17	16	件/千克		Jerseys or pullovers, piled, tricolette turn-down collar, open-necked collar, high-necked collar, of cotton, knitted
6110. 2000 32	棉制针织起绒男紧身衫及套头衫(轻薄细针翻领、开领、高领,但平床机生产、直接针织成形除外)	14	90	17	16	件/千克		Men's or boys' jerseys, pullovers, piled, tricolette turn-down collar, open-necked collar, high-necked collar, of cotton, knitted
6110. 2000 33	棉制针织起绒女紧身衫及套头衫(轻薄细针翻领、开领、高领,但平床机生产、直接针织成形除外)	14	90	17	16	件/千克		Women's or girls' jerseys, pullovers, piled, tricolette turn-down collar, open-necked collar, high-necked collar, of cotton knitted
6110. 2000 41	棉制针织或钩编起绒其他毛衫	14	90	17	16	件/千克		Other sweater, piled, of cotton, knitted or crocheted
6110. 2000 42	棉制针织或钩编起绒男套头衫等(包括开襟衫、背心及类似品,但平床机生产、直接针织成形除外)	14	90	17	16	件/千克		Men's or boys' pullovers, cardigans, waistcoats and similar articles, piled, of cotton, knitted or crocheted
6110. 2000 43	棉制针织或钩编起绒女套头衫等(包括开襟衫、背心及类似品,但平床机生产、直接针织成形除外)	14	90	17	16	件/千克		Women's or girls' pullovers, cardigans, waistcoats and similar articles, piled, of cotton, knitted or crocheted

税则号列	货品名称	最惠(%)	普通	增值税率	出口退税	计量单位	监管条件	Article Description
6110.2000 51	其他棉制儿童游戏套装紧身及套头衫(针织、非起绒、轻薄细针翻领、开领、高领)	14	90	17	16	件/千克	A	Other boys' or girls' playsuit, jerseys, pullovers, tricolette turn-down collar, open-necked collar, high-necked collar, not piled, of cotton, knitted
6110.2000 52	其他棉制儿童游戏套装套头衫等(针织或钩编、非起绒、包括开襟衫、背心及类似品)	14	90	17	16	件/千克	A	Other boys' or girls' playsuit pullovers, cardigans, waistcoats and similar articles, of cotton, knitted or crocheted not piled
6110.2000 60	其他棉制针织或钩编非起绒马甲(毛衫、背心除外)	14	90	17	16	件/千克		Other waistcoats, other than sweater, not piled, of cotton, knitted or crocheted
6110.2000 71	棉制针织非起绒男紧身及套头衫等(轻薄细针翻领、开领、高领)	14	90	17	16	件/千克		Men's or boys' jerseys, pullovers, tricolette turn-down collar, open-necked collar, high-necked collar, knitted, not piled, of cotton, knitted
6110.2000 72	棉制非起绒男紧身衫及套头衫(轻薄细针翻领、开领、高领,但平床机生产、直接针织成形除外)	14	90	17	16	件/千克		Men's or boys' jerseys, pullovers, tricolette turn-down collar, open-necked collar, high-necked collar, not piled, of cotton
6110.2000 73	棉制针织非起绒女紧身衫及套头衫(轻薄细针翻领、开领、高领,但平床机生产、直接针织成形除外)	14	90	17	16	件/千克		Women's or girls' jerseys, pullovers, tricolette turn-down collar, open-necked collar, high-necked collar, knitted, not piled, of cotton, knitted
6110.2000 91	其他棉制针织或钩编非起绒毛衫	14	90	17	16	件/千克		Other sweater, not piled, of cotton, knitted or crocheted
6110.2000 92	其他针织钩编棉制非起绒男套头衫等(包括开襟衫、背心及类似品,但平床机生产、直接针织成形除外)	14	90	17	16	件/千克		Other men's or boys' pullovers, cardigans, waistcoats and similar articles, not piled, of cotton, knitted or crocheted
6110.2000 93	棉制针织或钩编女套头衫等(包括开襟衫、背心及类似品,但平床机生产、直接针织成形除外)	14	90	17	16	件/千克		Women's or girls' pullovers, cardigans, waistcoats and similar articles, not piled, of cotton, knitted or crocheted
6110.2000 99	其他棉制针织钩编套头衫等(包括开襟衫、背心及类似品)	14	90	17	16	件/千克		Other pullovers, cardigans, waistcoats and similar articles, not piled, of cotton, knitted or crocheted
6110.3000	-化学纤维制	16	130	17	16	件/千克		-Of man-made fibres
6110.3000 11	化纤儿童游戏套装紧身衫及套头衫(针织起绒,轻薄细针翻领、开领、高领毛<23%,丝<30%)	16	130	17	16	件/千克	A	Boys' or girls' playsuit, jerseys, pullovers, tricolette turn-down collar, open-necked collar, high-necked collar, containing < 23% by weight of wool or fine animal hair, containing < 30% by weight of silk or silk waste, of man-made fibres, knitted, piled
6110.3000 12	化纤起绒儿童游戏套装及套头衫等(针织或钩编包括开襟衫、背心及类似品含毛<23%,含丝<30%)	16	130	17	16	件/千克	A	Boys' or girls' playsuit, jerseys, pullovers, tricolette turn-down collar, open-necked collar, high-necked collar, containing < 23% by weight of wool or fine animal hair, containing < 30% by weight of silk or silk waste, of man-made fibres knitted, piled
6110.3000 21	化纤制针织或钩编起绒马甲(含羊毛或动物细毛23%及以上)	16	130	17	16	件/千克		Waistcoats, piled, containing ≥ 23% by weight of wool or fine animal hair, of man-made fibres, knitted or crocheted
6110.3000 22	化纤制针织起绒男紧身及套头毛衫(含羊毛或动物细毛23%及以上,轻薄细针翻领、开领、高领)	16	130	17	16	件/千克		Men's or boys' jerseys, pullovers, piled, knitted, containing≥23% by weight of wool or fine animal hair, tricolette turn-down collar, open-necked collar, high-necked collar, of man-made fibres
6110.3000 23	化纤制针织或钩编起绒男毛衫(含羊毛或动物细毛23%及以上)	16	130	17	16	件/千克		Men's or boys' sweater, piled, containing ≥ 23% by weight of wool or fine animal hair, of man-made fibres, knitted or crocheted
6110.3000 24	化纤制针织起绒女紧身及套头毛衫	16	130	17	16	件/千克		Women's or girls' jerseys, pullovers, piled, knitted, of man-made fibres
6110.3000 25	化纤制针织或钩编起绒女毛衫(含羊毛或动物细毛23%及以上)	16	130	17	16	件/千克		Women's or girls' sweater, piled, containing ≥ 23% by weight of wool or fine animal hair, of man-made fibres, knitted or crocheted
6110.3000 26	其他化纤针织起绒套头衫(含羊毛或动物细毛≥23%,轻薄细针翻领、开领、高领)	16	130	17	16	件/千克		Other pullovers, piled, knitted, containing≥23% by weight of wool or fine animal hair, of man-made fibres, tricolette turn-down collar, open-necked collar, high-necked collar

税则号列	货品名称	最惠(%)	普通	增值税率	出口退税	计量单位	监管条件	Article Description
6110. 3000 29	其他化纤针织或钩编起绒开襟衫等(含羊毛或动物细毛≥23%,包括背心及类似品)	16	130	17	16	件/千克		Other cardigans, waistcoats and similar articles, piled, containing ≥23% by weight of wool or fine animal hair, of man-made fibres, knitted or crocheted
6110. 3000 31	其他化纤制针织或钩编起绒马甲	16	130	17	16	件/千克		Other waistcoats, piled, of man-made fibres, knitted or crocheted
6110. 3000 32	化纤针织或起绒男紧身及套头毛衫(轻薄细针翻领、开领、高领)	16	130	17	16	件/千克		Men's or boys' jerseys, pullovers, knitted or piled, tricolette turn-down collar, open-necked collar, high-necked collar, of man-made fibres
6110. 3000 33	其他化纤制针织或钩编起绒男毛衫	16	130	17	16	件/千克		Other men's or boys' sweater, of man-made fibres, knitted or crocheted
6110. 3000 34	化纤制针织起绒女紧身及套头毛衫(轻薄细针、翻领、开领、高领)	16	130	17	16	件/千克		Women's or girls' jerseys, pullovers, piled, knitted, tricolette turn-down collar, open-necked collar, high-necked collar, of man-made fibres
6110. 3000 35	其他化纤制针织或钩编起绒女毛衫	16	130	17	16	件/千克		Other women's or girls' sweater, piled, of man-made fibres knitted or crocheted
6110. 3000 36	其他化纤针织起绒男套头衫(轻薄细针翻领、开领、高领,但平床机生产、直接针织成形除外)	16	130	17	16	件/千克		Other men's or boys' pullovers, piled, tricolette turn-down collar, open-necked collar, high-necked collar, of man-made fibres, knitted or crocheted
6110. 3000 37	其他化纤针织钩编起绒男开襟衫等(包括背心及类似品,但平床机生产、直接针织成形除外)	16	130	17	16	件/千克		Other men's or boys' cardigans, piled, including waistcoats and similar articles, of man-made fibres, knitted or crocheted
6110. 3000 38	其他化纤起绒针织女套头衫(轻薄细针翻领、开领、高领,但平床机生产、直接针织成形除外)	16	130	17	16	件/千克		Other women's or girls' pullovers, piled, tricolette turn-down collar, open-necked collar, high-necked collar, of man-made fibres, knitted
6110. 3000 39	其他化纤制针织或钩编女开襟衫等(起绒,包括背心及类似品,但平床机生产、直接针织成形除外)	16	130	17	16	件/千克		Other women's or girls' cardigans, including waistcoats and similar articles, piled, of man-made fibres, knitted or crocheted
6110. 3000 41	化纤其他儿童游戏套装紧身及套头衫(针织非起绒,轻薄细针翻领、开领、高领)	16	130	17	16	件/千克	A	Other boys' or girls' playsuit, jerseys, pullovers, knitted, tricolette turn-down collar, open-necked collar, high-necked collar, not piled, of man-made fibres, knitted
6110. 3000 42	化纤制其他儿童游戏套装套头衫等(针织或钩编,非起绒,包括开襟衫、背心及类似品)	16	130	17	16	件/千克	A	Other boys' or girls' playsuit, including cardigans, waistcoats and similar articles, not piled, of man-made fibres, knitted or crocheted
6110. 3000 51	其他化纤制针织或钩编非起绒马甲(含羊毛或动物细毛23%及以上)	16	130	17	16	件/千克		Other waistcoats, containing ≥ 23% by weight of wool or fine animal hair, not piled, of man-made fibres, knitted or crocheted
6110. 3000 52	化纤针织非起绒男紧身及套头毛衫(含羊毛或动物细毛23%及以上,轻薄细针翻领、开领、高领)	16	130	17	16	件/千克		Men's or boys' jerseys, pullovers, containing ≥23% by weight of wool or fine animal hair, tricolette turn-down collar, open-necked collar, high-necked collar, not piled, of man-made fibres, knitted
6110. 3000 53	化纤制针织或钩编非起绒男毛衫(含羊毛或动物细毛23%及以上)	16	130	17	16	件/千克		Men's or boys' sweater, containing≥23% by weight of wool or fine animal hair, not piled, of man-made fibres, knitted or crocheted
6110. 3000 54	化纤针织非起绒女紧身及套头毛衫(含羊毛或动物细毛23%及以上,轻薄细针翻领、开领、高领)	16	130	17	16	件/千克		Women's or girls' jerseys, pullovers, containing ≥ 23% by weight of wool or fine animal hair, tricolette turn-down collar, open-necked collar, high-necked collar, not piled, of man-made fibres, knitted
6110. 3000 57	化纤制针织钩编非起绒女毛衫(含羊毛或动物细毛23%及以上)	16	130	17	16	件/千克		Women's or girls' sweater, containing ≥ 23% by weight of wool or fine animal hair, not piled, of man-made fibres, knitted or crocheted
6110. 3000 58	其他化纤针织非起绒套头衫(含毛≥23%非起绒,轻薄细针翻领、开领、高领)	16	130	17	16	件/千克		Other pullovers, containing≥23% by weight of wool or fine animal hair, tricolette turn-down collar, open-necked collar, high-necked collar, not piled, of man-made fibres, knitted

税则号列	货品名称	最惠(%)	普通	增值税率	出口退税	计量单位	监管条件	Article Description
6110.3000 59	其他化纤针织或钩编开襟衫等(含羊毛或动物细毛≥23%,非起绒,包括背心及类似品)	16	130	17	16	件/千克		Other cardingans, including waistcoats and similar articles, containing≥23% by weight of wool or fine animal hair, not piled, of man-made fibres, knitted or crocheted
6110.3000 91	其他化纤针织男紧身及套头毛衫(非起绒,轻薄细针翻领、开领、高领)	16	130	17	16	件/千克		Other men's or boys' jerseys, pullovers, tricolette turn-down collar, open-necked collar, high-necked collar, not piled, of man-made fibres, knitted
6110.3000 92	其他化纤针织或钩编非起绒男毛衫	16	130	17	16	件/千克		Other men's or boys' sweater, not piled, of man-made fibres, knitted or crocheted
6110.3000 93	化纤针织非起绒女紧身及套头毛衫(轻薄细针翻领、开领、高领)	16	130	17	16	件/千克		Other women's or girls' jerseys, pullovers, tricolette turn-down collar, open-necked collar, high-necked collar, not piled, of man-made fibres, knitted
6110.3000 94	其他化纤针织或钩编非起绒女毛衫	16	130	17	16	件/千克		Other women's or girls' sweater, not piled, of man-made fibres, knitted or crocheted
6110.3000 95	其他化纤针织非起绒男套头衫(轻薄细针翻领、开领、高领,但平床机生产、直接针织成形除外)	16	130	17	16	件/千克		Other men's or boys' pullovers, tricolette turn-down collar, open-necked collar, high-necked collar, not piled, of man-made fibres, knitted
6110.3000 96	其他化纤针织或钩编男开襟衫等(非起绒,包括外穿背心及类似品,但平床机生产、直接针织成形除外)	16	130	17	16	件/千克		Other men's or boys' cardigans, waistcoats and similar articles, not piled, of man-made fibres, knitted or crocheted
6110.3000 97	其他化纤制针织非起绒女套头衫(轻薄细针翻领、开领、高领,但平床机生产、直接针织成形除外)	16	130	17	16	件/千克		Other women's or girls' pullovers, tricolette turn-down collar, open-necked collar, high-necked collar, not piled of man-made fibres, knitted
6110.3000 98	其他化纤制针织或钩编女开襟衫等(包括外穿背心及类似品,但平床机生产、直接针织成形除外)	16	130	17	16	件/千克		Other women's or girls' cardigans, waistcoats and similar articles of man-made fibres, knitted or crocheted
6110.3000 99	其他化纤制针织钩编套头衫等(包括开襟衫,背心及类似品)	16	130	17	16	件/千克		Other pullovers, of man-made fibres, knitted or crocheted, including cardingams, waistcoats and similar articles
	-其他纺织材料制:							-Of other textile materials:
6110.9010	---丝及绢丝制	14	130	17	16	件/千克		---Of silk or spun silk
6110.9010 11	丝及绢丝制针织或钩编起绒毛衫等(含丝≥70%,含开衫、马甲)	14	130	17	16	件/千克		Sweater, including cardigans, waistcoats, piled, containing≥70% by weight of silk or silk waste, knitted or crocheted
6110.9010 19	丝及绢丝制针织或钩编起绒毛衫等(含丝<70%,含开衫、马甲)	14	130	17	16	件/千克		Sweater, including cardigans, waistcoats, piled, knitted or crocheted, containing<70% by weight of silk or spun silk
6110.9010 91	其他丝及绢丝针织或钩编毛衫等(非起绒,含丝≥70%,含开衫、马甲)	14	130	17	16	件/千克		Other sweater, including cardigans, waistcoats, containing≥70% by weight of silk or spun silk, not piled, knitted or crocheted
6110.9010 99	其他丝及绢丝针织或钩编毛衫等(非起绒,含丝<70%,含开衫、马甲)	14	130	17	16	件/千克		Other sweater, including cardigans, waistcoats, not piled, knitted or crocheted, containing < 70% by weight of silk or spun silk
6110.9090	---其他	14	130	17	16	件/千克		---Other
6110.9090 11	其他纺织材料针织或钩编起绒马甲(棉限内,毛衫背心除外)	14	130	17	16	件/千克		Waistcoats, piled, other than sweater or sleeveless, knitted or crocheted, of other textile materials, cotton within limitations
6110.9090 12	其他纺织材料针织或钩编起绒马甲(羊毛限内,毛衫背心除外)	14	130	17	16	件/千克		Waistcoats, piled, other than sweater or sleeveless, knitted or crocheted, of other textile materials, wool within limitations
6110.9090 13	其他纺织材料针织或钩编起绒马甲(化纤限内,毛衫背心除外)	14	130	17	16	件/千克		Waistcoats, piled, other than sweater or sleeveless sweater, knitted or crocheted, of other textile materials, man-made fibres within limitations
6110.9090 19	其他纺织材料起绒针织或钩编马甲(毛衫背心除外)	14	130	17	16	件/千克		Waistcoats, piled, other than sweater or sleeveless sweater, knitted or crocheted, of other textile materials

税则号列	货品名称	最惠(%)	普通	增值税率	出口退税	计量单位	监管条件	Article Description
6110.9090 21	其他纺织材料制针织或钩编非起绒马甲(棉限内,毛衫背心除外)	14	130	17	16	件/千克		Waistcoats, not piled, other than sweater or sleeveless sweater, knitted or crocheted, of other textile materials, cotton within limitations
6110.9090 22	其他纺织材料制针织或钩编非起绒马甲(羊毛限内,毛衫背心除外)	14	130	17	16	件/千克		Waistcoats, not piled, other than sweater or sleeveless sweater, knitted or crocheted, of other textile materials, wool within limitations
6110.9090 23	其他纺织材料制针织或钩编非起绒马甲(化纤限内,毛衫、背心除外)	14	130	17	16	件/千克		Waistcoats, not piled, other than sweater or sleeveless sweater, knitted or crocheted, of other textile materials, man-made fibres within limitations
6110.9090 29	其他纺织材料制针织或钩编马甲(非起绒,毛衫、背心除外)	14	130	17	16	件/千克		Waistcoats, not piled, other than sweater or sleeveless sweater, knitted or crocheted, of other textile materials
6110.9090 31	其他纺织材料制针织或钩编起绒毛衫(棉限内)	14	130	17	16	件/千克		Sweater, piled, knitted or crocheted, of other textile materials, cotton within limitations
6110.9090 33	其他纺织材料制针织或钩编起绒男毛衫(羊毛限内)	14	130	17	16	件/千克		Men's or boys' sweater, piled, knitted or crocheted, of other textile materials, wool within limitations
6110.9090 34	其他纺织材料制针织或钩编起绒女毛衫(羊毛限内)	14	130	17	16	件/千克		Women's or girls' sweater, piled, knitted or crocheted, of other textile materials, wool within limitations
6110.9090 35	其他纺织材料制针织或钩编起绒男毛衫(化纤限内)	14	130	17	16	件/千克		Men's or boys' sweater, knitted or crocheted, of other textile materials, man-made fibres within limitations
6110.9090 36	其他纺织材料制针织或钩编起绒女毛衫(化纤限内)	14	130	17	16	件/千克		Women's or girls' sweater, piled, knitted or crocheted, of other textile materials, man-made fibres within limitations
6110.9090 39	其他纺织材料制针织或钩编毛衫(起绒)	14	130	17	16	件/千克		Other sweater, piled, knitted or crocheted, of other textile materials
6110.9090 41	其他纺材针织或钩编起绒男套头衫等(棉限内,包括开襟衫、马甲及类似品,但平床机生产、直接针织成形除外)	14	130	17	16	件/千克		Men's or boys' pullovers, cardigans, waistcoats and similar articles, piled, knitted or crocheted, of other textile materials, cotton within limitations
6110.9090 42	其他纺织材料针织或钩编起绒女套头衫等(棉限内,包括开襟衫、马甲及类似品,但平床机生产、直接针织成形除外)	14	130	17	16	件/千克		Women's or girls' pullovers, cardigans, waistcoats and similar articles, piled, knitted or crocheted, of other textile materials, cotton within limitations
6110.9090 43	其他纺织材料针织或钩编起绒套头衫等(羊毛限内,包括开襟衫、马甲及类似品)	14	130	17	16	件/千克		Pullovers, cardigans, waistcoats and similar articles, piled, knitted or crocheted, of other textile materials, wool within limitations
6110.9090 45	其他纺织材料针织或钩编起绒男套头衫等(化纤限内,包括开襟衫、马甲及类似品,但平床机生产、直接针织成形除外)	14	130	17	16	件/千克		Men's or boys' pullovers, cardigans, waistcoats and similar articles, piled, knitted or crocheted, of other textile materials, man-made fibres within limitations
6110.9090 46	其他纺织材料针织或钩编起绒女套头衫等(化纤限内,包括开襟衫、马甲及类似品,但平床机生产、直接针织成形除外)	14	130	17	16	件/千克		Women's or girls' pullovers, cardigans, waistcoats and similar articles, piled, knitted or crocheted, of other textile materials, man-made fibres within limitations
6110.9090 49	其他纺织材料针织或钩编套头衫等(起绒,包括开襟衫、马甲及类似品)	14	130	17	16	件/千克		Pullovers, cardigans, waistcoats and similar articles, piled, knitted or crocheted, of other textile materials
6110.9090 51	其他纺织材料针织或钩编非起绒毛衫(棉限内)	14	130	17	16	件/千克		Sweater, not piled, knitted or crocheted, of other textile materials, cotton within limitations
6110.9090 53	其他纺织材料针织或钩编非起绒男毛衫(羊毛限内)	14	130	17	16	件/千克		Men's or boys' sweater, not piled, knitted or crocheted, of other textile materials, wool within limitations
6110.9090 54	其他纺织材料针织或钩编非起绒女毛衫(羊毛限内)	14	130	17	16	件/千克		Women's or girls' sweater, not piled, knitted or crocheted, of other textile materials, wool within limitations
6110.9090 57	其他纺织材料针织或钩编非起绒男毛衫(化纤限内)	14	130	17	16	件/千克		Men's or boys' sweater, not piled, knitted or crocheted, of other textile materials, man-made fibres within limitations
6110.9090 58	其他纺织材料针织或钩编非起绒女毛衫(化纤限内)	14	130	17	16	件/千克		Women's or girls' sweater, not piled, knitted or crocheted, of other textile materials, man-made fibres within limitations

税则号列	货品名称	最惠(%)	普通	增值税率	出口退税	计量单位	监管条件	Article Description
6110.9090 59	其他纺织材料针织或钩编毛衫(非起绒)	14	130	17	16	件/千克		Sweater, not piled, knitted or crocheted, of other textile materials
6110.9090 61	其他纺织材料制针织或钩编非起绒男套衫等(包括开襟衫、背心及类似品,但平床机生产、直接针织成形除外)	14	130	17	16	件/千克		Men's or boys' pullovers, cardigans, waistcoats and similar articles, not piled, knitted or crocheted, of other textile materials, cotton within limitations
6110.9090 62	其他纺织材料制针织或钩编非起绒女套衫等(包括开襟衫、背心及类似品,但平床机生产、直接针织成形除外)	14	130	17	16	件/千克		Women's or girls' pullovers, cardigans, waistcoats and similar articles, not piled, knitted or crocheted, of other textile materials, cotton within limitations
6110.9090 63	其他纺织材料制针织或钩编非起绒套头衫等(羊毛限内,包括开襟衫、背心及类似品)	14	130	17	16	件/千克		Other pullovers, cardigans, waistcoats and similar articles, not piled, knitted or crocheted of other textile materials, wool within limitations
6110.9090 65	其他纺织材料制针织或钩编非起绒男套衫等(化纤限内,包括开襟衫、背心及类似品,但平床机生产、直接针织成形除外)	14	130	17	16	件/千克		Men's or boys' pullovers, cardigans, waistcoats and similar articles, not piled, knitted or crocheted, of other textile materials, man-made fibres within limitations
6110.9090 66	其他纺织材料制针织或钩编非起绒女套衫等(化纤限内,包括开襟衫、背心及类似品,但平床机生产、直接针织成形除外)	14	130	17	16	件/千克		Women's or girls' pullovers, cardigans, waistcoats and similar articles, not piled, knitted or crocheted, of other textile materials, man-made fibres within limitations
6110.9090 69	其他纺织材料针织或钩编套头衫等(非起绒,包括开襟衫、背心及类似品)	14	130	17	16	件/千克		Other pullovers, cardigans, waistcoats and similar articles, not piled, knitted or crocheted, of other textile materials
6110.9090 90	其他纺织材料针织或钩编套头衫等(包括开襟衫、背心及类似品)	14	130	17	16	件/千克		Other pullovers, cardisans, waistcoats and similar articles, knities or crocheied, of other textile materials
61.11	针织或钩编的婴儿服装及衣着附件:							**Babies' garments and clothing accessories, knitted or crocheted:**
6111.2000	-棉制	14	90	17	16	千克		-Of cotton
6111.2000 10	棉制针织或钩编婴儿袜	14	90	17	16	千克	A	Babies' hosiery of cotton, knitted or crocheted
6111.2000 20	棉制婴儿分指、连指、露指手套(针制或钩编)	14	90	17	16	千克	A	Babies' gloves, mittens and mitts of cotton, knitted or crocheted
6111.2000 40	棉制针织婴儿外衣、雨衣、滑雪装(针制或钩编,包括夹克类似品)	14	90	17	16	千克	A	Babies' coat, raincoat, ski suit, including jacked and similar articles, of cotton, knitted or crocheted
6111.2000 50	棉制针织钩编婴儿其他服装	14	90	17	16	千克	A	Other babies' garments of cotton, knitted or crocheted
6111.2000 90	棉制针织钩编婴儿衣着附件	14	90	17	16	千克	A	Babies' clothing accessories of cotton, knitted or crocheted
6111.3000	-合成纤维制	16	130	17	16	千克		-Of synthetic fibres
6111.3000 10	合纤制针织或钩编婴儿袜	16	130	17	16	千克	A	Babies' hosiery of synthetic fibres, knitted or crocheted
6111.3000 20	合纤婴儿分指、连指及露指手套(针制或钩编)	16	130	17	16	千克	A	Babies' gloves, mittens and mitts of synthetic fibres, knitted or crocheted
6111.3000 40	合纤婴儿外衣、雨衣、滑雪装(针制或钩编,包括夹克类似服装)	16	130	17	16	千克	A	Babies' coat, raincoat, ski suit, jacked and similar articles, of synthetic fibres, knitted or crocheted
6111.3000 50	合纤针织或钩编婴儿其他服装(包括衣着附件)	16	130	17	16	千克	A	Other babies' garments of synthetic fibres, knitted or crocheted
6111.3000 90	合纤针织或钩编婴儿衣着附件	16	130	17	16	千克	A	Babies' clothing accessories of synthetic fibres, knitted or crocheted
	-其他纺织材料制:							-Of other textile materials
6111.9010	---羊毛或动物细毛制	14	130	17	16	千克	A	---Of wool or fine animal hair
6111.9090	---其他	14	130	17	16	千克		---Other
6111.9090 10	人造纤维针织或钩编婴儿袜	14	130	17	16	千克	A	Babies' hosiery of artificial fibres, knitted or crocheted
6111.9090 90	其他纺织材料制婴儿服装及衣着附件(针织或钩编)	14	130	17	16	千克	A	Babies' garments and clothing accessories, of other textile materials, knitted or crocheted
61.12	针织或钩编的运动服、滑雪服及游泳服:							**Track suits, ski suits and swimwear, knitted or crocheted:**
	-运动服:							-Track suits:
6112.1100	--棉制	16	90	17	16	套/千克		--Of cotton

税则号列	货品名称	最惠(%)	普通	增值税率	出口退税	计量单位	监管条件	Article Description
6112.1100 11	棉制针织或钩编男式运动套装	16	90	17	16	套/千克		Men's or boys' track suits of cotton, knitted or crocheted
6112.1100 19	棉制针织或钩编女式运动套装	16	90	17	16	套/千克		Women's or girls' track suits of cotton, knitted or crocheted
6112.1200	--合成纤维制	17.5	130	17	16	套/千克		--Of synthetic fibres
6112.1200 21	合纤制针织或钩编男式运动服	17.5	130	17	16	套/千克		Men's or boys' track suits of synthetic fibres, knitted or crocheted
6112.1200 29	合纤制针织或钩编女式运动套装	17.5	130	17	16	套/千克		Women's or girls' track suits of synthetic fibres, knitted or crocheted
6112.1900	--其他纺织材料制	16	130	17	16	套/千克		--Of other textile materials
6112.1900 31	人造纤维制针织或钩编男式运动服	16	130	17	16	套/千克		Men's or boys' track suits of artificial fibres, knitted or crocheted
6112.1900 39	人造纤维制针织或钩编女运动套装	16	130	17	16	套/千克		Women's or girls' track suits of artificial fibres, knitted or crocheted
6112.1900 41	羊毛制男式运动套装(针织或钩编,含丝70%以下)	16	130	17	16	套/千克		Men's or boys' track suits of wool, knitted or crocheted, containing <70% by weight of silk
6112.1900 49	羊毛制女式运动套装(针织或钩编,含丝70%以下)	16	130	17	16	套/千克		Women's or girls' track suits of wool, knitted or crocheted, containing <70% by weight of silk
6112.1900 51	动物细毛制男式运动套装(针织或钩编,含丝70%以下)	16	130	17	16	套/千克		Men's or boys' track suits of other fine animal hair, knitted or crocheted, containing <70% by weight of silk
6112.1900 59	动物细毛制女式运动套装(针织或钩编,含丝70%以下)	16	130	17	16	套/千克		Women's or girls' track suits of other fine animal hair, knitted or crocheted, containing < 70% by weight of silk
6112.1900 61	其他纺织材料制男式运动套装(针织或钩编,含丝70%以下)	16	130	17	16	套/千克		Men's or boys' track suits of other textile materials, knitted or crocheted, containing <70% by weight of silk
6112.1900 69	其他纺织材料制女式运动套装(针织或钩编,含丝70%以下)	16	130	17	16	套/千克		Women's or girls' track suits of other textile materials, knitted or crocheted, containing < 70% by weight of silk
6112.1900 90	其他纺织材料制运动套装(针织或钩编,含丝70%以上)	16	130	17	16	套/千克		Track suits of other textile materials, knitted or crocheted, containing <70% by weight of silk
	-滑雪服:							-Ski suits:
6112.2010	---棉制	16	90	17	16	套/千克		---Of cotton
6112.2090	---其他	19	130	17	16	套/千克		---Other
6112.2090 10	羊毛或动物细毛针织或钩编滑雪套装	19	130	17	16	套/千克		Ski suits of wool or fine animal hair, knitted or crocheted
6112.2090 21	化学纤维制针织或钩编男式滑雪套装	19	130	17	16	套/千克		Men's or boys' ski suits of man-made fibres, knitted or crocheted
6112.2090 29	化学纤维制针织或钩编女式滑雪套装	19	130	17	16	套/千克		Women's or girls' ski suits of man-made fibres, knitted or crocheted
6112.2090 90	其他纺织材料针织或钩编滑雪套装	19	130	17	16	套/千克		Ski suits of other textile materials, knitted or crocheted
	-男式游泳服:							-Men's or boys' swimwear:
6112.3100	--合成纤维制	17.5	130	17	16	件/千克	A	--Of synthetic fibres
6112.3900	--其他纺织材料制	16	130	17	16	件/千克	A	--Of other textile materials
	-女式游泳服:							-Women's or girls' swimwear:
6112.4100	--合成纤维制	17.5	130	17	16	件/千克	A	--Of Synthetic fibres
6112.4900	--其他纺织材料制	16	130	17	16	件/千克	A	--Of other textile materials
61.13	**用税目59.03、59.06或59.07的针织物或钩编织物制成的服装:**							**Garments, made up of knitted or crocheted fabrics of heading No. 59.03, 59.06 or 59.07:**
6113.0000	用税目59.03、59.06或59.07的针织物或钩编织物制成的服装	16	130	17	16	件/千克		Carments, made up of knitted or crocheted fabrics of heading No. 59.03, 59.06 or 59.07
6113.0000 11	用橡胶处理的服装(针织或钩编,织物外表面由橡胶完全覆盖)	16	130	17	16	件/千克		Garments knitted or crocheted, rubber processed, with fabric surface covered with rubber completely
6113.0000 13	用塑料处理的毛、棉及化纤制服装(针织或钩编毛指羊动物细毛织物外表面由塑料完全覆盖)	16	130	17	16	件/千克		Garments knitted or crocheted, plastic processed, of wool or fine animal hair, of cotton, or of man-made fibres, with fabric surface covered with plastics completely

税则号列	货品名称	最惠(%)	普通	增值税率	出口退税	计量单位	监管条件	Article Description
6113.0000 19	用塑料处理的其他纺织材料制服装(针织或钩编,织物外表面由塑料完全覆盖)	16	130	17	16	件/千克		Garments of other textile materials, plastic processed, with fabric surface covered with plastics completely, knitted or crochetey
6113.0000 21	其他橡胶处理的棉制针织或钩编男上衣	16	130	17	16	件/千克		Other men's or boys' jackets and blazers of cotton, rubber processed, knitted or crocheted
6113.0000 22	其他塑料等处理的棉制针织男上衣(包括钩编,包括用其他材料处理的)	16	130	17	16	件/千克		Other men's or boys' jackets and blazers of cotton, plastic of other materials processed, knitted or crocheted
6113.0000 23	其他橡胶处理的棉针织或钩编女上衣	16	130	17	16	件/千克		Other women's or girls' jackets and blazers of cotton, rubber processed, knitted or crocheted
6113.0000 28	其他塑料等处理的棉针织女上衣(包括钩编,包括用其他材料处理的)	16	130	17	16	件/千克		Other women's or girls' jackets and blazers of cotton, plastic or other materials processed, knitted or crocheted
6113.0000 31	其他橡胶处理的纺织材料制男上衣(针织或钩编)	16	130	17	16	件/千克		Other men's or boys' jackets and blazers of textile materials, rubber processed, knitted or crocheted
6113.0000 32	其他塑料等处理的毛制男上衣(针织或钩编,羊毛或动物细毛制,包括用其他材料处理的)	16	130	17	16	件/千克		Other men's or boys' jackets and blazers of wool or fine animal hair, plastic or other materials processed, knitted or crocheted
6113.0000 33	其他塑料等处理的毛、化纤男上衣(针织或钩编,包括用其他材料处理的)	16	130	17	16	件/千克		Other men's or boys' jackets and blazers of wool or of man-made fibres, plastic or other materials processed, knitted or crocheted
6113.0000 34	其他塑料等处理的纺织材料制男上衣(针织或钩编,包括用其他材料处理的)	16	130	17	16	件/千克		Other men's or boys' jackets and blazers of textile materials, plastic of other materials processed, knitted or crocheted
6113.0000 35	其他橡胶处理的纺织材料制女上衣(针织或钩编)	16	130	17	16	件/千克		Other women's or girls' jackets and blazers of textile materials, rubber processed, knitted or crocheted
6113.0000 36	其他塑料等处理的毛制女上衣(针织或钩编,羊毛或动物细毛制,包括用其他材料处理的)	16	130	17	16	件/千克		Other women's or girls' jackets and blazers of wool or fine animal hair, plastic or other materials processed, knitted or crocheted
6113.0000 37	其他塑料等处理的化纤制女上衣(针织或钩编,包括用其他材料处理的)	16	130	17	16	件/千克		Other women's or girls' jackets and blazers of man-made fibres, plastic or other materials processed knitted or crocheted
6113.0000 38	其他塑料等处理的纺织材料制女上衣(针织或钩编,包括用其他材料处理的)	16	130	17	16	件/千克		Other women's or girls' jackets and blazers of textile materials, plastic or other materials processed, knitted or crocheted
6113.0000 41	其他橡胶等处理的棉制男式长短裤(针织或钩编)	16	130	17	16	件/千克		Other men's or boys' trousers and shorts of cotton, rubber processed, knitted or crocheted
6113.0000 42	其他塑料等处理的棉制男式长短裤(针织或钩编,包括用其他材料处理的)	16	130	17	16	件/千克		Other men's or boys' trousers and shorts of cotton, plastic or other materials processed, knitted or crocheted
6113.0000 43	其他橡胶等处理的棉制女式长短裤(针织或钩编)	16	130	17	16	件/千克		Other women's or girls' trousers and shorts of cotton, rubber processed, knitted or crocheted
6113.0000 44	其他塑料等处理的棉制女式长短裤(针织或钩编,包括用其他材料处理的)	16	130	17	16	件/千克		Other women's or girls' trousers and shorts of cotton, plastic or other materials processed, knitted or crocheted
6113.0000 51	其他橡胶处理纺织材料制男长短裤(针织或钩编)	16	130	17	16	件/千克		Ohter men's or boys' trousers and shorts of textile materials, rubber processed, knitted or crocheted
6113.0000 53	其他塑料等处理的毛化纤制男裤(针织或钩编长短裤包括用其他材料处理的)	16	130	17	16	件/千克		Other men's or boys' trousers and shorts of wool or of man-made fibres, plastic or other materials processed, knitted or crocheted
6113.0000 54	其他塑料等处理纺织材料男长短裤(针织或钩编长、短裤,包括用其他材料处理的)	16	130	17	16	件/千克		Other men's or boys' trousers and shorts of textile materials, plastic or other materials processed, knitted or crocheted
6113.0000 57	其他橡胶处理纺织材料制女长短裤(针织或钩编)	16	130	17	16	件/千克		Other women's or girls' trousers and shorts of textile materials, rubber processed, knitted or crocheted

税则号列	货品名称	最惠(%)	普通	增值税率	出口退税	计量单位	监管条件	Article Description
6113.0000 58	其他塑料等处理的毛、化纤制女裤(针织或钩编长、短裤,包括用其他材料处理的)	16	130	17	16	件/千克		Other women's or girls' trousers and shorts of wool or of man-made fibres, plastic or other materials processed knitted or crocheted
6113.0000 59	其他塑料等处理纺织材料制女长短裤(针织或钩编,包括用其他材料处理)	16	130	17	16	件/千克		Other women's or girls' trousers and shorts of textile materials, plastic or other materials processed, knitted or crocheted
6113.0000 91	其他橡胶处理棉针织或钩编服装	16	130	17	16	件/千克		Other garments of cotton, rubber processed, knitted or crocheted
6113.0000 92	其他塑料处理棉针织或钩编服装(包括用其他材料处理的)	16	130	17	16	件/千克		Other garments of cotton, plastic or other materials processed, knitted or crocheted
6113.0000 93	其他橡胶处理纺织材料针织服装(包括钩编服装)	16	130	17	16	件/千克		Other garments of textile materials, rubber processed, knitted or crocheted
6113.0000 94	其他塑料等处理毛化纤制针织服装(包括钩编服装、包括用其他材料处理的)	16	130	17	16	件/千克		Other garments of wool or of man-made fibres, plastic or other materials processed, knitted or crocheted
6113.0000 98	其他塑料等处理纺织材料针织服装(包括钩编服装,包括用其他材料处理的)	16	130	17	16	件/千克		Other garments of textile materials, plastic or other materials processed, knitted or crocheted
61.14	针织或钩编的其他服装:							**Other garments, knitted or crocheted:**
6114.2000	-棉制	16	90	17	16	件/千克		-Of cotton
6114.2000 11	棉制针织或钩编儿童非保暖连身裤	16	90	17	16	件/千克	A	Boys' or girls' overall, not thermal, knitted or crocheted, of cotton
6114.2000 19	棉制针织或钩编其他连身裤	16	90	17	16	件/千克		Other overall, knitted or crocheted, of cotton
6114.2000 21	棉制针织或钩编男成人及男童 TOPS(指8-18号男童 TOPS)	16	90	17	16	件/千克	A	Men's TOPS or boys' TOPS No. 8 ~ No. 18, knitted or crocheted, of cotton
6114.2000 22	棉制针织或钩编其他男童 TOPS	16	90	17	16	件/千克	A	Other boys' TOPS, knitted or crocheted, of cotton
6114.2000 29	棉制针织或钩编女式 TOPS	16	90	17	16	件/千克		Women's or girls' TOPS, knitted or crocheted, of cotton
6114.2000 30	棉制针织或钩编其他运动服	16	90	17	16	件/千克		Other sports suits, knitted or crocheted, of cotton
6114.2000 40	棉制针织或钩编夏服、水洗服(包括女成人、女童及男童)	16	90	17	16	件/千克	A	Women's or girls' and boys' summer wear, wash wear, knitted or crocheted, of cotton
6114.2000 90	棉制针织或钩编其他服装	16	90	17	16	件/千克		Other garments, knitted or crocheted, of cotton
6114.3000	-化学纤维制	17.5	130	17	16	件/千克		-Of man-made fibres
6114.3000 11	化纤制针织或钩编连身衣(含羊毛或动物细毛23%及以上)	17.5	130	17	16	件/千克		Overall, containing≥23% by weight of wool or fine animal hair, knitted or crocheted, of man-made fibres
6114.3000 12	化纤制针织或钩编紧身服及衬衫(含羊毛或动物细毛23%及以上,包括无袖罩衫)	17.5	130	17	16	件/千克		Jerseys and shirts, including cloaks, containing ≥ 23% by weight of wool or fine animal hair, knitted or crocheted, of man-made fibres
6114.3000 13	化纤制针织或钩编其他连身衣	17.5	130	17	16	件/千克		Other overall, knitted or crocheted, of man-made fibres
6114.3000 19	化纤制针织或钩编紧身服及衬衫(包括无袖罩衫)	17.5	130	17	16	件/千克		Jerseys and shirts, including cloaks, knitted or crocheted, of man-made fibres
6114.3000 21	化纤针织或钩编男成人及男 TOPS(指8-18号男童 TOPS)	17.5	130	17	16	件/千克	A	Men's TOPS or boys' TOPS No. 8 ~ No. 18, knitted or crocheted, of man-made fibres
6114.3000 22	化纤针织或钩编其他男童 TOPS	17.5	130	17	16	件/千克	A	Other boys' TOPS, knitted or crocheted, of man-made fibres
6114.3000 29	化纤针织或钩编女式 TOPS	17.5	130	17	16	件/千克		Women's or girls' TOPS, knitted or crocheted, of man-made fibres
6114.3000 30	化纤针织或钩编其他运动服	17.5	130	17	16	件/千克		Other sports suits, knitted or crocheted, of man-made fibres
6114.3000 40	化纤针织或钩编夏服、水洗服(包括女成人、女童及男童)	17.5	130	17	16	件/千克		Women's or girls' and boys' summer wear, wash wear, knitted or crocheted, of man-made fibres
6114.3000 90	化纤针织或钩编其他服装	17.5	130	17	16	件/千克		Other garments, knitted or crocheted, of man-made fibres
	-其他纺织材料制:							-Of other textile materials:
6114.9010	---羊毛或动物细毛制	16	130	17	16	件/千克		---Of wool or fine animal hair
6114.9090	---其他	16	130	17	16	件/千克		---Other

税则号列	货品名称	最惠(%)	普通	增值税率	出口退税	计量单位	监管条件	Article Description
61.15	针织或钩编的连裤袜、紧身裤袜、长筒袜、短袜及其他袜类，包括渐紧压袜类（例如用以治疗静脉曲张的长筒袜）和无外绱鞋底的鞋类：							**Panty hose, tights, stockings, socks and other hosiery, including graduate compression hosiery (for example, stockings for varicose veins) and footwear without applied soles, knitted or crocheted:**
6115.1000	-渐紧压袜类（例如用以治疗静脉曲张的长筒袜，针织或钩编）	16	130	17	16	双/千克		-Graduated compression hosiery (for example, stockings for varicose veins)
	-其他连裤袜及紧身裤袜：							-Other panty hose and tights:
6115.2100	--每根单丝细度在67分特以下的合成纤维制	16	130	17	16	双/千克		--Of synthetic fibres, measuring per single yarn less than 67 decitex
6115.2200	--每根单丝细度在67分特及以上的合成纤维制	16	130	17	16	双/千克		--Of synthetic fibres, measuring per single yarn 67 decitex or more
	--其他纺织材料制：							--Of other textile materials:
6115.2910	---棉制	14	90	17	16	双/千克		---Of cotton
6115.2990	---其他	14	130	17	16	双/千克		---Other
6115.3000	-其他女式长筒袜及中筒袜，每根单丝细度在67分特以下	14	130	17	16	双/千克		-Women's full-length or knee-length hosiery, measuring per single yarn less than 67 decitex
6115.3000 21	合纤制针织或钩编女长筒袜（单丝细度在67分特以下）	14	130	17	16	双/千克		Women's or girls' full-length hosiery of synthetic fibres, measuring per single yarn < 67 decitex, knitted or crocheted
6115.3000 29	合纤制针织或钩编女中筒袜（单丝细度在67分特以下）	14	130	17	16	双/千克		Women's or girls' knee-length hosiery of synthetic fibres, measuring per single yarn < 67 decitex, knitted or crocheted
6115.3000 90	其他材料制女筒袜（单丝细度在67分特以下）	14	130	17	16	双/千克		Women's or girls' full-length or knee-length hosiery, of other textile materials measuring per single yarn < 67 decitex
	-其他：							-Other:
6115.9400	--羊毛或动物细毛制	14	130	17	16	双/千克		--Of wool or fine animal hair
6115.9500	--棉制	14	90	17	16	双/千克		--Of cotton
6115.9500 11	棉制针织或钩编矫正袜（外科用带压缩刻度）	14	90	17	16	双/千克		Orthopedic stockings, with surgical restriction scale, of cotton, knitted or crocheted
6115.9500 19	棉制针织或钩编短袜及其他袜类	14	90	17	16	双/千克		Socks and other hosiery of cotton, knitted or crocheted
6115.9600	--合成纤维制	16	130	17	16	双/千克		--Of synthetic fibres
6115.9600 11	合纤制针织或钩编矫正袜（外科用带压缩刻度）	16	130	17	16	双/千克		Orthopedic stockings, with surgical restriction scale, of synthentic fibres, knitted or crocheted
6115.9600 12	合纤制女长筒袜（针织或钩编含羊毛或动物细毛23%及以上）	16	130	17	16	双/千克		Women's or girls' full-length hosiery of synthetic fibres, containing≥23% by weight of wool or fine animal hair, knitted or crocheted
6115.9600 13	合成纤维制短袜及其他袜类（针织或钩编含羊毛或动物细毛23%及以上）	16	130	17	16	双/千克		Socks and other hosiery of synthetic fibres, containing ≥23% by weight of wool or fine animal hair, knitted or crocheted
6115.9600 14	其他合成纤维制女长筒袜（针织或钩编）	16	130	17	16	双/千克		Women's or girls' full-length hosiery of synthetic fibres, knitted or crocheted
6115.9600 19	其他合成纤维制短袜及其他袜类（针织或钩编）	16	130	17	16	双/千克		Socks and other hosiery of synthetic fibres, knitted or crocheted
6115.9900	--其他纺织材料制	14	130	17	16	双/千克		--Of other textile materials
6115.9900 11	人造纤维制短袜及其他袜类（针织或钩编，含羊毛或动物细毛23%及以上）	14	130	17	16	双/千克		Socks or other hosiery of artificial fibres, containing ≥23% by weight of wool or fine animal hair, knitted or crocheted
6115.9900 19	其他人造纤维制短袜及其他袜类（针织或钩编）	14	130	17	16	双/千克		Socks or other hosiery of artificial fibres, knitted or crocheted
6115.9900 91	其他纺织材料制短袜及其他袜类（针织或钩编，含丝70%及以上）	14	130	17	16	双/千克		Socks or other hosiery of other textile materials, containing≥70% by weight of silk, knitted or crocheted
6115.9900 99	其他纺织材料制短袜及其他袜类（针织或钩编，含丝70%及以下）	14	130	17	16	双/千克		Socks or other hosiery of other textile materials, containing < 70% by weight of silk, knitted or crocheted

税则号列	货品名称	最惠(%)	普通	增值税率	出口退税	计量单位	监管条件	Article Description
61.16	针织或钩编的分指手套、连指手套及露指手套：							**Gloves, mittens and mitts, knitted or crocheted:**
6116.1000	-用塑料或橡胶浸渍、涂布或包覆的	14	130	17	16	双/千克		-Gloves impregnated, coated or covered with plastics or rubber
6116.1000 10	塑料或橡胶浸渍的运动手套	14	130	17	16	双/千克		Sports gloves impregnated, coated or covered with plastics or rubber
6116.1000 91	塑料或橡胶浸渍的非运动手套(含塑料或橡胶超过50%及以上)	14	130	17	16	双/千克		Nonsports gloves impregnated, coated or covered with plastics or rubber, containing≥50% by weight of plastics or rubber
6116.1000 92	塑料或橡胶浸渍的非运动手套(含塑料或橡胶不超过50%,棉限内)	14	130	17	16	双/千克		Nonsports gloves impregnated, coated or covered with plastics or rubber, containing < 50% by weight of plastics or rubber, cotton within limitations
6116.1000 93	塑料或橡胶浸渍的非运动手套(含塑料或橡胶不超过50%,毛限内)	14	130	17	16	双/千克		Nonsports gloves impregnated, coated or covered with plastics or rubber, containing < 50% by weight of plastics or rubber, wool within limitations
6116.1000 94	塑料或橡胶浸渍的其他非运动手套(含塑料或橡胶不超过50%,化纤限内)	14	130	17	16	双/千克		Nonsports gloves impregnated, coated or covered with plastics or rubber, containing < 50% by weight of plastics or rubber, man-made fibres within limitations
6116.1000 99	塑料或橡胶浸渍的其他非运动手套(含塑料或橡胶不超过50%)	14	130	17	16	双/千克		Other nonsports gloves impregnated, coated or covered with plastics or rubber, containing < 50% by weight of plastics or rubber
	-其他:							-Other:
6116.9100	--羊毛或动物细毛制	14	130	17	16	双/千克		--Of wool of fine animal hair
6116.9200	--棉制	14	90	17	16	双/千克		--Of cotton
6116.9300	--合成纤维制	16	130	17	16	双/千克		--Of synthetic fibres
6116.9300 10	合纤制其他针织或钩编手套(含羊毛或动物细毛23%及以上)	16	130	17	16	双/千克		Mittens and mitts, containing ≥ 23% by weight of wool or fine animal hair, knitted or crocheted, of synthetic fibres
6116.9300 90	合纤制其他针织或钩编手套(含羊毛或动物细毛23%以下)	16	130	17	16	双/千克		Mittens and mitts, containing < 23% by weight of wool or fine animal hair, knitted or crocheted, of synthetic fibres
6116.9900	--其他纺织材料制	14	130	17	16	双/千克		--Of other textile materials
6116.9900 11	人造纤维制其他针织或钩编手套(运动手套)	14	130	17	16	双/千克		Sports gloves, mittens and mitts, of artificial fibres, knitted or crocheted
6116.9900 19	人造纤维制其他针织或钩编手套(非运动手套)	14	130	17	16	双/千克		Nonsports gloves, mittens and mitts, of artificial fibres, knitted or crocheted
6116.9900 20	丝或绢丝制其他针织或钩编手套(含丝70%及以上)	14	130	17	16	双/千克		Gloves, mittens and mitts of silk or spun silk containing≥70% by weight of silk, knitted or crocheted
6116.9900 91	其他纺材制其他针织或钩编手套(棉限内)	14	130	17	16	双/千克		Gloves, mittens and mitts of other textile materials, knitted or crocheted, cotton within limitations
6116.9900 92	其他纺材制其他针织或钩编手套(毛限内)	14	130	17	16	双/千克		Gloves, mittens and mitts of other textile materials, knitted or crocheted, wool within limitations
6116.9900 93	其他纺材制其他针织或钩编手套(化纤限内)	14	130	17	16	双/千克		Gloves, mittens and mitts of other textile materials, knitted or crocheted, man-made fibres within limitations
6116.9900 99	未列名纺材制其他针织或钩编手套	14	130	17	16	双/千克		Other gloves, mittens and mitts of other textile materials, knitted or crocheted, not elsewhere specified or included
61.17	其他制成的针织或钩编的衣着附件;服装或衣着附件的针织或钩编的零件:							**Other made up clothing accessories, knitted or crocheted; knitted or crocheted parts of garments or of clothing accessories:**
	-披巾、头巾、围巾、披纱、面纱及类似品:							-Shawls, scarves, mufflers, mantillas, veils and the like:
	---动物细毛制:							---Of fine animal hair:
6117.1011	----山羊绒制	14	130	17	16	条/千克		----Of goats
6117.1019	----其他	14	130	17	16	条/千克		---Other

税则号列	货品名称	最惠(%)	普通	增值税率	出口退税	计量单位	监管条件	Article Description
6117.1020	---羊毛制	14	130	17	16	条/千克		----Of wool
6117.1090	---其他	14	130	17	16	条/千克		---Other
	-其他附件:							-Other、accessories:
6117.8010	---领带及领结	14	130	17	16	千克/条		---Ties, bow ties and cravats
6117.8090	---其他	14	130	17	16	千克		---Other
6117.9000	-零件	14	130	17	16	千克		-Parts
6117.9000 10	保暖型衬里(针织或钩编)	14	130	17	16	千克		Thermal lining, knitted or crocheted
6117.9000 21	毛制针织毛衫的零件(针织或钩编,羊毛或动物细毛)	14	130	17	16	千克		Parts of sweaters of wool or fine animal hair, knitted or crocheted
6117.9000 22	毛制针织衬衫的零件(针织或钩编,羊毛或动物细毛)	14	130	17	16	千克		Parts of shirts of wool or fine animal hair, knitted or crocheted
6117.9000 23	毛制针织上衣的零件(针织或钩编,羊毛或动物细毛)	14	130	17	16	千克		Parts of jackets or blazers of wool or fine animal hair, knitted or crocheted
6117.9000 24	毛制针织长裤、马裤、短裤的零件(针织或钩编,羊毛或动物细毛)	14	130	17	16	千克		Parts of trousers, breeches, shorts, of wool or fine animal hair, knitted or crocheted
6117.9000 29	毛制其他未列名针织服装零件(针织或钩编,羊毛或动物细毛)	14	130	17	16	千克		Other part of garments of wool or fine animal hair, not elsewhere specified or included, knitted or crocheted
6117.9000 31	棉制针织毛衫的零件(针织或钩编)	14	130	17	16	千克		Parts of sweaters of cotton, knitted or crocheted
6117.9000 32	棉制针织衬衫的零件(针织或钩编)	14	130	17	16	千克		Parts of shirts of cotton, knitted or crocheted
6117.9000 33	棉制针织上衣的零件(针织或钩编)	14	130	17	16	千克		Parts of jackets or blazers of cotton, knitted or crocheted
6117.9000 34	棉制针织长裤、马裤、短裤的零件(针织或钩编)	14	130	17	16	千克		Parts of trousers, breeches, shorts, of cotton, knitted or crocheted
6117.9000 39	棉制其他未列名针织服装零件(针织或钩编)	14	130	17	16	千克		Other parts, of cotton, not elsewhere specified or included, knitted or crocheted
6117.9000 41	化纤制针织毛衫的零件(针织或钩编)	14	130	17	16	千克		Parts of sweaters of man-made fibres, knitted or crocheted
6117.9000 42	化纤制针织衬衫的零件(针织或钩编)	14	130	17	16	千克		Parts of shirts of man-made fibres, knitted or crocheted
6117.9000 43	化纤制针织上衣的零件(针织或钩编)	14	130	17	16	千克		Parts of jackets or blazers of man-made fibres, knitted or crocheted
6117.9000 44	化纤制针织长裤、马裤、短裤零件(针织或钩编)	14	130	17	16	千克		Parts of trousers, breeches, shorts, of man-made fibres, knitted or crocheted
6117.9000 49	化纤制其他未列名针织服装零件(针织或钩编)	14	130	17	16	千克		Other parts of garments of man-made fibres not elsewhere specified or included, knitted or crocheted
6117.9000 91	其他材料制衣着零件(针织或钩编,含丝70%及以上)	14	130	17	16	千克		Parts of garments of other textile materials, containing≥70% by weight of silk, knitted or crocheted
6117.9000 92	其他材料制针织毛衫的零件(针织或钩编)	14	130	17	16	千克		Parts of sweaters of other textile materials, knitted or crocheted
6117.9000 93	其他材料制针织衬衫的零件(针织或钩编)	14	130	17	16	千克		Parts of shirts of other textile materials, knitted or crocheted
6117.9000 94	其他材料制针织上衣的零件(针织或钩编)	14	130	17	16	千克		Parts of jackets or blazers of other textile materials, knitted or crocheted
6117.9000 95	其他材料制长裤、马裤、短裤零件(针织或钩编)	14	130	17	16	千克		Parts of trousers, breeches, shorts of other textile materials, knitted or crocheted
6117.9000 99	其他材料制未列名针织服装零件(针织或钩编)	14	130	17	16	千克		Other parts of garments of other textile materials not elsewhere specified or included, knitted or crocheted

第六十二章
非针织或非钩编的服装及衣着附件

注释：

一、本章仅适用于除絮胎以外任何纺织物的制成品，但不适用于针织品或钩编织品(税目62.12的除外)。

二、本章不包括：

(一)税目63.09的旧衣服及其他旧物品；

(二)矫形器具、外科手术带、疝气带及类似品(税目90.21)。

三、税目62.03及62.04所称：

(一)"西服套装"，是指面料用相同的织物制成的两件套或三件套的下列成套服装：

一件人体上半身穿着的外套或短上衣，除袖子外，应由四片或四片以上面料组成；也可附带一件马甲(西服背心)，这件马甲(西服背心)的前片面料应与套装其他各件的面料相同，后片料则应与外套或短上衣的衬里料相同；

以及一件人体下半身穿着的服装，即不带背带或护胸的长裤、马裤、短裤(游泳裤除外)、裙子或裙裤。

西服套装各件面料质地、颜色及构成必须完全相同，其款式、尺寸大小也须相互般配，但套装的各件可以用不同织物滚边(缝口上缝入长条织物)。

如果数件人体下半身穿着的服装同时进口或出口(例如，两条长裤、长裤与短裤、裙子或裙裤与长裤)，构成西服套装下装的应是一条长裤，而对于女式西服套装，则应是一条裙子或裙裤，其他服装应分别归类。

所称"西服套装"，包括不论是否完全符合上述条件的下列配套服装：

1. 常礼服，由一件后襟下垂并下端开圆弧形叉的素色短上衣和一条条纹长裤组成；
2. 晚礼服(燕尾服)，一般用黑色织物制成，上衣前襟较短且不闭合，背后有燕尾；
3. 无燕尾套装夜礼服，其中上衣款式与普通上衣相似(可以更为显露衬衣前胸)，但有光滑丝质或仿丝质的翻领。

(二)"便服套装"，是指面料相同并作零售包装的下列成套服装(西服套装及税目62.07或62.08的物品除外)

一件人体上半身穿着的服装，但背心除外，因为背心可作为内衣；以及一件或两件不同的人体下半身穿着的服装，即长裤、护胸背带工装裤、马裤、短裤(游泳裤除外)、裙子或裙裤。

便服套装各件面料质地、款式、颜色及构成必须相同；尺寸大小也须相互般配。所称"便服套装"不包括税目62.11的运动服及滑雪服。

Chapter 62
Articles of apparel and clothing accessories, not knitted or crocheted

Notes:

1. This Chapter applies only to made up articles of any textile fabric other than wadding, excluding knitted or crocheted articles (other than those of heading No. 62.12).
2. This Chapter does not cover:
   (a) Worn clothing or other worn articles of heading No. 63.09; or
   (b) Orthopaedic appliances, surgical belts, trusses or the like (heading No. 90.21).
3. For the purposes of headings Nos. 62.03 and 62.04:
   (a) The term "suit" means a set of garments composed of two or three pieces made up in hespect of their outer surface, in identical fabric and comprising:
   -One suit coat or jacket the outer shell of which, exclusive of sleeves, consists of four or more panels, designed to cover the upper part of the body, possibly with a tailored waistcoat in addition whose front is made from the same fabric as the outer shell of the other components of the set and whose back is made from the same fabric as the lining of the suit coat or jacket, and
   One garment designed to cover the lower part of the body and consisting of trousers, breeches or shorts (other than swimwear), a skirt or a divided skirt, having neither braces nor bibs.
   All of the components of a suit must be of the same fabric construction, colour and composition; they must also be of the same style and of corresponding or compatible size. However, these components may have piping (a strip of fabric sewn into the seam) in a different fabric.
   If several separate components to cover the lower part of the body are presented together (for example two palls of trousers or, trousers and shorts, or a skirt or divided skirt and trousers), the constituent lower part shall be one pair of trousers, or, in the case of women's or girls' suits, the skirt or divided skirt, the other garments being considered separately.
   The term "suit" includes the following sets of garments, whether or not they fulfil all the above conditions:
   (1) morning dress, comprising a plain jacket (cutaway) with rounded tails hanging well down at the back and striped trousers;
   (2) evening dress (tailcoat), generally made of black cloth, the jacket of which is relatively short at the front, does not close and has narrow skirts cut in at the hips and hanging down behind;
   (3) dinner jacket suits, in which the jacket is similar in style to an ordinary jacket (though perhaps revealing more of the shirt front), but has shiny silk or imitation silk lapels.
   (b) The term "ensemble" means a set of garments (other than suits and articles of heading No. 62.07 or 62.08) composed of several pieces made up in identical fabric, put up for retail sale, and comprising:
   -one garment designed to cover the upper part of the body, with the exception of waistcoats which may also form a second upper garment, and one or two different garments, designed to cover the lower part of the body and consisting of trousers, bib and brace overalls, breeches, shorts (other than swimwear), a skirt or a divided skirt.
   All of the components of an ensemble must be of the same fabric construction, style, colour and composition; they also must be of corresponding or compatible size. The term "ensemble" does not apply to track suits or ski suits, of heading No. 62.11.

四、对于税目62.09:

(一)所称"婴儿服装及衣着附件",是指用于身高不超过86厘米幼儿的服装;

(二)既可归入税目62.09,也可归入本章其他税目的物品,应归入税目62.09;

五、既可归入税目62.10,也可归入本章其他税目的服装,除税目62.09所列的仍归入该税目外,其余的应一律归入税目62.10。

六、税目62.11所称"滑雪服",是指从整个外观和织物质地来看,主要在滑雪(速度滑雪和高山滑雪)时穿着的下列服装或成套服装:

(一)"滑雪连身服",即上下身连在一起的单件服装;除袖子和领子外,滑雪连身服可有口袋或脚带;或

(二)"滑雪套装",即由两件或三件构成一套并作零售包装的下列服装:

一件用一条拉链扣合的带风帽的厚夹克、防风衣、防风短上衣或类似的服装,可以附带一件背心;以及一条不论是否过腰的长裤、一条马裤或一条护胸背带工装裤。

"滑雪套装"也可由一件类似以上(一)款所述的类似连身服和一件可套在连身服外面的有胎料背心组成。

"滑雪套装"各件颜色可以不同,但面料质地、款式及构成必须相同;尺寸大小也须相互般配。

七、正方形或近似正方形的围巾及围巾式样的物品,如果每边均不超过60厘米,应作为手帕归类(税目62.13)。任何一边超过60厘米的手帕,应归入税目62.14。

八、本章的服装,凡门襟为左压右的,应视为男式;右压左的,应视为女式。但本规定不适用于其式样已明显为男式或女式的服装。无法区别是男式还是女式的服装,应按女式服装归入有关税目。

九、本章物品可用金属线制成。

4. For the purposes of heading No. 62. 09:

(a) The expression "babies' garments and clothing accessories" means articles for young children of a body height not exceeding 86cm;

(b) Articles which are, *prima facie*, classifiable both in heading 62. 09 and in other headings of this Chapter are to be classified in heading No. 62. 09.

5. Garments which are, *prima facie*, classifiable both in heading No. 62. 10 and in other headings of this Chapter, excluding heading No. 62. 09, are to be classified in heading No. 62. 10.

6. For the purposes of heading No. 62. 11, "ski suits" means garments or sets of garments which, by their general appearance and texture, are identifiable as intended to be worn principally for skiing (cross-country or alpine).

They consist either of:

(a) a "ski overall", that is, a one-piece garment designed to cover the upper and the lower parts of the body; in addition to sleeves and a collar the ski overall may have pockets or footstraps; or

(b) a "ski ensemble", that is, a set of garments composed of two or three pieces, put up for retail sale and comprising:

-one garment such as an anorak, wind-cheater, wind-jacket or similar article, closed by a slide fastener (zipper), possibly with a waistcoat in addition, and one pair of trousers whether or not extending above waist-level, one pair of breeches or one bib and brace overall.

The "ski ensemble" may also consist of an overall similar to the one mentioned in paragraph (a) above and a type of padded, sleeveless jacket worn over the overall.

All the components of a "ski ensemble" must be made up in a fabric of the same texture, style and composition whether or not of the same colour; they also must be of corresponding or compatible size.

7. Scarves and articles of the scarf type, square or approximately square, of which no side exceeds 60cm, are to be classified as handkerchiefs (heading No. 62. 13). Handkerchiefs of which any side exceeds 60cm are to be classified in heading No. 62. 14.

8. Garments of this Chapter designed for left over right closure at the front shall be regarded as men's or boys' garments, and those designed for right over left closure at the front as women's or girls' garments. these provisions do not apply where the cut of the garment clearly indicates that it is designed for one or other of the sexes. Garments which cannot be identified as either men's or boys' garments or as women's or girls' garments are to be classified in the headings covering women's or girls' garments.

9. Articles of this Chapter may be made of metal thread.

税则号列	货品名称	最惠(%)	普通	增值税率	出口退税	计量单位	监管条件	Article Description
62.01	**男式大衣、短大衣、斗篷、短斗篷、带风帽的防寒短上衣(包括滑雪短上衣)、防风衣、防风短上衣及类似品,但税号62.03的货品除外:**							**Men's or boys' overcoats, car-coats, capes, cloaks, anoraks (including ski-jackets), wind-cheaters, wind-jackets and similar articles, other than those of heading No. 62.03:**
	-大衣、雨衣、短大衣、斗篷、短斗篷及类似品:							-Overcoats, raincoats, car-coats, capes, cloaks and similar articles:
6201.1100	--羊毛或动物细毛制	16	130	17	16	件/千克		--Of wool or fine animal hair
6201.1100 10	毛制男式雨衣(羊毛或动物细毛制)	16	130	17	16	件/千克		Men's or boys' raincoats, of wool or fine animal hair
6201.1100 90	毛制男式大衣,斗篷及类似品(含短大衣、短斗篷,羊毛或动物细毛制)	16	130	17	16	件/千克		Men's or boys' overcoats, car-coats, capes, cloak and similar articles, of wool or fine animal hair
	--棉制:							--Of cotton:
6201.1210	---羽绒服	16	90	17	16	件/千克		---Padded with feathers or down
6201.1290	---其他	16	90	17	16	件/千克		---Other
6201.1290 10	棉制男式雨衣	16	90	17	16	件/千克		Men's or boys' raincoats of cotton

税则号列	货品名称	最惠(%)	普通	增值税率	出口退税	计量单位	监管条件	Article Description
6201.1290 20	棉制男式连风帽派克大衣等(含带风帽的防寒短上衣、防风衣、防风短上衣及类似品)	16	90	17	16	件/千克		Men's or boys' hooded parka, anoraks, wind-cheaters, wind-jackets and similar articles, of cotton
6201.1290 90	棉制男式大衣、斗篷及类似品(包括短大衣、短斗篷)	16	90	17	16	件/千克		Men's or boys' overcoats, car-coats, capes, cloaks and similar articles, of cotton
	--化学纤维制:							--Of man-made fibres:
6201.1310	---羽绒服	17.5	130	17	16	件/千克		---Padded with feathers or down
6201.1390	---其他	17.5	130	17	16	件/千克		---Other
6201.1390 10	化纤制男式雨衣	17.5	130	17	16	件/千克		Men's or boys' raincoats, of man-made fibres
6201.1390 20	化纤制男式连风帽派克大衣等(羊毛或动物细毛≥36%,带风帽防寒短上衣、防风衣等)	17.5	130	17	16	件/千克		Men's or boys' hooded parka, anoraks, wind-cheaters wind-jackts and similar articles, containing ≥36% by weight of wool or fine animal hair, of man-made fibres
6201.1390 30	化纤制男大衣、斗篷及类似品(包括短大衣、短斗篷,含羊毛或动物细毛36%及以上)	17.5	130	17	16	件/千克		Men's or boys' overcoats, car-coats, capes, cloak and similar articles, containing≥36% by weight of wool or fine animal hair, of man-made fibres
6201.1390 40	化纤制男式连风帽派克大衣等(羊毛或动物细毛<36%,带风帽防寒短上衣、防风衣等)	17.5	130	17	16	件/千克		Men's or boys' hooded parka, anoraks, wind-jackets and similar articles, containing <36% by weight of wool or fine animal hair, of man-made fibres
6201.1390 90	化纤制男大衣、斗篷及类似品(包括短大衣、短斗篷,含羊毛或动物细毛36%以下)	17.5	130	17	16	件/千克		Men's or boys' overcoats, car-coats, capes, cloak and similar articles, containing <36% by weight of wool or fine animal hair, of man-made fibres
6201.1900	--其他纺织材料制	16	100	17	16	件/千克		--Of other textile materials
6201.1900 10	其他材料制男雨衣	16	100	17	16	件/千克		Men's or boys' raincoats, of other textile materials
6201.1900 21	其他材料制男大衣、斗篷及类似品(含短大衣、斗篷、短斗篷,含丝70%及以上)	16	100	17	16	件/千克		Men's or boys' overcoats, car-coats, capes, cloak and similar articles, containing≥70% by weight of silk, of other textile materials
6201.1900 29	其他材料制男大衣、斗篷及类似品(含短大衣、斗篷、短斗篷,含丝<70%)	16	100	17	16	件/千克		Men's or boys' overcoats, car-coats, capes, cloak and similar articles, containing <70% by weight of silk, of other textile materials
6201.1900 30	其他材料制男大衣等,羊毛限内(含短大衣、斗篷、短斗篷)	16	100	17	16	件/千克		Men's or boys' overcoats, car-coats, capes, cloak and similar articles, of other textile materials, wool within limitations
6201.1900 40	其他材料制男大衣等,棉限内(含短大衣、斗篷、短斗篷)	16	100	17	16	件/千克		Men's or boys' overcoats, car-coats, capes, cloak and similar articles, of other textile materials, cotton within limitations
6201.1900 50	其他材料制男大衣等,化纤限内(含短大衣、斗篷、短斗篷)	16	100	17	16	件/千克		Men's or boys' overcoats, car-coats, capes, cloak and similar articles, of other textile materials, man-made fibres within limitations
6201.1900 90	其他材料制男大衣等(含短大衣、斗篷、短斗篷)	16	100	17	16	件/千克		Men's or boys' overcoats, car-coats, capes, cloak and similar articles, of other textile materials
	-其他:							-Other:
6201.9100	--羊毛或动物细毛制	16	130	17	16	件/千克		--Of wool or fine animal hair
6201.9100 10	毛制男式有填料无袖上衣(羊毛或动物细毛制)	16	130	17	16	件/千克		Men's or boys' cloaks, padded, of wool or fine animal hair
6201.9100 20	毛制男式带防寒衬里防风衣(羊毛或动物细毛制,含防风短上衣)	16	130	17	16	件/千克		Men's or boys' wind-cheaters, wind-jackets, with thermal lining, of wool or fine animal hair
6201.9100 30	毛制男式带风帽、有填料短上衣(羊毛或动物细毛制,含防风上衣,衬衫式样,特制领)	16	130	17	16	件/千克		Men's or boys' anoraks, wind-jackets, shirt style, padded, of wool or fine animal hair
6201.9100 90	毛制男式其他防寒上衣(羊毛或动物细毛制)	16	130	17	16	件/千克		Other men's or boys' anoraks, of wool or fine animal hair
	--棉制:							--Of cotton:
6201.9210	---羽绒服	16	90	17	16	件/千克		---Padded with feathers or down
6201.9290	---其他	16	90	17	16	件/千克		---Other

税则号列	货品名称	最惠(%)	普通	增值税率	出口退税	计量单位	监管条件	Article Description
6201.9290 10	棉制男式有填料无袖上衣(不带可连接袖子配件)	16	90	17	16	件/千克		Men's or boys' cloaks, padded, of cotton (not with fasteners of detachable sleeves)
6201.9290 20	棉制男式带防寒衬里防风衣(含防风短上衣)	16	90	17	16	件/千克		Men's or boys' wind-cheaters, wind-jackets, with thermal lining, of cotton
6201.9290 30	棉制男式带风帽、有填料上衣(包括防风上衣,衬衫式样,特制领)	16	90	17	16	件/千克		Men's or boys' anoraks, wind-jackets, shirt style, having made-to-order collar, padded, with hood
6201.9290 90	棉制男式其他防寒上衣(包括滑雪短上衣、防风短上衣及类似品)	16	90	17	16	件/千克		Other men's or boys' anoraks, ski-jackets, wind-cheaters, wind-jackets and similar articles, of cotton
	--化学纤维制:							--Of man-made fibres:
6201.9310	---羽绒服	17.5	130	17	16	件/千克		---Padded with feathers or down
6201.9390	---其他	17.5	130	17	16	件/千克		---Other
6201.9390 10	化纤制男式有填料无袖上衣(不带可连接袖子配件)	17.5	130	17	16	件/千克		Men's or boys' sleeveless tops, padded, of man-made fibres
6201.9390 20	化纤制男式带风帽防寒短上衣(羊毛或动物细毛36%及以上)	17.5	130	17	16	件/千克		Men's or boys' anoraks, containing≥36% by weight of wool or fine animal hair, of man-made fibres
6201.9390 30	化纤制男式带防寒衬里防风衣(含防风短上衣)	17.5	130	17	16	件/千克		Men's or boys' wind-cheaters, wind-jackets with thermal lining, of man-made fibres
6201.9390 40	化纤制男式带风帽、有填料上衣(包括防风上衣,衬衫式样,特制领)	17.5	130	17	16	件/千克		Men's or boys' anoraks, wind-jackets, shirt style, having made-to-order collar, padded, of man-made fibres
6201.9390 90	化纤制其他防寒上衣(包括带风帽防寒短上衣、防风短上衣及其他类似品)	17.5	130	17	16	件/千克		Other men's or boys' anoraks, wind-cheaters, wind-jackets and similar articles, of man-made fibres
6201.9900	--其他纺织材料制	16	100	17	16	件/千克		--Of other textile materials
6201.9900 11	丝制男式带防寒衬里短上衣(含丝70%及以上,含防风上衣、防风短上衣)	16	100	17	16	件/千克		Men's or boys' wind-cheaters, wind-jackets, with thermal lining, containing≥70% by weight of silk
6201.9900 12	丝制男式带特制领、有填料短上衣(含丝70%及以上,含防风上衣,衬衫式样,带风帽)	16	100	17	16	件/千克		Men's or boys' tops, wind-cheaters, with specially made cdlar, padded, containing≥70% by weight of silk, having made-to-order collar, shirt style, with hood
6201.9900 19	丝制其他防寒上衣(含丝70%及以上)	16	100	17	16	件/千克		Other men's or boys' anoraks, containing≥70% by weight of silk
6201.9900 21	丝制男式带防寒衬里短上衣(含丝70%以下,含防风上衣、防风短上衣)	16	100	17	16	件/千克		Men's or boys' wind-cheaters, wind-jackets, containing<70% by weight of silk, with thermal lining
6201.9900 22	丝制男式带特制领、有填料短上衣(含丝70%以下,含防风上衣,衬衫式样,带风帽)	16	100	17	16	件/千克		Men's or boys'tops wind-cheaters, with specially made collar, padded, containing<70% by weight of silk, shirt style, with hood
6201.9900 29	丝制其他防寒上衣(含丝70%以下)	16	100	17	16	件/千克		Other men's or boys' anoraks, containing<70% by weight of silk
6201.9900 31	其他材料制男式带风帽防寒短上衣(棉限内,带防寒衬里)	16	100	17	16	件/千克		Men's or boys' anoraks, with thermal lining, of other textile materials, cotton within limitations
6201.9900 32	其他材料制男式带风帽防寒短上衣(羊毛限内,带防寒衬里)	16	100	17	16	件/千克		Men's or boys' anoraks, with thermal lining, of other textile materials, wool within limitations
6201.9900 33	其他材料制男式带风帽防寒短上衣(化纤限内,带防寒衬里)	16	100	17	16	件/千克		Men's or boys' anoraks, with thermal lining, of other textile materials, man-made fibres within limitations
6201.9900 39	其他材料制男式带风帽防寒短上衣(其他纺织材料制,带防寒衬里)	16	100	17	16	件/千克		Men's or boys' anoraks, with thermal lining, of other textile materials
6201.9900 41	其他材料制男式带风帽短上衣(棉限内,带特制领,有填料,衬衫式样)	16	100	17	16	件/千克		Men's or boys' anoraks, padded, with specially made collar, shirt style, of other textile materials, cotton within limitations
6201.9900 42	其他材料制男式带风帽短上衣(羊毛限内,带特制领,有填料,衬衫式样)	16	100	17	16	件/千克		Men's or boys' anoraks, padded, with specially made collar, shirt style, of other textile materials, wool within limitations
6201.9900 43	其他材料制男式带风帽短上衣(化纤限内,带特制领,有填料,衬衫式样)	16	100	17	16	件/千克		Men's or boys' anoraks, padded, with specially made collar, shirt style, of other textile materials, man-made fibres within limitations
6201.9900 49	其他材料制男式带风帽短上衣(其他材料制,带特制领,有填料,衬衫式样)	16	100	17	16	件/千克		Men's or boys' anoraks, padded, with specially made collar, shirt style, of other textile materials

税则号列	货品名称	最惠(%)	普通	增值税率	出口退税	计量单位	监管条件	Article Description
6201.9900 91	其他材料制男式防寒短上衣(棉限内,含防风衣、防风短上衣类似品)	16	100	17	16	件/千克		Men's or boys' wind-cheaters, wind-jackets and similar articles, of other textile materials, cotton within limitations
6201.9900 92	其他材料制男式防寒短上衣(羊毛限内,含防风衣、防风短上衣类似品)	16	100	17	16	件/千克		Men's or boys' wind-cheaters, wind-jackets and similar articles, of other textile materials, wool within limitations
6201.9900 93	其他材料制男式防寒短上衣(化纤限内,含防风衣、防风短上衣类似品)	16	100	17	16	件/千克		Men's or boys' wind-cheaters, wind-jackets and similar articles, of other textile materials, man-made fibres within limitations
6201.9900 99	其他材料制男式其他防寒短上衣(含防风衣、防风短上衣类似品)	16	100	17	16	件/千克		Other men's or boys' anoraks, wind-cheaters, wind-jackets and similar articles, of other textile materials
62.02	**女式大衣、短大衣、斗篷、短斗篷、带风帽的防寒短上衣(包括滑雪短上衣)、防风衣、防风短上衣及类似品,但税目62.04的货品除外:**							**Women's or girls' overcoats, car-coats, capes, cloaks, anoraks (including ski-jackets), wind-cheaters, wind-jackets and similar articles, other than those of heading No. 62.04:**
	-大衣、雨衣、短大衣、斗篷、短斗篷及类似品:							-Overcoats, raincoats, car-coats, capes, cloaks and similar articles:
6202.1100	--羊毛或动物细毛制	16	130	17	16	件/千克		--Of wool or fine animal hair
6202.1100 10	毛制女式雨衣(羊毛或动物细毛制)	16	130	17	16	件/千克		Women's or girls' raincoats, of wool or fine animal hair
6202.1100 90	毛制女式大衣、斗篷及类似品等(包括短大衣、短斗篷,羊毛或动物细毛制)	16	130	17	16	件/千克		Women's or girls' overcoats, car-coats, capes, cloak and similar articles, of wool or fine animal hair
	--棉制:							--Of cotton:
6202.1210	---羽绒服	16	90	17	16	件/千克		---Padded with feathers or down
6202.1290	---其他	16	90	17	16	件/千克		---Other
6202.1290 10	棉制女式雨衣	16	90	17	16	件/千克		Women's or girls' raincoats, of cotton
6202.1290 20	棉制女式连风帽派克大衣等(含带风帽的防寒短上衣、防风衣、防风短上衣及类似品)	16	90	17	16	件/千克		Women's or girls' hooded parka, wind-cheaters, wind-jackets and similar articles, of cotton
6202.1290 90	棉制女式大衣、斗篷及类似品(包括短大衣、短斗篷)	16	90	17	16	件/千克		Women's or girls' overcoats, car-coats, capes, cloak and similar articles, of cotton
	--化学纤维制:							--Of man-made fibres:
6202.1310	---羽绒服	19	130	17	16	件/千克		---Padded with feathers or down
6202.1390	---其他	19	130	17	16	件/千克		---Other
6202.1390 10	化纤制女雨衣(含羊毛或动物细毛<36%,含带风帽防寒上衣、防风衣及类似品)	19	130	17	16	件/千克		Women's or girls' raincoats, anoraks, wind-cheaters, wind-jackets, containing <36% by weight of wool or fine animal hair, of man-made fibres
6202.1390 20	化纤制女式连风帽派克大衣(含短大衣、短斗篷,含羊毛或动物细毛36%及以上)	19	130	17	16	件/千克		Women's or girls' hooded parka, wind-cheaters, wind-jackets and similar articles, containing ≥36% by weight of wool or fine animal hair, of man-made fibres
6202.1390 30	化纤制女大衣、斗篷及类似品(含短大衣、短斗篷,含羊毛或动物细毛36%及以上)	19	130	17	16	件/千克		Women's or girls' overcoats, car-coats, capes, cloak and similar articles, containing ≥36% by weight of wool or fine animal hair, of man-made fibres
6202.1390 40	化纤制女式连风帽派克大衣(含羊毛或动物细毛<36%,含带风帽防寒上衣、防风衣及类似品)	19	130	17	16	件/千克		Women's or girls' hooded parka, wind-cheaters, wind-jackets and similar articles, containing <36% by weight of wool or fine animal hair, of man-made fibres
6202.1390 90	化纤制女大衣、斗篷及类似品(含短大衣、短斗篷,含羊毛或动物细毛36%以下)	19	130	17	16	件/千克		Women's or girls' overcoats, car-coats, capes, cloak and similar articles, containing <36% by weight of wool or fine animal hair, of man-made fibres
6202.1900	--其他纺织材料制	16	100	17	16	件/千克		--Of other textile materials
6202.1900 10	其他材料制女雨衣	16	100	17	16	件/千克		Women's or girls' raincoats of other textile materials

税则号列	货品名称	最惠(%)	普通	增值税率	出口退税	计量单位	监管条件	Article Description
6202.1900 21	其他材料制女大衣、斗篷及类似品(含短大衣、短斗篷,含丝70%及以上)	16	100	17	16	件/千克		Women's or girls' overcoats, car-coats, capes, cloak and similar articles, containing ≥70% by weight of silk, of other textile materials
6202.1900 29	其他材料制女大衣、斗篷及类似品(含短大衣、短斗篷,含丝70%及以下)	16	100	17	16	件/千克		Women's or girls' overcoats, car-coats, capes, cloak and similar articles, containing <70% by weight of silk, of other textile materials
6202.1900 30	其他材料制女大衣等,羊毛限内(含短大衣、斗篷、短斗篷)	16	100	17	16	件/千克		Women's or girls' overcoats, car-coats, capes, cloak and similar articles, of other textile materials, wool within limitations
6202.1900 40	其他材料制女大衣等,棉限内(含短大衣、斗篷、短斗篷)	16	100	17	16	件/千克		Women's or girls' overcoats, car-coats, capes, cloak and similar articles, of other textile materials, cotton within limitations
6202.1900 50	其他材料制女大衣等,化纤限内(含短大衣、斗篷、短斗篷)	16	100	17	16	件/千克		Women's or girls' overcoats, car-coats, capes, cloak and similar articles, of other textile materials, man-made fibres within limitations
6202.1900 90	其他材料制女大衣(含短大衣、斗篷、短斗篷)	16	100	17	16	件/千克		Women's or girls' overcoats, car-coats, capes, clock, of other textile materials
	-其他:							-Other:
6202.9100	--羊毛或动物细毛制	16	130	17	16	件/千克		--Of wool or fine animal hair
6202.9100 10	毛制女式有填料无袖上衣(羊毛或动物细毛制)	16	130	17	16	件/千克		Women's or girls' cloaks, padded, of wool or fine animal hair
6202.9100 20	毛制女式带防寒衬里的短上衣(羊毛或动物细毛制,含防风衣、防风短上衣)	16	130	17	16	件/千克		Women's or girls' wind-cheaters, wind-jackets, with thermal lining, of wool or fine animal hair
6202.9100 90	毛制女式其他防寒上衣(羊毛或动物细毛制)	16	130	17	16	件/千克		Other women's or girls' anoraks, of wool or fine animal hair
	--棉制:							--Of cotton:
6202.9210	---羽绒服	16	90	17	16	件/千克		---Padded with feathers or down
6202.9290	---其他	16	90	17	16	件/千克		---Other
6202.9290 10	棉制女式有填料无袖上衣(不带可连接袖子配件)	16	90	17	16	件/千克		Women's or girls's sleevelsee tops, padded, of cotton (not with fasteners of detachable sleeves)
6202.9290 20	棉制女式带防寒衬里的短上衣(含防风衣、防风短上衣)	16	90	17	16	件/千克		Women's or girls' wind-cheaters, wind-jackets, with thermal lining, of cotton
6202.9290 90	棉制女式其他防寒上衣	16	90	17	16	件/千克		Other women's or girls' anoraks of cotton
	--化学纤维制:							--Of man-made fibres:
6202.9310	---羽绒服	17.5	130	17	16	件/千克		---Padded with feathers or down
6202.9390	---其他	17.5	130	17	16	件/千克		---Other
6202.9390 10	化纤制女式有填料无袖上衣(不带可连接袖子配件)	17.5	130	17	16	件/千克		Women's or girls's sleeveless tops, padded, of man-made fibres
6202.9390 20	化纤制女式带风帽防寒短上衣(含羊毛或动物细毛36%及以上)	17.5	130	17	16	件/千克		Women's or girls' anoraks, containing≥36% by weight of wool or fine animal hair, of man-made fibres
6202.9390 30	化纤制女式带防寒衬里的短上衣(含防风衣、防风短上衣)	17.5	130	17	16	件/千克		Women's or girls' wind-cheaters, wind-jackets, with thermal lining, of man-made fibres
6202.9390 90	化纤制女式其他防寒上衣	17.5	130	17	16	件/千克		Other women's or girls' anoraks of man-made fibres
6202.9900	--其他纺织材料制	16	100	17	16	件/千克		--Of other textile materials
6202.9900 11	丝制女式带防寒衬里的短上衣(含丝70%及以上,含防风衣、防风短上衣)	16	100	17	16	件/千克		Women's or girls' wind-cheaters, wind-jackets, with thermal lining, containing≥70% by weight of silk
6202.9900 19	丝制女式其他防寒上衣(含丝70%及以上)	16	100	17	16	件/千克		Other women's or girls' anoraks of silk, containing ≥ 70% by weight of silk
6202.9900 21	丝制女式带防寒衬里的短上衣(含丝70%以下,含防风衣、防风短上衣)	16	100	17	16	件/千克		Women's or girls' wind-cheaters, wind-jackets, with thermal lining, containing <70% by weight of silk
6202.9900 29	丝制女式其他防寒上衣(含丝70%以下)	16	100	17	16	件/千克		Other women's or girls' anoraks of silk, containing < 70% by weight of silk
6202.9900 31	其他材料制女式带风帽防寒短上衣(棉限内,带防寒衬里)	16	100	17	16	件/千克		Women's or girls' anoraks, with thermal lining, of other textile materials, cotton within limitations

税则号列	货品名称	最惠(%)	普通	增值税率	出口退税	计量单位	监管条件	Article Description
6202.9900 32	其他材料制女式带风帽防寒短上衣(羊毛限内,带防寒衬里)	16	100	17	16	件/千克		Women's or girls' anoraks, wind-jackets, with thermal lining, of other textile materials, wool within limitations
6202.9900 33	其他材料制女式带风帽防寒短上衣(化纤限内,带防寒衬里)	16	100	17	16	件/千克		Women's or girls' anoraks, wind-jackets, with thermal lining, of other textile materials, man-made fibres within limitations
6202.9900 39	其他材料制女式带风帽防寒短上衣(其他纺织材料制,带防寒衬里)	16	100	17	16	件/千克		Women's or girls' anoraks, with thermal lining, of other textile materials
6202.9900 91	其他材料制女式防寒短上衣等(棉限内,含防风衣、防风短上衣及类似品)	16	100	17	16	件/千克		Women's or girls' wind-cheaters, wind-jackets and similar articles, of other textile materials, cotton within limitations
6202.9900 92	其他材料制女式防寒短上衣等(羊毛限内,含防风衣、防风短上衣及类似品)	16	100	17	16	件/千克		Women's or girls' wind-cheaters, wind-jackets and similar articles, of other textile materials, wool within limitations
6202.9900 93	其他材料制女式防寒短上衣等(化纤限内,含防风衣、防风短上衣及类似品)	16	100	17	16	件/千克		Women's or girls' wind-cheaters, wind-jackets and similar articles, of other textile materials, man-made fibres within limitations
6202.9900 99	其他材料制女式其他防寒短上衣等(含防风衣、防风短上衣及类似品)	16	100	17	16	件/千克		Other women's or girls' anoraks, wind-cheaters, wind-jackets and similar articles, of other textile materials
62.03	男式西服套装、便服套装、上衣、长裤、护胸背带工装裤、马裤及短裤(游泳裤除外):							**Men's or boys' suits, ensembles, jackets, blazers, trousers, bib and brace overalls, breeches and shorts (other than swim wear):**
	-西服套装:							-Suits:
6203.1100	--羊毛或动物细毛制	17.5	130	17	16	套/千克		--Of wool or fine animal hair
6203.1200	--合成纤维制	17.5	130	17	16	套/千克		--Of synthetic fibres
6203.1200 10	合成纤维制男式西服套装(含羊毛或动物细毛36%及以上)	17.5	130	17	16	套/千克		Men's or boys' suits, containing ≥36% by weight of wool or fine animal hair, of synthetic fibres
6203.1200 90	其他合纤制男式西服套装	17.5	130	17	16	套/千克		Other men's or boys' suits of synthetic fibres
	--其他纺织材料制:							--Of other textile materials:
6203.1910	---丝及绢丝制	17.5	100	17	16	套/千克		---Of silk or spun silk
6203.1910 10	丝及绢丝制男式西服套装(含丝70%及以上)	17.5	100	17	16	套/千克		Men's or boys' suits, containing ≥70% by weight of silk
6203.1910 90	其他丝及绢丝制男式西服套装(含丝70%以下)	17.5	100	17	16	套/千克		Other men's or boys' suits, containing < 70% by weight of silk
6203.1990	---其他	17.5	100	17	16	套/千克		---Other
6203.1990 10	棉制男式西服套装	17.5	100	17	16	套/千克		Men's or boys' suits of cotton
6203.1990 21	人造纤维制男式西服套装(含羊毛或动物细毛36%及以上)	17.5	100	17	16	套/千克		Men's or boys' suits of artificial fibres, containing ≥36% by weight of wool or fine animal hair
6203.1990 29	其他人造纤维制男式西服套装	17.5	100	17	16	套/千克		Men's or boys' suits of other artificial fibres
6203.1990 91	其他材料制男式西服套装(棉限内)	17.5	100	17	16	套/千克		Men's or boys' suits of other textile materials, cotton within limitations
6203.1990 92	其他材料制男式西服套装(毛限内)	17.5	100	17	16	套/千克		Men's or boys' suits of other textile materials, wool within limitations
6203.1990 93	其他材料制男式西服套装(化纤限内)	17.5	100	17	16	套/千克		Men's or boys' suits of other textile materials, man-made fibres within limitations
6203.1990 99	其他材料制其他男式西服套装	17.5	100	17	16	套/千克		Men's or boys' suits of other textile materials
	-便服套装:							-Ensembles:
6203.2200	--棉制	17.5	90	17	16	套/千克		--Of cotton
6203.2200 10	棉制男式便服套装(工业及职业用)	17.5	90	17	16	套/千克		Men's or boys' ensembles of cotton, industrial and career apparel
6203.2200 90	其他棉制男式便服套装	17.5	90	17	16	套/千克		Other men's or boys' ensembles of cotton
6203.2300	--合成纤维制	17.5	130	17	16	套/千克		--Of synthetic fibres
6203.2300 11	合成纤维制其他男式便服套装(含羊毛或动物细毛≥36%,工业及职业用)	17.5	130	17	16	套/千克		Other men's or boys' ensembles, containing ≥36% by weight of wool or fine animal hair industrial and career apparel, of synthetic fibres

税则号列	货品名称	最惠(%)	普通	增值税率	出口退税	计量单位	监管条件	Article Description
6203.2300 19	合成纤维制其他男式便服套装(含羊毛或动物细毛≥36%)	17.5	130	17	16	套/千克		Other men's or boys' ensembles, containing ≥36% by weight of wool or fine animal hair, of synthetic fibres
6203.2300 91	其他合成纤维制其他男式便服套装(工业及职业用)	17.5	130	17	16	套/千克		Other men's or boys' ensembles, industrial and career apparel, of synthetic fibres
6203.2300 99	其他合成纤维制其他男式便服套装	17.5	130	17	16	套/千克		Other men's or boys' ensembles of synthetic fibres
	--其他纺织材料制:							--Of other textile materials:
6203.2910	---丝及绢丝制	17.5	130	17	16	套/千克		---Of silk or spun silk
6203.2910 10	丝制男式便服套装(含丝70%及以上)	17.5	130	17	16	套/千克		Men's or boys' ensembles, containing ≥ 70% by weight of silk
6203.2910 90	丝制其他男式便服套装(含丝70%以下)	17.5	130	17	16	套/千克		Other men's or boys' ensembles, containing < 70% by weight of silk
6203.2920	---羊毛或动物细毛制	17.5	130	17	16	套/千克		---Of wool or fine animal hair
6203.2990	---其他	17.5	100	17	16	套/千克		---Other
6203.2990 11	人造纤维制其他男式便服套装(工业及职业用)	17.5	100	17	16	套/千克		Other men's or boys' ensembles of artificial fibres, industrial and career apparel
6203.2990 19	人造纤维制其他男式便服套装	17.5	100	17	16	套/千克		Other men's or boys' ensembles of artificial fibres
6203.2990 90	其他材料制其他男式便服套装	17.5	100	17	16	套/千克		Other men's or boys' ensembles of other textile materials
	-上衣:							-Jackets and blazers:
6203.3100	--羊毛或动物细毛制	16	130	17	16	件/千克		--Of wool or fine animal hair
6203.3100 10	毛制男式西服式上衣(羊毛或动物细毛制)	16	130	17	16	件/千克		Men's or boys' suit jackets and blazers, of wool or fine animal hair
6203.3100 90	毛制男式其他上衣(羊毛或动物细毛制)	16	130	17	16	件/千克		Other men's or boys' jackets and blazers, of wool or fine animal hair
6203.3200	--棉制	16	90	17	16	件/千克		--Of cotton
6203.3200 10	棉制工业及职业用男式上衣	16	90	17	16	件/千克		Men's or boys' jackets and blazers of cotton, industrial and career apparel
6203.3200 90	棉制其他男式上衣	16	90	17	16	件/千克		Men's or boys' jackets and blazers of cotton
6203.3300	--合成纤维制	17.5	130	17	16	件/千克		--Of synthetic fibres
6203.3300 11	合成纤维制男式西服式上衣(含羊毛或动物细毛36%及以上,工业及职业用)	17.5	130	17	16	件/千克		Men's or boys' suit jacket, containing ≥ 36% by weight of wool or fine animal hair, industrial and career apparel, of synthetic fibres
6203.3300 19	合成纤维制男式西服式上衣(含羊毛或动物细毛36%及以上)	17.5	130	17	16	件/千克		Men's or boys' suit jacket, containing ≥ 36% by weight of wool or fine animal hair, of synthetic fibres
6203.3300 21	合成纤维制男式其他上衣(含羊毛或动物细毛36%及以上,工业及职业用)	17.5	130	17	16	件/千克		Other men's or boys' jackets and blazers of synthetic fibres, containing ≥36% by weight of wool or fine animal hair, industrial and career apparel
6203.3300 29	合成纤维制男式其他上衣(含羊毛或动物细毛36%及以上)	17.5	130	17	16	件/千克		Other men's or boys' jackets and blazers of synthetic fibres, containing ≥36% by weight of wool or fine animal hair
6203.3300 91	其他合成纤维制男式上衣(工业及职业用)	17.5	130	17	16	件/千克		Other men's or boys' jackets and blazers of synthetic fibres, industrial and career apparel
6203.3300 99	其他合成纤维制男式上衣	17.5	130	17	16	件/千克		Other men's or boys' jackets and blazers of synthetic fibres
	--其他纺织材料制:							--Of other textile materials:
6203.3910	---丝及绢丝制	16	130	17	16	件/千克		---Of silk or spun silk
6203.3910 10	丝制男式上衣(含丝70%及以上)	16	130	17	16	件/千克		Men's or boys' jackets and blazers of silk, containing ≥70% by weight of silk
6203.3910 90	丝制男式上衣(含丝70%以下)	16	130	17	16	件/千克		Men's or boys' jackets and blazers of silk, containing <70% by weight of silk
6203.3990	---其他	16	100	17	16	件/千克		---Other
6203.3990 11	人造纤维制男式西服式上衣(含羊毛或动物细毛36%及以上,工业及职业用)	16	100	17	16	件/千克		Men's or boys' suit-type jacket, of artificial fibres, industrial and career apparel, containing ≥ 36% by weight of wool or fine animal hair
6203.3990 19	人造纤维制男式西服式上衣(含羊毛或动物细毛36%及以上)	16	100	17	16	件/千克		Men's or boys' suit-type jacket, of artificial fibres, containing≥36% by weight of wool or fine animal hair

税则号列	货品名称	最惠(%)	普通	增值税率	出口退税	计量单位	监管条件	Article Description
6203.3990 21	人造纤维制男式其他上衣(含羊毛或动物细毛36%及以上,工业及职业用)	16	100	17	16	件/千克		Other men's or boys' jackets and blazers of artificial fibres, containing ≥36% by weight of wool or fine animal hair, industrial and career apparel
6203.3990 29	人造纤维制男式其他上衣(含羊毛或动物细毛36%及以上)	16	100	17	16	件/千克		Other men's or boys' jackets and blazers of artificial fibres, containing ≥36% by weight of wool or fine animal hair
6203.3990 31	其他人造纤维制男式上衣(工业及职业用)	16	100	17	16	件/千克		Men's or boys' jackets and blazers of artificial fibres, industrial and career apparel
6203.3990 39	其他人造纤维制男式上衣	16	100	17	16	件/千克		Men's or boys' jackets and blazers of artificial fibres
6203.3990 91	其他材料制男式上衣(棉限内)	16	100	17	16	件/千克		Other men's or boys' jackets and blazers of other textile materials, cotton within limitations
6203.3990 92	其他材料制男式上衣(毛限内)	16	100	17	16	件/千克		Other men's or boys' jackets and blazers of other textile materials, wool within limitations
6203.3990 93	其他材料制男式上衣(化纤限内)	16	100	17	16	件/千克		Other men's or boys' jackets and blazers of other textile materials, man-made fibres within limitations
6203.3990 99	其他材料制男式上衣	16	100	17	16	件/千克		Other men's or boys' jackets and blazers of other textile materials
	-长裤、护胸背带工装裤、马裤及短裤:							-Trousers, bib and brace overalls, breeches and shorts:
6203.4100	--羊毛或动物细毛制	16	130	17	16	条/千克		--Of wool or fine animal hair
6203.4100 11	毛制男式护胸背带工装裤(羊毛或动物细毛制,带防寒衬里)	16	130	17	16	条/千克		Men's or boys' bib and brace overalls, with thermal lining, of wool or fine animal hair
6203.4100 19	毛制男式护胸背带工装裤(羊毛或动物细毛制)	16	130	17	16	条/千克		Men's or boys' bib and brace overalls, of wool or fine animal hair
6203.4100 21	毛制男式长裤、马裤(羊毛或动物细毛制,带防寒衬里)	16	130	17	16	条/千克		Men's or boys' trousers, breeches, with thermal lining, of wool or fine animal hair
6203.4100 22	毛制男式长裤、马裤(羊毛或动物细毛制,含8-18号男童)	16	130	17	16	条/千克	A	Men's trousers, breeches, including boys' No. 8 ~ No. 18, of wool or fine animal hair
6203.4100 29	毛制其他男童长裤、马裤(羊毛或动物细毛制)	16	130	17	16	条/千克	A	Other boys' trousers, breeches, of wool or fine animal hair
6203.4100 90	毛制男式短裤(羊毛或动物细毛制)	16	130	17	16	条/千克		Men's or boys' shorts, of wool or fine animal hair
	--棉制:							--Of cotton:
6203.4210	---阿拉伯裤	16	90	17	16	条/千克		---Arabian trousers
6203.4210 10	棉制男式阿拉伯裤(羽绒和水禽毛≥15%且含绒率≥35%,或含羽绒≥10%)	16	90	17	16	条/千克		Men's or boys' Arabian trousers of cotton, containing ≥15% by weight of down or feathers and water fowl, down content rate≥35%, or containing≥10% by weight of down or feathers
6203.4210 90	棉制男式阿拉伯裤	16	90	17	16	条/千克		Men's or boys' Arabian trousers of cotton
6203.4290	---其他	16	90	17	16	条/千克		---Other
6203.4290 11	工业、职业用棉男护胸背带工装裤(羽绒和水禽毛≥15%且含绒率≥35%,或含羽绒≥10%)	16	90	17	16	条/千克		Men's or boys' bib and brace overalls, industrial and career apparel, containing≥15% by weight of down or feathers and water fowl, down content rate ≥ 35%, or containing ≥ 10% by weight of down or feathers, of cotton
6203.4290 12	棉制男式护胸背带工装裤(羽绒和水禽毛≥15%且含绒率≥35%,或含羽绒≥10%)	16	90	17	16	条/千克		Men's or boys' bib and brace overalls, containing ≥ 15% by weight of down or feathers and water fowl, down content rate ≥ 35%, or containing ≥ 10% by weight of down or feathers, of cotton
6203.4290 13	棉制其他男成人护胸背带工装裤(带防寒衬里,工业及职业用)	16	90	17	16	条/千克		Other men's bib and brace overalls, with thermal lining, of cotton, industrial and career apparel
6203.4290 14	棉制其他男成人护胸背带工装裤(带防寒衬里)	16	90	17	16	条/千克		Other men's bib and brace overalls, with thermal lining, of cotton, industrial and career apparel
6203.4290 15	棉制其他男童护胸背带工装裤(带防寒衬里)	16	90	17	16	条/千克	A	Other boys' bib and brace overalls, with thermal lining, of cotton
6203.4290 16	棉制其他男成人护胸背带工装裤(工业及职业用)	16	90	17	16	条/千克		Other men's bib and brace overalls, of cotton, industrial and career apparel

税则号列	货品名称	最惠(%)	普通	增值税率	出口退税	计量单位	监管条件	Article Description
6203.4290 17	棉制其他男成人护胸背带工装裤	16	90	17	16	条/千克		Other men's bib and brace overalls of cotton
6203.4290 19	棉制其他男童护胸背带工装裤	16	90	17	16	条/千克	A	Other boys' bib and brace overalls of cotton
6203.4290 21	工业、职业用棉男长裤、马裤(羽绒和水禽毛≥15%且含绒率≥35%,或含羽绒≥10%)	16	90	17	16	条/千克		Men's or boys' trousers, breeches, containing≥15% by weight of down or feathers and water fowl, down content rats≥35%, industrial and career apparel, or containing≥10% by weight of down or feathers, of cotton
6203.4290 29	棉制男式长裤、马裤(羽绒和水禽毛≥15%且含绒率≥35%,或含羽绒≥10%)	16	90	17	16	条/千克		Men's or boys' trousers, breeches, containing≥15% by weight of down or feathers and water fowl, down content rate≥35%, or containing≥10% by weight of down or feathers, of cotton
6203.4290 30	棉制男式长裤、马裤(游戏装,带防寒衬里)	16	90	17	16	条/千克		Men's or boys' trousers, breeches, playsuit, with thermal lining, of cotton
6203.4290 41	棉制男式长裤、马裤(游戏装,不带防寒衬里,含8-18号男童)	16	90	17	16	条/千克		Men's or boys' trousers, breeches, playsuit, including boys' No. 8 ~ No. 18, of cotton, playsuit, without thermal lining
6203.4290 49	棉制其他男童长裤、马裤(游戏装,不带防寒衬里)	16	90	17	16	条/千克	A	Other boys' trousers, breeches, of cotton, playsuit, without thermal lining
6203.4290 51	棉制男式长裤、马裤(非游戏装,带防寒衬里,工业及职业用)	16	90	17	16	条/千克		Men's or boys' trousers, breeches, of cotton, with thermal lining, industrial and career apparel (other than playsuit)
6203.4290 59	棉制男式长裤、马裤(非游戏装,带防寒衬里)	16	90	17	16	条/千克		Men's or boys' trousers, breeches, of cotton, with thermal lining, other than playsuit
6203.4290 61	棉制男成人长裤、马裤(非游戏装,不带防寒衬里,工业及职业用)	16	90	17	16	条/千克		Men's trousers, breeches, of cotton, industrial and career apparel, other than playsuit, without thermal lining
6203.4290 62	棉制男式长裤、马裤(非游戏装,不带防寒衬里,含8-18号男童)	16	90	17	16	条/千克	A	Men's trousers, breeches, including boys' No. 8 ~ No. 18, of cotton, other than playsuit, without thermal lining
6203.4290 69	棉制其他男童长裤、马裤(非游戏装,不带防寒衬里)	16	90	17	16	条/千克	A	Other boys' trousers, breeches, of cotton, other than playsuit, without thermal lining
6203.4290 91	棉制男式短裤(羽绒和水禽毛≥15%且含绒率≥35%,或含羽绒≥10%)	16	90	17	16	条/千克		Men's or boys' shorts of cotton, containing≥15% by weight of down or feathers and water fowl, down content rate≥35%, or containing≥10% by weight of down or feathers
6203.4290 92	棉制其他男式短裤(游戏装)	16	90	17	16	条/千克		Other men's or boys' shorts of cotton, playsuit
6203.4290 99	棉制其他男式短裤(非游戏装)	16	90	17	16	条/千克		Other men's or boys' shorts of cotton, other than playsuit
	--合成纤维制:							--Of synthetic fibres:
6203.4310	---阿拉伯裤	17.5	130	17	16	条/千克		---Arabian trousers
6203.4310 10	合成纤维制男式阿拉伯裤(羽绒和水禽毛≥15%且含绒率≥35%,或含羽绒≥10%)	17.5	130	17	16	条/千克		Men's or boys' Arabian trousers of synthetic fibres, containing≥15% by weight of down or feathers and water fowl, down content rate≥35%, or containing ≥10% by weight of down or feathers
6203.4310 90	合成纤维制男式阿拉伯裤	17.5	130	17	16	条/千克		Men's or boys' Arabian trousers of synthetic fibres
6203.4390	---其他	17.5	130	17	16	条/千克		---Other
6203.4390 11	工业、职业用合纤制男护胸背带工裤(羽绒和水禽毛≥15%且含绒率≥35%,或含羽绒≥10%)	17.5	130	17	16	条/千克		Men's or boys' bib and brace overalls, industrial and career apparel, containing≥15% by weight of down or feathers and water fowl, down content rate ≥35%, or containing ≥10% by weight of down or feathers, of synthetic fibres
6203.4390 12	合纤制男式护胸背带工裤(羽绒和水禽毛≥15%且含绒率≥35%,或含羽绒≥10%)	17.5	130	17	16	条/千克		Men's or boys' bib and brace overalls, containing≥15% by weight of down or feathers and water fowl, down content rate≥35%, or containing≥10% by weight of down or feathers, of synthetic fibres
6203.4390 13	其他合纤制男成人护胸背带工装裤(带防寒衬里,工业及职业用)	17.5	130	17	16	条/千克		Other men's bib and brace overalls, with thermal lining, industrial and career apparel, of synthetic fibres

税则号列	货品名称	最惠(%)	普通	增值税率	出口退税	计量单位	监管条件	Article Description
6203.4390 14	其他合纤制男成人护胸背带工装裤(带防寒衬里)	17.5	130	17	16	条/千克		Other men's bib and brace overalls, with thermal lining, of synthetic fibres
6203.4390 15	其他合纤制男童护胸背带工装裤(带防寒衬里)	17.5	130	17	16	条/千克	A	Other boys' bib and brace overalls, with thermal lining of synthetic fibres
6203.4390 16	其他合纤制男成人护胸背带工装裤(工业及职业用)	17.5	130	17	16	条/千克		Other men's bib and brace overalls, industrial and career apparel, of synthetic fibres
6203.4390 17	其他合纤制男成人护胸背带工装裤	17.5	130	17	16	条/千克		Other men's bib and brace overalls of synthetic fibres
6203.4390 19	其他合纤制男童护胸背带工装裤	17.5	130	17	16	条/千克	A	Other boys' bib and brace overalls of synthetic fibres
6203.4390 21	工业、职业用合纤制男长裤、马裤(羽绒和水禽毛≥15%且含绒率≥35%,或含羽绒≥10%)	17.5	130	17	16	条/千克		Men's or boys' trousers, breeches, industrial apparel containing≥15% by weight of down or feathers and water fowl, down content rate≥35% or containing≥10% by weight of down or feathers, of synthetic fibres
6203.4390 29	合纤制男式长裤、马裤(羽绒和水禽毛≥15%且含绒率≥35%,或含羽绒≥10%)	17.5	130	17	16	条/千克		Men's or boys' trousers, breeches, containing≥15% by weight of down or feathers and water fowl, down content rate≥35% or containing≥10% by weight of down or feathers, of synthetic fibres
6203.4390 31	其他合纤制男式长裤、马裤(带防寒衬里,含羊毛或动物细毛36%及以上,工职业用)	17.5	130	17	16	条/千克		Men's or boys' trousers, breeches, containing≥36% by weight of wool or fine animal hair, with thermal lining, industrial and career apparel, of synthetic fibres
6203.4390 39	其他合纤制男式长裤、马裤(带防寒衬里,含羊毛或动物细毛36%及以上)	17.5	130	17	16	条/千克		Men's or boys' trousers, breeches, containing≥36% by weight of wool or fine animal hair, with thermal lining, of synthetic fibres
6203.4390 41	其他合纤制男成人长裤、马裤(不带防寒衬里,含羊毛或动物细毛36%及以上,工/职业用)	17.5	130	17	16	条/千克		Men's trousers, breeches, containing ≥ 36% by weight of wool or fine animal hair, industrial and career apparel, without thermal lining, of synthetic fibres
6203.4390 42	其他合纤制男式长裤、马裤(不带防寒衬里,含羊毛或动物细毛36%及以上,指8-18号男童)	17.5	130	17	16	条/千克		Men's trousers, breeches, including boys' No. 8 ~ No. 18, containing≥36% by weight of wool or fine animal hair, without thermal lining, of synthetic fibres
6203.4390 49	其他合纤制男童长裤、马裤(不带防寒衬里,含羊毛或动物细毛36%及以上)	17.5	130	17	16	条/千克	A	Boys' trousers, breeches, containing≥36% by weight of wool or fine animal hair, without thermal lining, of synthetic fibres
6203.4390 50	其他合纤制男式长裤、马裤(带防寒衬里,游戏装)	17.5	130	17	16	条/千克		Other men's or boys' trousers, breeches, with thermal lining, playsuit, of synthetic fibres
6203.4390 61	其他合纤制男式长裤、马裤(不带防寒衬里,游戏装,含8-18号男童)	17.5	130	17	16	条/千克	A	Other men's trousers, breeches, of synthetic fibres, without thermal lining, including boys' No. 8 ~ No. 18, playsuit
6203.4390 69	其他合纤制其他男童长裤、马裤(不带防寒衬里,游戏装)	17.5	130	17	16	条/千克	A	Other boys' trousers, breeches, playsuit, of synthetic fibres, without thermal lining
6203.4390 71	其他合纤制男式长裤、马裤(带防寒衬里,非游戏装和滑雪裤,工业及职业用)	17.5	130	17	16	条/千克		Other men's or boys' trousers, breeches, with thermal lining, industrial and career apparel, other than playsuit, of synthetic fibres
6203.4390 79	其他合纤制男式长裤、马裤(带防寒衬里,非游戏装和滑雪裤)	17.5	130	17	16	条/千克		Other men's or boys' trousers, breeches, with thermal lining, other than playsuit or ski trousers of synthetic fibres
6203.4390 81	其他合纤制男成人长裤、马裤(不带防寒衬里,非游戏装和滑雪裤,工业及职业用)	17.5	130	17	16	条/千克		Other men's trousers, breeches, industrial and career apparel, of synthetic fibres, other than playsuit or ski trousers without thermal lining
6203.4390 82	其他合纤制男童长裤、马裤(不带防寒衬里,非游戏装和滑雪裤,指8-18号男童)	17.5	130	17	16	条/千克	A	Other men's trousers, breeches, including boys' No. 8 ~ No. 18, of synthetic fibres, other than playsuit or ski trousers without thermal lining
6203.4390 89	其他合纤制其他男童长裤、马裤(不带防寒衬里,非游戏装和滑雪裤)	17.5	130	17	16	条/千克	A	Other boys' trousers, breeches of synthetic fibres, other than playsuit or ski trousers without thermal lining

税则号列	货品名称	最惠(%)	普通	增值税率	出口退税	计量单位	监管条件	Article Description
6203.4390 91	合纤制男式短裤(羽绒和水禽毛≥15%且含绒率≥35%,或含羽绒≥10%)	17.5	130	17	16	条/千克		Men's or boys' shorts, containing≥15% by weight of down or feathers and water fowl, down content rate≥35% or containing ≥10% by weight of down or feathers
6203.4390 92	其他合纤制男式短裤(游戏装)	17.5	130	17	16	条/千克		Men's or boys' shorts, playsuit, of synthetic fibres
6203.4390 93	其他合纤制男式短裤(非游戏装)	17.5	130	17	16	条/千克		Other men's or boys' shorts, other than playsuit, of synthetic fibres
6203.4390 99	其他合纤制男裤	17.5	130	17	16	条/千克		Other men's or boys' trousers of synthetic fibres
	--其他纺织材料制:							--Of other textile materials:
6203.4910	---阿拉伯裤	16	100	17	16	条/千克		---Arabian trousers
6203.4910 10	人纤制男式阿拉伯裤(羽绒和水禽毛≥15%且含绒率≥35%,或含羽绒≥10%)	16	100	17	16	条/千克		Men's or boys' Arabian trousers of artificial fibres, containing≥15% by weight of down or feathers and water fowl, down content rate≥35%, or containing ≥10% by weight of down or feathers
6203.4910 20	人纤制男式阿拉伯裤	16	100	17	16	条/千克		Men's or boys' Arabian trousers of artificial fibres
6203.4910 30	其他材料制男式阿拉伯裤(羽绒和水禽毛≥15%且含绒率≥35%,或含羽绒≥10%)	16	100	17	16	条/千克		Men's or boys' Arabian trousers of other textile materials, containing≥15% by weight of down or feathers and water fowl, down content rate≥35%, or containing≥10% by weight of down or feathers
6203.4910 90	其他材料制男式阿拉伯裤	16	100	17	16	条/千克		Men's or boys' Arabian trousers of other textile materials
6203.4990	---其他	16	100	17	16	条/千克		---Other
6203.4990 11	人纤制男成人护胸背带工装裤(带防寒衬里)	16	100	17	16	条/千克		Men's bib and brace overalls, with thermal lining, of artificial fibres
6203.4990 12	人纤制男童护胸背带工装裤(带防寒衬里)	16	100	17	16	条/千克	A	Boys' bib and brace overalls, with thermal lining, of artificial fibres
6203.4990 13	人纤制男成人护胸背带工装裤	16	100	17	16	条/千克		Men's bib and brace overalls, of artificial fibres
6203.4990 19	人纤制男童护胸背带工装裤	16	100	17	16	条/千克	A	Boys' bib and brace overalls, of artificial fibres
6203.4990 21	人纤制男式长裤、马裤(带防寒衬里,含羊毛或动物细毛36%及以上)	16	100	17	16	条/千克		Men's or boys' trousers, breeches, with thermal lining, containing≥36% by weight of wool or fine animal hair, of artificial fibres
6203.4990 22	人纤制其他男式长裤、马裤(不带防寒衬里,含羊毛或动物细毛36%及以上)	16	100	17	16	条/千克		Men's or boys' trousers, breeches, containing≥36% by weight of wool or fine animal hair, of artificial fibres, without thermal lining
6203.4990 23	人纤制男式长裤、马裤(带防寒衬里,游戏装)	16	100	17	16	条/千克		Men's or boys' trousers, breeches, with thermal lining, playsuit, of artificial fibres
6203.4990 24	人纤制其他男式长裤、马裤(不带防寒衬里,游戏装)	16	100	17	16	条/千克		Men's or boys' trousers, breeches, playsuit, of artificial fibres, without thermal lining
6203.4990 25	人纤制男式长裤、马裤(带防寒衬里,非游戏装)	16	100	17	16	条/千克		Men's or boys' trousers, breeches, with thermal lining, of artificial fibres, other than playsuits
6203.4990 26	人纤制其他男式长裤、马裤(不带防寒衬里,非游戏装)	16	100	17	16	条/千克		Men's or boys' trousers, breeches, of artificial fibres, without thermal lining, other than playsuits
6203.4990 27	人纤制男式短裤(含羊毛或动物细毛36%及以上)	16	100	17	16	条/千克		Men's or boys' shorts of artificial fibres, containing≥36% by weight of wool or fine animal hair
6203.4990 28	人纤制男式短裤(游戏装)	16	100	17	16	条/千克		Men's or boys' shorts, playsuit, of artificial fibres
6203.4990 29	人纤制男式短裤(非游戏装)	16	100	17	16	条/千克		Men's or boys' shorts of artificial fibres, other than playsuit
6203.4990 31	丝制男式护胸背带工装裤(含丝70%及以上)	16	100	17	16	条/千克		Men's or boys' bib and brace overalls, containing≥70% by weight of silk
6203.4990 32	丝制男式长裤、马裤(含丝70%及以上,带防寒衬里)	16	100	17	16	条/千克		Men's or boys' trousers, breeches, containing≥70% by weight of silk, with thermal lining
6203.4990 33	丝制男式长裤、马裤(含丝70%及以上,不带防寒衬里)	16	100	17	16	条/千克		Men's or boys' trousers, breeches, containing≥70% by weight of silk, without thermal lining
6203.4990 34	丝制男式短裤(含丝70%及以上)	16	100	17	16	条/千克		Men's or boys' shorts, containing≥70% by weight of silk
6203.4990 35	丝制男式护胸背带工装裤(含丝70%以下,带防寒衬里)	16	100	17	16	条/千克		Men's or boys' bib and brace overalls, containing < 70% by weight of silk, with thermal lining

税则号列	货品名称	最惠(%)	普通	增值税率	出口退税	计量单位	监管条件	Article Description
6203.4990 36	丝制男式护胸背带工装裤(含丝70%以下,不带防寒衬里)	16	100	17	16	条/千克		Men's or boys' bib and brace overalls, containing <70% by weight of silk, without thermal lining
6203.4990 37	丝制男式长裤、马裤(含丝70%以下,带防寒衬里)	16	100	17	16	条/千克		Men's or boys' trousers, breeches, containing <70% by weight of silk, with thermal lining
6203.4990 38	丝制男式长裤、马裤(含丝70%以下,不带防寒衬里)	16	100	17	16	条/千克		Men's or boys' trousers, breeches, containing <70% by weight of silk, without thermal lining
6203.4990 39	丝制男式短裤(含丝70%以下)	16	100	17	16	条/千克		Men's or boys' shorts, containing <70% by weight of silk
6203.4990 41	其他材料制男式长裤、马裤(棉限内,带防寒衬里)	16	100	17	16	条/千克		Men's or boys' trousers, breeches, cotton within limitations, with thermal lining, of other textile materials
6203.4990 42	其他材料制男式长裤、马裤(棉限内,不带防寒衬里)	16	100	17	16	条/千克		Men's or boys' trousers, breeches, cotton within limitations, of other textile materials without thermal lining
6203.4990 49	其他材料制男式短裤(棉限内)	16	100	17	16	条/千克		Men's or boys' shorts, cotton within limitations, of other textile materials
6203.4990 51	其他材料制男式长裤、马裤(毛限内,带防寒衬里)	16	100	17	16	条/千克		Men's or boys' trousers, breeches, wool within limitations, with thermal lining, of other textile materials
6203.4990 52	其他材料制男式长裤、马裤(毛限内,不带防寒衬里)	16	100	17	16	条/千克		Men's or boys' trousers, breeches, wool within limitations, of other textile materials, without thermal lining
6203.4990 59	其他材料制男式短裤(毛限内)	16	100	17	16	条/千克		Men's or boys' shorts of other textile materials, wool within limitations
6203.4990 61	其他材料制男式长裤、马裤(化纤限内,带防寒衬里)	16	100	17	16	条/千克		Men's or boys' trousers, breeches, with thermal lining, of other textile materials, man-made fibres within limitations
6203.4990 62	其他材料制男式长裤、马裤(化纤限内,不带防寒衬里)	16	100	17	16	条/千克		Men's or boys' trousers, breeches without thermal lining, of other textile materials, man-made fibres within limitations
6203.4990 69	其他材料制男式短裤(化纤限内)	16	100	17	16	条/千克		Men's or boys' shorts, of other textile materials, man-made fibres within limitations
6203.4990 91	其他材料制男式护胸背带工装裤(带防寒衬里)	16	100	17	16	条/千克		Men's or boys' bib and brace overalls, with thermal lining, of other textile materials
6203.4990 92	其他材料制男式护胸背带工装裤(不带防寒衬里)	16	100	17	16	条/千克		Men's or boys' bib and brace overalls, of other textile materials, without thermal lining
6203.4990 93	其他材料制男式长裤、马裤(带防寒衬里)	16	100	17	16	条/千克		Men's or boys' trousers, breeches, with thermal lining, of other textile materials
6203.4990 94	其他材料制男式长裤、马裤(不带防寒衬里)	16	100	17	16	条/千克		Men's or boys' trousers, breeches of other textile materials, without thermal lining
6203.4990 99	其他材料制男式短裤	16	100	17	16	条/千克		Men's or boys' shorts of other textile materials
62.04	**女式西服套装、便服套装、上衣、连衣裙、裙子、裙裤、长裤、护胸背带工装裤、马裤及短裤(游泳服除外):**							**Women's or girls' suits, ensembles, jackets, blazers, dresses, skirts, divided skirts, trousers, bib and brace overalls, breeches and shorts (other than swimwear):**
	-西服套装:							-Suits:
6204.1100	--羊毛或动物细毛制	17.5	130	17	16	套/千克		--Of wool or fine animal hair
6204.1200	--棉制	17.5	90	17	16	套/千克		--Of cotton
6204.1200 10	含裤子的棉制女式西服套装	17.5	90	17	16	套/千克		Women's or girls' suits, including trousers, of cotton
6204.1200 90	不含裤子的棉制女式西服套装	17.5	90	17	16	套/千克		Women's or girls' suits, not including trousers, of cotton
6204.1300	--合成纤维制	17.5	130	17	16	套/千克		--Of synthetic fibres
6204.1300 10	合纤制女式西服套装(含羊毛或动物细毛36%及以上)	17.5	130	17	16	套/千克		Women's or girls' suits, containing ≥36% by weight of wool or fine animal hair, of synthetic fibres
6204.1300 90	其他合纤制女式西服套装	17.5	130	17	16	套/千克		Other women's or girls' suits of synthetic fibres
	--其他纺织材料制:							--Of other textile materials:
6204.1910	---丝及绢丝制	17.5	100	17	16	套/千克		---Of silk or spun silk
6204.1910 10	丝及绢丝制女式西服套装(含丝70%及以上)	17.5	100	17	16	套/千克		Women's or girls' suits of silk and silk waste, containing≥70% by weight of silk or spun silk

税则号列	货品名称	最惠(%)	普通	增值税率	出口退税	计量单位	监管条件	Article Description
6204.1910 90	其他丝及绢丝制女式西服套装(含丝70%以下)	17.5	100	17	16	套/千克		Women's or girls' suits of silk and spun silk waste containing <70% by weight of silk
6204.1990	---其他	17.5	100	17	16	套/千克		---Other
6204.1990 11	人造纤维制女式西服套装(含羊毛或动物细毛36%及以上)	17.5	100	17	16	套/千克		Women's or girls' suits of artificial fibres, containing ≥36% by weight of wool or fine animal hair
6204.1990 19	其他人造纤维制女式西服套装	17.5	100	17	16	套/千克		Other women's or girls' suits of artificial fibres
6204.1990 91	含裤子的其他材料制女式西服套装(棉限内)	17.5	100	17	16	套/千克		Women's or girls' suits of other textile materials, cotton within limitations
6204.1990 92	其他材料制女式西服套装(毛限内)	17.5	100	17	16	套/千克		Women's or girls' suits of other textile materials, wool within limitations
6204.1990 93	其他材料制女式西服套装(化纤限内)	17.5	100	17	16	套/千克		Women's or girls' suits of other textile materials, man-made fibres within limitations
6204.1990 99	其他材料制其他女式西服套装	17.5	100	17	16	套/千克		Women's or girls' suits of other textile materials
	-便服套装:							-Ensembles:
6204.2100	--羊毛或动物细毛制	17.5	130	17	16	套/千克		--Of wool or fine animal hair
6204.2200	--棉制	17.5	90	17	16	套/千克		--Of cotton
6204.2200 11	含裤子的棉制女式便服套装(工业及职业用)	17.5	90	17	16	套/千克		Women's or girls' ensembles of cotton, including trousers, industrial and career apparel
6204.2200 19	不含裤子的棉制女式便服套装(工业及职业用)	17.5	90	17	16	套/千克		Women's or girls' ensembles of cotton, excluding trousers, industrial and career apparel
6204.2200 91	含裤子的棉制非工业及职业用女式便服套装	17.5	90	17	16	套/千克		Women's or girls' ensembles of cotton, including trousers, non – industrial or career apparel
6204.2200 99	不含裤子的棉制非工业及职业用女式便服套装	17.5	90	17	16	套/千克		Women's or girls' ensembles of cotton, not including trousers, non – industrial or career apparel
6204.2300	--合成纤维制	20	130	17	16	套/千克		--Of synthetic fibres
6204.2300 11	工业、职业用合纤制女式便服套装(含羊毛或动物细毛≥36%)	20	130	17	16	套/千克		Women's or girls' ensembles of synthetic fibres, industrial and career apparel, containing ≥ 36% by weight of wool or fine animal hair
6204.2300 19	合成纤维制其他女式便服套装(含羊毛或动物细毛≥36%)	20	130	17	16	套/千克		Women's or girls' ensembles of synthetic fibres, containing≥36% by weight of wool or fine animal hair
6204.2300 91	其他合成纤维制含裤子的女式便服套装	20	130	17	16	套/千克		Women's or girls' ensembles of synthetic fibres, including trousers, industrial and career apparel
6204.2300 99	其他合成纤维制其他女式便服套装	20	130	17	16	套/千克		Women's or girls' ensembles of synthetic fibres
	--其他纺织材料制:							--Of other textile materials:
6204.2910	---丝及绢丝制	20	130	17	16	套/千克		---Of silk or spun silk
6204.2910 10	丝制女式便服套装(含丝及绢丝≥70%)	20	130	17	16	套/千克		Women's or girls' ensembles, containing ≥ 70% by weight of silk or spun silk
6204.2910 90	丝制其他女式便服套装(含丝及绢丝<70%)	20	130	17	16	套/千克		Women's or girls' ensembles, containing < 70% by weight of silk or spun silk
6204.2990	---其他	14	100	17	16	套/千克		---Other
6204.2990 11	含裤子的人纤制女便服套装	14	100	17	16	套/千克		Women's or girls' ensembles of artificial fibres, including trousers
6204.2990 19	不含裤子的人纤制女便服套装	14	100	17	16	套/千克		Women's or girls' ensembles of artificial fibres, excluding trousers
6204.2990 21	含裤子的其他材料制女式便服套装(棉限内)	14	100	17	16	套/千克		Women's or girls' ensembles of other textile materials, including trousers, cotton within limitations
6204.2990 29	不含裤子的其他材料制女式便服套装(棉限内)	14	100	17	16	套/千克		Women's or girls' ensembles of other textile materials, excluding trousers, cotton within limitations
6204.2990 30	其他材料制女式便服套装(毛限内)	14	100	17	16	套/千克		Women's or girls' ensembles of other textile materials, wool within limitations
6204.2990 41	含裤子的其他材料制女式便服套装(化纤限内)	14	100	17	16	套/千克		Women's or girls' ensembles of other textile materials, including trousers, man-made fibres within limitations
6204.2990 49	不含裤子的其他材料制女式便服套装(化纤限内)	14	100	17	16	套/千克		Women's or girls' ensembles, excluding trousers, of other textile material, man – made fibres within limitations

税则号列	货品名称	最惠(%)	普通	增值税率	出口退税	计量单位	监管条件	Article Description
6204.2990 91	含裤子的其他材料制女式便服套装	14	100	17	16	套/千克		Women's or girls' ensembles, including trousers, of other textile material
6204.2990 99	不含裤子的其他材料制女式便服套装	14	100	17	16	套/千克		Women's and girls' ensembles of other textile materials, excluding trousers
	-上衣:							-Jackets and blazers:
6204.3100	--羊毛或动物细毛制	16	130	17	16	件/千克		--Of wool or fine animal hair
6204.3200	--棉制	16	90	17	16	件/千克		--Of cotton
6204.3200 10	棉制女式上衣(工业及职业用)	16	90	17	16	件/千克		Women's or girls' jackets and blazers of cotton, industrial and career apparel
6204.3200 90	棉制其他女式上衣	16	90	17	16	件/千克		Women's or girls' jackets and blazers of cotton
6204.3300	--合成纤维制	17.5	130	17	16	件/千克		--Of synthetic fibres
6204.3300 10	合成纤维制女式上衣(含羊毛或动物细毛36%及以上,工业及职业用)	17.5	130	17	16	件/千克		Women's or girls' jackets and blazers of synthetic fibres, containing≥36% by weight of wool or fine animal hair, industrial and career apparel
6204.3300 20	合成纤维制其他女式上衣(含羊毛或动物细毛36%及以上)	17.5	130	17	16	件/千克		Women's or girls' jackets and blazers of synthetic fibres, containing≥36% by weight of wool or fine animal hair
6204.3300 30	合成纤维制女式上衣(工业及职业用)	17.5	130	17	16	件/千克		Women's or girls' jackets and blazers of synthetic fibres, industrial and career apparel
6204.3300 90	合成纤维制其他女式上衣	17.5	130	17	16	件/千克		Other women's or girls' jackets and blazers of synthetic fibres
	--其他纺织材料制:							--Of other textile materials:
6204.3910	---丝及绢丝制	16	130	17	16	件/千克		---Of silk or spun silk
6204.3910 10	丝制女式上衣(含丝及绢丝70%及以上)	16	130	17	16	件/千克		Women's or girls' jackets and blazers of silk, containing≥70% by weight of silk or spun silk
6204.3910 90	丝制其他女式上衣(含丝及绢丝70%以下)	16	130	17	16	件/千克		Women's or girls' jackets and blazers of silk, containing<70% by weight of silk or spun silk
6204.3990	---其他	16	100	17	16	件/千克		---Other
6204.3990 11	人纤制女式上衣(含羊毛或动物细毛≥36%,工业及职业用)	16	100	17	16	件/千克		Women's or girls' jackets and blazers of artificial fibres, containing≥36% by weight of wool or fine animal hair, industrial and career apparel
6204.3990 12	人纤制其他女式上衣(含羊毛或动物细毛≥36%)	16	100	17	16	件/千克		Women's or girls' jackets and blazers of artificial fibres, containing≥36% by weight of wool or fine animal hair
6204.3990 13	人纤制女式上衣(工业及职业用)	16	100	17	16	件/千克		Women's or girls' jackets and blazers of artificial fibres, industrial and career apparel
6204.3990 19	人纤制其他女式上衣	16	100	17	16	件/千克		Women's or girls' jackets and blazers, of artificial fibres
6204.3990 91	其他材料制女式上衣(棉限内)	16	100	17	16	件/千克		Women's or girls' jackets and blazers of other textile materials, cotton within limitations
6204.3990 92	其他材料制女式上衣(毛限内)	16	100	17	16	件/千克		Women's or girls' jackets and blazers of other textile materials, wool within limitations
6204.3990 93	其他材料制女式上衣(化纤限内)	16	100	17	16	件/千克		Women's or girls' jackets and blazers of other textile materials, man-made fibres within limitations
6204.3990 99	其他材料制女式上衣	16	100	17	16	件/千克		Women's or girls' jackets and blazers of other textile materials
	-连衣裙:							-Dresses:
6204.4100	--羊毛或动物细毛制	16	130	17	16	件/千克		--Of wool or fine animal hair
6204.4200	--棉制	16	90	17	16	件/千克		--Of cotton
6204.4300	--合成纤维制	17.5	130	17	16	件/千克		--Of synthetic fibres
6204.4300 10	合成纤维制女式连衣裙(含羊毛或动物细毛≥36%)	17.5	130	17	16	件/千克		Women's or girls' dresses of synthetic fibres, containing≥36% by weight of wool or fine animal hair
6204.4300 90	合成纤维制其他女式连衣裙	17.5	130	17	16	件/千克		Other women's or girls' dresses of synthetic fibres
6204.4400	--人造纤维制	16	130	17	16	件/千克		--Of artificial fibres
6204.4400 10	人造纤维制女式连衣裙(含羊毛或动物细毛≥36%)	16	130	17	16	件/千克		Women's or girls' dresses of artificial fibres, containing≥36% by weight of wool or fine animal hair
6204.4400 90	人造纤维制其他女式连衣裙	16	130	17	16	件/千克		Other women's or girls' dresses of artificial fibres

税则号列	货 品 名 称	最惠(%)	普通	增值税率	出口退税	计量单位	监管条件	Article Description
	--其他纺织材料制：							--Of other textile materials：
6204.4910	---丝及绢丝制	16	130	17	16	件/千克		---Of silk or spun silk
6204.4910 10	丝制女式连衣裙（含丝及绢丝70%及以上）	16	130	17	16	件/千克		Women's or girls' dresses of silk, containing ≥70% by weight of silk or spun silk
6204.4910 90	丝制其他女式连衣裙（含丝及绢丝70%以下）	16	130	17	16	件/千克		Other women's or girls' dresses of silk, containing <70% by weight of silk or spun silk
6204.4990	---其他	16	100	17	16	件/千克		---Other
6204.4990 91	其他材料制女式连衣裙（棉限内）	16	100	17	16	件/千克		Women's or girls' dresses of other textile materials, cotton within limitations
6204.4990 92	其他材料制女式连衣裙（毛限内）	16	100	17	16	件/千克		Women's or girls' dresses of other textile materials, wool within limitations
6204.4990 93	其他材料制女式连衣裙（化纤限内）	16	100	17	16	件/千克		Women's or girls' dresses of other textile materials, man-made fibres within limitations
6204.4990 99	其他材料制其他女式连衣裙	16	100	17	16	件/千克		Women's or girls' dresses of other textile materials
	-裙子及裙裤：							-Skirts and divided skirts：
6204.5100	--羊毛或动物细毛制	14	130	17	16	件/千克		--Of wool or fine animal hair
6204.5200	--棉制	14	90	17	16	件/千克		--Of cotton
6204.5300	--合成纤维制	16	130	17	16	件/千克		--Of synthetic fibres
6204.5300 10	合成纤维制女式裙子及裙裤（含羊毛或动物细毛≥36%）	16	130	17	16	件/千克		Women's or girls' skirts and divided skirts, of synthetic fibres, containing ≥36% by weight of wool or fine animal hair
6204.5300 90	合成纤维制其他女式裙子及裙裤	16	130	17	16	件/千克		Women's or girls' skirts and divided skirts, of synthetic fibres
	--其他纺织材料制：							--Of other textile materials
6204.5910	---丝及绢丝制	14	130	17	16	件/千克		---Of silk or spun silk
6204.5910 10	丝制女式裙子及裙裤（含丝70%及以上）	14	130	17	16	件/千克		Women's or girls' skirts and divided skirts, containing ≥70% by weight of silk
6204.5910 90	其他丝制女式裙子及裙裤（含丝70%以下）	14	130	17	16	件/千克		Women's or girls' skirts and divided skirts, containing <70% by weight of silk
6204.5990	---其他	14	100	17	16	件/千克		---Other
6204.5990 11	人造纤维制女式裙子及裙裤（含羊毛或动物细毛36%及以上）	14	100	17	16	件/千克		Women's or girls' skirts and divided skirts, of artificial fibres, containing ≥36% by weight of wool or fine animal hair
6204.5990 19	人造纤维制其他女式裙子及裙裤	14	100	17	16	件/千克		Women's or girls' skirts and divided skirts, of artificial fibres
6204.5990 91	其他材料制女式裙子及裙裤（棉限内）	14	100	17	16	件/千克		Women's or girls' skirts and divided skirts of other textile materials, cotton within limitations
6204.5990 92	其他材料制女式裙子及裙裤（毛限内）	14	100	17	16	件/千克		Women's or girls' skirts and divided skirts of other textile materials, wool within limitations
6204.5990 93	其他材料制女式裙子及裙裤（化纤限内）	14	100	17	16	件/千克		Women's or girls' skirts and divided skirts of other textile materials, man-made fibres within limitations
6204.5990 99	其他材料制其他女式裙子及裙裤	14	100	17	16	件/千克		Women's or girls' skirts and divided skirts of other textile materials
	-长裤、护胸背带工装裤、马裤及短裤：							-Trousers, bib and brace overalls, breeches and shorts：
6204.6100	--羊毛或动物细毛制	16	130	17	16	条/千克		--Of wool or fine animal hair
6204.6100 10	毛制女式护胸背带工装裤及短裤（带防寒衬里）	16	130	17	16	条/千克		Women's or girls' bib and brace overalls, with thermal lining, of wool or fine animal hair
6204.6100 90	毛制女式长裤、马裤	16	130	17	16	条/千克		Women's or girls' trousers, breeches, of wool or fine animal hair
6204.6200	--棉制	16	90	17	16	条/千克		--Of cotton
6204.6200 10	棉制女式护胸背带工装裤	16	90	17	16	条/千克		Women's or girls' bib and brace overalls of cotton

税则号列	货品名称	最惠(%)	普通	增值税率	出口退税	计量单位	监管条件	Article Description
6204.6200 21	棉制女式长裤、马裤(羽绒和水禽毛≥15%且含绒率≥35%,或含羽绒≥10%)	16	90	17	16	条/千克		Women's or girls' trousers, breeches of cotton, containing≥15% by weight of down or feathers and water fowl, down content rate≥35% or containing≥10% by weight of down or feathers
6204.6200 22	棉制女式长裤、马裤(游戏装)	16	90	17	16	条/千克		Women's or girls' trousers, breeches, of cotton(playsuit)
6204.6200 29	其他棉制女式长裤、马裤	16	90	17	16	条/千克		Other women's or girls' trousers, breeches of cotton
6204.6200 91	棉制女式短裤(羽绒和水禽毛≥15%且含绒率≥35%,或含羽绒≥10%)	16	90	17	16	条/千克		Women's or girls' shorts of cotton, containing≥15% by weight of down or feathers and water fowl, down content rate≥35% or containing≥10% by weight of down or feathers
6204.6200 92	棉制女式短裤(游戏装)	16	90	17	16	条/千克		Girls' shorts of cotton(playsuit)
6204.6200 99	其他棉制女式短裤	16	90	17	16	条/千克		Other women's shorts of cotton
6204.6300	--合成纤维制	17.5	130	17	16	条/千克		--Of synthetic fibres
6204.6300 10	合纤制女式护胸背带工装裤	17.5	130	17	16	条/千克		Women's or girls' bib and brace overalls of synthetic fibres
6204.6300 21	合纤女式长裤、马裤(羽绒和水禽毛≥15%且含绒率≥35%,或含羽绒≥10%)	17.5	130	17	16	条/千克		Women's or girls' trousers, breeches, containing≥15% by weight of down or feathers and water fowl, down content rate≥35% or containing≥10% by weight of down or feathers, of synthetic fibres
6204.6300 22	合纤制其他女式长裤、马裤(含羊毛或动物细毛36%及以上)	17.5	130	17	16	条/千克		Women's or girls' trousers, breeches, containing≥36% by weight of wool or fine animal hair, of synthetic fibres
6204.6300 23	合纤制女式长裤、马裤(游戏装)	17.5	130	17	16	条/千克		Women's or girl's trousers, breeches, of synthetic fibres(playsuit)
6204.6300 24	合纤制女式长裤、马裤(滑雪裤除外)	17.5	130	17	16	条/千克		Women's or girl's trousers, breeches, of synthetic fibres(other than ski pants)
6204.6300 29	合纤制女式其他长裤、马裤	17.5	130	17	16	条/千克		Other women's or girls' trousers, breeches, of synthetic fibres
6204.6300 91	合纤制女式短裤(羽绒和水禽毛≥15%且含绒率≥35%,或含羽绒≥10%)	17.5	130	17	16	条/千克		Women's or girls' shorts, containing≥15% by weight of down or feathers and water fowl, down content rate≥35% or containing≥10% by weight of down or feathers, of synthetic fibres
6204.6300 92	合纤制女式短裤(游戏装)	17.5	130	17	16	条/千克		Other wonen's or girls' shorts of synthetic fibres(playsuit)
6204.6300 99	其他合纤制女短裤	17.5	130	17	16	条/千克		Other women's or girls' trousers short, of synthefic fibres
6204.6900	--其他纺织材料制	16	100	17	16	条/千克		--Of other textile materials
6204.6900 11	人纤制女式护胸背带工装裤	16	100	17	16	条/千克		Women's bib and brace overalls of artificial fibres
6204.6900 12	人纤制女式长裤、马裤(含羊毛或动物细毛36%及以上)	16	100	17	16	条/千克		Women's or girls' trousers, breeches of artificial fibres(containing≥36% by weight of wool or fine animal hair)
6204.6900 13	人纤制女式短裤(含羊毛或动物细毛36%及以上)	16	100	17	16	条/千克		Women's or trousers, shorts, of artificial fibres(containing≥36% by weight of wool or fine animal hair)
6204.6900 14	人纤制女式长裤、马裤(游戏装)	16	100	17	16	条/千克		Women's or girls' trousers, breeches, shorts, of artificial fibres, playsuit
6204.6900 15	人纤制女式短裤(游戏装)	16	100	17	16	条/千克		Women's trousers, shorts, of artificial fibres(playsuit)
6204.6900 16	人纤制女式其他长裤、马裤	16	100	17	16	条/千克		Other women's trousers, breeches of artificial fibres
6204.6900 17	人纤制女式其他短裤	16	100	17	16	条/千克		Women's or girls' other tuousers, short, of artificial fibres
6204.6900 21	丝制女式护胸背带工装裤	16	100	17	16	条/千克		Women's or girls' bib and brace overalls, of silk
6204.6900 25	丝制女式其他长裤、马裤、短裤(含丝70%及以上)	16	100	17	16	条/千克		Women's or girls' other trousers, breeches, shorts, of silk, containing≥70% by weight of silk
6204.6900 26	丝制女式长裤、马裤、短裤(含丝70%及以下的游戏装)	16	100	17	16	条/千克		Women's or girls' trousers, breeches、shorts, of silk, containing≤70% by weight of silk (playsuit)

税则号列	货品名称	最惠(%)	普通	增值税率	出口退税	计量单位	监管条件	Article Description
6204.6900 29	丝制女式其他长裤、马裤、短裤(含丝70%以下)	16	100	17	16	条/千克		Women's or girls' other trousers, breeches, shorts, of silk, containing <70% by weight of silk
6204.6900 91	其他材料制女式护胸背带工装裤	16	100	17	16	条/千克		Women's or girls' bib and brace overalls of other textile materials
6204.6900 92	其他材料制女式长裤、马裤、短裤(游戏装)	16	100	17	16	条/千克		Women's or girls' trousers, breeches, shorts, playsuit of other textile materials
6204.6900 93	其他材料制女式长裤、马裤、短裤(棉限内)	16	100	17	16	条/千克		Women's or girls' trousers, breeches, shorts, cotton within limitations, of other textile materials
6204.6900 94	其他材料制女式长裤、马裤、短裤(羊毛限内)	16	100	17	16	条/千克		Women' s or girls trousers, breeches, shorts, of other textile materials, wool within limitations
6204.6900 95	其他材料制女式长裤、马裤、短裤(化纤限内)	16	100	17	16	条/千克		Wonmen' s or girls' trousers, breeches, shorts, of other textile materials, man-made fibres within limitations
6204.6900 99	其他材料制其他女式长、马、短裤	16	100	17	16	条/千克		Women's or girls' other trousers, bree-ches, shorts, of other textile materials
62.05	男衬衫:							**Men's or boys' shirts:**
6205.2000	-棉制	16	90	17	16	件/千克		-Of cotton
6205.2000 10	不带特制领的棉制男成人衬衫(含男童8-18号衬衫)	16	90	17	16	件/千克	A	Men's shirts and boys' No. 8 ~ No. 18, without specially made collar, of cotton
6205.2000 91	其他棉制男童游戏套装衬衫(不包括长衬衫)	16	90	17	16	件/千克	A	Boy's shirts, playsuit, other than long shirts, of cotton
6205.2000 99	其他棉制男式衬衫	16	90	17	16	件/千克	A	Other men's or boys' shirts, of cotton
6205.3000	-化学纤维制	16	130	17	16	件/千克		-Of man-made fibres
6205.3000 11	不带特制领的化学纤维制男式衬衫(含羊毛或动物细毛36%及以上,含男童8-18号衬衫)	16	130	17	16	件/千克	A	Men's or boys' shirts, without specially made collar, containing ≥36% by weight of wool or fine animal hair, including boys' No. 8 ~ No. 18, of man-made fibres
6205.3000 19	不带特制领的化纤制其他男童衬衫(含羊毛或动物细毛36%及以上)	16	130	17	16	件/千克	A	Boys' shirts, without specially made collar, containing ≥36% by weight of wool or fine animal hair, of man-made fibres
6205.3000 91	化学纤维制其他男成人及男童衬衫(不带特制领,男童衬衫指8-18号)	16	130	17	16	件/千克	A	Men's or boys' shirts without specially made collar, including boys' No. 8 ~ No. 18, of man-made fibres
6205.3000 92	化学纤维制其他男童游戏套装衬衫	16	130	17	16	件/千克	A	Other boy's shirts of playsuit, of man-made fibres
6205.3000 99	化纤制其他男成人衬衫	16	130	17	16	件/千克	A	Other men's shirts of man-made fibres
	-其他纺织材料制:							-Of other textile materials:
6205.9010	---丝及绢丝制	16	130	17	16	件/千克		---Of silk or spun silk
6205.9010 11	不带特制领的丝制非针织男式衬衫(含丝70%及以上,含男童8-18号衬衫)	16	130	17	16	件/千克	A	Men's or boys' shirts of silk, without specially made collar, not knitted, containing ≥70% by weight of silk, including boys' No. 8 ~ No. 18
6205.9010 19	丝制非针织其他男式衬衫(含丝70%及以上)	16	130	17	16	件/千克	A	Men's or boys' shirts of silk, not knitted, containing ≥70% by weight of silk
6205.9010 21	丝制其他非针织男式衬衫(棉限内,不带特制领的,含男童8-18号衬衫)	16	130	17	16	件/千克	A	Men's or boys' shirts of silk, not knitted, without specially made collar, including boys' No. 8 ~ No. 18, cotton within limitations
6205.9010 29	丝制其他非针织其他男式衬衫(棉限内)	16	130	17	16	件/千克	A	Men's or boys' shirts of silk, not knitted, cotton within limitations
6205.9010 31	丝制其他非针织男式衬衫(羊毛限内,不带特制领的,含男童8-18号衬衫)	16	130	17	16	件/千克	A	Men's or boys' shirts of silk, not knitted, without specially made collar, including boys' No. 8 ~ No. 18, wool within limitations
6205.9010 39	丝制其他非针织其他男式衬衫(羊毛限内)	16	130	17	16	件/千克	A	Men's or boys' shirts of silk, not knitted, wool within limitations
6205.9010 41	丝制非针织男式衬衫(化纤限内,不带特制领的,含男童8-18号衬衫)	16	130	17	16	件/千克	A	Men's or boys' shirts of silk, not knitted, without specially made collar, including boys' No. 8 ~ No. 18, man-made fibres within limitations
6205.9010 49	丝制其他非针织其他男式衬衫(化纤限内)	16	130	17	16	件/千克	A	Men's or boys' shirts of silk, not knitted, man-made fibres within limitations

税则号列	货品名称	最惠(%)	普通	增值税率	出口退税	计量单位	监管条件	Article Description
6205.9010 91	未列名丝制非针织男式衬衫(含丝70%以下,不带特制领的,含男童8-18号衬衫)	16	130	17	16	件/千克	A	Men's or boys' shirts of silk, not knitted, containing <70% by weight of silk, without specially made collar, including boys' No. 8 ~ No. 18, not elsewhere specified or included
6205.9010 99	未列名丝制非针织其他男式衬衫(含丝70%以下)	16	130	17	16	件/千克	A	Other men's or boys' shirts of silk, not knitted, containing <70% by weight of silk, not elsewhere specified or included
6205.9020	---羊毛或动物细毛制	16	100	17	16	件/千克	A	---Of wool or fine animal hair
6205.9090	---其他	16	100	17	16	件/千克		---Other
6205.9090 11	其他纺织材料制男式衬衫(棉限内,不带特制领的,含男童8-18号衬衫)	16	100	17	16	件/千克	A	Men's or boys' shirts of other textile materials, without specially made collar, including boys' No. 8 ~ No. 18, cotton within limitations
6205.9090 19	其他纺织材料制其他男式衬衫(棉纤限内)	16	100	17	16	件/千克	A	Men's or boys' shirts of other textile materials, cotton or man-made fibres within limitations
6205.9090 21	其他纺织材料制男式衬衫(羊毛限内,不带特制领的,含男童8-18号衬衫)	16	100	17	16	件/千克	A	Men's or boys' shirts of other textile materials, without specially made collar, including boys' No. 8 ~ No. 18, wool within limitations
6205.9090 29	其他纺织材料制其他男式衬衫(羊毛限内)	16	100	17	16	件/千克	A	Men's or boys' shirts of other textile materials, wool or man-made fibres within limitations
6205.9090 31	其他纺织材料制男式衬衫(化纤限内,不带制特领的,含男童8-18号衬衫)	16	100	17	16	件/千克	A	Men's or boys' shirts of other textile materials, without specially made collar, including boys' No. 8 ~ No. 18, man-made fibres within limitations
6205.9090 39	其他纺织材料制其他男式衬衫(化纤限内)	16	100	17	16	件/千克	A	Men's or boys' shirts of other textile materials, man-made fibres within limitations
6205.9090 91	未列名纺织材料制男式衬衫(不带特制领的,含男童8-18号衬衫)	16	100	17	16	件/千克	A	Men's or boys' shirts of other textile materials, without speciallymade collar, including boys' No.8 ~ No. 18, not elsewhere specified or included
6205.9090 99	未列名纺织材料制其他男式衬衫	16	100	17	16	件/千克	A	Other men's or boys' shirts of other textile materials, not elsewhere specified or included
62.06	女衬衫:							**Women's or girls' blouses, shirts and shirt-blouses:**
6206.1000	-丝及绢丝制	16	130	17	16	件/千克		-Of silk or spun silk
6206.1000 11	丝及绢丝制女式衬衫(棉限内,成人及7-16号女童衬衫)	16	130	17	16	件/千克	A	Women's or girls' shirts of silk or spun silk, cotton within limitations, including girls' No. 7 ~ No. 16
6206.1000 19	丝及绢丝制其他女童衬衫(棉限内)	16	130	17	16	件/千克	A	Other girls' shirts of silk or spun silk, cotton within limitations
6206.1000 21	丝及绢丝制女式衬衫(羊毛限内,成人及7-16号女童衬衫)	16	130	17	16	件/千克	A	Women's or girls' shirts of silk or spun silk, wool within limitations, including girls' No. 7 ~ No. 16
6206.1000 29	丝及绢丝制其他女童衬衫(羊毛限内)	16	130	17	16	件/千克	A	Other girls' shirts of silk and spun silk, wool within limitations
6206.1000 31	丝及绢丝制女式衬衫(化纤限内,成人及7-16号女童衬衫)	16	130	17	16	件/千克	A	Women's or girls' shirts of silk and spun silk, including girls' No. 7 ~ No. 16, man-made fibres within limitations
6206.1000 39	丝及绢丝制其他女童衬衫(化纤限内)	16	130	17	16	件/千克	A	Other girls' shirts of silk and spun silk, man-made fibres within limitations
6206.1000 41	丝制女成人及7-16号女童衬衫(含丝70%及以上)	16	130	17	16	件/千克	A	Women's shirts of silk, containing ≥70% by weight of silk, including girls' No. 7 ~ No. 16
6206.1000 49	其他丝及绢丝制女童衬衫(含丝70%及以上)	16	130	17	16	件/千克	A	Other girls' shirts of silk and spun silk, containing ≥70% by weight of silk
6206.1000 91	丝制女成人及7-16号女童衬衫(含丝70%以下)	16	130	17	16	件/千克	A	Women's shirts of silk, containing <70% by weight of silk, including girls' No. 7 ~ No. 16
6206.1000 99	其他丝及绢丝制女童衬衫(含丝70%以下)	16	130	17	16	件/千克	A	Other girls' shirts of silk and spun silk, containing <70% by weight of silk
6206.2000	-羊毛或动物细毛制	16	130	17	16	件/千克		-Of wool or fine animal hair
6206.2000 10	毛制女成人及7-16号女童衬衫	16	130	17	16	件/千克	A	Women's and girls No. 7 ~ No. 16 shirts, of wool or fine animal hair
6206.2000 90	其他羊毛或动物细毛制女童衬衫	16	130	17	16	件/千克	A	Other girls' shirts of wool or fine animal hair

税则号列	货品名称	最惠(%)	普通	增值税率	出口退税	计量单位	监管条件	Article Description
6206.3000	-棉制	16	90	17	16	件/千克		-Of cotton
6206.3000 10	棉制女成人及7-16号女童衬衫	16	90	17	16	件/千克	A	Women's and girls' No.7 ~ No.16 shirts, of cotton
6206.3000 20	棉制女童游戏套装衬衫(含游戏套装衬衫)	16	90	17	16	件/千克	A	Girls' shirt of playsuit, of cotton
6206.3000 90	其他棉制女式衬衫	16	90	17	16	件/千克	A	Other women's or girls' shirts of cotton
6206.4000	-化学纤维制	17.5	130	17	16	件/千克		-Of man-made fibres
6206.4000 11	化学纤维制女成人及女童衬衫(含羊毛或动物细毛36%及以上,成人及7-16号女童衬衫)	17.5	130	17	16	件/千克	A	Women's and girls' No.7 ~ No.16 shirts, containing ≥ 36% by weight of wool or fine animal hair, of man-made fibres
6206.4000 19	化学纤维制女成人及女童衬衫(含羊毛或动物细毛36%及以上)	17.5	130	17	16	件/千克	A	Other women's or girls' shirts, containing ≥ 36% by weight of wool or fine animal hair, of man-made fibres
6206.4000 20	化纤制女成人及7-16号女童衬衫	17.5	130	17	16	件/千克	A	Women's shirts and girls' No.7 ~ No.16, of man-made fibres
6206.4000 30	化学纤维制女童游戏套装衫	17.5	130	17	16	件/千克	A	Girls' shirts, playsuit, of man-made fibres
6206.4000 90	其他化学纤维制女式衬衫	17.5	130	17	16	件/千克	A	Other women's or girls' shirts of man-made fibres
6206.9000	-其他纺织材料制	16	100	17	16	件/千克		-Of other textile materials
6206.9000 10	其他纺织材料制女式衬衫(棉限内)	16	100	17	16	件/千克	A	Women's or girls' shirts of other textile materials, cotton within limitations
6206.9000 20	其他纺织材料制女式衬衫(羊毛限内)	16	100	17	16	件/千克	A	Women's or girls' shirts of other textile materials, wool within limitations
6206.9000 30	其他纺织材料制女式衬衫(化纤限内)	16	100	17	16	件/千克	A	Women's or girls' shirts of other textile materials, man-made fibres within limitations
6206.9000 91	其他纺织材料制女成人及女童衬衫(女童衬衫指7-16号)	16	100	17	16	件/千克	A	Women's and girls' No.7 ~ No.16, shirts of other textile materials
6206.9000 99	其他纺织材料制女成人及女童衬衫	16	100	17	16	件/千克	A	Other women's or girls' shirts of other textile materials
62.07	男式背心及其他内衣、内裤、三角裤、长睡衣、睡衣裤、浴衣、晨衣及类似品:							**Men's or boys' singlets and other vests, underpants, briefs, nightshirts, pyjamas, bathrobes, dressing gowns and similar articles:**
	-内裤及三角裤:							-Underpants and briefs:
6207.1100	--棉制	14	90	17	16	件/千克	A	--Of cotton
	--其他纺织材料制:							--Of other textile materials:
6207.1910	---丝及绢丝制	14	130	17	16	件/千克		---Of silk or spun silk
6207.1910 10	含丝70%及以上男式内裤及三角裤	14	130	17	16	件/千克	A	Men's or boys' underpants and briefs, containing ≥ 70% by weight of silk
6207.1910 90	含丝70%以下男式内裤及三角裤	14	130	17	16	件/千克	A	Men's or boys' underpants and briefs, containing < 70% by weight of silk
6207.1920	---化学纤维制	16	130	17	16	件/千克	A	---Of man-made fibres
6207.1990	---其他	14	100	17	16	件/千克		---Other
6207.1990 10	毛制男式内裤及三角裤	14	100	17	16	件/千克	A	Men's or boys' underpants and briefs of wool or fine animal hair
6207.1990 90	其他材料制男式内裤及三角裤	14	100	17	16	件/千克	A	Men's or boys' underpants and briefs of other textile materials
	-长睡衣及睡衣裤:							-Nightshirts and pyjamas:
6207.2100	--棉制	14	90	17	16	件/千克	A	--Of cotton
6207.2200	--化学纤维制	16	130	17	16	件/千克	A	--Of man-made fibres
	--其他纺织材料制:							--Of other textile materials:
6207.2910	---丝及绢丝制	14	130	17	16	件/千克		---Of silk or spun silk
6207.2910 11	含丝70%及以上男式长睡衣、睡衣裤(含8-18号男童长睡衣、睡衣裤)	14	130	17	16	件/千克	A	Men's nightshirts and pyjamas containing ≥ 70% by weight of silk, including boys' No.8 ~ No.18
6207.2910 19	含丝70%以下男式长睡衣、睡衣裤(含8-18号男童长睡衣、睡衣裤)	14	130	17	16	件/千克	A	Men's or boys' nightshirts and pyjamas, containing < 70% by weight of silk, including boys' No.8 ~ No.18
6207.2910 91	其他含丝≥70%男童长睡衣、睡衣裤	14	130	17	16	件/千克	A	Other boys' nightshirts and pyjamas, containing ≥ 70% by weight of silk
6207.2910 99	其他含丝<70%男童长睡衣、睡衣裤	14	130	17	16	件/千克	A	Other boys' nightshirts and pyjamas, containing < 70% by weight of silk
6207.2990	---其他	14	100	17	16	件/千克		---Other

税则号列	货品名称	最惠(%)	普通	增值税率	出口退税	计量单位	监管条件	Article Description
6207.2990 10	毛制男式长睡衣及睡衣裤	14	100	17	16	件/千克	A	Men's or boys' nightshirts and pyjamas, of wool or fine animal hair
6207.2990 91	其他材料制男式长睡衣及睡衣裤(含8-18号男童长睡衣及睡衣裤)	14	100	17	16	件/千克	A	Men's or boys' nightshirts and pyjamas, of other textile materials, including boys' No. 8 ~ No. 18
6207.2990 99	其他材料制男童长睡衣及睡衣裤	14	100	17	16	件/千克	A	Boys' nightshirts and pyjamas of other textile materials
	-其他:							-Other:
6207.9100	--棉制	14	90	17	16	件/千克		--Of cotton
6207.9100 11	棉制男式内衣式背心	14	90	17	16	件/千克	A	Men's or boys' singlets, vest style, of cotton
6207.9100 12	棉制男式非内衣式背心(男成人及8-18号男童背心)	14	90	17	16	件/千克	A	Men's and boys' No. 8 ~ No. 18 singlets, of cotton, non-vest style
6207.9100 19	棉制其他男童非内衣式背心	14	90	17	16	件/千克	A	Other boy's singlets of cotton, non-vests style
6207.9100 91	棉制男式浴衣、晨衣及类似品	14	90	17	16	件/千克	A	Men's or boys' bathrobes, dressing gowns and similar articles of cotton
6207.9100 92	棉制男式睡衣、睡裤(男成人及8-18号男童背心)	14	90	17	16	件/千克	A	Men's or boys' nightshirts and pyjamas, men's and boy's No. 8 ~ No. 18 singlets, of cotton
6207.9100 99	棉制男式其他内衣(男成人及8-18号男童背心)	14	90	17	16	件/千克	A	Other men's or boys' vests, men's and boys' No. 8 ~ No. 18 singlets, of cotton
	--其他纺织材料制:							--Of other textile materials:
6207.9910	---丝及绢丝制	14	130	17	16	件/千克		---Of silk or apun silk
6207.9910 11	丝制男式内衣式背心(含丝70%及以上)	14	130	17	16	件/千克	A	Men's or boys' singlets of silk, vest style, containing ≥70% by weight of silk
6207.9910 19	丝制其他男式内衣式背心	14	130	17	16	件/千克	A	Other men's or boys' singlets of sil, vest style
6207.9910 21	丝制男式非内衣式背心(含丝70%及以上)	14	130	17	16	件/千克	A	Men's or boys' singlets of silk, non-vest style, containing≥70% by weight of silk
6207.9910 29	丝制其他男式非内衣式背心	14	130	17	16	件/千克	A	Other men's or boys' singlets of silk, non-vests style
6207.9910 91	丝制男睡衣,浴衣,晨衣及类似品(含丝70%及以上)	14	130	17	16	件/千克	A	Men's or boys' bathrobes, dressing gowns and similar articles, of silk, containing≥70% by weight of silk
6207.9910 99	丝制其他男睡衣,浴衣,晨衣(含类似品)	14	130	17	16	件/千克	A	Other men's or boys' pyjamas, bathrobes, dressing gowns and similar articles, of silk
6207.9920	---化学纤维制	16	130	17	16	件/千克		---Of man-made fibres
6207.9920 11	化学纤维制男式内衣式背心	16	130	17	16	件/千克	A	Men's or boys' singlets, vest style, of man-made fibres
6207.9920 12	化学纤维制男式非内衣式背心(男成人及8-18号男童背心)	16	130	17	16	件/千克	A	Men's or boys' singlets, non-vests style, men's and boys' No. 8 ~ No. 18 singlets, of man-made fibres
6207.9920 19	化学纤维制其他男式非内衣式背心	16	130	17	16	件/千克	A	Other men's or boys' singlets, non-vests style, of man-made fibres
6207.9920 21	化纤制男式浴衣、晨衣(含羊毛或动物细毛36%及以上,含类似品)	16	130	17	16	件/千克	A	Men's or boys' bathrobes, dressing gowns and similar articles, containing≥36% by weight of wool or fine animal hair, of man-made fibres
6207.9920 29	其他化纤制男浴衣、晨衣(含类似品)	16	130	17	16	件/千克	A	Other men's or boys' bathrobes, dressing gowns and similar articles, of man-made fibres
6207.9920 91	化纤制男睡衣、睡裤(含类似品)	16	130	17	16	件/千克	A	Men's or boys' nightshirts, pyjamas and similar articles, of man-made fibres
6207.9920 99	化纤制男式其他内衣(含类似品)	16	130	17	16	件/千克	A	Other men's or boys' vest and similar articles of man-made fibres
6207.9990	---其他	14	100	17	16	件/千克		---Other
6207.9990 11	毛制男式内衣式背心	14	100	17	16	件/千克	A	Men's or boys' singlets, vests style, of wool or fine animal hair
6207.9990 12	毛制男式非内衣式背心(男成人及8-18号男童背心)	14	100	17	16	件/千克	A	Men's or boys' singlets, non-vests style, (men's and boys' No. 8 ~ No. 18), of wool or fine animal hair
6207.9990 13	毛制其他男式非内衣式背心	14	100	17	16	件/千克	A	Other men's or boys' singlets, non-vests style, of wool or fine animal hair
6207.9990 19	毛制男睡衣,浴衣,晨衣及类似品	14	100	17	16	件/千克	A	Men's or boys' bathrobes, dressing gowns and similar articles, of wool or fine animal hair
6207.9990 91	其他材料制男式内衣式背心	14	100	17	16	件/千克	A	Men's or boys' singlets, vests style, of other textile materials

税则号列	货品名称	最惠(%)	普通	增值税率	出口退税	计量单位	监管条件	Article Description
6207.9990 92	其他材料制男式非内衣式背心	14	100	17	16	件/千克	A	Men's or boys' singlets, non-vests style, of other textile materials
6207.9990 99	其他材料制男睡衣、浴衣、晨衣(含类似品)	14	100	17	16	件/千克	A	Other men's or boys' bathrobes, dressing gowns and similar articles, of other textile materials
62.08	**女式背心及其他内衣、长衬裙、衬裙、三角裤、短衬裤、睡衣、睡衣裤、浴衣、晨衣及类似品:**							**Women's or girls' singlets and other vests, slips, petticoats, briefs, panties, night-dresses, pyjamas, nègligès, bathrobes, dressing gowns and similar articles:**
	-长衬裙及衬裙:							-Slips and petticoats:
6208.1100	--化学纤维制	16	130	17	16	件/千克		--Of man-made fibres
	--其他纺织材料制:							--Of other textile materials:
6208.1910	---丝及绢丝制	14	130	17	16	件/千克		---Of silk or spun silk
6208.1910 11	丝制女式长衬裙及衬裙(含7-16号女童长衬裙及衬裙,含丝70%及以上)	14	130	17	16	件/千克		Women's or girls' slips and petticoats of silk, including girls' No. 7 ~ No. 16, containing ≥ 70% by weight of silk
6208.1910 19	丝制其他女式长衬裙及衬裙(含7-16号女童长衬裙及衬裙,含丝70%以下)	14	130	17	16	件/千克		Other women's or girls' slips and petticoats of silk, including girls' No. 7 ~ No. 16, containing < 70% by weight of silk
6208.1910 91	丝制女童长衬裙及衬裙(含丝70%及以上)	14	130	17	16	件/千克		Girls' slips and petticoats of silk, containing ≥70% by weight of silk
6208.1910 99	丝制其他女童长衬裙及衬裙(含丝70%以下)	14	130	17	16	件/千克		Girls' slips and petticoats of silk, containing < 70% by weight of silk
6208.1920	---棉制	14	90	17	16	件/千克		---Of cotton
6208.1990	---其他	14	100	17	16	件/千克		---Other
6208.1990 10	毛制女式长衬裙及衬裙	14	100	17	16	件/千克		Women's or girls' slips and petticoats of wool or fine animal hair
6208.1990 90	其他材料制女式长衬裙及衬裙	14	100	17	16	件/千克		Women's or girls' slips and petticoats of other textile materials
	-睡衣及睡衣裤:							-Nightdresses and pyjamas:
6208.2100	--棉制	14	90	17	16	件/千克	A	--Of cotton
6208.2200	--化学纤维制	16	130	17	16	件/千克	A	--Of man-made fibres
	--其他纺织材料制:							--Of other textile materials:
6208.2910	---丝及绢丝制	14	130	17	16	件/千克		---Of silk or spun silk
6208.2910 10	丝及绢丝≥70%女式睡衣及睡衣裤	14	130	17	16	件/千克	A	Women's or girls' night-dresses and pyjamas, containing≥70% by weight of silk or spun silk
6208.2910 90	丝及绢丝<70%女式睡衣及睡衣裤	14	130	17	16	件/千克	A	Women's or girls' night-dresses and pyjamas, containing < 70% by weight of silk or spun silk
6208.2990	---其他	14	100	17	16	件/千克		---Other
6208.2990 10	毛制女式睡衣及睡衣裤	14	100	17	16	件/千克	A	Women's or girls' night-dresses and pyjamas, of wool or fine animal hair
6208.2990 90	其他材料制女式睡衣及睡衣裤	14	100	17	16	件/千克	A	Women's or girls' nightdresses and pyjamas of other textile materials
	-其他:							-Other:
6208.9100	--棉制	14	90	17	16	件/千克		--Of cotton
6208.9100 10	棉制女式内衣式背心、三角裤等(包括短衬裤)	14	90	17	16	件/千克	A	Women's or girls' singlets, briefs, panties, vest style, of cotton
6208.9100 21	棉制女式非内衣式背心(女成人及7-16号女童背心)	14	90	17	16	件/千克	A	Women's or girls' singlets, non-vest style, (women's and girls No. 7 ~ No. 16) of cotton
6208.9100 29	棉制其他女式非内衣式背心	14	90	17	16	件/千克	A	Other women's or girls' singlets; non-vest style, of cotton
6208.9100 90	棉制女式浴衣、晨衣及类似品	14	90	17	16	件/千克	A	Women's or girls' bathrobes, dressing gowns and similar articles, of cotton
6208.9200	--化学纤维制	16	130	17	16	件/千克		--Of man-made fibres
6208.9200 10	化纤制女式内衣式背心、三角裤(含短衬裤)	16	130	17	16	件/千克	A	Women's or girls' singlets, vest style, briefs, panties, of man-made fibres

税则号列	货品名称	最惠(%)	普通	增值税率	出口退税	计量单位	监管条件	Article Description
6208.9200 21	化纤制女式非内衣式背心(女成人及7－16号女童背心)	16	130	17	16	件/千克	A	Women's or girls' singlets, non-vest style (women's and girls No. 7 ~ No. 16), of man-made fibres
6208.9200 29	化纤制其他女式非内衣式背心	16	130	17	16	件/千克	A	Other women's or girls' singlets, non-vest style, of man-made fibres
6208.9200 90	化纤制女式浴衣、晨衣及类似品	16	130	17	16	件/千克	A	Women's or girls' bathrobes, dressing gowns and similar articles, of man-made fibres
	--其他纺织材料制:							--Of other textile materials:
6208.9910	---丝及绢丝制	14	130	17	16	件/千克		---Of silk or spun silk
6208.9910 11	丝制女内衣式背心、三角裤等(含丝及绢丝≥70%,包括短衬裤)	14	130	17	16	件/千克	A	Women's or girls' singlets, vest style briefs, panties of silk, containing≥70% by weight of silk or spun silk
6208.9910 19	丝制女内衣式背心、三角裤等(含丝及绢丝<70%,包括短衬裤)	14	130	17	16	件/千克	A	Women's or girls' singlets, vest style briefs, panties of silk, containing<70% by weight of silk or spun silk
6208.9910 21	丝制女式非内衣式背心(含丝及绢丝70%及以上)	14	130	17	16	件/千克	A	Women's or girls' singlets of silk, non-vest style, containing≥70% by weight of silk or spun silk
6208.9910 29	丝制女式非内衣式背心(含丝70%以下)	14	130	17	16	件/千克	A	Women's or girls' singlets of silk, non-vest style, containing<70% by weight of silk or spun silk
6208.9910 91	丝制女式浴衣、晨衣及类似品(含丝及绢丝70%及以上)	14	130	17	16	件/千克	A	Women's or girls' bathrobes, dressing gowns and similar articles of silk, containing≥70% by weight of silk or spun silk
6208.9910 99	丝制女式浴衣、晨衣及类似品(含丝及绢丝70%以下)	14	130	17	16	件/千克	A	Women's or girls' bathrobes, dressing gowns and similar articles, of silk, containing<70% by weight of silk or spun silk
6208.9990	---其他	14	100	17	16	件/千克		---Other
6208.9990 11	毛制女式内衣式背心、三角裤等(包括短衬裤)	14	100	17	16	件/千克	A	Women's or girls' singlets, vest style briefs, panties, of wool or fine animal hair
6208.9990 12	毛制女式非内衣式背心(女成人及7－16号女童背心)	14	100	17	16	件/千克	A	Women's and girls' No. 7 – No. 16 singlets, non-vest style, of wool or fine animal hair
6208.9990 13	毛制其他女式非内衣式背心	14	100	17	16	件/千克	A	Other women's or girls' singlets, non-vest style, of wool or fine animal hair
6208.9990 19	毛制女式浴衣、晨衣及类似品	14	100	17	16	件/千克	A	Women's or girls' bathrobes, dressing gowns and similar articles, of wool or fine animal hair
6208.9990 90	其他材料制女式背心、三角裤、短衬裤	14	100	17	16	件/千克	A	Women's or girls' singlets, vest style briefs, panties, other textile materials
62.09	**婴儿服装及衣着附件:**							**Babies' garments and clothing accessories:**
6209.2000	-棉制	14	80	17	16	千克	A	-Of cotton
6209.3000	-合成纤维制	16	130	17	16	千克		-Of synthetic fibres
6209.3000 10	合成纤维制婴儿手套、袜子(含分指、连指及露指手套,长袜、短袜及其他袜)	16	130	17	16	千克	A	Babies' gloves, mittens, mitts, stockings, socks and similar articles, of synthetic fibres
6209.3000 20	合成纤维婴儿外衣、雨衣、滑雪装(包括夹克类似服装)	16	130	17	16	千克	A	Babies' coats, raincoats, ski-suits, jackets and similar articles, of synthetic fibres
6209.3000 30	合成纤维制婴儿其他服装(含裤子、衬衫、裙子、睡衣、内衣等)	16	130	17	16	千克	A	Babies' other garments, including trousers, shirt, skirt, night clothes, underwear, of synthetic fibres
6209.3000 90	合成纤维制婴儿衣着附件	16	130	17	16	千克	A	Babies' clothing accessories, of synthetic fibres
	-其他纺织材料制:							-Of other textile materials:
6209.9010	---羊毛或动物细毛制	14	130	17	16	千克	A	---Of wool or fine animal hair
6209.9090	---其他纺织材料制	14	100	17	16	千克	A	---Other textile materials
62.10	**用税目56.02、56.03、59.03、59.06或59.07的织物制成的服装:**							**Garments, made up of fabrics of heading No. 56.02, 56.03, 59.03, 59.06 or 59.07:**
	-用税目56.02或56.03的织物制成的服装:							-Of fabrics of heading No. 56.02 or 56.03:
6210.1010	---羊毛或动物细毛制	16	130	17	16	件/千克		---Of wool or fine animal hair
6210.1010 10	毛制纸衬背或覆盖的无纺布服装(羊毛或动物细毛制,包括毡呢或无纺织物制服装)	16	130	17	16	件/千克		Garments, made up of nonwovens or felt, paper backed or covered, of wool or fine animal hair
6210.1010 20	毛制一次性或医疗用无纺织物服装(羊毛或动物细毛制)	16	130	17	16	件/千克		Garments, made up of nonwovens, disposable or for medical use, of wool or fine animal hair

税则号列	货品名称	最惠(%)	普通	增值税率	出口退税	计量单位	监管条件	Article Description
6210.1010 90	毛制其他毡呢或无纺织物服装(羊毛或动物细毛制)	16	130	17	16	件/千克		Other garments, made up of felt or nonwovens, of wool or fine animal hair
6210.1020	---棉或麻制	16	90	17	16	件/千克		---Of cotton or bast fibres
6210.1020 10	棉或麻制纸衬或覆盖的无纺布服装(包括毡呢或无纺织物制服装)	16	90	17	16	件/千克		Garments, made up of felt or nonwovens, paper backed or covered, of cotton or bast fibres
6210.1020 20	棉或麻一次性或医用无纺织物服装	16	90	17	16	件/千克		Garments, made up of nonwovens, disposable or for, medical use of cotton or bast fibres
6210.1020 90	棉或麻制其他毡呢或无纺织物服装	16	90	17	16	件/千克		Other garments, made up of felt or nonwovens, of cotton or bast fibres
6210.1030	---化学纤维制	17.5	130	17	16	件/千克		---Of man-made fibres
6210.1030 10	化纤制纸衬背或覆盖的无纺布服装(包括毡呢或无纺织物制服装)	17.5	130	17	16	件/千克		Garments, made up of felt or nonwovens, paper backed or covered, of man-made fibres
6210.1030 20	化纤制一次性或医用无纺织物服装	17.5	130	17	16	件/千克		Garments made up, of nonwovens, disposable or for medical use, of man-made fibres
6210.1030 90	化纤制其他毡呢或无纺织物服装	17.5	130	17	16	件/千克		Other garments, made up of felt or nonwovens, of man-made fibres
6210.1090	---其他纺织材料制	16	100	17	16	件/千克		---Of other textile materials
6210.1090 10	其他纺织材料制纸衬背的无纺服装(包括纸覆盖的毡呢或无纺织物制服装)	16	100	17	16	件/千克		Garments, of felt or nonwovens, paper backed or covered, of other textile materials
6210.1090 20	其他材料制一次性或医用无纺织物服装	16	100	17	16	件/千克		Garments, of nonwovens, disposable or for medical use, of other textile materials
6210.1090 90	其他纺织材料制其他无纺织物服装(包括毡呢制服装)	16	100	17	16	件/千克		Other garments, made up of felt or nonwovens, of other textile materials
6210.2000	-子目号 6201.11 至 6201.19 所列类型的其他服装	16	100	17	16	件/千克		-Other garments, made up of the type described in subheadings No. 6201.11 to 6201.19
6210.2000 11	用塑料或橡胶处理的化纤制男外装(织物外表面由塑料或橡胶完全覆盖的大衣、雨衣、斗篷等)	16	100	17	16	件/千克		Men's or boys' outer garments of man-made fibres, including overcoat, raincoat, cape, outer surface of fabrics completely covered with plastics or rubber
6210.2000 19	其他用塑料或橡胶处理的化纤制男外装(含用其他材料处理的织物制大衣、雨衣、斗篷等)	16	100	17	16	件/千克		Other men's or boys' outer garments of man-made fibres, including overcoat, raincoat, cape, treated by plastics or rubber or other material
6210.2000 21	用塑料或橡胶处理的羊毛制男外装(织物外表面由塑料或橡胶完全覆盖的大衣、雨衣、斗篷等)	16	100	17	16	件/千克		Men's or boys' outer garments of wool, outer surface including overcoat, raincoat, cope, of fabrics completely covered with plastics or rubber
6210.2000 29	用塑料或橡胶处理的羊毛制男外装(含用其他材料处理的织物制大衣、雨衣、斗篷等)	16	100	17	16	件/千克		Other men's or boys' outer garments of wool, including overcoat, raincoat, cape, treated by plastics or rubber or other materials
6210.2000 31	用塑料或橡胶处理的棉制男外装(织物外表面由塑料或橡胶完全覆盖的大衣、雨衣、斗篷等)	16	100	17	16	件/千克		Men's or boys' outer garments of cotton, including overcoat, raincoat, cape, outer surface of fabrics completely covered with plastics or rubber
6210.2000 39	其他用塑料或橡胶等处理棉制男外装(含用其他材料处理的织物制大衣、雨衣、斗篷等)	16	100	17	16	件/千克		Other men's or boys' outer garments of cotton, including overcoat, raincoat, cape, treated by plastic or rubber or other materials
6210.2000 40	用塑料或橡胶处理的其他纺材男外装(织物外表面由塑料或橡胶完全覆盖的大衣、雨衣、斗篷等)	16	100	17	16	件/千克		Men's or boys' outer garments of other textile materials, including overcoat, raincoat, cape, outer surface of fabrics completely covered with plastics or rubber
6210.2000 91	用塑料或橡胶等处理的亚麻制男外装(含用其他材料处理的织物制大衣、雨衣、斗篷等)	16	100	17	16	件/千克		Men's or boys' outer garments of flax, including overcoat, raincoat, cape, treated by plastic or rubber or other materials
6210.2000 99	用塑料等处理的其他纺材制男外装(含用橡胶及其他材料处理的织物制大衣、雨衣、斗篷等)	16	100	17	16	件/千克		Other men's or boys' outer garments of other textile materials, including overcoat, raincoat, cape, treated by plastic or rubber or other materials
6210.3000	-子目号 6202.11 至 6202.19 所列类型的其他服装	16	100	17	16	件/千克		-Other garments, of the type described in subheadings No. 6202.11 to 6202.19

税则号列	货品名称	最惠(%)	普通	增值税率	出口退税	计量单位	监管条件	Article Description
6210.3000 11	用塑料或橡胶处理化纤制女外装(织物外表面由塑料或橡胶完全覆盖的大衣、雨衣、斗篷等)	16	100	17	16	件/千克		Women's or girls' outer garments of man-made fibres, including overcoat, raincoat, cape , outer surface of fabrics completely covered with plastics or rubber
6210.3000 19	其他用塑料或橡胶处理化纤制女外装(含用其他材料处理的织物制大衣、雨衣、斗篷等)	16	100	17	16	件/千克		Other women's or girls' outer garments of man-made fibres, including overcoat, raincoat, cape , treated by plastic or rubber or other materials
6210.3000 21	用塑料或橡胶处理的羊毛制女外装(织物外表面由塑料或橡胶完全覆盖的大衣、雨衣、斗篷等)	16	100	17	16	件/千克		Women's or girls' outer garments of wool, including overcoat, raincoat, cape , outer surface of fabrics completely covered with plastics or rubber
6210.3000 29	用塑料或橡胶处理的羊毛制女外装(含用其他材料处理的织物制大衣、雨衣、斗篷等)	16	100	17	16	件/千克		Other women's or girls' outer garments of wool, including overcoat, raincoat, cape , treated by plastic or rubber or other materials
6210.3000 31	用塑料或橡胶处理的棉制女外装(织物外表面由塑料或橡胶完全覆盖的大衣、雨衣、斗篷等)	16	100	17	16	件/千克		Women's or girls' outer garments of cotton, including overcoat, raincoat, cape , outer surface of fabrics completely covered with plastics or rubber
6210.3000 39	其他用塑料或橡胶等处理棉制女外装(含用其他材料处理的织物制大衣、雨衣、斗篷等)	16	100	17	16	件/千克		Other women's or girls' outer garments of cotton, including overcoat, raincoat, cape , treated by plastic or rubber or other materials
6210.3000 40	用塑料或橡胶处理的其他纺材女外装(织物外表面由塑料或橡胶完全覆盖的大衣、雨衣、斗篷等)	16	100	17	16	件/千克		Women's or girls' outer garments of other textile materials, including overcoat, raincoat, cape , outer surface of fabrics completely covered with plastics or rubber
6210.3000 91	用塑料或橡胶等处理的亚麻制女外装(含用其他材料处理的织物制大衣、雨衣、斗篷等)	16	100	17	16	件/千克		Women's or girls' outer garments of flax, including overcoat, raincoat, cape , treated by plastic or rubber or other materials
6210.3000 99	用塑料等处理的其他纺材制女外装(含用橡胶及其他材料处理的织物制大衣、雨衣、斗篷等)	16	100	17	16	件/千克		Other women's or girls' outer garments of other textile materials, including overcoat, raincoat, cape , treated by plastic or rubber or other materials
6210.4000	-其他男式服装	16	100	17	16	件/千克		-Other men's or boys' garments
6210.4000 11	用塑料或橡胶处理化纤制其他男式服装(织物外表面由塑料或橡胶完全覆盖)	16	100	17	16	件/千克		Men's or boys' garments of man-made fibre, outer surface of fabrics completely covered with plastic or rubber
6210.4000 12	用塑料等处理的化纤制男防风衣(含用橡胶及其他材料处理织物制带风帽防寒短上衣、风衣)	16	100	17	16	件/千克		Men's or boys' wind-cheaters, anoraks, wind-jackets, of man-made fibres, treated by plastic or rubber or other materials
6210.4000 13	用塑料等处理的化纤制男式长、短裤(滑雪裤除外)	16	100	17	16	件/千克		Men's or boys' trousers and shorts of man-made fibres, other than ski-pants, treated by plastic or rubber
6210.4000 19	用塑料等处理的化纤制其他男式服装(含用橡胶及其他材料处理的织物)	16	100	17	16	件/千克		Other men's or boys' garments, of man-made fibres, treated by plastic or rubber or other materials
6210.4000 21	用塑料或橡胶处理的毛制其他男外装(织物外表面由塑料或橡胶完全覆盖,羊毛或动物细毛制)	16	100	17	16	件/千克		Other men's or boys' garments, of wool or fine animal hair, outer surface of fabrics completely covered with plastic or rubber
6210.4000 22	用塑料等处理的毛制男式防风衣(含用橡胶及其他材料处理织物制带风帽防寒短上衣、风衣)	16	100	17	16	件/千克		Men's or boys' wind-cheaters, anoraks, wind-jackets, of wool or fine animal hair, treated by plastic or rubber or other materials
6210.4000 23	用塑料等处理的毛制男式长、短裤(含用橡胶及其他材料处理的毛制男式长、短裤)	16	100	17	16	件/千克		Men's or boys' trousers and shorts, of wool or fine animal hair, treated by rubber and other material
6210.4000 29	用塑料等处理的其他男式服装(用橡胶及其他材料处理的织物)	16	100	17	16	件/千克		Other men's or boys' garments, treated by plastic or rubber or other materials
6210.4000 31	用塑料或橡胶处理的棉制其他男外装(织物外表面由塑料或橡胶完全覆盖)	16	100	17	16	件/千克		Men's or boys' outer garments of cotton, outer surface of fabrics completely covered with plastic or rubber

税则号列	货品名称	最惠(%)	普通	增值税率	出口退税	计量单位	监管条件	Article Description
6210.4000 32	用塑料等处理的棉制男式防风衣(含用橡胶及其他材料处理织物制带风帽防寒短上衣、风衣)	16	100	17	16	件/千克		Men's or boys' wind-cheaters, anoraks, wind-jackets and similar articles of cotton, treated by plastic or rubber or other materials
6210.4000 33	用塑料等处理的棉制男式长、短裤(含用橡胶及其他材料处理的棉制男式长、短裤)	16	100	17	16	件/千克		Men's or boys' trousers and shorts of cotton, treated by plastic or rubber or other materials
6210.4000 39	用塑料等处理的棉制其他男式服装(含用橡胶及其他材料处理的织物)	16	100	17	16	件/千克		Other men's or boys' garments of cotton, treated by plastic or rubber or other materials
6210.4000 40	用塑料或橡胶处理其他纺材制其他男装	16	100	17	16	件/千克		Other men's or boys' garments of other textile materials
6210.4000 91	用塑料等处理的丝制其他男式服装(含用橡胶及其他材料处理的织物,含丝及绢丝70%及以上)	16	100	17	16	件/千克		Other men's or boys' garments of silk, treated by plastic or rubber or other materials, containing ≥ 70% by weight of silk or spun silk
6210.4000 92	用塑料等处理的其他纺材制男防风衣(含用橡胶及其他材料处理织物制带风帽防寒短上衣、风衣)	16	100	17	16	件/千克		Men's or boys' wind-cheaters, anoraks, wind-jackets, of other textile materials, treated by plastic or rubber or other materials
6210.4000 93	用塑料等处理其他纺材制男长、短裤(含用橡胶及其他材料处理的其他纺材制男长、短裤)	16	100	17	16	件/千克		Men's or boys' trousers and shorts, of other textile materials, treated by plastic or rubber or other materials
6210.4000 99	用塑料等处理的其他纺材制男服装(含用橡胶及其他材料处理的织物)	16	100	17	16	件/千克		Other men's or boys' garments, of other textile materials, treated by plastic or rubber
6210.5000	-其他女式服装	16	100	17	16	件/千克		-Other women's or girls' garments
6210.5000 11	用塑料或橡胶处理化纤制其他女装(织物外表面由塑料或橡胶完全覆盖)	16	100	17	16	件/千克		Other women's or girls' garments of man-made fibres, outer surface of fabrics completely covered with plastic or rubber
6210.5000 12	用塑料等处理的化纤制女防风衣(含用橡胶及其他材料处理织物制带风帽防寒短上衣、风衣)	16	100	17	16	件/千克		Women's or girls' garments wind-cheaters, anoraks, wind-jackets, of man-made fibres, treated by plastic or rubber or other materials
6210.5000 13	用塑料等处理的化纤制女式长、短裤(滑雪裤除外)	16	100	17	16	件/千克		Women's or girls' garments trousers and shorts, of man-made fibres, treated by plastic or rubber
6210.5000 19	用塑料等处理的化纤制其他女服装(含用橡胶及其他材料处理的织物)	16	100	17	16	件/千克		Other women's or girls' garments, of man-made fibres, treated by plastic or rubber or other materials
6210.5000 21	用塑料或橡胶处理的毛制其他女外装(织物外表面由塑料或橡胶完全覆盖,羊毛或动物细毛制)	16	100	17	16	件/千克		Other women's or girls' garments, of wool or fine animal hair, outer surface of fabrics completely covered with plastic or rubber
6210.5000 22	用塑料等处理的毛制女式防风衣(含用橡胶及其他材料处理织物制带风帽防寒短上衣、风衣)	16	100	17	16	件/千克		Women's or girls' wind-cheaters, anoraks, wind-jackets, of wool or fine animal hair, treated by plastic or rubber or other materials
6210.5000 23	用塑料等处理的毛制女式长、短裤(含用橡胶及其他材料处理的毛制女式长、短裤)	16	100	17	16	件/千克		Women's or girls' trousers and shorts, of wool or fine animal hair, treated by plastic or rubber or other materials
6210.5000 29	用塑料等处理的毛制其他女式服装(含用橡胶及其他材料处理的织物)	16	100	17	16	件/千克		Other women's or girls' garments, of wool or fine animal hair, treated by plastic or rubber or other materials
6210.5000 31	用塑料或橡胶处理的棉制其他女外装(织物外表面由塑料或橡胶完全覆盖)	16	100	17	16	件/千克		Other women's or girls' outer garments, of cotton, outer surface of fabrics completely covered with plastic or rubber
6210.5000 32	用塑料等处理的棉制女式防风衣(含用橡胶及其他材料处理织物制带风帽防寒短上衣、风衣)	16	100	17	16	件/千克		Women's or girls' wind-cheaters, anoraks, wind-jackets, of cotton, treated by plastic or rubber or other materials
6210.5000 33	用塑料等处理的棉制女式长、短裤(含用橡胶及其他材料处理的棉制女式长、短裤)	16	100	17	16	件/千克		Women's or girls' trousers and shorts of cotton, treated by plastic or rubber or other materials
6210.5000 39	用塑料等处理的棉制其他女式服装(含用橡胶及其他材料处理的棉制其他女式服装)	16	100	17	16	件/千克		Other women's or girls' garments of cotton, treated by plastic or rubber or other materials
6210.5000 40	用塑料或橡胶处理其他纺材其他女装(织物外表面由塑料或橡胶完全覆盖)	16	100	17	16	件/千克		Other women's or girls' garments of other textile materials, outer surface of fabrics completely covered with plastic or rubber

税则号列	货品名称	最惠(%)	普通	增值税率	出口退税	计量单位	监管条件	Article Description
6210.5000 91	用塑料等处理的丝制其他女式服装(含用橡胶及其他材料处理的织物,含丝及绢丝70%及以上)	16	100	17	16	件/千克		Other women's or girls' garments of silk, treated by plastic or rubber, containing≥70% by weight of silk or spun silk
6210.5000 92	用塑料等处理其他纺材制女防风衣(含用橡胶及其他材料处理织物制带风帽防寒短上衣、风衣)	16	100	17	16	件/千克		Women's or girls' wind-cheaters, anoraks, wind-jackets, of other textile materials, treated by plastic or rubber or other materials
6210.5000 93	用塑料等处理其他纺材制女长、短裤(含用橡胶及其他材料处理织物制带风帽防寒短上衣、风衣)	16	100	17	16	件/千克		Women's or girls' trousers and shorts, of other textile materials, treated by plastic or rubber or other materials
6210.5000 99	用塑料等处理的其他纺材制女服装(含用橡胶及其他材料处理的其他纺材制女服装)	16	100	17	16	件/千克		Other women's or girls' garments, of other textile materials, treated by plastic or rubber or other materials
62.11	**运动服、滑雪服及游泳服;其他服装:**							**Track suits, ski suits and swimwear; other garments:**
	-游泳服:							-Swimwear:
6211.1100	--男式	16	130	17	16	件/千克		--Men's or boys'
6211.1100 10	羊毛或动物细毛制男式游泳服	16	130	17	16	件/千克	A	Men's or boys' swimwear of wool or fine animal hair
6211.1100 41	丝制男式游泳服(含丝70%及以上)	16	130	17	16	件/千克	A	Men's or boys' swimwear of silk, containing ≥70% by weight of silk
6211.1100 49	丝制男式游泳服(含丝70%以下)	16	130	17	16	件/千克	A	Men's or boys' swimwear of silk, containing < 70% by weight of silk
6211.1100 90	其他纺织材料制男式游泳服	16	130	17	16	件/千克	A	Men's or boys' swimwear of other textile materials
6211.1200	--女式	16	130	17	16	件/千克		--Women's or girls'
6211.1200 10	羊毛或动物细毛制女式游泳服	16	130	17	16	件/千克	A	Women's or girls' swimwear of wool or fine animal hair
6211.1200 41	丝制女式游泳服(含丝70%及以上)	16	130	17	16	件/千克	A	Women's or girls' swimwear of silk, containing ≥ 70% by weight of silk
6211.1200 49	丝制女式游泳服(含丝70%以下)	16	130	17	16	件/千克	A	Women's or girls' swimwear of silk, containing < 70% by weight of silk
6211.1200 90	其他纺织材料制女式游泳服	16	130	17	16	件/千克	A	Women's or girls' swimwear of other textile materials
	-滑雪服:							-Ski suits:
6211.2010	---棉制	16	90	17	16	套/千克		---Of cotton
6211.2090	---其他纺织材料制	19	130	17	16	套/千克		---Of other textile materials
6211.2090 11	含滑雪男裤的羊毛制滑雪套装	19	130	17	16	套/千克		Ski suits of wool, including men's or boys' ski trousers
6211.2090 19	不含滑雪男裤的羊毛制滑雪套装	19	130	17	16	套/千克		Ski suitsof wool, excluding men's or boys' ski trousers
6211.2090 21	含滑雪短裤或不防水滑雪裤的化纤制滑雪套装	19	130	17	16	套/千克		Ski suits of man-made (including ski shorts or no water-proof trousers)
6211.2090 29	化纤制其他滑雪套装	19	130	17	16	套/千克		Other ski suits of man-made fibres
6211.2090 90	其他纺织材料制滑雪套装	19	130	17	16	套/千克		Ski suits of other textile materials
	-其他男式服装:							-Other garments, men's or boys' :
	--棉制:							--Of cotton:
6211.3210	---阿拉伯袍	16	90	17	16	件/千克		---Arabian robes
6211.3220	---运动服	16	90	17	16	套/千克		--- Track suits
6211.3220 11	棉制男式运动套装(面和衬里的面料相同的运动套装)	16	90	17	16	套/千克		Men's or boys' track suits, outside and underside being of same fabrics, of cotton
6211.3220 19	棉制其他男式运动套装	16	90	17	16	套/千克		Other men's or boys' track suits of cotton
6211.3290	---其他	16	90	17	16	件/千克		---Other
6211.3290 21	棉制男式连衣服及类似品	16	90	17	16	件/千克		Men's or boys' overall and similar articles, of cotton
6211.3290 29	棉制男式连衣裤及类似品	16	90	17	16	件/千克		Men's or boys' union suit and similar articles, of cotton
6211.3290 30	棉制男式水洗服,夏服,游戏装	16	90	17	16	件/千克		Men's or boys' summer wear, wash wear, playsuit, of cotton
6211.3290 40	棉制男式工业及职业衣着	16	90	17	16	件/千克		Men's or boys' garments of cotton, industrial and career apparel
6211.3290 51	棉制男式 TOPS(男成人及8-18号男童 TOPS)	16	90	17	16	件/千克		Men's TOPS and boys' TOPS No. 8 ~ No. 18, of cotton

税则号列	货 品 名 称	最惠(%)	普通	增值税率	出口退税	计量单位	监管条件	Article Description
6211.3290 59	棉制其他男式 TOPS	16	90	17	16	件/千克		Other men's or boys' TOPS, of cotton
6211.3290 60	棉制男式风雪套装及类似服装	16	90	17	16	件/千克		Men's or boys' ski suits and similar articles, of cotton
6211.3290 91	棉制男衬衫(品目6205的衬衫除外)	16	90	17	16	件/千克		Men's or boys' shirt, other than heading No. 62.05
6211.3290 99	棉制男式其他服装(含马甲,上衣)	16	90	17	16	件/千克		Other men's or boys' garments, including vests, coats, of cotton
	--化学纤维制:							--Of man-made fibres:
6211.3310	---阿拉伯袍	17.5	130	17	16	件/千克		---Arabian robes
6211.3320	---运动服	18	130	17	16	套/千克		---Track suits
6211.3320 11	化纤制男式运动套装(面和衬里的面料相同的运动套装)	18	130	17	16	套/千克		Men's or boys' track suits, outside and underside being of same fabrics, of man – made fibres
6211.3320 19	化纤制其他男式运动套装	18	130	17	16	套/千克		Other men's or boys' track suits of man – made fibres
6211.3390	---其他	17.5	130	17	16	件/千克		---Other
6211.3390 21	化纤制男式连衣服及类似品	17.5	130	17	16	件/千克		Men's or boys' overall and similar articles, of man-made fibres
6211.3390 29	化纤制男式连衣裤及类似品	17.5	130	17	16	件/千克		Men's or boys' union suit and similar articles, of man-made fibres
6211.3390 30	化纤制男式水洗服,夏服,游戏装(含类似服)	17.5	130	17	16	件/千克		Men's or boys' summer wear, wash wear, playsuit and similar articles, of man-made fibres
6211.3390 91	化纤制男式工业及职业衣着	17.5	130	17	16	件/千克		Men's or boys' garments of man-made fibres, industrial and career apparel
6211.3390 92	化纤制男式 TOPS(男成人及8-18号男童 TOPS)	17.5	130	17	16	件/千克		Men's TOPS and boys' TOPS No. 8 ~ No. 18, of man-made fibres
6211.3390 93	化纤制其他男式 TOPS	17.5	130	17	16	件/千克		Other men's or boys' TOPS, of man-made fibres
6211.3390 94	化纤制男式风雪套装及类似服装	17.5	130	17	16	件/千克		Men's or boys' ski suits and similar articles, of man-made fibres
6211.3390 95	化纤制男衬衫(品目6205的衬衫除外)	17.5	130	17	16	件/千克		Men's or boys' shirt of man – made fibres (other than the shirt of subheading No. 62.05)
6211.3390 99	化纤制男式其他服装(含马甲、上衣)	17.5	130	17	16	件/千克		Other men's or boys' garments, including vests, coats, of man-made fibres
	--其他纺织材料制:							--Of other textile materials:
6211.3910	---丝及绢丝制	16	130	17	16	件/千克		---Of silk or spun silk
6211.3910 11	丝及绢丝制男运动服(含丝70%及以上)	16	130	17	16	件/千克		Men's or boys' track suits of silk, containing ≥70% by weight of silk
6211.3910 19	丝及绢丝制男运动服(含丝70%以下)	16	130	17	16	件/千克		Men's or boys' track suits of silk, containing < 70% by weight of silk
6211.3910 21	丝或绢丝制男连衣裤及类似品(含丝70%及以上)	16	130	17	16	件/千克		Men's or boys' overall and similar articles, of silk or spun silk, containing ≥70% by weight of silk
6211.3910 29	丝或绢丝制男连衣裤及类似品(含丝70%以下)	16	130	17	16	件/千克		Men's or boys' union suit and similar articles, containing < 70% by weight of silk
6211.3910 91	丝或绢丝制男式 TOPS(含丝70%及以上)	16	130	17	16	件/千克		Men's or boys' TOPS of silk or silk waste, containing ≥70% by weight of silk
6211.3910 92	丝或绢丝制男式 TOPS(含丝70%以下)	16	130	17	16	件/千克		Men's or boys' TOPS of silk or silk waste, containing < 70% by weight of silk
6211.3910 93	丝或绢丝制男式风雪套装(含类似服装,含丝70%及以上)	16	130	17	16	件/千克		Men's or boys' ski suits and similar articles, of silk or silk waste, containing ≥70% by weight of silk
6211.3910 94	丝或绢丝制男式风雪套装(含类似服装,含丝70%以下)	16	130	17	16	件/千克		Men's or boys' ski suits and similar articles, of silk or silk waste, containing < 70% by weight of silk
6211.3910 95	丝或绢丝制男式其他服装(含衬衫、马甲、上衣,含丝70%及以上)	16	130	17	16	件/千克		Men's or boys' other shirts, vests, coats, of silk or silk waste, containing ≥70% by weight of silk
6211.3910 99	丝或绢丝制男式其他服装(含衬衫、马甲、上衣,含丝70%以下)	16	130	17	16	件/千克		Other men's or boys', vests, coats, of silk or silk waste, containing < 70% by weight of silk
6211.3920	---羊毛或动物细毛制	16	130	17	16	件/千克		--Of wool or fine animal hair
6211.3920 10	毛制男式运动套装	16	130	17	16	件/千克		Men's or boys' track suits of wool or fine animal hair
6211.3920 90	毛制男式其他服装	16	130	17	16	件/千克		Other men's or boys' garments, of wool or fine animal hair
6211.3990	---其他	16	100	17	16	件/千克		---Other

税则号列	货品名称	最惠(%)	普通	增值税率	出口退税	计量单位	监管条件	Article Description
6211.3990 10	其他纺织材料制男式运动套装	16	100	17	16	件/千克		Men's or boys' track suits of other textile materials
6211.3990 20	其他纺织材料制男连衣裤(含类似品)	16	100	17	16	件/千克		Men's or boys' union wear and similar articles of other textile materials
6211.3990 91	其他纺织材料制男式水洗服、夏服(含游戏装等类似服装)	16	100	17	16	件/千克		Men's or boys' summer wear, wash wear, including playsuit and similar articles, of other textile materials
6211.3990 92	其他纺织材料制男式 TOPS	16	100	17	16	件/千克		Men's or boys' TOPS, of other textile materials
6211.3990 93	其他纺织材料制男式风雪套装(含类似服装)	16	100	17	16	件/千克		Men's or boys' ski suits and similar articles of other textile materials
6211.3990 99	其他纺织材料制男式其他服装(含衬衫、马甲、上衣)	16	100	17	16	件/千克		Other men's or boys' shirts, vests, coats, of other textile materials
	-其他女式服装:							-Other garments, women's or girls':
	--棉制:							--Of cotton:
6211.4210	---运动服	16	90	17	16	套/千克		--- Track suits
6211.4210 10	棉制女式运动套装(面和衬里的面料相同的运动套装)	16	90	17	16	套/千克		Women's or girls' track suits, outside and underside being of same fabrics, of cotton
6211.4210 90	棉制其他女式运动套装	16	90	17	16	套/千克		Other Women's or girls' track suits of cotton
6211.4290	---其他	16	90	17	16	件/千克		---Other
	--化学纤维制:							--Of man-made fibres:
6211.4310	---运动服	17.5	130	17	16	套/千克		---Track suits
6211.4310 10	化纤制女式运动套装(面和衬里的面料相同的运动套装)	17.5	130	17	16	套/千克		Women's or girls' track suits, outside and underside being of same fabrics, of man-made fibres
6211.4310 90	化纤制其他女式运动套装	17.5	130	17	16	套/千克		Other Women's or girls' track suits of man-made fibres
6211.4390	---其他	17.5	130	17	16	件/千克		---Other
	--其他纺织材料制:							--Of other textile materials:
6211.4910	---丝及绢丝制	16	130	17	16	件/千克		---Of silk or spun silk
6211.4910 11	丝或绢丝制女式运动套装(含丝 70% 及以上)	16	130	17	16	件/千克		Women's or girls' track suits, of silk or spun silk, containing≥70% by weight of silk
6211.4910 19	丝或绢丝制女式运动套装(含丝 70% 以下)	16	130	17	16	件/千克		Women's or girls' track suits, of silk or spun silk, containing<70% by weight of silk
6211.4910 21	丝或绢丝制女连衣裤及类似品(含丝 70% 及以上)	16	130	17	16	件/千克		Women's or girls' union suit and similar articles, of silk or spun silk, containing≥70% by weight of silk
6211.4910 29	丝或绢丝制女连衣裤及类似品(含丝 70% 以下)	16	130	17	16	件/千克		Women's or girls' union suit and similar articles, of silk or spun silk, containing<70% by weight of silk
6211.4910 31	丝或绢丝制女式 TOPS(含丝 70% 及以上)	16	130	17	16	件/千克		Women's or girls' TOPS, of silk or spun silk, containing≥70% by weight of silk
6211.4910 39	丝或绢丝制女式 TOPS(含丝 70% 以下)	16	130	17	16	件/千克		Women's or girls' TOPS, of silk or spun silk, containing<70% by weight of silk
6211.4910 41	丝或绢丝制女式风雪套装(含类似服装,含丝 70% 及以上)	16	130	17	16	件/千克		Women's or girls' ski suits and similar articles, of silk or spun silk, containing≥70% by weight of silk
6211.4910 49	丝或绢丝制女式风雪套装(含类似服装,含丝 70% 以下)	16	130	17	16	件/千克		Women's or girls' ski suits and similar articles, of silk or spun silk, containing<70% by weight of silk
6211.4910 51	丝及绢丝制女式其他服装(含衬衫、马甲、上衣、无袖罩衫,含丝 70% 及以上)	16	130	17	16	件/千克		Other women's or girls' garments, including shirts vests coat, cloaks, of silk or spun silk, containing≥70% by weight of silk
6211.4910 59	丝及绢丝制女式其他服装(含衬衫、马甲、上衣和无袖罩衫,含丝 70% 以下)	16	130	17	16	件/千克		Other women's or girls' garments, including shirts vests coats, cloaks, of silk or spun silk, containing<70% by weight of silk
6211.4910 91	丝及绢丝制女式其他服装(含丝 70% 及以上)	16	130	17	16	件/千克		Other women's or girls' garments, of silk or spun silk, containing≥70% by weight of silk
6211.4910 99	丝及绢丝制女式其他服装(含丝 70% 以下)	16	130	17	16	件/千克		Other women's or girls' garments, of silk or spun silk, containing<70% by weight of silk
6211.4990	---其他	16	100	17	16	件/千克		---Other
6211.4990 10	其他纺织材料制女式运动套装	16	100	17	16	件/千克		Other women's or girls' track suits, of other textile materials
6211.4990 20	其他纺织材料制女连衣裤(含类似品)	16	100	17	16	件/千克		Other women's or girls' union suit and similar articles, of other textile materials

税则号列	货品名称	最惠(%)	普通	增值税率	出口退税	计量单位	监管条件	Article Description
6211.4990 30	其他纺织材料制女式其他服装(含游戏装,类似服装)	16	100	17	16	件/千克		Other women's or girls' garments, including playsuit and similar articles, of other textile materials
6211.4990 40	其他纺织材料制女式 TOPS	16	100	17	16	件/千克		Women's or girls' TOPS, of other textile materials
6211.4990 50	其他纺织材料制女式风雪套装(含类似服装)	16	100	17	16	件/千克		Women's or girls' ski suits and similar articles, of other textile materials
6211.4990 90	其他纺织材料制女式其他服装(含衬衫、马甲、上衣、无袖罩衫)	16	100	17	16	件/千克		Other women's or girls' garments including shirts, vests, coats, cloaks, of other textile materials
62.12	**胸罩、束腰带、紧身胸衣、吊裤带、吊袜带、束袜带和类似品及其零件,不论是否针织或钩编的:**							**Brassières, girdles, corsets, braces, suspenders, garters and similar articles and parts thereof, whether or not knitted or crocheted:**
	-胸罩:							-Brassières:
6212.1010	---化学纤维制	16	130	17	16	件/千克	A	---Of man-made fibres
6212.1090	---其他纺织材料制	14	100	17	16	件/千克		---Of other textile materials
6212.1090 10	毛制其他胸罩(不论是否针织或钩编)	14	100	17	16	件/千克	A	Brassieres of wool or fine animal hair(whether or not knitted or crocheted)
6212.1090 20	棉制其他胸罩(不论是否针织或钩编)	14	100	17	16	件/千克	A	Brassières, whether or not knitted or crocheted, of cotton
6212.1090 31	丝制胸罩(不论是否针织或钩编,含丝70%及以上)	14	100	17	16	件/千克	A	Brassieres of silk, whether or not knitted or crocheted, containing≥70% by weight of silk
6212.1090 39	丝制其他胸罩(不论是否针织或钩编,含丝70%以下)	14	100	17	16	件/千克	A	Brassières of silk, whether or not knitted or crocheted, containing<70% by weight of silk
6212.1090 90	其他纺织材料制其他胸罩(不论是否针织或钩编)	14	100	17	16	件/千克	A	Brassières, whether or not knitted or crocheted, of other textile materials
	-束腰带及腹带:							-Girdles and panty-girdles:
6212.2010	---化学纤维制	16	130	17	16	件/千克	A	---Of man-made fibres
6212.2090	---其他纺织材料制	14	100	17	16	件/千克		---Of other textile materials
6212.2090 10	毛制束胸带及腹带(不论是否针织或钩编)	14	100	17	16	件/千克	A	Girdles and panty-girdles, whether or not knitted or crocheted, of wool or fine animal hair
6212.2090 20	棉制束腰带及腹带(不论是否针织或钩编)	14	100	17	16	件/千克	A	Girdles and panty-girdles of cotton, whether or not knitted or crocheted
6212.2090 31	丝制束腰带及腹带(不论是否针织或钩编,含丝70%及以上)	14	100	17	16	件/千克	A	Girdles and panty-girdles of silk, whether or not knitted or crocheted, containing≥70% by weight of silk
6212.2090 39	丝制束腰带及腹带(不论是否针织或钩编,含丝70%以下)	14	100	17	16	件/千克	A	Girdles and panty-girdles of silk, whether or not knitted or crocheted, containing<70% by weight of silk
6212.2090 90	其他材料制束胸带及腹带(不论是否针织或钩编)	14	100	17	16	件/千克	A	Girdles and panty-girdles, whether or not knitted or crocheted, of other textile materials
	-束腰胸衣:							-Corselettes:
6212.3010	---化学纤维制	16	130	17	16	件/千克	A	---Of man-made fibres
6212.3090	---其他纺织材料制	14	100	17	16	件/千克		---Of other textile materials
6212.3090 10	毛制紧身胸衣(不论是否针织或钩编)	14	100	17	16	件/千克	A	Croselettes, of wool or fine animal hair
6212.3090 20	棉制紧身胸衣(不论是否针织或钩编)	14	100	17	16	件/千克	A	Croselettes, whether or not knitted or crocheted, of cotton
6212.3090 31	丝制紧身胸衣(不论是否针织或钩编,含丝70%及以上)	14	100	17	16	件/千克	A	Croselettes of silk, whether or not knitted or crocheted, containing≥70% by weight of silk
6212.3090 39	丝制其他紧身胸衣(不论是否针织或钩编,含丝70%以下)	14	100	17	16	件/千克	A	Croselettes of silk, whether or not knitted or crocheted, containing<70% by weight of silk
6212.3090 90	其他材料制紧身胸衣(不论是否针织或钩编)	14	100	17	16	件/千克	A	Croselettes of other textile materials, whether or not knitted or crocheted
	-其他:							-Other:
6212.9010	---化学纤维制	16	130	17	16	件/千克		---Of man-made fibres
6212.9090	---其他纺织材料制	14	100	17	16	件/千克		---Of other textile materials
6212.9090 10	毛制吊裤带、吊袜带、束袜带等(不论是否针织或钩编,含羊毛与橡胶/塑料制的)	14	100	17	16	件/千克		Braces, suspenders, garters and similar articles, of wool and plastics or rubber, whether or not knitted or crocheted

税则号列	货品名称	最惠(%)	普通	增值税率	出口退税	计量单位	监管条件	Article Description
6212.9090 20	棉制吊裤带、吊袜带、束袜带等(不论是否针织或钩编,含棉与橡胶/塑料制的)	14	100	17	16	件/千克		Braces, suspenders, garters and similar articles, of cotton and plastics/rubber, whether or not knitted or crocheted
6212.9090 31	丝制吊裤带、吊袜带、束袜带等(不论是否针织或钩编,含丝70%及以上)	14	100	17	16	件/千克		Braces, suspenders, garters and similar articles, of silk, containing≥70% by weight of silk, whether or not knitted or crocheted
6212.9090 39	丝制吊裤带、吊袜带、束袜带等(不论是否针织或钩编,含丝70%以下)	14	100	17	16	件/千克		Braces, suspenders, garters and similar articles, of silk, containing<70% by weight of silk, whether or not knitted or crocheted
6212.9090 90	其他材料制吊裤带、吊袜带等(不论是否针织或钩编、包括束袜带和类似品及其零件)	14	100	17	16	件/千克		Braces, suspenders, garters and similar articles and parts thereof, of other textile materials, whether or not knitted or crocheted
62.13	手帕:							**Handkerchiefs:**
	-棉制:							-Of cotton:
6213.2010	---刺绣的	14	90	17	16	条/千克		---Embroidered
6213.2090	---其他	14	90	17	16	条/千克		---Other
	-其他纺织材料制:							-Of other textile materials:
6213.9020	---刺绣的	14	100	17	16	条/千克		---Embroidered
6213.9090	---其他	14	100	17	16	条/千克		---Other
6213.9090 10	化纤制其他手帕	14	100	17	16	条/千克		Other handkerchiefs of man-made fibres
6213.9090 20	麻制其他手帕	14	100	17	16	条/千克		Other handkerchiefs of flax
6213.9090 90	其他材料制手帕	14	100	17	16	条/千克		Handkerchiefs of other textile materials
62.14	披巾、领巾、围巾、披纱、面纱及类似品:							**Shawls, scarves, mufflers, mantillas, veils and the like:**
6214.1000	-丝或绢丝制	14	130	17	16	条/千克		-Of silk or spun silk
6214.1000 10	含丝70%及以上的披巾、头巾、围巾(包括披纱、面纱等及类似品)	14	130	17	16	条/千克		Shawls, scarves, mufflers, mantillas, veils and the like, containing≥70% by weight of silk
6214.1000 90	含丝70%以下的披巾、头巾、围巾(包括披纱、面纱等及类似品)	14	130	17	16	条/千克		Shawls, scarves, mufflers, mantillas, veils and the like, containing<70% by weight of silk
	-羊毛或动物细毛制:							-Of wool or fine animal hair:
6214.2010	---羊毛制	14	130	17	16	条/千克		---Of wool
6214.2020	---山羊绒制	14	130	17	16	条/千克		---Of goats
6214.2090	---其他	14	130	17	16	条/千克		---Other
6214.3000	-合成纤维制	16	130	17	16	条/千克		-Of synthetic fibres
6214.4000	-人造纤维制	14	130	17	16	条/千克		-Of artificial fibres
6214.9000	-其他纺织材料制	14	100	17	16	条/千克		-Of other textile materials
6214.9000 10	棉制披巾、头巾及类似品(包括围巾、披纱、面纱)	14	100	17	16	条/千克		Shawls, scarves, mufflers, mantillas, veils and the like, of cotton
6214.9000 90	其他材料制披巾、头巾及类似品(包括围巾、披纱、面纱及类似品)	14	100	17	16	条/千克		Shawls, scarves, mufflers, mantillas, veils and the like, of other textile materials
62.15	领带及领结:							**Ties, bow ties and cravats:**
6215.1000	-丝或绢丝制	14	130	17	16	条/千克		-Of silk or spun silk
6215.1000 11	丝及绢丝制领带及领结(非丝纺织材料含量50%及以上)	14	130	17	16	条/千克		Ties, bow ties and cravats of silk and spun silk, containing≥50% by weight of non-silk textile fabrics
6215.1000 19	丝及绢丝制领带及领结(非丝纺织材料含量50%以下,外层织物含丝70%及以上)	14	130	17	16	条/千克		Ties, bow ties and cravats of silk and spun silk, containing<50% by weight of non-silk textile fabrics, outside fabrics containing≥70% by weight of silk
6215.1000 90	其他丝及绢丝制领带及领结(非丝纺织材料含量50%以下)	14	130	17	16	条/千克		Other ties, bow ties and cravats of silk and spun silk, containing<50% by weight of non-silk textile fabrics
6215.2000	-化学纤维制	16	130	17	16	条/千克		-Of man-made fibres
6215.9000	-其他纺织材料制	14	100	17	16	条/千克		-Of other textile materials
6215.9000 10	毛制领带及领结	14	100	17	16	条/千克		Ties, bow ties and cravats, of wool or fine animal hair
6215.9000 20	棉制领带及领结	14	100	17	16	条/千克		Ties, bow ties and cravats, of cotton
6215.9000 90	其他材料制领带及领结	14	100	17	16	条/千克		Ties, bow ties and cravats, of other textile materials
62.16	**分指手套、连指手套及露指手套:**							**Gloves, mittens and mitts:**

税则号列	货品名称	最惠(%)	普通	增值税率	出口退税	计量单位	监管条件	Article Description
6216.0000	分指手套、连指手套及露指手套	14	100	17	16	双/千克		Gloves, mittens and mitts
6216.0000 11	非针织物裁剪缝制成的运动手套(已浸渍塑料/橡胶,但含量不超过50%;棉限内;并四指)	14	100	17	16	双/千克		Sports mittens, not-knitted, making-up, impregnated, rubber or plastics content≤50% (W), cotton within limitations
6216.0000 12	非针织物裁剪缝制成的非运动手套(已浸渍塑料/橡胶,但含量不超过50%;棉限内;并四指)	14	100	17	16	双/千克		Other mittens, not-knitted, making-up, impregnated, rubber or plastics content≤50% (W), cotton within limitations, other than sport mittens
6216.0000 13	非针织物裁剪缝制成的运动手套(已浸渍塑料/橡胶,但含量不超过50%;化纤限内;并四指)	14	100	17	16	双/千克		Sports mittens, not-knitted, making-up impregnated, rubber or plastics content≤50% (W), man-made fibres within limitations
6216.0000 14	非针织物裁剪缝制成的非运动手套(已浸渍塑料、橡胶,但含量不超过50%;化纤限内;并四指)	14	100	17	16	双/千克		Other mittens, not-knitted making-up, impregnated, rubber or plastics content≤50% (W), man-made fibres within limitations
6216.0000 15	其他非针织物裁剪缝成的运动手套(已浸渍塑料、橡胶,但含量不超过50%;并四指)	14	100	17	16	双/千克		Other sports mittens, not-knitted, making-up, impregnated, rubber or plastics content≤50% (W)
6216.0000 19	其他非针织物制成的非运动手套(已浸渍塑料、橡胶,但含量不超过50%;并四指)	14	100	17	16	双/千克		Other mittens, not-knitted making-up, impregnated, rubber or plastics content ≤ 50% (W), other than sports mittens
6216.0000 21	其他浸渍塑料/橡胶非针织运动手套(含棉、化学纤维及其他纺织纤维50%及以上;棉限内)	14	100	17	16	双/千克		Other gloves, mittens not-knitted, impregnated with rubber or plastics, cotton, man-made fibres or other textile fibres content≥50% (W), cotton within limitations, other than sports mittens
6216.0000 22	其他浸渍塑料/橡胶非针织非运动手套(含棉、化学纤维及其他纺织纤维50%及以上;棉限内)	14	100	17	16	双/千克		Other gloves, mittens, not-knitted, impregnated with rubber or plastics, cotton, man-made fibres or other textile fibres content≥50% (W), cotton within limitations
6216.0000 23	其他浸渍塑料/橡胶非针织运动手套(含棉、化学纤维及其他纺织纤维50%及以上,化纤限内)	14	100	17	16	双/千克		Other gloves, mittens sports, not-knitted, impregnated with rubber or plastics, cotton, man-made fibres or other textile fibres content ≥ 50% (W), man-made fibres within limitations
6216.0000 24	其他浸渍塑料/橡胶非针织非运动手套(含棉、化学纤维及其他纺织纤维50%及以上;化纤限内)	14	100	17	16	双/千克		Other gloves, mittens, not-knitted, impregnated with rubber or plastics, cotton, man-made fibres or other textile fibres content ≥ 50% (W), man-made fibres within limitations, other than sports mittens
6216.0000 25	未列名浸渍塑料/橡胶非针织运动手套(含棉、化学纤维及其他纺织纤维50%及以上)	14	100	17	16	双/千克		Other gloves, mittens sports, not-knitted, impregnated, rubber or plastics, cotton, man-made fibres or other textile fibres content≥50% (W)
6216.0000 29	未列名浸渍塑料/橡胶非针织非运动手套(含棉、化学纤维及其他纺织纤维50%及以上)	14	100	17	16	双/千克		Other gloves, not-knitted, impregnated with rubber or plastics, cotton, man-made fibres or other textile fibres content≥50% (W), not elsewhere specified or included, other than sports mittens
6216.0000 31	棉的非针织物制的运动手套(非浸渍塑料、橡胶;含并四指、分四指)	14	100	17	16	双/千克		Other sports gloves, mittens, not-knitted, of cotton, not impregnated with rubber or plastics
6216.0000 39	棉的非针织物制的非运动手套(非浸渍塑料、橡胶;含并四指、分四指)	14	100	17	16	双/千克		Other gloves, mittens, not-knitted, of cotton, not impregnated with rubber or plastics, other than sports mittens
6216.0000 41	化纤制非针织物制的运动手套(非浸渍塑料/橡胶;含并/分四指;含羊毛或动物细毛≥36%)	14	100	17	16	双/千克		Other sports gloves, mittens, not-knitted, of man-made fibres, containing ≥ 36% by weight of wool or fine animal hair, not impregnated with rubber or plastics
6216.0000 42	化纤制非针织物制的非运动手套(非浸渍塑料/橡胶;含并/分四指;含羊毛或动物细毛≥36%)	14	100	17	16	双/千克		Other gloves, mittens, not-knitted, of man-made fibres, containing≥36% by weight of wool or fine animal hair, not impregnated with rubber or plastics, other than sports mittens
6216.0000 43	其他化纤制非针织运动手套(非浸渍塑料、橡胶的;含并四指、分四指)	14	100	17	16	双/千克		Other sports gloves, mittens, not-knitted, of man-made fibres, not impregnated with rubber or plastics

税则号列	货品名称	最惠(%)	普通	增值税率	出口退税	计量单位	监管条件	Article Description
6216.0000 49	其他化纤制非针织非运动手套(非浸渍塑料、橡胶的;含并四指、分四指)	14	100	17	16	双/千克		Other gloves, mittens, not-knitted, of man-made fibres, not impregnated with rubber or plastics other than sports mittens
6216.0000 51	毛制非针织运动手套(非浸渍塑料、橡胶的;含并四指、分四指)	14	100	17	16	双/千克		Other sports gloves, mittens, not-knitted, of wool or fine animal hair, not impregnated with rubber or plastics
6216.0000 59	毛制非针织非运动手套(非浸渍塑料、橡胶的;含并四指、分四指)	14	100	17	16	双/千克		Other gloves, mittens, not-knitted, of wool or fine animal hair, not impregnated with rubber or plastics, other than sports mittens
6216.0000 91	其他纺织材料制非针织运动手套(非浸渍塑料、橡胶的;含分指手套、连指手套及露指手套)	14	100	17	16	双/千克		Other sports gloves, mittens and mitts, not-knitted, of other textile materials, not impregnated with rubber or plastics
6216.0000 99	其他纺织材料制非针织非运动手套(非浸渍塑料、橡胶的;含分指手套、连指手套及露指手套)	14	100	17	16	双/千克		Other gloves, mittens and mitts, not-knitted, of other textile materials, not impregnated with rubber or plastics, other than sports mittens
62.17	**其他制成的衣着附件;服装或衣着附件的零件,但税号62.12的货品除外:**							**Other made up clothing accessories; parts of garments or of clothing accessories, other than those of heading No. 62.12:**
	-附件:							-Accessories:
6217.1010	---袜子及袜套	14	130	17	16	千克/双		---Stocking, socks and sockettes
6217.1020	---和服腰带	14	100	17	16	千克/双		---Kimono belts
6217.1090	---其他	14	100	17	16	千克		---Other
6217.1090 10	毛制服装或衣着附件(指非针织非钩编)	14	100	17	16	千克		Garments or clothing accessories of wool or fine animal hair, not knitted or crocheted
6217.1090 20	棉制服装或衣着附件(指非针织非钩编)	14	100	17	16	千克		Garments or clothing accessories of cotton, not knitted or crocheted
6217.1090 30	化纤制服装或衣着附件(指非针织非钩编)	14	100	17	16	千克		Garments or clothing accessories of man-made fibres, not knitted or crocheted
6217.1090 41	丝制服装或衣着附件(指非针织非钩编,含丝70%及以上)	14	100	17	16	千克		Garments or clothing accessories of silk, not knitted or crocheted, containing≥70% by weight of silk
6217.1090 49	丝制服装或衣着附件(指非针织非钩编,含丝70%以下)	14	100	17	16	千克		Garments or clothing accessories of silk, not knitted or crocheted, containing <70% by weight of silk
6217.1090 90	其他服装或衣着附件(指非针织非钩编)	14	100	17	16	千克		Other garments or clothing accessories other, not knitted or crocheted
6217.9000	-零件	14	100	17	16	千克		-Parts
6217.9000 11	羊毛或动物细毛制保暖型衬里	14	100	17	16	千克		Thermal lining of wool or fine animal hair
6217.9000 12	毛制非针织或非钩编衬衫的零件	14	100	17	16	千克		Parts of shirts, not knitted or crocheted, of wool or fine animal hair
6217.9000 13	毛制非针织或非钩编上衣的零件	14	100	17	16	千克		Parts of jackets and blazers, not knitted or crocheted, of wool or fine animal hair
6217.9000 14	毛制长裤及马裤的零件(指非针织非钩编)	14	100	17	16	千克		Parts of trousers or breeches, not knitted or crocheted, of wool or fine animal hair
6217.9000 19	其他毛制服装或衣着零件(指非针织非钩编)	14	100	17	16	千克		Other parts of other garments, not knitted or crocheted, of wool or fine animal ha-ir
6217.9000 21	棉制保暖型衬里	14	100	17	16	千克		Thermal lining of cotton
6217.9000 22	棉制非针织非钩编衬衫的零件	14	100	17	16	千克		Parts of shirts, not knitted or crocheted, of cotton
6217.9000 23	棉制非针织非钩编上衣的零件	14	100	17	16	千克		Parts of jackets and blazers, not knitted or crocheted, of cotton
6217.9000 24	棉制长裤及马裤的零件(指非针织非钩编)	14	100	17	16	千克		Parts of trousers or breeches, not knitted or crocheted, of cotton
6217.9000 29	棉制服装或衣着零件(指非针织非钩编)	14	100	17	16	千克		Other parts of garments, not knitted or crocheted, of cotton
6217.9000 31	化纤制保暖型衬里	14	100	17	16	千克		Thermal lining, of man-made fibres
6217.9000 32	化纤制非针织非钩编衬衫的零件	14	100	17	16	千克		Parts of shirts, not knitted or crocheted, of man-made fibres

税则号列	货品名称	最惠(%)	普通	增值税率	出口退税	计量单位	监管条件	Article Description
6217.9000 33	化纤制非针织非钩编上衣的零件	14	100	17	16	千克		Parts of jackets and blazers, not knitted or crocheted, of man-made fibres
6217.9000 34	化纤制长裤及马裤的零件(指非针织非钩编)	14	100	17	16	千克		Parts of trousers or breeches, not knitted or crocheted, of man-made fibres
6217.9000 39	化纤制服装或衣着零件(指非针织非钩编)	14	100	17	16	千克		Other parts of garments, not knitted or crocheted, of man-made fibres
6217.9000 41	丝制保暖型衬里	14	100	17	16	千克		Thermal lining of silk, not knitted or crocheted
6217.9000 42	丝制服装或衣着零件(指非针织非钩编,含丝70%及以上)	14	100	17	16	千克		Parts of garments of silk, containing ≥ 70% by weight of silk, not knitted or crocheted
6217.9000 49	丝制服装或衣着零件(指非针织非钩编,含丝70%以下)	14	100	17	16	千克		Parts of garments of silk, containing < 70% by weight of silk, not knitted or crocheted
6217.9000 91	其他材料制保暖型衬里	14	100	17	16	千克		Thermal lining of other textile materials
6217.9000 92	其他材料制衬衫零件(非针织非钩编)	14	100	17	16	千克		Parts of shirts of other textile materials, not knitted or crocheted
6217.9000 93	其他材料制上衣零件(指非针织非钩编)	14	100	17	16	千克		Parts of jackets and blazers, of other textile materials, not knitted or crocheted
6217.9000 94	其他材料制长裤及马裤的零件(指非针织非钩编)	14	100	17	16	千克		Parts of trousers or breeches, of other textile materials, not knitted or crocheted
6217.9000 99	其他材料制服装或衣着附件(指非针织或非钩编,含各种附件的零件)	14	100	17	16	千克		Garments or clothing accessories, parts of clothing accessories, of other textile materials, not knitted or crocheted

第六十三章
其他纺织制成品；成套物品；旧衣着及旧纺织品；碎织物

注释：

一、第一分章仅适用于各种纺织物制成的物品。

二、第一分章不包括：

（一）第五十六章至第六十二章的货品；

（二）税目 63.09 的旧衣着或其他旧物品。

三、税目 63.09 仅适用于下列货品：

（一）纺织材料制品：

1. 衣着和衣着附件及其零件；
2. 毯子及旅行毯；
3. 床上、餐桌、盥洗及厨房用的织物制品；
4. 装饰用织物制品，但税目 57.01 至 57.05 的地毯及税目 58.05 的装饰毯除外。

（二）用石棉以外其他任何材料制成的鞋帽类。

上述物品只有同时符合下列两个条件才能归入本税目：

1. 必须明显看得出穿用过；
2. 必须以散装、捆装、袋装或类似的大包装形式进口或出口。

Chapter 63
Other made up textile articles; sets; worn clothing and worn textile articles; rags

Notes:

1. Sub-Chapter 1 applies only to made uparticles, of any textile fabric.
2. Sub-Chapter 1 does not cover:
   (a) Goods of Chapters 56 to 62; or
   (b) Worn clothing or other worn articles of heading No. 63.09.
3. Heading No. 63.09 applies only to the following goods:
   (a) Articles of textile materials:
   (1) Clothing and clothing accessories, and parts thereof;
   (2) Blankets and travelling rugs;
   (3) Bed linen, table linen, toilet lined and kitchen linen;
   (4) Furnishing articles, other than carpets of headings No. 57.01 to 57.05 and tapestries of heading No. 58.05;
   (b) Footwear and headgear of any material other than asbestos.
   In order to be classified in this heading, the articles mentioned above must comply with both of the following requirements:
   (1) They must show signs of appreciable wear; and
   (2) They must be presented in bulk or in bales, sacks or similar packings.

税则号列	货 品 名 称	最惠(%)	普通	增值税率	出口退税	计量单位	监管条件	Article Description
	第一分章　其他纺织制成品							Ⅰ. -OTHER MADE UP TEXTILE ARTICLES
63.01	毯子及旅行毯：							**Blankets and travelling rugs:**
6301.1000	-电暖毯	16	100	17	16	条/千克	A	-Electric blankets
6301.2000	-羊毛或动物细毛制的毯子（电暖毯除外）及旅行毯	16	130	17	16	条/千克		-Blankets (other than electric blankets) and travelling rugs, of wool or of fine animal hair
6301.2000 10	毛制毯子及旅行毯（羊毛或动物细毛制，非电暖的，长度不超过 3 米）	16	130	17	16	条/千克		Blankets (other than electric blankets) and travelling rugs, of wool or fine animal hair, length≤3m
6301.2000 20	其他毛制毯子及旅行毯（羊毛或动物细毛制，非电暖的，长度超过 3 米）	16	130	17	16	条/千克		Other blankets (other than electric blankets) and travelling rugs, of wool or of fine animal hair, length >3m
6301.3000	-棉制的毯子（电暖毯除外）及旅行毯	16	90	17	16	条/千克		-Blankets (other than electric blankets) and travelling rugs, of cotton
6301.4000	-合成纤维制的毯子（电暖毯除外）及旅行毯	17.5	130	17	16	条/千克		-Blankets (other than electric blankets) and travelling rugs, of synthetic fibres
6301.9000	-其他毯子及旅行毯	16	90	17	16	条/千克		-Other blankets and travelling rugs
6301.9000 10	人造纤维制的毯子及旅行毯（非电暖的）	16	90	17	16	条/千克		Blankets (other than electric blankets) and travelling rugs of artificial fibres
6301.9000 20	丝制毯子及旅行毯（非电暖的，含丝及绢丝 85% 及以上）	16	90	17	16	条/千克		Blankets (other than electric blankets) and travelling rugs of silk, containing≥85%, by weight of silk or spun silk
6301.9000 90	其他纺织材料制毯子及旅行毯（非电暖的）	16	90	17	16	条/千克		Other blankets (other than electric blankets) and travelling rugs, of other textile materials
63.02	床上、餐桌、盥洗及厨房用的织物制品：							**Bed linen, table linen, toilet linen and kitchen linen:**
	-针织或钩编的床上用织物制品：							-Bed linen, knitted or crocheted:
6302.1010	---棉制	14	90	17	16	条/千克		---Of cotton
6302.1090	---其他纺织材料制	14	130	17	16	条/千克		---Other
	-其他印花的床上用织物制品：							-Other bed linen, printed:
	--棉制：							--Of cotton:
6302.2110	---床单	14	90	17	16	条/千克		---Bed sheets
6302.2190	---其他	14	90	17	16	条/千克		---Other
6302.2190 10	棉制印花枕套	14	90	17	16	条/千克		Pillowcases, of cotton, printed
6302.2190 20	棉制印花枕罩	14	90	17	16	条/千克		Pillow cover, of cotton, printed
6302.2190 90	其他棉制印花床上用织物制品	14	90	17	16	条/千克		Other bed linen, of cotton, printed

税则号列	货品名称	最惠(%)	普通	增值税率	出口退税	计量单位	监管条件	Article Description
	--化学纤维制:							--Of man-made fibres:
6302.2210	---床单	16	130	17	16	条/千克		---Bed sheets
6302.2290	---其他	16	130	17	16	条/千克		---Other
6302.2290 10	化纤制印花枕套	16	130	17	16	条/千克		Pillowcases of man-made fibres, printed
6302.2290 20	化纤无纺织物制印花床用织物制品	16	130	17	16	条/千克		Bed linen, made up of nonwoven, of man-made fibres, printed
6302.2290 90	其他化纤制印花床上用织物制品	16	130	17	16	条/千克		Other bed linen of man-made fibres, printed
	--其他纺织材料制:							--Of other textile materials:
6302.2910	---丝及绢丝制	14	130	17	16	条/千克		---Of silk or spun silk
6302.2910 10	丝及绢丝制印花床上用织物制品(含丝85%及以上)	14	130	17	16	条/千克		Bed linen of silk or spun silk, containing ≥85% by weight of silk, printed
6302.2910 90	丝及绢丝制印花床上用织物制品(含丝85%以下)	14	130	17	16	条/千克		Bed linen of silk or spun silk, containing <85% by weight of silk, printed
6302.2920	---麻制	14	90	17	16	条/千克		---Of bast fibres
6302.2920 10	亚麻或苎麻制印花床上用织物制品	14	90	17	16	条/千克		Bed linen of flax or ramie, printed
6302.2920 90	其他麻制印花床上用织物制品	14	90	17	16	条/千克		Bed linen of other bast fibres, printed
6302.2990	---其他	14	100	17	16	条/千克		---Other
	-其他床上用织物制品:							-Other bed linen:
	--棉制:							--Of cotton:
6302.3110	---刺绣的	14	90	17	16	条/千克		---Embroidered
	---其他:							---Other:
6302.3191	----床单	14	90	17	16	条/千克		----Bed sheets
6302.3192	----毛巾被	14	90	17	16	条/千克		----Towelling coverlets
6302.3199	----其他	14	90	17	16	条/千克		----Other
6302.3199 10	棉制其他枕套	14	90	17	16	条/千克		Other pillowcases of cotton
6302.3199 20	其他棉与亚麻混纺床上用织物制品	14	90	17	16	条/千克		Other bed linen of blended fabrics, mixed with cotton and flax
6302.3199 30	棉制其他枕罩	14	90	17	16	条/千克		Other pillow cover of cotton
6302.3199 90	棉制其他床上用织物制品	14	90	17	16	条/千克		Other bed linen of cotton
	--化学纤维制:							--Of man-made fibres:
6302.3210	---刺绣的	16	130	17	16	条/千克		---Embroidered
6302.3290	---其他	16	130	17	16	条/千克		---Other
6302.3290 10	化纤制其他床单	16	130	17	16	条/千克		Bed sheets of man-made fibres
6302.3290 20	化纤制其他枕套	16	130	17	16	条/千克		Other pillowcases of man-made fibres
6302.3290 30	其他化纤无纺织物制床上织物制品	16	130	17	16	条/千克		Other bed linen of nonwoven fabrics, of man-made fibres
6302.3290 90	化纤制其他床上用织物制品	16	130	17	16	条/千克		Other bed linen, of man-made fibres
	--其他纺织材料制:							--Of other textile materials:
6302.3910	---丝及绢丝制	14	130	17	16	条/千克		---Of silk or spun silk
6302.3910 10	丝及绢丝制其他床上用织物制品(含丝85%及以上)	14	130	17	16	条/千克		Other bed linen of silk and spun silk, containing silk ≥85%
6302.3910 90	丝及绢丝制其他床上用织物制品(含丝85%以下)	14	130	17	16	条/千克		Other bed linen of silk and spun silk, containing silk <85%
	---麻制:							---Of bast fibres:
6302.3921	----刺绣的	14	90	17	16	条/千克		----Embroidered
6302.3921 10	亚麻或苎麻制其他床上用织物制品(刺绣的)	14	90	17	16	条/千克		Other bed linen of flax or ramie, embroidered
6302.3921 90	其他麻制其他床上用织物制品(刺绣的)	14	90	17	16	条/千克		Other bed linen of other bast fibres, embroidered
6302.3929	----其他	14	90	17	16	条/千克		----Other
6302.3929 10	亚麻或苎麻制其他床上用织物制品	14	90	17	16	条/千克		Other bed linen of flax or ramie
6302.3929 90	其他麻制其他床上用织物制品	14	90	17	16	条/千克		Other bed linen of other bast fibres
	---其他:							---Other:
6302.3991	----刺绣的	14	100	17	16	条/千克		----Embroidered
6302.3991 10	毛制刺绣床上用织物制品	14	100	17	16	条/千克		Other bed linen of wool or fine animal hair, embroidered

税则号列	货　品　名　称	最惠(%)	普通	增值税率	出口退税	计量单位	监管条件	Article Description
6302.3991 90	其他材料制刺绣床上用织物制品	14	100	17	16	条/千克		Other bed linen of other textile materials, embroidered
6302.3999	----其他	14	100	17	16	条/千克		----Other
6302.3999 10	毛制非刺绣床上用织物制品	14	100	17	16	条/千克		Other bed linen of wool or fine animal hair, embroidered
6302.3999 90	其他材料制其他床上用织物制品	14	100	17	16	条/千克		Other bed linen of other textile materials
	-针织或钩编的餐桌用织物制品:							-Table linen, knitted or crocheted:
6302.4010	---手工制	14	100	17	16	件/千克		---Hand-worked
6302.4010 10	手工棉制餐桌用织物制品(指针织或钩编类的)	14	100	17	16	件/千克		Table linen of cotton, hand-worked, knitted or crocheted
6302.4010 20	手工植物纺织纤维制餐桌用制品(指针织或钩编类的)	14	100	17	16	件/千克		Table linen of other vegetable textile fibres, hand-worked, knitted or crocheted
6302.4010 90	手工其他纺织材料制餐桌用制品(指针织或钩编类的)	14	100	17	16	件/千克		Other table linen of other textile materials, hand-worked, knitted or crocheted
6302.4090	---其他	14	100	17	16	件/千克		---Other
6302.4090 10	棉制餐桌用织物制品(针织或钩编的,非手工)	14	100	17	16	件/千克		Table linen, of cotton, knitted or crocheted, other than hand-worked
6302.4090 20	植物纺织纤维制的餐桌用织物制品(针织或钩编的,非手工)	14	100	17	16	件/千克		Table linen, of other vegetable textile fibres, knitted or crocheted, other than hand-worked
6302.4090 90	其他纺织材料制餐桌用织物制品(针织或钩编的,非手工)	14	100	17	16	件/千克		Table linen, of other textile materials, knitted or crocheted, other than hand-worked
	-其他餐桌用织物制品:							-Other table linen:
	--棉制:							--Of cotton:
6302.5110	---刺绣的	14	90	17	16	件/千克		---Embroidered
6302.5190	---其他	14	90	17	16	件/千克		---Other
	--化学纤维制:							--Of man-made fibres:
6302.5310	---刺绣的	14	130	17	16	件/千克		---Embroidered
6302.5390	---其他	16	130	17	16	件/千克		---Other
6302.5390 10	化纤无纺织物制餐桌用织物制品	16	130	17	16	件/千克		Table linen made up of nonwoven fabrics of man-made fibres
6302.5390 90	化纤制其他餐桌用织物制品	16	130	17	16	件/千克		Other table linen of man-made fibres
	--其他纺织材料制:							--Of other textile materials:
	---亚麻制:							---Of flax:
6302.5911	----刺绣的	14	90	17	16	件/千克		----Embroidered
6302.5919	----其他	14	90	17	16	件/千克		----Other
6302.5990	---其他	14	100	17	16	件/千克		---Other
6302.5990 10	羊毛或动物细毛制餐桌用织物制品	14	100	17	16	件/千克		Table linen of wool or other fine animal hair
6302.5990 90	其他纺织材料制餐桌用织物制品	14	100	17	16	件/千克		Table linen of other textile materials
	-盥洗及厨房用棉制毛巾织物或类似的毛圈织物的制品:							-Toilet linen and kitchen linen, of terry towelling or similar terry fabrics, of cotton:
6302.6010	---浴巾	14	90	17	16	条/千克		---Bath towels
6302.6010 10	棉制针织或钩编毛巾织物浴巾(含类似毛圈织物的制品)	14	90	17	16	条/千克		Bath towels, of terry towelling or similar terry fabrics, of cotton, knitted or crocheted
6302.6010 90	棉制非针织或非钩编毛巾织物浴巾(含类似毛圈织物的制品)	14	90	17	16	条/千克		Bath towels, of terry towelling or similar terry fabrics, of cotton, not knitted or crocheted
6302.6090	---其他	14	90	17	16	条/千克		---Other
6302.6090 11	棉制针织或钩编毛巾织物茶巾(包括类似毛圈织物的制品)	14	90	17	16	条/千克		Tea cloth, knitted or crocheted, of terry towelling or similar terry fabrics, of cotton
6302.6090 19	棉制非针织或非钩编毛巾织物茶巾(包括类似毛圈织物的制品)	14	90	17	16	条/千克		Tea cloth, not knitted or crocheted, of terry towelling or similar terry fabrics, of cotton
6302.6090 91	棉制其他盥洗及厨房用毛巾制品(包括类似毛圈织物的制品,针织或钩编)	14	90	17	16	条/千克		Other toilet linen and kitchen linen, of terry towelling or similar terry fabrics, of cotton, knitted or crocheted
6302.6090 99	棉制其他盥洗及厨房用毛巾制品(含类似毛圈织物的制品,非针织或非钩编)	14	90	17	16	条/千克		Other toilet linen and kitchen linen, of terry towelling or similar terry fabrics, of cotton, not knitted or crocheted
	-其他:							-Other:

税则号列	货品名称	最惠(%)	普通	增值税率	出口退税	计量单位	监管条件	Article Description
6302.9100	--棉制	14	90	17	16	条/千克		--Of cotton
6302.9100 10	棉制茶巾(毛巾织物或类似毛圈织物的除外)	14	90	17	16	条/千克		Tea cloth of cotton, other than of terry towelling or similar terry fabrics
6302.9100 20	棉制毛巾(毛巾织物或类似毛圈织物的除外)	14	90	17	16	条/千克		Towels of cotton, other than of terry towelling or similar terry fabrics
6302.9100 90	棉制其他盥洗及厨房织物制品(毛巾织物或类似毛圈织物的除外)	14	90	17	16	条/千克		Other toilet linen and kitchen linen of cotton, other than of terry towelling or similar terry fabrics
6302.9300	--化学纤维制	16	130	17	16	条/千克		--Of man-made fibres
6302.9300 10	化纤无纺织物制盥洗及厨房制品	16	130	17	16	条/千克		Toilet linen and kitchen linen of nonwoven fabrics of man - made fibres
6302.9300 90	化纤制其他盥洗及厨房织物制品	16	130	17	16	条/千克		Other toilet linen and kitchen linen of man - made fibres
	--其他纺织材料制:							--Of other textile materials:
6302.9910	---亚麻制	14	90	17	16	条/千克		---Of flax
6302.9990	---其他	14	100	17	16	条/千克		---Other
6302.9990 10	毛制盥洗及厨房用织物制品	14	100	17	16	条/千克		Other toilet linen and kitchen linen, of wool or fine animal hair
6302.9990 90	其他材料制盥洗及厨房织物制品	14	100	17	16	条/千克		Other toilet linen and kitchen linen of other textile materials
63.03	窗帘(包括帷帘)及帐幔;帘帷或床帷:							**Curtains (including drapes) and interior blinds; curtain or bed valances:**
	-针织或钩编的:							-Knitted or crocheted:
	--合成纤维制:							--Of synthetic fibres:
6303.1210	---针织的	16	130	17	16	千克		---Knitted
6303.1210 10	合纤制针织百叶窗、卷帘和窗幔	16	130	17	16	千克		Shutter, valance, roller shutter, of knitted, of synthetic fibres
6303.1210 90	其他合纤制针织窗帘等(包括帷帘,帐幔,帘帷及床帷)	16	130	17	16	千克		Curtains, of knitted, of synthetic fibres (including drapes, interior blinds, curtain and bed valances)
6303.1220	---钩编的	16	130	17	16	千克		---Crocheted
6303.1220 10	合纤制钩编百叶窗,卷帘和窗幔	16	130	17	16	千克		Shutter, valance, roller shutter, of crocheted, of synthetic fibres
6303.1220 90	其他合纤制钩编的窗帘等(包括帷帘,帐幔,帘帷及床帷)	16	130	17	16	千克		Other curtains of crocheted, of synthetic fibres etc (including drapes, inter, or blinds, curtain and bed valances)
	--其他纺织材料制:							--Of other textile materials:
	---棉制:							---Of cotton:
6303.1931	----针织的	14	90	17	16	千克		----Knitted
6303.1932	----钩编的	14	90	17	16	千克		----Crocheted
	---其他纺织材料制:							---Of other textile materials:
6303.1991	----针织的	14	130	17	16	千克		----Knitted
6303.1992	----钩编的	14	130	17	16	千克		----Crocheted
	-其他:							-Other:
6303.9100	--棉制	14	90	17	16	千克		--Of cotton
6303.9100 10	棉制非针织网眼窗帘(包括帷帘、帐幔、帘帷及床帷)	14	90	17	16	千克		Curtains (including drapes, interior blinds, curtain or bed valances) of cotton, nets, not knitted
6303.9100 90	棉制非针织非钩编窗帘(包括帷帘、帐幔、帘帷及床帷)	14	90	17	16	千克		Curtains (including drapes, interior blinds, curtain or bed valances) of cotton, nets, not knitted or crocheted
6303.9200	--合成纤维制	16	130	17	16	千克		--Of synthetic fibres
6303.9200 10	合纤百叶窗、卷帘和窗幔(非针织非钩编)	16	130	17	16	千克		Shutter, valance, roller shutter, of synthetic fibres, not knittedor crocheted
6303.9200 90	其他合纤制非针织非钩编窗帘等(包括帷帘、帐幔、帘帷及床帷)	16	130	17	16	千克		Curtains (including drapes) and interior blinds; curtain or bed valances, of synthetic fibres, not knitted or crocheted
6303.9900	--其他纺织材料制	14	100	17	16	千克		--Of other textile materials

税则号列	货品名称	最惠(%)	普通	增值税率	出口退税	计量单位	监管条件	Article Description
6303.9900 10	毛制非针织非钩编窗帘(包括帷帘、帐幔、帘帷及床帷)	14	100	17	16	千克		Curtains (including drapes, interior blinds, curtain or bed valances) not knitted or crocheted, of wool or fine animal hair
6303.9900 20	人造纤维制非针织非钩编窗帘(包括帷帘、帐幔、帘帷及床帷)	14	100	17	16	千克		Curtains (including drapes, interior blinds, curtain or bed valances) not knitted or crocheted, of artificial fibres
6303.9900 31	丝制非针织非钩编窗帘(包括帷帘、帐幔、帘帷及床帷,含丝85%及以上)	14	100	17	16	千克		Curtains (including drapes, interior blinds, curtain or bed valances) not knitted or crocheted, containing silk≥85%, of silk
6303.9900 39	丝制非针织非钩编窗帘(含帷帘、帐幔、帘帷及床帷,含丝85%以下)	14	100	17	16	千克		Curtains (including drapes, interior blinds, curtain or bed valances) not knitted or crocheted, containing silk <85%, of silk
6303.9900 40	其他纺织材料无纺织物制窗帘(包括帷帘、帐幔、帘帷及床帷)	14	100	17	16	千克		Curtains (including drapes, interior blinds, curtain or bed valances) of non-woven fabrics of other textile materials
6303.9900 50	亚麻或苎麻制非针织非钩编窗帘(包括帷帘、帐幔、帘帷及床帷)	14	100	17	16	千克		Curtains (including drapes, interior blinds, curtain or bed valances) not knitted or crocheted, of flax or ramie
6303.9900 60	其他纺织材料制非针织网眼窗帘(包括帷帘、帐幔、帘帷及床帷)	14	100	17	16	千克		Curtains (including drapes, interior blinds, curtain or bed valances) of other textile materials, not knitted, nets
6303.9900 90	其他纺织材料制非针织非钩编窗帘(包括帷帘、帐幔、帘帷及床帷)	14	100	17	16	千克		Curtains (including drapes, interior blinds, curtain or bed valances) of other textile materials, not knitted or crocheted
63.04	**其他装饰用织物制品,但税目94.04的货品除外:**							**Other furnishing articles, excluding those of heading No. 94.04:**
	-床罩:							-Bedspreads:
	--针织或钩编的:							--Knitted or crocheted:
	---针织的:							---Knitted:
6304.1121	----手工制	14	100	17	16	件/千克		----Hand-worked
6304.1121 10	棉制手工针织床罩	14	100	17	16	件/千克		Bedspreads, knitted, hand-worked, of cotton
6304.1121 20	化纤制手工针织床罩	14	100	17	16	件/千克		Bedspreads, knitted, hand-worked, of man-made fibres
6304.1121 90	其他纺织材料制手工针织床罩	14	100	17	16	件/千克		Bedspreads, knitted, hand-worked, of other textile materials
6304.1129	----其他	14	100	17	16	件/千克		----Other
6304.1129 10	棉制非手工针织床罩	14	100	17	16	件/千克		Bedspreads, knitted, other than hand-worked, of cotton
6304.1129 20	化纤制非手工针织床罩	14	100	17	16	件/千克		Bedspreads, knitted, other than hand-worked, of man-made fibres
6304.1129 90	其他纺织材料制非手工针织床罩	14	100	17	16	件/千克		Bedspreads, knitted, other than hand-worked, of other textile materials
	---钩编的:							---Crocheted:
6304.1131	----手工制	14	100	17	16	件/千克		----Hand-worked
6304.1131 10	棉制手工钩编床罩	14	100	17	16	件/千克		Bedspreads, crocheted, hand-worked, of cotton
6304.1131 20	化纤制手工钩编床罩	14	100	17	16	件/千克		Bedspreads, crocheted, hand-worked, of man-made fibres
6304.1131 90	其他纺织材料制手工钩编床罩	14	100	17	16	件/千克		Bedspreads, crocheted, hand-worked, of other textile materials
6304.1139	----其他	14	100	17	16	件/千克		----Other
6304.1139 10	棉制非手工钩编床罩	14	100	17	16	件/千克		Bedspreads, crocheted, other than hand-worked, of cotton
6304.1139 20	化纤制非手工钩编床罩	14	100	17	16	件/千克		Bedspreads, crocheted, other than hand-worked, of man-made fibres
6304.1139 90	其他纺织材料制非手工钩编床罩	14	100	17	16	件/千克		Bedspreads, crocheted, other than hand-worked, of other textile materials
	--其他:							--Other:
6304.1910	---丝及绢丝制	14	130	17	16	件/千克		---Of silk or spun silk

税则号列	货品名称	最惠(%)	普通	增值税率	出口退税	计量单位	监管条件	Article Description
6304.1910 10	丝及绢丝制非针织非钩编床罩(含丝85%及以上)	14	130	17	16	件/千克		Bedspreads of silk or spun silk, containing silk ≥ 85%, not knitted or crocheted
6304.1910 90	丝及绢丝制非针织非钩编床罩(含丝85%以下)	14	130	17	16	件/千克		Bedspreads of silk or spun silk, containing silk < 85%, not knitted or crocheted
	---棉或麻制:							---Of cotton or bast fibres:
6304.1921	----刺绣的	14	90	17	16	件/千克		----Embroidered
6304.1921 10	亚麻或苎麻制刺绣床罩(指非针织非钩编)	14	90	17	16	件/千克		Bedspreads, embroidered, not knitted or crocheted, of flax or ramie
6304.1921 20	其他麻制非针织非钩编刺绣床罩	14	90	17	16	件/千克		Bedspreads, embroidered, not knitted or crocheted, of other bast fibres
6304.1921 90	棉制非针织非钩编刺绣床罩	14	90	17	16	件/千克		Bedspreads, embroidered, not knitted or crocheted, of cotton
6304.1929	----其他	14	90	17	16	件/千克		----Other
6304.1929 10	亚麻或苎麻制非针织非钩编床罩	14	90	17	16	件/千克		Bedspreads, not knitted or crocheted, of flax or ramie
6304.1929 91	其他麻制其他非针织非钩编床罩	14	90	17	16	件/千克		Bedspreads, not knitted or crocheted, of other bast fibres
6304.1929 99	棉制其他非针织非钩编床罩	14	90	17	16	件/千克		Bedspreads, not knitted or crocheted, of cotton
	---化学纤维制:							---Of man-made fibres:
6304.1931	----刺绣的	16	130	17	16	件/千克		----Embroidered
6304.1939	----其他	16	130	17	16	件/千克		----Other
	---其他纺织材料制:							---Of other textile materials:
6304.1991	----刺绣的	14	100	17	16	件/千克		----Embroidered
6304.1991 10	毛制非针织非钩编刺绣床罩(羊毛或动物细毛制)	14	100	17	16	件/千克		Bedspreads, not knitted or crocheted, embroidered, of wool or fine animal hair
6304.1991 90	其他纺织材料制非针织刺绣床罩(含非钩编的)	14	100	17	16	件/千克		Bedspreads, not knitted or crocheted, embroidered, of other textile materials
6304.1999	----其他	14	100	17	16	件/千克		----Other
6304.1999 10	毛制其他非针织非钩编床罩(羊毛或动物细毛制)	14	100	17	16	件/千克		Bedspreads, not knitted or crocheted, embroidered, of wool or fine animal hair
6304.1999 90	其他材料制非针织非钩编其他床罩	14	100	17	16	件/千克		Bedspreads, not knitted or crocheted, embroidered, of other textile materials
	-其他:							-Other:
	--针织或钩编的:							--Knitted or crocheted:
	---针织的:							---Knitted:
6304.9121	----手工制	14	100	17	16	千克		----Hand-worked
6304.9121 10	棉制手工针织的其他装饰制品	14	100	17	16	千克		Other furnishing articles, knitted, hand-worked, of cotton
6304.9121 20	毛制手工针织的其他装饰制品(羊毛或动物细毛制)	14	100	17	16	千克		Other furnishing articles, knitted, hand-worked, of wool or fine animal hair
6304.9121 31	丝制手工针织的其他装饰制品(含丝85%及以上)	14	100	17	16	千克		Other furnishing articles, knitted, hand-worked, containing silk≥85%
6304.9121 39	丝制手工针织的其他装饰制品(含丝85%以下)	14	100	17	16	千克		Other furnishing articles, knitted, hand-worked, containing silk > 85%
6304.9121 40	化纤制手工针织的其他装饰制品	14	100	17	16	千克		Other furnishing articles, knitted, hand-worked, of man-made fibres
6304.9121 90	其他纺织材料制手工针织其他装饰制品	14	100	17	16	千克		Other furnishing articles, knitted, hand-worked, of other textile materials
6304.9129	----其他	14	100	17	16	千克		----Other
6304.9129 10	棉制非手工针织的其他装饰制品	14	100	17	16	千克		Other furnishing articles, knitted, not hand-worked, of cotton
6304.9129 20	毛制非手工针织的其他装饰制品(羊毛或动物细毛制)	14	100	17	16	千克		Other furnishing articles, knitted, not hand-worked, of wool or fine animal hair
6304.9129 31	丝制非手工针织的其他装饰制品(含丝85%及以上)	14	100	17	16	千克		Other furnishing articles, knitted, not hand-worked, containing silk≥85%
6304.9129 39	丝制非手工针织的其他装饰制品(含丝85%以下)	14	100	17	16	千克		Other furnishing articles, knitted, not hand-worked, containing silk < 85%

税则号列	货品名称	最惠(%)	普通	增值税率	出口退税	计量单位	监管条件	Article Description
6304.9129 40	化纤制非手工针织其他装饰制品	14	100	17	16	千克		Other furnishing articles, knitted, not hand-worked, of man-made fibres
6304.9129 90	其他纺织材料制非手工针织其他装饰制品	14	100	17	16	千克		Other furnishing articles, knitted, not hand-worked, of other textile materials
	---钩编的:							---Crocheted:
6304.9131	----手工制	14	100	17	16	千克		----Hand-worked
6304.9131 10	棉制手工钩编的其他装饰制品	14	100	17	16	千克		Other furnishing articles, crocheted, hand-worked, of cotton
6304.9131 20	毛制手工钩编的其他装饰制品(羊毛或动物细毛制)	14	100	17	16	千克		Other furnishing articles, crocheted, hand-worked, of wool or fine animal hair
6304.9131 31	丝制手工钩编的其他装饰制品(含丝85%及以上)	14	100	17	16	千克		Other furnishing articles of silk, crocheted, hand-worked, containing silk≥85%
6304.9131 39	丝制手工钩编的其他装饰制品(含丝85%以下)	14	100	17	16	千克		Other furnishing articles of silk, crocheted, hand-worked, containing silk <85%
6304.9131 40	化纤制手工钩编的其他装饰制品	14	100	17	16	千克		Other furnishing articles, crocheted, hand-worked, of man-made fibres
6304.9131 90	其他制手工钩编的其他材料装饰制品	14	100	17	16	千克		Other furnishing articles, crocheted, hand-worked, of other textile materials
6304.9139	----其他	14	100	17	16	千克		----Other
6304.9139 10	棉制非手工钩编的其他装饰制品	14	100	17	16	千克		Other furnishing articles, crocheted, not hand-worked, of cotton
6304.9139 20	毛制非手工钩编的其他装饰制品(羊毛或动物细毛制)	14	100	17	16	千克		Other furnishing articles, crocheted, not hand-worked, of wool or fine animal hair
6304.9139 31	丝制非手工钩编的其他装饰制品(含丝85%及以上)	14	100	17	16	千克		Other furnishing articles of silk, crocheted, not hand-worked, containing silk≥85%
6304.9139 39	丝制非手工钩编的其他装饰制品(含丝85%以下)	14	100	17	16	千克		Other furnishing articles of silk, crocheted, not hand-worked, containing silk <85%
6304.9139 40	化纤制非手工钩编其他装饰制品	14	100	17	16	千克		Other furnishing articles, crocheted, not hand-worked, of man-made fibres
6304.9139 90	其他纺织材料制非手工钩编其他装饰品	14	100	17	16	千克		Other furnishing articles, crocheted, not hand-worked, of other textile materials
	--非针织或非钩编的,棉制:							--Not knitted or crocheted, of cotton:
6304.9210	---刺绣的	14	90	17	16	千克		---Embroidered
6304.9290	---其他	14	90	17	16	千克		---Other
	--非针织或非钩编的,合成纤维制:							--Not knitted or crocheted, of synthetic fibres:
6304.9310	---刺绣的	16	130	17	16	千克		---Embroidered
6304.9390	---其他	16	130	17	16	千克		---Other
	--非针织或非钩编的,其他纺织材料制:							--Not knitted or crocheted, of other textile materials:
6304.9910	---丝及绢丝制	14	130	17	16	千克		---Of silk or spun silk
6304.9910 10	丝制非针织非钩编的装饰制品(含绢丝制品,含丝85%及以上)	14	130	17	16	千克		Other furnishing articles of silk or spun silk, not knitted or crocheted, containing silk≥85%
6304.9910 90	丝制非针织非钩编的装饰制品(含绢丝制品,含丝85%以下)	14	130	17	16	千克		Other furnishing articles of silk or spun silk, not knitted or crocheted, containing silk <85%
	---麻制:							---Of bast fibres:
6304.9921	----刺绣的	14	90	17	16	千克		----Embroidered
6304.9921 10	亚麻或苎麻非针织其他刺绣装饰品(含非钩编制品)	14	90	17	16	千克		Other furnishing articles, not knitted or crocheted, embroidered, of flax or ramie
6304.9921 90	其他麻制非针织其他刺绣装饰品(包括非钩编的)	14	90	17	16	千克		Other furnishing articles, not knitted or crocheted, embroidered, of other bast fibres
6304.9929	----其他	14	90	17	16	千克		----Other
6304.9929 10	亚麻或苎麻制其他非针织的装饰品(含非钩编制品)	14	90	17	16	千克		Other furnishing articles, not knitted or crocheted, of flax or ramie
6304.9929 90	其他麻制其他非针织的装饰制品(含非钩编制品)	14	90	17	16	千克		Other furnishing articles not knitted or crocheted, of other bast fibres
6304.9990	---其他	14	100	17	16	千克		---Other

税则号列	货品名称	最惠(%)	普通	增值税率	出口退税	计量单位	监管条件	Article Description
6304.9990 10	毛制非针织非钩编装饰制品(羊毛或动物细毛制)	14	100	17	16	千克		Other furnishing articles, not knitted or crocheted, of wool or fine animal hair
6304.9990 20	人造纤维制非针织非钩编装饰品	14	100	17	16	千克		Other furnishing articles, not knitted or crocheted, of man-made fibres
6304.9990 90	其他材料制非针织非钩编装饰品	14	100	17	16	千克		Other furnishing articles, not knitted or crocheted, of other textile materials
63.05	货物包装用袋:							**Sacks and bags, of a kind used for the packing of goods:**
6305.1000	-黄麻或税目53.03的其他韧皮纺织纤维制	10	40	17	16	条/千克		-Of jute or of other textile bast fibres of heading No. 53.03
6305.1000 10	黄麻制旧的货物包装袋(含品目5303的其他韧皮纤维制)	10	40	17	16	条/千克		Sacks and bags, of a kind used for the packing of goods, of jute or of other textile bast fibres of heading No. 53.03
6305.1000 90	黄麻制其他货物包装袋(含品目5303的其他韧皮纤维制)	10	40	17	16	条/千克		Other sacks and bags, of a kind used for the packing of goods, of jute or of other textile bast fibres of heading No. 53.03
6305.2000	-棉制	16	90	17	16	条/千克		-Of cotton
	-化学纤维材料制:							-Of man-made textile materials:
6305.3200	--散装货物储运软袋	16	100	17	16	条/千克		--Flexible intermediate bulk containers
6305.3200 11	聚乙烯或聚丙烯制软袋(针织或钩编的,用扁条及类似材料制成,散装货物周转用)	16	100	17	16	条/千克		Sacks and bags, of a kind used for the packing of goods, flexible intermediate bulk containers of PE or PP strip or the like, knitted or crocheted
6305.3200 19	聚乙烯或聚丙烯制软袋(非针织或钩编的,扁条及类似材料制成,散装货物周转用)	16	100	17	16	条/千克		Sacks and bags, of a kind used for the packing of goods, flexible intermediate bulk containers of PE or PP strip or the like, not knited or crocheted
6305.3200 90	化纤制的散装货物周转软袋	16	100	17	16	条/千克		Sacks and bags, of a kind used for the packing of goods, flexible intermediate bulk containers, of man-made fibres
6305.3300	--其他,聚乙烯、聚丙烯扁条或类似材料制	16	100	17	16	条/千克		--Other, of polyethylene or polypropylene strip or the like
6305.3300 10	聚乙烯或聚丙烯制其他货物包装袋(针织或钩编的,用扁条及类似材料制成)	16	100	17	16	条/千克		Sacks and bags, of a kind used for the packing of goods, of PE or PP strip or the like, knitted or crocheted
6305.3300 90	聚乙烯或聚丙烯制其他货物包装袋(非针织或钩编的,用扁条及类似材料制成)	16	100	17	16	条/千克		Sacks and bags, of a kind used for the packing of goods, of PE or PP strip or the like, not knitted or crocheted
6305.3900	--其他	16	100	17	0	条/千克		--Other
6305.9000	-其他纺织材料制	14	90	17	16	条/千克		-Of other textile materials
6305.9000 11	亚麻制旧货物包装袋(针织或钩编的)	14	90	17	16	条/千克		Sacks and bags, of a kind used for the packing of goods, of flax, knitted or crocheted
6305.9000 19	其他亚麻制旧货物包装袋	14	90	17	16	条/千克		Sacks and bags, of a kind used for the packing of goods of flax, not knitted or crocheted
6305.9000 90	其他纺织材料制其他货物包装袋	14	90	17	16	条/千克		Other sacks and bags, of a kind used for the packing of goods, of other textile materials
63.06	油苫布、天篷及遮阳篷;帐篷;风帆;野营用品:							**Tarpaulins, awnings and sunblinds; tents; sails for boats, sailboards or landcraft; camping goods:**
	-油苫布、天篷及遮阳篷:							-Tarpaulins, awnings and sunblinds:
6306.1200	--合成纤维制	16	130	17	16	件/千克		--Of synthetic fibres
	--其他纺织材料制:							--Of other textile materials:
6306.1910	---麻制	14	80	17	16	件/千克		---Of bast fibres
6306.1920	---棉制	14	80	17	16	件/千克		---Of cotton
6306.1990	---其他	14	100	17	16	件/千克		---Other
6306.1990 10	人造纤维制油苫布、天篷及遮阳篷	14	100	17	16	件/千克		Tarpaulins, awnings and sunblinds, of artificial fibres
6306.1990 90	其他材料制油苫布、天篷及遮阳篷	14	100	17	16	件/千克		Tarpaulins, awnings and sunblinds, of other textile materials

税则号列	货 品 名 称	最惠(%)	普通	增值税率	出口退税	计量单位	监管条件	Article Description
	-帐篷:							-Tents:
6306.2200	--合成纤维制	16	130	17	16	件/千克		--Of synthetic fibres
6306.2200 10	合纤制移动帐篷	16	130	17	16	件/千克		Moveable, of synthetic fibres
6306.2200 90	合纤制帐篷	16	130	17	16	件/千克		Other tents of synthetic fibres:
	--其他纺织材料制:							--Of other textile materials:
6306.2910	---棉制	14	80	17	16	件/千克		---Of cotton
6306.2990	---其他	14	100	17	16	件/千克		---Other
	-风帆:							-Sails:
6306.3010	---合成纤维制	16	130	17	16	件/千克		---Of synthetic fibres
6306.3090	---其他纺织材料制	14	100	17	16	件/千克		---Of other textile materials
	-充气褥垫:							-Pneumatic mattresses:
6306.4010	---棉制	14	80	17	16	件/千克		--Of cotton
6306.4020	---化学纤维制	16	130	17	16	件/千克		---Of man-made fibres
6306.4090	---其他纺织材料制	14	100	17	16	件/千克		---Of other textile materials
	-其他:							-Other:
6306.9010	--棉制	14	80	17	16	件/千克		--Of cotton
6306.9020	---麻制	14	80	17	16	件/千克		---Of bast fibres
6306.9030	---化学纤维制	16	130	17	16	件/千克		---Of man-made fibres
6306.9090	---其他	14	100	17	16	件/千克		---Other
63.07	**其他制成品,包括服装裁剪样:**							**Other made up articles, including dress patterns:**
6307.1000	-擦地布、擦碗布、抹布及类似擦拭用布	14	130	17	16	千克		-Floor-cloths, dish-cloths, dusters and similar cleaning cloths
6307.2000	-救生衣及安全带	14	70	17	16	千克/件		-Life-jackets and life-belts
6307.9000	-其他	14	100	17	16	千克		-Other
6307.9000 11	棉制标签、服饰辫线及流苏(含紧身胸衣、鞋及类似品的系带)	14	100	17	16	千克		Label, chain-off thread and fringes, including laces of corsets, shoelaces and similar articles, of cotton
6307.9000 19	其他制标签、服饰辫线及流苏(含紧身胸衣、鞋及类似品的系带)	14	100	17	16	千克		Label, chain-off thread and fringes, including laces of corsets, shoelaces and similar articles, of other textile materials
6307.9000 20	棉制起绒或簇绒织物制毛巾	14	100	17	16	千克		Towel, made up of napping or tufted, of cotton
6307.9000 30	棉制枕壳	14	100	17	16	千克		Outershell of pillow, of cotton
6307.9000 40	棉制被壳、羽绒被壳、盖被壳(含类似品,含棉85%以下)	14	100	17	16	千克		Outershell of down quilt or comforter, of cotton, containing cotton <85%
6307.9000 51	棉制手术用巾及其他毛巾	14	100	17	16	千克		Towel for operation and other towel, of cotton
6307.9000 59	化学纤维制未列名毛巾	14	100	17	16	千克		Towel of man-made fibres, not elsewhere specified or included
6307.9000 61	以棉做面的冷藏包	14	100	17	16	千克		Cotton facing refrigerating bag
6307.9000 62	以化纤纺织材料做面的冷藏包	14	100	17	16	千克		Man-made textile materials facing refrigerating bag
6307.9000 69	其他纺织材料做面的冷藏包	14	100	17	16	千克		Other textile materials facing refrigerating bag
6307.9000 90	纺织材料制未列名制品	14	100	17	16	千克		Other made up articles, not elsewhere specified or included, of other textile materials
	第二分章 成套物品							Ⅱ. -SETS
63.08	**由机织物及纱线构成的零售包装成套物品,不论是否带附件,用以制作小地毯、装饰毯、绣花台布、餐巾或类似的纺织物品:**							**Sets consisting of woven fabric and yarn, whether or not with accessories, for making up into rugs, tapestries, embroidered table cloths or serviettes, or similar textile articles, put up in packings for retail sale:**
6308.0000	由机织物及纱线构成的零售包装成套物品,不论是否带附件,用以制作小地毯、装饰毯、绣花台布、餐巾或类似的纺织物品	14	130	17	16	千克		Sets consisting of woven fabric and yarn, whether or not with accessories, for making up into rugs, tapestries, embroidered table cloths or serviettes, or similar textile articles, put up in packings for retail sale
6308.0000 10	机织物及纱线制零售包装成套物品(内含羊毛纱的)	14	130	17	16	千克		Sets consisting of woven fabric and yarn, containing wool yarn, put up in packings for retail sale

税则号列	货品名称	最惠(%)	普通	增值税率	出口退税	计量单位	监管条件	Article Description
6308.0000 20	机织物及纱线制零售包装成套物品(由普通棉机织物及棉绗缝被褥织物与纱线构成的)	14	130	17	16	千克		Sets consisting of woven fabric, guilted textile products by stitching and yarn, of cotton, put up in packings for retail sale
6308.0000 30	机织物及纱线制零售包装成套物品(由合成纤维普通机织物及绗缝被褥织物与纱线构成)	14	130	17	16	千克		Sets consisting of woven fabric, guilted textile products by stitching and yarn, of synthetic fibres, put up in packings for retail sale
6308.0000 90	其他机织物及纱线构成的成套物品(零售包装的)	14	130	17	16	千克		Other sets consisting of woven fabric and yarn, put up in packing for retail sale
	第三分章　旧衣着及旧纺织品;碎织物							Ⅲ.-WORN CLOTHING AND WORN TEXTILE ARTICLES; RAGS
63.09	旧衣物:							**Worn clothing and other worn articles:**
6309.0000	旧衣物	14	130	17	16	千克	9	Worn clothing and other worn articles
63.10	**纺织材料的新的或旧的碎织物及废线、绳、索、缆及其制品:**							**Used or new rags, scrap twine, cordage, rope and cables and worn out articles of twine, cordage, rope or cables, of textile materials:**
6310.1000	-经分拣的	14	50	17	16	千克		-Sorted
6310.1000 10	新的或未使用过的纺织材料制经分拣的碎织物等(新的或未使用过的,包括废线、绳、索、缆及其制品)	14	50	17	0	千克	AP	Not used or new rags, scrap twine, cordage, rope and cables and worn out articles of twine, cordage, rope or cables, of textile materials, sorted
6310.1000 90	其他纺织材料制经分拣的碎织物等(包括废线、绳、索、缆及其制品)	14	50	17	0	千克	9	
6310.9000	-其他	14	50	17	16	千克		-Other
6310.9000 10	新的或未使用过的纺织材料制其他碎织物等(新的或未使用过的,包括废线、绳、索、缆及其制品)	14	50	17	16	千克	AP	Not used or new rags, scrap twine, cordage, rope and cables and worn out articles of twine, cordage, rope or cables, of textile materials
6310.9000 90	其他纺织材料制碎织物等(包括废线、绳、索、缆及其制品)	14	50	17	16	千克	9	Other rags, scrap twine, cordage, rope and cables and worn out articles of twine, cordage, rope or cables, of textile materials

第十二类
鞋、帽、伞、杖、鞭及其零件；已加工的羽毛及其制品；人造花；人发制品

SECTION Ⅻ
FOOTWEAR, HEADGEAR, UMBRELLAS, SUN UMBRELLAS, WALKING-STICKS, SEAT-STICKS, WHIPS, RIDING-CROPS AND PARTS THEREOF; PREPARED FEATHERS AND ARTICLES MADE THEREWITH; ARTIFICIAL FLOWERS; ARTICLES OF HUMAN HAIR

第六十四章
鞋靴、护腿和类似品及其零件

注释：

一、本章不包括：

（一）易损材料（例如，纸、塑料薄膜）制的无外绱鞋底的一次性鞋靴罩或套，这些产品应按其构成材料归类；

（二）纺织材料制的鞋靴，没有用粘、缝或其他方法将外底固定或安装在鞋面上的（第十一类）；

（三）税目63.09的旧鞋靴；

（四）石棉制品（税目68.12）；

（五）矫形鞋靴或其他矫形器具及其零件（税目90.21）；

（六）玩具鞋及装有冰刀或轮子的滑冰鞋；护胫或类似的运动防护服装（第九十五章）。

二、税目64.06所称"零件"，不包括鞋钉、护鞋铁掌、鞋眼、鞋钩、鞋扣、饰物、编带、鞋带、绒球或其他装饰带（应分别归入相应税目）及税目96.06的钮扣或其他货品。

三、本章所称：

（一）"橡胶"及"塑料"，包括能用肉眼辨出其外表有一层橡胶或塑料的机织物或其他纺织产品，运用本款时，橡胶或塑料仅引起颜色变化的不计在内；

（二）"皮革"，是指税目41.07及41.12至41.14的货品。

四、除本章注释三另有规定的以外：

（一）鞋面的材料应以占表面面积最大的那种材料为准，计算表面面积可不考虑附件及加固件，例如，护踝、裹边、饰物、扣子、拉襻、鞋眼或类似附属件。

（二）外底的主要材料应以与地面接触最广的那种材料为准，计算接触面时可不考虑鞋底钉、铁掌或类似附属件；

子目注释：

子目6402.12、6402.19、6403.12、6403.19及6404.11所称"运动鞋靴"，仅适用于：

一、带有或可装鞋底钉、止滑柱、夹钳、马蹄掌或类似品的体育专用鞋靴。

二、滑冰靴，滑雪靴及越野滑雪用鞋靴、滑雪板靴、角力靴、拳击靴及赛车鞋。

Chapter 64
Footwear, gaiters and the like; parts of such articles

Notes:

1. This Chapter does not cover:

(a) Disposable foot or shoe coverings of flimsy material (for example, paper, sheeting of plastics) without applied soles. These products are classified according to their constituent material;

(b) Footwear of textile material, without an outer sole glued, sewn or otherwise affixed or applied to the upper (Section Ⅺ);

(c) Worn footwear of heading No. 63.09;

(d) Articles of asbestos (heading No. 68.12);

(e) Orthopaedic footwear or other orthopaedic appliances, or parts thereof (heading No. 90.21) or;

(f) Toy footwear or skating boots with ice or roller skates attached; shin-guards or similar protective sportswear (Chapter 95).

2. For the purposes of heading No. 64.06, the term "parts" does not include pegs, protectors, eyelets, hooks, buckles, ornaments, braid, laces, pompons or other trimmings (which are to be classified in their appropriate headings) or buttons or other goods of heading No. 96.06.

3. For the purposes of this Chapter:

(a) the terms "rubber" and "plastics" include woven fabrics or other textile products with an external layer of rubber or plastics being visible to the naked eye; for the purpose of this provision, no account should be taken of any resulting change of colour;

(b) the term "leather" refers to the goods of headings No. 41.07 and 41.12 to 41.14.

4. Subject to Note 3 to this Chapter:

(a) the material of the upper shall be taken to be the constituent material having the greatest external surface area, no account being taken of accessories or reinforcements such as ankle patches, edging, ornamentation, buckles, tabs, eyelet stays or similar attachments;

(b) the constituent material of the outer sole shall be taken to be the material having the greatest surface area in contact with the ground, no account being taken of accessories or reinforcements such as spikes, bars, nails, protectors or similar attachments.

Subheading Notes:

For the purposes of subheadings No. 6402.12, 6402.19, 6403.12, 6403.19 and 6404.11, the expression "sports footwear" applies only to:

(1) footwear which is designed for a sporting activity and has, or has provision for the attachment of, spikes, sprigs, stops, clips, bars or the like;

(2) skating boots, ski-boots and cross-country ski footwear, snowboard boots, wrestling boots, boxing boots and cycling shoes.

税则号列	货品名称	最惠(%)	普通	增值税率	出口退税	计量单位	监管条件	Article Description
64.01	橡胶或塑料制外底及鞋面的防水鞋靴，其鞋面不是用缝、铆、钉、旋、塞或类似方法固定在鞋底上的：							**Waterproof footwear with outer soles and uppers of rubber or of plastics, the uppers of which are neither fixed to the sole nor assembled by stitching, riveting, nailing, screwing, plugging or similar processes:**
	-装有金属防护鞋头的鞋靴：							-Footwear incorporating a protective metal toe-cap:
6401.1010	---橡胶制鞋面的	24	100	17	16	千克/双		---With uppers of rubber
6401.1090	---塑料制鞋面的	24	100	17	15	千克/双		---With uppers of plastics
	-其他鞋靴：							-Other footwear:
	--中、短统靴(过踝但未到膝)：							--Covering the ankle but not covering the knee:
6401.9210	---橡胶制鞋面的	24	100	17	15	千克/双		---With uppers of rubber
6401.9290	---塑料制鞋面的	24	100	17	15	千克/双		---With uppers of plastics
6401.9900	--其他	24	100	17	15	千克/双		--Other
64.02	橡胶或塑料制外底及鞋面的其他鞋靴：							**Other footwear with outer soles and uppers of rubber or plastics:**
	-运动鞋靴：							-Sports footwear:
6402.1200	--滑雪靴、越野滑雪鞋靴及滑雪板靴	10	100	17		千克/双		--Ski-boots, cross-country ski footwear and snow-board boots
6402.1200 10	含濒危动物毛皮橡胶、塑料底及面滑雪靴(包括越野滑雪鞋靴及滑雪板靴)	10	100	17	15	千克/双	EF	Inverted skiing boot with rubber、plastic sole and hair of endangered animals(including cross-counory skiing boots and boots for skin)
6402.1200 90	其他橡胶、塑料底及面滑雪靴(包括越野滑雪鞋靴及滑雪板靴)	10	100	17	0	千克/双		Other ski-boots cross-country ski footwear and snoroboard boots, with outer soles and upper of rubber or plastics
6402.1900	--其他	24	100	17		千克/双		--Other
6402.1900 10	含濒危动物毛皮其他运动鞋靴(橡胶、塑料制底及面)	24	100	17	15	千克/双	EF	Other sports shoes and boots containing endangered animal hair and hide (rubbor and plastic shoes and inverced)
6402.1900 90	橡胶、塑料制底及面的其他运动鞋靴	24	100	17	0	千克/双		Other sport footwear, with outer soles and uppers of rubber or plastics (rubber and plastic shoes and inverted)
6402.2000	-用栓塞方法将鞋面条带装配在鞋底上的鞋	24	100	17	15	千克/双		-Footwear with upper straps or thongs assembled to the sole by means of plugs
	-其他鞋靴：							-Other footwear:
6402.9100	--短筒靴(过踝)	24	100	17	15	千克/双		--Covering the ankle
	--其他：							--Other:
6402.9910	---橡胶制鞋面的	24	100	17	15	千克/双		---With uppers of rubber
	---塑料制鞋面的：							---With uppers of plastics:
6402.9921	----其他以机织物或其它纺织材料做衬底的	24	100	17	15	千克/双		----With substrate of woven fabrics or other textile materials
6402.9929	----其他	24	100	17	15	千克/双		----Other
64.03	橡胶、塑料、皮革或再生皮革制外底，皮革制鞋面的鞋靴：							**Footwear with outer soles of rubber, plastics, leather or composition leather and upers of leather:**
	-运动鞋靴：							-Sports footwear:
6403.1200	--滑雪靴、越野滑雪鞋靴及滑雪板靴	24	100	17	15	千克/双		--Ski-boots, cross-country ski footwear and snow-board boots
6403.1200 10	野生动物皮革制鞋面的滑雪靴	24	100	17	15	千克/双	EF	Ski-boots, with uppers of leather of wild animals
6403.1200 90	其他皮革制鞋面的滑雪靴(包括橡胶、塑料、皮革制外底和越野滑雪鞋靴及板靴)	24	100	17	15	千克/双		Ski-boots, cross-country sik footwear and snowboard boots, with outer soles of rubber, plastics, leather or composition leather and upers of leather
6403.1900	--其他	15	100	17	15	千克/双		--Other
6403.1900 10	野生动物皮革制鞋面其他运动鞋靴	15	100	17	15	千克/双	EF	Other sports footwear with uppers of leather of wild animals

税则号列	货品名称	最惠(%)	普通	增值税率	出口退税	计量单位	监管条件	Article Description
6403.1900 90	皮革制鞋面的其他运动鞋靴(橡胶、塑料、皮革或再生皮革制外底)	15	100	17	15	千克/双		Other sports footwear with outer soles of rubber, plastics, leather or composition leather and uppers of leather
6403.2000	-皮革制外底,由交叉于脚背并绕大脚趾的皮革条带构成鞋面的鞋	24	100	17	15	千克/双		-Footwear with outer soles of leather, and uppers which consist of leather straps across the instep and around the big toe
6403.2000 10	野生动物皮革条带为鞋面的皮底鞋	24	100	17	15	千克/双	EF	Footwear with outer soles of leather and with uppers of leather straps of wild animals
6403.2000 90	其他皮革条带为鞋面的皮底鞋(皮革条带交叉于脚背并绕大脚趾的)	24	100	17	15	千克/双		Footwear with outer soles of leather and with uppers which consist of leather straps across the instep and around the big toe
6403.4000	-装有金属防护鞋头的其他鞋靴	24	100	17	15	千克/双		-Other footwear, incorporating a protective metal toe-cap
6403.4000 10	其他含野生动物皮革面鞋靴(装有金属护鞋头的)	24	100	17	15	千克/双	FE	Other footwear, incorporating a protective metal toe-cap with uppers of leather of wild animals
6403.4000 90	装有金属护鞋头的其他皮革面鞋靴(橡胶、塑料、皮革或再生皮革制外底)	24	100	17	15	千克/双		Other footwear, incorporating a protective metal toe-cap, with outer soles of rubber, plastics, leather or composition leather and uppers of leather
	-皮革制外底的其他鞋靴:							-Other footwear with outer soles of leather:
	--短统靴(过踝):							--Covering the ankle:
	---过脚踝但低于小腿的短统靴,按内底长度分类:							---Covering the ankle but not covering the calf, by length of inner soles:
6403.5111	----小于24cm的	10	100	17	15	千克/双		----Less than 24cm
6403.5111 10	野生动物皮革制外底皮革面过脚踝但低于小腿的短筒靴(内底长度小于24cm,运动用靴除外)	10	100	17	15	千克/双	FE	Other footwear with outer soles of leather and uppers of leather, covering the ankle but lower than crus, with uppers of leather of wild animals (inner sole length <24cm, other than sports boots)
6403.5111 90	皮革制外底皮革面过脚踝但低于小腿的短筒靴(内底长度小于24cm,运动用靴除外)	10	100	17	15	千克/双		Footwear, with outer soles of leather and uppers of leather, covering the ankle but lower than crus, with uppers of leather (inner sole length < 24cm, other than sports boots)
6403.5119	----其他	10	100	17	15	千克/双		----Other
6403.5119 10	其他野生动物皮革制外底皮革面过脚踝但低于小腿短筒靴(运动用靴除外)	10	100	17	15	千克/双	EF	Other footwear with outer soles of leather and uppers of leather, covering the ankle but lower than crus, with uppers of leather of wild animals, other than sports footwear
6403.5119 90	其他皮革制外底皮革面过脚踝但低于小腿短筒靴(运动用靴除外)	10	100	17	15	千克/双		Other footwear with outer soles of leather and uppers of leather, covering the ankle but lower than crus, other than sports footwear
	---其他,按内底长度分类:							---Other, by length of inner soles:
6403.5191	----小于24cm的	10	100	17	15	千克/双		----Less than 24cm
6403.5191 10	野生动物皮革制外底皮革面短筒靴(内底长度小于24cm,运动用靴除外)	10	100	17	15	千克/双	EF	Footwear with outer soles of leather and uppers of leather, covering the ankle, with uppers of leather of wild animals (inner soles < 24cm, other than sports footwear)
6403.5191 90	皮革制外底的皮革面短筒靴(过踝)(内底长度小于24cm,运动用靴除外)	10	100	17	15	千克/双		Footwear with outer soles of leather and uppers of leather, covering the ankle (inner soles < 24cm other than sports footwear)
6403.5199	----其他	10	100	17	15	千克/双		----Other
6403.5199 10	野生动物皮革制外底皮革面短筒靴(运动用靴除外)	10	100	17	15	千克/双	FE	Footwear with outer soles of leather and uppers of leather, covering the ankle, with uppers of leather of wild animals (other than sports footwear)
6403.5199 90	皮革制外底的皮革面短筒靴(过踝)(运动用靴除外)	10	100	17	15	千克/双		Footwear with outer soles of leather and uppers of leather, covering the ankle, with uppers of leather (other than sports footwear)
6403.5900	--其他	10	100	17	15	千克/双		--Other

税则号列	货品名称	最惠(%)	普通	增值税率	出口退税	计量单位	监管条件	Article Description
6403.5900 10	野生动物皮革制外底皮革面其他鞋(包括靴,运动用鞋靴除外)	10	100	17	15	千克/双	EF	Other footwear with outer soles of leather and upers of leather of wild animals (other than sports footwear)
6403.5900 90	皮革制外底的皮革面其他鞋靴(运动用鞋靴除外)	10	100	17	15	千克/双		Other footwear with outer soles of leather and upers of leather of other animals (other than sports footwear)
	-其他鞋靴:							-Other footwear:
	--短筒靴(过踝):							--Covering the ankle:
	---过脚踝但低于小腿的短筒靴,按内底长度分类:							---Covering the ankle but not covering the calf, by length of inner soles
6403.9111	----小于24cm的	10	100	17	15	千克/双		----Less than 24cm
6403.9111 10	其他野生动物皮革制面过脚踝但低于小腿的短筒靴(内底<24cm,橡胶、塑料、再生皮革制外底,运动用靴除外)	10	100	17	15	千克/双	EF	Footwear with outer uper of feather, covering the ankle but lower than crus, with upers of wild animal leather, inner soles of rubber or plastic and the length < 24cm, outer soles of composition leather, other than sports footwear
6403.9111 90	其他皮革制面过脚踝但低于小腿的短筒靴(内底<24cm,橡胶、塑料、再生皮革制外底,运动用靴除外)	10	100	17	15	千克/双		Footwear with outer uper of feather, lovering the ankle but lower than crus, with inner soles of rubber or plastic and the length < 24cm, outer soles of composition leather, other than sports footwear
6403.9119	----其他	10	100	17	15	千克/双		----Other
6403.9119 10	其他野生动物皮革制面过脚踝但低于小腿的短筒靴(橡胶、塑料、再生皮革制外底,运动用靴除外)	10	100	17	15	千克/双	EF	Footwear covering the ankle but lower than crus, with outer soles of rubber, plastics, leather of composition leather and upers of wild animal feather, other than sports footwear
6403.9119 90	其他皮革制面过脚踝但低于小腿的短筒靴(橡胶、塑料、再生皮革制外底,运动用靴除外)	10	100	17	15	千克/双		Footwear covering the ankle but lower than crus, with outer soles of rubber, plastics, leather of composition leather and upers of leather, other than sports footwear
	---其他,按内底长度分类:							---Other, by length of inner soles:
6403.9191	----小于24cm的	10	100	17	15	千克/双		----Less than 24cm
6403.9191 10	其他野生皮革制面的短筒靴(过踝)(内底<24cm,橡胶、塑料、再生皮革制外底,运动用靴除外)	10	100	17	15	千克/双	EF	Footwear covering ankle, with outer upers of leather of wild animal, inner soles of rubber, plastic and the length < 24cm, outer soles of composition leather, other than sports footwear
6403.9191 90	其他皮革制面的短筒靴(过踝)(内底<24cm,橡胶、塑料、再生皮革制外底,运动用靴除外)	10	100	17	15	千克/双		Footwear covering ankle, with outer upers of leather, inner soles of rubber, plastic and the length < 24cm, outer soles of composition leather, other than sports footwear
6403.9199	----其他	10	100	17	15	千克/双		----Other
6403.9199 10	其他野生皮革制面的短筒靴(过踝)(橡胶、塑料、再生皮革制外底,运动用靴除外)	10	100	17	15	千克/双	EF	Footwear covering the ankle with outer soles of rubber, plastics, leather or composition leather and upers of leather, of wild animals, other than sports footwear
6403.9199 90	其他皮革制面的短筒靴(过踝)(橡胶、塑料、再生皮革制外底,运动用靴除外)	10	100	17	15	千克/双		Footwear covering the ankle with outer soles of rubber, plastics, leather or composition leather and upers of leather, of other animals, other than sports footwear
6403.9900	--其他	10	100	17	15	千克/双		--Other
6403.9900 10	野生动物皮革制面的其他鞋靴(橡胶、塑料、再生皮革制外底,运动用鞋靴除外)	10	100	17	15	千克/双	FE	Other footwear with outer soles of rubber, plastics, leather or composition leather and upers of leather of wild animals, other than sports footwear
6403.9900 90	其他皮革制面的其他鞋靴(橡胶、塑料、再生皮革制外底,运动用鞋靴除外)	10	100	17	15	千克/双		Other footwear with outer soles of rubber, plastics, leather or composition leather and upers of leather of other animals, other than sports footwear

税则号列	货品名称	最惠(%)	普通	增值税率	出口退税	计量单位	监管条件	Article Description
64.04	**橡胶、塑料、皮革或再生皮革制外底，用纺织材料制鞋面的鞋靴：**							**Footwear with outer soles of rubber, plastics, leather or composition leather and uppers of textile materials:**
	-橡胶或塑料制外底的鞋靴：							-Footwear with outer soles of rubber or plastics:
6404.1100	--运动鞋靴；网球鞋、篮球鞋、体操鞋、训练鞋及类似鞋	24	100	17	15	千克/双		--Sports footwear, tennis shoes, basketball shoes, gym shoes, training shoes and the like
6404.1900	--其他	24	100	17	15	千克/双		--Other
6404.2000	-皮革或再生皮革制外底的鞋靴	24	100	17	15	千克/双		-Footwear with outer soles of leather or composition leather
64.05	**其他鞋靴：**							**Other footwear:**
	-皮革或再生皮革制鞋面的：							-With uppers of leather or composition leather:
6405.1010	---橡胶、塑料、皮革及再生皮革制外底的	24	100	17	15	千克/双		---Outer soles of rubber, plastics, leather or composition leather
6405.1090	---其他材料制外底的	24	100	17	15	千克/双		---Outer soles of other materials
6405.1090 10	野生动物皮革制面的其他鞋靴（外底用橡胶、塑料、皮革及再生皮革以外的材料制成）	24	100	17	15	千克/双	EF	Other footwear with uppers of leather or composition leather of wid andimds(with outer soles of materials other than rubber, plastics , leather or composition leather)
6405.1090 90	其他皮革或再生皮革制面的其他鞋靴（外底用橡胶、塑料、皮革及再生皮革以外的材料制成）	24	100	17	15	千克/双		Other footwear eieh uppers of leather or composition leather(with outer soles of materials other than rubber, plastics, leather or composition leather)
6405.2000	-纺织材料制鞋面的	22	100	17	15	千克/双		-With uppers of textile materials
6405.2000 10	羊毛毡呢制内底及鞋面的鞋靴（外底用橡胶，塑料，皮革或再生皮革制以外材料制成）	22	100	17	15	千克/双		Footwear with inner soles and uppers of wool felt, outer soled of materials other than rubber, plastics, leather or composition leather
6405.2000 90	纺织材料制鞋面的其他鞋靴（外底用橡胶，塑料，皮革或再生皮革制以外材料制成）	22	100	17	15	千克/双		Other footwear with uppers of textile materials, outer soles of materials other than rubber, plastics, leather or composition leather
	-其他：							-Other:
6405.9010	---橡胶、塑料、皮革及再生皮革制外底的	15	100	17	15	千克/双		---With outer soles of rubber, plastics, leather or composition leather
6405.9090	---其他材料制外底的	15	100	17	15	千克/双		---Outer soles of other materials
64.06	**鞋靴零件（包括鞋面，不论是否带有除外底以外的其他鞋底）；活动式鞋内底、跟垫及类似品；护腿、裹腿和类似品及其零件：**							**Parts of footwear (including uppers whether or not attached to soles other than outer soles); removable in-soles, heel cushions and similar articles; gaiters, leggings and similar articles, and parts thereof:**
6406.1000	-鞋面及其零件，但硬衬除外	15	90	17	15	千克		-Uppers and parts thereof, other than stiffeners
6406.1000 10	含野生动物皮的鞋面及其零件	15	90	17	15	千克	FE	Uppers and parts thereof, consist of leather of wild animals
6406.1000 90	其他鞋面及其零件（不包括硬衬及毡呢制品）	15	90	17	15	千克		Other uppers and parts thereof(other than stiffeners and articles of felt)
	-橡胶或塑料制的外底及鞋跟：							-Outer soles and heels, of rubber or plastics:
6406.2010	---橡胶制的	15	90	17	15	千克		---Of rubber
6406.2020	---塑料制的	15	90	17	15	千克		---Of plastics
	-其他：							-Other:
6406.9010	--木制	15	90	17	15	千克	A	--Of wood
	--其他材料制：							--Of other materials:
6406.9091	----活动式鞋内底、跟垫及类似品	15	90	17	15	千克		----Removable in-soles, heel cushions and similar articles
6406.9092	----护腿、裹脚和类似品及其零件	15	90	17	15	千克		----Gaiters, leggings and similar articles, and parts thereof
6406.9099	----其他材料制其他鞋靴零件	9		17	15	千克		----Other parts of footwear of other materials

第六十五章
帽类及其零件

注释：

一、本章不包括：

（一）税目 63.09 的旧帽类；

（二）石棉制帽类（税目 68.12）；

（三）第九十五章的玩偶帽、其他玩具帽或狂欢节用品。

二、税目 65.02 不包括缝制的帽坯，但仅将条带缝成螺旋形的除外。

Chapter 65
Headgear and parts thereof

Notes:

1. This Chapter does not cover:

(a) Worn headgear of heading No. 63.09;

(b) Asbestos headgear (Heading No. 68.12) or;

(c) Dolls' hats, other toy hats or carnival articles of Chapter 95.

2. Heading No. 65.02 does not cover hat-shapes made by sewing, other than those obtained simply by sewing strips in spirals.

税则号列	货品名称	最惠(%)	普通	增值税率	出口退税	计量单位	监管条件	Article Description
65.01	**毡呢制的帽坯、帽身及帽兜，未楦制成形，也未加帽边；毡呢制的圆帽片及制帽用的毡呢筒（包括裁开的毡呢筒）：**							**Hat-forms, hat bodies and hoods of felt, neither blocked to shape nor with made brims; plateaux and manchons (including slit manchons), of felt:**
6501.0000	毡呢制的帽坯、帽身及帽兜，未楦制成形，也未加帽边；毡呢制的圆帽片及制帽用的毡呢筒（包括裁开的毡呢筒）	22	100	17	15	千克		Hat-forms, hat bodies and hoods of felt, neither blocked to shape nor with made brims; plateaux and manchons (including slit manchons), of felt
65.02	**编结的帽坯或用任何材料的条带拼制而成的帽坯，未楦制成形，也未加帽边、衬里或装饰物：**							**Hat-shapes, plaited or made by assembling strips of any material, neither blocked to shape, nor with made brims, nor lined, nor trimmed:**
6502.0000	编结的帽坯或用任何材料的条带拼制成而的帽坯，未楦制成形，也未加帽边、衬里或装饰物	20	100	17	15	千克		Hat-shapes, plaited or made by assembling strips of any material, neither blocked to shape, nor with made brims, nor lined, nor trimmed
65.04	**编结帽或用任何材料的条带拼制而成的帽类，不论有无衬里或装饰物：**							**Hats and other headgear, plaited or made by assembling strips of any material, whether or not lined or trimmed:**
6504.0000	编结帽或用任何材料的条带拼制而成的帽类，不论有无衬里或装饰物	20	130	17	15	个/千克		Hats and other headgear, plaited or made by assembling strips of any material, whether or not lined or trimmed
65.05	**针织或钩编的帽类，用成匹的花边、毡呢或其他纺织物（条带除外）制成的帽类，不论有无衬里或装饰物；任何材料制的发网，不论有无衬里或装饰物：**							**Hats and other headgear, knitted or crocheted, or made up from lace, felt or other textile fabric, in the piece (but not in strips), whether or not lined or trimmed; hair-nets of any material, whether or not lined or trimmed:**
6505.0010	-发网	10	130	17	15	个/千克		-Hair-nets
6505.0020	---钩编的帽类	20	130	17	15	个/千克		---Hats and other headgear, knitted or crocheted
	---其他：							---Other:
6505.0091	----用税目 65.01 的帽身、帽兜或圆帽片制成的毡呢帽类，无论有无衬里或装饰物	22	130	17	15	个/千克		----Felt hats and other felt headgear, made from the hat bodies, hoods or plateaux of heading No. 65.01, whether or not lined or trimmed
6505.0099	----其他	20	130	17	15	个/千克		----Other
65.06	**其他帽类，不论有无衬里或装饰物：**							**Other headgear, whether or not lined or trimmed:**
6506.1000	-安全帽	10	100	17	15	个/千克		-Safety headgear
6506.1000 10	防护面罩（带有能够滤除生物因子滤器的面罩）	10	100	17	15	个/千克	3	Protecting cover (with veil and colander that can screen biological elements)
6506.1000 90	其他安全帽（不论有无衬里或饰物）	10	100	17	15	个/千克		Other safety caps (whether or not lined or trimmed)
	-其他：							-Other:
6506.9100	--橡胶或塑料制	10	100	17	15	个/千克		--Of rubber or of plastics
	--其他材料制：							--Of other materials:
6506.9910	---皮革制	10	130	17	15	个/千克		---Of leather
6506.9910 10	野生动物皮革制帽类	10	130	17	15	个/千克	EF	Other headgear, of leather of wild animals
6506.9910 90	其他皮革制帽类	10	130	17	15	个/千克		Other headgear, of leather of other animals
6506.9920	---毛皮制	10	130	17	15	个/千克		---Of furskin

税则号列	货 品 名 称	最惠(%)	普通	增值税率	出口退税	计量单位	监管条件	Article Description
6506.9920 10	野生动物毛皮制的帽类(无论有无衬里或饰物)	10	130	17	15	个/千克	EF	Other headgear, of leather of wild animals (whether or not lined or trimmed)
6506.9920 90	其他毛皮制的帽类(无论有无衬里或饰物)	10	130	17	15	个/千克		Other headgear, of leather of other animals (whether or not lined or trimmed)
6506.9990	---其他	24	100	17	15	个/千克		---Other
65.07	**帽圈、帽衬、帽套、帽帮、帽骨架、帽舌及帽颏带:**							**Head-bands, linings, covers, hat foundations, hat frames, peaks and chinstraps, for headgear:**
6507.0000	帽圈、帽衬、帽套、帽帮、帽骨架、帽舌及帽颏带	24	100	17	15	千克		Head-bands, linings, covers, hat foundations, hat frames, peaks and chinstraps, for headgear
6507.0000 10	含野生动物成分的帽类附件(指帽圈、衬、套、帮、骨架、舌及颏带)	24	100	17	15	千克	FE	Headwear accessories (including head-bands, linings, covers, hat foundations, hat frames, peaks and chinstraps) containing materials of wild animals
6507.0000 90	其他帽类附件(指帽圈、衬、套、帮、骨架、舌及颏带)	24	100	17	15	千克		Other headwear accessories (including head-bands, linings, covers, hat foundations, hat frames, peaks and chinstraps)

第六十六章
雨伞、阳伞、手杖、鞭子、马鞭及其零件

Chapter 66
Umbrellas, sun umbrellas, walking-sticks, seat-sticks, whips, riding-crops and parts thereof

注释：

一、本章不包括：

（一）丈量用杖及类似品（税目90.17）；

（二）火器手杖、刀剑手杖、灌铅手杖及类似品（第九十三章）；

（三）第九十五章的货品（例如，玩具雨伞、玩具阳伞）。

二、税目66.03不包括纺织材料制的零件、附件及装饰品或者任何材料制的罩套、流苏、鞭梢、伞套及类似品。此类货品即使与税目66.01或66.02的物品一同进口或出口，只要未装配在一起，则不应视为上述税目所列物品的组成零件，而应分别归入各有关税目。

Notes:

1. This Chapter does not cover:

(a) Measure walking-sticks or the like (heading No. 90.17);

(b) Firearm-sticks, sword-sticks, loaded walking-sticks or the like (Chapter 93) or;

(c) Goods of Chapter 95 (for example, toy umbrellas, toy sun umbrellas).

2. Heading No. 66.03 does not cover parts, trimmings or accessories of textile material, or covers, tassels, thongs, umbrella cases or the like, of any material. Such goods presented with, but not fitted to, articles of heading No. 66.01 or 66.02 are to be classified separately and not to be treated as forming part of those articles.

税则号列	货品名称	最惠(%)	普通	增值税率	出口退税	计量单位	监管条件	Article Description
66.01	雨伞及阳伞(包括手杖伞、庭园用伞及类似伞)：							**Umbrellas and sun umbrellas (including walking-stick umbrellas, garden umbrellas and similar umbrellas):**
6601.1000	-庭院用伞及类似伞	14	130	17	15	千克/把		-Garden or similar umbrellas
	-其他：							-Other:
6601.9100	--折叠伞	10	130	17	15	千克/把		--Having a telescopic shaft
6601.9900	--其他	10	130	17	15	千克/把		--Other
66.02	手杖、带座手杖、鞭子、马鞭及类似品：							**Walking-sticks, seat-sticks, whips, riding-crops and the like:**
6602.0000	手杖、带座手杖、鞭子、马鞭及类似品	10	130	17	15	千克/把		Walking-sticks, seat-sticks, whips, riding-crops and the like
6602.0000 11	含野生动物成分的手杖、带座手杖(包括马鞭、鞭子及类似品)	10	130	17	15	千克/把	EF	Walking-sticks, seat-sticks, whips, riding-crops and the like, containing materials of wild animals
6602.0000 19	动植物材料制手杖、鞭子及类似品(包括带座手杖)	10	130	17	15	千克/把		Walking-sticks, seat-sticks, whips, riding-crops and the like, of plant materials or animal materials
6602.0000 90	其他手杖、带座手杖、鞭子及类似品	10	130	17	15	千克/把		Other walking-sticks, seat-sticks, whips, riding-crops and the like
66.03	税目66.01或66.02所列物品的零件及装饰品：							**Parts, trimmings and accessories of articles of heading No. 66.01 or 66.02:**
6603.2000	-伞骨，包括装在伞柄上的伞骨	14	130	17	15	千克		-Umbrella frames, including frames mounted on shafts (sticks)
6603.9000	-其他	14	130	17	15	千克		-Other
6603.9000 10	含野生动物成分的伞、手杖的零件及装饰品(包括鞭子的其他零件及饰品)	14	130	17	15	千克	EF	Parts, trimmings and accessories of articles, containing materials of wild animals
6603.9000 90	伞、手杖及鞭子的其他零件及饰品(罩套、流苏、鞭梢及纺织材料制品除外)	14	130	17	15	千克		Other parts, trimmings and accessories of articles, other than covers, tassels, thongs and other articles of textile material

第六十七章
已加工羽毛、羽绒及其制品；人造花；人发制品

Chapter 67
Prepared feathers and down and articles made of feathers or of down; artificial flowers; articles of human hair

注释：

一、本章不包括：

（一）人发制滤布（税目 59.11）；

（二）花边、刺绣品或其他纺织物制成的花卉图案（第十一类）；

（三）鞋靴（第六十四章）；

（四）帽类及发网（第六十五章）；

（五）玩具、运动用品或狂欢节用品（第九十五章）；

（六）羽毛掸帚、粉扑及人发制的筛子（第九十六章）。

二、税目 67.01 不包括：

（一）羽毛或羽绒仅在其中作为填充料的物品（例如税目 94.04 的寝具）；

（二）羽毛或羽绒仅作为饰物或填充料的衣服或衣着附件；

（三）税目 67.02 的人造花、叶及其部分品，以及它们的制成品。

三、税目 67.02 不包括：

（一）玻璃制品（第七十章）；

（二）用陶器、石料、金属、木料或其他材料经模铸、锻造、雕刻、冲压或用其他方法整件制成形的人造花、叶或果实；用捆扎、胶粘及类似方法以外的其他方法将部分品组合而成的上述制品。

Notes:

1. This Chapter does not cover:

(a) Straining cloth of human hair (heading No. 59. 11);

(b) Floral motifs of lace, of embroidery or other textile fabric (Section XI);

(c) Footwear (Chapter 64);

(d) Headgear or hair-nets (Chapter 65);

(e) Toys, sports requisites or carnival articles (Chapter 95); or

(f) Feather dusters, powder-puffs or hair sieves (Chapter 96).

2. Heading No. 67. 01 does not cover:

(a) Articles in which feathers or down constitute only filling or padding (for example, bedding of heading No. 94. 04);

(b) Articles of apparel or clothing accessories in which feathers or down constitute no more than mere trimming or padding; or

(c) Artificial flowers or foliage or parts thereof or made up articles of heading No. 67. 02.

3. Heading No. 67. 02 does not cover:

(a) Articles of glass (Chapter 70); or

(b) Artificial flowers, foliage or fruit of pottery, stone, metal, wood or other materials, obtained in one piece by moulding, forging, carving, stamping or other process, or consisting of parts assembled otherwise than by binding, glueing, fitting into one another or similar methods.

税则号列	货品名称	最惠(%)	普通	增值税率	出口退税	计量单位	监管条件	Article Description
67.01	**带羽毛或羽绒的鸟皮及鸟体其他部分、羽毛、部分羽毛、羽绒及其制品(税目 05.05 的货品和经加工的羽管及羽轴除外)：**							**Skins and other parts of birds with their feathers or down, feathers, parts of feathers, down and articles thereof (other than goods of heading No. 05. 05 and worked quills and scapes):**
6701.0000	带羽毛或羽绒的鸟皮及鸟体其他部分、羽毛、部分羽毛、羽绒及其制品(税目 05.05 的货品和经加工的羽管及羽轴除外)	20	130	17	15	千克		Skins and other parts of birds with their feathers or down, feathers, parts of feathers, down and articles thereof (other than goods of heading No. 05. 05 and worked quills and scapes)
6701.0000 10	已加工野禽羽毛、羽绒及其制品	20	130	17	15	千克	AFEB	Worked feathers, down and articles thereof, of wild birds
6701.0000 90	其他已加工羽毛、羽绒及其制品(税号 0505 的货品及经加工的羽管及羽轴除外)	20	130	17	15	千克	AB	Other worked feathers, down and articles thereof (other than goods of heading No. 0505 and worked quills and scapes)
67.02	**人造花、叶、果实及其零件；用人造花、叶或果实制成的物品：**							**Artificial flowers, foliage and fruit and parts thereof; articles made of artificial flowers, foliage or fruit:**
6702.1000	-塑料制	20	130	17	15	千克		-Of plastics
	-其他材料制：							-Of other materials:
6702.9010	---羽毛制	20	130	17	15	千克		---Of feathers or down
6702.9010 10	野禽羽毛制花、叶、果实及其制品	20	130	17	15	千克	AFEB	Flowers, foliage and fruit and articles thereof, of feathers or down of wild birds
6702.9010 90	其他羽毛制花、叶、果实及其制品(包括花、叶、果实的零件)	20	130	17	15	千克	AB	Flowers, foliage and fruit and parts thereof; articles made of artificial flowers, foliage or fruit, of other feathers or down
6702.9020	---丝及绢丝制	24	130	17	15	千克		---Of silk or spun silk
6702.9030	---化学纤维制	24	130	17	15	千克		---Of man-made fibres
6702.9090	---其他	20	130	17	15	千克		---Other

税则号列	货 品 名 称	最惠(%)	普通	增值税率	出口退税	计量单位	监管条件	Article Description
67.03	经梳理、稀疏、脱色或其他方法加工的人发;作假发及类似品用的羊毛、其他动物毛或其他纺织材料:							**Human hair, dressed, thinned, bleached or otherwise worked; wool or other animal hair or other textile materials, prepared for use in making wigs or the like:**
6703.0000	经梳理、稀疏、脱色或其他方法加工的人发或作假发及类似品用的羊毛、其他动物毛或其他纺织材料	20	100	17	15	千克		Human hair, dressed, thinned, bleached or otherwise worked; wool or other animal hair or other textile materials, prepared for use in making wigs or the like
67.04	人发、动物毛或纺织材料制的假发、假胡须、假眉毛、假睫毛及类似品;其他税目未列名的人发制品:							**Wigs, false beards, eyebrows and eyelashes, switches and the like, of human or animal hair or of textile materials; articles of human hair not elsewhere specified or included:**
	-合成纤维纺织材料制:							-Of synthetic textile materials:
6704.1100	--整头假发	25	130	17	15	千克		--Complete wigs
6704.1900	--其他	25	130	17	15	千克		--Other
6704.2000	-人发制	15	130	17	15	千克		-Of human hair
6704.9000	-其他材料制	25	130	17	15	千克		-Of other materials

第十三类
石料、石膏、水泥、石棉、云母及类似材料的制品；陶瓷产品；玻璃及其制品

SECTION XIII
ARTICLES OF STONE, PLASTER, CEMENT, ASBESTOS, MICA OR SIMILAR MATERIALS; CERAMIC PRODUCTS; GLASS AND GLASSWARE

第六十八章
石料、石膏、水泥、石棉、云母及类似材料的制品

注释：

一、本章不包括：

（一）第二十五章的货品；

（二）税目48.10或48.11的经涂布、浸渍或覆盖的纸及纸板（例如，用云母粉或石墨涂布的纸及纸板、沥青纸及纸板）；

（三）第五十六章或第五十九章的经涂布、浸渍或包覆的纺织物（例如，用云母粉、沥青涂布或包覆的织物）；

（四）第七十一章的物品；

（五）第八十二章的工具及其零件；

（六）税目84.42的印刷用石板；

（七）绝缘子（税目85.46）或绝缘材料制的零件（税目85.47）；

（八）牙科用磨锉（税目90.18）；

（九）第九十一章的物品（例如，钟及钟壳）；

（十）第九十四章的物品（例如，家具、灯具及照明装置、活动房屋）；

（十一）第九十五章的物品（例如，玩具、游戏品及运动用品）；

（十二）用第九十六章注释二（二）所述材料制成的税目96.02的物品或税目96.06的物品（例如钮扣）、税目96.09的物品（例如石笔）或税目96.10的物品（例如绘画石板）；

（十三）第九十七章的物品（例如艺术品）。

二、税目68.02所称"已加工的碑石或建筑用石"，不仅适用于已加工的税目25.15、25.16的各种石料，也适用于所有经类似加工的其他天然石料（例如，石英岩、燧石、白云石及冻石），但不适用于板岩。

Chapter 68
Articles of stone, plaster, cement, asbestos, mica or similar materials

Notes:

1. This Chapter does not cover:

(a) Goods of Chapter 25;

(b) Coated, impregnated or covered paper and paperboard of heading No. 48.10 or 48.11 (for example, paper and paperboard coated with mica powder or graphite, bituminized or asphalted paper and paperboard);

(c) Coated, impregnated or covered textile fabric of Chapter 56 or 59 (for example, fabric coated or covered with mica powder, bituminized or asphalted fabric);

(d) Articles of Chapter 71;

(e) Tools or parts of tools, of Chapter 82;

(f) Lithographic stones of heading No. 84.42;

(g) Electrical insulators (heading No. 85.46) or fittings of insulating material of heading No. 85.47;

(h) Dental burrs (heading No. 90.18);

(i) Articles of Chapter 91 (for example, clocks and clock cases);

(j) Articles of Chapter 94 (for example, furniture, lamps and lighting fittings, prefabricated buildings);

(k) Articles of Chapter 95 (for example, toys, games and sports requisites);

(l) Articles of heading No. 96.02, if made of materials specified in Note 2 (b) to Chapter 96, or of heading No. 96.06 (for example, buttons), No. 96.09 (for example, slate pencils) or No. 96.10 (for example, drawing slates); or

(m) Articles of Chapter 97 (for example, works of art).

2. In heading No. 68.02, the expression "worked monumental or building stone" applies not only to the varieties of stone referred to in heading No. 25.15 or 25.16, but also to all other natural stone (for example, quartzite, flint, dolomite and steatite) similarly worked; it does not, however, apply to slate.

税则号列	货品名称	最惠(%)	普通	增值税率	出口退税	计量单位	监管条件	Article Description
68.01	由天然石料(不包括板岩)制的长方砌石、路缘石、扁平石:							**Setts, curbstones and flagstones, of natural stone (except slate):**
6801.0000	天然石料(不包括板岩)制的长方砌石、路缘石、扁平石	12	70	17		千克		Setts, curbstones and flagstones, of natural stone (except slate)
68.02	已加工的碑石或建筑用石(不包括板岩)及其制品,但税目68.01的货品除外;天然石料(包括板岩)制的镶嵌石(马赛克)及类似品,不论是否有衬背;天然石料(包括板岩)制的人工染色石粒、石片及石粉:							**Worked monumental or building stone (except slate) and articles thereof, other than goods of heading No. 68.01; mosaic cubes and the like, of natural stone (including slate), whether or not on a backing; artificially coloured granules, chippings and powder, of natural stone (including slate):**
	-砖、瓦、方块及类似品,不论是否为矩形(包括正方形),其最大表面积以可置入边长小于7厘米的方格为限;人工染色的石粒、石片及石粉:							-Tiles, cubes and similar articles, whether or not rectangular (including square), the largest surface area of which is capable of being enclosed in a square the side of which is less than 7cm; artificially coloured granules, chippings and powder:
6802.1010	---大理石	24	90	17		千克		---Marble
6802.1090	---其他	20	90	17		千克		---Other
	-简单切削或锯开并具有一个平面的其他碑石或建筑用石及其制品:							-Other monumental or building stone and articles thereof, simply cut or sawn, with a flat or even surface:
	--大理石、石灰华及蜡石:							--Marble, travertine and alabaster:
6802.2110	---大理石	10	90	17		千克		---Marble
6802.2120	---石灰华	24	90	17	9	千克		---Travertine
6802.2190	---其他	24	90	17		千克		---Other
6802.2300	--花岗岩	10	90	17		千克	A	--Granite
	--其他石:							--Other stone:
6802.2910	---其他石灰石	24	90	17		千克		---Other calcareous stone
6802.2990	---其他	15	90	17		千克		---Other
	-其他:							-Other:
	--大理石、石灰华及蜡石:							--Marble, travertine and alabaster:
6802.9110	---石刻	24	90	17	13	千克		---Carvings
6802.9190	---其他	10	90	17	9	千克		---Other
	--其他石灰石:							--Other calcareous stone:
6802.9210	---石刻	24	90	17	13	千克		---Carvings
6802.9290	---其他	10	90	17	9	千克		---Other
	--花岗岩:							--Granite:
	---石刻:							---Carvings:
6802.9311	----墓碑石	24	90	17	13	千克	A	----Tombstone (gravestone)
6802.9319	----其他	24	90	17	13	千克	A	----Other
6802.9390	---其他	10	90	17	9	千克	A	---Other
	--其他石:							--Other stone:
6802.9910	---石刻	24	90	17	13	千克		---Carvings
6802.9990	---其他	24	90	17	9	千克		---Other
68.03	已加工的板岩及板岩或粘聚板岩的制品:							**Worked slate and articles of slate or of agglomerated slate:**
6803.0010	---板岩制	20	80	17	5	千克		---Of slate
6803.0090	---其他	20	80	17	5	千克		---Other
68.04	未装支架的石磨、石碾、砂轮和类似品及其零件,用于研磨、磨刃、抛光、整形或切割,以及手用磨石、抛光石及其零件,用天然石料、粘聚的天然磨料、人造磨料或陶瓷制成,不论是否装有其他材料制成的零件:							**Millstones, grindstones, grinding wheels and the like, without frameworks, for grinding, sharpening, polishing, trueing or cutting, hand sharpening or polishing stones, and parts thereof, of natural stone, of agglomerated natural or artificial abrasives, or of ceramics, with or without parts of other materials:**
6804.1000	-碾磨或磨浆用石磨、石碾	8	40	17	5	千克		-Millstones and grindstones for milling, grinding or pulping

税则号列	货品名称	最惠(%)	普通	增值税率	出口退税	计量单位	监管条件	Article Description
	-其他石磨、石碾、砂轮及类似品:							-Other millstones, grindstones, grinding wheels and the like:
6804.2100	--粘聚合成或天然金刚石制	8	17	17	5	千克		--Of agglomerated synthetic or natural diamond
	--其他粘聚磨料制或陶瓷制:							--Of other agglomerated abrasives or of ceramics:
6804.2210	---砂轮	8	17	17	5	千克		---Grinding wheels
6804.2290	---其他	8	40	17	5	千克		---Other
	--天然石料制:							--Of natural stone:
6804.2310	---砂轮	8	17	17	5	千克		---Grinding wheels
6804.2390	---其他	8	40	17	5	千克		---Other
	-手用磨石及抛光石:							-Hand sharpening or polishing stones:
6804.3010	---琢磨油石	8	17	17	5	千克		---Oilstones
6804.3090	---其他	8	40	17	5	千克		---Other
68.05	**砂布、砂纸及以其他材料为底的类似品,不论是否裁切、缝合或用其他方法加工成形:**							**Natural or artificial abrasive powder or grain, on a base of textile material, of paper, of paperboard or of other materials, whether or not cut to shape or sewn or otherwise made up:**
6805.1000	-砂布	8	40	17	5	千克		-On a base of woven textile fabric only
6805.2000	-砂纸	8	40	17	5	千克		-On a base of paper or paperboard only
6805.3000	-其他	8	40	17	5	千克		-On a base of other materials
68.06	**矿渣棉、岩石棉及类似的矿质棉;页状蛭石、膨胀粘土、泡沫矿渣及类似的膨胀矿物材料;具有隔热、隔音或吸音性能的矿物材料的混合物及制品,但税目68.11、68.12或第六十九章的货品除外:**							**Slag wool, rock wool and similar mineral wools; exfoliated vermiculite, expanded clays, foamed slag and similar expanded mineral materials; mixtures and articles of heat-insulating, sound-insulating or sound-absorbing mineral materials, other than those of heading No. 68.11 or 68.12 or of Chapter 69:**
	-矿渣棉、岩石棉及类似的矿质棉(包括其相互混合物),块状、成片或成卷:							-Slag wool, rock wool and similar mineral wools (including intermixtures thereof), in bulk, sheets or rolls:
6806.1010	---硅酸铝纤维及其制品	10.5	40	17	5	千克		---Aluminum silicate fiber and its products
6806.1090	---其他		40	17	5	千克		---Other
6806.1090暂 01	其他矿物纤维,渣球含量小于5%	5	40	17	5	千克		Other mineral fibre, containing slag, <5%
6806.1090 90	矿渣棉,岩石棉及类似矿质棉(包括相互混合物,块状、成片或成卷)	10.5	40	17	5	千克		Slag wool, rock wool and similar mineral wools (including intermixtures thereof, inbulk, sheets or rolls)
6806.2000	-页状硅石、膨胀粘土、泡沫矿渣及类似的膨胀矿物材料(包括其相互混合物)	10.5	40	17		千克		-Exfoliated vermiculite, expanded clays, foamed slag and similar expanded mineral materials (including intermixtures thereof)
6806.9000	-其他	10	50	17		千克		-Other
68.07	**沥青或类似原料(例如,石油沥青或煤焦油沥青)的制品:**							**Articles of asphalt or of similar material (for example, petroleum bitumen or coal tar pitch):**
6807.1000	-成卷		50	17		千克		-In rolls
6807.1000暂 01	聚酯-铜复合胎基改性沥青根阻防水卷材	1	50	17		千克		Polyester-waterproofing modified bitumen coiled material with copper composite base
6807.1000 90	成卷的沥青或类似原料的制品(如:石油沥青或煤焦油沥青)	12	50	17		千克		Articles of asphalt or of similar material in rolls (for example, petroleum bitumen or coal tar pitch)
6807.9000	-其他	12	50	17		千克		-Other
68.08	**镶板、平板、瓦、砖及类似品,用水泥、石膏及其他矿物粘合材料粘合植物纤维、稻草、刨花、木片屑、木粉、锯末或木废料制成:**							**Panels, boards, tiles, blocks and similar articles of vegetable fibre, of straw or of shavings, chips, particles, sawdust or other waste, of wood, agglomerated with cement, plaster or other mineral binders:**
6808.0000	镶板、平板、瓦、砖及类似品,用水泥、石膏及其他矿物粘合材料粘合植物纤维、稻草、刨花、木片屑、木粉、锯末或木废料制成	10.5	40	17	5	千克		Panels, boards, tiles, blocks and similar articles of vegetable fibre, of straw or of shavings, chips, particles, sawdust or other waste, of wood, agglomerated with cement, plaster or other mineral binders
68.09	**石膏制品及以石膏为基本成分的混合材料制品:**							**Articles of plaster or of compositions based on plaster:**

税则号列	货品名称	最惠(%)	普通	增值税率	出口退税	计量单位	监管条件	Article Description
	-未经装饰的板、片、砖、瓦及类似品:							-Boards, sheets, panels, tiles and similar articles, not ornamented:
6809.1100	--仅用纸、纸板贴面或加强的	28	100	17	5	千克		--Faced or reinforced with paper or paper-board only
6809.1900	--其他	25	100	17	5	千克		--Other
6809.9000	-其他制品	25	100	17	5	千克		-Other articles
68.10	**水泥、混凝土或人造石制品,不论是否加强:**							**Articles of cement, of concrete or of artificial stone, whether or not reinforced:**
	-砖、瓦、扁平石及类似品:							-Tiles, flagstones, bricks and similar articles:
6810.1100	--建筑用砖及石砌块	10.5	40	17	5	千克		--Building blocks and bricks
	--其他:							--Other:
6810.1910	---人造石制	10.5	70	17	5	千克		---Of artificial stone
6810.1990	---其他	10.5	70	17	5	千克		---Other
	-其他制品:							-Other articles:
	--建筑或土木工程用的预制结构件:							--Prefabricated structural components for building or civil engineering:
6810.9110	---钢筋混凝土和预应力混凝土管、杆、板、桩等	10.5	40	17	5	千克		---Reinforced concrete and prestressed concrete tubes, pipes, rods, plates, piles and similar articles
6810.9190	---其他	10.5	40	17	5	千克		---Other
	--其他:							--Other:
6810.9910	---铁道用水泥枕	8	14	17	5	千克		---Railway sleepers of concrete
6810.9990	---其他	10.5	70	17	5	千克		---Other
68.11	**石棉水泥、纤维素水泥或类似材料的制品:**							**Articles of asbestos-cement, of cellulose fibre-cement or the like:**
	-含石棉的:							- Containing aspestos:
6811.4010	---瓦楞板	5	40	17	5	千克		---Corrugated sheets
6811.4020	---其他片、板、砖、瓦及类似制品	10.5	40	17	5	千克		---Other sheets, panels, tiles and similar articles
6811.4030	---管子及管子附件	8	40	17	5	千克		---Tubes, pipes and tube or pipe fittings
6811.4090	---其他制品	8.4	40	17	5	千克		---Other articles
	-不含石棉的:							-Not containing asbestos:
6811.8100	--瓦楞板	5	40	17	5	千克		--Corrugated sheets
6811.8200	--其他片、板、砖、瓦及类似制品	10.5	40	17	5	千克		--Other sheets, panels, tiles and similar articles
	--其他制品:							--Other articles:
6811.8910	---管子及管子附件	8	40	17	5	千克		---Tubes, pipes and tube or pipe fittings
6811.8990	---其他	8.4	40	17	5	千克		---Other
68.12	**已加工的石棉纤维;以石棉为基本成分或以石棉和碳酸镁为基本成分的混合物;上述混合物或石棉的制品(例如,纱线、机织物、服装、帽类、鞋靴、衬垫),不论是否加强,但税号 68.11 或 68.13 的货品除外:**							**Fabricated asbestos fibres; mixtures with a basis of asbestos or with a basis of asbestos and magnesium carbonate; articles of such mixtures or of asbestos (for example, thread, woven fabric, clothing, headgear, footwear, gaskets), whether or not reinforced, other than goods of heading No. 68.11 or 68.13:**
6812.8000	-青石棉的	10.5	40	17	5	千克		-Of crocidolite
	-其他:							-Other:
6812.9100	--服装、衣着附件、帽类及鞋靴	10.5	40	17	5	千克		--Clothing, clothing accessories, footwear and headgear
6812.9200	--纸、麻丝板及毡子	10.5	40	17	5	千克		--Paper, millboard and felt
6812.9300	--成片或成卷的压缩石棉纤维接合材料	10.5	40	17	5	千克		--Compressed asbestos fibre jointing, in sheets or rolls
6812.9900	--其他	10	40	17	5	千克		--Other
68.13	**以石棉、其他矿物质或纤维素为基本成分的未装配摩擦材料及其制品(例如,片、卷、带、盘、圈、垫及扇形),适于作制动器、离合器及类似品,不论是否与织物或其他材料结合而成:**							**Friction material and articles thereof (for example, sheets, rolls, strips, segments, discs, washers, pads), not mounted, for brakes, for clutches or the like, with a basis of asbestos, of other mineral substances or of cellulose, whether or not combined with textile or other materials:**

税则号列	货品名称	最惠(%)	普通	增值税率	出口退税	计量单位	监管条件	Article Description
	-含石棉的：							-Containing asbestos：
6813.2010	--闸衬、闸垫	10	40	17	5	千克		--Brake linings and pads
6813.2090	---其他	12	40	17	5	千克		---Other
	-不含石棉的：							-Not containing asbestos：
6813.8100	--闸衬、闸垫	10	40	17	5	千克		--Brake linings and pads
6813.8900	--其他	12	40	17	5	千克		--Other
68.14	**已加工的云母及其制品，包括粘聚或复制的云母，不论是否附于纸、纸板或其他材料上：**							**Worked mica and articles of mica, including agglomerated or reconstituted mica, whether or not on a support of paper, paperboard or other meterials：**
6814.1000	-粘聚或复制云母制的板、片、带，不论是否附于其他材料上	10.5	35	17	5	千克		-Plates, sheets and strips of agglomerated or reconstituted mica, whether or not on a support
6814.9000	-其他	10.5	35	17	5	千克		-Other
68.15	**其他税号未列名的石制品及其他矿物制品(包括碳纤维及其制品和泥煤制品)：**							**Articles of stone or of other mineral substances (including carbon fibres, articles of carbon fibres and articles of peat), not elsewhere specified or included：**
6815.1000	-非电器用的石墨或其他碳精制品	15	70	17		千克	3	-Non-electrical articles of graphite or other carbon
6815.2000	-泥煤制品	15	70	17		千克		-Articles of peat
	-其他制品：							-Other articles：
6815.9100	--含有菱镁矿、白云石或铬铁矿的	15	70	17		千克		--Containing magnesite, dolomite or chromite
	--其他：							--Other：
6815.9920	---碳纤维	17.5	70	17	5	千克		---Carbon fibres
	---碳纤维制品：							---Articles of carbon fibres：
6815.9920 10	两用物项管制的碳纤维(比模量≥12.7×10^6 m，或比抗拉强度≥23.5×10^4 m)	17.5	70	17	5	千克	3	Carbon fibres, fual - use items control, modulus atio ≥12.7×106m, specific ultimate tensile strength≥23.5×104m
6815.9920 90	其他碳纤维	17.5	70	17	5	千克		Other carbon fibres
6815.9931	----碳布	17.5	70	17	5	千克		----Carbon fabric
6815.9932	----碳纤维预浸料(制品)	17.5	70	17	5	千克		----Carbon fiber prepreg(articles)
6815.9932 10	两用物项管制的碳纤维预浸料(制品)	17.5	70	17	5	千克	3	Carbon fiber pripreg(articles), fual - use items control
6815.9932 90	其他碳纤维预浸料(制品)	17.5	70	17	5	千克		Other carbon fiber pripreg(articles)
6815.9939	----其他		70	17	5	千克		----Other
6815.9939暂 21	碳含量>90%特种碳纤维纱线(比模量≥12.3×10^6米，比抗拉强度≥23.5×10^4米)	15	70	17	5	千克		
6815.9939 29	碳含量≤90%特种碳纤维(比模量≥12.3×10^6米，比抗拉强度≥23.5×10^4米)	17.5	70	17	5	千克		
6815.9939暂 91	碳含量>90%的碳纤维纱线	15	70	17	5	千克		Carbon fibres yarn, cantaining≤90% by weight of carbon
6815.9939 99	其他碳纤维制品	17.5	70	17	5	千克		Other carbon fibres articles
6815.9940	---玄武岩纤维及其制品	17.5	70	17		千克		---Basalt fiber and its products
6815.9990	---其他	17.5	70	17		千克		---Other

第六十九章
陶瓷产品

注释：

一、本章仅适用于成形后经过烧制的陶瓷产品。税目69.04至69.14仅适用于不能归入税目69.01至69.03的产品。

二、本章不包括：

（一）税目28.44的产品；

（二）税目68.04的物品；

（三）第七十一章的物品（例如，仿首饰）；

（四）税目81.13的金属陶瓷；

（五）第八十二章的物品；

（六）绝缘子（税目85.46）或绝缘材料制的零件（税目85.47）；

（七）假牙（税目90.21）；

（八）第九十一章的物品（例如，钟及钟壳）；

（九）第九十四章的物品（例如，家具、灯具及照明装置、活动房屋）；

（十）第九十五章的物品（例如，玩具、游戏品及运动用品）；

（十一）税目96.06的物品（例如，钮扣）或税目96.14的物品（例如，烟斗）；

（十二）第九十七章的物品（例如，艺术品）。

Chapter 69
Ceramic products

Notes:

1. This Chapter applies only to ceramic products which have been fired after shaping. Headings Nos. 69.04 to 69.14 apply only to such products other than those classifiable in headings Nos. 69.01 to 69.03.

2. This Chapter does not cover:

(a) Products of heading No. 28.44;

(b) Articles of heading No. 68.04;

(c) Articles of Chapter 71 (for example, imitation jewellery);

(d) Cermets of heading No. 81.13;

(e) Articles of Chapter 82;

(f) Electrical insulators (heading No. 85.46) or fittings of insulating material of heading No. 85.47;

(g) Artificial teeth (heading No. 90.21);

(h) Articles of Chapter 91 (for example, clocks and clock cases);

(i) Articles of Chapter 94 (for example, furniture, lamps and lighting fittings, prefabricated buildings);

(j) Articles of Chapter 95 (for example, toys, games and sports requisites);

(k) Articles of heading No. 96.06 (for example, buttons) or of heading No. 96.14 (for example, smoking pipes); or

(l) Articles of Chapter 97 (for example, works of art).

税则号列	货品名称	最惠(%)	普通	增值税率	出口退税	计量单位	监管条件	Article Description
	第一分章　硅化石粉或类似硅土及耐火材料制品							Ⅰ.-GOODS OF SILICEOUS FOSSIL MEALS OR OF SIMILAR SILICEOUS EARTHS, AND REFRACTORY GOODS
69.01	**硅质化石粉(例如各种硅藻土)或类似硅土制的砖、块、瓦及其他陶瓷制品:**							**Bricks, blocks, tiles and other ceramic goods of siliceous fossil meals (for example, kieselguhr, tripolite or diatomite) or of similar siliceous earths:**
6901.0000	硅质化石粉(例如各种硅藻土)或类似硅土制的砖、瓦、块及其他陶瓷制品	8	50	17		千克		Bricks, blocks, tiles and other ceramic goods of siliceous fossil meals (for example, kieselguhr, tripolite or diatomite) or of similar siliceous earths
69.02	**耐火砖、块、瓦及类似耐火陶瓷建材制品，但硅质化石粉及类似硅土制的除外:**							**Refractory bricks, blocks, tiles and similar refractory ceramic constructional goods, other than those of siliceous fossil meals or similar siliceous earths:**
6902.1000	-单独或同时含有按重量计超过50%的镁、钙或铬(分别以氧化镁、氧化钙及三氧化二铬的含量计)	8	30	17		千克		-Containing by weight, singly or together, more than 50% of the elements Mg, Ca or Cr, expressed as MgO, CaO or Cr_2O_3
6902.2000	-含有按重量计超过50%的三氧化二铝、二氧化硅或其混合物或化合物	8	30	17		千克		-Containing by weight more than 50% of alumina (Al_2O_3), of silica (SiO_2) or of a mixture or compound of these products
6902.9000	-其他	8	30	17		千克		-Other
69.03	**其他耐火陶瓷制品(例如，甑、坩埚、马弗罩、喷管、栓塞、支架、烤钵、管子、护套及棒条)，但硅质化石粉及类似硅土制的除外:**							**Other refractory ceramic goods (for example, retorts, crucibles, muffles, nozzles, plugs, supports, cupels, tubes, pipes, sheaths and rods), other than those of siliceous fossil meals or of similar siliceous earths:**
6903.1000	-含有按重量计超过50%的石墨、其他碳或其混合物	8	20	17		千克		-Containing by weight more than 50% of graphite or other carbon or of a mixture of these products

税则号列	货品名称	最惠(%)	普通	增值税率	出口退税	计量单位	监管条件	Article Description
6903.2000	-含有按重量计超过50%的三氧化二铝或三氧化二铝和二氧化硅的混合物或化合物	8	20	17		千克		-Containing by weight more than 50% of alumina (AL_2O_3) or of a mixture of compound of alumina and of silica (SiO_2)
6903.9000	-其他	8	20	17	9	千克		-Other
	第二分章 其他陶瓷产品							Ⅱ.-OTHER CERAMIC PRODUCTS
69.04	**陶瓷制建筑用砖、铺地砖、支撑或填充用砖及类似品:**							**Ceramic building bricks, flooring blocks, support or filler tiles and the like:**
6904.1000	-建筑用砖	15	90	17	9	千克/千块		-Building bricks
6904.9000暂	-其他	15	90	17	9	千克		-Other
69.05	**屋顶瓦、烟囱罩、通风帽、烟囱衬壁、建筑装饰物及其他建筑用陶瓷制品:**							**Roofing tiles, chimney-pots, cowls, chimney liners, architectural ornaments and other ceramic constructional goods:**
6905.1000暂	-屋顶瓦	15	90	17	9	千克		-Roofing tiles
6905.9000暂	-其他	15	90	17	9	千克		-Other
69.06	**陶瓷套管、导管、槽管及管子附件:**							**Ceramic pipes, conduits, guttering and pipe fittings:**
6906.0000暂	陶瓷套管、导管、槽管及管子附件	10	90	17	9	千克		Ceramic pipes, conduits, guttering and pipe fittings
69.07	**未上釉的陶瓷贴面砖、铺面砖,包括炉面砖及墙面砖;未上釉的陶瓷镶嵌砖(马赛克)及类似品,不论是否有衬背:**							**Unglazed ceramic flags and paving, hearth or wall tiles; unglazed ceramic mosaic cubes and the like, whether or not on a backing:**
6907.1000暂	-砖、瓦、块及类似品,不论是否矩形,其最大表面积以可置入边长小于7厘米的方格为限	12	90	17	9	千克/平方米		-Tiles, cubes and similar articles, whether or not rectangular, the largest surface area of which is capable of being enclosed in a square, the side of which is less than 7cm
6907.1000暂 10	瓷砖、陶瓷等产品,未打磨上釉陶瓷(表面最宽<7cm)	12	90	17	9	千克/平方米		Ceramic tile, ceramics products, unglazed, unpolished(the widest side of surface square<7cm)
6907.1000暂 90	未上釉的小陶瓷砖、瓦、块及类似品(小指最大表面积可置入边长<7cm的方格为限)	12	90	17	9	千克/平方米		Unglazed small ceramic tiles, cubes and similar articles(thelargest surface area of which is capable of being enclosed in a square side<7cm)
6907.9000暂	-其他	8	90	17	9	千克/平方米		-Other
69.08	**上釉的陶瓷贴面砖、铺面砖,包括炉面砖及墙面砖;上釉的陶瓷镶嵌砖(马赛克)及类似品,不论是否有衬背:**							**Glazed ceramic flags and paving, hearth or wall tiles; glazed ceramic mosaic cubes and the like, whether or not on a backing:**
6908.1000	-砖、瓦、块及类似品,不论是否矩形,其最大表面积以可置入边长小于7厘米的方格为限	12	100	17	9	千克/平方米		-Tiles, cubes and similar articles, whether or not rectangular, the largest surface area of which is capable of being enclosed in a square, the side of which is less than 7cm
6908.9000	-其他	12	100	17	9	千克/平方米		-Other
69.09	**实验室、化学或其他专门技术用途的陶瓷器;农业用陶瓷槽、缸及类似容器;通常供运输及盛装货物用的陶瓷罐、坛及类似品:**							**Ceramic wares for laboratory, chemical or other technical uses; ceramic troughs, tubs and similar receptacles of a kind used in agriculture; ceramic pots, jars and similar articles of a kind used for the conveyance or packing of goods:**
	-实验室、化学或其他专门技术用途的陶瓷器:							-Ceramic wares for laboratory, chemical or other technical uses:
6909.1100	--瓷制	8	30	17	13	千克		--Of porcelain or china
6909.1200	--摩氏硬度为9或以上的物品	8	30	17	13	千克		--Articles having a hardness equivalent to 9 or more on the Mohs scale
6909.1900	--其他	8	30	17	13	千克		--Other
6909.9000暂	-其他	15	90	17	9	千克		-Other
69.10	**陶瓷洗涤槽、脸盆、脸盆座、浴缸、坐浴盆、抽水马桶、水箱、小便池及类似的固定卫生设备:**							**Ceramic sinks, wash basins, wash basin pedestals, baths, bidets, water closet pans, flushing cisterns, urinals and similar sanitary fixtures:**
6910.1000	-瓷制	10	100	17	9	千克/件		-Of porcelain or china
6910.9000	-其他	10	100	17	9	千克/件	A	-Other

税则号列	货品名称	最惠(%)	普通	增值税率	出口退税	计量单位	监管条件	Article Description
69.11	瓷餐具、厨房器具及其他家用或盥洗用瓷器：							**Tableware, kitchenware, other household articles and toilet articles, of porcelain or china:**
	-餐具及厨房器具：							-Tableware and kitchenware:
	---餐具：							---Tableware:
6911.1011暂	----骨瓷	8	100	17	13	千克	A	----Bone china
6911.1019暂	----其他	8	100	17	13	千克	A	----Other
	---厨房器具：							---Kitchenware:
6911.1021暂	----刀具	10	100	17	13	千克	A	----Knife tool
6911.1029暂	----其他	10	100	17	13	千克	A	----Other
6911.9000	-其他	24.5	100	17	13	千克		-Other
69.12	陶餐具、厨房器具及其他家用或盥洗用陶器：							**Ceramic tableware, kitchenware, other household articles and toilet articles, other than of procelain or china:**
6912.0010暂	---餐具	10	100	17	13	千克	A	---Tableware
6912.0090暂	---其他	10	100	17	13	千克	A	---Other
69.13	塑像及其他装饰用陶瓷制品：							**Statuettes and other ornamental ceramic articles:**
6913.1000	-瓷制	15	100	17	13	千克		-Of porcelain or china
6913.9000	-其他	15	100	17	13	千克		-Other
69.14	其他陶瓷制品：							**Other ceramic articles:**
6914.1000	-瓷制	24.5	100	17	9	千克		-Of porcelain or china
6914.9000	-其他	10	100	17	9	千克		-Other

第七十章
玻璃及其制品

注释：

一、本章不包括：

（一）税目 32.07 的货品（例如，珐琅和釉料、搪瓷玻璃料及其他玻璃粉、粒或粉片）；

（二）第七十一章的物品（例如，仿首饰）；

（三）税目 85.44 的光缆、税目 85.46 的绝缘子或税目 85.47 所列绝缘材料制的零件；

（四）光导纤维、经光学加工的光学元件、注射用针管、假眼、温度计、气压计、液体比重计或第九十章的其他物品；

（五）有永久固定电光源的灯具及照明装置、灯箱标志或铭牌和类似品及其零件（税目94.05）；

（六）玩具、游戏品、运动用品、圣诞树装饰品及第九十五章的其他物品（供玩偶或第九十五章其他物品用的无机械装置的玻璃假眼珠除外）；

（七）钮扣、保温瓶、香水喷雾器和类似的喷雾器及第九十六章的其他物品。

二、对于税目 70.03、70.04 及 70.05：

（一）玻璃在退火前的各种处理都不视为“已加工”；

（二）玻璃切割成一定形状并不影响其作为板片归类；

（三）所称“吸收、反射或非反射层”，是指极薄的金属或化合物（例如金属氧化物）镀层，该镀层可以吸收红外线等光线或可以提高玻璃的反射性能，同时仍然使玻璃具有一定程度的透明性或半透明性；或者该镀层可以防止光线在玻璃表面的反射。

三、税目 70.06 所述产品，不论是否具有制成品的特性仍归入该税目。

四、税目 70.19 所称“玻璃棉”，是指：

（一）按重量计二氧化硅的含量在 60% 及以上的矿质棉；

（二）按重量计二氧化硅的含量在 60% 以下，但碱性氧化物（氧化钾或氧化钠）的含量在 5% 以上或氧化硼的含量在 2% 以上的矿质棉。

不符合上述规定的矿质棉归入税目 68.06。

五、本协调制度所称“玻璃”，包括熔融石英及其他熔融硅石。

子目注释：

子目号 7013.22、7013.33 及 7013.41 及 7013.91 所称“铅晶质玻璃”，仅指按重量计氧化铅含量不低于 24% 的玻璃。

Chapter 70
Glass and glassware

Notes:

1. This Chapter does not cover:

(a) Goods of heading No. 32.07 (for example, vitrifiable enamels and glazes, glass frit, other glass in the form of powder, granules or flakes);

(b) Articles of Chapter 71 (for example, imitation jewellery);

(c) Optical fibre cables (heading No. 85.44), electrical insulators (heading 85.46) or fitting of insulating material of heading No. 85.47;

(d) Optical fibres, optically worked optical elements, hypodermic syringes, artificial eyes, thermometers, barometers, hydrometers or other articles of Chapter 90;

(e) Lamps or lighting fittings, illuminated signs, illuminated nameplates or the like, having a permanently fixed light source, or parts thereof of heading No. 94.05;

(f) Toys, games, sports requisites, Christmas tree ornaments or other articles of Chapter 95 (excluding glass eyes without mechanisms for dolls or for other articles of Chapter 95); or

(g) Buttons, fitted vacuum flasks, scent or similar sprays or other articles of Chapter 96.

2. For the purposes of headings Nos. 70.03, 70.04 and 70.05:

(a) glass is not regarded as "worked" by reason of any process it has undergone before annealing;

(b) cutting to shape does not affect the classification of glass in sheets;

(c) the expression "absorbent, reflecting or non-reflecting layer" means a microscopically thin coating of metal or of a chemical compound (for example, metal oxide) which absorbs, for example, infra-red light or improves the reflecting qualities of the glass while still allowing it to retain a degree of transparency or translucency; or which prevents light from being reflected on the surface of the glass.

3. The products referred to in heading No. 70.06 remain classified in that heading whether or not they have the character of articles.

4. For the purposes of heading No. 70.19, the expression "glass wool" means:

(a) Mineral wools with a silica (SiO_2) content not less than 60% by weight;

(b) Mineral wools with a silica (SiO_2) content less than 60% but with an alkaline oxide (K_2O or Na_2O) content exceeding 5% by weight or a boric oxide (B_2O_3) content exceeding 2% by weight.

Mineral wools which do not comply with the above specifications fall in heading No. 68.06.

5. Throughout the Nomenclature, the expression "glass" includes fused quartz and other fused silica.

Subheading Note:

For the purposes of subheadings Nos. 7013.22, 7013.33, 7013,41and 7013.91, the expression "lead crystal" means only glass having a minimum lead monoxide (PbO) content by weight of 24%.

税则号列	货品名称	最惠(%)	普通	增值税率	出口退税	计量单位	监管条件	Article Description
70.01	**碎玻璃及废玻璃;玻璃块料:**							**Cullet and other waste and scrap of glass; glass in the mass:**
7001.0000	碎玻璃及废玻璃;玻璃块料	12	50	17		千克		Cullet and other waste and scrap of glass; glass in the mass
7001.0000 10	废碎玻璃	12	50	17		千克	9	Waster and scrap of slass
7001.0000 90	玻璃块料	12	50	17		千克		Glass in the mass
70.02	**未加工的玻璃球、棒及管(税目70.18的微型玻璃球除外):**							**Glass in balls (other than microspheres of heading No. 70.18), rods or tubes, unworked:**
7002.1000	-玻璃球	12	50	17		千克		-Balls
	-玻璃棒:							-Rods:
7002.2010	---光导纤维预制棒	6	50	17	13	千克		---Preformed bars for drawing optical fibre
7002.2090	---其他	12	50	17		千克		---Other
	-玻璃管:							-Tubes:
	--熔融石英或其他熔融硅石制:							--Of fused quartz or other fused silica:
7002.3110暂	---光导纤维用波导级石英玻璃管	1	17	17	13	千克		---Waveguide quartz tubes for optical fibres use
7002.3190	---其他	14	50	17		千克		---Other
7002.3200	--温度在0℃至300℃时线膨胀系数不超过5×10^{-6}/开尔文的其他玻璃制	12	50	17	13	千克		--Of other glass having a linear coefficient of expansion not exceeding 5×10^{-6} per Kelvin within a temperature range of 0℃ to 300℃
7002.3900	--其他		50	17	13	千克		--Other
7002.3900暂 01	光通信用微光组件的玻璃毛细管、定位管(外径小于3mm)	3	50	17	13	千克		Glass capillaries of micro-optical assemblies used in optical communications (external diameter < 3mm)
7002.3900 90	未列名、未加工的玻璃管	12	50	17	13	千克		Glass tubes, not elsewhere specified or included, unworked
70.03	**铸制或轧制玻璃板、片或型材及异型材,不论是否有吸收、反射或非反射层,但未经其他加工:**							**Cast glass and rolled glass, in sheets or profiles, whether or not having an absorbent, reflecting or non-reflecting layer, but not otherwise worked:**
	-非夹丝玻璃板、片:							-Non-wired sheets:
7003.1200	--整块着色、不透明、镶色或具有吸收、反射或非反射层的	15	50	17		千克/平方米		--Coloured throughout the mass (body tinted), opacified, flashed or having an absorbent, or non-reflecting reflecting layer
7003.1900	--其他		50	17		千克/平方米		--Other
7003.1900暂 01	液晶或有机发光二极管(OLED)显示屏用原板玻璃,包括保护屏用含碱玻璃(铸、轧制的非夹丝玻璃板、片,未着色,透明及不具吸收层的,未经其他加工)	3	50	17	5	千克/平方米		Original plate glass using for liquid crystal or an organic light - emitting diode (OLED) displayincluding the protection screen containing alkali glass(cast and rolled other non - wired glass, in sheets or parcel, not colored, transparent and without absorbing layer, not processed in other way)
7003.1900 90	铸、轧制的其他非夹丝玻璃板、片(未着色,透明及不具吸收层的,未经其他加工)	17.5	50	17		千克/平方米		Cast and rolled other non-wired glass, in sheets or parcel (not colored, transparent and without absorbing layer, not processed in other way)
7003.2000	-夹丝玻璃板、片	15	50	17		千克/平方米		-Wired sheets
7003.3000	-型材及异型材	15	50	17		千克/平方米		-Profiles
70.04	**拉制或吹制玻璃板、片,不论是否有吸收、反射或非反射层,但未经其他加工:**							**Drawn glass and blown glass, in sheets, whether or not having an absorbent, reflecting or non-reflecting layer, but not otherwise worked:**
7004.2000	-整块着色、不透明、镶色或具有吸收、反射或非反射层的	17.5	50	17		千克/平方米		-Glass, coloured throughout the mass (body tinted), opacified, flashed or having an absorbent, reflecting or non-reflecting layer
7004.9000	-其他玻璃		50	17		千克/平方米		-Other glass

税则号列	货品名称	最惠(%)	普通	增值税率	出口退税	计量单位	监管条件	Article Description
7004.9000暂 01	光学平板玻璃,厚度0.7mm以下(未着色,透明及不具吸收层的,未经其他加工)	9	50	17		千克/平方米		Optic plane glass, thickness < 0.7mm (not coloured, transparent and not having an absorbent, not otherwise worked)
7004.9000 90	拉、吹制的其他玻璃板、片(未着色,透明及不具吸收层的,未经其他加工)	17.5	50	17		千克/平方米		Other glass plate and piece made by blowing and pulling (not colonred, transparent and not having an absorbent not othermie worked)
70.05	**浮法玻璃板、片及表面研磨或抛光玻璃板、片,不论是否有吸收、反射或非反射层,但未经其他加工:**							**Float glass and surface ground or polished glass, in sheets, whether or not having an absorbent, reflecting or non-reflecting layer, but not otherwise worked:**
7005.1000	-具有吸收、反射或非反射层的非夹丝玻璃	15	50	17		千克/平方米		-Non-wired glass, having an absorbent, reflecting or non-reflecting layer
	-其他非夹丝玻璃:							-Other non-wired glass:
7005.2100	--整块着色、不透明、镶色或仅表面研磨的	15	50	17		千克/平方米		--Coloured throughout the mass (body tinted), opacified, flashed or merely surface ground
7005.2900	--其他		50	17		千克/平方米		--Other
7005.2900暂 02	液晶或有机发光二极管(OLED)显示屏用原板玻璃,包括保护屏用含碱玻璃(非夹丝浮法玻璃板、片)	3	50	17	5	千克/平方米		Lidquid cry stal or organic luminous diode (OLED) original plate glass used for display including the protection screen containing alkali glass (Non – wired float slass and piece
7005.2900 90	其他非夹丝浮法玻璃板、片	15	50	17		千克/平方米		Other float non-wired glass, in sheets
7005.3000	-夹丝玻璃	17.5	50	17		千克/平方米		-Wired glass
70.06	**经弯曲、磨边、镂刻、钻孔、涂珐琅或其他加工的税目70.03、70.04或70.05的玻璃,但未用其他材料镶框或装配:**							**Glass of heading No. 70.03, 70.04 or 70.05, bent, edge-worked, engraved, drilled, enamelled or otherwise worked, but not framed or fitted with other materials:**
7006.0000	经弯曲、磨边、镂刻、钻孔、涂珐琅或其他加工的税目70.03、70.04或70.05的玻璃,但未用其他材料镶框或装配		50	17	13	千克		Glass of heading No. 70.03, 70.04 or 70.05, bent, edge-worked, engraved, drilled, enamelled or otherwise worked, but not framed or fitted with other materials
7006.0000暂 01	液晶玻璃基板,6代(1850mm * 1500mm)以上,不含6代(经弯曲、磨边、镂刻、钻孔、涂珐琅等加工,款镶框或装配)	4	50	17	13	千克		LCD glass base plate, more than 6 generation, (1850mm * 1500mm), other than 6 generation (bent, edge – worked, engraved, drilled, enamelled or otherwise worked, but not framed or fitted)
7006.0000暂 02	液晶玻璃基板,6代(1850mm * 1500mm)及以下(经弯曲、磨边、镂刻、钻孔、涂珐琅等加工,款镶框或装配)	6	50	17	13	千克		LCD glass base plate, 6 generation and less than, (1850mm * 1500mm), other than 6 generation (bent, edge – worked, engraved, drilled, enamelled or otherwise worked, but not framed or fitted)
7006.0000 90	经其他加工编号7003－7005的玻璃(经弯曲、磨边、镂刻、钻孔、涂珐琅等加工、未镶框或装配)	15	50	17	13	千克		Glass in other process Nos. from 7003 to 7005 (after being bent, edged, carved, holed and painted with enamel, not mounted in cabinet or fixed)
70.07	**钢化或层压玻璃制的安全玻璃:**							**Safety glass, consisting of toughened (tempered) or laminated glass:**
	-钢化安全玻璃:							-Toughened (tempered) safety glass:
	--规格及形状适于安装在车辆、航空器、航天器及船舶上:							--Of size and shape suitable for incorporation in vehicles, aircraft, spacecraft or vessels:
7007.1110	---航空器、航天器及船舶用		11	17	13	千克		---For aircraft, spacecraft or vessels
7007.1110暂 01	空载重量≥25吨飞机的挡风玻璃	1	11	17	13	千克		Toughened (tempered) safety glass, of size and shape suitable for incorporation in aircraft, W≥25 tons
7007.1110 90	航空航天器及船舶用钢化安全玻璃(其他规格及形状适于安装在航空航天器及船上的)	2	11	17	13	千克		Toughened safety glass for aircraft, spacecraft and ships (other specs and forms suitable for installation in aircraft, spacecraft and ships)
7007.1190	---其他	10	50	17	13	千克	A	---Other
7007.1900	--其他		50	17	13	千克/平方米		--Other

税则号列	货品名称	最惠(%)	普通	增值税率	出口退税	计量单位	监管条件	Article Description
7007.1900暂 01	低铁钢化太阳能电池组件封装专用玻璃(指最大含铁量 0.02% Fe_2O_3,厚度为 2.5mm-3.5mm 的玻璃)	12	50	17	13	千克/平方米		Low-ferrous toughened safety glass, specified for sealing of solar cell assemblies, (maximum ferrous content: 0.02% Fe_2O_3, thickness: 2.5mm~3.5mm)
7007.1900 90	其他钢化安全玻璃	14	50	17	13	千克/平方米		Other toughened (tempered) safety glass
	-层压安全玻璃:							-Laminated safety glass:
	--规格及形状适于安装在车辆、航空器、航天器及船舶上:							--Of size and shape suitable for incorporation in vehicles, aircraft, spacecraft or vessels:
7007.2110	---航空器、航天器及船舶用	2	11	17	13	千克		---for aircraft, spacecraft or vessels
7007.2190	---其他	20	50	17	13	千克	A	---Other
7007.2900	--其他	14	50	17	13	千克/平方米		--Other
70.08	**多层隔温、隔音玻璃组件:**							**Multiple-walled insulating units of glass:**
7008.0010	---中空或真空隔温、隔音玻璃	14	50	17	13	千克		---Sealed or vacuum insulating glass
7008.0090	---其他	14	50	17	13	千克		---Other
70.09	**玻璃镜(包括后视镜),不论是否镶框:**							**Glass mirrors, whether or not framed, including rear-view mirrors:**
7009.1000	-车辆后视镜	10	100	17	13	千克		-Rear-view mirrors for vehicles
	-其他:							-Other:
7009.9100	--未镶框		70	17	13	千克		--Unframed
7009.9100暂 01	槽式太阳能抛物面反射镜	10	70	17	13	千克		Reflecting mirror of trench type solar paraboloid
7009.9100 90	其他未镶框玻璃镜(包括后视镜)	21	70	17	13	千克		Other class mirrors, not framed (including rear-view mirrors)
7009.9200	--已镶框	12	100	17	13	千克		--Framed
70.10	**玻璃制的坛、瓶、缸、罐、安瓿及其他容器,用于运输或盛装货物;玻璃制保藏罐;玻璃塞、盖及类似的封口器:**							**Carboys, bottles, flasks, jars, pots, phials, ampoules and other containers, of glass, of a kind used for the conveyance or packing of goods; preserving jars of glass; stoppers, lids and other closures, of glass:**
7010.1000	-安瓿	14	50	17	13	千克		-Ampoules
7010.2000	-塞、盖及类似的封口器	14	50	17	13	千克		-Stoppers, lids and other closures
	-其他:							-Other:
7010.9010	---超过1升	14	50	17	13	千克		---Exceeding 1L
7010.9020	---超过0.33升,但不超过1升	14	50	17	13	千克		---Exceeding 0.33L but not exceeding 1L
7010.9030	---超过0.15升,但不超过0.33升	14	50	17	13	千克		---Exceeding 0.15L but not exceeding 0.33L
7010.9090	---不超过0.15升	14	50	17	13	千克		---Not exceeding 0.15L
70.11	**制灯泡、阴极射线管及类似品用的未封口玻璃外壳(包括玻璃泡及管)及其玻璃零件,但未装有配件:**							**Glass envelopes (including bulbs and tubes), open, and glass parts thereof, without fittings, for electric lamps, cathode-ray tubes or the like:**
7011.1000	-电灯用	21	80	17		千克		-For electric lighting
	-阴极射线管用:							-For cathode-ray tubes:
7011.2010	---显像管玻壳及其零件	10	35	17	13	千克	6	---Glass envelopes for kinescope and glass parts thereof
7011.2090	---其他		35	17	5	千克		---Other
7011.2090暂 01	显示管玻壳及其零件(包括零件,但未装有配件)	6	35	17	5	千克	6	Glass envelopes for display tubes and glass parts (including parts thereof, without fittings)
7011.2090 90	其他阴极射线管用的未封口玻壳(包括零件,但未装有配件)	10	35	17	5	千克	6	Glass envelopes for cathode-ray tules open (including parts thereof, without fittings)
	-其他:							-Other:
7011.9010	---电子管用(阴极射线管用的除外)	8	35	17	5	千克		---For electronic tubes and valves (other than cathode-ray tubes)
7011.9090	---其他	21	80	17		千克		---Other
70.13	**玻璃器,供餐桌、厨房、盥洗室、办公室、室内装饰或类似用途(税号 70.10 或 70.18 的货品除外):**							**Glassware of a kind used for table, kitchen, toilet, office, indoor decoration or similar purposes (other than that of heading No. 70.10 or 70.18):**
7013.1000	-玻璃陶瓷制	24.5	100	17	13	千克		-Of glass-ceramics
	-高脚杯,但玻璃陶瓷制的除外:							-Stemware drinking glasses, other than of glass-ceramics:
7013.2200暂	--铅晶质玻璃制	15	100	17	13	千克		--Of lead crystal
7013.2800	--其他	8	100	17	13	千克	A	--Other
	-其他杯子,但玻璃陶瓷制的除外:							-Other drinking glasses, other than of glass-ceramics:

税则号列	货　品　名　称	最惠(%)	普通	增值税率	出口退税	计量单位	监管条件	Article Description
7013.3300[暂]	--铅晶质玻璃制	15	100	17	13	千克		--Of lead crystal
7013.3700	--其他	8	100	17	13	千克	A	--Other
	-餐桌或厨房用玻璃器皿(不包括杯子),但玻璃陶瓷制的除外:							-Classware of a kind used for table (other than drinkings glasses) or kitchen purposes other than of glass-ceramics:
7013.4100[暂]	--铅晶质玻璃剂	15	100	17	13	千克	A	--Of lead crystal
7013.4200	--温度在0℃至300℃时线膨胀系数不超过5×10^{-6}/开尔文的其他玻璃制	10	100	17	13	千克	A	--Of glasc having a linear coefficient of expansion not exceeding 5×10^{-6} perkelvin within a temperature range of 0℃ to 300℃
7013.4900	--其他	10	100	17	13	千克	A	--Other
	-其他玻璃器:							-Other glassware:
7013.9100	--铅晶质玻璃制	10	100	17	13	千克		--Of lead crystal
7013.9900	--其他	10	100	17	13	千克		--Other
70.14	**未经光学加工的信号玻璃器及玻璃制光学元件(税目70.15的货品除外):**							**Signalling glassware and optical elements of glass (other than thoseof heading No. 70.15), not optically worked:**
7014.0010	---光学仪器用光学元件毛坯	10	40	17	13	千克		---Blanks of optical elements, for optical instruments
7014.0090	---其他		80	17	13	千克		---Other
7014.0090[暂] 01	滤波玻璃(带有抗红外和防反射薄膜的)	9	80	17	13	千克		Wave filtering glass (with anti-infrared and anti-radiation film)
7014.0090 90	其他未经光学加工的信号玻璃器(包括玻璃制光学元件,编号7015的物品除外)	17.5	80	17	13	千克		Other signaling glassware and optical elements of glass (including glass optical elements, other than thoseof heading No. 70.15)
70.15	**钟表玻璃及类似玻璃、视力矫正或非视力矫正眼镜用玻璃,呈弧面、弯曲、凹形或类似形状但未经光学加工的;制造上述玻璃用的凹面圆形及扇形玻璃:**							**Clock or watch glasses and similar glasses, glasses for non-corrective or corrective spectacles, curved, bent, hollowed or the like, not optically worked; hollow glass spheres and their segments, for the manufacture of such glasses:**
	-视力矫正眼镜用玻璃:							-Glasses for corrective spectacles:
7015.1010	---变色镜片坯件	21	80	17	13	千克		---Blanks for photochromic spectacles
7015.1090	---其他	17.5	70	17	13	千克		---Other
	-其他:							-Other:
7015.9010	---钟表玻璃	17.5	70	17		千克		---Clock and watch glasses
7015.9020	---平光变色镜片坯件	18	80	17	13	千克		---Blanks for plane photochromic spectacles
7015.9090	---其他	12	80	17		千克		---Other
70.16	**建筑用压制或模制的铺面用玻璃块、砖、片、瓦及其他制品,不论是否夹丝;供镶嵌或类似装饰用的玻璃马赛克及其他小件玻璃品,不论是否有衬背;花饰铅条窗玻璃及类似品;多孔或泡沫玻璃块、板、片及类似品:**							**Paving blocks, slabs, bricks, squares, tiles and other articles of pressed or moulded glass, whether or not wired, of a kind used for building or construction purposes; glass cubes and other glass smallwares, whether or not on a backing, for mosaics or similar decorative purposes; leaded lights and the like; multicellular or foam glass in blocks, panels, plates, shells or similar forms:**
7016.1000	-供镶嵌或类似装饰用的玻璃马赛克及其他小件玻璃品,不论是否有衬背	22	100	17	13	千克		-Glass cubes and other glass smallwares, whether or not on a backing, for mosaics or similar decorative purposes
	-其他:							-Other:
7016.9010	---花饰铅条窗玻璃及类似品	24	90	17	13	千克		---Leaded lights and the like
7016.9090	---其他	18	90	17	13	千克		---Other
70.17	**实验室、卫生及配药用的玻璃器,不论有无刻度或标量:**							**Laboratory, hygienic or pharmaceutical glassware, whether or not graduated or calibrated:**
7017.1000	-熔融石英或其他熔融硅石制	0	30	17	13	千克		-Of fused quartz or other fused silica
7017.2000	-温度在0℃至300℃时线膨胀系数不超过5×10^{-6}/开尔文的其他玻璃制	8	30	17	13	千克		-Of other glass having a linear coefficient of expansion not exceeding 5×10^{-6} per Kelvin within a temperature range of 0℃ to 300℃
7017.9000	-其他	8	30	17	13	千克		-Other

税则号列	货 品 名 称	最惠(%)	普通	增值税率	出口退税	计量单位	监管条件	Article Description
70.18	玻璃珠、仿珍珠、仿宝石或仿半宝石和类似小件玻璃品及其制品,但仿首饰除外;玻璃假眼,但医用假眼除外;灯工方法制作的玻璃塑像及其他玻璃装饰品,但仿首饰除外;直径不超过1毫米的微型玻璃球:							**Glass beads, imitation pearls, imitation precious or semi-precious stones and similar glass smallwares, and articles thereof other than imitation jewellery; glass eyes other than prosthetic articles; statuettes and other ornaments of lampworked glass, other than imitation jewellery; glass microspheres not exceeding 1mm in diameter:**
7018.1000	-玻璃珠、仿珍珠、仿宝石或仿半宝石及类似小件玻璃品	10	100	17	13	千克		-Glass beads, imitation pearls, imitation precious or semi-precious stones and similar glass smallwares
7018.2000	-直径不超过1毫米的微型玻璃珠		100	17	13	千克		-Glass microspheres, diameter≤1mm
7018.2000暂 01	熔融球形二氧化硅微粉,直径≤100um	5.5	100	17	13	千克		Molten spherical silica powder, diameter ≤ 100um
7018.2000 90	其他直径≤1毫米的微型玻璃珠	20	100	17	13	千克		Other glass microspheres not exceeding lmm in diameler
7018.9000暂	-其他	10	100	17	13	千克		-Other
70.19	**玻璃纤维(包括玻璃棉)及其制品(例如,玻璃纤维纱线及其织物):**							**Glass fibres (including glass wool) and articles thereof (for example, yarn, woven fabrics):**
	-梳条、粗纱、纱线及短切纤维:							-Slivers, rovings, yarn and chopped strands:
7019.1100	--长度不超过50毫米的短切纤维	12	50	17	5	千克		--Chopped strands, of a length of not more than 50mm
7019.1100 10	两用物项管制的长度不超过50mm的短切玻璃纤维(比模量≥3.18×10^6 m,以及比抗拉强度≥7.62×10^4 m)	12	50	17		千克	3	Chopped fibres, fual - use items control, length ≤ 50mm, modulus atio≥3.18×10^6m, specific ultimate tensile strength≥7.62×10^4m
7019.1100 90	其他长度不超过50mm的短切玻璃纤维	12	50	17	5	千克		Other chopped fibres, fual - use items control, length ≤50mm
7019.1200	--粗纱	12	50	17	5	千克		--Rovings
7019.1200 20	两用物项管制的玻璃纤维粗纱(比模量≥3.18×10^6 m,以及比抗拉强度≥7.62×10^4 m)	12	50	17	5	千克	3	Glass fibres rovings, fual - use items control, modulus atio≥3.18×10^6m, specific ultimate tensile strength ≥7.62×10^4m
7019.1200 90	其他玻璃纤维粗纱	12	50	17	5	千克		Other glass fibres rovings
7019.1900	--其他	10	50	17	5	千克		--Other
7019.1900 11	间苯二酚甲醛胶浸渍的玻璃纤维纱(用于生产非导电玻璃纤维长丝粗纱机织轮胎帘子布的)	10	50	17	5	千克		Glass fibers yarn impregnated with resorcinol formaldehydeglue (for manufacturing woven tyre cord fabrics of non-conductive fibre glass roving)
7019.1900 12	玻璃纤维或纤丝材料(其"比模量"为3.18×10^6米或更大和"比抗拉强度"为7.62×10^4米或更大的玻璃纤维或纤丝材料)	10	50	17	5	千克	3	Glass fibre or filaments (specific modulus ≥3.18×10^6 m, specific ultimate tensile strength≥7.62×10^4 m)
7019.1900 19	其他玻璃纱线(包括长度超过50mm的短切纤维)	10	50	17	5	千克		Other glass yarn (including chopped fibres which length >50mm)
7019.1900 90	其他玻璃纤维(含长度超过50mm的短切纤维)	10	50	17	5	千克		Other glass fibres (including chopped fibres which length >50mm)
	-薄片(巴厘纱)、纤维网、席、垫、板及类似无纺产品:							-Thin sheets (voiles), webs, mats, mattresses, boards and similar nonwoven products:
7019.3100	--席	5	40	17	5	千克		--Mats
7019.3200	--薄片(巴厘纱)	14	40	17	5	千克		--Thin sheets (voiles)
	--其他:					千克		--Other:
7019.3910	---垫	10.5	40	17	5	千克		---Mattresses
7019.3990	---其他	10.5	40	17	5	千克		---Other
7019.4000	-粗纱机织物	12	40	17	5	千克		-Woven fabrics of rovings
	-其他机织物:							-Other woven fabrics:
7019.5100	--宽度不超过30厘米的	12	40	17	5	千克		--Of a width not exceeding 30cm
7019.5100 10	两用物项管制的宽度≤15mm的玻璃纤维机织物	12	40	17	5	千克	3	Glass fibres woven fabrics, fual - use items control, width≤15mm
7019.5100 90	其他宽度≤30cm的玻璃纤维机织物	12	40	17	5	千克		Other glass fibres woven fabrics, width≤30cm
7019.5200	--宽度超过30厘米的长丝平纹织物,每平方米重量不超过250克,单根纱线细度不超过136特克斯		40	17	5	千克		--Of a width exceeding 30cm, plain weave, weighing less than 250g/m², of filaments measuring per single yarn not more than 136 tex

税则号列	货品名称	最惠(%)	普通	增值税率	出口退税	计量单位	监管条件	Article Description
7019.5200暂 01	覆铜板用玻璃纤维长丝平纹布,开纤或每平米重≤180克(宽度>30cm,单根纱线细度≤136特)	10	40	17	5	千克		Glass fibres filament plain weave for CCL (width > 30cm, of filaments measuring per single yarn ≤ 136 tex)
7019.5200 90	其他平米重≤250g玻璃长丝平纹布(宽度超过30cm,单根纱线细度不超过136特)	12	40	17	5	千克		Other class fibrels filament plain weave (width > 30cm, of filaments measuring per single yarn ≤ 136 tex)
7019.5900	--其他	12	40	17	5	千克		--Other
	-其他:					千克		-Other:
7019.9010	---玻璃棉及其制品	7	40	17	5	千克		---glass wool and its articles
	---玻璃纤维布浸胶制品:							---Glass fiber cloth dipped articles:
7019.9021	----每平方米重量<450克	7	40	17	5,13	千克		----Weight<450g/m²
7019.9029	----其他	7	40	17	5	千克		----Other
7019.9090	---其他	7	40	17	13	千克		---Other
70.20	**其他玻璃制品:**							**Other articles of glass:**
	---工业用:							---For technical use:
7020.0011暂	----导电玻璃	7	40	17	13	千克		----Conductivity glass
7020.0012	----绝缘子用玻璃伞盘	10.5	40	17		千克		----Glass umbrella for insulator
7020.0013	----熔融石英或其他熔融硅石制	10.5	40	17		千克		----Of fused quartz or other fused silica
7020.0013 01	半导体晶片生产用石英反应管及夹持器(熔融石英或其他熔融硅石制)(用于插入熔化和氧化炉内)	0	40	17		千克	s	Quartz reactor tubes and holders for production of semiconductor wafers, of fused quartz or other fused silica (for inserting in melting and oxidation)
7020.0013 90	熔融石英或其他熔融硅石制工业用其他玻璃制品(导电玻璃及绝缘子用玻璃伞盘除外)	10.5	40	17	0	千克		Other articles of fused quartz or other fused silica (other than glass umbrella for insulator)
7020.0019	----其他		40	17		千克		----Other
7020.0019 01	半导体晶片生产用石英反应管及夹持器(用于插入熔化和氧化炉内)	0	40	17		千克	s	Quartz reactor tubes and holders for production of semiconductor wafers (for inserting in melting and oxidation)
7020.0019 02	等离子模块生产用高应变点玻璃(应变点在550℃及以上)	10.5	40	17	5	千克		High strain-point glass for producing plasma module (strain point≥550℃)
7020.0019 90	其他工业用玻璃制品	10.5	40	17		千克		Other galss articles for other technical use
	---其他:							---Other:
7020.0091	----保温瓶或其他保温容器用的玻璃胆	21	100	17	13	千克/个	A	----Glass inners for vacuum flasks or for other vacuum vessels
7020.0099	----其他		100	17		千克		----Other
7020.0099暂 01	石英玻璃,平整度小于等于1微米	4	100	17		千克		Quartz glass, levelling degree ≤1 μm
7020.0099 90	其他非工业用玻璃制品	15	100	17		千克		Other glass articles not for other technical use

第十四类
天然或养殖珍珠、宝石或半宝石、贵金属、包贵金属及其制品；仿首饰；硬币

第七十一章
天然或养殖珍珠、宝石或半宝石、贵金属、包贵金属及其制品；仿首饰；硬币

注释：

一、除第六类注释一（一）及下列各款另有规定的以外，凡制品的全部或部分由下列物品构成，均应归入本章：

（一）天然或养殖珍珠、宝石或半宝石（天然、合成或再造）；

（二）贵金属或包贵金属。

二、（一）税目 71.13、71.14 及 71.15 不包括带有贵金属或包贵金属制的小附件或小装饰品（例如，交织字母、套、圈、套环）的制品，上述注释一（二）也不适用于这类制品；

（二）税目 71.16 不包括含有贵金属或包贵金属（仅作为小附件或小装饰品的除外）的制品。

三、本章不包括：

（一）贵金属汞齐及胶态贵金属（税目 28.43）；

（二）第三十章的外科用无菌缝合材料、牙科填料或其他货品；

（三）第三十二章的货品（例如光瓷釉）；

（四）载体催化剂（税目 38.15）；

（五）第四十二章注释三（二）所述的税目 42.02 或 42.03 的物品；

（六）税目 43.03 或 43.04 的物品；

（七）第十一类的货品（纺织原料及纺织制品）；

（八）第六十四章或第六十五章的鞋靴、帽类及其他物品；

（九）第六十六章的伞、手杖及其他物品；

（十）税目 68.04 或 68.05 及第八十二章含有宝石或半宝石（天然或合成）粉末的研磨材料制品；第八十二章装有宝石或半宝石（天然、合成或再造）工作部件的器具；第十六类的机器、机械器具、电气设备及其零件。然而，完全以宝石或半宝石（天然、合成或再造）制成的物品及其零件，除未安装的唱针用已加工蓝宝石或钻石外（税目 85.22），其余仍应归入本章；

（十一）第九十章、第九十一章或第九十二章的物品（科学仪器、钟表及乐器）；

SECTION XIV
NATURAL OR CULTURED PEARLS, PRECIOUS OR SEMI-PRECIOUS STONES, PRECIOUS METALS, METALS CLAD WITH PRECIOUS METAL, AND ARTICLES THEREOF; IMITATION JEWELLERY; COIN

Chapter 71
Natural or cultured pearls, precious or semi-precious stones, precious metals, metals clad with precious metal, and articles thereof; imitation jewellery; coin

Notes:

1. Subject to Note 1 (a) to Section Ⅵ and except as provided below, all articles consisting wholly or partly:

(a) Of natural or cultured pearls or of precious or semi-precious stones (natural, synthetic or reconstructed), or

(b) Of precious metal or of metal clad with precious metal, are to be classified in this Chapter.

2. (a) Headings Nos. 71.13, 71.14 and 71.15 do not cover articles in which precious metal or metal clad with precious metal is present as minor constituents only, such as minor fittings or minor ornamentation (for example, monograms, ferrules and rims), and paragraph Note 1 (b) of the foregoing Note does not apply to such articles;

(b) Heading No. 71.16 does not cover articles containing precious metal or metal clad with precious metal (other than as minor constituents)

.

3. This Chapter does not cover:

(a) Amalgams of precious metal, or colloidal precious metal (heading No. 28.43);

(b) Sterile surgical suture materials, dental fillings or other goods of Chapter 30;

(c) Goods of Chapter 32 (for example, lustres);

(d) Supported catalysts (heading No. 38.15);

(e) Articles of heading No. 42.02 or 42.03 referred to in Note 3(B) to Chapter 42;

(f) Articles of heading No. 43.03 or 43.04;

(g) Goods of Section Ⅺ (textiles and textile articles);

(h) Footwear, headgear or other articles of Chapter 64 or 65;

(i) Umbrellas, walking-sticks or other articles of Chapter 66;

(j) Abrasive goods of heading 68.04 or 68.05 or Chapter 82, containing dust or powder of precious or semi-precious stones (natural or synthetic); articles of Chapter 82 with a working part of precious or semi-precious stones (natural, synthetic or reconsturcted); machinery, mechanical appliances or electrical goods, or parts thereof, of Section ⅩⅥ. However, articles and parts thereof, wholly of precious or semi-precious stones (natural, synthetic or reconstructed) remain classified in this Chapter, except unmounted worked sapphires and diamonds for styli (heading No. 85.22);

(k) Articles of Chapter 90, 91 or 92 (scientific instruments, clocks and watches, musical instruments);

（十二）武器及其零件（第九十三章）；

（十三）第九十五章注释二所述物品；

（十四）根据第九十六章注释四应归入该章的物品；

（十五）雕塑品原件（税目97.03）、收藏品（税目97.05）或超过一百年的古物（税目97.06）、但天然或养殖珍珠、宝石及半宝石除外。

四、（一）所称“贵金属”，是指银、金及铂；

（二）所称“铂”，是指铂、铱、锇、钯、铑及钌；

（三）所称“宝石或半宝石”，不包括第九十六章注释二（二）所述任何物质。

五、含有贵金属的合金（包括烧结及化合的），只要其中任何一种贵金属的含量达到合金重量的2%，即应视为本章的贵金属合金。贵金属合金应按下列规则归类：

（一）按重量计含铂量在2%及以上的合金，应视为铂合金；

（二）按重量计含金量在2%及以上，但不含铂或按重量计含铂量在2%以下的合金，应视为金合金；

（三）按重量计含银量在2%及以上的其他合金，应视为银合金。

六、除条文另有规定的以外，本协调制度所称贵金属应包括上述注释五所规定的贵金属合金，但不包括包贵金属或表面镀以贵金属的贱金属及非金属。

七、本协调制度所称“包贵金属”，是指以贱金属为底料，在其一面或多面用焊接、熔接、热轧或类似机械方法覆盖一层贵金属的材料。除条文另有规定的以外，也包括镶嵌贵金属的贱金属。

八、除第六类注释一（一）另有规定的以外，凡符合税目71.12规定的货品，应归入该税目而不归入本协调制度的其他税目。

九、税目71.13所称“首饰”，是指：

（一）个人用小饰物（例如，戒指、手镯、项圈、饰针、耳环 表链、表链饰物、垂饰、领带别针、袖扣、饰扣、宗教性或其他勋章及徽章）；

（二）通常放置在衣袋、手提包或佩戴在身上的个人用品（例如，雪茄盒、烟盒、鼻烟盒、口香糖或药丸盒、粉盒、链袋或念珠）。

这些物品可以和下列物品组合或镶嵌下列物品：例如，天然或养殖珍珠、宝石或半宝石、合成或再造的宝石或半宝石、玳瑁壳、珍珠母、兽牙、天然或再生琥珀、黑玉或珊瑚

十、税目71.14所称“金银器”，包括装饰品、餐具、梳妆用具、吸烟用具及类似的家庭、办公室或宗教用的其他物品。

(l) Arms or parts thereof (Chapter 93);

(m) Articles covered by Note 2 to Chapter 95;

(n) Articles classified in Chapter 96 by virtue of Note 4 to that Chapter;

(o) Original sculptures or statuary (heading No. 97.03), collectors' pieces (heading No. 97.05) or antiques of an age exceeding one hundred years (heading No. 97.06), other than natural or cultured pearls or precious or semi-precious stones.

4. (a) The expression "precious metal" means silver, gold and platinum.

(b) The expression "platinum" means platinum, iridium, osmium, palladium, rhodium and ruthenium.

(c) The expression "precious or semi-precious stones" does not include any of the substances specified in Note 2 (b) to Chapter 96.

5. For the purposes of this Chapter, any alloy (including a sintered mixture and an inter-metallic compound) containing precious metal is to be treated as an alloy of precious metal if any one precious metal constitutes as much as 2%, by weight, of the alloy. Alloys of precious metal are to be classified according to the following rules:

(a) An alloy containing 2% or more, by weight, of platinum is to be treated as an alloy of platinum;

(b) An alloy containing 2% or more, by weight, of gold but no platinum, or less than 2%, by weight, of platinum, is to be treated as an alloy of gold;

(c) Other alloys containing 2% or more, by weight, of silver are to be treated as alloys of silver.

6. Except where the context otherwise requires, any reference in the Nomenclature to precious metal or to any particular precious metal includes a reference to alloys treated as alloys of precious metal or of the particular metal in accordance with the rules in Note 5 above, but not to metal clad with precious metal or to base metal or nonmetals plated with precious metal.

7. Throughout the Nomenclature the expression "metal clad with precious metal" means material made with a base of metal upon one or more surfaces of which there is affixed by soldering, brazing, welding, hot-rolling or similar mechanical means a covering of precious metal. Except where the context otherwise requires, the expression also covers base metal inlaid with precious metal.

8. Subject to Note 1 (a) to Section Ⅵ, goods answering to a description in heading No. 71.12 are to be classified in that heading and in no other heading of the Nomenclature.

9. For the purposes of heading No. 71.13, the expression "articles of jewellery" means:

(a) Any small objects of personal adornment (for example, rings, bracelets, necklaces, brooches, ear-rings, watch-chains, fobs, pendants, tie-pins, cuff-links, dress-studs, religious or other medals and insignia); and

(b) Articles of personal use of a kind normally carried in the pocket, in the handbag or on the person (for example) cigar or cigarette cases snuffboxes cachou or pill boxes, powder boxes chain purses or prayer beads.

These articles may be combined or set, for example, with natural or cultured pearls, precious or semiprecious stone, synthetic or reconstructed precious or semi-precious stones, tortoise shell, mother-of-pearl, ivory, natural or reconstituted amber, jet or coral.

10. For the purposes of heading No. 71.14, the expression "articles of goldsmiths' or silversmiths' wares" includes such articles as ornaments, tableware, toilet-ware, smokers' requisites and other articles of household, office or religious use.

十一、税目71.17所称"仿首饰"，是指不含天然或养殖珍珠、宝石或半宝石（天然、合成或再造）及贵金属或包贵金属（仅作为镀层或小附件、小装饰品的除外）的上述注释九（一）所述的首饰（不包括税目96.06的钮扣及其他物品或税目96.15的梳子、发夹及类似品）。

11. For the purposes of heading No. 71.17, the expression "imitation jewellery" means articles of jewellery within the meaning of Note 9(a) above (but not including buttons or other articles of heading 96.06, or dress-combs, hair-slides or the like, or hairpins, of heading No. 96.15), not incorporating natural or cultured pearls, precious or semi-precious stones (natural synthetic, or reconstructed) nor (except as plating or as minor constituents) precious metal or metal clad with precious metal.

子目注释：

一、子目号7106.10、7108.11、7110.11、7110.21、7110.31及7110.41所称"粉末"，是指按重量计90%及以上可从网眼孔径为0.5毫米的筛子通过的产品；

二、子目号7110.11及7110.19所称"铂"，可不受本章注释四（二）的规定约束，不包括铱、锇、钯、铑及钌。

三、对于税目71.10项下的子目所列合金的归类，按其所含铂、钯、铑、铱、锇或钌中重量最大的一种金属归类。

Subheading Notes:

1. For the purposes of subheadings Nos. 7106.10, 7108.11, 7110.11, 7110.21, 7110.31 and 7110.41, the expressions "powder" and "in powder form" mean products of which 90% or more by weight passes through a sieve having a mesh aperture of 0.5mm.
2. Notwithstanding the provisions of Chapter Note 4 (b), for the purposes of subheadings Nos. 7110.11 and 7110.19, the expression "platinum" does not include iridium, osmium, palladium, rhodium or ruthenium.
3. For the classification of alloys in the subheadings of heading No. 71.10, each alloy is to be classified with that metal, platinum, palladium, rhodium, iridium, osmium or ruthenium which predominates by weight over each other of these metals.

税则号列	货品名称	最惠(%)	普通	增值税率	出口退税	计量单位	监管条件	Article Description
	第一分章　天然或养殖珍珠、宝石或半宝石							Ⅰ.-NATURAL OR CULTURED PEARLS AND PRECIOUS OR SEMI-PRECIOUS STONES
71.01	**天然或养殖珍珠，不论是否加工或分级，但未成串或镶嵌；天然或养殖珍珠，为便于运输而暂穿成串：**							**Pearls, natural or cultured, whether or not worked or graded but not strung, mounted or set; ungraded pearls, natural or cultured, temporarily strung for convenience of transport:**
	-天然珍珠：							-Natural pearls:
	---未分级：							---Ungraded:
7101.1011[暂]	----黑珍珠	0	100	17	5	克	AB	----Tahitian pearls
7101.1019	----其他	21	100	17	5	克	AB	----Other
	---其他：							---Other:
7101.1091[暂]	----黑珍珠	0	130	17	5	克	AB	----Tahitan pearls
7101.1099	----其他	21	130	17	5	克	AB	----Other
	-养殖珍珠：							-Cultured pearls:
	--未加工：							--Unworked:
7101.2110	---未分级		100	17	5	千克		---Ungraded
7101.2110[暂] 01	未分级、未加工的养殖黑珍珠（未制成制品）	0	100	17	5	千克	AB	Ungraded and unworked cultured tahitan pearls(semi-manufactured)
7101.2110 90	其他未分级、未加工的养殖珍珠（未制成制品）	21	100	17	5	千克	AB	Other uagraded and unworked cultured pearls(semi-manufactured)
7101.2190	---其他		130	17	5	千克	AB	---Other
7101.2190[暂] 01	其他未加工的养殖黑珍珠（未制成制品）	0	130	17	5	千克	AB	Other unworked cultured tahitan pearls(semi – manufactured)
7101.2190 90	其他未加工的养殖珍珠（未制成制品）	21	130	17	5	千克	AB	Other unworked cultured pearls (semi – manufactured)
	--已加工：							--Worked:
7101.2210	---未分级		100	17	5	千克		---Ungraded
7101.2210[暂] 01	未分级，已加工的养殖黑珍珠（未制成制品）	0	100	17	5	千克		Cultured Tahitan pearls, ungraded, worlced (semi – manufactured)
7101.2210 90	其他未分级，已加工的养殖珍珠（未制成制品）	21	100	17	5	千克		Other cultured pearls, ungraded, worked (semi – manufactured)
7101.2290	---其他		130	17	5	千克		---Other
7101.2290[暂] 01	其他已加工的养殖黑珍珠（未制成制品）	0	130	17	5	千克		Other worked cultured tahitan pearls(semi – manufactured)
7101.2290 90	其他已加工的养殖珍珠（未制成制品）	21	130	17	5	千克		Other worked cultured pearls(semi – manufactured)

税则号列	货品名称	最惠(%)	普通	增值税率	出口退税	计量单位	监管条件	Article Description
71.02	钻石，不论是否加工，但未镶嵌：							**Diamonds, whether or not worked, but not mounted or set:**
7102.1000	-未分级	3	14	17		克拉	D	-Unsorted
	-工业用：							-Industrial:
7102.2100	--未加工或经简单锯开、劈开或粗磨	0	14	17	5	克拉	D	--Unworked or simply sawn, cleaved or bruted
7102.2900	--其他	0	14	17	5	克拉		--Other
	-非工业用：							-Non-industrial:
7102.3100	--未加工或经简单锯开、劈开或粗磨	3	14	17		克拉	D	--Unworked or simply sawn, cleaved or bruted
7102.3900	--其他	8	35	17		克拉		--Other
71.03	宝石(钻石除外)或半宝石，不论是否加工或分级，但未成串或镶嵌；未分级的宝石(钻石除外)或半宝石，为便于运输而暂穿成串：							**Precious stones (other than diamonds) and semi-precious stones, whether or not worked or graded but not strung, mounted or set; ungraded precious stones (other than diamonds) and semi-precious stones, temporarily strung for covenience of transport:**
7103.1000	-未加工或经简单锯开或粗制成形	3	14	17	5	千克		-Unworked or simply sawn or roughly shaped
	-经其他加工：							-Otherwise worked:
7103.9100	--红宝石、蓝宝石、祖母绿	8	35	17	5	克拉		--Rubies, sapphires and emeralds
	--其他：							--Other:
7103.9910	---翡翠	8	35	17	5	克拉		---Jadeite
7103.9920	---水晶	8	35	17	5	克拉		---Crystal
7103.9930	---碧玺	8	35	17	5	克拉		---Tourmaline
7103.9940	---软玉	8	35	17	5	克拉		---Nephrite
7103.9990	---其他	8	35	17	5	克拉		---Other
71.04	合成或再造的宝石或半宝石，不论是否加工或分级，但未成串或镶嵌的；未分级的合成或再造的宝石或半宝石，为便于运输而暂穿成串：							**Synthetic or reconstructed precious or semi-precious stones, whether or not worked or graded but not strung, mounted or set; ungraded synthetic or reconstructed precious or semi-precious stones, temporarily strung for convenience of transport:**
7104.1000	-压电石英	6	14	17	5	克		-Piezo-electric quartz
	-其他，未加工或经简单锯开或粗制成形：							-Other, unworked or simply sawn or roughly shaped:
7104.2010	---钻石	0	14	17		克		---Diamonds
7104.2090	---其他	0	14	17	5	克		---Other
	-其他：							-Other:
	---工业用：							---For technical use:
7104.9011	----钻石	6	14	17	5	克		----Diamonds
7104.9012	----蓝宝石		14	17	5	克		----Sapphires
7104.9012暂 01	蓝宝石衬底(由人造刚玉加工而成，厚度<0.5mm)	1	14	17	5	克		Precious or semi - precious stones underlay with sapphirel, made of man - made corundum (with thickness <0.5mm)
7104.9012 90	其他工业用蓝宝石(合成或再造宝石、半宝石)	6	14	17	5	克		Other sapphire used for Industry (synthetic or reconstructed precious or semi-precious stones)
7104.9019	----其他	6	14	17	5	克		----Other
	---其他：							---Other:
7104.9091	----钻石	8	35	17		克		----Diamonds
7104.9099	----其他	8	35	17	5	克		----Other
71.05	天然或合成的宝石或半宝石的粉末：							**Dust and powder of natural orsynthetic precious or semi-precious stones:**
	-钻石的：							-Of diamonds:
7105.1010	---天然的	0	17	17		克拉		---Natural
7105.1020	---人工合成的	0	17	17	5	克拉		---Synthetic
7105.9000	-其他	0	17	17	5	克		-Other
	第二分章　贵金属及包贵金属							Ⅱ.-PRECIOUS METALS AND METALS CLAD WITH PRECIOUS METAL

税则号列	货品名称	最惠(%)	普通	增值税率	出口退税	计量单位	监管条件	Article Description
71.06	银(包括镀金、镀铂的银),未锻造、半制成或粉末状:							**Silver (including silver plated with gold or platinum), unwrought or in semi-manufactured forms, or in powder form:**
	-银粉:							-Powder:
	---非片状粉末:							---Not Flake:
7106.1011	----平均粒径小于3微米	0	0	17		克	A4xy	----Average diameter less than 3 micron
7106.1019	----其他	0	0	17		克	A4xy	----Other
	---片状粉末:							---Flake:
7106.1021	----平均粒径小于10微米	0	0	17		克	4xy	----Average diameter less than 10 micron
7106.1029	----其他	0	0	17		克	4xy	----Other
	-其他							-Other:
	--未锻造:							--Unwrought:
7106.9110	---纯度达99.99%及以上	0	0	17		克	4xy	---of a purity of 99.99 or more
7106.9190	---其他	0	0	17		克	4xy	---Other
	--半制成:							--Semi-manufactured:
7106.9210	---纯度达99.99%及以上	0	50	17		克	4xy	---of a purity of 99.99 or more
7106.9290	---其他	0	50	17		克	4xy	---Other
71.07	以贱金属为底的包银材料:							**Base metals clad with silver, not further worked than semi-manufactured:**
7107.0000	以贱金属为底的包银材料	10.5	50	17	5	千克		Base metals clad with silver, not further worked than semi-manufactured
71.08	金(包括镀铂的金),未锻造、半制成或粉末状:							**Gold (including gold plated with platinum) unwrought or in semi-manufactured forms, or in powder form:**
	-非货币用:							-Non-monetary:
7108.1100	--金粉	0	0	0		克	J	--Powder
7108.1200	--其他未锻造形状	0	0	0		克	J	--Other unwrought forms
7108.1300	--其他半制成形状	0	50	0		克	J	--Other semi-manufactured forms
7108.2000	-货币用	0	0	0		克	J	-Monetary
71.09	以贱金属或银为底的包金材料:							**Base metals or silver, clad with gold, not further worked than semi-manufactured:**
7109.0000	以贱金属或银为底的包金材料	10.5	50	17	5	克		Base metals or silver, clad with gold, not further worked than semi-manufactured
71.10	铂,未锻造、半制成或粉末状:							**Platinum, unwrought or in semi-manufactured forms, or in powder form:**
	-铂:							-Platinum:
7110.1100	--未锻造或粉末状	0	0	0		克	8x	--Unwrought or in powder form
	--其他:							--Other:
7110.1910	---板、片	0	0	0		克	8x	---Plates and sheets
7110.1990	---其他	3	11	0		克	4xy	---Other
	-钯:							-Palladium:
7110.2100	--未锻造或粉末状	0	10	17		克	4xy	--Unwrought or in powder form
	--其他:							--Other:
7110.2910	---板、片	0	0	17		克	4xy	---Plates and sheets
7110.2990	---其他	3	11	17		克	4xy	---Other
	-铑:							-Rhodium:
7110.3100	--未锻造或粉末状	0	0	17		克	4xy	--Unwrought or in powder form
	--其他:							--Other:
7110.3910	---板、片	0	0	17		克	4xy	---Plates and sheets
7110.3990	---其他	3	11	17		克	4xy	---Other
	-铱、锇及钌:							-Iridium, osmium and ruthenium:
7110.4100	--未锻造或粉末状	0	0	17		克	4xy	--Unwrought or in powder form
	--其他:							--Other:
7110.4910	---板、片	0	0	17		克	4xy	---Plates and sheets
7110.4990	---其他	3	11	17		克	4xy	---Other

税则号列	货品名称	最惠(%)	普通	增值税率	出口退税	计量单位	监管条件	Article Description
71.11	**以贱金属、银或金为底的包铂材料:**							**Base metals, silver or gold, clad with platinum, not further worked than semi-manufactured:**
7111.0000	以贱金属、银或金为底的包铂材料	3	11	17	0,5	克	4xy	Base metals, silver or gold, clad with platinum, not further worked than semi-manufactured
71.12	**贵金属或包贵金属的废碎料;含有贵金属或贵金属化合物的其他废碎料,主要用于回收贵金属:**							**Waste and scrap of precious metal or of metal clad with precious metal; other waste and scrap containing precious metal or precious metal compounds, of a kind used principally for the recovery of precious metal:**
	-含有贵金属或贵金属化合物的灰:							-Ash containing precious metal or precious metal compounds:
7112.3010	---含有银或银化合物的	8	50	17	5	克	9	---Of silver or silver compounds
7112.3090	---其他	6	50	17		克	9	---Other
	-其他:							-Other:
	--金及包金的废碎料,但含有其他贵金属的除外:							--Of gold, including metal clad with gold but excluding sweepings containing other precious metals:
7112.9110	---金及包金的废碎料	0	0	17		克		---Of gold, or gold compounds
7112.9110 10	金的废碎料	0	0	17		克	AP	Waster and scrap of gold
7112.9110 90	包金的废碎料(但含有其他贵金属的除外)	0	0	17		克	AP	Waster and scrap of including metal clad with gold, but excluding sweepings containing other precious metals
7112.9120	---含有金或金化合物的废碎料	6	35	17		克	9	---Waste and scrap with gold or gold compounds
	--铂及包铂的废碎料,但含有其他贵金属的除外:							--Of platinum, including metal clad with platinum but excluding sweepings containing other precious metals:
7112.9210	---铂及包铂的废碎料	0	0	17		克	4APxy	---Of platinum
7112.9220	---含有铂或铂化合物的废碎料		35	17		克		---Wastes and scrap with platinum
7112.9220暂 01	铂含量在3%以上的其他含有铂或铂化合物的废碎料(但含有其他贵金属除外,主要用于回收铂)	0	35	17		克	4xy	Other waste and scraps with platinum and its compounds, containing > 3% of platinum (but excluding sweeping contcaining other precious metals, used for recycling platinum)
7112.9220 90	其他含有铂及铂化合物的废碎料(但含有其他贵金属除外,主要用于回收铂)	6	35	17		克	4xy	Other waste and scraps containing platinum (but excluding sweepings containing other precious metals, used for recycling platinum)
	--其他:							--Other:
7112.9910	---含有银或银化合物的废碎料	8	35	17	5	克	9	---Waste and scrap with silver or silver compounds
7112.9920	---含有其他贵金属或贵金属化合物的废碎料	6	35	17		克	9	---Waste and scrap with other precious metals
7112.9990	---其他	0	50	17		克		---Other
	第三分章 珠宝首饰、金银器及其他制品							Ⅲ.-JEWELLERY, GOLDSMITHS' AND SILVERSMITHS' WARES AND OTHER ARTICLES
71.13	**贵金属或包贵金属制的首饰及其零件:**							**Articles of jewellery and parts thereof, of precious metal or of metal chad with precious metal:**
	-贵金属制,不论是否包、镀贵金属:							-Of precious metal whether or not plated or clad with precious metal:
	--银制,不论是否包、镀其他贵金属:							--Of silver, whether or not plated or clad with other precious metal:
7113.1110	---镶嵌钻石的	20	130	17		克		---Diamond mounted of set
7113.1190	---其他	20	130	17		克		---Other
7113.1190 10	镶嵌濒危物种制品的银首饰及零件(不论是否包、镀其他贵金属)	20	130	17		克	FE	Silver jewellery and parts thereof, inlaid with articles of endangered species (whether or not plated or clad with other precious metal)
7113.1190 90	其他银首饰及其零件(不论是否包、镀其他贵金属)	20	130	17	5	克		Other silver jewellery and parts thereof (whether or not plated or clad with other precious metal)
	--其他贵金属制,不论是否包、镀贵金属:							--Of other precious metal, whether or not plated or clad with predious metal:

税则号列	货品名称	最惠(%)	普通	增值税率	出口退税	计量单位	监管条件	Article Description
	---金制:							---Of gold:
7113.1911	----镶嵌钻石的	20	130	17		克	J	----Diomond mounted
7113.1919	----其他	20	130	17		克		----Other
7113.1919 10	镶嵌濒危物种制品的金首饰及零件(不论是否包、镀其他贵金属)	20	130	17		克	FE	Gold jewellery and parts thereof, inlaid with articles of endangered species (whether or not plated or clad with other precious metal)
7113.1919 90	其他黄金制首饰及其零件(不论是否包、镀其他贵金属)	20	130	17		克	J	Other gold jewellery and parts thereof(whether or not plated or clad with other precious metal)
	--其他:							--Other:
	---铂制:							---Of platinum
7113.1921	----镶嵌钻石的	35	130	17		克		----Diomond mounted
7113.1929	----其他	35	130	17		克		----Other
7113.1929 10	镶嵌濒危物种制品的铂金首饰及零件(不论是否包、镀其他贵金属)	35	130	17		克	EF	Platinum jewellery and parts thereof, inlaid with articles of endangered species, whether or not plated or clad with other precious metal
7113.1929 90	其他铂金制首饰及其零件(不论是否包、镀其他贵金属)	35	130	17		克		Other platinum jewellery and parts thereof, whether or not plated or clad with other precious metal
7113.1991	----镶嵌钻石的	35	130	17		克		----Diomond mounted or set
7113.1999	----其他	35	130	17		克		----Other
7113.1999 10	镶嵌濒危物种制品其他贵金属首饰(不论是否包、镀其他贵金属)	35	130	17		克	FE	Jewellery and parts thereof, of precious metal, inlaid with articles of endangered species (whether or not plated or clad with other precious metal)
7113.1999 90	其他贵金属制首饰及其零件(不论是否包、镀其他贵金属)	35	130	17		克		Other jewellery and parts thereof of precious metal (whether or not plated or clad with other precious metal)
	-以贱金属为底的包贵金属制:							-Of base metal clad with precious metal:
7113.2010	---镶嵌钻石的	35	130	17		克		---Diamond mounted or set
7113.2090	---其他	35	130	17		克		---Other
7113.2090 10	镶嵌濒危物种制品以贱金属为底的包贵金属制首饰(包括零件)	35	130	17		克	FE	Jewellery and parts thereof, of base metal clad with precious metal, inlaid with articles of endangered species
7113.2090 90	其他以贱金属为底的包贵金属制首饰(包括零件)	35	130	17	5	克		Other jewellery and parts thereof, of base metal clad with precious metal
71.14	**贵金属或包贵金属制的金银器及其零件:**							**Articles of goldsmiths' or silversmiths' wares and parts thereof, of precious metal or of metal clad with precious metal:**
	-贵金属制,不论是否包、镀贵金属:							-Of precious metal whether or not plated or clad with precious metal:
7114.1100	--银制,不论是否包、镀其他贵金属	35	100	17		克		--Of silver, whether or not plated or clad with other precious metal
7114.1100 10	镶嵌濒危物种制品的银器及零件(不论是否包、镀贵金属)	35	100	17		克	FE	Silversmiths' wares and parts thereof, inlaid with articles of endangered species (whether or not plated or clad with other precious metal)
7114.1100 90	其他银器及零件(不论是否包、镀贵金属)	35	100	17	5	克		Other silversmiths' wares and parts thereof(whether or not plated or clad with other precious metal)
7114.1900	--其他贵金属制,不论是否包、镀贵金属	35	100	17		克		--Of other precious metal, whether or not plated or clad with precious metal
7114.1900 10	镶嵌濒危物种制品的金银器及零件(不论是否包,镀贵金属)	35	100	17		克	FE	Goldsmiths' or silversmiths' wares and parts thereof, inlaid with articles of endangered species (whether or not plated or clad with other precious metal)
7114.1900 20	其他贵金属制金器及零件(不论是否包,镀贵金属)	35	100	17		克	J	Of other precious metal gold and parts (regardless of whether the packet, plated with precious metal)
7114.1900 90	其他贵金属制金银器及零件(不论是否包,镀贵金属)	35	100	17		克		Other goldsmiths' or silversmiths' wares and parts thereof, of precious metal (whether or not plated or clad with other precious metal)

税则号列	货　品　名　称	最惠(%)	普通	增值税率	出口退税	计量单位	监管条件	Article Description
7114.2000	-以贱金属为底的包贵金属制	35	100	17		克		-Of base metal clad with precious metal
7114.2000 10	以贱金属为底的包贵金属制金银器(镶嵌濒危物种制品,包括零件)	35	100	17		克	FE	Goldsmiths' or silversmiths' wares and parts thereof, inlaid with articles of endangered species, of base metal cald with precious metal
7114.2000 90	其他贱金属为底包贵金属制金银器(包括零件)	35	100	17	0,5	克		Other goldsmiths' or silversmiths' wares and parts thereof, of base metal cald with precious metal
71.15	**贵金属或包贵金属的其他制品:**							**Other articles of precious metal or of metal clad with precious metal:**
7115.1000	-金属丝布或格栅形状的铂催化剂	3	11	17		克	4xy	-Catalysts in the form of wire cloth or grill, of platinum
	-其他:							-Other:
7115.9010暂	---工业或实验室用	0	11	17		克		---For technical or laboratory use
7115.9010暂 10	银制工业、实验室用制品	0	11	17	5	克		Articles of silver for industrial or laboratory use
7115.9010暂 20	金制工业、实验室用制品	0	11	17		克	J	Articles of gold for industrial or laboratory use
7115.9010暂 90	其他工业、实验室用贵金或包贵金制品	0	11	17	0,5	克		Articles of precious metal or of metal clad with precious metal for industrial or laboratory use
7115.9090	---其他	35	100	17	0,5	克		---Other
71.16	**用天然或养殖珍珠、宝石或半宝石(天然、合成或再造)制成的物品:**							**Articles of natural or cultured pearls, precious or semi-precious stones (natural, synthetic or reconstructed):**
7116.1000	-天然或养殖珍珠制	35	130	17	5	千克		-Of natural or cultured pearls
7116.2000	-宝石或半宝石(天然、合成或再造)制	35	130	17	0,5	千克		-Of precious or semi-precious stones (natural, synthetic or reconstructed)
71.17	**仿首饰:**							**Imitation jewellery:**
	-贱金属制,不论是否镀贵金属:							-Of base metal, whether or not plated with precious metal:
7117.1100	--袖扣、饰扣	35	130	17	9	千克	A	--Cuff-links and studs
7117.1900	--其他	17	130	17	9	千克	A	--Other
7117.9000	-其他	35	130	17	9	千克	A	-Other
71.18	**硬币:**							**Coin:**
7118.1000	-非法定货币的硬币(金币除外)	0	0	17	5	千克		-Coin (other than gold coin), not being legal tender
7118.9000	-其他	0	0	17		千克		-Other
7118.9000 10	金质铸币(金质贵金属纪念币)	0	0	17		千克	J	Gold coins (gold precious metal commemorative coins)
7118.9000 90	其他硬币	0	0	17		千克		Other coins

第十五类
贱金属及其制品

注释：

一、本类不包括：

（一）以金属粉末为基本成分的调制油漆、油墨或其他产品（税目 32.07 至 32.10、32.12、32.13 或 32.15）；

（二）铈铁或其他引火合金（税目 36.06）；

（三）税目 65.06 或 65.07 的帽类及其零件；

（四）税目 66.03 的伞骨及其他物品；

（五）第七十一章的货品（例如，贵金属合金、以贱金属为底的包贵金属、仿首饰）；

（六）第十六类的物品（机器、机械器具及电气设备）；

（七）已装配的铁路或电车轨道（税目 86.08）或第十七类的其他物品（车辆、船舶、航空器）；

（八）第十八类的仪器及器具，包括钟表发条；

（九）做弹药用的铅弹（税目 93.06）或第十九类的其他物品（武器、弹药）；

（十）第九十四章的物品（例如，家具、弹簧床垫、灯具及照明装置、发光标志、活动房屋）；

（十一）第九十五章的物品（例如，玩具、游戏品及运动用品）；

（十二）手用筛子、钮扣、钢笔、铅笔套、钢笔尖或第九十六章的其他物品（杂项制品）

（十三）第九十七章的物品（例如，艺术品）。

二、本协调制度所称"通用零件"，是指：

（一）税目 73.07、73.12、73.15、73.17 或 73.18 的物品及其他贱金属制的类似品；

（二）贱金属制的弹簧及弹簧片，但钟表发条（税目 91.14）除外；

（三）税目 83.01、83.02、83.08、83.10 的物品及税目 83.06 的贱金属制的框架及镜子。

第七十三章至第七十六章（税目 73.15 除外）及第七十八章至第八十二章所列货品的零件，不包括上述的通用零件。

除上段及第八十三章注释一另有规定的以外，第七十二章至第七十六章及第七十八章至第八十一章不包括第八十二章、第八十三章的物品。

三、本协调制度所称"贱金属"是指：铁及钢、铜、镍、铝、铅、锌、锡、钨、钼、钽、镁、钴、铋、镉、钛、锆、锑、锰、铍、铬、锗、钒、镓、铪、铟、铌、铼及铊。

四、本协调制度所称"金属陶瓷"，是指金属与陶瓷成分的极细微粒不均匀结合而成的产品。"金属陶瓷"包括硬质合金（金属碳化物与金属烧结而成）。

SECTION XV
BASE METALS AND ARTICLES OF BASE METAL

Notes:

1. This Section does not cover:

(a) Prepared paints, inks or other products with a basis of metallic flakes or powder (headings Nos. 32.07 to 32.10, 32.12, 32.13 or 32.15);

(b) Ferro-cerium or other pyrophoric alloys (heading No. 36.06);

(c) Headgear or parts thereof of heading No. 65.06 or 65.07;

(d) Umbrella frames or other articles of heading No. 66.03;

(e) Goods of Chapter 71 (for example, precious metal alloys, base metal clad with precious metal, imitation Jewelry);

(f) Articles of Section XVI (machinery, mechanical appliances and electrical goods);

(g) Assembled railway or tramway track (heading No. 86.08) or other articles of Section XVII (vehicles, ships and boats, aircraft);

(h) Instruments or apparatus of Section XVIII, including clock or watch springs;

(ij) Lead shot prepared for anmmunition (heading No. 93.06) or other articles of Section XIX (arms and ammunition);

(k) Articles of Chapter 94 (for example, furniture, mattress supports, lamps and lighting fittings, illuminated signs, prefabricated buildings);

(L) Articles of Chapter 95 (for example, toys, games, sports requisites);

(m) Hand sieves, buttons, pens, pencil-holders, pen nibs or other articles of Chapter 96 (miscellaneous manufactured articles); or

(n) Articles of Chapter 97 (for example, works of art).

2. Throughout the Nomenclature, the expression "parts of general use" means:

(a) Articles of heading No. 73.07, 73.12, 73.15, 73.17 or 73.18 and similar articles of other base metal;

(b) Springs and leaves for springs, of base metal, other than clock or watch springs (heading No. 91.14); and

(c) Articles of headings Nos. 83.01, 83.02, 83.08, 83.10 and frames and mirrors, of base metal, of heading No. 83.06.

In Chapters 73 to 76 and 78 to 82 (but not in heading No. 73.15) references to parts of goods do not include references to parts of general use as defined above.

Subject to the preceding paragraph and to Note 1 to Chapter 83, the articles of Chapter 82 or 83 are excluded from Chapters 72 to 76 and 78 to 81.

3. Throughout the Nomenclature, the expression "base metals" means: iron and steel, copper, nickel, aluminium, lead, zinc, tin, tungsten (wolfram), molybdenum, tantalum, magnesium, cobalt, bismuth, cadmium, titanium, zirconium, antimony, manganese, beryllium, chromium, germanium, vanadium, gallium, hafnium, indium, niobium (columbium), rhenium and thallium.

4. Throughout the Nomenclature, the term "cermets" means products containing a microscopic heterogeneous combination of a metallic component and a ceramic component. The term "cermets" includes sintered metal carbides (metal carbides sintered with a metal).

五、合金的归类规则(第七十二章、第七十四章所规定的铁合金及母合金除外):

(一)贱金属的合金按其所含重量最大的金属归类;

(二)由本类的贱金属和非本类的元素构成的合金,如果所含贱金属的总重量等于或超过所含其他元素的总重量,应作为本类贱金属合金归类;

(三)本类所称"合金",包括金属粉末的烧结混合物、熔化而得的不均匀紧密混合物(金属陶瓷除外)及金属间化合物。

六、除条文另有规定的以外,本协调制度所称的贱金属包括贱金属合金,这类合金应按上述注释五的规则进行归类。

七、复合材料制品的归类规则:

除各税目另有规定的以外,贱金属制品(包括根据"归类总规则"作为贱金属制品的混合材料制品)如果含有两种或两种以上贱金属的,按其所含重量最大的贱金属的制品归类。为此:

(一)钢、铁或不同种类的钢铁,均视为一种金属;

(二)按照注释五的规定作为某一种金属归类的合金,应视为一种金属;

(三)税目 81.13 的金属陶瓷,应视为一种贱金属。

八、本类所用有关名词解释如下:

(一)废碎料

在金属生产或机械加工中产生的废料及碎屑以及因破裂、切断、磨损及其他原因而明显不能作为原物使用的金属货品。

(二)粉末

按重量计 90% 及以上可从网眼孔径为 1 毫米的筛子通过的产品。

5. Classification of alloys (other than ferro-alloys and master alloys as defined in Chapters 72 and 74):

(a) An alloy of base metals is to be classified as an alloy of the metal which predominates by weight over each of the other metals;

(b) An alloy composed of base metals of this Section and of elements not falling within this Section is to be treated as an alloy of base metals of this Section if the total weight of such metals equals or exceeds the total weight of the other elements present;

(c) In this Section the term "alloys" includes sintered mixtures of metal powders, heterogeneous intimate mixtures obtained by melting (other than cermets) and intermetallic compounds.

6. Unless the context otherwise requires, any reference in the Nomenclature to a base metal includes a reference to alloys which, by virtue of Note 5 above, are to be classified as alloys of that metal.

7. Classification of composite articles:

Except where the headings otherwise require, articles of base metal (including articles of mixed materials treated as articles of base metal under the Interpretative Rules) containing two or more base metals are to be treated as articles of the base metal predominating by weight over each of the other metals. For this purpose:

(a) Iron and steel, or different kinds of iron or steel, are regarded as one and the same metal;

(b) An alloy is regarded as being entirely composed of that metal as an alloy of which, by virtue of Note 5, it is classified; and

(c) A cermet of heading No. 81.13 is regarded as a single base metal.

8. In this Section, the following expressions have the meanings hereby assigned to them:

(a) Waste and scrap

Metal waste and scrap from the manufacture or mechanical working of metals, and metal goods definitely not usable as such because of breakage, cutting-up, wear or other reasons.

(b) Powders

Products of which 90% or more by weight passes through a sieve having a mesh aperture of 1mm.

第七十二章
钢　铁

注释:

一、本章所述有关名词解释如下(本条注释(四)、(五)、(六)适用于本协调制度其他各章):

(一)生铁

无实用可锻性的铁碳合金,按重量计含碳量在 2% 以上并可含有一种或几种下列含量范围的其他元素:

铬不超过 10%;

锰不超过 6%;

磷不超过 3%;

硅不超过 8%;

其他元素合计不超过 10%。

(二)镜铁

按重量计含锰量在 6% 以上,但不超过 30% 的铁碳合金,其他方面符合上述(一)款所列标准。

Chapter 72
Iron and steel

Notes:

1. In this Chapter and, in the case of Notes (d), (e) and (f) throughout the Nomenclature, the following expressions have the meanings hereby assigned to them:

(a) Pig iron

Iron-carbon alloys not usefully malleable, containing more than 2% by weight of carbon and which may contain by weight one or more other elements within the following limits:

-not more than 10% of chromium

-not more than 6% of manganese

-not more than 3% of phosphorus

-not more than 8% of silicon

-a total of not more than 10% of other elements.

(b) Spiegeleisen

Iron-carbon alloys containing by weight more than 6% but not more than 30% of manganese and otherwise conforming to the specification at (a) above.

（三）铁合金

锭、块、团或类似初级形状、连续铸造而形成的各种形状及颗粒、粉末状的合金，不论是否烧结，通常用于其他合金生产过程中的添加剂或在黑色金属冶炼中作除氧剂、脱硫剂及类似用途，一般无实用可锻性，按重量计铁元素含量在4%及以上并含有下列一种或几种元素：

铬超过10%；
锰超过30%；
磷超过3%；
硅超过8%；
除碳以外的其他元素，合计超过10%，但最高含铜量不得超过10%。

（四）钢

除税目72.03以外的黑色金属材料（某些铸造而成的种类除外），具有实用可锻性，按重量计含碳量在2%及以下，但铬钢可具有较高的含碳量。

（五）不锈钢

按重量计含碳量在1.2%及以下，含铬量在10.5%及以上的合金钢，不论是否含有其他元素。

（六）其他合金钢

不符合以上不锈钢定义的钢，含有一种或几种按重量计符合下列含量比例的元素：

铝0.3%及以上；
硼0.0008%及以上；
铬0.3%及以上；
钴0.3%及以上；
铜0.4%及以上；
铅0.4%及以上；
锰1.65%及以上；
钼0.08%及以上；
镍0.3%及以上；
铌0.06%及以上；
硅0.6%及以上；
钛0.05%及以上；
钨0.3%及以上；
钒0.1%及以上；
锆0.05%及以上；
其他元素（硫、磷、碳及氮除外）单项含量在0.1%及以上。

（七）供再熔的碎料钢铁锭

粗铸成形无缩孔或冒口的锭块产品，表面有明显瑕疵，化学成分不同于生铁、镜铁及铁合金。

（八）颗粒

按重量计不到90%可从网眼孔径为1毫米的筛子通过，而90%及以上可从网眼孔径为5毫米的筛子通过的产品。

(c) Ferro-alloys

Alloys in pigs, blocks, lumps or similar primary forms, in forms obtained by continuous casting and also in granular or powder forms, whether or not agglomerated, commonly used as an additive in the manufacture of other alloys or as de-oxidants, de-sulphurizing agents or for similar uses in ferrous metal-lurgy and generally not usefully malleable, containing by weight 4% or more of the element iron and one or more of the following:

-more than 10% of chromium
-more than 30% of manganese
-more than 3% of phosphorus
-more than 8% of silicon
-a total of more than 10% of other elements, excluding carbon, subject to a maximum content of 10% in the case of copper.

(d) Steel

Ferrous materials other than those of heading 72.03 which (with the exception of certain types produced in the form of castings) are usefully malleable and which contain by weight 2% or less of carbon. However, chromium steels may contain higher proportions of carbon.

(e) Stainless steel

Alloy steels containing, by weight, 1.2% or less of carbon and 10.5% or more of chromium, with or without other elements.

(f) Other alloy steel

Steels not complying with the definition of stainless steel and containing by weight one or more of the following elements in the proportion shown:

-0.3% or more of aluminium
-0.0008% or more of boron
-0.3% or more of chromium
-0.3% or more of cobalt
-0.4% or more of copper
-0.4% or more of lead
-1.65% or more of manganese
-0.08% or more of molybdenum
-0.3% or more of nickel
-0.06% or more of niobium
-0.6% or more of silicon
-0.05% or more of titanium
-0.3% or more of tungsten (wolfram)
-0.1% or more of vanadium
-0.05% or more of zirconium
-0.1% or more of other elements (except sulphur, phosphorus, carbon and nitrogen), taken separately.

(g) Remelting scrap ingots of iron or steel

Products roughly cast in the form of ingots without feeder-heads or hot tops, or of pigs, having obvious surface faults and not complying with the chemical composition of pig iron, spiegeleisen or ferro-alloys.

(h) Granules

Products of which less than 90% by weight passes through a sieve with a mesh aperture of 1mm and of which 90% or more by weight passes through a sieve with a mesh aperture of 5mm.

（九）半制成品

连续铸造的实心产品，不论是否初步热轧；其他实心产品，除经初步热轧或锻造粗制成形以外未经进一步加工，包括角材、型材及异型材的坯件。

本类产品不包括成卷的产品。

（十）平板轧材

截面为矩形（正方形除外）并且不符合以上第（九）款所述定义的下列形状实心轧制产品：

1. 层叠的卷材；
2. 平直形状，其厚度如果在4.75毫米以下，则宽度至少是厚度的十倍；其厚度如果在4.75毫米及以上，其宽度应超过150毫米，并且至少应为厚度的两倍。

平板轧材包括直接轧制而成并有凸起式样（例如，凹槽、肋条形、格槽、珠粒、菱形）的产品以及穿孔、抛光或制成瓦楞形的产品，但不具有其他税目所列制品或产品的特征。

各种规格的平板轧材（矩形或正方形除外），但不具有其他税目所列制品或产品的特征，都应作为宽度为600毫米及以上的产品归类。

（十一）不规则盘绕的热轧条、杆

经热轧不规则盘绕的实心产品，其截面为圆形、扇形、椭圆形、矩形（包括正方形）、三角形及其他外凸多边形（包括"扁圆形"及"变形矩形"，即相对两边为弧拱形，另外两边为等长平行直线形）。这类产品可带有在轧制过程中产生的凹痕、凸缘、槽沟或其他变形（钢筋）。

（十二）其他条、杆

不符合上述（九）、（十）、（十一）款或"丝"定义的实心产品，其全长截面均为圆形、扇形、椭圆形、矩形（包括正方形）三角形或其他外凸多边形（包括"扁圆形"及"变形矩形"，即相对两边为弧拱形，另两边为等长平行直线形）。这些产品可以：

1. 带有在轧制过程中产生的凹痕、凸缘、槽沟或其他变形（钢筋）；
2. 轧制后扭曲的。

（十三）角材、型材及异型材

不符合上述（九）、（十）、（十一）、（十二）款或"丝"定义，但其全长截面均为同样形状的实心产品。

第七十二章不包括税目73.01或73.02的产品。

（十四）丝

不符合平板轧材定义但全长截面均为同样形状的盘卷冷成形实心产品。

(i) Semi-finished products

Continuous cast products of solid section, whether or not subjected to primary hot-rolling; and other products of solid section, which have not been further worked than subjected to primary hot-rolling or roughly shaped by forging, including blanks for angles, shapes or sections.

These products are not presented in coils.

(j) Flat-rolled products

Rolled products of solid rectangular (other than square) cross-section, which do not conform to the definition at (ij) above in the form of:

-coils of successively superimposed layers; or

-straight lenghths, which if of a thickness less than 4.75mm are of a width measuring at least ten times the thickness or if of a thickness of 4.75mm or more are of a width which exceeds 150mm and measures at least twice the thickness.

Flat-rolled products include those with patterns in relief derived directly from rolling (for example, grooves, ribs, chequers, tears, buttons, lozenges) and those which have been perforated, corrugated or polished, provided that they do not thereby assume the character of articles or products of other headings.

Flat-rolled products of a shape other than rectangular or square, of any size, are to be classified as products of a width of 600mm or more, provided that they do not assume the character of articles or products of other headings.

(k) Bars and rods, hot-rolled, in irregularly wound coils

Hot-rolled products in irregularly wound coils, which have a solid cross-section in the shape of circles, segments of circles, ovals, rectangles (including squares), triangles or other convex polygons (including "flattened circles" and modified rectangles of which two opposite sides are convex arcs, the other two sides being straight, of equal length and paralled). These products may have indentations, ribs, grooves or other deformations produced during the rolling process (reinforcing bars and rods).

(l) Other bars and rods

Products which do not conform to any of the definitions at (i), (i) or (j) above or to the definition of wire, which have a uni-form solid cross-section along their whole length in the shape of circles, segments of circles, ovals, rectangles (including squares), triangles or other convex polygons (including "flattened circles" and "modified rectangles", of which two opposite sides are convex arcs, the other two sides being straight, of equal length and parallel). These products may:

-have indentations, ribs, grooves or other deformations produced during the rolling process (reinforcing bars and rods);

-be twisted after rolling.

(m) Angles, shapes and sections

Products having a uniform solid cross-section along their whole length which do not conform to any of the definitions at (i), (j), (k) or (l) above or to the definition of wire.

Chapter 72 does not include products of heading No. 73.01 or 73.02.

(n) Wire

Cold-formed products in coils, of any uniform solid cross-section along their whole length, which do not conform to the definition of flat-rolled products.

（十五）空心钻钢

适合钻探用的各种截面的空心条、杆，其最大外形尺寸超过15毫米但不超过52毫米，最大内孔尺寸不超过最大外形尺寸的二分之一。不符合本定义的钢铁空心条、杆应归入税目73.04。

二、用一种黑色金属包覆不同种类的黑色金属，应按其中重量最大的材料归类。

三、用电解沉积法、压铸法或烧结法所得的钢铁产品，应按其形状、成分及外观归入本章类似热轧产品的相应税目。

子目注释：

一、本章所用有关名词解释如下：

（一）合金生铁

按重量计含有一种或几种下列比例的元素的生铁：

铬0.2%以上；

铜0.3%以上；

镍0.3%以上；

0.1%以上的任何下列元素：

铝、钼、钛、钨、钒。

（二）非合金易切削钢

按重量计含有一种或几种下列比例的元素的非合金钢：

硫0.08%及以上；

铅0.1%及以上；

硒0.05%以上；

碲0.01%以上；

铋0.05%以上。

（三）硅电钢

按重量计含硅量至少为0.6%但不超过6%，含碳量不超过0.08%的合金钢。这类钢还可含有按重量计不超过1%的铝，但所含其他元素的比例并不使其具有其他合金钢的特性。

（四）高速钢

不论是否含有其他元素，但至少含有按重量计合计含量在7%及以上的钼、钨、钒中两种元素的合金钢，按重量计其含碳量在0.6%及以上，含铬量在3%～6%。

（五）硅锰钢

按重量计同时含有下列元素的合金钢：

碳不超过0.7%；

锰0.5%及以上，但不超过1.9%；

硅0.6%及以上，但不超过2.3%。但所含其他元素的比例并不使其具有其他合金钢的特性。

二、税目72.02项下的子目所列铁合金，应按照下列规则归类：

对于只有一种元素超出本章注释一（三）规定的最低百分比的铁合金，应作为二元合金归入相应的子目号。以此类推，如果有两种或三种合金元素超出了最低百分比的，则可分别作为三元或四元合金。在运用本规定时，本章注释一（三）所述的未列名的“其他元素”，按重量计单项含量必须超过10%。

(o) Hollow drill bars and rods

Hollow bars and rods of any cross-section, suitable for drills, of which the greatest external dimension of the cross-section exceeds 15mm but does not exceed 52mm, and of which the greatest internal dimension does not exceed one half of the greatest external dimension. Hollow bars and rods of iron or steel not conforming to this definition are to be classified in heading No. 73. 04.

2. Ferrous metals clad with another ferrous metal are to be classified as products of the ferrous metal predominating by weight.

3. Iron or steel products obtained by electrolytic deposition, by pressure casting or by sintering are to be classified, according to their form, their composition and their appearance, in the headings of this Chapter appropriate to similar hot-rolled products.

Subheading Notes:

1. In this Chapter the following expressions have the meanings hereby assigned to them:

(a) Alloy pig iron

Pig iron containing, by weight, one or more of the following elements in the specified proportions:

-more than 0. 2% of chromium

-more than 0. 3% of copper

-more than 0. 3% of nickel

-more than 0. 1% of any of the following elements:

aluminium, molybdenum, titanium, tungsten (wolfram), vanadium.

(b) Non-alloy free-cutting steel

Non-alloy steel containing, by weight, one or more of the following elements in the specified proportions:

-0. 08% or more of sulphur

-0. 1% or more of lead

-more than 0. 05% of selenium

-more than 0. 01% of tellurium

-more than 0. 05% of bismuth.

(c) Silicon-electrical steel

Alloy steels containing by weight at least 0. 6% but not more than 6% of silicon and not more than 0. 08% of carbon. They may also contain by weight not more than 1% of aluminium but no other element in a proportion that would give the steel the characteristics of another alloy steel.

(d) High speed steel

Alloy steels containing, with or without other elements, at least two of the three elements molybdenum, tungsten and vanadium with a combined content by weight of 7% or more, 0. 6% or more of carbon and 3% to 6% of chromium.

(e) Silico-manganese steel

Alloy steels containing by weight:

-not more than 0. 7% of carbon,

-0. 5% or more but not more than 1. 9% of manganese, and

-0. 6% or more but not more than 2. 3% of silicon, but no other element in a proportion that would give the steel the characteristics of another alloy steel.

2. For the classification of ferro-alloys in the subheadings of heading 72. 02 the following rule should be observed: A ferro-alloy is considered as binary and classified under the relevant subheading (if it exists) if only one of the alloy elements exceeds the minimum percentage laid down in Chapter Note 1 (c); by analogy, it is considered respectively as ternary or quaternary if two or three alloy elements exceed the minimum percentage. For the application of this rule the unspecified "other elements" referred to in Chapter Note 1 (c) must each exceed 10% by weight.

税则号列	货 品 名 称	最惠(%)	普通	增值税率	出口退税	计量单位	监管条件	Article Description
	第一分章　原料；粒状及粉状产品							Ⅰ. -PRIMARY MATERIALS; PRODUCTS IN GRANULAR OR POWDER FORM
72.01	**生铁及镜铁，锭、块或其他初级形状：**							**Pig iron and spiegeleisen in pigs, blocks or other primary forms:**
7201.1000	-非合金生铁，按重量计含磷量在0.5%及以下	1	8	17		千克		-Non-alloy pig iron containing by weight 0.5% or less of phosphorus
7201.2000	-非合金生铁，按重量计含磷量在0.5%以上	1	8	17		千克		-Non-alloy pig iron containing by weight more than 0.5% of phosphorus
7201.5000	-合金生铁；镜铁	1	8	17		千克		-Alloy pig iron; spiegeleisen
7201.5000 10	合金生铁	1	8	17		千克		Alloy pig iron
7201.5000 90	镜铁	1	8	17		千克		Spiegeleisen
72.02	**铁合金：**							**Ferro-alloys:**
	-锰铁：							-Ferro-manganese:
7202.1100	--按重量计含碳量在2%以上	2	11	17		千克	4xy	--Containing by weight more than 2% of carbon
7202.1900	--其他	2	11	17		千克	4xy	--Other
	-硅铁：							-Ferro-silicon:
7202.2100	--按重量计含硅量在55%以上	2	11	17		千克		--Containing by weight more than 55% of silicon
7202.2100 10	硅铁，含硅量大于55%，小于90%	2	11	17		千克	4ABxy	Ferro – silicon, containing more than 55% but less than 90% of silicon
7202.2100 90	硅铁，含硅量大于90%	2	11	17		千克	4xy	Ferro-silicon, containing more than 90% of silicon
7202.2900	--其他	2	11	17		千克		--Other
7202.2900 10	硅铁，含硅量大于等于30%且不超过55%	2	11	17		千克	4ABxy	Ferro – silicon, containing more than 30% but less than 55% of silicon
7202.2900 90	硅铁，含硅量小于30%	2	11	17		千克	4xy	Ferro – silicon, containing less than 30% of silicon
7202.3000	-硅锰铁	2	11	17		千克	4xy	-Ferro-silico-manganese
	-铬铁：							-Ferro-chromium:
7202.4100[暂]	--按重量计含碳量在4%以上	0	8	17		千克	4xy	--Containing by weight more than 4% of carbon
7202.4900[暂]	--其他	1	8	17		千克	4xy	--Other
7202.5000	-硅铬铁	2	11	17		千克	4xy	-Ferro-silico-chromium
7202.6000[暂]	-镍铁	0	11	17		千克	4xy	-Ferro-nickel
7202.7000[暂]	-钼铁	1	11	17		千克	4xy	-Ferro-molybdenum
	-钨铁及硅钨铁：							-Ferro-tungsten and ferro-silico-tungsten:
7202.8010[暂]	---钨铁	1	11	17		千克	4xy	---Ferro-tungsten
7202.8020	---硅钨铁	2	11	17		千克	4xy	---Ferro-silico-tungsten
	-其他：							-Other:
7202.9100	--钛铁及硅钛铁	2	11	17		千克	4xy	--Ferro-titanium and ferro-silico-titanium
	--钒铁：							--Ferro-vanadium:
7202.9210	---按重量计含钒量在75%及以上	9	30	17		千克	4xy	---Containing by weight more than 75% of ranadium
7202.9290	---其他	9	30	17		千克	4xy	---Other
7202.9300[暂]	--铌铁	1	11	17		千克		--Ferro-niobium
7202.9300[暂] 10	铁钽铌合金（钽含量<10%）	1	11	17		千克	4xy	Ferro-tantalum-niobium alloy (containing < 10% by weight of tantalum)
7202.9300[暂] 90	其他铌铁	1	11	17		千克	4xy	Other ferro-niobium
	--其他：							--Other:
	---钕铁硼合金：							---Na-Fe-B alloy:
7202.9911	----速凝永磁片	2	11	17		千克	4xy	----Rapid setting permanent magnet film
7202.9912	----磁粉	2	11	17		千克	4xy	----Magnetic powder
7202.9919	----其他	2	11	17		千克	4xy	----Other
	---其他：							---Other:
7202.9991	----按重量计稀土元素总含量在10%以上的	2	11	17		千克	4xy	----Containing by weight more than 10% of rate eath elements
7202.9991 10	按重量计中重稀土总含量≥30%的铁合金（按重量计稀土元素总含量在10%以上）	2	11	17		千克	4xy	Containing by weight more than 30% of middle heavy rare – earth, alloy iron (containing by weight more than 10% of rare – earth element)
7202.9991 91	稀土硅铁合金（按重量计稀土元素总含量在10%以上）	2	11	17		千克	4xy	Rare earth ferrosilicon alloy (containing by weight more than 10% of rare – earth element)

税则号列	货 品 名 称	最惠(%)	普通	增值税率	出口退税	计量单位	监管条件	Article Description
7202.9991 99	其他按重量计稀土元素总含量在10%以上的铁合金	2	11	17		千克	4xy	Containing weight by more than 10% of rare－earth element, alloy iron
7202.9999	----其他	2	11	17		千克	4xy	----Other
72.03	**直接从铁矿还原所得的铁产品及其他海绵铁产品,块、团、团粒及类似形状;按重量计纯度在99.94%及以上的铁,块、团、团粒及类似形状:**							**Ferrous products obtained by direct reduction of iron ore and other spongy ferrous products, in lumps, pellets or similar forms; iron having a minimum purity by weight of 99.94%, in lumps, pellets or similar forms:**
7203.1000	-直接从铁矿还原所得的铁产品		8	17		千克		-Ferrous products obtained by direct reduction of iron ore
7203.1000暂 01	热压铁块	0	8	17		千克		Hot－birquetted iron
7203.1000 90	直接从铁矿还原的铁产品(铁团、铁粒及类似形状)	2	8	17		千克		Other ferrous products obtained by direct reduction of iron ore(in lumps, pellets or similar forms)
7203.9000	-其他	2	8	17		千克		-Other
72.04	**钢铁废碎料;供再熔的碎料钢铁锭:**							**Ferrous waste and scrap; remelting scrap ingots of iron steel:**
7204.1000暂	-铸铁废碎料	0	8	17		千克	AP	-Waste and scrap of cast iron
	-合金钢废碎料:							-Waste and scrap of alloy steel:
7204.2100	--不锈钢废碎料	0	8	17		千克	AP	--Of stainless steel
7204.2900	--其他	0	8	17		千克	AP	--Other
7204.3000暂	-镀锡钢铁废碎料	0	8	17		千克	AP	-Waste and scrap of tinned iron or steel
	-其他废碎料:							-Other waste and scrap:
7204.4100暂	--车、刨、铣、磨、锯、锉、剪、冲加工过程中产生的废料,不论是否成捆	0	8	17		千克	AP	--Turnings, shavings, chips, milling waste, sawdust, filings, trimmings and stampings, whether or not in bundles
7204.4900	--其他	0	8	17		千克		--Other
7204.4900 10	废汽车压件	0	8	17		千克	AP	Compressed piece of scrap automobile
7204.4900 20	以回收钢铁为主的废五金电器	0	8	17		千克	AP	Waste hardware and electric appliance mainly for recovering steel and iron
7204.4900 90	未列名钢铁废碎料	0	8	17		千克	AP	Other ferrous waste and scrap, not elsewhere specifiled or included
7204.5000	-供再熔的碎料钢铁锭	0	8	17		千克	AP	-Remelting scrap ingots
72.05	**生铁、镜铁及钢铁的颗粒和粉末:**							**Granules and powders, of pig iron, spiegeleiseniron or steel:**
7205.1000	-颗粒	2	30	17		千克		-Granules
7205.1000 01	棱角钢砂(不带球弧面的棱角形颗粒数量大于80%)	2	30	17		千克		Steel emery with angular (grain with angular, without Spherical Arc, grain quantity >80%)
7205.1000 02	铸钢丸和铸钢砂(筛网孔径在0.3－2.8mm的铸钢丸和铸钢砂)	2	30	17		千克		Cast steel shot, cast steel grit (mesh size in the 0.3－2.8mm steel shot and Zhu Gangsha)
7205.1000 90	其他生铁、镜铁及钢铁颗粒	2	30	17		千克		Other granules, of pig iron, spiegeleisen, iron or steel
	-粉末:							-Powders:
7205.2100	--合金钢的	2	17	17		千克		--Of alloy steel
7205.2900	--其他	2	17	17		千克		--Other
7205.2900 01	生铁、镜铁及其他钢铁粉末(平均粒径<10μm的超细铁粉的除外)	2	17	17		千克		Powders, of pig iron, spiegeleiseniron or steel(other than average particle diameter of less than 10μm superfine iron powder)
7205.2900 90	生铁、镜铁及其他钢铁粉末(平均粒径<10μm的超细铁粉)	2	17	17		千克		Powders, of pig iron, spiegeleiseniron or steel(average particle diameter of less than 10μm superfine iron powder)
	第二分章　铁及非合金钢							Ⅱ-IRON AND NON-ALLOY STEEL
72.06	**铁及非合金钢,锭状或其他初级形状(税目72.03的铁除外):**							**Iron and non-alloy steel in ingots or other primary forms (excluding iron of heading No. 72.03):**
7206.1000	-锭状	2	11	17		千克		-Ingots
7206.9000	-其他	2	11	17		千克		-Other
72.07	**铁及非合金钢的半制成品:**							**Semi-finished products of iron or non-alloy steel:**

税则号列	货 品 名 称	最惠(%)	普通	增值税率	出口退税	计量单位	监管条件	Article Description
	-按重量计含碳量在0.25%以下:							-Containing by weight less than 0.25% of carbon:
7207.1100	--矩形(包括正方形)截面,宽度小于厚度的两倍	2	11	17		千克		--Of rectangular (including square) cross-section, the width measuring less than twice the thickness
7207.1200	--其他矩形(正方形除外)截面的	2	11	17		千克		--Other, of rectangular (other than square) cross-section
7207.1900	--其他	2	11	17		千克		--Other
7207.2000	-按重量计含碳量在0.25%及以上	2	11	17		千克		-Containing by weight 0.25% or more of carbon
72.08	**宽度在600毫米及以上的铁或非合金钢平板轧材,经热轧,但未经包覆、镀层或涂层:**							**Flat-rolled products of iron or non-alloy steel, of a width of 600mm or more, hot-rolled, not clad, plated or coated:**
7208.1000	-除热轧外未经进一步加工的卷材,已轧压花纹	5	14	17		千克	A	-In coils, not further worked than hot-rolled, with patterns in relief
	-其他经酸洗的卷材,除热轧外未经进一步加工:							-Other, in coils, not further worked than hot-rolled, pickled:
7208.2500	--厚度在4.75毫米及以上	5	14	17		千克	A	--Of a thickness of 4.75mm or more
	--厚度在3毫米及以上,但小于4.75毫米:							--Of a thickness of 3mm or more but less than 4.75mm:
7208.2610	---屈服强度大于355牛顿/平方毫米	5	14	17		千克	A	---Of a yield strength exceeding 355N/mm²
7208.2690	---其他	5	14	17		千克	A	---Other
	--厚度小于3毫米:							--Of a thickness of less than 3mm:
7208.2710	---厚度小于1.5毫米	5	14	17		千克	A	---Of a thickness of less than 1.5mm
7208.2790	---其他	5	14	17		千克	A	---Other
	-其他卷材,除热轧外未经进一步加工:							-Other, in coils, not further worked than hot-rolled:
7208.3600	--厚度超过10毫米	6	14	17		千克	A	--Of a thickness exceeding 10mm
7208.3700	--厚度在4.75毫米及以上,但不超过10毫米	5	14	17		千克	A	--Of a thickness of 4.75mm or more but not exceeding 10mm
	--厚度在3毫米及以上,但小于4.75毫米:							--Of a thickness of 3mm or more but less than 4.75mm:
7208.3810	---屈服强度大于355牛顿/平方毫米	5	14	17		千克	A	---Of a yield strength exceeding 355N/mm²
7208.3890	---其他	5	14	17		千克	A	---Other
	--厚度小于3毫米:							--Of a thickness of less than 3mm:
7208.3910	---厚度小于1.5毫米	3	14	17		千克	A	---Of a thickness of less than 1.5mm
7208.3990	---其他	3	14	17		千克	A	---Other
7208.4000	-已轧压花纹的非卷材,除热轧外未经进一步加工	6	17	17		千克	A	-Not in coils, not further worked than hot-rolled, with patterns in relief
	-其他非卷材,除热轧外未经进一步加工:							-Other, not in coils, not further worked than hot-rolled:
	--厚度超过10毫米:							--Of a thickness exceeding 10mm:
7208.5110	---厚度超过50毫米	6	17	17		千克	A	---Of a thickness exceeding 50mm
7208.5120	---厚度在20毫米以上,但不超过50毫米	6	17	17		千克	A	---Of a thickness exceeding 20mm but not exceeding 50mm
7208.5190	---其他	6	17	17		千克	A	---Other
7208.5200	--厚度在4.75毫米及以上,但不超过10毫米	6	17	17		千克	A	--Of a thickness of 4.75mm or more but not exceeding 10mm
	--厚度在3毫米及以上,但小于4.75毫米:							--Of a thickness of 3mm or more but less than 4.75mm:
7208.5310	---屈服强度大于355牛顿/平方毫米	6	17	17		千克	A	---Of a yield strength exceeding 355N/mm²
7208.5390	---其他	6	17	17		千克	A	---Other
	--厚度小于3毫米:							--Of a thickness of less than 3mm:
7208.5410	---厚度小于1.5毫米	6	17	17		千克	A	---Of a thickness of less than1.5mm:
7208.5490	---其他	6	17	17		千克	A	---Other
7208.9000	-其他	6	17	17		千克	A	-Other
72.09	**宽度在600毫米及以上的铁或非合金钢平板轧材,经冷轧,但未经包覆、镀层或涂层:**							**Flat-rolled products of iron or non-alloy steel, of a width of 600mm or more, cold-rolled (cold-reduced), not clad, plated or coated:**

税则号列	货品名称	最惠(%)	普通	增值税率	出口退税	计量单位	监管条件	Article Description
	-卷材,除冷轧外未经进一步加工:							-In coils, not further worked than cold-rolled (cold-reduced):
	--厚度在3毫米及以上:							--Of a thickness of 3mm or more:
7209.1510	---屈服强度大于355牛顿/平方毫米	6	17	17		千克	A	---Of a yield strength exceeding 355N/mm^2
7209.1590	---其他	6	17	17	13	千克	A	---Other
	--厚度超过1毫米,但小于3毫米:							--Of a thickness exceeding 1mm but less than 3mm:
7209.1610	---屈服强度大于275牛顿/平方毫米	6	17	17	13	千克	A	---Of a yield strength exceeding 275N/mm^2
7209.1690	---其他	6	17	17	13	千克	A	---Other
	--厚度在0.5毫米及以上,但不超过1毫米:							--Of a thickness of 0.5mm or more but not exceeding 1mm:
7209.1710	---屈服强度大于275牛顿/平方毫米	3	17	17	13	千克	A	---Of a yield strength exceeding 275N/mm^2
7209.1790	---其他	3	17	17	13	千克	A	---Other
	--厚度小于0.5毫米:							--Of a thickness of less than 0.5mm:
7209.1810暂	---厚度小于0.3毫米	4	17	17	13	千克	A	---Of a thickness less than 0.3mm
7209.1890	---其他	6	17	17	13	千克	A	---Other
	-非卷材,除冷轧外未经进一步加工:							-Not in coils, not further worked than cold-rolled (cold-reduced):
7209.2500	--厚度在3毫米及以上	6	17	17	13	千克	A	--Of a thickness of 3mm or more
7209.2600	--厚度超过1毫米,但小于3毫米	6	17	17	13	千克	A	--Of a thickness exceeding 1mm but less than 3mm
7209.2700	--厚度在0.5毫米及以上,但不超过1毫米	6	17	17	13	千克	A	--Of a thickness of 0.5mm or more but not exceeding 1mm
7209.2800	--厚度小于0.5毫米	6	17	17	13	千克	A	--Of a thickness of less than 0.5mm
7209.9000	-其他	6	17	17	13	千克	A	-Other
72.10	**宽度在600毫米及以上的铁或非合金钢平板轧材,经包覆、镀层或涂层:**							**Flat-rolled products of iron or non-alloy steel, of a width of 600mm or more, clad, plated or coated:**
	-镀或涂锡的:							-Plated or coated with tin:
7210.1100	--厚度在0.5毫米及以上	10	20	17	13	千克	A	--Of a thickness of 0.5mm or more
7210.1200	--厚度小于0.5毫米	5	20	17	13	千克	A	--Of a thickness of less than 0.5mm
7210.2000	-镀或涂铅的,包括镀铅锡钢板	4	20	17	13	千克		-Plated or coated with lead, including terneplate
7210.3000	-电镀锌的	8	20	17	13	千克	A	-Electrolytically plated or coated with zinc
	-用其他方法镀或涂锌的:							-Otherwise plated or coated with zinc:
7210.4100	--瓦楞形	8	20	17	13	千克	A	--Corrugated
7210.4900	--其他	4	20	17	13	千克	A	--Other
7210.5000	-镀或涂氧化铬或铬及氧化铬的	8	20	17	13	千克		-Plated or coated with chromium oxides or with chromium and chromium oxides
	-镀或涂铝的:							-Plated or coated with aluminium:
7210.6100	--镀或涂铝锌合金的	8	20	17	13	千克		--Plated or coated with aluminium-zinc alloys
7210.6900	--其他	8	20	17	13	千克		--Other
	-涂漆或涂塑的:							-Painted, varnished or coated with plastics:
7210.7010	---厚度小于1.5毫米	4	20	17	13	千克		---Of a thickness of less than 1.5mm
7210.7090	---其他	4	20	17	13	千克		---Other
7210.9000	-其他	8	20	17	13	千克		-Other
72.11	**宽度小于600毫米的铁或非合金钢平板轧材,但未经包覆、镀层或涂层:**							**Flat-rolled products of iron or non-alloy steel, of a width of less than 600mm, not clad, plated or coated:**
	-除热轧外未经进一步加工:							-Not further worked than hot-rolled:
7211.1300	--经四面轧制或在闭合匣内轧制的非卷材,宽度超过150毫米,厚度不小于4毫米,未轧压花纹	6	30	17		千克	A	--Rolled on four faces or in a closed box pass, of a width exceeding 150mm and a thickness of not less than 4mm, not in coils and without patterns in relief
7211.1400	--其他,厚度在4.75毫米及以上	6	30	17		千克	A	--Other, of a thickness of 4.75mm or more
7211.1900	--其他	6	30	17		千克	A	--Other
	-除冷轧外未经进一步加工:							-Not further worked than cold-rolled (cold-reduced):
7211.2300	--按重量计含碳量低于0.25%	6	30	17		千克	A	--Containing by weight less than 0.25% of carbon
7211.2900	--其他	6	30	17		千克	A	--Other
7211.9000	-其他	6	30	17		千克	A	-Other
72.12	**宽度小于600毫米的铁或非合金钢平板轧材,经包覆、镀层或涂层:**							**Flat-rolled products of iron or non-alloy steel, of a width of less than 600mm, clad, plated or coated:**
7212.1000	-镀或涂锡的	5	20	17		千克	A	-Plated or coated with tin
7212.2000	-电镀锌的	8	20	17		千克	A	-Electrolytically plated or coated with zinc

税则号列	货品名称	最惠(%)	普通	增值税率	出口退税	计量单位	监管条件	Article Description
7212.3000	-用其他方法镀或涂锌的	8	20	17		千克	A	-Otherwise plated or coated with zinc
7212.4000	-涂漆或涂塑的	4	20	17		千克		-Painted, varnished or coated with plastics
7212.5000	-镀或涂其他材料的	8	20	17		千克		-Otherwise plated or coated
7212.6000	-经包覆的	8	20	17		千克		-Clad
72.13	**不规则盘卷的铁及非合金钢的热轧条、杆：**							**Bars and rods, hot-rolled, in irregularly wound coils, of iron or non-alloy steel:**
7213.1000	-带有轧制过程中产生的凹痕、凸缘、槽沟及其他变形的	3	20	17		千克	A	-Containing indentations, ribs, grooves or other deformations produced during the rolling process
7213.2000	-其他，易切削钢制	3	20	17		千克	A	-Other, of free-cutting steel
	-其他：							-Other:
7213.9100	--直径小于14毫米圆形截面的	5	20	17		千克	A	--Of circular cross-section measuring less than 14mm in diameter
7213.9900	--其他	5	20	17		千克	A	--Other
72.14	**铁或非合金钢的其他条、杆，除锻造、热轧、热拉拔或热挤压外未经进一步加工，包括轧制后扭曲的：**							**Other bars and rods of iron or non-alloy steel, not further worked than forged, hot-rolled, hot-drawn or hot-extruded, but including those twisted after rolling:**
7214.1000	-锻造的	7	10	17	9	千克	A	-Forged
7214.2000	-带有轧制过程中产生的凹痕、凸缘、槽沟或其他变形以及轧制后扭曲的	3	20	17		千克	A	-Containing indentations, ribs, grooves or other deformations produced during the rolling process or twisted after rolling
7214.3000	-其他，易切削钢制	7	20	17		千克	A	-Other, of free-cutting steel
	-其他：							-Other:
7214.9100	--矩形(正方形除外)截面的	3	20	17		千克	A	--Of rectangular cross section (other than square)
7214.9900	--其他	3	20	17		千克	A	--Other
72.15	**铁及非合金钢的其他条、杆：**							**Other bars and rods of iron or non-alloy steel:**
7215.1000	-易切削钢制，除冷成形或冷加工外未经进一步加工	7	20	17		千克	A	-Of free-cutting steel, not further worked than cold-formed or cold-finished
7215.5000	-其他，除冷成形或冷加工外未经进一步加工	7	20	17		千克	A	-Other, not further worked than cold-formed or cold-finished
7215.9000	-其他	3	20	17		千克	A	-Other
72.16	**铁或非合金钢的角材、型材及异型材：**							**Angles, shapes and sections of iron or non-alloy steel:**
	-槽钢、工字钢及H型钢，除热轧、热拉拔或热挤压外未经进一步加工，截面高度低于80毫米：							-U, I or H sections, not further worked than hot-rolled, hot-drawn or extruded, of a height of less than 80mm:
7216.1010	---H型钢	3	14	17		千克	A	---H sections
7216.1020	---工字钢	3	14	17		千克	A	---I sections
7216.1090	---其他	3	14	17		千克	A	---Other
	-角钢及丁字钢，除热轧、热拉拔或热挤压外未经进一步加工，截面高度低于80毫米：							-L or T sections, not further worked than hot-rolled, hot-drawn or extruded, of a height of less than 80mm:
7216.2100	--角钢	6	17	17		千克	A	--L sections
7216.2200	--丁字钢	6	14	17		千克	A	--T sections
	-槽钢、工字钢及H型钢，除热轧、热拉拔或热挤压外未经进一步加工，截面高度在80毫米及以上：							-U, I or H sections, not further worked than hot-rolled, hot-drawn or extruded of a height of 80mm or more:
7216.3100	--槽钢	6	14	17		千克	A	--U sections
	--工字钢：							--I sections:
7216.3210	---截面高度在200毫米以上	6	14	17		千克	A	---Of a height exceeding 200mm
7216.3290	---其他	6	14	17		千克	A	---Other
	--H型钢：							--H sections:
	---截面高度在200毫米以上：							---Of a height exceeding 200mm:
7216.3311	----截面高度在800毫米以上	6	14	17		千克	A	----Of a height exceeding 800mm
7216.3319	----其他	6	14	17		千克	A	----Other
7216.3390	---其他	6	14	17		千克	A	---Other

税则号列	货品名称	最惠(%)	普通	增值税率	出口退税	计量单位	监管条件	Article Description
	-角钢及丁字钢,除热轧、热拉拔或热挤压外未经进一步加工,截面高度在80毫米及以上:							-L or T sections, not further worked than hot-rolled, hot-drawn or extruded, of a height of 80mm or more:
7216.4010	---角钢	3	17	17		千克	A	---L sections
7216.4020	---丁字钢	3	14	17		千克	A	---T sections
	-其他角材、型材及异型材,除热轧、热拉拔或热挤压外未经进一步加工:							-Other angles, shapes and sections, not further worked than hot-rolled, hot-drawn or extruded:
7216.5010	---乙字钢	6	14	17		千克	A	---Z sections
7216.5020	---球扁钢	3	20	17		千克	A	---Bulb flat steel
7216.5090	---其他	3	20	17		千克	A	---Other
	-角材、型材及异型材,除冷成形或冷加工外未经进一步加工:							-Angles, shapes and sections, not further worked than cold-formed or cold-finished:
7216.6100	--平板轧材制的	3	20	17		千克	A	--Obtained from flat-rolled products
7216.6900	--其他	3	20	17		千克	A	--Other
	-其他:							-Other:
7216.9100	--平板轧材经冷成形或冷加工制的	3	20	17		千克	A	--Cold-formed or cold-finished from flat-rolled products
7216.9900	--其他	3	20	17		千克	A	--Other
72.17	**铁丝或非合金钢丝:**							**Wire of iron or non-alloy steel:**
7217.1000	-未经镀或涂层,不论是否抛光	8	40	17		千克		-Not plated or coated, whether or not polished
7217.2000	-镀或涂锌的	8	40	17	9	千克		-Plated or coated with zinc
	-镀或涂其他贱金属的:							-Plated or coated with other base metals
7217.3010	---镀或涂铜的	8	40	17	9	千克		---Plated or coated with copper
7217.3090	---其他	8	40	17	9	千克		---Other
7217.9000	-其他	8	40	17		千克		-Other
	第三分章　不锈钢							Ⅲ.-STAINLESS STEEL
72.18	**不锈钢,锭状或其他初级形状;不锈钢半制成品:**							**Stainless steel in ingots or other primary forms; semi-finished products of stainless steel:**
7218.1000	-锭状及其他初级形状	2	11	17		千克		-Ingots and other primary forms
	-其他:							-Other:
7218.9100	--矩形(正方形除外)截面的	2	11	17		千克		--Of rectangular (other than square) cross-section
7218.9900	--其他	2	11	17		千克		--Other
72.19	**不锈钢平板轧材,宽度在600毫米及以上:**							**Flat-rolled products of stainless steel, of a width of 600mm or more:**
	-除热轧外未经进一步加工的卷材:							-Not further worked than hot-rolled, in coils:
7219.1100	--厚度超过10毫米	4	14	17	13	千克	A	--Of a thickness exceeding 10mm
7219.1200	--厚度在4.75毫米及以上,但不超过10毫米	4	14	17	13	千克	A	--Of a thickness of 4.75mm or more but not exceeding 10mm
	--厚度在3毫米及以上,但小于4.75毫米:							--Of a thickness of 3mm or more but less than 4.75mm:
	---未经酸洗的:							---Not acid pickled:
7219.1312	----按重量计含锰量在5.5%及以上铬锰系不锈钢	4	14	17		千克	A	----Containing more than 5.5% by weight of manganese of Ferro-chromium-manganese steel
7219.1319	----其他	4	14	17	13	千克	A	----Other
	---经酸洗的:							---Acid pickled:
7219.1322	----按重量计含锰量在5.5%及以上铬锰系不锈钢	4	14	17		千克	A	----Containing more than 5.5% by weight of manganese of Ferro-chromiam-manganese steel
7219.1329	----其他	4	14	17	13	千克	A	----Other
	--厚度小于3毫米:							--Of a thickness of less than 3mm:
	---未经酸洗的:							---Not acid pickled:
7219.1412	----按重量计含锰量在5.5%及以上铬锰系不锈钢	4	14	17		千克	A	----Containing more than 5.5% by weight of manganese of Ferro-chromium-marganese steel
7219.1419	----其他	4	14	17	13	千克	A	----Other
	---经酸洗的:							---Acid Pickled:
7219.1422	----按重量计含锰量在5.5%及以上铬锰系不锈钢	4	14	17		千克	A	----Containing more than 5.5% by weight of manganese of ferro chromium-manganese steel
7219.1429	----其他	4	14	17	13	千克	A	----Other

税则号列	货品名称	最惠(%)	普通	增值税率	出口退税	计量单位	监管条件	Article Description
	-除热轧外未经进一步加工的非卷材:							-Not further worked than hot-rolled, not in coils:
7219.2100	--厚度超过10毫米	10	40	17	13	千克	A	--Of a thickness exceeding 10mm
7219.2200	--厚度在4.75毫米及以上,但不超过10毫米	10	40	17	13	千克	A	--Of a thickness of 4.75mm or more but not exceeding 10mm
7219.2300	--厚度在3毫米及以上,但小于4.75毫米	10	40	17	13	千克	A	--Of a thickness of 3mm or more but less than 4.75mm
	--厚度小于3毫米:							--Of a thickness of less than 3mm:
7219.2410	---厚度超过1毫米但小于3毫米	10	40	17	13	千克	A	---Of a thickness exceeding 1mm, but less than 3mm
7219.2420	---厚度在0.5毫米及以上,但不超过1毫米	10	40	17	13	千克	A	---Of a thickness of 0.5mm or more but not exceeding 1mm
7219.2430	---厚度小于0.5毫米	10	40	17	13	千克	A	---Of a thickness of less than 0.5mm
	-除冷轧外未经进一步加工:							-Not further worked than cold-rolled (cold-reduced):
7219.3100	--厚度在4.75毫米及以上	10	40	17	13	千克	A	--Of a thickness of 4.75mm or more
7219.3200	--厚度在3毫米及以上,但小于4.75毫米	10	40	17	13	千克	A	--Of a thickness of 3mm or more but less than 4.75mm
	--厚度超过1毫米,但小于3毫米:							--Of a thickness exceeding 1mm but less than 3mm:
7219.3310	---按重量计含锰量在5.5%及以上的铬锰系不锈钢	10	40	17	13	千克	A	---Containing more than 5.5% by weight of manganese of ferro chromium-manganese steel
7219.3390	---其他	10	40	17	13	千克	A	---Other
7219.3400	--厚度在0.5毫米及以上,但不超过1毫米	10	40	17	13	千克	A	--Of a thickness of 0.5mm or more but not exceeding 1mm
7219.3500	--厚度小于0.5毫米	10	40	17	13	千克	A	--Of a thickness of less than 0.5mm
7219.9000	-其他	10	40	17	13	千克	A	-Other
72.20	**不锈钢平板轧材,宽度小于600毫米:**							**Flat-rolled products stainless steel, of a width of less than 600mm:**
	-除热轧外未经进一步加工:							-Not further worked than hot-rolled:
7220.1100	--厚度在4.75毫米及以上	10	20	17	9	千克	A	--Of a thickness of 4.75mm or more
7220.1200	--厚度小于4.75毫米	10	20	17	9	千克	A	--Of a thickness of less than 4.75mm
	-除冷轧外未经进一步加工:							-Not further worked than cold-rolled (cold-reduced):
7220.2020	---厚度在0.35毫米及以下	10	20	17	9	千克	A	---Of a thickness of 0.35mm orless
7220.2030	---厚度在0.35毫米及以上但小于3毫米	10	20	17	9	千克	A	---Of a thickness of more than 0.35mm but less than 3mm
7220.2040	---厚度在3毫米及以上	10	20	17	9	千克	A	---Of a thickness of 3mm or more
7220.9000	-其他	10	20	17	9	千克	A	-Other
72.21	**不规则盘卷的不锈钢热轧条、杆:**							**Bars and rods, hot-rolled, in irregularly wound coils, of stainless steel:**
7221.0000	不规则盘卷的不锈钢热轧条、杆	10	20	17	13	千克	A	Bars and rods, hot-rolled, in irregularly wound coils, of stainless steel
72.22	**不锈钢其他条、杆;不锈钢角材、型材及异型材:**							**Other bars and rods of stainless steel; angles, shapes and sections of stainless steel:**
	-条、杆,除热轧、热拉拔或热挤压外未经进一步加工:							-Bars and rods, not further worked than hot-rolled, hot-drawn or extruded:
7222.1100	--圆形截面的	10	40	17	5	千克	A	--Of circular cross-section
7222.1900	--其他	10	40	17	5	千克	A	--Other
7222.2000	-条、杆,除冷成形或冷加工外未经进一步加工	10	40	17	5	千克		-Bars and rods, not further worked than cold-formed or cold-finished
7222.3000	-其他条、杆	10	40	17	5	千克		-Other bars and rods
7222.4000	-角材、型材及异型材	10	17	17	5	千克	A	-Angles, shapes and sections
72.23	**不锈钢丝:**							**Wire of stainless steel:**
7223.0000	不锈钢丝	10	20	17	5	千克		Wire of stainless steel
	第四分章　其他合金钢;合金钢或非合金钢制的空心钻钢							Ⅳ. OTHER ALLOY STEEL; HOLLOW DRILL BARS AND RODS, OF ALLOY OR NON-ALLOY STEEL
72.24	**其他合金钢,锭状或其他初级形状;其他合金钢制的半制成品:**							**Other alloy steel in ingots or other primary forms; semi-finished products of other alloy steel:**
7224.1000	-锭状及其他初级形状	2	11	17		千克		-Ingots and other primary forms
	-其他:							-Other:

税则号列	货 品 名 称	最惠(%)	普通	增值税率	出口退税	计量单位	监管条件	Article Description
7224.9010	---单件重量在10吨及以上的粗铸锻件坯	2	11	17		千克		---Raw casting forging stocks, individual piece weight of 10t or more
7224.9090	---其他	2	11	17		千克		---Other
72.25	**其他合金钢平板轧材,宽度在600毫米及以上:**							**Flat-rolled products of other alloy steel, of a width of 600mm or more:**
	-硅电钢制:							-Of silicon-electrical steel:
7225.1100	--取向性硅电钢	3	20	17	13	千克	A7	--Grain-oriented
7225.1900	--其他	6	20	17	13	千克	A	--Other
7225.3000	-其他卷材,除热轧外未经进一步加工	3	14	17	9	千克	A	-Other, not further worked than hot-rolled, in coils
	-其他非卷材,除热轧外未经进一步加工:							-Other, not further worked than hot-rolled, not in coils
7225.4010	---工具钢	3	17	17	13	千克	A	---Tool steel
	---其他:							---Other:
7225.4091	----含硼合金钢	3	17	17	13	千克	A	----Alloy steel containing boron
7225.4099	----其他	3	17	17	13	千克	A	----Other
7225.5000	-其他,除冷轧外未经进一步加工	3	17	17	13	千克	A	-Other, not further worked than cold-rolled (cold-reduced)
	-其他:							-Other:
7225.9100	--电镀或涂锌的	7	17	17	9	千克	A	--Electrolytically plated or coated with zinc
7225.9200	--用其他方法镀或涂锌的	7	17	17	9	千克	A	--Otherwise plated or coated with zinc
	--其他:							--Other:
7225.9910	---高速钢制	3	17	17	9	千克	A	---Of high speed steel
7225.9990	---其他	7	17	17	9	千克	A	---Other
72.26	**其他合金钢平板轧材,宽度小于600毫米:**							**Flat-rolled products of other alloy steel, of a width of less than 600mm:**
	-硅电钢制:							-Of silicon-electrical steel:
7226.1100	--取向性硅电钢	3	20	17	13	千克	A	--Grain-oriented
7226.1900	--其他	3	20	17	13	千克	A	--Other
7226.2000	-高速钢制	3	20	17	9	千克	A	-Of high speed steel
	-其他:							-Other:
	--除热轧外未经进一步加工:							--Not further worked than hot-rolled:
7226.9110	---工具钢	3	20	17	9	千克	A	---Tool steel
	---其他:							---Other:
7226.9191	----含硼合金钢	3	20	17	9	千克	A	----Alloy steel containing boron
7226.9199	----其他	3	20	17	9	千克	A	----Other
7226.9200	--除冷轧外未经进一步加工	3	20	17	9	千克	A	--Not further worked than cold-rolled (cold-reduced)
	--其他:							--Other:
7226.9910	---电镀锌的	7	20	17	9	千克	A	---Electrolytically plated or coated with zinc
7226.9920	---用其他方法镀或涂锌的	7	20	17	9	千克	A	---Otherwise plated or coated with zinc
7226.9990	---其他		20	17	9	千克		---Other
7226.9990暂 01	铁镍合金带材(生产集成电路框架用)(宽度<600mm)	4	20	17	9	千克	A	Other flat-rolled products of other alloy steel, Fe-Ni alloys strip, width < 600mm (production of the frame for electronic integrated circuits)
7226.9990 90	其他合金板材(宽度<600mm)	7	20	17	9	千克	A	Other flat-rolled products of other alloy steel, width < 600mm
72.27	**不规则盘卷的其他合金钢热轧条、杆:**							**Bars and rods, hot-rolled, in irregularly wound coils, of other alloy steel:**
7227.1000	-高速钢制	3	20	17	9	千克	A	-Of high speed steel
7227.2000	-硅锰钢制	6	20	17	9	千克	A	-Of silico-manganese steel
	-其他:							-Other:
7227.9010	---含硼合金钢制	3	20	17	9	千克	A	---Of containing boron alloy steel
7227.9090	---其他	3	20	17	9	千克	A	---Other

税则号列	货品名称	最惠(%)	普通	增值税率	出口退税	计量单位	监管条件	Article Description
72.28	**其他合金钢条、杆;其他合金钢角材、型材及异型材;合金钢或非合金钢制的空心钻钢:**							**Other bars and rods of other alloy steel; angles, shapes and sections, of other alloy steel; hollow drill bars and rods, of alloy or non-alloy steel:**
7228.1000	-高速钢条、杆	3	20	17	13	千克	A	-Bars and rods, of high speed steel
7228.2000	-硅锰钢条、杆	6	20	17		千克	A	-Bars and rods, of silico-manganese steel
	-其他条、杆,除热轧、热拉拔或热挤压外未经进一步加工:							-Other bars and rods, not further worked than hot-crolled, hot-drawn or extruded:
7228.3010	---含硼合金钢制	3	20	17	13	千克	A	---Of containing boron alloy steel
7228.3090	---其他	3	20	17	13	千克	A	---Other
7228.4000	-其他条、杆,除锻造外未经进一步加工	3	20	17	13	千克	A	-Other bars and rods, not further worked than forged
7228.5000	-其他条、杆,除冷成形或冷加工外未经进一步加工	3	20	17	13	千克	A	-Other bars and rods, not further worked than cold-formed of cold-finished
7228.6000	-其他条、杆	3	20	17	9	千克	A	-Other bars and rods
	-角材、型材及异型材:							-Angles, shapes and sections:
7228.7010	---履带板型钢	6	17	17	9	千克	A	---Shapes of crawler tread
7228.7090	---其他	6	17	17	9	千克	A	---Other
7228.8000	-空心钻钢	7	35	17	13	千克	A	-Hollow drill bars and rods
72.29	**其他合金钢丝:**							**Wire of other alloy steel:**
7229.2000	-硅锰钢丝	7	20	17		千克		-Of silico-manganese steel
	-其他:							-Other:
7229.9010	---高速钢丝	3	20	17	13	千克		---Of high speed steel
7229.9090	---其他	7	20	17	9	千克		---Other

第七十三章
钢铁制品

Chapter 73
Articles of iron or steel

注释：

一、本章所称"铸铁"，适用于经铸造而得的产品，按重量计其铁元素含量超过其他元素单项含量并与第七十二章注释一（四）所述的钢的化学成分不同。

二、本章所称"丝"，是指热或冷成形的任何截面形状的产品，但其截面尺寸均不超过16毫米。

Notes:

1. In this Chapter the expression "cast iron" applies to products obtained by casting in which iron predominates by weight over each of the other elements and which do not comply with the chemical composition of steel as defined in Note 1 (d) to Chapter 72.
2. In this Chapter the word "wire" means hot or cold-formed products of any cross-sectional shape, of which no cross-sectional dimension exceeds 16mm.

税则号列	货品名称	最惠(%)	普通	增值税率	出口退税	计量单位	监管条件	Article Description
73.01	钢铁板桩，不论是否钻孔、打眼或组装；焊接的钢铁角材、型材及异型材：							**Sheet piling of iron or steel, whether or not drilled, punched or made from assembled elements; welded angles, shapes and sections, of iron or steel:**
7301.1000	-钢铁板桩	7	20	17	9	千克		-Sheet piling
7301.2000	-角材、型材及异型材	7	30	17	9	千克		-Angles, shapes and sections
73.02	铁道及电车道铺轨用钢铁材料（钢轨、护轨、齿轨、道岔尖轨、辙叉、尖轨拉杆及其他岔道段体、轨枕、鱼尾板、轨座、轨座楔、钢轨垫板、钢轨夹、底板、固定板及其他专门用于连接或加固路轨的材料）：							**Railway or tramway track construction material of iron or steel, the following: rails, check-rails and rack rails, switch blades, crossing frogs, point rods and other crossing pieces, sleepers (cross-ties), fish-plates, chairs, chair wedges, sole plates (base plates), rail clips, bedplates, ties and other material specialized for jointing or fixing rails:**
7302.1000	-钢轨	6	14	17	9	千克	A	-Rails
7302.3000	-道岔尖轨、辙叉、尖轨拉杆及其他岔道段体	8	17	17	9	千克	A	-Switch blades, crossing frogs, point rods and other crossing pieces
7302.4000	-鱼尾板及钢轨垫板	7	17	17	9	千克	A	-Fish-plates and sole plates
	-其他：							-Other:
7302.9010	---轨枕	6	14	17	9	千克	A	---Sleepers (cross-ties)
7302.9090	---其他	7	17	17	9	千克	A	---Other
73.03	铸铁管及空心异型材：							**Tubes, pipes and hollow profiles, of cast iron:**
7303.0010	---内径在500毫米及以上的圆形截面管	4	40	17	9	千克		---Tubes and pipes of circular cross-section, of the internal diameter of 500mm or more
7303.0090	---其他	4	40	17	9	千克		---Other
73.04	无缝钢铁管及空心异型材（铸铁的除外）：							**Tubes, pipes and hollow profiles, seamless, of iron (other than cast iron) or steel:**
	-石油或天然气管道管：							-Line pipe of a kind used for oil or gas pipelines:
	--不锈钢制：							--Of stainless steel:
7304.1110	---外径大于等于215.9毫米，但不超过406.4毫米	5	17	17	13	千克	A	---Having an outside diameter of 215.9mm or more but not exceeding 406.4mm
7304.1120	---外径超过114.3毫米，但小于215.9毫米	5	17	17	13	千克	A	---Having an outside diameter exceeding 114.3mm but less than 215.9mm
7304.1130	---外径不超过114.3毫米	5	17	17	13	千克	A	---Having an outside diameter≤114.3mm
7304.1190	---其他	5	17	17	13	千克	A	---Other
	--其他：							--Other:
7304.1910	---外径大于等于215.9毫米，但不超过406.4毫米	5	17	17	13	千克	A	---Having an outside diameter of 215.9mm or more but not exceeding 406.4mm
7304.1920	---外径超过114.3毫米，但小于215.9毫米	5	17	17	13	千克	A	---Having an outside diameter exceeding 114.3mm but less than 215.9mm
7304.1930	---外径不超过114.3毫米	5	17	17	13	千克	A	---Having an outside diameter not exceeding 114.3mm
7304.1990	---其他	5	17	17	13	千克	A	---Other

税则号列	货品名称	最惠(%)	普通	增值税率	出口退税	计量单位	监管条件	Article Description
	-钻探石油及天然气用的套管、导管及钻管:							-Casing, tubing and drill pipe, of a kind used in drilling for oil or gas:
	--不锈钢钻管:							--Drill pipe, of stainless steel:
7304.2210	---外径不超过168.3毫米	4	17	17	13	千克	A	---Having an outside diameter≤168.3mm
7304.2290	---其他	4	17	17	13	千克	A	---Other
	--其他钻管:							--Other drill pipe:
7304.2310	---外径不超过168.3毫米	4	17	17	13	千克	A	---Having an outside diameter ≤168.3mm
7304.2390	---其他	4	17	17	13	千克	A	---Other
7304.2400	--其他不锈钢管	4	17	17	13	千克	A	--Other pipe, of stainless steel
	--其他:							--Other:
7304.2910	---屈服强度小于552兆帕的	4	17	17	13	千克	A	---Yield strength <552MPA
7304.2920	---屈服强度大于等于552兆帕,但小于758兆帕的	4	17	17	13	千克	A	---552MPA≤Yield strength <758MPA
7304.2930	---屈服强度大于等于758兆帕的	4	17	17	13	千克	A	---Yield strength >758MPA
	-铁或非合金钢的其他圆形截面管:							-Other, of circular cross-section, of iron or non-alloy steel:
	--冷拔或冷轧的:							--Cold-drawn or cold-rolled (cold-reduced):
7304.3110	---锅炉管	4	17	17	9	千克	A	---Boiler tubes and pipes
7304.3120	---地质钻管、套管	8	17	17	9	千克	A	---Geological casing and drill pipes
7304.3190	---其他	4	17	17	9	千克	A	---Other
	--其他:							--Other:
7304.3910	---锅炉管	4	17	17	9	千克	A	---Boiler tubes and pipes
7304.3920	---地质钻管、套管	5	17	17	9	千克	A	---Geological casing and drill pipes
7304.3990	---其他	4	17	17	9	千克	A	---Other
	-不锈钢的其他圆形截面管:							-Other, of circular cross-section, of stainless steel:
	--冷拔或冷轧的:							--Cold-drawn or cold-rolled (cold-reduced):
7304.4110	---锅炉管	10	17	17	9	千克		---Boiler tubes and pipes
7304.4110 01	冷轧的不锈钢制无缝锅炉管(抗拉强度大于等于550Mpa屈服强度大于200Mpa)	10	17	17	9	千克	A	Boiler tube of cold rolled stainless steel (tensile strength ≥550Mpa, Yield strength >200Mpa)
7304.4110 90	其他冷轧的不锈钢制无缝锅炉管(冷拔或冷轧的,包括内螺纹)	10	17	17	9	千克	A	Other boiler tube of cold rolled stainless steel, clod-drawn or cold-rolled (including internal thread)
7304.4190	---其他	10	40	17	13	千克	A	---Other
	--其他:							--Other:
7304.4910	---锅炉管	10	17	17	13	千克		---Boiler tubes and pipes
7304.4910 01	非冷轧(拔)不锈钢制无缝锅炉管(抗拉强度大于等于550Mpa屈服强度大于200Mpa)	10	17	17	13	千克	A	Boiler tube of non-cold rolled stainless steel (tensile strength≥550Mpa, Yield strength >200Mpa)
7304.4910 90	其他非冷轧(拔)不锈钢制无缝锅炉管(包括内螺纹)	10	17	17	13	千克	A	Other boiler tube of non-cold rolled stainless steel (including internal thread)
7304.4990	---其他	10	40	17	9	千克	A	---Other
	-其他合金钢的其他圆形截面管:							-Other, of circular cross-section, of other alloy steel:
	--冷拔或冷轧的:							--Cold-drawn or cold-rolled (cold-reduced):
7304.5110	---锅炉管	4	17	17	9	千克	A	---Boiler tubes and pipes
7304.5110 01	高温承压用合金钢无缝钢管(抗拉强度≧620MPa、屈服强度≧440MPa)(锅炉管外径≧127mm,化学成分(wt%)0.07≦C≦0.13、8.5≦Cr≦9.5、0.3≦Mo≦0.6、1.5≦W≦2.0,冷拔或冷轧,不论是否经进一步加工,包括内螺纹)	4	17	17	9	千克	A	Alloy steel seamless steel tubes for pressure and high temperature (tensile strength, yield strength ≥620MPa ≥ 440MPa ≥ 127mm) (boiler tube, the chemical composition (wt%) 0.07 ≤ C ≤ 0.13, 8.5 ≤ Cr ≤ 9.5, 0.3 ≤ Mo ≤ 0.6, 1.5 ≤ W ≤ 2, cold drawn or cold rolled, whether or not after further processing, including the internal thread)
7304.5110 90	冷轧的其他合金钢无缝锅炉管(冷拔或冷轧的,包括内螺纹)	4	17	17	9	千克	A	Other alloy steel seamless boiler tubes (cold cold drawn or cold rolled, including internal thread)
7304.5120	---地质钻管、套管	4	17	17	9	千克	A	---Geological casing and drill pipes
7304.5190	---其他	4	17	17	9	千克	A	---Other

税则号列	货品名称	最惠(%)	普通	增值税率	出口退税	计量单位	监管条件	Article Description
7304.5190 01	高温承压用合金钢无缝钢管(抗拉强度≧620MPa、屈服强度≧440MPa)(外径≧127mm,化学成分(wt%)0.07≦C≦0.13、8.5≦Cr≦9.5、0.3≦Mo≦0.6、1.5≦W≦2.0,冷拔或冷轧,不论是否经进一步加工)	4	17	17	9	千克	A	Alloy steel seamless steel tubes for pressure and high temperature (≥620MPa, tensile strength, yield strength ≥440MPa) (chemical composition diameter ≥127mm, (wt%) 0.07≤C≤0.13, 8.5≤Cr≤9.5, 0.3≤Mo≤0.6, 1.5≤W≤2, cold drawn or cold rolled, whether or not after further processing)
7304.5190 90	冷轧的其他合金钢制其他无缝管(冷拔或冷轧的)	4	17	17	9	千克	A	Other alloy steel cold rolling for other seamless tubes (cold drawn or cold-rolled)
	--其他:							--Other:
7304.5910	---锅炉管	4	17	17	9	千克	A	---Boiler tubes and pipes
7304.5910 01	高温承压用合金钢无缝钢管(抗拉强度≧620MPa、屈服强度≧440MPa)(锅炉管外径≧127mm,化学成分(wt%)0.07≦C≦0.13、8.5≦Cr≦9.5、0.3≦Mo≦0.6、1.5≦W≦2.0,非冷拔或冷轧,不论是否经进一步加工)	4	17	17	9	千克	A	Alloy steel seamless steel tubes for pressure and high temperature (tensile strength, yield strength ≥620MPa ≥440MPa ≥127mm) (boiler tube, the chemical composition (wt%) 0.07≤C≤0.13, 8.5≤Cr≤9.5, 0.3≤Mo≤0.6, 1.5≤W≤2, non cold drawn or cold rolled, whether or not the further engineering)
7304.5910 90	非冷轧其他合金钢无缝锅炉管(非冷拔或冷轧的)	4	17	17	9	千克	A	Other non rolled alloy steel seamless boiler tubes (non cold drawn or cold)
7304.5920	---地质钻管、套管	4	17	17	9	千克	A	---Geological casing and drill pipes
7304.5990	---其他	4	17	17	9	千克	A	---Other
7304.5990 01	高温承压用合金钢无缝钢管(抗拉强度≧620MPa、屈服强度≧440MPa)(外径≧127mm,化学成分(wt%)0.07≦C≦0.13、8.5≦Cr≦9.5、0.3≦Mo≦0.6、1.5≦W≦2.0,非冷拔或冷轧,不论是否经进一步加工)	4	17	17	9	千克	A	Alloy steel seamless steel tubes for pressure and high temperature (≥620MPa, tensile strength, yield strength ≥440MPa) (chemical composition diameter ≥127mm, (wt%) 0.07≤C≤0.13, 8.5≤Cr≤9.5, 0.3≤Mo≤0.6, 1.5≤W≤2, non cold drawn or cold-rolled, whether or not after further processing)
7304.5990 90	非冷轧其他合金钢制无缝圆形截面管(非冷拔或冷轧的)	4	17	17	9	千克	A	Other non rolled alloy steel seamless pipe (non circular cross section of cold drawn or cold rolled)
7304.9000	-其他	4	17	17	9	千克	A	-Other
73.05	**其他圆形截面钢铁管(例如,焊、铆及用类似方法接合的管),外径超过406.4毫米:**							**Other tubes and pipes (for example, welded, riveted or similarly closed), having circular cross-sections, the external diameter of which exceeds 406.4mm, of iron or steel:**
	-石油或天然气管道管:							-Line pipe of a kind used for oil or gas pipelines:
7305.1100	--纵向埋弧焊接的	7	17	17	13	千克	A	--Longitudinally submerged arc welded
7305.1200	--其他纵向焊接的	3	17	17	13	千克	A	--Other, longitudinally welded
7305.1900	--其他	7	17	17	13	千克	A	--Other
7305.2000	-钻探石油或天然气用套管	7	17	17	13	千克	A	-Casing of a kind used in drilling for oil or gas
	-其他焊接的:							-Other, welded:
7305.3100	--纵向焊接的	6	30	17	9	千克	A	--Longitudinally welded
7305.3900	--其他	6	30	17	9	千克	A	--Other
7305.9000	-其他	6	30	17	9	千克	A	-Other
73.06	**其他钢铁管及空心异型材(例如,辊缝、焊、铆及类似方法接合的):**							**Other tubes, pipes and hollow profiles (for example, open seam or welded, riveted or similarly closed), of iron or steel:**
	-石油及天然气管道管:							-Line pipe of a kind used for oil or gas pipelines:
7306.1100	--不锈钢焊缝管	7	17	17	13	千克	A	--Welded, of stainless steel
7306.1900	--其他	7	17	17	13	千克	A	--other
	-钻探石油及天然气用的套管及导管:							-Casing and tubing of a kind used in drilling for oil or gas:
7306.2100	--不锈钢焊缝管	3	17	17	13	千克	A	--Welded of stainless steel
7306.2900	--其他	3	17	17	13	千克	A	--Welded other
	-铁或非合金钢的其他圆形截面焊缝管:							-Other, welded, of circular cross-section, of iron or non-alloy steel:

税则号列	货品名称	最惠(%)	普通	增值税率	出口退税	计量单位	监管条件	Article Description
	---外径不超10毫米的:							---Having an Outeside diameter not exceedins 10mm:
7306.3011	----壁厚在0.7毫米及以下	3	30	17	13	千克		----Having a wall thickness of 0.7mm or less
7306.3019	----其他	3	30	17	9	千克		----Other
7306.3090	---其他	3	30	17	9	千克		---Other
7306.4000	-不锈钢的其他圆形截面细焊缝管	6	30	17	9	千克		-Other, welded, of circular cross-section, of stainless steel
7306.5000	-其他合金钢的圆形截面细焊缝管	3	30	17	9	千克		-Other, welded, of circular cross-section, of other alloy steel
	-非圆形截面的其他焊缝管:							-Other, welded, of non-circular cross-section:
7306.6100	--矩形或正方形截面的	3	30	17	9	千克		--Of square or rectangular cross-section
7306.6900	--其他非圆形截面的	3	30	17	9	千克		--Of other non-circular cross section
7306.9000	-其他	6	30	17	9	千克		-Other
7306.9000 10	多壁式管道(直接与化学品接触表面由特殊耐腐蚀材料制成)	6	30	17	9	千克	3A	Multiple – wall channel (produced by special erosion-proof materials)
7306.9000 90	未列名其他钢铁管及空心异型材	6	30	17	9	千克	A	Other tubes, pipes and hollow profiles, not elsewhere specified or included
73.07	**钢铁管子附件(例如,接头、肘管、管套):**							**Tube or pipe fittings (for example, couplings, elbows, sleeves), of iron or steel:**
	-铸件:							-Cast fittings:
7307.1100	--无可锻性铸铁制	5	20	17	9	千克		--Of non-malleable cast iron
7307.1900	--其他	8	20	17	9	千克		--Other
	-其他,不锈钢制:							-Other, of stainless steel:
7307.2100	--法兰	8.4	20	17	9	千克		--Flanges
7307.2200	--螺纹肘管、弯管及管套	8.4	20	17	9	千克		--Threaded elbows, bends and sleeves
7307.2300	--对焊件	8.4	20	17	9	千克		--Butt welding fittings
7307.2900	--其他	8.4	20	17	9	千克		--Other
	-其他:							-Other:
7307.9100	--法兰	7	20	17	9	千克		--Flanges
7307.9200	--螺纹肘管、弯管及管套	4	20	17	9	千克		--Threaded elbows, bends and sleeves
7307.9300	--对焊件	7	20	17	9	千克		--Butt welding fittings
7307.9900	--其他	4	20	17	9	千克		--Other
73.08	**钢铁结构体(税目94.06的活动房屋除外)及其部件(例如,桥梁及桥梁体段、闸门、塔楼、格构杆、屋顶、屋顶框架、门窗及其框架、门槛、百叶窗、栏杆、支柱及立柱);上述结构体用的已加工钢铁板、杆、角材、型材、异型材、管子及类似品:**							**Structures (excluding prefabricated buildings of heading No. 94.06) and parts of structures (for example, bridges and bridge-sections, lockgates, towers, lattice masts, roofs, roofing frameworks, doors and windows and their frames and thresholds for doors, shutters, balustrades, pillars and columns), of iron or steel; plates, rods, angles, shapes, sections, tubes and the like, prepared for use in structures, of iron or steel:**
7308.1000	-桥梁及桥梁体段	8	30	17	9	千克		-Bridges and bridge-sections
7308.2000	-塔楼及格构杆	8.4	30	17	9	千克		-Towers and lattice masts
7308.3000	-门窗及其框架、门槛	10	50	17	9	千克		-Doors, windows and their frames and thresholds for doors
7308.4000	-脚手架、模板或坑道支撑用的支柱及类似设备	8.4	30	17	9	千克		-Equipment for scaffolding, shuttering, propping or pit-propping
7308.9000	-其他	4	30	17	9	千克		-Other
73.09	**盛装物料用的钢铁囤、柜、罐、桶及类似容器(装压缩气体或液化气体的除外),容积超过300升,不论是否衬里或隔热,但无机械或热力装置:**							**Reservoirs, tanks, vats and similar containers for any material (other than compressed or liquefied gas), of iron or steel, of a capacity exceeding 300 L, whether or not lined or heat-insulated, but not fitted with mechanical or thermal equipment:**
7309.0000	盛装物料用的钢铁囤、柜、罐、桶及类似容器(装压缩气体或液化气体的除外),容积超过300升,不论是否衬里或隔热,但无机械或热力装置	10.5	35	17	5	千克		Reservoirs, tanks, vats and similar containers for any material (other than compressed or liquefied gas), of iron or steel, of a capacity exceeding 300L whether or not lined or heat-insulated, but not fitted with mechanical or thermal equipment

税则号列	货品名称	最惠(%)	普通	增值税率	出口退税	计量单位	监管条件	Article Description
73.10	盛装物料用的钢铁柜、桶、罐、听、盒及类似容器（装压缩气体或液化气体的除外），容积不超过300升，不论是否衬里或隔热，但无机械或热力装置：							**Tanks, casks, drums, cans, boxes and similar containers, for any material (other than compressed or liquefied gas), of iron or steel, of a capacity not exceeding 300L whether or not lined or heat-insulated, but not fitted with mechanical or thermal equipment:**
7310.1000	-容积在50升及以上	10.5	40	17	5	千克		-Of a capacity of 50L or more
7310.1000 10	总容积大于100升不超过300升的容器（与所处理或盛放的化学品接触表面由特殊耐腐蚀材料制成）	10.5	40	17	5	千克	3	Containers, 100L < capacity ≤ 300L (surface in contact with chemicals treated or contained is made of special corrosion - resistant materials)
7310.1000 90	50L≤容积≤300L的其他钢铁制盛物容器（钢铁柜、桶、罐、听及类似容器）	10.5	40	17	5	千克		Tanks, casks, drums, cans, boxes and similar containers, 50L≤capacity≤300L, of iron or steel
	-容积在50升以下：							-Of a capacity of less than 50L:
	--焊边或卷边接合的罐：							--Cans which are to be closed by soldering or crimping:
7310.2110	---易拉罐及罐体	17.5	70	17	5	千克	A	---Cans and tank
7310.2190	---其他	17.5	70	17	5	千克		---Other
	--其他：							--Other:
7310.2910	---易拉罐及罐体	17.5	70	17	9	千克	A	---Pop can and tank
7310.2990	---其他	17.5	70	17	9	千克	A	---Other
73.11	装压缩气体或液化气体用的钢铁容器：							**Containers for compressed or liquefied gas, of iron or steel:**
7311.0010	---零售包装用	17.5	70	17	5	千克	6A	---For retail packing
7311.0090	---其他	8	17	17	13	千克	6A	---Other
73.12	非绝缘的钢铁绞股线、绳、缆、编带、吊索及类似品：							**Stranded wire, ropes, cables, plaited bands, slings and the like, of iron or steel, not electrically insulated:**
7312.1000	-绞股线、绳、缆	4	20	17	5	千克	A	-Stranded wire, ropes and cables
7312.9000	-其他	4	20	17	5	千克		-Other
73.13	带刺钢铁丝；围篱用的钢铁绞带或单股扁丝（不论是否带刺）及松绞的双股丝：							**Barbed wire of iron or steel; twisted hoop or single flat wire, barbed or not, and loosely twisted double wire, of a kind used for fencing, of iron or steel:**
7313.0000	带刺钢铁丝；围篱用的钢铁绞带或单股扁丝（不论是否带刺）及松绞的双股丝	7	70	17	5	千克		Barbed wire of iron or steel; twisted hoop or single flat wire, barbed or not, and loosely twisted double wire, of a kind used for fencing, of iron or steel
73.14	钢铁丝制的布（包括环形带）、网、篱、格栅；网眼钢铁板：							**Cloth (including endless bands), grill, netting and fencing, of iron or steel wire; expanded metal of iron or steel:**
	-机织品：							-Woven cloth:
7314.1200	--不锈钢制的机器用环形带	12	20	17	5	千克		--Endless bands for machinery, of stainless steel
7314.1400	--不锈钢制的其他机织品	12	20	17	5	千克		--Other woven cloth, of stainless steel
7314.1900	--其他	7	20	17	5	千克		--Other
7314.2000	-交点焊接的网、篱及格栅，其丝的最大截面尺寸在3毫米及以上，网眼尺寸在100平方厘米及以上	7	70	17	5	千克		-Grill, netting and fencing, welded at the intersection, of wire with a maximum cross-sectional dimension of 3mm or more and having a mesh size of 100cm^2 or more
	-其他交点焊接的网、篱及格栅：							-Other grill, netting and fencing, welded at the intersection:
7314.3100	--镀或涂锌的	7	70	17	5	千克		--Plated or coated with zinc
7314.3900	--其他	7	70	17	5	千克		--Other
	-其他网、篱及格栅：							-Other grill, netting and fencing:
7314.4100	--镀或涂锌的	8	20	17	5	千克		--Plated or coated with zinc
7314.4200	--涂塑的	8	20	17	5	千克		--Coated whith plastics
7314.4900	--其他	8	20	17	5	千克		--Other
7314.5000	-网眼钢铁板	8	70	17	5	千克		-Expanded metal
73.15	钢铁链及其零件：							**Chain and parts thereof, of iron or steel:**
	-铰接链及其零件：							-Articulated link chain and parts thereof:
	--滚子链：							--Roller chain:
7315.1110	---自行车用	12	80	17	9	千克		---For bicycles
7315.1120	---摩托车用	12	80	17	5	千克		---For motorcycles

税则号列	货品名称	最惠(%)	普通	增值税率	出口退税	计量单位	监管条件	Article Description
7315.1190	---其他	12	80	17	13	千克		---Other
7315.1200	--其他链	12	80	17	5	千克		--Other chain
7315.1900	--零件	12	80	17	5	千克		--Parts
7315.2000	-防滑链	12	80	17	5	千克		-Skid chain
	-其他链:							-Other chain:
7315.8100	--日字环节链	12	80	17	13	千克		--Stud-link
7315.8200	--其他焊接链	12	80	17	13	千克		--Other, welded link
7315.8900	--其他	12	80	17	13	千克		--Other
7315.9000	-其他零件	10	80	17	5	千克		-Other parts
73.16	**钢铁锚、多爪锚及其零件:**							**Anchors, grapnels and parts thereof, of iron or steel:**
7316.0000	钢铁锚、多爪锚及其零件	10	40	17	9	千克		Anchors, grapnels and parts thereof, of iron or steel
73.17	**钢铁制的钉、平头钉、图钉、波纹钉、U形钉(税目83.05的货品除外)及类似品,不论钉头是否用其他材料制成,但不包括铜头钉:**							**Nails, tacks, drawing pins, corrugated nails, staples (other than those of heading No. 83.05) and similar articles, of iron or steel, whether or not with heads of other material, but excluding such articles with heads of copper:**
7317.0000	钢铁制的钉、平头钉、图钉、波纹钉、U形钉(税目83.05的货品除外)及类似品,不论钉头是否用其他材料制成,但不包括铜头钉	10	80	17	5	千克		Nails, tacks, drawing pins, corrugated nails, staples (other than those of heading No. 83.05) and similar articles, of iron or steel, whether or not with heads of other material, but excluding such articles with heads of copper
73.18	**钢铁制的螺钉、螺栓、螺母、方头螺钉、钩头螺钉、铆钉、销、开尾销、垫圈(包括弹簧垫圈)及类似品:**							**Screws, bolts, nuts, coach screws, screw hooks, rivets, cotters, cotter-pins, washers (including spring washers) and similar articles, of iron of steel:**
	-螺纹制品:							-Threaded articles:
7318.1100	--方头螺钉	10	80	17	5	千克		--Coach screws
7318.1200	--其他木螺钉	10	80	17	5	千克		--Other wood screws
7318.1200 01	非用于民用航空器维护和修理的其他木螺钉	10	80	17	5	千克		Other screws of wood not for civil aircraft maintenance and repair
7318.1200 90	其他木螺钉	10	80	17	5	千克		Other screws of wood
7318.1300	--钩头螺钉及环头螺钉	10	80	17	5	千克		--Screw hooks and screw rings
7318.1400	--自攻螺钉	10	80	17	5	千克		--Self-tapping screws
7318.1400 01	非用于民用航空器维护和修理的自攻螺钉	10	80	17	5	千克		Self - tapping screws of wood not for civil aircraft maintenance and repair
7318.1400 90	其他自攻螺钉	10	80	17	5	千克		Other self - tapping screws
	--其他螺钉及螺栓,不论是否带有螺母或垫圈:							--Other screws and bolts, whether or not with their nuts or washers:
7318.1510	---抗拉强度≥800兆帕的	8	80	17	5	千克		---Tensile strength≥800MPA
7318.1510 01	抗拉强度≥800兆帕,杆径>6mm的其他螺钉及螺栓(不论是否带有螺母或垫圈,非用于民用航空器维护和修理的)	8	80	17	5	千克		Other screws and bolts, tensile strength ≥ 800MPA, shank diameters >6mm (whether or not with their nuts or washers, not for civil aircraft maintenance and repair)
7318.1510 90	其他抗拉强度≥800兆帕的螺钉及螺栓(不论是否带有螺母或垫圈)	8	80	17	5	千克		Other screws and bolts, tensile strength ≥ 800MPA (whether or not with their nuts or washers)
7318.1590	---其他	8	80	17	5	千克		---Other
7318.1590 01	杆径>6mm的其他螺钉及螺栓(不论是否带有螺母或垫圈,非用于民用航空器维护和修理的)	8	80	17	5	千克		Other screws and bolts, shank diameters > 6mm (whether or not with their nuts or washers, not for civil aircraft maintenance and repair)
7318.1590 90	其他螺钉及螺栓(不论是否带有螺母或垫圈)	8	80	17	5	千克		Other screws and bolts, (whether or not with their nuts or washers)
7318.1600	--螺母	8	80	17	5	千克		--Nuts
7318.1900	--其他	5	80	17	5	千克		--Other
	-无螺纹制品:							-Non-threaded articles:
7318.2100	--弹簧垫圈及其他防松垫圈	10	80	17	5	千克		--Spring washers and other lock washers

税则号列	货品名称	最惠(%)	普通	增值税率	出口退税	计量单位	监管条件	Article Description
7318.2100 01	弹簧垫圈及其他防松垫圈(非用于民用航空器维护和修理的)	10	80	17	5	千克		Spring washers and other lock washers (not for civil aircraft maintenance and repair)
7318.2100 90	其他弹簧垫圈及其他防松垫圈	10	80	17	5	千克		Other spring washers and other lock washers
7318.2200	--其他垫圈	10	80	17	5	千克		--Other washers
7318.2200 01	其他垫圈(非用于民用航空器维护和修理的)	10	80	17	5	千克		Other screws and bolts (whether or not with their nuts or washers)
7318.2200 90	其他垫圈	10	80	17	5	千克		Other washers
7318.2300	--铆钉	10	80	17	5	千克		--Rivets
7318.2400	--销及开尾销	10	80	17	5	千克		--Cotters and cotter-pins
7318.2900	--其他	10	80	17	5	千克		--Other
73.19	**钢铁制的手工缝针、编织针、引针、钩针、刺绣穿孔锥及类似制品;其他税目未列名的钢铁制安全别针及其他别针:**							**Sewing needles, knitting needles, bodkins, crochet hooks, embroidery stilettos and similar articles, for use in the hand, of iron or steel; safety pins and other pins of iron or steel, not elsewhere specified or included:**
	-安全别针及其他别针:							-Safety pins and other pins:
7319.4010	---安全别针	10	90	17	5	千克		---Safety pins
7319.4090	---其他	10	90	17	5	千克		---Other
7319.9000	-其他	10	80	17	5	千克		-Other
73.20	**钢铁制弹簧及弹簧片:**							**Springs and leaves for springs, of iron or steel:**
	-片簧及簧片:							-Leaf-springs and leaves thereof:
7320.1010	---铁道车辆用	6	14	17	5	千克		---For railway locomotives and rollingstock
7320.1020	---汽车用	10	14	17	5	千克		---For motor vehicles
7320.1090	---其他	10	50	17	5	千克		---Other
	-螺旋弹簧:							-Helical springs:
7320.2010	---铁道车辆用	6	14	17	5	千克		---For railway locomotives and rollingstock
7320.2090	---其他	10	50	17	5	千克		---Other
	-其他:							-Other:
7320.9010	---铁道车辆用	6	14	17	5	千克		---For railway locomotives and rollingstock
7320.9090	---其他	12	50	17	5	千克		---Other
73.21	**非电热的钢铁制家用炉、灶(包括附有集中供暖用的热水锅的炉)、烤肉架、烤炉、煤气灶、加热板和类似非电热的家用器具及其零件:**							**Stoves, ranges, grates, cookers (including those with subsidiary boilers for central heating), barbecues, braziers, gas-rings, plate warmers and similar non-electric domestic appliances, and parts thereof, of iron or steel:**
	-炊事器具及加热板:							-Cooking appliances and plate warmers:
7321.1100	--使用气体燃料或可使用气体燃料及其他燃料的	15	80	17	9	千克/个	6	--For gas fuel or for both gas and other fuels
	--使用液体燃料的:							--For liquid fuel:
7321.1210	---煤油炉	21	80	17	5	千克/个		---Kerosene cooking stoves
7321.1290	---其他	21	80	17	9	千克/个		---Other
7321.1900	--其他,包括使用固体燃料的	21	80	17	9	千克/个		--Other including appliances for solid fuel
	-其他器具:							-Other appliances:
7321.8100	--使用气体燃料或可使用气体燃料及其他燃料的	23	80	17	5	千克/个	6	--For gas fuel or for both gas and other fuels
7321.8200	--使用液体燃料的	21	80	17	5	千克/个		--For liquid fuel
7321.8900	--其他,包括使用固体燃料的	21	80	17	9	千克/个		--Other induding appliances for solid fuel
7321.9000	-零件	12	80	17	9	千克		-Parts
73.22	**非电热的钢铁制集中供暖用散热器及其零件;非电热的钢铁制空气加热器、暖气分布器(包括可分布新鲜空气或调节空气的)及其零件,装有电动风扇或鼓风机:**							**Radiators for central heating, not electrically heated, and parts thereof, of iron or steel; air heaters and hot air distributors (including distributors which can also distribute fresh or conditioned air), not electrically heated, incorporating a motor-dirven fan or blower, and parts thereof, of iron or steel:**
	-散热器及其零件:							-Radiators and parts thereof:
7322.1100	--铸铁制	21	80	17	5	千克		--Of cast iron
7322.1900	--其他	21	80	17	5	千克		--Other
7322.9000	-其他	20	80	17	5	千克		-Other

税则号列	货品名称	最惠(%)	普通	增值税率	出口退税	计量单位	监管条件	Article Description
73.23	餐桌、厨房或其他家用钢铁器具及其零件;钢铁丝绒;钢铁制擦锅器、洗刷擦光用的块垫、手套及类似品:							**Table, kitchen or other household articles and parts thereof, of iron or steel; iron or steel wool; pot scourers and scouring or polishing pads, gloves and the like, of iron or steel:**
7323.1000	-钢铁丝绒;擦锅器及洗刷擦光用的块垫、手套及类似品	14	80	17	5	千克	A	-Iron or steel wool; pot scourers and scouring or polishing pads, gloves and the like
	-其他:							-Other:
7323.9100暂	--铸铁制,未搪瓷	10	80	17	9	千克	A	--Of cast iron, not enamelled
7323.9200暂	--铸铁制,已搪瓷	10	100	17	9	千克	A	--Of cast iron, enamelled
7323.9300	--不锈钢制	12	80	17	9	千克	A	--Of stainless steel
	--钢铁(铸铁除外)制,已搪瓷:							--Of iron (other than cast iron) or steel, enamelled:
7323.9410暂	---面盆	10	100	17	9	千克	A	---Basin
7323.9420暂	---烧锅	10	100	17	9	千克	A	---Casserole
7323.9490	---其他	20	100	17	9	千克	A	---Other
7323.9900	--其他	20	80	17	9	千克	A	--Other
73.24	**钢铁制卫生器具及其零件:**							**Sanitary ware and parts thereof, of iron or steel:**
7324.1000暂	-不锈钢制洗涤槽及脸盆	10	80	17	9	千克		-Sinks and wash basins, of stainless steel
	-浴缸:							-Baths:
7324.2100	--铸铁制,不论是否搪瓷	10	100	17	9	千克		--Of cast iron, whether or not enamelled
7324.2900暂	--其他	15	100	17	9	千克		--Other
7324.9000暂	-其他,包括零件	15	100	17	9	千克		-Other, including parts
73.25	**其他钢铁铸造制品:**							**Other cast articles of iron or steel:**
	-无可锻性铸铁制:							-Of non-malleable cast iron:
7325.1010	---工业用	7	40	17	5	千克		---For technical use
7325.1090	---其他	20	90	17	5	千克		---Other
	-其他:							-Other:
7325.9100	--研磨机用的研磨球及类似品	10.5	40	17	5	千克		--Grinding balls and similar articles for mills
	--其他:							--Other:
7325.9910	---工业用	10.5	40	17	5	千克		---For technical use
7325.9990	---其他	20	90	17	5	千克		---Other
73.26	**其他钢铁制品:**							**Other articles of iron or steel:**
	-经锻造或冲压,但未经进一步加工:							-Forged or stamped, but not further worked:
7326.1100	--研磨机用的研磨球及类似品	10.5	40	17	5	千克		--Grinding balls and similar articles for mills
	--其他:							--Other:
7326.1910	---工业用	10.5	40	17	5	千克		---For technical use
7326.1990	---其他	20	90	17	5	千克		---Other
	-钢铁丝制品:							-Articles of iron or steel wire:
7326.2010	---工业用	10	40	17	5	千克		---For technical use
7326.2090	---其他	18	90	17	9	千克		---Other
	-其他:							-Other:
	---工业用:							---For technical use:
7326.9011	----钢铁纤维及其制品	10.5	40	17	5	千克		----Steel fiber and its products
7326.9019	----其他	10.5	40	17	5	千克		----Other
7326.9090	---其他	8	90	17	9	千克		---Other

第七十四章
铜及其制品

注释：

本章所用有关名词解释如下：

一、精炼铜

按重量计含铜量至少为99.85%的金属；或按重量计含铜量至少为97.5%，但其他各种元素的含量不超过下表中规定的限量的金属：

其他元素表

元	素	所含重量百分比
Ag	银	0.25
As	砷	0.5
Cd	镉	1.3
Cr	铬	1.4
Mg	镁	0.8
Pb	铅	1.5
S	硫	0.7
Sn	锡	0.8
Te	碲	0.8
Zn	锌	1
Zr	锆	0.3
其他元素*，每种		0.3

*其他元素，例如，铝、铍、钴、铁、锰、镍、硅。

二、铜合金

除未精炼铜以外的金属物质，按重量计含铜量大于其他元素单项含量，但：

1. 按重量计至少有一种其他元素的含量超过上表中规定的限量；
2. 按重量计其他元素的总含量超过2.5%。

三、铜母合金

含有其他元素，但按重量计含铜量超过10%的合金，该合金无实用可锻性，通常用作生产其他合金的添加剂或用作冶炼有色金属的脱氧剂、脱硫剂及类似用途。但按重量计含磷量超过15%的磷化铜归入税目28.48。

Chapter 74
Copper and articles thereof

Notes:

In this Chapter the following expressions have the meanings hereby assigned to them:

1. Refined copper

Metal containing at least 99.85% by weight of copper; or metal containing at least 97.5% by weight of copper, provided that the content by weight of any other element does not exceed the limit specified in the following table:

TABLE - Other elements

Element		Limiting content % by weight
Ag	Silver	0.25
As	Arsenic	0.5
Cd	Cadmium	1.3
Cr	Chromium	1.4
Mg	Magnesium	0.8
Pb	Lead	1.5
S	Sulphur	0.7
Sn	Tin	0.8
Te	Tellurium	0.8
Zn	Zinc	1
Zr	Zirconium	0.3
Other elements*, each		0.3

* Other elements are, for example, Al, Be, Co, Fe, Mn, Ni, Si.

2. Copper alloys

Metallic substances other than unrefined copper in which copper predominates by weight over each of the other elements, provided that:

(a) the content by weight of at least one of the other elements is greater than the limit specified in the foregoing table; or

(b) the total content by weight of such other elements exceeds 2.5%.

3. Master alloys

Alloys containing with other elements more than 10% by weight of copper, not usefully malleable and commonly used as an additive in the manufacture of other alloys or as de-oxidants, de-sulphurizing agents or for similar uses in the metallurgy of non-ferrous metals. However, copper phosphide (phosphor copper) containing more than 15% by weight of phosphorus falls in heading No. 28.48.

四、条、杆

轧、挤、拔或锻制的实心产品，非成卷的，其全长截面均为圆形、椭圆形、矩形（包括正方形）、等边三角形或规则外凸多边形（包括相对两边为弧拱形，另外两边为等长平行直线的“扁圆形”及“变形矩形”）。对于矩形（包括正方形）、三角形或多边形截面的产品，其全长边角可经磨圆。矩形（包括“变形矩形”）截面的产品，其厚度应大于宽度的十分之一。所述条、杆也包括同样形状及尺寸的铸造或烧结产品。该产品在铸造或烧结后再经加工（简单剪修或去氧化皮的除外），但不具有其他税目所列制品或产品的特征。

线锭及坯段已具锥形尾端或经其他简单加工以便送入机器制成盘条或管子等的，仍应作为未锻轧铜归入税目 74.03。

4. Bars and rods

Rolled, extruded, drawn or forged products, not in coils, which have a uniform solid cross-section along their whole length in the shape of circles, ovals, rectangles (including squares), equilateral triangles or regular convex polygons (including “flattened circles” and “modified rectangles”, of which two opposite sides are convex arcs, the other two sides being straight, of equal length and parallel). Products, with a rectangular (including square), triangular or polygonal cross-section may have corners rounded along their whole length. The thickness of such products which have a rectangular (including “modified rectangular”) cross-section exceeds one-tenth of the width. The expression also covers cast or sintered products, of the same forms and dimensions, which have been subsequently worked after production (otherwise than by simple trimming or de-scaling), provided that they have not thereby assumed the character of articles or products of other headings.

Wire-bars and billets with their ends tapered or otherwise worked simply to facilitate their entry into machines for converting them into, for example, drawing stock (wire-rod) or tubes, are however to be taken to be unwrought copper of heading No. 74. 03.

五、型材及异型材

轧、挤、拔、锻制的产品或其他成型产品，不论是否成卷，其全长截面相同，但与条、杆、丝、板、片、带、箔、管的定义不相符合。同时也包括同样形状的铸造或烧结产品。该产品在铸造或烧结后再经加工（简单剪修或去氧化皮的除外），但不具有其他税目所列制品或产品的特征。

5. Profiles

Rolled, extruded, drawn, forged or formed pruducts, coiled or not, of a uniform cross-section along their whole length, which do not conform to any of the definitions of bars, rods, wire, plates, sheets, strip, foil, tubes or pipes. The expression also covers cast or sintered products, of the same forms, which have been subsequently worked after production (otherwise than by simple trimming or de-scaling), provided that they have not thereby assumed the character of articles or products of other headings.

六、丝

盘卷的轧、挤或拔制实心产品，其全长截面均为圆形、椭圆形、矩形（包括正方形）、等边三角形或规则外凸多边形（包括相对两边为弧拱形，另外两边为等长平行直线的“扁圆形”及“变形矩形”）。对于矩形（包括正方形）、三角形或多边形截面的产品，其全长边角可经磨圆。矩形（包括“变形矩形”）截面的产品，其厚度应大于宽度的十分之一。

6. Wire

Rolled, extruded or drawn products, in coils, which have a uniform solid cross-section along their whole length in the shape of circles, ovals, rectangles (including squares), equilateral triangles or regular convex polygons (including “flattened circles” and “modified rectangles”, of which two opposite sides are convex arcs, the other two sides being straight, of equal length and parallel). Products with a rectangular (including square), triangular or polygonal cross-section may have corners rounded along their whole length. The thickness of such products which have a rectangular (including “modified rectangular”) cross-section exceeds one-tenth of the width.

七、板、片、带、箔

成卷或非成卷的平面产品（税目 74.03 的未锻轧产品除外），截面均为厚度相同的实心矩形（不包括正方形），不论边角是否磨圆（包括相对两边为弧拱形，另外两边为等长平行直线的“变形矩形”），并且符合以下规格：

1. 矩形（包括正方形）的，厚度不超过宽度的十分之一；
2. 矩形或正方形以外形状的，任何尺寸，但不具有其他税目所列制品或产品的特征。

7. Plates, sheets, strip and foil

Flat-surfaced products (other than the unwrought products of heading No. 74. 03), coiled or not, of soild rectangular (other than square) cross-section with or without rounded corners (including “modified rectangles” of which two opposite sides are convex arcs, the other two sides being straight, of equal length and parallel) of a uniform thickness, which are:

-of rectanglular (including square) shape with a thickness not exceeding one-tenth of the width,
-of a shape other than rectangular or square, of any size, provided that they do not assume the character of articles or products of other headings.

税目74.09及74.10还适用于具有花样(例如,凹槽、肋条形、格槽、珠粒及菱形)的板、片、带、箔以及穿孔、抛光、涂层或制成瓦楞形的这类产品,但不具有其他税目所列制品或产品的特征。

八、管

全长截面及管壁厚度相同并只有一个闭合空间的空心产品,成卷或非成卷的,其截面为圆形、椭圆形、矩形(包括正方形)、等边三角形或规则外凸多边形。对于截面为矩形(包括正方形)、等边三角形或规则外凸多边形的产品,不论全长边角是否磨圆,只要其内外截面为同一圆心并为同样形状及同一轴向,也可视为管子。上述截面的管子可经抛光、涂层、弯曲、攻丝、钻孔、缩腰、胀口、成锥形或装法兰、颈圈或套环。

Headings Nos. 74.09 and 74.10 apply, *inter alia*, to plates, sheets, strip and foil with patterns (for example, grooves, ribs, chequers, tears, buttons, lozenges) and to such products which have been perforated, corrugated, polished or coated, provided that they do not thereby assume the character of articles or products of other headings.

8. Tubes and pipes

Hollow products, coiled or not, which have a uniform cross-section with only one enclosed void along their whole length in the shape of circles, ovals, rectangles (including squares), equilateral triangles or regularconvex polygons, and which have a uniform wall thickness. Products with a rectangular (including square), equilateral triangular or regular convex polygonal cross-section, which may have corners rounded along their whole length, are also to be taken to be tubes and pipes provided the inner and outer cross-sections are concentric and have the same form and orientation. Tubes and pipes of the foregoing cross-sections may be polished, coated, bent, threaded, drilled, waisted, expanded, cone-shaped or fitted with flanges, collars or rings.

子目注释:

本章所用有关名词解释如下:

一、铜锌合金(黄铜)

铜与锌的合金,不论是否含有其他元素。含有其他元素时:

(一)按重量计含锌量应大于其他各种元素的单项含量;

(二)按重量计含镍量应低于5%[参见铜镍锌合金(德银)];

(三)按重量计含锡量应低于3%[参见铜锡合金(青铜)]。

二、铜锡合金(青铜)

铜与锡的合金,不论是否含有其他元素。含有其他元素时,按重量计含锡量应大于其他各种元素的单项含量。当按重量计含锡量在3%及以上时,锌的含量可大于锡的含量,但必须小于10%。

三、铜镍锌合金(德银)

铜、镍、锌的合金,不论是否含有其他元素,按重量计含镍量在5%及以上[参见铜锌合金(黄铜)]。

四、铜镍合金

铜与镍的合金,不论是否含有其他元素,但按重量计含锌量不得大于1%。含有其他元素时,按重量计含镍量应大于其他各种元素的单项含量。

Subheading Note:

In this Chapter the following expressions have the meanings hereby assigned to them:

1. Copper-zinc base alloys (brasses)

Alloys of copper and zinc, with or without other elements. When other elments are present:

(a) zinc predominates by weight over each of such other elements;

(b) any nickel content by weight is less than 5% (see copper-nickel-zinc alloys (nickel silvers)); and

(c) any tin content by weight is less than 3% (see copper-tin alloys (bronzes)).

2. Copper-tin base alloys (bronzes)

Alloys of copper and tin, with or without other elements. When other elements are present, tin predominates by weight over each of such other elements, except that when the tin content is 3% or more the zinc content by weight may exceed that of tin but must be less than 10%.

3. Copper-nickel-zinc base alloys (nickel silvers)

Alloys of copper, nickel and zinc, with or without other elements. The nickel content is 5% or more by weight (see copper-zinc alloys (brasses)).

4. Copper-nickel base alloys

Alloys of copper and nickel, with or without other elements but in any case containing by weight not more than 1% of zinc. When other elements are present, nickel predominates by weight over each of such other elements.

税则号列	货品名称	最惠(%)	普通	增值税率	出口退税	计量单位	监管条件	Article Description
74.01	铜锍;沉积铜(泥铜):							**Copper mattes; cement copper (precipitated copper):**
7401.0000	铜锍,沉积铜(泥铜)		11	17		千克		Copper mattes; cement copper (precipitated copped)
7401.0000 10	沉积铜(泥铜)	2	11	17		千克	9A	cement copper (precipitated copped)
7401.0000[暂] 90	铜锍	0	11	17		千克		Copper mattes
74.02	未精炼铜;电解精炼用的铜阳极:							**Unrefined copper; copper anodes for electrolytic refining:**
7402.0000[暂]	未精炼铜;电解精炼用的铜阳极	0	11	17		千克		Unrefined copper; copper anodes for electrolytic refining
7402.0000[暂] 01	未精炼铜、电解精炼用铜阳极(含黄金价值部分)	0	11	0		千克		Unrefined copper, copper anodes for electrolytic refining(containing gold value part)

税则号列	货 品 名 称	最惠(%)	普通	增值税率	出口退税	计量单位	监管条件	Article Description
7402.0000暂 90	未精炼铜、电解精炼用铜阳极（非黄金价值部分）	0	11	17		千克		Unrefined copper, copper anodes for electrolytic refining (not containing gold value part)
74.03	**未锻轧的精炼铜及铜合金：**							**Refined copper and copper alloys, unwrought:**
	-精炼铜：							-Refined copper:
	--阴极及阴极型材：							--Cathodes and sections of cathodes:
	---阴极：							---Cathodes:
7403.1111暂	----按重量计铜含量超过99.9935%的	0	11	17		千克		----Containing at least 99.9935% by weight of copper
7403.1111暂 01	高纯阴极铜（99.9999% ＞铜含量＞99.9935%）（未锻轧的）	0	11	17		千克		Higher purity copper cathode (99.9999% > copper content > 99.9935%)
7403.1111暂 90	高纯阴极铜（铜含量≥99.9999%）未锻轧的	0	11	17		千克		Higher purity copper cathode (copper content ≥99.9999%), unwrought
7403.1119暂	----其他	0	11	17		千克		----Other
7403.1190暂	---阴极型材	0	11	17		千克		---Sections of cathodes
7403.1200暂	--线锭	0	11	17		千克		--Wire-bars
7403.1300暂	--坯段	0	11	17		千克		--Billets
7403.1900暂	--其他	0	11	17		千克		--Other
	-铜合金：							-Copper alloys:
7403.2100	--铜锌合金（黄铜）	1	14	17		千克		--Copper-zinc base alloys (brass)
7403.2200	--铜锡合金（青铜）	1	17	17		千克		--Copper-tin base alloys (bronze)
7403.2900	--其他铜合金（税目74.05的铜母合金除外）	1	17	17		千克		--Other copper alloys (other than master alloys of heading No. 74.05)
74.04	**铜废碎料：**							**Copper waste and scrap:**
7404.0000暂	铜废碎料	0	11	17		千克		Copper waste and scrap
7404.0000暂 10	以回收铜为主的废电机等（包括废电机、电线、电缆、五金电器）	0	11	17		千克	AP	Waste electric machines, waste wires, cables, mainly for recoverying copper
7404.0000暂 90	其他铜废碎料	0	11	17		千克	AP	Other copper waste and scrap
74.05	**铜母合金：**							**Master alloys of copper:**
7405.0000	铜母合金	4	17	17		千克		Master alloys of copper
74.06	**铜粉及片状粉末：**							**Copper powders and flakes:**
	-非片状粉末：							-Powders of non-lamellar structure:
7406.1010	---精炼铜制	3	14	17		千克		---Of refined copper
7406.1020	---铜镍合金（白铜）或铜镍锌合金（德银）制	6	40	17		千克		---Of copper-nickel base alloys (cupronickel) or copper-nickel-zinc base alloys (nickel silver)
7406.1030	---铜锌合金（黄铜）制	6	30	17		千克		---Of copper-zinc base alloys (brass)
7406.1040	---铜锡合金（青铜）制	6	30	17		千克		---Of copper-tin base alloys (bronze)
7406.1090	---其他铜合金制	6	30	17		千克		---Other
	-片状粉末：							-Powders of lamellar structure; flakes:
7406.2010	---精炼铜制	4	14	17		千克		---Of refined copper
7406.2020	---铜镍合金（白铜）或铜镍锌合金（德银）制	6	40	17		千克		---Of copper-nickel base alloys (cupronick el) or copper-nickel-zinc base alloys (nickel silver)
7406.2090	---其他铜合金制	6	30	17		千克		---Other
74.07	**铜条、杆、型材及异型材：**							**Copper bars, rods and profiles:**
	-精炼铜制：							-Of refined copper:
7407.1010	---铬锆铜制	4	14	17		千克		---Chrome-zircorium-copper
7407.1090	---其他	4	14	17		千克		---Other
	-铜合金制：							-Of copper alloys:
	--铜锌合金（黄铜）							--Of copper-zinc base alloys (brass):
	---铜条、杆：							---Of copper bars, rods:
7407.2111	----直线度≤0.5mm/米	7	20	17		千克		----Linearity ≤0.5mm/m
7407.2119	----其他	7	20	17		千克		----Other
7407.2190	---其他	7	20	17		千克		---Other
7407.2900	--其他	7	20	17		千克		--Other
74.08	**铜丝：**							**Copper wire:**
	-精炼铜制：							-Of refined copper:

税则号列	货 品 名 称	最惠(%)	普通	增值税率	出口退税	计量单位	监管条件	Article Description
7408.1100	--最大截面尺寸超过6毫米	4	14	17		千克		--Of which the maximum cross-sectional dimension exceeds 6mm
7408.1900	--其他		14	17		千克		--Other
7408.1900[暂] 01	其他含氧量<5PPM的精炼铜丝(截面尺寸≤6mm)	2	14	17		千克		Other refined copper wire, containing oxygen less than 5PPM(cross-sectional dimension≤6mmm)
7408.1900 90	其他截面尺寸≤6mm的精炼铜丝	4	14	17		千克		Other refined copper wire, cross-sectional dimension ≤6mm
	-铜合金制:							-Of copper alloys:
7408.2100	--铜锌合金(黄铜)	7	20	17		千克		--Of copper-zinc base alloys (brass)
	--铜镍合金(白铜)或铜镍锌合金(德银):							--Of copper-nickel base alloys (cupronickel) or copper-nickel-zinc base alloys (nickel silver):
7408.2210	---铜镍锌铅合金(加铅德银)丝	8	40	17		千克		---Wire of nickel copper zinc lead base alloy
7408.2290	---其他	8	40	17		千克		---Other
7408.2900	--其他	7	20	17		千克		--Other
74.09	**铜板、片及带,厚度超过0.15毫米:**							**Copper plates, sheets and strip, of a thickness exceeding 0.15mm:**
	-精炼铜制:							-Of refined copper:
	--盘卷的:							--In coils:
7409.1110	---含氧量不超过10PPM的	4	14	17	9	千克		--Containing oxygen not exceeding 10ppm
7409.1190	--其他	4	14	17	9	千克		--Other
7409.1900	--其他	4	14	17	9	千克		--Other
	-铜锌合金(黄铜)制:							-Of copper-zinc base alloys (brass)
7409.2100	--盘卷的	7	20	17	9	千克		--In coils
7409.2900	--其他	7	20	17	9	千克		--Other
	-铜锡合金(青铜)制:							-Of copper-tin base alloys (bronze):
7409.3100	--盘卷的	7	20	17	9	千克		--In coils
7409.3900	--其他	7	20	17	9	千克		--Other
7409.4000	-铜镍合金(白铜)或铜镍锌合金(德银)制	7	40	17	9	千克		-Of copper-nickel base alloys (cupro-nickel) or copper-nickel-zinc base alloys (nickel silver)
7409.9000	-其他铜合金制	7	20	17	9	千克		-Of other copper alloys
74.10	**铜箔(不论是否印花或用纸、纸板、塑料或类似材料衬背),厚度(衬背除外)不超过0.15毫米:**							**Copper foil (whether or not printed or backed with paper, paperboard, plastics or similar backing materials) of a thickness (excluding any backing) not exceeding 0.15mm:**
	-无衬背:							-Not backed:
7410.1100	--精炼铜制	4	14	17	13	千克		--Of refined copper
	--铜合金制:							--Of copper alloys:
7410.1210	---铜镍合金(白铜)或铜镍锌合金(德银)	7	40	17	13	千克		---Of copper-nickel base alloys (cupronickel) or copper-nickel-zinc base alloys (nickel silver)
7410.1290	---其他	7	20	17	13	千克		---Other
	-有衬背:							-Backed:
	--精炼铜制:							--Of refined copper:
7410.2110	---印制电路用覆铜板	4	14	17	17	千克		---Copper – clad board used to print circuit
7410.2190	---其他	4	14	17	13	千克		---Other
	--铜合金制:							--Of copper alloys:
7410.2210	---铜镍合金(白铜)或铜镍锌合金(德银)	7	40	17	13	千克		---Of copper-nickel base alloys (cupronickel) or copper-nickel-zinc base alloys (nickel silver)
7410.2290	---其他	7	20	17	13	千克		---Other
74.11	**铜管:**							**Copper tubes and pipes:**
	-精炼铜制:							-Of refined copper:
	---外径不超过25毫米的:							---Having an outside diameter not exceeding 25mm:
7411.1011	----带有螺纹或翅片的	4	14	17	13	千克		----Threaded or with fins
7411.1019	----其他		14	17	13	千克		----Other
7411.1019[暂] 01	其他含氧量<5PPM,外径≤25mm的精炼铜管	2	14	17	13	千克		Other refined copper wire, containing oxygen less than 5PPM, having an outside diameter not exceeding 25mm

税则号列	货品名称	最惠(%)	普通	增值税率	出口退税	计量单位	监管条件	Article Description
7411.1019 90	外径≤25mm 的其他精炼铜管	4	14	17	13	千克		Refined copper tubing, outer diameter≤25mm
7411.1020	---外径超过70毫米的	4	14	17	13	千克		---Having an outside diameter exceeding 70mm
7411.1090	---其他	4	14	17	13	千克		---Other
	-铜合金制:							-Of copper alloys:
	--铜锌合金(黄铜):							--Of copper-zinc base alloys(brass):
7411.2110	---盘卷的	7	20	17	13	千克		---In coils
7411.2190	---其他	7	20	17	13	千克		---Other
7411.2200	--铜镍合金(白铜)或铜镍锌合金(德银)	7	40	17	13	千克		--Of copper-nickel base alloys (cupronickel) or copper-nickel-zinc base alloys (nickel silver)
7411.2900	--其他	7	20	17	13	千克		--Other
74.12	**铜制管子附件(例如,接头、肘管、管套):**							**Copper tube or pipe fittings (for example, couplings, elbows, sleeves):**
7412.1000	-精炼铜制	4	14	17		千克		-Of refined copper
	-铜合金制:							-Of copper alloys:
7412.2010	---铜镍合金(白铜)或铜镍锌合金(德银)	7	40	17		千克		---Of copper-nickel base alloys (cupronickel) or copper-nickel-zinc base alloys (nickel silver)
7412.2090	---其他	7	20	17		千克		---Other
74.13	**非绝缘的铜丝绞股线、缆、编带及类似品:**							**Stranded wire, cables, plaited bands and the like, of copper, not electrically insulated:**
7413.0000	非绝缘的铜丝绞股线、缆、编带及类似品	5	14	17		千克	A	Stranded wire, cables, plaited bands and the like, of copper, not electrically insulated
74.15	**铜制或钢铁制带铜头的钉、平头钉、图钉、U形钉(税目83.05的货品除外)及类似品;铜制螺钉、螺栓、螺母、钩头螺钉、铆钉、销、开尾销、垫圈(包括弹簧垫圈)及类似品:**							**Nails, tacks, drawing pins, staples (other than those of heading No. 83.05) and similar articles, of copper or of iron or steel with heads of copper; screws, bolts, nuts, screw hooks, rivets, cotters, cotter-pins, washers (including spring washers) and similar articles, of copper:**
7415.1000	-钉、平头钉、图钉、U形钉及类似品	8	80	17		千克		-Nails and tacks, drawing pins, staples and similar articles
	-其他无螺纹制品:							-Other articles, not threaded:
7415.2100	--垫圈(包括弹簧垫圈)	10	80	17		千克		--Washers (including spring washers)
7415.2900	--其他	10	80	17		千克		--Other
	-其他螺纹制品:							-Other threaded articles:
	--螺钉;螺栓及螺母:							--Screws; bolts and nuts:
7415.3310	---木螺钉	8	80	17		千克		---Screws for wood
7415.3390	---其他	8	80	17		千克		---Other
7415.3900	--其他	10	80	17		千克		--Other
74.18	**餐桌、厨房或其他家用铜制器具及其零件;铜制擦锅器、洗刷擦光用的块垫、手套及类似品;铜制卫生器具及其零件:**							**Table, kitchen or other household articles and parts thereof, of copper; pot scourers and scouring or polishing pads, gloves and the like, of copper; sanitary ware and parts thereof, of copper:**
	-餐桌、厨房或其他家用器具及其零件;擦锅器及洗刷擦光用的块垫、手套及类似品:							-Table, kitchen or other household articles and parts thereof; pot scourers and scouring or polishing pads, gloves and the like:
7418.1010	--擦锅器及洗刷擦光用的块垫、手套及类似品	18	80	17	9	千克	A	--Pot scourers and scouring or polishing pads, gloves and the like
7418.1020	---非电热的铜制家用烹饪器具及其零件	20	80	17	9	千克	A	---Cooking apparatus of a kind used for domestic purposes, non-electric, and parts thereof, of copper
7418.1090暂	---其他	10	80	17	9	千克	A	---Other
7418.2000暂	-卫生器具及其零件	10	80	17	9	千克		-Sanitary ware and parts thereof
74.19	**其他铜制品:**							**Other articles of copper:**
7419.1000	-链条及其零件	14	80	17		千克		-Chain and parts thereof
	-其他:							-Other:
	--铸造、模压、冲压或锻造,但未经进一步加工的:							--Cast, moulded, stamped or forged, but not further worked:

税则号列	货品名称	最惠(%)	普通	增值税率	出口退税	计量单位	监管条件	Article Description
7419.9110	---工业用	10	40	17		千克		---For technical use
7419.9190	---其他	20	80	17	5	千克		---Other
	--其他:							--Other:
7419.9920	---铜弹簧	10	40	17	5	千克		---Copper springs
7419.9930	---铜丝制的布(包括环形带)	7	20	17	5	千克		---Cloth (cincluding endless bands), of copper wire
7419.9940	---铜丝制的网,格栅、网眼铜板	8	20	17	5	千克		---Grill and netting、of copper wire expanded metal of copper
7419.9950	---非电热的铜制家用供暖器具及其零件	20	80	17	5	千克		---Heating apparatus of a kind used for dimestic purposes, non-electric, and parts thereof, of copper
	---其他:							---Other:
7419.9991	----工业用	10	40	17		千克		----For technical use
7419.9999	----其他	20	80	17	5	千克		----Other

第七十五章
镍及其制品

注释:

本章所用有关名词解释如下:

一、条、杆

轧、挤、拔或锻制的实心产品,非成卷的,其全长截面均为圆形、椭圆形、矩形(包括正方形)、等边三角形或规则外凸多边形(包括相对两边为弧拱形,另外两边为等长平行直线的"扁圆形"及"变形矩形")。对于矩形(包括正方形)、三角形或多边形截面的产品,其全长边角可经磨圆。矩形(包括"变形矩形")截面的产品,其厚度应大于宽度的十分之一。所述条、杆也包括同样形状及尺寸的铸造或烧结产品。该产品在铸造或烧结后再经加工(简单剪修或去氧化皮的除外),但不具有其他税目所列制品或产品的特征。

二、型材及异型材

轧、挤、拔、锻制的产品或其他成型产品,不论是否成卷,其全长截面相同,但与条、杆、丝、板、片、带、箔、管的定义不相符合。同时也包括同样形状的铸造或烧结产品。该产品在铸造或烧结后再经加工(简单剪修或去氧化皮的除外),但不具有其他税目所列制品或产品的特征。

三、丝

盘卷的轧、挤或拔制实心产品,其全长截面均为圆形、椭圆形、矩形(包括正方形)、等边三角形或规则外凸多边形(包括相对两边为弧拱形,另外两边为等长平行直线的"扁圆形"及"变形矩形")。对于矩形(包括正方形)、三角形或多边形截面的产品,其全长边角可经磨圆。矩形(包括"变形矩形")截面的产品,其厚度应大于宽度的十分之一。

四、板、片、带、箔

成卷或非成卷的平面产品(税目75.02的未锻轧产品除外),截面均为厚度相同的实心矩形(不包括正方形),不论边角是否磨圆(包括相对两边为弧拱形,另外两边为等长平行直线的"变形矩形"),并且符合以下规格:

1. 矩形(包括正方形)的,厚度不超过宽度的十分之一;
2. 矩形或正方形以外形状的,任何尺寸,但不具有其他税目所列制品或产品的特征。

税目75.06还适用于具有花样(例如,凹槽、肋条形、格槽、珠粒及菱形)的板、片、带、箔以及穿孔、抛光、涂层或制成瓦楞形的这类产品,但不具有其他税目所列制品或产品的特征。

Chapter 75
Nickel and articles thereof

Notes:

In this Chapter the following expressions have the meanings hereby assigned to them:

1. Bars and rods

Rolled, extruded, drawn or forged products, not in coils, which have a uniform soild cross-section along their whole length in the shape of circles, ovals, rectangles (including squares), equilateral triangles or regular convex polygons (including "flattened circles" and "modified rectangles", of which two opposite sides are convex arcs, the other two sides being straight, of equal length and parallel). Products with a rectangular (including square), triangular or polygonal cross-section may have corners rounded along their whole length. The thickness of such products which have a rectangular (including "modified rectangular") cross-section exceeds one-tenth of the width. The expression also covers cast or sintered products, of the same forms and dimensions, which have been subsequently worked after production (otherwise than by simple trimming or de-scaling), provided that they have not thereby assumed the character of articles or products of other headings.

2. Profiles

Rolled, extruded, drawn, forged or formed products, coiled or not, of a uniform cross-section along their whole length, which do not conform to any of the definitions of bars, rods, wire, plates, sheets, strip, foil, tubes or pipes. The expression also covers cast or sintered products, of the same forms, which have been subsequently worked after production (otherwise than by simple trimming or de-scaling), provided that they have not thereby assumed the character of articles or products of other headings.

3. Wire

Rolled, extruded or drawn products, in coils, which have a uniform soild cross-section along their whole length in the shape of circles, ovals, rectangles (in cluding squares), equilateral triangles or regular convexpolygons (including "flattened circles" and "modified rectangles", of which two opposite sides are convex arcs, the other two sides being straight, of equal length and parallel). Products with a rectangular (including square), triangular or polygonal cross-section may have corners rounded along their whole length. The thickness of such products which have a rectangular (including "modified rectangular") cross-section exceeds one-tenth of the width.

4. Plates, sheets, strip and foil

Flat-surfaced products (other than the unwrought products of heading 75.02), coiled or not, of soild rectangular (other than square) cross-section with or without rounded corners (including "modified rectangles" of which two opposite sides are convex arcs, the other two sides being straight, of equal length and parallel) of a uniform thickness, which are:

(a) of rectanglular (including square) shape with a thickness not exceeding one-tenth of the width,

(b) of a shape other than rectangular or square, of any size, provided that they do not assume the character of articles or products of other headings.

Heading 75.06 applies, *inter alia*, to plates, sheets, strip and foil with patterns (for example, grooves, ribs, chequers, tears, buttons, lozenges) and to such products which have been perforated, corrugated, polished or coated, provided that they do not thereby assume the character of articles or products of other headings.

五、管

全长截面及管壁厚度相同并只有一个闭合空间的空心产品,成卷或非成卷的,其截面为圆形、椭圆形、矩形(包括正方形)、等边三角形或规则外凸多边形。对于截面为矩形(包括正方形)、等边三角形或规则外凸多边形的产品,不论全长边角是否磨圆,只要其内外截面为同一圆心并为同样形状及同一轴向,也可视为管子。上述截面的管子可经抛光、涂层、弯曲、攻丝、钻孔、缩腰、胀口、成锥形或装法兰、颈圈或套环。

5. Tubes and pipes

Hollow products, coiled or not, which have a uniform cross-section with only one enclosed void along their whole length in the shape of circles, ovals, rectangles (including squares), equilateral triangles of regular convex polygons, and which have a uniform wall thickness. Products with a rectangular (including square), equilateral triangular, or regular convex polygonal cross-section, which may have corners rounded along their whole length, are also to be considered as tubes and pipes provided the inner and outer cross-sections are concentric and have the same form and orientation. Tubes and pipes of the foregoing crosssections may be polished, coated, bent, threaded, drilled, waisted, expanded, cone-shaped or fitted with flanges, collars or rings.

子目注释:

一、本章所用有关名词解释如下:

(一)非合金镍

按重量计镍及钴的含量至少为99%的金属,但:

1. 按重量计含钴量不超过1.5%;
2. 按重量计其他各种元素的含量不超过下表中规定的限量:

其他元素表

元素		所含重量百分比
Fe	铁	0.5
O	氧	0.4
其他元素,每种		0.3

(二)镍合金

按重量计含镍量大于其他元素单项含量的金属物质,但:

1. 按重量计含钴量超过1.5%;
2. 按重量计至少有一种其他元素的含量超过上表中规定的限量;
3. 除镍及钴以外,按重量计其他元素的总含量超过1%。

二、子目号7508.10所称"丝",不受本章注释三的限制,仅适用于截面尺寸不超过6毫米的任何截面形状的产品,不论是否盘卷。

Subheading Notes:

1. In this Chapter the following expressions have the meanings hereby assigned to them:

(a) Nickel, not alloyed

Metal containing by weight at least 99% of nickel plus cobalt, provided that:

(1) the cobalt content by weight does not exceed 1.5%, and
(2) the content by weight of any other element does not exceed the limit specified in the following table:

TABLE - Other elements

Element		Limiting content % by weight
Fe	Iron	0.5
O	Oxygen	0.4
Other elements, each		0.3

(b) Nickel alloys

Metallic substances in which nickel predominates by weight over each of the other elements provided that:

(1) the content by weight of cobalt exceeds 1.5%,
(2) the content by weight of at least one of the other elements is greater than the limit specified in the foregoing table, or
(3) the total content by weight of elements other than nickel plus cobalt exceeds 1%.

2. Notwithstanding the provisions of Chapter Note 3, for the purposes of subheading No. 7508.10 the term "wire" applies only to products, whether or not in coils, of any cross-sectional shape, of which no cross-sectional dimension exceeds 6mm.

税则号列	货品名称	最惠(%)	普通	增值税率	出口退税	计量单位	监管条件	Article Description
75.01	**镍锍、氧化镍烧结物及镍冶炼的其他中间产品:**							**Nickel mattes, nickel oxide sinters and other intermediate products of nickel metallurgy**
7501.1000暂	-镍锍	0	11	17		千克	4xy	-Nickel mattes
	-氧化镍烧结物及镍冶炼的其他中间产品:							-Nickel oxide sinters and other intermediate products of nickel metallurgy:
7501.2010暂	---镍湿法冶炼中间品	0	11	17		千克	4xy	---Intermediate products of nickel metallurgy by wet process
7501.2090暂	---其他	0	11	17		千克	4xy	---Other
75.02	**未锻轧镍:**							**Unwrought nickel:**
	-非合金镍:							-Nickel, not alloyed:
7502.1010暂	---按重量计镍、钴总量在99.99%及以上的,但钴含量不超过0.005%	1	11	17		千克	4xy	---Containing 99.99% or more than by total weight of nickel and cobalt, but containing cobalt not exceeding 0.005%
7502.1090暂	---其他	1	11	17		千克	4xy	---Other
7502.2000	-镍合金	3	11	17		千克	4xy	-Nickel, alloys

税则号列	货　品　名　称	最惠(%)	普通	增值税率	出口退税	计量单位	监管条件	Article Description
75.03	**镍废碎料：**							**Nickel waste and scrap:**
7503.0000[暂]	镍废碎料	1	11	17		千克	4APxy	Nickel waste and scrap
75.04	**镍粉及片状粉末：**							**Nickel powders and flakes:**
7504.0010	---非合金镍粉及片状粉末	4	17	17		千克	3	---Nickel powders and flakes, not alloyed
7504.0020	---合金镍粉及片状粉末	4	17	17		千克		---Nickel powders and flakes, alloys
75.05	**镍条、杆、型材及异型材或丝：**							**Nickel bars, rods, profiles and wire:**
	-条、杆、型材及异型材：							-Bars, rods and profiles:
7505.1100	--非合金镍制	6	14	17	5	千克		--Of nickel, not alloyed
7505.1200	--镍合金制	6	14	17	13	千克		--Of nickel alloys
	-丝：							-Wire:
7505.2100	--非合金镍制	6	17	17	5	千克		--Of nickel, not alloyed
7505.2200	--镍合金制	6	17	17	13	千克		--Of nickel alloys
75.06	**镍板、片、带、箔：**							**Nickel plates, sheets, strip and foil:**
7506.1000	-非合金镍制	6	14	17	5	千克		-Of nickel, not alloyed
7506.2000	-镍合金制	6	14	17		千克		-Of nickel alloys
75.07	**镍管及管子附件(例如，接头、肘管、管套)：**							**Nickel tubes, pipes and tube or pipe fittings (for example, couplings, elbows, sleeves):**
	-镍管：							-Tubes and pipes:
7507.1100	--非合金镍制	6	17	17		千克		--Of nickel, not alloyed
7507.1200	--镍合金制	6	17	17	13	千克		--Of nickel alloys
7507.2000	-管子附件	6	17	17		千克		-Tube or pipe fittings
75.08	**其他镍制品：**							**Other articles of nickel:**
	-镍丝布、网及格栅：							-Cloth, grill and netting, of nickel wire:
7508.1010	---镍丝布	6	20	17		千克		---Wire cloth
7508.1080	---其他工业用镍制品	6	40	17		千克		---Other articles of nickel, for technical use
7508.1090	---其他	6	70	17		千克		---Other
	-其他：							-Other:
7508.9010	---电镀用镍阳极	4	14	17		千克		---Electroplating anodes
7508.9080	---其他工业用镍制品	6	40	17		千克		---Other articles of nickel, for technical use
7508.9090	---其他	6	70	17		千克		---Other

第七十六章
铝及其制品

注释：

本章所用有关名词解释如下：

一、条、杆

轧、挤、拔或锻制的实心产品，非成卷的，其全长截面均为圆形、椭圆形、矩形（包括正方形）、等边三角形或规则外凸多边形（包括相对两边为弧拱形，另外两边为等长平行直线的“扁圆形”及“变形矩形”）。对于矩形（包括正方形）、三角形或多边形截面的产品，其全长边角可经磨圆。矩形（包括“变形矩形”）截面的产品其厚度应大于宽度的十分之一。所述条、杆也包括同样形状及尺寸的铸造或烧结产品。该产品在铸造或烧结后再经加工（简单剪修或去氧化皮的除外），但不具有其他税目所列制品或产品的特征。

二、型材及异型材

轧、挤、拔、锻制的产品或其他成型产品，不论是否成卷，其全长截面相同，但与条、杆、丝、板、片、带、箔、管的定义不相符合。同时也包括同样形状的铸造或烧结产品。该产品在铸造或烧结后再经加工（简单剪修或去氧化皮的除外），但不具有其他税目所列制品或产品的特征。

三、丝

盘卷的轧、挤或拔制实心产品，其全长截面均为圆形、椭圆形、矩形（包括正方形）等边三角形或规则外凸多边形（包括相对两边为弧拱形，另外两边为等长平行直线的“扁圆形”及“变形矩形”）。对于矩形（包括正方形）、三角形或多边形截面的产品，其全长边角可经磨圆。矩形（包括“变形矩形”）截面的产品，其厚度应大于宽度的十分之一。

四、板、片、带、箔

成卷或非成卷的平面产品（税目76.01的未锻轧产品除外），截面均为厚度相同的实心矩形（不包括正方形），不论边角是否磨圆（包括相对两边为弧拱形，另外两边为等长平行直线的“变形矩形”），并且符合以下规格：

1. 矩形（包括正方形）的，厚度不超过宽度的十分之一；
2. 矩形或正方形以外形状的，任何尺寸，但不具有其他税目所列制品或产品的特征。

税目76.06和76.07还适用于具有花样（例如，凹槽、肋条形、格槽、珠粒及菱形）的板、片、带、箔以及穿孔、抛光、涂层或制成瓦楞形的这类产品，但不具有其他税目所列制品或产品的特征。

Chapter 76
Aluminium and articles thereof

Notes:

In this Chapter the following expressions have the meanings hereby assigned to them:

1. Bars and rods

Rolled, extruded, drawn or forged products, not in coils, which have a uniform solid cross-section along their whole length in the shape of circles, ovals, rectangles (including squares), equilateral triangles or regular convex polygons (including "flattened circles" and "modified rectangles", of which two opposite sides are convex arcs, the other two sides being straight, of equal length and parallel). Products with a rectangular (including square), triangular or polygonal cross-section may have corners rounded along their whole length. The thickness of such products which have a rectangular (including "modified rectangular") cross-section exceeds one-tenth of the width. The expression also covers cast or sintered products, of the same forms and dimensions, which have been subsequently worked after production (otherwise than by simple trimming or de-scaling), provided that they have not thereby assumed the character of articles or products of other headings.

2. Profiles

Rolled, extruded, drawn, forged or formed products, coiled or not, of a uniform cross-section along their whole length, which do not conform to any of the definitions of bars, rods, wire, plates, sheets, strip, foil, tubes or pipes. The expression also covers cast or sintered products, of the same forms, which havebeen subsequently worked after production (otherwise than by simple trimming or de-scaling), provided that they have not thereby assumed the character of articles or products of other headings.

3. Wire

Rolled, extruded or drawn products, in coils, which have a uniform soild cross-section along their whole length in the shape of circles, ovals, rectangles (including squares), equilateral triangles or regular convex polygons (including "flattened circles" and "modified rectangles", of which two opposite sides are convex arcs, the other two sides being straight, of equal length and parallel). Products with a rectangular (including square), triangular or polygonal cross-section may have corners rounded along their whole length. The thickness of such products which have a rectangular (including "modified rectangular") cross-section exceeds one-tenth of the width.

4. Plates, sheets, strip and foil

Flat-surfaced products (other than the unwrought products of heading No. 76.01), coiled or not, of solid rectangular (other than square) cross-section with or without rounded corners (including "modified rectangles" of which two opposite sides are convex arcs, the other two sides being straight, of equal length and parallel) of a uniform thickness, which are:

-of rectanglular (including square) shape with a thickness not exceeding one-tenth of the width,

-of a shape other than rectangular or square, of any size, provided that they do not assume the character of articles or products of other headings.

Headings No. 76.06 and 76.07 apply, *inter alia*, to plates, sheets, strip and foil with patterns (for example, grooves, ribs, chequers, tears, buttons, lozenges) and to such products which have been perforated, corrugated, polished or coated, provided that they do not thereby assume the character of articles or products of other headings.

五、管

全长截面及管壁厚度相同并只有一个闭合空间的空心产品，成卷或非成卷的，其截面为圆形、椭圆形、矩形（包括正方形）、等边三角形或规则外凸多边形。对于截面为矩形（包括正方形）、等边三角形或规则外凸多边形的产品，不论全长边角是否磨圆，只要其内外截面为同一圆心并为同样形状及同一轴向，也可视为管子。上述截面的管子可经抛光、涂层、弯曲、攻丝、钻孔、缩腰、胀口、成锥形或装法兰、颈圈或套环。

5. Tubes and pipes

Hollow products, coiled or not, which have a uniform cross-section with only one enclosed void along their whole length in the shape of circles, ovals, rectangles (including squares), equilateral triangles or regular convex polygons, and which have a uniform wall thickness. Products with a rectangular (including square), equilateral triangular or regular convex polygonal cross-section, which may have corners rounded along their whole length, are also to be considered as tubes and pipes provided the inner and outer cross-sections are concentric and have the same form and orientation. Tubes and pipes of the foregoing cross-sections may be polished, coated, bent, threaded, drilled, waisted, expanded, cone-shaped or fitted with flanges, collars or rings.

子目注释：

一、本章所用有关名词解释如下：

（一）非合金铝

按重量计含铝量至少为99%的金属，但其他各种元素的含量不超过下表中规定的限量：

其他元素表

元　　素	所含重量百分比
Fe + Si（铁 + 硅）	1
其他元素(1)，每种	0.1(2)

（1）其他元素，例如，铬、铜、镁、锰、镍、锌。

（2）含铜成分可大于0.1%，但不得大于0.2%，且铬和锰的含量均不得超过0.05%。

（二）铝合金

按重量计含铝量大于其他元素单项含量的金属物质，但：

1. 按重量计至少有一种其他元素或铁加硅的含量大于上表中规定的限量；

2. 按重量计其他元素的总含量超过1%。

二、子目7616.91所称"丝"，不受本章注释三的限制，仅适用于截面尺寸不超过6毫米的任何截面形状产品，不论是否盘卷。

Subheading Notes:

1. In this Chapter the following expressions have the meanings hereby assigned to them:

(a) Aluminium, not alloyed

Metal containing by weight at least 99% of aluminium, provided that the content by weight of any other element does not exceed the limit specified in the following table:

TABLE - Other elements

Element	Limiting content % by weight
Fe + Si (iron plus silicon)	1
Other elements (1), each	0.1(2)

(1) Other elements are, for example, Cr, Cu, Mg, Mn, Ni, Zn.

(2) Copper is permitted in a proportion greater than 0.1% but not more than 0.2%, provided that neither the chromium nor manganese content exceeds 0.05%.

(b) Aluminium alloys

Metallic substances in which aluminium predominates by weight over each of the other elements, provided that:

(1) the content by weight of at least one of the other elements or of iron plus silicon taken together is greater than the limit specified in the foregoing table;

(2) the total content by weight of such other elements exceeds 1%.

2. Notwithstanding the provisions of Chapter Note 1 (c), for the purposes of subheading No. 7616.91 the term "wire" applies only to products, whether or not in coils, of any cross-sectional shape, of which no cross-sectional dimension exceeds 6mm.

税则号列	货品名称	最惠(%)	普通	增值税率	出口退税	计量单位	监管条件	Article Description
76.01	未锻轧铝：							**Unwrought aluminium:**
	-非合金铝：							-Aluminium, not alloyed:
7601.1010	---按重量计含铝量在99.95%及以上	5	14	17		千克		---Containing by weight 99.95% or more of aluminium
7601.1090暂	---其他	0	14	17		千克		---Other
7601.2000	-铝合金	7	14	17		千克		-Aluminium alloys
7601.2000 10	碱金属含量（钠+钾+钙）<10ppm，氢含量<0.12毫升/100克铝的低碱精炼铝合金	7	14	17		千克		The content of alkali metals (Na + K + calcium) < 10ppm, low alkali hydrogen content of < 0.12 ml /100 grams of aluminum in the refining process of aluminum alloy
7601.2000 90	其他未锻轧铝合金	7	14	17		千克		Other unwrought aluminum alloy
76.02	铝废碎料：							**Aluminium waste and scrap:**
7602.0000暂	铝废碎料	0	14	17		千克		Aluminium waste and scrap
7602.0000暂 10	以回收铝为主的废电线等（包括废电线、电缆、五金电器）	0	14	17		千克	AP	Aluminium waste wires, cables, hardware and electric appliance, mainly for recoverying aluminium

税则号列	货品名称	最惠(%)	普通	增值税率	出口退税	计量单位	监管条件	Article Description
7602.0000[暂] 90	其他铝废碎料	0	14	17		千克	AP	Aluminium waste and scrap
76.03	铝粉及片状粉末:							**Aluminium powders and flakes:**
7603.1000	-非片状粉末	6	30	17		千克		-Powders of non-lamellar structure
7603.1000 10	颗粒<500μm 的微细球形铝粉(颗粒均匀,铝含量≥97%)	6	30	17		千克	3A	Microspherical aluminum powder, granularity < 500μm, containing≥97% by weight of aluminium
7603.1000 90	其他非片状铝粉	6	30	17		千克	AB	Other powders of non-lamellar structure, of aluminium
7603.2000	-片状铝粉末	7	30	17		千克		-Powders of lamellar structure; flakes
76.04	铝条、杆、型材及异型材:							**Aluminium bars, rods and profiles:**
	-非合金铝制:							-Of aluminium, not alloyed:
7604.1010	---铝条、杆	5	30	17		千克		---Bars and rods
7604.1090	---其他	5	30	17		千克		---Other
	-铝合金制:							-Of aluminium alloys:
7604.2100	--空心异型材	5	30	17	13	千克	A	--Hollow profiles
	--其他:							--Other:
7604.2910	---铝合金条、杆	5	30	17		千克		---Bars and rods
7604.2910 11	柱形实心体铝合金[在293K(20摄氏度)时的极限抗拉强度能达到460兆帕(0.46×10⁹牛顿/平方米)或更大(截面周长大于等于210毫米)]	5	30	17		千克	3A	Column solid aluminum alloy[tensile strength reaches at least 460 mega - P(0.46×10⁹Newton/Square Meters) at 293K(20degree centigrade) cross - sectional Perimeter ≥210mm]
7604.2910 19	柱形实心体铝合金[在293K(20摄氏度)时的极限抗拉强度能达到460兆帕(0.46×10⁹牛顿/平方米)或更大(截面周长小于210毫米)]	5	30	17		千克	3A	Column solid aluminum alloy[tensile strength reaches at least 460 mega - P(0.46×10⁹Newton/Square Meters) at 293K(20degree centigrade) cross - sectional Perimeter <210mm]
7604.2910 91	其他铝合金制条、杆(截面周长大于等于210毫米)	5	30	17		千克	A	Other bars, rods and profiles, of aluminium alloys (cross - sectional Perimeter ≥210mm)
7604.2910 99	其他铝合金制条、杆(截面周长小于210毫米)	5	30	17		千克	A	Other bars, rods and profiles, of aluminium alloys (cross - sectional Perimeter <210mm)
7604.2990	---其他	5	30	17	13	千克	A	-Other
76.05	**铝丝:**							**Aluminium wire:**
	-非合金铝制:							-Of aluminium, not alloyed:
7605.1100	--最大截面尺寸超过7毫米	8	17	17		千克		--Of which the maximum cross-sectional dimension exceeding 7mm
7605.1900	--其他	8	17	17		千克		--Other
	-铝合金制:							-Of aluminium alloys:
7605.2100	--最大截面尺寸超过7毫米	8	17	17		千克		--Of which the maximum cross-sectional dimension exceeding 7mm
7605.2900	--其他	8	17	17		千克		--Other
76.06	**铝板、片及带,厚度超过0.2毫米:**							**Aluminium plates, sheets and strip, of a thickness exceeding 0.2mm:**
	-矩形(包括正方形):							-Rectangular (including square):
	--非合金铝制:							--Of aluminium, not alloyed:
	---厚度在0.30毫米及以上,但不超过0.36毫米:							---Of a thickness of 0.30mm or more but not exceeding 0.36mm:
7606.1121	----铝塑复合的	6	50	17	13	千克	A	----Aluminum-plastic composite
7606.1129[暂]	----其他	4	50	17	13	千克	A	----Other
	---其他:							---Other:
7606.1191	----铝塑复合的	6	30	17	13	千克	A	----Aluminum-plastic composite
7606.1199	----其他	6	30	17	13	千克	A	----Other
	--铝合金制:							--Of aluminium alloys:
7606.1220	---厚度小于0.28毫米	6	30	17	13	千克	A	---Of a thickness less than 0.28mm
7606.1230	---厚度在0.28毫米及以上,但不超过0.35毫米	6	30	17	13	千克	A	---Of a thickness of 0.28mm or more but not exceeding 0.35mm
	---厚度在超过0.35毫米以上,但不超过4毫米:							---Of a thickness more than 0.35mm but not exceeding 4mm:
7606.1251	----铝塑复合的	6	50	17	13	千克	A	----Aluminum-plastic composite
7606.1259	----其他	6	50	17	13	千克	A	----Other

税则号列	货品名称	最惠(%)	普通	增值税率	出口退税	计量单位	监管条件	Article Description
7606.1290	---其他	6	50	17	13	千克	A	---Other
	-其他:							-Other:
7606.9100	--非合金铝制	6	30	17	13	千克		--Of aluminium, not alloyed
7606.9200	--铝合金制	10	30	17	13	千克	A	--Of aluminium alloys
76.07	**铝箔(不论是否印花或用纸、纸板、塑料或类似材料衬背),厚度(衬背除外)不超过0.2毫米:**							**Aluminium foil (whether or not printed or backed with paper, paperboard, plastics or similar backing materials) of a thickness (excluding any backing) not exceeding 0.2mm:**
	-无衬背:							-Not backed:
	--轧制后未经进一步加工的:							--Rolled but not further worked:
7607.1110	---厚度不超过0.007毫米	6	35	17	15	千克		---Of a thickness not exceeding 0.007mm
7607.1120	---厚度大于0.007毫米,但不超过0.01毫米	6	35	17	15	千克		---Of a thickness exceeding 0.007mm, but not exceeding 0.01mm
7607.1190	---其他	6	35	17	15	千克		---Other
7607.1900	--其他		35	17	15	千克		--Other
7607.1900暂 01	化成箔(厚度≤0.2mm)	3	35	17	15	千克		Formed foils (thickness≤0.2mm)
7607.1900 90	其他无衬背铝箔(厚度≤0.2mm)	6	35	17	15	千克		Other aluminum foils without lining back (thickness≤0.2mm)
7607.2000	-有衬背	6	35	17	15	千克		-Backed
76.08	**铝管:**							**Aluminium tubes and pipes:**
7608.1000	-非合金铝制	8	30	17	13	千克		-Of aluminium, not alloyed
	-铝合金制:							-Of aluminium alloys:
7608.2010	---外径不超过10厘米的	8	30	17	13	千克		---Having an outside diameter not exceeding locm
7608.2010 10	外径≤10厘米的管状铝合金[在293K(20摄氏度)时的极限抗拉强度能达到460兆帕(0.46×10^9牛顿/平方米)或更大]	8	30	17	13	千克	3A	Tube aluminum alloy, outer diameter ≤ 10cm, can reach at least 460 mega-Pa (0.46×10^9 Newton/Square Meters) at 293K(20 degree centigrade)
7608.2010 90	外径≤10厘米的其他合金制铝管	8	30	17	13	千克	A	Other alloy aluminum pipes, outer diameter≤10 cm
	---其他:							---Other:
7608.2091	----壁厚不超过25毫米	8	30	17	13	千克		----Having a wall thickness not exceeding 25mm
7608.2091 10	外径>10厘米,壁厚≤25毫米的管状铝合金[在293K(20摄氏度)时的极限抗拉强度能达到460兆帕(0.46×10^9牛顿/平方米)或更大]	8	30	17	13	千克	3A	Tubular aluminum alloy, outer diameter > 10 cm, wall thickness ≤25mm, can reach at least 460 mega - Pa (0.46×10^9Newton /Square Meters) at 293K (20 degree centigrade)
7608.2091 90	外径>10厘米,壁厚≤25毫米的其他合金制铝管	8	30	17	13	千克	A	Other alloy aluminum pipes, outer diameter > 10 cm, wall thickness ≤25mm
7608.2099	----其他	8	30	17	13	千克		----Ohter
7608.2099 10	外径>10厘米,其他管状铝合金[在293K(20摄氏度)时的极限抗拉强度能达到460兆帕(0.46×10^9牛顿/平方米)或更大]	8	30	17	13	千克	3A	The tensile strength of tube aluminum alloy can reach at least 460 mega - Pa (0.46×10^9Newton /Square Meters) at 293K (20 degree centigrade)
7608.2099 90	外径>10厘米,其他合金制铝管	8	30	17	13	千克	A	Other aluminium tubes and pipes, alloys
76.09	**铝制管子附件(例如,接头、肘管、管套):**							**Aluminium tube or pipe fittings (for example, couplings, elbows, sleeves):**
7609.0000	铝制管子附件(例如,接头、肘管、管套)	8	35	17	13	千克		Aluminium tube or pipe fittings (for example, couplings, elbows, sleeves)
76.10	**铝制结构体(税目94.06的活动房屋除外)及其部件(例如,桥梁及桥梁体段、塔、格构杆、屋顶、屋顶框架、门窗及其框架、门槛、栏杆、支柱及立柱);上述结构体用的已加工铝板、杆、型材、异型材、管子及类似品:**							**Aluminium structures (excluding prefabricated buildings of heading 94.06) and parts of structures (for example, bridges and bridge-sections, towers, lattice masts, roofs, roofing frameworks, doors and windows and their frames and thresholds for doors, balustrades, pillars and columns); aluminium plates, rods, profiles, tubes and the like, prepared for use in structures:**
7610.1000	-门窗及其框架、门槛	25	80	17	13	千克		-Doors, windows and their frames and thresholds for doors
7610.9000	-其他	6	50	17	13	千克		-Other

税则号列	货品名称	最惠(%)	普通	增值税率	出口退税	计量单位	监管条件	Article Description
76.11	**盛装物料用的铝制囤、柜、罐、桶及类似容器(装压缩气体或液化气体的除外),容积超过300升,不论是否衬里或隔热,但无机械或热力装置:**							**Aluminium reservoirs, tanks, vats and similar containers, for any material (other than compressed or liquefied gas), of a capacity exceeding 300L, whether or not lined or heat-insulated, but not fitted with mechanical or thermal equipment:**
7611.0000	盛装物料用的铝制囤、柜、罐、桶及类似容器(装压缩气体或液化气体的除外),容积超过300升,不论是否衬里或隔热,但无机械或热力装置	12	35	17	13	千克		Aluminium reservoirs, tanks, vats and similar containers, for any material (other than compressed or liquefied gas), of a capacity exceeding 300L whether or not lined or heat-insulated, but not fitted with mechanical or thermal equipment
76.12	**盛装物料用的铝制桶、罐、听、盒及类似容器,包括软管容器及硬管容器(装压缩气体或液化气体的除外),容积不超过300升,不论是否衬里或隔热,但无机械或热力装置:**							**Aluminium casks, drums, cans, boxes and similar containers (including rigid or collapsible tubular containers), for any material (other than compressed or liquefied gas), of a capacity not exceeding 300 l, whether or not lined or heat-insulated, but not fitted with mechanical or thermal equipment:**
7612.1000	-软管容器	12	50	17	13	千克		-Collapsible tubular containers
	-其他:							-Other:
7612.9010	---易拉罐及罐体	30	100	17	13	千克	A	---Tear tab ends and bodies thereof
7612.9090	---其他	12	70	17	13	千克		---Other
76.13	**装压缩气体或液化气体用的铝制容器:**							**Aluminium containers for compressed or liquefied gas:**
7613.0010	---零售包装用	12	70	17	13	千克		---For retail packing
7613.0090	---其他	6	17	17	13	千克	6	---Other
76.14	**非绝缘的铝制绞股线、缆、编带及类似品:**							**Stranded wire, cables, plaited bands and the like, of aluminium, not electrically insulated:**
7614.1000	-带钢芯的	6	20	17	13	千克	A	-With steel core
7614.9000	-其他	6	20	17	13	千克		-Other
76.15	**餐桌、厨房或其他家用铝制器具及其零件;铝制擦锅器、洗刷擦光用的块垫、手套及类似品;铝制卫生器具及其零件:**							**Table, kitchen or other household articles and parts thereof, of aluminium; pot scourers and scouring or polishing pads, gloves and the like, of aluminium; sanitary ware and parts thereof, of aluminium:**
	-餐桌、厨房或其他家用器具及其零件;擦锅器及洗刷擦光用的块垫、手套及类似品:							-Table, kitchen or other household articles and parts thereof; pot scourers and scouring or polishing pads, gloves and the like:
7615.1010	--擦锅器、洗刷、擦光用的块垫、手套及类似品	18	90	17	13	千克	A	--Pot scourers and scouring or polishing pads, gloves and the like
7615.1090暂	--其他	10	90	17	13	千克		--Other
7615.1090暂 10	铝制高压锅	10	90	17	13	千克	A	Aluminum pressure cooker
7615.1090暂 90	其他餐桌厨房等家用铝制器具及其零件	10	90	17	13	千克	A	Other household aluminum utensils used on dining tables and in kitchens and parts thereof
7615.2000	-卫生器具及其零件	18	90	17	13	千克		-Sanitary ware and parts thereof
76.16	**其他铝制品:**							**Other articles of aluminium:**
7616.1000	-钉、平头钉、U形钉(税目83.05的货品除外)、螺钉、螺栓、螺母、钩头螺钉、铆钉、销、开尾销、垫圈及类似品	10	40	17	13	千克		-Nails, tacks, staples (other than those of heading 83.05), screws, bolts, nuts, screw hooks, rivets, cotters, cotter-pins, washers and similar articles
	-其他:							-Other:
7616.9100	--铝丝制的布、网、篱及格栅	10	40	17	13	千克		--Cloth, grill, netting and fencing, of aluminium wire
	--其他:							--Other:
7616.9910	---工业用	10	40	17	13	千克		---For technical use

税则号列	货　品　名　称	最惠(%)	普通	增值税率	出口退税	计量单位	监管条件	Article Description
7616.9910 10	高度小于直径的柱形实心体铝合金[在293K(20摄氏度)时的极限抗拉强度能达到460兆帕(0.46×10^9牛顿/平方米)或更大]	10	40	17	13	千克	3	Aluminum of cylinder shape with height less than diameter[tensile strengh can reach 460 MPa (0.46×10^9N/m^2) or more at 293k (20℃)]
7616.9910 90	其他工业用铝制品(不包括铝丝布、网、格栅及栅栏)	10	40	17	13	千克		Other articles of alumnum for thechnical use (other than cloth, grill, netting and fencing, of aluminum wire)
7616.9990	---其他	15	80	17	13	千克		---Other

第七十八章
铅及其制品

注释：

本章所用有关名词解释如下：

一、条、杆

轧、挤、拔或锻制的实心产品，非成卷的，其全长截面均为圆形、椭圆形、矩形（包括正方形）、等边三角形或规则外凸多边形（包括相对两边为弧拱形，另外两边为等长平行直线的“扁圆形”及“变形矩形”）。对于矩形（包括正方形）、三角形或多边形截面的产品，其全长边角可经磨圆。矩形（包括“变形矩形”）截面的产品，其厚度应大于宽度的十分之一。所述条、杆也包括同样形状及尺寸的铸造或烧结产品。该产品在铸造或烧结后再经加工（简单剪修或去氧化皮的除外），但不具有其他税目所列制品或产品的特征。

二、型材及异型材

轧、挤、拔、锻制的产品或其他成型产品，不论是否成卷，其全长截面相同，但与条、杆、丝、板、片、带、箔、管的定义不相符合。同时也包括同样形状的铸造或烧结产品。该产品在铸造或烧结后再结加工（简单剪修或去氧化皮的除外），但不具有其他税目所列制品或产品的特征。

三、丝

盘卷的轧、挤或拔制实心产品，其全长截面均为圆形、椭圆形、矩形（包括正方形）、等边三角形或规则外凸多边形（包括相对两边为弧拱形，另外两边为等长平行直线的“扁圆形”及“变形矩形”）。对于矩形（包括正方形）、三角形或多边形截面的产品，其全长边角可经磨圆。矩形（包括“变形矩形”）截面的产品，其厚度应大于宽度的十分之一。

四、板、片、带、箔

成卷或非成卷的平面产品（税目 78.01 的未锻轧产品除外），截面均为厚度相同的实心矩形（不包括正方形），不论边角是否磨圆（包括相对两边为弧拱形，另外两边为等长平行直线的“变形矩形”），并且符合以下规格：

1. 矩形（包括正方形）的，厚度不超过宽度的十分之一，
2. 矩形或正方形以外形状的，任何尺寸，但不具有其他税目所列制品或产品的特征。

税目 78.04 还适用于具有花样（例如，凹槽、肋条形、格槽、珠粒及菱形）的板、片、带、箔以及穿孔、抛光、涂层或制成瓦楞形的这类产品，但不具有其他税目所列制品或产品的特征。

Chapter 78
Lead and articles thereof

Notes:

In this Chapter the following expressions have the meanings hereby assigned to them:

1. Bars and rods

Rolled, extruded, drawn or forged products, not in coils, which have a uniform solid cross-section along their whole length in the shape of circles, ovals, rectangles (including squares), equilateral triangles or regular convex polygons (including "flattened circles" and "modified rectangles", of which two opposite sides are convex arcs, the other two sides being straight, of equal length and parallel). Products with a rectangular (including square), triangular or polygonal cross-section may have corners rounded along their whole length. The thickness of such products which have a rectangular (including "modified rectangular") cross-section exceeds one-tenth of the width. The expression also covers cast or sintered products, of the same forms and dimensions, which have been subsequently worked after production (otherwise than by simple trimming or de-scaling), provided that they have not thereby assumed the character of articles or products of other headings.

2. Profiles

Rolled, extruded, drawn, forged or formed products, coiled or not, of a uniform cross-section along their whole length, which do not conform to any of the definitions of bars, rods, wire, plates, sheets, strip, foil, tubes or pipes. The expression also covers cast or sintered products, of the same forms, which have been subsequently worked after production (otherwise than by simple trimming or de-scaling), provided that they have not thereby assumed the character of articles or products of other headings.

3. Wire

Rolled, extruded or drawn products, in coils, which have a uniform solid cross-section along their whole length in the shape of circles, ovals, rectangles (including squares), equilateral triangles or regular convex polygons (including "flattened circles" and "modified rectangles", of which two opposite sides are convex arcs, the other two sides being straight, of equal length and parallel). Products with a rectangular (including square), triangular or polygonal cross-section may have corners rounded along their whole length. The thickness of such products which have a rectangular (including "modified rectangular") cross-section exceeds one-tenth of the width.

4. Plates, sheets, strip and foil

Flat-surfaced products (other than the unwrought products of heading No. 78.01), coiled or not, of solid rectangular (other than square) cross-section with or without rounded corners (including "modified rectangles" of which two opposite sides are convex arcs, the other two sides being straight, of equal length and parallel) of a uniform thickness, which are:

- of rectangular (including square) shape with a thickness not exceeding one-tenth of the width,
- of a shape other than rectangular or square, of any size, proviede that they do not assume the character of articles or products of other headings.

Heading No. 78.04 applies, *inter alia*, to plates, sheets, strip and foil with patterns (for example, grooves, ribs, chequers, tears, buttons, lozenges) and to such products which have been perforated, corrugated, polished or coated, provided that they do not thereby assume the character of articles or products of other headings.

五、管

全长截面及管壁厚度相同并只有一个闭合空间的实心产品，成卷或非成卷的，其截面为圆形、椭圆形、矩形（包括正方形）、等边三角形或规则外凸多边形。对于截面为矩形（包括正方形）、等边三角形或规则外凸多边形的产品，不论全长边角是否磨圆，只要其内外截面为同一圆心并为同样形状及同一轴向，也可视为管子。上述截面的管子可经抛光、涂层、弯曲、攻丝、钻孔、缩腰、胀口、成锥形或装法兰、颈圈或套环。

5. Tubes and pipes

Hollow products, coiled or not, which have a uniform cross-section with only one enclosed void along their whole langth in the shape of circles, ovals, rectangles (including squares), equilateral triangles or regular convex polygons, and which have a uniform wall thickness. Products with a rectangular (including square), equilateral triangular or regular convex polygonal cross-section, which may have corners rounded along their whole length, are also to be considered as tubes and pipes provided the inner and outer cross-sections are concentric and have the same form and orientation. Tubes and pipes of the foregoing cross-sections may be polished, coated, bent, threaded, drilled, waisted, expanded, cone-shaped or fitted with flanges, collars or rings.

子目注释：

本章所称“精炼铅”，是指：

按重量计含铅量至少为 99.9% 的金属，但其他各种元素的含量不超过下表中规定的限量：

其他元素表

元素		所含重量百分比
Ag	银	0.02
As	砷	0.005
Bi	铋	0.05
Ca	钙	0.002
Cd	镉	0.002
Cu	铜	0.08
Fe	铁	0.002
S	硫	0.002
Sb	锑	0.005
Sn	锡	0.005
Zn	锌	0.002
其他(例如碲)，每种		0.001

Subheading Note:

In this Chapter the expression “refined lead” means:

Metal containing by weight at least 99.9% of lead, provided that the content by weight of any other element does not exceed the limit specified in the following table:

TABLE — Other elements

Element		Limiting centen% by weight
Ag	Silver	0.02
As	Arsenic	0.005
Bi	Bismuth	0.05
Ca	Calcium	0.002
Cd	Cadmium	0.002
Cu	Copper	0.08
Fe	Iron	0.002
S	Sulphur	0.002
Sb	Antimony	0.005
Sn	Tin	0.005
Zn	Zinc	0.002
Other (for example Te), each		0.001

税则号列	货品名称	最惠(%)	普通	增值税率	出口退税	计量单位	监管条件	Article Description
78.01	**未锻轧铅：**							**Unwrought lead:**
7801.1000	-精炼铅	3	20	17		千克		-Refined lead
	-其他：							-Other:
7801.9100	--按重量计所含其他元素是以锑为主的	3	20	17		千克		--Containing by weight antimony as the principal other element
7801.9900	--其他	3	20	17		千克		--Other
78.02	**铅废碎料：**							**Lead waste and scrap:**
7802.0000	铅废碎料	1.5	10	17		千克	9	Lead waste and scrap
78.04	**铅板、片、带、箔；铅粉及片状粉末：**							**Lead plates sheets, strip and foil; lead powders and flakes:**
	-板、片、带、箔：							-Plates, sheets, strip and foil:
7804.1100	--片、带及厚度(衬背除外)不超过 0.2 毫米的箔	6	30	17	5	千克		--Sheets, strip and foil of a thickness (excluding any backing) not exceeding 0.2mm
7804.1900	--其他	6	30	17		千克		--Other
7804.2000	-粉末及片状粉末	6	35	17		千克		-Powders and flakes
78.06	**其他铅制品：**							**Other articles of lead:**
7806.0010	---铅条、杆、型材及异型材或丝	6	30	17		千克		---Lead bars, rods, profiles and wire
7806.0090	---其他	6	40	17		千克		---Other

第七十九章
锌及其制品

注释：

本章所用名词解释如下：

一、条、杆

轧、挤、拔或锻制的实心产品，非成卷的，其全长截面均为圆形、椭圆形、矩形（包括正方形）、等边三角形或规则外凸多边形（包括相对两边为弧拱形，另外两边为等长平行直线的“扁圆形”及“变形矩形”）。对于矩形（包括正方形）、三角形或多边形截面的产品，其全长边角可经磨圆。矩形（包括“变形矩形”）截面的产品，其厚度应大于宽度的十分之一。所述条、杆也包括同样形状及尺寸的铸造或烧结产品。该产品在铸造烧结后再经加工（简单剪修或去氧化皮的除外），但不具有其他税目所列制品或产品的特征。

二、型材及异型材

轧、挤 拔、锻制的产品或其他成型产品，不论是否成卷，其全长截面相同，但与条、杆、丝、板、片、带、箔、管的定义不相符合。同时也包括同样形状的铸造或烧结产品。该产品在铸造或烧结后再经加工（简单剪修或去氧化皮的除外），但不具有其他税目所列制品或产品的特征。

三、丝

盘卷的轧、挤或拔制实心产品，其全长截面均为圆形、椭圆形、矩形（包括正方形）、等边三角形或规则外凸多边形（包括相对两边为弧拱形，另外两边为等长平行直线的“扁圆形”及“变形矩形”）。对于矩形（包括正方形）、三角形或多边形截面的产品，其全长边角可经磨圆。矩形（包括“变形矩形”）截面的产品，其厚度应大于宽度的十分之一。

四、板、片、带、箔

成卷或非成卷的平面产品（税目 79.01 的未锻轧产品除外），截面均为厚度相同的实心矩形（不包括正方形），不论边角是否磨圆（包括相对两边为弧拱形，另外两边为等长平行直线的“变形矩形”），并且符合以下规格：

1. 矩形（包括正方形）的，厚度不超过宽度的十分之一；
2. 矩形或正方形以外形状的，任何尺寸，但不具有其他税目所列制品或产品的特征。

税目 79.05 还适用于具有花样（例如，凹槽、肋条形、格槽、珠粒及菱形）的板、片、带、箔以及穿孔、抛光、涂层或制成瓦楞形的这类产品，但不具有其他税目所列制品或产品的特征。

Chapter 79
Zinc and articles thereof

Notes:

In this Chapter the following expressions have the meanings hereby assigned to them:

1. Bars and rods

Rolled, extruded, drawn or forged products, not in coils, which have a uniform solid cross-section along their whole length in the shape of circles, ovals, rectangle (including squares), equilateral triangles or regular convex polygons (including "flattened circles" and "modified rectangles", of which two opposite sides are convex arcs, the other two sides being straight, of equal length and parallel). Products with a rectangular (including square), triangular or polygonal cross-section may have corners rounded along their whole length. The thickness of such products which have a rectangular (including "modified rectangular") cross-section exceeds one-tenth of the width. The expression also covers cast or sintered products, of the same forms and dimensions, which have been subsequently worked after production (otherwise than by simple trimming or de-scaling), provided that they have not thereby assumed the character of articles or products of other headings.

2. Profiles

Rolled, extruded, drawn, forged or formed products, coiled or not, of a uniform cross-section along their whole length, which do not conform to any of the definitions of bars, rods, wire, plates, sheets, strip, foil, tubes or pipes. The expression also covers cast or sintered products, of the same forms, which have been subsequently worked after production (otherwise than by simple trimming or de-scaling), provided that they have not thereby assumed the character of articles or products of other headings.

3. Wire

Rolled, extruded or drawn products, in coils, which have a uniform solid cross-section along their whole length in the shape of circles, ovals, rectangles (including squares), equilateral triangles or regular convex polygons (including "flattened circles" and "modified rectangles", of which two opposite sides are convex arcs, the other two sides being straight, of equal length and parallel). Products with a rectangular (including square), triangular or polygonal cross-section may have corners rounded along their whole length. The thickness of such products which have a rectangular (including "modified rectangular") cross-section exceeds one-tenth of the width

4. Plates, sheets, strip and foil

Flat-surfaced products (other than the unwrought products of heading No. 79.01), coiled or not, of solid rectangular (other than square) cross-section with or without rounded corners (including "modified rectangles" of which two opposite sides are convex arcs, the other two sides being straight, of equal length and parallel) of a uniform thickness, which are:

(1) of rectangular (including square) shape with a thickness not exceeding one-tenth of the width,

(2) of a shape other than rectangular or square, of any size, provided that they do not assume the character of articles or products of other headings.

Heading No. 79.05 applies, *inter alia*, to plates, sheets strip and foil with patterns (for example, grooves, ribs chequers, tears, buttons, lozenges) and to such products which have been perforated, corrugated, polished or coated, provided that they do not thereby assume the character of articles or products of other headings.

五、管

全长截面及管壁厚度相同并只有一个闭合空间的空心产品，成卷或非成卷的，其截面为圆形、椭圆形、矩形（包括正方形）、等边三角形或规则外凸多边形。对于截面为矩形（包括正方形）、等边三角形或规则外凸多边形的产品，不论全长边角是否磨圆，只要其内外截面为同一圆心并为同样形状及同一轴向，也可视为管子。上述截面的管子可经抛光、涂层、弯曲、攻丝、钻孔、缩腰、胀口、成锥形或装法兰、颈圈或套环。

5. Tubes and pipes

Hollow products, coiled or not, which have a uniform cross-section with only one enclosed void along their whole length in the shape of circles, ovals, rectangles (including squares), equilateral triangles or regular convex polygons, and which have a uniform wall thickness. Products with a rectangular (including square), equilateral triangular or regular convex polygonal cross-section, which may have corners rounded along their whole length, are also to be considered as tubes and pipes provided the inner and outer cross-sections are concentric and have the same form and orientation. Tubes and pipes of the foregoing cross-sections may be polished, coated, bent, threaded, drilled, waisted, expanded, cone-shaped or fitted with flanges, collars or rings.

子目注释：

本章所用有关名词解释如下：

一、非合金锌

按重量计含锌量至少为97.5%的金属。

二、锌合金

按重量计含锌量大于其他元素单项含量的金属物质，但按重量计其他元素的总含量超过2.5%。

三、锌末

冷凝锌雾所得的锌末。该产品由球形微粒组成，比锌粉更为精细，按重量计至少80%的微粒可以通过孔径为63微米的筛子，而且必须含有按重量计至少为85%的金属锌。

Subheading Note:

In this Chapter the following expressions have the meanings hereby assigned to them:

1. Zinc, not alloyed

Metal containing by weight at least 97.5% of zinc.

2. Zinc alloys

Metallic substances in which zinc predominates by weight over each of the other elements, provided that the total content by weight of such other elements exceeds 2.5%.

3. Zinc dust

Dust obtained by condensation of zinc vapour, consisting of spherical particles which are finer than zinc powders. At least 80% by weight of the particles pass through a sieve with 63 micrometres (microns) mesh. It must contain at least 85% by weight of metallic zinc.

税则号列	货品名称	最惠(%)	普通	增值税率	出口退税	计量单位	监管条件	Article Description
79.01	未锻轧锌：							**Unwrought zinc:**
	-非合金锌：							-Zinc, not alloyed:
	--按重量计含锌量在99.99%及以上：							--Containing by weight 99.99% or more of zinc:
7901.1110暂	---按重量计含锌量在99.995%及以上	1	20	17		千克		---Containing by weight 99.995% or more of zinc
7901.1190暂	---其他	1	20	17		千克		---Other
7901.1200暂	--按重量计含锌量低于99.99%	1	20	17		千克		--Containing by weight less than 99.99% of zinc
7901.2000暂	-锌合金	1	20	17		千克		-Zinc alloys
79.02	锌废碎料：							**Zinc waste and scrap:**
7902.0000暂	锌废碎料	1	20	17		千克	AP	Zinc waste and scrap
79.03	锌末、锌粉及片状粉末：							**Zinc dust, powders and flakes:**
7903.1000	-锌末	6	20	17		千克	A	-Zinc dust
7903.9000	-其他	6	20	17		千克		-Other
7903.9000 10	颗粒＜500μm的锌及其合金（含量≥97%，不论球形、椭球体、雾化、片状、研碎金属燃料）	6	20	17		千克	3A	Zinc and its alloys, granularity＜500μm (containing zinc≥97%, whether spheroid, ellipsoid, atomized, flake formed, ground metallic fuels)
7903.9000 90	其他锌粉及片状粉末	6	20	17		千克	AB	Other zine powders and flakes
79.04	锌条、杆、型材及异型材或丝：							**Zinc bars, rods, profiles and wire:**
7904.0000	锌条、杆、型材及异型材或丝	6	30	17		千克		Zinc bars, rods, profiles and wire
79.05	锌板、片、带、箔：							**Zinc plates, sheets, strip and foil:**
7905.0000	锌板、片、带、箔	6	30	17		千克		Zinc plates, sheets, strip and foil
79.07	其他锌制品：							**Other articles of zinc:**
7907.0020	---锌管及锌制管子附件（例如，接头、肘管、管套）	6	30	17		千克		---Zinc tubes pipes and tube or pipe fittings (for example, couplings, elbows, sleeves)
7907.0030	---电池壳体坯料（锌饼）	6	40	17		千克		---Cellpacking blanks (zinc biscuits)
7907.0090	---其他	6	40	17		千克		---Other

第八十章
锡及其制品

注释：

本章所用有关名词解释如下：

一、条、杆

轧、挤、拔或锻制的实心产品，非成卷的，其全长截面均为圆形、椭圆形、矩形（包括正方形）、等边三角形或规则外凸多边形（包括相对两边为弧拱形，另外两边为等长平行直线的"扁圆形"及"变形矩形"）。对于矩形（包括正方形）、三角形或多边形截面的产品，其全长边角可经磨圆。矩形（包括"变形矩形"）截面的产品，其厚度应大于宽度的十分之一。所述条、杆也包括同样形状及尺寸的铸造或烧结产品。该产品在造铸或烧结后再经加工（简单剪修或去氧化皮的除外），但不具有其他税目所列制品或产品的特征。

二、型材及异型材

轧、挤、拔、锻制的产品或其他成型产品，不论是否成卷，其全长截面相同，但与条、杆、丝、板、片、带、箔、管的定义不相符合。同时也包括同样形状的铸造或烧结产品。该产品在铸造或烧结后再经加工（简单剪修或去氧化皮的除外），但不具有其他税目所列制品或产品的特征。

三、丝

盘卷的轧、挤或拔制实心产品，其全长截面均为圆形、椭圆形、矩形（包括正方形）、等边三角形或规则外凸多边形（包括相对两边为弧拱形，另外两边为等长平行直线的"扁圆形"及"变形矩形"）。对于矩形（包括正方形）、三角形或多边形截面的产品，其全长边角可经磨圆。矩形（包括"变形矩形"）截面的产品，其厚度应大于宽度的十分之一。

四、板、片、带、箔

成卷或非成卷的平面产品（税目 80.01 的未锻轧产品除外），截面均为厚度相同的实心矩形（不包括正方形），不论边角是否磨圆（包括相对两边为弧拱形，另外两边为等长平行直线的"变形矩形"），并且符合以下规格：

1. 矩形（包括正方形）的，厚度不超过宽度的十分之一；
2. 矩形或正方形以外形状的，任何尺寸，但不具有其他税目所列制品或产品的特征。

Chapter 80
Tin and articles thereof

Notes:

In this Chapter the following expressions have the meanings hereby assigned to them:

1. Bars and rods

Rolled, extruded, drawn or forged products, not in coils, which have a uniform solid cross-section along their whole length in the shape of circles, ovals, rectangles (including squares), equilateral triangles or regular convex polygons (including "flattened circles" and "modified rectangles", of which two opposite sides are convex arcs, the other two sides being straight, of equal length and parallel). Products with a rectangular (including square), triangular or polygonal cross-section may have corners rounded along their whole length. The thickness of such products which have a rectangular (including "modified rectangular") cross-section exceeds one-tenth of the width. The expression also covers cast or sintered products, of the same forms and dimensions, which have been subsequently worked after production (otherwise than by simple trimming or de-scaling), provided that they have not thereby assumed the character of articles or products of other headings.

2. Profiles

Rolled, extruded, drawn, forged or formed products, coiled or not, of a uniform cross-section along their whole length, which do not conform to any of the definitions of bars, rods, wire, plates, sheets, strip, foil, tubes or pipes. The expression also covers cast or sintered products, of the same forms, which have been subsequently worked after production (otherwise than by simple trimming or de-scaling), provided that they have not thereby assumed the character of articles or products of other headings.

3. Wire

Rolled, extruded or drawn products, in coils, which have a uniform solid cross-section along their whole length in the shape of circles, ovals, rectangles (including squares), equilateral triangles or regular convex polygons (including "flattened circles" and "modified rectangles", of which two opposite sides are convex arcs, the other two sides being straight, of equal length and parallel). Products with a rectangular (including square), triangular or polygonal cross-section may have corners rounded along their whole length. The thickness of such products which have a rectangular (including "modified rectangular") cross-section exceeds one-tenth of the width.

4. Plates, sheets, strip and foil

Flat-surfaced products (other than the unwrought products of heading No. 80.01), coiled or not, of solid rectangular (other than square) cross-section with or without rounded corners (including "modified rectangles" of which two opposite sides are convex arcs, the other two sides being straight, of equal length and parallel) of a uniform thickness, which are:

(1) of rectangular (including square) shape with a thickness not exceeding one-tenth of the width,

(2) of a shape other than rectangular or square, of any size, proviede that they do not assume the character of articles or products of other headings.

五、管

全长截面及管壁厚度相同并只有一个闭合空间的实心产品,成卷或非成卷的,其截面为圆形、椭圆形、矩形(包括正方形)、等边三角形或规则外凸多边形。对于截面为矩形(包括正方形)、等边三角形或规则外凸多边形的产品,不论全长边角是否磨圆,只要其内外截面为同一圆心并为同样形状及同一轴向,也可视为管子。上述截面的管子可经抛光、涂层、弯曲、攻丝、钻孔、缩腰、胀口、成锥形或装法兰、颈圈或套环。

5. Tubes and pipes

Hollow products, coiled or not, which have a uniform cross-section with only one enclosed void along their whole length in the shape of circles, ovals, rectangles (including squares), equilateral triangles or regular convex polygons, and which have a uniform wall thickness. Products with a rectangular (including square), equilateral triangular or regular convex polygonal cross-section, which may have corners rounded along their whole length, are also to be considered as tubes and pipes provided the inner and outer cross-sections are concentric and have the same form and orientation. Tubes and pipes of the foregoing cross-sections may be polished, coated, bent, threaded, drilled, waisted, expanded, cone-shaped or fitted with flanges, collars or rings.

子目注释:

本章所用有关名词解释如下:

一、非合金锡

按重量计含锡量至少为99%的金属,但含铋量或含铜量不超过下表中规定的限量:

其他元素表

元素		所含重量百分比
Bi	铋	0.1
Cu	铜	0.4

二、锡合金

按重量计含锡量大于其他元素单项含量的金属物质,但:

(一)按重量计其他元素的总含量超过1%;或

(二)按重量计含铋量或含铜量应等于或大于上表中规定的限量。

Subheading Note:

In this Chapter the following expressions have the meanings hereby assigned to them:

1. Tin, not alloyed.

Metal containing by weight at least 99% of tin, provided that the content by weight of any bismuth or copper is less than the limit specified in the following table:

TABLE — Other elements

Element		Limiting content % by weight
Bi	Bismuth	0.1
Cu	Copper	0.4

2. Tin alloys

Metallic substances in which tin predominates by weight over each of the other elements, provided that:

(a) the total content by weight of such other elements exceeds 1%; or

(b) the content by weight of either bismuth or copper is equal to or greater than the limit specified in the foregoing table.

税则号列	货品名称	最惠(%)	普通	增值税率	出口退税	计量单位	监管条件	Article Description
80.01	**未锻轧锡:**							**Unwrought tin:**
8001.1000	-非合金锡	3	20	17		千克	4xy	-Tin, not alloyed
	-锡合金:							-Tin alloys:
8001.2010	---锡基巴毕脱合金	3	20	17		千克	4xy	---Babbitt metal
	---焊锡:							---solder:
8001.2021	----按重量计含铅量在0.1%以下的	3	30	17		千克	4xy	----Containing by weight less than 0.1% of lead
8001.2029	----其他	3	30	17		千克	4xy	----Other
8001.2090	---其他	3	30	17		千克	4xy	---Other
80.02	**锡废碎料:**							**Tin waste and scrap:**
8002.0000	锡废碎料	1.5	30	17		千克	4APxy	Tin waste and scrap
80.03	**锡条、杆、型材及异型材或丝:**							**Tin bars, rods, profiles and wire:**
8003.0000	锡条、杆、型材及异型材或丝	8	40	17		千克	4xy	Tin bars, rods, profiles and wire
80.07	**其他锡制品:**							**Other articles of tin:**
8007.0020	---锡板、片及带,厚度超过0.2毫米	8	40	17		千克	4xy	---Tin plates, sheets and strip, of a thickness exceeding 0.2mm
8007.0030	---锡箔(不论是否印花或用纸、纸板、塑料或类似材料衬背),厚度(衬背除外)不超过0.2毫米;锡粉及片状粉末	8	40	17	5	千克		---Tin foil (whether or not printed or backed with paper, paperboard, plastics or similar backing materials), of a thickness (excluding and backing) not exceeding 0.2mm; tin powders and flakes
8007.0040	---锡管及管子附件(例如,接头、肘管、管套)	8	45	17		千克	4xy	---Tin tubes, pipes and tube or pipe fittings (for example, couplings, elbows, sleeves)
8007.0090	---其他	8	80	17		千克		---Other

第八十一章 其他贱金属、金属陶瓷及其制品

Chapter 81 Other base metals; cermets; artiles thereof

子目注释：

第七十四章注释中有关“条、杆”、“型材及异型材”、“丝”及“板、片、带、箔”的规定也适用于本章。

Subheading Note:

Notes 1 to Chapter 74, defining "bars and rods", "profiles", "wire" and "plates, sheets, strip and foil" applies, *mutatis mutandis*, to this Chapter.

税则号列	货品名称	最惠(%)	普通	增值税率	出口退税	计量单位	监管条件	Article Description
81.01	**钨及其制品，包括废碎料：**							**Tungsten (wolfram) and articles thereof, including waste and scrap:**
8101.1000	-粉末	6	20	17		千克		-Powders
8101.1000 10	颗粒＜500μm 的钨及其合金（含量≥97%，不论球形、椭球体、雾化、片状、研碎金属燃料）	6	20	17		千克	3	Tungesten and tungsten alloys, granularity＜500μm, (containing tungsten≥97%, whether in the form of spheroid, elipsoid, flakes, atomized or pulverized metallic fuel)
8101.1000 90	其他钨粉末	6	20	17		千克	4xy	Other tungsten powders
	-其他：							-Other:
8101.9400	--未锻轧钨，包括简单烧结而成的条、杆	3	20	17		千克	4xy	--Unwrought tungsten, including bars and rods obtained simply by sintering
8101.9600	--丝	8	20	17	5	千克		--Wire
8101.9700[暂]	--废碎料	1	20	17		千克	4APxy	--Waste and scrap
	--其他：							--Other:
8101.9910	---条、杆，但简单烧结而成的除外；型材及异型材、板、片、带、箔	5	30	17		千克		---Bars and rods, other than those obtained simply by sintering, profiles, plates, sheets, strip and foil
8101.9990	---其他	8	70	17		千克		---Other
81.02	**钼及其制品，包括废碎料：**							**Molybdenum and articles thereof, including waste and scrap:**
8102.1000	-粉末	6	20	17		千克	4xy	-Powders
	-其他：							-Other:
8102.9400	--未锻轧钼，包括简单烧结而成的条、杆	3	20	17		千克	4xy	--Unwrought molybdenum, including bars and rods obtained simply by sintering
8102.9500	--条、杆，但简单烧结而成的除外；型材及异型材、板、片、带、箔	8	30	17		千克		--Bars and rods, other than those obtained simply by sintering, profiles, plates, sheets, strip and foil
8102.9600	--丝	8	20	17	5	千克		--Wire
8102.9700	--废碎料	3	20	17		千克	49xy	--Waste and scrap
8102.9900	--其他	8	70	17		千克	4xy	--Other
81.03	**钽及其制品，包括废碎料：**							**Tantalum and articles thereof, including waste and scrap:**
	-未锻轧钽，包括简单烧结而成的条、杆；粉末：							-Unwrought tantalum, including bars and rods obtained simply by sinteing; powders:
	---钽粉：							---Powders:
8103.2011	----松装密度小于 2.2g/cm³ 的	6	14	17	13	千克	4xy	----Loose density less than 2.2g/cm³
8103.2019	----其他	6	14	17		千克	4xy	----Other
8103.2090	---其他	6	14	17		千克	4xy	---Other
8103.3000[暂]	-废碎料	0	14	17		千克	4APxy	-Waste and scrap
	-其他：							-Other:
	---钽丝：							---Wire of tantalum
8103.9011	----直径小于 0.5mm	8	30	17	13	千克	4xy	----Diameter less than 0.5mm
8103.9019	----其他	8	30	17	9	千克	4xy	----Other
8103.9090	---其他	8	30	17		千克		---Other
8103.9090 10	钽坩埚（容积在 50ml 至 2L 之间、钽纯度≥98%）	8	30	17		千克	3	Tantalum crucible, of a volune between 50 milliliter and 2 litre, tantaium≥98%
8103.9090 90	其他锻轧钽及其制品	8	30	17	9	千克	4xy	Other wrought tantalum and articles thereof
81.04	**镁及其制品，包括废碎料：**							**Magnesium and articles thereof, including waste and scrap:**
	-未锻轧镁：							-Unwrought magnesium:

税则号列	货　品　名　称	最惠(%)	普通	增值税率	出口退税	计量单位	监管条件	Article Description
8104.1100	--按重量计含镁量至少为99.8%	6	20	17		千克		--Containing at least 99.8% by weight of magnesium
8104.1900	--其他	6	20	17		千克		--Other
8104.2000	-废碎料	1.5	20	17		千克	AP	-Waste and scrap
8104.3000	-锉屑、车屑及颗粒,已按规格分级的;粉末	8	30	17		千克		-Raspings, turnings and granules, graded according to size; powders
8104.3000 10	颗粒<500μm的镁及其合金(含量≥97%,不论球形、椭球体、雾化、片状、研碎金属燃料)	8	30	17		千克	3	Magnesium and magnesium alloys, granularity <500μm (containing magnesium ≥97%, whether spheroid, ellipsoid, atomized, flake formed, ground metallic fuels)
8104.3000 90	其他已分级的镁锉屑,车屑,颗粒;粉末	8	30	17		千克		Other magnesium raspings, turnings and granules, graded according to size; powders
	-其他:							-Other:
8104.9010	---锻轧镁	8	30	17		千克		---Wrought magnesium
8104.9020	---镁制品	8.4	70	17		千克		---Magnesium articles
8104.9020 10	镁金属基复合材料(包括各种结构件和制品、各种预成形件,其中增强材料的比拉伸强度大于7.62×10^4m和比模量大于3.18×10^6m)	8.4	70	17	5	千克	3	Masnesium composite materials (including various structural parts and products, various prefabricated parts and their specific tensile strength is bigger than 7.62×10^4m and specific modulus bigger than 3.18×10^6m)
8104.9020 90	其他镁制品	8.4	70	17		千克		Other magnesium articlec
81.05	**钴锍及其他冶炼钴时所得的中间产品;钴及其制品,包括废碎料:**							**Cobalt mattes and other intermediate products of cobalt matallurgy; cobalt and articles thereof, including waste and scrap:**
	-钴锍及其他冶炼钴时所得的中间产品;未锻轧钴;粉末:							-Cobalt mattes and other intermediate products of cobalt matallurgy; unwrought cobalt; powders:
8105.2010暂	---钴湿法冶炼中间品	0	14	17		千克	4xy	---Intermediate products of cobalt metallurgy by wet process
8105.2020	---未锻轧钴	4	14	17		千克	4xy	---Unwrought cobalt
8105.2090	---其他		14	17		千克		---Other
8105.2090暂 01	钴锍及其他冶炼钴时所得中间产品	0	14	17		千克	4xy	Mid-product smelted with cobalt and sulfur and others
8105.2090 10	钴≥99.5%的超细钴粉(费氏粒度0.8-1.5μm,松装密度0.4-0.8g/立方厘米)	4	14	17		千克		Supper-fine cobalt powders, containing ≥99.5% by weight of cobalt (fischer granularinty 0.8~1.5μm. bulk package density 0.4~0.8g/cm^3)
8105.2090 90	其他钴锍、粉末	4	14	17		千克	4xy	Other cobalt mattes; powders
8105.3000	-废碎料	4	14	17		千克	49xy	-Waste and scrap
8105.9000	-其他	8	30	17		千克	4xy	-Other
81.06	**铋及其制品,包括废碎料:**							**Bismuth and articles thereof, including waste and scrap:**
8106.0010	---未锻轧铋;废碎料;粉末		20	17		千克		---Unwroght bismuth; waste and scrap; powders
8106.0010暂 11	高纯度未锻轧的铋(纯度≥99.99%含银量低于十万分之一)	1	20	17		千克	3	Highly-pure unwroght bismuth, purity≥99.99% (containing silver quality <1.0×10^{-6})
8106.0010 19	高纯度未锻轧的铋废料、粉末(纯度≥99.99%含银量低于十万分之一)	3	20	17		千克	3	Highly-pure unwroght bismuth, waste and scrap, powders, purity≥99.99% (containing silver quality <1.0×10^{-6})
8106.0010暂 91	其他未锻轧铋	1	20	17		千克	4xy	Other unwroght bismuth
8106.0010 92	其他未锻轧铋废碎料	3	20	17		千克	4APxy	Other unwroght bismuth waste and scap
8106.0010 99	其他未锻轧铋粉末	3	20	17		千克	4xy	Other unwroght bismuth powders
8106.0090	---其他	8	30	17		千克		---Other
8106.0090 10	高纯度铋及铋制品(纯度≥99.99%,含银量低于十万分之一)	8	30	17	5	千克	3	Highly-pure unwrought bismuth and aricles thereof (Purity≥99.99%, purity containing silver quantity is lower than 1/100,000)
8106.0090 90	其他铋及铋制品	8	30	17		千克	4xy	Other bismuth and articles thereof
81.07	**镉及其制品,包括废碎料:**							**Cadmium and articles thereof, including waste and scrap:**
8107.2000	-未锻轧镉;粉末	3	14	17		千克		-Unwrought cadmium; powders
8107.3000	-废碎料	3	14	17		千克	9	-Waste and scrap

税则号列	货 品 名 称	最惠(%)	普通	增值税率	出口退税	计量单位	监管条件	Article Description
8107.9000	-其他	8	30	17		千克		-Other
81.08	钛及其制品,包括废碎料:							**Titanium and articles thereof, including waste and scrap:**
	-未锻轧钛;粉末:							-Unwrought titanium; powders:
	---未锻轧钛:							---Unwrousht titanium:
8108.2021	----海绵钛	3	14	17		千克	4xy	----Sponge titanium
8108.2029	----其他	3	14	17		千克		----Other
8108.2029 10	颗粒<500μm的钛及其合金(含量≥97%,不论球形、椭球体、雾化、片状、研碎金属燃料)	3	14	17		千克	3A	Titanium and its alloy with the particles <500μm (containing ≥97%, whether in balls, atomized, in sheet or in pulverized metal fuel)
8108.2029 90	其他未锻轧钛	3	14	17		千克	4xy	Other unwrought titanium; powders
8108.2030	---粉末	3	14	17		千克	A4xy	---Powders
8108.3000	-废碎料	3	14	17		千克	4APxy	-Waste and scrap
	-其他:							-Other:
8108.9010	---条、杆、型材及异型材	8	30	17	13	千克		---Bars, rods, shapes and sections
8108.9010 10	钛合金,实心圆柱体,包括锻件(20℃下极限抗拉强度≥900兆帕,外径超过75mm)	8	30	17	13	千克	3	Titanium alloys, solid cylinder, including castings (ultimate tensile strength≥900MPa at 20℃, outer diameter >75mm)
8108.9010 20	钛金属基复合材料的条、杆、型材及异型材(其中增强材料的比拉伸强度大于 7.62×10^6 米和比模量大于 3.18×10^7 米)	8	30	17	13	千克	3	Bars, rods, shaps and sections, made of composite material with titanium metal (the degree of streangth of intensity waterial $>7.62\times10^6$m, and specific modulus $>3.18\times10^7$m)
8108.9010 90	其他钛条、杆、型材及异型材	8	30	17	13	千克		Other bars, rods, shapes and sections, of titanium
8108.9020	---丝	8	30	17	13	千克		---Wire
	---板、片、带、箔:							---Plates, sheets, strap, foil:
8108.9031暂	----厚度不超过0.8毫米	4	30	17	13	千克		----Of a thickness not more than 0.8mm
8108.9032暂	----厚度超过0.8毫米	4	30	17	13	千克		----Of a thickness more than 0.8mm
8108.9032暂 10	钛金属基复合材料的板、片、带、箔(其中增强材料的比拉伸强度大于 7.62×10^4 米和比模量大于 3.18×10^7 米,厚度大于0.8毫米)	4	30	17	13	千克	3	Plates. sheets, strip and foil made of conyosite material with titanium metal (the degree of strength of intensity material $>7.62\times10^4$m, and specific mondulus $>3.18\times10^7$mm, thickness >0.8mm)
8108.9032暂 90	其他厚度>0.8毫米的钛板、片、带、箔	4	30	17	13	千克		Other plates, sheets, strap, foil of titanium thickness >0.8mm
8108.9040	---管	8	30	17	13	千克		---Tubes or pipes
8108.9040 10	钛合金管(20℃下极限抗拉强度≥900MPa,外径>75mm)	8	30	17	13	千克	3	Tubes or pipes of titanium (ultimate tensile strength ≥900MPa at 20℃, outer diameter >75mm)
8108.9040 90	其他钛管	8	30	17	13	千克		Other titanium tubes or pipes
8108.9090	---其他	8	30	17	13	千克		---Other
81.09	锆及其制品,包括废碎料:							**Zirconium and articles thereof, including waste and scrap:**
8109.2000	-未锻轧锆;粉末	3	20	17		千克		-Unwrought zirconium; powders
8109.2000 10	颗粒<500μm的锆及其合金(含量≥97%,不论球形、椭球体、雾化、片状、研碎金属燃料)	3	20	17		千克	3A	Zirconium and alloys, granularity <500μm (containing zirconium≥97%, whether spheroid, ellipsoid, atomized, flake formed, ground metallic fuels)
8109.2000 90	其他未锻轧锆;粉末	3	20	17		千克	3A	Other unwrought zirconium; powders
8109.3000	-废碎料	3	20	17		千克	3AP	-Waste and scrap
8109.9000	-其他	8	30	17		千克		-Other
8109.9000 10	锆管(铪与锆重量比低于1:500的锆金属和合金的管或组件)	8	30	17	5	千克	3	Tubes or pipes of zirconium and its alloys (ratio of hafnium and zirconium <1:500 by weight)
8109.9000 90	其他锻轧锆及锆制品	8	30	17		千克	3	Other wrought zirconium and articles thereof
81.10	锑及其制品,包括废碎料:							**Antimony and articles thereof, including waste and scrap:**
	-未锻轧锑;粉末:							-Unwrought antimony; powders:
8110.1010暂	---未锻轧锑	1	30	17		千克	4xy	---Unwrought antimony
8110.1020	---粉末	3	30	17		千克	4Axy	---Powders

税则号列	货　品　名　称	最惠(%)	普通	增值税率	出口退税	计量单位	监管条件	Article Description
8110.2000	-废碎料	3	30	17		千克	49xy	-Antimony waste and scrap
8110.9000	-其他	8	40	17		千克	4xy	-Other
81.11	**锰及其制品,包括废碎料:**							**Manganese and articles thereof, including waste and scrap:**
8111.0010	---未锻轧锰;废碎料;粉末	3	20	17		千克		---Unwrought manganese; waste and scrap; powders
8111.0010 10	锰废碎料	3	20	17		千克	49xy	Unwrought manganese waste and scraps
8111.0010 90	未锻轧锰;粉末	3	20	17		千克	4Axy	Unwrought manganese powders
8111.0090	---其他	8	30	17		千克	4xy	---Other
81.12	**铍、铬、锗、钒、镓、铪、铟、铼、铌、铊及其制品,包括废碎料:**							**Beryllium, chromium, germanium, vanadium, gallium, hafnium, indium, niobium (columbium), rhenium and thallium, and articles of these metals, including waste and scrap:**
	-铍:							-Beryllium:
8112.1200	--未锻轧铍;粉末	3	30	17		千克	3A	--Unwrought; powders
8112.1300	--废碎料	3	30	17		千克	39	--Waste and scrap
8112.1900	--其他	8	30	17		千克	3	--Other
	-铬:							-Chromium:
8112.2100	--未锻轧铬;粉末	3	20	17		千克	4xy	--Unwrought; powders
8112.2200	--废碎料	3	20	17		千克	49xy	--Waste and scrap
8112.2900	--其他	3	20	17		千克	4xy	--Other
	-铊:							-Thallium:
8112.5100	--未锻轧铊;粉末	3	20	17		千克	AB	--Unwrought; powders
8112.5200	--废碎料	3	20	17		千克	9	--Waste and scrap
8112.5900	--其他	8	30	17		千克		--Other
	-其他:							-Other:
	--未锻轧的;废碎料;粉末:							--Unwrought; waste and scrap; powders:
8112.9210	---锗	3	20	17		千克		---Germanium
8112.9210 10	未锻轧锗废碎料	3	20	17		千克	4APxy	Unwrought germanium waste and scraps
8112.9210 90	未锻轧的锗;锗粉末	3	20	17		千克	4xy	Unwrought germanium; powders
8112.9220	---钒		20	17		千克		---Vanadium
8112.9220[暂] 01	未锻轧、废碎料或粉末状的钒氮合金	0	20	17		千克	4xy	Unwrought, waste and scrap, powders, vanadium - nitrogen alloys
8112.9220 10	未锻轧的钒废碎料	3	20	17		千克	4APxy	Unwrought, vanadium waste and scraps
8112.9220 90	未锻轧的钒;钒粉末	3	20	17		千克	4xy	Unwrought vanadium; Powders
8112.9230	---铟	3	20	17		千克	4xy	---Indium
8112.9230 01	未锻轧的铟	3	20	17		千克	4xy	Unwrought indium
8112.9230 02	铟粉末	3	20	17		千克	4xy	Indium powders
8112.9230 90	未锻轧的铟废碎料	3	20	17		千克	49xy	Unwrought indium waste and scrap
8112.9240[暂]	---铌	1	20	17		千克		---Niobium
8112.9240[暂] 10	铌废碎料	1	20	17		千克	4APxy	Unwrought niobium waste and scrap
8112.9240[暂] 90	未锻轧的铌;铌粉末	1	20	17		千克	4xy	Unwrought niobium; powders
8112.9290	---其他	3	20	17		千克		---Other
8112.9290 11	未锻轧的铪废碎料	3	20	17		千克	3AP	Unwrought hafnium waste and scrap
8112.9290 19	未锻轧的铪;粉末	3	20	17		千克	3A	Unwrought hafnium; powders
8112.9290 91	未锻轧的镓、铼废碎料	3	20	17		千克	4APxy	Unwrought gallium, rhenium sawte and scraps
8112.9290 99	未锻轧的镓、铼;粉末	3	20	17		千克	4xyA	Unwrought gallium, rhenium; powders
	--其他:							--Other:
8112.9910	---锗	3	20	17	5	千克	4xy	---Germanium
8112.9920	---钒		20	17		千克		---Vanadium
8112.9920[暂] 01	其他钒氮合金	0	20	17		千克	4xy	Other vanadium - nitrogen alloys
8112.9920 90	其他钒及其制品	3	20	17		千克	4xy	Other vanadium and articles thereof
8112.9930	---铟	8	20	17		千克	4xy	---Indium
8112.9940	---铌	8	20	17		千克	4xy	---Niobium
8112.9990	---其他	8	30	17		千克		---Other
8112.9990 10	锻轧的铪及其制品	8	30	17		千克	3	Wrought hafnium and articles thereof
8112.9990 90	锻轧的镓、铼及其制品	8	30	17		千克	4xy	Other wrought gallium, rhenium and articles therof

税则号列	货 品 名 称	最惠(%)	普通	增值税率	出口退税	计量单位	监管条件	Article Description
81.13	金属陶瓷及其制品,包括废碎料:							**Cermets and articles thereof, including waste and scrap:**
	金属陶瓷及其制品包括废碎料:							Cermets and articles thereof, including waste and scrap:
8113.0010	---颗粒;粉末	8.4	30	17		千克		---Granules, powder
8113.0010 10	颗粒或粉末状碳化钨废碎料	8.4	30	17		千克	AP	Waster and scrap of tungsten carbide, granules or powders
8113.0010 90	颗粒或粉末状其他金属陶瓷及其制品	8.4	30	17		千克		Other metal cermets and articles thereof, granules or powders
8113.0090	---其他	8.4	30	17		千克		---Other
8113.0090 10	其他碳化钨废碎料,颗粒或粉末除外	8.4	30	17		千克	AP	Other tungsten carbide waste and scrap, other than granules or powders
8113.0090 90	其他金属陶瓷及其制品,颗粒或粉末除外(包括废料)	8.4	30	17		千克		Other metal cermets and articles thereof, other than grainor powders (including waster and scrap)

第八十二章
贱金属工具、器具、利口器、餐匙、餐叉及其零件

Chapter 82
Tools, implements, cutlery, spoons and forks, parts thereof of base metal

注释:

一、除喷灯、轻便锻炉、带支架的砂轮、修指甲和修脚用器具及税目82.09的货品外,本章仅包括带有用下列材料制成的刀片、工作刃、工作面或其他工作部件的物品:
(一)贱金属;
(二)硬质合金或金属陶瓷;
(三)装于贱金属、硬质合金或金属陶瓷底座上的宝石或半宝石(天然、合成或再造);
(四)附于贱金属底座上的磨料,当附上磨料后,所具有的切齿、沟、槽或类似结构仍保持其特性及功能。

二、本章所列物品的贱金属零件,应与该制品归入同一税号,但具体列名的零件及手工工具的工具夹具(税目84.66)除外。第十五类注释二所述的通用零件,均不归入本章。电动剃须刀及电动毛发推剪的刀头、刀片应归入税目85.10。

三、由税号82.11的一把或多把刀具与税号82.15至少数量相同的物品构成的成套货品应归入税号82.15。

Notes:

1. Apart from blow lamps, portable forges, grinding wheels with frameworks, manicure or pedicure sets, and goods of heading No. 82.09, this Chapter covers only articles with a blade, working No. edge, working surface or other working part of :
(a) Base metal;
(b) Metal carbides or cermets;
(c) Precious or semi-precious stones (natural, synthetic or reconstructed) on a support of base metal, metal carbide or cermet; or
(d) Abrasive materials on a support of base metal, provided that the articles have cutting teeth, flutes, grooves, or the like, of base metal, which retain their identity and function after the application of the abrasive.
2. Parts of base metal of the articles of this Chapter are to be classified with the articles of which they are parts, except parts separately specified as such and tool-holders for hand tools (heading No. 84.66). However, parts of general use as defined in Note 2 to Section XV are in all cases excluded from this Chapter. Heads, blades and cutting plates for electric shavers and electric hair clippers are to be classified in heading No. 85.10.
3. Sets consisting of one or more knives of heading No. 82.11 and at least an equal number of articles of heading No. 82.15 are to be classified in heading No. 82.15.

税则号列	货品名称	最惠(%)	普通	增值税率	出口退税	计量单位	监管条件	Article Description
82.01	锹、铲、镐、锄、叉及耙;斧子、钩刀及类似砍伐工具;各种修枝用剪刀;镰刀、秣刀、树篱剪、伐木楔子及其他农业、园艺或林业用手工工具:							Hand tools, the following: spades, shovels, mattocks, picks, hoes, forks and rakes; axes, bill hooks and similar hewing tools; secateurs and prundrs of any kind; scythes, hay knives, hedge shears, timber wedges and other tools of a kind used in agriculture, horticulture or forestry:
8201.1000	-锹及铲	8	50	13	5	千克/把		-Spades and shovels
8201.1000 10	含植物性材料的锹及铲	8	50	13	5	千克/把	AB	Spades and shovels with vegetable materials
8201.1000 90	其他锹及铲	8	50	13	5	千克/把		Other spades and shovels
8201.3000	-镐、锄及耙	8	50	13	5	千克/把		-Mattocks, picks, hoes and rakes
8201.3000 10	含植物性材料的镐、锄、耙	8	50	13	5	千克/把	AB	Mattocks, picks, hoes and rakes with vegetable materials
8201.3000 90	其他镐、锄、耙	8	50	13	5	千克/把		Other mattocks, picks, hoes and rakes
8201.4000	-斧子、钩刀及类似砍伐工具	8	50	13	5	千克/把		-Axes, bill hooks and similar hewing tools
8201.4000 10	含植物性材料的砍伐工具(包括斧子、钩刀及类似砍伐工具)	8	50	13	5	千克/把	AB	Hewing tools with vegetable materials (including axes, bill hooks and similar hewing tools)
8201.4000 90	其他斧子、钩刀及类似砍伐工具	8	50	13	5	千克/把		Other axes, bill hooks and similar hewing tools
8201.5000	-修枝剪及类似的单手操作剪刀(包括家禽剪)	8	50	13	5	千克/把		-Secateurs and similar one-handed pruners and shears (including poultry shears)
8201.5000 10	含植物性材料的单手操作农用剪(包括家禽剪)	8	50	13	5	千克/把	AB	Secateurs and similar one-handed pruners and shears (including poultry shears), with vegetable materials, of a kind used in agriculture
8201.5000 90	其他修枝剪等单手操作农用剪(包括家禽剪)	8	50	13	5	千克/把		Other secateurs and similar one-handed pruners and shears (including poultry shears), of a kind used in agriculture

税则号列	货品名称	最惠(%)	普通	增值税率	出口退税	计量单位	监管条件	Article Description
8201.6000	-树篱剪、双手修枝剪及类似的双手操作剪刀	8	50	13		千克/把		-Hedge shears, two-handed pruning shears and similar two-handed shears
8201.6000 10	含植物性材料的双手操作农用剪	8	50	13	5	千克/把	AB	Hedge shears, two-handed pruning shears and similar two-handed shears, with vegetable materials, of a kind used in agriculture
8201.6000 90	其他修枝等双手操作农用剪	8	50	13	9	千克/把		Other hedge shears, two-handed pruning shears and similar two-handed shears, of a kind used in agriculture
	-用于农业、园艺或林业的其他手工工具:							-Other hand tools of a kind used in agriculture, horticulture or forestry:
8201.9010	---叉	8	50	13	5	千克/把		---Forks
8201.9010 10	含植物性材料的农业、园艺、林业用叉	8	50	13	5	千克/把	AB	Forks of a kind used in argiculture, horticulture or forestry, with vegetable materials
8201.9010 90	其他农业、园艺、林业用叉	8	50	13	5	千克/把		Other forks of a kind used in argiculture, horticulture or forestry
8201.9090	---其他	8	50	13	5	千克/把		---Other
8201.9090 10	含植物性材料的农林、园艺、林业用手工工具	8	50	13	5	千克/把	AB	Hand tools of a kind used in agriculture, horticulture or forestry, with vegetable materials
8201.9090 90	其他农业、园艺、林业用手工工具	8	50	13	5,9	千克/把		Other hand tools of a kind used in agriculture, horticulture or forestry
82.02	**手工锯;各种锯的锯片(包括切条、切槽或无齿锯片):**							**Hand saws; blades for saws of all kinds (including slitting, slotting or toothless saw blades):**
8202.1000	-手工锯	8.4	50	17	9	千克/把		-Hand saws
	-带锯片:							-Band saw blades:
8202.2010	---双金属带锯条	8	20	17	9	千克		---Double metal band saw blade
8202.2090	---其他	8	20	17	9	千克		---Other
	-圆锯片(包括切条或切槽锯片):							-Circular saw blades (including slitting or slotting saw blades):
8202.3100	--带有钢制工作部件	8	20	17	9	千克		--With working part of steel
	--其他,包括部件:							--Other, including parts:
8202.3910	---带有天然或合成金刚石、立方氮化硼制的工作部件	8	20	17	9	千克		---with working part of natural or synthetic diamond, cubic boron nitride
8202.3990	---其他	8	20	17	9	千克		---Other
8202.4000	-链锯片	8	20	17	9	千克		-Chain saw blades
	-其他锯片:							-Other saw blades:
	--直锯片,加工金属用:							--Straight saw blades, for working metal:
8202.9110	---机械锯用	8	20	17	9	千克		---For sawing machines
8202.9190	---其他	8	50	17	9	千克		---Other
	--其他:							--Other:
8202.9910	---机械锯用	8.4	20	17	9	千克		---For sawing machines
8202.9990	---其他	10.5	50	17	9	千克		---Other
82.03	**钢锉、木锉、钳子(包括剪钳)、镊子、白铁剪、切管器、螺栓切头器、打孔冲子及类似手工工具:**							**Files, rasps, pliers (including cutting pliers), pincers, tweezers, metal cutting shears, pipe-cutters, bolt croppers, perforating punches and similar hand tools:**
8203.1000	-钢锉、木锉及类似工具	10.5	50	17	9	千克/把		-Files, rasps and similar tools
8203.2000	-钳子(包括剪钳)、镊子及类似工具	10.5	50	17	9	千克/把		-Pliers (including cutting pliers), pincers, tweezers and similar tools
8203.3000	-白铁剪及类似工具	10.5	50	17	9	千克/把		-Metal cutting shears and similar tools
8203.4000	-切管器、螺栓切头器、打孔冲子及类似工具	10.5	50	17	9	千克/把		-Pipe-cutters, bolt croppers, perforating punches and similar tools
82.04	**手动扳手及扳钳(包括转矩扳手,但不包括丝锥扳手);可互换的扳手套筒,不论是否带手柄:**							**Hand-operated spanners and wrenches (including torque meter wrenches but not including tap wrenches); interchangeable spanner sockets, with or without handles:**
	-手动扳手及扳钳:							-Hand-operated spanners and wrenches:
8204.1100	--固定的	10.5	50	17	9	千克/把		--Non-adjustable

税则号列	货品名称	最惠(%)	普通	增值税率	出口退税	计量单位	监管条件	Article Description
8204.1200	--可调的	10	50	17	9	千克/把		--Adjustable
8204.2000	-可互换的扳手套筒，不论是否带手柄	10	50	17	9	千克/套		-Interchangeable spanner sockets, with or without handles
82.05	**其他税目未列名的手工工具(包括玻璃刀)；喷灯；台钳、夹钳及类似品，但作为机床附件或零件的除外；砧；轻便锻炉；带支架的手摇或脚踏砂轮：**							**Hand tools (including glaziers' diamonds), not elsewhere specified or included; blow lamps; vices, clamps and the like, other than accessories for and parts of, machine tools; anvils; portable forges; hand or pedal operated grinding wheels with frame works:**
8205.1000	-钻孔或攻丝工具	10	50	17	9	千克/个		-Drilling, threading or tapping tools
8205.2000	-锤子	10	50	17	9	千克/个		-Hammers and sledge hammers
8205.3000	-木工用刨子、凿子及类似切削工具	10.5	50	17	9	千克/个		-Planes, chisels, gouges and similar cutting tools for working wood
8205.4000	-螺丝刀	10.5	50	17	9	千克/个		-Screwdrivers
	-其他手工工具(包括玻璃刀)：							-Other hand tools (including glaziers' diamonds):
8205.5100	--家用工具	10.5	50	17	9	千克/个		--Household tools
8205.5900	--其他	10	50	17	9	千克/个		--Other
8205.6000	-喷灯	10	50	17	9	千克/个		-Blow lamps
8205.7000	-台钳、夹钳及类似品	10.5	50	17	9	千克/个		-Vices, clamps and the like
8205.9000	-其他，包括由本税目项下两个或多个子目所列物品组成的成套货品	10.5	50	17	9	千克		-Other, including sets of articles of two or more the foregoing subheadings
82.06	**由税目82.02至82.05中两个或多个税目所列工具组成的零售包装成套货品：**							**Tools of two or more of the headings Nos. 82.02 to 82.05, put up in sets for retail sale:**
8206.0000	由税目82.02至82.05中两个或多个税目所列工具组成的零售包装成套货品	10.5	50	17	9	千克		Tools of two or more of the headings Nos. 82.02 to 82.05, put up in sets for retail sale
82.07	**手工工具(不论是否有动力装置)及机床(例如，锻压、冲压、攻丝、钻孔、镗孔、铰孔及铣削、车削或上螺丝用的机器)的可互换工具，包括金属拉拔或挤压用模以及凿岩或钻探工具：**							**Interchangeable tools for hand tools, whether or not power-operated, or for machine-tools (for example, for pressing, stamping, punching, tapping, threading, drilling, boring, broaching, milling, turning or screw driving), including dies for drawing or extruding metal, and rock drilling or earth boring tools:**
	-凿岩或钻探工具：							-Rock drilling or earth boring tools:
8207.1300	--带有金属陶瓷制的工作部件	8	20	17	13	千克		--With working part of cermets
	--其他，包括部件：							--Other, including parts:
8207.1910	---带有天然或合成金钢石、立方氮化硼制的工作部件	8	20	17	13	千克		---With working part of natural or synthetic diamonds or cubic boronnitride
8207.1990	---其他	8	20	17	13	千克		---Other
	-金属拉拔或挤压用模：							-Dies for drawing or extruding metal:
8207.2010	---带有天然或合成金刚石、立方氮化硼制的工作部件	8	20	17	13	千克/套		---With working part of natural or synthetic diamonds or cubic boronnitride
8207.2090	---其他	8	20	17	13	千克/套		---Other
8207.3000	-锻压或冲压工具		20	17	13	千克		-Tools for pressing, stamping or punching
8207.3000暂 01	加工小轿车车身冲压件用的4种关键模具(侧围外板模具、翼子板模具、拼接整体侧围内板模具、拼焊整体侧围加强板模具)	4	20	17	13	千克		Four Special mold stamping for processing cars Body used (mold used for body side, fender, splice whole of inner plate side, welding, splice whole side strengthen plate)
8207.3000暂 02	加工小轿车车身冲压件用的4种特种模具($\sigma b \geq 980N/mm^2$的冷冲压、热成型、内高压成型模具和铝板用模具)	4	20	17	13	千克		Four Special mold stamping for processing cars Body used (used for $\sigma b \geq 980N/mm^2$ kaltpressen, warmformgebung, high pressure formation and aluminium plate)
8207.3000 90	其他锻压或冲压工具	8	20	17	13	千克		Other tools for pressing, stamping or punching
8207.4000	-攻丝工具	8	20	17	13	千克/件		-Tools for tapping or threading
	-钻孔工具，但凿岩及钻探用的除外：							-Tools for drilling, other than for rock drilling:
8207.5010	---带有天然或合成金刚石、立方氮化硼制的工作部件	8	20	17	13	千克/件		---With working part of natural or synthetic diamonds or cubic boronnitride

税则号列	货品名称	最惠(%)	普通	增值税率	出口退税	计量单位	监管条件	Articie Description
8207.5090	---其他	8	20	17	13	千克/件		---Other
	-镗孔或铰孔工具:							-Tools for boring or broaching:
8207.6010	---带有天然或合成金刚石、立方氮化硼制的工作部件	8	20	17	13	千克/件		---With working part of natural or synthetic diamonds or cubic boronnitride
8207.6090	---其他	8	20	17	13	千克/件		---Other
	-铣削工具:							-Tools for milling:
8207.7010	---带有天然或合成金刚石、立方氮化硼制的工作部件	8	20	17	13	千克/件		---With working part of natural or synthetic diamonds or cubic boronnitride
8207.7090	---其他	8	20	17	13	千克/件		---Other
	-车削工具:							-Tools for turning:
8207.8010	---带有天然或合成金刚石、立方氮化硼制的工作部件	8	20	17	13	千克/件		---With working part of natural or synthetic diamonds or cubic boronnitride
8207.8090	---其他	8	20	17	13	千克/件		---Other
	-其他可互换工具:							-Other interchangeable tools:
8207.9010	---带有天然或合成金刚石、立方氮化硼制的工作部件	8	20	17	13	千克/件		---With working part of natural or synthetic diamonds or cubic boronnitride
8207.9090	---其他	8	20	17	13	千克/件		---Other
82.08	**机器或机械器具的刀及刀片:**							**Knives and cutting blades, for machines or for mechanical appliances:**
	-金属加工用:							-For metal working:
	---硬质合金制的:							---Of metal carbides:
8208.1011	----经镀或涂层的	8	20	17	13	千克		----Plated or coated
8208.1019	----其他	8	20	17	13	千克		----Other
8208.1090	---其他	8	20	17	5	千克		---Other
8208.2000	-木器加工用	8	20	17	5	千克		-For wood working
8208.3000	-厨房器具或食品工业机器用	8	20	17	5	千克	A	-For kitchen appliances or for machines used by the food industry
8208.4000	-农业、园艺或林业机器用	8	20	13	5	千克		-For agricultural, horticultural or forestry machines
8208.9000	-其他	8	20	17	5	千克		-Other
82.09	**未装配的工具用金属陶瓷板、杆、刀头及类似品:**							**Plates, sticks, tips and the like for tools, unmounted, of cermets:**
8209.0010	---板	8	20	17	9	千克		---plates
	---条、杆:							---Bar, rod:
8209.0021	----晶粒度<0.8微米	8	20	17	9	千克		----Grain size <0.8um
8209.0029	----其他	8	20	17	9	千克		----Other
8209.0030	---刀头	8	20	17	9	千克		---Tips
8209.0090	---其他	8	20	17	9	千克		---Other
82.10	**用于加工或调制食品或饮料的手动机械器具,重量不超过10公斤:**							**Hand-operated mechanical appliances, weighing 10g or less, used in the preparation, conditioning or serving of food or drink:**
8210.0000	用于加工或调制食品或饮料的手动机械器具,重量不超过10公斤	18	80	17	5	千克	A	Hand-operated mechanical appliances, weighing 10kg or less, used in the preparation, conditioning or serving of food or drink
82.11	**有刃口的刀及其刀片,不论是否有锯齿(包括整枝刀),但税目82.08的刀除外:**							**Knives with cutting blades, serrated or not (including pruning knives), other than knives of heading No. 82.08, and blades therefor:**
8211.1000[暂]	-成套货品	10	80	17	9	千克/套		-Sets of assorted articles
	-其他:							-Other:
8211.9100[暂]	--刃面固定的餐刀	10	80	17	9	千克/把	A	--Table knives having fixed blades
8211.9200	--刃面固定的其他刀	12	80	17	9	千克/把		--Other knives having fixed blades
8211.9300[暂]	--刃面不固定的刀	10	80	17	9	千克/把		--Knives having other than fixed blades
8211.9400	--刀片	14	80	17	9	千克		--Blades
8211.9500	--贱金属制的刀柄	12	80	17	5	千克		--Handles of base metal
82.12	**剃刀及其刀片(包括未分开的刀片条):**							**Razors and razor blades (including razor blade blanks in strips):**
8212.1000	-剃刀	12	80	17	9	千克/把		-Razors
8212.2000	-安全刀片,包括未分开的刀片条	14	80	17	9	千克/片		-Safety razor blades, including razor blade blanks in strips
8212.9000	-其他零件	12	80	17	9	千克		-Other parts

税则号列	货品名称	最惠(%)	普通	增值税率	出口退税	计量单位	监管条件	Article Description
82.13	剪刀、裁缝剪刀及类似品、剪刀片：							**Scissors, tailors' shears and similar shears, and blades therefor:**
8213.0000	剪刀、裁缝剪刀及类似品、剪刀片	12	80	17	9	千克		Scissors, tailors' shears and similar shears, and blades therefor
82.14	其他利口器(例如,理发推剪、屠刀、砍骨刀、切肉刀、切菜刀、裁纸刀);修指甲及修脚用具(包括指甲锉):							**Other articles of cutlery (for example, hair clippers, butchers' or kitchen cleavers, choppers and mincing knives, paper knives); manicure or pedicure sets and instruments (including nail files):**
8214.1000	-裁纸刀、开信刀、改错刀、铅笔刀及其刀片	12	80	17	5	千克		-Paper knives, letter openers, erasing knives, pencil sharpeners and blades therefor
8214.2000	-修指甲及修脚用具(包括指甲锉)	18	90	17	9	千克		-Manicure or pedicure sets and instruments (including nail files)
8214.9000	-其他	18	80	17	9	千克		-Other
8214.9000 10	切菜刀等厨房用利口器	18	80	17	9	千克	A	Kitchen cleavers, choppers mincing knives and other articles of cutlery
8214.9000 90	理发推子等其他利口器	18	80	17	9	千克		Hair clippers and other articles of cutlery
82.15	餐匙、餐叉、长柄勺、漏勺、糕点夹、鱼刀、黄油刀、糖块夹及类似的厨房或餐桌用具:							**Spoons, forks, ladles, skimmers, cakeservers, fish-knives, butter-knives, sugar tongs and similar kitchen or tableware:**
8215.1000	-成套货品,至少其中一件物品是镀贵金属的	18	80	17	5	千克	A	-Sets of assorted articles containing at least one article plated with precious metal
8215.2000	-其他成套货品	18	80	17	9	千克	A	-Other sets of assorted articles
	-其他:							-Other:
8215.9100	--镀贵金属的	18	80	17	5	千克	A	--Plated with precious metal
8215.9900[暂]	--其他	10	80	17	9	千克	A	--Other

第八十三章 贱金属杂项制品

Chapter 83 Miscellaneous articles of base metal

注释：

一、在本章，贱金属零件应与制品一同归类。但税目73.12、73.15、73.17、73.18及73.20的钢铁制品或其他贱金属（第七十四章至第七十六章及第七十八章至第八十一章）制的类似物品不应视为本章制品的零件。

二、税目83.02所称"脚轮"，是指直径（对于有胎的，连胎计算在内，下同）不超过75毫米的或直径虽超过75毫米，但所装轮或胎的宽度必须小于30毫米的脚轮。

Notes:

1. For the purposes of this Chapter, parts of base metal are to be classified with their parent artcles. However, articles of iron or steel of heading Nos. 73.12, 73.15, 73.17, 73.18 or 73.20, or similar articles of other base metal (Chapters 74 to 76 and 78 to 81) are not to be taken as parts of articles of this Chapter.
2. For the purposes of heading No. 83.02, the word "castors" means those having a diameter (including, where appropriate, tyres) not exceeding 75mm, or those having a diameter (including, where appropriate, tyres) exceeding 75mm provided that the width of the wheel or tyre fitted thereto is less than 30mm.

税则号列	货品名称	最惠(%)	普通	增值税率	出口退税	计量单位	监管条件	Article Description
83.01	**贱金属制的锁（钥匙锁、数码锁及电动锁）；贱金属制带锁的扣环及扣环框架；上述锁的贱金属制钥匙：**							**Padlocks and locks (key, combination or electrically operated), of base metal; clasps and frames with clasps, incorporating locks, of base metal; keys for any of the foregoing articles, of base metal:**
8301.1000	-挂锁	14	80	17	9	千克/把		-Padlocks
	-机动车用锁：							-Locks of a kind used for motor vehicles:
8301.2010	---中央控制门锁	10	80	17	13	千克/套		---Central controll door lock
8301.2090	---其他	10	80	17	9	千克/套		---Other
8301.3000	-家具用锁	14	80	17	9	千克/个		-Locks of a kind used for furniture
8301.4000	-其他锁	14	80	17	9	千克/个		-Other locks
8301.5000	-带锁的扣环及扣环框架	14	80	17	9	千克		-Clasps and frames with clasps, incorporating locks
8301.6000	-锁零件	12	80	17	9	千克		-Parts of locks
8301.7000	-钥匙	10	80	17	9	千克		-Keys presented separately
83.02	**用于家具、门窗、楼梯、百叶窗、车厢、鞍具、衣箱、盒子及类似品的贱金属附件及架座；贱金属制帽架、帽钩、托架及类似品；用贱金属做支架的小脚轮；贱金属制的自动闭门器：**							**Base metal mountings, fittings and similar articles suitable for furniture, doors, staircases, windows, blinds, coachwork, saddlery, trunks, chests, caskets, or the like; base metal hat-racks, hat-pegs, brackets and similar fixtures; castors with mountings of base metal; automatic door closers of base metal:**
8302.1000	-铰链（折叶）	10	80	17	5	千克		-Hinges
8302.2000	-小脚轮	12	80	17	9	千克		-Castors
8302.3000	-机动车辆用的其他附件及架座	10	80	17	5	千克		-Other mountings, fittings and similar articles suitable for motor vehicles
	-其他附件及架座：							-Other mountings, fittings and similar articles:
8302.4100	--建筑用	14	80	17	5	千克		--Suitable for buildings
8302.4200	--其他，家具用	12	80	17	5	千克		--Other, suitable for furniture
8302.4900	--其他	12	80	17	5	千克		--Other
8302.5000	-帽架、帽钩、托架及类似品	14	80	17	9	千克		-Hat-racks, hat-pegs, brackets and similar fixtures
8302.6000	-自动闭门器	12	80	17	5	千克/个		-Automatic door closers
83.03	**装甲或加强的贱金属制保险箱、保险柜及保险库的门和带锁保险储存橱、钱箱、契约箱及类似品：**							**Armoured or reinforced safes, strong-boxes and doors and safe deposit lockers for strong-rooms, cash or deed boxes and the like, of base metal:**
8303.0000	装甲或加强的贱金属制保险箱、保险柜及保险库的门和带锁保险储存橱、钱箱、契约箱及类似品	14	50	17	5	千克/个		Armoured or reinforced safes, strong-boxes and doors and safe deposit lockers for strong-rooms, cash or deed boxes and the like, of base metal

税则号列	货　品　名　称	最惠(%)	普通	增值税率	出口退税	计量单位	监管条件	Article Description
83.04	**贱金属制的档案柜、卡片索引柜、文件盘、文件篮、笔盘、公章架及类似的办公用具,但税目94.03的办公室家具除外:**							**Filing cabinets, card-index cabinets, paper trays, paper rests, pen trays, office-stamp stands and similar office or desk equipment, of base metal, other than office furniture of heading No. 94.03:**
8304.0000	贱金属制的档案柜、卡片索引柜、文件盘、文件篮、笔盘、公章架及类似的办公用具,但税目94.03的办公室家具除外	10.5	80	17	5	千克		Filing cabinets, card-index cabinets, paper trays, paper rests, pen trays, office-stamp stands and similar office or desk equipment, of base metal, other than office furniture of heading No. 94.03
83.05	**活页夹、卷宗夹的贱金属附件,贱金属制的信夹、信角、文件夹、索引标签及类似的办公用品;贱金属制的成条钉书钉(例如,供办公室、室内装饰或包装用):**							**Fittings for loose-leaf binders or files, letter clips, letter corners, paper clips, indexing tags and similar office articles, of base metal; staples in strips (for example, for offices, upholstery, packaging), of base metal:**
8305.1000	-活页夹或宗卷夹的附件	10.5	80	17	5	千克		-Fittings for loose-leaf binders of files
8305.2000	-成条订书钉	10.5	80	17	5	千克		-Staples in strips
8305.9000	-其他,包括零件	10.5	80	17	5	千克		-Other, including parts
83.06	**非电动的贱金属铃、钟、锣及类似品;贱金属雕塑像及其他装饰品;贱金属相框或画框及类似框架;贱金属镜子:**							**Bells, gongs and the like, non-electric, of base metal; statuettes and other ornaments, of base metal; photograph, picture or similar frames, of base metal; mirrors of base metal:**
8306.1000	-铃、钟、锣及类似品	8	80	17	5	千克		-Bells, gongs and the like
	-雕塑像及其他装饰品:							-Statuettes and other ornaments:
8306.2100	--镀贵金属的	8	100	17	5	千克		--Plated with precious metal
	--其他:							--Other:
8306.2910	---景泰蓝的	8	100	17	9	千克		---Cloisonne
8306.2990	---其他	8	100	17	13	千克		---Other
8306.3000	-相框、画框及类似框架、镜子	8	100	17	5	千克		-Photograph, picture or similar frames; mirrors
83.07	**贱金属软管,不论是否有附件:**							**Flexible tubing of base metal, with or without fittings:**
8307.1000	-钢铁制	8.4	35	17	5	千克		-Of iron or steel
8307.9000	-其他贱金属制	8.4	35	17	5	千克		-Of other base metal
83.08	**贱金属制的扣、钩、环、眼及类似品,用于衣着、鞋靴、天篷、提包、旅行用品或其他制成品;贱金属制的管形铆钉及开口铆钉;贱金属制的珠子及亮晶片:**							**Clasps, frames with clasps, buckles, buckle-clasps, hooks, eyes, eyelets and the like, of base metal, of a kind used for clothing, footwear, awnings, handbags, travel goods or other made up articles; tubular or bifurcated rivets, of base metal; beads and spangles, of base metal:**
8308.1000	-钩、环及眼	10.5	80	17	9	千克		-Hooks, eyes and eyelets
8308.2000	-管形铆钉及开口铆钉	10.5	80	17	5	千克		-Tubular or bifurcated rivets
8308.9000	-其他,包括零件	10.5	80	17	5	千克		-Other, including parts
83.09	**贱金属制的塞子、盖子(包括冠形瓶塞、螺口盖及倒水塞)、瓶帽、螺口塞、塞子帽、封志及其他包装用附件:**							**Stoppers, caps and lids (including crown corks, screw caps and pouring stoppers), capsules for bottles, threaded bungs, bung covers, seals and other packing accessories, of base metal:**
8309.1000	-冠形瓶塞	18	90	17	5	千克		-Crown corks
8309.9000	-其他	12	80	17	5	千克		-Other
83.10	**贱金属制的标志牌、铭牌、地名牌及类似品、号码、字母及类似标志,但税目94.05的货品除外:**							**Sign-plates, name-plates, address-plates and similar plates, numbers, letters and other symbols, of base metal, excluding those of heading No. 94.05:**
8310.0000	贱金属制的标志牌、铭牌、地名牌及类似品、号码、字母及类似标志,但税目94.05的货品除外	18	80	17	5	千克		Sign-plates, name-plates, address-plates and similar plates, numbers, letters and other symbols, of base metal, excluding those of heading No. 94.05

税则号列	货品名称	最惠(%)	普通	增值税率	出口退税	计量单位	监管条件	Article Description
83.11	**贱金属或硬质合金制的丝、条、管、板、电极及类似品,以焊剂涂面或以焊剂为芯,用于焊接或沉积金属、硬质合金;贱金属粉粘聚而成的丝或条,供金属喷镀用:**							**Wire, rods, tubes, plates, electrodes and similar products, of base metal or of metal carbides, coated or cored with flux material, of a kind used for soldering, brazing, welding or deposition of metal or of metal carbides; wire and rods, of agglomerated base metal powder, used for metal spraying:**
8311.1000	-以焊剂涂面的贱金属制电极,电弧焊用	8	30	17	13	千克		-Coated electrodes of base metal, for electric arc-welding
8311.2000	-以焊剂为芯的贱金属制焊丝,电弧焊用	8	30	17	13	千克		-Cored wire of base metal, for electric arc-welding
8311.3000	-以焊剂涂面或以焊剂为芯的贱金属条或丝,钎焊或气焊用	8	30	17	13	千克		-Coated rods and cored wire, of base metal, for soldering, brazing or welding by flame
8311.9000	-其他	8	30	17	13	千克		-Other

第十六类
机器、机械器具、电气设备及其零件；录音机及放声机、电视图像、声音的录制和重放设备及其零件、附件

SECTION XVI
MACHINERY AND MECHANICAL APPLIANCES; ELECTRICAL EQUIPMENT; PARTS THEREOF; SOUND RECORDERS AND REPRODUCERS, TELEVISION IMAGE AND SOUND RECORDERS AND REPRODUCERS, AND PARTS AND ACCESSORIES OF SUCH ARTICLES

注释：

一、本类不包括：

(一)第三十九章的塑料或税目40.10的硫化橡胶制的传动带、输送带；除硬质橡 胶以外的硫化橡胶制的机器、机械器具、电气器具或其他专门技术用途的物品(税目40.16)；

(二)机器、机械器具或其他专门技术用途的皮革、再生皮革(税目42.05)或毛皮（税目43.03)的制品；

(三)各种材料（例如，第三十九章、第四十章、第四十四章、第四十八章及第十五类的材料)制的筒管、卷轴、纡子、锥形筒管、芯子、线轴及类似品；

(四)提花机及类似机器用的穿孔卡片（例如，归入第三十九章、第四十八章或第十五类的)；

(五)纺织材料制的传动带、输送带或带料(税目59.10)或专门技术用途的其他纺织材料制品(税目59.11)；

(六)税目71.02至71.04的宝石或半宝石(天然、合成或再造）或税目71.16的完全以宝石或半宝石制成的物品，但已加工未装配的唱针用蓝宝石和钻石除外（税目85.22)；

(七)第十五类注释二所规定的贱金属制通用零件(第十五类)及塑料制的类似品(第三十九章)；

(八)钻管(税目73.04)；

(九)金属丝、带制的环形带(第十五类)；

(十)第八十二章或第八十三章的物品；

(十一)第十七类的物品；

(十二)第九十章的物品；

(十三)第九十一章的钟、表及其他物品；

(十四)税目82.07的可互换工具及作为机器零件的刷子(税目96.03)；类似的可互换工具应按其构成工作部件的材料归类(例如，归入第四十章、第四十二章、第四十三章、第四十五章、第五十九章或税目68.04、69.09)；

(十五)第九十五章的物品。

(十六)打字机色带或类似色带，不论是否装轴或装盒(应按其材料属性归类；如已上油或经其他方法处理能着色的，应归入税目96.12)。

二、除本类注释一、第八十四章注释一及第八十五章注释一另有规定的以外，机器零件（不属于税目84.84、85.44、85.45、85.46或85.47所列物品的零件)应按下列规定归类：

Notes:

1. This Section does not cover:

(a) Transmission or conveyor belts or belting, of plastics of Chapter 39, or of vulcanized rubber (heading No. 40. 10); or other articles of a kind used in machinery or mechanical or electrical appliances or for other technical uses, of vulcanized rubber other than hard rubber (heading No. 40. 16);

(b) Articles of leather or of composition leather (heading No. 42. 05) or of furskin (heading No. 43. 03), of a kind used in machinery or mechanical appliances or for other technical uses;

(c) Bobbins, spools, cops, cones, cores, reels or similar supports of any material (for example, Chapter 39, 40, 44 or 48 or Section XV);

(d) Perforated cards for Jacquard or similar machines (for example, Chapter 39 or 48 Section XV);

(e) Transmission or conveyor belts or belting of textile material (heading No. 59. 10) or other articles of textile material for technical uses (heading No. 59. 11);

(f) Precious or semi-precious stones (natural, synthetic or reconstructed) of headings Nos. 71. 02 to 71. 04, or articles wholly of such stones of heading 71. 16, except unmounted worked sapphires and diamonds for styli (heading No. 85. 22);

(g) Parts of general use, as defined in Note 2 to Section XV, of base metal (Section XV), or similar goods of plastics (Chapter 39);

(h) Drill pipe (heading No. 73. 04);

(ij) Endless belts of metal wire or strip (Section XV);

(k) Articles of Chapter 82 or 83;

(L) Articles of Section XVII;

(m) Articles of Chapter 90;

(n) Clocks, watches or other articles of Chapter 91;

(o) Interchangeable tools of headingNo. 82. 07 or brushes of a kind used as parts of machines (heading No. 96. 03), similar interchangable tools are to be classified according to constituent material of their working part (for example in Chapter 40, 42, 43, 45, 59 or heading No. 68. 04, or 69. 09);

(p) Articles of Chapter 95; or

(q) Typewriter or similar ribbons, whether or not on spools or in cartridges (classified according to their constituent material, or in heading No. 96. 12 if inked or otherwise prepared for giving impressions).

2. Subject to Note 1 to this Section, Note 1 to Chapter 84 and Note 1 to Chapter 85, parts of machines (not being parts of the articles of heading No. 84. 84, 85. 44, 85. 45, 85. 46 or 85. 47) are to be classified according to the following rules:

（一）凡在第八十四章、第八十五章的税目（税目84.09、84.31、84.48、84.66、84.73、84.87、85.03、85.22、85.29、85.38及85.48除外）列名的货品，均应归入该两章的相应税目；

（二）专用于或主要用于某一种机器或同一税目的多种机器（包括税目84.79或85.43的机器）的零件，应与该种机器一并归类，或酌情归入税目84.09、84.31、84.48、84.66、84.73、85.03、85.22、85.29或85.38。但能同时主要用于税目85.17和85.25至85.28所列机器的零件，应归入税目85.17；

（三）所有其他零件应酌情归入税目84.09、84.31、84.48、84.66、84.73、85.03、85.22、85.29或85.38，如不能归入上述税目，则应归入税目84.87或85.48。

三、由两部及两部以上机器装配在一起形成的组合式机器，或具有两种及两种以上互补或交替功能的机器，除条文另有规定的以外，应按具有主要功能的机器归类。

四、由不同独立部件（不论是否分开或由管道、传动装置、电缆或其他装置连接）组成的机器（包括机组），如果组合后明显具有一种第八十四章或第八十五章某个税号所列功能，则全部机器应按其功能归入有关税目。

五、上述各注释所称"机器"，是指第八十四章或第八十五章各税目所列的各种机器、设备、装置及器具。

第八十四章
核反应堆、锅炉、机器、机械器具及其零件

注释：

一、本章不包括：

（一）第六十八章的石磨、石碾及其他物品；

（二）陶瓷材料制的机器或器具（例如泵）及供任何材料制的机器或器具用的陶瓷零件（第六十九章）；

（三）实验室用玻璃器（税目70.17）；玻璃制的机器、器具或其他专门技术用途的物品及其零件（税目70.19或70.20）；

（四）税目73.21或73.22的物品或其他贱金属制的类似物品（第七十四章至第七十六章或第七十八章至第八十一章）。

（五）税目85.08的真空吸尘器。

（六）税目85.09的家用电动器具；或税目85.25的数字照相机；

（七）非机动的手工操作地板清扫器（税目96.03）。

二、除第十六类注释三及本章注释九另有规定的以外，如果某种机器或器具既符合税目84.01至84.24或税目84.46中一个或几个税目的规定，又符合税目84.25至84.80中一个或几个税目的规定，则应酌情归入税目84.01至84.24或税目84.86中的相应税目，而不归入税目84.25至84.80中的有关税目。

(a) Parts which are goods included in any of the headings of Chapter 84 or 85 (other than headingsNo. 84.09, 84.31, 84.48, 84.66, 84.73, 84.87, 85.03, 85.22, 85.29, 85.38, and 85.48) are in all cases to be classified in their respective headings;

(b) Other parts, if suitable for use solely or principally with a particular kind of machine, or with a number of machines of the same heading (including a machine of heading No. 84.79 or 85.43) are to be classified with the machines of that kind or in heading No. 84.09, 84.31, 84.48, 84.66, 84.73, 85.03, 85.22, 85.29 or 85.38 as appropriate. However, parts which are equally suitable for use principally with the goods of headings No. 85.17 and 85.25 to 85.28 are to be classified in headingNo. 85.17;

(c) All other parts are to be classified in heading No. 84.09, 84.31, 84.48, 84.66, 84.73, 85.03, 85.22, 85.29 or 85.38 as appropriate or, failing that, in heading No. 84.87 or 85.48.

3. Unless the context otherwise requires, composite machines consisting of two or more machines fitted together to form a whole and other machines adapted for the purpose of performing two or more complementary or alternative functions are to be classified as if consisting only of that component or as being that machine which performs the principal function.

4. Where a machine (including a combination of machines) consists of individual components (whether separate or interconnected by piping, by transmission devices, by electric cables or by other devices) intended to contribute together to a clearly defined function covered by one of the headings in Chapter 84 or Chapter 85, then the whole falls to be classified in the heading appropriate to that function.

5. For the purposes of these Notes, the expression "machine" means any machine, machinery, plant, equipment, apparatus or appliance cited in the headings of Chapter 84 or 85.

Chapter 84
Nuclear reactors, boilers, machinery and mechanical appliances; parts thereof

Notes:

1. This Chapter does not cover:

(a) Millstones, grindstones and other articles of Chapter 68;

(b) Machinery or appliances (for example, pumps) of ceramic material and ceramic parts of machinery or appliances of any material (Chapter 69);

(c) Laboratory glassware (heading No. 70.17); machinery, appliances or other articles for technical uses or parts thereof, of glass (heading No. 70.19 or 70.20);

(d) Articles of heading No. 73.21 or 73.22 or similar articles of other base metals (Chapters 74 to 76 or 78 to 81);

(e) Vacuum cleaners of heading No. 85.08

(f) Electro-mechanical domestic appliances of heading No. 85.09; digital cameras of heading No. 85.25; or

(g) Hand-operated mechanical floor sweepers, not motorized (heading No. 96.03).

2. Subject to the operation of Note 3 to Section XVI and subject to Note9 to this chapter, a machine or appliance which answers to a description in one or more of the headings No. 84.01 to 84.24 or heading 84.46 and at the same time to a description in one or other of the headings Nos. 84.25 to 84.80 is to be classified under the appropriate headings of the former group or under heading 84.86, as the case may be, and not the latter.

但税目 84.19 不包括：
（一）催芽装置、孵卵器或育雏器（税目 84.36）；
（二）谷物调湿机（税目 84.37）；
（三）萃取糖汁的浸提装置（税目 84.38）；
（四）纱线、织物及纺织制品的热处理机器（税目 84.51）；
（五）温度变化（即使必不可少）仅作为辅助功能的机器设备。
税目 84.22 不包括：
（一）缝合袋子或类似品用的缝纫机；
（二）税目 84.72 的办公室用机器。
税目 84.24 不包括：
（一）喷墨印刷（打印）机器（税目 84.43）。
（二）水射流切割机（税目 84.56）。

三、如果用于加工各种材料的某种机床既符合税目 84.56 的规定，又符合税目 84.57、84.58、84.59、84.60、84.61、84.64 或 84.65 的规定，则应归入税目 84.56。

四、税目 84.57 仅适用于可以完成下列不同形式机械操作的金属加工机床，但车床（包括车削中心）除外：
（一）按照机械加工程序从刀具库中自动更换刀具（加工中心）；
（二）同时或顺序地自动使用不同的动力头对固定不动的工件进行加工（单工位组合机床）；
（三）自动将工件送向不同的动力头（多工位组合机床）。

五、（一）税目 84.71 所称“自动数据处理设备”，是指：具有如下功能的机器：
1. 存储处理程序和执行程序直接需要的起码的数据；
2. 按照用户的要求随意编辑程序；
3. 按照用户指令进行算术计算；以及
4. 在运行过程中，可不需人为干预而通过逻辑判断，执行一个处理程序，这个处理程序可改变计算机指令的执行。
（二）自动数据处理设备可以是一套由若干单独部件所组成的系统。
（三）除本条注释（四）及（五）另有规定以外，一个部件如果符合下列所有规定，即可视为自动数据处理系统的一部分：
1. 专用于或主要用于自动数据处理系统；
2. 可以直接或通过一个或几个其他部件同中央处理机相联接；
3. 能够以本系统所使用的方式（代码或信号）接收或传送数据。
自动数据处理设备的部件如果单独报验，应归入税目 84.71
但是，键盘、X－Y 座标输入装置及盘（片）式存储部件，只要符合上述注释（三）2 及（三）3 所列的规定，应一律作为税目 84.71 的部件归类；
（四）税目 84.71 不包括单独报验的下述设备，即使该设备符合上述注释五（三）的所有规定：

HeadingNo. 84. 19 does not, however, cover:
(a) Germination plant, incubators or brooders (headingNo. 84. 36);
(b) Grain dampening machines (heading No. 84. 37);
(c) Diffusing apparatus for sugar juice extraction (headingNo. 84. 38);
(d) Machinery for the heat-treatment of textile yarns, fabrics or made up textile articles (heading No. 84. 51); or
(e) Machinery or plant, designed for mechanical operation, in which a change of temperature, even if necessary, is subsidiary.
Heading No. 84. 22 does not cover:
(a) Sewing machines for closing bags or similar containers ;
(b) Office machinery of heading No. 84. 72.
Heading No. 84. 24 does not cover:
(a) Ink-jet printing machines (heading No. 84. 43).
(b) Water-jet cutting machines (heading No. 84. 56).

3. A machine-tool for working any material which answers to a description in heading No. 84. 56 and at the same time to a description in heading Nos. 84. 57, 84. 58, 84. 59, 84. 60, 84. 61, 84. 64 or 84. 65 is to be classified in heading No. 84. 56.

4. Heading No. 84. 57 applies only to machine-tools for working metal other than lathes (including turning centres), which can carry out different types of machining operations either:
(a) by automatic tool change from a magazine or the like in conformity with a machining programme (machining centres),
(b) by the automatic use, simultaneously or sequentially, of different unit heads working on a fixed position workpiece (unit construction machines, single station), or
(c) by the automatic transfer of the workpiece to different unit heads (multi-station transfer machines).

5. (a) For the purposes of heading No. 84. 71, the expression "automatic data processing machines" means machines capable of:
(1) Storing the processing program or programs and at least the data immediately necessary for the execution of the program;
(2) being freely programmed in accordance with the requirements of the user;
(3) performing arthmetical computations specified by the user; and,
(4) executing, without human intervention, a processing program which requires them to modify their execution, by logical decision during the processing run;
(b) Automatic data processing machines may be in the form of systems consisting of a variable number of separate units.
(c) Subject to paragraph (d) and (e) below, a unit is to be rgearded as being a part of an automatic data processing system if it meets all of the following condition
(1) It is of a kind solehy or praincipally used in an automatic data processing system;
(2) It is connectable to the central processing unit either directly or through one or more other units; and
(3) It is able to accept or delirer data in afrom (codes or signals), which can be used by the system.
Separatly presented units of an automatic data processing malhine are to be classified heading 84. 71.
However keybards X－Y co-ordinate input devices and disk storage units which satisfy the cond it ions of paragraphs (c)(2) and (c)(3) above are in all cases to be dassified as anits of heading No. 84. 71
(d) Heading 84. 71 does not cover the following when prestented separateby eren if they meet all of conditions set forth in Notes (c) above:

1. 打印机、复印机、传真机，不论是否组合式；
2. 发送或接收声音、图像或其他数据的设备，包括无线或有线网络；（例如，局域网或广域网）通信设备
3. 扬声器及传声器（麦克风）；
4. 电视摄相机、数字照相机及视频摄录一体机；
5. 监视器及投影机，未装有电视接收装置。

（五）装有自动数据处理设备或与自动数据处理设备连接使用，但却从事数据处理以外的某项专门功能的机器，应按其功能归入相应的税目，对于无法按功能归类的，应归入未列名税目。

六、税目84.82还包括最大直径及最小直径与标称直径相差均不超过1%或0.05毫米（以相差数值较小的为准）的抛光钢珠，其他钢珠归入税目73.26。

七、具有一种以上用途的机器在归类时，其主要用途可作为唯一的用途对待。除本章注释二、第十六类注释三另有规定的以外，凡任何税目都未列明其主要用途的机器，以及没有哪一种用途是主要用途的机器，均应归入税目84.79。税目84.79还包括将金属丝、纺织纱线或其他各种材料以及它们的混合材料制成绳、缆的机器（例如，捻股机、绞扭机、制缆机）。

八、税目84.70所称"袖珍式"，仅适用于外形尺寸不超过170毫米×100毫米×45毫米的机器。

九、（一）第八十五章注释八（一）及（二）同样适用于本条注释及税目84.86中所称的"半导体器件"及"集成电器"。但本条注释及税目84.86所称"半导体器件"，也包括光敏半导体器件及发光二极管。

（二）本条注释和税目84.86所称"平板显示器的制造"，包括将各层基片制造成平板，但不包括玻璃的制造或将印刷电路板或其他电子元件装配在平板上。所称"平板显示"不包括阴极射线管技术。

（三）税目84.86也包括专用于或主要用于下列用途的机器及装置：
1. 制造或修补掩膜版及刻线；
2. 组装半导体器件或集成电路；
3. 升降、搬运、装卸单晶柱、圆片、半导体器件、集成电路及平板显示器。

（四）除十六类注释一及第八十四章注释一另有规定的以外，符合税目84.86规定的机器及装置，应归入该税目而不归入本协调制度的其他税目。

子目注释：

一、子目号8471.49所称"系统"，是指各部件符合第八十四章注释五（三）所列条件，并且至少由一个中央处理部件、一个输入部件（例如，键盘或扫描仪）及一个输出部件（例如，视频显示器或打印机）组成的自动数据处理设备。

(1) printers copying machines facsimile machines whether or not combined.
(2) Apparats for the transmission or reception of voice images or other data including apparatus for communication in a wired or wireless network (Such as alocal or wide area netaork)
(3) Loud speakers and microphones
(4) Television camera, digital cemera and video camera recorders
(5) Monitors and projectors not incorp orating television reception apparatus recezvers.

(e) Machines performing a specific function other than data processing and incorporating or working in conjunction with an automatic data processing machine are to be classified in the headings appropriate to their respective functions or, failing that, in residual headings.

6. Heading No. 84.82 applies, *inter alia*, to polished steel balls, the maximum and minimum diameters of which do not differ from the nominal diameter by more than 1% or by more than 0.05mm, whichever is less. Other steel balls are to be classified in heading No. 73.26.

7. A machine which is used for more than one purpose is, for the purposes of classification, to be treated as if its principal purpose were its sole purpose. Subject to Note 2 to this Chapter and Note 3 to Section XVI, a machine, the principal purpose of which is not described in any heading or for which no one purpose is the principal purpose, unless the context otherwise requires, is to be classified in heading No. 84.79. Heading No. 84.79 also covers machines for making rope or cable (for example, stranding, twisting or cabling machines) from metal wire, textile yarn or any other material or from a combination of such materials.

8. For the purposes of headingNo. 84.70, the term "pocket-size" applies only to machines the dimensions of which do not exceed 170mm × 100mm × 45mm.

9 (a) Notes 8(a) and 8(b) to chapter 85 also apply with respect to the expressions "semicoiductor devices and electonic integrated circuits" respectively, as used in this Note and in heading 84.86. However for the parposes of this Note and of heading 84.86. the expression semicondutor devices also covers photo sensitive semicondactor devices and light emitting diodes.

(b) For the purposes of this Note and of heading 84.86 the expression "manufacture of flat pane displays" covers the fabrication of substrtes into aftat panel. It does not cover the manufacture of glass or the assembly of plinted circuit boards or other electronie components onto the flat panel The expression "flat panel display" does not cover calhoderay tube technology.

(c) Heading No. 84.86 also includes machines apparatus solely or principally of a kind used for
(1) The manafactre or rapair of masks and retides
(2) Assemb semiconductor devices or electronic: integrated circuits; and
(3) Lifting handing loadingor unlading of boules, wafers, semicondu ctor devices electonic integrated circuits and flat panel displays.

(d) Subject to Notel to section XVI and Note I to chapter 84. machines and apparatus answring to the description in heading 84.86 are to be classfied in that heading and in no other heading of the Nomenclature.

Subheading Notes:

1. For the purposes of subheading No. 8471.49, the term "systems" means automatic data processing machines whose units satisfy the conditions laid down in Note 5 (b) to Chapter 84 and which comprise at least a central processing unit, one input unit (for example: a keyboard or a scanner), and one output unit (for example: a visual display unit or a printer).

二、子目号 8482.40 仅包括滚柱直径相同，最大不超过 5 毫米，且长度至少是直径三倍的圆滚柱轴承，滚柱的两端可以磨圆。

2. Subheading No. 8482.40 applies only to bearings with cylindrical rollers of a uniform diameter not exceeding 5mm and having a length which is at least three times the diameter. The ends of the rollers may be rounded.

税则号列	货品名称	最惠(%)	普通	增值税率	出口退税	计量单位	监管条件	Article Description
84.01	核反应堆；核反应堆的未辐照燃料元件（释热元件）；同位素分离机器及装置：							**Nuclear reactors; fuel elements (cartridges), non-irradiated, for nuclear reactors; machinery and apparatus for isotopic separation:**
8401.1000	-核反应堆	2	8	17	17	千克	3	-Nuclear reactors
8401.2000	-同位素分离机器、装置及其零件	1	8	17	17	个/千克	3	-Machinery and apparatus for isotopic separation, and parts thereof
	-未辐照燃料元件（释热元件）：							-Fuel elements (cartridges), non-irradiated:
8401.3010	---未辐照燃料元件	2	8	17	17	千克		---Fuel elements, non-irrdadiated
8401.3090	---未辐照燃料元件的零件	1	8	17	17	千克		---Parts for fuel elements non-irradiated
	-核反应堆零件：							-Parts of nuclear reactors:
8401.4010	---未辐照相关组件	1	8	17	17	千克		---Non-irradiated Associated Assembly
8401.4020	---堆内构件	1	8	17	17	千克	3	---Reactor internals
8401.4090	---其他	1	8	17	17	千克		---Other
8401.4090 10	核反应堆压力容器（包括其顶板）（专门设计或制造来用于容纳核反应堆的堆芯）	1	8	17	17	千克	3	Pressure vessels for nuclear reactors (including top slabs) specially designed or produced to hold the reactor core of the nuclear reactors
8401.4090 20	核反应堆控制棒和设备（专用于核反应堆裂变控制棒、支承结构或悬吊结构等）	1	8	17	17	千克	3	Control rods and devices of nuclear reactors (fission control rod and support and suspension structures thereof, specified for nuclear reactors)
8401.4090 30	核反应堆压力管（专用于容纳核燃料元件和一次冷却剂的，压力 >5.1MPa）	1	8	17	17	千克	3	Pressure tubes of nuclear reactors (specified for holding fuel elements or primary coolants, pressure >5.1MPa)
8401.4090 90	其他核反应堆零件	1	8	17	17	千克		Other parts of nuclear reactors
84.02	蒸汽锅炉（能产生低压水蒸汽的集中供暖用的热水锅炉除外）；过热水锅炉：							**Steam or other vapour generating boilers (other than central heating hot water boilers capable also of producting low pressure steam); superheated water boilers:**
	-蒸汽锅炉：							-Steam or other vapour generating boilers:
	--蒸发量超过 45 吨/时的水管锅炉：							--Watertube boilers with a steam production exceeding 45t per hour:
8402.1110	---蒸发量在 900 吨/时及以上的发电用锅炉	3	11	17	17	台/千克	6A	---Boilers for generating electricity with a steam production 900t or more per hour
8402.1190	---其他	14	35	17	17	台/千克	6A	---Other
8402.1200	--蒸发量不超过 45 吨/时的水管锅炉	5	35	17	17	台/千克		--Watertube boilers with a steam production not exceeding 45t per hour
8402.1200 10	纸浆厂废料锅炉（蒸发量≤45 吨/时蒸汽水管锅炉）	5	35	17	17	台/千克	6A	Waster material boiler of pulp mill (steam water tube boilers with their evaporation≤45tons/hour)
8402.1200 90	其他蒸发量未超 45 吨/时水管锅炉	5	35	17	17	台/千克	6A	Other wate tube boilers with the evaporation ≤45tons/hour
8402.1900	--其他蒸汽锅炉，包括混合式锅炉	5	35	17	17	台/千克	6A	--Other vapour generating boilers, including hybrid boilers
8402.2000	-过热水锅炉	16	35	17	17	台/千克	6A	-Super-heated water boilers
8402.9000	-零件	2	11	17	17	千克		-Parts
84.03	集中供暖用的热水锅炉，但税目 84.02 的货品除外：							**Central heating boilers other than those of headingNo. 84.02:**
	--锅炉：							--Boilers:
8403.1010	---家用型	10	80	17	17	台/千克	6A	---Household type
8403.1090	---其他	10	80	17	17	台/千克	6A	---Other
8403.9000	-零件	6	80	17	17	千克		-Parts

税则号列	货 品 名 称	最惠(%)	普通	增值税率	出口退税	计量单位	监管条件	Article Description
84.04	税目84.02或84.03所列锅炉的辅助设备(例如,节热器、过热器、除灰器、气体回收器);水蒸汽或其他蒸汽动力装置的冷凝器:							**Auxiliary plant for use with boilers of heading No. 84.02 or 84.03 (for example, economizers, super-heaters, soot removers, gas recoverers); condensers for steam or other vapour power units:**
	-税目84.02或84.03所列锅炉的辅助设备:							-Auxiliary plant for use with boilers of headingNo. 84.02 or 84.03:
8404.1010	---税目84.02所列锅炉的辅助设备	7	35	17	17	千克	6A	---For use with boilers of headingNo. 84.02
8404.1020	---税目84.03所列锅炉的辅助设备	10	80	17	17	千克	6A	---For use with boilers of headingNo. 84.03
8404.2000	-水蒸汽或其他蒸汽动力装置的冷凝器	14	35	17	17	千克	6A	-Condensers for steam or other vapour power units
	-零件:							-Parts:
8404.9010	---子目8404.1020所列设备的零件	10	80	17	17	千克		---Of the auxiliary plant of subheading No. 8404.1020
8404.9090	---其他	7	35	17	17	千克		---Other
84.05	煤气发生器,不论有无净化器;乙炔发生器及类似的水解气体发生器,不论有无净化器:							**Producer gas or water gas generators, with or without their purifiers; acetylene gas generators and similar water process gas generators, with or without their purifiers:**
8405.1000	-煤气发生器,不论有无净化器;乙炔发生器及类似的水解气体发生器,不论有无净化器	14	30	17	17	千克	A	-Producer gas or water gas generators, with or without their purifiers; acetylene gas generators and similar water process gas generators, with or without their purifiers
8405.9000	-零件	8	30	17	17	千克		-Parts
84.06	汽轮机:							**Steam turbines and other vapour turbines:**
8406.1000	-船舶动力用汽轮机	5	35	17	17	台/千瓦		-Turbines for marine propulsion
	-其他汽轮机:							-Other turbines:
	--输出功率超过40兆瓦的:							--Of an output exceeding 40 MW:
8406.8110	---输出功率不超过100兆瓦的	5	35	17	17	台/千瓦		---Of an output not exceeding 100 MW
8406.8120	---输出功率超过100兆瓦,但不超过350兆瓦的	5	35	17	17	台/千瓦		---Of an output exceeding 100 MW but not exceeding 350 MW
8406.8130	---输出功率超过350兆瓦的	6	11	17	17	台/千瓦		---Of an output exceeding 350 MW
8406.8200	--输出功率不超过40兆瓦的	5	35	17	17	台/千瓦	O	--Of an output not exceeding 40 MW
8406.9000	-零件	2	11	17	17	千克		-Parts
84.07	点燃往复式或旋转式活塞内燃发动机:							**Spark-ignition reciprocating or rotary internal combustion piston engines:**
	-航空器发动机:							-Aircraft engines:
8407.1010[暂]	---输出功率不超过298千瓦	1	11	17	17	台/千瓦	6	---Of an output not exceeding 298kW
8407.1020[暂]	---输出功率超过298千瓦	1	11	17	15	台/千瓦	6	---Of an output exceeding 298kW
	-船舶发动机:							-Marine propulsion engines:
8407.2100	--舷外发动机	8	35	17	17	台/千瓦	6	--Outboard motors
8407.2900	--其他	8	20	17	17	台/千瓦	6	--Other
	-用于第八十七章所列车辆的往复式活塞发动机:							-Reciprocating piston engines of a kind used for the propulsion of vehicles of Chapter 87:
8407.3100	---气缸容量(排气量)不超过50毫升	10	35	17	15	台/千瓦	y4xA6	---Of a cylinder capacity not exceeding 50cc
8407.3200	--气缸容量(排气量)超过50毫升,但不超过250毫升	10	35	17	15	台/千瓦	y4xA6	--Of a cylinder capacity exceeding 50cc but not exceeding 250cc
8407.3300	--气缸容量(排气量)超过250毫升,但不超过1000毫升	10	70	17	15	台/千瓦	AO6	--Of a cylinder capacity exceeding 250cc but not exceeding 1000cc
	--气缸容量(排气量)超过1000毫升:							--Of a cylinder capacity exceeding 1000cc:
8407.3410	---气缸容量(排气量)超过1000毫升,但不超过3000毫升	10	70	17	17	台/千瓦	A6O	---Of a cylinder capacity exceeding 1000cc but not exceeding 3000cc

税则号列	货　品　名　称	最惠(%)	普通	增值税率	出口退税	计量单位	监管条件	Article Description
8407.3420	---气缸容量(排气量)超过3000毫升	10	35	17	17	台/千瓦		---Of a cylinder capacity exceeding 3000cc
8407.3420 10	排气量≥5.9升的天然气发动机(第87章所列车辆用的点燃往复式活塞发动机)	10	35	17	17	台/千瓦	A6O	Natural gas engines with displacement≥5.9L(spark – ignition reciprocating piston engines for the vehicles listed in Chapter 87)
8407.3420 90	其他排气量超3000cc车用往复式活塞引擎(第87章所列车辆用的点燃往复式活塞发动机)	10	35	17	17	台/千瓦	A6O	Other vehicle use reciprocating piston engines with displacement > 3000cc(spark – ignition reciprocating piston engines for the vehicles listed in Chapter 87)
	-其他发动机:							-Other engines:
8407.9010	---沼气发动机	12	35	17	17	台/千瓦	6	---Friedamp engines
8407.9090	---其他		35	17	17	台/千瓦		---Other
8407.9090 10	转速<3600r/min汽油发动机(发电机用)	18	35	17	17	台/千瓦	O6	Speed < 3600r/min gasoline engine (generator)
8407.9090 20	转速<4650r/min汽油发动机(品目8426、8428–8430所列机械用)	18	35	17	17	台/千瓦	O6	Speed < 4650r/min gasoline engine (heading 8426, 8428 – 8430 listed machinery)
8407.9090[暂] 31	叉车用汽油发动机(800转/分≤转速≤3400转/分)(立式输出轴汽油发动机除外)	9	35	17	17	台/千瓦	O6	Gasoline engine forklift (800 rpm is less than or equal to the speed below 3400RPM) (except for vertical output shaft of the gasoline engine)
8407.9090 39	其他转速<4650转/分汽油发动机(品目84.27所列机械用,立式输出轴汽油发动机除外)	18	35	17	17	台/千瓦	O6	Other speed <4650 RPM gasoline engine (heading 84.27 column machinery, vertical output shaft of the gasoline engine except)
8407.9090[暂] 40	立式输出轴汽油发动机(非第八十七章所列车辆用其他往复式活塞发动机)	9	35	17	17	台/千瓦	6	Vertical output shaft of the gasoline engine (the eighty – seventh chapter car trainnon other reciprocating piston engines)
8407.9090 90	其他往复或旋转式活塞内燃引擎(非第87章所列车辆用其他点燃往复式或旋转式活塞发动机)	18	35	17	17	台/千瓦	6	Other reciprocating or rotary internal combustion piston engines(spark-ignition reciprocating or rotary piston engines for the vehicles not listed in Chapter 87)
84.08	压燃式活塞内燃发动机(柴油或半柴油发动机):							**Compression-ignition internal combustion piston engines (diesel or semi-diesel engines):**
8408.1000	-船舶发动机	5	11	17	17	台/千瓦	O6	-Marine propulsion engines
	-用于第八十七章所列车辆的发动机:							-Engines of a kind used for the propulsion of vehicles of Chapter 87:
8408.2010	---输出功率在132.39千瓦(180马力)及以上		14	17	17	台/千瓦		---Of an output of 132.39kW (180HP) or more
8408.2010[暂] 01	输出功率在441千瓦及以上的柴油发动机(600马力)	4	14	17	17	台/千瓦	O6	Diesel genines, output power≥441kW(600HP)
8408.2010 10	功率≥132.39kW拖拉机用柴油机	9	14	17	17	台/千瓦	6	Diesel engines for tractors, output power≥132.39kW
8408.2010 90	功率≥132.39kW其他用柴油机[指87章车辆用压燃式活塞内燃发动机(132.39kW=180马力)]	9	14	17	17	台/千瓦	O6	Other diesel engines, output power≥132.39kW(refers to compression – ignition internal combustion piston engines for the vehicles listed in Chaper 87)
8408.2090	---其他		35			台/千瓦		---Other
8408.2090 10	功率<132.39千瓦拖拉机用柴油机	25	35	13	13,17	台/千瓦	6	Diesel engines for tractors, output power < 132.39kW
8408.2090[暂] 20	升功率≥50千瓦,输出功率<132.39千瓦的轿车用柴油发动机	15	35	17	15	台/千瓦	60	L power more than 50 kilowatts, diesel engine power output of132.39 kilowatts of car "
8408.2090 90	功率<132.39千瓦其他用柴油机(指第87章车辆用压燃式活塞内燃发动机)	25	35	17	15	台/千瓦	60	Other diesel engines, output power < 132.39kw (refers to compression – ignition internal combustion piston engines for the vehicles listed in Chapter 87)
	-其他发动机:							-Other engines:
8408.9010	---机车发动机	6	11	17	17	台/千瓦	O6	---Locomotive engines
	---其他:							---Other:
8408.9091	----输出功率不超过14千瓦	5	35		13	台/千瓦		----Of an output not exceeding 14kW

税则号列	货品名称	最惠(%)	普通	增值税率	出口退税	计量单位	监管条件	Article Description
8408.9091 11	功率≤14千瓦农业用单缸柴油机[非87章车辆用压燃式活塞内燃发动机(14kW=19.05马力)]	5	35	13	13	台/千瓦	6	Single-cylinder diesel engines for agricultural use, output power≤14kW (19.05PS) (other than compression-ignition internal combustion piston engines for the vehicles of chapter 87)
8408.9091 19	功率≤14千瓦农业用柴油发动机[非87章车辆用压燃式活塞内燃发动机(14千瓦=19.05马力)]	5	35	17	13	台/千瓦	6	Diesel engines for agricultural use, output power≤14kW (19.05PS) (other than compression-ignition internal combustion piston engines for the vehicles of chapter 87)
8408.9091 91	功率≤14千瓦其他用单缸柴油机[非87章车辆用压燃式活塞内燃发动机(14千瓦=19.05马力)]	5	35	17	13	台/千瓦	6	Single-cyclinder diesel engines for other use, output power≤14kW (19.05PS), (other than compression-ignition internal combustion piston engines for the vehicles of chapter 87)
8408.9091 99	功率≤14千瓦其他用柴油发动机[非87章车辆用压燃式活塞内燃发动机(14千瓦=19.05马力)]	5	35	17	13	台/千瓦	6	Other diesel engines, output power ≤ 14kW (19.05PS) (other than compression-ignition internal combustion piston engines for the vehicles of chapter 87)
8408.9092	----输出功率超过14千瓦,但小于132.39千瓦(180马力)	8.4	35			台/千瓦		----Of an output exceeding 14kW but not exceeding 132.39kW(180PS)
8408.9092 10	转速<4650r/min柴油发动机,14千瓦<功率<132.39千瓦(税号8426-8430所列工程机械用)	8.4	35	17	17	台/千瓦	60	Diesel engines, rotational speed < 4650 r/min, 14kW < output power < 132.39 kW (for engineering machinery listed in heading No. 8426 to 8430)
8408.9092 20	14千瓦<功率<132.39千瓦的农业用柴油机[非87章车辆用压燃式活塞内燃发动机(1千瓦=1.36马力)]	8.4	35	13	13,17	台/千瓦	6	Diesel engines for agricutural use, 14kW < output powder < 132.39kW (compression - ignition internal combustion piston engines for the vehicles not listed in Chapter87) (1kW = 1.36PS)
8408.9092 90	14千瓦<功率<132.39千瓦的其他用柴油机[非87章车辆用压燃式活塞内燃发动机(1千瓦=1.36马力)]	8.4	35	17	17	台/千瓦	6	Diesel engine for other use, 14kW < output powder < 132.39kW (compression - ignition internal combustion piston engines for the vehicles not listed in Chapter87) (1kW = 1.36PS)
8408.9093	----输出功率在132.39千瓦(180马力)及以上	5	14		17	台/千瓦		----Of an output of 132.39KW (180HP) or more
8408.9093 10	功率≥132.39千瓦的农业用柴油机[非87章用压燃式活塞内燃发动机(132.39千瓦=180马力)]	5	14	13	17	台/千瓦	6	Diesel engines for agricutural use, output powder≥132.39kW (180PS) (compression - ignition internal combustion piston engines for the vehicles not listed in Chapter 87)
8408.9093 90	功率≥132.39千瓦其他用柴油发动机[非87章用压燃式活塞内燃发动机(132.39千瓦=180马力)]	5	14	17	17	台/千瓦	O6	Diesel engine for other use, output powder≥132.39kW (180PS) (compression - ignition internal combustion piston engines for the vehicles not listed in Chapter 87)
84.09	专用于或主要用于品目**84.07**或**84.08**所列发动机的零件:							**Parts suitable for use solely or principally with the engines of headingNo. 84.07 or 84.08:**
8409.1000	-航空器发动机用	2	11	17	17	千克		-For aircraft engines
	-其他:							-Other:
	--专用于或主要用于点燃式活塞内燃发动机的:							--Suitable for use solely or principally with spark-ignition internal combustion piston engines:
8409.9110	---船舶发动机用	6	17	17	17	千克		---For marine propulsion engines
	---其他:							---Other:
8409.9191	----电控燃油喷射装置	5	35	17	17	千克/套	O	----Electric fuel injection devices
8409.9199	----其他	5	35	17	15,17	千克		----Other
8409.9199 20	废气再循环(EGR)装置(专用或主要用于内燃发动机)	5	35	17	15,17	千克		Exhaust gas recycling apparatuses (EGR) (suitable for use solely or principally with combustion piston engines)
8409.9199 30	连杆(专用或主要用于内燃发动机)	5	35	17	15,17	千克		Links (connecting rods) (suitable for use solely or principally with combustion piston engines)
8409.9199 40	喷嘴(专用或主要用于内燃发动机)	5	35	17	15,17	千克		Nozzles (suitable for use solely or principally with combustion piston engines)

税则号列	货品名称	最惠(%)	普通	增值税率	出口退税	计量单位	监管条件	Article Description
8409.9199 50	气门摇臂(专用或主要用于内燃发动机)	5	35	17	15,17	千克		Valve rockers arms(suitable for use solely or principally with combustion piston engines)
8409.9199 90	其他点燃式活塞内燃发动机用零件	5	35	17	15,17	千克		Other parts of spark-ignition internal combustion piston engines
	--其他:							--Other:
8409.9910	---船舶发动机用	5	11	17	17	千克		---For marine propulsion engines
8409.9920	---机车发动机用	2	11	17	17	千克		---For locomotive engines
	---其他:							---Other:
8409.9991	----输出功率在132.39千瓦(180马力)及以上的发动机用	2	11	17	17	千克		----For engines with an output of 132.39KW (180HP) or more
8409.9999	----其他		35	17	17	千克		----Other
8409.9999暂 01	电控柴油喷射装置(指编号8408所列的其他发动机用)	5	35	17	17	千克	O	Electronically controlled diesel injection systems (other engines listed in Heading No. 84.08)
8409.9999 90	其他发动机的专用零件(指编号8407或8408所列的其他发动机)	8.4	35	17	17	千克		Special parts for other engines(other engines listed in Heding No. 84.07 or 84.08)
84.10	**水轮机、水轮及其调节器:**							**Hydraulic turbines, water wheels, and regulators therefor:**
	-水轮机及水轮:							-Hydraulic turbines and water wheels:
8410.1100	--功率不超过1000千瓦	10	35	17	17	台/千克		--Of a power not exceeding 1000KW
8410.1200	--功率超过1000千瓦,但不超过10000千瓦	10	35	17	17	台/千克		--Of a power exceeding 1000KW but not exceeding 10000KW
	--功率超过10000千瓦:							--Of a power exceeding 10000KW:
8410.1310	---功率超过30000千瓦的冲击式水轮机及水轮	10	35	17	17	台/千克		---Impulse hydraulic turbines and water wheels of a power exceeding 30000 kW
8410.1320	---功率超过35000千瓦的贯流式水轮机及水轮	10	35	17	17	台/千克		---Radial hydraulic turbines and water wheels of a power exceeding 35000 kW
8410.1330	---功率超过200000千瓦的水泵水轮机及水轮	10	35	17	17	台/千克		---Pumping hydraulic turbines and water wheels of a power exceeding 200000kW
8410.1390	---其他	10	35	17	17	台/千克		---Other
	-零件,包括调节器:							-Parts, including regulators:
8410.9010	---调节器	6	35	17	17	千克/套		---Regulators
8410.9090	---其他	6	35	17	17	千克		---Other
84.11	**涡轮喷气发动机,涡轮螺桨发动机及其他燃气轮机:**							**Turbo-jets, turbo-propellers and other gas turbines:**
	-涡轮喷气发动机:							-Turbo-jets:
	--推力不超过25千牛顿:							--Of a thrust not exceeding 25kN:
8411.1110	---涡轮风扇发动机	1	11	17	17	台	3	---Turbofan engines
8411.1190	---其他	1	11	17	17	台		---Other
	--推力超过25千牛顿:							--Of a thrust exceeding 25kN:
8411.1210	---涡轮风扇发动机	1	11	17	17	台	3	---Turbofan engines
8411.1290	---其他	1	11	17	17	台		---Other
8411.1290 10	小型燃烧率高轻型涡轮喷气发动机(推力大于或等于90千牛顿的涡轮喷气发动机)	1	11	17	17	台	3	Minitype turbo - jets with high combustion rate(turo-jets with propulsive force≥90kN)
8411.1290 90	其他涡轮喷气发动机(推力超过25kN)	1	11	17	17	台		Other turbo-jets(propulsive force >25kN)
	-涡轮螺桨发动机:							-Turbo-propellers:
8411.2100	--功率不超过1100千瓦	2	11	17	17	台/千瓦		--Of a power not exceeding 1100kW
	--功率超过1100千瓦:							--Of a power exceeding 1100kW:
8411.2210	---功率超过1100千瓦,但不超过2238千瓦	2	11	17	17	台/千瓦		---Of a power exceeding 1100kW but not exceeding 2238kW
8411.2220	---功率超过2238千瓦,但不超过3730千瓦	2	11	17	17	台/千瓦		---Of a power exceeding 2238kW but not exceeding 3730kW
8411.2230	---功率超过3730千瓦	2	11	17	17	台/千瓦		---Of a power exceeding 3730kW
	-其他燃气轮机:							-Other gas turbines:
8411.8100	--功率不超过5000千瓦		35	17	17	台/千瓦		--Of a power not exceeding 5000kW
8411.8100暂 01	涡轮轴航空发动机(功率≤5000kw)	1	35	17	17	台/千瓦		Turbine shaft aeroengine(power≤5000kw)
8411.8100 90	功率≤5000kw的其他燃气轮机	15	35	17	17	台/千瓦		

税则号列	货品名称	最惠(%)	普通	增值税率	出口退税	计量单位	监管条件	Article Description
8411.8200	--功率超过5000千瓦	3	35	17	17	台/千瓦	O	--Of a power exceeding 5000kW
	-零件：							-Parts:
8411.9100	--涡轮喷气发动机或涡轮螺桨发动机用	1	11	17	17	千克		--Of turbo-jets or turbo-propellers
	--其他：							--Other:
8411.9910	---涡轮轴发动机用		35	17	17	千克		---Of turbine shaft engines
8411.9910暂 01	涡轮轴航空发动机用零件	0	35	17	17	千克		Parts of turbine shaft aeroengine
8411.9910 90	其他涡轮轴发动机用零件	5	35	17	17	千克		Other part of turbine shaft engines
8411.9990	---其他	5	35	17	17	千克		---Other
84.12	其他发动机及动力装置：							**Other engines and motors:**
	-喷气发动机，但涡轮喷气发动机除外：							-Jet engines other than turbo-jets:
8412.1010	---航空器及航天器用	3	11	17	17	台/千克		---For aircraft or spacecraft
8412.1010 10	冲压喷气发动机（包括超燃冲压喷气发动机）	3	11	17	17	台/千克	3	Ramjet engines (including scramjet engines)
8412.1010 20	脉冲喷气发动机	3	11	17	17	台/千克	3	Pulse jet engines
8412.1010 30	组合循环发动机	3	11	17	17	台/千克	3	Combined cycle engines
8412.1010 90	其他航空、航天器用喷气发动机（涡轮喷气发动机除外）	3	11	17	17	台		Other jet engines (other than turbo-jets) for aircraft or spacecraft
8412.1090	---其他	10	35	17	17	台/千克		---Other
	-液压动力装置：							-Hydraulic power engines and motors:
8412.2100	--直线作用（液压缸）的	12	35	17	17	台/千克		--Linear acting (cylinders)
	--其他：							--Other:
8412.2910	---液压马达	10	35	17	17	台/千克		---Hydraulic motors
8412.2990	---其他		35	17	17	台/千克	O	---Other
8412.2990暂 01	抓桩器（抱桩器）	7	35	17	17	台/千克	O	Catch pile device
8412.2990 90	其他液压动力装置	14	35	17	17	台/千克	O	Other hydrulic power engines and motors
8412.3100	--直线作用（气压缸）的		35	17	17	台/千克		--Linear acting (cylinders)
8412.3100暂 01	三坐标测量机用平衡气缸	7	35	17	17	台/千克		Balance cylinder for three – dimensional measuring machine
8412.3100 90	其他直线作用的气压动力装置（气压缸）	14	35	17	17	台/千克		Other pneumatic power engines and motors of straightening (cylinders)
8412.3900	--其他	14	35	17	17	台/千克	O	--Other
8412.8000	-其他	10	35	17	17	台/千克		-Other
8412.8000 10	液体火箭发动机（推力大于或等于90千牛顿可贮存推进剂的）	10	35	17	17	台/千克	3	Liquid-propellant rocket engines (thrust ≥ 90kN, capable of storing propellant)
8412.8000 20	固体火箭发动机（总冲大于或等于1100千牛顿每秒的）	10	35	17	17	台/千克	3	Solid-propellant rocket engine (of a total impulse ≥ 1100kN)
8412.8000 90	其他发动机及动力装置	10	35	17	17	台/千克		Other engines and motors
	-零件：							-Parts:
8412.9010	---子目8412.1010所列机器的零件	2	11	17	17	千克		---For machines of subheading No. 8412.1010
8412.9010 10	燃烧调节装置（冲压或脉冲喷气发动机的）	2	11	17	17	千克	3	Combustion control devices (for ramjet engine or pulse jet engines)
8412.9010 20	火箭发动机的壳体	2	11	17	17	千克	3	Shells of rocket engines
8412.9010 90	航空、航天器用喷气发动机的零件（涡轮喷气发动机的零件，编号8412901010除外）	2	11	17	17	千克		Parts of jet engines for aircraft or spacecraft, (other than parts of turbo-jets engines and parts of subheading No. 8412.9010 10)
8412.9090	---其他	8	35	17	17	千克		---Other
84.13	液体泵，不论是否装有计量装置；液体提升机：							**Pumps for liquids, whether or not fitted with a measuring device; liquid elevators:**
	-装有或可装计量装置的泵：							-Pumps fitted or designed to be fitted with a measuring device:
8413.1100暂	--分装燃料或润滑油的泵，用于加油站或车库	6	30	17	15	台/千克		--Pumps for dispensing fuel or lubricants, of the type used in filling-stations or in garages
8413.1900暂	--其他	6	30	17	15	台/千克		--Other
8413.2000	-手泵，但子目8413.11或8413.19的货品除外	10	30	17	15	台/千克		-Hand pumps, other than those of subheadingNo. 8413.11 or 8413.19
	-活塞式内燃发动机用的燃油泵、润滑油泵或冷却剂泵：							-Fuel, lubricating or cooling medium pumps for internal combustion piston engines:

税则号列	货品名称	最惠(%)	普通	增值税率	出口退税	计量单位	监管条件	Article Description
	---燃油泵:							---Fuel pumps:
8413.3021	----输出功率在132.39千瓦(180马力)及以上的发动机用燃油泵	3	30	17	15	台/千克		----Fuel pumps for engines of an output of 132.39KW (180PS) or more
8413.3029	----其他	3	30	17	15	台/千克		----Other
8413.3030	---润滑油泵	3	30	17	15	台/千克		---Lubricating oil pumps
8413.3090	---其他	3	30	17	15	台/千克		---Other
8413.4000	-混凝土泵	8	30	17	15	台/千克		-Concrete pumps
	-其他往复式排液泵:							-Other reciprocating positive displacement pumps:
8413.5010暂	---气动式	6	40			台/千克		---Pneumatic
8413.5010暂 10	农业用气动往复式排液泵	6	40	13	13	台/千克		Pneumatic reciprocating positive displacement pumps for agricultural use
8413.5010暂 20	气动式耐腐蚀波纹或隔膜泵(流量大于0.6m³/h,接触表面由特殊耐腐蚀材料制成)	6	40	17	15	台/千克	3	Pneumatic corrosion-resisting bellows or diaphragm pumps (flow capacity > 0.6m³/h, with a contact surface of special corrosion-resisting material)
8413.5010暂 90	其他非农业用气动往复式排液泵	6	40	17	15	台/千克		Pneumatic reciprocating positive displacement pumps for non – agricultural use
8413.5020暂	---电动式	6	40			台/千克		---Electric
8413.5020暂 10	农业用电动往复式排液泵	6	40	13	13	台/千克		Electric reciprocating positive displacement pumps for agricutlural use
8413.5020暂 20	电动式耐腐蚀波纹或隔膜泵(流量大于0.6m³/h,接触表面由特殊耐腐蚀材料制成)	6	40	17	15	台/千克	3	Electric corrosion-resisting bellows diaphragm pumps (flow capacity > 0.6m³/h with a contact-surface of special corrosion-resisting materials)
8413.5020暂 30	电动往复式排液多重密封泵(两用物项管制)	6	40	17	15	台/千克	3	Electric reciprocating multiple – sealed positive displacement pumps for non – agricultural use
8413.5020暂 90	其他非农业用电动往复式排液泵	6	40	17	15	台/千克		Other electric reciprocating positive displacement pumps for non – argricultlral use
	---液压式:							---Hydraulic:
8413.5031暂	----柱塞泵	6	40			台/千克		----Plunger pumps
8413.5031暂 01	农业用柱塞泵	6	40	13	13	台/千克		Plunger pumps for agriculture use
8413.5031暂 90	其他非农业用柱塞泵	6	40	17	15	台/千克		Other plunger pumps for non – agriculture use
8413.5039暂	----其他	6	40			台/千克		----Other
8413.5039暂 01	其他农业用液压往复式排液泵	6	40	13	13	台/千克		Other hydraulic reciprocating positive displacement pumps for agricultural use
8413.5039暂 20	液压式耐腐蚀波纹或隔膜泵(流量大于0.6m³/h,接触表面由特殊耐腐蚀材料制成)	6	40	17	15	台/千克	3	Hydraulic corrosion-resisting bellows or diaphragm pumps(flow capacity > 0.6m³/h with a contact-surface of special corrosion-resisting materials)
8413.5039暂 90	其他非农业用液压往复式排液泵	6	40	17	15	台/千克		Other hydraulic reciprocating positive displacement pumps for non – agricultural use
8413.5090暂	---其他	6	40			台/千克		---Other
8413.5090暂 10	其他农用往复式排液泵	6	40	13	13	台/千克		Other reciprocating positive displacement pumps for agricutural use
8413.5090暂 20	其他耐腐蚀波纹或隔膜泵(流量大于0.6m³/h,接触表面由特殊耐腐蚀材料制成)	6	40	17	15	台/千克	3	Other corrosion-resisting bellows or diaphragm pumps(flow capacity > 0.6m³/h with a contact-surface of special corrosion-resisting materials)
8413.5090暂 90	其他非农用往复式排液泵	6	40	17	15	台/千克		Other reciprocating positive displacement pumps for non – agricultural use
	-其他回转式排液泵:							-Other rotary positive displacement pumps:
	---齿轮泵							---Gear pumps
8413.6021暂	----电动式	6	40			台/千克		----Electric
8413.6021暂 01	农业用电动齿轮泵(回转式排液泵)	6	40	13	13	台/千克		Electric gear pumps for agricultural use(rotary positive displacement pumps)
8413.6021暂 10	电动齿轮多重密封泵(非农业用回转式排液泵)	6	40	17	15	台/千克	3	Electric multiple – sealed gear pumps (rotary positive displacement pumps for non – agricultural use)
8413.6021暂 90	其他非农业用电动齿轮泵(回转式排液泵,多重密封泵除外)	6	40	17	15	台/千克		Other electric gear pumps for non – agricultural use (rotary positive displacement pumps for non-agricultural use)

税则号列	货品名称	最惠(%)	普通	增值税率	出口退税	计量单位	监管条件	Article Description
8413.6022暂	----液压式		40			台/千克		----Hydraulic
8413.6022暂 01	农业用回转式液压油泵(输入转速>2000r/min,输入功率>190kW,最大流量>2×280L/min)	3	40	13	13	台/千克		Rotary hydraulic oil pumps for agricultural use (input speed >2000 r/min, input power >190 kW, maximum flow quantity >2×280L/min)
8413.6022暂 02	非农业用回转式液压油泵(输入转速>2000r/min,输入功率>190kW,最大流量>2×280L/min)	3	40	17	15	台/千克		Rotary hydraulic oil pumps for non-agricultural use (input speed >2000 r/min, input power >190 kW, maximum flow quantity >2×280L/min)
8413.6022暂 10	其他农业用液压齿轮泵(回转式排液泵)	6	40	13	13	台/千克		Other hydraulic gear pumps for agricultural use (rotary positive displacement pumps)
8413.6022暂 20	液压齿轮多重密封泵(非农业用回转式排液泵)	6	40	17	15	台/千克	3	Hydraulic gear multiple – sealed pumps (rotary positive discharging hydraulic pump for non – agricultural use)
8413.6022暂 90	其他非农业用液压齿轮泵(回转式排液泵,多重密封泵除外)	6	40	17	15	台/千克		Other hydraulic gear pumps for non – agricultural use (except rotary positive displacement pumps, multiple – sealed pumps)
8413.6029暂	----其他	6	40			台/千克		----Other
8413.6029暂 01	其他农业用齿轮泵(回转式排液泵)	6	40	13	13	台/千克		Other gear pumps for agricultural use (rotary positive displacement pumps)
8413.6029暂 90	其他非农业用齿轮泵(回转式排液泵)	6	40	17	15	台/千克		Other gear pumps for non – agricultural use (rotary positive displacement pumps)
	---叶片泵:							---Vane pumps:
8413.6031暂	----电动式	6	40			台/千克		----Electric
8413.6031暂 01	农业用电动叶片泵(回转式排液泵)	6	40	13	13	台/千克		Electric vane pumps for agricultural use (rotary positive displacement pumps)
8413.6031暂 10	电动叶片多重密封泵(非农业用回转式排液泵)	6	40	17	15	台/千克	3	Electric multiple-sealed vane pumps (rotary positive displacement pumps for non – agricultural use)
8413.6031暂 90	其他非农业用电动叶片泵(回转式排液泵,多重密封泵除外)	6	40	17	15	台/千克		Other electric vane pumps for non – agricultural use (except rotary positive displacement pumps, multiple – sealed pumps)
8413.6032暂	----液压式	6	40			台/千克		----Hydraulic
8413.6032暂 01	农业用液压叶片泵(回转式排液泵)	6	40	13	13	台/千克		Hydraulic vane pumps for agricultural use (rotary positive displacement pumps)
8413.6032暂 10	液压叶片多重密封泵(非农业用回转式排液泵)	6	40	17	15	台/千克	3	Hydraulic vane multiple – sealed pumps (rotary positive displacement pumps for non – agricultural use)
8413.6032暂 90	其他非农业用液压叶片泵(回转式排液泵,多重密封泵除外)	6	40	17	15	台/千克		Other hydraulic vane pumps for non – agricultural use (except rotary positive displacement pumps, multiple – sealed pumps)
8413.6039暂	----其他	6	40			台/千克		----Other
8413.6039暂 01	其他农业用叶片泵(回转式排液泵)	6	40	13	13	台/千克		Other vane pumps for agricultural use (rotary positive displacement pumps)
8413.6039暂 90	其他非农业用叶片泵(回转式排液泵)	6	40	17	15	台/千克		Other vane pumps for non – agricultural use (rotary positive displacement pumps)
8413.6040暂	---螺杆泵	6	40			台/千克		---Screw pumps
8413.6040暂 01	农业用螺杆泵(回转式排液泵)	6	40	13	13	台/千克		Screw pumps for agricultural use (rotary positive displacement pumps)
8413.6040暂 10	螺杆多重密封泵(非农业用回转式排液泵)	6	40	17	15	台/千克	3	Screw pumps (rotary positive multiple-sealed displacement pumps for non – agricultural use.)
8413.6040暂 90	其他非农业用螺杆泵(回转式排液泵,多重密封泵除外)	6	40	17	15	台/千克		Other screw pumps for non – agricultural use (except rotary positive displacement pumps, multiple – sealed pumps)
8413.6050暂	---径向柱塞泵	6	40			台/千克		---Radial plunger pumps
8413.6050暂 01	农业用径向柱塞泵(回转式排液泵)	6	40	13	13	台/千克		Radial plunger pumps for agricultural use (rotary positive displacement pumps)
8413.6050暂 90	其他非农业用径向柱塞泵(回转式排液泵)	6	40	17	15	台/千克		Other radial plunger pumps for non – agricultural use (rotary positive displacement pumps)

税则号列	货品名称	最惠(%)	普通	增值税率	出口退税	计量单位	监管条件	Article Description
8413.6060暂	---轴向柱塞泵	6	40			台/千克		---Axial plunger pumps
8413.6060暂 01	农业用轴向柱塞泵(回转式排液泵)	6	40	13	13	台/千克		Axial plunger pumps for agricultural use(rotary positive displacement pumps)
8413.6060 90	其他非农业用轴向柱塞泵(回转式排液泵)	6	40	17	15	台/千克		Other axial plunger pumps for non – agricultural use (rotary positive displacement pumps)
8413.6090暂	---其他	6	40			台/千克		---Other
8413.6090暂 10	农业用其他回转式排液泵	6	40	13	13	台/千克		Other rotary positive displacement pumps for agricutural use
8413.6090暂 90	其他回转式排液泵	6	40	17	15	台/千克		Other rotary positive displacement pumps
	-其他离心泵:							-Other centrifugal pumps:
8413.7010	---转速在10000转/分及以上	8	40			台/千克		---Rotational speed no less than 10000r/min
8413.7010 10	农业用其他离心泵(转速在10000转/分及以上)	8	40	13	13	台/千克		Other centrifugal pumps for agricutural use, rotational speed≥10000r/min
8413.7010 20	液体推进剂用泵(转速≥10000转/分,出口压力≥7000千帕的)	8	40	17	15	台/千克	3	Liquid – propellant pumps, rotational speed ≥ 10000r/min, outlet pressure≥7000KPa
8413.7010 30	离心泵多重密封泵(两用物项管制)	8	40	17	15	台/千克	3	centrifugal Multiple sealedg pumps(subject to regulation of sensitive items)
8413.7010 90	其他非农用离心泵(转速在10000转/分及以上)	8	40	17	15	台/千克		Other centrifugal pumps, for non – agricultural use rotational speed≥10000r/min,
	---其他							---Other
8413.7091暂	----电动潜油泵及潜水电泵	8	40			台/千克		----Electric submersible oil pumps and electric submrsible pumps
8413.7091暂 10	农业用电动潜油泵及潜水电泵(转速在10000转/分以下)	8	40	13	13	台/千克		Electric submersible oil pumps and electric submrsible pumps for agricultural use (rotational speed ≥ 10000r/min)
8413.7091暂 90	其他非农业用电动潜油泵及潜水电泵(转速在10000转/分以下)	8	40	17	15	台/千克		Other electric submersible oil pumps and electric submrsible pumps for non – agricultural use (rotational speed≥10000r/min)
8413.7099	----其他	8	40			台/千克		----Other
8413.7099 10	其他农业用离心泵(转速在10000转/分以下)	8	40	13	13	台/千克		Other centrifugal pumps for agricultural use (rotational speed < 10000r/min)
8413.7099 20	一次冷却剂泵(全密封驱动泵,有惯性质量系统的泵,及鉴定为NC-1泵等)	8	40	17	15	台/千克	3	Primary coolant pumps (completely-sealed driving pumps, pumps with inertia mass system, approved NC-1pumps)
8413.7099 30	转速小于10000转/分的离心式屏蔽泵(流量大于0.6m³/h,接触表面由特殊耐腐蚀材料制成)	8	40	17	15	台/千克	3	Canned centrifugal pumps, rotational speed < 10000r/min (flow capacity > 0.6m³/h with a contact-surface of special corrosion-resisting materials)
8413.7099 40	转速小于10000转/分的离心式磁力泵(流量大于0.6m³/h,接触表面由特殊耐腐蚀材料制成)	8	40	17	15	台/千克	3	Magnetically – driven centrifugal pumps, rotational speed < 10000r/min (flow capacity > 0.6m³/h with a contact-surface of special corrosion-resisting materials)
8413.7099 50	液体推进剂用泵(8000转/分<转速<10000转/分,出口压力≥7000kPa的)	8	40	17	15	台/千克	3	Liquid – propellant pumps (8000r/min < rotational speed < 10000r/min, outlet pressure≥7000KPa)
8413.7099 60	其他离心泵多重密封泵(两用物项管制)	8	40	17	15	台/千克	30	Other centrifugal pumps and multiple – sealed pumps(subject to regulation of sensitive items)
8413.7099 90	其他非农业用离心泵(转速在10000转/分以下)	8	40	17	15	台/千克		Other centrifugal pumps for non – agricultural use, rotational speed < 10000r/min
	-其他泵;液体提升机:							-Other pumps; liquid elevators:
8413.8100	--泵	8	40			台/千克		--Pumps
8413.8100 10	农业用其他液体泵	8	40	13	13	台/千克		Other liquid pumps for agricultural use
8413.8100 20	生产重水用多级泵(专门为利用氨-氢交换法生产重水而设计或制造的多级泵)	8	40	17	15	台/千克	3	Multiple-staged pumps specified for heavy water (specially designed or manufactured for heavy water production with ammonia-hydrogen exchange)
8413.8100 90	其他非农用液体泵	8	40	17	15	台/千克		Other liquid pump for non – agricultural use
8413.8200	--液体提升机	8	30	17	15	台/千克		--Liquid elevators
	-零件:							-Parts:

税则号列	货品名称	最惠(%)	普通	增值税率	出口退税	计量单位	监管条件	Article Description
8413.9100	--泵用	5	30	17	15	千克		--Of pumps
8413.9200暂	--液体提升机用	4	30	17	15	千克		--Of liquid elevators
84.14	空气泵或真空泵、空气及其他气体压缩机、风机、风扇；装有风扇的通风罩或循环气罩，不论是否装有过滤器：							**Air or vacuum pumps, air or other gas compressors and fans; ventilating or recycling hoods incorporating a fan, whether or not fitted with filters:**
8414.1000暂	-真空泵	5	30	17	15	台/千克		-Vacuum pumps
8414.1000暂 10	耐腐蚀真空泵（流量大于5m^3/h，接触表面由特殊耐腐蚀材料制成）	5	30	17	15	台/千克	3	Corrosion-resisting vacuum pumps (flow capacity > 5m^3/h, with a contact-surface of special corrosion-resisting materials)
8414.1000暂 20	真空泵（抽气口≥38厘米，速度≥15m^3/秒，产生<10^{-4}托极限真空度	5	30	17	15	台/千克	3	Vacucm pumps (aspirating hole ≥ 38cm, speed ≥ 15kl/s, capacity < 10^{-4} absolute vaccum degree
8414.1000暂 30	能在含UF_6气氛中使用的真空泵（用铝、镍或含镍高于60%的合金制成或为衬里的）	5	30	17	15	台/千克	3	Vacuum pumps, suitable to be used in UF_6 atmosphere (made of or lined with aluminum, nickel or alloys containing more than 60% nickel)
8414.1000暂 40	专门设计或制造的抽气能力≥5m^3/min的真空泵（专用于同位素气体扩散浓缩）	5	30	17	15	台/千克	3	Vacuum pump whose specially designed or produced air - exhausting capacity ≥ 5m^3/min (especially used for the diffusion and concentration of isotope gas)
8414.1000暂 50	能在含UF_6气氛中使用的真空泵（耐UF_6腐蚀的，也可用氟碳密封和特殊工作流体）	5	30	17	15	台/千克	3	Vacuum pumps, suitable to be used in UF_6 atmosphere (can be sealed with fluorine-carbon or can be used with other special working fluid)
8414.1000暂 90	其他真空泵	5	30	17	15	台/千克		Other vacuum pumps
8414.2000	-手动或脚踏式空气泵	8	30	17	15	台/千克		-Handor footoperated pumps
	-用于制冷设备的压缩机：							-Compressors of a kind used in refrigerating equipment:
	---电动机驱动的压缩机：							---Driven by a motor:
8414.3011	----冷藏箱或冷冻箱用，电动机额定功率不超过0.4千瓦	8	80	17	17	台	A	----For refrigerators or freezers, of a motor power not exceeding 0.4kW
8414.3012	----冷藏箱或冷冻箱用，电动机额定功率超过0.4千瓦，但不超过5千瓦	10	80	17	17	台	A	----For refrigerators or freezers, of a motor power exceeding 0.4kW but not exceeding 5kW
8414.3013	----空气调节器用，电动机额定功率超过0.4千瓦，但不超过5千瓦	10	80	17	17	台	A	----For air conditioning machines, of a motor power exceeding, 0.4kW but not exceeding 5kW
8414.3014	----空气调节器用，电动机额定功率超过5千瓦	10	80	17	17	台	A	----For air conditioning machines, motor power > 5kW
8414.3015	----冷冻或冷藏设备用，电动机额定功率超过5千瓦	10	30	17	17	台	A	----For refrigerators or freezers, motor power > 5kW
8414.3019	----其他	10	30	17	17	台/千克	A	----Other
8414.3090	---非电动机驱动的压缩机	9	80	17	17	台/千克		---Comptessor by a non-motor
8414.3090 10	汽车空调压缩机	9	80	17	17	台/千克		Compressors for auto air conditioners
8414.3090 90	非电机驱动其他制冷设备用压缩机	9	80	17	17	台/千克		Other non - motor - driven compressors for refrigeration equipments
8414.4000	-装在拖车底盘上的空气压缩机	8	30	17	17	台/千克		-Air compressors mounted on a wheeled chassis for towing
	-风机、风扇：							-Fans:
	--台扇、落地扇、壁扇、换气扇或吊扇，包括风机，本身装有一个输出功率不超过125瓦的电动机：							--Table, floor, wall, window, ceiling or roof fans, with a self-contained electric motor of an output not exceeding 125W:
8414.5110	---吊扇	20	130	17	15	台/千克	A	---Ceiling or roof fans
8414.5120	---换气扇	20	130	17	15	台/千克	A	---Window fans
8414.5130	---具有旋转导风轮的风扇	12	130	17	15	台/千克		---Repeating front louver fan
	---其他：							---Other:
8414.5191	----台扇	10	130	17	15	台/千克	A	----Table fans
8414.5192	----落地扇	10	130	17	15	台/千克	A	----Floor fans
8414.5193	----壁扇	10	130	17	15	台/千克	A	----Wall fans
8414.5199	----其他	10	130	17	15	台/千克		----Other

税则号列	货品名称	最惠(%)	普通	增值税率	出口退税	计量单位	监管条件	Article Description
	--其他:							--Other:
8414.5910	---吊扇	8	30	17	15	台/千克	A	---Ceiling or roof fans
8414.5920	---换气扇	8	30	17	15	台/千克	A	---Window fans
8414.5930	---离心通风机	10	30	17	17	台/千克		---Centrifugal ventilation fans
8414.5990	---其他	8	30	17		台/千克		---Other
8414.5990 10	罗茨式鼓风机	8	30	17	17	台/千克	A	Root's blower
8414.5990 20	吸气＞1m^3/min 的耐 UF_6 腐蚀的鼓风机(轴向离心式或正排量鼓风机,压力比在2:1 和6:1 之间)	8	30	17	15	台/千克	3A	Blower, suitable to be used in UF_6 atmosphere, extraction capability ≥1m^3/min (axial centrifugal fans or positive-discharge fans, pressure ratio between 2:1 ~ 6:1)
8414.5990 30	吸气≥2m^3/min 的耐 UF_6 腐蚀鼓风机(轴向离心式或正排量鼓风机,压力比在 1.2:1 和6:1 之间)	8	30	17	15	台/千克	3A	Blower, suitable to be used in UF_6 atmosphere, extraction capability ≥2m^3/min (axial centrifugal fans or positive-discharge fans, pressure ratio between 1.2:1 and 6:1)
8414.5990 40	吸气≥56m^3/s 的鼓风机(用于循环硫化氢气体的单级、低压头离心式鼓风机)	8	30	17	15	台/千克	3A	Blower, extraction capability ≥56m^3/s (one-stage, low-pressure centrifugal blowers used for cycling hydrogen sulphide gas)
8414.5990 50	电子产品散热用轴流风扇	8	30	17	17	台/千克	A	Axial flow fans for heat elimination of electronic products
8414.5990 91	其他台扇、落地扇、壁扇(电动机输出功率超过125 瓦的)	8	30	17	15	台/千克	A	Other desk fans, floor – standing fans and wall – mounted fans (electric output power > 125w)
8414.5990 99	其他风机、风扇	8	30	17	15	台/千克	A	Other fans
	-罩的平面最大边长不超过 120 厘米的通风罩或循环气罩:							-Hoods having a maximum horizontal side not exceeding 120cm:
8414.6010暂	---抽油烟机	6	130	17	15	台/千克		---Range hoods
8414.6090	---其他	10	130	17	15	台/千克		---Other
8414.6090 11	生物安全柜(符合世界卫生组织规定的生物安全水平三级标准,罩的最大边长≤120 厘米)	10	130	17	15	台/千克	3	Biological safety cabinets (conform to the biological safety criterion of level – Ⅲ as stipulated by WHO, the longest sides covered ≤120 cm)
8414.6090 12	活动(柔软的)隔离装置;手套箱(具有与三级生物安全柜类似标准,罩的最大边长≤120 厘米)	10	130	17	15	台/千克	3	Active (soft) isolating device, glove boxes (up to standards similar to biological safety criterion of level – Ⅲ, the longest sides covered ≤120 cm)
8414.6090 13	层流罩(柜)(垂直流密闭通风柜,具有三级生物安全柜类似标准,罩的最大边长≤120厘米)	10	130	17	15	台/千克	3	Laminar flow hoods (vertical closed ventilation hoods, up to standards similar to biological safety criterion of level – Ⅲ, the longest sides covered ≤ 120 cm)
8414.6090 14	吸收塔(两用物项管制,罩的最大边长≤120 厘米)	10	130	17	15	台/千克	3	Absorbing tower (subject to regulation of sensitive items, the longest sides covered ≤120 cm)
8414.6090 15	带有风扇的高效空气粒子过滤单元的封闭洁净设备(高效空气粒子过滤单元(HEPA),罩的最大边长≤120 厘米)	10	130	17	15	台/千克	3	HEPA closed cleaning equipment with fans (HEPA referring high efficiency particulate air filter, the longest sides covered ≤120cm)
8414.6090 16	厌氧微生物柜(具有与三级生物安全柜类似标准,罩的最大边长≤120 厘米)	10	130	17	15	台/千克	3	Anaerobe Cabinet (conform to the biological safety criterion of level – Ⅲ, hoods having a maximum horizontal side not exceeding 120cm)
8414.6090 90	其他≤120 厘米的通风罩或循环气罩(指罩的平面最大边长不超过 120 厘米,装有风扇的)	10	130	17	15	台/千克		Other ventilating or recycling hoods with the side length ≤ 120cm (meaning the maximum side length ≤120cm, fitted with a fan)
	-其他:							-Other:
8414.8010	---燃气轮机用的自由活塞式发生器	8	50	17	15	台/千克		---Free piston generators for gas turbines
8414.8020	---二氧化碳压缩机	7	30	17	15	台/千克		---CO_2 compressors
8414.8030	---发动机用增压器		30	17	15	台/千克		---Supercharger for engines
8414.8030暂 01	乘用车机械增压器	5	30	17	15	台/千克		Passenger car mechanical supercharger
8414.8030 90	发动机用增压器	7	30	17	15	台/千克		Supercharger for engine
8414.8040	---空气及其他气体压缩机	7	30	17	15	台/千克		"---Air and other gases compressors"

税则号列	货品名称	最惠(%)	普通	增值税率	出口退税	计量单位	监管条件	Article Description
8414.8040 10	吸气>1立方米/分的耐UF6腐蚀压缩机(轴向离心式或正排量压缩机,压力比在2:1和6:1之间)	7	30	17	15	台/千克	3	Aspirated > 1 cubic meters / min of corrosion resistance to UF6 (axial compressorcentrifugal or positive displacement compressor, pressure than in 2:1 and 6:1)
8414.8040 20	MLIS用UF6/载气压缩机(能在UF6环境中长期操作UF6/载气混合气压缩机)	7	30	17	15	台/千克	3	The carrier gas compressor with UF6/ MLIS (long - term operation of UF6/ carrier gas mixed gas compressor in the UF6 environment)
8414.8040 30	吸气≥56立方米/秒的压缩机(用于循环硫化氢气体的单级、低压头离心式压缩机)	7	30	17	15	台/千克	3	The compressor suction is more than 56 m3 / S (for single level, low headcentrifugal compressor cycle of hydrogen sulfide gas)
8414.8040 40	吸气≥2立方米/分的耐UF6腐蚀压缩机(轴向离心式或正排量压缩机,压力比在1.2:1和6:1之间)	7	30	17	15	台/千克	3	UF6 corrosion resistance than the compressor suction of 2 cubic meters / min(axial centrifugal or positive displacement compressor, pressure ratio in 1.2:1 and6:1 between)
8414.8040 90	其他空气及气体压缩机	7	30	17	15	台/千克		Other air and gas compressors
8414.8090	---其他	7	30	17		台/千克		---Other
8414.8090 51	其他生物安全柜(符合世界卫生组织规定的生物安全水平三级标准)	7	30	17	17	台/千克	3	Other biological safety cabinet (conform to the biological safety criterion of level - III as stipulated by WHO)
8414.8090 52	其他活动(柔软的)隔离装置与其他手套箱(具有与三级生物安全柜类似标准)	7	30	17	17	台/千克	3	Other active (soft) isolating device and other glove boxes (up to standard similar to biological safety cabinet of level Ⅲ)
8414.8090 53	其他层流罩(柜)(垂直流密闭通风柜,具有与三级生物安全柜类似标准)	7	30	17	17	台/千克	3	Other Laminar flow hoods (vertical closed ventilation hoods, up to standards similar to biological safety criterion of level - III)
8414.8090 54	其他吸收塔(两用物项管制)	7	30	17	17	台/千克	3	Absorbing tower (subject to regulation of sensitive items)
8414.8090 55	其他带有风扇的高效空气粒子过滤单元的封闭洁净设备[高效空气粒子过滤单元(HEPA)]	7	30	17	17	台/千克	3	Other HEPA closed cleaning equipment with fans (HEPA referring high efficiency particulate air filter.)
8414.8090 56	其他厌氧微生物柜(具有与三级生物安全柜类似标准)	7	30	17	15	台/千克	3	Other anaerobe Cabinet (conform to the biological safety criterion of level-Ⅲ)
8414.8090 90	其他空气泵、气体压缩机及通风罩(通风罩指装有风扇的通风罩或循环气罩,平面边长>120cm)	7	30	17	17	台/千克		Other air pumps, air compressors and ventilating hoods (ventilating or recycling hoods incorporating fan, having a maximum horizontal side > 120cm)
	-零件:							-Parts:
	---子目8414.3011至8414.3014及8414.3090所列机器的零件:							---Of the machines of subheadings No. 8414.3011 to 8414.3014 and 8414.3090:
8414.9011[暂]	----压缩机进、排气阀片	5	80	17	15	千克		----In take valve leaf or discharge valve leaf
8414.9019[暂]	----其他	5	80	17	15	千克		----Other
8414.9020[暂]	---子目8414.5110至8414.5199及8414.6000所列机器的零件	6	130	17	15	千克		---Of the machines of subheadings No. 8414.5110 to 8414.5199 and 8414.6000
8414.9090[暂]	---其他	4	30	17	15	千克		---Other
8414.9090[暂] 10	分子泵(气体离心机的静态部件,专门设计或制造的内部有已加工或挤压的螺纹槽和已加工的腔的泵体)	4	30	17	15	千克	3	Molec ular pumpcstatic component of gas centrifuge, Specialized design and manufacture, interior has been processing extrusion screw groove and processing chamber of the pump body
8414.9090[暂] 90	编号8414其他未列名零件	4	30	17	15	千克		Other parts ont listed in Heading No. 8414

税则号列	货品名称	最惠(%)	普通	增值税率	出口退税	计量单位	监管条件	Article Description
84.15	空气调节器,装有电扇及调温、调湿装置,包括不能单独调湿的空调器:							**Air conditioning machines, comprising a motor-driven fan and elements for changing the temperature and humidity, including those machines in which the humidity cannot be separately regulated:**
	-窗式或壁式,独立的或分体的:							-Window or wall types, self-contained or "split-system":
8415.1010	---独立式	15	130	17	17	台	A	---Self-contained
	---分体式:							---Split-system:
8415.1021	----制冷量不超过4000大卡/时	15	130	17	17	台	A	----Of a refrigerating effect not exceeding 4000 Cal per hour
8415.1022	----制冷量超过4000大卡/时	15	90	17	17	台		----Of a refrigerating effect exceeding 4000 Cal per hour
8415.1022 01	4000大卡/时<制冷量≤12046大卡/时(14000W)分体式空调,窗式或壁式(装有电扇及调温、调湿装置,包括不能单独调湿的空调器)	15	90	17	17	台	A	Split type air conditioner, 4000Cal/hour < refrigerating effect≤12046Cal/hour, window type or wall type (comprising a motordriven fan and elements for changing the temperature and humidity, including those machines in which the humidity cannot be separately regutated)
8415.1022 90	其他制冷量>12046大卡/时(14000W)分体式空调,窗式或壁式(装有电扇及调温、调湿装置,包括不能单独调湿的空调器)	15	90	17	17	台	A	Other split type air conditioner, refrigerating effect >12046Cal/hour, window type or wall type (comprising a motordriven fan and elements for changing the temperature and humidity, including those machines in which the humidity cannot be separately regutated)
8415.2000[暂]	-机动车辆上供人使用的	10	110	17	17	台	A	-Of a kind used for persons, in motor vehicles
	-其他:							-Other:
	--装有制冷装置及一个冷热循环换向阀的(可逆式热泵):							--Incorporating a refrigerating unit and a valve for reversal of the cooling/heat cycle (reversible heat pumps):
8415.8110	---制冷量不超过4000大卡/时	15	130	17	17	台	A	---Of a refrigerating effect not exceeding 4000 Cal per hour
8415.8120[暂]	---制冷量超过4000大卡/时	12	90	17	17	台	A	---Of a refrigerating effect exceeding 4000 Cal per hour
8415.8120[暂] 01	4000大卡/时<制冷量≤12046大卡/时(14000W)热泵式空调器(装有制冷装置及一个冷热循环换向阀的)	12	90	17	17	台	A	Heat pump type air conditioner, 4000Cal/hour < refrigerating effect≤12046Cal/hour (incorporating a refrigerating unit and a valve for reversal of the cooling/beat cycle)
8415.8120[暂] 90	其他制冷量>12046大卡/时(14000W)热泵式空调器(装有制冷装置及一个冷热循环换向阀的)	12	90	17	17	台	A	Other heat pump type air conditioner, refrigerating effect >12046Cal/hour (incorporating a refrigerating unit and a valve for reversal of the cooling/beat cycle)
	--其他,装有制冷装置的:							--Other, incorporating a refrigerating unit:
8415.8210	---制冷量不超过4000大卡/时	15	130	17	17	台	A	---Of a refrigerating effect not exceeding 4000 Cal per hour
8415.8220[暂]	---制冷量超过4000大卡/时	12	90	17	17	台		---Of a refrigerating effect exceeding 4000 Cal per hour
8415.8220[暂] 01	4000大卡/时<制冷量≤12046大卡/时(14000W)的其他空调(仅装有制冷装置,而无冷热循环装置的)	12	90	17	17	台	A	Other air conditioner, 4000Cal/hour < refrigerating effect≤12046Cal/hour, incorporating a refrigerating unit, No thermal cycling device
8415.8220[暂] 90	其他制冷量>12046大卡/时(14000W)的其他空调(仅装有制冷装置,而无冷热循环装置的)	12	90	17	17	台	A	Other air conditioner, refrigerating effect >12046Cal/hour, incorporating a refrigerating unit, No thermal cycling device
8415.8300	--未装有制冷装置的	10	90	17	17	台	A	--Not incorporating a refrigerating unit
	-零件:							-Parts:

税则号列	货 品 名 称	最惠(%)	普通	增值税率	出口退税	计量单位	监管条件	Article Description
8415.9010[暂]	---子目8415.1010、8415.1021、8415.8110及8415.8210所列设备的零件	6	130	17	15	千克		---Of the machines of subheading No. 8415.1010, 8415.1021, 8415.8110 and 8415.8210
8415.9090[暂]	---其他	6	90	17	15	千克		---Other
84.16	**使用液体燃料、粉状固体燃料或气体燃料的炉用燃烧器；机械加煤机，包括其机械炉箅、机械出灰器及类似装置：**							**Furnace burners for liquid fuel, for pulverzied solid fuel or for gas; mechanical stokers, including their mechanical grates, mechanical ash dischargers and similar appliances:**
8416.1000	-使用液体燃料的炉用燃烧器	10	35	17	15	千克	6	-Furnace burners for liquid fuel
	-其他炉用燃烧器，包括复式燃烧器：							-Other furnace burners, including combination burners:
	---气体的：							---For gas:
8416.2011	----使用天然气的		35	17	15	千克		----Of using natural gas
8416.2011[暂] 01	溴化锂空调用天然气燃烧机	5	35	17	15	千克	6	Natural gas burners for lithium bromide air conditioners
8416.2011 90	其他使用天然气的炉用燃烧器	10.5	35	17	15	千克	6	Other natural gas furnace burners
8416.2019	----其他	10.5	35	17	15	千克	6	----Other
8416.2090	---其他		35	17	15	千克	6	---Other
8416.2090[暂] 01	溴化锂空调用复式燃烧机	5	35	17	15	千克	6	Combination burners for lithium bromide air conditioner
8416.2090 90	其他使用粉状固体燃料炉用燃烧器（包括其他复式燃烧器）	10.5	35	17	15	千克	6	Other furnace burners for pulverzied solid fuel (including other combination burners)
8416.3000	-机械加煤机，包括其机械炉箅、机械出灰器及类似装置	8.4	35	17	15	千克	6	-Mechanical stokers, including their mechanical grates, mechanical ash dischargers and similar appliances
8416.9000	-零件	6	35	17	15	千克		-Parts
84.17	**非电热的工业或实验室用炉及烘箱，包括焚烧炉：**							**Industrial or laboratory furnaces and ovens, including incinerators, non-electric:**
8417.1000	-矿砂、黄铁矿或金属的焙烧、熔化或其他热处理用炉及烘箱	10	35	17	15	台	6OA	-Furnaces and ovens for the roasting, melting or other heat-treatment of ores, pyrites or of metals
8417.2000	-面包房用烤炉及烘箱，包括做饼干用的	10	35	17	15	台	A	-Bakery ovens, including biscuit ovens
	-其他：							-Other:
8417.8010	---炼焦炉	10	35	17	15	台	6A	---Coke ovens
8417.8020	---放射性废物焚烧炉	5	35	17	15	台	6A	---Burn furnaces for radioactive waste
8417.8030	---水泥回转窑	10	35	17	15	台	AO	---Cement rotary kilns
8417.8040	---石灰石分解炉	10	35	17	15	台	A	---Limestone decomposition furnace
8417.8050	---垃圾焚烧炉	10	35	17	15	台/千克	6AO	---Refuse incinerator
8417.8090	---其他	10	35	17	15	台		---Other
8417.8090 10	平均温度>1000℃的耐腐蚀焚烧炉（为销毁管制化学品或化学弹药用）	10	35	17	15	台	36AO	Corrosion-resisting incinerators, average temperature > 1000℃ (for incinerating controlled chemicals or chemical ammunitions)
8417.8090 90	其他非电热的工业用炉及烘箱（包括实验室用炉、烘箱和焚烧炉）	10	35	17	15	台	6OA	Other non-electric industrial furnaces and ovens (including laboratory furnaces, ovens and incinerators)
	-零件：							-Parts:
8417.9010	---海绵铁回转窑用	7	35	17	15	千克		---For sponge iron rotary kiln
8417.9020	---炼焦炉用	7	35	17	15	千克		---For coke ovens
8417.9090	---其他	7	35	17	15	千克		---Other
84.18	**电气或非电气的冷藏箱、冷冻箱及其他制冷设备；热泵，但税目84.15的空气调节器除外：**							**Refrigerators, freezers and other refrigerating or freezing equipment, electric or other; heat pumps other than air conditioning machines of headingNo. 84.15:**
	-冷藏-冷冻组合机，各自装有单独外门的：							-Combined refrigerator-freezers, fitted with separate external doors:
8418.1010	---容积超过500升	10	100	17	17	台/千克	A	---Of a capacity exceeding 500 L
8418.1020	---容积超过200升，但不超过500升	15	130	17	17	台/千克	A	---Of a capacity exceeding 200 L, not exceeding 500 L
8418.1030	---容积不超过200升	15	130	17	17	台/千克	A	---Of a capacity not exceeding 200 L
	-家用型冷藏箱：							-Refrigerators, household type:

税则号列	货品名称	最惠(%)	普通	增值税率	出口退税	计量单位	监管条件	Article Description
	--压缩式:							--Compression-type:
8418.2110	---容积超过150升	10	130	17	17	台/千克	A	---Of a capacity exceeding 150 L
8418.2120	---容积超过50升,但不超过150升	10	130	17	17	台/千克	A	---Of a capacity exceeding 50 L, not exceeding 150 L
8418.2130	---容积不超过50升	10	130	17	17	台/千克	A	---Of a capacity not exceeding 50 L
	--其他:							--Other:
8418.2910	---半导体制冷式	30	130	17	17	台/千克	A	---Semiconductor freezing type
8418.2920	---电气吸收式	15	130	17	17	台/千克	A	---Absorption-type, electrical
8418.2990	---其他	30	130	17	17	台/千克	A	---Other
	-柜式冷冻箱,容积不超过800升:							-Freezers of the chest type, not exceeding 800L capacity:
8418.3010	---制冷温度在-40℃及以下	9	50	17	17	台/千克	A	---Of a refrigerating temperature of -40℃ or lower
	---制冷温度在-40℃以上:							---Of a refrigerating temperature higher than -40℃:
8418.3021	----容积超过500升	23	100	17	17	台/千克	A	----Of a capacity exceeding 500 L
8418.3029	----其他	30	130	17	17	台/千克	A	----Other
	-立式冷冻箱,容积不超过900升:							-Freezers of the upright type, not exceeding 900L capacity:
8418.4010	---制冷温度在-40℃及以下	9	50	17	17	台/千克	A	---Of a refrigerating temperature of -40℃ or lower
	---制冷温度在-40℃以上:							---Of a refrigerating temperature higher than -40℃:
8418.4021	----容积超过500升	15	100	17	17	台/千克	A	----Of a capacity exceeding 500 L
8418.4029	----其他	30	130	17	17	台/千克	A	----Other
8418.5000	-装有冷藏或冷冻装置的其他设备(柜、箱、展示台、陈列箱及类似品)用于存储及展示	10	100	17	17	台/千克	A	-Other furniture (chests, cabinets, display counters, show cases and the like) for storage and display, incorporating refrigerating or freeezing equipment
	-其他制冷设备;热泵:							-Other refrigerating or freezing equipment; heat pumps:
	--热泵,税目84.15的空气调节器除外:							--Heat pumps other than air conditioning madimes of heading 84.15:
8418.6120	---压缩式	10	90	17	17	台/千克		---Compression-type
8418.6120 10	压缩式制冷机组的热泵(介质为氢、氦的可冷却到≤23K且排热>150W)	10	90	17	17	台/千克	3	Hot pump for compression-type refrigerating units (medium being hydrogen or helium, and can be cooled to temperature ≤23K, and remove heat >150W)
8418.6120 90	其他压缩式热泵,税目8415的空气调节器除外	10	90	17	17	台/千克		Other compression-type hot pumps, excluding air conditioning machines listed in heading No. 8415
8418.6190	---其他	15	130	17	17	台/千克		---Other
	--其他:							--Other:
8418.6920	---制冷机组	10	90	17	17	台/千克		---Refigerating units
8418.6920 10	其他压缩式制冷设备(介质为氦或氢,可冷却到≤23K且排热>150W)	10	90	17	17	台/千克	3	Other compression-type refrigerating equipment (medium being hydrogen or helium, and can be cooled to temperature ≤23K, and remove heat >150W)
8418.6920 90	其他制冷机组	10	90	17	17	台/千克		Other refrigerating units
8418.6990	---其他	10	130	17	17	台/千克		---Other
8418.6990 10	带制冷装置的发酵罐(不发散气溶胶,且容积大于20升)	10	130	17	17	台/千克	3	Fermenters with refrigeration appliances (not divergent aerosol, capacity >20L)
8418.6990 20	制冰机、冰激凌机	10	130	17	17	台/千克	A	Ice-making machine, ice cream machine
8418.6990 90	其他制冷设备	10	130	17	17	台/千克		Other refrigrating equipments
	-零件							-Parts:
8418.9100	--冷藏或冷冻设备专用的特制家具	18	130	17	15	千克		--Furniture designed to receive refrigerating or freezing equipment
	--其他:							--Other:
8418.9910暂	---制冷机组及热泵用	6	90	17	17	千克		---Of refrigerating units and heat pumps
	---其他:							---Other:
8418.9991暂	----制冷温度在-40℃及以下的冷冻设备用	6	50	17	15	千克		----Of freezing equipment of a refrigerating temperature of -40℃ or lower

税则号列	货品名称	最惠(%)	普通	增值税率	出口退税	计量单位	监管条件	Article Description
8418.9992暂	----制冷温度在 -40℃以上,但容积超过500升的冷藏或冷冻设备用	6	100	17	15	千克		----Of refrigerating or freezing equipment of a refrigerating temperature higher than -40℃ and a capacity exceeding 500 L
8418.9999暂	----其他	6	130	17	15	千克		----Other
8418.9999暂 10	耐腐蚀冷凝器(20平方米>换热面积>0.15平方米)	6	130	17	15	千克	3	Corrosion-resisting condensers ($20m^2$ > area of heat-exchange > $0.15m^2$)
8418.9999暂 90	编号8418其他制冷设备用零件	6	130	17	15	千克		Parts of other refrigerating equipment of heading No. 8418
84.19	利用温度变化处理材料的机器、装置及类似的实验室设备,例如,加热、烹煮、烘炒、蒸馏、精馏、消毒、灭菌、汽蒸、干燥、蒸发、气化、冷凝、冷却的机器设备,不论是否电热的(不包括税目85.14的炉,烘箱及其他设备),但家用的除外;非电热的快速热水器或贮备式热水器:							**Machinery, plant or laboratory equipment, whether or not electrically heated (excluding furnaces, ovens and other equipment of headingNo. 85.14), for the treatment of materials by a process involving a change of temperature such as heating, cooking, roasting, distilling, rectifying, sterilizing, pasteurizing, steaming, drying, evaporating, vaporizing, condensing or cooling, other than machinery or plant of a kind used for domestic purposes; instantaneous or storage water heaters, non-electric:**
	-非电热的快速热水器或贮备式热水器:							-Instantaneous or storage water heaters, non-electric:
8419.1100	--燃气快速热水器	35	100	17	15	台	A	--Instantaneous gas water heaters
	--其他:							--Other:
8419.1910	---太阳能热水器	35	100	17	17	台	A	---Solar water heater
8419.1990	---其他	35	100	17	17	台	A	---Other
8419.2000	-医用或实验室用消毒器具	4	30	17	15	台	A	-Medical, surgical or laboratory sterilizers
	-干燥器:							-Dryers:
8419.3100	--农产品干燥器	8	30	13	13	台	A	--For agricultural products
8419.3200	--木材、纸浆、纸或纸板干燥器	9	30	17	15	台	A	--For wood, paper pulp, paper or paperboard
	--其他:							--Other:
8419.3910	---微空气流动陶瓷坯件干燥器	9	30	17	15	台	A	---Breeze pottery blanks dryers
8419.3990	---其他		30	17	15	台		---Other
8419.3990暂 01	生产奶粉用干燥器	4	30	17	15	台	A	Dryers, of a kind uced in powdered milk producing
8419.3990暂 02	污泥涡轮干燥机	4	30	17	15	台	A	Sludge turbo dryer
8419.3990 10	冻干设备(10千克≤24小时凝冰量≤1000千克,并可蒸汽消毒)	9	30	17	15	台	3A	Freezer-dryers (10kg/24h ≤ volume of icing ≤ 1000 kg/24h, capable of be sterilized by steam)
8419.3990 20	烟丝烘干机	9	30	17	15	台	AO	Tobacco dryer
8419.3990 30	干燥箱(具有与三级生物安全柜类似标准)	9	30	17	15	台	3A	Drying tunnel (conform to the biological safety criterion of level - Ⅲ)
8419.3990 90	其他用途的干燥器	9	30	17	15	台	A	Dryers for other use
	-蒸馏或精馏设备:							-Distilling or rectifying plant:
8419.4010	---提净塔	10	30	17	15	台	A	---Stripping towers
8419.4020	---精馏塔	10	30	17	15	台	A	---Rectifying towers
8419.4090	---其他	10	30	17	15	台		---Other
8419.4090 10	氢-低温蒸馏塔(温度≤-238℃,压力为0.5-5兆帕,内径≥1米等条件)	10	30	17	15	台	3AO	Hydrogen-low temperature distilling towers (temperature ≤ -238℃, pressure = 0.5MPa ~ 5MPa, inside diameter ≥ 1m)
8419.4090 20	耐腐蚀蒸馏塔(内径大于0.1米,接触表面由特殊耐腐蚀材料制成)	10	30	17	15	台	3AO	Corrosion-resisten distilling towers (inside diameter > 0.1m, with a contact surface of special corrosion-resisten materials)
8419.4090 90	其他蒸馏或精馏设备	10	30	17	15	台	AO	Other distillation or rectification equipment
8419.5000	-热交换装置	10	30	17	15	台		-Heat exchange units
8419.5000 10	热交换器(专用于核反应堆的一次冷却剂回路的)	10	30	17	15	台	3O	Heat exchanger (used exclusively for nuclear reactor primary coolant loop)
8419.5000 20	蒸汽发生器(专用于核反应堆内生成的热量输送到进水以产生蒸汽的)	10	30	17	15	台	3	Steam generators (used exclusively to transmit the heat generated within nuclear reactors to the inlet to produce vapors)

税则号列	货品名称	最惠(%)	普通	增值税率	出口退税	计量单位	监管条件	Article Description
8419.5000 30	冷却 UF_6 的热交换器(在压差为 100kPa 下渗透压力变化率小于 10Pa/h)	10	30	17	15	台	3A	Heat exchangers for cooling UF_6 (rate of change of osmotic pressure change rate <10Pa/h under differential pressure of less than 100kPa)
8419.5000 40	冷却气体用热交换器(用耐 UF_6 腐蚀材料制成或加以保护的)	10	30	17	15	台	3AO	Heat exchangers for cooling gases (made of or protected with UF_6-resistant materials)
8419.5000 50	耐腐蚀热交换器(0.15 平方米<换热面积<20 平方米)	10	30	17	15	台	3AO	Corrosion-resisting heat exchangers ($20m^2$ > area of heat-exchange area > $0.15m^2$)
8419.5000 90	其他热交换装置	10	30	17	15	台	A	Other heat exchange devices
	-液化空气或其他气体的机器:							-Machinery for liquefying air or other gases:
	---制氧机:							---Oxygen producers:
8419.6011	----制氧量在 15000 立方米/小时及以上	12	30	17	17	台	A	----Oxygen preparation volume no less than $15000m^3/h$
8419.6019	----其他	13	30	17	17	台	A	----Other
8419.6090	---其他	10	30	17	15	台		---Other
8419.6090 10	液化器(将来自级联的 UF_6 气体压缩并冷凝成液态 UF_6)	10	30	17	15	台	3AO	Liquefiers (to compress and condense gaseous UF_6 from cascade into liquefied UF_6)
8419.6090 90	其他液化空气或其他气体用的机器	10	30	17	15	台	AO	Other machinery for liquefying air or other gases
	-其他机器设备:							-Other machinery, plant and equipment:
8419.8100暂	--加工热饮料或烹调、加热食品用	6	30	17	15	台	A	--For making hot drinks of for cooking or heating food
	--其他:							--Other:
8419.8910	---加氢反应器	0	30	17	15	台	A	---Hydroformer vessels
8419.8990	---其他	0	30	17	15	台		---Other
8419.8990 10	带加热装置的发酵罐(不发散气溶胶,且容积大于 20 升)	0	30	17	15	台	3AO	Fermenter fitted with heat devices (not diverging aerosol, volume >20L)
8419.8990 21	凝华器(或冷阱)(从扩散级联中取出 UF_6 并可再蒸发转移)	0	30	17	15	台	3AO	Sublimator (or cold trap) (take out UF_6 diffusion cascade and can transfer by evaporation)
8419.8990 22	低温制冷设备(能承受-120℃或更低的温度)	0	30	17	15	台	3A	Low - temperature refrigeration equipment (bearing -120℃ or evem lower temperature)
8419.8990 23	UF_6 冷阱(能承受-20℃或更低的温度)	0	30	17	15	台	3AO	UF_6 cold traps (bearing -120℃ or even lower temperature)
8419.8990 90	其他利用温度变化处理材料的机器(包括类似的实验室设备)	0	30	17	15	台	A	Other machinery for the treatment of materials by a process involving a change of temperature (including similar laboratory equipment)
	-零件:							-Parts:
8419.9010	---热水器用	0	100	17	17	千克		---Of water heaters
8419.9090	---其他	4	30	17	15	千克		---Other
84.20	**研光机或其他滚压机器及其滚筒,但加工金属或玻璃用的除外:**							**Calendering or other rolling machines, other than for metals or glass, and cylinders therefor:**
8420.1000	-研光机或其他滚压机器		30	17	15	台		-Calendering or other rolling machines
8420.1000暂 01	织物轧光机	6	30	17	15	台		Textile calenders
8420.1000 90	其他研光机或滚压机器(加工金属或玻璃用的除外)	8.4	30	17	15	台		Other calendar or rolling machines (excluding those for processing metals or glass)
	-零件:							-Parts:
8420.9100	--滚筒	8	30	17	15	个/千克		--Cylinders
8420.9900	--其他	8	30	17	15	千克		--Other
84.21	**离心机,包括离心干燥机;液体或气体的过滤、净化机器及装置:**							**Centrifuges, including centrifugal dryers; filtering or purifying machinery and apparatus, for liquids or gases:**
	-离心机,包括离心干燥机:							-Centrifuges, including centrifugal dryers:
8421.1100	--奶油分离器	8.4	30	17	15	台	A	--Cream separators
	--干衣机:							--Clothes-dryers:
8421.1210	---干衣量不超过 10 公斤	17.5	70	17	15	台		---Of a dry linen capacity not exceeding 10kg
8421.1290	---其他	8	30	17	15	台		---Other
	--其他:							--Other:

税则号列	货品名称	最惠(%)	普通	增值税率	出口退税	计量单位	监管条件	Article Description
8421.1910暂	---脱水机	6	30	17	15	台		---Dewaterers
8421.1920	---固液分离机	10	30	17	15	台		---Solid-liquor separators
8421.1990	---其他	10	30	17	15	台		---Other
8421.1990 20	液-液离心接触器(为化学交换过程的铀浓缩而专门设计或制造的)	10	30	17	15	台	3	Liquid-liquid centrifugal contactors (specially designed or manufactured for uranium concentration in chemical exchange process)
8421.1990 30	离心分离器,包括倾析器(不发散气溶胶、可对致病性微生物进行连续分离的)	10	30	17	15	台	3	Centrifugal separator including decanters (not diverging aerosol, capable of continuously separating disease microorganism)
8421.1990 90	其他离心机及离心干燥机	10	30	17	15	台		Other centrifuges and centrifugal dryers
	-液体的过滤、净化机器及装置:							-Filtering or purifying machinery and apparatus for liquids:
	--过滤或净化水用:							--For filtering or purifying water:
8421.2110暂	---家用型	12	63	17	15	台/千克	A	---Of the household type
8421.2191	----船舶压载水处理设备	5	50	17	15	台/千克		----Ship ballast water treatment equipment
8421.2199	----其他		50	17	15	台/千克		----Other
8421.2199暂 01	喷灌设备用叠式净水过滤器	0	50	17	15	台/千克		Cascade water purifying filters for sprinkler irrigation equipment
8421.2199暂 02	船舶压载水处理设备用过滤器	2	50	17	15	台/千克		Ballast water treatment equipment filter useds to vessel
8421.2199 90	其他非家用型过滤或净化水的装置	5	50	17	15	台/千克		Other non-household filtering or purifying water equipment
8421.2200	--过滤或净化饮料(水除外)用	12	40	17	15	台	A	--For filtering or purifying beverages other than water
8421.2300	--内燃发动机的滤油器	10	40	17	15	个		--Oil or petrol-filters for internal combustion engines
	--其他:							--Other:
8421.2910	---压滤机	5	40	17	15	个	O	---Press filters
8421.2990	---其他	5	40	17	15			---Other
8421.2990 40	液体截流过滤设备(可连续分离致病性微生物、毒素和细胞培养物)	5	40	17	15	个	3	Liquid closure filtration equipment (which can continuously separate pathogenic microorganisms, toxins and cell culture)
8421.2990 90	其他液体的过滤、净化机器及装置	5	40	17	15	个		Other filtering, purifying machinery and apparatuses for other liquids
	-气体的过滤、净化机器及装置:							-Filtering or purifying machinery and apparatus for gases:
8421.3100	--内燃发动机的进气过滤器	10	40	17	15	个		--Intake air filters for internal combustion engines
	--其他:							--Other:
8421.3910暂	---家用型	8	100	17	15	个		---Of the household type
	---工业用除尘器:							---Dust collectors for industry uses:
8421.3921	----静电除尘器	5	40	17	15	个		----Electrostatic
8421.3922	----袋式除尘器	5	40	17	15	个		----Baghoused
8421.3923	----旋风式除尘器	5	40	17	15	个		----Cyclone
8421.3924	----电袋复合除尘器	5	40	17	15	个/千克		----Electric bag composite dust collector
8421.3929	----其他	5	40	17	15	个		----Other
8421.3930	---内燃发动机排气过滤及净化装置		40	17	15	个		---Exhaust air filtering or purifyirg apparatus for internal combustion engines
8421.3930暂 01	摩托车发动机排气过滤及净化装置	3	40	17	15	个		Exhaust air filtering or purifying apparatus for motorcycle engine
8421.3930 90	其他内燃发动机排气过滤及净化装置	5	40	17	15	个		Other exhast air filtering or purifying appratus internal combustion engines
8421.3940	---烟气脱硫装置	5	40	17	15	个		---Flue gas desulpharisation apparatus
8421.3950	---烟气脱硝装置	5	40	17	15	个		---Flue gas denitration apparatus
8421.3990	---其他	5	40	17	15	个		---Other
	-零件:							-Parts:
	--离心机用,包括离心干燥机用:							--Of centrifuges, including centrifugal dryers:
8421.9110	---干衣量不超过10公斤的干衣机用	0	70	17	15	千克		---Of clothes-dryers of a dry linen capacity not exceeding 10kg
8421.9190	---其他	0	30	17	15	千克		---Other

税则号列	货品名称	最惠(%)	普通	增值税率	出口退税	计量单位	监管条件	Article Description
8421.9190 11	离心机壳/收集器(容纳气体离心机的转筒组件的耐 UF_6 部件)	0	30	17	15	千克	3	Centrifugal cover/collectors (accommodate gas centrifuge rotor components to UF_6 resistance)
8421.9190 12	收集器(由内径不同的同心管组成用于供取 UF_6 气体的管件)	0	30	17	15	千克	3	Collectors (parts of tube used for providing air of UF_6, made up of concentric tubes with different radiuses)
8421.9190 13	气体扩散膜(由耐 UF_6 材料制成的多细孔过滤薄膜)	0	30	17	15	千克	3	Air diffusion membrances (multiple stoma filtration membrane made of UF_6 resistance materials)
8421.9190 14	扩散室(含一个进气管两个出气管的容纳气体扩散膜的密闭式容器)	0	30	17	15	千克	3	Diffusion rooms (a closed spectacle that accommodate other diffusion membrances, with one inlet pipe and two outlet pipes)
8421.9190 90	其他离心机用零件	0	30	17	15	千克		Other parts of centrifuge machines
	--其他:							-Other:
8421.9910暂	---家用型过滤、净化装置用	6	100	17	15	千克		---Of household-type filtering or purifying machines
8421.9990	---其他	5	40	17	15	千克		---Other
84.22	**洗碟机;瓶子及其他容器的洗涤或干燥机器;瓶、罐、箱、袋或其他容器装填、封口、密封、贴标签的机器;瓶、罐、管、筒或类似容器的包封机器;其他包装或打包机器(包括热缩包装机器);饮料充气机:**							**Dish washing machines; machinery for cleaning or drying bottles or other containers; machinery for filling, closing, sealing or labelling bottles, cans, boxes, bags or other containers; machinery for capsuling bottles, jars, tubes and similar containers other packing or wrapping machinery (including heat-shrink wrapping machinery); machinery for aerating beverages:**
	-洗碟机:							-Dish washing machines:
8422.1100暂	--家用型	6	90	17	15	台/千克		--Of the household type
8422.1900	--其他	14	90	17	15	台/千克		--Other
8422.2000	-瓶子或其他容器的洗涤或干燥机器	10	35	17	15	台		-Machinery for cleaning or drying bottles or other containers
	-瓶、罐、箱、袋或其他容器的装填、封口、密封、贴标签的机器;瓶、罐、管、筒或类似容器的包封机器;饮料充气机:							-Machinery for filling, closing, sealing, or labelling bottles, cans, boxes, bags or other containers; machinery for capsuling bottles, jars, tubes and similar containers; machinery for aerating beverages:
8422.3010	---饮料及液体食品灌装设备		45	17	15	台		---Bottling or canning machinery for beverages or liquid food
8422.3010暂 01	乳品加工用自动化灌装设备	6	45	17	15	台	OA	Automatic bottling or canning machinery for dairy goods producing
8422.3010 90	其他饮料及液体食品灌装设备	12	45	17	15	台	OA	Other botting or canning machinery for beverages or liquid food
	---水泥包装机:							---Machinery for packing cement:
8422.3021	----全自动灌包机	12	45	17	15	台		----Automatic filling and sacking machines
8422.3029	----其他	12	45	17	15	台		----Other
8422.3030	---其他包装机		35	17	15	台		---Other packing machines
8422.3030暂 01	全自动无菌灌装生产线用包装机(加工速度≥20000 只/小时)	6	35	17	15	台	OA	Packing machines for fully automatic aseptic filling production lines (processing speed ≥2000 bottles/hour)
8422.3030 90	其他包装机	10	35	17	15	台	OA	Other packing machines
8422.3090	---其他		35	17	15	台		---Other
8422.3090暂 01	全自动无菌灌装生产线用贴吸管机(加工速度≥22000 只/小时)	6	35	17	15	台	A	Pipette machines for fully automatic filling production lines (processing speed ≥2000 bottles/hour)
8422.3090 10	充装设备(两用物项管制)	10	35	17	15	台	3A	Filling equipment (Subject to regulation of sensitive items)
8422.3090 90	饮料充气机及其他包封机	10	35	17	15	台	A	Machinery for aerating beverages and other encapsulation machinery
8422.4000	-其他包装或打包机器(包括热缩包装机器)	10	35	17	13,15	台		-Other packing or wrapping machinery (including heat-shrink wrapping machinery)
	-零件:							-Parts:
8422.9010暂	---洗碟机用	6	90	17	15	千克		---Of dish washing machines

税则号列	货品名称	最惠(%)	普通	增值税率	出口退税	计量单位	监管条件	Article Description
8422.9020	---饮料及液体食品灌装设备用	8.5	45	17	15	千克	A	---Of bottling or canning machinery for beverages or liquid food
8422.9090	---其他	8.5	35	17	15	千克		---Other
84.23	衡器(感量为50毫克或更精密的天平除外),包括计数或检验用的衡器;衡器用的各种砝码、秤砣:							**Weighing machinery (excluding balances of a sensitivity of 50 mg or better), including weight operated counting or checking machines; weighing machine weights of all kinds:**
8423.1000	-体重计,包括婴儿秤;家用秤	10.5	80	17	15	台		-Personal weighing machines, including baby scales; household scales
	-输送带上连续称货的秤:							-Scales for continuous weighing of goods on conveyors:
8423.2010	---电子皮带秤	10	80	17	15	台		---Electronic belt weighing machines
8423.2090	---其他	10	80	17	15	台		---Other
	-恒定秤、物料定量装袋或装容器用的秤,包括库秤:							-Constant weight scales and scales for discharging a predetermined weight of material into a bag or container, including hopper scales:
8423.3010	---定量包装秤	10.5	80	17	15	台		---Rationed packing scales
8423.3020	---定量分选秤	10.5	80	17	15	台		---Rationed sorting scales
8423.3030	---配料秤	10.5	80	17	15	台		---Proporating scales
8423.3090	---其他	10.5	80	17	15	台		---Other
	-其他衡器:							-Other weighing machinery:
	--最大称量不超过30公斤:							--Having a maximum weighing capacity not exceeding 30kg:
8423.8110	---计价秤	10.5	80	17	15	台		---Account balances
8423.8120	---弹簧秤	10.5	80	17	15	台		---Spring balances
8423.8190	---其他	10.5	80	17	15	台		---Other
	--最大称量超过30公斤,但不超过5000公斤:							--Having a maximum weighing capacity exceeding 30kg but not exceeding 5000kg:
8423.8210	---地中衡	10.5	80	17	15	台		---Weighbridges
8423.8290	---其他	10.5	80	17	15	台		---Other
	--其他:							--Other:
8423.8910	---地中衡	10	80	17	15	台		---Weighbridges
8423.8920	---轨道衡	10	80	17	15	台		---Track scales
8423.8930	---吊秤	10	80	17	15	台		---Hanging scales
8423.8990	---其他	10	80	17	15	台		---Other
8423.9000	-衡器用的各种砝码、秤砣;衡器的零件	10	80	17	15	千克		-Weighing machine weights of all kinds; parts of weighing machinery
84.24	液体或粉末的喷射、散布或喷雾的机械器具(不论是否手工操作);灭火器,不论是否装药;喷枪及类似器具;喷汽机、喷砂机及类似的喷射机器:							**Mechanical appliances (whether or not hand-operated) for projecting, dispersing or spraying liquids or powders; fire extinguishers, whether or not charged; spray guns and similar appliances; steam or sand blasting machines and similar jet projecting machines:**
8424.1000	-灭火器,不论是否装药	8.4	70	17	15	个	A	-Fire extinguishers, whether or not charged
8424.2000	-喷枪及类似器具	8.4	40	17	15	个		-Spray guns and similar appliances
8424.3000	-喷气机、喷砂机及类似的喷射机器	8.4	40	17	15	台		-Steam or sand blasting machines and similar jet projecting machines
	-其他器具:							-Other appliances:
8424.8100	--农业或园艺用	8	30	13	13	台		--Agricultural or horticul tural
	--其他:							--Other:
8424.8910	---家用型	0	80	17	15	台/千克		---Of the household type
8424.8920	---喷涂机器人	0	80	17	15	台/千克		---Spraying robot
	---其他:							---Other:
8424.8991	----船用洗舱机	0	30	17	15	台		----Marine cabinet washer
8424.8999	----其他	0	30	17	15	台		----Other

税则号列	货品名称	最惠(%)	普通	增值税率	出口退税	计量单位	监管条件	Article Description
8424.8999 10	分离喷嘴(由狭缝状、曲率半径极小的弯曲通道组成,内有分离楔尖)	0	30	17	15	台	3	Separating nozzles (composed of slik-like curved and channels of very small curvature radius, with separation of wedge tip)
8424.8999 90	其他用途的喷射、喷雾机械器具	0	30	17	15	台		Mechanical appliances for projecting, or spraying for other use
	-零件:							-Parts:
8424.9010	---子目8424.1000所列器具的零件	0	70	17	15	千克		---Of the apparatus of subheading No. 8424.1000
8424.9020	---子目8424.8910所列器具的零件	0	80	17	15	千克		---Of the apparatus of subheading No. 8424.8910
8424.9090	---其他	0	30	17	13,15	千克		---Other
84.25	**滑车及提升机,但倒卸式提升机除外;卷扬机及绞盘;千斤顶:**							**Pulley tackle and hoists other than skip hoists; winches and capstans; jacks:**
	-滑车及提升机,但倒卸式提升机及提升车辆用的提升机除外:							-Pulley tackle and hoists other than skip hoists or hoists of a kind used for raising vehicles:
8425.1100	--电动的	6	30	17	17	台		--Powered by electric motor
8425.1900	--其他	5	30	17	17	台		--Other
	-卷扬机;绞盘:							-Winches; capstans:
	--电动的:							--Powered by electric motor:
8425.3110	---矿井口卷扬装置;专为井下使用设计的卷扬机	10	30	17	17	台		---Pit-head winding gear; winches specially designed for use underground
8425.3190	---其他	5	30	17	17	台		---Other
	--其他:							--Other:
8425.3910	---矿井口卷扬装置;专为井下使用设计的卷扬机	10	30	17	17	台		---Pit-head winding gear; winches specially designed for use underground
8425.3990	---其他	5	30	17	17	台		---Other
	-千斤顶;提升车辆用的提升机:							-Jacks; hoists of a kind used for raising vehicles:
8425.4100	--车库中使用的固定千斤顶系统	3	30	17	17	台		--Built-in jacking systems of a type used in garages
	--其他液压千斤顶及提升机:							--Other jacks and hoists, hydraulic:
8425.4210	---液压千斤顶	3	30	17	17	台		---Hydraulic jacks
8425.4290	---其他	5	30	17	17	台		---Other
	--其他:							--Other:
8425.4910	---其他千斤顶	5	30	17	17	台		---Other jacks
8425.4990	---其他	10	30	17	17	台		---Other
84.26	**船用桅杆式起重机;起重机,包括缆式起重机;移动式吊运架、跨运车及装有起重机的工作车:**							**Ships derricks; cranes, including cable cranes; mobile lifting frames, straddle carriers and works trucks fitted with a crane:**
	-高架移动式起重机、桁架桥式起重机、龙门起重机、桥式起重机、移动式吊运架及跨运车:							-Overhead travelling cranes, transporter cranes, gantry cranes, bridge cranes, mobile lifting frames and straddle carriers:
	--固定支架的高架移动式起重机:							--Overhead travelling cranes on fixed support:
8426.1120	---通用桥式起重机	8	30	17	17	台		---Bridge cranes, all-purpose
8426.1190	---其他	8	30	17	17	台		---Other
8426.1200	--带胶轮的移动式吊运架及跨运车	6	30	17	17	台		--Mobile lifting frames on tyres and straddle carriers
	--其他:							--Other:
8426.1910	---装船机	5	30	17	17	台		---Ship loading cranes
	---卸船机:							---Ship unloading cranes:
8426.1921	----抓斗式	5	30	17	17	台		----Grab ship unloading cranes
8426.1929	----其他	5	30	17	17	台	O	----Other
8426.1930	---龙门式起重机	10	30	17	17	台		---Gantry cranes
	---装卸桥:							---Loading and unlcading bridges:
8426.1941	----门式装卸桥	10	30	17	17	台		----Frame loading and unloading bridges
8426.1942	----集装箱装卸桥	10	30	17	17	台		----Container loading and unloading bridges
8426.1943	----其他动臂式装卸桥	10	30	17	17	台		----Derrick loading and unloading bridges
8426.1949	----其他	10	30	17	17	台		----Other
8426.1990	---其他	10	30	17	17	台		---Other
8426.2000	-塔式起重机	10	30	17	17	台	O	-Tower cranes
8426.3000	-门座式起重机及座式旋臂起重机	6	30	17	17	台		-Portal or pedestal jib cranes

税则号列	货品名称	最惠(%)	普通	增值税率	出口退税	计量单位	监管条件	Article Description
	-其他自推进机械：							-Other machinery, self-propelled:
	--带胶轮的：							--On tyres:
8426.4110	---轮胎式起重机	5	30	17	17	台	O	---Wheel-mounted cranes
8426.4190	---其他	5	30	17	17	台		---Other
	--其他：							--Other:
8426.4910	---履带式起重机	8	30	17	17	台	O	---Crawler cranes
8426.4990	---其他	13	30	17	17	台		---Other
	-其他机械：							-Other machinery:
8426.9100	--供装于公路车辆的	10	30	17	17	台		--Designed for mounting on road vehicles
8426.9900	--其他	6	30	17	17	台		--Other
84.27	**叉车；其他装有升降或搬运装置的工作车：**							**Fork-lift trucks; other works trucks fitted with lifting or handling equipment:**
	-电动机推进的机动车：							-Self-propelled trucks powered by an electric motor:
8427.1010	---有轨巷道堆垛机	9	30	17	17	台	A	---Track alleyway stackers
8427.1020	---无轨巷道堆垛机	9	30	17	17	台	A	---Trackless alleyway stackers
8427.1090	---其他	9	30	17	17	台	A	---Other
	-其他机动车：							-Other self-propelled trucks:
8427.2010	---集装箱叉车	9	30	17	17	台	A	---Fork-lift trucks cranes
8427.2090	---其他	9	30	17	17	台	A	---Other
8427.9000	-其他车	9	30	17	17	台	A	-Other trucks
84.28	**其他升降、搬运、装卸机械（例如，升降机、自动梯、输送机、缆车）：**							**Other lifting, handling, loading or unloading machinery (for example, lifts, escalators, conveyors, teleferics):**
	-升降机及倒卸式起重机：							-Lifts and skip hoists:
8428.1010	---载客电梯		30	17	17	台		---Designed for the transport of persons
8428.1010暂 01	无障碍升降机	4	30	17	17	台	A	Accessibility lifts
8428.1010 90	其他载客电梯	8	30	17	17	台	A	Other passenger elevators
8428.1090	---其他	6	30	17	17	台	A	---Other
8428.2000	-气压升降机及输送机	5	30	17	17	台		-Pneumatic elevators and conveyors
	-其他用于连续运送货物或材料的升降机及输送机：							-Other continuous-action elevators and conveyors, for goods or materials:
8428.3100	--地下专用的	5	30	17	17	台		--Specially designed for underground use
8428.3200	--其他，斗式	5	30	17	17	台		--Other, bucket type
8428.3300	--其他，带式	5	30	17	17	台		--Other, belt type
	--其他：							--Other:
8428.3910	---链式	5	30	17	17	台		---Chain type
8428.3920	---辊式	5	30	17	17	台		---Roller type
8428.3990	---其他	5	30	17	17	台		---Other
8428.4000	-自动梯及自动人行道	5	30	17	17	台	A	-Escalators and moving walkways
	-缆车、座式升降机、滑雪拉索、索道用牵引装置：							-Teleferics, chair-lifts, ski-draglines; traction mechanisms for funiculars:
8428.6010	---货运架空索道	8	30	17	17	台		---Cargo aerial cableways
	---客运架空索道：							---Passanger aerial cableways:
8428.6021	----单线循环式	8	30	17	17	台		----Monocable endless
8428.6029	----其他	8	30	17	17	台		----Other
8428.6090	---其他	8	30	17	17	台		---Other
	-其他机械							-Other machinery
8428.9010	---矿车推动机、铁道机车或货车的转车台、货车倾卸装置及类似的铁道货车搬运装置	10	30	17	17	台		---Mine wagon pushers, locmotive or wagon traversers, wagon tippers and similar railway wagon handling equipment
8428.9020	---机械式停车设备	5	30	17	17	台		---Machinery parking equipment
	---装卸机械：							---Unloading machinery:
8428.9031	----堆取料机械	5	30	17	17	台		----Stacker reclaimers machinery
8428.9039	----其他装卸机械	5	30	17	17	台		----Other unloading machinery

税则号列	货品名称	最惠(%)	普通	增值税率	出口退税	计量单位	监管条件	Article Description
8428.9040	---搬运机器人	5	30	17	17	台		---Handling robot
8428.9090	---其他	5	30	17	17	台		---Other
8428.9090 10	放化分离作业和热室用遥控机械手(能贯穿0.6米以上热室壁或壁厚为0.6米以上热室顶)	5	30	17	17	台	3	Remote manipulators for radioactive chemical separating operation and hot cell (capable of penetrating wall of hot cell thickness >0.6m or top of hot cell thickness >0.6m)
8428.9090 20	核反应堆燃料装卸机(用于在核反应堆中插入或取出燃料的操作设备)	5	30	17	17	台	3	nuclear reactor fuel loader and unloader (operational appliances used for putting inor taking out the fuels in nuclear reactor)
8428.9090 90	其他升降、搬运、装卸机械	5	30	17	17	台		Other lifting, carrying, loading or unloading machinery
84.29	**机动推土机、侧铲推土机、筑路机、平地机、铲运机、机械铲、挖掘机、机铲装载机、捣固机械及压路机:**							**Self-propelled bulldozers, angledozers, graders, levellers, scrapers, mechanical shovels, excavators, shovel loaders, tamping machines and road rollers:**
	-推土机及侧铲推土机:							-Bulldozers and angledozers:
	--履带式:							--Track laying:
8429.1110	---发动机输出功率超过235.36千瓦(320马力)的	7	17	17	17	台	A	---With an engine of an output exceeding 235.36KW (320hs)
8429.1190	---其他	7	30	17	17	台	A	---Other
	--其他:							--Other:
8429.1910	---发动机输出功率超过235.36千瓦(320马力)的	7	17	17	17	台	A	---With an engine of an output exceeding 235.36KW (320hp)
8429.1990	---其他	7	30	17	17	台	A	---Other
	-筑路机及平地机:							-Graders and levellers:
8429.2010	---发动机输出功率超过235.36千瓦(320马力)的	5	17	17	13,17	台	A	---With an engine of an output exceeding 235.36KW (320hp)
8429.2090	---其他	5	30	17	13,17	台	A	---Other:
	-铲运机:							-Scrapers:
8429.3010	---斗容量超过10立方米的	3	17	17	17	台	A	---Having a capacity of shovel exceeding $10m^3$
8429.3090	---其他	5	30	17	17	台	A	---Other
	-捣固机械及压路机:							-Tamping machines and road rollers:
	---机动压路机:							---Self-propelled road rollers:
8429.4011	----机重18吨及以上的振动压路机	7	20	17	17	台	OA	----Vibration type, of a deadweight of 18t or more
8429.4019	----其他	8	40	17	17	台	OA	----Other
8429.4090	---其他	6	30	17	17	台	A	---Other
	-机械铲、挖掘机及机铲装载机:							-Mechanical shovels, excavators and shovel loaders:
8429.5100	--前铲装载机	5	30	17	17	台	A	--Front-end shovel loaders
	--上部结构可旋转360度的机械:							--Machinery with a 360° revolving super-structure:
	---挖掘机:							---Excavators:
8429.5211	----轮胎式	8	30	17	17	台	OA	----Tyre-mounted
8429.5212	----履带式	8	30	17	17	台	OA	----Track-mounted
8429.5219	----其他	8	30	17	17	台	OA	----Other
8429.5290	---其他	8	30	17	17	台	OA	---Other
8429.5900	--其他	8	30	17	17	台	OA	--Other
84.30	**泥土、矿物或矿石的运送、平整、铲运、挖掘、捣固、压实、开采或钻探机械;打桩机及拔桩机;扫雪机及吹雪机:**							**Other moving, grading, levelling, scraping, excavating, tamping, compacting, extracting or boring machinery, for earth, minerals or ores; pile-drivers and pile-extractors; snow-ploughs and snow-blowers:**
8430.1000	-打桩机及拔桩机	10	30	17	17	台		-Pile-drivers and pile-extranctors
8430.2000	-扫雪机及吹雪机	10	30	17	17	台		-Snow-ploughs and snow-blowers
	-截煤机、凿岩机及隧道掘进机:							-Coal or rock cutters and tunnelling machinery:
	--自推进的:							--Self-propelle:
8430.3110	---采(截)煤机	10	30	17	17	台/千克	O	---Mining (cutting) coal machine
8430.3120	---凿岩机	10	30	17	17	台/千克	O	---Rock drilling machine
8430.3130	---隧道掘进机	10	30	17	17	台/千克	O	---Tunnel boring machine
8430.3900	--其他	6	30	17	17	台		--Other
	-其他钻探或凿井机械:							-Other boring or sinking machinery:

税则号列	货品名称	最惠(%)	普通	增值税率	出口退税	计量单位	监管条件	Article Description
	--自推进的:							--Self-propelled:
	---石油及天然气钻探机:							---Oil and natural gas drilling machinery:
8430.4111	----钻探深度在6000米及以上的	5	11	17	17	台		----Of drilling depth of 6000m or more
8430.4119	----其他	5	17	17	17	台		----Other
	---其他钻探机:							---Other drilling machinery:
8430.4121	----钻探深度在6000米及以上的	5	11	17	17	台		----Of drilling depth of 6000m or more
8430.4122	----钻探深度在6000米以下的履带式自推进钻机	5	17	17	17	台		----Crawler boring machinery of drilling depth not exceeding 6000 m
8430.4129	----钻探深度在6000米以下的其他钻探机	5	17	17	17	台		----Other boring machinery of drilling depth exceeding 6000 m
8430.4190	---其他	5	30	17	17	台		---Other
8430.4900	--其他	5	30	17	17	台		--Other
	-其他自推进机械:							-Other machinery, self-propelled:
8430.5010	---其他采油机械	3	17	17	17	台		---For oil production
8430.5020	---矿用电铲	7	30	17	17	台		---Mining power shovels
	---采矿钻机:							---Mining drills:
8430.5031	----牙轮直径380毫米及以上	5	30	17	17	台		----Gear wheel diameter more than 380mm
8430.5039	----其他	5	30	17	17	台		----Other
8430.5090	---其他	5	30	17	17	台		---Other
	-其他非自推进机械:							-Other machinery, not self-propelled:
8430.6100	--捣固或压实机械	6	30	17	17	台		--Tamping or compacting machinery
	--其他:							--Other:
	---工程钻机:							---Engineering drills:
8430.6911	----钻筒直径在3米及以上	6	30	17	17	台		----Boring casing diameter more than 3m
8430.6919	----其他	6	30	17	17	台		----Other
8430.6920	---铲运机	6	30	17	17	台		---Serapers
8430.6990	---其他	6	30	17	17	台		---Other
84.31	**专用于或主要用于税目84.25至84.30所列机械的零件:**							**Parts suitable for use solely or principally with the machinery of headings No. 84.25 to 84.30:**
8431.1000	-税目84.25所列机械的零件	3	30	17	15	千克		-Of machinery of heading No. 84.25
	-税目84.27所列机械的零件							-Of machinery of heading No. 84.27:
8431.2010	---装有差速器的驱动桥及其零件,不论是否装有传动部件	6	30	17	15	千克/个		---Drive-axle with differential and parts thereof, whether or not provided transmussion components
8431.2090[暂]	---其他	3	30	17	15	千克		---Other
	-税目84.28所列机械的零件:							-Of machinery of heading No. 84.28:
8431.3100	--升降机、倒卸式起重机或自动梯的零件		30	17	15	千克		--Of lifts, skip hoists or escalators
8431.3100[暂] 01	无障碍升降机的零件	1	30	17	15	千克		Parts of accessibility lifts
8431.3100 90	其他升降机、倒卸式起重机零件(包括自动梯零件)	3	30	17	15	千克		Other lifters, unloading crane parts (including automatic elevator parts)
8431.3900	--其他	5	30	17	15	千克		--Other
	-税目84.26、84.29、或84.30所列机械的零件:							-Of machinery of headingNo. 84.26, 84.29 or 84.30:
8431.4100	--戽斗、铲斗、抓斗、及夹斗	6	17	17	15	千克/个		--Buckets, shovels, grabs and grips
8431.4200	--推土机或侧铲推土机用铲	6	17	17	15	千克/个		--Bulldozer or angledozer blades
	--子目8430.41或8430.49所列钻探或凿井机械的零件:							--Parts of boring or sinking machinery of subheading No. 8430.41 or 8430.49:
8431.4310	---石油或天然气钻探机用	4	11	17	15	千克		---Of oil and natural gas drilling machinery
8431.4320	---其他钻探机用	4	11	17	15	千克		---Of other drilling machinery
8431.4390	---其他	5	17	17	15	千克		---Other
	--其他:							--Other:
8431.4920	---装有差速器的驱动桥及其零件,不论是否装有传动部件	5	17	17	15	千克/个		---Drive-axle with differential and parts thereof, whether or not provided transmussion components
	---其他:							---Other:
8431.4991	----矿用电铲用	5	17	17	15	千克		----For electrical shovels for mining
8431.4999	----其他:	5	17	17	15	千克		----Other:
84.32	**农业、园艺及林业用整地或耕作机械;草坪及运动场地滚压机:**							**Agricultural, horticultural or forestry machinery for soil preparation or cultivation; lawn or sports-ground rollers:**
8432.1000	-犁	5	30	13	13	台/千克		-Ploughs
	-耙、松土机、中耕机、除草机及耕耘机:							-Harrows, scarifiers, cultivators, weeders and hoes:

税则号列	货　品　名　称	最惠(%)	普通	增值税率	出口退税	计量单位	监管条件	Article Description
8432.2100	--圆盘耙	5	30	13	13	台/千克		--Disc harrows
8432.2900	--其他	4	30	13	13	台/千克		--Other
	-播种机、种植机及移植机							-Seeders, planters and transplanters:
	---播种机:							---Operating-seeder:
8432.3011	----谷物播种机	4	30	13	13	台		----Grain operating-seeder
8432.3019	----其他	4	30	13	13	台		----Other
	---种植机:							---Planter:
8432.3021	----马铃薯种植	4	30	13	13	台		----Potato planter
8432.3029	----其他	4	30	13	13	台		----Other
	---移植机(栽植机):							---Transplanter:
8432.3031	----水稻插秧机	4	30	13	13	台		----Rice transplanter
8432.3039	----其他	4	30	13	13	台		----Other
8432.4000	-施肥机	4	30	13	13	台		-Manure spreaders and fertilizer distributors
	-其他机械:							-Other machinery:
8432.8010	---草坪及运动场地滚压机	7	40	17	15	台		---Lawn or sports-ground rollers
8432.8090	---其他	4	30	13	13,15	台		---Other
8432.9000	-零件	4	17	17	15	千克		-Parts
84.33	**收割机、脱粒机,包括草料打包机;割草机;蛋类、水果或其他农产品的清洁、分选、分级机器,但税目84.37的机器除外:**							**Harvesting or threshing machinery, including straw or fodder balers; grass or hay mowers; machines for cleaning, sorting or grading eggs, fruit or other agricultural produce, other than machinery of heading No. 84.37:**
	-草坪、公园或运动场地用的割草机:							-Mowers for lawns, parks or sports grounds:
8433.1100	--机动的,切割装置在同一水平面上旋转的	6	30	13	15	台		--Powered, with the cutting device rotating in a horizontal plane
8433.1900	--其他	6	30	17	15	台		--Other
8433.2000	-其他割草机,包括牵引装置用的刀具杆	4	30	13	13	台		-Other mowers, including cutter bars for tractor mounting
8433.3000	-其他干草切割、翻晒机器	5	30	13	13	台		-Other haymaking machinery
8433.4000	-草料打包机,包括收集打包机	5	30	13	13	台		-Straw or fodder balers, including pick-up balers
	-其他收割机;脱粒机:							-Other harvesting machinery; threshing machinery:
8433.5100	--联合收割机		17	13	13	台		--Combine harvester-threshers
8433.5100[暂] 01	功率≥160马力的联合收割机	5	17	13	13	台		Combine harvester-threshers, power≥160PS
8433.5100 90	功率<160马力的联合收割机	8	17	13	13	台		Combine harvester-threshers, power<160PS
8433.5200	--其他脱粒机	8	30	13	13	台		--Other threshing machinery
8433.5300	--根茎或块茎收获机		30	13	13	台		--Root or tuber harvesting machines
8433.5300[暂] 01	功率≥160马力的土豆、甜菜收获机	4	30	13	13	台		Potatoes, beets harvesting machines, power ≥ 160Hp
8433.5300 90	其他根茎或块茎收获机	8	30	13	13	台		Other root or tuber harvesting machines
	--其他:							--Other:
8433.5910	---甘蔗收获机		30	13	13	台		---Sugarcane harvesters
8433.5910[暂] 01	功率≥160马力的甘蔗收获机	4	30	13	13	台		Sugarcane harvesting machines, power ≥160Hp
8433.5910 90	其他甘蔗收获机	8	30	13	13	台		Other sugarcane harvesters
8433.5920[暂]	---棉花采摘机	5	30	13	13	台		---Cotton picker
8433.5990	---其他		30	13	13	台		---Other
8433.5990[暂] 01	自走式青储饲料收获机	5	30	13	13	台		Self-propelled silage harvester
8433.5990[暂] 02	茶叶采摘机	4	30	13	13	台		Tea picker
8433.5990 90	其他收割机及脱粒机	8	30	13	13	台		Other harvesers and threshers
8433.6000	-蛋类、水果或其他农产品的清洁、分选、分级机器	5	30	13	13	台		-Machines for cleaning, sorting or grading eggs, fruit or other agricultural produce
	-零件:							-Parts:
8433.9010	---联合收割机用	5	11	17	15	千克		---Of combine harvester-threshers
8433.9090	---其他	3	17	17	15	千克		---Other
84.34	**挤奶机及乳品加工机器:**							**Milking machines and dairy machinery:**
8434.1000	-挤奶机	10	20	13	13	台		-Milking machines
8434.2000[暂]	-乳品加工机器	2	30	17	15	台	A	-Dairy machinery
8434.9000	-零件	5	17	17	15	千克	A	-Parts

税则号列	货品名称	最惠(%)	普通	增值税率	出口退税	计量单位	监管条件	Article Description
84.35	**制酒、制果汁或制类似饮料用的压榨机、轧碎机及类似机器：**							**Presses, crushers and similar machinery used in the manufacture of wine, cider, fruit juices or similar beverages:**
8435.1000	-机器	10	30	17	15	台	A	-Machinery
8435.9000	-零件	6	30	17	15	千克	A	-Parts
84.36	**农业、园艺、林业、家禽饲养业或养蜂业用的其他机器，包括装有机械或热力装置的催芽设备；家禽孵卵器及育雏器：**							**Other agricultural, horticultural, forestry, poultry-keeping or bee-keeping machinery, including germination plant fitted with mechanical or thermal equipment; poultry incubators and brooders:**
8436.1000	-动物饲料配制机	7	30	13	13	台		-Machinery for preparing animal feeding stuffs
	-家禽饲养用的机器；家禽孵卵器及育雏器：							-Poultry-keeping machinery; poultry incubators and brooders:
8436.2100	--家禽孵卵器及育雏器	5	30	13	13	台		--Poultry incubators and brooders
8436.2900	--其他	10	30	13	13	台		--Other
8436.8000	-其他机器		30	13	13,15	台		-Other machinery
8436.8000暂 01	青储饲料切割上料机	3	30	13	13,15	台		Silage cutting feeders
8436.8000暂 02	自走式饲料搅拌投喂车	5	30	13	13,15	台		self-propelled type feed mixing and feeding vehicle
8436.8000 90	农、林业、园艺等用的其他机器（包括装有机械或热力装置的催芽设备）	10	30	13	13,15	台		Other machines for agricultural, horticultural, forestry (lincluding germination equipments fitted with mechanical or thermal equipment)
	-零件：							-Parts:
8436.9100	--家禽饲养用机器的零件或家禽孵卵器及育雏器的零件	6	17	17	15	千克		--Of poultry-keeping machinery or poultry incubators and brooders
8436.9900	--其他	6	17	17	15	千克		--Other
84.37	**种子、谷物或干豆的清洁、分选或分级机器；谷物磨粉业加工机器或谷物、干豆加工机器，但农业用机器除外：**							**Machines for cleaning, sorting or grading seed, grain or dried leguminous vegetables; machinery used in the milling industry or for the working of cereals or dried leguminous vegetables, other than farm-type machi-nery:**
	-种子、谷物或干豆的清洁、分选或分级机器：							-Machines for cleaning, sorting or grading seed, grain or dried leguminous vegetables:
8437.1010	---光学色差颗粒选别机（色选机）	10	30	13	13,15	台		---Optical color granule sorter(color sorter)
8437.1090	---其他	10	30	13	13	台		---Other
8437.8000	-其他机器	10	30	17	13	台	A	-Other machinery
8437.9000	-零件	6	30	17	15	千克		-Parts
84.38	**本章其他税目未列名的食品、饮料工业用的生产或加工机器，但提取、加工动物油脂或植物固定油脂的机器除外：**							**Machinery, not specified or included else-where in this Chapter, for the industrial preparation or manufacture of food or drink, other than machinery for the extraction or preparation of animal or fixed vegetable fats or oils:**
8438.1000	-糕点加工机器及生产通心粉、面条或类似产品的机器	7	30	17	15	台		-Bakery machinery and machinery for the manufacture of macaroni, spaghetti or similar products
8438.1000 10	糕点生产线	7	30	17	15	台	A	Bakery production lines
8438.1000 90	通心粉，面条的生产加工机器（包括类似产品的加工机）	7	30	17	15	台	A	Machines for producing and processing macaroni and noodles (including processing machine of similar products)
8438.2000	-生产糖果、可可粉、巧克力的机器	8	30	17	15	台	A	-Machinery for the manufacture of confectionery, cocoa or chocolate
8438.3000	-制糖机器	10	30	17	15	台	A	-Machinery for sugar manufacture
8438.4000	-酿酒机器	7	30	17	15	台	A	-Brewery machinery
8438.5000	-肉类或家禽加工机器	7	30	17	15	台/千克	A	-Machinery for the preparation of meat or poultry
8438.6000	-水果、坚果或蔬菜加工机器	10	30	17	15	台/千克	A	-Machinery for the preparation of fruits, nuts or vegetables

税则号列	货品名称	最惠(%)	普通	增值税率	出口退税	计量单位	监管条件	Article Description
8438.8000	-其他机器	8.5	30	17	15	台/千克	A	-Other machinery
8438.9000	-零件	5	30	17	15	千克	A	-Parts
84.39	纤维素纸浆、纸及纸板的制造或整理机器:							**Machinery for making pulp of fibrous cellulosic material or for making or finishing paper or paperboard:**
8439.1000	-制造纤维素纸浆的机器	8.4	30	17	15	台	O	-Machinery for making pulp of fibrous cellulosic material
8439.2000	-纸或纸板的抄造机器	8.4	30	17	15	台	O	-Machinery for making paper or paper board
8439.3000	-纸或纸板的整理机器	8.4	30	17	15	台	O	-Machinery for finishing paper or paper board
	-零件:							-Parts:
8439.9100	--制造纤维素纸浆的机器用	6	30	17	15	千克		--Of machinery for making pulp of fibrous cellulosic material
8439.9900	--其他	6	30	17	15	千克		--Other
84.40	**书本装订机器,包括锁线订书机:**							**Book-binding machinery, including book-sewing machines:**
	-机器:							-Machinery:
8440.1010	---锁线装订机	10	35	17	15	台		---Sewing bookbinders
8440.1020	---胶订机	12	35	17	15	台		---Glueing bookbinders
8440.1090	---其他	12	35	17	15	台		---Other
8440.9000	-零件	8	35	17	15	千克		-Parts
84.41	**其他制造纸浆制品、纸制品或纸板制品的机器,包括各种切纸机:**							**Other machinery for making up paper pulp, paper or paperboard, including cutting machines of all kinds:**
8441.1000	-切纸机	12	50	17	15	台		-Cutting machines
8441.2000	-制造包、袋或信封的机器	12	30	17	15	台		-Machines for making bags, sacks or envelopes
	-制造箱、盒、管、桶或类似容器的机器,但模制成型机器除外:							-Machines for making cartons, boxes, cases, tubes, drums or similar containers, other than by moulding:
8441.3010	---制造纸塑铝复合罐的生产设备	13.5	30	17	15	台		---Machines for paper, plastic and aluminium composite can manufacture
8441.3090	---其他	13.5	30	17	15	台		---Other
8441.4000	-纸浆、纸或纸板制品模制成型机器	12	30	17	15	台	O	-Machines for moulding articles in paper pulp, paper or paperboard
	-其他机器:							-Other machinery:
8441.8010	---制造纸塑铝软包装的生产设备	12	30	17	15	台		---Machines for paper plastic and aluminium flexible packaging manufacture
8441.8090	---其他	12	30	17	15	台	O	---Other
	-零件:							-Parts:
8441.9010	---切纸机用		50	17	15	千克		---Of cutting machines
8441.9010暂 01	切纸机用弧形辊	4	50	17	15	千克		Bowed roll, of a kind used in paper cutter
8441.9010暂 02	切纸机用横切刀单元	3	50	17	15	千克		Crosscut knife unit, of a kind used in paper cutter
8441.9010 90	其他切纸机零件	8	50	17	15	千克		Other parts of paper cutter
8441.9090	---其他	8.4	30	17	15	千克		---Other
84.42	**制版用的机器、器具及设备(税目84.56至84.65的机床除外);印刷用版(片)滚筒及其他部件;制成供印刷用(例如,刨平、压纹或抛光)的版(片)滚筒及石板:**							**Machinery, apparatus and equipment (other than the machine-tools of headingsNOS. 84.56 to 84.65), for preparing or making plates, cylinders or other printing components; plates, cylinders and other printing components; plates, cylinders and lithographic stones, prepared for printing purposes (for example, planed, grained or polished):**
	-机器、器具及设备:							-Machinery, apparatus and equipment:
8442.3010	---铸字机	9	35	17	15	台		---Type casters
	---制版机器、器具及设备:							---Other machinery, apparatus and equipment for typesetting:
8442.3021暂	----计算机直接制版设备		35	17	15	台		----Machines for preparing CTP plates

税则号列	货品名称	最惠(%)	普通	增值税率	出口退税	计量单位	监管条件	Article Description
8442.3021[暂] 10	凹版式计算机直接制版设备(CTP)	3	35	17	15	台		Concave layout of computer direct plate making equipment(CTP)
8442.3021[暂] 90	除凹版式以外的其他计算机直接制版设备(CTP)	5	35	17	15	台		Other computer direct plate making equipment in addition to outside the concaveformat (CTP)
8442.3029	----其他	9	35	17	15	台		----Other
8442.3090	---其他	9	35	17	15	台		---Other
8442.4000	-上述机器、器具及设备的零件		20	17	15	千克		-Parts of the foregoing machinery, apparatus or equipment
8442.4000[暂] 01	计算机直接制版机器用零件	0	20	17	15	千克		Parts of computer – to – plate machines
8442.4000 90	其他铸字、排字、制版机器的零件	7	20	17	15	千克		Other components of typecasting, typesetting and platemaking machines
8442.5000	-印刷用版、滚筒及其他印刷部件;制成供印刷用(例如,刨平、压纹或抛光)的板、滚筒及石板	7	35	17	15	千克		-Plates, cylinders and other printing components; plates, cylinders and lithographic stones, prepared for printing purposes (for example, planed, grained or polished)
84.43	**用于税目84.42的印刷用版(片)、滚筒及其他印刷部件进行印刷的机器;其他打印机、复印机及传真机,不论是否组合式;上述机器的零件及附件:**							**Printing machinery used for printing, cylinders and other printing components of heading84.42; other printers Copying mechines and facsimile machines,whether or not combined;Part and accessories there of:**
	-用税目84.42的印刷用版(片)、滚筒及其他印刷部件进行印刷的机器:							-Printing machinery used for printing by means of plates, cylinders and other printing components of heading No.84.42:
8443.1100	--卷取进料式胶印机	10	35	17	15	台		--Offset printing machinery reel-fed
8443.1200	--办公室用片取进料式胶印机(片尺寸一边长不超过22cm,另一边长不超过36cm)	12	35	17	15	台		--Offset printhg machinery sheet-fed, office type (using sheets with one side not exceeding 22cm and the other side not exceedig 36cm in the unfoldool state)
	--其他胶印机:							--Other offset printing machinery:
	---平张纸进料式:							---Sheet fed:
8443.1311	----单色机	10	35	17	15	台		----Single color
8443.1312	----双色机	10	35	17	15	台		----Double colors
8443.1313	----四色机		35	17	15	台		----Four colors
8443.1313[暂] 01	四色平张纸胶印机(对开单张单面印刷速度≥16000张/小时)	7	35	17	15	台		Four – color sheet fed offset printing presses(single folio double side printing speed≥16000 folio/hour)
8443.1313[暂] 02	四色平张纸胶印机(对开单张双面印刷速度≥13000张/小时)	7	35	17	15	台		Four – color sheet fed offset printing press(single folio double sides printing speed≥13000pcs/hr)
8443.1313[暂] 03	四色平张纸胶印机(全张或超全张单张单面印刷速度≥13000张/小时)	7	35	17	15	台		Four – color sheet fed offset printing press(sheetwise or full – sheet one piece single side printing speed≥13000pcs/hr)
8443.1313 90	其他四色平张纸胶印机(用税目84.42项下商品进行印刷的机器)	10	35	17	15	台		Other four – color sheet fed offset printing press (machines printing with commodities in Duty item 84.42)
8443.1319	----其他		35	17	15	台		----Other
8443.1319[暂] 01	五色及以上平张纸胶印机(对开单张单面印刷速度≥17000张/小时)	7	35	17	15	台		Five(or higher) – color sheet fed offset printing press(speed≥16000pcs/h)
8443.1319[暂] 02	五色及以上平张纸胶印机(对开单张双面印刷速度≥13000张/小时)	7	35	17	15	台		Five(or higher) – color sheet fed offset printing press (single folio double sides printing speed ≥13000pcs/hr)
8443.1319[暂] 03	五色及以上平张纸胶印机(全张或超全张单张单面印刷速度≥13000张/小时)	7	35	17	15	台		Five(or higher) – color sheet fed offset printins press(sheetwise or full – sheet one piece single side printing speed≥13000pcs/hr)
8443.1319 90	其他平张纸进料式胶印机(用税目84.42项下商品进行印刷的机器)	10	35	17	15	台		Other sheet fed offset printing press (machines printing with commodities under heading No. 84.42)
8443.1390	---其他	10	35	17	15	台		---Other
8443.1400	--卷取进料式凸版印刷机,但不包括苯胺印刷机	12	35	17	15	台		--Letterpress printing machinery, reelfed, excluding flexographic printing

税则号列	货品名称	最惠(%)	普通	增值税率	出口退税	计量单位	监管条件	Article Description
8443.1500	--除卷取进料式以外的凸版印刷机,但不包括苯胺印刷机	12	35	17	15	台		--Letterpress printing machinery other than reelfed, excluding flexographic printing
8443.1600	--苯胺印刷机		35	17	15	台		--Flexographic printing machinery
8443.1600暂 01	苯胺印刷机,线速度≥350 米/分钟,幅宽≥800 毫米(柔性版印刷机,用税目 84.42 项下商品进行印刷的机器)	3	35	17	15	台		Flexographic pringting machinery, linear speed ≥ 300m/min, Wide ≥800mm flexographic persses, using good in heading No. 84.42 to printing
8443.1600暂 02	机组式柔性版印刷机,线速度≥160m/min,250mm≤幅宽<800mm(具有烫印或全息或丝网印刷功能单元的)	5	35	17	15	台		Flexographic press, unit-Type, linear speed≥160m/min, 250mm ≤ width < 800mm (with function of stamping or holography or screen printing)
8443.1600 90	其他苯胺印刷机(柔性版印刷机,用税目 84.42 项下商品进行印刷的机器)	10	35	17	15	台		Other flexographic printing machinery (flexographic press and machines printing with commodities under heading No. 84.42)
8443.1700	--凹版印刷机		35	17	15	台		--Gravure printing machinery
8443.1700暂 01	凹版印刷机,印刷速度≥350 米/分钟(用税目 84.42 项下商品进行印刷的机器)	9	35	17	15	台		Gravure printing machinery, linear speed ≥ 350m/min, using goods in heading No. 84.42 to printing
8443.1700 90	其他凹版印刷机(用税目 84.42 项下商品进行印刷的机器)	18	35	17	15	台		Other gravure printing machinery, using goods in heading No. 84.42 to printing
	--其他:							--Other:
	---网式印刷机:							---Screen printing machinery:
8443.1921	----圆网印刷机		35	17	15	台		----Cylinder screen press
8443.1921暂 01	纺织用圆网印花机	6	35	17	15	台	O	Rotary screen printing machines for textile
8443.1921 90	其他圆网印刷机(用税目84.42项下商品进行印刷的机器)	10	35	17	15	台	O	Other rotary screen printing machines (printing machinery using the commodities under heading No. 84.42)
8443.1922	----平网印刷机		35	17	15	台		----Platen screen press
8443.1922暂 01	纺织用平网印花机	6	35	17	15	台	O	Flat screen printing machines for textile
8443.1922 10	用于光盘生产的盘面印刷机(用税目 84.42 项下商品进行印刷的机器)	10	35	17	15	台	6	Disk presser for producing compact disks (machines using the commodities under heading No. 84.42 for printing)
8443.1922 90	其他平网印刷机(用税目 84.42 项下商品进行印刷的机器)	10	35	17	15	台	O	Other platen screen presses (printing machinery using the commodities under heading No. 84.42)
8443.1929	----其他	10	35	17	15	台	O	----Other
8443.1980	---其他	8	35	17	15	台	O	---Other
	-其他印刷(打印)机、复印机及传真机,不论是否组合式:							-Other printers, copying machines and facsimile machines, whether or not combined:
	--具有打印、复印或传真中两种及以上功能的机器,可与自动数据处理设备或网络连接:							--Machines which perform two or more of the functions of printing, copying or facsimile transmission, capable of connecting to an automatic data processing machine or to a network:
8443.3110暂	---静电感光式	3	70	17	17	台		---Electrostatic photosensitive-type
8443.3110暂 10	静电感光式多功能一体加密传真机(可与自动数据处理设备或网络连接)	3	70	17	17	台	M	Electrostatic - sensitive multifunctional integrated encrypting facsimile machines (capable of connecting to an automatic data processing machine or to a network)
8443.3110暂 90	其他静电感光式多功能一体机(可与自动数据处理设备或网络连接)	3	70	17	17	台		Other electrostatic - sensitive multifunctional integrated machines (capable of cconnecting to an automatic data processing machine or to a network)
8443.3190	---其他	0	17	17	17	台		---Other
8443.3190 10	其他具有打印和复印两种功能的机器(可与自动数据处理设备或网络连接)	0	17	17	17	台	A	Other machines which perform two of the function of printing, copying (capable of connecting to an automatic data processing machine or to a network)
8443.3190 20	其他多功能一体加密传真机(兼有打印、复印中一种及以上功能的机器)	0	17	17	17	台	AM	Other multifunctional integrated encrypting facsimile machines (machines with the function of printing, copying or both)

税则号列	货品名称	最惠(%)	普通	增值税率	出口退税	计量单位	监管条件	Article Description
8443.3190 90	其他具有打印、复印或传真中两种及以上功能的机器(具有打印和复印两种功能的机器除外,可与自动数据处理设备或网络连接)	0	17	17	17	台	A	Other machines which perform two or more of the function of printing, copying, facsimile transmission (other than machines which perform two of the function of printing, copying, capable of connecting to an automatic data processing machine or to a network)
	--其他,可与自动数据处理设备或网络连接:							--Other, capable of connecting to an automatic data processing machine or to a net work:
	---专用于税目8471所列设备的打印机:							---Printer of a kind solely used in the machines of heading No. 8471:
8443.3211	----针式打印机	0	14	17	17	台	A	----Stylus printers
8443.3212	----激光打印机	0	14	17	17	台	A	----Laser printers
8443.3213	----喷墨打印机	0	14	17	17	台	A	----Ink-jet-printers
8443.3214	----热敏打印机	0	14	17	17	台	A	----Thermal printers
8443.3219	----其他	0	14	17	17	台	A	----Other
	---数字式印刷设备:							---Digital printing machines:
8443.3221[暂]	----喷墨印刷机	5	30	17	17	台		----Ink-jet printing machines
8443.3222[暂]	----静电照相印刷机(激光印刷机)	5	35	17	15	台		----Electrostatic photographic printing machines (laser printing machines)
8443.3229	----其他	8	30	17	15	台		----Other
8443.3290	---其他	0	17	17	15	台		---Other
8443.3290 10	其他加密传真机(可与自动数据处理设备或网络连接)	0	17	17	15	台	AM	Other encryption facsimile machine (capable commecting to an automatic data processing machine or to a network)
8443.3290 90	其他印刷(打印)机、复印机、传真机和电传打字机(可与自动数据处理设备或网络连接)	0	17	17	15	台	A	Other presses (pinters), copying machine, facsimile machine, and teleprinters (capable of connecting to an automatic data processing machine or to a network)
	--其他:							--Other:
	---静电感光复印设备:							---Electrostatic photo-copying appcocrtus
8443.3911	----将原件直接复印的(直接法)	0	70	17	15	台		----Operating by reproducing the original image directly onto the capy (direct process)
8443.3912	----将原件通过中间体转印的(间接法)	10	70	17	15	台		----Operating by reproducing the original image via an intermediate onto the copy (indirect process)
	---其他感光复印设备:							---Other photocopying apparatus:
8443.3921	----带有光学系统的	0	70	17	15	台		----Incorporoting an optical system
8443.3922	----接触式的	20	70	17	15	台		----Of the contact type
8443.3923	----热敏复印设备	20	70	17	15	台		----Thermo copying apparatus
8443.3924	----热升华复印设备	20	70	17	15	台		----Thermo - sublime copying apparatus
	---数字式印刷设备:							---Digital printing machines:
8443.3931	----喷墨印刷机	8	30	17	15	台		----Ink-jet printing machines
8443.3932	----静电照相印刷机(激光印刷机)	8	35	17	15	台		----Electrostatic photographic printing machine (Laser printing machines)
8443.3939	----其他	8	30	17	15	台		----Other
8443.3990	---其他	0	30	17	15	台		---Other
	-零件及附件:							-Parts and accessories:
	--用税目84.42的印刷版、滚筒及其他印刷部件进行印刷的机器零件及附件:							--Parts and accessories of printing machinery used for printing by means of plates, cylinders and other printing components of heading 84.42:
	---印刷用辅助机器:							---Machines for uses ancillary to printing:
8443.9111	----卷筒料给料机		35	17	15	台		----Roll material feeder
8443.9111[暂] 01	卷筒料自动给料机,给料线速度≥12m/s	4	35	17	15	千克/台	O	Automatic roll material feeder, feeding speed≥12m/s
8443.9111 90	其他卷筒料给料机	12	35	17	15	千克/台	O	Other roll material feeder
8443.9119[暂]	----其他	6	35	17	15	千克/台	O	----Other
8443.9190[暂]	---其他		20	17	15	千克		---Other
8443.9190[暂] 01	胶印机用墨量遥控装置(包括墨色控制装置,墨量调节装置、墨斗体等组成部分)	0	20	17	15	千克/个	O	Remote controllers for controlling the use of ink by offset printing machine (including ink-color control devices, ink amount regulation elevices and ink fountain containers)

税则号列	货品名称	最惠(%)	普通	增值税率	出口退税	计量单位	监管条件	Article Description
8443.9190[暂] 90	传统印刷机用零件及附件(胶印机墨量遥控装置除外)	3	20	17	15	千克/个		Traditional printing machine with spare parts and accessories (except for offset printing ink quantity remote control device)
	--其他:							--Other:
8443.9910	---数字印刷设备用辅助机器	12	35	17	15	千克/台	O	---Machines for uses ancillary to digital printing machines
	---数字印刷设备的零件:							---Parts of digital printing machines:
8443.9921	----热敏打印头	6	20	17	15	千克/个		----Thermal print heads
8443.9929	----其他		20	17	15	千克		----Other
8443.9929[暂] 01	压电式喷墨头(非用品目84.42项下商品进行印刷的机器零件)	3	20	17	15	千克		Piezoelectric ink gun(other than parts and accessories of machinery using the commodities under heading No. 8422 for printing)
8443.9929 90	其他数字印刷设备的零件(非用品目84.42项下商品进行印刷的机器零件)	6	20	17	15	千克		Other parts of digital printing machine (other than parts and accessories of machinery using the commodities under heading No. 8422 for printing)
8443.9990	---其他	0	35	17	15	千克		---Other
8443.9990 10	其他印刷(打印)机、复印机及传真机的感光鼓和含感光鼓的碳粉盒	0	35	17	15	千克		Photosensitive drums and toner cartridges containing photosensitive drums for other presses(printer), copying machine and facsinile machine
8443.9990 90	其他印刷(打印)机、复印机及传真机的零件和附件	0	35	17	15	千克		Spare parts and accessories for other presses (printer), copying machine and facsinile machine
84.44	**化学纺织纤维挤压、拉伸、变形或切割机器:**							**Machines for extruding, drawing, texturing or cutting man-made textile materials:**
8444.0010	---合成纤维长丝纺丝机	10	30	17	17	台		---Synthetic filaments spinning jets
8444.0020	---合成纤维短丝纺丝机	10	30	17	17	台		---Synthetic staple fibres spinning jets
8444.0030	---人造纤维纺丝机	10	30	17	17	台		---Artificial fibres spinning jets
8444.0040	---化学纤维变形机	10	30	17	17	台		---Man-made filaments crimping machinery
8444.0050	---化学纤维切断机	10	30	17	17	台		---Man-made filaments cutting machinery
8444.0090	---其他	10	30	17	17	台		---Other
84.45	**纺织纤维的预处理机器;纺纱机、并线机、加捻机及其他生产纺织纱线的机器;摇纱机、络纱机(包括卷纬机)及处理税目84.46或84.47所列机器用的纺织纱线的机器:**							**Machines for preparing textile fibres; spinning, doubling or twisting machines and other machinery for producing textile yarns; textile reeling or winding (including weft-winding) machines and machines for preparing textile yarns for use on the machines of headingNo. 84.46 or 84.47:**
	-纺织纤维的预处理机器:							-Machines for preparing textile fibres:
	--梳理机:							--Carding machines:
	---棉纤维型:							---For cotton type fibres:
8445.1111	----清梳联合机	10	30	17	17	台	A	----Blowing-carding-Machinery
8445.1112	----自动抓棉机	10	30	17	17	台	A	----Bale Pucker
8445.1113	----梳棉机	10	30	17	17	台	A	----Card or carding Machine
8445.1119	----其他	10	30	17	17	台	A	----Other
8445.1120	---毛纤维型	10	30	17	17	台	A	---For wool type fibres
8445.1190	---其他		30	17	17	台		---Other
8445.1190[暂] 01	宽幅非织造布梳理机(工作幅宽>3.5米,工作速度>120米/分钟)	6	30	17	17	台	A	Extra - width non - woven cloth carding machine (working width > 3.5m, working speed > 120m/min)
8445.1190 90	其他纺织纤维梳理机	10	30	17	17	台	A	Other carding machines for textile fibres
	--精梳机:							--Combing Machines:
8445.1210	---棉精梳机	10	30	17	17	台	A	---Cotton Comber
8445.1220	---毛精梳机	10	30	17	17	台	A	---Worsted Comber
8445.1290	---其他	10	30	17	17	台	A	---Other
	--拉伸机或粗纱机:							--Drawing or roving machines:
8445.1310	---拉伸机	10	30	17	17	台	A	---Drawing machines

税则号列	货品名称	最惠(%)	普通	增值税率	出口退税	计量单位	监管条件	Article Description
	---粗纱机:							---Roving machines:
8445.1321	----棉纺粗纱机	10	30	17	17	台	A	----Cotton Roving Frames
8445.1322	----毛纺粗纱机	10	30	17	17	台	A	----Worsted Roving Machines
8445.1329	----其他	10	30	17	17	台	A	----Other
8445.1900	--其他	10	30	17	17	台	A	--Other
	-纺纱机:							-Textile spinning machines:
	---自由端纺纱机:							---Open-end spinner:
8445.2031	----转杯纺纱机		30	17	17	台		----Rotor spinning machine
8445.2031暂 01	全自动转杯纺纱机	5	30	17	17	台	AO	Fully automatic rotor spinning machines
8445.2031 90	其他自由端转杯纺纱机	10	30	17	17	台	AO	Other open - end spinner machine
8445.2032	----喷气纺纱机	10	30	17	17	台	A	----Jet spinner
8445.2039	----其他	10	30	17	17	台	A	----Other
	---环锭细纱机:							---Ring spining frames:
8445.2041	----棉细纱机	10.5	40	17	17	台	AO	----Cotton Ring Spinning Frame
8445.2042	----毛细纱机	10	40	17	17	台	A	----Worsted Ring Spinning Frame
8445.2049	----其他	10	40	17	17	台	A	----Other
8445.2090	---其他	10	30	17	17	台	A	---Other
8445.3000	-并线机或加捻机	10	30	17	17	台	A	-Textile doubling or twisting machines
	-络纱机(包括卷纬机)或摇纱机:							-Textile winding (including weft-winding) or reeling machines:
8445.4010暂	---自动络筒机	6	30	17	17	台	AO	---Automatic bobbin winders
8445.4090	---其他	10	30	17	17	台	A	---Other
	-其他:							-Other:
8445.9010	---整经机	10	30	17	17	台	A	---Warping machines
8445.9020	---浆纱机	10	30	17	17	台	A	---Sizing machines
8445.9090	---其他	10	30	17	17	台	OA	---Other
84.46	**织机:**							**Weaving machines(looms):**
8446.1000	-所织织物宽度不超过30厘米的织机	8	30	17	17	台	A	-For weaving fabrics of a width not exceeding 30cm
	-所织织物宽度超过30厘米的梭织机:							-For weaving fabrics of width exceeding 30cm, shuttle type:
	--动力织机:							--Power looms:
8446.2110	---地毯织机	12	35	17	17	台	A	---For making carpets or rugs
8446.2190	---其他	10	30	17	17	台	A	---Other
8446.2900	--其他	10	30	17	17	台	A	--Other
	-所织织物宽度超过30厘米的无梭织机:							-For weaving fabrics of a width exceeding 30cm, shuttleless type:
8446.3020	---剑杆织机	8	30	17	17	台	AO	---Rapier looms
8446.3030	---片梭织机	8	30	17	17	台	AO	---Carrier looms
8446.3040	---喷水织机	8	30	17	17	台	OA	---Water jet looms
8446.3050暂	---喷气织机	0	30	17	17	台	AO	---Air jet looms
8446.3090	---其他	8	30	17	17	台	A	---Other
84.47	**针织机、缝编机及制粗松螺旋花线、网眼薄纱、花边、刺绣品、装饰带、编织带或网的机器及簇绒机:**							**Knitting machines, stitch-bonding machines and machines for making gimped yarn, tulle lace, embroidery, trimmings, braid or net and machines for tufting:**
	-圆型针织机:							-Circular knitting machines:
8447.1100	--圆筒直径不超过165毫米	8	30	17	17	台	A	--With cylinder diameter not exceeding 165mm
8447.1200	--圆筒直径超过165毫米	8	30	17	17	台	A	--With cylinder diameter exceeding 165mm
	-平型针织机;缝编机:							-Flat knitting machines; stitch-bonding machines:
	---经编机:							---Warp knitting machines:
8447.2011	----特里科经编机	8	30	17	17	台	A	----Tricot machines
8447.2012	----拉舍尔经编机	8	30	17	17	台	A	----Raschel machines
8447.2019	----其他	8	30	17	17	台	A	----Other
8447.2020	---平型纬编机	8	30	17	17	台	A	---Flat weft rnitting machimes
8447.2030	---缝编机	8	30	17	17	台	A	---Stitch-bonding machines
	-其他:							-Other:
	---簇绒机:							---Tufting machines:
8447.9011	----地毯织机	7	35	17	17	台	A	----For making carpets or rugs

税则号列	货品名称	最惠(%)	普通	增值税率	出口退税	计量单位	监管条件	Article Description
8447.9019	----其他	8	30	17	17	台	A	----Other
8447.9020	---绣花机	8	30	17	17	台	A	---Embroidery machines
8447.9090	---其他	10	30	17	17	台	A	---Other
84.48	**税目84.44、84.45、84.46或84.47所列机器的辅助机器(例如,多臂机、提花机、自停装置及换梭装置);专用于或主要用于税目84.44、84.45、84.46或84.47所列机器的零件、附件(例如,锭子、锭壳、钢丝针布、梳、喷丝头、梭子、综丝、综框、针织机用针):**							**Auxiliary machinery for use with machines of headingNos. 84.44, 84.45, 84.46 or 84.47 (for example, dobbies, Jacquards, automatic stop motions, shuttle changing mechanisms); parts and accessories suitable for use solely or principally with the machines of this heading or of headingNos. 84.44, 84.45, 84.46 or 84.47 (for example, spindles and spindle flyers, card clothing, combs, extruding nipples, shuttles, healds and heald-frames, hosiery needles):**
	-税目84.44、84.45、84.46或84.47所列机器的辅助机器:							-Auxiliary machinery for machines of heading No. 84.44, 84.45, 84.46 or 84.47:
8448.1100	--多臂机或提花机及其所用的卡片缩小、复制、穿孔或汇编机器		20	17	17	千克		--Dobbies and Jacquards; card reducing, copying, punching or assembling machines for use there with
8448.1100暂 01	多臂机或提花机(转速指标500转/分以上)	4	20	17	17	千克		Dobbies or jacquards (index of revolution speed > 500r/min)
8448.1100 90	多臂机或提花机所用卡片缩小、复制、穿孔或汇编机器(包括其所用的卡片缩小、复制、穿孔或汇编机器)	8	20	17	17	千克		Card narrowing ,copying, perforation, or compilation machines used by dobbies or jacquards (including the use of card narrowing, copying, perforation or compilation machines)
8448.1900	--其他	8	20	17	17	千克		--Other
	-税目84.44所列机器及其辅助机器的零件、附件:							-Parts and accessories of machines of heading No. 84.44 or of their auxiliary machinery:
8448.2020	---喷丝头或喷丝板	6	14	17	17	个/千克		---Extruding nipples or spinnerets
8448.2090	---其他	6	17	17	17	千克		---Other
	-税目84.45所列机器及其辅助机器的零件、附件:							-Parts and accessories of machines of headingNo. 84.45 or of their auxiliary machinery:
8448.3100	--钢丝针布	6	17	17	17	千克		--Card clothing
8448.3200	--纺织纤维预处理机器的零件、附件,但钢丝针布除外	6	17	17	17	千克		--Of machines for preparing textile fibres, other than card clothing
	--锭子、锭壳、纺丝环、钢丝圈:							--Spindles, spindle flyers, spinning rings and ring travellers:
8448.3310	---络筒锭	6	17	17	17	个/千克		---Winding spindle
8448.3390	---其他	6	17	17	17	千克		---Other
	--其他:							--Other:
8448.3910	---气流杯	6	14	17	17	个/千克		---Open-end rotors
8448.3920暂	---电子清纱器	3	17	17	17	个/千克		---Electronic yarn clearers
8448.3930暂	---空气捻接器	3	17	17	17	个/千克		---Air twisting devices
8448.3940暂	---环锭细纱机紧密纺装置	0	17	17	17	个/千克		---Compact set of ring spinning frames
8448.3990暂	---其他	3	17	17	17	千克		---Other
	-织机及其辅助机器的零件、附件:							-Parts and accessories of weaving machines (looms) or of their auxiliary machinery:
8448.4200	--织机用筘、综丝及综框	6	50	17	17	千克		--Reeds for looms, healds and heald-frames
	--其他:							--Other:
8448.4910	---接、投梭箱	6	17	17	17	个/千克		---Catching and throwing shuttle boxes
8448.4920暂	---引纬、送经装置	3	17	17	17	个/千克		---Weft insertion and let-off motions
8448.4930	---梭子	6	50	17	17	个/千克		---Shuttles
8448.4990暂	---其他	3	17	17	17	千克		---Other
	-税目84.47所列机器及其辅助机器的零件、附件:							-Parts and accessories of machines of heading No. 84.47 or of their auxiliary machinery:
	--沉降片、织针及其他成圈机件:							--Sinkers, needles and other articles used in forming stitches:

税则号列	货品名称	最惠(%)	普通	增值税率	出口退税	计量单位	监管条件	Article Description
8448.5120	---针织机用28号以下的弹簧针、钩针及复合针	6	50	17	17	千克		---Barbered needles, crotchet hooks and complex needles for knitting machines, smaler than gauge No. 28
8448.5190	---其他	6	17	17	17	千克		---Other
8448.5900暂	--其他	3	17	17	17	千克		--Other
84.49	**成匹、成形的毡呢或无纺织物制造或整理机器,包括制毡呢帽机器;帽模:**							**Machinery for the manufacture or finishing of felt or nonwovens in the piece or in shapes, including machinery for making felt hats; blocks for making hats:**
8449.0010	---针刺机		30	17	17	台/千克		---Machinery for stitch
8449.0010暂 01	高速针刺机,针刺频率>2000次/分钟	6	30	17	17	台/千克		High – speed needle – punching machines, stroke frequency >2000time/min
8449.0010 90	其他针刺机	8	30	17	17	台/千克		Other needle – punching machines
8449.0020	---水刺设备		30	17	17	台/千克		---Spunlaced Equipment
8449.0020暂 01	高速宽幅水刺设备(工作幅宽>3.5米,工作速度>250米/分钟,水刺压力≥400帕)	6	30	17	17	台/千克		High – speed width spun-laced equipment (working width >3.5m, working speed >250m/min, spun – laced pressure ≥400 Pa)
8449.0020 90	其他水刺设备	8	30	17	17	台/千克		Other spun-laced equipment
8449.0090	---其他	8	30	17	17	千克		---Other
84.50	**家用型或洗衣房用洗衣机,包括洗涤干燥两用机:**							**Household or laundry-type washing machines, including machines which both wash and dry:**
	-干衣量不超过10千克的洗衣机:							-Machines, each of a dry linen capacity not exceeding 10kg:
	--全自动的:							--Fully-automatic machines:
8450.1110	---波轮式	10	130	17	17	台	A	---Of the continuously rotating impeller
8450.1120	---滚筒式	10	130	17	17	台	A	---Of the drum type
8450.1190	---其他	10	130	17	17	台	A	---Other
8450.1200	--其他机器,装有离心甩干机	30	130	17	17	台	A	--Other machines, with built-in centrifugal drier
8450.1900	--其他	30	130	17	17	台	A	--Other
	-干衣量超过10千克的洗衣机:					台		-Machines, each of a dry linen capacity exceeding 10kg:
	---全自动的:							---Full automatic :
8450.2011	----波轮式	10	80	17	17	台		----wave – wheel type
8450.2012	----滚筒式	10	80	17	17	台		----Drum – type
8450.2019	----其他	10	80	17	17	台		----Other
8450.2090	---其他	10	80	17	17	台		---Other
	-零件:							-Parts:
8450.9010	---干衣量不超过10千克的洗衣机用	5	130	17	15	千克		---Of the machines, each of a dry linen capacity not exceeding 10kg
8450.9090暂	---其他	5	80	17	15	千克		---Other
84.51	**纱线、织物及纺织制品的洗涤、清洁、绞拧、干燥、熨烫、挤压、(包括熔压)、漂白、染色、上浆、整理、涂布或浸渍机器(税目84.50的机器除外);列诺伦(亚麻油地毡)及类似铺地制品的布基或其他底布的浆料涂布机器;纺织物的卷绕、退绕、折叠、剪切或剪齿边机器:**							**Machinery (other than machines of headingNo. 84.50) for washing, cleaning, wringing, drying, ironing, pressing (including fusing presses), bleaching, dyeing, dressing, finishing, coating or impregnating textile yarns, fabrics or made up textile articles and machines for applying the paste to the base fabric or other support used in the manufacture of floor coverings such as linoleum; machines for reeling, unreeling, folding, cutting or pinking textile fabrics:**
8451.1000	-干洗机	21	80	17	15	台		-Dry-cleaning machines
	-干燥机:							-Drying machines:
8451.2100	--干衣量不超过10千克	15	80	17	15	台		--Each of a dry linen capacity not exceeding 10kg
8451.2900	--其他	8	30	17	15	台		--Other
8451.3000	-熨烫机及挤压机(包括熔压机)	8	30	17	15	台		-Ironing machines and presses (including fusing presses)
8451.4000	-洗涤、漂白或染色机器	8.4	20	17	15	台		-Washing, bleaching or dyeing machines

税则号列	货品名称	最惠(%)	普通	增值税率	出口退税	计量单位	监管条件	Article Description
8451.5000	-纺织物的卷绕、退绕、折叠、剪切或剪齿边机器	8	20	17	15	台		-Machines for reeling, unreeling, folding, cutting or pinking textile fabrics
8451.8000	-其他机器		30	17	15	台		-Other machinery
8451.8000暂 01	服装定型焙烘炉；服装液氨整理机；预缩机；罐蒸机	10	30	17	15	台		Baking furnaces for finalizing the design of clothes; machine with liquid ammonia for finishing clothes; pre－shrinkage machine; tank vapor
8451.8000暂 02	剪绒，洗缩联合机；剪毛联合机；柔软整理机	10	30	17	15	台		Pile shearing and shrinking combine, potting steamer, sheepshearing combination machine, supple finishing machine
8451.8000暂 03	定型机；精练机；丝光机；磨毛机	10	30	17	15	台		Boarding machine; refining machine; mercerizing range; napping grinder
8451.8000暂 04	涂层机	8	30	17	15	台		Coating machine
8451.8000 90	编号84.51未列名的其他机器	12	30	17	15	台		Other machinery of heading No. 8451, not elsewhere specified or included
8451.9000	-零件	8	20	17	15	千克		-Parts
84.52	**缝纫机，但税目84.40的锁线订书机除外；缝纫机专用的特制家具、底座及罩盖；缝纫机针：**							**Sewing machines, other than book-sewing machines of heading No. 84.40; furniture, bases and covers specially designed for sewing machines; sewing machine needles:**
	-家用型缝纫机：							-Sewing machines of household type:
8452.1010	---多功能型	21	80	17	17	台		---Multifuncitonal
	---其他：							---Other:
8452.1091	----手动式	21	80	17	17	台		----Hand ooperated
8452.1099	----其他	21	80	17	17	台		----Other
	-其他缝纫机：							-Other sewing machines:
	--自动的：							--Automatic units:
8452.2110	---平缝机	12	40	17	17	台		---Flatseam
8452.2120	---包缝机	12	40	17	17	台		---Overlock machine
8452.2130	---绷缝机	12	40	17	17	台		---Interlock machine
8452.2190	---其他	12	40	17	17	台		---Other
8452.2900	--其他	12	40	17	17	台		--Other
8452.3000	-缝纫机针	14	100	17	15	千克		-Sewing machine needles
	-缝纫机专用的特制家具、底座和罩盖及其零件；缝纫机的其他零件：							-Furniture, bases and covers for sewing machines and parts thereof; other parts of sewing machines:
	---家用型缝纫机用：							---Of sewing machines of the household type:
8452.9011	----旋梭	14	80	17	15	千克		----Rotating shuttles
8452.9019	----其他	14	80	17	15	千克		----Other
	---其他：							---Other:
8452.9091	----旋梭	14	80	17	15	千克		----Rotating shuttles
8452.9092	----缝纫机专用的特制家具、底座和罩盖及其零件	14	100	17	15	千克		---Furniture, bases and covers for sewing machines and parts thereof
8452.9099	----其他	14	80	17	15	千克		----Other
84.53	**生皮、皮革的处理、鞣制或加工机器，鞋靴、毛皮及其他皮革制品的制作或修理机器，但缝纫机除外：**							**Machinery for preparing, tanning or working hides, skins or leather or for making or repairing footwear or other articles of hides, skins or leather, other than sewing machines:**
8453.1000	-生皮、皮革的处理、鞣制或加工机器	8.4	30	17	15	台		-Machinery for preparing, tanning or working hides, skins or leather
8453.2000	-鞋靴制作或修理机器	8.4	30	17	15	台		-Machinery for making or repairing footwear
8453.8000	-其他机器	8.4	30	17	15	台		-Other machinery
8453.9000	-零件	8	30	17	15	千克		-Parts
84.54	**金属冶炼及铸造用的转炉、浇包、锭模及铸造机：**							**Converters, ladles, ingot moulds and casting machines, of a kind used in metallurgy or in metal foundries:**

税则号列	货品名称	最惠(%)	普通	增值税率	出口退税	计量单位	监管条件	Article Description
8454.1000	-转炉	8.4	35	17	17	台		-Converters
	-锭模及浇包:							-Ingot moulds and ladles:
8454.2010	---炉外精炼设备	8.4	35	17	17	台		---Fining equipments, outside of converters
8454.2010 10	VOD 炉(真空脱气炉)	8.4	35	17	17	台	O	VOD furnaces(vacuum degassing furnaces)
8454.2010 90	其他炉外精炼设备	8.4	35	17	17	台	O	Other secondary refining equipments
8454.2090	---其他	8.4	35	17	17	台		---Other
	-铸造机:							-Casting machines:
8454.3010	---冷室压铸机	12	35	17	17	台	O	---Cold chamber die-casting machines
	---钢坯连铸机:							---Ingot continuous casting machines:
8454.3021	----方坯连铸机	10	35	17	17	台		----Ingot block
8454.3022	----板坯连铸机	12	35	17	17	台	O	----Ingot slab
8454.3029	----其他	12	35	17	17	台	O	----Other
8454.3090	---其他	12	35	17	17	台		---Other
	-零件:							-Parts:
8454.9010	---炉外精炼设备用	8	20	17	17	千克		---For the fining equipments outside of converters
	---钢坯连铸机用:							---For ingot continuous casting machines:
8454.9021	----结晶器	8	20	17	17	千克		----Crystallizers
8454.9022	----振动装置	8	20	17	17	千克		----Vibrating devices
8454.9029	----其他	8	20	17	17	千克		----Other
8454.9090	---其他	8	20	17	17	千克		---Other
84.55	**金属轧机及其轧辊:**							**Metal-rolling mills and rolls therefof:**
	-轧管机:							-Tube mills:
8455.1010	---热轧管机	12	35	17	17	台		---Tube mills, for hot-rolled
8455.1020	---冷轧管机	12	35	17	17	台	O	---Tube mills for cold-rolled
8455.1030	---定减径轧管机	12	35	17	17	台	O	---Fixed and reduced tube mills
8455.1090	---其他	12	35	17	17	台	O	---Other
	-其他轧机:							-Other rolling mills:
	--热轧机或冷热联合轧机:							--Hot or combination hot and cold:
8455.2110	---板材热轧机	15	35	17	17	台	O	---Sheet mills, hot-rolled
8455.2120	---型钢轧机	15	35	17	17	台	O	---Rolled-steel section mills
8455.2130	---线材轧机	15	35	17	17	台	O	---Wire mills
8455.2190	---其他	15	35	17	17	台	O	---Other
	--冷轧机:							--Cold mills:
8455.2210	---板材冷轧机	10	35	17	17	台	O	---Sheet mills
8455.2290	---其他	15	35	17	17	台		---Other
8455.2290 10	铝箔粗轧机	15	35	17	17	台		Aluminium foil roughing mills
8455.2290 90	其他金属冷轧机	15	35	17	17	台		Other cold rolling mills of metal
8455.3000	-轧机用轧辊	8.4	20	17	17	个		-Rolls for rolling mills
8455.9000	-其他零件	8	20	17	17	千克		-Other parts
84.56	用激光、其他光、光子束、超声波、放电、电化学法、电子束、离子束或等离子弧处理各种材料的加工机床;水射流切割机:							**Machine-tools for working any material by removal of material, by laser or other light or photon beam, ultrasonic, electro-discharge, electro-chemical, electron beam, ionic-beam or plasma arc processes; water-jet cutting machines**
8456.1000	-用激光、其他光或光子束处理的	0	30	17	17	台		-Operated by laser or other light or photon beam processes
8456.1000 10	辐照元件激光切割机(切割燃料包壳以使辐照核材料能熔解,含遥控设备)	0	30	17	17	台	3A	Irradiated - component laser cutting machines (cutting the fuel claddings to make the irradated nuclear materials to melt down, with a remote control)
8456.1000 90	其他用激光或其他光或光子束处理的机床	0	30	17	17	台	A	Other machine tools using laser or other light or photon beam
8456.2000	-用超声波处理的	10	30	17	17	台	A	-Operated by ultrasonic processes
	-用放电处理的:							-Operated by electro-discharge processes:
8456.3010	---数控的	9.7	30	17	17	台		---Numerically controlled

税则号列	货品名称	最惠(%)	普通	增值税率	出口退税	计量单位	监管条件	Article Description
8456.3010 10	数控放电加工机床(2轴或多轴成形控制的无线型放电加工机床)	9.7	30	17	17	台	3AO	CNC EDM machne tools (wireless – type EDM machine tools controlled by 2 – axis or multi – axis contours)
8456.3010 90	其他数控的放电处理加工机床	9.7	30	17	17	台	AO	Other CNC processing machine tools
8456.3090	---其他	10	30	17	17	台		---Other
8456.3090 10	非数控放电加工机床(2轴或多轴成形控制的无线型放电加工机床)	10	30	17	17	台	3A	Non – CNC EDM machine tools (wireless – type EDM machine tools controlled by 2 – axis or multi – axis contours)
8456.3090 90	其他非数控的放电处理加工机床	10	30	17	17	台	A	Other non – CNC EDM machine Tools
	-其他:							-Other:
8456.9010	---等离子切割机	0	30	17	17	台	A	---Cutting machines of plasma arc
8456.9020	---水射流切割机	0	30	17	15	台	A	---Water-jet cutting machines
8456.9090	---其他	0	30	17	17	台	A	---Other
84.57	**加工金属的加工中心、单工位组合机床及多工位组合机床:**							**Machining centres, unit construction machines (single station) and multi-station transfer machines, for working metal:**
	-加工中心:							-Machining centres:
8457.1010	---立式	9.7	20	17	17	台	AO	---Vertical
8457.1020	---卧式	9.7	20	17	17	台	AO	---Horizontal
8457.1030	---龙门式	9.7	20	17	17	台	AO	---Plano
	---其他:							---Other:
8457.1091	----铣车复合	9.7	20	17	17	台	AO	----Milling and turning composite
8457.1099	----其他	9.7	20	17	17	台	AO	----Other
8457.2000	-单工位组合机床	8	20	17	17	台	OA	-Unit construction machines (single station)
8457.3000	-多工位组合机床	5	20	17	17	台	OA	-Multi-station transfer machines
84.58	**切削金属的车床(包括车削中心):**							**Lathes (including turning centres) for removing metal:**
	-卧式车床:							-Horizontal lathes:
8458.1100	--数控的	9.7	20	17	17	台		--Numerically controlled
8458.1100 10	两用物项管制的切削金属的卧式数控车床(包括车削中心)	9.7	20	17	17	台	3AO	Lathes for removing metal, fual – use items control, horizontal lathes, numerically controlled (including turning centres)
8458.1100 90	其他切削金属的卧式数控车床(包括车削中心)	9.7	20	17	17	台	AO	Other lathes for removing metal, horizontal lathes, numerically controlled(including turning centres)
8458.1900	--其他	12	50	17	17	台	A	--Other
	-其他车床:							-Other lathes:
	--数控的:							--Numerically controlled:
8458.9110	---立式	5	20	17	17	台		---Vertical
8458.9110 10	两用物项管制的切削金属立式数控车床(包括车削中心)	5	20	17	17	台/千克	3AO	Lathes for removing metal, fual – use items control, vertical, numerically controlled (including turning centres)
8458.9110 90	其他切削金属的立式数控车床(包括车削中心)	5	20	17	17	台/千克	AO	Lathes for removing metal, numerically controlled (including turning centres)
8458.9120	---其他	5	20	17	17	台		---Other
8458.9120 10	其他两用物项管制的切削金属数控车床(包括车削中心)	5	20	17	17	台/千克	3AO	Other lathes for removing metal, fual – use items control, (including turning centres)
8458.9120 90	其他切削金属的数控车床(包括车削中心)	5	20	17	17	台/千克	AO	Other lathes for removing metal (including turning centres)
8458.9900	--其他	12	50	17	17	台	A	--Other
84.59	**切削金属的钻床、镗床、铣床、攻丝机床(包括直线移动式动力头钻床),但税目84.58的车床(包括车削中心)除外:**							**Machine-tools (including way-type unit head machines) for drilling, boring, milling, threading or tapping by removing metal, other than lathes (including turning centres) of heading No. 84.58:**
8459.1000	-直线移动式动力头钻床	15	50	17	17	台	A	-Way-type unit head machines
	-其他钻床:							-Other drilling machines:

税则号列	货品名称	最惠(%)	普通	增值税率	出口退税	计量单位	监管条件	Article Description
8459.2100	--数控的	9.7	20	17	17	台	AO	--Numerically controlled
8459.2900	--其他	15	50	17	17	台	A	--Other
	-其他镗铣机床：							-Other boring-milling machines:
8459.3100	--数控的	9.7	20	17	17	台	OA	--Numerically controlled
8459.3900	--其他	10	50	17	17	台	A	--Other
	-其他镗床：							-Other boring machines:
8459.4010	---数控的	9.7	20	17	17	台	OA	---Numerically controlled
8459.4090	---其他	15	50	17	17	台	A	---Other
	-升降台式铣床：							-Milling machines, knee-type:
8459.5100	--数控的	9.7	20	17	17	台	OA	--Numerically controlled
8459.5900	--其他	15	50	17	17	台	A	--Other
	-其他铣床：							-Other milling machines:
	--数控的：							--Numerically controlled:
8459.6110	---龙门铣床	5	20	17	17	台	OA	---Planomilling machines
8459.6190	---其他	5	20	17	17	台	OA	---Other
	--其他：							--Other:
8459.6910	---龙门铣床	12	50	17	17	台	A	---Planomilling machines
8459.6990	---其他	12	50	17	17	台	A	---Other
8459.7000	-其他攻丝机床	12	50	17	17	台	A	-Other threading or tapping machines
84.60	**用磨石、磨料或抛光材料对金属或金属陶瓷进行去毛刺、刃磨、磨削、珩磨、研磨、抛光或其他精加工的机床，但税目84.61的切齿机、齿轮磨床或齿轮精加工机床除外：**							**Machine-tools for deburring, sharpening, grinding, honing, lapping, polishing or otherwise finishing metal or cermets by means of grinding stones, abrasives or polishing products, other than gear cutting, gear grinding or gear finishing machines of heading No. 84.61:**
	-平面磨床，在任一坐标的定位精度至少是0.01毫米：							-Flat-surface grinding machines, in which the positioning in any one axis can be set up to an accuracy of at least 0.01mm:
8460.1100	--数控的	9.7	20	17	17	台	OA	--Numerically controlled
8460.1900	--其他	15	50	17	17	台		--Other
	-其他磨床，在任一坐标的定位精度至少是0.01毫米：							-Other grinding machines, in which the positioning in any one axis can be set up to an accuracy of at least 0.01mm:
	--数控的：							--Numerically controlled:
	---外圆磨床：	9.7	20	17	17	台	OA	---Cylindrical grinding machines:
8460.2111	----曲轴磨床	9.7	20	17	17	台	AO	----Crank shaft grinder
8460.2119	----其他	9.7	20	17	17	台	AO	----Other
8460.2120	---内圆磨床	9.7	20	17	17	台	OA	---Internal grinding machines
8460.2190	---其他	9.7	20	17	17	台	OA	---Other
	--其他：							--Other:
8460.2910	---外圆磨床	15	50	17	17	台	A	---Cylindrical grinding machines
8460.2920	---内圆磨床	15	50	17	17	台	A	---Internal grinding machines
8460.2930	---轧辊磨床	13	50	17	17	台		---Grinding machines of roll
8460.2990	---其他	13	50	17	17	台	A	---Other
	-刃磨（工具或刀具）机床：							-Sharpening (tool or cutter grinding) machines:
8460.3100	--数控的	9.7	20	17	17	台	A	--Numerically controlled
8460.3900	--其他	15	50	17	17	台	A	--Other
	-珩磨或研磨机床：							-Honing or lapping machines:
8460.4010	---珩磨	13	50	17	17	台	A	---Honing
8460.4020	---研磨	13	50	17	17	台	A	---Lapping
	-其他：							-Other:
8460.9010	---砂轮机	15	50	17	17	台		---Grinding wheel machines
8460.9020	---抛光机床	15	50	17	17	台	A	---Polishing machines
8460.9090	---其他	15	50	17	17	台	A	---Other

税则号列	货品名称	最惠(%)	普通	增值税率	出口退税	计量单位	监管条件	Article Description
84.61	切削金属或金属陶瓷的刨床、牛头刨床、插床、拉床、切齿机、齿轮磨床或齿轮精加工机床、锯床、切断机及其他税目未列名的切削机床：							**Machine-tools for planing, shaping, slotting, broaching, gear cutting, gear grinding or gear finishing, sawing, cutting-off and other machine-tools working by removing metal or cermets, not elsewhere specified or included:**
	-牛头刨床或插床：							-Shaping or slotting machines:
8461.2010	---牛头刨床	15	50	17	17	台		---Shaping machines
8461.2020	---插床	15	50	17	17	台		---Slotting machines
8461.3000	-拉床	12	50	17	17	台		-Broaching machines
	-切齿机、齿轮磨床或齿轮精加工机床：							-Gear cutting, gear grinding or gear finishing machines:
	---数控的：							---Numerically controlled:
8461.4011	----齿轮磨床	9.7	20	17	17	台	OA	----Gear grinder
8461.4019	----其他	9.7	20	17	17	台	OA	----Other
8461.4090	---其他	15	50	17	17	台	A	---Other
8461.5000	-锯床或切断机	12	50	17	17	台		-Sawing or cutting-off machines
8461.5000 10	辐照元件刀具切割机［切割燃料包壳以使辐照核材料能溶解（含遥控设备）］	12	50	17	17	台	3	Irradiated-component cutting machine toole［cutting the fuel claddings to make the irradiated nuclear materials to melt down(including remote control)］
8461.5000 90	其他锯床或切断机	12	50	17	17	台		Other sawing or cutting-off
	-其他：							-Other:
	---刨床：							---Planing machines:
8461.9011	----龙门刨床	15	50	17	17	台		----Double-column (open-side) planing machines
8461.9019	----其他	15	50	17	17	台		----Other
8461.9090	---其他	12	50	17	17	台		---Other
84.62	加工金属的锻造（包括模锻）或冲压机床；加工金属的弯曲、折叠、矫直、矫平、剪切、冲孔或开槽机床；其他加工金属或硬质合金的压力机：							**Machine-tools (including presses) for working metal by forging, hammering or die-stamping; machine-tools (including presses) for working metal by bending, folding, straightening, flattening, shearing, punching or notching; presses for working metal or metal carbides, not specified above:**
	-锻造（包括模锻）或冲压机床及锻锤：							-Forging or die-stamping machines (including presses) and hammers:
8462.1010	---数控的	9.7	20	17	17	台		---Numerically controlled
8462.1090	---其他	12	50	17	17	台		---Other
	-弯曲、折叠、矫直或矫平机床：							-Bending, folding, straightening or flattening machines (including presses):
	--数控的：							--Numerically controlled:
8462.2110	---矫直机	9.7	20	17	17	台		---Straightening machines
8462.2190	---其他	9.7	20	17	17	台		---Other
	--其他：							--Other:
8462.2910	---矫直机	10	50	17	17	台		---Straightening machines
8462.2990	---其他	10	50	17	17	台		---Other
	-剪切机床，但冲剪两用机除外：							-Shearing machines (including presses), other than combined punching and shearing machines:
	--数控的：							--Numerically controlled:
8462.3110	---板带纵剪机	7	20	17	17	台		---Shearing lengthwise
8462.3120	---板带横剪机	7	20	17	17	台		---Shearing transverse
8462.3190	---其他	7	20	17	17	台		---Other
	--其他：							--Other:
8462.3910	---板带纵剪机	10	50	17	17	台		---Shearing lengthwise
8462.3920	---板带横剪机	10	50	17	17	台		---Shearing transverse
8462.3990	---其他	10	50	17	17	台		---Other

税则号列	货品名称	最惠(%)	普通	增值税率	出口退税	计量单位	监管条件	Article Description
	-冲孔或开槽机床,包括冲剪两用机:							-Punching or notching machines (including presses), including combined punching and shearing machines:
	--数控的:							--Numerically controlled:
	---冲床:							---Punch press
8462.4111	----自动模式数控步冲压力机	9.7	20	17	17	台		----CNC automatic tool change punch press
8462.4119	----其他	9.7	20	17	17	台		----Other
8462.4190	---其他	9.7	20	17	17	台		---Other
8462.4900	--其他	10	50	17	17	台		--Other
	-其他:							-Other:
	--液压压力机:							--Hydraulic presses:
8462.9110	---金属型材挤压机	10	50	17	17	台		---Metal section squeezing machine
8462.9190	---其他	10	50	17	17	台		---Other
	--其他:							--Other:
8462.9910	---机械压力机	10	50	17	17	台		---Mechanical presses
8462.9990	---其他	10	50	17	17	台		---Other
84.63	**金属或金属陶瓷的其他非切削加工机床:**							**Other machine-tools for working metal or cermets, without removing material:**
	-杆、管、型材、异型材、丝及类似品的拉拔机:							-Draw-benches for bars, tubes, profiles, wire or the like:
	---冷拔管机:							---Cold-drawing tube benches:
8463.1011	----拉拔力为300吨及以下	10	50	17	17	台		----With 300t or less
8463.1019	----其他	10	50	17	17	台		----Other
8463.1020	---拔丝机	10	50	17	17	台		---Wiredrawing machines
8463.1090	---其他	10	50	17	17	台		---Other
8463.2000	-螺纹滚轧机	15	50	17	17	台		-Thread rolling machines
8463.3000	-金属丝加工机	10	50	17	17	台		-Machines for working wire
8463.9000	-其他	10	50	17	17	台		-Other
8463.9000 10	滚压成形机床(数控,装3个以上压辊)	10	50	17	17	台	3	Roll forming machine tools (CNC with three or more rollers)
8463.9000 20	具有滚压功能的旋压成形机床(数控,装3个以上压辊)	10	50	17	17	台	3	Spin forming machines with roll forming function (CNC with three or more rollers)
8463.9000 90	其他非切削加工机床(是指加工金属或金属陶瓷的)	10	50	17	17	台		Other non – cutting machine tools (for processing metals or metal ceramics)
84.64	**石料、陶瓷、混凝土、石棉水泥或类似矿物材料的加工机床、玻璃冷加工机床:**							**Machine-tools for working stone, ceramics, concrete, asbestos-cement or like mineral materials or for cold working glass:**
	-锯床:							-Sawing machines:
8464.1010	---圆盘锯	0	30	17	17	台		---Of disk saw
8464.1020	---钢丝锯	0	30	17	17	台		---Of scroll saw
8464.1090	---其他	0	30	17	17	台		---Other
	-研磨或抛光机床:							-Grinding or polishing machines:
8464.2010	---玻璃研磨或抛光机床	0	30	17	17	台		---Machines for grinding or polishing glass or glassware
8464.2090	---其他	0	30	17	17	台		---Other
	-其他:							-Other:
	---玻璃的其他冷加工机床:							---Other machines for cold-working glass or glassware:
8464.9011	----切割机	0	30	17	17	台		----Cutting-off machines
8464.9012	----刻花机	0	30	17	17	台		----Carving machines
8464.9019	----其他	0	30	17	17	台		----Other
8464.9090	---其他	0	30	17	17	台		---Other
84.65	**木材、软木、骨、硬质橡胶、硬质塑料或类似硬质材料的加工机床(包括用打钉或打U形钉、胶粘或其他方法组合前述材料的机器):**							**Machine-tools (including machines for nailing, stapling, glueing or otherwise assembling) for working wood, cork, bone, hard rubber, hard plastics or similar hard materials:**

税则号列	货品名称	最惠(%)	普通	增值税率	出口退税	计量单位	监管条件	Article Description
8465.1000	-不需更换工具即可进行不同机械加工的机器	10	30	17	17	台		-Machines which can carry out different types of machining operations without tool change between such operations
	-其他：							-Other:
8465.9100	--锯床	10	30	17	17	台		--Sawing machines
8465.9200	--刨、铣或切削成形机器	10	30	17	17	台		--Planing, milling or moulding (by cutting) machines
8465.9300	--研磨、砂磨或抛光机器	10	30	17	17	台		--Grinding, sanding or polishing machines
8465.9400	--弯曲或装配机器	10	30	17	17	台		--Bending or assembling machines
8465.9500	--钻孔或凿榫机器	10	30	17	17	台		--Drilling or mortising machines
8465.9600	--剖开、切片或刮削机器	10	30	17	17	台		--Splitting, slicing or paring machines
8465.9900	--其他	10	30	17	17	台		--Other
84.66	**专用于或主要用于税目 84.56 至 84.65 所列机器的零件、附件，包括工件或工具的夹具、自启板牙切头、分度头及其他专用于机床的附件；各种手提工具的工具夹具：**							**Parts and accessories suitable for use solely or principally with the machines of headings No. 84.56 to 84.65, including work or tool holders, self-opening dieheads, dividing heads and other special attachments for machine-tools; tool holders for any type of tool for working in the hand:**
8466.1000	-工具夹具及自启板牙切头	7	17	17	15	千克		-Tool holders and self-opening dieheads
8466.2000	-工件夹具	7	17	17	15	千克		-Work holders
8466.3000	-分度头及其他专用于机床的附件	7	17	17	15	千克		-Dividing heads and other special attachments for machine-tools
	-其他：							-Other:
8466.9100	--税目 84.64 所列机器用	0	17	17	15	千克		--For machines of heading No. 84.64
8466.9200	--税目 84.65 所列机器用	6	17	17	15	千克		--For machines of heading No. 84.65
	--税目 84.56 至 84.61 所列机器用：							--For machines of headings No. 84.56 to 84.61:
8466.9310	---刀库及自动换刀装置	0	17	17	15	千克		---Tool storage ond automatic tool change machine
8466.9390	---其他	0	17	17	15	千克		---Other
8466.9400	--税目 84.62 或 84.63 所列机器用	6	17	17	15	千克		--For machines of heading No. 84.62 or 84.63
8466.9400 10	滚压成形机床用芯轴（转筒成形用的芯轴，内径在 75 毫米至 400 毫米之间）	6	17	17	15	千克	3	Mandrels for roll forming machines tools (mandrel for forming of revolving drum, inner diameter 75mm ~ 400mm)
8466.9400 20	有滚压功能的旋压成形机用芯轴（转筒成形用的芯轴，内径在 75 毫米至 400 毫米之间）	6	17	17	15	千克	3	Mandrels for spin forming machines with roll forming functions (spindles for forming of revolving drum, inner diameter 75mm ~ 400mm)
8466.9400 90	编号 84.62 - 84.63 机器用其他零件	6	17	17	15	千克		Other parts for machines of heading No. 84.62 or 84.63
84.67	**手提式风动或液压工具及本身装有电动或非电动动力装置的手提式工具：**							**Tools for working in the hand, pneumatic and hydraulic and with self-contained electric or non-electric motor:**
	-风动的：							-Pneumatic:
8467.1100	--旋转式（包括旋转冲击式的）	8	30	17	15	台		--Rotary type (including combined rotary-percussion)
8467.1900	--其他	8	30	17	15	台		--Other
	-本身装有电动动力装置的：							-With self-contained electric motor:
8467.2100	--各种钻	10	30	17	15	台	A	--Drills of all kinds
	--锯：							--Saws:
8467.2210	---链锯	10	30	17	15	台	A	---Chain saws
8467.2290	---其他	10	30	17	15	台	A	---Other
	--其他：							--Other:
8467.2910	---砂磨工具（包括磨光机、砂光机、砂轮机等）	10	30	17	15	台	A	---Grinding tools (including burnisher, belt sander, wheel-sander)
8467.2920	---电刨	10	30	17	15	台	A	---Planings
8467.2990	---其他	10	30	17	15	台	A	---Other
	-其他工具：							-Other tools:

税则号列	货品名称	最惠(%)	普通	增值税率	出口退税	计量单位	监管条件	Article Description
8467.8100	--链锯	8	30	17	15	台		--Chain saws
8467.8900	--其他	8	30	17	15	台		--Other
	-零件:							-Parts:
	--链锯用:							--Of chain saws
8467.9110	---电动的	6	30	17	15	千克		---With self-contained electric motor
8467.9190	---其他	6	30	17	15	千克		---Other
8467.9200	--风动工具用	6	30	17	15	千克		--Of pneumatic tools
	--其他:							--Other:
8467.9910	---电动工具用	10	30	17	15	千克		---With self-contained elecric motor
8467.9990	---其他	6	30	17	15	千克		---Other
84.68	**焊接机器及装置,不论是否兼有切割功能,但税目85.15的货品除外;气体加温表面回火机器及装置:**							**Machinery and apparatus for soldering, brazing or welding, whether or not capable of cutting, other than those of headingNo. 85.15; gas-operated surface tempering machines and appliances:**
8468.1000	-手提喷焊器	12	30	17	15	台		-Hand-held blow pipes
8468.2000	-其他气体焊接或表面回火机器及装置	12	30	17	15	台		-Other gas-operated machinery and apparatus
8468.2000 10	自动焊接机[将端塞焊接于燃料细棒(或棒)的自动焊接机]	12	30	17	15	台	3	Automatic welding machine [the automatic welder machine that joint the end plug with the fuel thin-stick (or stick)]
8468.2000 90	其他气体焊接或表面回火机器及装置	12	30	17	15	台		Other gas welding or surface tempering machines and equipments
8468.8000	-其他机器及装置	12	30	17	15	台		-Other machinery and apparatus
8468.9000暂	-零件	3	30	17	15	千克		-Parts
84.69	**打字机,但税目84.43的打印机除外;文字处理机:**							**Typewriters other than printers of headingNo. 84.43; word-processing machines:**
	---自动打字机及文字处理机:							---Automatic typewriters and word-processing machines:
8469.0011	----文字处理机	0	40	17	15	台		----Word-processing machines
8469.0012	----自动打字机	12	40	17	15	台		----Automatic typewriters
8469.0020	---其他电动打字机	12	40	17	15	台		----Other typewriters, electric
8469.0030	---其他非电动打字机	12	40	17	15	台		---Other typewriters, non-electric
84.70	**计算机器及具有计算功能的袖珍式数据记录、重现及显示机器;装有计算装置的会计计算机、邮资盖戳机、售票机及类似机器;现金出纳机:**							**Calculating machines and pocket-size data recording, reproducing and displaying machines with calculating functions; accounting machines, postage-franking machines, ticket-issuing machines and similar machines, incorporating a calculating device; cash registers:**
8470.1000	-不需外接电源的电子计算器及具有计算功能的袖珍式数据记录、重现及显示机器	0	80	17	15	台		-Electronic calculators capable of operation without an external source of electric power and pocket-size data recording, reproducing and displaying machines with caluclating functions
	-其他电子计算器:							-Other electronic calculating machines:
8470.2100	--装有打印装置的	0	80	17	15	台		--Incorporating a printing device
8470.2900	--其他	0	80	17	15	台		--Other
8470.3000	-其他计算机器	0	40	17	15	台		-Other calculating machines
	-现金出纳机:							-Cash registers:
8470.5010	---销售点终端出纳机	0	40	17	15	台		---Terminal registers for market
8470.5090	---其他	0	40	17	15	台		---Other
8470.9000	-其他	0	40	17	15	台		-Other
84.71	**自动数据处理设备及其部件;其他税目未列名的磁性或光学阅读机、将数据以代码形式转录到数据记录媒体的机器及处理这些数据的机器:**							**Automatic data processing machines and units thereof; magnetic or optical readers, machines for transcribing data onto data media in coded form and machines for processing such data, not elsewhere specified or included:**

税则号列	货品名称	最惠(%)	普通	增值税率	出口退税	计量单位	监管条件	Article Description
	-重量不超过10公斤的便携自动数据处理设备,至少由一个中央处理部件、一个键盘及一个显示器组成:							-Portable automatic data processing machines, weighing not more than 10kg, consisting of at least a central processing unit, a keyboard and a display:
8471.3010	---平板电脑	0	70	17	17	台	A	---Panel computer
8471.3090	---其他	0	70	17	17	台	A	---Other
	-其他自动数据处理设备:							-Other automatic data processing machines:
	--同一机壳内至少有一个中央处理部件及一个输入和输出部件,不论是否组合式:							--Comprising in the same housing at least a central processing unit and an input and output unit, whether or not combined:
8471.4110	---巨型机、大型机及中型机	0	14	17	17	台	3	---mainframes
8471.4120	---小型机	0	14	17	17	台	3	---Mini-computers
8471.4140	---微型机	0	70	17	17	台	A	---Microprocessings
8471.4190	---其他	0	70	17	17	台		---Other
	--其他,以系统形式进口或出口的:							--Other, presented in the form of systems:
8471.4910	---巨型机、大型机及中型机	0	29	17	17	台	3	---Mainframes
8471.4920	---小型机	0	29	17	17	台	3	---Mini-computers
8471.4940	---微型机	0	70	17	17	台		---Microprocessings
	---其他:							---Other:
8471.4991	----分散型工业过程控制设备	0	70	17	17	台		----Processing machines for the distributed control system
8471.4999	----其他	0	70	17	17	台		----Other
	-子目号8471.41或8471.49所列以外的处理部件,不论是否在同一机壳内有一个或两个下列部件:存储部件、输入部件、输出部件:							-Processing units other than those of subheading No. 8471.41 or 8471.49, whether or not containing in the same housing one or two of the following types of unit: storage units, input units, output units:
8471.5010	---巨型机、大型机及中型机的	0	14	17	17	台	3	---Mainframes
8471.5020	---小型机的	0	14	17	17	台	3	---Mini-computers
8471.5040	---微型机的	0	70	17	17	台		---Microprocessings
8471.5040 01	含显示器和主机的微型机(不论是否在同一机壳内有一或两个存储,输入或输出部件)	0	70	17	17	台		Microprocessings, with display and host (whether or not containing in the same housing one or two ofstorage nuits, input or output units)
8471.5040 90	其他的微型机的处理部件(不论是否在同一机壳内有一或两个存储,输入或输出部件)	0	70	17	17	台		Other processing unit of microprocessings (whether or not containing in the same housing one or two ofstorage nuits, input or output units)
8471.5090	---其他	0	70	17	17	台		---Other
	-输入或输出部件,不论是否在同一机壳内有存储部件:							-Input or output units, whether or not containing storage units in the same housing:
8471.6040	---巨型机、大型机、中型机及小型机用终端	0	14	17	17	台		---Terminating machines for the huge computers, mainframes and mini-computers
8471.6050	---扫描仪	0	14	17	17	台		---Scanner
8471.6060	---数字化仪	0	14	17	17	台		---Digitizer
	---键盘、鼠标器:							---Keyboards, mouses:
8471.6071	----键盘	0	40	17	17	个		----Keyboards
8471.6072	----鼠标器	0	40	17	17	个		----Mouses
8471.6090	---其他	0	14	17	17	台		---Other
	-存储部件:							-Storage units:
8471.7010	---硬盘驱动器	0	14	17	17	台		---Rigid disk drivers
8471.7020	---软盘驱动器	0	14	17	17	台		---Floppy disk drivers
8471.7030	---光盘驱动器	0	14	17	17	台		---CD drivers
8471.7030 10	具有刻录功能的光盘驱动器(自动数据处理设备的光盘驱动器)	0	14	17	17	台		CD-R drivers (for automatic data processing machines)
8471.7030 90	其他光盘驱动器(自动数据处理设备的光盘驱动器)	0	14	17	17	台		Other CD drivers (for automatic data processing machines)
8471.7090	---其他	0	14	17	17	台		---Other

税则号列	货品名称	最惠(%)	普通	增值税率	出口退税	计量单位	监管条件	Article Description
8471.8000	-自动数据处理设备的其他部件	0	40	17	17	台		-Other units of automatic data processing machines
8471.9000	-其他	0	40	17	17	台		-Other
8471.9000 10	专用于复制的光盘刻录机(也称光盘复读机)	0	40	17	17	台		CD－R machines used exclusively for copying(also called CD repeaters)
8471.9000 90	未列名的磁性或光学阅读器(包括将数据以代码形式转录的机器及处理这些数据的机器)	0	40	17	17	台		Magnetic or optical readers, not elsewhere specified or included(including machines for transcribing data onto data media in coded form and machines for processing such data)
84.72	其他办公室用机器(例如,胶版复印机、油印机、地址印写机、自动付钞机、硬币分类、计数及包装机、削铅笔机、打洞机或订书机):							**Other office machines (for example, hectograph or stencil duplicating machines, addressing machines, automatic banknote dispensers, coin-sorting machines, coin-counting or wrapping machines, pencil-sharpening machines, perforating or stapling machines):**
8472.1000	-胶版复印机、油印机	14	40	17	15	台		-Duplicating machines
	-信件分类或折叠机或信件装封机、信件开封或闭封机、粘贴或盖销邮票机:							-Machines for sorting or folding mail or for inserting mail in envelopes or bands, machines for opening, closing or sealing mail and machines for affixing or cancelling postage stamps:
8472.3010	---邮政信件分拣及封装设备	10	40	17	15	台		---Machines for sorting or banding mail
8472.3090	---其他	14	40	17	15	台		---Other
	-其他:							-Other:
8472.9010	---自动柜员机	0	40	17	15	台		---Automated teller
	---装订用机器:							---Stapling machines:
8472.9021	----打洞机	0	40	17	15	台		----Perforator
8472.9022	----订书机	0	40	17	15	台		----Stapler
8472.9029	----其他	0	40	17	15	台		----Other
8472.9030	---碎纸机	0	40	17	15	台		---Paper shrudders
8472.9040	---地址印写机及地址铭牌压印机	14	40	17	15	台		---Addressing machines and address plate embossing machines
8472.9090	---其他	0	40	17	15	台		---Other
84.73	**专用于或主要用于税目84.69至84.72所列机器的零件、附件(罩套、提箱及类似品除外):**							**Parts and accessories (other than covers, carrying cases and the like) suitable for use solely or principally with machines of headings No.84.69 to 84.72:**
8473.1000	-税目84.69所列机器的零件、附件	8	35	17	15	千克		-Parts and accessories of the machines of heading No.84.69
	-税目84.70所列机器的零件、附件:							-Parts and accessories of the machines of heading No.84.70:
8473.2100	--子目号8470.10、8470.21或8470.29所列电子计算器的零件、附件	0	50	17	15	千克		--Of the electronic calculating machines of subheading No.8470.10, 8470.21 or 8470.29
8473.2900	--其他	0	35	17	15	千克		--Other
	-税目84.71所列机器的零件、附件:							-Parts and accessories of the machines of heading No.84.71:
8473.3010	---子目号8471.4110、8471.4120、8471.4910、8471.4920、8471.5010、8471.5020、8471.6090、8471.7010、8471.7020、8471.7030及8471.7090所列机器及装置的零件、附件	0	14	17	17	千克		---Of the machines of subheading 8471.4110, 8471.4120, 8471.4910, 8471.4920, 8471.5010, 8471.5020, 8471.6090, 8471.7010, 8471.7020, 8471.7030 and 8471.7090
8473.3090	---其他	0	40	17	17	千克		---Other
	-税目84.72所列机器的零件、附件:							-Parts and accessories of the machines of heading No.84.72:
8473.4010[暂]	---自动柜员机用出钞器	5	35	17	15	千克		---Banknote dispenser of automated teller
8473.4090	---其他		35	17	15	千克		---Other

税则号列	货品名称	最惠(%)	普通	增值税率	出口退税	计量单位	监管条件	Article Description
8473.4090暂 01	钞票清分机零附件	3	35	17	15	千克		Parts and accessories of banknote sorters
8473.4090 90	其他办公室用机器零附件	10.5	35	17	15	千克		Parts and accessories of other office machines
8473.5000	-同样适用于税目84.69至84.72中两个或两个以上税目所列机器的零件、附件	0	35	17	15	千克		-Parts and accessories equally suitable for use with machines of two or more of the heading No. 84.69 to 84.72
84.74	**泥土、石料、矿石或其他固体(包括粉状、浆状)矿物质的分类、筛选、分离、洗涤、破碎、磨粉、混合或搅拌机器;固体矿物燃料、陶瓷坯泥、未硬化水泥、石膏材料或其他粉状、浆状矿产品的粘聚或成形机器;铸造用砂模的成形机器:**							**Machinery for sorting, screening, separating, washing, crushing, grinding, mixing or kneading earth, stone, ores or other mineral substances, in solid (including powder or paste) form; machinery for agglomerating, shaping or moulding solid mineral fuels, ceramic paste unhardned cements plastering materials or other mineral products in powder or paste form, machines for forming foundry moulds of sand**
8474.1000	-分类、筛选、分离或洗涤机器	5	30	17	15	台		-Sorting, screening, separating or washing machines
	-破碎或磨粉机器:							-Crushing or grinding machines:
8474.2010	---齿辊式	5	30	17	15	台		---Toothing roller type
8474.2020	---球磨式	5	30	17	15	台		---Em-Peters type
8474.2090	---其他	5	30	17	15	台		---Other
	-混合或搅拌机器:							-Mixing or kneading machines:
8474.3100	--混凝土或砂浆混合机器	7	30	17	17	台		--Concrete or mortar mixers
8474.3200	--矿物与沥青的混合机器	7	30	17	17	台		--Machines for mixing mineral substances with bitumen
8474.3900	--其他	5	30	17	17	台		--Other
	-其他机器:							-Other machinery:
8474.8010	---辊压成型机	5	30	17	17	台		---Rolling forming machines
8474.8020	---模压成型机	5	30	17	17	台		---Molud pressing machines
8474.8090	---其他	5	30	17	17	台		---Other
8474.8090 10	纸面角线石膏板搅拌成型机	5	30	17	17	台		Paper faced angle line gypsum board mixing machines
8474.8090 90	编号8474未列名的其他机器(如矿产品的粘聚或成型机器及铸造用砂模的成型机器)	5	30	17	17	台		Other machines, not elsewhere specified or included of heading No. 8474 (for example, machinery for agglomerating, shaping or moulding or machines for forming foundry moulds of sand)
8474.9000	-零件	5	30	17	15	千克		-Parts
84.75	**白炽灯泡、灯管、放电灯管、电子管、闪光灯泡及类似品的封装机器;玻璃或玻璃制品的制造或热加工机器:**							**Machines for assembling electric or electronic lamps, tubes or valves or flash-bulbs, in glass envelopes; machines for manufacturing or hot working glass or glassware:**
8475.1000	-白炽灯泡、灯管、放电灯管、电子管、闪光灯泡及类似品的封装机器	8	30	17	15	台		-Machines for assembling electric or electronic lamps, tubes or valves or flashbulbs, in glass envelopes
	-玻璃或玻璃制品的制造或热加工机器:							-Machines for manufacturing or hot working glass or glassware:
8475.2100	--制造光导纤维及其预制棒的机器	10	30	17	15	台		--Machines for making optical fibres and preforms thereof
	--其他:							--Other:
	---玻璃的热加工设备:							---Equipments for hot working glass or glasswares:
8475.2911	----连续式玻璃热弯炉	10	30	17	15	台		----Continuous hot bending furnaces
8475.2912	----玻璃纤维拉丝机(光纤拉丝机除外)	10	30	17	15	台		----Fiber glass winder(excluding opticae fiber winder)
8475.2919	----其他	10	30	17	15	台		----Other
8475.2990	---其他	10	30	17	15	台		---Other
8475.9000	-零件	8	30	17	15	千克		-Parts
84.76	**自动售货机(例如,出售邮票、香烟、食品或饮料的机器),包括钱币兑换机:**							**Automatic goods-vending machines (for example, postage stamp, cigarette, food or beverage machines), including money-changing machines:**
	-饮料自动销售机:							-Automatic beverage-vending machines:

税则号列	货品名称	最惠(%)	普通	增值税率	出口退税	计量单位	监管条件	Article Description
8476.2100	--装有加热或制冷装置的	14	50	17	15	台	A	--Incorporating heating or refrigerating devices
8476.2900	--其他	15	50	17	15	台	A	--Other
	-其他机器:							-Other machines:
8476.8100	--装有加热或制冷装置的	14	50	17	15	台		--Incorporating heating or refrigerating devices
8476.8900	--其他	15	50	17	15	台		--Other
8476.9000	-零件	10	50	17	15	千克		-Parts
84.77	**本章其他税目未列名的橡胶或塑料及其产品的加工机器:**							**Machinery for working rubber or plastics or for the manufacture of products from these materials, not specified or included elsewhere in this Chapter:**
	-注射机:							-Injection-moulding machines:
8477.1010	---注塑机	0	45	17	15	台		---For working plastics
8477.1010 10	用于光盘生产的精密注塑机(加工塑料的)	0	45	17	15	台	6	Precision injection-moulders for disks production (for working plastics)
8477.1010 90	其他注塑机	0	45	17	15	台		Other working plastics machines
8477.1090	---其他	0	30	17	15	台		---Other
	-挤出机:							-Extruders:
8477.2010	---塑料造粒机	5	30	17	15	台		---Plastic pelletizers
8477.2090	---其他	5	30	17	15	台		---Other
	-吹塑机							-Blow moulding machines:
8477.3010	---挤出吹塑机	5	30	17	15	台		---Extruders blow moulding machines
8477.3020	---注射吹塑机	5	30	17	15	台		---Injection blow moulding machines
8477.3090	---其他	5	30	17	15	台		---Other
	-真空模塑机器及其他热成型机器:							-Vacuum moulding machines and other thermoforming machines:
8477.4010	---塑料中空成型机	5	30	17	15	台		---Plastics brideg-die-forming machines
8477.4020	---塑料压延成型机	5	30	17	15	台		---Plastics calender-forming machines
8477.4090	---其他	5	30	17	15	台		---Other
	-其他模塑或成型机器:							-Other machinery for moulding or otherwise forming:
8477.5100	--用于充气轮胎模塑或翻新的机器及内胎模塑或用其他方法成型的机器	5	30	17	15	台		--For moulding or retreading pneumatic tyres or for moulding or otherwise forming inner tubes
	--其他:							--Other:
8477.5910	---三维打印机(3D打印机)	5	30	17	15	台		---3D printing
8477.5990	---其他	5	30	17	15	台		---Other
8477.8000	-其他机器	5	30	17	15	台		-Other machinery
8477.9000	-零件	0	30	17	15	千克		-Parts
84.78	**本章其他税目未列名的烟草加工及制作机器:**							**Machinery for preparing or making up tobacco, not specified or included elsewhere in this Chapter:**
8478.1000	-机器	5	30	17	15	台	O	-Machinery
8478.9000暂	-零件	5	30	17	15	千克	O	-Parts
84.79	**本章其他税目未列名的具有独立功能的机器及机械器具:**							**Machines and mechanical appliances having individual functions, not specified or included elsewhere in this Chapter:**
	-公共工程用机器:							-Machinery for public works, building or the like:
	---摊铺机:							---Spreading machines:
8479.1021	----沥青混凝土摊铺机	8	30	17	17	台	O	----Machines for spreading bituminous concrete
8479.1022	----稳定土摊铺机	8	30	17	17	台		----Stabilizer spreading machines
8479.1029	----其他	8	30	17	17	台	O	----Other
8479.1090	---其他	8	30	17	17	台		---Other
8479.2000	-提取、加工动物油脂或植物固定油脂的机器	10	30	17	15	台	A	-Machinery for the extraction or preparation of animal or fixed vegetable fats or oils
8479.3000	-木碎料板或木纤维板的挤压机及其他木材或软木处理机	10	30	17	15	台		-Presses for the manufacture of particle board or fibre building board or wood or other ligneous materials and other machinery for treating wood or cork
8479.4000暂	-绳或缆的制造机器	5	30	17	15	台		-Rope or cable-making machines

税则号列	货品名称	最惠(%)	普通	增值税率	出口退税	计量单位	监管条件	Article Description
	-未列名工业机器人:							-Industrial robots, not elsewhere specified or included:
8479.5010	---多功能工业机器人	0	20	17	17	台		---Industrial robots for multiple uses
8479.5090	---其他	0	30	17	17	台		---Other
8479.5090 10	机器人,末端操纵装置[能处理高能炸药或能抗大于5×10^4戈瑞(硅)辐射的]	0	30	17	17	台	3	Robots, end - control devices (capable of handling high-energy explosives or resisting radiance > 5×10^4Gy (Si))
8479.5090 90	其他工业机器人(多功能工业机器人除外)	0	30	17	17	台		Other industrial robots (other than multiple-functional industrial robots)
8479.6000	-蒸发式空气冷却器	10	30	17	15	台	A	-Evaporative air coolers
	-旅客登机(船)桥:							-Passenger boarding (boats) bridge use at airport:
8479.7100	--用于机场的	0	30	17	15	台	A	--Of a kind used in airports
8479.7900	--其他	0	30	17	15	台	A	--Other
	-其他机器及机械器具:							-Other machines and mechanical appliances:
	--处理金属的机械,包括线圈绕线机:							--For treating metal, including electric wire coil-winders:
8479.8110	---绕线机	9.5	30	17	15	台		---Filament winding machines
8479.8190	---其他	9.5	30	17	15	台		---Other
8479.8200	--混合、搅拌、轧碎、研磨、筛选、均化或乳化机器	7	30	17	15	台		--Mixing, kneading, crushing, grinding, screening, sifting, homogenizing, emulsifying or stirring machines
8479.8200 10	两用物项管制搅拌器(耐腐蚀热交换器、搅拌器用,带搅拌的发酵罐)	7	30	17	15	台	3	Beaters subject to regulations of sensitive item (Rot-proof heat exchanger and ferment jar for use of beater)
8479.8200 90	其他混合、搅拌、轧碎、研磨机器(包括筛选、均化、乳化机器)	7	30	17	15	台		Other mixing, kneading, crushing, grinding, screening, sifting, homogenizing, emulsifying or stirring machines
	--其他:							--Other:
8479.8910	---船舶用舵机及陀螺稳定器	0	14	17	15	台		---Steering and rudder equipment or gyroscopic stabilizers for ships
8479.8920	---空气增湿器及减湿器	0	70	17	15	台		---Air humidifiers or dehumidifiers
8479.8940	---邮政用包裹、印刷品分拣设备	0	30	17	15	台	A	---Bundle and printed matter sorting machines used in post offices
8479.8950	---放射性废物压实机	0	30	17	15	台		---Presses for radioactive waste material
	---在印刷电路电路板上装配元器件的机器:							---Machines for assemblying elements on printed circuit boards:
8479.8961	----自动插件机	0	30	17	15	台	A	----Automatic plug-in machines
8479.8962	----自动贴片机	0	30	17	15	台	A	----Automatic coreslice adhering machines
8479.8969	----其他	0	30	17	15	台	A	----Other
	---其他:							---Other:
8479.8992	----自动化立体仓储设备	0	30	17	15	台	A	----Three - dimensional automatic warehouse equipmentt
8479.8999	----其他	0	30	17	15	台		----Other
8479.8999 10	用于光盘生产的金属母盘生产设备(具有独立功能的)	0	30	17	15	台	6A	Metal master production equipment for CD production (having independent functions)
8479.8999 20	用于光盘生产的粘合机(具有独立功能的)	0	30	17	15	台	6A	Fusing machine for CD production (having independent functions)
8479.8999 30	用于光盘生产的真空金属溅镀机(具有独立功能的)	0	30	17	15	台	6A	Vacuum metal-splashers for CD production (having independent functions)
8479.8999 40	保护胶涂覆机及染料层旋涂机(光盘生产用,具有独立功能的)	0	30	17	15	台	6A	Protective rubber-coating machine and dye-layer spin-coating machine (for CD production, having independent functions)
8479.8999 51	等静压压力机(两用物项管制机器及机械器具)	0	30	17	15	台	3A	Isostatic press (Dual - use items control machines and mechanical appliances)
8479.8999 52	生物反应器(两用物项管制机器及机械器具)	0	30	17	15	台	3A	Biological reactor (Dual - use items control machines and mechanical appliances)

税则号列	货品名称	最惠(%)	普通	增值税率	出口退税	计量单位	监管条件	Article Description
8479.8999 53	恒化器(两用物项管制机器及机械器具)	0	30	17	15	台	3A	Chemostat(Dual - use items control machines and mechanical appliances)
8479.8999 54	连续灌流系统(两用物项管制机器及机械器具)	0	30	17	15	台	3A	Continuous langendorff (Dual - use items control machines and mechanical appliances)
8479.8999 55	三坐标或多坐标联动和程控的纤维缠绕机(两用物项管制机器及机械器具)	0	30	17	15	台	3A	Filament winding Machines coordinated and programmed in three or more axes, (Dual - use items control machines and mechanical appliances)
8479.8999 59	其他两用物项管制机器及机械器具	0	30	17	15	台	3A	Other dual-use items control machines and mechanical appliances
8479.8999 60	绕线机(能卷绕直径在75mm至400mm、长度为600mm或更长的)	0	30	17	15	台	3A	winding machines(capable of winding wire diameter 75mm~400mm, length≥600mm)
8479.8999 90	本章其他未列名机器及机械器具(具有独立功能的)	0	30	17	15	台	A	Machines and mechanical appliances having independent functions, not specified or included elsewhere in this Chapter
	-零件:							-Parts:
8479.9010	---船舶用舵机及陀螺稳定器用	0	14	17	15	千克		---Of the machines of subheading No. 8479.8910
8479.9020	---空气增湿器及减湿器用	0	70	17	15	千克		---Of the machines of subheading No. 8479.8920
8479.9090	---其他	0	20	17	15	千克		---Other
8479.9090 10	绕线机的精密芯轴(专用于编号8479899060绕线机的精密芯轴)	0	20	17	15	千克	3	Precision mandrels for winding machines(precision mandrels used exclusively for No. 84798990.60 winding machines)
8479.9090 90	编号8479所列机器的其他零件	0	20	17	15	千克		Other parts of machiners of heading No. 8479
84.80	**金属铸造用型箱;型模底板;阳模;金属用型模(锭模除外)、硬质合金、玻璃、矿物材料、橡胶或塑料用型模:**							**Moulding boxes for metal foundry; mould bases; moulding patterns; moulds for metal (other than ingot moulds), metal carbides, glass, mineral materials, rubber or plastics:**
8480.1000	-金属铸造用型箱	10	20	17	15	千克		-Moulding boxes for metal foundry
8480.2000	-型模底板	8	20	17	15	千克		-Mould bases
8480.3000	-阳模	10	20	17	15	千克		-Moulding patterns
	-金属、硬质合金用型模:							-Moulds for metal or metal carbides:
	--注模或压模:							--Injection or compression types:
8480.4110	---压铸模	8	20	17	15	千克		---Die-casting mould
8480.4120	---粉末冶金用压模	8	20	17	15	千克		---Die-casting mould use for powder metallurgy
8480.4190	---其他	8	20	17	15	千克		---Other
8480.4900	--其他	8	20	17	15	千克		--Other
8480.5000	-玻璃用型模	8.4	20	17	15	套/千克		-Moulds for glass
8480.6000	-矿物材料用型模	8.4	20	17	15	套/千克		-Moulds for mineral materials
	-塑料或橡胶用型模:							-Moulds for rubber or plastics:
	--注模或压模:							--Other:
8480.7110	---硫化轮胎用囊式型模	0	20	17	15	套		---Tyre vulcanizing mould for capsule type(injection or compression types)
8480.7190	---其他	0	20	17	15	套/千克		---Other
8480.7190 10	用于光盘生产的专用模具(注模或压模)	0	20	17	15	套/千克	6	Injection molds for CD production(injection or compression types)
8480.7190 90	其他塑料或橡胶用注模或压模	0	20	17	15	套/千克		Other injection or compression types for rubber or plastics
8480.7900	--其他	5	20	17	15	套/千克		--Other
8480.7900 10	农用双壁波纹管生产线用其他模具	5	20	17	15	套/千克		Other molds for agricultural double-wall corrugated pipe production lines
8480.7900 90	塑料或橡胶用其他型模	5	20	17	15	套/千克		Other moulds for rubber plastics
84.81	**用于管道、锅炉、罐、桶或类似品的龙头、旋塞、阀门及类似装置,包括减压阀及恒温控制阀:**							**Taps, cocks, valves and similar appliances for pipes, boiler shells, tanks, vats or the like, including pressure-reducing valves and thermostatically controlled valves:**
8481.1000	-减压阀		30	17	15	套/千克		-Pressure-reducing valves

税则号列	货品名称	最惠(%)	普通	增值税率	出口退税	计量单位	监管条件	Article Description
8481.1000[暂] 01	喷灌设备用减压阀(用于管道、锅炉、罐、桶或类似品的)	2	30	17	15	套/千克		Pressure-reducing valves for spray irrigation equipment(used in pipes, boiler shells, tanks, vats or similar products)
8481.1000 90	其他减压阀(用于管道、锅炉、罐、桶或类似品的)	5	30	17	15	套/千克		Other pressure-reducing valves(used in pipes, boiler shells, thanks, vats or similar products)
	-油压或气压传动阀:							-Valves for oleohydraulic or pneumatic transmissions:
8481.2010	---油压的	5	30	17	15	套/千克		---For oleohydraulic transmissions
8481.2020	---气压的	5	30	17	15	套/千克		---For pneumatic transmissions
8481.3000[暂]	-止回阀	3	30	17	15	套/千克		-Check (nonreturn) valves
8481.4000	-安全阀或溢流阀	5	30	17	15	套/千克		-Safety or relief valves
	-其他器具:							-Other appliances:
	---换向阀:							---Directional valve:
8481.8021	----电磁式	7	30	17	15	套/千克		----Electromagnetic
8481.8021 10	两用物项管制的电磁式换向阀	7	30	17	15	套/千克	3	Electromagnetic directional valve of dual – use items control
8481.8021 90	其他电磁式换向阀(用于管道、锅炉、罐、桶或类似品的)	7	30	17	15	套/千克		Other electromagnetic selector valve(used for tubing, boilers, Cans, barrels or similar products)
8481.8029	----其他	7	30	17	15	套/千克		----Other
8481.8029 10	两用物项管制的其他换向阀	7	30	17	15	套/千克	3	Other selector valve of dual – use items control
8481.8029 90	其他换向阀(用于管道、锅炉、罐、桶或类似品的)	7	30	17	15	套/千克		Other selector valve(used for tubing, boilers, Cans, barrels or similar products)
	---流量阀:							---Flow control valves:
8481.8031	----电子膨胀阀	7	30	17	15	套/千克		----Electronic expansion valves
8481.8031 10	两用物项管制的电子膨胀流量阀	7	30	17	15	套/千克	3	Electronic expansion flow valve of dual – use items control
8481.8031 90	其他电子膨胀流量阀(用于管道、锅炉、罐、桶或类似品的)	7	30	17	15	套/千克		Other electronic expansion flow valve(used for tubing, boilers, Cans, barrels or similar products)
8481.8039	----其他	7	30	17	15	套/千克		----Other
8481.8039 10	两用物项管制的其他流量阀	7	30	17	15	套/千克	3	Other flow control valve of sensitive items control
8481.8039 90	其他流量阀(用于管道、锅炉、罐、桶或类似品的)	7	30	17	15	套/千克		Other flow control valve (used for tubing, boilers, Cans, barrels or similar products)
8481.8040[暂]	---其他阀门	3	30	17	15	套/千克		---Other valve
8481.8040[暂] 10	两用物项管制的其他阀门	3	30	17	15	套/千克	3	Other valve of sensitive items control
8481.8040[暂] 90	其他阀门(用于管道、锅炉、罐、桶或类似品的)	3	30	17	15	套/千克		Other valve(used for tubing, boilers, Cans, barrels or similar products)
8481.8090	---其他	5	50	17	15	套/千克		---Other
	-零件:							-Parts:
8481.9010[暂]	---阀门用	4	30	17	15	千克		---Of valves
8481.9090	---其他	8	50	17	15	千克		---Other
84.82	**滚动轴承:**							**Ball or roller bearings:**
	-滚珠轴承							-Ball bearings
8482.1010	---调心球轴承	8	20	17	15	套		---Self – aliging ball bearing
8482.1020	---深沟球轴承	8	20	17	15	套		---Deep groove ball bearing
8482.1030	---角接触轴承	8	20	17	15	套		---Angular contact ball bearing
8482.1040	---推力球轴承	8	20	17	15	套		---Thrust ball bearing
8482.1090	---其他	8	20	17	15	套		---Other
8482.2000	-锥形滚子轴承,包括锥形滚子组件	8	20	17	15	套		-Tapered roller bearings, including cone and tapered roller assemblies
8482.3000[暂]	-鼓形滚子轴承	6	20	17	15	套		-Spherical roller bearings
8482.4000[暂]	-滚针轴承	6	20	17	15	套		-Needle roller bearings
8482.5000[暂]	-其他圆柱形滚子轴承	8	20	17	15	套		-Other cylindrical roller bearings
8482.5000[暂] 01	三环、二环偏心滚动轴承	4	20	17	15	套		Tricyclic, bicyclic eccentric rolling bearing

税则号列	货品名称	最惠(%)	普通	增值税率	出口退税	计量单位	监管条件	Article Description
8482.5000 90	其他圆柱形滚子轴承	8	20	17	15	套		Other cylindrical roller bearings
8482.8000	-其他,包括球、柱混合轴承	8	20	17	15	套		-Other, including combined ball/roller bearings
	-零件:							-Parts:
8482.9100[暂]	--滚珠、滚针及滚柱	6	20	17	15	千克		--Balls, needles and rollers
8482.9900[暂]	--其他	3	20	17	15	千克		--Other
84.83	**传动轴(包括凸轮轴及曲柄轴)及曲柄;轴承座及滑动轴承;齿轮及齿轮传动装置;滚珠或滚子螺杆传动装置;齿轮箱及其他变速装置,包括扭矩变换器;飞轮及滑轮,包括滑轮组;离合器及联轴器(包括万向节):**							**Transmission shafts (including cam shafts and crank shafts) and cranks; bearing housings and plain shaft bearings; gears and gearing ball or roller screws; gear boxes and other speed changers, including torque converters; flywheels and pulleys, including pulley blocks; clutches and shaft couplings (including universal joints):**
	-传动轴(包括凸轮轴及曲柄轴)及曲柄:							-Transmission shafts (including cam shafts and crank shafts) and cranks:
	---船舶用传动轴:							---Transmission shafts for ships:
8483.1011	----柴油机曲轴	6	14	17	17	个		----Crank shaft for diesel engine
8483.1019	----其他	6	14	17	17	个		----Other
8483.1090	---其他	6	30	17	17	个		---Other
8483.2000	-装有滚珠或滚子轴承的轴承座	6	30	17	15	个		-Bearing housings, incorporating ball or roller bearings
8483.3000[暂]	-未装滚珠或滚子轴承的轴承座;滑动轴承	3	30	17	15	个		-Bearing housings, not incorporating ball or roller bearings; plain shaft bearings
8483.3000[暂] 10	磁悬浮轴承(轴承组合件,由悬浮在充满阻尼介质的环形磁铁组成)	3	30	17	15	个	3	Magnetic suspension bearing (assembly of bearing, compased of circular magnets of supending in filled with damping mediun)
8483.3000[暂] 20	轴承/阻尼器(安装在阻尼器上的具有枢轴/盖的轴承)	3	30	17	15	个	3	Bearings dampers (installed on the bearing with a pivot lid on the damper)
8483.3000[暂] 90	其他未装有滚珠或滚子轴承的轴承座;其他滑动轴承	3	30	17	15	个		Other bearing housing not incorporalins ball or rouer bearings; other plain shaft bearins
	-齿轮及齿轮传动装置,但单独进口或出口的带齿的轮、链轮及其他传动元件除外;滚珠或滚子螺杆传动装置;齿轮箱及其他变速装置,包括扭矩变换器:							-Gears and gearing, other than toothed wheels, chain sprockets and other transmission elements presented separately; ball or roller screws; gear boxes and other speed changers, including torque converters:
8483.4010	---滚子螺杆传动装置	8	30	17	15	个		---Roller Screws
8483.4020	---行星齿轮减速器		30	17	15	个		---Planet decelerators
8483.4020[暂] 01	磨煤机用行星齿轮减速器(由螺旋伞齿轮加行星齿轮二级立式减速机构组成,转盘外圆直径为1300mm至2400mm)	2	30	17	15	个		Plantary gear reducers for coal - grinding machines (consisting of a spiral bevel gear and a two - stage vertical planetary gear reducing structure, rotary cylindrical diameter is 1300mm ~ 2400mm)
8483.4020 90	其他行星齿轮减速器	8	30	17	15	个		Other planetary gear reducers
8483.4090	---其他	8	30	17	17	个		---Other
8483.5000	-飞轮及滑轮,包括滑轮组	8	30	17	15	个		-Flywheels and pulleys, including pulley blocks
8483.6000	-离合器及联轴器(包括万向节)		30	17	17	个		-Clutches and shaft couplings (including universal joints)
8483.6000[暂] 01	压力机用组合式湿式离合/制动器(离合扭矩为60kNM-300kNM,制动扭矩为30kNM-100kNM)	4	30	17	17	个		Combined wet clutches / brakes for presses (the on-off torque is 60KNM ~ 300KNM and the braking torque is 30KNM ~ 100KNM)
8483.6000 90	离合器及联轴器(包括万向节)	8	30	17	17	个		Clutches and shaft couplings (including universal joints)
8483.9000	-单独报验的带齿的轮、链轮及其他传动元件;零件		30	17	17	千克		-Toothed wheels, chain sprockets and other transmission elements presented separately; parts
8483.9000[暂] 10	车用凸轮轴相位调节器(汽车发动机用)	4	30	17	17	千克		Car camshaft phase regulator (car engine)

税则号列	货　品　名　称	最惠(%)	普通	增值税率	出口退税	计量单位	监管条件	Article Description
8483.9000 90	品目84.83所列货品用其他零件(包括单独报验的带齿的轮、链轮及其他传动元件)	8	30	17	17	千克		Other components for goods of heading 84.83 goods (toothed wheels, chain sprockets and other transmission components including separately presented)
84.84	**密封垫或类似接合衬垫,用金属片与其他材料制成或用双层或多层金属片制成;成套或各种不同材料的密封垫或类似接合衬垫,装于袋、套或类似包装内;机械密封件:**							**Gaskets and similar joints of metal sheeting combined with other material or of two or more layers of metal; sets or assortments of gaskets and similar joints, dissimilar in composition, put up in pouches, envelopes or similar packings mechanical seals:**
8484.1000暂	-密封垫或类似接合衬垫(用金属片与其他材料制成或用双层或多层金属片制成)	5	30	17	17	千克		-Gaskets and similar joints of metal sheeting combined with other material or of two or more layers of metal
8484.2000暂	-机械密封件	5	30	17		千克		-Mechanical seals
8484.2000暂 10	耐UF_6腐蚀的转动轴封(专门设计的真空密封装置,缓冲气体泄漏率1000cm^3/min)	5	30	17	17	千克	3	UF_6 resisting rotary shaft seals (specially designed vacuum airtight devices, rate of leakage of buffer gas 1000cm^3/min)
8484.2000暂 20	转动轴封(专门设计的带有密封式进气口和出气口的转动轴封)	5	30	17	17	千克	3	Rotary shalt seals (specially designed shaft seals with an airtight inlet and outlet)
8484.2000暂 30	MLIS用转动轴封(专门设计的带密封进气口和出气口的转动轴封)	5	30	17	15	千克	3	Rotary shalt seals for MLIS(specially designed, shaft seals an airtight inlet and outlet)
8484.2000暂 90	其他机械密封件	5	30	17	15	千克		Other mechanical seals
8484.9000暂	-其他	5	30	17	15	千克		-Other
84.86	**专用于或主要用于制造半导体单晶柱或晶圆、半导体器件、集成电路或平板显示器的机器及装置;本章注释九(三)规定的机器及装置,零件及附件:**							**Machines and apparatus of a kind used soldy or principally for the manufacture of semiconductor boules or wafers, semiconductor devices, electronic integrated circuits or flat panel displays; machines and apparatus specified in Note 9(C) to this chapter; Parts and accessories**
	-制造单晶柱或晶圆用的机器及装置:							-Machines and apparatus for the manvifacture of boules or wafers:
8486.1010	---利用温度变化处理单晶硅的机器及装置	0	30	17	17	台		---Machines and apparatus for the treatment of monocrystalline sillicon by aprocess involving a change of temperature
8486.1020	---研磨设备	0	30	17	17	台		---Grinding machines
8486.1030	---切割设备	0	30	17	17	台		---Sawing machines
8486.1040	---化学机械抛光设备(CMP)	0	30	17	17	台		---Chemical mechanical polishers (CMP)
8486.1090	---其他	0	30	17	17	台		---other
	-制造半导体器件或集成电路用的机器及装置:							-Machines and apparatus for the manufacture of semiconductor devices or of electronic integrated circuis:
8486.2010	---氧化、扩散、退火及其他热处理设备	0	30	17	17	台		---Diffusion, oxidatation annealing and other heat treatment equipment
	---薄膜沉积设备:							---Film deposition ouqipment:
8486.2021	----化学气相沉积装置(CVD)	0	30	17	17	台		----Chemical Vapor Deposition (CVD) equipment
8486.2022	----物理气相沉积装置(PVD)	0	30	17	17	台		----Physical Vapour Deposition (PVD) equipment
8486.2029	----其他	0	30	17	17	台		----Other
	---将电路图投影或绘制到感光半导体材料上的装置:							---Apparatus for the projection or drawing of circuit patterns on sensitized semiconductor materials:
8486.2031	----分步重复光刻机(步进光刻机)	0	100	17	17	台		----step and repeat alignersw
8486.2039	----其他	0	100	17	17	台		----Other
	---刻蚀及剥离设备:							---Etching and stripoing equipment:
8486.2041	----等离子体干法刻蚀机	0	30	17	17	台		----Dry plasma etching
8486.2049	----其他	0	30	17	17	台		----Other
8486.2050	---离子注入机	0	11	17	17	台		---Ion Implanters
8486.2090	---其他	0	30	17	17	台		---Other

税则号列	货品名称	最惠(%)	普通	增值税率	出口退税	计量单位	监管条件	Article Description
	-制造平板显示器用的机器及装置：							-Machines and apparatus for the manufacture of flat panel displays:
8486.3010	---扩散、氧化、退火及其他热处理设备	0	30	17	17	台		---Oxidatation diffusinon annealing and other heat treatment equipment
	---薄膜沉积设备：							---Film deposition equipment:
8486.3021	----化学气相沉积设备(CVD)	0	30	17	17	台		---- Chemical vapour deposition (CVD) equipment
8486.3022	----物理气相沉积设备(PVD)	0	30	17	17	台		----Physical Vapour Deposition (PVD) equipment
8486.3029	----其他	0	30	17	17	台		----Other
	---将电路图投影或绘制到感光半导体材料上的装置：							---Apparatus for the projection or drawing of circuit patterns on sensitized stmiconductor materials:
8486.3031	----分布重复光刻机	0	100	17	17	台		----Step and repeat alignersw
8486.3039	----其他	0	100	17	17	台		---Other
	---湿法蚀刻、显影、剥离、清洗装置：							---Apparatus for wet-etching developing stripping or cleaning:
8486.3041暂	----超声波清洗装置	5	30	17	17	台		----Ultrasonic apparatus for cleaning
8486.3049	----其他	0	30	17	17	台		----Other
8486.3090	---其他	0	30	17	17	台		---Other
	-本章注释九(三)规定的机器及装置：							-Machines and apparatus specified in Note 9 (c) to this chapter:
8486.4010	---主要用于或专用于制作和修复掩膜版或投影掩膜版的装置	0	70	17	17	台		---Apparatus solely or principally of a kind used for the manufacture or repair of masks and reticles
	---主要用于或专有于装配与封装半导体器件或集成电路的设备：							---Machines solely or principally of a kind used for assembling or encapsulating semiconductor devices or electronic integrated circuits:
8486.4021	----塑封机	5	30	17	17	台		----Plastics encapsulating machines
8486.4022	----引线键合装置		30	17	17	台		----Wire bonders
8486.4022暂 10	全自动铝丝焊接机(主要用于或专用于装配与封装半导体器件和集成电路的设备)	6	30	17	17	台		Automatic aluminum foil welding apparatus (machines solely or principally of a kind used for assembling or encapsulating semiconductor devices or electronic integrated circuits)
8486.4022暂 20	全自动铜丝焊接机(主要用于或专用于装配与封装半导体器件和集成电路的设备)	6	30	17	17	台		Full automatic wire welding machine (mainly for or dedicated to the assembly and packaging of semiconductor devices and integrated circuits equipment)
8486.4022暂 30	全自动金丝焊接机(主要用于或专用于装配与封装半导体器件和集成电路的设备)	4	30	17	17	台		Fully automatic gold wire welding machine (mainly for or dedicated to theassembly and packaging of semiconductor devices and integrated circuitsequipment)
8486.4022 90	其他引线键合装置(主要用于或专用于装配与封装半导体器件和集成电路的设备)	8	30	17	17	台		Other wire bonders(machines solely or principally of a kind used for assembling or encapsulating semiconductor devices or electronic integrated circuits)
8486.4029	----其他	0	17	17	17	台		----Other
	---主要用于或专用于升降、装卸、搬运单晶柱、晶圆、半导体器件、集成电路或平板显示器的装置：							---Apparatus solely or principally of a kind used for lifting, handling, loading or unloading of boules, wafers, semiconductor devices, electronic integrated circuits and flat panel displays:
8486.4031	----集成电路工厂专用的自动搬运机器人	0	20	17	17	台		----Automated material handling machines solely or principally of a kind used in the electronic integrated circuits factories
8486.4039	----其他	5	30	17	17	台		----Other
	-零件及附件：							-Parts and accessories:
8486.9010	---升降、搬运、装卸机器用(自动搬运设备用除外)	5	30	17	17	千克		---Of machines for lifting, handling, loading or unloading (other than automated material handling machines)
8486.9020	---引线键合装置用	6	30	17	17	千克		---Of wire bonders
	---其他：							---Other:

税则号列	货　品　名　称	最惠(%)	普通	增值税率	出口退税	计量单位	监管条件	Article Description
8486.9091	----带背板的溅射靶材组件	0	17	17	17	千克		With the backplane of the sputtering target assembly
8486.9099	----其他品目 8486 项下商品用零件和附件	0	17	17	17	千克		----Parts and accessories of heading No. 8486
84.87	**本章其他税目未列名的机器零件,不具有电气接插件、绝缘体,线圈、触点或其他电气器材特征的:**							**Machinery parts, not containing electrical connectors insulators, coils, contacts or other eledrical features, not specified or included cleswhere in this chopter:**
8487.1000	-船用推进器及桨叶	6	14	17	17	千克		-Ships'or boats'propellers and blades therefor
8487.9000	-其他	8	30	17	15	千克	-other	

第八十五章
电机、电气设备及其零件；录音机及放声机、电视图像、声音的录制和重放设备及其零件、附件

注释：

一、本章不包括：

（一）电暖的毯子、褥子、足套及类似品，电暖的衣服、靴、鞋、耳套或其他供人穿戴的电暖物品；

（二）税目70.11的玻璃制品；

（三）税目84.86的机器及装置；

（四）用于医疗、外科、牙科或兽医的真空设备（税目90.18）

（五）第九十四章的电热家具。

二、税目85.01至85.04不适用于税目85.11、85.12、85.40、85.41或85.42的货品，但金属槽汞弧整流器仍归入税目85.04。

三、税目85.09仅包括通常供家用的下列电动器具：

（一）任何重量的地板打蜡机、食品研磨机及食品搅拌器、水果或蔬菜的榨汁机；

（二）重量不超过20千克的其他机器。

但该税目不适用于风机、风扇或装有风扇的通风罩及循环气罩（不论是否装有过滤器）（税目84.14）、离心干衣机（税目84.21）、洗碟机（税目84.22）、家用洗衣机（税目84.50）、滚筒式或其他形式的熨烫机器（税目84.20或84.51）、缝纫机（税目84.52）、电剪子（税目84.67）或电热器具（税目85.16）。

四、税目85.23所称：

（一）"固态、非易决性存储器件"（例如，"闪存卡"或"电子闪存卡"，是指带有接口的存储器件，共在同一壳体内包含一块或多块闪存（FLASH E^2 PROM），以集成电路的形式装配在一块印刷电路板上。它们可以包括一个集成电路形式的控制器及分立无源元件，例如，电容器及电阻器；

（二）所称"智能卡"是指装有一块或多块集成电路微处理器、随机存取存储器（RAM）或只读存储器（ROM）芯片的卡。这些卡可带有触点、磁条或嵌入式天线，但不包含任何其他有源或无源电路元件。

五、税目85.34所称"印刷电路"，是指采用各种印制方法（例如，压印、覆镀、腐蚀）或采用"膜电路"工艺，将导线、接点或其他印制元件（例如，电感器、电阻器、电容器）按预定的图形单独或互相连接地印制在绝缘基片上的电路，但能够产生、整流、调制或放大电信号的元件（例如，半导体元件）除外。

所称"印刷电路"，不包括装有非印制元件的电路，也不包括单个的分立式电阻器、电容器及电感器，但印刷电路可配有非经印刷的连接元件。

Chapter 85
Electrical machinery and equipment and parts thereof; sound recorders and reproducers, television image and sound recorders and reproducers, and parts and accessories of such articles

Notes:

1. This Chapter does not cover:

(a) Electrically warmed blankets, bed pads, foot-muffs or the like; electrically warmed clothing, footwear or ear pads or other electrically warmed articles worn on or about the person;

(b) Articles of glass of heading No. 70.11.

(c) Machines and apparaatus of heading 84.86;

(d) Vacuum apparatus of a kind used in medical, surgical, dencal or veterinary purposes (Heading No. 90.18);

(e) Electrically heated furniture of Chapter 94.

2. HeadingsNo. 85.01 to 85.04 do not apply to goods described in headingNo. 85.11, 85.12, 85.40, 85.41 or 85.42. However, metal tank mercury arc rectifiers remain classified in headingNo. 85.04.

3. HeadingNo. 85.09 covers only the following electro-mechanical machines of the kind commonly used for domestic purposes:

(a) Floor polishers, food grinders and mixers, and fruit or vegetable juice extractors, of any weight;

(b) Other machines provided the weight of such machines does not exceed 20 kg.

The heading does not, however, apply to fans or ventilating or recycling hoods incorporating a fan, whether or not fitted with filters (headingNo. 84.14), centrifugal clothes-dryers (headingNo. 84.21), dish washing machines (headingNo. 84.22), household washing machines (headingNo. 84.50), roller or other ironing machines (headingNo. 84.20 or 84.51), sewing machines (headingNo. 84.52), electric scissors (headingNo. 84.67) or to electro-thermic appliances (headingNo. 85.16).

4. For the purposes of heading 85.23:

(a) "Solid – state non-volatile storage devices" (for example, "flash memory cards" or "flash electronic storage cards") are storage devices with a connecting socket, comprising in the same housing one or more flash memories (for example, "FLASH E^2PROM") in the form of integrated circuits mounted on a printed circuit board. They may include a controller in the form of an integrated circuit and discrete passive components, such as capacitors and resistors;

(b) The term "smart cards" means cards which have embedded in them one or more electronic integrated circuits (a microprocessor, random access memory (RAM) or readonly memory (ROM)) in the form of chips. These cards may contain contacts, a magnetic stripe or an embedded antenna but do not contain any other active or passive circuit elements.

5. For the purposes of headingNo. 85.34 "printed circuits" are circuits obtained by forming on an insulating base, by any printing process (for example, embossing, plating-up, etching) or by the "film circuit" technique, conductor elements, contacts or other printed components (for example, inductances, resistors, capacitors) alone or interconnected according to a pre-established pattern, other than elements which can produce, rectify, modulate or amplify an electrical signal (for example, semiconductor elements).

The expression "printed circuits" does not cover circuits combined with elements other than those obtained during the printing process, nor does it cover individual, discrete resistors, capacitors or inductances.

用同样工艺制得的无源元件及有源元件组成的薄膜电路或厚膜电路应归入税目85.42。

Thinor thick-film circuits comprising passive and active elements obtained during the same technological process are to be classified in heading No. 85. 42.

六、税目85.36所称"光导纤维、光导纤维束或光缆用连接器",是指在有线数字通讯设备中,简单机械地把光纤端部相连成一线的连接器。它们不具备请如对信号进行放大、再生或修正等其他功能。

6. For the purpose of heading 85. 36. "connectors for opticalfl bres, optical fibre bundles or cables" means connectors that simply mechanically align optical fibres end to end in a ligital line system. They perform on other function, such as the am plification, regeneration or modification of a signal.

七、税目85.37不包括电视接收机或其他电气设备用的无绳红外遥控器(税目85.43)

7. Heading 85. 37 does not include cordless infrared devices for the remote control of television receivers or other elcctrical quipment (heading 85. 43).

八、税目85.41及85.42所称:

(一)"二极管、晶体管及类似的半导体器件",是指那些依靠外加电场引起电阻率的变化而进行工作的半导体器件。

(二)"集成电路",是指:

1. 单片集成电路,即电路元件(二极管、晶体管、电阻器、电容器、电感器等)主要整体制作在一片半导体材料或化合物半导体材料(例如掺杂硅砷化镓、硅锗或磷化铟)基片的表面,并不可分割地连接在一起的电路。

2. 混合集成电路,即通过薄膜或厚膜工艺制得的无源元件(电阻器、电容器、电感器等)和通过半导体工艺制得的有源元件(二极管、晶体管、单片集成电路等)用互连或连接线不可分割地组合在同一绝缘基片(玻璃、陶瓷等)上的电路。这种电路也可包括分立元件。

3. 多芯片集成电路是由两个或多个单片集成电路不可分割地组合在一片或多片的绝缘基片上构成的电路,不论是否带有引线框架,但不带有其他有源或无源的电路元件。

本注释所述物品在归类时,即使本目录其他税目涉及到上述物品,尤其是物品的功能,仍应优先考虑归入税目85.41及85.42。

8. For the purposes of headings No. 85. 41 and 85. 42:

(a) "Diodes, transistors and similar semiconductor devices" are semiconductor devices the operation of which depends on variations in resistivity on the application of an electric field;

(b) "Electronic integrated circuits" are:

(1) Monolithic integrated circuits in which the circuit elements (diodes, transistors resistors capacitors, interconnections, etc) are created in the mass (essentially) and on the surface of a semiconductor or compound semiconductor materical (for example, doped silicon, gallium arsenide silicon, gemanium indium phospide) and are inseparably associated;

(2) Hybrid integrated circuits in which passive elements (resistors, capacitors, inductances, etc), obtained by thin-or thick-film technology, and active elements (diodes, transistors, monolithic integrated circuits, etc.), obtained by semiconductor technology, are combined to all intents and purposes indivisibly, by interconne cltions or interconnecting cables on a single insulating substrate (glass, ceramic, etc.). These circuits may also include discrete components;

(3) Multichip integrated circuits consisting of two or more interconnected monolithic integrated circuits combined to all intents and purposes indivisibly, whether or not on one or more insulating substrates, with or without leadframes, but with no other active or passive circuit elements.

For the classification of the articles defined in this Note, headings-No. 85. 41 and 85. 42 shall take precedence over any other heading in the Nomenclature which might cover them by reference to, in particular, their function.

九、税目85.48所称"废原电池、废原电池组及废蓄电池",是指因破损、拆解、耗尽或其他原因而不能再使用,也不能再充电的电池。

9. For the purposes of headingNo. 85. 48, spent primary cells, "spent primary batteries and spent electric accumulators" are those which are neither usable as such because of breakage, cutting-up, wear or other reasons, nor capable of being recharged.

子目注释:

一、子目号8527.12仅包括有内置放大器但无内置扬声器的盒式磁带放声机,不需外接电源即能工作,且外型尺寸不超过170毫米×100毫米×45毫米。

Subheading Notes:

1. Subheadings 8527. 12 cover only cassetteplayers with built-in amplifier, without built-in loudspeaker, capable of operating without an external source of electric power and the dimensions of which do not exceed 170mm×100mm×45mm.

税则号列	货品名称	最惠(%)	普通	增值税率	出口退税	计量单位	监管条件	Article Description
85.01	**电动机及发电机(不包括发电机组):**							**Electric motors and generators (excluding generating sets):**
	-输出功率不超过37.5瓦的电动机:							-Motors of an output not exceeding 37.5W:
8501.1010	---玩具用	24.5	80	17	17	台		---For use in toys
	---其他:							---Other:
8501.1091	----微电机,机座尺寸在20毫米及以上,但不超过39毫米		70	17	17	台		----Micromotors with a housing size of 20mm or more but not exceeding 39mm

税则号列	货品名称	最惠(%)	普通	增值税率	出口退税	计量单位	监管条件	Article Description
8501.1091暂 01	激光视盘机机芯精密微型电机(1瓦≤功率<18瓦,20mm≤直径≤30mm)	5	70	17	17	台		Precision micromotors for the movement of laser disc players(1W≤power≤18W,20mm≤diameter≤30mm)
8501.1091暂 02	摄像机、摄录一体机用精密微型电机(0.5瓦≤功率≤10瓦),20mm≤直径≤39mm)	5	70	17	17	台		Micro motor with a video camera, camcorder (≤0.5 watt power ≤ 10 watts), 20mm ≤ diameter ≤ 39mm)
8501.1091 90	其他机座最大尺寸在20mm至39mm微电机(输出功率不超过37.5瓦)	9	70	17	17	台		Other micromotors with a housing size of 20mm or more but not exceeding 39mm (output≤37.5W)
8501.1099	----其他		35	17	17	台		----Other
8501.1099暂 01	功率≤0.5W非用于激光视盘机机芯的微型电机(圆柱型直径≤6mm,高≤25mm;扁圆型直径≤15mm,厚≤5mm)	5	35	17	17	台		Micromotors,power≤0.5W, not for movements of laser disc players(cylindricd diameter≤6mm, high ≤25mm; oblate diameter≤15mm, thick≤5mm)
8501.1099暂 02	激光视盘机机芯用精密微型电机(0.5瓦≤功率≤2瓦),5mm≤直径≤20mm	5	70	17	17	台		Precision micro motor with laser videodisc (≤ 0.5 watt power ≤ 2 watts), 5mm ≤ diameter ≤ 20mm
8501.1099暂 03	摄像机、摄录一体机、激光视盘机机芯用精密微型电机(0.5瓦≤功率≤2瓦,5mm≤直径<20mm或39mm<直径≤40mm)	5	35	17	17	台		Precision micromotors for video camera,camcorder, movement of laser discplayers(0.5W≤power≤2W, 5mm≤Diameter<20mm Or < 39 mm diameter≤ 40 mm)
8501.1099 90	其他微电机(输出功率不超过37.5瓦)	9	35	17	17	台		Other micromotors(output power≤37.5W)
8501.2000	-交直流两用电动机,输出功率超过37.5瓦	12	35	17	17	台		-Universal AC/DC motors of an output exceeding 37.5 W
	-其他直流电动机;直流发电机:							-Other DC motors; DC generators:
8501.3100	--输出功率不超过750瓦	12	35	17	17	台		--Of an output not exceeding 750 W
8501.3200	--输出功率超过750瓦,但不超过75千瓦	10	35	17	17	台		--Of an output exceeding 750 W but not exceeding 75 KW
8501.3300	--输出功率超过75千瓦,但不超过375千瓦	5	35	17	17	台		--Of an output exceeding 75 KW but not exceeding 375 KW
8501.3400	--输出功率超过375千瓦	12	35	17	17	台		--Of an output exceeding 375 KW
8501.4000	-其他单相交流电动机	12	35	17	17	台		-Other AC motors, single-phase
	-其他多相交流电动机:							-Other AC motors, multi-phase:
8501.5100	--输出功率不超过750瓦	5	35	17	17	台		--Of an output not exceeding 750 W
8501.5100 10	发电机(功率≥40瓦特,频率600至2000赫兹,谐波畸变低于10%等)	5	35	17	17	台	3	Generators (power ≥ 40W, frequency = 600 ~ 2000Hz, harmonic distortion<10%)
8501.5100 90	其他输出功率≤750W多相交流电动机	5	35	17	17	台		Other AC motors, multi-phase, output power ≤ 750W
8501.5200	--输出功率超过750瓦,但不超过75千瓦	10	35	17	17	台		--Of an output exceeding 750 W but not exceeding 75 KW
8501.5300	--输出功率超过75千瓦		35	17	17	台		--Of an output exceeding 75 KW
8501.5300暂 01	高速电力机车交流异步牵引电动机[用于(200KM/h)电力机车]	3	35	17	17	台		AC asyncronous traction motor for high speed electric locomotive (for electric locomo tives with the speed of 200KM/h)
8501.5300 90	其他功率>75KW多相交流电动机	12	35	17	17	台		Other AC electric motors, multi-phase, output power>75KW
	-交流发电机:							-AC generators (alternators):
8501.6100	--输出功率不超过75千伏安	5	30	17	17	台/千瓦		--Of an output not exceeding 75 KVA
8501.6200	--输出功率超过75千伏安,但不超过375千伏安	12	30	17	17	台/千瓦		--Of an output exceeding 75 KVA but not exceeding 375 KVA
8501.6300	--输出功率超过375千伏安,但不超过750千伏安	12	30	17	17	台/千瓦		--Of an output exceeding 375 KVA but not exceeding 750 KVA
	--输出功率超过750千伏安:							--Of an output exceeding 750 KVA:
8501.6410	---输出功率超过750千伏安,但不超过350兆伏安	10	30	17	17	台/千瓦	O	---Of an output exceeding 750 KVA but not exceeding 350 MVA
8501.6420	---输出功率超过350兆伏安,但不超过665兆伏安	5.8	14	17	17	台/千瓦	O	---Of an output exceeding 350 MVA but not exceeding 665 MVA
8501.6430	---输出功率超过665兆伏安	6	11	17	17	台/千瓦	O	---Of an output exceeding 665 MVA

税则号列	货品名称	最惠(%)	普通	增值税率	出口退税	计量单位	监管条件	Article Description
85.02	**发电机组及旋转式变流机：**							**Electric generating sets and rotary converters:**
	-装有压燃式活塞内燃发动机（柴油或半柴油发动机）的发电机组：							-Generating sets with compression-ignition internal combustion piston engines (diesel or semi-diesel engines):
8502.1100	--输出功率不超过75千伏安	10	45	17	17	台/千瓦		--Of an output not exceeding 75 KVA
8502.1200	--输出功率超过75千伏安，但不超过375千伏安	10	45	17	17	台/千瓦	O	--Of an output exceeding 75 KVA but not exceeding 375 KVA
	--输出功率超过375千伏安：							--Of an output exceeding 375 KVA:
8502.1310	---输出功率超过375千伏安，但不超过2兆伏安	10	45	17	17	台/千瓦	O	---Of an output exceeding 375 KVA but not exceeding 2 MVA
8502.1320	---输出功率超过2兆伏安	10	30	17	17	台/千瓦	O	---Of an output exceeding 2 MVA
8502.2000	-装有点燃式活塞内燃发动机的发电机组	10	45	17	17	台/千瓦		-Generating sets with spark-ignition internal combustion piston engines
	-其他发电机组：							-Other generating sets:
8502.3100	--风力驱动的	8	30	17	17	台/千瓦		--Wind-powered
8502.3900	--其他	10	30	17	17	台/千瓦		--Other
8502.4000	-旋转式变流机	10	30	17	17	台		-Electric rotary converters
85.03	**专用于或主要用于税目85.01或85.02所列机器的零件：**							**Parts suitable for use solely or principally with the machines of headingNo. 85.01 or 85.02:**
8503.0010	---子目8501.1010及8501.1091所列电动机用	12	70	17	17	千克		---Of the motors of subheading No. 8501.1010 and 8501.1091
8503.0020	---子目8501.6420及8501.6430所列发电机用	3	11	17	17	千克		---Of the generators of subheading No. 8501.6420 and 8501.6430
8503.0030暂	---子目8502.3100所列发电机组用	1	30	17	17	千克		---Of the generating sets of subheading No. 8502.3100
8503.0090	---其他	8	30	17	17	千克		---Other
8503.0090 10	电动机定子（用于真空中频率600－2000Hz、功率50－1000VA条件下）	8	30	17	17	千克	3	Motor stator(used under vacuum conditions, frequency range = 600Hz ~ 2000Hz, power = 50VA ~ 1000VA)
8503.0090 90	其他电动机、发电机（组）零件	8	30	17	17	千克		Other parts of electric motors, generators and generating sets
85.04	**变压器、静止式变流器（例如整流器）及电感器：**							**Electrical transformers, static converters (for example, rectifiers) and inductors:**
	-放电灯或放电管用镇流器：							-Ballasts for discharge lamps or tubes:
8504.1010	---电子镇流器	10	35	17	17	个		---Electronic ballats
8504.1090	---其他	10	35	17	17	个		---Other
	-液体介质变压器：							-Liquid dielectric transformers:
8504.2100	--额定容量不超过650千伏安	10.5	50	17	17	个		--Having a power handling capacity not exceeding 650 KVA
8504.2200	--额定容量超过650千伏安，但不超过10兆伏安	12.6	50	17	17	个		--Having a power handling capacity exceeding 650 KVA but not exceeding 10 MVA
	--额定容量超过10兆伏安：							--Having a power handling capacity exceeding 10 MVA:
	---额定容量超过10兆伏安，但小于400兆伏安：							---Having a power handling capacity exceeding 10MVA but less than 400MVA:
8504.2311	----额定容量超过10兆伏安，但小于220兆伏安	10	50	17	17	个		----Having a power handling capacity exceding 10MVA but less than 220MVA
8504.2312	----额定容量在220兆伏安及以上，但小于330兆伏安	10	50	17	17	个		----Having a power handling capacity exceding 220MVA but less than 330MVA
8504.2313	----额定容量在330兆伏安及以上，但小于400兆伏安	10	50	17	17	个		----Having a power handling capacity exceding 330MVA but less than 400MVA
	---额定容量在400兆伏安及以上：							---Having a power handling capacity of 400 MVA or more:
8504.2321	----额定容量在400兆伏安及以上，但小于500兆伏安	6	11	17	17	个		----Having a power handling capacity exceding 400MVA but less than 500MVA
8504.2329	----其他	6	11	17	17	个		----Other
	-其他变压器：							-Other transformers:
	--额定容量不超过1千伏安：							--Having a power handling capacity not exceeding 1 KVA:
8504.3110	---互感器	5	50	17	17	个		---Mutual inductor

税则号列	货品名称	最惠(%)	普通	增值税率	出口退税	计量单位	监管条件	Article Description
8504.3190	---其他	5	50	17	17	个		---Other
	--额定容量超过1千伏安,但不超过16千伏安:							--Having a power handling capacity exceeding 1KVA but not exceeding 16KVA:
8504.3210	---互感器	5	50	17	17	个		---Mutual inductor
8504.3290	---其他	5	50	17	17	个		---Other
	--额定容量超过16千伏安,但不超过500千伏安:							--Having a power handling capacity exceeding 16 KVA but not exceeding 500 KVA:
8504.3310	---互感器	5	50	17	17	个/千克		---Mutual inductor
8504.3390	---其他	5	50	17	17	个/千克		---Other
	--额定容量超过500千伏安:							--Having a power handling capacity exceeding 500 KVA:
8504.3410	---互感器	14	50	17	17	个/千克		---Mutual inductor
8504.3490	---其他	14	50	17	17	个/千克		---Other
	-静止式变流器:							-Static converters:
	---稳压电源:							---Voltage-stabilized suppliers:
8504.4013	----税目84.71所列机器用	0	40	17	17	个	A	----Of the machines of heading No. 84.71
8504.4014[暂]	----其他直流稳压电源,功率小于1千瓦,精度低于万分之一	3	80	17	17	个		----Other DC voltage-stabilized suppliers, of a power of less than 1 KW and an accuracy of not better than 0.0001
8504.4015	----其他交流稳压电源,功率小于10千瓦,精度低于千分之一	0	80	17	17	个		----Other AC voltage-stabilized suppliers, of a power of less than 10 KW and an accuracy of not better than 0.001
8504.4019	----其他	0	50	17	17	个		----Other
8504.4019 10	同位素电磁分离器离子源磁体电源(高功率直流型)	0	50	17	17	个	3	Ion source magnetic power suppliers of isotopioes electromagnetic separators (high-power, DC type)
8504.4019 20	直流高功率电源(能8小时连续产生100V,500A电流,稳定度优于0.1%)	0	50	17	17	个	3	High-power DC power suppliers (capable of generating 100V, 500A current uninterrupted in 8 hours, stability better than 0.1%)
8504.4019 30	高压直流电源(能8小时连续产生20KV,1A电流,稳定度优于0.2%)	0	50	17	17	个	3	High-voltage DC power suppliers (capable of generating 20KV, 1A current uninterrupted in 8 hours, stability better than 0.2%)
8504.4019 40	同位素电磁分离器离子源高压电源	0	50	17	17	个	3	Ion source high-voltage power suppliers of isotopies electromagnetic separators
8504.4019 90	其他稳压电源	0	50	17	17	个		Other voltage-stabilized suppliers
8504.4020	---不间断供电电源(UPS)	10	50	17	17	台		---Uninterrupted power suppliers
8504.4030	---逆变器		30	17	17	个		---Inverter
8504.4030[暂] 01	电动汽车用逆变器模块(功率密度≥8千瓦/升)	6	30	17		个		Inverter module for electric vehicle. Power density≥8KW/L
8504.4030 10	两用物项管制的逆变器(功率≥40瓦特,频率600至2000赫兹,谐波畸变低于10%等)	10	30	17	17	个	3	Inverter of sensitive items control(power≥40w, frequency = 600hz ~ 2000hz, harmonic distortion < 10%)
8504.4030 90	其他逆变器	10	30	17	17	个		Other inverter
	---其他:							---Other:
8504.4091[暂]	----具有变流功能的半导体模块		30	17	17	个		----Semiconductor modules with a converting function
8504.4091 01	具有变流功能的半导体模块(自动数据处理设备机器及组件、电讯设备用的)	0	30	17	17	个	s	Semi-conductor modules with a converting function (for automatic data processing machines and units thereof and telecommunication apparatus)
8504.4091[暂] 09	其他具有变流功能的半导体模块	3	30	17	17	个		Other semiconductor modules with a converting function
8504.4099	----其他		30	17	17	个		----Other
8504.4099 10	静止式变流器(自动数据处理设备机器及组件、电讯设备用)	0	30	17	17	个	s	Static converters(for automatic data processing machines and units thereof and telecommunication apparatus)

税则号列	货品名称	最惠(%)	普通	增值税率	出口退税	计量单位	监管条件	Article Description
8504.4099 20	ITA 产品用的印刷电路组件(包括外接组件,如符合 PCMCIA 标准的卡)	0	30	17	17	个	s	Printed circuit assemblies for products falling within the ITA (including external assemblies, for example, cards in accordance with PCMCIA)
8504.4099 30	频率变换器(专用85030090.10电动机定子的频率变换器)	10	30	17	17	个	3	Frequency converters, specially, for stators of heading 85030090.10
8504.4099 40	两用物项管制的频率变换器(功率≥40瓦特,频率600至2000赫兹,谐波畸变低于10%等)	10	30	17	17	个	3	Frequency converters (power≥40W, frequency = 600Hz～2000Hz, harmonic distortion＜10%)
8504.4099 50	电源(真空或受控环境感应炉用电源,额定输出功率≥5千瓦)	10	30	17	17	个	3	Power suppliers (for vacuum or atmosphere-controlled induction furnace, rated output power≥5KW)
8504.4099 60	模块式电脉冲发生器(在15ms内输出电流＞100A,密封在防尘罩内,温宽范围大)	10	30	17	17	个	3	Module－type electric pulse generator (output electric current＞100A in 15ms and greater in temperature span when sealed in dustproof cover)
8504.4099暂 70	高速电力机车的牵引变流器[用于(200千米/时)电力机车]	3	30	17	17	个		High speed electric locomotive traction converter (for (200 km / h) electric locomotive)
8504.4099暂 80	汽车冲压线用压力机变频调速装置	5	30	17	17	个		Press of variable frequency speed regulating device in automobile press line
8504.4099暂 91	纯电动汽车及混合动力汽车用电机控制器	6	30	17	17	个		Pure electric vehicle and hybrid electric vehicle with motor controller
8504.4099暂 92	纯电动汽车或插电式混合动力汽车用车载充电机	6	30	17	17	个		Pure electric vehicle or a plug in hybrid electric vehicle on－board charger
8504.4099 99	其他未列名静止式变流器	10	30	17	17	个		Other static converters, not elsewhere specified or included
8504.5000	-其他电感器	0	35	17	17	个		-Other inductors
	-零件:							-Parts:
	---变压器用:							---Of transformers:
8504.9011	----子目号8504.2321,8504.2329所列变压器用	5	11	17	17	千克		----Of the transformers of subheading No. 8504.2321, 8504.2329
8504.9019	----其他	8	50	17	17	千克		----Other
8504.9020	---稳压电源及不间断供电电源用	8	50	17	17	千克		---Of voltage-stabilized suppliers and uninterrupted power suppliers
8504.9090	---其他	8	30	17	17	千克		---Other
85.05	**电磁铁;永磁铁及磁化后准备制永磁铁的物品;电磁铁或永磁铁卡盘、夹具及类似的工件夹具;电磁联轴节、离合器及制动器;电磁起重吸盘:**							**Electro-magnets; permanent magnets and articles intended to become permanent magnets after magnetization; electro-magnetic or permanent magnet chucks, clamps and similar holding devices; electro-magnetic couplings, clutches and brakes; electro-magnetic lifting heads:**
	-永磁铁及磁化后准备制永磁铁的物品:							-Permanent magnets and articles intended to become permanent magnets after magnetization:
	--金属的:							--Of metal:
8505.1110	---稀土的	7	20	17	17	千克		---Of rare-earth
8505.1190	---其他	7	20	17	17	千克		---Other
8505.1900	--其他	7	20	17	17	千克		--Other
8505.1900 10	磁极块(直径大于2m,用在同位素电磁分离器内)	7	20	17	17	千克	3	Magnet pole pieces (diameter＞2m, used for electromagnetic isotope separator)
8505.1900 90	其他非金属永磁铁及永磁体	7	20	17	17	千克		Non-metal permanent magnets
8505.2000	-电磁联轴节、离合器及制动器	8	20	17	17	千克		-Electro-magnetic couplings, clutches and brakes
	-其他,包括零件:							-Other, including parts:
8505.9010	---电磁起重吸盘	8	20	17	17	个/千克		---Electro-magnetic lifting heads
8505.9090	---其他	8	20	17	17	个/千克		---Other

税则号列	货品名称	最惠(%)	普通	增值税率	出口退税	计量单位	监管条件	Article Description
8505.9090 10	超导螺线电磁体(产生超过2个泰斯拉磁场,长径比≥2mm,内径≥300mm 等)	8	20	17	17	个/千克	3	Superconduction spiral electro magnets (capable of generating more than two Tesla magnetic fields, L/D ≥2, inside diameter≥300mm)
8505.9090 90	其他电磁夹具等及编号8505的零件	8	20	17	17	个/千克		Other electro magnetic clamping apparatus and parts of headingNo. 8505
85.06	原电池及原电池组:							**Primary cells and primary batteries:**
	-二氧化锰的:							-Manganese dioxide:
	---碱性锌锰的:							---Alkaline zinc-manganese dioxide:
8506.1011	----扣式	20	80	17	0,15	个	A	----Button shape
8506.1012	----圆柱形	20	80	17	0,15	个	A	----Cycinder shape
8506.1019	----其他	20	80	17	15	个	A	----Other
8506.1090	---其他	20	80	17	15	个	A	---Other
8506.3000	-氧化汞的	14	40	17		个	A	-Mercuric oxide
8506.4000	-氧化银的	14	40	17	15	个	A	-Silver oxide
8506.5000	-锂的	14	40	17	15	个	A	-Lithium
8506.6000	-锌空气的	14	40	17	15	个	A	-Air-zinc
8506.8000	-其他原电池及原电池组	14	40	17	15	个	A	-Other primary cells and primary batteries
	-零件:							-Parts:
8506.9010	---子目8506.1000所列电池用	14	80	17	15	千克	A	---Of the cells of subheading No. 8506.1000
8506.9090	---其他	10	40	17	15	千克	A	---Other
85.07	**蓄电池,包括隔板,不论是否矩形(包括正方形):**							**Electric accumulators, including separators therefor, whether or not rectangular (including square):**
8507.1000	-铅酸蓄电池,用于起动活塞式发动机	10	90	17		个	AB	-Lead-acid, of a kind used for starting piston engines
8507.2000	-其他铅酸蓄电池	10	90	17		个	A	-Other lead-acid accumulators
8507.3000	-镍镉蓄电池	10	40	17		个	A	-Nickel-cadmium
8507.4000	-镍铁蓄电池	12	40	17	15	个	A	-Nickel-iron
8507.5000	-镍氢蓄电池	12	40	17	15	个	A	-Nickel-metal hydride
8507.6000	-锂离子蓄电池		40	17	17	个		-Lithium ion
8507.6000暂 10	纯电动汽车或插电式混合动力汽车用锂离子蓄电池单体(容量≥10Ah,比能量≥110Wh/kg)	8	40	17	17	个	A	Pure electric vehicle or a plug in hybrid electric vehicle lithium ion batterymonomer (capacity is greater than or equal to 10Ah, ratio of energy is higher than or equal to 110Wh/kg)
8507.6000暂 20	纯电动汽车或插电式混合动力汽车用锂离子蓄电池系统(包含蓄电池模块、容器、盖、冷却系统、管理系统等,比能量≥80Wh/kg)	10	40	17	17	个	A	Pure electric vehicles and plug - in hybrid vehicle lithium ion battery (includedbattery module, container, cover, cooling system, management system, specific energy is greater than or equal to 80Wh/kg)
8507.6000 90	其他锂离子蓄电池	12	40	17	17	个	A	Other lithium ion
	-其他蓄电池:							-Other accumulators
8507.8030	---全钒液流电池	12	40	17	15	个/千克	A	---Vanadium redox flow battery
8507.8090	---其他	12	40	17	15	个/千克	AB	---Other
	-零件:							-Parts:
8507.9010	---铅酸蓄电池用		90	17		千克	A	---Of lead-acid accumulators
8507.9010暂 01	铅酸蓄电池电极	5	90	17		千克	A	Electrode of lead - acid battery
8507.9010 90	其他铅酸蓄电池零件	10	90	17		千克	A	Other lead - acid battery parts
8507.9090暂	---其他	5	40	17	15	千克	A	---Other
85.08	**真空吸尘器:**							**Vacuum cleaners:**
	-电动的:							-With self-contained electric-motor:
8508.1100	--功率不超过1500瓦,且带有容积不超过20升的集尘袋或其他集尘容积器	10	130	17	17	台/千克	A	--Of a power not exceeding 1500W and hawing a dust bag or other receptade capaeity not excecding 20L
8508.1900	--其他	0	30	17	17	台/千克	A	--Other
8508.6000	-其他真空吸尘器	0	30	17	17	台/千克	A	-Other vacuum cleaners
	-零件:							-Parts:
8508.7010	---子目8508.1100所列吸尘器用	12	100	17	17	千克		---Of the deamers of subheading No. 8508.1100
8508.7090	---其他	0	20	17	17	千克		---Other

税则号列	货品名称	最惠(%)	普通	增值税率	出口退税	计量单位	监管条件	Article Description
85.09	家用电动器具,税目85.08的真空吸尘器除外:							**Electro-mechanical domestic appliances, with self-contained electric motor, other than vacuum cleaners of heading No. 85.08:**
	-食品研磨机及搅拌器;水果或蔬菜的榨汁机:							-Food grinders and mixers; fruit or vegetable juice extractors:
8509.4010[暂]	---水果或蔬菜的榨汁机	6	100	17	17	台/千克	A	---Fruit or vegetable juice extractors
8509.4090[暂]	---其他	6	100	17	17	台/千克	A	---Other
	-其他器具:							-Other appliances:
8509.8010	---地板打蜡机	30	100	17	17	台/千克		---Floor polishers
8509.8020	---厨房废物处理器	20	100	17	17	台/千克		---Kitchen waste disposers
8509.8090[暂]	---其他	15	100	17	17	台/千克	A	---Other
8509.9000[暂]	-零件	6	100	17	17	千克		-Parts
85.10	电动剃须刀、电动毛发推剪及电动脱毛器:							**Shavers, hair clippers and hair-removing appliances, with self-contained electric motor:**
8510.1000[暂]	-剃须刀	15	100	17	17	个		-Shavers
8510.2000	-毛发推剪	30	100	17	17	个		-Hair clippers
8510.3000	-脱毛器	20	100	17	17	个		-Hair-removing appliances
8510.9000[暂]	-零件	12	100	17	17	千克		-Parts
85.11	点燃式或压燃式内燃发动机用的电点火及电启动装置(例如,点火磁电机、永磁直流发电机、点火线圈、火花塞、电热塞及起动电机);附属于上述内燃发动机的发电机(例如,直流发电机、交流发电机)及断流器:							**Electrical ignition or starting equipment of a kind used for spark-ignition or compression-ignition internal combustion engines (for example, ignition magnetos, magneto-dynamos, ignition coils, sparking plugs and glow plugs, starter motors); generators (for example, dynamos, alternators) and cut-outs of a kind used in conjunction with such engines:**
8511.1000	-火花塞	10	30	17	17	个		-Sparking plugs
	-点火磁电机;永磁直流发电机;磁飞轮:							-Ignition magnetos; magneto-dynamos; magnetic flywheels:
8511.2010	---机车、航空器及船舶用	5	11	17	17	个		---For locomotives, aircraft or ships
8511.2090	---其他	10	30	17	17	个		---Other
	--分电器;点火线圈:							--Distributors; ignition coils:
8511.3010	---机车、航空器及船舶用	5	11	17	17	个		---For locomotives, aircraft or ships
8511.3090	---其他	8.4	30	17	17	个		---Other
	-启动电机及两用启动发电机:							-Starter motors and dual purpose starter-generators:
8511.4010	---机车、航空器及船舶用	5	11	17	17	个		---For locomotives, aircraft or ships
	---其他:							---Other:
8511.4091	----输出功率在132.39千瓦(180马力)及以上的发动机用启动电机	8.4	30	17	17	个		----Starter motors for engines of an output of 132.39kW(180HP) or more
8511.4099	----其他	8.4	30	17	17	个		----Other
	-其他发电机:							-Other generators:
8511.5010	---机车、航空器及船舶用	5	11	17	17	个		---For locomotives, aircraft or ships
8511.5090	---其他	8.4	30	17	17	个		---Other
8511.8000	-其他装置	8.4	30	17	17	个		-Other equipment
	-零件:							-Parts:
8511.9010	---税号85.11所列供机车、航空器及船舶用的各种装置的零件	4.5	11	17	17	千克		---Of the equipment of headingNo. 85.11 used for locomotives, aircraft or ships
8511.9090	---其他	5	30	17	17	千克		---Other
85.12	自行车或机动车辆用的电气照明或信号装置(税目85.39的物品除外)、风挡刮水器、除霜器及去雾器:							**Electrical lighting or signalling equipment (excluding articles of headingNo. 85.39), windscreen wipers, defrosters and demisters, of a kind used for cycles or motor vehicles:**
8512.1000	-自行车用照明或视觉信号装置	10.5	45	17	17	个		-Lighting or visual signalling equipment of a kind used on bicycles
	-其他照明或视觉信号装置:							-Other lighting or visual signalling equipment:
8512.2010	---机动车辆用照明装置	10	45	17	17	个		---Lighting equipment of a kind used for motor vehicles
8512.2090	---其他	10	45	17	17	个		---Other
	-音响信号装置:							-Sound signalling equipment:

税则号列	货品名称	最惠(%)	普通	增值税率	出口退税	计量单位	监管条件	Article Description
	---机动车辆用:							---For motor vehicles:
8512.3011	----喇叭、蜂鸣器	10	45	17	17	个		----Loudspeaker, buzzers
8512.3012	----防盗报警器	10	40	17	17	个		----Burglay alarm
8512.3019	----其他	10	45	17	17	个		----Other
8512.3090	---其他	10	45	17	17	个		---Other
8512.4000	-风挡刮水器、除霜器及去雾器	10	45	17	17	个		-Windscreen wipers, defrosters and demisters
8512.9000	-零件	8	45	17	17	千克		-Parts
85.13	**自供能源(例如,使用干电池、蓄电池、永磁发电机)的手提式电灯,但税目85.12的照明装置除外:**							**Portable electric lamps designed to function by their own source of energy (for example, dry batteries, accumulators, magnetos), other than lighting equipment of headingNo. 85.12:**
	-灯:							-Lamps:
8513.1010	---手电筒	15	100	17	17	个		---Portable electric torches designed to function by dry batteries
8513.1090	---其他	17.5	70	17	17	个		---Other
	-零件:							-Parts:
8513.9010	---手电筒用	14	100	17	17	千克		---Of the torches of subheading No. 8513.1010
8513.9090	---其他	14	70	17	17	千克		---Other
85.14	**工业或实验室用电炉及电烘箱(包括通过感应或介质损耗工作的);工业或实验室用其他通过感应或介质损耗对材料进行热处理的设备:**							**Industrial or laboratory electric furnaces and ovens (including those functioning by induction or dielectric loss); other industrial or laboratory equipment for the heat treatment of materials by induction or dielectric loss:**
	-电阻加热的炉及烘箱:							-Resistance heated furnaces and ovens:
8514.1010	---可控气氛热处理炉	0	30	17	17	台		---Furnaces for heat treatment, atmosphere controllable
8514.1090	---其他	0	30	17	17	台		---Other
8514.2000	-通过感应或介质损耗工作的炉及烘箱	0	30	17	17	台		-Furnaces and ovens functioning by induction or dielectric loss
8514.2000 10	真空感应炉或受控环境感应炉(工作温度>850℃,感应线圈直径≤600mm,功率≥5千瓦)	0	30	17	17	台	3	Vacuum induction furnaces or controlled atmosphere induction furnaces (rated output power≥5KW, diameter of induction coil≤600mm, working temperature>850℃)
8514.2000 90	其他感应或介质损耗工作炉及烘箱(包括实验室用)	0	30	17	17	台		Other furnaces and ovens functioning by induction or dielectric loss (including laboratory)
8514.3000	-其他炉及烘箱	0	30	17	17	台		-Other furnaces and ovens
8514.3000 20	电弧重熔炉和铸造用炉(容量1千—2万立方厘米,使用自耗电极,工作温度1700℃以上)	0	30	17	17	台	3	Arc remelting furnaces and casting furnaces (capacity = 1000 ~ 20000cm^3, with consumable electrode, working temperature>1700℃)
8514.3000 30	电子束熔化炉(功率≥50千瓦,能在>1200℃的熔化温度工作)	0	30	17	17	台	3	Electron-beam melting furnaces (power≥50KW, capable of working at smelting temperature >1200℃)
8514.3000 40	等离子体雾化和熔化炉(功率≥50千瓦,能在>1200℃的熔化温度工作)	0	30	17	17	台	3	Plasma atomization and melting furnaces (power≥50KW, capable of working at smelting temperature >1200℃)
8514.3000 90	工业用其他电炉及电烘箱(包括实验室用)	0	30	17	17	台		Other industrial or laboratory electric furnaces and ovens
8514.4000	-其他通过感应或介质损耗对材料进行热处理的设备		30	17	17	台		-Other equipment for the heat treatment of materials by induction or dielectric loss
8514.4000暂 01	焊缝中频退火装置	7	30	17	17	台		Welding seam intermediate frequency annealing device
8514.4000 90	其他感应或介质损耗的加热设备(包括实验室用)	10	30	17	17	台		Other equipment for the heat treatment of materials by induction or dielectric loss
	-零件:							-Parts:
8514.9010	---炼钢电炉用	8	30	17	17	千克		---Of steel making electric furnaces
8514.9090	---其他	0	30	17	17	千克		---Other

税则号列	货品名称	最惠(%)	普通	增值税率	出口退税	计量单位	监管条件	Article Description
85.15	电气(包括电热气体)、激光、其他光、光子束、超声波、电子束、磁脉冲或等离子弧焊接机器及装置,不论是否兼有切割功能;用于热喷金属或金属陶瓷的电气机器及装置:							**Electric (including electrically heated gas), laser or other light or photon beam, ultrasonic, electron beam, magnetic pulse or plasma arc soldering, brazing or welding machines and apparatus, whether or not capable of cutting; electric machines and apparatus for hot spraying of metals or cermets:**
	-钎焊机器及装置:							-Brazing or soldering machines and apparatus:
8515.1100	--烙铁及焊枪	10	30	17	17	个		--Soldering irons and guns
8515.1900	--其他	10	30	17	17	台		--Other
	-电阻焊接机器及装置:							-Machines and apparatus for resistance welding of metals:
	--全自动或半自动的:							--Fully or partly automatic:
8515.2120	---机器人	10	30	17	17	台	AO	---Robot
8515.2120暂 01	汽车生产线电阻焊接机器人	5	30	17	17	台	AO	Resistance of automotive production line welding robot
8515.2120 90	其他电阻焊接机器人	10	30	17	17	台	AO	Other resistance welding robot
	---其他:							---Other:
	---其他:							---Other:
8515.2191	----直缝焊管机	10	30	17	17	台		Straight seam pipemill
8515.2199	---其他	10	30	17	17	台	AO	----Other:
8515.2900	--其他	10	30	17	17	台	A	--Other
	-电弧(包括等离子弧)焊接机器及装置:							-Machines and apparatus for arc (including plasma arc) welding of metals:
	--全自动或半自动的:							--Fully or partly automatic:
8515.3120	---机器人	10	30	17	17	台	AO	---Robot
	---其他:							---Other:
8515.3191	----螺旋焊管机	10	30	17	17	台		----Spiral weld pipe mill
8515.3199	----其他	10	30	17	17	台	AO	----Other
8515.3900	--其他	10	30	17	17	台	A	--Other
	-其他机器及装置:							-Other machines and apparatus:
8515.8010	---激光焊接机器人	8	30	17	17	台		---Laser welding robot
8515.8010暂 01	汽车生产线激光焊接机器人	5	30	17	17	台		Laser welding robot used for auto production line
8515.8010 90	其他激光焊接机器人	8	30	17	17	台		Other laser wdlding robot
8515.8090	----其他	8	30	17	17	台		---Other
8515.8090 10	电子束、激光自动焊接机(将端塞焊接于燃料细棒(或棒)的自动焊接机)	8	30	17	17	台	3	Automatic electron beam, laser wdlding machine (automatic welding machine for welding end plug onto fuelpins or rods)
8515.8090 90	其他焊接机器及装置	8	30	17	17	台		Other welding machines and devices
8515.9000暂	-零件	3	30	17	17	千克		-Parts
85.16	电热的快速热水器、储存式热水器、浸入式液体加热器;电气空间加热器及土壤加热器;电热的理发器具(例如,电吹风机、电卷发器、电热发钳)及干手器;电熨斗;其他家用电热器具;加热电阻器,但税目85.45的货品除外:							**Electric instantaneous or storage water heaters and immersion heaters; electric space heating apparatus and soil heating apparatus; electro-thermic hair-dressing apparatus (for example, hair dryers, hair curlers, curling tong heaters) and hand dryers; electric smoothing irons; other electro-thermic appliances of a kind used for domestic purposes; electric heating resistors, other than those of headingNo. 85.45:**
	-电热的快速热水器、储存式热水器、浸入式液体加热器:							-Electric instantaneous or storage water heaters and immersion heaters:
8516.1010	---储存式电热水器	10	100	17	17	个	A	---Electric storage water heaters
8516.1020	---即热式电热水器	10	100	17	17	个	A	---Electric instantaneous water heaters
8516.1090	---其他	10	100	17	17	个	A	---Other
	-电气空间加热器及土壤加热器:							-Electric space heating apparatus and electric soil heating apparatus:
8516.2100	--储存式散热器	35	100	17	17	个		--Storage heating radiators
	--其他:							--Other:
8516.2910	---土壤加热器	10	40	17	17	个		---Electric soil heating apparatus
8516.2920	---辐射式空间加热器	10	100	17	17	个		---Radiat space heating apparatus

税则号列	货品名称	最惠(%)	普通	增值税率	出口退税	计量单位	监管条件	Article Description
	---对流式空间加热器							---Convectiom space heating apparatus
8516.2931	----风扇式	10	100	17	17	个		---Fan type
8516.2932	----充液式	10	100	17	17	个		---Oil-filled type
8516.2939	----其他	10	100	17	17	个		---Other
8516.2990	---其他	10	100	17	17	个		---Other
	-电热的理发器具及干手器:							-Electro-thermic hair-dressing or hand-drying apparatus:
8516.3100	--吹风机	10	100	17	17	个	A	--Hair dryers
8516.3200	--其他理发器具	35	100	17	17	个	A	--Other hair-dressing apparatus
8516.3300	--干手器	35	100	17	17	个	A	--Hand-drying apparatus
8516.4000[暂]	-电熨斗	17	100	17	17	个	A	-Electric smoothing irons
8516.5000[暂]	-微波炉	8	130	17	17	个	A	-Microwave ovens
	-其他炉;电锅、电热板、加热环、烧烤炉及烘烤器:							-Other ovens; cookers, cooking plates, boiling rings, grillers and roasters:
8516.6010	---电磁炉	15	130	17	17	个	A	---Electromagnetic ovens
8516.6030[暂]	---电饭锅	8	130	17	17	个	A	---Electric rice cookers
8516.6040	---电炒锅	15	130	17	17	个	A	---Electric frying pans
8516.6050[暂]	---电烤箱	8	130	17	17	个	A	---Roaster oven
8516.6090[暂]	---其他	8	130	17	17	个	A	---Other
	-其他电热器具:							-Other electro-thermic appliances:
	--咖啡壶或茶壶:							--Coffee or tea makers:
8516.7110[暂]	---滴液式咖啡机	16	130	17	17	个	A	---Drip coffee maker
8516.7120[暂]	---蒸馏渗滤式咖啡机	16	130	17	17	个	A	---Steam espresso makers
8516.7130[暂]	---泵压式咖啡机	16	130	17	17	个	A	---Pump-espresso makers
8516.7190[暂]	---其他	16	130	17	17	个	A	---Other
	--烤面包器:							--Toasters:
8516.7210	---家用自动面包机	32	130	17	17	个	A	---Household automated bread makers
8516.7220	---片式烤面包机(多士炉)	32	130	17	17	个	A	---Slice pop-up toasters
8516.7290	---其他	32	130	17	17	个	A	---Other
	--其他:							--Other:
8516.7910	---电热饮水机	32	100	17	17	台	A	---Electro-thermic water dispensers
8516.7990[暂]	---其他	16	100	17	17	个	A	---Other
8516.8000	-加热电阻器	10	40	17	17	个		-Electric heating resistors
	-零件:							-Parts:
8516.9010	---土壤加热器及加热电阻器用	8	40	17	17	千克		---For electric soil heating apparatus or electric heating resistors
8516.9090[暂]	---其他	8	100	17	17	千克		---Other
85.17	**电话机,包括用于蜂窝网络或其他无线网络的电话机;其他发送或接收声音、图像或其他数据用的设备,包括有线或无线网络(例如,局域网或广域网)的通信设备,税目84.43、85.25、85.27或85.28的发送或接收设备除外:**							**Telephone sets, including telephones for cellular networks or for other wireless networks; other apparatus for the transmission or reception of voice, images or other data, including apparatus for communication in a wired or wireless network (such as a local or wide are network), other than transmission or reception apparatus of heading 84.43, 85.25, 85.27 or 85.28:**
	-电话机,包括蜂窝网络或其他无线网络用电话机:							-Telephone sets, including telephones for cellular networks or for other wireless networks:
8517.1100	--无绳电话机	0	30	17	17	台		--Line telephone sets with cordless handsets
8517.1100 10	无绳加密电话机	0	30	17	17	台	AM	Cordless encrypting telephones
8517.1100 90	其他无绳电话机	0	30	17	17	台	A	Other cordless telephones
	--用于蜂窝网络或其他无线网络的电话机:							--Telephones for cellular net works or for other wireless networks:
8517.1210	---手持(包括车载)式无线电话机	0	20	17	17	台		---Wirelrss telephone handsets (including vehicle installed)
8517.1210 11	GSM数字式手持无线电话整套散件	0	20	17	17	台	AO	Full set of parts of GSM digital wireless telephones handheld
8517.1210 19	其他GSM数字式手持无线电话机	0	20	17	17	台	AO	Other GSM digital wireless telephones handsets
8517.1210 21	CDMA数字式手持无线电话整套散件	0	20	17	17	台	AO	Full set of parts of CDMA digital wireless phones handheld

税则号列	货品名称	最惠(%)	普通	增值税率	出口退税	计量单位	监管条件	Article Description
8517.1210 29	其他CDMA数字式手持无线电话机	0	20	17	17	台	AO	Other CDMA wirelesst elephones handheld
8517.1210 90	其他手持式无线电话机(包括车载式无线电话机)	0	20	17	17	台	AO	Other wireless telephones handsets (including vehicle installed)
8517.1220	---对讲机	0	17	17	17	台		---Walkie-talkie
8517.1290	---其他	0	14	17	17	台	O	---Other
8517.1800	--其他	0	30	17	17	台		--Other
8517.1800 10	其他加密电话机	0	30	17	17	台	AM	Other encrypting telephones
8517.1800 90	其他电话机	0	30	17	17	台	A	Other telephones
	-其他发送或接收声音、图像或其他数据用的设备,包括有线或无线网络(例如,局域网或广域网)的通信设备:							-Other apparatus for tromsmission or reception of voice, images or other data including apparatus for communication in a wired or wireless network (such as a local or wide area network):
	--基站:							--Base stations:
8517.6110	---移动通信基站	0	14	17	17	台		---Mobile communication base station
8517.6110 10	GSM式移动通信基地站	0	14	17	17	台	O	GSM mobile communication base station
8517.6110 20	CDMA式移动通信基地站	0	14	17	17	台	O	CDMA mobile communication base station
8517.6110 30	TACS式移动通信基地站	0	14	17	17	台		TACS mobile communication base station
8517.6110 90	其他移动通信基地站	0	14	17	17	台	O	Other mobile communication base station
8517.6190	---其他	0	14	17	17	台	O	---Other
	--接收、转换并且发送或再生声音、图像或其他数据用的设备,包括交换及路由设备:							--Machines for the reception, conversion and transmission or regeneration of voice images or other data, induding switchig and routing apparatus:
	---数字式程控电话或电报交换机:							---Digital program - controlled telephonic or telephooic switching apparatus:
8517.6211	----局用电话交换机;长途电话交换机;电报交换机	0	17	17	17	台		----Public telephonic switching apparatus, toll telephonic switching apparatus telegrapbic switching apparatus
8517.6212	----移动通信交换机	0	40	17	17	台	O	----Mobile communication switching system
8517.6219	----其他电话交换机	0	40	17	17	台	A	----Other telephonic switching appatatus
	---光通讯设备:							---Optical communication equipments:
8517.6221	----光端机及脉冲编码调制设备(PCM)	0	17	17	17	台	O	----Optical line terminal equipments and pulse code modulation equipments
8517.6222	----波分复用光传输设备	0	30	17	17	台	O	----Optical transmission equipments for wave-division multlplexing
8517.6229	----其他	0	30	17	17	台		----Other
8517.6229 10	光通迅加密路由器	0	30	17	17	台	AMO	Optical communication encrypting routers
8517.6229 90	其他光通讯设备	0	30	17	17	台	OA	Other optical communication equipment
	---其他有线数字通信设备:							---Other telecommunication apparatus for digit line system:
8517.6231	----通信网络时钟同步设备	0	30	17	17	台		----Communication network synchronization equipments
8517.6232	----以太网络交换机	0	30	17	17	台		----Ethernet exchangers
8517.6232 10	非光通讯加密以太网络交换机	0	30	17	17	台	M	Non - optical communication encypting ethernet exchangers
8517.6232 90	其他非光通讯以太网络交换机	0	30	17	17	台		Other non - optical communication ethernet exchangers
8517.6233	----IP电话信号转换设备	0	30	17	17	台	A	----IP telephone signal converters
8517.6234	----调制解调器	0	30	17	17	台	A	----Modem
8517.6235	----集线器	0	40	17	17	台	A	----Hubs
8517.6236	----路由器	0	40	17	17	台		----Routers
8517.6236 10	非光通讯加密路由器	0	40	17	17	台	M	Non - optical communication encrypting routers
8517.6236 90	其他路由器	0	40	17	17	台		Other routers
8517.6237	----有线网络接口卡	0	30	17	17	台		----Wired network interface card
8517.6239	----其他	0	30	17	17	台	O	----Other
	---其他:							---Other:
8517.6292	----无线网络接口卡	0	14	17	17	台		----Wireless network interface cards
8517.6293	----无线接入固定台	0	14	17	17	台		----Fixed wireless access station
8517.6294	----无线耳机	0	14	17	17	个		----Wireless headset
8517.6299	----其他	0	14	17	17	台		----Other
	--其他:							--Other:

税则号列	货品名称	最惠(%)	普通	增值税率	出口退税	计量单位	监管条件	Article Description
8517.6910	---其他无线设备		14	17	17	台		---Other equipments in a wireless network
8517.6910 01	用于呼叫、提示和寻呼的便携式接收器	0	14	17	17	台	As	Portable receivers for calling ,promoting and paging
8517.6910 90	其他无线通信设备	9	14	17	17	台	AO	Other wireless communication equipments
8517.6990	---其他有线设备	0	30	17	17	台		---Other equipments in a wired network
	-零件:							-Parts:
8517.7010	---数字式程控电话或电报交换机用	0	14	17	17	千克		---Of digital program-controlled telephonic or telegraphic switching appootus
8517.7020	---光端机及脉冲编码调制设备(PCM)用	0	14	17	17	千克		---Of optical line terminal equipments and pulse code modulation equipments
8517.7030	---手持式无线电话机用(天线除外)	0	17	17	17	千克		---Of wireless tevephone handsets (other than aerials)
8517.7040	---对讲机用(天线除外)	8	20	17	17	千克		---of walkle-talkie(other than aerials)
8517.7060	---光通信设备的激光收发模块	0	30	17	17	千克		---Laser receiving and transmitting unit of optical communication equipments
8517.7070	---税号 8517 所列设备用天线及其零件		20	17	17	千克		---Antenna and parts thereof of heading No. 85.17
8517.7070 01	无线电话电报装置的天线	0	20	17	17	千克	s	Antenna for wireless telephones and telegrams
8517.7070 90	编号 8517 所列设备用其他天线及其零件	2	20	17	17	千克		Other antenna and parts thereof of heading No. 85.17
8517.7090	---其他	0	20	17	17	千克		---Other
85.18	**传声器(麦克风)及其座架;扬声器,不论是否装成音箱;耳机、耳塞机,不论是否装有传声器,由传声器及一个或多个扬声器组成的组合机,音频扩大器;电气扩音机组:**							**Microphones and stands therefor; loudspeakers, whether or not mounted in their enclosures; headphones earphones, whether or not combined with a microphone, and sets consisting of a microphone and one or more loudspeakers; audio-frequency electric amplifiers; electric sound amplifier sets:**
8518.1000	-传声器(麦克风)及其座架		40	17	17	个		-Microphones and stands therefor
8518.1000 01	电讯用频率在 300～3400Hz 麦克风(直径不超过 10mm,高不超过 3mm)	0	40	17	17	个	s	Microphones, telecommunication use, frequency between 300Hz～3400Hz(with a diameter≤10mm and a height≤3mm)
8518.1000暂 90	其他传声器(麦克风)及其座架	6	40	17	17	个		Other microphones and stands therefor
	-扬声器,不论是否装成音箱							-Loudspeakers, whether or not mounted in their enclosures:
8518.2100暂	--单喇叭音箱	6	40	17	17	个	A	--Single loudspeakers, mounted in their enclosures
8518.2200暂	--多喇叭音箱	6	40	17	17	个	A	--Multiple loudspeakers, mounted in the same enclosure
8518.2900	--其他	0	40	17	17	个		--Other
8518.3000	-耳机、耳塞机,不论是否装有传声器,以及由传声器及一个或多个扬声器组成的组合机	0	40	17	17	个		-Headphones and earphones, whether or not combined with a microphone, and sets consisting of a microphone and one or more loudspeakers:
8518.4000	-音频扩大器		40	17	17	台		-Audio-frequency electric amplifiers
8518.4000 01	电器扩音器(列入 ITA 的有线电话重复器用的)	0	40	17	17	台	s	Amplifiers for electric equipment
8518.4000 90	其他音频扩大器	12	40	17	17	台	A	Other audio-frequency electric amplifiers
8518.5000	-电气扩音机组	10	40	17	17	套		-Electric sound amplifier sets
8518.9000	-零件		40	17	17	千克		-Parts
8518.9000 01	编号 8518400001 所列货品的零件(列入 ITA 的有线电话重复器用的)	0	40	17	17	千克	s	Parts for goods of heading No. 8518400001 (for telephone repeaters falling within ITA)
8518.9000 90	编号 8518 所列货品的其他零件	10.5	40	17	17	千克		Other parts of goods of heading No. 8518
85.19	**声音录制或重放设备:**							**Sound recording or reproducing apparatus**
8519.2000	-用硬币、钞票、银行卡、代币或其他支付方式使其工作的设备	20	80	17	17	台		-Apparatus oporated by coins barknotes, bank cards tokens or by other means of payment
8519.2000 10	以特定支付方式使其工作的激光唱机(用硬币、钞票、银行卡、代币或其他支付方式使其工作)	20	80	17	17	台	A	Laser phonographs that work by special means of payment (coins, notes, bank card, token coins or other means of payment are used to make it work)
8519.2000 90	其他以特定支付方式使其工作的声音录制或重放设备(用硬币、钞票、银行卡、代币或其他支付方式使其工作)	20	80	17	17	台		Other sound recording or reproducing apparatus that work by special means of payment (coins, notes, bank card, token coins or other means of payment are used to make it work)

税则号列	货品名称	最惠(%)	普通	增值税率	出口退税	计量单位	监管条件	Article Description
8519.3000	-转盘(唱机唱盘)	30	130	17	17	台		-Tuntables(record-decks)
8519.5000	-电话应答机	0	80	17	17	台		-Telephone answering machines
	-其他设备:							-Other apparatus:
	--使用磁性、光学或半导体媒体:							--Using magnetic, optical or semiconductor media:
	---使用磁性媒体的:							---Using magnetic media:
8519.8111	----未装有声音录制装置的盒式磁带型声音重放装置,编辑节目用放声机除外	17	130	17	17	台	A	----Cassette-type sound reproducing apparatus not incorporating a sound recording device, other than transchibing machines
8519.8112	----装有声音重放装置的盒式磁带录音机	30	130	17	17	台	A	----Cassette-type magnetic tape recorders in corporating sound reproducing apparatus
8519.8119	----其他	20	80	17	17	台	6A	----Other
	---使用光学媒体的:							---Using optical media:
8519.8121	----激光唱机,未装有声音录制装置	30	80	17	17	台	A	----Compact disc players, not in corporating a sound re condig devices
8519.8129	----其他	20	80	17	17	台		----Other
8519.8129 10	具有录音功能的激光唱机	20	80	17	17	台	6A	Recordable laser phonographs
8519.8129 90	其他使用光学媒体的声音录制或重放设备	20	80	17	17	台	A	Other sound recording or reproducing apparontus using optics media
	---使用半导体媒体:							---Using semiconductor media:
8519.8131暂	----装有声音重放装置的闪速存储器型声音录制设备	12	80	17	17	台	6A	----Flash memory type recorders incorporating sound reproducing apparatus
8519.8139暂	----其他	12	80	17	17	台	6A	----Other
	--其他:							--Other:
8519.8910	---不带录制装置的其他唱机,不论是否带有扬声器	30	130	17	17	台	A	---Other record-players, not incorporating a sound recording device with or without loudspeaker
8519.8990暂	---其他声音录制或重放设备	12	80	17	17	台	6A	---Other sound recording or reproducing apparatus
85.21	**视频信号录制或重放设备,不论是否装有高频调谐器:**							**Video recording or reproducing apparatus, whether or not incorporating a video tuner:**
	-磁带型:							-Magnetic tape-type:
	---录像机:							---Video tape recorders:
8521.1011暂	----广播级	①	T2	17	17	台	A	----Broadcast quality
8521.1019	----其他	T2	T2	17	17	台	A	----Other
8521.1020	---放像机	T2	T2	17	17	台	A	---Video tape reproducers
	-其他:							-Other:
	---激光视盘机:							---Laser video compact disk player:
8521.9011	----视频高密光盘(VCD)播放机	20	130	17	17	台		----Video Compact Disc player
8521.9011 10	具有录制功能的视频高密光盘(VCD)播放机(不论是否装有高频调谐放大器)	20	130	17	17	台	A	Recordable video compact Disc (VCD) player (whether or not incorporating with a high-frequency amplifier tuner)
8521.9011 90	其他视频高密光盘(VCD)播放机(不论是否装有高频调谐放大器)	20	130	17	17	台	A	Other video compact disc(VCD) player(whether or not incorporating with ahigh-frequency ammelifer tuner)
8521.9012	----数字化视频光盘(DVD)播放机	20	130	17	17	台		----Digital Video Disc player
8521.9012 10	具有录制功能的数字化视频光盘(DVD)播放机(不论是否装有高频调谐放大器)	20	130	17	17	台	A	Recordable Digital video Disc(DVD) player(whether or not in corporating with a high-frequency tuner)
8521.9012 90	其他数字化视频光盘(DVD)播放机(不论是否装有高频调谐放大器)	20	130	17	17	台	A	Other Digital video Disc(DVD) player(whether or not incorporating with a high - frequency tuned amplifier)
8521.9019	----其他	20	130	17	17	台		----Other
8521.9019 10	具有录制功能的其他激光视盘播放机(不论是否装有高频调谐放大器)	20	130	17	17	台	A	Laser video compact disk (VCD) player with CD-R drivers (whether or not incorporating with a high - frequency tuned amplifier)
8521.9019 90	其他激光视盘播放机(不论是否装有高频调谐放大器)	20	130	17	17	台	A	Other laser video compact disk (VCD) player (whether or not incorporating with a high - frequency tuned amplifier)
8521.9090	---其他		130	17	17	台		---Other
8521.9090暂 01	光盘型广播级录像机	②	130	17	17	台	6A	Disc - type broadcast - quailty video recorders

① 8521.1011 暂定税率为:完税价格不超过5000美元/台:15%;完税价格高于5000美元/台:3%,加3648元。

② 8521.9090 01 暂定税率为:完税价格不超过7000美元/台:15%;完税价格高于7000美元/台:5%,加4256元。

税则号列	货品名称	最惠(%)	普通	增值税率	出口退税	计量单位	监管条件	Article Description
8521.9090 10	用于光盘生产的金属母盘生产设备(不论是否装有高频调谐放大器)	20	130	17	17	台	6A	Metal master disc production equipments for CD production (whether or not incorporating with a high-frequency tuned amplifier)
8521.9090 90	其他视频信号录制或重放设备(不论是否装有高频调谐放大器)	20	130	17	17	台	6A	Other video recording or reproducing apparatus, whether or not incorporating with a high-frequency tuner amlifier
85.22	**专用于或主要用于税目85.19或85.21所列设备的零件、附件:**							**Parts and accessories suitable for use solely or principally with the apparatus of headings No. 85.19 or 85.21:**
8522.1000	-拾音头	35	130	17	17	个/千克		-Pick-up cartridges
	-其他:							-Other:
8522.9010	---转盘或唱机用	25	130	17	17	千克		---Of turntables (record decks) or record-players
	---盒式磁带录音机或放声机用:							---Of cassette magnetic tape recorders or reproducers:
8522.9021	----走带机构(机芯),不论是否装有磁头	25	100	17	17	千克		----Transport mechanisms, whether or not incorporating a magnetic head
8522.9022	----磁头	25	100	17	17	个/千克		----Magnetic heads
8522.9023	----磁头零件	20	100	17	17	千克		----Parts of magnetic heads
8522.9029	----其他	30	100	17	17	千克		----Other
	---视频信号录制或重放设备用:							---Of video recording or reproducing apparatus:
8522.9031	----激光视盘机的机芯		100	17	17	千克		----Movements for laser video compact disk player
8522.9031[暂] 02	车载导航仪视频播放机机芯	17	100	17	17	千克		Movement of video player, used for car navigator
8522.9031 90	其他激光视盘机的机芯	30	100	17	17	千克		Other movements for laser video compact disk player
8522.9039	----其他		100	17	17	千克		----Other
8522.9039[暂] 02	激光视盘机激光收发装置用零件	8	100	17	17	千克		Parts of laser receiver-transmitter specified for laser video disk set
8522.9039[暂] 09	其他视频信号录制或重放设备的零件	15	100	17	17	千克		Parts of other video recording or reproducing apparatus
	---其他:							---Other:
8522.9091[暂]	----车载音频转播器或发射器	10	80	17	17	台/千克		----Tone converters or transmission apparatus of a kind used for vehides
8522.9099[暂]	----其他	10	80	17	17	千克		----Other
85.23	**录制声音或其他信息用的圆盘、磁带、固态非易失性数据存储器件、"智能卡"及其他媒体,不论是否已录制,包括供复制圆盘用的母片及母带,但不包括第三十七章的产品:**							**Discs, tapes, solid-state nonvolatile storage devices, "smart cards" and other media for the recording of sound or of other phenomena whether or not recorded including matrices and masters for the production of discs, but excluding products of chopter 37:**
	-磁性媒体:							-Magnetic media:
	--磁条卡:							--Cads incorporating a magnetic stripe:
8523.2110	---未录制	17.5	70	17	17	个/千克		---Unrecorded
8523.2120	---已录制	15	130	13	13,17	个/千克		---Recorded
	--其他:							--Other:
	---磁盘:							---Magnetic discs:
8523.2911	----未录制	0	14	17	17	个/千克		----Unrecorded
8523.2919	----其他	0	14	13	13,17	个/千克		----Other
	---磁带:							---Magnetic tapes:
8523.2921	----未录制的宽度不超过4毫米磁带	0	130	17	17	盘/千克	A	----Of a width not exceedig 4mm unrecorded
8523.2922	----未录制的宽度超过4毫米,但不超过6.5毫米的磁带	0	130	17	17	盘/千克		----Of a width excecdig 4mm. but not exceedig 6.5mm unrecorded
8523.2923	----未录制的宽度超过6.5毫米的磁带	0	20	17	17	盘/千克		----Of a width exceeding 6.5mm unrecorded
8523.2928[暂]	----重放声音或图像信息的磁带	6	130	13	13,17	盘/千克	Z	----For reproducing sound or image phencomena
8523.2929	----已录制的其他磁带	0	14	17	13,17	盘/千克	Z	----Other recorded magnetic tapes
8523.2990	---其他	0	14	17	13,17	盘/千克	Z	---Other
	-光学媒体:							-Optical media:
8523.4100	--未录制	0	14	17	17	张/千克		--Unrecorded
	--其他:							--Other:
8523.4910[暂]	---仅用于重放声音信息的	6	130	13	13,17	张/千克	Z	---For reproducing sound

税则号列	货品名称	最惠(%)	普通	增值税率	出口退税	计量单位	监管条件	Article Description
8523.4920	---用于重放声音、图像以外信息的,税目84.71所列机器用	0	14	13	13,17	张/千克		---Forreproducing phenomena other than sound or image for the machines of heading 84.71
8523.4990	---其他	0	14	17	13,17	张/千克	Z	---Other
	-半导体媒体:							-Semiconductor media:
	--固态非易失性存储器件(闪速存储器):							--Solid-state non-volatile storage devices(flash memorizer):
8523.5110	---未录制	0	70	17	17	个/千克		---Unrecorded
8523.5120	---已录制	0	14	13	13,17	个/千克		---Recorded
	--"智能卡":							--"Smart cards":
8523.5210	---未录制	0	21	13	17	个/千克		---Unrecorded
8523.5290	---其他	0	21	13	13,17	个/千克		---Other
	--其他:							--Other:
8523.5910	---未录制	0	70	17	17	个/千克		---Unrecorded
8523.5920	---已录制	0	14	13	13,17	个/千克		---Recorded
	-其他:							-Other:
	---唱片:							---Gramophone recorols:
8523.8011	----已录制	15	130	13	13,17	张/千克	Z	----Recorded
8523.8019	----其他	0	70	17	13,17	张/千克		----Other
	---税号84.71所列机器用:							---For the machines of heading No. 84.71:
8523.8021	----未录制	0	14	17	17	张/千克		----Unrecorded
8523.8029	----其他	0	14	17	13,17	张/千克		----Other
	---其他:							---Other:
8523.8091	----未录制	0	14	13	17	张/千克		----Unrecorded
8523.8099	----其他	0	14	13	13,17	张/千克	Z	----Other
85.25	**无线电广播、电视发送设备,不论是否装有接收装置或声音的录制、重放装置;电视摄像机、数字照相机及视频摄录一体机:**							**Transmission apparatus for radio-broadcasting or television, whether or not incorporating reception apparatus or sound recording or reproducing apparatus; television cameras; digital cameras and video camera recorders;**
8525.5000	-发送设备	0	30	17	17	台	O	-Transmission apparatus
	-装有接收装置的发送设备:							-Transmission apparatus incorporating reception apparatus:
8525.6010	---卫星地面站设备	0	14	17	17	台	O	---Satellite earth station
8525.6090	---其他	0	30	17	17	台	O	---Other
	-电视摄像机、数字照相机及视频摄录一体机:							-Television cameras、digital cameras and video camera recorders:
	---电视摄像机:							---Telvision cameras:
8525.8011	----特种用途的	10	17	17	17	台		----For special purposes
8525.8011 10	抗辐射电视摄像机[能抗 5×10^4 戈瑞(硅)以上辐射而又不会降低使用质量]	10	17	17	17	台	3A	Radiation-resistant telvision cameras (capable of resisting fradiance $>5\times10^4$GY(Si) and not lowering operation quality)
8525.8011 90	其他特种用途电视摄像机	10	17	17	17	台	A	Other telveision cameras for special use
8525.8012	----非特种用途的广播级	T2	T2	17	17	台	A	----Broodcast quality not for special purposes
8525.8013	----非特种用途的其他类型		T2	17	17	台		----Other not for special purposes
8525.8013暂 01	手机用摄像组件(由镜头+CCD/CMOS+数字信号处理电路三部分构成)	4	T2	17	17	台		Camera components for cellphones(including lens + CCD/CMOS + digital signal processing electric circuit)
8525.8013暂 02	高清摄像头(必须满足以下三个条件:1.镜头元件必须使用5层玻璃镜头;2.使用USB2.0高速接口;3.硬件传感器像素达到130万及以上)	10	T2	17	17	台		High definition cameras (Must meet the following three conditions: 1. lens element must used Five floors Glass lenses; 2. used USB2.0 high speed interface; 3. hardware sensor pixel ≥130W)
8525.8013 90	其他非特种用途电视摄像机及其他摄像组件(其他摄像组件由非广播级镜头+CCD/CMOS+数字信号处理电路构成)	T2	T2	17	17	台		Other telecameras not for special use and other camera components (the latter is composed of non-broadcast-quality lens + CCD/CMOS + digital signal processing electric circuit)
	---数字照相机:							---Digital cameras:

税则号列	货品名称	最惠(%)	普通	增值税率	出口退税	计量单位	监管条件	Article Description
8525.8021	----特种用途的	0	17	17	17	台		----For special purposes
8525.8022	----非特种用途的,单镜头反光型	T2	T2	17	17	台		----Single lens reflex not for special purposes
8525.8025	----非特种用途其他可换镜头数字照相机	T2	T2	17	17	台		Not special purpose other interchangeable lens digital camera
8525.8029	----非特种用途的其他类型	T2	T2	17	17	台		----Other not for special purposes
	---视频摄录一体机:							---Video camera recorders:
8525.8031	----特种用途	0	17	17	17	台	A	----For special puposes
8525.8032	----非特种用途的广播级	T2	T2	17	17	台	A	----Broadcast quality not for special purposes
8525.8033	----非特种用途的家用型	0	130	17	17	台	A	----Householdtype not for special purposes
8525.8039	----非特种用途的其他类型	T2	T2	17	17	台	A	----Other not for special purposes
85.26	**雷达设备、无线电导航设备及无线电遥控设备:**							**Radar apparatus, radio navigational aid apparatus and radio remote control apparatus:**
	-雷达设备:							-Radar apparatus:
8526.1010	---导航用	2	8	17	17	台		---For navigational aid
8526.1010 10	用于导弹、火箭等的导航雷达设备(用于弹道导弹、运载火箭、探空火箭等的目标探测)	2	8	17	17	台	3	Navigational radar equipments for missiles or rockets (for target detection of ballistic missiles, carrier rockets, sounding rockets)
8526.1010 90	其他导航用雷达设备	2	8	17	17	台	O	Other radar apparatus for navigational aid
8526.1090	---其他		14	17	17	台		---Other
8526.1090暂 01	飞机机载雷达(包括气象雷达、地形雷达和空中交通管制应答系统)	1	14	17	17	台		Air borne radars (including meteorological radars, topographic radar and air traffic control answering system)
8526.1090暂 02	雷达生命探测仪	2	14	17	17	台	O	Radar life detector
8526.1090 11	用于导弹、火箭等的机载雷达设备(用于弹道导弹、运载火箭、探空火箭等的目标探测)	5	14	17	17	台	3	Air borne radars equipment for missiles or rockets (suitable for target detection of ballistic missiles, carrier rockets, sounding rockets)
8526.1090 91	用于导弹、火箭等的其他雷达设备(用于弹道导弹、运载火箭、探空火箭等的目标探测)	5	14	17	17	台	3	Other radars equipment for missiles or rockets (target detection of ballistic missiles, carrier rockets, sounding rockets)
8526.1090 99	其他雷达设备	5	14	17	17	台	O	Other radar equipments
	-其他:							-Other:
	--无线电导航设备:							--Radio navigational aid apparatus:
8526.9110	---机动车辆用	2	8	17	17	台		---For motor vehicles
8526.9190	---其他	2	8	17	17	台		---Other
8526.9190 10	制导装置(使300km射程导弹达到≤10km圆公算偏差)	2	8	17	17	台	3O	Guidance devices (making 300km-range misslies, circle probability or estimated chances deviation ≤10km)
8526.9190 90	其他无线电导航设备	2	8	17	17	台	O	Other radio navigational aid apparatus
8526.9200	--无线电遥控设备	5	14	17	17	台	O	--Radio remote control apparatus
85.27	**无线电广播接收设备,不论是否与声音的录制、重放装置或时钟组合在同一机壳内:**							**Reception apparatus for radio-broadcasting, whether or not combined, in the same housing, with sound recording or reproducing apparatus or a clock:**
	-不需外接电源的无线电收音机:							-Radio-broadcast receivers capable of operating without an external source of power:
8527.1200	--袖珍盒式磁带收放机	20	130	17	17	台		--Pocket-size radio cassette-players
8527.1300	--其他收录(放)音组合机	15	130	17	17	台		--Other apparatus combined with sound recording or reproducing apparatus
8527.1900	--其他	15	130	17	17	台		--Other
	-需外接电源的汽车用无线电收音机:							-Radio-broadcast receivers not capable of operating without an external source of power, of a kind used in motor vehicles:
8527.2100	--收录(放)音组合机	15	130	17	17	台		--Combined with sound recording or reproducing apparatus
8527.2900	--其他	15	130	17	17	台		--Other
	-其他:							-Other:

税则号列	货品名称	最惠(%)	普通	增值税率	出口退税	计量单位	监管条件	Article Description
8527.9100	--收录(放)音组合机	15	130	17	17	台	A	--Combined with sound recording or reproducing apparatus
8527.9200	--带时钟的收音机	15	130	17	17	台		--Not combined with sound recording or reproducing apparatus but combined with a clock
8527.9900	--其他	27	130	17	17	台	A	--Other
85.28	**监视器及投影机,未装电视接收装置;电视接收装置,不论是否装有无线电收音装置或声音、图像的录制或重放装置:**							**Monitors and projectors, not incorporatig television reception apparatus: reception apparatus for tele vision, whether or not incorporating radiobroad cast receivers or sound or video recordig or reproducing apparatus:**
	-阴极射线管监视器:							-Cathode-ray tube monitors:
8528.4100	--专用于或主要用于税目84.71商品的自动数据处理系统的	0	40	17	17	台	6A	--Of a kind solely or principally used in an automatic data processing system of heading No. 84.71
	--其他:							--Other:
8528.4910	---彩色的	30	130	17	17	台	6A	---Colour
8528.4990	---单色的	19	100	17	17	台	6A	---monochrone
	-其他监视器:							-Other monitors:
	--专用于或主要用于税目84.71的自动数据处理系统的:							--Of a kind solely or principally used in an auto matic data processing system of heading No. 84.71:
8528.5110	---液晶监视器的	0	40	17	17	台	A	---With liquid crystal display
8528.5190	---其他	0	40	17	17	台	A	---Other
	--其他:							--Other:
8528.5910	---彩色的		130	17	17	台		---Colour
8528.5910暂 01	专用于车载导航仪的液晶监视器	15	130	17	17	台	6A	LCD monitors of special use vehicle navigator
8528.5910 90	其他彩色的监视器	30	130	17	17	台	6A	Other colors monitors
8528.5990	---单色的	19	100	17	17	台	6A	---monochrome
	-投影机:							-Projectors:
8528.6100	--专用于或主要用于税目84.71的自动数据处理系统的	0	14	17	17	台		--Of a kind solely or principally used in an auto matic data processing system of heading No. 84.71
8528.6100 10	专用或主要用于税目84.71商品的彩色投影机	0	14	17	17	台	A	Specially used or mainly used for color projector of heading No. 84.71
8528.6100 90	其他专用或主要用于税目84.71商品的投影机	0	14	17	17	台	A	Specially used or mainly used for projector of heading No. 84.71
	--其他:							--Other:
8528.6910	---彩色的	30	130	17	17	台	6A	---Colour
8528.6990	---单色的	15	100	17	17	台	A	---monochrome
	-电视接收装置,不论是否装有无线电收音装置或声音、图像的录制或重放装置:							-Reception apparatus for television, whether or not incorporating radio-broadcast receivers or sound or video recording or reproducing apparatus:
	--在设计上不带有视频显示器或屏幕的:							--Not designed to incorporate a video display or screen:
8528.7110	---彩色卫星电视接收机	30	130	17	17	台	AO	---Colour satellite television receivers
8528.7180	---其他彩色的	30	130	17	17	台	A	---Other colour
8528.7190	---单色的	15	100	17	17	台	A	---monochrome
	--其他,彩色的:							--Other, colour:
	---阴极射线显像管的:							---Of cathode-ray tube monitors:
8528.7211	----模拟电视接收机	30	130	17	17	台	6A	----Analogue
8528.7212	----数字电视接收机	30	130	17	17	台	6A	----Digital
8528.7219	----其他	30	130	17	17	台	6A	----Other
	---液晶显示器的:							---Of LCD
8528.7221	----模拟电视接收机	30	130	17	17	台	A	----Analogue
8528.7222	----数字电视接收机	30	130	17	17	台	A	----Digital
8528.7229	----其他	30	130	17	17	台	A	----Other
	---等离子显示器的:							---Of plasma:
8528.7231	----模拟电视接收机	30	130	17	17	台	A	----Analogue

税则号列	货品名称	最惠(%)	普通	增值税率	出口退税	计量单位	监管条件	Article Description
8528.7232	----数字电视接收机	30	130	17	17	台	A	----Digital
8528.7239	----其他	30	130	17	17	台	A	----Other
	---其他:							---Other:
8528.7291	----模拟电视接收机	30	130	17	17	台	A	----Analogue
8528.7292	----数字电视接收机	30	130	17	17	台	A	----Digital
8528.7299	----其他	30	130	17	17	台	A	----Other
8528.7300	--其他,单色的	15	100	17	17	台	6A	--Other, monchrome
85.29	**专用于或主要用于税目85.25至85.28所列装置或设备的零件:**							**Parts suitable for use solely or principally with the apparatus of headingsNo. 85.25 to 85.28:**
	-各种天线或天线反射器及其零件:							-Aerials and aerial reflectors of all kinds; parts suitable for use therewith:
8529.1010	---雷达设备及无线电导航设备用	1.5	8	17	17	千克		---For radar apparatus and radio navigational aid apparatus
8529.1020	---无线电收音机及其组合机、电视接收机用	0	90	17	17	千克		---For radio-broadcast receivers and their combinations, television receivers
8529.1090	---其他	2	20	17	17	千克/个		---Other
8529.1090 21	卫星电视接收用天线	2	20	17	17	千克/个	O	Satellite TV receiving antenna
8529.1090 29	其他无线广播电视用天线(品目8525至8528所列其他装置或设备的,包括天线反射器)	2	20	17	17	千克/个	O	Other radio broadcasting and television antenna (suitable for use solely or principally with the apparatus of heading No. 8525 to 8528, including antenna reflectors)
8529.1090 90	其他无线电设备天线及其零件(品目8525至8528所列其他装置或设备的,包括天线反射器)	2	20	17	17	千克/个		Other radio antennas and parts (suitable for use solely or principally with the apparatus of heading No. 8525 to 8528, including antenna reflectors)
	-其他:							-Other:
8529.9010	---电视发送、差转设备及卫星电视地面接收转播设备用	0	30	17	17	千克		---Of television transmission or translation apparatus, satellite television ground receiving and relaying apparatus
8529.9010 11	卫星电视接收用解码器	0	30	17	17	千克/个	O	Decoders for statellite TV recervers
8529.9010 12	卫星电视接收用收视卡	0	30	17	17	千克/个	O	CA card for receiving satellite television
8529.9010 13	卫星电视接收用器件板卡	0	30	17	17	千克/个	O	CRD cards for receiving statellite TV
8529.9010 14	卫星电视接收用专用零件	0	30	17	17	千克/个	O	Parts exclusive for receiving statellite TV signals
8529.9010 90	其他电视发送,差转等设备零件(包括其他卫星电视地面接收转播设备零件)	0	30	17	17	千克/个		Parts of other television tronsmission or translation apparatus (including parts of satellite television ground receiving and relaying apparatus)
	---电视摄像机、静像视频摄像机及其他视频摄录一体机、数字照相机用:							---Of television cameras、still image rideo cameras other video camera recorders and igital cameras:
8529.9041	----特种用途的	8	17	17	17	千克		----Of special purpose
8529.9042	----非特种用途的取像模块		100	17	17	千克		----Cameera modules without special pnrpose
8529.9042[暂] 10	摄录一体机、数码相机、用取像模块	3	100	17	17	千克		Video camera recorders, digital camera, with image capture module
8529.9042[暂] 20	手机、平板电脑用取像模块	4	100	17	17	千克		Mobile phone, tablet computer with image capture module
8529.9042 90	其他非特种用途的取像模块	12	100	17	17	千克		Other cameera modules not for special purpose
8529.9049[暂]	----其他	2	100	17	17	千克		----Other
8529.9050	---雷达设备及无线电导航设备用	1.5	8	17	17	千克		---Of radar apparatus and radio navigational aid apparatus
8529.9060[暂]	---无线电收音机及其组合机用	7	130	17	17	千克		---Of radio-broadcast receivers and their combinations
	---电视接收机用(高频调谐器除外):							---Of television receivers (Other than H. F tuners):
8529.9081[暂]	----彩色电视接收机用(等离子显像组件及其零件、有机发光显示屏除外)	6	80	17	17	千克		----Of colour television receivers (other than plasma display modules or parts thereof, organic light emitting diode display screen)
8529.9082[暂]	----等离子显像组件及其零件	5	80	17	17	千克		----Plasma display modules and parts thereof
8529.9083[暂]	----有机发光二极管显示屏	5	80	17	17	千克/个		----Organic light emitting diode display screen
8529.9089	----其他	0	50	17	17	千克		----Other

税则号列	货品名称	最惠(%)	普通	增值税率	出口退税	计量单位	监管条件	Article Description
8529.9090	---其他	0	57	17	17	千克/个		---Other
8529.9090 11	卫星电视接收用高频调谐器	0	57	17	17	千克/个	O	High – frequency tuners for satellite television
8529.9090 19	其他高频调谐器	0	57	17	17	千克/个		Other high – frepuency tuners
8529.9090 90	品目 8525 至 8528 所列设备其他零件	0	57	17	17	千克/个		Other parts of apparatus of headings No. 8525 ~ 8528
85.30	**铁道、电车道、道路或内河航道、停车场、港口或机场用的电气信号、安全或交通管理设备(税目 86.08 的货品除外):**							**Electrical signalling, safety or traffic control equipment for railways, tramways, roads, inland waterways, parking facilities, port installations or airfields (other than those of heading No. 86.08):**
8530.1000	-铁道或电车道用的设备	10	20	17	17	个	O	-Equipment for railways or tramways
8530.8000	-其他设备	8	20	17	17	个	O	-Other equipment
8530.9000	-零件	8	20	17	17	千克		-Parts
85.31	**电气音响或视觉信号装置(例如,电铃、电笛、显示板、防盗或防火报警器),但税目 85.12 或 85.30 的货品除外:**							**Electric sound or visual signalling apparatus (for example, bells, sirens, indicator panels, burglar or fire alarms), other than those of heading Nos. 85.12 or 85.30:**
8531.1000	-防盗或防火报警器及类似装置	10	40	17	17	个	A	-Burglar or fire alarms and similar apparatus
8531.2000	-装有液晶装置(LCD)或发光二极管(LED)的显示板	0	70	17	17	个		-Indicator panels incorporating liquid crystal devices (LCD) or light emitting diodes (LED)
	-其他装置:							-Other apparatus:
8531.8010	---蜂鸣器		70	17	17	个		---Buzzers
8531.8010暂 01	音量不超过 110db 的小型蜂鸣器	7.5	70	17	17	个		Small buzzers, volue <110dB
8531.8010 90	其他蜂鸣器	15	70	17	17	个		Other buzzers
8531.8090	---其他	10	70	17	17	个		---Other
	-零件:							-Parts:
8531.9010	---防盗或防火报警器及类似装置用	0	40	17	17	千克	A	---Of burglar or fire alarms and similar apparatus
8531.9090	---其他	0	70	17	17	千克		---Other
85.32	**固定、可变或可调(微调)电容器:**							**Electrical capacitors, fixed, variable or adjustable (preset):**
8532.1000	-固定电容器,用于 50/60 赫兹电路,其额定无功功率不低于 0.5 千瓦(电力电容器)	0	20	17	17	千克/千个		-Fixed capacitors designed for use in 50/60 Hz circuits and having a reactive power handling capacity of not less than 0.5 kVar (power capacitors)
	-其他固定电容器:							-Other fixed capacitors:
	--钽电容器:							--Tantalum:
8532.2110	---片式	0	35	17	17	千克/千个		---Laminate
8532.2190	---其他	0	35	17	17	千克/千个		---Other
	--铝电介电容器:							--Aluminium electrolytic:
8532.2210	---片式	0	35	17	17	千克/千个		---Laminate
8532.2290	---其他	0	35	17	17	千克/千个		---Other
8532.2300	--单层瓷介电容器	0	35	17	17	千克/千个		--Ceramic dielectric, single layer
	--多层瓷介电容器:							--Ceramic dielectric, multilayer:
8532.2410	---片式	0	35	17	17	千克/千个		---Laminate
8532.2490	---其他	0	35	17	17	千克/千个		---Other
	--纸介质或塑料介质电容器:							--Dielectric of paper or plastics:
8532.2510	---片式	0	35	17	17	千克/千个		---Laminate
8532.2590	---其他	0	35	17	17	千克/千个		---Other
8532.2900	--其他	0	35	17	17	千克/千个		--Other
8532.3000	-可变或可调(微调)电容器	0	35	17	17	千克/千个		-Variable or adjustable (pre-set) capacitors
	-零件:							-Parts:
8532.9010	---子目号 85321000 所列电容器用	0	20	17	17	千克		---Of the capacitors of subheadingNo. 8532.1000
8532.9090	---其他	0	35	17	17	千克		---Other
85.33	**电阻器(包括变阻器及电位器),但加热电阻器除外:**							**Electrical resistors (including rheostats and potentiometers), other than heating resistors:**
8533.1000	-固定碳质电阻器,合成或薄膜式	0	50	17	17	千克/千个		-Fixed carbon resistors, composition or film types
	-其他固定电阻器:							-Other fixed resistors:
	--额定功率不超过 20 瓦:							--For a power handling capacity not exceeding 20W:

税则号列	货品名称	最惠(%)	普通	增值税率	出口退税	计量单位	监管条件	Article Description
8533.2110	---片式	0	50	17	17	千克/千个		---Laminate
8533.2190	---其他	0	50	17	17	千克/千个		---Other
8533.2900	--其他	0	50	17	17	千克/千个		--Other
	-线绕可变电阻器,包括变阻器及电位器:							-Wirewound variable resistors, including rheostats and potentiometers:
8533.3100	--额定功率不超过20瓦	0	50	17	17	千克/千个		--For a power handling capacity not exceeding 20 W
8533.3900	--其他	0	50	17	17	千克/千个		--Other
8533.4000	-其他可变电阻器,包括变阻器及电位器	0	50	17	17	千克/千个		-Other variable resistors, including rheostats and potentiometers
8533.9000	-零件	0	50	17	17	千克		-Parts
85.34	**印刷电路:**							**Printed circuits:**
8534.0010	---4层以上的	0	35	17	17	块/千克		---Of more than 4 layers
8534.0090	---其他	0	50	17	17	块/千克		---Other
85.35	**电路的开关、保护或连接用的电气装置(例如,开关、熔断器、避雷器、电压限幅器、电涌抑制器、插头及其他连接器、接线盒),用于电压超过1000伏的线路:**							**Electrical apparatus for switching or protecting electrical circuits, or for making connections to or in electrical circuits (for example, switches, fuses, lightning arresters, voltage limiters, surge suppressors, plugs and other conneltors, junction boxes), for a voltage exceeding 1,000 volts:**
8535.1000	-熔断器	14	50	17	17	个/千克	A	-Fuses
	-自动断路器:							-Automatic circuit breakers:
8535.2100	--用于电压低于72.5千伏的线路:	14	50	17	17	个/千克	A	--For a voltage of less than 72.5 kV
	--其他:							--Other:
8535.2910	---用于72.5千伏≤电压≤220千伏的线路	10	50	17	17	个/千克		---For72.5Kv≤Voltage≤220Kv
8535.2920	---用于220千伏＜电压≤750千伏的线路	10	50	17	17	个/千克		---For220Kv≤Voltage≤750Kv
8535.2990	---用于电压＞750千伏的	10	50	17	17	个/千克		---For Voltage＞750Kv
	-隔离开关及断续开关:							-Isolating switches and make-and-break switches:
8535.3010	---用于72.5千伏≤电压≤220千伏的	10	50	17	17	个/千克		---For72.5Kv≤Voltage≤220Kv
8535.3020	---用于220千伏＜电压≤750千伏的	10	50	17	17	个/千克		---For220Kv≤Voltage≤750Kv
8535.3090	---其他(用于电压超过1000伏的线路)	10	50	17	17	个/千克	A	---Other
8535.4000	-避雷器、电压限幅器及电涌抑制器	18	50	17	17	个/千克		-Lightning arresters, voltage limiters and surge suppressors
8535.9000	-其他	10	50	17	17	千克		-Other
8535.9000 10	触发式火花隙(阳极延迟时间≤15ms,阳极峰值额定电流≥500A)	10	50	17	17	千克	3	Triggered spark gap (time for delay of anode ≤15ms, rating current of anode's peak value≥500A)
8535.9000 20	具有快速开关功能的模件或组件(阳极峰值电压≥2KV;电流≥500A;接通时间为1微秒或更短)	10	50	17	17	千克	3	Module or groupware that can be speedily switched on or off (peak voltage value of anode≥2KV, current≥500A, time for switching on 1 ms)
8535.9000 90	其他电压＞1000伏电路开关等电气装置	10	50	17	17	千克		Other electrical apparatuses for switching or protecting electrical circuits, or for making connections to or in electrical circuits, for a voltage exceeding 1000 volts)
85.36	**电路的开关、保护或连接用的电器装置(例如,开关、继电器、熔断器、电涌抑制器、插头、插座、灯座及其他连接器、接线盒),用于电压不超过1000伏的线路;光导纤维、光导纤维束或光缆用连接器:**							**Electrical apparatus for switching or protecting electrical circuits, or for making connections to or in electricalcircuits (for example, switches, relays, fuses, surge suppressors, plugs, sockets, lamp-holders, and other conneltors junction boxes), for a voltage not exceeding 1000 volts; connectors for optical fibres. optical fibre bundles or cables:**
8536.1000	-熔断器	10	50	17	17	个/千克	A	-Fuses
8536.2000	-自动断路器	9	50	17	17	个/千克	A	-Automatic circuit breakers
8536.3000	-其他电路保护装置	9	50	17	17	个/千克	A	-Other apparatus for protecting electrical circuits
	-继电器:							-Relays:
	--用于电压不超过60伏的线路:							--For a voltage not exceeding 60 V:

税则号列	货　品　名　称	最惠(%)	普通	增值税率	出口退税	计量单位	监管条件	Article Description
8536.4110	---用于电压不超过36伏的线路	10	50	17	17	个/千克		---For a voltage not exceeding 36V
8536.4190	---其他	10	50	17	17	个/千克	A	---Other
8536.4900	--其他	10	50	17	17	个/千克	A	--Other
8536.5000	-其他开关	0	50	17	17	个/千克	A	-Other switches
	-灯座、插头及插座：							-Lamp-holders, plugs and sockets:
8536.6100	--灯座	10	50	17	17	个/千克		--Lamp-holders
8536.6900	--其他	0	50	17	17	个/千克		--Other
8536.7000	-光导纤维、光导纤维束或光缆用连接器	8	30	17	17	千克		-Connectors for optical fibres, optical fibre bundles or cables
	-其他装置：							-Other apparatus:
	---接插件：							---Connector:
8536.9011	----工作电压不超过36伏的	0	50	17	17	千克		----Working voltage not exceeding 36 volts
8536.9019	----其他	0	50	17	17	千克	A	----Other
8536.9090	---其他	0	50	17	17	千克	A	---Other
85.37	**用于电气控制或电力分配的盘、板、台、柜及其他基座，装有两个或多个税目85.35或85.36所列的装置，包括装有第九十章所列的仪器或装置，以及数控装置，但税目85.17的交换机除外：**							**Boards, panels, consoles, desks, cabinets and other bases, equipped with two or more apparatus of headingNo. 85.35 or 85.36, for electric control or the distribution of electricity, including those incorporating instruments or apparatus of Chapter 90, and numerical control apparatus, other than switching apparatus of heading No. 85.17:**
	-用于电压不超过1000伏的线路：							-For a voltage not exceeding 1,000 V:
	---数控装置：							---Numerical control panels:
8537.1011	----可编程序控制器		14	17	17	个/千克		----Programmable logic controuers(PLC)
8537.1011暂 01	机床用可编程序控制器(PLC)	3	14	17	17	个/千克		Programmable logic controuers for machine tools
8537.1011 10	调节和编程控制器(8479　899960绕线机用)	5	14	17	17	个/千克	3	Adiusting and programming controllers for winding machine of subbeading No. 8479.899060
8537.1011 90	其他可编程控制器(用于电压不超过1000伏的线路)	5	14	17	17	个/千克		Other programming logic controllers (for the circuit with its voltage≤1000V)
8537.1019	----其他		14	17	17	个/千克		----Other
8537.1019暂 01	机床用其他数控单元(包括单独进口的CNC操作单元)	3	14	17	17	个/千克		Other digital control units for machine tool (CNC operating unit with separate import)
8537.1019 90	其他非机床用数控装置(用于电压不超过1000伏的线路)	5	14	17	17	个/千克		Other digital controller not for machine tool (for a voltage≤1000 volts)
8537.1090	---其他		50	17	17	个/千克		---Other
8537.1090暂 01	电梯用控制柜及控制柜专用印刷电路板(用于电压不超过1000伏的线路)	4	50	17	17	个/千克		Control cabinet (electric cabinet) for elevators and circuit board for control cabinet (for the circuit with its voltage≤1000V)
8537.1090 21	控制器[用于机器人或末端操纵装置(详见核两用清单)]	8.4	50	17	17	个/千克	3	Controllers (use for roloots or end - operation devices, see the dual - purpose nuclear goods list for details)
8537.1090 22	数字控制器(专用于编号8479899959电动式振动试验系统)	8.4	50	17	17	个/千克	3	Digital controllers (only use of electric vibration test system subweading No. 8479899959)
8537.1090 90	其他电力控制或分配的装置(电压不超过1000伏的线路)	8.4	50	17	17	个/千克	A	Other power contorl or distribution devices (for the circuit with its voltage≤1000V)
	-用于电压超过1000伏的线路：							-For a voltage exceeding 1,000 V:
8537.2010	---全封闭组合式高压开关装置，用于电压在500千伏及以上的线路	8.4	30	17	17	台/千克		---Gas insulated switchgear, for a voltage of 500 KV or more
8537.2090	---其他	8.4	50	17	17	千克		---Other
85.38	**专用于或主要用于税目85.35、85.36或85.37所列装置的零件：**							**Parts suitable for use solely or principally with the apparatus of headingNo. 85.35, 85.36 or 85.37:**
	-税目85.37所列货品用的盘、板、台、柜及其他基座，但未装有关装置：							-Boards, panels, consoles, desks, cabinets and other bases for the goods of headingNo. 85.37, not equipped with their apparatus:

税则号列	货品名称	最惠(%)	普通	增值税率	出口退税	计量单位	监管条件	Article Description
8538.1010	---税目8537.2010所列货品用	8.4	50	17	17	千克		---For the goods of headingNo. 8537.2010
8538.1090	---其他	7	50	17	17	千克		---Other
8538.9000	-其他	7	50	17	17	千克		-Other
85.39	白炽灯泡、放电灯管，包括封闭式聚光灯及紫外线灯管或红外线灯泡；弧光灯：							**Electric filament or discharge lamps, including sealed beam lamp units and ultra-violet or infra-red lamps; arc-lamps:**
8539.1000	-封闭式聚光灯	10	45	17	17	只		-Sealed beam lamp units
	-其他白炽灯泡，但不包括紫外线灯管或红外线灯泡：							-Other filament lamps, excluding ultra-violet or infra-red lamps:
	--卤钨灯：							--Tungsten halogen:
8539.2110	---科研、医疗专用	8	20	17	17	只		---For scientific or medical uses only
8539.2120	---火车、航空器及船舶用	8	20	17	17	只		---For locomotives and rolling-stock, aircraft or ships
8539.2130	---机动车辆用	10	45	17	17	只		---For motor vehicles
8539.2190	---其他	10.5	70	17	17	只		---Other
	--其他灯，功率不超过200瓦，但额定电压超过100伏：							--Other, of a power not exceeding 200 W and for a voltage exceeding 100 V:
8539.2210	---科研、医疗专用	10.5	20	17	17	只		---For scientific or medical uses only
8539.2290	---其他	5	70	17	17	只		---Other
	--其他：							--Other:
8539.2910	---科研、医疗专用	5	20	17	17	只		---For scientific or medical uses only
8539.2920	---火车、航空器及船舶用	10.5	20	17	17	只		---For locomotives and rolling-stock, aircraft or ships
8539.2930	---机动车辆用	5	45	17	17	只		---For motor vehicles
	---其他：							---Other:
8539.2991	----12伏及以下的	12	70	17	17	只		----Of a voltage 12 V or less
8539.2999	----其他	12	70	17	17	只		----Other
	-放电灯管，但紫外线灯管除外：							-Discharge lamps, other than ultra-violet lamps:
	--热阴极荧光灯：							--Fluorescent, hot cathode:
8539.3110	---科研、医疗专用	8	20	17	17	只		---For scientific or medical uses only
8539.3120	---火车、航空器及船舶用	8	20	17	17	只		---For locomotives and rolling-stock, aircraft or ships
	---其他：							---Other:
8539.3191	----紧凑型	8	70	17	17	只		----Compact type
8539.3199	----其他	8	70	17	17	只		----Other
	--汞或钠蒸汽灯；金属卤化物灯：							--Mercury or sodium vapour lamps; metal halide lamps:
8539.3230	---钠蒸气灯	8	20	17	17	只		---Sodium vapour lamps
8539.3240	---汞蒸气灯		20	17	17	只		---Mercury vapour lamps
8539.3240暂 01	彩色投影机用的照明光源（汞蒸汽灯）	3	20	17	17	只		Mercury vapor light for color LCD projectors
8539.3240 90	其他汞蒸汽灯	8	20	17	17	只		Other mercury vapor light
8539.3290	---其他	8	70	17	17	只		---Other
	--其他：							--Other:
8539.3910	---科研、医疗专用	8	20	17	17	只		---For scientific or medical uses only
8539.3920	---火车、航空器及船舶用	8	20	17	17	只		---For locomotives and rolling-stock, aircraft or ships
8539.3990	---其他		70	17	17	只		---Other
8539.3990暂 01	液晶显示器背光模组用冷阴极灯管	3	70	17	17	只		Cold cathode flourescent lamps for component modules at the back of LCD
8539.3990 90	其他用途的其他放电灯管	8	70	17	17	只		Other discharge lamps of other purposes
	-紫外线灯管或红外线灯泡；弧光灯：							-Ultraviolet or infrared lamps; arc-lamps:
8539.4100	--弧光灯	8	20	17	17	只		--Arc-lamps
8539.4900	--其他	8	20	17	17	只		--Other
8539.9000	-零件	8	20	17	17	千克		-Parts

税则号列	货品名称	最惠(%)	普通	增值税率	出口退税	计量单位	监管条件	Article Description
85.40	热电子管、冷阴极管或光阴极管(例如,真空管或充气管、汞弧整流管、阴极射线管、电视摄像管):							**Thermionic, cold cathode or photo-cathode valves and tubes (for example, vacuum or vapour or gas filled valves and tubes, mercury arc rectifying valves and tubes, cathode-ray tubes, television camera tubes):**
	-阴极射线电视显像管,包括视频监视器用阴极射线管:							-Cathode-ray television picture tubes, including video monitor cathode-ray tubes:
8540.1100	--彩色的	12	40	17	17	只	6A	--Colour
8540.1200	--单色的	15	40	17	17	只	6A	--Monochrome
	-电视摄像管;变像管及图像增强管;其他光阴极管:							-Television camera tubes; image converters and intensifiers; other photo-cathode tubes:
8540.2010	---电视摄像管	12	35	17	17	只		---Television camera tubes
8540.2090	---其他	8	17	17	17	只		---Other
8540.2090 10	电子条纹相机的条纹显像管(专用于编号9006.5900 40的条纹显像管)	8	17	17	17	只	3	Stripe kinescope of electronic stripe camera (striation kinescope tube specially used for Serial Number 9006.5900 40)
8540.2090 90	其他电视摄像管;其他变像管及图像增强管;其他光阴极管	8	17	17	17	只		Other television camera tubes, other image converter tube and image intensifier tubes, other photo cathode tubes
	-单色的数据/图形显示管;彩色的数据/图形显示管,屏幕荧光点间距小于0.4毫米:							-Data/graphic display tubes, monochrome; data/graphic displaytubes, colour, with a phosphor dot screen pitch smaller than 0.4mm
8540.4010	---彩色的数据/图形显示管,屏幕荧光点间距小于0.4毫米	8	17	17	17	只	6	-Data/graphic displaytubes, colour, with a phosphor dot screen pitch smaller than 4mm
8540.4020	---单色的数据/图形显示管	8	17	17	17	只	6	---Data/graphic display tubes, monochrome
	-其他阴极射线管:							-Other cathode-ray tubes:
8540.6010	---雷达显示管	6	14	17	17	只		---Radar display tubes
8540.6090	---其他	8	17	17	17	只	6	---Other
	-微波管(例如,磁控管、速调管、行波管、返波管),但不包括栅控管:							-Microwave tubes (for example, magnetrons, klystrons, travelling wave tubes, carcinotrons), excluding grid-controlled tubes:
8540.7100	--磁控管	8	17	17	17	只		--Magnetrons
	--其他:							--Other:
8540.7910	---速调管	8	17	17	17	只		---Klystrons
8540.7990	---其他	8	17	17	17	只		---Other
	-其他管:							-Other valves and tubes:
8540.8100	--接收管或放大管	8	17	17	17	只		--Receiver or amplifier valves and tubes
8540.8900	--其他	8	17	17	17	只		--Other
8540.8900 10	光电倍增管(光电阴极面积大于20平方厘米,并且阳极脉冲上升时间小于1纳秒)	8	17	17	17	只	3	Electron-multiplier phototube (Photoelectric cathode area greater than 20 square centimeters, and the anode pulse rise time less than 1ns)
8540.8900 90	其他电子管(包括光阴极管或汞弧整流管	8	17	17	17	只		Other electron tube (including photo - cathode valves and mercury arc rectifying valves and tubes)
	-零件:							-Parts:
	--阴极射线管用:							--Of cathode-ray tubes:
8540.9110暂	---电视显像管用	3	40	17	17	千克		---Of television picture tubes
8540.9120	---雷达显示管用	5	14	17	17	千克		---Of radar display tubes
8540.9190暂	---其他	4	17	17	17	千克		---Other
	--其他:							--Other:
8540.9910	---电视摄像管用	8	35	17	17	千克		---Of television camera tubes
8540.9990	---其他	8	17	17	17	千克		---Other

税则号列	货品名称	最惠(%)	普通	增值税率	出口退税	计量单位	监管条件	Article Description
85.41	**二极管、晶体管及类似的半导体器件;光敏半导体器件,包括不论是否装在组件内或组装成块的光电池;发光二极管;已装配的压电晶体:**							**Diodes, transistors and similar semi-conductor devices; photosensitive semi-conductor devices, including photovoltaic cells whether or not assembled in modules or made up into panels; light emitting diodes; mounted piezo-electric crystals:**
8541.1000	-二极管,但光敏二极管或发光二极管除外	0	30	17	17	个/千克		-Diodes, other than photosensitive or light emitting diodes
	-晶体管,但光敏晶体管除外:							-Transistors, other than photosensitive transistors:
8541.2100	--耗散功率小于1瓦的	0	30	17	17	个/千克		--With a dissipation rate of less than 1 W
8541.2900	--其他	0	30	17	17	个/千克		--Other
8541.3000	-半导体开关元件、两端交流开关元件及三端双向可控硅开关元件,但光敏器件除外	0	30	17	17	个/千克		-Thyristors, diacs and triacs, other than photosensitive devices
	-光敏半导体器件,包括不论是否装在组件内或组装成块的光电池;发光二极管:							-Photosensitive semiconductor devices, including photovoltaic cells whether or not assembled in modules or made up into panels; light emitting diodes:
8541.4010	---发光二极管	0	30	17	17	个/千克		---Light emitting diodes
8541.4020	---太阳能电池	0	30	17	17	个/千克		---Solar cells
8541.4090	---其他	0	30	17	17	个/千克		---Other
8541.5000	-其他半导体器件	0	30	17	17	个/千克		-Other semiconductor devices
8541.6000	-已装配的压电晶体	0	30	17	17	个/千克		-Mounted piezo-electric crystals
8541.9000	-零件	0	30	17	17	千克		-Parts
85.42	**集成电路:**							**Electronic integrated circuits**
	-集成电路:							-Electronic integrated circuits
8542.3100	--处理器及控制器,不论是否带有存储器、转换器、逻辑电路、放大器、时钟及时序电路或其他电路	0	24	17	17	个/千克		--Proceosors and controuers, whether or not combined with memories, converter, logic circuit, amplifier, clock and timing circuit or other circuit
8542.3200	--存储器	0	24	17	17	个/千克		--Memories
8542.3300	--放大器	0	24	17	17	个/千克		--Amplifier
8542.3900	--其他	0	24	17	17	个/千克		--Other
8542.9000	-零件	0	30	17	17	千克		-Parts
85.43	**本章其他税目未列名的具有独立功能的电气设备及装置:**							**Electrical machines and apparatus, having individual functions, not specified or included elsewhere in this Chapter:**
8543.1000	-粒子加速器:	5	11	17	17	台		-Particle accelerators:
8543.1000 10	脉冲电子加速器(峰值能量为500千电子伏或更高)	5	11	17	17	台	3	Pulsed electron accelerators (peak value power ≥500KEV)
8543.1000 20	中子发生器系统,包括中子管(真空下,利用静电加速来诱发氚-氘核反应)	5	11	17	17	台	3	Neutron generator systems, including neutron tubes (in vacuum condition, induce the tritium-deuteron reaction through acceleration of static)
8543.1000 90	其他粒子加速器	5	11	17	17	台		Other particle accelerator
	-信号发生器:							-Signal generators:
8543.2010	---输出信号频率在1500兆赫兹以下的通用信号发生器	15	80	17	17	台		---Universal signal generators, with a frequency range of less than 1500 MHz
8543.2090	---其他	8	20	17	17	台		---Other
8543.2090 10	高速脉冲发生器(脉冲上升时间小于500ps)	8	20	17	17	台	3	High-speed pulse generator (risetime of pulse <500ps)
8543.2090 90	其他输出信号频率≥1500Mhz的通用信号发生器	8	20	17	17	台		Other versatile signal generators with the ouput signal frequency≥1500Mhz
8543.3000	-电镀、电解或电泳设备及装置	0	35	17	17	台		-Machines and apparatus for electro-plating, electrolysis or electrophoresis
8543.3000 10	电化学还原槽;锂汞齐电解槽(电化学还原槽为化学交换过程的铀浓缩设计的)	0	35	17	17	台	3	Electrochemical lithium amalgam electrolysis cells reduction cells (specially designed for uranium concentration in chemical exchange process)
8543.3000 20	产氟电解槽(每小时产250克以上)	0	35	17	17	台	3	Fluorine generating electrolytic cells (produce more than 250 grams/hour)

税则号列	货品名称	最惠(%)	普通	增值税率	出口退税	计量单位	监管条件	Article Description
8543.3000 90	其他电镀、电解或电泳设备及装置	0	35	17	17	台		Other machines and equipment for electro-plating, electrolysis or electrophoresis
	-其他设备及装置:							-Other machines and apparatus:
8543.7091	----金属、矿藏探测器	0	17	17	17	台		----Metal or mine detectors
8543.7092	----高、中频放大器	0	17	17	17	台		----High or intermediate frequency amplifiers
8543.7093	----电篱网激发器	10	35	17	17	台		---Electric fence energizers
8543.7099	----其他	0	35	17	17	台		----Other
8543.7099 10	飞行数据记录器、报告器	0	35	17	17	台		Flying data recorders and reporters
8543.7099 20	无线广播电视用激励器(具有独立功能)	0	35	17	17	台	O	Exciters for wireless television broadcasting (having independently functions)
8543.7099 30	模/数转换器(能设计或改进成军用、或设计成抗辐射的)	0	35	17	17	台	3	Analog/digital converters (capable of being designed or improved for military uses or being designed to resist radiation)
8543.7099 40	质谱仪用的离子源(原子质量单位≥230,分辨率>2/230)	0	35	17	17	台	3	Ion source for mass spectrogragh (atomic quality unit≥230, exculpation>2/230)
8543.7099 50	密码机、密码卡(不包括数字电视智能卡、蓝牙模块、用于知识产权保护的加密狗)	0	35	17	17	台	M	Cipher, cipher card (not including the intelligent digital TV card, Bluetooth module, for intellectual property protection dongle)
8543.7099 90	其他未列名的具有独立功能的电气设备及装置	0	35	17	17	台		Other unisted electrical equipment and devices, having independently functions
	-零件:							-Parts:
8543.9010	---粒子加速器用	0	11	17	17	千克		---Of particle accelerators
	---信号发生器用:							---Of signal generators:
8543.9021	----输出信号频率在1500兆赫兹以下的通用信号发生器用	0	80	17	17	千克		----Of the generators of subheading No. 8543.2010
8543.9029	----其他	0	20	17	17	千克		----Other
8543.9030	---金属、矿藏探测器用	0	17	17	17	千克		---Of metal or mine detectors
8543.9040	---高、中频放大器用	0	17	17	17	千克		---Of high or intermediate frequency amplifiers
8543.9090	---其他	0	35	17	17	千克		---Other
85.44	绝缘(包括漆包或阳极化处理)电线、电缆(包括同轴电缆)及其他绝缘电导体,不论是否有接头;由每根被覆光纤组成的光缆,不论是否与电导体装配或装有接头:							**Insulated (including enamelled or anodized) wire, cable (including co-axial cable) and other insulated electric conductors, whether or not ritted with connectors; optical fibre cables, made up of individually sheathed fibres, whether or not assembled with electric conductors or fitted with connectors:**
	-绕组电线:							-Winding wire:
8544.1100[暂]	--铜制	6	70	17	17	千克	A	--Of copper
8544.1900	--其他	20	70	17	17	千克	A	--Other
8544.2000	-同轴电缆及其他同轴电导体	10	20	17	17	千克	A	-Co-axial cable and other co-axial electric conductors
	-车辆、航空器、船舶用点火布线组及其他布线组:							-Ignition wiring sets and other wiring sets of a kind used in vehicles, aircraft or ships:
8544.3020	---机动车辆用		20	17	17	千克		---For motor vehicles
8544.3020[暂] 01	车辆用电控柴油机的线束	5	20	17	17	千克	A	Wiring harness for electronic control diesel engines of vehicles
8544.3020 90	机动车辆用其他点火布线组及其他布线组	10	20	17	17	千克	A	Other ignition wiring sets and other wiring sets of a king used for motor vehicles
8544.3090	---其他	5	70	17	17	千克	A	---Other
	-其他电导体,额定电压不超过1000伏:							-Other electric conductors, for a voltage not exceeding 1000 V:
	--有接头:							--Fitted with connectors:
	---额定电压不超过80伏:							---For a voltage not exceeding 80 V:
8544.4211	----电缆	0	20	17	17	千克	A	----Electric cable
8544.4219	----其他	0	70	17	17	千克	A	----Other

税则号列	货品名称	最惠(%)	普通	增值税率	出口退税	计量单位	监管条件	Article Description
	---额定电压超过80伏,但不超过1000伏:							---for a voltage exceeding 80V but not exceeding 1000 V:
8544.4221	----电缆	0	20	17	17	千克	A	----Electric cable
8544.4229	----其他	0	70	17	17	千克	A	----Other
	--其他:							--Other:
	---额定电压不超过80伏:							---For a voltage not exceeding 80 V:
8544.4911	----电缆	0	20	17	17	千克	A	----Electric cable
8544.4919	----其他	0	70	17	17	千克	A	----Other
	---额定电压超过80伏,但不超过1000伏:							---for a voltage exceeding 80 V but not exceeding 1000 V:
8544.4921	----电缆	6	20	17	17	千克	A	----Electric cable
8544.4929	----其他	12	70	17	17	千克	A	----Other
	-其他电导体,额定电压超过1000伏:							-Other electric conductors, for a voltage exceeding 1000 V:
	---电缆:							---Electric cable:
8544.6012	----额定电压不超过35千伏	10	50	17	17	千克	A	----For a voltage not execedding 35 KV
8544.6013	----额定电压超过35千伏,但不超过110千伏	8.4	20	17	17	千克	A	----For a voltage execedding 35 KV, but not execedding 110 KV
8544.6014	----额定电压超过110千伏,但不超过220千伏	8.4	20	17	17	千克	A	----For a voltage execedding 110 KV, but not execedding 220 KV
8544.6019	----其他	8.4	20	17	17	千克	A	----Other
8544.6090	---其他		70	17	17	千克		---Other
8544.6090暂 01	额定电压≥500千伏的气体绝缘金属封闭输电线	10	70	17	17	千克	A	gas - insulated transmission electric wire, rated voltage≥500Kv
8544.6090 90	额定电压>1千伏的其他电导线	21	70	17	17	千克	A	
8544.7000	-光缆	0	20	17	17	千克	A	-Optical fibre cables
85.45	碳电极、碳刷、灯碳棒、电池碳棒及电气设备用的其他石墨或碳精制品,不论是否带金属:							**Carbon electrodes, carbon brushes, lamp carbons, battery carbons and other articles of graphite or other carbon, with or without metal, of a kind used for electrical purposes:**
	-碳电极:							-C arbon Electrodes:
8545.1100	--炉用	8	35	17		千克	3	--Of a kind used for furnaces
8545.1900	--其他	10.5	35	17		千克	3	--Other
8545.2000	-碳刷	10.5	35	17	17	千克		-Brushes
8545.9000	-其他	10.5	35	17	17	千克	3	-Other
85.46	各种材料制的绝缘子:							**Electrical insulators of any material:**
8546.1000	-玻璃制	10.5	35	17	17	千克		-Of glass
	-陶瓷制:							-Of ceramics:
8546.2010	---输变电线路绝缘瓷套管	6	35	17	17	千克		---Power transmission and converting ceramic bushings
8546.2090	---其他		35	17	17	千克		---Other
8546.2090暂 01	输变电架空线路用长棒形瓷绝缘子瓷件(单支长度为1—2米,实芯)	3	35	17	17	千克		Porcelain parts of long - rod porcelain insulators for electric transmission and transformation overhead lines (length of a single rod: 1 ~ 2m, solid)
8546.2090 90	其他陶瓷制绝缘子(包括非输变电线路绝缘瓷套管)	12	35	17	17	千克		Other electrical insulators of ceramics (including not power transmission and transformation and converting ceramic bushings)
8546.9000	-其他	10	35	17	17	千克		-Other
85.47	电气机器、器具或设备用的绝缘零件,除了为装配需要而在模制时装入的小金属零件(例如螺纹孔)以外,全部用绝缘材料制成,但税目85.46的绝缘子除外;内衬绝缘材料的贱金属制线路导管及其接头:							**Insulating fittings for electrical machines, appliances or equipment, being fittings wholly of insulating material apart from any minor components of metal (for example, threaded sockets) incorporated during moulding solely for purposes of assembly, other than insulators of headingNo. 85.46; electrical conduit tubing and joints therefor, of base metal lined with insulating material:**
8547.1000	-陶瓷制绝缘零件	8	35	17	17	千克		-Insulating fittings of ceramics
8547.2000	-塑料制绝缘零件	8	35	17	17	千克		-Insulating fittings of plastics

税则号列	货 品 名 称	最惠(%)	普通	增值税率	出口退税	计量单位	监管条件	Article Description
	-其他:							-Other:
8547.9010	---内衬绝缘材料的贱金属制线路导管及其接头	10	50	17	17	千克		---Electrical conduit tubing and joints therefor, of base metal lined with insulating material
8547.9090	---其他	8	35	17	17	千克		---Other
85.48	**原电池、原电池组及蓄电池的废碎料;废原电池、废原电池组及废蓄电池;机器或设备的本章其他税目未列名的电气零件:**							**Waste and scrap of primary cells, primary batteries and electric accumulators; spent primary cells, spent primary batteries and spent electric accumulators; electrical parts of machinery or apparatus, not specified or included elsewhere in this Chapter:**
8548.1000	-原电池、原电池组及蓄电池的废碎料;废原电池、废原电池组及废蓄电池	8	36	17	17	千克	9	-Waste and scrap of primary cells, primary batteries and electric accumulators; spent primary cells, spent primary batteries and spent electric accumulators
8548.9000	-其他		40	17		千克		-Other
8548.9000[暂] 01	电磁干扰滤波器	3	40	17	17	千克		Patch filters
8548.9000[暂] 02	非电磁干挠滤波器	6	40	17	15	千克		Non electromagnetic interference filter
8548.9000 10	可调脉冲单模染料振荡器(平均输出功率 >1 W,重复率 >1 kHZ,脉宽 < 100ns 可见光范围)	12	40	17	17	千克	3	Ingle - mode tunable pulsed dye oscillators(average output power > 1w, repetition rate > 1khz, pulse width < 100ns of wavelength range of visible light)
8548.9000 20	可调脉冲染料激光放大器和振荡器(不包括单模振荡器)(平均输出功率 > 30 W,重复率 > 1kHZ,脉宽 < 100ns 可见光范围)	12	40	17	17	千克	3	Single - mode tunable pulsed dye amplifiers and oscillators(average output power > 30w, repetition rate > 1khz, pulse width < 100ns of wavelength range of visible light, excluding single transverse - mode oscillators)
8548.9000 90	第85章其他编号未列名的电气零件	12	40	17	15	千克		Other electrical parts, not specified or included elsewhere in the Chapter 85

第十七类
车辆、航空器、船舶
及有关运输设备

注释：

一、本类不包括税目 95.03 或 95.08 的物品以及税目 95.06 的长雪橇、平底雪橇及类似品。

二、本类所称"零件"及"零件、附件"，不适用于下列货品，不论其是否确定为供本类货品使用：

(一)各种材料制的接头、垫圈或类似品(按其构成材料归类或归入税目 84.84)或硫化橡胶(硬质橡胶除外)的其他制品(税目 40.16)；

(二)第十五类注释二所规定的贱金属制通用零件(第十五类)或塑料制的类似品(第三十九章)；

(三)第八十二章的物品(工具)；

(四)税目 83.06 的物品；

(五)税目 84.01 至 84.79 的机器或装置及其零件；税目 84.81 或 84.82 的物品及税目 84.83 的物品(这些物品是构成发动机或其他动力装置所必需的)；

(六)电机或电气设备(第八十五章)；

(七)第九十章的物品；

(八)第九十一章的物品；

(九)武器(第九十三章)；

(十)税目 94.05 的灯具或照明装置；

(十一)作为车辆零件的刷子(税目 96.03)。

三、第八十六章至第八十八章所称"零件"或"附件"，不适用于那些非专用于或非主要用于这几章所列物品的零件、附件。同时符合这几章内两个或两个以上税目规定的零件、附件，应按其主要用途归入相应的税目。

四、在本类中：

(一)既可在道路上，又可在轨道上行驶的特殊构造的车辆，应归入第八十七章的相应税目；

(二)水陆两用的机动车辆，应归入第八十七章的相应税目；

(三)可兼作地面车辆使用的特殊构造的航空器，应归入第八十八章的相应税目。

五、气垫运输工具应按本类最相似的运输工具归类，其规定如下：

(一)在导轨上运行的(气垫火车)，归入第八十六章；

(二)在陆地行驶或水陆两用的，归入第八十七章；

(三)在水上航行的，不论能否在海滩或浮码头登陆及能否在冰上行驶，一律归入第八十九章。

气垫运输工具的零件、附件，应按照上述规定，与最相类似的运输工具的零件、附件一并归类。

SECTION XVII
VEHICLES, AIRCRAFT, VESSELS AND ASSOCIATED TRANSPORT EQUIPMENT

Notes:

1. This Section does not cover articles of headingNo. 95.03 or 95.08, or bobsleighs, toboggans or the like of heading. 95.06.

2. The expressions "parts" and "parts and accessories" do not apply to the following articles, whether or not they are identifiable as for the goods of this Section:

(a) Joints, washers or the like of any material (classified according to their constituent material or in headingNo. 84.84) or other articles of vulcanized rubber other than hard rubber (heading. 40.16);

(b) Parts of general use, as defined in Note 2 to Section XV, of base metal (Section XV), or similar goods of plastics (Chapter 39);

(c) Articles of Chapter 82 (tools);

(d) Articles of headingNo. 83.06;

(e) Machines or apparatus of headings No. 84.01 to 84.79, or parts thereof; articles of heading. 84.81 or 84.82 or, provided they constitute integral parts of engines or motors, articles of headingNo. 84.83;

(f) Electrical machinery or equipment (Chapter 85);

(g) Articles of Chapter 90;

(h) Articles of Chapter 91;

(i) Arms (Chapter 93);

(j) Lamps or lighting fittings of headingNo. 94.05;

(k) Brushes of a kind used as parts of vehicles (headingNo. 96.03).

3. References in Chapters 86 to 88 to "parts" or "accessories" do not apply to parts or accessories which are not suitable for use solely or principally with the articles of those Chapters. A part or accessory which answers to a description in two or more of the headings of those Chapters is to be classified under that heading which corresponds to the principal use of that part or accessory.

4. For the purposes of this Section:

(a) Vehicles specially constructed to travel on both road and rail are classified under the appropriate heading of Chapter 87;

(b) Amphibious motor vehicles are classified under the appropriate heading of Chapter 87;

(c) Aircraft specially constructed so that they can also be used as road vehicles are classified under the appropriate heading of Chapter 88.

5. Air-cushion vehicles are to be classified within this Section with the vehicles to which they are most akin as follows:

(a) In Chapter 86 if designed to travel on a guide-track (hover-trains);

(b) In Chapter 87 if designed to travel over land or over both land and water;

(c) In Chapter 89 if designed to travel over water, whether or not able to land on beaches or landingstages or also able to travel over ice.

Parts and accessories of air-cushion vehicles are to be classified in the same way as those of vehicles of the heading in which the air-cushion vehicles are classified under the above provisions.

气垫火车的导轨固定装置及附件应与铁道轨道固定装置及附件一并归类。气垫火车运行系统的信号、安全或交通管理设备应与铁路的信号、安全或交通管理设备一并归类。

Hovertrain track fixtures and fittings are to be classified as railway track fixtures and fittings, and signalling, safety or traffic control equipment for hovertrain transport systems as signalling, safety or traffic control equipment for railways.

第八十六章
铁道及电车道机车、车辆及其零件；铁道及电车道轨道固定装置及其零件、附件；各种机械(包括电动机械)交通信号设备

Chapter 86
Railway or tramway locomotives, rolling-stock and parts thereof; railway or tramway track fixtures and fittings and parts thereof; mechanical (including electro-mechanical) traffic signalling equipment of all kinds

注释：

一、本章不包括：

(一)木制或混凝土制的铁道或电车道轨枕及气垫火车用的混凝土导轨(税目44.06或68.10)；

(二)税目73.02的铁道及电车道辅轨用钢铁材料；

(三)税目85.30的电气信号、安全或交通管理设备。

二、税目86.07主要适用于：

(一)轴、轮、行走机构、金属轮箍、轮圈、毂及轮子的其他零件；

(二)车架、底架、转向架；

(三)轴箱；制动装置；

(四)车辆缓冲器；钩或其他联结器及车厢走廊联结装置；

(五)车身。

三、除上述注释一另有规定的以外，税目86.08包括：

(一)已装配的轨道、转车台、站台缓冲器、量载规；

(二)铁道及电车道、道路、内河航道、停车场、港口或机场用的臂板信号机、机械信号盘、平交道口控制器、信号及道岔控制器及其他机械(包括电动机械)信号、安全或交通管理设备，不论是否装有电力照明装置。

Notes:

1. This Chapter does not cover:

(a) Railway or tramway sleepers of wood or of concrete, or concrete guide-track sections for hovertrain (heading No. 44.06 or 68.10);

(b) Railway or tramway track construction material of iron or steel of heading No. 73.02;

(c) Electrical signalling, safety of traffic control equipment of heading No. 85.30.

2. Heading No. 86.07 applies, *inter alia*, to:

(a) Axles, wheels, wheel sets (running gear), metal tyres, hoops and hubs and other parts of wheels;

(b) Frames, underframes, bogies and bissel-bogies;

(c) Axle boxes; brake gear;

(d) Buffers for rolling-stock; hooks and other coupling gear and corridor connections;

(e) Coachwork.

3. Subject to the provisions of Note 1 above, headingNo. 86.08 applies, *inter alia*, to:

(a) Assembled track, turntables, platform buffers, loading gauges;

(b) Semaphores, mechanical signal discs, level crossing control gear, signal and point controls, and other mechanical (including electro-mechanical) signalling, safety or traffic control equipment, whether or not fitted with electric lighting, for railways, tramways, roads, inland waterways, parking facilities, port installations or airfields.

税则号列	货品名称	最惠(%)	普通	增值税率	出口退税	计量单位	监管条件	Article Description
86.01	**铁道电力机车，由外部电力或蓄电池驱动：**							**Rail locomotives powered from an external source of electricity or by electric accumulators:**
	-由外部电力驱动：							-Powered from an external source of electricity:
	---直流电机驱动的：							---Drived by DC motors:
8601.1011	----微型机控制的	3	11	17	17	辆		----Controlled by microprocessings
8601.1019	----其他	3	11	17	17	辆		----Other
8601.1020	---交流电机驱动的	3	11	17	17	辆	O	---Drived by AC motors
8601.1090	---其他	3	11	17	17	辆	O	---Other
8601.2000	-由蓄电池驱动	3	11	17	17	辆		-Powered by electric accumulators
86.02	**其他铁道机车；机车煤水车：**							**Other rail locomotives; locomotive tenders:**
	-柴油电力机车：							-Diesel-electric locomotives:
8602.1010	---微型机控制的	3	11	17	17	辆		---Controled by microprocessings
8602.1090	---其他	3	11	17	17	辆		---Other
8602.9000	-其他	3	11	17	17	辆		-Other

税则号列	货品名称	最惠(%)	普通	增值税率	出口退税	计量单位	监管条件	Article Description
86.03	铁道及电车道用的机动客车、货车、敞车，但税目**86.04**的货品除外：							**Self-propelled railway or tramway coaches, vans and trucks, other than those of heading No. 86.04:**
8603.1000	-由外部电力驱动	3	11	17	17	辆	O	-Powered from an external source of electricity:
8603.9000	-其他	3	11	17	17	辆		-Other
86.04	铁道及电车道用的维修或服务车，不论是否机动（例如，工场车、起重机车、道碴捣固车、轨道校正车、检验车及查道车）：							**Railway or tramway maintenance or service vehicles, whether or not self-propelled (for example, workshops, cranes, ballast tampers, trackliners, testing coaches and track inspection vehicles):**
	---检验车及查道车：							---Testing coaches and track inspection vehicles:
8604.0011	----隧道限界检查车	3	14	17	17	辆		----Inspection vehicles for tunnel clearance
8604.0012	----钢轨在线打磨列车	3	14	17	17	辆		----Sanding vehicles for on-line rails
8604.	----其他	5	14	17	17	辆	O	----Other
	---其他：							---Other:
8604.0091	----电气化接触网架线机（轨行式）	5	20	17	17	辆		----Installing vehicles for suspension of contact wire (running on rails)
8604.0099	----其他	7	20	17	17	辆		----Other
86.05	铁道及电车道用的非机动客车；行李车、邮政车和其他铁道及电车道用的非机动特殊用途车辆（税目**86.04**的货品除外）：							**Railway or tramway passenger coaches, not self-propelled; luggage vans, post office coaches and other special purpose railway or tramway coaches, not self-propelled (excluding those of headingNo. 86.04):**
8605.0010	---铁道客车	5	14	17	17	辆		---Railway passenger coaches
8605.0090	---其他	5	14	17	17	辆		---Other
86.06	铁道及电车道用的非机动有篷及无篷货车：							**Railway or tramway goods vans and wagons, not self-propelled:**
8606.1000	-油罐货车及类似车	5	14	17	17	辆		-Tank wagons and the like
8606.3000	-自卸货车，但子目号8606.1000的货品除外	5	14	17	17	辆		-Self-discharging vans and wagons, other than those of subheadingNo. 8606.1000
	-其他：							-Other:
8606.9100	--带篷及封闭的	5	14	17	17	辆		--Covered and closed
8606.9200	--敞篷的，厢壁固定且高度超过60厘米	5	14	17	17	辆		--Open, with non-removable sides of a hight exceeding 60 cm
8606.9900	--其他	5	14	17	17	辆		--Other
86.07	铁道及电车道机车或其他车辆的零件：							**Parts of railway or tramway locomotives or rolling-stock:**
	-转向架、轴、轮及其零件：							-Bogies, bissel-bogies, axles and wheels, and parts thereof:
8607.1100	--驾驶转向架	3	11	17	15	套/千克		--Driving bogies and bissel-bogies
8607.1200	--其他转向架	3	11	17	15	套/千克		--Other bogies and bissel-bogies
	--其他，包括零件：							--Other, including parts:
8607.1910	---轴	3	11	17	17	根/千克	A	---Axles
8607.1990	---其他	3	11	17	17	千克	A	---Other
	-制动装置及其零件：							-Brakes and parts thereof:
8607.2100	--空气制动器及其零件	3	11	17	17	千克		--Air brakes and parts thereof
8607.2900	--其他	3	11	17	17	千克		--Other
8607.3000	-钩、其他联结器、缓冲器及其零件	3	11	17	17	千克		-Hooks and other coupling devices, buffers, and parts thereof
	-其他：							-Other:
8607.9100	--机车用	3	11	17	17	千克		--Of locomotives
8607.9900	--其他	3	11	17	17	千克		--Other

税则号列	货品名称	最惠(%)	普通	增值税率	出口退税	计量单位	监管条件	Article Description
86.08	铁道及电车道轨道固定装置及附件;供铁道、电车道、道路、内河航道、停车场、港口或机场用的机械(包括电动机械)信号、安全或交通管理设备;上述货品的零件:							**Railway or tramway track fixtures and fittings; mechanical (including electro-mechanical) signalling, safety or traffic control equipment for railways, tramways, roads, inland waterways, parking facilities, port installations or airfields; parts of the foregoing:**
8608.0010	---轨道自动计轴设备	3	20	17	17	千克/台		---Rail automatic axle counting equipments
8608.0090	---其他	4	20	17	17	千克		---Other
86.09	集装箱(包括运输液体的集装箱),经特殊设计、装备适用于各种运输方式:							**Containers (including containers for the transport of fluids) specially designed and equipped for carriage by one or more modes of transport:**
	---20 英尺的:							---Of 20 feet:
8609.0011	----保温式	10.5	35	17	15	个	AB	----Insulated
8609.0012	----罐式	10.5	35	17	15	个	AB	----Tank type
8609.0019	----其他	10.5	35	17	15	个	AB	----Other
	---40 英尺的:							---Of 40 feet:
8609.0021	----保温式的	10.5	35	17	15	个	AB	----Insulated
8609.0022	----罐式	10.5	35	17	15	个	AB	----Tank type
8609.0029	----其他	10.5	35	17	15	个	AB	----Other
8609.0030	---45、48、53 英尺的	10.5	35	17	15	个	AB	---Of 45, 48, 53 feet
8609.0090	---其他	10.5	35	17	15	个	AB	---Other

第八十七章
车辆及其零件、附件，但铁道及电车道车辆除外

Chapter 87
Vehicles other than railway or tramway rolling-stock, and parts and accessories thereof

注释：

一、本章不包括仅可在钢轨上运行的铁道及电车道车辆。

二、本章所称“牵引车、拖拉机”，是指主要为牵引或推动其他车辆、器具或重物的车辆。除了上述主要用途以外，不论其是否还具有装运工具、种子、肥料或其他货品的辅助装置。

用于安装在税目 87.01 的牵引车、拖拉机上，作为可替换设备的机器或作业工具，即使与牵引车、拖拉机一同进口或出口，不论是否已安装在车(机)上，仍应归入其各自相应的税目。

三、装有驾驶室的机动车辆底盘，应归入税目 87.02 至 87.04，而不归入税目 87.06。

四、税目 87.12 包括所有儿童两轮车，其他儿童脚踏车归入税目 95.03。

Notes:

1. This Chapter does not cover railway or tramway rolling-stock designed solely for running on rails.

2. For the purposes of this Chapter, “tractors” means vehicles constructed essentially for hauling or pushing another vehicle, appliance or load, whether or not they contain subsidiary provision for the transport, in connection with the main use of the tractor, of tools, seeds, fertilizers or other goods.

   Machines and working tools designed for fitting to tractors of heading No. 87. 01 as interchangeable equipment remain classified in their respective headings even if presented with the tractor, and whether or not mounted on it.

3. Motor chassis fitted with cabs fall in headings No. 87. 02 to 87. 04, and not in headingNo. 87. 06.

4. HeadingNo. 87. 12 includes all children's bicycles. Other children's cycles fall in headingNo. 95. 03.

税则号列	货品名称	最惠(%)	普通	增值税率	出口退税	计量单位	监管条件	Article Description
87. 01	**牵引车、拖拉机(税目 87. 09 的牵引车除外)：**							**Tractors (other than tractors of h eading No. 87. 09):**
8701. 1000	-手扶拖拉机	9	20	13	13	辆	6	-Pedestrian controlled tractors
8701. 2000	-半挂车用的公路牵引车	6	20	17	17	辆	46AOxy	-Road tractors for semi-trailers
8701. 3000	-履带式牵引车、拖拉机	6	20		13,17	辆		-Track-laying tractors
8701. 3000 10	履带式拖拉机	6	20	13	13,17	辆	A6	Track-laying tractors
8701. 3000 90	履带式牵引车	6	20	17	13,17	辆	A6	Track-laying tractors
	-其他：							-Other:
	---拖拉机：							---Tractors:
8701. 9011	----轮式		20	13	13,17	辆		----Wheeled
8701. 9011[暂] 01	功率大于 150 马力的轮式拖拉机	5	20	13	13,17	辆	6A	Wheeled tractors, power > 150H. P.
8701. 9011 90	其他轮式拖拉机	8	20	13	13,17	辆	6A	Other wheeled tractors (tyre)
8701. 9019	----其他		20	13	13,17	辆		----Other
8701. 9019[暂] 01	其他功率大于 150 马力的拖拉机	5	20	13	13,17	辆	6A	Other tractors, power > 150H. P.
8701. 9019 90	其他拖拉机	8	20	13	13,17	辆	A6	Other tractors
8701. 9090	---其他	8	20	17	13,17	辆	A6	---Other
87. 02	**客运机动车辆，10 座及以上(包括驾驶座)：**							**Motor vehicles for the transport of ten or more persons, including the driver:**
	-装有压燃式活塞内燃发动机(柴油或半柴油发动机)的车辆：							-With compression-ignition internal combustion piston engine (diesel or semi-diesel):
8702. 1020	---机坪客车(机场专用车)	4	90	17	17	辆	6AO	---Buses for transport passengers at airport
	---其他：							---Other:
8702. 1091	----30 座及以上(大型客车)	25	90	17	17	辆	46AOxy	----With 30 seats or more
8702. 1092	----20 座及以上，但不超过 29 座	25	230	17	17	辆		----With 20 seats or more, but not exceeding 29 seats
8702. 1092 01	20≤座≤23 装有压燃式活塞内燃发动机的客车	25	230	17	17	辆	46AOxy	Buses for transport passengers, with compression –ignition internal combustion piston engine, with 20 ~ 23 seats
8702. 1092 90	24≤座≤29 装有压燃式活塞内燃发动机的客车	25	230	17	17	辆	46AOxy	Buses for transport passengers, with compression –ignition internal combustion piston engine, with 24 ~ 29 seats
8702. 1093	----10 座及以上，但不超过 19 座	25	230	17	17	辆	46AOxy	With 10 Seats or more, but not exceeding 19 seats
	-其他：							-Other:
8702. 9010	---30 座及以上(大型客车)	25	90	17	17	辆	46AOxy	---With 30 seats or more

税则号列	货　品　名　称	最惠(%)	普通	增值税率	出口退税	计量单位	监管条件	Article Description
8702.9020	---20 座及以上,但不超过 29 座	25	230	17	17	辆		---With 20 seats or more, but not exceeding 29 seats
8702.9020 01	20≤座≤23 装有非压燃式活塞内燃发动机的客车	25	230	17	17	辆	46AOxy	Buses for transport passengers, with non-compression-ignition internal combustion piston engine, with 20～23 seats
8702.9020 90	24≤座≤29 装有非压燃式活塞内燃发动机的客车	25	230	17	17	辆	46AOxy	Buses for transport passengers, with non-compression-ignition internal combustion piston engine, with 24～29 seats
8702.9030	---10 座及以上,但不超过 19 座	25	230	17	17	辆	46AOxy	---With 10 seats or more, but not exceeding 19 seats
87.03	**主要用于载人的机动车辆(税目 87.02 的货品除外),包括旅行小客车及赛车:**							**Motor cars and other motor vehicles principally designed for the transport of persons (other than those of headingNo. 87.02), including station wagons and racing cars:**
	-雪地行走专用车;高尔夫球车及类似车辆:							-Vehicles specially designed for travelling on snow; golf cars and similar vehicles:
	---高尔夫球车及类似车辆:							---Golf cars and similar vehicles
8703.1011	----全地形车	25	150	17	15	辆	46xy	----All terrain vehicle
8703.1019	----其他	25	150	17	15	辆	6	----Other
8703.1090	---其他	25	150	17	15	辆	6	---Other
	-装有点燃往复式活塞内燃发动机的其他车辆:							-Other vehicles, with spark-ignition internal combustion reciprocating piston engine:
	--气缸容量(排气量)不超过 1000 毫升:							--Of a cylinder capacity not exceeding 1000 cc:
8703.2130	---小轿车	25	230	17	17	辆		---Saloon cars
8703.2130 01	排气量≤1 升的装有点燃往复式活塞内燃发动机的小轿车	25	230	17	17	辆	46AOxy	Saloon cars with spark-ignition internal combustion reciprocating piston engine, cylinder capacity≤1L
8703.2130 90	排气量≤1 升的装有点燃往复式活塞内燃发动机小轿车的成套散件	25	230	17	17	辆	46Oxy	Complete parts of saloon cars with spark-ignition internal combustion reciprocating piston engine, cylinder capacity≤1L
8703.2140	---越野生(4 轮驱动)	25	230	17	17	辆		---Gross-country cars (4WD)
8703.2140 01	排气量≤1 升的装有点燃往复式活塞内燃发动机的(四轮驱动)越野车	25	230	17	17	辆	46AOxy	Gross-country cars (4WD) with spark-ignition internal combustion reciprocating piston engine, cylinger capacity≤1L
8703.2140 90	排气量≤1 升的装有点燃往复式活塞内燃发动机的(四轮驱动)越野车成套散件	25	230	17	17	辆	46AOxy	Complete parts of gross-country cars (4WD) with spark-ignition internal combustion reciprocating piston engine, cylinger capacity≤1L
8703.2150	---9 座及以下的小客车	25	230	17	17	辆		---Station wagons (with 9 seats or less)
8703.2150 01	排气量≤1 升的装有点燃往复式活塞内燃发动机的小客车(≤9 座)	25	230	17	17	辆	46AOxy	Station wagons, with spark-ignition internal combustion reciprocating piston engine, cylinder capacity≤1L (with 9 seats or less)
8703.2150 90	排气量≤1 升的装有点燃往复式活塞内燃发动机的小客车的成套散件(≤9 座)	25	230	17	17	辆	46AOxy	Complete parts of station wagons (with 9 seats or less) with spark-ignition internal combustion reciprocating piston engine, cylinder capacity≤1L
8703.2190	---其他	25	230	17	17	辆		---Other
8703.2190 01	排气量≤1 升的装有点燃往复式活塞内燃发动机的其他车辆	25	230	17	17	辆	46AOxy	Other vehicles with spark-ignition internal combustion reciprocating piston engine, cylinder capacity≤1L
8703.2190 90	排气量≤1 升的装有点燃往复式活塞内燃发动机的其他车辆的成套散件	25	230	17	17	辆	46AOxy	Complete parts of other vehicles with spark-ignition internal combustion reciprocating piston engine, cylinder capacity≤1L
	--气缸容量(排气量)超过 1000 毫升,但不超过 1500 毫升:							--Of a cylinder capacity exceeding 1000ccc but not exceeding 1500cc:
8703.2230	---小轿车	25	230	17	17	辆		---Saloon cars
8703.2230 01	1 升＜排气量≤1.5 升的装有点燃往复式活塞内燃发动机的小轿车	25	230	17	17	辆	46AOxy	Saloon cars with spark-ignition internal combustion reciprocating piston engine, 1L＜cylinder capacity≤1.5L

税则号列	货品名称	最惠(%)	普通	增值税率	出口退税	计量单位	监管条件	Article Description
8703.2230 90	1升＜排气量≤1.5升的装有点燃往复式活塞内燃发动机的小轿车的成套散件	25	230	17	17	辆	46AOxy	Complete parts of saloon car with spark-igition internal combustion reciprocating piston engine, 1L < cylinder capacity ≤ 1.5L
8703.2240	---越野车(4轮驱动)	25	230	17	17	辆		---Cross-country cars (4WD)
8703.2240 01	1升＜排气量≤1.5升的装有点燃往复式活塞内燃发动机的四轮驱动越野车	25	230	17	17	辆	46AOxy	Crass-country cars (4WD) with spark-ignition internal combustion reciprocating piston engine, 1L < cylinder capacity ≤ 1.5L
8703.2240 90	1升＜排气量≤1.5升的装有点燃往复式活塞内燃发动机的四轮驱动越野车的成套散件	25	230	17	17	辆	46AOxy	Complete parts of cross-country cars (4WD) with spark-ignition inernal combustion reciprocating piston engine, 1L < cylinder capacity ≤ 1.5L
8703.2250	---9座及以下的小客车	25	230	17	17	辆		---Station wagons (with 9 seats or less)
8703.2250 01	1升＜排气量≤1.5升的装有点燃往复式活塞内燃发动机的小客车(≤9座)	25	230	17	17	辆	46AOxy	Station wagons (with 9 seats or less) with spark-ignition internal combustion reciprocation piston engine, 1L < cylinder capacity ≤ 1.5L
8703.2250 90	1升＜排气量≤1.5升的装有点燃往复式活塞内燃发动机的小客车的成套散件(≤9座)	25	230	17	17	辆	46AOxy	Complete parts of station wagons (with 9seats or less) with spark-ignition internal combustion reciprocating piston engine, 1L < cylinder capacity ≤ 1.5L
8703.2290	---其他	25	230	17	17	辆		---Other
8703.2290 01	1升＜排气量≤1.5升的装有点燃往复式活塞内燃发动机的其他车	25	230	17	17	辆	46AOxy	Other vehicles with spark-ignition internal combustion reciprocating piston engine, 1L < cylinder capacity ≤ 1.5L
8703.2290 90	1升＜排气量≤1.5升的装有点燃往复式活塞内燃发动机的其他车辆的成套散件	25	230	17	17	辆	46AOxy	Complete parts of other vehicles with spark-ingition internal combustion reciprocating piston engine, 1L < cylinder capacity ≤ 1.5L
	--气缸容量(排气量)超过1500毫升,但不超过3000毫升:							--Of a cylinder capacity exceeding 1500cc but not exceeding 3000cc:
	---气缸容量(排气量)超过1500毫升,但不超过2000毫升:							---Of a cylinder capacity exceeding 1500cc but not exceeding 2000cc:
8703.2341	----小轿车	25	230	17	17	辆		----Saloon cars
8703.2341 01	1.5升＜排气量≤2升装点燃往复式活塞内燃发动机小轿车	25	230	17	17	辆	46AOxy	Saloon cars with spark - ignition internal combustion reciprocating piston engine, 1.5L < cylinder capacity ≤ 2L
8703.2341 90	1.5升＜排气量≤2升装点燃往复式活塞内燃发动机小轿车的成套散件	25	230	17	17	辆	46AOxy	Complete parts of saloon cars with spark-ignition internal cmbustion reciprocating piston engine, 1.5L < cylinder capacity ≤ 2L
8703.2342	----越野车(4轮驱动)	25	230	17	17	辆		----Cross-country cars (4WD)
8703.2342 01	1.5升＜排气量≤2升装点燃往复式活塞内燃发动机四轮驱动越野车	25	230	17	17	辆	46AOxy	Cross - country cars (4WD) with spark - ignition internal combustion reciprocating piston engine, 1.5L < cylinder capacity ≤ 2L
8703.2342 90	1.5升＜排气量≤2升装点燃往复式活塞内燃发动机四轮驱动越野车的成套散件	25	230	17	17	辆	46AOxy	Complete parts of cross-country cars (4WD) with spark-ignition internal combustion reciprocating piston engine, 1.5L < cylinder capacity ≤ 2L
8703.2343	----9座及以下的小客车	25	230	17	17	辆		----Station wagons (with 9 seats or less)
8703.2343 01	1.5升＜排气量≤2升装点燃往复式活塞内燃发动机小客车(≤9座)	25	230	17	17	辆	46AOxy	Station wagons (with 9 seats or less) with spark - ignition internal combustion reciprocating piston engine, 1.5L < cylinder capacity ≤ 2L
8703.2343 90	1.5升＜排气量≤2升装点燃往复式活塞内燃发动机小客车的成套散件(≤9座)	25	230	17	17	辆	46AOxy	Complete parts of station wagons (with 9 seats or less) with spark-ignition internal combustion reciprocating piston engine, 1.5L < cylinder capacity ≤ 2L
8703.2349	----其他	25	230	17	17	辆		----Other
8703.2349 01	1.5升＜排气量≤2升装点燃往复式活塞内燃发动机的其他载人车辆	25	230	17	17	辆	46AOxy	Other motor vehicles principally designed for transport of persons with spark - ignition internal combustion reciprocating piston engine, 1.5L < cylinder capacity ≤ 2L

税则号列	货品名称	最惠(%)	普通	增值税率	出口退税	计量单位	监管条件	Article Description
8703.2349 90	1.5 升＜排气量≤2 升装点燃往复式活塞内燃发动机的其他载人车辆的成套散件	25	230	17	17	辆	46AOxy	Complete parts of other motor vehicles principally designed for the transport of person's with spark-ignition internal combustion reciprocating piston engine, 1.5L < cylinder capacity≤2L
	---气缸容量(排气量)超过 2000 毫升,但不超过 2500 毫升:							---Of a culinder capacity exceeding 2000cc but not exceeding 2500cc:
8703.2351	----小轿车	25	230	17	17	辆		----Saloon cars
8703.2351 01	2 升＜排气量≤2.5 升装点燃往复式活塞内燃发动机小轿车	25	230	17	17	辆	46AOxy	Saloon cars with spark-ignition internal combustion reciprocating pistorl engine, 2L < cylinder capacity≤2.5L
8703.2351 90	2 升＜排气量≤2.5 升装点燃往复式活塞内燃发动机小轿车的成套散件	25	230	17	17	辆	46AOxy	Complete parts of saloon cars with spark-ignition internal combustion reciprocating piston engine, 2L < cylinder capacity≤2.5L
8703.2352	----越野车(4 轮驱动)	25	230	17	17	辆		----Cross-country cars (4WD)
8703.2352 01	2 升＜排气量≤2.5 升装点燃往复式活塞内燃发动机越野车(4 轮驱动)	25	230	17	17	辆	46AOxy	Cross-country cars (4WD) with spark-ignition internal combustion reciprocating piston engine, 2L < cylinder capacity≤2.5L
8703.2352 90	2 升＜排气量≤2.5 升装点燃往复式活塞内燃发动机越野车的成套散件(4 轮驱动)	25	230	17	17	辆	46AOxy	Complete parts of crass-country cars (4WD) with spark-ignition internal combustion reciprocating piston engine, 2L < cylinder capacity≤2.5L
8703.2353	----9 座及以下的小客车	25	230	17	17	辆		----Station wagons (with 9 seats or less)
8703.2353 01	2 升＜排气量≤2.5 升装点燃往复式活塞内燃发动机小客车(≤9 座)	25	230	17	17	辆	46AOxy	Station wagons (with 9 seats or less) with spark-ignition internal combustion reciprocating piston engine, 2L < cylinder capacity≤2.5L
8703.2353 90	2 升＜排气量≤2.5 升装点燃往复式活塞内燃发动机小客车的成套散件(≤9 座)	25	230	17	17	辆	46AOxy	Complete parts of station wagons (with 9 seats or less) with spark-ignition internal combustion reciprocating piston engine, 2L < cylinder capacity≤2.5L
8703.2359	----其他	25	230	17	17	辆		----Other
8703.2359 01	2 升＜排气量≤2.5 升带点燃往复式活塞内燃发动机的其他载人车辆	25	230	17	17	辆	46AOxy	Other motor vehicles (with 9 seats or less) principally designed for transport of person's with spark-ignition internal combustion reciprocationg piston engine, 2L < cylinder capacity≤2.5L
8703.2359 90	2 升＜排气量≤2.5 升带点燃往复式活塞内燃发动机的其他载人车辆的成套散件	25	230	17	17	辆	46AOxy	Complete parts of other motor vehicles (with 9 seats or less) designed for transport of person's, with spark-ignition internal combustion reciprocating piston engine, 2L < cylinder capacity≤2.5L
	---气缸容量(排气量)超过 2500 毫升,但不超过 3000 毫升:							---Of a cylinder capacity exceeding 2500cc but not exceeding 3000cc:
8703.2361	----小轿车	25	270	17	17	辆		----Saloon cars
8703.2361 01	2.5 升＜排气量≤3 升带点燃往复式活塞内燃发动机小轿车	25	270	17	17	辆	46AOxy	Saloon cars with spark-ignition internal combustion reciprocating piston engine, 2.5L < cylinder capacity≤3L
8703.2361 90	2.5 升＜排气量≤3 升带点燃往复式活塞内燃发动机小轿车的成套散件	25	270	17	17	辆	46Oxy	Complete parts of saloon cars with spark-ignition internal combustion reciprocating piston engine, 2.5L < cylinder capacity≤3L
8703.2362	----越野车(4 轮驱动)	25	270	17	17	辆		----Cross-country cars (4WD)
8703.2362 01	2.5 升＜排气量≤3 升带点燃往复式活塞内燃发动机越野车(4 轮驱动)	25	270	17	17	辆	46AOxy	Cross - country cars (4WD) with spark-ignition internal combustion reciprocating piston engine, 2.5L < cylinder capacity≤3L
8703.2362 90	2.5 升＜排气量≤3 升带点燃往复式活塞内燃发动机越野车的成套散件(4 轮驱动)	25	270	17	17	辆	46Oxy	Complete parts of cross-country cars (4WD) with spark-ignition internal combustion reciprocating piston engine, 2.5L < cylinder capacity≤3L
8703.2363	----9 座及以下的小客车	25	270	17	17	辆		----Station wagons (with 9 seats or less)
8703.2363 01	2.5 升＜排气量≤3 升带点燃往复式活塞内燃发动机的小客车(≤9 座)	25	270	17	17	辆	46AOxy	Station wagons (with 9 seats or less) with spark - ignition internal combustion reciprocating piston engine, 2.5L < cylinder capacity≤3L

税则号列	货品名称	最惠(%)	普通	增值税率	出口退税	计量单位	监管条件	Article Description
8703.2363 90	2.5升<排气量≤3升带点燃往复式活塞内燃发动机小客车的成套散件(≤9座)	25	270	17	17	辆	46Oxy	Complete parts of station wagons(with 9 seats or less) with spark-ignition internal combustion reciporcating piston engine,2.5L<cylinder capacity≤3L
8703.2369	----其他	25	270	17	17	辆		----Other
8703.2369 01	2.5升<排气量≤3升带点燃往复式活塞内燃发动机的其他载人车辆(不包括非4轮驱动越野车)	25	270	17	17	辆	46AOxy	Other motor vehicles principally designed for transport of person's with spark-ignition internal combustion reciprocating piston engine,2.5L<cylinder capacity≤3L
8703.2369 99	2.5<排量≤3升装点燃往复式活塞内燃发动机的其他载人车辆的成套散件(不包括非4轮驱动越野车的成套散件)	25	270	17	17	辆	46Oxy	Complete parts of motor vehicles principally designed for transport of person's with spark-ignition internal combustion reciprocating piston engine, 2.5L<cylinder capacity≤3L(excluding not four wheel drive off-road vehicle)
	---气缸容量(排气量)超过3000毫升,但不超过4000毫升:							---Of a cylinder capacity exceeding 3000cc but not exceeding 4000cc:
8703.2411	----小轿车	25	270	17	17	辆		----Saloon cars
8703.2411 01	3升<排气量≤4升带点燃往复式活塞内燃发动机小轿车	25	270	17	17	辆	46AOxy	Saloon cars with spark-ignition internal combustion reciprocating piston engine,3L<cylinder capacity≤4L
8703.2411 90	3升<排气量≤4升带点燃往复式活塞内燃发动机小轿车的成套散件	25	270	17	17	辆	46AOxy	Complete parts of saloon cars with spark-ignition internal combustion reciprocating piston engine,3L<cylinder capacity≤4L
8703.2412	----越野车(4轮驱动)	25	270	17	17	辆		----Cross-country cars (4WD)
8703.2412 01	3升<排气量≤4升带点燃往复式活塞内燃发动机越野车(4轮驱动)	25	270	17	17	辆	46AOxy	Cross-country cars(4WD) with spark-ignition internal combustion reciprocating piston engine,3L<cylinder capacity≤4L
8703.2412 90	3升<排气量≤4升带点燃往复式活塞内燃发动机越野车的成套散件(4轮驱动)	25	270	17	17	辆	46Oxy	Complete parts of crass-country cars(4WD) with spark-ignition internal combustion reciprocating piston engine,3L<cylinder capacity≤4L
8703.2413	----9座及以下的小客车	25	270	17	17	辆		----Station wagons (with 9 seats or less)
8703.2413 01	3升<排气量≤4升带点燃往复式活塞内燃发动机的小客车(≤9座)	25	270	17	17	辆	46AOxy	Station wagons(with 9 seats or less) with spark-ignition internal cmobustion reciprocating piston engine, 3L<cylinder capacity≤4L
8703.2413 90	3升<排气量≤4升带点燃往复式活塞内燃发动机的小客车的成套散件(≤9座)	25	270	17	17	辆	46AOxy	Complete parts of station wagons(with 9 seats or less) with spark-ignition internal combustion reciprocating piston engine,3<cylinder capacity≤4L
8703.2419	----其他	25	270	17	17	辆		----Other
8703.2419 01	3升<排气量≤4升带点燃往复式活塞内燃发动机的其他载人车辆(不包括非4轮驱动越野车)	25	270	17	17	辆	46AOxy	Other motor vehicles(with 9 seats or less) designed for transport of person's with spark-ignition internal combustion reciprocationg piston engine,3L<cylinder capacity≤4L
8703.2419 99	3<排量≤4升装点燃往复式活塞内燃发动机的其他载人车辆的成套散件(不包括非4轮驱动越野车成套散件)	25	270	17	17	辆	46AOxy	Complete parts of motor vehicles principally designed for transport of person's with spark-ignition internal combustion reciprocating piston engine,3L<cylinder capacity≤4L(excluding not four wheel drive off-road vehicle)
	---气缸容量(排气量)超过4000毫升:							---Of a cylinder capacity exceeding 4000cc:
8703.2421	----小轿车	25	270	17	17	辆		----Saloon cars
8703.2421 01	排气量>4升带点燃往复式活塞内燃发动机小轿车	25	270	17	17	辆	46AOxy	Saloon cars with spark-ignition internal combustion reciprocating piston engine,cylinder capacity>4L
8703.2421 90	排气量>4升带点燃往复式活塞内燃发动机小轿车的成套散件	25	270	17	17	辆	46AOxy	Complete parts of saloon cars with spork-ignition internal combustion reciprocating piston engine,cylinder capacity>4L
8703.2422	----越野车(4轮驱动)	25	270	17	17	辆		----Cross-country cars (4WD)

税则号列	货品名称	最惠(%)	普通	增值税率	出口退税	计量单位	监管条件	Article Description
8703.2422 01	排气量>4升带有点燃往复式活塞内燃发动机越野车(4轮驱动)	25	270	17	17	辆	46AOxy	Cross - country cars with spark - ignition internal combustion reciprocating piston engine, cylinder capacity >4L
8703.2422 90	排气量>4升带点燃往复式活塞内燃发动机越野车的成套散件(4轮驱动)	25	270	17	17	辆	46Oxy	Complete parts of cross-country cars with spark-ignition internal combustion reciprocating piston engine, cylinder capacity >4L
8703.2423	----9座及以下的小客车	25	270	17	17	辆		----Station wagons (with 9 seats or less)
8703.2423 01	排气量>4升带有点燃往复式活塞内燃发动机的小客车(≤9座)	25	270	17	17	辆	46AOxy	Station wagons with spark - ignition internal combustion reciprocating piston engine, cylinder capacity >4L
8703.2423 90	排气量>4升带有点燃往复式活塞内燃发动机的小客车的成套散件(≤9座)	25	270	17	17	辆	46AOxy	Complete parts of station wagons with spark-ignition internal combustion reciporcating piston engine, cylinder capacity >4L
8703.2429	----其他	25	270	17	17	辆		----Other
8703.2429 01	排气量>4升装点燃往复式活塞内燃发动机的其他载人车辆(不包括非4轮驱动越野车)	25	270	17	17	辆	46AOxy	Other motor vehicles designed for transport of person's with spark - ignition internal combustion reciprocating piston engine, cylinder capacity >4L
8703.2429 99	排量>4升装点燃往复式活塞内燃发动机的其他载人车辆的成套散件(不包括非4轮驱动越野车成套散件)	25	270	17	17	辆	46AOxy	Complete parts of motor vehicles principally designed for transport of person's with spark - ignition internal combustion reciprocating piston engine, cylinder capacity >4L(excluding not four wheel drive off - road vehicle)
	-装有压燃式活塞内燃发动机(柴油或半柴油发动机)的其他车辆:							-Other vehicles, with compression-ignition internal combustion piston engine(diesel or semi-diesel):
	--气缸容量(排气量)不超过1500毫升:							--Of a cylinder capacity not exceedlirg 1500cc:
	---气缸容量(排气量)不超过1000毫升:							---Of a cylinder capacity not exceeding 1000 cc:
8703.3111	----小轿车	25	230	17	17	辆		----Saloon cars
8703.3111 01	排气量≤1升带有压燃往复式活塞内燃发动机小轿车	25	230	17	17	辆	46AOxy	Saloon cars with compression-ignition internal combustion piston engine, cyclinder capacity≤1L
8703.3111 90	排气量≤1升带有压燃往复式活塞内燃发动机小轿车的成套散件	25	230	17	17	辆	46AOxy	Complete parts of saloon cars with compression-ignition internal combustion piston engine, cylinder capacity≤1L
8703.3119	----其他	25	230	17	17	辆		----Other
8703.3119 01	排气量≤1升带有压燃往复式活塞内燃发动机其他载人车辆	25	230	17	17	辆	46AOxy	Other motor vehicles designed for transport of person's with compression-ignition internal combustion piston engine, cylinder cpacity≤1L
8703.3119 90	排气量≤1升带有压燃往复式活塞内燃发动机其他载人车辆的成套散件	25	230	17	17	辆	46AOxy	Complete parts of other moter vehicles designed for transport of person's with compression-ignition internal cmobustion piston engine, cylinder capaeity≤1L
	---气缸容量(排气量)超过1000毫升,但不超过1500毫升:							---Of a cylinder capacity exceeding 1000cc but not exceeding 1500cc:
8703.3121	----小轿车	25	230	17	17	辆		----Saloon cars
8703.3121 01	1升<排气量≤1.5升带有压燃往复式活塞内燃发动机小轿车	25	230	17	17	辆	46AOxy	Saloon cars with compression - ignition internal combustion piston engine, 1L < cylinder capacity≤1.5L
8703.3121 90	1升<排气量≤1.5升带有压燃往复式活塞内燃发动机小轿车的成套散件	25	230	17	17	辆	46AOxy	Complete parts of salotn cars with compression-ignition internal combustion piston engine, 1L < cylinder capacity≤1.5L
8703.3122	---越野车(4轮驱动)	25	230	17	17	辆		---Cross-country cars (4WD)
8703.3122 01	1升<排气量≤1.5升带有压燃式活塞内燃发动机越野车(4轮驱动)	25	230	17	17	辆	46AOxy	Cross - country cars(4WD) with compression - ignition internal combustion piston engine, 1L < cylinder capacity≤1.5L
8703.3122 90	1升<排气量≤1.5升带有压燃式活塞内燃发动机越野车的成套散件(4轮驱动)	25	230	17	17	辆	46AOxy	Complete parts of cross-country cars (4WD) with compression-ignition internal combustion piston engine, 1L < cylinder≤1.5L
8703.3123	----9座及以下的小客车	25	230	17	17	辆		----Station wagons (with 9 seats or less)

税则号列	货品名称	最惠(%)	普通	增值税率	出口退税	计量单位	监管条件	Article Description
8703.3123 01	1升<排气量≤1.5升带有压燃往复式活塞内燃发动机小客车(指≤9座)	25	230	17	17	辆	46AOxy	Station wagons(with 9 seats or less) with compression – ignition internal combustion piston engine, 1L < cylinder capacity≤1.5L
8703.3123 90	1升<排气量≤1.5升带有压燃往复式活塞内燃发动机小客车的成套散件(指≤9座)	25	230	17	17	辆	46AOxy	Complate parts of station wagons (with 9 seats or less) with compression-ignition internal combustion piston engine, 1L < cylinder capacity≤1.5L
8703.3129	----其他	25	230	17	17	辆		----Other
8703.3129 01	1升<排气量≤1.5升带有压燃往复式活塞内燃发动机其他载人车辆	25	230	17	17	辆	46AOxy	Other motor vehicles designed for the transport of person's with compression-ignition internal combustion piston engine, 1L < cylinder capacity ≤1.5L
8703.3129 90	1升<排气量≤1.5升带有压燃往复式活塞内燃发动机的其他载人车辆的成套散件	25	230	17	17	辆	46AOxy	Complete parts of other motor vehicles designed for the transport of person's with compression-ignition internal combustion piston engine, 1L < cylinder capacity≤1.5L
	--气缸容量(排气量)超过1500毫升,但不超过2500毫升:							---Of a cylinder capaity exceeding 1500cc but not exceeding 2500cc:
	---气缸容量(排气量)超过1500毫升,但不超过2000毫升:							---Of a cylinder capacity exceeding 1500cc, but not exceeding 2000cc:
8703.3211	----小轿车	25	230	17	17	辆		----Saloon cars
8703.3211 01	1.5升<排气量≤2升带有压燃往复式活塞内燃发动机小轿车	25	230	17	17	辆	46AOxy	Saloon cars with compression-ignition internal combustion piston engine, 1.5L < cylinder capacity ≤2L
8703.3211 90	1.5升<排气量≤2升带有压燃往复式活塞内燃发动机小轿车的成套散件	25	230	17	17	辆	46AOxy	Complete parts of saloon cars with compression-ignition internal combustion piston engine, 1.5L < cylinder capacity≤2L
8703.3212	----越野车(4轮驱动)	25	230	17	17	辆		----Cross-country cars (4WD)
8703.3212 01	1.5升<排气量≤2升带有压燃往复式活塞内燃发动机越野车(4轮驱动)	25	230	17	17	辆	46AOxy	Cross – country cars(4WD) with compression ignition internal combustion piston engine, 1.5L < cylinder capacity≤2L
8703.3212 90	1.5升<排气量≤2升带有压燃往复式活塞内燃发动机四轮驱动越野车的成套散件	25	230	17	17	辆	46AOxy	Complete parts of cross-country cars (4WD) with compression-ignition internal combustion piston engine, 1.5L < cylinder capcity≤2L
8703.3213	----9座及以下的小客车	25	230	17	17	辆		----Station wagons (with 9 seats or less)
8703.3213 01	1.5升<排气量≤2升带有压燃往复式活塞内燃发动机小客车(≤9座)	25	230	17	17	辆	46AOxy	Station wagons with compression – ignition internal combustion piston engine, 1.5L < cylinder capacity ≤2L(with 9 seats or less)
8703.3213 90	1.5升<排气量≤2升带有压燃往复式活塞内燃发动机小客车的成套散件(≤9座)	25	230	17	17	辆	46AOxy	Complete parts of station wagons with compression-ignition internel combustion piston engine, 1.5L < cylinder capacity≤2L(with 9 seats or less)
8703.3219	----其他	25	230	17	17	辆		----Other
8703.3219 01	1.5升<排气量≤2升带有压燃往复式活塞内燃发动机的其他载人车辆	25	230	17	17	辆	46AOxy	Motor cars and other motor vehicles principally designed for the transport of person's with compression-ignition internal combustion piston engine, 1.5L < cylinder capacity ≤2L
8703.3219 90	1.5升<排气量≤2升带有压燃往复式活塞内燃发动机的其他载人车辆的成套散件	25	230	17	17	辆	46AOxy	Complete parts of other motor vehicles principally designed for the transport of persons with compression-ignition internal combustion piston engine, 1.5L < cylinder capacity ≤2L
	---气缸容量(排气量)超过2000毫升,但不超过2500毫升:							---Of a cylinder capacity exceeding 2000cc, but not exceeding 2500cc:
8703.3221	----小轿车	25	230	17	17	辆		----Saloon cars
8703.3221 01	2升<排气量≤2.5升带有压燃往复式活塞内燃发动机小轿车	25	230	17	17	辆	46AOxy	Saloon cars with compression-ignition internal combustion piston engine, 2L < cylinder capacity ≤2.5L
8703.3221 90	2升<排气量≤2.5升带有压燃往复式活塞内燃发动机小轿车的成套散件	25	230	17	17	辆	46AOxy	Complete parts of saloon cars with compression – ignition internal combustion piston engine, 2L < cylinder capacity ≤2.5L

税则号列	货品名称	最惠(%)	普通	增值税率	出口退税	计量单位	监管条件	Article Description
8703.3222	----越野车(4轮驱动)	25	230	17	17	辆		----Cross-country cars (4WD)
8703.3222 01	2升<排气量≤2.5升带有压燃往复式活塞内燃发动机越野车(4轮驱动)	25	230	17	17	辆	46AOxy	Cross – country cars(4WD) with compression – ignition internal combustion piston engine, 2L < cylinder capacity≤2.5L
8703.3222 90	2升<排气量≤2.5升带有压燃往复式活塞内燃发动机越野车的成套散件(4轮驱动)	25	230	17	17	辆	46AOxy	Complete parts of cross-country cars (4WD) with compression-ignition internal combustion piston engine, 2L < cylinder capcity≤2.5L
8703.3223	----9座及以下的小客车	25	230	17	17	辆		----Station wagons (with 9 seats or less)
8703.3223 01	2升<排气量≤2.5升带有压燃往复式活塞内燃发动机的小客车(≤9座)	25	230	17	17	辆	46AOxy	Station wagons with compression – ignition internal combustion piston engine, 2L < cylinder capacity ≤ 2.5L(with 9 seats or less)
8703.3223 90	2升<排气量≤2.5升带有压燃往复式活塞内燃发动机的小客车的成套散件(≤9座)	25	230	17	17	辆	46AOxy	Complete parts of station wagons with compression-ignition internel combustion piston engine, 2L < cylinder capacity≤2.5L(with 9 seats or less)
8703.3229	----其他	25	230	17	17	辆		----Other
8703.3229 01	2升<排气量≤2.5升带有压燃往复式活塞内燃发动机的其他载人车辆	25	230	17	17	辆	46AOxy	Other motor vehicles designed for the transport of person's with compression-ignition internal combustion piston engine, 2L < cylinder capacity ≤2.5L
8703.3229 90	2升<排气量≤2.5升带有压燃往复式活塞内燃发动机的其他载人车辆的成套散件	25	230	17	17	辆	46AOxy	Complete parts of other motor vehicles designed for the transport of person's with compression-ignition internal combustion piston engine, 2L < cylinder capacity ≤2.5L
	--气缸容量(排气量)超过2500毫升:							--Of a cyhinder capacity exceeding 2500cc:
	---气缸容量(排气量)超过2500毫升,但不超过3000毫升:							---Of a cylinder capacity exceeding 2500cc, but not exceeding 3000cc:
8703.3311	----小轿车	25	270	17	17	辆		----Saloon cars
8703.3311 01	2.5升<排气量≤3升带有压燃往复式活塞内燃发动机小轿车	25	270	17	17	辆	46AOxy	Saloon cars with compression-ignition internal combustion piston engine, 2.5L < cylinder capacity ≤3L
8703.3311 90	2.5升<排气量≤3升带有压燃往复式活塞内燃发动机小轿车的成套散件	25	270	17	17	辆	46AOxy	Complete parts of saloon cars with compression – ignition internal combustion piston engine, 2.5L < cylinder capacity ≤3L
8703.3312	----越野车(4轮驱动)	25	270	17	17	辆		----Gross-country cars(4wd)
8703.3312 01	2.5升<排气量≤3升带有压燃往复式活塞内燃发动机越野车(4轮驱动)	25	270	17	17	辆	46AOxy	Cross – country cars(4WD) with compression – ignition internal combustion piston engine, 2.5L < cylinder capacity≤3L
8703.3312 90	2.5升<排气量≤3升带有压燃往复式活塞内燃发动机越野车的成套散件(4轮驱动)	25	270	17	17	辆	46AOxy	Complete parts of cross-country cars (4WD) with compression-ignition internal combustion piston engine, 2.5L < cylinder capacity≤3L
8703.3313	----9座及以下的小客车	25	270	17	17	辆		----Station wagons (with 9 seats or less)
8703.3313 01	2.5升<排气量≤3升带有压燃往复式活塞内燃发动机小客车(≤9座)	25	270	17	17	辆	46AOxy	Station wagons(with 9 seats or less) with compression-ignition internal combustion piston engine, 2.5L < cylinder capacity≤3L
8703.3313 90	2.5升<排气量≤3升带有压燃往复式活塞内燃发动机小客车的成套散件(≤9座)	25	270	17	17	辆	46AOxy	Complate parts of station wagon(with 9 seats or less) with compression-ignition internal combustion piston engine, 2.5L < cylinder capacity≤3L
8703.3319	----其他	25	270	17	17	辆		----Other
8703.3319 01	2.5升<排气量≤3升带有压燃往复式活塞内燃发动机的其他载人车辆(不包括非4轮驱动越野)	25	270	17	17	辆	46AOxy	Other motor vehicles designed for the transport of person's with compression-ignition internal combustion piston engine, 2.5L < cylinder capacity ≤3L
8703.3319 99	2.5<排量≤3升装压燃往复式活塞内燃发动机的其他载人车辆的成套散件(不包括非4轮驱动越野车成套散件)	25	270	17	17	辆	46AOxy	Complete parts of motor vehicles principally designed for transport of person's with compression – ignition internal combustion reciprocating piston engine, 2.5L < cylinder capacity ≤ 3L (excluding not four wheel drive off – road vehicle)

税则号列	货品名称	最惠(%)	普通	增值税率	出口退税	计量单位	监管条件	Article Description
	---气缸容量(排气量)超过3000毫升,但不超过4000毫升:							---Of a cylinder capacity exceeding 3000cc, but not exceeding 4000cc:
8703.3321	----小轿车	25	270	17	17	辆		----Saloon cars
8703.3321 01	3升<排气量≤4升装有压燃往复式活塞内燃发动机小轿车	25	270	17	17	辆	46AOxy	Saloon cars with compression-ignition internal combustion piston engine, 3L < cylinder capacity ≤4L
8703.3321 90	3<排量≤4升装压燃往复式活塞内燃发动机小轿车的成套散件	25	270	17	17	辆	46AOxy	Complate parts of station saloon cars with compression - ignition internal combustion piston egnine, 3L < cylinder capacity≤4L
8703.3322	----越野车(4轮驱动)	25	270	17	17	辆		----Cross-country cars (4WD)
8703.3322 01	3升<排气量≤4升带有压燃往复式活塞内燃发动机越野车(4轮驱动)	25	270	17	17	辆	46AOxy	Cross - country cars(4WD) with compression - ignition internal combustion piston engine, 3L < cylinder capacity≤4L
8703.3322 90	3升<排气量≤4升带有压燃往复式活塞内燃发动机越野车的成套散件(4轮驱动)	25	270	17	17	辆	46AOxy	Complete parts of cross-country cars (4WD) with compression-ignition internal combustion piston engine, 3L < cylinder capacity ≤4L
8703.3323	----9座及以下的小客车	25	270	17	17	辆		----Station wagons (with 9 seats or less)
8703.3323 01	3升<排气量≤4升带有压燃往复式活塞内燃发动机小客车(≤9座)	25	270	17	17	辆	46AOxy	Station wagons (with 9 seats or less) with compression - ignition internal combustion piston engine, 3L < cylinder capacity≤4L
8703.3323 90	3升<排气量≤4升带有压燃往复式活塞内燃发动机小客车的成套散件(≤9座)	25	270	17	17	辆	46AOxy	Complate parts of station wagons (with 9 seats or less) with compression-ignition internal combustion piston engine, 3L < cylinder capacity≤4L
8703.3329	----其他	25	270	17	17	辆		----Other
8703.3329 01	3升<排气量≤4升装有压燃往复式活塞内燃发动机其他载人车辆(不包括非4轮驱动越野车)	25	270	17	17	辆	46AOxy	Other motor vehicles designed for the transport of person's with compression - ignition internal combustion piston engine, 3L < cylinder capacity ≤4L
8703.3329 99	3<排量≤4升装压燃往复式活塞内燃发动机的其他载人车辆的成套散件(不包括非4轮驱动越野车成套散件)	25	270	17	17	辆	46AOxy	Complete parts of motor vehicles principally designed for transport of person's with compression - ignition internal combustion reciprocating piston engine, 3L < cylinder capacity≤4L (excluding not four wheel drive off - road vehicle)
	---气缸容量(排气量)超过4000毫升:							---Of a cylinder capacity exceeding 4000cc:
8703.3361	----小轿车	25	270	17	17	辆		----Saloon cars
8703.3361 01	排气量>4升带有压燃往复式活塞内燃发动机小轿车	25	270	17	17	辆	46AOxy	Saloon cars with compression-ignition internal combustion piston engine, cylinder capacity ≥4L
8703.3361 90	排气量>4升带有压燃往复式活塞内燃发动机小轿车的成套散件	25	270	17	17	辆	46AOxy	Complete parts of saloon cars with compression - ignition internal combustion piston engine, cylinder capacity ≥4L
8703.3362	----越野车(4轮驱动)	25	270	17	17	辆		----Cross-country cars (4WD)
8703.3362 01	排气量>4升带有压燃往复式活塞内燃发动机越野车(4轮驱动)	25	270	17	17	辆	46AOxy	Cross - country cars(4WD) with compression - ignition internal combustion piston engine, cylinder capacity >4L
8703.3362 90	排气量>4升带有压燃往复式活塞内燃发动机越野车的成套散件(4轮驱动)	25	270	17	17	辆	46AOxy	Complete parts of cross-country cars (4WD) with compression-ignition internal combustion piston engine, cylinder capacity >4L
8703.3363	----9座及以下的小客车	25	270	17	17	辆		----Station wagons (with 9 seats or less)
8703.3363 01	排气量>4升装有压燃往复式活塞内燃发动机小客车(指≤9座)	25	270	17	17	辆	46AOxy	Station wagons (with 9 seats or less) with compression-ignition internal combustion piston engine, cylinder capacity >4L
8703.3363 90	排气量>4升带压燃往复式活塞内燃发动机小客车的成套散件(指≤9座)	25	270	17	17	辆	46AOxy	Complete parts of station wagons(with 9 seats or less) with compression-ignition internal combustion piston engine, cylinder capacity >4L
8703.3369	----其他	25	270	17	17	辆		----Other
8703.3369 01	排气量>4升装有压燃往复式活塞内燃发动机其他载人车辆(不包括非4轮驱动越野车)	25	270	17	17	辆	46AOxy	Other motor vehicles designed for the transport of person's with compression - ignition internal combustion piston engine, cylinder capacity >4L

税则号列	货　品　名　称	最惠(%)	普通	增值税率	出口退税	计量单位	监管条件	Article Description
8703.3369 99	排量>4升装压燃往复式活塞内燃发动机其他载人车辆的成套散件(不包括非4轮驱动越野车成套散件)	25	270	17	17	辆	46AOxy	Complete parts of motor vehicles principally designed for transport of person's with compression – ignition internal combustion reciprocating piston engine, cylinder capacity > 4L (excluding not four wheel drive off – road vehicle)
8703.9000	-其他	25	270	17	17	辆		-Other
8703.9000 01	其他型排气量≤1升的其他载人车辆	25	270	17	17	辆	46AOxy	Other motor vehicles designed for transport of person's, cylinder capacity≤1.5L
8703.9000 02	其他型1.5升<排气量≤2升的其他载人车辆	25	270	17	17	辆	46AOxy	Other motor vehicles designed for transport of person's, 1.5L<cylinder capacity≤2L
8703.9000 03	其他型2升<排气量≤2.5升的其他载人车辆	25	270	17	17	辆	46AOxy	Other motor vehicles designed for transport of person's, 2L<cylinder capacity≤2.5L
8703.9000 04	其他型2.5升<排气量≤3升的其他载人车辆(不包括编号8703 9000 14所述小轿车和越野车)	25	270	17	17	辆	46AOxy	Other motor vehicles principally for transport of person's, 2.5L<cylinder capacity≤3L
8703.9000 05	其他型3升<排气量≤4升的其他载人车辆(不包括编号8703 9000 15所述小轿车和越野车)	25	270	17	17	辆	46AOxy	Other motor vehicles designed for transport of person's, 3L<cylinder capacity≤4L
8703.9000 06	其他型排气量>4升的其他载人车辆(不包括编号8703 9000 16所述小轿车和越野车)	25	270	17	17	辆	46AOxy	Other motor vehicles designed for transport of person's, cylinder capacity >4L
8703.9000 07	其他型1升<排气量≤1.5升的其他载人车辆	25	270	17	17	辆	46AOxy	Other motor vehicles designed for transport of person's, 1L<cylinder capacity≤1.5L
8703.9000 10	电动汽车和其他无法区分排气量的载人车辆	25	270	17	17	辆	6AO	Electric vehicles and other motor vehicles designed for transport of person's, can not distinguished cylinder capacity
8703.9000 99	其他型载人车辆的成套散件	25	270	17	17	辆	6AO	Complete parts of motor vehicles designed for transport of person's
87.04	货运机动车辆:							**Motor vehicles for the transport of goods:**
	-非公路用自卸车:							-Dumpers designed for off-highway use:
8704.1030	---电动轮货运自卸车	6	20	17	17	辆	6A	---Electromobile dumpers for the transport of goods
8704.1090	---其他	6	20	17	17	辆	6A	---Other
	-装有压燃式活塞内燃发动机(柴油或半柴油发动机)的其他货车:							-Other, with compression-ignition internal combustion piston engine (diesel or semidiesesl):
8704.2100	--车辆总重量不超过5吨	25	70	17	17	辆	46Axy	--G. v. w. not exceeding 5 tons
	--车辆总重量超过5吨,但不超过20吨:							--G. v. w. exceeding 5 tons but not exceeding 20 tons:
8704.2230	---车辆总重量超过5吨,但小于14吨	20	70	17	17	辆	46Axy	---G. v. w. exceeding 5 tons but notexceeding 14 tons
8704.2240	---车辆总重量在14吨及以上,但不超过20吨	20	40	17	17	辆	46Axy	---G. v. w. of 14 tons or more but not exceeding 20 tons
8704.2300	--车辆总重量超过20吨		40	17	17	辆		--G. v. w. exceeding 20 tons
8704.2300[暂] 10	固井水泥车、压裂车、混砂车、连续油管车、液氮泵车用底盘(车辆总重量>35吨,装驾驶室)	10	40	17	17	辆	46AOxy	Cementing truck, car, fracturing sand mixing truck, coiled tubing unit, liquid nitrogen pump vehicle chassis (gross vehicle weight > 35 tons, installed cab)
8704.2300[暂] 20	起重≥55吨汽车起重机用底盘(装有压燃式活塞内燃发动机)	8	40	17	17	辆	46AOxy	Chassis for crane lorries, lifting capacity≥55tons, with compression-ignition internal combustion piston engine
8704.2300[暂] 30	车辆总重量≥31吨清障车专用底盘	10	40	17	17	辆	46AOxy	Special chassis for wreckers truck with total vehicle G. v. w≥31 tons
8704.2300 90	柴油型的其他超重型货车(装有压燃式活塞内燃发动机,超重型指车辆总重量>20吨)	15	40	17	17	辆	46AOxy	Other overweight truck, with compression-ignition internal combustion piston engine (diesel or semi-diesel, G. v. w>20 tons)

税则号列	货品名称	最惠(%)	普通	增值税率	出口退税	计量单位	监管条件	Article Description
	-装有点燃式活塞内燃发动机的其他货车：							-Other, with spark-ignition internal combustion piston engine:
8704.3100	--车辆总重量不超过5吨	25	70	17	17	辆	46Axy	--G. v. w. not exceeding 5 tons
	--车辆总重量超过5吨：							--G. v. w. exceeding 5 tons:
8704.3230	---车辆总重量超过5吨,但不超过8吨	20	70	17	17	辆	46Axy	---G. v. w. exceeding 5 tons, but not exceeding 8 tons.
8704.3240	---车辆总重量超过8吨	20	70	17	17	辆	46Axy	---G. v. w. exceeding 8 tons
8704.9000	-其他	25	70	17	17	辆	46Axy	-Other
87.05	特殊用途的机动车辆(例如,抢修车、起重车、救火车、混凝土搅拌车、道路清洁车、喷洒车、流动工场车及流动放射线检查车),但主要用于载人或运货的车辆除外：							**Special purpose motor vehicles, other than those principally designed for the transport of persons or goods (for example, breakdown lorries, crane lorries, fire fighting vehicles, concrete-mixer lorries, road sweeper lorries, spraying lorries, mobile workshops, mobile radiological units):**
	-起重车：							-Crane lorries:
	---全路面起重车：							---All-road crane lorries:
8705.1021	----最大起重重量不超过50吨	15	30	17	17	辆	6A	----Of a maxium lifting capacity not more than 50tons
8705.1022	----最大起重重量超过50吨,但不超过100吨	10	30	17	17	辆	6A	----Of a maxium lifting capacity exceeding 50tons but not exceeding 100tons
8705.1023	----最大起重重量超过100吨	10	30	17	17	辆	6A	----Of a maxium lifting capacity exceeding 100tons
	---其他：							---Other:
8705.1091	----最大起重重量不超过50吨	15	30	17	17	辆	6A	----Of a maxium lifting capacity not more than 50tons
8705.1092	----最大起重重量超过50吨,但不超过100吨	10	30	17	17	辆	6A	----Of a maxium lifting capacity exceeding 50tons but not exceeding 100 tons
8705.1093	----最大起重重量超过100吨	10	30	17	17	辆	6A	----Of a maxium lifting capacity exceeding 100 tons
8705.2000	-钻探车	12	17	17	17	辆	6A	-Mobile drilling derricks
	-救火车：							-Fire fighting vehicles:
8705.3010	---装有云梯的救火车	3	8	17	17	辆	A6	---Mounted with scaling ladder
8705.3090	---其他	3	8	17	17	辆	A6	---Other
8705.4000	-混凝土搅拌车	15	35	17	17	辆	A6	-Concrete-mixer lorries
	-其他：							-Other:
8705.9010	---无线电通信车	9	35	17	17	辆	A6	---Radio communication vans
8705.9020	---放射线检查车	9	14	17	17	辆	6A	---Mobile radiological units
8705.9030	---环境监测车	12	20	17	17	辆	6A	---Mobile environmental monitoring units
8705.9040	---医疗车	12	30	17	17	辆	6A	---Mobile clinics
	---电源车：							---Mobile electric generator sets:
8705.9051	----航空电源车(频率为400赫兹)	12	30	17	17	辆	6	----Airplane charging vehicles (frequency 400Hz)
8705.9059	----其他	12	30	17	17	辆	6A	----Other
8705.9060	---飞机加油车、调温车、除冰车	12	35	17	17	辆	A6	---Mobile vehicles for aircraft refuelling, air-conditioning or deicing
8705.9070	---道路(包括跑道)扫雪车	12	35	17	17	辆	A6	---Snow sweep vehicles for cleansing streets or airfield runways
8705.9080	---石油测井车、压裂车、混沙车	12	35	17	17	辆	A6	---Petrolcum well logging trucks, fracturing unit trucks and mixing sand trucks
	---其他：							---Other:
8705.9091	----混凝土泵车	12	35	17	17	辆/千克	A6	----Truck mounted concrete pump
8705.9099	----其他		35	17	17	辆/千克		----Other
8705.9099[暂] 01	跑道除冰车	10	35	17	17	辆/千克	A6	Runway deicing vehicle
8705.9099 30	用于导弹、火箭等的车辆(为弹道导弹、运载火箭等运输、装卸和发射而设计的)	12	35	17	17	辆/千克	36A	Vehicles for carrying missiles or rockets (specially designed for transporting, handling and launching of ballistic missiles or carrier rockets)
8705.9099 90	其他特殊用途的机动车辆(主要用于载人或运货的车辆除外)	12	35	17	17	辆/千克	A6	Other special purpose motor vehicles (other than those principally designed for the transport of person's or goods)

税则号列	货品名称	最惠(%)	普通	增值税率	出口退税	计量单位	监管条件	Article Description
87.06	**装有发动机的机动车辆底盘，税目87.01至87.05所列车辆用：**							**Chassis fitted with engines, for the motor vehicles of headings No. 87.01 to 87.05:**
8706.0010	---非公路用自卸车底盘	8	14	17	17	台	6	---Chassis fitted of off-highway dumpers
	---货车底盘：							---Chassis fitted of trucks
8706.0021	----车辆总重量在14吨及以上的	10	30	17	17	台	46AOxy	----For vehicles g. v. w of 14tons or more:
8706.0022	----车辆总重量在14吨以下的	10	45	17	17	台	46AOxy	----For vehicles g. v. w less than 14 tons
8706.0030	---大型客车底盘	20	70	17	17	台	46Oxy	---For passenger motor vehicles with 30 seats or more
8706.0040	---汽车起重机底盘	20	100	17	17	台	6AO	---For crane lorries
8706.0090	---其他	10	100	17	17	台	46AOxy	---Other
87.07	**机动车辆的车身（包括驾驶室），税目87.01至87.05所列车辆用：**							**Bodies (including cabs), for the motor vehicles of headings No. 87.01 to 87.05:**
8707.1000	-税目87.03所列车辆用	10	100	17	17	台	6O	-For the vehicles of headingNo. 87.03
	-其他：							-Other:
8707.9010	---税目8702.1092、8702.1093、8702.9020及8702.9030所列车辆用	10	70	17	17	台	6O	---For the vehicles of subheadingNo. 8702.1092、8702.1093、8702.9020 or 8702.9030
8707.9090	---其他	10	70	17	17	台	6O	---Other
87.08	**机动车辆的零件、附件，税目87.01至87.05所列车辆用：**							**Parts and accessories of the motor vehicles of headings No. 87.01 to 87.05:**
8708.1000	-缓冲器（保险杠）及其零件	10	100	17	17	千克	6	-Bumpers and parts thereof
	-车身（包括驾驶室）的其他零件、附件：							-Other parts and accessories of bodies (including cabs):
8708.2100	--座椅安全带	10	100	17	17	千克	6A	--Safety seat belts
	--其他：							--Other:
8708.2930	---车窗玻璃升降器	10	100	17	15	千克	6	---Windowpane raiser
	---天窗：							---Sunroofs:
8708.2941	----电动的	10	100	17	17	千克/套	6	----Electric
8708.2942	----手动的	10	100	17	17	千克/套	6	----Hand-operated
	---其他车身覆盖件：							---Other covered parts of bodies:
8708.2951	----侧围	10	100	17	17	千克	6	----Side appearance of bodies
8708.2952	----车门	10	100	17	17	千克/个	6	----doors
8708.2953	----发动机罩盖	10	100	17	17	千克	6	----Bonnets
8708.2954	----前围	10	100	17	17	千克	6	----Frontal appearance of bodies
8708.2955	----行李箱盖（或背门）	10	100	17	17	千克	6	----Rear compartment covers(or rear door)
8708.2956	----后围	10	100	17	17	千克	6	----Rear appearance of bodies
8708.2957	----翼子板（或叶子板）	10	100	17	17	千克	6	----Running-boards
8708.2959	----其他	10	100	17	17	千克	6	----Other
8708.2990	---其他	10	100	17	17	千克	6	---Other
	-制动器、助力制动器及其零件：							-Brakes and servo-brakes and parts thereof:
8708.3010	---装在蹄片上的制动摩擦片	10	100	17	17	千克	6	---Mounted brake linings
	---防抱死制动系统（ABS）：							---Anti-skid brake system:
8708.3021	----子目号87.01、8704，1030及8704.1090所列车辆用	6	11	17	17	千克	6	----Of the rehicles of heading 87.01、8704,1030 and 8704.1090
8708.3029	----其他	10	100	17	17	千克	6	----Other
	---其他：							---Other:
8708.3091	----税目87.01所列车辆用	6	14	17	17	千克	6	----Of the vehicles of heading No. 87.01
8708.3092	----子目号8702.1091及8702.9010所列车辆用	10	70	17	17	千克	6	----Of the vehicles of subheading No. 8702.1091 and 8702.9010
8708.3093	----子目号8704.1030及8704.1090所列车辆用	6	11	17	17	千克	6	----Of the vehicles of subheading No. 8704.1030 and 8704.1090
8708.3094	----子目号8704.2100、8704.2230、8704.3100及8704.3230所列车辆用	10	45	17	17	千克	6	----Of the vehicles of subheading No. 8704.2100, 8704.2230, 8704.3100 and 8704.3230
8708.3095	----子目号8704.2240、8704.2300及8704.3240所列车辆用	10	30	17	17	千克	6	----Of the vehicles of subheading No. 8704.2240, 8704.2300 and 8704.3240
8708.3096	----税目87.05所列车辆用	10	100	17	17	千克	6	----Of the vehicles of heading No. 87.05
8708.3099	----其他车辆用	10	100	17	17	千克		----Other

税则号列	货品名称	最惠(%)	普通	增值税率	出口退税	计量单位	监管条件	Article Description
8708.3099暂 11	纯电动或混合动力汽车用电动制动器(由制动器电子控制单元、踏板行程模拟器、制动执行器等组成)	5	100	17	17	千克/个	60	Electric brake for pure electric or hybrid vehicles (electronic control unit, composed of a brake pedal travel simulator, the brake actuator etc.)
8708.3099 19	其他机动车辆用制动器(包括助力制动器)	10	100	17	17	千克/个	60	Brakes of other vehicles (including booster brake)
8708.3099 90	其他机动车辆用制动器(包括助力制动器)的零件	10	100	17	17	千克/个	6	Parts of brakes for other motor vehicles (including servo-brakes)
	-变速箱及其零件:							-Gear boxes and parts thereof:
8708.4010	---税目87.01所列车辆用	6	14	17	17	个/千克	6	---Of the vehicles of heading of No. 87.01
8708.4020	---子目号8702.1091及8702.9010所列车辆用	10	70	17	17	个/千克	6	---Of the vehicles of subheading No. 8702.1091 and 8702.9010
8708.4030	---子目号8704.1030及8704.1090所列车辆用		11	17	17	个/千克		---Of the vehicles of subheading No. 8704.1030 and 8704.1090
8708.4030暂 01	扭矩>1500Nm非公路自卸车用变速箱	3	11	17	17	个/千克	6	Gear boxes for off-highway dumpers use, troque > 1500mm
8708.4030 90	其他非公路自卸车用变速箱及其零件	6	11	17	17	个/千克	6	Other gear boxes and parts for off-highway dumpers use
8708.4040	---子目号8704.2100、8704.2230、8704.3100及8704.3230所列车辆用	10	45	17	17	个/千克	6	---Of the vehicles of subheading No. 8704.2100, 8704.2230, 8704.3100 and 8704.3230
8708.4050	---子目号8704.2240、8704.2300及8704.3240所列车辆用	10	30	17	17	个/千克	6	---Of the vehicles of subheading No. 8704.2240, 8704.2300 and 8704.3240
8708.4060	---税目87.05所列车辆用	10	100	17	17	个/千克	6	---Of the vehicles of heading No. 87.05
	---其他:							---Other:
8708.4091	----小轿车用自动换挡变速箱及其零件		100	17	17	个/千克		----Automatic gearshift for saloon cars and parts thereof
8708.4091暂 01	小轿车用自动换挡变速箱(6挡及6挡以上)	6.5	100	17	17	个/千克	60	Automatic gearshift for saloon car (with the excluding of hydraulic machines with 6 or fewer sears)
8708.4091暂 04	小轿车用自动换挡变速箱的零件(6挡及6挡以上)	6.5	100	17	17	个/千克	6	Automatic gearshift other parts for saloon cars (with the exception of hydraulic machines with 6 or fewer gears)
8708.4091 91	其他小轿车用自动换挡变速箱	10	100	17	17	个/千克	60	Other automatic gearshift for saloon cars
8708.4091 99	其他小轿车用自动换挡变速箱的零件	10	100	17	17	个/千克	6	Parts of automatic gearshift for saloon cars
8708.4099	----其他	10	100	17	17	个/千克		----Other
8708.4099 10	其他未列名机动车辆用变速箱	10	100	17	17	个/千克	60	Other gearboxes for other not else where specified vehicles
8708.4099 90	其他未列名机动车辆用变速箱的零件	10	100	17	17	个/千克	6	Spare parts for gearboxes for other not elsewhere specified vehicles
	-装有差速器的驱动桥及其零件,不论是否装有其他传动部件;非驱动桥及其零件:							-Drive-axles with differential, whether or not provided with other transmission components and non-driving axles and parts thereof:
	---装有差速器的驱动桥及其零件,不论是否装有其他传动部件:							---Drive-axles with differential and part thereof, whether or not provided with other transmission components:
8708.5071	----税目87.01所列车辆用	6	14	17	17	个/千克	6	----Of the vehicles of heading No. 87.01
8708.5072	----子目号8702.1091及8702.9010所列车辆用		70	17	17	个/千克		----Of the vehicles of subheading No. 8702.1091 and 8702.9010
8708.5072暂 01	轴荷≥10吨的中后驱动桥的零件	8	70	17	17	个/千克	6	Parts of middle and rear drive-axles and parts thereof, axle loading capacity≥10t
8708.5072 91	其他大型客车用驱动桥(装有差速器的,不论是否装有其他传动件)	10	70	17	17	个/千克	60	Other drive-axles for other buses (with differential, whether or not provided with other transmission components)

税则号列	货品名称	最惠(%)	普通	增值税率	出口退税	计量单位	监管条件	Article Description
8708.5072 99	其他大型客车用驱动桥的零件(装有差速器的,不论是否装有其他传动件)	10	70	17	17	个/千克	6	Parts of drive - axles with differential for other large buses(whether or not provided with other transmission components)
8708.5073	----子目号 8704.1030 及 8704.1090 所列车辆用	6	11	17	17	个/千克	6	----Of the vehicles of subheading No. 8704.1030 and 8704.1090
8708.5074	----子目号 8704.2100、8704.2230、8704.3100 及 8704.3230 所列车辆用	10	45	17	17	个/千克		----Of the vehicles of subheading No. 8704.2100, 8704.2230, 8704.3100 and 8704.3230
8708.5074 10	柴、汽油型轻型货车用驱动桥(8704.2100,2230,3100,3230 所列总重量≤14 吨车辆用,装差速器)	10	45	17	17	个/千克	60	Drive-axles for diesel oil and gasoline light trucks (used by ≤14 ton vehicles listed in 8707.2100, 2300,3100 and 3230 and with differential gears)
8708.5074 90	柴、汽油型轻型货车用驱动桥的零件(8704.2100,2230,3100,3230 所列总重量≤14 吨车辆用,装差速器)	10	45	17	17	个/千克	6	Parts of drive-axles for diesel oil and gasoline light trucks(used by ≤14 tons vehicles of subheading No. 8707.2100,2300,3100 and 3230 and with differential)
8708.5075	----子目号 8704.2240、8704.2300 及 8704.3240 所列车辆用	10	30	17	17	个/千克		----Of the vehicles of subheading No. 8704.2240, 8704.2300 and 8704.3240
8708.5075 10	其他柴、汽油型重型货车用驱动桥(指编号 87042240,87042300 及 87043240 所列车辆用)	10	30	17	17	个/千克	60	Drive-axles for other diesel oil and gasoline heavy trucks (referring to vehicles subheading No. 87042240,87042300 and 87043240)
8708.5075 90	其他柴、汽油型重型货车用驱动桥的零件(指编号 87042240,87042300 及 87043240 所列车辆用)	10	30	17	17	个/千克	6	Parts of drive-axles bridges for other diesel oil and gasoline heavy trucks (referring to vehicles subheading No. 87042240,87042300 and 87043240)
8708.5076	----税目 87.05 所列车辆用	10	100	17	17	个/千克		----Of the vehicles of heading No. 87.05
8708.5076 10	特种车用驱动桥(指 8705 所列车辆用,装有差速器,不论是否装有其他传动件)	10	100	17	17	个/千克	60	Drive-axles for special vehicles(referring to vehicles of heading No. 8705, with differential, whether or not provided transmussion components)
8708.5076 90	特种车用驱动桥的零件(指 8705 所列车辆用,装有差速器,不论是否装有其他传动件)	10	100	17	17	个/千克	6	Parts of drive-axles for special vehicles(referring to vehicles of heading No. 8705, with differential, whether or not provided transmussion components)
8708.5079	----其他	10	100	17	17	个/千克		----Other
8708.5079 10	未列名机动车辆用驱动桥(装有差速器的,不论是否装有其他传动件)	10	100	17	17	个/千克	60	Drive-axles for unlisted motor vehicles (with differential, whether or not provided transmussion components)
8708.5079 90	未列名机动车辆用驱动桥的零件(装有差速器的,不论是否装有其他传动件)	10	100	17	17	个/千克	6	Parts of drive-axles of unlisted motor vehicles (with differential, whether or not provided transmussion components)
	---非驱动桥及其零件:							---Non-driving axles and parts thereof:
8708.5081	----税目 87.01 所列车辆用	6	14	17	17	千克	6	----Of the vehicles of heading No. 87.01
8708.5082	----子目号 8702.1091 及 8702.9010 所列车辆用	15	70	17	17	千克	6	----Of the vehicles of subheading No. 8702.1091 and 8702.9010
8708.5083	----子目号 8704.1030 及 8704.1090 所列车辆用	6	11	17	17	千克	6	----Of the vehicles of subheading No. 8704.1030 and 8704.1090
8708.5084	----子目号 8704.2100、8704.2230、8704.3100 及 8704.3230 所列车辆用	10	45	17	17	千克	6	----Of the vehicles of subheading No. 8704.2100, 8704.2230, 8704.3100 and 8704.3230
8708.5085	----子目号 8704.2240、8704.2300 及 8704.3240 所列车辆用	10	30	17	17	千克	6	----Of the vehicles of subheading No. 8704.2240, 8704.2300 and 8704.3240
8708.5086	----税目 87.05 所列车辆用	10	100	17	17	千克	6	----Of the vehicles of heading No. 87.05
8708.5089	----其他	10	100	17	17	千克		----Other
8708.5089 10	未列名机动车辆用非驱动桥	10	100	17	17	千克/个	60	Non - drive-axles for not specified motor vehicles
8708.5089 90	未列名机动车辆用非驱动桥的零件	10	100	17	17	千克/个	6	Parts of non - drive-axles for not specified motor vehicles
	-车轮及其零件、附件:							-Road wheels and parts and accessories thereof:
8708.7010	---子目号 87.01 所列车辆用	6	14	17	17	千克	6	---Of the vehicles of heading No. 87.01
8708.7020	---子目号 8702.1091 及 8702.9010 所列车辆用	10	70	17	17	千克	6	---Of the vehicles of subheadings No. 8702.1091 and 8702.9010

税则号列	货品名称	最惠(%)	普通	增值税率	出口退税	计量单位	监管条件	Article Description
8708.7030	---子目8704.1030及8704.1090所列车辆用	6	11	17	17	千克	6	---Of the vehicles of subheadings No. 8704.1030 and 8704.1090
8708.7040	---子目8704.2100、8704.2230、8704.3100及8704.3230所列车辆用	10	45	17	17	千克	6	---Of the vehicles of subheadings No. 8704.2100, 8704.2230, 8704.3100 and 8704.3230
8708.7050	---子目8704.2240、8704.2300及8704.3240所列车辆用	10	30	17	17	千克	6	---Of the vehicles of subheadings No. 8704.2240, 8704.2300 and 8704.3240
8708.7060	---税目87.05所列车辆用	10	100	17	17	千克	6	---Of the vehicles of heading No. 87.05
	---其他:							---Other:
8708.7091	----铝合金制的	10	100	17	17	千克	6	----Of aluminium alloy
8708.7099	----其他	10	100	17	17	千克	6	----Other
	-悬挂系统及其零件(包括减振器):							-Suspension systems and parts there of (in-cluding shock-absorbers):
8708.8010	---税目87.03所列车辆用	10	100	17	17	千克	6	---Of the vehicles of heading No. 87.03
8708.8090	---其他	10	100	17	17	千克	6	---Other
	-其他零件、附件:							-Other parts and accessories:
	--散热器及其零件:							--Radiators and parts therof:
8708.9110	---水箱散热器	10	100	17	17	个/千克	6	---Water tank radiators
8708.9120	---机油冷却器	10	100	17	17	个/千克	6	---Oil coolers
8708.9190	---其他	10	100	17	17	个/千克	6	---Other
8708.9200	--消声器(消音器)排气管及零件	10	100	17	17	千克	6	--Silencers (mufflers) and exhaust pipes, parts therof
	--离合器及其零件:							--Clutches and parts thereof:
8708.9310	---税目87.01所列车辆用	6	14	17	17	千克	6	---Of the vehicles of heading No. 87.01
8708.9320	---子目8702.1091及8702.9010所列车辆用	10	70	17	17	千克	6	---Of the vehicles of subheadings No. 8702.1091 and 8702.9010
8708.9330	---子目号8704.1030及8704.1090所列车辆用	6	11	17	17	千克	6	---Of the vehicles of subheadings No. 8704.1030 and 8704.1090
8708.9340	---子目8704.-2100、8704.-2230、8704.3100及8704.3230所列车辆用	10	45	17	17	千克	6	---Of the vehicles of subheadings No. 8704.2100, 8704.2230, 8704.3100 and 8704.3230
8708.9350	---子目号8704.2240、8704.2300及8704.3240所列车辆用	10	30	17	17	千克	6	---Of the vehicles of subheadings No. 8704.2240, 8704.2300 and 8704.3240
8708.9360	---税目87.05所列车辆用	10	100	17	17	千克	6	---Of the vehicles of heading No. 87.05
8708.9390	---其他	10	100	17	17	千克	6	---Other
	--转向盘、转向柱及转向器及其零件:							--Steering wheels, steering columns and steering bo-xes parts thereof:
8708.9410	---税目87.01所列车辆用	6	14	17	17	千克	6	---Of the vehicles of heading No. 87.01
8708.9420	---子目8702.1091及8702.9010所列车辆用		70	17	17	千克		---Of the vehicles of subheadings No. 8702.1091 and 8702.9010
8708.9420[暂] 01	座位≥30位的客车用转向器零件	8	70	17	17	千克	6	Parts of steering boxes for the buses with 30 seats or more
8708.9420 90	大型客车用其他转向盘、转向柱及其零件(包括转向器)	10	70	17	17	千克	6	Other steering wheels, steering columns and parts thereof for large buses
8708.9430	---子目号8704.1030及8704.1090所列车辆用	6	11	17	17	千克	6	---Of the vehicles of subheadings No. 8704.1030 and 8704.1090
8708.9440	---子目号8704.2100、8704.2230、8704.3100及8704.3230所列车辆用	10	45	17	17	千克	6	---Of the vehicles of subheadings No. 8704.2100, 8704.2230, 8704.3100 and 8704.3230
8708.9450	---子目号8704.2240、8704.2300及8708.3240所列车辆用		30	17	17	千克		---Of the vehicles of subheadings No. 8704.2240, 8704.2300 and 8704.3240
8708.9450[暂] 01	总重≥14吨柴油型货车转向器的零件	8	30	17	17	千克	6	Redirector components of diesel oil trucks whose weight≥14 tons
8708.9450 90	其他重型货车用转向盘、转向柱、转向器及其零件(指编号87042240、87042300及87043240所列车辆用)	10	30	17	17	千克	6	Steering wheels, steering columns, steering boxes and parts thereof for the vehicles of subheading No. 8704.2240, 8704.2300 and 8704.3240
8708.9460	---税目87.05所列车辆用转向器	10	100	17	17	千克	6	---Of the vehicles of heading No. 87.05
8708.9490	---其他		100	17	17	千克		---Other

税则号列	货品名称	最惠(%)	普通	增值税率	出口退税	计量单位	监管条件	Article Description
8708.9490[暂] 01	采用电动转向系统的转向盘、转向柱、转向器及其零件	8	100	17	17	千克	6	Steering wheels, steering columns, steering boxes and thereof parts, with electric power steering system
8708.9490 90	其他未列名机动车辆用转向盘、转向柱及其零件(包括转向器)	10	100	17	17	千克	6	Steering wheels, steering columns, steering gears and thereof parts for other unlisted motor vehicles
8708.9500	--带充气系统的安全气囊及其零件	10	100	17	17	千克	6	--Safety air-bags with inflater system; parts thereof
	--其他:							--Other:
8708.9910	---税目87.01所列车辆用	6	14	17	17	千克	6	---Of the vehicles of heading No. 87.01
	---子目号8702.1091及8702.9010所列车辆用:							---Of the vehicles of subheadings No. 8702.1091 and 8702.9010:
8708.9921	----车架	25	70	17	17	千克	6	----Frames
8708.9929	----其他	25	70	17	17	千克	6	----Other
	---子目8704.1030及8704.1090所列车辆用:							---Of the vehicles of subheading No. 8704.1030 and 8704.1090:
8708.9931	----车架	6	11	17	17	千克	6	----Frames
8708.9939[暂]	----其他	3	11	17	17	千克	6	----Other
	---子目8704.2100、8704.2230、8704.3100及8704.3230所列车辆用:							---Of the vehicles of subheadings No. 8704.2100, 8704.2230, 8704.3100 and 8704.3230:
8708.9941	----车架	25	45	17	17	千克	6	----Frames
8708.9949	----其他	25	45	17	17	千克	6	----Other
	---子目8704.2240、8704.2300及8704.3240所列车辆用:							---Of the vehicles of subheadings No. 8704.2240, 8704.2300 and 8704.3240:
8708.9951	----车架	10	30	17	17	千克	6	----Frames
8708.9959	----其他	10	30	17	17	千克	6	----Other
8708.9960	---税目87.05所列车辆用	15	100	17	17	千克	6	---Of the vehicles of heading No. 87.05
	---其他:							---Other:
8708.9991	----车架	10	100	17	17	千克/个	60	----Frames
8708.9992	----传动轴	10	100	17	17	千克	6	----Transmission shafts
8708.9999	----其他		100	17	17	千克		----Other
8708.9999[暂] 10	混合动力汽车动力传动装置及其零件(由发电机、电动机和动力分配装置等组成,编号8701至8704所列车辆用)	6	100	17	17	千克	6	Transmission device of hybrid electric vehicle and part (made of generators, motor and power spilt device, of vehicles of subheading No. 8701 to 8704)
8708.9999 90	机动车辆用未列名零件、附件(编号8701至8704所列车辆用)	10	100	17	17	千克	6	Parts and accessories of motor vehicles, not elsewhere specified or included (of the vehicles of subheading No. 87.01 to 87.04)
87.09	**短距离运输货物的机动车辆,未装有提升或搬运设备,用于工厂、仓库、码头或机场;火车站台上用的牵引车;上述车辆的零件:**							**Works trucks, self-propelled, not fitted with lifting or handling equipment, of the type used in factories, warehouses, dock areas or airports for short distance transport of goods; tractors of the type used on railway station platforms; parts of the foregoing vehicles:**
	-车辆:							-Vehicles:
	--电动的:							--Electrical:
8709.1110	---牵引车	10	30	17	15	辆	6	---Tractors
8709.1190	---其他	10	30	17	15	辆	6	---Other
	--其他:							--Other:
8709.1910	---牵引车	10.5	30	17	15	辆	6	---Tractors
8709.1990	---其他	10.5	30	17	15	辆	6	---Other
8709.9000	-零件	8.4	17	17	15	千克	6	-Parts
87.10	**坦克及其他机动装甲战斗车辆,不论是否装有武器;上述车辆的零件:**							**Tanks and other armoured fighting vehicles, motorized, whether or not fitted with weapons, and parts of such vehicles:**
8710.0010	---整车	15	100	17		辆	6	---Assembled
8710.0090	---零件	15	100	17		千克	6	---Parts and accessories
87.11	**摩托车(包括机器脚踏两用车)及装有辅助发动机的脚踏车,不论有无边车;边车:**							**Motorcycles (including mopeds) and cycles fitted with an auxiliary motor, with or without side-cars; side-cars:**

税则号列	货 品 名 称	最惠(%)	普通	增值税率	出口退税	计量单位	监管条件	Article Description
8711.1000	-装有往复式活塞内燃发动机,气缸容量(排气量)不超过50毫升	45	150	17	15	辆		-With reciprocating internal combustion piston engine of a cylinder capacity not exceeding 50 cc
8711.1000 10	微马力摩托车及脚踏两用车(装有往复式活塞发动机,微马力指排气量=50cc)	45	150	17	15	辆	y4xA6	Micro horsepower motorcycles and mopeds(with reciprocating internal combustion piston engine, micro horsep ower cylinder capacity =50cc)
8711.1000 90	微马力摩托车及脚踏两用车(装有往复式活塞发动机,微马力指排气量<50cc)	45	150	17	15	辆	6A	Micro horsepower motorcycles and mopeds(with reciprocating internal combustion piston engine, micro horsepower cylinder capacity <50cc)
	-装有往复式活塞内燃发动机,气缸容量(排气量)超过50毫升,但不超过250毫升							-With reciprocating internal combustion piston engine of a cylinder capacity exceeding 50 cc but not exceeding 250cc
8711.2010	---气缸容量超过50毫升,但不超过100毫升	45	150	17	15	辆	y4xA6	---Of a cylinder capacity exceeding 50cc but not exceeding 100cc
8711.2020	---气缸容量超过100毫升,但不超过125毫升	45	150	17	15	辆	y4xA6	---Of a cylinder capacity exceeding 100cc but not exceeding 125cc
8711.2030	---气缸容量超过125毫升,但不超过150毫升	45	150	17	15	辆	y4xA6	---Of a cylinder capacity exceeding 125cc but not exceeding 150cc
8711.2040	---气缸容量超过150毫升,但不超过200毫升	45	150	17	15	辆	y4xA6	---Of a cylinder capacity exceeding 150cc < but not exceeding 200cc
8711.2050	---气缸容量超过200毫升,但不超过250毫升	45	150	17	15	辆		---Of a cylinder capacity exceeding 200cc < but not exceeding 250cc
8711.2050 10	200<排气量<250毫升装往复式活塞内燃发动机摩托车及脚踏两用车	45	150	17	15	辆	46Axy	200 < < 250 ml loaded exhaust volume of reciprocating piston internal combustion engine for motorcycles and mopeds
8711.2050 90	排气量=250毫升装往复式活塞内燃发动机摩托车及脚踏两用车	45	150	17	15	辆	46Axy	Displacement = 250 ml with reciprocating internal combustion piston engine for motorcycles and mopeds
	-装有往复式活塞内燃发动机,气缸容量(排气量)超过250毫升,但不超过500毫升:							-With reciprocating internal combustion piston engine of a cylinder capacity exceeding 250cc but not exceeding 500cc:
8711.3010	---气缸容量超过250毫升,但不超过400毫升	45	150	17	15	辆	46Axy	---Of a cylinder capacity exceeding 250cc but not exceeding 400cc
8711.3020	---气缸容量超过400毫升,但不超过500毫升	45	150	17	15	辆	46Axy	---Of a cylinder capacity exceeding 400cc but not exceeding 500cc
8711.4000	-装有往复式活塞内燃发动机,气缸容量(排气量)超过500毫升,但不超过800毫升	40	150	17	15	辆	46Axy	-With reciprocating internal combustion piston engine of a cylinder capacity exceeding 500 cc < but not exceeding 800 cc
8711.5000	-装有往复式活塞内燃发动机,气缸容量(排气量)超过800毫升	30	150	17	15	辆	46Axy	-With reciprocating internal combustion piston engine of a cylinder capacity exceeding 800 cc
	-其他:							-Other:
8711.9010	---电动及电动助力的	45	150	17	15	辆		---Electric or with electrical assistant
8711.9010 10	电动自行车	45	150	17	15	辆	A6	Electric bicycle
8711.9010 90	其他电动及电动助力的摩托车及边车(包括机器脚踏两用车;脚踏车)	45	150	17	15	辆	A6	Other electric and electric auxiliary motorcycles and side-cars (incldling mopeds, bicycle)
8711.9090	---其他	45	150	17	15	辆		---Other
8711.9090 01	排气量≤250毫升摩托车及脚踏两用车	45	150	17	15	辆	6A	Motorcycles and mopedes, cylinder capacity≤250cc
8711.9090 02	排气量>250毫升摩托车及脚踏两用车	45	150	17	15	辆	6A	Motorcycles and mopedes, cylinder capacity >250cc
8711.9090 09	其他无法区分排气量的摩托车及脚踏两用车	45	150	17	15	辆	6A	Other motorcycles and mopedes, of can not distinction cylinder capacity
8711.9090 90	装有其他辅助发动机的脚踏车及边车	45	150	17	15	辆	6A	Motor-assisted bicycle and side-cars
87.12	自行车及其他非机动脚踏车(包括运货三轮脚踏车):							**Bicycles and other cycles (including delivery tricycles), not motorized:**
8712.0020	---竞赛型自行车	13	130	17	15	辆	6	---Racing bicycle

税则号列	货品名称	最惠(%)	普通	增值税率	出口退税	计量单位	监管条件	Article Description
8712.0030	---山地自行车	13	130	17	15	辆	6	---Mountain bicycle
	---越野自行车:							---Cross-country bicycles:
8712.0041	----16、18、20英寸	13	130	17	15	辆	6	----16inchs, 18inchs and 20inchs
8712.0049	----其他	13	130	17	15	辆	6	----Other
	---其他自行车:							---Other cycles:
8712.0081	----16英寸及以下	13	130	17	15	辆		----Not larger than 16inchs
8712.0081 10	12~16英寸的未列名自行车	13	130	17	15	辆	6	Bicycles, 12inches~16inches, not elsewhere specified or included
8712.0081 90	11英寸及以下的未列名自行车	13	130	17	15	辆	6	Bicycles, 11inchs or less, not elsewhere specified or included
8712.0089	----其他	13	130	17	15	辆	6	----Other
8712.0090	---其他	23	130	17	15	辆	6	---Other
87.13	**残疾人用车,不论是否机动或其他机械驱动:**							**Carriages for disabled persons, whether or not motorised or otherwise mechanically propelled:**
8713.1000	-非机械驱动	6	20	0	15	辆	6	-Not mechanically propelled
8713.9000	-其他	4	20	0	15	辆	6	-Other
87.14	**零件、附件,税目87.11至87.13所列车辆用:**							**Parts and accessories of vehicles of headings No. 87.11 to 87.13:**
8714.1000	-摩托车(包括机器脚踏两用车)用		100	17	15	千克		-Of motorcycles (including mopeds)
8714.1000暂 01	星型轮及碟刹件	10	100	17	15	千克	6	Star-shaped wheels and disc brakes
8714.1000 10	摩托车架	30	100	17	15	千克	46xy	Frams of motorcycles
8714.1000 90	摩托车其他零件,附件(包括机动脚踏两用车的零件、附件)	30	100	17	15	千克	6	Other parts and accessories thereof, of motorcycles and mopeds
8714.2000	-残疾人车辆用	5	17	17	15	千克	6	-Of carriages for disabled persons
	-其他:							-Other:
8714.9100	--车架、轮叉及其零件	12	80	17	15	千克	6	--Frames and forks, and parts thereof
	--轮圈及辐条:							--Wheel rims and spokes:
8714.9210	---轮圈	12	80	17	15	千克	6	Wheel rims
8714.9290	---辐条	12	80	17	15	千克	6	Spokes
	--轮毂(倒轮制动毂及毂闸除外);飞轮、链轮:							--Hubs, other than coaster braking hubs and hub brakes, and free-wheel, sprocket wheels:
8714.9310	---轮毂	12	80	17	15	千克	6	---Hubs
8714.9320	---飞轮	12	80	17	15	千克	6	---Free-wheel
8714.9390	---其他	12	80	17	15	千克	6	---Other
8714.9400	--制动器(包括倒轮制动毂及毂闸)及其零件	12	80	17	15	千克	6	--Brakes, including coaster braking hubs and hub brakes, and parts thereof
8714.9500	--鞍座	12	80	17	15	千克/个	6	--Saddles
	--脚蹬、曲柄链轮及其零件:							--Pedals and crank-gear, and parts thereof:
8714.9610	---脚蹬及其零件	12	80	17	15	千克	6	---Pedals and parts thereof
8714.9620	---曲柄链轮及其零件	12	80	17	15	千克	6	---Crank-gear and parts thereof
8714.9900	--其他	12	80	17	15	千克	6	--Other
87.15	**婴孩车及其零件:**							**Baby carriages and parts thereof:**
8715.0000	婴孩车及其零件	20	80	17	15	千克	6AB	Baby carriages and parts thereof
87.16	**挂车及半挂车或其他非机械驱动车辆及其零件:**							**Trailers and semi-trailers; other vehicles, not mechanically propelled; parts thereof:**
8716.1000	-供居住或野营用厢式挂车及半挂车	10	35	17	15	辆	6	-Trailers and semi-trailers of the caravan type, for housing or camping
8716.2000	-农用自装或自卸式挂车及半挂车	10	35	17	13,15	辆	6	-Self-loading or self-unloading trailers and semi-trailers for agricultural purposes
	-其他货运挂车及半挂车:							-Other trailers and semi-trailers for the transport of goods:
	--罐式挂车及半挂车:							--Tanker trailers and tanker semi-trailers:
8716.3110	---油罐挂车及半挂车	10	20	17	15	辆	6A	---Oil tanker trailers and semi-trailers
8716.3190	---其他	10	35	17	15	辆	6A	---Other
	--其他:							--Other:

税则号列	货品名称	最惠(%)	普通	增值税率	出口退税	计量单位	监管条件	Article Description
8716.3910	---货柜挂车及半挂车	10	20	17	15	辆	6A	---Van trailers and semi-trailers
8716.3990	---其他	10	35	17	15	辆	6A	---Other
8716.4000	-其他挂车及半挂车	10	35	17	15	辆	6A	-Other trailers and semi-trailers
8716.8000	-其他车辆	10	80	17	15	辆	6	-Other vehicles
8716.9000	-零件	10	35	17	15	千克	6	-Parts

第八十八章
航空器、航天器及其零件

Chapter 88
Aircraft, spacecraft, and parts thereof

子目注释：

子目 8802.11 至 8802.40 所称"空载重量"，是指航空器在正常飞行状态下，除去机组人员、燃料及非永久性安装设备后的重量。

Subheading Note:

For the purposes of subheadings Nos. 8802.11 to Nos. 8802.40, the expression "unladen weight" means the weight of the machine in normal flying order, excluding the weight of the crew and of fuel and equipment other than permanently fitted items of equipment.

税则号列	货品名称	最惠(%)	普通	增值税率	出口退税	计量单位	监管条件	Article Description
88.01	气球及飞艇；滑翔机、悬挂滑翔机及其他无动力航空器：							**Balloons and dirigibles; gliders, hang gliders and other non-powered aircraft:**
8801.0010	---滑翔机、及悬挂滑翔机：	3	11	17	17	架		---Cliders and hang gliders
8801.0090	---其他	3	11	17	17	架		---Other
88.02	**其他航空器（例如，直升机、飞机）；航天器（包括卫星）及其运载工具、亚轨道运载工具：**							**Other aircraft (for example, helicopters, aeroplanes); spacecraft (including satellites) and suborbital and spacecraft launch vehicles:**
	-直升机：							-Helicopters:
8802.1100	--空载重量不超过 2000 千克	2	11	17	17	架	O	--Of an unladen weight not exceeding 2000kg
	--空载重量超过 2000 千克：							--Of an unladen weight exceeding 2000kg:
8802.1210	---空载重量超过 2000 千克，但不超过 7000 千克	2	11	17	17	架	O	---Of an unladen weight exceeding 2000kg but not exceeding 7000kg
8802.1220	---空载重量超过 7000 千克	2	11	17	17	架	O	---Of an unladen weight exceeding 7000kg
8802.2000	-飞机及其他航空器，空载重量不超过 2000 千克	5	11	17	17	架		-Aeroplanes and other aircraft, of an unladen weight not exceeding 2000kg
8802.2000 10	无人驾驶航空飞行器（空载重量小于 2000 千克）	5	11	17	17	架	30	Pilotless aircraft (unladen weight ≤2000kg)
8802.2000 90	其他小型飞机及其他航空器（小型指空载重量不超过 2000 千克的）	5	11	17	17	架		Other small planes and other aircrafts (unladen weight≤2000kg)
8802.3000	-飞机及其他航空器，空载重量超过 2000 千克，但不超过 15000 千克	4	11	17	17	架	O	-Aeroplanes and other aircraft, of an unladen weight exceeding 2000kg but not exceeding 15000kg
	-飞机及其他航空器，空载重量超过 15000 千克：							-Aeroplanes and other aircraft, of an unladen weight exceeding 15000kg:
8802.4010	---空载重量超过 15000 千克，但不超过 45000 千克	5	11	17	17	架	O	---Of an unladen weight exceeding 15000kg but not exceeding 45000kg
8802.4020	---空载重量超过 45000 千克	1	11	17	17	架	O	---Of an unladen weight exceeding 45000kg
8802.6000	-航天器（包括卫星）及其运载工具、亚轨道运载工具	2	11	17	17	架		-Spacecraft (including satellites) and suborbital and spacecraft launch vehicles
88.03	**税目 88.01 或 88.02 所列货品的零件：**							**Parts of goods of heading No. 88.01 or 88.02:**
8803.1000	-推进器、水平旋翼及其零件	1	11	17	17	千克		-Propellers and rotors and parts thereof
8803.2000	-起落架及其零件	1	11	17	17	千克		-Under-carriages and parts thereof
8803.3000	-飞机及直升机的其他零件	1	11	17	17	千克		-Other parts of aeroplanes or helicopters
8803.9000	-其他	0	11	17	17	千克		-Other
8803.9000 10	两用物项管制的火箭及其零部件	0	11	17	17	千克	3	Missile and parts and accessories thereof, of sensitive items control
8803.9000 90	其他未列名的航空器、航天器零件（指编号 8801 或 8802 所列货品用的）	0	11	17	17	千克		Parts of other aircraft, sfacecraft, not elsewhere specified or included (parts of goods of heading No. 88.01 or 88.02)
88.04	**降落伞（包括可操纵降落伞及滑翔伞）、旋翼降落伞及其零件、附件：**							**Parachutes (including dirigible parachutes and paragliders) and rotochutes; parts thereof and accessories thereto:**
8804.0000	降落伞（包括可操纵降落伞及滑翔伞）、旋翼降落伞及其零件、附件	2	11	17	17	千克		Parachutes (including dirigible parachutes and paragliders) and rotochutes; parts thereof and accessories thereto
88.05	**航空器的发射装置、甲板停机装置或类似装置和地面飞行训练器及其零件：**							**Aircraft launching gear; deck-arrestor or similar gear; ground flying trainers; parts of the foregoing articles:**

税则号列	货 品 名 称	最惠(%)	普通	增值税率	出口退税	计量单位	监管条件	Article Description
8805.1000	-航空器的发射装置及其零件;甲板停机装置或类似装置及其零件	1.5	11	17	17	千克		-Aircraft launching gear and parts thereof; deck-arrestor or similar gear and parts thereof
	-地面飞行训练器及其零件:							-Ground flying trainers and parts thereof:
8805.2100	--空战模拟器及其零件	1.5	11	17	17	千克		--Air combat simulators and parts thereof
8805.2900	--其他	1.5	11	17	17	千克	O	--Other

第八十九章
船舶及浮动结构体

Chapter 89
Ships, boats and floating structures

注释:

已装配、未装配或已拆卸的船体、未完工或不完整的船舶以及未装配或已拆卸的完整船舶,如果不具有某种船舶的基本特征,应归入税目 89.06。

Note:

A hull, an unfinished or incomplete vessel, assembled, unassembled or disassembled, or a complete vessel unassembled or disassembled, is to be classified in heading No. 89.06 if it does not have the essential character of a vessel of a particular kind.

税则号列	货品名称	最惠(%)	普通	增值税率	出口退税	计量单位	监管条件	Article Description
89.01	巡航船、游览船、渡船、货船、驳船及类似的客运或货运船舶:							**Cruise ships, excursion boats, ferry-boats, cargo ships, barges and similar vessels for the transport of persons or goods:**
	-巡航船、游览船及主要用于客运的类似船舶;各式渡船:							-Cruise ships, excursion boats and similar vessels principally designed for the transport of persons; ferry-boats of all kinds:
8901.1010	---机动船舶	5	14	17	17	艘		---Motor vessels
8901.1010 10	高速客船(包括主要用于客运的类似船舶)	5	14	17	17	艘	O	High-speed passenger vessels (similar vessels principally designed for the transport of persons)
8901.1010 90	其他机动巡航船游览船及各式渡船(包括主要用于客运的类似船舶)	5	14	17	17	艘	O	Other cruise ships, excursion boats ferry – boats of all kinds (similar vessels principally designed for the transport of persons)
8901.1090	---非机动船舶	8	30	17	17	艘		---Other
	-液货船:							-Tankers:
	---成品油船:							---Finished oil tankers:
8901.2011	----载重量不超过 10 万吨	9	14	17	17	艘	O	----Loading not exceeding 100000t
8901.2012	----载重量超过 10 万吨,但不超过 30 万吨	9	14	17	17	艘		----Loading exceeding 100000t, but not exceeding 300000t
8901.2013	----载重量超过 30 万吨	6	14	17	17	艘		----Loading exceeding 300000t
	---原油船:							---Crude oil tankers
8901.2021	----载重量不超过 15 万吨	9	14	17	17	艘	O	----Loading not exceeding 150000t
8901.2022	----载重量超过 15 万吨,但不超过 30 万吨	9	14	17	17	艘		----Loading exceeding 150000t, but not exceeding 300000t
8901.2023	----载重量超过 30 万吨	6	14	17	17	艘		----Loading exceeding 300000t
	---液化石油气船:							---Liquified petroleum gas carriers:
8901.2031	----容积在 20000 立方米及以下	9	14	17	17	艘	O	----Volume with 20000m^3 or less
8901.2032	----容积在 20000 立方米以上	6	14	17	17	艘		----Volume more than 20000m^3
	---液化天然气船:							---Liquified natural gas carriers:
8901.2041	----容积在 20000 立方米及以下	9	14	17	17	艘		----Volume with 20000m^3 or less
8901.2042	----容积在 20000 立方米以上	6	14	17	17	艘		----Volume more than 20000m^3
8901.2090	---其他	9	14	17	17	艘	O	---Other
8901.3000	-冷藏船,但子目 8901.20 的船舶除外	9	14	17	17	艘		-Refrigerated vessels, other than those of subheading No. 8901.20
	-其他货运船舶及其他客货兼运船舶:							-Other vessels for the transport of goods and other vessels for the transport of both persons and goods:
	---机动集装箱船:							---Motor container vessels:
8901.9021	----可载标准集装箱在 6000 箱及以下	9	14	17	17	艘	O	----Capable loading standard containers with 6000 or less
8901.9022	----可载标准集装箱在 6000 箱以上	6	14	17	17	艘		----Capable loading standard containers more than 6000
	---机动滚装船:							---Motor Ro-Ro carriers:
8901.9031	----载重量在 2 万吨及以下	9	14	17	17	艘	O	----Loading with 20000t or less
8901.9032	----载重量在 2 万吨以上的	6	14	17	17	艘		----Loading more than 20000t
	---机动散货船:							---Motor bulk carriers:
8901.9041	----载重量不超过 15 万吨	9	14	17	17	艘	O	----Loading not exceeding 150000t
8901.9042	----载重量超过 15 万吨,但不超过 30 万吨	9	14	17	17	艘		----Loading exceeding 150000t, not exceeding 300000t
8901.9043	----载重量超过 30 万吨	9	14	17	17	艘		----Loading exceeding 300000t
8901.9050	---机动多用途船	9	14	17	17	艘	O	---Multi-purposes motor vessels

税则号列	货 品 名 称	最惠(%)	普通	增值税率	出口退税	计量单位	监管条件	Article Description
8901.9080	---其他机动船舶	9	14	17	17	艘	O	---Other motor vessels
8901.9090	---非机动船舶	8	30	17	15,17	艘	O	---Other non-motor vessels
89.02	**捕鱼船;加工船及其他加工保藏鱼类产品的船舶:**							**Fishing vessels; factory ships and other vessels for processing or preserving fishery products:**
8902.0010	---机动船舶	7	14	17	17	艘	O	---Motor vessels
8902.0090	---非机动船舶	8	30	17	13,17	艘		---Other
89.03	**娱乐或运动用快艇及其他船舶;划艇及轻舟:**							**Yachts and other vessels for pleasure or sports; rowing boats and canoes:**
8903.1000	-充气的	10	30	17	15	艘		-Inflatable
	-其他:							-Other:
8903.9100	--帆船,不论是否装有辅助发动机	8	30	17	15	艘		--Sailboats, with or without auxiliary motor
8903.9100 01	8 米 < 长度 < 90 米的机动帆船	8	30	17	15	艘		Motor vessels, 8m < length < 90m
8903.9100 90	其他帆船(不论是否装有辅助发动机)	8	30	17	15	艘		Other sailboats (with or without auxiliary motor)
8903.9200	--汽艇,但装有舷外发动机的除外	10.5	30	17	15	艘		--Motorboats, other than outboard motorboats
8903.9200 01	8 米 < 长度 < 90 米的汽艇(装有舷外发动机的除外)	10.5	30	17	15	艘		Motorboats, 8m < length < 90m (other than outboard motorboats)
8903.9200 90	其他汽艇(装有舷外发动机的除外)	10.5	30	17	15	艘		Other motorboats (other than outboard motorboats)
8903.9900	--其他	10	30	17	15	艘		--Other
8903.9900 01	8 米 < 长度 < 90 米的娱乐或运动用其他机动船舶或快艇	10	30	17	15	艘		Yachts and other vessels for pleasure or sports, 8m < length < 90m
8903.9900 90	娱乐或运动用其他船舶或快艇(包括划艇及轻舟)	10	30	17	15	艘		Other yachts and other vessels for pleasure or sports (including rowing boats and canoes)
89.04	**拖轮及顶推船:**							**Tugs and pusher craft:**
8904.0000	拖轮及顶推船	9	14	17	17	艘	O	Tugs and pusher craft
89.05	**灯船、消防船、挖泥船、起重船及其他不以航行为主要功能的船舶;浮船坞;浮动或潜水式钻探或生产平台:**							**Light-vessels, fire-floats, dredgers, floating cranes, and other vessels the navigability of which is subsidiary to their main function; floating docks; floating or submersible drilling or roduction platforms:**
8905.1000	-挖泥船	3	11	17	17	艘	O	-Dredgers
8905.2000	-浮动或潜水式钻探或生产平台	6	11	17	17	座	O	-Floating or submersible drilling or production platforms
	-其他:							-Other:
8905.9010	---浮船坞	8	30	17	17	个	O	---Floating docks
8905.9090	---其他	3	11	17	17	个	O	---Other
89.06	**其他船舶,包括军舰及救生船,但划艇除外:**							**Other vessels, including warships and lifeboats other than rowing boats:**
8906.1000	-军舰	5	14	17	17	艘		-Warships
	-其他:							-Other:
8906.9010	---机动船舶	5	14	17	17	艘		---Motor vessels
8906.9020	---非机动船舶	8	30	17		艘		---Not-motorized vessels
8906.9030	---未制成或不完整的船舶,包括船舶分段	8	30	17		艘		---Unfinished or incomplete vessels, including subsections of vessels
89.07	**其他浮动结构体(例如,筏、柜、潜水箱、浮码头、浮筒及航标):**							**Other floating structures (for example, rafts, tanks, coffer-dams, landing-stages, buoys and beacons):**
8907.1000	-充气筏	8	30	17	15	艘		-Inflatable rafts
8907.9000	-其他	8	30	17	15	个		-Other
8907.9000 10	含植物性材料的浮动结构体(例如,筏、柜、潜水箱、浮筒及航标)	8	30	17	15	个		Floating structures (for example, rafts, tanks, coffer-dams, buoys and beacons) with parts of vegetable materials
8907.9000 90	其他浮动结构体(例如,筏、柜、潜水箱、浮筒及航标)	8	30	17	15	个		Other floating structures (for example, rafts, tanks, coffer-dams, buoys and beacons)
89.08	**供拆卸的船舶及其他浮动结构体:**							**Vessels and other floating structures for breaking up:**
8908.0000	供拆卸的船舶及其他浮动结构体	3	11	17	15	艘/千克	ABP	Vessels and other floating structures for breaking up

第十八类
光学、照相、电影、计量、检验、医疗或外科用仪器及设备、精密仪器及设备；钟表；乐器；上述物品的零件、附件

第九十章
光学、照相、电影、计量、检验、医疗或外科用仪器及设备、精密仪器及设备；上述物品的零件、附件

注释：

一、本章不包括：

（一）机器、设备或其他专门技术用途的硫化橡胶（硬质橡胶除外）制品（税目 40.16）、皮革或再生皮革制品（税目 42.04）或纺织材料制品（税目 59.11）；

（二）纺织材料制的承托带及其他承托物品，其承托器官的作用仅依靠自身的弹性（例如，孕妇用的承托带，用于胸部、腹部、关节或肌肉的承托绷带）（第十一类）；

（三）税目 69.03 的耐火材料制品；税目 69.09 的实验室、化学或其他专门技术用途的陶瓷器；

（四）税目 70.09 的未经光学加工的玻璃镜及税目 83.06 或第七十一章的非光学元件的贱金属或贵金属制的镜子；

（五）税目 70.07、70.08、70.11、70.14、70.15 或 70.17 的货品；

（六）第十五类注释二所规定的贱金属制通用零件（第十五类）或塑料制的类似品（第三十九章）；

（七）税目 84.13 的装有计量装置的泵；计数和检验用的衡器或单独进口或出口的天平砝码（税目 84.23）；升降、起重及搬运机械（税目 84.25 至 84.28）；纸张或纸板的各种切割机器（税目 84.41）；税目 84.66 的用于机床上调整工件或工具的附件，包括具有读度用的光学装置的附件（例如，“光学”分度头），但其本身主要是光学仪器的除外（例如，校直望远镜）；计算机器（税目 84.70）；税目 84.81 的阀门及其他装置；税目 84.86 的机器及装置（包括将电路图投影或绘制到感光半导体材料上的装置）；

SECTION XVIII
OPTICAL, PHOTOGRAPHIC, CINEMATOGRAPHIC, MEASURING, CHECKING, PRECISION, MEDICAL OR SURGICAL INSTRUMENTS AND APPARATUS; CLOCKS AND WATCHES; MUSICAL INSTRUMENTS; PARTS AND ACCESSORIES THEREOF

Chapter 90
Optical, photographic, cinematographic, measuring, checking, precision, medical or surgical instruments and apparatus; parts and accessories thereof

Notes:

1. This Chapter does not cover:

(a) Articles of a kind used in machines, appliances or for other technical uses, of vulcanized rubber other than hard rubber (heading No. 40.16), of leather or of composition leather (heading No. 42.05) or of textile material (heading No. 59.11);

(b) Supporting belts or other support articles of textile material, whose intended effect on the organ to be supported or held derives solely from their elasticity (for example, maternity belts, thoracic support bandages, abdominal support bandages, supports for joints or muscles) (Section XI);

(c) Refractory goods of heading No. 69.03; ceramic wares for laboratory, chemical or other technical uses, of heading No. 69.09;

(d) Glass mirrors, not optically worked, of heading No. 70.09, or mirrors of base metal or of precious metal, not being optical elements (heading No. 83.06 or Chapter 71);

(e) Goods of heading No. 70.07, 70.08, 70.11, 70.14, 70.15 or 70.17;

(f) Parts of general use, as defined in Note 2 to Section XV, of base metal (Section XV) or similar goods of plastics (Chapter 39);

(g) Pumps incorporating measuring devices, of heading No. 84.13; weight-operated counting or checking machinery, or separately presented weights for balances (heading No. 84.23); lifting or handling machinery (headings No. 84.25 to 84.28); paper or paperboard cutting machines of all kinds (heading No. 84.41); fittings for adjusting work or tools on machine-tools, of heading No. 84.66, including fittings with optical devices for reading the scale (for example, "optical" dividing heads) but not those which are in themselves essentially optical instruments (for example, alignment telescopes); calculating machines (heading No. 84.70); valves or other appliances of heading 84.81; machines and apparats (including opparatus for the projection or dralving of circuit pattern on sensitized semiconductor materials) of heading 84.86.

（八）自行车或机动车辆用探照灯或聚光灯（税目85.12）；税目85.13的手提式电灯；电影录音机、还音机及转录机（税目85.19）；拾音头或录音头（税目85.22）；电视摄像机、及数字照相机视频摄录一体机（税目85.25）；雷达设备、无线电导航设备或无线电遥控设备（税目85.26）；光导纤维、光导纤维束或光缆用连接器（税目85.36）；税目85.37的数控制装置；税目85.39的封闭式聚光灯；税目85.44的光缆；

（九）税目94.05的探照灯及聚光灯；

（十）第九十五章的物品；

（十一）容量的计量器具（按其构成的材料归类）；

（十二）卷轴、线轴及类似芯子（按其构成材料归类，例如，归入税目39.23或第十五类）。

二、除上述注释一另有规定的以外，本章各税目所列机器、设备、仪器或器具的零件、附件，应按下列规定归类：

（一）凡零件、附件本身已构成本章或第八十四章、第八十五章或第九十一章各税目（税目84.87、85.48或90.33除外）所包括的货品，应一律归入其相应的税目；

（二）其他零件、附件，如果专用于或主要用于某种或同一税目项下的多种机器、仪器或器具（包括税目90.10、90.13或90.31的机器、仪器或器具），应归入相应机器、仪器或器具的税目；

（三）所有其他零件、附件均应归入税目90.33。

三、第十六类注释三、四也适用于本章。

四、税目90.05不包括武器用望远镜瞄准具、潜艇或坦克上的潜望镜式望远镜及本章或第十六类的机器、设备、仪器或器具用的望远镜；这类望远镜瞄准具及望远镜应归入税目90.13。

五、计量或检验用的光学仪器、器具或机器，如果既可归入税目90.13，又可归入税目90.31，则应归入税目90.31。

六、税目90.21所称“矫形器具”，是指下列用途的器具：

预防或矫正人体畸变；

生病、手术或受伤后人体部位的支撑或固定；

矫形器具包括用于矫正畸形的鞋及特种鞋垫，但需符合下列任一条件：

1. 定制的

2. 成批生产的、单独报验、且不成双的、设计为左右两脚同样适用。

(h) Searchlights or spotlights of a kind used for cycles or motor vehicles (heading No. 85.12); portable electric lamps of heading 85.13; cinematographic sound recording, reproducing or re-recording apparatus (heading No. 85.19); sound-heads (heading No. 85.22); television cameras digital cameras and video camera retorders (heading No. 85.25) radar apparatus, radio navigational aid apparatus or radio remote control apparatus (heading No. 85.26); coneltors for optical fibres optical fibre bundles or cables (heading 85.36); numerical control apparatus of heading No. 85.37; sealed beam lamp units of heading No. 85.39; optical fibre cables of heading No. 85.44;

(i) Searchlights or spotlights of heading No. 94.05;

(j) Articles of Chapter 95;

(k) Capacity measures, which are to be classified according to their constituent material;

(l) Spools, reels or similar supports (which are to be classified according to their constituent material, for example, in heading No. 39.23 or Section XV).

2. Subject to Note 1 above, parts and accessories for machines, apparatus, instruments or articles of this Chapter are to be classified according to the following rules:

(a) Parts and accessories which are goods included in any of the headings of this Chapter or of Chapter 84, 85 or 91 (other than heading No. 84.87, 87.48 or 90.33) are in all cases to be classified in their respective headings;

(b) Other parts and accessories, if suitable for use solely or principally with a particular kind of machine, instrument or apparatus, or with a number of machines, instruments or apparatus of the same heading (including a machine, instrument or apparatus of heading No. 90.10, 90.13 or 90.31) are to be classified with the machines, instruments or apparatus of that kind;

(c) All other parts and accessories are to be classified in heading No. 90.33.

3. The provisions of Notes 3 and 4 to Section Ⅲ or ⅩⅥ apply also to this Chapter.

4. Heading No. 90.05 does not apply to telescopic sights for fitting to arms, periscopic telescopes for fitting to submarines or tanks, or to telescopes for machines, appliances, instruments or apparatus of this Chapter of Section ⅩⅦ; such telescopic sights and telescopes are to be classified in heading No. 90.13.

5. Measuring or checking optical instruments, appliances or machines which, but for this Note, could be classified both in heading No. 90.13 and in heading No. 90.31 are to be classified in heading No. 90.31.

6. For the purposes of heading No. 90.21, the expression "orthopaedic appliances" means appliances for:

Preventing or correcting bodily deformities;

Supporting or holding parts of the body following an illness, operation or injury.

Orthopaedic appliances include footwear and special insoles designed to correct orthopaedic conditions, provided that they are either:

(1) made to measure or

(2) mass-produced, presented singly. and not in pairs and designed to fit either foot equally

七、税目90.32仅适用于：

（一）液体或气体的流量、液位、压力或其他变化量的自动控制仪器及装置或温度自动控制装置，不论其是否依靠要被自控的因素所发生的电现象来进行工作，这些仪器或装置将被自控因素调到并保持在一设定值上，通过持续或定期测量实际值来保持稳定，修正偏差；

（二）电量自动调节器及自动控制非电量的仪器或装置，依靠要被控制的因素所发生的电现象来进行工作，这些仪器或装置将被控制的因素调到并保持在一设定值上，通过持续或定期测量实际值来保持稳定，修正偏差。

7. Heading No. 90.32 applies only to:

(a) Instruments and apparatus for automatically controlling the flow, level, pressure or other variables of liquids or gases, or for automatically controlling temperature, whether or not their operation depends on an electrical phenomenon which varies according to the factor to be automatically controlled; which are designed to bring this factor to, and maintain it at, a desired value, stabilised against disturbances, by constantly or periodically measuring its actual value;

(b) Automatic regulators of electrical quantities, and instruments or apparatus for automatically controlling non-electrical quantities the operation of which depends on an electrical phenomenon varying according to the factor to be controlled, which are designed to bring this factor to, and maintain it at, a desired value, stabilised against disturbances, by constantly or periodically measuring its actual value.

税则号列	货品名称	最惠(%)	普通	增值税率	出口退税	计量单位	监管条件	Article Description
90.01	**光导纤维及光导纤维束；光缆，但税目85.44的货品除外；偏振材料制的片及板；未装配的各种材料制透镜（包括隐形眼镜片）、棱镜、反射镜及其他光学元件，但未经光学加工的玻璃制上述元件除外：**							**Optical fibres and optical fibre bundles; optical fibre cables, other than those of heading No 85.44; sheets and plates of polarizing material; lenses (including contact lenses), prisms, mirrors and other optical elements, of any material, unmounted, other than such elements of glass not optically worked:**
9001.1000	-光导纤维、光导纤维束及光缆	5	20	17	15	千克		-Optical fibres, optical fibre bundles and cables
9001.1000 01	非色散位移单模光纤（G.652，包括G652A、G652B、G652C、G652D等）	5	20	17	15	千克		Dispersion-unshifted single-mode fibers (G.652 including G652A、G652B、G652C、G652D)
9001.1000 02	其他单模光纤	5	20	17	15	千克		Other single - mode fibers
9001.1000 09	其他光导纤维（但编号8544的货品除外）	5	20	17	15	千克		Other optical fibres (other than goods of heading No. 85.44)
9001.1000 90	光导纤维束及光缆（但编号8544的货品除外）	5	20	17	15	千克		Optical fibres bundles and cables (other than goods of heading No. 85.44)
9001.2000	-偏振材料制的片及板		20	17	15	千克		-Sheets and plates of polarizing material
9001.2000[暂] 02	液晶投射仪用偏光板	6	20	17	15	千克		Plates of polarizing material for LCD projector
9001.2000[暂] 03	数字电影放映机用偏光板	6	20	17	15	千克		Plates of polarizing material for digital film projector
9001.2000 90	其他偏振材料制的片及板	8	20	17	15	千克		Other sheets and plates of polarizing material
9001.3000[暂]	-隐形眼镜片	6	70	17	15	片		-Contact lenses
	-玻璃制眼镜片：							-Spectacle lenses of glass:
9001.4010[暂]	---变色镜片	15	90	17	15	片		---Photochromic
	---其他：							---Other:
9001.4091	----太阳镜片	20	90	17	15	片		----For sunglasses
9001.4099	----其他	20	70	17	15	片		----Other
	-其他材料制眼镜片：							-Spectacle lenses of other materials:
9001.5010[暂]	---变色镜片	15	90	17	15	片		---Photochromic
	---其他：							---Other:
9001.5091	----太阳镜片	20	90	17	15	片		----For sunglasses
9001.5099[暂]	----其他	12	70	17	15	片		----Other
	-其他：							-Other:
9001.9010	---彩色滤光片	8	20	17	15	千克		---Color filter
9001.9090	---其他		20	17	15	千克		---Other
9001.9090[暂] 01	光通信用微光组件的光学元件（包括波长800—1700nm薄膜滤光片，自聚焦透镜，法拉第旋转片）	0	20	17	15	千克		Optical elements of micro-optical assemblies for optical communications (thin film filters with working wave-length 800nm ~ 1700nm, automatic selfoc lens, faraday rotation isolator)
9001.9090[暂] 02	微型镜片（激光视盘机激光收发装置用）	3	20	17	15	千克		Micro-lens (laser transceiver devices for laser video disc)
9001.9090[暂] 03	非涅耳透镜投影屏（屏幕对角线≥80英寸，投射比≤0.26，增益比≥0.8，镜头间距≤100微米）	6	20	17	15	千克		Fresnel lens projection screen (screen diagonal ≥ 80 inches, projection ratio ≤ 0.26, gain ratio ≥ 0.8, lens spacing ≤ 100 micron)

税则号列	货品名称	最惠(%)	普通	增值税率	出口退税	计量单位	监管条件	Article Description
9001.9090暂 04	液晶显示屏背光模组的光学元件(包括导光板、反射板、扩散片、增亮片)	2	20	17	15	千克		Optical components for back-light modules of LCD (induding light guide baffle-boord, diffusion sheet, brightening sheet)
9001.9090暂 05	液晶投影仪用偏光元件	6	20	17	15	千克		Polarizer for LCD projector
9001.9090暂 06	数字电影放映机用偏光元件	6	20	17	15	千克		Polarizing element with digital movie projector
9001.9090 90	编号9001未列名的其他光学元件(未经光学加工的玻璃制元件除外)	8	20	17	15	千克		Other optical elements, not specified or included elsewhere in the heading No. 9001 (other than of glass made elements not optically processed)
90.02	**已装配的各种材料制透镜、棱镜、反射镜及其他光学元件,作为仪器或装置的零件、配件,但未经光学加工的玻璃制上述元件除外:**							**Lenses, prisms, mirrors and other optical elements, of any material, mounted, being parts of or fittings for instruments or apparatus, other than such elements of glass not optically worked:**
	-物镜:							-Objective lenses:
	--照相机、投影仪、照片放大机及缩片机用:							--For cameras, projectors or photographic enlargers or reducers:
9002.1110	---子目号9006.1010至9006.3000所列照相机用	8	14	17	15	千克/个		---For the photographic cameras of subheadings No. 9006.1010 to 9006.3000
9002.1120	---缩微阅读机用	8	14	17	15	千克/个		---For microfilm, microfiche or other microform readers
	---其他照相机用:							---For other cameras:
9002.1131暂	----单反相机镜头	3	80	17	15	千克/个		----Lens for single lens reftex cameras
9002.1131暂 10	单反相机镜头(整机)	3	80	17	15	千克/个		SLR camera lens (machine)
9002.1131暂 90	单反相机镜头的零件及附件	3	80	17	15	千克/个		Parts and accessories of SLR camera lens
9002.1139暂	----其他	3	80	17	15	千克/个		----Other
9002.1190	---其他		80	17	15	千克/个		---Other
9002.1190暂 10	彩色投影机和数字光处理器的镜头及镜头组件	3	80	17	15	千克/个		Lenses and lens components for colour crystal projector and digital light processor
9002.1190 90	其他照相机,投影仪等用物镜(包括照片放大机用物镜)	15	80	17	15	千克/个		Other objective lenses for cameras, projectors (including lenses for photographic enlargers)
	--其他:							--Other:
9002.1910	---摄影机或放映机用	15	40	17	15	千克/个		---For cinematographic cameras or projectors
9002.1990	---其他		50	17	15	千克/个		---Other
9002.1990暂 10	摄像机、摄录一体机的镜头	3	50	17	15	千克/个		Lenses for vidicon and amcorder
9002.1990暂 20	手机、平板电脑用物镜(800万像素及以上)	6	50	17	15	千克/个		Mobile phone, tablet computer in an objective lens (8000000 pixels and above)
9002.1990 90	编号9002未列名的其他物镜	15	50	17	15	千克/个		Other objective lenses not specified or included
	-滤色镜:							-Filters:
9002.2010	---照相机用	15	80	17	15	千克/个		---For cameras
9002.2090	---其他	15	40	17	15	千克/个		---Other
	-其他:							-Other:
9002.9010	---照相机用		80	17	15	千克		---For cameras
9002.9010暂 01	照相机用带屈光度调节装置的目镜(但物镜,滤色镜除外)	10	80	17	15	千克		Eyepiece of diopter adjustment device for camera (other than objective, filters)
9002.9010 90	其他照相机用未列名光学元件(但物镜,滤色镜除外)	15	80	17	15	千克		Other optical elements for cameras (other than objective, filters)
9002.9090	---其他		40	17	15	千克		---Other
9002.9090暂 01	其他带屈光度调节装置的目镜	10	40	17	15	千克		Other eyepiece of diopter adjustment device for camera
9002.9090暂 02	掩膜版	10	40	17	15	千克		Mask plate

税则号列	货品名称	最惠(%)	普通	增值税率	出口退税	计量单位	监管条件	Article Description
9002.9090 10	抗辐射镜头[能抗 5×10^4 戈瑞(硅)以上辐射而又不会降低使用质量]	15	40	17	15	千克	3	Radiation resistance lenses (capable of resisting radiance > 5×10^4Gy (Si) and not lowering operation quality)
9002.9090 90	其他光学仪器用未列名光学元件(但物镜,滤色镜除外)	15	40	17	15	千克		Other unlisted optical elements for optical instruments (other than objective lenses and filters)
90.03	**眼镜架及其零件:**							**Frames and mountings for spectacles, goggles or the like, and parts thereof:**
	-眼镜架:							-Frames and mountings:
9003.1100暂	--塑料制	12	70	17	15	千克/副		--Of plastics
	--其他材料制:							--Of other materials:
9003.1910暂	---金属材料制	6	70	17	15	千克/副		---Of metal materials
9003.1920	---天然材料制	10	70	17		千克/副		---Of natural materials
9003.1920 10	濒危动植物产品制眼镜架	10	70	17		千克/副	FE	Frames and mountings of product of endangered animals and plants
9003.1920 90	其他天然材料制眼镜架	10	70	17	15	千克/副		Frames and mountings of other natural materials
9003.1990	---其他	10	70	17	15	千克/副		---Other
9003.9000暂	-零件	6	70	17	15	千克		-Parts
90.04	**矫正视力、保护眼睛或其他用途的眼镜、挡风镜及类似品:**							**Spectacles, goggles and the like, corrective, protective or other:**
9004.1000暂	-太阳镜	12	100	17	15	千克/副		-Sunglasses
	-其他:							-Other:
9004.9010暂	---变色镜	10	100	17	15	千克/副		---Photochromic spectacles
9004.9090暂	---其他	12	90	17	15	千克/副		---Other
90.05	**双筒望远镜、单筒望远镜、其他光学望远镜及其座架;其他天文仪器及其座架,但不包括射电天文仪器:**							**Binoculars, monoculars, other optical telescopes, and mountings therefor; other astronomical instruments and mountings therefor, but not including instruments for radio-astronomy:**
9005.1000	-双筒望远镜	15	50	17	15	个		-Binoculars
	-其他仪器:							-Other instruments:
9005.8010	---天文望远镜及其他天文仪器	3	8	17	17	台		---Astronomical telescopes and other astronomical instruments
9005.8090	---其他	12	50	17	15	台		---Other
	-零件、附件(包括座架):							-Parts and accessories (including mountings):
9005.9010	---天文望远镜及其他天文仪器用	2	8	17	15	千克		---For astronomical telescopes and other astronomica instruments
9005.9090	---其他	8	30	17	15	千克		---Other
90.06	**照相机(电影摄影机除外);照相闪光灯装置及闪光灯泡,但税目85.39的放电灯泡除外:**							**Photographic (other than cinematographic) cameras; photographic fla-shlight apparatus and flashbulbs, other than discharge lamps of heading No. 85.39:**
	-制版照相机:							-Cameras of a kind used for preparing printing plates or cylinders:
9006.1010	---电子分色机	12	20	17	15	台		---Electronic colour scanners
9006.1090	---其他	10	20	17	15	台	A	---Other
9006.3000	-水下、航空测量或体内器官检查用的特种照相机;法庭或犯罪学用的比较照相机	9	17	17	15	台		-Cameras specially designed for underwater use, for aerial survey or for medical or surgical examination of internal organs; comparison cameras for forensic or criminological purposes
9006.4000	-一次成像照相机	5	70	17	15	台		-Instant print cameras
	-其他照相机:							-Other cameras:
9006.5100	--通过镜头取景(单镜头反光式(SLR)),使用胶片宽度不超过35mm	25	100	17	15	架		--With a through-the-lens viewfinder (single lens reflex (SLR)), for roll film of a width not exceeding 35 mm
	--其他,使用胶片宽度小于35mm							--Other, for roll film of a width less than 35 mm

税则号列	货品名称	最惠(%)	普通	增值税率	出口退税	计量单位	监管条件	Article Description
9006.5210	---缩微照相机,使用缩微胶卷,胶片或其他缩微品的	9	17	17	15	架		---Cameras of a kind used for recording documents on microfilm, microfiche or other microforms
9006.5290	---其他	25	100	17	15	架		---Other
9006.5300	--其他,使用胶片宽度为35mm	20	100	17	15	架		--Other, for roll film of a width of 35mm
	--其他:							--Other:
9006.5910	---激光照相排版设备	9	35	17	15	台	A	---Laser photo typesetting equipment
9006.5990	---其他	25	100	17	15	架		---Other
9006.5990 10	分幅相机(记录速率超过每秒225000帧)	25	100	17	15	架	3A	Frame cameras (rate of recording > 225000 frame/sec)
9006.5990 20	电子(或电子快门)分幅相机(帧曝光时间为51纳秒或更短)	25	100	17	15	架	3A	Electromc (or electromc shutter) framing cameras (frane exposure time≤51 nanoseconds)
9006.5990 30	条纹相机(书写速度超过每微秒0.5mm)	25	100	17	15	架	3A	Stripe cameras (speed of writing >0.5mm/microsec)
9006.5990 40	电子条纹相机(时间分辨率为51纳秒或更小)	25	100	17	15	架	3A	Electron stripe cameras (rate of time discrimination≤51nanoseconds)
9006.5990 90	使用胶片宽>35mm的其他照相机	25	100	17	15	架		Other cameras, for roll film of a width >35mm
	-照相闪光灯装置及闪光灯泡:							-Photographic flashlight apparatus and flashbulbs:
9006.6100	--放电式(电子式)闪光灯装置		80	17	15	个		--Discharge lamp ("electronic") flashlight apparatus
9006.6100暂 01	照相手机用闪光灯组件	4	80	17	15	个		Flashlight component for camera mobile phone
9006.6100暂 02	照相机外置式电子闪光灯(闪光指数GN≥30,具有无线闪光功能,支持自动变焦)	15	8	17	15	个		Camera external electronic flash (flash index GN ≥ 30, with wireless flash function, support auto zoom)
9006.6100 90	其他放电式(电子式)闪光灯装置	18	80	17	15	个		Other discharge lamp("electronic") flashlight apparatus
	--其他:							--Other:
9006.6910	---闪光灯泡	18	80	17	15	个		---Flasbbulbs
9006.6990	---其他	18	80	17	15	个		---Other
	-零件、附件:							-Parts and accessories:
	--照相机用:							--For cameras:
9006.9110	---子目号9006.1010至9006.3000所列相机用	8	17	17	15	千克		---For cameras of subheadings No.9006.1010 to 9006.3000
9006.9120	----一次成像照相机用	5	100	17	15	千克		---For instant print cameras
	---其他:							---Other:
9006.9191暂	----自动调焦组件	6	100	17	15	千克/套		----Automatic focal setting units
9006.9192暂	----快门组件	6	100	17	15	千克/套		----Shutter units
9006.9199暂	----其他	6	100	17	15	千克		----Other
9006.9900	--其他	12	80	17	15	千克		--Other
90.07	**电影摄影机、放映机,不论是否带有声音的录制或重放装置:**							**Cinematographic cameras and projectors, whether or not incorporating sound recording or reproducing apparatus:**
	-摄影机:							-Cameras:
9007.1010	---高速摄影机	14	40	17	15	台		---High speed cameras
9007.1090	---其他	14	40	17	15	台		---Other
	-放映机:							-Projectors:
9007.2010	---数字式		40	17	15	台		---Digital
9007.2010暂 01	2K及以上分辨率的硬盘式数字电影放映机	8	40	17	15	台		Digital film projector ,resolution ≥2K,disk type
9007.2010 90	其他数字式放映机	14	40	17	15	台		Other digital projectors
9007.2090	---其他	14	40	17	15	台		---Other
	-零件、附件:							-Parts and accessories:
9007.9100暂	--摄影机用	5	40	17	15	千克		--For cameras
9007.9200暂	--放映机用	5	40	17	15	千克		--For projectors
90.08	**影像投影仪,但电影用除外;照片(电影片除外)放大机及缩片机:**							**Image projectors, other than cinematographic; photographic (other than cinematographic) enlargers and reducers:**
	-投影仪、放大机及缩片机:							-Image projectors、enlargers and reducers:

税则号列	货品名称	最惠(%)	普通	增值税率	出口退税	计量单位	监管条件	Article Description
9008.5010	---幻灯机	14	40	17	15	台		---Slide projectors
9008.5020	---缩微胶卷、缩微胶片或其他缩微品的阅读机,不论是否可以进行复制	10	17	17	15	台		---Microfilm, microfiche or other microform readers, whether or not capable of producing copies
	---其他影像投影仪:							---Other image projectors:
9008.5031	----正射投影仪	18	40	17	15	台		----Orthographical projectors
9008.5039	---其他	18	40	17	15	台		----Other
9008.5040	---照片(电影片除外)放大机及缩片机	20	80	17	15	台		---Photographic(other than cinematographic) enlargers and reducers
	-零件、附件:							-Parts and accessories:
9008.9010	---缩微阅读机用	8	17	17	15	千克		---Of microfilm, microfiche or other microform readers
9008.9020	---照片放大机及缩片机用	14	80	17	15	千克		---Of photographic enlargers and reducers
9008.9090	---其他	14	40	17	15	千克		---Other
90.10	**本章其他税目未列名的照相(包括电影)洗印用装置及设备;负片显示器;银幕及其他投影屏幕:**							**Apparatus and equipment for photographic (including cinematographic) laboratories, not specified or included elsewhere in this Chapter; negatoscopes; projection screens:**
	-照相(包括电影)胶卷或成卷感光纸的自动显影装置及设备或将已冲洗胶卷自动曝光到成卷感光纸上的装置及设备:							-Apparatus and equipment for automatically developing photographic (including cinematographic) film or paper in rolls or for automatically exposing developed film to rolls of photographic paper:
9010.1010	---电影用	14	40	17	15	台		---Of a kind used in cinematographic film
9010.1020	---特种照相用	8.4	20	17	15	台		---Of a kind used in special photographic film or paper
	---其他:							---Other:
9010.1091	----彩色胶卷用	25	100	17	15	台		----For the colour photographic film in rolls
9010.1099	----其他	15	100	17	15	台		----Other
	-照相(包括电影)洗印用其他装置及设备;负片显示器:							-Other apparatus and equipment for photographic (including cinematographic) laboratories; negatoscope:
9010.5010	---负片显示器	14	50	17	15	台		---Negatoscopes
	---其他:							---Other:
9010.5021	----电影用	14	40	17	15	台		----Of a kind used in cinematographic film
9010.5022	----特种照相用	8.4	20	17	15	台		----Of a kind used in special photographic film or paper
9010.5029	----其他	17	100	17	15	台		----Other
9010.6000	-银幕及其他投影屏幕	14	50	17	15	个		-Projection screens
	-零件、附件:							-Parts and accessories:
9010.9010	---电影用	0	40	17	15	千克		---Of a kind used in cinematographic film
9010.9020	---特种照相用	0	20	17	15	千克		---Of a kind used in special photographic film or paper
9010.9090	---其他	0	100	17	15	千克		---Other
90.11	**复式光学显微镜,包括用于缩微照相、显微电影摄影及显微投影的:**							**Compound optical microscopes, including those for photomicrography, cinephotomi-crography or microprojection:**
9011.1000	-立体显微镜	0	14	17	17	台		-Stereoscopic microscopes
9011.2000	-缩微照相、显微电影摄影及显微投影用的其他显微镜	0	14	17	15	台		-Other microscopes, for photomicrography, cinephotomicrography or microprojection
9011.8000	-其他显微镜		14	17	15	台		-Other microscopes
9011.8000暂 01	高倍测量显微镜,放大倍数≥1000倍,分辨率≤0.08微米	3	14	17	15	台		High power microscope, amplification factor ≥1000times, resolution≤0.08μm
9011.8000 90	其他显微镜	7	14	17	15	台		Other microscopes
9011.9000	-零件、附件	0	14	17	15	千克		-Parts and accessories
90.12	**显微镜,但光学显微镜除外;衍射设备:**							**Microscopes other than optical microscopes; diffraction apparatus:**
9012.1000	-显微镜,但光学显微镜除外;衍射设备	0	14	17	15	台		-Microscopes other than optical microscopes and diffraction apparatus
9012.9000	-零件、附件	0	14	17	15	千克		-Parts and accessories

税则号列	货品名称	最惠(%)	普通	增值税率	出口退税	计量单位	监管条件	Article Description
90.13	**其他税目未列名的液晶装置;激光器,但激光二极管除外;本章其他税目未列名的光学仪器及器具:**							**Liquid crystal devices not constituting articles provided for more specifically in other headings; lasers, other than laser diodes; other optical appliances and instruments, not specified or included elsewhere in this Chapter:**
9013.1000	-武器用望远镜瞄准具;潜望镜式望远镜;作为本章或第十六类的机器、设备、仪器或器具部件的望远镜	8	14	17	15	个		-Telescopic sights for fitting to arms; periscopes; telescopes designed to form parts of machines, appliances, instruments or apparatus of this Chapter or Section XVI
9013.2000	-激光器,但激光二极管除外		11	17	17	个		-Lasers, other than laser diodes
9013.2000暂 10	激光切割机用气体激光发生器、切割功率≥2千瓦	3	11	17	17	个		Gas laser generators for laser cutting machines, cutting power ≥ 2 kW
9013.2000 20	AVLIS、MLIS和CRISLA激光系统	6	11	17	17	个	3	AVLIS, MLIS, CRISLA laser systems
9013.2000 30	氩离子激光器(平均输出功率≥40瓦特、工作波长400纳米—515纳米)	6	11	17	17	个	3	Argon ion lasers (average output power≥40W, working wavelength = 400nm ~ 515nm)
9013.2000 40	紫翠玉激光器(带宽≤0.005纳米,重复率>125赫兹,功率>30瓦特等)	6	11	17	17	个	3	Alexandrite lasers (bandwidth ≤ 0.005nm, repetition rate > 125Hz, power > 30W)
9013.2000 50	脉冲二氧化碳激光器(重复率>250赫兹,功率>500瓦,脉冲宽度<200纳秒等)	6	11	17	17	个	3	Pulsed carbon dioxide lasers (repetition rate > 250Hz, power > 500W, pules width < 200ns)
9013.2000 60	脉冲受激准分子激光器(XeF、XeCl、KrF型,重复率>250赫兹,功率>500瓦等)	6	11	17	17	个	3	Pulsed excimer lasers (XeF、XeCl or KrF type, recurrent rate > 250Hz, power > 500W)
9013.2000 70	铜蒸汽激光器(平均输出功率≥40瓦特、工作波长500纳米—600纳米)	6	11	17	17	个	3	Copper vapor lasers (average output power ≥ 40W, working wavelength = 500nm ~ 600nm)
9013.2000 80	掺钕激光器(非玻璃激光器,两用物项管制商品)	6	11	17	17	个	3	Neodymium doped laser (not glass laser) (Dual-use items controlled commodity)
9013.2000 90	其他激光器(但激光二极管除外)	6	11	17	17	个		Other lasers (other than laser diodes)
9013.2000暂 91	2.5GB/S及以上SDH、波分复用光传输设备980纳米、1480纳米的泵浦激光器	3	11	17	17	个		980nm, 1480nm pump laser of SDH≥2.5GB/s, optical transmission equipment for wave-divison multicomplexing
9013.2000暂 92	用于2.5GB/S及以上光通信设备的850纳米、1260～1625纳米,且功率≤200毫瓦的激光器(泵浦激光机除外)	3	11	17	17	个		For the? 850 nm, 1260 ~ 1625 nm and above 2.5GB/S optical communicationdevice, and the laser power less than 200 MW (excluding pumped laser machine)
	-其他装置、仪器及器具:							-Other devices, appliances and instruments:
9013.8010	---放大镜	12	50	17	15	个		---Hand magnifying glasses
9013.8020	---光学门眼	12	50	17	15	个		---"Door eyes"
9013.8030	---液晶显示板	5	50	17	17	个/千克		---Liquid crystal display panel
9013.8030 10	10.1英寸及以下的液晶显示板	5	50	17	17	个/千克		size ≤ 10.1 inch liquid crystal display panel
9013.8030 20	10.1英寸<尺寸≤32英寸的液晶显示板	5	50	17	17	个/千克		10.1 inch < size ≤ 32 inch liquid crystal display panel
9013.8030 90	其他液晶显示板(90章其他品目未列名的)	5	50	17	17	个/千克		Other liquid crystal display panel(90 chapter not else where specified or included)
9013.8090	---其他	5	17	17	15	个		---Other
	-零件、附件:							-Parts and accessories:
9013.9010	---子目录9013.1000及9013.2000所列货品用	6	11	17	17	千克		---For goods of subhedding No. 9013.1000 and 9013.2000
9013.9020	---子目录9013.8030所列货品用	8	17	17	17	千克		---For goods of subhedding No. 9013.8030
9013.9090	---其他	8	17	17	17	千克		---Other
90.14	**定向罗盘;其他导航仪器及装置:**							**Direction finding compasses; other navigational instruments and appliances:**
9014.1000	-定向罗盘	2	8	17	17	个		-Direction finding compasses
	-航空或航天导航仪器及装置(罗盘除外):							-Instruments and appliances for aeronautical or space navigation (other than compasses):
9014.2010暂	---自动驾驶仪	1	8	17	17	个		---Automatic pilot
9014.2010暂 10	无人航空飞行器的自动驾驶仪	1	8	17	17	个	3	Automatic piolt for unmanned aircrafts
9014.2010暂 90	其他自动驾驶仪	1	8	17	17	个		Other navigational automatic pilot

税则号列	货品名称	最惠(%)	普通	增值税率	出口退税	计量单位	监管条件	Article Description
9014.2090	---其他		8	17	17	个		---Other
9014.2090暂 11	航空惯性导航仪	1	8	17	17	个	3	Inertial navigation instruments for airplanes
9014.2090 12	其他航天惯性导航仪(天文陀螺盘及其他利用天体或卫星进行导航的装置)	2	8	17	17	个	3	Other space inertial navigational instument(astronomical gyrocompass and astronomical or satellite navigational devices thereof)
9014.2090 13	陀螺稳定平台	2	8	17	17	个	3	Gyro stabilized platforms
9014.2090 15	陀螺仪(额定漂移率小于0.5度/小时的陀螺仪)	2	8	17	17	个	3	Gyroscopes (rated drift rate <0.5 degree/h)
9014.2090 16	专门设计的导航信息处理机(用于弹道导弹、运载火箭、探空火箭等的目标探测)	2	8	17	17	个	3	Specially-designed navigation information processors (for target detection of ballistic missiles, carrier rockets or sounding rockets)
9014.2090 17	地形等高线绘制设备(用于弹道导弹、运载火箭、探空火箭等的目标探测)	2	8	17	17	个	3	Terrain contour mapping equipments for target detection of ballistic missiles, carrier rockets or sounding rockets
9014.2090 18	场景绘图及相关设备(用于弹道导弹、运载火箭、探空火箭等的目标探测)	2	8	17	17	个	3	Scene mapping equipments and relative equipments (for target detection of ballistic missiles, carrier rockets or sounding rockets)
9014.2090 90	其他航空或航天导航仪器及装置(但罗盘除外)	2	8	17	17	个		Other instruments and appliances for aeronautical or space navigation (other than compasses)
9014.8000	-其他仪器及装置	2	8	17	17	个		-Other instruments and appliances
9014.8000 10	比例误差小于0.25%的加速度表	2	8	17	17	个	3	Accelerometers, proportion error <0.25%
9014.8000 20	高度表(用于弹道导弹、运载火箭、探空火箭等的目标探测)	2	8	17	17	个	3	Altimeters (for target detection of ballistic missiles, carrier rockets or sounding rockets)
9014.8000 90	其他导航仪器及装置	2	8	17	17	个		Other navigational instruments and appliances
	-零件、附件:							-Parts and accessories:
9014.9010暂	---自动驾驶仪用	1	8	17	17	千克		---For automatic pilot
9014.9090	---其他	1.5	8	17	17	千克		---Other
90.15	大地测量(包括摄影测量)、水道测量、海洋、水文、气象或地球物理用仪器及装置,不包括罗盘;测距仪:							**Surveying (including photogrammetrical surveying), hydrographic, oceanographic, hydrological, meteorological or geophysical instruments and appliances, excluding compasses; rangefinders:**
9015.1000	-测距仪	9	14	17	17	台		-Rangefinders
9015.2000	-经纬仪及视距仪	9	14	17	17	台		-Theodolites and tachymeters(tacheometers)
9015.3000	-水平仪	9	14	17	17	台		-Levels
9015.4000	-摄影测量用仪器及装置	9	14	17	17	千克		-Photogrammetrical surveying instruments and appliances
9015.8000	-其他仪器及装置	5	14	17	17	台		-Other instruments and appliances
9015.8000 10	机载或舰载重力仪(精度为1毫伽或更好、稳态记录时间至多为2分钟的)	5	14	17	17	台	3	Air-borne or ship-borne gravimeters (accuracy 1 milligamma or more better, duration of static recording ≤ 2 min)
9015.8000 20	机载或舰载重力梯度仪(精度为1毫伽或更好、稳态记录时间至多为2分钟的)	5	14	17	17	台	3	Air-borne or ship-borne gravity gradiometers (accuracy 1 milligamma or more better, duration of static recording ≤2 min)
9015.8000 90	其他测量仪器及装置	5	14	17	17	台		Other instruments and appliances
9015.9000	-零件、附件	5	14	17	17	千克		-Parts and accessories
9015.9000 10	机、舰载重力仪和重力梯度仪部件	5	14	17	17	千克	3	Parts and components of airborne or ship-borne gravity meters and gradiometers
9015.9000 90	其他大地测量仪及装置的零、附件	5	14	17	17	千克		Other parts and accessories of geodetic instruments and appliances
90.16	**感量为50毫克或更精密的天平,不论是否带有砝码:**							**Balances of a sensitivity of 50 mg or better, with or without weights:**
9016.0010	---感量为0.1毫克或更精密的天平	9	14	17	17	台/千克		---Of a sensitivity of 0.1 mg or better
9016.0090	---其他	10.5	30	17	17	台/千克		---Other

税则号列	货品名称	最惠(%)	普通	增值税率	出口退税	计量单位	监管条件	Article Description
90.17	绘图、划线或数学计算仪器及器具(例如,绘图机、比例缩放仪、分度规、绘图工具、计算尺及盘式计算器);本章其他税目未列名的手用测量长度的器具(例如,量尺、量带、千分尺及卡尺):							**Drawing, marking-out or mathematical-calculating instruments (for example, drafting machines, pantographs, protractors, drawing sets, slide rules, disc calculators); instruments for measuring length, for use in the hand (for example, measuring rods and tapes, micrometers, callipers), not specified or included elsewhere in this Chapter:**
9017.1000	-绘图台及绘图机,不论是否自动	8	20	17	15	台		-Drafting tables and machines, whether or not automatic
9017.2000	-其他绘图、划线或数学计算器具	0	70	17	15	个		-Other drawing, marking-out or mathematical calculating instruments
9017.3000	-千分尺、卡尺及量规	8	20	17	15	个		-Micrometers, callipers and gauges
9017.8000	-其他仪器及器具	8	20	17	15	个		-Other instruments
9017.9000	-零件、附件	0	20	17	15	千克		-Parts and accessories
90.18	医疗、外科、牙科或兽医用仪器及器具,包括闪烁扫描装置、其他电气医疗装置及视力检查仪器:							**Instruments and appliances used in medical, surgical, dental or veterinary sciences, including scintigraphic apparatus, other electro-medical apparatus and sight-testing instruments:**
	-电气诊断装置(包括功能检查或生理参数检查用装置):							-Electro-diagnostic apparatus (including apparatus for functional exploratory examination or for checking physiological parameters):
9018.1100	--心电图记录仪	5	17	17	17	台/千克	6O	--Electro-cardiographs
	--超声波扫描装置:							--Ultrasonic scanning apparatus:
9018.1210	---B型超声波诊断仪	7	35	17	17	台/千克	6OA	---B-ultrasonic diagnostic equipment
	---其他:							---Other:
9018.1291	----彩色超声波诊断仪	5	17	17	17	台/千克		----Chromoscope ultrasonic diagnostice-quipment
9018.1291 10	彩色超声波诊断仪(整机)	5	17	17	17	台/千克	6OA	Color ultrasonic diagnostic apparatus (machine)
9018.1291 90	彩色超声波诊断仪的零件及附件	5	17	17	17	台/千克	6OA	Parts and accessories of color ultrasonic diagnostic instrument
9018.1299	----其他	5	17	17	17	台/千克	6A	----Other
	--核磁共振成像装置:							--Magnetic resonance imaging apparatus:
9018.1310	---成套的	4	17	17	17	套/千克	6OA	---Complete sets
9018.1390	---零件	4	17	17	17	个/千克	6OA	---Parts
9018.1400	--闪烁摄影装置	5	17	17	17	台/千克	6A	--Scintigraphic apparatus
	--其他:							--Other:
9018.1930	---病员监护仪	4	17	17	17	台/千克		---Patient monitors
9018.1930 10	病员监护仪(整机)	4	17	17	17	台/千克	6A	The patient monitor (machine)
9018.1930 90	病员监护仪的零件及附件	4	17	17	17	台/千克	6A	Parts and accessories of patient monitor
	---听力诊断装置:							---Hearing diagnostic apparatas:
9018.1941	----听力计	4	17	17	17	台/千克	6A	----Andiometer
9018.1949	----其他	4	17	17	17	台/千克	6A	----Other
9018.1990	---其他	4	17	17	17	台/千克	6A	---Other
9018.2000	-紫外线及红外线装置	4	17	17	17	台/千克	6A	-Ultra-violet or infra-red ray apparatus
	-注射器、针、导管、插管及类似品:							-Syringes, needles, catheters, cannulae and the like:
9018.3100	--注射器,不论是否装有针头	8	50	17	17	个/千克	6A	--Syringes, with or without needles
	--管状金属针头及缝合用针:							--Tubular metal needles and needles for sutures:
9018.3210	---管状金属针头	8	50	17	17	千克	6A	---Tubular metal needles
9018.3220	---缝合用针	4	17	17	17	千克	6A	---Needles for sutures
9018.3900	--其他	4	17	17	17	个/千克	6A	--Other
	-牙科用其他仪器及器具:							-Other instruments and appliances, used in dental sciences:
9018.4100	--牙钻机,不论是否与其他牙科设备组装在同一底座上	4	17	17	17	台/千克	6A	--Dental drill engines, whether or not combined on a single base with other dental equipment
	--其他:							--Other:
9018.4910	---装有牙科设备的牙科用椅	4	17	17	17	台/千克	6A	---Dentists' chairs incorporating dental equipment
9018.4990	---其他	4	17	17	17	台/千克	6A	---Other

税则号列	货品名称	最惠(%)	普通	增值税率	出口退税	计量单位	监管条件	Article Description
9018.5000	-眼科用其他仪器及器具	4	17	17	17	千克	6A	-Other ophthalmic instruments and appliances
	-其他仪器及器具:							-Other instruments and appliances:
9018.9010	---听诊器	4	17	17	17	个/千克	6	---Stethoscopes
9018.9020	---血压测量仪器及器具	4	17	17	17	个/千克	6A	---Sphygmomanometers and appliances
9018.9030	---内窥镜	4	17	17	17	台/千克		---Endoscopes
9018.9030 10	内窥镜(整机)	4	17	17	17	台/千克	6A	Endoscope (machine)
9018.9030 90	内窥镜的零件及附件	4	17	17	17	台/千克	6A	Parts and accessories of endoscope mirror
9018.9040	---肾脏透析设备(人工肾)	4	17	17	17	台/千克	6A	---Artificial kidney (dialysis) apparatus
9018.9050	---透热疗法设备	4	17	17	17	台/千克	6A	---Diathermy apparatus
9018.9060	---输血设备	4	17	17	17	台/千克	6A	---Blood transfusion apparatus
9018.9070	---麻醉设备	4	17	17	17	台/千克	6A	---Anaesthetic apparatus and instruments
9018.9080	---宫内节育器	4	17			个/千克	6A	---Intrauterine contraceptive device
9018.9090	---其他	4	17	17	17	台/千克		---Other
9018.9090 10	其他医疗、外科或兽医用仪器器具(整机)	4	17	17	17	台/千克	6A	Instruments and apparatus for other medical, surgical or veterinary (machine)
9018.9090 90	其他医疗、外科或兽医用仪器器具的零件及附件	4	17	17	17	台/千克	6A	Parts and accessories for instruments and apparatus for other medical, surgical or veterinary
90.19	**机械疗法器具;按摩器具;心理功能测验装置;臭氧治疗器;氧气治疗器、喷雾治疗器、人工呼吸器及其他治疗用呼吸器具:**							**Mechano-therapy appliances; massage apparatus; psychological aptitude-testing apparatus; ozone therapy, oxygen therapy, aerosol therapy, artificial respiration or other therapeutic respiration apparatus:**
	-机械疗法器具;按摩器具;心理功能测验装置:							-Mechano-therapy appliances; massage apparatus; psychological aptitude-testing apparatus:
9019.1010	---按摩器具	15	40	17	17	台/千克	A	---Massage apparatus
9019.1090	---其他	4	30	17	17	台/千克		---Other
9019.2000	-臭氧治疗器、氧气治疗器、喷雾治疗器、人工呼吸器及其他治疗用呼吸器具	4	17	17	17	台/千克		-Ozone therapy, oxygen therapy, aerosol therapy, artificial respiration or other therapeutic respiration apparatus
90.20	**其他呼吸器具及防毒面具,但不包括既无机械零件又无可互换过滤器的防护面具:**							**Other breathing appliances and gas masks, excluding protective masks having neither mechanical parts nor replaceable filters:**
9020.0000[暂]	其他呼吸器具及防毒面具(但不包括既无机械零件又无可互换过滤器的防护面具)	4	30	17	17	千克		Other breathing appliances and gas masks, excluding protective masks having neither mechanical parts nor replaceable filters
90.21	**矫形器具,包括支具、外科手术带、疝气带;夹板及其他骨折用具;人造的人体部分;助听器及为弥补生理缺陷或残疾而穿戴、携带或植入人体内的其他器具:**							**Orthopaedic appliances, including crutches, surgical belts and trusses; splints and other fracture appliances; artificial parts of the body; hearing aids and other appliances which are worn or carried, or implanted in the body, to compensate for a defect or disability:**
9021.1000	-矫形或骨折用器具	4	17	17	15	千克		-Orthopaedic or fracture appliances:
	-假牙及牙齿固定件:							-Artificial teeth and dental fittings:
9021.2100	--假牙	4	17	17	15	千克		--Artificial teeth
9021.2900	--其他	4	17	17	15	千克		--Other
	-其他人造的人体部分:							-Other artificial parts of the body:
9021.3100	--人造关节	4	17	17	15	千克/套		--Artificial joints
9021.3900	--其他	4	17	17	15	千克		--Other
9021.4000	-助听器,不包括零件、附件	4	17	17	15	个		-Hearing aids, excluding parts and accessories
9021.5000[暂]	-心脏起搏器,不包括零件、附件	2	17	17	15	个	A	-Pacemakers for stimulating heart muscles, excluding parts and accessories
	-其他:							-Other:
	---支架:							---Brace:
9021.9011[暂]	----血管支架	2	17	17	15	千克/个		---Intravascular stents
9021.9019[暂]	----其他	2	17	17	15	千克/个		----Other bracket
9021.9090	---其他		17	17	15	千克		---Other
9021.9090[暂] 01	人工耳蜗植入装置	0	17	17	15	千克		Artificial cochlear implant device

税则号列	货品名称	最惠(%)	普通	增值税率	出口退税	计量单位	监管条件	Article Description
9021.9090 90	其他弥补生理缺陷、残疾用器具等(包括穿戴、携带或植入人体内的器具及零件)	4	17	17	15	个/千克		Other appliances to compensate for a defect or disability (including appliances and parts which are worn or carried, or implanted in the body)
90.22	**X射线或α射线、β射线、γ射线的应用设备,不论是否用于医疗、外科、牙科或兽医,包括射线照相及射线治疗设备,X射线管及其他X射线发生器、高压发生器、控制板及控制台、荧光屏、检查或治疗用的桌、椅及类似品:**							**Apparatus based on the use of X-rays or of alpha, beta or gamma radiations, whether or not for medical, surgical, dental or veterinary uses, including radiography or radiotherapy apparatus, X-ray tubes and other X-ray generators, high tension generators, control panels and desks, screens, examination or treatment tables, chairs and the like:**
	-X射线的应用设备,不论是否用于医疗、外科、牙科或兽医,包括射线照相或射线治疗设备:							-Apparatus based on the use of X-rays, whether or not for medical, surgical, dental or veterinary uses, including radiography or radiotherapy apparatus:
9022.1200	--X射线断层检查仪	4	11	17	17	台	6OA	--Computed tomography apparatus
9022.1300	--其他,牙科用	4	11	17	17	台	6OA	--Other, for dental uses
9022.1400	--其他,医疗、外科或兽医用	4	11	17	17	台		--Other, for medical, surgical or veterinary uses
9022.1400 10	医用直线加速器	4	11	17	17	台	6OA	Linear accelerators for medical use
9022.1400 90	其他医疗或兽医用X射线应用设备	4	11	17	17	台	6OA	Other apparatus based on the use of X-rays, for medical or veterinary uses
	--其他:							--For other uses:
9022.1910	---低剂量X射线安全检查设备	4	11	17	15	台	6A	---Low dosage X-ray security inspecting equipment
9022.1910 01	采用X光机技术或X射线加速器技术的X射线安全检查设备(能量大于100千电子伏,不包括采用X射线交替双能加速器技术的第二代X射线安全检查设备)	4	11	17	15	台	6A	X – ray security inspecting equipment of adopt X – ray aparatus technology and X – ray accelerator technology(energy >100KeV, excluding of adopt X – ray alternate dual – energy accelerator technology)
9022.1910 90	其他低剂量X射线安全检查设备	4	11	17	15	台	6A	Other low dosage X – ray security inspecting equipment
9022.1920	---X射线无损探伤检测仪	4	11	17	17	台	6A	---X-ray non-destructive testing appliances
9022.1990	---其他	4	11	17	17	台		---Other:
9022.1990 10	X射线全自动燃料芯块检查台(专门设计或制造用于检验燃料芯块的最终尺寸和表面缺陷)	4	11	17	17	台	36A	X-ray fully-automatic fuel core exouiwins table (Specially designed or made to inspect final dimensions and superficial defects of fuel core)
9022.1990 90	其他X射线应用设备	4	11	17	17	台	6A	Other apparatus based on the use of X-rays
	-α射线、β射线、γ射线的应用设备,不论是否用于医疗、外科、牙科或兽医,包括射线照相或射线治疗设备:							-Apparatus based on the use of alpha, beta or gamma radiations, whether or not for medical, surgical, dental or veterinary uses, including radiography or radiothe rapy apparatus:
9022.2100	--医疗、外科、牙科或兽医用	4	11	17	17	台	6A	--For medical, surgical, dental or veterinary uses
	--其他:							--Other
9022.2910	---γ射线无损探伤检测仪	6	11	17	15	台	6A	---γ-Ray non-destructivetesting appliances
9022.2990	---其他	6	11	17	15	台		---Other
9022.2990 10	γ射线全自动燃料芯块检查台(专门设计或制造用于检验燃料芯块的最终尺寸和表面缺陷)	6	11	17	15	台	36A	γ – Ray fully – automatic fuel core examiwins table (specially designed or made to inspect final dimensions and superficial defects of fuel core)
9022.2990 90	其他非医疗用α、β、γ射线设备	6	11	17	15	台	6A	Other α – rays、β – rays、γ – rays, not for medical uses
9022.3000	-X射线管	2	11	17	15	个	6A	-X-ray tubes
	-其他,包括零件、附件:							-Other, including parts and accessories:
9022.9010	---X射线影像增强器	6	11	17	15	个/千克	6OA	---X-ray intensifiers
9022.9090	---其他		11	17	15	个/千克		---Other
9022.9090暂 01	射线发生器的零部件	1	11	17	15	个/千克	6	Parts and components of radiation generators
9022.9090 20	闪光X射线发生器(峰值能量≥500千电子伏)	6	11	17	15	个/千克	36O	Flash X-ray generators (peak value power≥500KeV)
9022.9090 30	X射线断层检查仪专用探测器	6	11	17	15	个/千克	6O	Detectors specified for X-ray tomography instruments
9022.9090 90	编号9022所列其他设备及零件(包括高压发生器、控制板及控制台、荧光屏等)	6	11	17	15	个/千克	6	Other apparatus and its parts of heading 90.22, (including high voltage generators, control panels and console, screens)

税则号列	货品名称	最惠(%)	普通	增值税率	出口退税	计量单位	监管条件	Article Description
90.23	**专供示范(例如,教学或展览)而无其他用途的仪器、装置及模型:**							**Instruments, apparatus and models, designed for demonstrational purposes (for example, in education or exhibitions), unsuitable for other uses:**
	专供示范的仪器、装置及模型[(例如,教学或展览)而无其他用途]:							Instruments, apparatus and models, designed for demonstrational purposes (for example, in education or exhibitions), unsuitable for other uses:
9023.0010	---教习头	7	20	17	15	千克		---Training head
9023.0090	---其他	7	20	17	15	千克		---Other
90.24	**各种材料(例如,金属、木材、纺织材料、纸张、塑料)的硬度、强度、压缩性、弹性或其他机械性能的试验机器及器具:**							**Machines and appliances for testing the hardness, strength, compressibility, elasticity or other mechanical properties of materials (for example, metals, wood, textiles, paper, plastics):**
	-金属材料的试验用机器及器具:							-Machines and appliances for testing metals:
9024.1010	---电子万能试验机	7	20	17	15	台		---Electric multitesting machines
9024.1020	---硬度计	7	20	17	15	台		---Machiness and applinances for testing hardness
9024.1090	---其他	7	20	17	15	台		---Other
9024.8000	-其他机器及器具	5	20	17	15	台		-Other machines and appliances
9024.9000	-零件、附件	6	20	17	15	千克		-Parts and accessories
90.25	**记录式或非记录式的液体比重计及类似的浮子式仪器、温度计、高温计、气压计、湿度计、干湿球湿度计及其组合装置:**							**Hydrometers and similar floating instruments, thermometers and pyrometers, barometers, hygrometers and psychrometers, recording or not, and any combination of these instruments:**
	-温度计及高温计,未与其他仪器组合:							-Thermometers and pyrometers, not combined with other instruments:
9025.1100	--液体温度计,可直接读数	4	40	17	15	个		--Liquid-filled, for direct reading
	--其他:							--Other:
9025.1910	---工业用	8.4	20	17	15	个		---For technical use
9025.1990	---其他		80	17	15	个		---Other
9025.1990[暂] 01	红外线人体测温仪	4	80	17	15	个		Infrared ray human - body thermometer
9025.1990 90	非液体的其他温度计,高温计	8.4	80	17	15	个		Other thermometers and pyrometers, non - liquid
9025.8000	-其他仪器	11	30	17	15	个		-Other instruments
9025.9000	-零件、附件		20	17	15	千克		-Parts and accessories
9025.9000[暂] 01	红外线测温仪传感器元件	3	20	17	15	千克		Infrared thermometer sensor elements
9025.9000 90	其他比重计,温度计等类似仪器的零件	8	20	17	15	千克		Parts of other hydrometers, thermometers and similar instruments
90.26	**液体或气体的流量、液位、压力或其他变化量的测量或检验仪器及装置(例如,流量计、液位计、压力表、热量计),但不包括税目90.14、90.15、90.28或90.32的仪器及装置:**							**Instruments and apparatus for measuring or checking the flow, level, pressure or other variables of liquids or gases (for example, flow meters, level gauges, manometers, heat meters), excluding instruments and apparatus of heading No. 90.14, 90.15, 90.28 or 90.32:**
9026.1000	-测量、检验液体流量或液位的仪器及装置	0	17	17	17	个		-For measuring or checking the flow or level of liquids
	-测量、检验压力的仪器及装置:							-For measuring or checking pressure:
9026.2010	---压力/差压变送器	0	17	17	15	个		---Pressure/differential pressure transducers
9026.2010 10	锰铜压力计(压力超过10GPa)	0	17	17	15	个	3	Manganese-copper pressure gauges (pressure > 10GPa)
9026.2010 90	其他压力,差压变送器	0	17	17	15	个		Other pressure、differential pressure transducers
9026.2090	---其他	0	17	17	15	个		---Other
9026.2090 10	压力传感器(两用物项管制商品)	0	17	17	15	个	3	Pressure sensor (not glass laser) (Dual - use items controlled commodity)
9026.2090 90	其他测量、检验压力的仪器及装置	0	17	17	15	个		Other instruments and equipment for measuring or checking pressure
	-其他仪器及装置:							-Other instruments or apparatus:
9026.8010	---测量气体流量的仪器及装置	0	17	17	15	个/千克		---Measurement of gas flowapparatus and device
9026.8090	---其他	0	17	17	15	个/千克		---Other

税则号列	货品名称	最惠(%)	普通	增值税率	出口退税	计量单位	监管条件	Article Description
9026.9000	-零件、附件	0	17	17	15	千克		-Parts and accessories
90.27	理化分析仪器及装置(例如,偏振仪、折光仪、分光仪、气体或烟雾分析仪);测量或检验粘性、多孔性、膨胀性、表面张力及类似性能的仪器及装置;测量或检验热量、声量或光量的仪器及装置(包括曝光表);检镜切片机:							**Instruments and apparatus for physical or chemical analysis (for example, polarimeters, refractometers, spectrometers, gas or smoke analysis apparatus); instruments and apparatus for measuring or checking viscosity, porosity, expansion, surface tension or the like; instruments and apparatus for measuring or checking quantities of heat, sound or light (including exposure meters); microtomes:**
9027.1000	-气体或烟雾分析仪	7	17	17	15	台		-Gas or smoke analysis apparatus
9027.1000 10	用于连续操作的气体检测器[可用于出口管制的化学品或有机化合物(含有磷、硫、氟或氯,其浓度低于0.3mg/m³)的检测,或为检测受抑制的胆碱酯酶的活性而设计]	7	17	17	15	台	3	Used in continuously operating gas tester [for testing chemicals or organic compounds under export control (containing phosphor, sulfur, fluorine or chlorine with concentration lower than 0.3mg/m³) or for testing the activity of cholinesterase under control]
9027.1000 90	其他气体或烟雾分析仪	7	17	17	15	台		Other gas or smoke analysis apparatus
	-色谱仪及电泳仪:							-Chromatographs and electrophoresis instruments:
	---色谱仪:							---Chromatographs instruments:
9027.2011	----气相色谱仪	0	17	17	17	台		----Gas chromatographs instruments
9027.2012	----液相色谱仪	0	17	17	17	台		----Liquid chromatosraphs instruments
9027.2019	----其他	0	17	17	17	台		----Other
9027.2020	---电泳仪	0	17	17	17	台		---Electrophoresis instruments
9027.3000	-使用光学射线(紫外线、可见光、红外线)的分光仪、分光光度计及摄谱仪	0	17	17	17	台		-Spectrometers, spectrophotometers and spectrographs using optical radiations (UV, visible, IR)
9027.5000	-使用光学射线(紫外线、可见光、红外线)的其他仪器及装置	0	17	17	15	台		-Other instruments and apparatus using optical radiations (UV, visible, IR)
	-其他仪器及装置:							-Other instruments and apparatus:
	---质谱仪:							---Mass spectrograph:
9027.8011	----集成电路生产用氦质谱检漏台	0	17	17	15	台		----Integrated circuit belium spectra leak detectors
9027.8012	----质谱联用仪	0	17	17	15	台		----Mass spectrometer
9027.8019	----其他	0	17	17	15	台		----Other
9027.8019 10	UF_6质谱仪/离子源(能从UF_6气流中在线取得供料、产品或尾料样品谱仪)	0	17	17	15	台	3	UF_6 mass spectrographs/ion sources (capable of online taking samples of charging gas, product gas or tail gas from UF_6 flow)
9027.8019 20	测大于230质量单位离子质谱仪(分辨率高于2/230)	0	17	17	15	台	3	Ion mass spectrographs (resolution $>2/230$)
9027.8019 90	其他质谱仪	0	17	17	15	台		Other mass spectrograph
	---其他:							---Other:
9027.8091	----曝光表	14	70	17	15	个		----Exposure meters
9027.8099	----其他	0	17	17	15	台		----Other
9027.9000	-检镜切片机;零件、附件	0	17	17	15	千克		-Microtomes; parts and accessories
90.28	生产或供应气体、液体及电力用的计量仪表,包括它们的校准仪表:							**Gas, liquid or electricity supply or production meters, including calibrating meters therefor:**
	-气量计:							-Gas meters:
9028.1010	---煤气表	10	30	17	15	个		---Coal gas meters
9028.1090	---其他	10	30	17	15	个		---Other
	-液量计:							-Liquid meters:
9028.2010	---水表	10	30	17	15	个		---Water meters
9028.2090	---其他	10	30	17	15	个		---Other
	-电量计:							-Electricity meters:
	---电度表:							---Watt-hour meter:
9028.3011	----单相感应式	10	30	17	15	个		----Single- phase inductions type
9028.3012	----三相感应式	10	30	17	15	个		----Threephase inductions type
9028.3013	----单相电子式(静止式)	10	30	17	15	个		----Single-phase induction type(motionless type)
9028.3014	----三相电子式(静止式)	10	30	17	15	个		----Three-phase induction type(motionless type)

税则号列	货品名称	最惠(%)	普通	增值税率	出口退税	计量单位	监管条件	Article Description
9028. 3019	----其他	10	30	17	15	个		----Other
9028. 3090	---其他	10	30	17	15	个		---Other
	-零件、附件：							-Parts and accessories:
9028. 9010	---工业用	8. 4	30	17	15	千克		---For technical use
9028. 9090	---其他	8. 4	50	17	15	千克		---Other
90. 29	**转数计、产量计数器、车费计、里程计、步数计及类似仪表；速度计及转速表，税目90. 14及90. 15的仪表除外；频闪观测仪：**							**Revolution counters, production counters, taximeters, mileometers, pedometers and the like; speed indicators and tachometers, other than those of heading No. 90. 14 or 90. 15; stroboscopes:**
	-转数计、产量计数器、车费计、里程计、步数计及类似仪表：							-Revolution counters, production counters, taximeters, mileometers, pedometers and the like:
9029. 1010	---转数计	15	50	17	15	个		---Revolution counters
9029. 1020	---车费计、里程计	15	35	17	15	个		---Taximeters and mileometers
9029. 1090	---其他	15	35	17	15	个		---Other
	-速度计及转速表，频闪观测仪：							-Speed indicators and tachometers; stroboscopes:
9029. 2010	---车辆用速度计	10	35	17	15	个		---Speed indicators for motor vehicles
9029. 2090	---其他	10	35	17	15	个		---Other
9029. 9000	-零件、附件	6	35	17	15	千克		-Parts and accessories
90. 30	**示波器、频谱分析仪及其他用于电量测量或检验的仪器和装置，但不包括税目90. 28的各种仪表；α射线、β射线、γ射线、X射线、宇宙射线或其他离子射线的测量或检验仪器及装置：**							**Oscilloscopes, spectrum analysers and other instruments and apparatus for measuring or checking electrical quantities, excluding meters of heading No. 90. 28; instruments and apparatus for measuring or detecting alpha, beta, gamma, X-ray, cosmic or other ionizing radiations:**
9030. 1000	-离子射线的测量或检验仪器及装置	5	20	17	17	台		-Instruments and apparatus for measuring or detecting ionizing radiations
	-示波器：							-Oscilloscopes and oscillographs:
9030. 2010	---测试频率在300兆赫兹以下的通用示波器	8	80	17	15	台		---For general use, of test frequency less than 300 MHz
9030. 2090	---其他	5	20	17	15	台		---Other
	-检测电压、电流、电阻或功率的其他仪器及装置：							-Other instruments and apparatus, for measuring or checking voltage, current, resistance or power,
	--万用表，不带记录装置：							--Multimeters without a recording device:
9030. 3110	---量程在五位半及以下的数字万用表	15	130	17	15	台		---Digital, of measuring range of 5. 5 or less
9030. 3190	---其他	5	20	17	15	台		---Other
9030. 3200	--万用表，带记录装置.	8	20	17	15	台		--Multimeters with a recording device
	--其他，不带记录装置：							--other without a recording device:
9030. 3310	---量程在五位半及以下的数字电流表、电压表	15	130	17	15	台		---Digital ammeters or voltmeters. of measuing rang of 5. 5or less
9030. 3320	---电阻测试仪	14	80	17	15	台		---Resistnace measaring instruments
9030. 3390	---其他	9	20	17	15	台		---Other
9030. 3900	--其他，带记录装置	8	20	17	15	台		--Other with a recordins device
	-通讯专用的其他仪器及装置（例如，串音测试器、增益测量仪、失真度表、噪声计）：							-Other instruments and apparatus, specially designed for telecommunications (for example, cross-talk meters, gain measuring instruments, distortion factor meters, psophometers):
9030. 4010	---测试频率在12. 4千兆赫兹以下的数字式频率计	0	80	17	17	台		---Digital frequency meters, of test frequency less than 12. 4 GHz
9030. 4090	---其他	0	20	17	17	台		---Other
	-其他仪器及装置：							-Other instruments and apparatus:
9030. 8200	--测试或检验半导体晶片或器件用	0	20	17	15	台		--For measuring or checking semiconductor wafers or devices
	--其他，带有记录装置：							--Other, with a recording device:
9030. 8410	---电感及电容测试仪	10	80	17	17	台		---For measuring inductances or capacitances
9030. 8490	---其他	8	20	17	17	台		---Other
	--其他：							--Other:
9030. 8910	---电感及电容测试仪	14	80	17	15	台		---For measuring inductances or capacitances

税则号列	货品名称	最惠(%)	普通	增值税率	出口退税	计量单位	监管条件	Article Description
9030.8990	---其他	8	20	17	15	台		---Other
9030.8990 10	中子探测和测量仪表(专用于测定核反应堆堆芯内中子通量的)	8	20	17	15	台	3	Neutron detection and measurement instruments (used exclusively to measure the neutron flux of the reactor cores)
9030.8990 90	其他电量的测量或检验仪器及装置(未装有记录装置的)	8	20	17	15	台		Other instruments and apparatus for measuring or checking electrical quantities (without a recording device)
9030.9000	-零件、附件	0	17	17	15	千克		-Parts and accessories
9030.9000 01	检测半导体晶片及器件的仪器零件(包括附件)	0	17	17	15	千克	s	Parts of instruments for measuring or checking semiconductor wafers or devices
9030.9000 02	ITA 产品用的印刷电路组件(包括外接组件,如符合 PCMCIA 标准的卡)	0	17	17	15	千克	s	Printed circuit components for products falling within the ITA (including such components for external connections such as cards that conform to the PCMCLA standard)
9030.9000 90	编号 9030 所属货品的零件及附件	7	17	17	15	千克		Parts and accessories of goods of heading 90.30
90.31	**本章其他税目未列名的测量或检验仪器、器具及机器;轮廓投影仪:**							**Measuring or checking instruments, appliances and machines, not specified or included elsewhere in this Chapter; profile projectors:**
9031.1000	-机械零件平衡试验机	7	17	17	15	台		-Machines for balancing mechanical parts
9031.1000 10	陀螺动态平衡测试仪	7	17	17	15	台	3	Gyro dynamic balancing testers
9031.1000 90	其他机械零件平衡试验机	7	17	17	15	台		Other machines for balancing mechanical parts
9031.2000	-试验台	7	17	17	15	台		-Test benches
9031.2000 10	陀螺/马达运转试验台	7	17	17	15	台	3	Gyro/motor running test-benches
9031.2000 20	加速度表测试台	7	17	17	15	台	3	Accelerometer test-benches
9031.2000 30	试车台(能试推力>90KN 火箭发动机的或同时测量三个推力分量的)	7	17	17	15	台	3	Testbed (capable of testing rocket engine with a thrust>90KN or testing three individual thrust forces at the same time)
9031.2000 40	惯性平台测试台(测试平台包括高精度离心机和转台)	7	17	17	15	台	3	Inertial platform test-benches (including high-precision centrifuge and turntable)
9031.2000 90	其他试验台	7	17	17	15	台		Other test benches
	-其他光学仪器及器具:							-Other optical instruments and appliances:
9031.4100	--制造半导体器件时检验半导体晶片、器件或检测光掩模或光栅用	0	17	17	15	台		--For inspecting semiconductor wafers or devices or for inspecting photomasks or reticles used in manufacturing semiconductor devices:
	--其他:							--Other:
9031.4910	---轮廓投影仪	10	20	17	15	台		---Profile proiecters
9031.4920	---光栅测量装置	0	17	17	15	台		---Measuring grating device
9031.4990	---其他	0	17	17	15	台		---Other
9031.4990 10	光盘质量在线检测仪及离线检测仪	0	17	17	15	台	6	Automatic inspection detectors (AID) for CD production
9031.4990 90	其他光学测量或检验仪器和器具(第 90 章其他编号未列名的)	0	17	17	15	台		Other measuring or checking optical instruments and appliances, not elsewhere specified or included in chapter 90
	-其他仪器、器具及机器:							-Other instruments, appliances and machines:
9031.8010	---光纤通信及光纤性能测试仪	5	17	17	17	台		---Optical telecommunication and optical fibre performance testing instruments
9031.8020	---坐标测量仪	5	17	17	17	台		---Coordinate measuring machine
	---无损探伤检测仪器(射线探伤仪除外):							---Apparatus for exanimations, without damaging structure (other than apparatus for radiological examinations):
9031.8031	----超声波探伤检测仪	5	17	17	17	台		----Apparatus for ultrasonic examinations
9031.8032	----磁粉探伤检测仪	5	17	17	17	台		----Apparatus for magnetic examinations
9031.8033[暂]	----涡流探伤检测仪	3	17	17	17	台		----Apparatus for eddy examinations
9031.8039	----其他	5	17	17	17	台		----Other
9031.8090	---其他		17	17	17	台		---Other
9031.8090[暂] 01	跑道摩擦系数测试仪	3	17	17	17	台		Runway friction coefficient tester
9031.8090[暂] 02	音频生命探测仪	2	17	17	17	台		Audio life detection instrument
9031.8090[暂] 03	音视频生命探测仪	2	17	17	17	台		Audio and video life detection instrument
9031.8090 10	惯性测量单元测试仪	5	17	17	17	台	3	Inertial measurement unit testers

税则号列	货品名称	最惠(%)	普通	增值税率	出口退税	计量单位	监管条件	Article Description
9031.8090 90	其他测量,检验仪器,器具及机器(指第90章其他编号未列名的)	5	17	17	17	台		Other measuring or checking instruments, appliances and machines (not elsewhere specified or included in Chapter 90)
9031.9000	-零件、附件	0	17	17	15	千克		-Parts and accessories
9031.9000 20	惯性测量单元稳定元件加工夹具	0	17	17	15	千克	3	Processing clamps for stabling element of inertial measurement unit
9031.9000 30	惯性平台平衡夹具	0	17	17	15	千克	3	Inertial platform balancing clamps
9031.9000 90	编号9031的仪器及器具的其他零件(第90章其他编号未列名的)	0	17	17	15	千克		Other parts of instruments, appliances and machines of heading No. 90.31, not elsewhere specified or included in chapter 90
90.32	**自动调节或控制仪器及装置:**							**Automatic regulating or controlling instruments and apparatus:**
9032.1000	-恒温器	7	17	17	15	台		-Thermostats
9032.2000	-恒压器	7	17	17	15	台		-Manostats
	-其他仪器及装置:							-Other instruments and apparatus:
9032.8100	--液压或气压的	7	17	17	17	台		--Hydraulic or pneumatic
	--其他:							--Other:
	---列车自动控制系统(ATC)车载设备:							---Automatic control systems(ATC)for train apparatus:
9032.8911	----列车自动防护系统(ATP)车载设备	7	17	17	17	台		----Automatic protective systems(ATP)for train apparatus
9032.8912	----列车自动运行系统(ATO)车载设备	7	17	17	17	台		----Automatic motion systems(ATO)for train apparatus
9032.8919	----其他	7	17	17	17	台		----Other:
9032.8990	---其他		17	17	17	台		---Other
9032.8990[暂] 01	三坐标测量机用自动控制柜	3	17	17	17	台		Automatic control cabinet for three coordinates measurer
9032.8990[暂] 02	飞机自动驾驶系统(包括自动驾驶、电子控制飞行、自动故障分析、警告系统配平系统及推力监控设备及其相关仪表)	1	17	17	17	台		Automatic pilotting systems for aircraft (including instruments of automatic pilotting, electronic flight control, automatic failure analysis, warning systems, balancing system and thrust monitoring equipment and related instruments and meters)
9032.8990[暂] 03	机床用成套数控伺服装置(包括CNC操作单元,带有配套的伺服放大器和伺服电机)	3	17	17	17	台		Numerically - controlled servo devices for machine tools (including CNC operating units, with complete a set servo amplifiers and servo motors)
9032.8990[暂] 04	风力发电设备用控制器	4	17	17	17	台		Controlling instruments for wind turbine equipment
9032.8990[暂] 06	电喷点火程序控制单元(自动控制、调节装置)	3	17	17	17	台		Eleetron ignition process controllers (automatic control、regulating apparatus)
9032.8990[暂] 07	印刷机用成套数控伺服传动装置(包括运动控制器或可编程序自动控制器、人机界面单元,带有配套的伺服驱动器和伺服电机)	3	17	17	17	台		Printing machine with complete sets of numerical control servo drive device (including motion controller or automatic programmable controller, man - machine interface unit, servo drive and servo motor) that contains form a complete set
9032.8990 20	组合喷气发动机的燃烧调节装置(自动控制、调节装置)	7	17	17	17	台	3	Combustion adjusting device for combined jet engine (automatic control and regulating devices)
9032.8990 90	其他自动调节或控制仪器及装置	7	17	17	17	台		Other automatic regulating or controlling instruments and devices
9032.9000	-零件、附件		17	17	17	千克		-Parts and accessories
9032.9000[暂] 01	飞机自动驾驶系统的零件(包括自动驾驶、电子控制飞行、自动故障分析、警告系统配平系统及推力监控设备及其相关仪表的零件)	1	17	17	17	千克		Parts of automatic pilotting systems for aircraft (including instruments of automatic pilotting, electronic flight control, automatic failure analysis, warning systems balancing system and thrust monitoring equipment and in struments and meters)
9032.9000 90	其他自动调节或控制仪器零件、附件	5	17	17	17	千克		Other parts and acessories of automatic regulating or controlling instruments
90.33	**第九十章所列机器、器具、仪器或装置用的本章其他税目未列名的零件、附件:**							**Parts and accessories (not specified or included elsewhere in this Chapter) for machines, appliances, instruments or apparatus of Chapter 90:**
9033.0000	第九十章所列机器、器具、仪器或装置用的本章其他税目未列名的零件、附件	6	17	17	17	千克		Parts and accessories (not specified or included elsewhere in this Chapter) for machines, appliances, instruments or apparatus of Chapter 90

第九十一章 钟表及其零件

Chapter 91 Clocks and watches and parts thereof

注释:

一、本章不包括:

(一)钟表玻璃及钟锤(按其构成材料归类);

(二)表链(根据不同情况,归入税目71.13或71.17);

(三)第十五类注释二所规定的贱金属制通用零件(第十五类)、塑料制的类似品(第三十九章)及贵金属或包贵金属制的类似品(一般归入税目71.15);但钟、表发条则应作为钟、表的零件归类(税目91.14);

(四)轴承滚珠(根据不同情况,归入税目73.26或84.82);

(五)税目84.12的物品,不需擒纵器可以工作的;

(六)滚珠轴承(税目84.82);

(七)第八十五章的物品,本身未组装在或未与其他零件组装在钟、表机芯内,也未组装成专用于或主要用于钟、表机芯零件的(第八十五章)。

二、税目91.01仅包括表壳完全以贵金属或包贵金属制的表,以及用贵金属或包贵金属与税目71.01至71.04的天然、养殖珍珠或宝石、半宝石(天然、合成或再造)合制的表。用贱金属上镶嵌贵金属制成表壳的表应归入税目91.02。

三、本章所称"表芯",是指由摆轮及游丝、石英晶体或其他能确定时间间隔的装置来进行调节的机构,并带有显示器或可装机械指示器的系统。表芯的厚度不超过12毫米,长、宽或直径不超过50毫米。

四、除注释一另有规定的以外,钟、表的机芯及其他零件,既适用于钟或表,又适用于其他物品(例如精密仪器)的,均应归入本章。

Notes:

1. This Chapter does not cover:

(a) Clock or watch glasses or weights (classified according to their constituent material);

(b) Watch chains (heading No. 71.13 or 71.17, as the case may be);

(c) Parts of general use defined in Note 2 to Section XV, of base metal (Section XV), or similar goods of plastics (Chapter 39) or of precious metal or metal clad with precious metal (generally heading No. 71.15); clock or watch springs are, however, to be classified as clock or watch parts (heading No. 91.14);

(d) Bearing balls (heading No. 73.26 or 84.82, as the case may be);

(e) Articles of heading No. 84.12 constructed to work without an escapement;

(f) Ball bearings (heading No. 84.82);

(g) Articles of Chapter 85, not yet assembled together or with other components into watch or clock movements or into articles suitable for use solely or principally as parts of such movements (Chapter 85).

2. Heading 91.01 covers only watches with case wholly of precious metal or of metal clad with precious metal, or of the same materials combined with natural or cultured pearls, or precious or semiprecious stones (natural, synthetic or reconstructed) of headings 71.01 to 71.04. Watches with case of base metal inlaid with precious metal fall in heading 91.02.

3. For the purposes of this Chapter, the expression "watch movements" means devices regulated by a balance-wheel and hairspring, quartz crystal or any other system capable of determining intervals of time, with a display or a system to which a mechanical display can be incorporated. Such watch movements shall not exceed 12 mm in thickness and 50 mm in width, length or diameter.

4. Except as provided in Note 1, movements and other parts suitable for use both in clocks or watches and in other articles (for example, precision instruments) are to be classified in this Chapter.

税则号列	货品名称	最惠(%)	普通	增值税率	出口退税	计量单位	监管条件	Article Description
91.01	手表、怀表及其他表,包括秒表,表壳用贵金属或包贵金属制成的:							**Wrist-watches, pocket-watches and other watches, including stop-watches, with case of precious metal or of metal clad with precious metal:**
	-电力驱动的手表,不论是否附有秒表装置:							-Wrist-watches, electrically operated whether or not incorporating a stop-watch facility:
9101.1100	--仅有机械指示器的	11	100	17	13	只		--With mechanical display only
	--其他:							--Other:
9101.1910	---仅有光电显示器的	16	100	17	13	只		---With optoelectronic display only
9101.1990	---其他	15	100	17	13	只		---Other
	-其他手表,不论是否附有秒表装置:							-Other wrist-watches, whether or not incorporating a stop-watch facility:
9101.2100	--自动上弦的	11	80	17		只		--Automatic winding
9101.2100 10	含濒危动物皮自动上弦贵金属机械手表(表壳用贵金属或包贵金属制成的)	11	80	17		只	EF	Mechanical-watches of precious metal, containing endangered animals skins, automatic winding (with case of precious metal or of metal clad with precious metal)
9101.2100 90	其他自动上弦贵金属机械手表(表壳用贵金属或包贵金属制成的)	11	80	17	13	只		Other mechanical-watches of precious metal, automatic winding (with case of precious metal or of metal clad with precious metal)
9101.2900	--其他	15	80	17		只		--Other

税则号列	货品名称	最惠(%)	普通	增值税率	出口退税	计量单位	监管条件	Article Description
9101.2900 10	含濒危动物皮非自动上弦贵金属机械手表(表壳用贵金属或包贵金属制成的)	15	80	17		只	EF	Mechanical - watches of precious metal, containing endangered animals skins, non - automatic winding, (with case of precious metal or of metal clad with precious metal)
9101.2900 90	其他非自动上弦贵金属机械手表(表壳用贵金属或包贵金属制成的)	15	80	17	13	只		Other mechanical-watches of precious metal, non-automatic winding, (with case of precious metal or metalclad with precious meta)
	-其他:							-Other:
9101.9100	--电力驱动的	15	100	17	13	只		--Electrically operated
9101.9900	--其他	20	80	17	13	只		--Other
91.02	**手表、怀表及其他表,包括秒表,但税目91.01的货品除外:**							**Wrist-watches, pocket-watches and other watches, including stop-watches, other than those of heading No. 91.01:**
	-电力驱动的手表,不论是否附有秒表装置:							-Wrist-watches, electrically operated, whether or not incorporating a stop-watch facility:
9102.1100	--仅有机械指示器的	12.5	100	17	13	只		--With mechanical display only
9102.1200	--仅有光电显示器的	23	100	17	13	只		--With optoelectronic clisplay only
9102.1900	--其他	15	100	17	13	只		--Other
	-其他手表,不论是否装有秒表装置:							-Other wrist-watches, whether or not incorporating a stop-watch facility:
9102.2100	--自动上弦的	11	80	17		只		--Automatic winding
9102.2100 10	含濒危动物皮其他自动上弦的机械手表(用贵金属或包贵金属制壳的除外)	11	80	17		只	EF	Mechanical-watches, containing endangered animals skins, automatic winding(other than with case of precious metal or metal clad with precious metal)
9102.2100 90	其他自动上弦的机械手表(用贵金属或包贵金属制壳的除外)	11	80	17	13	只		Other mechanical-watches, automatic winding (other than with case of precious metal or of metal clad with precious metal)
9102.2900	--其他	15	80	17		只		--Other
9102.2900 10	含濒危动物皮其他非自动上弦机械手表(用贵金属或包贵金属制壳的除外)	15	80	17		只	EF	Othe mechanical-watches, containing endangered animals skins, non-automatic winding(other than with case of precious metal or of metal clad with precious metal)
9102.2900 90	其他非自动上弦的机械手表(用贵金属或包贵金属制壳的除外)	15	80	17	13	只		Other mechanical - watches, non - automatic winding, (other than with case of precious metal or metalclad with precious metal)
	-其他:							-Other:
9102.9100	--电力驱动的	15	100	17	13	只		--Electrically operated
9102.9900	--其他	20	80	17	13	只		--Other
91.03	**以表芯装成的钟,但不包括税目91.04的钟:**							**Clocks with watch movements, excluding clocks of heading No. 91.04:**
9103.1000	-电力驱动的	23	100	17	13	只		-Electrically operated
9103.9000	-其他	20	100	17	13	只		-Other
91.04	**仪表板钟及车辆、航空器、航天器或船舶用的类似钟:**							**Instrument panel clocks and clocks of a similar type for vehicles, aircraft, spacecraft or vessels:**
9104.0000	仪表板钟及车辆、航空器、航天器或船舶用的类似钟	10	100	17	13	只		Instrument panel clocks and clocks of a similar type for vehicles, aircraft, spacecraft or vessels
91.05	**其他钟:**							**Other clocks:**
	-闹钟:							-Alarm clocks:
9105.1100	--电力驱动的	23	100	17	13	只		--Electrically operated
9105.1900	--其他	20	100	17	13	只		--Other
	-挂钟:							-Wall clocks:
9105.2100	--电力驱动的	23	100	17	13	只		--Electrically operated
9105.2900	--其他	20	100	17	13	只		--Other
	-其他:							-Other:
	--电力驱动的:							--Electrically operated:
9105.9110	---天文钟	3	8	17	13	只		---Astronomical chronometer
9105.9190	---其他	23	100	17	13	只		---Other

税则号列	货品名称	最惠(%)	普通	增值税率	出口退税	计量单位	监管条件	Article Description
9105.9900	--其他	16	100	17	13	只		--Other
91.06	时间记录器以及测量、记录或指示时间间隔的装置，装有钟、表机芯或同步电动机的（例如，考勤钟、时刻记录器）：							**Time of day recording apparatus and apparatus for measuring, recording or otherwise indicating intervals of time, with clock or watch movement or with synchronous motor (for example, time-registers, time-recorders):**
9106.1000	-考勤钟、时刻记录器	16	50	17	13	只		-Time-registers; time-recorders
9106.9000	-其他	16	50	17	13	只		-Other
91.07	装有钟、表机芯或同步电动机的定时开关：							**Time switches with clock or watch movement or with synchronous motor:**
9107.0000	装有钟、表机芯或同步电动机的定时开关	12	50	17	13	个		Time switches with clock or watch movement or with synchronous motor
91.08	已组装的完整表芯：							**Watch movements, complete and assembled:**
	-电力驱动的：							-Electrically operated:
9108.1100暂	--仅有机械指示器或有可装机械指示器的装置的	10	80	17	13	只		--With mechanical display only or with a device to which a mechanical display can be incorporated
9108.1200	--仅有光电显示器的	16	80	17	13	只		--With optoelectronic display only
9108.1900	--其他	16	80	17	13	只		--Other
9108.2000	-自动上弦的	16	80	17	13	只		-Automatic winding
	-其他：							-Other:
9108.9010	---表面尺寸在33.8毫米及以下	16	80	17	13	只		---Measuring 33.8mm or less
9108.9090	---其他	16	80	17	13	只		---Other
91.09	已组装的完整钟芯：							**Clock movements, complete and assembled:**
9109.1000	-电力驱动的	16	100	17	13	只		-Eletrically operated
9109.9000	-其他	16	100	17	13	只		-Other
91.10	未组装或部分组装的完整钟、表机芯（机芯套装件）；已组装的不完整钟、表机芯；未组装的不完整钟、表机芯：							**Complete watch or clock movements, unassembled or partly assembled (movement sets); incomplete watch or clock movements, assembled; rough watch or clock movements:**
	-表的：							-Of watches:
9110.1100	--未组装或部分组装的完整机芯（机芯套装件）	16	80	17	13	只		--Complete movements, unassembled or partly assembled (movement sets)
9110.1200	--已组装的不完整表机芯	16	70	17	13	千克		--Incomplete movements, assembled
9110.1900	--未组装的不完整表机芯	16	70	17	13	千克		--Rough movements
	-其他：							-Other:
9110.9010	---未组装或部分组装的完整钟芯	16	100	17	13	千克/只		---Complete movements, unassembled or partly assembled
9110.9090	---其他	16	80	17	13	千克		---Other
91.11	表壳及其零件：							**Watch cases and parts thereof:**
9111.1000	-贵金属表壳或包贵金属表壳	14	80	17		只		-Cases of precious metal or of metal clad with precious metal
9111.1000 10	按重量计含金量在80%及以上的黄金表壳	14	80	17		只	J	Watch-cases of gold, containing 80% or more by weight of gold
9111.1000 90	其他贵金属或包贵金属制的表壳	14	80	17	0,13	只		Other watch-cases of precious metal or of metal clad with precious metal
9111.2000	-贱金属表壳，不论是否镀金或镀银	14	80	17	13	只		-Cases of base metal, whether or not gold-plated silver-plated
9111.8000	-其他表壳	14	80	17	13	只		-Other cases
9111.9000	-零件	14	80	17	0,13	千克		-Parts
91.12	钟壳和本章所列其他货品的类似外壳及其零件：							**Clock cases and cases of a similar type for other goods of this Chapter, and parts thereof:**
9112.2000	-壳	14	80	17	13	只		-Cases
9112.9000	-零件	12	80	17	13	千克		-Parts
91.13	表带及其零件：							**Watch straps, watch bands and watch bracelets, and parts thereof:**
9113.1000	-贵金属或包贵金属制	20	130	17		千克		-Of precious metal or of metal clad with pecious metal

税则号列	货品名称	最惠(%)	普通	增值税率	出口退税	计量单位	监管条件	Article Description
9113.1000 10	按重量计含金量在80%及以上的黄金表带	20	130	17		千克	J	Gold watch straps, containing 80% or more of gold by weight of gold
9113.1000 90	其他贵金属或包贵金属制的表带及零件	20	130	17	0,13	千克		Other watch straps and parts thereof of precious metals or of metal clad with precious metal
9113.2000	-贱金属制,不论是否镀金或镀银	14	100	17	13	千克		-Of base metal, whether or not gold-plated or silver-plated
9113.9000	-其他	14	100	17		千克		-Other
9113.9000 10	濒危动物皮制的表带及其零件	14	100	17		千克	FE	Watch straps, watch bands and watch bracelets, and parts thereof, of endangered animals skins
9113.9000 90	其他非金属制的表带及其零件	14	100	17	13	千克		Other watch straps, watch bands and watch bracelets and parts thereof, of non-metal
91.14	**钟、表的其他零件:**							**Other clock or watch parts:**
9114.1000	-发条,包括游丝	14	50	17	13	千克		-Springs, including hair-springs
9114.3000	-钟面或表面	14	50	17	13	千克		-Dials
9114.4000	-夹板及横担(过桥)	14	50	17	13	千克		-Plates and bridges
	-其他:							-Other:
9114.9010	---宝石轴承	14	50	17	13	千克		---Jewel bearings
9114.9090	---其他	14	70	17	13	千克		---Other

第九十二章
乐器及其零件、附件

注释：

一、本章不包括：

（一）第十五类注释二所规定的贱金属制通用零件（第十五类）或塑料制的类似品（第三十九章）；

（二）第八十五章或第九十章的传声器、扩大器、扬声器、耳机、开关、频闪观测仪及其他附属仪器、器具或设备，虽用于本章物品但未与该物品组成一体或安装在同一机壳内；

（三）玩具乐器或器具（税目 95.03）；

（四）清洁乐器用的刷子（税目 96.03）；

（五）收藏品或古物（税目 97.05 或 97.06）。

二、用于演奏税目 92.02、92.06 所列乐器的弓、槌及类似品，如果与该乐器一同进口或出口，数量合理，用途明确，应归入有关乐器的相应税目。

税目 92.09 的卡片、盘或卷，即使与乐器一同进口或出口，也不视为该乐器的组成部分，而应作为单独进口或出口的物品对待。

Chapter 92
Musical instruments; parts and accessories of such articles

Notes:

1. This Chapter does not cover:

(a) Parts of general use, as defined in Note 2 to Section XV, of base metal (Section XV), or similar goods of plastics (Chapter 39);

(b) Microphones, amplifiers, loudspeakers, headphones, switches, stroboscopes or other accessory instruments, apparatus or equipment of Chapter 85 or 90, for use with but not incorporated in or housed in the same cabinet as instruments of this Chapter;

(c) Toy instruments or apparatus (heading No. 95.03);

(d) Brushes for cleaning musical instruments (heading No. 96.03); or

(e) Collectors' pieces or antiques (heading No. 97.05 or 97.06).

2. Bows and sticks and similar devices used in playing the musical instruments of headings No. 92.02 and 92.06 presented with such instruments in numbers normal thereto and clearly intended for use therewith, are to be classified in the same heading as the relative instruments.

Cards, discs and rolls of heading No. 92.09 presented with an instrument are to be treated as separate articles and not as forming a part of such instrument.

税则号列	货品名称	最惠(%)	普通	增值税率	出口退税	计量单位	监管条件	Article Description
92.01	**钢琴，包括自动钢琴、拨弦古钢琴及其他键盘弦乐器：**							**Pianos, including automatic pianos; harpsichords and other keyboard stringed instruments:**
9201.1000	-竖式钢琴	17.5	70	17	13	台		-Upright pianos
9201.2000	-大钢琴		70	17	13	台		-Grand pianos
9201.2000暂 01	完税价格≥5 万美元的大钢琴	1	70	17	13	台		Grand pianos, duty-paid price≥USD 50000/set
9201.2000 90	其他大钢琴	17.5	70	17	13	台		Other grand pianos
9201.9000	-其他	17.5	70	17	13	台		-Other
92.02	**其他弦乐器（例如，吉他、小提琴、竖琴）：**							**Other string musical instruments (for example, guitars, violins, harps):**
9202.1000	-弓弦乐器		70	17		只		-Played with a bow
9202.1000暂 11	完税价格≥1.5 万美元的含濒危动物皮及濒危木的弓弦乐器	1	70	17		只	FE	Played with a bow, duty-paid price ≥ USD 15000/set, containing endangered animals skins and endangered wood
9202.1000 19	其他含濒危动物皮及濒危木的弓弦乐器	17.5	70	17		只	FE	Other played with a bow, containing endangered animals skins and endangered wood
9202.1000暂 91	完税价格≥1.5 万美元的不含野生动物皮弓弦乐器	1	70	17	13	只		Played with a bow, duty-paid price ≥ USD 15000/set, other than endangered animals skins
9202.1000 99	其他弓弦乐器	17.5	70	17	13	只		Other played with a bow
9202.9000	-其他	17.5	70	17		只		-Other
9202.9000 10	含濒危物种成分的其他弦乐器	17.5	70	17		只	FE	Other played with a bow, containing endangered species composition
9202.9000 90	其他弦乐器	17.5	70	17	13	只		Other string musical instruments
92.05	**管乐器（例如，键盘管风琴、手风琴、单簧管、小号、风笛），但游艺场风琴及手摇风琴除外：**							**Wind musical instruments (for example keyboard pipe organs、accordions、clarinets、trumpets、bag pipes) other than fairground or gans and mechanical street organs:**
9205.1000	-铜管乐器		70	17	13	只		-Brass-wind instruments
9205.1000暂 01	完税价格≥2000 美元的铜管乐器	1	70	17	13	只		Brass – wind instruments, duty-paid price ≥ USD 2000/set
9205.1000 90	其他铜管乐器	17.5	70	17	13	只		Other brass – wind instruments
	-其他：							-Other:

税则号列	货品名称	最惠(%)	普通	增值税率	出口退税	计量单位	监管条件	Article Description
9205.9010	---键盘管风琴、簧风琴及类似乐器(包括游离金属簧片键盘乐器)	20	80	17	13	只		---Keyboard pipe organs; harmoniums and similar keyboard instruments with free metal reeds
9205.9020	---手风琴及类似乐器	21	80	17	13	只		---Accordions and similar instruments
9205.9030	---口琴	21	80	17	13	只		---mouth organs
9205.9090	---其他		80	17	13	只		---Other
9205.9090暂 01	完税价格≥1万美元的其他管乐器(但游艺场风琴及手摇风琴除外)	1	70	17	13	只		Other brass-wind instruments, duty-paid price ≥USD 10000/set
9205.9090 90	其他管乐器(但游艺场风琴及手摇风琴除外)	17.5	70	17	13	只		Other brass-wind instruments (other than fairgrou organs and mechanical street organs)
92.06	**打击乐器(例如,鼓、木琴、铙、钹、响板、响葫芦):**							**Percussion musical instruments (for example, drums, xylophones, cymbals, castanets, maracas):**
9206.0000	打击乐器(例如,鼓、木琴、铙、钹、响板、响葫芦)	17.5	70	17		只		Percussion musical instruments (for example, drums, xylophones, cymbals, castanets, maracas)
9206.0000 10	含濒危动物皮及濒危木的打击乐器(例如,鼓、木琴、钹、响板)	17.5	70	17		只	AFE	Percussion musical instruments (for example, drums, xylophones, cymbals, castanets, maracas) containing endangered animal skins and endangered wood
9206.0000 90	其他打击乐器(例如,鼓、木琴、钹、响板)	17.5	70	17	13	只		Other percussion musical instruments (for example, drums, xylophones, cymbals, castanets, maracas)
92.07	**通过电产生或扩大声音的乐器(例如,电风琴、电吉他、电手风琴):**							**Musical instruments, the sound of which is produced or must be amplified electrically (for example, organs, guitars, accordions):**
9207.1000暂	-键盘乐器,但手风琴除外	15	100	17	13	只		-Keyboard instruments, other than accordions
9207.9000	-其他	30	100	17	13	个		-Other
92.08	**百音盒、游艺场风琴、手摇风琴、机械鸣禽、乐锯及本章其他税目未列名的其他乐器;各种媒诱音响器、哨子、号角、口吹音响信号器:**							**Musical boxes, fairground organs, mechanical street organs, mechanical singing birds, musical saws and other musical instruments not falling within any other heading of this Chapter; decoy calls of all kinds; whistles, call horns and other mouth-blown sound signalling instruments:**
9208.1000	-百音盒	22	80	17	13	个		-Musical boxes
9208.9000	-其他	22	80	17	13	个		-Other
92.09	**乐器的零件(例如百音盒的机械装置)、附件(例如,机械乐器用的卡片、盘及带卷);节拍器、音叉及各种定音管:**							**Parts (for example, mechanisms for musical boxes) and accessories (for example, cards, discs and rolls for mechanical instruments) of musical instruments; metronomes, tuning forks and pitch pipes of all kinds:**
9209.3000	-乐器用的弦	17.5	70	17	13	千克		-Musical instrument strings
	-其他:							-Other:
9209.9100	--钢琴的零件、附件	17.5	70	17	13	千克		--Parts and accessories for pianos
9209.9200	--税目92.02所列乐器的零件、附件	17.5	70	17	13	千克		--Parts and accessories for the musical instruments of heading No. 92.02
9209.9400暂	--税目92.07所列乐器的零件、附件	10	70	17	13	千克		--Parts and accessories for the musical instruments of heading No. 92.07
	--其他:							--Other
9209.9910	---节拍器、音叉及定音管	17.5	70	17	13	千克		---Metsonomes tuning froks and pitch pipes
9209.9920	---百音盒的机械装置	17.5	70	17	13	千克		---Mechanisms for musicol boxes
9209.9990	---其他	17.5	70	17	13	千克		---Other

第十九类
武器、弹药及其零件、附件

SECTION XIX
ARMS AND AMMUNITION; PARTS AND ACCESSORIES THEREOF

第九十三章
武器、弹药及其零件、附件

Chapter 93
Arms and ammunition; parts and accessories thereof

注释：

一、本章不包括：

（一）第三十六章的货品（例如，火帽、雷管、信号弹）；

（二）第十五类注释二所规定的贱金属制通用零件（第十五类）或塑料制的类似品（第三十九章）；

（三）装甲战斗车辆（税目87.10）；

（四）武器用的望远镜瞄准具及其他光学装置（第九十章），但安装在武器上或与武器一同进口或出口以备安装在该武器上的除外；

（五）弓、箭、钝头击剑或玩具（第九十五章）；

（六）收藏品及古物（税目97.05或97.06）。

二、税目93.06所称"零件"，不包括税目85.26的无线电设备及雷达设备。

Notes:

1. This Chapter does not cover:

(a) Goods of Chapter 36 (for example, percussion caps, detonators, signalling flares);

(b) Parts of general use, as defined in Note 2 to Section XV, of base metal (Section XV), or similar goods of plastics (Chapter 39);

(c) Armoured fighting vehicles (heading No. 87.10);

(d) Telescopic sights and other optical devices suitable for use with arms, unless mounted on a firearm or presented with the firearm on which they are designed to be mounted (Chapter 90);

(e) Bows, arrows, fencing foils or toys (Chapter 95);

(f) Collectors' pieces or antiques (heading No. 97.05 or 97.06).

2. In heading No. 93.06, the reference to "parts thereof" does not include radio or radar apparatus of heading No. 85.26.

税则号列	货品名称	最惠(%)	普通	增值税率	出口退税	计量单位	监管条件	Article Description
93.01	**军用武器，但左轮手枪、其他手枪及税目93.07的兵器除外：**							**Military weapons, other than revolvers, pistols and the arms of heading No. 93.07:**
	-火炮武器（例如，榴弹炮及迫击炮）：							-Artillery weapons (for example, guns, howitzers and mortars):
9301.1010	--自推进的	13	80	17		座		--Self-propelled
9301.1090	--其他	13	80	17		座		--Other
9301.2000	-火箭发射装置；火焰喷射器；手榴弹发射器；鱼雷发射管及类似发射装置自推进的	13	80	17		个		-Rocket launchers; flame-throwers; grenade launchers; torpedo tubes and similar projectors
9301.9000	-其他	13	80	17		支		-Other
93.02	**左轮手枪及其他手枪，但税目93.03或93.04的货品除外：**							**Revolvers and pistols, other than those of heading 93.03 or 93.04:**
9302.0000	左轮手枪及其他手枪，但税目93.03或93.04的货品除外	13	80	17		支		Revolvers and pistols, other than those of heading No. 93.03 or 93.04
93.03	**靠爆炸药发射的其他火器及类似装置（例如，运动用猎枪及步枪、前装枪、维利式信号枪及其他专为发射信号弹的装置、发射空包弹的左轮手枪和其他手枪、弩枪式无痛捕杀器、抛缆枪）：**							**Other firearms and similar devices which operate by the firing of an explosive charge (for example, sporting shotguns and rifles, muzzle-loading firearms, Very pistols and other devices designed to project only signal flares, pistols and revolvers for firing blank ammunition, captive-bolt humane killers, linethrowing guns):**
9303.1000	-前装枪	13	80	17	13	支		-Muzzle-loading firearms
9303.2000	-其他运动、狩猎或打靶用猎枪，包括组合式滑膛来复枪	13	80	17	13	支		-Other sporting, hunting or target shooting shotguns, including combination shotgunrifles
9303.3000	-其他运动、狩猎或打靶用步枪	13	80	17	13	支		-Other sporting, hunting or target shooting rifles
9303.9000	-其他	13	80	17	13	支		-Other
93.04	**其他武器（例如，弹簧枪、气枪、气手枪、警棍），但不包括税目93.07的货品：**							**Other arms (for example, spring, air or gas guns and pistols, truncheons), excluding those of heading No. 93.07:**
9304.0000	其他武器（例如，弹簧枪、气枪、警棍），但不包括税目93.07的货品	13	80	17	13	支		Other arms (for example, spring, air or gas guns and pistols, truncheons), excluding those of heading No. 93.07
93.05	**税目93.01至93.04所列物品的零件、附件：**							**Parts and accessories of articles of headings No. 93.01 to 93.04:**

税则号列	货品名称	最惠(%)	普通	增值税率	出口退税	计量单位	监管条件	Article Description
9305.1000	-左轮手枪或其他手枪用	13	80	17	0,13	千克		-Of revolvers or pistols
9305.2000	-税目93.03的猎枪或步枪用	13	80	17	0,13	千克		-Of shotguns or rifles of heading No. 93.03:
	-其他:							-Other:
9305.9100	--税目93.01的军用武器用	13	80	17		千克		--Of military weapons of heading No. 93.01
9305.9900	--其他	13	80	17	0,13	千克		--Other
93.06	**炸弹、手榴弹、鱼雷、地雷、水雷、导弹及类似武器及其零件;子弹、其他弹药和射弹及其零件,包括弹丸及弹垫:**							**Bombs, grenades, torpedoes, mines, missiles, and similar munitions of war and parts thereof; cartridges and other ammunition and projectiles and parts thereof, including shot and cartridge wads:**
	-猎枪子弹及其零件;气枪弹丸:							-Shotgun cartridges and parts thereof; air gun pellets:
9306.2100	--猎枪子弹	13	80	17	13	千克		--Cartridges
9306.2900	--其他	13	80	17	13	千克		--Other
	-其他子弹及其零件:							-Other cartridges and parts thereof:
9306.3080	---铆接机或类似工具用及弩枪式无痛捕杀器用子弹及其零件	13	80	17	0,13	千克		---Cartridges for riveting or similar tools or for captivebolt humane killers and parts thereof
9306.3090	--其他	13	80	17	0,13	千克		---Other
9306.9000	-其他	13	80	17		千克		-Other
9306.9000 10	两用物项管制的导弹及其零件(能把500千克以上有效载荷投掷到300千米以上的)	13	80	17		千克	3	Missiles and parts thereof under contorol of sensitive item (capable of throwing an available load over 500kg beyond 300km)
9306.9000 20	运载火箭(能把500千克以上有效载荷投掷到300千米以上的)	13	80	17		千克	3	Carrier rockets (capable of throwing an available load over 500kg beyond 300km)
9306.9000 30	探空火箭(能把500千克以上有效载荷投掷到300千米以上的)	13	80	17		千克	3	Sounding rockets (capable of throwing an available load over 500kg beyond 300km)
9306.9000 40	巡航导弹(能把500千克以上有效载荷投掷到300千米以上的)	13	80	17		千克	3	Cruise missiles (capable of throwing an available load over 500kg beyond 300km)
9306.9000 90	其他弹药和射弹及其零件(包括炸弹、手榴弹、鱼雷、地雷、水雷、导弹等)	13	80	17	0,13	千克		Other ammunition and projectiles and parts thereof (including bombs, grenades, torpedoes, mines, missiles)
93.07	**剑、短弯刀、刺刀、长矛和类似的武器及其零件;刀鞘、剑鞘:**							**Swords, cutlasses, bayonets, lances and similar arms and parts thereof and scabbards and sheaths therefor:**
	剑、短弯刀、刺刀、长矛和类似的武器及其零件;刀鞘、剑鞘:							Swords, cutlasses, bayonets, lances and similar arms and parts thereof and scabbards and sheaths therefor:
9307.0010	---军用	13	80	17		千克/件		---For military
9307.0010 10	军用刀鞘、剑鞘、濒危动物制	13	80	17		千克/件	FF	Scabbards and sheaths of endangered animals, for military
9307.0010 90	其他军用剑、刀、长矛和类似的武器及其零件(包括刀鞘、剑鞘)	13	80	17		千克/件		Other swords, cutlasses, lances and similar arms and parts thereof (including scabbards and sheaths), for military
9307.0090	---其他	13	80	17		千克/件		---Other
9307.0090 10	其他濒危动物制的刀鞘、剑鞘	13	80	17		千克/件	FE	Scabbards and sheaths of endangered animals
9307.0090 90	其他剑,刀,长矛和类似的武器及其零件(包括刀鞘、剑鞘)	13	80	17		千克/件		Other swords, cutlasses, lances and similar arms and parts thereof (including scabbards and sheaths)

第二十类
杂 项 制 品

第九十四章
家具;寝具、褥垫、弹簧床垫、软座垫及类似的填充制品;未列名灯具及照明装置;发光标志、发光铭牌及类似品;活动房屋

注释:

一、本章不包括:

(一)第三十九章、第四十章或第六十三章的充气或充水的褥垫、枕头及座垫;

(二)落地镜[例如税目70.09的试衣镜(旋转镜)];

(三)第七十一章的物品;

(四)第十五类注释二所规定的贱金属制通用零件(第十五类)、塑料制的类似品(第三十九章)或税目83.03的保险箱;

(五)冷藏或冷冻设备专用的特制家具(税目84.18);缝纫机专用的特制家具(税目84.52);

(六)第八十五章的灯具及照明装置;

(七)税目85.18、85.19、85.21或税目85.25至85.28所列装置专用的特制家具(应分别归入税目85.18、85.22或85.29);

(八)税目87.14的物品;

(九)装有税目90.18所列牙科用器具或漱口盂的牙科用椅(税目90.18);

(十)第九十一章的物品(例如,钟及钟壳);

(十一)玩具家具、玩具灯或玩具照明装置(税目95.03)、台球桌或其他供游戏用的特制家具(税目95.04)、魔术用的特制家具或中国灯笼及类似的装饰品(电气彩灯串除外)(税目95.05)。

二、税目94.01至94.03的物品(零件除外),只适用于落地式的物品。

对下列物品,即使是悬挂的、固定在墙壁上的或叠摞的,仍归入上述各税目:

(一)碗橱、书柜、其他架式家具(包括与将其固定于墙上的支撑物一同报验的单层搁架)及组合家具。

(二)坐具及床。

三、(一)税目94.01至94.03所列货品的零件,不包括玻璃(包括镜子)、大理石或其他石料以及第六十八章及第六十九章所列任何其他材料的片、块(不论是否切割成形,但未与其他零件组装);

(二)税目94.04的货品,如果单独进口或出口,不能作为税目94.01、94.02或94.03所列货品的零件归类。

SECTION XX
MISCELLANEOUS MANUFACTURED ARTICLES

Chapter 94
Furniture; bedding, mattresses, mattress supports, cushions and similar stuffed furnishings; lamps and lighting fittings, not elsewhere specified or included; illuminated signs, illuminated name-plates and the like; prefabricated buildings

Notes:

1. This Chapter does not cover:

(a) Pneumatic or water mattresses, pillows or cushions, of Chapter 39, 40 or 63;

(b) Mirrors designed for placing on the floor or ground (for example, cheval-glasses (swing-mirrors) of heading No. 70.09);

(c) Articles of Chapter 71;

(d) Parts of general use as defined in Note 2 to Section XV, of base metal (Section XV), or similar goods of plastics (Chapter 39), or safes of heading NO. 83.03;

(e) Furniture specially designed as parts of refrigerating or freezing equipment of heading No. 84.18; furniture specially designed for sewing machines (heading NO. 84.52);

(f) Lamps or lighting fittings of Chapter 85;

(g) Furniture specially designed as parts of apparatus of heading No. 85.18 (heading No. 85.18), of headings No. 85.19 to 85.21 (heading 85.22) or of headings Nos. 85.25 to 85.28 (heading No. 85.29);

(h) Articles of heading No. 87.14;

(i) Dentists' chairs incorporating dental appliances of heading 90.18 or dentists' spittoons (heading No. 90.18);

(j) Articles of Chapter 91 (for example, clocks and clock cases);

(k) Toy furniture or toy lamps or lighting fittings (heading No. 95.03), billiard tables or other furniture specially constructed for games (heading No. 95.04), furniture for conjuring tricks or decorations (other than electric garlands) such as Chinese lanterns (heading No. 95.05).

2. The articles (other than parts) referred to in headings No. 94.01 to 94.03 are to be classified in those headings only if they are designed for placing on the floor or ground.

The following are, however, to be classified in the above-mentioned headings even if they are designed to be hung, to be fixed to the wall or to stand one on the other:

(a) Cupboards, bookcases, other shelved furniture (including single shelves presented with supports for fixing them to the wall) and unit furniture

(b) Seats and beds.

3. (a) In headings No. 94.01 to 94.03 references to parts of goods do not include references to sheets or slabs (whether or not cut to shape but not combined with other parts) of glass (including mirrors), marble or other stone or of any other material referred to in Chapter 68 and 69.

(b) Goods described in heading No. 94.04, presented separately, are not to be classified in heading No. 94.01, 94.02 or 94.03 as parts of goods.

四、税目94.06所称"活动房屋"，是指在工厂制成成品或制成部件并一同进口或出口，供以后在有关地点上组装的房屋，例如，工地用房、办公室、学校、店铺、工作棚、车房或类似的建筑物。

4. For the purposes of heading No. 94.06, the expression "prefabricated buildings" means buildings which are finished in the factory or put up as elements, presented together, to be assembled on site, such as housing or worksite accommodation, offices, schools, shops, sheds, garages or similar buildings.

税则号列	货品名称	最惠(%)	普通	增值税率	出口退税	计量单位	监管条件	Article Description
94.01	**坐具(包括能作床用的两用椅，但税目94.02的货品除外)及其零件：**							**Seats (other than those of heading No. 94.02), whether or not convertible into beds, and parts thereof:**
9401.1000	-飞机用坐具	0	100	17	15	个/千克		-Seats of a kind used for aircraft
	-机动车辆用座具：							-Seats of a kind used for motor vehicles:
9401.2010	---皮革或再生皮革面的	10	100	17	15	个/千克		---With outer surface of leather or composition leather
9401.2090	---其他	10	100	17	15	个/千克		---Other
9401.3000	-可调高度的转动坐具	0	100	17	15	个/千克		-Swivel seats with variable height adjustment
	-能做床用的两用椅，但庭园坐具或野营设备除外：							-Seats other than garden seats or camping equipment, convertible into beds:
9401.4010	---皮革或再生皮革面的	0	100	17	15	个/千克		---With outer surface of leather or composition leather
9401.4090	---其他	0	100	17	15	个/千克		---Other
	-藤、柳条、竹及类似材料制的坐具：							-Seats of cane, osier, bamboo or similar materials:
9401.5100	--竹制或藤制的	0	100	17	15	个/千克	AB	--Of bamboo or rattan
9401.5900	--其他	0	100	17	15	个/千克	AB	--Other
	-木框架的其他坐具：							-Other seats, with wooden frames:
	--装软垫的：							--Upholstered:
9401.6110	---皮革或再生皮革面的	0	100	17	15	个/千克	AB	---With outer surface of leather or composition leather
9401.6190	---其他	0	100	17	15	个/千克	AB	---Other
9401.6900	--其他	0	100	17		个/千克		--Other
9401.6900 10	其他濒危木框架的坐具	0	100	17		个/千克	ABEF	Other seats, with endangered wood frames
9401.6900 90	其他木框架的坐具(不包括编号94011000－94015000的坐具)	0	100	17	15	个/千克	AB	Other seats, with wood frames (other than seats of No. 94011000～94015000)
	-金属框架的其他坐具：							-Other seats, with metal frames:
	--装软垫的：							--Upholstered:
9401.7110	---皮革或再生皮革面的	0	100	17	15	个/千克		---With outer surface of leather or composition leather
9401.7190	---其他	0	100	17	15	个/千克		---Other
9401.7900	--其他	0	100	17	15	个/千克		--Other
	-其他坐具：							-Other seats:
9401.8010	---石制的	0	100	17	15	个/千克		---Of stone
9401.8090	---其他	0	100	17		个/千克		---Other
9401.8090 10	其他濒危木制坐具	0	100	17		个/千克	EF	Other seats of endangered wood
9401.8090 91	儿童用汽车安全坐椅	0	100	17	17	个/千克	AB	Automobile safety seat for children
9401.8090 99	其他坐具	0	100	17	15	个/千克		Other seats
	-零件：							-Parts:
	---机动车辆用：							--Of the motor Vehicles:
9401.9011	----坐椅调角器	10	100	17	15	套/千克		----Seat angle requlating devices
9401.9019	----其他	0	100	17	15	千克		----Other
9401.9090	---其他	0	100	17	15	千克		---Other
94.02	**医疗、外科、牙科或兽医用家具(例如，手术台、检查台、带机械装置的病床、牙科用椅)；有旋转、倾斜、升降装置的理发用椅及类似椅；上述物品的零件：**							**Medical, surgical, dental or veterinary furniture (for example, operating tables, examination tables, hospital beds with mechanical fittings, dentists' chairs); barbers' chairs and similar chairs, having rotating as well as both reclining and elevating movements; parts of the foregoing articles:**
	-牙科、理发及类似用途的椅及其零件：							-Dentists', barbers' or similar chairs and parts thereof:
9402.1010	---理发用椅及其零件	0	100	17	15	个/千克		---Barbers chairs and parts thereof
9402.1090	---其他	0	30	17	15	个/千克		---Other
9402.9000	-其他	0	30	17	15	件/千克		-Other

税则号列	货品名称	最惠(%)	普通	增值税率	出口退税	计量单位	监管条件	Article Description
94.03	**其他家具及其零件：**							**Other furniture and parts thereof:**
9403.1000	-办公室用金属家具	0	100	17	15	件/千克		-Metal furniture of a kind used in offices
9403.2000	-其他金属家具	0	100	17	15	件/千克		-Other metal furniture
9403.3000	-办公室用木家具	0	100	17		件/千克		-Wooden furniture of a kind used in offices
9403.3000 10	濒危木制办公室用木家具	0	100	17		件/千克	ABFE	Furniture of endangered wood, of a kind used in offices
9403.3000 90	其他办公室用木家具	0	100	17	15	件/千克	AB	Other wooden furniture of a kind used in offices
9403.4000	-厨房用木家具	0	100	17		件/千克		-Wooden furniture of a kind used in the kitchen
9403.4000 10	濒危木制厨房用木家具	0	100	17		件/千克	ABFE	Furniture of endangered wood, of a kind used in the kitchen
9403.4000 90	其他厨房用木家具	0	100	17	15	件/千克	AB	Other wooden furniture of a kind used in the kitchen
	-卧室用木家具：							-Wooden furniture of a kind used in the bedroom:
9403.5010	---红木制	0	100	17		件/千克		---Of rose wood
9403.5010 10	卧室用濒危红木制家具	0	100	17		件/千克	ABFE	Furniture of endangered rose wood, of a kind used in the bedroom
9403.5010 90	其他卧室用红木制家具	0	100	17	15	件/千克	AB	Other furniture of rose wood, of a kind used in the bedroom
	---其他：							---Other:
9403.5091	----天然漆(大漆)漆木家具	0	100	17	15	件/千克	AB	----Lacquer, lacquer wood furniture
9403.5099	----其他	0	100	17		件/千克		----Other
9403.5099 10	卧室用其他濒危木家具	0	100	17		件/千克	ABFE	Furniture of other endangered wood, of a kind used in the bedroom
9403.5099 90	卧室用其他木家具	0	100	17	15	件/千克	AB	Furniture of other wood, of a kind used in the bedroom
	-其他木家具：							-Other wooden furniture:
9403.6010	---红木制	0	100	17		件/千克		---Of rose wood
9403.6010 10	濒危红木制其他家具(非卧室用)	0	100	17		件/千克	ABFE	Other furniture of rose endangered wood (other than use in the bedroom)
9403.6010 90	其他红木制家具(非卧室用)	0	100	17	15	件/千克	AB	Other furniture of rose wood (use in the bedroom)
	---其他：							---Other:
9403.6091	----天然漆(大漆)漆木家具	0	100	17		件/千克	AB	----Lacquer, lacquer wood furniture
9403.6099	----其他	0	100	17		件/千克		----Other
9403.6099 10	濒危木制其他家具(非卧室用)	0	100	17		件/千克	ABFE	Other furniture of endangered wood(other than use in the bedroom)
9403.6099 90	其他木家具(非卧室用)	0	100	17	15	件/千克	AB	Other furniture of wood(other than use in the bedroom)
9403.7000	-塑料家具	0	100	17	15	件/千克		-Furniture of plastics
	-其他材料制的家具，包括藤、柳条、竹或类似材料制的：							-Furniture of other materials, including cane, osier, bamboo or similar materials:
9403.8100	--竹制或藤制的	0	100	17	15	件/千克	AB	--Of bamboo or rattan
	--其他：							---Other:
9403.8910	---柳条及类似材料制的	0	100	17	15	件/千克	AB	---Of osier or similar materials
9403.8920	---石制的	0	100	17	15	件/千克		---Of stone
9403.8990	---其他	0	100	17	15	件/千克		---Other
9403.9000	-零件	0	100	17	15	千克		-Parts
9403.9000 10	飞机内厨房家具零件	0	100	17	15	千克		Parts of furnitures in kitchens of airplanes
9403.9000 90	其他编号9403所列物品的零件	0	100	17	15	千克		Parts of the articles of heading No. 94.03
94.04	**弹簧床垫；寝具及类似用品，装有弹簧、内部用任何材料填充、衬垫或用海绵橡胶、泡沫塑料制成，不论是否包面(例如，褥垫、棉被、羽绒被、靠垫、座垫及枕头)：**							**Mattress supports; articles of bedding and similar furnishing (for example, mattresses, quilts, eiderdowns, cushions, pouffes and pillows) fitted with springs or stuffed or internally fitted with any material or of cellular rubber or plastics, whether or not covered:**
9404.1000暂	-弹簧床垫	10	100	17	15	个/千克		-Mattress supports
	-褥垫：							-Mattresses:

税则号列	货品名称	最惠(%)	普通	增值税率	出口退税	计量单位	监管条件	Article Description
9404.2100暂	--海绵橡胶或泡沫塑料制,不论是否包面	10	100	17	15	个/千克		--Of cellular rubber or plastics, whether or not covered
9404.2100暂 10	蔺草包面的垫子(单件面积大于1平方米,无论是否包边)	10	100	17	15	个/千克	4ABxy	Mattresses covered with rush (area of single piece > $1m^2$, whether or not edged)
9404.2100暂 90	海绵橡胶或泡沫塑料制褥垫(不论是否包面)	10	100	17	15	个/千克		Mattresses of foam rubber or foamed plastics (whether or not covered)
9404.2900暂	--其他材料制	10	100	17	16	个/千克		--Of other materials
	-睡袋:							-Sleeping bags:
9404.3010暂	---羽毛或羽绒填充的	10	130	17		个/千克		---Stunffed with feathers or down
9404.3010暂 10	濒危野禽羽毛或羽绒填充的睡袋	10	130	17		个/千克	FE	Sleeping bags stuffed with feathers or down of endangered wild birds
9404.3010暂 90	其他羽毛或羽绒填充的睡袋	10	130	17	16	个/千克		Sleeping bags, stuffed with other feathers or down
9404.3090暂	---其他	10	100	17	16	个/千克		---Other
	-其他:							-Other:
9404.9010暂	---羽毛或羽绒填充的	10	130	17		千克		---Stuffed with feathers or down
9404.9010暂 10	濒危野禽羽绒和羽毛填充其他寝具(含类似品)	10	130	17		千克	EF	Other articles of bedding and similar furnishing, stuffed with feathers of down of endangered wild birds
9404.9010暂 90	其他羽绒和羽毛填充的其他寝具(含类似品)	10	130	17	16	千克		Other articles of bedding and similar furnishing, stuffed with pther feathers of down
9404.9020暂	---兽毛填充的	10	130	17		千克		---Stuffed with animal hair
9404.9020暂 10	濒危兽毛填充的寝具(用野生兽毛填充的,含盖被及类似品)	10	130	17		千克	EF	Articles of bedding, stuffed with endangered wild animal hair(including quilt and similar furnishing)
9404.9020暂 90	其他兽毛填充的其他寝具(含类似品)	10	130	17	16	千克		Articles of bedding and similar furnishing, stuffed with other animal hair
9404.9030暂	---丝棉填充的	10	130	17	16	千克		---Stuffed with silk wadding
9404.9040暂	---化纤棉填充的	10	130	17	16	千克		---Stuffed with man-made fibres
9404.9090暂	---其他	10	130	17	16	千克		---Other
94.05	其他税目未列名的灯具及照明装置,包括探照灯、聚光灯及其零件;装有固定光源的发光标志、发光铭牌及类似品,以及其他税目未列名的这些货品的零件:							**Lamps and lighting fittings including searchlights and spotlights and parts thereof, not elsewhere specified or included; illuminated signs, illuminated name-plates and the like, having apermanently fixed light source, andparts thereof not elsewhere specified or included:**
9405.1000	-枝形吊灯及天花板或墙壁上的其他电气照明装置,但不包括公共露天场所或街道上的电气照明装置	10	80	17	13	个/千克		-Chandeliers and other electric ceiling or wall lighting fittings, excluding those of a kind used for lighting public open spaces or thorough-fares
9405.2000	-电气的台灯、床头灯或落地灯	20	80	17		台/千克		-Electric table, desk, bedeside or floor-standing lamps
9405.2000 10	含濒危物种成分的电气台灯、床头灯、落地灯	20	80	17		台/千克	EF	Endangered species composition containing electric lamp, bedside lamp, floor lamp
9405.2000 90	其他电气台灯、床头灯、落地灯	20	80	17	13	台/千克		Other electric lamp, bedside lamp, floor lamp
9405.3000	-圣诞树用的成套灯具	16	100	17	13	套/千克		-Lighting sets of a kind used for Christmas trees
	-其他电灯及照明装置:							-Other electric lamps and lighting fittings:
9405.4010	---探照灯	17.5	70	17	13	台/千克		---Searchlights
9405.4020	---聚光灯	17.5	70	17	13	台/千克	A	---Spotlights
9405.4090	---其他	10	80	17	13	千克	A	---Other
9405.5000	-非电气的灯具及照明装置	20	80	17	13	千克		-Non-electrical lamps and lighting fittings
9405.6000	-发光标志、发光铭牌及类似品	20	80	17	13	千克		-Illuminated signs, illuminated name plates and the like
	-零件:							-Parts:
9405.9100	--玻璃制	20	70	17	13	千克		--Of glass
9405.9200	--塑料制	20	70	17	13	千克		--Of plastics
9405.9900	--其他	20	70	17	13	千克		--Other
94.06	**活动房屋:**							**Prefabricated buildings:**
9406.0000	活动房屋	10	70	17	13	千克		Prefabricated buildings

税则号列	货品名称	最惠(%)	普通	增值税率	出口退税	计量单位	监管条件	Article Description
9406.0000 10	用动植物材料制作的活动房屋	10	70	17	13	千克	AB	Prefabricated buildings of animal or vegetable materials
9406.0000 20	带有风扇的高效空气粒子过滤单元(HEPA)的封闭洁净室	10	70	17	13	千克	3	Sealed clean room, with fan, for filtering unit of high efficiency particulate air
9406.0000 90	其他活动房屋	10	70	17	13	千克		Other prefabricated buildings

第九十五章
玩具、游戏品、运动用品及其零件、附件

注释：

一、本章不包括：

（一）蜡烛（税目 34.06）；

（二）税目 36.04 的烟花、爆竹或其他烟火制品；

（三）已切成一定长度但未制成钓鱼线的纱线、单丝、绳、肠线及类似品（第三十九章、税目 42.06 或第十一类）；

（四）税目 42.02、43.03 或 43.04 的运动用袋或其他容器；

（五）第六十一章或第六十二章的纺织品制的运动服或化装舞会服装；

（六）第六十三章的纺织品制的旗帜及帆板或滑行车用帆；

（七）第六十四章的运动鞋靴（装有冰刀或滑轮的溜冰鞋除外）或第六十五章的运动用帽；

（八）手杖、鞭子、马鞭或类似品（税目 66.02）及其零件（税目 66.03）；

（九）税目 70.18 的未装配的玩偶或其他玩具用的玻璃假眼；

（十）第十五类注释二所规定的贱金属制通用零件（第十五类）或塑料制的类似货品（第三十九章）；

（十一）税目 83.06 的铃、钟、锣及类似品；

（十二）液体泵（税目 84.13）、液体或气体的过滤净化机器及装置（税目 84.21）、电动机（税目 85.01）、变压器（税目 84.04）；录制声音或其他信息用的圆盘、磁带、固态非易失性数据存储器件、“智能卡”及其他媒体，不论是否已录制（税目 85.23）；无线电遥控设备（税目 85.26）或无绳红外线遥控器件（85.43）；

（十三）第十七类的运动用车辆（长雪橇、平底雪橇及类似品除外）；

（十四）儿童两轮车（税目 87.12）；

（十五）运动用船艇，例如，轻舟、赛艇（第八十九章）及其桨、橹和类似品（木制的归入第四十四章）；

（十六）运动及户外游戏用的眼镜、护目镜及类似品（税目 90.04）；

（十七）媒诱音响器及哨子（税目 92.08）；

（十八）第九十三章的武器及其他物品；

（十九）各种电气彩灯串（税目 94.05）；

（二十）球拍线、帐篷或类似的野营用品、手套、棒球手套和露指手套（按其构成材料归类）；或

（二十一）餐具、厨房用具、盥洗用品、地毯及纺织材料制的其他铺地制品、服装、床上及餐桌用织物制品、盥洗及厨房用织物制品及具有实用功能的类似货品（按其构成材料归类）。

二、本章包括天然或养殖珍珠、宝石或半宝石（天然、合成或再造）、贵金属或包贵金属只作为小零件的物品。

Chapter 95
Toys, games and sports requisites; parts and accessories thereof

Notes:

1. This Chapter does not cover:

(a) Candles (heading No. 34.06);

(b) Fireworks or other pyrotechnic articles of heading No. 36.04;

(c) Yarns, monofilament, cords or gut or the like for fishing, cut to length but not made up into fishing lines, of Chapter 39, heading No. 42.06 or Section XI;

(d) Sports bags or other containers of heading No. 42.02, 43.03 or 43.04;

(e) Sports clothing or fancy dress, of textiles, of Chapter 61 or 62;

(f) Textile flags or bunting, or sails for boats, sailboards or land craft, of Chapter 63;

(g) Sports footwear (other than skating boots with ice or roller skates attached) of Chapter 64, or sports headgear of Chapter 65;

(h) Walking-sticks, whips, riding-crops or the like (heading No. 66.02), or parts thereof (heading No. 66.03);

(i) Unmounted glass eyes for dolls or other toys, of heading No. 70.18;

(j) Parts of general use, as defined in Note 2 to Section XV, of base metal (Section XV), or similar goods of plastics (Chapter 39);

(k) Bells, gongs or the like of heading No. 83.06;

(l) Pumps for liquids (heading No. 84.13), filtering or purifying machinery and apparatus for liquids or gases (heading No. 84.21), electric motors (heading No. 85.01), electric transformers (heading No. 85.04); discs, tapes, solid - state non - volatile storage devices, “smart cards” and other media for the recording of sound or of other phenomena, wheter or not recorded (heading 85.23), radio remote control apppratus (heading85.26) or cordless infrared remote control devices (heading85.43)

(m) Sports vehicles (other than bobsleighs, toboggans and the like) of Section XVII;

(n) Children's bicycles (heading No. 87.12);

(o) Sports craft such as canoes and skiffs (Chapter 89), or their means of propulsion (Chapter 44 for such articles made of wood);

(p) Spectacles, goggles or the like, for sports or outdoor games (heading No. 90.04);

(q) Decoy calls or whistles (heading No. 92.08);

(r) Arms or other articles of Chapter 93;

(s) Electric garlands of all kinds (heading No. 94.05);

(t) Racket strings, tents or other camping goods, or gloves, mittens and mitts (classified according to their constituent material). or

(u) Tableware, kitchenware, toilet articles, carpetsand other textile floor coverings, apparel, bed linen, table linen, toilet linen, kitchen linen and similar articles having a utilitarian function (classified according to their constituent material).

2. This Chapter includes articles in which natural or cultured pearls, precious or semi-precious stones (natural, synthetic or reconstructed), precious metal or metal clad with precious metal constitute only minor consistuents.

三、除上述注释一另有规定的以外，凡专用于或主要用于本章各税目所列物品的零件、附件，应与有关物品一并归类。

四、税目95.03不包括因其设计、形状或构成材料可确认为专供动物使用的物品，例如"宠物玩具"归入其相应的税目

3. Subject to Note 1 above, parts and accessories which are suitable for use solely or principally with articles of this Chapter are to be classified with those articles.

4. Heading 95.03 does not cover articles which, on account of their design, shape or constituent material, are identifiable as intended exclusively for animals, for example, "pet toys" (classification in their own appropriate heading).

子目注释：

一、子目9504.50包括：

（一）在电视机、监视器或其他外部屏幕或表面上重放图像的视频游戏控制器；

（二）自带显示屏的视频游戏设备，不论是否便携式。

本子目不包括用硬币、钞票、银行卡、代币或任何其他支付方式使其工作的视频游戏控制器或设备（子目9504.30）

Subheading Note:

1. Subheading 9504.50 covers:

(a) Video game consoles from which the image is reproduced on a television receiver, a monitor or other external screen or surface;

(b) Video game machines having a self-contained video screen, whether or not portable.

This subheading does not cover video game consoles or machines operated by coins, banknotes, bank cards, tokens or by any other means of payment (subheading9504.30)

税则号列	货品名称	最惠(%)	普通	增值税率	出口退税	计量单位	监管条件	Article Description
95.03	**三轮车、踏板车、踏板汽车和类似的带轮玩具；玩偶车；玩偶；其他玩具；缩小（按比例缩小）的模型及类似的娱乐用模型，不论是否活动；各种智力玩具：**							**Tricycles, scooters, pedal cars and similar wheeled toys; dals carriages; dolls; Other toys; re duced-size ("scale") models and similar recreational models working or not; puzzles of all kinds;**
9503.0010	---三轮车、踏板车、踏板汽车和类似的带轮玩具；玩偶车	0	80	17	15	千克	B	---Tricycles, scooters, pedal cars and similar wheeled toys; doll's carriage
	---玩偶，不论是否着装；玩具动物							---Dolls, whether or not dressed; toy representing animals or non-human creatures:
9503.0021	----动物	0	80	17	15	个/千克	AB	----Animals
9503.0029	----其他	0	80	17	15	个/千克	AB	----Other
	---缩小（按比例缩小）的全套模型组件，不论是否活动：							---Reduced-size ("scale") model assembly kits, whether or not working models:
9503.0031	----电动火车	0	80	17	15	千克	AB	----Electric trains
9503.0039	----其他	0	80	17	15	套/千克	AB	----Other
9503.0040	---其他建筑套件及建筑玩具	0	80	17	15	套/千克	AB	---Other constructrom sets and constructional toys
9503.0050	---玩具乐器	0	80	17	15	千克	AB	---Toy musical instruments and apparatus
9503.0060	---智力玩具	0	80	17	15	套/千克	AB	---Puzzles
	---其他玩具：							---Other toys:
9503.0081	----组装成套或全套的	0	80	17	15	套/千克	AB	----Put up in sets or outfies
9503.0082	----其他带动力装置的玩具及模型	0	80	17	15	个/千克	AB	----Other toys and models incorporating a motor
9503.0089	----其他	0	80	17	15	个/千克	AB	----Other
9503.0090	---零件、附件	0	80	17	15	千克	AB	---Parts and accessories
95.04	**视频游戏控制器及设备、游艺场所、桌上或室内游戏用品，包括弹球机、台球、娱乐专用桌及保龄球自动球道设备：**							**Vide game controller、Articles for funfair, table or parlour games, including pintables, billiards, special tables for casino games and automatic bowling alley equipment:**
9504.2000	-各种台球用品及附件	0	80	17		千克		-Articles and accessories for billiards of all kinds
9504.2000 10	濒危木制的台球用品及附件	0	80	17		千克	EF	Articles and accessories for billiards of endangered wood
9504.2000 90	其他台球用品及附件	0	80	17	13	千克		Other articles and accessories for billiards of au kinds
	-用硬币、钞票、银行卡、代币及任何其他支付方式使其工作的其他游戏用品，但保龄球自动球道设备除外：							-Other games, operated by coins, banknotes bank cords, tokens or by other means of payment, other than automatic bowing alley equipment
9504.3010	---电子游戏机	0	130	17	13	台/千克	60	---Video games
9504.3090	---其他	0	80	17	13	台/千克	60	---Other
9504.4000	-扑克牌	0	80	17	13	副		-Playing cards
	-视频游戏控制器及设备，但子目9504.30的货品除外：							-Video game consoles or machines operated, other than heading 9504.30:
	---与电视接收机配套使用的：							---Video games of a kind used with a television receiver:
9504.5011	----零件及附件	0	130	17	15	个/千克	60	----Articles and accessories

税则号列	货品名称	最惠(%)	普通	增值税率	出口退税	计量单位	监管条件	Article Description
9504.5019	----其他	0	130	17	15	台/千克	60	----Other
	---其他:							---Other:
9504.5091	----零件	0	130	17	13	个/千克	60	----Part
9504.5099	----其他	0	130	17	13	台/千克	60	----Other
	-其他:							-Other:
9504.9010	---其他电子游戏机	0	130	17	13	台/千克	60	---Other video games
	---保龄球自动球道设备及器具:							---Automatic bowling alley equipments and appliances:
9504.9021	----保龄球自动分瓶机	0	80	17	13	台/千克		----Automatic bowling pin distributing machines
9504.9022	----保龄球	0	80	17	13	个		----Bowling balls
9504.9023	----保龄球瓶	0	80	17	13	个		----Bowling pins
9504.9029	----其他	0	80	17	13	台/千克		----Other
9504.9030	---中国象棋、国际象棋、跳棋等棋类用品	0	80	17	13	副/千克		---Chess and other board games, including Chinese chess, international chess, Chinese cherkers and draughts
9504.9040	---麻将及类似桌上游戏用品	0	80	17	13	副/千克		---Mahjong and similiar table games
9504.9090	---其他	0	80	17	13	台/千克		---Other
95.05	**节日(包括狂欢节)用品或其他娱乐用品,包括魔术道具及嬉戏品:**							**Festive, carnival or other entertainment articles, including conjuring tricks and novelty jokes:**
9505.1000	-圣诞节用品	0	100	17	13	千克		-Articles for Christmas festivities
9505.1000 10	含动植物性材料的圣诞用品(不包括成套圣诞节灯具)	0	100	17	13	千克	AB	Articles for Christmas festivities containing animals or vegetable materials (other than lighting sets of a kind used for Christmas)
9505.1000 90	其他圣诞节用品(不包括成套圣诞节灯具)	0	100	17	13	千克		Other articles for Christmas festivities (other than lighting sets of a kind used for Christmas)
9505.9000	-其他	0	100	17	13	千克	B	-Other
95.06	**一般的体育活动、体操、竞技及其他运动(包括乒乓球运动)或户外游戏用的本章其他税目未列名用品及设备;游泳池或戏水池:**							**Articles and equipment for general physical exercise, gymnastics, athletics, other sports (including table-tennis) or out door games, not specified or included elsewhere in this Chapter; swimming pools and paddling pools:**
	-滑雪屐及其他滑雪用具:							-Snow-skis and other snow-ski equipment:
9506.1100	--滑雪屐	14	50	17	13	双		--Skis
9506.1200	--滑雪屐扣件(滑雪屐带)	14	50	17	13	千克		--Ski-fastenings (ski-bindings)
9506.1900	--其他	14	50	17	13	千克		--Other
	-滑水板、冲浪板、帆板及其他水上运动用具:							-Water-skis, surf-boards, sailboards and other water-sport equipment:
9506.2100	--帆板	12	50	17	13	个/千克		--Sailboards
9506.2900	--其他	14	50	17	13	个/千克		--Other
	-高尔夫球棍及其他高尔夫球用具:							-Golf clubs and other golf equipment:
9506.3100	--棍,全套	14	50	17	13	根		--Clubs, complete
9506.3200	--球	12	50	17	13	个		--Balls
9506.3900	--其他	14	50	17	13	千克		--Other
	-乒乓球运动用品及器械:							-Articles and equipment for table-tennis:
9506.4010	---乒乓球	12	50	17	13	百个/千克		---Table-tennis balls
9506.4090[暂]	---其他	7	50	17	13	千克		---Other
	-网球拍、羽毛球拍或类似的球拍,不论是否装弦:							-Tennis, badminton or similar rackets, whether or not strung:
9506.5100	--草地网球拍,不论是否装弦	14	50	17	13	支		--Lawn-tennis rackets, whether or not strung
9506.5900	--其他	14	50	17	13	支		--Other
	-球,但高尔夫球及乒乓球除外:							-Balls, other than golf balls and tabletennis balls:
9506.6100	--草地网球	12	50	17	13	个		--Lawn-tennis balls
	--可充气的球:							--Inflatable:
9506.6210[暂]	---篮球、足球、排球	6	50	17	13	个		---Basketballs, footballs or volleyballs
9506.6290	---其他	12	50	17	13	个		---Other
9506.6900	--其他	12	50	17	13	个		--Other

税则号列	货品名称	最惠(%)	普通	增值税率	出口退税	计量单位	监管条件	Article Description
	-溜冰鞋及旱冰鞋,包括装有冰刀的溜冰靴:							-Ice skates and roller skates, including skating boots with skates attached:
9506.7010	---溜冰鞋	14	50	17	13	双/千克		---Ice skates
9506.7020	---旱冰鞋	14	50	17	13	双/千克		---Roller skates
	-其他:							-Other:
	--一般的体育活动、体操或竞技用品及设备:							--Articles and equipment for general physical exercise, gymnastics or athletics:
	---健身及康复器械:							---Equipment for exercise and recovery:
9506.9111暂	----跑步机	6	50	17	13	台/千克		----Runing machines
9506.9111暂 10	跑步机(整机)	6	50	17	13	台/千克		The treadmill (machine)
9506.9111暂 90	跑步机的零件及附件	6	50	17	13	台/千克		Parts and accessories of treadmill
9506.9119暂	----其他	6	50	17	13	千克		----Other
9506.9120暂	---滑板	6	50	17	13	个/千克		---Skateboards
9506.9190暂	---其他	6	50	17	13	千克		---Other
9506.9900	--其他	12	50	17	13	个/千克		--Other
95.07	**钓鱼竿、钓鱼钩及其他钓鱼用品;捞鱼网、捕蝶网及类似网;化子"鸟"(税目92.08或97.05的货品除外)以及类似的狩猎用品:**							**Fishing rods, fish-hooks and other line fishing tackle; fish landing nets, butterfly nets and similar nets; decoy "birds" (other than those of heading 92.08 or 97.05) and similar hunting or shooting requisites:**
9507.1000	-钓鱼竿	21	80	17	13	副/千克		-Fishing rods
9507.1000 10	用植物性材料制作的钓鱼竿	21	80	17	13	副/千克	AB	Fishing rods of vegetable materials
9507.1000 90	其他钓鱼竿	21	80	17	13	副/千克		Other fishing rods
9507.2000	-钓鱼钩,不论有无系钩丝	21	80	17	13	千克		-Fish-hooks, whether or not snelled
9507.3000	-钓线轮	21	80	17	13	个/千克		-Fishing reels
9507.9000	-其他	21	80	17	13	千克		-Other
95.08	**旋转木马、秋千、射击用靶及其他游乐场的娱乐设备;流动马戏团及流动动物园;流动剧团:**							**Roundabouts, swings, shooting galleries and other fairground amusements; travelling circuses and travelling menageries; travelling theatres:**
9508.1000	-流动马戏团及流动动物园	15	100	17		千克		-Travelling circuses and travelling menageries
9508.1000 10	有濒危动物的流动马戏团(包括流动动物园)	15	100	17		千克	FEAB	Travelling circuses and travelling menageries, having endangered animals
9508.1000 90	其他流动马戏团及流动动物园	15	100	17	13	千克	AB	Other travelling circuses and travelling menageries
9508.9000	-其他	15	100	17	13	千克	AB	-Other

第九十六章
杂 项 制 品

注释：

一、本章不包括：

(一)化妆盥洗用笔(第三十三章)；

(二)第六十六章的制品(例如，伞或手杖的零件)；

(三)仿首饰(税目71.17)；

(四)第十五类注释二所规定的贱金属制通用零件(第十五类)或塑料制的类似品(第三十九章)；

(五)第八十二章的利口器及其他物品，其柄或其他零件是雕刻或模塑材料制的；但税目96.01或96.02适用于单独进口或出口的上述物品的柄或其他零件；

(六)第九十章的物品，例如，眼镜架(税目90.03)、数学绘图笔(税目90.17)、各种牙科、医疗、外科或兽医专用刷子(税目90.18)；

(七)第九十一章的物品(例如，钟壳或表壳)；

(八)乐器及其零件、附件(第九十二章)；

(九)第九十三章的物品(武器及其零件)；

(十)第九十四章的物品(例如，家具、灯具及照明装置)；

(十一)第九十五章的物品(玩具、游戏品、运动用品)；

(十二)艺术品、收藏品及古物(第九十七章)。

二、税目96.02所称"植物质或矿物质雕刻材料"，是指：

(一)用于雕刻的硬种子、硬果核、硬果壳、坚果及类似植物材料(例如，象牙果及棕榈子)；

(二)琥珀、海泡石、粘聚琥珀、粘聚海泡石、黑玉及其矿物代用品。

三、税目96.03所称"制帚、制刷用成束、成簇的材料"，仅指未装配的成束、成簇的兽毛、植物纤维或其他材料。这些成束、成簇的材料无需分开即可安装在帚、刷之上，或只需经过简单加工(例如将顶端修剪成形)即可安装的。

四、除税目96.01至96.06或96.15的货品以外，本章的物品还包括全部或部分用贵金属、包贵金属、天然或养殖珍珠、宝石或半宝石(天然、合成或再造)制成的物品。而且，税目96.01至96.06及96.15包括天然或养殖珍珠、宝石或半宝石(天然、合成或再造)、贵金属或包贵金属只作为小零件的物品。

Chapter 96
Miscellaneous manufactured articles

Notes:

1. This Chapter does not cover:

(a) Pencils for cosmetic or toilet uses (Chapter 33);

(b) Articles of Chapter 66 (for example, parts of umbrellas or walking-sticks);

(c) Imitation jewellery (heading No. 71.17);

(d) Parts of general use, as defined in Note 2 to Section XV, of base metal (Section XV), or similar goods of plastics (Chapter 39);

(e) Cutlery or other articles of Chapter 82 with handles or other parts of carving or moulding materials; heading No. 96.01 or 96.02 applies, however, to separately pressented handles or other parts of such articles;

(f) Articles of Chapter 90 (for exampple, spectacle frames (heading No. 90.03), mathematical drawing pens (heading No. 90.17), brushes of a kind specialized for use in dentistry or for medical, surgical or veterinary purposes (heading No. 90.18);

(g) Articles of Chapter 91 (for example, clock or watch cases);

(h) Musical instruments or parts or accessories thereof (Chapter 92);

(i) Articles of Chapter 93 (arms and parts thereof);

(j) Articles of Chapter 94 (for example, furniture, lamps and lighting fittings);

(k) Articles of Chapter 95 (toys, games, sports requisites);

(l) Works of art, collectors' pieces or antiques (Chapter 97).

2. In heading No. 96.02 the expression "vegetable or mineral carving material" means:

(a) Hard seeds, pips, hulls and nuts and similar vegetable materials of a kind used for carving (for example, corozo and dom);

(b) Amber, meerschaum, agglomerated amber and agglomerated meerschaum, jet and mineral substitutes for jet.

3. In heading No. 96.03 the expression "prepared knots and tufts for broom or brush making" applies only to unmounted knots and tufts of animal hair, vegetable fibre or other material, which are ready for incorporation without division in brooms or brushes, or which require only such further minor processes as trimming to shape at the top, to render them ready for such incorporation.

4. Articles of this Chapter, other than those of headings No. 96.01 to 96.06 or 96.15, remain classified in the Chapter whether or not composed wholly or partly of precious metal or metal clad with precious metal, of natural or cultured pearls, or precious or semiprecious stones (natural, synthetic or reconstructed). However, headings No. 96.01 to 96.06 and 96.15 include articles in which natural or cultured pearls, precious or semi-precious stones (natural, synthetic or reconstructed), precious metal or metal clad with precious metal constitute only minor constituents.

税则号列	货品名称	最惠(%)	普通	增值税率	出口退税	计量单位	监管条件	Article Description
96.01	已加工的兽牙、骨、玳瑁壳、角、鹿角、珊瑚、珍珠母及其他动物质雕刻材料及其制品(包括塑模制品):							**Worked ivory, bone, tortoise-shell, horn, antlers, coral, mother-of-pearl and other animal carving material and articles of these materials (including articles obtained by moulding):**
9601.1000	-已加工的兽牙及其制品	20	100	17		千克		-Worked ivory and articles of ivory
9601.1000 10	已加工的濒危兽牙及其制品	20	100	17		千克	AFEB	Worked ivory and articles of ivory, of endangered animals
9601.1000 90	其他已加工的兽牙及其制品	20	100	17	13	千克	AB	Other worked ivory and articles of ivory
9601.9000	-其他	20	100	17		千克		-Other
9601.9000 10	其他已加工濒危动物质雕刻料(包括其制品)	20	100	17		千克	AFEB	Other worked carving material and articles of these materials of endangered animals
9601.9000 90	其他已加工动物质雕刻料及其制品	20	100	17	13	千克	AB	Other worked animal carving material and articles of these materials
96.02	已加工的植物质或矿物质雕刻材料及其制品;蜡、硬脂、天然树胶、天然树脂或塑型膏制成的模塑或雕刻制品以及其他税目未列名的模塑或雕刻制品;已加工的未硬化明胶(税目35.03的明胶除外)及未硬化明胶制品:							**Worked vegetable or mineral carving material and articles of these materials; moulded or carved articles of wax, of stearin, of natural gums or natural resins or of modelling pastes, and other moulded or carved articles, not elsewhere specified or included; worked, unhardened gelatin (except gelatin of heading No35.03) and articles of unhardened gelatin:**
9602.0010	---装药用胶囊	10.5	40	17	13	千克		---Pharmaceutical capsules
9602.0090	---其他	25	100	17	13	千克	AB	---Other
96.03	帚、刷(包括作为机器、器具、车辆零件的刷)、非机动的手工操作地板清扫器、拖把及毛掸;供制帚、刷用的成束或成簇的材料;油漆块垫及滚筒;橡皮扫帚(橡皮辊除外):							**Brooms, brushes (including brushes constituting parts of machines, appliances or vehicles), hand-operated mechanical floor sweepers, not motorized, mops and feather dusters; prepared knots and tufts for broom or brush making; paint pads and rollers; squeegees (other than roller squeegees):**
9603.1000	-用枝条或其他植物材料捆扎而成的帚及刷,不论是否有把	25	100	17	13	把	AB	-Brooms and brushes, consisting of twigs or other vegetable materials bound together, with or without handles
	-牙刷、剃须刷、发刷、指甲刷、睫毛刷及其他人体化妆用刷,包括作为器具零件的上述刷:							-Tooth brushes, shaving brushes, hair brushes, nail brushes, eyelash brushes and other toilet brushes for use on the person, including such brushes constituting parts of appliances:
9603.2100暂	--牙刷,包括齿板刷	10	100	17	13	把		--Tooth brushes, including dental-plate brushes
9603.2900	--其他	15	100	17	13	支		--Other
9603.2900 10	野生动物毛制剃须刷,发刷(包括睫毛刷等人体化妆刷)	15	100	17	13	支	FE	Shaving brushes, hair brushes(including eyelash brushes and other toilet brushes for use on the person) of wild animal hair
9603.2900 90	剃须刷,发刷,睫毛刷等人体化妆刷(包括作为器具零件的编号960329所属的刷)	15	100	17	13	支		Shaving brushes, hair brushes, eyelash brushes and other toilet brushes for use on the person (including parts and appliances of subheading No. 960329)
	-画笔、毛笔及化妆用的类似笔:							-Artists' brushes, writing brushes and similar brushes for the application of cosmetics:
9603.3010	---画笔	25	100	17		支		---Artists' brushes
9603.3010 10	濒危动物毛制的画笔	25	100	17		支	FE	Artists' brushes of endangered animal hair
9603.3010 90	其他画笔	25	100	17	13	支		Other artists' brushes
9603.3020	---毛笔	20	100	17		支		---Writing brushes
9603.3020 10	濒危动物毛制的毛笔	20	100	17		支	FE	Writing brushes of endangered animal hair
9603.3020 90	其他毛笔	20	100	17	13	支		Other writing brushes
9603.3090	---其他	25	100	17		支		---Other
9603.3090 10	濒危动物毛制化妆用的类似笔	25	100	17		支	FE	Similar brushes for the application of cosmetics, of endangered animal hair
9603.3090 90	其他化妆用的类似笔	25	100	17	13	支		Other similar brushes for the application of cosmeties

税则号列	货品名称	最惠(%)	普通	增值税率	出口退税	计量单位	监管条件	Article Description
	-油漆刷、涂料刷、清漆刷及类似的刷(子目号9603.30的货品除外);油漆块垫及滚筒:							-Paint, distemper, varnish or similar brushes (other than brushes of subheading No. 9603.30); paint pads and rollers:
	---漆刷及类似刷:							---Paint, distemper, varnish or similar brushes:
9603.4011	----猪鬃制	20	100	17	13	把		----Of pigs', hogs' or boars' bristle
9603.4019	----其他	23	100	17	13	把		----Other
9603.4020	---油漆块垫及滚筒	23	100	17	13	个		---Paint pads and rollers
	-作为机器、器具、车辆零件的刷:							-Other brushes constituting parts of machines, appliances or vehicles:
	---金属丝刷:							---Brushes of metal wire:
9603.5011	----作为机器、器具零件的刷	14	50	17	13	个		----Constituting parts of machines or appliances
9603.5019	----其他	14	100	17	13	个		----Other
	---其他:							---Other:
9603.5091	----作为机器、器具零件的刷	14	50	17		个		----Constituting parts of machines or appliances
9603.5091 10	濒危动物毛制作为机器零件其他刷(包括器具零件的其他刷)	14	50	17		个	FE	Other brushes constituting parts of machines or appliances, of endangered animal hair
9603.5091 90	其他作为机器、器具零件的其他刷	14	50	17	13	个		Other brushes constituting parts of machines or appliances
9603.5099	----其他	14	100	17		个		----Other
9603.5099 10	濒危动物毛制作为车辆零件其他刷	14	100	17		个	FE	Other brushes constituting parts of vehicles, of endangered animal hair
9603.5099 90	其他作为车辆零件的其他刷	14	100	17	13	个		Other brushes constituting parts of vehicles
	-其他:							-Other:
9603.9010	---羽毛掸	21	130	17		个		---Feather dusters
9603.9010 10	濒危野禽羽毛掸	21	130	17		个	AFEB	Feather dusters of endangered wild birds
9603.9010 90	其他羽毛掸	21	130	17	13	个	AB	Other feather dusters
9603.9090	---其他	15	100	17		个		---Other
9603.9090 10	濒危动物毛、鬃、尾制其他帚,刷(包括拖把及其他毛掸)	15	100	17		个	AFEB	Other brooms, brushes (including mops, feather dusters), of hair, bristles or tails, of endangered animals
9603.9090 20	其他动植物材料制帚,刷,拖把等(包括动植物材料制非机动的手工操作地板清扫器、毛掸)	15	100	17	13	个	AB	Brooms, brushes, mops (including feather dusters, hand-operated mechanical floor sweepers, not motorized) of other animal or vegetable materials
9603.9090 90	其他材料制帚,刷,拖把及毛掸(包括其他材料制非机动的手工操作地板清扫器等)	15	100	17	13	个		Brooms, brushes, mops and feather dusters (incluelding hand-operated mechanical floor sweepers, not motorized, of other materials)
96.04	**手用粗筛、细筛:**							**Hand sieves and hand riddles:**
9604.0000	手用粗筛、细筛	21	100	17	13	个	AB	Hand sieves and hand riddles
96.05	**个人梳妆、缝纫或清洁鞋靴、衣服用的成套旅行用具:**							**Travel sets for personal toilet, sewing or shoe or clothes cleaning:**
9605.0000	个人梳妆、缝纫或清洁鞋靴、衣服用的成套旅行用具	15	100	17	13	套		Travel sets for personal toilet, sewing or shoe or clothes cleaning
96.06	**钮扣、揿扣、钮扣芯及钮扣和揿扣的其他零件;钮扣坯:**							**Buttons, press-fasteners, snap-fasteners and press-studs, button moulds and other parts of these articles; button blanks:**
9606.1000	-揿扣及其零件	21	100	17	13	千克		-Press-fasteners, snap-fasteners and press-studs and parts thereof
	-钮扣:							-Buttons:
9606.2100	--塑料制,未用纺织材料包裹	21	100	17	13	千克		--Of plastics, not covered with textile material
9606.2200	--贱金属制,未用纺织材料包裹	15	100	17	13	千克		--Of base metal, not covered with textile material
9606.2900	--其他	15	100	17		千克		--Other
9606.2900 10	含濒危动物成分的其他钮扣	15	100	17		千克	FE	Other buttons containing materials of endangered animals
9606.2900 90	其他钮扣	15	100	17	13	千克		Other buttons
9606.3000	-钮扣芯及钮扣的其他零件;钮扣坯	15	100	17	13	千克		-Button moulds and other parts of buttons; button blanks
96.07	**拉链及其零件:**							**Slide fasteners and parts thereof:**

税则号列	货品名称	最惠(%)	普通	增值税率	出口退税	计量单位	监管条件	Article Description
	-拉链:							-Slide fasteners:
9607.1100	--装有贱金属制咪牙齿的	21	130	17	13	米/千克		--Fitted with chain scoops of base metal
9607.1900	--其他	21	130	17	13	米/千克		--Other
9607.2000	-零件	21	130	17	13	千克		-Parts
96.08	**圆珠笔;毡尖和其他渗水式笔尖笔及唛头笔;自来水笔、铁笔型自来水笔及其他钢笔;蜡纸铁笔;活动铅笔;钢笔杆、铅笔套及类似的笔套;上述物品的零件(包括帽、夹),但税目96.09的货品除外:**							**Ball point pens; felt tipped and other porous-tipped pens and markers; fountain pens, stylograph pens and other pens; duplicating stylos; propelling or sliding pencils; pen-holders, pencil-holders and similar holders; parts (including caps and clips) of the foregoing articles, other than those of heading No. 96.09:**
9608.1000	-圆珠笔	15	80	17	13	支		-Ball point pens
9608.2000	-毡尖和其他渗水式笔尖笔及唛头笔	21	80	17	13	支		-Felt tipped and other porous-tipped pens and markers
	-自来水笔、铁笔型自来水笔及其他钢笔:							-Fountain pens, stylograph pens and other pens:
9608.3010	---墨汁画笔	21	80	17	13	支		---Indian ink drawing pens
9608.3020	---自来水笔	21	80	17	13	支		---Fountain pens
9608.3090	---其他	21	80	17	13	支		---Other
9608.4000	-活动铅笔	21	80	17	13	支		-Propelling or sliding pencils
9608.5000	-由上述两个或多个子目所列物品组成的成套货品	21	80	17	13	套		-Sets of articles from two or more of the foregoing sub-headings
9608.6000	-圆珠笔芯,由圆珠笔头和墨芯构成	21	80	17	13	支		-Refills for ball point pens, comprising the ball point and ink-reservoir
	-其他:							-Other:
9608.9100	--钢笔头及笔尖粒	12	70	17	13	支		--Pen nibs and nib points
	--其他:							--Other:
9608.9910	---机器、仪器用笔	17.5	40	17	13	支/千克		---Of a kind used on machines or instruments
9608.9920	---蜡纸铁笔;钢笔杆、铅笔杆及类似的笔杆	21	80	17	13	支/千克		---Duplicating stylos; pen-holders, pencil-holders and similar holders
9608.9990	---其他	21	80	17	13	千克		---Other
96.09	**铅笔(税目96.08的铅笔除外)、颜色铅笔、铅笔芯、蜡笔、图画碳笔、书写或绘画用粉笔及裁缝划粉:**							**Pencils (other than pencils of heading No. 96.08), crayons, pencil leads, pastels, drawing charcoals, writing or drawing chalks and tailors' chalks:**
	-铅笔及颜色铅笔:							-Pencils and crayons, with leads encased in a rigid sheath:
9609.1010	---铅笔	21	80	17	13	千克/百支		---Pencils
9609.1020	---颜色铅笔	21	80	17	13	千克		---Crayons
9609.2000	-铅笔芯,黑的或其他颜色的	21	80	17	13	千克		-Pencil leads, black or coloured
9609.9000	-其他	15	80	17	13	千克		-Other
96.10	**具有书写或绘画面的石板、黑板及类似板,不论是否镶框:**							**Slates and boards, with writing or drawing surfaces, whether or not framed:**
9610.0000	具有书写或绘画面的石板、黑板及类似板,不论是否镶框	15	80	17	13	千克		Slates and boards, with writing or drawing surfaces, whether or not framed
96.11	**手用日期戳、封缄戳、编号戳及类似印戳(包括标签压印器);手工操作的排字盘及带有排字盘的手印器:**							**Date, sealing or numbering stamps, and the like (including devices for printing or embossing labels), designed for operating in the hand; hand-operated composing sticks and hand printing sets incorporating such composing sticks:**
9611.0000	手用日期戳、封缄戳、编号戳及类似印戳(包括标签压印器);手工操作的排字盘及带有排字盘的手印器	21	80	17		千克		Date, sealing or numbering stamps, and the like (including devices for printing or embossing labels), designed for operating in the hand; hand-operated composing sticks and hand printing sets incorporating such composing sticks
9611.0000 10	含濒危动物成分的手用日期戳(包括封缄戳及类似印戳)	21	80	17		千克	FE	Date, sealing, and the like, designed for operating in the hand, containing materials of endangered animals

税则号列	货品名称	最惠(%)	普通	增值税率	出口退税	计量单位	监管条件	Article Description
9611.0000 90	手用日期戳、封缄戳及类似印戳(包括编号戳、标签压印器;手工排字盘及带有字盘的手印器)	21	80	17	13	千克		Other date, sealing or numbering stamps, and the like (including devices for printing or embossing labels), designed for operating in the hand; hand-operated composing sticks and hand printing sets incorporating such composing sticks
96.12	**打字机色带或类似色带,已上油或经其他方法处理能着色的,不论是否装轴或装盒;印台,不论是否已加印油或带盒子:**							**Typewriter or similar ribbons, inked or otherwise prepared for giving impressions, whether or not on spools or in cartridges; ink-pads, whether or not inked, with or without boxes:**
9612.1000	-色带	10.5	35	17	13	个/千克		-Inked ribbons
9612.2000	-印台	25	100	17	13	个		-Ink-pads
96.13	**香烟打火机和其他打火器(不论是机械的,还是电气的)及其零件,但打火石及打火机芯除外:**							**Cigarette lighters and other lighters, whether or not mechanical or electrical, and parts thereof other than flints and wicks:**
9613.1000	-袖珍气体打火机,一次性的	25	130	17	13	个	B	-Pocket lighters, gas fuelled, non refillable
9613.2000	-袖珍气体打火机,可充气的	25	130	17	13	个	B	-Pocket lighters, gas fuelled, refillable
9613.8000	-其他打火器	25	130	17	13	个	B	-Other lighters
9613.9000	-零件	25	130	17	13	千克		-Parts
96.14	**烟斗(包括烟斗头)和烟嘴及其零件:**							**Smoking pipes (including pipe bowls) and cigar or cigarette holders, and parts thereof:**
9614.0010	---烟斗及烟斗头	25	130	17		个/千克		---Pipes and pipe bowls
9614.0010 10	含濒危动物成分的烟斗及烟斗头(仅指野生哺乳类牙齿制产品)	25	130	17		个/千克	ABFE	Smoking pipes (including pipe bowls) containing materials of endangered animals (only referring to products made of ivory of wild mammals)
9614.0010 20	用植物性材料制作的烟斗及烟斗头	25	130	17	13	个/千克	AB	Smoking pipes and pipe bowls, of vegetable materials
9614.0010 90	其他烟斗及烟斗头	25	130	17	13	个/千克		Other smoking pipes and pipe bowls
9614.0090	---其他	25	130	17		千克		---Other
9614.0090 10	含濒危野生动物成分的烟嘴及其零件(仅指野生哺乳类牙齿制产品)	25	130	17		千克	FE	Cigar or cigarette holders, and parts thereof, containing endangered wild animal materials (only referring to products made of ivory of wild mammals)
9614.0090 90	其他烟嘴及其零件	25	130	17	13	千克		Other cigar or cigarette holders, and parts thereof
96.15	**梳子、发夹及类似品;发卡、卷发夹、卷发器或类似品及其零件,但税目85.16的货品除外:**							**Combs, hair-slides and the like; hairpins, curling pins, curling grips, hair-curlers and the like, other than those of heading No. 85.16, and parts thereof:**
	-梳子、发夹及类似品:							-Combs, hair-slides and the like:
9615.1100	--硬质橡胶或塑料制	18	130	17	13	千克		--Of hard rubber or plastics
9615.1900	--其他	18	130	17		千克		--Other
9615.1900 10	含濒危动物成分的其他材料制梳子(包括角质发夹等,金属、塑料及家畜来源的产品除外)	18	130	17		千克	FE	Combs containing endangered animals materials (including hair-slides made of horns, but not including products made of metal, plastic or material of domestic animals)
9615.1900 20	用其他动植物材料制的梳子(包括角质发夹等,金属、塑料及家畜来源的产品除外)	18	130	17	13	千克		Combs, of other animal or vegetable materials (including hair-slides made of horns, but not including products made of metal, plastic or material of domestic animals)
9615.1900 90	其他材料制梳子、角质发夹等(包括类似品,但橡胶、塑料制的除外)	18	130	17	13	千克		Combs and hair-slides of other materials (lincluding simials goods, but excluding products made of metal, plastic or material of domestic animals)
9615.9000	-其他	18	130	17	13	千克		-Other
96.16	**香水喷雾器或类似的化妆用喷雾器及其座架、喷头;粉扑及粉拍,施敷脂粉或化妆品用:**							**Scent sprays and similar toilet sprays, and mounts and heads therefor; powderpuffs and pads for the application of cosmetics or toilet preparations:**
9616.1000	-香水喷雾器或类似的化妆用喷雾器及其座架、喷头	18	130	17	13	千克		-Scent sprays and similar toilet sprays, and mounts and heads therefor

税则号列	货品名称	最惠(%)	普通	增值税率	出口退税	计量单位	监管条件	Article Description
9616.2000	-粉扑及粉拍,施敷脂粉或化妆品用	18	130	17	13	千克		-Powder-puffs and pads for the application of cosmetics or toilet preparations
96.17	**带壳的保温瓶和其他真空容器及其零件,但玻璃瓶胆除外:**							**Vacuum flasks and other vacuum vessels, complete with cases; parts thereof, other than glass inners:**
	---保温瓶:							---Vacuum flasks:
9617.0011	----玻璃内胆制	24	130	17	13	个/千克		----Glass bottle
9617.0019	----其他	24	130	17	13	个/千克		----Other
9617.0090	---其他	18	130	17	13	千克		---Other
96.18	**裁缝用人体模型及其他人体活动模型;橱窗装饰用的自动模型及其他活动陈列品:**							**Tailors' dummies and other lay figures; automata and other animated displays used for shop window dressing:**
9618.0000	裁缝用人体模型及其他人体活动模型;橱窗装饰用的自动模型及其他活动陈列品	21	80	17	13	千克		Tailors' dummies and other lay figures; automata and other animated displays used for shop window dressing
9618.0000 10	用植物性材料制作的人体模型	21	80	17	13	千克	AB	Dummies of vegetable materials
9618.0000 90	裁缝用其他人体模型(包括橱窗装饰用的自动模型及其他活动陈列品)	21	80	17	13	千克		Tailors' other dummies (including automaton and other animated displays used for shop window dressing)
96.19	**任何材料制的卫生巾(护垫)及止血塞、婴儿尿布及尿布衬里和类似品:**							**Sanitary towels(Pads) and tampons, napkins and napkin liners for babies and similar articles, of any material:**
9619.0010	---尿裤及尿布	7.5	80	17	13	千克	A	---Napkins and napkin liners
9619.0020	---卫生巾(护垫)及止血塞	10	80	17	13	千克	A	---Sanitary towels(Pads) and tampons
9619.0090	---其他	14	80	17	13	千克	A	---Other

第二十一类
艺术品、收藏品及古物

SECTION XXI
WORKS OF ART, COLLECTORS' PIECES AND ANTIQUES

第九十七章
艺术品、收藏品及古物

Chapter 97
Works of art, collectors' pieces and antiques

注释：

一、本章不包括：

(一)品目49.07的未经使用的邮票、印花税票，邮政信笺(印有邮票的纸品)及类似的票证

(二)作舞台、摄影的布景及类似用途的已绘制画布(税目59.07)，但可归入税目97.06的除外；

(三)天然或养殖珍珠、宝石或半宝石(税目71.01至71.03)。

二、税目97.02所称"雕版画、印制画、石印画的原本"，是指以艺术家完全手工制作的单块或数块印版直接印制出来的黑白或彩色原本，不论艺术家使用何种方法或材料，但不包括使用机器或照相制版方法制作的。

三、税目97.03不适用于成批生产的复制品及具有商业性质的传统手工艺品，即使这些物品是艺术家设计或创造的。

四、(一)除上述注释一至三另有规定的以外，可归入本章各税目的物品，均应归入本章的相应税目而不归入本目录的其他税目；

(二)税目97.06不适用于可以归入本章其他各税目的物品。

五、已装框的油画、粉画及其他绘画、版画、拼贴画及类似装饰板，如果框架的种类及价值与作品相称，应与作品一并归类。如果框架的种类及价值与作品不相称，应分别归类。

Notes:

1. This Chapter does not cover:

(a) Unused postage or revenue stamps, postal stationery (stamped paper) or the like, of heading 49.07;

(b) Theatrical scenery, studio back-cloths or the like, of painted canvas (heading No. 59.07) except if they may be classified in heading No. 97.06;

(c) Pearls, natural or cultured, or precious or semi-precious stones (headings No. 71.01 to 71.03).

2. For the purposes of heading No. 97.02, the expression "original engravings, prints and lithographs" means impressions produced directly, in black and white or in colour, of one or of several plates wholly executed by hand by the artist, irrespective of the process or of the material employed by him, but not including any mechanical or photomechanical process.

3. Heading No. 97.03 does not apply to mass-produced reproductions or works of conventional craftsmanship of a commercial character, even if these articles are designed or created by artists.

4. (a) Subject to Notes 1 to 3 above, articles of this Chapter are to be classified in this Chapter and not in any other Chapter of the Nomenclature.

(b) heading No. 97.06 does not apply to articles of the preceding headings of this Chapter.

5. Frames around paintings, drawings, pastels, collages or similar decorative plaques, engravings, prints or lithographs are to be classified with those articles, provided they are of a kind and of a value normal to those articles. Frames which are not of a kind or of a value normal to the articles referred to in this Note are to be classified separately.

税则号列	货品名称	最惠(%)	普通	增值税率	出口退税	计量单位	监管条件	Article Description
97.01	油画、粉画及其他手绘画，但带有手工绘制及手工描饰的制品或税目49.06的图纸除外；拼贴画及类似装饰板：							**Paintings, drawings and pastels, executed entirely by hand, other than drawings of heading No. 49.06 and other than hand-painted or hand-decorated manufactured articles; collages and similar decorative plaques:**
	-油画、粉画及其他手绘画：							-Paintings, drawings and pastels:
	---原件：							---The originals:
9701.1011暂	----唐卡	6	50	17		幅		----Thangka
9701.1019暂	----其他	6	50	17		幅		----Other
9701.1020	---复制品	14	50	17		幅		---Reproductions
9701.9000	-其他	14	50	17		千克		-Other
9701.9000 10	含濒危动物成分的拼贴画(包括类似装饰板，指一切源自濒危动物的产品)	14	50	17		千克	ABFE	Collages and similar decorative plaques, containing materials of endangered animals (referring to collages of materials of all kinds of endangered animals)
9701.9000 20	用其他动植物材料制作的拼贴画(包括类似装饰板，指一切源自野生动物的产品)	14	50	17		千克	AB	Collages and similar decorative plaques of other animal or vegetable materials (referring to collages of materials of all kinds of wild animals)

税则号列	货品名称	最惠(%)	普通	增值税率	出口退税	计量单位	监管条件	Article Description
9701.9000 90	其他拼贴画及类似装饰板	14	50	17		千克		Other collages and similar decorative plaques
97.02	**雕版画、印制画、石印画的原本：**							**Original engravings, prints and lithographs:**
9702.0000暂	雕版画、印制画、石印画的原本	6	50	17		幅		Original engravings, prints and lithographs
97.03	**各种材料制的雕塑品原件：**							**Original sculptures and statuary, in any material:**
9703.0000暂	各种材料制的雕塑品原件	6	50	17		幅		Original sculptures and statuary, in any material
9703.0000暂 10	濒危动植物材料制的雕塑品原件（指一切源自濒危动植物的产品）	6	50	17		幅	FE	Original sculptures and statuary, in endangered animals and vegetable material (referring to articles from endangered animals and vegetable)
9703.0000暂 90	其他各种材料制的雕塑品原件	6	50	17		幅		Other original sculptures and statuary, in any materials
97.04	**使用过或未使用过的邮票、印花税票、邮戳印记、首日封、邮政信笺（印有邮票的纸品）及类似品，但税目49.07的货品除外：**							**Used or unused postage or revenue stamps, stamp-postmarks, first-day covers, postal stationery (stamped paper), and the like, other than those of heading No. 49.07:**
9704.0010	---邮票	8	50	17		千克		---Postage
9704.0090	---其他	14	50	17		千克		---Other
97.05	**具有动物学、植物学、矿物学、解剖学、历史学、考古学、古生物学、人种学或钱币学意义的收集品及珍藏品：**							**Collections and collectors pieces of zoological, botanical, mineralogical, anatomical, historical, archaeological, palaeontological, ethnographic or numismatic interest:**
9705.0000	具有动物学、植物学、矿物学、解剖学、历史学、考古学、古生物学、人种学或钱币学意义的收集品及珍藏品	0	0	17		千克		Collections and collectors' pieces of zoological, botanical, mineralogical, anatomical, historical, archaeological, palaeontological, ethnographic or numismatic interest
9705.0000 10	含濒危动植物的收藏品（具有动植物学意义的）	0	0	17		千克	ABFE	Collections and collectors' pieces, containing endangered plants or animal (with zoological and botanical interest)
9705.0000 90	具有动、植、矿物学意义的收藏品（还包括具有解剖、历史、考古、古生物学意义的收藏品）	0	0	17		千克	AB	Collections and collectors' pieces (with zoological, botanical, mineralogical, anatomical, historical, archaeological, palaeontological, ethnographic or numismatic interest)
97.06	**超过一百年的古物：**							**Antiques of an age exceeding one hundred years:**
9706.0000	超过一百年的古物	0	0	17		千克		Antiques of an age exceeding one hundred years
9706.0000 10	超过一百年的濒危野生动植古物（具收藏或文史价值的）	0	0	17		千克	ABFE	Antiques of an age exceeding one hundred years of endangered wild animal or vegetable (having literary or historical collection value)
9706.0000 90	其他超过一百年的古物	0	0	17		千克		Other antiques of an age exceeding one hundred years

第二十二类
特殊交易品及未分类商品

SECTION XXII
ARTICLES OF SPECIAL TRADE AND GOOD UNCLASSIFIED

第九十八章
特殊交易品及未分类商品

Chapter 98
Articles of Special Trade and Good Unclassified

税则号列	货品名称	最惠(%)	普通	增值税率	出口退税	计量单位	监管条件	Article Description
98.01	**未分类商品**							**Good unclassified**
9801.0010	≤2000 元 RMB 的非税，非证进口商品	0	0			千克		Import goods exempted from the levy of customs duties and not subject to license control, value ≤ 2000RMB
9801.0090	其他未分类商品	0	0		13	千克		Other unclassified commodities
9801.3000	流通中的货币现钞（包括纸币及硬币）	0	0			千克	T	Official currencies (negotiable paper notes and coins)
98.03	**出口计算机软件（仅用于出口，不包括与产品固化或集成为一体的软件）**							**Computer software, not including software hard-wired or integrated in products**
9803.0010	定制型系统软件	0	0			套		System software
9803.0020	定制型支撑软件	0	0			套		Support software
9803.0030	定制型应用软件	0	0			套		Application software
9803.0090	其他定制型软件	0	0			套		Other software

2

中华人民共和国海关进出口货物报关单填报规范和报关自动化系统常用代码表及说明

Standards for Filling Import/Export Goods Declaration Form and Code list to Supporting Documents subject to Customs of the People's Republic of China

(1)中华人民共和国海关进出口货物报关单填制规范 739
(1)Standards for Filling Import/Export Goods Declaration Form
(2)海关总署关于优惠贸易协定项下进口货物的报关单填制规范公告 751
(2)General Administration of Customs P. R. C. Announcement for Standards of Filling Declaration for Import Goods Stipulated Under Preferential Trading Agreements
(3)报关自动化系统常用代码表说明 753
(3)Explantlons about table of codes often use in customs clearance system
(4)报关自动化系统常用代码表 802
(4)Common Codes for Automated Customs Declartion System(EDI)
监管方式代码表 802
Codes for Customs Procedures (Modes of International Trade)
征免性质代码表 805
Codes for the Nature of Levy, Reduction and Exemption of Customs Duties and Taxes
征减免税方式代码表 806
Codes For Type of Levy, Reduction and Exemption of Customs Duties and Taxes
运输方式代码表 806
Codes for Modes of Transport
关区代码表 806
Codes for International Trade Ports (Customs Establishment)
国内地区代码表 814
Codes for Sub-entity of the P. R. C.
★监管证件名称代码表 821
Code list of Supporting Documents Subject to Customs Control of the People's Republic of China
结汇方式代码表 822
Codes for Modes of Bank's Exchange Settlement
用途代码表 823
Codes for Use of Imported Goods
货币代码表 823
Codes for the Representation of Currencies
计量单位代码表 823
Codes for Units of Measure Used in International Trade
成交方式代码表 824
Codes for Trade Terms
国别(地区)代码表 824
Codes for the Representation of Names of Countries and Regions
地区性质代码表 827
Codes for the Nature of Designated Areas
企业性质代码表 827
Codes for Class of Enterprises

中华人民共和国海关进出口货物报关单填制规范

为规范进出口货物收发货人的申报行为，统一进出口货物报关单填制要求，保证报关单数据质量，根据《中华人民共和国海关法》及有关法规，制定本规范。

《中华人民共和国海关进（出）口货物报关单》在本规范中采用“报关单”、“进口报关单”、“出口报关单”的提法。

报关单各栏目的填制规范如下：

一、预录入编号

本栏目填报预录入报关单的编号，预录入编号规则由接受申报的海关决定。

二、海关编号

本栏目填报海关接受申报时给予报关单的编号，一份报关单对应一个海关编号。

报关单海关编号为18位，其中第1－4位为接受申报海关的编号（海关规定的《关区代码表》中相应海关代码），第5－8位为海关接受申报的公历年份，第9位为进出口标志（"1"为进口，"0"为出口；集中申报清单"I"为进口，"E"为出口），后9位为顺序编号。在海关H883/EDI通关系统向H2000通关系统过渡期间，后9位的编号规则同H883/EDI通关系统的要求，即1－2位为接受申报海关的编号（海关规定的《关区代码表》中相应海关代码的后2位），第3位为海关接受申报公历年份4位数字的最后1位，后6位为顺序编号。

三、进口口岸/出口口岸

本栏目应根据货物实际进出境的口岸海关，填报海关规定的《关区代码表》中相应口岸海关的名称及代码。特殊情况填报要求如下：

进口转关运输货物应填报货物进境地海关名称及代码，出口转关运输货物应填报货物出境地海关名称及代码。按转关运输方式监管的跨关区深加工结转货物，出口报关单填报转出地海关名称及代码，进口报关单填报转入地海关名称及代码。

在不同海关特殊监管区域或保税监管场所之间调拨、转让的货物，填报对方特殊监管区域或保税监管场所所在的海关名称及代码。

其他无实际进出境的货物，填报接受申报的海关名称及代码。

四、备案号

本栏目填报进出口货物收发货人在海关办理加工贸易合同备案或征、减、免税备案审批等手续时，海关核发的《中华人民共和国海关加工贸易手册》、电子账册及其分册（以下统称《加工贸易手册》）、《进出口货物征免税证明》（以下简称《征免税证明》）或其他备案审批文件的编号。

一份报关单只允许填报一个备案号。具体填报要求如下：

（一）加工贸易项下货物，除少量低值辅料按规定不使用《加工贸易手册》及以后续补税监管方式办理内销征税的外，填报《加工贸易手册》编号。

使用异地直接报关分册和异地深加工结转出口分册在异地口岸报关的，本栏目应填报分册号；本地直接报关分册和本地深加工结转分册限制在本地报关，本栏目应填报总册号。

加工贸易成品凭《征免税证明》转为减免税进口货物的，进口报关单填报《征免税证明》编号，出口报关单填报《加工贸易手册》编号。

Standards for Filling Import/Export Goods Declaration Form

In order to regulate declaration of consigners and consignees, unify the requirements for filling the import/export goods declaration form and ensure the quality of data given in the declaration form, this standard is laid down according to the Customs Law of the People's Republic of China and relevant regulations.

The Import/Export Goods Declaration Form of the People's Republic of China is mentioned as the "declaration form", "import declaration form" or "export declaration form" in this standard.

The rule on filling the columns of the declaration form is as follows:

1. Pre - entry No.

Fill the No. of the pre - entry declaration form in this column and the rule on pre - entry Nos. is decided by the Customs office which accepts declaration.

2. Customs No.

Fill in this column the No. of the declaration form given by the Customs office when it accepts declaration and one declaration form corresponds to one Customs No.

The Customs No. consists of 18 digits. Therein the first four are the code No. of the Customs office which accepts declaration (its corresponding Customs code in the Table of Customs Codes prepared by the Customs), the 5th to the 8th digits are the Gregorian calendar year when the Customs office accepts declaration and the 9th digit is the import and export sign ("1" means import, "0" means export; "I" means import and "E" means export in the collective declaration form). The last 9 digits is the serial No. When the H883/EDI Customs clearance system transits to the H2000 Customs clearance system, the rule of numbering the last 9 digits is the same as the requirement of the H883/EDI Customs clearance, i. e. the 1st and 2nd digits are the No. of the Customs office which accepts declaration (the last two digits of its corresponding Customs code in the Table of Customs Codes prepared by the Customs), the 3rd digit is the last digit of the four digits of the Gregorian calendar year when the Customs office accepts declaration and the last six digits are the serial No.

3. Import port/export port

Fill the name and code of the Customs office at the port where goods are actually imported or exported according to the Table of Customs Codes prepared by the Customs. The requirements for filling special circumstances are as follows:

In the case of import goods in Customs transfer, fill the name and code of the Customs office via which goods are imported; in the case of export goods in Customs transfer, fill the name and code of the Customs office via which goods will be exported. Fill the name and code of the Customs office of exit on the export declaration form and fill the name and code of the Customs office of entry on the import declaration form in the case of goods transferred from one Customs area to another for deep processing according to the procedure of Customs transfer.

In the case of goods allocated or transferred between special supervision areas or bonded areas of different Customs offices, fill the name and code of the destination Customs office.

If goods are transferred without actual import or export, fill the name and code of the Customs office which accepts declaration.

4. Registration No.

Fill in this column the Processing Trade Handbook of the Customs of the People's Republic of China, electronic account book and its sub - book (referred to as the Processing Trade Handbook collectively hereunder), the Certificate of Collection of and Exemption of Import and Export Goods from Duties (shortened to the Certificate of Collection of and Exemption from Duties hereunder) or other recording or approving documents issued by the Customs when consigners and consignees of import and export goods have their processing trade contracts recorded or go through recording and approving formalities for collection and reduction of and exemption from duties with the Customs.

For one declaration form, only one registration No. is to be filled. Specific requirements are as follows:

(1) Fill the No. of the Processing Trade Handbook for goods under processing trade except a small quantity of low - value auxiliary materials and goods which are to be sold domestically after paying duties retrospectively.

Fill the No. of the sub - book when declaring to another port using the declaration sub - book for direct declaration at the other port and the sub - book for reexporting at another port goods deep processed in another place; fill the general No. of the declaration book when the sub - book for local direct declaration and the sub - book for local processing are limited to the local Customs.

Fill the No. of the certificate in the import declaration form and fill the No. of the Processing Trade Handbook in the export declaration form when finished products under processing trade are turned into imports of whose duties are reduced or exempted based on the Certificate of Collection of and Exemption from Duties.

对加工贸易设备之间的结转，转入和转出企业分别填制进、出口报关单，在报关单"备案号"栏目填报《加工贸易手册》编号。

For transference of processing trade equipment, transferors and transferees fill import and export declaration forms respectively and fill the No. of the Processing Trade Handbook in the column of "No. of Record" in the export declaration form.

（二）涉及征、减、免税备案审批的报关单，填报《征免税证明》编号。

(2) Fill the No. of the Certificate of Collection of and Exemption from Duties when the declaration form involves record and approval of collection and reduction of and exemption from duties.

（三）涉及优惠贸易协定项下实行原产地证书联网管理（香港CEPA、澳门CEPA，下同）的报关单，填报原产地证书代码"Y"和原产地证书编号。

(3) Fill the code "Y" and the No. of the place of origin certificate in the declaration form which involves networked management of the place of origin certificate under the preferential trade protocol (Hong Kong CEPA and Macao CEPA).

（四）减免税货物退运出口，填报《减免税进口货物同意退运证明》的编号；减免税货物补税进口，填报《减免税货物补税通知书》的编号；减免税货物结转进口（转入），填报《征免税证明》的编号；相应的结转出口（转出），填报《减免税进口货物结转联系函》的编号。

(4) Fill the No. of the Certificate of Agreeing to Returning Imports Granted Reduction of and Exemption from Duties when returning imports granted reduction of and exemption from duties; fill the No. of the Notice about Supplementing Duties for Imports Granted Reduction of and Exemption from Duties when supplementing duties for imports; fill the No. of the Certificate of Collection of and Exemption from Duties when imports granted reduction of and exemption from duties are imported (turn in); fill the No. of the Letter on Imports Granted Reduction of and Exemption from Duties for corresponding export (turn out).

（五）涉及构成整车特征的汽车零部件的报关单，填报备案的Q账册编号。

(5) Fill the No. of the Q account book for record when the declaration form involves auto parts which constitute the characteristics of a whole car.

五、合同协议号

5. Contract/agreement No.

本栏目填报进出口货物合同（包括协议或订单）编号。

Fill the No. of import and export contracts (including agreements or orders).

六、进口日期/出口日期

6. Date of import/date of export

进口日期填报运载进口货物的运输工具申报进境的日期。

Fill the date when the means of transport which carries imports is declared for entry as the date of import.

出口日期指运载出口货物的运输工具办结出境手续的日期，本栏目供海关签发打印报关单证明联用，在申报时免予填报。

The date of export is the date when the formalities for the means of transport which carried exports to clear the Customs are gone through. This column is for the Customs to print the declaration form certificate and it's unnecessary to fill it in declaration.

无实际进出境的报关单填报海关接受申报的日期

Fill the date when the Customs accepts declaration in the declaration form in the case of no actual import and export.

本栏目为8位数字，顺序为年（4位）、月（2位）、日（2位）。

This column consists of eight digits and the sequence is the year (four digits), month(disits) and days (two digits)

七、申报日期

7. Date of declaration

申报日期指海关接受进出口货物收发货人、受委托的报关企业申报数据的日期。以电子数据报关单方式申报的，申报日期为海关计算机系统接受申报数据时记录的日期。以纸质报关单方式申报的，申报日期为海关接受纸质报关单并对报关单进行登记处理的日期。

The date of declaration is the date when the Customs accepts data declared by consigners and consignees of imports and exports or their trusted declaring agents. When declaration is made electronically, the date of declaration is the date when the computer system of the Customs receives declaration data. When declaration is made in paper, the date of declaration is the date when the Customs receives declaration forms in paper and records and processes them.

申报日期为8位数字，顺序为年（4位）、月（2位）、日（2位）。本栏目在申报时免予填报。

The date of declaration consists of eight digits and the sequence is the year ((four digits), month (2 digits) and days (two digits). It's unnecessary to fill this column in declaration.

八、经营单位

8. Operating unit

本栏目填报在海关注册登记的对外签订并执行进出口贸易合同的中国境内法人、其他组织或个人的名称及海关注册编码。

Fill in this column the name of the legal person, other organization or individual in China that has been registering with the Customs and signed and implemented import and export contracts as well as its Customs registration code.

特殊情况下填制要求如下：

Requirements for filling in special cases are as follows:

（一）进出口货物合同的签订者和执行者非同一企业的，填报执行合同的企业。

(1) Fill the enterprise which implements an import or export contract when the signer and implementer of the contract is not the same.

（二）外商投资企业委托进出口企业进口投资设备、物品的，填报外商投资企业，并在标记唛码及备注栏注明"委托某进出口企业进口"。

(2) If a foreign – invested enterprise trusts an import and export enterprise with import of invested equipment and articles, fill the name of the foreign – invested enterprise and indicate "trust an import and export enterprise with import" in the mark and equipment column.

（三）有代理报关资格的报关企业代理其他进出口企业办理进出口报关手续时，填报委托的进出口企业的名称及海关注册编码。

(3) Fill the name of the trusted import and export enterprise and the Customs registration code if a declaring agent with the qualification for declaration handles import and export declaration formalities for other import and export enterprises.

九、收货单位/发货单位

9. Consigners/consigners

（一）收货单位填报已知的进口货物在境内的最终消费、使用单位的名称，包括：

(1) The name of the end user of imports filled by consignees, including:

1. 自行从境外进口货物的单位。

2. 委托进出口企业进口货物的单位。

a. Units which import goods by themselves.

b. Units which trust import and export enterprises with import.

（二）发货单位填报出口货物在境内的生产或销售单位的名称，包括：

(2) Consigners fill the name of the manufacturer or sales unit of exports, including:

1. 自行出口货物的单位。

2. 委托进出口企业出口货物的单位。

a. Units which exports goods by themselves.

b. Units which trusts import and export enterprises with export.

（三）有海关注册编码或加工企业编码的收、发货单位，本栏目应填报其中文名称及编码；没有编码的应填报其中文名称。使用《加工贸易手册》管理的货物，报关单的收、发货单位应与《加工贸易手册》的"经营企业"或"加工企业"一致；减免税货物报关单的收、发货单位应与《征免税证明》的"申请单位"一致。

(3) Consignees and consigners which have the Customs registration code or processing enterprise code fill their Chinese names and codes in this column or fill their Chinese names if they don't have codes. Consigners and consignees in declaration forms for goods managed by the Processing Trade Handbook should be consistent with "operating enterprises" or "processing enterprises" in the Processing Trade Handbook; consigners and consignees in declaration forms for goods granted reduction of and exemption from duties should be consistent with "applicants" in the Certificate of Collection of and Exemption from Duties.

十、申报单位

10. Declaring units

自理报关的，本栏目填报进出口企业的名称及海关注册编码；委托代理报关的，本栏目填报经海关批准的报关企业名称及海关注册编码。

Import and export enterprises which declare to the Customs by themselves fill their names and Customs registration codes in this column; those that trust agents with declaration to the Customs fill names and Customs registration codes of approved declaring enterprises in this column.

本栏目还包括报关单左下方用于填报申报单位有关情况的相关栏目，包括报关员、报关单位地址、邮政编码和电话号码等栏目。

This column also includes the relevant column in the lower left side of the declaration form for filling conditions of declaring units, such as declarers, addresses of declaring units, post codes and telephone Nos.

十一、运输方式

11. Means of transport

运输方式包括实际运输方式和海关规定的特殊运输方式，前者指货物实际进出境的运输方式，按进出境所使用的运输工具分类；后者指货物无实际进出境的运输方式，按货物在境内的流向分类。

Means of transport include actual means of transport and special means of transport stipulated by the Customs. The former refers to the actual means of transport for import and export and is classified according to means of transport for import and export; the latter refers to means of transport without actual import and export and is classified according to the flow direction of goods in China.

本栏目应根据货物实际进出境的运输方式或货物在境内流向的类别，按照海关规定的《运输方式代码表》选择填报相应的运输方式。

Fill corresponding means of transport in this column according to the actual means of transport for import and export or the classification of the flow direction of goods in China and based on the Table of Codes of Means of Transport prepared by the Customs.

（一）特殊情况填报要求如下：

1. 非邮件方式进出境的快递货物，按实际运输方式填报；

2. 进出境旅客随身携带的货物，按旅客所乘运输工具填报；

3. 进口转关运输货物，按载运货物抵达进境地的运输工具填报；出口转关运输货物，按载运货物驶离出境地的运输工具填报；

4. 不复运出（入）境而留在境内（外）销售的进出境展览品、留赠转卖物品等，填报“其他运输”（代码9）；

（1）The requirements for filling special circumstances are as follows:

a. Fill according to the actual means of transport for express goods not imported or exported by post;

b. Fill according to means of transport taken by inbound and outbound passengers for goods carried by them personally;

c. Fill according to means of transport which carry goods into China for goods transferred to other Customs offices after import; fill according to means of transport which carry goods out of China for goods transferred to other Customs offices before export;

d. Fill "other transport" (the code 9) for import and export exhibits which will not be reexported or reimported, articles retained, presented or sold, etc.;

（二）无实际进出境货物在境内流转时填报要求如下：

1. 境内非保税区运入保税区货物和保税区退区货物，填报"非保税区"（代码0）；

2. 保税区运往境内非保税区货物，填报"保税区"（代码7）；

3. 境内存入出口监管仓库和出口监管仓库退仓货物，填报"监管仓库"（代码1）；

4. 保税仓库转内销货物，填报"保税仓库"（代码8）；

5. 从境内保税物流中心外运入中心或从中心运往境内中心外的货物，填报"物流中心"（代码W）；

6. 从境内保税物流园区外运入园区或从园区运往境内园区外的货物，填报"物流园区"（代码X）；

7. 从境内保税港区外运入港区（不含直通）或从港区运往境内港区外（不含直通）的货物，填报"保税港区"（代码Y），综合保税区比照保税港区填报；

8. 从境内出口加工区、珠澳跨境工业区珠海园区（以下简称珠海园区）外运入加工区、珠海园区或从加工区、珠海园区运往境内区外的货物，区外企业填报“出口加工区”（代码Z），区内企业填报“其他运输”（代码9）；

9. 境内运入深港西部通道港方口岸区的货物，填报"边境特殊海关作业区"（代码H）；

10. 其他境内流转货物，填报"其他运输"（代码9），包括特殊监管区域内货物之间的流转、调拨货物，特殊监管区域、保税监管场所之间相互流转货物，特殊监管区域外的加工贸易余料结转、深加工结转、内销等货物。

（2）If goods circulate in China without actual import and export, the requirements for filling the declaration form are as follows:

a. Fill "non - bonded areas" (the code 0) for goods transported into bonded areas from non - bonded areas and for goods returned from bonded areas;

b. Fill "bonded areas" (the code 7) for goods transported from bonded areas to non - bonded areas in China;

c. Fill "warehouses under supervision" (the code 1) for goods stored domestically in warehouses under export supervision and for goods returned from such warehouses;

d. Fill "bonded warehouses" (the code 8) for goods leaving bonded warehouses and sold domestically;

e. Fill "centers for flow of goods" (the code W) for goods transported into centers from domestic bonded centers for flow of goods or for goods transported out of such centers;

f. Fill "parks for flow of goods" (the code X) for goods transported into domestic bonded parks for flow of goods or for goods transported out of such parks;

g. Fill "bonded ports" (the code Y) for goods transported into domestic bonded ports (not including through bonded ports) or goods transported out of such ports (not including through bonded ports) and fill likewise in the case of comprehensive bonded areas;

h. Enterprises outside domestic export processing areas and the Zhuhai Section of the Cross - Zhuhai and Macao Industrial Park (shortened to the Zhuhai Section) fill "export processing areas" (the code Z) and enterprises inside them fill "other transport" (the code 9) for goods transported into or out of them;

i. Fill the "special Customs area in the border" (the code H) for goods transported into the Hong Kong port at the western passage between Shenzhen and Hong Kong;

j. Fill "other transport" (the code 9) for other goods circulating domestically, including flow and allocation of goods in areas under special supervision, flow of goods between areas under special supervision and bonded areas and carry - over of leftover materials, carry - over of deep processing and internally sold goods outside areas under special supervision.

十二、运输工具名称

12. Names of means of transport

本栏目填报载运货物进出境的运输工具名称或编号。填报内容应与运输部门向海关申报的舱单（载货清单）所列相应内容一致。具体填报要求如下：

Fill names or serial Nos. of means of transport for carrying goods into and out of China. The filled content should be consistent with the corresponding content listed in the cargo manifest. The specific requirements for filling this column are as follows:

（一）直接在进出境地或采用“属地申报，口岸验放”通关模式办理报关手续的报关单填报要求如下：

1. 水路运输：填报船舶编号（来往港澳小型船舶为监管簿编号）或者船舶英文名称。

2. 公路运输：填报该跨境运输车辆的国内行驶车牌号，深圳提前报关模式的报关单填报国内行驶车牌号+"/"+"提前报关"。

3. 铁路运输：填报车厢编号或交接单号。

（1）The requirements for filling the declaration form when handling declaration formalities directly at import and export ports or adopting the customs clearance mode of "declaring goods in the local place and having them examined and cleared at ports" are as follows:

a. Waterway transport: fill the No. of ships (Nos. in the supervision book for small ships ferrying between Hong Kong and Macao) or English names of ships.

b. Road transport: fill plate license Nos. of domestic vehicles engaged in cross - border transport and fill plate Nos. of domestic vehicles + "/" + "declaring to the Customs in advance" in the declaration form in the case of declaring to the Customs in advance in Shenzhen.

c. Railway transport: fill Nos. of cars or takeover and handover list Nos.

4. 航空运输:填报航班号。
5. 邮件运输:填报邮政包裹单号。
6. 其他运输:填报具体运输方式名称,例如:管道、驮畜等。
(二)转关运输货物的报关单填报如下:

1. 进口
(1)水路运输:直转、提前报关填报"@"+16位转关申报单预录入号(或13位载货清单号);中转填报进境英文船名。

(2)铁路运输:直转、提前报关填报"@"+16位转关申报单预录入号;中转填报车厢编号。

(3)航空运输:直转、提前报关填报"@"+16位转关申报单预录入号(或13位载货清单号);中转填报"@"。

(4)公路及其他运输:填报"@"+16位转关申报单预录入号(或13位载货清单号)。
(5)以上各种运输方式使用广东地区载货清单转关的提前报关货物填报"@"+13位载货清单号。

2. 出口
(1)水路运输:非中转填报"@"+16位转关申报单预录入号(或13位载货清单号)。如多张报关单需要通过一张转关单转关的,运输工具名称字段填报"@"。

中转货物,境内水路运输填报驳船船名;境内铁路运输填报车名(主管海关4位关别代码+"TRAIN");境内公路运输填报车名(主管海关4位关别代码+"TRUCK")。
(2)铁路运输:填报"@"+16位转关申报单预录入号(或13位载货清单号),如多张报关单需要通过一张转关单转关的,填报"@"。

(3)航空运输:填报"@"+16位转关申报单预录入号(或13位载货清单号),如多张报关单需要通过一张转关单转关的,填报"@"。

(4)其他运输方式:填报"@"+16位转关申报单预录入号(或13位载货清单号)。
(三)采用"集中申报"通关方式办理报关手续的,报关单本栏目填报"集中申报"。

(四)无实际进出境的报关单,本栏目免予填报。

十三、航次号
本栏目填报载运货物进出境的运输工具的航次编号。
具体填报要求如下:
(一)直接在进出境地或采用"属地申报,口岸验放"通关模式办理报关手续的报关单

1. 水路运输:填报船舶的航次号。
2. 公路运输:填报运输车辆的8位进出境日期〔顺序为年(4位)、月(2位)、日(2位),下同〕。
3. 铁路运输:填报列车的进出境日期。
4. 航空运输:免予填报。
5. 邮件运输:填报运输工具的进出境日期。
6. 其他运输方式:免予填报。
(二)转关运输货物的报关单
1. 进口
(1)水路运输:中转转关方式填报"@"+进境干线船舶航次。直转、提前报关免予填报。
(2)公路运输:免予填报。
(3)铁路运输:"@"+8位进境日期。
(4)航空运输:免予填报。
(5)其他运输方式:免予填报。
2. 出口
(1)水路运输:非中转货物免予填报。中转货物:境内水路运输填报驳船航次号;境内铁路、公路运输填报6位起运日期〔顺序为年(2位)、月(2位)、日(2位)〕。

d. Air transport: fill flight Nos.
e. Post transport: fill Nos. of postal parcels.
f. Other transport: fill names of specific means of transport, such as pipelines, beasts of burden, etc.
(2) The requirement for filling the declaration form for soods transferred to another customs office are as follows:
a. Import
a) Waterway transport: fill "@" +16 - digit pre - entry No. of the Customs transfer declaration form (or 13 - digit No. of the cargo manifest) in the case of direct transfer and declaring in advance; fill English names of entry ships in the case of transit.
b) Railway transport: fill "@" +16 - digit pre - entry No. of the Customs transfer declaration form in the case of direct transfer and declaring in advance; fill Nos. of cars in the case of transit.
c) Air transport: fill "@" +16 - digit pre - entry No. of the Customs transfer declaration form (or 13 - digit No. of the cargo manifest) in the case of direct transfer and declaring in advance; fill "@" in the case of transit.
d) Road and other transport: fill "@" +16 - digit pre - entry No. of the Customs transfer declaration form (or 13 - digit No. of the cargo manifest).
e) Fill "@" + 13 - digit No. of the cargo manifest for goods transported by the above means of transport, transferred to another Customs office by cargo manifests of Guangdong and declared to the Customs in advance.
b. Export
a) Waterway transport: fill "@" +16 - digit pre - entry No. of the Customs transfer declaration form (or 13 - digit No. of the cargo manifest) in the case of non transit; if many declaration forms have to be transferred to other Customs offices by one Customs transfer form, fill "@" in the name section of means of transport.
Fill names of ships for transit goods and domestic waterway transport; fill names of trains in the case of domestic railway transport (four Customs class codes of competent Customs + "TRAIN"); fill names of vehicles in the case of domestic road transport (four Customs class codes of competent Customs + "Truck").
b) Railway transport: fill "@" +16 - digit pre - entry No. of the Customs transfer declaration form (or 13 - digit No. of the cargo manifest); if many declaration forms have to be transferred to other Customs offices by one Customs transfer form, fill "@" in the name section of means of transport.
c) Air transport: fill "@" +16 - digit pre - entry No. of the Customs transfer declaration form (or 13 - digit No of the cargo manifest); if many declaration forms have to be transferred to other Customs offices by one Customs transfer form, fill "@" in the name section of means of transport.
d) Other means of transport: fill "@" +16 - digit pre - entry No. of the Customs transfer declaration form (or 13 - digit No. of the cargo manifest).
(3) Fill "collective declaration" in this column of the declaration form when handling Customs declaration formalities by the clearance way of "collective declaration".
(4) It's unnecessary to fill this column for the declaration form without actual import and export.

13. Journey Nos.
Fill journey Nos. of means of transport which carry goods into and out of China in this column.
The specific requirements for filling this column are as follows:
(1) Declaration form for handling declaration formalities directly at import and export ports or adopting the customs clearance mode of "declaring goods in the local place and having them examined and cleared at ports"
a. Waterway transport: fill voyage Nos. of ships.
b. Road transport: fill the 8 - digit import and export date when transport vehicles enter or leave China (the sequence is the year (four digits), month (two digits), days (two digits), the same below).
c. Railway transport: fill the date when trains enter or leave China.
d. Air transport: dont fill.
e. Post transport: fill the date when means of transport enter or leave China.
f. Other means of transport: dont fill.
(2) Declaration form for goods transferred to another port
a. Import
a) Waterway transport: fill "@" + voyage Nos. of entry ships on main routes in the case of transit and Customs transfer. Don't fill in the case of direct transfer and declaration in advance.
b) Road transport: dont fill.
c) Railway transport: "@" + 8 - digit date of entry.
d) Air transport: dont fill.
e) Other means of transport: dont fill.
b. Export
a) Waterway transport: dont fill for non - transit goods. Transit goods: fill voyage Nos. of barges for domestic waterway transport; fill the 6 - digit date when domestic railway and road transport start (the sequence is the year (two digits), month (two digits), month (two digits and days (two digits).

(2)铁路拼车拼箱捆绑出口:免予填报。
(3)航空运输:免予填报。
(4)其他运输方式:免予填报。
(三)无实际进出境的报关单,本栏目免予填报。

十四、提运单号

本栏目填报进出口货物提单或运单的编号。

一份报关单只允许填报一个提单或运单号,一票货物对应多个提单或运单时,应分单填报。

具体填报要求如下:

(一)直接在进出境地或采用"属地申报,口岸验放"通关模式办理报关手续的。

1. 水路运输:填报进出口提单号。如有分提单的,填报进出口提单号+"*"+分提单号。

2. 公路运输:免予填报。
3. 铁路运输:填报运单号。
4. 航空运输:填报总运单号+"_"+分运单号,无分运单的填报总运单号。

5. 邮件运输:填报邮运包裹单号。

(二)转关运输货物的报关单

1. 进口

(1)水路运输:直转、中转填报提单号。提前报关免予填报。

(2)铁路运输:直转、中转填报铁路运单号。提前报关免予填报。

(3)航空运输:直转、中转货物填报总运单号+"_"+分运单号。提前报关免予填报。

(4)其他运输方式:免予填报。

(5)以上运输方式进境货物,在广东省内用公路运输转关的,填报车牌号。

2. 出口

(1)水路运输:中转货物填报提单号;非中转货物免予填报;广东省内汽车运输提前报关的转关货物,填报承运车辆的车牌号。

(2)其他运输方式:免予填报。广东省内汽车运输提前报关的转关货物,填报承运车辆的车牌号。

(三)采用"集中申报"通关方式办理报关手续的,报关单填报归并的集中申报清单的进出口起止日期〔按年(4位)月(2位)日(2位)年(4位)月(2位)日(2位)〕。

(四)无实际进出境的,本栏目免予填报。

十五、贸易方式(监管方式)

本栏目应根据实际对外贸易情况按海关规定的《监管方式代码表》选择填报相应的监管方式简称及代码。一份报关单只允许填报一种监管方式。

特殊情况下加工贸易货物监管方式填报要求如下:

(一)进口少量低值辅料(即5000美元以下,78种以内的低值辅料)按规定不使用《加工贸易手册》的,填报"低值辅料"。使用《加工贸易手册》的,按《加工贸易手册》上的监管方式填报。

(二)外商投资企业为加工内销产品而进口的料件,属非保税加工的,填报"一般贸易"。

外商投资企业全部使用国内料件加工的出口成品,填报"一般贸易"。

(三)加工贸易料件结转或深加工结转货物,按批准的监管方式填报。

(四)加工贸易料件转内销货物以及按料件办理进口手续的转内销制成品、残次品、半成品,应填制进口报关单,填报"来料料件内销"或"进料料件内销";加工贸易成品凭《征免税证明》转为减免税进口货物的,应分别填制进、出口报关单,出口报关单本栏目填报"来料成品减免"或"进料成品减免",进口报关单本栏目按照实际监管方式填报。

(五)加工贸易出口成品因故退运进口及复运出口

b) LCL tied – together rail car and box export: dont fill.
c) Air transport: dont fill.
d) Other means of transport: dont fill.
e) Dont fill this column in the declaration form if no import or export occurs actually.

14. Nos. of bills of lading

Fill the No. of the import and export bill of lading or waybill in this column.

Fill the No. of only one bill of lading or waybill in a declaration form and fill forms separately when one bill of goods corresponds to many bills of lading or waybills.

The specific requirements for filling this column are as follows:

(1) Handling declaration formalities directly at import and export ports or adopting the customs clearance mode of "declaring goods in the local place and having them examined and cleared at ports

a. Waterway transport: fill Nos. of import and export bills of lading. Fill import and export bills of lading + "+" + separate bills of lading if there are separate bills of lading.

b. Road transport: dont fill.

c. Railway transport: fill Nos. of bills of lading.

d. Air transport: fill the No. of the general bill of lading + " – " + Nos. of separate bills of lading. Fill the No. of the general bill of lading if there are not separate bills of lading.

e. Post transport: fill Nos. of postal parcels.

(2) Declaration form for goods transferred to another port

a. Import

a) Waterway transport: fill Nos. of bills of lading for direct transfer and transit. Dont fill when declaring to the Customs in advance.

b) Railway transport: fill Nos. of railway bills of lading for direct transfer and transit. Dont fill when declaring to the Customs in advance.

c) Air transport: fill the No. of the general bill of lading for direct transfer and transit + " – " + separate bills of lading. Dont fill when declaring to the Customs in advance.

d) Other means of transport: dont fill.

e) Fill the license plate No. if goods are imported by the above means of transport and transferred to other Customs offices by road transport in Guangdong Province.

b. Export

a) Waterway transport: fill Nos. of bills of lading for transit goods; dont fill for non – transit goods; fill license plate Nos. of transport vehicles for transit goods transported by road and declared to the Customs in advance.

b) Other means of transport: dont fill. Fill license plate Nos. of transport vehicles for transit goods transported by road and declared to the Customs in advance.

(3) When handling the declaring formalities by the clearance method of "collective declaration, fill the combined collective starting and stopping import and export dates in the declaration form (according to the year (four digits), month (two digits), days (two digits).

(4) Dont fill this column if there are no actual import and export.

15. Way of trade (way of supervision)

Fill the abbreviation and code of the corresponding way of supervision according to the Table of Codes of Ways of Supervision stipulated by the Customs based on actual foreign trade circumstances. Fill only one way of supervision in one declaration form.

The requirements for filling the way of supervision for processing trade under special circumstances are as follows:

(1) When the Processing Trade Handbook is not used according to the regulation when importing a small quantity of low – value auxiliary materials (i. e. under US $5000 and low – value auxiliary materials within the 78 varieties), fill "low – value auxiliary materials". If the Processing Trade Handbook is used, fill according to the way of supervision in the manual.

(2) Fill "general trade" for materials and parts imported by foreign – invested enterprises for producing products to be sold domestically in non – bonded processing.

When foreign – invested enterprises producing finished products by domestic materials and parts, fill "general trade".

(3) Fill according to the approved way of supervision for carry – over of materials and parts or carry – over of goods for deep processing in processing trade.

(4) Materials and components for processing inward to be declared for domestic use (including making up an import declaration afterward for the materials and components of finished products which to be declared for domestic use), fill in "supplied/imported materials and components for domestic use" on import declaration; finished products of inward processing to be declared for domestic use with the Certificate of Collection of and Exemption from Duties, fill in "supplied/imported materials and components for domestic use with the Certificate of Collection of and Exemption from Duties" both on import declaration and export declaration.

(5) Fill "exchange of finished products with supplied materials" or "finished

的，填报"来料成品退换"或"进料成品退换"；加工贸易进口料件因换料退运出口及复运进口的，填报"来料料件退换"或"进料料件退换"；加工贸易过程中产生的剩余料件、边角料退运出口，以及进口料件因品质、规格等原因退运出口且不再更换同类货物进口的，分别填报"来料料件复出"、"来料边角料复出"、"进料料件复出"、"进料边角料复出"。

（六）备料《加工贸易手册》中的料件结转转入加工出口《加工贸易手册》的，填报"来料加工"或"进料加工"。

（七）保税工厂加工贸易进出口货物，根据《加工贸易手册》填报"来料加工"或"进料加工"。

（八）加工贸易边角料内销和副产品内销，应填制进口报关单，填报"来料边角料内销"或"进料边角料内销"。

（九）加工贸易进口料件不再用于加工成品出口，或生产的半成品（折料）、成品因故不再出口，主动放弃交由海关处理时，应填制进口报关单，填报"料件放弃"或"成品放弃"。

十六、征免性质

本栏目应根据实际情况按海关规定的《征免性质代码表》选择填报相应的征免性质简称及代码，持有海关核发的《征免税证明》的，应按照《征免税证明》中批注的征免性质填报。一份报关单只允许填报一种征免性质。

加工贸易货物报关单应按照海关核发的《加工贸易手册》中批注的征免性质简称及代码填报。特殊情况填报要求如下：

（一）保税工厂经营的加工贸易，根据《加工贸易手册》填报"进料加工"或"来料加工"。

（二）外商投资企业为加工内销产品而进口的料件，属非保税加工的，填报"一般征税"或其他相应征免性质。

（三）加工贸易转内销货物，按实际情况填报（如一般征税、科教用品、其他法定等）。

（四）料件退运出口、成品退运进口货物填报"其他法定"（代码0299）。

（五）加工贸易结转货物，本栏目免予填报。

十七、征税比例/结汇方式

进口报关单本栏目免予填报。

出口报关单填报结汇方式，按海关规定的《结汇方式代码表》选择填报相应的结汇方式名称或代码。

十八、许可证号

本栏目填报以下许可证的编号：进（出）口许可证、两用物项和技术进（出）口许可证、两用物项和技术出口许可证（定向）、纺织品临时出口许可证、出口许可证（加工贸易）、出口许可证（边境小额贸易）。

一份报关单只允许填报一个许可证号。

十九、起运国（地区）/运抵国（地区）

起运国（地区）填报进口货物启始发出直接运抵我国或者在运输中转国（地）未发生任何商业性交易的情况下运抵我国的国家（地区）。

运抵国（地区）填报出口货物离开我国关境直接运抵或者在运输中转国（地区）未发生任何商业性交易的情况下最后运抵的国家（地区）。

不经过第三国（地区）转运的直接运输进出口货物，以进口货物的装货港所在国（地区）为起运国（地区），以出口货物的指运港所在国（地区）为运抵国（地区）。

经过第三国（地区）转运的进出口货物，如在中转国（地区）发生商业性交易，则以中转国（地区）作为起运/运抵国（地区）。

本栏目应按海关规定的《国别（地区）代码表》选择填报相应的起运国（地区）或运抵国（地区）中文名称及代码。

无实际进出境的，填报"中国"（代码142）。

二十、装货港/指运港

装货港填报进口货物在运抵我国关境前的最后一个

products with imported materials" if finished exports are returned and reexported for some reason in processing trade, fill "exchange of supplied materials and parts" or "exchange of imported materials and parts" if imported materials and parts are returned for exchange in processing trade; fill "reexport of supplied materials and parts", "reexport of supplied scraps", "reexport of imported materials and parts" and "reexport of imported scraps" respectively if leftover materials, parts and scraps produced in processing trade are reexported and if imported materials and parts are returned for reasons of quality and specifications and not in exchange for similar goods.

(6) To close and transfer materials and components of Processing Trade Handbook for reservation into Processing Trade Handbook for inward processing, fill in corresponding Mode of Trade of inward processing with supplied/imported materials.

(7) Import/export goods for inward processing by bonded factory, fill in corresponding Mode of Trade of inward processing with supplied/imported materials, which should be in accordance with Processing Trade Handbook.

(8) Leftover scraps or by - products of processing trade to be declared for domestic use, fill in "scraps to be declared for domestic use" on import declaration.

(9) Materials/components or finished products of processing trade to be abandoned, fill in "Materials/components or finished products to be abandoned on import declaration.

16. Nature of levy and reduction of and exemption from Customs duties

Fill this column in accordance with the nature of levy, reduction and exemption marked on the Certificate of Collection of and Exemption from Duties, or on basis of fact choice the suitable abbreviation or code from "Codes for the Nature of Levy, Reduction of and Exemption from Customs Duties prescribed by the Customs.

Declaration for inward processing, fill the column in accordance with the nature of levy, reduction and exemption marked on R handbook. Specific requirements are as follows:

(1) Inward processing performed by bonded factory, fill in "inward processing with supplied/imported materials, which should be in accordance with Processing Trade Handbook.

(2) To import materials and components by foreign - invested enterprise for the purpose of processing products for domestic use proportionally or wholly, fill in "Levy according to regulations: or other suitable Nature of Levy, Reduction of and Exemption from Customs Duties.

(3) Goods for inward processing to be declared for domestic use, on basis of fact fill in the suitable Nature of Levy, Reduction of and Exemption from Customs Duties (for example, levy according to regulations, educational and scientific materials, other legal reduction and remission, etc.)

(4) Materials and components sending back outward, or finished products sending back inward, fill in "other legal reduction and remission" (the code 0299).

(5) Dont fill this column in the case of carried over goods in processing trade.

17. Rate of levy/way of settlement

Dont fill this column in the import declaration form.

Fill the way of settlement in the export declaration form by selecting the name of the corresponding way of settlement or code according to the Table of Codes of Ways of Settlement stipulated by the Customs.

18. No. of the license

Fill Nos. of the following licenses in this column: import (export) license, dual - use material and technology import (export) license, dual - use material and technology export license (oriented), temporary textile export license, export license (processing trade) and export license (boundary small - amount trade).

Fill the No. of only one license for one declaration form.

19. Starting country (region)/destination country (region)

The starting country (region) means the country (region) from which imports are transported to our country directly or via a country (region) without any commercial transaction.

The destination country (region) is the country (region) to which exports are transported directly from our country or via a country (region) without any commercial transaction.

The country where the loading port of imports transported directly instead of indirectly via a third country is located is the starting country (region) and the country where the destination port of exports transported directly instead of indirectly via a third country is located is the destination country (region).

If imports and exports undergo commercial transactions when transported via a third country (region), the third country (region) is the starting/destination country (region).

Fill the Chinese name and code of the corresponding starting country (region) or destination country (region) according to the Table of Codes of Countries (Regions) stipulated by the Customs.

Fill "China" (the code 142) if there are actual import and export.

20. Loading port/designated port

The loading port is the last overseas loading port for imports before they arrive at

境外装运港。

指运港填报出口货物运往境外的最终目的港；最终目的港不可预知的，按尽可能预知的目的港填报。

本栏目应根据实际情况按海关规定的《港口航线代码表》选择填报相应的港口中文名称及代码。装货港/指运港在《港口航线代码表》中无港口中文名称及代码的，可选择填报相应的国家中文名称或代码。

无实际进出境的，本栏目填报"中国境内"（代码142）。

二十一、境内目的地/境内货源地

境内目的地填报已知的进口货物在国内的消费、使用地或最终运抵地，其中最终运抵地为最终使用单位所在的地区。最终使用单位难以确定的，填报货物进口时预知的最终收货单位所在地。

境内货源地填报出口货物在国内的产地或原始发货地。出口货物产地难以确定的，填报最早发运该出口货物的单位所在地。

本栏目按海关规定的《国内地区代码表》选择填报相应的国内地区名称及代码。

二十二、批准文号

进口报关单中本栏目免予填报。

出口报关单中本栏目填报出口收汇核销单编号。

二十三、成交方式

本栏目应根据进出口货物实际成交价格条款，按海关规定的《成交方式代码表》选择填报相应的成交方式代码。

无实际进出境的报关单，进口填报 CIF，出口填报 FOB。

二十四、运费

本栏目填报进口货物运抵我国境内输入地点起卸前的运输费用，出口货物运至我国境内输出地点装载后的运输费用。进口货物成交价格包含前述运输费用或者出口货物成交价格不包含前述运输费用的，本栏目免于填报。

运费可按运费单价、总价或运费率三种方式之一填报，注明运费标记（运费标记"1"表示运费率，"2"表示每吨货物的运费单价，"3"表示运费总价），并按海关规定的《货币代码表》选择填报相应的币种代码。

运保费合并计算的，填报在本栏目。

二十五、保费

本栏目填报进口货物运抵我国境内输入地点起卸前的保险费用，出口货物运至我国境内输出地点装载后的保险费用。进口货物成交价格包含前述保险费用或者出口货物成交价格不包含前述保险费用的，本栏目免于填报。

保费可按保险费总价或保险费率两种方式之一填报，注明保险费标记（保险费标记"1"表示保险费率，"3"表示保险费总价），并按海关规定的《货币代码表》选择填报相应的币种代码。

运保费合并计算的，本栏目免予填报。

二十六、杂费

本栏目填报成交价格以外的、按照《中华人民共和国进出口关税条例》相关规定应计入完税价格或应从完税价格中扣除的费用。可按杂费总价或杂费率两种方式之一填报，注明杂费标记（杂费标记"1"表示杂费率，"3"表示杂费总价），并按海关规定的《货币代码表》选择填报相应的币种代码。

应计入完税价格的杂费填报为正值或正率，应从完税价格中扣除的杂费填报为负值或负率。

二十七、件数

本栏目填报有外包装的进出口货物的实际件数。特殊情况填报要求如下：

（一）舱单件数为集装箱的，填报集装箱个数。

a Chinese port.

The designated port is the final overseas destination port for exports. If the final destination is unforeseeable, fill the most likely destination port.

Fill the Chinese name and code of the corresponding port in this column according to the actual situation and based on the Table of Codes of Port Routes stipulated by the Customs. If there is no Chinese name and code of the loading/designated port in the Table of Codes of Port Routes, fill the Chinese name or code of the corresponding country.

If there are no actual import and export, fill " in China: in this column (the code 142).

21. Domestic destination/domestic place of origin of goods

For domestic destination, fill the known place of consumption or use or the final destination of imports in China. Therein the final destination is the place where the end user is located. If the final destination is where the end user is located and it is hard to determine the end user, fill the final place where the final consignee is located as known in importation.

For domestic place of origin of exports, fill the place of origin of exports or the original place where exports are sent from. If it's hard to determine the place of origin of exports, fill the place where the unit which sent the exports earliest is located.

Fill the corresponding name and code China in this column according to the Table of Codes of Domestic Regions stipulated by the Customs.

22. No. of the approving document

Don't fill this column in the import declaration form.

Fill the export proceeds writing – off certificate in this column of the export declaration form.

23. Way of transaction

Fill the code of the corresponding way of transaction in this column according to the Table of Codes of Way of Transactions stipulated by the Customs based on the article on the actual transaction price of imports and exports.

Fill CIF for imports and FOB for exports for declaration forms without actual import and export.

24. Freight

Fill the transport cost before imports are unloaded at ports in our country and that after exports are loaded at ports in our country. If the transaction price of imports includes the above transport cost or if the transaction price of exports doesn't include the above transport cost, don't fill this column.

Fill the unit transport price, total transport price or transport rate. Indicate the mark of transport cost ("1" indicates the transport rate, "2" indicates the unit transport price per ton and "3" indicate the total transport price). Fill the corresponding code of the currency according to the Table of Codes of Currencies stipulated by the Customs.

Fill transport cost and insurance premium in this column if they are calculated together.

25. Insurance premium

International insurance premium for the declared goods should be declared in case the transaction price of imports doesn't cover insurance premium, or in case the transaction price of exports covers insurance premium. It could be declared in two ways: insurance premium rate or total insurance premium. Meanwhile, fill the category of mark of insurance premium and the code of the currency. The latter should be in accordance with the "Codes for Representation of Currencies" stipulated by the Customs.

In case freight and insurance premium are calculated together, fill freight and insurance premium in the column of freight. The category marks of insurance premium are as follows: 1 refers to insurance premium rate, 3 refers to total insurance premium.

Don't fill transport cost and in surance premium in this column if theyare calulated together.

26. Incidental expenses

The term means other expenses incurred for the goods which should be included in or deducted from the dutiable price in accordance with the "Regulations of the People's Republic of China on Import and Export Duties". It could be declared in two ways: incidental expense rate, or total incidental expenses. Meanwhile, fill the category mark of incidental expenses and the code of currency. The latter should be in accordance with the "Codes for Representation of Currencies" stipulated by the Customs. The category marks of inciden tal expenses are as follows: 1 refers to in cidental expense rate and 3 refers to total incidental expenses

Incidental expenses should be included in the dutiable price. Fill positive value or positive rate, incidental expenses should be deducted from the dutiable price, fill negative value or negative rate.

27. Number of packages

Fill the actual number of packages of imports and exports in this column. The requirements for filling under special circumstances are as follows:

(1) If the number of packages in manifest is the number of containers, fill the number of containers.

（二）舱单件数为托盘的，填报托盘数。

本栏目不得填报为零，裸装货物填报为"1"。

二十八、包装种类

本栏目应根据进出口货物的实际外包装种类，按海关规定的《包装种类代码表》选择填报相应的包装种类代码。

二十九、毛重（千克）

本栏目填报进出口货物及其包装材料的重量之和，计量单位为千克，不足一千克的填报为"1"。

三十、净重（千克）

本栏目填报进出口货物的毛重减去外包装材料后的重量，即货物本身的实际重量，计量单位为千克，不足一千克的填报为"1"。

三十一、集装箱号

本栏目填报装载进出口货物（包括拼箱货物）集装箱的箱体信息。一个集装箱填一条记录，分别填报集装箱号（在集装箱箱体上标示的全球唯一编号）、集装箱的规格和集装箱的自重。非集装箱货物填报为"0"。

三十二、随附单证

本栏目根据海关规定的《监管证件代码表》选择填报除本规范第十八条规定的许可证件以外的其他进出口许可证件或监管证件代码及编号。

本栏目分为随附单证代码和随附单证编号两栏，其中代码栏应按海关规定的《监管证件代码表》选择填报相应证件代码；编号栏应填报证件编号。

（一）加工贸易内销征税报关单，随附单证代码栏填写"c"，随附单证编号栏填写海关审核通过的内销征税联系单号。

（二）含预归类商品报关单，随附单证代码项下填写"r"，随附单证编号项下填写XX关预归类书XX号。

（三）优惠贸易协定项下进出口货物

"Y"为原产地证书代码。优惠贸易协定代码选择"01"、"02"、"03"、"04"、"05"、"06"、"07"、"08"、"09"填报：

"01"为"亚太贸易协定"项下的进口货物；

"02"为"中国－东盟自贸区"项下的进口货物；

"03"为"内地与香港紧密经贸关系安排"（香港CEPA）项下的进口货物；

"04"为"内地与澳门紧密经贸关系安排"（澳门CEPA）项下的进口货物；

"05"为"对非洲特惠待遇"项下的进口货物；

"06"为"台湾农产品零关税措施"项下的进口货物；

"07"为"中巴自贸区"项下的进口货物；

"08"为"中智自贸区"项下的进口货物；

"09"为"对也门等国特惠待遇"项下的进口货物。

具体填报要求如下：

1. 实行原产地证书联网管理的，随附单证代码栏填写"Y"，随附单证编号栏的"< >"内填写优惠贸易协定代码。例如香港CEPA项下进口商品，应填报为："Y"和"<03>"。一票进口货物中如涉及多份原产地证书或含有非原产地证书商品，应分单填报。

2. 未实行原产地证书联网管理的，随附单证代码栏填写"Y"，随附单证编号栏"< >"内填写优惠贸易协定代码＋"："＋需证商品序号。例如《亚太贸易协定》项下进口报关单中第1到第3项和第5项为优惠贸易协定项下商品，应填报为："<01:1-3,5>"。

优惠贸易协定项下出口货物，本栏目填报原产地证书代码和编号。

三十三、用途/生产厂家

进口货物本栏目填报用途，应根据进口货物的实际用途按海关规定的《用途代码表》选择填报相应的用途代码。

出口货物本栏目填报其境内生产企业。

三十四、标记唛码及备注

本栏目填报要求如下：

（一）标记唛码中除图形以外的文字、数字。

(2) If the number of packages in manifest is the number of pallets, fill the number of pallets.

It's not allowed to fill 0 in this column and fill "1" for unpacked goods.

28. Kind of packages

Fill the actual kind of packages according to the "Codes for Kind of Packages" stipulated by the Customs.

29. Gross weight (kilogram)

Fill the total weight of imports and exports and their packing materials in this column. The calculation unit is kilogram and fill "1" for less than 1 kilogram.

30. Net weight (kilogram)

Fill the weight of imports and exports without the weight of packages, i. e. the actual weight of goods, in this column. The calculation unit is kilogram and fill "1" for less than 1 kilogram.

31. No. of containers

Fill information on container bodies of imports and exports (including LCL goods). Fill one record for one container and fill Nos. of containers separately (the only No. of a container worldwide which is indicated on its body), the specification of containers and the net weight of containers. Fill "0" if goods are not carried in containers.

32. Attached documents

Fill export licenses in this column except those stipulated by Article 18 of this standard or codes of supervision certificates and codes according to the Table of Codes of Supervision Certificates.

This column is divided into the code of attached documents and No. of attached documents. Therein fill the code of corresponding certificates in the sub - column of the code according to the Table of Codes of Supervision Certificates stipulated by the Customs and fill the No. of documents in the column of the No.

(1) Fill "c" in the column of the code of attached documents for the declaration form for domestic sale taxation under processing trade and fill the No. of the liaison sheet for domestic sale taxation approved by the Customs in the column of the No. of attached documents.

(2) Fill "r" in the column of the No. of attached documents for the declaration form containing pre - retained commodities and fill No. XX, pre - retaining book, XX Customs in the column of the No. of attached documents.

(3) Imports and exports under preferential trade protocols

"Y" is the code of the place of origin certificate. Select and fill"01","02","03","04","05","06","07","08" or"09.

"01" means imports under the "Asia - Pacific Trade Protocol".

"02" means imports under "China - ASEAN Free Trade Zone".

"03" means imports under Hong Kong CEPA.

"04" means imports under Macao CEPA".

"05: means imports under "Preferential Treatment for Africa".

"06" means imports under "Zero Duty Measure for Taiwan Agricultural Products".

"07" means imports under "China - Brazil Free Trade Zone".

"08" means imports under "China - Chile Free Trade Zone:.

"09" means imports under "Preferential Treatment for Yemen and Other Countries".

The specific requirements for filling this column are as follows:

a. Fill "Y" in the column of the No. of attached documents for those under online management of place of origin certificates, fill the code of the preferential trade protocol in "< >". For example, fill "Y" and "<03>" for imports under Hong Kong CEPA. If imports in an order involve many place of origin certificates or include non - place - of - origin - certificate commodities, fill them in separate declaration forms.

b. Fill "Y" in the column of attached documents for those not under online management of place of origin certificates, fill the code of the preferential trade protocol in "< >" + the No. of commodities which need certificates. For example Item 1 to 2 and Item 5 in the export declaration form under the Asia - Pacific Trade Protocol are commodities under the preferential trade protocol and "<01:1 - 3,5>" should be filled.

Fill the code and No. of the place of origin certificate in this column for exports under preferential trade protocols.

33. Use/manufacturer

Fill the corresponding code of use of imports in this column according to the Table of Codes of Use stipulated by the Customs based on actual use of imports.

Fill names of manufacturers of exports in this column.

34. Mark and remark

The specific requirements for filling this colum are as follows:

(1) Characters and numbers except graphics in mark

（二）受外商投资企业委托代理其进口投资设备、物品的进出口企业名称。

（三）与本报关单有关联关系的，同时在业务管理规范方面又要求填报的备案号，填报在电子数据报关单中"关联备案"栏。

加工贸易结转货物及凭《征免税证明》转内销货物，其对应的备案号应填报在"关联备案"栏。

减免税货物结转进口（转入），报关单"关联备案"栏应填写本次减免税货物结转所申请的《减免税进口货物结转联系函》的编号。

减免税货物结转出口（转出），报关单"关联备案"栏应填写与其相对应的进口（转入）报关单"备案号"栏中《征免税证明》的编号。

（四）与本报关单有关联关系的，同时在业务管理规范方面又要求填报的报关单号，填报在电子数据报关单中"关联报关单"栏。

加工贸易结转类的报关单，应先办理进口报关，并将进口报关单号填入出口报关单的"关联报关单"栏。

办理进口货物直接退运手续的，除另有规定外，应当先填写出口报关单，再填写进口报关单，并将出口报关单号填入进口报关单的"关联报关单"栏。

减免税货物结转出口（转出），应先办理进口报关，并将进口（转入）报关单号填入出口（转出）报关单的"关联报关单"栏。

（五）办理进口货物直接退运手续的，本栏目填报《准予直接退运决定书》或者《责令直接退运通知书》编号。

（六）申报时其他必须说明的事项填报在本栏目。

三十五、项号

本栏目分两行填报及打印。第一行填报报关单中的商品顺序编号；第二行专用于加工贸易、减免税等已备案、审批的货物，填报和打印该项货物在《加工贸易手册》或《征免税证明》等备案、审批单证中的顺序编号。

优惠贸易协定项下实行原产地证书联网管理的报关单，第一行填报报关单中的商品顺序编号，第二行填报该项商品对应的原产地证书上的商品项号。

加工贸易项下进出口货物的报关单，第一行填报报关单中的商品顺序编号，第二行填报该项商品在《加工贸易手册》中的商品项号，用于核销对应项号下的料件或成品数量。其中第二行特殊情况填报要求如下：

（一）深加工结转货物，分别按照《加工贸易手册》中的进口料件项号和出口成品项号填报。

（二）料件结转货物（包括料件、制成品和半成品折料），出口报关单按照转出《加工贸易手册》中进口料件的项号填报；进口报关单按照转进《加工贸易手册》中进口料件的项号填报。

（三）料件复出货物（包括料件、边角料、来料加工半成品折料），出口报关单按照《加工贸易手册》中进口料件的项号填报；如边角料对应一个以上料件项号时，填报主要料件项号。料件退换货物（包括料件、不包括半成品），进出口报关单按照《加工贸易手册》中进口料件的项号填报。

（四）成品退换货物，退运进境报关单和复运出境报关单按照《加工贸易手册》原出口成品的项号填报。

（五）加工贸易料件转内销货物（以及按料件办理进口手续的转内销制成品、半成品、残次品）应填制进口报关单，填报《加工贸易手册》进口料件的项号；加工贸易边角料、副产品内销，填报《加工贸易手册》中对应的进口料件项号。如边角料或副产品对应一个以上料件项号时，填报主要料件项号。

(2) Names of import and export enterprises trusted by foreign - invested enterprises with importing of invested equipment and articles.

(3) Fill the column of "associated record" in the electronic data declaration form when the record No. is associated with this declaration form and has to be filled to regulate business management.

Fill the record No. in the "associated record" for goods turned over from processing trade and goods sold domestic instead of exported against the Certificate of Collection of and Exemption from Duties.

Fill the No. of the Liaison Letter on Turnover of Exports Granted Exemption and Reduction of Duties applied for in turnover of goods granted reduction of and exemption from duties in the column of the "Associated Record" of the declaration form to turn goods granted reduction of and exemption from duties into imports (turn in).

Fill the No. of the Certificate of Collection of and Exemption from Duties in the column of the "Associated Record" of the corresponding import (turn in) declaration form to turn goods granted reduction of and exemption from duties into exports (turn out).

(4) When the No. of the declaration form is associated with this declaration form and has to be filled according to business management norm, fill it in the "association declaration" column of the electronic data declaration form.

For declaration forms in the category of processing trade carry - over, declare for import first and fill the No. of the import declaration form in the column of "associated declaration form" of the export declaration form.

To handle formalities for direct return of imports, first fill the export declaration, then fill the import declaration and export declaration forms and fill in the No. of the export declaration form in the column of "associated declaration form" of the export declaration except as otherwise provided.

For carry - over of exports (turn out) granted reduction of and exemption from duties, declare for import first and fill the No. of import (turn in) declaration form in the column of "associated declaration form" of the import declaration form.

(5) To handle formalities for direct return of imports, fill the No. of Decision on Approval of Direct Return or Notice about Ordering Direct Return in this column.

(6) Fill other matters that have to be explained in declaration in this column.

35. Item No.

This column is divided into two lines and printed. Fill the No. of commodities in the declaration form in the first line; fill and print the No. of the commodities in the recording or approving document for the Processing Trade Handbook or the Certificate of Collection of and Exemption from Duties in the second line for recorded and approved goods which are specially used in processing trade or granted reduction of and exemption from duties.

For the declaration form under online management of the place of origin certificate under preferential trade protocol, fill the No. of commodities in the declaration form in the first line and the No. of commodities in the corresponding place of origin certificate of the commodities.

For the declaration form for imports and exports under processing trade, fill the No. of commodities in the declaration form in the first line and the No. of the commodities in the Processing Trade Handbook in the second line to write off the quantity of materials or finished products under the corresponding Item No. The requirements for filling special circumstances in the second line are as follows:

(1) Fill the No. of imported materials and parts and the No. of finished exports according to the Processing Trade Handbook for carry - over of deep processed goods.

(2) Fill goods carried over from materials and parts (including materials, parts, finished products and materials from semi - finished products) in the export declaration form according to the Item No. of imported materials and parts in the turn - out part of Processing Trade Handbook; fill the import declaration form according to the Item No. of imported materials and parts in the turn - in part of the Processing Trade Handbook.

(3) To return materials and components (including scraps, materials and components converted from semi - finished products), fill the item No. of import materials and components in the export declaration form according to Processing Trade Handbook; to replace materials and components (not including semi - finished products) fill the item No. of import materials and components in the export declaration form according to the Processing Trade Handbook.

(4) To return finished goods, fill the item No. of the original finished exports in the import return declaration form and the reexport declaration form according to the Processing Trade Handbook.

(5) Inward processing materials and components to be declared for domestic use (including making up import declaration for materials and components of finished products which are declared for domestic use, semi - finished products and defective goods), fill the item No. of import materials and components in the import declaration form according to the Processing Trade Handbook. Scraps and byproducts of inward processing to be declared for domestic use, fill the item No. of import materials and components in the import declaration form according to the Processing Trade Handbook. In the case of scraps and byproducts related to more than one Item Nos.,

fill the main item No.

（六）加工贸易成品凭《征免税证明》转为减免税货物进口的，应先办理进口报关手续。进口报关单填报《征免税证明》中的项号，出口报关单填报《加工贸易手册》原出口成品项号，进、出口报关单货物数量应一致。

(6) Finished products of inward processing to be declared for domestic use with the Certificate of Collection of and Exemption from Duties, import declaration formalities should be gone through first. Fill the item No. of the Certificate of Collection of and Exemption from Duties in the import declaration form, fill the Item No. of original finished exports in the export declaration form. The quantity in the import and export declaration forms should be consistent.

（七）加工贸易料件放弃或成品放弃，本栏目应填报《加工贸易手册》中的进口料件或出口成品项号。半成品放弃的应按单耗折回料件，以料件放弃申报，本栏目填报《加工贸易手册》中对应的进口料件项号。

(7) To abandon materials and components of inward processing, fill the item No. filed in the Processing Trade Handbook. To abandon semi - finished products, they should be converted into materials and components first, then to declare abandonment of materials and components, fill the Item No. filed in the Processing Trade Manual.

（八）加工贸易副产品退运出口、结转出口或放弃，本栏目应填报《加工贸易手册》中新增的变更副产品的出口项号。

(8) To return, close and export or abandon byproducts of inward processing, fill the item No. of alternated byproducts newly added to the Processing Trade Handbook.

（九）经海关批准实行加工贸易联网监管的企业，按海关联网监管要求，企业需申报报关清单的，应在向海关申报进出口（包括形式进出口）报关单前，向海关申报"清单"。一份报关清单对应一份报关单，报关单上的商品由报关清单归并而得。加工贸易电子账册报关单中项号、品名、规格等栏目的填制规范比照《加工贸易手册》。

(9) Approved enterprises under processing trade networking Customs supervision should declare a detailed list of goods to the Customs before declaring import/exports. One detailed list matches one declaration form. Commodities in the declaration form come from the declaration list. Item Nos., names, specifications and other columns in the electronic account declaration form for processing trade should be filled according to the Processing Trade Handbook.

三十六、商品编号

本栏目应填报由《中华人民共和国进出口税则》确定的进出口货物的税则号列和《中华人民共和国海关统计商品目录》确定的商品编码，以及符合海关监管要求的附加编号组成的10位商品编号。

36. Nos. of commodities

This column should be filled according to the tariff Nos. of imports and exports in the Import and Export Tariffs of the People's Republic of China and the codes of commodities in the Customs Statistics Commodity Catalog of the People's Republic of China and in line with the 10 - digit commodity code composed of the additional No. as required for Customs supervision.

三十七、商品名称、规格型号

本栏目分两行填报及打印。第一行填报进出口货物规范的中文商品名称，第二行填报规格型号。

37. Names, specifications and models of commodities

This column is to be filled and printed in two lines. Fill the Chinese standard names of imports and exports in the first line and fill the specifications and models in the second line.

具体填报要求如下：

The specific requirements for filling this column are as follows:

（一）商品名称及规格型号应据实填报，并与进出口货物收发货人或受委托的报关企业所提交的合同、发票等相关单证相符。

(1) Fill names, specifications and models of commodities according to facts and in line with contracts and invoices submitted by consigners and consignees of imports and exports or declaring agents.

（二）商品名称应当规范，规格型号应当足够详细，以能满足海关归类、审价及许可证件管理要求为准，可参照《中华人民共和国海关进出口商品规范申报目录》中对商品名称、规格型号的要求进行填报。

(2) Names of commodities should be standard and their specifications and models should be detailed enough to satisfy the Customs' requirements for classification, estimate and license management. Fill according to the requirements of the Import and Export Customs Declaration Norm Directory of the People's Republic of China for names, specifications and models of commodities.

（三）加工贸易等已备案的货物，填报的内容必须与备案登记中同项号下货物的商品名称一致。

(3) Fill recorded goods in processing trade in line with the commodity names of the goods under the same Item No. in record registration.

（四）对需要海关签发《货物进口证明书》的车辆，商品名称栏应填报"车辆品牌+排气量（注明cc）+车型（如越野车、小轿车等）"。进口汽车底盘不填报排气量。车辆品牌应按照《进口机动车辆制造厂名称和车辆品牌中英文对照表》中"签注名称"一栏的要求填报。规格型号栏可填报"汽油型"等。

(4) To import motor vehicles for which the Certificate of Import should be issued by the Customs, fill the first line with "brand + cylinder capacity (cc) + type (for example cross - country cars, saloon cars, etc.). to import chassis of motor vehicles, the column of cylinder capacity doesn't need filling. The brand should be filled according to the requirements stipulated by the Chinese - English list of Names of Manufacturers and Brand of Import Motor Vehicles. Fill specifications in the second line, for example, with spark - ignition international combustion reciprocating piston engine.

（五）由同一运输工具同时运抵同一口岸并且属于同一收货人、使用同一提单的多种进口货物，按照商品归类规则应当归入同一商品编号的，应当将有关商品一并归入该商品编号。商品名称填报一并归类后的商品名称；规格型号填报一并归类后商品的规格型号。

(5) Many imports which are transported by the same means of transport to the same port at the same time, belong to the same consignee, have the same bill of lading and should be classified into the same commodities No. according to the commodity classification rule should be put into the commodity No. Fill the classified commodity name as the commodity name and fill classified commodity specifications and models as the specifications and models.

（六）加工贸易边角料和副产品内销，边角料复出口，本栏目填报其报验状态的名称和规格型号。

(6) Fill the names, specifications and models of scraps and byproducts for domestic sale and reexport of scraps in processing trade in this column.

（七）进口货物收货人以一般贸易方式申报进口属于《需要详细列名申报的汽车零部件清单》（海关总署2006年第64号公告）范围内的汽车生产件的，应按以下要求填报：

(7) Fill auto parts in the List of Auto Parts That Have to Be Declared (Bulletin No. 64 of the General Administration of Customs imported by consignees in general trade according to the following requirements:

1.商品名称填报进口汽车零部件的详细中文商品名称和品牌，中文商品名称与品牌之间用"/"相隔，必要时加注英文商业名称；进口的成套散件或者毛坯件应在品牌后加注"成套散件"、"毛坯"等字样，并与品牌之间用"/"相隔。

a. Fill the Chinese commodity names and brands of imported auto parts as the commodity names, partition the Chinese commodity names and brands with "/" and add English commodity names when necessary; indicate "complete spare parts", "semi - finished product", etc. for imported complete spare parts or semi - finished products after their brands and partition brands with "/".

2.规格型号填报汽车零部件的完整编号。在零部件编号前应当加注"S"字样，并与零部件编号之间用"/"相隔，零部件编号之后应当依次加注该零部件适用的汽车品牌和车型。

b. Fill the complete No. of auto parts as their specifications and models. Add "S" before the No. of spare parts and partition it and No. of spare parts with "/". Add car brands models of auto parts are applicable to successively after No. of spare parts.

汽车零部件属于可以适用于多种汽车车型的通用零部件的，零部件编号后应当加注"TY"字样，并用"/"与零部件编号相隔。

When auto spare parts are applicable to many car models, add "TY" after the No. of spare parts and partition it and the No. of spare parts with "/".

与进口汽车零部件规格型号相关的其他需要申报的

Other elements that need declaration in connection with specifications and mod-

要素,或者海关规定的其他需要申报的要素,如"功率"、"排气量"等,应当在车型或"TY"之后填报,并用"/"与之相隔。

汽车零部件报验状态是成套散件的,应当在"标记唛码及备注"栏内填报该成套散件装配后的最终完整品的零部件编号。

(八)进口货物收货人以一般贸易方式申报进口属于《需要详细列名申报的汽车零部件清单》(海关总署2006年第64号公告)范围内的汽车维修件的,填报规格型号时,应当在零部件编号前加注"W",并与零部件编号之间用"/"相隔;进口维修件的品牌与该零部件适用的整车厂牌不一致的,应当在零部件编号前加注"WF",并与零部件编号之间用"/"相隔。其余申报要求同上条执行。

三十八、数量及单位

本栏目分三行填报及打印。

(一)第一行应按进出口货物的法定第一计量单位填报数量及单位,法定计量单位以《中华人民共和国海关统计商品目录》中的计量单位为准。

(二)凡列明有法定第二计量单位的,应在第二行按照法定第二计量单位填报数量及单位。无法定第二计量单位的,本栏目第二行为空。

(三)成交计量单位及数量应填报并打印在第三行。

(四)法定计量单位为"千克"的数量填报,特殊情况下填报要求如下:

1. 装入可重复使用的包装容器的货物,应按货物扣除包装容器后的重量填报,如罐装同位素、罐装氧气及类似品等。

2. 使用不可分割包装材料和包装容器的货物,按货物的净重填报(即包括内层直接包装的净重重量),如采用供零售包装的罐头、化妆品、药品及类似品等。

3. 按照商业惯例以公量重计价的商品,应按公量重填报,如未脱脂羊毛、羊毛条等。

4. 采用以毛重作为净重计价的货物,可按毛重填报,如粮食、饲料等大宗散装货物。

5. 采用零售包装的酒类、饮料,按照液体部分的重量填报。

(五)成套设备、减免税货物如需分批进口,货物实际进口时,应按照实际报验状态确定数量。

(六)根据《商品名称及编码协调制度》归类规则,零部件按整机或成品归类的,法定计量单位是非重量的,其对应的法定数量填报"0.1"。

(七)具有完整品或制成品基本特征的不完整品、未制成品,根据《商品名称及编码协调制度》归类规则应按完整品归类的,按照构成完整品的实际数量填报。

(八)加工贸易等已备案的货物,成交计量单位必须与《加工贸易手册》中同项号下货物的计量单位一致,加工贸易边角料和副产品内销、边角料复出口,本栏目填报其报验状态的计量单位。

(九)优惠贸易协定项下进出口商品的成交计量单位必须与原产地证书上对应商品的计量单位一致。

(十)法定计量单位为立方米的气体货物,应折算成标准状况(即摄氏零度及1个标准大气压)下的体积进行填报。

三十九、原产国(地区)/最终目的国(地区)

原产国(地区)应依据《中华人民共和国进出口货物原产地条例》、《中华人民共和国海关关于执行〈非优惠原产地规则中实质性改变标准〉的规定》以及海关总署关于各项优惠贸易协定原产地管理规章规定的原产地确定标准填报。同一批进口货物的原产地不同的,应分别填报原产国(地区)。进口货物原产国(地区)无法确定的,填报"国别不详"(代码701)。

最终目的国(地区)填报已知的出口货物的最终实际消费、使用或进一步加工制造国家(地区)。不经过第三国(地区)转运的直接运输货物,以运抵国(地区)为最终目的国(地区);经过第三国(地区)转运的货物,以最后运往国(地区)为最终目的国(地区)。同一批出口货物的最终目的国(地区)不同的,应分别填报最终目的国(地区)。出口货物不能确定最终目的国(地区)时,以尽可能预知的最后运往国(地区)为最终目的国(地区)。

els of spare parts of imported cars or other elements that the Customs requires to be declared, such as "power", "displacement", etc. should be filled after car models or "TY" and partitioned with that by "/".

If the state of auto spare parts is in complete spare parts, fill the No. of spare parts of the final complete products after assembly in the column of "mark No. and remark".

(8) Fill specifications and models of auto parts imported by consignees in general trade in the List of Auto Spare Parts that Need Detailed Declaration (Bulletin No. 64 of the General Administration of the Customs and add "W" before the No. of spare parts and partition it and the No. of spare parts with "/". When the brand of imported maintenance parts and the auto brand of spare parts which the imported maintenance parts are inconsistent, add "WF" before the No. of spare parts and partition it and the No. of spare parts with "/". The other declaration requirements are the same as those in the above.

38. Quantity and unit

This column is filled and printed in three lines.

(1) Fill the quantity and unit according to the first legal unit of measurement of imports and exports in the first line. The legal unit of measurement is based on the units of measurements in the Customs Statistics Catalog of the People's Republic of China.

(2) When a legal second unit of measurement is indicated, fill the quantity and unit according to the second unit of measurement in the second line. If there is no second legal unit of measurement, leave the second line blank.

(3) Fill the transaction unit of measurement and quantity in the third line.

(4) When the legal unit of measurement is "kilogram", the special requirements for filling this column are as follows:

a. Fill the weight after deducting the package and container of goods for goods that are put into reusable package or container, such as canned isotope, canned oxygen and similar products.

b. Fill the net weight of goods for goods put into undividable packing materials and packing containers (i. e. the net weight including inner direct packing), such as cans, cosmetics, drugs and similar products packed for retail.

c. Fill metric weight of commodities priced according to metric weight based on commercial rules, such as greased wool, wool tops, etc.

d. Fill gross weight of goods priced according to gross weight as net weight, such as grain, fodder and other staple bulk cargo.

e. Fill the weight of liquid for wine and beverages packed for retail.

(5) If complete equipment and goods granted reduction and exemption of duties have to be imported in batches, determine the weight according to the actual state when such goods are actually imported.

(6) Fill "01" according to the classification rule of the Coordination System of Commodity Names and Codes when spare parts are classified as a whole machine or finished product and the legal unit of measurement is not based on weight.

(7) Fill the actual quantity of complete products for those incomplete products or unfinished products which constitute the basic characteristics of complete products or finished products and should be classified into complete products according to the Coordination System of Commodity Names and Codes.

(8) The transaction unit of measurement of goods recorded in processing trade must be consistent with the unit of measurement of goods under the same Item No. in the Processing Trade Handbook. Fill the unit of measurement of the state of scraps and byproducts sold domestically and reexport of scraps in this column.

(9) The transaction unit of measurement of imports and exports under preferential trade protocol must be consistent with the corresponding unit of measurement of the products in their place of origin certificates.

(10) Gaseous goods whose legal unit of measurement is m3 should be converted into the volume under the standard state (i. e. 00C and one standard atmosphere) before filling.

39. Country (region) of origin/final destination country (region)

1. Fill the country (region) of origin according to the Origin of Imports and Exports Regulations of the Republic of China, the Standard on Substantial Change in Implementation of Non – Preferential Place of Origin Rule of the Customs of People's Republic of China and the standard of the General Administration of Customs on determination of the place of origin in the regulations on management of the place of origin of various preferential trade protocols. If the place of origin of the same batch of imports is different, fill the country (region) of origin separately. If it's impossible to determine the country (region) of origin, fill "the country is unknown" (code 701).

Fill the known final consumer, user or further processor country (region) of exports as the final destination country (region). The destination country (region) of goods directly transported without passing a third country (region) is the country (region) the goods arrive at; the final destination country (region) of goods transported via a third country (region) is the last country (region) the goods arrive at. When the final destination countries (regions) of a batch of exports are different, fill them separately. When the final destination country (region) of exports cannot be determined, take the predictable final country (region) arrived at as the final destination

本栏目应按海关规定的《国别(地区)代码表》选择填报相应的国家(地区)名称及代码。

四十、单价

本栏目填报同一项号下进出口货物实际成交的商品单位价格。无实际成交价格的,本栏目填报单位货值。

四十一、总价

本栏目填报同一项号下进出口货物实际成交的商品总价格。无实际成交价格的,本栏目填报货值。

四十二、币制

本栏目应按海关规定的《货币代码表》选择相应的货币名称及代码填报,如《货币代码表》中无实际成交币种,需将实际成交货币按申报日外汇折算率折算成《货币代码表》列明的货币填报。

四十三、征免

本栏目应按照海关核发的《征免税证明》或有关政策规定,对报关单所列每项商品选择海关规定的《征减免税方式代码表》中相应的征减免税方式填报。

加工贸易货物报关单应根据《加工贸易手册》中备案的征免规定填报;《加工贸易手册》中备案的征免规定为"保金"或"保函"的,应填报"全免"。

四十四、税费征收情况

本栏目供海关批注进(出)口货物税费征收及减免情况。

四十五、录入员

本栏目用于记录预录入操作人员的姓名。

四十六、录入单位

本栏目用于记录预录入单位名称。

四十七、填制日期

本栏目填报申报单位填制报关单的日期。本栏目为8位数字,顺序为年(4位)、月(2位)、日(2位)。

四十八、海关审单批注及放行日期(签章)

本栏目供海关作业时签注。

本规范所述尖括号(< >)、逗号(,)、连接符(-)、冒号(:)等标点符号及数字,填报时都必须使用非中文状态下的半角字符。

相关用语的含义:

报关单录入凭单:指申报单位按报关单的格式填写的凭单,用作报关单预录入的依据。该凭单的编号规则由申报单位自行决定。

预录入报关单:指预录入单位按照申报单位填写的报关单凭单录入、打印由申报单位向海关申报,海关尚未接受申报的报关单。

报关单证明联:指海关在核实货物实际进出境后按报关单格式提供的,用作进出口货物收发货人向国税、外汇管理部门办理退税和外汇核销手续的证明文件。

country (region).

Fill the name and code of the country (region) according to the Table of Codes of Countries and Regions stipulated by the Customs.

40. Vnit price

Fill the unit price of actually traded imports and exports under the same item No. in this column. If there is no actual transaction price, fill the unit value of goods in this column.

41. Total price

Fill the total price of actually traded imports and exports under the same item No. in this column. If there is no actual transaction price, fill the unit value of goods in this column.

42. Currency system

Fill the name and code of corresponding currency in this column according to the Table of Currencies stipulated by the Customs. If the actual transaction currency cannot be found in the Table of Codes of Currencies, fill the currency by converting it into a currency listed in the Table of Codes of Currencies according to the exchange rate on the date of declaration.

43. Exemption of duties

For goods of each item No. of the declaration, on the basis of the Certificate of Collection of and Exemption from Duties issued by the Customs or on the basis of relative policies stipulated by national legislation, fill a corresponding procedure according to the " Codes for Type of Levy, Reduction and Exemption of Customs Duties and Taxes" stipulated by the Customs.

Declaration for goods of processing trade, fill the Certificate of Collection of and Exemption from Duties procedure registered in the Processing Trade Handbook. In case of the certificate of collection of and Exemption from Duties procedure resistered in the processing Trade Hamdbook is" security deposit "or" cetter of suarancce" ,fill" relief from all duites and "taxes" other than" reduction and remission according to resistered procedure.

44. State of LRE

This column leaves for the Customs to remark the state of levy, reduction and exemption of Customs duties and taxes to the import/export goods.

45. Declaration maker (natural person)

The columnis specially used for recording the name of the natural person who made the pre-entry declaration.

46. Declaration maker (legal person)

The column is specially used for recording the name of the legal person who made the electronic data declaration.

47. Date of making

Fill the date when the declaring unit fills the declaration form. This column is composed of 8 digits and the sequence is the year (four digits), month (two digits) and date (two digits).

48. Date when the Customs examines, makes comments on and clears (seal)

This column is for the Customs to make comments in operation.

The pointed brackets (< >), comma (,), dash (-), colon (:) and other punctuation marks and figures described in this standard must be filled by using half - angle characters in the non - Chinese state.

Meanings of relevant terms:

Declaration entry voucher: referring to the voucher the declaring unit fills according to the format of the declaration form. It's the basis for making pre - entries in the declaration form. The rule of numbering the voucher is up to the declaring unit.

Pre - entry declaration form: referring to the declaration form filled and printed by the pre - entry unit according to the declaration voucher filled by the declaring unit, to be declared to the Customs by the declaring unit and not accepted by the Customs yet.

Declaration form certificate: referring to the certificate provided by the Customs according to the format of the declaration form after checking actual import and export goods for consignees and consigners of imports and exports to go through drawback and foreign exchange cancellation formalities with the national tax bureau and the foreign exchange administration.

海关总署关于优惠贸易协定项下进口货物的报关单填制规范公告

2005 年第 69 号

为保证优惠贸易协定项下进口货物顺利通关，根据2006 年《中华人民共和国进出口税则》，现将优惠贸易协定项下进口货物的报关单填制规范公告如下：

一、报关单填制规范中的“原产地证书代码”和“优惠贸易协定代码”

“原产地证书代码”为“Y”。

“优惠贸易协定代码”目前为：“01”、“02”、“03”、“04”、“05”、“06”、“07”、“08”。

填制要求：

属于“亚太贸易协定”项下的进口货物填“01”；

属于“中国—东盟自贸区”项下的进口货物填“02”；

属于“内地与香港紧密经贸关系安排”（香港 CEPA）项下的进口货物填“03”；

属于“内地与澳门紧密经贸关系安排”（澳门 CEPA）项下的进口货物填“04”。

属于“对非洲特惠待遇”项下的进口货物填“05”；

属于“台湾水果零关税措施”项下的进口货物填“06”；

属于“中巴自贸区”项下的进口货物填“07”；

属于“中智自贸区”项下的进口货物填“08”。

二、实行原产地证书联网管理的具体填制要求

（一）“备案号”栏：填写“Y”+原产地证书编号。香港、澳门 CEPA 项下进口报关单填写“Y”+11 位原产地证书编号。

（二）“随附单据”栏：使用海关 H2000 通关系统申报的，在本栏随附单证代码项下填写“Y”，在随附单证编号项下的“< >”内填写“优惠贸易协定代码”。使用海关 H883/EDI 通关系统申报的，此栏不填报原产地证书相关内容。

（三）“备注”栏：使用海关 H883/EDI 通关系统申报的，填写“<”+“协”+“优惠贸易协定代码”+“>”。例如香港 CEPA 项下进口报关单应填为：“< 协 03 >”。使用海关 H2000 通关系统申报的，此栏不填报原产地证书相关内容。

（四）“项号”栏：分两行填写。第一行填写报关单中商品排列序号，第二行填写对应的原产地证书上的“商品项号”。

三、未实行原产地证书联网管理的具体填制要求

（一）“备案号”栏：未实行原产地证书联网管理的货物本栏目免予填报。

（二）“随附单据”栏：使用海关 H2000 通关系统申报的，在报关单“随附单据”栏随附单证代码项下填写“Y”，在随附单证编号项下“〈 〉”内填写“优惠贸易协定代码”+“：”+“需证商品序号”。例如《亚太贸易协定》项下进口报关单中第 1 到第 3 项和第 5 项为优惠贸易协定项下商品，应填为：“< 01:1-3,5 >”。使用海关 H883/EDI 通关系统申报的，此栏不填报原产地证书相关内容。

（三）“备注”栏：使用海关 H883/EDI 通关系统申报的，在报关单“备注”栏中填“<”+“协”+“优惠贸易协

General Administration of Customs P. R. C. Announcement for Standards of Filling Declaration for Import Goods Stipulated Under Preferential Trading Agreements

No. 69 2005

For the purpose of ensuring import goods stipulated under preferential trading agreements to pass the Customs expeditiously, herein the standards of filling declaration for import goods stipulated under preferential trading agreements are announced as follows:

1. Supplement the standards of filling declaration with “Code for Certificate of Origin” and “Codes for Preferential Trading Agreements”

Code for Certificate of Origin is “Y”.

At present, Codes for Preferential Trading Agreements are “01”, “02”, “03”, “04”、“05”、“06”、“07”、“08”. Specific filling requirements are as follows:

For import goods stipulated under Asia – pacific Trade Treaty, fill in 01;

For import goods stipulated under China – ASEAN Free Trade Zone fill in 02;

For import goods stipulated under “Mainland-Hong Kong Close Economic and Trade Relationship Promotion Arrangement”(Hong Kong CEPA), fill in 03;

For import goods stipulated under “Mainland-Macao Close Economic and Trade Relationship Promotion Arrangement”(Macao CEPA), fill in 04;

For import goods stipulated under“Special Preferential for African” ,fill in 05

For import goods stipulated under“ Taiwan fruit zero customs duties measure”, fill in 06;

For import goods stipulated under“China and Pakistan Trade Treaty”,fill in 07;

For import goods stipulated under“China and Chile Trade Treaty”,fill in 08.

2. Where Certificate of Origin internet control has been put into practice, specific requirements are as follows:

(1) In the box of Filing No, fill in Y + No. of Certificate of Origin. To import goods stipulated under Hong Kong/Macao CEPA, fill in Y + 11 digits No. of Certificate of Origin.

(2) In the box of other documents attached, declaring via Customs H2000 Declaration System, fill in the particular of code with Y, and fill in < > of No. of document with code for preferential trading agreement. Declaring via Customs H883/EDI Declaration System, should not fill relative contents of Certificate of Origin in this box.

(3) In the box of remarks, declaring via Customs H883/EDI Declaration System, fill in < +“协” + code for preferential trading agreement + >. For example, to import goods stipulated under Hong Kong CEPA, fill in < 协 03 >. Declaring via Customs H2000 Declaration System, should not fill relative contents of Certificate of Origin in this box.

(4) In the box of item No., fill in two lines. Fill in the first line with the item No. of the declaration, fill in the second line with corresponding item No. of Certificate of Origin.

3. Where Certificate of Origin internet control has not been put into practice yet, specific requirements are as follows:

(1) The column exempts from not put into effect administrative networked country of origin certificate goods fill in a form and report to the leadership

(2) In the box of other documents attached, declaring via Customs H2000 Declaration System, fill in the particular of code with Y, and fill in ◇ of No. of document with code for preferential trading agreement + “:” + “item Nos.”. For example, declaration for goods stipulated under “Asia – Pacific Agreement”, which item Nos. are 1-3 and 5, fill in < 01:1-3,5 >. Declaring via Customs H883/EDI Declaration System, should not fill relative contents of Certificate of Origin in this box.

(3) In the box of remarks, declaring via Customs H883/EDI Declaration System, fill in < +“协” + code for preferential trading agreement + : + item Nos.

定代码"+":"+"需证商品序号"+">"。例如《亚太贸易协定》项下进口报关单中第1项到第3项和第5项为优惠贸易协定项下商品，应填为："<协01:1-3,5>"。使用海关H2000通关系统申报的，此栏不填报原产地证书相关内容。

四、其他填制要求

（一）一份原产地证书只能对应一份报关单。同一份报关单上的商品不能同时享受协定税率和减免税。

（二）在一票进口货物中，对于实行原产地证书联网管理的，如涉及多份原产地证书或含非原产地证书商品，应分单填报。

（三）原产地证书实行"一批一证"，不能重复使用和逐次扣减。

（四）报关单上申报商品的计量单位必须与原产地证书上对应商品的计量单位一致。

（五）上述所有尖括号"〈　〉"、逗号","、连接符"-"及数字都必须使用非中文状态下的半角字符。

（六）其他栏目填制要求，仍按海关总署2004年第34号公告《中华人民共和国海关进出口货物报关单填制规范》填制。

五、本公告中"优惠贸易协定"的具体名称如下：

（一）"亚太贸易协定"是指《曼谷协定》，《曼谷协定》第一届部长级理事会上正式更名为《亚太贸易协定》。

（二）"中国－东盟自贸区"是指《中国－东盟全面经济合作框架协议货物贸易协议》。

（三）"内地与香港紧密经贸关系安排"是指《内地与香港关于建立更紧密经贸关系的安排》。

（四）"内地与澳门紧密经贸关系安排"是指《内地与澳门关于建立更紧密经贸关系的安排》。

（五）"对非洲特惠待遇"是指中国给予非洲最不发达国家部分输华商品免关税待遇。

（六）"台湾水果零关税措施"是指自2005年8月1日起对原产于台湾地区的15种进口鲜水果实施零关税的措施。

（七）"中巴自贸区"是指《中国－巴基斯坦关于自由贸易协定早期收获计划的协议》。

（八）"中智自贸区"是指《中国－智利自由贸易协定》。

本公告自2006年1月1日起执行，2003年12月18日海关总署发布的2003年第72号公告同时废止。

特此公告。

中华人民共和国海关总署
二〇〇五年十二月三十一日

\+ >. For example, declaration for goods stipulated under Asia - Pacific Agreement, which item Nos. are 1-3 and 5, fill in <协01:1-3,5>. Declaring via Customs H2000 Declaration System, should not fill relative contents of Certificate of Origin in this box.

4. Other filling requirements

(1) One Certificate of Origin corresponds to only on declaration. For goods of the same one declaration should not claim preferential rate and also claim other reduction or exemption of duties and taxes.

(2) Where Certificate of Origin internet control has been put into practice, goods of one consignment involve many Certificates of Origin or include goods which are not controlled with Certificate of Origin, the goods should be declared separately.

(3) The Control of Certificate of Origin exercises "one consignment, one certificate", which could not be used repeatedly or deducted time by time.

(4) The measure unit of the declaration should be in accordance with the measure unit of Certificate of Origin.

(5) The above mentioned angle brackets(< >), comma(,), hyphen(-) and numerals should be printed with half-angle characters in non-Chinese input state.

(6) Requirements for other particulars are same as "Standards for Filling Import/Export Goods Declaration" (No. 34, 2004) announced by the Customs General Administration.

5. The announcement is hit by concrete "preferential trade agreement" name as follows

(1) "The Asia - Pacific trade agreement " is to point to "the Bangkok agreement ", "Bangkok changes " Asia - Pacific trade agreement ' s name formally on agreement " the first minister level council"

(2) "Chinese - ASEAN is to point to the all - round economic cooperation of " Chinese - ASEAN frame agreement goods trade agreement from trade area "

(3) "The inland and the rapid and intense economic and trade relationship of Hong Kong are arranged to be to point to " inland and Hong Kong arrangement about rapid and intense economic and trade relationship of building - up "

(4) "The inland and the rapid and intense economic and trade relationship of Macao are arranged to be to point to " inland and Macao arrangement about rapid and intense economic and trade relationship of building - up "

(5) "Pay is to refer to China give Africa least developed countries a part convey the China commodity to Africa preference" dispense with customs duties pay.

(6) "Taiwan fruit zero customs duties measure " is to refer to the measure implementing zero customs duties to 15 kinds fresh entrance fruit that the plain produces in Taiwan area starting from August 1, 2005.

(7) "The medium - size bus is to refer to " Chinese - Pakistan ' s agreement about free trade agreement early phase gains plan from trade area "

(8) "Being hit by wisdom is to point to the "Chinese - Chile free trade agreement from trade area "

The announcement 72nd in 2003 that General tration of Customs announces on December 18, 2003 is shed at the same time.

It is hereby announced.

The Customs General Administration
On 31 December 2005

报关自动化系统常用代码表说明

EXPLANATIONS ABOUT TABLE OF CODES OFTEN USED IN CUSTOMS CLEARANCE SYSTEM

监管方式代码表说明

Explanations about Table of Codes of Ways of Supervision

进出口货物海关监管方式(以下简称监管方式),即现行进出口货物报关单“监管方式”,是以国际贸易中进出口货物的交易方式为基础,结合海关对进出口货物的征税、统计及监管条件综合设定的海关对进出口货物的管理方式。

The Customs ways of supervision for imports and exports, i. e. the current "ways of supervision" for declaration forms of imports and exports, are the Customs ways of management of imports and exports established comprehensively based on the ways of transactions for imports and exports in international trade and in light of the Customs levy, statistics and supervision conditions.

由于海关对不同监管方式下进出口货物的监管、征税、统计作业的要求不尽相同,因此为满足海关管理的要求,H2000通关管理系统的监管方式代码采用四位数字结构,其中前二位是按海关监管要求和计算机管理需要划分的分类代码,后二位为海关统计代码。

As the Customs´requirements for supervision, levy and statistics of imports and exports under different ways of supervision are not all the same, the four - digit structure is adopted for the codes of ways of supervision of the H2000 clearance management system to satisfy the Customs´needs of management; therein the first two digits are classification codes classified according to the Customs´requirements for supervision and the needs of computerized management and the last two digits are the statistic codes of the Customs.

●一般贸易

一、定义与代码

一般贸易是指我国境内有进出口经营权的企业单边进口或单边出口的贸易。

本监管方式代码为“0110”,简称:一般贸易。

二、适用范围

(一)本监管方式包括:

1.以正常交易方式成交的进出口货物。

2.贷款援助的进出口货物。

3.外商投资企业进口供加工内销产品的料件。

4.外商投资企业用国产原材料加工成品出口或采购产品出口。

5.供应外国籍船舶、飞机等运输工具的国产燃料、物料及零配件。

6.保税仓库进口供应给中国籍国际航行运输工具使用的燃料、物料等保税货物。

7.境内企业在境外投资以实物投资带出的设备、物资。

8.来料养殖、来料种植的进出口货物。

(二)本监管方式不适用:

1.进出口货样广告品,监管方式为“货样广告品A”(3010)、“货样广告品B”(3039)。

2.没有对外贸易经营资格的单位获准临时进出口货物,监管方式为.“其他贸易”(9739)。

3.境外劳务合作项目,对方以实物产品抵偿我劳务人员工资所进口的货物(如钢材、木材、化肥、海产品等),对外承包工程期间在国外获取及在境外购买的设备、物资等,监管方式为“承包工程进口”(3410)。

● General trade

1. Definition and codes

General trade refers to trade of unilateral import and unilateral export of enterprises in China which have the import and export right.

The code of this way of supervision is "0110" and the shortened form of it is: " general trade".

1. Scope of application

(1) This way of supervision includes:

a. Imports and exports traded in normal way of transaction.

b. Imports and exports aided by loans.

c. Materials and parts imported by foreign - invested enterprises for processing domestically sold products.

d. Exports made with domestic raw materials or procured by foreign - invested enterprises.

e. Domestic fuel, materials and spare parts for foreign ships, aeroplanes and other means of transport. ;

f. Bonded goods such as fuel and materials imported and supplied by bonded for Chinese means of transport for international voyage and transport.

g. Equipment and materials invested by domestic enterprises abroad.

h. Imports and exports bred or plants with foreign materials.

(2) This way of supervision is not applicable to:

a. Imported and exported samples of goods and advertising product, the way of supervision for which is "Samples of Goods and Advertising Products A" (3010) and "Samples of Goods and Advertising Products B" (3039).

b. Imports and exports units that don't have the foreign trade qualification are permitted to import and export and the way of supervision is "other trade" (9739).

c. Goods paid our laborers in overseas labor cooperative projects in kind (such as steel, wood, chemical fertilizers, marine products, etc.), equipment and materials secured and purchased abroad during contracted foreign projects and the way of supervision is "imports in contracted projects (3410).

●易货贸易

一、定义与代码

易货贸易是指不通过货币媒介而直接用出口货物交换进口货物的贸易。

● Barter trade

1. Definition and code

Barter trade refers to the trade of exchanging exports for imports directly without the medium of currencies.

本监管方式代码为“0130”，简称：易货贸易。

The code of this way of supervision is "0130" and the shortened form of it is barter trade".

二、适用范围

本监管方式仅适用于易货贸易经营企业在核准的范围内易货贸易的进出口货物。

以下情况不适用本监管方式

(一)对台小额贸易中签订易货合同的贸易，监管方式为“对台小额”(4039)。

(二)边境小额贸易企业易货贸易进出口货物，监管方式为“边境小额贸易”(4019)。

2. Scope of application

This way of supervision is only applicable to goods barter trade enterprises import and export in the approved scope.

This way of supervision is not applicable to the following circumstances:

(1) Trade in small - amount barter trade contracts with Taiwan and its way of supervision is "small amounts with Taiwan" (4039).

(2) The way of supervision for imports and exports barter traded by frontier trading companies in small amounts is "small - amount frontier trade" (4019).

●旅游购物商品

● Tourist shopping commodities

一、定义与代码

旅游购物商品是指境外旅游者用自带外汇购买的或委托境内企业托运出境5万美元以下的旅游商品或小批量订货。

本监管方式代码为“0139”，简称：“旅游购物商品”。

1. Definition and code

Tourist shopping commodities refer to tourist shopping commodities or ordered goods in small amounts under 50,000 US $ bought by overseas tourists with their own foreign exchange or entrusted domestic enterprises with overseas consignment.

The code of this way of supervision is "0139" and the shortened form of it is "tourist shopping commodities".

二、适用范围

以下情况不适用本监管方式：

(一)出口5万美元以上旅游购物商品。出口旅游商品5万美元以上的，有进出口经营权的企业，按“一般贸易”(0110)申报出口，没有进出口经营权的企业，按“其他贸易”(9739)申报出口。

(二)入境旅游者(包括外籍运输工具服务人员)自带出境用外汇购买旅游纪念品、工艺品、中药材和中成药，由出境地海关旅检部门按照规定限值、限量办理。

2. Scope of application

This way of supervision is not applicable to the following circumstances:

(1) Export of tourist shopping commodities above the value of 50,000 US $. Those enterprises that export tourist commodities above 50,000 US $ and have the import and export right declare for export according to "general grade" (0110) and those enterprises that don't have import and export right declare for export according to "other trade" (9739).

(2) Tourist souvenirs, handcrafts, Chinese herbal medicines and Chinese patent medicines bought by inbound tourists (including service staffs of foreign means of transport) with foreign exchange are handled by the Customs' tourist inspection department at the exit according to limited value and quantity.

●加工贸易料件、成品放弃

● Materials, parts and finished products given up in processing trade

一、定义与代码

(一)加工贸易料件放弃是指加工贸易企业来料加工或进料加工进口的料件，不再用于加工成品出口，主动放弃交由海关处理。

本监管方式的代码为“0200”，简称“料件放弃”。

(二)加工贸易成品放弃是指加工贸易企业来料加工或进料加工生产的成品因故不再出口，主动放弃交由海关处理。

本监管方式的代码为“0400”，简称“成品放弃”。

1. Definition and code

(1) Give - up of materials and parts means materials and parts imported for processing with supplied materials or imported materials by processing trade enterprises are no longer used for making finished products and given up voluntarily to the Customs for disposal.

The code of this way of supervision is "0200" and the shortened form of it is "given - up of materials and parts".

(2) Give - up of finished products in processing trade means finished products made by processing trade enterprises with imported materials or supplied materials will not be exported for some reason and given up voluntarily to the Customs for disposal.

The code of this way of supervision is "0400" and the shortened form of it is "give - up of finished products".

二、适用范围

(一)料件放弃包括：加工贸易进口料件、剩余料件和边角料。

(二)成品放弃包括：加工贸易进口料件加工的成品、半成品、残次品。

2. Scope of application

(1) Give - up of materials and parts includes: imported materials and parts, leftover materials and parts and scraps in processing trade.

(2) Give - up of finished products includes: finished products, semi - finished products and defective products made with imported materials and parts in processing trade.

●来料加工

● Processing of supplied materials

一、定义与代码

来料加工是指进口料件由境外企业提供，经营企业不需要付汇进口，按照境外企业的要求进行加工或者装配，只收取加工费，制成品由境外企业销售的经营活动。

监管方式代码“0214”，简称：“来料加工”。

1. Definition and code

Processing of supplied materials means imported materials and parts are provided by overseas enterprises and operating enterprises don't need to pay foreign exchange for import and only process or assemble according to the requirements of overseas enterprises and charge for processing while overseas enterprises are responsible for sale.

The code of this way of supervision is "0214" and the shortened form of it is "processing of supplied materials".

二、适用范围

（一）本监管方式包括：

1. 来料加工项下进口的料件和加工出口的成品。

2. 设立保税工厂的加工贸易企业来料加工进口料件和出口成品。

（二）以下情况不适用本监管方式：

1. 国营企业代理来料加工企业进口加工生产用柴油，监管方式为“加工专用油”（0314）。

2. 由特定企业以加工贸易进口原油加工成品油，不返销出境，供应国内市场的，监管方式为“成品油”（0642）。

3. 进口5000美元以下、78种列名辅料，监管方式为“低值辅料”（0815）。

2. Scope of application

(1) This way of supervision includes:

a. Materials and parts imported for processing of supplied materials and finished products made for export.

b. Imported materials and parts and finished exports of processing trade enterprises, which have established bonded factories, in processing of supplied materials.

(2) This way of supervision is not applicable to the following circumstances:

a. Diesel oil imported by state - owned enterprises for enterprises which process with supplied materials for production and the way of supervision is "oil for processing" (0314).

b. Crude oil imported by given enterprises for production of finished oil in processing trade, which will not be reexported but supply the domestic market. The way of supervision is "refined oil product" (0642).

c. Import 78 listed auxiliary materials under the value of 5000 US $ and the way of supervision is "low - value auxiliary materials" (0815).

●加工贸易保税货物深加工结转

一、定义与代码

加工贸易保税货物深加工结转是指来料加工、进料加工经营企业将保税进口料件加工的产品不直接出口，在境内结转给另一个加工贸易企业再加工后复出口。

来料深加工结转货物监管方式的代码为“0255”，简称“来料深加工”。

进料深加工结转货物监管方式的代码为“0654”，简称“进料深加工”。

二、适用范围

（一）本监管方式适用：

1. 非海关特殊监管区域加工贸易经营企业之间来料、进料深加工货物结转。

2. 非海关特殊监管区域加工贸易经营企业转自海关特殊监管区域加工贸易经营企业加工的货物。

（二）本监管方式不适用：

1. 保税区、保税物流园区等海关特殊监管区域之间结转的货物，监管方式为“保税间货物”（1200）。

2. 出口加工区企业生产的产品结转至其他出口加工区或非海关特殊监管区域加工复出口，加工区企业转出、转入报关单监管方式为“出口加工区成品进出区”（5100）。

3. 经营企业进料加工产品转给享受减免税优惠的企业，监管方式为“进料成品转减免”（0744）。

● Carry - over of bonded goods in processing trade

1. Definition and code

Processing of suppllied materials and processing imported materials enterproese not directly exported bonded materials imported for processing products; enterproses transfer imported materials and parts to other processing trade enterproses for further processing and reexports. s

The code of the way of supervision for goods carried over in deep processing of supplied materials is "0255" and the shortened form of it is "deep processing of supplied materials".

The code of the way of supervision for goods carried over in deep processing of imported materials is "0654" and the shortened form of it is "deep processing of imported materials".

2. Scope of application

(1) This way of supervision is applicable to:

a. Carry - over of goods deep processed with supplied and imported materials between processing trade enterprises in non - Customs special supervision areas.

b. Processed goods carried over by processing trade enterprises in non - Customs special supervision areas from processing trade enterprises in Customs special supervision areas.

(2) This way of supervision is not applicable to:

a. Goods carried over between bonded areas, bonded parks for flow of goods and other areas under the Customs´ special supervision and the way of supervision is "goods between bonded areas" (1200).

b. When products produced by enterprises in export processing areas are carried over to other export processing areas or non - Customs supervision areas for processing and reexport, the way of supervision for turn in and turn out declaration forms of enterprises in processing areas is "finished product export areas in export processing areas" (5100).

c. When enterprises´ products produced with imported materials are transferred to enterprises granted reduction and exemption of duties, the way of supervision is "finished products with imported materials are granted reduction and exemption of duties (0744).

●加工贸易余料结转

加工贸易余料结转是指加工贸易企业在经营来料加工、进料加工复出口业务过程中剩余的、可以继续用于加工制成品的加工贸易进口料件，结转到同一经营单位、同一加工企业、同样进口料件和同一加工监管方式的另一个加工贸易合同项下继续加工复出口。

来料余料结转监管方式的代码为“0258”，简称“来料余料结转”。

进料余料结转监管方式的代码为“0657”，简称“进料余料结转”。

● Carry - over of leftover materials in processing trade

Carry - over of leftover materials in processing trade means processing trade enterprises carry over imported materials which are left over in processing with supplied and imported materials for reexport in processing trade and can be used for producing finished products continually for further processing and reexport under another processing trade contract with the same enterprise, the same processing enterprise, the same imported materials and parts and the same way of supervision for processing.

The code of the way of supervision for leftover of supplied materials is "0258" and the shortened form of it is "carry - over of leftover of supplied materials".

The code of the way of supervision for leftover of imported materials is "0657" and the shortened form of it is "carry - over of leftover of imported materials".

●加工贸易料件复出

一、定义与代码

加工贸易料件复出是指来料加工、进料加工进口的保税料件因品质、规格等原因退运，以及加工过程中产生的剩余料件、边角料、废料退运出境。

来料加工料件复出监管方式的代码为“0265”，简称“来料料件复出”。

来料加工边角料复出监管方式的代码为“0865”，简称“来料边角料复出”。

进料加工料件复出监管方式的代码为“0664”，简称“进料料件复出”。

进料加工边角料复出监管方式的代码为“0864”，简称“进料边角料复出”。

二、适用范围

（一）加工贸易料件复出适用：

1. 来料加工、进料加工进口的保税料件因品质、规格等原因退运，以及加工过程中产生的剩余料件、边角料、废料退运出境。

2. 经营企业因加工贸易出口产品售后服务需要，申请出口加工贸易手册项下进口的保税料件。

（二）本监管方式不适用：

加工贸易进口料件、剩余料件及边角料、废料复运出境后更换同类货物进口，监管方式为“来料料件退换”（0300）、“进料料件退换”（0700）。

● Reexport of materials and parts in processing trade

1. Definition and code

Reexport of materials and parts in processing trade means bonded materials and parts imported for processing trade with supplied and imported materials are returned for the reason of quality and specifications and outbound return of leftover materials, parts, scraps and waste produced in the processing process.

The code of the way of supervision for reexport of materials and parts in processing with supplied materials is "0265" and the shortened form of it is "reexport of supplied materials and parts".

The code of the way of supervision for reexport of scraps in processing with supplied materials is "0865" and the shortened form of it is "reexport of supplied scraps".

The code of the way of supervision for reexport of materials and parts in processing with imported materials is "0664" and the shortened form of it is "reexport of imported materials and parts".

The code of the way of supervision for reexport of scraps in processing with imported materials is "0864" and the shortened form of it is "reexport of imported scraps".

1. Scope of application

(1) Reexport of materials and parts in processing trade is applicable to:

a. Bonded materials and parts imported for processing with supplied and imported materials are returned for quality and specifications and outbound return of leftover materials and parts, scraps and waste produced in the processing process.

b. Enterprises apply for export of bonded materials and parts imported in the processing trade handbook for after-sale service of exports in processing trade.

(1) This way of supervision is not applicable to:

Imported materials and parts, leftover materials and parts, scraps and waste in processing trade are exported in exchange of same kinds of imports and the way of supervision is "return and exchange of supplied materials and parts" (0300) and "return and exchange of imported materials and parts" (0700).

●加工贸易货物退换

一、定义与代码

（一）加工贸易料件退换

加工贸易料件退换是指来料、进料加工进口的保税料件因品质、规格等原因退运出境，更换料件复进口。

来料加工料件退换监管方式的代码为“0300”，简称“来料料件退换”。

进料加工料件退换监管方式的代码为“0700”，简称“进料料件退换”。

（二）加工贸易成品退换

加工贸易成品退换是指来料、进料加工出口的成品因品质、规格或其他原因退运进境，经加工、维修或更换同类商品复出口。

来料加工成品退换监管方式的代码为“4400”．简称“来料成品退换”。

进料加工成品退换监管方式的代码为“4600”，简称“进料成品退换”。

二、适用范围

该监管方式不适用于来料加工、进料加工过程中产生的剩余料件、边角料、废料退运出境，以及进口料件因品质、规格等原因退运出境且不再更换同类货物进境。这几类货物分别适用以下监管方式：“来料料件复出”（0265）、“来料边角料复出”（0865）、“进料料件复出”（0664）、“进料边角料复出”（0864）。

● Return and exchange of goods in processing trade

1. Definition and code

(1) Return and exchange of materials and parts in processing trade

Return and exchange of materials and parts in processing trade means bonded materials and parts imported in processing with supplied and imported materials are returned overseas for quality and specifications for new materials and parts.

The code of the way of supervision for materials and parts in processing with supplied materials is "0300" and the shortened form of it is "return and exchange of supplied materials and parts".

The code of the way of supervision for materials and parts in processing with imported materials is "0700" and the shortened form of it is "return and exchange of imported materials and parts".

(2) Return and exchange of finished products in processing trade

Return and exchange of finished products in processing trade means finished exports with supplied and imported materials are returned for quality, specifications or other reasons and reexported after processing, maintenance or exchange for similar commodities.

The code of the way of supervision for finished products in processing with supplied materials is "4400" and the shortened form of it is "return and exchange of finished products with supplied materials".

The code of the way of supervision for finished products in processing with imported materials is "4600" and the shortened form of it is "return and exchange of finished products with imported materials".

2. Scope of application

This way of supervision is not applicable to outbound return of leftover materials and parts, scraps, waste produced in processing with supplied and imported materials and outbound return of imported materials and parts for quality and specifications not in exchange of similar imports. The following way of supervision is applicable to these varieties of goods: "reexport of supplied materials and parts" (0265), "reexport of supplied scraps" (0865), "reexport of imported materials and parts" (0664) and "reexport of imported scraps" (0864).

●加工贸易保税货物转内销

包括以下监管方式：来料料件内销（0245）、来料成品转减免（0345）、进料料件内销（0644）、进料成品转减免（0744）、进料边角料内销（0844）、来料边角料内销（0845）

一、定义与代码

（一）加工贸易保税料件转内销是指经营企业来料、进料加工过程中产生的剩余料件或用剩余料件生产的制成品、半成品、残次品以及受灾保税货物，经批准转为国内销售，不再加工复出口，包括海关事后发现有关企业擅自转内销并准予补办进口手续的货物。

来料加工料件转内销监管方式代码“0245”，简称“来料料件内销”。

进料加工料件转内销监管方式代码“0644”，简称进料料件内销”。

（二）加工贸易保税货物减免是指来料、进料加工成品在境内销售给凭《征免税证明》进口货物的企业。

来料加工成品转减免监管方式的代码为“0345”，简称“来料成品转减免”。

进料加工成品转减免监管方式的代码为“0744”，简称“进料成品转减免”。

（三）加工贸易边角料内销是指经批准在境内销售的来料、进料加工过程中有形损耗产生的、仍有商业价值的边角料，包括来料、进料加工副产品。

来料加工边角料转内销监管方式的代码为“0845”，简称“来料边角料内销”。

进料加工边角料转内销监管方式的代码为“0844”，简称“进料边角料内销”。

二、适用范围

（一）加工贸易保税货物内销监管方式适用于边角料、剩余料件、残次品、副产品和受灾保税货物。

1. 边角料，是指加工贸易企业经营来料加工、进料加工业务，在海关核定的单耗内、加工过程中产生的、无法再用于加工该合同项下出口制成品的数量合理的废、碎及下脚料件。

2. 剩余料件，是指加工贸易企业在经营业务过程中剩余的、可以继续用于加工制成品的加工贸易进口料件。

3. 残次品，是指加工贸易企业经营来料加工、进料加工业务，在生产过程中产生的有严重缺陷或者达不到出口合同标准，无法复出口的制品（包括完成品和未完成品）。

4. 副产品，是指加工贸易企业经营来料加工、进料加工业务，在加工生产出口合同规定的制成品（即主产品）过程中同时产生的，且出口合同未规定应当复出口的一个或者一个以上的其他产品。

5. 受灾保税货物，是指加工贸易企业经营业务过程中，因不可抗力原因或者其他经海关审核认可的正当理由造成灭失、短少、损毁等导致无法复出口的保税进口料件和制品。

● Domestic sale of bonded goods in processing trade

including following supervision: domestic sale of supplied materials and parts (0245), reduction of and exemption from dutied os finished products with supplied materials(0345), domestic sale of imported materials and parts(0644), reduction of and exemption from duties of finished products with improted materials(0744), domestic sale of improted scraps(0844), domestic sale of supplied scraps(0845)

1. Definition and code

(1) Domestic sale of bonded materials and parts in processing trade means approved domestic sale of finished products, semi－finished products, defective products and bonded goods after disaster produced with leftover materials produced in enterprises´processing with supplied or imported materials instead of being processed for reexport, including goods whose unapproved domestic sale is found by the Customs after the event and retrospective handling of whose import formalities are approved.

The code of the way of supervision for supplied materials and parts is "0245" and the shortened form of it is "domestic sale of supplied materials and parts".

The code of the way of supervision for imported materials and parts is "0644" and the shortened form of it is "domestic sale of imported materials and parts".

(2) Reduction of and exemption from duties of bonded goods in processing trade means domestic sale of finished products in processing with supplied or imported materials to enterprises which import against the certificate of collection of and exemption from duties.

The code of the way of supervision for reduction of and exemption from duties of finished products in processing with imported materials is "0345" and the shortened form of it is "reduction of and exemption from duties of finished products with supplied materials".

The code of the way of supervision for reduction of and exemption from duties of finished products in processing with supplied materials is "0744" and the shortened form of it is "reduction of and exemption from duties of finished products with imported materials".

(3) Domestic sale of scraps in processing trade means scraps whose domestic sale is approved and which is produced in tangible consumption of processing with supplied and imported materials still have commercial value, including byproducts in processing with supplied and imported materials.

The code of the way of supervision for domestic sale of scraps in processing with supplied materials is "0845" and the shortened form of it is "domestic sale of supplied scraps".

The code of the way of supervision for domestic sale of scraps in processing with imported materials is "0844" and the shortened form of it is "domestic sale of imported scraps".

1. Scope of application

(1) The way of supervision for bonded goods in processing trade applies to scraps, leftover materials and parts, defective products, byproducts and bonded goods after disaster.

a. Scraps refer to waste, broken and scrap materials in reasonable quantity in enterprises´processing with supplied and imported materials, within the unit consumption determined by the Customs, produced in the processing process and unable to be further used to produce finished products under contracts.

b. Leftover materials and parts refer to imported materials and parts in processing trade left over from processing trade enterprises´operation and able to be further used to produce finished products.

c. Defective products refer to serious defective or not－up－to－standard and not reexportable finished products (including finished products and unfinished products) produced in production of processing trade enterprises´processing with supplied and imported materials.

d. Byproducts refer to one or more than one other products which are produced by processing trade enterprises in production of finished products (i. e. main products) stipulated by export contracts in processing with supplied and imported materials and which are not to be reexported according to export contracts.

e. Boned goods after disaster refer to bonded imported materials and parts and finished products which are lost, reduced or damaged in processing trade enterprises´operation because of force of majeure or other justifiable reasons examined and recognized by the Customs and cannot be reexported.

（二）以下情况不适用加工贸易保税货物转内销的监管方式：

1. 特定企业以加工贸易的方式进口原油炼制成品油，不返销出境而供应国内市场，其监管方式为“成品油”（0642）。

2. 保税区、出口加工区加工贸易转内销货物，其监管方式为“保税区进料料件”（0544）、“保税区来料料件”（0545）。

3. 企业擅自内销加工贸易保税货物，按走私或违规处理的。

(2) The way of supervision for domestic sale of bonded goods in processing trade is not applicable to the following circumstances:

a. The way of supervision for given enterprises to import crude oil to produce finished oil in processing trade for the domestic market instead of exporting it is "refined oil product" (0642).

b. The way of supervision for domestically sold goods from processing trade in bonded areas and export processing areas is "imported materials and parts of bonded areas" (0544) and supplied materials and parts of bonded areas" (0545).

c. Bonded goods in processing trade sold by enterprises without approval will be treated as contrabands or goods in violation of regulations.

● 加工专用油

加工专用油是指指定国营贸易企业代理来料加工企业进口来料加工生产用柴油。

本监管方式代码“0314”，简称“加工专用油”。

● Oil for processing

Oil for processing means designated state – owned trading enterprises import oil for processing for enterprises with supplied materials.

The code of this way of supervision is "0314" and the shortened form of it is "oil for processing".

● 加工贸易设备

包括以下监管方式：不作价设备（0320）、加工贸易设备（0420）、加工设备内销（0446）、加工设备结转（0456）、加工设备退运（0466）

一、定义与代码

（一）外商提供的加工贸易不作价设备是指境外企业与境内企业开展来料、进料加工业务，外商免费向境内加工贸易经营单位提供加工生产所需设备，境内经营单位不需支付外汇、不需用加工费或差价偿还。

外商提供的加工贸易不作价设备监管方式的代码为“0320”，简称“不作价设备”。

（二）加工贸易设备是指来料加工、进料加工贸易项下外商作价提供、不扣减企业投资总额的进口设备。

加工贸易设备监管方式的代码为“0420”，简称“加工贸易设备”。

（三）加工贸易设备转内销是指在海关监管期内的加工贸易免税进口设备经批准转售给境内非加工贸易企业。

加工贸易设备转内销监管方式的代码为“0446”，简称“加工设备内销”。

（四）加工贸易设备结转是指海关监管期内的加工贸易免税进口设备经批准转让给另一加工企业，或从本企业一本《加工贸易手册》结转入另一本《加工贸易手册》。

加工贸易设备结转监管方式的代码为“0456”，简称“加工设备结转”。

（五）加工贸易设备退运是指加工贸易免税进口设备退运出境。

加工贸易设备退运监管方式的代码为“0466”，简称“加工设备退运”。

二、适用范围

以下情况不适用本节监管方式：

（一）暂时进口（期限在半年以内）加工贸易生产所需不作价设备（限模具、单台设备），按暂时进口货物办理。

（二）外商投资企业投资总额内资金进口的设备，其监管方式为“合资合作设备”（2025）、“外资设备物品”（2225）。

（三）外商投资企业自有资金（投资总额以外）进口设备，监管方式为“一般贸易”（0110）。

（四）出口加工区的设备进口、退运及结转，分别适用“境外设备进区”（代码5335）、“区内设备退运”（代码5361）和“设备进出区”（代码5300）。

● Processing trade equipment

Including following supervision: equipment not priced (0320), processing trade equipment (0420), domestic sale of processing equipment (0446), carry – over of processing equipment (0456), return of processing equipment (0466)

1. Definition and code

(1) Processing trade equipment not priced which is supplied by foreign businessmen refers to equipment for production supplied by foreign businessmen free of charge to domestic processing trade units in their processing with supplied and imported materials without the need of paying foreign exchange and repaying with processing cost or price difference.

The code of the way of supervision for this is "0320" and the shortened form of it is "equipment not priced".

(2) Processing trade equipment refers to imported equipment supplied by foreign businessmen not free of charge and without deduction of the total investment in enterprises in processing with supplied and imported materials.

The code of the way of supervision for this is "0420" and the shortened form of it is "processing trade equipment".

(3) Domestic sale of processing trade equipment refers to duty – free imported equipment in processing trade is sold to domestic non – processing trade enterprises with approval during the Customs' supervision period.

The code of the way of supervision for this is "0446" and the shortened form of it is "domestic sale of processing equipment".

(4) Carry – over of processing trade equipment refers to transfer of duty – free imported equipment in processing trade to another processing enterprise with approval during the Customs' supervision period or carry – over from one Processing Trade Handbook to another of the same enterprise.

The code of the way of supervision for this is "0456" and the shortened form of it is "carry – over of processing equipment".

(5) Return of processing trade equipment refers to outbound return of duty – free imported equipment in processing trade.

The code of the way of supervision for this is "0466" and the shortened form of it is "return of processing equipment".

1. Scope of application

The way of supervision is not applicable to the following circumstances:

(1) Equipment not priced for processing trade production (limited to molds and single set of equipment) imported temporarily (within half a year) is handled as temporary imports.

(2) The way of supervision for equipment imported in the total investment by foreign – invested enterprises is "equipment for joint ventures and cooperative ventures" (2025) and "foreign – funded equipment and articles" (2225).

(3) The way of supervision for equipment imported with self – owned funds of foreign – invested enterprises is "general trade" (0110).

(4) "Overseas equipment import" (code 5335), "return of equipment from areas" (code 5361) and "equipment import and export" (code 5300) are applicable respectively to import, return and carry – over of equipment to export processing areas.

●监管年限内减免税设备结转

一、定义与代码

监管年限内减免税设备结转是指进口企业在减免税设备监管年限内转让给另一享受减免税待遇的企业。

本监管方式代码"0500",简称"减免设备结转"。

二、适用范围

本监管方式不适用于加工贸易项下进口设备结转给另一加工贸易企业,监管方式为"加工设备结转"(0456)。

● Carry – over of equipment granted reduction of and exemption from duties within the supervision years

1. **Definition and code**

Carry – over of equipment granted reduction of and exemption from duties within the supervision years refers to transfer of equipment by import enterprises within the years of reduction of and exemption from duties and supervision to another enterprise which enjoys the treatment of reduction of and exemption from duties.

The code of the way of supervision is "0500" and the shortened form of it is "carry – over of equipment granted reduction of and exemption from duties".

1. **Scope of application**

This way of supervision is not applicable to carry – over of equipment imported in processing trade to another processing trade enterprise and the way of supervision is "carry – over of processing equipment" (0456).

●保税区加工贸易内销货物

保税区进料加工、来料加工加工成品不复运出境,转为国内使用,按征税方式区分,适用以下监管方式:

一区内加工企业来料、进料加工全部用境外运入料件加工的制成品销往非保税区,以及来料、进料加工内销制成品所含进口料件的品名、数量、价值难以区分的,按照制成品征税,监管方式为:

(一)按成品征税的保税区来料加工成品转内销货物,监管方式代码为"0445",简称"保区来料成品"。

(二)按成品征税保税区进料加工成品转内销货物,监管方式代码为"0444",简称"保区进料成品"。

二区内企业来料、进料加工用含有部分境外运入料件加工的制成品销往非保税区时,对其制成品按照所含进口料件征税,其监管方式为:

(一)按料件征税的保税区来料加工成品转内销货物,监管方式代码为"0545",简称"保区来料料件"。

(二)按料件征税的保税区进料加工成品转内销货物,监管方式代码为"0544",简称"保区进料料件"。

● Domestically sold goods from processing trade in bonded areas

Finished products produced with supplied and imported materials in bonded areas which are not reexported and used domestically are supervised according to the following way of supervision based on the way of collection duties:

1 Materials and parts are all imported for enterprises´ processing with supplied and imported materials. whan finished products produced one sold to non-bonded areas and it' s hard to disting wish the name, quantity and value of imported materials con tained in finished products produced with supphed and imported materials for domestic sale, duties on then will be levied as finished products . The way of supervision is:

(1) The code of the way of supervision for domestically sold finished products that are produced with supplied materials in bonded areas and duties on which are levied as finished products is "0445" and the shortened form of it is "finished products with supplied materials in bonded areas".

(2) The code of the way of supervision for domestically sold finished products that are produced with imported materials in bonded areas and duties on which are levied as finished products is "0444" and the shortened form of it is "finished products with supplied materials in bonded areas".

2 When finished products produced by enterprises in bonded areas with some of materials and parts imported from overseas in processing with supplied and imported materials are sold to non – bonded areas, duties on the finished products are levied based on imported materials and parts contained in them. The way of supervision is:

(1) The code of the way of supervision for domestically sold finished products that are produced with supplied materials in bonded areas and duties on which are levied based on materials and parts is "0545" and the shortened form of it is "materials and parts with supplied materials in bonded areas".

(2) The code of the way of supervision for domestically sold finished products that are produced with imported materials in bonded areas and duties on which are levied based on materials and parts is "0544" and the shortened form of it is "materials and parts with imported materials in bonded areas".

●补偿贸易

一、定义与代码

补偿贸易是指由境外厂商提供或者利用国外出口信贷进口生产技术或设备,我方企业(包括"外商投资企业")进行生产,以返销其产品的方式分期偿还对方技术、设备价款或贷款本息的交易方式。包括经经贸主管部门批准,使用该企业(包括企业联合体)所生产的其他产品返销给对方,进行间接补偿。

补偿贸易偿还对方技术、设备价款或贷款本息的方式一般有两种:

(一)产品出口先偿还设备价款,还清本息后再出口收汇。

● Compensation trade

1. **Definition and code**

Compensation trade means overseas manufacturers provide production technology or equipment or production technology or equipment is imported by using foreign export credit and our enterprises (including "foreign – invested enterprises") engage in production and repay the cost of the other side's technology, equipment or principal of and interest on loans in installments by products, including repayment by other products produced by such enterprises (including corporate conglomerates) to the other side for indirect compensation as approved by the competent economic and trade department.

There are generally two ways to repay the cost of the other side's technology, equipment or principal of and interest on loans:

(1) Repay the cost of equipment by exporting products first and collect foreign exchange after principal and interest are repaid.

(二)设备价款本息在每批出口货物价款中扣还一部分。直到还清为止。

本监管方式代码为"0513",简称"补偿贸易"。

二、适用范围

本监管方式包括补偿贸易中对方有偿或免费提供的机器设备、模具等。

本监管方式不包括:

(一)直接用国内产品同国外厂商交换设备、料件或成品,以货换货,其监管方式为"易货贸易"(0130)。

(二)出口产品收取外汇,其监管方式为"一般贸易"(0110)。

(三)在补偿贸易合同中同时订有来料加工合同的,来料加工合同部分,其监管方式为"来料加工"(0214)。

(2) Repay the principal of and interest on the cost of equipment by part of the cost of every batch of exports till all is repaid.

The code of the way of supervision for this is "0513" and the shortened form of it is "compensation trade".

2. Scope of application

This way of supervision includes machinery, equipment and molds the other side supplies free or not free of charge in compensation trade.

This way of supervision doesnt include:

(1) Exchange domestic products for equipment, materials, parts or finished products directly with foreign manufacturers in barter trade and the way of supervision is "barter trade" (0130).

(2) Collect foreign exchange by export and the way of supervision is "general trade" (0110).

(3) When compensation trade contracts are accompanied by contracts on processing with supplied materials, the way of supervision for the latter is "processing with supplied materials" (0214).

●进料加工贸易

一、定义与代码

进料加工贸易,是指进口料件由经营企业付汇进口,制成品由经营企业外销出口的经营活动。进料加工贸易按照对外签约形式分为"进料加工非对口合同"和"进料加工对口合同"。

"进料加工非对口合同"是指我方有外贸进出口经营权的企业动用外汇购买进口原料、材料、元器件、零部件、配套件和包装物料(以下简称料件),加工成品或半成品再返销出口的交易形式。

本监管方式代码为"0715",简称"进料非对口"。

"进料加工对口合同"是指买卖双方分别签订进出口对口合同,料件进口时,我方先付料件款,加工成品出口时再向对方收取出口成品款项的交易形式,包括动用外汇的对口合同或不同客户的对口的联号合同以及对开信用证的对口合同。

本监管方式代码为"0615",简称"进料对口"。

境外客户为境内企业加工复出口产品提供进口5000美元及以下、数量零星的辅料或包装物料以及数量合理直接用于服装生产车间的小型易耗性生产工具。

本监管方式代码为"0815",简称"低值辅料"。

二、适用范围

(一)本监管方式包括:

1. 进料加工项下进口料件和加工出口产品。

2. 设立保税工厂的加工贸易企业进料加工进口料件和出口成品

(二)本监管方式不适用出口加工区加工贸易进出口货物,其监管方式为"区内加工货物"(5015)。

● Processing trade with imported materials

1. Definition and code

Processing trade with imported materials means imported materials and parts are imported with foreign exchange and finished products are exported by operating enterprises. Processing trade with imported materials is divided into "non - compatible contracts on processing with imported materials" and "compatible contracts on processing with imported materials" according to the agreement form signed.

"Non - compatible contracts on processing with imported materials" is the transaction form in which our enterprises with the import and export right use foreign exchange to import raw materials, materials, components, spare parts, accessories and packing materials (shortened to materials and parts hereunder) to produce finished products or semi - finished products for reexport.

The code of the way of supervision for this is "0715" and the shortened form of it is "non - compatible import of materials".

"Compatible contracts on processing with imported materials" is the transaction form in which buyers and sellers sign compatible import and export contracts. Our side pays for materials and parts first in their import and then collect the cost of finished products in export, including compatible contracts using foreign exchange or joint compatible contracts signed with different customers and compatible contracts using LC.

The code of the way of supervision for this is "0615" and the shortened form of it is "compatible import of materials".

Overseas customers provide domestic enterprises´ reexport with auxiliary materials or packing materials in small quantities under the value of US $ 5000 or under and small consumable production tools in reasonable quantities and directly usable in garment workshops.

The code of the way of supervision for this is "0815" and the shortened form of it is "low - value auxiliary materials".

2. Scope of application

(1) This way of supervision includes:

a. Imported materials and parts and exports in processing with imported materials.

b. Bonded factory processing trade enterprises imported materials and export finished products

(2) This way of supervision is not applicable to imports and exports in processing trade in export processing areas, the way of supervision for which is "processed goods in areas (5015).

●加工贸易成品油以产顶进

加工贸易成品油以产顶进是指特定企业以加工贸易形式进口原油,加工供国内市场的成品油。

本监管方式代码为"0642",简称"成品油"。

● Substitute imports with finished oil in processing trade

Substituting imports with finished oil in processing trade means given enterprises import crude oil in processing trade and refine it into finished oil for the domestic market.

The code of this way of supervision is "0642" and the shortened form of it is "importing materials to substitute imports with products".

●国轮油物料

一、定义与代码

国轮油物料指中国籍国际航行的运输工具在境内添加的保税仓库进口仓储的油料、物料。

本监管方式代码为"1139",简称"国轮油物料"。

二、适用范围

本监管方式适用于从保税仓库提取,供应航行国际航线的中国籍船舶、民用航空器等运输工具的进口燃料、物料及零配件等。

本监管方式不适用从设在非海关特殊监管区域的保税仓库提取,供应航行国际航线的外国籍船舶、飞机等运输工具的进口燃料、物料,其监管方式为"保税仓库货物"(1233)。

●保税区间及保税仓库间货物结转

一、定义与代码

保税区间及保税仓库间货物结转是指保税区、保税物流园区、出口加工区、出口监管仓库、保税仓库、保税物流中心(A、B型)等海关特殊监管区域、保税监管场所间往来的货物。

本监管代码为"1200",简称"保税间货物"

二、适用范围

本监管方式不适用出口加工区间结转货物,不同出口加工区企业结转货物适用"出口加工区成品进出区"(5100)和"料件进出区"(5000)。

●保税仓库进出境仓储、转口货物

一、定义与代码

保税仓库进出境仓储及转口货物,指从境外进口直接存入保税仓库和保税仓库出境的仓储、转口货物,以及出口监管仓库出境的货物。

本监管方式代码为"1233",简称"保税仓库货物"。

二、适用范围

(一)本监管方式适用于经批准设立的保税仓库进出境和出口监管仓库的出境货物。包括从保税仓库提取用于外国籍国际航行运输工具的物料。

(二)下列情况不适用本监管方式:

1.保税仓库、出口监管仓库进口自用的货架、办公用品、管理用具、运输车辆、搬运、起重和包装设备以及改装用的机器等,其监管方式为"一般贸易"(0110)。

2.从保税仓库提取用于本国籍运输工具或用于维修境内设备的仓储货物,按进口申报,其监管方式为"一般贸易"(0110)。

3.保税仓库进境货物销往境内,按货物运出保税仓库的实际用途填报相应的监管方式。

4.境内存入出口监管仓库和出口监管仓库的退仓货物分各种监管方式。

5.保税区、保税物流中心进出境仓储、转口货物,监管方式分别为"保税区仓储、转口"(1234)、"物流中心进出境货物"(6033)。

6.保税仓库货物出仓运往境内其他地方转为正式进

● Guolun oil and materials

1. Definition and code

Guolun oil and materials means Chinese means of transport for international navigation is refueled domestically with oil and materials imported and stored in bonded warehouses.

The code of the way of supervision for this is "1139" and the shortened form of it is "Guolun oil and materials".

1. Scope of application

This way of supervision is applicable to imported fuel, materials and spare and accessory parts taken from bonded warehouses for Chinese ships and civil aircrafts on international routes.

This way of supervision is not applicable to imported fuel, materials and spare and accessory parts taken from bonded warehouses not in the Customs supervision areas for foreing ships and civil aircrafts on international routes, the way of supervision for which is "goods in bonded warehouses" (1233).

● Carry - over of goods between bonded areas and bonded warehouses

1. Definition and code

Carry - over of goods between bonded areas and bonded warehouses means goods transferred between bonded areas, bonded parks for flow of goods, export processing areas, warehouses under export supervision, bonded warehouses, bonded centers for flow of goods (Type A and B) and other areas and places under the Customs supervision.

The code of the way of supervision for this is "1200" and the shortened form of it is "goods between bonded areas".

1. Scope of application

This way of supervision is not applicable to goods carried over between export processing areas and "import and export areas for finished products in export processing areas" (5100) and "import and export areas for materials" (5000) are applicable to goods carried over between different export processing areas.

● Warehoused and transit imports and exports in bonded warehouses

1. Definition and code

Warehoused and transit imports and exports in bonded warehouses refers to imports directly stored in bonded warehouses, stored and transit exports from bonded warehouses and exports from warehouses under export supervision.

The code of the way of supervision for this is "1233" and the shortened form of it is "goods in bonded warehouses".

2. Scope of application

(1) This way of supervision is applicable to imports into and exports from bonded warehouses established with approval and exports from warehouses under export supervision, including materials taken from bonded warehouses for foreign means of transport for international navigation.

(2) The way of supervision doesn't apply to the following Circumstances:

a. The way of supervision for shelves, office supplies, management appliances, transport vehicles, equipment for carrying, lifting and packing and machines for refitting used by bonded warehouses and warehouses under export supervision is "general trade" (0110).

b. Warehoused goods taken from bonded warehouses for means of transport of this country or for maintenance of domestic equipment shall be declared as imports and the way of supervision for them is "general trade" (0110).

c. When imports in bonded warehouses are sold domestically, fill the corresponding way of supervision according to the actual use of goods after being transported out of bonded warehouses.

d. Returned goods stored in warehouses under export supervision and import supervision have various ways of supervision.

e. The ways of supervision for bonded areas, warehoused and transit imports and exports in bonded centers for flow of goods are "warehousing and transit in bonded areas" (1234) and "imports and exports in centers for flow of goods (6033).

f. When goods in bonded warehouses are transported to other domestic places and

口的,在仓库主管海关办结出仓报关手续,填制出口报关单,监管方式填写"1200",进口报关单按实际进口监管方式填报。

7. 保税仓库寄售维修零部件申请免税出仓的,进口报关单贸易方式应为"无代价抵偿货物"(代码为"3100")

●保税区进出境仓储、转口货物

一、定义与代码

保税区进出境仓储、转口货物是指从境外存入保税区、保税物流园区和从保税区、保税物流园区运出境的仓储、转口货物。

本监管方式代码为"1234",简称"保税区仓储转口"。

二、适用范围

下列情况不适用本监管方式:

(一)保税区、保税物流园区除仓储、转口货物以外的其他进出境货物,按实际监管方式填报。

(二)从境内非海关特殊监管区域、保税监管场所运入保税区、保税物流园区的货物,按实际监管方式填报。

从境内非海关特殊监管区域、保税监管场所运入保税区、保税物流园区的货物退回境内,按实际监管方式填报。

(三)从保税区、保税物流园区运往境内非海关特殊监管区域、保税监管场所的货物,按实际监管方式填报。

●寄售代销贸易

一、定义与代码

寄售代销贸易是指寄售人把货物运交事先约定的代销人,由代销人按照事先约定或根据寄售代销协议规定的条件,在当地市场代为销售,所得货款扣除代销人的佣金和其他费用后,按协议规定方式将余款付给寄售人的交易形式。寄售人与代销人之间不是买卖关系,而是委托关系,代销人对货物没有所有权。

本监管方式代码为"1616",简称"寄售代销"。

二、适用范围

本监管方式包括寄售代销贸易进出口的货物及进口寄售货物的增发部分。

本监管方式不包括:

(一)经营寄售代销业务的企业,接受国外免费提供的样品,其监管方式应为"货样广告品B"(3039);

(二)委托我驻港澳机构代销的鲜活商品,其监管方式应为"一般贸易"(0110)。

●进出境修理物品

一、定义与代码

进出境修理物品是指进境或出境维护修理的货物、物品。

本监管方式代码"1300",简称"修理物品"。

二、适用范围

本监管方式适用于各类进出境维修的货物以及修理货物维修所用的原材料、零部件。

以下情况不适用本监管方式:

(一)按加工贸易保税货物管理的进境维修业务。

turned into imports, go through declaration formalities with the competent Customs office, fill the export declaration form and fill "1200" as the way of supervision and fill the import declaration form according to the actual way of supervision for imports.

7. Bonded warehouse consignment maintenance Spare parts apply for tax – free to take out of storage, the way of import declaration trade is" Unpriced offset goods" (the code is" 3100")

● Warehoused and transit imports and exports in bonded areas

1. Definition and code

Warehoused and transit imports and exports in bonded areas refers to warehoused and transit goods stored into bonded areas and bonded parks for flow of goods from overseas and transported overseas from bonded areas and bonded parks for flow of goods.

The code of the way of supervision for this is "1234" and the shortened form of it is "warehouse transit in bonded areas".

1. Scope of application

This way of supervision is not applicable to the following circumstances:

(1) Declare imports and exports in bonded areas and bonded parks for flow of goods according to the actual way of supervision except warehoused and transit goods.

(2) Fill goods transported from domestic areas not under the Customs supervision and non – bonded supervision areas into bonded areas and bonded parks for flow of goods according to the actual way of supervision.

When goods transported from domestic areas not under the Customs supervision and non – bonded supervision areas into bonded areas and bonded parks for flow of goods according to the actual way of supervision are returned domestically, fill according to the actual way of supervision.

(3) Fill good transported from bonded areas and bonded parks into doinestic arease not under the customs supervision and non-bonded supervision areas in for flow of goods according to the actual way of supervision.

● Consignment trade

1. Definition and code

Consignment trade refers to the transaction form in which consignors consign goods to consignees appointed beforehand and the latter sell them on the local market according to the prior agreement or the conditions stipulated in consignment agreement and pay consignors the extra after deducting commissions and other expenses from the payments for goods. The relationship between consignors and consignees is not the relationship between buyers and sellers but the relationship of trust. Consignees dont have ownership of the goods.

The code of the way of supervision for this is "1616" and the shortened form of it is "consignment".

2. Scope of application

This way of supervision includes imports and exports in consignment trade and the addition of imported consignment goods.

This way of supervision doesnt include:

(1) Free samples received by enterprises which engage in consignment business and the way of supervision for this shall be "advertisement sample B" (3039).

(2) Fresh and live commodities consigned to our organizations in Hong Kong and Macao and the way of supervision for this shall be "general trade" (0110).

● Goods imported and exported for maintenance

1. Definition and code

Goods imported and exported for maintenance refer to goods and articles imported or exported for maintenance.

The code of the way of supervision for this is "1300" and the shortened form of it is "goods for maintenance"

2. Scope of application

This way of supervision is applicable to various kinds of goods imported and exported for maintenance and raw materials and spare parts for maintaining goods.

This way of supervision is not applicable to the following circumstances:

(1) Maintenance of imported goods managed as bonded goods in processing

（二）加工贸易进口料件和出口成品进出境维修，分别适用“来料料件退换”（0300）、“来料成品退换”（4400）、“进料料件退换”（0700）、“进料成品退换”（4600）。

trade.

(2) "Return and exchange of supplied materials and parts" (0300), "return and exchange of finished products with supplied materials" (4400) and return and exchange of "return and exchange of imported materials and parts" (0700) and "return and exchange of finished products with imported materials" (4600) are applicable to maintenance of imported materials and parts and finished exports in processing trade respectively.

●出料加工贸易

一、定义及代码

出料加工贸易是指境内企业将境内原辅料、零部件、元器件或半成品交由境外厂商按我方要求进行加工或装配，成品复运进口，我方支付加工费的交易方式。

本监管方式代码为1427，简称：出料加工。

二、适用范围

本监管方式不包括：

（一）运往境外维修的货物以及石化生产过程中所需催化剂需运至国外添加氢以增加活性后复运进境继续投入生产使用，不改变其物理和化学性质，未产生新的产品，其监管方式为“修理物品”（1300）。

（二）出料加工，原则上不改变原出口货物的物理形态。对完全改变原出口货物的物理形态，如出口废钢进口钢材，出口废铝进口铝合金板材等，不属出料加工，应按一般贸易货物办理进出口手续。

● Processing trade for exported materials

1. Definition and code

Processing trade for exported materials refers to the transaction form in which domestic enterprises deliver domestic auxiliary materials, spare parts, components or semi - finished products to overseas manufacturers for processing or assembly according to our requirements with processing fees and sending back finished products.

The code of the way of supervision for this is 1427 and the shortened form of it is processing for exported materials.

2. Scope of application

This way of supervision doesnt include:

(1) Goods transported overseas for maintenance and catalyst for petrochemical production that has to be transported overseas for addition of hydrogen and enhancement of its activity, without changing its physical and chemical properties and producing new products, before being reimported and put again into production, the way of supervision for which is "maintained goods" (1300).

(2) Processing for exported materials doesnt change exports´original physical form in principle. If exports´original physical form is totally changed, for example exporting steel scraps and reimporting steel products, exporting aluminum scraps and reimporting aluminum alloy sheets, etc., import and export formalities shall be handled as for goods in general trade instead of processing for exported materials.

●租赁贸易

一、定义及代码

租赁贸易是指经营租赁业务的企业与外商签订国际租赁合同项下境内企业租赁进口或出租出口的货物。

租赁期在一年及以上的进出口货物，其监管方式代码为“1523”，简称“租赁贸易”。

租赁期在一年及以上的进出口货物分期办理征税手续时，每期征税适用监管方式代码为“9800”，简称“租赁征税”。

租赁期不满一年的进出口货物，其监管方式代码为“1500”，简称“租赁不满一年”。

二、适用范围

以下情况不适用本监管方式：

（一）经营租赁业务的企业进口自用的设备、办公用品，其监管方式为“一般贸易”（0110）。

（二）加工贸易租赁进口的机器设备，其监管方式应为“加工贸易设备”（0420）。

（三）补偿贸易租借进口的货物，其监管方式应为“补偿贸易”（0513）。

（四）“租赁贸易”（1523）期满复运出（进）口的货物，其监管方式为“退运货物”（4561）；“租赁不满一年”（1500）期满复运出（进）境的货物，其监管方式为“租赁不满一年”（1500）。

● Leasing trade

1. Definition and code

Leasing trade means enterprises which engage in leasing trade sign international leasing contracts with foreign businessmen to import or export leased goods.

The code of the way of supervision for imports and exports with the leasehold of one year or more is "1523" and the shortened form of it is "leasing trade".

When duty levy formalities are handled for imports and exports with the leasehold of one year or more in phases, the code of the way of supervision for every phase is "9800" and the shortened form of it is "lease levy".

The code of the way of supervision for imports and exports with the leasehold of less than one year is "1500" and the shortened form of it is "leasehold of less than one year".

2. Scope of application

This way of supervision doesnt apply to the following circumstances:

(1) Equipment and office supplies that enterprises which engage in leasing business import for themselves and the way of supervision is "general trade" (0110).

(2) Machines and equipment leased and imported in processing trade and the way of supervision shall be "equipment in processing trade" (0420).

(3) Goods leased and imported in compensation trade and the way of supervision shall be "compensation trade (0513).

(4) Goods reexported (reimported) after the leasehold expires and the way of supervision is "returned goods" (4561); goods reexported (reimported) when the leasehold of less than one year expires and the way of supervision is "leasehold of less than one year" (1500).

●免税品

一、定义及代码

免税品是指设在国际机场、港口、车站和过境口岸的免税品商店进口，按有关规定销售给办完出境手续的旅客的免税商品，供外国籍船员和我国远洋船员购买送货上船出售的免税商品，供外交人员购买的免税品，以及在我国际航机，国际班轮上向国际旅客出售的免税商品。

● Duty - free articles

1. Definition and code

Duty - free goods refer to duty - free commodities of passengers who import them in duty - free shops at international airports, ports, railway stations and cross - border ports and have gone through exit formalities according to regulations, duty - free commodities sold and delivered on board to foreign crew members and our ocean - going crew members, duty - free articles for diplomatic personnel and duty - free com-

本监管方式代码为“1741”,简称“免税品”。

modities sold to international passengers on international airliners and international liners.

The code of the way of supervision for this is "1741" and the shortened form of it is "duty - free articles".

二、适用范围

(一)本监管方式适用于:

1. 免税店范围:进出境口岸免税店、运输工具免税店、市内免税店、外交人员免税店和供船免税店等五类免税店进口核定品种的免税品。

2. 供应对象:办结出境手续的出境旅客、国际航行运输工具服务人员、外交人员。

(二)本监管方式不适用:

1. 境内免税外汇商店销售给为我出国人员、华侨的免税外汇商品,其监管方式为“免税外汇商品”(1831)。

2. 经营免税品业务的单位进口的供维修使用的零部件、工具、展台、货架,其监管方式为“一般贸易”(0110)。

3. 免税品退运出境,其监管方式为“其他”(9900)。

2. **Scope of application**

(1) This way of supervision is applicable to:

a. The scope of duty - free shops: the approved varieties of duty - free articles imported by duty - free shops at import and export ports, duty - free shops on means of transport, duty - free shops in cities, duty - free shops for diplomatic personnel and duty - free shops on ships.

b. Objects of supply: outbound passengers who have gone through outbound formalities, service staffs on means of transport for international navigation and diplomatic personnel.

(2) This way of supervision is not applicable to:

a. Duty - free commodities sold by domestic duty - free foreign exchange shops to our outbound personnel and overseas Chinese and the way of supervision is "duty - free foreign exchange commodities" (1831).

b. Spare parts, tools, booths and shelves imported by units which engage in the business of duty - free articles for maintenance and the way of supervision is "general trade" (0110).

c. The way of supervision for outbound return of duty - free articles is "other (9900).

●免税外汇商品

一、定义及代码

免税外汇商品是指由经批准的经营单位进口,销售专供入境的我国特定出国人员和驻华外交人员的免税外汇商品。

本监管方式代码“1831”,简称“免税外汇商品”。

二、适用范围

(一)本监管方式适用:

1. 免税外汇商品供应对象是指我国驻外外交机构人员、留学人员、访问学者、赴境外劳务人员、援外人员和远洋船员。

2. 上述人员用结存外汇在境内免税外汇商品店购买限定品种的免税外汇商品。

3. 专供外国驻华外交人员免税商品的特定公司进口的免税外汇商品。

(二)本监管方式不适用:

1. 设在国际机场、港口、车站和过境口岸的免税品商店所进口的,按有关规定销售给办结出境手续的旅客的免税商品,供外国籍船员和我国远洋船员购买送货上船出售的免税商品,供外交人员购买的免税品,以及在我国际航班,国际班轮上向国际旅客出售的免税商品。其监管方式为“免税品”(1741)。

2. 经营免税外汇商品的单位进口供商品维修用的零部件、工具和商场自用的货架、手推车等。其监管方式为“一般贸易”(0110)。

3. 因故经批准转内销进口免税外汇商品,其监管方式为“一般贸易”(0110)。

4. 免税外汇商品退运出境,其监管方式为“退运货物”(4561)。

● Duty - free foreign exchange commodities

1. **Definition and code**

Duty - free foreign exchange commodities refer to duty - free foreign exchange commodities imported by approved operating units and sold to inbound specific Chinese personnel and diplomatic personnel stationed in China.

The code of the way of supervision is 1831 and the shortened form of it is duty - free foreign exchange commodities.

1. **Scope of application**

(1) This way of supervision applies to:

a. The objects of supply of duty - free foreign exchange commodities are Chinese diplomatic personnel in foreign countries, students studying abroad, visiting scholars, laborers working overseas, personnel for foreign aid and ocean - going crew members.

b. Duty - free foreign exchange commodities in limited varieties bought by the above people with foreign exchange they saved at domestic duty - free shops.

c. Duty - free foreign exchange commodities imported by designated companies for foreign diplomatic personnel in China.

(1) This way of supervision does not apply to:

a. Duty - free commodities of passengers who import them in duty - free shops at international airports, ports, railway stations and cross - border ports and have gone through exit formalities according to regulations, duty - free commodities sold and delivered on board to foreign crew members and our ocean - going crew members, duty - free articles for diplomatic personnel and duty - free commodities sold to international passengers on international airliners and international liners. The way of supervision is "duty - free articles (1741).

b. Spare parts and tools imported by duty - free foreign exchange shops for maintenance of commodities and shelves and handcarts used by the shops. The way of supervision is "general trade" (0110).

c. Imported duty - free foreign exchange commodities approved for domestic sale for some reason. The way of supervision is "general trade" (0110).

d. Outbound return of duty - free foreign exchange commodities. The way of supervision is "returned goods" (4561).

外商投资企业作为投资进口的设备、物品

一、定义及代码

外商投资企业作为投资进口的设备、物品是指外商投资企业投资总额内的资金(包括中方投资)进口的机器设备、零部件和其他建厂(场)物料,安装、加固机器所需材料,以及进口本企业自用合理数量的交通工具、生产用车辆、办公用品(设备)(以下简称"设备物品")。

中外合资、合作企业进口设备、物品,监管方式代码"2025",简称"合资合作设备"。

外商独资企业(以下简称"外资企业")进口设备、物品,监管方式代码为"2225",简称"外资设备物品"。

二、适用范围

(一)外商投资企业是指中外合资企业、中外合作企业、外商独资企业,包括华侨、港、澳、台同胞投资企业。

(二)"设备"是指外商投资企业在其投资总额内进口本企业自用的机器设备、零部件和其他物料[指建厂(场)以及安装、加固机器所需材料]及生产用车辆。

(三)"物品"是指外商投资企业进口自用合理数量的办公用品(设备)和交通工具。

(四)下列情况不适用本监管方式:

1. 鼓励类和限制类外商投资企业、外商投资研究开发中心、先进技术型和产品出口型外商投资企业以及符合中西部省、自治区、直辖市利用外资优势产业和优势项目目录的项目、企业自有资金(投资总额以外,具体是指企业储备基金、发展基金、折旧和税后利润),在原批准的生产经营范围内,对设备进行更新维修,进口国内不能生产或性能不能满足需要的自用设备及其配套的技术、配件、备件,其监管方式为"一般贸易"(0110)。

2. 外商投资企业经营来料加工、进料加工、租赁贸易等进口的设备物品,分别适用"不作价设备"(0320)、"加工贸易设备"(0420)、"租赁不满一年"(1500)、"租赁贸易"(1523)。

3. 外国常驻机构进口自用合理数量的公用物品,其监管方式为"常驻机构公用"(2439)。

4. 没有实际进出境,在境内结转的减免税设备,其监管方式为"减免设备结转"(0500)。

5. 出口加工区外商投资企业进口设备物品,其监管方式为"出口加工区进口设备"(5035)。

Equipment and articles imported by foreign – invested enterprises as investments

1. Definition and code

Equipment and articles imported by foreign – invested enterprises as investments refer to machines, equipment, spare parts, other materials needed for establishing factories (workshops) and materials needed for installing and reinforcing machines, means of transport in reasonable quantities for self – use, vehicles for production and office supplies (equipment) which are imported with the funds in the total investment (including investments from the Chinese side) [(shortened to" equipment and articles" hereunder)].

The code of the way of supervision for equipment and articles imported by Sino – foreign joint ventures and cooperative ventures is "2025" and the shortened form of it is "joint venture and cooperative equipment".

The code of the way of supervision for equipment and articles imported by solely foreign – funded enterprises (shortened to "foreign enterprises" hereunder) is "2225" and the shortened form of it is "foreign funded equipment and articles".

2. Scope of application

(1) Foreign – invested enterprises refer to Sino – foreign joint ventures, Sino – foreign cooperative enterprises and solely foreign – funded enterprises, including enterprises with investments of overseas Chinese and Hong Kong, Macao and Taiwan compatriots.

(2) "Equipment" refers to machines and equipment, spare parts, other materials [i. e. materials needed for establishing factories (workshops) and installing and reinforcing machines] and vehicles for production imported by foreign – invested enterprises for self use with funds in their total investment.

(3) "Articles" refer to office supplies (equipment) and means of transport imported by foreign – invested enterprises for self use in reasonable quantities.

(4) The way of supervision is not applicable to the following circumstances:

a. Foreign – invested enterprises in the encouragement and restriction categories, foreign investment R&D centers, high – tech and export – oriented foreign – funded enterprises, projects in line with the directory of appropriate industries and appropriate projects for foreign investments of provinces and autonomous regions in the central and western China and municipalities directly under the Central Government, enterprises´own funds (beyond the total investment, specifically corporate reserve funds, development funds, depreciation and after – tax profits), updating and maintenance of equipment within the originally approved production and operation scope, import of equipment and auxiliary technology, accessories and spare parts which cannot be produced domestically or whose domestic counterparts cannot meet needs for self use. The way of supervision is "general trade" (0110).

b. "Unpriced equipment" (0320), "equipment for processing trade" (0420), "leasehold of less than one year" (1500) and "leasing trade" (1523) are applicable to and articles imported by foreign – invested enterprises for processing with supplied materials, processing with imported materials and leasing trade respectively.

c. The way of supervision for public articles imported by foreign permanent institutions in reasonable quantities is "public use for permanent institutions" (2439).

d. The way of supervision for equipment granted reduction of and exemption from duties which are carried over domestically instead of being actually imported and exported is "carry – over of equipment granted reduction of and exemption from duties" (0500).

e. The way of supervision for equipment and articles imported by foreign – invested enterprises in export processing areas is "imported equipment of export processing areas" (5035).

退运货物

一、定义及代码

退运货物是指原进出口货物因残损、短少、品质不良或者规格不符、延误交货或其他原因退运出、进境的

Returned goods

1. Definition and code

Returned goods refer to imports or exports returned abroad or home for defects, damages, shortages, poor quality, improper specifications, delayed delivery or other

货物。

本监管方式代码“4561”，简称“退运货物”。

二、适用范围

（一）本监管方式适用以下监管方式进出口货物退运出进境：

代码	名　称	代　码	名　称
0110	一般贸易	0130	易货贸易
0139	旅游购物商品	1523	租赁贸易
1616	寄售代销	2025	外商投资企业
		2225	设备物品
1831	外汇免税商品	3010	货样广告品 A
		3039	货样广告品 B
3339	其他进出口免费	3410	承包工程进口
3422	对外承包出口	3511	无偿援助
3612	捐赠物资	4019	边境小额
4039	对台小额	9739	其他贸易

（二）本监管方式不适用：

1. 货物进境后、放行结关前退运的货物，其监管方式为“直接退运”（4500）。

2. 加工贸易进出口货物退运，其监管方式为“来料料件退换”（0300）、“进料料件退换”（0700）、“来料成品退换”（4400）、“进料成品退换”（4600）。

3. 加工贸易设备退运，其监管方式为“加工设备退运”（0466）。

4.“租赁不满一年”（1500）、“免税品”（1741）退运出境，其监管方式为“其他”（9900）。

5. 出口加工区进口设备退运出境，其监管方式为“区内设备退运”（5361）。

6. 进出口无代价抵偿货物，被更换的原进口货物退运出境，其监管方式为“其他”（9900）。

●外国常驻机构进出境公用物品

一、定义及代码

外国常驻机构进出境公用物品是指境外（地区）企业、新闻机构、经贸机构、文化团体及其他境外（地区）法人经我国政府主管部门批准，在境内设立的常驻代表机构为开展公务活动所需进出境的物品。

本监管方式代码为“2439”，简称“常驻机构公用”。

二、适用范围

（一）本监管方式包括常驻机构进境自用且数量合理的办公用机器设备、家具、文具、机动车辆等及复运出境的原进境的公用物品。

（二）本监管方式适用于以下机构：

1. 外国企业和其他经济组织常驻机构。

2. 外国民间经济贸易团体常驻机构。

reasons.

The code of the way of supervision for this is "4561" and the shortened form of it is "returned goods".

1. Scope of application

(1) This way of supervision is applicable to outbound and inbound return of imports and exports in the following ways of supervision:

Code	Name	Code	Name
0110	General trade	0130	Barter trade
0139	Tourist shopping commodities	1523	Leasing trade
1616	寄售代销	2025	Foreign - invested enterprises
		2225	Equipment and articles
1831	Foreign exchange dutyfree commodities	3010	Samples of Goods and Advertising Product A
		3039	Samples of Goods and Advertising Product B
3339	Other duty - free imports and exports	3410	Imports for contracted projects
3422	Exports for contracted foreign projects	3511	Free aid
3612	Donated materials	4019	Small - amount frontier trade
4039	Small amounts with Taiwan	9739	Other trade

(1) This way of supervision is not applicable to:

a. Goods returned after import and before clearance, the way of supervision for which is "direct return (4500).

b. Return of imports and exports for processing trade, the way of supervision for which is "return and exchange of imported materials" (0300), "return and exchange of imported materials" (0700), "return and exchange of finished products with supplied materials" (4400) and "return and exchange of finished products with imported materials" (4600).

c. Return of processing trade equipment, the way of supervision for which is "return of processing equipment" (0466).

d. "Leasehold of less than one year" (1500). "duty - free articles" (1741), the way of supervision for which is "other" (9900).

e. Outbound of imported equipment in export processing areas, the way of supervision for which is "return of equipment in areas" (5361).

f. Unpriced offset imports and exports and return of original imports replaced, the way of supervision for which is "other" (9900).

● Public articles imported and exported by foreign permanent institutions

1. Definition and code

Public articles imported and exported by foreign permanent institutions refer to articles imported and exported by permanent institutions established in China by overseas (regional) enterprises, press institutions, economic and trade organizations, cultural bodies and other overseas (regional) legal persons with approval of competent departments of our government for conducting public activities.

The code of the way of supervision for this is "2439" and the shortened form of it is "public use for permanent institutions".

1. Scope of application

(1) This way of supervision includes equipment, furniture, stationery and motor vehicles imported by permanent institutions for self use and in reasonable quantities and reexported public articles.

(2) This regulatory way applies to the following organizations:

1. Foreign enterprises and permanent officesof f oreign Economic organization agencies.

2. permanent officesof f oreign Foreign non - governmental economic and Trade

3. 外国常驻新闻机构。
4. 其他外国常驻机构。
5. 华侨、港澳同胞、台湾同胞经营的企业常驻机构。

（三）不适用本监管方式的监管业务
1. 外国驻中国使馆、领馆，联合国及其专门机构，以及其他与中国政府签有协议的国际组织驻中国代表机构进出境物品填报“外国使领馆公私用物品进出境申报单”。
2. 外国人员子女学校进出境物品，其监管方式为“其他贸易”（9739）。
3. 常驻机构人员进境自用的汽车，其监管方式为“其他贸易”（9739）。
4. 外国驻华使、领馆在我国内购运出境的货物，其监管方式为“其他”（9900）。
5. 暂时进出境的公用物品，其监管方式为“暂时进出口”（2600）。

Group organization agencies.
3. permanent officesof f oreign news agencies.
4. other permanent officesof f oreign agencies.
5. Overseas Chinese, Hong Kong and Macao compatriots, Taiwan compatriots of enterprises permanent agencies.
(3) Supervision business to which this way of supervision is not applicable:
a. Foreign embassies, consulates, the UN, its institutions and representative organizations of international organizations which have signed agreements with the Chinese government in China shall fill the Import and Export Declaration Form for Private Articles of Foreign Embassies and Consulates for Imported and Exported Articles.
b. Articles imported and exported by schools for foreign personnel's children, the way of supervision for which is "other trade" (9739).
c. Cars imported by foreign institutions for self use, the way of supervision for which is "other trade" (9739).
d. Goods purchased and exported by foreign embassies and consulates in our country, the way of supervision for which is "other trade" (9900).
e. Public articles imported and exported temporarily, the way of supervision for which is "temporary imports and exports" (2600).

●暂时进出境货物

一、定义及代码
暂时进出境货物是指经海关批准，暂时进出关境并且在规定的期限内复运出境、进境的货物。

本监管方式代码有“2600”，简称“暂时进出货物”。

（一）本监管方式包括：
1. 文化、体育交流活动中使用的表演、比赛用品；
2. 进行新闻报道或者摄制电影、电视节目使用的仪器、设备及用品；
3. 开展科研、教学、医疗活动使用的仪器、设备及用品；
4. 在本款第1至第3项所列活动中使用的交通工具及特种车辆；
5. 货样；
6. 慈善活动使用的仪器、设备及用品；
7. 供安装、调试、检测、修理设备时使用的仪器及工具；
8. 盛装货物的容器；
9. 旅游用自驾交通工具及其用品；
10. 工程施工中使用的设备、仪器及其用品；
11. 海关批准的其他暂时进出境货物。

（二）以下情况不适用本监管方式：
1. 进出境展览品，监管方式为“展览品”（2700）；
2. 驻华商业机构不复运出口的进口陈列样品，其监管方式为“陈列样品”（2939）；
3. 对外承包工程出口物资，其监管方式为“对外承包出口”（3422）；
4. 进出境修理物品，其监管方式为“修理物品”（1300）；
5. 租赁贸易进出口货物，其监管方式为“租期不满一年”（1500）、“租期一年及以上”（1523）；
6. 企业使用旧钢瓶容器进口燃料、物料，按进口燃

● Temporary imports and exports

1. Definition and code
Temporary imports and exports are goods temporarily imported and exported with the approval of the Customs and shall be reexported and reimported within the prescribed period.
The code of the way of supervision for this is "2600" and the shortened form of it is "temporary imports and exports"; The code of the way of supervision for this is.
(1) This way of supervision includes:
a. Performance and competition articles used in cultural and sports exchange activities;
b. Instruments, equipment and articles used in news reporting and movie and TV program shooting;
c. Instruments, equipment and articles used in scientific research, teaching and medical activities;
d. Means of transport and special vehicles used in activities mentioned in Item 1 to 3 of this clause;
e. Sample goods;
f. Instruments, equipment and articles used in charitable activities;
g. Instruments and tools used in installation, adjustment, testing and maintenance of equipment;
h. Containers for goods;
i. Tourists' cars and related articles;
j. Equipment, instruments and articles used in construction;
k. Other goods imported and exported temporarily with the approval of the Customs.
(2) This way of supervision is not applicable to the following circumstances;
a. Imported and exported exhibits, the way of supervision for which is "exhibits" (2700);
b. Samples for display imported by foreign commercial organizations in China which will not be reexported, the way of supervision for which is "samples for display" (2939);
c. Materials exported for contracted foreign projects, the way of supervision for which is "exports for contracted foreign projects" (3422);
d. Goods imported and exported for maintenance, the way of supervision for which is "goods for maintenance" (1300);
e. Goods imported and exported in leasing trade, the way of supervision for which is "leasehold of less than one year" (1500) and "leasehold of one year or more" (1523);
f. Enterprises using the old cylinder container imported fuels, materials, accord-

料、物料的监管方式申报，报关单“包装种类”栏目填报“旧钢瓶”。旧钢瓶容器凭“入境货物通关单”验放，复运出境时监管方式填报“其他”(9900)

ing to import fuel, materials supervision mode declaration, customs declaration" type of package " column fill in the " old cylinder". The old cylinder container with a" certificate of inspection for goods outward" , re – shipped out fill in the " other ways of supervision

7. 从境外暂时进境的货物转入保税区、出口加工区等海关特殊监管区域和保税监管场所的，不属于复运出境；

g. Transfer of temporarily imported goods to bonded areas, export processing areas and other areas and bonded places under the Customs supervision is not reexport;

8. 用于装载海关监管货物的进出境集装箱；

h. Outbound and inbound containers for goods under the Customs supervision;

9. 享有外交特权和豁免的外国驻华机构或者人员暂时进出境物品。

i. Temporarily imported articles of foreign institutions or their staffs in China that enjoy diplomatic privileges and immunity.

●进出境展览品

● Imported and exported exhibits

一、定义及代码

进出境展览品是指外国来华或我国为到国外举办经济、文化、科技等展览或参加博览会而进出口的展览品及展览品有关的宣传品、布置品、招待品、小卖品和其他物品。

本监管方式代码为“2700”，简称“展览品”。

1. Definition and code

Imported and exported exhibits refer to exhibits imported by foreign exhibitors or exported by Chinese exhibitors for economic, cultural, scientific and technological exhibitions and fairs as well as related promotional materials, decoration articles, entertaining articles, small items for sale and other articles.

The code of this way of supervision is "2700" and the shortened form of it is " exhibits".

二、适用范围

(一)进出境展览品主要包括：

1. 在展览会、交易会、会议及类似活动中展示或者使用的货物，包括：

(1)为了示范展览会展出机器或者器具所使用的货物；

(2)设置临时展台的建筑材料及装饰材料；

(3)宣传展示货物的电影片、幻灯片、录像带、录音带、说明书、广告、光盘、显示器材等。

2. 上述所列活动中使用的交通工具及特种车辆。

3. 其他经海关批准用于展示的进出境货物、物品。

(二)以下情况不适用本监管方式：

1. ATA 单证册项下的暂准进出口展览品，持证人免填报关单。

2. 不复运出(进)境而留在国内(外)销售的进出境展览品，按实际监管方式填报。

3. 在商店或者其他营业场所以销售国外货物为目的而组织的非公共展览会。

2. Scope of application

(1) Imported and exported exhibits mainly include:

a. Goods exhibited or used in exhibitions, fairs, conferences and similar activities, including:

a) Goods for demonstrating machines or devices shown in exhibitions;

b) Building materials and decoration materials for setting up temporary booths;

c) Movies, lantern slides, video tapes, audio tapes, instructions for use, ads, discs and displaying devices for promoting goods;

b. Means of transport and special vehicles used in the above activities.'

c. Imported and exported goods and articles for display approved by the Customs.

(2) This way of supervision is not applicable to the following circumstances:

a. Exhibits whose import and export are temporarily allowed under the ATA carnet. Holders of the ATA carnet dont need to fill the declaration form.

b. Imported and exported exhibits which will not be reexported (reimported) but sold domestically (abroad). Fill the declaration form according to the actual way of supervision.

c. Non – public exhibitions organized in shops or other business premises for selling foreign goods.

●货样、广告品

● Samples of goods and advertising products

一、定义及代码

进出口货样是指专供订货参考的进出口货物样品；广告品是指用以宣传有关商品的进出口广告宣传品。

有进出口经营权的企业价购或价售进出口货样广告品，监管方式代码为“3010”，简称“货样广告品 A”。

没有进出口经营权的企业(单位)进出口及免费提供进出口的货样广告品，监管方式代码“3039”，简称“货样广告 B”。

1. Definition and code

Imported and exported samples of goods refer to those for reference in ordering and advertising products refer to imported and exported advertising promotional products for promotion of related commodities.

The code of the way of supervision for imported and exported samples of goods and advertising products sold and bought by enterprises which have the import and export right is "3010" and the shortened form of it is "Samples of Goods and Advertising Products A".

The code of the way of supervision for imported and exported samples of goods and advertising products sold and bought by enterprises which have not the import and export right is“3039”and the shortened from of it is“Samples of Goods and Advertising Products B”

二、适用范围

上述监管方式除以上定义所述范围外，还包括寄售代销贸易中外商免费提供的货样广告品。

下列情况不适用本监管方式：

(一)暂时进出口的货样、广告品，其监管方式为“暂

2. Scope of application

Apart from the scope stated in the above definition, the above way of supervision also includes samples of goods and advertising products provided free of charge by foreign businessmen in consignment trade.

This way of supervision is not applicable to the following circumstances:

(1) Temporarily imported and exported samples of goods and advertising prod-

时进出口货物”(2600)。

(二)驻华商业机构不复运出口的进口陈列样品,其监管方式应为“陈列样品”(2939)。

●无代价抵偿进出口货物

一、定义及代码

无代价抵偿货物是指进出口货物海关放行后,因残损、短少、品质不良或者规格不符原因,由进出口货物的发货人、承运人或保险公司免费补偿或更换的与原货物相同或者与合同规定相符的货物。

本监管方式代码为“3100”,简称“无代价抵偿”。

二、适用范围

下列情况不适用本监管方式:

(一)来料加工、进料加工贸易进口料件和出口成品因残损、短少、品质不良或者规格不符原因,由进出口货物的发货人、承运人或保险公司免费补偿或更换的与原货物相同或者与合同规定相符的货物,分别适用具体列名的料件或成品退换的监管方式。

(二)与无代价抵偿进出口货物相关的原进出口货物退运出进境,其监管方式为“其他”(9900)。

●其他免费提供的进出口货物

一、定义及代码

其他免费提供货物指除已具体列名的礼品、无偿援助和赠送物资、捐赠物资、无代价抵偿进口货物、国外免费提供的货样、广告品等及归入列名监管方式的免费提供货物以外,进出口其他免费提供的货物。

本监管方式代码为“3339”,简称“其他进出口免费”。

二、适用范围

(一)本监管方式包括:

1. 外商在经贸活动中赠送的物品。

2. 外国人捐赠品。

3. 驻外中资机构向国内单位赠送的物资。

4. 经贸活动中,由外商免费提供的试车材料、消耗性物品等。

(二)下列情况不适用本监管方式:

1. 保税仓库中由外商免费提供进口的机械设备、手工工具、运输工具、办公用品等,其监管方式为“其他贸易”(9739)。

2. 免税店由外商免费提供进口的货架、柜台、手推车等,其监管方式为“其他贸易”(9739)。

3. 来料加工、进料加工贸易项下外商免费提供的机械设备,其监管方式为“不作价设备”(0320)。

4. 免费提供进出口的货样广告品,其监管方式为“货样广告品 B”(3039)。

5. 国家和国际组织无偿援助物资,其监管方式为“援助物资”(3511)。

6. 捐赠物资,其监管方式为“捐赠物资”(3612)。

ucts, the way of supervision for which is "temporarily imported goods" (2600).

(2) Samples for display imported by foreign commercial institutions in China that will not be reexported, the way of supervision for which shall be "samples for display (2939).

● Unpriced offset import and export goods

1. Definition and code

Unpriced offset import and export goods means goods provided free of charge by consignors and carriers of imports and exports or insurance companies in compensation or in exchange for original goods that are found having defects, damages, shortages, poor quality or improper specifications after being cleared.

The way of supervision for this is "3100" and the shortened form of it is "unpriced offset".

2. Scope of application

This way of supervision is not applicable to the following circumstances:

(1) Goods provided free of charge by consignors and carriers of imports and exports or insurance companies in compensation or in exchange for imported materials and parts and finished exports in processing with supplied and imported materials that have defects, damages, shortages, poor quality or improper specifications, to which the ways of supervision for specifically named materials and parts or return of finished products are applicable respectively.

(2) Outbound and inbound return of imports and exports related to unpriced offset imports and exports, the way of supervision for which is "other" (9900).

● Other imports and exports provided free of charge

1. Definition and code

Other imports and exports provided free of charge refer to other imports and exports provided free of charge apart from specifically named gifts, materials given and presented free of charge, materials donated, unpriced offset imports, foreign samples of goods provided free of charge, advertising products and goods provided free of charge and listed in the specifically named way of supervision.

The code of the way of supervision for this is "3339" and the shortened form of it is "other free imports and exports".

1. Scope of application

(1) This way of supervision includes:

a. Articles presented by foreign businessmen in economic and trade activities.

b. Articles presented by foreigners.

c. Materials presented by Chinese institutions in other countries to domestic units;

d. Materials for commissioning and consumable materials provided by foreign businessmen free of charge in economic and trade activities.

(2) This way of supervision is not applicable to the following circumstances:

a. Imported machines, equipment, manual tools, means of transport, office supplies, etc. in bonded warehouses that are provided by foreign businessmen free of charge, the way of supervision for which is "other trade" (9739).

b. Shelves, counters, handcarts, etc. in duty - free shops that are provided by foreign businessmen free of charge, the way of supervision for which is "other trade" (9739).

c. Machines and equipment provided by foreign businessmen free of charge in processing with supplied and imported materials, the way of supervision for which is "unpriced equipment" (0320).

d. Imported and exported samples of goods and advertising products provided free of charge, the way of supervision for which is "Samples of Goods and Advertising Products B" (3039).

e. Materials provided by other countries and international organizations free of charge, the way of supervision for which is "materials in aid" (3511).

f. Donated materials, the way of supervision for which is "donated materials" (3612).

7. 无代价抵偿进出口货物，其监管方式为“无代价抵偿”(3100)。

g. Unpriced offset imports and exports, the way of supervision for which is "unpriced offset" (3100).

●对外承包工程进出口物资

● Imported and exported materials for contracted foreign projects

一、定义及代码

对外承包工程出口物资是指经商务部批准的有对外承包工程经营权的公司为承包国外建设工程和开展劳务合作等对外合作项目而出口的设备、物资。

承包工程出口物资监管方式代码为“3422”，简称“对外承包出口”。

对外承包工程进口物资是指承包工程期间在国外获取的设备、物资，以及境外劳务合作项目对方以实物产品抵偿我劳务人员工资所进口的货物。

监管方式代码为“3410”，简称“承包工程进口”。

1. Definition and code

Exported materials for contracted foreign projects refer to equipment and materials exported by companies granted the right of contracting foreign projects by the Ministry of Commerce for contracting foreign construction projects and developing labor cooperation and other external cooperative projects.

The code of the way of supervision for exported materials for contracted foreign projects is "3422" and the shortened form of it is "exports for contracted foreign projects".

Foreign contracting engineering materials imported refers toEquipment and materials secured abroad during the period of contracted projects and imports paid by the foreign side of overseas labor cooperative projects to our laborers in kind.

The code of the way of supervision is "3410" and the shortened form of it is "imports for contracted foreign projects".

二、适用范围

(一)本监管方式不包括我劳务人员带出的自用生活物资，监管方式为“其他”(9900)。

(二)援外成套项目出口的货物应根据无偿援助或贷款援助，监管方式代码分别选用“援助物资”(3511)或“一般贸易”(0110)。

(三)边境地区有对外经济技术合作经营权的企业与毗邻国家边境地区开展承包工程和劳务合作项下出口的工程设备、物资(包括在外购买及换回的)运回境内时，监管方式代码为“边境小额贸易”(4019)。

(四)承包工程结束后复运进境原从国内运出的承包工程项下的设备、物资，其监管方式为“退运货物”(4561)。

1. Scope of application

(1) This way of supervision does not include the living materials for self use brought by our laborers, the way of supervision for which is "other" (9900).

(2) The way of supervision for goods exported for aiding complete projects is "materials in aid" (3511) or "general trade" (0110) based on free aid or loan aid.

(3) The code of the way of supervision for engineering equipment and materials exported by enterprises in border areas which have the external economic and technical cooperation right to carry out contracted projects and labor cooperation with border areas of adjoining countries, including what is purchased or exchanged abroad, is "small - amount frontier trade" (4019).

(4) The way of supervision for reimported equipment and materials that were shipped originally from China for contracted projects in the end is "returned goods" (4561).

●国家或国际组织无偿援助和赠送的物资

● Materials given and presented free of charge by other countries or international organizations

一、定义及代码

国家或国际组织无偿援助和赠送的物资是指我国根据两国政府间的协议或临时决定，对外提供无偿援助的物资、捐赠品或我国政府、组织基于友好关系向对方国家政府、组织赠送的物资，以及我国政府、组织接受国际组织、外国政府、组织无偿援助、捐赠或赠送的物资。

本监管方式代码为“3511”，简称“无偿援助”。

1. Definition and code

Materials given and presented free of charge by other countries or international organizations refer to materials and donations provided free of charge by our country according to bilateral agreements or temporary decisions or materials donated by our country and organizations to other countries and organizations based on friendly relations and materials given free of charge, donated or presented by international organizations, foreign governments or organizations to our country.

The code of this way of supervision is "3511" and the shortened form of it is "free aid".

二、适用范围

(一)有关名词：

外国政府，是指外国国家的中央政府。

国际组织，是指联合国各专门机构以及长期与我国有合作关系的其他国际组织。

国际条约，是指依据《中华人民共和国缔结条约程序法》以“中华人民共和国”、“中华人民共和国政府”以及“中华人民共和国政府部门”名义同外国缔结协定或协议以及参加的国际条约。

(二)以下情况不适用本监管方式：

1. 贷款援助的进出口货物(包括我方利用贷款或援助款项自行采购进口的货物)，其监管方式为“一般贸易”(0110)。

2. Scope of application

(1) Relevant terms:

Foreign governments refer to central governments of foreign countries.

International organizations refer to special organizations of the US and other international organizations with long - term cooperative relationship with our country.

International treaties are protocols, agreements and international treaties concluded in the names of the "People's Republic of China", the "government of the People's Republic of China and a department of the "government of the People's Republic of China with foreign countries according to the Procedural Law of the People's Republic of China on Conclusion of Treaties.

(2) This way of supervision is not applicable to the following circumstances:

a. Imports and exports funded by loans (including goods our side purchases by ourselves with loans or supporting funds), the way of supervision for which is "general trade" (0110).

2. 来(出)访的团体和人员相互馈赠的礼品，监管方式为“其他”(9900)。

3. 经济贸易往来关系赠送的物资，监管方式为“其他进出口免费提供”(3339)。

4. 随援外物资一并出口或另外发运的批量出口的生活物资应按照“其他贸易”(9739)报关。

5. 以扶贫、慈善、救灾为目的向我国境内或向境外捐赠的直接用于扶贫、救灾、兴办公益福利事业的物资，其监管方式为“捐赠物资”(3612)。

b. Gifts presented mutually by incoming (outgoing) delegations and personnel, the way of supervision for which is "other" (9900).

c. Materials presented in economic and trade exchanges, the way of supervision for which is "other imports and exports provided free of charge" (3339).

d. Living materials in quantity which are exported with materials in foreign aid or sent separately shall be declared according to "other trade" (9379).

e. Materials donated to our country or overseas for poverty alleviation, charity and disaster relief and used directly in poverty alleviation, disaster relief and contribution to the public welfare cause, the way of supervision for which is "donated materials" (3612).

●进出口捐赠物资

一、定义及代码

进出口捐赠物资是指境外捐赠人以扶贫、慈善、救灾为目的向我国境内捐赠的直接用于扶贫、救灾、兴办公益福利事业的物资，以及境内捐赠人以扶贫、慈善、救灾为目的向境外捐赠的直接用于扶贫、救灾、兴办公益福利事业的物资。

本监管方式代码“3612”，简称“捐赠物资”。

二、适用范围

(一)本监管方式适用范围：

1. 捐赠人

(1)境外捐赠人包括华侨、港、澳、台同胞、外籍人，包括法人。

(2)境内捐赠人，包括法人。

2. 扶贫、慈善公益性事业的物资

(1)新的衣服、被褥、鞋帽、账篷、手套、睡袋、毛毯及其他维持基本生活的必需用品等。

(2)食品类及饮用品(调味品、水产品、水果、饮料、烟酒等除外)。

(3)医疗类包括直接用于治疗特困患者疾病或贫困地区治疗地方病及基本医疗卫生、公共环境卫生所需的基本医疗药品、基本医疗器械、医疗书籍和资料。

(4)直接用于公共图书馆、公共博物馆、各类职业学校、高中、初中、小学、幼儿园教育的教学仪器、器材、图书、资料和一般学习用品。

(5)直接用于环境保护的专用仪器。

(6)经国务院批准的其他直接用于扶贫、慈善事业的物资。

3. 受赠人和使用人

受赠人是指国务院有关部门和各省、自治区、直辖市人民政府，以及从事人道救助和发展扶贫、慈善事业为宗旨的全国性的社会团体。包括中国红十字会总会、全国妇女联合会、中国残疾人联合会、中华慈善总会、中国初级卫生保健基金会和宋庆龄基金会。

使用人(使用单位)是指捐赠物资的直接使用者或负责分配该捐赠物资的单位或个人。

(二)下列情况不适用本监管方式：

1. 国家间、国际组织无偿援助和赠送的物资，其监管方式为“援助物资”(3611)。

2. 经贸往来中赠送的物品、外国人捐赠品、我驻外(包括驻港澳)中资机构向国内单位赠送的物资等，其监

● Imported and exported materials donated

1. Definition and code

Imported and exported materials donated refer to materials donated by overseas donors to our country for poverty alleviation, charity and disaster relief and used directly in poverty alleviation, disaster relief and contribution to the public welfare cause and materials donated overseas by domestic donors for poverty alleviation, charity and disaster relief and used directly in poverty alleviation, disaster relief and contribution to the public welfare cause.

The code of the way of supervision for this is "3612" and the shortened form of it is "donated materials".

2. Scope of application

(1) Scope of application this way of supervision is applicable to:

a. Donors

a) Overseas donors include overseas Chinese, Hong Kong, Macao and Taiwan compatriots, foreigners, inclusive of legal persons.

b) Domestic donors, inclusive of legal persons.

b. Materials for poverty alleviation, charities and the public welfare cause

a) New clothes, quilts, cotton-padded mattress, shoes, caps, tents, gloves, sleeping bags, blankets and other necessities for maintaining basic living.

b) Food and beverages (seasoning, aquatic products, fruits and beverages, excluding cigarettes and wine).

c) Medical category, including basic medicines, basic medical devices and medical books and materials directly used for treating extremely poor patients or local diseases in poverty-stricken areas and required for basic health and public environment sanitation.

d) Teaching instruments, devices, books, materials and ordinary learning appliances directly used in public libraries, public museums, various kinds of vocational schools, senior high schools, junior high schools, primary schools and kindergartens.

e) Specialized instruments directly used in environmental protection.

f) Other materials used directly in poverty alleviation and charities with the approval of the State Council.

c. Donees and users

Donees refer to relevant departments of the State Council, people's governments of provinces, autonomous regions and municipalities directly under the Central Government, nationwide social bodies engaged in humanitarian assistance and development of the poverty alleviation cause and charities, including the Red Cross Society of China, All-China Women's Federation, China Disabled Persons' Association, China Charity Federation, Primary HealthCare Foundation of China and Song Qingling Foundation.

Users (using units) refer to end users of donated materials or units or individuals in charge of distributing donated materials.

(2) This way of supervision is not applicable to the following circumstances:

a. Materials given and presented between countries and international organizations, the way of supervision for which is "materials in aid (3611).

b. Articles presented in economic and trade exchanges, presents given by foreigners and materials presented by Chinese organizations stationed overseas (inclu-

管方式为“其他进出口免费提供货物”(3339)。

ding in Hong Kong and Macao), the way of supervision for which is "other imports and exports provided free of charge" (3339).

●边境小额贸易

● Small – amount frontier trade

一、定义及代码

边境小额贸易指我国沿陆地边境线经国家批准对外外放的边境县(旗)、边境城市辖区内(以下简称边境地区)经批准有边境小额贸易经营权的企业,通过国家指定的陆地边境口岸,与毗邻国家边境地区的企业或其他贸易机构进行的贸易活动。

本监管方式代码“4019”,简称“边境小额”。

二、适用范围

(一)本监管方式包括:

1. 边境地区有对外经济技术合作经营权的企业与我国毗邻国家边境地区以易货贸易、现汇贸易形式开展的边境小额贸易。

2. 边境地区有对外经济技术合作经营权的企业与我国毗邻国家边境地区经济合作(工程承包、劳务输出)项下进出口物资及原出口工程设备、物资(包括在境外购买及换回的)运回境内。

(二)下列情况不适用本监管方式:

1. 边民互市贸易(互市进口商品),每人每日价值人民币3000元以下免征进口关税和进口环节税,超出部分照章征税,监管方式“其他贸易”(9739)。

2. 未获准经营边境小额贸易的企业进出口货物。

3. 对台湾居民同大陆对台小额贸易公司成交用台湾船只直接运进产自台湾的产品和运出大陆产品到台湾,其监管方式为“对台小额”(4039)。

1. Definition and code

Small – amount frontier trade means trade activities conducted by Chinese frontier counties (banners) along land borderlines which are open to the outside world with the approval of the state and enterprises in areas under the jurisdiction of frontier cities (shortened to frontier regions) which have the right to engage in small – amount frontier trade with enterprises or other trading institutions in frontier areas of adjoining countries via land frontier ports designated by the state.

The code of the way of supervision for this is "4019" and the shortened form of it is "frontier small amounts".

2. Scope of application

(1) This way of supervision includes:

a. Small – amount frontier trade conducted by enterprises with the external economic and technological cooperation right in frontier areas with frontier areas of countries adjoining our country by barter trade or spot trade.

b. Materials imported and exported by enterprises in frontier areas which have the external economic and technological cooperation right in economic cooperation with frontier areas of countries adjoining our country (project contracting and labor export) and inbound return of originally exported engineering equipment and materials (including what's purchased or exchanged abroad).

(2) This way of supervision is not applicable to the following circumstances:

a. Frontier citizens´ exchange market trade (imports from exchange markets), where no more than RMB 3000/person/day is exempted from the import duty and import link tax and the duty and tax will be levied on the extra amount. The way of supervision is "other trade" (9739).

b. Goods imported and exported by enterprises which are not permitted to engage in small – amount frontier trade.

c. Products made in Taiwan and transported directly to the mainland and products made on the mainland and transported directly to Taiwan by Taiwanese ships in transactions between Taiwanese citizens and companies on the mainland which engage in small – amount trade with Taiwan, the way of supervision for which is "small amounts with Taiwan" (4039).

●对台小额

● Small – amount trade with Taiwan

一、定义及代码

对台湾小额贸易是指台湾地区居民与大陆批准的企业依照有关规定进行的货物交易

本监管方式代码“4039”,简称“对台小额”。

二、适用范围

本监管方式不适用进入厦门大嶝对台小额商品交易市场的人员带出台湾产品,每人每日价值人民币3000元以下免征进口关税和进口环节税,超出部分照章征税,监管方式“其他贸易”(9739)。

1. Definition and code

Small – amount trade with Taiwan refers to residents in Taiwan area and the mainland approved enterprise in accordance with the relevant provisions of trade goods.

This regulatory way is coded “4039” and abbreviated to “petty trade with Taiwan”.

2. This woy doesn't apply to the following:

Everybody who brings products made in Taiwan from the market of petty trade with Taiwan in Dayu, Xiamen can be exempted 3000 yuan of import duty and import link tax per day, beyond part subject to taxation and the supervision way is “Other trade” (4139).

●对台小额商品交易市场

● Market for small – amount commodity trade with Taiwan

一、定义及代码

对台小额商品交易市场是经国家批准设立,用于开展对台民间小额贸易交易活动,并实行封闭管理的特定区域,以下简称“交易市场”。

二、适用范围

本监管方式仅限于厦门大嶝岛对台小额商品交易市场。

1. Definition and code

On Taiwan petty commodities trading market is the country approved the establishment of, for the nongovernmental small – volume trade transactions, and the implementation of closure in the management of specific regions, hereinafter referred to as " trading market "

2. Scope of application

This way of supervision is only applicable to the Xiamen Dachen Market for Small – Amount Commodity Trade with Taiwan.

下列情况不适用本监管方式：

（一）对台湾居民同大陆对台小额贸易公司成交用台湾船只直接运进产自台湾的产品和运出大陆产品到台湾，其监管方式为“对台小额”（4039）。

（二）我国沿陆地边境线经国家批准对外开放的边境县（旗）、边境城市辖区内（以下简称边境地区）经批准有边境小额贸易经营权的企业，通过国家指定的陆地边境口岸，与毗邻国家边境地区的企业或其他贸易机构进行的贸易活动，其监管方式为“边境小额”（4019）。

This way of supervision is not applicable to the following circumstances:

(1) Products made in Taiwan and transported directly to the mainland and products made on the mainland and transported directly to Taiwan by Taiwanese ships in transactions between Taiwanese citizens and companies on the mainland which engage in small - amount trade with Taiwan, the way of supervision for which is "small amounts with Taiwan" (4039).

(2) Small - amount frontier trade means trade activities conducted by Chinese frontier counties (banners) along land borderlines which are open to the outside world with the approval of the state and enterprises in areas under the jurisdiction of frontier cities (shortened to frontier regions) which have the right to engage in small - amount frontier trade with enterprises or other trading institutions in frontier areas of adjoining countries via land frontier ports designated by the state. The way of supervision for this is "frontier small amounts" (4019).

●驻外机构运回旧公用物品

一、定义及代码

驻外机构运回旧公用物品是指我驻各国（地区）使、领馆，驻国外、港澳地区的经济、贸易机构，驻国际组织代表处等我驻外机构更新且闲置不用而运回或因机构撤销而运回的物品，包括临时出国展览团、考察团等运回的生产资料和公用物品。

本监管方式代码“4200”，简称“驻外机构运回”。

二、适用范围

本监管方式不适用暂时进出境公用物品。

● Old public articles transported back by institutions stationed abroad

1. Definition and code

Old public articles transported back by institutions stationed abroad refer to articles transported back by our institutions stationed abroad, such as embassies, consulates, economic and trading institutions in foreign countries, Hong Kong and Macao and representative offices in international organizations, because of updating or disuse or articles transported back because of withdrawal of institutions, including means of production and public articles transported back by delegations and inspection delegations which stay abroad for a short period.

The code of the way of supervision for this is "4200" and the shortened from of it is "carried back by organizations stationed overseas".

2. Scope of application

This way of supervision is not applicable to temporarily imported and exported public articles.

●直接退运货物

一、定义及代码

直接退运货物是指进口货物收发货人、原运输工具负责人或者其代理人（以下统称：当事人）在有关货物进境后、办结海关放行手续前，因海关责令或有正当理由获准退运境外的货物。

本监管方式代码为“4500”，简称“直接退运货物”。

二、适用范围

（一）在货物进境后、办结海关放行手续前，有下列情形之一的，当事人可以向海关申请办理直接退运手续：

1. 因国家贸易管理政策调整，收货人无法提供相关证件的；

2. 属于错发、误卸或者溢卸货物，能够提供发货人或者承运人书面证明文书的；

3. 收发货人双方协商一致同意退运，能够提供双方同意退运的书面证明文书的；

4. 有关贸易发生纠纷，能够提供法院判决书、仲裁机构仲裁决定书或者无争议的有效货物所有权凭证的；

5. 货物残损或者国家检验检疫不合格，能够提供国家检验检疫部门根据收货人申请而出具的相关检验证明文书的。

（二）在货物进境后、办结海关放行手续前，有下列情形之一，依法应当退运的，由海关责令当事人将进口货物直接退运境外：

1. 进口国家禁止进口的货物，经海关依法处理后的；

2. 违反国家检验检疫政策法规，经国家检验检疫部

● Directly returned goods

1. Definition and code

Directly returned goods refer to goods returned abroad by consignors, consignees, persons responsible for the original means of transport or their agents (called parties concerned collectively hereunder) after they are imported and before they are cleared as ordered by the Customs or approved with justification approval.

The code of the way of supervision for this is "4500" and the shortened form of it is "directly returned goods".

2. Scope of application

(1) Parties concerned can apply to the Customs for direct return in one of the following circumstances after goods enter and before they are cleared.

a. Consignors cannot provide relevant certificates when the state trade management policy is adjusted.

b. Consignors or carriers' written certificates can be produced for wrongly sent, wrongly unloaded or excessively unloaded goods.

c. Consignors and consignees' written agreements can be produced if both parties agree to return goods.

d. Court judgments, arbitration decisions or indisputable effective documents of title to goods can be produced if disputes arise from relevant trade;

e. Relevant inspection certificates issued by the state inspection and quarantine department at the request of consignors can be produced if goods are defective or unqualified in state inspection and quarantine.

(2) The Customs orders parties concerned to return imported goods abroad directly according to law in one of the following circumstances after goods are imported and before they are cleared:

a. Import goods whose import is banned by the state and the Customs has dealt with it in accordance with the law;

b. Violate the state inspection and quarantine policy and regulation and the state

门处理并且出具《检验检疫处理通知书》或者其他证明文书后的；

3. 未经许可擅自进口属于限制进口的固体废物用作原料，经海关依法处理后的；

4. 违反国家有关法律、行政法规，应当责令直接退运的其他情形。

（三）保税区、出口加工区及其他海关特殊监管区域和保税监管场所进口货物的直接退运。

（四）下列情况不适用本监管方式：

1. 放行后的进口货物退运出境，其监管方式为"退运货物"（4561）。

2. 进口转关货物在进境地海关放行后，当事人申请办理退运手续的，应当按照一般退运手续办理。

inspection and quarantine department has dealt with it and issued the Notice of Inspection and Quarantine Treatment or other certificates;

c. Solid waste whose import is restricted is imported as raw materials presumptuously without approval and the Customs has dealt with it according to law;

d. Other circumstances of direct return ordered for violating relevant laws and administrative regulations.

(3) Direct return of goods imported by bonded areas, export processing areas and other areas and bonded places under the Customs supervision.

(4) This way of supervision is not applicable to the following circumstances:

a. Outbound return of imported goods after they are cleared, the way of supervision for which is "returned goods" (4561).

b. It shall be handled according to the ordinary return formalities if parties concerned apply for return after imported transit goods are cleared with the Customs at ports of import.

●区内加工货物

区内加工货物是指出口加工区内企业经营加工贸易业务从境外进口料件及加工出口的成品。

本监管方式代码"5015"简称"区内加工货物"。

●Goods processed in zones

Goods processed in zones refer to the export processing zone enterprises operating overseas processing trade business from imported materials and processing of finished products for export.

The way of supervision code is "5015" and the shortened form of it is "Goods processed in zones".

●区内仓储货物

区内仓储货物是指出口加工区内仓储企业从境外进口供区内企业加工的仓储货物。

本监管方式代码"5033"，简称"区内仓储货物"。

●Goods in warehouse zones

Good in warehouse zones refer to the export processing zone warehouse enterprises to import for the enterprises within the area of the warehouse processing goods.

The way of supervision code is "5033" and the shortened form of it is "Goods in warehouse zones".

●境外设备进区

境外设备进区指加工区内企业从境外进口用于区内加工生产所需的机器设备和工模具、区内建设所需的基建物资，以及区内企业和行政管理机构自用合理数量的办公用品等。

本监管方式代码"5335"，简称"境外设备进区"。

●Outside equipment into zone

Outside equipment into zone refers to processing zone enterprises imports from import for processing zone production of the required equipment and tooling, zone needed for construction materials, enterprises and administrative agencies use the reasonable amount of office supplies.

The way of supervision code is "5335" and the shortened form of it is "outside equipment into zone".

●区内设备退运

区内设备退运指出口加工区内退运境外的设备。

本监管方式代码"5361"，简称"区内设备退运"。

●Equipment returned in Zone

Equipment returned in Zone refers to the export processing zone returned outside equipment.

The way of supervision code is "5361" and the shortened form of it is "Equipment returned in zone".

●加工贸易料件进出出口加工区

加工贸易料件进出出口加工区指出口加工区内加工贸易料件在境内结转、销售，包括从区外购进或加工区内企业经批准销往区外的料件，同一出口加工区或不同出口加工区内的企业之间相互结转（调拨）的料件，深加工结转转入的料件，加工区内企业为区外加工的料件进区，以及上述料件在境内的退运，但不包括退换货物。

本监管方式代码"5000"，简称"料件进出区"。

●Processing trade materials import and export processing zone

Processing trade materials import and export processing zone refers to processing the export processing zone of materials carry – over, sales, including from outsid import or processing zone enterprises approved sold outside of materials o , the same export processing zone or different export processing zone enterprises between the carry – over (transfer) of materials ,deep processing carry – over into materials , processing zone enterprises for outside processing import materials , and the above – mentioned returned materials , but not including exchanges and refunds goods.

The way of supervision code is "5000" and the shortened form of it is "Processing trade materials import and export processing zone".

●加工贸易成品进出出口加工区

加工贸易成品进出出口加工区指出口加工区内加工贸易成品在境内结转、销售，包括销往区外、结转到同一出口加工区或另一出口加工区内的企业，以及加工区内企业为区外加工的成品出区、销往区外的成品因故退运

●Processing trade finished products import and export processing zone

Processing trade finished products import and export processing zone refers to the processing trade finished products of export processing zone carry – over, sales ,including sold to outside, transferred to the same export processing zone or another export processing zone enterprises, and enterprises of processing zone for outside processing

进区,不包括退换货物。

本监管方式代码"5100",简称"成品进出区"。

finished out of zone, sold to outside For some reason returned into zone, not including returned goods.

The way of supervision code is "5300" and the shortened form of it is "Processing trade finished products import and export processing zone".

●设备进出区

设备进出区指出口加工区内企业设备、物资在境内结转、销售,包括从区外购进设备、物资,设备因故销往区外,设备结转到同一出口加工区或另一出口加工区内的企业,以及上述设备、物资在境内的退运、退换。

本监管方式代码"5300",简称"设备进出区"。

●Equipment import and export zone

Equipment import and export zone refers to the export processing zones of enterprises equipment, materials . Equipment for some resons sold form outside and carry - over into the same export processing zone another export processing zone of enterprises , including the above - mentioned equipment and materials returned , exchanges and refunds.

The way of supervision code is "5300" and the shortened form of it is "Equipment import and export zone".

●出口加工区加工贸易边角料出区

出口加工区加工贸易边角料出区指出口加工区内企业边角料结转到同一加工区或不同加工区的另一企业,或经批准销售到区外。

本监管方式代码"5200",简称"区内边角调出"。

●Export processing zones of processing trade scrap material outside the zone

Export processing zones of processing trade scrap material outside the zone refers to export processing zone of enterprises scrap material carry - over to the same processing zone or different processing zone of enterprises, or approved sales to the outside.

The way of supervision code is "5200" and the shortened form of it is "Export processing zones of processing trade scrap material outside the zone ".

●物流中心进出境货物

一、定义及代码

保税物流中心进出境仓储货物是指从境外直接存入保税物流中心(A、B型)和从保税物流中心(A、B型)运出境的仓储、转口货物。

本监管方式代码为"6033",简称"物流中心进出境货物"。

二、适用范围

(一)保税物流中心(A型)是指经海关批准,由中国境内企业法人经营、专门从事保税仓储物流业务的海关监管场所。保税物流中心(A型)按照服务范围分为公用型物流中心和自用型物流中心。

1. 公用型物流中心是指由专门从事仓储物流业务的中国境内企业法人经营,向社会提供保税仓储物流综合服务的海关监管场所。

2. 自用型物流中心是指中国境内企业法人经营,仅向本企业或者本企业集团内部成员提供保税仓储物流服务的海关监管场所。

(二)保税物流中心(B型)(以下简称物流中心)是指经海关批准,由中国境内一家企业法人经营、多家企业进入并从事保税仓储物流业务的海关集中监管场所。

(三)下列情况不适用本监管方式:

1. 从境内(海关特殊监管区域除外)运入保税物流中心(A、B型)货物和从保税物流中心(A、B型)提取运往境内的货物。

2. 保税物流中心(A、B型)与保税区、出口加工区、保税物流园区、保税仓库、出口监管仓库及保税物流中心(A、B型)之间等海关特殊监管区域或保税监管场所之间往来的货物,其监管方式填报为"保税间货物"(1200)。

3. 保税仓库进出境仓储、转口货物,其监管方式为

● Goods imported and exported by centers for flow of goods

1. Definition and code

Goods imported and exported by centers for flow of goods refers to warehoused and transit goods imported directly into bonded centers for flow of goods (Type A and B) and exported from bonded centers for flow of goods (Type A and B).

The code of the way of supervision for this is "6033" and the shortened form of it is "Goods imported and exported by centers for flow of goods".

2. Scope of application

(1) Bonded centers for flow of goods (Type A) refer to venues under the Customs supervision which are approved by the Customs, operated by corporate legal persons in China and devoted to bonded warehousing and flow of goods. Bonded centers for flow of goods (Type A) are divided into public centers for flow of goods and private centers for flow of goods.

a. Public centers for flow of goods refer to venues under the Customs supervision devoted to bonded warehousing and flow of goods, operated by corporate legal persons in China and providing comprehensive bonded warehoused flow of goods service.

b. Private centers for flow of goods refer to venues under the Customs supervision operated by corporate legal persons in China and only providing bonded warehoused flow of goods service for the owner enterprises or internal members of the owner enterprise groups.

(2) Bonded centers for flow of goods (Type B) (shortened to centers for flow of goods hereunder) refer to venues under the Customs supervision operated by a corporate legal person in China, entered by many enterprises and are devoted to bonded warehoused flow of goods.

(3) This way of supervision is not applicable to the following circumstances:

a. Goods transported into bonded centers for flow of goods (Type A and B) from within China (not including areas under the Customs supervision) and goods transported to other places in China from bonded centers for flow of goods (Type A and B).

b. Goods transferred between bonded centers for flow of goods (Type A and B) and bonded areas, export processing areas, bonded parks for flow of goods, bonded warehouses, warehouses under export supervision and bonded centers for flow of goods (Type A and B), the way of supervision for which is "goods between bonded" (1200).

c. Warehoused and transit goods imported into and exported from bonded ware-

"保税仓库货物"(1233)。

4. 保税区、保税物流园区进出境仓储、转口货物，其监管方式为"保税区仓储、转口"(1234)。

●内贸货物跨境运输

一、定义及代码

内贸货物跨境运输是指国内贸易货物由我国关境内一口岸启运，通过境外运至我国关境内另一口岸的业务，以下简称"跨境运输"。

本监管方式代码为"9600"，简称"内贸跨境"。

二、适用范围

经海关总署批准的进出境口岸、所经境外口岸、运输方式等实行跨境运输的货物。

●海关处理货物

一、定义及代码

海关处理货物是指由海关提取变卖处理的超期未报关进口货物、误卸、溢卸货物、放弃进口货物，以及走私违规案件查处的货物。

本监管方式代码为"9639"，简称"海关处理货物"。

二、适用范围

本监管方式适用以下定义的货物：

(一)超期未报关货物，是指进口货物的收货人自运输工具申报进境之日起超过3个月未向海关申报，由海关提取依法变卖处理的进口货物。

超期未报关货物还包括保税货物、暂时进口货物超过规定的期限3个月，未向海关办理复运出境或者其他有关手续，以及过境、转运和通运货物超过规定的期限3个月，未运输出境，由海关提取依法变卖处理。

(二)误卸、溢卸货物，是指未列入进境运输工具载货清单、运单申报进境的误卸或者溢卸的货物，运输工具负责人或进口货物收货人未向海关办理退运出境或申报进口手续，由海关提取依法变卖处理的进口货物。

(三)放弃进口货物，是指进口货物的收货人或其所有人声明放弃，由海关提取依法变卖处理的进口货物。

(四)超期未报关进口货物、误卸或者溢卸进口货物属于危险品或者鲜活、易腐、易烂、易失效、易变质、易贬值等不宜长期保存的货物的，海关根据实际情况，提前提取依法变卖处理。

(五)进出境物品所有人声明放弃的物品，在海关规定期限内未办理海关手续或者无人认领的物品，以及无法投递又无法退回的进境邮递物品，由海关提取依法变卖处理。

(六)走私违法案件予以没收，由海关依法变卖处理的货物。

●无原始报关单的后续补税

无原始报关单的后续补税是指无法获得原始报关单的后续退补税货物，包括调查、稽查补税及审价、归类等各种原因的后续退补税货物。

houses and bonded parks for flow of goods, the way of supervision for which is "warehousing and transit in bonded areas" (1234).

● Cross - border transport of domestic trade goods

1. Definition and code

Cross - border transport of domestic trade goods refers to the business where domestic trade goods are transported from a port in China to another port in China via a foreign place, which is shortened to "cross - border transport".

The code of the way of supervision for this is "9600" and the shortened form of it is "cross - border domestic trade".

2. Scope of application

Goods transported across borders via import and export ports, overseas ports and means of transport approved by the Customs.

● Goods disposed of by the Customs

1. Definition and code

Goods disposed of by the Customs refer to imported goods confiscated and sold off by the Customs which are not declared within the prescribed period, wrongly unloaded, excessively unloaded, abandoned or confiscated in dealing with smuggling and irregular cases.

The code of the way of supervision for this is "9639" and the shortened form of it is "goods disposed of by the Customs".

2. Scope of application

This way of supervision is applicable to goods in the following definitions:

(1) Goods not declared within the prescribed period refer to imported goods which havent been declared to the Customs by consignees within 3 months after the date when means of transport were declared for entry and confiscated and sold off by the Customs according to law.

Goods not declared within the prescribed period also include bonded goods and temporarily imported goods not going through the reexport or other relevant formalities with the Customs within the prescribed three months and transit, transshipped and through goods not transported abroad within the prescribed three months, which will be confiscated and sold off by the Customs according to law.

(2) Wrongly unloaded and excessively unloaded goods refer to wrongly unloaded and excessively unloaded goods not declarable according to the manifest or waybill of inbound means of transport and not returned or declared to the Customs for import by responsible persons of means of transport or consignees, which will be confiscated and sold off by the Customs according to law.

(3) Abandoned imports refer to goods that consignors or owners declare they give up and are taken and sold off by the Customs according to law.

(4) If imports not declared within the prescribed period, wrongly unloaded or excessively unloaded imports are dangerous goods or goods which are fresh, live, easy to decay, rot, expire, deteriorate and depreciate and cannot be kept for long, the Customs will take and sell them off in advance as necessary according to law.

(5) Articles that their owners declare they give up, articles for which the Customs formalities have not been gone through within the period prescribed by the Customs, articles not claimed by anybody and posted imports both undeliverable and unreturnable will be taken and sold off by the Customs according to law.

(6) Goods confiscated in dealing with smuggling and illicit cases will be confiscated and sold off by the Customs.

● Retrospective supplementation of duties for goods without original declaration forms

Retrospective supplementation of duties for goods without original declaration forms involves goods for which original declaration forms cannot be obtained, including goods for which duties are supplemented retrospectively due to investigation, check, estimate of prices and classification.

本监管方式代码为“9700”，简称“后续补税”。

The code of the way of supervision for this is "9700" and the shortened form of it is "retrospective supplementation of duties".

●其他贸易

● Other trade

一、定义及代码

其他贸易是指除本章上述各节列名的监管方式以外，列入海关“其他贸易”统计的进出口货物。

本监管方式代码为“9739”，简称“其他贸易”。

二、适用范围

（一）本监管方式适用：

1. 我国境内经批准临时进出口货物的机关、团体、学校、企事业单位等进出口货物、物品。

2. 外国驻华使、领馆在我国内购买货物出口。

3. 外商投资企业外方常驻人员和外国驻华机构的常驻人员，以及持有长期居留证件和来华定居的引进专家等进口自用汽车。

4. 进入厦门大嶝对台小额商品交易市场的人员带出台湾产品，每人每日价值人民币1000元以下免征进口关税和进口环节税，超出部分照章征税，监管方式为“其他贸易”。

5. 外国企业常驻我国办事机构进口不复运出境的陈列用企业产品样品。

6. 未列入运输工具进口载货清单、提（运）单，或多于进口载货清单、提（运）单所列数量的货物，运输工具负责人或溢卸货物的收货人申请办理进口溢卸货物。

（二）本监管方式不包括：

1. 入境旅客在境内购买5万美元以内的旅游商品托运出境，其监管方式为“旅游购物商品”（0139）。

2. 本国籍运输工具在境内添加进口保税油、物料，其监管方式为“国轮油物料”（1139）。

3. 外国常驻机构进口办公用品，其监管方式为“常驻机构公用”（2439）。

4. 驻华商业机构进口不复运出口的陈列样品，其监管方式为“陈列样品”（2939）。

5. 对台湾小额贸易，其监管方式为“对台小额”（4039）。

6. 没有进出口经营权的企业或单位进出口货样广告品，其监管方式为“货样广告品B”（3039）。

7. 除援助、捐赠以外进出口其他免费提供的货物，其监管方式为“其他进出口免费”（3339）。

8. 我国驻外机构在境外购买的公务用品、机动车辆运回境内，其监管方式为“驻外机构购进”（4239）。

9. 海关拍卖处理超期未报货物、走私违规货物，其监管方式为“海关处理货物”（9639）。

10. 驻华外交机构转售境内非外交机构或个人，国际文体交流活动进口物品获准留赠或放弃，其监管方式为“留赠、转卖物品”（9839）。

1. Definition and code

Other trade refers to imports and exports listed in the statistics of "other trade" by the Customs among the ways of supervision listed in the above sections of this chapter.

The code of the way of supervision for this is "9739" and the shortened form of it is "other trade".

2. Scope of application

(1) This way of supervision is applicable to:

a. Goods and articles imported and exported by organs, bodies, schools, enterprises and institutions in China which are permitted to import and export temporarily.

b. Goods purchased in our country and exported by foreign embassies and consulates stationed in China.

c. Cars imported by foreign permanent staffs of foreign - invested enterprises, permanent staffs of foreign institutions stationed in China and foreign experts who have long - term residence permits and settled down in China for self use.

d. Everybody who bring products made in Taiwan from the market of petty trade with Taiwan in Dayu, xiamen can be exempted 1000 yuan of import duty and import link tax per day and the way of supervision is "Other trade".

e. Samples of products imported for display and not to be reexported by permanent offices of foreign enterprises in China.

f. Excluded in the transportation of import manifest, carried (carry), or more than the import manifest, carried (carry) a single list the quantity of the goods, transportation of person in charge or overlanded cargo of consignee.

(2) This way of supervision does not include:

a. Inbound tourists buy tourist commodities worth no more than US $ 50000 domestically and consign them overseas and the way of supervision is "tourist shopping commodities (0139).

b. Chinese means of transport is supplied with imported bonded oil and materials and the way of supervision is "guolun oil and materials" (1139).

c. Foreign permanent institutions import office supplies and the way of supervision is "public use for permanent institutions" (2439).

d. Foreign commercial organizations in China import and don't reexport samples for display and the way of supervision is "samples for display" (2939).

e. Small - amount trade with Taiwan and the way of supervision is "small amounts with Taiwan" (4039).

f. Enterprises or units that don't have the import and export right import and export samples of goods and advertising products and the way of supervision is "Samples of Goods and Advertising Products B" (3039).

g. Import and export other free goods besides contributions and donations and the way of supervision is "other duty - free imports and exports" (3339).

h. Chinese institutions purchase public articles and motor vehicles abroad and transport them to China and the way of supervision is "purchase and import by institutions abroad" (4239).

i. The Customs auction goods not declared within the prescribed period and smuggled and illicit goods and the way of the supervision is "" goods disposed of by the Customs" (9639).

j. Diplomatic institutions in China resell articles of non - diplomatic institutions and individuals and imported articles for international cultural and sports exchange activities which are left as presents or given up and the way of supervision is "articles left as presents or resold" (9839).

●留赠、转卖物品

● Articles left as presents or resold

留赠转卖物品是指外国（地区）驻我国外交机构转

Articles left as presents or resold means diplomatic institutions in China resell ar-

售境内非外交机构或国际文体活动留赠、放弃的特批进口物品。

本监管方式代码为"9839",简称"留赠转卖物品"。

ticles of non – diplomatic institutions and individuals and imported articles for international cultural and sports exchange activities which are left as presents or given up.

The way of supervision for this is "9839" and the shortened form of it is "articles left as presents or resold".

●其他

一、定义及代码

指除已具体列名监管方式以外其他不列入海关统计的进出境货物、物品。

本监管方式代码为"9900",简称"其他"。

二、适用范围

(一)从货运渠道进出境的个人行李物品。

(二)中国驻外国使领馆出口公务或自用物品。

(三)在境内结转的进出口货物:

1. 以出顶进货物,指经批准在国内以外汇向有关进出口公司购买出口商品顶替其应进口的同一商品。

2. 供应国内外汇免税商店并收取外汇的出口商品。

3. 经批准将来料加工、进料加工贸易项下加工的成品转为免税外汇商品。

4. 经批准内销征税的进口免税品。

(四)边民互市贸易进出境货物。

(五)我国远洋渔业企业进口自捕水产品。

(六)国有文物收藏单位经国家文物局核准后,接受境外捐赠、归还和从境外追索的文物进口。

国有文物收藏单位秕系指国家文物局审核批准从事文物收藏和研究的博物馆(院)、展览馆、研究所(院)等单位。

(七)与无代价抵偿进出口货物相关的原进口货物退运出境或原出口货物退运进境。

(八)我国各银行总行调运进出境的人民币、外币现钞。

● Other

1. Definition and code

Referring to imported and exported goods and articles not listed in the Customs statistics among specifically named ways of supervision.

The code of the way of supervision for this is "9900" and the shortened form of it is "other".

2. Scope of application

(1) Personal luggage and articles imported and exported from freight transport channels.

(2) Public or self – use articles exported by Chinese embassies and consulates in other countries.

(3) Imports and exports carried over domestically.

a. Substituting imports with exports refers to buying exports at home from relevant import and export companies with foreign exchange to substitute the same commodities that should be imported.

b. Exports sold in domestic duty – free shops for foreign exchange.

c. Finished products produced with supplied and imported materials and turned into duty – free foreign exchange commodities with approval.

d. Imported duty – free articles that are turned with approval into dutiable articles for domestic sale.

(4) Goods imported and exported from frontier citizens´exchange markets.

(5) Aquatic products caught and imported by our deep – sea fishing enterprises.

(6) The state – owned cultural relics collection entities by the State Cultural Relics Bureau approval, to accept outside donations, return and recourse from overseas imports of cultural relics. The state – owned cultural relics collection.

Entities blighted refers to the State Bureau of cultural relics for examination and approval in the cultural relics collection and research Museum (Institute), exhibition hall, the unit such as Institute (Academy).

(7) Outbound return of original imports and inbound return of original exports related to unpriced offset imports and exports.

(8) Renminbi and foreign currencies transferred across the border by Chinese banks.

征免性质代码表说明

Explanations about Table of Codes for Collection and Exemption Natures

征免性质是指海关对进出口货物实施征、减、免税管理的性质类别。

征免性质分为照章征税、法定减免税、特定减免税和临时减免税四部分。其中特定减免税又分为按地区实施的税收政策、按用途实施的税收政策、按贸易性质实施的税收政策、按企业性质和资金来源实施的税收政策等五类。

一份报关单只允许填报一种征免性质,涉及多个征免性质的,应分单填报。

Collection and exemption natures refer to the categories of natures in the Customs´management of collection and reduction of and exemption from duties on imports and exports.

Collection and exemption natures are divided into collection of duties according to regulations, legal reduction of and exemption from duties, specific reduction of and exemption from duties and temporary reduction of and exemption from duties. Therein specific reduction of and exemption from duties is divided further into five categories, i. e. local taxation policies, taxation policies based on use, taxation policies based on natures of trade, taxation policies based on corporate natures and sources of funds.

Fill only one collection and exemption nature in one declaration form or one other Customs business document. When many collection and exemption natures are involved, fill the declaration form separately.

●一般征税进出口货物

一、定义及代码

● Generally dutiable imports and exports

1. Definition and code

一般征税进出口货物指海关根据《中华人民共和国海关法》、《中华人民共和国进出口关税条例》(国务院令第392号)、《中华人民共和国进出口税则》及其他法律、行政法规、规章的规定征收进出口关税、进口环节税的进出口货物。

本征免性质代码为“101”,简称“一般征税”。

二、适用范围

本征免性质限于海关依据法律、行政法规、规章规定的法定税率征收进出口关税、进口环节税的进出口货物,包括按照公开暂定、关税配额、反倾销、反补贴、保障措施等税率、税额征税或补税的进出口货物。

执行ITA税率的货物(征免性质代码“499”)不适用本征免性质。

Generally dutiable imports and exports refer to imports and exports on which the Customs levies import and export duties and the import link tax according to the Customs Law of the People's Republic of China, Regulations of the People's Republic of China on Import and Export Duties, Import and Export Tariffs of the People's Republic of China and other laws, administrative regulations and rules.

The code of this collection and exemption nature is "101" and the shortened form of it is "general collection".

2. **Scope of application**

This collection and exemption nature is limited to imports and exports on which the Customs levies import and export duties and the import link tax according to legal tax rates stipulated by the laws and administrative regulations and rules, including imports and exports on which duties are levied or supplemented according to the tax rates and tax amounts stipulated in the public provisional, tariff quota, anti-dumping, anti-subsidy and guarantee measures.

This collection and exemption nature is not applicable to goods the ITA tariff rate applies to (the code of the collection and exemption nature is "499").

●无偿援助进出口物资

一、定义及代码

无偿援助进出口物资指外国政府、国际组织对我国无偿赠送及我关履行国际条约规定进口的物资,或我国对国外无偿援助或赠送的物资。

本征免性质代码“201”,简称“无偿援助”。

二、适用范围

(一)本征免性质所称外国政府是指外国国家的中央政府;国际组织是指联合国各专门机构以及长期与我国有合作关系的其他国际组织;国际条约是指依据《中华人民共和国缔结条约程序法》以“中华人民共和国”、“中华人民共和国政府”、“中华人民共和国政府部门”名义同外国缔结协定或协议以及参加的国际条约。

(二)免税范围

1. 根据中国与外国政府、国际组织间的协定或协议,由外国政府、国际组织直接无偿赠送的物资或由其提供无偿赠款,由我国受赠单位按照协定或协议规定用途自行采购进口的物资。

2. 外国地方政府或民间组织受外国政府委托无偿赠送的物资。

3. 国际组织成员受国际组织委托无偿赠送的物资。

4. 我国履行国际条约规定免税进口的物资。

(三)外国民间团体、企业、友好人士和华侨、香港居民、台湾、澳门同胞及外籍华人无偿向我境内受灾地区捐赠的直接用于救灾的物资(征免性质代码“801”),境外捐赠人无偿向我国境内捐赠的直接用于扶贫、慈善事业的进口物资(征免性质代码“802”)不适用本征免性质。

● Imported and exported materials for free aid

1. **Definition and code**

Imported and exported materials for free aid refer to materials foreign governments and international organizations donate to our country free of charge and materials our country imports to fulfill international treaties or our country gives or presents to foreign countries free of charge.

The code of this collection and exemption nature is 201 and the shortened form of it is free aid.

2. **Scope of application**

(1) Foreign countries mentioned in this collection and exemption nature refer to central governments of foreign countries; international organizations refer to the UN agencies and other international organizations which have long-term cooperative relationship with our country; international treaties refer to treaties or protocols concluded with foreign countries and international treaties joined in the names of the People's Republic of China, the Government of the People's Republic of China and departments of the Government of the People's Republic of China according to the Procedural Law of the People's Republic of China on Conclusion of Treaties.

(2) Scope of exemption

a. Materials or grants donated directly by foreign governments and international organizations free of charge according to pacts or protocols between China and foreign governments or international organizations and materials purchased and imported by recipient units of China themselves according to use prescribed in such pacts or protocols.

b. Materials presented by foreign local governments or non-governmental organizations free of charge as trusted by foreign governments.

c. Materials presented by members of international organizations as trusted by international organizations.

d. Materials our country imports duty-freely to fulfill international treaties.

(3) Materials donated by foreign non-governmental bodies, enterprises and friendly persons and overseas Chinese, Hong Kong residents, Taiwan and Macao compatriots and Chinese of foreign nationalities to disaster areas directly for disaster relief (the code of the collection and exemption code is "801"). This collection and exemption nature is not applicable to imported materials donated by overseas donors to our country directly for poverty alleviation and charities (the code of the collection and exemption code is "802".

●其他法定减免税进出口货物

一、定义及代码

其他法定减免税进出口货物指海关依照《海关法》、《中华人民共和国进出口关税条例》,对除无偿援助进出口

● Other imported and exported goods granted reduction of and exemption from duties by law

1. **Definition and code**

Other imported and exported goods granted reduction of and exemption from duties by law refer to other imported and exported goods granted reduction of and

物资外的其他实行法定减免税的进出口货物,以及根据有关规定按非全额货值征税的部分进出口货物。

本征免性质代码“299”,简称“其他法定”。

二、适用范围

本征免性质仅限无代价抵偿货物、货样和广告品、暂时进出境货物、展览会货物、退运货物、残损货物、进出境运输工具装载的途中必需的燃料、物料和饮食用品、我国缔结或者参加的国际条约规定减免税款的货物、因不可抗力因素造成的受灾保税货物等不按《进出口货物征免税证明》管理的减免税货物。

●保税区进出口自用物资

一、定义及代码

保税区进出口货物是指对保税区单独实施征减免税政策的进口自用物资和出口货物。

本征免性质代码“307”,简称“保税区”。

二、适用范围

本征免性质仅限保税区进口的自用物资,包括区内生产性基础设施建设物资、区内企业自用的生产、管理设备和自用合理数量的办公用品、建设生产厂房、仓储设施所需的物资设备、保税区行政管理机构自用合理数量的管理设备和办公用品等。

保税区内加工贸易进出口货物、仓储货物、转口货物和外商投资企业按照外商投资企业进口税收政策进口的设备等不适用本征免性质。

●其他执行特殊政策地区进出口货物

一、定义及代码

其他执行特殊政策地区进出口货物指除保税区外单独实施特殊税收政策地区进出口的货物。

本征免性质代码“399”,简称“其他地区”。

二、适用范围

(一)本征免性质仅限出口加工区、保税港区、综合保税区、珠澳跨境工业园区等海关特殊监管区进口的基建、生产和管理设备、物资、区内出口货物,以及从境内区外进入上述海关特殊监管区(包括中哈霍尔果斯国际边境合作中心)的基建物资或区内生产企业在国内采购用于生产出口产品的原材料。

(二)本征免性质不适用:

1.特殊区域内加工贸易进出口货物、仓储货物、转口货物和外商投资企业按照外商投资企业进口税收政策进口的设备等。

2.保税区进出口货物,征免性质代码“307”。

exemption from goods by the Customs according to the Customs Law and the Regulations of the People's Republic of China on Import and Export Duties besides those provided free of charge and some imported and exported goods held partially dutiable according to relevant regulations.

The code of this collection and exemption nature is 299 and the shortened form of it is other legal exemption.

2. Scope of application

This collection and exemption nature is only applicable to unpriced offset goods, samples of goods, advertising products, temporarily imported and exported goods, exhibition goods, returned goods, defective and damaged goods, fuel, materials, beverages and food necessary for import and export transport, goods whose reduction of and exemption from duties is prescribed by international treaties our country concluded or joined, disaster - stricken bonded goods due to force majeure and other goods which are not administered according to the Certificate of Collection of and Exemption from Duties on Imports and Exports.

●Imports and exports personal material in bonded zones

1. Definition and code

Imports and exports in bonded zones refer to goods imported by enterprises in the zones for themselves and exported by them and whose duties are reduced or exempted according to policies for bonded zones.

This levy and exemption nature is coded “307” and abbreviated to “bonded zones”.

2. Application scope

This levy and exemption nature is only limited to goods imported by enterprises in the zones for themselves and exported by them, including materials for construction of productive infrastructure in the zones, production and management equipment used by enterprises in the zones themselves and office supplies for themselves in a reasonable quantity, materials and equipment for construction of workshops and warehouses, management equipment and office supplies for administrative bodies of bonded zones.

This levy and exemption nature does not apply to imports and exports of bonded zones in processing trade, warehoused goods, transit goods and equipment imported by foreign - funded enterprises according to the policy on import duties on foreign - funded enterprises.

●Imports and exports of other zones which implement special policies

1. Definition and code

Imports and exports of other zones which implement special policies refer to goods imported and exported by non - bonded zones which implement other special policies on duties.

This levy and exemption nature is coded “399” and abbreviated to “other zones”.

2. Application scope

(1) This levy and exemption nature is only limited to capital construction, production and management equipment and materials imported by export - oriented processing zones, bonded zones, comprehensive bonded zones, Zhuhai - Macao Industrial Park and other zones under special customs surveillance, exports from the above and capital construction materials coming into the above from outside (include the Sino - Kazakhstan Horgos International Border Cooperation Center) or raw materials purchased by producers in the zones domestically for producing exports.

(2) This levy and exemption nature does not apply to the following:

a. Imports and exports of special zones in processing trade, warehoused goods, transit goods and equipment imported by foreign - funded enterprises according to the policy on import duties on foreign - funded enterprises.

b. The levy and exemption nature for imports and exports in bonded zones is coded "307".

●科教用品和科技开发用品

一、定义及代码

科教用品指为促进科学研究和教育事业的发展，推动科教兴国战略的实施，科学研究机构和学校以科学研究和教学为目的，在合理数量范围内进口国内不能生产或者性能不能满足需要的科学研究和教学用品。

科技开发用品指为鼓励科学研究和技术开发，促进科技进步，科学研究、技术开发机构，在 2010 年 12 月 31 日前，在合理数量范围内进口国内不能生产或者性能不能满足需要的科技开发用品。

本征免性质代码"401"，简称"科教用品"。

二、适用范围

（一）本征免性质所称科研机构和学校是指：

1. 国务院部委、直属机构和省、自治区、直辖市、计划单列市所属专门从事科学研究工作的各类科研院所。

2. 国家承认学历的实施专科及以上高等学历教育的高等学校。

3. 财政部会同国务院有关部门核定的其他科学研究机构和学校。

（二）本征免性质所称科学研究、技术开发机构是指：

1. 科技部会同财政部、海关总署和国家税务总局核定的科技体制改革过程中转制为企业和进入企业的主要从事科学研究和技术开发工作的机构。

2. 国家发展和改革委员会会同财政部、海关总署和国家税务总局核定的国家工程研究中心。

3. 国家发展和改革委员会会同财政部、海关总署、国家税务总局和科技部核定的企业技术中心。

4. 科技部会同财政部、海关总署和国家税务总局核定的国家重点实验室和国家工程技术研究中心。

5. 财政部会同国务院有关部门核定的其他科学研究、技术开发机构。

（三）具体免税范围限于《免税进口科学研究和教学用品清单》和《免税进口科技开发用品清单》。

（四）转制科研机构进口国家鼓励发展的内外资项目技术和设备（征免性质代码"789"）不适用本征免性质。

● Scientific and educational appliances and technical development appliances

1. Definition and code

Scientific and educational appliances and technical development appliances refer to scientific research and educational appliances imported by scientific research institutes and schools in reasonable quantities for scientific researches and education since they cannot be produced domestically or their domestic counterparts cannot meet needs to promote development of scientific researches and the educational cause and help implement the strategy of invigorating the country science and education.

Technical development appliances refer to technical development appliances imported by scientific research institutes and technical development institutions in reasonable quantities before December 31, 2010 since they cannot be produced domestically or their counterparts cannot meet needs to encourage scientific researches and technical development and promote scientific and technical progress.

The code of this collection and exemption nature is 401 and the shortened form of it is scientific and educational appliances.

2. Scope of application

(1) Scientific research institutes and schools mentioned in this nature refer to:

a. Various scientific research academies and institutes under ministries, commission and institutions of the State Council, provinces, autonomous regions, municipalities directly under the Central Government and cities with a separate plan.

b. Institutions of higher learning which offer three - year or longer education with a diploma recognized by the state.

c. Other scientific research institutes and schools recognized by the Ministry of Finance jointly with other departments of the State Council.

(2) Scientific research and technical development institutions mentioned in this collection and exemption nature refer to:

a. Institutions mainly engaged in scientific researches and technical development and turned into enterprises systematically and entering into enterprises which are recognized by the Ministry of Science and Technology jointly with the Ministry of Finance, the General Administration of Customs and the State Administration of Taxation.

b. State engineering research centers recognized by the State Development and Reform Commission jointly with the Ministry of Finance, the General Administration of Customs and the State Administration of Taxation.

c. Corporate technical centers recognized by the State Development and Reform Commission jointly with the Ministry of Finance, the General Administration of Customs and the State Tax Bureau.

d. State key labs and state engineering and technical research centers recognized by the Ministry of Science and Technology jointly with the Ministry of Finance, the General Administration of Customs and the State Tax Bureau.

e. Other scientific research and technical development institutions recognized by the Ministry of Finance jointly with other departments of the State Council.

(3) The specific scope of exemption is limited to the List of Appliances Imported Duty - Freely for Scientific Researches and Education and List of Appliances Imported Duty - Freely for Scientific Development.

(4) This collection and exemption nature is not applicable to technology and equipment advocated by the state which are imported by scientific research institutes transformed systematically (the code of the collection and exemption nature is "789").

●国家重大项目进口货物

一、定义及代码

国家重大项目进口货物指经国务院批准的国家重大建设项目项下进口的设备，以及安装所需材料等。

● Imported goods for key projects of the state

1. Definition and code

Imported goods for key projects of the state refer to imported equipment and installation materials for key construction projects approved by the State Council.

本征免性质代码为"406",简称"重大项目"。

二、适用范围

(一)本征免性质仅限1996年4月1日前经国务院批准可行性研究报告中列明减免税条款或另有减免税批准文件的重大建设项目。

(二)利用政府贷款、世界银行贷款等外资贷款建设的重大项目(征免性质代码"609")不适用于本征免性质。

This collection and exemption nature is "406" and the shortened form of it is "key projects".

2. Scope of application

(1) This collection and exemption nature is only applicable to key construction projects whose feasibility study reports are approved by the State Council and contain a reduction and exemption article or which have a separate document approving reduction and exemption.

(2) This collection and exemption nature is not applicable to significant projects using government loans and World Bank loans (the code of the collection and exemption nature is "609").

●进口残疾人专用品和专用设备

一、定义及代码

进口残疾人专用品和专用设备指为支持残疾人康复工作、帮助残疾人自立,免税进口的残疾人专用品和有关福利机构、康复机构、企业按照国家有关规定免税进口的国内不能生产的残疾人专用设备及专用生产设备。

本征免性质代码为"413",简称"残疾人"。

二、适用范围

(一)本征免性质仅限进口的残疾人专用品和残疾人福利机构、康复机构、企业进口的残疾人专用设备及专用生产设备。

(二)免税货物范围

1.残疾人个人专用品

(1)假肢及其零部件:上肢假肢包括部分手、前臂、上臂、假手、肘关节;下肢假肢包括部分足、小腿、大腿、膝关节等。

(2)假眼。

(3)假鼻。

(4)内脏托带:肾托、胃托、疝气带、疝气腰带等。

(5)矫形器:包括脊柱、上肢、下肢、功能性电子刺激器和复合力源矫形器系统等。

(6)矫形鞋:成品矫形鞋、订做的矫形鞋、适配的标准鞋。

(7)非机动助行器:包括单臂操作助行器(手杖、肘拐、前臂支撑拐、腋拐、三脚及多脚拐杖等)、双臂操作助行器(助行架、轮式助行架、助行椅、助行台等)及助行器的附件等。

(8)代步工具(不包括汽车、摩托车):包括轮椅车(手动、电动、机动)、残疾人专业自行车(如手摇三轮车、串翼自行车、助行自行车手扒推轮椅等)。

(9)辅助器具:移动用辅助器具、翻身用辅助器具(如翻身垫、翻身床单、翻身毯等)、升降用辅助器具(如轮椅爬楼梯装置、升降架等)。

(10)生活自助具:包括残疾人专用服装(如轮椅使用者的连裤服、雨衣、手套,鞋和靴的防滑装置等)、安全防护辅助器具(如用于头部、面部、上肢、下肢及全身的防护装置等)、穿脱衣服的辅助器具,画图和书写辅助器具(如书写板、书写框等)、日常生活用辅助器具(如罐头开启器、防洒碗等)。

(11)专用卫生用品。

(12)视力残疾者用盲杖。

● Special articles and equipment imported for the disabled

1. Definition and code

Special articles and equipment imported for the disabled refer to special articles imported duty - freely to support rehabilitation of the disabled and help self - reliance of the disabled and special equipment and production equipment imported by enterprises duty - freely according to the relevant regulation of the state which cannot be produced domestically.

The code of this collection and exemption nature is "413" and the shortened form of it is "the disabled".

2. Scope of application

(1) This collection and exemption nature is only limited to imported special articles for the disabled and special equipment and production equipment imported by welfare and rehabilitation institutions and enterprises for the disabled.

(2) Scope of duty - free goods

a. Special personal articles for the disabled

a) Artificial limbs and spare parts: upper artificial limbs include some hands, forearms, upper arms, artificial hands and elbow joints; the lower artificial limbs include some feet, shanks, thighs, knee joints, etc.

b) Artificial eyes

c) Artificial noses

d) Visceral balteums: kidney balteums, stomach balteums, hernia bandages, hernia cestuses, etc.

e) Orthoses: including spines, upper limbs, lower limbs, functional electronic stimulators, complex power source orthotic systems, etc.

f) Orthotic shoes: finished orthotic shoes, custom - made orthotic shoes and adaptive standard shoes.

g) Non - motorized walking aids: including single arm - operated walking aids (walking sticks, elbow crutches, forearm crutches, three - foot and multi - foot crutches, etc.), two arms - operated walking aids (walking frames, wheeled walking frames, walking chairs, walking tables, etc.) and accessories.

h) Means of riding instead of walking (not including autos and motorcycles): including wheeled chairs (manual, electric and motor wheelchairs), special bicycles for the disabled (such as manual tricycles, string wing bikes, aided bicycles and hand - pulled wheelchairs).

i) Assistive devices: mobile assistive devices, assistive devices for turnover (such as turnover pads, turnover bed sheets and turnover blankets), lifting assistive devices (such as devices for climbing staircases and lifting racks).

j) Self - help devices for life: special clothes for the disabled (such as connected coats and pants for wheelchair users, raincoats, gloves and anti - skid devices for shoes and boots), security assistive devices (such as guards for the head, face, upper and lower limbs and whole body), assistive devices for wearing and taking off clothes, drawing and writing assistive devices (such as writing boards and writing frames), assistive devices for daily life (such as can openers and anti - sprinkling bowls).

(k) Special health supplies.

(l) Blind sticks for persons with visual disabilities.

(13)导盲镜。

(14)助视器。

(15)盲人阅读器:电子盲文书写器、手动盲文书写器等。

(16)语言、听力残疾者用的语言训练器:言语训练辅助器具。

(17)智力残疾者用的行为训练器。

(18)生活能力训练用品。

2. 残疾人专用设备和专用生产设备

(1)残疾人康复及专用设备:包括床旁监护设备、中心监护设备、生化分析仪和超声诊断仪。

(2)残疾人特殊教育设备和职业教育设备:指对残疾人进行义务教育、学历教育、职业教育所需的各类设备(如聋人助听设备、智力残疾检测设备等)。

(3)残疾人职业能力评估测试设备(如手腕作业检查盘、注意力集中能力测试仪等)。

(4)残疾人专用劳动设备和劳动保护设备(如某种肢残人操作的特殊机床、聋人专用的特殊报警装置等),以及为残疾人就业设立的福利企业进口的适合残疾人操作的生产设备。

(5)残疾人文体活动专用设备:指残疾人进行文化、娱乐、体育活动和体育竞赛所需的专用设备(如各种运动轮椅、盲人门球等)。

(6)假肢专用生产、装配、检测设备,包括假肢专用铣磨机、假肢专用真空成型机、假肢专用平板加热器和假肢综合检测仪。

(7)听力残疾者用的助听器:包括各类助听器等。

(三)境外捐赠人无偿向我国境内捐赠的直接用于扶贫、慈善事业的进口物资(征免性质代码"802")不适用本征免性质。

(m) Glasses for the blind.

(n) Assistive glasses for vision

(o) Readers for the blind: electronic and manual Braille writers, etc.

(p) Language training devices for those with language and hearing disabilities: language training aids.

(q) Behavior training devices for persons with intellectual disabilities.

(r) Training supplies for living abilities.

b. Special equipment and special production equipment for the disabled

a) Special equipment for rehabilitation of the disabled: including bedside monitoring devices, central monitoring devices, biochemical analyzers and ultrasonic diagnostic instruments.

b) Special education equipment and vocational education equipment for the disabled refer to various types of equipment for carrying out compulsory education, academic education, vocational education required for the disabled (such as hearing aids for the deaf and equipment for testing intellectual disabilities).

c) Equipment for testing and assessing the vocational ability of the handicapped (such as disks for checking wrist operations and the instrument for testing the ability to focus attention).

d) Special working equipment and labor protection equipment for the disabled (such as special machine tools for a kind of physically disabled persons and special alarm devices for the deaf) and production equipment fit to be operated by the disabled which are imported by welfare enterprises established to employ the disabled.

e) Special equipment for cultural and sports activities of the disabled refers to special equipment for cultural, entertainment, sports and competition activities of the disabled (such as various sports wheelchairs and the blind's gate balls).

f) Special equipment for production, assembly and testing of artificial limbs, including milling and grinding machines for production of artificial limbs, special vacuum forming machines for production of artificial limbs, special flat heater for production of artificial limbs and comprehensive tester for artificial limbs.

(g) Hearing aids for people with hearing disability: including all types of hearing aids.

3. This collection and exemption nature is not applicable to mported materials donated by overseas donors free of charge to our country directly for poverty alleviation and charities (the code of the collection and exemption nature is "802").

●远洋渔业自捕水产品

一、定义及代码

远洋渔业自捕水产品是指根据国家远洋渔业企业运回自捕水产品的原产地规则,我国远洋渔业企业在公海或按照有关协议规定,在国外海域捕获并运回国内销售的自捕水产品及其加工制品,视同国内产品,免征关税和进口环节税。

本征免性质代码为"417",简称"远洋渔业"。

二、适用范围

本征免性质仅限经农业部批准,获得"农业部远洋渔业企业资格证书"的我国远洋渔业企业。运回的水产品及其加工制品限于在公海或按照有关协议规定,在国外海域自捕,并符合原产地规则的认定。

● Aquatic products caught by deep - sea fishery

1. Definition and code

Aquatic products caught by deep - sea fishery means aquatic products caught in the high seas or in foreign seas according to relevant agreements and transported back home by our deep - sea fishing enterprises and their processed products are regarded as domestic products and exempted from duties and import link tax based on the place of origin principle of the state on aquatic products caught and transported back by deep - sea fishing enterprises.

The code of this collection and exemption nature is "417" and the shortened form of it is "deep - sea fishery".

2. Scope of application

This collection and exemption nature is only applicable to deep - sea fishing enterprises granted by the Ministry of Finance the " Qualification Certificate of Deep - Sea Fishing Enterprises of Ministry of Agriculture". Aquatic products transported back and their processed products are only limited to those caught in the high seas or in foreign seas according to the relevant agreements and recognized by the place of origin principle.

●远洋船舶及设备部件

一、定义及代码

远洋船舶及设备部件是指中央关于制定国民经济和社

● Ocean - going ships and their equipment and components

1. Definition and code

Ocean - going ships and their equipment and components means the preferen-

会发展第十一个五年规划期间(以下简称"十一五"期间)在国内订造、改造远洋渔船进口船用关键设备和部件,进口少量带有入渔配额的二手远洋渔船以及进口国内不能建造的特种渔船,实施进口税收优惠政策。

本征免性质代码为"420",简称"远洋船舶"。

二、适用范围

(一)本征免性质仅适用于"十一五"期间(2006年1月1日至2010年12月31日)经农业部批准的在国内订造、改造远洋渔船所需进口的船用关键设备和部件、国内尚不能建造的特种渔船及少量带有入渔配额的二手远洋渔船。

(二)本征免性质不适用于"十一五"期间为建造内销远洋船所需进口的国内不能生产或性能不能满足要求的关键设备及部件,征免性质代码为"421"。

tial import duty policy is implemented for import of key equipment and components for custom building and transforming deep - sea fishing vessels domestically, import of a small quantity of second - hand deep - sea fishing vessels with a fishing quota and import of special fishing vessels which cannot be built domestically during the period of the central authorities' 11th Five - Year Plan for National Economy and Social Development (shortened to "11th Five - Year" period hereunder).

The code of this collection and exemption nature is "420" and the shortened form of it is "deep - sea ships".

2. Scope of application

(1) This collection and exemption nature is only applicable to key equipment and components imported with approval of the Ministry of Agriculture to custom build and transform deep - sea fishing vessels domestically, special shipping vessels that cannot be built domestically and a small quantity of second - hand deep - sea fishing vessels with a fishing quota during the "11th Five - Year Plan" period (from January 1, 2006 to December 31, 2010).

(2) This collection and exemption nature is not applicable to key equipment and components imported to build ocean - going ships for domestic sale that cannot be built domestically or whose domestic counterparts cannot meet needs during the "11th Five - Year Plan" period, the code of the collection and exemption nature for which is "421".

●内销远洋船用设备及关键部件

一、定义及代码

内销远洋船用设备及关键部件是指为建造内销远洋船所需进口的国内不能生产或性能不能满足要求的关键设备及部件。

征免性质代码为"421",简称"内销设备"。

二、适用范围

(一)本征免性质仅适用于"十一五"期间(2006年1月1日至2010年12月31日)经国家有关部门共同审定,为建造内销远洋船所需进口的国内不能生产或性能不能满足要求的关键部件及设备。

内销远洋船是指中国远洋运输(集团)总公司、中国海运(集团)总公司、中国对外贸易运输(集团)总公司和长江航运(集团)总公司委托中国船舶工业集团公司和中国船舶重工集团公司所属企业(包括造船企业和配套造船企业)建造的远洋船舶。

(二)本征免性质不适用于远洋渔业企业、国内船舶及船用设备制造企业在国内订造、改造远洋渔船所需进口的船用关键设备和部件,征免性质代码为"420"。

● Equipment and key parts for ocean - going ships for domestic sale

1. Definition and code

Equipment and key parts for ocean - going ships for domestic sale refer to key equipment and components imported to build ocean - going ships for domestic sale that cannot be built domestically or whose domestic counterparts cannot meet needs.

The code of the collection and exemption nature is "421" and the shortened form of it is "domestically sold equipment".

2. Scope of application

(1) This collection and exemption nature is only applicable to key components and equipment imported with joint approval of the relevant departments of the state during the 11th Five - Year Plan" period (from January 1, 2006 to December 31, 2010) to build ocean - going ships for domestic sale that cannot be built domestically or whose domestic counterparts cannot meet needs.

Domestically sold ocean - going ships refer to ocean - going ships built by enterprises under China State Shipbuilding Corporation and China State Shipbuilding Heavy Industry Corporation (including shipbuilding enterprises and auxiliary shipbuilding enterprises) for the China Ocean Shipping (Group) Company, China Shipping (Group) Company, China National Foreign Trade Transportation (Group) Corporation and China Changjiang National Shipping (Group) Corp.

(2) This collection and exemption nature is not applicable to key equipment and components imported by deep - sea fishing enterprises, domestic ship and ship equipment manufacturers to custom build and transform deep - sea fishing vessels domestically, the code of the collection and exemption nature for which is "420".

●集成电路生产企业进口货物

一、定义及代码

集成电路生产企业进口货物是指在中国境内设立的经审核符合条件的集成电路生产企业进口国内无法生产的自用生产性原材料、消耗品、净化室专用建筑材料、配套系统和集成电路生产设备零、配件。

本征免性质代码为"422",简称"集成电路"。

二、适用范围

本征免性质仅适用于集成电路线宽小于0.8微米

● Goods imported by integrated circuit makers

1. Definition and code

Goods imported by integrated circuit makers refer to productive raw materials, consumables, building materials for decontamination chambers, auxiliary systems and spare parts and accessories of integrated circuit production equipment imported by qualified integrated circuit makers in China which cannot be produced domestically.

The code of this collection and exemption nature is "422: and the shortened form of it is "integrated circuit".

2. Scope of application

This collection and exemption nature is only applicable to productive raw ma-

(含)集成电路生产企业进口自用生产性原材料、消耗品和集成电路线宽小于0.25微米或投资额超过80亿元的集成电路生产企业进口自用生产性原材料、消耗品、净化室专用建筑材料、配套系统和集成电路生产设备零、配件。

terials, consumables and integrated circuits with the line width of less than 0.25 microns imported by makers of integrated circuits with the lines width of less than 0.8 microns (included) for self use or productive raw materials, building materials for decontamination chambers, auxiliary systems and spare parts and accessories of integrated circuit production equipment imported by integrated circuit makers with an investment of more than RMB 80 billion for self use.

●薄膜晶体管液晶显示器件生产企业进口货物

一、定义及代码

薄膜晶体管液晶显示器件生产企业进口货物是指薄膜晶体管液晶显示器件生产企业进口国内不能生产的净化室专用建筑材料、配套系统、维修生产设备用的零配件、自用生产性原材料和消耗品。

本征免性质代码"423",简称:"膜晶显"。

二、适用范围

本征免性质仅适用于经国务院有关部门共同审核确定,可享受本税收政策的薄膜晶体管液晶显示器件的生产企业(以下简称膜晶显生产企业),进口国内不能生产的净化室专用建筑材料、配套系统、维修生产设备用的零配件、自用生产性原材料和消耗品。

第一批符合条件的膜晶显生产企业是:北京京东方光电科技有限公司(以下简称京东方)、上海广电NEC液晶显示器公司(以下简称上广电)和吉林北方彩晶数码电子有限公司。

●Goods imported by producers of thin film transistor – liquid crystal display

1. Definition and code

Goods imported by producers of thin film transistor – liquid crystal display refer to special construction materials for clean rooms, supporting systems, spare parts for maintenance of production equipment, own production raw materials and consumables that cannot be made domestically.

This levy and exemption nature is coded "423" and abbreviated to new – type displays.

2. Application scope

This levy and exemption nature only applies to special construction materials for clean rooms, supporting systems, spare parts for maintenance of thin film transistor – liquid crystal display production equipment, own production raw materials (including R & D use) and consumables that cannot be made domestically and imported by producers that are designated by relevant departments under the State Council together and can enjoy this tax policy.

The first batch of qualified film crystal display manufacturers are: Beijing BOE Optoelectronics Technology Co., Ltd. (hereinafter referred to as the BOE), Shanghai radio and television NEC liquid crystal display company (hereinafter referred to as the SVA) and North Jilin color crystal digital electronics company limited.

●非全税号信息技术产品

一、定义及代码

非全税号信息技术产品是指为执行"信息技术产品协议",海关核定用途后执行ITA税率的部分用于信息技术产品生产的商品。

本征免性质代码为"499",简称"ITA产品"。

二、适用范围

本征免性质仅适用于进口《中华人民共和国进出口税则》所列的ITA产品。

● Non – all tax No. IT products

1. Definition and code

Non – all tax No. IT products refer to some commodities used in production of IT products for which the ITA tariff rate is implemented after the Customs checks use to fulfill the "ITA".

The code of this collection and exemption nature is "499" and the shortened form of it is "ITA products".

2. Scope of application

This collection and exemption nature is only applicable to import of ITA products listed in the Import and Export Tariffs of the People's Republic of China.

●加工贸易外商提供的不作价进口设备

一、定义及代码

加工贸易外商提供的不作价进口设备是指与经营企业开展加工贸易(包括来料加工、进料加工)的境外企业,以免费即不需经营企业付汇进口、也不需用加工费或差价偿还方式,向经营企业提供的加工生产所需设备。

本征免性质代码为"501",简称"加工设备"。

二、适用范围

(一)本征免性质仅适用于加工贸易项下境外企业免费提供的不作价进口设备。

(二)本征免性质不适用按暂时进出口货物监管(监管方式:"暂时进出口"、代码"2600")的加工贸易生产所需的不作价设备(限模具、单台设备),征免性质为"法定减免"

● Unpriced imported equipment provided by foreign businessmen in processing trade

1. Definition and code

Unpriced imported equipment provided by foreign businessmen in processing trade refers to processing equipment provided by overseas enterprises which develop processing trade with operating enterprises in processing trade (including processing with supplied and processing with imported materials) for operating enterprises free of charge, i. e. neither charging operating enterprises for foreign exchange nor reducing processing fees or price difference as repayments.

The code of this collection and exemption nature is "501" and the shortened form of it is "processing equipment".

2. Scope of application

(1) This collection and exemption nature is only applicable to unpriced imported equipment provided by overseas enterprises free of charge in processing trade.

(2) This collection and exemption nature is not applicable to unpriced equipment (only molds and single set of equipment) for processing trade which is supervised as temporarily imported and exported goods (the way of supervision: "tempo-

(299)。

rary imports and exports" and the code: "2600"). The collection and exemption nature is "legal reduction and exemption" (299).

●来料加工贸易进口料件及出口成品

一、定义及代码

来料加工贸易进口料件及出口成品是指由境外企业提供,经营企业不需要付汇进口的来料加工业务所需全部或部分原辅材料、零部件、元器件和包装物料(以下简称料件),以及经加工或者装配后复出口的成品。

本征免性质代码为"502",简称"来料加工"。

二、适用范围

(一)本征免性质仅限来料加工项下进口的用于加工复出口成品所需的料件,以及经加工或者装配后复出口的成品。

(二)进口料件或制成品内销的,不适用本征免性质,征免性质为"照章征税"(101)。

● Imported materials and parts and finished exports in processing trade with supplied materials

1. Definition and code

Imported materials and parts and finished exports in processing trade with supplied materials refer to all or part raw and auxiliary materials, parts, components and packing materials (shortened to materials and parts hereunder) provided by overseas enterprises for operating enterprises free of charge for processing with supplied materials and finished reexports after processing or assembly.

The code of this collection and exemption nature is "502" and the shortened form of it is "processing with supplied materials".

2. Scope of application

(1) This collection and exemption nature is only applicable to materials and parts imported in processing with supplied materials for producing finished reexports and finished reexports after processing or assembly.

(2) This collection and exemption nature is not applicable to imported materials and parts or finished products for domestic sale. The collection and exemption nature is "collection of duties according to regulations" (101).

●进料加工贸易进口料件及出口成品

一、定义及代码

进料加工贸易进口料件及出口成品是指经营企业付汇进口的进料加工所需的全部或者部分原辅材料、零部件、元器件、包装物料(以下简称:料件),以及经过加工或者装配后复出口的成品。

本征免性质代码为"503",简称"进料加工"。

二、适用范围

(一)本征免性质仅限进料加工项下进口的用于加工复出口成品所需的料件,以及经加工后复出口的成品。

(二)进口料件或制成品内销的,按规定不予保税备案的消耗性物料,不适用本征免性质。征免性质为"照章征税"(101)。

● Imported materials and parts in processing trade with imported materials and finished exports

1. Definition and code

Imported materials and parts and finished exports in processing trade with supplied materials refer to all or part raw and auxiliary materials, parts, components and packing materials (shortened to materials and parts hereunder) imported by operating enterprises with foreign exchange for processing with imported materials and finished reexports after processing or assembly.

The code of this collection and exemption nature is "503" and the shortened form of it is "processing with imported materials".

2. Scope of application

(1) This collection and exemption nature is only applicable to materials and parts imported in processing with imported materials for producing finished reexports and finished reexports after processing or assembly.

(2) This collection and exemption nature is not applicable to imported materials and parts or finished products for domestic sale and consumable materials not recoded as bonded according to regulations. The collection and exemption nature is "collection of duties according to regulations (101).

●边境小额贸易进口货物

一、定义及代码

边境小额贸易进口货物是指我国边境地区经批准有小额贸易经营权的企业通过国家指定的陆路边境口岸,进口原产于毗邻国家的货物,包括边境地区开展易货贸易、现汇贸易、互利经济合作(工程承包、劳务输出),以及除边民互市贸易以外的其他各类边境贸易形式进口的货物。

本征免性质代码为"506",简称:边境小额。

二、适用范围

(一)本征免性质适用于边境小额贸易企业通过国家指定的陆路边境口岸进口原产于毗邻国家的货物及边境地区外经贸企业与毗邻国家边境地区开展承包工程和劳务合作项下换回的原产于毗邻国家的物资。

(二)本征免性质不适用边民互市贸易、通过边境口岸

● Imported and exported goods in small - amount frontier trade

1. Definition and code

Imported and exported goods in small - amount frontier trade means goods produced in adjoining countries and imported by enterprises in frontier areas of our country which are granted the right to engage in small - amount frontier trade via land ports designated by the state, including barter trade, spot trade, mutually beneficial economic cooperation (project contracting and labor export) and goods imported in various types of frontier trade except frontier citizens' exchange market trade.

The code of this collection and exemption nature is "506" and the shortened form of it is frontier small amounts.

2. Scope of application

(1) This collection and exemption nature is applicable to goods produced in adjoining countries and imported by small - amount frontier trade enterprises via land ports designated by the state and materials produced by adjoining countries and exchanged back by frontier foreign trade enterprises in developing contracted projects and labor cooperation with frontier areas of adjoining countries.

(2) This collection and exemption nature is not applicable to frontier citizens

进口第三国贸易的商品。

´exchange market trade and commodities produced in a third country and imported via land ports.

●外商投资企业进出口货物

一、定义及代码

外商投资企业进出口货物指1997年12月31日前按国家规定程序批准设立的国内企业与境外企业在中国境内合资经营的企业、合作经营的企业，以及境外企业在中国境内独资经营的企业在投资总额内进口的设备，以及外商投资企业（不受批准时间限制）生产的出口产品（加工贸易除外）。

中外合资经营企业进出口货物的征免性质代码为“601”，简称“中外合资”。

中外合作经营企业进出口货物的征免性质代码为“602”，简称“中外合作”。

外商独资企业进出口货物的征免性质代码为“603”，简称“外资企业”。

二、适用范围

（一）征免性质为“601”、“602”、“603”适用以下经批准设立的外商投资企业、外商投资项目在项目额度或投资总额内进口的自用设备及其按照合同随设备进口的技术及配套件、备件，以及所有外商投资企业生产（加工贸易除外）的出口产品：

1.1996年3月31日前成立的外商投资企业，包括依法批准增资及原外经贸部颁发批准证书的外商投资企业。

2.1995年10月1日至1996年3月31日依照程序经原外经贸部、原国家计委、原国家经贸委备案审核合格并经海关总署关税司转发各海关清单内的外商投资企业。

3.1995年9月30日前地方依法审批报原外经贸部备案的外商投资企业。

4.1996年4月1日至1997年12月31日按国家规定程序批准设立的外商投资项目。

（二）本征免性质不适用：

1.外商投资企业开展加工贸易进口的不作价设备，征免性质代码为“501”。

2.国家鼓励发展的外资项目项下进口的货物，征免性质代码为“789”。

3.外商投资额度外利用自有资金进口的货物，征免性质代码为“799”。

● Goods imported and exported by foreign - invested enterprises

1. Definition and code

Goods imported and exported by foreign - invested enterprises refer to equipment imported by joint ventures and cooperative ventures set up by domestic enterprises and overseas enterprises according to the prescribed procedure of the state before December 31, 1997 and solely foreign - funded enterprises in China within their total investments and products produced and exported (processing trade apart) by foreign - invested enterprises (not limited by the time of approval).

The collection and exemption nature for goods imported and exported by Sino - foreign joint ventures is "601" and shortened form of it is "Sino - foreign joint ventures".

The collection and exemption nature for goods imported and exported by Sino - foreign cooperative ventures is "602" and shortened form of it is "Sino - foreign cooperative ventures".

The collection and exemption nature for goods imported and exported by foreign - funded enterprises is "603" and shortened form of it is "foreign - funded enterprises".

2. Scope of application

(1) The collection and exemption natures "601", "602" and "603" are applicable to equipment imported by the following approved foreign - funded enterprises and foreign - funded projects in total investments in projects or total investments for self use, technology, accessories and spare parts imported with the equipment according to contracts and products produced and exported (processing trade apart) by all foreign - funded enterprises:

a. Foreign - invested enterprises established before March 31, 1996, including those whose addition of investments is approved and those whose approving certificates were issued by the former Ministry of Foreign Trade and Economic Cooperation.

b. Foreign - invested enterprises approved by the former Ministry of Foreign Trade and Economic Cooperation, the former State Planning Commission, the former State Economic and Trade Commission according to the procedure from October 1, 1995 to March 31, 1996 and on the list circulated by the Tariff Dept. of the General Administration of Customs to all Customs offices.

c. Foreign - funded enterprises reported to the former Ministry of Foreign Trade and Economic Cooperation for record by local places according to law before September 30, 1995.

d. Foreign - funded projects established according to the prescribed procedure of the state from April 1, 1996 to December 31, 1997.

(2) This collection and exemption nature is not applicable to:

a. Unpriced equipment imported by foreign - funded enterprises for processing trade, the code of the collection and exemption nature for which is "501".

b. Goods imported for foreign - funded projects encouraged by the state, the code of the collection and exemption nature for which is "789".

c. Goods imported with self funds beyond foreign investments, the code of the collection and exemption nature for which is "799".

●勘探开发煤层气进口物资

一、定义及代码

勘探开发煤层气进口物资指勘探开发煤层气项目的单位在我国境内进行煤层气勘探开发所需进口的设备、仪器、零附件和专用工具。

本征免性质代码：605，简称：勘探开发煤层气。

● Materials imported to explore and develop coal bed gas.

1. Definition and code

Materials imported to explore and develop coal bed methane refer to equipment, instruments, spare parts and special tools imported by units engaged in exploration and development of coal bed methane for exploration and development of coal bed methane in China.

The code of this collection and exemption nature is 605 and the shortened form of it is exploration and development of coal bed gas.

二、适用范围

勘探开发煤层气所需进口物资的免税政策执行期限为"十一五"期间。勘探开发煤层气项目的单位为中联煤层气有限责任公司及其他经财政部商海关总署和税务总局审核认定的单位。

具体免税范围限于国内不能生产或国内产品性能不能满足要求,并直接用于勘探开发作业的设备、仪器、零附件和专用工具。上述物资应符合《勘探开发煤层气免税进口物资清单》。

2. Scope of application

The exemption policy for materials imported for exploration and development of coal bed methane is implemented in the "11th Five - Year Plan" period. The units which are engaged in exploration and development of coal bed methane are China United Coalbed Methane Co. Ltd. and other units recognized by the Ministry of Finance together with the General Administration of Customs and the State Administration of Taxation.

The specific exemption scope is limited to equipment, instruments, spare parts, accessories and special tools directly used in exploration which cannot be produced domestically or whose domestic counterparts cannot meet needs. The above materials shall accord with the List of Duty - Free Imports for Exploration and Development of Coal Bed Methane.

●开采海洋、陆上石油(天然气)进口物资

一、定义及代码

开采海洋、陆上石油(天然气)进口物资指在我国海洋或陆上特定地区进行石油和天然气开采作业所需进口的设备、仪器、零附件和专用工具。

海洋指我国内海、领海、大陆架以及其他海洋资源管辖海域,包括浅海滩涂。

陆上特定地区指我国领土内的沙漠、戈壁荒漠和中外合作开采经国家批准的陆上石油、天然气中标区块。

开采海洋石油、天然气进口物资的征免性质代码"606",简称"海洋石油"。

开采陆上石油、天然气进口物资的征免性质代码"608",简称"陆上石油"。

二、适用范围

开采海洋、陆上石油(天然气)所需进口物资的免税政策执行期限为"十一五"期间。

具体免税范围限于国内不能生产或性能不能满足要求,并直接用于开采作业的设备、仪器、零附件、专用工具。上述物资应符合《开采海洋石油(天然气)免税进口物资清单》或《开采陆上特定地区石油(天然气)免税进口物资清单》。

● Materials imported to mine oil (natural gas) in ocean and on land

1. Definition and code

Materials imported to exploit oil (natural gas) in ocean and on land refer to equipment, instruments, spare parts, accessories and special tools imported for exploitation of oil and natural gas in specific Chinese marine and land areas.

Ocean refers to domestic seas, territorial seas, continental shelves and other waters which have marine resources, including shallow beaches.

Specific land areas refer to deserts, Gobi desert and exploitation of land oil and gas blocks by successful Sino - foreign cooperative bidders with approval of the state.

The code of the collection and exemption nature for materials imported to exploit ocean oil and natural gas is 606 and the shortened form of it is ocean oil.

The code of the collection and exemption nature for materials imported to exploit land oil and natural gas is 608 and the shortened form of it is land oil.

2. Scope of application

The exemption policy for materials imported for exploration of ocean and land oil (natural gas) is implemented in the "11th Five - Year Plan" period.

The specific exemption scope is limited to equipment, instruments, spare parts, accessories and special tools directly used in exploitation which cannot be produced domestically or whose domestic counterparts cannot meet needs. The above materials shall accord with the List of Duty - Free Imports for Exploration of Ocean Oil (Natural Gas) or the List of Duty - Free Imports for Exploration of Oil (Natural Gas) in Specific Land Areas.

●利用贷款进口货物

一、定义及代码

外国政府贷款和国际金融组织贷款项目进口设备指1997年12月31日前按国家规定程序批准的利用外国政府贷款和国际金融组织(世界银行、亚洲开发银行、联合国农业发展基金)贷款项目所进口的自用设备,以及按合同随设备进口的技术及数量合理的配套件、备件。

本征免性质代码为"609",简称"贷款项目"。

二、适用范围

(一)本征免性质仅限1997年12月31日前按国家规定程序批准的利用外国政府贷款和国际金融组织贷款项目。

(二)本征免性质不适用:

1. 利用国际金融组织贷款、外国政府贷款生产中标机电设备所需进口的零部件,其征免性质代码为"611"。

2. 纳入国家鼓励发展内外资项目的利用外国政府贷款

● Goods imported with loans

1. Definition and code

Equipment imported with loans from foreign government and loans from international financial organization refers to equipment imported with loans from foreign governments and international financial organizations (World Bank, Asian Development Bank and the United Nations Development Fund for Agriculture) for self use as well as technology and accessories and spare parts in reasonable quantities imported together with the equipment according to contracts.

The code of this collection and exemption nature is "609" and the shortened form of it is "loan projects".

2. Scope of application

(1) This collection and exemption nature is only applicable to use of loans of foreign governments and international financial organizations approved according to the prescribed procedure of the state before December 31, 1997.

(2) This collection and exemption nature is not applicable to:

a. Spare parts and components imported with loans from international financial organizations and foreign governments to produce electrical and mechanical equipment bid for successfully, the code of the collection and exemption nature for which is "611".

b. Loans from foreign governments and international financial organizations lis-

和国际金融组织贷款项目，其征免性质代码为“789”。

ted in the domestic and foreign fund categories encouraged by the state, the code of the collection and exemption nature is "789".

●中标机电设备零部件

● spare parts of mechanical and electrical equipment

一、定义及代码

国际金融组织贷款、外国政府贷款中标机电设备零部件指国内中标单位利用国际金融组织贷款、外国政府贷款，为生产中标机电设备而进口国内不能生产或性能不能满足需要的零部件。

本征免性质代码“611”，简称“贷款中标”。

1. Definition and code

Spare parts of mechanical and electrical equipment winning bids in purchases with loans of international financial organizations and foreign governments refer to spare parts imported by domestic successful bidders with loans of international financial organizations and foreign governments for production of mechanical and electrical equipment winning bids because those spare parts cannot be made domestically or their domestic counterparts cannot meet requirements.

This levy and exemption nature is coded “611” and abbreviated to “winning bids and loans”.

二、适用范围

（一）本征免性质适用于利用国际金融组织贷款、外国政府贷款（世界银行贷款、亚洲开发银行贷款、日本国际协力银行贷款，以及上述组织的赠款）为生产中标机电设备所需进口的零部件。

中标机电设备限于在国际招标中国内企业直接中标、中外联合中标生产的机电设备，以及中标的境外企业、国内企业将中标项目再分包给国内其他企业制造的机电设备，不包括《外商投资项目不予免税的进口商品目录》中所列设备。

（二）本征免性质不适用1997年12月31日前按国家规定程序批准的利用外国政府贷款和国际金融组织贷款项目，征免性质代码“609”。

2. Application scope

(1) This levy and exemption nature applies to spare parts imported with loans of international financial organizations and foreign governments (loans and donations from the World Bank, Asian Development Bank and Japan Bank for International Cooperation) for production of mechanical and electrical equipment winning bids.

Mechanical and electrical equipment winning bids is limited to the equipment bid for successfully in international bidding by domestic enterprises directly or jointly with foreign enterprises and the equipment subcontracted to other domestic enterprises by successful bidding foreign enterprises or domestic enterprises and doesn't include equipment listed in the Catalogue of Import Goods Not Exempted from Duties for Foreign Investment Projects.

(2) This levy and exemption nature does not apply to the projects approved according to the procedure stipulated by the state before December 31, 1997 for use of loans of foreign governments and international financial organizations and this levy and exemption nature is coded “609”.

●国家鼓励发展的内外资项目进口设备

● Equipment imported for domestic and foreign – funded projects encouraged by the state

一、定义及代码

国家鼓励发展的内外资项目进口设备指自1998年1月1日起对按国家规定程序审批并出具确认书的国家鼓励发展的国内投资项目和外商投资项目，以及从1999年9月1日起按国家规定程序审批的外商投资研究开发中心、中西部省、自治区、直辖市利用外资优势产业和优势项目目录的项目，在投资总额内进口的自用设备和按合同随设备进口的技术及数量合理的配套件、备件。

本征免性质代码为“789”，简称“鼓励项目”。

1. Definition and code

Equipment imported for domestic and foreign – funded projects encouraged by the state refers to equipment imported within total investments for self use for domestic and foreign – funded projects approved according to the prescribed procedure of the state with a confirmation from January 1, 1998 and for projects in the directories of industries and projects fit for foreign investments published by foreign investment study and development centers, provinces and autonomous regions in Central and West China and municipalities directly under the Central Government and approved according to the prescribed procedure of the state from September 1, 1999 as well as technology, accessories and spare parts imported together with the equipment in reasonable quantities according to contracts.

The code of this collection and exemption nature is "789" and the shortened form of it is "encouraged projects".

二、适用范围

（一）本征免性质适用于1998年1月1日后国家鼓励发展的国内投资项目和外商投资项目，以及从1999年9月1日起，按国家规定程序审批的外商投资研究开发中心、中西部省、自治区、直辖市利用外资优势产业和优势项目目录的项目，在投资总额内进口的自用设备和按合同随设备进口的技术及数量合理的配套件、备件。

（二）本征免性质不适用：

1. 1997年12月31日前批准设立的外商投资企业进口货物，其征免性质代码为“601”、“602”、“603”。

2. 1997年12月31日前按国家规定程序批准的利用外

2. Scope of application

(1) This collection and exemption nature is applicable to domestic and foreign – invested projects encouraged by the state since January 1, 1998 and projects fit for foreign investments published by foreign investment study and international financial organizations and West China and municipalities directly under the Central Government and approved according to the prescribed procedure of the state from September 1, 1999 as well as technology, accessories and spare parts imported together with the equipment in reasonable quantities according to contracts.

(2) This collection and exemption nature is not applicable to:

a. Goods imported by foreign – invested enterprises established with approval before December 31, 1997, the code of the collection and exemption nature for which is "601", "602" and "603".

b. Loans from foreign governments and international financial organizations ap-

国政府贷款和国际金融组织贷款项目,其征免性质代码为“609”。

3. 外商投资企业投资额度外利用自有资金进口货物,其征免性质代码为“799”。

●外商投资额度外利用自有资金进口设备、备件、配件

一、定义及代码

外商投资额度外利用自有资金进口设备、备件、配件是指已设立的鼓励类和原限制乙类外商投资企业、外商投资研究开发中心、先进技术型和产品出口型外商投资企业技术改造,在投资总额以外利用自有资金,在原批准的生产经营范围内进口国内不能生产或性能不能满足需要的自用设备及其配套的技术、配件、备件。

本征免性质代码为“799”,简称“自有资金”。

二、适用范围

(一)本征免性质适用于已设立的鼓励类和原限制乙类外商投资企业、外商投资研究开发中心、先进技术型和产品出口型外商投资企业(以下简称“五类企业”)技术改造。

在投资总额以外利用自有资金,在原批准的生产经营范围内进口国内不能生产或性能不能满足需要的自用设备及其配套的技术、配件、备件。

1. 资金来源

“五类企业”投资总额以外的自有资金,具体是指企业储备基金、发展基金、折旧和税后利润。

2. 进口商品用途

在原批准的生产经营范围内,对本企业原有设备更新(不包括成套设备和生产线)或维修。

成套设备是指以完成某零、部件或产品生产加工或装配全部过程所有工序所需的全部设备,生产线是指用于完成某种产品一道或多道工序的、有一定节拍要求的、以一定方式连续生产的设备组合。

3. 进口商品范围

国内不能生产或性能不能满足需要的设备(即不属于《国内投资项目不予免税的进口商品目录》的商品),以及与上述设备配套的技术、配件、备件,包括随设备进口或单独进口的。

(二)本征免性质不适用

1. 1997年12月31日前批准设立的外商投资企业进口货物,征免性质代码为“601”、“602”、“603”。

2. 国家鼓励发展的外资项目项下进口货物,其征免性质代码为“789”。

●救灾捐赠进口物资

一、定义及代码

救灾捐赠进口物资指外国民间团体、企业、友好人士和华侨、香港居民、台湾、澳门同胞及外籍华人无偿向我境内受灾地区捐赠的直接用于救灾的物资。

proved according to the prescribed procedure of the state before December 31, 1997, the code of the collection and exemption nature for which is "609".

c. Goods imported with self funds beyond total investments of foreign - invested enterprises, the code of the collection and exemption nature for which is "799".

● Equipment, spare parts and accessories imported with self funds beyond total foreign investments

1. Definition and code

Equipment, spare parts and accessories imported with self funds beyond total foreign investments mean equipment and related technology, accessories and spare parts imported by established foreign - invested enterprises in the encouraged category and originally restricted Category B, foreign investment study and development centers, advanced technology and export - oriented foreign - invested enterprises, for technical transformation, with self funds beyond total investments for self use in the originally approved production scope, which cannot be produced domestically or whose domestic counterparts cannot meet needs.

The code of this collection and exemption nature is "799" and the shortened form of it is "self funds".

2. Scope of application

(1) This collection and exemption nature is applicable to established foreign - invested enterprises in the encouraged category and originally restricted Category B, foreign investment study and development centers and advanced technology and export - oriented foreign - invested enterprises for technical transformation (shortened to "five categories of enterprises hereunder).

Equipment and related technology, accessories and spare parts imported with self funds beyond total investments for self use in the originally approved production scope, which cannot be produced domestically or whose domestic counterparts cannot meet needs.

a. Sources of funds

Self funds beyond total investments in the "five categories of enterprises" refer specifically to enterprises´reserve funds, development funds, depreciation and after - tax profits.

b. Use of imported commodities

Updating or maintenance of original equipment of an enterprise in the originally approved production scope (not including complete equipment and production lines).

Complete equipment refers to all equipment needed to finish all the process of producing or assembling a spare part, a component or product and production lines refer to the combination of production equipment for finishing one or more processes of producing a product continuously in a certain rhythm and by a certain way.

c. Scope of imported commodities

Equipment which cannot be produced domestically or whose domestic counterparts cannot meet needs (i. e. not commodities falling into the Catalogue of Not Duty - Free Commodities for Foreign - Invested Projects and related technology, accessories and spare parts imported together with the above equipment or imported separately.

(2) This collection and exemption nature is not applicable to:

a. Goods imported by foreign - invested enterprises established with approval before December 31, 1997, the code of the collection and exemption nature is "601","602" and"603".

b. Goods imported for foreign - invested projects encouraged by the state, the code of the collection and exemption nature for which is "789".

● Donations imported for disaster relief

1. Definition and code

Donations imported for disaster relief refer to materials donated free of charge by foreign non - governmental bodies, enterprises, friendly persons, overseas Chinese, Hong Kong residents, Taiwan and Macao compatriots and Chinese of foreign

本征免性质代码为“801”，简称“救灾捐赠”。

nationalities to domestic disaster areas directly for disaster relief.

The code of this collection and exemption nature is "801" and the shortened form of it is "donations for disaster relief".

二、适用范围

2. Scope of application

（一）本征免性质适用范围

(1) This collection and exemption nature is applicable to:

1. 外国民间团体、企业、友好人士和华侨、香港居民、台湾、澳门同胞及外籍华人无偿向我境内受灾地区捐赠的直接用于救灾的物资。

a. Materials donated free of charge by foreign non – governmental bodies, enterprises, friendly persons, overseas Chinese, Hong Kong residents, Taiwan and Macao compatriots and Chinese of foreign nationalities to domestic disaster areas directly for disaster relief.

2. 享受救灾捐赠物资进口免税的区域限于新华社对外发布和民政部《中国灾情信息》公布的受灾地区。

b. Areas which can import disaster relief donations duty – freely are those published by the Xinhua News Agency and Information on Disasters in China published by the Ministry of Civil Affairs.

●境外向我境内无偿捐赠用于扶贫慈善的免税进口物资

● Duty – free overseas materials donated to our country for poverty alleviation and charities

一、定义代码

1. Definition and code

扶贫、慈善性捐赠物资是指境外捐赠人无偿向我国境内捐赠的直接用于扶贫、慈善事业的进口物资。

Materials donated to our country for poverty alleviation and charities refer to imported materials donated by overseas donors free of charge directly for poverty alleviation and charities in our country.

征免性质代码为“802”，简称“扶贫慈善”。

The code of the collection and exemption nature is "802" and the shortened form of it is "poverty alleviation and charities".

二、适用范围

2. Scope of application

（一）本征免性质适用于境外捐赠人无偿向我国境内捐赠的直接用于扶贫、慈善事业的进口物资。

(1) This collection and exemption nature is applicable to imported materials donated by overseas donors free of charge directly for poverty alleviation and charities in our country.

1. 境外捐赠人应为中华人民共和国关境外的自然人、法人或者其他组织。

a. Overseas donors shall be natural persons, legal persons or other organizations outside the People's Republic of China.

2. 受赠人应为国务院有关部门和各省、自治区、直辖市人民政府，以及从事人道救助和发展扶贫、慈善事业为宗旨的全国性的社会团体，包括中国红十字会总会、全国妇女联合会、中国残疾人联合会、中华慈善总会、中国初级卫生保健基金会和宋庆龄基金会。

b. Donees shall be departments under the State Council, people's governments of provinces, autonomous regions and municipalities directly under the Central Government and national social bodies for humanitarian relief and development of the poverty alleviation cause and charities, including the Red Cross Society of China, All – China Women's Federation, China Disabled Persons' Association, China Charity Federation, Primary HealthCare Foundation of China and Song Qingling Foundation.

3. 使用人应为捐赠物资的直接使用者或负责分配该捐赠物资的单位或个人。

c. Users shall be direct uses of donated materials or units or individuals in charge of distributing donated materials.

（二）扶贫、慈善公益性事业物资包括：

(2) Materials for poverty alleviation and charities include:

1. 新的衣服、被褥、鞋帽、帐篷、手套、睡袋、毛毯及其他维持基本生活的必需用品等。

a. New clothes, quilts, cotton – padded mattress, shoes, caps, tents, gloves, sleeping bags, blankets and other necessities for maintaining basic living.

2. 食品类及饮用品（调味品、水产品、水果、饮料、烟酒等除外）。

b. Food and beverages (seasoning, aquatic products, fruits and beverages, excluding cigarettes and wine).

3. 医疗类包括直接用于治疗特困患者疾病或贫困地区治疗地方病及基本医疗卫生、公共环境卫生所需的基本医疗药品、基本医疗器械、医疗书籍和资料。

c. Medical category, including basic medicines, basic medical devices and medical books and materials directly used for treating extremely poor patients or local diseases in poverty – stricken areas and required for basic health and public environment sanitation.

其中，“基本医疗药品”是指用于急救、治疗、防疫、消毒、抗菌等用途的药品和人体移植用的器官，但不包括保健药和营养药；“基本医疗器械”是指诊疗器械、手术器械、卫生检测器械、伤残修复器械、防疫防护器械、消毒灭菌器械。

Therein "basic medicines" refer to medicines used for first aid, treatment, epidemic prevention, disinfection and bacterial resistance and organs used for human transplants, excluding healthcare and nutritional medicines; "basic medical devices" refer to diagnostic instruments, surgical instruments, health testing equipment, equipment for repairing disabilities, epidemic prevention equipment, disinfection and sterilization equipment.

4. 直接用于公共图书馆、公共博物馆、各类职业学校、高中、初中、小学、幼儿园教育的教学仪器、教材、图书、资料和一般学习用品。

d. Teaching instruments, teaching materials, books, materials and ordinary learning appliances directly used in public libraries, public museums, various kinds of vocational schools, senior high schools, junior high schools, primary schools, and kindergartens.

其中，“公共图书馆和公共博物馆”是指经省级以上文化行政管理部门认定、向社会开放的县（市）级以上单位管理的公益性图书馆或经省级以上文物行政管理部门认定、向公众开放的县（市）级以上单位管理的各类公益性博

Therein "public libraries and public museums" refer to public welfare libraries managed by units at the county (municipal) or higher level and opened to the society which are recognized by cultural administrations at the provincial or higher level or public welfare museums managed by units at the county (municipal) or

物馆；

higher level and opened to the society which are recognized by cultural administrations at the provincial or higher level.

“教学仪器”是指《扶贫、慈善性捐赠物资免征进口税收暂行办法》规定的学校、幼儿园专用于教学的检验、观察、计量、演示用的仪器和器具；“一般学习用品”是指《扶贫、慈善性捐赠物资免征进口税收暂行办法》规定的学校、幼儿园教学和学生专用的文具、教具、婴幼儿玩具、标本、模型、切片、各类学习软件、实验室用器皿和试剂、学生服装（含鞋帽）和书包等。

"Teaching instruments" refer to testing, observation, measurement and demonstration instruments and devices used for teaching by schools and kindergartens mentioned in the Interim Measure Concerning Import – duty Exemption to Poverty – relief and Charity Donation Materials; "ordinary learning articles" refer to stationery, teaching aids, toys for infants, specimens, models, slices, various software for learning, laboratory vessels and reagents, students´ clothes (including shoes and caps) and schoolbags used by schools and kindergartens mentioned in the Interim Measure Concerning Import – duty Exemption to Poverty – relief and Charity Donation Materials for teaching and used by students.

5. 直接用于环境保护的专用仪器。具体是指环保系统专用的空气质量与污染源废气监测仪器及治理设备、环境水质与污水监测仪器及治理设备、环境污染事故应急监测仪器、固体废物监测仪器及处置设备、辐射防护与电磁辐射监测仪器及设备、生态保护监测仪器及设备、噪声及振动监测仪器和实验室通用分析仪器及设备。

e. Instruments directly for environmental protection refer specifically to environmental protection system, air quality and pollution source gas monitoring instruments and treatment equipment, environmental water quality and sewage monitoring and treatment equipment, environmental pollution emergency monitoring instruments, solid waste monitoring instruments and disposal equipment, radiation protection and electromagnetic radiation monitoring instruments and equipment, ecological protection monitoring instruments and equipment, noise and vibration monitoring instruments and universal laboratory analytic instruments and equipment.

6. 经国务院批准的其他直接用于扶贫、慈善事业的物资。

f. Other materials approved by the State Council directly for poverty alleviation and charities.

上述物资不包括国家停止减免税的 20 种商品、汽车、生产性设备、生产性原材料及半成品等。

The above materials dont include 20 kinds of commodities, vehicles, productive equipment, productive raw materials and semi – finished products whose reduction of and exemption from duties are stopped by the state.

捐赠物资应为新品，在捐赠物资内不得夹带有害环境、公共卫生和社会道德及政治渗透等违禁物品。

Donated materials shall be new products and shall not contain prohibited articles which endanger environment, public health and social morality and are used for political penetration.

（三）本征免性质不适用：

1. 无偿援助物资，其征免性质代码为“201”。

2. 残疾人专用品、残疾人专用设备及专用生产设备，其征免性质代码为“413”。

(3) This collection and exemption nature is not applicable to:

a. Materials donated free of charge, the code of the collection and exemption nature for which is "201".

b. Articles, equipment and production equipment for the disabled, the code of the collection and exemption nature for which is "412".

●进口艾滋病病毒药品

进口抗艾滋病病毒药品指对于卫生部委托进口的抗艾滋病病毒药品免进口关税和进口环节增值税政策。

本征免性质代码“803”，简称“抗艾滋病药品”。

● Imported AIDS virus drugs

Imported anti – AIDS drugs refers to the Ministry of Health commissioned by the import of anti – HIV drugs free of import tariffs and import value – added tax policy

The code of this collection and exemption nature is "803" and the shortened form of it is "anti AIDS drugs "

●享受进口税收优惠政策的进口种子（苗）、种畜（禽）、鱼种（苗）和种用野生动植物种源

享受进口税收优惠政策的进口种子（苗）、种畜（禽）、鱼种（苗）和种用野生动植物种源指根据规定进口种子（苗）、种畜（禽）、鱼种（苗）和种用野生动植物种源免征进口环节增值税政策。

本征免性质代码“811”，简称“种苗种畜”

● Enjoy the preferential import tax policies of imported seed (seedling), animal (avian), fish (seedlings) and a wildlife species source

Enjoy the preferential import tax policies of imported seed (seedling), animal (avian), fish (seedlings) and a wildlife provenance refers to according to the provisions of imported seed (seedling), animal (avian), fish (seedlings) and a wildlife species source of exemption of import value – added tax policy.

The code of this collection and exemption nature is "811" and the shortened form of it is "Seedling and breeding stock "

●中央储备粮油免征进口环节增值税政策

中央储备粮油免征进口环节增值税政策指对中储粮总公司及其子公司在免税进口额度范围内进口的粮油，予以免征进口环节增值税。

本征免性质代码“818”，简称“中央储备粮油”。

● The central reserve grain and oil of exemption of import value – added tax policy

The central reserve grain and oilof exemption of import value – added tax policy refers to the Grain and oil reserves corporation and its subsidiaries in the duty – free import quota import of grain, to be exempt from vat.

The code of this collection and exemption nature is "818" and the shortened form of it is "The central reserve Grain and oil"

●进口科研教学用图书资料

一、定义及代码

进口科研教学用图书资料指根据规定对中国图书进出口(集团)总公司等7家图书进出口公司为科研单位、大专院校进口用于科教学的图书、文献、报刊及其他资料(包括只读光盘、缩微平片、胶卷、地球资料卫星照片、科技和教学声像制品)免征进口环节增值税。

本征免性质代码“819”,简称“科教图书”。

二、适用范围

享受该项进口税收优惠政策的企业为中国图书进出口(集团)总公司及其具有独立法人资格的子公司、中国出版对外贸易总公司、北京中科进出口有限责任公司、中国科技资料进出口总公司和中国国际图书贸易集团有限公司等7家图书进出口公司。

● Import scientific research teaching Library information

1. Definition and code

Import scientific research teaching books according to provisions of the China Book Import and export (Group) Corporation 7 Book Import and export company for scientific research units, universities and colleges are imported for teaching books, literature, the press and other information (including CD - ROM, microfiche, microfilm, earth resources satellite photos, science and teaching audio - visual products shall be exempted from import link) value added tax.

The code of this collection and exemption nature is "819" and the shortened form of it is "Science books"

2. Scope of application

Enjoy the preferential import tax policies of enterprise for China Book Import and export (Group) Corporation and has an independent legal personality of the company, the China National Publishing Industry Trading Corp, Beijing branch in the import and export of a limited liability company, information science and technology of China Import and Export Corporation and the China International Book Trading Corporation company 7 Books Import and export corporation.

●经核准的航空公司进口维修用航空器材

一、定义及代码

经核准的航空公司进口维修用航空器材是指经国务院批准,由民航总局确认的营运国际和港澳航线的国内航空公司进口的维修用航空器材。

本征免性质代码“888”,简称“航材减免”。

二、适用范围

(一)本征免性质仅限经国务院批准,由民航总局确认的营运国际和港澳航线的国内航空公司。

(二)进口维修用航空器材限于甩于维修飞机机载设备及其零部件所进口的航空器材,以及维修飞机所必需的消耗材料,包括:

1. 发动机及其零部件、附件。
2. 辅助动力装置(APU)及其零部件、附件。
3. 起落架及其零部件、附件。
4. 其他飞机零部件、附件。
5. 维修飞机所必需的润滑油、油漆。
6. 上述设备、装置和附件送境外维修时所更换的零部件及附件。

进口维修用的飞机驾驶舱内的设备及其零部件,以及固定安装在飞机上且为飞行和载客、载货运输所必须的设备及其零部件(例如,飞机上的液晶显示屏、机上用照明灯具、飞机轮胎等),属于可享受进口税收优惠政策的商品范围。但移动式餐车等非固定安装在飞机上的物品不属于减税商品范围。

● Aviation supplies imported by approved airlines for maintenance

1. Definition and code

Aviation supplies imported by approved airlines for maintenance refer to aviation supplies imported for maintenance by domestic airlines which run international, Hong Kong and Macao routes with approval of the State Council and confirmation of CAAC.

The code of this collection and exemption nature is 888 and the shortened form of it is reduction and exemption for aviation supplies.

2. Scope of application

(1) This collection and exemption nature is only applicable to domestic airlines which run international, Hong Kong and Macao routes with approval of the State Council and confirmation of CAAC.

(2) Aviation supplies imported for maintenance are limited to those imported for maintenance of equipment carried by aeroplanes and consumables needed for maintenance of aeroplanes, including:

a. Engines and related spare parts, components and accessories.
b. Auxiliary power units and related spare parts, components and accessories.
c. Undercarriages and related spare parts, components and accessories.
d. Other spare parts, components and accessories of aeroplanes.
e. Lubricating oil and paint needed for maintenance of aeroplanes
f. Spare parts, components and accessories changed when the above equipment, devices and accessories are sent abroad for maintenance.

Equipment and related spare parts and components imported for maintenance of aircraft cockpits and equipment and related spare parts and components imported for mounting on aeroplanes which are necessary for carrying passengers and cargos (such as LCD, lighting and tyres) fall into the scope of commodities which enjoy the preferential import duty policy. But movable dining cars and other articles which are not mounted on aeroplanes dont fall into this scope.

●国务院特准减免税的进出口货物

一、定义及代码

国务院特准减免税的进出口货物指经国务院特案批准予以减免税的进出口货物。

本征免性质代码“898”,简称“国批减免”。

二、适用范围

本征免性质仅限国务院特案批准予以减免税的特殊行

● Duty - free imports and exports with special approval of the State Council

1. Definition and code

Duty - free imports and exports with special approval of the State Council refer to goods imported and exported duty - freely with special approval of the State Council.

This collection and exemption nature is "898" and the shortened form of it is "reduction and exemption with state approval".

2. Scope of application

This collection and exemption nature is only applicable to industries or impor-

业或进出口货物，如国家计划内进口的化肥、饲料、图书资料、种子（苗）、种畜（禽）、鱼苗和非盈利性种用野生动植物、航空公司进口或租赁的飞机等。

ted and exported goods which are granted reduction of and exemption from duties specially by the State Council, such as chemical fertilizers, fodders, books and materials, seeds (seedlings), breeding stock (poultry), fries, non－profitable wild animals and plants for breeding and aeroplanes imported or leased by airlines.

●例外减免税进出口货物

● Goods whose import and export duties are reduced or exempted exceptionally

一、定义及代码

例外减免税进出口货物指无法归入以上各类列名征免性质的减免税进出口货物。

本征免性质代码“999”，简称“例外减免”。

二、管理规定

（一）按海关总署文件或通知的具体内容执行。

（二）减免税办理程序：

申请减免税的企业或单位持批准文件和其他有关单证，到所在地海关办理减免税审批手续。

海关核发“进出口货物征免税证明”，进出口地海关凭以办理货物的减免税手续。

1. Definition and code

Goods whose import and export duties are reduced or exempted exceptionally refer to duty－free imports and exports which cannot be classified into any of the above－mentioned collection and exemption natures.

The code of this collection and exemption nature is "999" and the shortened form of it is "exceptional reduction and exemption".

"2、Management regulations

(1) According to the General Administration of Customs document or notice the specific content implementation.

(2) Tax reduction and exemption Handling procedures.

Tax relief for enterprises or units with the approval documents and other relevant documents, to the local customs for approval of duty reduction or exemption formalities.

" Exemption certificate for import and export goods" by the customs Issued, import and export customs with the tax reduction and exemption for goods.

征减免税方式代码表说明

Table of Levy mode

征减免税方式是指进出口货物征税、减税、免税或特案处理的方式。

一、征减免税方式的分类

征减免税方式分为照章征税、折半征税、全免、特案减免、随征免性质、保证金、保证函、折半补税，各种方式分别用不同的代码标识。

二、征减免税方式代码说明

（一）照章征税

指对进出口货物依照法定税率计征各类税、费。代码“1”

（二）折半征税

指依照主管海关签发的《进出口货物征免税证明》或海关总署的通知，对进出口货物依照法定税率折半计征收税款。代码“2”

（三）全免

指依照主管海关签发的《进出口货物征免税证明》或其他有关规定，对进出口货物免征关税和增值税，但消费税是否免征依批文规定办理。代码“3”

（四）特案减免

指依照主管海关签发的《进出口货物征免税证明》或其他有关规定的税率或完税价计征关税、增值税和消费税。代码“4”。

（五）随征免性质

用于特定监管方式进出口的货物按特殊计税公式或税率计征关税、增值税和消费税。代码“5”。

Levy and exemption ways refer to levy, reduction and exemption of duties on imported and exported goods or treatments for special cases.

1. Classification of levy modes

Levy modes include levy taxation according to tax rules, duty reduction by half, exemption, exemption and reduction in special cases, of exemption nature, deposit, guarantee, overdue tax by half, Various ways of respectively different identification code.

2. Explanation on the codes of Levy modes

1. Levy taxation according to rules in force

Import and export goods should be levied according to lawful duty rate. The code is"1".

2. Duty reduction by half

It refers to the levy of tariff and value-added tax on import and export goods on half duty rate, but levy of excise according to rules. The code is"2".

3. Exemption

It refers to the exemption of tariff and value-added tax on import and export goods but whether or not tax levy excise according to the *Tax Levy and Exemption Certificate of the Customs of the People's Republic of China* issued by the Customs in charge or notices issued by Custom of the People's Republic of China. The code is"3".

4. Reduction and exemption in special cases

Refer to calculation and collection of duties, VAT and consumption tax according to the Certificate of Levy and Exemption of Duties on Imported and Exported Goods issued by the competent customs office or other relevant tariff rates or duty－paid prices. The code is "4".

5. Levy taxation on goods of exemption nature

Used to calculate and levy customs duties, VAT and consumption tax on goods imported and exported in special regulatory ways according to special tax formulas or tax rates. The code is "5".

（六）保证金

经海关准予担保放行的货物收取保证金。代码“6”。

（七）保证函

经海关准予担保放行的货物凭保函办理。代码“7”。

6. Deposit

Collect security deposits for goods that can be cleared by the Customs with securities. The code is "6".

7. Guarantee

Handle goods that can be cleared by the Customs with securities against letters of guarantee. The code is "7".

运输方式代码表说明

一、定义

运输方式包括实际运输方式和海关规定的特殊运输方式，前者指货物实际进出境的运输方式，按进出境所使用的运输工具分类；后者指货物无实际进出境的运输方式，按货物在境内的流向分类。

二、运输方式分类说明

（一）水路运输：代码“2”，指利用船舶在国内外港口之间，通过固定的航区和航线进行货物运输的一种方式。

（二）铁路运输：代码“3”，指利用铁路承担进出口货物运输的一种方式。

（三）公路运输：代码“4”，指利用汽车承担进出口货物运输的一种方式。

（四）航空运输：代码“5”，指利用航空器承运进出口货物的一种方式。

（五）邮件运输：代码“6”，指通过邮局寄运货物进出口的一种方式。

（六）其他运输：代码“9”，除上述几种运输方式以外的货物进出口运输方式。

包括电缆、电网、管道（包括输油、输水管道）、输送带、人力、驮畜等。

（七）用于标志境内进出和退回保税区或保税仓库等区域的运输方式代码如下：

1. 境内非保税区运入保税区货物和保税区退区货物，填报“非保税区”（代码0）；

2. 境内存入出口监管仓库和出口监管仓库退仓货物，填报“监管仓库”（代码1）；

3. 保税区运往境内非保税区货物，填报“保税区”（代码7）；

4. 保税仓库转内销货物，填报“保税仓库”（代码8）；

5. 境内运入深港西部通道港方口岸区的货物，填报“边境特殊海关作业区”（代码H）；

6. 从境内保税物流中心外运入中心或从中心运往境内中心外的货物，填报“物流中心”（代码W）；

7. 从境内运入园区或从园区运往境内的货物，填报“物流园区”（代码X）；

8. 从保税港区（不包括直通港区）运往区外和区外运入保税港区的货物。填报“保税港区”（代码Y）

9. 出口加工区：代码“Z”，指出口加工区运往境内加工区外和区外运入出口加工区的货物。

Code table of Mode of Transport

1. **Definition**

Mode of transport refers to the categorizations of means of transportation when goods cross borders. It includes non-bonded area, supervised warehouse, by sea, by rail, by road, by air, bonded area by post, bonded warehouse and others, ten categories in all.

2. **Explanation on the categorization of mode of transport**

(1) By sea: it refers to the mode of transportation of goods by means of fixed sailing areas and courses between ports home and abroad

(2) By rail: it refers to the mode of transportation of goods by means of railways.

(3) By road: it refers to the mode of transportation of goods by means of trucks.

(4) By air: it refers to the mode of transportation of import and export goods by means of aircrafts.

(5) By post: it refers to the mode of transportation of import and export goods by mailing through the post office.

(6) Other modes of transport: it refers to the other modes of transportation of import and export goods except the ones above mentioned.

Include cables, grids, pipelines (including oil and water pipelines), conveyance belts, manpower, beasts of burden, etc.

(7) Used for marking within borders import and export , returned to bonded zone or bonded warehouse of code of mode of transport as follows:

a. Fill "non – bonded zone" (code 0) for goods transported from domestic non – bonded zones into bonded zones and goods returned from bonded zones;

b. Fill "warehouse under surveillance" (code 1) for goods transported from non – bonded zones into warehouses under export surveillance and goods returned from warehouses under export surveillance;

c. Fill "bonded zone" (code 7) for goods transported into domestic non – bonded zones;

d. Fill "bonded warehouse" (code 8) for goods to be sold domestically in bonded warehouses;

e. Fill "special customs operation area in the border" (code H) for goods transported from the inland to the Hong Kong port of the Shenzhen – Hong Kong West Passage.

f. Fill "logistics center" (code W) for goods transported from outside domestic bonded logistics centers into the centers or vice versa;

g. Fill "logistics park" (code X) for goods transported from outside domestic bonded logistics parks into the parks or vice versa;

h. Fill"Bonded Port zone"(code Y) for goods transport from outside domestic bonded prots into ports(excluding direct ports) and goods transported outside from the ports.

i. Export processing zones code"Z" refer to export processing zones to the domestic processing zone and zone carried into export processing zone goods.

关区代码表说明

一、关区代码表用于填报进出口报关单的进出口口岸海关的名称。

《关区代码表》由两部分组成，即关区代码和关区名称。

关区代码由四位数字组成，前两位采用海关统计的直属海关关别代码，后两位为隶属海关的代码。

关区名称即各口岸海关中文名称。

二、使用关区代码时应注意的问题。

代码表中只有直属海关关别和代码的，可以填报直属海关名称和代码（见例1）；如果有隶属海关关别和代码时，必须填报隶属海关关别和代码（见例2）。

例1：在太原海关办理货物进出口报关手续，本栏目可填报“太原海关”，代码“0500”。

例2：在上海浦江海关办理货物进出口报关手续，本栏目不得填报“上海海关”，代码“2200”，必须填报“上海浦江海关”、代码“2201”。

Code Table of Mainland Customs Port

1. Code Table of Mainland Customs Port is used for filling in the names of the customs ports in Customs Declaration Form.

Code Table of Mainland Customs Port consists of two parts, one is code of customs port and the other is name of customs port.

Code of customs port consists of a figure of four digits, the first two of which regards the code for the direct customs port in customs statistics; the second two of which regards the code for the subject customs.

Name of customs port is the Chinese name of the customs port.

2. Points worth attention regarding the use of codes of customs ports.

Filling the Code Table on Mainland Customs Port, if there is only direct customs port, only the name and code of the direct customs port is required (see Sample 1); if there is only subject customs port, only the name and code of the subject customs port required (see Sample 2).

Sample 1: at Taiyuan Customhouse,“太原海关”, Code “0500” is sufficient in import and export declaration procedures.

Sample 2: at Shanghai Pujiang Customhouse, “上海海关”,Code“2200” is insufficient thus prohibited. “上海浦江海关”, Code“2201” is required.

国内地区代码表说明

一、国内地区代码表用于填报进出口报关单的境内目的地和境内货源地。

国内地区代码由5位数构成，1至4位数为行政区划代码，其中第1、2位数表示省（自治区、直辖市）；第3、4位数表示省辖市（地区、省直辖行政单位）、包括省会城市、计划单列城市，沿海开放城市。

国内地区代码第5位数为省辖市（地区、省直辖行政单位）经济区划代码：

“1”表示经济特区；

“2”表示经济技术开发区：（包括上海浦东新区、海南洋浦经济开发区）；

“3”表示高新技术开发区；

“4”表示保税区；

“5”出口加工区；

“6”保税港区；

“7”保税物流园区

“9”其他地区。

Code Table of Mainland District

1. Code Table on Mainland District is used for filling in the domestic destination and domestic origin of goods in the Customs Declaration Form.

Mainland district code consists of a figure of five digits. The first four is the administrative district code of where the company is situated. Among them, the first and second digits represent province (municipality and autonomous region); the third and fourth ones represent cities of province (district, administrative units under direct government of the province) 、cities、separate planning cities、coastal cities open to the outside world. The code used is in accordance to the national standards.

The fifth digits in domestic area codes are the economic division codes of cities directly under provinces (regions and administrative units directly under provinces):

“1” represents special economic zone;

“2” represents economic and technological development district;

“3” represents high technology development district;

“4” represents bonded area;

“5” represents export processing zones;

“6” represents bonded port;

“7” represents bornded logistics zones;

“9” represents others except the ones above mentioned.

结汇方式代码表说明

一、定义

结汇方式是出口货物发货人或其代理通过银行收结外汇的方式。

Code Table of Mode of Foreign Exchange Collection

1. Definition

Mode of foreign exchange collection refers to the ways for the goods shipper or its agent to get foreign exchange through banks

二、《结汇方式代码表》结构及说明

(一)《结汇方式代码表》由两部分组成,即结汇方式代码和结汇方式名称。

(二)结汇方式代码分为汇付、托收、信用证和其他。

1. 汇付包括:

(1)信汇:买方将货款交给进口地银行,由银行开具付款委托书,邮寄出口地银行,委托其向卖方付款。代码"1"

(2)电汇:进口地银行应买方申请,直接用电报发出付款委托书,委托出口地银行向卖方付款。代码"2"

(3)票汇:买方向进口地银行购买银行汇票径寄卖方,由卖方或其指定的人持票向出口地有关银行取款。代码"3"

汇付从时间上分预付和后付。预付即卖方装运货物前,买方先将货款汇结卖方;后付即卖方先交货,在买方收到货物或单据后才汇付货款。

2. 托收包括:

(1)付款交单(D/P):指卖方托收时指示托收行,只有在买方付清货款时才交出单据。代码"4"

(2)承兑交单(D/A):指买方承兑汇票后即可取得单据,提取货物,待汇票到期时才付货款。代码"5"

3. 信用证(L/C):信用证是银行在买卖双方之间保证付款的凭证。银行根据买方的申请书,向卖方开出保证付款的信用证,即只要卖方提交符合信用证要求的单据,银行就保证付款。代码"6"

4. 先出后结:代码"7"

5. 先结后出:代码"8"

6. 其他:指除上述以外的结汇方式。代码"9"

2. Structure of and explanation about Code Table of Mode of Foreign Exchange Collection

(1) Code Table of Mode of Foreign Exchange Collection consists of two parts: the code for mode of foreign exchange collection and the designation for mode of foreign exchange collection.

(2) The code for mode of foreign exchange collection includes remittance, collection, letter of credit and others.

a. Remittance includes:

(a) Mail transfer: the buyer sends money to a bank in the import country. The bank opens a payment order and mails it to the relevant bank in the export country, consigning the latter to pay the seller.

(b) Telegraphic transfer: the buyer applies to a bank in the import country and telegraphs the payment order and consigns the relevant bank in the export country to pay the seller.

(c) Demand draft: the buyer purchases bank draft in a bank in the import country and mails it to the seller. The seller or the one appointed by the seller that holds the bank draft withdraws money from the relevant bank in the export country.

Temporally speaking, remittance includes advance payment and deferred payment. Advance payment is to pay the seller through remittance before the seller ships the goods; deferred payment is that the seller ships goods first before getting paid and the buyer pays after receiving the goods or the receipt

b. Collection includes:

(a) Documents against payment (D/P): upon the direction of the seller, the collection bank gives the documents to the buyer only if the purchaser pays off.

(b) Documents against acceptance (D/A): upon acceptance the buyer gets the documents to pick up goods and pays off when the acceptance is due.

c. Letter of Credit (L/C): letter of credit is a payment warrant made by a bank between the buyer and the seller. Upon the request of the buyer, the bank opens a letter of credit to the seller to assure payment. Once the seller submits the required documents for L/C, the bank will assure payment.

d. Settlement after export.

e. Settlement before export.

f. Other: other means of foreign exchange collection except the one mentioned above.

监管证件代码表说明

一、定义

监管证件名称代码是海关依据我国外贸法律、法规及规章,为便于实施计算机系统管理和便捷通关需求,对实行进出口许可证件管理的货物在海关管理环节须验核的各种进出口许可证件的分类标识。其总和称为监管证件名称代码表。

二、《监管证件名称代码表》结构

《监管证件名称代码表》由两部分组成,即监管证件代码和监管证件名称。例如:代码"1",为进口许可证,如果某一商品编号后注有监管证件"1",则说明在一般贸易项下进口该种商品需申领进口许可证。

三、监管证件名称代码说明

(一)代码"1"——进口许可证:指商务部配额许可证事务局或其授权机关签发的进口许可证。

(二)代码"2"——两用物项和技术进口许可证:指列入《两用物项和技术进口许可证管理目录》的商品,进口时由商务部签发的《两用物项和技术进口许可证》。

(三)代码"3"——两用物项和技术出口许可证:根据

Code Table of the Licensed

1. Definition

Code for the Licensed refers to the categorization, according to relevant customs laws, rules and regulations, of all kinds of import and export licenses which need to be checked in customs management procedures regarding the goods which require import and export licenses, for the purpose of computer system management and efficient customs clearance.

2. The structure of Code Table of the Licensed

Code Table on Licensed consists of two parts: the code for the licensed and the designation for the licensed.

3. Explanations about the codes and designations of the licensed.

(1) Code "1"—— Import License: Import License issued by Quota Licensing Bureau of the Ministry of Commerce or its authorized departments.

(2) Code"2"—— Import License for Dual - use Items and Technologies: Import License for Dual - use Items and Technologies issued by the Ministry of Commerce for importing items listed in the List of Import License for Dual -use Items and Technologies Management.

(3) Code "3"—dual - use item and technical export license: get the license

商务部会同海关总署联合发布《敏感物项和技术出口许可证暂行管理办法》及《敏感物项和技术出口许可证管理目录》,凭商务部签发的敏感物项和技术出口批复到商务部授权的发证机构领取敏感物项和技术出口许可证。

(四)代码"4"——出口许可证:指商务部配额许可证事务局或其授权机关签发的出口许可证。

(五)代码"6"——旧机电产品禁止进口:商品编码后有此代码的商品,其旧品禁止进口。

(六)代码"7"——自动进口许可证或重要工业品证明:指进口商品实行自动进口许可管理,由商务部及其授权机构按责分工签发自动进口许可证。

(七)代码"8"——禁止出口商品:指国务院授权商务部门会同有关部门,依照《中华人民共和国对外贸易法》等有关法律法规,制定、调整并公布的禁止出口货物目录所列商品。商品编码后有此代码的商品禁止出口。

(八)代码"9"——禁止进口商品:指国务院授权对商务部门会同有关部门,依照《中华人民共和国对外贸易法》等有关法律法规,制定、调整并公布的禁止进口货物目录所列商品。商品编码后有此代码的商品禁止进口。

(九)代码"A"——入境货物通关单:指国家质量监督检验检疫机构根据《中华人民共和国进出口商品检验法》、《中华人民共和国动植物检疫法》和《中华人民共和国食品卫生法》等有关法律、法规,对列入《出入境检验检疫机构实施检验检疫的进出境商品目录》的进口商品签发的入境货物通关单。

(十)代码"B"——出境货物通关单:指国家质量监督检验检疫机构根据《中华人民共和国进出口商品检验法》、《中华人民共和国动植物检疫法》和《中华人民共和国食品卫生法》等有关法律、法规,对列入《出入境检验检疫机构实施检验检疫的进出境商品目录》的出口商品签发的出境货物通关单。

(十一)代码"D"——出/入境货物通关单:为履行我国国际义务,制止"冲突钻石"非法交易,国家质检总局、海关总署等六部委联合发布2002年第132号公告,对毛坯钻石进出口实施管理,毛坯钻石进出口时,授权检验检疫机构签发出/入境货物通关单。

(十二)代码"E"——濒危物种允许出口证明书:指根据《中华人民共和国野生动物保护法》及相关法律法规,对列入《国家重点保护野生动物名录》的货物,出口时由国家濒危物种进出口管理办公室或其办事机构签发的濒危物种出口允许证。

(十三)代码"F"——濒危物种允许进口证明书:指根据《中华人民共和国野生动物保护法》及相关法律法规,对列入《国家重点保护野生动物名录》的货物,进口时由国家濒危物种进出口管理办公室或其办事机构签发的濒危物种允许进口证明书。

(十四)代码"G"——易制毒化学品定向出口许可证:

for export of sensitive items and technologies from the licensing body authorized by the Ministry of Commerce with the letter of the ministry approving export of sensitive items and technologies according to the Tentative Measures for Management of License for Export of Sensitive Items and Technologies and the Catalogue for Management of License for Export of Sensitive Items and Technologies published jointly by the Ministry of Commerce and the General Administration of Customs.

(4) Code"4"—— Export License: Export license issued by Quota Licensing Bureau of the Ministry of Commerce or its authorized departments.

(5) Code"6"—— used electro-mechanical products import prohibited: the importing of used electro-mechanical products with this code at the end of its code of goods is prohibited.

(6) Code"7"——Automatic Import License: Importing products are under automatic import license management. The license is issued by the Ministry of Commerce.

(7) Code"8"——export forbidden items: It refers to all the listed items in the export forbidden items list regulated and declared by commerce department and relevant departments authorized by State Department in accordance with such relevant laws and regulations as*Foreign Trade Law of People 's Republic of China* . Products with this code are prohibited to be exported.

(8) Code"9"—— import forbidden items: It refers to all the listed items in the import forbidden items list regulated and declared by commerce department and relevant departments authorized by State Department in accordance with such relevant laws and regulations as*Foreign Trade Law of People 's Republic of China* . Products with this code are prohibited to be imported.

(9) Code "A"—— Customs Clearance of Entry Commodities: It refers to the Customs Clearance of Entry Commodities issued by the administrations of quality supervision, inspection and quarantine for commodities listed in the List of Entry-Exit Commodities under Quality Supervision, Inspection and Quarantine in accordance with such relevant laws and regulations as*Law of the P. R. C. on Import and Export Commodity Inspection* ,*Law of the P. R. C. on Animal and Plant Quarantine* , and*Food Hygiene Law of the People's Republic of China*

(10) Code "B"—— Customs Clearance of Exit Commodities: It refers to the Customs Clearance of Exit Commodities issued by the administrations of quality supervision, inspection and quarantine for commodities listed in the List of Entry-Exit Commodities under Quality Supervision, Inspection and Quarantine in accordance with such relevant laws and regulations as*Law of the P. R. C. on Import and Export Commodity Inspection* ,*Law of the P. R. C. on Animal and Plant Quarantine* , and*Food Hygiene Law of the People's Republic of China* .

(11) Code "D"——Customs Clearance of Entry/Exit Commodities: In order to fulfill our international obligations and to prevent illegal "conflict diamonds" transaction, six departments including State Quality Inspection and Quarantine Bureau and the Custom of the P. R. C. issued Notice No. 132 in 2002 to implement rough diamond import management. Customs Clearance of Entry/Exit Commodities is issued by authorized inspection and quarantine institutes for importing and exporting rough diamonds.

(12) Code "E"—— export permit for endangered wild animals: it refers to the export permit for endangered wild animals issued by the administrative bureau of the Import and Export of Endangered Wild Animals or by other relevant administrative bureaus for exporting items listed in the List of Import/Export Animals and Plants in accordance with*Law of the People's Republic of China on the Protection of Wildlife* and other relevant rules and regulations.

(13) Code "F"—— Import permit for endangered wild animals: it refers to the import permit for endangered wild animals issued by the administrative bureau of the Import and Export of Endangered Wild Animals or by other relevant administrative bureaus for exporting items listed in the List of Import/Export Animals and Plants in accordance with*Law of the People's Republic of China on the Protection of Wildlife* and other relevant rules and regulations.

(14) Code "G" ——Toxic Chemicals Directional License: It refers to the

指列入《向特定国家(地区)出口易制毒化学品管理目录》的商品,向特定国家出口时由商务部签发《易制毒化学品定向出口许可证》。

Toxic Chemicals Directional License issued by the Ministry of Commerce allowing exporting to appointed countries items listed in the List of Toxic Chemicals Management to be exported to appointed countries or regions.

(十五)代码"I"——精神药物进(出)口准许证:根据《中华人民共和国药品管理法》和国务院《精神药品管理办法》及相关法律法规,国家对精神药品的进(出)口实行进(出)口准许证管理制度。对列入"精神药品管制品种目录"的商品,国家药品监督管理局核发《精神药品进(出)口准许证》或《携带麻醉药品、精神药品证明》。

(15) Code "I"—— Psychotropic drug import and export license: according to*Pharmaceutical Administration Law of the People 's Republic of China* and*Management Regulations on Psychotropic Drug* issued by the State Council and other relevant laws and regulations, Psychotropic drug import and export is under licensed management. For the items listed in the List of Controlled Psychotropic Drug,*Psychotropic Drug Import and Export License* or Certificate for holding anesthesia and psychotropic drugs issued by State Drug Administration is required.

(十六)代码"J"——黄金及其制品进出口准许可证或批件:指根据《中华人民共和国金银管理条例》及相关法律法规,对进出口黄金及其制品,由中国人民银行签发的准许进出境证件。

(16) Code "J"—— Gold product export license or the approval of import issued by the People's Bank of China: according to Regulations of the People's Republic of China on the Control of Gold and Silver and other relevant laws and regulations, the importing and exporting of gold and gold products requires the approvals issued by the People's Bank of China.

(十七)代码"L"——药品进(出)口准许证:根据《中华人民共和国反兴奋条例》,国家食品监督管理部门依法对列入兴奋剂目录的蛋白同化制剂、肽类激素等供医疗用的兴奋剂实施进出口管理,签发准予进(出)口的许可证件。

(17) Code "L"—drug import (export) license: the State Food and Drug Administration controls anabolic agents, peptide hormones and other stimulants for medical use according to the Anti - Doping Regulations of the PRC and issues the import (export) license.

(十八)代码"M"——密码产品和设备进口许可证:根据《商用密码管理条例》,对列入《密码产品和含有密码技术的设备进口管理目录》的商品,由国家密码管理局签发进口许可证件。

(18) Code "M"— import license for products and equipment: the State Encryption Administration issues the import license for commodities listed in the Catalogue for Management of Import of Encryption Products and Equipment Containing Cryptography according to the Management Regulations on Commercial Codes.

(十九)代码"O"——自动进口许可证(新旧机电产品):根据商务部、海关总署、国家质检总局2001年第10号令《机电产品进口管理办法》和《机电产品自动进口许可管理实施细则》,进口实行自动进口许可管理的机电产品,进口单位应当在办理海关报关手续前,向商务部或地方外经贸主管机构、部门机电办申领自动进口许可证。

(19) Code "O"—automatic import license (new and old mechanical and electrical products): according to the Measures for Management of Mechanical and Electrical Products (Decree 10, 2001) and the Implementation Rules on Management of Automatic Import Licensing of Mechanical and Electrical Products published by the Ministry of Commerce, the General Administration of Customs and the General Administration of Quality Supervision, Inspection and Quarantine, import units shall apply to the Ministry of Commerce or local foreign economic and trade authorities or departmental mechanical and electrical offices for the automatic import license to import mechanical and electrical products under automatic import licensing management before declaring them to the Customs.

(二十)代码"P"——进口废物批准证书:根据《中华人民共和国固体废物污染环境防治法》和《废物进口环境保护管理暂行规定》及相关法律法规,对列入《国家限制进口的可用作原料的废物目录》的进品商品,由国家环保总局签发固体废物进口许可证。

(20) Code "P"——Certificate of approval for import of wastes: according to law of the People's Republic of China on the Prevention and contrd of Environmental pdlution by Soild Wastes and Temporary Management Regulation on the Protection of Environmental. Pollution by Imported Wastes and other relevant laws and regulations, for imported items listed in the List of Restricted Waste Import used as Materials and in the List of Waste Import Used as Materials undoer Automatil Import license Management, Waste import license issued by the Sate Environmental Protection Administration is repuired.

(二十一)代码"Q"——进口药品通关单:根据《中华人民共和国药品管理法》及相关法律法规,对列入《进口药品管理目录》的药品,国家食品药品监督管理局及其授权机构签发进口药品通关单。

(21) Code "Q"——drug import customs clearance: according to*Pharmaceutical Administration Law of the People 's Republic of China* and other relevant laws and regulations. For drugs listed in the List of Drug Import Management to be imported, Drug Import Customs Clearance issued by the State Drug Administration or the authorized bureaus is required.

(二十二)代码"R"——进口兽药通关单:根据《兽药管理条例》,农业部或兽药进口口岸所在地省级人民政府兽医行政管理部门对列入《进口兽药管理目录》的进口兽药实施监督管理,签发准予进口的许可证件。

(22) Code "R"— customs clearance form for imported veterinary drugs: according to the Regulations on Veterinary Drugs, the Ministry of Agriculture or veterinary administrations of provincial people's governments in charge of the port where veterinary drugs are imported supervises and manages import of veterinary drugs listed in the Catalogue for Management of Imported Drugs and issues the import license.

(二十三)代码"S"——进出口农药登记证明:根据《农药管理条例》及有关法律法规,《中华人民共和国进出口农药登记证明管理名录》和《中华人民共和国进出口列入事先知情同意程序(PIC)农药登记证明管理名录》的商品,进出口时,农业部签发进出口农药登记证明。

(23) Code "S"——pesticide import registration certificate: According to Management Regulations of Pesticides and other relevant laws and regulations, the import and export of items, listed in the List of Import/Export Pesticides Registration Certificate Management of P. R. C. and in the List of Import/Export Pesticides listed in PIC for registration certificate management, require registration cer-

(二十四)代码"T"——银行调运外币现钞进出境许可证:指国家外汇管理局和中国人民银行根据《银行调运外币现钞进出境管理规定》等法律、法规,对允许进出境的外币和人民币现钞签发的许可证件。

(二十五)代码"U"——合法捕捞产品通关证明:进口"实施合法捕捞证明的水产品清单"所列的鱼类,由农业部签发"合法捕捞产品通关证明"。

(二十六)代码"W"——麻醉药品进出口准许证:根据《中华人民共和国药品管理法》和国务院《麻醉药品管理办法》及相关法律法规,国家对麻醉药品的进(出)口实行进(出)口准许证管理制度。对列入"麻醉药品管制品种目录"的商品,国家食品药品监督管理局核发《麻醉药品进(出)口准许证》、或《携带麻醉药品、精神药品证明》。

(二十七)代码"X"——有毒化学品环境管理放行通知单:指列入《中国严格限制的有毒化学品名录》的进出口化学品,由国家环境保护部签发的放行通知单。

(二十八)代码"Y"——原产地证明:是指受惠国政府指定部门签发的证明该货物原产于该国的证明文书。

(二十九)代码"Z"——进口音像制品批准单或节目提取单:指国家实行进口管理的音像制品,由文化部签发的《文化部进口音像制品批准单》或广播电影电视总局及其授权部门签发的《进口广播电影电视节目带(片)提取单》。

(三十)代码"e"——关税配额外优惠关税税率进口棉花配额证:指对于一定数量的关税配额外报关进口的棉花,按"暂定优惠关税税率"征收进口关税,由国家发展改革委授权机构出具《关税配额外优惠关税税率进口棉花配额证》。

(三十一)代码"q"——国别关税配额证明:进口原产于新西兰并享受协定税率的羊毛或毛条时,应单独向海关申报,并按照海关总署令第175号规定提交原产地证明文件和商务部及其授权机构签发的在备注栏注明"新西兰羊毛、毛条国别配额"字样的《农产品进口关税配额证》,该证简称"国别关税配额证明"。

(三十二)代码"t"——关税配额证明:是指列入实施《关税配额目录》的商品,进口时由商务部签发《关税配额证明》。

(三十三)代码"v"——自动进口许可证(加工贸易):适用于加工贸易方式下自动进口许可证管理的商品。

(三十四)代码"x"——出口许可证(加工贸易):适用于加工贸易方式下出口许可证管理的商品。

(三十五)代码"y"——出口许可证:边境小额贸易项下需凭出口许可证办理有关手续。

tificate of import and export pesticides issued by the Ministry of Agriculture.

(24) Code "T"—— license for bank transfer of cash across borders: it refers to the approval of cash transfer across borders issued by the State Administration of Foreign Exchange and the People's Bank of China according to Management Regulations on bank transfer of cash across borders and other relevant laws and regulations.

(25) Code "U" ——Legal fishing products clearance certificate: import implementation " legal fishing clearance aquatic product list" listed in fishes by the Minstry of Agriculture of the people's Republic

(26) Code "W" ——license for import and export of narcotic drugs: According to *Pharmaceutical Administration Law of the People 's Republic of China* , *Management Regulations on Narcotic Drugs* and other relevant laws and regulations, narcotic drugs are under import and export licensed management. The import and export of items listed in the List of Controlled Narcotic Drugs require Narcotic drugs Import and Export License or certificate of holding narcotic and psychotropic drugs issued by the State Drug Administration.

(27) Code "X" —— release notice of import/export of toxic chemicals: The import and export of chemicals listed in the List of Toxic Chemicals Banned or Severely Restricted in People's Republic of China require release notice issued by the State Environmental Protection Administration.

(28) Code "Y"—the certificate of origin refers to the certificate issued by the department designated by a beneficiary government proving the goods are made in the country.

(29) Code "Z"—— audio – visual product import approval or program deliver order: It refers to the audio – visual product import approval issued by the Ministry of Culture or the delivery order of broadcasting, film and television program tapes and video import issued by

(30) Code "e"—— quota certificate for cotton import beyond tariff quota to enjoy preferential duties: It refers to the import quota certificate for cotton beyond tariff quota with preferential duties issued by institutions authorized by National Development and Reform Commission for certain amount of cotton imports beyond tariff rate quota to enjoy preferential duties.

(31) Code "q" – – country – specific tariff quota certificate: declare to the Customs separately, submit the certificate of origin according to the Regulation No. 175 of the General Administration of Customs and fill the words "New Zealand wool and country – specific top quota" in the remark column of the import tariff quota permit for agricultural products (abbreviated to "country – specific tariff quota certificate") issued by the Ministry of Commerce and its authorized agency when importing wool or tops that are originated in New Zealand and enjoy agreement rates.

(32) Code "t"—— tariff rate quota certificate: It refers to the Tariff Rate Quota Certificate issued by the Ministry of Commerce for items listed in the List of Tariff Rate Quota to be imported.

(33) Code "v"—automatic import license (processing trade): applicable to commodities subject to automatic import licensing in processing trade.

(34) Code "x"—— export license: Applicable to goods of under export license management

(35) Code "y"—— export license: Export License is required for procedures of petty trade in the border areas.

用途代码说明

一、定义

指进口货物的实际用途,以此对征免税和监管条件进行辅助检查和处理。

二、用途分类代码及说明

(一)外贸自营内销:代码"01",指有外贸进出口经营权的企业,在其经营范围内以正常方式成交的进口货物。

(二)特区内销:代码"02",指特区内有外贸进出口经营权的企业在其经营范围内进口在特区内销售的货物。

(三)其他内销:代码"03",指进料加工转内销部分、来料加工转内销货物及外商投资企业进口供加工内销产品的料件。

(四)企业自用:代码:"04",指进口供本单位(企业)自用的货物,如外商投资企业及特区内的企业、事业和机关单位进口自用的机器设备等。

(五)加工返销:代码:"05",指来料加工、进料加工、补偿贸易和外商投资企业为履行产品出合同从国外进口料件，用于在国内加工后返销到境外。

（六）借用：代码“06”，指从境外租借进口，在规定的使用期满后退运出境外的进口货物，如租赁贸易进口货物。

（七）收保证金：代码“07”，指由担保人向海关缴纳现金的一种担保形式。

（八）免费提供：代码“08”，指免费提供的进口货物，如无偿援助、捐赠、礼品等进口货物。

（九）作价提供：代码“09”，指我方与外商签订合同（协议），规定由外商作价提供进口的货物，事后由我方支付或从我方出口货物款中或出口加工成品的加工费中扣除，如来料加工贸易进口设备等。

（十）货样、广告品：代码“10”，指进口专供订货参考的货物样品及用以宣传有关商品内容的广告宣传品。

（十一）其他：代码“11”，指用途代码表中未具体列名的其他用途。

报关自动化系统常用代码表

Common Codes for Automated Customs Declaration System (EDI)

监管方式代码表

Codes for Customs Procedures (Modes of International Trade)

监管方式代码 Code	监管方式简称	监管方式全称	Customs Procedures (Modes of International Trade)
0110	一般贸易	一般贸易	Normal transaction (Lateral import/export by entitled legal person)
0130	易货贸易	易货贸易	Barter trade
0139	旅游购物商品	用于旅游者5万美元以下的出口小批量订货	Exportation of tourist commodities on an order not more than USD50,000
0200	料件销毁	加工贸易料件、残次品(折料)销毁	Processing and international trade, incomplete destroyed fold (material)
0214	来料加工	来料加工装配贸易进口料件及加工出口货物	Inward processing/assembling with supplied materials/components
0245	来料料件内销	来料加工料件转内销	Supplied materials/components for inward processing to be declared for home use
0255	来料深加工	来料深加工结转货物	To close and transfer accounts of supplied materials for supplementary processing
0258	来料余料结转	来料加工余料结转	To close and transfer accounts of surplus supplied materials
0265	来料料件复出	来料加工复运出境的原进口料件	Re-exportation of supplied materials/components in the same state
0300	来料料件退换	来料加工料件退换	Replacement of supplied materials/components
0314	加工专用油	国营贸易企业代理来料加工企业进口柴油	Diesel oil imported by state - run trading enterprises on behalf of processors on order with supplied materials
0320	不作价设备	加工贸易外商提供的不作价进口设备	Non-pricing equipment supplied for inward processing
0345	来料成品减免	来料加工成品凭征免税证明转减免税	Finished products with supplied materials to be declared for home use with "Certificate of Levy/Exemption of Customs Duties and Taxes"
0400	边角料销毁	加工贸易边角料、副产品(按状态)销毁	Processing trade leftover material, by - products (by state)
0420	加工贸易设备	加工贸易项下外商提供的进口设备	Importation of equipment for inward processing supplied at a fixed price
0444	保区进料成品	按成品征税的保税区进料加工成品转内销货物	Finished products processed in bonded warehouse zone with purchased materials to be declared for home use against payment Custom duties on the basis of finished products
0445	保区来料成品	按成品征税的保税区来料加工成品转内销货物	Finished products processed in bonded warehouse zone with supplied materials to be declared for home use against payment Custom duties on the basis of finished products
0446	加工设备内销	加工贸易免税进口设备转内销	Duty-free equipment imported for inward processing trade to be declared for home use
0456	加工设备结转	加工贸易免税进口设备结转	To close and transfer accounts of duty-free equipment supplied for inward processing trade
0466	加工设备退运	加工贸易免税进口设备退运出境	Sending back duty-free equipment supplied for inward processing trade
0500	减免设备结转	用于监管年限内减免税设备的结转	To close and transfer accounts of equipment bearing reduced Customs duties and taxes or be allowed conditional relief from duties and taxes within certain control duration
0513	补偿贸易	补偿贸易	Compensation trade
0544	保区进料料件	按料件征税的保税区进料加工成品转内销货物	Finished products processed in bonded warehouse zone with purchased materials to be declared for home use against payment Customs duties on the basis of materials

监管方式代码 Code	监管方式简称	监管方式全称	Customs Procedures (Modes of International Trade)
0545	保区来料料件	按料件征税的保税区来料加工成品转内销货物	Finished products processed in bonded warehouse zone with supplied materials to be declared for home use against payment Custom duties on the basis of materials
0615	进料对口	进料加工(对口合同)	Inward processing with purchased materials under a reciprocal contract
0642	进料以产顶进	进料加工成品以产顶进	Finished products obtained from purchased materials imported for import substitution
0644	进料料件内销	进料加工料件转内销	Purchased materials for inward processing to be declared for home use
0654	进料深加工	进料深加工结转货物	To close and transfer accounts of purchased materials for supplementary processing
0657	进料余料结转	进料加工余料结转	To close and transfer accounts of surplus purchased materials
0664	进料料件复出	进料加工复运出境的原进口料件	Re-exportation of purchased materials for inward processing
0700	进料料件退换	进料加工料件退换	Replacement of purchased materials for inward processing
0715	进料非对口	进料加工(非对口合同)	Inward processing with purchased materials under a non-reciprocal contract
0744	进料成品减免	进料加工成品凭征免税证明转减免税	Finished products with purchased materials to be declared for home use
0815	低值辅料	低值辅料	Low-value auxiliary materials
0844	进料边角料内销	进料加工项下边角料转内销	Leftover scraps of purchased materials for processing to be declared for home use
0845	来料边角料内销	来料加工项下边角料转内销	Leftover scraps of supplied materials for processing to be declared for home use
0864	进料边角料复出	进料加工项下边角料复出口	Re-exportation of leftover scraps of purchased materials for processing
0865	来料边角料复出	来料加工项下边角料复出口	Re-exportation of leftover scraps of supplied materials for processing
1039	市场采购	市场采购	The market purchase
1139	国轮油物料	中国籍运输工具境内添加的保税油料、物料	Chinese transport means to be filled with bonded fuel
1200	保税间货物	海关保税场所及保税区域之间往来的货物	Goods transit between Customs bonded areas
1210	保税电商	保税跨境贸易电子商务	Bonded cross – border trade e – commerce
1215	保税工厂	保税工厂	Inward processing in bonded factory with purchased materials
1233	保税仓库货物	保税仓库进出境货物	Entering and leaving bonded warehouse
1234	保税区仓储转口	保税区进出境仓储转口货物	Entering and leaving bonded warehouse zone
1300	修理物品	进出境修理物品	Articles to be imported/exported for repair
1371	保税维修	保税维修	Bonded repair
1427	出料加工	出料加工	Outward processing
1500	租赁不满一年	租期不满一年的租赁贸易货物	Leasing trade, lease term less than one year
1523	租赁贸易	租期在一年及以上的租赁贸易货物	Leasing trade, lease term one year or more
1616	寄售代销	寄售、代销贸易	Consignment trade
1741	免税品	免税品	Duty-free goods
1831	外汇商品	免税外汇商品	Duty-free foreign-currency goods
2025	合资合作设备	合资合作企业作为投资进口设备物品	Importation of equipment/articles purchased by Chinese-foreign equity joint ventures or Chinese-foreign contractual joint ventures
2225	外资设备物品	外资企业作为投资进口的设备物品	Importation of equipment/articles purchased by foreign wholly-owned enterprises
2439	常驻机构公用	外国常驻机构进口办公用品	Communal articles of foreign resident institutions
2600	暂时进出货物	暂时进出口货物	Temporary admission subject to re-exportation in the same state
2700	展览品	进出境展览品	Articles for exhibition
2939	陈列样品	驻华商业机构不复运出口的进口陈列样品	Samples for display keeping within the Customs territory
3010	货样广告品 A	有经营权单位进出口的货样广告品	Commercial samples of advertising imported by authorized organizations
3039	货样广告品 B	无经营权单位进出口的货样广告品	Commercial samples of advertising imported by non-authorized organizations
3100	无代价抵偿	无代价抵偿进出口货物	Free replacement goods
3339	其他进出口免费	其他进出口免费提供货物	Other free imports

监管方式代码 Code	监管方式简称	监管方式全称	Customs Procedures (Modes of International Trade)
3410	承包工程进口	对外承包工程进口物资	Importation of machines or equipments gained during undertaking contracted construction abroad
3422	对外承包出口	对外承包工程出口物资	Exports for undertaking contracted construction abroad
3511	援助物资	国家和国际组织无偿援助物资	Goods and materials rendered gratis by foreign governments or international organizations
3611	无偿军援	无偿军援	Free of charge military aid
3612	捐赠物资	进出口捐赠物资	Import and export donate goods and materials
3910	军事装备	军事装备	Military equipment
4019	边境小额	边境小额贸易(边民互市贸易除外)	Petty frontier trade (other than frontier traffics)
4039	对台小额	对台小额贸易	Petty trade between the Mainland and Taiwan
4139	对台小额商品交易市场	进入对台小额商品交易专用市场的货物	The goods entered the thawan small commodities trading market
4200	驻外机构运回	我驻外机构运回旧公用物品	Re-importation of used articles of Chinese resident institutions abroad
4239	驻外机构购进	我驻外机构境外购买运回国的公务用品	Importation of communal articles purchased outside by Chinese resident institutions abroad
4400	来料成品退换	来料加工成品退换	Sending back finished products processed with supplied materials
4500	直接退运	直接退运	Outright sending back
4539	进口溢误卸	进口溢卸、误卸货物	Dutiable overlanded or mislanded goods
4561	退运货物	因质量不符、延误交货等原因退运进出境货物	Sending back goods not in accordance with the agreed specification, delayed delivery or due to other causes
4600	进料成品退换	进料成品退换	Sending back finished products obtained from purchased materials
5000	料件进出区	料件进出海关特殊监管区域	Materials and parts transported into and out of zones under special customs
5010	特殊区域研发货物	海关特殊监管区域与境外之间进出的研发货物	R&D goods transported between zones under special customs
5014	区内来料加工	海关特殊监管区域与境外之间进出的来料加工货物	goods processed with supplied materials and transported between zones under special customs
5015	区内进料加工货物	海关特殊监管区域与境外之间进出的进料加工货物	goods processed with imported materials and transported between zones under special customs
5033	区内仓储货物	加工区内仓储企业从境外进口的货物	Storage of imported goods operated by warehousing enterprises established in processing zone
5034	区内物流货物	海关特殊监管区域与境外之间进出的物流货物	goods circulated between zones under special customs surveillance and overseas and apply to warehoused, allocated, distributed and transit goods imported or exported by enterprises in zones under special customs
5100	成品进出区	成品进出海关特殊监管区域	Finished goods in and out of the areas under special customs supervision
5200	区内边角调出	用于区内外非实际进出境货物	Leftover scraps removal from processing zone within the Customs territory
5300	设备进出区	设备及物资进出海关特殊监管区域	equipment and materials transported into or out of zones under special customs
5335	境外设备进区	海关特殊监管区域从境外进口的设备及物资	equipment and goods imported from overseas into zones under special customs
5361	区内设备退运	海关特殊监管区域设备及物资退运境外	equipment and goods returned overseas from zones under special customs surveillance and applies to equipment and goods returned by enterprises in zones under special customs
6033	物流中心进出境货物	保税物流中心与境外之间进出仓储货物	Import and export of storage goods by bonded center of commodities interflow
9600	内贸货跨境运输	内贸货物跨境运输	Cross-border transport for Internal goods
9610	电子商务	跨境贸易电子商务	Cross – border trade e – commerce
9639	海关处理货物	海关变卖处理的超期未报货物,走私违规货物	Customs sell goods which have not been declared within the time allowed, or which have involved in acts of smuggling or Customs offence
9700	后续补税	无原始报关单的后续补税	To recover Customs duties subsequently
9739	其他贸易	其他贸易	Other modes of trade
9800	租赁征税	租赁期1年及以上的租赁贸易货物的租金	Dutiable rental charge of leasing trade, lease term one year or more
9839	留赠转卖物品	外交机构转售境内或国际活动留赠放弃特批货物	Diplomatic institutions resell/Cultural or sports articles abandoned as donations in case of prior authority granted
9900	其他	其他	Other

征免性质代码表
Codes for the Nature of Levy, Reduction and Exemption of Customs Duties and Taxes

征免性质代码 Code	征免性质简称	征免性质全称	Nature of Levy, Reduction and Exemption of Customs Duties and Taxes
101	一般征税	一般征税进出口货物	Levy Customs duties and taxes according to regulations
118	整车征税	构成整车特征的汽车零部件纳税	Pay taxes to automobile Components and parts Featuring Complete Vehicles
119	零部件征税	不构成整车特征的汽车零部件纳税	Pay taxes to not automobile components and parts featuring complete vehicles
201	无偿援助	无偿援助进出口物资	Aid provided free of charge
299	其他法定	其他法定减免税进出口货物	Other legal reduction and remission
301	特定区域	特定区域进口自用物资及出口货物	Goods imported into or exported out of designated areas
307	保税区	保税区进口自用物资	Imports intended to be used within bonded warehouse zone
399	其他地区	其他执行特殊政策地区出口货物	Reduction and remission according to incentive policy for particular areas
401	科教用品	大专院校及科研机构进口科教用品	Importation of educational and scientific materials
402	示范平台用品		Demonstration platform
403	技术改造	企业技术改造进口货物	Imports for technical reform of enterprises
405	科技开发用品	科学研究、技术开发机构进口科技开发用品	Scientifie researches institutes and technical development imported technical development appliances
406	重大项目	国家重大项目进口货物	Imports for major projects of the state
407	动漫用品	动漫开发生产用品	Animation development and production Supplies
408	重大技术装备	生产重大技术装备进口关键零部件及原材料	key spare parts and raw materials for production of significant technical equipment and products
409	科技重大专项	科技重大专项进口关键设备、零部件和原材料	Key spare parts and raw materials for technical key projects
412	基础设施	通信、港口、铁路、公路、机场建设进口设备	Imports for infrastructure (such as communication, port, railway, highway, airport)
413	残疾人	残疾人组织和企业进出口货物	Imports/exports by organizations or enterprises of disabled persons
417	远洋渔业	远洋渔业自捕水产品	Deep-sea fishing
418	国产化	国家定点生产小轿车和摄录机企业进口散件	Importation of assemblies of compact cars/camcorders by enterprises designated by the state
419	整车特征	构成整车特征的汽车零部件进口	Import of automobile components parts featuring complete vehicles.
420	远洋船舶	远洋船舶及设备部件	Oceangoing vessels and equipment thereof
421	内销设备	内销远洋船用设备及关键部件	Equipment and key parts for Chinese oceangoing vessels
422	集成电路	集成电路生产企业进口货物	Imports by IC manufacturing enterprises
423	新型显示器件	新型显示器件生产企业进口物资	Imports for production companies of novel display devices
499	ITA 产品	非全税号信息技术产品	Reduction according to interim duty rate of IT articles
501	加工设备	加工贸易外商提供的不作价进口设备	Equipment imported for contract processing/assembling and compensation trade
502	来料加工	来料加工装配和补偿贸易进口料件及出口成品	Imports/exports of processing/assembling with supplied materials/components
503	进料加工	进料加工贸易进口料件及出口成品	Imports/exports of inward processing with self-bought materials
506	边境小额	边境小额贸易进口货物	Petty frontier trade
510	港澳 OPA	港澳在内地加工的纺织品获证出口	Hong Kong and Macao in the processing of textiles export licence from mainland China
601	中外合资	中外合资经营企业进出口货物	Chinese-foreign equity joint ventures
602	中外合作	中外合作经营企业进出口货物	Chinese-foreign contractual joint ventures
603	外资企业	外商独资企业进出口货物	Foreign wholly-owned enterprises
605	勘探开发煤层气	勘探开发煤层气	Explorate and exploit gas layer
606	海洋石油	勘探、开发海洋石油进口货物	Exploiting offshore petroleum resources
608	陆上石油	勘探、开发陆上石油进口货物	Exploiting inland petroleum resources
609	贷款项目	利用贷款进口货物	Importation of goods purchased with international loans
611	贷款中标	国际金融组织贷款、外国政府贷款中标机电设备零部件	Goods exported on the basis of winning international bids and using loans from international organizations or foreign government
698	公益收藏	国有公益性收藏单位进口藏品	Collections imported by state - owned public welfare collection units
789	鼓励项目	国家鼓励发展的内外资项目进口设备	Imports for projects encouraged by the state
799	自有资金	外商投资额度外利用自有资金进口设备、备件、配件	Foreign investment quota by using its own funds of imported equipment, spare parts and accessories
801	救灾捐赠	救灾捐赠进口物资	Donations of relief nature

征免性质代码 Code	征免性质简称	征免性质全称	Nature of Levy, Reduction and Exemption of Customs Duties and Taxes
802	扶贫慈善	境外向我境内无偿捐赠用于扶贫慈善的免税进口物资	Goods sent to charitable or philanthropic organizations for distribution to needy persons
803	抗艾滋病药物	进口抗艾滋病病毒药物	Import HIV drug resistance
811	种子种源	进口种子(苗)、种蓄(禽)、鱼种(苗)和种用野生动植物种源。	Imported species (seeding), storage (birds), fishs (seeding) and for wild animals
818	中央储备粮油	中央储备粮油免征进口环节增值税政策	Central reserve grain of exemption of import value-added tax policy
819	科教用书	进口科研教学用图书资料	Import research teaching books
888	航材减免	经核准的航空公司进口维修用航空器材	Import preserving of the approved airline use the aviation material
898	国批减免	国务院特准减免税的进出口货物	Reduction and remission according to special approval by the State Council
899	选择征税	选择征税	Choice of Taxation
997	自贸协定		
998	内部暂定	享受内部暂定税率的进出口货物	Provisional reduction according to interim duty rate
999	例外减免	例外减免税进出口货物	Reduction and remission of Customs duties granted by the Customs

征减免税方式代码表

Codes For Type of Levy, Reduction and Exemption of Customs Duties and Taxes

征减免税方式代码 Code	征减免税方式名称	Type of Levy, Reduction and Exemption of Customs Duties and Taxes
1	照章征税	Levy according to regulations
2	折半征税	Reduction by half
3	全免	Relief from all duties and taxes
4	特案	Special case
5	随征免性质	Reduction and remission according to the different nature of objects
6	保证金	Security deposit
7	保函	Letter of guarantee
8	折半补税	Pay an overdue tax by half
9	全额退税	A full refund

运输方式代码表

Codes for Modes of Transport

运输方式代码 Code	运输方式名称	Modes of Transport
0	非保税区	Entry and release of bonded warehouse zone
1	监管仓库	Temporary storage of export goods
2	水路运输	Maritime transport/Inland water transport
3	铁路运输	Railway transport
4	公路运输	Road transport
5	航空运输	Airway transport
6	邮件运输	Mail transport
7	保税区	Shipment out of bonded warehouse zone to non-bonded area
8	保税仓库	Goods in bonded warehouse to be declared for home use
9	其他运输	Other transport
H	边境特殊海关作业区	Border especial custom operation zone
T	综合实验区	Experimentaiont arer
W	物流中心	center of commodities interflow
X	物流园区	Goods flow zones
Y	保税港区	Bonded harbor zones
Z	出口加工区	Entry and release of export processing zone

关区代码表

Codes for International Trade Ports (Customs Establishment)

关区代码 Code	关区名称 Name of International Trade Port (Customs Establishment)	关区代码 Code	关区名称 Name of International Trade Port (Customs Establishment)	关区代码 Code	关区名称 Name of International Trade Port (Customs Establishment)
0000	海关总署	0000	平谷海关	0123	机场调技
0100	北京关区	0111	京五里店	0124	北京站
0101	机场单证	0112	京邮办处	0125	西客站
0102	京监管处	0113	京中关村	0126	京加工区
0103	京关展览	0114	京国际局	0127	京快件
0104	京一处	0115	京东郊站	0128	京顺义办
0105	京二处	0116	京信		
0106	京关关税	0117	京开发区		
0107	机场库区	0118	十八里店		
0108	京通关处	0119	机场物流		
0109	机场旅检	0121	京稽查处		

关区代码 Code	关区名称 Name of International Trade Port (Customs Establishment)
0128	京顺义办
0129	北京海关天竺综合保税区(京关天竺)
0130	北京亦庄保税物流中心
0200	**天津关区**
0201	天津海关
0202	新港海关
0203	津开发区
0204	东港海关
0205	津塘沽办
0206	津驻邮办
0207	津机场办
0208	津保税区
0209	蓟县海关
0210	武清海关
0211	津加工区
0212	天津保税物流园区(津物流园)
0213	天津东疆保税港区(天津东疆)
0214	天津滨海新区综合保税区(津滨综保)
0215	天津机场海关快件监管中心(津机快件)
0216	天津经济技术开发区保税物流中心(津开物流)
0217	东疆港区
0218	静海海关
0220	津关税处
0400	**石家庄区**
0401	石家庄关
0402	秦皇岛关
0403	唐山海关
0404	廊坊海关
0405	保定海关
0406	石家庄海关驻邯郸办事处(石关邯办)
0407	秦加工区
0408	中华人民共和国沧州海关(沧州海关)
0409	廊坊海关驻出口加工区办事处(廊加工区)
0410	石家庄海关驻机场办事处(石机场办)
0411	中华人民共和国张家口海关(张家口海关)
0412	石家庄海关驻曹妃甸港区办事处(石关曹办)
0413	邢台海关
0414	曹综保区
0415	衡水海关
0500	**太原海关**
0501	并关监管
0502	太原机场海关(并机场关)
0503	大同海关
0504	侯马海关
0505	山西方略保税物流中心(方略物流)
0506	太原综保
0600	**满洲里关**
0601	海拉尔关
0602	额尔古纳
0603	满十八里
0604	满赤峰办
0605	满通辽办
0606	满哈沙特
0607	满室韦
0608	满互贸区
0609	满铁路
0610	满市区
0611	满洲里海关驻西郊机场办事处满关机办
0612	阿尔山关
0613	赤峰物流
0700	**呼特关区**
0701	呼和浩特
0702	二连海关
0703	包头海关
0704	呼关邮办
0705	二连公路
0706	包头海关驻国际集装箱中转站办事处(包头箱站)
0707	额济纳海关
0708	乌拉特海关(乌拉特关)
0709	满都拉口岸(满达口岸)
0710	东乌海关
0711	呼和浩特海关驻白塔机场办事处(呼关机办)
0712	呼和浩特海关驻出口加工区办事处(呼加工区)
0713	鄂尔多斯海关(鄂尔多斯)
0714	集宁海关
0800	**沈阳关区**
0801	沈阳海关
0802	锦州海关
0803	沈驻邮办
0804	沈驻抚顺
0805	沈开发区
0806	沈驻辽阳
0807	沈机场办
0808	沈综保区
0809	沈快件
0810	葫芦岛关
0811	沈阳海关驻辽宁沈阳出口加工区办事处(辽沈加区)
0812	沈阳海关驻张士出口加工区办事处(沈张出加)
0813	沈阳保税物流中心(沈阳物流)
0900	**大连海关**
0901	大连港湾海关(大连港湾)
0902	大连机场
0903	连开发区
0904	连加工区
0905	大窑湾海关驻北良港办事处(窑北良办)
0906	连保税区
0907	大连保税物流园区(连物流园)
0908	连大窑湾
0909	大连邮办
0910	大连大窑湾保税港区(连保税港)
0912	大连国际快件监管中心(大连快件)
0915	庄河海关
0917	大连海关驻旅顺办事处(大连旅办)
0930	丹东海关
0931	大连海关驻本溪办事处(大连本办)
0932	太平湾海关(丹太平湾)
0940	营口海关
0941	营口海关驻盘锦办事处(营盘锦办)
0950	鲅鱼圈关
0951	营口港保税物流中心(营港物流)
0960	大东港关
0980	鞍山海关
1500	**长春关区**
1501	长春海关
1502	长开发区
1503	长白海关
1504	临江海关
1505	图们海关
1506	通化海关
1507	珲春海关
1508	吉林海关
1509	延吉海关
1510	长春综保
1511	长春机办
1515	图们车办
1516	通海关村
1517	珲长岭子
1518	吉林海关驻车站办事处(吉关车办)
1519	延吉三合
1521	一汽场站
1525	图们桥办
1526	通集青石
1527	珲春圈河
1529	延吉南坪
1531	长春东站
1536	通集铁路
1537	珲沙坨子
1539	延开山屯
1547	珲加工区
1549	延古城里
1557	珲春海关驻车站办事处(珲春车办)

关区代码 Code	关区名称 Name of International Trade Port (Customs Establishment)
1559	延吉邮办
1569	延吉海关驻机场办事处(延吉机办)
1591	长春邮办
1593	长白邮办
1595	图们邮办
1596	通集邮办
1900	哈尔滨区
1901	哈尔滨关
1902	绥关铁路
1903	黑河海关
1904	同江海关
1905	佳木斯关
1906	牡丹江关
1907	东宁海关
1908	逊克海关
1909	齐齐哈尔
1910	大庆海关
1911	密山海关
1912	虎林海关
1913	富锦海关
1914	抚远海关
1915	漠河海关
1916	萝北海关
1917	嘉荫海关
1918	饶河海关
1919	哈内陆港
1920	哈开发区
1921	黑龙江绥芬河综合保税区(绥综保区)
1922	哈关邮办
1923	哈关车办
1924	哈关机办
1925	绥关公路
2200	上海海关
2201	浦江海关
2202	吴淞海关
2203	沪机场关
2204	闵开发区
2205	沪车站办
2206	沪邮局办
2207	沪稽查处
2208	宝山海关
2209	龙吴海关
2210	浦东海关
2211	卢湾监管
2212	奉贤海关
2213	莘庄海关
2214	漕河泾发
2215	世博中心
2216	上海浦东机场综合保税区(浦机综保)
2217	嘉定海关
2218	外高桥关
2219	杨浦监管
2220	金山海关
2221	松江海关
2222	青浦海关
2223	南汇海关
2224	崇明海关
2225	外港海关
2226	贸易网点
2227	普陀区站
2228	长宁区站
2229	航交办
2230	徐汇区站
2231	洋山海关驻市内报关点(洋山市内)
2232	嘉定海关驻出口加工区办事处(嘉定出口)
2233	浦东机场
2234	沪钻交所
2235	松江加工
2236	洋山海关驻芦潮港铁路集装箱中心站监管点(洋山芦潮)
2237	上海松江出口加工区 B 区(松江 B 区)
2238	上海青浦出口加工区(青浦加工)
2239	上海闵行出口加工区(闵行加工)
2240	上海漕河泾出口加工区(漕河泾加)
2241	沪业一处
2242	沪业二处
2243	沪业三处
2244	上海快件
2245	沪金桥办
2246	上海保税物流园区(保税物流)
2247	上海海关驻化学工业区办事处(沪化工区)
2248	洋山海关(港区)(洋山港区)
2249	洋山海关(保税)(洋山保税)
2300	南京海关
2301	连云港关
2302	南通海关
2303	苏州海关
2304	无锡海关
2305	张家港关
2306	常州海关
2307	镇江海关
2308	新生圩关
2309	盐城海关
2310	扬州海关
2311	徐州海关
2312	江阴海关
2313	张保税区
2314	苏工业区
2315	淮安海关
2316	泰州海关
2317	禄口机办
2318	南京现场
2319	如皋海关
2320	无锡海关驻机场办事处(锡关机办)
2321	常溧阳办
2322	镇丹阳办
2323	金陵海关
2324	常熟海关
2325	昆山海关
2326	吴江海关
2327	太仓海关
2328	苏吴县办
2329	通启东办
2330	泰州海关驻泰兴办事处(泰泰兴办)
2331	锡宜兴办
2332	锡锡山办
2333	南通关办
2335	昆山加工
2336	苏园加工
2337	连开发办
2338	苏关邮办
2339	南通海关驻出口加工区办事处(南通加工)
2340	无锡海关驻出口加工区办事处(无锡加工)
2341	连云港海关驻连云港出口加工区办事处(连关加工)
2342	南京海关驻江苏南京出口加工区办事处(南京加工)
2343	南京海关驻江苏南京出口加工区(南区)办事处(宁南加工)
2344	苏州海关驻苏州高新区出口加工区办事处(苏高加工)
2345	镇江海关驻镇江出口加工区办事处(镇江加工)
2346	苏州工业园区海关保税物流中心(苏园物流)
2347	苏州工业园区海关驻苏州工业园区出口加工区 B 区办事处(苏园 B 区)
2348	张家港保税物流园区(张物流园)
2349	南京海关驻邮局办事处(宁关邮办)
2350	苏州高新区保税物流中心(B 型)(苏高物流)
2351	南京海关驻江宁经济技术开发区办事处(江宁办)

关区代码 Code	关区名称 Name of International Trade Port (Customs Establishment)
2352	南京龙潭保税物流中心(B型)(龙潭物流)
2353	常州海关驻出口加工区办事处(常关出加)
2354	扬州海关驻出口加工区办事处(扬关出加)
2355	常熟海关驻出口加工区办事处(常熟出加)
2356	吴江海关驻出口加工区办事处(吴江出加)
2357	常州海关驻武进办事处(常关武办)
2358	苏州工业园综合保税区(苏园保税)
2359	苏州海关驻吴中出口加工区办事处(吴中出加)
2360	盐城海关驻大丰港办事处(盐关港办)
2361	淮安海关驻出口加工区办事处(淮关出加)
2362	江阴保税物流中心(澄关物流)
2363	太仓保税物流中心(太仓物流)
2364	江苏武进出口加工区(武进出加)
2365	张家港保税港区(张保税港)
2366	中华人民共和国宿迁海关(宿迁海关)
2367	泰州海关驻出口加工区办事处(泰出加区)
2368	苏州高新技术产业开发区综合保税区(苏高综保)
2369	昆山综合保税区(昆山综保)
2370	连云港保税物流中心(连关物流)
2371	盐城海关驻机场办事处(盐机场办)
2373	淮安综保
2374	锡高综保
2375	靖江海关
2376	南通综保
2377	龙潭综保
2378	江宁综保
2379	苏州海关驻相城办事处(苏相城办)
2380	太仓港综合保税区(太仓综保)
2900	**杭州关区**
2901	杭州海关
2903	温州海关
2904	舟山海关
2905	台州海关
2906	绍兴海关
2907	湖州海关
2908	嘉兴海关
2909	杭经开关
2910	杭州萧山机场海关(杭州机场)
2911	杭关邮办
2912	杭关萧办
2915	丽水海关
2916	杭州萧山机场海关快件监管中心(杭州快件)
2917	衢州海关
2918	杭关余办
2919	杭富阳办
2920	金华海关
2921	义乌海关
2922	金华海关驻永康办事处(金关永办)
2903	义乌物流
2928	杭关电商
2931	温关邮办
2932	温经开关
2933	温关机办
2934	温关鳌办
2935	温州海关驻瑞安办事处(温关瑞办)
2936	温州海关驻乐清办事处(温关乐办)
2941	舟山海关驻嵊泗办事处(舟关嵊办)
2942	舟关金塘
2943	舟关综保
2951	台州海关驻临海办事处(台关临办)
2952	台州海关驻温岭办事处(台关温办)
2961	绍兴海关驻上虞办事处(绍关虞办)
2962	绍兴海关驻诸暨办事处(绍关诸办)
2963	绍关新办
2981	嘉关乍办
2982	嘉兴海关驻嘉善办事处(嘉关善办)
2983	嘉兴海关驻出口加工区办事处(嘉兴加工)
2984	嘉兴海关驻海宁办事处(嘉关宁办)
2985	嘉兴海关驻桐乡办事处(嘉兴桐办)
2986	嘉兴海关驻出口加工区(B)区办事处(嘉加B区)
2991	杭州经济技术开发区海关驻出口加工区办事处(杭加工区)
2992	杭州保税物流中心(B型)(杭州物流)
3100	**宁波关区**
3101	宁波海关
3102	镇海海关
3103	甬开发区
3104	北仑海关
3105	甬保税区
3106	大榭海关
3107	甬驻余办
3108	甬驻慈办
3109	宁波机场海关(甬机场关)
3110	象山海关
3111	宁波保税区海关驻出口加工区办事处(甬加工区)
3112	宁波保税物流园区(甬物流区)
3113	浙江慈溪出口加工区(慈加工区)
3114	宁波海关驻鄞州办事处(甬驻鄞办)
3115	宁波海关驻鄞州办事处栎社保税物流中心(栎社物流)
3116	宁波梅山保税港区港口功能区(梅山港区)
3117	宁波梅山保税港区保税加工物流功能区(梅山保税)
3300	**合肥海关**
3301	芜湖海关
3302	安庆海关
3303	马鞍山海关(马鞍山关)
3304	黄山海关
3305	蚌埠海关
3306	铜陵海关
3307	阜阳海关
3308	池州海关
3309	滁州海关
3310	合肥现场
3311	合肥海关驻骆岗机场办事处(合肥机场)
3312	芜湖海关驻出口加工区办事处(芜关加办)
3500	**福州关区**
3501	马尾海关
3502	福清海关
3503	宁德海关
3504	三明海关
3505	福保税区
3506	莆田海关
3507	福关机办
3508	福州新港
3509	福关邮办
3510	南平海关
3511	武夷山关
3513	福现业处
3515	平潭港区
3516	平潭海关
3520	福州出口加工区海关(福州加工)
3521	福清出口加工区海关(福清加工)
3522	福州保税物流园区(福物流园)
3523	福保税港
3700	**厦门关区**
3701	厦门海关

关区代码 Code	关区名称 Name of International Trade Port (Customs Establishment)
3702	泉州海关
3703	漳州海关
3704	东山海关
3705	石狮海关
3706	龙岩海关
3707	厦肖厝关
3708	厦门海沧保税港区港口功能区（海沧港区）
3709	厦门海沧保税港区保税加工物流功能区（海沧保税）
3710	厦高崎办
3711	厦门东渡海关（东渡海关）
3712	厦海沧办
3713	厦驻邮办
3714	象屿保税
3715	高崎机场海关（机场海关）
3716	厦同安办
3717	象屿保税物流园区（厦物流园）
3718	泉州出口加工区（泉州加工）
3719	厦门加工
3720	厦门火炬（翔安）保税物流中心（厦门物流）
3722	厦门海关驻同安办事处大嶝监管科（大嶝监管）
3723	泉州海关驻晋江办事处（泉晋江办）
3724	油轮办
3777	厦稽查处
3788	厦侦查局
4000	**南昌关区**
4001	南昌海关
4002	九江海关
4003	赣州海关
4004	景德镇关
4005	吉安海关
4006	昌北机办
4007	南昌海关驻高新技术产业开发区办事处（洪关高新）
4008	南昌海关驻龙南办事处（洪关龙南）
4009	新余海关
4010	九江海关驻出口加工区办事处（浔关区办）
4011	南昌海关驻出口加工区办事处（洪关区办）
4012	赣州海关驻出口加工区办事处（虔关区办）
4013	上饶海关
4014	南昌保税物流中心（南昌物流）
4015	吉井加工
4016	鹰潭海关
4200	**青岛海关**
4201	烟台海关
4202	日照海关
4203	龙口海关
4204	威海海关
4205	济南海关（暂时）
4206	潍坊海关（暂时）
4207	淄博海关（暂时）
4208	烟台海关驻出口加工区B区办事处（烟加B区）
4209	荣成海关
4210	青保税区
4211	济宁海关
4212	泰安海关（暂时）
4213	临沂海关
4214	青前湾港
4215	青菏泽办
4216	东营海关（暂时）
4217	青枣庄办
4218	青开发区
4219	蓬莱海关
4220	青机场关
4221	烟机场办
4222	莱州海关
4223	青邮局办
4224	龙长岛办
4225	威开发区
4226	青聊城办（暂时）
4227	青岛大港
4228	烟关快件
4229	德州海关（暂时）
4230	青岛保税物流园区（青物流园）
4231	烟开发区
4232	日岚山办
4233	济机场办（暂时）
4234	济南海关驻出口加工区办事处（济加工区）（暂时）
4235	济邮局办
4236	荣成海关驻龙眼港办事处（荣龙眼办）
4237	现场业务
4238	威海关驻威海邮局办事处（威海快件）
4239	潍诸城办（暂时）
4240	青岛海关快件监管中心（青关快件）
4241	烟加工区
4242	威加工区
4243	济宁海关驻曲阜办事处（济曲阜办）
4244	青岛海关驻滨州办事处（青滨州办）（暂时）
4245	烟台海关驻邮局办事处（烟台邮办）
4246	青加工区
4247	威海海关驻机场办事处（威机场办）
4248	青岛海关驻莱芜办事处（青莱芜办）（暂时）
4249	潍坊海关驻出口加工区办事处（潍加工区）（暂时）
4250	青岛西海岸出口加工区（青西加区）
4251	淄博保税物流中心（暂时）
4253	日照保税物流中心（日照物流）
4254	青岛保税物流中心（青岛物流）
4255	潍坊海关驻寿光办事处（潍寿光办）（暂时）
4258	青岛前湾保税港区（青保税港）
4300	**济南海关**
4301	现场业务
4302	济机场办
4303	济综保区
4305	济邮局办
4310	潍坊海关
4311	潍诸城办
4312	潍综保区
4313	潍寿光办
4320	淄博海关
4321	淄博物流
4330	泰安海关
4341	济关快件
4350	东营海关
4360	济聊城办
4370	德州海关
4380	济滨州办
4381	滨州保税物流中心（并州物流）
4390	济莱芜办
4600	**郑州关区**
4601	郑州海关
4602	洛阳海关
4603	南阳海关
4604	郑州机办
4605	郑州邮办
4606	郑铁东办
4607	安阳海关
4608	郑州海关驻出口加工区办事处（郑加工区）
4609	郑州海关驻商丘办事处（郑关商办）
4610	周口海关
4611	河南保税物流中心（河南物流）
4612	郑州新郑综合保税区（新郑综保）
4613	郑州空港
4614	焦作海关
4615	三门峡关
4616	新乡海关
4617	信阳海关
4618	鹤壁海关
4700	**武汉海关**
4701	宜昌海关
4702	荆州海关
4703	襄阳海关
4704	黄石海关

关区代码 Code	关区名称 Name of International Trade Port (Customs Establishment)
4705	武汉沌口
4706	宜三峡办
4707	鄂加工区
4708	武汉海关现场业务处(武业务处)
4709	武汉海关驻汉办事处东西湖保税物流中心(武江物流)
4710	武关货管
4711	武关江岸
4712	武关机场
4713	武关邮办
4716	十堰海关
4718	武汉东湖新技术开发区海关(东湖海关)
4719	东湖综保
4720	黄石棋盘洲保税物流中心(黄石物流)
4900	**长沙关区**
4901	衡阳海关
4902	岳阳海关
4903	长沙海关驻林州办事处(湘关郴办)
4904	常德海关
4905	长沙海关
4906	株洲海关
4907	韶山海关
4908	湘关机办
4909	株洲海关驻醴陵办事处(株关醴办)
4910	长沙海关驻郴州出口加工区办事处(郴加工区)
4911	衡阳海关永州监管组(衡关永办)
4913	长沙金霞保税物流中心(金霞物流)
4914	**张家界海关(张家界关)**
4915	衡阳综保
4916	星沙海关(星沙海关)
5000	**广东分署**
5100	**广州海关**
5101	内港新风
5103	清远海关
5104	清远英德
5105	广州海关现场业务处(广州现场)
5106	南沙海关小虎监管点(南沙小虎)
5107	肇庆高新区大旺进出境货运车辆检查场(肇庆大旺)
5108	肇庆德庆
5109	内港窖心
5110	南海海关
5111	南海官窑
5112	南海九江
5113	南海北村
5114	南海平洲
5116	南海业务
5117	桂江货柜车场(桂江车场)
5118	平洲旅检
5119	南海三山
5120	广州内港
5121	内港芳村
5122	内港洲嘴
5123	内港四仓
5125	从化海关
5126	内港赤航
5130	广州萝岗
5131	花都海关
5132	花都码头
5133	穗知识城
5134	穗保税处
5135	广州海关现场业务处驻市政务中心监管点(穗现场处)
5136	穗统计处
5137	穗价格处
5138	高明食出
5139	穗监管处
5140	穗关税处
5141	广州机场
5142	民航快件
5143	广州车站
5144	穗机宗保
5145	广州邮办
5146	亚运物资通关服务中心(穗亚运会)
5147	穗邮办监
5148	穗大郎站
5149	大铲海关
5150	顺德海关
5151	顺德海关加工贸易监管科(顺德保税)
5152	顺德食出
5153	顺德车场
5154	北窖车场
5155	顺德旅检
5157	顺德陈村港澳货柜车检查场(陈村车场)
5158	顺德勒流
5160	番禺海关
5161	沙湾车场
5162	番禺旅检
5163	番禺货柜
5164	番禺船舶
5165	南沙保税
5166	南沙新港
5167	南沙货港
5168	南沙汽车
5169	南沙海关
5170	肇庆海关
5171	肇庆高要
5172	肇庆车场
5173	肇庆新港
5174	肇庆旅检
5175	肇庆码头
5176	肇庆四会
5177	肇庆三榕
5178	云浮海关
5179	罗定海关
5180	佛山海关
5181	高明海关
5182	佛山澜石
5183	三水码头
5184	佛山窖口
5185	佛山海关快件监管现场(佛山快件)
5186	佛山保税
5187	佛山车场
5188	佛山火车
5189	佛山新港
5190	韶关海关
5191	韶关乐昌
5192	三水海关
5193	三水车场
5194	三水港
5195	审单中心
5196	云浮新港
5197	广州联邦快递亚太转运中心(转运中心)
5198	穗河源关
5199	穗技术处
5200	**黄埔关区**
5201	黄埔老港海关(埔老港关)
5202	黄埔新港海关(埔新港关)
5203	新塘海关
5204	东莞海关
5205	太平海关
5206	惠州海关
5207	黄浦海关驻凤岗办事处(埔凤岗办)
5208	黄埔海关驻广州经济技术开发区办事处(埔开发区)
5210	埔红海办
5211	河源海关
5212	新沙海关
5213	黄埔海关驻长安办事处(埔长安办)
5214	黄埔海关驻常平办事处(埔常平办)
5216	黄埔海关驻沙田办事处(埔沙田办)
5217	东莞海关寮步车检场(寮步车场)
5218	新塘海关江龙车检场(江龙车场)
5219	广州保税物流园区(埔物流园)
5220	东莞保税物流中心(B 型)(东莞物流)
5221	新塘车检场(新塘车场)
5300	**深圳海关**
5301	皇岗海关
5302	罗湖海关

关区代码 Code	关区名称 Name of International Trade Port (Customs Establishment)
5303	沙头角关
5304	蛇口海关
5305	深关现场
5306	笋岗海关
5307	南头海关
5308	沙湾海关
5309	布吉海关
5310	淡水办
5311	深关车站
5312	深监管处
5313	深调查局
5314	深关邮办
5315	惠东海关
5316	大鹏海关
5317	深关机场
5318	梅林海关
5319	同乐海关
5320	文锦渡关
5321	福保税关
5322	沙保税关
5323	深审单处
5324	深审价办
5325	深关税处
5326	深数统处
5327	深法规处
5328	深规范处
5329	深保税处
5330	盐保税关
5331	三门岛办
5332	深财务处
5333	深侦查局
5334	深稽查处
5335	深技术处
5336	深办公室
5337	大亚湾核
5338	惠州港关
5339	深加工区
5340	深关特办
5341	深惠州关
5342	深红海办
5343	深圳盐田港保税物流园区（深盐物流）
5344	惠州港海关驻大亚湾石化区办事处（惠石化办）
5345	深圳湾海关（深圳湾关）
5346	深圳机场海关快件监管中心（深机快件）
5348	大铲湾海关（深关大铲）
5349	深圳前海湾保税区（深关前海）
5351	深圳前海湾保税港区保税功能区（前海保税）
5700	**拱北关区**
5701	拱稽查处
5710	拱关闸办
5720	中山海关

关区代码 Code	关区名称 Name of International Trade Port (Customs Establishment)
5721	中山港
5724	中石岐办
5725	坦洲货场
5726	中山保税物流中心（中山物流）
5727	中小榄办
5728	中山海关驻神湾港办事处（神湾办）
5729	中山快件
5730	拱香洲办
5740	湾仔海关
5741	湾仔船舶
5750	九洲海关
5760	拱白石办
5770	斗门海关
5771	斗井岸办
5772	斗平沙办
5780	高栏海关
5790	拱监管处
5791	珠澳跨境工业区珠海园区海关办事机构（拱跨工区）
5792	拱保税区
5793	万山海关
5795	横琴海关
5796	澳门大学新校区临时监管区（澳大校区）
5798	拱行监邮
5799	拱行监处
6000	**汕头海关**
6001	汕关货一
6002	汕关货二
6003	汕关行邮
6004	汕关机场
6006	汕关保税
6007	汕关业务
6008	汕保税区
6009	汕关邮包
6011	揭阳海关
6012	汕关普宁
6013	澄海海关
6014	广澳海关
6015	南澳海关
6018	汕关惠来
6019	汕关联成
6020	汕关港口
6021	潮州海关
6022	饶平海关
6023	潮州海润快件监管中心（饶平快件）
6028	潮阳海关
6031	汕尾海关
6032	汕关海城
6033	汕关陆丰

关区代码 Code	关区名称 Name of International Trade Port (Customs Establishment)
6038	汕头海关外砂快件监管中心（汕关快件）
6041	梅州海关
6042	梅州兴宁
6400	**海口关区**
6401	海口海关
6402	三亚海关
6403	八所海关
6404	洋浦经济开发区海关（洋浦区关）
6405	海保税区
6406	清澜海关
6407	美兰机场
6408	洋浦保税港口海关（洋浦港区）
6409	海口综合保税区海关（海口综保）
6410	马村港监管点（马村监管）
6411	海口海关现场业务处（海口现场）
6700	**湛江关区**
6701	湛江海关
6702	茂名海关
6703	徐闻海关
6704	湛江南油
6705	湛江水东
6706	湛江吴川
6707	湛江廉江
6708	湛江高州
6709	湛江信宜
6710	东海岛组
6711	霞山海关
6712	湛江霞海
6713	湛江机场
6714	湛江博贺
6715	湛江进出境快件监管中心（湛江快件）
6800	**江门关区**
6810	江门海关
6811	江门高沙
6812	江门外海
6813	江门旅检
6816	江门市进出境货运车辆检查场（江门车场）
6817	江门保税
6820	新会海关
6821	新会港
6827	新会稽查
6830	台山海关
6831	台公益港
6837	台山稽查
6840	开平海关
6841	开平码头
6847	开平稽查
6850	恩平海关
6851	恩平港
6857	恩平稽查
6860	鹤山海关

关区代码 Code	关区名称 Name of International Trade Port (Customs Establishment)
6861	鹤山码头
6867	鹤山稽查
6870	阳江海关
6871	阳江港
6872	阳江车场
6877	阳江稽查
7200	**南宁关区**
7201	邕州海关
7202	北海海关
7203	梧州海关
7204	桂林海关
7205	柳州海关
7206	防城海关
7207	东兴海关
7208	凭祥海关
7209	贵港海关
7210	水口海关
7211	龙邦海关
7212	钦州海关
7213	桂林机办
7214	北海海关驻出口加工区办事处（北海加工）
7215	广西钦州保税港区（南关钦保）
7216	南宁保税物流中心（南宁物流）
7217	广西钦州保税港（口岸）（钦保口岸）
7218	南宁海关驻玉林办事处（玉林办）
7219	广西凭祥综合保税区（南凭综保）
7220	友谊关
7900	**成都关区**
7901	成都海关
7902	成都双流机场海关（蓉机场关）
7903	乐山海关
7904	攀枝花关
7905	绵阳海关
7906	成关邮办
7907	成都自贡
7908	成都加工
7909	成都公路国际物流中心监管场站（公路场站）
7910	成都双流机场海关非邮政快件监管点（蓉机快件）
7911	成都海关驻泸州办事处（泸州办）
7912	成都海关驻宜宾办事处（宜宾办）
7913	成都海关驻南充办事处（南充办）
7914	绵阳出口加工区（绵阳出口）
7915	成都保税物流中心（B型）（成都物流）
7916	成都高新综合保税区（成都综保）
7917	遂宁海关
7918	德阳海关
7919	成都空港
7920	成空物流
8000	**重庆关区**
8001	重庆海关
8002	南坪开发
8003	重庆机场
8004	重庆邮办
8005	万州海关
8006	重庆铁路

关区代码 Code	关区名称 Name of International Trade Port (Customs Establishment)
8007	九龙坡港
8008	渝加工区
8009	重庆海关驻涪陵办事处（渝涪陵办）
8010	重庆两路寸滩保税港区水港功能区（寸滩水港）
8011	重庆两路寸滩保税港区空港功能区（两路空港）
8012	重庆两路寸滩保税港区保税加工物流功能区（重庆保税）
8013	重庆西永综合保税区（西永综保）
8014	西永海关
8300	**贵阳海关**
8301	贵阳总关
8302	贵阳海关驻机场办事处（贵关机办）
8303	中华人民共和国遵义海关（遵义海关）
8304	贵高新办
8600	**昆明关区**
8601	昆明海关
8602	畹町海关
8603	瑞丽海关
8604	章凤海关
8605	盈江海关
8606	孟连海关
8607	南伞海关
8608	孟定海关
8609	打洛海关
8610	腾冲海关
8611	沧源海关
8612	勐腊海关
8613	河口海关
8614	金水河关
8615	天保海关
8616	田蓬海关
8617	大理海关
8618	芒市海关
8619	保山监管
8620	昆明机场
8621	昆明邮办
8622	西双版纳
8623	昆丽江办
8624	思茅海关
8625	河口海关驻山腰办事处（河口山腰）
8626	六库监管
8627	昆明海关现场业务处开发区监管科（昆明高新）
8628	云南昆明出口加工区（昆明加工）
8629	昆明香办
8631	勐康海关
8632	昆明快件
8800	**拉萨海关**
8801	聂拉木关
8802	日喀则关
8803	狮泉河关
8804	拉萨机办
8805	拉萨现场
8808	吉隆海关

关区代码 Code	关区名称 Name of International Trade Port (Customs Establishment)
9000	**西安关区**
9001	西安陆港
9002	咸阳机场
9003	宝鸡海关
9004	西安海关邮局办事处（西关邮办）
9007	西安保税物流中心（西安物流）
9005	陕西西安出口加工区 A 区（陕加工 A）
9006	陕西西安出口加工区 B 区（陕加工 B）
9007	西安保税物流中心（西安综保）
9008	高新综保
9009	西安高新
9010	延安海关
9400	**乌关区**
9401	乌鲁木齐海关现场业务处（乌关现场）
9402	霍尔果斯
9403	吐尔尕特
9404	阿拉山口
9405	塔城海关
9406	伊宁海关
9407	吉木乃办
9408	喀什海关
9409	红其拉甫
9410	乌鲁木齐海关隶属阿勒泰海关（阿勒泰关）
9411	塔克什肯
9412	乌拉斯太
9413	老爷庙
9414	红山嘴
9415	伊尔克什
9416	库尔勒办
9417	乌鲁木齐机场海关（乌机场关）
9418	乌鲁木齐海关驻出口加工区办事处（乌加工区）
9419	都拉塔海关（都拉塔关）
9420	乌鲁木齐海关驻车站办事处（乌关车办）
9421	霍尔果斯国际边境合作中心海关（霍中心 A）
9422	石河子关
9423	山口综保
9500	**兰州关区**
9501	兰州海关
9502	酒泉海关
9503	甘肃机场集团空港国际物流中心海关监管组（兰州空港）
9504	武威物流
9505	兰州海关驻天水监管组（天水监管）
9600	**银川海关**
9601	银川海关业务现场（银川现场）
9602	银川海关驻机场办事处（银机办）
9603	银川海关驻惠农监管组（惠农监管）
9604	银川综保
9700	**西宁关区**
9701	西宁海关现场（西宁海关）
9900	**政法司**

国内地区代码表

Codes for Sub-entity of the P. R. C.

地区代码 Code	地区名称 Name of Sub-entity	地区性质标记 ID of Designated Area
11013	中关村国家自主创新示范区（东城园）	
11019	东城区	9
11023	中关村国家自主创新示范区（西城园）	
11029	西城区	9
11039	崇文区	9
11049	宣武区	9
11053	中关村国家自主创新示范区（朝阳园）	B
11059	朝阳区	9
11063	中关村国家自主创新示范区（丰台园）	B
11069	丰台区	9
11073	中关村国家自主创新示范区（石景山园）	B
11079	石景山	9
11083	中关村国家自主创新示范区（海淀园）	B
11089	海淀区其他	9
11093	中关村国家自主创新示范区（门头沟园）	B
11099	门头沟	9
11103	中关村国家自主创新示范区（房山园）	
11109	房山	9
11113	中关村国家自主创新示范区（顺义园）	
11115	北京天竺出口加工区	
11116	北京天竺综合保税区	
11119	顺义	9
11123	中关村国家自主创新示范区（昌平园）	B
11129	昌平	9
11132	北京经济技术开发区	3
11133	中关村国家自主创新示范区（大兴－亦庄园）	B
11139	大兴其他	9
1113w	北京亦庄保税物流中心	
11143	中关村国家自主创新示范区（通州园）	B
11149	通县	9
11153	中关村国家自主创新示范区（怀柔园）	
11159	怀柔	9
11163	中关村国家自主创新示范区（平谷园）	
11169	平谷	9
11173	中关村国家自主创新示范区（延庆园）	B
11179	延庆	9
11183	中关村国家自主创新示范区（密云园）	B
11189	密云	9
11909	北京其他	9
12019	和平区	2
12029	河东区	2
12039	河西区	2
12043	天津新技术产业园区	B
12049	南开区其他	2
12059	河北区	2
12069	红桥区	2
12072	天津经济技术开发区	3
12074	天津港保税区	A
12075	天津出口加工区	
12076	天津东疆保税港区	2
12077	天津保税物流园	2
12079	滨海新区（塘沽其他）	2
1207W	天津经济技术开发保税物流中心	
12089	滨海新区（汉沽）	2
12099	滨海新区（大港）	2
12106	天津滨海新区综合保税区	6
12109	东丽区	2
12119	西青区	2
12129	津南区	2
12139	北辰区	2
12149	宁河县	2
12159	武清县	2
12169	静海县	2
12179	宝坻县	2
12189	蓟县	2
12909	天津其他	2
13013	石家庄高新技术产业开发实验区	B
13019	石家庄其他	2
13022	曹妃甸经济技术开发区	
13026	曹妃甸综合保税区	
13029	唐山	
13032	秦皇岛经济技术开发区	3
13035	河北秦皇岛出口加工区	2
13039	秦皇岛其他	2
13049	邯郸	
13059	邢台	
13063	保定高新技术产业开发区	B
13069	保定其他	
13079	张家口	
13089	承德	
13099	沧州	
13105	河北廊坊出口加工区	
13109	廊坊	
13119	衡水	
13129	武安	
13909	河北其他	
14012	山西太原经济技术开发区	3
14013	太原高新技术产业开发区	B
14016	太原武宿综合保税区	
14019	太原其他	2
14022	大同经济技术开发区	
14029	大同	
14039	阳泉	
14049	长治	
14059	晋城	
14069	朔州	
14079	雁北	
14089	忻州	
14099	吕梁	
14102	晋中经济技术开发区	
14109	晋中	
14119	临汾	
1411W	山西方略保税物流中心	
14129	运城	

地区代码 Code	地区名称 Name of Sub-entity	地区性质标记 ID of Designated Area
14139	古交	
14909	山西其他	
15015	内蒙古呼和浩特出口加工区	
15019	呼和浩特	
15023	包头高新技术产业开发区	B
15029	包头其他	
15039	乌海	
15049	赤峰	
1504W	赤峰保税物流中心	
15059	二连	2
15069	满洲里	2
15079	呼伦贝尔盟	
15089	哲里木盟	
15099	兴安盟	
15109	乌兰察布盟	
15119	巴彦淖尔市	
15129	伊克昭盟	
15139	阿拉善盟	
15149	锡林郭勒盟	
15909	内蒙古其他	
21012	沈阳经济技术开发区	3
21013	沈阳南湖科技开发区	B
21015	辽宁沈阳、张士出口加工区	
21016	沈阳综合保税区	
21019	沈阳其他	
21022	大连经济技术开发区	3
21023	大连高新技术产业园区	B
21024	大连大窑湾保税区	A
21025	辽宁大连出口加工区	
21026	大窑湾保税港区	
21027	大连保税物流园区	2
21029	大连其他	2
21033	鞍山高新技术产业开发区	B
21039	鞍山其他	
21049	抚顺	
21059	本溪	
21069	丹东	
21079	锦州	
21089	营口	
2108W	营口港保税物流中心	
21099	阜新	
21109	辽阳	
21119	盘锦	
21129	铁岭	
21139	朝阳	
21149	葫芦岛市	
21159	瓦房店	
21169	海城	
21179	兴城	
21189	铁法	
21199	北票	
21209	开源	
21909	辽宁其他	
22012	长春经济技术开发区	3
22013	长春南湖-南岭新技术产业园区	B
22016	长春兴隆综合保税区	
22019	长春其他	2
22023	吉林高新技术产业开发区	B
22029	吉林其他	
22039	四平	
22049	辽源	
22059	通化	
22069	白山	
22075	吉林珲春出口加工区	
22079	珲春	2
22089	图们	
22099	白城	
22109	延边	
22119	公主岭	
22129	梅河口	
22139	集安	
22149	桦甸	
22159	九台	
22169	蛟河	
22179	松原	
22189	延吉市	
22909	吉林其他	
23012	哈尔滨经济技术开发区	3
23013	哈尔滨高技术开发区	B
23019	哈尔滨其他	2
23029	齐齐哈尔	
23039	鸡西	
23049	鹤岗	
23059	双鸭山	
23063	大庆高新技术产业开发区	B
23069	大庆其他	
23079	伊春	
23089	佳木斯	
23099	七台河	
23109	牡丹江	
23119	黑河	2
23126	绥芬河综合保税区	
23129	绥芬河	2
23139	松花江	
23149	绥化	
23159	大兴安岭	
23169	阿城	
23179	同江	
23189	富锦	
23199	铁力	
23209	密山	
23909	黑龙江其他	
31019	黄浦	2
31029	南市	2
31039	卢湾	2
31043	上海漕河泾新技术开发区	B
31049	徐汇其他	2
31052	上海经济技术开发区	3
31059	长宁	2
31069	静安	2
31079	普陀	2
3107W	上海西北物流园区保税物流中心	
31089	闸北	2
31099	虹口	2
31109	杨浦	2
31112	上海闵行经济技术开发区	2
31113	上海浦江高科技园区	B
31115	上海漕河泾出口加工区	2
31119	闵行其他	2
31129	宝山	2
31145	上海嘉定出口加工区	2
31149	嘉定	2
31159	川沙	2
31162	上海闵行经济技术开发区（临港新城）	3

地区代码 Code	地　区　名　称 Name of Sub-entity	地区性质标记 ID of Designated Area	地区代码 Code	地　区　名　称 Name of Sub-entity	地区性质标记 ID of Designated Area
31166	洋山保税港区	2	32189	丹阳	
31169	南汇	2	32199	东台	
31175	上海闵行出口加工区	2	32209	兴化	
31179	奉贤	2	32229	宜兴	
31185	上海松江出口加工区		32235	江苏昆山出口加工区	
31189	松江	2	32236	昆山综合保税区	
31199	金山	2	32239	昆山	
31205	上海青浦出口加工区	2	32249	启东	
31209	青浦	2	32255	江苏吴江出口加工区	
31219	崇明	2	32259	吴江市	
31222	上海浦东新区	3	32269	太仓市	
31224	上海外高桥保税区	A	3226W	太仓保税物流中心	
31225	上海金桥出口加工区(南区)		32909	江苏其他	
31226	上海浦东机场综合保税区	2	33012	杭州经济技术开发区	3
31227	上海保税物流园区	2	33013	杭州高新技术产业开发区	B
31229	浦东其他	2	33015	浙江杭州出口加工区	
31909	上海其他	2	33019	杭州其他	
32013	南京浦口高新技术外向型开发区	B	33022	宁波经济技术开发区	3
32015	江苏南京出口加工区		33023	宁波高新技术产业开发区	
32016	南京综合保税区		33024	浙江宁波北仑港保税区	A
32019	南京其他		33025	浙江宁波出口加工区	2
3201W	南京龙潭港保税物流中心		33026	宁波梅山保税港区	2
32023	无锡高新技术产业开发区	B	33027	宁波保税物流园	2
32025	江苏无锡出口加工区		33029	宁波其他	2
32026	无锡高新区综合保税区		3302W	宁波栎社保税物流中心	
32029	无锡其他		33032	温州经济技术开发区	3
32039	徐州		33039	温州其他	2
32043	常州高新技术产业开发区	B	33045	浙江嘉兴出口加工区	
32045	江苏常州出口加工区		33049	嘉兴	
32049	常州其他		33059	湖州	
32052	苏州工业园区	3	33069	绍兴	
32053	苏州高新技术产业开发区	B	33072	金华经济技术开发区	
32055	江苏苏州工业园区加工区		33079	金华	
32056	苏州工业园综合税区、苏州高新综保区		33089	衢州	
			33096	舟山港综合保税区	
32059	苏州其他		33099	舟山	
32062	南通经济技术开发区	3	33109	丽水	
32065	江苏南通出口加工区		33119	台州	
32066	南通综合保税区		33129	余姚	
32069	南通其他	2	33139	海宁	
32072	连云港经济技术开发区	3	33149	兰溪	
32075	江苏连云港出口加工区	2	33159	瑞安	
32079	连云港其他	2	33169	萧山	
3207W	连云港保税物流中心	2	3316W	杭州保税物流中心	
32085	江苏省淮安出口加工区		33179	江山	
32086	淮安综合保税区		33189	义乌	
32089	淮安市		3318W	义乌保税物流中心	
32096	盐城综合保税区		33199	东阳	
32099	盐城		33205	浙江慈溪出口加工区	
32105	江苏扬州出口加工区		33209	慈溪	
32109	扬州		33219	奉化	
32115	江苏镇江出口加工区		33229	诸暨	
32119	镇江		33239	黄岩	
32125	江苏泰州出口加工区		33909	浙江其他	
32129	泰州		34012	合肥经济技术开发区	3
32139	仪征		34013	合肥科技工业园区	B
32145	江苏常熟出口加工区		34015	安徽合肥出口加工区	
32149	常熟		34019	合肥其他	2
32154	江苏张家港保税区	A	34022	芜湖经济技术产业开发区	3
32156	张家港保税港区		34023	芜湖高新技术开发区	
32157	张家港保税物流园		34025	安徽芜湖出口加工区	
32159	张家港其他		34029	芜湖其他	2
32169	江阴		34033	蚌埠高新技术产业开发区	
3216W	江阴保税物流中心		34039	蚌埠	
32179	宿迁		34042	安徽淮南经济技术开发区	

地区代码 Code	地区名称 Name of Sub-entity	地区性质标记 ID of Designated Area
34049	淮南	
34052	马鞍山经济技术开发区	3
34053	马鞍山慈湖高新技术产业开发区	
34059	马鞍山	
34069	淮北	
34072	铜陵经济技术开发区	3
34079	铜陵	
34082	安庆经济技术开发区	3
34089	安庆	
34099	黄山	
34109	阜阳	
34119	宿州	
34122	滁州经济技术开发区	3
34129	滁州	
34132	安徽六安经济技术开发区	
34139	六安	
34142	安徽宁国经济技术开发区	
34149	宣城	
34159	巢湖	
34162	池州经济技术开发区	3
34169	池州	
34179	亳州	
34909	安徽其他	
35012	福州经济技术开发区	3
35013	福州市科技园区	B
35014	福建马尾保税区	A
35015	福建福州、福清出口加工区	8
35016	福州保税港区	
35017	福州保税物流园区	2
35019	福州其他	2
35021	厦门特区	1
35023	厦门火炬高技术产业开发区	B
35024	厦门象屿保税区	A
35025	福建厦门出口加工区	
35026	厦门海沧保税港区	
35027	厦门象屿保税物流园	1
35029	厦门其他	2
3502W	厦门火炬(翔安)保税物流中心	
35039	莆田	8
35049	三明	
35055	福建泉州出口加工区	8
35059	泉州	8
35069	漳州	8
35079	南平	8
35089	宁德	8
35099	龙岩	8
35109	永安	8
35119	石狮	8
35128	平潭综合试验区	8
35129	平潭	
35909	福建其他	8
36012	南昌经济技术开发区	12
36013	南昌高新技术产业开发区	B
36015	江西南昌出口加工区	
36019	南昌其他	
3601W	南昌保税物流中心	
36023	景德镇高新技术产业开发区	B
36029	景德镇	
36032	萍乡经济技术开发区	3
36039	萍乡	
36042	九江经济技术开发区	3
36045	江西九江出口加工区	2
36049	九江	2
36053	新余高新技术产业开发区	B

地区代码 Code	地区名称 Name of Sub-entity	地区性质标记 ID of Designated Area
36059	新余	
36063	鹰潭高新技术产业开发区	
36069	鹰潭	
36072	赣州经济技术开发区	3
36075	江西赣州出口加工区	
36079	赣州	
36082	宜春经济技术开发区	
36089	宜春	
36092	上饶经济技术开发区	3
36099	上饶	
36102	井冈山经济技术开发区	3
36105	井冈山出口加工区	
36109	吉安	
36119	抚州	
36129	瑞昌	
36909	江西其他	
37013	济南高新技术产业开发区	B
37015	山东济南出口加工区	
37016	济南综合保税区	
37019	济南其他	
37022	青岛经济技术开发区	3
37023	青岛高新技术产业开发区	B
37024	青岛保税区	A
37025	山东青岛出口加工区	
37026	青岛前湾保税港区	2
37027	青岛保税物流园区	2
3702W	青岛保税物流中心	
37029	青岛其他	2
37033	淄博高新技术产业开发区	B
37039	淄博	
3703W	淄博保税物流中心	
37049	枣庄	
37059	东营	
37062	烟台经济技术开发区	3
37065	山东烟台出口加工区	
37069	烟台其他	2
37073	潍坊高新技术产业开发区	B
37075	山东潍坊出口加工区	
37076	潍坊综合保税区	
37079	潍坊其他	
37089	济宁	
37099	泰安	
37103	威海火炬高技术产业开发区	B
37105	山东威海出口加工区	
37109	威海其他	
37119	日照	
3711W	日照保税物流中心	
37129	惠民	
37139	德州	
37149	聊城	
37159	临沂	
37169	菏泽	
37179	青州	
37189	龙口	
37199	曲阜	
37209	莱芜	
37219	新泰	
37229	胶州	
37239	诸城	
37249	莱阳	
37259	滕州	
37269	文登	
37279	荣城	
37289	即墨	
37299	平度	

地区代码 Code	地 区 名 称 Name of Sub-entity	地区性质标记 ID of Designated Area
37909	山东其他	
41012	郑州经济技术开发区	2
41013	郑州高新技术开发区	B
41015	河南郑州出口加工区	
41016	新郑综合保税区	
41018	郑州航空港经济综合试验区	
41019	郑州其他	2
4101W	河南保税物流中心	
41029	开封	
41033	洛阳高新技术产业开发区	B
41039	洛阳其他	
41049	平顶山	
41059	安阳	
41069	鹤壁	
41079	新乡	
41089	焦作	
41099	濮阳	
41109	许昌	
41119	漯河	
41129	三门峡	
41139	商丘	
41149	周口	
41159	驻马店	
41169	南阳	
41179	信阳	
41189	义马	
41199	汝州	
41209	济源	
41219	禹州	
41229	卫辉	
41239	辉县	
41249	泌阳	
41909	河南其他	
42012	武汉经济技术开发区	3
42013	武汉东湖新技术开发区	B
42015	湖北武汉出口加工区	
42016	武汉东湖综合保税区	
42019	武汉其他	2
4201W	武汉东西湖保税物流中心	2
42022	黄石经济技术开发区	3
42029	黄石	
42039	十堰	
42049	沙市	
42059	宜昌	
42062	襄阳经济技术开发区	3
42063	襄阳高新技术产业开发区	B
42069	襄阳其他	
42079	鄂州	
42089	荆门	
42099	黄冈	
42109	孝感	
42119	咸宁	
42122	荆州经济技术开发区	3
42129	荆州	
42139	郧阳	
42149	鄂西	
42159	随州	
42169	老河口	
42179	枣阳	
42189	神农架	
42909	湖北其他	
43013	长沙科技开发区	B
43019	长沙其他	2
4301W	长沙金霞保税物流中心	
43023	株州高新技术产业开发区	B
43029	株州其他	
43039	湘潭	
43046	衡阳综合保税区	
43049	衡阳	
43059	邵阳	
43069	岳阳	2
43079	常德	
43089	张家界	
43099	益阳	
43109	娄底	
43115	湖南郴州出口加工区	
43119	郴州	
43129	永州	
43139	怀化	
43149	湘西	
43159	醴陵	
43169	湘乡	
43179	耒阳	
43189	汨罗	
43199	津市	
43909	湖南其他	
44012	广州经济技术开发区	3
44013	广州天河高新技术产业开发区	B
44014	广州保税区	A
44015	广东广州出口加工区	
44016	广州白云机场综合保税区	
44017	广州保税物流园区	7
44019	广州其他	2
44029	韶关	7
44031	深圳特区	1
44033	深圳科技工业园区	B
44034	福田盐田沙头角保税区	A
44035	广东深圳出口加工区	
44036	深圳前湾保税港区	
44037	深圳盐田保税物流园区	1
4403W	深圳机场保税物流中心	
44039	深圳其他	7
4403W	深圳机场保税物流中心	
44041	珠海特区	1
44043	珠海高新技术产业开发区	B
44044	珠海保税区	A
44045	珠澳跨境工业区珠海园区	7
44048	珠海横琴新区	
44049	珠海其他	7
44051	汕头特区	1
44054	汕头保税区	A
44059	汕头其他	7
44063	佛山高新技术产业开发区	B
44069	佛山其他	7
44079	江门	7
44082	湛江经济技术开发区	3
44089	湛江其他	2
44099	茂名	7
44129	肇庆	7
44133	惠州高新技术产业开发区	B
44139	惠州其他	7
44149	梅州	7
44159	汕尾	7
44169	河源	7
44179	阳江	7
44189	清远	7
44193	东莞松山湖高薪技术产业开发区	
44199	东莞	7
4419W	东莞保税物流中心	

地区代码 Code	地区名称 Name of Sub-entity	地区性质标记 ID of Designated Area
44203	中山火炬高技术产业开发区	B
44209	中山其他	7
4420W	中山保税物流中心	
44219	潮州	7
44229	顺德	7
44235	广东南沙出口加工区	7
44236	广州浦沙保税港区	
44239	番禺	7
44249	揭阳	7
44289	南海	7
44299	云浮市	7
44306	广州南沙保税港区	
44309	南沙其他	
44909	广东其他	7
45013	南宁高新技术产业开发区	B
45019	南宁其他	2
4501W	南宁保税物流中心	
45029	柳州	
45033	桂林高新技术产业开发区	B
45039	桂林其他	
45049	梧州	
45055	广西北海出口加工区	
45059	北海	2
45069	玉林	
45079	百色	
45089	河池	
45096	广西钦州保税港区	
45099	钦州	
45106	广西凭祥综合保税区	
45109	凭祥	2
45119	东兴	2
45129	防城港市	
45139	贵港市	
45149	崇左	
45159	来宾	
45169	贺州	
45909	广西其他	
46011	海口	1
46013	海南国际科技园区	B
46014	海南海口保税区	A
46016	海口综合保税区	1
46021	三亚	5
46031	三沙	
46041	五指山	
46051	琼海	
46061	儋州	
46062	洋浦经济开发区	
46066	洋浦保税港区	
46071	文昌	
46081	万宁	
46091	东方	
46101	定安	
46111	屯昌	
46121	澄迈	
46131	临高	
46141	白沙	
46151	昌江	
46161	乐东	
46171	陵水	
46181	保亭	
46191	琼中	
46901	海南其他	1
46902	海南洋浦经济技术开发区	3
46906	海南洋浦保税港区	5
50012	万州经济技术开发区	
50019	万州区	
50029	涪陵区	
50039	渝中区	
50049	大渡口区	
50052	重庆两江新区江北区	3
50056	重庆两路寸滩保税港区(水港)	
50059	江北区	
50066	重庆西永综合保税区	
50069	沙坪坝区	
50073	重庆高新技术产业开发区	B
50079	九龙坡区	
50082	重庆经济技术开发区	3
50089	南岸区	
50092	重庆两江新区北碚区	3
50099	北碚区	
50109	万盛区	
50119	双桥区	
50122	重庆两江新区渝北区	3
50125	重庆出口加工区	
50126	重庆两路寸滩保税港区(空港)	
50129	渝北区	
50139	巴南区	
50212	长寿经济技术开发区	2
50219	长寿县	
50229	綦江区	
50239	潼南县	
50249	重庆市铜梁区　铜梁区	
50259	大足区	
50269	荣昌县	
50279	重庆市璧山区　璧山区	
50289	梁平县	
50299	城口县	
50309	丰都县	
50319	垫江县	
50329	武隆县	
50339	忠县	
50349	开县	
50359	云阳县	
50369	奉节县	
50379	巫山县	
50389	巫溪县	
50399	黔江	
50409	石柱土家族自治区	
50419	秀山土家族苗族自治县	
50429	酉阳土家族苗族自治县	
50439	彭水苗族土家族自治县	
50819	江津市	
50829	合川市	
50839	永川市	
50849	南川市	
51012	成都经济技术开发区	3
51013	成都高新技术产业开发区	B
51015	四川成都出口加工区	
51016	成都高新综合保税区	
51019	成都其他	2
5101W	成都空港保税物流中心	
51039	自贡	
51049	攀枝花	
51059	泸州	
51069	德阳	
51072	绵阳经济技术开发区	
51073	绵阳高新技术产业开发区	B
51075	四川绵阳出口加工区	
51079	绵阳其他	
51082	广元经济技术开发区	
51089	广元	
51099	遂宁	
51109	内江	
51119	乐山	

地区代码 Code	地区名称 Name of Sub-entity	地区性质标记 ID of Designated Area
51142	宜宾临港经济开发区	
51149	宜宾	
51159	南充	
51169	达县	
51179	雅安	
51189	阿坝	
51199	甘孜	
51209	凉山	
51229	广汉	
51239	江油	
51249	都江堰	
51259	峨眉山	
51269	资阳(资阳)	
51279	眉山(眉山)	
51289	广安(广安)	
51299	巴中(巴中)	
51909	四川其他	
52013	贵阳高新技术产业开发区	B
52016	贵阳综合保税区	
52019	贵阳其他	2
52029	六盘水	
52039	遵义	
52049	铜仁	
52059	黔西南	
52069	毕节	
52079	安顺	
52089	黔东南	
52099	黔南	
52909	贵州其他	
53012	昆明经济技术开发区	3
53013	昆明高新技术产业开发区	B
53015	云南昆明出口加工区	
53019	昆明其他	
53029	东川	
53039	昭通	
53042	曲靖经济技术开发区	3
53049	曲靖	
53059	楚雄	
53069	玉溪	
53079	红河	
53089	文山	
53099	普洱	
53109	西双版纳	
53119	大理	
53129	保山	
53139	德宏	
53149	丽江	
53159	怒江	
53169	迪庆	
53179	临沧	
53189	畹町	2
53199	瑞丽	2
53209	河口	2
53909	云南其他	
54019	拉萨	6
54029	昌都	6
54039	山南	6
54049	日喀则	6
54059	那曲	6
54069	阿里	6
54079	林芝	6
54909	西藏其他	6
61012	陕西航天经济技术开发区	
61013	西安新技术产业开发区	B
61015	陕西西安出口加工区	
61016	西安综合保税区和西安高新综合保税区	
61019	西安其他	2
61029	铜川	
61033	宝鸡高新技术产业开发区	B
61039	宝鸡其他	
61049	咸阳	
61059	渭南	
61062	汉中经济技术开发区	
61069	汉中	
61079	安康	
61089	商洛	
61099	延安	
61109	榆林	
61909	陕西其他	
62013	兰州宁卧庄新技术产业开发区	B
62019	兰州其他	2
62029	嘉峪关	
62039	金昌	
62049	白银	
62059	天水	
62069	酒泉	
62079	张掖	
62089	武威	
6208W	武威保税物流中心	
62099	定西	
62109	陇南	
62119	平凉	
62129	庆阳	
62139	临夏	
62149	甘南	
62909	甘肃其他	
63012	西宁经济技术开发区	3
63013	青海高新技术产业开发区	B
63019	西宁	2
63029	海东	
63039	海北	
63049	黄南	
63059	海南	
63069	果洛	
63079	玉树	
63089	海西	
63909	青海其他	
64012	银川经济技术开发区	3
64016	银川综合保税区	
64019	银川	2
64029	石嘴山	
64039	吴中	
64049	固原	
64059	中卫	
64909	宁夏其他	
65012	乌鲁木齐经济技术开发区	3
65013	乌鲁木齐高新技术产业开发区	B
65015	新疆乌鲁木齐出口加工区	9
65019	乌鲁木齐其他	9
65029	克拉玛依	9
65036	阿拉山口综合保税区	
65039	博乐	9
65049	巴音	9
65059	阿克苏	9
65069	克孜	9
65079	喀什	9
65089	和田	9
65099	伊宁	9
65109	塔城	2
65119	阿勒泰	9
65122	石河子经济技术开发区	3
65129	石河子	9
65219	吐鲁番	9
65229	哈密	9
65239	昌吉回族自治州	9
65909	新疆其他	9

监管证件名称代码表

Code list of Supporting Documents Subject to Customs Control of the People's Republic of China

许可证或批文代码 Code	许可证或批文名称	Name of Licences or Instruments of Ratification	监管证件签发机构	Name of Licences or Instruments of Ratification
1	进口许可证	Import licence	商务部配额许可证事务局或其授权机关	Quota & Licence Administrative Bureau Ministry of Commerce or its authorized institution
2	两用物项和技术进口许可证	Import licence for dualuse item and techndog – ines	商务部	Ministry of commerce
3	两用物项和技术出口许可证	Export licence for dualuse item and technologines	商务部	Ministry of commerce
4	出口许可证	Export licence	商务部配额许可证事务局或其授权机关	Quota & Licence Administrative Bureau Ministry of Commerce or its authorized institution
5	纺织品临时出口许可证	Deep processing Transfer application form	商务部	Ministry of commerce
6	旧机电产品禁止进口	Used machinery and electrical products are on the list of prohibited import goods	商品编码后有此代码的,其旧产品禁止进口	the importing of used electro – mechanical products with this code at the end of its code of goods is prohibited.
7	自动进口许可证	Automatic import licence	商务部	Ministry of commerce
8	禁止出口商品	Articles on the list of prohibited export goods	商品编码后有此代码的,禁止出口	Products with this code are prohibited to be exported.
9	禁止进口商品	Articles on the list of prohibited import goods	商品编码后有此代码的,禁止进口	Products with this code are prohibited to be eximport.
A	入境货物通关单	Certificate of inspection for goods inward	国家质量监督检验检疫机构	the administrations of quality supervision
B	出境货物通关单	Certificate of inspection for goods outward	国家质量监督检验检疫机构	the administrations of quality supervision
D	出/入境货物通关单(毛坯钻石用)	Certificate of inspection for goods inward/outward (for semifi-nished diamonds)	国家质量监督检验检疫机构	the administrations of quality supervision
E	濒危物种允许出口证明书	Export licencing certificate for endangeted species	国家濒危物种进出口管理办公室或其办事机构	the administrative bureau of the Import and Export of Endangered Wild Animals or by other relevant administrative
F	濒危物种允许进口证明书	Import licencing certificate for endangeted species	国家濒危物种进出口管理办公室或其办事机构	the administrative bureau of the Import and Export of Endangered Wild Animals or by other relevant administrative
G	两用物项和技术出口许可证(定向)	Export permit for dual-use item and technologines	商务部	Ministry of commerce
H	港澳 OPA 纺织品证明	Hong Kong and Macao OPA textiles prove	香港工业贸易署或澳门经济局	Hongkong Department of trade and Industry
I	精神药物进(出)口准许证	Import or export permit for psychotropic drugs	国家食品药品监督管理局	State food and drug administration
J	黄金及其制品进出口准许证或批件	Import or export permit for gold products	中国人民银行	The people's bank of china
K	深加工结转申请表	Deep processing carry – over application form	外经贸主管部门	Foreign trade department
L	药品进出口准许证	Import or export of medicines permit licence	国家食品药品监督管理局及其授权机构	State food and drug administration and its authorized in atitution
M	密码产品和设备进口许可证	Import permit for encryption products and equipment	国家密码管理局	National password administration
O	自动进口许可证(新旧机电产品)	Automatic import licence (machinery and electrical products, whether used or not)	商务部或地方商务主管机构、部门机电办	Business Department, local institutions in charge of foreign trade or department of Electrical and Mechanical Serivecs
P	固体废物进口许可证	Import permit for solid wastes	国家环保总局	State environmental protection administration of china
Q	进口药品通关单	Report of inspection of soundness on import medicines	国家食品药品监督管理局及其授权机构	State food and drug administration and its authorized institution
R	进口兽药通关单	Clearance form for import veterinary drugs	农业部	Ministry of Agriculture of the people's Republic

许可证或批文代码 Code	许可证或批文名称	Name of Licences or Instruments of Ratification	监管证件签发机构	Name of Licences or Instruments of Ratification
S	进出口农药登记证明	Import or export registration certificate for pesticides	农业部	Ministry of Agriculture of the people's Republic
T	银行调运现钞进出境许可证	Entry or exit permit for foreign currency cash transfer and reallocation between banks	(1)外币现钞进出境,外汇管理局核发的"银行调运外币现钞进出境许可证;(2)人民币现钞进出境,中国人民银行货币金银局的批件	(1)"License for banks to transfer foreign currencies" released by state Administration of Foreign Exchange is required for the entry and exit of foreign currency; (2)Sanction from the Silver, Gold & Currency" Department of Peoples Bank of China is required for the entry and exit of RMB".
U	合法捕捞产品通关证明	Lawfu fish for products clearance certificate	农业部	Minstry of Agriculture of the people's Republic
W	麻醉药品进出口准许证	Import or export permit for narcolic drugs	国家食品药品监督管理局	State food and drug administration
X	有毒化学品环境管理放行通知单	Enyironment control release notice for poisonous chemicals	国家环保总局	State environmental protection administration of china
Y	原产地证明	certificate of origin	各地出入境检验检疫局	State environmental protection administration of china
Z	音像制品进口批准单或节目提取单	Issuance permit for audio/or video products, release for protolype tape	(1)文化部签发《文化部进口音像制品批准单》(2)广播电影电视总局及其授权部门签发的《进口广播电影电视节目带(片)提取单》	(1) License for Importing and Exporting Visual Product released by the Department of Academy and Culture; (2) List of Imported Movies and Television Programmes released by the State Association of Broadcasting, Films & Television.
c	内销征税联系单	Domestic taxation contact list	所在地海关	Local Customs
e	关税配额外优惠税率进口棉花配额证	Quota certificate for importing cotton beyond the tariff quota at a preferention rate.	商务部配额许可证事务局或其授权机关	Quota & Licence Administrative Bureau Ministry of Commerce or its authorized institution
h	核增核扣表			
q	国别关税配额证明	Country – specific tariff quota certificates	国家发展和改革委员会	National development and Reform commission
r	预归类标志	Pre classification symbol	海关总署或其授权部门	Customs of P. R. china or its authorized institution
s	适用ITA税率的商品用途认定证明	Application of apply to ITA rates goods certificate	所在地海关	Local customs
t	关税配额证明	Certificate of customs quota	商务部配额许可证事务局或其授权机关	Quota & Licence Administrative Bureau Ministry of Commerce or its authorized institution
v	自动进口许可证(加工贸易)	Automatic import license (processing trade volume)	商务部配额许可证事务局或其授权机关	Quota & Licence Administrative Bureau Ministry of Commerce or its authorized institution
x	出口许可证(加工贸易)	Export license (processing trade)	商务部配额许可证事务局或其授权机关	Quota & Licence Administrative Bureau Ministry of Commerce or its authorized institution
y	出口许可证(边境小额贸易)	Export license (Small frantier trade volume)	商务部配额许可证事务局或其授权机关	Quota & Licence Administrative Bureau Ministry of Commerce or its authorized institution

结汇方式代码表
Codes for Modes of Bank's Exchange Settlement

结汇方式代码 Code	结汇方式名称	Modes of Bank's Exchange Settlement
1	信汇	M/T (Mail transfer)
2	电汇	T/T (Telegraphic transfer)
3	票汇	D/D (Demand draft)
4	付款交单	D/P (Documents against payment)
5	承兑交单	D/A (Documents against acceptance)
6	信用证	L/C (Letter of credit)
7	先出后结	Settlement after export
8	先结后出	Settlement before export
9	其他	Other

用途代码表
Codes for Use of Imported Goods

用途代码 Code	用途名称	Name of Usage
01	外贸自营内销	Autonomous imports of authorized enterprises for home use
02	特区内销	Imports of SEZ for home use
03	其他内销	Other imports for home use
04	企业自用	Autonomous imports of authorized enterprises for one's own use
05	加工返销	For processing export
06	借用	Leased or borrowed
07	收保证金	Security deposit
08	免费提供	Supplied free of charge
09	作价提供	Supplied at a fixed price
10	货样,广告品	Samples and advertising matters
11	其它	Other
13	以产顶进	Enter in order to produce a top

货币代码表
Codes for the Representation of Currencies

货币代码 Code	货币符号 Symbol	货币名称 Name of Currency	货币代码 Code	货币符号 Symbol	货币名称 Name of Currency
110	HKD	港币	305	FRF	法国法郎
116	JPY	日本元	307	ITL	意大利里拉
121	MOP	澳门元	312	ESP	西班牙比赛塔
129	PHP	菲律宾比索	315	ATS	奥地利先令
132	SGD	新加坡元	318	FIM	芬兰马克
133	KRW	韩国圆	326	NOK	挪威克朗
136	THB	泰国铢	330	SEK	瑞典克朗
142	CNY	人民币	331	CHF	瑞士法郎
300	EUR	欧元	501	CAD	加拿大元
302	DKK	丹麦克朗	502	USD	美元
303	GBP	英镑	601	AUD	澳大利亚元
304	DEM	德国马克	609	NZD	新西兰元

计量单位代码表
Codes for Units of Measure Used in International Trade

计量单位代码 Code	计量单位名称	Name of Unit
001	台	set
002	座	set
003	辆	unit
004	艘	unit
005	架	set
006	套	assortment/kit/outfit/set/suit
007	个	piece
008	只	piece
009	头	head/piece
010	张	sheet
011	件	piece
012	支	piece
013	枝	piece
014	根	stick
015	条	bar
016	把	piece
017	块	block/cake/piece
018	卷	coil/reel/roll/spool
019	副	pair/set
020	片	piece/slice
021	组	group/set/unit
022	份	ration
023	幅	piece

计量单位代码 Code	计量单位名称	Name of Unit
025	双	pair
026	对	couple/pair/set
027	棵	piece
028	株	piece
029	井	*jing*
030	米	meter
031	盘	coil/disk
032	平方米	square meter
033	立方米	cubic meter
034	筒	cone/reel/sleeve/tube
035	千克	kilogram
036	克	gram
037	盆	basin/pot
038	万个	ten thousand pie-ces
039	具	piece/set
040	百副	hundred pairs/sets
041	百支	hundred piece
042	百把	hundred piece
043	百个	hundred piece
044	百片	hundred sheet
045	刀	hundred sheet/quire

计量单位代码 Code	计量单位名称	Name of Unit
046	疋	bolt
047	公担	quintal
048	扇	piece
049	百枝	hundred piece
050	千只	thousand piece
051	千块	thousand block
052	千盒	thousand box
053	千枝	thousand piece
054	千个	thousand piece
055	亿支	hundred million piece
056	亿个	hundred million piece
057	万套	ten thousand set
058	千张	thousand sheet
059	万张	ten thousand sheet
060	千伏安	kilovolt-ampere
061	千瓦	kilowatt
062	千瓦时	kilowatt-hour
063	千升	kilolitre, thousand liter
067	英尺	foot
070	吨	metric ton
071	长吨	long ton
072	短吨	short ton
073	司马担	picul

计量单位代码 Code	计量单位名称	Name of Unit
074	司马斤	catty
075	斤	*jin*
076	磅	pound
077	担	hundred pounds
078	英担	UK hundred-weight
079	短担	short hundred-weight
080	两	*liang*
081	市担	*dan*
083	盎司	ounce
084	克拉	carat
085	市尺	*chi*
086	码	yard
088	英寸	inch
089	寸	*cun*
095	升	liter/*sheng*
096	毫升	milliliter
097	英加仑	UK gallon
098	美加仑	US gallon
099	立方英尺	cubic foot
101	立方尺	cubic *chi*
110	平方码	square yard
111	平方英尺	square foot
112	平方尺	square *chi*
115	英制马力	UK horsepower
116	公制马力	metric horsepower
118	令	link/ream
120	箱	box/carton/case/cassette/chest/crate
121	批	batch/lot/panel
122	罐	can/jar/tin
123	桶	barrel/bucket/cask/drum/keg/pail
124	扎	bundle
125	包	bag/bale/pack/packet
126	箩	basket
127	打	dozen
128	筐	basket/pannier
129	罗	gross/twelve dozen
130	匹	bolt/piece
131	册	book/copy
132	本	book/copy
133	发	shell/round
134	枚	piece
135	捆	bundle
136	袋	bag/sack
139	粒	grain
140	盒	box/capsule
141	合	*he*
142	瓶	bottle/carboy/cylinder/flask/jar/vial
143	千支	thousand piece
144	万双	ten thousand pair
145	万粒	ten thousand grain
146	千粒	thousand grain
147	千米	kilometer
148	千英尺	thousand feet
149	百万贝可	Million Ba
163	部	set/unit
164	亿株	set/unit

成交方式代码表
Codes for Trade Terms

成交方式代码 Code	成交方式名称	Codes for Trade Terms
1	CIF	CIF
2	C&F	CFR/CNF/C&F
3	FOB	FOB
4	C&I	C&I
5	市场价	Market price
6	垫仓	Dunnage charge

国别(地区)代码表
Codes for the Representation of Names of Countries and Regions

代码 Code	中文名 Chinese Name	英文名 English Name	最惠/普标记 Preferential/General tariff rate	船舶吨税优/普标记
100	亚洲	**Asia**		
101	阿富汗	Afghanistan	L	H
102	巴林	Bahrian	L	H
103	孟加拉国	Bangladesh	L	L
104	不丹	Bhutan	H	H
105	文莱	Brunei	L	H
106	缅甸	Myanmar	L	H
107	柬埔寨	Cambodia	L	H
108	塞浦路斯	Cyprus	L	L
109	朝鲜	Korea, DPR	L	L
110	香港	Hong Kong	L	L
111	印度	India	L	L
112	印度尼西亚	Indonesia	L	L
113	伊朗	Iran	L	L
114	伊拉克	Iraq	L	H
115	以色列	Israel	L	L
116	日本	Japan	L	L
117	约旦	Jordan	L	H
118	科威特	Kuwait	L	H
119	老挝	Lao PDR	L	H
120	黎巴嫩	Lebanon	L	L
121	澳门	Macau	L	L
122	马来西亚	Malaysia	L	L
123	马尔代夫	Maldives	L	H
124	蒙古	Mongolia	L	L
125	尼泊尔联邦民主共和国	Nepal, FDR	L	H
126	阿曼	Oman	L	L
127	巴基斯坦	Pakistan	L	L
128	巴勒斯坦	Palestine	H	H
129	菲律宾	Philippines	L	L
130	卡塔尔	Qatar	L	H
131	沙特阿拉伯	Saudi Arabia	L	H
132	新加坡	Singapore	L	L
133	韩国	Korea, Rep.	L	L
134	斯里兰卡	Sri Lanka	L	L
135	叙利亚	Syrian Arab Republic	L	H
136	泰国	Thailand	L	L
137	土耳其	Turkey	L	L
138	阿联酋	United Arab Emirates	L	H

代码 Code	中文名 Chinese Name	英文名 English Name	最惠/普标记 Preferential/General tariff rate	船舶吨税优/普标记
139	也门	Yemen	L	L
141	越南	Viet Nam	L	L
142	中国	China	L	L
143	台澎金马关税区	Taiwan, Prov. of China	L	H
144	东帝汶	Timor – Leste	L	H
145	哈萨克斯坦	Kazakhstan	L	H
146	吉尔吉斯斯坦	Kyrgyzstan	L	H
147	塔吉克斯坦	Tajikistan	L	H
148	土库曼斯坦	Turkmenistan	L	H
149	乌兹别克斯坦	Uzbekistan	L	H
199	亚洲其他国家(地区)	Oth. Asia nes		H
101	非洲			
201	阿尔及利亚	Algeria	L	L
202	安哥拉	Angola	L	H
203	贝宁	Benin	L	H
204	博茨瓦纳	Botswana	L	H
205	布隆迪	Burundi	L	H
206	喀麦隆	Cameroon	L	H
207	加那利群岛	Canary Islands	H	H
208	佛得角	Cape Verde	L	H
209	中非	Central African Republic.	L	H
210	塞卜泰(休达)	Ceuta	H	H
211	乍得	Chad	L	H
212	科摩罗	Comoros	H	H
213	刚果(布)	Congo	L	L
214	吉布提	Djibouti	L	H
215	埃及	Egypt	L	L
216	赤道几内亚	Equatorial Guinea	L	H
217	埃塞俄比亚	Ethiopia	L	L
218	加蓬	Gabon	L	H
219	冈比亚	Gambia	L	H
220	加纳	Ghana	L	L
221	几内亚	Guinea	L	H
222	几内亚比绍	Guinea – Bissau	L	H
223	科特迪瓦	Cote dlvoire	L	H
224	肯尼亚	Kenya	L	L
225	利比里亚	Liberia	L	H
226	利比亚	Libyan Arab Jamahiriya	L	H
227	马达加斯加	Madagascar	L	H
228	马拉维	Malawi	L	H
229	马里	Mali	L	H
230	毛里塔尼亚	Mauritania	L	H
231	毛里求斯	Mauritius	L	H
232	摩洛哥	Morocco	L	L
233	莫桑比克	Mozambique	L	H
234	纳米比亚	Namibia	L	H
235	尼日尔	Niger	L	H
236	尼日利亚	Nigeria	L	H
237	留尼汪	Reunion	H	H
238	卢旺达	Rwanda	L	H
239	圣多美和普林西比	Sao Tome and Principe	H	H
240	塞内加尔	Senegal	L	H
241	塞舌尔	Seychelles	H	H
242	塞拉利昂	Sierra Leone	L	H
243	索马里	Somalia	L	H
244	南非	South Africa	L	L
245	西撒哈拉	Western Sahara	H	H
246	苏丹	Sudan	L	L
247	坦桑尼亚	Tanzania	L	H
248	多哥	Togo	L	H
249	突尼斯	Tunisia	L	L
250	乌干达	Uganda	L	H
251	布基纳法索	Burkina Faso	L	H
252	刚果(金)	Congo, DR	L	L
253	赞比亚	Zambia	L	H
254	津巴布韦	Zimbabwe	L	H
255	莱索托	Lesotho	L	H
256	梅利利亚	Melilla	H	H
257	斯威士兰	Swaziland	L	H
258	厄立特里亚	Eritrea	L	H
259	马约特	Mayotte	L	H
260	南苏单共和国	**Rcpuplic of south sudan**	普通	H
260	南苏丹共和国	Republic of South Sudan	H	H
299	非洲其他国家(地区)	Oth. Afr. nes		H
300	欧洲			
301	比利时	Belgium	L	L
302	丹麦	Denmark	L	L
303	英国	United Kingdom	L	L
304	德国	Germany	L	L
305	法国	France	L	L
306	爱尔兰	Ireland	L	L
307	意大利	Italy	L	L
308	卢森堡	Luxembourg	L	L
309	荷兰	Netherlands	L	L
310	希腊	Greece	L	L
311	葡萄牙	Portugal	L	L
312	西班牙	Spain	L	L
313	阿尔巴尼亚	Albania	L	L
314	安道尔	Andorra	H	H
315	奥地利	Austria	L	L
316	保加利亚	Bulgaria	L	L
318	芬兰	Finland	L	L
320	直布罗陀	Gibraltar	H	L
321	匈牙利	Hungary	L	L
322	冰岛	Iceland	L	H
323	列支敦士登	Liechtenstein	L	H
324	马耳他	Malta	L	L
325	摩纳哥	Monaco	L	H
326	挪威	Norway	L	L
327	波兰	Poland	L	L
328	罗马尼亚	Romania	L	L

代码 Code	中文名 Chinese Name	英文名 English Name	最惠/普标记 Preferential/General tariff rate	船舶吨税优/普标记
329	圣马力诺	San Marino	L	H
330	瑞典	Sweden	L	L
331	瑞士	Switzerland	L	H
334	爱沙尼亚	Estonia	L	L
335	拉脱维亚	Latvia	L	L
336	立陶宛	Lithuania	L	L
337	格鲁吉亚	Georgia	L	L
338	亚美尼亚	Armenia	L	H
339	阿塞拜疆	Azerbai jan	L	H
340	白俄罗斯	Belarus	L	H
343	摩尔多瓦	Moldova	L	H
344	俄罗斯联邦	Russian Federation	L	L
347	乌克兰	Ukraine	L	L
349	塞尔维亚和黑山		H	H
350	斯洛文尼亚	Slovenia	L	L
351	克罗地亚	Croatia	L	L
352	捷克	Czech Republic	L	L
353	斯洛伐克	Slovakia	L	L
354	前南马其顿	Macedonia, FYR	L	H
355	波黑	Bosnia and Hercegovina	L	H
356	梵蒂冈城国	Vatican City State	H	H
357	法罗群岛	Faroe Islands	L	H
358	塞尔维亚	Serbia	L	H
359	黑山	Montenegro	L	H
399	欧洲其他国家(地区)	Oth. Eur. nes		H
400	**拉丁美洲**			
401	安提瓜和巴布达	Antigua & Barbuda	L	H
402	阿根廷	Argentina	L	L
403	阿鲁巴	Aruba	H	H
404	巴哈马	Bahamas	H	L
405	巴巴多斯	Barbados	L	H
406	伯利兹	Belize	L	H
408	多民族玻利维亚国	Estado Plurinacionalde Bolivia	L	H
409	博内尔	Bonaire	H	H
410	巴西	Brazil	L	L
411	开曼群岛	Cayman Islands	H	L
412	智利	Chile	L	L
413	哥伦比亚	Colombia	L	H
414	多米尼克	Dominica	L	H
415	哥斯达黎加	Costa Rica	L	H
416	古巴	Cuba	L	L
417	库腊索岛	Curacao	H	H
418	多米尼加共和国	Dominican Republic	L	H
419	厄瓜多尔	Ecuador	L	H
420	法属圭亚那	French Guiana	H	H
421	格林纳达	Grenada	L	H
422	瓜德罗普	Guadeloupe	H	H
423	危地马拉	Guatemala	L	H
424	圭亚那	Guyana	L	H
425	海地	Haiti	L	H
426	洪都拉斯	Honduras	L	H
427	牙买加	Jamaica	L	H
428	马提尼克	Martinique	H	H
429	墨西哥	Mexico	L	L
430	蒙特塞拉特	Montserrat	H	H
431	尼加拉瓜	Nicaragua	L	H
432	巴拿马	Panama	L	H
433	巴拉圭	Paraguay	L	H
434	秘鲁	Peru	L	L
435	波多黎各	Puerto Rico	L	H
436	萨巴	Saba	H	H
437	圣卢西亚	Saint Lucia	L	H
438	圣马丁岛	Saint Martin Islands	H	H
439	圣文森特和格林纳丁斯	Saint Vincent and Grenadines	L	H
440	萨尔瓦多	El Salvador	H	H
441	苏里南	Suriname	L	H
442	特立尼达和多巴哥	Trinidad and Tobago	L	H
443	特克斯和凯科斯群岛	Turks and Caicos Islands	H	H
444	乌拉圭	Uruguay	L	H
445	委内瑞拉	Venezuela	L	H
446	英属维尔京群岛	Virgin Islands, British	H	H
447	圣其茨和尼维斯	Saint Kitts and Nevis	L	H
448	圣皮埃尔和密克隆	Saint. Pierre and Miquelon	L	H
449	荷属安地列斯	Netherlands Antilles	H	H
499	拉丁美洲其他国家(地区)	Oth. L. Amer. nes		H
500	**北美洲**			
501	加拿大	Canada	L	L
502	美国	United States	L	L
503	格陵兰	Greenland	L	H
504	百慕大	Bermuda	H	L
599	北美洲其他国家(地区)	Oth. N. Amer. nes		H
600	**大洋洲**			
601	澳大利亚	Australia	L	H
602	库克群岛	Cook Islands	L	H
603	斐济	Fiji	L	H
604	盖比群岛	Gambier Islands	H	H
605	马克萨斯群岛	Marquesas Islands	H	H
606	瑙鲁	Nauru	H	H

代码 Code	中文名 Chinese Name	英文名 English Name	最惠/普标记 Preferential/General tariff rate	船舶吨税优/普标记
607	新喀里多尼亚	New Caledonia	L	H
608	瓦努阿图	Vanuatu	L	H
609	新西兰	New Zealand	L	L
610	诺福克岛	Norfolk Island	H	H
611	巴布亚新几内亚	Papua New Guinea	L	H
612	社会群岛	Society Islands	H	H
613	所罗门群岛	Solomon Islands	L	H
614	汤加	Tonga	L	H
615	土阿莫土群岛	Tuamotu Islands	H	H
616	土布艾群岛	Tubai Islands	H	H
617	萨摩亚	Samoa	L	H
618	基里巴斯	Kiribati	H	H
619	图瓦卢	Tuvalu	H	H
620	密克罗尼西亚联邦	Micronesia, Fs	L	H
621	马绍尔群岛	Marshall Islands	H	H
622	帕劳	Palau	H	H
623	法属波利尼西亚	French Polynesia	L	H
625	瓦利斯和浮图纳	Wallis and Futuna	L	H
699	大洋洲其他国家(地区)	Oth. Ocean. nes		H
701	国(地)别不详	Countries(reg.) unknown	H	H
702	联合国及机构和国际组织	UN and oth. intl org.		
999	中性包装原产国别	Conutries of Neutral Package	H	H

地区性质代码表
Codes for the Nature of Designated Areas

地区性质代码 Code	地区性质名称	Name of the Nature of Designated Areas
1	经济特区	Special economic zone (SEZ)
2	沿海开放城市	Coastal open city
3	经济技术开发区	Development zone of economy and technology
4	经济开放区	Open-door economic zone
5	海南省	Hainan
6	西藏自治区	Xizang autonomous region
7	广东省	Guangdong
8	福建省	Fujian
9	北京市、新疆	Beijing municipality, Xinjiang autonomous region
A	保税工业区	Bonded industrial zone
B	新技术开发园区	New-technology development parks

企业性质代码表
Codes for Class of Enterprises

企业性质代码 Code	企业性质名称	Class of enterprises
1	国有	State-owned enterprises
2	合作	Chinese-foreign contractual joint ventures
3	合资	Chinese-foreign equity joint ventures
4	独资	Foreign wholly-owned enterprises
5	集体	Collective owned enterprises
6	私营	Privately owned enterprises
7	个体工商户	Individual business
8	报关	Customs clearing agent
9	其他	Other

3

中华人民共和国海关进口关税税率附表

（2015 年 1 月 1 日起实施）

Import tariff attached table

(Enforced from January 1, 2015)

附表 1：

Attached table 1：

2015 年进口商品协定、特惠税目税率表

Conventional、special preferential Duty Item and Duty Rate for Import 2015

（2015 年 1 月 1 日起实施）

(Enforced from January 1,2015)

税则号列	货品名称	最惠国	协定税率 东盟统一	亚太5国	智利	巴基斯坦	新加坡	新西兰	秘鲁	哥达	香港	澳门	台湾	瑞士	冰岛	特惠税率 亚太2国	老挝	柬埔寨	缅甸	LDC1	LDC2	LDC3
01012100	改良种用马	0																				
01012900	其他马	10	0		0	5		0	4	0				6	0					0	0	0
01013010	改良种用驴	0																		0	0	0
01013090	其他驴	10	0		0	5		0	4	0				6	0					0	0	0
01019000	骡	10	0		0	5		0	4	0				6	0					0	0	0
01022100	改良种用家牛	0																		0	0	0
01022900	其他家牛	10	0		0	5		0	4	0				6	0		0	0	0	0	0	0
01023100	改良种用水牛	0																		0	0	0
01023900	其他水牛	10	0		0	5		0	4	0				6	0		0	0	0	0	0	0
01029010	改良种用其他牛	0																		0	0	0
01029090	其他牛	10	0		0	5		0	4	0				6	0		0	0	0	0	0	0
01031000	改良种用猪	0																		0	0	0
01039110	重量<10kg 的猪	10	0		0	5		0	0	0				6	0			0	0	0	0	0
01039120	重量在 10－50kg 的猪，包括 10kg	10	0		0	5		0	0	0				6	0			0	0	0	0	0
01039200	重量≥50kg 的猪	10	0		0	5		0	0	0				6	0		0	0	0	0	0	0
01041010	改良种用的绵羊	0																		0	0	0
01041090	其他绵羊	10	0		0	5		0	0	0				6	0					0	0	0
01042010	改良种用的山羊	0																		0	0	0
01042090	其他山羊	10	0		0	5		0	0	0				6	0					0	0	0
01051110	重量≤185g 的改良种用鸡	0																		0	0	0
01051190	重量≤185g 的其他鸡	10	0		0	5		0	4	0				6	0		0		0	0	0	0
01051210	重量≤185g 的改良种用火鸡	0																		0	0	0
01051290	重量≤185g 的其他火鸡	10	0		0	5		0	4	0				6	0					0	0	0
01051310	重量不超过 185 克的改良种用鸭	0																		0	0	0
01051390	重量不超过 185 克的其他鸭	10	0		0	5		0	0	0				6	0		0			0	0	0
01051410	重量不超过 185 克的改良种用鹅	0																		0	0	0
01051490	重量不超过 185 克的其他鹅	10	0		0	5		0	0	0				6	0		0			0	0	0
01051510	重量不超过 185 克的改良种用珍珠鸡	0																		0	0	0
01051590	重量不超过 185 克的其他珍珠鸡	10	0		0	5		0	0	0				6	0		0			0	0	0
01059410	重量>185g 的改良种用鸡	0																		0	0	0
01059490	重量>185g 的其他鸡	10	0		0	5		0	0	0				6	0					0	0	0
01059910	重量>185g 的其他改良种用家禽	0																		0	0	0
01059991	重量>185g 的非改良种用鸭	10	0		0	5		0	0	0				6	0					0	0	0
01059992	重量>185g 的非改良种用鹅	10	0		0	5		0	0	0				6	0					0	0	0
01059993	重量>185g 的非改良种用珍珠鸡	10	0		0	5		0	0	0				6	0					0	0	0
01059994	重量>185g 的非改良种用火鸡	10	0		0	5		0	0	0				6	0					0	0	0
01061110	改良种用灵长目动物	0																		0	0	0
01061190	其他灵长目动物	10	0		0	5		0	0	0				6	0					0	0	0
01061211	改良种用鲸、海豚及鼠海豚；海牛及儒艮	10	0		0	5		0	0	0				6	0					0	0	0
01061219	其他鲸、海豚及鼠海豚；海牛及儒艮	10	0		0	5		0	0	0				6	0					0	0	0
01061221	改良种用海豹、海狮及海象	0																		0	0	0
01061229	其他海豹、海狮及海象	10	0		0	5		0	4	0				6	0					0	0	0
01061310	改良种用骆驼及其他骆驼科动物	0																		0	0	0
01061390	其他骆驼及其他骆驼科动物	10	0		0	5		0	4	0				6	0					0	0	0
01061410	改良种用家兔及野兔	0																		0	0	0
01061490	其他家兔及野兔	10	0		0	5		0	4	0				6	0					0	0	0
01061910	改良种用哺乳动物	0																		0	0	0
01061990	其他哺乳动物	10	0		0	5		0	4	0				6	0					0	0	0
01062011	改良种用鳄鱼苗	0																		0	0	0
01062019	其他改良种用爬行动物	0																		0	0	0
01062020	食用爬行动物	10	0		0	5		0	0	0				6	0				0	0	0	0
01062090	其他爬行动物	10	0		0	5		0	0	0				6	0					0	0	0
01063110	改良种用猛禽	0																		0	0	0
01063190	其他猛禽	10	0		0	5		0	0	0				6	0					0	0	0
01063210	改良种用鹦形目鸟	0																		0	0	0
01063290	其他鹦形目鸟	10	0		0	5		0	0	0				6	0					0	0	0
01063310	改良种用鸵鸟；鸸鹋	0																		0	0	0

税则号列	货 品 名 称	最惠国	协定税率													特惠税率						
			东盟统一	亚太5国	智利	巴基斯坦	新加坡	新西兰	秘鲁	哥达	香港	澳门	台湾	瑞士	冰岛	亚太2国	老挝	柬埔寨	缅甸	LDC1	LDC2	LDC3
01063390	其他鸵鸟；鸸鹋	10	0		0	5		0	0	0				6	0					0	0	0
01063910	其他改良种用鸟	0																		0	0	0
01063921	乳鸽	10	0		0	5		0	0	0				6	0				0	0	0	0
01063923	野鸭	10	0		0	5		0	0	0				6	0				0	0	0	0
01063929	其他食用鸟	10	0		0	5		0	0	0				6	0				0	0	0	0
01063990	其他鸟	10	0		0	5		0	0	0				6	0					0	0	0
01064110	改良种用蜂	0																		0	0	0
01064190	其他蜂	10	0	9	0	5		0	4	0				6	0					0	0	0
01064910	改良种用其他昆虫	0																		0	0	0
01064990	其他昆虫	10	0	9	0	5		0	4	0				6	0					0	0	0
01069011	改良种用蛙苗	0																		0	0	0
01069019	其他改良种用动物	0																		0	0	0
01069090	其他动物	10	0	9	0	5		0	4	0				6	0					0	0	0
02011000	整头及半头鲜、冷牛肉	20	0		0			2.2	12	13.3				16	0		0	0		0	0	0
02012000	鲜、冷的带骨牛肉	12	0		0	6		1.3	7.8	8				9.6	0		0	0		0	0	0
02013000	鲜、冷的去骨牛肉	12	0		0	6		1.3	7.8	8				9.6	0			0		0	0	0
02021000	冻的整头及半头牛肉	25	0		0			2.8	15	0				20	0		0	0		0	0	0
02022000	冻的带骨牛肉	12	0		0	6		1.3	7.8	0				9.6	0		0	0		0	0	0
02023000	冻的去骨牛肉	12	0		0	6		1.3	7.8	0				9.6	0			0		0	0	0
02031110	鲜、冷的整头及半头乳猪肉	20	0		0			0	8	0				16	0		0	0		0	0	0
02031190	其他鲜、冷的整头及半头猪肉	20	0		0			0	0	0				16	0		0	0		0	0	0
02031200	鲜、冷的带骨猪前腿、后腿及其肉块	20	0		0			0	8	0				16	0		0	0		0	0	0
02031900	其他鲜、冷猪肉	20	0		0			0	0	0				16	0		0	0		0	0	0
02032110	冻整头及半头乳猪肉	12	0		0	6		0	4.8	0				9.6	0		0	0		0	0	0
02032190	其他冻整头及半头猪肉	12	0		0	6		0	4.8	0				9.6	0		0	0		0	0	0
02032200	冻的带骨猪前腿、后腿及其肉块	12	0		0	6		0	0	0				9.6	0		0	0		0	0	0
02032900	其他冻猪肉	12	0		0	6		0	7.2	0				9.6	0			0		0	0	0
02041000	鲜或冷的整头及半头羔羊	15	0		0	12		1.7	9	10				12	0					0	0	
02042100	鲜或冷的整头及半头绵羊肉	23	0		0			2.6	13.8	15.3				18.4	0					0	0	
02042200	鲜或冷的带骨绵羊肉	15	0		0	12		1.7	9	10				12	0					0	0	
02042300	鲜或冷的去骨绵羊肉	15	0		0	12		1.7	7.5	10				12	0					0	0	
02043000	冻的整头及半头羔羊	15	0		0	12		1.7	9.7	10				12	0					0	0	
02044100	冻的整头及半头绵羊肉	23	0		0			2.6	14.9	15.3				18.4	0					0	0	
02044200	冻的其他带骨绵羊肉	12	0		0	6		1.3	7.8	8				9.6	0					0	0	
02044300	冻的其他去骨绵羊肉	15	0		0	12		1.7	9.7	10				12	0					0	0	
02045000	鲜、冷、冻的山羊肉	20	0		0			2.2	10	13.3				16	0					0	0	
02050000	鲜、冷、冻的马、驴、骡肉	20	0		0			0	8	0				16	0					0	0	
02061000	鲜、冷的牛杂碎	12	0		0	6		1.3	6	0				9.6	0		0	0		0	0	0
02062100	冻牛舌	12	0		0	6		0	4.8	0				9.6	0		0	0		0	0	0
02062200	冻牛肝	12	0		0	6		0	0	0				9.6	0		0	0		0	0	0
02062900	其他冻牛杂碎	12	0		0	6		0	4.8	0				9.6	0		0	0		0	0	0
02063000	鲜、冷的猪杂碎	20	0		0			0	8	0				16	0		0	0	0	0	0	0
02064100	冻猪肝	20	0		0			0	8	0				16	0		0	0		0	0	0
02064900	其他冻猪杂碎	12	0		0	6		0	4.8	0				9.6	0		0	0		0	0	0
02068000	鲜、冷的羊、马、驴、骡杂碎	20	0		0			2.2	10	0				16	0			0		0	0	0
02069000	冻的羊、马、驴、骡杂碎	18	0		0	14.4		2	11.6	0				14.4	0			0		0	0	0
02071100	整只，鲜或冷的鸡	20	0		0			0	0	0				16	0		0	0	0	0	0	0
02071200	整只，冻的鸡	20	0		0			0	8	0				16	0		0	0	0	0	0	0
02071311	鲜或冷的带骨鸡块	20	0		0			0	0	0				16	0		0	0	0	0	0	0
02071319	鲜或冷的其他鸡块	20	0		0			0	0	0				16	0		0	0	0	0	0	0
02071321	鲜或冷的鸡翼(不包括翼尖)	20	0		0			0	0	0				16	0		0	0	0	0	0	0
02071329	鲜或冷的其他鸡杂碎	20	0		0			0	0	0				16	0		0	0	0	0	0	0
02071411	冻的的带骨鸡块	10	0		0	0.3元/千克		0	0	0				6	0		0	0	0	0	0	0
02071419	冻的其他鸡块	10	0		0	0.35元/千克		0	4	0				6	0		0	0	0	0	0	0
02071421	冻的鸡翼(不包括翼尖)	10	0		0	0.4元/千克		0	0	0				6	0		0	0	0	0	0	0

税则号列	货品名称	最惠国	协定税率													特惠税率						
			东盟统一	亚太5国	智利	巴基斯坦	新加坡	新西兰	秘鲁	哥达	香港	澳门	台湾	瑞士	冰岛	亚太2国	老挝	柬埔寨	缅甸	LDC1	LDC2	LDC3
02071422	鲜、冷、冻鸡爪	10	0		0	0.25元/千克		0	4	0				6	0		0	0	0	0	0	0
02071429	冻的其他鸡杂碎	10	0		0	0.25元/千克		0	4	0				6	0		0	0	0	0	0	0
02072400	整只,鲜或冷的火鸡	20	0		0			0	0	0				16	0		0			0	0	0
02072500	整只,冻的火鸡	20	0		0			0	8	0				16	0		0			0	0	0
02072600	鲜或冷的火鸡块及杂碎	20	0		0			0	0	0				16	0		0			0	0	0
02072700	冻的火鸡块及杂碎	10	0		0	5		0	4	0				6	0		0			0	0	0
02074100	鲜或冷的整只鸭	20	0		0			0	8	0				16	0		0	0	0	0	0	0
02074200	冻的整只鸭	20	0		0			0	8	0				16	0		0	0	0	0	0	0
02074300	鲜或冷的鸭肥肝	20	0		0			0	8	0				16	0		0	0		0	0	0
02074400	鲜或冷的其他鸭	20	0		0			0	8	0				16	0		0	0	0	0	0	0
02074500	冻的其他鸭	20	0		0			0	8	0				16	0		0	0	0	0	0	0
02075100	鲜或冷的整只鹅	20	0		0			0	8	0				16	0		0	0	0	0	0	0
02075200	冻的整只鹅	20	0		0			0	8	0				16	0		0	0	0	0	0	0
02075300	鲜或冷的鹅肥肝	20	0		0			0	8	0				16	0		0	0		0	0	0
02075400	鲜或冷的其他鹅	20	0		0			0	8	0				16	0		0	0	0	0	0	0
02075500	冻的其他鹅	20	0		0			0	8	0				16	0		0	0	0	0	0	0
02076000	鲜、冷、冻珍珠鸡	20	0		0			0	8	0				16	0		0	0		0	0	0
02081010	鲜或冷藏的家兔肉或野兔,不包括兔头	20	0		0			0	8	0				16	0					0	0	
02081020	冻家兔或野兔,不包括兔头	20	0		0			0	8	0				16	0					0	0	
02081090	鲜、冷、冻的家兔及野兔食用杂碎	20	0		0			0	8	0				16	0					0	0	
02083000	鲜、冷、冻的灵长目动物的肉及其食用杂碎	23	0		0			0	9.2	0				18.4	0					0	0	
02084000	鲜、冷、冻鲸、海豚及鼠海豚;鲜、冷、冻海牛及儒艮;鲜、冷、冻海豹、海狮及海象	23	0		0			0	9.2	0				18.4	0					0	0	
02085000	鲜、冷、冻的爬行动物的肉及其食用杂碎	23	0		0			0	9.2	0				18.4	0					0	0	
02086000	鲜、冷、冻骆驼及其他骆驼科动物	23	0		0			0	9.2	0				18.4	0					0	0	
02089010	鲜、冷、冻的乳鸽肉及其食用杂碎	20	0		0			0	8	0				16	0					0	0	
02089090	其他鲜、冷、冻肉及食用杂碎	23	0		0			0	9.2	0				18.4	0					0	0	
02091000	未炼制猪脂肪	20	0		0			0	8	0				16	0					0	0	
02099000	未炼制家禽脂肪	20	0		0			0	8	0				16	0					0	0	
02101110	干、熏、盐制的带骨猪腿	25	0		0			0	0	0					0		0	0		0	0	0
02101190	干、熏、盐制的带骨猪腿肉块	25	0		0			0	0	0					0		0	0		0	0	0
02101200	干、熏、盐制的猪腹肉	25	0		0			0	0	0					0		0	0		0	0	0
02101900	干、熏、盐制的其他猪肉	25	0		0			0	10	0					0			0	0	0	0	0
02102000	干、熏、盐制的牛肉	25	0		0			0	10	0				15	0		0	0		0	0	0
02109100	干、熏、盐制的灵长目动物肉及食用杂碎	25	0		0			0	10	0				20	0		0	0		0	0	0
02109200	鲸、海豚及鼠海豚的;海牛及儒艮的;海豹、海狮及海象的肉及食用杂碎	25	0		0			0	10	0				20	0		0	0		0	0	0
02109300	干、熏、盐制的爬行动物肉及食用杂碎	25	0		0			0	10	0				20	0		0	0		0	0	0
02109900	干、熏、盐制的其他肉及食用杂碎	25	0		0			0	10	0				20	0		0	0		0	0	0
03011100	淡水观赏鱼	17.5	0		0	14		0	0	8.8	0			14	0					0	0	0
03011900	其他观赏鱼	17.5	0		0	14		0	0	8.8	0			14	0					0	0	0
03019110	鳟鱼苗	0																		0	0	0
03019190	其他活鳟鱼	10.5	0	8	0	5		0	0	5.3				8.4	0					0	0	0
03019210	鳗鱼苗	0																		0	0	0
03019290	其他活鳗鱼	10	0	6.7	0	5		0	0	5				6	0			0	0	0	0	0
03019310	鲤科鱼鱼苗	0																		0	0	0
03019390	其他鲤科鱼	10.5	0	8	0	5		0	0	5.3				8.4	0			0	0	0	0	0
03019410	大西洋及太平洋蓝鳍金枪鱼鱼苗	0																		0	0	0
03019491	大西洋蓝鳍金枪鱼	10.5	0	8	0	5		0	0	5.3	0			8.4	0			0	0	0	0	0
03019492	太平洋蓝鳍金枪鱼	10.5	0	8	0	5		0	4.2	5.3	0		0	8.4	0			0	0	0	0	0
03019510	南方蓝鳍金枪鱼鱼苗	0																		0	0	0
03019590	其他活南方蓝鳍金枪鱼	10.5	0	8	0	5		0	0	5.3	0			8.4	0			0	0	0	0	0
03019911	鲈鱼鱼苗	0																		0	0	0
03019912	鲟鱼鱼苗	0																		0	0	0
03019919	其他鱼苗	0																		0	0	0
03019991	活罗非鱼	10.5	0		0	5		0	4.2	5.3	0			8.4	0			0	0	0	0	0

税则号列	货品名称	最惠国	协定税率 东盟统一	亚太5国	智利	巴基斯坦	新加坡	新西兰	秘鲁	哥达	香港	澳门	台湾	瑞士	冰岛	特惠税率 亚太2国	老挝	柬埔寨	缅甸	LDC1	LDC2	LDC3
03019992	活鲀	10.5	0	8	0	5		0	0	5.3	0			8.4	0			0	0	0	0	0
03019993	其他鲤科鱼	10.5	0	8	0	5		0	0	5.3				8.4	0			0	0	0	0	0
03019999	其他活鱼	10.5	0	8	0	5		0	4.2	5.3	0		0	8.4	0			0	0	0	0	0
03021100	鲜、冷鳟鱼	12	0		0	6		0	4.8	6				9.6	0					0	0	0
03021300	鲜、冷大麻哈鱼	10	0		0	5		0	4	5				6	0					0	0	0
03021410	鲜、冷大西洋鲑鱼	10	0		0	5		0	4	5				6	0					0	0	0
03021420	鲜、冷多瑙哲罗鱼	10	0		0	5		0	4	5				6	0					0	0	0
03021900	其他鲜、冷鲑鱼	12	0	8	0	5		0	0	6				9.6	0					0	0	0
03022100	鲜、冷庸鲽鱼	12	0	9	0	5		0	0	6				9.6	0					0	0	0
03022200	鲜、冷鲽鱼	12	0	9	0	5		0	0	6				9.6	0					0	0	0
03022300	鲜、冷鳎鱼	12	0	9	0	5		0	0	6				9.6	0					0	0	0
03022400	鲜、冷大菱鲆	12	0	6	0	5		0	4.8	6				9.6	0			0		0	0	0
03022900	其他鲜、冷比目鱼	12	0	6	0	5		0	4.8	6				9.6	0			0		0	0	0
03023100	鲜、冷长鳍金枪鱼	12	0	9	0	5		0	4.8	6				9.6	0			0		0	0	0
03023200	鲜、冷黄鳍金枪鱼	12	0	9	0	5		0	0	6	0			9.6	0					0	0	0
03023300	鲜、冷鲣鱼或狐鲣	12	0	8	0	5		0	0	6				9.6	0					0	0	0
03023400	鲜、冷大眼金枪鱼	12	0		0	6		0	0	6				9.6	0			0	0	0	0	0
03023510	鲜、冷大西洋蓝鳍金枪鱼	12	0		0	6		0	0	6				9.6	0			0	0	0	0	0
03023520	鲜、冷太平洋蓝鳍金枪鱼	12	0	8	0	5		0	0	6				9.6	0			0	0	0	0	0
03023600	鲜、冷南方蓝鳍金枪鱼	12	0		0	6		0	0	6				9.6	0			0	0	0	0	0
03023900	其他鲜、冷金枪鱼	12	0	8	0	5		0	0	6				9.6	0			0	0	0	0	0
03024100	鲜、冷鲱鱼(大西洋鲱鱼、太平洋鲱鱼)	12	0	8	0	5		0	0	6				9.6	0					0	0	0
03024200	鲜、冷鳀鱼	12	0	8	0	5		0	0	6	0		0	9.6	0			0	0	0	0	0
03024300	鲜、冷沙丁鱼(沙丁鱼、沙瑙鱼属)、小沙丁鱼属、黍鲱或西鲱	12	0	8	0	5		0	0	6				9.6	0					0	0	0
03024400	鲜、冷鲭鱼	12	0	8	0	5		0	0	6				9.6	0					0	0	0
03024500	鲜、冷对称竹荚鱼、新西兰竹荚鱼及竹荚鱼	12	0	8	0	5		0	0	6	0		0	9.6	0			0	0	0	0	0
03024600	鲜、冷军曹鱼	12	0	8	0	5		0	0	6	0		0	9.6	0			0	0	0	0	0
03024700	鲜、冷剑鱼	12	0	8	0	5		0	0	6	0			9.6	0					0	0	0
03025100	鳕鱼(大西洋鳕鱼、格陵兰鳕鱼、太平洋鳕鱼)	12	0	8	0	5		0	0	6				9.6	0					0	0	0
03025200	鲜、冷黑线鳕鱼	12	0	8	0	5		0	0	6				9.6	0					0	0	0
03025300	鲜、冷绿青鳕鱼	12	0	8	0	5		0	0	6				9.6	0					0	0	0
03025400	鲜、冷狗鳕鱼	12	0	8	0	5		0	0	6	0		0	9.6	0			0	0	0	0	0
03025500	鲜、冷狭鳕鱼	12	0	8	0	5		0	0	6	0		0	9.6	0			0	0	0	0	0
03025600	鲜、冷蓝鳕鱼	12	0	8	0	5		0	0	6	0		0	9.6	0			0	0	0	0	0
03025900	鲜、冷其他鳕科鱼	12	0	8	0	5		0	0	6	0		0	9.6	0			0	0	0	0	0
03027100	鲜、冷罗非鱼	12	0		0	6		0	4.8	6				9.6	0			0	0	0	0	0
03027200	鲜、冷鲶鱼	12	0	8	0	5		0	0	6	0		0	9.6	0			0	0	0	0	0
03027300	鲜、冷鲤科鱼	12	0	8	0	5		0	0	6	0		0	9.6	0			0	0	0	0	0
03027400	鲜、冷鳗鱼	12	0	8	0	5		0	0	6	0			9.6	0				0	0	0	0
03027900	鲜、冷尼罗河鲈鱼及黑鱼	12	0	8	0	5		0	0	6	0		0	9.6	0			0	0	0	0	0
03028100	鲜、冷角鲨及其他鲨鱼	12	0	9	0	5		0	4.8	6	0			9.6	0					0	0	0
03028200	鲜、冷魟鱼及鳐鱼	12	0	8	0	5		0	0	6	0		0	9.6	0			0	0	0	0	0
03028300	鲜、冷南极犬牙鱼	12	0	8	0	5		0	0	6	0			9.6	0			0	0	0	0	0
03028400	鲜、冷尖吻鲈鱼	12	0	8	0	5		0	0	6	0		0	9.6	0			0	0	0	0	0
03028500	鲜、冷菱羊鲷	12	0	8	0	5		0	0	6	0		0	9.6	0			0	0	0	0	0
03028910	鲜、冷带鱼	12	0	8	0	8		0	4.8	6	0			9.6	0					0	0	0
03028920	鲜、冷黄鱼	12	0	8	0	5		0	4.8	6	0			9.6	0					0	0	0
03028930	鲜、冷鲳鱼	12	0	8	0	5		0	4.8	6	0			9.6	0					0	0	0
03028940	鲜、冷鲀	12	0	8	0	5		0	4.8	6	0			9.6	0			0	0	0	0	0
03028990	鲜、冷其他鱼	12	0	8	0	5		0	0	6	0		0	9.6	0			0	0	0	0	0
03029000	鲜、冷鱼肝及鱼卵	12	0		0	6		0	0	6				9.6	0			0		0	0	0
03031100	冻红大麻哈鱼	10	0	6.7	0	5		0	4	5				6	0			0		0	0	0
03031200	冻其他大麻哈鱼	10	0	6.7	0	5		0	4	5				6	0			0		0	0	0
03031300	冻大西洋鲑鱼及多瑙哲罗鱼	10	0		0	5		0	4	5				6	0					0	0	0
03031400	冻鳟鱼	12	0		0	6		0	4.8	6				9.6	0					0	0	0
03031900	冻其他鲑科鱼	10	0	6.7	0	5		0	0	5				6	0					0	0	0
03032300	冻罗非鱼	10	0	5	0	5		0	4	5				6	0	0		0	0	0	0	0

税则号列	货品名称	最惠国	协定税率													特惠税率						
			东盟统一	亚太5国	智利	巴基斯坦	新加坡	新西兰	秘鲁	哥达	香港	澳门	台湾	瑞士	冰岛	亚太2国	老挝	柬埔寨	缅甸	LDC1	LDC2	LDC3
03032400	冻鲶鱼	10	0	5	0	5		0	2.5	5	0		0	6	0	0		0	0	0	0	0
03032500	冻鲤科鱼	10	0	5	0	5		0	2.5	5	0		0	6	0	0		0	0	0	0	0
03032600	冻鳗鱼	12	0	8	0	8		0	4.8	6	0			9.6	0					0	0	0
03032900	冻尼罗河鲈鱼及黑鱼	10	0	5	0	5		0	2.5	5	0		0	6	0	0		0	0	0	0	0
03033110	冻格陵兰庸鲽鱼	10	0	6.7	0	5		0	0	5	0			6	0					0	0	0
03033190	冻庸鲽鱼	10	0	6.7	0	5		0	0	5	0			6	6.7					0	0	0
03033200	冻鲽鱼	12	0	8	0	8		0	0	6				9.6	8					0	0	0
03033300	冻鳎鱼	12	0	8	0	8		0	0	6				9.6	0					0	0	0
03033400	冻大菱鲆	10	0	8	0	8		0	4	5				6	0					0	0	0
03033900	其他冻比目鱼	10	0	8	0	8		0	4	5				6	6.7					0	0	0
03034100	冻长鳍金枪鱼	12	0	9	0	5		0	0	6				9.6	0					0	0	0
03034200	冻黄鳍金枪鱼	12	0	9	0	5		0	0	6				9.6	0					0	0	0
03034300	冻鲣鱼或狐鲣	12	0	9	0	5		0	0	6				9.6	0					0	0	0
03034400	冻大眼金枪鱼,但鱼肝及鱼卵除外	12	0		0	6		0	0	6	0			9.6	0			0	0	0	0	0
03034510	冻大西洋蓝鳍金枪鱼	12	0		0	6		0	0	6				9.6	0			0	0	0	0	0
03034520	冻太平洋蓝鳍金枪鱼	12	0	9	0	5		0	0	6				9.6	0			0	0	0	0	0
03034600	冻南方蓝鳍金枪鱼,但鱼肝及鱼卵除外	12	0		0	6		0	0	6				9.6	0			0	0	0	0	0
03034900	其他冻金枪鱼,但鱼肝及鱼卵除外	12	0	9	0	5		0	0	6				9.6	0			0	0	0	0	0
03035100	冻鲱鱼(大西洋鲱鱼、太平洋鲱鱼),但鱼肝及鱼卵除外	10	0	6.7	0	5		0	0	5				6	0					0	0	0
03035300	冻沙丁鱼、小沙丁鱼属、黍鲱或西鲱	12	0	8	0	5		0	4.8	6				9.6	0					0	0	0
03035400	冻鲭鱼	10	0	6.7	0	6.7		0	2.5	5				6	0					0	0	0
03035500	冻对称竹荚鱼、新西兰竹荚鱼及竹荚鱼	10	0	5	0	5		0	2.5	5	0		0	6	0	0		0	0	0	0	0
03035600	冻军曹鱼	10	0	5	0	5		0	2.5	5	0		0	6	0	0		0	0	0	0	0
03035700	冻剑鱼	10	0	5	0	5		0	0	5	0			6	0	0				0	0	0
03036300	鳕鱼(大西洋鳕鱼、格陵兰鳕鱼、太平洋鳕鱼)	10	0	6.7	0	5		0	0	5				6	6.7					0	0	0
03036400	冻黑线鳕鱼	12	0	8	0	5		0	0	6				9.6	8					0	0	0
03036500	冻绿青鳕鱼	12	0	8	0	5		0	0	6				9.6	0					0	0	0
03036600	冻狗鳕鱼	12	0		0	6		0	4.8	6				9.6	0					0	0	0
03036700	冻狭鳕鱼	10	0	5	0	5		0	2.5	5	0		0	6	0	0		0	0	0	0	0
03036800	冻蓝鳕鱼	10	0	5	0	5		0	2.5	5	0		0	6	0	0		0	0	0	0	0
03036900	其他冻鳕鱼	10	0	5	0	5		0	2.5	5	0		0	6	0	0		0	0	0	0	0
03038100	冻角鲨及其他鲨鱼	12	0	9	0	9		0	4.8	6				9.6	0					0	0	0
03038200	冻魟鱼及鳐鱼	10	0	5	0	5		0	2.5	5	0		0	6	0	0		0	0	0	0	0
03038300	冻南极犬牙鱼	10	0	5	0	5		0	0	5	0			6	0	0		0	0	0	0	0
03038400	冻尖吻鲈鱼	12	0	8	0	5		0	0	6	0			9.6	0					0	0	0
03038910	冻带鱼	10	0	5	0	5		0	4	5	0			6	8.2	0		0	0	0	0	0
03038920	冻黄鱼	10	0	5	0	5		0	4	5	0			6	0	0		0	0	0	0	0
03038930	冻鲳鱼	10	0	5	0	5		0	4	5	0			6	0	0		0	0	0	0	0
03038990	其他冻鱼	10	0	5	0	5		0	2.5	5	0		0	6	0	0		0	0	0	0	0
03039000	冻鱼肝及鱼卵	10	0	9	0	5		0		5				6	6.7					0	0	0
03043100	鲜、冷罗非鱼片	12	0	9	0	5		0	4.8	0	0			9.6	0				0	0	0	0
03043200	鲜、冷鲶鱼片	12	0	9	0	5		0	4.8	0	0			9.6	0				0	0	0	0
03043300	鲜、冷尼罗河鲈鱼片	12	0	9	0	5		0	4.8	0	0			9.6	0				0	0	0	0
03043900	鲜、冷鲤科鱼、鳗鱼、黑鱼片	12	0	9	0	5		0	4.8	0	0			9.6	0				0	0	0	0
03044100	鲜、冷大麻哈鱼片	12	0	9	0	5		0	4.8	0	0			9.6	0				0	0	0	0
03044200	鲜、冷鳟鱼片	12	0	9	0	5		0	4.8	0	0			9.6	0				0	0	0	0
03044300	鲜、冷比目鱼片	12	0	9	0	5		0	4.8	0	0			9.6	0				0	0	0	0
03044400	鲜、冷犀鳕科等鳕科鱼片	12	0	9	0	5		0	4.8	0	0			9.6	0				0	0	0	0
03044500	鲜、冷剑鱼片	12	0	9	0	5		0	0	0	0			9.6	0				0	0	0	0
03044600	鲜、冷南极犬牙鱼片	12	0	9	0	5		0	0	0	0			9.6	0				0	0	0	0
03044900	鲜、冷其他鱼片	12	0	9	0	5		0	4.8	0	0			9.6	0				0	0	0	0
03045100	鲜、冷罗非鱼等鱼鱼肉	12	0	9	0	5		0	4.8	0	0			9.6	0				0	0	0	0
03045200	鲜、冷鲑科鱼肉	12	0	9	0	5		0	4.8	0	0			9.6	0				0	0	0	0
03045300	鲜、冷犀鳕科等鳕科鱼肉	12	0	9	0	5		0	4.8	0	0			9.6	0				0	0	0	0
03045400	鲜、冷剑鱼肉	12	0	9	0	5		0	0	0	0			9.6	0				0	0	0	0
03045500	鲜、冷南极犬牙鱼肉	12	0	9	0	5		0	0	0	0			9.6	0				0	0	0	0
03045900	鲜、冷其他鱼肉	12	0	9	0	5		0	4.8	0	0			9.6	0				0	0	0	0

税则号列	货品名称	最惠国	协定税率													特惠税率						
			东盟统一	亚太5国	智利	巴基斯坦	新加坡	新西兰	秘鲁	哥达	香港	澳门	台湾	瑞士	冰岛	亚太2国	老挝	柬埔寨	缅甸	LDC1	LDC2	LDC3
03046100	冻罗非鱼等鱼鱼片	10	0		0	5		0	0	0	0			6	0			0	0	0	0	0
03046211	冻斑点叉尾鮰鱼片	10	0		0	5		0	0	0	0			6	0					0	0	0
03046219	冻其他叉尾鮰鱼片	10	0		0	5		0	0	0	0			6	0					0	0	0
03046290	冻其他鲶鱼片	10	0		0	5		0	2.5	0	0		0	6	0			0	0	0	0	0
03046300	冻尼罗河鲈鱼片	10	0		0	5		0	2.5	0	0		0	6	0			0	0	0	0	0
03046900	冻鲤科鱼、鳗鱼、黑鱼片	10	0		0	5		0	2.5	0	0		0	6	0			0	0	0	0	0
03047100	鳕鱼(大西洋鳕鱼、格陵兰鳕鱼、太平洋鳕鱼)	10	0		0	5		0	2.5	0	0		0	6	0			0	0	0	0	0
03047200	冻黑线鳕鱼片	10	0		0	5		0	2.5	0	0		0	6	0			0	0	0	0	0
03047300	冻绿青鳕鱼片	10	0		0	5		0	2.5	0	0		0	6	0			0	0	0	0	0
03047400	冻狗鳕鱼片	10	0		0	5		0	2.5	0	0		0	6	0			0	0	0	0	0
03047500	冻狭鳕鱼片	10	0		0	5		0	2.5	0	0		0	6	0			0	0	0	0	0
03047900	冻其他鳕鱼片	10	0		0	5		0	2.5	0	0		0	6	0			0	0	0	0	0
03048100	冻大麻哈鱼、大西洋鲑鱼及多瑙哲罗鱼片	10	0		0	5		0	2.5	0	0		0	6	0			0	0	0	0	0
03048200	冻鳟鱼片	10	0		0	5		0	2.5	0	0		0	6	0			0	0	0	0	0
03048300	冻比目鱼片	10	0		0	5		0	2.5	0	0		0	6	0			0	0	0	0	0
03048400	冻剑鱼片	10	0		0	5		0	0	0	0			6	0			0	0	0	0	0
03048500	冻南极犬牙鱼片	10	0		0	5		0	0	0	0			6	0			0	0	0	0	0
03048600	冻鲱鱼片	10	0		0	5		0	2.5	0	0		0	6	0			0	0	0	0	0
03048700	冻金枪鱼、鲣鱼或狐鲣(鲣)片	10	0		0	5		0	2.5	0	0		0	6	0			0	0	0	0	0
03048900	冻其他鱼片	10	0		0	5		0	2.5	0	0		0	6	0			0	0	0	0	0
03049100	冻的剑鱼肉	10	0		0	5		0	0	0				6	0	0			0	0	0	0
03049200	冻的南极犬牙鱼肉	10	0		0	5		0	0	0				6	0	0			0	0	0	0
03049300	冻罗非鱼等鱼鱼肉	10	0		0	5		0	0	0				6	0	0			0	0	0	0
03049400	冻狭鳕鱼肉	10	0		0	5		0	0	0				6	0	0			0	0	0	0
03049500	冻犀鳕科等鳕科鱼肉	10	0		0	5		0	0	0				6	0	0			0	0	0	0
03049900	其他冻鱼肉	10	0		0	5		0	0	0				6	0	0			0	0	0	0
03051000	供人食用的鱼粉及团粒	10	0		0	5		0	0	0		0		6	0					0	0	0
03052000	干、熏、盐制的鱼肝及鱼卵	10	0		0	5		0		5					0					0	0	0
03053100	干、盐腌罗非鱼等鱼鱼片	10	0	7.8	0	5		0	4	0	0	0			0	0			0	0	0	0
03053200	干、盐腌犀鳕科等鳕科鱼片	10	0	7.8	0	5		0	4	0	0	0			0	0			0	0	0	0
03053900	干、盐腌其他鱼片	10	0	7.8	0	5		0	4	0	0	0			0	0			0	0	0	0
03054110	熏大西洋鲑鱼,食用杂碎除外	14	0		0	7		0	0	0	0				0					0	0	
03054120	熏鲱鱼,食用杂碎除外	14	0		0	11.2		0	0	0					0					0	0	
03054200	熏鲱鱼,食用杂碎除外	16	0		0	12.8		0	0	0					0					0	0	
03054300	熏鳟鱼,食用杂碎除外	14	0		0	11.2		0	5.6	0		0			0	0			0	0	0	0
03054400	熏罗非鱼等鱼,食用杂碎除外	14	0		0	11.2		0	5.6	0		0			0	0			0	0	0	0
03054900	熏其他鱼,食用杂碎除外	14	0		0	11.2		0	5.6	0		0			0	0			0	0	0	0
03055100	鳕鱼(大西洋鳕鱼、格陵兰鳕鱼、太平洋鳕鱼)	16	0		0	12.8		0	0	0		0		12.8	0					0	0	
03055910	干海马、干海龙	2	0		0	0		0	0	0				0	0	0		0	0	0	0	0
03055990	干其他鱼,食用杂碎除外	16	0		0			0	6.4	8	0	0		12.8	0	0			0	0	0	0
03056100	盐腌及盐渍的鲱鱼,食用杂碎除外	16	0	11.1	0	8		0	0	0				12.8	0					0	0	
03056200	鳕鱼(大西洋鳕鱼、格陵兰鳕鱼、太平洋鳕鱼)	16	0	12	0	8		0	0	0				12.8	0					0	0	0
03056300	盐腌及盐渍的鳀鱼,食用杂碎除外	16	0	12	0	8		0	6.4	0				12.8	0					0	0	
03056400	盐腌及盐渍的罗非鱼等鱼,食用杂碎除外	16	0		0	12.8		0	6.4	0	0			12.8	0	0			0	0	0	0
03056910	盐腌及盐渍的带鱼,食用杂碎除外	16	0		0	12.8		0	6.4	0	0			12.8	0	0			0	0	0	0
03056920	盐腌及盐渍的黄鱼,食用杂碎除外	16	0		0	12.8		0	6.4	0	0			12.8	0	0			0	0	0	0
03056930	盐腌及盐渍的鲳鱼,食用杂碎除外	16	0		0	12.8		0	6.4	0	0			12.8	0	0			0	0	0	0
03056990	盐腌及盐渍的其他鱼,食用杂碎除外	16	0		0	12.8		0	6.4	0	0			12.8	0	0			0	0	0	0
03057100	鲨鱼翅	15	0		0			0	6	7.5		0		12	0	0		0	0	0	0	0
03057200	鱼头、鱼尾、鱼鳔	16	0		0	12.8		0	0	0					0					0	0	
03057900	其他可食用杂碎	16	0		0	12.8		0	0	0					0					0	0	
03061100	岩礁虾和其他龙虾(真龙虾属、龙虾属、岩龙虾属)	10	0		0	5		0	0	0				6	0			0	0	0	0	0
03061200	鳌龙虾(鳌龙虾属)	10	0	7.2	0	5		0	0	0				6	0			0		0	0	0
03061410	冻梭子蟹	10	0		0	5		0	4	0				6	0	0		0	0	0	0	0
03061490	其他冻蟹	10	0		0	5		0	4	0				6	0	0		0	0	0	0	0
03061500	冻挪威海鳌虾	16	0		0	12.8		0	6.4	0				12.8	0			0		0	0	0

税则号列	货品名称	最惠国	协定税率													特惠税率						
			东盟统一	亚太5国	智利	巴基斯坦	新加坡	新西兰	秘鲁	哥达	香港	澳门	台湾	瑞士	冰岛	亚太2国	老挝	柬埔寨	缅甸	LDC1	LDC2	LDC3
03061611	冻冷水小虾虾仁	8	0	4	0	0		0	0	0	0			4.8	0			0	0	0	0	0
03061612	冻北方长额虾虾仁	5	0	2.5	0	0		0	0	0	0			0	0			0	0	0	0	0
03061619	冻其他冷水小虾	5	0	2.5	0	0		0	0	0	0			0	3.3			0	0	0	0	0
03061621	冻冷水对虾虾仁	8	0	4	0	0		0	0	0	0			4.8	0			0	0	0	0	0
03061629	冻其他冷水对虾	5	0	2.5	0	0		0	0	0	0			0	0			0	0	0	0	0
03061711	冻小虾虾仁	8	0	4	0	0		0	0	0	0			4.8	0			0	0	0	0	0
03061719	冻其他小虾	5	0	2.5	0	0		0	0	0	0			0	3.3			0	0	0	0	0
03061721	冻对虾虾仁	8	0	4	0	0		0	0	0	0			4.8	0			0	0	0	0	0
03061729	冻其他对虾	5	0	2.5	0	0		0	0	0	0			0	0			0	0	0	0	0
03061911	冻淡水小龙虾仁	16	0		0	12.8		0	0	0				12.8	0			0		0	0	0
03061919	冻带壳淡水小龙虾	16	0		0	12.8		0	0	0				12.8	0			0		0	0	0
03061990	其他冻甲壳动物	16	0		0	12.8		0	6.4	0				12.8	0			0		0	0	0
03062110	岩礁虾和其他龙虾(真龙虾属、龙虾属、岩龙虾属)种苗	0																		0	0	0
03062190	其他岩礁虾和其他龙虾(真龙虾属、龙虾属、岩龙虾属)	15	0		0			0	0	0	0			12	0			0	0	0	0	0
03062210	鳌龙虾(鳌龙虾属)种苗	0																		0	0	0
03062290	其他鳌龙虾(鳌龙虾属)	15	0		0	12		0	0	0	0			12	0			0	0	0	0	0
03062410	蟹种苗	0																		0	0	0
03062491	未冻的中华绒毛蟹(大闸蟹)	14	0		0	7		0	0	0				11.2	0			0		0	0	0
03062492	未冻的梭子蟹	14	0		0	11.2		0	5.6	0	0			11.2	0			0		0	0	0
03062499	未冻的其他蟹	14	0		0			0	5.6	0	0			11.2	0			0		0	0	0
03062510	未冻的挪威海螯虾种苗	0																		0	0	0
03062590	未冻的其他挪威海螯虾	14	0		0	11.2		0	0	0	0			11.2	0			0	0	0	0	0
03062610	未冻的冷水小虾及对虾种苗	0																		0	0	0
03062620	鲜、冷冷水对虾	15	0		0	12		0	0	0	0			12	0			0	0	0	0	0
03062690	未冻的其他冷水小虾及对虾	12	0		0	6		0	0	0	0			9.6	0			0	0	0	0	0
03062710	未冻的其他小虾及对虾种苗	0																		0	0	0
03062720	鲜、冷对虾	15	0		0	12		0	0	0	0			12	0			0	0	0	0	0
03062790	未冻的其他小虾及对虾	12	0		0	6		0	0	0	0			9.6	0			0	0	0	0	0
03062910	其他食用甲壳动物种苗	0																		0	0	0
03062990	其他带壳或去壳的未冻的甲壳动物	14	0		0	11.2		0	0	0	0			11.2	0			0	0	0	0	0
03071110	活、鲜或冷的牡蛎(蚝)种苗	0																		0	0	0
03071190	活、鲜或冷的其他牡蛎(蚝)	14	0		0	11.2		0	5.6	0	0			11.2	0				0	0	0	0
03071900	冻、干、盐腌或盐渍的牡蛎(蚝)	14	0		0	11.2		0	5.6	0	0			11.2	0				0	0	0	0
03072110	扇贝(包括海扇)种苗	0																		0	0	0
03072190	其他活、鲜、冷扇贝	14	0		0	11.2		0	5.6	0	0			11.2	0				0	0	0	0
03072900	其他冻、干、盐腌或盐渍的扇贝	14	0		0	11.2		0	3.5	0				11.2	0				0	0	0	0
03073110	贻贝种苗	0																		0	0	0
03073190	其他活、鲜、冷贻贝	14	0		0	11.2		0	0	0	0			11.2	0			0	0	0	0	0
03073900	其他冻、干、盐制的贻贝	14	0	9.8	0	7		0	5.6	0				11.2	0			0	0	0	0	0
03074110	墨鱼及鱿鱼种苗	0																		0	0	0
03074190	其他活、鲜或冷墨鱼及鱿鱼	12	0		0	6		0	4.8	0	0			9.6	0			0	0	0	0	0
03074900	其他冻、干、盐制的墨鱼及鱿鱼	12	0	10	0	10		0	4.8	0	0	0		9.6	0			0	0	0	0	0
03075100	活、鲜、冷章鱼	17	0		0	13.6		0	6.8	0	0			13.6	0					0	0	
03075900	其他冻、干、盐制的章鱼	17	0		0	13.6		0	6.8	0	0	0		13.6	0					0	0	0
03076010	蜗牛及螺的种苗,海螺种苗除外	0																		0	0	0
03076090	其他蜗牛及螺,海螺除外	14	0		0	11.2		0	0	0				11.2	0			0		0	0	0
03077110	活、鲜或冷的蛤、鸟蛤及舟贝种苗	0																		0	0	0
03077191	活、鲜或冷的蛤	14	0		0	11.2		0	0	0	0			11.2	0					0	0	
03077199	活、鲜或冷的鸟蛤及舟贝	14	0		0	11.2		0	5.6	0	0			11.2	0			0	0	0	0	0
03077910	冻、干、盐腌或盐渍的蛤	10	0		0			0		0				6	0					0	0	0
03077990	冻、干、盐腌或盐渍的鸟蛤及舟贝	10	0		0			0	4	0		0		6	0			0	0	0	0	0
03078110	活、鲜或冷的鲍鱼种苗	0																		0	0	0
03078190	活、鲜或冷的其他鲍鱼	14	0		0	11.2		0	5.6	0	0			11.2	0			0	0	0	0	0
03078900	冻、干、盐腌或盐渍的鲍鱼	10	0		0	5		0		0	0	0		6	0			0	0	0	0	0
03079110	活、鲜或冷的其他软体动物种苗	0																		0	0	0
03079190	活、鲜或冷的其他软体动物	14	0		0	11.2		0	5.6	0	0			11.2	0			0	0	0	0	0
03079900	冻、干、盐腌或盐渍的软体动物	10	0		0			0	4	0		0		6	0			0	0	0	0	0
03081110	活、鲜或冷的海参种苗	0																		0	0	0
03081190	活、鲜或冷的其他海参	14	0		0	11.2		0	5.6	0	0			11.2	0			0	0	0	0	0

税则号列	货品名称	最惠国	协定税率													特惠税率						
			东盟统一	亚太5国	智利	巴基斯坦	新加坡	新西兰	秘鲁	哥达	香港	澳门	台湾	瑞士	冰岛	亚太2国	老挝	柬埔寨	缅甸	LDC1	LDC2	LDC3
03081900	冻、干、盐腌或盐渍的海参	10	0		0			0	4	0				6	6.7			0	0	0	0	0
03082110	活、鲜或冷的海胆种苗	0																		0	0	0
03082190	活、鲜或冷的其他海胆	14	0		0	11.2		0	5.6	0	0			11.2	0			0	0	0	0	0
03082900	冻、干、盐腌或盐渍的海胆	10	0		0			0	4	0		0		6	0			0	0	0	0	0
03083011	活、鲜或冷的海蜇种苗	0																		0	0	0
03083019	活、鲜或冷的其他海蜇	14	0		0	11.2		0	5.6	0	0			11.2	0			0	0	0	0	0
03083090	冻、干、盐腌或盐渍的海蜇	10	0		0			0	4	0		0		6	0			0	0	0	0	0
03089011	活、鲜或冷的其他水生无脊椎动物种苗	0																		0	0	0
03089012	活、鲜或冷的其他沙蚕	14	0		0	11.2		0	5.6	0	0			11.2	0			0	0	0	0	0
03089019	活、鲜或冷的其他水生无脊椎动物	14	0		0	11.2		0	5.6	0	0			11.2	0			0	0	0	0	0
03089090	冻、干、盐腌或盐渍的其他水生无脊椎动物	10	0		0			0	4	0		0		6	0			0	0	0	0	0
04011000	脂肪含量未超1%未浓缩及未加糖的乳及奶油	15	0		0	12		0	6	10		0		12	0					0	0	0
04012000	脂肪含量在1-6%未浓缩及未加糖的乳及奶油	15	0		0	12		3	6	10	0	0		12	0					0	0	0
04014000	按重量计脂肪含量超过6%,但不超过10%的未浓缩及未加糖或其他甜物质的乳及奶油	15	0		0	12		3	6	10		0		12	0					0	0	0
04015000	按重量计脂肪含量超过10%的未浓缩及未加糖或其他甜物质的乳及奶油	15	0		0	12		3	6	10		0		12	0					0	0	0
04021000	脂肪含量≤1.5%固状乳及奶油	10	0	7	0	5		3.3	6.5	6.7	0	0		6	0					0	0	0
04022100	脂肪量>1.5%未加糖固状乳及奶油	10	0	7	0	7		3.3	6.5	6.7	0	0			0					0	0	0
04022900	脂肪量>1.5%的加糖固状乳及奶油	10	0		0	5		3.3	6.5	6.7	0	0		6	0					0	0	0
04029100	浓缩但未加糖的非固状乳及奶油	10	0		0	5		3.3	4	6.7	0	0			0					0	0	0
04029900	浓缩并已加糖的非固状乳及奶油	10	0		0	5		0	6.5	6.7					0					0	0	0
04031000	酸乳	10	0		0	5		0	4	6.7	0	0		8.3	0					0	0	0
04039000	酪乳及其他发酵或酸化的乳及奶油	20	0		0			0	8	13.3	0	0			0					0	0	
04041000	乳清及改性乳清	6	0		0	5		0	0	4					0					0	0	
04049000	其他编号未列名的含天然乳的产品	20	0		0			0	8	13.3					0					0	0	
04051000	黄油	10	0		0	5		2	4	6.7				6	0					0	0	0
04052000	乳酱	10	0	8.1	0	5		0	0	6.7		0		6	0					0	0	0
04059000	其他从乳中提取的脂和油	10	0		0	5		2	4	6.7					0					0	0	0
04061000	鲜乳酪(未熟化或未固化的)	12	0		0	6		2.4	4.8	8	0	0		9.2	0					0	0	0
04062000	各种磨碎或粉化的乳酪	12	0		0	6		0	7.2	8	0			9.2	0					0		
04063000	经加工的乳酪,但磨碎或粉化的除外	12	0		0	6		2.4	7.2	8				9.2	0					0	0	
04064000	蓝纹乳酪和娄地青霉生产的带有纹理的其他乳酪	15	0		0	12		0	6	10					0					0	0	
04069000	其他乳酪	12	0		0	6		2.4	4.8	8				9.2	0					0	0	0
04071100	种用鸡蛋	0																		0	0	0
04071900	种用其他禽蛋	0																		0	0	0
04072100	鲜鸡蛋	20	0		0			0	8	0				16	0			0	0	0	0	0
04072900	其他鲜禽蛋	20	0		0			0	8	0				16	0			0	0	0	0	0
04079010	咸蛋	20	0		0			0	0	0				16	0				0	0	0	0
04079020	皮蛋	20	0		0			0	0	0				16	0					0	0	
04079090	其他蛋	20	0		0			0	0	0				16	0					0	0	
04081100	干蛋黄	20	0		0			0	8	0				16	0					0	0	
04081900	其他蛋黄	20	0		0			0	8	0				16	0					0	0	
04089100	干的其他去壳禽蛋	20	0		0			0	8	0				16	0					0	0	
04089900	其他去壳禽蛋	20	0		0			0	8	0	0			16	0					0	0	
04090000	天然蜂蜜	15	0		0	12		0	6	0				12	0		0	0		0	0	0
04100010	燕窝	25	0		0			0	10	0	0	0		20	0			0	0	0	0	0
04100041	鲜蜂王浆	15	0		0	12		0	6	0				12	0					0	0	
04100042	鲜蜂王浆粉	15	0		0	12		0	6	0				12	0					0	0	
04100043	蜂花粉	20	0		0			0	8	0				16	0					0	0	
04100049	其他蜂产品	20	0		0			0	8	0				16	0					0	0	
04100090	其他编号未列名的食用动物产品	20	0		0			0	8	0			0	16	0				0	0	0	0
05010000	未经加工的人发;废人发	15	0		0	12		0	6	0				12	0					0	0	
05021010	猪鬃	20	0		0			0	8	0				16	0					0	0	
05021020	猪毛	20	0		0			0	8	0				16	0					0	0	

税则号列	货品名称	最惠国	协定税率													特惠税率						
			东盟统一	亚太5国	智利	巴基斯坦	新加坡	新西兰	秘鲁	哥达	香港	澳门	台湾	瑞士	冰岛	亚太2国	老挝	柬埔寨	缅甸	LDC1	LDC2	LDC3
05021030	猪鬃或猪毛的废料	20	0		0			0	8	0				16	0					0	0	
05029011	山羊毛	20	0		0			0	8	0				16	0					0	0	
05029012	黄鼠狼尾毛	20	0		0			0	8	0				16	0					0	0	
05029019	獾毛及其他制刷用兽毛	20	0		0			0	8	0				16	0					0	0	
05029020	獾毛及其他制刷用兽毛的废料	20	0		0			0	8	0				16	0					0	0	
05040011	整个或切块的盐渍猪肠衣(猪大肠头除外)	20	0	10	0	10		0	8	0				12	0					0	0	
05040012	整个或切块的盐渍绵羊肠衣	18	0	9	0	9		0	7.2	0				14.4	0					0	0	
05040013	整个或切块的盐渍山羊肠衣	18	0	9	0	9		0	7.2	0				14.4	0					0	0	
05040014	整个或切块的盐渍猪大肠头	20	0	10	0	10		0	8	0				16	0					0	0	
05040019	整个或切块的其他动物肠衣	18	0	9	0	9		0	7.2	0				14.4	0					0	0	
05040021	冷和冻的鸡肫	20	0	0.65元/千克	0	0.65元/千克		0	8	0				16	0					0	0	
05040029	鲜、冷、冻、干、盐制的其他动物胃	20	0	10	0	10		0	8	0				16	0					0	0	0
05040090	鲜、冷、冻、干、盐制的其他动物肠、膀胱、胃	20	0	10	0	10		0	8	0				12	0					0	0	
05051000	填充用羽毛;羽绒	10	0	7.5	0	5		0	0	0				6	0					0	0	0
05059010	羽毛或不完整羽毛的粉末及废料	10	0		0	5		0	0	0				6	0					0	0	0
05059090	其他羽毛,羽绒,带有羽毛,羽绒,的鸟皮及鸟体其他部分	10	0		0	5		0	0	0				6	0					0	0	0
05061000	经酸处理的骨胶原及骨	12	0		0	6		0	0	0				9.6	0		0			0	0	0
05069011	含牛羊成分的骨粉及骨废料	12	0		0	6		0	4.8	0				9.6	0		0			0	0	0
05069019	骨粉及骨废料	12	0		0	6		0	4.8	0				9.6	0		0			0	0	0
05069090	其他骨及角柱	12	0		0	6		0	4.8	6		0		9.6	0		0			0	0	0
05071000	兽牙;兽牙粉末及废料	10	0		0	5		0	0	0				6	0					0	0	0
05079010	羚羊角及其粉末和废料	3	0		0	0		0	0	0				0	0					0	0	0
05079020	鹿茸及其粉末	11	0		0	5		0	0	0				8.8	0					0	0	0
05079090	龟壳、鲸须、鲸须毛、鹿角及其他角	10	0		0	5		0	0	0				6	0					0	0	0
05080010	珊瑚及水产品壳、骨的粉末及废料	12	0		0			0	4.8	0	0			9.6	0					0	0	0
05080090	珊瑚及介、贝、棘皮动物的壳、骨	12	0		0	6		0	4.8	0	0			9.6	0					0	0	0
05100010	黄药	3	0		0	0		0	0	0				0	0					0	0	0
05100020	龙涎香、海狸香、灵猫香	7	0		0	5		0	0	0				4.2	0					0	0	
05100030	麝香	7	0		0	5		0	0	0				4.2	0					0	0	
05100040	斑蝥	7	0		0	5		0	0	0				4.2	0					0	0	0
05100090	胆汁,配药用腺体及其他动物产品	6	0		0	5		0	0	0				3.6	0					0	0	0
05111000	牛的精液	0																		0	0	0
05119111	受精鱼卵	12	0		0	6		0	0	0				9.6	0					0	0	0
05119119	其他鱼产品	12	0		0			0	4.8	0				9.6	9.8					0	0	0
05119190	其他未列名水产品;第三章的死动物	12	0		0	6		0	4.8	0				9.6	0					0	0	0
05119910	动物精液(牛的精液除外)	0																		0	0	0
05119920	动物胚胎	0																		0	0	0
05119930	蚕种	0																		0	0	0
05119940	马毛及废马毛,不论是否制成有或无衬垫的毛片	15	0		0	12		0	6	0				12	0					0	0	
05119990	其他编号未列名的动物产品;不适合供人食用的第一章的死动物	12	0		0	6		0	4.8	0				9.6	0					0	0	0
06011010	休眠的番红花球茎	4	0	2	0	0		0	0	0				0	0		0			0	0	0
06011021	种用百合球茎	0																		0	0	0
06011029	其他百合球茎	5	0	2.5	0	0		0	0	0				0	0		0			0	0	0
06011091	种用休眠的鳞茎、块茎、块根等	0																		0	0	0
06011099	其它休眠的鳞茎、块茎、块根等	5	0	2.5	0	0		0	0	0				0	0		0			0	0	0
06012000	生长或开花的鳞茎等及菊苣植物	15	0	7.5	0	7.5		0	6	0				12	0					0	0	
06021000	无根插枝及接穗	0																		0	0	0
06022010	食用水果及坚果树的种用苗木	0																		0	0	0
06022090	其他食用水果及坚果树及灌木	10	0	5	0	5		0	4	0				6	0					0	0	0
06023010	种用杜鹃	0																		0	0	0
06023090	其他杜鹃	15	0		0	12		0	6	0				12	0					0	0	
06024010	种用玫瑰	0																		0	0	0

税则号列	货品名称	最惠国	协定税率												特惠税率						
			东盟统一	亚太5国	智利	巴基斯坦	新加坡	新西兰	秘鲁	哥达	香港	澳门	台湾	瑞士	冰岛	亚太2国	老挝	柬埔寨	缅甸	LDC1	LDC2	LDC3
06024090	其他玫瑰	15	0		0	12		0	6	0				12	0					0	0	
06029010	蘑菇菌丝	0																		0	0	0
06029091	其他种用苗木	0																		0	0	0
06029092	兰花	10	0		0	5		0	4	0				6	0					0	0	0
06029093	菊花	10	0		0	5		0	4	0				6	0					0	0	0
06029094	百合	10	0		0	5		0	4	0				6	0					0	0	0
06029095	康乃馨	10	0		0	5		0	4	0				6	0					0	0	0
06029099	其他非种用活植物	10	0	5	0	5		0	4	0				6	0					0	0	0
06031100	鲜玫瑰	10	0	5	0	5		0	0	0				6	0		0			0	0	0
06031200	鲜康乃馨	10	0	5	0	5		0	0	0				6	0		0			0	0	0
06031300	鲜兰花	10	0	5	0	5		0	0	0			0	6	0		0			0	0	0
06031400	鲜菊花	10	0	5	0	5		0	0	0				6	0		0			0	0	0
06031500	鲜百合花	10	0	5	0	5		0	0	0				6	0		0			0	0	0
06031900	其他鲜花	10	0	5	0	5		0	0	0				6	0		0			0	0	0
06039000	干的及经过染色等加工的插花及花蕾	23	0	11.5	0	11.5		0	9.2	0	0			18.4	0		0			0	0	0
06042010	鲜苔藓及地衣	23	0		0			0	9.2	0				18.4	0					0	0	
06042090	鲜植物枝、叶等	10	0		0	5		0	4	0				6	0					0	0	0
06049010	其他苔藓及地衣	23	0		0			0	9.2	0				18.4	0					0	0	
06049090	其他植物枝、叶等	10	0		0	5		0	0	0	0			6	0					0	0	0
07011000	种用马铃薯	13	0		0	6.5		0	0	0				10.4						0	0	0
07019000	其他鲜或冷的马铃薯	13	0	9	0	5		0	0	0				10.4	0			0		0	0	0
07020000	鲜或冷藏的番茄	13	0		0	6.5		0	0	0				10.4	0					0	0	0
07031010	鲜或冷的洋葱	13	0	6.5	0	5		0	0	0				10.4	0			0	0	0	0	0
07031020	鲜或冷的青葱	13	0	6.5	0	5		0	0	0				10.4	0			0	0	0	0	0
07032010	鲜或冷藏的大蒜头	13	0	6.5	0	0		0	0	0				10.4	0					0	0	
07032020	鲜或冷藏的大蒜蒜台及蒜苗(青蒜)	13	0	6.5	0	0		0	0	0				10.4	0					0	0	
07032090	其他鲜或冷藏的大蒜	13	0	6.5	0	0		0	0	0				10.4	0					0	0	
07039010	鲜或冷的韭葱	13	0		0	6.5		0	0	0				10.4	0			0		0	0	0
07039020	鲜或冷的大葱	13	0		0	6.5		0	0	0				10.4	0			0		0	0	0
07039090	鲜或冷的其他葱属蔬菜	13	0		0	6.5		0	0	0				10.4	0			0		0	0	0
07041000	鲜或冷的菜花及硬花甘蓝	10	0		0	5		0	0	0				6						0	0	0
07042000	鲜或冷的抱子甘蓝	13	0		0	6.5		0	0	0				10.4	0					0	0	
07049010	卷心菜	13	0		0	6.5		0	0	0				10.4	0		0			0	0	0
07049020	西兰花	13	0		0	6.5		0	0	0				10.4	0		0			0	0	0
07049090	鲜或冷的其他食用芥菜类蔬菜	13	0		0	6.5		0	0	0				10.4	0		0			0	0	0
07051100	鲜或冷的结球莴苣(包心生菜)	10	0		0	0		0	0	0				6	0					0	0	0
07051900	鲜或冷的其他莴苣	10	0		0	0		0	0	0				6	0					0	0	0
07052100	鲜或冷的维特罗夫菊苣	13	0		0	0		0	0	0				10.4	0					0	0	
07052900	鲜或冷的其他菊苣	13	0		0	0		0	0	0				10.4	0					0	0	
07061000	鲜或冷的胡萝卜及萝卜	13	0		0	6.5		0	0	0				10.4						0	0	
07069000	鲜或冷的小萝卜及类似食用根茎	13	0		0	6.5		0	0	0				10.4	0					0	0	
07070000	鲜或冷的黄瓜及小黄瓜	13	0	6.5	0	5		0	0	0				10.4	0			0		0	0	0
07081000	鲜或冷的豌豆	13	0	6.5	0	0		0	0	0				10.4	0			0		0	0	0
07082000	鲜或冷的豇豆及菜豆	13	0	6.5	0	0		0	0	0				10.4	0		0	0		0	0	0
07089000	鲜或冷的其他豆类蔬菜	13	0	6.5	0	0		0	0	0				10.4	0			0		0	0	0
07092000	鲜或冷的芦笋	13	0	6.5	0	0		0	0	0				10.4	0					0	0	0
07093000	鲜或冷的茄子	13	0	6.5	0	0		0	0	0				10.4	0					0	0	0
07094000	鲜或冷的芹菜,但块根芹除外	10	0		0	0		0	0	0				6	0					0	0	0
07095100	鲜或冷的其他伞菌属蘑菇	13	0		0	0		0	0	0	0			10.4	0			0		0	0	0
07095910	鲜或冷的松茸	13	0		0	0		0	0	0				10.4	0			0		0	0	0
07095920	鲜或冷的香菇	13	0		0	0		0	0	0				10.4	0			0		0	0	0
07095930	鲜或冷的金针菇	13	0		0	0		0	0	0			0	10.4	0			0		0	0	0
07095940	鲜或冷的草菇	13	0		0	0		0	0	0				10.4	0			0		0	0	0
07095950	鲜或冷的口蘑	13	0		0	0		0	0	0				10.4	0			0		0	0	0
07095960	鲜或冷的块菌	13	0		0	0		0	0	0				10.4	0					0	0	
07095990	鲜或冷的其他蘑菇	13	0		0	0		0	0	0				10.4	0			0		0	0	0
07096000	鲜或冷的辣椒,包括甜椒	13	0	6.5	0	0		0	0	0				10.4	0			0		0	0	0
07097000	鲜或冷的菠菜	13	0		0	0		0	0	0	0			10.4	0					0	0	0
07099100	鲜或冷藏的洋蓟	13	0		0	0		0	0	0	0			10.4	0			0		0	0	0
07099200	鲜或冷藏的油橄榄	13	0		0	0		0	0	0	0			10.4	0			0		0	0	0
07099300	鲜或冷藏的南瓜、笋瓜及瓠瓜	13	0		0	0		0	0	0	0			10.4	0			0		0	0	0

税则号列	货品名称	最惠国	协定税率													特惠税率						
			东盟统一	亚太5国	智利	巴基斯坦	新加坡	新西兰	秘鲁	哥达	香港	澳门	台湾	瑞士	冰岛	亚太2国	老挝	柬埔寨	缅甸	LDC1	LDC2	LDC3
07099910	鲜或冷藏的竹笋	13	0		0	0		0	0	0				10.4	0		0	0		0	0	0
07099990	鲜或冷藏的其他蔬菜	13	0		0	0		0	0	0	0			10.4	0			0		0	0	0
07101000	冷冻马铃薯	13	0		0	6.5		0	0	0				10.4						0	0	
07102100	冷冻豌豆	13	0		0	6.5		0	0	0				10.4	0					0	0	
07102210	红小豆(赤豆)	13	0		0	6.5		0	0	0				10.4	0			0		0	0	0
07102290	其他冷冻豇豆及菜豆	13	0		0	6.5		0	0	0				10.4	0			0		0	0	0
07102900	冷冻其他豆类蔬菜	13	0		0	6.5		0	0	0				10.4	0			0		0	0	0
07103000	冷冻菠菜	13	0		0	6.5		0	0	0				10.4	0					0	0	
07104000	冷冻甜玉米	10	0		0	5		0	0	0				6	0					0	0	0
07108010	冷冻松茸	13	0		0	6.5		0	0	0				10.4	0			0		0	0	0
07108020	冻其他蒜台及蒜苗(青蒜)	13	0		0	6.5		0	0	0				10.4	0			0		0	0	0
07108030	冻蒜头	13	0		0	6.5		0	0	0				10.4	0			0		0	0	0
07108040	冻牛肝菌	13	0		0	6.5		0	0	0				10.4	0			0		0	0	0
07108090	冷冻未列名蔬菜	13	0		0	6.5		0	0	0				10.4	0			0		0	0	0
07109000	冷冻什锦蔬菜	10	0		0	5		0	0	0				6	0			0		0	0	0
07112000	暂时保藏的油橄榄	13	0		0	0		0	0	0				10.4	0					0	0	
07114000	暂时保藏的黄瓜及小黄瓜	13	0		0	0		0	0	0				10.4	0					0	0	
07115112	盐水小白蘑菇	13	0		0	0		0	0	0				10.4	0					0	0	
07115119	盐水的其他伞菌属蘑菇	13	0		0	0		0	0	0				10.4	0					0	0	
07115190	其他伞菌属蘑菇	13	0		0	0		0	0	0				10.4	0					0	0	
07115911	盐水松茸	13	0		0	0		0	0	0				10.4	0					0	0	
07115919	盐水其他蘑菇及菌块	13	0		0	0		0	0	0				10.4	0					0	0	
07115990	暂时保藏的其他蘑菇及菌块	13	0		0	0		0	0	0				10.4	0					0	0	
07119031	盐水竹笋	13	0	6.5	0	0		0	0	0				10.4	0					0	0	
07119034	盐水大蒜	13	0	6.5	0	0		0	0	0				10.4	0					0	0	
07119039	盐水其他蔬菜;什锦蔬菜	13	0	6.5	0	0		0	0	0				10.4	0					0	0	
07119090	暂时保藏的其他蔬菜;什锦蔬菜	13	0	6.5	0	0		0	0	0				10.4	0					0	0	
07122000	干制洋葱	13	0		0	6.5		0	0	0				10.4	0					0	0	0
07123100	干伞菌属蘑菇	13	0	9	0	5		0	0	0				10.4	0					0	0	0
07123200	干木耳	13	0		0	6.5		0	0	0				10.4	0					0	0	
07123300	干银耳	13	0		0	6.5		0	0	0				10.4	0					0	0	
07123910	干香菇	13	0	9	0	5		0	0	0				10.4	0					0	0	
07123920	干金针菇	13	0	9	0	5		0	0	0				10.4	0					0	0	
07123930	干草菇	13	0	9	0	5		0	0	0				10.4	0					0	0	
07123940	干口蘑	13	0	9	0	5		0	0	0				10.4	0					0	0	
07123950	干牛肝菌	13	0	9	0	5		0	0	0				10.4	0					0	0	
07123990	其他干制蘑菇及块菌	13	0	9	0	9		0	0	0				10.4	0					0	0	
07129010	笋干丝	13	0		0	6.5		0	0	0				10.4	0					0	0	0
07129020	紫萁(薇菜干)	13	0		0	6.5		0	0	0				10.4	0					0	0	
07129030	干金针菜(黄花菜)	13	0		0	6.5		0	0	0				10.4	0					0	0	
07129040	蕨菜干	13	0		0	6.5		0	0	0				10.4	0					0	0	
07129050	干制的大蒜	13	0		0	6.5		0	0	0				10.4	0					0	0	
07129091	干制的辣根	13	0		0	6.5		0	0	0				10.4	0					0	0	0
07129099	干制的其他蔬菜及什锦蔬菜	13	0		0	6.5		0	0	0				10.4	0					0	0	0
07131010	种用豌豆	0																		0	0	0
07131090	其他干豌豆	5	0		0	0		0	0	0				0	0					0	0	0
07132010	种用鹰嘴豆	0																		0	0	0
07132090	其他干鹰嘴豆	7	0		0	5		0	0	0				4.2	0					0	0	0
07133110	种用绿豆	0																		0	0	0
07133190	其他干绿豆	3	0	1.5	0	0		0	0	0				0	0			0	0	0	0	0
07133210	种用红小豆(赤豆)	0																		0	0	0
07133290	其他红小豆(赤豆)	3	0		0	0		0	0	0				0	0			0		0	0	0
07133310	种用芸豆	0																		0	0	0
07133390	其他干芸豆	7.5	0		0	5		0	0	0				4.5	0			0		0	0	0
07133400	干巴姆巴拉豆	7	0	3.5	0	0		0	0	0				4.2	0			0		0	0	0
07133500	干牛豆	7	0	3.5	0	0		0	0	0				4.2	0			0		0	0	0
07133900	干豇豆及菜豆	7	0	3.5	0	0		0	0	0				4.2	0			0		0	0	0
07134010	种用扁豆	0																		0	0	0
07134090	其他干扁豆	7	0		0	5		0	0	0				4.2	0					0	0	0
07135010	种用蚕豆	0																		0	0	0
07135090	其他干蚕豆	7	0		0	5		0	0	0				4.2	0					0	0	0

税则号列	货品名称	最惠国	协定税率													特惠税率						
			东盟统一	亚太5国	智利	巴基斯坦	新加坡	新西兰	秘鲁	哥达	香港	澳门	台湾	瑞士	冰岛	亚太2国	老挝	柬埔寨	缅甸	LDC1	LDC2	LDC3
07136010	种用干木豆	0																		0	0	0
07136090	其他干木豆	7	0		0	5		0	0	0				4.2	0					0	0	0
07139010	种用干豆	0																		0	0	0
07139090	其它干豆	7	0		0	5		0	0	0				4.2	0					0	0	0
07141010	鲜木薯	10	0		0	5		0	0	0				6	0		0	0		0	0	0
07141020	干木薯	5	0		0	0		0	0	0				0	0		0	0		0	0	0
07141030	冷或冻的木薯	10	0		0	5		0	0	0				6	0		0	0		0	0	0
07142011	种用鲜甘薯	0															0	0		0	0	0
07142019	其他鲜甘薯	13	0	6.5	0	5		0	0	0				10.4	0		0	0		0	0	0
07142020	干甘薯	13	0	6.5	0	5		0	0	0				10.4	0		0	0		0	0	0
07142030	冷或冻的甘薯	13	0	6.5	0	5		0	0	0				10.4	0		0	0		0	0	0
07143000	山药	13	0	6.5	0	5		0	0	0				10.4	0		0	0		0	0	0
07144000	芋头	13	0	6.5	0	5		0	0	0				10.4	0					0	0	
07145000	箭叶黄体芋	13	0	6.5	0	5		0	0	0				10.4	0		0	0		0	0	0
07149010	鲜、干或冷、冻的荸荠	13	0	6.5	0	5		0	0	0				10.4	0		0	0		0	0	0
07149021	种用藕	0																		0	0	0
07149029	其他藕	13	0	6.5	0	5		0	0	0				10.4	0		0	0		0	0	0
07149090	含有高淀粉或菊粉的其他类似根茎	13	0	6.5	0	5		0	0	0				10.4	0		0	0		0	0	0
08011100	干的椰子	12	0	6	0	5		0	0	8		0		9.6	0			0		0	0	0
08011200	未去内壳的鲜椰子	12	0	6	0	5		0	0	8				9.6	0			0		0	0	0
08011910	种用椰子	0																		0	0	0
08011990	其他鲜椰子	12	0	6	0	5		0	0	8				9.6	0			0		0	0	0
08012100	鲜或干的未去壳巴西果	10	0		0	5		0	0	6.7		0		6	0					0	0	0
08012200	鲜或干的去壳巴西果	10	0		0	5		0	0	6.7		0		6	0					0	0	0
08013100	鲜或干的未去壳腰果	20	0		0			0	8	13.3		0		16	0			0		0	0	0
08013200	鲜或干的去壳腰果	10	0		0	5		0	0	6.7		0		6	0			0	0	0	0	0
08021100	未去壳扁桃仁	24	0		0			0	9.6	16		0		19.2	0					0	0	
08021200	其他扁桃仁	10	0		0	5		0	4	6.7		0		6	0					0	0	0
08022100	鲜或干的未去壳榛子	25	0		0			0	10	16.7		0		20	0					0	0	
08022200	鲜或干的去壳榛子	10	0		0	5		0	0	6.7		0		6	0					0	0	0
08023100	鲜或干的未去壳核桃	25	0		0			0	10	16.7		0		20	0					0	0	
08023200	鲜或干的去壳核桃	20	0		0			0	8	13.3		0		16	0					0	0	
08024110	未去壳板栗	25	0		0			0	10	16.7		0		20	0					0	0	
08024190	未去壳其他栗子	25	0		0			0	10	16.7		0		20	0					0	0	
08024210	去壳板栗	25	0		0			0	10	16.7		0		20	0					0	0	
08024290	去壳其他栗子	25	0		0			0	10	16.7		0		20	0					0	0	
08025100	未去壳阿月浑子果	10	0		0	5		0	0	6.7		0		6	0					0	0	
08025200	去壳阿月浑子果	10	0		0	5		0	0	6.7		0		6	0					0	0	
08026110	未去壳种用马卡达姆坚果	0																		0	0	0
08026190	未去壳其他马卡达姆坚果	24	0		0			0	9.6	16		0		19.2	0					0	0	
08026200	去壳马卡达姆坚果	24	0		0			0	9.6	16		0		19.2	0					0	0	
08027000	可乐果	24	0		0			0	9.6	16		0		19.2	0					0	0	
08028000	槟榔果	10	0	5	0	5		0	0	6.7		0		6	0					0	0	0
08029020	鲜或干的白果	25	0		0			0	10	16.7		0		20	0					0	0	
08029030	鲜或干的松子仁	25	0		0			0	10	16.7		0		20	0					0	0	
08029090	其他鲜或干坚果	24	0		0			0	9.6	16		0		19.2	0					0	0	
08031000	鲜或干的芭蕉	10	0	6.9	0	5		0	4	6.7		0	0	6	0		0	0		0	0	0
08039000	鲜或干的其他香蕉	10	0	6.9	0	5		0	4	6.7		0	0	6	0		0	0		0	0	0
08041000	鲜或干的椰枣	15	0		0	0		0	6	10		0		12	0					0	0	
08042000	鲜或干的无花果	30	0		0	0		0	12	20		0		23.1	0					0	0	
08043000	鲜或干菠萝	12	0	7.9	0	0		0	0	8	0	0		9.6	0			0		0	0	0
08044000	鲜或干鳄梨	25	0	12.5	0	0		0	0	16.7		0		20	0			0		0	0	0
08045010	鲜或干番石榴	15	0	7.5	0	0		0	6	10		0		12	0					0	0	
08045020	鲜或干芒果	15	0	10.6	0	0		0	0	10		0		12	0					0	0	0
08045030	鲜或干山竹果	15	0	7.5	0	0		0	0	10		0		12	0					0	0	
08051000	鲜或干橙	11	0		0	0		1.2	2.8	7.3		0	0	8.8	0					0	0	0
08052010	鲜或干蕉柑	12	0		0	0		1.3	4.8	8		0		9.6	0					0	0	
08052020	阔叶柑橘	12	0		0	0		1.3	4.8	8		0		9.6	0					0	0	
08052090	其他鲜或干的柑桔及杂交柑桔	12	0		0	0		1.3	3	8		0		9.6	0					0	0	
08054000	鲜或干的葡萄柚,包括柚	12	0		0	0		0	4.8	8	0	0		9.6	0					0	0	0
08055000	鲜或干的柠檬及酸橙	11	0	5.5	0	0		1.2	2.8	7.3		0	0	8.8	0					0	0	0

税则号列	货品名称	最惠国	协定税率													特惠税率						
			东盟统一	亚太5国	智利	巴基斯坦	新加坡	新西兰	秘鲁	哥达	香港	澳门	台湾	瑞士	冰岛	亚太2国	老挝	柬埔寨	缅甸	LDC1	LDC2	LDC3
08059000	其他鲜或干的柑桔属水果	30	0	15	0	0		0	0	20		0		23.1	0					0	0	
08061000	鲜葡萄	13	0		0	6.5		0	0	0				10.4	0					0	0	
08062000	葡萄干	10	0		0	5		0	4	0		0		6	0					0	0	
08071100	鲜西瓜	25	0	12.5	0	12.5		0	10	0				20	0					0		
08071910	鲜哈密瓜	12	0	6	0	5		0	0	0			0	9.6	0					0	0	0
08071920	鲜罗马甜瓜及加勒比甜瓜	12	0	6	0	5		0	4.8	0				9.6	0					0	0	0
08071990	其他鲜甜瓜	12	0	6	0	5		0	4.8	6				9.6	0					0	0	0
08072000	鲜木瓜	25	0		0			0	10	0				20	0			0		0	0	0
08081000	鲜苹果	10	0		0	5		0	4	0				6	0					0	0	0
08083010	鲜鸭梨及雪梨	12	0	10	0	5		0	4.8	0				9.6	0					0	0	
08083020	鲜香梨	12	0	10	0	5		0	4.8	0				9.6	0					0	0	
08083090	其他鲜梨	10	0		0	5		0	4	0				6	0					0	0	
08084000	鲜榅桲	16	0		0	12.8		0	6.4	0				12.8	0					0	0	
08091000	鲜杏	25	0		0			0	10	0				20	0					0	0	
08092100	鲜欧洲酸樱桃	10	0		0	5		0	4	0				6	0					0	0	0
08092900	其他鲜樱桃	10	0		0	5		0	4	0				6	0					0	0	0
08093000	鲜桃,包括鲜油桃	10	0		0	5		0	4	0				6	0					0	0	0
08094000	鲜梅及李	10	0		0	5		0	4	0				6	0					0	0	
08101000	鲜草莓	14	0		0			0	0	0				11.2	0					0	0	0
08102000	鲜的木莓、黑莓、桑椹及罗甘莓	25	0		0			0	10	0				20	0					0	0	
08103000	鲜黑、白或红的穗醋栗(加仑子)及醋栗	25	0		0			0	10	0				20	0					0	0	
08104000	鲜蔓越桔及越桔	30	0		0			0	0	0				23.1	0					0		
08105000	鲜猕猴桃	20	0	16.5	0	16		2.2	8	0				16	0					0	0	
08106000	鲜榴莲	20	0		0			0	8	0				16	0			0		0	0	0
08107000	鲜柿子	20	0	16.4	0	16		0	0	0	0			16	0					0	0	
08109010	鲜荔枝	30	0	20	0	20		0	12	0				23.1	0					0	0	
08109030	鲜龙眼	12	0		0	6		0	0	0				9.6	0			0		0	0	0
08109040	鲜红毛丹	20	0		0			0	8	0				16	0					0	0	
08109050	鲜番荔枝	20	0		0			0	0	0				16	0					0	0	
08109060	鲜杨桃	20	0		0			0	0	0				16	0					0	0	
08109070	莲雾	20	0	16.4	0	16		0	8	0				16	0					0	0	
08109080	火龙果	20	0	16.4	0	16		0	8	0			0	16	0					0	0	
08109090	其他鲜果	20	0	16.4	0	16		0	0	0	0			16	0					0	0	
08111000	冷冻草莓	30	0		0			0	12	0					0					0	0	
08112000	冷冻其他浆果	30	0		0			0	12	0					0					0	0	
08119010	未去壳的冷冻栗子	30	0		0			0	12	0					0					0	0	
08119090	其他冷冻水果及坚果	30	0		0			0	12	0					0					0		
08121000	暂时保藏的樱桃	30	0		0			0	12	0					0					0		
08129000	暂时保藏的其他水果及坚果	25	0		0			0	11	0				20	0					0	0	
08131000	杏干	25	0		0			0	10	0		0		20	0					0	0	
08132000	梅干及李干	25	0		0			0	10	0		0		20	0					0	0	
08133000	苹果干	25	0		0			0	10	0		0		20	0					0	0	
08134010	龙眼干、肉	20	0		0			0	8	0		0		16	0			0		0	0	0
08134020	柿饼	25	0		0			0	10	0		0		20	0			0		0	0	0
08134030	干红枣	25	0		0			0	10	0		0		20	0			0		0	0	0
08134040	荔枝干	25	0		0			0	10	0		0		20	0			0		0	0	0
08134090	其他干果	25	0		0			0	10	0		0		20	0			0		0	0	0
08135000	本章的什锦坚果或干果	18	0		0	14.4		0	7.2	0		0		14.4	0					0	0	
08140000	柑桔属水果或甜瓜的果皮	25	0		0			0	10	0		0		20	0					0	0	
09011100	未浸除咖啡碱的未焙炒咖啡	8	8		0			0		4				4.8	0		0	0		0	0	0
09011200	已浸除咖啡碱的未焙炒咖啡	8	8		0			0						4.8	0		0	0		0	0	0
09012100	未浸除咖啡碱的已焙炒咖啡	15	15		0			0		7.5	0	0		13.2	0		0	0		0	0	0
09012200	已浸除咖啡碱的已焙炒咖啡	15	0		0	12		0				0		12	0		0	0		0	0	0
09019010	咖啡豆荚及咖啡豆皮	10	0		0	5	0	0	0	0				6	0		0	0		0	0	0
09019020	含咖啡的咖啡代用品	30	0		0		0	0				0			0		0	0		0	0	0
09021010	每件净重≤3kg 的花茶	15	0	7.5	0	7.5	0	0	6	0		0		12	0					0	0	
09021090	每件净重≤3kg 的其他绿茶	15	0	7.5	0	7.5	0	0	6	0		0	0	12	0					0	0	0
09022010	每件净重>3kg 的花茶	15	0	7.5	0	7.5	0	0	6	0		0		12	0					0	0	
09022090	每件净重>3kg 的其他绿茶	15	0	7.5	0	7.5	0	0	6	0		0	0	12	0					0	0	0
09023010	每件净重≤3kg 的乌龙茶	15	0	7.5	0	7.5	0	0	6	0	0	0	0	12	0					0	0	
09023020	每件净重≤3kg 的普洱茶	15	0	7.5	0	7.5	0	0	6	0	0	0		12	0					0	0	

税则号列	货品名称	最惠国	协定税率 东盟统一	亚太5国	智利	巴基斯坦	新加坡	新西兰	秘鲁	哥达	香港	澳门	台湾	瑞士	冰岛	特惠税率 亚太2国	老挝	柬埔寨	缅甸	LDC1	LDC2	LDC3
09023090	每件净重≤3kg 的其他发酵、半发酵红茶	15	0	7.5	0	7.5	0	0	6	0	0	0	0	12	0					0	0	0
09024010	每件净重 >3kg 的乌龙茶	15	0	7.5	0	7.5	0	0	6	0	0	0	0	12	0		0	0	0	0	0	0
09024020	每件净重 >3kg 的普洱茶	15	0	7.5	0	7.5	0	0	6	0	0	0		12	0		0	0	0	0	0	0
09024090	每件净重 >3kg 的其他红茶(已发酵)及半发酵茶	15	0	7.5	0	7.5	0	0	6	0	0	0	0	12	0		0	0	0	0	0	0
09030000	马黛茶	10	0		0	5	0	0	0	0				6	0					0	0	0
09041100	未磨胡椒	20	20		0			0	8	0				16	0					0	0	
09041200	已磨胡椒	20	20	10	0	10		0	8	0	0			16	0					0	0	
09042100	未磨干辣椒	20	0	10	0	10	0	0	0	0	0			16	0					0	0	
09042200	已磨辣椒	20	0	10	0	10	0	0	0	0	0			16	0					0	0	
09051000	未磨香子兰豆	15	0		0	12	0	0	6	0				12	0					0	0	0
09052000	已磨香子兰豆	15	0		0	12	0	0	6	0				12	0					0	0	0
09061100	未磨锡兰肉桂	5	0		0	0		0	0	0				0	0					0	0	0
09061900	其他未磨的肉桂及肉桂花	5	0		0	0		0	0	0				0	0					0	0	0
09062000	已磨肉桂及肉桂花	15	0		0	12	0	0	6	0	0			12	0					0	0	
09071000	未磨丁香	3	0		0	0		0	0	0				0	0			0		0	0	0
09072000	已磨丁香	3	0		0	0		0	0	0				0	0			0		0	0	0
09081100	未磨肉豆蔻	8	0		0	5		0	0	0				4.8	0		0	0		0	0	0
09081200	已磨肉豆蔻	8	0		0	5		0	0	0				4.8	0		0	0		0	0	0
09082100	未磨肉豆蔻衣	8	0		0	5		0	0	0				4.8	0		0	0		0	0	0
09082200	已磨肉豆蔻衣	8	0		0	5		0	0	0				4.8	0		0	0		0	0	0
09083100	未磨豆蔻	3	0		0	0		0	0	0				0	0		0	0		0	0	0
09083200	已磨豆蔻	3	0		0	0		0	0	0				0	0		0	0		0	0	0
09092100	未磨芫荽子	15	0		0	12	0	0	6	0				12	0					0	0	
09092200	已磨芫荽子	15	0		0	12	0	0	6	0				12	0					0	0	
09093100	未磨枯茗子	15	0	7.5	0	7.5	0	0	6	0				12	0					0	0	
09093200	已磨枯茗子	15	0	7.5	0	7.5	0	0	6	0				12	0					0	0	
09096110	未磨八角茴香	20	0		0		0	0	8	0				16	0					0	0	
09096190	未磨其他茴香	15	0		0	12	0	0	6	0				12	0					0	0	
09096210	已磨八角茴香	20	0		0		0	0	8	0				16	0					0	0	
09096290	已磨其他茴香	15	0		0	12	0	0	6	0				12	0					0	0	
09101100	未磨姜	15	0	7.5	0	7.5	0	0	6	0				12	0		0	0		0	0	0
09101200	已磨姜	15	0	7.5	0	7.5	0	0	6	0				12	0		0	0		0	0	0
09102000	番红花	2	0		0	0		0	0	0				0	0					0	0	0
09103000	姜黄	15	0	7.5	0	7.5	0	0	6	0	0			12	0			0		0	0	0
09109100	混合调味香料	15	0	7.5	0	7.5	0	0	6	0	0	0		12	0					0	0	0
09109900	其他调味香料	15	0		0	12	0	0	6	0	0			12	0					0	0	0
10011100	种用硬粒小麦	65	20																			
10011900	其他硬粒小麦	65	20																			
10019100	种用其他小麦及混合麦	65	20																			
10019900	其他小麦及混合麦	65	20																			
10021000	种用黑麦	0																		0	0	0
10029000	其他黑麦	3	0		0	0		0	0	0				0	0					0	0	0
10031000	种用大麦	0																		0	0	0
10039000	其他大麦	3	0	0	0	0		0	0	0				0	0					0	0	0
10041000	种用燕麦	0																		0	0	0
10049000	其他燕麦	2	0		0	0		0	0	0				0	0					0	0	0
10051000	种用玉米	20	20																			
10059000	其他玉米	65	50																			
10061011	种用籼米稻谷	65	50																			
10061019	种用稻谷	65	20																			
10061091	其他籼米稻谷	65	50																			
10061099	其他稻谷	65	20																			
10062010	籼型糙米	65	50																			
10062090	其他糙米	65	20																			
10063010	籼型精米	65	50																			
10063090	其他精米	65	20																			
10064010	籼米碎米	65	20																			
10064090	其他碎米	65	20																			
10071000	种用高粱	0																		0	0	0
10079000	其他高粱	2	0		0	0		0	0	0				0	0					0	0	

税则号列	货品名称	最惠国	协定税率													特惠税率						
			东盟统一	亚太5国	智利	巴基斯坦	新加坡	新西兰	秘鲁	哥达	香港	澳门	台湾	瑞士	冰岛	亚太2国	老挝	柬埔寨	缅甸	LDC1	LDC2	LDC3
10081000	荞麦	2	0		0	0		0	0	0				0	0					0	0	0
10082100	种用谷子	2	0		0	0		0	0	0				0	0		0			0	0	0
10082900	其他谷子	2	0		0	0		0	0	0				0	0		0			0	0	0
10083000	加那利草子	2	0		0	0		0	0	0				0	0		0			0	0	0
10084010	种用直长马唐	0																		0	0	0
10084090	其他直长马唐	3	0		0	0		0	0	0				0	0		0			0	0	0
10085010	种用昆诺阿藜	0																		0	0	0
10085090	其他昆诺阿藜	3	0		0	0		0	0	0				0	0		0			0	0	0
10086010	种用黑小麦	0																		0	0	0
10086090	其他黑小麦	3	0		0	0		0	0	0				0	0		0			0	0	0
10089010	其他种用谷物	0																		0	0	0
10089090	其他谷物	3	0		0	0		0	0	0				0	0		0			0	0	0
11010000	小麦或混合麦的细粉	65	50																			
11022000	玉米细粉	40	40																			
11029011	籼米大米细粉	40	40																			
11029019	其他大米细粉	40	20																			
11029090	其他谷物细粉	5	0		0	0		0	0	0				0	0			0		0	0	0
11031100	小麦粗粒及粗粉	65	50																			
11031300	玉米粗粒及粗粉	65	50																			
11031910	燕麦粗粒及粗粉	5	0		0	0		0	0	0				0	0					0	0	0
11031921	籼米大米粗粒及粗粉	10	10																			
11031929	其他大米粗粒及粗粉	10	10																			
11031990	其他谷物粗粒及粗粉	5	0		0	0		0	0	0				0	0			0		0	0	0
11032010	小麦团粒	65	50																			
11032090	其他谷物团粒	20	0		0		0	0	8	0				16	0					0	0	
11041200	滚压或制片的燕麦	20	0		0		0	0	8	0				16	0					0	0	
11041910	滚压或制片的大麦	20	0		0		0	0	8	0				16	0					0	0	
11041990	滚压或制片的其他谷物	20	0		0		0	0	8	0				16	0					0	0	
11042200	经其他加工的燕麦	20	0		0		0	0	8	0				16	0					0	0	
11042300	经其他加工的玉米	65	50																			
11042910	经其他加工的大麦	65	0		0		0	0	26	0										0	0	
11042990	经其他加工的其他谷物	20	0		0		0	0	8	0				16	0					0	0	
11043000	整粒或经加工的谷物胚芽	20	0		0		0	0	8	0				16	0					0	0	
11051000	马铃薯细粉、粗粉及粉末	15	0		0	12	0	0	0	0				12	0					0	0	
11052000	马铃薯粉片、颗粒及团粒	15	0		0	12	0	0	6	0				12	0					0	0	
11061000	干豆细粉、粗粉及粉末	10	0		0		0	0	0	0				6	0			0		0	0	0
11062000	用品目0714的西谷茎髓、植物根茎、块茎制成的细粉、粗粉、粉末	20	0		0		0	0	0	0				16	0		0	0	0	0	0	0
11063000	水果及坚果的细粉、粗粉及粉末	20	0	10	0	10	0	0	8	0				16	0					0	0	
11071000	未焙制麦芽	10	0		0	5	0	0	4	0				6	0					0	0	
11072000	已焙制麦芽	10	0		0	5	0	0	4	0				6	0					0	0	
11081100	小麦淀粉	20	0		0		0	0	8	0				16	0					0	0	
11081200	玉米淀粉	20	0		0		0	0	0	0				16	0					0	0	
11081300	马铃薯淀粉	15	0		0	12	0	0	6	0				12	0					0	0	
11081400	木薯淀粉	10	0		0	5	0	0	0	0				6	0					0	0	0
11081900	其他淀粉	20	0		0		0	0	8	0				16	0					0	0	
11082000	菊粉	20	0		0		0	0	8	0				16	0					0	0	
11090000	面筋,不论是否干制	18	0		0	14.4	0	0	7.2	0				14.4	0					0	0	
12011000	种用大豆	0																		0	0	0
12019010	黄大豆	3	0	0	0	0		0	0	0				0	0		0	0		0	0	0
12019020	黑大豆	3	0	0	0	0		0	0	0				0	0		0	0		0	0	0
12019030	青大豆	3	0	0	0	0		0	0	0				0	0		0	0		0	0	0
12019090	其他大豆	3	0	0	0	0		0	0	0				0	0					0	0	0
12023000	种用花生	0																		0	0	0
12024100	去壳花生	15	0		0	12	0	0	6	0				12	0		0			0	0	0
12024200	未去壳花生	15	0		0	12	0	0	6	0				12	0		0			0	0	0
12030000	干椰子肉	15	0	7.5	0	7.5	0	0	6	0				12	0			0		0	0	0
12040000	亚麻子	15	0		0	12	0	0	6	0				12	0					0	0	
12051010	种用的低芥子酸油菜子	0																		0	0	0
12051090	其他低芥子酸油菜子	9	0	0	0	0		0	0	0				5.4	0					0	0	
12059010	其他种用油菜子	0																		0	0	0

税则号列	货品名称	最惠国	协定税率													特惠税率						
			东盟统一	亚太5国	智利	巴基斯坦	新加坡	新西兰	秘鲁	哥达	香港	澳门	台湾	瑞士	冰岛	亚太2国	老挝	柬埔寨	缅甸	LDC1	LDC2	LDC3
12059090	其他油菜子	9	0	0	0	0		0	0	0				5.4	0					0	0	
12060010	种用葵花籽	0																		0	0	0
12060090	其他葵花籽	15	0		0	12	0	0	6	0				12	0					0	0	
12071010	种用棕榈果及棕榈仁	0																		0	0	0
12071090	其他棕榈果及棕榈仁	10	0		0	5	0	0	0	0				6	0			0		0	0	0
12072100	种用棉子	0																		0	0	0
12072900	其他棉子	15	0		0	12	0	0	6	0				12	0					0	0	
12073010	种用蓖麻子	0																		0	0	0
12073090	其他蓖麻子	15	0		0		0	0	6	0				12	0		0	0	0	0	0	0
12074010	种用芝麻	0																		0	0	0
12074090	其他芝麻	10	0	9	0	9	0	0	0	0				6	0		0	0	0	0	0	0
12075010	种用芥子	0																		0	0	0
12075090	其他芥子	15	0		0	12	0	0	6	0				12	0					0	0	
12076010	种用红花子	0																		0	0	0
12076090	其他红花子	20	0		0		0	0	8	0				16	0					0	0	
12077010	种用甜瓜子	0																		0	0	0
12077091	黑瓜子	20	0		0		0	0	8	0				16	0					0	0	
12077092	红瓜子	20	0		0		0	0	8	0				16	0					0	0	
12077099	其他瓜子	30	0		0			0	12	0					0					0	0	0
12079100	罂粟子	20	0		0		0	0	8	0				16	0					0	0	
12079910	其他种用含油子仁及果实	0																		0	0	0
12079991	牛油树果	20	0		0		0	0	8	0				16	0				0	0	0	0
12079999	其他含油子仁及果实	10	0		0	5	0	0	4	0				6	0		0	0	0	0	0	0
12081000	大豆粉	9	0		0	5		0	0	0				5.4	0			0		0	0	0
12089000	其他含油子仁或果实的细粉及粗粉	15	0		0	12	0	0	6	0	0			12	0			0		0	0	0
12091000	糖甜菜子	0																		0	0	0
12092100	紫苜蓿子	0																		0	0	0
12092200	三叶草子	0																		0	0	0
12092300	羊茅子	0																		0	0	0
12092400	草地早熟禾子	0																		0	0	0
12092500	黑麦草种子	0																		0	0	0
12092910	甜菜籽,糖甜菜子除外	0																		0	0	0
12092990	其他饲料植物种子	0																		0	0	0
12093000	草本花卉植物种子	0																		0	0	0
12099100	蔬菜种子	0																		0	0	0
12099900	其他种植用的种子、果实及孢子	0																		0	0	0
12101000	未研磨也未制成团粒的啤酒花	20	0		0		0	0	8	0				16	0					0	0	
12102000	已研磨或制成团粒的啤酒花;蛇麻腺	10	0		0	5	0	0	0	0				6	0					0	0	0
12112010	鲜或干的西洋参	7.5	0		0	5	0	0	0	0	0	0		4.5	0					0	0	0
12112020	鲜或干的野山参(西洋参除外)	20	0	16.4	0	16	0	0	8	0				16	0					0	0	
12112091	其他鲜人参	20	0		0		0	0	8	0	0			16	0					0	0	
12112099	其他干人参	20	0		0		0	0	8	0	0			16	0					0	0	
12113000	古柯叶	9	0		0	5		0	0	0				5.4	0			0		0	0	0
12114000	罂粟杆	9	0		0	5		0	0	0				5.4	0			0		0	0	0
12119011	鲜或干的当归	6	0	3	0	0		0	0	0				3.6	0			0		0	0	0
12119012	三七(田七)	6	0	3	0	0		0	0	0				3.6	0			0		0	0	0
12119013	鲜或干的党参	6	0	3	0	0		0	0	0				3.6	0					0	0	0
12119014	鲜或干的黄连	6	0	3	0	0		0	0	0				3.6	0					0	0	0
12119015	鲜或干的菊花	6	0	3	0	0		0	0	0				3.6	0			0		0	0	0
12119016	鲜或干的冬虫夏草	6	0	3	0	0		0	0	0		0		3.6	0			0		0	0	0
12119017	鲜或干的贝母	6	0	3	0	0		0	0	0				3.6	0			0		0	0	0
12119018	鲜或干的川芎	6	0	3	0	0		0	0	0				3.6	0			0		0	0	0
12119019	鲜或干的半夏	6	0	3	0	0		0	0	0				3.6	0			0		0	0	0
12119021	鲜或干的白芍	6	0	3	0	0		0	0	0				3.6	0			0		0	0	0
12119022	鲜或干的天麻	6	0	3	0	0		0	0	0				3.6	0			0		0	0	0
12119023	鲜或干的黄芪	6	0	3	0	0		0	0	0				3.6	0			0		0	0	0
12119024	鲜或干的大黄、籽黄	6	0	3	0	0		0	0	0				3.6	0			0		0	0	0
12119025	鲜或干的白术	6	0	3	0	0		0	0	0				3.6	0			0		0	0	0
12119026	鲜或干的地黄	6	0	3	0	0		0	0	0				3.6	0			0		0	0	0
12119027	鲜或干的槐米	6	0	3	0	0		0	0	0				3.6	0			0		0	0	0
12119028	鲜或干的杜仲	6	0	3	0	0		0	0	0				3.6	0			0		0	0	0

税则号列	货品名称	最惠国	协定税率													特惠税率						
			东盟统一	亚太5国	智利	巴基斯坦	新加坡	新西兰	秘鲁	哥达	香港	澳门	台湾	瑞士	冰岛	亚太2国	老挝	柬埔寨	缅甸	LDC1	LDC2	LDC3
12119029	鲜或干的茯苓	6	0	3	0	0		0	0	0				3.6	0		0	0	0	0	0	0
12119031	鲜或干的枸杞	6	0	3	0	0		0	0	0				3.6	0			0		0	0	0
12119032	鲜或干的大海子	6	0	3	0	0		0	0	0				3.6	0			0		0	0	0
12119033	鲜或干的沉香	3	0	1.5	0	0		0	0	0				0	0			0		0	0	0
12119034	鲜或干的沙参	6	0	3	0	0		0	0	0				3.6	0			0		0	0	0
12119035	鲜或干的青蒿	6	0		0	5		0	0	0				3.6	0			0		0	0	0
12119036	鲜或干的甘草	6	0		0	5		0	0	0				3.6	0					0	0	0
12119037	鲜或干的黄芩	6	0	3	0	0		0	0	0				3.6	0		0	0	0	0	0	0
12119038	椴树(欧椴)花及叶	6	0	3	0	0		0	0	0				3.6	0		0	0	0	0	0	0
12119039	其他主要用作药料的鲜或干的植物	6	0	3	0	0		0	0	0				3.6	0		0	0	0	0	0	0
12119050	主要用作香料的植物	8	0	4	0	0		0	0	0				4.8	0			0		0	0	0
12119091	鲜或干的鱼藤根、除虫菊	3	0	1.5	0	0		0	0	0				0	0			0		0	0	0
12119099	其他鲜或干的杀虫、杀菌用植物	9	0	4.5	0	4.5		0	0	0				5.4	0			0		0	0	0
12122110	适合供人食用的海带	20	0	10	0	10	0	0	8	0				16	0					0	0	
12122120	适合供人食用的发菜	20	0	10	0	10	0	0	8	0				16	0					0	0	
12122131	适合供人食用的干裙带菜	15	0	7.5	0	7.5	0	0	7.5	0				12	0					0	0	
12122132	适合供人食用的鲜裙带菜	15	0	7.5	0	7.5	0	0	7.5	0				12	0					0	0	
12122139	适合供人食用的其他裙带菜	15	0	7.5	0	7.5	0	0	7.5	0				12	0					0	0	
12122141	适合供人食用的干紫菜	15	0	7.5	0	7.5	0	0	7.5	0				12	0					0	0	
12122142	适合供人食用的鲜紫菜	15	0	7.5	0	7.5	0	0	7.5	0				12	0					0	0	
12122149	适合供人食用的其他紫菜	15	0	7.5	0	7.5	0	0	7.5	0				12	0					0	0	
12122161	适合供人食用的干麒麟菜	15	0	7.5	0	7.5		0	7.5	0				12	0					0	0	0
12122169	适合供人食用的其他麒麟菜	15	0	7.5	0	7.5		0	7.5	0				12	0					0	0	
12122171	适合供人食用的干江蓠	15	0	7.5	0	7.5		0	7.5	0				12	0					0	0	
12122179	适合供人食用的其他江蓠	15	0	7.5	0	7.5		0	7.5	0				12	0					0	0	
12122190	其他适合供人食用的海草及其他藻类	15	0	7.5	0	7.5	0	0	7.5	0				12	0					0	0	0
12122990	其他不适合供人食用的海草及其他藻类	15	0	7.5	0	7.5	0	0	7.5	0				12	0					0	0	0
12122910	马尾藻	15	0	7.5	0	7.5	0	0	7.5	0				12	0					0	0	0
12129100	鲜、冷、冻或干的甜菜	20	0		0		0	0	8	0				16	0					0	0	
12129200	刺槐豆	20	0	10	0	10	0	0	8	0				16	0					0	0	
12129300	甘蔗	20	0		0			0	8	0				16	0		0	0	0	0	0	0
12129400	菊苣根	20	0		0			0	12	0					0					0	0	0
12129911	主要供人食用的苦杏仁	20	0		0		0	0	8	0				16	0					0	0	
12129912	主要供人食用的甜杏仁	20	0		0		0	0	8	0	0			16	0					0	0	
12129919	主要供人食用的桃(包括油桃)、梅或李的核及核仁	20	0		0		0	0	8	0				16	0					0	0	
12129993	鲜、冷、冻或干的白瓜子	20	0		0		0	0	8	0				16	0					0	0	
12129994	鲜、冷、冻或干的莲子	20	0		0		0	0	8	0				16	0					0	0	
12129996	甜叶菊叶	30	0		0		0	0	12	0					0					0	0	0
12129999	鲜、冷、冻或干的其他主要供人食用的其他税号未列明的果核、果仁及植物产品	30	0		0		0	0	12	0					0					0	0	0
12130010	未经处理的稻草的茎、杆	12	0		0	6	0	0	0	0				9.6	0			0		0	0	0
12130090	其他未经处理的谷类植物茎、杆及谷壳	12	0		0	6	0	0	0	0				9.6	0			0		0	0	0
12141000	紫苜蓿粗粉及团粒	5	0		0	0		0	0	0				0	0			0		0	0	0
12149000	芜菁甘蓝、饲料甜菜等其他植物饲料	9	0		0	5		0	0	0				5.4	0			0		0	0	0
13012000	阿拉伯胶	15	0		0	0	0	0	0	0				12	0					0	0	0
13019010	胶黄耆树胶	15	0		0	0	0	0	0	0				12	0					0	0	0
13019020	乳香、没药及血竭	3	0		0	0		0	0	0				0	0					0	0	0
13019030	阿魏	3	0		0	0		0	0	0				0	0					0	0	0
13019040	松脂	15	0		0	0	0	0	0	0				12	0					0	0	0
13019090	其他天然树胶、树脂	15	0		0	0	0	0	0	0				12	0					0	0	0
13021100	鸦片液汁及浸膏	0																		0	0	0
13021200	甘草液汁及浸膏	6	0		0	5		0	0	0				3.6	0					0	0	0
13021300	啤酒花液汁及浸膏	10	0		0	5	0	0	0	0				6	0					0	0	0
13021910	生漆	20	0		0		0	0	8	0				16	0					0	0	
13021920	印楝素	3	0		0	0		0	0	0				0	0					0	0	0
13021930	除虫菊或含鱼藤酮植物根茎的液汁及浸膏	3	0		0	0		0	0	0				0	0					0	0	0
13021940	银杏的液汁及浸膏	20	0	15	0	15	0	0	8	0				12	0					0	0	

税则号列	货品名称	最惠国	协定税率												特惠税率						
			东盟统一	亚太5国	智利	巴基斯坦	新加坡	新西兰	秘鲁	哥达	香港	澳门	台湾	瑞士	冰岛	亚太2国	老挝	柬埔寨	缅甸	LDC1	LDC2	LDC3
13021990	其他植物液汁及浸膏	20	0	15	0	15	0	0	8	0				12	0					0	0	
13022000	果胶、果胶酸盐及果胶酸酯	20	0		0		0	0	8	0				16	0					0	0	
13023100	琼脂	10	0		0	5	0	0	4	0				6	0					0	0	0
13023200	刺槐豆、刺槐豆子或瓜尔豆制得的胶液及增稠剂	15	0	10	0	0	0	0	6	0				12	0					0	0	
13023911	卡拉胶	15	0		0	12	0	0	6	0				12	0					0	0	
13023912	褐藻胶	15	0		0	12	0	0	6	0				12	0					0	0	
13023919	其他海草及藻类制品	15	0		0	12	0	0	9.7	0				12	0					0	0	
13023990	其他植物胶液及增稠剂	15	0		0	12	0	0	7.5	0				12	0					0	0	
14011000	竹	10	0		0	5	0	0	0	0				6	0		0	0		0	0	0
14012000	藤	10	0		0	5	0	0	0	0				6	0		0	0		0	0	0
14019010	谷类植物的茎秆(麦秸除外)	10	0		0	5	0	0	4	0				6	0			0		0	0	0
14019020	芦苇	10	0		0	5	0	0	0	0				6	0			0		0	0	0
14019031	蔺草	10	0		0	5	0	0	0	0				6	0			0		0	0	0
14019039	灯芯草属的其他主要作编结用的植物材料	10	0		0	5	0	0	0	0				6	0			0		0	0	0
14019090	未列名主要用作编结用的植物材料	10	0		0	5	0	0	4	0				6	0			0		0	0	0
14042000	棉短绒	4	0		0	0		0	0	0				0	0					0	0	0
14049010	主要供染料或鞣料用的植物原料	5	0	4.3	0	0		0	2.5	0				0	0					0	0	0
14049090	其他植物产品	15	0		0		0	0	0	0				12	0					0	0	0
15011000	猪油	10	0		0		0	0	0	0	0	0		6	0					0	0	0
15012000	其他猪脂肪	10	0		0		0	0	0	0	0	0		6	0					0	0	0
15019000	家禽脂肪	10	0		0		0	0	0	0	0	0		6	0					0	0	0
15021000	牛、羊油脂	8	0	0	0	0		0	0	0		0		4.8	0					0	0	0
15029000	其他牛、羊脂肪	8	0	0	0	0		0	0	0		0		4.8	0					0	0	0
15030000	未经制作的猪油硬脂、油硬脂等	10	0		0		0	0	0	0		0		6	0					0	0	0
15041000	鱼肝油及其分离品	12	0		0		0	0	0	0		0		9.6	0					0	0	
15042000	其他鱼油、脂及其分离品	12	0		0		0	0	3	0		0		9.2	0					0	0	
15043000	海生哺乳动物的油、脂及其分离品	14.4	0		0		0	0	0	0		0		11.5	0					0	0	
15050000	羊毛脂及羊毛脂肪物质	20	0		0		0	0	8	0				16	0					0	0	
15060000	其他动物油、脂及其分离品	20	0		0		0	0	8	0		0		16	0					0	0	
15071000	初榨豆油的分离品	9	9																			
15079000	精制的豆油及其分离品	9	9																			
15081000	初榨花生油的分离品	10	0				0															
15089000	精制的花生油及其分离品	10	0				0															
15091000	初榨油橄榄油及其分离品	10	0		0		0	0	4	0		0		6	0					0	0	
15099000	精制的油橄榄油及其分离品	10	0		0		0	0	0	0	0	0		6	0					0	0	
15100000	其他橄榄油及其分离品	10	0		0		0	0	0	0		0		6	0					0	0	
15111000	初榨棕榈油的分离品	9	9																			
15119010	精制的棕榈液油(熔点19－24度)	9	9																			
15119020	精制的棕榈硬脂(熔点44－56度)	8	8																			
15119090	其他精制的棕榈油及其分离品	9	9																			
15121100	初榨葵花油或红花油的分离品	9	0									0										
15121900	精制的葵花油或红花油及其分离品	9	0									0										
15122100	初榨棉子油的分离品	10	0				0					0										
15122900	精制的棉子油及其分离品	10	0				0					0										
15131100	初榨椰子油分离品	9	0	4.5	0	4.5		0	0	0		0		5.4	0					0	0	
15131900	椰子油及其分离品	9	0	4.5	0	4.5		0	0	0		0		5.4	0					0	0	0
15132100	初榨棕榈仁油或巴巴苏棕榈果油及其分离品	9	0		0			0	0	0		0		5.4	0					0	0	
15132900	精制的棕榈仁油或巴巴苏棕榈果油及其分离品	9	0		0			0	0	0		0		5.4	0					0	0	
15141100	初榨低芥子酸菜子油及其分离品	9	9																			
15141900	其他低芥子酸菜子油或芥子油及其分离品	9	9																			
15149110	初榨菜子油及其分离品	9	9																			
15149190	初榨芥子油及其分离品	9	9																			
15149900	其他菜子油或芥子油及其分离品	9	9																			
15151100	初榨亚麻子油及其分离品	15	0		0		0	0	6	0		0		12	0					0	0	
15151900	精制的亚麻子油及其分离品	15	0		0		0	0	6	0		0		12	0					0	0	

税则号列	货品名称	最惠国	协定税率													特惠税率						
			东盟统一	亚太5国	智利	巴基斯坦	新加坡	新西兰	秘鲁	哥达	香港	澳门	台湾	瑞士	冰岛	亚太2国	老挝	柬埔寨	缅甸	LDC1	LDC2	LDC3
15152100	初榨玉米油的分离品	10	0				0					0					0	0		0	0	0
15152900	精制的玉米油及其分离品	10	0				0					0					0	0		0	0	0
15153000	蓖麻油及其分离品	10	0		0		0	0	0	0		0		6	0		0	0		0	0	0
15155000	芝麻油及其分离品	12	0		0		0	0	0	0		0		9.6	0		0	0		0	0	0
15159010	希蒙得木油及其分离品	20	0		0		0	0		0		0		16	0			0		0	0	0
15159020	印楝油及其分离品	20	0		0		0	0		0		0		16	0					0	0	
15159030	桐油及其分离品	20	0		0		0	0		0		0		16	0			0		0	0	0
15159090	其他固定植物油、脂及其分离品	20	0		0		0	0		0		0		16	0		0	0	0	0	0	0
15161000	氢化、酯化或反油酸化动物油、脂及其分离品,但未进一步加工的	5	0		0			0	0	0		0		0	0					0	0	0
15162000	氢化、酯化或反油酸化植物油、脂及其分离品,但未进一步加工的	25	0		0			0	10	0		0			0					0	0	
15171000	人造黄油,非液态	30	0		0		0	0		0		0										
15179010	起酥油	25	0		0			0	10	0	0	0		20	0					0	0	
15179090	混合制成的食用油脂或制品	25	0		0			0	10	0	0	0		19.3	0					0	0	
15180000	化学改性的动、植物油、脂及其制品;其他税号未列名的非食用油、脂或制品	10	0		0		0	0	4	0		0		6	0					0	0	0
15200000	粗甘油,甘油水及甘油碱液	20	0		0		0	0	8	0	0	0		16	0					0	0	
15211000	植物蜡	20	0		0		0	0	8	0				16	0					0	0	
15219010	蜂蜡	20	0		0		0	0	8	0				16	0					0	0	
15219090	其他虫蜡及鲸蜡	20	0		0		0	0	8	0				16	0					0	0	
15220000	油鞣回收脂;加工处理油脂及动、植物蜡所剩残渣	20	0		0		0	0	8	0				16	0					0	0	
16010010	用天然肠衣做外包装的香肠及类似产品	15	0		0	12	0	0	6	0	0	0		12	0					0	0	
16010020	其他香肠及类似产品	15	0		0	12	0	0	6	0	0	0		12	0					0	0	
16010030	用香肠制成的食品	15	0		0	12	0	0	6	0		0		12	0					0	0	
16021000	肉或食用杂碎的均化食品	15	0		0	12	0	0	6	0				12	0					0	0	
16022000	制作或保藏的动物肝	15	0		0	12	0	0	6	0	0			12	0					0	0	
16023100	制作或保藏的火鸡肉及杂碎	15	0		0	12	0	0	6	0				12	0					0	0	
16023210	鸡罐头	15	0		0	12	0	0	6	0		0		12	0					0	0	
16023291	鸡胸肉	15	0		0	12	0	0	6	0	0			12	0					0	0	
16023292	鸡腿肉	15	0		0	12	0	0	6	0	0			12	0					0	0	
16023299	其他鸡肉	15	0		0	12	0	0	6	0	0	0		12	0					0	0	
16023910	其他品目 0105 所列家禽肉及杂碎的罐头	15	0		0	12	0	0	6	0		0		12	0					0	0	
16023991	鸭肉	15	0		0	12	0	0	6	0	0			12	0					0	0	
16023999	经制作或保藏的其他品目 0105 所列家禽肉及杂碎	15	0		0	12	0	0	6	0		0		12	0					0	0	
16024100	制作或保藏的猪后腿及其肉块	15	0		0	12	0	0	6	0		0		12	0					0	0	
16024200	制作或保藏的猪前腿及其肉块	15	0		0	12	0	0	6	0		0		12	0					0	0	
16024910	其他猪肉及杂碎的罐头	15	0		0	12	0	0	6	0		0		12	0					0	0	
16024990	制作或保藏的其他猪肉、杂碎及血	15	0		0	12	0	0	6	0	0	0		12	0					0	0	
16025010	牛肉及牛杂碎罐头	12	0		0	6	0	0	4.8	0	0	0		9.6	0					0	0	
16025090	其他制作或保藏的牛肉、杂碎及血	12	0		0	6	0	0	4.8	0	0	0		9.6	0					0	0	
16029010	其他肉及杂碎罐头	15	0		0	12	0	0	6	0		0		12	0					0	0	
16029090	经制作或保藏的其他肉、杂碎及血	15	0		0	12	0	0	6	0		0		12	0					0	0	
16030000	肉及水产品的精、汁	23	0		0		0	0	9.2	0	0			18.4	0					0	0	
16041110	制作或保藏的大西洋鲑鱼,整条或切块,但未绞碎	12	0		0	6	0	0		0	0				0					0	0	
16041190	制作或保藏的其他鲑鱼,整条或切块,但未绞碎	12	0		0	6	0	0		0					0					0	0	
16041200	制作或保藏的鲱鱼,整条或切块,但未绞碎	12	0		0	6	0	0	0	0				9.6	0					0	0	
16041300	制作或保藏的沙丁鱼、小沙丁鱼属、黍鲱或西鲱	5	0		0	0		0	1.3	0		0		0	0			0		0	0	0
16041400	制作或保藏的金枪鱼、鲣鱼及狐鲣	5	0		0	0		0	0	0	0			0	0			0		0	0	0
16041500	制作或保藏的鲭鱼,整条或切块,但未绞碎	12	0		0	6	0	0	3	0				9.6	0					0	0	

税则号列	货品名称	最惠国	协定税率 东盟统一	亚太5国	智利	巴基斯坦	新加坡	新西兰	秘鲁	哥达	香港	澳门	台湾	瑞士	冰岛	特惠税率 亚太2国	老挝	柬埔寨	缅甸	LDC1	LDC2	LDC3
16041600	制作保藏的 Anchovies(醍鱼),整条或切块,但未绞碎	12	0		0	6	0	0	3	0				9.6	0					0	0	
16041700	制作或保藏的鳗鱼	12	0	9.9	0	5	0	0		0	0			9.6	0					0	0	0
16041920	制作或保藏的罗非鱼,整条或切块,但未绞碎	12	0		0	6	0	0		0	0			9.6	0					0	0	
16041931	制作或保藏的斑点叉尾鮰鱼	12	0	9.9	0	5	0	0		0	0			9.6	0					0	0	0
16041939	制作或保藏的其他叉尾鮰鱼	12	0	9.9	0	5	0	0		0	0			9.6	0					0	0	0
16041990	制作或保藏的其他鱼,整条或切块,但未绞碎	12	0	9.9	0	5	0	0		0	0	0		9.6	0					0	0	0
16042011	鱼翅罐头	12	0	9.9	0	5	0	0	4.8	0	0	0		9.6	0					0	0	
16042019	其他制作或保藏的鱼罐头	12	0	9.9	0	5	0	0	4.8	0	0	0		9.6	0					0	0	
16042091	鱼翅	12	0	9.9	0	5	0	0	4.8	0	0	0		9.6	0					0	0	
16042099	其他制作或保藏的鱼	12	0	9.9	0	5	0	0	4.8	0	0	0		9.6	0					0	0	
16043100	鲟鱼子酱	12	0		0	6	0	0	0	0				9.6	0					0	0	
16043200	鲟鱼子酱代用品	12	0		0	6	0	0	0	0				9.6	0					0	0	
16051000	制作或保藏的蟹	5	0		0	0		0	0	0	0			0	0					0	0	0
16052100	制作或保藏的非密封包装小虾及对虾	5	0		0	0		0	0	0	0			0	0			0		0	0	0
16052900	制作或保藏的其他小虾及对虾	5	0		0	0		0.	0	0	0			0	0			0		0	0	0
16053000	制作或保藏的龙虾	5	0		0	0		0	0	0	0			0	0			0		0	0	0
16054011	制作或保藏的淡水小龙虾仁	5	0		0	0		0	0	0				0	0			0		0	0	0
16054019	制作或保藏的带壳淡水小龙虾	5	0		0	0		0	0	0				0	0			0		0	0	0
16054090	制作或保藏的其他甲壳动物	5	0		0	0		0	0	0		0		0	0			0		0	0	0
16055100	制作或保藏的牡蛎	5	0	3.9	0	0		0	1.3	0	0	0		0	0					0	0	0
16055200	制作或保藏的扇贝	5	0	3.9	0	0		0	1.3	0	0	0		0	0					0	0	0
16055300	制作或保藏的贻贝	5	0	3.9	0	0		0	1.3	0	0	0		0	0					0	0	0
16055400	制作或保藏的墨鱼及鱿鱼	5	0	3.9	0	0		0	1.3	0	0	0		0	0					0	0	0
16055500	制作或保藏的章鱼	5	0	3.9	0	0		0	1.3	0	0	0		0	0					0	0	0
16055610	制作或保藏的蛤	5	0	3.9	0	0		0		0	0			0	0					0	0	0
16055620	制作或保藏的鸟蛤及舟贝	5	0	3.9	0	0		0	1.3	0	0	0		0	0					0	0	0
16055700	制作或保藏的鲍鱼	5	0	3.9	0	0		0	1.3	0	0	0		0	0					0	0	0
16055800	制作或保藏的蜗牛及螺	5	0	3.9	0	0		0	1.3	0	0	0		0	0					0	0	0
16055900	制作或保藏的其他软体动物	5	0	3.9	0	0		0	1.3	0	0	0		0	0					0	0	0
16056100	制作或保藏的海参	5	0	3.9	0	0		0	1.3	0	0	0		0	0					0	0	0
16056200	制作或保藏的海胆	5	0	3.9	0	0		0	1.3	0	0	0		0	0					0	0	0
16056300	制作或保藏的海蜇	15	0		0	12	0	0		0	0			12	0					0	0	0
16056900	制作或保藏的其他水生无脊椎动物	5	0	3.9	0	0		0	1.3	0	0	0		0	0					0	0	0
17011200	未加香料或着色剂的甜菜原糖	50	50																			
17011300	本章子目注释二所述的甘蔗糖	50	50																			
17011400	其他甘蔗糖	50	50																			
17019100	加有香料或着色剂的糖	50	50																			
17019910	砂糖	50	50																			
17019920	绵白糖	50	50																			
17019990	其他精制糖	50	50																			
17021100	无水乳糖,按重量计含量>99%	10	0		0	5	0	0	0	0		0		6						0	0	0
17021900	其他乳糖及乳糖浆	10	0		0	5	0	0	0	0		0		6						0	0	0
17022000	槭糖及槭糖浆	30	0		0		0	0	12	0		0								0		
17023000	低果糖含量的葡萄糖及糖浆	30	0		0		0	0	12	0	0	0								0		
17024000	中果糖含量的葡萄糖及糖浆	30	0		0		0	0	12	0		0								0		
17025000	化学纯果糖	30	0		0		0	0	12	0		0			0					0		
17026000	其他果糖及糖浆	30	0		0		0	0	12	0		0			0					0		
17029000	其他固体糖;人造蜜;焦糖	30	0		0		0	0	19.4	0	0	0		23.1	0					0	0	0
17031000	甘蔗糖蜜	8	0		0	5		0	0	0				4.8	0					0	0	0
17039000	其他糖蜜	8	0		0	5		0	0	0				4.8	0					0	0	0
17041000	口香糖,不论是否裹糖	12	0	9.5	0	5	0	0	7.8	0	0			9.6	0					0	0	0
17049000	其他不含可可的糖食	10	0	8.2	0	8.2	0	0	4	0	0	0		0	0					0	0	0
18010000	生或焙炒的整颗或破碎的可可豆	8	0		0	5		0	0	0				4.8	0					0	0	0
18020000	可可荚、壳、皮及废料	10	0		0	5	0	0	0	0				6	0					0	0	0
18031000	未脱脂可可膏	10	0		0	5		0	0	0				6	0					0	0	
18032000	全脱脂或部分脱脂的可可膏	10	0		0	5		0	0	0				6	0					0	0	
18040000	可可油,可可脂	22	0		0			0	8.8	0				17.6	0					0	0	0

税则号列	货品名称	最惠国	协定税率													特惠税率						
			东盟统一	亚太5国	智利	巴基斯坦	新加坡	新西兰	秘鲁	哥达	香港	澳门	台湾	瑞士	冰岛	亚太2国	老挝	柬埔寨	缅甸	LDC1	LDC2	LDC3
18050000	未加糖或其他甜物质的可可粉	15	0		0	12		0	6	0				12	0					0	0	
18061000	含糖或其他甜物质的可可粉	10	0		0	5		0	4	0				6	0					0	0	
18062000	每件净重>2kg的含可可食品	10	0	7.7	0	5	0	0	4	0	0	0		0	0					0	0	
18063100	其他夹心块状或条状的含可可食品	8	0	6.4	0	5		0	0	0	0	0		4.8	0					0	0	0
18063200	其他不夹心块状或条状含可可食品	10	0	7.7	0	5	0	0	4	0	0	0		0	0					0	0	
18069000	其他巧克力及含可可的食品	8	0	6.4	0	5		0	0	0	0	0		6.4	0					0	0	0
19011010	配方奶粉	15	0		0	12	0	0	6	0		0		12	0					0	0	
19011090	其他供婴幼儿食用的零售包装食品	15	0		0	12	0	0	6	0		0		12	0					0	0	
19012000	供焙烘面包糕点用的调制品及面团	25	0		0		0	0	10	0	0	0		20	0					0	0	
19019000	其他麦精制的其他税号未列名食品	10	0		0	5	0	0	4	0	0	0		6	0					0	0	
19021100	未包馅或未制作的含蛋生面食	15	0		0	12	0	0	6	0	0	0		12						0	0	0
19021900	其他未包馅或未制作的生面食	15	0		0	12	0	0	6	0	0	0		12						0	0	0
19022000	包馅面食	15	0		0	12	0	0	6	0	0	0			0					0	0	0
19023010	米粉干	15	0		0	12	0	0	6	0		0		12	0					0	0	
19023020	粉丝	15	0		0	12	0	0	6	0		0		12	0					0	0	
19023030	即食或快熟面条	15	0	13.1	0	7.5	0	0	6	0	0	0		12	0					0	0	0
19023090	其他面食	15	0	13.1	0	7.5	0	0	6	0	0	0			0					0	0	
19024000	古斯古斯面食	25	0		0		0	0	10	0		0		20	0					0	0	
19030000	珍粉及淀粉制成的珍粉代用品	15	0		0	12	0	0	6	0		0		12	0					0	0	0
19041000	谷物或谷物产品经膨化或烘炒制的食品	25	0		0		0	0	10	0		0		20.8	0					0	0	
19042000	未烘炒谷物片制成的食品	30	0		0		0	0	18	0				18	0					0		
19043000	碾碎的干小麦	30	0		0		0	0	18	0		0			0					0		
19049000	其他谷物制品	30	0		0		0	0	15	0	0	0		18	0					0		
19051000	黑麦脆面包片	20	0		0		0	0	8	0		0		16	0					0	0	
19052000	姜饼及类似品	20	0		0		0	0	8	0		0		16	0					0	0	
19053100	甜饼干	15	0	12.4	0	12.4	0	0	6	0	0	0		12.5	0	7.5				0	0	0
19053200	华夫饼干及圣餐饼	15	0	12.4	0	7.5	0	0	6	0	0	0		0	0	7.5				0	0	0
19054000	面包干、吐司及类似的烤面包	20	0		0		0	0	8	0		0		16						0	0	
19059000	其他面包、糕点、饼干及其焙烘糕饼	20	0	17.1	0	16	0	0	8	0	0	0		16	0	10				0	0	
20011000	用醋或醋酸制作的黄瓜及小黄瓜	25	0		0		0	0	10	0				20	0					0	0	
20019010	用醋制作的大蒜	25	0		0		0	0	10	0				20	0	12.5				0	0	
20019090	用醋制作的其他果、菜及食用植物	25	0		0		0	0	10	0		0		20	0	12.5				0	0	
20021010	非用醋制作的整个或切片番茄罐头	19	0		0		0	0	7.6	0		0		15.2	0					0	0	
20021090	非用醋制作的其他整个或切片番茄	25	0		0		0	0	10	0				20	0					0	0	
20029011	重量不超过5kg的番茄酱罐头	20	0		0		0	0	0	0		0		16	0					0	0	
20029019	重量大于5kg的番茄酱罐头	20	0		0		0	0	0	0		0		16	0					0	0	
20029090	非用醋制作的绞碎番茄	18	0		0	14.4	0	0	0	0		0		14.4	0					0	0	
20031011	伞菌属小白蘑菇罐头	25	0		0		0	0	10	0		0		20	0					0	0	
20031019	其他非用醋制作的伞菌属蘑菇罐头	25	0		0		0	0	10	0		0		20	0					0	0	
20031090	非用醋制作的其他伞菌属蘑菇	25	0		0		0	0	10	0		0		20	0					0	0	
20039010	其他蘑菇及块菌罐头	25	0		0		0	0	10	0		0		20	0					0	0	
20039090	其他蘑菇及块菌	25	0		0		0	0	10	0		0		20	0					0	0	
20041000	非用醋制作的冷冻马铃薯	13	0		0	6.5	0	0	5.2	0				10.4						0	0	0
20049000	非用醋制作的其他冷冻蔬菜	25	0		0		0	0	10	0				20	0					0	0	
20051000	非用醋制作的未冷冻均化蔬菜	25	0		0		0	0	10	0				20	0					0	0	
20052000	非用醋制作的未冷冻马铃薯	15	0		0	12	0	0	6	0	0			12						0	0	
20054000	非用醋制作的未冷冻豌豆	25	0		0		0	0	10	0				20	0					0	0	
20055111	非用醋或醋酸制作或保藏的未冷冻的赤豆馅罐头	25	0		0		0	0	10	0	0	0		20	0					0	0	
20055119	非用醋或醋酸制作或保藏的未冷冻的其他脱荚豇豆及菜豆罐头	25	0		0		0	0	10	0	0	0		20	0					0	0	
20055191	非用醋或醋酸制作或保藏的未冷冻的赤豆馅,不包括罐头	25	0		0		0	0	10	0				20	0					0	0	
20055199	非用醋或醋酸制作或保藏的未冷冻的其他脱荚豇豆及菜豆	25	0		0		0	0	10	0	0			20						0	0	
20055910	非用醋制作的其他豇豆及菜豆罐头	25	0		0		0	0	10	0		0		20						0	0	
20055990	非用醋制作的其他豇豆及菜豆	25	0		0		0	0	10	0				20						0	0	
20056010	非用醋制作的芦笋罐头	25	0		0		0	0	10	0		0		20						0	0	
20056090	非用醋制作的其他芦笋	25	0		0		0	0	10	0				20	0					0	0	
20057000	非用醋制作的未冷冻油橄榄	10	0		0	5	0	0	4	0				6	0					0	0	

税则号列	货品名称	最惠国	协定税率													特惠税率						
			东盟统一	亚太5国	智利	巴基斯坦	新加坡	新西兰	秘鲁	哥达	香港	澳门	台湾	瑞士	冰岛	亚太2国	老挝	柬埔寨	缅甸	LDC1	LDC2	LDC3
20058000	非用醋制作的未冷冻甜玉米	10	0		0	5	0	0	0	0				6	0					0	0	
20059110	非用醋制作或保藏的竹笋罐头	25	0		0		0	0	10	0		0		20	0					0	0	
20059190	非用醋制作或保藏的未冷冻的其他竹笋	25	0		0		0	0	10	0				20	0					0	0	
20059920	蚕豆罐头	25	0		0		0	0	10	0		0		20	0					0	0	
20059940	榨菜	25	0		0		0	0	10	0				20	0					0	0	
20059950	咸蕨菜	25	0		0		0	0	10	0				20	0					0	0	
20059960	咸荞头	25	0		0		0	0	10	0				20	0					0	0	
20059991	其他蔬菜及什锦蔬菜罐头	25	0		0		0	0	0	0		0		20	0					0	0	
20059999	非用醋制作的其他蔬菜及什锦蔬菜	25	0		0		0	0	0	0				19.3	0					0	0	
20060010	蜜枣	30	0		0		0	0	12	0	0				0				0	0	0	0
20060020	糖渍制橄榄	30	0		0		0	0	19.4	0	0				0				0	0	0	0
20060090	其他糖渍蔬菜、水果、坚果、果皮	30	0		0		0	0	19.4	0	0	0		0	0				0	0	0	0
20071000	烹煮制成的果子均化食品	30	0		0		0	0	19.4	0				18	0					0		
20079100	烹煮制成的柑桔属水果	30	0		0		0	0	12	0		0		0	0				0	0	0	0
20079910	烹煮制成的其他果酱、果冻罐头	5	0		0	0		0	2	0		0		0	0	2.5				0	0	0
20079990	烹煮制成的其他果酱、果冻	5	0		0	0		0	2	3.3		0		3	0	2.5				0	0	0
20081110	花生米罐头	30	0		0		0	0		0	0	0			0					0		
20081120	烘焙花生	30	0		0		0	0		0	0	0			0			0		0	0	0
20081130	花生酱	30	0		0		0	0		0					0					0		
20081190	其他非用醋制作的花生	30	0		0		0	0		0	0	0			0					0		
20081910	核桃仁罐头	20	0	10	0	10	0	0	8	0	0	0		16	0		0	0		0	0	0
20081920	其他果仁罐头	13	0	6.5	0	5	0	0	5.2	0	0	0		10.4	0		0	0		0	0	0
20081991	栗仁	10	0	5	0	5	0	0	4	0	0	0		7.7	0		0	0		0	0	0
20081992	用其他方法制作或保藏的芝麻	10	0	5	0	5	0	0	0	0	0	0		6						0	0	
20081999	其他坚果及子仁	10	0	5	0	5	0	0	4	0	0	0		6	0		0	0		0	0	0
20082010	菠萝罐头	15	15		0			0	6	10		0		12	0		0			0	0	0
20082090	非用醋制作的其他菠萝	15	15		0			0	6	10				12	0		0			0	0	0
20083010	柑桔属水果罐头	20	0		0		0	0	0	13.3		0		16	0		0			0	0	0
20083090	非用醋制作的其他柑桔属水果	20	0		0		0	0	0	0	0			16	0		0			0	0	0
20084010	梨罐头	20	0		0		0	0	8	0		0		16	0		0			0	0	0
20084090	非用醋制作的其他梨	20	0		0		0	0	8	0				16	0		0			0	0	0
20085000	非用醋制作的杏	20	0		0		0	0	8	0				16	0					0	0	
20086010	用其他方法制作或保藏的樱桃罐头	20	0		0		0	0	8	0				16	0					0	0	
20086090	用其他方法制作或保藏的其他樱桃	20	0		0		0	0	8	0				16	0					0	0	
20087010	桃罐头	10	0		0	5	0	0	4	0		0		6	0		0			0	0	0
20087090	非用醋制作的其他桃	20	0		0		0	0	8	0	0			16	0		0			0	0	0
20088000	非用醋制作的草莓	15	0		0	12	0	0	6	0				12	0					0	0	
20089100	非用醋制作的棕榈芯	5	0		0	0		0	0	0				0	0			0		0	0	0
20089300	用其他方法制作或保藏的蔓越橘	15	0		0	12	0	0	6	0	0	0		9	0			0		0	0	0
20089700	用其他方法制作或保藏的什锦果实	10	0		0	5	0	0	4	0		0		6	0			0		0	0	0
20089910	荔枝罐头	20	0		0		0	0	8	0	0	0		16	0					0	0	
20089920	龙眼罐头	15	15		0			0	6	0	0	0		12	0			0		0	0	0
20089931	调味紫菜	15	0		0		0	0	6	0	0	0		12	0			0		0	0	0
20089932	盐渍海带	15	0		0	12		0	6	0	0	0		12	0			0		0	0	0
20089933	盐渍裙带菜	15	0		0	12		0	6	0	0	0		12	0			0		0	0	0
20089939	其他海草及藻类制品	15	0		0	12		0	6	0	0	0		12	0			0		0	0	0
20089940	清水荸荠(马蹄)罐头	25	0		0		0	0	10	0		0		20	0					0	0	
20089990	未列名制作或保藏的水果、坚果	15	0		0	12	0	0	6	0	0	0		9	0			0		0	0	0
20091100	冷冻的橙汁	7.5	0		0	5		0.8	3	0	0	0		4.5	0		0	0		0	0	0
20091200	非冷冻的，白利糖度值不超过20的橙汁	30	0		0		0	3.3	12		0	0		0	0		0	0		0	0	0
20091900	其他橙汁	30	0		0		0	3.3	12			0			0		0	0		0	0	0
20092100	白利糖度值不超过20的葡萄柚(包括柚)汁	15	0		0	12	0	0	0	0	0	0		12	0		0			0	0	0
20092900	其他葡萄柚(包括柚)汁	15	0		0	12	0	0	0	0		0		12	0		0			0	0	0
20093110	白利糖度不超过20的柠檬汁	18	0	16.8	0	14.4	0	0	7.2	0	0	0		14.4	0	9		0		0	0	0
20093190	其他未混合的白利糖度值不超过20的柑桔属水果汁	18	0	16.8	0	14.4	0	0	7.2	0	0	0		14.4	0	9		0		0	0	0
20093910	白利糖度超过20的柠檬汁	18	0	16.8	0	14.4	0	0	0	0		0		14.4	0	9		0		0	0	0
20093990	其他未混合的柑桔属水果汁，白利糖度值不超过20	18	0	16.8	0	14.4	0	0	0	0		0		14.4	0	9		0		0	0	0

税则号列	货品名称	最惠国	协定税率 东盟统一	亚太5国	智利	巴基斯坦	新加坡	新西兰	秘鲁	哥达	香港	澳门	台湾	瑞士	冰岛	特惠税率 亚太2国	老挝	柬埔寨	缅甸	LDC1	LDC2	LDC3
20094100	白利糖度值不超过20的菠萝汁	10	10		0			0	0	0	0	0		6	0		0	0		0	0	0
20094900	其他菠萝汁	10	10		0			0	0	0		0		6	0		0	0		0	0	0
20095000	番茄汁	30	0		0		0	0	12	0		0			0	15	0			0	0	0
20096100	白利糖度值不超过30的的葡萄汁,包括酿酒葡萄汁	20	0		0		0	0	10	0	0	0		16	0					0	0	
20096900	葡萄汁,包括酿酒葡萄汁	20	0		0		0	0	10	0		0		16	0					0	0	
20097100	白利糖度值不超过20的苹果汁	20	0		0		0	0	0	0	0	0		16	0					0	0	
20097900	其他苹果汁	20	0		0		0	0	8	0		0		16	0					0	0	
20098100	蔓越橘汁	20	0	10	0	10	0	0	8	0	0	0		16	0		0		0	0	0	0
20098912	芒果汁	20	0	17.4	0	16	0	0	8	0	0	0		16	0		0		0	0	0	0
20098913	西番莲果汁	20	0	17.4	0	16	0	0	8	0	0	0		16	0		0		0	0	0	0
20098914	番石榴果汁	20	0	17.4	0	16	0	0	8	0	0	0		16	0		0		0	0	0	0
20098915	梨汁	20	0	10	0	10	0	0	8	0	0	0		16	0		0		0	0	0	0
20098919	其他未混合的水果汁	20	0	10	0	10	0	0	8	0	0	0		16	0		0		0	0	0	0
20098920	其他未混合蔬菜汁	20	0	10	0	10	0	0	8	0	0	0		16	0				0	0	0	0
20099010	混合水果汁	20	0	17.4	0	16	0	0	0	0	0	0		16	0	10	0	0		0	0	0
20099090	混合蔬菜汁、水果与蔬菜的混合汁	20	0		0		0	0	0	0	0	0		16	0	10	0	0		0	0	0
21011100	咖啡浓缩精汁	17	0		0	13.6	0	0		0	0	0			0					0	0	0
21011200	以咖啡浓缩精汁或咖啡为基本成分的制品	30	0		0		0	0		0	0	0			0					0		
21012000	茶、马黛茶浓缩精汁及其制品	32	0	16	0	16	0	0	12.8	0	0	0		19.2	0					0	0	
21013000	烘焙咖啡代用品及其浓缩精汁	32	0		0		0	0		0										0	0	
21021000	活性酵母	25	0		0		0	0	10	0	0	0		15	0					0	0	
21022000	非活性酵母;已死的其他单细胞微生物	25	0		0		0	0	10	0		0		15	0					0	0	
21023000	发酵粉	25	0		0		0	0	10	0		0			0					0	0	
21031000	酱油	28	0		0		0	0	11.2	0	0	0		22.4	0			0		0	0	0
21032000	番茄沙司及其他番茄调味汁	15	0		0	12	0	0	6	0	0	0		12				0		0	0	0
21033000	芥子粉及其调味品	15	0		0	12	0	0	6	0		0		12				0		0	0	0
21039010	味精	21	0	18.2	0	18.2	0	0	8.4	0	0	0		16.8	0					0	0	
21039020	别特油(Aromatic bitters)	21	0		0		0	0	13.6	0	0	0		16.8	0					0	0	
21039090	其他调味品	21	0	18.4	0	18.4	0	0	10.5	0	0	0		17.5	0					0	0	0
21041000	汤料及其制品	15	0		0	12	0	0	6	0	0	0		12	0					0	0	
21042000	均化混合食品	32	0		0		0	0	12.8	0		0								0	0	
21050000	冰淇淋及其他冰制食品不论是否含可可	19	0		0		0	0	7.6	0	0	0		0	0					0	0	
21061000	浓缩蛋白质及人造蛋白物质	10	0		0	5	0	0	4	0		0		6	0					0	0	
21069010	制造碳酸饮料的浓缩物	35	0		0		0	0	14	0	0	0			0					0	0	
21069020	制造饮料用的复合酒精制品	20	0		0		0	0	8	0	0	0		16	0					0	0	
21069030	蜂王浆制剂	3	0		0	0		0	0	0	0	0		0	0		0			0	0	0
21069040	椰子汁	10	10	9	0	9		0	4	0	0	0		6	0		0		0	0	0	0
21069050	海豹油胶囊	20	0	18.4	0	18.4	0	0	8	0	0	0		16.7	0					0	0	
21069090	其他税号未列名的食品	20	0	18.4	0	18.4	0	0	8	0	0	0		16.7	0					0	0	
22011010	未加糖及未加味的矿泉水	20	0		0		0	0	8	0	0	0		16	0					0	0	0
22011020	未加糖及未加味的汽水	20	0		0		0	0	8	0		0		16	0					0	0	0
22019010	天然水	10	0		0	5	0	0	0	0	0	0		6	0					0	0	
22019090	其他水、冰及雪	10	0		0	5	0	0	0	0	0			6	0					0	0	
22021000	加味、加糖或其他甜物质的水	20	0		0		0	0	8	0	0	0		16	0					0	0	
22029000	其他无酒精饮料	35	0	29.5	0	29.5	0	0	14	0	0	0		29.2	0					0	0	0
22030000	麦芽酿造的啤酒	0																		0	0	0
22041000	葡萄汽酒	14	0		0	11.2	0	0	5.6	0				11.2	0					0	0	
22042100	小包装的鲜葡萄酿造的酒	14	0		0	11.2	0	0	8.4	0	0			11.2	0					0	0	
22042900	其他包装的鲜葡萄酿造的酒	20	0		0		0	0	12	0				16	0					0	0	
22043000	其他酿酒葡萄汁	30	0		0		0	0	15	0					0							
22051000	小包装的味美思酒及类似酒	65	0		0		0	0	32.5	0												
22059000	其他包装的味美思酒及类似酒	65	0		0		0	0	32.5	0												
22060010	黄酒	40	0		0		0	0	16	0	0	0			0					0	0	
22060090	其他发酵饮料	40	0		0		0	0	16	0	0	0			0					0	0	
22071000	浓度≥80%的未改性乙醇	40	0		0	0	0	0	16	0		0			0					0	0	
22072000	任何浓度的改性乙醇及其他酒精	30	0		0	0	0	0	0	0					0					0	0	
22082000	蒸馏葡萄酒制得的烈性酒	10	0		0	5	0	0	4	0				6	0					0	0	0
22083000	威士忌酒	10	0		0	5	0	0	4	0				6	0					0	0	0

税则号列	货品名称	最惠国	协定税率												特惠税率						
			东盟统一	亚太5国	智利	巴基斯坦	新加坡	新西兰	秘鲁	哥达	香港	澳门	台湾	瑞士	冰岛	亚太2国	老挝	柬埔寨	缅甸	LDC1	LDC2	LDC3
22084000	朗姆酒及蒸馏已发酵甘蔗产品制得的其他烈性酒	10	0		0	5	0	0	0	0				6	0					0	0	0
22085000	杜松子酒	10	0		0	5	0	0	0	0				6						0	0	0
22086000	伏特加酒	10	0	8.8	0	5	0	0	0	0				6						0	0	0
22087000	利口酒及柯迪尔酒	10	0	8.8	0	5	0	0	4	0				6	0					0	0	0
22089010	龙舌兰酒	10	0	8.8	0	5	0	0	0	0				6	0					0	0	
22089020	白酒	10	0	8.8	0	5	0	0	4	0		0		6	0					0	0	0
22089090	其他蒸馏酒及酒精饮料	10	0	8.8	0	5	0	0	4	0		0		6	0					0	0	0
22090000	醋及醋酸制得的醋代用品	20	0		0		0	0	8	0	0	0		16	0					0	0	
23011011	含牛羊成分的肉骨粉	2	0		0	0		0	0	0				0	0					0	0	0
23011019	其他动物的肉骨粉	2	0		0	0		0	0	0				0	0					0	0	0
23011020	油渣	5	0		0	0		0	0	0	0			0	0					0	0	0
23011090	其他不适于供人食用的肉渣粉	5	0		0	0		0	0	0				0	0					0	0	0
23012010	饲料用鱼粉	2	0	0	0	0		0	0	1	0			0	0					0	0	0
23012090	其他不适于供人食用的水产品渣粉	5	0	0	0	0		0	1.3	0	0			0	0					0	0	0
23021000	玉米糠、麸及其他残渣	5	0		0	0		0	0	0				0	0					0	0	0
23023000	小麦糠、麸及其他残渣	3	0		0	0		0	0	0				0	0					0	0	0
23024000	其他谷物糠、麸及其他残渣	5	0		0	0		0	0	0				0	0					0	0	0
23025000	豆类植物糠、麸及其他残渣	5	0		0	0		0	0	0	0			0	0					0	0	0
23031000	制造淀粉过程中的残渣及类似品	5	0		0	0		0	0	0				0	0					0	0	0
23032000	甜菜渣、甘蔗渣及制糖过程中的其他残渣	5	0		0	0		0	0	0				0	0					0	0	0
23033000	酿造及蒸馏过程中的糟粕及残渣	5	0		0	0		0	0	0				0	0					0	0	0
23040010	提炼豆油所得的油渣饼(豆饼)	5	0	0	0	0		0	0	0				0	0					0	0	0
23040090	提炼豆油所得的其他固体残渣	5	0	0	0	0		0	0	0				0	0					0	0	0
23050000	花生饼及类似油渣	5	0		0	0		0	0	0				0	0					0	0	0
23061000	棉子油渣饼及固体残渣	5	0		0	0		0	0	0				0	0					0	0	0
23062000	亚麻子油渣饼及固体残渣	5	0		0	0		0	0	0				0	0		0			0	0	0
23063000	葵花子油渣饼及固体残渣	5	0		0	0		0	0	0				0	0					0	0	0
23064100	低芥子酸的油菜子油渣饼及固体残渣	5	0		0	0		0	0	0				0	0					0	0	
23064900	油菜子油渣饼及固体残渣	5	0		0	0		0	0	0				0	0					0	0	
23065000	椰子或干椰肉油渣饼及固体残渣	5	0	2.5	0	0		0	0	0				0	0			0		0	0	0
23066000	油棕果或油棕仁油渣饼及固体残渣	5	0		0	0		0	0	0				0	0			0		0	0	0
23069000	其他油渣饼及固体残渣	5	0		0	0		0	0	0				0	0		0			0	0	0
23070000	葡萄酒渣、粗酒石	5	0		0	0		0	0	0				0	0					0	0	0
23080000	动物饲料用其他植物产品	5	0		0	0		0	0	0				0	0					0	0	
23091010	零售包装的狗食或猫食罐头	15	0		0	12	0	0	6	0	0	0		12	0					0	0	
23091090	零售包装的其他狗食或猫食	15	0		0	12	0	0	6	0	0	0		12	0					0	0	
23099010	制成的饲料添加剂	5	0	2.5	0	0		0	2	0	0			3	0					0	0	0
23099090	其他配制的动物饲料	6.5	0	3.3	0	0		0	2.6	0	0	0		3.9	0					0	0	0
24011010	未去梗的烤烟	10	10	9.4	0	9.4		0														
24011090	其他未去梗的烟草	10	10		0			0														
24012010	部分或全部去梗的烤烟	10	10		0			0														
24012090	部分或全部去梗的其他烟草	10	10		0			0														
24013000	烟草废料	10	10		0			0	4											0	0	0
24021000	烟草制的雪茄烟	25	25		0			0														
24022000	烟草制的卷烟	25	25		0			0														
24029000	烟草代用品制的雪茄烟及卷烟	25	25		0			0														
24031100	本章子目注释所述的水烟料	57	50	50	0	50		0														
24031900	其他供吸用的烟草	57	50	50	0	50		0														
24039100	“均化”或“再造”烟草	57	50		0			0														
24039900	其他烟草及烟草代用品的制品;烟草精汁	57	50		0			0														
25010011	食用盐	0																		0	0	0
25010019	其他盐	0																		0	0	0
25010020	纯氯化钠	3	0		0	0		0	0	0				0	0		0			0	0	0
25010030	海水	0																		0	0	0
25020000	未焙烧的黄铁矿	3	0		0	0		0	0	0				0	0					0	0	0
25030000	硫磺,但升华硫磺、沉淀硫磺及胶态硫磺除外	3	0		0	0		0	0	0				0	0					0	0	
25041010	鳞片状天然石墨	3	0		0	0		0	0	0				2.4	0					0	0	0
25041091	球化石墨	3	0		0	0		0	0	0				0	0					0	0	0
25041099	其他粉末状天然石墨	3	0		0	0		0	0	0				0	0					0	0	0

税则号列	货品名称	最惠国	协定税率													特惠税率						
			东盟统一	亚太5国	智利	巴基斯坦	新加坡	新西兰	秘鲁	哥达	香港	澳门	台湾	瑞士	冰岛	亚太2国	老挝	柬埔寨	缅甸	LDC1	LDC2	LDC3
25049000	其他天然石墨	3	0		0	0		0	0	0				0	0					0	0	0
25051000	硅砂及石英砂,不论是否着色	3	0		0	0		0	0	0				0	0					0	0	0
25059000	其他天然砂,不论是否着色	3	0		0	0		0	0	0				0	0					0	0	0
25061000	石英	3	0		0	0		0	0	0				0	0					0	0	0
25062000	石英岩,不论是否切割成矩形板、块	3	0		0	0		0	0	0				0	0					0	0	0
25070010	不论是否煅烧的高岭土	3	0		0	0		0	0	0				0	0					0	0	0
25070090	不论是否煅烧的类似土	3	0		0	0		0	0	0				0	0					0	0	0
25081000	膨润土,不论是否煅烧	3	0		0	0		0	0	0				0	0					0	0	0
25083000	耐火粘土,不论是否煅烧	3	0		0	0		0	0	0				0	0					0	0	0
25084000	其他粘土,不论是否煅烧	3	0		0	0		0	0	0				0	0					0	0	0
25085000	红柱石,蓝晶石及硅线石,不论是否煅烧	3	0		0	0		0	0	0				0	0					0	0	0
25086000	富铝红柱石	3	0		0	0		0	0	0				0	0					0	0	0
25087000	火泥及第纳斯土	3	0		0	0		0	0	0				2.4	0					0	0	0
25090000	白垩	3	0		0	0		0	0	0				0	0					0	0	0
25101010	未碾磨磷灰石	3	0		0	0		0	0	0				0	0					0	0	0
25101090	未碾磨天然磷酸钙、天然磷酸铝钙及磷酸盐白垩,磷灰石除外	3	0		0	0		0	0	0				0	0					0	0	0
25102010	已碾磨磷灰石	3	0		0	0		0	0	0				0	0					0	0	0
25102090	已碾磨天然磷酸钙、天然磷酸铝钙及磷酸盐白垩,磷灰石除外	3	0		0	0		0	0	0				0	0					0	0	0
25111000	天然硫酸钡(重晶石)	3	0		0	0		0	0	0				0	0					0	0	
25112000	天然碳酸钡(毒重石),不论是否煅烧	3	0		0	0		0	0	0				0	0					0	0	
25120010	硅藻土	3	0		0	0		0	0	0				0	0					0	0	0
25120090	其他硅质化石粗粉及类似的硅质土	3	0		0	0		0	0	0				0	0					0	0	0
25131000	浮石	3	0		0	0		0	0	0				0	0					0	0	0
25132000	刚玉岩、天然刚玉砂、天然石榴石及其他天然磨料	3	0		0	0		0	0	0				0	0					0	0	0
25140000	板岩,不论是否粗加修整或切割成矩形板块	3	0		0	0		0	0	0				0	0					0	0	0
25151100	原状或粗加修整大理石及石灰华	4	0		0	0		0	0	0				0	0					0	0	0
25151200	矩形大理石及石灰华	4	0		0	0		0	0	0				0	0					0	0	0
25152000	其他石灰质碑用或建筑用石;蜡石,不论是否粗加修整或切割成矩形板块	3	0		0	0		0	0	0				0	0					0	0	0
25161100	原状或粗加修整的花岗岩	4	0	2	0	0		0	0	0				0	0					0	0	0
25161200	矩形或正方形的花岗岩	4	0	2	0	0		0	0	0				0	0					0	0	0
25162000	砂岩,不论是否粗加修整或切割成矩形板块	3	0	2.1	0	0		0	0	0				0	0					0	0	0
25169000	其他碑用或建筑用石,不论是否粗加修整或切割成矩形板块	3	0	2.1	0	0		0	0	0				0	0					0	0	0
25171000	通常做混凝土粒料、铺路、铁道路基或其他路基用的卵石、砾石及碎石,圆石子及燧石,不论是否热处理	4	0		0	0		0	0	0				0	0					0	0	0
25172000	矿渣、浮渣及类似的工业残渣	3	0		0	0		0	0	0				0	0					0	0	0
25173000	沥青碎石	3	0		0	0		0	0	0				0	0					0	0	0
25174100	大理石碎粒、碎屑及粉末,不论是否热处理	3	0		0	0		0	0	0				0	0					0	0	0
25174900	税目 2515 及 2616 所列各种石料的碎粒、碎屑及粉末,大理石的除外,不论是否热处理	3	0		0	0		0	0	0				0	0					0	0	0
25181000	未煅烧或烧结的白云石,不论是否粗加修整或切割成矩形板块	3	0		0	0		0	0	0				0	0					0	0	0
25182000	已煅烧或烧结的白云石,不论是否粗加修整或切割成矩形板块	3	0		0	0		0	0	0				0	0					0	0	0
25183000	夯混白云石	3	0		0	0		0	0	0				0	0					0	0	0
25191000	天然碳酸镁(菱镁矿)	3	0		0	0		0	0	0				0	0					0	0	0
25199010	熔凝镁氧矿	3	0		0	0		0	0	0				0	0					0	0	0
25199020	烧结镁氧矿(重烧镁)	3	0		0	0		0	0	0				0	0					0	0	0
25199030	碱烧镁(轻烧镁)	3	0		0	0		0	0	0				0	0					0	0	0
25199091	化学纯氧化镁	3	0		0	0		0	0	0				0	0					0	0	0
25199099	非纯氧化镁	3	0		0	0		0	0	0				0	0					0	0	0

税则号列	货品名称	最惠国	协定税率												特惠税率						
			东盟统一	亚太5国	智利	巴基斯坦	新加坡	新西兰	秘鲁	哥达	香港	澳门	台湾	瑞士	冰岛	亚太2国	老挝	柬埔寨	缅甸	LDC1	LDC2	LDC3
25201000	生石膏;硬石膏	5	0		0	0		0	0	0	0			0	0		0			0	0	0
25202010	牙科用熟石膏,不论是否着色及带有少量促凝剂或缓凝剂	5	0		0	0		0	0	0				0	0		0			0	0	0
25202090	其他熟石膏,不论是否着色及带有少量促凝剂或缓凝剂	5	0		0	0		0	0	0				0	0		0			0	0	0
25210000	石灰石助熔剂;通常用于制造石灰或水泥的石灰石及其他钙质石	5	0		0	0		0	0	0	0			0	3.3					0	0	0
25221000	生石灰	5	0		0	0		0	0	0				0	0					0	0	0
25222000	熟石灰	5	0		0	0		0	0	0				0	0					0	0	0
25223000	水硬石灰	5	0		0	0		0	0	0				0	0					0	0	0
25231000	水泥熟料,不论是否着色	8	0		0	5		0	0	0	0		0	4.8	0					0	0	0
25232100	白水泥,不论是否人工着色	6	0	4.5	0	0		0	0	0			0	3.6	0					0	0	0
25232900	其他硅酸盐水泥,不论是否着色	8	0	6	0	5		0	0	0	0	0	0	4.8	0					0	0	0
25233000	矾土水泥,不论是否着色	6	0		0	5		0	0	0				3.6	0					0	0	0
25239000	其他水凝水泥,不论是否着色	8	0		0	5		0	0	0				4.8	0					0	0	0
25241000	青石棉	5	0		0	0		0	0	0				0	0					0	0	
25249010	其他长纤维石棉	5	0		0	0		0	0	0				0	0					0	0	
25249090	其他石棉	5	0		0	0		0	0	0				0	0					0	0	
25251000	原状云母及劈开的云母片	5	0		0	0		0	0	0				0	0					0	0	0
25252000	云母粉	5	0		0	0		0	0	0				0	0					0	0	0
25253000	云母废料	5	0		0	0		0	0	0				0	0					0	0	0
25261010	未破碎及未研粉的天然冻石,不论是否粗加修整或切割成矩形板块	3	0		0	0		0	0	0				0	0					0	0	0
25261020	未破碎及未研粉的滑石,不论是否粗加修整或切割成矩形板块	3	0		0	0		0	0	0				0	0					0	0	0
25262010	已破碎或已研粉的天然冻石	3	0		0	0		0	0	0				0	0					0	0	0
25262020	已破碎或已研粉的天然滑石	3	0		0	0		0	0	0				0	0					0	0	0
25280010	天然硼砂及其精矿,不论是否煅烧	3	0		0	0		0	0	0				0	0					0	0	0
25280090	硼酸盐(硼砂除外),不论是否煅烧;天然粗硼酸,含硼酸干重不超85%	5	0		0	0		0	2	0				0	0					0	0	0
25291000	长石	3	0		0	0		0	0	0				0	0					0	0	0
25292100	按重量计氟化钙含量≤97%的萤石	3	0		0	0		0	0	0				0	0					0	0	0
25292200	按重量计氟化钙含量>97%的萤石	3	0		0	0		0	0	0				0	0					0	0	0
25293000	白榴石;霞石及霞石正长岩	5	0		0	0		0	0	0				0	0					0	0	0
25301010	未膨胀的绿泥石	5	0		0	0		0	0	0				0	0					0	0	0
25301020	未膨胀的蛭石及珍珠岩	5	0		0	0		0	0	0				0	0					0	0	0
25302000	硫镁矾矿及泻盐矿(天然硫酸镁)	3	0		0	0		0	0	0				0	0					0	0	0
25309010	矿物性药材	3	0		0	0		0	0	0				0	0					0	0	0
25309020	稀土金属矿	0																		0	0	0
25309091	硅灰石	3	0		0	0		0	0	0				0	0					0	0	0
25309099	其他矿产品	3	0		0	0		0	0	0				0						0	0	0
26011110	平均粒径小于0.8毫米的未煅烧铁矿砂及其精矿;但焙烧黄铁矿除外	0																		0	0	0
26011120	平均粒径不小于0.8毫米,但不大于6.3毫米的未煅烧铁矿砂及其精矿;但焙烧黄铁矿除外	0																		0	0	0
26011190	平均粒径大于6.3毫米的未烧结铁矿砂及其精矿,但焙烧黄铁矿除外	0																		0	0	0
26011200	已烧结铁矿砂及其精矿	0																		0	0	0
26012000	焙烧黄铁矿	0																		0	0	0
26020000	锰矿砂及其精矿,包括以干重计含锰量在20%及以上的锰铁砂及其精矿	0																		0	0	0
26030000	铜矿砂及其精矿	0																		0	0	0
26040000	镍矿砂及其精矿	0																		0	0	0
26050000	钴矿砂及其精矿	0																		0	0	0
26060000	铝矿砂及其精矿	0																		0	0	0
26070000	铅矿砂及其精矿	0																		0	0	0
26080000	锌矿砂及其精矿	0																		0	0	0
26090000	锡矿砂及其精矿	0																		0	0	0

税则号列	货品名称	最惠国	协定税率													特惠税率						
			东盟统一	亚太5国	智利	巴基斯坦	新加坡	新西兰	秘鲁	哥达	香港	澳门	台湾	瑞士	冰岛	亚太2国	老挝	柬埔寨	缅甸	LDC1	LDC2	LDC3
26100000	铬矿砂及其精矿	0																		0	0	0
26110000	钨矿砂及其精矿	0																		0	0	0
26121000	铀矿砂及其精矿	0																		0	0	0
26122000	钍矿砂及其精矿	0																		0	0	0
26131000	已焙烧钼矿砂及其精矿	0																		0	0	0
26139000	其他钼矿砂及其精矿	0																		0	0	0
26140000	钛矿砂及其精矿	0																		0	0	0
26151000	锆矿砂及其精矿	0																		0	0	0
26159010	水合钽铌原料(钽铌富集物)	0																		0	0	0
26159090	其他铌钽钒矿砂及其精矿	0																		0	0	0
26161000	银矿砂及其精矿	0																		0	0	0
26169000	其他贵金属矿砂及其精矿	0																		0	0	0
26171010	生锑(锑精矿,选矿产品)	0																		0	0	0
26171090	其他锑矿砂及其精矿	0																		0	0	0
26179010	朱砂(辰砂)	3	0		0	0		0	0	0				0	0					0	0	0
26179090	其他矿砂及其精矿	0																		0	0	0
26180010	冶炼钢铁产生的锰渣	4	0		0	0		0	0	0				0	0					0	0	
26180090	冶炼钢铁产生的其他粒状熔渣(熔渣砂)	4	0		0	0		0	0	0				0	0					0	0	
26190000	冶炼钢铁产生的熔渣、浮渣、氧化皮及其他废料	4	0		0	0		0	0	0				0	0					0	0	
26201100	含硬锌的矿灰及残渣	4	0		0	0		0	0	0				0	0					0	0	0
26201900	含其他锌的矿灰及残渣	4	0		0	0		0	0	0				0	0					0	0	0
26202100	含铅汽油的淤渣及含铅抗震化合物的淤渣	4	0		0	0		0	0	0				0	0					0	0	0
26202900	其他主要含铅的矿灰及残渣	4	0		0	0		0	0	0				0	0					0	0	0
26203000	主要含铜的矿灰及残渣	4	0		0	0		0	0	0				0	0					0	0	0
26204000	主要含铝的矿灰及残渣	4	0		0	0		0	0	0				0	0					0	0	0
26206000	含砷、汞、铊及其混合物,用于提取或生产砷、汞、铊及其化合物的矿灰及残渣	4	0		0	0		0	0	0				0	0					0	0	0
26209100	含锑、铍、镉、铬及其混合物的矿灰及残渣	4	0		0	0		0	0	0				0	0					0	0	0
26209910	主要含钨的矿灰及残渣	4	0		0	0		0	0	0				0	0					0	0	0
26209990	含其他金属及化合物的矿灰及残渣	4	0		0	0		0	0	0				0	0					0	0	0
26211000	焚化城市垃圾所产生的灰、渣	4	0		0	0		0	0	0				0	0					0	0	0
26219000	其他矿渣及矿灰	4	0		0	0		0	0	0	0			0	0					0	0	0
27011100	未制成型的无烟煤,不论是否粉化	3	0		0	0		0	0	0				0	0		0			0	0	0
27011210	未制成型的炼焦烟煤,不论是否粉化	3	0		0	0		0	0	0				0	0		0			0	0	0
27011290	未制成型的其他烟煤,不论是否粉化	6	0		0	5		0	0	0				3.6	0		0			0	0	0
27011900	未制成型的其他煤,不论是否粉化	5	0	3.5	0	0		0	0	0				0	0		0			0	0	0
27012000	煤砖、煤球及类似用煤制固体燃料	5	0		0	0		0	0	0				0	0		0			0	0	0
27021000	褐煤	3	0		0	0		0	0	0				0	0					0	0	0
27022000	制成型的褐煤	3	0		0	0		0	0	0				0	0					0	0	0
27030000	泥煤(包括肥料用泥煤)不论是否成型	5	0		0	0		0	0	0				0	0					0	0	
27040010	煤制焦炭及半焦炭不论是否成型	5	0	2.5	0	0		0	0	0				0	0					0	0	
27040090	甑炭	5	0	2.5	0	0		0	0	0				0	0					0	0	
27050000	煤气、水煤气、炉煤气及类似气体,石油气及其他烃类气除外	5	0		0	0		0	0	0				0	0					0	0	
27060000	从煤、褐煤、或泥煤蒸馏所得的焦油及矿物焦油,不论是否脱水或部分蒸馏,包括再造焦油	6	0		0	5		0	0	0				3.6	0					0	0	
27071000	粗苯	6	0		0	5		0	0	0				3.6	0					0	0	0
27072000	粗甲苯	6	0		0	5		0	0	0				3.6	0					0	0	0
27073000	粗二甲苯	6	0		0	5		0	0	0				3.6	0					0	0	0
27074000	萘	7	0	6	0	5		0	0	0				4.2	0					0	0	0
27075000	其他芳烃混合物,温度在250℃时蒸馏出的芳烃含量以体积计(包括损耗)在65%及以上(以美国标准实验法D86为准)	7	0		0	5		0	0	0				4.2	0					0	0	0
27079100	杂酚油	7	0		0	5		0	0	0				4.2	0					0	0	0
27079910	酚	7	0		0	5		0	0	0				4.2	0					0	0	0

税则号列	货品名称	最惠国	协定税率												特惠税率						
			东盟统一	亚太5国	智利	巴基斯坦	新加坡	新西兰	秘鲁	哥达	香港	澳门	台湾	瑞士	冰岛	亚太2国	老挝	柬埔寨	缅甸	LDC1	LDC2	LDC3
27079990	蒸馏煤焦油所得的其他产品;芳族成分重量超过非芳族成分的类似产品	7	0		0	5		0	0	0				4.2	0					0	0	0
27081000	从煤焦油或其他矿物焦油所得的沥青	7	0		0	5		0	0	0				4.2	0					0	0	
27082000	从煤焦油或其他矿物焦油所得的沥青焦	6	0		0	5		0	0	0				3.6	0					0	0	
27090000	石油原油及从沥青矿物提取的原油	0																		0	0	0
27101210	车用汽油及航空汽油	5	0		0	0	0	0		0				0	0					0	0	
27101220	石脑油	6	0	5.4	0	0	0	0		0				3.6	0					0	0	
27101230	橡胶溶剂油、油漆溶剂油、抽提溶剂油	6	6		0			0		0				3.6	0					0	0	
27101291	壬烯	9	9		0			0		0				5.4	0					0		
27101299	其他轻油馏分产品	9	9		0			0		0				5.4	0					0		
27101911	航空煤油	9	0		0	5	0	0	0	0			0	5.4	0					0	0	
27101912	灯用煤油	9	9		0			0	3.6	0				5.4	0					0		
27101919	其他煤油馏分产品	6	0		0	5	0	0	0	0			0	3.6	0					0	0	
27101922	5－7号燃料油	6	0		0	5	0	0	0	0				3.6	0					0	0	
27101923	柴油	6	6		0			0	2.4	0				3.6	0					0		
27101929	其他柴油及其他燃料油	6	0		0	5	0	0	2.4	0		0		3.6	0					0	0	
27101991	润滑油	6	0	5.4	0	0		0	0	0	0	0		3.6	0					0	0	0
27101992	润滑脂	6	0	5.4	0	0		0	0	0				3.6	0					0	0	
27101993	润滑油基础油	6	0		0	5		0	0	0			0	3.6	0					0	0	
27101994	液体石蜡和重质液体石蜡	6	0	5.4	0	0		0	0	0			0	3.6	0					0	0	
27101999	其他重油及重油制品	6	0		0	5		0	0	0	0			3.6	0					0	0	
27102000	石油及从沥青矿物提取的油类以及以上述油为基本成分(按重量计不低于70%)的其他税目未列名制品,含有生物柴油,但废油除外	6	0		0	0	0	0		0			0	0	0					0	0	
27109100	含多氯联苯(PCBs)、多氯三联苯(PCTs)或多溴联苯(PBBs)的废油	6	0		0	5		0	0	0				3.6	0					0	0	
27109900	其他废油	6	0		0	5		0	0	0				3.6	0					0	0	
27111100	液化天然气	0																		0	0	0
27111200	液化丙烷	5	0	3.5	0	0		0	0	0				0	0					0	0	
27111310	直接灌注香烟打火机及类似打火器用,其包装容器的容积超过300立方厘米的液化丁烷	11	0		0	5	0	0	0	0				8.8	0					0	0	
27111390	其他液化丁烷	5	0		0	0		0	2	0				0	0					0		
27111400	液化的乙烯、丙烯、丁烯及丁二烯	5	0		0	0		0	0	0				0	0					0	0	
27111910	直接灌注香烟打火机及类似打火器用,其包装容器的容积超过300立方厘米的其他液化燃料	10	0	7	0	5		0	0	0				6	0					0	0	
27111990	其他液化石油气及烃类气	3	0	2.1	0	0		0	1.2	0				0	0					0		
27112100	气态天然气	0																		0	0	0
27112900	其他气态石油气及烃类气	6	0		0	5		0	0	0				3.6	0					0	0	
27121000	凡士林	8	0		0	5		0	0	0				4.8	0					0	0	0
27122000	石蜡,不论是否着色,按重量计含油小于0.75%	8	0		0	5		0	0	0				4.8	0					0	0	0
27129010	微晶石蜡,不论是否着色	8	0		0	5		0	0	0				4.8	0					0	0	0
27129090	其他矿物蜡及用合成或其他方法制得的类似产品,不论是否着色	8	0		0	5		0	0	0				4.8	0					0	0	0
27131110	硫的重量百分比小于3%的未煅烧石油焦	3	0		0	0		0	0	0				0	0					0	0	0
27131190	未煅烧石油焦	3	0		0	0		0	0	0				0	0					0	0	0
27131210	硫的重量百分比小于0.8%的已煅烧石油焦	3	0		0	0		0	0	0				0	0					0	0	0
27131290	已煅烧石油焦	3	0		0	0		0	0	0				0	0					0	0	0
27132000	石油沥青	8	0	5.6	0	5		0	0	0				4.8	0					0	0	0
27139000	其他石油或从沥青矿物提取油类的残渣	6	0		0	5		0	0	0				3.6	0					0	0	0
27141000	沥青页岩、油页岩及焦油砂	6	0		0	5		0	0	0				3.6	0					0	0	0
27149010	天然沥青(地沥青)	8	0		0	5		0	0	0				4.8	0					0	0	0
27149020	乳化沥青	0																		0	0	0
27149090	沥青岩	3	0		0	0		0	0	0				0	0					0	0	0

税则号列	货品名称	最惠国	协定税率													特惠税率						
			东盟统一	亚太5国	智利	巴基斯坦	新加坡	新西兰	秘鲁	哥达	香港	澳门	台湾	瑞士	冰岛	亚太2国	老挝	柬埔寨	缅甸	LDC1	LDC2	LDC3
27150000	以天然沥青(地沥青)、石油沥青、矿物焦油或矿物焦油沥青为基本成分的沥青混合物	8	0		0	5		0	0	0		0		4.8	0					0	0	0
27160000	电力	0																		0	0	0
28011000	氯	5.5	0		0	5		0	0	0				3.3	0					0	0	
28012000	碘	5.5	0			5		0		0				3.3	0					0	0	
28013010	氟	5.5	0		0	0		0	0	0				3.3	0					0	0	
28013020	溴	5.5	0		0	0		0	0	0				3.3	0					0	0	
28020000	升华、沉淀、胶态硫磺	5.5	0		0	0		0	0	0				3.3	0					0	0	
28030000	碳(碳黑及其他税号未列名的其他形状的碳)	5.5	0	4.4	0	0		0	0	0	0		0	3.3						0	0	0
28041000	氢	5.5	0		0	0		0	0	0	0			3.3	0					0	0	0
28042100	氩	5.5	0		0	5		0	0	0	0			3.3	0					0	0	0
28042900	其他稀有气体	5.5	0		0	5		0	0	0	0			3.3	0					0	0	0
28043000	氮	5.5	0		0	5		0	0	0	0			3.3	0					0	0	0
28044000	氧	5.5	0		0	5		0	0	0	0			3.3	0					0	0	0
28045000	硼、碲	5.5	0		0	0		0	0	0				3.3	0					0	0	0
28046117	电子工业用直径≥30cm单晶硅棒	4	0		0	0		0	0	0				0	0					0	0	0
28046119	电子工业用7.5≤直径<30cm单晶硅棒	4	0		0	0		0	0	0				0	0					0	0	0
28046120	电子工业用直径<7.5cm单晶硅棒	4	0		0	0		0	0	0				0	0					0	0	0
28046190	其他含硅量≥99.99%的硅	4	0		0	0		0	0	0				2.4	0					0	0	0
28046900	其他含硅量<99.99%的硅	4	0		0	0		0	0	0				0	0					0	0	0
28047010	黄磷(白磷)	5.5	0		0	0		0	0	0				3.3	0					0	0	0
28047090	其他磷	5.5	0		0	0		0	0	0				3.3	0					0	0	0
28048000	砷	5.5	0		0	0		0	0	0				3.3	0					0	0	0
28049010	经掺杂用于电子工业的硒晶体棒	4	0		0	0		0	1.6	0				0	0					0	0	0
28049090	其他硒	5.5	0		0	0		0	3.9	0				3.3	0					0	0	
28051100	钠	5.5	0		0	0		0	0	0				3.3	0					0	0	
28051200	钙	5.5	0		0	0		0	0	0				3.3	0					0	0	
28051900	其他碱金属及碱土金属	5.5	0		0	0		0	0	0				3.3	0					0	0	
28053011	钕	5.5	0		0	0		0	0	0				3.3	0					0	0	
28053012	镝	5.5	0		0	0		0	0	0				3.3	0					0	0	
28053013	铽	5.5	0		0	0		0	0	0				3.3	0					0	0	
28053014	镧	5.5	0		0	0		0	0	0				3.3	0					0	0	
28053015	铈	5.5	0		0	0		0	0	0				3.3	0					0	0	
28053016	镨	5.5	0		0	0		0	0	0				3.3	0					0	0	
28053017	钇	5.5	0		0	0		0	0	0				3.3	0					0	0	
28053019	其他未相互混合或熔合的稀土金属、钪及钇	5.5	0		0	0		0	0	0				3.3	0					0	0	
28053021	已相互混合或熔合的稀土金属、钪及钇,电池级	5.5	0		0	0		0	0	0				3.3	0					0	0	
28053029	其他已相互混合或熔合的稀土金属、钪及钇	5.5	0		0	0		0	0	0				3.3	0					0	0	
28054000	汞	5.5	0		0	0		0	0	0				3.3	0					0	0	
28061000	氯化氢(盐酸)	5.5	0		0	5		0	0	0				3.3	0					0	0	
28062000	氯磺酸	5.5	0		0	0		0	0	0				3.3	0					0	0	
28070000	硫酸、发烟硫酸	5.5	0		0	5		0	0	0				3.3	0					0	0	
28080000	硝酸及磺硝酸	5.5	0		0	5		0	0	0				3.3	0					0	0	
28091000	五氧化二磷	1	0		0	0		0	0	0				0	0					0	0	
28092011	食品级磷酸	1	0		0	0		0	0	0				0	0					0	0	
28092019	其他磷酸及偏磷酸、焦磷酸	1	0		0	0		0	0	0				0	0					0	0	
28092090	其他多磷酸	5.5	0		0	5		0	0	0				3.3	0					0	0	
28100010	硼的氧化物	5.5	0		0	0		0	2.2	0				3.3	0					0	0	
28100020	硼酸	5.5	0		0	0		0	2.2	0				3.3	0					0	0	
28111100	氟化氢(氢氟酸)	5.5	0		0	0		0	0	0				3.3	0					0	0	0
28111910	氢氰酸	5.5	0		0	0		0	0	0				3.3	0					0	0	0
28111920	硒化氢	5.5	0		0	5		0	0	0				3.3	0					0	0	0
28111990	其他无机酸	5.5	0		0	5		0	0	0				3.3	0					0	0	0
28112100	二氧化碳	5.5	0		0	5		0	0	0	0			3.3	0					0	0	0
28112210	硅胶	5.5	0		0	5		0	0	0		0		3.3	0					0	0	0

税则号列	货品名称	最惠国	协定税率													特惠税率						
			东盟统一	亚太5国	智利	巴基斯坦	新加坡	新西兰	秘鲁	哥达	香港	澳门	台湾	瑞士	冰岛	亚太2国	老挝	柬埔寨	缅甸	LDC1	LDC2	LDC3
28112290	其他二氧化硅	5.5	0		0	5		0	0	0		0		3.3	0					0	0	0
28112900	其他非金属无机氧化物	5.5	0		0	5		0	0	0	0			3.3	0					0	0	0
28121010	氯化亚砜	5.5	0		0	5		0	0	0				3.3	0					0	0	
28121020	氧氯化磷(磷酰氯;三氯氧磷)	5.5	0		0	5		0	0	0				3.3	0					0	0	
28121030	碳酰二氯(光气)	5.5	0		0	0		0	0	0				3.3	0					0	0	
28121041	一氯化硫(氯化硫)	5.5	0		0	0		0	0	0				3.3	0					0	0	
28121042	二氯化硫	5.5	0		0	0		0	0	0				3.3	0					0	0	
28121043	三氯化磷	5.5	0		0	0		0	0	0				3.3	0					0	0	
28121044	三氯化砷	5.5	0		0	0		0	0	0				3.3	0					0	0	
28121045	五氯化磷	5.5	0		0	0		0	0	0				3.3	0					0	0	
28121049	其他非金属氯化物	5.5	0		0	5		0	0	0				3.3	0					0	0	
28121090	其他非金属氯化物及氯氧化物	5.5	0		0	0		0	0	0				3.3	0					0	0	
28129011	三氟化氮	5.5	0		0	0		0	0	0				3.3	0					0	0	
28129019	其他氟化物及氟氧化物	5.5	0		0	0		0	0	0				3.3	0					0	0	
28129090	其他非金属卤化物及卤氧化物	5.5	0		0	0		0	0	0				3.3	0					0	0	
28131000	二硫化碳	5.5	0		0	0		0	0	0	0			3.3	0					0	0	
28139000	其他非金属硫化物,商品三硫化二磷	5.5	0		0	0		0	0	0				3.3	0					0	0	
28141000	氨	5.5	0		0	0		0	0	0				3.3	0					0	0	0
28142000	氨水	5.5	0		0	0		0	0	0				3.3	0					0	0	0
28151100	固体氢氧化钠	10	10	7	0	7		0	0	0				6	0					0	0	0
28151200	氢氧化钠水溶液及液体烧碱	8	8	5.6	0	5.6		0	0	0				4.8	0					0	0	0
28152000	氢氧化钾(苛性钾)	5.5	0		0	5		0	0	0				3.3	0					0	0	0
28153000	过氧化钠及过氧化钾	5.5	0		0	0		0	0	0				3.3	0					0	0	0
28161000	氢氧化镁及过氧化镁	5.5	0		0	5		0	0	0				3.3	0					0	0	
28164000	锶或钡的氧化物、氢氧化物及过氧化物	5.5	0		0	5		0	0	0				3.3	0					0	0	
28170010	氧化锌	5.5	0		0	0		0	1.4	0				3.3	0					0	0	0
28170090	过氧化锌	5.5	0		0	0		0	2.2	0				3.3	0					0	0	0
28181010	棕刚玉	5.5	0		0	0		0	0	0				3.3	0					0	0	0
28181090	其他人造刚玉,不论是否已有化学定义	5.5	0		0	0		0	0	0				3.3	0					0	0	0
28182000	氧化铝,但人造刚玉除外	8	0		0	5	0	0	0	0				4.8	0					0	0	0
28183000	氢氧化铝	5.5	0		0	0		0	0	0				3.3	0					0	0	0
28191000	三氧化铬	5.5	0		0	0		0	0	0				3.3	0					0	0	0
28199000	其他铬的氧化物及氢氧化物	5.5	0		0	0		0	0	0				3.3	0					0	0	0
28201000	二氧化锰	5.5	0		0	0		0	0	0				3.3	0					0	0	0
28209000	其他锰的氧化物	5.5	0		0	0		0	0	0				3.3	0					0	0	0
28211000	铁的氧化物及氢氧化物	5.5	0		0	0		0	0	0				3.3	0					0	0	0
28212000	土色料	5.5	0		0	0		0	0	0				3.3	0					0	0	0
28220010	四氧化三钴	5.5	0		0	0		0	0	0				3.3	0					0	0	
28220090	其他钴的氧化物及氢氧化物;商品氧化钴	5.5	0		0	0		0	0	0				3.3	0					0	0	
28230000	钛的氧化物	5.5	0		0	0		0	0	0				3.3	0					0	0	
28241000	一氧化铅(铅黄、黄丹)	5.5	0		0	0		0	0	0				3.3	0					0	0	
28249010	铅丹及铅橙	5.5	0		0	0		0	0	0				3.3	0					0	0	
28249090	其他铅的氧化物	5.5	0		0	0		0	0	0				3.3	0					0	0	
28251010	水合肼	5.5	0		0	0		0	0	0				3.3	0					0	0	0
28251020	硫酸羟胺	5.5	0		0	5		0	0	0				3.3	0					0	0	0
28251090	其他肼、胲及其无机盐	5.5	0		0	5		0	0	0				3.3	0					0	0	0
28252010	氢氧化锂	5.5	0		0	0		0	0	0				3.3	0					0	0	0
28252090	锂的氧化物	5.5	0		0	0		0	0	0				3.3	0					0	0	0
28253010	五氧化二钒	5.5	0		0	0		0	0	0				3.3	0					0	0	0
28253090	其他钒的氧化物及氢氧化物	5.5	0		0	0		0	0	0				3.3	0					0	0	0
28254000	镍的氧化物及氢氧化物	5.5	0		0	0		0	0	0				3.3	0					0	0	0
28255000	铜的氧化物及氢氧化物	5.5	0		0	0		0	0	0				3.3	0					0	0	0
28256000	锗的氧化物及二氧化锆	5.5	0		0	0		0	0	0				3.3	0					0	0	0
28257000	钼的氧化物及氢氧化物	5.5	0		0	0		0	0	0				3.3	0					0	0	0
28258000	锑的氧化物	5.5	0		0	0		0	0	0				3.3	0					0	0	0
28259011	钨酸	5.5	0		0	0		0	0	0				3.3	0					0	0	0
28259012	三氧化钨	5.5	0		0	5		0	0	0				3.3	0					0	0	0
28259019	其他钨的氧化物及氢氧化物	5.5	0		0	0		0	0	0				3.3	0					0	0	0
28259021	三氧化二铋	5.5	0		0	0		0	0	0				3.3	0					0	0	0
28259029	其他铋的氧化物及氢氧化物	5.5	0		0	0		0	0	0				3.3	0					0	0	0
28259031	二氧化锡	5.5	0		0	0		0	0	0				3.3	0					0	0	0

税则号列	货品名称	最惠国	协定税率													特惠税率						
			东盟统一	亚太5国	智利	巴基斯坦	新加坡	新西兰	秘鲁	哥达	香港	澳门	台湾	瑞士	冰岛	亚太2国	老挝	柬埔寨	缅甸	LDC1	LDC2	LDC3
28259039	其他锡的氧化物及氢氧化物	5.5	0		0	0		0	0	0				3.3	0					0	0	0
28259041	一氧化铌	5.5	0		0	0		0	0	0				3.3	0					0	0	0
28259049	其他铌的氧化物及氢氧化物	5.5	0		0	0		0	0	0				3.3	0					0	0	0
28259090	其他无机碱;其他金属的氧化物及氢氧化物及过氧化物	5.5	0		0	0		0	0	0				3.3	0					0	0	0
28261210	无水氟化铝	5.5	0		0	0		0	0	0				3.3	0					0	0	0
28261290	其他氟化铝	5.5	0		0	0		0	0	0				3.3	0					0	0	0
28261910	铵的氟化物	5.5	0		0	0		0	0	0				3.3	0					0	0	0
28261920	钠的氟化物	5.5	0		0	0		0	0	0				3.3	0					0	0	0
28261990	其他氟化物	5.5	0		0	5		0	0	0				3.3	0					0	0	0
28263000	六氟铝酸钠(人造冰晶石)	5.5	0		0	0		0	0	0				3.3	0					0	0	0
28269010	氟硅酸盐	5.5	0		0	5		0	0	0	0			3.3	0					0	0	0
28269090	氟铝酸盐及其他氟络盐	5.5	0		0	5		0	0	0				3.3	0					0	0	0
28269020	六氟磷酸锂	5.5	0		0	5		0	0	0				3.3	0					0	0	0
28271010	肥料用氯化铵	4	0		0	0		0	0	0				0	0					0	0	0
28271090	非肥料用氯化铵	5.5	0		0	5		0	0	0				3.3	0					0	0	0
28272000	氯化钙	5.5	0		0	5		0	0	0				3.3	0					0	0	0
28273100	氯化镁	5.5	0		0	5		0	0	0				3.3	0					0	0	0
28273200	氯化铝	5.5	0		0	5		0	0	0				3.3	0					0	0	0
28273500	氯化镍	5.5	0		0	5		0	0	0				3.3	0					0	0	0
28273910	氯化锂	5.5	0	4.4	0	0		0		0				3.3	0					0	0	0
28273920	氯化钡	5.5	0	4.4	0	0		0		0					0					0	0	0
28273930	氯化钴	5.5	0	4.4	0	0		0	0	0				3.3	0					0	0	0
28273990	其他未列名氯化物	5.5	0	4.4	0	0		0		0				3.3	0					0	0	0
28274100	铜的氯氧化物及氢氧基氯化物	5.5	0		0	0		0	2.2	0				3.3	0					0	0	0
28274910	锆的氯氧化物及氢氧基氯化物	5.5	0		0	5		0	0	0				3.3	0					0	0	0
28274990	其他氯氧化物及氢氧基氯化物	5.5	0		0	5		0	0	0				3.3	0					0	0	0
28275100	溴化钠及溴化钾	5.5	0		0	0		0	0	0				3.3	0					0	0	0
28275900	其他溴化物及溴氧化物	5.5	0		0	5		0	0	0				3.3	0					0	0	0
28276000	碘化物及碘氧化物	5.5	0		0	5		0		0				3.3	0					0	0	0
28281000	商品次氯酸钙及其他钙的次氯酸盐	12	0	8.4	0	5	0	0	0	0				9.6	0					0	0	
28289000	次氯酸盐;亚氯酸盐及次溴酸盐	5.5	0		0	5		0	0	0				3.3	0					0	0	
28291100	氯酸钠	12	0		0	6	0	0	0	0				9.6	0					0	0	
28291910	氯酸钾(洋硝)	5.5	0		0	0		0	0	0				3.3	0					0	0	
28291990	其他氯酸盐	5.5	0		0	0		0	0	0				3.3	0					0	0	
28299000	高氯酸盐;溴酸盐及过溴酸盐;碘酸盐及高碘酸盐	5.5	0		0	5		0	0	0				3.3	0					0	0	
28301010	硫化钠	5.5	0		0	5		0	0	0				3.3	0					0	0	0
28301090	其他钠的硫化物	5.5	0		0	0		0	0	0				3.3	0					0	0	0
28309020	硫化锑	5.5	0		0	0		0	0	0				3.3	0					0	0	0
28309030	硫化钴	5.5	0		0	0		0	0	0				3.3	0					0	0	0
28309090	其他硫化物、多硫化物	5.5	0		0	5		0	0	0				3.3	0					0	0	0
28311010	钠的连二硫酸盐	5.5	0		0	5		0	0	0				3.3	0					0	0	
28311020	钠的次硫酸盐	5.5	0		0	5		0	0	0				3.3	0					0	0	
28319000	其他连二亚硫酸盐及次硫酸盐	5.5	0		0	5		0	0	0				3.3	0					0	0	
28321000	钠的亚硫酸盐	5.5	0		0	5		0	0	0				3.3	0					0	0	
28322000	其他亚硫酸盐	5.5	0		0	0		0	0	0				3.3	0					0	0	
28323000	硫代硫酸盐	5.5	0		0	0		0	0	0				3.3	0					0	0	
28331100	硫酸钠	5.5	0		0	5		0	0	0				4.4	0					0	0	
28331900	钠的其他硫酸盐	5.5	0		0	5		0	0	0				3.3	0					0	0	
28332100	硫酸镁	5.5	0		0	5		0	0	0				3.3	0					0	0	0
28332200	硫酸铝	5.5	0		0	5		0	0	0				3.3	0					0	0	0
28332400	镍的硫酸盐	5.5	0		0	0		0	0	0				3.3	0					0	0	0
28332500	铜的硫酸盐	5.5	0		0	5		0	0	0				3.3	0					0	0	0
28332700	硫酸钡	5.5	0		0	5		0	0	0				3.3	0					0	0	0
28332910	硫酸亚铁	5.5	0		0	5		0	0	0				3.3	0					0	0	0
28332920	铬的硫酸盐	5.5	0		0	0		0	0	0				3.3	0					0	0	0
28332930	硫酸锌	5.5	0		0	5		0	0	0				3.3	0					0	0	0
28332990	其他硫酸盐	5.5	0		0	5		0	0	0				4.4	0					0	0	0
28333010	钾铝矾	5.5	0		0	0		0	0	0				3.3	0					0	0	0
28333090	其他矾	5.5	0		0	0		0	0	0				3.3	0					0	0	0

税则号列	货品名称	最惠国	协定税率													特惠税率						
			东盟统一	亚太5国	智利	巴基斯坦	新加坡	新西兰	秘鲁	哥达	香港	澳门	台湾	瑞士	冰岛	亚太2国	老挝	柬埔寨	缅甸	LDC1	LDC2	LDC3
28334000	过硫酸盐	5.5	0		0	5		0	0	0				3.3	0					0	0	0
28341000	亚硝酸盐	5.5	0		0	5		0	0	0				3.3	0					0	0	0
28342110	肥料用硝酸钾	4	0		0	0		0	0	0				0	0					0	0	0
28342190	非肥料用硝酸钾	5.5	0		0	5		0	0	0				3.3	0					0	0	0
28342910	硝酸钴	5.5	0		0	0		0	0	0				3.3	0					0	0	0
28342990	其他硝酸盐	5.5	0		0	5		0	0	0				3.3	0					0	0	0
28351000	次磷酸盐及亚磷酸盐	5.5	0		0	5		0	0	0				3.3	0					0	0	0
28352200	磷酸一钠及磷酸二钠	5.5	0		0	5		0	0	0				3.3	0					0	0	0
28352400	钾的磷酸盐	5.5	0		0	5		0	0	0				3.3	0					0	0	0
28352510	饲料级的正磷酸氢钙(磷酸二钙)	5.5	0		0	5		0	0	0				3.3	0					0	0	0
28352520	食品级的正磷酸氢钙(磷酸二钙)	5.5	0		0	5		0	0	0				3.3	0					0	0	0
28352590	其他正磷酸氢钙(磷酸二钙)	5.5	0		0	5		0	0	0				4.2	0					0	0	0
28352600	其他磷酸钙	5.5	0		0	5		0	0	0				3.3	0					0	0	0
28352910	磷酸三钠	5.5	0		0	5		0	0	0				3.3	0					0	0	0
28352990	其他磷酸盐	5.5	0		0	5		0	0	0				3.3	0					0	0	0
28353110	食品级的三磷酸钠(三聚磷酸钠)	5.5	0		0	5		0	0	0				3.3	0					0	0	0
28353190	其他三磷酸钠(三聚磷酸钠)	5.5	0		0	5		0	0	0				3.3	0					0	0	0
28353911	食品级的六偏磷酸钠	5.5	0		0	5		0	0	0				3.3	0					0	0	0
28353919	其他六偏磷酸钠	5.5	0		0	5		0	0	0				3.3	0					0	0	0
28353990	其他多磷酸盐	5.5	0		0	5		0	0	0				3.3						0	0	0
28362000	碳酸钠(纯碱)	5.5	0		0	5		0	0	0				3.3	0					0	0	0
28363000	碳酸氢钠(小苏打)	5.5	0		0	5		0	0	0				3.3	0					0	0	0
28364000	钾的碳酸盐	5.5	0		0	5		0	0	0				3.3	0					0	0	0
28365000	碳酸钙	5.5	0		0	5		0	0	0				3.3	0					0	0	0
28366000	碳酸钡	5.5	0		0	5		0	0	0				3.3	0					0	0	0
28369100	锂的碳酸盐	5.5	0		0	5		0		0				3.3	0					0	0	0
28369200	锶的碳酸盐	5.5	0		0	5		0	0	0				3.3	0					0	0	0
28369910	碳酸镁	5.5	0		0	5		0	0	0				3.3	0					0	0	0
28369930	碳酸钴	5.5	0		0	5		0	0	0				3.3	0					0	0	0
28369940	商品碳酸铵及其他铵的碳酸盐	5.5	0		0	0		0	0	0				3.3	0					0	0	0
28369950	碳酸锆	5.5	0		0	5		0	0	0				3.3	0					0	0	0
28369990	其他碳酸盐;过碳酸盐	5.5	0		0	5		0	0	0		0		3.3	0					0	0	0
28371110	氰化钠	5.5	0		0	0		0	0	0				3.3	0					0	0	
28371120	氧氰化钠	5.5	0	5	0	0		0	0	0				3.3	0					0	0	
28371910	氰化钾	5.5	0		0	0		0	0	0				3.3	0					0	0	
28371990	其他氰化物及氧氰化物	5.5	0		0	0		0	0	0				3.3	0					0	0	
28372000	氰络合物	5.5	0		0	0		0	0	0				3.3	0					0	0	
28391100	偏硅酸钠	5.5	0		0	5		0	0	0				3.3	0					0	0	
28391910	硅酸钠	5.5	0		0	5		0	0	0				3.3	0					0	0	
28391990	其他钠的硅酸盐;商品硅酸钠	5.5	0		0	5		0	0	0				3.3	0					0	0	
28399000	其他硅酸盐;商品碱金属硅酸盐	5.5	0		0	5		0	0	0				4.4	0					0	0	
28401100	无水四硼酸钠	5.5	0		0	0		0	0	0				3.3	0					0	0	
28401900	其他四硼酸钠	5.5	0		0	0		0	0	0				3.3	0					0	0	
28402000	其他硼酸盐	5.5	0		0	0		0	0	0				3.3	0					0	0	
28403000	过硼酸盐	5.5	0		0	0		0	0	0				3.3	0					0	0	
28413000	重铬酸钠	5.5	0		0	0		0	0	0				3.3	0					0	0	0
28415000	其他铬酸盐及重铬酸盐;过铬酸盐	5.5	0		0	5		0	0	0				3.3	0					0	0	0
28416100	高锰酸钾	5.5	0		0	5		0	0	0				3.3	0					0	0	0
28416910	锰酸锂	5.5	0		0	0		0	0	0				3.3	0					0	0	0
28416990	其他亚锰酸盐、锰酸盐及高锰酸盐	5.5	0		0	0		0	0	0				3.3	0					0	0	0
28417010	钼酸铵	5.5	0		0	5		0	0	0				3.3	0					0	0	0
28417090	其他钼酸盐	5.5	0		0	5		0	0	0				3.3	0					0	0	0
28418010	仲钨酸铵	5.5	0		0	0		0	0	0				3.3	0					0	0	0
28418020	钨酸钠	5.5	0		0	0		0	0	0				3.3	0					0	0	0
28418030	钨酸钙	5.5	0		0	0		0	0	0				3.3	0					0	0	0
28418040	偏钨酸铵	5.5	0		0	0		0	0	0				3.3	0					0	0	0
28418090	其他钨酸盐	5.5	0		0	0		0	0	0				3.3	0					0	0	0
28419000	其他金属酸盐及过金属酸盐	5.5	0		0	5		0	0	0				3.3	0					0	0	0
28421000	硅酸复盐及硅酸络盐(包括不论是否已有化学定义的硅铝酸盐)	5.5	0		0	5		0	0	0	0			4.2	0					0	0	
28429011	硫氰酸钠	5.5	0		0	5		0	0	0				3.3	0					0	0	

税则号列	货品名称	最惠国	协定税率													特惠税率						
			东盟统一	亚太5国	智利	巴基斯坦	新加坡	新西兰	秘鲁	哥达	香港	澳门	台湾	瑞士	冰岛	亚太2国	老挝	柬埔寨	缅甸	LDC1	LDC2	LDC3
28429019	其他雷酸盐、氰酸盐及硫氰酸盐	5.5	0		0	5		0	0	0				3.3	0					0	0	
28429020	碲化镉	5.5	0		0	5		0	0	0				3.3	0					0	0	
28429030	锂镍钴锰氧化物	5.5	0		0	5		0	0	0				3.3	0					0	0	
28429040	磷酸铁锂	5.5	0		0	5		0	0	0				3.3	0					0	0	
28429050	硒酸盐及亚硒酸盐	5.5	0		0	5		0	0	0				3.3	0					0	0	
28429090	其他无机酸盐及过氧酸盐,叠氮化物除外	5.5	0		0	5		0	0	0				3.3	0					0	0	
28431000	胶态贵金属	5.5	0		0	0		0	0	0				3.3	0					0	0	
28432100	硝酸银	5.5	0		0	0		0	0	0	0			3.3	0					0	0	
28432900	其他银化合物,不论是否已有化学定义	5.5	0		0	0		0	0	0	0			3.3	0					0	0	
28433000	金化合物,不论是否已有化学定义	5.5	0		0	0		0	0	0	0			3.3	0					0	0	
28439000	其他贵金属化合物,不论是否已有化学定义;贵金属汞齐	5.5	0		0	5		0	0	0	0				0					0	0	
28441000	天然铀及其化合物(包括其合金,分散体,陶瓷产品及混合物)	5.5	0		0	0		0	0	0				3.3	0					0	0	0
28442000	U235浓缩铀、钚及它们的化合物(包括其合金,分散体,陶瓷产品及混合物)	5.5	0		0	0		0	0	0				3.3	0					0	0	0
28443000	U235贫化铀、钍及它们的化合物(包括其合金,分散体,陶瓷产品及混合物)	5.5	0		0	0		0	0	0				3.3	0					0	0	0
28444010	镭及镭盐(包括其合金,分散体,陶瓷产品及混合物)	4	0		0	0		0	0	0				0	0					0	0	0
28444020	放射性钴及放射性钴盐(包括其合金,分散体,陶瓷产品及混合物)	4	0		0	0		0	0	0				0	0					0	0	0
28444090	其他放射性元素同位素及其化合物(包括其合金,分散体,陶瓷产品及混合物);放射性残渣	5.5	0		0	0		0	0	0				3.3	0					0	0	0
28445000	核反应堆已耗尽的燃料元件	5.5	0		0	0		0	0	0				3.3	0					0	0	
28451000	重水(氧化氘)	5.5	0		0	0		0	0	0				3.3	0					0	0	
28459000	其他同位素及其化合物,不论是否已有化学定义	5.5	0		0	0		0	0	0				3.3	0					0	0	
28461010	氧化铈	5.5	0	3.9	0	0		0	0	0				3.3	0					0	0	
28461020	氢氧化铈	5.5	0	3.9	0	0		0	0	0				3.3	0					0	0	
28461030	碳酸铈	5.5	0	3.9	0	0		0	0	0				3.3	0					0	0	
28461090	铈的其他化合物	5.5	0	3.9	0	0		0	0	0				3.3	0					0	0	
28469011	氧化钇	5.5	0		0	0		0	0	0				3.3	0					0	0	
28469012	氧化镧	5.5	0		0	0		0	0	0				3.3	0					0	0	
28469013	氧化钕	5.5	0		0	0		0	0	0				3.3	0					0	0	
28469014	氧化铕	5.5	0		0	0		0	0	0				3.3	0					0	0	
28469015	氧化镝	5.5	0		0	0		0	0	0				3.3	0					0	0	
28469016	氧化铽	5.5	0		0	0		0	0	0				3.3	0					0	0	
28469017	氧化镨	5.5	0		0	0		0	0	0				3.3	0					0	0	
28469019	其他氧化稀土	5.5	0		0	0		0	0	0				3.3	0					0	0	
28469021	氯化铽	5.5	0		0	0		0	0	0				3.3	0					0	0	
28469022	氯化镝	5.5	0		0	0		0	0	0				3.3	0					0	0	
28469023	氯化镧	5.5	0		0	0		0	0	0				3.3	0					0	0	
28469024	氯化钕	5.5	0		0	0		0	0	0				3.3	0					0	0	
28469025	氯化镨	5.5	0		0	0		0	0	0				3.3	0					0	0	
28469026	氯化钇	5.5	0		0	0		0	0	0				3.3	0					0	0	
28469028	混合氯化稀土	5.5	0		0	0		0	0	0				3.3	0					0	0	
28469029	未混合氯化稀土	5.5	0		0	0		0	0	0				3.3	0					0	0	
28469031	氟化铽	5.5	0		0	0		0	0	0				3.3	0					0	0	
28469032	氟化镝	5.5	0		0	0		0	0	0				3.3	0					0	0	
28469033	氟化镧	5.5	0		0	0		0	0	0				3.3	0					0	0	
28469034	氟化钕	5.5	0		0	0		0	0	0				3.3	0					0	0	
28469035	氟化镨	5.5	0		0	0		0	0	0				3.3	0					0	0	
28469036	氟化钇	5.5	0		0	0		0	0	0				3.3	0					0	0	
28469039	其他氟化稀土	5.5	0		0	0		0	0	0				3.3	0					0	0	
28469041	碳酸镧	5.5	0		0	0		0	0	0				3.3	0					0	0	
28469042	碳酸铽	5.5	0		0	0		0	0	0				3.3	0					0	0	
28469043	碳酸镝	5.5	0		0	0		0	0	0				3.3	0					0	0	
28469044	碳酸钕	5.5	0		0	0		0	0	0				3.3	0					0	0	

税则号列	货品名称	最惠国	协定税率													特惠税率						
			东盟统一	亚太5国	智利	巴基斯坦	新加坡	新西兰	秘鲁	哥达	香港	澳门	台湾	瑞士	冰岛	亚太2国	老挝	柬埔寨	缅甸	LDC1	LDC2	LDC3
28469045	碳酸镨	5.5	0		0	0		0	0	0				3.3	0					0	0	
28469046	碳酸钇	5.5	0		0	0		0	0	0				3.3	0					0	0	
28469048	混合碳酸稀土	5.5	0		0	0		0	0	0				3.3	0					0	0	
28469049	未混合碳酸稀土	5.5	0		0	0		0	0	0				3.3	0					0	0	
28469091	镧的其他化合物	5.5	0		0	0		0	0	0				3.3	0					0	0	
28469092	钕的其他化合物	5.5	0		0	0		0	0	0				3.3	0					0	0	
28469093	铽的其他化合物	5.5	0		0	0		0	0	0				3.3	0					0	0	
28469094	镝的其他化合物	5.5	0		0	0		0	0	0				3.3	0					0	0	
28469095	镨的其他化合物	5.5	0		0	0		0	0	0				3.3	0					0	0	
28469096	钇的其他化合物	5.5	0		0	0		0	0	0				3.3	0					0	0	
28469099	稀土金属、钇、钪的其他化合物	5.5	0		0	0		0	0	0				3.3	0					0	0	
28470000	过氧化氢(不论是否用尿素固化)	5.5	0		0	5		0	0	0				3.3	0					0	0	
28480000	磷化物,不论是否已有化学定义,,但不包括磷铁	5.5	0		0	0		0	0	0				3.3	0					0	0	
28491000	碳化钙,不论是否已有化学定义,	5.5	0		0	0		0	0	0				3.3	0					0	0	
28492000	碳化硅,不论是否已有化学定义,	5.5	0		0	5		0	0	0				3.3	0					0	0	
28499010	碳化硼,不论是否已有化学定义,	5.5	0		0	0		0	0	0				3.3	0					0	0	
28499020	碳化钨,不论是否已有化学定义,.	5.5	0		0	0		0	0	0				3.3	0					0	0	
28499090	其他碳化物,不论是否已有化学定义,	5.5	0		0	0		0	0	0				3.3	0					0	0	
28500011	氮化锰	5.5	0	3.9	0	0		0	0	0	0			3.3	0					0	0	
28500019	其他氮化物	5.5	0	3.9	0	0		0	0	0	0			3.3	0					0	0	
28500012	氮化硼	5.5	0	3.9	0	0		0	0	0	0			3.3	0					0	0	
28500090	氢化物、迭氮化物、硅化物及硼化物,不论是否已有化学定义,但可归入税号28.49的碳化物除外;	5.5	0	3.9	0	0		0	0	0	0			3.3	0					0	0	
28521000	汞的有机或无机化合物,汞齐除外	5.5	0		0	0		0	0	0				3.3	0					0	0	
28529000	无化学定义的汞化合物	5.5	0		0	5		0	0	0				3.3	0					0	0	0
28530010	饮用蒸馏水	5.5	0		0	0		0	0	0	0	0		3.3	0					0	0	
28530020	氯化氰	5.5	0		0	0		0	0	0				3.3	0					0	0	
28530030	镍钴锰氢氧化物	6.5	0		0	5		0	0	0	0	0		3.3	0					0	0	
28530090	其他无机化合物、液态空气、压缩空气,汞齐,但贵金属汞齐除外	5.5	0		0	5		0	0	0	0	0		3.3	0					0	0	
29011000	饱和无环烃	2	0		0	0		0	0	0	0			0	0					0	0	
29012100	乙烯	2	0		0	0		0	0	0				0	0					0	0	
29012200	丙烯	2	0		0	0		0	0	0			0	0	0					0	0	
29012310	1-丁烯	2	0		0	0		0	0	0				0	0					0	0	
29012320	2-丁烯	2	0		0	0		0	0	0				0	0					0	0	
29012330	2-甲基丙稀	2	0		0	0		0	0	0				0	0					0	0	
29012410	1,3-丁二烯	2	0		0	0		0	0	0			0	0	0					0	0	
29012420	异戊二烯	2	0		0	0		0	0	0			0	0	0					0	0	
29012910	异戊烯	2	0		0	0		0	0	0				0	0					0	0	
29012920	乙炔	2	0		0	0		0	0	0				0	0					0	0	
29012990	其他不饱和无环烃	2	0		0	0		0	0	0				0	1.3					0	0	
29021100	环己烷	2	0		0	0		0	0	0				0	0					0	0	
29021910	蒎烯	2	0		0	0		0	0	0				0	1.3					0	0	
29021920	－－－4-烷基-4′-烷基双环己烷	2	0		0	0		0	0	0				0	1.3					0	0	
29021990	其他环烷烃、环烯及环萜烯	2	0		0	0		0	0	0				0	1.3					0	0	
29022000	苯	2	0		0	0		0	0	0				0	0					0	0	
29023000	甲苯	2	0		0	0		0	0	0				0	0					0	0	
29024100	邻二甲苯	2	0		0	0		0	0	0			0	0	0					0	0	
29024200	间二甲苯	2	0		0	0		0	0	0			0	0	0					0	0	
29024300	对二甲苯	2	0		0	0		0	0	0			0	1.6	0					0	0	
29024400	混合二甲苯异构体	2	0		0	0		0	0	0			0	0	0					0	0	
29025000	苯乙烯	2	2	1.4	0	0		0	0	0				1.6	0							
29026000	乙苯	2	0		0	0		0	0	0				0	0					0	0	
29027000	异丙基苯	2	0		0	0		0	0	0				0	0					0	0	
29029010	四氢萘	2	0		0	0		0	0	0				0	0					0	0	
29029020	精萘	2	0		0	0		0	0	0				0	0					0	0	
29029030	十二烷基苯	2	0		0	0		0	0	0			0	0	0					0	0	
29029040	4-(4′-烷基环己基)环己基乙烯	2	0		0	0		0	0	0				0	0					0	0	

税则号列	货品名称	最惠国	协定税率													特惠税率						
			东盟统一	亚太5国	智利	巴基斯坦	新加坡	新西兰	秘鲁	哥达	香港	澳门	台湾	瑞士	冰岛	亚太2国	老挝	柬埔寨	缅甸	LDC1	LDC2	LDC3
29029090	其他芳香烃	2	0		0	0		0	0	0				0	0					0	0	
29031100	一氯甲烷及氯乙烷	5.5	0		0	0		0	0	0				3.3	0					0	0	
29031200	二氯甲烷	8	0		0	5		0	0	0	0			4.8	0					0	0	
29031300	氯仿(三氯甲烷)	10	0	9	0	5		0	0	0			0	6	0					0	0	
29031400	四氯化碳	8	0		0	5		0	0	0				4.8	0					0	0	
29031500	1,2－二氯乙烷(ISO)	5.5	5.5		0			0		0				3.3	0					0		
29031910	1,1,1－三氯乙烷(甲基氯仿)	8	0		0	5		0	0	0				4.8	0					0	0	
29031990	其他无环烃的饱和氯化衍生物	5.5	0		0	5		0	0	0				3.3	0					0	0	
29032100	氯乙烯	5.5	0	3.9	0	0		0	0	0			0	3.3	0					0	0	
29032200	三氯乙烯	8	0		0	5		0	0	0				4.8	0					0	0	
29032300	四氯乙烯	5.5	0		0	0		0	0	0				3.3	0					0	0	
29032910	3－氯－1－丙稀(氯丙稀)	5.5	0		0	0		0	0	0				3.3	0					0	0	
29032990	其他无环烃的不饱和氯化衍生物	5.5	0		0	0		0	0	0				3.3	0					0	0	
29033100	1,2－二溴乙烷(ISO)	5.5	0		0	5		0	0	0	0			3.3	0					0	0	
29033910	全氟异丁烯(八氟异丁烯)	5.5	0		0	0		0	0	0				3.3	0					0	0	
29033990	其他无环烃的氟化、溴化或碘化衍生物	5.5	0		0	5		0	0	0	0			3.3	0					0	0	
29037100	一氯二氟甲烷	5.5	0		0	5		0	0	0				3.3	0					0	0	
29037200	二氯三氟乙烷	5.5	0		0	5		0	0	0				3.3	0					0	0	
29037300	二氯一氟乙烷	5.5	0		0	5		0	0	0				3.3	0					0	0	
29037400	一氯二氟乙烷	5.5	0		0	5		0	0	0				3.3	0					0	0	
29037500	二氯五氟丙烷	5.5	0		0	5		0	0	0				3.3	0					0	0	
29037600	溴氯二氟甲烷、溴三氟甲烷及二溴四氟乙烷	5.5	0		0	0		0	0	0				3.3	0					0	0	
29037710	三氯氟甲烷	5.5	0		0	5		0	0	0				3.3	0					0	0	
29037720	其他仅含氟和氯的甲烷、乙烷及丙烷的全卤化物	5.5	0		0	0		0	0	0				3.3	0					0	0	
29037790	其他仅含氟氯的无环烃全卤化衍生物	5.5	0		0	5		0	0	0				3.3	0					0	0	
29037800	其他无环烃全卤化衍生物	5.5	0		0	0		0	0	0				3.3	0					0	0	
29037910	其他仅含氟和氯的甲烷、乙烷及丙烷的卤化衍生物	5.5	0		0	5		0	0	0				3.3	0					0	0	
29037990	其他含有两种或两种以上不同卤素的无环烃卤化衍生物	5.5	0		0	0		0	0	0				3.3	0					0	0	
29038100	1,2,3,4,5,6－六氯环己烷[六六六(ISO)],包括林丹(ISO,INN)	5.5	0		0	0		0	0	0				3.3	0					0	0	
29038200	艾氏剂(ISO)、氯丹(ISO)及七氯(ISO)	5.5	0		0	0		0	0	0				3.3	0					0	0	
29038900	其他环烷烃或环烯烃等卤化衍生物	5.5	0		0	0		0	0	0				3.3	0					0	0	
29039110	邻二氯苯	5.5	0		0	0		0	0	0				3.3	0					0	0	
29039190	氯苯及对二氯苯	5.5	0		0	5		0	0	0				3.3	0					0	0	
29039200	六氯苯(ISO)及滴滴涕(ISO,INN)	5.5	0		0	0		0	0	0				3.3	0					0	0	
29039910	对氯甲苯	5.5	0		0	0		0	0	0				3.3	0					0	0	
29039920	3,4－二氯三氟甲苯	5.5	0		0	0		0	0	0				3.3	0					0	0	
29039930	4－(4′－烷基苯基)－1－(4′－烷基苯基)－2－氟苯	5.5	0		0	5		0	0	0				3.3	0					0	0	
29039990	其他芳烃卤化衍生物	5.5	0		0	5		0	0	0				3.3	0					0	0	
29041000	仅含磺基的衍生物及其盐和乙酯	5.5	0		0	5		0	0	0	0			3.3	0					0	0	
29042010	硝基苯	5.5	0		0	0		0	0	0				3.3	0					0	0	
29042020	硝基甲苯	5.5	0		0	0		0	0	0				3.3	0					0	0	
29042030	二硝基甲苯	5.5	0		0	0		0	0	0				3.3	0					0	0	
29042040	三硝基甲苯(TNT)	5.5	0		0	0		0	0	0				3.3	0					0	0	
29042090	其他仅含硝基或亚硝基衍生物	5.5	0		0	5		0	0	0				3.3	0					0	0	
29049011	邻硝基氯化苯	5.5	0		0	0		0	0	0				3.3	0					0	0	
29049012	间硝基氯化苯	5.5	0		0	0		0	0	0				3.3	0					0	0	
29049013	对硝基氯化苯	5.5	0		0	0		0	0	0				3.3	0					0	0	
29049020	二硝基氯化苯	5.5	0		0	0		0	0	0				3.3	0					0	0	
29049030	三氯硝基甲烷(氯化苦;硝基氯仿)	5.5	0		0	0		0	0	0				3.3	0					0	0	
29049090	其他烃的磺化、硝化、亚硝化衍生物,不论是否卤化	5.5	0		0	5		0	0	0				3.3	0					0	0	
29051100	甲醇	5.5	0		0	0		0		0	0	0		3.3	0							
29051210	丙醇	5.5	0		0	0		0	0	0				3.3	0					0	0	

税则号列	货品名称	最惠国	协定税率													特惠税率						
			东盟统一	亚太5国	智利	巴基斯坦	新加坡	新西兰	秘鲁	哥达	香港	澳门	台湾	瑞士	冰岛	亚太2国	老挝	柬埔寨	缅甸	LDC1	LDC2	LDC3
29051220	异丙醇	5.5	0		0	0		0	0	0			0	3.3	0					0	0	
29051300	正丁醇	5.5	0		0	0		0	0	0			0	3.3	0					0	0	
29051410	异丁醇	5.5	0		0	0		0	0	0			0	3.3	0					0	0	
29051420	仲丁醇	5.5	0		0	0		0	0	0				3.3	0					0	0	
29051430	叔丁醇	5.5	0		0	0		0	0	0				3.3	0					0	0	
29051610	正辛醇	5.5	0		0	5		0		0				3.3	0							
29051690	其他辛醇	5.5	0		0	5		0		0				3.3	0							
29051700	十二醇、十六醇及十八醇	7	0		0	5		0	0	0				4.2	0					0	0	
29051910	3,3－二甲基丁－2－醇(频哪基醇)	5.5	0		0	0		0	0	0				3.3	0					0	0	
29051990	其他饱和一元醇	5.5	0		0	5		0	0	0				4.4	0					0	0	
29052210	香叶醇、橙花醇	5.5	0		0	0		0	0	0				3.3	0					0	0	
29052220	香茅醇	5.5	0		0	5		0	0	0				3.3	0					0	0	
29052230	芳樟醇	5.5	0		0	5		0	0	0					0					0	0	
29052290	其他无环萜烯醇	5.5	0		0	5		0	0	0				4.2	0					0	0	
29052900	其他不饱和一元醇(无环萜烯醇除外)	5.5	0		0	5		0	0	0				3.3	0					0	0	
29053100	1,2－乙二醇	5.5	5.5		0			0		0					0							
29053200	丙二醇	5.5	0		0	5		0	0	0				3.3	0					0	0	
29053910	2,5－二甲基己二醇	4	0		0	0		0	0	0				0	0					0	0	
29053990	其他二元醇	5.5	0		0	5		0	0	0				3.3	0					0	0	
29054100	三羟甲基丙烷	5.5	0		0	0		0	0	0				3.3	0					0	0	
29054200	季戊四醇	5.5	0		0	5		0	0	0				3.3	0					0	0	
29054300	甘露糖醇	8	0		0	5		0	0	0				4.8	0					0	0	0
29054400	山梨醇	14	0		0	11.2	0	0	0	0				11.2	0					0	0	
29054500	丙三醇(甘油)	14	0	11.2	0	7	0	0	0	0		0		11.2	0					0	0	
29054910	木糖醇	5.5	0		0	5		0	0	0				3.3	0					0	0	
29054990	其他多元醇	5.5	0		0	5		0	0	0				3.3	0					0	0	
29055100	乙氯维诺	5.5	0		0	0		0	0	0				3.3	0					0	0	
29055900	无环醇的卤化、磺化、硝化、或亚硝化的衍生物(乙氯维诺除外)	5.5	0		0	5		0	0	0				3.3	0					0	0	
29061100	薄荷醇	5	0		0	0		0	0	0				0	0					0	0	
29061200	环己醇、甲基环己醇、二甲基环己醇	5.5	0		0	5		0	0	0				3.3	0					0	0	
29061310	固醇	5.5	0		0	0		0	0	0				3.3	0					0	0	
29061320	肌醇	5.5	0		0	5		0	0	0				3.3	0					0	0	
29061910	萜品醇	5.5	0		0	5		0	0	0				3.3	0					0	0	
29061990	其他环烷醇、环烯醇及环萜烯醇	5.5	0		0	5		0	0	0					0					0	0	
29062100	苄醇	5	0		0	0		0	0	0				0	0					0	0	
29062910	2－苯基乙醇	5.5	0		0	5		0	0	0				3.3	0					0	0	
29062990	其他芳香醇及它们的衍生物	5.5	0		0	5		0	0	0				4.2	0					0	0	
29071110	苯酚	5.5	0		0	0		0	0	0				3.3	0					0	0	0
29071190	苯酚的盐	5.5	0		0	0		0	0	0				4.4	0					0	0	0
29071211	间甲酚	5.5	0		0	0		0	0	0				3.3	0					0	0	0
29071212	邻甲酚	5.5	0		0	0		0	0	0				3.3	0					0	0	0
29071219	其他甲酚(对甲酚)	5.5	0		0	5		0	0	0				3.3	0					0	0	0
29071290	甲酚的盐	5.5	0		0	0		0	0	0				3.3	0					0	0	0
29071310	壬基酚	5.5	0		0	0		0	0	0				3.3	0					0	0	0
29071390	辛基酚及其异构体的盐和壬基酚盐	5.5	0		0	0		0	0	0				3.3	0					0	0	0
29071510	β－萘酚(2－萘酚)	5.5	0		0	0		0	0	0				3.3	0					0	0	0
29071590	其他萘酚及其盐	5.5	0		0	5		0	0	0				3.3	0					0	0	0
29071910	邻仲丁基酚、邻异丙基酚	4	0		0	0		0	0	0				3.2	0					0	0	0
29071990	其他一元酚	5.5	0		0	5		0	0	0				4.4	0					0	0	0
29072100	间苯二酚及其盐	5.5	0		0	5		0	0	0				3.3	0					0	0	0
29072210	对苯二酚	5.5	0		0	5		0	0	0				3.3	0					0	0	0
29072290	对苯二酚的盐	5.5	0		0	0		0	0	0				3.3	0					0	0	0
29072300	4,4′－异亚丙基联苯酚(双酚A)及其盐	5.5	0		0	5		0	0	0				3.3	0					0	0	0
29072910	邻苯二酚	4	0		0	0		0	0	0				0	0					0	0	0
29072990	其他多元酚；酚醇	5.5	0		0	5		0	0	0				3.3	0					0	0	0
29081100	五氯苯酚(ISO)	5.5	0		0	5		0	0	0				3.3	0					0	0	
29081910	对氯苯酚	4	0		0	0		0	0	0				0	0					0	0	
29081990	其他仅含卤素取代基的酚及酚醇衍生物及其盐	5.5	0		0	5		0	0	0				3.3	0					0	0	
29089100	地乐酚(ISO)及其盐	5.5	0		0	5		0	0	0				3.3	0					0	0	

税则号列	货品名称	最惠国	协定税率 东盟统一	亚太5国	智利	巴基斯坦	新加坡	新西兰	秘鲁	哥斯达	香港	澳门	台湾	瑞士	冰岛	特惠税率 亚太2国	老挝	柬埔寨	缅甸	LDC1	LDC2	LDC3
29089200	4,6—二硝基邻甲酚〔二硝酚(ISO)〕及其盐	5.5	0		0	5		0	0	0				3.3	0					0	0	
29089910	对硝基酚、对硝基酚钠	5.5	0		0	0		0	0	0				3.3	0					0	0	
29089990	其他酚及酚醇的卤化、磺化、硝化、或亚硝化的等衍生物	5.5	0		0	5		0	0	0				3.3	0					0	0	
29091100	乙醚	5.5	0		0	0		0	0	0				3.3	0					0	0	0
29091910	甲醚	5.5	0		0	5		0		0				3.3	0					0		
29091990	其他无环醚及其卤化、磺化、硝化或亚硝化衍生物:	5.5	0		0	5		0		0				3.3	0					0		
29092000	环烷醚、环烯醚或环萜烯醚及其卤化、磺化、硝化或亚硝化衍生物	5.5	0		0	0		0	0	0				3.3	0					0	0	0
29093010	---1-烷氧基-4-(4-乙烯基环己基)-2,3-二氟苯	5.5	0		0	5		0	0	0				3.3	0					0	0	0
29093090	其他芳香醚及其卤化、磺化、硝化或亚硝化衍生物	5.5	0		0	5		0	0	0				3.3	0					0	0	0
29094100	2,2′-氧联二乙醇(二甘醇)	5.5	0		0	0		0		0			0	3.3	0					0		
29094300	乙二醇或二甘醇的单丁醚	5.5	0		0	5		0	0	0		0	0	3.3	0					0	0	0
29094400	乙二醇或二甘醇的其他单烷基醚	5.5	0		0	5		0	0	0				3.3	0					0	0	0
29094910	间苯氧基苄醇	4	0		0	0		0	0	0				0	0					0	0	0
29094990	其他醚醇及其卤化、磺化、硝化、或亚硝化的衍生物	5.5	0		0	5		0	0	0				3.3	0					0	0	0
29095000	醚酚、醚醇酚及其卤化、磺化、硝化、或亚硝化的衍生物	5.5	0		0	5		0	0	0				3.3						0	0	0
29096000	过氧化醇、过氧化醚、过氧化酮及其卤化、磺化、硝化、或亚硝化的衍生物	5.5	0		0	5		0	0	0				3.3	0					0	0	0
29101000	环氧乙烷(氧化乙烯)	5.5	0		0	0		0	0	0				3.3	0					0	0	
29102000	甲基环氧乙烷(氧化丙烯)	5.5	0		0	0		0	0	0				3.3	0					0	0	
29103000	1-氯-2,3-环氧丙烷(表氯醇)	5.5	0		0	5		0	0	0			0	3.3	0					0	0	
29104000	狄氏剂(ISO,INN)	5.5	0		0	5		0	0	0				3.3	0					0	0	
29109000	三节环环氧化物,环氧醇(酚、醚)及其卤化、磺化、硝化、或亚硝化的衍生物	5.5	0		0	5		0	0	0		0		4.2	0					0	0	
29110000	缩醛、半缩醛,不论是否含有其它含氧基,及其卤化、磺化、硝化、或亚硝化的衍生物	5.5	0		0	5		0	0	0				4.2	0					0	0	
29121100	甲醛	5.5	0		0	0		0	0	0				3.3	0					0	0	
29121200	乙醛	5.5	0		0	0		0	0	0				3.3	0					0	0	
29121900	其他无环醛(不含其他含氧基)	5.5	0		0	5		0	0	0				4.4	0					0	0	
29122100	苯甲醛	5.5	0		0	5		0	0	0				3.3	0					0	0	
29122910	铃兰醛(对叔丁基-α-甲基-氧化肉桂醛)	5.5	0		0	5		0	0	0				3.3	0					0	0	
29122990	其他环醛(不含其他含氧基)	5.5	0		0	5		0	0	0				4.2	0					0	0	
29124100	香草醛(3-甲氧基-4-羟基苯甲醛)	5.5	0		0	5		0	0	0				3.3	0					0	0	
29124200	乙基香草醛	5.5	0		0	5		0	0	0				3.3	0					0	0	
29124910	醛醇	5.5	0		0	5		0	0	0				3.3	0					0	0	
29124990	其他醛醚、醛酚、其他含氧基的醛	5.5	0		0	5		0	0	0				3.3	0					0	0	
29125000	环聚醛	5.5	0		0	0		0	0	0					0					0	0	
29126000	多聚甲醛	5.5	0		0	5		0	0	0				3.3	0					0	0	
29130000	税目2912所列产品的卤化、磺化、硝化、或亚硝化的衍生物	5.5	0		0	5		0	0	0				3.3	0					0	0	
29141100	丙酮	5.5	0		0	0		0	0	0				3.3	0					0	0	
29141200	丁酮	5.5	0		0	0		0	0	0		0		3.3	0					0	0	
29141300	4-甲基-2-戊酮	5.5	0		0	0		0	0	0				3.3	0					0	0	
29141900	其他不含其他含氧基的无环酮	5.5	0		0	5		0	0	0				3.3	0					0	0	
29142200	环己酮及甲基环己酮	5.5	0		0	0		0	0	0				3.3	0					0	0	
29142300	芷香酮及甲基芷香酮	5.5	0		0	0		0	0	0					0					0	0	
29142910	樟脑	5.5	0		0	5		0	0	0				3.3	0					0	0	
29142990	其他不含含氧基环烷酮、环烯酮或环萜烯酮	5.5	0		0	5		0	0	0					0					0	0	

税则号列	货品名称	最惠国	协定税率												特惠税率						
			东盟统一	亚太5国	智利	巴基斯坦	新加坡	新西兰	秘鲁	哥达	香港	澳门	台湾	瑞士	冰岛	亚太2国	老挝	柬埔寨	缅甸	LDC1	LDC2	LDC3
29143100	苯丙酮(苯基丙-2-酮)	5.5	0		0	0		0	0	0				3.3	0					0	0	
29143910	苯乙酮	4	0		0	0		0	0	0				0	0					0	0	
29143990	其他不含其他含氧基的芳香酮	5.5	0		0	5		0	0	0				4.4	0					0	0	
29144000	酮醇及酮醛	5.5	0		0	5		0	0	0				4.4	0					0	0	
29145011	覆盆子酮	5.5	0		0	0		0	0	0				3.3	0					0	0	
29145019	其他酮酚	5.5	0		0	5		0	0	0				4.4	0					0	0	
29145020	2-羟基-4-甲氧基二苯甲酮	5.5	0		0	5		0	0	0				3.3	0					0	0	
29145090	酮酚及含其他含氧基酮	5.5	0		0	5		0	0	0				3.3	0					0	0	
29146100	蒽醌	5.5	0		0	5		0	0	0				3.3	0					0	0	
29146910	辅酶Q10	5.5	0		0	0		0	0	0				3.3	0					0	0	
29146990	其他醌,不论是否含有其他含氧基,及其卤化、磺化、硝化或亚硝化衍生物	5.5	0		0	0		0	0	0				3.3	0					0	0	
29147000	其他酮及醌的卤化、磺化、硝化、或亚硝化的衍生物	5.5	0		0	5		0	0	0					0					0	0	
29151100	甲酸	5.5	0		0	5		0	0	0				3.3	0					0	0	0
29151200	甲酸盐	5.5	0		0	5		0	0	0				3.3	0					0	0	0
29151300	甲酸酯	5.5	0		0	5		0	0	0				3.3	0					0	0	0
29152111	食品级冰乙酸	5.5	0		0	5		0	0	0			0	3.3	0					0	0	0
29152119	其他冰乙酸(冰醋酸)	5.5	0		0	5		0	0	0			0	3.3	0					0	0	0
29152190	其他乙酸	5.5	0		0	5		0	0	0				3.3	0					0	0	0
29152400	乙酸酐	5.5	0		0	0		0	0	0				3.3	0					0	0	0
29152910	乙酸钠	5.5	0		0	5		0	0	0				3.3	0					0	0	0
29152990	其他乙酸盐	5.5	0		0	5		0	0	0				3.3	0					0	0	0
29153100	乙酸乙酯	5.5	0		0	5		0	0	0				3.3	0					0	0	0
29153200	乙酸乙烯酯	5.5	0		0	5		0	0	0			0	3.3	0					0	0	0
29153300	乙酸正丁酯	5.5	0		0	0		0	0	0				3.3	0					0	0	0
29153600	地乐酚(ISO)乙酸酯	5.5	0		0	5		0	0	0				3.3	0					0	0	0
29153900	其他乙酸酯	5.5	0		0	5		0	0	0				4.4	0					0	0	0
29154000	一、二、三氯代乙酸及其盐和酯	5.5	0		0	5		0	0	0				3.3	0					0	0	0
29155010	丙酸	5.5	0		0	5		0	0	0				3.3	0					0	0	0
29155090	丙酸盐和酯	5.5	0		0	5		0	0	0				3.3	0					0	0	0
29156000	丁酸、戊酸及其盐和酯	5.5	0		0	5		0	0	0				3.3	0					0	0	0
29157010	硬脂酸	7	0		0	5		0	0	0				4.2	0					0	0	0
29157090	棕榈酸及其盐和酯、硬脂酸盐、酯	5.5	0		0	5		0	0	0				3.3	0					0	0	0
29159000	其他饱和无环一元羧酸及其酸酐	5.5	0		0	5		0	0	0		0		4.4	0					0	0	0
29161100	丙烯酸及其盐	6.5	0		0	0		0	0	0				3.9	0					0	0	
29161210	丙烯酸甲酯	6.5	0		0	5	0	0	0	0				5	0					0	0	
29161220	丙烯酸乙酯	6.5	0		0	5	0	0	0	0				3.9	0					0	0	
29161230	丙烯酸丁酯	6.5	0		0	5	0	0	0	0				3.9	0					0	0	
29161240	丙烯酸异辛酯	6.5	0		0	5	0	0	0	0				3.9	0					0	0	
29161290	其他丙烯酸酯	6.5	0		0	5	0	0	0	0				3.9	0					0	0	
29161300	甲基丙烯酸及其盐	6.5	0		0	5		0	0	0			0	3.9	0					0	0	
29161400	甲基丙烯酸酯	6.5	0		0	5		0	0	0			0	3.9	0					0	0	
29161500	油酸、亚油酸或亚麻酸及其盐和酯	6.5	0		0	5		0	0	0	0			3.9	0					0	0	
29161600	乐杀螨(ISO)	6.5	0		0	5		0	0	0				3.9	0					0	0	
29161900	其他不饱和无环一元羧酸(包括其酸酐,酰卤化物,过氧化物和过氧酸及它们的衍生物)	6.5	0		0	5		0	0	0					0					0	0	
29162010	DV菊酸甲酯、二溴菊酸	4	0		0	0		0	0	0				0	0					0	0	
29162090	其他(环烷、环烯、环萜烯)一元羧酸(包括其酸酐,酰卤化物,过氧化物和过氧酸及它们的衍生物)	6.5	0		0	5		0	0	0				5	0					0	0	
29163100	苯甲酸及其盐和酯	6.5	0		0	5		0	0	0					0					0	0	
29163200	过氧化苯甲酰及苯甲酰氯	6.5	0		0	5		0	0	0				3.9	0					0	0	
29163400	苯乙酸及其盐	6.5	0		0	5		0	0	0					0					0	0	
29163910	邻甲基苯甲酸	6.5	0		0	5		0	0	0				3.9	0					0	0	
29163920	布洛芬	6.5	0		0	5		0	0	0				3.9	0					0	0	

税则号列	货品名称	最惠国	协定税率												特惠税率						
			东盟统一	亚太5国	智利	巴基斯坦	新加坡	新西兰	秘鲁	哥达	香港	澳门	台湾	瑞士	冰岛	亚太2国	老挝	柬埔寨	缅甸	LDC1	LDC2	LDC3
29163990	其他芳香一元羧酸(包括其酸酐,酰卤化物,过氧化物和过氧酸及它们的衍生物)	6.5	0		0	5		0	0	0				5	0					0	0	
29171110	草酸	6.5	0		0	5		0	0	0				3.9	0					0	0	
29171120	草酸钴	9	0		0	5		0	0	0				5.4	0					0	0	
29171190	其他草酸盐和酯	6.5	0		0	5		0	0	0				3.9	0					0	0	
29171200	己二酸及其盐和酯	6.5	0		0	5		0	0	0				3.9	0					0	0	
29171310	癸二酸及其盐和酯	6.5	0		0	5		0	0	0				3.9	0					0	0	
29171390	壬二酸及其盐和酯	6.5	0		0	5		0	0	0				3.9	0					0	0	
29171400	马来酐	6.5	0		0	5		0	0	0				3.9	0					0	0	
29171900	其他无环多元羧酸(包括其酸酐,酰卤化物,过氧化物和过氧酸及它们的衍生物)	6.5	0		0	5		0	0	0		0		3.9	0					0	0	
29172010	四氢苯酐	4	0		0	0		0	0	0				0	0					0	0	
29172090	其他(环烷、环烯、环萜烯)多元羧酸(包括其酸酐,酰卤化物,过氧化物和过氧酸及它们的衍生物)	6.5	0		0	5		0	0	0				3.9	0					0	0	
29173200	邻苯二甲酸二辛酯	6.5	0		0	5		0	0	0			0	3.9	0					0	0	
29173300	邻苯二甲酸二壬酯,邻苯二甲酸二癸酯	6.5	0		0	5		0	0	0			0	3.9	0					0	0	
29173410	邻苯二甲酸二丁酯	6.5	0		0	5		0	0	0				3.9	0					0	0	
29173490	其他邻苯二甲酸酯	6.5	0		0	5		0	0	0			0	3.9	0					0	0	
29173500	邻苯二甲酸酐(苯酐)	6.5	0		0	5		0	0	0				3.9	0					0	0	
29173611	精对苯二甲酸	6.5	0	6	0	6	0	0		0				5	0					0	0	
29173619	其他对苯二甲酸	6.5	0	6	0	6	0	0	0	0				5	0					0	0	
29173690	对苯二甲酸盐	6.5	0		0	5		0	0	0				3.9	0					0	0	
29173700	对苯二甲酸二甲酯	6.5	0		0	5		0	0	0				3.9	0					0	0	
29173910	间苯二甲酸	6.5	0		0	5		0	0	0				3.9	0					0	0	
29173990	其他芳香多元羧酸(包括其酸酐,酰卤化物,过氧化物和过氧酸及它们的衍生物)	6.5	0		0	5		0	0	0				3.9	0					0	0	
29181100	乳酸及其盐和酯	6.5	0		0	5		0	0	0				3.9	0					0	0	
29181200	酒石酸	6.5	0		0	5		0	0	0				3.9	0					0	0	
29181300	酒石酸盐及酒石酸酯	6.5	0		0	5		0	0	0				3.9	0					0	0	
29181400	柠檬酸	6.5	0		0	5		0	0	0				3.9	0					0	0	
29181500	柠檬酸盐及柠檬酸酯	6.5	0		0	5		0	0	0				3.9	0					0	0	
29181600	葡糖酸及其盐和酯	6.5	0		0	5		0	0	0				3.9	0					0	0	
29181800	乙酯杀螨醇(ISO)	6.5	0		0	5		0	0	0				3.9	0					0	0	
29181910	2,2－二苯基－2－羟基乙酸	6.5	0		0	5		0	0	0				3.9	0					0	0	
29181990	其他含醇基但不含其他含氧基的羧酸(包括其酸酐,酰卤化物,过氧化物和过氧酸及它们的衍生物)	6.5	0		0	5		0	0	0				3.9	0					0	0	
29182110	水杨酸、水杨酸钠	6.5	0		0	5		0	0	0				5	0					0	0	
29182190	其他水杨酸盐	6.5	0		0	5		0	0	0				3.9	0					0	0	
29182210	邻乙酰水杨酸(阿斯匹林)	6	0		0	5		0	0	0				3.6	0					0	0	
29182290	邻乙酰水杨酸盐和酯	6.5	0		0	5		0	0	0				3.9	0					0	0	
29182300	水杨酸其他酯及其盐	6.5	0		0	5		0	0	0					0					0	0	
29182900	其他含酚基但不含其他含氧基羧酸及其酸酐(酰卤化物,过氧化物和过氧酸及它们的衍生物)	6.5	0		0	5		0	0	0		0		3.9	0					0	0	
29183000	含醛基或酮基不含其他含氧基羧酸及其酸酐(酰卤化物,过氧化物和过氧酸及它们的衍生物)	6.5	0		0	5		0	0	0				5	0					0	0	
29189100	2,4,5－涕(ISO)(2,4,5－三氯苯氧基乙酸)及其盐或酯	6.5	0		0	5		0	0	0				3.9	0					0	0	
29189900	其他含其他附加含氧基羧酸及其酸酐(酰卤化物,过氧化物和过氧酸及它们的衍生物)	6.5	0		0	5		0	0	0				5	0					0	0	
29191000	三(2,3－二溴丙基)磷酸酯	6.5	0		0	5		0	0	0				3.9	0					0	0	

税则号列	货品名称	最惠国	协定税率 东盟统一	亚太5国	智利	巴基斯坦	新加坡	新西兰	秘鲁	哥达	香港	澳门	台湾	瑞士	冰岛	特惠税率 亚太2国	老挝	柬埔寨	缅甸	LDC1	LDC2	LDC3
29199000	其他磷酸酯及其盐(包括乳磷酸盐),及它们的卤化、磺化、硝化、或亚硝化的衍生物	6.5	0		0	5		0	0	0				3.9	0					0	0	
29201100	对硫磷(ISO)及甲基对硫磷(ISO)	6.5	0		0	5		0	0	0				3.9	0					0	0	
29201900	其他硫代磷酸酯及其盐,及它们的卤化、磺化、硝化、或亚硝化的衍生物	6.5	0		0	5		0	0	0				3.9	0					0	0	
29209011	亚磷酸三甲酯	6.5	0		0	5		0	0	0				3.9	0					0	0	
29209012	亚磷酸三乙酯	6.5	0		0	5		0	0	0				3.9	0					0	0	
29209013	亚磷酸二甲酯	6.5	0		0	5		0	0	0				3.9	0					0	0	
29209014	亚磷酸二乙酯	6.5	0		0	5		0	0	0				3.9	0					0	0	
29209019	其他亚磷酸酯	6.5	0		0	5		0	0	0				3.9	0					0	0	
29209090	其他无机酸酯(不包括卤化氢的酯)及其盐,及它们的卤化、磺化、硝化、或亚硝化的衍生物	6.5	0		0	5		0	0	0				3.9	0					0	0	
29211100	甲胺、二甲胺或三甲胺及其盐	6.5	0		0	5		0	0	0				3.9	0					0	0	
29211910	二正丙胺	4	0		0	0		0	0	0				0	0					0	0	
29211920	异丙胺	6.5	0		0	5		0	0	0				3.9	0					0	0	
29211930	N,N-二(2-氯乙基)乙胺	6.5	0		0	5		0	0	0				3.9	0					0	0	
29211940	N,N-二(2-氯乙基)甲胺	6.5	0		0	5		0	0	0				3.9	0					0	0	
29211950	三(2-氯乙基)胺	6.5	0		0	5		0	0	0				3.9	0					0	0	
29211960	二烷氨基乙基-2-氯及其质子化盐	6.5	0		0	5		0	0	0				3.9	0					0	0	
29211990	其他无环单胺及其衍生物,及它们的盐	6.5	0		0	5		0	0	0				3.9	0					0	0	
29212110	乙二胺	6.5	0		0	5		0	0	0				3.9	0					0	0	
29212190	乙二胺盐	6.5	0		0	5		0	0	0				5	0					0	0	
29212210	已二酸已二胺盐(尼龙-66盐)	6.5	0		0	5		0	0	0				3.9	0					0	0	
29212290	六亚甲基二胺及其他盐	6.5	0		0	5		0	0	0				3.9	0					0	0	
29212900	其他无环多胺及其衍生物,及它们的盐	6.5	0		0	5		0	0	0				3.9	0					0	0	
29213000	环(烷、烯、萜烯)单胺或多胺及衍生物,及它们的盐	6.5	0		0	5		0	0	0				3.9	0					0	0	
29214110	苯胺	6.5	0		0	5		0	0	0				3.9	0					0	0	
29214190	苯胺盐	6.5	0		0	5		0	0	0					0					0	0	
29214200	苯胺衍生物及其盐	6.5	0		0	5		0	0	0					0					0	0	
29214300	甲苯胺及其衍生物,及它们的盐	6.5	0		0	5		0	0	0				3.9	0					0	0	
29214400	二苯胺及其衍生物,及它们的盐	6.5	0		0	5		0	0	0					0					0	0	
29214500	1-萘胺、2-萘胺及其衍生物及其盐	6.5	0		0	5		0	0	0					0					0	0	
29214600	安非他明、苄非他明、右苯丙胺、乙非他明、芬坎法明、利非他明、左苯丙胺、美芬雷司、芬特明以及它们的盐	6.5	0		0	5		0	0	0				3.9	0					0	0	
29214910	对异丙基苯胺	4	0		0	0		0	0	0				0	0					0	0	
29214920	二甲基苯胺	6.5	0		0	5		0	0	0				3.9	0					0	0	
29214930	2,6-甲基乙基苯胺	4	0		0	0		0	0	0				0	0					0	0	
29214940	2,6-二乙基苯胺	6.5	0		0	5		0	0	0					0					0	0	
29214990	其他芳香单胺及衍生物及它们的盐	6.5	0		0	5		0	0	0					0					0	0	
29215110	邻苯二胺	4	0		0	0		0	0	0				0	0					0	0	
29215190	间-、对-苯二胺、二氨基甲苯及其衍生物及它们的盐	6.5	0		0	5		0	0	0				3.9	0					0	0	
29215900	其他芳香多胺及衍生物及它们的盐	6.5	0		0	5		0	0	0					0					0	0	
29221100	单乙醇胺及其盐	6.5	0		0	5		0	0	0				3.9	0					0	0	
29221200	二乙醇胺及其盐	6.5	0		0	5		0	0	0				3.9	0					0	0	
29221310	三乙醇胺	6.5	0		0	5		0	0	0				3.9	0					0	0	
29221320	三乙醇胺盐	6.5	0		0	5		0	0	0				3.9	0					0	0	
29221400	右丙氧吩及其盐	6.5	0		0	5		0	0	0				3.9	0					0	0	
29221910	乙胺丁醇	6.5	0		0	5		0	0	0				3.9	0					0	0	
29221921	二甲氨基乙醇及其质子化盐	6.5	0		0	5		0	0	0				3.9	0					0	0	
29221922	二乙氨基乙醇及其质子化盐	6.5	0		0	5		0	0	0				3.9	0					0	0	
29221929	其他二烷氨基乙-2-醇及其质子化	6.5	0		0	5		0	0	0				3.9	0					0	0	
29221930	乙基二乙醇胺	6.5	0		0	5		0	0	0				3.9	0					0	0	
29221940	甲基二乙醇胺	6.5	0		0	5		0	0	0				3.9	0					0	0	

税则号列	货品名称	最惠国	协定税率													特惠税率						
			东盟统一	亚太5国	智利	巴基斯坦	新加坡	新西兰	秘鲁	哥达	香港	澳门	台湾	瑞士	冰岛	亚太2国	老挝	柬埔寨	缅甸	LDC1	LDC2	LDC3
29221950	本芴醇	6.5	0		0	5		0	0	0				3.9	0					0	0	
29221990	其他氨基醇及其醚、酯和它们的盐(但含有一种以上含氧基的除外)	6.5	0		0	5		0	0	0				3.9	0					0	0	
29222100	氨基羟基萘磺酸及其盐	6.5	0		0	5		0	0	0				3.9	0					0	0	
29222910	茴香胺、二茴香胺、氨基苯乙醚及其盐	6.5	0		0	5		0	0	0				3.9	0					0	0	
29222990	其他氨基(萘酚、酚)及醚、酯、盐(但含有一种以上含氧基的除外)	6.5	0		0	5		0	0	0				3.9	0					0	0	
29223100	安非拉酮、美沙酮和去甲美沙酮以及它们的盐	6.5	0		0	5		0	0	0				3.9	0					0	0	
29223910	4-甲基甲卡西酮	6.5	0		0	5		0	0	0				3.9	0					0	0	
29223990	其他氨基醛、氨基酮、氨基醌及其盐(但含有一种以上含氧基的除外)	6.5	0		0	5		0	0	0				3.9	0					0	0	
29224110	赖氨酸	5	0		0	0		0	0	0				0	0					0	0	
29224190	赖氨酸酯和赖氨酸盐	6	0		0	5		0	0	0				3.6	0					0	0	
29224210	谷氨酸	10	0	8.6	0	5	0	0	0	0				6	0					0	0	
29224220	谷氨酸钠	10	0		0	5	0	0	0	0	0			6	0					0	0	
29224290	其他谷氨酸盐	6.5	0		0	5		0	0	0				3.9	0					0	0	
29224310	邻氨基苯甲酸(氨茴酸)	6.5	0		0	5		0	0	0				3.9	0					0	0	
29224390	邻氨基苯甲酸(氨茴酸)盐	6.5	0		0	5		0	0	0				3.9	0					0	0	
29224400	替利定及其盐	6.5	0		0	5		0	0	0				3.9	0					0	0	
29224911	氨甲环酸	6.5	0		0	5		0	0	0				3.9	0					0	0	
29224919	其他氨基酸	6.5	0		0	5		0	0	0				3.9	0					0	0	
29224991	普鲁卡因	6	0		0	5		0	0	0				3.6	0					0	0	
29224999	其他氨基酸及其酯及它们的盐(但含有一种以上含氧基的除外)	6.5	0		0	5		0	0	0				3.9	0					0	0	
29225010	对羟基苯甘氨酸及其邓甲盐	6.5	0		0	5		0	0	0				3.9	0					0	0	
29225020	莱克多巴胺和盐酸莱克多巴胺	6.5	0		0	5		0	0	0				3.9	0					0	0	
29225090	其他氨基醇酚、氨基酸酚及其他含氧基氨基化合物	6.5	0		0	5		0	0	0				3.9	0					0	0	
29231000	胆碱及其盐	6.5	0		0	5		0	0	0				3.9	0					0	0	
29232000	卵磷脂及其他磷氨基类脂	6.5	0		0	5		0	0	0				3.9	0					0	0	
29239000	其他季铵盐及季铵碱	6.5	0		0	5		0	0	0				3.9	0					0	0	
29241100	甲丙氨酯	6.5	0		0	5		0	0	0				3.9	0					0	0	
29241200	氯乙酰胺(ISO)、久效磷(ISO)及磷胺(ISO)	6.5	0		0	5		0	0	0				3.9	0					0	0	
29241910	二甲基甲酰胺	6.5	0		0	5		0	0	0	0		0	3.9	0					0	0	
29241990	其他无环酰胺及其衍生物以及他们的盐	6.5	0		0	5		0	0	0				3.9	0					0	0	
29242100	酰脲及其衍生物,及它们的盐	6.5	0		0	5		0	0	0				3.9	0					0	0	
29242300	2-乙酰氨基苯甲酸(N-乙酰邻氨基苯甲酸)及其盐	6.5	0		0	5		0	0	0					0					0	0	
29242400	炔己蚁胺	6.5	0		0	5		0	0	0				3.9	0					0	0	
29242910	对乙酰氨基苯乙醚(非那西丁)	6	0		0	5		0	0	0				3.6	0					0	0	
29242920	对乙酰氨基酚(扑热息痛)	6	0		0	5		0	0	0				3.6	0					0	0	
29242930	阿斯巴甜	6.5	0		0	5		0	0	0		0		5.2	0					0	0	
29242990	其他环酰胺(包括环氨基甲酸酯)	6.5	0		0	5		0	0	0		0		5.2	0					0	0	
29251100	糖精及其盐	9	0		0	5		0	0	0				5.4	0					0	0	
29251200	格鲁米特	6.5	0		0	5		0	0	0				3.9	0					0	0	
29251900	其他酰亚胺及其衍生物、盐	6.5	0		0	5		0	0	0				5	0					0	0	
29252100	杀虫脒	6.5	0		0	5		0	0	0				3.9	0					0	0	
29252900	其他亚胺及其衍生物以及它们的盐	6.5	0		0	5		0	0	0				3.9	0					0	0	
29261000	丙烯腈	6.5	6.5		0			0	0	0				3.9	0					0	0	
29262000	1-氰基胍(双氰胺)	6.5	0		0	5		0	0	0				3.9	0					0	0	
29263000	芬普雷司及其盐;美沙酮中间体(4-氰基-2-二甲氨基-4,4-二苯基丁烷)	6.5	0		0	5		0	0	0				3.9	0					0	0	
29269010	对氯氰苄	4	0		0	0		0	0	0				0	0					0	0	
29269020	间苯二甲腈	6.5	0		0	5		0	0	0				3.9	0					0	0	
29269090	其他腈基化合物	6.5	0		0	5		0	0	0	0			5.2	0					0	0	
29270000	重氮化合物、偶氮化合物及氧化偶氮化合物	6.5	0		0	5		0	0	0		0		3.9	0					0	0	
29280000	肼(联氨)及胲(羟胺)的有机衍生物	6.5	0		0	5		0	0	0				3.9	0					0	0	

税则号列	货品名称	最惠国	协定税率													特惠税率						
			东盟统一	亚太5国	智利	巴基斯坦	新加坡	新西兰	秘鲁	哥达	香港	澳门	台湾	瑞士	冰岛	亚太2国	老挝	柬埔寨	缅甸	LDC1	LDC2	LDC3
29291010	2,4和2,6甲苯二异氰酸酯混合物(甲苯二异氰酸酯TDI)	6.5	0		0	5		0	0	0			0	3.9	0					0	0	
29291020	二甲苯二异氰酸酯(TODI)	6.5	0		0	5		0	0	0					0					0	0	
29291030	二苯基甲烷二异氰酸酯(纯MDI)	6.5	0		0	5		0	0	0				5.2	0					0	0	
29291040	六亚甲基二异氰酸酯	6.5	0		0	5		0	0	0				3.9	0					0	0	
29291090	其他异氰酸酯	6.5	0		0	5		0	0	0				3.9	0					0	0	
29299010	环已基氨基磺酸钠(甜蜜素)	9	0		0	5		0	0	0				5.4	0					0	0	
29299020	二烷(甲、乙、正丙或异丙)氨基膦酰二卤	6.5	0		0	5		0	0	0				3.9	0					0	0	
29299030	二烷氨基膦酸二烷酯	6.5	0		0	5		0	0	0				3.9	0					0	0	
29299040	乙酰甲胺磷	6.5	0		0	5		0	0	0				3.9	0					0	0	
29299090	其他含氮基化合物	6.5	0		0	5		0	0	0				3.9	0					0	0	
29302000	其他硫代氨基甲酸盐(或酯)	6.5	0		0	5		0	0	0				3.9	0					0	0	
29303000	(一硫化、二硫化、三硫化)二烃氨基硫羰	6.5	0		0	5		0	0	0				3.9	0					0	0	
29304000	甲硫氨酸(蛋氨酸)	6.5	0		0	5		0	0	0				3.9	0					0	0	
29305000	敌菌丹(ISO)及甲胺磷(ISO)	6.5	0		0	5		0	0	0				3.9	0					0	0	
29309010	双巯丙氨酸(胱氨酸)	6.5	0		0	5		0	0	0				3.9	0					0	0	
29309020	二硫代碳酸酯(或盐)[黄原酸酯(或盐)]	6.5	0		0	5		0	0	0				3.9	0					0	0	
29309090	其他有机硫化合物	6.5	0		0	5		0	0	0	0			3.9	0					0	0	
29311000	四甲基铅及四乙基铅	6.5	0		0	5		0	0	0				3.9	0					0	0	
29312000	三丁基锡化合物	6.5	0		0	5		0	0	0				3.9	0					0	0	
29319011	双甘膦	6.5	0		0	5		0	0	0				3.9	0					0	0	
29319019	其他含有磷原子的有机－无机化合物	6.5	0		0	5		0	0	0				3.9	0					0	0	
29319090	其他有机－无机化合物	6.5	0		0	5		0	0	0				3.9	0					0	0	
29321100	四氢呋喃	6	0		0	5		0	0	0	0		0	3.6	0					0	0	
29321200	2－糠醛	6	0		0	5		0	0	0				3.6	0					0	0	
29321300	糠醇及四氢糠醇	6	0		0	5		0	0	0				3.6	0					0	0	
29321900	其他结构上有非稠合呋喃环化合物(不论是否氢化)	6.5	0		0	5		0	0	0					0					0	0	
29322010	香豆素、甲基香豆素及乙基香豆素	6.5	0		0	5		0	0	0				3.9	0					0	0	
29322090	其他内酯	6.5	0		0	5		0	0	0				5.2	0					0	0	
29329100	4－丙烯基－1,2－亚甲二氧基苯	6.5	0		0	5		0	0	0				3.9	0					0	0	
29329200	1－(1,3－苯并二恶茂－5－基)丙－2－酮	6.5	0		0	5		0	0	0				3.9	0					0	0	
29329300	3,4－亚甲二氧基苯甲醛(胡椒醛)	6.5	0		0	5		0	0	0				3.9	0					0	0	
29329400	4－烯丙基－1,2－亚甲二氧基苯(黄樟脑)	6.5	0		0	5		0	0	0				3.9	0					0	0	
29329500	四氢大麻酚(所有异构体)	6.5	0		0	5		0	0	0				3.9	0					0	0	
29329910	7－羟基苯并呋喃(呋喃酚)	4	0		0	0		0	0	0				0	0					0	0	
29329920	联苯双酯	6.5	0		0	5		0	0	0				3.9	0					0	0	
29329930	蒿甲醚	6.5	0		0	5		0	0	0				5.2	0					0	0	
29329990	其他仅含氧杂原子的杂环化合物	6.5	0		0	5		0	0	0				5.2	0					0	0	
29331100	二甲基苯基吡唑酮(安替比林)及其衍生物	6.5	0	6	0	5		0	0	0				3.9	0					0	0	
29331920	安乃近	6	0		0	5		0	0	0				3.6	0					0	0	
29331990	其他结构上有非稠合吡唑环化合物(不论是否氢化)	6.5			0	5		0	0	0				3.9	0					0	0	
29332100	乙内酰脲及其衍生物	6.5	0		0	5		0	0	0				3.9	0					0	0	
29332900	其他结构上有非稠合咪唑环化合物(不论是否氢化)	6.5			0	5		0	0	0				5	0					0	0	
29333100	吡啶及其盐	6	0		0	5		0	0	0			0	3.6	0					0	0	
29333210	哌啶(六氢吡啶)	4	0		0	0		0	0	0				0	0					0	0	
29333220	哌啶(六氢吡啶)盐	6.5	0		0	5		0	0	0				3.9	0					0	0	
29333300	阿芬太尼、阿尼利定、氰苯双哌酰胺、溴西泮、地芬诺新、地芬诺酯、地匹哌酮、芬太尼、凯托米酮、哌醋甲酯、喷他左辛、哌替啶、哌替啶中间体A、苯环利定、苯哌利定、哌苯甲醇、哌氰米特、丙吡兰和三甲利定以及它们的盐	6.5	0		0	5		0	0	0				3.9	0					0	0	
29333910	二苯乙醇酸－3－奎宁环脂	6.5	0		0	5		0	0	0				3.9	0					0	0	

税则号列	货品名称	最惠国	协定税率													特惠税率						
			东盟统一	亚太5国	智利	巴基斯坦	新加坡	新西兰	秘鲁	哥达	香港	澳门	台湾	瑞士	冰岛	亚太2国	老挝	柬埔寨	缅甸	LDC1	LDC2	LDC3
29333920	奎宁环-3-醇	6.5	0		0	5		0	0	0				3.9	0					0	0	
29333990	其他结构上有非稠合吡啶环化合物(不论是否氢化)	6.5	0		0	5		0	0	0				5.2	0					0	0	
29334100	左非诺及其盐	6.5	0		0	5		0	0	0				3.9	0					0	0	
29335920	环丙氟哌酸	6.5	0	6	0	5		0	0	0				3.9	0					0	0	
29334990	其他含喹啉或异喹啉环系的化合物(但未经进一步稠合)	6.5	0		0	5		0	0	0				3.9	0					0	0	
29335200	丙二酰脲(巴比土酸)及其盐	6.5	0		0	5		0	0	0				3.9	0					0	0	
29335300	阿洛巴比妥、异戊巴比妥、巴比妥、布他比妥、正丁巴比妥、环己巴比妥、甲苯巴比妥、戊巴比妥、苯巴比妥、仲丁巴比妥、司可巴比妥和乙烯比妥以及他们的盐	6.5	0		0	5		0	0	0				3.9	0					0	0	
29335400	其他丙二酰脲的衍生物以及他们的盐	6.5	0		0	5		0	0	0				3.9	0					0	0	
29335500	氯普唑仑、甲氯喹酮等以及他们的盐	6.5	0		0	5		0	0	0				3.9	0					0	0	
29335910	胞嘧啶	6.5	0	4.6	0	0		0	0	0				3.9	0					0	0	
29335990	其他结构上有嘧啶环或哌嗪环的化合物(不论是否氢化)	6.5	0	4.6	0	0		0	0	0				5.2	0					0	0	
29336100	三聚氰胺(蜜胺)	6.5	0		0	5		0	0	0				3.9	0					0	0	
29336910	三聚氰氯	6	0		0	5		0	0	0		0		3.6	0					0	0	
29336921	二氯异氰脲酸	6.5	0		0	5		0	0	0		0		3.9	0					0	0	
29336922	三氯异氰脲酸	6.5	0		0	5		0	0	0		0		3.9	0					0	0	
29336929	其他异氰脲酸氯化衍生物	6.5	0		0	5		0	0	0		0		3.9	0					0	0	
29336990	其他结构上含非稠合三嗪环化合物(不论是否氢化)	6.5	0		0	5		0	0	0		0		3.9	0					0	0	
29337100	6-己内酰胺	9	9		0			0		0				5.4	0							
29337200	氯巴占和甲乙哌酮	9	0		0	5		0	0	0				5.4	0					0	0	
29337900	其他内酰胺	9	0		0	5		0	0	0					0					0	0	
29339100	阿普唑仑、卡马西泮等以及它们的盐	6.5	0		0	5		0	0	0				3.9	0					0	0	
29339900	其他仅含氮杂原子的杂环化合物	6.5	0		0	5		0	0	0				5	0					0	0	
29341000	结构上含有非稠合噻唑环的化合物(不论是否氢化)	6.5	0		0	5		0	0	0				3.9	0					0	0	
29342000	含一个苯并噻唑环系的化合物(但未经进一步稠合,不论是否氢化)	6.5	0		0	5		0	0	0				3.9	0					0	0	
29343000	含一个吩噻嗪环系的化合物(但未经进一步稠合,不论是否氢化)	6.5	0		0	5		0	0	0				3.9	0					0	0	
29349100	阿米雷司、溴替唑仑、氯噻西泮等以及他们的盐	6.5	0		0	5		0	0	0				3.9	0					0	0	
29349910	磺内酯及磺内酰胺	6.5	0		0	5		0	0	0				3.9	0					0	0	
29349920	呋喃唑酮	6	0		0	5		0	0	0					0					0	0	
29349930	核酸及其盐	6.5	0		0	5		0	0	0				3.9	0					0	0	
29349940	奈韦拉平、依发韦仑、利托那韦及它们的盐	6.5	0		0	5		0	0	0				3.9	0					0	0	
29349950	克拉维酸及其盐	6.5	0		0	5		0	0	0				3.9	0					0	0	
29349960	7-苯乙酰氨基-3-氯甲基-4-头孢烷酸对甲氧基苄酯、7-氨基头孢烷酸、7-氨基脱乙酰氧基头孢烷酸	6	0	5	0	0		0	0	0				3.6	0					0	0	
29349990	其他杂环化合物	6.5	0		0	5		0	0	0				3.9	0					0	0	
29350010	磺胺嘧啶	6.5	0		0	5		0	0	0				3.9	0					0	0	
29350020	磺胺双甲基嘧啶	6.5	0		0	5		0	0	0				3.9	0					0	0	
29350030	磺胺甲恶唑	6.5	0		0	5		0	0	0				3.9	0					0	0	
29350090	其他磺(酰)胺	6.5	0		0	5		0	0	0				5	0					0	0	
29362100	未混合的维生素 A 及其衍生物	4	0		0	0		0	0	0		0		3.1	0					0	0	0
29362200	未混合的维生素 B1 及其衍生物	4	0		0	0		0	0	0		0		0	0					0	0	0
29362300	未混合的维生素 B2 及其衍生物	4	0		0	0		0	0	0		0		0	0					0	0	0
29362400	未混合的 D 或 DL-泛酸及其衍生物	4	0		0	0		0	0	0		0		0	0					0	0	0
29362500	未混合的维生素 B6 及其衍生物	4	0		0	0		0	0	0		0		0	0					0	0	0
29362600	未混合的维生素 B12 及其衍生物	4	0		0	0		0	0	0		0		3.2	0					0	0	0
29362700	未混合的维生素 C 及其衍生物	4	0		0	0		0	0	0		0		0	0					0	0	0
29362800	未混合的维生素 E 及其衍生物	4	0		0	0		0	0	0		0		3.2	0					0	0	0
29362900	其他未混合的维生素及其衍生物	4	0		0	0		0	0	0		0		3.2	0					0	0	0

税则号列	货品名称	最惠国	协定税率 东盟统一	亚太5国	智利	巴基斯坦	新加坡	新西兰	秘鲁	哥达	香港	澳门	台湾	瑞士	冰岛	特惠税率 亚太2国	老挝	柬埔寨	缅甸	LDC1	LDC2	LDC3
29369000	维生素原、混合维生素及其衍生物	4	0		0	0		0	0	0		0		0	0					0	0	0
29371100	生长激素及其衍生物和类似结构物	4	0		0	0		0	0	0				0	0					0	0	
29371210	重组人胰岛素及其盐	4	0		0	0		0	0	0				0	0					0	0	
29371290	其他胰岛素及其盐	4	0		0	0		0	0	0				0	0					0	0	
29371900	其他多肽激素、蛋白激素、糖蛋白激素及其衍生物和类似结构物	4	0		0	0		0	0	0				3.2	0					0	0	
29372100	可的松、氢化可的松及脱氢可的松及脱氢皮质(甾)醇	4	0		0	0		0	0	0				0	0					0	0	
29372210	地塞米松	4	0		0	0		0	0	0				0	0					0	0	
29372290	其他皮质(甾)激素的卤化衍生物	4	0		0	0		0	0	0				0	0					0	0	
29372311	孕马结合雌激素	4	0		0	0		0	0	0				0	0					0	0	
29372319	其他动物源的雌(甾)激素和孕激素	4	0		0	0		0	0	0				0	0					0	0	
29372390	其他皮质甾类激素的卤化衍生物	4	0		0	0		0	0	0				0	0					0	0	
29372900	其他甾族激素及其衍生物和类似结构物	4	0		0	0		0	0	0				0	0					0	0	
29375000	前列腺素、血栓烷和白细胞三烯及其衍生物和结构类似物	4	0		0	0		0	0	0				0	0					0	0	
29379000	其他天然或合成再制的激素及其衍生物和结构类似物,包括主要用作激素的改性链多肽	4	0		0	0		0	0	0				0	0					0	0	
29381000	芸香苷及其衍生物	6.5	0		0	5		0	0	0				3.9	0					0	0	
29389010	齐多夫定、拉米夫定、司他夫定、地达诺新及它们的盐	6.5	0		0	5		0	0	0				3.9	0					0	0	
29389090	其他天然或合成再制的苷及其盐、醚、酯和其他衍生物	6.5	0		0	5		0	0	0				3.9	0					0	0	
29391100	罂粟杆浓缩物、丁丙诺啡、可待因等以及他们的盐	4	0		0	0		0	0	0				0	0					0	0	0
29391900	其他鸦片碱及其衍生物,及它们的盐	4	0		0	0		0	0	0				0	0					0	0	0
29392000	其他金鸡纳生物碱及其衍生物,及它们的盐	4	0		0	0		0	0	0				0	0					0	0	0
29393000	咖啡因及其盐	4	0		0	0		0	0	0				0	0					0	0	0
29394100	麻黄碱及其盐	4	0		0	0		0	0	0				0	0					0	0	0
29394200	假麻黄碱及其盐	4	0		0	0		0	0	0				0	0					0	0	0
29394300	d-去甲麻黄碱(INN)及其盐	4	0		0	0		0	0	0				0	0					0	0	0
29394400	去甲麻黄碱及其盐	4	0		0	0		0	0	0				0	0					0	0	0
29394900	其他麻黄碱类及其盐	4	0		0	0		0	0	0				0	0					0	0	0
29395100	芬乙茶碱(INN)及其盐	4	0		0	0		0	0	0				0	0					0	0	0
29395900	其他茶碱和氨茶碱及其衍生物,及它们的盐	4	0		0	0		0	0	0				0	0					0	0	0
29396100	麦角新碱及其盐	4	0		0	0		0	0	0				0	0					0	0	0
29396200	麦角胺及其盐	4	0		0	0		0	0	0				0	0					0	0	0
29396300	麦角酸及其盐	4	0		0	0		0	0	0				0	0					0	0	0
29396900	其他麦角生物碱及其衍生物,及它们的盐	4	0		0	0		0	0	0				3.2	0					0	0	0
29399110	可卡因及其盐	4	0		0	0		0	0	0				0	0					0	0	0
29399190	芽子碱、左甲苯丙胺、去氧麻黄碱、去氧麻黄碱外消旋体,它们的盐、酯及其他衍生物;可卡因的酯及其他衍生物	4	0		0	0		0	0	0				0	0					0	0	0
29399910	烟碱及其盐	4	0		0	0		0	0	0				0	0					0	0	0
29399920	番木鳖碱(士的年)及其盐	4	0		0	0		0	0	0				0	0					0	0	0
29399990	其他天然或合成再制的生物碱及其盐、醚、酯和其他衍生物	4	0		0	0		0	0	0				3.2	0					0	0	0
29400090	其他化学纯糖	6	0		0	5		0	0	0				3.6	0					0	0	0
29400010	木糖	6	0		0	5		0	0	0				3.6	0					0	0	0
29411011	氨苄青霉素	6	0	5	0	0		0	0	0				3.6	0					0	0	0
29411012	氨苄青霉素三水酸	6	0	5	0	0		0	0	0				3.6	0					0	0	0
29411019	其他氨苄青霉素盐	6	0	5	0	0		0	0	0				3.6	0					0	0	0
29411091	羟氨苄青霉素	4	0		0	0		0	0	0				0	0					0	0	0
29411092	羟氨苄青霉素三水酸	4	0		0	0		0	0	0				0	0					0	0	0
29411093	6氨基青霉烷酸(6APA)	4	0		0	0		0	0	0				0	0					0	0	0
29411094	青霉素V	4	0		0	0		0	0	0				0	0					0	0	0

税则号列	货品名称	最惠国	协定税率													特惠税率						
			东盟统一	亚太5国	智利	巴基斯坦	新加坡	新西兰	秘鲁	哥达	香港	澳门	台湾	瑞士	冰岛	亚太2国	老挝	柬埔寨	缅甸	LDC1	LDC2	LDC3
29411095	磺苄青霉素	4	0		0	0		0	0	0				0	0					0	0	0
29411096	邻氯青霉素	4	0		0	0		0	0	0				0	0					0	0	0
29411099	其他青霉素及其衍生物,及它们的盐	4	0		0	0		0	0	0				0	0					0	0	0
29412000	链霉素及其衍生物,及它们的盐	4	0		0	0		0	0	0				0	0					0	0	0
29413011	四环素	4	0		0	0		0	0	0		0		0	0					0	0	0
29413012	四环素盐	4	0		0	0		0	0	0		0		0	0					0	0	0
29413020	四环素衍生物及其盐	4	0		0	0		0	0	0		0		0	0					0	0	0
29414000	氯霉素及其衍生物,及它们的盐	4	0		0	0		0	0	0				0	0					0	0	0
29415000	红霉素及其衍生物,及它们的盐	4	0		0	0		0	0	0		0		0	0					0	0	0
29419010	庆大霉素及其衍生物,及它们的盐	4	0		0	0		0	0	0				0	0					0	0	0
29419020	卡那霉素及其衍生物,及它们的盐	4	0		0	0		0	0	0				0	0					0	0	0
29419030	利福平及其衍生物,及它们的盐	4	0		0	0		0	0	0				0	0					0	0	0
29419040	林可霉素及其衍生物,及它们的盐	4	0		0	0		0	0	0				0	0					0	0	0
29419052	头孢氨苄及其盐	6	0	5	0	0		0	0	0				3.6	0					0	0	0
29419053	头孢唑啉及其盐	6	0	5	0	0		0	0	0				3.6	0					0	0	0
29419054	头孢拉啶及其盐	6	0	5	0	0		0	0	0				3.6	0					0	0	0
29419055	头孢三嗪(头孢曲松)及其盐	6	0	5	0	0		0	0	0				4.6	0					0	0	0
29419056	头孢哌酮及其盐	6	0	5	0	0		0	0	0				3.6	0					0	0	0
29419057	头孢噻肟及其盐	6	0	5	0	0		0	0	0				3.6	0					0	0	0
29419058	头孢克罗及其盐	6	0	5	0	0		0	0	0				3.6	0					0	0	0
29419059	其他头孢菌素及其衍生物以及它们的盐	6	0	5	0	0		0	0	0				3.6	0					0	0	0
29419060	麦迪霉素及其衍生物,及它们的盐	6	0	4.2	0	0		0	0	0				3.6	0					0	0	0
29419070	乙酰螺旋霉素及其衍生物,及它们的盐	4	0		0	0		0	0	0				0	0					0	0	0
29419090	其他抗菌素	6	0	5	0	0		0	0	0				3.6	0					0	0	0
29420000	其他有机化合物	6.5	0		0	5		0	0	0				3.9	0					0	0	0
30012000	腺体、其他器官及其分泌物提取物	3	0		0	0		0	0	0				0	0					0	0	
30019010	肝素及其盐	3	0		0	0		0	0	0				0	0					0	0	
30019090	其他未列名的人体或动物制品(供治疗或预防疾病用)	3	0		0	0		0	0	0				0	0					0	0	
30021000	抗血清、其他血份及免疫制品(不论是否修饰通过生物工艺加工制得)	3	0		0	0		0	0	0				2.3	0					0	0	0
30022000	人用疫苗	3	0		0	0		0	0	0				2.4	0					0	0	0
30023000	兽用疫苗	3	0		0	0		0	0	0				0	0					0	0	0
30029010	石房蛤毒素	3	0		0	0		0	0	0				0	0					0	0	0
30029020	蓖麻毒素	3	0		0	0		0	0	0				0	0					0	0	0
30029030	细菌及病毒	3	0		0	0		0	0	0				2.4	0					0	0	0
30029040	遗传物质和基因修饰生物体	3	0		0	0		0	0	0				0	0					0	0	0
30029090	人血;治病、防病或诊断用动物血制品;其他毒素、培养微生物(不包括酵母)及类似产品	3	0		0	0		0	0	0	0			0	0					0	0	0
30031011	含有氨苄青霉素的混合药品(两种或两种以上成分混合而成的,治病或防病用,未配定剂量或非零售包装)	6	0	4.5	0	0		0	0	0				3.6	0					0	0	0
30031012	含有羟氨苄青霉素的混合药品(两种或两种以上成分混合而成的,治病或防病用未配定剂量或非零售包装)	6	0	4.5	0	0		0	0	0				3.6	0					0	0	0
30031013	含有青霉素V的混合药品(两种或两种以上成分混合而成的,治病或防病用未配定剂量或非零售包装)	6	0	4.5	0	0		0	0	0				3.6	0					0	0	0
30031019	含有其他青霉素及具有青霉烷酸结构的青霉素衍生物的混合药品(两种或两种以上成分混合而成的,治病或防病用未配定剂量或非零售包装)	6	0	4.5	0	0		0	0	0				3.6	0					0	0	0
30031090	含有含有链霉素的混合药品(两种或两种以上成分混合而成的,治病或防病用未配定剂量或非零售包装)	6	0	4.5	0	0		0	0	0				3.6	0					0	0	0

税则号列	货品名称	最惠国	协定税率													特惠税率						
			东盟统一	亚太5国	智利	巴基斯坦	新加坡	新西兰	秘鲁	哥达	香港	澳门	台湾	瑞士	冰岛	亚太2国	老挝	柬埔寨	缅甸	LDC1	LDC2	LDC3
30032011	含有头孢噻肟的混合药品(两种或两种以上成分混合而成的,治病或防病用未配定剂量或非零售包装)	6	0	5.4	0	0		0	0	0				3.6	0					0	0	0
30032012	含有头孢他啶的混合药品(两种或两种以上成分混合而成的,治病或防病用未配定剂量或非零售包装)	6	0	5.4	0	0		0	0	0				3.6	0					0	0	0
30032013	含有头孢西丁的混合药品(两种或两种以上成分混合而成的,治病或防病用未配定剂量或非零售包装)	6	0	5.4	0	0		0	0	0				3.6	0					0	0	0
30032014	含有头孢替唑的混合药品(两种或两种以上成分混合而成的,治病或防病用未配定剂量或非零售包装)	6	0	5.4	0	0		0	0	0				3.6	0					0	0	0
30032015	含有头孢克罗的混合药品(两种或两种以上成分混合而成的,治病或防病用未配定剂量或非零售包装)	6	0	5.4	0	0		0	0	0				3.6	0					0	0	0
30032016	含有头孢呋辛的混合药品(两种或两种以上成分混合而成的,治病或防病用未配定剂量或非零售包装)	6	0	5.4	0	0		0	0	0				3.6	0					0	0	0
30032017	含有头孢三嗪(头孢曲松)的混合药品(两种或两种以上成分混合而成的,治病或防病用未配定剂量或非零售包装)	6	0	5.4	0	0		0	0	0				3.6	0					0	0	0
30032018	含有头孢哌酮的混合药品(两种或两种以上成分混合而成的,治病或防病用未配定剂量或非零售包装)	6	0	5.4	0	0		0	0	0				3.6	0					0	0	0
30032019	含有其他头孢菌素的混合药品(两种或两种以上成分混合而成的,治病或防病用未配定剂量或非零售包装)	6	0	5.4	0	0		0	0	0				3.6	0					0	0	0
30032090	其他含有其他抗菌素的混合药品(两种或两种以上成分混合而成的,治病或防病用未配定剂量或非零售包装)	6	0	4.2	0	0		0	0	0				3.6	0					0	0	0
30033100	含有胰岛素但不含抗菌素的混合药品(两种或两种以上成分混合而成的,治病或防病用未配定剂量或非零售包装)	5	0	3.5	0	0		0	0	0				0	0					0	0	0
30033900	含激素(胰岛素除外)或税目29.37其他产品,但不含抗菌素的混合药品(两种或两种以上成分混合而成的,治病或防病用未配定剂量或非零售包装)	6	0	4.2	0	0		0	0	0				3.6	0					0	0	0
30034010	含奎宁或其盐,但不含抗菌素及税目2937的产品的混合药品(两种或两种以上成分混合而成的,治病或防病用未配定剂量或非零售包装)	5	0		0	0		0	0	0				0	0					0	0	0
30034090	含生物碱及其衍生物(奎宁或其盐除外),但不含抗菌素及税目2937的激素或其他产品的混合药品(两种或两种以上成分混合而成的,治病或防病用未配定剂量或非零售包装)	5	0		0	0		0	0	0				0	0					0	0	0
30039010	含磺胺类的混合药品(两种或两种以上成分混合而成的,治病或防病用未配定剂量或非零售包装)	6	0	4.2	0	0		0	0	0		0		3.6	0					0	0	0
30039020	含有青蒿素及其衍生物药品	5	0		0	0		0	0	0		0		0	0					0	0	0
30039090	含其他成份混合药品(两种或两种以上成分混合而成的,治病或防病用未配定剂量或非零售包装)	5	0		0	0		0	0	0		0		3.9	0					0	0	0
30041011	氨苄青霉素制剂(混合,治病或防病用,已配定剂量或制成零售包装)	6	0	4.5	0	0		0	0	0	0	0		3.6	0					0	0	0

税则号列	货品名称	最惠国	协定税率												特惠税率						
			东盟统一	亚太5国	智利	巴基斯坦	新加坡	新西兰	秘鲁	哥达	香港	澳门	台湾	瑞士	冰岛	亚太2国	老挝	柬埔寨	缅甸	LDC1	LDC2	LDC3
30041012	羟氨苄青霉素制剂(两种或两种以上成分混合而成的,治病或防病用,已配定剂量或制成零售包装)	6	0	4.5	0	0		0	0	0	0	0		3.6	0					0	0	0
30041013	青霉素V制剂(两种或两种以上成分混合而成的,治病或防病用,已配定剂量或制成零售包装)	6	0	4.5	0	0		0	0	0	0	0		3.6	0					0	0	0
30041019	其他青霉素制剂(混合或非混合,治病或防病用,已配定剂量或制成零售包装)	6	0	4.5	0	0		0	0	0	0	0		3.6	0					0	0	0
30041090	含有其他青霉素及具有青霉烷酸结构的青霉素衍生物或链霉素及其衍生物的药品(混合或非混合,治病或防病用,已配定剂量或制成零售包装)	6	0	4.5	0	0		0	0	0	0	0		3.6	0					0	0	0
30042011	头孢噻肟制剂(混合或非混合,治病或防病用已配定剂量或制成零售包装)	6	0	5	0	0		0	0	0	0			3.6	0					0	0	0
30042012	头孢他啶制剂(混合或非混合,治病或防病用,已配定剂量或制成零售包装)	6	0	5	0	0		0	0	0	0			3.6	0					0	0	0
30042013	头孢西丁制剂(混合或非混合,治病或防病用,已配定剂量或制成零售包装)	6	0	5	0	0		0	0	0	0			3.6	0					0	0	0
30042014	头孢替唑制剂(混合或非混合,治病或防病用,已配定剂量或制成零售包装)	6	0	5	0	0		0	0	0	0			3.6	0					0	0	0
30042015	头孢克罗制剂(混合或非混合,治病或防病用,已配定剂量或制成零售包装)	6	0	5	0	0		0	0	0	0			3.6	0					0	0	0
30042016	头孢呋辛制剂(混合或非混合,治病或防病用,已配定剂量或制成零售包装)	6	0	5	0	0		0	0	0	0			3.6	0					0	0	0
30042017	头孢三嗪(头孢曲松)制剂(混合或非混合,治病或防病用,已配定剂量或制成零售包装)	6	0	5	0	0		0	0	0	0			3.6	0					0	0	0
30042018	头孢哌酮制剂(混合或非混合,治病或防病用,已配定剂量或制成零售包装)	6	0	5	0	0		0	0	0	0			3.6	0					0	0	0
30042019	含有其他头孢菌素制剂(混合或非混合,治病或防病用,已配定剂量或制成零售包装)	6	0	5	0	0		0	0	0	0			3.6	0					0	0	0
30042090	含有其他抗菌素的药品(混合或非混合,治病或防病用,已配定剂量或制成零售包装)	6	0	4.2	0	0		0	0	0	0	0		4.8	0					0	0	0
30043110	含有重组人胰岛素但不含抗菌素的药品(混合或非混合,治病或防病用已配定剂量或零售包装)	5	0	3.5	0	0		0	0	0				0	0					0	0	0
30043190	含有其他胰岛素但不含抗菌素的药品(混合或非混合,治病或防病用已配定剂量或零售包装)	5	0	3.5	0	0		0	0	0				0	0					0	0	0
30043200	含肾上腺皮混合或非混合质激素但不含抗菌素的药品(,治病或防病用已配定剂量或零售包装)	5	0	3.5	0	0		0	0	0	0			0	0					0	0	0
30043900	含有税目29.37其他产品但不含抗菌素的药品(混合或非混合,治病或防病用已配定剂量或零售包装)	5	0	3.5	0	0		0	0	0	0			4	0					0	0	0
30044010	含有奎宁或其盐,但不含抗菌素及税目29.37的产品的药品(混合或非混合,治病或防病用已配定剂量或零售包装)	5	0	4	0	0		0	0	0	0			0	0					0	0	0
30044090	含有其他生物碱及其衍生物,但不含抗菌素及税目29.37的产品的药品(混合或非混合,治病或防病用已配定剂量或零售包装)	5	0		0	0		0	0	0	0			0	0					0	0	0
30045000	含有维生素或税目29.36其他产品的其他药品(混合或非混合,治病或防病用已配定剂量或零售包装)	6	0	5	0	0		0	0	0		0		3.6	0					0	0	0

税则号列	货品名称	最惠国	协定税率													特惠税率					
			东盟统一	亚太5国	智利	巴基斯坦	新加坡	新西兰	秘鲁	哥达	香港	澳门	台湾	瑞士	冰岛	亚太2国	老挝	柬埔寨	缅甸	LDC1	LDC2	LDC3
30049010	含有磺胺类的药品(两种或两种以上成分混合而成的,治病或防病用已配定剂量或零售包装)	6	0	4.2	0	0		0	0	0	0	0		3.6	0					0	0	0
30049020	含联苯双酯的药品(混合或非混合,治病或防病用已配定剂量或零售包装)	4	0	2.8	0	0		0	0	0		0		0	0					0	0	0
30049051	中药酒(混合或非混合,治病或防病用已配定剂量或零售包装)	3	0	2	0	0		0	0	0	0	0		0	0					0	0	0
30049052	片仔癀(混合或非混合,治病或防病用已配定剂量或零售包装)	3	0	2	0	0		0	0	0	0	0		0	0					0	0	0
30049053	白药(混合或非混合,治病或防病用已配定剂量或零售包装)	3	0	2	0	0		0	0	0	0	0		0	0					0	0	0
30049054	清凉油(混合或非混合,治病或防病用已配定剂量或零售包装)	3	0	2	0	0		0	0	0	0	0		0	0					0	0	0
30049055	安宫牛黄丸	3	0	2	0	0		0	0	0	0	0		0	0					0	0	0
30049059	其他中式成药(混合或非混合,治病或防病用已配定剂量或零售包装)	3	0	2	0	0		0	0	0	0	0		0	0					0	0	0
30049060	含有青蒿素及其衍生物的中成药	4	0		0	0		0	0	0	0	0		0	0					0	0	0
30049090	其他药品(混合或非混合,治病或防病用已配定剂量或零售包装)	4	0	2.8	0	0		0	0	0	0	0		3.2	0					0	0	
30051010	橡皮膏(经药物浸涂或制定零售包装供医疗、外科、牙科或兽医用)	5	0		0	0		0	0	0		0		0	0					0	0	0
30051090	其他胶粘敷料及有胶粘涂层的物品(经药物浸涂或制定零售包装供医疗、外科、牙科或兽医用)	5	0		0	0		0	0	0		0		0						0	0	0
30059010	药棉、纱布、绷带(经药物浸涂或制定零售包装供医疗、外科、牙科或兽医用)	5	0	3	0	0		0	0	0	0			0	0					0	0	0
30059090	其他医用软填料及类似物品(经药物浸涂或制定零售包装供医疗、外科、牙科或兽医用)	5	0		0	0		0	0	0	0	0		0						0	0	0
30061000	无菌外科肠线;无菌昆布、无菌粘合胶布、无菌吸收性止血材料、外科或牙科用无菌抗粘连阻隔材料及类似无菌材料	5	0		0	0		0	0	0	0	0		3	0					0	0	0
30062000	血型试剂	3	0		0	0		0	0	0				2.4	0					0	0	0
30063000	X光检查造影剂;诊断试剂	4	0		0	0		0	0	0				2.4	0					0	0	0
30064000	牙科粘固剂及其他牙科填料(包括骨骼粘固剂)	5	0		0	0		0	0	0				3	0					0	0	0
30065000	急救药箱、药包	5	0		0	0		0	0	0				0	0					0	0	0
30066010	以激素等为基本成分的化学避孕药	0																		0	0	0
30066090	其他化学避孕药物	0																		0	0	0
30067000	专用于人类或作兽药用的凝胶制品,作为外科手术或体检时躯体部位的润滑剂,或者作为躯体和医疗器械之间的偶合剂	6.5	0		0	5		0	0	0	0			3.9	0					0	0	0
30069100	可确定用于造口术用具	10	0	9.2	0	9.2	0	0	0	0	0	0		6	0					0	0	0
30069200	废药物	5	0		0	0		0	0	0				0	0					0	0	0
31010011	未经化学处理的鸟粪	3	0		0	0		0	0	0				0	0					0	0	0
31010019	未经化学处理的其他动植物肥料	6.5	0		0	5		0	0	0		0		3.9	0					0	0	0
31010090	动植物产品经混合或化学处理的制成的肥料	4	0		0	0		0	0	0	0			0	0					0	0	0
31021000	尿素(不论是否水溶液)	50	50	40		40					0											
31022100	硫酸铵	4	0		0	0		0	0	0				0	0					0	0	
31022900	硫酸铵和硝酸铵的复盐及混合物	4	0		0	0		0	0	0				0	0					0	0	
31023000	硝酸铵(不论是否水溶液)	4	0		0	0		0	0	0				0	0					0	0	
31024000	硝酸铵与碳酸钙或其他无肥效无机物的混合物	4	0		0	0		0	0	0				0	0					0	0	
31025000	硝酸钠	4	0		0	0		0	0	0				0	0					0	0	
31026000	硝酸钙和硝酸铵的复盐及混合物	4	0		0	0		0	0	0				0	0					0	0	
31028000	尿素及硝酸铵混合物的水溶液或氨水溶液	4	0		0	0		0	0	0				0	0					0	0	
31029010	氰氨化钙	4	0		0	0		0	0	0				0	0					0	0	

税则号列	货品名称	最惠国	协定税率													特惠税率						
			东盟统一	亚太5国	智利	巴基斯坦	新加坡	新西兰	秘鲁	哥斯达	香港	澳门	台湾	瑞士	冰岛	亚太2国	老挝	柬埔寨	缅甸	LDC1	LDC2	LDC3
31029090	其他矿物氮肥及化学氮肥,包括上述子目未列名的混合物	4	0		0	0		0	0	0				0	0					0	0	
31031010	重过磷酸钙	4	0		0	0		0	0	0				0	0					0	0	
31031090	其他过磷酸钙	4	0		0	0		0	0	0				0	0					0	0	
31039000	其他矿物磷肥或化学磷肥	4	0		0	0		0	0	0				0	0					0	0	
31042020	纯氯化钾	3	0		0	0		0	0	0				0	0					0	0	
31042090	其他氯化钾	3	0		0	0		0	0	0				0	0					0	0	
31043000	硫酸钾	3	0		0	0		0	0	0				0	0					0	0	
31049010	光卤石、钾盐及其他天然粗钾盐	3	0		0	0		0	0	0				0	0					0	0	
31049090	其他矿物钾肥及化学钾肥	3	0		0	0		0	0	0				0	0					0	0	
31051000	制成片状及类似形状或每包毛重不超过10公斤的31章各货品	4	0		0	0		0	0	0	0			0	0					0	0	
31052000	含氮、磷、钾三种肥效元素的肥料	50	50								0											
31053000	磷酸氢二铵	50	50																			
31054000	磷酸二氢铵及磷酸二氢铵与磷酸氢二铵的混合物	4	0		0	0		0	0	0				0	0					0	0	
31055100	含有硝酸盐及磷酸盐的肥料	4	0		0	0		0	0	0	0			0	0					0	0	
31055900	其他含氮、磷两种肥效元素的矿物肥料或化学肥料	4	0		0	0		0	0	0				0	0					0	0	
31056000	含磷、钾两种元素的肥料	4	0		0	0		0	0	0	0			0	0					0	0	
31059000	其他肥料	4	0		0	0		0	0	0	0			0	0					0	0	
32011000	坚木浸膏	5	0		0	0		0	0	0				0	0					0	0	
32012000	荆树皮浸膏	6.5	0		0	5		0	0	0				3.9	0					0	0	
32019010	其他植物鞣料浸膏	6.5	0		0	5		0	0	0				3.9	0					0	0	
32019090	鞣酸及其盐、醚、酯和其他衍生物	6.5	0		0	5		0	0	0				3.9	0					0	0	
32021000	有机合成鞣料	6.5	0		0	5		0	0	0	0			3.9	0					0	0	
32029000	无机鞣料;鞣料制剂等,不论是否含有天然鞣料;预鞣用酶制剂	6.5	0		0	5		0	0	0	0	0		3.9	0					0	0	
32030011	天然靛蓝及以其为基本成分的制品,包括染料浸膏(不论是否已有化学定义)	6.5	0		0	5		0	4.6	0				3.9	0					0	0	0
32030019	其他植物质着色料及以其为基本成分的制品包括染料浸膏(不论是否已有化学定义);32章注释三所述的以植物质着色料为基本成分的制品	6.5	0		0	5		0	4.6	0		0		3.9	0					0	0	0
32030020	动物质着色料及以其为基本成分的制品包括染料浸膏(不论是否已有化学定义,但动物炭黑除外);32章注释三所述的以动物质着色料为基本成分的制品	6.5	0		0	5		0	4.6	0				3.9	0					0	0	0
32041100	分散染料及以其为基本成分的制品(不论是否已有化学定义)	6.5	0	5.8	0	0		0	0	0					0					0	0	0
32041200	酸性染料(不论是否预金属络合)及以其为基本成分的制品(不论是否已有化学定义);媒染染料及以其为基本成分的制品(不论是否已有化学定义)	6.5	0	5.8	0	0		0	0	0	0		0	5	0					0	0	0
32041300	碱性染料及以其为基本成分的制品(不论是否已有化学定义)	6.5	0	6	0	0		0	0	0				3.9	0					0	0	0
32041400	直接染料及以其为基本成分的制品(不论是否已有化学定义)	6.5	0	6	0	0		0	0	0			0	5.2	0					0	0	0
32041510	合成靛蓝(还原靛蓝)(不论是否已有化学定义)	6.5	0	6	0	0		0	0	0				3.9	0					0	0	0
32041590	其他瓮染料(包括颜料用的)及以其为基本成分的制品(不论是否已有化学定义)	6.5	0	6	0	0		0	0	0				3.9	0					0	0	0
32041600	活性染料及以其为基本成分的制品(不论是否已有化学定义)	6.5	0	5.8	0	0		0	0	0	0		0	5	0					0	0	0
32041700	颜料及以其为基本成分的制品(不论是否已有化学定义)	6.5	0	4.6	0	0		0	0	0	0		0	5.2	0					0	0	0
32041911	硫化黑(硫化青)及以其为基本成分的制品(不论是否已有化学定义)	6.5	0	6	0	0		0	0	0				3.9	0					0	0	0
32041919	其他硫化染料及以其为基本成分的制品(不论是否已有化学定义)	6.5	0	6	0	0		0	0	0				3.9	0					0	0	0

税则号列	货品名称	最惠国	协定税率 东盟统一	亚太5国	智利	巴基斯坦	新加坡	新西兰	秘鲁	哥达	香港	澳门	台湾	瑞士	冰岛	特惠税率 亚太2国	老挝	柬埔寨	缅甸	LDC1	LDC2	LDC3
32041990	由子目号3204.11至3204.19中两个或多个子目所列着色料组成的混合物,(不论是否已有化学定义)	6.5	0	6	0	0		0	0	0			0		0					0	0	0
32042000	用作萤光增白剂的有机合成产品(不论是否已有化学定义)	6.5	0	6	0	0		0	0	0	0		0	5	0					0	0	0
32049010	生物染色剂及染料指示剂(不论是否已有化学定义)	6.5	0	6	0	0		0	0	0				5.2	0					0	0	0
32049090	其他用作发光体的有机合成产品(不论是否已有化学定义)	6.5	0	6	0	0		0	0	0				3.9	0					0	0	0
32050000	色淀及32章注释三所述的以色淀为基本成分的制品	6.5	0		0	5		0	0	0				3.9	0					0	0	0
32061110	钛白粉	6.5	0		0	5		0	0	0			0	3.9	0					0	0	0
32061190	干量计二氧化钛≥80%的颜料及制品,钛白粉除外	6.5	0		0	5		0	0	0				3.9	0					0	0	0
32061900	二氧化钛为基料的颜料及制品,干量计二氧化钛<80%	10	0		0	5	0	0	0	0	0		0	6	0					0	0	0
32062000	铬化合物为基本成分的颜料及制品	6.5	0		0	5		0	0	0				3.9	0					0	0	0
32064100	群青及以其为基本成分的制品	6.5	0		0	5		0	0	0				3.9	0					0	0	0
32064210	锌钡白	6.5	0		0	5		0	0	0				3.9	0					0	0	0
32064290	其他以硫化锌为基本成份的颜料和制品	6.5	0		0	5		0	0	0				3.9	0					0	0	0
32064911	以钒酸铋为基本成分的颜料及制品	6.5	0	3.3	0	0		0	0	0	0		0	3.9	0					0	0	0
32064919	其他以铋化合物为基本成分的颜料及制品	6.5	0	3.3	0	0		0	0	0	0		0	3.9	0					0	0	0
32064990	其他着色料及其他制品	6.5	0	3.3	0	0		0	0	0	0		0	3.9	0					0	0	0
32065000	用作发光体的无机产品,不论是否已有化学定义	6.5	0	5.9	0	5		0	0	0				3.9	0					0	0	0
32071000	调制颜料、遮光剂、着色剂及类似制品(用于陶瓷、搪瓷及玻璃工业)	5	0		0	0		0	0	0				0	0					0	0	0
32072000	珐琅和釉料、釉底料及类似制品(用于陶瓷、搪瓷及玻璃工业)	5	0		0	0		0	0	0				0	0					0	0	0
32073000	光瓷釉及类似制品(用于陶瓷、搪瓷及玻璃工业)	5	0		0	0		0	0	0				0	0					0	0	0
32074000	呈粉、粒状搪瓷玻璃料及其他玻璃	5	0		0	0		0	0	0				0	0					0	0	0
32081000	分散或溶于非水介质的聚酯油漆及清漆等	10	0	9	0	5	0	0	4	0	0	0	0	6	0					0	0	0
32082010	分散或溶于非水介质的丙烯酸聚合物油漆及清漆	10	0	9	0	5	0	0	4	0			0	6	0					0	0	
32082020	分散或溶于非水介质的乙烯聚合物油漆及清漆	10	0	9	0	5		0	4	0				6	0					0	0	
32089010	分散或溶于非水介质的聚胺酯类油漆及清漆	10	0	9	0	5	0	0	4	0				6	0					0	0	
32089090	分散或溶于非水介质其他油漆、清漆溶液	10	0	9	0	5	0	0	4	0	0	0	0	8	0					0	0	
32091000	分散或溶于水介质的丙烯酸聚合物或乙烯聚合物油漆及清漆	10	0	9	0	5	0	0	4	0		0		6	0					0	0	0
32099010	以环氧树脂为基本成分的溶于水介质其他聚合物油漆及清漆	10	0		0	5	0	0	0	0			0	6	0					0	0	
32099020	以氟树脂为基本成分的溶于水介质其他聚合物油漆及清漆	10	0		0	5	0	0	0	0				6	0					0	0	
32099090	溶于水介质其他聚合物油漆及清漆	10	0		0	5	0	0	0	0	0		0	8	0					0	0	
32100000	其他油漆及清漆(包括瓷漆\大漆及水浆涂料);皮革用水性颜料	10	0	9	0	5	0	0	4	0	0	0	0	6	0					0	0	0
32110000	配制的催干剂	10	0		0	5	0	0	0	0				8	0					0	0	
32121000	压印箔	15	0		0	12	0	0	6	0				12	0					0	0	
32129000	制漆用颜料(分散于非水介质中呈液状或浆状的)及零售形状或零售包装的染料、色料	10	0		0	5	0	0	0	0				6	0					0	0	
32131000	成套的颜料(艺术家、学生和广告美工用的)	10	0		0	5		0	4	0				6	0					0	0	

税则号列	货品名称	最惠国	协定税率													特惠税率						
			东盟统一	亚太5国	智利	巴基斯坦	新加坡	新西兰	秘鲁	哥达	香港	澳门	台湾	瑞士	冰岛	亚太2国	老挝	柬埔寨	缅甸	LDC1	LDC2	LDC3
32139000	非成套颜料、调色料及类似品(艺术家、学生和广告美工用的,片状、管装、罐装、瓶装、扁盒装等类似形状或包装的)	10	0	9	0	5		0	0	0				6	0					0	0	0
32141010	半导体器件封装材料	9	0		0	5		0	0	0				5.4	0					0	0	0
32141090	其他安装玻璃用油灰、接缝用油灰、树脂胶泥、嵌缝胶及其他类似胶粘剂;漆工用填料	9	0		0	5		0	0	0				7.2	0					0	0	0
32149000	非耐火涂面制剂,涂门面、内墙、地板、天花板等用	9	0		0	5		0	0	0	0			5.4	0					0	0	0
32151100	黑色印刷油墨(不论是否固体或浓缩)	6.5	0	4.6	0	0		0	0	0	0	0		3.9	0					0	0	0
32151900	其他印刷油墨(不论是否固体或浓缩),黑色印刷油墨除外	6.5	0	4.6	0	0		0	0	0	0	0	0	5.2	0					0	0	0
32159010	书写墨水(不论是否固体或浓缩)	6.5	0		0	5		0	0	0	0	0		3.9	0					0	0	0
32159020	水性喷墨墨水	10	0		0	5	0	0	0	0	0	0		8	0					0	0	0
32159090	绘图墨水及其他墨类(不论是否固体或浓缩)	10	0		0	5	0	0	0	0	0	0		8	0					0	0	0
33011200	橙油(包括浸膏及净油)	20	0		0		0	0	8	0		0		16.7	0					0	0	
33011300	柠檬油(包括浸膏及净油)	20	0		0		0	0	0	0		0		12	0					0	0	0
33011910	白柠檬油(酸橙油)(包括浸膏及净油)	20	0		0		0	0	0	0		0		16	0					0	0	
33011990	其他柑桔属果实的精油(包括浸膏及净油)	20	0		0		0	0	0	0		0		16	0					0	0	
33012400	胡椒薄荷油(包括浸膏及净油)	20	0		0		0	0	8	0		0		16	0					0	0	
33012500	其他薄荷油(包括浸膏及净油)	15	0	14	0	12	0	0	6	0		0		12	0					0	0	0
33012910	樟脑油(包括浸膏及净油)	20	0		0		0	0	8	0		0		16	0					0	0	
33012920	香茅油(包括浸膏及净油)	15	0		0	12	0	0	6	0		0		12	0					0	0	0
33012930	茴香油(包括浸膏及净油)	20	0		0		0	0	8	0		0		16	0					0	0	
33012940	桂油(包括浸膏及净油)	20	0		0		0	0	8	0		0		16	0					0	0	
33012950	山苍子油(包括浸膏及净油)	20	0		0		0	0	8	0		0		16	0					0	0	
33012960	桉叶油(包括浸膏及净油)	20	0		0		0	0	8	0		0		16	0					0	0	
33012991	老鹳草油(香叶油)(包括浸膏及净油)	20	0		0		0	0	8	0		0		16	0					0	0	
33012999	其他非柑桔属果实的精油(包括浸膏及净油)	15	0		0	12	0	0	0	0		0		12	0					0	0	0
33013010	鸢尾凝脂	20	0		0		0	0	8	0		0		16	0					0	0	
33013090	其他香膏	20	0		0		0	0	8	0		0		16	0					0	0	
33019010	提取的油树脂	20	0	18	0	18	0	0	0	0		0		16	0					0	0	
33019020	柑桔属果实的精油脱萜所得的萜烯副产品	20	0	18	0	18	0	0	0	0		0		16	0					0	0	
33019090	用花香吸取法或浸渍法制定的含浓缩精油的脂肪、固定油、蜡及类似品;精油脱萜所得的萜烯副产品(柑桔属果实的除外);精油水溶液及水馏液	20	0	18	0	18	0	0	0	0		0		16	0					0	0	0
33021010	生产饮料用的混合香料以及以香料为基本成分的制品,按容量计酒精浓度≤0.5%	15	0	12.8	0	7.5	0	0	6	0		0		12	0					0	0	
33021090	其他食品或饮料工业用混合香料以及以香料为基本成分的制品	15	0		0	12	0	0	6	0		0		12	0					0	0	0
33029000	其他工业用混合香料及以香料为基本成分的混合物和制品	10	0		0	5	0	0	4	0	0	0		6	0					0	0	0
33030000	香水及花露水	10	0	8.2	0	5	0	0	0	0	0	0		6	0					0	0	0
33041000	唇用化妆品	10	0		0	5	0	0	0	0	0	0		6	0					0	0	
33042000	眼用化妆品	10	0		0	5	0	0	0	0	0	0		6	0					0	0	
33043000	指(趾)甲化妆品	15	0		0	12	0	0	6	0	0	0		12	0					0	0	
33049100	香粉,不论是否压紧	10	0		0	5	0	0	0	0	0	0		6	0					0	0	
33049900	其他美容品或化妆品及护肤品	6.5	0		0	5.2	0	0	0	0	0	0		3.9	4.3					0	0	

税则号列	货品名称	最惠国	协定税率													特惠税率						
			东盟统一	亚太5国	智利	巴基斯坦	新加坡	新西兰	秘鲁	哥达	香港	澳门	台湾	瑞士	冰岛	亚太2国	老挝	柬埔寨	缅甸	LDC1	LDC2	LDC3
33051000	洗发剂(香波)	6.5	0	5.4	0	5	0	0	0	0	0	0		3.9						0	0	0
33052000	烫发剂	15	0		0	12	0	0	6	0		0		12	0					0	0	
33053000	定型剂	15	0		0	12	0	0	6	0		0		12	0					0	0	
33059000	其他护发品	10	0	8.5	0	5	0	0	0	0	0	0		6						0	0	0
33061010	牙膏	10	0	7	0	5	0	0	0	0	0	0		6	0					0	0	0
33061090	其他洁齿品	10	0	7	0	5	0	0	0	0				6	0					0	0	
33062000	牙线	10	0	9.2	0	5		0	0	0				6	0					0	0	
33069000	其他口腔及牙齿清洁剂	10	0		0	5	0	0	0	0	0	0		6	0					0	0	
33071000	剃须用制剂	10	0	7	0	5	0	0	0	0				6	0					0	0	
33072000	人体除臭剂及止汗剂	10	0	7	0	5	0	0	0	0		0		6	0					0	0	
33073000	香浴盐及其他沐浴用制剂	10	0	8.5	0	5	0	0	0	0	0	0		6	0					0	0	
33074100	神香及其他通过燃烧散发香气制品	10	0		0	5	0	0	0	0	0			6	0					0	0	0
33074900	室内除臭制品	10	0		0	5	0	0	0	0	0			6	0					0	0	0
33079000	脱毛剂、其他编号未列名的芳香料制品及化妆盥洗品	9	0	6.3	0	5		0	0	0		0		5.4	0					0	0	0
34011100	盥洗用肥皂及有机表面活性产品,条状、块状或模制形状的,以及用肥皂或洗涤剂浸渍、涂面或包覆的纸、絮胎、毡呢及无纺织物	10	0	8.3	0	8.3	0	0	0	0	0	0		6	0	0				0	0	0
34011910	洗衣皂	10	0		0	5	0	0	0	0		0		6	0					0	0	0
34011990	其他用肥皂及有机表面活性产品,条状、块状或模制形状的,以及用肥皂或洗涤剂浸渍、涂面或包覆的纸、絮胎、毡呢及无纺织物	15	0		0	12		0	6	0				12	0					0	0	
34012000	其他形状的肥皂	15	0	12.4	0	7.5		0	6	0	0	0		12	0	0				0	0	0
34013000	洁肤用的有机表面活性产品及制品,液状或膏状并制成零售包装的,不论是否含有肥皂	10	0		0	5	0	0	0	0		0		6	0					0	0	0
34021100	阴离子型有机表面活性剂	6.5	0	6	0	5		0	0	0	0	0		3.9	0					0	0	0
34021200	阳离子型有机表面活性剂	6.5	0	6	0	5		0	0	0	0	0		3.9	0					0	0	0
34021300	非离子型有机表面活性剂	6.5	0	5.9	0	5		0	0	0	0	0	0	5.2	0					0	0	0
34021900	其他有机表面活性剂	6.5	0	6	0	5		0	0	0		0		3.9	0					0	0	0
34022010	零售包装的合成洗涤粉	10	0	8.5	0	5	0	0	0	0		0		6	0					0	0	
34022090	零售包装有机表面活性剂制品(合成洗涤粉除外)	10	0	8.5	0	5	0	0	0	0	0	0		6	0					0	0	
34029000	非零售包装有机表面活性剂制品、洗涤剂及清洁剂	9	0	7.8	0	5	0	0	0	0	0	0		7.2	0					0	0	0
34031100	用于纺织材料、皮革、毛皮或其他材料油脂处理的制剂(含有石油或从沥青矿物提取的油类且按重量计<70%)	10	0	9.5	0	5	0	0	0	0	0			6	0					0	0	
34031900	润滑剂(含有石油或从沥青矿物提取的油类且按重量计<70%)	10	0		0	5	0	0	0	0	0			0	0					0	0	0
34039100	用于纺织、皮革、毛皮或其他材料油脂处理的制剂(不含有石油或从沥青矿物提取的油类)	10	0		0	5	0	0	4	0	0			6	0					0	0	
34039900	润滑剂(不含有石油或从沥青矿物提取的油类)	10	0		0	5	0	0	4	0		0		8	0					0	0	
34042000	聚乙二醇蜡	10	0		0	5		0	0	0				6	0					0	0	
34049000	其他人造蜡及调制蜡	10	0		0	5		0	4	0				6	0					0	0	0
34051000	鞋靴或皮革用的上光剂及类似制品	10	0		0	5	0	0	4	0	0			6	0					0	0	
34052000	保养木制品的上光剂及类似制品	10	0		0	5	0	0	4	0	0			6	0					0	0	
34053000	车身用的上光剂及类似制品	10	0		0	5	0	0	4	0				6	0					0	0	
34054000	擦洗膏、去污粉及类似制品	10	0		0	5		0	0	0				6	0					0	0	
34059000	玻璃或金属用的光洁剂	10	0	8.5	0	5	0	0	4	0	0			6	0					0	0	
34060000	各种蜡烛及类似品	10	0		0	5	0	0	0	0		0		6	0					0	0	
34070010	牙科用蜡及造型膏	6.5	0		0	5		0	0	0				5.2	0					0	0	0
34070020	以熟石膏为成分的牙科用其他制品	6.5	0		0	5		0	0	0				3.9	0					0	0	0
34070090	塑型用膏	10	0		0	5		0	0	0				6	0					0	0	
35011000	酪蛋白	10	0		0	5	0	0	0	0				6	0					0	0	
35019000	酪蛋白衍生物;酪蛋白胶	10	0		0	5		0	4	0				6	0					0	0	

税则号列	货品名称	最惠国	协定税率												特惠税率						
			东盟统一	亚太5国	智利	巴基斯坦	新加坡	新西兰	秘鲁	哥达	香港	澳门	台湾	瑞士	冰岛	亚太2国	老挝	柬埔寨	缅甸	LDC1	LDC2	LDC3
35021100	干的卵清蛋白	10	0		0	5		0	0	0				6	0					0	0	
35021900	其他卵清蛋白	10	0		0	5		0	0	0				6	0					0	0	
35022000	乳白蛋白,包括两种或两种以上的乳清蛋白浓缩物	10	0		0	5		0	0	0				6	0					0	0	
35029000	其他白蛋白及白蛋白盐及其衍生物	10	0		0	5		0	4	0	0			6	0					0	0	
35030010	明胶及其衍生物	12	0		0	6	0	0	0	0				9.6	0					0	0	
35030090	鱼胶;其他动物胶	12	0		0	6	0	0	0	0				9.6	0					0	0	
35040010	蛋白胨	3	0		0	0		0	0	0		0		0	0					0	0	0
35040090	其他税号未列名蛋白质及其衍生物,皮粉	8	0		0	5		0	0	0		0		4.8	0					0	0	0
35051000	糊精及其他改性淀粉	12	0		0	6	0	0	4.8	0	0	0		9.6	0					0	0	
35052000	以淀粉、糊精或其他改性淀粉为基本成分的胶	20	0		0		0	0	8	0				16	0					0	0	
35061000	适于作胶或粘合剂的产品,零售包装每件净重≤1kg	10	0	9.2	0	5	0	0	4	0	0		0	8						0	0	0
35069110	以聚酰胺为基本成份的粘合剂	10	0	7	0	5	0	0	4	0	0	0	0	6	0					0	0	0
35069120	以环氧树脂为基本成分的粘合剂	10	0	7	0	5	0	0	4	0	0	0	0	8	0					0	0	0
35069190	以其他橡胶或塑料为基本成分的粘合剂	10	0	7	0	5	0	0	4	0	0	0	0	8	0					0	0	0
35069900	其他调制胶、粘合剂	10	0	8.6	0	5	0	0	4	0	0	0	0	8	0					0	0	0
35071000	粗制凝乳酶及其浓缩物	6	0		0	5		0	0	0				3.6	0					0	0	0
35079010	碱性蛋白酶	6	0		0	5		0	0	0				3.6	0					0	0	0
35079020	碱性脂肪酶	6	0		0	5		0	0	0				3.6	0					0	0	0
35079090	其他酶及未列名的酶制品	6	0		0	5		0	0	0		0		3.6	0					0	0	0
36010000	发射药	9	0		0	5		0	0	0				5.4	0					0	0	
36020010	硝铵炸药,但发射药除外	9	0		0	5		0	0	0				5.4	0					0	0	
36020090	其他配制炸药,但发射药除外	9	0		0	5		0	0	0				5.4	0					0	0	
36030000	安全导火索、导爆索;火帽或雷管;引爆器;电雷管	9	0		0	5		0	0	0				5.4	0					0	0	0
36041000	烟花、爆竹	6	0		0	5		0	0	0				3.6	0					0	0	
36049000	信号弹、降雨火箭、浓雾信号弹及其他烟火制品	6	0		0	5		0	0	0				3.6	0					0	0	
36050000	火柴,但税目3604的烟火制品除外	6	0		0	5		0	0	0				3.6	0					0	0	0
36061000	灌注打火机等用的液体或液化气体燃料,其包装容器的容积≤300cm3	10	0		0	5		0	0	0	0			6	0					0	0	
36069011	已切成形可直接使用的铈铁及其他引火合金	9	0		0	5		0	0	0				5.4	0					0	0	0
36069019	未切成形不可直接使用的铈铁及其他引火合金	9	0		0	5		0	0	0				5.4	0					0	0	0
36069090	其他易燃材料制品	9	0		0	5		0	0	0				5.4	0					0	0	0
37011000	未曝光的X光感光硬片及平面软片,用纸、纸板及纺织物以外任何材料制成	20	20		0			0	8	0				16	0					0	0	
37012000	未曝光的一次成像感光平片,用纸、纸板及纺织物以外任何材料制成	5	0		0	0		0	0	0				3.9	0					0	0	0
37013021	激光照排片(任何一边超过255mm),用纸、纸板及纺织物以外任何材料制成	10	10		0			0	0	0		0		8	0					0	0	
37013022	PS版(预涂感光版)(任何一边超过255mm),用纸、纸板及纺织物以外任何材料制成	10	10		0			0	0	0		0		6	0					0	0	
37013024	CTP版	10	0		0	5		0	0	0		0		6	0					0	0	
37013025	柔性印刷版	10	10		0			0	0	0		0		8	0					0	0	
37013029	其他未曝光照相制版用感光硬片及软片(任何一边超过255mm),用纸、纸板及纺织物以外任何材料制成	10	10		0			0	0	0		0		8	0					0	0	
37013090	未曝光其他用途的感光硬片及软片(任何一边超过255mm),用纸、纸板及纺织物以外任何材料制成	20	0		0		0	0	8	0				16	0					0	0	
37019100	彩色摄影用未曝光彩色硬片及平面软片,用纸、纸板及纺织物以外任何材料制成,任何一边≤255mm	22	0		0		0	0	8.8	0				17.6	0					0	0	

税则号列	货品名称	最惠国	协定税率													特惠税率						
			东盟统一	亚太5国	智利	巴基斯坦	新加坡	新西兰	秘鲁	哥达	香港	澳门	台湾	瑞士	冰岛	亚太2国	老挝	柬埔寨	缅甸	LDC1	LDC2	LDC3
37019920	照相制版用其他未曝光软片及硬片,用纸、纸板及纺织物以外任何材料制成,任何一边≤255mm	10	0		0	5		0	4	0				6	0					0	0	
37019990	其他用未曝光软片及硬片,用纸、纸板及纺织物以外任何材料制成,任何一边≤255mm	25	0		0		0	0	10	0				20	0					0	0	
37021000	成卷的未曝光的X光感光胶片,用纸、纸板及纺织物以外任何材料制成	10	10		0			0	0	0				6	0					0	0	
37023110	彩色摄影用未曝光一次成像感光卷片,宽度≤105 mm,用纸、纸板及纺织物以外任何材料制成	5	0		0	0		0	0	0				0	0					0	0	0
37023190	彩色摄影用未曝光无齿孔彩色胶卷,宽度≤105 mm,用纸、纸板及纺织物以外任何材料制成	40	0		0		0	0	16	0					0					0	0	
37023210	照相制版用未曝光涂卤化银液无齿孔一次成像感光卷片,宽度≤105 mm,用纸、纸板及纺织物以外任何材料制成	5	0		0	0		0	0	0				0	0					0	0	0
37023220	照相制版用未曝光涂卤化银液无齿孔胶卷,宽度≤105 mm,用纸、纸板及纺织物以外任何材料制成	10	0		0	2.25元/平方米		0	0	0				6	0					0	0	
37023290	其他未曝光涂乳液无齿孔胶卷,宽度≤105 mm,用纸、纸板及纺织物以外任何材料制成	22	0		0		0	0	8.8	0				17.6	0					0	0	
37023920	照相制版用未曝光未涂卤化银无齿孔感光胶卷,宽度≤105 mm,用纸、纸板及纺织物以外任何材料制成	10	0		0	6元/平方米		0	0	0				6	0					0	0	
37023990	其他未曝光未涂卤化银无齿孔感光胶卷,宽度≤105 m,用纸、纸板及纺织物以外任何材料制成	22	0		0		0	0	8.8	0				17.6	0					0	0	
37024100	彩色摄影用未曝光无齿孔彩色胶卷,宽度>610 mm,长度>200m,用纸、纸板及纺织物以外任何材料制成	16	16		0			0	6.4	0				12.8	0					0	0	
37024221	印刷电路板制造用未曝光光致抗蚀干膜,宽度>610 mm,长度>200m,用纸、纸板及纺织物以外任何材料制成	10	0		0	0.3元/平方米	0	0	0	0				6	0					0	0	
37024229	照相制版用其他未曝光无齿孔胶卷,宽度>610 mm,长度>200m,用纸、纸板及纺织物以外任何材料制成	10	0		0	0.8元/平方米		0	0	0				6	0					0	0	
37024292	红色或红外激光胶片	16	0		0		0	0	6.4	0				12.8	0					0	0	
37024299	其他未曝光无齿孔宽长胶卷	16	0		0		0	0	6.4	0				12.8	0					0	0	
37024321	照相制版用未曝光无齿孔激光照排片,宽度>610 mm,长度≤200m,用纸、纸板及纺织物以外任何材料制成	10	0		0	0.9元/平方米		0	0	0				6	0					0	0	
37024329	其他照相制版用未曝光无齿孔胶卷,宽度>610 mm,长度≤200m,用纸、纸板及纺织物以外任何材料制成	10	0		0	1.85元/平方米		0	0	0				6	0					0	0	
37024390	其他用未曝光无齿孔胶卷,宽度610 mm,长度≤200m,用纸、纸板及纺织物以外任何材料制成	20	0		0		0	0	8	0				16	0					0	0	
37024421	照相制版用无齿孔未曝光激光照排片,105mm<宽度≤610mm,用纸、纸板及纺织物以外任何材料制成	10	0		0	1.0元/平方米		0	0	0				6	0					0	0	
37024422	印刷电路板制造用未曝光光致抗蚀干膜,105mm<宽度≤610mm,用纸、纸板及纺织物以外任何材料制成	10	0		0	0.45元/平方米		0	0	0				6	0					0	0	
37024429	其他照相制版用无齿孔未曝光胶卷,105mm<宽度≤610mm,用纸、纸板及纺织物以外任何材料制成	10	0		0	1.45元/平方米		0	0	0				6	0					0	0	
37024490	其他用无齿孔未曝光胶卷,105mm<宽度≤610mm,用纸、纸板及纺织物以外任何材料制成	20	0		0		0	0	8	0				16	0					0	0	

税则号列	货品名称	最惠国	协定税率													特惠税率						
			东盟统一	亚太5国	智利	巴基斯坦	新加坡	新西兰	秘鲁	哥达	香港	澳门	台湾	瑞士	冰岛	亚太2国	老挝	柬埔寨	缅甸	LDC1	LDC2	LDC3
37025200	彩色摄影用未曝光彩色胶卷，宽度≤16 mm	47	0		0		0	0	18.8	0					0					0	0	
37025300	幻灯片用未曝光彩色摄影胶卷，16 mm＜宽度≤35 mm，长度＜30m，用纸、纸板及纺织物以外任何材料制成	47	0		0		0	0	18.8	0	0				0					0	0	
37025410	非幻灯片用未曝光彩色胶卷，宽度35mm，长度≤2 m，用纸、纸板及纺织物以外任何材料制成	18	18		0			0	7.2	0	0			14.4	0					0	0	
37025490	非幻灯片用彩色摄影用未曝光彩色胶卷，16 mm＜宽度＜35 mm，2 m＜长度≤30m，用纸、纸板及纺织物以外任何材料制成	18	18		0			0	7.2	0	0			14.4	0					0	0	
37025520	未曝光的彩色电影胶片，16mm＜宽度≤35mm，长度＞30m，用纸、纸板及纺织物以外任何材料制成	26	20		0			0	10.4	0					0					0	0	
37025590	未曝光彩色摄影用胶卷，16mm＜宽度≤35mm，长度＞30m，用纸、纸板及纺织物以外任何材料制成，电影胶片除外	40	20		0			0		0					0					0		
37025620	未曝光的彩色电影胶片，宽度＞35mm，用纸、纸板及纺织物以外任何材料制成	24	0		0		0	0	9.6	0				19.2	0					0	0	
37025690	未曝光的彩色摄影用胶卷，宽度＞35mm，用纸、纸板及纺织物以外任何材料制成，电影胶片除外	40	0		0		0	0	16	0					0					0	0	
37029600	未曝光非彩色胶卷，宽度≤35mm，长度≤30m，用纸、纸板及纺织物以外任何材料制成	20	20					0	8	0				16	0					0	0	
37029700	未曝光的非彩色胶卷，宽度≤35mm，长度＞30m，用纸、纸板及纺织物以外任何材料制成	18	18		0	9元/平方米		0	7.2	0				14.4	0					0	0	
37029800	未曝光的非彩色胶卷，宽度＞35mm，用纸、纸板及纺织物以外任何材料制成	18	0		0	8元/平方米	0	0	7.2	0				14.4	0					0	0	
37031010	成卷未曝光的感光纸及纸板，宽度＞610mm	18	18		0			0	7.2	0				14.4	0					0	0	
37031090	成卷未曝光的感光布，宽度＞610mm	18	18		0			0	7.2	0				14.4	0					0	0	
37032010	未曝光的彩色摄影用感光纸及纸板，非成卷或宽度≤610mm	35	20		0			0		0	0				0					0		
37032090	未曝光的彩色摄影用感光布，非成卷或宽度≤610mm	18	18		0			0	7.2	0	0			14.4	0					0	0	
37039010	未曝光的非彩色摄影用感光纸及纸板，非成卷或宽度≤610mm	35	20		0			0		0					0					0		
37039090	未曝光的非彩色摄影用感光布，非成卷或宽度≤610mm	18	18		0			0	7.2	0				14.4	0					0	0	
37040010	已曝光未冲洗的电影胶片	6.5	0		0	5		0	0	0				3.9	0					0	0	
37040090	已曝光未冲洗的摄影硬片、软片、纸、纸板及纺织物，电影胶片除外	18	0		0	14.4	0	0	7.2	0				14.4	0					0	0	
37051000	已曝光已冲洗供复制胶版用摄影硬片及软片	18	0		0	14.4	0	0	7.2	0				14.4	0					0	0	
37059010	已曝光已冲洗的教学专用幻灯片	0																		0	0	0
37059021	书籍、报刊用的已曝光已冲洗的缩微胶片	0																		0	0	0
37059029	已曝光已冲洗的缩微胶片，书籍、报刊用除外	4	0		0	0		0	0	0				0	0					0	0	
37059090	已曝光已冲洗的其他摄影硬片及软片	18	0		0	14.4	0	0	7.2	0				14.4	0					0	0	
37061010	已曝光已冲洗的教学专用电影胶片，宽度≥35mm，不论是否配有声道或仅有声道	0																		0	0	0
37061090	已曝光已冲洗的电影胶片，宽度≥35mm，不论是否配有声道或仅有声道，教学专用除外	5	0		0	0		0	0	0	0			0	0					0	0	0

税则号列	货品名称	最惠国	协定税率													特惠税率						
			东盟统一	亚太5国	智利	巴基斯坦	新加坡	新西兰	秘鲁	哥达	香港	澳门	台湾	瑞士	冰岛	亚太2国	老挝	柬埔寨	缅甸	LDC1	LDC2	LDC3
37069010	已曝光已冲洗的教学专用电影胶片,宽度<35mm,不论是否配有声道或仅有声道	0																		0	0	0
37069090	已曝光已冲洗的电影胶片,宽度<35mm,不论是否配有声道或仅有声道,教学专用除外	4	0		0	0		0	0	0	0			0	0					0	0	0
37071000	摄影用感光乳液	8	0		0	5		0	0	0		0		6.4	0					0	0	0
37079010	冲洗胶卷及相片用化学制剂或摄影用未混合品(定量包装或零售包装可立即使用的)	16	0		0	12.8	0	0	6.4	0	0			12.8	0					0	0	
37079020	复印机用化学制剂或摄影用未混合品(定量包装或零售包装可立即使用的)	10	0		0	5	0	0	4	0	0	0		6	0					0	0	0
37079090	其他摄影用化学制剂或摄影用未混合品(定量包装或零售包装可立即使用的)	8	0		0	5		0	0	0	0	0		6.4	0					0	0	0
38011000	人造石墨	6.5	0		0	5		0	0	0	0			5.2	0					0	0	0
38012000	胶态或半胶态石墨	6.5	0		0	5		0	0	0				3.9	0					0	0	0
38013000	电极用碳糊及炉衬用的类似糊	6.5	0		0	5		0	0	0				5.2	0					0	0	0
38019010	表面处理的球化石墨	6.5	0		0	5		0	0	0				3.9	0					0	0	0
38019090	其他石墨	6.5	0		0	5		0	0	0				3.9	0					0	0	0
38021010	木质活性碳	6.5	0	5.5	0	5		0	0	0				3.9	0					0	0	
38021090	其他活性碳	6.5	0	5.5	0	5		0	0	0				3.9	0					0	0	
38029000	活性天然矿产品;动物炭黑(包括废动物炭黑)	10	0		0	5	0	0	4	0				6	0					0	0	
38030000	妥尔油,不论是否精炼	6.5	0		0	5		0	0	0				3.9	0					0	0	0
38040000	木浆残余碱液,不论是否浓缩、脱糖或经化学处理,包括木素磺酸盐,但不包括税目38.03的妥尔油	6.5	0		0	5		0	0	0				3.9	0					0	0	
38051000	脂松节油、木松节油和硫酸松节油	6.5	0		0	5		0	0	0				3.9	0					0	0	0
38059010	以α萜品醇为基本成分的松油,用蒸馏或其他方法从针叶木制得	6.5	0		0	5		0	0	0				3.9	0					0	0	0
38059090	粗制二聚戊烯;亚硫酸盐松节油及其他粗制对异丙基苯甲烷;其他萜烯油,用蒸馏或其他方法从针叶木制得	6.5	0		0	5		0	0	0				3.9	0					0	0	0
38061010	松香	10	0		0	5	0	0	0	0		0		6	0					0	0	
38061020	树脂酸	10	0		0	5		0	0	0		0		6	0					0	0	
38062010	松香盐及树脂酸盐	6.5	0		0	5		0	0	0		0		3.9	0					0	0	
38062090	松香或树脂酸衍生物的盐,但松香加合物的盐除外	6.5	0		0	5		0	0	0		0		3.9	0					0	0	
38063000	酯胶	6.5	0		0	5		0	0	0		0		3.9	0					0	0	
38069000	其他松香和树脂酸的衍生物;松香精及松香油;再熔胶	6.5	0		0	5		0	0	0		0		3.9	0					0	0	
38070000	木焦油;精制木焦油;木杂酚油;粗木精;植物沥青;以松香、树脂酸或植物沥青为基本成分的啤酒桶沥青及类似制品	6.5	0		0	5		0	0	0				3.9	0					0	0	
38085010	零售包装的本章注释一规定货物	9	0		0	5		0	0	0	0			5.4	0					0	0	0
38085090	非零售包装的本章注释一规定货物	5	0		0			0	0	0	0			0	0					0	0	0
38089111	蚊香	10	0	0	0	0		0	0	0		0		6	0					0	0	0
38089112	生物杀虫剂	10	0	7	0	5		0	0	0	0	0		6	0					0	0	0
38089119	零售包装杀虫剂	10	0	7	0	5		0	0	0	0	0		6	0					0	0	0
38089190	非零售包装杀虫剂	6	0	4.2	0	0		0	0	0	0	0		4.8	0					0	0	0
38089210	零售包装的杀菌剂	9	0		0	5		0	0	0	0			7.2	0					0	0	0
38089290	非零售包装的杀菌剂	6	0		0	5		0	0	0				4.8	0					0	0	0
38089311	零售包装的除草剂	9	0		0	5		0	0	0				5.4	0					0	0	0
38089319	非零售包装的除草剂	5	0	4.5	0	0		0	0	0				4	0					0	0	0
38089391	零售包装抗萌剂及植物生长调节剂	9	0	8.3	0	5		0	0	0				5.4	0					0	0	0
38089399	非零售抗萌剂及植物生长调节剂	6	0	5.5	0	5		0	0	0				3.6	0					0	0	0
38089400	消毒剂	9	0		0	5		0	0	0	0			7.2	0					0	0	0

税则号列	货品名称	最惠国	协定税率 东盟统一	亚太5国	智利	巴基斯坦	新加坡	新西兰	秘鲁	哥达	香港	澳门	台湾	瑞士	冰岛	特惠税率 亚太2国	老挝	柬埔寨	缅甸	LDC1	LDC2	LDC3
38089910	零售包装的杀鼠剂及其他类似产品	9	0		0	5		0	0	0	0			5.4	0					0	0	0
38089990	非零售包装的杀鼠剂及其他类似产品	9	0		0	5		0	0	0		0		5.4	0					0	0	0
38091000	以淀粉物质为基本成分,纺织、造纸、制革及类似工业用的其他税号未列名的整理剂、染料加速着色或固色助剂及其他产品和制剂	10	0		0	0	0	0	0	0				6	0					0	0	0
38099100	纺织工业及类似工业用其他税号未列名整理剂、染料加速着色剂或固色助剂及其他产品和制剂	6.5	0	6	0	0		0	0	0	0			5.2	0					0	0	0
38099200	造纸工业用其他税号未列名整理剂、染料加速着色剂或固色助剂及其他产品和制剂	6.5	0		0	0		0	0	0	0			3.9	0					0	0	0
38099300	制革工业用其他税号未列名整理剂、染料加速着色剂或固色助剂及其他产品和制剂	6.5	0		0	0		0	0	0	0			3.9	0					0	0	0
38101000	金属表面酸洗剂；金属及其他材料制成的焊粉或焊膏	6.5	0	6	0	5		0	0	0	0	0		3.9	0					0	0	0
38109000	焊接用的焊剂及其他辅助剂;作焊条芯子或焊条涂料用的制品	6.5	0		0	5		0	0	0				3.9	0					0	0	0
38111100	以铅化合物为基本成分的抗震剂,用于矿物油或与矿物油同样用途的其他液体	6.5	0		0	5		0	0	0				3.9	0					0	0	
38111900	抗震剂(以铅化合物为基本成分的除外),用于矿物油或与矿物油同样用途的其他液体	6.5	0		0	5		0	0	0				3.9	0					0	0	
38112100	含有石油或从沥青矿物提取的油类的润滑油添加剂	6.5	0		0	5		0	0	0				3.9	0					0	0	
38112900	不含石油或从沥青矿物提取的油类的润滑油添加剂	6.5	0	5.5	0	5		0	0	0		0		3.9	0					0	0	
38119000	抗氧剂、防胶剂、粘度改良剂、防腐剂配制添加剂,用于矿物油或与矿物油同样用途的其他液体	6.5	0		0	5		0	0	0	0	0		3.9	0					0	0	
38121000	配制的橡胶促进剂	6	0		0	5		0	0	0				3.6	0					0	0	0
38122000	橡胶或塑料用复合增塑剂	6.5	0		0	5		0	0	0				3.9	0					0	0	0
38123010	橡胶的防老剂	6	0		0	5		0	0	0	0			3.6	0					0	0	0
38123090	其他橡胶、塑料用抗氧剂及其他稳定剂	6.5	0	4.6	0	0		0	0	0	0			5.2	0					0	0	0
38130010	灭火器的装配药	6.5	0		0	5		0	0	0				3.9	0					0	0	0
38130020	已装药的灭火弹	10	0		0	5		0	0	0				6	0					0	0	0
38140000	其他税号未列名的有机复合溶剂及稀释剂;除漆剂	10	0	9	0	5	0	0	4	0	0	0		8	0					0	0	0
38151100	以镍及其化合物为活性物的载体催化剂	6.5	0		0	5		0	0	0				3.9	0					0	0	0
38151200	以贵金属及其化合物为活性物的载体催化剂	6.5	0		0	5		0	0	0	0			3.9	0					0	0	0
38151900	其他载体催化剂	6.5	0	4.6	0	0		0	0	0				3.9	0					0	0	0
38159000	其他未列名的反应引发剂、促进剂	6.5	0	6	0	5		0	0	0		0		5.2	0					0	0	0
38160000	耐火水泥、灰泥、混凝土及类似耐火材料,但税目38.01的产品除外	6.5	0		0	5		0	0	0				3.9	0					0	0	
38170000	混合烷基苯及混合烷基萘,但税目27.07及29.02的产品除外	6.5	0		0	5		0	0	0			0	3.9	0					0	0	0
38180011	7.5 cm≤直径≤15.24 cm 的单晶硅切片	0																		0	0	0
38180019	经掺杂用于电子工业的,已切成圆片、薄片或类似形状,直径>15.24cm 的单晶硅片	0																		0	0	0
38180090	经掺杂用于电子工业的化学元素，,已切成圆片、薄片或类似形状,单晶硅片除外;经掺杂用于电子工业的化合物	0																		0	0	0

税则号列	货品名称	最惠国	协定税率													特惠税率						
			东盟统一	亚太5国	智利	巴基斯坦	新加坡	新西兰	秘鲁	哥达	香港	澳门	台湾	瑞士	冰岛	亚太2国	老挝	柬埔寨	缅甸	LDC1	LDC2	LDC3
38190000	闸用液压油及其他液压传动用液体,不含石油或从沥青矿物提取的油类,或者按重量计石油或从沥青矿物提取的油类含量低于70%	6.5	0		0	5		0	0	0		0		3.9	0					0	0	
38200000	防冻剂及解冻剂	10	0		0	5	0	0	0	0		0		6	0					0	0	0
38210000	制成的微生物培养基	3	0		0	0		0	0	0	0			0	0					0	0	
38220010	附于衬背上的诊断或实验用试剂,但税目32.02,32.06的货品除外	4	0		0	0		0	0	0	0			2.4	2.7					0	0	0
38220090	无论是否附于衬背上的诊断或实验用配制试剂,但税目32.02,32.06的货品除外	5	0		0	0		0	0	0	0			3	3.3					0	0	0
38231100	硬脂酸	16	0		0	12.8		0	6.4	0				12.8						0	0	
38231200	油酸	16	0		0	12.8	0	0	6.4	0	0			12.8						0	0	
38231300	妥尔油脂肪酸	16	0		0	12.8	0	0	6.4	0				12.8	0					0	0	
38231900	其他工业用单羧脂肪酸;精炼所得的酸性油	16	0		0	12.8	0	0	6.4	0	0	0		12.8	0					0	0	
38237000	工业用脂肪醇	13	0		0	6.5	0	0	0	0				10.4	0					0	0	
38241000	铸模及铸芯用粘合剂	6.5	0		0	5		0	0	0				3.9	0					0	0	0
38243000	自身混合或与金属粘合剂混合的未烧结金属碳化物	6.5	0		0	5		0	0	0				3.9	0					0	0	0
38244010	高效减水剂	6.5	0		0	5		0	0	0	0			3.9	0					0	0	0
38244090	其他水泥、灰泥及混凝土用添加剂	6.5	0		0	5		0	0	0	0			3.9	0					0	0	0
38245000	非耐火的灰泥及混凝土	6.5	0		0	5		0	0	0	0	0		3.9	0					0	0	0
38246000	子目号2905.44以外的山梨醇	14	0		0	11.2	0	0	0	0				11.2	0					0	0	
38247100	含全氯氟烃的,不论是否含氢氯氟烃、全氟烃或氢氟烃的含有甲烷、乙烷、丙烷卤化衍生物混合物	6.5	0		0	5		0	0	0	0	0		3.9	0					0	0	0
38247200	含溴氯二氟甲烷、溴三氟甲烷或二溴四氟乙烷的含有甲烷、乙烷、丙烷卤化衍生物混合物	6.5	0		0	5		0	0	0				3.9	0					0	0	0
38247300	含氢溴氟烃的含有甲烷、乙烷、丙烷卤化衍生物混合物	6.5	0		0	5		0	0	0	0	0		3.9	0					0	0	0
38247400	含氢氯氟烃的,不论是否含全氟烃或氢氟烃,但不含全氯氟烃的含有甲烷、乙烷、丙烷卤化衍生物混合物	6.5	0		0	5		0	0	0	0	0		3.9	0					0	0	0
38247500	含四氯化碳的含有甲烷、乙烷、丙烷卤化衍生物混合物	6.5	0	6	0	5		0	0	0	0	0		3.9	0					0	0	0
38247600	含1,1,1-三氯乙烷(甲基氯仿)的含有甲烷、乙烷、丙烷卤化衍生物混合物	6.5	0	6	0	5		0	0	0	0	0		3.9	0					0	0	0
38247700	含溴化甲烷(甲基溴)或溴氯甲烷的含有甲烷、乙烷、丙烷卤化衍生物混合物	6.5	0		0	5		0	0	0	0	0		3.9	0					0	0	0
38247800	含全氟烃或氢氟烃的,但不含全氯氟烃或氢氯氟烃的含有甲烷、乙烷、丙烷卤化衍生物混合物	6.5	0	6	0	5		0	0	0	0	0		3.9	0					0	0	0
38247900	其他含有甲烷、乙烷、丙烷卤化衍生物的混合物	6.5	0		0	5		0	0	0	0	0		3.9	0					0	0	0
38248100	含环氧乙烷的混合物及制品	6.5	0	6	0	5		0	0	0	0	0		3.9	0					0	0	0
38248200	含多氯联苯、多氯三联苯或多溴联苯的混合物及制品	6.5	0	6	0	5		0	0	0	0	0		3.9	0					0	0	0
38248300	含三(2,3-二溴丙基)磷酸酯的混合物及制品	6.5	0	6	0	5		0	0	0	0	0		3.9	0					0	0	0
38249010	杂醇油	6.5	0	5.5	0	5		0	0	0				3.9	0					0	0	0
38249020	除墨剂、蜡纸改正液及类似品	9	0	8.3	0	5	0	0	0	0				5.4	0					0	0	0
38249030	增炭剂	6.5	0		0	5		0	0	0				3.9	0					0	0	0
38249091	含滑石50%以上的混合物	6.5	0	6	0	5		0	0	0	0	0		3.9	0					0	0	0
38249092	按重量计含氧化镁70%以上的混合物	6.5	0	6	0	5		0	0	0	0	0		3.9	0					0	0	0
38249093	表层包覆钴化合物的氢氧化镍(掺杂炭)	6.5	0	6	0	5		0	0	0	0	0			0					0	0	0

税则号列	货品名称	最惠国	协定税率													特惠税率						
			东盟统一	亚太5国	智利	巴基斯坦	新加坡	新西兰	秘鲁	哥达	香港	澳门	台湾	瑞士	冰岛	亚太2国	老挝	柬埔寨	缅甸	LDC1	LDC2	LDC3
38249099	其他税目未列名的化学工业及其相关工业的化学产品及配制品	6.5	0	6	0	5		0	0	0	0	0			0					0	0	0
38251000	城市垃圾	6.5	0		0	5		0	0	0				3.9	0					0	0	
38252000	下水道淤泥	6.5	0		0	5		0	0	0				3.9	0					0	0	
38253000	医疗废物	6.5	0		0	5		0	0	0				3.9	0					0	0	
38254100	含卤化物的废有机溶剂	6.5	0		0	5		0	0	0				3.9	0					0	0	
38254900	其他废有机溶剂	6.5	0		0	5		0	0	0				3.9	0					0	0	
38255000	废的金属酸洗液、液压油、制动油及防冻液	6.5	0		0	5	0	0	0	0				3.9	0					0	0	
38256100	主要含有机成分的化工及相关工业废物	6.5	0		0	5		0	0	0				3.9	0					0	0	
38256900	其他税目未列名的化工及相关工业废物	6.5	0		0	5		0	0	0				3.9	0					0	0	
38259000	其他税目未列名的化学工业及相关工业的副产品	6.5	0		0	5		0	0	0	0			3.9	0					0	0	
38260000	生物柴油及其混合物,不含或含有按重量计低于70%的石油或从沥青矿物提取的油类	6.5	0	6	0	5		0	0	0	0	0			0					0	0	0
39011000	初级形状比重<0.94的聚乙烯	6.5	6.5	6	0	6		0		0	0	0		5	0							
39012000	初级形状比重≥0.94的聚乙烯	6.5	6.5	6	0	6		0		0	0	0		5	0							
39013000	初级形状乙烯-乙酸乙烯酯共聚物	6.5	0	6	0	5		0	0	0	0			3.9	0					0	0	
39019010	初级形状的乙烯丙烯共聚物(乙丙橡胶,乙烯单体单元的含量大于丙烯单体单元)	6.5	0		0	5	0	0	0	0				3.9	0					0	0	
39019020	线型低密度聚乙烯	6.5	0		0	5	0	0		0					0					0	0	0
39019090	其他初级形状的乙烯聚合物	6.5	0	6.3	0	5	0	0	0	0	0	0		3.9	0					0	0	
39021000	初级形状的聚丙烯	6.5	0		0	5	0	0		0	0	0		5	0							
39022000	初级形状的聚异丁烯	6.5	0		0	5		0	0	0				3.9	0					0	0	0
39023010	初级形状的乙烯丙烯共聚物(乙丙橡胶丙烯单体单元的含量大于乙烯单体单元)	6.5	0	6	0	5	0	0	0	0	0		0	3.9	0					0	0	0
39023090	初级形状的其他丙烯共聚物	6.5	0	6	0	5	0	0	0	0	0			3.9	0					0	0	0
39029000	其他初级形状的烯烃聚合物	6.5	0		0	5	0	0	0	0			0	3.9	0					0	0	0
39031100	初级形状的可发性聚苯乙烯	6.5	0	6	0	5	0	0	0	0				3.9	0					0	0	0
39031910	初级形状的改性非可发性聚苯乙烯	6.5	0	6	0	5	0	0	0	0	0			3.9	0					0	0	0
39031990	初级形状的其他聚苯乙烯	6.5	0	6	0	5	0	0	0	0	0			3.9	0					0	0	0
39032000	初级形状苯乙烯-丙烯腈共聚物	12	0		0	6	0	0	0	0			0	9.6	0					0	0	
39033010	初级形状的改性丙烯腈-丁二烯-苯乙烯共聚物	6.5	0	6	0	5	0	0	0	0	0	0		5	0					0	0	0
39033090	其它丙烯腈-丁二烯-苯乙烯共聚物	6.5	0	6	0	5	0	0	0	0	0	0		5.2	0					0	0	0
39039000	初级形状的其他苯乙烯聚合物	6.5	0	6	0	5	0	0	0	0	0		0	3.9	0					0	0	0
39041010	聚氯乙烯糊树脂	6.5	0	6	0	6	0	0	0	0				3.9	0					0	0	0
39041090	其他初级形状的纯聚氯乙烯	6.5	0	6	0	6	0	0	0	0				3.9	0					0	0	0
39042100	初级形状未塑化的聚氯乙烯	6.5	0		0	5	0	0	0	0	0			3.9	0					0	0	0
39042200	初级形状已塑化的聚氯乙烯	6.5	0		0		0	0	0	0	0			3.9	0					0	0	0
39043000	氯乙烯-乙酸乙烯酯共聚物	9	0	8.6	0	5		0	0	0				5.4	0					0	0	0
39044000	初级形状的其他氯乙烯共聚物	12	0	11.4	0	6	0	0	4.8	0				9.6	0					0	0	
39045000	初级形状的偏二氯乙烯聚合物	6.5	0		0	5		0	0	0				3.9	0					0	0	0
39046100	初级形状的聚四氟乙烯	10	0		0	5	0	0	0	0				6	0					0	0	0
39046900	初级形状的其他氟聚合物	6.5	0		0	5		0	0	0				3.9	0					0	0	0
39049000	初级形状的其他卤化烯烃聚合物	10	0		0	5		0	0	0				6	0					0	0	0
39051200	聚乙酸乙烯酯的水分散体	10	0		0		0	0	4	0				6	0					0	0	
39051900	其他初级形状聚乙酸乙烯酯	10	0		0	5		0	0	0				6	0					0	0	
39052100	乙酸乙烯酯共聚物的水分散体	10	0		0	5	0	0	0	0			0	6	0					0	0	
39052900	其他初级形状的乙酸乙烯酯共聚物	10	0		0	5	0	0	0	0					0					0	0	
39053000	初级形状的聚乙烯醇(不论是否含有未水解的乙酸酯基)	14	0		0	11.2	0	0	0	0			0	11.2	0					0	0	
39059100	其他乙烯酯或乙烯基的共聚物	10	0		0	5		0	0	0				6	0					0	0	
39059900	其他乙烯酯或乙烯基的聚合物	10	0		0			0	4	0	0			6	0					0	0	
39061000	初级形状的聚甲基丙烯酸甲酯	6.5	0	6	0	5		0	0	0	0		0	3.9	0					0	0	0
39069010	聚丙稀酰胺	6.5	0	6	0	5		0	0	0	0		0	3.9	0					0	0	0
39069090	其他初级形状的丙烯酸聚合物	6.5	0	6	0	5		0	0	0	0		0	5.2	0					0	0	0

税则号列	货品名称	最惠国	协定税率 东盟统一	亚太5国	智利	巴基斯坦	新加坡	新西兰	秘鲁	哥达	香港	澳门	台湾	瑞士	冰岛	特惠税率 亚太2国	老挝	柬埔寨	缅甸	LDC1	LDC2	LDC3
39071010	初级形状的聚甲醛	6.5	0	6	0	5	0	0	0	0	0		0	3.9	0					0	0	0
39071090	其他初级形状的聚缩醛	6.5	0	6	0	5	0	0	0	0	0			3.9	0					0	0	0
39072010	聚四亚甲基醚二醇	6.5	0	6	0	5	0	0	0	0			0	3.9	0					0	0	0
39072090	其他初级形状的聚醚	6.5	0	6	0	5	0	0	0	0				5.2	0					0	0	0
39073000	初级形状的环氧树脂	6.5	0	6	0	5	0	0	0	0	0		0	5	0					0	0	0
39074000	初级形状的聚碳酸酯	6.5	0	6.1	0	5		0	0	0	0		0	5.2	0					0	0	0
39075000	初级形状的醇酸树脂	10	0	9.5	0	5	0	0	4	0			0	6	0					0	0	0
39076011	高粘度聚对苯二甲酸乙二酯切片	6.5	6.5		0			0	0	0				3.9	0					0	0	0
39076019	其他聚对苯二甲酸乙二酯切片	6.5	6.5		0			0	0	0	0	0		3.9	0					0	0	0
39076090	其他初级形状聚对苯二甲酸乙二酯	6.5	0		0			0	0	0		0		3.9	0					0	0	0
39077000	聚乳酸	6.5	0	6.2	0	5		0	0	0	0	0		3.9	0					0	0	0
39079100	初级形状的不饱和聚酯	6.5	0		0	5	0	0	0	0			0	3.9	0					0	0	0
39079910	聚对苯二甲酸丁二酯	6.5	0	6.2	0	5		0	0	0	0	0		3.9	0					0	0	0
39079991	聚对苯二甲酸-己二醇-丁二醇酯	6.5	0	6.2	0	5		0	0	0	0	0	0	3.9	0					0	0	0
39079999	其他聚酯	6.5	0	6.2	0	5		0	0	0	0	0	0	3.9	0					0	0	0
39081011	聚酰胺-6,6切片	6.5	0		0	5	0	0	0	0	0			5.2	0					0	0	0
39081012	聚酰胺-6切片	6.5	0		0	5	0	0	0	0	0			5	0					0	0	0
39081019	初级形状聚酰胺切片	6.5	0		0	5	0	0	0	0	0			5	0					0	0	0
39081090	其他初级形状的聚酰胺	6.5	0		0	5		0	0	0	0			5.2	0					0	0	0
39089000	初级形状的其他聚酰胺	10	0		0	5	0	0	0	0	0				0					0	0	0
39091000	初级形状的尿素树脂及硫尿树脂	6.5	0	6.1	0	5		0	0	0			0	3.9	0					0	0	0
39092000	初级形状的蜜胺树脂	6.5	0	6.1	0	5		0	0	0			0	3.9	0					0	0	0
39093010	聚合MDI	6.5	0	6	0	5	0	0	0	0	0			3.9	0					0	0	0
39093090	其他初级形状的其他氨基树脂	6.5	0		0	5	0	0	0	0			0	3.9	0					0	0	0
39094000	初级形状的酚醛树脂	6.5	0	6.1	0	5		0	0	0			0	3.9	0					0	0	0
39095000	初级形状的聚亚氨酯	6.5	0	6	0	5	0	0	0	0	0	0	0	3.9	0					0	0	0
39100000	初级形状的聚硅氧烷	6.5	0	6.1	0	5		0	0	0	0		0	3.9	0					0	0	0
39111000	初级形状的石油树脂、苯并呋喃-茚树脂、多萜树脂	6.5	0	6.1	0	5		0	0	0			0	3.9	0					0	0	0
39119000	其他初级形状的多硫化物、聚砜及39章注释3所规定的其他税号未列名新产品	6.5	0		0	5		0	0	0				3.9	0					0	0	0
39121100	初级形状的未塑化醋酸纤维素	6.5	0		0	5		0	0	0				3.9	0					0	0	
39121200	初级形状的已塑化醋酸纤维素	6.5	0		0	5		0	0	0				3.9	0					0	0	
39122000	初级形状的硝酸纤维素	6.5	0		0	5		0	0	0				3.9	0					0	0	
39123100	初级形状的羧甲基纤维素及其盐	6.5	0		0	5		0	0	0				3.9	0					0	0	
39123900	初级形状的其他纤维素醚	6.5	0		0	5		0	0	0				3.9	0					0	0	
39129000	初级形状的其他未列名的纤维素(包括化学衍生物)	6.5	0		0	5		0	0	0	0			3.9	0					0	0	
39131000	初级形状的藻酸及盐和酯	10	0		0	5	0	0		0				6	0					0	0	0
39139000	初级形状的其他未列名天然聚合物(包括改性天然聚合物)	6.5	0		0	5		0	0	0				3.9	4.3					0	0	0
39140000	初级形状的离子交换剂	6.5	0		0	5		0	0	0				3.9						0	0	0
39151000	乙烯聚合物的废碎料及下脚料	6.5	0		0	5	0	0	0	0	0	0		3.9	0					0	0	0
39152000	苯乙烯聚合物的废碎料及下脚料	6.5	0		0	5	0	0	0	0	0	0		3.9	0					0	0	0
39153000	氯乙烯聚合物的废碎料及下脚料	6.5	0		0	5	0	0	0	0	0	0		3.9	0					0	0	0
39159010	聚对苯二甲酸乙二酯的塑料废碎料及下脚料	6.5	0		0	5	0	0	0	0	0	0		5.2	0					0	0	0
39159090	其他塑料的废碎料及下脚料	6.5	0		0	5	0	0	0	0	0	0		5.2	0					0	0	0
39161000	乙烯聚合物制单丝、条、杆及型材	10	0		0	5	0	0	4	0				6	0					0	0	
39162010	聚氯乙烯异型材	10	0	7	0	5		0	0	0				6	0					0	0	
39162090	氯乙烯聚合物制单丝、条、杆及型材	10	0	7	0	5		0	0	0				6	0					0	0	
39169010	聚酰胺制的单丝、条、杆及型材	10	0		0	5	0	0	0	0	0			6	0					0	0	
39169090	其他塑料制单丝、条、杆及型材	10	0		0	5	0	0	0	0				6	0					0	0	
39171000	硬化蛋白或纤维素材料制人造肠衣	10	0		0	5		0	0	0				6	0					0	0	
39172100	乙烯聚合物制的硬管	10	0		0	5	0	0	4	0				6	0					0	0	0
39172200	丙烯聚合物制的硬管	10	0		0	5		0	0	0				6	0					0	0	0
39172300	氯乙烯聚合物制的硬管	10	0		0	5	0	0	4	0	0			6	0					0	0	0
39172900	其他塑料制的硬管	10	0		0	5	0	0	0	0				8	0					0	0	0
39173100	塑料制的软管	10	0	7	0	5	0	0	0	0	0			6	0					0	0	0
39173200	其他未装有附件的塑料制管子	6.5	0	4.6	0	0		0	0	0				5.2	0					0	0	0

税则号列	货品名称	最惠国	协定税率													特惠税率						
			东盟统一	亚太5国	智利	巴基斯坦	新加坡	新西兰	秘鲁	哥达	香港	澳门	台湾	瑞士	冰岛	亚太2国	老挝	柬埔寨	缅甸	LDC1	LDC2	LDC3
39173300	其他装有附件的塑料管子	6.5	0	4.6	0	0		0	0	0				3.9	0					0	0	0
39173900	塑料制的其他管子	6.5	0	4.5	0	4.5	0	0	0	0				3.9	0					0	0	0
39174000	塑料制的管子附件	10	0	7	0	5	0	0	4	0				8	0					0	0	0
39181010	氯乙烯聚合物制糊墙品	10	0		0	5		0	4	0				6	0					0	0	
39181090	氯乙烯聚合物制的铺地制品	10	0		0	5		0	4	0				8	0					0	0	
39189010	其他塑料制的糊墙品	10	0		0	5		0	0	0	0			6	0					0	0	
39189090	其他塑料制的铺地制品	10	0		0	5		0	0	0	0			6	0					0	0	
39191010	丙烯酸树脂为基本成份的成卷胶粘板片条等,宽度≤20cm	6.5	0		0	5		0	0	0				3.9	0					0	0	0
39191091	宽度≤20cm 成卷的胶囊型反光膜	6.5	0		0	5		0	0	0				3.9	0					0	0	0
39191099	其他材料制的,宽度≤20cm 的其他成卷塑料胶粘板片等	6.5	0		0	5		0	0	0			0	5.2	0					0	0	0
39199010	其他胶囊型反光膜	6.5	0	4.6	0	0		0	0	0	0			3.9	0					0	0	0
39199090	其他自粘塑料板、片、膜等材料	6.5	0	4.6	0	0		0	0	0	0		0	3.9	0					0	0	0
39201010	乙烯聚合物制电池隔膜	6.5	0	4.6	0	0		0	0	0	0			3.9	0					0	0	0
39201090	其他乙烯聚合物制板、片、带	6.5	0	4.6	0	0		0	0	0	0	0	0	5.2	0					0	0	0
39202010	丙烯聚合物制电池隔膜	6.5	0		0	5		0	0	0	0			3.9	0					0	0	0
39202090	其他丙烯聚合物制板、片、带	6.5	0		0	5		0	0	0	0	0	0	5.2	0					0	0	0
39203000	非泡沫聚苯乙烯板、片、膜、箔及扁条	6.5	0	4.6	0	0		0	0	0	0		0	3.9	0					0	0	0
39204300	按重量计增塑剂含量不小于6%的聚氯乙烯板、片、膜、箔及扁条	6.5	0	4.5	0	4.5	0	0	0	0	0		0	3.9	0					0	0	0
39204900	按重量计增塑剂含量小于6%的聚氯乙烯板、片、膜、箔及扁条	6.5	0	4.5	0	4.5		0	0	0	0	0	0	5.2	0					0	0	0
39205100	聚甲基丙烯酸甲酯板片膜箔及扁条	6.5	0	4.6	0	0		0	0	0			0	3.9	0					0	0	0
39205900	其他丙烯酸聚合物板片膜箔及扁条	6.5	0		0	5		0	0	0				3.9	0					0	0	0
39206100	聚碳酸酯制板、片、膜、箔及扁条	6.5	0	4.6	0	0		0	0	0			0	3.9	0					0	0	0
39206200	聚对苯二甲酸乙二酯板片膜箔扁条	6.5	0	4.6	0	0		0	0	0	0	0	0	3.9	0					0	0	0
39206300	不饱和聚酯板、片、膜、箔及扁条	10	0		0	5		0	0	0				6	0					0	0	0
39206900	其他聚酯板、片、膜、箔及扁条	10	0	9	0	5	0	0	4	0			0	6	0					0	0	0
39207100	再生纤维素制板、片、膜、箔及扁条	6.5	0		0	5		0	0	0				3.9	0					0	0	0
39207300	醋酸纤维素制板、片、膜、箔及扁条	6.5	0		0	5		0	0	0	0			3.9	0					0	0	0
39207900	纤维素衍生物制板、片、膜箔及扁条	10	0		0	5		0	0	0				6	0					0	0	0
39209100	聚乙烯醇缩丁醛板、片、膜、箔及扁条	6.5	0		0	5		0	0	0				3.9	0					0	0	0
39209200	聚酰胺板、片、膜、箔及扁条	10	0		0	5	0	0	0	0				6	0					0	0	0
39209300	氨基树脂板、片、膜、箔及扁条	6.5	0		0	5		0	0	0				3.9	0					0	0	0
39209400	酚醛树脂板、片、膜、箔及扁条	10	0	7	0	5	0	0	0	0				6	0					0	0	0
39209910	聚四氟乙烯制的非泡沫塑料板片	6.5	0		0	5		0	0	0				3.9	0					0	0	0
39209990	其他塑料制的非泡沫塑料板片	6.5	0		0	5		0	0	0	0		0	3.9	0					0	0	0
39211100	泡沫聚苯乙烯板、片、带、箔及扁条	10	0	9	0	5		0	0	0				6	0					0	0	0
39211210	泡沫聚氯乙烯人造革及合成革	9	0		0	5	0	0	0	0	0		0	5.4	0					0	0	0
39211290	泡沫聚氯乙烯板、片、带、箔及扁条	6.5	0		0	5		0	0	0	0			5.2	0					0	0	0
39211310	泡沫聚氨酯制人造革及合成革	9	0	6.3	0	5	0	0	0	0	0		0	5.4	0					0	0	0
39211390	泡沫聚氨酯板、片、带、箔及扁条	6.5	0	4.6	0	0		0	0	0	0			3.9	0					0	0	0
39211400	泡沫再生纤维素板、片、膜、箔及扁条	10	0		0	5		0	0	0				6	0					0	0	0
39211910	其他泡沫塑料制人造革及合成革	9	0	6.3	0	5		0	0	0				5.4	0					0	0	0
39211990	其他泡沫塑料板、片、膜、箔及扁条	6.5	0	4.6	0	0		0	0	0			0	5.2	0					0	0	0
39219020	嵌有玻璃纤维的聚乙烯板、片	6.5	0	4.6	0	0		0	0	0	0			5.2	0					0	0	0
39219030	聚异丁烯为基本成分的附有人造毛毡的板、片、卷材	6.5	0	4.6	0	0		0	0	0	0			3.9	0					0	0	0
39219090	未列名塑料板、片、膜、箔及扁条	6.5	0	4.6	0	0		0	0	0	0		0	5.2	0					0	0	0
39221000	塑料浴缸、淋浴盘及盥洗盆	10	0		0	5		0	0	0		0		6	0		0			0	0	0
39222000	塑料马桶坐圈及盖	10	0		0	5		0	4	0		0		6	0		0			0	0	0
39229000	塑料便盆、抽水箱等类似卫生洁具	10	0		0	5		0	0	0				6	0					0	0	0
39231000	塑料制盒、箱及类似品	10	0	7	0	5	0	0	4	0	0	0	0	6	0					0	0	0
39232100	乙烯聚合物制袋及包	10	0		0	5	0	0	4	0	0	0		6	0					0	0	
39232900	其他塑料制的袋及包	10	0		0	5	0	0	4	0	0	0		6	0					0	0	0
39233000	塑料制坛、瓶及类似品	6.5	0		0	5	0	0		0	0			3.9	0					0	0	0
39234000	塑料制卷轴、纡子、筒管及类似品	10	0	7	0	5	0	0	0	0				6	0					0	0	
39235000	塑料制塞子、盖子及类似品	10	0		0	5	0	0	4	0	0		0	8	0					0	0	0

税则号列	货品名称	最惠国	协定税率													特惠税率						
			东盟统一	亚太5国	智利	巴基斯坦	新加坡	新西兰	秘鲁	哥达	香港	澳门	台湾	瑞士	冰岛	亚太2国	老挝	柬埔寨	缅甸	LDC1	LDC2	LDC3
39239000	供运输或包装货物用其他塑料制品	10	0	7	0	5	0	0	4	0	0	0	0	6	0					0	0	
39241000	塑料制餐具及厨房用具	10	0		0	5	0	0	4	0	0	0		6	0	0				0	0	0
39249000	塑料制其他家庭用具及卫生或盥洗用具	10	0		0	5	0	0	4	0	0	0		6	0					0	0	0
39251000	塑料制囤、柜、罐、桶及类似容器	10	0		0	5		0	4	0				6	0					0	0	0
39252000	塑料制门、窗及其框架、门槛	10	0	7	0	5		0	4	0				6	0					0	0	
39253000	塑料制窗板、百叶窗及类似制品	10	0		0	5		0	0	0				6	0					0	0	
39259000	其他未列名的建筑用塑料制品	10	0		0	5		0	4	0	0			7.7	0					0	0	
39261000	办公室或学校用塑料制品	10	0		0	5	0	0	0	0				6	0					0	0	0
39262011	聚氯乙稀制手套(包括分指手套、连指手套及露指手套)	10	0		0		0	0	0	0	0			6	0					0	0	
39262019	其他手套(包括分指手套、连指手套及露指手套)	10	0		0		0	0	0	0	0			6	0					0	0	
39262090	其他塑料制衣服及衣着附件	10	0		0		0	0	0	0	0			6	0					0	0	0
39263000	塑料制家具、车厢及类似品的附件	10	0		0	5	0	0	4	0				6	0					0	0	0
39264000	塑料制小雕塑品及其他装饰品	10	0	8.3	0	5		0	0	0				6	0					0	0	0
39269010	塑料制机器及仪器用零件	10	0	9	0	5	0	0	4	0	0	0	0	8	0					0	0	0
39269090	其他塑料制品	10	0	9.2	0	9.2	0	0	4	0	0	0	0	8	0					0	0	0
40011000	天然胶乳	20	20		0			0		0				16	0							
40012100	天然橡胶烟胶片	20	20	17	0	17		0		0				16	0							
40012200	技术分类天然橡胶(TSNR)	20	20		0			0		0				16	0							
40012900	其他初级形状的天然橡胶	20	20	17	0	17		0		0				16	0							
40013000	巴拉塔胶、古塔波胶、银胶菊胶、糖胶树胶及类似的天然树胶	20	0		0		0	0	8	0				16	0					0	0	
40021110	羧基丁苯橡胶胶乳	7.5	0		0	5		0	0	0	0			4.5	0					0	0	0
40021190	丁苯橡胶胶乳	7.5	0		0	5		0	0	0	0			4.5	0					0	0	0
40021911	未经任何加工的丁苯橡胶(溶聚的除外)	7.5	0		0	5		0	0	0	0			4.5	0					0	0	0
40021915	未经任何加工的溶聚丁苯橡胶	7.5	0		0	5		0	0	0	0			4.5	0					0	0	0
40021912	充油丁苯橡胶(溶聚的除外)	7.5	0		0	5		0	0	0	0			4.5	0					0	0	0
40021916	充油溶聚丁苯橡胶	7.5	0		0	5		0	0	0	0			4.5	0					0	0	0
40021913	初级形状的热塑丁苯橡胶	7.5	0		0	5		0	0	0	0			4.5	0					0	0	0
40021914	初级形状的充油热塑丁苯橡胶	7.5	0		0	5		0	0	0	0			4.5	0					0	0	0
40021919	初级形状的其他丁苯橡胶及羧基丁苯橡胶	7.5	7.5		0			0	0	0	0			4.5	0					0	0	0
40021990	丁苯橡胶及羧基丁苯橡胶板、片、带	7.5	0	7.1	0	5		0	0	0	0			4.5	0					0	0	0
40022010	初级形状的丁二烯橡胶	7.5	0		0	5		0	0	0				4.5	0					0	0	0
40022090	丁二烯橡胶板、片、带	7.5	0	7	0	5		0	0	0				4.5	0					0	0	0
40023110	初级形状的异丁烯－异戊二烯橡胶	6	0	5.6	0	5		0	0	0				3.6	0					0	0	0
40023190	异丁烯－异戊二烯橡胶板、片、带	7.5	0	7.1	0	5		0	0	0				4.5	0					0	0	0
40023910	初级形状的其他卤代丁基橡胶	7.5	0		0	5		0	0	0				4.5	0					0	0	0
40023990	卤代丁基橡胶板、片、带	7.5	0	7.1	0	5		0	0	0				4.5	0					0	0	0
40024100	氯丁二烯橡胶胶乳	7.5	0	7.1	0	5		0	0	0				4.5	0					0	0	0
40024910	初级形状的氯丁二烯橡胶	7.5	0		0	5		0	0	0				4.5	0					0	0	0
40024990	氯丁二烯橡胶板、片、带	7.5	0	7.1	0	5		0	0	0				4.5	0					0	0	0
40025100	丁腈橡胶胶乳	7.5	0	7.1	0	5		0	0	0				4.5	0					0	0	0
40025910	初级形状的丁腈橡胶	7.5	0		0	5		0	0	0				4.5	0					0	0	0
40025990	丁腈橡胶板、片、带	7.5	0		0	5		0	0	0				4.5	0					0	0	0
40026010	初级形状的异戊二烯橡胶	3	0		0	0		0	0	0				0	0					0	0	0
40026090	异戊二烯橡胶板、片、带	5	0	4.5	0	0		0	0	0				0	0					0	0	0
40027010	初级形状的乙丙非共轭二烯橡胶	7.5	0		0	5		0	0	0				4.5	0					0	0	0
40027090	乙丙非共轭二烯橡胶板、片、带	7.5	0	7.1	0	5		0	0	0				4.5	0					0	0	0
40028000	天然橡胶与合成橡胶的混合物	7.5	0		0	5		0	0	0				4.5	0					0	0	0
40029100	其他未列名的合成橡胶胶乳	7.5	0		0	5		0	0	0				4.5	0					0	0	0
40029911	其他初级形状的合成橡胶	7.5	0		0	5		0	0	0	0		0	4.5	0					0	0	0
40029919	其他合成橡胶板、片、带	7.5	0		0	5		0	0	0	0			4.5	0					0	0	0
40029990	从油类提取的油膏	4	0		0	0		0	0	0				0	0					0	0	0
40030000	初级形状或板、片、带状再生橡胶	8	0		0	5		0	0	0	0			4.8	0					0	0	0
40040000	橡胶(硬质橡胶除外)废碎料及下脚料及其粉、粒	8	0	7.6	0	5		0	0	0				4.8	0					0	0	
40051000	与碳黑等混合的未硫化复合橡胶	8	0		0	5		0	0	0		0		4.8	0					0	0	0
40052000	未硫化的复合橡胶溶液及分散体	8	0		0	5		0	0	0				4.8	0					0	0	0

税则号列	货品名称	最惠国	协定税率													特惠税率						
			东盟统一	亚太5国	智利	巴基斯坦	新加坡	新西兰	秘鲁	哥达	香港	澳门	台湾	瑞士	冰岛	亚太2国	老挝	柬埔寨	缅甸	LDC1	LDC2	LDC3
40059100	其他未硫化的复合橡胶板、片、带	8	0		0	5		0	0	0				4.8	0					0	0	0
40059900	其他未硫化的初级形状复合橡胶	8	0		0	5		0	0	0	0			4.8	0					0	0	0
40061000	未硫化轮胎翻新用胎面补料胎条	8	0		0	5		0	0	0				4.8	0					0	0	0
40069010	未硫化橡胶的杆、管或型材及异型材	8	0		0	5		0	0	0				4.8	0					0	0	0
40069020	未硫化橡胶制品	14	0		0	11.2	0	0	0	0				11.2	0					0	0	
40070000	硫化橡胶线及绳	14	0		0	11.2	0	0	0	0	0			11.2	0					0	0	
40081100	海绵硫化橡胶制的板、片及带	8	0		0	5		0	0	0				4.8	0					0	0	
40081900	海绵硫化橡胶制型材、异型材及杆	8	0		0	5		0	0	0				4.8	0					0	0	0
40082100	非海绵硫化橡胶制板、片及带	8	0		0	5		0	0	0				4.8	0					0	0	0
40082900	非海绵硫化橡胶型材、异型材及杆	8	0		0	5		0	0	0				4.8	0					0	0	0
40091100	未加强或未与其他材料合制硫化橡胶管,未装有附件	10.5	0		0	5	0	0	0	0				8.4	0					0	0	
40091200	未加强或未与其他材料合制硫化橡胶管,装有附件	10	0		0	5		0	0	0				6	0					0	0	
40092100	用金属加强或只与金属合制的硫化橡胶管,未装有附件	10.5	0		0	5	0	0	4.2	0				8.4	0					0	0	
40092200	用金属加强或只与金属合制的硫化橡胶管,装有附件	10	0		0	5	0	0	0	0				6	0					0	0	
40093100	用纺织材料加强或只与纺织材料合制硫化橡胶管,未装有附件	10.5	0		0	5	0	0	4.2	0				8.4	0					0	0	
40093200	用纺织材料加强或只与纺织材料合制硫化橡胶管,装有附件	10	0		0	5		0	0	0				6	0					0	0	
40094100	用其他材料加强或与其他材料合制硫化橡胶管,未装有附件	10.5	0		0	5	0	0	4.2	0				8.4	0					0	0	
40094200	用其他材料加强或与其他材料合制硫化橡胶管,装有附件	10	0		0	5	0	0	4	0				6	0					0	0	
40101100	金属加强的硫化橡胶输送带及带料	10	0		0	5		0	4	0	0			8.3	0					0	0	
40101200	纺织材料加强的硫化橡胶输送带及带料	10	0		0	5		0	4	0				0	0					0	0	
40101900	其他硫化橡胶制的输送带及带料	10	0		0	5		0	4	0				0	0					0	0	
40103100	梯形截面的环形传动带(三角带),V形肋状的,外周长超过60厘米,但不超过180厘米	8	0		0	5		0	0	0				4.8	0					0	0	0
40103200	梯形截面的环形传动带(三角带),V形肋状的除外,外周长超过60厘米,但不超过180厘米	8	0		0	5		0	0	0				4.8	0					0	0	0
40103300	180CM<外周长≤240CM的三角带,V形肋状的	8	0		0	5		0	0	0				4.8	0					0	0	0
40103400	180CM<外周长≤240CM的三角带,V形肋状的除外	8	0		0	5		0	0	0				4.8	0					0	0	0
40103500	60CM<外周长≤150CM的环形同步带	10	0		0	5	0	0	0	0				6	0					0	0	
40103600	150CM<外周长≤198CM的环形同步带	10	0		0	5		0	0	0				6	0					0	0	
40103900	其他硫化橡胶制的传动带及带料	8	0	7.6	0	5		0	0	0				0	0					0	0	0
40111000	机动小客车用新的充气橡胶轮胎	10	0	9.4	0	5	0	0		0			0	6	0					0	0	0
40112000	客或货运车用新的充气橡胶轮胎	10	0	9.4	0	5	0	0	4	0			0	6	0					0	0	
40113000	航空器用新的充气橡胶轮胎	1	0		0	0		0	0	0				0	0					0	0	0
40114000	摩托车用新的充气橡胶轮胎	15	0		0	12	0	0	6	0			0	12	0					0	0	
40115000	自行车用新的充气橡胶轮胎	20	0		0		0	0	8	0			0	16	0					0	0	
40116100	农业或林业车辆及机器用人字形胎面或类似胎面的新充气橡胶轮胎	17.5	0		0	14	0	0	7	0			0	14	0					0	0	
40116200	辋圈尺寸不超过61CM的建筑或工业搬运车辆及机器用人字形胎面或类似胎面的新充气橡胶轮胎	17.5	0		0	14	0	0	7	0				14						0	0	
40116300	辋圈>61CM建筑或工业搬运车辆及机器用人字形胎面或类似胎面的新充气橡胶轮胎	17.5	0		0	14	0	0	7	0				14	0					0	0	
40116900	其他人字形胎面或类似胎面的新充气橡胶轮胎	17.5	0		0	14	0	0	7	0			0	14	0					0	0	
40119200	农业或林业车辆及机器用非人字形胎面或类似胎面的新充气橡胶轮胎	25	0		0		0	0		0			0		0					0	0	0

税则号列	货品名称	最惠国	协定税率													特惠税率						
			东盟统一	亚太5国	智利	巴基斯坦	新加坡	新西兰	秘鲁	哥达	香港	澳门	台湾	瑞士	冰岛	亚太2国	老挝	柬埔寨	缅甸	LDC1	LDC2	LDC3
40119300	辋圈尺寸不超过61CM的建筑或工业搬运车辆及机器用非人字形胎面或类似胎面的新充气橡胶轮胎	25	0		0		0	0		0					0					0		
40119400	辋圈>61CM建筑或工业搬运车辆及机器用非人字形胎面或类似胎面的新充气橡胶轮胎	25	0		0		0	0		0					0					0		
40119900	其他新的充气橡胶轮胎	25	0		0		0	0		0					0					0		
40121100	机动小客车(包括旅行小客车及赛车)用翻新轮胎	20	0		0		0	0	8	0				16	0					0	0	
40121200	机动大客车或货运机动车用翻新轮胎	20	0		0		0	0	8	0	0			16	0					0	0	
40121300	航空器用翻新轮胎	20	0		0		0	0	8	0	0			16	0					0	0	
40121900	其他翻新轮胎	20	0		0		0	0	8	0				16	0					0	0	
40122010	汽车用旧的充气橡胶轮胎	25	0		0		0	0		0	0				0							
40122090	其他用途旧的充气橡胶轮胎	25	0		0		0	0		0	0				0							
40129010	航空器用实心或半实心橡胶轮胎	3	0		0	0		0	0	0				0	0					0	0	
40129020	汽车用实心或半实心橡胶轮胎	22	0		0		0	0	8.8	0				17.6	0					0	0	
40129090	其他用实心或半实心橡胶轮胎	22	0		0		0	0	8.8	0				17.6	0					0	0	
40131000	汽车用橡胶内胎	15	0	13	0	7.5	0	0	6	0				12	0					0	0	
40132000	自行车用橡胶内胎	15	0		0	12	0	0	6	0				12	0					0	0	
40139010	航空器用橡胶内胎	3	0		0	0		0	0	0				0	0					0	0	0
40139090	其他用橡胶内胎	15	0		0	12	0	0	6	0				12	0					0	0	
40141000	硫化橡胶制避孕套	0																		0	0	0
40149000	硫化橡胶制其他卫生及医疗用品	17.5	0		0	14	0	0	7	0		0		14	0					0	0	
40151100	硫化橡胶制外科用手套	8	0		0	5		0	0	0				4.8	0					0	0	0
40151900	硫化橡胶制其他手套	18	0		0		0	0	7.2	0				14.4	0					0	0	0
40159010	医疗用硫化橡胶衣着用品及附件	8	0		0	5		0	0	0				4.8						0	0	0
40159090	其他硫化橡胶制衣着用品及附件	15	0		0		0	0	6	0				12	0					0	0	
40161010	硫化海绵橡胶制机器及仪器用零件	8	0		0	5		0	0	0				4.8	0					0	0	0
40161090	硫化海绵橡胶制其他制品	15	0		0	12	0	0	6	0				12	0					0	0	
40169100	硫化橡胶制铺地制品及门垫	18	0		0		0	0	7.2	0	0			14.4	0					0	0	
40169200	硫化橡胶制橡皮擦	18	0		0			0	7.2	0				14.4	0					0	0	
40169310	硫化橡胶制机器、仪器用垫片、垫圈及其他密封垫	8	0		0	5		0	0	0	0			6.4	0					0	0	0
40169390	硫化橡胶制其他用垫片、垫圈、及其他密封垫	15	0		0		0	0	6	0	0			12	0					0	0	0
40169400	硫化橡胶制船舶或码头的碰垫	18	0		0		0	0	7.2	0				14.4	0					0	0	
40169500	硫化橡胶制其他可充气制品	18	0		0		0	0	7.2	0		0		14.4	0					0	0	
40169910	硫化橡胶制机器及仪器用其他零件	8	0	7.6	0	5		0	0	0		0		6.4	0					0	0	0
40169990	其他未列名硫化橡胶制品	10	0	9.5	0	5	0	0	4	0		0		8	0					0	0	0
40170010	各种形状的硬质橡胶(包括废碎料)	8	0		0	5		0	0	0		0		4.8	0					0	0	
40170020	硬质橡胶制品	15	0		0	12	0	0	6	0		0		12	0					0	0	
41012011	规定重量范围内的未剖层整张生牛皮,经逆鞣处理的	8	0	6	0	5		0	0	0	0			4.8	0					0	0	0
41012019	规定重量范围内的未剖层整张生牛皮,经逆鞣处理的除外	5	0		0	0		0	0	0	0			0	0		0	0		0	0	0
41012020	规定重量范围内的未剖层整张生马皮	5	0		0	0		0	0	2.5	0			0	0		0	0		0	0	0
41015011	经逆鞣处理的重量>16公斤的整张生牛皮	8.4	0	7	0	5		0	0	0				5	0					0	0	0
41015019	重量>16公斤的整张生牛皮,经逆鞣处理的除外	5	0		0	0		0	0	0				0	0		0	0		0	0	0
41015020	重量>16公斤的整张生马皮	5	0		0	0		0	0	2.5				0	0		0	0		0	0	0
41019011	其他(包括整张或半张的背皮及腹皮)经逆鞣处理的生牛皮	8.4	0	7	0	5		0	0	0				5	0					0	0	0
41019019	其他(包括整张或半张的背皮及腹皮)生牛皮,经逆鞣处理的除外	5	0		0	0		0	0	0				0	0		0	0		0	0	0
41019020	其他(包括整张或半张的背皮及腹皮)生马皮	5	0		0	0		0	0	2.5				0	0		0	0		0	0	0
41021000	带毛的绵羊或羔羊生皮	7	0		0	5		0		3.5				4.2	0					0	0	0
41022110	浸酸的不带毛绵羊或羔羊生皮,经逆鞣处理的	14	0		0	11.2	0	1.6		7				11.2	0					0	0	

税则号列	货品名称	最惠国	协定税率 东盟统一	亚太5国	智利	巴基斯坦	新加坡	新西兰	秘鲁	哥达	香港	澳门	台湾	瑞士	冰岛	特惠税率 亚太2国	老挝	柬埔寨	缅甸	LDC1	LDC2	LDC3
41022190	浸酸的不带毛绵羊或羔羊生皮,经逆鞣处理的除外	9	0	8	0	5		0	0	4.5				5.4	0					0	0	0
41022910	其他不带毛的绵羊或羔羊生皮,经逆鞣处理的	14	0		0	7	0	0	0	7				11.2	0					0	0	
41022990	其他不带毛的绵羊或羔羊生皮,经逆鞣处理的除外	7	0	6	0	5		0	0	3.5				4.2	0					0	0	0
41032000	爬行动物的生皮	9	0		0	5		0	0	4.5				5.4	0					0	0	0
41033000	生猪皮	9	0		0	5		0	0	4.5				5.4	0				0	0	0	0
41039011	经逆鞣处理的山羊板皮	14	0		0	7	0	0	0	7				11.2	0					0	0	
41039019	山羊板皮,经逆鞣处理的除外	9	0		0	5		0	0	4.5				5.4	0					0	0	0
41039021	经逆鞣处理的其他山羊或小山羊皮	14	0		0	7	0	0	0	7				11.2	0					0	0	
41039029	其他山羊或小山羊皮,经逆鞣处理的除外	9	0		0	5		0	0	4.5				5.4	0					0	0	0
41039090	其他生皮	9	0		0	5		0	0	4.5	0			5.4	0				0	0	0	0
41041111	全粒面未剖层或粒面剖层蓝湿牛皮	7	0	3.5	0	0		0	0	3.5				4.2	0	1.4				0	0	0
41041119	其他全粒面未剖层或粒面剖层湿牛皮革	8	0	4	0	0		0	0	4	0			4.8	0	2				0	0	0
41041120	全粒面未剖层或粒面剖层马皮革	5	0	2.5	0	0		0	0	2.5	0			0	0	2				0	0	0
41041911	其他蓝湿牛皮	6	0	3	0	3		0	0	3.5				3.6	0	1.4				0	0	0
41041919	其他湿牛皮革	7	0	3.5	0	0		0	0	3.5	0			4.2	0	1.8				0	0	0
41041920	其他湿马皮革	7	0	3.5	0	0		0	0	3.5	0			4.2	0	2.1				0	0	0
41044100	全粒面未剖层或粒面剖层干革(坯革)	5	0	3.5	0	0		0	0	2.5	0			0	0	2				0	0	0
41044910	其他机器带用干革(坯革)	5	0	3.5	0	0		0	0	2.5				0	0	0				0	0	0
41044990	其他干革(坯革)	7	0	4.9	0	4.9		0	0	3.5	0			4.2	0	2.1				0	0	0
41051010	蓝湿绵羊或羔羊皮	14	0	7	0	5	0	1.6		7				11.2	0	2.1				0	0	0
41051090	其他他绵羊或羔羊湿皮革	10	0	5	0	5		0	0	5				6	0	2				0	0	0
41053000	绵羊或羔羊干革(坯革)	8	0	5.6	0	5.6		0	0	4				4.8	0	4.8				0	0	0
41062100	山羊或小山羊皮湿革	14	0	12	0	12	0	0	0	7				11.2	0	2.1				0	0	0
41062200	山羊或小山羊皮干革(坯革)	14	0	9.8	0	9.8	0	1.6		7				11.2	0	8.4				0	0	0
41063110	蓝湿猪皮	14	0		0	11.2	0	0	0	7				11.2	0	4.2				0	0	
41063190	其他猪皮湿革	14	0		0	7	0	0	0	7				11.2	0	4.2				0	0	
41063200	猪皮干革(坯革)	14	0		0	11.2	0	0	0	7				11.2	0	4.2				0	0	
41064000	爬行动物皮革	14	0		0	7	0	0	0	7				11.2	0	0				0	0	0
41069100	其他未列名动物皮湿革(包括蓝湿皮革)	14	0		0	11.2	0	0	0	7				11.2	0	0				0	0	0
41069200	其他未列名动物皮干革(坯革)	14	0		0	11.2	0	0	0	7				11.2	0	0				0	0	0
41071110	已鞣全粒面未剖层整张牛皮革	8	0		0			0		4	0			4.8	0							
41071120	已鞣全粒面未剖层整张马皮革	5	0		0	0		0	0	2.5	0			0	0					0	0	0
41071210	已鞣粒面剖层整张牛皮革	8	0		0			0		4	0			4.8	0							
41071220	已鞣粒面剖层整张马皮革	5	0		0	0		0	0	2.5	0			0	0					0	0	0
41071910	已鞣机器带用整张牛马皮革	5	0		0	0		0	0	2.5				0	0					0	0	0
41071990	其他已鞣整张牛马皮革	7	0		0			0		3.5	0			4.2	0					0	0	0
41079100	已鞣全粒面未剖层非整张牛马皮革	5	0		0	0		0	0	2.5				0	0					0	0	0
41079200	已鞣粒面剖层非整张牛马皮革	5	0		0			0	0	2.5				3	0					0	0	0
41079910	已鞣机器带用非整张牛马皮革	5	0		0	0		0	0	2.5				0	0					0	0	0
41079990	其他已鞣非整张牛马皮革	7	0		0			0	0	3.5	0			4.2	0					0	0	0
41120000	已鞣进一步加工的不带毛绵羊或羔羊皮革	8	0	5.6	0	5.6		0	0	4	0			4.8	0					0	0	0
41131000	已鞣进一步加工的不带毛山羊或小山羊皮革	14	0	9.8	0	9.8	0	1.6		7	0			11.2						0	0	0
41132000	已鞣进一步加工的不带毛猪皮革	14	0		0		0	0	0	7	0			11.2	0					0	0	
41133000	已鞣进一步加工的不带毛爬行动物皮革	14	0		0	11.2	0	0	0	7				11.2						0	0	0
41139000	其他已鞣进一步加工的不带毛动物皮革	14	0		0		0	0	0	7				11.2	9.3					0	0	0
41141000	油鞣皮革	14	0		0		0	0	5.6	7				11.2	0					0	0	
41142000	漆皮及层压漆皮;镀金属皮革	10	0	9	0	9	0	0		5				6	0							
41151000	以皮革或皮革纤维为基本成分的再生皮革,成块、成张或成条,不论是否成卷	14	0		0		0	0		7				11.2	0							
41152000	皮革或再生皮革边角料;皮革粉末	14	0		0		0	0	0	7				11.2	0	4.2				0	0	
42010000	各种材料制成的鞍具及挽具,适合各种动物用	20	0	12	0	10	0	0	8	0		0		16	0	8				0	0	0
42021110	以皮革、再生皮革作面的衣箱	15	0		0	12	0	0	6	0				12	0	8.3				0	0	
42021190	以皮革、再生皮革作面的箱包	10	0		0	5		0	0	0				8	0	8				0	0	0

税则号列	货品名称	最惠国	协定税率													特惠税率						
			东盟统一	亚太5国	智利	巴基斯坦	新加坡	新西兰	秘鲁	哥达	香港	澳门	台湾	瑞士	冰岛	亚太2国	老挝	柬埔寨	缅甸	LDC1	LDC2	LDC3
42021210	以塑料或纺织材料作面的衣箱	20	0	17	0	16	0	0	8	0			0	16	0					0	0	
42021290	塑料或纺织材料作面的其他箱包	20	0	17	0	16	0	0	8	0		0	0	16	0					0	0	0
42021900	其他材料制箱包	20	0		0		0	0	8	0			0	16	0	8				0	0	0
42022100	以皮革、再生皮革作面的手提包	10	0	6.9	0	5		0	4	0	0	0		8	0					0	0	0
42022200	以塑料片或纺织材料作面的手提包	10	0	8.2	0	5	0	0	4	0		0	0	8	0					0	0	0
42022900	以钢纸或纸板作面的手提包	20	0	14	0	14	0	0	8	0		0		16	0	8				0	0	
42023100	以皮革、再生皮革作面的钱包等物品	10	0	6.9	0	5		0	0	0		0		8	0					0	0	0
42023200	以塑料或纺织品作面的钱包等物品	20	0	14	0	14	0	0	8	0		0		16	0					0	0	0
42023900	以钢纸或纸板作面的钱包等物品	20	0	14	0	14	0	0	8	0				16	0	8				0	0	
42029100	皮革、再生皮革作面的其他容器	10	0	8.5	0	5		0	0	0		0		8	0					0	0	0
42029200	以塑料或纺织材料作面的其他容器	10	0	8.5	0	5	0	0	4	0	0	0		6	0					0	0	0
42029900	以钢纸或纸板作面的其他容器	20	0		0		0	0	8	0		0		15.4	0					0	0	
42031000	皮革或再生皮革制的衣服	10	0		0	0		0	4	0	0	0		6	0	8				0	0	0
42032100	皮革或再生皮革制专供运动用手套	20	0	14	0	0	0	0	8	0	0	0		16						0	0	
42032910	皮革或再生皮革制的劳保手套	20	0		0	0	0	0	8	0	0	0		16		8				0	0	
42032990	皮革或再生皮革制的其他手套	20	0		0	0	0	0	8	0	0	0		16		8				0	0	
42033010	皮革或再生皮革制腰带	10	0		0	0		0	4	0	0	0		6	0	8				0	0	0
42033020	皮革或再生皮革制的腰带及子弹带	10	0		0	0		0	4	0	0			6	0	8				0	0	0
42034000	皮革或再生皮革制的其他衣着附件	20	0		0	0	0	0	8	0	0	0		16		8				0	0	
42050010	皮革或再生皮革制坐具套	12	0		0	6	0	0	0	0	0			9.6	0	7.8				0	0	0
42050020	机器、机械器具或其他专门技术用途的皮革或再生皮革制品	8	0		0	5		0	0	0				6.2	0					0	0	0
42050090	皮革或再生皮革的其他制品	12	0		0	6	0	0	4.8	0	0			9.6	0	7.8				0	0	0
42060000	肠线、肠膜、膀胱或筋腱制品	20	0		0		0	0	8	0				16	0					0	0	
43011000	整张生水貂皮	15	0		0	12	0	0	6	0	0			12	0					0	0	
43013000	阿斯特拉罕等羔羊的整张生毛皮，不论是否带头、尾或爪	20	0		0		0	0	8	0	0			16	0					0	0	
43016000	整张生狐皮	20	0		0		0	0	8	0	0			16	0					0	0	
43018010	整张生兔皮	20	0		0		0	0	8	0	0			16	0					0	0	
43018090	整张的其他生毛皮	20	0		0		0	0	8	0	0			16	0					0	0	
43019010	黄鼠狼尾	20	0		0		0	0	8	0	0			16	0					0	0	
43019090	适合加工皮货用的其他未鞣头、尾、爪	20	0		0		0	0	8	0	0			16	0					0	0	
43021100	已鞣未缝制的整张水貂皮	12	0		0	6	0	0	0	0	0			9.6	0					0	0	
43021910	已鞣未缝制的贵重毛皮（貂皮、狐皮、水獭及旱獭等）	10	0		0	5		0	0	0	0			6	0					0	0	
43021920	已鞣未缝制的整张兔皮	10	0		0	5		0	0	0	0			6	0					0	0	0
43021930	已鞣未缝制阿斯特拉罕等羔羊皮，不论是否带头、尾或爪	20	0		0		0	0	8	0	0			16						0	0	0
43021990	已鞣未缝制的其他毛皮	10	0		0			0	0	0	0			6	0					0	0	0
43022000	已鞣未缝制的头、尾、爪及其他块片	20	0		0		0	0	8	0	0			16	0					0	0	
43023010	已鞣已缝制的贵重毛皮及其块、片	20	0		0		0	0	8	0	0			16	0					0	0	
43023090	已鞣已缝制的其他整张毛皮及块片	20	0		0		0	0	8	0	0			16						0	0	
43031010	毛皮衣服	23	0		0		0	0	9.2	0	0			18.4		10.4				0	0	
43031020	毛皮衣着附件	18	0		0		0	0	7.2	0	0			14.4		9.9				0	0	
43039000	毛皮制其他物品	18	0		0	14.4	0	0	0	0	0			14.4		9.9				0	0	
43040010	人造毛皮	18	0		0		0	0	7.2	0	0			14.4		10.8				0	0	
43040020	人造毛皮制品	18	0		0	14.4	0	0	7.2	0	0			14.4		10.8				0	0	
44011000	薪柴	0																		0	0	0
44012100	针叶木木片或木粒	0																		0	0	0
44012200	非针叶木木片或木粒	0																		0	0	0
44013100	木屑棒	0																		0	0	0
44013900	其他锯末、木废料及碎片，不论是否粘结成原木段、块、片或类似形状	0																		0	0	0
44021000	竹炭	10.5	0		0	5	0	0	0	0				8.4	0					0	0	
44029000	木炭	10.5	0		0	5	0	0	0	0				8.4	0					0	0	
44031000	用油漆、着色剂、防腐剂等处理的原木	0																		0	0	0
44032010	红松和樟子松	0																		0	0	0
44032020	白松（云杉和冷杉）	0																		0	0	0
44032030	辐射松	0																		0	0	0
44032040	落叶松	0																		0	0	0

税则号列	货品名称	最惠国	协定税率													特惠税率						
			东盟统一	亚太5国	智利	巴基斯坦	新加坡	新西兰	秘鲁	哥达	香港	澳门	台湾	瑞士	冰岛	亚太2国	老挝	柬埔寨	缅甸	LDC1	LDC2	LDC3
44032050	花旗松	0																		0	0	0
44032090	其他针叶木	0																		0	0	0
44034100	深红色红柳桉木、浅红色红柳桉木及巴栲红柳桉木原木	0																		0	0	0
44034910	柚木原木	0																		0	0	0
44034920	奥克曼(奥克榄)原木	0																		0	0	0
44034930	龙脑香木原木	0																		0	0	0
44034940	山樟(香木)原木	0																		0	0	0
44034950	印加木(波罗格)原木	0																		0	0	0
44034960	大干巴豆(门格里斯或康派斯)原木	0																		0	0	0
44034970	异翅香木原木	0																		0	0	0
44034990	其他方法处理的其他热带原木	0																		0	0	0
44039100	栎木原木	0																		0	0	0
44039200	山毛榉木原木	0																		0	0	0
44039910	楠木原木	0																		0	0	0
44039920	樟木原木	0																		0	0	0
44039930	红木原木	0																		0	0	0
44039940	泡桐木原木	0																		0	0	0
44039950	水曲柳原木	0																		0	0	0
44039960	北美硬阔叶木原木(包括樱桃木、黑胡桃木、枫木)	0																		0	0	0
44039980	其他未列名的温带非针叶原木	0																		0	0	0
44039990	其他未列名非针叶原木	0																		0	0	0
44041000	针叶木的箍木、木劈条、木桩、木棒及类似品,木片条	8	0		0	5	0	0	0	0				4.8	0					0	0	
44042000	非针叶木箍木、木劈条、木桩、木棒及类似品,木片条	8	0		0	5	0	0	0	0				4.8	0					0	0	
44050000	木丝及木粉	8	0		0	5	0	0	0	0				4.8	0					0	0	0
44061000	未浸渍的铁道及电车道枕木	0																		0	0	0
44069000	已浸渍的铁道及电车道枕木	0																		0	0	0
44071010	红松和樟子松厚板材	0																		0	0	0
44071020	白松(云杉和冷杉)厚板材	0																		0	0	0
44071030	辐射松厚板材	0																		0	0	0
44071040	花旗松厚板材	0																		0	0	0
44071090	其他针叶木厚板材	0																		0	0	0
44072100	桃花心木板材,经纵锯、纵切、刨切,不论是否刨平、砂光或指榫结合,厚度超过6mm	0																		0	0	0
44072200	维罗蔻、细孔绿心樟、轻木板材,经纵锯、纵切、刨切,不论是否刨平、砂光或指榫结合,厚度超过6mm	0																		0	0	0
44072500	深红色红柳桉木、浅红色红柳桉木及巴栲红柳桉木板材,经纵锯、纵切、刨切,不论是否刨平、砂光或指榫结合,厚度超过6mm	0																		0	0	0
44072600	白柳桉木、白色红柳桉木、白色柳桉木、黄色红柳桉木及阿兰木,经纵锯、纵切、刨切,不论是否刨平、砂光或指榫结合,厚度超过6mm	0																		0	0	0
44072700	卡雅楝木板材,经纵锯、纵切、刨切,不论是否刨平、砂光或指榫结合,厚度超过6mm	0																		0	0	0
44072800	绿柄桑木板材,经纵锯、纵切、刨切,不论是否刨平、砂光或指榫结合,厚度超过6mm	0																		0	0	0
44072910	柚木板材,经纵锯、纵切、刨切,不论是否刨平、砂光或指榫结合,厚度超过6mm	0																		0	0	0
44072920	非洲桃花心木板材	0																		0	0	0
44072930	波罗格板材	0																		0	0	0

税则号列	货品名称	最惠国	协定税率													特惠税率						
			东盟统一	亚太5国	智利	巴基斯坦	新加坡	新西兰	秘鲁	哥达	香港	澳门	台湾	瑞士	冰岛	亚太2国	老挝	柬埔寨	缅甸	LDC1	LDC2	LDC3
44072990	其他列名的热带木板材，经纵锯、纵切、刨切，不论是否刨平、砂光或指榫结合，厚度超过6mm	0																		0	0	0
44079100	栎木板材，经纵锯、纵切、刨切，不论是否刨平、砂光或指榫结合，厚度超过6mm	0																		0	0	0
44079200	山毛榉木板材，经纵锯、纵切、刨切，不论是否刨平、砂光或指榫结合，厚度超过6mm	0																		0	0	0
44079300	枫木厚板材	0																		0	0	0
44079400	樱桃木厚板材	0																		0	0	0
44079500	白蜡木厚板材	0																		0	0	0
44079910	樟木、楠木、红木板材，经纵锯、纵切、刨切，不论是否刨平、砂光或指榫结合，厚度超过6mm	0																		0	0	0
44079920	泡桐木板材，经纵锯、纵切、刨切，不论是否刨平、砂光或指榫结合，厚度超过6mm	0																		0	0	0
44079930	北美硬阔叶木（含樱桃木、枫木、黑胡桃木）厚板材	0																		0	0	0
44079980	其他温带非针叶木厚板材	0																		0	0	0
44079990	其他木板材，经纵锯、纵切、刨切，不论是否刨平、砂光或指榫结合，厚度超过6mm	0																		0	0	0
44081011	用胶合板等多层板制的饰面用针叶木薄板，不论是否刨平、砂光或指榫结合	8	8		0			0	0	0				4.8	0					0		
44081019	饰面用针叶木薄板，不论是否刨平、砂光或指榫结合，用胶合板等多层板制的除外	4	0		0	0	0	0	0	0				0	0					0	0	
44081020	制胶合板用针叶木薄板，不论是否刨平、砂光或指榫结合	4	0		0	0	0	0	0	0				0	0					0	0	
44081090	其他针叶木薄板材，不论是否刨平、砂光或指榫结合	4	0		0	0	0	0	0	0				0	0					0	0	
44083111	用胶合板等多层板制的深红色红柳桉木、浅红色红柳桉木及巴栲红柳桉木制的饰面用薄板，不论是否刨平、砂光或指榫结合	10	10		0			0	0	0				6	0					0		
44083119	深红色红柳桉木、浅红色红柳桉木及巴栲红柳桉木制的饰面用薄板，不论是否刨平、砂光或指榫结合，用胶合板等多层板制的除外	4	0		0	0	0	0	0	0				0	0					0	0	
44083120	深红色红柳桉木、浅红色红柳桉木及巴栲红柳桉木制的胶合板用薄板，不论是否刨平、砂光或指榫结合	4	0		0	0	0	0	0	0				0	0					0	0	
44083190	深红色红柳桉木、浅红色红柳桉木及巴栲红柳桉木制的其他薄板，不论是否刨平、砂光或指榫结合	4	0		0	0	0	0	0	0				0	0					0	0	
44083911	用胶合板等多层板制的其他列名的热带木制的饰面用薄板，不论是否刨平、砂光或指榫结合	10	10		0			0	0	0				6	0					0		
44083919	其他列名的热带木制的饰面用薄板，不论是否刨平、砂光或指榫结合，用胶合板等多层板制的除外	4	0		0	0	0	0	0	0				0	0					0	0	
44083920	其他列名热带木制的胶合板用薄板，不论是否刨平、砂光或指榫结合	4	0		0	0	0	0	0	0				0	0					0	0	
44083990	其他列名的热带木制的其他薄板材，不论是否刨平、砂光或指榫结合	4	0		0	0	0	0	0	0				0	0					0	0	
44089011	用胶合板等多层板制的其他木制饰面用薄板，不论是否刨平、砂光或指榫结合	4	4		0			0	0	0				0	0					0		
44089012	温带非针叶木制饰面用单板	3	0		0	0	0	0	0	0				0	0					0	0	
44089013	竹制饰面用单板	4	4		0			0	0	0				0	0					0		

税则号列	货品名称	最惠国	协定税率													特惠税率						
			东盟统一	亚太5国	智利	巴基斯坦	新加坡	新西兰	秘鲁	哥达	香港	澳门	台湾	瑞士	冰岛	亚太2国	老挝	柬埔寨	缅甸	LDC1	LDC2	LDC3
44089019	其他木制饰面用薄板,不论是否刨平、砂光或指榫结合,用胶合板等多层板制的除外	3	0		0	0	0	0	0	0				0	0					0	0	
44089021	其他温带非针叶木制胶合板用单板	3	0		0	0	0	0	0	0				0	0					0	0	
44089029	其他木制胶合板用单板	3	0		0	0	0	0	0	0				0	0					0	0	
44089091	其他温带非针叶木制木材	3	0		0	0	0	0	0	0				0	0					0	0	
44089099	其他木材	3	0		0	0	0	0	0	0				0	0					0	0	
44091010	针叶木地板条(块)	7.5	0		0	5	0	0	0	0				4.5	0					0	0	0
44091090	一边或面制成连续形状的针叶木材,不论是否刨平、砂光或指榫结合	7.5	0		0	5	0	0	0	0				4.5	0					0	0	0
44092110	竹制地板条	4	0		0	0	0	0	0	0				0	0					0	0	0
44092190	一边或面制成连续形状的竹材,不论是否刨平、砂光或指榫结合	4	0		0	0	0	0	0	0				0	0					0	0	0
44092910	其他非针叶木地板条	4	0		0	0	0	0	0	0				0	0					0	0	0
44092990	一边或面制成连续形状的其他非针叶木材,不论是否刨平、砂光或指榫结合	4	0		0	0	0	0	0	0				0	0					0	0	
44101100	木制碎料板	4	4											0								
44101200	木制定向刨花板	4	4											0								
44101900	木制其他材料板	4	4											2.4								
44109011	麦稻秸秆制碎料板	7.5	7.5																			
44109019	其他类似木质碎料板	7.5	7.5																			
44109090	类似木质碎料的木质材料板	7.5	7.5																			
44111211	厚度不超过5毫米的中密度木纤维板,密度超过每立方厘米0.8克,未经机械加工或盖面的	4	4											0								
44111219	厚度不超过5毫米的中密度木纤维板,密度超过每立方厘米0.8克,经机械加工或盖面的	7.5	7.5											4.5								
44111221	辐射松制的厚度不超过5毫米的中密度木纤维板,密度超过每立方厘米0.5克,但未超过每立方厘米0.8克	4	4					0						0						0		
44111229	其他厚度不超过5毫米的中密度木纤维板,密度超过每立方厘米0.5克,但未超过每立方厘米0.8克	4	4											0								
44111291	厚度不超过5毫米的其他中密度木纤维板,未经机械加工或盖面的	7.5	7.5											4.5								
44111299	厚度不超过5毫米的其他中密度木纤维板,经机械加工或盖面的	4	4											0								
44111311	厚度超过5毫米但未超过9毫米的中密度木纤维板,密度超过每立方厘米0.8克,未经机械加工或盖面的	4	4											0								
44111319	厚度超过5毫米但未超过9毫米的中密度木纤维板,密度超过每立方厘米0.8克,经机械加工或盖面的	7.5	7.5											5.8								
44111321	辐射松制的厚度超过5毫米但未超过9毫米的中密度木纤维板,密度超过每立方厘米0.5克,但未超过每立方厘米0.8克	4	4					0						0						0		
44111329	其他厚度超过5毫米但未超过9毫米的中密度木纤维板,密度超过每立方厘米0.5克,但未超过每立方厘米0.8克	4	4											0								
44111391	厚度超过5毫米但未超过9毫米的其他中密度木纤维板,未经机械加工或盖面的	7.5	7.5											4.5								
44111399	厚度超过5毫米但未超过9毫米的其他中密度木纤维板,经机械加工或盖面的	4	4											0								

税则号列	货品名称	最惠国	协定税率													特惠税率						
			东盟统一	亚太5国	智利	巴基斯坦	新加坡	新西兰	秘鲁	哥达	香港	澳门	台湾	瑞士	冰岛	亚太2国	老挝	柬埔寨	缅甸	LDC1	LDC2	LDC3
44111411	厚度超过9毫米的中密度木纤维板,密度超过每立方厘米0.8克,未经机械加工或盖面的	4	4											0								
44111419	厚度超过9毫米的中密度木纤维板,密度超过每立方厘米0.8克,经机械加工或盖面的	7.5	7.5											5.8								
44111421	辐射松制的厚度超过9毫米的中密度木纤维板,密度超过每立方厘米0.5克,但未超过每立方厘米0.8克	4	4					0						0						0		
44111429	其他厚度超过9毫米的中密度木纤维板,密度超过每立方厘米0.5克,但未超过每立方厘米0.8克	4	4											0								
44111491	厚度超过9毫米的其他中密度木纤维板,未经机械加工或盖面的	7.5	7.5											4.5								
44111499	厚度超过9毫米的其他中密度木纤维板,经机械加工或盖面的	4	4											0								
44119210	其他木纤维板,密度超过每立方厘米0.8克,未经机械加工或盖面的	4	4											0								
44119290	其他木纤维板,密度超过每立方厘米0.8克,经机械加工或盖面的	7.5	7.5											4.5								
44119310	辐射松制的其他木纤维板,密度超过每立方厘米0.5克,但未超过每立方厘米0.8克	4	4					0						0						0		
44119390	其他木纤维板,密度超过每立方厘米0.5克,但未超过每立方厘米0.8克	4	4											0								
44119410	其他木纤维板,密度超过每立方厘米0.35克,但未超过每立方厘米0.5克	7.5	7.5											4.5								
44119421	其他木纤维板,密度未超过每立方厘米0.35,未经机械加工或盖面的	7.5	7.5											4.5								
44119429	其他木纤维板,密度未超过每立方厘米0.35,经机械加工或盖面的	4	4											0								
44121011	至少有一表层为热带木的竹胶合板	12	12		0			0	0	0				9.6	0					0		
44121019	其他仅由薄板制竹胶合板	4	4											0								
44121020	竹面多层板	10	10			5		0	0	0				6						0		
44121091	至少一层为热带木的竹面多层板	8	8											4.8								
44121092	至少一层为木碎板的竹面多层板	10	10											6								
44121099	其他竹面多层板	4	0		0	0	0	0	0	0				0	0					0	0	0
44123100	其他至少有一表层为热带木薄板制的胶合板	12	12		0			0	0	0				9.6	0					0		
44123210	其他至少有一表层为温带非针叶木单板制的胶合板	4	4											0								
44123290	其他至少有一表层为非针叶木单板制的胶合板	4	4											0								
44123900	其他仅由薄木板制胶合板	4	0		0	0	0	0	0	0				0	0					0	0	0
44129410	木块芯胶合板,侧板条芯胶合板及板条芯胶合板,至少有一表层是非针叶木	10	10			5								6								
44129491	木块芯胶合板,侧板条芯胶合板及板条芯胶合板,至少有一层是热带木	8	8											4.8								
44129492	木块芯胶合板,侧板条芯胶合板及板条芯胶合板,至少含有一层木碎料	10	10											6								

税则号列	货品名称	最惠国	协定税率													特惠税率						
			东盟统一	亚太5国	智利	巴基斯坦	新加坡	新西兰	秘鲁	哥达	香港	澳门	台湾	瑞士	冰岛	亚太2国	老挝	柬埔寨	缅甸	LDC1	LDC2	LDC3
44129499	其他木块芯胶合板,侧板条芯胶合板及板条芯胶合板	4	0		0	0	0	0	0	0				0	0					0	0	0
44129910	至少有一表层是非针叶木的其他木面多层板	10	10			5								6								
44129991	至少有一层是热带木的其他木面多层板	8	8											4.8								
44129992	至少含有一层木碎料板的其他木面多层板	10	10											6								
44129999	其他木面多层板	4	0		0	0	0	0	0	0				0	0					0	0	
44130000	强化木	6	0		0	5	0	0	0	0				3.6	0					0	0	0
44140010	辐射松制的画框、相框、镜框及类似品	20	20					0												0		
44140090	其他木制的画框、相框、镜框及类似品	20	20																			
44151000	木箱及类似的包装容器;电缆卷筒	7.5	0		0	5	0	0	0	0				4.5	0					0	0	0
44152010	辐射松制的木托板、箱形托盘及其他装载用木板;辐射松制制的托盘护框	7.5	7.5					0												0		
44152090	其他木托板、箱形托盘及其他装载用木板;其他木制的托盘护框	7.5	7.5																			
44160010	辐射松制的大桶、琵琶桶、盆和其他辐射松制箍桶及其零件,包括桶板	16	16					0												0		
44160090	其他木制大桶、琵琶桶、盆和其他木制箍桶及其零件,包括桶板	16	16																			
44170010	辐射松制的工具、工具支架、工具柄、扫帚及刷子的身及柄;辐射松制鞋靴楦及楦头	16	16					0												0		
44170090	其他木制的工具、工具支架、工具柄、扫帚及刷子的身及柄;木制鞋靴楦及楦头	16	16																			
44181010	辐射松制的窗、法兰西式(落地)窗及其框架	4	4					0												0		
44181090	其他木制的窗、法兰西式(落地)窗及其框架	4	4									0								0		
44182000	木门及其框架和门槛	4	0		0	0	0	0	0	0		0		0	0					0	0	0
44184000	水泥构件的木模板	4	0		0	0		0	0	0				0	0					0	0	0
44185000	木瓦及盖屋板	7.5	0		0	5		0	0	0				4.5	0					0	0	0
44186000	柱和梁	4	0		0	0	0	0	0	0				0	0					0	0	0
44187100	已拼装的马赛克地板	4	0		0	0	0	0	0	0				0	0					0	0	0
44187210	竹制已拼装的多层地板	4	0		0	0	0	0	0	0				0	0					0	0	
44187290	其他已拼装的多层地板	4	0		0	0	0	0	0	0				0	0					0	0	
44187910	竹制已拼装的地板	4	0		0	0	0	0	0	0				0	0					0	0	
44187990	其他已拼装的地板	4	0		0	0	0	0	0	0				0	0					0	0	
44189010	竹制建筑用制品	4	0		0	0	0	0	0	0				0	0					0	0	0
44189090	其他建筑用木工制品	4	0		0	0	0	0	0	0				0	0					0	0	0
44190031	木制一次性筷子	0																		0	0	0
44190032	竹制一次性筷子	0																		0	0	0
44190091	竹制其他餐具及厨房用具	0																		0	0	0
44190099	其他木制餐具及厨房用具	0																		0	0	0
44201011	木刻	0																		0	0	0
44201012	竹刻	0																		0	0	0
44201020	木扇	0																		0	0	0
44201090	其他木制小雕像及其他装饰品	0																		0	0	0
44209010	镶嵌木	0																		0	0	0
44209090	木盒子及类似品;非落地式木家具	0																		0	0	0
44211000	木衣架	0																		0	0	0
44219010	木卷轴、纡子、筒管、线轴及类似品	0																		0	0	0
44219021	木制园签、园棒、冰果棒、压舌片及类似一次性制品	0																		0	0	0
44219022	竹制园签、园棒、冰果棒、压舌片及类似一次性制品	0																		0	0	0
44219090	其他未列名的木制品	0																		0	0	0
45011000	未加工或简单加工的天然软木	6	0		0	5		0	0	0				3.6	0					0	0	
45019010	软木废料	0																		0	0	0

税则号列	货品名称	最惠国	协定税率 东盟统一	亚太5国	智利	巴基斯坦	新加坡	新西兰	秘鲁	哥达	香港	澳门	台湾	瑞士	冰岛	特惠税率 亚太2国	老挝	柬埔寨	缅甸	LDC1	LDC2	LDC3
45019020	软木废料及碎、粒、粉状的软木	0																		0	0	0
45020000	除去表皮或粗切成方形或成块、板、片或条状的天然软木	8	0		0	5		0	0	0				4.8	0					0	0	0
45031000	天然软木塞子	8	0		0	5		0	0	0				4.8	0					0	0	0
45039000	其他天然软木制品	10.5	0		0	5	0	0	0	0				8.4	0					0	0	0
45041000	块、板、片及条状压制软木;任何形状的砖、瓦;实心圆柱体,包括原片	8.4	0		0	5		0	0	0				5	0					0	0	0
45049000	其他压制软木及其制品	0																		0	0	0
46012100	竹制的席子、席料、帘子	9	0		0	5		0	0	0		0		5.4	0		0			0	0	0
46012200	藤制的席子、席料及帘子	9	0		0	5		0	0	0		0		5.4	0		0			0	0	0
46012911	蔺草制的席子、席料及帘子	9	0		0	5		0	0	0		0		5.4	0		0			0	0	0
46012919	其他草制的席子、席料及帘子	9	0		0	5		0	0	0				5.4	0		0			0	0	0
46012921	苇帘	9	0		0	5		0	0	0				5.4	0		0			0	0	0
46012929	芦苇制的席子、席料	9	0		0	5		0	0	0				5.4	0		0			0	0	0
46012990	其他植物材料制席子、席料及帘子	9	0		0	5		0	0	0				5.4	0		0			0	0	0
46019210	竹缏条及类似产品,不论是否缝合成宽条	9	0		0	5		0	0	0		0		5.4	0		0			0	0	0
46019290	其他竹编结产品	9	0		0	5		0	0	0		0		5.4	0					0	0	0
46019310	藤缏条及类似产品,不论是否缝合成宽条	9	0		0	5		0	0	0		0		5.4	0		0			0	0	0
46019390	其他藤编结产品	9	0		0	5		0		0		0		5.4	0					0		
46019411	稻草制的鞭条(绳)	10	0		0	5		0	0	0				6	0					0	0	
46019419	稻草制的其他编结材料产品	10	0		0	5		0	0	0				6	0					0	0	
46019491	其他植物编结材料的缏条及类似产品,不论是否缝合成宽条	9	0		0	5		0	0	0				5.4	0		0			0	0	0
46019499	其他植物编结材料产品	9	0		0	5		0	0	0				5.4	0					0	0	0
46019910	其他非植物编结材料的缏条及类似产品,不论是否缝合成宽条	9	0		0	5		0	0	0				5.4	0		0			0	0	0
46019990	其他非植物编结材料产品	9	0		0	5		0	0	0				5.4	0					0	0	
46021100	竹编制的篮筐及其他制品	9	0		0	5		0	0	0				5.4	0			0		0	0	0
46021200	藤编制的篮筐及其他制品	9	0		0	5		0		0				5.4	0			0		0	0	0
46021910	草编制的篮筐及其他制品	9	0		0	5		0	0	0				5.4	0			0		0	0	0
46021920	玉米皮编制的篮筐及其他制品	9	0		0	5		0	0	0				5.4	0			0		0	0	0
46021930	柳条编制的篮筐及其他制品	9	0		0	5		0	0	0				5.4	0			0		0	0	0
46021990	其他植物材料编制篮筐及其他制品	9	0		0	5		0		0				5.4	0			0		0	0	0
46029000	其他编结材料制品及其他制品	9	0	8	0	5		0	0	0		0		5.4	0			0		0	0	0
47010000	机械木浆	0																		0	0	0
47020000	化学木浆,溶解级	0																		0	0	0
47031100	未漂白针叶木碱木浆或硫酸盐木浆	0																		0	0	0
47031900	未漂白非针叶木碱木浆或硫酸盐木浆	0																		0	0	0
47032100	漂白针叶木碱木浆或硫酸盐木浆	0																		0	0	0
47032900	漂白非针叶木碱木浆或硫酸盐木浆	0																		0	0	0
47041100	未漂白的针叶木亚硫酸盐木浆	0																		0	0	0
47041900	未漂白的非针叶木亚硫酸盐木浆	0																		0	0	0
47042100	漂白的针叶木亚硫酸盐木浆	0																		0	0	0
47042900	漂白的非针叶木亚硫酸盐木浆	0																		0	0	0
47050000	半化学木浆	0																		0	0	0
47061000	棉短绒纸浆	0																		0	0	0
47062000	从回收纸或纸板提取的纤维浆	0																		0	0	0
47063000	竹浆	0																		0	0	0
47069100	其他纤维状纤维素机械浆	0																		0	0	0
47069200	其他纤维状纤维素化学浆	0																		0	0	0
47069300	用机械和化学联合法制得的浆	0																		0	0	0
47071000	未漂白牛皮、瓦楞纸或纸板废碎品	0																		0	0	0
47072000	漂白化学木浆制的未经本体染色纸和纸板废碎品	0																		0	0	0
47073000	机械木浆制的纸或纸板的废碎品	0																		0	0	0
47079000	其他回收纸或纸板	0																		0	0	0
48010000	成卷或成张的新闻纸	5	5																			
48021010	宣纸	7.5	7.5																			
48021090	其他手工制纸及纸板	7.5	7.5																			
48022010	照相原纸	7.5	7.5								0									0		

税则号列	货品名称	最惠国	协定税率													特惠税率						
			东盟统一	亚太5国	智利	巴基斯坦	新加坡	新西兰	秘鲁	哥达	香港	澳门	台湾	瑞士	冰岛	亚太2国	老挝	柬埔寨	缅甸	LDC1	LDC2	LDC3
48022090	光敏、热敏、电敏纸,纸板的原纸、板	7.5	7.5								0									0		
48024000	墙壁纸原纸	7.5	7.5								0									0		
48025400	书写、印刷等用未涂布薄纸及纸板,不含用机械方法制得的纤维或所含前述纤维不超过全部纤维重量的10%	7.5	7.5								0									0		
48025500	其他书写印刷等用未涂中厚纸(板),不含用机械方法制得的纤维或所含前述纤维不超过全部纤维重量的10%,成卷	5	5								0									0		
48025600	书写、印刷等用未涂布中厚纸及纸板,不含用机械方法制得的纤维或所含前述纤维不超过全部纤维重量的10%,成张,一边≤435mm,另一边≤297mm	5	5								0									0		
48025700	其他书写印刷等用未涂中厚纸(板),不含用机械方法制得的纤维或所含前述纤维不超过全部纤维重量的10%,其他成张	5	5								0									0		
48025800	书写、印刷等用未涂布厚纸及纸板,不含用机械方法制得的纤维或所含前述纤维不超过全部纤维重量的10%	5	5								0									0		
48026110	其他书写、印刷等用未涂布纸及纸板,所含用机械方法制得的纤维超过全部纤维重量的10%,成卷的新闻纸	7.5	7.5																			
48026190	其他书写、印刷等用未涂布纸及纸板,所含用机械方法制得的纤维超过全部纤维重量的10%,成卷的其他纸	5	5								0									0		
48026200	其他书写、印刷等用未涂布纸及纸板,所含用机械方法制得的纤维超过全部纤维重量的10%,成张的,一边≤435mm、另一边≤297mm(以未折叠计)	5	5								0									0		
48026910	其他书写、印刷等用未涂布纸及纸板,所含用机械方法制得的纤维超过全部纤维重量的10%,成张的新闻纸	7.5	7.5																			
48026990	其他书写、印刷等用未涂布纸及纸板,所含用机械方法制得的纤维超过全部纤维重量的10%,成张的其他纸	5	5								0									0		
48030000	卫生纸、面巾纸、餐巾纸及类似纸	7.5	7.5																			
48041100	成卷或成张的未经涂布未漂白的牛皮挂面纸	5	5																			
48041900	成卷或成张的未经涂布的漂白的牛皮挂面纸	5	5																			
48042100	未漂白的袋用牛皮纸	5	5																			
48042900	漂白的袋用牛皮纸	5	5																			
48043100	未漂白的其他薄牛皮纸及纸板	2	2																			
48043900	漂白的薄牛皮纸及纸板	2	2																			
48044100	未漂白的其他中厚牛皮纸及纸板	2	2																			
48044200	本体均匀漂白的中厚牛皮纸及纸板	5	5																			
48044900	其他漂白的中厚牛皮纸及纸板	2	2																			
48045100	未漂白的其他厚牛皮纸及纸板 、	2	2																			
48045200	本体均匀漂白的厚牛皮纸及纸板	5	5																			
48045900	其他漂白的厚牛皮纸及纸板	2	2																			
48051100	半化学的瓦楞纸(瓦楞原纸)	7.5	7.5								0									0		
48051200	草浆瓦楞原纸	7.5	7.5								0									0		
48051900	其他瓦楞原纸	7.5	7.5								0									0		
48052400	薄强韧箱纸板	7.5	7.5								0									0		
48052500	厚强韧箱纸板	7.5	7.5								0									0		
48053000	亚硫酸盐包装纸	7.5	7.5																			
48054000	滤纸及纸板	7.5	7.5																			
48055000	毡纸及纸板	7.5	7.5																			

税则号列	货品名称	最惠国	协定税率													特惠税率						
			东盟统一	亚太5国	智利	巴基斯坦	新加坡	新西兰	秘鲁	哥达	香港	澳门	台湾	瑞士	冰岛	亚太2国	老挝	柬埔寨	缅甸	LDC1	LDC2	LDC3
48059110	每平方米重量在150克及以下的电解电容器原纸	7.5	7.5								0									0		
48059190	每平方米重量在150克及以下的薄纸及纸板	7.5	7.5								0									0		
48059200	其他未经涂布中厚纸及纸板	7.5	7.5																			
48059300	其他未经涂布厚纸及纸板	7.5	7.5								0									0		
48061000	植物羊皮纸	7.5	7.5																			
48062000	防油纸	7.5	7.5																			
48063000	描图纸	7.5	7.5																			
48064000	高光泽透明或半透明纸	7.5	7.5																			
48070000	成卷或成张的复合纸及纸板,未经表面涂布或未浸渍	7.5	7.5																			
48081000	瓦楞纸及纸板	7.5	7.5											5.8								
48084000	皱纹牛皮纸	7.5	7.5																			
48089000	其他皱纹纸及纸板、纹纸及纸板	7.5	7.5																			
48092000	大张(卷)的自印复写纸	7.5	7.5																			
48099000	其他大张(卷)的拷贝纸或转印纸	7.5	7.5																			
48101300	涂无机物书写(印刷)纸(板),不含用机械方法制得的纤维或所含前述纤维不超过全部纤维重量的10%,成卷的	5	5								0									0		
48101400	涂无机物书写(印刷)纸(板),不含用机械方法制得的纤维或所含前述纤维不超过全部纤维重量的10%,成张的,一边≤435mm,另一边≤297mm(以未折叠计)	5	5								0									0		
48101900	其他涂无机物书写(印刷)纸(板),不含用机械方法制得的纤维或所含前述纤维不超过全部纤维重量的10%,成张的	5	5								0									0		
48102200	轻质涂布无机物的书写、印刷纸,所含用机械方法制得的纤维超过全部纤维重量的10%	5	5																			
48102900	其他涂无机物的书写、印刷纸及纸板,所含用机械方法制得的纤维超过全部纤维重量的10%	5	5								0									0		
48103100	涂无机物的薄漂白牛皮纸及纸板,书写、印刷或类似用途的除外	5	5								0	0								0		
48103200	涂无机物的厚漂白牛皮纸及纸板,书写、印刷或类似用途的除外	5	5								0	0								0		
48103900	涂无机物的其他牛皮纸及纸板,书写、印刷或类似用途的除外	5	5								0	0								0		
48109200	其他涂无机物的多层纸及纸板	5	5								0	0								0		
48109900	其他涂无机物的纸及纸板	7.5	7.5								0	0								0		
48111000	焦油纸及纸板、沥青纸及纸板	7.5	7.5								0	0								0		
48114100	自粘的胶粘纸及纸板	7.5	7.5								0	0								0		
48114900	其他胶粘纸及纸板	7.5	7.5								0	0								0		
48115110	漂白的彩色相纸用双面涂塑厚纸	7.5	7.5								0	0								0		
48115199	其他漂白的,每平方米重量超过150克的纸、纸板、纤维素絮纸及纤维素纤维网纸	7.5	7.5								0	0								0		
48115191	纸塑铝复合材料	7.5	7.5								0	0								0		
48115910	绝缘纸及纸板	7.5	7.5								0	0								0		
48115991	镀铝的用塑料涂布、浸渍的其他纸及纸板	7.5	7.5								0	0								0		
48115999	其他用塑料涂布、浸渍的其他纸及纸板	7.5	7.5								0	0								0		
48116010	用蜡或油等涂布的绝缘纸及纸板	7.5	7.5								0	0								0		
48116090	用蜡或油等涂布的其他纸及纸板	7.5	7.5								0	0								0		
48119000	其他经涂布、浸渍、覆盖的纸及纸板	7.5	7.5								0	0								0		
48120000	纸浆制的滤块、滤板及滤片	7.5	7.5																			
48131000	成小本或管状的卷烟纸	7.5	7.5																			
48132000	宽度≤5cm成卷的卷烟纸	7.5	7.5																			
48139000	其他卷烟纸	7.5	7.5																			

税则号列	货品名称	最惠国	协定税率 东盟统一	亚太5国	智利	巴基斯坦	新加坡	新西兰	秘鲁	哥达	香港	澳门	台湾	瑞士	冰岛	特惠税率 亚太2国	老挝	柬埔寨	缅甸	LDC1	LDC2	LDC3
48142000	用塑料涂面或盖面的壁纸及类似品	7.5	7.5																			
48149000	其他壁纸及类似品;窗用透明纸	7.5	7.5																			
48162000	小卷(张)自印复写纸	7.5	7.5																			
48169010	小卷(张)热敏转印纸	7.5	7.5																			
48169090	小卷(张)胶印版纸及其他拷贝纸或	7.5	7.5																			
48171000	信封	7.5	7.5																			
48172000	封缄信片、素色明信片及通信卡片	7.5	7.5																			
48173000	纸或纸板制的盒子、袋子及夹子	7.5	7.5																			
48181000	小卷(张)卫生纸	7.5	7.5																			
48182000	小卷(张)纸手帕及纸面巾	7.5	7.5																			
48183000	小卷(张)纸台布及纸餐巾	7.5	7.5																			
48185000	纸制衣服及衣着附件	7.5	0		0	5		0	0	0				4.5	0					0	0	0
48189000	纸床单及类似家庭、卫生、医院用品	7.5	7.5																			
48191000	瓦楞纸或纸板制的箱、盒、匣	5	5								0	0								0		
48192000	非瓦楞纸或纸板制可折叠箱、盒、匣	5	5								0	0								0		
48193000	底宽≥40cm 的纸袋	7.5	0		0	5	0	0	0	0				4.5	0					0	0	0
48194000	其他纸袋	7.5	7.5																			
48195000	其他纸包装容器	7.5	7.5																			
48196000	纸卷宗盒、信件盘、存储盒及类似品	7.5	7.5																			
48201000	登记本、帐本、笔记本、定货本、收据本、信笺本、记事本、日记本及类似品	7.5	7.5																			
48202000	练习本	7.5	7.5																			
48203000	纸制活动封面、文件夹及卷宗皮	7.5	7.5																			
48204000	多联商业表格纸、页间夹有复写纸的本	7.5	0		0	5		0	0	0				4.5	0					0	0	0
48205000	纸制样品簿及粘贴簿	7.5	7.5																			
48209000	其他纸制文具用品,书籍封面	7.5	7.5																			
48211000	纸或纸板印制的各种标签	7.5	7.5								0	0								0		
48219000	纸或纸板制的其他各种标签	7.5	7.5																			
48221000	纺织纱线用纸制的筒管、卷轴、纡子	7.5	7.5																			
48229000	纸制的其他筒管、卷轴、纡子	7.5	7.5																			
48232000	切成形的滤纸及纸板	7.5	7.5																			
48234000	已印制的自动记录器用打印纸	7.5	7.5																			
48236100	竹浆纸、纸板制的盘、碟、盆、杯及类似品	7.5	0		0	5		0	0	0				4.5	0					0	0	0
48236910	非木植物浆制	7.5	0		0	5		0	0	0				4.5	0					0	0	0
48236990	其他纸或纸板制的盘、碟、盆、杯及类似品	7.5	0		0	5		0	0	0				4.5	0					0	0	0
48237000	压制或模制纸浆制品	7.5	7.5																			
48239010	以纸或纸板为底制成的铺地制品	7.5	7.5											4.5								
48239020	神纸及类似用品	7.5	0		0	5		0	0	0				4.5	0					0	0	0
48239030	纸扇	7.5	0		0	5		0	0	0				4.5	0					0	0	0
48239090	其他纸及纸制品	7.5	7.5								0	0								0		
49011000	单张的书籍、小册子及类似印刷品	0																		0	0	0
49019100	字典、百科全书	0																		0	0	0
49019900	其他书籍、小册子及类似的印刷品	0																		0	0	0
49021000	每周至少出版四次的报纸、杂志	0																		0	0	0
49029000	其他报纸、杂志及期刊	0																		0	0	0
49030000	儿童图画书、绘画或涂色书	0																		0	0	0
49040000	乐谱原稿或印本	0																		0	0	0
49051000	地球仪、天体仪	0																		0	0	0
49059100	成册的各种印刷的地图及类似图表	0																		0	0	0
49059900	其他各种印刷的地图及类似图表	0																		0	0	0
49060000	设计图纸原稿或手稿及其复制件	0																		0	0	0
49070010	指运国流通新发行未使用的邮票	7.5	7.5											4.5						0	0	
49070020	钞票	0																		0	0	0
49070030	证券凭证	0																		0	0	0
49070090	指运国流通新发行未使用的印花税票及类似票证;印有邮票或印花税票的纸品;空白支票	7.5	7.5											4.5						0	0	
49081000	釉转印贴花纸	7.5	7.5											4.5						0	0	
49089000	其他转印贴花纸	7.5	7.5								0			4.5						0	0	

税则号列	货品名称	最惠国	协定税率													特惠税率						
			东盟统一	亚太5国	智利	巴基斯坦	新加坡	新西兰	秘鲁	哥达	香港	澳门	台湾	瑞士	冰岛	亚太2国	老挝	柬埔寨	缅甸	LDC1	LDC2	LDC3
49090010	印刷或有图画的明信片	7.5	7.5											4.5						0	0	
49090090	其他致贺或通告卡片	7.5	7.5											4.5						0	0	
49100000	印刷的各种日历,包括日历芯	7.5	7.5											6						0	0	0
49111010	无商业价值的广告品及类似印刷品	0																		0	0	0
49111090	其他商业广告品及类似印刷品	7.5	7.5								0			6						0	0	
49119100	印刷的图片、设计图样及照片	7.5	7.5											4.5						0	0	
49119910	纸质的其他印刷品	7.5	7.5								0			5.8	0					0	0	
49119990	其他印刷品	7.5	7.5								0			5.8	0					0	0	
50010010	适于缫丝的桑蚕茧	6	0		0	5		0	0	0				3.6	0					0	0	0
50010090	适于缫丝的其他蚕茧	6	0		0	5		0	0	0				3.6	0					0	0	0
50020011	厂丝	9	0		0	5		0	0	0				5.4	0					0	0	0
50020012	土丝	9	0		0	5		0	0	0				5.4	0					0	0	0
50020013	双宫丝	9	0		0	5		0	0	0				5.4	0					0	0	0
50020019	其他未加捻桑蚕丝	9	0		0	5		0	0	0				5.4	0					0	0	0
50020020	未加捻柞蚕丝	9	0		0	5		0	0	0				5.4	0					0	0	0
50020090	未加捻其他生丝	9	0		0	5		0	0	0				5.4	0					0	0	0
50030011	下茧、茧衣、长吐、滞头	9	0		0	5		0	0	0				5.4	0					0	0	0
50030012	回收纤维	9	0		0	5		0	0	0				5.4	0					0	0	0
50030019	其他	9	0		0	5		0	0	0				5.4	0					0	0	0
50030091	绵球	9	0		0	5		0	0	0				5.4	0					0	0	0
50030099	其他	9	0		0	5		0	0	0				5.4	0					0	0	0
50040000	非供零售用丝纱线	6	0		0	5		0	0	0		0		3.6	0					0	0	0
50050010	非供零售用绸丝纱线	6	0		0	5		0	0	0		0		3.6	0					0	0	0
50050090	非供零售用其他绢纺纱线	6	0		0	5		0	0	0		0		3.6	0					0	0	0
50060000	零售用丝纱线、绢纺纱线;蚕胶丝	6	0		0	5		0	0	0		0		3.6	0					0	0	0
50071010	未漂白或漂白的绸丝机织物	10	0		0	5		0	0	0				6	0		0			0	0	0
50071090	其他绸丝机织物	10	0		0	5		0	0	0				6	0		0			0	0	0
50072011	未漂白或漂白的纯桑蚕丝机织物	10	0	9	0	5		0	0	0				6	0		0			0	0	0
50072019	其他纯桑蚕丝机织物	10	0	9	0	5		0	0	0	0			6	0		0			0	0	0
50072021	未漂白或漂白的纯柞蚕丝机织物	10	0	9	0	5		0	0	0				6	0		0			0	0	0
50072029	其他纯柞蚕丝机织物	10	0	9	0	5		0	0	0				6	0		0			0	0	0
50072031	未漂白或漂白的纯绢丝机织物	10	0	9	0	5		0	0	0				6	0		0			0	0	0
50072039	其他纯绢丝机织物	10	0	9	0	5		0	0	0				6	0		0			0	0	0
50072090	其他纯丝机织物	10	0	9	0	5		0	0	0				6	0		0			0	0	0
50079010	未漂白或漂白其他丝机织物	10	0	8.5	0	5		0	0	0				6	0		0			0	0	0
50079090	其他丝机织物	10	0	8.5	0	5		0	4	0				6	0		0			0	0	0
51011100	未梳的含脂剪羊毛	38	20																			
51011900	未梳的其他含脂羊毛	38	20																			
51012100	未梳的脱脂剪羊毛(未碳化)	38	20																			
51012900	未梳的其他脱脂羊毛(未碳化)	38	20																			
51013000	未梳碳化羊毛	38	20									0										
51021100	未梳喀什米尔山羊毛	9	0		0	5		0	0	0				5.4	0					0	0	0
51021910	未梳兔毛	9	0		0	5		0	0	0				5.4	0					0	0	0
51021920	未梳其他山羊绒	9	0		0	5		0	0	0				5.4	0					0	0	0
51021930	未梳骆驼毛、骆驼绒	9	0		0	5		0	0	0				5.4	0					0	0	0
51021990	未梳的其他动物细毛	9	0		0	5		0	0	0				5.4	0					0	0	
51022000	未梳的动物粗毛	9	0		0	5		0	0	0				5.4	0					0	0	0
51031010	羊毛落毛	38	20																			
51031090	其他动物细毛落毛	9	0		0	5		0	0	0				5.4	0					0	0	0
51032010	羊毛废料	13.5	0		0	6.8	0	0	5.4	0				10.8	0					0	0	
51032090	其他动物细毛废料	9	0		0	5		0	0	0				5.4	0					0	0	
51033000	动物粗毛废料	9	0		0	5		0	0	0				5.4	0					0	0	0
51040010	羊毛回收纤维	15	0		0	12	0	0	6	0				12	0					0	0	
51040090	其他动物细毛或粗毛的回收纤维	5	0		0	0		0	0	0				0	0					0	0	0
51051000	粗梳羊毛	38	38																			
51052100	精梳羊毛片毛	38	38																			
51052900	羊毛条及其他精梳羊毛	38	38																			
51053100	已梳喀什米尔山羊毛	5	0		0	0		0	0	0				0	0					0	0	0
51053910	已梳兔毛	5	0		0	0		0		0				0	0					0	0	0
51053921	已梳无毛山羊绒	5	0		0	0		0		0				0	0					0	0	0
51053929	其他已梳山羊绒	5	0		0	0		0		0				0	0					0	0	0

税则号列	货品名称	最惠国	协定税率													特惠税率						
			东盟统一	亚太5国	智利	巴基斯坦	新加坡	新西兰	秘鲁	哥达	香港	澳门	台湾	瑞士	冰岛	亚太2国	老挝	柬埔寨	缅甸	LDC1	LDC2	LDC3
51053990	其他已梳动物细毛	5	0		0	0		0		0				0	0					0	0	
51054000	已梳动物粗毛	5	0		0	0		0		0				0	0					0	0	0
51061000	非供零售用粗梳纯羊毛纱线	5	0		0	0		0	0	0	0	0		0	0					0	0	0
51062000	非供零售用粗梳混纺羊毛纱线	5	0		0	0		0	0	0	0	0		0	0					0	0	0
51071000	非供零售用精梳纯羊毛纱线	5	0	2.5	0	0		0	0	0	0	0		0						0	0	0
51072000	非供零售用精梳混纺羊毛纱线	5	0		0	0		0	0	0		0		0	0					0	0	0
51081011	按重量计山羊绒的含量在85%及以上的非供零售用的粗梳纱线	5	0	4.3	0	0		0	0	0		0		0	0					0	0	0
51081019	按重量计其他动物细毛含量在85%及以上的非供零售用的粗梳纱线	5	0	4.3	0	0		0	0	0		0		0	0					0	0	0
51081090	按重量计动物细毛含量在85%以下的非供零售用的粗梳纱线	5	0	4.3	0	0		0	0	0		0		0	0					0	0	0
51082011	按重量计山羊绒含量在85%及以上的非供零售用的精梳纱线	5	0		0	0		0		0		0		0	0					0	0	0
51082019	按重量计其他动物细毛含量在85%及以上的非供零售用的精梳纱线	5	0		0	0		0		0		0		0	0					0	0	0
51082090	按重量计动物细毛含量在85%以下的非供零售用的精梳纱线	5	0		0	0		0		0		0		0	0					0	0	0
51091011	按重量计山羊绒含量在85%及以上的供零售用的纱线	6	0		0	5		0	0	0				3.6	0					0	0	0
51091019	按重量计其他动物细毛含量在85%及以上的供零售用的纱线	6	0		0	5		0	0	0		0		3.6	0					0	0	0
51091090	按重量计羊毛含量在85%及以上的供零售用的纱线	6	0		0	5		0	0	0		0		3.6	0					0	0	0
51099011	供零售用的其他山羊绒纱线	6	0		0	5		0		0		0		3.6	0					0	0	0
51099019	供零售用的其他动物细毛纱线	6	0		0	5		0		0		0		3.6	0					0	0	0
51099090	供零售用的羊毛纱线	6	0		0	5		0		0		0		3.6	0					0	0	0
51100000	动物粗毛或马毛的纱线	6	0		0	5		0	0	0		0		3.6	0					0	0	0
51111111	按重量计山羊绒含量在85%及以上,每平方米重量不超过300克的山羊绒机织物	10	0	8.5	0	5	0	0	0	0				6	0					0	0	
51111119	按重量计其他动物细毛含量在85%及以上,每平方米重量不超过300克的其他动物细毛机织物	10	0	8.5	0	5	0	0	0	0				6	0					0	0	
51111190	按重量计羊毛含量在85%及以上,每平方米重量不超过300克的羊毛机织物	10	0	8.5	0	5	0	0	4	0		0		6	0					0	0	
51111911	按重量计山羊绒含量在85%及以上,每平方米重量超过300克的山羊绒的机织物	10	0	8.5	0	5	0	0	0	0				6	0					0	0	
51111919	按重量计其他动物细毛含量在85%及以上,每平方米超过300克的其他动物细毛机织物	10	0	8.5	0	5	0	0	0	0				6	0					0	0	
51111990	按重量计羊毛含量在85%及以上,每平方米超过300克的羊毛机织物	10	0	8.5	0	5	0	0	4	0				6	0					0	0	
51112000	与化纤长丝混纺粗梳毛布	10	0		0	5	0	0	0	0				6	0					0	0	
51113000	与化纤短纤混纺粗梳毛布	10	0	8.5	0	5	0	0	0	0				6	0					0	0	
51119000	与其他纤维混纺的粗梳毛布	10	0		0	5	0	0	0	0				6						0	0	
51121100	重量≤200g/平米精梳全毛布	10	0	5	0	5	0	0	4	0	0	0		6	0					0	0	0
51121900	重量>200g/平米精梳全毛布	10	0	5	0	5	0	0	4	0	0	0		6	0		0	0	0	0	0	0
51122000	与化纤长丝混纺精梳毛布	10	0		0	5	0	0	0	0		0		6	0					0	0	0
51123000	与化纤短纤混纺精梳毛布	10	0		0	5	0	0	0	0		0		6	0					0	0	0
51129000	与其他纤维混纺精梳毛布	10	0		0	5	0	0	4	0		0		6	0					0	0	0
51130000	动物粗毛或马毛机织物	10	0		0	5	0	0	0	0		0		6	0					0	0	0
52010000	未梳的棉花	40	20																			
52021000	废棉纱线	10	0		0		0	0	4	0				6	0					0	0	
52029100	棉的回收纤维	10	0		0		0	0	0	0	0			6	0					0	0	0
52029900	其他废棉	10	0		0		0	0		0				6	0							
52030000	已梳的棉花	40	40																			
52041100	非供零售用全棉缝纫线	5	0		0			0	0	0		0		0	0		0			0	0	0
52041900	非供零售用其他棉缝纫线	5	0		0			0	0	0		0		0	0					0	0	0

税则号列	货品名称	最惠国	协定税率												特惠税率						
			东盟统一	亚太5国	智利	巴基斯坦	新加坡	新西兰	秘鲁	哥达	香港	澳门	台湾	瑞士	冰岛	亚太2国	老挝	柬埔寨	缅甸	LDC1	LDC2	LDC3
52042000	零售用棉制缝纫线	5	0		0			0	0	0		0		0	0		0			0	0	0
52051100	非零售粗梳粗支纯棉单纱	5	0	3.5	0	3.5		0	0	0	0	0	0	0	0		0	0	0	0	0	0
52051200	非零售粗梳中支纯棉单纱	5	0	3.5	0	3.5		0	0	0	0		0	0	0		0	0	0	0	0	0
52051300	非零售粗梳细支纯棉单纱	5	0	3.5	0	3.5		0	0	0	0			0	0					0	0	0
52051400	非零售粗梳较细支纯棉单纱	5	0	3.5	0	3.5		0	0	0	0			0	0		0		0	0	0	0
52051500	非零售粗梳特细支纯棉单纱	5	0	3.5	0	3.5		0	0	0				0	0					0	0	0
52052100	非零售精梳粗支纯棉单纱	5	0	3.5	0	3.5		0	0	0	0			0	0				0	0	0	0
52052200	非零售精梳中支纯棉单纱	5	0	3.5	0	3.5		0	0	0	0			0	0					0	0	0
52052300	非零售精梳细支纯棉单纱	5	0	3.5	0	3.5		0	0	0	0			0	0					0	0	0
52052400	非零售精梳较细支纯棉单纱	5	0	3.5	0	3.5		0	0	0	0			0	0		0		0	0	0	0
52052600	非零售精梳较特细支纯棉单纱	5	0		0			0	0	0	0			0	0					0	0	0
52052700	非零售精梳特细支纯棉单纱	5	0		0			0	0	0	0			0	0					0	0	0
52052800	非零售精梳超细支纯棉单纱	5	0		0			0	0	0	0			0	0					0	0	0
52053100	非零售粗梳粗支纯棉多股纱	5	0	4.5	0	4.5		0		0	0	0		0	0							
52053200	非零售粗梳中支纯棉多股纱	5	0	3.5	0	3.5		0	0	0	0	0		0	0					0	0	0
52053300	非零售粗梳细支纯棉多股纱	5	0		0			0	0	0	0	0		0	0					0	0	0
52053400	非零售粗梳较细支纯棉多股纱	5	0		0			0	0	0	0	0		0	0					0	0	0
52053500	非零售粗梳特细支纯棉多股纱	5	0		0			0	0	0		0		0	0					0	0	0
52054100	非零售精梳粗支纯棉多股纱	5	0	4.5	0	4.5		0		0	0	0		0	0					0	0	
52054200	非零售精梳中支纯棉多股纱	5	5	3.5	0	3.5		0	0	0	0	0		3	0					0	0	0
52054300	非零售精梳细支纯棉多股纱	5	0		0			0		0	0	0		0	0					0	0	0
52054400	非零售精梳较细支纯棉多股纱	5	0		0			0	0	0	0	0		0	0					0	0	0
52054600	非零售精梳较特细支纯棉多股纱	5	0	4.5	0	4.5		0	0	0	0	0		0	0					0	0	0
52054700	非零售精梳特细支纯棉多股纱	5	0	4.5	0	4.5		0	0	0	0	0		0	0					0	0	0
52054800	非零售精梳超细支纯棉多股纱	5	0	4.5	0	4.5		0	0	0	0	0		0	0					0	0	0
52061100	非零售粗梳粗支混纺棉单纱	5	0	3.5	0	3.5		0		0	0	0		0	0							
52061200	非零售粗梳中支混纺棉单纱	5	0	3.5	0	3.5		0	0	0	0	0	0	0	0					0	0	
52061300	非零售粗梳细支混纺棉单纱	5	0		0			0	0	0	0	0		0	0					0	0	0
52061400	非零售粗梳较细支混纺棉单纱	5	0		0			0	0	0	0	0		0	0					0	0	0
52061500	非零售粗梳特细支混纺棉单纱	5	0	3.5	0	3.5		0	0	0	0	0		0	0					0	0	0
52062100	非零售精梳粗支混纺棉单纱	5	0	4.5	0	4.5		0	0	0	0	0		0	0					0	0	
52062200	非零售精梳中支混纺棉单纱	5	0		0			0	0	0	0	0	0	0	0					0	0	
52062300	非零售精梳细支混纺棉单纱	5	0		0			0	0	0	0	0		0	0					0	0	0
52062400	非零售精梳较细支混纺棉单纱	5	0		0			0	0	0	0	0	0	0	0					0	0	0
52062500	非零售精梳特细支混纺棉单纱	5	0		0			0	0	0	0	0		0	0					0	0	0
52063100	非零售粗梳粗支混纺棉多股纱	5	0		0			0	0	0	0	0		0	0					0	0	
52063200	非零售粗梳中支混纺棉多股纱	5	0		0			0	0	0	0	0		0	0					0	0	
52063300	非零售粗梳细支混纺棉多股纱	5	0		0			0	0	0	0	0		0	0					0	0	0
52063400	非零售粗梳较细混纺棉多股纱	5	0		0			0	0	0	0	0		0	0					0	0	0
52063500	非零售粗梳特细混纺棉多股纱	5	0		0			0	0	0	0	0		0	0					0	0	0
52064100	非零售精梳粗支混纺棉多股纱	5	0		0			0	0	0	0	0		0	0					0	0	
52064200	非零售精梳中支混纺棉多股纱	5	0		0			0	0	0	0	0		0	0					0	0	
52064300	非零售精梳细支混纺棉多股纱	5	0		0			0	0	0	0	0		0	0					0	0	0
52064400	非零售精梳较细混纺棉多股纱	5	0		0			0	0	0	0	0		0	0					0	0	0
52064500	非零售精梳特细混纺棉多股纱	5	0		0			0	0	0	0	0		0	0					0	0	0
52071000	供零售用纯棉纱线	6	0	5	0	5		0	0	0		0		3.6	0					0	0	
52079000	供零售用混纺棉纱线	6	0		0	5		0	0	0		0		3.6	0					0	0	0
52081100	未漂白轻质全棉平纹布	10	0		0	0		0	0	0	0			6	0					0	0	
52081200	未漂白较轻质全棉平纹布	10	0		0	0	0	0	0	0	0			6	0					0	0	
52081300	未漂白轻质全棉三、四线斜纹布	10	0	8.5	0	0		0	0	0	0			6	0					0	0	
52081900	未漂白轻质其他全棉机织物	10	0		0	0	0	0	0	0	0			6	0					0	0	
52082100	漂白的轻质全棉平纹布	10	0		0	0		0	0	0	0			6	0					0	0	
52082200	漂白的较轻质全棉平纹布	10	0		0	0	0	0	0	0	0			6	0		0	0	0	0	0	0
52082300	漂白的轻质全棉三、四线斜纹布	12	0		0	0	0	0	0	0	0			9.2	0					0	0	
52082900	漂白的轻质其他全棉机织物	10	0		0	0		0	0	0	0			6	0					0	0	
52083100	染色的轻质全棉平纹布	10	0		0	0		0	0	0	0		0	6	0					0	0	0
52083200	染色的较轻质全棉平纹布	10	0	8.5	0	0	0	0	0	0	0		0	6	0					0	0	0
52083300	染色的轻质全棉三、四线斜纹布	10	0	8.5	0	0		0	0	0	0			6	0		0	0	0	0	0	0
52083900	染色的轻质其他全棉机织物	10	0	8.5	0	0	0	0	0	0	0		0	6	0					0	0	0
52084100	色织的轻质全棉平纹布	10	0		0	0	0	0	0	0	0			8	0					0	0	
52084200	色织的较轻质全棉平纹布	10	0	7	0	0	0	0	0	0	0		0	8	0					0	0	0

税则号列	货品名称	最惠国	协定税率													特惠税率						
			东盟统一	亚太5国	智利	巴基斯坦	新加坡	新西兰	秘鲁	哥达	香港	澳门	台湾	瑞士	冰岛	亚太2国	老挝	柬埔寨	缅甸	LDC1	LDC2	LDC3
52084300	色织的轻质全棉三、四线斜纹布	10	0		0	0		0	0	0	0			8	0					0	0	
52084900	色织的轻质其他全棉机织物	10	0	9	0	0	0	0	0	0	0			6	0		0	0	0	0	0	0
52085100	印花的轻全棉平纹布	10	0		0	0		0	0	0	0			6	0					0	0	0
52085200	印花的较轻全棉平纹布	10	0	8.5	0	0	0	0	0	0	0			6	0					0	0	0
52085910	印花的轻质全棉三、四线斜纹布	10	0		0	0		0	0	0	0			6	0					0	0	
52085990	印花的轻质其他全棉机织物	10	0	8.5	0	0		0	0	0			0	6	0					0	0	
52091100	未漂白重质全棉平纹布	10	10		0	0		0		0	0			6	0					0	0	0
52091200	未漂白重质全棉三、四线斜纹布	10	0	7	0	0	0	0	0	0	0			6	0					0	0	
52091900	未漂白重质其他全棉机织物	10	0		0	0	0	0	0	0	0			6	0					0	0	0
52092100	漂白的重质全棉平纹布	12	0		0	0	0	0	0	0	0			9.6	0					0	0	0
52092200	漂白的重质全棉三、四线斜纹布	12	0		0	0	0	0	0	0	0			9.6	0					0	0	
52092900	漂白的重质其他全棉机织物	12	0		0	0	0	0	0	0	0			9.6	0					0	0	
52093100	染色的重质全棉平纹布	10	0	8.5	0	0	0	0	0	0	0		0	6	0		0	0	0	0	0	0
52093200	染色的重质全棉三、四线斜纹布	10	0	8.5	0	0	0	0	0	0	0		0	6	0		0	0	0	0	0	0
52093900	染色的重质其他全棉机织物	10	0	8.5	0	0	0	0	0	0	0		0	6	0		0	0	0	0	0	0
52094100	色织的重质全棉平纹布	10	0		0	0	0	0	0	0	0		0	6	0					0	0	
52094200	色织的重质全棉粗斜纹布(劳动布)	10	0	8.5	0	0	0	0	0	0	0	0	0	6	0		0	0	0	0	0	0
52094300	其他三线或四线斜纹机织物,包括双面斜纹机织物	10	0	9.3	0	0		0	0	0	0			6	0					0	0	
52094900	色织的重质其他全棉机织物	10	0		0	0	0	0	0	0	0			6	0					0	0	
52095100	印花的重质全棉平纹布	10	0	9.3	0	0	0	0	0	0	0			6	0					0	0	0
52095200	印花的重质全棉三、四线斜纹布	10	0		0	0		0	0	0	0			6	0					0	0	
52095900	印花的重质其他全棉机织物	10	0	8.5	0	0		0	0	0	0			6	0					0	0	0
52101100	与化纤混纺未漂白轻质平纹棉布	12	0	10.2	0	0	0	0	0	0	0			9.6	0					0	0	0
52101910	化纤混纺未漂白轻质3、4线斜纹棉布	12	0		0	0	0	0	0	0	0			9.6	0					0	0	
52101990	与化纤混纺未漂白轻质其他棉布	12	0		0	0	0	0	0	0	0			9.6	0					0	0	0
52102100	与化纤混纺漂白的轻质平纹棉布	14	0		0	0	0	0	0	0	0			11.2	0					0	0	0
52102910	化纤混纺漂白的轻质三线或线斜纹棉布	14	0		0	0	0	0	0	0	0			11.2	0					0	0	
52102990	与化纤混纺漂白的轻质其他棉布	14	0		0	0	0	0	0	0				11.2	0					0	0	
52103100	与化纤混纺染色的轻质平纹棉布	10	0	8.5	0	0	0	0	0	0	0		0	6	0					0	0	0
52103200	化纤混纺染色的轻质三线或四线斜纹棉布	10	0	8.5	0	0	0	0	0	0	0			6	0					0	0	
52103900	与化纤混纺染色的轻质其他棉布	10	0	8.5	0	0	0	0	4	0	0		0	6	0					0	0	
52104100	与化纤混纺色织的轻质平纹棉布	10	0		0	0	0	0	0	0	0		0	6	0					0	0	
52104910	化纤混纺色织的轻质三线或四线斜纹棉布	10	0		0	0	0	0	0	0	0			6	0					0	0	
52104990	与化纤混纺色织的轻质其他棉布	10	0		0	0	0	0	0	0	0		0	6	0					0	0	0
52105100	与化纤混纺印花的轻质平纹棉布	10	0		0	0		0	0	0				6	0·					0	0	0
52105910	化纤混纺印花的轻质三线或四线斜纹棉布	10	0		0	0		0	0	0				6	0					0	0	
52105990	与化纤混纺印花的轻质其他棉布	10	0		0	0		0	0	0				6	0					0	0	0
52111100	与化纤混纺未漂白重质平纹棉布	12	0		0	0	0	0	0	0	0			9.6	0					0	0	0
52111200	化纤混纺未漂白重质三线或四线斜纹棉布	12	0		0	0	0	0	0	0	0			9.6	0					0	0	0
52111900	与化纤混纺未漂白重质其他棉布	12	0		0	0	0	0	0	0	0			9.6	0					0	0	0
52112000	与化纤混纺漂白的重质其他棉布	14	0		0	0	0	0	0	0	0			11.2	0					0	0	
52113100	与化纤混纺染色的重质平纹棉布	10	0	8.5	0	0	0	0	0	0	0			6	0					0	0	0
52113200	化纤混纺染色的重质三线或四线斜纹棉布	10	0	8.5	0	0	0	0	0	0	0			6	0					0	0	
52113900	与化纤混纺染色的重质其他棉布	10	0	8.5	0	0	0	0	4	0	0		0	6	0					0	0	0
52114100	与化纤混纺色织的重质平纹棉布	10	0		0	0		0	0	0	0			6	0					0	0	
52114200	与化纤混纺色织的重质粗斜纹棉布	10	0		0	0	0	0	0	0	0			6	0					0	0	
52114300	其他三线或四线斜纹机织物,包括双面斜纹机织物	10	0		0	0		0	0	0	0			6	0					0	0	
52114900	与化纤混纺色织的重质其他棉布	10	0		0	0	0	0	0	0				6	0					0	0	
52115100	与化纤混纺印花的重质平纹棉布	10	0		0	0		0	0	0				6	0					0	0	
52115200	化纤混纺印花的重质三线或四线斜纹棉布	10	0		0	0		0	0	0				6	0					0	0	
52115900	与化纤混纺印花的重质其他棉布	10	0	8.5	0	0		0	0	0				6	0					0	0	

税则号列	货品名称	最惠国	协定税率													特惠税率						
			东盟统一	亚太5国	智利	巴基斯坦	新加坡	新西兰	秘鲁	哥达	香港	澳门	台湾	瑞士	冰岛	亚太2国	老挝	柬埔寨	缅甸	LDC1	LDC2	LDC3
52121100	未漂白的其他混纺轻质棉布	12	0		0	0	0	0	0	0	0			9.6	0					0	0	0
52121200	漂白的其他混纺轻质棉布	14	0		0	0	0	0	0	0	0			11.2	0					0	0	
52121300	染色的其他混纺轻质棉布	10	0		0	0		0	0	0	0			6	0					0	0	
52121400	色织的其他混纺轻质棉布	10	0		0	0		0	0	0				6	0					0	0	
52121500	印花的其他混纺轻质棉布	10	0		0	0		0	0	0				6	0					0	0	
52122100	未漂白的其他混纺重质棉布	12	0		0	0	0	0	0	0	0			9.6	0					0	0	0
52122200	漂白的其他混纺重质棉布	14	0		0	0	0	0	0	0	0			11.2	0					0	0	
52122300	染色的其他混纺重质棉布	10	0		0	0		0	0	0	0			6	0					0	0	
52122400	色织的其他混纺重质棉布	10	0		0	0		0	0	0				6	0					0	0	
52122500	印花的其他混纺重质棉布	10	0		0	0		0	0	0				6	0					0	0	0
53011000	生的或沤制的亚麻	6	0		0	5		0	0	0				3.6	0					0	0	0
53012100	破开或打成的亚麻	6	0		0	5		0	0	0				3.6	0					0	0	0
53012900	栉梳或经其他加工未纺制的亚麻	6	0		0	5		0	0	0				3.6	0					0	0	0
53013000	亚麻短纤及废麻	6	0		0	5		0	0	0				3.6	0					0	0	0
53021000	生的或沤制的大麻	6	0		0	5		0	0	0				3.6	0					0	0	0
53029000	经加工、未纺的大麻、大麻短纤及废麻	6	0		0	5		0	0	0				3.6	0					0	0	0
53031000	生或沤制黄麻,其他纺织用韧皮纤维	5	0		0	0		0	0	0				0	0	0	0	0	0	0	0	0
53039000	经加工、未纺的黄麻及其他纺织用韧皮纤维	5	0		0	0		0	0	0				0	0		0	0	0	0	0	0
53050011	生的苎麻	5	0		0	0		0	0	0				0	0					0	0	0
53050012	经加工、未纺制的苎麻	5	0		0	0		0	0	0				0	0					0	0	0
53050013	苎麻的短纤及废麻	5	0		0	0		0	0	0				0	0					0	0	0
53050019	其他苎麻	5	0		0	0		0	0	0				0	0					0	0	0
53050020	经加工、未纺制的蕉麻及蕉麻废料	3	0		0	0		0	0	0				0	0					0	0	0
53050091	经加工、未纺的西沙尔麻及其他龙舌兰类纤维	5	0		0	0		0	0	0				0	0					0	0	0
53050092	加工、未纺的椰壳纤维及椰壳纤维废料	5	0	4	0	0		0	0	0				0	0		0	0	0	0	0	0
53050099	经加工的其他未列名纺织用植物纤维及其废麻	5	0		0	0		0	0	0				0	0					0	0	0
53061000	亚麻单纱	6	0		0	5		0	0	0	0	0		3.6	0					0	0	0
53062000	亚麻多股纱线或缆线	10	0		0	5		0	0	0	0	0		6	0					0	0	0
53071000	黄麻及其他纺织用韧皮纤维单纱	6	0		0	5		0	0	0		0		3.6	0	3		0		0	0	0
53072000	黄麻及其他纺织用韧皮纤维多股纱或缆线	6	0		0	5		0	0	0		0		3.6	0	3		0		0	0	0
53081000	椰壳纤维纱线	6	0		0	5		0	0	0		0		3.6	0					0	0	0
53082000	大麻纱线	6	0		0	5		0	0	0		0		3.6	0					0	0	0
53089011	未漂白或漂白的全苎麻纱线	6	0		0	5		0	0	0		0		3.6	0					0	0	0
53089012	全苎麻色纱线	6	0		0	5		0	0	0		0		3.6	0					0	0	0
53089013	未漂白或漂白的混纺苎麻纱线	6	0		0	5		0	0	0		0		3.6	0					0	0	0
53089014	混纺苎麻色纱线	6	0		0	5		0	0	0		0		3.6	0					0	0	0
53089091	纸纱线	6	0		0	5		0	0	0		0		3.6	0					0	0	0
53089099	其他植物纺织纤维纱线	6	0		0	5		0	0	0		0		3.6	0					0	0	0
53091110	未漂白全亚麻机织物	10	0		0	0		0	0	0				6	0					0	0	0
53091120	漂白的全亚麻机织物	10	0		0	0		0	0	0				6	0					0	0	0
53091900	其他全亚麻机织物	10	0	9.3	0	0		0	0	0	0			6	0					0	0	0
53092110	未漂白的混纺亚麻机织物	10	0		0	0		0	0	0		0		6	0					0	0	0
53092120	漂白的混纺亚麻机织物	10	0		0	0		0	0	0		0		6	0					0	0	0
53092900	其他混纺亚麻机织物	10	0	8.5	0	0		0	0	0	0	0		6	0					0	0	0
53101000	未漂白黄麻或其他韧皮纤维织物	10	0		0	5		0	0	0				6	0	5		0		0	0	0
53109000	其他黄麻机织物或韧皮鲜为纤维织物	10	0		0	5		0	0	0				6	0	5		0		0	0	0
53110012	未漂白全苎麻机织物	10	0		0	5		0	0	0		0		6	0					0	0	0
53110013	其他全苎麻机织物	12	0		0	6	0	0	0	0		0		9.6	0					0	0	0
53110014	未漂白混纺苎麻机织物	10	0		0	5		0	0	0				6	0					0	0	0
53110015	其他混纺苎麻机织物	12	0		0	6	0	0	0	0		0		9.6	0					0	0	
53110020	纸纱线机织物	10	0		0	5		0	0	0				6	0					0	0	0
53110030	大麻的机织物	10	0	9.3	0	5		0	0	0				6	0					0	0	0

税则号列	货品名称	最惠国	协定税率													特惠税率						
			东盟统一	亚太5国	智利	巴基斯坦	新加坡	新西兰	秘鲁	哥达	香港	澳门	台湾	瑞士	冰岛	亚太2国	老挝	柬埔寨	缅甸	LDC1	LDC2	LDC3
53110090	其他纺织用植物纤维机织物	10	0	9.3	0	5		0	0	0				6	0					0	0	0
54011010	非供零售用合成纤维长丝缝纫线	5	0		0	0		0	0	0	0	0	0	3	0					0	0	0
54011020	供零售用合成纤维长丝缝纫线	5	0		0	0		0	0	0				0	0					0	0	0
54012010	非供零售用人纤长丝缝纫线	5	0		0	0		0	0	0				0	0					0	0	0
54012020	供零售用人纤长丝缝纫线	5	0		0	0		0	0	0				0	0					0	0	0
54021110	非零售用聚间苯二甲酰间苯二胺纺制的长丝高强力纱	5	0		0	0		0	0	0		0		0	0					0	0	0
54021120	非零售用聚对苯二甲酰对苯二胺纺制的长丝高强力纱	5	0		0	0		0	0	0		0		0	0					0	0	0
54021190	非零售用其他芳香族聚酰胺纺制的长丝高强力纱	5	0		0	0		0	0	0		0		0	0					0	0	0
54021910	非零售用聚酰胺-6纺制的长丝高强力纱	5	0		0	0		0	0	0		0		0	0					0	0	0
54021920	非零售用聚酰胺-66纺制的长丝高强力纱	5	0		0	0		0	0	0		0		0	0					0	0	0
54021990	非零售用其他尼龙长丝高强纱	5	0		0	0		0	0	0		0		0	0					0	0	0
54022000	非零售聚酯长丝高强力纱	5	0		0	0		0	0	0		0	0	3	0					0	0	0
54023111	非零售用聚酰胺-6纺制的细弹力丝	5	0		0	0		0	0	0	0	0		0	0					0	0	0
54023112	非零售用聚酰胺-66纺制的细弹力丝	5	0		0	0		0	0	0	0	0		0	0					0	0	0
54023113	非零售用芳香族聚酰胺纺制的细弹力丝	5	0		0	0		0	0	0	0	0		0	0					0	0	0
54023119	非零售其他细尼龙弹力丝	5	0		0	0		0	0	0	0	0		0	0					0	0	0
54023190	非零售其他细尼龙变形纱线	5	0		0	0		0	0	0	0	0		0	0					0	0	0
54023211	非零售用聚酰胺-6纺制的粗弹力丝	5	0		0	0		0	0	0	0	0		0	0					0	0	0
54023212	非零售用聚酰胺-66纺制的粗弹力丝	5	0		0	0		0	0	0	0	0		0	0					0	0	0
54023213	非零售用芳香族聚酰胺纺制的粗弹力丝	5	0		0	0		0	0	0	0	0		0	0					0	0	0
54023219	非零售其他粗尼龙弹力丝	5	0		0	0		0	0	0	0	0		0	0					0	0	0
54023290	非零售其他粗尼龙变形纱线	5	0	4.5	0	0		0	0	0	0	0		0	0					0	0	0
54023310	非零售聚酯弹力丝	5	0		0	0		0	0	0		0	0	0	0					0	0	0
54023390	非零售其他聚酯变形纱线	5	5		0	0		0	0	0		0		0	0					0	0	0
54023400	非零售用聚丙烯变形纱线	5	0		0	0		0	0	0		0		0	0					0	0	0
54023900	非零售其他合成纤维长丝变形纱线	5	0		0	0		0	0	0		0		0	0					0	0	0
54024410	弹性氨纶纱线,未加捻或捻度每米不超过50转	5	0		0	0		0	0	0		0		0	0					0	0	0
54024490	其他弹性纱线,未加捻或捻度每米不超过50转	5	0	4.7	0	0		0	0	0	0	0		0	0					0	0	0
54024510	聚酰胺-6纺制的其他单纱,未加捻或捻度每米不超过50转	5	0	4.7	0	0		0	0	0		0		0	0					0	0	0
54024520	聚酰胺-6,6纺制的其他单纱,未加捻或捻度每米不超过50转	5	0	4.7	0	0		0	0	0		0		0	0					0	0	0
54024530	芳香族聚酰胺纺制的其他单纱,未加捻或捻度每米不超过50转	5	0	4.7	0	0		0	0	0		0		0	0					0	0	0
54024590	其他尼龙或聚酰胺纱线纺制的,未加捻或捻度每米不超过50转的单纱	5	0	4.7	0	0		0	0	0		0		0	0					0	0	0
54024600	其他部分定向聚酯纱线,未加捻或捻度每米不超过50转	5	5		0	0		0	0	0		0		0	0					0	0	0
54024700	其他聚酯纱线,未加捻或捻度每米不超过50转	5	5	4.7	0	0		0	0	0		0		4	0					0	0	0
54024800	其他聚丙烯纱线,未加捻或捻度每米不超过50转	5	0		0	0		0	0	0		0		0	0					0	0	0
54024910	断裂强度大于等于22cN/dtex,且初始模量大于等于750cN/dtex的聚乙烯纱线	5	0		0	0		0	0	0		0		0	0					0	0	0
54024990	其他纱线,未加捻或捻度每米不超过50转	5	0		0	0		0	0	0		0		0	0					0	0	0
54025110	非零售用聚酰胺-6纺制的加捻单纱	5	5		0	0		0	0	0		0		0	0					0	0	0
54025120	非零售用聚酰胺-66纺制的加捻单纱	5	0		0	0		0	0	0		0		0	0					0	0	0
54025130	非零售用芳香族聚酰胺纺制的加捻单纱	5	0		0	0		0	0	0		0		0	0					0	0	0
54025190	非零售用其他尼龙加捻单纱	5	0		0	0		0	0	0		0		0	0					0	0	0
54025200	非零售加捻的其他聚酯加捻单纱	5	5	4.3	0	0		0	0	0		0		0	0					0	0	0
54025910	非零售用聚丙烯加捻单纱	5	0		0	0		0	0	0		0		0	0					0	0	0

税则号列	货品名称	最惠国	协定税率													特惠税率						
			东盟统一	亚太5国	智利	巴基斯坦	新加坡	新西兰	秘鲁	哥达	香港	澳门	台湾	瑞士	冰岛	亚太2国	老挝	柬埔寨	缅甸	LDC1	LDC2	LDC3
54025920	断裂强度大于等于22cN/dtex,且初始模量大于等于750cN/dtex的聚乙烯纱线	5	0		0	0		0	0	0		0		0	0					0	0	0
54025990	非零售加捻的其他合成纤维长丝单纱	5	0		0	0		0	0	0		0		0	0					0	0	0
54026110	非零售用聚己内酰胺(尼龙-6)制多股纱线	5	0		0	0		0	0	0		0		0	0					0	0	0
54026120	非零售用聚酰胺-66制多股纱线	5	0		0	0		0	0	0		0		0	0					0	0	0
54026130	非零售用芳香族聚酰胺制多股纱线	5	0		0	0		0	0	0		0		0	0					0	0	0
54026190	非零售用其他尼龙制多股纱线	5	0		0	0		0	0	0		0		0	0					0	0	0
54026200	非零售聚酯多股纱线	5	0		0	0		0	0	0		0	0	0	0					0	0	0
54026910	非零售用聚丙烯多股纱线	5	0		0	0		0	0	0		0		0	0					0	0	0
54026920	非零售用氨纶多股纱线	5	0		0	0		0	0	0		0		0	0					0	0	0
54026990	非零售其他合成纤维长丝多股纱线	5	0		0	0		0	0	0		0		0	0					0	0	0
54031000	非零售粘胶纤维高强力纱	5	0		0	0		0	0	0		0		0	0					0	0	0
54033110	竹制非零售未捻的粘胶纤维单纱	5	0		0	0		0	0	0		0		0	0					0	0	0
54033190	其他非零售未捻的粘胶纤维单纱	5	0		0	0		0	0	0		0		0	0					0	0	0
54033210	竹制非零售加捻的粘胶纤维单纱	5	0		0	0		0	0	0		0		0	0					0	0	0
54033290	其他非零售加捻的粘胶纤维单纱	5	0		0	0		0	0	0		0		0	0					0	0	0
54033310	非零售二醋酸纤维单纱	5	0		0	0		0	0	0		0		0	0					0	0	0
54033390	非零售其他醋酸纤维单纱	5	0		0	0		0	0	0		0		0	0					0	0	0
54033900	非零售其他人造纤维长丝单纱	5	0		0	0		0	0	0		0		0	0					0	0	0
54034100	非零售粘胶长丝多股纱线或缆线	5	0		0	0		0	0	0		0		0	0					0	0	0
54034200	非零售醋酸长丝多股纱线或缆线	5	0		0	0		0	0	0		0		0	0					0	0	0
54034900	非零售其他人造纤维长丝多股纱或缆线	5	0		0	0		0	0	0		0		0	0					0	0	0
54041100	细度≥67分特、≤1mm的弹性单丝	5	0		0	0		0	0	0	0			0	0					0	0	0
54041200	细度≥67分特、≤1mm的的聚丙烯单丝	5	0		0	0		0	0	0	0			0	0					0	0	0
54041900	细度≥67分特、≤1mm的其他合成纤维单丝	5	0		0	0		0	0	0	0			3	0					0	0	0
54049000	其他宽≤5mm合成纺织材料制扁条及类似品	5	0		0	0		0	0	0		0		0	0					0	0	0
54050000	细度≥67分特、≤1mm人造纤维单丝;宽≤5mm扁条及类似品	5	0		0	0		0	0	0		0		0	0					0	0	0
54060010	供零售用合成纤维长丝纱线	5	0		0	0		0	0	0		0		0	0					0	0	0
54060020	供零售用人造纤维长丝纱线	5	0		0	0		0	0	0		0		0	0					0	0	0
54071010	尼龙或其他聚酰胺高强力纱制机织物	10	0		0	0	0	0	0	0	0		0	6	0					0	0	
54071020	聚酯高强力纱制机织物	10	0		0	0	0	0	0	0			0	6	0					0	0	
54072000	合成纤维扁条及类似品的机织物	10	0		0	0	0	0	0	0				6	0					0	0	
54073000	多层平行纱线相互层迭并粘合机织物	10	0		0	0	0	0	0	0				6	0					0	0	
54074100	未漂白或漂白的纯尼龙布	10	0		0	0	0	0	0	0	0		0	6	0					0	0	
54074200	染色的纯尼龙布	10	0	9.5	0	0	0	0	0	0	0	0	0	6	0		0	0	0	0	0	0
54074300	色织的纯尼龙布	10	0	7	0	0	0	0	0	0	0		0	6	0					0	0	
54074400	印花的纯尼龙布	10	0		0	0	0	0	0	0				6	0					0	0	
54075100	未漂白或漂白纯聚酯变形长丝布	10	0	7	0	0	0	0	0	0			0	6	0					0	0	
54075200	染色的纯聚酯变形长丝布	10	0	9.5	0	0	0	0	0	0	0		0	6	0		0	0	0	0	0	0
54075300	色织的纯聚酯变形长丝布	10	0		0	0	0	0	0	0			0	6	0					0	0	
54075400	印花的纯聚酯变形长丝布	10	0		0	0	0	0	0	0			0	6	0					0	0	
54076100	其他纯聚酯非变形长丝布	10	0	9.5	0	0	0	0	0	0	0	0	0	6	0					0	0	0
54076900	其他纯聚酯长丝布	10	0	9.5	0	0	0	0	0	0			0	6	0					0	0	0
54077100	未漂白或漂白其他纯合成纤维长丝布	10	0	8.8	0	0	0	0	0	0	0		0	6	0					0	0	
54077200	染色的其他纯合成纤维长丝布	10	0	9.5	0	0	0	0	0	0	0		0	6	0		0	0	0	0	0	0
54077300	色织的其他纯合成纤维长丝布	10	0		0	0	0	0	0	0				6	0					0	0	
54077400	印花的其他纯合成纤维长丝布	10	0	9.5	0	0	0	0	0	0				6	0					0	0	
54078100	未漂或漂白的与棉混纺合成纤维长丝布	10	0		0	0	0	0	0	0	0			6	0					0	0	
54078200	染色的与棉混纺合成纤维长丝布	10	0		0	0	0	0	0	0	0		0	6	0					0	0	0
54078300	色织的与棉混纺合成纤维长丝布	10	0		0	0	0	0	0	0			0	6	0					0	0	
54078400	印花的与棉混纺合成纤维长丝布	10	0		0	0	0	0	0	0				6	0					0	0	
54079100	未漂或漂白的其他混纺合成纤维长丝布	10	0		0	0	0	0	0	0	0			6	0					0	0	
54079200	染色的其他混纺合成纤维长丝布	10	0		0	0	0	0	0	0	0		0	6	0		0	0	0	0	0	0
54079300	色织的其他混纺合成纤维长丝布	10	0		0	0	0	0	0	0			0	6	0					0	0	
54079400	印花的其他混纺合成纤维长丝布	10	0		0	0	0	0	0	0				6	0					0	0	
54081000	粘胶长丝高强力纱的机织物	10	0		0	0	0	0	0	0				6	0					0	0	

税则号列	货品名称	最惠国	协定税率												特惠税率						
			东盟统一	亚太5国	智利	巴基斯坦	新加坡	新西兰	秘鲁	哥达	香港	澳门	台湾	瑞士	冰岛	亚太2国	老挝	柬埔寨	缅甸	LDC1	LDC2	LDC3
54082110	粘胶长丝制未漂白或漂白的机织物	12	0		0	0	0	0	0	0				9.6	0					0	0	
54082120	醋酸长丝制未漂白或漂白的机织物	12	0		0	0	0	0	0	0				9.6	0					0	0	
54082190	其他人造长丝制未漂白或漂白的机织物	12	0		0	0	0	0	0	0				9.6	0					0	0	
54082210	纯粘胶长丝制染色机织物	10	0		0	0	0	0	0	0	0			6	0					0	0	
54082220	纯醋酸长丝制染色机织物	10	0		0	0	0	0	0	0	0		0	6	0					0	0	
54082290	纯其他人造长丝制染色机织物	10	0		0	0	0	0	0	0	0		0	6	0					0	0	
54082310	纯粘胶长丝制色织机织物	10	0		0	0	0	0	0	0				6	0					0	0	
54082320	纯醋酸长丝制色织机织物	10	0		0	0	0	0	0	0				6	0					0	0	
54082390	纯其他人造长丝制色织机织物	10	0		0	0	0	0	0	0			0	6	0					0	0	
54082410	纯粘胶长丝制印花机织物	10	0		0	0	0	0	0	0	0			6	0					0	0	
54082420	纯醋酸长丝制印花机织物	10	0		0	0	0	0	0	0	0			6	0					0	0	
54082490	纯其他人造长丝制印花机织物	10	0		0	0	0	0	0	0	0			6	0					0	0	
54083100	未漂白或漂白人造纤维长丝混纺布	10	0		0	0	0	0	0	0				6	0					0	0	
54083200	染色的人纤长丝混纺布	10	0	9.5	0	0	0	0	0	0			0	6	0					0	0	0
54083300	色织的人纤长丝混纺布	10	0		0	0	0	0	0	0				6	0					0	0	
54083400	印花的人纤长丝混纺布	10	0		0	0	0	0	0	0				6	0					0	0	
55011000	尼龙或其他聚酰胺长丝丝束	5	0		0	0		0	0	0				0	0					0	0	0
55012000	聚酯长丝丝束	5	5		0	0		0	0	0				0	0					0	0	0
55013000	聚丙烯腈长丝丝束	5	5	4.5	0	0		0		0				0	0					0	0	0
55014000	聚丙烯长丝丝束	5	0		0	0		0	0	0	0			0	0					0	0	0
55019000	其他合成纤维长丝丝束	5	0		0	0		0	0	0	0			0	0					0	0	0
55020010	二醋酸纤维丝束	3	0	2.1	0	0		0	0	0				0	0					0	0	0
55020090	其他人造纤维长丝丝束	5	0	3.5	0	0		0	0	0				0	0					0	0	0
55031110	未梳的聚间苯二甲酰间苯二胺纺制的合成纤维短纤	5	0		0	0		0	0	0				0	0					0	0	0
55031120	未梳的聚对苯二甲酰对苯二胺纺制的合成纤维短纤	5	0		0	0		0	0	0				0	0					0	0	0
55031190	未梳的其他芳香聚酰胺纺制的合成纤维短纤	5	0		0	0		0	0	0				4	0					0	0	0
55031900	未梳的尼龙或其他聚酰胺合成纤维短纤	5	0		0	0		0	0	0				4	0					0	0	0
55032000	未梳的聚酯合成纤维短纤	5	5	4.5	0	0		0	0	0				0	0					0	0	0
55033000	未梳的聚丙烯腈合成纤维短纤	5	5	4.5	0	0		0	0	0				0	0					0	0	0
55034000	未梳的聚丙烯合成纤维短纤	5	0		0	0		0	0	0				0	0					0	0	0
55039010	聚苯硫醚制未梳的纤维短纤	5	0		0	0		0	0	0			0	0	0					0	0	0
55039090	未梳的其他合成纤维短纤	5	0		0	0		0	0	0			0	0	0					0	0	0
55041010	竹制未梳的粘胶纤维短纤	5	0		0	0		0	0	0				0	0					0	0	0
55041021	木制未梳的阻燃的粘胶纤维短纤	5	0		0	0		0	0	0				0	0					0	0	0
55041029	其他木制未梳的粘胶纤维短纤	5	0		0	0		0	0	0				0	0					0	0	0
55041090	其他未梳的粘胶纤维短纤	5	0		0	0		0	0	0				0	0					0	0	0
55049000	未梳的其他人造纤维短纤	5	0		0	0		0	0	0			0	0	0					0	0	0
55051000	合成纤维废料	5	0		0	0		0	0	0				0	0					0	0	0
55052000	人造纤维废料	5	0		0	0		0	0	0	0			0	0					0	0	0
55061011	已梳的聚间苯二甲酰间苯二胺纤维短纤	5	0		0	0		0	0	0				0	0					0	0	0
55061012	已梳的聚对苯二甲酰对苯二胺纤维短纤	5	0		0	0		0	0	0				0	0					0	0	0
55061019	已梳的其他芳香族聚酰胺纤维短纤	5	0		0	0		0	0	0				0	0					0	0	0
55061090	已梳的尼龙或其他聚酰胺纤维短纤	5	0		0	0		0	0	0				0	0					0	0	0
55062000	已梳的聚酯纤维短纤	5	5	4.5	0	4.5		0	0	0				0	0					0	0	0
55063000	已梳的聚丙烯腈及其变性纤维短纤	5	5	4.5	0	4.5		0	0	0				0	0					0	0	0
55069010	聚苯硫醚制已梳的纤维短纤	5	0		0	0		0	0	0				0	0					0	0	0
55069090	已梳的其他合成纤维短纤	5	0		0	0		0	0	0				0	0					0	0	0
55070000	已梳的人造纤维短纤	5	0		0	0		0	0	0				0	0					0	0	0
55081000	合成纤维短纤纺制的缝纫线	5	0	4.5	0	0		0	0	0	0	0		0	0					0	0	0
55082000	人造纤维短纤纺制的缝纫线	5	0		0	0		0	0	0				0	0					0	0	0
55091100	非零售纯尼龙短纤单纱	5	0		0	0		0	0	0	0	0		0	0					0	0	0
55091200	非零售纯尼龙短纤多股纱线	5	0		0	0		0	0	0	0	0		0	0					0	0	0
55092100	非零售纯聚酯短纤单纱	5	0		0	0		0	0	0	0	0		0	0					0	0	0
55092200	非零售纯聚酯短纤多股纱线	5	0		0	0		0	0	0	0	0		0	0					0	0	0
55093100	非零售纯聚丙烯腈短纤单纱	5	0		0	0		0	0	0	0	0		0	0					0	0	0
55093200	非零售纯聚丙烯腈短纤多股纱线	5	0	4.8	0	0		0	0	0	0	0	0	0	0					0	0	0

税则号列	货品名称	最惠国	协定税率 东盟统一	亚太5国	智利	巴基斯坦	新加坡	新西兰	秘鲁	哥达	香港	澳门	台湾	瑞士	冰岛	特惠税率 亚太2国	老挝	柬埔寨	缅甸	LDC1	LDC2	LDC3
55094100	非零售纯其他合成纤维短纤单纱	5	0		0	0		0	0	0	0	0		0	0					0	0	0
55094200	非零售纯其他合成纤维短纤多股纱线	5	0		0	0		0	0	0	0	0		0	0					0	0	0
55095100	非零售与人造纤维短纤混纺聚酯短纤纱	5	0		0	0		0	0	0	0	0		0	0					0	0	0
55095200	非零售与毛混纺聚酯短纤纱线	5	0		0	0		0	0	0	0	0		0	0					0	0	0
55095300	非零售与棉混纺聚酯短纤纱线	5	0	3.5	0	0		0	0	0	0	0	0	0	0					0	0	0
55095900	非零售其他混纺聚酯短纤纱线	5	0		0	0		0	0	0	0	0		0	0					0	0	0
55096100	非零售与毛混纺腈纶短纤纱线	5	0		0	0		0	0	0	0	0		0	0					0	0	0
55096200	非零售与棉混纺腈纶短纤纱线	5	0	4.8	0	0		0	0	0	0	0		0	0					0	0	0
55096900	非零售与其他混纺腈纶短纤纱线	5	0		0	0		0	0	0	0	0		0	0					0	0	0
55099100	非零售与毛混纺其他合成纤维短纤纱线	5	0		0	0		0	0	0	0	0		0	0					0	0	0
55099200	非零售与棉混纺其他合成纤维短纤纱线	5	0		0	0		0	0	0	0	0	0	0	0					0	0	0
55099900	非零售与其他混纺合成纤维短纤纱线	5	0		0	0		0	0	0	0	0		0	0					0	0	0
55101100	非零售纯人造纤维短纤单纱	5	0	4.5	0	0		0	0	0	0	0	0	0	0					0	0	0
55101200	非零售纯人造纤维短纤多股纱线	5	0		0	0		0	0	0	0	0	0	0	0					0	0	0
55102000	非零售与毛混纺人造纤维短纤纱线	5	0		0	0		0	0	0	0	0		0	0					0	0	0
55103000	非零售与棉混纺人造纤维短纤纱线	5	0	3.5	0	0		0	0	0	0	0	0	0	0					0	0	0
55109000	非零售与其他混纺人造纤维短纤纱线	5	0	4.5	0	0		0	0	0	0	0		0	0					0	0	0
55111000	零售用纯合成纤维短纤纱线	5	0		0	0		0	0	0				0	0					0	0	0
55112000	零售用混纺合成纤维短纤纱线	5	0		0	0		0	0	0				0	0					0	0	0
55113000	零售用人造纤维短纤纱线	5	0		0	0		0	0	0				0	0					0	0	0
55121100	未漂或漂白的纯聚酯布	15	0	10.5	0	0	0	0	7	0			0	12	0					0	0	0
55121900	其他纯聚酯布	10	0		0	0	0	0	4	0	0		0	6	0					0	0	0
55122100	未漂或漂白的纯腈纶布	13	0		0	0	0	0	0	0				10.4	0					0	0	0
55122900	其他纯腈纶布	10	0	9.3	0	0	0	0	0	0				6	0					0	0	
55129100	未漂或漂白的纯其他合成纤维布	18	0		0	0	0	0	7.2	0				14.4	0					0	0	
55129900	其他纯合成纤维布	10	0		0	0	0	0	0	0	0	0	0	6	0		0	0	0	0	0	0
55131110	与棉混纺未漂白的轻质聚酯平纹布	16	0		0	0	0	0	6.4	0	0			12.8	0					0	0	
55131120	与棉混纺漂白的轻质聚酯平纹布	15	0		0	0	0	0	6	0	0			12	0					0	0	
55131210	与棉混纺未漂白的轻质聚酯斜纹布	16	0		0	0	0	0	6.4	0	0			12.8	0					0	0	
55131220	与棉混纺漂白的轻质聚酯斜纹布	18	0		0	0	0	0	7.2	0	0			14.4	0					0	0	
55131310	与棉混纺未漂白的其他轻质聚酯布	16	0		0	0	0	0	6.4	0				12.8	0					0	0	
55131320	与棉混纺漂白的其他轻质聚酯布	18	0		0	0	0	0	7.2	0				14.4	0					0	0	
55131900	与棉混纺未漂白或漂白的轻质其他合成纤维布	18	0		0	0	0	0	7.2	0				14.4	0					0	0	
55132100	与棉混纺染色的轻质聚酯平纹布	10	0	9.1	0	0	0	0	0	0	0	0	0	6	0					0	0	
55132310	与棉混纺染色的轻质聚酯斜纹布	10	0		0	0	0	0	0	0	0			6	0					0	0	
55132390	与棉混纺染色的其他轻质聚酯布	10	0		0	0	0	0	0	0				6	0					0	0	
55132900	与棉混纺染色的轻质其他合成纤维布	10	0		0	0	0	0	0	0				6	0					0	0	0
55133100	与棉混纺色织的轻质聚酯平纹布	10	0		0	0	0	0	0	0	0			6	0					0	0	
55133910	与棉混纺色织的轻质聚酯斜纹布	10	0	8.8	0	0	0	0	0	0	0			6	0					0	0	
55133920	与棉混纺色织的其他轻质聚酯布	10	0		0	0	0	0	0	0	0			6	0					0	0	
55133990	与棉混纺色织的轻质其他合成纤维布	10	0		0	0	0	0	0	0				6	0					0	0	
55134100	与棉混纺印花的轻质聚酯平纹布	10	0		0	0	0	0	0	0				6	0		0	0	0	0	0	0
55134910	与棉混纺印花的轻质聚酯斜纹布	10	0		0	0	0	0	0	0				6	0					0	0	
55134920	与棉混纺印花的其他轻质聚酯布	10	0		0	0	0	0	0	0				6	0					0	0	
55134990	与棉混纺印花的轻质其他合成纤维布	10	0		0	0	0	0	0	0				6	0					0	0	
55141110	与棉混纺未漂白的重质聚酯平纹布	16	0	14.4	0	0	0	0	6.4	0				12.8	0					0	0	
55141120	与棉混纺漂白的重质聚酯平纹布	18	0		0	0	0	0	7.2	0				14.4	0					0	0	
55141210	与棉混纺未漂白的重质聚酯斜纹布	16	0		0	0	0	0	6.4	0	0			12.8	0					0	0	
55141220	与棉混纺漂白的重质聚酯斜纹布	18	0		0	0	0	0	7.2	0	0			14.4	0					0	0	
55141911	与棉混纺未漂白的重质其他聚酯布	16	0		0	0	0	0	6.4	0				12.8	0					0	0	
55141912	与棉混纺漂白的重质其他聚酯布	18	0		0	0	0	0	7.2	0				14.4	0					0	0	
55141990	与棉混纺未漂白或漂白的重质其他合成纤维布	16	0	15.2	0	0	0	0	6.4	0				12.8	0					0	0	
55142100	与棉混纺染色的重质聚酯平纹布	10	0		0	0	0	0	0	0	0			6	0					0	0	
55142200	与棉混纺染色的重质聚酯斜纹布	10	0		0	0	0	0	0	0	0			6	0					0	0	
55142300	与棉混纺染色的其他重质聚酯布	10	0		0	0	0	0	0	0				6	0		0	0	0	0	0	0
55142900	与棉混纺染色的重质其他合成维纤布	10	0		0	0	0	0	0	0				6	0					0	0	0
55143010	与棉混纺色织的重质聚酯平纹布	10	0		0	0	0	0	0	0	0			6	0					0	0	
55143020	与棉混纺色织的重质聚酯斜纹布	10	0		0	0	0	0	0	0	0			6	0					0	0	
55143030	与棉混纺色织的其他重质聚酯布	10	0		0	0	0	0	0	0				6	0					0	0	

税则号列	货品名称	最惠国	协定税率													特惠税率						
			东盟统一	亚太5国	智利	巴基斯坦	新加坡	新西兰	秘鲁	哥达	香港	澳门	台湾	瑞士	冰岛	亚太2国	老挝	柬埔寨	缅甸	LDC1	LDC2	LDC3
55143090	与棉混纺色织的重质其他合成纤维布	10	0		0	0	0	0	0	0				6	0					0	0	
55144100	与棉混纺印花的重质聚酯平纹布	10	0		0	0	0	0	0	0				6	0					0	0	
55144200	与棉混纺印花的重质聚酯斜纹布	10	0		0	0	0	0	0	0				6	0					0	0	
55144300	与棉混纺印花的其他重质聚酯布	10	0		0	0	0	0	0	0				6	0					0	0	
55144900	与棉混纺印花的重质其他合成纤维布	10	0		0	0	0	0	0	0				6	0					0	0	
55151100	与粘胶纤维短纤混纺的聚酯布	10	0	8.8	0	0	0	0	0	0			0	6	0					0	0	
55151200	与化纤长丝混纺的聚酯布	10	0	9	0	0	0	0	0	0			0	6	0					0	0	
55151300	与毛混纺的聚酯布	10	0		0	0	0	0	0	0				6	0					0	0	
55151900	与其他纤维混纺的聚酯布	10	0	9	0	0	0	0	0	0				6	0					0	0	
55152100	与化纤长丝混纺的腈纶布	10	0		0	0	0	0	0	0				6	0					0	0	
55152200	与毛混纺的腈纶布	12	0		0	0	0	0	0	0				9.6	0					0	0	0
55152900	与其他纤维混纺的腈纶布	10	0		0	0	0	0	0	0				6	0					0	0	
55159100	与化纤长丝混纺的其他合成纤维短纤布	10	0		0	0	0	0	0	0				6	0					0	0	
55159900	与其他纤维混纺的其他合成纤维短纤布	10	0	9	0	0	0	0	0	0				6	0					0	0	
55161100	未漂白或漂白的纯人造纤维短纤布	12	0		0	0	0	0	0	0	0			9.6	0					0	0	0
55161200	染色的纯人造纤维短纤布	10	0		0	0	0	0	0	0	0		0	6	0					0	0	
55161300	色织的纯人造纤维短纤布	10	0		0	0	0	0	0	0	0			6	0					0	0	
55161400	印花的纯人造纤维短纤布	10	0		0	0	0	0	0	0	0			6	0					0	0	
55162100	与化纤长丝混纺未漂白或漂白的人造纤维布	12	0		0	0	0	0	0	0	0			9.6	0					0	0	
55162200	与化纤长丝混纺的染色人造纤维布	10	0	9.5	0	0	0	0	0	0	0		0	6	0					0	0	
55162300	与化纤长丝混纺的色织人造纤维布	10	0		0	0	0	0	0	0	0			6	0					0	0	
55162400	与化纤长丝混纺的印花人造纤维布	10	0		0	0	0	0	0	0	0			6	0					0	0	
55163100	与毛混纺的未漂或漂白人造纤维布	12	0		0	0	0	0	0	0	0			9.6	0					0	0	
55163200	与毛混纺的染色人造纤维布	10	0		0	0	0	0	0	0	0			6	0					0	0	
55163300	与毛混纺的色织人造纤维布	10	0		0	0	0	0	0	0	0			6	0					0	0	
55163400	与毛混纺的印花人造纤维布	10	0		0	0	0	0	0	0	0			6	0					0	0	
55164100	与棉混纺的未漂或漂白人造纤维布	12	0		0	0	0	0	0	0	0			9.6	0					0	0	
55164200	与棉混纺的染色人造纤维布	12	0		0	0	0	0	0	0	0			9.6	0					0	0	
55164300	与棉混纺的色织人造纤维布	10	0		0	0	0	0	0	0	0			6	0					0	0	
55164400	与棉混纺的印花人造纤维布	10	0		0	0	0	0	0	0	0			6	0					0	0	
55169100	与其他纤维混纺未漂白或漂白的人造纤维布	12	0		0	0	0	0	0	0	0			9.6	0					0	0	
55169200	与其他纤维混纺的染色人造纤维布	10	0		0	0	0	0	0	0	0			6	0					0	0	0
55169300	与其他纤维混纺的色织人造纤维布	10	0		0	0	0	0	0	0	0			6	0					0	0	
55169400	与其他纤维混纺的印花人造纤维布	10	0	9.4	0	0	0	0	0	0	0			6	0					0	0	
56012100	棉制的絮胎及其他絮胎制品	10	0		0	5	0	0	0	0		0		6	0					0	0	
56012210	化学纤维制的卷烟滤嘴	12	0		0	6	0	0	0	0				9.6	0					0	0	
56012290	化学纤维制的絮胎及其他絮胎制品	12	0		0		0	0	0	0			0	9.6	0					0	0	0
56012900	其他材料制絮胎及其他絮胎制品	10	0		0	5	0	0	0	0				6	0					0	0	0
56013000	纺织纤维屑、纤维粉末及球结	10	0		0	5	0	0	0	0				6	0					0	0	
56021000	针刺机制毡呢及纤维缝编织物	10	0		0	5	0	0	0	0				6	0					0	0	
56022100	未浸、涂的毛制其他毡呢	10	0		0	5	0	0	0	0				6	0					0	0	
56022900	未浸、涂的其他纺织材料制其他毡呢	10	0		0	5	0	0	0	0				6	0					0	0	
56029000	经浸、涂、包覆或层压的其他毡呢	10	0		0	5	0	0	0	0				6	0					0	0	0
56031110	每平米≤25g 经浸渍化纤长丝无纺织物	10	0	8.5	0	0	0	0	0	0			0	6	0		0	0	0	0	0	0
56031190	每平米≤25g 的其他化纤长丝无纺织物	10	0	8.5	0	0	0	0	0	0				6	0					0	0	
56031210	25g ＜每平米≤70g 浸渍化纤长丝无纺织物	10	0	8.5	0	0	0	0	0	0	0	0		6	0		0	0	0	0	0	0
56031290	25g ＜每平米≤70g 其他化纤长丝无纺织物	10	0		0	0	0	0	0	0	0	0	0	6	0					0	0	0
56031310	70g＜每平米≤150g 浸渍化纤长丝无纺织物	10	0	8.5	0	0	0	0	0	0		0	0	6	0					0	0	
56031390	70g ＜每平米≤150g 其他化纤长丝无纺织物	10	0		0	0	0	0	0	0		0	0	6	0					0	0	0
56031410	每平米＞150g 经浸渍化纤长丝无纺织物	10	0	8.5	0	0	0	0	0	0			0	6	0					0	0	
56031490	每平米＞150g 的其他化纤长丝无纺织物	10	0	7	0	0	0	0	0	0			0	6	0					0	0	0
56039110	每平米≤25g 经浸渍其他无纺织物	10	0	8.5	0	0	0	0	0	0				6	0					0	0	
56039190	每平米≤25g 的其他无纺织物	10	0	8.5	0	0	0	0	0	0				6	0					0	0	
56039210	25g ＜每平米≤70g 浸渍其他无纺织物	10	0	8.5	0	0	0	0	0	0	0	0		6	0					0	0	

税则号列	货品名称	最惠国	协定税率 东盟统一	亚太5国	智利	巴基斯坦	新加坡	新西兰	秘鲁	哥达	香港	澳门	台湾	瑞士	冰岛	特惠税率 亚太2国	老挝	柬埔寨	缅甸	LDC1	LDC2	LDC3
56039290	25g <每平米≤70g 其他无纺织物	10	0	9.3	0	0		0	0	0	0	0	0	6	0		0	0	0	0	0	0
56039310	70g <每平米≤150g 浸渍其他无纺织物	10	0	8.5	0	0	0	0	0	0	0	0		6	0					0	0	
56039390	70g <每平米≤150g 的其他无纺织物	10	0	9.3	0	0	0	0	0	0	0	0	0	6	0					0	0	
56039410	每平米>150g 经浸渍其他无纺织物	10	0	8.5	0	0	0	0	0	0	0		0	6	0					0	0	
56039490	每平米>150g 的其他无纺织物	10	0	9.3	0	0	0	0	0	0	0		0	6	0		0	0	0	0	0	0
56041000	用纺织材料包覆的橡胶线及绳	5	0		0	0		0	0	0		0		0	0		0	0	0	0	0	0
56049000	用橡、塑浸渍涂布的其他纺织纱线	5	0		0	0		0	0	0		0		0	0					0	0	0
56050000	含金属纱线	5	0		0	0		0	0	0		0		0	0					0	0	0
56060000	绳绒线及粗松螺旋花线	5	0		0	0		0	0	0		0		0	0					0	0	0
56072100	剑麻或其他龙舌兰纤维制包扎用绳	5	0		0	0		0	0	0		0		0	0					0	0	0
56072900	剑麻或龙舌兰纤维制其他线绳索缆	5	0		0	0		0	0	0		0		0	0					0	0	0
56074100	聚乙烯或聚丙烯制包扎用绳	5	0		0	0		0	0	0		0		0	0					0	0	0
56074900	聚乙烯或聚丙烯制线、绳、索、缆	5	0		0	0		0	0	0		0		0	0					0	0	0
56075000	其他合纤制线、绳、索、缆	5	0		0	0		0	0	0		0	0	3	0					0	0	0
56079010	蕉麻或硬质纤维制线、绳、索、缆	5	0		0	0		0	0	0		0		0	0					0	0	0
56079090	其他纺织材料制线、绳、索、缆	5	0		0	0		0	0	0		0		0	0	2.5	0	0	0	0	0	0
56081100	化纤材料制成的渔网	10	0		0	5		0	4	0				6	0					0	0	0
56081900	化纤材料制成的其他网	12	0		0	6	0	0	0	0			0	9.6	0					0	0	
56089000	其他纤维制成的渔网及其他网	10	0		0	5		0	0	0	0			6	0					0	0	0
56090000	用纱线、扁条、绳、索、缆制其他物品	10	0		0	5		0	0	0				6	0	0				0	0	0
57011000	羊毛结织栽绒地毯及其他铺地制品	14	0		0		0	0	0	0				11.2	0					0	0	0
57019010	化纤结织栽绒地毯及其他铺地制品	16	0		0	12.8	0	0	6.4	0				12.8	0					0	0	0
57019020	丝制结织栽绒地毯及铺地制品	14	0		0	7	0	0	0	0				11.2	0					0	0	
57019090	其他材料结织栽绒地毯及铺地制品	14	0		0	7	0	0	0	0				11.2	0					0	0	
57021000	"开来姆"等手织地毯	14	0		0	0	0	0	0	0				11.2	0	0				0	0	0
57022000	椰壳纤维制的铺地制品	14	0		0	0	0	0	0	0				11.2	0					0	0	
57023100	未制成的毛制起绒地毯及铺地制品	10	0		0	0	0	0	0	0				8	0					0	0	0
57023200	未制成的化纤起绒地毯及铺地制品	16	0		0	0	0	0	6.4	0				12.8	0					0	0	
57023900	未制成其他纺织材料起绒铺地制品	14	0		0	0	0	0	0	0				11.2	0	0				0	0	0
57024100	制成的毛制起绒地毯及铺地制品	10	0		0	0	0	0	0	0				6	0					0	0	0
57024200	制成的化纤起绒地毯及铺地制品	10	0		0	0	0	0	0	0				6	0					0	0	0
57024900	制成的其他纺织材料起绒铺地制品	14	0	9.3	0	0	0	0	0	0				11.2	0					0	0	
57025010	未制成毛制非起绒地毯及铺地制品	14	0		0	0	0	0	0	0				11.2	0					0	0	
57025020	未制成化纤非起绒地毯及铺地制品	16	0		0	0	0	0	6.4	0				12.8	0					0	0	
57025090	未制成其他纺织材料非起绒地毯及铺地制品	14	0		0	0	0	0	0	0				11.2	0					0	0	
57029100	制成的毛制非起绒地毯及铺地制品	14	0		0	0	0	0	0	0				11.2	0					0	0	
57029200	制成的化纤非起绒地毯及铺地制品	16	0		0	0	0	0	6.4	0				12.8	0					0	0	
57029900	制成的其他纺织材料非起绒地毯及铺地制品	14	0		0	0	0	0	0	0				11.2	0					0	0	
57031000	毛制簇绒地毯及其他簇绒铺地制品	14	0		0		0	0	0	0				11.2	0					0	0	0
57032000	尼龙簇绒地毯及其他簇绒铺地制品	10	0		0	5	0	0	0	0				6	0					0	0	0
57033000	化纤簇绒地毯及其他簇绒铺地制品	10	0		0		0	0	0	0				6	0					0	0	0
57039000	其他纺织材料簇绒地毯及其他簇绒铺地制品	14	0		0	11.2	0	0	0	0				11.2	0	0				0	0	0
57041000	小块毡呢地毯及其他毡呢铺地制品	14	0		0	7	0	0	0	0				11.2	0					0	0	
57049000	大块毡呢地毯及其他毡呢铺地制品	10	0		0	5	0	0	0	0				6	0					0	0	0
57050010	毛制其他地毯及其他铺地制品	14	0		0	11.2	0	0	0	0				11.2	0	0				0	0	0
57050020	化纤制其他地毯及其他铺地制品	10	0		0	5	0	0	0	0				6	0	0				0	0	0
57050090	其他纺织材料制其他地毯及铺地制品	14	0		0	11.2	0	0	0	0				11.2	0	0				0	0	0
58011000	毛制起绒机织物及绳绒织物	10	0		0	0	0	0	0	0				6	0					0	0	0
58012100	不割绒的棉制纬起绒织物	12	0		0	0	0	0	0	0				9.6	0					0	0	
58012200	割绒的棉制灯芯绒	10	0		0	0		0	0	0	0		0	6	0					0	0	0
58012300	其他棉制纬起绒织物	10	0		0	0		0	0	0				6	0					0	0	0
58012600	棉制绳绒织物	10	0		0	0		0	0	0				6	0					0	0	0
58012710	棉制的不割绒的经起绒织物(棱纹绸)	10	0		0	0		0	0	0				6	0					0	0	0
58012720	棉制的割绒的经起绒织物	10	0		0	0		0	0	0	0			6	0					0	0	0
58013100	不割绒的化纤制纬起绒织物	10	0		0	0	0	0	0	0				6	0					0	0	0
58013200	割绒的化纤制灯芯绒	10	0		0	0	0	0	0	0				6	0					0	0	0
58013300	其他化纤纬起绒织物	10	0		0	0	0	0	0	0			0	6	0		0	0	0	0	0	0

税则号列	货品名称	最惠国	协定税率													特惠税率						
			东盟统一	亚太5国	智利	巴基斯坦	新加坡	新西兰	秘鲁	哥达	香港	澳门	台湾	瑞士	冰岛	亚太2国	老挝	柬埔寨	缅甸	LDC1	LDC2	LDC3
58013600	化纤绳绒织物	10	0		0	0	0	0	0	0				6	0					0	0	0
58013710	化学纤维制的不割绒的经起绒织物(棱纹绸)	10	0		0	0	0	0	0	0				6	0					0	0	0
58013720	化学纤维制的割绒的经起绒织物	10	0		0	0	0	0	0	0				6	0					0	0	0
58019010	丝及绢丝制起绒机织物及绳绒织物	10	0		0	0	0	0	0	0				6	0					0	0	0
58019090	其他材料制起绒机织物及绳绒织物	10	0		0	0	0	0	0	0				6	0					0	0	0
58021100	未漂白棉毛巾织物及类似毛圈机织物	12	0		0	0	0	0	0	0		0		9.6	0	0				0	0	0
58021900	其他棉毛巾织物及类似毛圈机织物	10	0		0	0		0	0	0		0		6	0					0	0	0
58022010	丝及绢丝毛巾织物及类似毛圈机织物	12	0		0	0	0	0	0	0		0		9.6	0	0				0	0	0
58022020	羊毛等毛巾织物及类似毛圈机织物	12	0		0	0	0	0	0	0		0		9.6	0	0				0	0	0
58022030	化纤毛巾织物及类似毛圈机织物	14	0		0	0	0	0	0	0		0		11.2	0	0				0	0	0
58022090	其他纺织材料毛巾织物及类似毛圈织物	12	0		0	0	0	0	0	0		0		9.6	0	0				0	0	0
58023010	丝及绢丝制簇绒织物	10	0		0	0	0	0	0	0				6	0					0	0	0
58023020	羊毛或动物细毛制簇绒织物	10	0		0	0	0	0	0	0				6	0					0	0	0
58023030	棉或麻制簇绒织物	10	0		0	0		0	0	0				6	0					0	0	0
58023040	化学纤维制簇绒织物	10	0		0	0	0	0	4	0				6	0					0	0	0
58023090	其他纺织材料制簇绒织物	10	0		0	0	0	0	0	0				6	0					0	0	0
58030010	棉制纱罗	10	0		0	5		0	0	0				6	0					0	0	0
58030020	丝及绢丝制纱罗	10	0		0	5	0	0	0	0				6	0					0	0	0
58030030	化学纤维制纱罗	10	0		0	5	0	0	0	0				6	0					0	0	0
58030090	其他纺织材料制纱罗	10	0		0	5	0	0	0	0				6	0					0	0	0
58041010	丝及绢丝网眼薄纱及其他网眼织物	10	0	7	0	5	0	0	0	0				6	0					0	0	0
58041020	棉制网眼薄纱及其他网眼织物	10	0	7	0	5		0	0	0				7.7	0					0	0	0
58041030	化纤制网眼薄纱及其他网眼织物	12	0	8.4	0	5	0	0	0	0			0	9.6	0		0	0	0	0	0	0
58041090	其他纺织材料网眼薄纱及其他网眼织物	10	0	7	0	5	0	0	0	0			0	6	0					0	0	0
58042100	化纤机制花边	10	0		0	5	0	0	0	0	0	0	0	6	0					0	0	0
58042910	丝及绢丝机制花边	10	0		0	5	0	0	0	0				6	0					0	0	0
58042920	棉机制花边	10	0		0	5		0	0	0				6	0		0	0	0	0	0	0
58042990	其他纺织材料制机制花边	10	0		0	5	0	0	0	0				6	0					0	0	0
58043000	手工制花边	10	0		0	5	0	0	0	0				6	0					0	0	0
58050010	手工针绣嵌花装饰毯	12	0		0	6	0	0	0	0				9.6	0					0	0	0
58050090	"哥白林"等手织装饰毯	12	0		0	6	0	0	0	0				9.6	0					0	0	0
58061010	棉或麻狭幅起绒机织物及绳绒织物	10	0		0	5		0	0	0				6	0					0	0	0
58061090	其他材料狭幅起绒织物及绳绒织物	10	0	9.1	0	5	0	0	0	0			0	6	0		0	0	0	0	0	0
58062000	含弹性纱线≥5%的狭幅织物	10	0		0	5	0	0	0	0	0	0	0	6	0		0	0	0	0	0	0
58063100	棉制其他狭幅机织物	10	0		0	5		0	0	0				6	0		0	0	0	0	0	0
58063200	化纤制其他狭幅机织物	10	0	7	0	5	0	0	0	0		0	0	6	0		0	0	0	0	0	0
58063910	丝及绢丝制其他狭幅机织物	10	0		0	5	0	0	0	0				6	0					0	0	0
58063920	毛制其他狭幅机织物	10	0		0	5	0	0	0	0				6	0					0	0	0
58063990	其他材料制其他狭幅机织物	10	0		0	5	0	0	0	0				6	0					0	0	0
58064010	棉或麻粘合有经纱无纬纱狭幅织物	10	0		0	5		0	0	0				6	0					0	0	0
58064090	其他材料粘合有经纱无纬纱狭幅织物	10	0		0	5	0	0	0	0				6	0					0	0	0
58071000	机织非绣制纺织材料标签、徽章等	10	0	8.5	0	8.5	0	0	4	0	0	0	0	6	0		0	0	0	0	0	0
58079000	非机织非绣制纺织材料标签徽章等	10	0		0	5	0	0	0	0				6	0					0	0	0
58081000	成匹的编带	10	0		0		0	0	0	0		0		6	0					0	0	0
58089000	非绣制成匹装饰带、流苏、绒球	10	0		0	5	0	0	0	0		0		6	0		0	0	0	0	0	0
58090010	与棉混制金属线布及含金属纱线布	10	0		0	5	0	0	0	0				6	0					0	0	0
58090020	与化纤混制金属线布及含金属纱布	10	0		0	5	0	0	0	0				6	0					0	0	0
58090090	其他金属线布及含金属纱线布	10	0		0	5	0	0	0	0				6	0					0	0	0
58101000	不见底布的刺绣品	10	0		0	5	0	0	0	0				6	0					0	0	0
58109100	棉制见底布的刺绣品	10	0		0		0	0	4	0				6	0					0	0	0
58109200	化学纤维制见底布刺绣品	10	0		0	5	0	0	0	0			0	6	0					0	0	0
58109900	其他纺织材料制见底布刺绣品	10	0		0	5	0	0	0	0				6	0					0	0	0
58110010	丝及绢丝制绗缝被褥状纺织品	10	0		0	0	0	0	0	0				6	0					0	0	0
58110020	羊毛或动物细毛制绗缝被褥状纺织品	10	0		0	0	0	0	0	0				6	0					0	0	0
58110030	棉制绗缝被褥状纺织品	10	0		0	0	0	0	0	0				6	0					0	0	0
58110040	化学纤维制绗缝被褥状纺织品	12	0		0	0	0	0	0	0				9.6	0					0	0	0
58110090	其他纺织材料制绗缝被褥状纺织品	10	0		0	0	0	0	0	0				6	0					0	0	0
59011010	用胶或淀粉涂布的棉或麻纺织物	10	0		0	5	0	0	0	0				6	0					0	0	0
59011020	用胶或淀粉涂布的化纤纺织物	10	0		0	5	0	0	0	0				6	0					0	0	0
59011090	用胶或淀粉涂布的其他纤维纺织物	10	0		0	5	0	0	0	0				6	0					0	0	0

税则号列	货品名称	最惠国	协定税率													特惠税率						
			东盟统一	亚太5国	智利	巴基斯坦	新加坡	新西兰	秘鲁	哥达	香港	澳门	台湾	瑞士	冰岛	亚太2国	老挝	柬埔寨	缅甸	LDC1	LDC2	LDC3
59019010	制成的油画布	10	0		0	5		0	0	0				6	0					0	0	0
59019091	棉或麻制描图布、帽里硬衬布等	10	0		0	5		0	0	0				6	0		0	0	0	0	0	0
59019092	化纤制描图布、帽里硬衬布等	10	0		0	5		0	0	0				6	0					0	0	0
59019099	其他纺织纤维制描图布、帽里硬衬布等	10	0		0	5		0	0	0				6	0					0	0	0
59021010	聚酰胺-6(尼龙-6)制的帘子布	10	0	9	0	5	0	0	0	0				6	0					0	0	0
59021020	聚酰胺-6,6(尼龙-6,6)制的帘子布	10	0	9	0	5	0	0	0	0				6	0					0	0	0
59021090	其他尼龙等高强力纱制的帘子布	10	0	9	0	5	0	0	0	0				6	0					0	0	0
59022000	聚酯高强力纱制的帘子布	10	0	9	0	5	0	0	0	0				6	0					0	0	0
59029000	粘胶纤维高强力纱制帘子布	10	0		0	5		0	0	0				8	0					0	0	0
59031010	用聚氯乙烯浸、涂的绝缘布或带	10	0	8.5	0	5		0	0	0				6	0					0	0	0
59031020	用聚氯乙烯浸、涂的人造革	10	0	8.5	0	5	0	0	0	0	0		0	6	0					0	0	0
59031090	用聚氯乙烯浸、涂的其他纺织物	10	0	8.5	0	5	0	0	0	0	0		0	6	0					0	0	0
59032010	用聚氨基甲酸酯浸、涂的绝缘布或带	10	0	8.5	0	5		0	0	0				6	0					0	0	0
59032020	用聚氨基甲酸酯浸、涂的人造革	10	0	8.5	0	5	0	0	0	0			0	6	0					0	0	0
59032090	用聚氨基甲酸酯浸、涂的其他纺织物	10	0	8.5	0	8.5	0	0	0	0	0		0	6	0					0	0	0
59039010	用其他塑料浸、涂的绝缘布或带	10	0	8.5	0	5		0	0	0				8	0					0	0	0
59039020	用其他塑料浸、涂的人造革	10	0	8.5	0	5	0	0	0	0			0	6	0					0	0	0
59039090	用其他塑料浸、涂的其他纺织物	10	0	8.5	0	8.5	0	0	0	0	0		0	6	0		0	0	0	0	0	0
59041000	列诺伦(亚麻油地毡)	14	0		0	11.2	0	0	0	0				11.2	0					0	0	
59049000	以织物为底涂布的铺地品	14	0		0	7	0	0	0	0				11.2	0					0	0	
59050000	糊墙织物	10	0		0	5	0	0	0	0				6	0					0	0	0
59061010	用橡胶处理宽≤20cm纺织绝缘胶粘带	10	0		0	5		0	0	0				6	0					0	0	0
59061090	用橡胶处理宽≤20cm其他纺丝胶粘带	10	0		0	5	0	0	0	0				6						0	0	0
59069100	用橡胶处理的针织或钩编的纺织物	10	0		0	5	0	0	0	0			0	6	0					0	0	0
59069910	用橡胶处理宽其他绝缘布或带	10	0		0	5		0	0	0				6	0					0	0	0
59069990	用橡胶处理的其他纺织物	10	0		0	5	0	0	0	0			0	6	0					0	0	0
59070010	用其他材料浸、涂的绝缘布或带	10	0	8.5	0	5		0	0	0				8	0					0	0	0
59070020	用其他材料浸、涂的已绘制画布	10	0	8.5	0	5		0	0	0	0			6	0					0	0	0
59070090	用其他材料浸、涂的其他纺织物	10	0	8.5	0	5	0	0	0	0				6	0					0	0	0
59080000	纺织材料制灯芯、炉芯等和煤气灯纱筒及纱罩	10	0		0	5		0	0	0				6	0					0	0	0
59090000	纺织材料制水龙软管及类似管子	8	0		0	5		0	0	0		0		4.8	0					0	0	0
59100000	纺织材料制的传动带或输送带及带料	8	0		0	5		0	0	0			0	4.8	0					0	0	0
59111010	包覆纺锤用浸胶的起绒狭幅织物	8	0	7.2	0	5		0	0	0				4.8	0					0	0	0
59111090	其他涂胶等针布及专门技术用途的纺织物起绒狭幅织物	8	0		0	5		0	0	0				4.8	0					0	0	0
59112000	筛布	8	0		0	5		0	0	0				0	0					0	0	0
59113100	造纸等机器用轻的环状或有联接装置的布或毡呢	8	0		0	5		0	0	0				4.8	0					0	0	0
59113200	造纸等机器用重的环状或有联接装置的布或毡呢	8	0		0	5		0	0	0				6.4	0					0	0	0
59114000	用于榨油机器或类似机器的滤布	8	0		0	5		0	0	0				4.8	0					0	0	0
59119000	其他专门技术用途纺织产品及制品	8	0		0	5		0	0	0				4.8	0					0	0	0
60011000	针织或钩编的长毛绒织物	10	0	8.5	0	0	0	0	0	0				6	0					0	0	0
60012100	棉制针织或钩编的毛圈绒头织物	10	0	8.5	0	0		0	0	0				6	0					0	0	0
60012200	化纤制针织或钩编毛圈绒头织物	10	0	8.5	0	0	0	0	0	0				6	0					0	0	0
60012900	其他材料制针织或钩编毛圈绒头布	12	0		0	0	0	0	0	0				9.6	0					0	0	
60019100	棉制针织或钩编起绒织物	10	0	7	0	0		0	0	0				6	0					0	0	0
60019200	化纤制针织或钩编起绒织物	10	0	8.5	0	0	0	0	0	0	0	0	0	6	0					0	0	0
60019900	其他纤维制针织或钩编起绒织物	12	0		0	0	0	0	0	0				9.6	0					0	0	
60024010	宽≤30cm,弹性纱线≥5%棉针织、钩编织物	10	0	8.5	0	0		0	0	0				6	0					0	0	0
60024020	宽≤30cm,弹性纱线≥5%丝及绢丝制针织、钩编织物	10	0	8.5	0	0	0	0	0	0				6	0					0	0	0
60024030	宽≤30cm,弹性纱线≥5%合成纤维制针织、钩编织物	10	0		0	0	0	0	0	0				6	0					0	0	0
60024040	宽≤30cm,弹性纱线≥5%人造纤维制针织、钩编织物	10	0		0	0	0	0	0	0				6	0					0	0	0
60024090	宽≤30cm,弹性纱线≥5%其他纺织材料针织、钩编织物	10	0	7	0	0	0	0	0	0				6	0					0	0	0

税则号列	货品名称	最惠国	协定税率													特惠税率						
			东盟统一	亚太5国	智利	巴基斯坦	新加坡	新西兰	秘鲁	哥达	香港	澳门	台湾	瑞士	冰岛	亚太2国	老挝	柬埔寨	缅甸	LDC1	LDC2	LDC3
60029010	宽≤30cm 含橡胶线的棉针织、钩编织物	10	0	8.5	0	0		0	0	0				6	0		0	0	0	0	0	0
60029020	宽≤30cm 含橡胶线的丝及绢丝制针织、钩编织物	10	0	8.5	0	0	0	0	0	0				6	0					0	0	0
60029030	宽≤30cm 含橡胶线的合成纤维制针织、钩编织物	10	0	5	0	0	0	0	0	0				6	0		0	0	0	0	0	0
60029040	宽≤30cm 含橡胶线的人造纤维制针织、钩编织物	10	0	5	0	0	0	0	0	0				6	0					0	0	0
60029090	宽≤30cm 含橡胶线的其他纺织材料针织、钩编织物	10	0	8.5	0	0	0	0	0	0				6	0					0	0	0
60031000	宽≤30cm 羊毛或动物细毛制的针织、钩编织物	10	0		0	0	0	0	0	0				6	0					0	0	0
60032000	宽≤30cm 其他棉制的针织、钩编织物	10	0		0	0		0	0	0				6	0					0	0	0
60033000	宽≤30cm 合成纤维制的针织、钩编织物	10	0	9.4	0	0	0	0	0	0				6	0					0	0	0
60034000	宽≤30cm 人造纤维制的针织、钩编织物	10	0	9.4	0	0	0	0	0	0				6	0					0	0	0
60039000	宽≤30cm 其他针织、钩编织物	10	0		0	0	0	0	0	0				6	0					0	0	0
60041010	宽>30cm,弹性纱线≥5% 棉针织、钩编织物	10	0	7	0	0	0	0	0	0	0			6	0		0	0	0	0	0	0
60041020	宽>30cm,弹性纱线≥5% 丝及绢丝制针织、钩编织物	10	0	8.5	0	0	0	0	0	0				6	0					0	0	0
60041030	宽>30cm,弹性纱线≥5% 合成纤维制针织、钩编织物	10	0		0	0	0	0	0	0	0	0	0	6	0					0	0	0
60041040	宽>30cm,弹性纱线≥5% 人造纤维制针织、钩编织物	10	0		0	0	0	0	0	0	0	0		6	0					0	0	0
60041090	宽>30cm,弹性纱线≥5% 其他纺织材料针织、钩编织物	10	0	8.5	0	0	0	0	0	0	0	0	0	6	0					0	0	0
60049010	宽>30cm 含橡胶线的棉针织、钩编织物	10	0	8.5	0	0		0	0	0	0			6	0					0	0	0
60049020	宽>30cm 含橡胶线的丝及绢丝制针织、钩编织物	10	0	8.5	0	0	0	0	0	0				6	0					0	0	0
60049030	宽>30cm 含橡胶线的合成纤维制针织、钩编织物	10	0		0	0	0	0	0	0	0	0	0	6	0					0	0	0
60049040	宽>30cm 含橡胶线的人造纤维制针织、钩编织物	10	0		0	0	0	0	0	0	0	0		6	0					0	0	0
60049090	宽>30cm 含橡胶线的其他纺织材料针织、钩编织物	10	0	7	0	0	0	0	0	0	0	0	0	6	0					0	0	0
60052100	未漂白或漂白棉制的其他经编织物	10	0		0	0		0	0	0	0			6	0					0	0	0
60052200	染色棉制的其他经编织物	10	0		0	0		0	0	0	0			6	0					0	0	0
60052300	色织棉制的其他经编织物	10	0		0	0		0	0	0	0			6	0					0	0	0
60052400	印花棉制的其他经编织物	10	0		0	0		0	0	0	0			6	0					0	0	0
60053100	未漂白或漂白合成纤维制的其他经编织物	10	0	8.5	0	0	0	0	0	0			0	6	0					0	0	0
60053200	染色合成纤维制的其他经编织物	10	0	8.5	0	0	0	0	0	0			0	6	0		0	0	0	0	0	0
60053300	色织合成纤维制的其他经编织物	10	0	8.5	0	0	0	0	0	0				6	0					0	0	0
60053400	印花合成纤维制的其他经编织物	10	0	8.5	0	0	0	0	0	0				6	0					0	0	0
60054100	未漂白或漂白人造纤维制的其他经编织物	10	0	8.5	0	0	0	0	0	0				6	0					0	0	0
60054200	染色人造纤维制的其他经编织物	10	0	8.5	0	0	0	0	0	0				6	0					0	0	0
60054300	色织人造纤维制的其他经编织物	10	0	8.5	0	0	0	0	0	0				6	0					0	0	0
60054400	印花人造纤维制的其他经编织物	10	0	8.5	0	0	0	0	0	0				6	0					0	0	0
60059010	羊毛或动物细毛制的其他经编织物	12	0		0	0	0	0	0	0				9.6	0					0	0	
60059090	其他纺织材料经编织物	12	0		0	0	0	0	0	0				9.6	0					0	0	
60061000	羊毛或动物细毛制的其他针织、钩编织物	12	0		0	0	0	0	0	0				9.6	0					0	0	
60062100	未漂白或漂白棉制的其他针织、钩编织物	10	0	7	0	0		0	0	0	0	0		6	0					0	0	0
60062200	染色棉制的其他针织、钩编织物	10	0	8.5	0	0	0	0	0	0	0	0		6	0		0	0	0	0	0	0
60062300	色织棉制的其他针织、钩编织物	10	0	7	0	0	0	0	0	0	0	0		6	0		0	0	0	0	0	0
60062400	印花棉制的其他针织、钩编织物	10	0	8.5	0	0		0	0	0	0	0	0	6	0					0	0	0

税则号列	货品名称	最惠国	协定税率 东盟统一	亚太5国	智利	巴基斯坦	新加坡	新西兰	秘鲁	哥达	香港	澳门	台湾	瑞士	冰岛	特惠税率 亚太2国	老挝	柬埔寨	缅甸	LDC1	LDC2	LDC3
60063100	未漂白或漂白合成纤维制的其他针织、钩编织物	10	0	8.5	0	0	0	0	0	0	0	0	0	6	0					0	0	0
60063200	染色合成纤维制的其他针织、钩编织物	10	0	8.5	0	0	0	0	0	0	0	0	0	6	0					0	0	0
60063300	色织合成纤维制的其他针织、钩编织物	10	0	8.5	0	0	0	0	0	0	0	0	0	6	0					0	0	0
60063400	印花合成纤维制的其他针织、钩编织物	10	0	8.5	0	0	0	0	0	0	0	0	0	6	0					0	0	0
60064100	未漂白或漂白人造纤维制的其他针织、钩编织物	10	0	8.5	0	0	0	0	0	0	0	0		6	0					0	0	0
60064200	染色人造纤维制的其他针织、钩编织物	10	0	8.5	0	0	0	0	0	0	0	0	0	6	0					0	0	0
60064300	色织人造纤维制的其他针织、钩编织物	10	0	8.5	0	0	0	0	0	0	0	0		6	0					0	0	0
60064400	印花人造纤维制的其他针织、钩编织物	10	0	8.5	0	0	0	0	0	0	0	0		6	0					0	0	0
60069000	未列名针织、钩编织物	12	0	10.2	0	0	0	0	0	0				9.6	0					0	0	
61012000	棉制针织或钩编男式大衣、防风衣	17.5	0	14	0	14	0	0	7	0	0	0		14	0					0	0	0
61013000	化纤制针织或钩编男式大衣等	17.5	0	12.3	0	8.8	0	0	7	0	0	0		14	0					0	0	0
61019010	毛制针织或钩编男式大衣、防风衣	25	0	18	0	18	0	0	10	0	0	0		20	0					0	0	
61019090	其他纺织材料制针织或钩编男式大衣、防风衣	17.5	0	12.3	0	8.8	0	0	7	0	0	0		14	0					0	0	
61021000	毛制针织或钩编女式大衣、防风衣	25	0	18	0	18	0	0	10	0	0	0		20	0					0	0	
61022000	棉制针织或钩编女式大衣、防风衣	17.5	0	14	0	14	0	0		0	0	0		14	0					0	0	0
61023000	化纤制针织或钩编女式大衣等	17.5	0	12.3	0	8.8	0	0	7	0	0	0		14	0					0	0	0
61029000	其他纺织材料制针织或钩编女式大衣、防风衣	20	0	13.8	0	10	0	0	8	0	0	0		16	0					0	0	
61031010	毛制针织或钩编男式西服套装	25	0	18	0	18	0	0	10	0	0	0		20	0					0	0	
61031020	合纤制针织或钩编男西服套装	25	0	18	0	18	0	0	10	0	0	0		20	0					0	0	
61031090	其他纺织材料制针织或钩编男式西服套装	17.5	0	12.3	0	8.8	0	0	7	0	0	0		14	0		0			0	0	0
61032200	棉制针织或钩编男式便服套装	20	0	14.8	0	14.8	0	0	8	0	0	0		16	0		0			0	0	0
61032300	合纤制针织或钩编男便服套装	25	0	18	0	18	0	0	10	0	0	0		20	0					0	0	
61032910	毛制针织或钩编男式便服套装	25	0	18	0	18	0	0	10	0	0	0		20	0					0	0	
61032990	其他纺织材料制针织或钩编男式便服套装	25	0	18	0	18	0	0	10	0		0		20	0		0			0	0	0
61033100	毛制针织或钩编男式上衣	16	0	11.7	0	8	0	0	6.4	0	0	0		12.8	0					0	0	
61033200	棉制针织或钩编男式上衣	16	0	12	0	8	0	0	6.4	0	0	0		12.8	0		0	0	0	0	0	0
61033300	合纤制针织或钩编男式上衣	19	0	13.6	0	9.5	0	0	7.6	0	0	0		15.2	0			0		0	0	0
61033900	其他纺织材料制针织或钩编男式上衣	16	0	11.7	0	8	0	0	6.4	0	0	0		12.8	0		0	0		0	0	0
61034100	毛制针织或钩编男长裤、工装裤等	16	0	11.7	0	8	0	0	6.4	0	0	0		12.8	0	0				0	0	0
61034200	棉制针织或钩编男长裤、工装裤等	16	0	13.6	0	8	0	0	6.4	0	0	0		12.8	0	6.4	0	0	0	0	0	0
61034300	合纤制针织或钩编男长裤等	17.5	0	12.3	0	8.8	0	0	7	0	0	0		14	0	0		0		0	0	0
61034900	其他纺织材料制针织或钩编男长裤等	16	0	11.7	0	8	0	0	6.4	0	0	0		12.8	0	0	0	0		0	0	0
61041300	合纤制针织或钩编女西服套装	25	0	18	0	18	0	0	10	0	0	0		20	0					0	0	
61041910	毛制针织或钩编女式西服套装	17.5	0	12.3	0	8.8	0	0	7	0	0	0		14	0					0	0	0
61041920	棉制针织或钩编女式西服套装	17.5	0	14	0	14	0	0	7	0	0	0		14	0		0			0	0	0
61041990	其他纺织材料制针织或钩编女式西服套装	17.5	0	12.3	0	8.8	0	0	7	0	0	0		14	0		0			0	0	0
61042200	棉制针织或钩编女式便服套装	17.5	0	14	0	14	0	0	7	0	0	0		14	0		0			0	0	0
61042300	合纤制针织或钩编女便服套装	25	0	18	0	18	0	0	10	0	0	0		20	0					0	0	
61042910	毛制针织或钩编女式便服套装	17.5	0	12.3	0	8.8	0	0	7	0	0	0		14	0					0	0	
61042990	其他纺织材料制针织或钩编女式便服套装	15	0	10.4	0	7.5	0	0	6	0	0	0		12	0					0	0	0
61043100	毛制针织女式上衣	16	0	11.7	0	8	0	0	6.4	0	0	0		12.8	0					0	0	0
61043200	棉制针织女式上衣	16	0	13.6	0	13.6	0	0	6.4	0	0	0		12.8	0		0	0	0	0	0	0
61043300	合纤制针织女上衣	19	0	13.6	0	9.5	0	0	7.6	0	0	0		15.2	0			0		0	0	0
61043900	其他纺织材料制针织女上衣	16	0	11.7	0	8	0	0	6.4	0	0	0		12.8	0			0		0	0	0
61044100	毛制针织或钩编连衣裙	16	0	11.7	0	8	0	0	6.4	0	0	0		12.8	0					0	0	
61044200	棉制针织或钩编连衣裙	16	0	13.6	0	8	0	0	6.4	0	0	0		12.8	0					0	0	0
61044300	合纤制针织或钩编连衣裙	17.5	0	12.3	0	8.8	0	0	7	0	0	0		14	0			0		0	0	0
61044400	人纤制针织或钩编连衣裙	16	0	11.7	0	8	0	0	6.4	0	0	0		12.8	0			0		0	0	0
61044900	其他纺织材料制针织或钩编连衣裙	16	0	11.7	0	8	0	0	6.4	0	0	0		12.8	0			0		0	0	0
61045100	毛制针织或钩编裙子及裙裤	14	0	10.8	0	7	0	0	0	0	0	0		11.2	0					0	0	
61045200	棉制针织裙子及裙裤	14	0	10.3	0	7	0	0	0	0	0	0		11.2	0					0	0	0
61045300	合纤制针织或钩编裙子及裙裤	16	0	11.7	0	8	0	0	6.4	0	0	0		12.8	0			0		0	0	0

税则号列	货品名称	最惠国	协定税率													特惠税率						
			东盟统一	亚太5国	智利	巴基斯坦	新加坡	新西兰	秘鲁	哥达	香港	澳门	台湾	瑞士	冰岛	亚太2国	老挝	柬埔寨	缅甸	LDC1	LDC2	LDC3
61045900	其他纺织材料制针织或钩编裙子及裙裤	14	0	10.8	0	7	0	0	0	0	0	0		11.2	0		0	0	0	0	0	0
61046100	毛制针织或钩编女长裤、工装裤等	16	0	11.7	0	8	0	0	6.4	0	0	0		12.8	0					0	0	0
61046200	棉制针织或钩编女长裤、工装裤等	16	0	13.6	0	8	0	0	6.4	0	0	0		12.8	0	6.4				0	0	0
61046300	合纤制针织或钩编女长裤等	17.5	0	12.3	0	8.8	0	0	7	0	0	0		14	0					0	0	0
61046900	其他纺织材料制针织或钩编女长裤等	16	0	12	0	8	0	0	6.4	0	0	0		12.8	0	0				0	0	0
61051000	棉制针织或钩编男衬衫	16	0	13.6	0	13.6	0	0		0	0	0	0	12.8	0	11.2	0	0	0	0	0	0
61052000	化纤制针织或钩编男衬衫	17.5	0	12.3	0	8.8	0	0	7	0	0	0		14	0	0				0	0	0
61059000	其他纺织材料制针织或钩编男衬衫	16	0	11.7	0	8	0	0	6.4	0	0	0		12.8	0	0				0	0	0
61061000	棉制针织或钩编女衬衫	16	0	13.6	0	8	0	0	6.4	0	0	0		12.8	0	6.4	0	0	0	0	0	0
61062000	化纤制针织或钩编女衬衫	17.5	0	12.3	0	8.8	0	0	7	0	0	0		14	0	0				0	0	0
61069000	其他纺织材料制针织或钩编女衬衫	16	0	11.7	0	8	0	0	6.4	0	0	0	0	12.8	0	0				0	0	0
61071100	棉制针织或钩编男内裤及三角裤	14	0		0	11.2	0	0	5.6	0	0	0		11.2	0	5.6	0	0	0	0	0	0
61071200	化纤制针织或钩编男内裤及三角裤	16	0	10.9	0	8	0	0	6.4	0	0	0		12.8	0					0	0	
61071910	丝及绢丝制针织或钩编男内裤及三角裤	14	0	9.3	0	7	0	0	0	0	0	0		11.2	0					0	0	
61071990	其他纺织材料制针织或钩编男内裤及三角裤	14	0	9.3	0	7	0	0	0	0	0	0		11.2	0					0	0	
61072100	棉制针织或钩编男长睡衣及睡衣裤	14	0		0	11.2	0	0		0	0	0		11.2	0	5.6	0	0	0	0	0	0
61072200	化纤制针织或钩编男睡衣裤	16	0	10.9	0	8	0	0	6.4	0	0	0		12.8	0	0				0	0	0
61072910	丝及绢丝制针织或钩编男长睡衣及睡衣裤	14	0	9.3	0	7	0	0	0	0	0			11.2	0	0				0	0	0
61072990	其他纺织材料制针织或钩编男长睡衣及睡衣裤	14	0	9.3	0	7	0	0	0	0	0			11.2	0	0	0	0	0	0	0	0
61079100	棉制针织或钩编男浴衣、晨衣	14	0		0	7	0	0	0	0	0			11.2	0					0	0	
61079910	化纤制针织或钩编男浴衣、晨衣	16	0	10.9	0	8	0	0	6.4	0	0			12.8	0					0	0	
61079990	其他纺织材料制针织或钩编男浴衣、晨衣	14	0	9.3	0	7	0	0	0	0				11.2	0					0	0	
61081100	化纤制针织或钩编长衬裙及衬裙	16	0	10.9	0	8	0	0	6.4	0	0			12.8	0					0	0	
61081910	棉制针织或钩编女式长衬裙及衬裙	14	0		0	7	0	0	0	0	0			11.2	0					0	0	0
61081920	丝及绢丝制针织或钩编女式长衬裙及衬裙	14	0		0	7	0	0	0	0	0			11.2	0					0	0	
61081990	其他纺织材料制针织或钩编女式长衬裙及衬裙	14	0	9.3	0	7	0	0	0	0	0			11.2	0					0	0	
61082100	棉制针织或钩编女三角裤及短衬裤	14	0		0	11.2	0	0	0	0	0	0		11.2	0		0	0	0	0	0	0
61082200	化纤制针织或钩编女三角裤及短衬裤	16	0	10.9	0	8	0	0	6.4	0	0	0		12.8	0					0	0	0
61082910	丝及绢丝制针织或钩编女三角裤及短衬裤	14	0	9.3	0	7	0	0	0	0	0	0		11.2	0					0	0	
61082990	其他纺织材料制针织或钩编女三角裤及短衬裤	14	0	9.3	0	7	0	0	0	0	0	0		11.2	0					0	0	
61083100	棉制针织或钩编女睡衣及睡衣裤	14	0		0	11.2	0	0	5.6	0	0	0		11.2	0	5.6	0	0	0	0	0	0
61083200	化纤制针织或钩编女睡衣及睡衣裤	16	0	10.9	0	8	0	0	6.4	0	0	0		12.8	0	0				0	0	0
61083910	丝及绢丝制针织或钩编女睡衣及睡衣裤	14	0	9.3	0	7	0	0	0	0	0			11.2	0	0				0	0	0
61083990	其他纺织材料制针织或钩编女睡衣及睡衣裤	14	0	9.3	0	7	0	0	0	0	0			11.2	0	0				0	0	0
61089100	棉制针织或钩编女浴衣、晨衣	14	0		0	11.2	0	0	5.6	0	0	0		11.2	0		0	0	0	0	0	0
61089200	化纤制针织或钩编女浴衣、晨衣	16	0	10.9	0	8	0	0	6.4	0	0	0		12.8	0					0	0	0
61089900	其他纺织材料制针织或钩编女浴衣、晨衣	14	0	9.3	0	7	0	0	0	0	0	0		11.2	0					0	0	
61091000	棉制针织或钩编T恤衫、汗衫等	14	0	9.4	0	9.4	0	0	5.6	0	0	0		11.2	0		0	0	0	0	0	0
61099010	丝及绢丝制针织或钩编T恤衫、汗衫等	14	0	9.3	0	7	0	0	0	0	0	0		11.2	0	0				0	0	0
61099090	其他纺织材料制针织或钩编T恤衫、汗衫等	14	0	9.3	0	9.3	0	0	5.6	0	0	0		11.2	0	0	0	0	0	0	0	0
61101100	羊毛制针织或钩编套头衫等	14	0	9.3	0	0	0	0	5.6	0	0	0	0	11.2	0	0	0	0	0	0	0	0
61101200	喀什米尔山羊细毛制针织或钩编套头衫等	14	0	9.3	0	0	0	0	0	0	0	0		11.2	0					0	0	0
61101910	其他山羊细毛制针织或钩编套头衫等	14	0	9.3	0	0	0	0	0	0	0	0		11.2	0					0	0	0
61101920	兔毛制针织或钩编套头衫等	14	0	9.3	0	0	0	0	0	0	0	0		11.2	0					0	0	
61101990	其他毛制针织或钩编套头衫等	14	0	9.3	0	0	0	0	5.6	0	0	0		11.2	0					0	0	0
61102000	棉制针织或钩编套头衫等	14	0	11	0	0	0	0	5.6	0	0	0	0	11.2	0	5.6	0	0	0	0	0	0
61103000	化纤制针织或钩编套头衫等	16	0	10.9	0	0	0	0	6.4	0	0	0	0	12.8	0	0				0	0	0
61109010	丝及绢丝制针织或钩编套头衫等	14	0	9.3	0	0	0	0	0	0	0	0		11.2	0	0				0	0	0
61109090	其他纺织材料制针织或钩编套头衫等	14	0	9.3	0	0	0	0	5.6	0	0	0		11.2	0	0				0	0	0

税则号列	货品名称	最惠国	协定税率 东盟统一	亚太5国	智利	巴基斯坦	新加坡	新西兰	秘鲁	哥达	香港	澳门	台湾	瑞士	冰岛	特惠税率 亚太2国	老挝	柬埔寨	缅甸	LDC1	LDC2	LDC3
61112000	棉制针织或钩编婴儿服装及附件	14	0		0	11.2	0	0	0	0	0	0		11.2	0					0	0	0
61113000	合纤制针织婴儿服装及附件	16	0	10.9	0	8	0	0	6.4	0	0	0		12.8	0					0	0	0
61119010	毛制针织或钩编婴儿服装及附件	14	0	9.3	0	7	0	0	0	0	0	0		11.2	0					0	0	0
61119090	其他纺织材料制针织或钩编婴儿服装及附件	14	0	9.3	0	7	0	0	5.6	0	0	0		11.2	0					0	0	
61121100	棉制针织或钩编运动服	16	0	13.6	0	8	0	0	6.4	0	0	0		12.8	0					0	0	
61121200	合纤制针织或钩编运动服	17.5	0	12.3	0	8.8	0	0	7	0	0	0		14	0					0	0	0
61121900	其他纺织材料制针织或钩编运动服	16	0	11.7	0	8	0	0	6.4	0	0	0		12.8	0					0	0	
61122010	棉制针织或钩编滑雪服	16	0	13.6	0	8	0	0	6.4	0				12.8	0					0	0	0
61122090	其他纺织材料制针织或钩编滑雪服	19	0	13.6	0	9.5	0	0	7.6	0				15.2	0					0	0	
61123100	合纤制针织或钩编男式游泳服	17.5	0	12.3	0	8.8	0	0	7	0	0			14	0					0	0	
61123900	其他纺织材料制针织或钩编男式游泳服	16	0	11.7	0	8	0	0	6.4	0	0			12.8	0					0	0	
61124100	合纤制针织或钩编女式游泳服	17.5	0	12.3	0	8.8	0	0	7	0	0		0	14	0					0	0	
61124900	其他纺织材料针织或钩编女式游泳服	16	0	11.7	0	8	0	0	6.4	0	0			12.8	0					0	0	
61130000	涂层经处理针织或钩编织物制服装	16	0	11.7	0	8	0	0	6.4	0	0	0		12.8	0	0				0	0	0
61142000	棉制针织或钩编的其他服装	16	0		0	12.8	0	0		0	0	0		12.8	0	6.4				0	0	0
61143000	化纤制针织或钩编的其他服装	17.5	0		0	14	0	0	7	0	0	0		14	0					0	0	0
61149010	毛制针织或钩编的其他服装	16	.0		0	12.8	0	0	6.4	0	0			12.8	0					0	0	
61149090	其他纺织材料制针织或钩编的其他服装	16	0		0	12.8	0	0	6.4	0	0			12.8	0					0	0	
61151000	渐紧压袜类连裤袜	16	0	9.3	0	8	0	0	6.4	0	0			12.3	0					0	0	
61152100	单丝<67 分特合纤制连裤袜等	16	0	14.4	0	12.8	0	0	6.4	0	0	0		12.8	0					0	0	
61152200	单丝≥67 分特合纤制连裤袜等	16	0	10.9	0	8	0	0	6.4	0		0	0	12.8	0					0	0	
61152910	棉制针织或钩编连裤袜及紧身裤袜	14	0		0	11.2	0	0	0	0		0		11.2	0					0	0	0
61152990	其他纺织材料制针织连裤袜及紧身裤袜	14	0	9.3	0	7	0	0	0	0		0	0	11.2	0					0	0	
61153000	单丝<67 分特制针织或钩编女统袜	14	0	9.3	0	7	0	0	0	0				11.2	0	0				0	0	0
61159400	毛制针织或钩编短袜及其他袜类	14	0		0	11.2	0	0	0	0	0			11.2	0					0	0	
61159500	棉制针织或钩编短袜及其他袜类	14	0		0	11.2	0	0	5.6	0	0			11.2	0					0	0	0
61159600	合纤制针织或钩编短袜及其他袜类	16	0	10.9	0	8	0	0	6.4	0	0			12.8	0					0	0	0
61159900	其他纺织材料制针织或钩编短袜及其他袜类	14	0	9.3	0	7	0	0	0	0	0		0	11.2	0					0	0	
61161000	塑料或橡胶浸渍的针织或钩织手套	14	0		0		0	0	0	0	0			11.2	0					0	0	0
61169100	毛制其他针织或钩编手套	14	0		0	7	0	0	0	0	0			11.2	0					0	0	0
61169200	棉制其他针织或钩编手套	14	0		0		0	0	0	0	0	0		11.2	0					0	0	
61169300	合纤制其他针织或钩编手套	16	0	10.9	0	8	0	0	6.4	0	0	0		12.8	0					0	0	0
61169900	其他纺织材料制针织或钩编手套	14	0	9.3	0	9.3	0	0	5.6	0	0			11.2	0					0	0	0
61171011	山羊绒制披巾、头巾、围巾、披纱、面纱及类似品	14	0	9.3	0	0	0	0	5.6	0	0			11.2	0					0	0	0
61171019	其他动物细毛制披巾、头巾、围巾、披纱、面纱及类似品	14	0	9.3	0	0	0	0	5.6	0	0			11.2	0					0	0	0
61171020	羊毛制披巾、头巾、围巾、披纱、面纱及类似品	14	0	9.3	0	0	0	0	5.6	0	0			11.2	0					0	0	0
61171090	其他制的披巾、头巾、围巾、披纱、面纱及类似品	14	0	9.3	0	0	0	0	5.6	0	0			11.2	0					0	0	0
61178010	针织或钩编领带及领结	14	0	9.3	0	0	0	0	0	0	0		0	11.2	0					0	0	0
61178090	针织或钩编其他衣着附件	14	0	9.3	0	0	0	0	5.6	0	0		0	11.2	0					0	0	0
61179000	其他针织或钩编衣着零件	14	0	7	0	0	0	0	0	0	0	0	0	11.2	0					0	0	0
62011100	毛制男式大衣、斗篷及类似品	16	0	11.7	0	8	0	0	6.4	0	0	0		12.8	0					0	0	0
62011210	棉制男式羽绒服	16	0		0	12.8	0	0	6.4	0	0	0		12.8	0					0	0	
62011290	棉制男式大衣、斗篷及类似品	16	0		0	12.8	0	0	6.4	0	0	0		12.8	0					0	0	0
62011310	化纤制男式羽绒服	17.5	0	12.3	0	8.8	0	0	7	0	0	0		14	0					0	0	0
62011390	化纤制男式大衣、斗篷及类似品	17.5	0	12.3	0	8.8	0	0	7	0	0	0		14	0					0	0	0
62011900	其他纺织材料制男式大衣、斗篷及类似品	16	0	11.7	0	8	0	0	6.4	0	0	0		12.8	0					0	0	0
62019100	毛制男式带风帽防寒短上衣、防风衣	16	0	11.7	0	8	0	0	6.4	0	0	0		12.8	0					0	0	0
62019210	棉制男式其他羽绒服	16	0		0	12.8	0	0	6.4	0	0	0		12.8	0					0	0	0
62019290	棉制男式带风帽防寒短上衣、防风衣	16	0		0	12.8	0	0	6.4	0	0	0		12.8	0		0	0	0	0	0	0
62019310	化纤制男式其他羽绒服	17.5	0	12.3	0	8.8	0	0	7	0	0	0		14	0					0	0	0
62019390	化纤制男式防寒短上衣、防风衣	17.5	0	12.3	0	8.8	0	0	7	0	0	0		14	0					0	0	0
62019900	其他纺织材料制男式防寒短上衣、防风衣	16	0	11.7	0	8	0	0	6.4	0	0	0		12.8	0				0	0	0	0
62021100	毛制女式大衣、斗篷及类似品等	16	0	11.7	0	8	0	0	6.4	0	0	0		12.8	0					0	0	0
62021210	棉制女式羽绒服	16	0		0	12.8	0	0	6.4	0	0	0		12.8	0					0	0	

税则号列	货品名称	最惠国	协定税率													特惠税率						
			东盟统一	亚太5国	智利	巴基斯坦	新加坡	新西兰	秘鲁	哥达	香港	澳门	台湾	瑞士	冰岛	亚太2国	老挝	柬埔寨	缅甸	LDC1	LDC2	LDC3
62021290	棉制女式大衣、斗篷及类似品等	16	0		0	12.8	0	0	6.4	0	0	0		12.8	0					0	0	0
62021310	化纤制女式羽绒服	19	0	13.6	0	9.5	0	0	7.6	0	0	0		15.2	0					0	0	0
62021390	化纤制女式大衣、斗篷及类似品	19	0	13.6	0	9.5	0	0	7.6	0	0	0		15.2	0					0	0	0
62021900	其他纺织材料制女式大衣、斗篷及类似品	16	0	11.7	0	8	0	0	6.4	0	0	0		12.8	0					0	0	0
62029100	毛制女式带风帽防寒短上衣、防风衣	16	0	11.7	0	8	0	0	6.4	0	0	0		12.8	0					0	0	
62029210	棉制女式其他羽绒服	16	0		0	12.8	0	0	6.4	0	0	0		12.8	0					0	0	
62029290	棉制女式带风帽防寒短上衣、防风衣	16	0		0	12.8	0	0	6.4	0	0	0		12.8	0					0	0	0
62029310	化纤制女式其他羽绒服	17.5	0	12.3	0	8.8	0	0	7	0	0	0		14	0					0	0	0
62029390	化纤制女式防风衣等	17.5	0	12.3	0	8.8	0	0	7	0	0	0		14	0					0	0	0
62029900	其他纺织材料制防风衣、防风短上衣等	16	0	11.7	0	8	0	0	6.4	0	0	0		12.8	0					0	0	0
62031100	毛制男式西服套装	17.5	0	12.3	0	8.8	0	0	7	0	0	0		0	0					0	0	0
62031200	合纤制男式西服套装	17.5	0	12.3	0	8.8	0	0	7	0	0	0		14	0					0	0	0
62031910	丝及绢丝制男式西服套装	17.5	0	12.3	0	8.8	0	0	7	0	0	0		14	0					0	0	
62031990	其他纺织材料制男式西服套装	17.5	0	12.3	0	8.8	0	0	7	0	0	0		13.5	0					0	0	
62032200	棉制男式便服套装	17.5	0		0	14	0	0	7	0	0	0		14	0					0	0	0
62032300	合纤制男式便服套装	17.5	0	12.3	0	8.8	0	0	7	0	0	0		14	0					0	0	0
62032910	丝及绢丝制男式便服套装	17.5	0	12.3	0	8.8	0	0	7	0		0		14	0					0	0	
62032920	毛制男式便服套装	17.5	0	12.3	0	8.8	0	0	7	0	0	0		14	0					0	0	
62032990	其他纺织材料制男式便服套装	17.5	0	12.3	0	8.8	0	0	7	0	0	0		14	0					0	0	
62033100	毛制男式上衣	16	0	11.7	0	8	0	0	6.4	0	0	0		12.8	0	9.6	0	0	0	0	0	0
62033200	棉制男式上衣	16	0	14.4	0	12.8	0	0	6.4	0	0	0		12.8	0	11.2	0	0	0	0	0	0
62033300	合纤制男式上衣	17.5	0	12.3	0	8.8	0	0	7	0	0	0		14	0					0	0	0
62033910	丝及绢丝制男式上衣	16	0	11.7	0	8	0	0	6.4	0	0	0		12.8	0	9.6				0	0	0
62033990	其他纺织材料制男式上衣	16	0	11.7	0	8	0	0	6.4	0	0	0		12.8	0	9.6				0	0	0
62034100	毛制男式长裤、工装裤等	16	0	11.7	0	8	0	0	6.4	0	0	0		0	0	0				0	0	0
62034210	棉制男式阿拉伯裤	16	0	12.9	0	8	0	0	6.4	0	0	0		12.8	0	11.2				0	0	
62034290	棉制男式长裤、工装裤等	16	0	12.9	0	8	0	0	6.4	0	0	0		12.8	0	11.2	0	0	0	0	0	0
62034310	合成纤维制男式阿拉伯裤	17.5	0	13.1	0	8.8	0	0	7	0	0	0		14	0					0	0	
62034390	合纤制男式长裤、工装裤等	17.5	0	13.1	0	8.8	0	0	7	0	0	0		14	0					0	0	0
62034910	其他纺织材料制男式阿拉伯裤	16	0	11.7	0	8	0	0	6.4	0	0	0		12.8	0	0				0	0	0
62034990	其他纺织材料制男童裤、工装裤	16	0	11.7	0	8	0	0	6.4	0	0	0		12.8	0	0				0	0	0
62041100	毛制女式西服套装	17.5	0	12.3	0	8.8	0	0	7	0	0	0		14	0					0	0	
62041200	棉制女式西服套装	17.5	0		0	14	0	0	7	0	0	0		14	0					0	0	
62041300	合纤制女式西服套装	17.5	0	12.3	0	8.8	0	0	7	0	0	0		14	0					0	0	
62041910	丝及绢丝制女式西服套装	17.5	0	12.3	0	8.8	0	0	7	0	0	0		14	0					0	0	
62041990	其他纺织材料制女式西服套装	17.5	0	12.3	0	8.8	0	0	7	0	0	0		14	0					0	0	
62042100	毛制女式便服套装	17.5	0	12.3	0	8.8	0	0	7	0	0	0		14	0					0	0	
62042200	棉制女式便服套装	17.5	0		0	14	0	0	7	0	0	0		14	0					0	0	
62042300	合纤制女式便服套装	20	0	13.8	0	10	0	0	8	0	0	0		16	0					0	0	
62042910	丝及绢丝制女式便服套装	20	0	13.8	0	10	0	0	8	0		0		16	0					0	0	
62042990	其他纺织材料制女式便服套装	14	0	9.9	0	7	0	0	0	0	0	0		11.2	0					0	0	
62043100	毛制女式上衣	16	0	11.7	0	8	0	0	6.4	0	0	0		12.8	0					0	0	0
62043200	棉制女式上衣	16	0		0	12.8	0	0	6.4	0	0	0		12.8	0	6.4	0	0	0	0	0	0
62043300	合纤制女式上衣	17.5	0	12.3	0	8.8	0	0	7	0	0	0		14	0	0				0	0	0
62043910	丝及绢丝制女式上衣	16	0	11.7	0	8	0	0	6.4	0	0	0		12.8	0	0				0	0	0
62043990	其他纺织材料制女式上衣	16	0	11.7	0	8	0	0	6.4	0	0	0		12.8	0	0				0	0	0
62044100	毛制连衣裙	16	0	11.7	0	8	0	0	6.4	0	0	0		12.8	0					0	0	0
62044200	棉制连衣裙	16	0		0	12.8	0	0	6.4	0	0	0		12.8	0		0	0	0	0	0	0
62044300	合纤制女式连衣裙	17.5	0	12.3	0	8.8	0	0	7	0	0	0		14	0					0	0	0
62044400	人纤制女式连衣裙	16	0	11.7	0	8	0	0	6.4	0	0	0		12.8	0					0	0	0
62044910	丝及绢丝制连衣裙	16	0	11.7	0	8	0	0	6.4	0	0	0		12.8	0					0	0	0
62044990	其他纺织材料制连衣裙	16	0	11.7	0	8	0	0	6.4	0	0	0		12.8	0					0	0	0
62045100	毛制裙子及裙裤	14	0	9.3	0	7	0	0	0	0	0	0		11.2	0					0	0	0
62045200	棉制裙子及裙裤	14	0		0	11.2	0	0	0	0	0	0		11.2	0					0	0	0
62045300	合纤制裙子及裙裤	16	0	11.7	0	8	0	0	6.4	0	0	0		12.8	0					0	0	0
62045910	丝及绢丝制裙子及裙裤	14	0	9.3	0	7	0	0	0	0	0	0		11.2	0					0	0	0
62045990	其他纺织材料制裙子及裙裤	14	0	9.3	0	7	0	0	5.6	0	0	0		11.2	0					0	0	0
62046100	毛制女式长裤、工装裤等	16	0	11.7	0	8	0	0	6.4	0	0	0		12.8	0					0	0	0
62046200	棉制女式长裤、工装裤等	16	0	14.4	0	12.8	0	0	6.4	0	0	0		12.8	0	11.2	0	0	0	0	0	0
62046300	合纤制女式长裤、工装裤等	17.5	0	12.3	0	8.8	0	0	7	0	0	0		14	0					0	0	0
62046900	其他纺织材料制女式长裤、工装裤等	16	0	12	0	8	0	0	6.4	0	0	0		12.8	0					0	0	0

税则号列	货品名称	最惠国	协定税率 东盟统一	亚太5国	智利	巴基斯坦	新加坡	新西兰	秘鲁	哥斯达	香港	澳门	台湾	瑞士	冰岛	特惠税率 亚太2国	老挝	柬埔寨	缅甸	LDC1	LDC2	LDC3
62052000	棉制男衬衫	16	0	8	0	8	0	0	6.4	0	0	0		12.8	0	6.4	0	0	0	0	0	0
62053000	化纤制男衬衫	16	0	11.7	0	8	0	0	6.4	0	0	0		12.8	0	0				0	0	0
62059010	丝及绢丝制男衬衫	16	0	11.7	0	8	0	0	6.4	0	0	0		12.8	0	0				0	0	0
62059020	毛制男衬衫	16	0	11.7	0	8	0	0	6.4	0	0	0		12.8	0	0				0	0	0
62059090	其他纺织材料制男衬衫	16	0	11.7	0	8	0	0	6.4	0	0	0		12.8	0	0				0	0	0
62061000	丝及绢丝制女式衬衫	16	0	11.7	0	8	0	0	6.4	0	0	0		12.8	0					0	0	0
62062000	毛制女衬衫	16	0	11.7	0	8	0	0	6.4	0	0	0		12.8	0					0	0	
62063000	棉制女衬衫	16	0	13.6	0	8	0	0	6.4	0	0	0		12.8	0	6.4	0	0	0	0	0	0
62064000	化纤制女衬衫	17.5	0	12.3	0	8.8	0	0	7	0	0	0		14	0					0	0	0
62069000	其他纺织材料制女衬衫	16	0	11.7	0	8	0	0	6.4	0	0	0		12.8	0	0				0	0	0
62071100	棉制男式内裤及三角裤	14	0	10.3	0	7	0	0	5.6	0	0	0		11.2	0					0	0	0
62071910	丝制男式内裤及三角裤	14	0		0	7	0	0	0	0	0	0		11.2	0					0	0	
62071920	化纤制男式内裤及三角裤	16	0		0	12.8	0	0	6.4	0	0	0		12.8	0					0	0	
62071990	其他纺织材料制男式内裤及三角裤	14	0		0	7	0	0	0	0	0	0		11.2	0					0	0	
62072100	棉制男式长睡衣及睡衣裤	14	0		0	11.2	0	0	0	0	0	0		11.2	0		0	0	0	0	0	0
62072200	化纤制男式长睡衣及睡衣裤	16	0		0	12.8	0	0	6.4	0	0	0		12.8	0					0	0	
62072910	丝及绢丝制男式长睡衣及睡衣裤	14	0		0	7	0	0	0	0				11.2	0					0	0	
62072990	其他纺织材料制男式长睡衣及睡衣裤	14	0		0	7	0	0	0	0				11.2	0		0	0	0	0	0	0
62079100	棉制男式浴衣、晨衣及类似品	14	0		0	11.2	0	0	0	0	0	0		11.2	0					0	0	0
62079910	丝及绢丝制男浴衣、晨衣及类似品	14	0	12.6	0	7	0	0	0	0	0	0		11.2	0					0	0	
62079920	化纤制男浴衣、晨衣及类似品	16	0		0	12.8	0	0	6.4	0	0	0		12.8	0					0	0	0
62079990	其他纺织材料制男浴衣、晨衣及类似品	14	0	12.6	0	7	0	0	0	0	0	0		11.2	0					0	0	0
62081100	化纤制长衬裙及衬裙	16	0		0	12.8	0	0	6.4	0	0			12.8	0					0	0	
62081910	丝及绢丝制长衬裙及衬裙	14	0		0	7	0	0	0	0	0			11.2	0					0	0	
62081920	棉制长衬裙及衬裙	14	0		0	7	0	0	0	0	0			11.2	0					0	0	0
62081990	其他纺织材料制长衬裙及衬裙	14	0		0	7	0	0	0	0	0			11.2	0					0	0	
62082100	棉制女式睡衣及睡衣裤	14	0	10.3	0	7	0	0	0	0	0	0		11.2	0		0	0	0	0	0	0
62082200	化纤制女式睡衣及睡衣裤	16	0		0	12.8	0	0	6.4	0	0	0		12.8	0		0	0	0	0	0	0
62082910	丝及绢丝制女式睡衣及睡衣裤	14	0		0	7	0	0	0	0	0			11.2	0					0	0	
62082990	其他纺织材料制女式睡衣及睡衣裤	14	0		0	7	0	0	0	0	0			11.2	0					0	0	
62089100	棉制女式背心.内衣.浴衣及类似品	14	0		0	11.2	0	0	5.6	0	0	0		11.2	0		0	0	0	0	0	0
62089200	化纤制女式背心、内衣及类似品	16	0		0	12.8	0	0	6.4	0	0	0	0	12.8	0		0	0	0	0	0	0
62089910	丝制女式背心、内衣及类似品	14	0	12.6	0	7	0	0	0	0	0	0		11.2	0					0	0	
62089990	其他纺织材料制女式背心、内衣及类似	14	0	12.6	0	7	0	0	0	0	0	0		11.2	0					0	0	0
62092000	棉制婴儿服装及衣着附件	14	0		0	7	0	0	0	0	0	0		11.2	0					0	0	0
62093000	合纤制婴儿服装及衣着附件	16	0		0	12.8	0	0	6.4	0	0	0		12.8	0					0	0	0
62099010	毛制婴儿服装及衣着附件	14	0		0	7	0	0	0	0	0	0		11.2	0					0	0	
62099090	其他纺织材料制婴儿服装及衣着附件	14	0		0	7	0	0	0	0	0	0		11.2	0					0	0	
62101010	毛制毡呢或无纺织物服装	16	0	11.7	0	8	0	0	6.4	0	0	0		12.8	0	0				0	0	0
62101020	棉或麻制毡呢或无纺织物服装	16	0		0	12.8	0	0	6.4	0	0	0		12.8	0	6.4				0	0	
62101030	化纤制毡呢或无纺织物服装	17.5	0	12.3	0	8.8	0	0	7	0	0	0		14	0	0				0	0	0
62101090	其他纺织材料制毡呢或无纺织物服装	16	0		0	12.8	0	0	6.4	0	0	0		12.8	0	0				0	0	0
62102000	用塑料、橡胶等处理的织物制男大衣等	16	0	11.7	0	8	0	0	6.4	0	0	0		12.8	0	0				0	0	0
62103000	用塑料、橡胶等处理的织物制女大衣等	16	0	11.7	0	8	0	0	6.4	0	0	0		12.8	0					0	0	0
62104000	用塑料、橡胶等处理的织物制的其他男式服装	16	0	11.7	0	8	0	0	6.4	0	0	0		12.8	0	0				0	0	0
62105000	用塑料、橡胶等处理的织物制的其他女式服装	16	0	11.7	0	8	0	0	6.4	0	0	0		12.8	0	0				0	0	0
62111100	男式游泳服	16	0	11.7	0	8	0	0	6.4	0	0	0		12.8	0					0	0	
62111200	女式游泳服	16	0	11.7	0	8	0	0	6.4	0	0			12.8	0					0	0	0
62112010	棉制滑雪服	16	0		0	12.8	0	0	6.4	0	0			12.8	0					0	0	0
62112090	其他纺织材料制滑雪服	19	0	13.6	0	9.5	0	0	7.6	0	0			15.2	0					0	0	
62113210	棉制男式阿拉伯袍	16	0		0	12.8	0	0	6.4	0	0			12.8	0					0	0	
62113220	棉制男式运动服	16	0		0		0	0	6.4	0	0	0		12.8	0					0	0	0
62113290	棉制其他男式服装	16	0		0		0	0	6.4	0	0	0		12.8	0					0	0	0
62113310	化纤制男式阿拉伯袍	17.5	0	12.3	0	8.8	0	0	7	0	0			14	0					0	0	
62113320	化纤制男式运动服	18	0	12.3	0	12.3	0	0	7.2	0	0	0		14.4	0					0	0	0
62113390	化纤制其他男式服装	17.5	0	12.3	0	12.3	0	0	7	0	0	0		14	0					0	0	0
62113910	丝及绢丝制男式运动服及其他服装	16	0	11.7	0	8	0	0	6.4	0	0	0		12.8	0					0	0	
62113920	毛制男式运动服及其他服装	16	0	11.7	0	8	0	0	6.4	0	0	0		12.8	0					0	0	
62113990	其他纺织材料制男式运动服及其他服装	16	0	11.7	0	8	0	0	6.4	0	0	0		12.8	0					0	0	

税则号列	货品名称	最惠国	协定税率													特惠税率						
			东盟统一	亚太5国	智利	巴基斯坦	新加坡	新西兰	秘鲁	哥达	香港	澳门	台湾	瑞士	冰岛	亚太2国	老挝	柬埔寨	缅甸	LDC1	LDC2	LDC3
62114210	棉制女式运动服	16	0		0	12.8	0	0	6.4	0	0	0		12.8	0					0	0	0
62114290	棉制其他女式服装	16	0		0	12.8	0	0	6.4	0	0	0		12.8	0					0	0	0
62114310	化纤制女式运动服	17.5	0	12.3	0	8.8	0	0	7	0	0	0		14	0					0	0	0
62114390	化纤制其他女式服装	17.5	0	12.3	0	8.8	0	0	7	0	0	0		14	0					0	0	0
62114910	丝及绢丝制女式运动服及其他服装	16	0	11.7	0	8	0	0	6.4	0	0	0		12.8	0					0	0	
62114990	其他纺织材料制女式运动服及其他服装	16	0	11.7	0	8	0	0	6.4	0	0	0		12.8	0					0	0	0
62121010	化纤制胸罩	16	0	14.4	0	12.8	0	0	6.4	0	0	0	0	12.8	0		0	0	0	0	0	0
62121090	其他纺织材料制胸罩	14	0	12.6	0	7	0	0	0	0	0	0	0	11.2	0					0	0	0
62122010	化纤制束腰带及腹带	16	0		0	12.8	0	0	6.4	0	0	0	0	12.8	0					0	0	
62122090	其他纺织材料制束腰带及腹带	14	0		0	11.2	0	0	0	0	0	0	0	11.2	0					0	0	0
62123010	化纤制紧身胸衣	16	0		0	12.8	0	0	6.4	0	0	0		12.8	0					0	0	
62123090	其他纺织材料制紧身胸衣	14	0		0	7	0	0	0	0	0	0		11.2	0					0	0	0
62129010	化纤制吊裤带、吊袜带等	16	0	14.4	0	12.8	0	0	6.4	0	0	0	0	12.8	0					0	0	
62129090	其他纺织材料制吊裤带、吊袜带等	14	0	12.6	0	7	0	0	0	0	0	0	0	11.2	0					0	0	
62132010	棉制刺绣手帕	14	0		0	7	0	0	0	0	0			11.2	0		0			0	0	0
62132090	其他棉制手帕	14	0		0	11.2	0	0	0	0	0			11.2	0		0			0	0	0
62139020	其他纺织材料制刺绣手帕	14	0		0	7	0	0	0	0				11.2	0		0			0	0	0
62139090	其他纺织材料制手帕	14	0		0	7	0	0	0	0	0			11.2	0		0			0	0	0
62141000	丝制披巾、头巾、围巾及类似品	14	0		0	11.2	0	0	0	0	0			11.2	0					0	0	0
62142010	羊毛制披巾、领巾、围巾、披纱、面纱及类似品	14	0		0	11.2	0	0	5.6	0	0			11.2	0					0	0	0
62142020	山羊绒制披巾、领巾、围巾、披纱、面纱及类似品	14	0		0	11.2	0	0	5.6	0	0			11.2	0					0	0	0
62142090	其他动物细毛制披巾、领巾、围巾、披纱、面纱及类似品	14	0		0	11.2	0	0	5.6	0	0			11.2	0					0	0	0
62143000	合纤制披巾、头巾及类似品	16	0		0	12.8	0	0	6.4	0	0			12.8	0					0	0	0
62144000	人纤制披巾、头巾及类似品	14	0		0	11.2	0	0	0	0	0			11.2	0					0	0	0
62149000	其他纺织材料制披巾、头巾及类似品	14	0		0	11.2	0	0	0	0	0			11.2	0					0	0	0
62151000	丝及绢丝制领带及领结	14	0		0	11.2	0	0	0	0	0			11.2	0					0	0	0
62152000	化纤制领带及领结	16	0	14.4	0	12.8	0	0	6.4	0	0			12.8	0					0	0	0
62159000	其他纺织材料制领带及领结	14	0		0	7	0	0	0	0	0			11.2	0					0	0	0
62160000	非针织非钩编手套	14	0		0		0	0	0	0	0	0		11.2	0					0	0	0
62171010	非针织非钩编袜子及袜套	14	0	12.2	0	7	0	0	0	0			0	11.2	0					0	0	
62171020	非针织非钩编和服腰带	14	0	12.2	0	7	0	0	0	0			0	11.2	0					0	0	0
62171090	非针织非钩编服装或衣着附件	14	0	12.2	0	12.2	0	0	0	0	0		0	11.2	0		0	0	0	0	0	0
62179000	非针织非钩编服装或衣着零件	14	0	12.6	0	12.6	0	0	0	0	0	0	0	11.2	0		0	0	0	0	0	0
63011000	电暖毯	16	0		0	12.8	0	0	6.4	0				12.8	0					0	0	
63012000	毛制毯子及旅行毯	16	0		0	12.8	0	0	6.4	0		0		12.8	0					0	0	0
63013000	棉制毯子及旅行毯	16	0		0	12.8	0	0	6.4	0		0		12.8	0					0	0	0
63014000	合纤制毯子及旅行毯	17.5	0		0	14	0	0	7	0		0		14	0					0	0	0
63019000	其他纺织材料制毯子及旅行毯	16	0		0	12.8	0	0	6.4	0		0	0	12.8	0					0	0	0
63021010	棉制针织或钩编的床上用织物制品	14	0		0	0	0	0	0	0				11.2	0					0	0	0
63021090	其他纺织材料制针织或钩编的床上用织物制品	14	0		0	0	0	0	0	0				11.2	0					0	0	
63022110	棉制印花床单	14	0		0	0	0	0	0	0				10.8	0					0	0	0
63022190	棉制印花床上用织物制品	14	0		0	0	0	0	0	0				11.2	0					0	0	0
63022210	化纤制印花床单	16	0		0	0	0	0	6.4	0				12.8	0					0	0	0
63022290	化纤制印花床上用织物制品	16	0		0	0	0	0	6.4	0				12.8	0					0	0	0
63022910	丝及绢丝制印花床上用织物制品	14	0		0	0	0	0	0	0				11.2	0					0	0	
63022920	麻制印花床上用织物制品	14	0		0	0	0	0	0	0				11.2	0					0	0	
63022990	其他纺织材料制印花床上用织物制品	14	0		0	0	0	0	0	0				11.2	0					0	0	
63023110	棉制刺绣其他床上用织物制品	14	0		0	0	0	0	0	0				11.2	0					0	0	0
63023191	棉制其他床单	14	0		0	0	0	0	0	0				11.2	0					0	0	0
63023192	棉制其他毛巾被	14	0		0	0	0	0	0	0				11.2	0					0	0	
63023199	棉制其他床上用织物制品	14	0		0	0	0	0	0	0				11.2	0					0	0	0
63023210	化纤制刺绣其他床上用织物制品	16	0		0	0	0	0	6.4	0				12.8	0					0	0	0
63023290	化纤制其他床上用织物制品	16	0		0	0	0	0	6.4	0				12.8	0					0	0	0
63023910	丝及绢丝制其他床上用织物制品	14	0		0	0	0	0	0	0				11.2	0					0	0	
63023921	麻制刺绣的其他床上用织物制品	14	0		0	0	0	0	0	0				11.2	0					0	0	
63023929	麻制其他床上用织物制品	14	0		0	0	0	0	0	0				11.2	0					0	0	

税则号列	货品名称	最惠国	协定税率													特惠税率						
			东盟统一	亚太5国	智利	巴基斯坦	新加坡	新西兰	秘鲁	哥达	香港	澳门	台湾	瑞士	冰岛	亚太2国	老挝	柬埔寨	缅甸	LDC1	LDC2	LDC3
63023991	其他纺织材料制刺绣床上用织物制品	14	0		0	0	0	0	0	0				11.2	0					0	0	
63023999	其他纺织材料制其他床上用织物制品	14	0		0	0	0	0	0	0				11.2	0					0	0	0
63024010	手工针织或钩编的餐桌用织物制品	14	0		0	0	0	0	0	0				11.2	0					0	0	
63024090	其他针织或钩编的餐桌用织物制品	14	0		0	0	0	0	0	0				11.2	0					0	0	0
63025110	棉制刺绣其他餐桌用织物制品	14	0		0	0	0	0	0	0	0			11.2	0					0	0	
63025190	棉制其他餐桌用织物制品	14	0		0	0	0	0	0	0	0	0		11.2	0					0	0	0
63025310	化纤制刺绣其他餐桌织物制品	14	0		0	0	0	0	0	0				11.2	0					0	0	
63025390	化纤制其他餐桌用织物制品	16	0		0	0	0	0	6.4	0				12.8	0					0	0	0
63025911	亚麻制刺绣其他餐桌用织物制品	14	0		0	0	0	0	0	0				11.2	0					0	0	
63025919	亚麻制其他餐桌用织物制品	14	0		0	0	0	0	0	0				11.2	0					0	0	
63025990	其他纺织材料制餐桌用织物制品	14	0		0	0	0	0	0	0				11.2	0					0	0	
63026010	棉制浴巾	14	0		0	0	0	0	0	0			0	11.2	0					0	0	0
63026090	棉制盥洗及厨房用毛巾织物	14	0		0	0	0	0	0	0			0	11.2	0					0	0	0
63029100	棉制其他盥洗及厨房织物制品	14	0		0	0	0	0	0	0				11.2	0					0	0	0
63029300	化纤制其他盥洗及厨房织物制品	16	0		0	0	0	0	6.4	0	0			12.8	0					0	0	
63029910	亚麻制其他盥洗及厨房织物制品	14	0		0	0	0	0	0	0				11.2	0					0	0	
63029990	其他材料制其他盥洗及厨房织物	14	0		0	0	0	0	0	0				11.2	0					0	0	
63031210	合纤制针织的窗帘等	16	0		0	0	0	0	6.4	0				12.8	0					0	0	
63031220	合纤制钩编的窗帘等	16	0		0	0	0	0	6.4	0				12.8	0					0	0	
63031931	棉制针织的窗帘等	14	0		0	0	0	0	0	0				11.2	0					0	0	0
63031932	棉制钩编的窗帘等	14	0		0	0	0	0	0	0				11.2	0					0	0	
63031991	其他纺织材料制针织的窗帘等	14	0		0	0	0	0	0	0				11.2	0					0	0	
63031992	其他纺织材料制钩编的窗帘等	14	0		0	0	0	0	0	0				11.2	0					0	0	
63039100	棉制非针织非钩编窗帘等	14	0		0	0	0	0	0	0				11.2	0					0	0	0
63039200	合纤制非针织非钩编窗帘等	16	0		0	0	0	0	6.4	0	0			12.8	0					0	0	0
63039900	其他纺织材料制非针织非钩编窗帘等	14	0		0	0	0	0	0	0				11.2	0					0	0	0
63041121	手工针织床罩	14	0		0	7	0	0	0	0		0		11.2	0					0	0	
63041129	非手工针织床罩	14	0		0	7	0	0	0	0		0		11.2	0					0	0	
63041131	手工钩编床罩	14	0		0	7	0	0	0	0				11.2	0					0	0	0
63041139	非手工钩编床罩	14	0		0	7	0	0	0	0				11.2	0					0	0	0
63041910	丝及绢丝制非针织非钩编床罩	14	0		0	7	0	0	0	0				11.2	0					0	0	
63041921	棉或麻制非针织非钩编刺绣床罩	14	0		0	7	0	0	0	0				11.2	0					0	0	
63041929	棉或麻制其他非针织非钩编床罩	14	0		0		0	0	0	0				11.2	0					0	0	0
63041931	化纤制非针织非钩编刺绣床罩	16	0		0	12.8	0	0	6.4	0				12.8	0					0	0	
63041939	化纤制其他非针织非钩编床罩	16	0		0	12.8	0	0	6.4	0				12.8	0					0	0	
63041991	其他纺织材料制非针织、非钩编刺绣床罩	14	0		0	7	0	0	0	0				11.2	0					0	0	
63041999	其他材料制其他非针织非钩编床罩	14	0		0	7	0	0	0	0				11.2	0					0	0	
63049121	手工针织的其他装饰制品	14	0		0	7	0	0	0	0				11.2	0					0	0	0
63049129	非手工针织的其他装饰制品	14	0		0	7	0	0	0	0		0		11.2	0					0	0	0
63049131	手工钩编的其他装饰制品	14	0		0	11.2	0	0	0	0				11.2	0					0	0	
63049139	非手工钩编的其他装饰制品	14	0		0	7	0	0	0	0				11.2	0					0	0	
63049210	棉制非针织、非钩编的其他刺绣装饰制品	14	0		0	7	0	0	0	0				11.2	0					0	0	
63049290	棉制非针织或钩编的其他装饰制品	14	0		0	11.2	0	0	0	0				11.2	0					0	0	0
63049310	合纤制非针织、非钩编其他刺绣装饰制品	16	0		0	12.8	0	0	6.4	0				12.8	0					0	0	
63049390	合纤制其他非针织、非钩编装饰制品	16	0		0	12.8	0	0	6.4	0				12.8	0					0	0	0
63049910	丝制非针织非钩编的装饰制品	14	0		0	7	0	0	0	0				11.2	0					0	0	0
63049921	麻制非针织、非钩编的其他刺绣装饰制品	14	0		0	7	0	0	0	0				11.2	0					0	0	
63049929	麻制其他非针织非钩编的装饰制品	14	0		0	7	0	0	0	0				11.2	0					0	0	
63049990	其他纺织材料制非针织非钩编装饰制品	14	0		0	7	0	0	0	0				11.2	0					0	0	0
63051000	黄麻或其他韧皮纤维制货物包装袋	10	0		0	5	0	0	0	0				6	0	0				0	0	0
63052000	棉制货物包装袋	16	0		0	12.8	0	0	6.4	0				12.8	0					0	0	0
63053200	化纤制的散装货物储运软袋	16	0		0	12.8	0	0	6.4	0				12.8	0					0	0	0
63053300	聚乙烯或聚丙烯扁条制其他货物包装袋	16	0	13.6	0	8	0	0	6.4	0				12.8	0					0	0	
63053900	其他化纤制货物包装袋	16	0		0	12.8	0	0	6.4	0				12.8	0					0	0	
63059000	其他纺织材料制货物包装袋	14	0		0	11.2	0	0	0	0				11.2	0					0	0	0
63061200	合纤制油苫布、天篷及遮阳篷	16	0		0	0	0	0	6.4	0				12.8	0					0	0	
63061910	麻制油苫布、天篷及遮阳篷	14	0		0	0	0	0	0	0				11.2	0					0	0	
63061920	棉制油苫布、天篷及遮阳篷	14	0		0	0	0	0	0	0				11.2	0					0	0	
63061990	其他纺织材料制油苫布、天篷及遮阳篷	14	0		0	0	0	0	0	0				11.2	0					0	0	
63062200	合纤制帐篷	16	0		0	0	0	0	6.4	0				12.8	0					0	0	0
63062910	棉制帐篷	14	0		0	0	0	0	0	0				11.2	0					0	0	

税则号列	货品名称	最惠国	协定税率													特惠税率						
			东盟统一	亚太5国	智利	巴基斯坦	新加坡	新西兰	秘鲁	哥达	香港	澳门	台湾	瑞士	冰岛	亚太2国	老挝	柬埔寨	缅甸	LDC1	LDC2	LDC3
63062990	其他纺织材料制帐篷	14	0		0	0	0	0	0	0				11.2	0					0	0	0
63063010	合纤制风帆	16	0		0	0	0	0	6.4	0	0			12.8	0					0	0	
63063090	其他纺织材料制风帆	14	0		0	0	0	0	0	0				11.2	0					0	0	
63064010	棉制充气褥垫	14	0		0	0	0	0	0	0				11.2	0					0	0	
63064020	化纤制充气褥垫	16	0		0	0	0	0	6.4	0				12.8	0					0	0	0
63064090	其他纺织材料制充气褥垫	14	0		0	0	0	0	0	0				11.2	0					0	0	
63069010	棉制其他野营用品	14	0		0	0	0	0	0	0				11.2	0					0	0	0
63069020	麻制其他野营用品	14	0		0	0	0	0	0	0				11.2	0					0	0	
63069030	化学纤维制其他野营用品	16	0		0	0	0	0	6.4	0				12.8	0					0	0	
63069090	其他野营用品	14	0		0	0	0	0	0	0				11.2	0					0	0	
63071000	擦地布、擦碗布等	14	0	11.9	0	7	0	0	0	0			0	11.2	0					0	0	
63072000	救生衣及安全带	14	0		0	11.2	0	0	0	0				11.2	0					0	0	0
63079000	其他纺织材料制成品	14	0		0	11.2	0	0	0	0	0	0		11.2	0		0	0	0	0	0	0
63080000	零售包装成套物品	14	0		0	7	0	0	0	0				11.2	0					0	0	
63090000	旧衣物	14	0		0	7	0	0	0	0				11.2	0					0	0	
63101000	经分拣的纺织材料制碎织物等	14	0		0	11.2	0	0	0	0				11.2	0					0	0	0
63109000	纺织材料制其他碎织物等	14	0		0		0	0	0	0				11.2	0		0	0	0	0	0	0
64011010	橡胶制鞋面的装金属护头的塑料、橡胶制防水鞋靴	24	0	12	0	12	0	0	9.6	0				19.2	0					0	0	
64011090	塑料制鞋面的装金属护头的塑料、橡胶制防水鞋靴	24	0	12	0	12	0	0	9.6	0				19.2	0					0	0	
64019210	橡胶制鞋面的橡胶、塑料底及面的中、短统防水靴	24	0	12	0	12	0	0	9.6	0				19.2	0					0	0	
64019290	塑料制鞋面的橡胶、塑料底及面的中、短统防水靴	24	0	12	0	12	0	0	9.6	0				19.2	0					0	0	
64019900	其他橡胶、塑料制外底及鞋面防水靴	24	0	12	0	12	0	0	9.6	0				19.2	0					0	0	
64021200	橡胶、塑料底及面的滑雪靴	10	0	5	0	5		0	0	0				6	0					0	0	0
64021900	橡胶、塑料制底及面的其他运动靴	24	0	12	0	12	0	0	9.6	0				19.2	0					0	0	
64022000	橡胶、塑料的将鞋面条带栓塞在鞋底上的鞋	24	0	12	0	12	0	0	9.6	0				19.2	0					0	0	
64029100	其他橡胶、塑料短统靴(过踝)	24	0	12	0	12	0	0	9.6	0		0		19.2	0					0	0	
64029910	橡胶制鞋面的其他橡胶、塑料鞋靴	24	0	12	0	12	0	0	9.6	0		0		19.2	0					0	0	0
64029921	以机织物或其他纺织材料作衬底的	24	0	12	0	12	0	0	9.6	0		0		19.2	0					0	0	0
64029929	塑料制鞋面的其他橡胶、塑料鞋靴	24	0	12	0	12	0	0	9.6	0		0		19.2	0					0	0	0
64031200	皮革制鞋面的滑雪靴	24	0		0		0	0	9.6	0				19.2	0			0		0	0	0
64031900	皮革制鞋面的其他运动鞋靴	15	0		0	12	0	0	6	0		0		12	0			0		0	0	0
64032000	皮革条带为鞋面的皮底鞋	24	0		0		0	0	9.6	0		0		19.2	0			0		0	0	0
64034000	装有金属护鞋头的其他皮革面鞋靴	24	0		0		0	0	9.6	0				19.2	0			0		0	0	0
64035111	低于小腿的内底长度<24cm 的皮革制外底皮革面的短统靴(过踝)	10	0		0	5		0	0	0		0		6	0			0		0	0	0
64035119	低于小腿的内底长度≥24cm 的皮革制外底皮革面的短统靴(过踝)	10	0		0	5		0	0	0				6	0			0		0	0	0
64035191	其他内底长度<24cm 的皮革制外底的皮革面短统靴(过踝)	10	0		0	5		0	0	0				6	0			0		0	0	0
64035199	其他内底长度≥24cm 的皮革制外底皮革面短统靴(过踝)	10	0		0	5		0	0	0				6	0			0		0	0	0
64035900	皮革制外底的皮革面其他鞋靴	10	0		0	5		0	4	0		0		8	0			0		0	0	0
64039111	其他低于小腿的内底长度<24cm 的皮革面的短统靴(过踝)	10	0		0	5	0	0	0	0		0		8	0			0		0	0	0
64039119	其他低于小腿的内底长度≥24cm 的皮革面的短统靴(过踝)	10	0		0	5	0	0	0	0		0		6	0			0		0	0	0
64039191	其他内底长度<24cm 的皮革面短统靴(过踝)	10	0		0	5	0	0	0	0		0		6	0			0		0	0	0
64039199	其他内底长度≥24cm 的皮革面短统靴(过踝)	10	0		0	5	0	0	0	0		0		6	0			0		0	0	0
64039900	皮革制面的其他鞋靴	10	0	8.5	0	5	0	0	0	0		0		8	0			0		0	0	0
64041100	纺织材料制鞋面的运动鞋靴	24	0	12	0	12	0	0	9.6	0		0		19.2	0					0	0	
64041900	纺织材料制鞋面胶底的其他鞋靴	24	0	12	0	12	0	0	9.6	0		0		19.2	0					0	0	
64042000	纺织材料制鞋面皮革底的鞋靴	24	0	12	0	12	0	0	9.6	0				19.2	0					0	0	

税则号列	货品名称	最惠国	协定税率													特惠税率						
			东盟统一	亚太5国	智利	巴基斯坦	新加坡	新西兰	秘鲁	哥达	香港	澳门	台湾	瑞士	冰岛	亚太2国	老挝	柬埔寨	缅甸	LDC1	LDC2	LDC3
64051010	橡胶、塑料、皮革及再生皮革制外底的皮革或再生皮革制面的其他鞋靴	24	0	12	0	12	0	0	9.6	0				19.2	0					0	0	
64051090	其他材料制外底的皮革或再生皮革制面的其他鞋靴	24	0	12	0	12	0	0	9.6	0				19.2	0					0	0	
64052000	纺织材料制面的其他鞋靴	22	0	11	0	11	0	0	8.8	0				17.6	0					0	0	
64059010	橡胶、塑料、皮革及再生皮革制外底的其他材料制面的鞋靴	15	0	10.5	0	7.5	0	0	6	0				12	0					0	0	
64059090	其他材料制外底的其他材料制面的鞋靴	15	0	10.5	0	7.5	0	0	6	0				12	0					0	0	
64061000	鞋面及其零件，硬衬除外	15	0	13.2	0	7.5	0	0	6	0			0	12	0					0	0	
64062010	橡胶制的外底及鞋跟	15	0		0	12	0	0	6	0			0	12	0					0	0	0
64062020	塑料制的外底及鞋跟	15	0		0	12	0	0	6	0				12	0					0	0	0
64069010	木制鞋靴零件，活动式鞋内底等	15	0	10.5	0	7.5	0	0	6	0				12	0					0	0	
64069091	活动式鞋内底、跟垫及类似品	15	0	10.5	0	7.5	0	0	6	0	0	0	0	12	0					0	0	
64069092	护腿、裹腿和类似品及其零件	15	0	10.5	0	7.5	0	0	6	0	0	0	0	12	0					0	0	
64069099	其他鞋靴零件(包括鞋面，不论是否带有除外底以外的其他鞋底)；活动式鞋内底、跟垫及类似品；护腿、裹腿和类似品及其零件	15	0	10.5	0	7.5	0	0	6	0	0	0	0	12	0					0	0	
65010000	毡呢制帽坯及圆帽片	22	0		0		0	0	8.8	0				17.6	0					0	0	
65020000	编结或用条带拼制的帽坯	20	0		0		0	0	8	0				16	0					0	0	
65040000	编结或用条带拼制成的帽类	20	0		0		0	0	8	0				16	0					0	0	
65050010	发网	10	0		0	5		0	0	0				6	0					0	0	0
65050020	钩编的帽类	20	0	19	0	19	0	0	8	0				16	0					0	0	0
65050091	成品毡呢帽类	22	0		0		0	0	8.8	0				17.6	0					0	0	
65050099	针织或成匹织物制成的帽类	20	0	19	0	19	0	0	8	0		0		16	0					0	0	0
65061000	安全帽	10	0		0	5		0	0	0				6	0					0	0	
65069100	橡胶或塑料制帽类	10	0		0	5		0	0	0				6	0					0	0	
65069910	皮革制帽类	10	0		0	5		0	0	0				6	0					0	0	
65069920	毛皮制帽类	10	0		0	5		0	0	0	0			6	0					0	0	0
65069990	其他材料制的未列名帽类	24	0		0		0	0	9.6	0				19.2	0					0	0	0
65070000	帽类附件	24	0		0		0	0	9.6	0		0		19.2	0					0	0	
66011000	庭园用伞及类似品	14	0		0	7	0	0	0	0				11.2	0					0	0	
66019100	折叠伞	10	0		0	5		0	0	0				6	0					0	0	0
66019900	其他伞	10	0		0	5		0	0	0				6	0					0	0	
66020000	手杖、带座手杖、鞭子及类似品	10	0		0	5		0	0	0				6	0					0	0	
66032000	伞骨	14	0		0	11.2	0	0	0	0				11.2	0					0	0	
66039000	伞、手杖及鞭子的其他零件及饰品	14	0		0	11.2	0	0	0	0				11.2	0					0	0	0
67010000	已加工羽毛、羽绒及其制品	20	0		0		0	0	8	0		0		16	0					0	0	
67021000	塑料制花、叶、果实及其制品	20	0		0		0	0	8	0				16	0					0	0	
67029010	羽毛制花、叶、果实及其制品	20	0		0		0	0	8	0				16	0					0	0	
67029020	丝或绢丝制花、叶、果实及其制品	24	0		0		0	0	9.6	0				19.2	0					0	0	
67029030	化学纤维制花、叶、果实及其制品	24	0		0		0	0	9.6	0				19.2	0					0	0	
67029090	其他材料制花、叶、果实及其制品	20	0		0		0	0	8	0				16	0					0	0	
67030000	经梳理、稀疏等方法加工的人发及假发材料	20	0	18	0	18	0	0	8	0				16	0					0	0	
67041100	合成纺织材料制整头假发	25	0		0		0	0	10	0				19.3	0					0	0	0
67041900	合成纺织材料制其他假发、须等	25	0		0		0	0	10	0		0		19.3	0					0	0	0
67042000	人发制假发、须、眉及类似品	15	0		0	12	0	0	6	0		0		12	0					0	0	0
67049000	其他材料制假发、须眉及类似品	25	0		0		0	0	10	0		0		19.3	0					0	0	0
68010000	长方砌石、路缘石、扁平石	12	0		0	6	0	0	0	0		0		9.6	0					0	0	
68021010	大理石制砖、瓦、方块及类似品	24	0	19.2	0	0	0	0	0	0	0	0		19.2	0					0	0	0
68021090	其他石料制砖瓦、方块及类似品	20	0	16	0	0	0	0	0	0	0	0		16	0					0	0	
68022110	具有一个平面的大理石及制品	10	0		0	0	0	0	0	0		0		6	0					0	0	0
68022120	石灰华	24	0		0	0	0	0	0	0		0		19.2	0					0	0	
68022190	具有一个平面石灰华及蜡石及制品	24	0		0	0	0	0	0	0				19.2	0					0	0	
68022300	具有一个平面的花岗岩及制品	10	0	9.2	0	0		0	0	0		0		6	0					0	0	0
68022910	具有一个平面的其他石灰石及制品	24	0		0	0	0	0	9.6	0		0		19.2	0					0	0	
68022990	具有一个平面的其他石及制品	15	0		0	0	0	0	6	0		0		12	0					0	0	0
68029110	大理石、石灰华及蜡石制石刻	24	0		0	0	0	0	0	0		0		19.2	0					0	0	

税则号列	货品名称	最惠国	协定税率													特惠税率						
			东盟统一	亚太5国	智利	巴基斯坦	新加坡	新西兰	秘鲁	哥达	香港	澳门	台湾	瑞士	冰岛	亚太2国	老挝	柬埔寨	缅甸	LDC1	LDC2	LDC3
68029190	其他大理石、石灰华及蜡石及制品	10	0		0	0		0	0	0	0	0		6	0					0	0	0
68029210	其他石灰石制石刻	24	0		0	0	0	0	9.6	0		0		19.2	0					0	0	
68029290	其他加工形式石灰石制品	10	0		0	0		0	4	0	0	0		6	0					0	0	0
68029311	花岗岩制墓碑石	24	0		0	0	0	0	9.6	0		0		19.2	0					0	0	
68029319	其他花岗岩制石刻	24	0		0	0	0	0	9.6	0	0	0		19.2	0					0	0	
68029390	其他加工形式花岗岩制品	10	0	9.2	0	0		0	0	0		0		6	0					0	0	0
68029910	其他石制成的石刻	24	0		0	0	0	0	0	0		0		19.2	0					0	0	
68029990	其他石及制品	24	0		0	0	0	0	0	0	0	0		19.2	0					0	0	0
68030010	板岩制品	20	0		0		0	0	8	0		0		16	0					0	0	
68030090	已加工板岩及板岩或粘聚板岩制品	20	0		0		0	0	8	0				16	0					0	0	
68041000	碾磨或磨浆用石磨、石碾	8	0		0	5		0	0	0				4.8	0					0	0	0
68042100	金刚石制石磨、石碾及砂轮	8	0		0	5		0	0	0	0			6.4	0					0	0	0
68042210	其他砂轮	8	0		0	5		0	0	0	0			6.4	0					0	0	0
68042290	其他石磨、石碾及类似品	8	0		0	5		0	0	0	0			4.8	0					0	0	0
68042310	天然石料制的砂轮	8	0		0	5		0	0	0				4.8	0					0	0	0
68042390	天然石料制其他石磨、石碾等	8	0		0	5		0	0	0				4.8	0					0	0	0
68043010	手用琢磨油石	8	0	6.4	0	5		0	0	0				4.8	0					0	0	0
68043090	手用其他磨石及抛光石	8	0	6.4	0	5		0	0	0				4.8	0					0	0	0
68051000	砂布	8	0		0	5		0	0	0				6.4	0					0	0	0
68052000	砂纸	8	0		0	5		0	0	0				6.4	0					0	0	0
68053000	其他材料为底的天然或人造研磨料	8	0		0	5		0	0	0				4.8	0					0	0	0
68061010	硅酸铝纤维及其制品	10.5	0		0	5	0	0	0	0				8.4	0					0	0	0
68061090	其他矿渣棉、岩石棉及类似的矿质棉(包括其相互混合物),块状、成片或成卷	10.5	0		0	5	0	0	0	0				8.4	0					0	0	0
68062000	页状硅石、膨胀粘土、泡沫矿渣	10.5	0		0	5	0	0	0	0				8.4	0					0	0	0
68069000	其他矿物材料的混合物及制品	10	0		0	5		0	0	0				6	0					0	0	0
68071000	成卷的沥青或类似原料的制品	12	0		0	6	0	0	0	0				9.6	0					0	0	
68079000	其他形状的沥青或类似原料的制品	12	0	9.6	0	5	0	0	0	0				9.6	0					0	0	
68080000	镶板、平板、瓦、砖及类似品	10.5	0		0	5	0	0	0	0				8.4	0					0	0	
68091100	纸贴面未饰的石膏板、片、砖、瓦及类似品	28	0		0		0	0	11.2	0				22.4	0					0	0	
68091900	以其他材料贴面加强的未饰石膏板	25	0		0		0	0	10	0		0			0					0	0	
68099000	其他石膏制品	25	0		0		0	0	10	0					0					0	0	
68101100	水泥制建筑用砖及石砌块	10.5	0	8.4	0	5	0	0	0	0	0			8.4	0					0	0	0
68101910	人造石制砖、瓦、扁平石及类似品	10.5	0	8.4	0	5	0	0	0	0		0		8.4	0					0	0	0
68101990	水泥制其他砖、瓦、扁平石	10.5	0	8.4	0	5	0	0	0	0				8.4	0					0	0	0
68109110	钢筋混凝土和预应力混凝土管、杆、板、桩等	10.5	0		0	5	0	0	0	0	0			8.4	0					0	0	0
68109190	其他水泥制建筑或土木工程用预制构件	10.5	0		0	5	0	0	0	0	0	0		8.4	0					0	0	0
68109910	铁道用水泥枕	8	0		0	5		0	0	0				4.8	0					0	0	0
68109990	水泥、混凝土或人造石制其他制品	10.5	0		0	5	0	0	0	0				8.4	0					0	0	0
68114010	含石棉的瓦楞板	5	0		0	0		0	0	0				0	0					0	0	
68114020	含石棉的片、板、砖、瓦及类似品	10.5	0		0	5	0	0	0	0				8.4	0					0	0	
68114030	含石棉的管子及管子配件	8	0		0	5		0	0	0				4.8	0					0	0	
68114090	含石棉的其他制品	8.4	0		0	5		0	0	0				5	0					0	0	
68118100	不含石棉的瓦楞板	5	0		0	0		0	0	0				0	0					0	0	
68118200	不含石棉的片、板、砖、瓦及类似品	10.5	0		0	5	0	0	0	0				8.1	0					0	0	
68118910	不含石棉的管子及管子配件	8	0		0	5		0	0	0				4.8	0					0	0	
68118990	不含石棉的其他制品	8.4	0		0	5		0	0	0				5	0					0	0	
68128000	青石棉或青石棉混合物制品	10.5	0		0	5	0	0	0	0				8.4	0					0	0	0
68129100	其他石棉或石棉混合物制的服装	10.5	0		0	5	0	0	0	0				8.4	0					0	0	0
68129200	其他石棉或石棉混合物制的纸、麻丝板	10.5	0		0	5	0	0	0	0				8.4	0					0	0	0
68129300	其他成片成卷的压缩石棉纤维接合材料	10.5	0		0	5	0	0	0	0				8.4	0					0	0	0
68129900	其他石棉或石棉混合物制品	10	0		0	5		0	0	0				6	0					0	0	0
68132010	含石棉的闸衬、闸垫	10	0		0	5		0	0	0				6	0					0	0	0
68132090	含石棉的磨擦料及其他用于制动等用途制品	12	0		0	6	0	0	0	0				9.6	0					0	0	
68138100	不含石棉的闸衬、闸垫	10	0		0	5		0	0	0				6	0					0	0	0
68138900	不含石棉的磨擦料及其他用于制动等用途制品	12	0		0	6	0	0	0	0				9.6	0					0	0	
68141000	粘聚或复制云母制的板、片、带	10.5	0		0	5	0	0	0	0				0	0					0	0	0

税则号列	货品名称	最惠国	协定税率 东盟统一	亚太5国	智利	巴基斯坦	新加坡	新西兰	秘鲁	哥达	香港	澳门	台湾	瑞士	冰岛	特惠税率 亚太2国	老挝	柬埔寨	缅甸	LDC1	LDC2	LDC3
68149000	其他已加工的云母及其制品	10.5	0		0	5	0	0	0	0				8.4	0					0	0	0
68151000	非电器用的石墨或其他碳精制品	15	0		0	12	0	0	6	0				12	0					0	0	0
68152000	泥煤制品	15	0		0	12	0	0	6	0				12	0					0	0	
68159100	含菱镁矿、白云石或铬铁矿的制品	15	0		0	12	0	0	6	0				12	0					0	0	
68159920	碳纤维	17.5	0		0		0	0	7	0				14	0					0	0	0
68159931	碳布	17.5	0		0		0	0	7	0				14	0					0	0	0
68159932	碳纤维预浸料	17.5	0		0		0	0	7	0				14	0					0	0	0
68159939	其他碳纤维制品	17.5	0		0		0	0	7	0				14	0					0	0	0
68159940	玄武岩纤维及其制品	17.5	0		0		0	0	7	0				14	0					0	0	0
68159990	其他未列名石制品及矿物制品	17.5	0		0		0	0	7	0				14	0					0	0	0
69010000	硅质化石粉或类似硅土制的砖、瓦	8	0	6.4	0	5		0	0	0				4.8	0					0	0	
69021000	含＞50%镁、钙、铬耐火砖及类似品	8	0		0	5		0	0	0				4.8	0					0	0	0
69022000	含＞50%氧化铝、硅耐火砖及类似品	8	0		0	5		0	0	0				6.4	0					0	0	0
69029000	其他耐火砖及耐火陶瓷建材制品	8	0		0	5		0	0	0				4.8	0					0	0	0
69031000	含＞50%石墨其他耐火陶瓷制品	8	0		0	5		0	0	0				4.8	0		0			0	0	0
69032000	含＞50%氧化铝其他耐火陶瓷制品	8	0		0	5		0	0	0				4.8	0		0			0	0	0
69039000	其他耐火陶瓷制品	8	0		0	5		0	0	0				4.8	0		0			0	0	0
69041000	陶瓷制建筑用砖	15	0		0	12	0	0	6	0				12	0					0	0	0
69049000	陶瓷制铺地砖、支撑或填充用砖	24.5	0		0		0	0	9.8	0				19.6	0					0	0	
69051000	陶瓷制屋顶瓦	24.5	0		0		0	0	9.8	0				19.6	0					0	0	
69059000	其他建筑用陶瓷制品	24.5	0		0		0	0	9.8	0				19.6	0					0	0	
69060000	陶瓷套管、导管、槽管及管子配件	15	0		0	12	0	0	6	0				12	0					0	0	
69071000	未上釉的小陶瓷砖、瓦、块及类似品	24.5	0		0		0	0	9.8	0				19.6	0					0	0	
69079000	未上釉的大陶瓷砖、瓦、块及类似品	12	0		0	6	0	0	0	0				9.6	0					0	0	
69081000	上釉的小陶瓷砖、瓦、块及类似品	12	0	10.4	0	5	0	0	0	0				9.6	0					0	0	
69089000	上釉的大陶瓷砖、瓦、块及类似品	12	0		0	6	0	0	0	0				9.6	0					0	0	
69091100	实验室、化学或其他技术用瓷器	8	0		0	5		0	0	0				4.8	0					0	0	0
69091200	莫氏硬度≥9的技术用陶瓷器	8	0		0	5		0	0	0				4.8	0					0	0	0
69091900	其他实验室、化学用陶瓷器	8	0		0	5		0	0	0				0	0					0	0	0
69099000	农业用、运输或盛装货物用陶瓷容器	21	0		0		0	0	8.4	0				16.8	0					0	0	
69101000	瓷制脸盆、浴缸及类似卫生器具	10	0	9	0	5	0	0	0	0				6	0					0	0	0
69109000	陶制脸盆、浴缸及类似卫生器具	10	0		0	5	0	0	0	0				6	0					0	0	0
69111011	骨瓷餐具	12	0	10	0	5	0	0	0	0				9.6	0					0	0	0
69111019	其他餐具	12	0	10	0	5	0	0	0	0				9.6	0					0	0	0
69111021	刀具	15	0	12.5	0	7.5	0	0	6	0				12	0					0	0	
69111029	其他厨房器具	15	0	12.5	0	7.5	0	0	6	0				12	0					0	0	
69119000	其他家用或盥洗用瓷器	24.5	0	20	0	20	0	0	9.8	0				19.6	0					0	0	
69120010	陶餐具	15	0		0	12	0	0	6	0				12	0					0	0	0
69120090	陶制厨房器具	15	0		0	12	0	0	6	0				12	0					0	0	
69131000	瓷塑像及其他装饰用瓷制品	15	0		0	12	0	0	6	0				12	0					0	0	0
69139000	陶塑像及其他装饰用陶制品	15	0		0	12	0	0	6	0				12	0					0	0	0
69141000	其他瓷制品	24.5	0		0		0	0	9.8	0				19.6	0					0	0	
69149000	其他陶制品	10	0		0	5	0	0	0	0				8	0					0	0	0
70010000	废碎玻璃及玻璃块料	12	0		0	6	0	0	0	0				9.6	0					0	0	
70021000	未加工的玻璃球	12	0		0	6	0	0	0	0				9.6	0					0	0	
70022010	光导纤维预制棒	6	0		0	5		0	0	0				3.6	0					0	0	
70022090	其他未加工的玻璃棒	12	0		0	6	0	0	0	0				9.6	0					0	0	
70023110	光导纤维用波导级石英玻璃管	5	0		0	0		0	0	0				0	0					0	0	
70023190	熔融石英或熔融硅石制其他玻璃管	14	0		0	11.2	0	0	0	0				11.2	0					0	0	
70023200	其他未加工的玻璃管	12	0		0	6	0	0	0	0				9.6	0					0	0	
70023900	未列名、未加工的玻璃管	12	0		0	6	0	0	0	0				9.6	0					0	0	
70031200	铸、轧制着色的非夹丝玻璃板、片	15	0		0	12	0	0	6	0				12	0					0	0	
70031900	铸、轧制的其他非夹丝玻璃板、片	17.5	0		0	14	0	0	7	0			0	14	0					0	0	
70032000	铸、轧制的夹丝玻璃板、片	15	0		0	12	0	0	6	0				12	0					0	0	
70033000	铸、轧制的玻璃型材及异型材	15	0		0	12	0	0	6	0				12	0					0	0	
70042000	拉、吹制的着色玻璃板、片	17.5	0		0	14	0	0	7	0				14	0					0	0	0
70049000	拉、吹制的其他玻璃板、片	17.5	0		0	14	0	0	7	0				14	0					0	0	
70051000	有吸收层非夹丝浮法或抛光玻璃板	15	0		0	12	0	0	6	0				12	0					0	0	
70052100	其他着色非夹丝浮法玻璃板、片	15	0		0	12	0	0	6	0				12	0					0	0	
70052900	其他非夹丝浮法玻璃板、片	15	0		0	12	0	0	6	0				12	0					0	0	
70053000	夹丝浮法玻璃板、片	17.5	0		0	14	0	0	7	0				14	0					0	0	

税则号列	货品名称	最惠国	协定税率													特惠税率						
			东盟统一	亚太5国	智利	巴基斯坦	新加坡	新西兰	秘鲁	哥达	香港	澳门	台湾	瑞士	冰岛	亚太2国	老挝	柬埔寨	缅甸	LDC1	LDC2	LDC3
70060000	经其他加工税号70.03－70.05的玻璃	15	0		0	12	0	0	6	0			0	12	0					0	0	
70071110	航空航天器及船舶用钢化安全玻璃	2	0		0	0		0	0	0	0			0	0					0	0	0
70071190	车辆用钢化安全玻璃	10	0		0	5		0	0	0	0			6	0					0	0	0
70071900	其他钢化安全玻璃	14	0		0	11.2	0	0	0	0				11.2	0					0	0	
70072110	航空航天器及船舶用层压安全玻璃	2	0		0	0		0	0	0				0	0					0	0	0
70072190	车辆用层压安全玻璃	20	0		0		0	0	8	0				16	0					0	0	0
70072900	其他层压安全玻璃	14	0		0	11.2	0	0	0	0				11.2	0					0	0	
70080010	中空或真空隔温、隔音玻璃	14	0		0	11.2	0	0	0	0				11.2	0					0	0	
70080090	其他多层隔温、隔音玻璃组件	14	0		0	11.2	0	0	0	0		0		11.2	0					0	0	
70091000	车辆后视镜	10	0		0	5	0	0	0	0			0	6	0					0	0	0
70099100	其他未镶框玻璃镜(包括后视镜)	21	0		0		0	0	8.4	0				16.8	0					0	0	
70099200	其他镶框玻璃镜(包括后视镜)	12	0	10.8	0	5	0	0	0	0				9.6	0					0	0	0
70101000	玻璃安瓿	14	0		0	11.2	0	0	0	0				11.2	0					0	0	
70102000	玻璃制的塞、盖及类似封口器	14	0		0	11.2	0	0	0	0				11.2	0					0	0	
70109010	装运货物或保藏用的玻璃大容器	14	0		0	11.2	0	0	0	0				11.2	0					0	0	
70109020	装运货物或保藏用的玻璃中容器	14	0		0	11.2	0	0	0	0				11.2	0					0	0	
70109030	装运货物或保藏用的玻璃小容器	14	0		0	11.2	0	0	0	0				11.2	0					0	0	
70109090	装运货物或保藏用的玻璃特小容器	14	0		0	11.2	0	0	0	0				11.2	0					0	0	0
70111000	电灯用未封口玻璃外壳及玻璃零件	21	0		0		0	0	8.4	0				16.8	0					0	0	
70112010	显象管玻壳及其零件	10	0	7	0	5		0	0	0				6	0					0	0	
70112090	阴极射线管用玻壳及零件	10	0	7	0	5		0	0	0				6	0					0	0	
70119010	电子管未封口玻璃外壳及玻璃零件	8	0		0	5		0	0	0				4.8	0					0	0	
70119090	其他类似品用未封口玻璃外壳零件	21	0		0		0	0	8.4	0				16.8	0					0	0	
70131000	玻璃陶瓷制玻璃器皿	24.5	0		0		0	0	9.8	0				19.6	0					0	0	0
70132200	铅晶质高脚杯	24.5	0		0		0	0	9.8	0				19.6	0					0	0	
70132800	其他高脚杯	8	0		0	5	0	0	0	0				4.8	0					0	0	0
70133300	其他铅晶质玻璃杯	24.5	0		0		0	0	9.8	0				19.6	0					0	0	
70133700	其他玻璃杯	8	0		0	5	0	0	0	0				4.8	0					0	0	0
70134100	铅晶质玻璃制餐桌、厨房用器皿	24.5	0		0		0	0	9.8	0				19.6	0					0	0	
70134200	低膨胀系数玻璃制餐桌厨房用器皿	10	0		0	5	0	0	0	0				6	0					0	0	0
70134900	其他玻璃制餐桌、厨房用器皿	10	0		0	5	0	0	0	0				6	0					0	0	0
70139100	其他铅晶质玻璃器皿	10	0		0	5	0	0	0	0				6	0					0	0	0
70139900	其他玻璃器皿	10	0		0	5	0	0	0	0				6	0					0	0	0
70140010	光学仪器用光学元件毛坯	10	0		0	5	0	0	0	0		0		6	0					0	0	0
70140090	其他未经光学加工的信号玻璃器	17.5	0		0	14	0	0	7	0				14	0					0	0	
70151010	视力矫正眼镜用变色镜片坯件	21	0		0		0	0	8.4	0				16.8	0					0	0	
70151090	其他视力矫正眼镜用镜片坯件	17.5	0		0	14	0	0	7	0				14	0					0	0	
70159010	钟表玻璃	17.5	0		0	14	0	0	7	0				14	0					0	0	
70159020	平光变色镜片坯件	18	0		0	14.4	0	0	7.2	0				14.4	0					0	0	
70159090	税号7015的其他未经光学加工玻璃	12	0		0	6	0	0	0	0				9.2	0					0	0	0
70161000	供镶嵌或装饰用玻璃马赛克	22	0		0		0	0	8.8	0				17.6	0					0	0	
70169010	花饰铅条窗玻璃及类似品	24	0		0		0	0	9.6	0				19.2	0					0	0	
70169090	建筑用压制或模制铺面玻璃块、砖	18	0		0		0	0	7.2	0				14.4	0					0	0	
70171000	实验室、卫生及配药用玻璃器	0																		0	0	0
70172000	其他玻璃制实验室等用玻璃器	8	0		0	5		0	0	0				6.2	0					0	0	0
70179000	其他实验室、卫生及配药用玻璃器	8	0		0	5		0	0	0				4.8	0					0	0	0
70181000	玻璃珠、仿珍珠及类似小件玻璃品	10	0		0	5	0	0	0	0				6	0					0	0	0
70182000	直径≤1mm的玻璃珠	20	0		0		0	0	8	0				16	0					0	0	
70189000	玻璃假眼;灯工方法制的玻璃塑像及玻璃饰品	20	0		0		0	0	8	0				16	0					0	0	
70191100	长度≤50mm的短切玻璃纤维	12	0		0	6	0	0	0	0			0	9.6	0					0	0	0
70191200	玻璃纤维粗纱	12	0		0	6	0	0	0	0				9.6	0					0	0	0
70191900	玻璃纤维、梳条、纱线	10	0		0	5	0	0	0	0		0	0	6	0					0	0	0
70193100	玻璃纤维(包括玻璃棉)制的席	5	0		0	0		0	0	0				0	0					0	0	0
70193200	玻璃纤维(包括玻璃棉)制的薄片	14	0		0	11.2	0	0	0	0				11.2	0					0	0	
70193910	垫	10.5	0		0	5	0	0	0	0			0	8.4	0					0	0	0
70193990	玻璃纤维(包括玻璃棉)及其制品	10.5	0		0	5	0	0	0	0			0	8.4	0					0	0	0
70194000	玻璃纤维粗纱机织物	12	0		0	6	0	0	0	0				9.6	0					0	0	0
70195100	宽度≤30mm的玻璃纤维机织物	12	0		0	6	0	0	0	0	0			9.6	0					0	0	0
70195200	每平米≤250g的玻璃长丝平纹织物	12	0		0	6	0	0	0	0	0	0		9.6	0					0	0	0
70195900	其他玻璃纤维机织物	12	0	8.4	0	5	0	0	0	0	0	0		9.6	0					0	0	0

税则号列	货品名称	最惠国	协定税率													特惠税率						
			东盟统一	亚太5国	智利	巴基斯坦	新加坡	新西兰	秘鲁	哥达	香港	澳门	台湾	瑞士	冰岛	亚太2国	老挝	柬埔寨	缅甸	LDC1	LDC2	LDC3
70199010	玻璃棉及其制品	7	0		0	5		0	0	0		0		4.2	0					0	0	0
70199021	每平方米重量小于450克的玻璃纤维布浸胶制品	7	0		0	5		0	0	0		0		4.2	0					0	0	0
70199029	其他玻璃纤维布浸胶制品	7	0		0	5		0	0	0		0		4.2	0					0	0	0
70199090	其他玻璃纤维及其制品	7	0		0	5		0	0	0		0		4.2	0					0	0	0
70200011	导电玻璃	10.5	0		0	5	0	0	0	0	0			8.4	0					0	0	0
70200012	绝缘子用玻璃伞盘	10.5	0	9.5	0	5	0	0	0	0				8.4	0					0	0	0
70200013	熔融石英或其他熔融硅石制	10.5	0	8.9	0	5	0	0	0	0				8.4	0					0	0	0
70200019	其他工业用玻璃制品	10.5	0	8.9	0	5	0	0	0	0				8.4	0					0	0	0
70200091	保温瓶或其他保温器用玻璃胆	21	0		0		0	0	8.4	0	0			16.8	0					0	0	
70200099	其他非工业用玻璃制品	15	0	12.8	0	7.5	0	0	6	0	0			12	0					0	0	0
71011011	未分级的天然黑珍珠	21	0		0		0	0	8.4	0				16.8	0					0	0	
71011019	其他未分级的天然珍珠	21	0		0		0	0	8.4	0				16.8	0					0	0	
71011091	其他天然黑珍珠	21	0		0		0	0	8.4	0				16.8	0					0	0	
71011099	其他天然珍珠	21	0		0		0	0	8.4	0				16.8	0					0	0	
71012110	未分级、未加工的养殖珍珠	21	0		0		0	0	8.4	0				16.8	0					0	0	
71012190	其他未加工的养殖珍珠	21	0		0		0	0	8.4	0				16.8	0					0	0	
71012210	未分级、已加工的养殖珍珠	21	0		0		0	0	8.4	0				16.8	0					0	0	
71012290	其他已加工的养殖珍珠	21	0		0		0	0	8.4	0				16.8	0					0	0	
71021000	未分级钻石	3	0		0	0		0	0	0				0	0					0	0	0
71022100	未加工或简单加工的工业用钻石	0																		0	0	0
71022900	其他工业用钻石	0																		0	0	0
71023100	未加工或简单加工非工业用钻石	3	0		0	0		0	0	0	0			2.4	0					0	0	0
71023900	其他非工业用钻石	8	0	0	0	0		0	0	0				6.4	0					0	0	0
71031000	未加工宝石或半宝石	3	0	2.8	0	0		0	0	0				0	0		0			0	0	0
71039100	经其他加工的红宝石、蓝宝石、祖母绿	8	0	4	0	0		0	0	0				6.4	0		0			0	0	0
71039910	经其他加工的翡翠	8	0	4	0	0		0	0	0				4.8	0					0	0	0
71039920	水晶	8	0	4	0	0		0	0	0				6.4	0					0	0	0
71039930	碧玺	8	0	4	0	0		0	0	0				6.4	0					0	0	0
71039940	软玉	8	0	4	0	0		0	0	0				6.4	0					0	0	0
71039990	经其他加工的其他宝石或半宝石	8	0	4	0	0		0	0	0				6.4	0					0	0	0
71041000	压电石英	6	0		0	5		0	0	0				3.6	0					0	0	0
71042010	未加工合成或再造钻石	0																		0	0	0
71042090	未加工合成或再造其他宝石或半宝石	0									0									0	0	0
71049011	其他工业用合成或再造的钻石	6	0		0	5		0	0	0				3.6	0					0	0	0
71049012	工业用蓝宝石	6	0		0	5		0	0	0	0			3.6	0					0	0	0
71049019	其他工业用合成或再造的其他宝石或半宝石	6	0		0	5		0	0	0				3.6	0					0	0	0
71049091	其他非工业用合成钻石	8	0		0	5		0	0	0				4.8	0					0	0	0
71049099	其他非工业用合成其他宝石或半宝石	8	0		0	5		0	0	0				4.8	0					0	0	0
71051010	天然钻石	0																		0	0	0
71051020	人工合成的钻石	0																		0	0	0
71059000	天然或合成宝石或半宝石粉末	0																		0	0	0
71061011	平均粒径小于3微米的非片状银粉	0																		0	0	0
71061019	平均粒径不小于3微米的非片状银粉	0																		0	0	0
71061021	平均粒径小于10微米的片状银粉	0																		0	0	0
71061029	其他银粉	0																		0	0	0
71069110	纯度达99.99%及以上的未锻造银	0																		0	0	0
71069190	其他未锻造银	0																		0	0	0
71069210	纯度达99.99%及以上的半制成银	0																		0	0	0
71069290	其他半制成银	0																		0	0	0
71070000	以贱金属为底的包银材料	10.5	0		0	5	0	0	0	0				8.4	0		0			0	0	0
71081100	非货币用金粉	0																		0	0	0
71081200	非货币用未锻造金	0																		0	0	0
71081300	非货币用半制成金	0															0			0	0	0
71082000	货币用未锻造金(包括镀铂的金)及金粉	0																		0	0	0
71090000	以贱金属或银为底的包金材料	10.5	0		0	5	0	0	0	0				8.4	0					0	0	0
71101100	未锻造或粉末状铂	0																		0	0	0
71101910	板、片状铂	0																		0	0	0
71101990	其他半制成铂	3	0		0	0		0	0	0	0			0	0					0	0	0
71102100	未锻造或粉末状钯	0																		0	0	0

税则号列	货品名称	最惠国	协定税率 东盟统一	亚太5国	智利	巴基斯坦	新加坡	新西兰	秘鲁	哥达	香港	澳门	台湾	瑞士	冰岛	特惠税率 亚太2国	老挝	柬埔寨	缅甸	LDC1	LDC2	LDC3
71102910	板、片状钯	0																		0	0	0
71102990	其他半制成钯	3	0		0	0		0	0	0	0			0	0					0	0	0
71103100	未锻造或粉末状铑	0																		0	0	0
71103910	板、片状铑	0																		0	0	0
71103990	其他半制成铑	3	0		0	0		0	0	0				0	0					0	0	0
71104100	未锻造或粉末状铱、锇、钌	0																		0	0	0
71104910	板、片状铱、锇、钌	0																		0	0	0
71104990	其他半制成铱、锇、钌	3	0		0	0		0	0	0				0	0					0	0	0
71110000	以贱金属、银或金为底的包铂材料	3	0		0	0		0	0	0				0	0					0	0	
71123010	含银或银化合物的灰	8	0		0	5		0	0	0				4.8	0					0	0	0
71123090	其他含贵金属或贵金属化合物的灰	6	0		0	5		0	0	0				3.6	0					0	0	0
71129110	金及包金的废碎料	0																		0	0	0
71129120	其他含金或金化合物的废碎料	6	0		0	5		0	0	0				3.6	0					0	0	0
71129210	铂及包铂的废碎料	0																		0	0	0
71129220	其他含铂或铂化合物的废碎料	6	0		0	5		0	0	0				3.6	0					0	0	0
71129910	含银及银化合物的废碎料	8	0		0	5		0	0	0				4.8	0					0	0	0
71129920	含有其他贵金属或贵金属化合物的废碎料	6	0		0	5		0	0	0				3.6	0					0	0	0
71129990	其他贵金属或包贵金属的废碎料	0																		0	0	0
71131110	镶嵌钻石的银首饰及其零件	20	0	16.5	0	16	0	0	8	0	0	0		15.4	0					0	0	
71131190	其他银首饰及其零件	20	0	16.5	0	16	0	0	8	0	0	0		12	0					0	0	0
71131911	镶嵌钻石的黄金制首饰及其零件	20	0	14	0	14	0	0	8	0	0	0		16.7	0					0	0	
71131919	其他黄金制首饰及其零件	20	0	16	0	16	0	0	8	0	0	0		12	0					0	0	
71131921	镶嵌钻石的铂制首饰及其零件	35	0	28	0	28	0	0	14	0	0	0			0					0	0	
71131929	其他铂制首饰及其零件	35	0	28	0	28	0	0	14	0	0	0		21	0					0	0	0
71131991	镶嵌钻石的其他贵金属制首饰及其零件	35	0	28	0	28	0	0	14	0	0	0			0					0	0	
71131999	其他贵金属制首饰及其零件	35	0	28	0	28	0	0	14	0	0	0		21	0					0	0	0
71132010	镶嵌钻石的以贱金属为底的包贵金属制首饰	35	0	30	0	30	0	0	14	0	0	0		26.6						0	0	
71132090	其他以贱金属为底的包贵金属制首饰	35	0	30	0	30	0	0	14	0	0	0			0					0	0	
71141100	银器及零件	35	0		0		0	0	0	0	0	0		21	0					0	0	0
71141900	其他贵金属制金银器及零件	35	0		0		0	0	14	0	0	0		29.2	0					0	0	
71142000	以贱金属为底的包贵金属制金银器	35	0		0		0	0	14	0	0	0		26.6	0					0	0	0
71151000	金属丝布或格栅状的铂催化剂	3	0		0	0		0	0	0	0			0	0					0	0	0
71159010	工业或实验室用贵或包贵金属制品	3	0		0	0		0	0	0	0	0		0	0					0	0	0
71159090	其他用途的贵或包贵金属制品	35	0		0		0	0	14	0	0	0			0					0	0	
71161000	天然或养殖珍珠制品	35	0		0		0	0	14	0	0	0		28	0					0	0	
71162000	宝石或半宝石制品	35	0		0		0	0	14	0	0	0		21	0					0	0	0
71171100	贱金属制袖扣、饰扣	35	0		0		0	0	14	0	0	0		26.6	0					0	0	
71171900	其他贱金属制仿首饰	17	0	15.3	0	13.6	0	0	6.8	0	0	0		13.6	0					0	0	0
71179000	未列名材料制仿首饰	35	0	30	0	30	0	0	14	0	0	0								0	0	0
71181000	非法定货币的硬币(金币除外)	0																		0	0	0
71189000	其他硬币	0																		0	0	0
72011000	非合金生铁,含磷量≤0.5%	1	0		0	0		0	0	0				0	0					0	0	0
72012000	非合金生铁,含磷量>0.5%	1	0		0	0		0	0	0				0	0					0	0	0
72015000	合金生铁、镜铁	1	0		0	0		0	0	0				0	0					0	0	0
72021100	锰铁,含碳量≥2%	2	0		0	0		0	0	0				0	0					0	0	0
72021900	锰铁,含碳量≤2%	2	0		0	0		0	0	0				0	0					0	0	0
72022100	硅铁,含硅量≥55%	2	0		0	0		0	0	0				0	0					0	0	0
72022900	硅铁,含硅量≤55%	2	0		0	0		0	0	0				0	0					0	0	0
72023000	硅锰铁	2	0		0	0		0	0	0				0	0					0	0	0
72024100	铬铁,含碳量≥4%	2	0		0	0		0	0	0				0	0					0	0	0
72024900	铬铁,含碳量≤4%	2	0		0	0		0	0	0				0	0					0	0	0
72025000	硅铬铁	2	0		0	0		0	0	0				0	0					0	0	0
72026000	镍铁	2	0		0	0		0	0	0				0	0					0	0	0
72027000	钼铁	2	0		0	0		0	0	0				0	0					0	0	0
72028010	钨铁	2	0		0	0		0	0	0				0	0					0	0	0
72028020	硅钨铁	2	0		0	0		0	0	0				0	0					0	0	0
72029100	钛铁及硅钛铁	2	0		0	0		0	0	0				0	0					0	0	0
72029210	按重量计含钒量在75%及以上的钒铁	9	0		0	5		0	0	0				5.4	0					0	0	0
72029290	其他钒铁	9	0		0	5		0	0	0				5.4	0					0	0	0

税则号列	货品名称	最惠国	协定税率													特惠税率						
			东盟统一	亚太5国	智利	巴基斯坦	新加坡	新西兰	秘鲁	哥达	香港	澳门	台湾	瑞士	冰岛	亚太2国	老挝	柬埔寨	缅甸	LDC1	LDC2	LDC3
72029300	铌铁	2	0		0	0		0	0	0				0	0					0	0	0
72029911	钕铁硼速凝永磁片	2	0		0	0		0	0	0				0	0					0	0	0
72029912	钕铁硼磁粉	2	0		0	0		0	0	0				0	0					0	0	0
72029919	其他钕铁硼合金	2	0		0	0		0	0	0				0	0					0	0	0
72029991	按重量计稀土元素总含量在10%以上的其他铁合金	2	0		0	0		0	0	0				0	0					0	0	0
72029999	其他铁合金	2	0		0	0		0	0	0				0	0					0	0	0
72031000	直接从铁矿还原的铁产品	2	0		0	0		0	0	0				0	0					0	0	
72039000	其他海绵铁,产品纯度>99.94%	2	0		0	0		0	0	0				0	0					0	0	
72041000	铸铁废碎料	2	0		0	0		0	0	0				0	0					0	0	0
72042100	不锈钢废碎料	0																		0	0	0
72042900	其他合金钢废碎料	0																		0	0	0
72043000	镀锡钢铁废碎料	2	0		0	0		0	0	0				0	0					0	0	0
72044100	机械加工中产生的废料	2	0		0	0		0	0	0				0	0					0	0	0
72044900	其他钢铁废碎料	0																		0	0	0
72045000	供再熔的碎料钢铁锭	0																		0	0	0
72051000	生铁、镜铁及钢铁颗粒	2	0		0	0		0	0	0				0	0					0	0	0
72052100	合金钢粉末	2	0		0	0		0	0	0				0	0					0	0	0
72052900	生铁、镜铁及其他钢铁粉末	2	0		0	0		0	0	0				0	0					0	0	0
72061000	铁及非合金钢锭	2	0		0	0		0	0	0				0	0					0	0	
72069000	其他初级形状的铁及非合金钢	2	0		0	0		0	0	0				0	0					0	0	
72071100	宽度<厚度两倍的矩形截面钢坯,C<0.25%	2	0		0	0		0	0	0				0	0					0	0	
72071200	其他矩形截面钢坯,C,0.25%	2	0		0	0		0	0	0				0	0					0	0	
72071900	其他含碳量<0.25%的钢坯	2	0		0	0		0	0	0				0	0					0	0	
72072000	含碳量≥0.25%的钢坯	2	0		0	0		0	0	0				0	0					0	0	
72081000	轧压花纹的热轧卷材	5	0		0	0		0	0	0				0	0					0	0	0
72082500	厚度≥4.75mm其他经酸洗的热轧卷材	5	0		0	0		0	0	0				0	0					0	0	0
72082610	屈服强度大于355牛顿/平方毫米,3mm≤厚度<4.75mm其他经酸洗热轧卷材	5	0		0	0		0	0	0				0	0					0	0	0
72082690	其他3mm≤厚度<4.75mm其他经酸洗热轧卷材	5	0		0	0		0	0	0				0	0					0	0	0
72082710	厚度<1.5mm的其他经酸洗的热轧卷材	5	0		0	0		0	0	0				0	0					0	0	0
72082790	其他厚度<3mm的其他经酸洗的热轧卷材	5	0		0	0		0	0	0			0	0	0					0	0	0
72083600	厚度>10mm的其他热轧卷材	6	0		0	5		0	0	0				3.6	0					0	0	0
72083700	4.75mm≤厚度≤10mm的其他热轧卷材	5	0		0	0		0	0	0				0	0					0	0	0
72083810	屈服强度大于355牛顿/平方毫米,3mm≤厚度<4.75mm的其他卷材	5	0		0	0		0	0	0				0	0					0	0	0
72083890	其他3mm≤厚度<4.75mm的其他卷材	5	0		0	0		0	0	0			0	0	0					0	0	0
72083910	厚度<1.5mm的其他热轧卷材	3	0		0	0		0	0	0				0	0					0	0	0
72083990	其他厚度<3mm的其他热轧卷材	3	0		0	0		0	0	0			0	0	0					0	0	0
72084000	轧有凸起花纹的热轧非卷材	6	0		0	5		0	0	0				3.6	0					0	0	0
72085110	厚度>50mm的其他热轧非卷材	6	0		0	5		0	0	0				3.6	0					0	0	0
72085120	厚度>20mm,但不超过50毫米的其他热轧非卷材	6	0		0	5		0	0	0				3.6	0					0	0	0
72085190	其他厚度>10mm的其他热轧非卷材	6	0		0	5		0	0	0				3.6	0					0	0	0
72085200	4.75mm≤厚度≤10mm的热轧非卷材	6	0		0	5		0	0	0				3.6	0					0	0	0
72085310	屈服强度大于355牛顿/平方毫米,3mm≤厚度<4.75mm的热轧非卷材	6	0	5.1	0	0		0	0	0				3.6	0					0	0	0
72085390	其他3mm≤厚度<4.75mm的热轧非卷材	6	0	5.1	0	0		0	0	0				3.6	0					0	0	0
72085410	厚度<1.5mm的热轧非卷材	6	0	5.1	0	0		0	0	0				3.6	0					0	0	0
72085490	其他厚度<3mm的热轧非卷材	6	0	5.1	0	0		0	0	0				3.6	0					0	0	0
72089000	其他热轧铁或非合金钢宽平板轧材	6	0		0	5		0	0	0				3.6	0					0	0	0
72091510	屈服强度大于355牛顿/平方毫米,厚度≥3mm的冷轧卷材	6	0		0	5		0	0	0				3.6	0					0	0	0

税则号列	货品名称	最惠国	协定税率													特惠税率						
			东盟统一	亚太5国	智利	巴基斯坦	新加坡	新西兰	秘鲁	哥达	香港	澳门	台湾	瑞士	冰岛	亚太2国	老挝	柬埔寨	缅甸	LDC1	LDC2	LDC3
72091590	其他厚度≥3mm 的冷轧卷材	6	0		0	5		0	0	0				3.6	0					0	0	0
72091610	屈服强度大于 275 牛顿/平方毫米,1mm<厚度<3mm 的冷轧卷材	6	0	4.2	0	0		0	0	0				3.6	0					0	0	0
72091690	其他 1mm<厚度<3mm 的冷轧卷材	6	0	4.2	0	0		0	0	0			0	3.6	0					0	0	0
72091710	屈服强度大于 275 牛顿/平方毫米,0.5mm≤厚度≤1mm 的冷轧卷材	3	0	2.1	0	0		0	0	0				0	0					0	0	0
72091790	其他 0.5mm≤厚度≤1mm 的冷轧卷材	3	0	2.1	0	0		0	0	0			0	0	0					0	0	0
72091810	厚度<0.3mm 的冷轧卷材	6	0	4.2	0	0		0	0	0				3.6	0					0	0	0
72091890	其他厚度<0.5mm 的冷轧卷材	6	0	4.2	0	0		0	0	0			0	3.6	0					0	0	0
72092500	厚度≥3mm 的冷轧非卷材	6	0		0	5		0	0	0				3.6	0					0	0	0
72092600	1mm<厚度<3mm 的冷轧非卷材	6	0		0	5		0	0	0				3.6	0					0	0	0
72092700	0.5mm≤厚度≤1mm 的冷轧非卷材	6	0	4.2	0	0		0	0	0				3.6	0					0	0	0
72092800	厚度<0.5mm 的冷轧非卷材	6	0		0	5		0	0	0				3.6	0					0	0	0
72099000	其他冷轧铁或非合金钢宽平板轧材	6	0	4.2	0	0		0	0	0				3.6	0					0	0	0
72101100	镀锡的铁或非合金钢厚宽平板轧材	10	0		0	5	0	0	0	0				6	0					0	0	0
72101200	镀锡的铁或非合金钢薄宽平板轧材	5	0		0	0		0	0	0				0	0					0	0	0
72102000	镀铅的铁或非合金钢宽平板轧材	4	0		0	0		0	0	0				0	0					0	0	0
72103000	电镀锌的铁或非合金钢宽板材	8	0		0	5		0	0	0			0	4.8	0					0	0	0
72104100	镀锌的瓦楞形铁或非合金钢宽板材	8	0		0	5		0	0	0				4.8	0					0	0	0
72104900	镀锌的其他形铁或非合金钢宽板材	4	0		0	0		0	0	0			0	0	0					0	0	0
72105000	镀氧化铬的铁或非合金钢宽板材	8	0		0	5		0	0	0				4.8	0					0	0	0
72106100	镀或涂铝锌合金的铁宽平板轧材	8	0		0	5		0	0	0				4.8	0					0	0	0
72106900	其他镀或涂铝的铁宽平板轧材	8	0		0	5		0	0	0				4.8	0					0	0	0
72107010	厚度小于 1.5 毫米涂漆或涂塑的宽度在 600 毫米及以上的铁或非合金钢平板轧材,经包覆、镀层或涂层	4	0		0	0		0	0	0	0			2.4	0					0	0	0
72107090	其他涂漆或涂塑的宽度在 600 毫米及以上的铁或非合金钢平板轧材,经包覆、镀层或涂层	4	0		0	0		0	0	0	0			2.4	0					0	0	0
72109000	涂镀其他材料铁或非合金钢宽板材	8	0		0	5		0	0	0				4.8	0					0	0	0
72111300	未轧花纹的四面轧制的热轧非卷材	6	0		0	5		0	0	0				3.6	0					0	0	0
72111400	厚度≥4.75mm 的其他热轧板材	6	0		0	5		0	0	0				3.6	0					0	0	0
72111900	其他热轧铁或非合金钢窄板材	6	0		0	5		0	0	0				3.6	0					0	0	0
72112300	冷轧含炭量<0.25%的板材	6	0		0	5		0	0	0				3.6	0					0	0	0
72112900	冷轧其他铁或非合金钢窄板材	6	0		0	5		0	0	0				3.6	0					0	0	0
72119000	冷轧的铁或非合金钢其他窄板材	6	0		0	5		0	0	0				3.6	0					0	0	0
72121000	镀或涂锡的铁或非合金钢窄板材	5	0		0	0		0	0	0				0	0					0	0	0
72122000	电镀锌的铁或非合金钢窄板材	8	0		0	5		0	0	0				4.8	0					0	0	0
72123000	其他镀或涂锌的铁窄板材	8	0		0	5		0	0	0				4.8	0					0	0	0
72124000	涂漆或涂塑的铁或非合金钢窄板材	4	0		0	0		0	0	0	0			0	0					0	0	0
72125000	涂镀其他材料铁或非合金钢窄板材	8	0		0	5		0	0	0				4.8	0					0	0	0
72126000	经包覆的铁或非合金钢窄板材	8	0		0	5		0	0	0				4.8	0					0	0	0
72131000	带有轧制花纹的热轧盘条	3	0		0	0		0	0	0				0	0					0	0	0
72132000	其他易切削钢制热轧盘条	3	0		0	0		0	0	0				0	0					0	0	0
72139100	直径<14mm 圆截面的其他热轧盘条	5	0	4.3	0	0		0	0	0				0	0					0	0	0
72139900	其他热轧盘条	5	0		0	0		0	0	0				0	0					0	0	0
72141000	锻造的铁或非合金钢条、杆	7	0		0	5		0	0	0				4.2	0					0	0	0
72142000	热加工带有轧制花纹的条、杆	3	0	0	0	0		0	0	0	0			0	0					0	0	0
72143000	热加工易切削钢的条、杆	7	0		0	5		0	0	0				4.2	0					0	0	0
72149100	热加工其他矩形截面的条杆	3	0		0	0		0	0	0				0	0					0	0	0
72149900	热加工其他条、杆	3	0		0	0		0	0	0				0	0					0	0	0
72151000	冷加工其他易切削钢制条、杆	7	0		0	5		0	0	0				5.6	0					0	0	0
72155000	冷加工或冷成形的其他条、杆	7	0		0	5		0	0	0				4.2	0					0	0	0
72159000	铁及非合金钢的其他条、杆	3	0		0	0		0	0	0				0	0					0	0	0
72161010	截面高度<80mm 的 H 型钢	3	0		0	0		0	0	0				0	0					0	0	0
72161020	截面高度低于 80 毫米的工字钢	3	0		0	0		0	0	0				0	0					0	0	0
72161090	截面高度<80mmU 型钢	3	0		0	0		0	0	0				0	0					0	0	0
72162100	热加工截面高度<80mm 角钢	6	0		0	5		0	0	0				3.6	0					0	0	0
72162200	热加工截面高度<80mm 丁字钢	6	0		0	5		0	0	0				3.6	0					0	0	0
72163100	热加工截面高度≥80mm 槽型钢	6	0		0	5		0	0	0				3.6	0					0	0	0

税则号列	货品名称	最惠国	协定税率													特惠税率						
			东盟统一	亚太5国	智利	巴基斯坦	新加坡	新西兰	秘鲁	哥达	香港	澳门	台湾	瑞士	冰岛	亚太2国	老挝	柬埔寨	缅甸	LDC1	LDC2	LDC3
72163210	截面高度在200毫米以上的工字钢	6	0		0	5		0	0	0				3.6	0					0	0	0
72163290	热加工截面高度≥80mm工字型钢	6	0		0	5		0	0	0				3.6	0					0	0	0
72163311	截面高度在800毫米以上的H型钲	6	0		0	5		0	0	0				3.6	0					0	0	0
72163319	截面高度≥200mmH型钢	6	0		0	5		0	0	0				3.6	0					0	0	0
72163390	其他截面高度≥80mmH型钢	6	0		0	5		0	0	0				3.6	0					0	0	0
72164010	热加工截面高度≥80mm角钢	3	0		0	0		0	0	0				0	0					0	0	0
72164020	热加工截面高度≥80mm丁字钢	3	0		0	0		0	0	0				0	0					0	0	0
72165010	热加工乙字钢	6	0		0	5		0	0	0				3.6	0					0	0	0
72165020	热加工球扁钢	3	0		0	0		0	0	0				0	0					0	0	0
72165090	热加工其他角材、型材及异型材	3	0		0	0		0	0	0				0	0					0	0	0
72166100	冷加工板材制的角材、型材及异型材	3	0		0	0		0	0	0				0	0					0	0	0
72166900	冷加工其他角材、型材及异型材	3	0		0	0		0	0	0				0	0					0	0	0
72169100	冷加工其他板材制角材、型材及异型材	3	0		0	0		0	0	0				0	0					0	0	0
72169900	其他角材、型材及异型材	3	0		0	0		0	0	0				0	0					0	0	0
72171000	未镀或涂层的铁或非合金钢丝	8	0		0	5		0	0	0			0	4.8	0					0	0	0
72172000	镀或涂锌的铁或非合金钢丝	8	0		0	5		0	0	0				4.8	0					0	0	0
72173010	镀或涂铜的铁丝和非合金钢丝	8	0	6.4	0	5		0	0	0				4.8	0					0	0	0
72173090	镀或涂其他贱金属的铁丝和非合金钢丝	8	0	6.4	0	5		0	0	0				4.8	0					0	0	0
72179000	其他铁丝或非合金钢丝	8	0		0	5		0	0	0	0			4.8	0					0	0	0
72181000	不锈钢锭及其他初级形状产品	2	0		0	0		0	0	0				0	0					0	0	0
72189100	矩形截面的不锈钢半制成品	2	0		0	0		0	0	0				0	0					0	0	0
72189900	其他不锈钢半制成品	2	0		0	0		0	0	0				0	0					0	0	0
72191100	厚度>10mm热轧不锈钢卷板	4	0		0	0		0	0	0				0	0					0	0	0
72191200	4.75mm≤厚度≤10mm热轧不锈钢卷板	4	0		0	0		0	0	0			0	0	0					0	0	0
72191312	按重量计含锰量在5.5%及以上的未经酸洗3mm≤厚度<4.75mm铬锰系不锈钢	4	0		0	0		0	0	0				0	0					0	0	0
72191319	厚度在3毫米及以上,但小于4.75毫米的未径酸洗的其他不锈钢卷板	4	0		0	0		0	0	0			0	0	0					0	0	0
72191322	按重量计含锰量在5.5%及以上的经酸洗3mm≤厚度<4.75mm铬锰系不锈钢	4	0		0	0		0	0	0				0	0					0	0	0
72191329	厚度在3毫米及以上,但小于4.75毫米的经酸洗的其他不锈钢卷板	4	0		0	0		0	0	0			0	0	0					0	0	0
72191412	按重量计含锰量在5.5%及以上的未经酸洗厚度<3mm的铬锰系不锈钢	4	0		0	0		0	0	0				0	0					0	0	0
72191419	厚度在3毫米以下的未径酸洗的其他不锈钢卷板	4	0		0	0		0	0	0				0	0					0	0	0
72191422	按重量计含锰量在5.5%及以上的经酸洗厚度<3mm的铬锰系不锈钢	4	0		0	0		0	0	0				0	0					0	0	0
72191429	厚度在3毫米以下的经酸洗的其他不锈钢卷板	4	0		0	0		0	0	0				0	0					0	0	0
72192100	厚度>10mm热轧不锈钢平板	10	0	9.3	0	5	0	0	0	0	0			6	0					0	0	
72192200	4.75mm≤厚度≤10mm热轧不锈钢平板	10	0	9.3	0	5	0	0	4	0	0			6	0					0	0	
72192300	3mm≤厚度<4.75mm热轧不锈钢平板	10	0	9.3	0	5	0	0	0	0			0	6	0					0	0	
72192410	1mm<厚度<3mm热轧不锈钢平板	10	0	9.3	0	5	0	0	0	0			0	6	0					0	0	
72192420	0.5mm≤厚度≤1mm热轧不锈钢平板	10	0	9.3	0	5	0	0	0	0				6	0					0	0	
72192430	厚度<0.5mm热轧不锈钢平板	10	0	9.3	0	5	0	0	0	0				6	0					0	0	
72193100	厚度≥4.75mm冷轧不锈钢板	10	0		0	5	0	0	4	0			0	6	0					0	0	
72193200	3mm≤厚度<4.75mm冷轧不锈钢板材	10	0		0	5	0	0	4	0			0	6	0					0	0	
72193310	1mm<厚度<3mm冷轧按重量计含锰量在5.5%及以上的铬锰系不锈钢板材	10	0		0	5	0	0	4	0	0		0	6	0					0	0	
72193390	其他1mm<厚度<3mm冷轧不锈钢板材	10	0		0	5	0	0	4	0	0		0	6	0					0	0	
72193400	0.5mm≤厚度≤1mm冷轧不锈钢板材	10	0		0	5	0	0	4	0	0		0	6	0					0	0	
72193500	厚度<0.5mm冷轧不锈钢板材	10	0		0	5	0	0	4	0	0		0	6	0					0	0	
72199000	其他不锈钢冷轧板材	10	0		0	5	0	0	0	0			0	6	0					0	0	
72201100	热轧不锈钢带材厚度≥4.75mm	10	0		0	5	0	0	0	0	0			6	0					0	0	
72201200	热轧不锈钢带材厚度<4.75mm	10	0		0	5	0	0	0	0				6	0					0	0	
72202020	厚度在0.35毫米及以下的冷轧不锈钢带材	10	0		0	5	0	0	0	0				6	0					0	0	

税则号列	货品名称	最惠国	协定税率												特惠税率						
			东盟统一	亚太5国	智利	巴基斯坦	新加坡	新西兰	秘鲁	哥达	香港	澳门	台湾	瑞士	冰岛	亚太2国	老挝	柬埔寨	缅甸	LDC1	LDC2	LDC3
72202030	厚度在0.35毫米以上但小于3毫米的冷轧不锈钢带材	10	0		0	5	0	0	0	0				6	0					0	0	
72202040	厚度在3毫米及以上的冷轧不锈钢带材	10	0		0	5	0	0	0	0				6	0					0	0	
72209000	其他不锈钢带材	10	0		0	5	0	0	0	0			0	6	0					0	0	
72210000	不锈钢热轧条、杆	10	0	8	0	5	0	0	0	0				6	0					0	0	
72221100	热加工的圆形截面不锈钢条、杆	10	0	9	0	5	0	0	0	0				6	0					0	0	
72221900	热加工其他截面形状不锈钢条杆	10	0	9	0	5	0	0	0	0				6	0					0	0	
72222000	冷成形或冷加工的不锈钢条、杆	10	0		0	5	0	0	0	0				6	0					0	0	
72223000	其他不锈钢条、杆	10	0	8.9	0	5	0	0	0	0				6	0					0	0	
72224000	不锈钢角材、型材及异型材	10	0		0	5	0	0	0	0				6	0					0	0	
72230000	不锈钢丝	10	0		0	5	0	0	0	0	0			6	0					0	0	0
72241000	其他合金钢锭及其他初级形状	2	0		0	0		0	0	0				0	0					0	0	0
72249010	单重≥10吨的粗铸锻件坯	2	0		0	0		0	0	0				0	0					0	0	0
72249090	其他合金钢坯	2	0		0	0		0	0	0				0	0					0	0	0
72251100	取向性硅电钢宽板	3	0	2.1	0	0		0	0	0				0	0					0	0	0
72251900	其他硅电钢宽板	6	0		0	5		0	0	0			0	3.6	0					0	0	0
72253000	宽度≥600mm热轧其他合金钢卷材	3	0		0	0		0	0	0				0	0					0	0	0
72254010	工具钢	3	0		0	0		0	0	0				0	0					0	0	0
72254091	含硼合金钢	3	0		0	0		0	0	0				0	0					0	0	0
72254099	其他非卷材,除热轧外未经进一步加工	3	0		0	0		0	0	0				0	0					0	0	0
72255000	宽度≥600mm冷轧其他合金钢板材	3	0		0	0		0	0	0				0	0					0	0	0
72259100	电镀锌的其他合金钢宽平板轧材	7	0		0	5		0	0	0				4.2	0					0	0	0
72259200	其他镀或涂锌的其他合金钢宽板材	7	0		0	5		0	0	0				4.2	0					0	0	0
72259910	宽度≥600mm的高速钢平板轧材	3	0		0	0		0	0	0				0	0					0	0	0
72259990	宽度≥600mm的其他合金钢平板轧材	7	0		0	5		0	0	0				4.2	0					0	0	0
72261100	取向性硅电钢窄板	3	0		0	0		0	0	0				0	0					0	0	0
72261900	其他硅电钢窄板	3	0		0	0		0	0	0				0	0					0	0	0
72262000	宽度<600mm的高速钢平板轧材	3	0		0	0		0	0	0				0	0					0	0	0
72269110	工具钢	3	0		0	0		0	0	0				0	0					0	0	0
72269191	含硼合金钢	3	0		0	0		0	0	0				0	0					0	0	0
72269199	其他除热轧外未经进一步加工的合金钢平板轧材,宽度小于600毫米	3	0		0	0		0	0	0				0	0					0	0	0
72269200	宽度<600mm冷轧其他合金钢板材	3	0		0	0		0	0	0				0	0					0	0	0
72269910	电镀锌的其他合金钢窄平板轧材	7	0		0	5		0	0	0				4.2	0					0	0	0
72269920	其他镀或涂锌的其他合金钢窄板材	7	0		0	5		0	0	0				4.2	0					0	0	0
72269990	宽度<600mm的其他合金板材	7	0		0	5		0	0	0				4.2	0					0	0	0
72271000	高速钢的热轧盘条	3	0		0	0		0	0	0				0	0					0	0	0
72272000	硅锰钢的热轧盘条	6	0		0	5		0	0	0				3.6	0					0	0	0
72279010	含硼合金钢制不规则盘卷的其他合金钢热轧条、杆	3	0		0	0		0	0	0				0	0					0	0	0
72279090	其他不规则盘卷的其他合金钢热轧条、杆	3	0		0	0		0	0	0				0	0					0	0	0
72281000	其他高速钢的条、杆	3	0		0	0		0	0	0				0	0					0	0	0
72282000	其他硅锰钢的条、杆	6	0		0	5		0	0	0				3.6	0					0	0	0
72283010	含硼合金钢制其他条、杆,除热轧、热拉拔或热挤压外未经进一步加工	3	0		0	0		0	0	0				0	0					0	0	0
72283090	其他条、杆,除热轧、热拉拔或热挤压外未经进一步加工	3	0		0	0		0	0	0				0	0					0	0	0
72284000	其他合金钢锻造条、杆	3	0		0	0		0	0	0				0	0					0	0	0
72285000	其他合金钢冷成形或冷加工条、杆	3	0		0	0		0	0	0				0	0					0	0	0
72286000	其他合金钢条、杆	3	0		0	0		0	0	0				0	0					0	0	0
72287010	履带板型钢	6	0		0	5		0	0	0				3.6	0					0	0	0
72287090	其他合金钢角材、型材及异型材	6	0		0	5		0	0	0				3.6	0					0	0	0
72288000	其他合金钢空心钻钢	7	0		0	5		0	0	0				4.2	0					0	0	0
72292000	硅锰钢丝	7	0		0	5		0	0	0				4.2	0					0	0	
72299010	高速钢丝	3	0		0	0		0	0	0				0	0					0	0	
72299090	其他合金钢丝	7	0		0	5		0	0	0				4.2	0					0	0	
73011000	钢铁板桩	7	0	6.3	0	5		0	0	0				4.2	0					0	0	0
73012000	焊接的钢铁角材、型材及异型材	7	0		0	5		0	0	0				4.2	0					0	0	0
73021000	钢轨	6	0		0	5		0	0	0				3.6	0					0	0	0

税则号列	货品名称	最惠国	协定税率													特惠税率						
			东盟统一	亚太5国	智利	巴基斯坦	新加坡	新西兰	秘鲁	哥达	香港	澳门	台湾	瑞士	冰岛	亚太2国	老挝	柬埔寨	缅甸	LDC1	LDC2	LDC3
73023000	道岔尖轨、辙叉、尖轨拉杆	8	0		0	5		0	0	0				4.8	0					0	0	0
73024000	钢铁制鱼尾板、钢轨垫板	7	0		0	5		0	0	0				4.2	0					0	0	0
73029010	钢铁轨枕	6	0	5.1	0	0		0	0	0				3.6	0					0	0	0
73029090	其他铁道电车道铺轨用钢铁材料	7	0	6	0	5		0	0	0				5.6	0					0	0	0
73030010	内径>500mm的铸铁圆型截面管	4	0		0	0		0	0	0				0	0					0	0	0
73030090	其他铸铁管及空心异型材	4	0		0	0		0	0	0				0	0					0	0	0
73041110	外径大于等于215.9毫米，但不超过406.4毫米的不锈钢制石油或天然气套管	5	0		0	0		0	0	0				0	0					0	0	0
73041120	外径大于114.3毫米，但小于215.9毫米的不锈钢制石油或天然气套管	5	0		0	0		0	0	0				0	0					0	0	0
73041130	外径不超过114.3毫米的不锈钢制石油或天然气套管	5	0		0	0		0	0	0				0	0					0	0	0
73041190	其他不锈钢制石油或天然气套管	5	0		0	0		0	0	0				0	0					0	0	0
73041910	外径大于等于215.9毫米，但不超过406.4毫米的非不锈钢制石油或天然气套管	5	0		0	0		0	0	0				0	0					0	0	0
73041920	外径大于114.3毫米，但小于215.9毫米的非不锈钢制石油或天然气套管	5	0		0	0		0	0	0				0	0					0	0	0
73041930	外径不超过114.3毫米的非不锈钢制石油或天然气套管	5	0		0	0		0	0	0				0	0					0	0	0
73041990	其他非不锈钢制石油或天然气套管	5	0		0	0		0	0	0				0	0					0	0	0
73042210	外径不超过168.3毫米的不锈钢制钻管	4	0		0	0		0	0	0				0	0					0	0	0
73042290	其他不锈钢制钻管	4	0		0	0		0	0	0				0	0					0	0	0
73042310	外径不超过168.3毫米的非不锈钢制钻管	4	0		0	0		0	0	0				0	0					0	0	0
73042390	其他非不锈钢制钻管	4	0		0	0		0	0	0				0	0					0	0	0
73042400	其他不锈钢制钻探石油用天然气套管、导管	4	0	2	0	0		0	0	0				0	0					0	0	0
73042910	屈服强度小于552兆帕的钻探石油及天然气用的套管、导管及钻管	4	0	2	0	0		0	0	0				0	0					0	0	0
73042920	屈服强度大于等于552兆帕，但小于758兆帕的钻探石油及天然气用的套管、导管及钻管	4	0	2	0	0		0	0	0				0	0					0	0	0
73042930	屈服强度大于等于758兆帕的钻探石油及天然气用的套管、导管及钻管	4	0	2	0	0		0	0	0				0	0					0	0	0
73043110	冷轧的钢铁制无缝锅炉管	4	0		0	0		0	0	0				0	0					0	0	0
73043120	冷轧的铁制无缝地质钻管、套管	8	0		0	5		0	0	0				4.8	0					0	0	0
73043190	其他冷轧的铁制无缝圆形截面管	4	0		0	0		0	0	0				2.4	0					0	0	0
73043910	非冷轧的铁制无缝锅炉管	4	0		0	0		0	0	0	0			0	0					0	0	0
73043920	非冷轧的铁制无缝地质钻管套管	5	0		0	0		0	0	0	0			0	0					0	0	0
73043990	非冷轧的铁制其他无缝管	4	0		0	0		0	0	0	0			0	0					0	0	0
73044110	冷轧的不锈钢制无缝锅炉管	10	0		0	5	0	0	0	0				6	0					0	0	
73044190	冷轧的不锈钢制的其他无缝管	10	0		0	5	0	0	0	0				6	0					0	0	
73044910	非冷轧的不锈钢制无缝锅炉管	10	0		0	5	0	0	0	0				6	0					0	0	
73044990	非冷轧的不锈钢制其他无缝管	10	0		0	5	0	0	0	0				6	0					0	0	
73045110	冷轧的其他合金钢无缝锅炉管	4	0		0	0		0	0	0				0	0					0	0	0
73045120	冷轧的其他合金钢无缝地质钻套管	4	0		0	0		0	0	0				0	0					0	0	0
73045190	冷轧的其他合金钢制其他无缝管	4	0		0	0		0	0	0				2.4	0					0	0	0
73045910	非冷轧其他合金钢无缝锅炉管	4	0		0	0		0	0	0				0	0					0	0	0
73045920	非冷轧其他合金钢无缝地质钻套管	4	0		0	0		0	0	0				0	0					0	0	0
73045990	非冷轧其他合金钢制无缝圆形截面	4	0		0	0		0	0	0				0	0					0	0	0
73049000	未列名无缝钢铁管及空心异型材	4	0		0	0		0	0	0				0	0					0	0	0
73051100	纵向埋弧焊接石油、天然气粗钢管	7	0		0	5		0	0	0				4.2	0					0	0	0
73051200	其他纵向焊接石油、天然气粗钢管	3	0		0	0		0	0	0				0	0					0	0	0
73051900	其他石油、天然气粗钢管	7	0		0	5		0	0	0				4.2	0					0	0	0
73052000	其他钻探石油、天然气用粗套管	7	0		0	5		0	0	0				4.2	0					0	0	0
73053100	纵向焊接的其他粗钢管	6	0		0	5		0	0	0				3.6	0					0	0	0
73053900	其他方法焊接其他粗钢铁管	6	0		0	5		0	0	0				3.6	0					0	0	0
73059000	未列名圆形截面粗钢铁管	6	0		0	5		0	0	0				3.6	0					0	0	0

税则号列	货品名称	最惠国	协定税率													特惠税率						
			东盟统一	亚太5国	智利	巴基斯坦	新加坡	新西兰	秘鲁	哥达	香港	澳门	台湾	瑞士	冰岛	亚太2国	老挝	柬埔寨	缅甸	LDC1	LDC2	LDC3
73061100	不锈钢焊缝石油、天然气管道管	7	0		0	5		0	0	0				4.2	0					0	0	0
73061900	其他石油、天然气管道管	7	0		0	5		0	0	0				4.2	0					0	0	0
73062100	不锈钢焊缝钻探石油天然气用套、导管	3	0		0	0		0	0	0				0	0					0	0	0
73062900	其他钻探石油天然气用套、导管	3	0		0	0		0	0	0				0	0					0	0	0
73063011	壁厚在0.7毫米及以下的外径不超过10毫米的其他铁或非合金钢圆形截面焊缝管	3	0		0	0		0	0	0				0	0					0	0	0
73063019	壁厚在0.7毫米以上外径不超过10毫米的其他铁或非合金钢圆形截面焊缝管	3	0		0	0		0	0	0				0	0					0	0	0
73063090	外径超过10毫米的其他铁或非合金钢圆形截面焊缝管	3	0		0	0		0	0	0				0	0					0	0	0
73064000	不锈钢其他圆形截面细焊缝管	6	0		0	5		0	0	0				3.6	0					0	0	0
73065000	其他合金钢的圆形截面细焊缝管	3	0		0	0		0	0	0				0	0					0	0	0
73066100	矩形或正方形截面的其他焊缝管	3	0		0	0		0	0	0				0	0					0	0	0
73066900	其他非圆形截面的其他焊缝管	3	0		0	0		0	0	0				0	0					0	0	0
73069000	未列名其他钢铁管及空心异型材	6	0		0	5		0	0	0				3.6	0					0	0	0
73071100	无可锻性铸铁制管子附件	5	0		0	0		0	0	0				0	0					0	0	0
73071900	可锻性铸铁及铸钢管子附件	8	0		0	5		0	0	0				6.4	0					0	0	0
73072100	不锈钢制法兰	8.4	0	6.7	0	5		0	0	0				5	0					0	0	0
73072200	不锈钢制螺纹肘管、弯管、管套	8.4	0		0	5		0	0	0	0			5	0					0	0	0
73072300	不锈钢制对焊件	8.4	0		0	5		0	0	0				5	0					0	0	0
73072900	不锈钢制其他管子附件	8.4	0		0	5		0	0	0	0			6.7	0					0	0	0
73079100	未列名钢铁制法兰	7	0		0	5		0	0	0				4.2	0					0	0	0
73079200	未列名钢铁制螺纹肘管、弯管、管套	4	0		0	0		0	0	0				2.4	0					0	0	0
73079300	未列名钢铁制对焊件	7	0		0	5		0	0	0				4.2	0					0	0	0
73079900	未列名钢铁制其他管子附件	4	0		0	0		0	0	0				2.4	0					0	0	0
73081000	钢铁制桥梁及桥梁体段	8	0		0	0		0	0	0				4.8	0					0	0	0
73082000	钢铁制塔楼及格构杆	8.4	0		0	0		0	0	0				5	0					0	0	0
73083000	钢铁制门窗及其框架、门槛	10	0		0	0	0	0	0	0	0	0		6	0					0	0	0
73084000	钢铁制脚手架模板坑凳用支柱及类	8.4	0		0	0		0	0	0				5	0					0	0	0
73089000	其他钢铁结构体及部件	4	0		0	0		0	0	0	0			2.4	0					0	0	0
73090000	容积>300L钢铁制盛物容器	10.5	0		0	5	0	0	4.2	0				8.4	0					0	0	0
73101000	容积50-300L钢铁制盛物容器	10.5	0		0	5	0	0	4.2	0	0			8.4	0					0	0	0
73102110	易拉罐及罐体	17.5	0		0	14	0	0	7	0	0			14	0					0	0	
73102190	其他容积在50升以下焊边或卷边接合的罐	17.5	0		0	14	0	0	7	0	0			14	0					0	0	
73102910	易拉罐及罐体	17.5	0		0	14	0	0	7	0	0			14.6	0					0	0	0
73102990	其他盛装物料用的钢铁柜、桶、罐、听、盒及类似容器(装压缩气体或液化气体的除外),容积不超过300升,不论是否衬里或隔热,但无机械或热力装置	17.5	0		0	14	0	0	7	0	0			14.6	0					0	0	0
73110010	装压缩或液化气的钢铁容器	17.5	0		0	14	0	0	7	0	0			14	0					0	0	
73110090	其他装压缩或液化气的容器	8	0		0	5		0	0	0	0			4.8	0					0	0	
73121000	非绝缘的钢铁绞股线、绳、缆	4	0		0	0		0	0	0				2.4	0					0	0	
73129000	非绝缘钢铁编带、吊索及类似品	4	0		0	0		0	0	0				2.4	0					0	0	0
73130000	带刺钢铁丝、围篱用钢铁绞带	7	0	6.3	0	5		0	0	0				4.2	0					0	0	0
73141200	不锈钢制的机器用环形带	12	0		0	6	0	0	0	0				9.2	0					0	0	0
73141400	不锈钢制的机织品	12	0		0	6	0	0	0	0				0	0					0	0	0
73141900	其他钢铁丝制机织品	7	0		0	3.5		0	0	0					0					0	0	0
73142000	交点焊接的粗钢铁丝网、篱及格栅	7	0		0	5		0	0	0	0			4.2	0					0	0	0
73143100	交点焊接的镀或涂锌细钢铁丝网	7	0		0	5		0	0	0	0			4.2	0					0	0	0
73143900	交点焊接的其他细钢铁丝网、篱	7	0		0	5		0	0	0	0			4.2	0					0	0	0
73144100	其他镀锌的钢铁丝网、篱及格栅	8	0	6	0	5		0	0	0				4.8	0					0	0	0
73144200	其他涂塑的钢铁丝网、篱及格栅	8	0		0	5		0	0	0				6.4	0					0	0	0
73144900	其他钢铁丝网、篱及格栅	8	0		0	5		0	0	0				6.4	0					0	0	0
73145000	网眼钢铁板	8	0		0	5		0	0	0	0			4.8	0					0	0	0
73151110	自行车滚子链	12	0		0	6	0	0	0	0	0			9.6	0					0	0	
73151120	摩托车滚子链	12	0		0	6	0	0	0	0	0			9.6	0					0	0	
73151190	其他滚子链	12	0		0	6	0	0	0	0	0			9.6	0					0	0	

税则号列	货品名称	最惠国	协定税率													特惠税率						
			东盟统一	亚太5国	智利	巴基斯坦	新加坡	新西兰	秘鲁	哥达	香港	澳门	台湾	瑞士	冰岛	亚太2国	老挝	柬埔寨	缅甸	LDC1	LDC2	LDC3
73151200	其他铰接链	12	0		0	6	0	0	0	0				9.6	0					0	0	
73151900	铰接链零件	12	0		0	6	0	0	0	0				9.6	0					0	0	
73152000	防滑链	12	0		0	6	0	0	0	0				9.6	0					0	0	
73158100	日字环节链	12	0		0	6	0	0	0	0				9.6	0					0	0	
73158200	其他焊接链	12	0		0	6	0	0	0	0				9.6	0					0	0	0
73158900	未列名链	12	0		0	6	0	0	4.8	0				9.6	0					0	0	
73159000	非铰接链零件	10	0		0	5		0	0	0				6	0					0	0	
73160000	钢铁锚、多爪锚及其零件	10	0		0	5		0	0	0				6	0					0	0	
73170000	铁钉、图钉、平头钉及类似品	10	0		0	5		0	4	0				6	0					0	0	
73181100	方头螺钉	10	0		0	5		0	4	0				6	0					0	0	
73181200	其他木螺钉	10	0		0	5		0	4	0				6	0					0	0	
73181300	钩头螺钉及环头螺钉	10	0		0	5		0	0	0				6	0					0	0	
73181400	自攻螺钉	10	0		0	5	0	0	4	0				8	0					0	0	
73181510	抗拉强度在800兆帕及以上的螺钉及螺栓,不论是否带有螺母或垫圈	8	0	4	0	0		0	0	0	0			6.4	0					0	0	0
73181590	其他螺钉及螺栓	8	0	4	0	0		0	0	0	0			6.4	0					0	0	0
73181600	螺母	8	0		0	5		0	0	0				6.4	0					0	0	0
73181900	未列名螺纹制品	5	0		0	0		0	0	0				3	0					0	0	0
73182100	弹簧垫圈及其他防松垫圈	10	0		0	5	0	0	0	0	0			6	0					0	0	0
73182200	其他垫圈	10	0		0	5	0	0	4	0				6	0					0	0	0
73182300	铆钉	10	0		0	5	0	0	0	0	0			6	0					0	0	0
73182400	销及开尾销	10	0		0	5	0	0	0	0				8	0					0	0	0
73182900	其他无螺纹紧固件	10	0		0	5	0	0	0	0				6	0					0	0	0
73194010	安全别针	10	0		0	5		0	0	0		0		6	0					0	0	0
73194090	其他别针	10	0		0	5		0	0	0				6	0					0	0	
73199000	未列名钢铁制针及类似品	10	0		0	5		0	4	0				8	0					0	0	0
73201010	铁道车辆用片簧及簧片	6	0		0	5		0	0	0				3.6	0					0	0	0
73201020	汽车用片簧及弹簧	10	0		0	5		0	0	0				6	0					0	0	0
73201090	其他片簧及簧片	10	0		0	5	0	0	0	0				8	0					0	0	0
73202010	铁道车辆用螺旋弹簧	6	0		0	5		0	0	0				3.6	0					0	0	0
73202090	其他螺旋弹簧	10	0	8.5	0	5	0	0	0	0				8	0					0	0	0
73209010	铁道车辆用其他弹簧	6	0		0	5		0	0	0				3.6	0					0	0	0
73209090	其他弹簧	12	0		0	6	0	0	0	0				9.6	0					0	0	0
73211100	可使用气体燃料的家用炉灶	15	0		0	12	0	0	6	0				12	0					0	0	
73211210	煤油炉	21	0		0		0	0	8.4	0				16.8	0					0	0	
73211290	其他使用液体燃料的家用炉灶	21	0		0		0	0	8.4	0				16.8	0					0	0	
73211900	其他炊事用具及加热板	21	0		0		0	0	8.4	0				16.8	0					0	0	
73218100	可使用气体燃料的其他家用器具	23	0	13.8	0	11.5	0	0	9.2	0				18.4	0					0	0	
73218200	使用液体燃料的其他家用器具	21	0		0		0	0	8.4	0				16.8	0					0	0	
73218900	其他非电热家用器具	21	0		0		0	0	8.4	0				16.8	0					0	0	
73219000	非电热家用器具零件	12	0	9.6	0	5	0	0	4.8	0				9.6	0					0	0	0
73221100	非电热铸铁制集中供暖用散热器	21	0		0		0	0	8.4	0				16.8	0					0	0	
73221900	非电热钢制集中供暖用散热器	21	0		0		0	0	8.4	0				16.8	0					0	0	
73229000	非电热空气加热器、暖气分布器	20	0		0		0	0	8	0				16	0					0	0	0
73231000	钢铁丝绒、擦锅器、洗擦用块垫等	14	0		0	11.2	0	0	5.6	0				11.2	0					0	0	
73239100	餐桌、厨房等家用铸铁制器具	20	0		0		0	0	8	0				16	0					0	0	
73239200	餐桌、厨房等家用铸铁制搪瓷器	20	0		0		0	0	8	0				16	0					0	0	
73239300	餐桌、厨房等家用不锈钢器具	12	0	8.4	0	5	0	0	0	0	0	0		9.6	0					0	0	0
73239410	钢铁制搪瓷面盆	20	0		0		0	0	8	0				16	0					0	0	
73239420	钢铁制搪瓷烧锅	20	0		0		0	0	8	0				16	0					0	0	
73239490	其他餐桌、厨房等家用钢铁制搪瓷器	20	0		0		0	0	8	0				16	0					0	0	
73239900	其他餐桌、厨房等用钢铁器具	20	0		0		0	0	8	0				16	0					0	0	
73241000	不锈钢制洗涤槽及脸盆	18	0		0		0	0	7.2	0	0			14.4	0					0	0	0
73242100	铸铁制浴缸	10	0		0	5	0	0	4	0				6	0					0	0	
73242900	其他钢铁制浴缸	30	0		0		0	0	12	0				24	0					0	0	
73249000	其他钢铁制卫生器具及零件	25	0		0		0	0	10	0				20	0					0	0	
73251010	工业用无可锻性制品	7	0		0	5		0	0	0				4.2						0	0	0
73251090	其他无可锻性铸铁制品	20	0		0		0	0	8	0				16	0					0	0	
73259100	可锻性铸铁及铸钢研磨机的研磨球	10.5	0		0	5	0	0	4.2	0				8.4	0					0	0	
73259910	工业用未列名可锻性铸铁制品	10.5	0	8.9	0	5	0	0	4.2	0				8.4	0					0	0	

税则号列	货品名称	最惠国	协定税率												特惠税率						
			东盟统一	亚太5国	智利	巴基斯坦	新加坡	新西兰	秘鲁	哥达	香港	澳门	台湾	瑞士	冰岛	亚太2国	老挝	柬埔寨	缅甸	LDC1	LDC2	LDC3
73259990	非工业用未列名可锻性铸铁制品	20	0	12	0	10	0	0	8	0				16	0					0	0	
73261100	钢铁制研磨机用研磨球及类似品	10.5	0		0	5	0	0	4.2	0				8.4	0					0	0	
73261910	工业用未列名钢铁制品	10.5	0		0	5	0	0	4.2	0				8.4	0					0	0	
73261990	非工业用未列名钢铁制品	20	0		0		0	0	8	0				16	0					0	0	
73262010	工业用钢铁丝制品	10	0	5	0	5		0	0	0				6	0					0	0	
73262090	非工业用钢铁丝制品	18	0	12.6	0	9	0	0	7.2	0				14.4	0					0	0	
73269011	钢铁纤维及其制品	10.5	0	8.9	0	5	0	0	4.2	0	0			8.4	0					0	0	0
73269019	其他工业用钢铁制品	10.5	0	8.9	0	5	0	0	4.2	0	0			8.4	0					0	0	0
73269090	其他非工业用钢铁制品	8	0	6.8	0	5	0	0	0	0	0			6.4	0					0	0	0
74010000	铜锍、沉积铜(泥铜)	2	0		0	0		0	0	0				0	0		0			0	0	0
74020000	未精炼铜、电解精炼用铜阳极	2	0		0	0		0		0				0	0					0	0	0
74031111	按重量计铜含量超过 99.9935% 的阴极精炼铜	2	0		0	0		0	0	0				0	0					0	0	0
74031119	其他阴极精炼铜	2	0		0	0		0	0	0				0	0					0	0	0
74031190	精炼铜阴极型材	2	0		0	0		0	0	0				0	0					0	0	0
74031200	精炼铜的线锭	2	0		0	0		0	0	0				1.6	0					0	0	0
74031300	精炼铜的坯段	2	0		0	0		0	0	0				0	0					0	0	0
74031900	其他未锻轧的精炼铜	2	0		0	0		0	0	0				0	0					0	0	0
74032100	未锻轧的铜锌合金(黄铜)	1	0		0	0		0	0	0		0		0	0					0	0	0
74032200	未锻轧的铜锡合金(青铜)	1	0		0	0		0	0	0				0	0					0	0	0
74032900	未锻轧的其他铜合金	1	0		0	0		0	0	0				0	0					0	0	0
74040000	铜废碎料	1.5	0		0	0		0		0	0			0	0		0			0	0	0
74050000	铜母合金	4	0		0	0		0	0	0	0			0	0					0	0	
74061010	精炼铜制非片状粉末	3	0		0	0		0	0	0				0	0					0	0	0
74061020	白铜或德银制非片状粉末	6	0		0	5		0	0	0				3.6	0					0	0	0
74061030	铜锌合金(黄铜)制非片状铜粉粉末	6	0		0	5		0	0	0				3.6	0					0	0	0
74061040	铜锡合金(青铜)制非片状铜粉粉末	6	0		0	5		0	0	0				3.6	0					0	0	0
74061090	其他铜合金制非片状粉末	6	0		0	5		0	0	0				3.6	0					0	0	0
74062010	精炼铜制片状粉末	4	0		0	0		0	0	0				0	0					0	0	0
74062020	白铜或德银制片状粉末	6	0		0	5		0	0	0				3.6	0					0	0	0
74062090	其他铜合金制片状粉末	6	0		0	5		0	0	0				3.6	0					0	0	0
74071010	铬锆铜制条、杆及型材及异型材	4	0		0	0		0	0	0			0	2.4	0					0	0	0
74071090	其他精炼铜条、杆及型材及异型材	4	0		0	0		0	0	0			0	2.4	0					0	0	0
74072111	直线度不大于 0.5 毫米/米铜锌合金条、杆	7	0		0	5		0	0	0		0	0	5.6	0					0	0	0
74072119	其他铜锌合金条、杆	7	0		0	5		0	0	0		0	0	5.6	0					0	0	0
74072190	其他黄铜条、杆及型材及异型材	7	0		0	5		0	0	0		0	0	5.6	0					0	0	0
74072900	其他铜合金条杆、型材及异型材	7	0		0	5		0	0	0			0	5.6	0					0	0	0
74081100	最大截面尺寸 >6mm 的精炼铜丝	4	0	2.8	0	0		0	1.6	0			0	0	0					0	0	0
74081900	截面尺寸≤6mm 的精炼铜丝	4	0	3.4	0	0		0	0	0	0		0	2.4	0					0	0	0
74082100	黄铜丝	7	0		0	5		0	0	0			0	4.2	0					0	0	0
74082210	铜镍锌铅合金(加铅德银)丝	8	0		0	5		0	0	0				4.8	0					0	0	0
74082290	其他白铜丝或德银(铜镍锌合金)丝	8	0		0	5		0	0	0				4.8	0					0	0	0
74082900	其他铜合金丝	7	0		0	5		0	0	0				4.2	0					0	0	0
74091110	含氧量不超过 10PPM,厚度超过 0.15mm 的盘卷精炼铜板、片、带	4	0		0	0		0	0	0				0	0					0	0	0
74091190	厚度超过 0.15mm 的其他盘卷精炼铜板、片、带	4	0		0	0		0	0	0				0	0					0	0	0
74091900	其他精炼铜板、片、带	4	0		0	0		0	0	0			0	2.4	0					0	0	0
74092100	成卷的黄铜板、片、带	7	0		0	5		0	0	0	0		0	5.6	0					0	0	0
74092900	其他黄铜板、片、带	7	0		0	5		0	0	0	0		0	4.2	0					0	0	0
74093100	成卷的青铜板、片、带	7	0		0	5		0	0	0			0	4.2	0					0	0	0
74093900	其他青铜板、片、带	7	0		0	5		0	0	0			0	4.2	0					0	0	0
74094000	白铜或德银制板、片、带	7	0		0	5		0	0	0			0	4.2	0					0	0	0
74099000	其他铜合金板、片、带	7	0		0	5		0	0	0	0		0	4.2	0					0	0	0
74101100	无衬背的精炼铜箔	4	0	2.8	0	0		0	0	0	0		0	2.4	0					0	0	
74101210	无衬背的白铜或德银铜箔	7	0		0	5		0	0	0			0	4.2	0					0	0	
74101290	无衬背的其他铜合金箔	7	0		0	5		0	0	0			0	4.2	0					0	0	
74102110	印刷电路用覆铜板	4	0	3.4	0	0		0	0	0	0	0	0	0	0					0	0	
74102190	有衬背的其他精炼铜箔	4	0	3.4	0	0		0	0	0	0	0	0	0	0					0	0	

税则号列	货品名称	最惠国	协定税率													特惠税率						
			东盟统一	亚太5国	智利	巴基斯坦	新加坡	新西兰	秘鲁	哥达	香港	澳门	台湾	瑞士	冰岛	亚太2国	老挝	柬埔寨	缅甸	LDC1	LDC2	LDC3
74102210	有衬背的白铜或德银铜箔	7	0		0	5		0	0	0				4.2	0					0	0	
74102290	有衬背的其他铜合金箔	7	0		0	5		0	0	0				4.2	0					0	0	
74111011	外径小于等于25mm的带有内(外)螺纹或翅片的精炼铜管	4	0	2.8	0	0		0	0	0				0	0					0	0	0
74111019	外径小于等于25mm的其他精炼铜管	4	0	2.8	0	0		0	0	0				0	0					0	0	0
74111020	外径超过70mm的精炼铜管	4	0	2.8	0	0		0	0	0				0	0					0	0	0
74111090	其他精炼铜管	4	0	2.8	0	0		0	0	0				3.2	0					0	0	0
74112110	盘卷黄铜管	7	0		0	5		0	0	0	0			4.2	0					0	0	0
74112190	铜锌合金(黄铜)管	7	0		0	5		0	0	0	0			4.2	0					0	0	0
74112200	白铜或德银管	7	0		0	5		0	0	0				4.2	0					0	0	0
74112900	其他铜合金管	7	0		0	5		0	0	0				4.2	0					0	0	0
74121000	精炼铜管子附件	4	0		0	0		0	0	0				3.2	0					0	0	0
74122010	白铜或德银管子配件	7	0	6	0	5		0	0	0				5.6	0					0	0	0
74122090	其他铜合金管子配件	7	0	6	0	5		0	0	0				4.2	0					0	0	0
74130000	非绝缘的铜丝绞股线、缆、编带等	5	0		0	0		0	0	0				3	0					0	0	0
74151000	铜钉、平头钉、图钉U型钉及类似品	8	0		0	5		0	0	0				4.8	0					0	0	0
74152100	铜垫圈(包括弹簧垫圈)	10	0		0	5	0	0	0	0	0			6	0					0	0	0
74152900	铜制其他无螺纹制品	10	0		0	5	0	0	0	0	0			6	0					0	0	0
74153310	铜制木螺钉	8	0		0	5		0	0	0	0			4.8	0					0	0	0
74153390	铜制其他螺钉螺栓螺母	8	0		0	5		0	0	0	0			4.8	0					0	0	0
74153900	其他铜制螺纹制品	10	0		0	5		0	0	0	0			6	0					0	0	0
74181010	擦锅器及洗刷擦光用的块垫、手套	18	0		0	14.4	0	0	7.2	0				14.4	0					0	0	0
74181020	非电热的铜制家用烹饪、供暖器具	20	0		0		0	0	8	0				16	0					0	0	
74181090	餐桌厨房等家用铜制器具及其零件	18	0		0	14.4	0	0	7.2	0				14.4	0					0	0	0
74182000	铜制卫生器具及其零件	18	0		0		0	0	7.2	0				14.4	0					0	0	0
74191000	铜链条及其零件	14	0		0	11.2	0	0	0	0	0			11.2	0					0	0	
74199110	工业用铸造、模压、冲压其他铜制品	10	0		0	5	0	0	0	0				6	6.7					0	0	0
74199190	非工业用铸造、模压、冲压铜制品	20	0		0		0	0	8	0				16	0					0	0	
74199920	铜弹簧	10	0		0	5		0	0	0				8	0					0	0	
74199930	铜丝制的布(包括环形带)	7	0		0	5.6		0	0	0				4.2	0					0	0	0
74199940	铜丝制的网、格删、网眼和铜板	8	0		0	6.4		0	0	0				4.8	0					0	0	0
74199950	非电热的铜制家用供暖器及其零件	20	0		0		0	0	8	0				16	0					0	0	
74199991	工业用其他铜制品	10	0	8.5	0	5	0	0	0	0				8						0	0	0
74199999	非工业用其他铜制品	20	0	17	0	16	0	0	8	0				16	0					0	0	0
75011000	镍锍	3	0		0	0		0	0	0				0	0					0	0	0
75012010	镍湿法冶炼中间品	3	0		0	0		0	0	0				0	0					0	0	0
75012090	氧化镍烧结物、镍的其他中间产品	3	0		0	0		0	0	0				0	0					0	0	0
75021010	按重量计镍、钴总量在99.99%及以上的,但钴含量不超过0.005%的非合金镍	3	0		0	0		0	0	0				0	0					0	0	0
75021090	其他非合金镍	3	0		0	0		0	0	0				0	0					0	0	0
75022000	未锻轧镍合金	3	0		0	0		0	0	0				0	0					0	0	0
75030000	镍废碎料	1.5	0		0	0		0	0	0				0	0					0	0	0
75040010	非合金镍粉及片状粉末	4	0		0	0		0	0	0				0	0					0	0	
75040020	合金镍粉及片状粉末	4	0		0	0		0	0	0				0	0					0	0	
75051100	纯镍条、杆、型材及异型材	6	0		0	5		0	0	0				3.6	0					0	0	0
75051200	合金镍条、杆、型材及异型材	6	0		0	5		0	0	0				3.6	0					0	0	0
75052100	纯镍丝	6	0		0	5		0	0	0				4.8	0					0	0	0
75052200	镍合金丝	6	0		0	5		0	0	0				3.6	0					0	0	0
75061000	纯镍板、片、带、箔	6	0		0	5		0	0	0				3.6	0					0	0	
75062000	镍合金板、片、带、箔	6	0		0	5		0	0	0	0			3.6	0					0	0	
75071100	纯镍管	6	0		0	5		0	0	0				4.6	0					0	0	
75071200	镍合金管	6	0		0	5		0	0	0				3.6	0					0	0	
75072000	镍及镍合金管子附件	6	0		0	5		0	0	0				3.6	0					0	0	
75081010	镍丝制的布	6	0		0	5		0	0	0				3.6	0					0	0	
75081080	工业用镍丝制的网及格栅	6	0		0	5		0	0	0				3.6	0					0	0	
75081090	其他镍丝制的网及格栅	6	0		0	5		0	0	0				3.6	0					0	0	
75089010	电镀用镍阳极	4	0		0	0		0	0	0				0	0					0	0	

税则号列	货品名称	最惠国	协定税率													特惠税率						
			东盟统一	亚太5国	智利	巴基斯坦	新加坡	新西兰	秘鲁	哥达	香港	澳门	台湾	瑞士	冰岛	亚太2国	老挝	柬埔寨	缅甸	LDC1	LDC2	LDC3
75089080	其他工业用镍制品	6	0		0	5		0	0	0				3.6	0					0	0	
75089090	其他非工业用镍制品	6	0		0	5		0	0	0				3.6	0					0	0	
76011010	按重量计含铝量在99.95%及以上的未煅轧非铝合金	5	0		0	0		0	0	0	0			0	0					0	0	0
76011090	其他非煅轧非铝合金	5	0		0	0		0	0	0	0			0	0					0	0	0
76012000	未锻轧铝合金	7	0	6	0	5		0	0	0		0		4.2	0					0	0	0
76020000	铝废碎料	1.5	0		0	0		0		0	0			0	0					0	0	0
76031000	非片状铝粉	6	0		0	5		0	0	0				3.6	0					0	0	0
76032000	片状铝粉末	7	0		0	5		0	0	0				4.2	0					0	0	0
76041010	非合金铝条、杆	5	0		0	0		0	0	0				0	0					0	0	0
76041090	非合金铝型材及异形材	5	0		0	0		0	0	0				0	0					0	0	0
76042100	铝合金制空心异型材	5	0		0	0		0	0	0				0	0					0	0	0
76042910	铝合金条、杆	5	0	3.5	0	0		0	0	0				3	0					0	0	0
76042990	铝合金型材及异形材	5	0	3.5	0	0		0	0	0				3	0					0	0	0
76051100	纯铝制的粗丝	8	0		0	5		0	0	0				4.8	0					0	0	
76051900	纯铝制的细丝	8	0	6.8	0	5		0	0	0	0			4.8	0					0	0	
76052100	铝合金制的粗丝	8	0		0	5		0	0	0				4.8	0					0	0	
76052900	铝合金制的细丝	8	0		0	5		0	0	0				4.8	0					0	0	
76061121	0.3mm≤厚度<0.36mm的非合金铝与塑料复合的矩形板片带	6	0	4.2	0	0		0	0	0				3.6	0					0	0	0
76061129	其他0.3mm≤厚度<0.36mm的非合金铝制矩形铝板片带	6	0	4.2	0	0		0	0	0				3.6	0					0	0	0
76061191	其他非合金铝与塑料复合的矩形板片带	6	0	4.2	0	0		0	0	0	0		0	3.6	0					0	0	0
76061199	纯铝制矩形的其他板、片及带	6	0	4.2	0	0		0	0	0	0		0	3.6	0					0	0	0
76061220	厚度<0.28mm的铝合金制矩形铝板片带	6	0	4.2	0	0		0	0	0	0		0	3.6	0					0	0	0
76061230	0.28mm≤厚度≤0.35mm的铝合金制矩形铝板片带	6	0	4.2	0	0		0	0	0	0		0	3.6	0					0	0	0
76061251	0.35mm<厚度≤0.4mm的铝合金与塑料复合的矩形板片带	6	0	4.2	0	0		0	0	0	0			4.8	0					0	0	0
76061259	其他0.35mm<厚度≤0.4mm的铝合金制矩形铝板片带	6	0	4.2	0	0		0	0	0	0			4.8	0					0	0	0
76061290	厚度>0.4mm的铝合金制矩形铝板片带	6	0	4.2	0	0		0	0	0	0			4.8	0					0	0	0
76069100	纯铝制非矩形的板、片及带	6	0		0	5		0	0	0	0		0	3.6	0					0	0	0
76069200	铝合金制非矩形的板、片及带	10	0		0	5	0	0	0	0	0		0	6	0					0	0	0
76071110	厚度不超过0.007毫米的无衬背铝箔	6	0	5.7	0	5		0	0	0				4.8	0					0	0	
76071120	厚度大于0.007毫米,但不超过0.01毫米的无衬背铝箔	6	0	5.7	0	5		0	0	0				3.6	0					0	0	
76071190	轧制后未进一步加工的无衬背铝箔	6	0	5.7	0	5		0	0	0			0	3.6						0	0	
76071900	其他无衬背铝箔	6	0	5.1	0	5		0	0	0			0	3.6						0	0	
76072000	有衬背铝箔	6	0		0	5		0	0	0	0		0	4.8						0	0	
76081000	纯铝管	8	0		0	5		0	0	0				4.8	0					0	0	0
76082010	外径不超过10厘米的铝合金管	8	0		0	5		0	0	0				4.8	0					0	0	0
76082091	外径超过10厘米壁厚不超过25毫米铝合金管	8	0		0	5		0	0	0				4.8	0					0	0	0
76082099	其他铝合金管	8	0		0	5		0	0	0				4.8	0					0	0	0
76090000	铝制管子附件	8	0		0	5		0	0	0				4.8	0					0	0	0
76101000	铝制门窗及其框架、门槛	25	0		0		0	0	10	0		0		20	0					0	0	
76109000	其他铝制结构体及其部件	6	0		0	5		0	0	0				3.6	0					0	0	0
76110000	容积>300L的铝制囤、罐等容器	12	0		0	6	0	0	0	0				9.6	0					0	0	
76121000	铝制软管容器	12	0		0	6	0	0	4.8	0				9.6	0					0	0	0
76129010	铝制易拉罐及罐体	30	0		0		0	0	12	0				24	0					0	0	
76129090	容积≤300L的铝制囤、罐等容器	12	0		0	6	0	0	4.8	0				9.6	0					0	0	0
76130010	零售包装装压缩、液化气体铝容器	12	0		0	6	0	0	0	0				9.2	0					0	0	
76130090	非零售装装压缩、液化气体铝容器	6	0		0	5		0	0	0				3.6	0					0	0	
76141000	带钢芯的铝制绞股线、缆、编带	6	0		0	5		0	0	0				3.6	0					0	0	0
76149000	不带钢芯的铝制绞股线、缆、编带	6	0		0	5		0	0	0				3.6	0					0	0	0
76151010	擦锅器及洗刷擦光用的块垫、手套	18	0		0	14.4	0	0	7.2	0				14.4	0					0	0	0

税则号列	货品名称	最惠国	协定税率 东盟统一	亚太5国	智利	巴基斯坦	新加坡	新西兰	秘鲁	哥达	香港	澳门	台湾	瑞士	冰岛	特惠税率 亚太2国	老挝	柬埔寨	缅甸	LDC1	LDC2	LDC3
76151090	餐桌厨房等家用铝制器具及其零件	15	0		0	12	0	0	6	0				12	0					0	0	0
76152000	铝制卫生器具及其零件	18	0		0	14.4	0	0	7.2	0				14.4	0					0	0	
76161000	铝钉、螺钉、螺母、垫圈等紧固件	10	0	8.5	0	5	0	0	0	0	0			6	0					0	0	0
76169100	铝丝制的布、网、篱及格栅	10	0		0		0	0	0	0				6	0					0	0	0
76169910	其他工业用铝制品	10	0	8.5	0	5	0	0	4	0				8	0					0	0	0
76169990	其他非工业用铝制品	15	0	12.8	0	7.5	0	0	6	0				12	0					0	0	0
78011000	未锻轧精炼铅	3	0		0	0		0	0	0				0	0					0	0	0
78019100	未锻轧铅锑合金	3	0		0	0		0	0	0				0	0					0	0	0
78019900	未锻轧的其他铅合金	3	0		0	0		0	0	0				0	0					0	0	0
78020000	铅废碎料	1.5	0		0	0		0	0	0				0	0					0	0	
78041100	铅片、带及厚度≤0.2mm的箔	6	0		0	5		0	0	0				3.6	0					0	0	0
78041900	铅及铅合金板、厚度>0.2mm的箔	6	0		0	5		0	0	0				3.6	0					0	0	0
78042000	铅及铅合金粉末、片状粉末	6	0		0	5		0	0	0				3.6	0					0	0	0
78060010	铅及铅合金条、杆、丝、型材	6	0		0	5		0	0	0				3.6	0					0	0	0
78060090	其他铅制品	6	0		0	5		0	0	0				3.6	0					0	0	0
79011110	按重量计含锌量在99.995%及以上的未煅轧锌	3	0		0	0		0	0	0				0	0					0	0	0
79011190	含锌量不小于99.99%，并小于99.995%的未煅轧锌	3	0		0	0		0	0	0				0	0					0	0	0
79011200	含锌量<99.99%的未锻轧锌	3	0		0	0		0	0	0				0	0					0	0	0
79012000	未锻轧锌合金	3	0		0	0		0	0	0	0			0	0					0	0	0
79020000	锌废碎料	1.5	0		0	0		0	0	0				0	0					0	0	0
79031000	锌末	6	0		0	5		0	0	0				3.6	0					0	0	0
79039000	锌粉及片状粉末	6	0		0	5		0	0	0				4.8	0					0	0	0
79040000	锌及锌合金条、杆、型材、丝	6	0		0	5		0	0	0				3.6	0					0	0	
79050000	锌板、片、带、箔	6	0		0	5		0	0	0				3.6	0					0	0	0
79070020	锌管及锌制管子附件	6	0		0	5		0	0	0				3.6	0					0	0	0
79070030	电池壳体坯料（锌饼）	6	0		0	5		0	4.2	0				3.6	0					0	0	0
79070090	其他非工业用锌制品	6	0		0	5		0	0	0				3.6	0					0	0	0
80011000	未锻轧非合金锡	3	0		0	0		0	0	0	0			0	0					0	0	0
80012010	锡基巴毕脱合金	3	0		0	0		0	0	0	0			0	0					0	0	0
80012021	按重量计含铅量在0.1%以下的焊锡	3	0		0	0		0	0	0	0	0		0	0					0	0	0
80012029	其他焊锡	3	0		0	0		0	0	0	0	0		0	0					0	0	0
80012090	其他锡合金	3	0		0	0		0	0	0	0			0	0					0	0	0
80020000	锡废碎料	1.5	0		0	0		0	0	0	0			0	0					0	0	
80030000	锡及锡合金条、杆、型材、丝	8	0		0	5		0	0	0	0			4.8	0					0	0	0
80070020	锡及锡合金板、片及带，厚度>0.2mm	8	0		0	5		0	0	0				4.8	0					0	0	
80070030	锡箔、锡粉及片状粉末	8	0		0	5		0	0	0				4.8	0					0	0	
80070040	锡及锡合金管、管子附件	8	0		0	5		0	0	0				6.4	0					0	0	
80070090	其他锡制品	8	0		0	6.4		0	0	0	0			4.8	0					0	0	
81011000	钨粉	6	0		0	5		0	0	0				3.6	0					0	0	
81019400	未锻轧钨	3	0		0	0		0	0	0				2.4	0					0	0	
81019600	钨丝	8	0		0	5		0	0	0				4.8	0					0	0	
81019700	钨废碎料	3	0		0	0		0	0	0				0	0					0	0	
81019910	锻轧钨条、杆、型材；废碎料	5	0		0	0		0	0	0				3	0					0	0	
81019990	其他钨制品	8	0		0	5		0	0	0				4.8	0					0	0	
81021000	钼粉	6	0		0	5		0	0	0				3.6	0					0	0	
81029400	未锻轧钼、钼废碎料	3	0		0	0		0	0	0				0	0					0	0	
81029500	锻轧钼条杆、型材、板片带箔	8	0		0	5		0	0	0				4.8	0					0	0	
81029600	钼丝	8	0		0	5		0	0	0				4.8	0					0	0	
81029700	钼废碎料	3	0		0	0		0	0	0				0	0					0	0	
81029900	钼制品	8	0		0	5		0	0	0				4.8	0					0	0	
81032011	松装密度小于2.2g/cm3的钽粉	6	0		0	5		0	0	0				3.6	0					0	0	
81032019	松装密度大于等于2.2g/cm3的钽粉	6	0		0	5		0	0	0				3.6	0					0	0	
81032090	未锻轧钽	6	0		0	5		0	0	0				3.6	0					0	0	
81033000	钽废碎料	6	0		0	5		0	0	0				3.6	0					0	0	
81039011	直径<0.5mm的钽丝	8	0		0	5		0	0	0				4.8	0					0	0	
81039019	直径≥0.5mm的钽丝	8	0		0	5		0	0	0				4.8	0					0	0	
81039090	其他锻轧钽及其制品	8	0		0	5		0	0	0				4.8	0					0	0	
81041100	含镁量≥99.8%的未锻轧镁	6	0	4.2	0	0		0	0	0				3.6	0					0	0	
81041900	其他未锻轧的镁及镁合金	6	0		0	5		0	0	0				3.6	0					0	0	

税则号列	货品名称	最惠国	协定税率													特惠税率						
			东盟统一	亚太5国	智利	巴基斯坦	新加坡	新西兰	秘鲁	哥达	香港	澳门	台湾	瑞士	冰岛	亚太2国	老挝	柬埔寨	缅甸	LDC1	LDC2	LDC3
81042000	镁废碎料	1.5	0		0	0		0	0	0				0	0					0	0	
81043000	已分级的镁锉屑、车屑、颗粒;粉末	8	0		0	5		0	0	0				4.8	0					0	0	
81049010	锻轧镁	8	0		0	5		0	0	0				4.8	0					0	0	
81049020	镁制品	8.4	0		0	5		0	0	0				5	0					0	0	
81052010	钴湿法冶炼中间品	4	0		0	0		0	0	0				0	0					0	0	0
81052020	未锻轧钴	4	0		0	0		0	0	0				0	0					0	0	0
81052090	钴锍及其他钴冶炼时所得的中间产品、粉末	4	0		0	0		0	0	0				0	0					0	0	0
81053000	钴锍废碎料	4	0		0	0		0	0	0				0	0					0	0	0
81059000	其他钴及制品	8	0		0	5		0	0	0				4.8	0					0	0	0
81060010	未锻轧铋、废碎料、粉末	3	0		0	0		0	0	0				0	0					0	0	
81060090	其他铋及铋制品	8	0		0	5		0	0	0				4.8	0					0	0	
81072000	未锻轧镉、粉末	3	0		0	0		0		0				0	0					0	0	
81073000	镉废碎料	3	0		0	0		0	0	0				0	0					0	0	
81079000	其他镉及镉制品	8	0		0	5		0	0	0				4.8	0					0	0	
81082021	海绵钛	3	0		0	0		0	0	0				0	0					0	0	
81082029	其他未锻轧钛	3	0		0	0		0	0	0				0	0					0	0	
81082030	钛粉末	3	0		0	0		0	0	0				0	0					0	0	
81083000	钛废碎料	3	0		0	0		0	0	0				0	0					0	0	
81089010	钛条、杆、型材及异型材	8	0		0	5		0	0	0				4.8	0					0	0	
81089020	钛丝	8	0		0	5		0	0	0				4.8	0					0	0	
81089031	厚度≤0.8mm 钛板、片、带、箔	8	0		0	5		0	0	0				4.8	0					0	0	
81089032	厚度>0.8mm 钛板、片、带、箔	8	0		0	5		0	0	0				4.8	0					0	0	
81089040	钛管	8	0		0	5		0	0	0				4.8	0					0	0	
81089090	其他钛及钛制品	8	0		0	5		0	0	0				4.8	0					0	0	
81092000	未锻轧锆、粉末	3	0		0	0		0	0	0				0	0					0	0	
81093000	锆废碎料	3	0		0	0		0	0	0				0	0					0	0	
81099000	锻轧锆及锆制品	8	0		0	5		0	0	0				4.8	0					0	0	
81101010	未锻轧锑	3	0		0	0		0	0	0				0	0					0	0	
81101020	锑粉末	3	0		0	0		0	0	0				0	0					0	0	
81102000	锑废碎料	3	0		0	0		0	0	0				0	0					0	0	
81109000	其他锑及锑制品	8	0		0	5		0	0	0				4.8	0					0	0	
81110010	未锻轧锰;锰废碎料;粉末	3	0		0	0		0	0	0				0	0					0	0	0
81110090	其他锰及制品	8	0		0	5		0	0	0				4.8	0					0	0	0
81121200	未锻轧铍、粉末	3	0		0	0		0	0	0				0	0					0	0	0
81121300	铍废碎料	3	0		0	0		0	0	0				0	0					0	0	0
81121900	其他铍及其制品	8	0		0	5		0	0	0				4.8	0					0	0	0
81122100	未锻轧铬、粉末	3	0		0	0		0	0	0				0	0					0	0	0
81122200	铬废碎料	3	0		0	0		0	0	0				0	0					0	0	0
81122900	其他铬制品	3	0		0	0		0	0	0				0	0					0	0	0
81125100	未锻轧铊、粉末	3	0		0	0		0	0	0				0	0					0	0	0
81125200	铊废碎料	3	0		0	0		0	0	0				0	0					0	0	0
81125900	其他铊制品	8	0		0	5		0	0	0				4.8	0					0	0	0
81129210	未锻轧锗	3	0		0	0		0	0	0				0	0					0	0	0
81129220	未锻轧钒	3	0		0	0		0	0	0				0	0					0	0	0
81129230	未锻轧铟、铟废碎料、粉末	3	0		0	0		0	0	0				0	0					0	0	0
81129240	未锻轧铌、铌废碎料、粉末	3	0		0	0		0	0	0				0	0					0	0	0
81129290	未锻轧的未列名贱金属及其制品	3	0		0	0		0	0	0				0	0					0	0	0
81129910	锗及其制品	3	0		0	0		0	0	0				0	0					0	0	0
81129920	钒及其制品	3	0		0	0		0	0	0				0	0					0	0	0
81129930	锻扎铟及其制品	8	0		0	5		0	0	0				4.8	0					0	0	0
81129940	锻扎铌及其制品	8	0		0	5		0	0	0				4.8	0					0	0	0
81129990	锻轧的未列名贱金属及其制品	8	0		0	0		0	0	0				4.8	0					0	0	0
81130010	金属陶瓷颗粒、粉末	8.4	0		0	5		0	0	0			0	5	0					0	0	
81130090	其他金属陶瓷及其制品,包括废碎料	8.4	0		0	5		0	0	0			0	5	0					0	0	
82011000	锹及铲	8	0		0	5		0	0	0				4.8	0					0	0	0
82013000	镐、锄、耙	8	0		0	5		0	0	0				4.8	0					0	0	0
82014000	斧子、钩刀及类似砍伐工具	8	0		0	5		0	0	0				4.8	0					0	0	0
82015000	修枝剪等单手操作农用剪	8	0		0	5		0	0	0				4.8	0					0	0	0
82016000	修枝等双手操作农用剪	8	0		0	5		0	0	0				4.8	0					0	0	0
82019010	农用叉	8	0		0	5		0	0	0				4.8	0					0	0	0

税则号列	货品名称	最惠国	协定税率													特惠税率						
			东盟统一	亚太5国	智利	巴基斯坦	新加坡	新西兰	秘鲁	哥达	香港	澳门	台湾	瑞士	冰岛	亚太2国	老挝	柬埔寨	缅甸	LDC1	LDC2	LDC3
82019090	其他农业、园艺、林业用手工工具	8	0		0	5		0	0	0				4.8	0					0	0	0
82021000	手工锯	8.4	0		0	5		0	0	0				5	0					0	0	0
82022010	双金属带锯条	8	0		0	5		0	0	0				6.4	0					0	0	0
82022090	其他带锯片手工锯	8	0		0	5		0	0	0				6.4	0					0	0	0
82023100	带有钢制工作部件的圆锯片	8	0		0	5		0	0	0				4.8	0					0	0	0
82023910	带有天然或合成金刚石、立方氮化硼制工作部件的圆锯片	8	0		0	5		0	0	0	0			4.8	0					0	0	0
82023990	其他圆锯片,包括部件	8	0		0	5		0	0	0	0			4.8	0					0	0	0
82024000	链锯片	8	0		0	5		0	0	0				6.4	0					0	0	0
82029110	加工金属用的机械锯的直锯片	8	0	7	0	5		0	0	0				6.4	0					0	0	0
82029190	加工金属用的非机械锯的直锯片	8	0		0	5		0	0	0				6.4	0					0	0	0
82029910	机械锯用的其他锯片	8.4	0		0	5		0	0	0				6.7	0					0	0	0
82029990	非机械锯用的其他锯片	10.5	0		0	5	0	0	0	0				8.4	0					0	0	
82031000	钢锉、木锉及类似工具	10.5	0		0	5	0	0	0	0				8.4	0					0	0	0
82032000	钳子、镊子及类似工具	10.5	0		0		0	0	0	0		0	0	8.4	0					0	0	
82033000	白铁剪及类似工具	10.5	0		0	5	0	0	0	0				8.4	0					0	0	
82034000	切管器、螺栓切头器、打孔冲子等	10.5	0		0	5	0	0	0	0				8.4	0					0	0	
82041100	固定式的手动扳手及板钳	10.5	0		0	5	0	0	0	0				8.4	0					0	0	0
82041200	可调式的手动扳手及板钳	10	0		0	5		0	0	0			0	6	0					0	0	0
82042000	可互换的扳手套筒	10	0		0	5		0	0	0				6	0					0	0	
82051000	手工钻孔或攻丝工具	10	0		0	5		0	0	0				6	0					0	0	
82052000	手工锤子	10	0		0	5		0	0	0			0	6	0					0	0	0
82053000	木工用刨子、凿子及类似切削工具	10.5	0		0	5	0	0	0	0				8.4	0					0	0	
82054000	手工螺丝刀	10.5	0		0	5	0	0	0	0			0	8.4	0					0	0	0
82055100	其他家用手工工具	10.5	0		0	5	0	0	0	0				8.4	0					0	0	
82055900	其他手工工具	10	0	8.5	0	5		0	0	0			0	8	0					0	0	
82056000	喷灯	10	0		0	5		0	0	0				8	0					0	0	
82057000	台钳、夹钳及类似品	10.5	0		0	5	0	0	0	0				8.1	0					0	0	
82059000	成套手工工具	10.5	0		0	5	0	0	0	0				8.4	0					0	0	
82060000	成套工具组成的零售包装货品	10.5	0		0	5	0	0	0	0				8.8	0					0	0	
82071300	带金属陶瓷工作部件的凿岩工具	8	0		0	5		0	0	0				4.8	0					0	0	0
82071910	带超硬材料部件的凿岩或钻探工具	8	0		0	5		0	0	0				4.8	0					0	0	0
82071990	带其他材料工作部件的凿岩工具	8	0		0	5		0	0	0				4.8	0					0	0	0
82072010	带超硬部件的金属拉拔或挤压用模	8	0		0	5		0	0	0			0	4.8	0					0	0	0
82072090	其他金属拉拔或挤压用模	8	0		0	5		0	0	0			0	6.4	0					0	0	0
82073000	锻压或冲压工具	8	0	6.8	0	5		0	0	0	0		0	4.8	0					0	0	0
82074000	攻丝工具	8	0		0	5		0	0	0			0	4.8	0					0	0	0
82075010	带超硬材料部件的钻孔工具	8	0		0	5		0	0	0	0		0	0	0					0	0	0
82075090	带其他材料工作部件的钻孔工具	8	0		0	5		0	0	0	0		0	4.8	0					0	0	0
82076010	带超硬材料部件的镗孔或铰孔工具	8	0		0	5		0	0	0			0	4.8	0					0	0	0
82076090	其他镗孔或铰孔工具	8	0		0	5		0	0	0				4.8	0					0	0	0
82077010	带有天然或合成金刚石、立方氮化硼制的工作部件的铣削工具	8	0		0	5		0	0	0	0		0	4.8	0					0	0	0
82077090	其他铣削工具	8	0		0	5		0	0	0	0		0	4.8	0					0	0	0
82078010	带有天然或合成金刚石、立方氮化硼制的车削工具	8	0	6.8	0	5		0	0	0			0	4.8	0					0	0	0
82078090	其他车削工具	8	0	6.8	0	5		0	0	0			0	4.8	0					0	0	0
82079010	带超硬材料部件的其他可互换工具	8	0	6.8	0	5		0	0	0	0		0	4.8	0					0	0	0
82079090	其他可互换工具	8	0	6.8	0	5		0	0	0	0		0	6.4	0					0	0	0
82081011	经镀或涂层的硬质合金制的金工机械用刀及刀片	8	0		0	5		0	0	0	0			6.4	0					0	0	
82081019	其他硬质合金制的金工机械用刀及刀片	8	0		0	5		0	0	0	0			6.4	0					0	0	
82081090	其他金工机械用刀及刀片	8	0		0	5		0	0	0	0			6.4	0					0	0	
82082000	木工机械用刀及刀片	8	0		0	5		0	0	0			0	4.8	0					0	0	0
82083000	厨房或食品加工机器用刀及刀片	8	0		0	5		0	0	0				4.8	0					0	0	0
82084000	农、林业机器用刀及刀片	8	0		0	5		0	0	0			0	6.4	0					0	0	
82089000	其他机器或机械器具用刀及刀片	8	0	7.2	0	5		0	0	0			0	6.4	0					0	0	
82090010	未装配的工具用金属陶瓷板	8	0	7.2	0	5		0	0	0				4.8	0					0	0	0
82090021	晶粒度小于0.8微米的金属陶瓷条、杆	8	0	7.2	0	5		0	0	0				6.4	0					0	0	0

税则号列	货品名称	最惠国	协定税率													特惠税率						
			东盟统一	亚太5国	智利	巴基斯坦	新加坡	新西兰	秘鲁	哥达	香港	澳门	台湾	瑞士	冰岛	亚太2国	老挝	柬埔寨	缅甸	LDC1	LDC2	LDC3
82090029	其他未装配的工具用金属陶瓷条、杆	8	0	7.2	0	5		0	0	0				6.4	0					0	0	0
82090030	未装配的工具用金属陶瓷刀头	8	0	7.2	0	5		0	0	0				4.8	0					0	0	0
82090090	其他未装配的工具用金属陶瓷类似品	8	0	7.2	0	5		0	0	0				4.8	0					0	0	0
82100000	加工调制食品、饮料用手动机械	18	0	16.2	0	14.4	0	0	7.2	0		0		14.4	0					0	0	
82111000	以刀为主的成套货品	18	0		0	0	0	0	7.2	0				14.4	0					0	0	
82119100	刃面固定的餐刀	18	0		0	0	0	0	7.2	0				14.4	0					0	0	
82119200	刃面固定的其他刀	12	0		0	0	0	0	0	0				10	0					0	0	0
82119300	可换刃面刀	18	0		0	0	0	0	7.2	0				10.8	0					0	0	
82119400	税号82.11所列刀的刀片	14	0		0	0	0	0	0	0				11.2	0					0	0	
82119500	贱金属制的刀柄	12	0		0	0	0	0	0	0				9.2	0					0	0	0
82121000	剃刀	12	0		0	0	0	0	0	0				9.6	0					0	0	0
82122000	安全剃刀片	14	0		0	0	0	0	0	0				11.2	0					0	0	
82129000	剃刀零件	12	0		0	0	0	0	0	0				9.6	0					0	0	0
82130000	剪刀、裁缝剪刀及类似品、剪刀片	12	0	10.8	0	0	0	0	0	0				9.6	0					0	0	0
82141000	裁纸刀、信刀、铅笔刀及刀片	12	0	10.8	0	5	0	0	0	0				9.6	0					0	0	0
82142000	修指甲及修脚用具(包括指甲锉)	18	0	16.2	0	16.2	0	0	7.2	0				14.4	0					0	0	0
82149000	理发推子、切菜刀等其他利口器	18	0		0		0	0	7.2	0				14.4	0					0	0	
82151000	成套含镀贵金属制厨房或餐桌用具	18	0		0	0	0	0	7.2	0				14.4	0					0	0	
82152000	成套的其他厨房或餐桌用具	18	0		0	0	0	0	7.2	0				14.4	0					0	0	
82159100	非成套镀贵金属制厨房或餐桌用具	18	0		0	0	0	0	7.2	0				14.4	0					0	0	
82159900	其他非成套的厨房或餐桌用具	18	0		0	0	0	0	7.2	0	0			14.4	0					0	0	0
83011000	挂锁	14	0		0	11.2	0	0	0	0				11.2	0					0	0	
83012010	机动车用中央控制门锁	10	10		0			0	0	0				6	0					0	0	0
83012090	其他机动车用锁	10	10		0			0	0	0				6	0					0	0	0
83013000	家具用锁	14	0		0	11.2	0	0	0	0				11.2	0					0	0	0
83014000	其他锁	14	0		0	11.2	0	0	0	0				11.2	0					0	0	0
83015000	带锁的扣环及扣环框架	14	0		0	11.2	0	0	0	0	0			11.2	0					0	0	0
83016000	锁零件	12	0		0	6	0	0	0	0				9.6	0					0	0	0
83017000	钥匙	10	0		0	5		0	0	0				6	0					0	0	0
83021000	铰链(折叶)	10	0		0	5		0	0	0	0			6	0					0	0	0
83022000	用贱金属支架的小脚轮	12	0		0	6	0	0	0	0				9.6	0					0	0	0
83023000	机动车辆用贱金属附件及架座	10	0		0	5		0	0	0				6	0					0	0	0
83024100	建筑用贱金属配件及架座	14	0		0	11.2	0	0	0	0				11.2	0					0	0	
83024200	家具用贱金属配件及架座	12	0		0	6	0	0	0	0				9.6	0					0	0	0
83024900	其他用贱金属配件及架座	12	0		0	6	0	0	0	0				9.6	0					0	0	0
83025000	帽架、帽钩、托架及类似品	14	0		0	11.2	0	0	0	0				11.2	0					0	0	
83026000	自动闭门器	12	0		0	6	0	0	0	0				9.6	0					0	0	0
83030000	保险箱、柜、保险库的门	14	0		0	11.2	0	0	0	0				11.2	0					0	0	
83040000	贱金属档案柜、文件箱等办公用具	10.5	0		0	5	0	0	0	0	0			8.4	0					0	0	0
83051000	活页夹或宗卷夹的附件	10.5	0		0	5	0	0	0	0				8.4	0					0	0	0
83052000	成条钉书钉	10.5	0		0	5	0	0	0	0				8.4	0					0	0	0
83059000	信夹、信角、文件夹等办公用品	10.5	0		0	5	0	0	0	0	0			8.4	0					0	0	0
83061000	非电动铃、钟、锣及其类似品	8	0		0	5		0	0	0				4.8	0					0	0	0
83062100	镀贵金属的雕塑像及其他装饰品	8	0		0	5		0	0	0				4.8	0					0	0	0
83062910	景泰兰雕塑像及其他装饰品	8	0		0	5		0	0	0				4.8	0					0	0	0
83062990	其他雕塑像及其他装饰品	8	0		0	5	0	0	0	0				4.8	0					0	0	0
83063000	相框、画框及类似框架、镜子	8	0		0	5		0	0	0				4.8	0					0	0	0
83071000	钢铁制软管、可有配件	8.4	0		0	5		0	0	0				6.7	0					0	0	0
83079000	其他贱金属软管,可有配件	8.4	0		0	5		0	0	0	0			5	0					0	0	0
83081000	贱金属制钩、环及眼	10.5	0		0	5	0	0	0	0				8.4	0					0	0	0
83082000	贱金属制管形铆钉及开口铆钉	10.5	0		0	5	0	0	0	0				8.4	0					0	0	0
83089000	贱金属制珠子及亮晶片	10.5	0		0	5	0	0	0	0				8.4	0					0	0	0
83091000	贱金属制冠形瓶塞	18	0		0	14.4	0	0	0	0				14.4	0					0	0	0
83099000	盖子瓶帽螺口塞封志等包装用配件	12	0		0	6	0	0	0	0	0			9.6	0					0	0	0
83100000	标志牌、铭牌、号码、字母等标志	18	0		0		0	0	7.2	0				14.4	0					0	0	
83111000	焊剂涂面的贱金属电极、电弧焊用	8	0		0	5		0	0	0	0			4.8	0					0	0	0
83112000	以焊剂为芯的贱金属制焊丝	8	0		0	5		0	0	0	0			4.8	0					0	0	0
83113000	以焊剂涂面或作芯的贱金属条或丝	8	0		0	5		0	0	0	0			4.8	0					0	0	0
83119000	贱金属粘聚成的丝或条	8	0	5.6	0	5		0	0	0	0			4.8	0					0	0	0
84011000	核反应堆	2	0		0	0		0	0	0				0	0					0	0	
84012000	同位素分离机器、装置及其零件	1	0		0	0		0	0	0				0	0					0	0	

税则号列	货品名称	最惠国	协定税率													特惠税率						
			东盟统一	亚太5国	智利	巴基斯坦	新加坡	新西兰	秘鲁	哥达	香港	澳门	台湾	瑞士	冰岛	亚太2国	老挝	柬埔寨	缅甸	LDC1	LDC2	LDC3
84013010	未辐照燃料元件(释热元件)	2	0		0	0		0	0	0				0	0					0	0	
84013090	未辐照燃料元件的零件	1	0		0	0		0	0	0				0	0					0	0	
84014010	未辐照相关组件	1	0		0	0		0	0	0				0	0					0	0	
84014020	堆内构件	1	0		0	0		0	0	0				0	0					0	0	
84014090	其他核反应堆零件	1	0		0	0		0	0	0				0	0					0	0	
84021110	蒸发量≥900t/hr 发电锅炉	3	0	2.5	0	0		0	0	0				0	0					0	0	
84021190	蒸发量>45t/hr,<900t/hr 发电锅炉	14	0	13.3	0	7	0	0	0	0				11.2	0					0	0	
84021200	蒸发量≤45t/hr 水管锅炉	5	0	3.9	0	0		0	0	0				0	0					0	0	
84021900	其他蒸汽锅炉	5	0		0	0		0	0	0				0	0					0	0	
84022000	过热水锅炉	16	0		0	12.8	0	0	6.4	0				12.8	0					0	0	
84029000	蒸汽锅炉及过热水锅炉的零件	2	0		0	0		0	0	0				0	0					0	0	
84031010	家用型集中供暖用热水锅炉	10	0	9.5	0	5		0	0	0				6	0					0	0	
84031090	其他集中供暖用的热水锅炉	10	0	9.5	0	5		0	0	0				6	0					0	0	
84039000	集中供暖用热水锅炉的零件	6	0		0	5		0	0	0				3.6	0					0	0	
84041010	蒸汽锅炉、过热水锅炉的辅助设备	7	0	3.5	0	0		0	0	0				5.6	0					0	0	
84041020	集中供暖用热水锅炉的辅助设备	10	0	5	0	5		0	0	0				6	0					0	0	
84042000	水及其他蒸汽动力装置的冷凝器	14	0		0	11.2	0	0	0	0				11.2	0					0	0	
84049010	集中供暖热水锅炉辅助设备的零件	10	0	0	0	0		0	0	0				6	0					0	0	
84049090	其他辅助设备用零件	7	0	0	0	0		0	0	0				4.2	0					0	0	
84051000	煤气、乙炔及类似水解气体发生器	14	0		0	11.2	0	0	0	0				11.2	0					0	0	
84059000	煤气、乙炔等气体发生器的零件	8	0		0	5		0	0	0				4.8	0					0	0	
84061000	船舶动力用汽轮机	5	0		0	0		0	0	0				0	0					0	0	0
84068110	40MW<输出功率≤100MW 的汽轮机	5	0		0	0		0	0	0				0	0					0	0	0
84068120	100MW<输出功率≤350MW 的汽轮机	5	0		0	0		0	0	0				0	0					0	0	0
84068130	输出功率>350MW 的汽轮机	6	0		0	5		0	0	0				3.6	0					0	0	0
84068200	输出功率≤40MW 的汽轮机	5	0		0	0		0	0	0				3.9	0					0	0	0
84069000	汽轮机用的零件	2	0		0	0		0	0	0				1.6	0					0	0	0
84071010	输出功率≤298kw 航空器点燃式发动机	2	0		0	0		0	0	0				0	0					0	0	
84071020	输出功率>298kw 航空器点燃式发动机	2	0		0	0		0	0	0				0	0					0	0	
84072100	船舶用舷外点燃式发动机	8	0		0	5		0	0	0				4.8	0					0	0	
84072900	船舶用其他未列名点燃式发动机	8	0		0	5		0	0	0				4.8	0					0	0	
84073100	排气量≤50cc 往复式活塞发动机	10	0		0	5		0	0	0				6	0					0	0	
84073200	排气量 50-250cc 往复式活塞发动机	10	0		0	5		0	0	0				6	0					0	0	
84073300	排气量 250-1000cc 往复式活塞发动机	10	0		0	8	0	0	0	0	0			6	0					0	0	
84073410	排气量 1000-3000cc 往复式活塞发动机	10	10	7	0	7		0		0	0			6	0							
84073420	排气量>3000cc 往复式活塞发动机	10	10	7	0	7		0		0	0			6	0					0		
84079010	沼气发动机	12	0		0	6	0	0	0	0				9.6	0					0	0	
84079090	其他点燃往复或旋转式内燃发动机	18	0		0		0	0	7.2	0				14.4	0					0	0	
84081000	船舶用压燃式内燃发动机	5	0	2.5	0	0	0	0	0	0				3	0					0	0	
84082010	输出功率≥132.39kw 车用柴油发动机	9	9	6.3	0	6.3		0	0	0	0			5.4	0					0	0	
84082090	输出功率<132.39kw 车用柴油发动机	25	20	17.5	0	17.5		0		0					0					0		
84089010	机车用柴油发动机	6	0	5.4	0	0		0	0	0				3.6	0					0	0	
84089091	功率≤14kw 其他用柴油发动机	5	0	4.5	0	0		0	0	0				0	0					0	0	
84089092	14kw<功率<132.39kw 其他柴油发动机	8.4	0	7.6	0	5		0	0	0				5	0					0	0	
84089093	功率≥132.39kw 其他用柴油发动机	5	0	4.5	0	0		0	0	0				3	0					0	0	
84091000	航空器发动机用零件	2	0		0	0		0	0	0				0	0					0	0	0
84099110	船舶用点燃式发动机专用零件	6	0	4.2	0	0		0	0	0				3.6	0					0	0	0
84099191	电控燃油喷射装置	5	0	3.5	0	0	0	0	0	0				0	0					0	0	0
84099199	其他点燃式活塞内燃发动机用零件	5	0	3.5	0	0	0	0	0	0				4	0					0	0	0
84099910	其他船舶发动机专用零件	5	0	4.5	0	0	0	0	0	0				4	0					0	0	0
84099920	其他机车发动机专用零件	2	0	1.5	0	0		0	0	0				0	0					0	0	0
84099991	功率≥132.39kw 发动机的专用零件	2	0	1.5	0	0		0	0	0				0	0					0	0	0
84099999	其他未列名发动机的专用零件	8.4	0	8	0	5	0	0	0	0				5	0					0	0	0
84101100	功率≤1000kw 的水轮机及水轮	10	0		0	5		0	0	0				6	0					0	0	
84101200	功率 1 千 kw-1 万 kw 的水轮机及水轮	10	0		0	5	0	0	0	0				6	0					0	0	
84101310	功率>3 万 kw 的冲击式水轮机及水轮	10	0		0	5	0	0	0	0				6	0					0	0	
84101320	功率>3.5 万 kw 的贯流水轮机及水轮	10	0		0	5	0	0	0	0				6	0					0	0	
84101330	功率>20 万 kw 的水泵式水轮机及水轮	10	0		0	5		0	0	0				6	0					0	0	
84101390	其他功率>1 万 kw 的水轮机及水轮	10	0		0	5		0	0	0				6	0					0	0	
84109010	水轮机及水轮的调节器	6	0		0	5		0	0	0				3.6	0					0	0	
84109090	水轮机及水轮的其他零件	6	0		0	5		0	0	0				3.6	0					0	0	

税则号列	货品名称	最惠国	协定税率												特惠税率						
			东盟统一	亚太5国	智利	巴基斯坦	新加坡	新西兰	秘鲁	哥达	香港	澳门	台湾	瑞士	冰岛	亚太2国	老挝	柬埔寨	缅甸	LDC1	LDC2	LDC3
84111110	推力≤25千牛顿的涡轮风扇发动机	1	0		0	0		0	0	0				0	0					0	0	0
84111190	推力≤25千牛顿的其他的涡轮喷气发动机	1	0		0	0		0	0	0				0	0					0	0	0
84111210	推力>25千牛顿的涡轮风扇发动机	1	0	0	0	0		0	0	0				0	0					0	0	0
84111290	推力>25千牛顿的其他涡轮喷气发动机	1	0	0.5	0	0		0	0	0				0	0					0	0	0
84112100	功率≤1100kw的涡轮螺桨发动机	2	0		0	0		0	0	0				0	0					0	0	0
84112210	功率1100-2238kw涡轮螺桨发动机	2	0		0	0		0	0	0				0	0					0	0	0
84112220	功率2238-3730kw涡轮螺桨发动机	2	0		0	0		0	0	0				0	0					0	0	0
84112230	功率>3730kw涡轮螺桨发动机	2	0		0	0		0	0	0				0	0					0	0	0
84118100	功率≤5000kw的其他燃气轮机	15	0		0	12	0	0	6	0				12	0					0	0	
84118200	功率>5000kw的其他燃气轮机	3	0		0	0		0	0	0				0	0					0	0	0
84119100	涡轮喷气或涡轮螺桨发动机用零件	1	0		0	0		0	0	0				0	0					0	0	0
84119910	涡轮轴发动机用零件	5	0		0	0		0	0	0				0	0					0	0	0
84119990	其他燃气轮机用零件	5	0		0	0		0	0	0				0	0					0	0	0
84121010	航空、航天器用喷气发动机	3	0		0	0		0	0	0				3	0					0	0	0
84121090	非航空、航天器用喷气发动机	10	0		0	5		0	0	0				0	0					0	0	0
84122100	直线作用的液压动力装置(液压缸)	12	0		0	6	0	0	4.8	0	0		0	9.6	0					0	0	
84122910	液压马达	10	0		0	5	0	0	0	0				8	0					0	0	
84122990	其他液压动力装置	14	0		0	11.2	0	0	0	0				11.2	0					0	0	
84123100	直线作用的气压动力装置(气压缸)	14	0	13.3	0	7	0	0	0	0			0	8.4	0					0	0	
84123900	其他气压动力装置	14	0		0	11.2	0	0	0	0				8.4	0					0	0	
84128000	其他发动机及动力装置	10	0		0	5		0	0	0				6	0					0	0	
84129010	航空、航天器用喷气发动机的零件	2	0		0	0		0	0	0				0	0					0	0	0
84129090	其他发动机及动力装置的零件	8	0		0	5		0	0	0				4.8	0					0	0	0
84131100	分装燃料或润滑油的泵	10	0		0	5	0	0	0	0				6	0					0	0	0
84131900	其他装有或可装计量装置的泵	10	0		0	5	0	0	0	0				8	0					0	0	0
84132000	手泵	10	0		0	5	0	0	0	0				6	0					0	0	0
84133021	输出功率在132.39千瓦(180马力)及以上的发动机用燃油泵	3	0	2.5	0	0		0	0	0				0	0					0	0	0
84133029	其他燃油泵	3	0		0	0		0	0	0				0	0					0	0	0
84133030	润滑油泵	3	0		0	0		0	0	0				0	0					0	0	0
84133090	其他燃油泵、润滑油泵或冷却剂泵	3	0	2.5	0	0		0	0	0				0	0					0	0	0
84134000	混凝土泵	8	0		0	5		0	0	0	0			4.8	0					0	0	0
84135010	气动式往复式排液泵	10	0		0	5	0	0	0	0				6	0					0	0	0
84135020	电动式往复式排液泵	10	0		0	5	0	0	0	0	0			8.3	0					0	0	0
84135031	往复式柱塞泵	10	0		0	5	0	0	0	0				6	0					0	0	0
84135039	其他液压式往复泵	10	0		0	5	0	0	0	0				6	0					0	0	0
84135090	其他往复式排液泵	10	0		0	5	0	0	4	0				6	0					0	0	0
84136021	电动式齿轮回转泵	10	0		0	5	0	0	0	0				6						0	0	0
84136022	液压式齿轮回转泵	10	0		0	5		0	0	0				6	0					0	0	0
84136029	其他齿轮回转泵	10	0		0	5		0	0	0				6	0					0	0	0
84136031	电动式叶片回转泵	10	0		0	5		0	0	0				6	0					0	0	0
84136032	液压式叶片回转泵	10	0		0	5		0	0	0				6	0					0	0	0
84136039	其他叶片回转泵	10	0		0	5		0	0	0				6	0					0	0	0
84136040	螺杆回转泵	10	0		0	5		0	0	0				6	0					0	0	0
84136050	径向柱塞泵	10	0		0	5		0	0	0				6	0					0	0	0
84136060	轴向柱塞泵	10	0		0	5		0	0	0				6	0					0	0	0
84136090	其他回转式排液泵	10	0		0	5	0	0	0	0				8	0					0	0	0
84137010	转速≥10000转/分离心泵	8	0	7.6	0	5		0	0	0				4.8	0					0	0	0
84137091	电动潜油泵及潜水电泵	10	0		0	5	0	0	0	0				6	0					0	0	0
84137099	其他离心泵	8	0	7.6	0	5		0	0	0	0			6.4	0					0	0	0
84138100	其他液体泵	8	0	4	0	0		0	0	0			0	6.4	0					0	0	0
84138200	液体提升机	8	0		0	5		0	0	0				6.2	0					0	0	0
84139100	液体泵用零件	5	0	2.5	0	0		0	0	0	0		0	4	0					0	0	0
84139200	液体提升机用零件	6	0		0	5		0	0	0				3.6	0					0	0	0
84141000	真空泵	8	0		0	5		0	0	0			0	6.4	0					0	0	
84142000	手动或脚踏式空气泵	8	0		0	5		0	0	0				4.8	0					0	0	
84143011	功率≤0.4kw的冷藏、冷冻箱用压缩机	8	0	5.9	0	5	0	0	0	0	0			4.8	0					0	0	0
84143012	功率0.4-5kw的冷藏、冷冻箱用压缩机	10	0	8.5	0	5	0	0	4	0	0			6	0					0	0	0
84143013	功率0.4-5kw的空气调节器用压缩机	10	0	8.5	0	5	0	0	4	0	0		0	6	0					0	0	0
84143014	功率>5kw的空气调节器用压缩机	10	0	8.5	0	5	0	0	4	0	0		0	6	0					0	0	0

税则号列	货品名称	最惠国	协定税率													特惠税率						
			东盟统一	亚太5国	智利	巴基斯坦	新加坡	新西兰	秘鲁	哥达	香港	澳门	台湾	瑞士	冰岛	亚太2国	老挝	柬埔寨	缅甸	LDC1	LDC2	LDC3
84143015	冷冻或冷藏设备用,电动机额定功率超过5千瓦的电动机驱动压缩机	10	0	9.2	0	5		0	4	0	0			6	0					0	0	0
84143019	其他制冷设备用压缩机	10	0	9	0	5	0	0	4	0	0			6	0					0	0	0
84143090	非电机驱动的压缩机	9	0	8.1	0	5	0	0	0	0	0			5.4	0					0	0	0
84144000	装在拖车底盘上的空气压缩机	8	0		0	5		0	0	0	0			4.8	0					0	0	
84145110	功率≤125瓦的吊扇	20	0		0		0	0	8	0				16	0		0			0	0	0
84145120	功率≤125瓦的换气扇	20	0		0		0	0	8	0			0	16	0		0			0	0	0
84145130	功率≤125瓦,有旋转导风轮的风扇	12	0		0	6	0	0	0	0				9.6	0		0			0	0	0
84145191	功率≤125瓦的台扇	10	0		0	5		0	0	0				6	0		0			0	0	0
84145192	功率≤125瓦的落地扇	10	0		0	5		0	0	0				6	0		0			0	0	0
84145193	功率≤125瓦的壁扇	10	0		0	5		0	0	0				6	0		0			0	0	0
84145199	功率≤125瓦其他风扇、风机	10	0		0	5	0	0	0	0			0	6	0		0			0	0	0
84145910	其他吊扇	8	0	7.2	0	5		0	0	0				4.8	0					0	0	
84145920	其他换气扇	8	0	7.2	0	5		0	0	0				4.8	0					0	0	
84145930	离心通风机	10	0	9.5	0	5	0	0	4	0				6	0					0	0	
84145990	其他扇,风机	8	0	7.2	0	5		0	0	0			0	6.4	0					0	0	0
84146010	抽油烟机	10	0		0	5		0	0	0				6	0		0			0	0	0
84146090	罩最大边长≤120cm的通风罩或循环气罩	10	0		·0	5	0	0	0	0				6	0		0			0	0	0
84148010	燃气轮机用的自由活塞式发生器	8	0	5.6	0	5		0	0	0				4.8	0					0	0	
84148020	二氧化碳压缩机	7	0	4.9	0	0		0	0	0				4.2	0					0	0	
84148030	发动机用增压器	7	0	4.9	0	0		0		0					0					0		
84148090	其他气体压缩机及通风罩或循环气罩	7	0	4.9	0	0		0	0	0	0		0	5.4	0					0	0	
84148040	空气及其他气体压缩机	7	0	4.9	0	0		0	0	0	0		0	5.4	0					0	0	
84149011	用于制冷设备的压缩机进、排气阀片	8	0	7.2	0	5		0	0	0				4.8	0		0			0	0	0
84149019	其他用于制冷设备的压缩机零件	8	0	7.2	0	5		0	0	0			0	6.4	0					0	0	
84149020	风机、风扇、通风罩及循环气罩零件	12	0	11.4	0	6	0	0	4.8	0			0	9.6	0					0	0	
84149090	税号84.14其他所列机器零件	7	0	6.5	0	5		0	0	0	0		0	5.4	0					0	0	
84151010	独立窗式或壁式空气调节器	15	0	13.5	0	7.5	0	0	6	0				12	0					0	0	
84151021	分体式制冷量制冷量≤4千大卡/时窗式或壁式空气调节器	15	0	13.5	0	7.5	0	0	6	0				12	0					0	0	
84151022	分体式制冷量制冷量>4千大卡/时窗式或壁式空气调节器	15	0	13.5	0	7.5	0	0	6	0				12	0					0	0	
84152000	机动车辆上供人使用的空气调节器	20	20		0			0		0	0			16	0					0		
84158110	制冷量≤4千大卡/时热泵式空调器	15	0		0	12	0	0	6	0				12	0					0	0	
84158120	制冷量>4千大卡/时热泵式空调器	20	0		0		0	0	8	0				16	0					0	0	
84158210	制冷量≤4千大卡/时的其他空调器	15	0		0	12	0	0	6	0				12	0					0	0	
84158220	制冷量>4千大卡/时的其他空调器	20	0		0		0	0	8	0				16	0					0	0	
84158300	未装有制冷装置的空调器	10	0		0	5	0	0	0	0				6	0					0	0	0
84159010	制冷量≤4千大卡/时等空调的零件	10	0	8	0	5	0	0	0	0	0			6	0					0	0	0
84159090	制冷量>4千大卡/时等空调的零件	10	0	8	0	5	0	0	0	0	0		0	6	0					0	0	0
84161000	使用液体燃料的炉用燃烧器	10	0	9.5	0	5	0	0	0	0				6	0					0	0	
84162011	使用天然气的燃烧器	10.5	0		0	5	0	0	0	0				8.4	0					0	0	
84162019	其他使用气体燃料的炉用燃烧器	10.5	0		0	5	0	0	0	0				8.4	0					0	0	
84162090	使用粉状固体燃料的炉用燃烧器	10.5	0		0	5	0	0	0	0				6.3	0					0	0	
84163000	机械加煤机及类似装置	8.4	0		0	5		0	0	0				5	0					0	0	
84169000	炉用燃烧器、机械加煤机等的零件	6	0		0	5		0	0	0				3.6	0					0	0	
84171000	矿砂、金属的热处理用炉及烤箱	10	0		0	5	0	0	0	0				6	0					0	0	
84172000	面包房用烤炉及烘箱等	10	0		0	5		0	0	0				6	0					0	0	
84178010	炼焦炉	10	0		0	5		0	0	0				6	0					0	0	
84178020	放射性废物焚烧炉	5	0		0	0		0	0	0				0	0					0	0	
84178030	水泥回转窑	10	0		0	5	0	0	0	0				6	0					0	0	
84178040	石灰石分解炉	10	0		0	5		0	0	0				6	0					0	0	
84178050	垃圾焚烧炉	10	0		0	5	0	0	0	0			0	8.3	0					0	0	
84178090	其他非电热的工业用炉及烘箱	10	0		0	5	0	0	0	0			0	8.3	0					0	0	
84179010	海绵铁回转窑的零件	7	0		0	5		0	0	0				4.2	0					0	0	
84179020	炼焦炉的零件	7	0		0	5		0	0	0				4.2	0					0	0	
84179090	其他非电热工业用炉及烘箱的零件	7	0		0	5		0	0	0				5.6	0					0	0	
84181010	容积>500L冷藏-冷冻组合机	10	0		0	5	0	0	4	0				6	0					0	0	0
84181020	200L<容积≤500L冷藏冷冻组合机	15	0		0	12	0	0	6	0				12	0					0	0	

税则号列	货品名称	最惠国	协定税率													特惠税率						
			东盟统一	亚太5国	智利	巴基斯坦	新加坡	新西兰	秘鲁	哥达	香港	澳门	台湾	瑞士	冰岛	亚太2国	老挝	柬埔寨	缅甸	LDC1	LDC2	LDC3
84181030	容积≤200L冷藏－冷冻组合机	15	0		0	12	0	0	6	0				12	0					0	0	
84182110	容积>150L压缩式家用型冷藏箱	10	0		0	5	0	0	0	0				6	0					0	0	0
84182120	50L<容积≤150L压缩式家用型冷藏箱	10	0	9	0	5	0	0	0	0				6	0					0	0	0
84182130	容积≤50L压缩式家用型冷藏箱	10	0	9	0	5	0	0	0	0				6	0					0	0	0
84182910	半导体制冷式家用型冷藏箱	30	0		0		0	0	12	0				24	0					0	0	
84182920	电气吸收式家用型冷藏箱	15	0		0	12	0	0	6	0				12	0					0	0	
84182990	其他家用型冷藏箱	30	0		0		0	0	12	0				24	0					0	0	
84183010	制冷温度≤－40℃，容积≤800L柜式冷冻箱	9	0		0	5		0	0	0		0		5.4	0					0	0	0
84183021	制冷温度>－40℃，容积500－800L柜式冷冻箱	23	0		0		0	0	9.2	0		0		18.4	0					0	0	
84183029	制冷温度>－40℃，容积≤500L柜式冷冻箱	30	0		0		0	0	12	0		0		23.1	0					0	0	
84184010	制冷温度≤－40℃，容积≤900L立式冷冻箱	9	0		0	5		0	0	0		0		5.4	0					0	0	0
84184021	制冷温度>－40℃，容积500－900L立式冷冻箱	15	0		0	12	0	0	6	0		0		12	0					0	0	
84184029	制冷温度>－40℃，容积≤500L立式冷冻箱	30	0		0		0	0	12	0		0			0					0	0	
84185000	其他装有冷藏或冷冻装置的柜、箱、展示台	10	0		0	5	0	0	4	0	0	0		6	0					0	0	0
84186120	压缩式热泵，税目8415的空气调节器除外	10	0	7	0	5	0	0	0	0				6	0					0	0	0
84186190	其他热泵，税目8415的空气调节器除外	15	0	7	0	7	0	0	6	0		0		12	0					0	0	
84186920	其他制冷机组	10	0	7	0	5	0	0	0	0		0		6	0					0	0	0
84186990	其他制冷设备	10	0	7	0	5	0	0	4	0		0		8	0					0	0	0
84189100	冷藏或冷冻设备用特制家具零件	18	0	17.1	0	14.4	0	0	7.2	0				14.4	0					0	0	
84189910	制冷机组及热泵用零件	10	0		0	5	0	0	4	0				6	0					0	0	0
84189991	制冷温度≤－40℃冷冻设备零件	9.5	0		0	5		0	0	0		0		5.7	0					0	0	0
84189992	制冷温度>－40℃，容积>500L冷藏设备零件	10	0		0	5		0	4	0		0		6	0					0	0	0
84189999	税号84.18其他制冷设备用零件	10	0		0	5	0	0	4	0		0		6	0					0	0	0
84191100	燃气快速热水器	35	0		0		0	0	14	0				26.6	0					0	0	
84191910	太阳能热水器	35	0		0		0	0	14	0			0	28	0					0	0	
84191990	其他非电热的快速或贮备式热水器	35	0		0		0	0	14	0			0	26.6	0					0	0	
84192000	医用或实验室用消毒器具	4	0		0	0		0	0	0				2.4	0					0	0	
84193100	农产品干燥器	8	0		0	5		0	0	0				4.8	0		0			0	0	0
84193200	木材、纸浆、纸或纸板用干燥器	9	0		0	5		0	0	0			0	5.4	0		0			0	0	0
84193910	微空气流动陶瓷坯件干燥器	9	0	4.5	0	4.5		0	0					5.4	0					0	0	
84193990	其他用途的干燥器	9	0	4.5	0	4.5		0	0				0	5.4	0					0	0	
84194010	提净塔	10	0		0	5	0	0	0					6	0					0	0	
84194020	精馏塔	10	0		0	5	0	0	0					6	0					0	0	
84194090	其他蒸馏或精馏设备	10	0		0	5	0	0	0					6	0					0	0	
84195000	热交换装置	10	0	9.5	0	5	0	0	4	0	0		0	8.3	0		0			0	0	0
84196011	制氧量≥15000立方米/小时制氧机	12	0		0	6	0	0	0	0	0			9.6	0					0	0	
84196019	制氧量<15000立方米/小时制氧机	13	0		0	6.5	0	0	0	0	0			10.4	0					0	0	
84196090	其他液化空气或其他气体的机器	10	0		0	5	0	0	0	0	0			6	0					0	0	
84198100	加工热饮料、烹调、加热食品的机器	10	0		0	5	0	0	4	0				0	0		0			0	0	0
84198910	加氢反应器	0															0			0	0	0
84198990	其他利用温度变化处理材料的机器	0															0			0	0	0
84199010	热水器用零件	0																		0	0	0
84199090	税号84.19的其他机器设备用零件	4	0		0	0		0	0	0	0		0	2.4	0					0	0	
84201000	研光机或其他滚压机器	8.4	0		0	5		0	0	0			0	5	0					0	0	0
84209100	研光机或其他滚压机器的滚筒	8	0		0	5		0	0	0				4.8	0					0	0	0
84209900	研光机或其他滚压机的未列名零件	8	0		0	5		0	0	0				4.8	0					0	0	0
84211100	奶油分离器	8.4	0		0	5		0	0	0				5	0					0	0	
84211210	干衣量≤10kg的离心干衣机	17.5	0		0	14	0	0	7	0				14	0					0	0	
84211290	干衣量>10kg的离心干衣机	8	0		0	5		0	0	0				4.8	0					0	0	
84211910	脱水机	10	0		0	5		0	0	0				6	0					0	0	

税则号列	货品名称	最惠国	协定税率												特惠税率						
			东盟统一	亚太5国	智利	巴基斯坦	新加坡	新西兰	秘鲁	哥达	香港	澳门	台湾	瑞士	冰岛	亚太2国	老挝	柬埔寨	缅甸	LDC1	LDC2	LDC3
84211920	固液分离机	10	0		0	5	0	0	0	0				6	0					0	0	
84211990	其他离心机	10	0		0	5	0	0	0	0				8	0					0	0	
84212110	家用型过滤或净化水的机器及装置	25	0	17.5	0	17.5	0	0	10	0	0	0		19.3	0					0	0	
84212191	船舶压载水处理设备	5	0	3.5	0	0		0	0	0	0	0	0	3	0					0	0	
84212199	其他过滤或净化水的装置	5	0	3.5	0	0		0	0	0	0	0	0	3	0					0	0	
84212200	过滤或净化饮料的机器及装置	12	0		0	6	0	0	0	0		0		7.2	0					0	0	
84212300	内燃发动机的燃油过滤器	10	0		0	5	0	0	4	0	0			6	0					0	0	
84212910	其他压滤机	5	0	3.5	0	0		0	0	0	0			0	0					0	0	
84212990	其他液体的过滤、净化机器及装置	5	0	3.5	0	0		0	0	0	0		0	4	0					0	0	0
84213100	内燃发动机的进气过滤器	10	0		0	5		0	4	0	0			6	0					0	0	
84213910	家用型气体过滤、净化机器及装置	15	0	10.5	0	7.5	0	0	6	0	0		0	12	0					0	0	
84213921	工业用静电除尘器	5	0	3.5	0	0		0	0	0	0		0	3	0					0	0	
84213922	工业用袋式除尘器	5	0	3.5	0	0		0	0	0	0			0	0					0	0	
84213923	工业用旋风式除尘器	5	0	3.5	0	0		0	0	0	0		0	3	0					0	0	
84213924	电袋复合除尘器	5	0	3.5	0	0		0	0	0	0		0	0	0					0	0	
84213929	工业用其他除尘器	5	0	3.5	0	0		0	0	0	0		0	0	0					0	0	
84213930	内燃发动机排气过滤及净化装置	5	0	3.5	0	0		0	0	0	0			0	0					0	0	0
84213940	烟气脱硫装置	5	0	3.5	0	0		0	0	0	0		0	0	0					0	0	0
84213950	烟气脱硝装置	5	0	3.5	0	0		0	0	0	0		0	3	0					0	0	0
84213990	其他气体的过滤、净化机器及装置	5	0	3.5	0	0		0	0	0	0		0	3	0					0	0	0
84219110	干衣量≤10kg 离心干衣机零件	0																		0	0	0
84219190	其他离心机用零件	0																		0	0	0
84219910	家用型过滤、净化装置用零件	10	0	9	0	5	0	0	4	0	0			6	0					0	0	
84219990	其他过滤、净化装置用零件	5	0	4.5	0	0		0	0	0	0		0	3	0					0	0	0
84221100	家用型洗碟机	10	0		0	5		0	0	0				6	0					0	0	0
84221900	非家用型洗碟机	14	0		0	11.2	0	0	0	0				0	0					0	0	
84222000	瓶子及其他容器的洗涤或干燥机器	10	0		0	5	0	0	4	0		0		6	0					0	0	0
84223010	饮料及液体食品罐装设备	12	0	8.4	0	5	0	0	0	0	0			9.6	0					0	0	0
84223021	水泥全自动灌包机	12	0	8.4	0	5	0	0	4.8	0	0			9.6	0					0	0	0
84223029	其他水泥包装机	12	0	8.4	0	5	0	0	4.8	0	0			9.6	0					0	0	0
84223030	其他包装机	10	0	7	0	5	0	0	4	0	0			6	0					0	0	0
84223090	其他装填密封等包封机器	10	0	7	0	5	0	0	4	0	0			0	0					0	0	0
84224000	其他包装或打包机器	10	0	9.5	0	5	0	0	4	0	0			6	0					0	0	0
84229010	洗碟机用零件	10.5	0		0	5	0	0	4.2	0				8.4	0					0	0	0
84229020	饮料及液体食品灌装设备用零件	8.5	0		0	5		0	0	0				5.1	0					0	0	0
84229090	税号 84.22 其他未列名机器零件	8.5	0		0	5		0	0	0	0			6.8						0	0	0
84231000	体重计、婴儿秤及家用秤	10.5	0		0	5	0	0	0	0		0		8.4	0					0	0	0
84232010	电子皮带秤	10	0		0	5		0	0	0				6	0					0	0	0
84232090	其他输送带上连续称货的秤	10	0		0	5		0	0	0				6	0					0	0	0
84233010	定量包装秤	10.5	0		0	5	0	0	0	0				8.4	0					0	0	0
84233020	定量分选秤	10.5	0		0	5	0	0	0	0				8.4	0					0	0	0
84233030	配料秤	10.5	0		0	5	0	0	0	0				8.4	0					0	0	0
84233090	其他恒定秤、物料定量装袋或容器用秤	10.5	0		0	5	0	0	0	0				8.4	0					0	0	0
84238110	最大称量≤30kg 的计价秤	10.5	0		0	5	0	0	0	0				8.4	0					0	0	0
84238120	最大称量≤30kg 的弹簧秤	10.5	0		0	5	0	0	0	0				8.4	0					0	0	0
84238190	最大称量≤30kg 的其他衡器	10.5	0		0	5	0	0	0	0				9.2	0					0	0	0
84238210	最大称量 30－5000kg 的地中衡	10.5	0		0	5	0	0	0	0				8.4	0					0	0	0
84238290	最大称量 30－5000kg 的其他衡器	10.5	0		0	5	0	0	0	0				0	0					0	0	0
84238910	其他地中衡	10	0		0	5		0	4	0				6	0					0	0	0
84238920	其他轨道衡	10	0		0	5		0	4	0				6	0					0	0	0
84238930	其他吊秤	10	0		0	5		0	4	0				6	0					0	0	0
84238990	其他衡器	10	0		0	5		0	4	0				6	0					0	0	0
84239000	衡器用的各种砝码、秤砣及其零件	10	0		0	5	0	0	0	0				8	0					0	0	0
84241000	灭火器	8.4	0		0	5		0	0	0				5	0					0	0	
84242000	喷枪及类似器具	8.4	0	8	0	5		0	0	0				5	0					0	0	
84243000	喷汽机、喷砂机及类似喷射机	8.4	0		0	5		0	0	0			0	6.7	0					0	0	
84248100	农业或园艺用喷射、喷雾机械器具	8	0	7.6	0	5		0	0	0	0			4.8	0					0	0	
84248910	家用型喷射、喷雾机械器具	0																		0	0	0
84248920	喷涂机器人	0																		0	0	0
84248991	船用洗舱机	0																		0	0	0
84248999	其他液体粉末喷射机械	0																		0	0	0

税则号列	货品名称	最惠国	协定税率 东盟统一	亚太5国	智利	巴基斯坦	新加坡	新西兰	秘鲁	哥达	香港	澳门	台湾	瑞士	冰岛	特惠税率 亚太2国	老挝	柬埔寨	缅甸	LDC1	LDC2	LDC3
84249010	灭火器用的零件	0																		0	0	0
84249020	家用型喷射、喷雾器具的零件	0																		0	0	0
84249090	其他喷雾器具及喷气机等用的零件	0																		0	0	0
84251100	电动滑车及提升机	6	0		0	5		0	0	0				3.6	0					0	0	0
84251900	非电动滑车及提升机	5	0		0	0		0	0	0				0	0					0	0	0
84253110	矿井口电动卷扬装置;专为井下使用设计的电动卷扬机	10	0		0	5		0	0	0				6	0					0	0	0
84253190	其他电动卷扬机及绞盘	5	0		0	0		0	0	0				3	0					0	0	0
84253910	其他矿井口卷扬装置;其他专为井下使用设计的卷扬机	10	0		0	5		0	0	0				6	0					0	0	0
84253990	其他非电动卷扬机及绞盘	5	0		0	0		0	0	0	0			0	0					0	0	0
84254100	车库中使用的固定千斤顶系统	3	0	2.5	0	0		0	0	0				0	0					0	0	0
84254210	其他液压千斤顶	3	0		0	0		0	0	0				0	0					0	0	0
84254290	提升车辆用液压提升机	5	0		0	0		0	0	0				0	0					0	0	0
84254910	其他千斤顶	5	0		0	0		0	0	0				3	0					0	0	0
84254990	其他提升车辆用提升机	10	0		0	5		0	4	0				6	0					0	0	0
84261120	通用桥式起重机	8	0		0	5		0	0	0				4.8	0					0	0	0
84261190	其他固定支架的高架移动式起重机	8	0		0	5		0	0	0				4.8	0					0	0	0
84261200	胶轮移动式吊运架及跨运车	6	0		0	5		0	0	0				3.6	0					0	0	0
84261910	装船机	5	0	2.5	0	0		0	0	0				0	0					0	0	0
84261921	抓斗式卸船机	5	0	3.5	0	0		0	0	0				0	0					0	0	0
84261929	其他卸船机	5	0	3.5	0	0		0	0	0				0	0					0	0	0
84261930	龙门式起重机	10	0	7	0	5		0	0	0				6	0					0	0	0
84261941	门式装卸桥	10	0	7	0	5		0	0	0				6	0					0	0	0
84261942	集装箱装卸桥	10	0	7	0	5		0	0	0				6	0					0	0	0
84261943	其他动臂式装卸桥	10	0	7	0	5		0	0	0				6	0					0	0	0
84261949	其他装卸桥	10	0	7	0	5		0	0	0				6	0					0	0	0
84261990	其他高架移动式起重机等	10	0	7	0	5	0	0	0	0				6	0					0	0	0
84262000	塔式起重机	10	0		0	5		0	0	0				6	0					0	0	0
84263000	门座式起重机及座式旋臂起重机	6	0		0	5		0	0	0				3.6	0					0	0	0
84264110	轮胎式起重机	5	0		0	0		0	0	0				0	0					0	0	0
84264190	其他带胶轮的自推进起重机	5	0		0	0		0	0	0				0	0					0	0	0
84264910	履带式起重机	8	0		0	5		0	0	0	0			4.8	0					0	0	0
84264990	其他不带胶轮的自推进起重机	13	0		0	6.5	0	0	5.2	0	0			10.4	0					0	0	
84269100	供装于公路车辆的其他起重机	10	0		0	5		0	0	0				6	0					0	0	0
84269900	其他起重设备	6	0		0	5		0	0	0				3.6	0					0	0	0
84271010	有轨巷道堆垛机	9	0		0	5		0	0	0				5.4	0					0	0	0
84271020	无轨巷道堆垛机	9	0		0	5		0	0	0				5.4	0					0	0	0
84271090	其他电动机推进的叉车及可升降工作车	9	0		0	5		0	0	0				5.4	0					0	0	0
84272010	集装箱叉车	9	0	8.6	0	5		0	0	0				5.4	0					0	0	0
84272090	其他机动叉车及有类似装置工作车	9	0	8.6	0	5		0	0	0				5.4	0					0	0	0
84279000	其他叉车及可升降的工作车	9	0		0	5		0	0	0				5.4	0					0	0	0
84281010	载客电梯	8	0	5.6	0	5	0	0	0	0	0	0		6.4	0					0	0	0
84281090	其他升降机及倒卸式起重机	6	0	4.2	0	0		0	0	0	0	0	0	3.6	0					0	0	0
84282000	气压升降机及输送机	5	0		0	0		0	0	0				3	0					0	0	0
84283100	地下连续运货或材料升降、输送机	5	0		0	0		0	0	0				0	0					0	0	0
84283200	其他斗式连续运货升降、输送机	5	0		0	0		0	0	0	0				0					0	0	0
84283300	其他带式连续运货升降、输送机	5	0	4.3	0	0		0	0	0	0		0	3	0					0	0	0
84283910	链式连续运送货物的升降机及输送机	5	0	3.5	0	0		0	0	0	0		0	0	0					0	0	0
84283920	辊式连续运送货物的升降机及输送机	5	0	3.5	0	0		0	0	0	0		0	0	0					0	0	0
84283990	其他未列名连续运货升降、输送机	5	0	3.5	0	0		0	0	0	0		0	3.9	0					0	0	0
84284000	自动梯及自动人行道	5	0		0	0		0	0	0				0	0					0	0	0
84286010	货运架空索道	8	0		0	5		0	0	0				4.8	0					0	0	0
84286021	单线循环式客运架空索道	8	0		0	5		0	0	0				4.8	0					0	0	0
84286029	其他客运架空索道	8	0		0	5		0	0	0				4.8	0					0	0	0
84286090	其他缆车、座式升降机用牵引装置	8	0		0	5		0	0	0				4.8	0					0	0	0
84289010	矿车推动机、铁道机车等的转车台	10	0		0	5		0	0	0				6	0					0	0	0
84289020	机械式停车设备	5	0		0	0		0	0	0	0			0	0					0	0	0
84289031	堆取料机械	5	0		0	0		0	0	0	0		0	4	0					0	0	0
84289039	其他装卸机械	5	0		0	0		0	0	0	0		0	4	0					0	0	0
84289040	搬运机器人	5	0		0	0		0	0	0	0		0	4	0					0	0	0

税则号列	货品名称	最惠国	协定税率													特惠税率						
			东盟统一	亚太5国	智利	巴基斯坦	新加坡	新西兰	秘鲁	哥达	香港	澳门	台湾	瑞士	冰岛	亚太2国	老挝	柬埔寨	缅甸	LDC1	LDC2	LDC3
84289090	其他升降、搬运、装卸机械	5	0		0	0		0	0	0	0		0	4	0					0	0	0
84291110	功率>235.36kw的履带式推土机	7	0		0	5		0	0	0				4.2	0					0	0	0
84291190	功率≤235.36kw的履带式推土机	7	0		0	5		0	0	0				4.2	0					0	0	0
84291910	功率>235.36kw的其他推土机	7	0		0	5		0	0	0				4.2	0					0	0	0
84291990	功率≤235.36kw的其他推土机	7	0		0	5		0	0	0				4.2	0					0	0	0
84292010	功率>235.36kw的筑路机及平地机	5	0		0	0		0	0	0				0	0					0	0	0
84292090	其他筑路机及平地机	5	0		0	0		0	0	0				0	0					0	0	0
84293010	斗容量>10立方米的铲运机	3	0		0	0		0	0	0				0	0					0	0	0
84293090	斗容量≤10立方米的铲运机	5	0		0	0		0	0	0				0	0					0	0	0
84294011	机重≥18吨的震动式压路机	7	0		0	5		0	0	0				4.2	0					0	0	0
84294019	其他机动压路机	8	0		0	5		0	0	0				4.8	0					0	0	0
84294090	其他未列名捣固机械及压路机	6	0		0	5		0	0	0				3.6	0					0	0	0
84295100	前铲装载机	5	0		0	0		0	0	0				0	0					0	0	0
84295211	轮胎式挖掘机	8	0	7.2	0	5		0	0	0				4.8	0					0	0	0
84295212	履带式挖掘机	8	0		0	5		0	0	0	0			4.8	0					0	0	0
84295219	其他挖掘机	8	0	7.2	0	5		0	0	0				4.8	0					0	0	0
84295290	其他上部结构可转360度的挖掘机类似机械	8	0	7.2	0	5		0	0	0				4.8	0					0	0	0
84295900	其他机械铲、挖掘机及机铲装载机	8	0		0	5		0	0	0				4.8	0					0	0	0
84301000	打桩机及拔桩机	10	0		0	5		0	0	0				6	0					0	0	0
84302000	扫雪机及吹雪机	10	0		0	5		0	0	0				6	0					0	0	0
84303110	采(截)煤机	10	0		0	5	0	0	4	0				6	0					0	0	0
84303120	凿岩机	10	0		0	5	0	0	4	0				6	0					0	0	0
84303130	隧道掘进机	10	0		0	5	0	0	4	0				6	0					0	0	0
84303900	其他非自推进截煤机、采石机及掘进机	6	0		0	5		0	0	0				3.6	0					0	0	0
84304111	钻探深度≥6000米的自推进石油钻探机	5	0		0	0		0	0	0	0			0	0					0	0	0
84304119	其他自推进石油及天然气钻探机	5	0		0	0		0	0	0	0			0	0					0	0	0
84304121	钻探深度≥6000米的其他钻探机	5	0		0	0		0	0	0	0			0	0					0	0	0
84304122	钻探深度<6000米履带式自推进钻机	5	0		0	0		0	0	0	0			0	0					0	0	0
84304129	钻探深度<6000米的其他自推进钻机	5	0		0	0		0	0	0	0			0	0					0	0	0
84304190	其他自推进的凿井机械	5	0		0	0		0	0	0	0			0	0					0	0	0
84304900	非自推进的钻探或凿井机械	5	0		0	0		0	0	0				0	0					0	0	0
84305010	其他自推进采油机械	3	0		0	0		0	0	0				0	0					0	0	0
84305020	矿用电铲	7	0		0	5		0	0	0				4.2	0					0	0	0
84305031	牙轮直径≥380mm的采矿牙轮钻机	5	0		0	0		0	0	0				0	0					0	0	0
84305039	牙轮直径<380mm的采矿牙轮钻机	5	0		0	0		0	0	0				0	0					0	0	0
84305090	其他自推进未列名机械	5	0		0	0		0	0	0				0	0					0	0	0
84306100	非自推进捣固或压实机械	6	0		0	5		0	0	0				3.6	0					0	0	0
84306911	钻筒直径>3m的工程钻机	6	0		0	5		0	0	0				3.6	0					0	0	0
84306919	钻筒直径≤3m的工程钻机	6	0		0	5		0	0	0				3.6	0					0	0	0
84306920	非自推进铲运机	6	0		0	5		0	0	0				3.6	0					0	0	0
84306990	其他非自推进未列名机械	6	0		0	5		0	0	0				3.6	0					0	0	0
84311000	滑车、绞盘、千斤顶等机械用零件	3	0		0	0		0	0	0				0	0					0	0	0
84312010	税号84.27所列机械的装有差速器的驱动桥及其零件,不论是否装有其他传动部件	6	0	5.4	0	0		0	0	0				3.6	0					0	0	0
84312090	其他税号84.27所列机械的零件	6	0	5.4	0	0		0	0	0				3.6	0					0	0	0
84313100	升降机、倒卸式起重机或自动梯的零件	3	0		0	0		0	0	0				0	0					0	0	0
84313900	税号84.28所列其他机械的零件	5	0	2.5	0	0		0	0	0	0			3	0					0	0	0
84314100	戽斗、铲斗、抓斗及夹斗	6	0	5.4	0	0		0	0	0				3.6	0					0	0	0
84314200	推土机或侧铲推土机用铲	6	0		0	5		0	0	0				3.6	0					0	0	0
84314310	石油或天然气钻探机用零件	4	0	2.8	0	0		0	0	0	0			0	0					0	0	0
84314320	其他钻探机用零件	4	0	2.8	0	0		0	0	0	0			0	0					0	0	0
84314390	其他凿井机用零件	5	0	3.5	0	0		0	0	0	0			0	0					0	0	0
84314920	税号84.26、84.29、或84.30所列机械的装有差速器的驱动桥及其零件,不论是否装有其他传动部件	5	0	4.5	0	0		0	0	0	0			3	0					0	0	0
84314991	矿用电铲用零件	5	0	4.5	0	0		0	0	0	0			0	0					0	0	0
84314999	其他税号84.26、84.29、或84.30所列机械的零件	5	0	4.5	0	0		0	0	0	0			3	0					0	0	0

税则号列	货品名称	最惠国	协定税率													特惠税率						
			东盟统一	亚太5国	智利	巴基斯坦	新加坡	新西兰	秘鲁	哥达	香港	澳门	台湾	瑞士	冰岛	亚太2国	老挝	柬埔寨	缅甸	LDC1	LDC2	LDC3
84321000	犁	5	0		0	0		0	0	0				0	0					0	0	0
84322100	圆盘耙	5	0		0	0		0	0	0				0	0					0	0	0
84322900	其他耙、松土机等耕作机械	4	0		0	0		0	0	0				0	0					0	0	
84323011	谷物播种机	4	0	3.5	0	0		0	0	0				0	0					0	0	
84323019	其他播种机	4	0	3.5	0	0		0	0	0				0	0					0	0	
84323021	马铃薯种植机	4	0	3.5	0	0		0	0	0				0	0					0	0	
84323029	其他种植机	4	0	3.5	0	0		0	0	0				0	0					0	0	
84323031	水稻插秧机	4	0	3.5	0	0		0	0	0				0	0					0	0	
84323039	其他移植机(栽植机)	4	0	3.5	0	0		0	0	0				0	0					0	0	
84324000	施肥机	4	0		0	0		0	0	0				0	0					0	0	
84328010	草坪及运动场地滚压机	7	0		0	5		0	0	0				4.2	0					0	0	
84328090	其他未列名整地或耕作机械	4	0		0	0		0	0	0				0	0					0	0	
84329000	整地或耕作机械、滚压机零件	4	0		0	0		0	0	0				0	0					0	0	
84331100	机动旋转式割草机	6	0		0	5		0	0	0				3.6	0					0	0	
84331900	草坪、公园等用其他割草机	6	0		0	5		0	0	0				3.6	0					0	0	
84332000	其他割草机	4	0		0	0		0	0	0				0	0					0	0	
84333000	其他干草切割、翻晒机器	5	0		0	0		0	0	0				0	0					0	0	
84334000	草料打包机	5	0		0	0		0	0	0				0	0					0	0	
84335100	联合收割机	8	0	7.6	0	5		0	0	0				4.8	0					0	0	
84335200	其他脱粒机	8	0		0	5		0	0	0				4.8	0					0	0	
84335300	根茎或块茎收获机	8	0		0	5		0	0	0				4.8	0					0	0	
84335910	甘蔗收获机	8	0		0	5		0	0	0				4.8	0					0	0	
84335920	棉花采摘机	8	0		0	5		0	0	0				4.8	0					0	0	
84335990	其他收割机	8	0		0	5		0	0	0				4.8	0					0	0	
84336000	蛋类、水果等清洁、分选、分级机	5	0		0	0		0	0	0				0	0					0	0	
84339010	联合收割机用零件	5	0		0	0		0	0	0				0	0					0	0	
84339090	税号84.33所列其他机械零件	3	0		0	0		0	0	0				0	0					0	0	0
84341000	挤奶机	10	0		0	5		1.1		0				6	0					0	0	
84342000	乳品加工机器	6	0		0	5		0	0	0				3.6	0					0	0	
84349000	挤奶机及乳品加工机器用零件	5	0		0	0		0	0	0				0	0					0	0	
84351000	制酒、果汁等的压榨、轧碎机	10	0		0	5		0	0	0		0		6	0					0	0	
84359000	制酒、果汁等压榨、轧碎机零件	6	0		0	5		0	0	0				3.6	0					0	0	
84361000	动物饲料配制机	7	0		0	5		0	0	0				5.4	0					0	0	
84362100	家禽孵卵器及育雏器	5	0		0	0		0	0	0				0	0					0	0	
84362900	家禽饲养用机器	10	0		0	5		0	0	0				6	0					0	0	
84368000	农、林业、园艺等用的其他机器	10	0		0	5		0	0	0				6	0					0	0	
84369100	家禽饲养机、孵卵器及育雏器零件	6	0		0	5		0	0	0				3.6	0					0	0	
84369900	税号84.36所列其他机器的零件	6	0		0	5		0	0	0				4.6	0					0	0	
84371010	光学色差颗粒选别机(色选机)	10	0		0	5		0	0	0				6	0					0	0	
84371090	其他种子、谷物或干豆的清洁、分选或分级机	10	0		0	5		0	0	0				6	0					0	0	
84378000	谷物磨粉业加工机器	10	0	8.5	0	5		0	0	0				6	0					0	0	
84379000	税号84.37所列机械的零件	6	0		0	5		0	0	0				4.8	0					0	0	
84381000	糕点、通心粉、面条的生产加工机器	7	0		0	5		0	0	0				5.6	0					0	0	0
84382000	生产糖果、可可粉、巧克力的机器	8	0		0	5		0	0	0				0	0					0	0	0
84383000	制糖机器	10	0		0	5		0	0	0					0					0	0	0
84384000	酿酒机器	7	0		0	5		0	0	0				4.2	0					0	0	0
84385000	肉类或家禽加工机器	7	0		0	5		0	0	0				4.2	0					0	0	0
84386000	水果、坚果或蔬菜加工机器	10	0		0	5	0	0	4	0				6	0					0	0	0
84388000	84章其他未列名食品等加工机器	8.5	0	8.1	0	5		0	0	0			0	6.8	0					0	0	0
84389000	食品、饮料工业用机器的零件	5	0		0	0		0	0	0				0	0					0	0	0
84391000	制造纤维素纸浆的机器	8.4	0		0	5		0	0	0				5	0					0	0	0
84392000	纸或纸板的抄造机器	8.4	0		0	5		0	0	0			0	6.7	0					0	0	0
84393000	纸或纸板的整理机器	8.4	0		0	5		0	0	0			0	5	0					0	0	0
84399100	制造纤维素纸浆的机器零件	6	0		0	5		0	0	0				3.6	0					0	0	0
84399900	制造或整理纸及纸板的机器零件	6	0	3	0	0		0	0	0				4.8	0					0	0	0
84401010	锁线装订机	10	0		0	5		0	0	0				6	0					0	0	
84401020	胶订机	12	0		0	6	0	0	0	0				7.2	0					0	0	
84401090	其他书本装订机器	12	0		0	6	0	0	0	0				0	0					0	0	
84409000	书本装订机器的零件	8	0		0	5		0	0	0				6.4	0					0	0	
84411000	切纸机	12	0		0	6	0	0	0	0			0		0					0	0	0

税则号列	货品名称	最惠国	协定税率													特惠税率						
			东盟统一	亚太5国	智利	巴基斯坦	新加坡	新西兰	秘鲁	哥达	香港	澳门	台湾	瑞士	冰岛	亚太2国	老挝	柬埔寨	缅甸	LDC1	LDC2	LDC3
84412000	制造包、袋或信封的机器	12	0	11.4	0	6	0	0	4.8	0				9.6	0					0	0	0
84413010	纸塑铝复合罐生产设备	13.5	0	12.8	0	6.8	0	0	5.4	0				10.8	0					0	0	
84413090	其他制造箱、盒、桶及类似容器的机器	13.5	0	12.8	0	6.8	0	0	5.4	0				10.8	0					0	0	
84414000	纸浆、纸或纸板制品模制成型机器	12	0		0	6	0	0	0	0				9.6	0					0	0	0
84418010	制造纸塑铝软包装的生产设备	12	0	11.4	0	6	0	0	0	0				9.6	0					0	0	0
84418090	其他制造纸浆制品、纸制品的机器	12	0	11.4	0	6	0	0	0	0			0	9.6	0					0	0	0
84419010	切纸机零件	8	0		0	5		0	0	0				4.8	0					0	0	0
84419090	其他制造纸浆、纸制品的机器零件	8.4	0		0	5		0	0	0					0					0	0	0
84423010	铸字机	9	0		0	5		0	0	0				5.4	0					0	0	0
84423021	计算机直接制版设备	9	0		0	5		0	0	0				7.2	0					0	0	0
84423029	去制版机器、器具及设备	9	0		0	5		0	0	0				5.4	0					0	0	0
84423090	其他铸字、制版用机器、器具及设备	9	0		0	5		0	0	0				5.4	0					0	0	0
84424000	铸字、排字、制版机器的零件	7	0		0	5		0	0	0				4.2	0					0	0	0
84425000	活字、印刷用版、片及其他部件	7	0		0	5		0	0	0	0			4.2	0					0	0	0
84431100	卷取进料式胶印机	10	0	7	0	5		0	4	0				6	0					0	0	0
84431200	办公室用片取进料式胶印机	12	0		0	6	0	0	0	0				9.6	0					0	0	0
84431311	平张纸进料式单色胶印机	10	0	7	0	5		0	0	0				6	0					0	0	0
84431312	平张纸进料式双色胶印机	.10	0	7	0	5		0	0	0				6	0					0	0	0
84431313	平张纸进料式四色胶印机	10	0	7	0	5		0	0	0				6	0					0	0	0
84431319	平张纸进料式其他胶印机	10	0	7	0	5		0	0	0				6	0					0	0	0
84431390	其他胶印机	10	0	7	0	5		0	0	0				6	0					0	0	0
84431400	卷取进料式凸版印刷机	12	0		0	6	0	0	0	0	0			9.6	0					0	0	0
84431500	其他凸版印刷机	12	0		0	6	0	0	0	0				9.6	0					0	0	0
84431600	苯胺印刷机	10	0		0	5		0	0	0				6	0					0	0	0
84431700	照像凹版印刷机	18	0	16.2	0	14.4	0	0	7.2	0				14.4	0					0	0	0
84431921	圆网印刷机	10	0	9	0	5		0	0	0				6	0					0	0	0
84431922	平网印刷机	10	0	9	0	5		0	0	0			0	8	0					0	0	0
84431929	其他网式印刷机	10	0	9	0	5	0	0	0	0			0	6	0					0	0	0
84431980	其它印刷机	8	0	7.2	0	5		0	0	0	0		0	4.8	0					0	0	0
84433110	静电感光式多功能机	10	0		0	5	0	0	0	0				6	0					0	0	0
84433190	其他多功能机	0																		0	0	0
84433211	针式打印机	0																		0	0	0
84433212	激光打印机	0																		0	0	0
84433213	喷墨打印机	0																		0	0	0
84433214	热敏打印机	0																		0	0	0
84433219	其他打印机	0																		0	0	0
84433221	可以网络连接的喷墨印刷机	8	0		0	5	0	0	0	0				4.8	0					0	0	0
84433222	可以网络连接的静电照相印刷机(激光印刷机)	8	0	7.2	0	5		0	0	0				4.8	0					0	0	0
84433229	可以网络连接的其他数字印刷设备	8	0	7.2	0	5		0	0	0				4.8	0					0	0	0
84433290	其他可与网络连接的传真机或打字机	0																		0	0	0
84433911	直接法静电感光复印设备	0																		0	0	0
84433912	间接法静电感光复印设备	10	0		0	5	0	0	0	0				6	0					0	0	0
84433921	带有光学系统的感光复印设备	0																		0	0	0
84433922	接触式感光复印设备	20	0		0		0	0	8	0				16	0					0	0	
84433923	热敏复印设备	20	0		0		0	0	8	0				16	0					0	0	
84433924	热升华复印设备	20	0		0		0	0	8	0				16	0					0	0	
84433931	其他独立的喷墨印刷机	8	0		0	5	0	0	0	0				4.8	0					0	0	0
84433932	其他独立的静电照相印刷机(激光印刷机)	8	0	7.2	0	5		0	0	0				4.8	0					0	0	0
84433939	其他独立的数字印刷设备	8	0	7.2	0	5	0	0	0	0				4.8	0					0	0	0
84433990	其他独立的电传打字机	0																		0	0	0
84439111	卷筒料给料机	12	0		0	6	0	0	0	0				9.6	0					0	0	0
84439119	其他传统印刷机用辅助机器	12	0		0	6	0	0	0	0				7.2	0					0	0	0
84439190	传统印刷机用零件及附件	6	0		0	5		0	0	0				4.8	0					0	0	0
84439910	数字印刷设备用辅助机器	12	0		0	6	0	0	0	0				7.2	0					0	0	0
84439921	热敏打印头	6	0		0	5		0	0	0				3.6	0					0	0	0
84439929	数字印刷设备的其他零件	6	0		0	5		0	0	0				3.6	0					0	0	0
84439990	其他打印机、复印机、传真机用零件	0																		0	0	0
84440010	合成纤维长丝纺丝机	10	0	7	0	5		0	0	0			0		0					0	0	
84440020	合成纤维短丝纺丝机	10	0	7	0	5		0	0	0				6	0					0	0	

税则号列	货品名称	最惠国	协定税率													特惠税率						
			东盟统一	亚太5国	智利	巴基斯坦	新加坡	新西兰	秘鲁	哥达	香港	澳门	台湾	瑞士	冰岛	亚太2国	老挝	柬埔寨	缅甸	LDC1	LDC2	LDC3
84440030	人造纤维纺丝机	10	0	7	0	5		0	0	0				6	0					0	0	
84440040	化学纤维变形机	10	0	7	0	5		0	0	0				8	0					0	0	
84440050	化学纤维切断机	10	0	7	0	5		0	0	0				8	0					0	0	
84440090	其他化学纤维挤压、拉伸、变形或切割机器	10	0	7	0	5		0	0	0				8	0					0	0	
84451111	棉纤维清梳联合机	10	0	9	0	5		0	0	0				6	0					0	0	0
84451112	棉纤维自动抓棉机	10	0	9	0	5		0	0	0					0					0	0	0
84451113	棉纤维梳棉机	10	0	9	0	5		0	0	0				8	0					0	0	0
84451119	其他棉纤维梳理机	10	0	9	0	5		0	0	0				6	0					0	0	0
84451120	毛纤维梳理机	10	0	9	0	5		0	0	0				6	0					0	0	0
84451190	其他纺织纤维梳理机	10	0	9	0	5		0	0	0				6	0					0	0	0
84451210	棉纺织纤维精梳机	10	0		0	5		0	0	0					0					0	0	0
84451220	毛纺织纤维精梳机	10	0		0	5		0	0	0				6	0					0	0	0
84451290	其他纺织纤维精梳机	10	0		0	5		0	0	0				6	0					0	0	0
84451310	拉伸机	10	0		0	5		0	0	0				6	0					0	0	0
84451321	棉纺粗纱机	10	0		0	5		0	0	0					0					0	0	0
84451322	毛纺粗纱机	10	0		0	5		0	0	0				6	0					0	0	0
84451329	其他粗纱机	10	0		0	5		0	0	0				6	0					0	0	0
84451900	纺织纤维的其他预处理机器	10	0	9	0	5		0	4	0					0					0	0	0
84452031	转杯纺纱机	10	0	9	0	5		0	0	0				6	0					0	0	0
84452032	喷气纺纱机	10	0		0	5		0	0	0					0					0	0	0
84452039	其他自由端纺纱机	10	0		0	5		0	0	0				6	0					0	0	0
84452041	棉环锭细纱机	10.5	0	9.5	0	5	0	0	0	0				8.4	0					0	0	0
84452042	毛环锭细纱机	10	0		0	5		0	0	0				6	0					0	0	0
84452049	其他环锭细纱机	10	0		0	5		0	0	0				6	0					0	0	0
84452090	其他纺纱机	10	0	9	0	5		0	0	0					0					0	0	0
84453000	并线机或加捻机	10	0	9	0	5		0	0	0				6	0					0	0	0
84454010	自动络筒机	10	0	9	0	5		0	4	0				6	0					0	0	0
84454090	其他络纱机(包括卷纬机)或摇纱机	10	0	9	0	5		0	4	0				6	0					0	0	0
84459010	整经机	10	0	9	0	5		0	0	0					0					0	0	0
84459020	浆纱机	10	0	9	0	5		0	0	0					0					0	0	0
84459090	其他生产及处理纺织纱线的机器	10	0	9	0	5		0	0	0				8	0					0	0	0
84461000	所织织物宽度≤30cm的织机	8	0	7.2	0	5		0	0	0				6.4	0					0	0	
84462110	所织织物宽度>30cm的梭织动力地毯织机	12	0	10.8	0	5	0	0	4.8	0				9.6	0					0	0	
84462190	所织织物宽度>30cm的其他梭织动力织机	10	0	9	0	5	0	0	4	0					0					0	0	
84462900	所织织物宽度>30cm的梭织非动力织机	10	0		0	5		0	4	0				6	0					0	0	
84463020	所织织物宽度>30cm的剑杆织机	8	0	6.8	0	5		0	0	0				6.4	0					0	0	
84463030	所织织物宽度>30cm的片梭织机	8	0	5.6	0	5		0	0	0					0					0	0	
84463040	所织织物宽度>30cm的喷水织机	8	0	6.8	0	5		0	0	0			0	4.8	0					0	0	
84463050	所织织物宽度>30cm的喷气织机	8	0	6.8	0	5		0	0	0				4.8	0					0	0	
84463090	所织织物宽度>30cm的其他无梭织机	8	0	6.8	0	5		0	0	0				4.8	0					0	0	
84471100	圆筒直径≤165mm的圆型针织机	8	0	7	0	5		0	0	0			0	4.8	0					0	0	0
84471200	圆筒直径>165mm的圆型针织机	8	0		0	5		0	0	0			0	4.8	0					0	0	0
84472011	特里科经编机	8	0	6.8	0	5		0	0	0				4.8	0					0	0	0
84472012	拉舍尔经编机	8	0	6.8	0	5		0	0	0				4.8	0					0	0	0
84472019	其他经编机	8	0	6.8	0	5		0	0	0				4.8	0					0	0	0
84472020	平型纬编机	8	0	6.8	0	5		0	0	0			0	6.4	0					0	0	0
84472030	缝编机	8	0	6.8	0	5		0	0	0				4.8	0					0	0	0
84479011	地毯织机	7	0	4.9	0	0		0	0	0				4.2	0					0	0	0
84479019	其他簇绒机	8	0	5.6	0	5		0	0	0				4.8	0					0	0	0
84479020	绣花机	8	0	6.8	0	5		0	0	0					0					0	0	0
84479090	税号84.47其他未列名机器	10	0	5	0	5		0	0	0					0					0	0	0
84481100	多臂机或提花机	8	0		0	5		0	0	0				4.8	0					0	0	0
84481900	税号84.44至84.47所列的其他辅助机器	8	0		0	5		0	0	0				6.4	0					0	0	0
84482020	喷丝头或喷丝板	6	0		0	5		0	0	0				4.8	0					0	0	0
84482090	纤维挤压机及其辅助机器的其他零附件	6	0		0	5		0	0	0				4.8	0					0	0	0
84483100	钢丝针布	6	0		0	5		0	0	0				5.2	0					0	0	0

税则号列	货品名称	最惠国	协定税率													特惠税率						
			东盟统一	亚太5国	智利	巴基斯坦	新加坡	新西兰	秘鲁	哥达	香港	澳门	台湾	瑞士	冰岛	亚太2国	老挝	柬埔寨	缅甸	LDC1	LDC2	LDC3
84483200	纺织纤维预处理机器的其他零附件	6	0		0	5		0	0	0				4.8	0					0	0	0
84483310	络筒锭	6	0		0	5		0	0	0				3.6	0					0	0	0
84483390	其他锭子、锭壳、纺丝环、钢丝圈	6	0		0	5		0	0	0				4.8	0					0	0	0
84483910	气流杯	6	0		0	5		0	0	0				3.6	0					0	0	0
84483920	电子清纱器	6	0		0	5		0	0	0				5.2	0					0	0	0
84483930	空气捻接器	6	0		0	5		0	0	0				3.6	0					0	0	0
84483940	环锭细纱机紧密纺装置	6	0		0	5		0	0	0				4.6	0					0	0	0
84483990	税号 84.45 所列机器的其他零附件	6	0		0	5		0	0	0				5.2	0					0	0	0
84484200	织机用筘、综丝及综框	6	0		0	5		0	0	0				4.8	0					0	0	0
84484910	接、投梭箱	6	0		0	5		0	0	0				4.8	0					0	0	0
84484920	引纬、送经装置	6	0		0	5		0	0	0				4.8	0					0	0	0
84484930	梭子	6	0		0	5		0	0	0				3.6	0					0	0	0
84484990	织机及其辅助机器用其他零附件	6	0		0	5		0	0	0				4.8	0					0	0	0
84485120	针织机用 28 号以下的弹簧针、钩针及复合针	6	0		0	5		0	0	0				3.6	0					0	0	0
84485190	沉降片、其他织针及成圈机件	6	0		0	5		0	0	0				3.6	0					0	0	0
84485900	税号 84.47 机器用的其他零附件	6	0		0	5		0	0	0	0		0	4.8	0					0	0	0
84490010	针刺机	8	0		0	5		0	0	0				4.8	0					0	0	
84490020	水刺设备	8	0		0	5		0	0	0				4.8	0					0	0	
84490090	其他毡呢或无纺织物制造或整理机器;帽模	8	0		0	5		0	0	0				4.8	0					0	0	
84501110	干衣量≤10kg 的波轮式全自动洗衣机	10	0	8.7	0	5	0	0	0	0				6	0					0	0	0
84501120	干衣量≤10kg 的滚筒式全自动洗衣机	10	0	8.7	0	5	0	0	0	0				6	0					0	0	0
84501190	干衣量≤10kg 的其他全自动洗衣机	10	0	8.7	0	5	0	0	0	0				6	0					0	0	0
84501200	装有离心甩干机的非全自动洗衣机	30	0	24.9	0	24.9	0	0	12	0				23.1	0					0	0	
84501900	干衣量≤10kg 的其他洗衣机	30	0		0		0	0	12	0				23.1	0					0	0	
84502011	波轮式洗衣机	10	0		0	5		0	0	0				6	0					0	0	0
84502012	滚筒式洗衣机	10	0		0	5		0	0	0				6	0					0	0	0
84502019	其他全自动洗衣机	10	0		0	5		0	0	0				6	0					0	0	0
84502090	其他干衣量超过 10 公斤的洗衣机	10	0		0	5		0	0	0				6	0					0	0	0
84509010	干衣量≤10kg 的洗衣机零件	5	0	4.2	0	0		0	0	0				0	0					0	0	0
84509090	干衣量 >10kg 的洗衣机零件	16	0	14.4	0	12.8	0	0	6.4	0				12.8	0					0	0	
84511000	干洗机	21	0	16	0	16	0	0	8.4	0				16.8	0					0	0	
84512100	干衣量≤10kg 的干燥机	15	0	13.5	0	7.5	0	0	6	0				12	0					0	0	
84512900	干衣量 >10kg 的干燥机	8	0	7.2	0	5		0	0	0				4.8	0					0	0	0
84513000	熨烫机及挤压机(包括熔压机)	8	0	7.2	0	5	0	0	0	0				4.8	0					0	0	0
84514000	洗涤、漂白或染色机器	8.4	0	7	0	5		0	0	0	0	0	0	5	0					0	0	0
84515000	纺织物卷绕、退绕、折叠、剪切或剪齿边机器	8	0	7.2	0	5		0	0	0			0	4.8	0					0	0	0
84518000	税号 84.51 所列其他未列名的机器	12	0	10.8	0	5	0	0	4.8	0	0		0		0					0	0	0
84519000	税号 84.51 所列机器的零件	8	0	7.2	0	5		0	0	0				4.8	0					0	0	0
84521010	多功能家用缝纫机	21	0	17	0	16.8	0	0	8.4	0				16.8	0					0	0	
84521091	手动式家用型缝纫机	21	0	17	0	16.8	0	0	8.4	0				16.8	0					0	0	
84521099	其他家用型缝纫机	21	0	17	0	16.8	0	0	8.4	0				16.8	0					0	0	
84522110	非家用自动平缝机	12	0	10.7	0	5	0	0	0	0				9.6	0					0	0	0
84522120	非家用自动包缝机	12	0	10.7	0	5	0	0	0	0			0	9.6	0					0	0	0
84522130	非家用自动绷缝机	12	0	10.7	0	5	0	0	0	0			0	9.6	0					0	0	0
84522190	其他非家用自动缝纫机	12	0	10.7	0	5	0	0	0	0			0	9.6	0					0	0	0
84522900	其他非家用非自动缝纫机	12	0	10.8	0	5	0	0	0	0	0			9.6	0					0	0	0
84523000	缝纫机针	14	0	12.6	0	7	0	0	0	0				11.2	0					0	0	
84529011	家用型缝纫机用旋梭	14	0	9.8	0	7	0	0	0	0				11.2	0					0	0	
84529019	家用型缝纫机用其他零件	14	0	9.8	0	7	0	0	0	0				11.2	0					0	0	
84529091	其他缝纫机用旋梭	14	0	9.8	0	7	0	0	0	0				11.2	0					0	0	0
84529092	其他缝纫机专用的特制家具、底座和罩盖及其零件	14	0		0	11.2	0	0	0	0				11.2	0					0	0	
84529099	其他缝纫机用其他零件	14	0	9.8	0	7	0	0	0	0			0	11.2	0					0	0	0
84531000	生皮、皮革的处理、鞣制或加工机器	8.4	0	8	0	5		0	0	0				5	0					0	0	
84532000	鞋靴制作或修理机器	8.4	0	8	0	5		0	0	0				5	0					0	0	
84538000	毛皮及其他皮革的制作或修理机器	8.4	0		0	5		0	0	0				5	0					0	0	
84539000	税号 84.53 所列机器的零件	8	0		0	5		0	0	0				4.8	0					0	0	

税则号列	货品名称	最惠国	协定税率 东盟统一	亚太5国	智利	巴基斯坦	新加坡	新西兰	秘鲁	哥达	香港	澳门	台湾	瑞士	冰岛	特惠税率 亚太2国	老挝	柬埔寨	缅甸	LDC1	LDC2	LDC3
84541000	金属冶炼及铸造用转炉	8.4	0		0	5		0	0	0				5	0					0	0	0
84542010	炉外精炼设备	8.4	0		0	5		0	0	0				5	0					0	0	0
84542090	其他金属冶炼及铸造用锭模及浇包	8.4	0		0	5		0	0	0					0					0	0	0
84543010	冷室压铸机	12	0	11.4	0	6	0	0	0	0				9.6	0					0	0	0
84543021	方坯连铸机	10	0	9.5	0	5		0	0	0				8	0					0	0	0
84543022	板坯连铸机	12	0	11.4	0	6	0	0	0	0				9.6	0					0	0	0
84543029	其他钢坯连铸机	12	0	11.4	0	6	0	0	0	0				9.6	0					0	0	0
84543090	其他金属冶炼及铸造用铸造机	12	0	11.4	0	6	0	0	0	0				9.6	0					0	0	0
84549010	炉外精炼设备用零件	8	0		0	5		0	0	0				4.8	0					0	0	0
84549021	结晶器	8	0		0	5		0	0	0				4.8	0					0	0	0
84549022	振动装置	8	0		0	5		0	0	0				4.8	0					0	0	0
84549029	其他钢坯连铸机用零件	8	0		0	5		0	0	0				6.4	0					0	0	0
84549090	其他冶炼等用转炉及铸造机的零件	8	0		0	5		0	0	0				6.4	0					0	0	0
84551010	热轧管机	12	0	8.4	0	5	0	0	0	0				9.6	0					0	0	0
84551020	冷轧管机	12	0	8.4	0	5	0	0	0	0				9.6	0					0	0	0
84551030	定、减径轧管机	12	0	8.4	0	5	0	0	0	0				9.6	0					0	0	0
84551090	其他金属轧管机	12	0	8.4	0	5	0	0	0	0				9.6	0					0	0	0
84552110	板材热轧机	15	0	10.5	0	7.5	0	0	6	0				12	0					0	0	
84552120	型钢轧机	15	0	10.5	0	7.5	0	0	6	0				12	0					0	0	
84552130	线材轧机	15	0	10.5	0	7.5	0	0	6	0				12	0					0	0	
84552190	其他金属热轧或冷热联合轧机	15	0	10.5	0	7.5	0	0	6	0				12	0					0	0	
84552210	板材冷轧机	10	0		0	5		0	0	0				6	0					0	0	
84552290	其他金属冷轧机	15	0		0	12	0	0	6	0				12	0					0	0	
84553000	金属轧机用轧辊	8.4	0		0	5		0	0	0				5	0					0	0	0
84559000	金属轧机的其他零件	8	0	4	0	0		0	0	0				4.8	0					0	0	0
84561000	用激光等处理各种材料的加工机床	0																		0	0	0
84562000	用超声波处理各种材料的加工机床	10	0		0	5	0	0	0	0					0					0	0	
84563010	数控的用放电处理各种材料的加工机床	9.7	0		0	5		0	0	0					0					0	0	
84563090	非数控的用放电处理各种材料的加工机床	10	0		0	5	0	0	0	0				6	0					0	0	
84569010	等离子切割机	0																		0	0	0
84569020	水射流切割机	0																		0	0	0
84569090	其他用电化学、电子束处理材料的加工机床	0																		0	0	0
84571010	立式加工中心	9.7	0	6.8	0	5		0	0	0					0					0	0	
84571020	卧式加工中心	9.7	0	8.8	0	5		0	0	0					0					0	0	
84571030	龙门式加工中心	9.7	0	6.8	0	5		0	0	0				5.8	0					0	0	
84571091	铣车复合加工中心	9.7	0	6.8	0	5		0	0	0					0					0	0	
84571099	其他加工中心	9.7	0	6.8	0	5		0	0	0					0					0	0	
84572000	加工金属的单工位组合机床	8	0		0	5		0	0	0				4.8	0					0	0	
84573000	加工金属的多工位组合机床	5	0		0	0		0	0	0					0					0	0	
84581100	切削金属的数控卧式车床	9.7	0		0	5		0	0	0	0		0	7.5	0					0	0	0
84581900	切削金属的非数控卧式车床	12	0		0	6	0	0	0	0	0			9.6	0					0	0	0
84589110	立式数控机床	5	0		0	0		0	0	0			0	3	0					0	0	0
84589120	其他数控机床	5	0		0	0		0	0	0			0	3	0					0	0	0
84589900	切削金属的其他车床	12	0		0	6	0	0	0	0				9.6	0					0	0	0
84591000	切削金属的直线移动式动力头钻床	15	0		0	12	0	0	6	0				12	0					0	0	
84592100	切削金属的数控钻床	9.7	0		0	5		0	0	0			0	5.8	0					0	0	0
84592900	切削金属的其他钻床	15	0		0	12	0	0	6	0				12	0					0	0	
84593100	切削金属的数控镗铣机床	9.7	0		0	5		0	0	0				7.8	0					0	0	0
84593900	切削金属的其他镗铣机床	10	0		0	5		0	0	0				6	0					0	0	0
84594010	切削金属的数控镗床	9.7	0		0	5		0	0	0				5.8	0					0	0	0
84594090	切削金属的其他镗床	15	0		0	12	0	0	6	0				12	0					0	0	
84595100	切削金属的升降台式数控铣床	9.7	0		0	5		0	0	0					0					0	0	0
84595900	切削金属的其他升降台式铣床	15	0		0	12	0	0	6	0				12	0					0	0	
84596110	切削金属的数控龙门铣床	5	0		0	0		0	0	0				0	0					0	0	0
84596190	切削金属的其他数控铣床	5	0		0	0		0	0	0				3	0					0	0	0
84596910	切削金属的非数控龙门铣床	12	0	10	0	5	0	0	0	0				9.6	0					0	0	0
84596990	切削金属的其他铣床	12	0	11	0	6	0	0	0	0				9.6	0					0	0	0
84597000	切削金属的其他攻丝机床	12	0		0	6	0	0	0	0					0					0	0	0
84601100	数控平面磨床	9.7	0		0	5		0	0	0			0	5.8	0					0	0	0

税则号列	货品名称	最惠国	协定税率												特惠税率						
			东盟统一	亚太5国	智利	巴基斯坦	新加坡	新西兰	秘鲁	哥达	香港	澳门	台湾	瑞士	冰岛	亚太2国	老挝	柬埔寨	缅甸	LDC1	LDC2	LDC3
84601900	其他平面磨床	15	0		0	12	0	0	6	0				12	0					0	0	
84602111	曲轴磨床	9.7	0		0	5		0	0	0					0					0	0	0
84602119	其他外圆磨床	9.7	0		0	5		0	0	0					0					0	0	0
84602120	数控内圆磨床	9.7	0		0	5		0	0	0					0					0	0	0
84602190	其他数控磨床	9.7	0		0	5		0	0	0				7.5	0					0	0	0
84602910	其他外圆磨床	15	0		0	12	0	0	6	0	0			12	0					0	0	
84602920	其他内圆磨床	15	0		0	12	0	0	6	0				12	0					0	0	
84602930	非数控轧辊磨床	13	0		0	6.5	0	0	0	0				10.4	0					0	0	
84602990	其他磨床	13	0		0	6.5	0	0	0	0					0					0	0	
84603100	数控刃磨(工具或刀具)机床	9.7	0		0	5		0	0	0					0					0	0	0
84603900	其他刃磨(工具或刀具)机床	15	0		0	12	0	0	6	0	0				0					0	0	
84604010	珩磨机床	13	0		0	6.5	0	0	0	0				10.4	0					0	0	
84604020	研磨机床	13	0		0	6.5	0	0	0	0			0	10.4	0					0	0	
84609010	砂轮机	15	0		0	12	0	0	6	0			0	12	0					0	0	
84609020	抛光机床	15	0		0	12	0	0	6	0			0	12	0					0	0	
84609090	其他磨削等精加工机床	15	0		0	12	0	0	6	0				12	0					0	0	
84612010	牛头刨床	15	0		0	12	0	0	6	0				12	0					0	0	
84612020	插床	15	0		0	12	0	0	6	0			0	12	0					0	0	
84613000	拉床	12	0		0	6	0	0	0	0			0	9.6	0					0	0	
84614011	齿轮磨床	9.7	0		0	5		0	0	0					0					0	0	0
84614019	其他数控的切齿机、齿轮磨床或齿轮精加工机床	9.7	0		0	5		0	0	0					0					0	0	0
84614090	非数控切齿机、齿轮磨床齿轮精加工机床	15	0		0	12	0	0	6	0					0					0	0	
84615000	锯床或切断机	12	0		0	6	0	0	0	0			0	9.6	0					0	0	
84619011	龙门刨床	15	0		0	12	0	0	6	0			0	12	0					0	0	
84619019	其他刨床	15	0		0	12	0	0	6	0			0	9	0					0	0	
84619090	税号84.61的未列名机床	12	0		0	6	0	0	0	0				9.6	0					0	0	
84621010	数控锻造或冲压机床及锻锤	9.7	0	6.8	0	5		0	0	0			0	7.8	0					0	0	0
84621090	非数控锻造或冲压机床及锻锤	12	0	8.4	0	5	0	0	4.8	0			0	9.6	0					0	0	0
84622110	数控矫直机	9.7	0		0	5		0	0	0				7.8	0					0	0	0
84622190	数控的其他弯曲、折迭、矫直或矫平机床	9.7	0		0	5		0	0	0				7.8	0					0	0	0
84622910	非数控矫直机	10	0		0	5		0	4	0				7.7	0					0	0	0
84622990	非数控的其他弯曲、折迭、矫直或矫平机床	10	0		0	5	0	0	4	0				6	0					0	0	0
84623110	数控的板带纵剪机	7	0		0	5		0	0	0				4.2	0					0	0	0
84623120	数控的板带横剪机	7	0		0	5		0	0	0				4.2	0					0	0	0
84623190	数控的其他剪切机床	7	0		0	5		0	0	0				4.2	0					0	0	0
84623910	非数控板带纵剪机	10	0	9.5	0	5		0	0	0				6	0					0	0	0
84623920	非数控板带横剪机	10	0	9.5	0	5		0	0	0				6	0					0	0	0
84623990	其他剪切机床	10	0	9.5	0	5		0	0	0				6	0					0	0	0
84624111	自动换模式数控步冲压力机	9.7	0		0	5		0	0	0				7.8	0					0	0	0
84624119	其他数控冲床	9.7	0		0	5		0	0	0				5.8	0					0	0	0
84624190	其他数控冲孔、开槽机、冲剪两用机	9.7	0		0	5		0	0	0				5.8	0					0	0	0
84624900	非数控冲孔、开槽机、冲剪两用机	10	0		0	5	0	0	0	0			0	6	0					0	0	0
84629110	金属型材挤压机	10	0	9.2	0	5		0	0	0				6	0					0	0	0
84629190	其他液压压力机	10	0	9.2	0	5	0	0	0	0				8	0					0	0	0
84629910	其他机械压力机	10	0	9.5	0	5	0	0	0	0			0	6	0					0	0	0
84629990	税号84.62的未列名机床	10	0	9.5	0	5	0	0	0	0				6	0					0	0	0
84631011	拉拔力为300吨及以下的冷拔管机	10	0		0	5		0	0	0				6	0					0	0	
84631019	其他冷拔管机	10	0		0	5	0	0	0	0			0	6	0					0	0	
84631020	拔丝机	10	0		0	5		0	0	0				6	0					0	0	
84631090	其他金属杆、管、型材及类似品的拉拔机	10	0		0	5		0	0	0				6	0					0	0	
84632000	金属或金属陶瓷的螺纹滚轧机	15	0		0	12	0	0	6	0				12	0					0	0	
84633000	金属丝加工机	10	0		0	5		0	0	0				6	0					0	0	
84639000	其他非切削加工机床	10	0		0	5		0	4	0				8	0					0	0	
84641010	圆盘锯	0																		0	0	0
84641020	钢丝锯	0																		0	0	0
84641090	其他加工矿物等材料的锯床	0																		0	0	0
84642010	玻璃研磨或抛光机床	0																		0	0	0

税则号列	货品名称	最惠国	协定税率													特惠税率						
			东盟统一	亚太5国	智利	巴基斯坦	新加坡	新西兰	秘鲁	哥达	香港	澳门	台湾	瑞士	冰岛	亚太2国	老挝	柬埔寨	缅甸	LDC1	LDC2	LDC3
84642090	其他加工矿物等材料的研磨或抛光机床	0																		0	0	0
84649011	切割机	0																		0	0	0
84649012	刻花机	0																		0	0	0
84649019	玻璃的其他冷加工机床	0																		0	0	0
84649090	其他税号 84.64 的未列名机床	0																		0	0	0
84651000	不需变换工具即可进行加工的机床	10	0		0	5	0	0	4	0	0			6	0					0	0	
84659100	加工木材等材料的锯床	10	0		0	5		0	4	0	0			6	0					0	0	
84659200	加工木材等材料的刨、铣或切削机器	10	0		0	5	0	0	0	0	0			6	0					0	0	
84659300	加工木材等材料的研磨或抛光机器	10	0		0	5		0	0	0	0			6	0					0	0	
84659400	加工木材等材料的弯曲或装配机器	10	0		0	5	0	0	0	0				6	0					0	0	
84659500	加工木材等材料的钻孔或凿榫机器	10	0		0	5	0	0	0	0	0			8	0					0	0	
84659600	加工木材等材料的剖、切或刮削机器	10	0		0	5	0	0	0	0				6	0					0	0	
84659900	加工木材等材料的其他机床	10	0		0	5	0	0	4	0	0			6	0					0	0	
84661000	工具夹具及自启板牙切头	7	0		0	5		0	0	0				5.6	0					0	0	0
84662000	工件夹具	7	0	4.9	0	0		0	0	0			0	5.6	0					0	0	0
84663000	分度头及其他专用于机床的附件	7	0		0	5		0	0	0				5.6	0					0	0	0
84669100	税号 84.64 所列机器用的零附件	0																		0	0	0
84669200	税号 84.65 所列机器用的零附件	6	0		0	5		0	0	0	0			3.6	0					0	0	0
84669310	刀库及自动换刀装置	0																		0	0	0
84669390	税号 84.56－84.61 机器用其他零附件	0																		0	0	0
84669400	税号 84.62－84.63 机器用其他零附件	6	0		0	5		0	0	0			0	4.8	0					0	0	0
84671100	旋转式手提风动工具	8	0		0	5		0	0	0				4.8	0					0	0	0
84671900	其他手提式风动工具	8	0		0	5		0	0	0				4.8	0					0	0	0
84672100	电动钻	10	0	9	0	5	0	0	4	0	0			6	0					0	0	0
84672210	电动链锯	10	0	9	0	5		0	4	0	0			6	0					0	0	0
84672290	其他电动锯	10	0	9	0	5	0	0	4	0	0			6	0					0	0	0
84672910	电动砂磨工具	10	0	8	0	5	0	0	4	0	0			7.7	0					0	0	0
84672920	电刨	10	0	8	0	5		0	4	0	0			6	0					0	0	0
84672990	其他电动工具	10	0	8	0	5	0	0	4	0	0			6	0					0	0	0
84678100	手提式液压或其他动力链锯	8	0		0	5		0	0	0				4.8	0					0	0	0
84678900	其他手提式液压或其他动力工具	8	0		0	5		0	0	0				4.8	0					0	0	0
84679110	电动链锯用零件	6	0	4.8	0	0		0	0	0	0			3.6	0					0	0	0
84679190	其他链锯用零件	6	0		0	5		0	0	0				4.8	0					0	0	0
84679200	风动工具零件	6	0		0	5		0	0	0				3.6						0	0	0
84679910	其他手提式电动工具用零件	10	0	9	0	5	0	0	0	0	0			8	0					0	0	0
84679990	其他手提式工具用零件	6	0		0	5		0	0	0				3.6	0					0	0	0
84681000	手提喷焊器	12	0		0	6	0	0	0	0				9.6	0					0	0	0
84682000	其他气体焊或表面回火机器及装置	12	0		0	6	0	0	0	0				7.2	0					0	0	0
84688000	其他焊接机器及装置	12	0		0	6	0	0	0	0				9.6	0					0	0	0
84689000	焊接机器用零件	7	0		0	5		0	0	0				4.2	0					0	0	0
84690011	文字处理机	0																		0	0	0
84690012	自动打字机	12	0		0	6	0	0	0	0				9.6	0					0	0	
84690020	其他电动打字机	12	0	10.8	0	5	0	0	0	0				9.6	0					0	0	
84690030	其他非电动打字机	12	0		0	6	0	0	0	0				9.6	0					0	0	
84701000	电子计算器及袖珍式数据录放机器	0																		0	0	0
84702100	装有打印装置的电子计算器	0																		0	0	0
84702900	其他电子计算器	0																		0	0	0
84703000	其他计算机器	0																		0	0	0
84705010	销售点终端出纳机	0																		0	0	0
84705090	其他现金出纳机	0																		0	0	0
84709000	邮资盖戳机、售票机及类似机器	0																		0	0	0
84713010	平板电脑	0																		0	0	0
84713090	其他重量不超过 10 公斤的便携数字式自动数据处理设备，至少由一个中央处理部件、一个键盘及一个显示器组成自动数据处理设备及其部件	0																		0	0	0
84714110	巨、大、中型计算机	0																		0	0	0
84714120	小型机	0																		0	0	0
84714140	微型机	0																		0	0	0
84714190	其他自动数据处理单体机	0																		0	0	0

税则号列	货品名称	最惠国	协定税率													特惠税率						
			东盟统一	亚太5国	智利	巴基斯坦	新加坡	新西兰	秘鲁	哥达	香港	澳门	台湾	瑞士	冰岛	亚太2国	老挝	柬埔寨	缅甸	LDC1	LDC2	LDC3
84714910	以系统形式进口的巨、大、中型计算机	0																		0	0	0
84714920	以系统形式进口的小型计算机	0																		0	0	0
84714940	以系统形式进口的微型机	0																		0	0	0
84714991	分散型工业过程控制设备	0																		0	0	0
84714999	以系统形式报验的其他计算机	0																		0	0	0
84715010	巨、大、中型机处理部件	0																		0	0	0
84715020	小型机的处理部件	0																		0	0	0
84715040	微型机的处理部件	0																		0	0	0
84715090	8471.41、8471.49 以外设备的其他处理部件	0																		0	0	0
84716040	巨、大、中及小型计算机用终端	0																		0	0	0
84716050	扫描仪	0																		0	0	0
84716060	数字化仪	0																		0	0	0
84716071	键盘	0																		0	0	0
84716072	鼠标器	0																		0	0	0
84716090	自动处理设备的其他输入或输出部件	0																		0	0	0
84717010	硬盘驱动器	0																		0	0	0
84717020	软盘驱动器	0																		0	0	0
84717030	光盘驱动器	0																		0	0	0
84717090	自动数据处理设备的其他存储部件	0																		0	0	0
84718000	其他自动数据处理设备的其他部件	0																		0	0	0
84719000	未列名的磁性或光学阅读器及其他数据处理设备	0																		0	0	0
84721000	胶版复印机、油印机	14	0		0	11.2	0	0	0	0				11.2	0					0	0	0
84723010	邮政信件分拣及封装设备	10	0		0	5		0	0	0					0					0	0	0
84723090	其他信件分类、折迭、信封装封机等机器	14	0		0	7	0	0	0	0				8.4	0					0	0	0
84729010	自动柜员机	0																		0	0	0
84729021	打洞机	0																		0	0	0
84729022	订书机	0																		0	0	0
84729029	其他装订用机器	0																		0	0	0
84729030	碎纸机	0																		0	0	0
84729040	地址印写机及地址铭牌压印机	14	0		0	11.2	0	0	0	0				11.2	0					0	0	0
84729090	其他办公室用机器	0																		0	0	0
84731000	打字机、文字处理机的零附件	8	0		0	5		0	0	0				4.8	0					0	0	0
84732100	税号 84.70 所列电子计算器的零附件	0																		0	0	0
84732900	税号 84.70 所列其他机器的零附件	0																		0	0	0
84733010	数字式大、中、小型计算机零附件	0																		0	0	0
84733090	税号 84.71 所列计算机的其他零附件	0																		0	0	0
84734010	自动柜员机用出钞器和循环出钞机	10.5	0		0	5	0	0	0	0				8.4	0					0	0	0
84734090	税号 84.72 所列其他办公室用机器零附件	10.5	0		0	5	0	0	0	0				8.4	0					0	0	0
84735000	税号 84.69－84.72 中所列机器零附件	0																		0	0	0
84741000	固体矿物的分类、筛选、分离或洗涤机器	5	0		0	0		0	0	0				3	0					0	0	0
84742010	齿辊式破碎及磨粉机器	5	0		0	0		0	0	0				0	0					0	0	0
84742020	球磨式破碎及磨粉机器	5	0		0	0		0	0	0				3	0					0	0	0
84742090	其他破碎及磨粉机器	5	0		0	0		0	0	0				3	0					0	0	0
84743100	混凝土或砂浆混合机器	7	0		0	5		0	0	0				4.2	0					0	0	0
84743200	矿物与沥青的混合机器	7	0		0	5		0	0	0					0					0	0	0
84743900	其他混合或搅拌机器	5	0		0	0		0	0	0				3.9	0					0	0	0
84748010	固体矿物的辊压成型机	5	0	4.5	0	0		0	0	0				0	0					0	0	0
84748020	模压成型机	5	0	4.5	0	0		0	0	0				0	0					0	0	0
84748090	税号 8474 所列的其他机器	5	0	4.5	0	0		0	0	0				0	0					0	0	0
84749000	税号 8474 所列机器的零件	5	0		0	0		0	0	0				4	0					0	0	0
84751000	白炽灯炮、灯管等的封装机	8	0		0	5		0	0	0				4.8	0					0	0	0
84752100	制造光导纤维及其预制棒的机器	10	0		0	5	0	0	0	0				6	0					0	0	0
84752911	连续式玻璃热弯炉	10	0		0	5		0	0	0				6	0					0	0	0
84752912	玻璃纤维拉丝机(光纤拉丝机除外)	10	0		0	5		0	0	0				6	0					0	0	0
84752919	其他玻璃热加工设备	10	0		0	5	0	0	0	0				6	0					0	0	0

税则号列	货品名称	最惠国	协定税率													特惠税率						
			东盟统一	亚太5国	智利	巴基斯坦	新加坡	新西兰	秘鲁	哥达	香港	澳门	台湾	瑞士	冰岛	亚太2国	老挝	柬埔寨	缅甸	LDC1	LDC2	LDC3
84752990	其他玻璃及其制品的制造或热加工机器	10	0		0	5		0	0	0				6	0					0	0	0
84759000	税号84.75所列机器的零件	8	0		0	5		0	0	0				4.8	0					0	0	0
84762100	装有加热或制冷装置的饮料自动销售机	14	0		0	11.2	0	0	0	0				11.2	0					0	0	
84762900	其他饮料自动销售机	15	0		0	12	0	0	6	0				12	0					0	0	
84768100	装有加热或制冷装置的自动售货机	14	0		0	7	0	0	0	0				11.2	0					0	0	
84768900	其他自动售货机	15	0		0	12	0	0	6	0				9	0					0	0	
84769000	税号8476所列机器的零件	10	0		0	5		0	0	0				0	0					0	0	0
84771010	注塑机	0																		0	0	0
84771090	其他加工橡胶或塑料的注射机	0																		0	0	0
84772010	塑料造粒机	5	0	4.5	0	0		0	0	0	0		0	0	0					0	0	0
84772090	其他加工橡胶或塑料的挤出机	5	0	4.5	0	0		0	0	0	0		0	3.9	0					0	0	0
84773010	挤出吹塑机	5	0		0	0		0	0	0	0			3	0					0	0	0
84773020	注射吹塑机	5	0		0	0		0	0	0	0			3	0					0	0	0
84773090	其他吹塑机	5	0		0	0		0	0	0	0			3	0					0	0	0
84774010	塑料中空成型机	5	0	4.5	0	0		0	0	0			0		0					0	0	0
84774020	塑料压延成型机	5	0	4.5	0	0		0	0	0			0	4	0					0	0	0
84774090	其他真空模塑及热成型机器	5	0	4.5	0	0		0	0	0			0	3.9	0					0	0	0
84775100	用于充气轮胎或内胎模塑或翻新的机器	5	0		0	0		0	0	0				0	0					0	0	0
84775910	三维打印机(3D打印机)	5	0	3.5	0	0		0	0	0	0		0	3	0					0	0	0
84775990	其他模塑或成型机器	5	0	3.5	0	0		0	0	0	0		0	3	0					0	0	0
84778000	其他橡胶或塑料加工机器	5	0	4.5	0	0		0	0	0	0		0	3.9	0					0	0	0
84779000	橡胶、塑料等加工机器的零件	0																		0	0	0
84781000	其他未列名的烟草加工及制作机器	5	0	2.5	0	0		0	0	0				0	0					0	0	
84789000	烟草加工及制作机器用的零件	10	0		0	5		0	0	0				6	0					0	0	
84791021	沥青混凝土摊铺机	8	0	5.6	0	5		0	0	0				4.8	0					0	0	0
84791022	稳定土摊铺机	8	0	5.6	0	5		0	0	0				4.8	0					0	0	0
84791029	其他摊铺机	8	0	5.6	0	5		0	0	0				4.8	0					0	0	0
84791090	其他公共工程用的机器	8	0	5.6	0	5		0	0	0				4.8	0					0	0	0
84792000	提取加工动物或植物油脂的机器	10	0		0	5	0	0	0	0				6	0					0	0	0
84793000	木碎料板或木纤维板的挤压机	10	0		0	5		0	0	0				6	0					0	0	0
84794000	绳或缆的制造机器	7	0		0	5		0	0	0				4.2	0					0	0	0
84795010	多功能工业机器人	0																		0	0	0
84795090	其他工业机器人	0																		0	0	0
84796000	蒸发式空气冷却器	10	0	9	0	5		0	0	0				6	0					0	0	0
84797100	机场用旅客登机桥	0																		0	0	0
84797900	其他旅客登机(船)桥	0																		0	0	0
84798110	绕线机	9.5	0	9	0	5		0	0	0	0		0	7.6	0					0	0	0
84798190	其他处理金属的机械	9.5	0	9	0	5		0	0	0	0		0	7.6	0					0	0	0
84798200	其他混合、研磨、筛选、均化等机器	7	0	4.9	0	0		0	0	0			0		0					0	0	0
84798910	船舶用舵机及陀螺稳定器	0																		0	0	0
84798920	空气增湿器及减湿器	0																		0	0	0
84798940	邮政用包裹、印刷品分拣设备	0																		0	0	0
84798950	放射性废物压实机	0																		0	0	0
84798961	自动插件机	0																		0	0	0
84798962	自动贴片机	0																		0	0	0
84798969	印刷电路电路板的其他加工设备	0																		0	0	0
84798992	自动化立体仓储设备	0																		0	0	0
84798999	本章其他税号未列名机器及机械器具	0																		0	0	0
84799010	船舶用舵机及陀螺稳定器零件	0																		0	0	0
84799020	空气增湿器及减湿器零件	0																		0	0	0
84799090	税号84.79所列机器的其他零件	0																		0	0	0
84801000	金属铸造用型箱	10	0		0	5		0	0	0				6	0					0	0	0
84802000	型模底板	8	0		0	5		0	0	0				4.8	0					0	0	0
84803000	阳模	10	0		0	5	0	0	0	0				6	0					0	0	0
84804110	压铸模	8	0	5.6	0	5		0	0	0	0		0	4.8	0					0	0	0
84804120	粉末冶金用压模	8	0	5.6	0	5		0	0	0	0		0	4.8	0					0	0	0
84804190	其他金属、硬质合金用注模或压模	8	0	5.6	0	5		0	0	0	0		0	4.8	0					0	0	0
84804900	金属、硬质合金用其他型模	8	0	5.6	0	5		0	0	0				4.8	0					0	0	0
84805000	玻璃用型模	8.4	0		0	5		0	0	0				5	0					0	0	0
84806000	矿物材料用型模	8.4	0		0	5		0	0	0				5	0					0	0	0
84807110	硫化轮胎用囊式型模	0																		0	0	0

税则号列	货品名称	最惠国	协定税率													特惠税率						
			东盟统一	亚太5国	智利	巴基斯坦	新加坡	新西兰	秘鲁	哥达	香港	澳门	台湾	瑞士	冰岛	亚太2国	老挝	柬埔寨	缅甸	LDC1	LDC2	LDC3
84807190	其他塑料或橡胶用注模或压模	0																		0	0	0
84807900	塑料或橡胶用其他型模	5	0	3.5	0	0		0	0	0	0		0	3						0	0	0
84811000	减压阀	5	0		0	0		0	0	0				4	0					0	0	0
84812010	油压传动阀	5	0		0	0		0	0	0			0	4	0					0	0	0
84812020	气压传动阀	5	0		0	0		0	0	0				4	0					0	0	0
84813000	止回阀	5	0		0	0		0	0	0			0	4	0					0	0	0
84814000	安全阀或溢流阀	5	0		0	0		0	0	0			0	3	0					0	0	0
84818021	电磁换向阀	7	0	4.9	0	0		0	0	0	0		0	5.6	0					0	0	0
84818029	其他换向阀	7	0	4.9	0	0		0	0	0	0		0	5.6	0					0	0	0
84818031	电子膨胀阀	7	0	4.9	0	0		0	0	0	0		0	4.2	0					0	0	0
84818039	其他流量阀	7	0	4.9	0	0		0	0	0	0		0	5.6	0					0	0	0
84818040	其他阀门	7	0	4.9	0	0		0	0	0	0		0	5.6	0					0	0	0
84818090	未列名龙头、旋塞及类似装置	5	0		0	0		0	0	0	0			3	0					0	0	0
84819010	阀门用零件	8	0		0	5		0	0	0			0	6.4	0					0	0	0
84819090	龙头、旋塞及类似装置的零件	8	0		0	5		0	0	0			0	4.8	0					0	0	0
84821010	调心球轴承	8	0	7.6	0	5	0	0	0	0	0			4.8	0					0	0	0
84821020	深沟球轴承	8	0	7.6	0	5	0	0	0	0	0			4.8	0					0	0	0
84821030	角接触轴承	8	0	7.6	0	5	0	0	0	0	0			4.8	0					0	0	0
84821040	推力球轴承	8	0	7.6	0	5	0	0	0	0	0			4.8	0					0	0	0
84821090	其他滚珠轴承	8	0	7.6	0	5	0	0	0	0	0			6.4	0					0	0	0
84822000	锥形滚子轴承	8	0		0	5		0	0	0				4.8	0					0	0	0
84823000	鼓形滚子轴承	8	0		0	5		0	0	0				4.8	0					0	0	0
84824000	滚针轴承	8	0		0	5		0	0	0			0	4.8						0	0	0
84825000	其他圆柱形滚子轴承	8	0		0	5	0	0	0	0				6.4	0					0	0	0
84828000	其他滚动轴承及球、柱混合轴承	8	0	5.6	0	5		0	0	0				6.4	0					0	0	0
84829100	滚珠、滚针及滚柱	8	0		0	5		0	0	0				4.8	0					0	0	0
84829900	滚动轴承的其他零件	6	0		0	5		0	0	0			0	4.8	0					0	0	0
84831011	船舶用柴油机曲轴	6	0	5.1	0	5		0	0	0	0	0		3.6	0					0	0	0
84831019	其他船舶用传动轴	6	0	5.1	0	5		0	0	0	0	0		3.6	0					0	0	0
84831090	其他传动轴及曲柄	6	0	5.4	0	5		0	0	0	0	0		4.8	0					0	0	0
84832000	装有滚珠或滚子轴承的轴承座	6	0		0	5		0	0	0		0		4.8	0					0	0	0
84833000	未装滚珠或滚子轴承的轴承座	6	0		0	5		0	0	0		0		4.8	0					0	0	0
84834010	滚子螺杆传动装置	8	0	5.6	0	5		0	0	0	0	0	0	6.4	0					0	0	0
84834020	行星齿轮减速器	8	0	5.6	0	5		0	0	0	0	0		6.4	0					0	0	0
84834090	其他齿轮及齿轮传动装置	8	0	5.6	0	5		0	0	0	0	0	0	6.4	0					0	0	0
84835000	飞轮、滑轮及滑轮组	8	0		0	5		0	0	0		0		6.4	0					0	0	0
84836000	离合器及联轴器(包括万向节)	8	0		0	5		0	0	0		0		6.4	0					0	0	0
84839000	单独报验的带齿的轮及其他传动元件;零件	8	0		0	5		0	0	0	0	0	0	6.4	0					0	0	0
84841000	金属片密封垫或类似接合衬垫	8	0		0	5		0	0	0			0	6.4	0					0	0	0
84842000	机械密封件	8	0		0	5		0	0	0				6.4	0					0	0	0
84849000	其他材料制密封垫及类似接合衬垫	8	0		0	5		0	0	0				4.8	0					0	0	0
84861010	利用温度变化处理单晶硅的机器及装置	0															0			0	0	0
84861020	制作单晶硅或晶圆的研磨设备	0																		0	0	0
84861030	制作单晶硅或晶圆的切割设备	0																		0	0	0
84861040	制作单晶硅或晶圆的化学机械抛光设备	0																		0	0	0
84861090	制作单晶硅或晶圆的其他设备	0																		0	0	0
84862010	制造半导体器件或集成电路用的热处理设备	0															0			0	0	0
84862021	制造半导体器件或集成电路用的化学气相沉积装置	0																		0	0	0
84862022	制造半导体器件或集成电路用的物理气相沉积装置	0																		0	0	0
84862029	制造半导体器件或集成电路用的其他薄膜沉积设备	0																		0	0	0
84862031	制造半导体器件或集成电路用的分步重复光刻机	0																		0	0	0
84862039	制造半导体器件或集成电路用的其他光刻设备	0																		0	0	0

税则号列	货品名称	最惠国	协定税率													特惠税率						
			东盟统一	亚太5国	智利	巴基斯坦	新加坡	新西兰	秘鲁	哥达	香港	澳门	台湾	瑞士	冰岛	亚太2国	老挝	柬埔寨	缅甸	LDC1	LDC2	LDC3
84862041	制造半导体器件或集成电路用的等离子体干法刻蚀机	0																		0	0	0
84862049	制造半导体器件或集成电路用的其他刻蚀及剥离设备	0																		0	0	0
84862050	制造半导体器件或集成电路用的离子注入机	0																		0	0	0
84862090	制造半导体器件或集成电路用的其他机器及装置	0																		0	0	0
84863010	制造平板显示器用的热处理设备	0															0			0	0	0
84863021	制造平板显示器用的化学气相沉积装置	0																		0	0	0
84863022	制造平板显示器用的物理气相沉积装置	0																		0	0	0
84863029	制造平板显示器用的其他薄膜沉积设备	0																		0	0	0
84863031	制造平板显示器用的分步重复光刻机	0																		0	0	0
84863039	制造平板显示器用的其他光刻设备	0																		0	0	0
84863041	制造平板显示器用的超声波清洗装置	10	0		0	5	0	0	0	0				6	0					0	0	0
84863049	制造平板显示器用的其他湿法蚀刻、显影、剥离、清洗装置	0																		0	0	0
84863090	制造平板显示器用的其他机器及装置	0																		0	0	0
84864010	专用于制作和修复掩膜版的装置	0																		0	0	0
84864021	专用于装配与封装半导体器件或集成电路的塑封机	5	0	4.5	0	0		0	0	0				0	0					0	0	0
84864022	专用于装配与封装半导体器件或集成电路的引线键合设备	8	0	7.6	0	5		0	0	0	0			6.4	0					0	0	0
84864029	专用于装配与封装半导体器件或集成电路的机器及装置	0																		0	0	0
84864031	集成电路工厂专用的自动搬运机器人	0																		0	0	0
84864039	其他集成电路或液晶显示屏工厂专用升降、装卸、搬运装置	5	0	3.5	0	0		0	0	0				3	0					0	0	0
84869010	升降、搬运、装卸机器用零件及附件(自动搬运设备用除外)	5	0	2.5	0	0		0	0	0				3	0					0	0	0
84869020	引线键合装置用零件及附件	6	0	5.7	0	5		0	0	0				3.6	0					0	0	0
84869091	带背板的溅射靶材组件	0																		0	0	0
84869099	其他半导体器件、集成电路、液晶显示器生产专用设备的零件及附件	0																		0	0	0
84871000	船用推进器及桨叶	6	0		0	5		0	0	0				3.6	0					0	0	0
84879000	本章其他税号未列名机器零件	8	0		0	5		0	0	0	0		0	6.4	0					0	0	0
85011010	输出功率≤37.5W 玩具电动机	24.5	0	23.3	0	23.3	0	0	9.8	0	0		0	19.6	0					0	0	
85011091	机座 20mm≤直径<39mm 微电机	9	0	8.6	0	.5	0	0	0	0	0			7.2	0					0	0	0
85011099	其他输出功率≤37.5W 微电机	9	0	8.6	0	5	0	0	0	0	0		0	7.2	0					0	0	0
85012000	输出功率>37.5W 交直流两用电动机	12	0		0	6	0	0	4.8	0				9.6	0					0	0	0
85013100	输出功率≤750 瓦直流电动机、发电机	12	0	11	0	6	0	0	0	0	0	0	0	7.2	0					0	0	0
85013200	750W<输出功率≤75KW 直流电动机、发电机	10	0		0	5	0	0	0	0				6	0					0	0	0
85013300	75KW<输出功率≤375KW 直流电动机、发电机	5	0		0	0		0	0	0				0	0					0	0	0
85013400	输出功率>375KW 直流电动机、发电机	12	0		0	6	0	0	0	0				9.6	0					0	0	0
85014000	单相交流电动机	12	0		0	6	0	0	4.8	0				9.6	0					0	0	0
85015100	输出功率≤750W 多相交流电动机	5	0		0	0		0	0	0				3	0					0	0	0
85015200	输出功率>750W≤75KW 多相交流电动机	10	0		0	5	0	0	0	0				8	0					0	0	0
85015300	输出功率>75KW 多相交流电动机	12	0	11.4	0	6	0	0	0	0				9.6	0					0	0	0
85016100	输出功率≤75KVA 交流发电机	5	0		0	0		0	0	0				0	0					0	0	0
85016200	75KVA<输出功率≤375KVA 交流发电机	12	0		0	6	0	0	4.8	0				9.6	0					0	0	0
85016300	375KVA<输出功率≤750KVA 交流发电机	12	0		0	6	0	0	4.8	0				9.6	0					0	0	0
85016410	750KVA<输出功率<350MVA 交流发电机	10	0		0	5	0	0	4	0				6	0					0	0	0

税则号列	货品名称	最惠国	协定税率												特惠税率						
			东盟统一	亚太5国	智利	巴基斯坦	新加坡	新西兰	秘鲁	哥达	香港	澳门	台湾	瑞士	冰岛	亚太2国	老挝	柬埔寨	缅甸	LDC1	LDC2	LDC3
85016420	350KVA≤输出功率＜665MVA 交流发电机	5.8	0		0	5		0	0	0				3.5	0					0	0	0
85016430	输出功率≥665MVA 交流发电机	6	0		0	5		0	0	0				3.6	0					0	0	0
85021100	输出功率≤75KVA 柴油发电机组	10	0		0	5	0	0	0	0	0			6	0					0	0	0
85021200	75KVA＜输出功率≤375KVA 柴油发电机组	10	0		0	5	0	0	4	0	0			6	0					0	0	0
85021310	375KVA＜输出功率≤2MVA 柴油发电机组	10	0	7	0	5	0	0	0	0	0			6	0					0	0	0
85021320	输出功率＞2MVA 柴油发电机组	10	0	7	0	5	0	0	0	0	0			6	0					0	0	0
85022000	装有点燃式活塞发动机的发电机组	10	0		0	5	0	0	0	0				6	0					0	0	0
85023100	风力驱动的发电机组	8	0		0	5		0	0	0				4.8	0					0	0	0
85023900	其他发电机组	10	0		0	5		0	0	0				6	0					0	0	0
85024000	旋转式变流机	10	0		0	5		0	0	0				6	0					0	0	0
85030010	玩具用电动机微电机零件	12	0	11.4	0	6	0	0	4.8	0	0		0	9.6	0					0	0	0
85030020	输出功率＞350MVA 交流发电机零件	3	0	2.5	0	0		0	0	0	0			2.4	0					0	0	0
85030030	风力驱动发电机组的零件	3	0	2.5	0	0		0	0	0	0			0	0					0	0	0
85030090	其他电动机、发电机(组)零件	8	0	7.6	0	5		0	0	0	0		0	6.4						0	0	0
85041010	电子镇流器	10	0		0	5	0	0	4	0		0		6	0					0	0	0
85041090	其他放电灯或放电管用镇流器	10	0		0	5		0	4	0		0		6	0					0	0	0
85042100	额定容量≤650KVA 的液体介质变压器	10.5	0		0	5	0	0	4.2	0				8.4	0					0	0	0
85042200	650KVA＜额定容量≤10MVA 的液体介质变压器	12.6	0		0	6.3	0	0	5	0				10.1	0					0	0	0
85042311	10MVA＜额定容量≤220MVA 的液体变压器	10	0	7	0	5		0	0	0					0					0	0	0
85042312	200MVA≤额定容量＜330MVA 的液体变压器	10	0	7	0	5		0	0	0				6	0					0	0	0
85042313	330MVA≤额定容量＜400MVA 的液体变压器	10	0	7	0	5		0	0	0				6	0					0	0	0
85042321	400MVA≤液体变压器额定容量＜500MVA	6	0	4.2	0	0		0	0	0				3.6	0					0	0	0
85042329	其他额定容量≥500MVA 的液体变压器	6	0	4.2	0	0		0	0	0				3.6	0					0	0	0
85043110	额定容量≤1KVA 的互感器	5	0	4.3	0	0		0	0	0		0	0	3	0					0	0	0
85043190	额定容量≤1KVA 的其他变压器	5	0	4.3	0	0	0	0	0	0	0	0	0	3	0					0	0	0
85043210	1KVA＜额定容量≤16KVA 的互感器	5	0		0	0		0	0	0		0		0	0					0	0	0
85043290	1KVA＜额定容量≤16KVA 的其他变压器	5	0		0	0		0	0	0		0		3	0					0	0	0
85043310	额定容量超过 16 千伏安,但不超过 500 千伏安的互感器	5	0		0	0		0	0	0		0		3	0					0	0	0
85043390	其他额定容量超过 16 千伏安,但不超过 500 千伏安的变压器、静止式变流器(例如整流器)及电感器	5	0		0	0		0	0	0		0		3	0					0	0	0
85043410	额定容量超过 500 千伏的安互感器	14	0		0	11.2	0	0	0	0		0		8.4	0					0	0	
85043490	其他额定容量超过 500 千伏安的变压器、静止式变流器(例如整流器)及电感器	14	0		0	11.2	0	0	0	0		0		8.4	0					0	0	
85044013	税号 84.71 所列机器用的稳压电源	0																		0	0	0
85044014	功率＜1KW 高精度直流稳压电源	7	0	5.6	0	5		0	0	0				5.6	0					0	0	0
85044015	功率＜10KW 高精度交流稳压电源	0																		0	0	0
85044019	其他稳压电源	0																		0	0	0
85044020	不间断供电电源(UPS)	10	0	8.5	0	5	0	0	0	0	0				0					0	0	0
85044030	逆变器	10	0		0	5	0	0	4	0	0	0		8	0					0	0	0
85044091	具有变流功能的半导体模块	10	0		0	5	0	0	4	0	0	0		8	0					0	0	0
85044099	其他未列名静止式变流器	10	0		0	5	0	0	4	0	0	0		8	0					0	0	0
85045000	其他电感器	0																		0	0	0
85049011	额定容量＞400KVA 液体介质变压器零件	5	0	4.5	0	0		0	0	0	0			4	0					0	0	0
85049019	其他变压器零件	8	0	4.5	0	4.5		0	0	0	0		0	6.4	0					0	0	0
85049020	稳压电源及不间断供电电源零件	8	0	5.6	0	5		0	0	0	0	0	0	6.4	0					0	0	0

税则号列	货品名称	最惠国	协定税率													特惠税率						
			东盟统一	亚太5国	智利	巴基斯坦	新加坡	新西兰	秘鲁	哥达	香港	澳门	台湾	瑞士	冰岛	亚太2国	老挝	柬埔寨	缅甸	LDC1	LDC2	LDC3
85049090	其他静止式变流器及电感器零件	8	0	5.6	0	5		0	0	0	0	0	0	6.4	0					0	0	0
85051110	稀土的永磁铁及磁化后准备制永磁铁的物品	7	0		0	5		0	0	0			0	4.2	0					0	0	0
85051190	其他金属的永磁体及磁化后准备制永磁体的物品	7	0		0	5		0	0	0	0		0	4.2	0					0	0	0
85051900	非金属永磁体	7	0	6.7	0	5		0	0	0	0			4.2	0					0	0	0
85052000	电磁联轴节、离合器及制动器	8	0	7.6	0	5		0	0	0				4.8	0					0	0	0
85059010	电磁起重吸盘	8	0		0	5		0	0	0				4.8	0					0	0	0
85059090	电磁夹具等及税号85.02的零件	8	0	7.6	0	5		0	0	0				6.4	0					0	0	0
85061011	扣式碱性锌锰电池	20	0		0		0	0	8	0	0			16	0					0	0	
85061012	圆柱型碱性锌锰电池	20	0		0		0	0	8	0	0			16	0					0	0	
85061019	其他碱性锌锰电池	20	0		0		0	0	8	0	0			16	0					0	0	
85061090	二氧化锰的原电池及原电池组	20	0		0		0	0	8	0	0			16	0					0	0	
85063000	氧化汞的原电池及原电池组	14	0		0	11.2	0	0	0	0				11.2	0					0	0	
85064000	氧化银的原电池及原电池组	14	0		0	11.2	0	0	0	0				11.2	0					0	0	
85065000	锂的原电池及原电池组	14	0		0	11.2	0	0	0	0				11.2	0					0	0	
85066000	锌空气的原电池及原电池组	14	0		0	11.2	0	0	0	0					0					0	0	
85068000	其他原电池及原电池组	14	0		0	11.2	0	0	0	0	0			11.2	0					0	0	0
85069010	二氧化锰原电池或原电池组的零件	14	0		0	11.2	0	0	0	0				11.2	0					0	0	
85069090	其他原电池组或原电池组的零件	10	0		0	5	0	0	0	0				6	0					0	0	
85071000	起动活塞式发动机用铅酸蓄电池	10	0	6.9	0	5	0	0	4	0		0		6	0					0	0	
85072000	其他铅酸蓄电池	10	0	6.9	0	5	0	0	0	0		0		6	0					0	0	
85073000	镍镉蓄电池	10	0	8	0	5	0	0	0	0	0			6	0					0	0	
85074000	镍铁蓄电池	12	0	9.6	0	5	0	0	0	0				9.6	0					0	0	
85075000	镍氢蓄电池	12	0	9.6	0	5	0	0	0	0	0			9.6	0					0	0	
85076000	锂离子蓄电池	12	0	9.6	0	5	0	0	0	0	0		0	9.6	0					0	0	
85078030	全钒液流电池	12	0	9	0	5	0	0	0	0	0			9.6	0					0	0	
85078090	其他蓄电池	12	0	9	0	5	0	0	0	0	0			9.6	0					0	0	
85079010	铅酸蓄电池零件	10	0		0	5		0	0	0	0			6	0	5				0	0	
85079090	其他蓄电池零件	8	0		0	5		0	0	0	0			4.8	0	4				0	0	0
85081100	功率不超过1500瓦，且带有容积不超过20升的电动真空吸尘器	10	0	8.2	0	5	0	0	0	0	0		0	6	0					0	0	0
85081900	其他电动真空吸尘器	0																		0	0	0
85086000	其他真空吸尘器	0																		0	0	0
85087010	税号8508.1100所列电动真空吸尘器用零件	12	0		0	6	0	0	0	0	0			9.6	0					0	0	
85087090	其他真空吸尘器用零件	0																		0	0	0
85094010	水果或蔬菜榨汁机	10	0		0	5	0	0	0	0		0		6	0					0	0	
85094090	食品研磨机及搅拌器或果、菜榨汁器	10	0		0	5	0	0	0	0			0	0	0					0	0	
85098010	地板打蜡机	30	0		0		0	0	12	0				23.1	0					0	0	
85098020	厨房废物处理器	20	0		0		0	0	8	0				16	0					0	0	
85098090	其他家用电动器具	30	0		0		0	0	12	0					0					0	0	
85099000	家用电动器具的零件	12	0		0	6	0	0	0	0	0			9.6	0					0	0	
85101000	电动剃须刀	30	0		0		0	0	12	0				23.1						0	0	
85102000	电动毛发推剪	30	0		0		0	0	12	0	0			23.1	0					0	0	
85103000	电动脱毛器	20	0		0		0	0	8	0		0		16	0					0	0	
85109000	税号85.10所列货品的零件	24.5	0		0		0	0	9.8	0				19.6	0					0	0	
85111000	火花塞	10	0		0	5	0	0	4	0				6	0					0	0	
85112010	车、船、飞机等用点火磁电机、永磁直流发电机、磁飞轮	5	0		0	0		0	0	0				0	0					0	0	0
85112090	其他点火磁电机、磁飞轮	10	0		0	5		0	0	0				6	0					0	0	0
85113010	分电器及点火线圈	5	0		0	0		0	0	0				0	0					0	0	0
85113090	其他用途用分电器、点火线圈	8.4	0		0	5		0	0	0				5	0					0	0	0
85114010	机车等用起动电机及两用起动发电机	5	0		0	0		0	0	0				0	0					0	0	0
85114091	输出功率≥132.39千瓦启动电机	8.4	0		0	5		0	0	0				5	0					0	0	0
85114099	其他用途的启动电机	8.4	0		0	5		0	0	0				5	0					0	0	0
85115010	其他机车、航空器、船舶用发电机	5	0		0	0		0	0	0				0	0					0	0	0
85115090	其他附属于内燃发动机的发电机	8.4	0		0	5		0	0	0				5	0					0	0	0
85118000	发动机用电点火、起动的其他装置	8.4	0		0	5		0	0	0				5	0					0	0	0

税则号列	货品名称	最惠国	协定税率													特惠税率						
			东盟统一	亚太5国	智利	巴基斯坦	新加坡	新西兰	秘鲁	哥达	香港	澳门	台湾	瑞士	冰岛	亚太2国	老挝	柬埔寨	缅甸	LDC1	LDC2	LDC3
85119010	机车、船、航空器用电点火、起动装置零件	4.5	0		0	0		0	0	0				0	0					0	0	0
85119090	其他用电点火、电起动装置的零件	5	0		0	0		0	0	0				0	0					0	0	0
85121000	自行车用照明或视觉信号装置	10.5	0		0	5	0	0	0	0				8.4	0					0	0	0
85122010	机动车辆用照明装置	10	10		0			0	0	0			0	6	0					0	0	0
85122090	其他机动车用照明或视觉信号装置	10	10		0			0	0	0				6	0					0	0	0
85123011	机动车辆用喇叭、蜂鸣器	10	10	8.5	0	8.5		0	0	0				6	0					0	0	0
85123012	防盗报警器	10	0	9	0	5		0	0	0				6	0					0	0	0
85123019	其他机动车辆用音响信号装置	10	10	8.5	0	8.5		0	0	0				6	0					0	0	0
85123090	其他车辆用音响信号装置	10	10	8.5	0	8.5		0	0	0				6	0					0	0	0
85124000	车辆风档刮水器、除霜器及去雾器	10	10		0			0	0	0				6	0					0	0	0
85129000	税号85.12所列装置的零件	8	0		0	5		0	0	0			0	4.8	0					0	0	0
85131010	手电筒	15	0	13.2	0	7.5	0	0	6	0		0		12	0					0	0	0
85131090	其他自供能源手提式电灯	17.5	0		0	14	0	0	7	0		0		14	0					0	0	
85139010	手电筒零件	14	0		0	11.2	0	0	0	0	0	0		11.2	0					0	0	0
85139090	其他自供能源手提式电灯零件	14	0		0	11.2	0	0	0	0	0	0		11.2	0					0	0	
85141010	可控气氛热处理炉	0																		0	0	0
85141090	工业、实验室用其他电阻加热炉及烘箱	0																		0	0	0
85142000	工业、实验室用通过感应或介质损耗工作的炉及烘箱	0																		0	0	0
85143000	工业、实验室用其他电炉及电烘箱	0																		0	0	0
85144000	其他通过感应或介质损耗工作的的加热设备	10	0		0	5	0	0	0	0				6	0					0	0	0
85149010	炼钢电炉用零件	8	0		0	5		0	0	0				4.8	0					0	0	0
85149090	工业用电阻加热炉及烘箱等零件	0																		0	0	0
85151100	钎焊机器及装置用烙铁及焊枪	10	0		0	5	0	0	0	0				6	0					0	0	0
85151900	其他钎焊机器及装置	10	0		0	5	0	0	0	0				8.7	0					0	0	0
85152120	电阻焊接机器人	10	0		0	5	0	0	0	0	0				0					0	0	0
85152191	直缝焊管机	10	0		0	5		0	0	0	0			6	0					0	0	0
85152199	其他全自动或半自动电阻焊接机器及装置	10	0		0	5	0	0	0	0	0				0					0	0	0
85152900	其他电阻焊接机器及装置	10	0	9.5	0	5	0	0	0	0				6	0					0	0	0
85153120	电弧(包括等离子弧)焊接机器人	10	10		0			0	0	0				6	0					0	0	0
85153191	螺旋焊管机	10	0		0	5		0	0	0				6	0					0	0	0
85153199	其他全自动或半自动的电弧(包括等离子弧)焊接机器及装	10	10		0			0	0	0				6	0					0	0	0
85153900	其他电弧焊接机器及装置	10	0		0	5		0	0	0				6	0					0	0	0
85158010	激光焊接机器人	8	0	7.6	0	5		0	0	0	0		0	6.9	0					0	0	0
85158090	其他机器及装置	8	0	7.6	0	5		0	0	0	0		0	6.9	0					0	0	0
85159000	电气等焊接机器及装置零件	6	0	5.7	0	5		0	0	0	0			4.8	0					0	0	0
85161010	储存式电热水器	10	0		0	5	0	0	0	0				6	0					0	0	0
85161020	即热式电热水器	10	0		0	5	0	0	0	0				6	0					0	0	0
85161090	其他电热的快速热水器、浸入式液体加热器	10	0		0	5	0	0	0	0				6	0					0	0	0
85162100	电气储存式散热器	35	0		0		0	0	14	0		0	0	26.6	0					0	0	
85162910	电气土壤加热器	10	0		0	5	0	0	0	0	0	0		6	0					0	0	0
85162920	辐射式空间加热器	10	0		0	5	0	0	0	0	0	0		6	0					0	0	0
85162931	风扇式对流式空间加热器	10	0		0	5	0	0	0	0	0	0		6	0					0	0	0
85162932	充液式对流式空间加热器	10	0		0	5	0	0	0	0	0	0		6	0					0	0	0
85162939	其他对流式空间加热器	10	0		0	5	0	0	0	0	0	0		6	0					0	0	0
85162990	电气空间加热器	10	0		0	5	0	0	0	0	0	0		6	0					0	0	0
85163100	电吹风机	10	0		0	5	0	0	0	0	0	0		8	0					0	0	0
85163200	其他电热理发器具	35	0		0		0	0	14	0		0		26.6	0					0	0	
85163300	电热干手器	35	0		0		0	0	14	0		0		26.6	0					0	0	
85164000	电熨斗	35	0		0		0	0	14	0		0	0	28	0					0	0	
85165000	微波炉	15	0	13.5	0	7.5	0	0	6	0				12	0					0	0	

税则号列	货品名称	最惠国	协定税率													特惠税率						
			东盟统一	亚太5国	智利	巴基斯坦	新加坡	新西兰	秘鲁	哥达	香港	澳门	台湾	瑞士	冰岛	亚太2国	老挝	柬埔寨	缅甸	LDC1	LDC2	LDC3
85166010	电磁炉	15	0		0	12	0	0	6	0		0		12	0					0	0	
85166030	电饭锅	15	0		0	12	0	0	6	0		0	0	12	0					0	0	
85166040	电炒锅	15	0		0	12	0	0	6	0		0		12	0					0	0	
85166050	电烤箱	15	0		0	12		0	6	0		0	0	12	0					0	0	
85166090	其他电热炉	15	0		0	12	0	0	6	0		0		12	0					0	0	
85167110	滴液式咖啡机	32	0		0		0	0	12.8	0		0		19.2						0	0	
85167120	蒸馏渗滤式咖啡机	32	0		0		0	0	12.8	0		0		19.2						0	0	
85167130	泵压式咖啡机	32	0		0		0	0	12.8	0		0		19.2	0					0	0	
85167190	其他电热咖啡机或茶壶	32	0		0		0	0	12.8	0		0		19.2	0					0	0	
85167210	家用自动面包机	32	0		0		0	0	12.8	0		0	0	24.6						0	0	
85167220	片式烤面包机(多士炉)	32	0		0		0	0	12.8	0		0		24.6						0	0	
85167290	电热烤面包器	32	0		0		0	0	12.8	0		0		24.6						0	0	
85167910	电热饮水机	32	0		0		0	0	12.8	0		0		25.6						0	0	
85167990	其他电热器具	32	0		0		0	0	12.8	0	0	0								0	0	
85168000	加热电阻器	10	0		0	5	0	0	0	0				8	0					0	0	0
85169010	土壤加热器及加热电阻器零件	8	0		0	5		0	0	0	0			4.8	0					0	0	0
85169090	税号85.16所列货品的其他零件	12	0		0	6	0	0	0	0	0			7.2	0					0	0	0
85171100	无绳电话机	0																		0	0	0
85171210	手持(包括车载)式无线电话机	0																		0	0	0
85171220	对讲机	0																		0	0	0
85171290	用于蜂窝网络或无线网络的其他电话机	0																		0	0	0
85171800	其他电话机	0																		0	0	0
85176110	移动通信基站	0																		0	0	0
85176190	其他通信基站	0																		0	0	0
85176211	数字式局用电话交换机;长途电话交换机;电报交换机	0																		0	0	0
85176212	数字式移动通信交换机	0																		0	0	0
85176219	数字式其他电话交换机	0																		0	0	0
85176221	光端机及脉冲编码调制设备	0																		0	0	0
85176222	波分复用光传输设备	0																		0	0	0
85176229	其他光通讯设备	0																		0	0	0
85176231	通信网络时钟同步设备	0																		0	0	0
85176232	以太网络交换机	0																		0	0	0
85176233	IP电话信号交换机	0																		0	0	0
85176234	调制解调器	0																		0	0	0
85176235	集线器	0																		0	0	0
85176236	路由器	0																		0	0	0
85176237	有线网络接口卡	0																		0	0	0
85176239	其他有线数字通信设备	0																		0	0	0
85176292	无线网络接口卡	0																		0	0	0
85176293	无线接入固定台	0																		0	0	0
85176294	无线耳机	0																		0	0	0
85176299	其他接收、转换并且发送或再生声音、图像或数据用的设备	0																		0	0	0
85176910	其他无线设备	9	0		0	0		0	0	0				5.4	0					0	0	0
85176990	其他有线设备	0																		0	0	0
85177010	数字式程控电话或电报交换机零件	0																		0	0	0
85177020	光端机、脉冲编码调制设备的零件	0																		0	0	0
85177030	手持式无线电话机用(天线除外)	0																		0	0	0
85177040	对讲机用(天线除外)	8	0	5.6	0	5		0	0	0	0			4.8	0					0	0	0
85177060	光通信设备的激光收发模块	0																		0	0	0
85177070	税号8517所列设备用天线及其零件	2	0		0	0		0	0	0				0	0					0	0	0

税则号列	货品名称	最惠国	协定税率													特惠税率					
			东盟统一	亚太5国	智利	巴基斯坦	新加坡	新西兰	秘鲁	哥斯达	香港	澳门	台湾	瑞士	冰岛	亚太2国	老挝	柬埔寨	缅甸	LDC1	LDC2	LDC3
85177090	发送或接收声音、图像或数据的设备用其他零件	0																		0	0	0
85181000	传声器(麦克风)及其座架	10	0		0	5	0	0	0	0	0		0	6	0					0	0	0
85182100	单喇叭音箱	10	0		0	5	0	0	0	0	0			6	0					0	0	0
85182200	多喇叭音箱	10	0		0	5	0	0	4	0	0			6	0					0	0	0
85182900	其他扬声器	0																		0	0	0
85183000	其他耳机、耳塞机	0																		0	0	0
85184000	音频扩大器	12	0		0	6	0	0	4.8	0	0		0	7.2	0					0	0	0
85185000	电气扩音机组	10	0		0	5	0	0	0	0				6	0					0	0	0
85189000	税号85.18所列货品的零件	10.5	0		0	5	0	0	0	0	0		0	8.4	0					0	0	0
85192000	用硬币、钞票、银行卡、代币使其工作的声音录放设备	20	0	16.4	0	16.4	0	0	8	0				16	0					0	0	
85193000	转盘(唱机唱盘)	30	0		0		0	0	12	0				23.1	0					0	0	
85195000	电话应答机	0																		0	0	0
85198111	不带录音功能的盒式磁带型声音重放装置,编辑节目用放声机除外	17	0		0	13.6	0	0	6.8	0				13.6	0					0	0	
85198112	装有声音重放装置的盒式磁带型录音机	30	0		0		0	0	12	0				23.1	0					0	0	
85198119	其他使用磁性媒体的声音录放机	20	0	16.4	0	16.4	0	0	8	0				16	0					0	0	
85198121	不带录音功能的激光唱机	30	0	26	0	26	0	0	12	0				23.1	0					0	0	
85198129	使用光学媒体的其他声音录放装置	20	0	16.4	0	16	0	0	8	0				16	0					0	0	
85198131	闪速存储器型声音录放机	20	0		0		0	0	8	0				16	0					0	0	
85198139	使用半导体媒体的其他声音录放装置	20	0	16.4	0	16.4	0	0	8	0				16	0					0	0	
85198910	不带录制装置的其他唱机,不论是否带有扬声器	30	0		0		0	0	12	0				23.1	0					0	0	
85198990	其他声音录制或重放设备	20	0	16.4	0	16	0	0	8	0				16	0					0	0	
85211011	广播级录像机	30	0	①	0	①	0	0	12	0				23.1	0					0	0	
85211019	其他磁带录像机	30	0	②	0	②	0	0	12	0				23.1	0					0	0	
85211020	磁带放像机	30	0	③	0	③	0	0	12	0				23.1	0					0	0	
85219011	视频高密光盘机VCD	20	0	16	0	16	0	0	8	0				16	0					0	0	
85219012	数字化视频光盘机DVD	20	0	16	0	16	0	0	8	0				16	0					0	0	
85219019	其他激光视盘放像机	20	0	16	0	16	0	0	8	0				16	0					0	0	
85219090	其他视频信号录制或重放设备	20	0	16	0	16	0	0	8	0	0			16	0					0	0	
85221000	拾音头	35	0		0		0	0	14	0	0			26.6	0					0	0	
85229010	转盘或唱机用零附件	25	0	20	0	20	0	0	10	0	0			19.3	0					0	0	
85229021	录音机走带机构(机芯)	25	0	22.5	0	22.5	0	0	10	0	0			19.3	0					0	0	
85229022	磁头	25	0	22.5	0	22.5	0	0	10	0	0			19.3	0					0	0	
85229023	磁头零件	20	0	18	0	18	0	0	8	0	0			16	0					0	0	
85229029	盒式磁带录音机或放声机其他零件	30	0	27	0	27	0	0	12	0	0			23.1	0					0	0	
85229031	激光视盘机的机芯	30	0	21	0	21	0	0	12	0	0			23.1	0					0	0	
85229039	其他视频信号录放设备的零件附件	30	0	21	0	21	0	0	12	0	0				0					0	0	
85229091	车载音频转播器或发射器	20	0	16	0	16	0	0	8	0	0			16	0					0	0	0
85229099	声音录制或重放设备用其他零件	20	0	16	0	16	0	0	8	0	0			16	0					0	0	0
85232110	未录制的磁条卡	17.5	0		0	14	0	0	7	0	0	0		14	0					0	0	
85232120	已录制的磁条卡	15	0		0	12	0	0	6	0	0	0		12	0					0	0	
85232911	未录制磁盘	0																		0	0	0
85232919	已录制磁盘	0																		0	0	0
85232921	宽度≤4mm的未录制磁带	0																		0	0	0
85232922	宽度>4mm且≤6.5mm的未录制磁带	0																		0	0	0
85232923	宽度>6.5mm的未录制磁带	0																		0	0	0
85232928	用于重放声音或图像信息的磁带	10	0		0	5	0	0	0	0	0			6	0					0	0	0
85232929	已录制其他信息的磁带	0																		0	0	0
85232990	其他磁性媒体	0																		0	0	0

税则号列	货品名称	最惠国	协定税率													特惠税率						
			东盟统一	亚太5国	智利	巴基斯坦	新加坡	新西兰	秘鲁	哥达	香港	澳门	台湾	瑞士	冰岛	亚太2国	老挝	柬埔寨	缅甸	LDC1	LDC2	LDC3
85234100	未录制的光学媒体	0																		0	0	0
85234910	仅用于重放声音信息的光学媒体	10	0		0	5		0	0	0	0	0		6	0					0	0	
85234920	用于重放声音、图像以外信息的,税号84.71所列机器用的光学媒体	0																		0	0	0
85234990	其他已录制的光学媒体	0																		0	0	0
85235110	未录制信息的闪速存储器	0																		0	0	0
85235120	已录制信息的闪速存储器	0																		0	0	0
85235210	未录制内容的"智能卡"	0																		0	0	0
85235290	已录制内容的"智能卡"	0																		0	0	0
85235910	未录制信息的其他半导体媒体	0																		0	0	0
85235920	已录制信息的其他半导体媒体	0																		0	0	0
85238011	已录制的唱片	15	0		0	12	0	0	6	0		0		12	0					0	0	
85238019	未录制的唱片	0																		0	0	0
85238021	税号84.71所列机器用未录制内容的其他媒体	0																		0	0	0
85238029	税号84.71所列机器用已录制内容的其他媒体	0																		0	0	0
85238091	其他未录制内容的媒体	0																		0	0	0
85238099	其他已录制内容的媒体	0																		0	0	0
85255000	广播电视发送设备	0																		0	0	0
85256010	卫星地面站设备	0																		0	0	0
85256090	其他装有接收装置的广播电视发送设备	0																		0	0	0
85258011	特种用途电视摄像机	10	0	9	0	5	0	0	0	0				6	0					0	0	
85258012	非特种用途的广播级电视摄像机	35	0	④	0	④	0	0	14	0				30.3	0					0	0	
85258013	非特种用途的其他电视摄像机	35	0	④	0	④	0	0	14	0	0	0	0	30.8	0					0	0	
85258021	特种用途的数字照相机	0																		0	0	0
85258022	非特种用途的单反数字照相机	0																		0	0	0
85258025	非特种用途的,其他可换镜头的数字照相机	0																		0	0	0
85258029	非特种用途的其他数字照相机	0																		0	0	0
85258031	特种用途的视频摄录一体机	0																		0	0	0
85258032	非特种用途的广播级视频摄录一体机	0																		0	0	0
85258033	非特种用途的家用视频摄录一体机	0																		0	0	0
85258039	非特种用途的其他视频摄录一体机	0																		0	0	0
85261010	导航用雷达设备	2	0		0	0		0	0	0				0	0					0	0	
85261090	其他雷达设备	5	0		0	0		0	0	0				0	0					0	0	
85269110	机动车辆用	2	0		0	0		0	0	0				0	0					0	0	
85269190	其他无线电导航设备	2	0		0	0		0	0	0				1.6	0					0	0	
85269200	无线电遥控设备	5	0		0	0		0	0	0				0	0					0	0	
85271200	不需外接电源袖珍盒式磁带收放机	20	0				0	0	8	0				16	0					0	0	
85271300	不需外接电源收录(放)音组合机	15	0		0	12	0	0	6	0				12	0					0	0	
85271900	不需外接电源无线电收音机	15	0		0	12	0	0	6	0				12	0					0	0	
85272100	需外接电源汽车收录(放)音组合机	15	0		0	12	0	0	6	0				12	0					0	0	
85272900	需外接电源汽车用无线电收音机	15	0		0	12	0	0	6	0				12	0					0	0	
85279100	其他收录(放)音组合机	15	0		0	12	0	0	6	0				12	0					0	0	
85279200	带时钟的收音机	15	0		0	12	0	0	6	0				12	0					0	0	
85279900	其他收音机	27	0		0		0	0	10.8	0				20.8	0					0	0	
85284100	计算机及其他自动数据处理设备用的阴极射线管监视器	0																		0	0	0
85284910	其他彩色阴极射线管监视器	30	0	26	0	26	0	0	12	0		0		24	0					0	0	
85284990	单色的阴极射线管监视器	19	0	15.2	0	15.2	0	0	7.6	0		0		15.2	0					0	0	
85285110	计算机及其他自动数据处理设备用的液晶显示器	0																		0	0	0
85285190	计算机及其他自动数据处理设备用的其他显示器	0																		0	0	0
85285910	其他彩色监视器	30	0	26	0	26	0	0	12		0	0			0					0	0	

税则号列	货品名称	最惠国	协定税率 东盟统一	亚太5国	智利	巴基斯坦	新加坡	新西兰	秘鲁	哥达	香港	澳门	台湾	瑞士	冰岛	特惠税率 亚太2国	老挝	柬埔寨	缅甸	LDC1	LDC2	LDC3
85285990	单色的其他监视器	19	0	15.2	0	15.2	0	0	7.6	0	0	0		15.2	0					0	0	
85286100	计算机及其他自动数据处理设备用的投影机	0																		0	0	0
85286910	其他彩色投影机	30	0	25.5	0	25.5	0	0	12	0	0	0			0					0	0	
85286990	单色的其他投影机	15	0		0	12	0	0	6	0		0		12	0					0	0	
85287110	不带显示屏的彩色卫星电视接收机	30	30	24	0	24		0		0					0					0		
85287180	不带显示屏的其他彩色电视接收机	30	0	21	0	21	0	0		0					0					0		
85287190	单色的不带视频显示器的电视接收机	15	0		0	12	0	0	6	0		0		12	0					0	0	
85287211	其他彩色模拟电视接收机，带阴极射线显像管的	30	30	21	0	21		0		0				23.1	0					0		
85287212	其他彩色数字电视接收机，带阴极射线显像管的	30	30	21	0	21		0		0				23.1	0					0		
85287219	其他彩色电视接收机，带阴极射线显像管的	30	30	21	0	21		0		0				23.1	0					0		
85287221	其他彩色模拟电视接收机，带液晶显示器的	30	20	21	0	21		0				0			0					0		
85287222	其他彩色数字电视接收机，带液晶显示器的	30	20	21	0	21		0							0					0		
85287229	其他彩色电视接收机，带液晶显示器的	30	20	21	0	21		0				0			0					0		
85287231	其他彩色模拟电视接收机，带等离子显示器的	30	20	21	0	21		0				0			0					0		
85287232	其他彩色数字电视接收机，带等离子显示器的	30	20	21	0	21		0							0					0		
85287239	其他彩色电视接收机，带等离子显示器的	30	20	21	0	21		0				0			0					0		
85287291	其他彩色模拟电视接收机	30	20	21	0	21		0	12	0					0					0	0	
85287292	其他彩色数字电视接收机	30	20	21	0	21		0							0					0		
85287299	其他彩色电视接收机	30	20	21	0	21		0		0					0					0		
85287300	其他单色的电视接收装置	15	0		0	12	0	0	6	0		0		12	0					0	0	
85291010	雷达及无线电导航设备天线及零件	1.5	0		0	0		0	0	0	0			0	0					0	0	
85291020	收音机、电视机天线及其零件	0																		0	0	0
85291090	其他无线电设备天线及其零件	2	0		0	0		0	0	0				0	0					0	0	
85299010	电视发送、差转等设备零件	0																		0	0	0
85299041	特种用途电视摄像机、静像视频摄像机及其他视频摄录一体机，数字相机零件	8	0	6.8	0	5		0	0	0	0			4.8	0					0	0	
85299042	非特种用途的取像模块	12	0	10.8	0	5	0	0	4.8	0	0		0	9.6	0					0	0	
85299049	其他电视摄像机、静像视频摄像机及其他视频摄录一体机、数字相机零件	12	0	10.8	0	5	0	0	0	0	0		0	9.6	0					0	0	
85299050	雷达及无线电导航设备零件	1.5	0	1.4	0	0		0	0	0				0	0					0	0	
85299060	收音机及其组合机的其他零件	15	0	12	0	7.5	0	0	6	0	0			12	0					0	0	0
85299081	彩色电视接收机用（等离子显像组件及其零件、有机发光二极管显示屏除外）	15	0	12	0	7.5	0	0	6					12	0					0	0	
85299082	等离子显像组件及其零件	15	0	12	0	7.5		0						12	0							
85299083	有机发光二极管显示屏	15	0	12	0	7.5	0	0	6					12	0					0	0	
85299089	其他电视机零件	0																		0	0	0
85299090	税号85.25至85.28所列设备的零件	0																		0	0	0
85301000	铁道或电车道用电气信号等设备	10	0		0	5		0	0	0				6	0					0	0	
85308000	其他用电气信号、安全、交通设备	8	0		0	5		0	0	0				4.8	0					0	0	0
85309000	税号85.30所列设备的零件	8	0		0	5		0	0	0				4.8	0					0	0	0
85311000	防盗或防火报警器及类似装置	10	0		0	5	0	0	0	0	0			6	0					0	0	0
85312000	有液晶装置或发光管的显示板	0																		0	0	0
85318010	蜂鸣器	15	0		0	12	0	0	6	0	0			12	0					0	0	
85318090	其他电气音响或视觉信号装置	10	0		0	5	0	0	0	0	0			6	0					0	0	
85319010	防盗、防火及类似装置用零件	0																		0	0	0
85319090	其他音响或视觉信号装置用零件	0																		0	0	0
85321000	固定电容器（电力电容器）	0																		0	0	0
85322110	片式钽电容器	0																		0	0	0
85322190	其他钽电容器	0																		0	0	0
85322210	片式铝电解电容器	0																		0	0	0
85322290	其他铝电解电容器	0																		0	0	0
85322300	单层瓷介电容器	0																		0	0	0
85322410	片式多层瓷介电容器	0																		0	0	0

税则号列	货品名称	最惠国	协定税率													特惠税率						
			东盟统一	亚太5国	智利	巴基斯坦	新加坡	新西兰	秘鲁	哥达	香港	澳门	台湾	瑞士	冰岛	亚太2国	老挝	柬埔寨	缅甸	LDC1	LDC2	LDC3
85322490	其他多层瓷介电容器	0																		0	0	0
85322510	片式纸介质或塑料介质电容器	0																		0	0	0
85322590	其他纸介质或塑料介质电容器	0																		0	0	0
85322900	其他固定电容器	0																		0	0	0
85323000	其他可变或可调(微调)电容器	0																		0	0	0
85329010	税号 8532.1000 所列电容器零件	0																		0	0	0
85329090	其他电容器零件	0																		0	0	0
85331000	合成或薄膜式固定碳质电阻器	0																		0	0	0
85332110	额定功率≤20W 片式固定电阻器	0																		0	0	0
85332190	额定功率≤20W 其他固定电阻器	0																		0	0	0
85332900	其他额定功率>20W 固定电阻器	0																		0	0	0
85333100	额定功率≤20W 线绕可变电阻器	0																		0	0	0
85333900	额定功率>20W 电位器	0																		0	0	0
85334000	其他可变电阻器	0																		0	0	0
85339000	各种电阻器零件	0																		0	0	0
85340010	>四层的印刷电路	0																		0	0	0
85340090	≤四层的印刷电路	0																		0	0	0
85351000	电路熔断器(电压>1000V)	14	0		0	11.2	0	0	0	0				11.2	0					0	0	
85352100	电压<72.5KV 自动断路器	14	0		0	11.2	0	0	0	0				8.4	0					0	0	
85352910	用于电压在 72.5 千伏及以上,但不高于 220 千伏的线路的自动断路器	10	0		0	5		0	0	0				6	0					0	0	0
85352920	用于电压高于 220 千伏,但不高于 750 千伏的线路的自动断路器	10	0		0	5		0	0	0				6	0					0	0	0
85352990	其他电压≥72.5KV 自动断路器	10	0		0	5		0	0	0				6	0					0	0	0
85353010	用于电压在 72.5 千伏及以上,但不高于 220 千伏的线路的隔离开关及断续开关	10	0		0	5		0	0	0				8.3	0					0	0	0
85353020	用于电压高于 220 千伏,但不高于 750 千伏的线路的隔离开关及断续开关	10	0		0	5		0	0	0				8.3	0					0	0	0
85353090	其他隔离开关及断续开关	10	0		0	5		0	0	0				8.3	0					0	0	0
85354000	避雷器、电压限幅器及电涌抑制器	18	0		0		0	0	7.2	0	0			14.4	0					0	0	
85359000	其他>1000V 电路开关等电气装置	10	0	9.5	0	5	0	0	4	0	0			8	0					0	0	0
85361000	熔断器(电压≤1000V)	10	0		0	5	0	0	0	0	0		0	8	0					0	0	0
85362000	电压≤1000V 自动断路器	9	0		0	5		0	0	0	0			7.2	0					0	0	0
85363000	电压≤1000V 其他电路保护装置	9	0		0	5		0	0	0	0			5.4	0					0	0	0
85364110	用于电压不超过 36 伏线路的继电器	10	0		0	5	0	0	0	0				6	0					0	0	0
85364190	用于电压超过 36 伏,但不超过 60 伏线路的继电器	10	0		0	5	0	0	0	0				6	0					0	0	0
85364900	电压>60V 的继电器	10	0		0	5	0	0	4	0	0			6	0					0	0	0
85365000	电压≤1000V 的其他开关	0																		0	0	0
85366100	电压≤1000V 的灯座	10	0		0	5	0	0	0	0				6	0					0	0	0
85366900	电压≤1000V 的插头及插座	0																		0	0	0
85367000	光导纤维、光导纤维束或光缆用连接器	8	0		0	5		0	0	0	0	0		6.4	0					0	0	0
85369011	工作电压不超过 36 伏的接插件	0																		0	0	0
85369019	其他接插件	0																		0	0	0
85369090	其他电路的开关、保护或连接用的电气装置	0																		0	0	0
85371011	可编程序控制器	5	0	2.5	0	0		0	0	0	0		0	4	0					0	0	0
85371019	其他数控装置	5	0	2.5	0	0		0	0	0	0		0	3.9	0					0	0	0
85371090	其他电力控制或分配的装置	8.4	0	4.2	0	0		0	0	0	0	0		6.5	0					0	0	0
85372010	电压≥500KV 高压开关装置	8.4	0	4.2	0	0		0	0	0				7	0					0	0	0
85372090	其他电力控制或分配装置	8.4	0	4.2	0	0		0	0	0	0			5	0					0	0	0
85381010	子目号 8537.2010 所列装置的零件	8.4	0	4.2	0	0		0	0	0				5	0					0	0	0
85381090	税号 85.37 货品用的其他盘、板等	7	0	3.5	0	0		0	0	0				5.6	0					0	0	0
85389000	税号 85.35、85.36 或 85.37 装置的零件	7	0		0	5		0	0	0	0		0	6	0					0	0	0
85391000	封闭式聚光灯	10	0		0	5		0	0	0				6	0					0	0	0
85392110	科研、医疗专用卤钨灯	8	0		0	5		0	0	0				4.8	0					0	0	0
85392120	火车、航空器及船舶用卤钨灯	8	0		0	5		0	0	0				4.8	0					0	0	0
85392130	机动车辆用卤钨灯	10	0		0	5		0	0	0				6	0					0	0	0
85392190	其他卤钨灯	10.5	0		0		0	0	0	0				8.4	0					0	0	0
85392210	科研、医疗用功率≤200W 白炽灯泡	10.5	0		0	5	0	0	0	0				8.4	0					0	0	0

税则号列	货品名称	最惠国	协定税率												特惠税率						
			东盟统一	亚太5国	智利	巴基斯坦	新加坡	新西兰	秘鲁	哥达	香港	澳门	台湾	瑞士	冰岛	亚太2国	老挝	柬埔寨	缅甸	LDC1	LDC2	LDC3
85392290	其他用功率≤200W白炽灯泡	5	0		0	0		0	0	0				0	0					0	0	0
85392910	科研、医疗专用其他白炽灯泡	5	0		0	0		0	0	0				0	0					0	0	0
85392920	火车、航空及船舶用其他白炽灯泡	10.5	0		0	5	0	0	0	0				8.4	0					0	0	0
85392930	机动车辆用其他白炽灯泡	5	0		0	0		0	0	0				0	0					0	0	0
85392991	电压≤12V未列名的白炽灯泡	12	0		0	6	0	0	0	0	0			9.6	0					0	0	0
85392999	其他未列名的白炽灯泡	12	0		0	6	0	0	0	0				9.6	0					0	0	0
85393110	科研、医疗专用热阴极荧光灯	8	0		0	5		0	0	0				4.8	0					0	0	0
85393120	火车、航空器、船舶用热阴极荧光灯	8	0		0	5		0	0	0				4.8	0					0	0	0
85393191	紧凑型荧光灯	8	0		0	5		0	0	0				4.8	0					0	0	0
85393199	其他热阴极荧光灯	8	0		0	5		0	0	0				4.8	0					0	0	0
85393230	钠蒸气灯	8	0		0	5		0	0	0				4.8	0					0	0	0
85393240	汞蒸气灯	8	0		0	5		0	0	0				4.8	0					0	0	0
85393290	金属卤化物灯	8	0		0	5		0	0	0				4.8	0					0	0	0
85393910	科研、医疗专用其他放电灯	8	0		0	5		0	0	0				4.8	0					0	0	0
85393920	火车、航空器、船舶用其他放电灯	8	0		0	5		0	0	0				4.8	0					0	0	0
85393990	其他用途的其他放电灯管	8	0		0	5		0	0	0		0	0	4.8	0					0	0	0
85394100	弧光灯	8	0		0	5		0	0	0				4.8	0					0	0	0
85394900	紫外线或红外线灯	8	0		0	5		0	0	0				4.8	0					0	0	0
85399000	税号85.39所列货品的零件	8	0		0	5		0	0	0			0	4.8	0					0	0	0
85401100	彩色阴极射线电视显像管	12	0		0	6	0	0	0	0				9.6	0					0	0	
85401200	黑白或单色阴极射线电视显像管	15	0		0	12	0	0	6	0				12	0					0	0	
85402010	电视摄像管	12	0		0	6	0	0	0	0				9.6	0					0	0	
85402090	变像管、图像增强管及光阴极管	8	0		0	5		0	0	0				4.8	0					0	0	0
85404010	彩色的数据/图形显示管,屏幕荧光点间距小于0.4毫米	8	0		0	5		0	0	0	0			4.8	0					0	0	0
85404020	单色的数据/图形显示管	8	0		0	5		0	0	0				4.8	0					0	0	0
85406010	雷达显示管	6	0		0	5		0	0	0				3.6	0					0	0	0
85406090	其他阴极射线管	8	0		0	5		0	0	0				4.8	0					0	0	0
85407100	磁控管	8	0		0	5		0	0	0				4.8	0					0	0	0
85407910	调速管	8	0		0	5		0	0	0				4.8	0					0	0	0
85407990	其他微波管	8	0		0	5		0	0	0				4.8	0					0	0	0
85408100	接收管或放大管	8	0		0	5		0	0	0				4.8	0					0	0	0
85408900	其他电子管	8	0		0	5		0	0	0			0	4.8	0					0	0	0
85409110	电视显像管零件	6	0		0	5		0	0	0				3.6	0					0	0	0
85409120	雷达显示管零件	5	0		0	0		0	0	0				0	0					0	0	0
85409190	其他阴极射线管零件	8	0		0	5		0	0	0				4.8	0					0	0	0
85409910	电视摄像管零件	8	0		0	5		0	0	0				4.8	0					0	0	0
85409990	其他热电子管、冷阴极管零件	8	0		0	5		0	0	0				4.8	0					0	0	0
85411000	二极管	0																		0	0	0
85412100	耗散功率<1W的晶体管	0																		0	0	0
85412900	耗散功率≥1W的晶体管	0																		0	0	0
85413000	半导体及可控硅等开关元件	0																		0	0	0
85414010	发光二极管	0																		0	0	0
85414020	太阳能电池	0																		0	0	0
85414090	其他光敏半导体器件,包括不论是否装在组件内或组装成块的光电池	0																		0	0	0
85415000	其他半导体器件	0																		0	0	0
85416000	已装配的压电晶体	0																		0	0	0
85419000	税号85.41所列货品零件	0																		0	0	0
85423100	集成电路处理器及控制器,不论是否带有存储器、转换器、逻辑电路、放大器、时钟及时序电路或其他电路	0																		0	0	0
85423200	集成电路存储器	0																		0	0	0
85423300	集成电路放大器	0																		0	0	0
85423900	其他集成电路	0																		0	0	0
85429000	集成电路的零件	0																		0	0	0
85431000	其他粒子加速器	5	0		0	0		0	0	0				0	0					0	0	0
85432010	输出信号频率<1500MHZ的通用信号发生器	15	0		0	12	0	0	6	0			0	12	0					0	0	

税则号列	货品名称	最惠国	协定税率													特惠税率						
			东盟统一	亚太5国	智利	巴基斯坦	新加坡	新西兰	秘鲁	哥达	香港	澳门	台湾	瑞士	冰岛	亚太2国	老挝	柬埔寨	缅甸	LDC1	LDC2	LDC3
85432090	输出信号频率≥1500MHZ 的通用信号发生器	8	0		0	5		0	0	0			0	4.8	0					0	0	0
85433000	电镀、电介或电泳设备及装置	0																		0	0	0
85437091	金属、矿藏探测器	0																		0	0	0
85437092	高、中频放大器	0																		0	0	0
85437093	电篱网激发器	10	0		0	5	0	0	0	0				6	0					0	0	0
85437099	未列名的电气设备及装置	0																		0	0	0
85439010	粒子加速器用零件	0																		0	0	0
85439021	输出信号频率＜1500MHZ 通用信号发生器零件	0																		0	0	0
85439029	输出信号频率≥1500MHZ 通用信号发生器零件	0																		0	0	0
85439030	金属、矿藏探测器用零件	0																		0	0	0
85439040	高、中频放大器用零件	0																		0	0	0
85439090	85 章其他未列名电气设备的零件	0																		0	0	0
85441100	铜制绕组电线	10	0	7	0	5	0	0	0	0	0	0	0	8	0					0	0	0
85441900	其他绕组电线	20	0		0		0	0	8	0				16	0					0	0	
85442000	同轴电缆及其他同轴电导体	10	0	9	0	5	0	0	4	0			0	8.7	0					0	0	0
85443020	机动车辆用点火布线组及其他布线组	10	10		0			0	0	0				6	0					0	0	0
85443090	车辆用点火布线组	5	5		0			0	0	0				3	0					0	0	0
85444211	耐压≤80V 有接头电缆	0																		0	0	0
85444219	耐压≤80V 有接头电导体	0																		0	0	0
85444221	1000V≥耐压＞80V 有接头电缆	0																		0	0	0
85444229	1000V≥耐压＞80V 有接头电导体	0																		0	0	0
85444911	耐压≤80V 无接头电缆	0																		0	0	0
85444919	耐压≤80V 无接头电导体	0																		0	0	0
85444921	1000V≥耐压＞80V 无接头电缆	6	0	4.2	0	0		0	0	0	0			4.8	0					0	0	0
85444929	1000V≥耐压＞80V 无接头电导体	12	0	8.4	0	5	0	0	0	0	0	0	0	9.6	0					0	0	0
85446012	额定电压不超过 35 千伏的电缆	10	0	8.9	0	5	0	0	0	0	0			8	0					0	0	0
85446013	额定电压超过 35 千伏，但不超过 110 千伏的电缆	8.4	0	8	0	5		0	0	0	0			5	0					0	0	0
85446014	额定电压超过 110 千伏，但不超过 220 千伏的电缆	8.4	0	8	0	5		0	0	0	0			5	0					0	0	0
85446019	其他额定电压超过 1000 伏的电缆	8.4	0	8	0	5		0	0	0	0				0					0	0	0
85446090	耐压＞1KV 的其他电导体	21	0	20	0	20	0	0	8.4	0	0			12.6	0					0	0	
85447000	光缆	0																		0	0	0
85451100	炉用碳电极	8	0		0	5		0	0	0				4.8	0					0	0	0
85451900	其他碳电极	10.5	0		0	5	0	0	0	0				8.4	0					0	0	0
85452000	碳刷	10.5	0		0	5	0	0	0	0				8.4	0					0	0	0
85459000	灯碳棒、电池碳棒及其他石墨制品	10.5	0		0	5	0	0	0	0				8.4	0					0	0	0
85461000	玻璃制绝缘子	10.5	0		0	5	0	0	0	0				8.4	0					0	0	0
85462010	输变电线路绝缘瓷套管	6	0		0	5		0	0	0				4.8	0					0	0	0
85462090	其他陶瓷制绝缘子	12	0		0	6	0	0	4.8	0				9.6	0					0	0	0
85469000	其他材料制绝缘子	10	0		0	5	0	0	0	0				8	0					0	0	0
85471000	陶瓷制绝缘零件	8	0		0	5		0	0	0				6.4	0					0	0	0
85472000	塑料制绝缘零件	8	0		0	5		0	0	0	0			6.4	0					0	0	0
85479010	内衬绝缘材料的贱金属导管及其接头	10	0		0	5	0	0	0	0				0	0					0	0	0
85479090	其他材料制绝缘配件	8	0		0	5		0	0	0				0	0					0	0	0
85481000	电池废碎料及废电池	8	0		0	5		0	0	0				4.8	0	4				0	0	
85489000	85 章其他未列名的电气零件	12	0		0	6	0	0	0	0				9.6	0					0	0	
86011011	微机控制的外部直流电动铁道机车	3	0		0	0		0	0	0				0	0					0	0	0
86011019	由外部直流电驱动的其他铁道机车	3	0		0	0		0	0	0				0	0					0	0	0
86011020	由外部交流电驱动的铁道机车	3	0		0	0		0	0	0				0	0					0	0	0
86011090	由其他外部电力驱动的铁道机车	3	0		0	0		0	0	0				0	0					0	0	0
86012000	由蓄电池驱动的铁道电力机车	3	0		0	0		0	0	0				0	0					0	0	0
86021010	微机控制的柴油电力铁道机车	3	0		0	0		0	0	0				0	0					0	0	0
86021090	其他柴油电力铁道机车	3	0		0	0		0	0	0				0	0					0	0	0
86029000	其他铁道机车及机车煤水车	3	0		0	0		0	0	0				0	0					0	0	0
86031000	由外电力驱动铁道及电车道用机动客车、货车、敞车	3	0		0	0		0	0	0				0	0					0	0	0

税则号列	货品名称	最惠国	协定税率													特惠税率						
			东盟统一	亚太5国	智利	巴基斯坦	新加坡	新西兰	秘鲁	哥达	香港	澳门	台湾	瑞士	冰岛	亚太2国	老挝	柬埔寨	缅甸	LDC1	LDC2	LDC3
86039000	其他铁道及电车道用机动客车、货车、敞车	3	0		0	0		0	0	0				0	0					0	0	0
86040011	隧道限界检查车	3	0		0	0		0	0	0				0	0					0	0	0
86040012	钢轨在线打磨列车	3	0		0	0		0	0	0				0	0					0	0	0
86040019	铁道及电车道用其他检验车及查道车	5	0		0	0		0	0	0				0	0					0	0	0
86040091	电气化接触网架线机(轨行式)	5	0		0	0		0	0	0				0	0					0	0	0
86040099	铁道及电车道用其他维修或服务车	7	0		0	5		0	0	0				4.2	0					0	0	0
86050010	铁道及电车道用非机动客车	5	0		0	0		0	0	0				0	0					0	0	0
86050090	铁道及电车道用其他非机动客车	5	0		0	0		0	0	0				0	0					0	0	0
86061000	铁道及电车道用非机动油罐货车及类似车	5	0		0	0		0	0	0				0	0					0	0	0
86063000	铁道及电车道用非机动自卸货车	5	0		0	0		0	0	0				0	0					0	0	0
86069100	铁道及电车道用非机动带篷及封闭货车	5	0		0	0		0	0	0				0	0					0	0	0
86069200	铁道及电车道用非机动厢高>60cm敞篷货车	5	0		0	0		0	0	0				0	0					0	0	0
86069900	税号86.06所列其他未列名非机动车	5	0		0	0		0	0	0				0	0					0	0	0
86071100	铁道及电车道机车的驾驶转向架	3	0		0	0		0	0	0				0	0					0	0	0
86071200	铁道及电车道机车非驾驶转向架	3	0		0	0		0	0	0				0	0					0	0	0
86071910	铁道及电车道机车用车轴	3	0		0	0		0	0	0				0	0					0	0	0
86071990	转向轮及其零件	3	0		0	0		0	0	0				0	0					0	0	0
86072100	铁道及电车道机车用空气制动器及其零件	3	0		0	0		0	0	0				0	0					0	0	0
86072900	铁道及电车道机车用非空气制动器	3	0		0	0		0	0	0				0	0					0	0	0
86073000	铁道及电车道机车用钩、联结器、缓冲器及其零件	3	0		0	0		0	0	0				0	0					0	0	0
86079100	铁道及电车道机车用其他零件	3	0		0	0		0	0	0				0	0					0	0	0
86079900	铁道及电车道非机车用其他零件	3	0		0	0		0	0	0				2.4	0					0	0	0
86080010	轨道自动计轴设备	3	0		0	0		0	0	0				0	0					0	0	0
86080090	铁道及电车道轨道固定装置及附件	4	0		0	0		0	0	0				2.4	0					0	0	0
86090011	20英尺保温式集装箱	10.5	0		0	5	0	0	0	0				8.4	0					0	0	0
86090012	20英尺罐式集装箱	10.5	0		0	5	0	0	0	0				8.4	0					0	0	0
86090019	20英尺其他集装箱	10.5	0		0	5	0	0	0	0				8.4	0					0	0	0
86090021	40英尺保温式集装箱	10.5	0		0	5	0	0	0	0				8.4	0					0	0	0
86090022	40英尺罐式集装箱	10.5	0		0	5	0	0	0	0				8.4	0					0	0	0
86090029	40英尺其他集装箱	10.5	0		0	5	0	0	0	0				8.4	0					0	0	0
86090030	45、48、53英尺的集装箱	10.5	0		0	5	0	0	0	0				8.4	0					0	0	0
86090090	其他集装箱	10.5	0		0	5	0	0	0	0				8.4	0					0	0	0
87011000	手扶拖拉机	9	0		0	5		0	0	0				5.4	0					0	0	
87012000	半挂车用的公路牵引车	6	6		0			0		0				3.6	0					0		
87013000	履带式牵引车、拖拉机	6	0		0	5		0	0	0				3.6	0					0	0	
87019011	轮式拖拉机	8	0		0	5		0	0	0				4.8	0					0	0	
87019019	其他拖拉机	8	0		0	5		0	0	0				4.8	0					0	0	
87019090	其他牵引车	8	0		0	5		0	0	0				4.8	0					0	0	
87021020	机坪客车	4	0		0	0		0	0	0				0	0					0	0	
87021091	≥30座大型客车(柴油型)	25	25		0			0		0					0					0		
87021092	≥20座,但≤29座的客车	25	25		0			0		0					0					0		
87021093	≥10座,但≤19座的客车	25	25		0			0		0					0					0		
87029010	≥30座大型客车(非柴油型)	25	20		0			0		0					0					0		
87029020	≥20座,但≤29座的客车(非柴油型)	25	20		0			0		0					0					0		
87029030	≥10座,但≤19座的客车(非柴油型)	25	20		0			0	10	0					0					0	0	
87031011	全地形车	25	0		0		0	0	10	0					0					0	0	
87031019	其他高尔夫球车及类似车辆	25	0		0		0	0	10	0					0					0	0	
87031090	雪地行走专用车	25	0		0		0	0	10	0					0					0	0	
87032130	排气量≤1000ml的小轿车	25	25	22.5	0	22.5		0		0					0							
87032140	排气量≤1000ml的越野车(4轮驱动)	25	25	22.5	0	22.5		0		0					0							
87032150	排气量≤1000ml的≤9座的小客车	25	25	22.5	0	22.5		0		0					0							
87032190	排气量≤1000ml的其他车辆	25	25	22.5	0	22.5		0		0					0							
87032230	1L<排气量≤1.5L的小轿车	25	25	22.5	0	22.5		0		0					0							
87032240	1L<排气量≤1.5L的越野车	25	25	22.5	0	22.5		0		0					0							

税则号列	货品名称	最惠国	协定税率													特惠税率						
			东盟统一	亚太5国	智利	巴基斯坦	新加坡	新西兰	秘鲁	哥达	香港	澳门	台湾	瑞士	冰岛	亚太2国	老挝	柬埔寨	缅甸	LDC1	LDC2	LDC3
87032250	1L＜排气量≤1.5L，≤9座的小客车	25	25	22.5	0	22.5		0		0					0							
87032290	1L＜排气量≤1.5L的其他车辆	25	25	22.5	0	22.5		0		0					0							
87032341	1.5L＜排气量≤2L的小轿车	25	25	22.5	0	22.5		0		0					0							
87032342	1.5L＜排气量≤2L的越野车	25	25	22.5	0	22.5		0		0					0							
87032343	1.5L＜排气量≤2L，≤9座的小客车	25	25	22.5	0	22.5		0		0					0							
87032349	1.5L＜排气量≤2L的其他车辆	25	25	22.5	0	22.5		0		0					0							
87032351	2L＜排气量≤2.5L的小轿车	25	25	22.5	0	22.5		0		0					0							
87032352	2L＜排气量≤2.5L的越野车	25	25	22.5	0	22.5		0		0					0							
87032353	2L＜排气量≤2.5L，≤9座的小客车	25	25	22.5	0	22.5		0		0					0							
87032359	2L＜排气量≤2.5L的其他车辆	25	25	22.5	0	22.5		0		0					0							
87032361	2.5L＜排气量≤3L的小轿车	25	25	22.5	0	22.5		0		0					0							
87032362	2.5L＜排气量≤3L的越野车	25	0	22.5	0	22.5	0	0		0					0							
87032363	2.5L＜排气量≤3L，≤9座的小客车	25	0	22.5	0	22.5	0	0		0					0							
87032369	2.5L＜排气量≤3L的其他车辆	25	0	22.5	0	22.5	0	0		0					0							
87032411	3L＜排气量≤4L的小轿车	25	25	22.5	0	22.5		0		0					0					0		
87032412	3L＜排气量≤4L的越野车	25	25	22.5	0	22.5		0		0					0					0		
87032413	3L＜排气量≤4L，≤9座的小客车	25	25	22.5	0	22.5		0		0					0					0		
87032419	3L＜排气量≤4L的其他车辆	25	25	22.5	0	22.5		0		0					0					0		
87032421	排气量＞4L的小轿车	25	25	22.5	0	22.5		0		0					0					0		
87032422	排气量＞4L的越野车	25	25	22.5	0	22.5		0		0					0					0		
87032423	排气量＞4L，≤9座的小客车	25	25	22.5	0	22.5		0		0					0					0		
87032429	排气量＞4L的其他车辆	25	25	22.5	0	22.5		0		0					0					0		
87033111	排气量≤1L的柴油型小轿车	25	25		0			0		0					0					0		
87033119	排气量≤1L的柴油型其他车辆	25	0		0		0	0	10	0					0					0	0	
87033121	1L＜排气量≤1.5L的柴油型小轿车	25	25		0			0		0					0							
87033122	1L＜排气量≤1.5L的柴油型越野车	25	25		0			0		0					0							
87033123	1L＜排气量≤1.5L，≤9座的柴油型小客车	25	25		0			0		0					0							
87033129	1L＜排气量≤1.5L的柴油型其他车辆	25	0		0		0	0	10	0					0					0	0	
87033211	1.5L＜排气量≤2L的柴油型小轿车	25	25	22.5	0	22.5		0		0					0							
87033212	1.5L＜排气量≤2L的柴油型越野车	25	25	22.5	0	22.5		0		0					0							
87033213	1.5L＜排气量≤2L，≤9座的柴油型小客车	25	25	22.5	0	22.5		0		0					0							
87033219	1.5L＜排气量≤2L的柴油型其他车辆	25	25	22.5	0	22.5		0		0					0							
87033221	2L＜排气量≤2.5L的柴油型小轿车	25	25	22.5	0	22.5		0		0					0							
87033222	2L＜排气量≤2.5L的柴油型越野车	25	25	22.5	0	22.5		0		0					0							
87033223	2L＜排气量≤2.5L，≤9座的柴油型小客车	25	25	22.5	0	22.5		0		0					0							
87033229	2L＜排气量≤2.5L的柴油型其他车辆	25	25	22.5	0	22.5		0		0					0							
87033311	2.5L＜排气量≤3L的柴油型小轿车	25	0	22.5	0	22.5	0	0		0					0							
87033312	2.5L＜排气量≤3L的柴油型越野车	25	0	22.5	0	22.5	0	0		0					0							
87033313	2.5L＜排气量≤3L，≤9座的柴油型小客车	25	0	22.5	0	22.5	0	0		0					0							
87033319	2.5L＜排气量≤3L的柴油型其他车辆	25	0	22.5	0	22.5	0	0		0					0							
87033321	3L＜排气量≤4L的柴油型小轿车	25	0	22.5	0	22.5	0	0		0					0					0		
87033322	3L＜排气量≤4L的柴油型越野车	25	0	22.5	0	22.5	0	0		0					0					0		
87033323	3L＜排气量≤4L，≤9座的柴油型小客车	25	0	22.5	0	22.5	0	0		0					0					0		
87033329	3L＜排气量≤4L的柴油型其他车辆	25	0	22.5	0	22.5	0	0		0					0					0		
87033361	排气量＞4L的柴油型小轿车	25	0	22.5	0	22.5	0	0		0					0					0		
87033362	排气量＞4L的柴油型越野车	25	0	22.5	0	22.5	0	0		0					0					0		
87033363	排气量＞4L，≤9座的柴油型小客车	25	0	22.5	0	22.5	0	0		0					0					0		
87033369	排气量＞4L的柴油型其他车辆	25	0	22.5	0	22.5	0	0		0					0					0		
87039000	装有压燃式内燃发动机的其他载人机动车辆	25	0	22.5	0	22.5	0	0	10	0					0					0	0	
87041030	非公路用电动轮货运自卸车	6	0		0	5		0	0	0				3.6	0					0	0	0
87041090	其他非公路用货运自卸车	6	0		0	5		0	0	0				3.6	0					0	0	0
87042100	柴油型其他小型货车	25	25		0			0		0					0					0		
87042230	柴油型其他中型货车	20	20	18	0	18		0	8					16	0					0	0	
87042240	柴油型其他重型货车	20	20	18	0	18		0	8					16	0					0	0	
87042300	柴油型的其他超重型货车	15	15		0			0		0				12	0					0		

税则号列	货品名称	最惠国	协定税率													特惠税率						
			东盟统一	亚太5国	智利	巴基斯坦	新加坡	新西兰	秘鲁	哥达	香港	澳门	台湾	瑞士	冰岛	亚太2国	老挝	柬埔寨	缅甸	LDC1	LDC2	LDC3
87043100	汽油型≤5 吨的其他货车	25	20		0			0		0					0					0		
87043230	5 吨<汽油型≤8 吨的其他货车	20	20		0			0	8	0				16	0					0	0	
87043240	汽油型>8 吨的其他货车	20	20		0			0	8	0				16	0					0	0	
87049000	装有其他发动机的货车	25	0		0		0	0	10	0					0					0	0	
87051021	最大起重重量≤50 吨的全路面汽车起重车	15	0		0	12	0	0	6	0				12	0					0	0	
87051022	50 吨<最大起重重量≤100 吨的全路面汽车起重车	10	0		0	5	0	0	0	0				6	0					0	0	0
87051023	最大起重重量>100 吨的全路面汽车起重车	10	0		0	5	0	0	0	0				6	0					0	0	0
87051091	最大起重重量≤50 吨的其他汽车起重车	15	0		0	12	0	0	6	0				12	0					0	0	
87051092	50 吨<最大起重重量≤100 吨的其他汽车起重车	10	0		0	5	0	0	0	0				6	0					0	0	0
87051093	最大起重重量>100 吨的其他汽车起重车	10	0		0	5	0	0	0	0				6	0					0	0	0
87052000	机动钻探车	12	0		0	6	0	0	0	0				9.6	0					0	0	0
87053010	装有云梯的救火车	3	0		0	0		0	0	0				0	0					0	0	0
87053090	其他机动救火车	3	0		0	0		0	0	0				0	0					0	0.	0
87054000	机动混凝土搅拌车	15	0	13.5	0	7.5	0	0	6	0				12	0					0	0	
87059010	无线电通信车	9	0	8.1	0	5	0	0	0	0				5.4	0					0	0	0
87059020	机动放射线检查车	9	0	8.1	0	5		0	0	0				5.4	0					0	0	0
87059030	机动环境监测车	12	0	10.8	0	5	0	0	0	0				9.6	0					0	0	
87059040	机动医疗车	12	0	10.8	0	5	0	0	0	0				9.6	0					0	0	
87059051	航空电源车(频率为 400 赫兹)	12	0	10.8	0	5	0	0	0	0				9.6	0					0	0	
87059059	其他机动电源车	12	0	10.8	0	5	0	0	0	0				9.6	0					0	0	
87059060	飞机加油车、调温车、除冰车	12	0	10.8	0	5	0	0	0	0				9.6	0					0	0	
87059070	道路(包括跑道)扫雪车	12	0	10.8	0	5	0	0	0	0				9.6	0					0	0	
87059080	石油测井车、压裂车、混沙车	12	0	10.8	0	5	0	0	0	0				9.6	0					0	0	
87059091	混凝土泵车	12	0	10.8	0	5	0	0	0	0				9.6	0					0	0	
87059099	其他特殊用途的机动车辆	12	0	10.8	0	5	0	0	0	0				9.6	0					0	0	
87060010	非公路用货运自卸车底盘	8	0		0	5		0	0	0				4.8	0					0	0	
87060021	车辆总重量≥14 吨的货车底盘	10	10		0			0		0				6	0					0		
87060022	车辆总重量<14 吨的货车底盘	10	10		0			0	0	0				6	0					0	0	
87060030	大型客车底盘	20	0		0		0	0		0				16	0					0		
87060040	汽车起重机底盘	20	0		0		0	0	8	0				16	0					0	0	
87060090	其他机动车辆底盘	10	0		0		0	0	0	0				6	0					0	0	
87071000	税号 87.03 所列车辆用车身(含驾驶室)	10	0		0		0	0	0	0				6	0					0	0	
87079010	税号 8702.1092、.1093、.9020 及.9030 所列车辆用车身	10	0	9	0	5	0	0	0	0				6	0					0	0	
87079090	其他车辆用车身(含驾驶室)	10	0	9	0	5	0	0	0	0				6	0					0	0	
87081000	缓冲器(保险杠)及其零件	10	0	9.6	0	5	0	0	0	0			0	6	0					0	0	0
87082100	座椅安全带	10	0		0	5	0	0	0	0		0		6	0					0	0	0
87082930	车窗玻璃升降器	10	10	9	0	9		0	0	0	0		0	6	0					0	0	0
87082941	汽车电动天窗	10	0	9	0	5	0	0	0	0	0		0	6	0					0	0	0
87082942	汽车手动天窗	10	0	9	0	5	0	0	0	0	0		0	6	0					0	0	0
87082951	侧围	10	0	9	0	5	0	0	0	0			0	6	0					0	0	0
87082952	车门	10	0	9	0	5	0	0	0	0			0	6	0					0	0	0
87082953	发动机罩盖	10	0	9	0	5	0	0	0	0			0	6	0					0	0	0
87082954	前围	10	0	9	0	5	0	0	0	0			0	6	0					0	0	0
87082955	行李箱盖(或背门)	10	0	9	0	5	0	0	0	0			0	6	0					0	0	0
87082956	后围	10	0	9	0	5	0	0	0	0			0	6	0					0	0	0
87082957	翼子板(或叶子板)	10	0	9	0	5	0	0	0	0			0	6	0					0	0	0
87082959	车身的其他覆盖件	10	0	9	0	5	0	0	0	0			0	6	0					0	0	0
87082990	车身的未列名零部件	10	0	9	0	5	0	0	0	0			0	8	0					0	0	0
87083010	装在蹄片上的制动摩擦片	10	0		0	5	0	0	4	0				6	0					0	0	0
87083021	牵引车、拖拉机、非公路自卸车用防抱死制动系统(ABS)	6	0	5.4	0	0		0	0	0				3.6	0					0	0	0
87083029	其他车辆用防抱死制动系统(ABS)	10	10	9	0	9		0	0	0				6	0					0	0	0
87083091	牵引车、拖拉机用制动器及其零件	6	0	5.4	0	0		0	0	0				3.6	0					0	0	0
87083092	大型客车用制动器及其零件	10	10	9	0	9		0	0	0				6	0					0	0	0

税则号列	货品名称	最惠国	协定税率 东盟统一	亚太5国	智利	巴基斯坦	新加坡	新西兰	秘鲁	哥达	香港	澳门	台湾	瑞士	冰岛	特惠税率 亚太2国	老挝	柬埔寨	缅甸	LDC1	LDC2	LDC3
87083093	非公路自卸车用制动器及其零件	6	0	5.4	0	0		0	0	0				3.6	0					0	0	0
87083094	柴、汽油轻型货车用制动器及零件	10	10	9	0	9		0	0	0				6	0					0	0	0
87083095	柴油型重型货车用制动器及其零件	10	0	9	0	5	0	0	0	0				6	0					0	0	0
87083096	特种车用制动器及其零件	10	0	9	0	5	0	0	0	0				6	0					0	0	0
87083099	其他未列名机动车辆用制动器及零件	10	10	9	0	9		0	0	0				8	0					0	0	0
87084010	牵引车、拖拉机用变速箱及零件	6	0		0	5		0	0	0			0	3.6	0					0	0	0
87084020	大型客车用变速箱及零件	10	10		0			0		0			0	6	0					0		
87084030	非公路自卸车用变速箱及零件	6	0		0	5		0		0			0	3.6	0					0		
87084040	柴、汽油轻型货车用变速箱及零件	10	10		0			0		0			0	6	0					0		
87084050	其他柴油型重型货车用变速箱及零件	10	10		0			0		0			0	6	0					0		
87084060	特种车用变速箱及零件	10	0		0	5	0	0	0	0			0	6	0					0	0	0
87084091	自动换档变速箱及零件	10	10		0			0		0				6	0					0		
87084099	未列名机动车辆用变速箱及零件	10	0		0		0	0		0			0	6	0					0		
87085071	牵引车、拖拉机用驱动桥及零件	6	0	5.4	0	0		0	0	0				3.6	0					0	0	0
87085072	其他大型客车用驱动桥及零件	10	10	9	0	9		0	0	0				6	0					0	0	0
87085073	非公路自卸车用驱动桥及零件	6	0	5.4	0	0		0	0	0				3.6	0					0	0	0
87085074	柴、汽油型轻型货车用驱动桥及零件	10	10	9	0	9		0	0	0				6	0					0	0	0
87085075	其他柴油型重型货车用驱动桥及零件	10	10	9	0	9		0	0	0				6	0					0	0	0
87085076	特种车用驱动桥及零件	10	0	9	0	5	0	0	0	0				6	0					0	0	0
87085079	未列名机动车辆用驱动桥及零件	10	10	9	0	9		0	0	0				8.7	0					0	0	0
87085081	牵引车、拖拉机用非驱动桥及零件	6	0		0	5		0	0	0				3.6	0					0	0	0
87085082	座位≥30 客车用非驱动桥及零件	15	0		0	9.7	0	0	6	0				12	0					0	0	
87085083	非公路自卸车用非驱动桥及零件	6	0		0	5		0	0	0				3.6	0					0	0	0
87085084	柴、汽油轻货车用非驱动桥及零件	10	0		0	5	0	0	0	0				6	0					0	0	0
87085085	柴油重型货车用非驱动桥及零件	10	0		0	5	0	0	0	0				6	0					0	0	0
87085086	特种车用非驱动桥及其零件	10	0		0	5	0	0	0	0				6	0					0	0	0
87085089	未列名机动车辆用非驱动桥及零件	10	0		0	5	0	0	0	0				6	0					0	0	0
87087010	牵引车及拖拉机用车轮及其零附件	6	0		0	5		0	0	0			0	3.6	0					0	0	0
87087020	大型客车用车轮及其零附件	10	0		0	5	0	0	0	0			0	6	0					0	0	0
87087030	非公路货运自卸车用车轮及其零件	6	0		0	5		0	0	0			0	3.6	0					0	0	0
87087040	中小型货车用车轮及其零件	10	0		0	5	0	0	0	0			0	6	0					0	0	0
87087050	大型货车用车轮及其零件	10	0		0	5	0	0	0	0			0	6	0					0	0	0
87087060	特种车用车轮及其零件	10	0		0	5	0	0	0	0			0	6	0					0	0	0
87087091	铝合金制的车轮及其零件、附件	10	0		0	5	0	0	0	0			0	6	0					0	0	0
87087099	其他车轮及其零件、附件	10	0		0	5	0	0	0	0			0	6	0					0	0	0
87088010	税号 87.03 所列车辆用的悬挂减震器及零件	10	0	9	0	5	0	0	0	0				6	0					0	0	0
87088090	机动车辆用的其他悬挂减震器及零件	10	0	9	0	5	0	0	0	0				6	0					0	0	0
87089110	水箱散热器	10	0		0	5	0	0	0	0				6	0					0	0	0
87089120	机油冷却器	10	0		0	5	0	0	0	0				6	0					0	0	0
87089190	其他散热器及其零件	10	0		0	5	0	0	0	0				6	0					0	0	0
87089200	机动车辆的消声器及排气管及零件	10	0		0	5	0	0	0	0				6	0					0	0	0
87089310	牵引车、拖拉机用离合器及其零件	6	0		0	5		0	0	0				3.6	0					0	0	0
87089320	座位≥30 客车用离合器及其零件	10	0		0	5	0	0	0	0				6	0					0	0	0
87089330	非公路自卸车用离合器及其零件	6	0		0	5		0	0	0				3.6	0					0	0	0
87089340	柴、汽油轻型货车用离合器及零件	10	0		0	5	0	0	0	0				6	0					0	0	0
87089350	总重≥14 吨柴油货车离合器及零件	10	0		0	5	0	0	0	0				6	0					0	0	0
87089360	特种车用的离合器及其零件	10	0		0	5	0	0	0	0				6	0					0	0	0
87089390	未列名机动车辆用离合器及其零件	10	0		0	5	0	0	0	0				6	0					0	0	0
87089410	牵引车、拖拉机用转向盘、转向柱及转向器及零件	6	0		0	5		0	0	0				3.6	0					0	0	0
87089420	大型客车用转向盘、转向柱及转向器及零件	10	0		0	5	0	0	0	0				6	0					0	0	0
87089430	非公路自卸车用转向盘、转向柱及转向器及零件	6	0		0	5		0	0	0				3.6	0					0	0	0
87089440	柴、汽油轻货车用转向盘、转向柱及转向器及零件	10	0		0	5	0	0	0	0				6	0					0	0	0
87089450	柴油型重型货车用转向盘、转向柱及转向器及零件	10	0		0	5	0	0	0	0				6	0					0	0	0

税则号列	货品名称	最惠国	协定税率 东盟统一	亚太5国	智利	巴基斯坦	新加坡	新西兰	秘鲁	哥达	香港	澳门	台湾	瑞士	冰岛	特惠税率 亚太2国	老挝	柬埔寨	缅甸	LDC1	LDC2	LDC3
87089460	特种车用转向盘、转向柱及转向器及零件	10	0		0	5	0	0	0	0				6	0					0	0	0
87089490	未列名机动车辆用转向盘、转向柱及转向器及零件	10	0		0	5	0	0	0	0				8.7	0					0	0	0
87089500	机动车辆的安全气囊装置	10	10	9	0	9		0		0	0			6	0					0		
87089910	牵引车及拖拉机用其他零附件	6	0		0	5		0	0	0				3.6	0					0	0	0
87089921	税号8702.1091及8702.9010所列车辆用车架	25	0		0		0	0	10	0					0					0	0	
87089929	大型客车用其他零附件	25	0		0		0	0	10	0					0					0	0	
87089931	税号8704.1030及8704.1090所列车辆用车架	6	0		0	5		0	0	0				3.6	0					0	0	0
87089939	非公路货运自卸车用其他零附件	6	0		0	5		0	0	0				3.6	0					0	0	0
87089941	税号8704.2100、8704.2230、8704.3100及8704.3230所列车辆用车架	25	0		0		0	0	10	0					0					0	0	
87089949	中小型货车用其他零附件	25	0		0		0	0	10	0					0					0	0	
87089951	税号8704.2240、8704.2300及8704.3240所列车辆用车架	10	0		0	5	0	0	0	0				6	0					0	0	0
87089959	总重≥14吨货车用其他零附件	10	0		0	5	0	0	0	0				6	0					0	0	0
87089960	特种车用其他零附件	15	0		0	12	0	0	6	0				12	0					0	0	
87089991	其他税号所列车辆用车架	10	0		0	5	0	0	0	0			0	6	0					0	0	0
87089992	汽车传动轴	10	0		0	5	0	0	0	0			0	6	0					0	0	0
87089999	机动车辆用未列名零附件	10	0		0	5	0	0	0	0			0	6	0					0	0	0
87091110	短距离运输货物电动牵引车	10	0		0	5	0	0	0	0				6	0					0	0	0
87091190	其他电动短矩离运货车	10	0		0	5	0	0	0	0				6	0					0	0	0
87091910	短距离运输货物其他牵引车	10.5	0		0	5	0	0	0	0				8.4	0					0	0	0
87091990	其他非电动短矩离运货车	10.5	0		0	5	0	0	0	0				8.4	0					0	0	0
87099000	短距离运货车、站台牵引车用零件	8.4	0		0	5		0	0	0				5	0					0	0	0
87100010	坦克及其他机动装甲战斗车辆	15	0		0	12	0	0	6	0				12	0					0	0	
87100090	坦克及其他机动装甲战斗车辆零件	15	0		0	12	0	0	6	0				12	0					0	0	
87111000	汽油型微马力摩托车及脚踏两用车	45	0		0		0	0	18	0				34.7	0					0	0	
87112010	装有往复式活塞发动机,气缸容量超过50毫升,但不超过100毫升的汽油型小马力摩托车及脚踏两用车	45	0		0		0	0	18	0				34.7	0					0	0	
87112020	装有往复式活塞发动机,气缸容量超过100毫升,但不超过125毫升的汽油型小马力摩托车及脚踏两用车	45	0		0		0	0	18	0				34.7	0					0	0	
87112030	装有往复式活塞发动机,气缸容量超过125毫升,但不超过150毫升的汽油型小马力摩托车及脚踏两用车	45	0		0		0	0	18	0				34.7	0					0	0	
87112040	装有往复式活塞发动机,气缸容量超过150毫升,但不超过200毫升的汽油型小马力摩托车及脚踏两用车	45	0		0		0	0		0				34.7	0					0		
87112050	装有往复式活塞发动机,气缸容量超过200毫升,但不超过250毫升的汽油型小马力摩托车及脚踏两用车	45	0		0		0	0		0				34.7	0					0		
87113010	汽油型中小马力摩托车及脚踏两用车	45	0	32.8	0	32.8	0	0		0					0					0		
87113020	汽油型中大马力摩托车及脚踏两用车	45	0	32.8	0	32.8	0	0		0					0					0		
87114000	汽油型大马力摩托车及脚踏两用车	40	0		0		0	0		0					0					0		
87115000	汽油型超大马力摩托车及类似车	30	0		0		0	0		0					0					0		
87119010	电动的或电动助力的摩托车(包括机器脚踏两用车)	45	0		0		0	0		0					0					0		
87119090	装有其他发动机的摩托车及边车	45	0		0		0	0		0					0					0		
87120020	竞赛型自行车	13	0	9.1	0	5	0	0	0	0			0	10.4	0					0	0	
87120030	山地自行车	13	0	9.1	0	5	0	0	0	0			0	10.4	0					0	0	
87120041	16、18、20英寸自行车	13	0	9.1	0	5	0	0	0	0			0	10.4	0					0	0	0
87120049	其他越野自行车	13	0	9.1	0	5	0	0	0	0			0	10.4	0					0	0	
87120081	≤16英寸的未列名自行车	13	0	9.1	0	5	0	0	0	0		0	0	10.4	0					0	0	
87120089	其他未列名自行车	13	0	9.1	0	5	0	0	0	0		0	0	10.4	0					0	0	
87120090	其他非机动脚踏车	23	0	16.1	0	16.1	0	0	9.2	0		0	0	18.4	0					0	0	
87131000	非机械驱动的残疾人用车	6	0		0	5		0	0	0				3.6	0					0	0	
87139000	其他机动残疾人用车	4	0		0	0		0	0	0				0	0					0	0	
87141000	摩托车及机动脚踏两用车用零附件	30	0		0		0	0	12	0					0					0	0	

税则号列	货品名称	最惠国	协定税率													特惠税率						
			东盟统一	亚太5国	智利	巴基斯坦	新加坡	新西兰	秘鲁	哥达	香港	澳门	台湾	瑞士	冰岛	亚太2国	老挝	柬埔寨	缅甸	LDC1	LDC2	LDC3
87142000	残疾人车辆用零附件	5	0		0	0		0	0	0				0	0					0	0	0
87149100	非机动脚踏车车架、轮叉及其零件	12	0		0	6	0	0	0	0			0	9.6	0					0	0	
87149210	轮圈	12	0		0	6	0	0	0	0			0	9.6	0					0	0	
87149290	辐条	12	0		0	6	0	0	0	0			0	9.6	0					0	0	
87149310	非机动脚踏车的轮毂	12	0		0	6	0	0	0	0			0	9.6	0					0	0	
87149320	飞轮	12	0		0	6	0	0	0	0			0	9.6	0					0	0	
87149390	其他非机动脚踏车的飞轮	12	0		0	6	0	0	0	0			0	9.6	0					0	0	
87149400	非机动脚踏车的制动器及其零件	12	0		0	6	0	0	0	0			0	9.6	0					0	0	
87149500	非机动脚踏车的鞍座	12	0		0	6	0	0	0	0			0	9.6	0					0	0	
87149610	非机动脚踏车脚蹬及其零件	12	0		0	6	0	0	0	0			0	9.6	0					0	0	
87149620	非机动脚踏车曲柄、链轮及其零件	12	0		0	6	0	0	0	0			0	9.6	0					0	0	
87149900	非机动脚踏车的其他零附件	12	0	8.4	0	5	0	0	0	0			0	9.6	0					0	0	
87150000	婴孩车及其零件	20	0		0		0	0	8	0		0		16	0					0	0	
87161000	供居住或野营用厢式挂车及半挂车	10	0		0	5	0	0	0	0				6	0					0	0	
87162000	农用自装或自卸式挂车及半挂车	10	0		0	5		0	0	0				6	0					0	0	
87163110	油罐挂车及半挂车	10	0		0	5	0	0	0	0				6	0					0	0	
87163190	其他罐式挂车及半挂车	10	0		0	5		0	0	0				6	0					0	0	
87163910	货柜挂车及半挂车	10	0		0	5		0	0	0				6	0					0	0	
87163990	其他货运挂车及半挂车	10	0		0	5		0	0	0				6	0					0	0	
87164000	其他未列名挂车及半挂车	10	0		0	5		0	0	0				6	0					0	0	
87168000	其他未列名非机械驱动车辆	10	0		0	5	0	0	0	0		0		6	0					0	0	
87169000	挂车、半挂车及非机动车用零件	10	0		0	5	0	0	0	0				6	0					0	0	0
88010010	滑翔机及悬挂滑翔机	3	0		0	0		0	0	0				0	0					0	0	0
88010090	汽球、飞艇及其他无动力航空器	3	0		0	0		0	0	0				0	0					0	0	0
88021100	空载重量≤2 吨的直升机	2	0		0	0		0	0	0				0	0					0	0	0
88021210	2 吨＜空载重量≤7 吨的直升机	2	0		0	0		0	0	0				0	0					0	0	0
88021220	空载重量＞7 吨的直升机	2	0		0	0		0	0	0				0	0					0	0	0
88022000	小型飞机及其他航空器	5	0		0	0		0	0	0				0	0					0	0	0
88023000	中型飞机及其他航空器	4	0		0	0		0	0	0				0	0					0	0	0
88024010	大型飞机及其他航空器	5	0	3.5	0	0		0	0	0				0	0					0	0	0
88024020	特大型飞机及其他航空器	1	0	0.7	0	0		0	0	0				0	0					0	0	0
88026000	航天器(包括卫星)及其运载工具	2	0		0	0		0	0	0				0	0					0	0	0
88031000	飞机等用推进器、水平旋翼及零件	1	0		0	0		0	0	0				0	0					0	0	0
88032000	飞机等用起落架及其零件	1	0		0	0		0	0	0				0	0					0	0	0
88033000	飞机及直升机的其他零件	1	0		0	0		0	0	0				0	0					0	0	
88039000	其他未列名的航空器、航天器零件	0																		0	0	0
88040000	降落伞及其零附件	2	0		0	0		0	0	0				0	0					0	0	0
88051000	航空器的发射装置及其零件等	1.5	0		0	0		0	0	0				0	0					0	0	0
88052100	空战模拟器及其零件	1.5	0		0	0		0	0	0				0	0					0	0	
88052900	其他地面飞行训练器及其零件	1.5	0		0	0		0	0	0				0	0					0	0	0
89011010	机动巡航船、游览船及各式渡船	5	0		0	0	0	0	0	0	0			0	0					0	0	
89011090	非机动巡航船、游览船及各式渡船	8	0		0	5		0	0	0				4.8	0					0	0	
89012011	载重≤10 万吨的成品油船	9	9		0			0	0	0				5.4	0					0	0	
89012012	10 万吨＜载重≤30 万吨的成品油船	9	9		0			0	0	0				5.4	0					0	0	
89012013	载重＞30 万吨的成品油船	6	6		0			0	0	0				3.6	0					0	0	
89012021	载重≤15 万吨的原油船	9	9		0			0	0	0				5.4	0					0	0	
89012022	15 万吨＜载重≤30 万吨的原油船	9	9		0			0	0	0				5.4	0					0	0	
89012023	载重＞30 万吨的原油船	6	6		0			0	0	0				3.6	0					0	0	
89012031	容积≤20000 立方米的液化石油气船	9	9		0			0	0	0				5.4	0					0	0	
89012032	容积＞20000 立方米的液化石油气船	6	6		0			0	0	0				3.6	0					0	0	
89012041	容积≤20000 立方米的液化天然气船	9	9		0			0	0	0				5.4	0					0	0	
89012042	容积＞20000 立方米的液化天然气船	6	6		0			0	0	0				3.6	0					0	0	
89012090	其他液货船	9	9		0			0	0	0				5.4	0					0	0	
89013000	冷藏船	9	0		0	5	0	0	0	0				5.4	0					0	0	
89019021	可载标准集装箱≤6000 箱的机动集装箱船	9	9		0			0	0	0				5.4	0					0	0	
89019022	可载标准集装箱＞6000 箱的机动集装箱船	6	6		0			0	0	0				3.6	0					0	0	
89019031	载重≤2 万吨的机动滚装船	9	9		0			0	0	0				5.4	0					0	0	

税则号列	货品名称	最惠国	协定税率													特惠税率						
			东盟统一	亚太5国	智利	巴基斯坦	新加坡	新西兰	秘鲁	哥达	香港	澳门	台湾	瑞士	冰岛	亚太2国	老挝	柬埔寨	缅甸	LDC1	LDC2	LDC3
89019032	载重＞2万吨的机动滚装船	6	6		0			0	0	0				3.6	0					0	0	
89019041	载重≤15万吨的机动散货船	9	9		0			0	0	0				5.4	0					0	0	
89019042	15万吨＜载重≤30万吨的机动散货船	9	9		0			0	0	0				5.4	0					0	0	
89019043	载重＞30万吨的机动散货船	9	9		0			0	0	0				5.4	0					0	0	
89019050	机动多用途船	9	9		0			0	0	0				5.4	0					0	0	
89019080	其他机动货运船舶	9	0		0	5	0	0	0	0				5.4	0					0	0	
89019090	非机动货运船舶及客货兼运船舶	8	0		0	5	0	0	0	0				4.8	0					0	0	
89020010	机动捕鱼船	7	0		0	5	0	0	0	0				4.2	0					0	0	
89020090	非机动捕鱼船	8	0		0	5		0	0	0				4.8	0					0	0	
89031000	充气的娱乐或运动用快艇	10	0		0	5		0	0	0				6	0					0	0	0
89039100	帆船	8	0		0	5		0	0	0				4.8	0					0	0	0
89039200	汽艇	10.5	0		0	5	0	0	4.2	0	0			8.4	0					0	0	0
89039900	娱乐或运动用其他船舶或快艇	10	0		0	5		0	0	0				6	0					0	0	0
89040000	拖轮及顶推船	9	0		0	5	0	0	0	0				5.4	0					0	0	0
89051000	挖泥船	3	0		0	0		0	0	0				0	0					0	0	0
89052000	浮动或潜水式钻探或生产平台	6	0		0	5		0	0	0				3.6	0					0	0	0
89059010	浮船坞	8	8		0			0	0	0				4.8	0					0	0	0
89059090	其他不以航行为主要功能的船舶	3	0		0	0		0	0	0				0	0					0	0	0
89061000	军舰	5	0		0	0		0	0	0				0	0					0	0	0
89069010	其他未列名的机动船舶	5	0		0	0		0	0	0				0	0					0	0	0
89069020	非机动船舶	8	0		0	5		0	0	0				4.8	0					0	0	0
89069030	未制成或不完整的船舶,包括船舶分段	8	0		0	5		0	0	0				4.8	0					0	0	0
89071000	充气筏	8	0		0	5		0	0	0				4.8	0					0	0	0
89079000	其他浮动结构体	8	0		0	5		0	0	0				4.8	0					0	0	0
89080000	供拆卸的船舶及其他浮动结构体	3	0		0	0		0	0	0				0	0					0	0	0
90011000	光导纤维束及光缆	5	0	4.5	0	0		0	0	0	0			3	0					0	0	0
90012000	偏振材料制的片及板	8	0	7.6	0	5		0	0	0	0			4.8	0					0	0	0
90013000	隐形眼镜片	10	0		0	5	0	0	0	0	0			6	0					0	0	0
90014010	玻璃制变色镜片	20	0		0		0	0	8	0	0			16	0					0	0	
90014091	玻璃制太阳镜片	20	0		0		0	0	8	0	0			16	0					0	0	
90014099	玻璃制其他眼镜片	20	0		0		0	0	8	0	0			16	0					0	0	
90015010	非玻璃材料制变色镜片	20	0		0		0	0	8	0	0			16	0					0	0	
90015091	非玻璃材料制太阳镜片	20	0		0		0	0	8	0	0			16	0					0	0	
90015099	非玻璃材料制其他眼镜片	20	0		0		0	0	8	0	0			16	0					0	0	
90019010	彩色滤光片	8	0	7.6	0	5		0	0	0	0			4.8	0					0	0	0
90019090	其他光学元件	8	0	7.6	0	5		0	0	0	0			6.4	0					0	0	0
90021110	特殊用途照相机用物镜	8	0		0	5		0	0	0				4.8	0					0	0	0
90021120	缩微阅读机用物镜	8	0		0	5		0	0	0				4.8	0					0	0	0
90021131	单反相机镜头	15	0		0	12	0	0	6	0				12	0					0	0	
90021139	其他照相机用镜头	15	0		0	12	0	0	6	0				12	0					0	0	0
90021190	其他照相机、投影仪等用物镜	15	0		0	12	0	0	6	0			0	12	0					0	0	0
90021910	摄影机或放映机用物镜	15	0		0	12	0	0	6	0				12	0					0	0	
90021990	税号90.02未列名的其他物镜	15	0		0	12	0	0	6	0	0		0	12	0					0	0	0
90022010	照相机用滤色镜	15	0	14.3	0	12	0	0	6	0				12	0					0	0	
90022090	其他光学仪器或装置滤色镜	15	0	14.3	0	12	0	0	6	0				12	0					0	0	
90029010	照相机用未列名光学元件	15	0		0	12	0	0	6	0	0		0	12	0					0	0	
90029090	其他光学仪器用未列名光学元件	15	0		0	12	0	0	6	0	0		0	12	0					0	0	0
90031100	塑料制眼镜架	18	0		0		0	0	7.2	0	0	0		14.4	0					0	0	
90031910	金属材料制眼镜架	10	0		0	5		0	0	0	0	0		6	0					0	0	
90031920	天然材料制眼镜架	10	0		0	5		0	0	0	0	0		6	0					0	0	
90031990	其他眼镜架	10	0		0	5		0	0	0	0	0		6	0					0	0	
90039000	眼镜架零件	10	0		0	5		0	0	0	0			6	0					0	0	
90041000	太阳镜	20	0		0		0	0	8	0	0	0		16	0					0	0	

税则号列	货品名称	最惠国	协定税率													特惠税率						
			东盟统一	亚太5国	智利	巴基斯坦	新加坡	新西兰	秘鲁	哥达	香港	澳门	台湾	瑞士	冰岛	亚太2国	老挝	柬埔寨	缅甸	LDC1	LDC2	LDC3
90049010	变色镜	16	0		0	12.8	0	0	6.4	0	0	0		12.8	0					0	0	
90049090	其他眼镜	20	0		0		0	0	8	0	0	0		16	0					0	0	
90051000	双筒望远镜	15	0		0	12	0	0	6	0				12	0					0	0	
90058010	天文望远镜及其他天文仪器	3	0		0	0		0	0	0				0	0					0	0	0
90058090	其他光学望远镜	12	0		0	6	0	0	0	0				9.6	0					0	0	0
90059010	天文望远镜及其他天文仪器用零件	2	0		0	0		0	0	0				0	0					0	0	0
90059090	其他望远镜零附件	8	0		0	5		0	0	0				4.8	0					0	0	0
90061010	电子分色机	12	0		0	6	0	0	0	0				9.6	0					0	0	0
90061090	其他制版照相机	10	0		0	5		0	0	0				6	0					0	0	0
90063000	特种用途的照相机	9	0		0	5		0	0	0				5.4	0					0	0	0
90064000	一次成相照相机	5	0		0	0		0	0	0				0	0					0	0	0
90065100	通过镜头取景的照相机	25	0		0		0	0		0				19.3	0					0		
90065210	缩微照相机	9	0		0	5		0	0	0				5.4	0					0	0	0
90065290	使用胶片宽 <35mm 的其他照相机	25	0		0		0	0		0				19.3						0		
90065300	其他照相机	20	0		0		0	0	8	0				16	0					0	0	
90065910	激光照排设备	9	0		0	5	0	0	0	0				5.4	0					0	0	0
90065990	其他照相机	25	0		0		0	0		0					0					0		
90066100	放电式(电子式)闪光灯装置	18	0		0		0	0	7.2	0				14.4	0					0	0	
90066910	闪光灯泡、方形闪光灯及类似品	18	0		0	14.4	0	0	7.2	0				14.4	0					0	0	
90066990	其他照相闪光灯装置	18	0		0	14.4	0	0	7.2	0				14.4	0					0	0	
90069110	特种用途照相机的零附件	8	0	5.6	0	5		0	0	0	0			4.8	0	0				0	0	0
90069120	一次成像照相机的零附件	5	0	3.5	0	0		0	0	0	0			0	0	0				0	0	0
90069191	照相机自动调焦组件	10	0	7	0	5	0	0	0	0	0			6	0	0				0	0	0
90069192	其他照相机的快门组件	10	0	7	0	5	0	0	0	0	0			6	0	0				0	0	0
90069199	其他照相机的其他零附件	10	0	7	0	5	0	0	0	0	0			6	0	0				0	0	0
90069900	照相闪光灯装置及闪光灯泡的零件	12	0		0	6	0	0	0	0				9.6	0					0	0	0
90071010	高速摄影机	14	0		0	7	0	0	0	0				11.2	0					0	0	
90071090	其他摄影机	14	0		0	11.2	0	0	0	0				11.2	0					0	0	
90072010	数字式放映机	14	0		0	11.2	0	0	0	0	0			11.2	0					0	0	
90072090	放映机	14	0		0	11.2	0	0	0	0				11.2	0					0	0	
90079100	电影摄影机用零附件	8.4	0		0	5		0	0	0				5	0					0	0	
90079200	电影放映机用零附件	8.4	0		0	5		0	0	0				5	0					0	0	
90085010	幻灯机	14	0		0	7	0	0	0	0				11.2	0					0	0	
90085020	缩微胶卷、缩微胶片或其他缩微品的阅读机,不论是否可以进行复制	10	0		0	5		0	0	0				6	0					0	0	
90085031	正射投影仪	18	0		0		0	0	7.2	0				14.4	0					0	0	
90085039	其他影像投影仪	18	0		0		0	0	7.2	0				14.4	0					0	0	
90085040	照片(电影片除外)放大机及缩片机	20	0		0		0	0	8	0				16	0					0	0	
90089010	缩微阅读机的零附件	8	0		0	5		0	0	0				4.8	0					0	0	
90089020	照片放大机及缩片机的零附件	14	0		0	7	0	0	0	0				11.2	0					0	0	
90089090	其他影像投影仪的零附件	14	0		0	11.2	0	0	0	0				11.2	0					0	0	
90101010	电影用胶卷的自动显影装置及设备	14	0		0	7	0	0	0	0	0			11.2	0					0	0	
90101020	特种照相胶卷自动显影装置及设备	8.4	0		0	5		0	0	0	0			5	0					0	0	0
90101091	彩色胶卷用自动显影及设备	25	0		0		0	0	10	0	0			19.3	0					0	0	
90101099	其他胶卷的自动显影装置及设备	15	0		0	12	0	0	6	0	0			12	0					0	0	
90105010	负片显示器	14	0		0	7	0	0	0	0				11.2	0					0	0	
90105021	电影用的洗印装置	14	0		0	11.2	0	0	0	0				11.2	0					0	0	
90105022	特种照相用的洗印装置	8.4	0		0	5		0	0	0				5	0					0	0	0
90105029	其他照相用的洗印装置	17	0		0	13.6	0	0	6.8	0				13.6	0					0	0	
90106000	银幕及其他投影屏幕	14	0		0	11.2	0	0	0	0				11.2	0					0	0	
90109010	电影洗印用洗印装置的零附件	0																		0	0	0
90109020	特种照相洗印用装置的零附件	0																		0	0	0
90109090	其他洗印用装置的零附件	0																		0	0	0

税则号列	货品名称	最惠国	协定税率 东盟统一	亚太5国	智利	巴基斯坦	新加坡	新西兰	秘鲁	哥达	香港	澳门	台湾	瑞士	冰岛	特惠税率 亚太2国	老挝	柬埔寨	缅甸	LDC1	LDC2	LDC3
90111000	立体显微镜	0																		0	0	0
90112000	缩微照相等用的其他显微镜	0																		0	0	0
90118000	其他显微镜	7	0		0	5		0	0	0				5.6	0					0	0	
90119000	复式光学显微镜的零附件	0																		0	0	0
90121000	其他非光学显微镜及衍射设备	0																		0	0	0
90129000	非光学显微镜及衍射设备的零件	0																		0	0	0
90131000	武器用望远镜瞄准具及其他望远镜	8	0		0	5		0	0	0				4.8	0					0	0	
90132000	激光器	6	0		0	5		0	0	0		0		4.8	0					0	0	
90138010	放大镜	12	0	8.4	0	5	0	0	0	0	0	0		9.6	0					0	0	
90138020	光学门眼	12	0	8.4	0	5	0	0	0	0				9.6	0					0	0	
90138030	液晶显示板	5	0		0	0		0			0	0			0							
90138090	其他液晶装置及光学仪器	5	0		0	0		0	0	0	0	0		3	0					0	0	
90139010	激光器、望远镜等装置的零附件	6	0		0	5		0	0	0	0	0		3.6	0					0	0	
90139020	子目录9013.8030所列货品用零附件	8	0		0	5		0	0	0	0	0		4.8	0					0	0	
90139090	税号90.13所列其他货品的零附件	8	0		0	5		0	0	0	0	0		4.8	0					0	0	
90141000	定向罗盘	2	0		0	0		0	0	0				0	0					0	0	0
90142010	自动驾驶仪	2	0		0	0		0	0	0				0	0					0	0	0
90142090	其他航空或航天导航仪器及装置(罗盘除外)	2	0		0	0		0	0	0				0	0					0	0	0
90148000	其他导航仪器及装置	2	0		0	0		0	0	0				0	0					0	0	0
90149010	自动驾驶仪用零件、附件	1.5	0		0	0		0	0	0				0	0					0	0	0
90149090	其他导航仪器及设备用零件、附件	1.5	0		0	0		0	0	0				0	0					0	0	
90151000	测距仪	9	0		0	5		0	0	0				7.5	0					0	0	0
90152000	经纬仪及视距仪	9	0		0	5		0	0	0				5.4	0					0	0	0
90153000	水平仪	9	0		0	5		0	0	0				5.4	0					0	0	0
90154000	摄影测量用仪器及装置	9	0		0	5		0	0	0				5.4	0					0	0	0
90158000	其他大地测量仪器及装置	5	0	3.5	0	0		0	0	0					0					0	0	0
90159000	大地测量仪器及装置的零附件	5	0		0	0		0	0	0				3	0					0	0	0
90160010	感量为0.1mg或更精密的天平	9	0		0	5		0	0	0					0					0	0	0
90160090	0.1mg<感量≤50mg的天平	10.5	0		0	5	0	0	0	0				6.3	0					0	0	0
90171000	绘图台及绘图机,不论是否自动	8	0		0	5		0	0	0				4.8	0					0	0	0
90172000	其他绘图、划线或数学计算器具	0																		0	0	0
90173000	千分尺、卡尺及量规	8	0		0	5		0	0	0				6.4	0					0	0	0
90178000	其他手用测量长度的器具	8	0		0	5		0	0	0				6.4	0					0	0	0
90179000	绘图计算器具等仪器的零附件	0																		0	0	0
90181100	心电图记录仪	5	0		0	0		0	0	0				3	0					0	0	0
90181210	B型超声波诊断仪	7	0	6	0	0		0	0	0				4.2	4.7					0	0	0
90181291	彩色超声波诊断仪	5	0	4.5	0	0		0	0	0				0	0					0	0	0
90181299	其他超声扫描装置	5	0	4.5	0	0		0	0	0				0	0					0	0	0
90181310	核磁共振成像成套装置	4	0		0	0		0	0	0	0			2.4	0					0	0	0
90181390	其他核磁共振成象装置	4	0		0	0		0	0	0	0			2.4	0					0	0	0
90181400	闪烁摄影装置	5	0		0	0		0	0	0				0	0					0	0	0
90181930	病员监护仪	4	0	3.5	0	0		0	0	0				2.4	0					0	0	0
90181941	听力计	4	0	3.5	0	0		0	0	0				0	0					0	0	0
90181949	其他听力诊断装置	4	0	3.5	0	0		0	0	0				0	0					0	0	0
90181990	其他电气诊断装置	4	0	3.5	0	0		0	0	0				2.4	0					0	0	0
90182000	紫外线及红外线装置	4	0		0	0		0	0	0				0	0					0	0	0
90183100	注射器	8	0	7.6	0	0		0	0	0				6.4	0					0	0	0
90183210	管状金属针头	8	0	7	0	0		0	0	0				4.8	0					0	0	0
90183220	缝合用针	4	0	3.5	0	0		0	0	0				0	0					0	0	0
90183900	导管、插管及类似品	4	0		0	0		0	0	0				3.2	2.7					0	0	0
90184100	牙钻机	4	0		0	0		0	0	0				2.4	0					0	0	0
90184910	装有牙科设备的牙科用椅	4	0		0	0		0	0	0				3.2	0					0	0	0

税则号列	货品名称	最惠国	协定税率													特惠税率						
			东盟统一	亚太5国	智利	巴基斯坦	新加坡	新西兰	秘鲁	哥达	香港	澳门	台湾	瑞士	冰岛	亚太2国	老挝	柬埔寨	缅甸	LDC1	LDC2	LDC3
90184990	牙科用其他仪器及器具	4	0		0	0		0	0	0				3.2	0					0	0	0
90185000	眼科用其他仪器及器具	4	0	3.5	0	0		0	0	0				3.2	0					0	0	0
90189010	听诊器	4	0	3.5	0	0		0	0	0	0			0	0					0	0	0
90189020	血压测量仪器及器具	4	0	3.5	0	0		0	0	0	0			0	0					0	0	0
90189030	内窥镜	4	0	3.5	0	0		0	0	0	0			2.4	0					0	0	0
90189040	肾脏透析设备(人工肾)	4	0	3.5	0	0		0	0	0	0			2.4	0					0	0	0
90189050	透热疗法设备	4	0	3.5	0	0		0	0	0	0			0	0					0	0	0
90189060	输血设备	4	0	3.5	0	0		0	0	0	0			3.2	0					0	0	0
90189070	麻醉设备	4	0	3.5	0	0		0	0	0	0			0	0					0	0	0
90189080	宫内节育器	4	0	2	0	0		0	0	0	0			0	0					0	0	0
90189090	税号90.18中未列名的医疗仪器	4	0	3.5	0	0		0	0	0	0	0		3.2	0					0	0	0
90191010	按摩器具	15	0		0	12	0	0	6	0	0			12	0					0	0	
90191090	机械疗法器具、心理功能测验装置	4	0		0	0		0	0	0	0			3.2	2.7					0	0	0
90192000	臭氧治疗器、氧气治疗器等器具	4	0		0	0		0	0	0		0		3.2	0					0	0	0
90200000	其他呼吸器具及防毒面具	8	0		0	5		0	0	0	0	0		4.8	0					0	0	0
90211000	矫形或骨折用器具	4	0		0	0		0	0	0				3.1	0					0	0	0
90212100	假牙	4	0		0	0		0	0	0	0			0	0					0	0	0
90212900	牙齿固定件	4	0		0	0		0	0	0				3.2	0					0	0	0
90213100	人造关节	4	0		0	0		0	0	0			0	3.2	0					0	0	0
90213900	其他人造的人体部分	4	0		0	0		0	0	0				2.4	0					0	0	0
90214000	助听器,不包括零附件	4	0		0	0		0	0	0				3.2	0					0	0	0
90215000	心脏起搏器,不包括零附件	4	0		0	0		0	0	0				3.2	0					0	0	0
90219011	血管支架	4	0		0	0		0	0	0				3.2	0					0	0	0
90219019	其他支架	4	0		0	0		0	0	0				3.2	0					0	0	0
90219090	其他税号90.21中未列名的矫形器具	4	0		0	0		0	0	0				3.2	2.7					0	0	0
90221200	X射线断层检查仪	4	0	2.8	0	0		0	0	0				0	0					0	0	0
90221300	其他牙科用x射线应用设备	4	0		0	0		0	0	0				0	0					0	0	0
90221400	其他医疗或兽医用x射线应用设备	4	0		0	0		0	0	0				2.4	0					0	0	0
90221910	低剂量x射线安全检查设备	4	0		0	0		0	0	0				0	0					0	0	0
90221920	X射线无损探伤检测仪	4	0		0	0		0	0	0	0			3.2	0					0	0	0
90221990	其他非医疗用X射线设备	4	0		0	0		0	0	0	0			3.2	0					0	0	0
90222100	医疗用α、β、γ射线设备	4	0		0	0		0	0	0				0	0					0	0	0
90222910	γ射线无损探伤检测仪	6	0		0	5		0	0	0				3.6	0					0	0	0
90222990	其他非医疗用α、β、γ射线设备	6	0		0	5		0	0	0				3.6	0					0	0	0
90223000	X射线管	2	0		0	0		0	0	0				0	0					0	0	0
90229010	X射线影像增强器	6	0		0	5		0	0	0				3.6	0					0	0	0
90229090	税号90.22所列其他设备及零件	6	0		0	5		0	0	0				4.8	4					0	0	0
90230090	其他专供示范(例如,教学或展览)而无其他用途的仪器、装置及模型	7	0		0	5		0	0	0				5.6	0					0	0	0
90230010	教习头	7	0		0	5		0	0	0				5.6	0					0	0	0
90241010	电子万能试验机	7	0	6.5	0	5		0	0	0				4.2	0					0	0	0
90241020	硬度计	7	0	6.5	0	5		0	0	0				5.6	0					0	0	0
90241090	其他金属材料的试验用机器及器具	7	0	6.5	0	5		0	0	0				4.2	0					0	0	0
90248000	非金属材料的试验用机器及器具	5	0		0	0		0	0	0				3	0					0	0	0
90249000	各种材料的试验用机器零附件	6	0		0	5		0	0	0				4.8	0					0	0	0
90251100	可直接读数的液体温度计	4	0		0	0		0	0	0		0		2.4	0					0	0	0
90251910	非液体的工业用温度计及高温计	8.4	0	8	0	5		0	0	0				5	0					0	0	0
90251990	非液体的其他温度计、高温计	8.4	0	8	0	5		0	0	0		0		5	0					0	0	0
90258000	其他温度计、比重计、湿度计等仪器	11	0		0	5	0	0	4.4	0				8.8	0					0	0	0
90259000	比重计、温度计等类似仪器的零件	8	0	7.6	0	5		0	0	0				6.4	0					0	0	0
90261000	测量、检验液体流量或液位的仪器	0																		0	0	0
90262010	压力/差压变送器	0																		0	0	0
90262090	测量、检验压力的仪器及装置	0																		0	0	0

税则号列	货品名称	最惠国	协定税率													特惠税率						
			东盟统一	亚太5国	智利	巴基斯坦	新加坡	新西兰	秘鲁	哥斯达	香港	澳门	台湾	瑞士	冰岛	亚太2国	老挝	柬埔寨	缅甸	LDC1	LDC2	LDC3
90268010	测量气体流量的仪器及装置	0																		0	0	0
90268090	测量或检验气体的除流量、压力以外其他变化量的仪器及装置	0																		0	0	0
90269000	液体或气体的测量或检验仪器零件	0																		0	0	0
90271000	气体或烟雾分析仪	7	0		0	5		0	0	0	0			5.6	0					0	0	0
90272011	气相色谱仪	0																		0	0	0
90272012	液相色谱仪	0																		0	0	0
90272019	其他色谱仪	0																		0	0	0
90272020	电泳仪	0																		0	0	0
90273000	分光仪、分光光度计及摄谱仪	0																		0	0	0
90275000	使用光学射线的其他仪器及装置	0																		0	0	0
90278011	集成电路生产用氦质谱检漏台	0																		0	0	0
90278012	质谱联用仪	0																		0	0	0
90278019	其他质谱仪	0																		0	0	0
90278091	曝光表	14	0		0	11.2	0	0	0	0				11.2	0					0	0	
90278099	其他理化分析仪器及装置	0																		0	0	0
90279000	检镜切片机;理化分析仪器零件	0																		0	0	0
90281010	煤气表	10	0		0	5		0	0	0				6	0					0	0	
90281090	其他气量计	10	0		0	5	0	0	0	0				6	0					0	0	
90282010	水表	10	0		0	5	0	0	0	0				6	0					0	0	
90282090	其他液量计	10	0		0	5	0	0	4	0				6	0					0	0	
90283011	单相感应式电度表	10	0		0	5		0	0	0	0			6	0					0	0	
90283012	三相感应式电度表	10	0		0	5		0	0	0	0			6	0					0	0	
90283013	单相电子式(静止式)电度表	10	0		0	5		0	0	0	0			6	0					0	0	
90283014	三相电子式(静止式)电度表	10	0		0	5		0	0	0	0				0					0	0	
90283019	其他电度表	10	0		0	5		0	0	0	0			6	0					0	0	
90283090	其他电量计	10	0		0	5	0	0	0	0	0			6	0					0	0	
90289010	工业用计量仪表零附件	8.4	0		0	5		0	0	0				5	0					0	0	0
90289090	非工业用计量仪表零附件	8.4	0		0	5		0	0	0				5	0					0	0	0
90291010	转数计	15	0		0	12	0	0	6	0				13	0					0	0	
90291020	车费计、里程计	15	0		0	12	0	0	6	0				12	0					0	0	
90291090	产量计数器、步数计及类似仪表	15	0		0	12	0	0	6	0				12	0					0	0	
90292010	车辆用速度计	10	0		0	5		0	0	0				6	0					0	0	
90292090	其他速度计及转速表、频闪观测仪	10	0		0	5		0	0	0				6	0					0	0	
90299000	转数计、车费计及类似仪表零件	6	0		0	5		0	0	0				4.8	0					0	0	0
90301000	离子射线的测量或检验仪器及装置	5	0		0	0		0	0	0				0	0					0	0	0
90302010	测试频率<300兆赫的通用示波器	8	0		0	5	0	0	0	0				4.8	0					0	0	0
90302090	其他阴极射线示波器	5	0		0	0		0	0	0				3	0					0	0	0
90303110	量程≤五位半的数字万用表,不带记录装置	15	0		0	12	0	0	6	0		0		12	0					0	0	
90303190	其他不带记录装置的万用表	5	0		0	0		0	0	0				0	0					0	0	0
90303200	带记录装置的万用表	8	0		0	5		0	0	0				4.8	0					0	0	0
90303310	量程≤五位半的数字电流表、电压表,不带记录装置	15	0		0	12	0	0	6	0	0			12	0					0	0	
90303320	不带记录装置的电阻测试仪	14	0		0	11.2	0	0	0	0	0			11.2	0					0	0	
90303390	检测电压、电流及功率的其他仪器,不带记录装置	9	0		0	5		0	0	0	0			7.2	0					0	0	0
90303900	检测电压、电流、电阻或功率的其他仪器,带记录装置	8	0		0	5		0	0	0				6.4	0					0	0	0
90304010	测试频率<12.4千兆赫兹数字式频率计	0																		0	0	0
90304090	其他无线电通讯专用仪器及装置	0																		0	0	0
90308200	检测半导体晶片或器件的仪器	0																		0	0	0
90308410	电感及电容测试仪	10	0		0	5	0	0	0	0				6	0					0	0	
90308490	其他电量的测量或检验仪器及装置	8	0		0	5		0	0	0				6.4	0					0	0	0
90308910	其他电感及电容测试仪	14	0		0	11.2	0	0	0	0				11.2	0					0	0	
90308990	其他电量的测量或检验仪器及装置	8	0		0	5		0	0	0				4.8	0					0	0	0

税则号列	货品名称	最惠国	协定税率 东盟统一	亚太5国	智利	巴基斯坦	新加坡	新西兰	秘鲁	哥达	香港	澳门	台湾	瑞士	冰岛	特惠税率 亚太2国	老挝	柬埔寨	缅甸	LDC1	LDC2	LDC3
90309000	税号90.30所属货品的零件及附件	7	0		0	5		0	0	0	0			5.6	0					0	0	0
90311000	机械零件平衡试验机	7	0	6.5	0	5		0	0	0				4.2	0					0	0	0
90312000	试验台	7	0		0	5		0	0	0				5.4	0					0	0	0
90314100	制造半导体器件时检验半导体晶片、器件或检验光掩模或光栅用	0																		0	0	0
90314910	轮廓投影仪	10	0		0	5		0	0	0				6	0					0	0	0
90314920	光栅测量装置	0																		0	0	0
90314990	其他光学测量或检验仪器和器具	0																		0	0	0
90318010	光纤通信及光纤性能测试仪	5	0	4	0	0		0	0	0	0			0	0					0	0	0
90318020	坐标测量仪	5	0		0	0		0	0	0	0			3	0					0	0	0
90318031	超声波探伤检测仪	5	0	4	0	0		0	0	0	0			0	0					0	0	0
90318032	磁粉探伤检测仪	5	0	4	0	0		0	0	0	0			0	0					0	0	0
90318033	涡流探伤检测仪	5	0	4	0	0		0	0	0	0			0	0					0	0	0
90318039	其他无损探伤检测仪器(射线探伤仪除外)	5	0	4	0	0		0	0	0	0			0	0					0	0	0
90318090	未列名测量、检验仪器器具及机器	5	0	4	0	0		0	0	0	0		0	3.9						0	0	0
90319000	税号90.31的仪器及器具的零件	0																		0	0	0
90321000	恒温器	7	0		0	5		0	0	0	0			5.6	0					0	0	0
90322000	恒压器	7	0		0	5		0	0	0	0			4.2	0					0	0	0
90328100	液压或气压的其他仪器及装置	7	0	6.5	0	5		0	0	0	0			5.6	0					0	0	0
90328911	列车自动防护系统(ATP)车载设备	7	0		0	5		0	0	0	0				0					0	0	0
90328912	列车自动运行系统(ATO)车载设备	7	0		0	5		0	0	0	0				0					0	0	0
90328919	其他列车自动控制系统(ATC)车载设备	7	0		0	5		0	0	0	0				0					0	0	0
90328990	非液压或气压的其他自动调节或控制仪器及装置	7	0		0	5		0	0	0	0				0					0	0	0
90329000	自动调节或控制仪器零附件	5	0		0	0		0	0	0				4	0					0	0	0
90330000	90章未列名零附件	6	0		0	5		0	0	0				4.8	0					0	0	0
91011100	机械指示式的贵金属电子手表	11	0	9.9	0	5	0	0	0	0				8.5	0					0	0	
91011910	光电显示式的贵金属电子手表	16	0		0	12.8	0	0	6.4	0				12.8	0					0	0	
91011990	其他贵金属电子手表	15	0		0	12	0	0	6	0				11.6	0					0	0	
91012100	自动上弦的贵金属机械手表	11	0		0	5	0	0	0	0				8.5	0					0	0	
91012900	非自动上弦贵金属机械手表	15	0		0	12	0	0	6	0				11.6	0					0	0	
91019100	贵金属电子怀表及其他电子表	15	0		0	12	0	0	6	0				12	0					0	0	
91019900	贵金属机械怀表及其他机械表	20	0		0		0	0	8	0				15.4	0					0	0	
91021100	机械指示式的其他电子手表	12.5	0	11.1	0	6.2	0	0	0	0	0	0		9.6	0					0	0	
91021200	光电显示式的其他电子手表	23	0		0		0	0	9.2	0	0	0		18.4	0					0	0	
91021900	其他电子手表	15	0		0	12	0	0	6	0				12	0					0	0	
91022100	其他自动上弦的机械手表	11	0		0	5	0	0	0	0	0			8.5	0					0	0	
91022900	其他非自动上弦的机械手表	15	0		0	12	0	0	6	0	0			11.6	0					0	0	
91029100	电力驱动的电子怀表及其他电子表	15	0		0	12	0	0	6	0				11.6	0					0	0	
91029900	其他机械怀表、秒表及其他表	20	0		0		0	0	8	0				15.4	0					0	0	
91031000	以表芯装成的电子钟	23	0		0		0	0	9.2	0	0	0		17.7	0					0	0	
91039000	以表芯装成的机械钟	20	0		0		0	0	8	0				15.4	0					0	0	
91040000	仪表板钟及车辆船舶等用的类似钟	10	0		0	5		0	0	0				6	0					0	0	
91051100	电子闹钟	23	0		0		0	0	9.2	0	0	0		17.7	0					0	0	0
91051900	机械闹钟	20	0		0		0	0	8	0				16	0					0	0	
91052100	电子挂钟	23	0		0		0	0	9.2	0				18.4	0					0	0	
91052900	机械挂钟	20	0		0		0	0	8	0				16	0					0	0	
91059110	电子天文钟	3	0		0	0		0	0	0				2.4	0					0	0	0
91059190	其他电子钟	23	0		0		0	0	9.2	0				18.4	0					0	0	
91059900	其他机械钟	16	0		0	12.8	0	0	6.4	0				12.3	0					0	0	
91061000	考勤钟、时刻记录器	16	0		0	12.8	0	0	6.4	0				12.8	0					0	0	
91069000	其他时间记录器及其他类似装置	16	0		0	12.8	0	0	6.4	0				12.3	0					0	0	
91070000	定时开关	12	0		0	6	0	0	0	0				9.6	0					0	0	
91081100	已组装的机械指示式完整电子表芯	16	0		0	12.8	0	0	6.4	0	0	0		12.8	0					0	0	
91081200	已组装的光电显示式完整电子表芯	16	0		0	12.8	0	0	6.4	0	0	0		12.3	0					0	0	
91081900	其他已组装的完整电子表芯	16	0	12	0	8	0	0	6.4	0	0	0		12.3	0					0	0	
91082000	已组装的自动上弦完整表芯	16	0		0	12.8	0	0	6.4	0				12.3	0					0	0	
91089010	已组装表面≤33.8mm机械完整表芯	16	0		0	12.8	0	0	6.4	0				12.3	0					0	0	

税则号列	货品名称	最惠国	协定税率													特惠税率						
			东盟统一	亚太5国	智利	巴基斯坦	新加坡	新西兰	秘鲁	哥达	香港	澳门	台湾	瑞士	冰岛	亚太2国	老挝	柬埔寨	缅甸	LDC1	LDC2	LDC3
91089090	其他已组装完整机械表芯	16	0		0	12.8	0	0	6.4	0	0	0		12.3	0					0	0	
91091000	已组装的完整电子钟芯	16	0		0	12.8	0	0	6.4	0				12.8	0					0	0	
91099000	已组装的完整机械钟芯	16	0		0	12.8	0	0	6.4	0				12.8	0					0	0	
91101100	未组装的完整表机芯	16	0		0	12.8	0	0	6.4	0				12.3	0					0	0	
91101200	已组装的不完整表机芯	16	0		0	12.8	0	0	6.4	0				12.8	0					0	0	
91101900	未组装的不完整表机芯	16	0		0	12.8	0	0	6.4	0				12.8	0					0	0	
91109010	未组装的完整的钟机芯	16	0		0	12.8	0	0	6.4	0				12.8	0					0	0	
91109090	不完整的钟机芯	16	0		0	12.8	0	0	6.4	0				12.8	0					0	0	
91111000	贵金属或包贵金属制的表壳	14	0		0	11.2	0	0	0	0				10.8	0					0	0	
91112000	贱金属制的表壳	14	0	10	0	7	0	0	0	0	0	0		11.2	0					0	0	
91118000	非金属制的表壳	14	0		0	11.2	0	0	0	0				11.2	0					0	0	
91119000	表壳的零件	14	0		0	11.2	0	0	0	0				11.2	0					0	0	
91122000	钟壳	14	0		0	11.2	0	0	0	0				11.2	0					0	0	
91129000	钟壳零件	12	0		0	6	0	0	0	0				9.6	0					0	0	
91131000	贵金属或包贵金属制的表带及零件	20	0		0		0	0	8	0					0					0	0	
91132000	贱金属制的表带及其零件	14	0		0	11.2	0	0	0	0	0	0		11.2	0					0	0	
91139000	非金属制的表带及其零件	14	0		0	11.2	0	0	0	0	0			11.2	0					0	0	0
91141000	钟、表的发条	14	0		0	7	0	0	0	0				11.2	0					0	0	
91143000	钟面或表面	14	0		0	11.2	0	0	0	0				10.8	0					0	0	
91144000	钟、表的夹板及横担(过桥)	14	0		0	11.2	0	0	0	0				11.2	0					0	0	
91149010	钟、表的宝石轴承	14	0		0	7	0	0	0	0				11.2	0					0	0	
91149090	钟、表的其他零件	14	0		0	11.2	0	0	0	0	0	0		10.8	0					0	0	
92011000	竖式钢琴	17.5	0		0	14	0	0	7	0		0		14	0					0	0	
92012000	大钢琴	17.5	0		0	14	0	0	7	0				14	0					0	0	
92019000	其他钢琴	17.5	0		0	14	0	0	7	0				14	0					0	0	
92021000	弓弦乐器	17.5	0		0	14	0	0	7	0				14	0					0	0	0
92029000	其他弦乐器	17.5	0		0	14	0	0	7	0				14	0					0	0	0
92051000	铜管乐器	17.5	0		0	14	0	0	7	0				14	0					0	0	0
92059010	键盘管风琴、簧风琴及类似乐器	20	0		0		0	0	8	0				16	0					0	0	
92059020	手风琴及类似乐器	21	0		0		0	0	8.4	0				16.8	0					0	0	
92059030	口琴	21	0		0		0	0	8.4	0				16.8	0					0	0	
92059090	其他管乐器,但游艺场风琴和手摇风琴除外	17.5	0		0	14	0	0	7	0				14	0					0	0	
92060000	打击乐器	17.5	0		0	14	0	0	0	0				14	0					0	0	0
92071000	通过电产生或扩大声音的键盘乐器	30	0		0		0	0	12	0				23.1	0					0	0	
92079000	其他通过电产生或扩大声音的乐器	30	0		0		0	0	12	0				23.1	0					0	0	
92081000	百音盒	22	0		0		0	0	8.8	0				17.6	0					0	0	
92089000	92 章未列名的其他乐器	22	0		0		0	0	8.8	0				17.6	0					0	0	
92093000	乐器用的弦	17.5	0		0	14	0	0	7	0				14	0					0	0	
92099100	钢琴的零附件	17.5	0		0	14	0	0	7	0				14	0					0	0	
92099200	编号 9202 所列乐器的零附件	17.5	0		0	14	0	0	7	0				14	0					0	0	0
92099400	编号 9207 所列乐器的零附件	17.5	0		0	14	0	0	7	0				14	0					0	0	
92099910	节拍器、音叉及定音管	17.5	0		0	14	0	0	7	0				14	0					0	0	
92099920	百音盒的机械装置	17.5	0		0	14	0	0	7	0				14	0					0	0	
92099990	本章其他编号未列名的乐器零件	17.5	0		0	14	0	0	7	0				14	0					0	0	0
93011010	自动推进的火炮武器	13	0		0	6.5	0	0	0	0				10.4	0					0	0	
93011090	其他火炮武器	13	0		0	6.5	0	0	0	0				10.4	0					0	0	
93012000	火箭发射装置、火焰喷射器等	13	0		0	6.5	0	0	0	0				10.4	0					0	0	
93019000	其他军用武器	13	0		0	6.5	0	0	0	0				10.4	0					0	0	
93020000	左轮手枪及其他手枪	13	0		0	6.5	0	0	0	0				10.4	0					0	0	
93031000	前装枪	13	0		0	6.5	0	0	0	0				10.4	0					0	0	
93032000	其他运动、狩猎或打靶用滑膛枪	13	0		0	6.5	0	0	0	0				10	0					0	0	
93033000	其他运动、狩猎或打靶用步枪	13	0		0	6.5	0	0	0	0				10.4	0					0	0	
93039000	其他火器及类似装置	13	0		0	6.5	0	0	0	0				10.4	0					0	0	
93040000	其他武器(如弹簧枪、气枪、警棍等)	13	0		0	6.5	0	0	0	0					0					0	0	
93051000	左轮手枪或其他手枪的零件及附件	13	0		0	6.5	0	0	0	0				10.4	0					0	0	
93052000	猎枪或步枪用零件及附件	13	0		0	6.5	0	0	0	0				10.4	0					0	0	
93059100	军用武器的零附件	13	0		0	6.5	0	0	0	0				10.4	0					0	0	
93059900	其他武器的零附件	13	0		0	6.5	0	0	0	0				10.4	0					0	0	

税则号列	货品名称	最惠国	协定税率 东盟统一	亚太5国	智利	巴基斯坦	新加坡	新西兰	秘鲁	哥达	香港	澳门	台湾	瑞士	冰岛	特惠税率 亚太2国	老挝	柬埔寨	缅甸	LDC1	LDC2	LDC3
93062100	猎枪弹	13	0		0	6.5	0	0	0	0				10.4	0					0	0	
93062900	猎枪弹的零件及气枪弹丸	13	0		0	6.5	0	0	0	0				10.4	0					0	0	
93063080	接机或类似工具用子弹及其零件	13	0		0	6.5	0	0	0	0				10.4	0					0	0	
93063090	其他子弹及其零件	13	0		0	6.5	0	0	0	0				10.4	0					0	0	
93069000	其他弹药和射弹及其零件	13	0		0	6.5	0	0	0	0				10.4	0					0	0	
93070010	军用剑、短弯刀、刺刀、长矛和类似的武器及其零件;军用刀鞘、剑鞘	13	0		0	6.5	0	0	0	0				10.4	0					0	0	0
93070090	其他剑、短弯刀、刺刀、长矛和类似的武器及其零件;其他刀鞘、剑鞘	13	0		0	6.5	0	0	0	0				10.4	0					0	0	0
94011000	飞机用坐具	0																		0	0	0
94012010	皮革或再生皮革面的机动车辆用坐具	10	10		0			0	0	0		0		6	0					0	0	
94012090	机动车辆用坐具	10	10		0			0	0	0		0		6	0					0	0	
94013000	可调高度的转动坐具	0																		0	0	0
94014010	皮革或再生皮革面的能作床用的两用椅	0																		0	0	0
94014090	能作床用的两用椅	0																		0	0	0
94015100	竹、藤制坐具	0															0			0	0	0
94015900	柳条及类似材料制的坐具	0															0			0	0	0
94016110	皮革或再生皮革面的装软垫的木框架其他坐具	0																		0	0	0
94016190	装软垫的木框架的其他坐具	0																		0	0	0
94016900	其他木框架的坐具	0																		0	0	0
94017110	皮革或再生皮革面的装软垫的金属框架其他坐具	0																		0	0	0
94017190	带软垫的金属框架的坐具	0																		0	0	0
94017900	其他金属框架的坐具	0																		0	0	0
94018010	石制坐具	0																		0	0	0
94018090	其他坐具	0																		0	0	0
94019011	机动车辆的座椅调角器	10	10		0			0	4	0	0			6	0					0	0	0
94019019	机动车辆用坐具的其他零件	0																		0	0	0
94019090	其他用途坐具的零件	0																		0	0	0
94021010	理发用椅及其零件	0																		0	0	0
94021090	牙科及类似用途的椅及其零件	0																		0	0	0
94029000	其他医疗、外科或兽医用家具及零件	0																		0	0	0
94031000	办公室用金属家具	0																		0	0	0
94032000	其他金属家具	0																		0	0	0
94033000	办公室用木家具	0															0	0		0	0	0
94034000	厨房用木家具	0																0		0	0	0
94035010	卧室用红木制家具	0																0		0	0	0
94035091	卧室用漆木家具	0																0		0	0	0
94035099	卧室用其他木家具	0																0		0	0	0
94036010	其他红木制家具	0																0		0	0	0
94036091	其他漆木家具	0																0		0	0	0
94036099	其他木家具	0																0		0	0	0
94037000	塑料家具	0																		0	0	0
94038100	竹、藤制家具	0																0		0	0	0
94038910	柳条及类似材料制家具	0																0		0	0	0
94038920	石制的家具	0																		0	0	0
94038990	其他材料制的家具	0																		0	0	0
94039000	税号 94.03 所列物品的零件	0																		0	0	0
94041000	弹簧床垫	20	0		0		0	0	8	0				16	0					0	0	0
94042100	海绵橡胶或泡沫塑料制褥垫	20	0		0		0	0	8	0	0	0		16	0					0	0	0
94042900	其他材料制褥垫	20	0	14	0	14	0	0	8	0	0	0		16	0					0	0	0
94043010	羽毛或羽绒填充的睡袋	20	0		0		0	0	8	0		0		16	0					0	0	0
94043090	其他睡袋	20	0		0		0	0	8	0		0		16	0					0	0	0
94049010	羽绒或羽毛填充的寝具及类似品	20	0		0		0	0	8	0	0	0		16						0	0	0
94049020	兽毛填充的寝具及类似品	20	0		0		0	0	8	0	0	0		16	0					0	0	0
94049030	丝棉填充的寝具及类似品	20	0		0		0	0	8	0	0	0		16	0					0	0	0
94049040	化纤棉填充的寝具及类似品	20	0		0		0	0	8	0	0	0		16	0					0	0	0
94049090	其他材料制的寝具及类似品	20	0		0		0	0	8	0	0	0		16	0					0	0	0

税则号列	货品名称	最惠国	协定税率													特惠税率						
			东盟统一	亚太5国	智利	巴基斯坦	新加坡	新西兰	秘鲁	哥达	香港	澳门	台湾	瑞士	冰岛	亚太2国	老挝	柬埔寨	缅甸	LDC1	LDC2	LDC3
94051000	枝形吊灯	10	0		0	5		0	0	0				6	0					0	0	0
94052000	电气台灯、床头灯、落地灯	20	0		0		0	0	8	0				16	0					0	0	0
94053000	圣诞树用的成套灯具	16	0		0	12.8	0	0	6.4	0				12.8	0					0	0	0
94054010	探照灯	17.5	0		0	14	0	0	7	0		0		14	0					0	0	0
94054020	聚光灯	17.5	0		0	14	0	0	7	0		0		14	0					0	0	0
94054090	其他电灯及照明装置	10	0		0	5	0	0	0	0	0	0		6	0					0	0	0
94055000	非电气灯具及照明装置	20	0		0		0	0	8	0				16	0					0	0	
94056000	发光标志、发光铭牌及类似品	20	0		0		0	0	8	0	0			16	0					0	0	
94059100	税号94.05所列物品的玻璃制零件	20	0		0		0	0	8	0				16	0					0	0	
94059200	税号94.05所列物品的塑料制零件	20	0		0		0	0	8	0		0		16	0					0	0	
94059900	税号94.05所列物品其他材料制零件	20	0		0		0	0	8	0		0		16	0					0	0	0
94060000	活动房屋	10	0	7	0	5	0	0	4	0		0		6	0					0	0	0
95030010	供儿童乘骑的带轮玩具及玩偶车	0																		0	0	0
95030021	玩具动物	0																		0	0	0
95030029	其他玩偶	0																		0	0	0
95030031	玩具电动火车	0																		0	0	0
95030039	其他缩小(按比例缩小)的全套模型组件	0																		0	0	0
95030040	其他建筑套件及建筑玩具	0																		0	0	0
95030050	玩具乐器	0																		0	0	0
95030060	智力玩具	0																		0	0	0
95030081	组装成套的其他玩具	0																		0	0	0
95030082	其他带动力装置的玩具及模型	0																		0	0	0
95030089	其他未列名玩具	0																		0	0	0
95030090	玩具的零件	0																		0	0	0
95042000	台球用品及附件	0																		0	0	0
95043010	投币式电子游戏机	0																		0	0	0
95043090	投币式其他游戏用品	0																		0	0	0
95044000	扑克牌	0																		0	0	0
95045011	与电视接收机配套使用的视频游戏控制器及设备零件及附件	0																		0	0	0
95045019	其他与电视接收机配套使用的游戏机	0																		0	0	0
95045091	其他视频游戏控制器及设备零件及附件	0																		0	0	0
95045099	其他游戏机	0																		0	0	0
95049010	其他电子游戏机	0																		0	0	0
95049021	保龄球自动分瓶机	0																		0	0	0
95049022	保龄球	0																		0	0	0
95049023	保龄球瓶	0																		0	0	0
95049029	其他保龄球自动球道设备及器具	0																		0	0	0
95049030	中国象棋、国际象棋、跳棋等棋类用品	0																		0	0	0
95049040	麻将及类似桌上游戏用品	0																		0	0	0
95049090	其他游艺场、桌上或室内游戏用品	0																		0	0	0
95051000	圣诞节用品	0																		0	0	0
95059000	其他节日用品或娱乐用品	0																		0	0	0
95061100	滑雪屐	14	0		0	0	0	0	0	0				11.2						0	0	
95061200	滑雪屐扣件(滑雪屐带)	14	0		0	0	0	0	0	0				11.2	0					0	0	
95061900	其他滑雪用具	14	0		0	0	0	0	0	0				11.2	0					0	0	
95062100	帆板	12	0		0	0	0	0	0	0				9.6	0					0	0	
95062900	其他水上运动用具	14	0		0	0	0	0	0	0	0			11.2	0					0	0	
95063100	完整的高尔夫球棍	14	0		0	0	0	0	0	0				11.2						0	0	0
95063200	高尔夫球	12	0		0	0	0	0	0	0				9.6	0					0	0	
95063900	其他高尔夫球用具	14	0		0	0	0	0	0	0			0	11.2						0	0	0
95064010	乒乓球	12	0		0	0	0	0	0	0				9.6	0					0	0	
95064090	其他乒乓球运动用品及器械	14	0		0	0	0	0	0	0				11.2	0					0	0	
95065100	草地网球拍	14	0		0	0	0	0	0	0				11.2	0					0	0	
95065900	其他网球拍、羽毛球拍或类似球拍	14	0		0	0	0	0	0	0				11.2	0					0	0	
95066100	草地网球	12	0		0	0	0	0	0	0				9.6	0					0	0	
95066210	篮球、足球、排球	12	0		0	0	0	0	0	0				9.6	0					0	0	
95066290	其他可充气的球	12	0		0	0	0	0	0	0				9.6	0					0	0	
95066900	其他球	12	0		0	0	0	0	0	0				9.6	0					0	0	
95067010	溜冰鞋	14	0	12	0	0	0	0	0	0				11.2	0					0	0	
95067020	旱冰鞋	14	0	12	0	0	0	0	0	0				11.2	0					0	0	
95069111	跑步机	12	0		0	0	0	0	0	0	0		0	9.6	0					0	0	
95069119	其他健身及康复器械	12	0		0	0	0	0	0	0	0		0	9.6	0					0	0	

税则号列	货品名称	最惠国	协定税率 东盟统一	亚太5国	智利	巴基斯坦	新加坡	新西兰	秘鲁	哥达	香港	澳门	台湾	瑞士	冰岛	特惠税率 亚太2国	老挝	柬埔寨	缅甸	LDC1	LDC2	LDC3
95069120	滑板	12	0		0	0	0	0	0	0	0			9.6	0					0	0	
95069190	一般的体育活动、体操或竞技用品	12	0		0	0	0	0	0	0	0	0		9.6	0					0	0	0
95069900	其他未列名的95章用品及设备	12	0		0	0	0	0	0	0	0	0		7.2	0					0	0	
95071000	钓鱼竿	21	0		0		0	0	8.4	0				16.8						0	0	
95072000	钓鱼钩	21	0		0		0	0	8.4	0				16.8						0	0	0
95073000	钓线轮	21	0		0		0	0	8.4	0				16.8						0	0	
95079000	其他钓鱼用品	21	0	18.9	0	18.9	0	0	8.4	0				16.8	0					0	0	
95081000	流动马戏团及流动动物园	15	0		0	12	0	0	6	0				12	0					0	0	
95089000	其他旋转木马、秋千等游乐场娱乐设备	15	0		0	12	0	0	6	0				12	0					0	0	
96011000	已加工的兽牙及其制品	20	0		0		0	0	8	0				16	0					0	0	
96019000	其他已加工动物质雕刻料及其制品	20	0		0		0	0	8	0				16	0					0	0	0
96020010	装药用胶囊	10.5	0		0	5	0	0	0	0				8.4	0					0	0	
96020090	已加工植物或矿物质雕刻料及制品	25	0		0		0	0	10	0				20	0					0	0	0
96031000	用枝条或其他植物材料捆扎成的帚	25	0		0		0	0	10	0		0		20	0					0	0	
96032100	牙刷,包括齿板刷	25	0		0		0	0	10	0	0	0		20	0					0	0	
96032900	剃须刷、发刷、睫毛刷等人体化妆用刷	15	0	13.5	0	7.5	0	0	6	0		0		12	0					0	0	0
96033010	画笔	25	0	15	0	15	0	0	10	0				20	0					0	0	
96033020	毛笔	20	0	18	0	18	0	0	8	0				16	0					0	0	
96033090	化妆用的类似笔	25	0	22.5	0	22.5	0	0	10	0				20	0					0	0	
96034011	猪鬃制漆刷及类似刷	20	0		0		0	0	8	0				16	0					0	0	
96034019	其他材料制漆刷及类似刷	23	0		0		0	0	9.2	0				18.4	0					0	0	
96034020	油漆块垫及滚筒	23	0		0		0	0	9.2	0				18.4	0					0	0	
96035011	作为机器、器具零件的金属丝刷	14	0		0	11.2	0	0	0	0				11.2	0					0	0	
96035019	作为车辆零件的金属丝刷	14	0		0	7	0	0	0	0				10.8	0					0	0	
96035091	作为机器、器具零件的其他刷	14	0		0	11.2	0	0	0	0				11.2	0					0	0	
96035099	作为车辆零件的其他刷	14	0		0	7	0	0	0	0				11.2	0					0	0	
96039010	羽毛掸	21	0	18.9	0	18.9	0	0	8.4	0				16.8	0					0	0	
96039090	其他帚、刷、拖把及其他毛掸	15	0		0		0	0	6	0				12	0					0	0	
96040000	手用粗筛、细筛	21	0		0		0	0	8.4	0				16.8	0					0	0	
96050000	个人梳妆、缝纫等用成套旅行用品	15	0		0	12	0	0	6	0				12	0					0	0	
96061000	揿扣及其零件	21	0		0		0	0	8.4	0				16.8	0					0	0	
96062100	塑料制钮扣,未用纺织材料包裹	21	0		0		0	0	8.4	0			0	16.8	0					0	0	0
96062200	贱金属制,未用纺织材料包裹的纽扣	15	0		0	12	0	0	6	0	0	0	0	12	0					0	0	0
96062900	其他钮扣	15	0		0	12	0	0	6	0	0			12	0					0	0	0
96063000	钮扣芯及钮扣的其他零件	15	0		0	12	0	0	6	0	0			12	0					0	0	0
96071100	装有贱金属齿的拉链	21	0		0		0	0	8.4	0	0	0		16.8	0					0	0	0
96071900	其他拉链	21	0	14.7	0	14.7	0	0	8.4	0	0	0		16.8	0					0	0	
96072000	拉链零件	21	0		0		0	0	8.4	0				16.8	0					0	0	
96081000	圆珠笔	15	0	13.5	0	7.5	0	0	6	0				12	0					0	0	0
96082000	毡尖和其他渗水式笔尖笔及唛头笔	21	0		0		0	0	8.4	0				16.8	0					0	0	
96083010	墨汁画笔	21	0		0		0	0	8.4	0				16.8	0					0	0	
96083020	自来水笔	21	0		0		0	0	8.4	0				16.8	0					0	0	0
96083090	其他钢笔	21	0		0		0	0	8.4	0				16.8	0					0	0	0
96084000	活动铅笔	21	0		0		0	0	8.4	0				16.8	0					0	0	
96085000	含有≥两种笔的成套货品	21	0		0		0	0	8.4	0				16.8	0					0	0	
96086000	圆珠笔芯	21	0		0		0	0	8.4	0	0	0		16.8	0					0	0	
96089100	钢笔头及笔尖粒	12	0		0	6	0	0	0	0	0	0		9.6	0					0	0	
96089910	机器、仪器用笔	17.5	0		0	14	0	0	7	0	0			14	0					0	0	
96089920	蜡纸铁笔、钢笔杆、铅笔杆等	21	0		0		0	0	8.4	0	0	0		16.8	0					0	0	
96089990	其他笔零件	21	0		0		0	0	8.4	0	0	0		0	0					0	0	
96091010	铅笔	21	0		0		0	0	8.4	0				16.8	0					0	0	0
96091020	颜色铅笔	21	0		0		0	0	8.4	0				16.8	0					0	0	
96092000	铅笔芯,黑的或其他颜色的	21	0		0		0	0	8.4	0				16.8	0					0	0	
96099000	蜡笔、图画碳笔、书写或绘画用粉笔	15	0		0	12	0	0	6	0				12	0					0	0	
96100000	具有书写或绘画面的石板、黑板	15	0		0	12	0	0	6	0				12	0					0	0	
96110000	手用日期戳、封缄戳、编号戳及类似印戳	21	0		0		0	0	8.4	0				16.8	0					0	0	
96121000	打字机色带或类似色带	10.5	0		0	5	0	0	0	0		0		8.4	0					0	0	0
96122000	印台	25	0		0		0	0	10	0				20	0					0	0	
96131000	一次性袖珍气体打火机	25	0		0		0	0	10	0				20	0					0	0	
96132000	可充气袖珍气体打火机	25	0		0		0	0	10	0				20	0					0	0	
96138000	其他打火器	25	0		0		0	0	10	0				20	0					0	0	
96139000	打火机及打火器零件	25	0		0		0	0	10	0				20	0					0	0	
96140010	烟斗及烟斗头	25	0		0		0	0	10	0				20	0					0	0	
96140090	烟嘴及其零件	25	0		0		0	0	10	0				20	0					0	0	
96151100	硬质橡胶或塑料制梳子、发夹及类似品	18	0	16.2	0	14.4	0	0	7.2	0				14.4	0					0	0	0
96151900	其他材料制梳子、发夹及类似品	18	0		0		0	0	7.2	0				14.4	0					0	0	0
96159000	其他发夹、卷发器等及其零件	18	0	16.2	0	14.4	0	0	7.2	0				14.4	0					0	0	0
96161000	香水喷雾器或类似的化妆用喷雾器	18	0	16.2	0	14.4	0	0	7.2	0				14.4	0					0	0	

税则号列	货品名称	最惠国	协定税率													特惠税率						
			东盟统一	亚太5国	智利	巴基斯坦	新加坡	新西兰	秘鲁	哥达	香港	澳门	台湾	瑞士	冰岛	亚太2国	老挝	柬埔寨	缅甸	LDC1	LDC2	LDC3
96162000	施敷脂粉或化妆品用粉扑及粉拍	18	0	16.2	0	14.4	0	0	7.2	0				14.4	0					0	0	
96170011	玻璃内胆制保温瓶	24	0		0		0	0	9.6	0	0			19.2	0					0	0	
96170019	其他保温瓶	24	0		0		0	0	9.6	0	0			19.2	0					0	0	
96170090	其他真空容器及零件	18	0		0		0	0	7.2	0	0			14.4	0					0	0	
96180000	裁缝用人体模型及其他人体模型	21	0		0		0	0	8.4	0				16.8	0					0	0	
96190010	尿布及尿裤	7.5	0		0			0	0	0	0	0	0							0	0	0
96190020	卫生巾(护垫)及止血塞	10	0		0	7.5		0	0	0	0	0	0	6	0					0	0	0
96190090	任何材料制的卫生巾或尿布的类似品	14	0	9.3	0	7.5	0	0	5.6	0	0	0	0	12.3	0					0	0	0
97011011	唐卡	12	0		0	6	0	0	4.8	0				9.6	0					0	0	0
97011019	其他手绘油画、粉画及其他画	12	0		0	6	0	0	4.8	0				9.6	0					0	0	0
97011020	手绘油画、粉画及其他画的复制品	14	0		0	11.2	0	0	0	0				11.2	0					0	0	0
97019000	拼贴画及类似装饰板	14	0		0	11.2	0	0	0	0				11.2	0					0	0	0
97020000	雕版画、印制画、石印画的原本	12	0		0	6	0	0	4.8	0				9.6	0					0	0	
97030000	各种材料制的雕塑品原件	12	0		0	6	0	0	0	0				9.6	0					0	0	0
97040010	使用或未使用的邮票	8	0		0	5		0	0	0	0	0		4.8	0					0	0	0
97040090	其他使用或未使用的印花税票及类似票证	14	0		0	7	0	0	0	0	0	0		11.2	0					0	0	
97050000	具有动、植、矿物学意义的收藏品	0																		0	0	0
97060000	超过一百年的古物	0																		0	0	0

注1:(1)亚太2国:孟加拉人民共和国、老挝人民民主共和国

(2)LDC1:埃塞俄比亚联邦民主共和国、布隆迪共和国、赤道几内亚共和国、刚果民主共和国、吉布提共和国、几内亚共和国、几内亚比绍共和国、莱索托王国、马达加斯加共和国、马拉维共和国、马里共和国、莫桑比克共和国、塞拉利昂共和国、塞内加尔共和国、苏丹共和国、南苏丹共和国、索马里联邦共和国、坦桑尼亚联合共和国、乌干达共和国、乍得共和国、中非共和国、阿富汗伊斯兰共和国、也门共和国、瓦努阿图共和国(共24国)

(3)LDC2:安哥拉共和国、贝宁共和国、多哥共和国、厄立特里亚国、科摩罗联盟、利比里亚共和国、卢旺达共和国、尼日尔共和国、赞比亚共和国、东帝汶民主共和国、柬埔寨王国、缅甸联邦共和国、尼泊尔联邦民主共和国、萨摩亚独立国(共14国)

(4)LDC3:毛里塔尼亚伊斯兰共和国、孟加拉人民共和国(共2国)

注2:①完税价格不高于2000美元/台,16%;完税价格高于2000美元/台:3%,加1581元。

②完税价格不高于2000美元/台:24.5%;完税价格高于2000美元/台:3%,加2614元。

③完税价格不高于2000美元/台:18%;完税价格高于2000美元/台:3%,加1824元。

④完税价格不高于5000美元:35%;完税价格高于5000美元,3%加9728元/台。

附表 2：

2015 年进口商品从量税、复合税税目、税率表

（2015 年 1 月 1 日起实施）

Attacjed table 2：

Specific、CompoundScaleDuties,2015

（EnforcedfromJanuary1,2015）

税则号列	货 品 名 称	普通税率	2015 年最惠国税率
02071200	冻的整只鸡	5.6 元/千克	1.3 元/千克
02071411	冻的带骨鸡块（包括鸡胸脯、鸡大腿等）	4.2 元/千克	0.6 元/千克
02071419	冻的不带骨鸡块（包括鸡胸脯、鸡大腿等）	9.5 元/千克	0.7 元/千克
02071421	冻的鸡翼（不包括翼尖）	8.1 元/千克	0.8 元/千克
02071422	冻的鸡爪	3.2 元/千克	1 元/千克
02071429	冻的其他食用鸡杂碎（包括鸡翼尖、鸡肝等）	3.2 元/千克	0.5 元/千克
05040021	冷、冻的鸡肫（即鸡胃）	7.7 元/千克	1.3 元/千克
22030000	麦芽酿造的啤酒	7.5 元/升	0
27090000	石油原油（包括从沥青矿物提取的原油）	85 元/吨	0
37023190	其他未曝光无齿孔彩色窄胶卷（窄胶卷指宽度≤105 毫米，彩色摄影用）	433 元/平方米	56 元/平方米
37023220	照相制版涂卤化银液无齿孔窄胶卷（成卷未曝光感光胶片，窄胶卷指宽度≤105 毫米）	104 元/平方米	4.5 元/平方米
37023290	其他涂卤化银乳液无齿孔窄胶卷（成卷未曝光感光胶片，窄胶卷指宽度≤105 毫米）	202 元/平方米	21 元/平方米
37023920	照相制版用其他无齿孔窄感光胶卷（成卷未曝光感光胶片，窄胶卷指宽度≤105 毫米）	104 元/平方米	12 元/平方米
37023990	其他用无齿孔窄感光胶卷（成卷未曝光感光胶片，窄胶卷指宽度≤105 毫米）	202 元/平方米	24 元/平方米
37024100	未曝光无齿孔宽长彩色胶卷（宽长胶卷指宽度＞610 毫米，长度＞200 米）	202 元/平方米	7.1 元/平方米
37024221	印刷电路板制造用光致抗蚀干膜（指宽度＞610 毫米，长度＞200 米）	110 元/平方米	0.6 元/平方米
37024229	照相制版其他未曝光无齿宽长胶卷（宽长指宽度＞610 毫米，长度＞200 米）	110 元/平方米	1.6 元/平方米
37024292	红色或红外激光胶片	213 元/平方米	2.4 元/平方米
37024299	黑白其他未曝光无齿孔宽长胶卷（宽长胶卷指宽度＞610 毫米，长度＞200 米）	213 元/平方米	7 元/平方米
37024321	照相制版用激光照排片（宽度＞610 毫米，长度≤200 米）	104 元/平方米	10%
37024329	其他照相制版用未曝光无齿孔胶卷（指宽度＞610 毫米，长度≤200 米）	104 元/平方米	3.7 元/平方米
37024390	彩色或黑白其他用未曝光无齿孔中长胶卷（中长胶卷指宽度＞610 毫米，长度≤200 米）	202 元/平方米	17 元/平方米
37024421	照相制版用未曝光激光照排片（宽度大于 105 毫米，小于等于 610 毫米）	115 元/平方米	2.0 元/平方米
37024422	印刷电路板制造用光致抗蚀干膜（宽度大于 105 毫米，小于等于 610 毫米）	115 元/平方米	5 元/平方米
37024429	其他照相制版用无齿孔未曝光胶卷（宽度大于 105 毫米，小于等于 610 毫米）	115 元/平方米	2.9 元/平方米
37024490	彩色或黑白其他用无齿孔未曝光中宽胶卷（中宽胶卷指宽度＞105 毫米，但≤610 毫米）	202 元/平方米	27 元/平方米
37025200	彩色摄影用未曝光彩色胶卷，宽度≤16 毫米	433 元/平方米	95 元/平方米
37025300	幻灯片用未曝光彩色摄影胶卷（宽度＞16 毫米，但≤35 毫米，长度≤30 米）	433 元/平方米	128 元/平方米
37025410	非幻灯片用彩色摄影胶卷（宽度＝35 毫米，长度≤2 米）	433 元/平方米	18 元/平方米

税则号列	货品名称	普通税率	2015年最惠国税率
37025490	其他非幻灯片用彩色摄影胶卷(宽度>16毫米,但≤35毫米,长度≤30米)	433元/平方米	24元/平方米
37025520	未曝光的窄长彩色电影胶卷(窄长胶卷指宽度>16毫米,但≤35毫米,长度>30米)	232元/平方米	9元/平方米
37025590	其他未曝光窄长彩色胶卷窄长胶卷指宽度>16毫米,但≤35毫米,长度>30米)	433元/平方米	27元/平方米
37025620	未曝光的中宽彩色电影胶卷(中宽胶卷指宽度>35毫米)	232元/平方米	13元/平方米
37025690	其他未曝光的中宽彩色胶卷(中宽胶卷指宽度>35毫米)	433元/平方米	74元/平方米
37029600	未曝光非彩色胶卷(宽度≤35毫米,长度≤30米)	210元/平方米	21元/平方米
37029700	未曝光非彩色胶卷(宽度≤35毫米,长度>30米)	210元/平方米	9元/平方米
37029800	未曝光的非彩色胶卷,宽度>35毫米	210元/平方米	10元/平方米
85211011	广播级磁带录像机	完税价格不高于2000美元/台:130%;完税价格高于2000美元/台:6%,加20600元	完税价格不高于2000美元/台:30%;完税价格高于2000美元/台:3%,加3283元
85211019	其他磁带录像机	完税价格不高于2000美元/台:130%;完税价格高于2000美元/台:6%,加20600元	完税价格不高于2000美元/台:30%;完税价格高于2000美元/台:3%,加3283元
85211020	磁带放像机	完税价格不高于2000美元/台:130%;完税价格高于2000美元/台:6%,加20600元	完税价格不高于2000美元/台:30%;完税价格高于2000美元/台:3%,加3283元
85258012	非特种用途的广播级电视摄像机	完税价格不高于5000美元/台:130%;完税价格高于5000美元/台:6%,加51500元	完税价格不高于5000美元/台,35%;完税价格高于5000美元/台:3%,加9728元
85258013	非特种用途的其他电视摄像机	完税价格不高于5000美元/台:130%;完税价格高于5000美元/台:6%,加51500元	完税价格不高于5000美元/台,35%;完税价格高于5000美元/台:3%,加9728元
85258022	非特种用途的单镜头反光型数字照相机	完税价格不高于5000美元/台:130%;完税价格高于5000美元/台:6%,加51500元	0
85258025	非特种用途的其他可换镜头的数字照相机	完税价格不高于5000美元/台:130%;完税价格高于5000美元/台:6%,加51500元	0
85258029	非特种用途的其他数字照相机	完税价格不高于5000美元/台:130%;完税价格高于5000美元/台:6%,加51500元	0
85258032	非特种用途的广播级视频摄录一体机	完税价格不高于5000美元/台:130%;完税价格高于5000美元/台:6%,加51500元	0
85258039	非特种用途的其他视频摄录一体机(家用型摄录一体机除外)	完税价格不高于5000美元/台:130%;完税价格高于5000美元/台:6%,加51500元	0

附表 3：

2015 年关税配额商品税目、税率表

（2015 年 1 月 1 日起实施）

说明：2015 年在国家规定配额内的进口货物，按下表配额内的税率执行；超过配额数量的进口货物，执行税则当中的法定关税税率，即配额外税率。

Attacjed table 3：

In-Quota Interim Duty Rate on Imported Goods, 2015

（Enforced from January 1, 2015）

Explanation：During 2015, according to the state regulations, goods imported within quota, will be processed using the In-Quota Duty Rate Schedule below; goods imported exceeding the quota amount, will be processed using Statutory Tariff Rate in the Tariff Schedule, that is, Out-Quota Tariff Rate.

序号 No.	货品名称 Description of Goods	税则号列 Tariff No.	2015 年进口税率（%） Import Duty Rate（%）			
			配额外税率 Out-Quota Duty Rate		配额内税率 In-Quota Duty Rate	"国别关税配额税率（中国－新西兰自贸区）（%）"
			最惠国税率 M. F. N.	普通税率 Gen.		
1	小麦 Wheat	10011100	65	180	1	
		10011900	65	180	1	
		10019100	65	180	1	
		10019900	65	180	1	
		11010000	65	130	6	
		11031100	65	130	9	
		11032010	65	180	10	
2	玉米 Maize（Corn）	10051000	20	180	1	
		10059000	65	180	1	
		11022000	40	130	9	
		11031300	65	130	9	
		11042300	65	180	10	
3	稻谷和大米 Rice, whether or not busked	10061011	65	180	1	
		10061019	65	180	1	
		10061091	65	180	1	
		10061099	65	180	1	
		10062010	65	180	1	
		10062090	65	180	1	
		10063010	65	180	1	
		10063090	65	180	1	
		10064010	65	180	1	
		10064090	65	180	1	
		11029011	40	130	9	
		11029019	40	130	9	
		11031921	10	70	9	
		11031929	10	70	9	
4	糖 Sugar	17011200	50	125	15	
		17011300	50	125	15	
		17011400	50	125	15	
		17019100	50	125	15	
		17019910	50	125	15	
		17019920	50	125	15	
		17019990	50	125	15	
5	羊毛 Wool	51011100	38	50	1	0
		51011900	38	50	1	0
		51012100	38	50	1	0
		51012900	38	50	1	0
		51013000	38	50	1	0
		51031010	38	50	1	0
6	毛条 Wool Tops	51051000	38	50	3	0
		51052100	38	50	3	0
		51052900	38	50	3	0

序号 No.	货品名称 Description of Goods	税则号列 Tariff No.	2015年进口税率(%) Import Duty Rate(%)			
			配额外税率 Out-Quota Duty Rate		配额内税率 In-Quota Duty Rate	"国别关税配额税率(中国－新西兰自贸区)(%)"
			最惠国税率 M.F.N.	普通税率 Gen.		
7	棉花 Cotton	52010000	40【注1】	125	1	
		52030000	40	125	1	
8	化肥 Chemical Fertilizer	31021000	50	150	4【注2】	
		31052000	50	150	4【注3】	
		31053000	50	150	4【注4】	

【注1】:

对配额外进口的一定数量棉花,适用滑准税形式暂定关税,具体方式如下:

1. 当进口棉花完税价格高于或等于15元/千克时,暂定从量税率为0.570元/千克;

2. 当进口棉花完税价格低于15元/千克时,暂定关税税率按下式计算:

$Ri = 9.377/Pi + 2.77\% \times Pi - 1 \ (Ri \leqslant 40\%)$

其中:Ri-暂定关锐税率,对上式计算结果小数点后第4位四舍五人保留前3位。

Pi-关税完税价格,单位为元/千克

【注2、3、4】:

暂定税率为1%。

附表4:
2015年非全税目信息技术产品税率表
（2015年1月1日起实施）

Attacjed table 4:
Duty Rate on Imported IT Goods (Incomplete), 2015
(Enforced from January 1, 2015)

ex	税则号列 Tariff No.	货品名称	最惠国税率 MFN(%)	EX项税率 EX rats(%)	Description of Goods
ex	70200013、70200019	用于插入熔化和氧化炉内以制备半导体晶片的石英反应管及夹持器	10.5	0	Quartz reactor tubes and holders designed for insertion into diffusion and oxidation furnaces for production of semiconductor wafers
ex	85044091	自动数据处理设备机器及组件、电讯设备用的具有变流功能的半导体模块	10	0	Semicondutor modules with converting function for automatic data processing machines and units thereof, and telecommunication apparatus
ex	85044099	自动数据处理设备机器及组件、电讯设备用的其他静止变流器;ITA产品用的印刷电路组件,包括外接组件,如符合PCMCIA标准的卡	10	0	Other stastic converters for automatic data processing machines and units thereof, and telecommunication apparatus; Printed Circuit Assemblies for products falling within the ITA, including such assemblies for external connections such as cards that conform to the PCMCIA standard
ex	85176910	用于呼叫、提示和寻呼的便携式接收器	9	0	Portable receivers for calling, alerting or paging
ex	85177070	无线电话电报装置的天线	2	0	Antenna device of wireless Telephone and tclegraph
ex	85181000	电讯用麦克风,频率范围在300赫兹到3.4千赫之间,直径不超过10毫米,高度不超过3毫米	10	0	Microphones having a frequency range of 300 Hz to 3,4 kHz with a diameter of not exceeding 10 mm and a height not exceeding 3 mm, for telecommunication use
ex	85184000	列入ITA的有线电话重复器用的电器扩音器	12	0	Electric amplifiers when used as repeaters in line telephony products falling within the ITA
ex	85189000	列入ITA的有线电话重复器用的电器扩音器的零件	10.5	0	Parts of electric amplifiers when used as repeaters in line telephony products falling within the ITA
ex	90309000	用于检测半导体晶片及器件的仪器的零件和附件;ITA产品用的印刷电路组件,包括外接组件,如符合PCMCIA标准的卡	7	0	Parts and accessories of instruments and apparatus for measuring or checking semiconductor wafers or devices; Printed Circuit Assemblies for products falling within the ITA, including such assemblies for external connections such as cards that conform to the PCMCIA standard

附表5：　　　　　　　　　　　　Attacjed table 5：

2015年进口商品消费税税率表　Consumption tax on Imported Goods 2015

税则号列	货品名称	进口从价税率	进口从量税率
2106902000	制造饮料用的复合酒精制品	5%	
2203000000	麦芽酿造的啤酒		进口完税价格≥370美元/吨的麦芽酿造啤酒，税率为250/吨；进口完税价格 < 370美元/吨的麦芽酿造啤酒，税率为220/吨
2204100000	葡萄汽酒	10%	
2204210000	小包装的鲜葡萄酿造的酒（小包装指装入两升及以下容器的）	10%	
2204290000	其他包装鲜葡萄酿造的酒（其他包装指装入两升以上容器的）	10%	
2204300000	其他酿酒葡萄汁（品目2009以外的）	10%	
2205100000	小包装的味美思酒及类似酒（两升及以下容器包装，加植物或香料的用鲜葡萄酿造的酒）	10%	
2205900000	其他包装的味美思酒及类似酒（两升以上容器包装，加植物或香料的用鲜葡萄酿造的酒）	10%	
2206001000	黄酒（以稻米、黍米、玉米、小米、小麦等为主要原料，经进一步加工制成）	（240元/吨）	1千克=0.962升
2206009000	其他发酵饮料（未列名的发酵饮料混合物及发酵饮料与无酒精饮料的混合物）	10%	
2208200000	蒸馏葡萄酒制得的烈性酒	（20% +1元/千克）	
2208300000	威士忌酒	20% +1元/千克	
2208400000	朗姆酒及蒸馏已发酵甘蔗产品制得的其他烈性酒	20% +1元/千克	
2208500000	杜松子酒	20% +1元/千克	
2208600000	伏特加酒	20% +1元/千克	1升=0.912千克
2208700000	利口酒及柯迪尔酒	20% +1元/千克	
2208901010	濒危龙舌兰酒	20% +1元/千克	
2208901090	其他龙舌兰酒	20% +1元/千克	
2208902000	白酒	20% +1元/千克	
2208909021	含濒危野生动植物成分的薯类蒸馏酒	20% +1元/千克	
2208909029	其他薯类蒸馏酒	20% +1元/千克	
2208909091	含濒危野生动植物成分的其他蒸馏酒及酒精	20% +1元/千克	
2208909099	其他蒸馏酒及酒精饮料	20% +1元/千克	
2402100000	烟草制的雪茄烟	36%	

税则号列	货品名称	进口从价税率	进口从量税率
2402200000	烟草制的卷烟		每标准条进口完税价格≥50元人民币,45%+150元/标准箱
			每标准条进口完税价格<50元人民币,30%+150元/标准箱
2402900001	烟草代用品制的卷烟		每标准条进口完税价格≥50元人民币,45%+150元/标准箱
			每标准条进口完税价格<50元人民币,30%+150元/标准箱
2402900009	烟草代用品制的雪茄烟	36%	
2403110000	供吸用的本章子目注释所述的水烟料(不论是否含有任何比例的烟草代用品)	30%	
2403190000	其他供吸用的烟草(不论是否含有任何比例的烟草代用品)	30%	
2403910010	再造烟草	30%	
2403910090	均化烟草	30%	
2403990090	其他烟草及烟草代用品的制品	30%	烟草精汁除外
2710122000	石脑油,不含生物柴油	1.4元/升	1千克=1.385升
2710123000	橡胶溶剂油、油漆溶剂油、抽提溶剂油,不含生物柴油	1.4元/升	1千克=1.282升
2710191100	航空煤油,不含生物柴油	1.1元/升(暂缓实施)	1千克=1.246升
2710191200	灯用煤油,不含生物柴油	1.1元/升	1千克=1.246升
2710191910	正构烷烃(C9-C13),不含生物柴油	1.1元/升	1千克=1.246升
2710191990	其他煤油馏分的油及制品,不含生物柴油	1.1元/升	1千克=1.246升
2710192200	5-7号燃料油,不含生物柴油	1.1元/升	1千克=1.015升
2710192300	车用、普通柴油,不含生物柴油	1.1元/升	1千克=1.176升
2710192910	蜡油,不含生物柴油(350℃以下馏出物体积<20%,550℃以下馏出物体积>80%)	1.1元/升	1千克=1.015升
2710192990	其他燃料油,不含生物柴油	1.1元/升	1千克=1.015升
2710199100	润滑油,不含生物柴油	1.4元/升	1千克=1.126升
2710199200	润滑脂,不含生物柴油	1.4元/升	1千克=1.126升
2710199300	润滑油基础油,不含生物柴油	1.4元/升	1千克=1.126升
2710199900	其他重油;其他重油制品,不含生物柴油(包括按重量计含油≥70%的制品)	1.1元/升	1千克=1.015升
2710200000	石油及从沥青矿物提取的油类(但原油除外)以及以上述油为基本成分(按重量计≥70%)的其他税目未列名制品(含生物柴油<30%,废油除外)	1.1元/升	
3302109001	生产食品、饮料用混合香料及制品(含以香料为基本成分的混合物,按容量计酒精浓度>0.5%)	5%	
3303000000	香水及花露水	30%	
3304100010	含濒危植物成分唇用化妆品	30%	
3304100090	其他唇用化妆品	30%	
3304200010	含濒危植物成分眼用化妆品	30%	
3304200090	其他眼用化妆品	30%	
3304300000	指(趾)甲化妆品	30%	
3304910090	粉,不论是否压紧	30%	
3304990091	其他含濒危植物成分美容品或化妆品	30%	不包括护肤品
3304990099	其他美容品或化妆品	30%	不包括护肤品
3604100000	烟花、爆竹	15%	
3826000090	其他生物柴油及其混合物	1.1元/升	
4013100000	汽车用橡胶内胎[机动小客车(包括旅行小客车及赛车)、客运车或货运车用]	3%	
4013909000	其他用橡胶内胎	3%	
4409101010	一边或面制成连续形状的濒危针叶木制地板条、块(包括未装拼的拼花地板用板条及缘板)	5%	

税则号列	货品名称	进口从价税率	进口从量税率
4409101090	一边或面制成连续形状的其他针叶木地板条,块(包括未装拼的拼花地板用板条及缘板)	5%	
4409291010	一边或面制成连续形状的拉敏木地板条、块(包括未装拼的拉敏木拼花地板用板条及缘板)	5%	
4409291020	一边或面制成连续形状的桃花心木地板条、块(包括未装拼的桃花心木拼花地板用板条及缘板)	5%	
4409291030	一边或面制成连续形状的其他濒危木地板条、块(包括未装拼的其他濒危木拼花地板用板条及缘板)	5%	
4409291090	一边或面制成连续形状的其他非针叶木地板条、块(包括未装拼的其他非针叶木拼花地板用板条及缘板)	5%	
4419003100	木制一次性筷子	5%	
7101101100	未分级的天然黑珍珠(不论是否加工,但未制成制品)	10%	
7101101900	其他未分级的天然珍珠(不论是否加工,但未制成制品)	10%	
7101109100	其他天然黑珍珠(不论是否加工,但未制成制品)	10%	
7101109900	其他天然珍珠(不论是否加工,但未制成制品)	10%	
7101211001	未分级,未加工的养殖黑珍珠(未制成制品)	10%	
7101211090	其他未分级,未加工的养殖珍珠(未制成制品)	10%	
7101219001	其他未加工的养殖黑珍珠(未制成制品)	10%	
7101219090	其他未加工的养殖珍珠(未制成制品)	10%	
7101221001	未分级,已加工的养殖黑珍珠(未制成制品)	10%	
7101221090	其他未分级,已加工的养殖珍珠(未制成制品)	10%	
7101229001	其他已加工的养殖黑珍珠(未制成制品)	10%	
7101229090	其他已加工的养殖珍珠(未制成制品)	10%	
7103100000	未加工宝石或半宝石(经简单锯开或粗制成形,未成串或镶嵌)	10%	
7103910000	经其他加工的红宝石,蓝宝石,祖母绿(未成串或镶嵌)	10%	
7103991000	经其他加工的翡翠(未成串或镶嵌)	10%	
7103992000	经其他加工的水晶(未成串或镶嵌)	10	
7103993000	经其他加工的碧玺(未成串或镶嵌)	10	
7103994000	经其他加工的软玉(未成串或镶嵌)	10	
7103999000	经其他加工的其他宝石或半宝石(未成串或镶嵌)	10%	
7104209000	未加工合成或再造其他宝石半宝石(经简单锯开或粗制成形,未成串或镶嵌)	10%	
7104901201	蓝宝石衬底(由人造刚玉加工而成)(厚度<0.5mm)	10%	
7104901290	其他工业用蓝宝石(合成或再造宝石、半宝石)	10%	
7104901900	其他工业用合成或再造宝石半宝石	10%	
7104909900	其他非工业用合成宝石或半宝石(未成串或镶嵌)	10%	
7105900000	其他天然或合成宝石或半宝石粉末	10%	
7113209010	镶嵌濒危物种制品以贱金属为底的包贵金属制首饰(包括零件)	10%	
7113209090	其他以贱金属为底的包贵金属制首饰(包括零件)	10%	
7116100000	天然或养殖珍珠制品	10%	
7116200000	宝石或半宝石制品(包括天然,合成或再造的)	10%	
8702109201	20≤座≤23 装有压燃式活塞内燃发动机的客车	5%	
8702109300	10≤座≤19 装有压燃式活塞内燃发动机的客车	5%	
8702902001	20≤座≤23 装有非压燃式活塞内燃发动机的客车	5%	
8702903000	10≤座≤19 装有非压燃式活塞内燃发动机的客车	5%	
8703213001	排气量≤1 升的装有点燃往复式活塞内燃发动机的小轿车	1%	
8703214001	排量≤1 升的带点燃往复式活塞内燃发动机的越野车(4 轮驱动)	1%	
8703215001	排量≤1 升的带点燃往复式活塞内燃发动机的小客车(9 座及以下)	1%	
8703219001	排量≤1 升的带点燃往复式活塞内燃发动机的其他车辆	1%	
8703223001	1<排量≤1.5 升带点燃往复式活塞内燃发动机小轿车	3%	
8703224001	1<排量≤1.5 升带点燃往复活塞内燃发动机四轮驱动越野车	3%	
8703225001	1<排量≤1.5 升带点燃往复式活塞内燃发动机小客车(≤9 座)	3%	
8703229001	1<排量≤1.5 升带点燃往复式活塞内燃发动机其他车	3%	
8703234101	1.5<排量≤2 升装点燃往复式活塞内燃发动机小轿车	5%	
8703234201	1.5<排量≤2 升装点燃往复式活塞内燃发动机越野车(4 轮驱动)	5%	
8703234301	1.5<排量≤2 升装点燃往复式活塞内燃发动机小客车(9 座及以下的)	5%	
8703234901	1.5<排量≤2 升装点燃往复式活塞内燃发动机的其他载人车辆	5%	
8703235101	2<排量≤2.5 升装点燃往复式活塞内燃发动机小轿车	9%	
8703235201	2<排量≤2.5 升装点燃往复式活塞内燃发动机越野车(4 轮驱动)	9%	
8703235301	2<排量≤2.5 升装点燃往复式活塞内燃发动机小客车(9 座及以下的)	9%	
8703235901	2<排量≤2.5 升装点燃往复式活塞内燃发动机的其他载人车辆	9%	

税则号列	货品名称	进口从价税率	进口从量税率
8703236101	2.5 < 排量≤3 升装点燃往复式活塞内燃发动机小轿车	12%	
8703236201	2.5 < 排量≤3 升装点燃往复式活塞内燃发动机越野车(4 轮驱动)	12%	
8703236301	2.5 < 排量≤3 升装点燃往复式活塞内燃发动机小客车(9 座及以下的)	12%	
8703236901	2.5 < 排量≤3 升装点燃往复式活塞内燃发动机的其他载人车辆(不包括非 4 轮驱动越野车)	12%	
8703236902	2.5 < 排量≤3 升装点燃往复式活塞内燃发动机的非 4 轮驱动越野车	12%	
8703241101	3 < 排量≤4 升装点燃往复式活塞内燃发动机小轿车	25%	
8703241201	3 < 排量≤4 升装点燃往复式活塞内燃发动机越野车(4 轮驱动)	25%	
8703241301	3 < 排量≤4 升装点燃往复式活塞内燃发动机的小客车(9 座及以下的)	25%	
8703241901	3 < 排量≤4 升装点燃往复式活塞内燃发动机的其他载人车辆(不包括非 4 轮驱动越野车)	25%	
8703241902	3 < 排量≤4 升装点燃往复式活塞内燃发动机的非 4 轮驱动越野车	25%	
8703242101	排气量 > 4 升装点燃往复式活塞内燃发动机小轿车	40%	
8703242201	排气量 > 4 升装点燃往复式活塞内燃发动机越野车(4 轮驱动)	40%	
8703242301	排气量 > 4 升装点燃往复式活塞内燃发动机的小客车(9 座及以下的)	40%	
8703242901	排量 > 4 升装点燃往复式活塞内燃发动机的其他载人车辆(不包括非 4 轮驱动越野车)	40%	
8703242902	排量 > 4 升装点燃往复式活塞内燃发动机的非 4 轮驱动越野车	40%	
8703311101	排气量≤1 升的装有压燃往复式活塞内燃发动机小轿车	1%	
8703311901	排量≤1 升的装有压燃往复式活塞内燃发动机的其他载人车辆	1%	
8703312101	1 升 <排气量≤1.5 升装压燃往复式活塞内燃发动机小轿车	3%	
8703312201	1 升 <排气量≤1.5 升装压燃式活塞内燃发动机越野车(4 轮驱动)	3%	
8703312301	1 升 <排气量≤1.5 升装压燃往复式活塞内燃发动机小客车(9 座及以下的)	3%	
8703312901	1 升 <排量≤1.5 升装压燃往复式活塞内燃发动机的其他载人车辆	3%	
8703321101	1.5 < 排量≤2 升装压燃往复式活塞内燃发动机小轿车	5%	
8703321201	1.5 < 排量≤2 升装压燃往复式活塞内燃发动机越野车(4 轮驱动)	5%	
8703321301	1.5 < 排量≤2 升装压燃往复式活塞内燃发动机小客车(9 座及以下的)	5%	
8703321901	1.5 < 排量≤2 升装压燃往复式活塞内燃发动机的其他载人车辆	5%	
8703322101	2 < 排量≤2.5 升装压燃往复式活塞内燃发动机小轿车	9%	
8703322201	2 < 排量≤2.5 升装压燃往复式活塞内燃发动机越野车(4 轮驱动)	9%	
8703322301	2 < 排量≤2.5 升装压燃往复式活塞内燃发动机小客车(9 座及以下的)	9%	
8703322901	2 < 排量≤2.5 升装压燃往复式活塞内燃发动机的其他载人车辆	9%	
8703331101	2.5 < 排量≤3 升装压燃往复式活塞内燃发动机小轿车	12%	
8703331201	2.5 < 排量≤3 升装压燃往复式活塞内燃发动机越野车(4 轮驱动)	12%	
8703331301	2.5 < 排量≤3 升装压燃往复式活塞内燃发动机小客车(9 座及以下的)	12%	
8703331901	2.5 < 排量≤3 升装压燃往复式活塞内燃发动机的其他载人车辆(不包括非 4 轮驱动越野车)	12%	
8703331902	2.5 < 排量≤3 升装压燃往复式活塞内燃发动机的非 4 轮驱动越野车	12%	
8703332101	3 < 排量≤4 升装压燃往复式活塞内燃发动机小轿车	25%	
8703332201	3 < 排量≤4 升装压燃往复式活塞内燃发动机越野车(4 轮驱动)	25%	
8703332301	3 < 排量≤4 升装压燃往复式活塞内燃发动机小客车(9 座及以下的)	25%	
8703332901	3 < 排量≤4 升装压燃往复式活塞内燃发动机的其他载人车辆(不包括非 4 轮驱动越野车)	25%	
8703332902	3 < 排量≤4 升装压燃往复式活塞内燃发动机的非 4 轮驱动越野车	25%	
8703336101	排量 > 4 升装压燃往复式活塞内燃发动机小轿车	40%	
8703336201	排量 > 4 升装压燃往复式活塞内燃发动机越野车(4 轮驱动)	40%	
8703336301	排量 > 4 升装压燃往复式活塞内燃发动机小客车(9 座及以下的)	40%	

税则号列	货品名称	进口从价税率	进口从量税率
8703336901	排量>4升装压燃往复式活塞内燃发动机其他载人车辆(不包括非4轮驱动越野车)	40%	
8703336902	排量>4升装压燃往复式活塞内燃发动机非4轮驱动越野车	40%	
8703900001	其他型排气量≤1升的其他载人车辆	1%	
8703900002	其他型1.5升<排气量≤2升的其他载人车辆	5%	
8703900003	其他型2升<排气量≤2.5升的其他载人车辆	9%	
8703900004	其他型2.5升<排气量≤3升的其他载人车辆(不包括编号8703900014所述小轿车和越野车)	12%	
8703900005	其他型3升<排气量≤4升的其他载人车辆(不包括编号8703900015所述小轿车和越野车)	25%	
8703900006	其他型排气量>4升的其他载人车辆(不包括编号8703900016所述小轿车和越野车)	40%	
8703900007	其他型1升 <排气量≤1.5升的其他载人车辆	3%	
8703900014	其他型2.5升<排气量≤3升的小轿车、越野车	12%	
8703900015	其他型3升<排气量≤4升的小轿车、越野车	25%	
8703900016	其他型排气量>4升的小轿车、越野车	40%	
8711205090	排量=250毫升装往复式活塞内燃发动机摩托车及脚踏两用车	3%	""
8711301000	250<排量≤400毫升装往复式活塞内燃发动机摩托车及脚踏两用车	10%	
8711302000	400<排量≤500毫升装往复式活塞内燃发动机摩托车及脚踏两用车	10%	
8711400000	500<排量≤800毫升装往复式活塞内燃发动机摩托车及脚踏两用车	10%	
8711500000	800毫升<排量装往复式活塞内燃发动机摩托车及脚踏两用车	10%	
8711909001	排气量≤250毫升摩托车及脚踏两用车	3%	
8711909002	排气量>250毫升摩托车及脚踏两用车	10%	
8711909009	其他无法区分排气量的摩托车及脚踏两用车	3%	
8903910001	8米<长度<90米的机动帆船	10%	
8903920001	8米<长度<90米的汽艇(装有舷外发动机的除外)	10%	
8903990001	8米<长度<90米的娱乐或运动用其他机动船舶或快艇	10%	
9101110000	机械指示式的贵金属电子手表(表壳用贵金属或包贵金属制成的)	进口关税完税价格在10000元人民币及以上时,税率为20%	
9101191000	光电显示式的贵金属电子手表(表壳用贵金属或包贵金属制成的)	进口关税完税价格在10000元人民币及以上时,税率为20%	
9101199000	其他贵金属电子手表(表壳用贵金属或包贵金属制成的)	进口关税完税价格在10000元人民币及以上时,税率为20%	
9101210010	含濒危动物皮自动上弦贵金属机械手表(表壳用贵金属或包贵金属制成的)	进口关税完税价格在10000元人民币及以上时,税率为20%	
9101210090	其他自动上弦贵金属机械手表(表壳用贵金属或包贵金属制成的)	进口关税完税价格在10000元人民币及以上时,税率为20%	
9101290010	含濒危动物皮非自动上弦贵金属机械手表(表壳用贵金属或包贵金属制成的)	进口关税完税价格在10000元人民币及以上时,税率为20%	
9101290090	其他非自动上弦贵金属机械手表(表壳用贵金属或包贵金属制成的)	进口关税完税价格在10000元人民币及以上时,税率为20%	
9102110000	机械指示式的其他电子手表(贵金属或包贵金属制壳的除外)	进口关税完税价格在10000元人民币及以上时,税率为20%	

税则号列	货品名称	进口从价税率	进口从量税率
9102120000	光电显示式的其他电子手表(贵金属或包贵金属制壳的除外)	进口关税完税价格在10000元人民币及以上时,税率为20%	
9102190000	其他电子手表(贵金属或包贵金属制壳的除外)	进口关税完税价格在10000元人民币及以上时,税率为20%	
9102210010	含濒危动物皮其他自动上弦的机械手表(用贵金属或包贵金属制壳的除外)	进口关税完税价格在10000元人民币及以上时,税率为20%	
9102210090	其他自动上弦的机械手表(用贵金属或包贵金属制壳的除外)	进口关税完税价格在10000元人民币及以上时,税率为20%	
9102290010	含濒危动物皮其他非自动上弦机械手表(用贵金属或包贵金属制壳的除外)	进口关税完税价格在10000元人民币及以上时,税率为20%	
9102290090	其他非自动上弦的机械手表(用贵金属或包贵金属制壳的除外)	进口关税完税价格在10000元人民币及以上时,税率为20%	
9506310000	完整的高尔夫球棍	10%	
9506320000	高尔夫球	10%	

附表 6：

中华人民共和国进境物品进口税率表

Attacjed table 6：

Duty Rate on Inward Articles of the People's Republic of China

税号 No.	物品名称	税率(%) Duty	货品名称 Article Description
1	书报、刊物、教育专用电影片、幻灯片、原版录音带、录像带 金、银及其制品 食品、饮料 本表税号 2、3、4 税号及备注不包含的其他商品	10	Book, newspaper, journal, movie, copy for educaiton, sliedo, cassette, video Gold, silver and article there of Food, beverage Other articles, other than item 2,3,4 and remark
2	纺织品及其制成品 摄像机、摄录一体机、数码像机及其他电器用具 照像机、自行车、手表、钟表(含配件、附件)	20	Textile product and finished products thereof Video camera, Camcorder, digital camera and other electric products Camera, bicycles, watch, clock (including accessories)
3	高尔夫球及球具、高档手表	30	Golf ball and golf equipment, slap-up watch
4	烟、酒、化妆品	50	Cigarettes; liquor, cosmetics

注：

避孕用具和避孕药品，超过海关规定的自用合理数量部分按有关规定予以退运或按货物进口程序办理报关及验放手续。

Note:

About contraceptive instruments and contraceptive medicines, the extra amount of which exceeding the reasonable self – using level set by customs regulations should be backtrack, or apply for customs registration and examination as required by goods – importing procedures

4

中华人民共和国海关出口税则

（2015年1月1日起实施）

Customs Export Tariff of the People's Republic of China

(Enforced from January 1,2015)

注释：

出口税则也采用《商品名称及编码协调制度》目录，进口税则的归类总规则同样适用于出口税则。

EX[①]	税则号列	商品名称（简称）	出口税率（%）	2015 年出口暂定税率（%）
	03019210	鳗鱼苗	20	
	05061000	经酸处理的骨胶原及骨	40	
	05069011	含牛羊成分的骨粉及骨废料	40	
	05069019	其他骨粉及骨废料	40	
ex	05069090	其他骨及角柱（已脱胶骨、角柱除外）	40	
ex	05069090	已脱胶骨、角柱	40	0
	25041010	鳞片状天然石墨		20
	25041099	其它粉末状天然石墨		20
	25049000	其他天然石墨		20
	25085000	红柱石，蓝晶石及硅线石，不论是否煅烧		10
	25086000	富铝红柱石		10
	25101010	未碾磨磷灰石		35
	25101090	未碾磨天然磷酸钙、天然磷酸铝钙及磷酸盐白垩，磷灰石除外		35
	25102010	已碾磨磷灰石		35
	25102090	已碾磨天然磷酸钙、天然磷酸铝钙及磷酸盐白垩，磷灰石除外		35
	25111000	天然硫酸钡（重晶石）		10
	25112000	天然碳酸钡（毒重石），不论是否煅烧		10
	25191000	天然碳酸镁（菱镁矿）		5
	25199010	熔凝镁氧矿		10
	25199020	烧结镁氧矿（重烧镁）		10
	25199030	碱烧镁（轻烧镁）		5
	25199099	非纯氧化镁		5
	25261020	未破碎及未研粉的滑石，不论是否粗加修整或切割成矩形板块		10
ex	25262020	已破碎或已研粉的天然滑石（体积百分比 90% 及以上的产品粒度小于等于 18 微米的滑石粉除外）		10
ex	25262020	体积百分比 90% 及以上的产品粒度小于等于 18 微米的滑石粉		5
	25301010	未膨胀的绿泥石		10
	25309020	稀土金属矿		15
ex	25309099	其他氧化镁含量在 70%（含 70%）以上的矿产品		5
	26011110	平均粒径小于 0.8 毫米的未煅烧铁矿砂及其精矿；但焙烧黄铁矿除外		10
	26011120	平均粒径不小于 0.8 毫米，但不大于 6.3 毫米的未煅烧铁矿砂及其精矿；但焙烧黄铁矿除外		10
	26011190	平均粒径大于 6.3 毫米的未烧结铁矿砂及其精矿，但焙烧黄铁矿除外		10
	26011200	已烧结铁矿砂及其精矿		10
	26012000	焙烧黄铁矿		10
	26030000	铜矿砂及其精矿		10
	26040000	镍矿砂及其精矿		15
	26050000	钴矿砂及其精矿		15
	26070000	铅矿砂及其精矿	30	
ex	26080000	锌矿砂及其精矿（氧化锌含量大于 80% 的灰色饲料氧化锌除外）	30	
ex	26080000	灰色饲料氧化锌（氧化锌 ZnO 含量大于 80%）	30	0
	26090000	锡矿砂及其精矿	50	20

EX①	税则号列	商品名称(简称)	出口税率(%)	2015年出口暂定税率(%)
	26100000	铬矿砂及其精矿		15
	26110000	钨矿砂及其精矿	20	
	26121000	铀矿砂及其精矿		10
	26122000	钍矿砂及其精矿		10
	26131000	已焙烧钼矿砂及其精矿		15
	26139000	其他钼矿砂及其精矿		15
	26140000	钛矿砂及其精矿		10
	26151000	锆矿砂及其精矿		10
	26159010	水合钽铌原料(钽铌富集物)	30	
	26159090	其他铌钽矿砂及其精矿	30	
	26161000	银矿砂及其精矿		10
	26169000	其他贵金属矿砂及其精矿		10
	26171010	生锑(锑精矿,选矿产品)	20	
	26171090	其他锑矿砂及其精矿		10
	26179010	朱砂(辰砂)		10
	26179090	其他矿砂及其精矿		10
	26180010	冶炼钢铁产生的锰渣		10
	26180090	冶炼钢铁产生的其他粒状熔渣(熔渣砂)		10
	26190000	冶炼钢铁产生的熔渣、浮渣、氧化皮及其他废料		10
	26202100	含铅汽油的淤渣及含铅抗震化合物的淤渣		10
	26202900	其他主要含铅的矿灰及残渣		10
	26203000	主要含铜的矿灰及残渣		10
	26206000	含砷、汞、铊及其混合物,用于提取或生产砷、汞、铊及其化合物的矿灰及残渣		10
	26209100	含锑、铍、镉、铬及其混合物的矿灰及残渣		10
	26209910	主要含钨的矿灰及残渣		10
	26209990	含其他金属及化合物的矿灰及残渣		10
	27011100	未制成型的无烟煤,不论是否粉化		3
	27011210	未制成型的炼焦烟煤,不论是否粉化		3
	27011290	未制成型的其他烟煤,不论是否粉化		3
	27011900	未制成型的其他煤,不论是否粉化		3
	27012000	煤砖、煤球及类似用煤制固体燃料		3
	27021000	褐煤		3
	27022000	制成型的褐煤		3
	27030000	泥煤(包括肥料用泥煤)不论是否成型		3
ex	27060000	从煤、褐煤、或泥煤蒸馏所得的焦油及矿物焦油,不论是否脱水或部分蒸馏,包括再造焦油(含蒽油≥50%及沥青≥40%的"炭黑油"除外)		15
	27071000	粗苯		10
	27090000	石油原油及从沥青矿物提取的原油		5
	28047010	黄磷(白磷)	20	
	28047090	其他磷	20	10
	28053011	钕		25
	28053012	镝		25
	28053013	铽		25
	28053014	镧		25
	28053015	铈		25
	28053016	镨		25
	28053017	钇		25

EX[①]	税则号列	商品名称(简称)	出口税率(%)	2015 年出口暂定税率(%)
	28053019	其他未相互混合或熔合的稀土金属、钪及钇		25
	28053021	已相互混合或熔合的稀土金属、钪及钇,电池级		25
	28053029	其他已相互混合或熔合的稀土金属、钪及钇		25
	28092019	磷酸		300 元/吨
	28111100	氢氟酸(氟化氢)		10
	28141000	氨		180 元/吨
	28142000	氨水		60 元/吨
	28220090	其他钴的氧化物及氢氧化物;商品氧化钴		10
	28253010	五氧化二钒		5
ex	28256000	锗的氧化物		5
	28257000	钼的氧化物及氢氧化物		5
	28259011	钨酸		5
	28259012	三氧化钨		5
	28259019	其他钨的氧化物和氢氧化物		5
	28261290	其他氟化铝		5
	28261920	钠的氟化物		5
	28261990	其他氟化物		5
ex	28269090	氟钽酸钾	30	
	28271010	肥料用氯化铵		5
	28331100	硫酸钠		5
	28342110	肥料用硝酸钾		5
	28417010	钼酸铵		5
	28417090	其他钼酸盐		5
	28418010	仲钨酸铵		5
	28418020	钨酸钠		5
	28418030	钨酸钙		5
	28418040	偏钨酸铵		5
	28418090	其他钨酸盐		5
	28461010	氧化铈		15
	28461020	氢氧化铈		15
	28461030	碳酸铈		15
	28461090	铈的其他化合物		15
	28469011	氧化钇		25
	28469012	氧化镧		15
	28469013	氧化钕		15
	28469014	氧化铕		25
	28469015	氧化镝		25
	28469016	氧化铽		25
	28469017	氧化镨		25
ex	28469019	其他氧化稀土(灯用红粉除外)		15
	28469021	氯化铽		25
	28469022	氯化镝		25
	28469023	氯化镧		25
	28469024	氯化钕		15
	28469025	氯化镨		15
	28469026	氯化钇		15

EX①	税则号列	商品名称(简称)	出口税率(%)	2015 年出口暂定税率(%)
	28469028	混合氯化稀土		15
	28469029	未混合氯化稀土		15
	28469031	氟化铽		15
	28469032	氟化镝		15
	28469033	氟化镧		15
	28469034	氟化钕		15
	28469035	氟化镨		15
	28469036	氟化钇		15
	28469039	其他氟化稀土		15
	28469041	碳酸镧		15
	28469042	碳酸铽		25
	28469043	碳酸镝		25
	28469044	碳酸钕		15
	28469045	碳酸镨		15
	28469046	碳酸钇		15
	28469048	混合碳酸稀土		15
	28469049	未混合碳酸稀土		15
	28469091	镧的其他化合物		25
	28469092	钕的其他化合物		25
	28469093	铽的其他化合物		25
	28469094	镝的其他化合物		25
	28469095	镨的其他化合物		25
ex	28469096	钇的其他化合物(LED 用荧光粉除外)		25
ex	28469099	稀土金属、钇、钪的其他化合物(LED 用荧光粉除外)		25
	28499020	碳化钨		5
	29022000	苯	40	0
	31021000	尿素		80 元/吨
	31029090	其他矿物氮肥及化学氮肥,包括上述子目未列名的混合物		5
	31031010	重过磷酸钙		5
	31031090	其他过磷酸钙		5
	31039000	其他矿物磷肥或化学磷肥		5
	31042090	其他氯化钾		600 元/吨
	31043000	硫酸钾		600 元/吨
	31049010	光卤石、钾盐及其他天然粗钾盐		30
	31049090	其他矿物钾肥及化学钾肥		30
	31051000	制成片状及类似形状或每包毛重不超过 10 公斤的 31 章各货品		5
	31052000	三元复合肥		30
	31053000	磷酸氢二铵		100 元/吨
	31054000	磷酸二氢铵及磷酸二氢铵与磷酸氢二铵的混合物		100 元/吨
	31055100	含有硝酸盐及磷酸盐的肥料		5
	31055900	其他含氮磷两种肥效元素的矿物肥料或化学肥料		5
	31056000	含磷钾两种元素的肥料		5
	31059000	其他肥料		5
	38249091	含滑石 50%以上的混合物		10
	41039011	经退鞣处理的山羊板皮	20	
	41039019	山羊板皮,经退鞣处理的除外	20	

EX[①]	税则号列	商品名称(简称)	出口税率(%)	2015年出口暂定税率(%)
	44012100	针叶木木片或木粒		15
	44012200	非针叶木木片或木粒		15
	44091010	针叶木地板条(块)		10
	44092910	其他非针叶木地板条		10
	44190031	木制一次性筷子		10
	44219021	木制圆签、圆棒、冰果棒、压舌片及类似一次性制品		10
	47010000	机械木浆		10
	47020000	化学木浆,溶解级		10
	47031100	未漂白针叶木碱木浆或硫酸盐木浆		10
	47031900	未漂白非针叶木碱木浆或硫酸盐木浆		10
	47032100	漂白针叶木碱木浆或硫酸盐木浆		10
	47032900	漂白非针叶木碱木浆或硫酸盐木浆		10
	47041100	未漂白的针叶木亚硫酸盐木浆		10
	47041900	未漂白的非针叶木亚硫酸盐木浆		10
	47042100	漂白的针叶木亚硫酸盐木浆		10
	47042900	漂白的非针叶木亚硫酸盐木浆		10
	47050000	半化学木浆		10
	47062000	从回收纸或纸板提取的纤维浆		10
	47063000	竹浆		10
	47069100	其他纤维状纤维素机械浆		10
	47069200	其他纤维状纤维素化学浆		10
	47069300	其他纤维状纤维素半化学浆		10
	72011000	非合金生铁,含磷量小于或等于0.5%	20	25
	72012000	非合金生铁,含磷量大于0.5%	20	25
	72015000	合金生铁	20	25
	72021100	锰铁,含碳量>2%	20	
	72021900	锰铁,含碳量≤2%	20	
	72022100	硅铁,含硅量>55%	25	
	72022900	硅铁,含硅量≤55%	25	
	72023000	硅锰铁	20	
	72024100	铬铁,含碳量>4%	40	20
	72024900	铬铁,含碳量≤4%	40	20
	72025000	硅铬铁		20
	72026000	镍铁		20
	72027000	钼铁		20
	72028010	钨铁		20
	72028020	硅钨铁		20
	72029100	钛铁及硅钛铁		20
	72029290	其他钒铁		20
	72029300	铌铁		20
	72029911	钕铁硼速凝永磁片		20
	72029919	其他钕铁硼合金		20
	72029991	按重量计含稀土元素10%以上的铁合金		25
	72029999	其他铁合金		20
	72031000	直接从铁矿还原的铁产品		25
	72039000	其他铁,海绵铁,产品纯度>99.94%		25

EX[①]	税则号列	商品名称(简称)	出口税率(%)	2015年出口暂定税率(%)
	72041000	铸铁废碎料	40	
	72042100	不锈钢废碎料	40	
	72042900	其他合金钢废碎料	40	
	72043000	镀锡钢铁废碎料	40	
	72044100	机械加工中产生的废料	40	
	72044900	其他钢铁废碎料	40	
	72045000	供再熔的碎料钢铁锭	40	
ex	72051000	生铁、镜铁及钢铁颗粒(不带球弧面的棱角形颗粒数量大于80%的棱角钢砂、筛网孔径在0.3-2.8mm的铸钢丸和铸钢砂除外)		25
ex	72052900	生铁、镜铁及其他钢铁粉末(平均粒径小于10μm的超细铁粉除外)		25
	72061000	铁及非合金钢锭		25
	72069000	其他初级形状的铁及非合金钢		25
	72071100	宽度<厚度两倍的矩形截面钢坯,C<0.25%		25
	72071200	其他矩形截面钢坯,C,0.25%		25
	72071900	其他含碳量<0.25%的钢坯		25
	72072000	含碳量≥0.25%的钢坯		25
	72131000	带有轧制花纹的热轧盘条		15
	72132000	其他易切削钢制热轧盘条		15
	72139100	直径<14mm圆截面的其他热轧盘条		15
	72139900	其他热轧盘条		15
	72142000	热加工带有轧制花纹的条、杆		15
	72143000	热加工易切削钢的条、杆		15
	72149100	热加工其他矩形截面的条杆		15
	72149900	热加工其他条、杆		15
	72151000	冷加工其他易切削钢制条、杆		15
	72155000	冷加工或冷成形的其他条、杆		15
	72159000	铁及非合金钢的其他条、杆		15
	72181000	不锈钢锭及其他初级形状产品		15
	72189100	矩形截面的不锈钢半制成品		15
	72189900	其他不锈钢半制成品		15
	72191312	厚度在3毫米及以上,但小于4.75毫米的未经酸洗的按重量计含锰量在5.5%及以上的铬锰系不锈钢卷板		10
	72191322	厚度在3毫米及以上,但小于4.75毫米的经酸洗的按重量计含锰量在5.5%及以上的铬锰系不锈钢卷板		10
	72191412	厚度小于3毫米的未经酸洗的按重量计含锰量在5.5%及以上的铬锰系不锈钢卷板		10
	72191422	厚度小于3毫米的经酸洗的按重量计含锰量在5.5%及以上的铬锰系不锈钢卷板		10
	72241000	合金钢锭及其他初级形状合金钢		15
	72249010	单重≥10吨的粗铸锻件坯		15
	72249090	其他合金钢坯		15
	74010000	铜锍、沉积铜(泥铜)		15
	74020000	未精炼铜,电解精炼用的铜阳极	30	15
ex	74031111	高纯阴极铜(铜含量不低于99.9999%)	30	0
ex	74031111	高纯阴极铜(铜含量高于99.9935%,但低于99.9999%)	30	5
	74031119	其他阴极精炼铜	30	10
	74031190	其他精炼铜的阴极型材	30	10

EX[①]	税则号列	商品名称(简称)	出口税率(%)	2015年出口暂定税率(%)
	74031200	精炼铜的线锭	30	10
	74031300	精炼铜的坯段	30	10
	74031900	其他未锻轧的精炼铜	30	10
	74032100	未锻轧的铜锌合金(黄铜)	30	5
	74032200	未锻轧的铜锡合金(青铜)	30	5
	74032900	未锻轧的其他铜合金	30	5
	74040000	铜废碎料	30	15
	74050000	铜母合金		10
	74071010	铬锆铜制条、杆及型材及异型材	30	0
	74071090	其他精炼铜制条、杆及型材及异型材	30	0
	74072111	直线度不大于0.5毫米/米铜锌合金条、杆	30	0
	74072119	其他铜锌合金条、杆	30	0
	74072190	其他铜锌合金型材及异型材	30	0
	74072900	其他铜合金条杆、型材及异型材	30	0
	74081100	最大截面尺寸>6mm的精炼铜丝	30	0
	74081900	其它精炼铜丝	30	0
	74082100	铜锌合金丝	30	0
	74082210	铜镍锌铅合金(加铅德银)丝	30	0
	74082290	其他白铜或德银丝	30	0
	74082900	其他铜合金丝	30	0
	74091110	含氧量不超过10PPM的成卷的精炼铜板、片、带	30	0
	74091190	其他成卷的精炼铜板、片、带	30	0
	74091900	其他精炼铜板、片、带	30	0
	74092100	成卷的铜锌合金板、片、带	30	0
	74092900	其他铜锌合金板、片、带	30	0
	74093100	成卷的铜锡合金板、片、带	30	0
	74093900	其他铜锡合金板、片、带	30	0
	74094000	铜镍合金或铜镍锌合金板、片、带	30	0
	74099000	其他铜合金板、片、带	30	0
	75021010	高纯镍(镍含量大于99.99%,钴含量不大于0.005%),	40	5
	75021090	未锻轧的非合金镍	40	15
	75022000	未锻轧镍合金	40	15
	75030000	镍废碎料		10
	75089010	电镀用镍阳极	40	15
	76011010	按重量计含铝量在99.95%及以上的非合金铝	30	0
	76011090	按重量计含铝量在99.95%以下的非合金铝	30	15
ex	76012000	碱金属含量(Na+K+Ca)<10ppm,氢含量<0.12ml/100gAl的低碱精炼铝合金	30	0
ex	76012000	其他未锻轧铝合金	30	15
	76020000	铝废碎料	30	15
	76041090	非合金铝型材及异型材	20	0
	76042100	铝合金制空心异型材	20	0
	76041010	非合金铝条、杆	20	0
ex	76042910	截面周长大于等于210毫米的铝合金制条、杆	20	0
ex	76042910	截面周长小于210毫米的铝合金条杆	20	0
	76042990	铝合金制其他型材及异型材	20	0
	76051100	最大截面尺寸超过7mm的非合金铝丝	20	0

EX①	税则号列	商品名称(简称)	出口税率(%)	2015年出口暂定税率(%)
	76051900	其他非合金铝丝	20	0
	76052100	最大截面尺寸超过7mm的铝合金丝	20	0
	76052900	其他铝合金丝	20	0
	76061121	厚度在0.3mm及以上,但不超过0.36mm的非合金铝与塑料复合的矩形铝板片带	20	0
	76061129	厚度在0.3mm及以上,但不超过0.36mm的其他非合金铝制矩形铝板片带	20	0
	76061191	非合金铝与塑料复合的矩形的其他板、片及带	20	0
	76061199	非合金铝制矩形的其他板、片及带	20	0
	76061220	厚度小于0.28mm的铝合金制矩形铝板片带	20	0
	76061230	厚度在0.28mm及以上,但不超过0.35mm的铝合金制矩形铝板片带	20	0
	76061251	厚度在0.35mm以上,但不超过4mm的铝合金与塑料复合的矩形铝板片带	20	0
	76061259	厚度在0.35mm以上,但不超过4mm的其他铝合金制矩形铝板片带	20	0
	76061290	厚度>4mm的铝合金制矩形铝板片带	20	0
	76069100	非合金铝制非矩形的板、片及带	20	0
	76069200	铝合金制非矩形的板、片及带	20	0
	78011000	未锻轧精炼铅		10
	78020000	铅废碎料		10
	79011110	按重量计含锌量在99.995%及以上的未锻轧锌	20	0
	79011190	99.99≤含锌量<99.995%的未锻轧锌	20	5
	79011200	含锌量<99.99%的未锻轧锌	20	15
	79012000	未锻轧锌合金	20	0
	80011000	非合金锡		10
	80020000	锡废碎料		10
	81011000	钨粉		5
	81019400	未锻轧钨		5
	81019700	钨废碎料		15
	81021000	钼粉		5
	81029400	未锻轧钼		5
	81029700	钼废碎料		15
	81033000	钽废碎料		10
	81101010	未锻轧锑	20	5
	81101020	锑粉末	20	
	81102000	锑废碎料	20	
	81122100	未锻轧铬、铬粉末		15
	81122200	铬废碎料		15
	81129230	未锻轧铟;铟废碎料;铟粉末		2

注①:"ex"表示实施暂定税率的商品应在该税号范围内,以具体商品描述为准。

5

中华人民共和国进出口关税税款计算方法

Calculation methods for import and Export Tax of the People's Republic of China

本书所列计算方法是根据《中华人民共和国关税条例》、《中华人民共和国增值税暂行条例》及《中华人民共和国消费税暂行条例》编制的。

为便于使用，现将有关问题说明如下：

一、所称进口税包括进口关税、进口环节增值税（简称增值税）、进口环节消费税（简称消费税），其中消费税仅对少数商品征收；出口税只含出口关税一项。

二、关税税率分为优惠关税税率和普通关税税率。凡原产地属于世贸组织成员或与我国签定有互惠双边贸易协定的国家或地区进口的商品，其进口关税税率使用优惠关税税率，否则使用普通关税税率。

三、税款计算公式

$$\text{进口关税税额} = \text{到岸价格} \times \text{进口关税税率}$$

$$\text{出口关税税额} = \frac{\text{离岸价格}}{1 + \text{出口税税率}} \times \text{出口关税税率}$$

$$\text{增值税税额} = (\text{到岸价} + \text{进口关税额} + \text{消费税额}) \times \text{增值税税率}$$

$$\text{从价消费税税额} = \left(\frac{\text{到岸价} + \text{关税额}}{1 - \text{消费税税率}}\right) \times \text{消费税税率}$$

$$\text{从量消费税税额} = \text{应征消费税的商品数量} \times \text{消费税单位税额}$$

其中，从量消费税商品计量单位的换算标准（按体积净重计）如下：

啤酒 1 吨 = 988 升

黄酒 1 吨 = 962 升

汽油 1 吨 = 1388 升

柴油 1 吨 = 1176 升

$$\text{进口税额} = \text{进口关税} + \text{增值税} + \text{消费税}$$

$$= \left(\frac{\text{进口关税率} + \text{消费税率} + \text{增值税率} + \text{进口关税率} \times \text{增值税率}}{1 - \text{消费税税率}}\right) \times \text{到岸价}$$

$$= \text{常数} \times \text{到岸价}$$

四、为便于计算进口税额，本书编制了《进口税计税系数表》，其使用方法如下：

（一）"系数表 1"适用于应征消费税税率不为 0 税率的商品。鉴于此类商品法定增值税率均为 17%，因此在本书中查出该商品的关税税率和消费税税率后，在"表 1"内找出这两个税率交叉栏内的常数，用进口货物的到岸价乘以该常数，即为应纳进口税额。

（二）"系数表 2"适用于消费税税率为 0 的进口商品。首先在本书中查出该商品的关税税率和增值税税率，然后在"表 2"内找出这两个税率的交叉栏内的常数，用进口货物的到岸价乘以该常数即为应纳进口税额。

五、对适用于暂定税率的商品，关税税率应用暂定关税税率。

The Calculation methods in this book is compiled in accordance with Regulations on Customs Tariff of the People's Republic of China, Provisional Regulations on Value-added Tax of the People's Republic of China and Provisional Regulations on Consumption Tax of the People's Republic of China.

For the convenience of usage, relevant explanations are listed below:

1. Import tax we mean consists of import customs duty (ICD), value-added tax (VAT), and consumption tax (CT) among which CT is levied on a few items of goods. Export tax consists of only export customs duty (ECD).

2. Import customs duty rates we mean fall into general duty rates and preferential duty rates. The preferential duty rates apply to goods originally produced or manufactured in countries with which the People's Republic of China has concluded trading agreement. Otherewise, the general duty rates will be applied.

3. Calculation formulae for tax collection

$$\text{ICD} = \text{CIF value} \times \text{ICD rate}$$

$$\text{ECD} = \frac{\text{FOB value}}{1 + \text{ECD rate}} \times \text{ECD rate}$$

$$\text{VAT} = (\text{CIF value} + \text{ICD} + \text{CT}) \times \text{VAT rate}$$

$$\textit{Ad Valorem CT} = \left(\frac{\text{CIF value} + \text{ICD}}{1 - \text{CT rate}}\right) \times \text{CT rate}$$

$$\text{Specific CT} = \text{Quantity of goods} \times \text{unit CT rate}$$

Note: The following is the conversion table of measurements of goods on which specific consumption tax is levied (net bulk)

Beer	1 ton = 988 litres
Millet wine	1 ton = 962 litres
Gasoline	1 ton = 1388 litres
Diesel	1 ton = 1176 litres

$$\text{Total Import Tax} = \text{ICD} + \text{VAT} + \text{CT}$$

$$= \left(\frac{\text{ICD rate} + \text{CT rate} + \text{VAT rate} + \text{ICD rate} \times \text{VAT rate}}{1 - \text{CT rate}}\right) \times \text{CIF value}$$

$$= \text{Coefficient} \times \text{CIF value}$$

4. To facilitate easy calculation, we compiled tables of import tax coefficients for reference. The following are the exemplary usage methods:

(1) The Table of Import Tax Coefficient (Consumption Taxes Applicable) applies to goods on which the consumption tax is levied. In viewof the statutory VAT rate is 17% for all goods in this table, the user may first find the duty rate and consumption tax rate of a particular type of goods in the table, then find the coefficient where those two rates meet in the table. The import tax payable equals the coefficient times the CIF value.

(2) The Table of Import Tax Cofficients (Consumption Taxes Not Applicable) applies to goods on which no consumption tax is levied. The user may first find the duty rate and VAT rate of a particular type of goods in the table, then find the coefficient where those two rates meet in the table. The total import tax is the coefficient times the CIF value.

5. As far as goods on which Interim Duty Rate is appliable, ICD rate is no other than Interim Duty Rate.

表1 进口关税与进口环节代征税(消费税及增值税)计税常数表

Table of import tariff and import tax (Consumption tax and value added tax)

关税税率(%)	消费税税率(%)											
	1	3	5	9	10	12	15	20	25	30	36	40
0	0.1818	0.2062	0.2316	0.2857	0.3000	0.3295	0.3765	0.4625	0.5600	0.6714	0.8281	0.9500
3.0	0.2173	0.2424	0.2685	0.3243	0.3390	0.3694	0.4178	0.5064	0.6068	0.7216	0.8830	1.0085
4.0	0.2291	0.2544	0.2808	0.3371	0.3520	0.3827	0.4315	0.5210	0.6224	0.7383	0.9013	1.0280
5.0	0.2049	0.2665	0.2932	0.3500	0.3650	0.3960	0.4453	0.5356	0.6380	0.7550	0.9195	1.0475
6.0	0.2527	0.2786	0.3055	0.3629	0.3780	0.4093	0.4591	0.5503	0.6536	0.7717	0.9378	1.0670
6.5	0.2586	0.2846	0.3116	0.3693	0.3845	0.4160	0.4659	0.5576	0.6614	0.7801	0.9470	1.0768
7.5	0.2705	0.2966	0.3239	0.3821	0.3975	0.4293	0.4797	0.5722	0.6770	0.7968	0.9652	1.0963
8.0	0.2764	0.3027	0.3301	0.3886	0.4040	0.4359	0.4866	0.5795	0.6848	0.8051	0.9744	1.1060
10.0	0.3000	0.3268	0.3457	0.4143	0.4300	04625	0.5141	0.6088	0.7160	0.8386	1.0109	1.1450
10.5	0.3059	0.3328	0.3609	0.4207	0.4365	0.4691	0.5210	0.6161	0.7238	0.8469	1.0201	1.1548
11.0	0.3118	0.3389	0.3671	0.4271	0.4430	0.4758	0.5279	0.6234	0.7316	0.8553	1.0292	1.1645
12.0	0.3236	0.3509	0.3794	0.4400	0.4560	0.4891	0.5416	0.6380	0.7472	0.8720	1.0475	1.1840
12.5	0.3295	0.3570	0.3855	0.4464	0.4625	0.4957	0.5485	0.6453	0.7550	0.8804	1.0566	1.1938
14.0	0.3473	0.3751	0.4040	0.4657	0.4820	0.5157	0.5692	0.6673	0.7784	0.9054	1.0841	1.2230
15.0	0.3591	0.3871	0.4163	0.4786	0.4950	0.5290	0.5829	0.6819	0.7940	0.9221	1.1023	1.2425
16.0	0.3709	0.3992	0.4286	0.4914	0.5080	0.5423	0.5967	0.6965	0.8096	0.9389	1.1206	1.2620
17.5	0.3848	0.4173	0.4471	0.5107	0.5275	0.5622	0.6174	0.7284	0.8330	0.9639	1.1480	1.2913
20.0	0.4182	0.4474	0.4779	0.5429	0.5600	0.5955	0.6518	0.7550	0.8720	1.0057	1.1938	1.3400
21.0	0.4300	0.4595	0.4902	0.5557	0.5730	0.6088	0.6655	0.7696	0.8876	1.0224	1.2120	1.3595
22.0	0.4418	0.4715	0.5025	0.5686	0.5860	0.622	0.6793	0.7843	0.9032	1.0391	1.2303	1.3790
23.0	0.4536	0.4836	0.5148	0.5814	0.5990	0.6353	0.6931	0.7989	0.9188	1.0559	1.2486	1.3985
25.0	0.4773	0.5077	0.5395	0.6071	0.6250	0.6619	0.7206	0.8281	0.9500	1.0893	1.2852	1.4375
30.0	0.5364	0.5680	0.6011	0.6714	0.6900	0.7284	0.7894	0.9013	1.0280	1.1729	1.3766	1.5350
35.0	0.5955	0.6284	0.6626	0.7357	0.7550	0.7949	0.8582	0.9744	1.1060	1.2564	1.4680	1.6325
40.0	0.6545	0.6887	0.7242	0.8000	0.8200	0.8614	0.9271	1.0475	1.1840	1.3400	1.5594	1.7300
45.0	0.7136	0.7490	0.7858	0.8643	0.8850	0.9278	0.9959	1.1206	1.2620	1.4236	1.6508	1.8275
57.0	0.8469	0.8937	0.9336	1.0186	1.0410	1.0874	1.1611	1.2961	1.4492	1.6241	1.8702	2.0615
65.0	0.9500	0.9902	1.0321	1.1214	1.1450	1.1938	1.2712	1.1431	1.5740	1.7579	2.0164	2.2175

注:

1. 鉴于应征消费税的进口商品的法定增值税税率均为17%,故本表省略了增值税税率一栏,但所列常数均已包括增值税在内。
2. 常数计算公式为:

$$常数=\frac{进口关税税率+消费税税率+增值税税率+进口关税税率\times增值税税率}{1-消费税税率}$$

表 2　进口关税与进口环节代征税(增值税)计税常数表
Table of Import Tariff and Import Tax(Value added Tax)

关税税率 Tariff (%)	增值税税率(%) VAT rate (%)		关税税率 Tariff (%)	增值税税率(%) VAT rate (%)		关税税率 Tariff (%)	增值税税率(%) VAT rate (%)	
	13	17		13	17		13	17
0	0.1300	0.1700	10.0	0.2430	0.2870	22.0	0.3786	0.4274
1.0	0.1413	0.1817	10.5	0.2487	0.2929	23.0	0.3899	0.4391
1.5	0.1470	0.1876	11.0	0.2543	0.2987	24.0	0.4012	0.4508
2.0	0.1526	0.1934	12.0	0.2656	0.3104	24.5	0.4069	0.4567
3.0	0.1639	0.2051	12.5	0.2713	0.3163	25.0	0.4125	0.4625
4.0	0.1752	0.2168	12.6	0.2724	0.3174	25.9	0.4227	0.4730
4.5	0.1809	0.2227	13.0	0.2769	0.3221	26.8	0.4328	0.4836
5.0	0.1865	0.2285	13.5	0.2826	0.3280	27.0	0.4351	0.4859
5.5	0.1922	0.2344	14.0	0.2882	0.3338	28.0	0.4464	0.4976
5.8	0.1955	0.2379	14.4	0.2927	0.3385	30.0	0.4690	0.5210
6.0	0.1978	0.2402	15.0	0.2995	0.3455	32.0	0.4916	0.5444
6.5	0.2035	0.2461	15.5	0.3052	0.3514	35.0	0.5255	0.5795
7.0	0.2091	0.2519	16.0	0.3108	0.3572	38.0	0.5594	0.6146
7.5	0.2148	0.2578	16.9	0.3201	0.3677	40.0	0.5820	0.6380
8.0	0.2204	0.2636	17.0	0.3221	0.3689	42.3	0.6080	0.6649
8.4	0.2249	0.2683	17.5	0.3278	0.3748	44.5	0.6329	0.6907
8.5	0.2261	0.2695	18.0	0.3334	0.3806	45.0	0.6385	0.6965
9.0	0.2317	0.2753	19.0	0.3447	0.3923	50.0	0.6950	0.7550
9.5	0.2374	0.2812	20.0	0.3560	0.4040	57.0	0.7741	0.8369
9.7	0.2396	0.2835	21.0	0.3673	0.4157	65.0	0.8645	0.9305

注:
常数 = 进口关税税率 + 增值税税率 + 进口关税税率 × 增值税税率

计量单位换算表

Conversion Table

面(地)积换算

公制		英美制			
平方米	平方厘米	平方码	平方英尺	平方英寸	平方尺
1	10000	1.1960	10.7639	1550	9
0.0001	1	0.00012	0.00108	0.155	0.0009
0.8361	8361	1	9	1296	7.525
0.0929	929	0.1111	1	144	0.836
0.00065	6.45	0.00077	0.00694	1	0.0058
0.111	0000	0.133	1.196	172.2	1

长度换算

公制		中国市制	英美制		
米	厘米	尺	码	英尺	英寸
1	100	3	1.094	3.2808	39.37
0.01	1	0.03	0.01094	0.03281	0.3937
0.3333	33.33	1	0.3646	1.094	13.123
0.9144	91.44	2.743	1	3	36
0.3048	30.48	0.9144	0.3334	1	12
0.0254	2.54	0.0762	0.0278	0.833	1

1 米 = 100 厘米 = 1000 毫米

重量换算(一)

公制	英制	美制	港制
公吨	长吨	短吨	司马担
1	0.9842	1.1023	16.535
1.016	1	1.12	16.8
0.9072	0.8929	1	15
0.05	0.04921	0.056	0.8267
0.0508	0.05	0.056	0.8402
0.0605	0.0594	0.0667	1

港制 1 司马担 = 100 司马斤

公制 1 公吨 = 10 公担

英制 1 长吨 = 20 英担(CWT)

1 英担 = 50.8024 千克

美制 1 短吨 = 20 短担(CWT)

1 短担 = 100 磅 = 45.36 千克

公制	中国市制	英美制
千克	斤	磅
1000	2000	2204.6
1016	2032	2242
907	1814	2000
50	100	110.23
50.8	101.6	112
60.48	120.96	133.33
1	2	2.2046
0.5	1	1.1023
0.4536	0.9072	1

重量换算(二)

公制		英美制常衡		英美制金衡或药衡		中国市制
千克	克	磅	唡	磅	唡	两
1	1000	2.2046	35.2736	2.697	31.1507	20
0.001	1	0.0022	0.03527	0.00268	0.0321	0.02
0.4536	453.59	1	16	1.2153	14.5833	9.072
0.02835	28.35	0.0625	1	0.07595	0.9114	0.567
0.3732	373.24	0.82286	13.1657	1	12	7.465
0.0311	31.10	0.06857	1.0971	0.08333	1	0.622
0.05	50	0.1102	1.76368	0.13396	1.6075	1

宝石:1 克拉 = 0.2 克　　　　1 金衡 = 155.5 克拉

容(体)积换算(一)

公制	中国市制	英制	美制
升	升	英加仑	美加仑
1	1	0.22	0.264
4.546	4.546	1	1.201
3.785	3.785	0.833	1

1000 升 = 1 立方米　　1 升 = 1000 毫升 = 1000 立方厘米(c. c.)

英制 1 加仑 = 277.42 立方英寸　　英制 1 加仑 = 231 立方英寸

容(体)积换算(二)

公制		英美制			中国市制
立方米	立方厘米	立方码	立方英尺	立方英寸	立方尺
1	1000000	1.303	35.3147	61024	27
0.000001	1	0.0000013	0.00004	0.06102	0.000027
0.7636	764555	1	27	46656	20.643
0.02832	28317	0.037	1	1728	0.7646
0.000016	16.387	0.00002	0.00058	1	0.00044
0.037	37037	0.0484	1.308	2260	1

木材体积单位换算

板(Board Foot Measure, BFM)

指厚一英寸、面积一平方英尺的木材

板材的换算:100 板 = 2.36 立方米

原木的换算:100 板 = 5 立方米(近似值)

功率换算

1 千瓦(kW) = 1.34 英制马力(hp) = 2.36 公制马力(hp)

1 英制马力 = 0.746 千瓦(kW)

1 公制马力 = 0.735 千瓦(kW)

1 千伏安(kVA) = $\frac{\text{千瓦(kW)}}{0.80}$

粮谷重量容积换算

品名	1 公吨折合蒲式耳	1 蒲式耳折合	
		磅	千克
小麦、大豆	36.743	60	27.216
玉米	39.368	56	25.402
大麦(英制)	44.092	50	22.68
大麦(美制)	45.931	48	21.773

1 英制蒲式耳(1.0321 美制蒲式耳)合 36.3677 升。

石(原)油重量、容积换算

国别	1 公吨折合			
	千升	美制桶	英制加仑	美制加仑
贡国、印度尼西亚	1.18	7.4	259.1	310.6
伊朗、沙特阿拉伯	1.19	7.49	261.8	314.5
日本	1.11	6.99	244.5	293.3
英国、科威特	1.16	7.31	255.8	306.7
委内瑞拉	1.09	6.84	239.2	287.4

注:世界平均比重的原油通常以 1 公吨 = 7.35 桶(每桶为 42 美制加仑)或 1174 升计。

常用度量衡英文名称和简写

名称	英文名称	简写	名称	英文名称	简写
克	gram	g.	码	yard	yd.
千克	kilogram	kg.	英尺	foot	ft.
公担	quintal	q.	英寸	inch	in
公吨	metric ton	m. t.	平方米	square metre	sq. m.
长吨	long ton	l. t.	平方英尺	square foot	sq. ft
短吨	short ton	sh. t.	平方码	square yard	sq. yd
英担	hundredweight	cwt.	立方米	cubic metre	cu. m.
美担	hundredweight	cwt.	立方英尺	cubic toor	cu. ft.
磅	pound	lb.	升	litre	l.
啢(常衡)	ounce	oz.	毫升	millilitre	ml.
(金衡)	ounce	oz. t	加仑	gallon	gal.
司马担	picul		蒲式耳	bushel	bu.
米	metre	m.	克拉	carat	car.
公里	kilomere	km.	马力	horse power	hp.
厘米	centimetre	cm.	千瓦	kilowatt	kw.
毫米	millimetre	mm.	公吨度	metric ton unit	m. t. u.

6

中华人民共和国海关进出口商品规范申报目录

Norm Declares Contents for the Customs Import and Export Goods of the People's Republic of China

中华人民共和国海关进出口商品规范申报目录

使 用 说 明

进出口品货物收货人或其代理人在填报海关进出品货物报关单的“商品名称、规格型号”栏目时，应按照本《申报目录》中所申报要素的内容填报。为方便《申报目录》的使用，特作说明如下：

一、《申报目录》采用了与《中华人民共和国海关进出品税则》（以下简称《税则》）一致的结构，所列商品按照类、章层次排列。除了《税则》中已有的类注释、章注释外，为了准确理解对商品规范申报的要求，在相关章前对应该章的共性问题用“注解”加以说明。在使用《申报目录》时，首先应阅读各章的注解，再查阅具体商品对应的规范申报内容。

二、《申报目录》正文由“商品编码”、“商品要素”、“备注详解\举例说明”栏组成。

三、《申报目录》的“商品描述”栏所列的全部编码与《税则》中“税则号列”栏所列全部编码保持一致；《申报目录》的“商品描述”与《税则》中“货品名称”内容相同。

四、《申报目录》对不同商品设置了特定的申报要素内容。报关单中的“商品名称、规格型号”栏应当按照《申报目录》中相应商品所列“申报要素”、“备注详解\举例说明”的各项内容填写。

五、《申报目录》属于结构性目录，其中所列商品按照不同位数编码所代表的层次进行排列，当某一层次编码商品所要求的申报要素与上一层次编码商品的申报要素相同时，则该商品的“商品编码”就不列示在书中，但表示该层次“商品编码”对应的商品使用上一层次编码商品所列的“申报要素”。例如：

（一）4位编码对应商品有“申报要素”的如下所示：

商品编码器	商品描述	申报要素/备注详解/举例说明
01.01	马、驴、骡：	1.品名；2.是否野生；3.是否改良种用举例；改良种用野马
	马	
~~0101.2100~~	~~改良种用~~	
~~0101.2900~~	~~其他~~	

“01.01”下面所属的“商品编码”所对应的商品的“申报要素”都与“01.01”一致，所以“01.01”下面所属的“商品编码”都省略，读者如有压根可参考《税则》。

（二）一级子目对应商品有“申报要素”的如下列示：

商品编码器	商品描述	申报要素/备注详解/举例说明
84.79	本章其他税目未列名的具有独立功能的机器及机器器具	
8479.1	-公共工程用机器：	1.品名；2.用途；3.功能
	~~--摊铺机：~~	
~~8479.1021~~	~~---沥青混凝土摊铺机~~	
~~8479.1022~~	~~---稳定土摊铺机~~	
~~8479.1029~~	~~---其他~~	
~~8479.1090~~	~~--其他~~	

“-公共工程用机器：”下面所属的“商品编码”所对应的商品的“申报要素”都与“-公共工程用机器：”一致，所以“-公共工程用机器：”下面所属的“商品编码”都省略列示，读者如有需要可参考《税则》。

依此类推二级子目、三有子目、四级子目都如上述列示。在《申报目录》中如低级子目有对应“申报要素”的，其上层子目对应的“申报要素”栏为空，但其上层子目的“商品编码”会一一列示。

为了更方便读者使用本“申报目录”，书中列示出5位、6位、7位编码，这样更加明确了商品归类的查询，更加专业的说明商品归类原则，以便读者对进出口商品进行正确归类。

《中华人民共和国海关进出口商品规范申报目录》使用说明 …… (1023)
第一类　活动物;动物产品 …… (1023)
第一章　活动物 …… (1023)
第二章　肉及食用杂碎 …… (1026)
第三章　鱼、甲壳动物、软体动物及其他水生无脊椎动物 …… (1027)
第四章　乳品;蛋品;天然蜂蜜;其他食用动物产品 …… (1031)
第五章　其他动物产品 …… (1034)
第二类　植物产品 …… (1035)
第六章　活树及其他活植物;鳞茎、根及类似品;插花及装饰用簇叶 …… (1035)
第七章　食用蔬菜、根及块茎 …… (1035)
第八章　食用水果及坚果;柑桔属水果或甜瓜的果皮 …… (1036)
第九章　咖啡、茶、马黛茶及调味香料 …… (1039)
第十章　谷物 …… (1039)
第十一章　制粉工业产品;麦芽;淀粉;菊粉;面筋 …… (1040)
第十二章　含油子仁及果实;杂项子仁及果实;工业用或药用植物;稻草、秸秆及饲料 …… (1041)
第十三章　虫胶;树胶、树脂及其他植物液、汁 …… (1043)
第十四章　编结用植物材料;其他植物产品 …… (1045)
第三类　动、植物油、脂及其分解产品;精制的食用油脂;动、植物蜡 …… (1045)
第十五章　动、植物油、脂及其分解产品;精制的食用油脂;动、植物蜡 …… (1045)
第四类　食品;饮料、酒及醋;烟草、烟草及烟草代用品的制品 …… (1048)
第十六章　肉、鱼、甲壳动物、软体动物及其他水生无脊椎动物的制品 …… (1048)
第十七章　糖及糖食 …… (1050)
第十八章　可可及可可制品 …… (1050)
第十九章　谷物、粮食粉、淀粉或乳的制品;糕饼点心 …… (1051)
第二十章　蔬菜、水果、坚果或植物其他部分的制品 …… (1052)
第二十一章　杂项食品 …… (1053)
第二十二章　饮料、酒及醋 …… (1054)
第二十三章　食品工业的残渣及废料;配制的动物饲料 …… (1056)
第二十四章　烟草、烟草及烟草代用品的制品 …… (1057)
第五类　矿产品 …… (1057)
第二十五章　盐;硫磺;泥土及石料;石膏料、石灰及水泥 …… (1057)
第二十六章　矿砂、矿渣及矿灰 …… (1061)
第二十七章　矿物燃料、矿物油及其蒸馏产品;沥青物质;矿物蜡 …… (1062)
第六类　化学工业及其相关工业的产品 …… (1065)
第二十八章　无机化学品;贵金属、稀土金属、放射性元素及其同位素的有机及无机化合物 …… (1065)
第二十九章　有机化学品 …… (1068)
第三十章　药　品 …… (1070)
第三十一章　肥　料 …… (1071)
第三十二章　鞣料浸膏及染料浸膏;鞣酸及其衍生物;染料、颜料及其他着色料;油漆及清漆;油灰及其他类似胶粘剂;墨水、油墨 …… (1071)
第三十三章　精油及香膏;芳香料制品及化妆盥洗品 …… (1073)
第三十四章　肥皂、有机表面活性剂、洗涤剂、润滑剂、人造蜡、调制蜡、光洁剂、蜡烛及类似品、塑型用膏、“牙科用蜡”及牙科用熟石膏制剂 …… (1073)
第三十五章　蛋白类物质;改性淀粉;胶;酶 …… (1074)
第三十六章　炸药;烟火制品;火柴;引火合金;易燃材料制品 …… (1075)
第三十七章　照相及电影用品 …… (1075)
第三十八章　杂项化学产品 …… (1076)
第七类　塑料及其制品;橡胶及其制品 …… (1078)
第三十九章　塑料及其制品 …… (1078)
第四十章　橡胶及其制品 …… (1080)
第八类　生皮、皮革、毛皮及其制品;鞍具及挽具;旅行用品、手提包及类似容器;动物肠线(蚕胶丝除外)制品 …… (1082)
第四十一章　生皮(毛皮除外)及皮革 …… (1082)
第四十二章　皮革制品;鞍具及挽具;旅行用品、手提包及类似容器;动物肠线(蚕胶丝除外)制品 …… (1084)
第四十三章　毛皮、人造毛皮及其制品 …… (1085)
第九类　木及木制品;木炭;软木及软木制品;稻草、秸秆、针茅或其他编结材料制品;篮筐及柳条编结品 …… (1086)
第四十四章　木及木制品;木炭 …… (1086)
第四十五章　软木及软木制品 …… (1088)
第四十六章　稻草、秸秆、针茅或其他编结材料制品;篮筐及柳条编结品 …… (1088)
第十类　木浆及其他纤维状纤维素浆;回收(废碎)纸或纸板;纸、纸板及其制品 …… (1089)
第四十七章　木浆及其他纤维状纤维素浆;回收(废碎)纸或纸板 …… (1089)
第四十八章　纸及纸板;纸浆、纸或纸板制品 …… (1090)
第四十九章　书籍、报纸、印刷图画及其他印刷品;手稿、打字稿及设计图纸 …… (1094)

第十一类　纺织原料及纺织制品 ……(1094)
第五十章　蚕丝 ……(1095)
第五十一章　羊毛、动物细毛或粗毛；马毛纱线及其机织物 ……(1095)
第五十二章　棉花 ……(1096)
第五十三章　其他植物纺织纤维；纸纱线及其机织物 ……(1097)
第五十四章　化学纤维长丝；化学纤维纺织材料制扁条及类似品 ……(1098)
第五十五章　化学纤维短纤 ……(1100)
第五十六章　絮胎、毡呢及无纺织物；特种纱线、绳、索、缆及其制品 ……(1101)
第五十七章　地毯纺织材料的其他铺地制品 ……(1103)
第五十八章　特种机织物；簇绒织物；花边；装饰毯；装饰带；刺绣品 ……(1103)
第五十九章　浸渍、涂布、包覆或层压的纺织物；工业用纺织物品 ……(1105)
第六十章　针织物及钩编织物 ……(1106)
第六十一章　针织或钩编的服装及衣着附件 ……(1106)
第六十二章　非针织或非钩编的服装及衣着附件 ……(1108)
第六十三章　其他纺织制成品；成套物品；旧衣着及旧纺织品；碎织物 ……(1109)
第十二类　鞋、帽、伞、杖、鞭及其零件；已加工的羽毛及其制品；人造花；人发制品 ……(1110)
第六十四章　鞋靴、护腿和类似品及其零件 ……(1110)
第六十五章　帽类及其零件 ……(1110)
第六十六章　雨伞、阳伞、手杖、鞭子、马鞭及其零件 ……(1111)
第六十七章　已加工羽毛、羽绒及其制品；人造花；人发制品 ……(1111)
第十三类　石料、石膏、水泥、石棉、云母及类似材料的制品；陶瓷产品；玻璃及其制品 ……(1112)
第六十八章　石料、石膏、水泥、石棉、云母及类似材料的制品 ……(1112)
第六十九章　陶瓷产品 ……(1113)
第七十章　玻璃及其制品 ……(1114)
第十四类　天然或养殖珍珠、宝石或半宝石、贵金属、包贵金属及其制品；仿首饰；硬币 ……(1117)
第七十一章　天然或养殖珍珠、宝石或半宝石、贵金属、包贵金属及其制品；仿首饰；硬币 ……(1117)
第十五类　贱金属及其制品 ……(1118)
第七十二章　钢铁 ……(1118)
第七十三章　钢铁制品 ……(1123)
第七十四章　铜及其制品 ……(1125)
第七十五章　镍及其制品 ……(1127)
第七十六章　铝及其制品 ……(1128)
第七十八章　铅及其制品 ……(1129)
第七十九章　锌及其制品 ……(1130)
第八十章　锡及其制品 ……(1130)
第八十一章　其他贱金属、金属陶瓷及其制品 ……(1130)
第八十二章　贱金属工具、器具、利口器、餐匙、餐叉及其零件 ……(1132)
第八十三章　贱金属杂项制品 ……(1133)
第十六类　机器、机械器具、电气设备及其零件；录音机及放声机、电视图像、声音的录制重设备及其零件、附件 ……(1134)
第八十四章　核反应堆、锅炉、机器、机械器具及其零件 ……(1134)
第八十五章　电机、电气设备及其零件；录音机及放声机、电视图像、声音的录制和重放设备及其零件、附件 ……(1146)
第十七类　车辆、航空器、船舶及有关运输设备 ……(1153)
第八十六章　铁道及电车道机车、车辆及其零件；铁道及电车道轨道固定装置及其零件、附件各种机械（包括电动机械）交通信号设备 ……(1153)
第八十七章　车辆及其零件、附件，但铁道及电车道车辆除外 ……(1154)
第八十八章　航空器、航天器及其零件 ……(1159)
第八十九章　船舶及浮动结构体 ……(1160)
第十八类　光学、照相、电影、计量、检验、医疗或外科用仪器及设备、精密仪器及设备；钟表；乐器；上述物品的零件、附件 ……(1161)
第九十章　光学、照相、电影、计量、检验、医疗或外科用仪器及设备、精密仪器及设备；上述物品的零件、附件 ……(1161)
第九十一章　钟表及其零件 ……(1166)
第九十二章　乐器及其零件、附件 ……(1167)
第十九类　武器、弹药及其零件、附件 ……(1167)
第九十三章　武器、弹药及其零件、附件 ……(1167)
第二十类　杂项制品 ……(1168)
第九十四章　家具；寝具、褥垫、弹簧床垫、软座垫及类似的填充制品；未列名灯具及照明装置；发光标志、发光铭牌及类似品；活动房屋 ……(1168)
第九十五章　玩具、游戏品、运动用品及其零件、附件 ……(1169)
第九十六章　杂项制品 ……(1170)
第二十一类　艺术品、收藏品及古物 ……(1172)
第九十七章　艺术品、收藏品及古物 ……(1172)

第一类　活动物;动物产品

第一章　活动物

税则号列	商品描述	规范申报要素 / 价格申报要素 / 其他申报要素 / 举例说明
01.01	马、驴、骡:	1.品名;2.是否改良种用;3.品种
01.02	牛:	1.品名;2.是否改良种用
01.03	猪:	
0103.1000	-改良种用	1.品名;2.是否改良种用
0103.9	-其他:	1.品名;2.个体重量
01.04	绵羊、山羊:	
0104.1010	---改良种用	1.品名;2.是否改良种用。注:改良种用绵羊
0104.1090	---其他	1.品名;2.是否改良种用。注:活绵羊
0104.2010	---改良种用	1.品名;2.是否改良种用。注:改良种用山羊
0104.2090	---其他	1.品名;2.是否改良种用。注:活山羊
01.05	家禽,即鸡、鸭、鹅、火鸡及珍珠鸡:	1.品名;2.是否改良种用;3.个体重量。注:不包括其他活禽(如鹧鸪、野鸡、鸽、野鸭、大雁)(税目01.06)
01.06	其他活动物:	
0106.1	-哺乳动物:	1.品名;2.是否改良种用
0106.201	---改良种用:	1.品名;2.是否改良种用
0106.2020	---食用	1.品名;2.用途(食用)
0106.2090	---其他	1.品名;2.用途
0106.31	--猛禽:	1.品名;2.是否改良种用
0106.32	--鹦形目(包括普通鹦鹉、长尾鹦鹉、金刚鹦鹉及美冠鹦鹉):	1.品名;2.是否改良种用
0106.33	--鸵鸟;鸸鹋:	1.品名;2.是否改良种用
0106.3910	---改良种用	1.品名;2.是否改良种用
0106.392	---食用:	1.品名;2.用途(食用)
0106.3990	---其他	1.品名
0106.4	-昆虫:	1.品名;2.是否改良种用
0106.9	-其他:	1.品名;2.是否改良种用
01.01	马、驴、骡:	1.品名;2.是否改良种用;3.品种
01.02	牛:	1.品名;2.是否改良种用
01.03	猪:	
0103.1000	-改良种用	1.品名;2.是否改良种用
0103.9	-其他:	1.品名;2.个体重量
01.04	绵羊、山羊:	
0104.1010	---改良种用	1.品名;2.是否改良种用。例:改良种用绵羊
0104.1090	---其他	1.品名;2.是否改良种用。例:活绵羊
0104.2010	---改良种用	1.品名;2.是否改良种用。例:改良种用山羊
0104.2090	---其他	1.品名;2.是否改良种用。例:活山羊
01.05	家禽,即鸡、鸭、鹅、火鸡及珍珠鸡:	1.品名;2.是否改良种用;3.个体重量。注:不包括其他活禽(如鹧鸪、野鸡、鸽、野鸭、大雁)(税目01.06)
01.06	其他活动物:	
0106.1	-哺乳动物:	1.品名;2.是否改良种用
0106.201	---改良种用:	1.品名;2.是否改良种用
0106.2020	---食用	1.品名;2.用途(食用)
0106.2090	---其他	1.品名
0106.31	--猛禽:	1.品名;2.是否改良种用
0106.32	--鹦形目(包括普通鹦鹉、长尾鹦鹉、金刚鹦鹉及美冠鹦鹉):	1.品名;2.是否改良种用
0106.33	--鸵鸟;鸸鹋:	1.品名;2.是否改良种用
0106.3910	---改良种用	1.品名;2.是否改良种用
0106.392	---食用:	1.品名;2.用途(食用)
0106.3990	---其他	1.品名
0106.4	-昆虫:	1.品名;2.是否改良种用
0106.9	-其他:	1.品名;2.是否改良种用

第二章　肉及食用杂碎

【注解】

1、本章中的“鲜的”包括运输途中用盐临时保藏的肉及杂碎；“冷的”即产品温度一般降至0℃左右，但未冻结的；“冻的”即冷却到产品的冰点以下，使产品全部冻结的。

2. 归入本章的杂碎及肉或杂碎的细粉、粗粉，应报明用途（食用）。

税则号列	商品描述	规范申报要素 / 价格申报要素 / 其他申报要素 / 举例说明
02.01	鲜、冷牛肉：	1.品名；2.制作或保存方法（鲜、冷）；3.加工方法（整头及半头、带骨或去骨等）；4.牛肉部位（如眼肉、腱子肉等）；5.包装规格
02.02	冻牛肉：	1.品名；2.制作或保存方法（冻）；3.加工方法（整头及半头、带骨或去骨等）；4.牛肉部位（如眼肉、腱子肉等）；5.包装规格
02.03	鲜、冷、冻猪肉：	1.品名；2.制作或保存方法（鲜、冷、冻）；3.加工方法（整头及半头、带骨或去骨等）；4.包装规格
02.04	鲜、冷、冻绵羊肉或山羊肉：	1.品名；2.制作或保存方法（鲜、冷、冻）；3.加工方法（整头及半头、带骨或去骨等）；
02.05	鲜、冷、冻马、驴、骡肉：	1.品名；2.制作或保存方法（鲜、冷、冻）；
02.06	鲜、冷、冻牛、猪、绵羊、山羊、马、驴、骡的食用杂碎：	1.品名；2.制作或保存方法（鲜、冷、冻）；3.种类（舌、肝、心管、板筋等）；4.包装规格
02.07	税目01.05所列家禽的鲜、冷、冻肉及食用杂碎：	
0207.1100	--整只，鲜或冷的	1.品名；2.制作或保存方法（鲜、冷）；3.加工方法（整只、带骨或去骨等）；4.厂号（名称或号码，饲养场或加工厂）；5.品牌
0207.1200	--整只，冻的	1.品名；2.制作或保存方法（冻）；3.加工方法（整只、带骨或去骨等）；4.厂号（名称或号码，饲养场或加工厂）；5.品牌
0207.13	--块及杂碎，鲜或冷的：	1.品名；2.制作或保存方法（鲜、冷）；3.加工方法（整只、带骨或去骨等）；4.厂号（名称或号码，饲养场或加工厂）；5.品牌
0207.141	---块：	1.品名；2.制作或保存方法（冻）；3.加工方法（整只、带骨或去骨等）；4.厂号（名称或号码，饲养场或加工厂）；5.品牌
0207.1421	----翼（不包括翼尖）	1.品名；2.制作或保存方法（冻）；3.加工方法（整只、带骨或去骨等）；4.厂号（名称或号码，饲养场或加工厂）；5.品牌
0207.1422	----鸡爪	1.品名；2.制作或保存方法（冻）；3.加工方法（整只、带骨或去骨等）；4.厂号（名称或号码，饲养场或加工厂）；5.品牌；6.规格（个体重量）
0207.1429	----其他	1.品名；2.制作或保存方法（冻）；3.加工方法（整只、带骨或去骨等）；4.种类（心、肝等）；5.厂号（名称或号码，饲养场或加工厂）；6.品牌
0207.2400	--整只，鲜或冷的	1.品名；2.制作或保存方法（鲜、冷）；3.加工方法（整只、带骨或去骨等）
0207.2500	--整只，冻的	1.品名；2.制作或保存方法（冻）；3.加工方法（整只、带骨或去骨等）
0207.2600	--块及杂碎，鲜或冷的	1.品名；2.制作或保存方法（鲜、冷）；3.加工方法（整只、带骨或去骨等）；4.杂碎请列明具体种类
0207.2700	--块及杂碎，冻的	1.品名；2.制作或保存方法（冻）；3.加工方法（整只、带骨或去骨等）；4.杂碎请列明具体种类
0207.4100	--整只，鲜或冷的	1.品名；2.制作或保存方法（鲜、冷）；3.加工方法（整只）
0207.4200	--整只，冻的	1.品名；2.制作或保存方法（冻）；3.加工方法（整只）
0207.4300	--肥肝，鲜或冷的	1.品名；2.制作或保存方法（鲜、冷）
0207.4400	--其他，鲜或冷的	1.品名；2.制作或保存方法（鲜、冷）；3.加工方法（带骨或去骨等）；4.杂碎请列明具体种类
0207.4500	--其他，冻的	1.品名；2.制作或保存方法（冻）；3.加工方法（带骨或去骨等）；4.杂碎请列明具体种类
0207.5100	--整只，鲜或冷的	1.品名；2.制作或保存方法（鲜、冷）；3.加工方法（整只）
0207.5200	--整只，冻的	1.品名；2.制作或保存方法（冻）；3.加工方法（整只）
0207.5300	--肥肝，鲜或冷的	1.品名；2.制作或保存方法（鲜、冷）
0207.5400	--其他，鲜或冷的	1.品名；2.制作或保存方法（鲜、冷）；3.加工方法（带骨或去骨等）；4.杂碎请列明具体种类
0207.5500	--其他，冻的	1.品名；2.制作或保存方法（冻）；3.加工方法（带骨或去骨等）；4.杂碎请列明具体种类
0207.6000	-珍珠鸡	1.品名；2.制作或保存方法（鲜、冷、冻）；3.加工方法（整只、带骨或去骨等）；4.杂碎请列明具体种类
02.08	其他鲜、冷、冻肉及食用杂碎：	
0208.1010	---鲜、冷兔肉，兔头除外	1.品名；2.制作或保存方法（鲜、冷）；3.包装规格

税则号列	商 品 描 述	规范申报要素 / 价格申报要素 / 其他申报要素 / 举例说明
0208.1020	---冻兔肉,兔头除外	1.品名;2.制作或保存方法(冻);3.包装规格
0208.1090	---其他	1.品名;2.制作或保存方法(鲜、冷、冻);3.杂碎请列明具体种类及用途;4.包装规格
0208.3000	-灵长目的	1.品名;2.制作或保存方法(鲜、冷、冻);3.杂碎请列明具体种类及用途;4.包装规格
0208.4000	-鲸、海豚及鼠海豚(鲸目哺乳动物)的;海牛及儒艮(海牛目哺乳动物)的;海豹、海 狮及海象(鳍足亚目哺乳动物)的	1.品名;2.制作或保存方法(鲜、冷、冻);3.杂碎请列明具体种类及用途;4.包装规格
0208.5000	-爬行动物(包括蛇及龟鳖)的	1.品名;2.制作或保存方法(鲜、冷、冻);3.杂碎请列明具体种类及用途;4.包装规格
0208.6000	-骆驼及其他骆驼科动物的	1.品名;2.制作或保存方法(鲜、冷、冻);3.杂碎请列明具体种类及用途;4.包装规格
0208.9	-其他:	1.品名;2.制作或保存方法(鲜、冷、冻);3.杂碎请列明具体种类及用途;4.包装规格
02.09	未炼制或用其他方法提取的不带瘦肉的肥猪肉、猪脂肪及家禽脂肪,鲜、冷、冻、干、熏、盐腌或盐渍的:	1.品名;2.制作或保存方法(未炼制、未提取脂肪、干、熏、盐腌、盐渍等)。注:不包括经炼制或用其他方法提取的脂肪(税目15.01);不包括海生哺乳动物的脂肪(第十五章)
02.10	肉及食用杂碎,干、熏、盐腌 或盐渍的;可供食用的肉或杂碎的细粉、粗粉:	
0210.1	-猪肉:	1.品名;2.制作或保存方法(带骨、腿肉、腹肉、干、熏、盐腌、盐渍等)。注:不包括未炼制或用其他方法提取的不带瘦肉的肥猪肉、猪脂肪或家禽脂肪(税目02.09);不包括不适合供人食用的肉或杂碎的粗粉或细粉(税目23.01)
0210.2000	-牛肉	1.品名;2.制作或保存方法(干、熏、盐腌、盐渍等)。注:不包括未炼制或用其他方法提取的不带瘦肉的肥猪肉、猪脂肪或家禽脂肪(税目02.09);不包括不适合供人食用的肉或杂碎的粗粉或细粉(税目23.01)
0210.9	-其他,包括可供食用的肉或杂碎的细粉、粗粉:	1.品名;2.用途;3.制作或保存方法(干、熏、盐腌、盐渍等);4.杂碎请列明具体种类。注:不包括未炼制或用其他方法提取的不带瘦肉的肥猪肉、猪脂肪或家禽脂肪(税目02.09);不包括不适合供人食用的肉或杂碎的粗粉或细粉(税目23.01)

第三章 鱼、甲壳动物、软体动物及其他水生无脊椎动物

【注解】

1、本章所称“冷”指产品的温度一般降至0℃左右,但产品尚未冻结的;“冻”指温度降至产品的冰点以下,使产品全部冻结的;“观赏鱼”指因其色彩或形态特殊而通常养于水族箱中以供观赏的活鱼;“鱼片”指顺鱼脊骨平切的长条肉片。

2、归入本章的细粉、粗粉、团粒应报明用途。

税则号列	商 品 描 述	规范申报要素 / 价格申报要素 / 其他申报要素 / 举例说明
03.01	活鱼:	
0301.1	-观赏鱼:	1.品名;2.用途(观赏用);3.状态(活);4.拉丁名称
0301.9110	---鱼苗	1.品名;2.状态(活);3.是否为鱼苗;4.拉丁名称
0301.9190	---其他	1.品名;2.状态(活);3.拉丁名称
0301.9210	---鱼苗	1.品名;2.状态(活);3.是否为鱼苗;4.拉丁名称
0301.9290	---其他	1.品名;2.状态(活);3.拉丁名称
0301.9310	---鱼苗	1.品名;2.状态(活);3.是否为鱼苗;4.拉丁名称
0301.9390	---其他	1.品名;2.状态(活);3.拉丁名称
0301.9410	---鱼苗	1.品名;2.状态(活);3.是否为鱼苗;4.拉丁名称
0301.949	---其他:	1.品名;2.状态(活);3.拉丁名称
0301.9510	---鱼苗	1.品名;2.状态(活);3.是否为鱼苗;4.拉丁名称
0301.9590	---其他	1.品名;2.状态(活);3.拉丁名称
0301.991	---鱼苗:	1.品名;2.状态(活);3.是否为鱼苗;4.拉丁名称
0301.999	---其他:	1.品名;2.状态(活);3.拉丁名称
03.02	鲜、冷鱼,但品目03.04的鱼片及其他鱼肉除外:	

税则号列	商品描述	规范申报要素 / 价格申报要素 / 其他申报要素 / 举例说明
0302.1	-鲑科鱼,但鱼肝及鱼卵除外:	1.品名;2.制作或保存方法(鲜、冷);3.拉丁名称;4.个体重量[如1000～2000克/条(块)等]。注:不包括鱼片及其他鱼肉(税目03.04)
0302.2	-比目鱼(鲽科、鲆科、舌鳎科、鳎科、菱鲆科、刺鲆科),但鱼肝及鱼卵除外:	1.品名;2.制作或保存方法(鲜、冷);3.拉丁名称;4.个体重量[如1000～2000克/条(块)等]。注:不包括鱼片及其他鱼肉(税目03.04)
0302.3	-金枪鱼(金枪鱼属)、鲣鱼或狐鲣(鲣),但鱼肝及鱼卵除外:	1.品名;2.制作或保存方法(鲜、冷);3.拉丁名称;4.个体重量[如1000～2000克/条(块)等]。注:不包括鱼片及其他鱼肉(税目03.04)
0302.4	-鲱鱼(大西洋鲱鱼、太平洋鲱鱼)、鳀鱼(鳀属)、沙丁鱼(沙丁鱼、沙瑙鱼属)、小沙丁鱼属、黍鲱或西鲱、鲭鱼〔大西洋鲭、澳洲鲭(鲐)、日本鲭(鲐)〕、对称竹荚鱼、新西兰竹荚鱼及竹荚鱼(竹荚鱼属)、军曹鱼及剑鱼,但鱼肝及鱼卵除外:	1.品名;2.制作或保存方法(鲜、冷);3.拉丁名称;4.个体重量[如1000～2000克/条(块)等]。注:不包括鱼片及其他鱼肉(税目03.04)
0302.5	-犀鳕科、多丝真鳕科、鳕科、长尾鳕科、黑鳕科、无须鳕科、深海鳕科及南极鳕科鱼,但鱼肝及鱼卵除外:	1.品名;2.制作或保存方法(鲜、冷);3.拉丁名称;4.个体重量[如1000～2000克/条(块)等]。注:不包括鱼片及其他鱼肉(税目03.04)
0302.7	-罗非鱼(口孵非鲫属)、鲶鱼(鲶属、鲶属、胡鲶属、真鮰属)、鲤科鱼(西鲤、黑鲫、草鱼、鲢属、鲮属、青鱼)、鳗鱼(鳗鲡属)、尼罗河鲈鱼(尼罗尖吻鲈)及黑鱼(鳢属),但鱼肝及鱼卵除外:	1.品名;2.制作或保存方法(鲜、冷);3.拉丁名称;4.个体重量[如1000～2000克/条(块)等]。注:不包括鱼片及其他鱼肉(税目03.04)
0302.8	-其他鱼,但鱼肝及鱼卵除外:	1.品名;2.制作或保存方法(鲜、冷);3.拉丁名称;4.个体重量[如1000～2000克/条(块)等]。注:不包括鱼片及其他鱼肉(税目03.04)
0302.9000	-鱼肝及鱼卵	1.品名;2.制作或保存方法(鲜、冷);3.拉丁名称。注:不包括鱼片及其他鱼肉(税目03.04)
03.03	冻鱼,但税目03.04的鱼片及其他鱼肉除外:	
0303.1	-鲑科鱼,但鱼肝及鱼卵除外:	1.品名;2.制作或保存方法(冻);3.拉丁名称;4.个体重量[如1000～2000克/条(块)等]。注:不包括鱼片及其他鱼肉(税目03.04)
0303.2	-罗非鱼(口孵非鲫属)、鲶鱼(鲶属、鲶属、胡鲶属、真鮰属)、鲤科鱼(西鲤、黑鲫、草鱼、鲢属、鲮属、青鱼)、鳗鱼(鳗鲡属)、尼罗河鲈鱼(尼罗尖吻鲈)及黑鱼(鳢属),但鱼肝及鱼卵除外:	1.品名;2.制作或保存方法(冻);3.拉丁名称;4.个体重量[如1000～2000克/条(块)等]。注:不包括鱼片及其他鱼肉(税目03.04)
0303.3	-比目鱼(鲽科、鲆科、舌鳎科、鳎科、菱鲆科、刺鲆科),但鱼肝及鱼卵除外:	1.品名;2.制作或保存方法(冻);3.拉丁名称;4.个体重量[如1000～2000克/条(块)等]。注:不包括鱼片及其他鱼肉(税目03.04)
0303.4	-金枪鱼(金枪鱼属)、鲣鱼或狐鲣(鲣),但鱼肝及鱼卵除外:	1.品名;2.制作或保存方法(冻);3.拉丁名称;4.个体重量[如1000～2000克/条(块)等]。注:不包括鱼片及其他鱼肉(税目03.04)
0303.5	-鲱鱼(大西洋鲱鱼、太平洋鲱鱼)、沙丁鱼(沙丁鱼、沙瑙鱼属)、小沙丁鱼属、黍鲱或西鲱、鲭鱼〔大西洋鲭、澳洲鲭(鲐)、日本鲭(鲐)〕、对称竹荚鱼、新西兰竹荚鱼及竹荚鱼(竹荚鱼属)、军曹鱼及剑鱼,但鱼肝及鱼卵除外:	1.品名;2.制作或保存方法(冻);3.拉丁名称;4.个体重量[如1000～2000克/条(块)等]。注:不包括鱼片及其他鱼肉(税目03.04)
0303.6	-犀鳕科、多丝真鳕科、鳕科、长尾鳕科、黑鳕科、无须鳕科、深海鳕科及南极鳕科鱼,但鱼肝及鱼卵除外:	1.品名;2.制作或保存方法(冻);3.拉丁名称;4.个体重量[如1000～2000克/条(块)等]。注:不包括鱼片及其他鱼肉(税目03.04)
0303.8	-其他鱼,但鱼肝及鱼卵除外:	1.品名;2.制作或保存方法(冻);3.拉丁名称;4.个体重量[如1000～2000克/条(块)等]。注:不包括鱼片及其他鱼肉(税目03.04)
0303.9000	-鱼肝及鱼卵	1.品名;2.制作或保存方法(冻);3.拉丁名称。注:不包括鱼片及其他鱼肉(税目03.04)
03.04	鲜、冷、冻鱼片及其他鱼肉(不论是否绞碎):	

税则号列	商品描述	规范申报要素 / 价格申报要素 / 其他申报要素 / 举例说明
0304.3	-鲜或冷的罗非鱼(口孵非鲫属)、鲶鱼(鲶属、鲶属、胡鲶属、真鮰属)、鲤科鱼(西鲤、黑鲫、草鱼、鲢属、鲮属、青鱼)、鳗鱼(鳗鲡属)、尼罗河鲈鱼(尼罗尖吻鲈)及黑鱼(鳢属)的鱼片:	1.品名;2.制作或保存方法(鲜、冷);3.拉丁名称;4.规格[克重/片(块)等]
0304.4	-鲜或冷的其他鱼片:	1.品名;2.制作或保存方法(鲜、冷);3.拉丁名称;4.规格[克重/片(块)等]
0304.5	-其他,鲜或冷的:	1.品名;2.制作或保存方法(鲜、冷);3.拉丁名称;4.规格[克重/片(块)等]
0304.6100	--罗非鱼(口孵非鲫属)	1.品名;2.制作或保存方法(冻);3.拉丁名称;4.规格[克重/片(块)等]
0304.621	---叉尾鮰鱼(真鮰属):	1.品名;2.制作或保存方法(冻);3.拉丁名称;4.规格[克重/片(块)等]
0304.6290	---其他	1.品名;2.制作或保存方法(冻);3.拉丁名称;4.规格[克重/片(块)等];5.是否带头、脏、皮、刺、鳞、鳍
0304.6300	--尼罗河鲈鱼(尼罗尖吻鲈)	1.品名;2.制作或保存方法(冻);3.拉丁名称;4.规格[克重/片(块)等];5.是否带头、脏、皮、刺、鳞、鳍
0304.6900	--其他	1.品名;2.制作或保存方法(冻);3.拉丁名称;4.规格[克重/片(块)等];5.是否带头、脏、皮、刺、鳞、鳍
0304.7	-冻的犀鳕科、多丝真鳕科、鳕科、长尾鳕科、黑鳕科、无须鳕科、深海鳕科及南极鳕科鱼的鱼片:	1.品名;2.制作或保存方法(冻);3.拉丁名称;4.规格[克重/片(块)等];5.是否带头、脏、皮、刺、鳞、鳍
0304.8100	--大麻哈鱼[红大麻哈鱼、细磷大麻哈鱼、大麻哈鱼(种)、大鳞大麻哈鱼、银大麻哈鱼、马苏大麻哈鱼、玫瑰大麻哈鱼]、大西洋鲑鱼及多瑙哲罗鱼	1.品名;2.制作或保存方法(冻);3.拉丁名称;4.规格[克重/片(块)等];5.是否带头、脏、皮、刺、鳞、鳍
0304.8200	--鳟鱼(河鳟、虹鳟、克拉克大麻哈鱼、阿瓜大麻哈鱼、吉雨大麻哈鱼、亚利桑那大麻哈鱼、金腹大麻哈鱼)	1.品名;2.制作或保存方法(冻);3.拉丁名称;4.规格[克重/片(块)等];5.是否带头、脏、皮、刺、鳞、鳍
0304.8300	--比目鱼(鲽科、鲆科、舌鳎科、鳎科、菱鲆科、刺鲆科)	1.品名;2.制作或保存方法(冻);3.拉丁名称;4.规格[克重/片(块)等];5.是否带头、脏、皮、刺、鳞、鳍
0304.8400	--剑鱼	1.品名;2.制作或保存方法(冻);3.拉丁名称;4.规格[克重/片(块)等]
0304.8500	--南极犬牙鱼(南极犬牙鱼属)	1.品名;2.制作或保存方法(冻);3.拉丁名称;4.规格[克重/片(块)等]
0304.8600	--鲱鱼(大西洋鲱鱼、太平洋鲱鱼)	1.品名;2.制作或保存方法(冻);3.拉丁名称;4.规格[克重/片(块)等];5.是否带头、脏、皮、刺、鳞、鳍
0304.8700	--金枪鱼(金枪鱼属)、鲣鱼或狐鲣(鲣)	1.品名;2.制作或保存方法(冻);3.拉丁名称;4.规格[克重/片(块)等];5.是否带头、脏、皮、刺、鳞、鳍
0304.8900	--其他	1.品名;2.制作或保存方法(冻);3.拉丁名称;4.规格[克重/片(块)等];5.是否带头、脏、皮、刺、鳞、鳍
0304.9	-其他,冻的:	1.品名;2.制作或保存方法(冻);3.拉丁名称;4.规格[克重/片(块)等]
03.05	干、盐腌或盐渍的鱼;熏鱼,不论在熏制前或熏制过程中是否烹煮;适合供人食用的鱼的细粉、粗粉及团粒:	
0305.1000	-适合供人食用的鱼的细粉、粗粉及团粒	1.品名;2.用途;3.拉丁名称
0305.2000	-干、熏、盐腌或盐渍的鱼肝及鱼卵	1.品名;2.制作或保存方法(干、熏、盐腌、盐渍);3.拉丁名称
0305.3	-干、盐腌或盐渍的鱼片,但熏制的除外:	1.品名;2.制作或保存方法(干、盐腌、盐渍);3.拉丁名称
0305.4	-熏鱼,包括鱼片,但食用杂碎除外:	1.品名;2.制作或保存方法(熏);3.拉丁名称
0305.5100	-干鱼(不包括食用杂碎),不论是否盐腌,但熏制的除外:	1.品名;2.制作或保存方法(干);3.拉丁名称
0305.59	--其他	1.品名;2.制作或保存方法(干);3.拉丁名称
0305.6	-盐腌及盐渍的鱼(不包括食用杂碎),但干或熏制的除外:	1.品名;2.制作或保存方法(盐腌、盐渍);3.拉丁名称
0305.7	-鱼鳍、鱼头、鱼尾、鱼鳔及其他可食用杂碎:	1.品名;2.用途;3.拉丁名称

税则号列	商品描述	规范申报要素 / 价格申报要素 / 其他申报要素 / 举例说明
03.06	带壳或去壳的甲壳动物,活、鲜、冷、冻、干、盐腌或盐渍的;熏制的带壳或去壳甲壳动物,不论在熏制前或熏制过程中是否烹煮;蒸过或用水煮过的带壳甲壳动物,不论是否冷、冻、干、盐腌或盐渍的;适合供人食用的甲壳动物的细粉、粗粉及团粒:	
0306.1100	--大螯虾及小龙虾	1.品名;2.制作或保存方法(冻);3.状态(带壳、去壳);4.拉丁名称;5.个体重量;6.包装规格
0306.1200	--龙虾	1.品名;2.制作或保存方法(冻);3.状态(带壳、去壳);4.拉丁名称;5.个体重量;6.包装规格
0306.14	--蟹:	1.品名;2.制作或保存方法(冻);3.状态(带壳、去壳);4.拉丁名称;5.个体重量;6.包装规格
0306.1500	--挪威海螯虾	1.品名;2.制作或保存方法(冻);3.状态(带壳、去壳);4.拉丁名称;5.个体重量;6.包装规格
0306.16	--冷水小虾及对虾(长额虾属、褐虾):	1.品名;2.制作或保存方法(冷水);3.状态(带壳、去壳);4.拉丁名称;5.规格(如41~50个/磅);6.包装规格
0306.17	--其他小虾及对虾:	1.品名;2.制作或保存方法(冻);3.状态(带壳、去壳);4.拉丁名称;5.规格(如41~50个/磅);6.包装规格
0306.19	--其他,包括适合供人食用的甲壳动物的细粉、粗粉及团粒:	1.品名;2.制作或保存方法(冻)
0306.2110	---种苗	1.品名;2.是否为种苗;3.拉丁名称
0306.2190	---其他	1.品名;2.制作或保存方法(活、鲜、冷、干等);3.状态(带壳、去壳);4.拉丁名称;5.个体重量;6.包装规格
0306.2210	---种苗	1.品名;2.是否为种苗;3.拉丁名称
0306.2290	---其他	1.品名;2.制作或保存方法(活、鲜、冷、干等);3.状态(带壳、去壳);4.拉丁名称
0306.2410	---种苗	1.品名;2.是否为种苗;3.拉丁名称
0306.249	---其他:	1.品名;2.制作或保存方法(活、鲜、冷、干等);3.状态(带壳、去壳);4.拉丁名称;5.个体重量;6.包装规格
0306.2510	---种苗	1.品名;2.是否为种苗;3.拉丁名称
0306.2590	---其他	1.品名;2.制作或保存方法(活、鲜、冷、干等);3.状态(带壳、去壳);4.拉丁名称;5.个体重量;6.包装规格
0306.2610	---种苗	1.品名;2.是否为种苗;3.拉丁名称
0306.2620	---鲜、冷对虾	1.品名;2.制作或保存方法(活、鲜、冷、干等);3.状态(带壳、去壳);4.拉丁名称;5.个体重量;6.包装规格
0306.2690	---其他	1.品名;2.制作或保存方法(活、鲜、冷、干等);3.状态(带壳、去壳);4.拉丁名称;5.个体重量;6.包装规格
0306.2710	---种苗	1.品名;2.是否为种苗;3.拉丁名称
0306.2720	---鲜、冷对虾	1.品名;2.制作或保存方法(活、鲜、冷、干等);3.状态(带壳、去壳);4.拉丁名称;5.个体重量;6.包装规格
0306.2790	---其他	1.品名;2.制作或保存方法(活、鲜、冷、干等);3.拉丁名称;4.状态(是否全虾、去头、去肠线、去尾、去壳、裹面粉等);5.个体重量;6.包装规格
0306.2910	---种苗	1.品名;2.是否为种苗
0306.2990	---其他	1.品名;2.制作或保存方法(活、鲜、冷、干等)
03.07	带壳或去壳的软体动物,活、鲜冷、冻、干、盐腌或盐渍的;熏制的带壳或去壳软体动物,不论在熏制前或熏制过程中是否烹煮;适合供人食用的软体动物的细粉、粗粉及团粒:	
0307.1110	---种苗	1.品名;2.是否为种苗;3.拉丁名称
0307.1190	---其他	1.品名;2.制作或保存方法(活、鲜、冷);3.状态(带壳、去壳);4.拉丁名称;5.个体重量;6.包装规格
0307.1900	--其他	1.品名;2.制作或保存方法(干、盐腌、盐渍等);3.状态(带壳、去壳);4.拉丁名称;5.个体重量;6.包装规格
0307.2110	---种苗	1.品名;2.是否为种苗;3.拉丁名称
0307.2190	---其他	1.品名;2.制作或保存方法(活、鲜、冷);3.状态(带壳、去壳);4.拉丁名称;5.个体重量;6.包装规格
0307.2900	--其他	1.品名;2.制作或保存方法(干、盐腌、盐渍等);3.状态(带壳、去壳);4.拉丁名称;5.个体重量;6.包装规格

税则号列	商品描述	规范申报要素 / 价格申报要素 / 其他申报要素 / 举例说明
0307.3110	---种苗	1.品名;2.是否为种苗;3.拉丁名称
0307.3190	---其他	1.品名;2.制作或保存方法(活、鲜、冷);3.状态(带壳、去壳);4.拉丁名称;5.个体重量;6.包装规格
0307.3900	--其他	1.品名;2.制作或保存方法(干、盐腌、盐渍等);3.状态(带壳、去壳);4.拉丁名称;5.个体重量;6.包装规格
0307.4110	---种苗	1.品名;2.是否为种苗;3.拉丁名称
0307.4190	---其他	1.品名;2.制作或保存方法(活、鲜、冷);3.拉丁名称;4.个体重量;5.包装规格
0307.4900	--其他	1.品名;2.制作或保存方法(干、盐腌、盐渍等);3.拉丁名称;4.个体重量;5.包装规格
0307.5	--活、鲜及冷的	1.品名;2.制作或保存方法(活、鲜、冷);3.拉丁名称;4.个体重量;5.包装规格
0307.5900	--其他	1.品名;2.制作或保存方法(活、鲜、冷);3.拉丁名称;4.个体重量;5.包装规格
0307.6010	---种苗	1.品名;2.是否为种苗;3.拉丁名称
0307.6090	---其他	1.品名;2.制作或保存方法(活、鲜、冷、冻、干、盐腌、盐渍等);3.拉丁名称;4.个体重量;5.包装规格
0307.7110	---种苗	1.品名;2.是否为种苗;3.拉丁名称
0307.719	---其他:	1.品名;2.制作或保存方法(活、鲜、冷);3.拉丁名称
0307.79	--其他:	1.品名;2.制作或保存方法(活、鲜、冷);3.拉丁名称
0307.8110	---种苗	1.品名;2.是否为种苗;3.拉丁名称
0307.8190	---其他	1.品名;2.制作或保存方法(活、鲜、冷);3.拉丁名称
0307.8900	--其他	1.品名;2.制作或保存方法(冻、干、盐腌、盐渍等);3.拉丁名称
0307.9110	---种苗	1.品名;2.是否为种苗;3.拉丁名称
0307.9190	---其他:	1.品名;2.制作或保存方法(活、鲜、冷);3.拉丁名称
0307.9900	--其他	1.品名;2.制作或保存方法(冻、干、盐腌、盐渍等);3.拉丁名称
03.08	不属于甲壳动物及软体动物的水生无脊椎动物,活、鲜、冷、冻 干、盐腌或盐渍的;熏制的不属 于甲壳动物及软体动物的水生无脊椎动物,不论在熏制前或熏制 过程中是否烹煮;适合供人食用 的不属于甲壳动物及软体动物的水生无脊椎动物的细粉、粗粉及 团粒:	
0308.1110	---种苗	1.品名;2.种苗请注明个体长度、尾数/千克等
0308.1190	---其他	1.品名;2.制作或保存方法(活、鲜、冷)
0308.1900	--其他	1.品名;2.制作或保存方法(冻、干、盐腌、盐渍等);3.是否经水煮;4.包装规格
0308.2110	---种苗	1.品名;2.种苗请注明个体长度、尾数/千克等
0308.2190	---其他	1.品名;2.制作或保存方法(活、鲜、冷)
0308.2900	--其他	1.品名;2.制作或保存方法(冻、干、盐腌、盐渍等);3.包装规格
0308.3011	----种苗	1.品名;2.种苗请注明个体长度、尾数/千克等
0308.3019	----其他	1.品名;2.制作或保存方法(活、鲜、冷)
0308.3090	---其他	1.品名;2.制作或保存方法(冻、干、盐腌、盐渍等);3.包装规格
0308.9011	----种苗	1.品名;2.种苗请注明个体长度、尾数/千克等
0308.9012	----沙蚕,种苗除外	1.品名;2.制作或保存方法(活、鲜、冷)
0308.9019	----其他	1.品名;2.制作或保存方法(活、鲜、冷)
0308.9090	---其他	1.品名;2.制作或保存方法(冻、干、盐腌、盐渍等);3.包装规格

第四章 乳品;蛋品;天然蜂蜜;其他食用动物产品

税则号列	商品描述	规范申报要素 / 价格申报要素 / 其他申报要素 / 举例说明
04.01	未浓缩及未加糖或其他甜物质的乳及奶油:	1.品名;2.制作或保存方法(未浓缩及未加糖或其他甜物质);3.脂肪含量(按重量计);4.成分含量;5.包装规格(如1升/盒);6.品牌
04.02	浓缩、加糖或其他甜物质的乳 及奶油:	1.品名;2.制作或保存方法(浓缩及加糖或其他甜物质);3.外观(粉状、粒状等);4.脂肪含量(按重量计);5.成分含量;6.包装规格(如25千克/包);7.品牌

税则号列	商　品　描　述	规范申报要素 / 价格申报要素 / 其他申报要素 / 举例说明
04.03	酪乳、结块的乳及奶油、酸乳、酸乳酒及其他发酵或酸化的 乳和奶油,不论是否浓缩、加 糖、加其他甜物质、加香料、加水果、加坚果或加可可:	1.品名;2.制作或保存方法(发酵、酸化、浓缩、加糖及其他甜物质、香料等);3.成分含量;4.包装规格;5.品牌
04.04	乳清,不论是否浓缩、加糖或 其他甜物质;其他税目未列名 的含天然乳的产品,不论是否加糖或其他甜物质:	
0404.1000	-乳清及改性乳清,不论是否 浓缩、加糖或其他甜物质	1.品名;2.用途;3.制作或保存方法(浓缩、加糖及其他甜物质);4.成分含量;5.品牌。注:美女牌低蛋白乳清粉(饲料用)蛋白3%、乳糖80%、灰粉9%、脂肪0.2%、其他2.8%、水分5%
0404.9000	-其他	1.品名;2.成分含量。注:该税则子目仅指其他税目未列名的含天然乳的产品
04.05	黄油及其他从乳中提取的脂 和油,乳酱:	1.品名;2.成分含量;3.包装规格;4.品牌。注:安佳牌无盐黄油乳脂含量85%(25千克/箱)
04.06	乳酪及凝乳:	
0406.1000	-鲜乳酪(未 熟化或未 固 化 的),包括乳清乳酪;凝乳	1.品名;2.制作或保存方法(未熟化、未固化等);3.成分含量;4.包装规格;5.品牌
0406.2000	-各种磨碎或粉化的乳酪	1.品名;2.制作或保存方法(未熟化、未固化等);3.乳脂含量;4.包装规格;5.品牌
0406.3000	-经加工的乳酪,但磨碎或粉 化的除外	1.品名;2.制作或保存方法(未熟化、未固化等);3.成分含量;4.包装规格;5.品牌
0406.4000	-蓝纹乳酪和娄地青霉生产的 带有纹理的其他乳酪	1.品名;2.制作或保存方法(熟化、固化、磨碎或粉化等);3.成分含量;4.是否带蓝纹或娄地青霉生产的带有纹理;5.包装规格;6.品牌
0406.9000	-其他乳酪	1.品名;2.制作或保存方法(熟化、固化、磨碎或粉化等);3.成分含量;4.包装规格;5.品牌
04.07	带壳禽蛋,鲜、腌制或煮过的	
0407.1	-孵化用受精禽蛋:	1.品名;2.是否孵化用受精禽蛋
0407.2	-其他鲜蛋:	1.品名;2.制作或保存方法(鲜、带壳)
0407.9	-其他:	1.品名;2.制作或保存方法(鲜、带壳、腌制、煮过)
04.08	去壳禽蛋及蛋黄,鲜、干、冻 蒸过或水煮、制成型或用其他方法保藏的,不论是否加糖或 其他甜物质:	1.品名;2.制作或保存方法(鲜、冻、干、去壳、蒸、水煮、制成型等)
04.09	天然蜂蜜:	1.品名;2.来源(天然);3.品牌。注:不包括人造蜜及天然蜜和人造蜜的混合制品(税目17.02)
04.10	其他品目未列名的食用动物 产品:	
0410.0010	---燕窝	1.品名;2.用途(食用);3.品种(燕子的品种);4.外形(燕盏或燕碎,燕条等);5.含水量。注:不包括海龟蛋油(税目15.06);不包括液态或干制的动物血,不论是否可供食用(税目05.11或税目30.02)
0410.0041	----鲜蜂王浆	1.品名;2.制作或保存方法(鲜);3.品牌。注:不包括海龟蛋油(税目15.06);不包括液态或干制的动物血,不论是否可供食用(税目05.11或税目30.02)
0410.0042	----鲜蜂王浆粉	1.品名;2.制作或保存方法(鲜);3.外观(粉);4.品牌。注:不包括海龟蛋油(税目15.06);不包括液态或干制的动物血,不论是否可供食用(税目05.11或税目30.02)
0410.0043	----蜂花粉	1.品名;2.外观(粉);3.品牌。注:不包括海龟蛋油(税目15.06);不包括液态或干制的动物血,不论是否可供食用(税目05.11或税目30.02)
0410.0049	----其他	1.品名;2.品牌。注:不包括海龟蛋油(税目15.06);不包括液态或干制的动物血,不论是否可供食用(税目05.11或税目30.02)
0410.0090	---其他	1.品名;2.用途(食用)。注:不包括海龟蛋油(税目15.06);不包括液态或干制的动物血,不论是否可供食用(税目05.11或税目30.02)
04.01	未浓缩及未加糖或其他甜物质的乳及奶油:	1.品名;2.制作或保存方法(未浓缩及未加糖或其他甜物质);3.脂肪含量(按重量计);4.成分含量;5.包装规格(如1升/盒);6.品牌
04.02	浓缩、加糖或其他甜物质的乳 及奶油:	1.品名;2.制作或保存方法(浓缩及加糖或其他甜物质);3.外观(粉状、粒状等);4.脂肪含量(按重量计);5.成分含量;6.包装规格(如25千克/包);7.品牌

税则号列	商 品 描 述	规范申报要素 / 价格申报要素 / 其他申报要素 / 举例说明
04.03	酪乳、结块的乳及奶油、酸乳、酸乳酒及其他发酵或酸化的 乳和奶油,不论是否浓缩、加 糖、加其他甜物质、加香料、加水果、加坚果或加可可:	1. 品名;2. 制作或保存方法(发酵、酸化、浓缩、加糖及其他甜物质、香料等);3. 成分含量;4. 包装规格;5. 品牌
04.04	乳清,不论是否浓缩、加糖或 其他甜物质;其他税目未列名 的含天然乳的产品,不论是否加糖或其他甜物质:	
0404.1000	-乳清及改性乳清,不论是否 浓缩、加糖或其他甜物质	1. 品名;2. 用途;3. 制作或保存方法(浓缩、加糖及其他甜物质);4. 成分含量;5. 品牌。例:美女牌低蛋白乳清粉(饲料用)蛋白 3%、乳糖 80%、灰粉 9%、脂肪 0.2%、其他 2.8%、水分 5%
0404.9000	-其他	1. 品名;2. 成分含量。注:该税则子目仅指其他税目未列名的含天然乳的产品
04.05	黄油及其他从乳中提取的脂 和油,乳酱:	1. 品名;2. 成分含量;3. 包装规格;4. 品牌。例:安佳牌无盐黄油乳脂含量 85%(25 千克/箱)
04.06	乳酪及凝乳:	
0406.1000	-鲜乳酪(未 熟化或未 固 化 的),包括乳清乳酪;凝乳	1. 品名;2. 制作或保存方法(未熟化、未固化等);3. 成分含量;4. 品牌
0406.2000	-各种磨碎或粉化的乳酪	1. 品名;2. 制作或保存方法(未熟化、未固化等);3. 乳脂含量;4. 包装规格;5. 品牌
0406.3000	-经加工的乳酪,但磨碎或粉 化的除外	1. 品名;2. 制作或保存方法(未熟化、未固化等);3. 成分含量;4. 包装规格;5. 品牌
0406.4000	-蓝纹乳酪和娄地青霉生产的 带有纹理的其他乳酪	1. 品名;2. 制作或保存方法(熟化、固化、磨碎或粉化等);3. 成分含量;4. 是否带蓝纹或娄地青霉生产的带有纹理;5. 包装规格;6. 品牌
0406.9000	-其他乳酪	1. 品名;2. 制作或保存方法(熟化、固化、磨碎或粉化等);3. 成分含量;4. 包装规格;5. 品牌
04.07	带壳禽蛋,鲜、腌制或煮过的	
0407.1	-孵化用受精禽蛋:	1. 品名;2. 是否孵化用受精禽蛋
0407.2	-其他鲜蛋:	1. 品名;2. 制作或保存方法(鲜、带壳)
0407.9	-其他:	1. 品名;2. 制作或保存方法(鲜、带壳、腌制、煮过)
04.08	去壳禽蛋及蛋黄,鲜、干、冻 蒸过或水煮、制成型或用其他方法保藏的,不论是否加糖或 其他甜物质:	1. 品名;2. 制作或保存方法(鲜、冻、干、去壳、蒸、水煮、制成型等)
04.09	天然蜂蜜:	1. 品名;2. 来源(天然);3. 品牌。注:不包括人造蜜及天然蜜和人造蜜的混合制品(税目 17.02)
04.10	其他品目未列名的食用动物 产品:	
0410.0010	---燕窝	1. 品名;2. 用途(食用);3. 品种(燕子的品种);4. 外形(燕盏或燕碎,燕条等);5. 含水量。注:不包括海龟蛋油(税目 15.06);不包括液态或干制的动物血,不论是否可供食用(税目 05.11 或税目 30.02)
0410.0041	----鲜蜂王浆	1. 品名;2. 制作或保存方法(鲜);3. 品牌。注:不包括海龟蛋油(税目 15.06);不包括液态或干制的动物血,不论是否可供食用(税目 05.11 或税目 30.02)
0410.0042	----鲜蜂王浆粉	1. 品名;2. 制作或保存方法(鲜);3. 外观(粉);4. 品牌。注:不包括海龟蛋油(税目 15.06);不包括液态或干制的动物血,不论是否可供食用(税目 05.11 或税目 30.02)
0410.0043	----蜂花粉	1. 品名;2. 外观(粉);3. 品牌。注:不包括海龟蛋油(税目 15.06);不包括液态或干制的动物血,不论是否可供食用(税目 05.11 或税目 30.02)
0410.0049	----其他	1. 品名;2. 品牌。注:不包括海龟蛋油(税目 15.06);不包括液态或干制的动物血,不论是否可供食用(税目 05.11 或税目 30.02)
0410.0090	---其他	1. 品名;2. 用途(食用)。注:不包括海龟蛋油(税目 15.06);不包括液态或干制的动物血,不论是否可供食用(税目 05.11 或税目 30.02)

第五章　其他动物产品

【注解】

本章所称"填充用羽毛"是指家禽(特别是鹅或鸭)、鸽子、鹧鸪或类似禽类的羽毛,但粗大的翼毛或尾毛及分级时摒弃的粗大的羽毛除外;"羽绒",主要指鹅或鸭毛中最为细小、柔软的绒毛,它与羽毛的区别在于没有硬羽轴。

税则号列	商品描述	规范申报要素 / 价格申报要素 / 其他申报要素 / 举例说明
05.01	未经加工的人发,不论是否洗涤;废人发:	1.品名;2.是否经加工。注:不包括经过简单洗涤以外加工(如稀疏、染色、漂白、卷曲或为制作假发进行加工)的人发及已按发根和发梢整理的人发(税目67.03)
05.02	猪鬃、猪毛;獾毛及其他制刷用兽毛;上述鬃毛的废料:	
0502.1	-猪鬃、猪毛及其废料:	1.品名。注:不包括成束或成簇的鬃毛(税目96.03)
0502.9	-其他:	1.品名;2.用途(制刷用)。注:不包括成束或成簇的鬃毛(税目96.03)
05.04	整个或切块的动物(鱼除外)的肠、膀胱及胃,鲜、冷、冻干、熏、盐腌或盐渍的:	
0504.001	---肠衣:	1.品名;2.制作或保存方法(鲜、冷、冻、干、熏、盐腌、盐渍)
0504.0021	----冷、冻的鸡胗	1.品名;2.制作或保存方法(冷、冻);3.品牌
0504.0029	----其他	1.品名;2.制作或保存方法(鲜、冷、冻、干、熏、盐腌、盐渍)
0504.0090	----其他	1.品名;2.制作或保存方法(鲜、冷、冻、干、熏、盐腌、盐渍)
05.05	带有羽毛或羽绒的鸟皮及鸟体其他部分;羽毛及不完整羽毛(不论是否修边)、羽绒,仅经洗涤消毒或为了保藏而做过处理,但未经进一步加工;羽毛或不完整 羽毛的粉末及废料:	
0505.1000	-填充用羽毛	1.品名;2.用途;3.制作或保存方法(仅经洗涤、消毒或为了保藏而做过处理);4.绒份;5.羽毛长度
0505.9	-其他	1.品名;2.用途;3.制作或保存方法(仅经洗涤、消毒或为了保藏而做过处理)
05.06	骨及角柱,未经加工或经脱 脂、简单整理(但未切割成 形)、酸处理或脱胶;上述产 品的粉末及废料:	
0506.1000	-经酸处理的骨胶原及骨	1.品名;2.处理方法(未经加工或经脱脂等)
0506.9011	----含牛羊成分的	1.品名;2.成分;3.处理方法(未经加工或经脱脂等);4.外观(粉末)5.是否废料
0506.9019	----其他	1.品名;2.处理方法(未经加工或经脱脂等)
0506.9090	---其他	1.品名;2.处理方法(未经加工或经脱脂等);3.是否脱胶
05.07	兽牙、龟壳、鲸须、鲸须毛、角 鹿角、蹄、甲、爪及喙,未经加 工或仅简单整理但未切割成形;上述产品的粉末及废料:	1.品名;2.处理方法(未经加工或经脱脂等);3.是否为粉末及废料
05.08	珊瑚及类似品,未经加工或仅 简单整理但未经进一步加工;软体动物壳、甲壳动物壳、棘 皮动物壳、墨鱼骨,未经加工 或仅简单整理但未切割成形,上述壳、骨的粉末及废料:	1.品名;2.处理方法(未经加工或经脱脂等);3.是否为粉末及废料
05.10	龙涎香、海狸香、灵猫香及麝 香;斑蝥;胆汁,不论是否干制;供配制药用的腺体及其他动物产品,鲜、冷、冻或用其 他方法暂时保藏的:	1.品名;2.制作或保存方法(鲜、冷、冻、干或用其他方法暂时保藏)。注:不包括胆汁精及制成干片后用安瓿封装的蛇或蜂的毒液(税目30.01)
05.11	其他品目未列名的动物产品;不适合供人食用的第一章或第三章的死动物:	
0511.1000	-牛的精液	1.品名。注:不包括食用鱼卵及食用鱼肝(第三章);不包括虫胶片、原胶、梗胶及其他虫胶(税目13.01)
0511.9111	----受精鱼卵	1.品名。注:不包括食用鱼卵及食用鱼肝(第三章);不包括虫胶片、原胶、梗胶及其他虫胶(税目13.01)
0511.9119	----其他	1.品名;2.用途。注:不包括食用鱼卵及食用鱼肝(第三章);不包括虫胶片、原胶、梗胶及其他虫胶(税目13.01)
0511.9190	---其他	1.品名;2.用途。注:不包括食用鱼卵及食用鱼肝(第三章);不包括虫胶片、原胶、梗胶及其他虫胶(税目13.01)

税则号列	商 品 描 述	规范申报要素 / 价格申报要素 / 其他申报要素 / 举例说明
0511.9910	---动物精液(牛的精液除外)	1.品名。注:不包括食用鱼卵及食用鱼肝(第三章);不包括虫胶片、原胶、梗胶及其他虫胶(税目13.01)
0511.9920	---动物胚胎	1.品名。注:不包括食用鱼卵及食用鱼肝(第三章);不包括虫胶片、原胶、梗胶及其他虫胶(税目13.01)
0511.9930	---蚕种	1.品名。注:不包括食用鱼卵及食用鱼肝(第三章);不包括虫胶片、原胶、梗胶及其他虫胶(税目13.01)
0511.9940	---马毛及废马毛,不论是否 制成有或无衬垫的毛片	1.品名。注:不包括食用鱼卵及食用鱼肝(第三章);不包括虫胶片、原胶、梗胶及其他虫胶(税目13.01)
0511.9990	---其他	1.品名;2.用途。注:不包括食用鱼卵及食用鱼肝(第三章);不包括虫胶片、原胶、梗胶及其他虫胶(税目13.01)

第二类 植物产品

第六章 活树及其他活植物;鳞茎、根及类似品;插花及装饰用簇叶

【注解】

本章所称"树、灌木"包括具有木质梗的藤本植物(例如,葡萄、杂交草莓、悬钩子属植物、弥猴桃树)及其带根插枝。

税则号列	商 品 描 述	规范申报要素 / 价格申报要素 / 其他申报要素 / 举例说明
06.01	鳞茎、块茎、块根、球茎、根颈及根茎,休眠、生长或开花 的;菊苣植物及其根,但品目12.12 的根除外:	1.品名;2.状态(休眠、生长、开花);3.种类(球茎、块茎、鳞茎、块根等);4.是否种用。注:不包括第七章的某些鳞茎、块茎、块根、球茎、根茎及根颈(如洋葱、青葱、大蒜、马铃薯、洋蓟);不包括生姜(税目09.10)
06.02	其他活植物(包括其根)、插枝及接穗;蘑菇菌丝:	
0602.1000	-无根插枝及接穗	1.品名;2.栽培方法(无根插枝、接穗等)
0602.2010	---种用苗木	1.品名;2.是否种用
0602.2090	---其他	1.品名
0602.3010	---种用	1.品名;2.是否种用
0602.3090	---其他	1.品名
0602.4010	---种用	1.品名;2.是否种用
0602.4090	---其他	1.品名
0602.9010	---蘑菇菌丝	1.品名
0602.9091	----种用苗木	1.品名;2.是否种用
0602.9092	----兰花	1.品名
0602.9093	----菊花	1.品名
0602.9094	----百合	1.品名
0602.9095	----康乃馨	1.品名
0602.9099	----其他	1.品名
06.03	制花束或装饰用的插花及花 蕾,鲜、干、染色、漂白、浸 渍或用其他方法处理的:	1.品名;2.用途(制花束或装饰用);3.制作或保存方法(鲜、干、染色、漂白、浸渍等)。注:不包括主要用作香料、药料、杀虫、杀菌或类似用途的花、花瓣及花蕾,如果其报验时的状态已不适合制花束或作装饰用(税目12.11);不包括税目97.01的拼贴画及类似的装饰板
06.04	制花束或装饰用的不带花及 花蕾的植物枝、叶或其他部分、草、苔藓及地衣,鲜、干 染色、漂白、浸渍或用其他方 法处理的:	1.品名;2.用途(制花束或装饰用);3.制作或保存方法(鲜且不带花及花蕾、干、染色、漂白、浸渍等)。注:不包括主要用作香料、药料、杀虫、杀菌或类似用途的植物及其部分品(包括草、苔藓及地衣)或供编结用的植物及其部分品,如果其报验时的状态已不适合制花束或作装饰用(税目12.11或14.01);不包括税目97.01的拼贴画及类似的装饰板

第七章 食用蔬菜、根及块茎

【注解】

本章所称"冷藏",是指产品的温度一般已降至0℃左右,但未冻结。然而,某些产品,例如,马铃薯,当温度降至并维持在10℃时,也可视作"冷藏";"冷冻",是指产品已冷却到本身冰点以下并且已经全部冻结。

税则号列	商品描述	规范申报要素 / 价格申报要素 / 其他申报要素 / 举例说明
07.01	鲜或冷藏的马铃薯:	1.品名;2.制作或保存方法(鲜、冷);3.是否种用。注:种用马铃薯
07.02	鲜或冷藏的番茄:	1.品名;2.制作或保存方法(鲜、冷)。注:鲜番茄
07.03	鲜或冷藏的洋葱、青葱、大 蒜、韭葱及其他葱属蔬菜:	1.品名;2.制作或保存方法(鲜、冷)本税目仅包括葱属蔬菜。注:鲜蒜头
07.04	鲜或冷藏的卷心菜、菜花、球茎甘蓝、羽衣甘蓝及类似的食用芥菜类蔬菜:	1.品名;2.制作或保存方法(鲜、冷)。注:冷藏菜花
07.05	鲜或冷藏的莴苣及菊苣:	1.品名;2.制作或保存方法(鲜、冷)。注:不包括菊苣植物及菊苣根(税目06.01或12.12)
07.06	鲜或冷藏的胡萝卜、萝卜、色 拉甜菜根、婆罗门参、块根芹 小萝卜及类似的食用根茎:	1.品名;2.制作或保存方法(鲜、冷)。注:冷藏胡萝卜
07.07	鲜或冷藏的黄瓜及小黄瓜:	1.品名;2.制作或保存方法(鲜、冷)。注:鲜黄瓜
07.08	鲜或冷藏的豆类蔬菜,不论 是否脱荚:	1.品名;2.制作或保存方法(鲜、冷)。注:不包括大豆(税目12.01)
07.09	鲜或冷藏的其他蔬菜:	1.品名;2.制作或保存方法(鲜、冷)。注:不包括荸荠属植物的可食用球茎(税目07.14)
07.10	冷冻蔬菜(不论是否蒸煮):	
0710.1000	-马铃薯	1.品名;2.制作或保存方法(冻)。注:冷冻马铃薯
0710.2	-豆类蔬菜,不论是否脱荚:	1.品名;2.制作或保存方法(冻)。注:冷冻马铃薯
0710.3000	-菠菜	1.品名;2.制作或保存方法(冻)。注:冷冻马铃薯
0710.4000	-甜玉米	1.品名;2.制作或保存方法(冻)。注:冷冻马铃薯
0710.8	-其他蔬菜:	1.品名;2.制作或保存方法(冻)。注:冷冻马铃薯
0710.9000	-什锦蔬菜	1.品名;2.制作或保存方法(冻);3.种类。注:冷冻马铃薯
07.11	暂时保藏(例如,使用二氧 化硫气体、盐水、亚硫酸水 或其他防腐液)的蔬菜,但 不适于直接食用的:	1.品名;2.用途(不适于直接食用);3.制作或保存方法(用盐水、二氧化硫气体、亚硫酸水或其他防腐液)。注:盐水松茸(不适于直接食用)
07.12	干蔬菜,整个、切块、切片、破碎或制成粉状,但未经进 一步加工的:	1.品名;2.制作或保存方法(干制,包括脱水、蒸干或冻干)
07.13	脱荚的干豆,不论是否去皮 或分瓣:	
0713.1010	---种用	1.品名;2.制作或保存方法(干制且脱荚);3.是否种用
0713.1090	---其他	1.品名;2.制作或保存方法(干制且脱荚);3.品种(黄豌豆、青豌豆、白豌豆等)
0713.2	-鹰嘴豆:	1.品名;2.制作或保存方法(干制且脱荚);3.是否种用
0713.3	-豇豆属及菜豆属:	1.品名;2.制作或保存方法(干制且脱荚);3.是否种用
0713.4	-扁豆:	1.品名;2.制作或保存方法(干制且脱荚);3.是否种用
0713.5	-蚕豆:	1.品名;2.制作或保存方法(干制且脱荚);3.是否种用
0713.6	-木豆(木豆属):	1.品名;2.制作或保存方法(干制且脱荚);3.是否种用
0713.9	-其他:	1.品名;2.制作或保存方法(干制且脱荚);3.是否种用
07.14	鲜、冷、冻或干的木薯、竹 芋、兰科植物块茎、菊芋、甘薯及含有高淀粉或菊粉的类似根茎,不论是否切片或 制成团粒;西谷茎髓:	1.品名;2.制作或保存方法(鲜、冷、冻、干);3.是否种用。注:干木薯

第八章　食用水果及坚果;柑桔属水果或甜瓜的果皮

【注解】

本章所称“冷藏”,是指产品的温度一般降至0℃左右,但未冻结的。但是有些产品(例如,甜瓜及某些柑桔属果实),其温度降至并维持在10℃时,也可视作“冷藏”;所称“冷冻”,是指温度降至产品的冰点以下,产品已全部冻结。

税则号列	商品描述	规范申报要素 / 价格申报要素 / 其他申报要素 / 举例说明
08.01	鲜或干的椰子、巴西果及腰果,不论是否去壳或去皮:	
0801.1	-椰子:	1.品名;2.制作或保存方法[鲜、干、未去内壳(内果皮)、去壳];3.是否种用。注:不包括用于榨取椰子油而不适合供人食用的干椰肉(税目12.03)
0801.2	-巴西果:	1.品名;2.制作或保存方法[鲜、干、未去内壳(内果皮)、去壳]。注:不包括用于榨取椰子油而不适合供人食用的干椰肉(税目12.04)

税则号列	商 品 描 述	规范申报要素 / 价格申报要素 / 其他申报要素 / 举例说明
0801.3100	--未去壳	1.品名;2.制作或保存方法[鲜、干、未去内壳(内果皮)、去壳]。注:不包括用于榨取椰子油而不适合供人食用的干椰肉(税目12.04)
0801.3200	--去壳	1.品名;2.制作或保存方法[鲜、干、未去内壳(内果皮)、去壳]。注:不包括用于榨取椰子油而不适合供人食用的干椰肉(税目12.04)
08.02	鲜或干的其他坚果,不论是否 去壳或去皮:	1.品名;2.制作或保存方法(鲜、干、未去壳、去壳)。注:不包括花生(税目12.02);不包括焙炒的花生或花生酱(税目20.08);不包括核桃壳及杏仁壳(税目14.04)
0802.1	-巴旦杏:	1.品名;2.制作或保存方法(鲜、干、未去壳、去壳)。注:不包括花生(税目12.02);不包括焙炒的花生或花生酱(税目20.08);不包括核桃壳及杏仁壳(税目14.04)
0802.2	-榛子:	1.品名;2.制作或保存方法(鲜、干、未去壳、去壳);3.品种。注:不包括花生(税目12.02);不包括焙炒的花生或花生酱(税目20.08);不包括核桃壳及杏仁壳(税目14.04)
0802.3	-核桃:	1.品名;2.制作或保存方法(鲜、干、未去壳、去壳);3.品种。注:不包括花生(税目12.02);不包括焙炒的花生或花生酱(税目20.08);不包括核桃壳及杏仁壳(税目14.04)
0802.4	-栗子:	1.品名;2.制作或保存方法(鲜、干、未去壳、去壳)。注:不包括花生(税目12.02);不包括焙炒的花生或花生酱(税目20.08);不包括核桃壳及杏仁壳(税目14.04)
0802.5	-阿月浑子果(开心果):	1.品名;2.制作或保存方法(鲜、干、未去壳、去壳)。注:不包括花生(税目12.02);不包括焙炒的花生或花生酱(税目20.08);不包括核桃壳及杏仁壳(税目14.04)
0802.6	-马卡达姆坚果(夏威夷果)	1.品名;2.制作或保存方法(鲜、干、未去壳、去壳);3.是否种用;4.签约日期。注:不包括花生(税目12.02);不包括焙炒的花生或花生酱(税目20.08);不包括核桃壳及杏仁壳(税目14.04)
0802.7000	-可乐果(可乐果属)	1.品名;2.制作或保存方法(鲜、干、未去壳、去壳)。注:不包括花生(税目12.02);不包括焙炒的花生或花生酱(税目20.08);不包括核桃壳及杏仁壳(税目14.04)
0802.8000	-槟榔果	1.品名;2.制作或保存方法(鲜、干、未去壳、去壳)。注:不包括花生(税目12.02);不包括焙炒的花生或花生酱(税目20.08);不包括核桃壳及杏仁壳(税目14.04)
0802.9	-其他:	1.品名;2.制作或保存方法(鲜、干、未去壳、去壳)。注:不包括花生(税目12.02);不包括焙炒的花生或花生酱(税目20.08);不包括核桃壳及杏仁壳(税目14.04)
08.03	鲜或干的香蕉,包括芭蕉:	1.品名;2.制作或保存方法(鲜、干);3.干制方法(脱水、蒸干或冻干);4.种类(大香蕉、蕉仔、皇帝蕉等);5.等级(A级、B级、C级等);6.品牌
08.04	鲜或干的椰枣、无花果、菠萝 鳄梨、番石榴、芒果及山竹果	
0804.1000	-椰枣	1.品名;2.制作或保存方法(鲜、干);3.等级
0804.2000	-无花果	1.品名;2.制作或保存方法(鲜、干);3.等级
0804.3000	-菠萝	1.品名;2.制作或保存方法(鲜、干);3.种类(如青菠萝、金菠萝等);4.等级
0804.4000	-鳄梨	1.品名;2.制作或保存方法(鲜、干);3.等级
0804.5	-番石榴、芒果及山竹果:	1.品名;2.制作或保存方法(鲜、干);3.等级
08.05	鲜或干的柑橘属水果:	
0805.1000	-橙	1.品名;2.制作或保存方法(鲜、干);3.种类(脐橙、夏橙等);4.等级;5.品牌。注:不包括柑橘皮(税目08.14)
0805.2	-柑橘;杂交柑橘:	1.品名;2.制作或保存方法(鲜、干);3.等级。注:不包括柑橘皮(税目08.14)

税则号列	商品描述	规范申报要素 / 价格申报要素 / 其他申报要素 / 举例说明
0805.4000	-葡萄柚,包括柚	1.品名;2.制作或保存方法(鲜、干);3.等级。注:不包括柑橘皮(税目08.14)
0805.5000	-柠檬及酸橙	1.品名;2.制作或保存方法(鲜、干);3.等级;4.品牌。注:不包括柑橘皮(税目08.14)
0805.9000	-其他	1.品名;2.制作或保存方法(鲜、干);3.等级。注:不包括柑橘皮(税目08.14)
08.06	鲜或干的葡萄:	
0806.1000	-鲜的	1.品名;2.制作或保存方法(鲜);3.种类;4.等级;5.品牌
0806.2000	-干的	1.品名;2.制作或保存方法(干);3.等级;4.品牌
08.07	鲜的甜瓜(包括西瓜)及木瓜	
0807.1100	--西瓜	1.品名;2.制作或保存方法(鲜);3.等级;4.品牌
0807.19	--其他:	1.品名;2.制作或保存方法(鲜);3.等级
0807.2000	-木瓜	1.品名;2.制作或保存方法(鲜);3.等级;4.品牌
08.08	鲜的苹果、梨及榅桲:	
0808.1000	-苹果	1.品名;2.制作或保存方法(鲜);3.种类(蛇果、加纳果、青苹果、富士等);4.等级;5.品牌
0808.3	-梨:	1.品名;2.制作或保存方法(鲜);3.等级
0808.4000	-榅桲	1.品名;2.制作或保存方法(鲜);3.等级
08.09	鲜的杏、樱桃、桃(包括油桃) 梅及李:	1.品名;2.制作或保存方法(鲜);3.等级
08.10	其他鲜果:	
0810.1000	-草莓	1.品名;2.制作或保存方法(鲜);3.等级
0810.2000	-木莓、黑莓、桑椹及罗甘莓	1.品名;2.制作或保存方法(鲜);3.等级
0810.3000	-黑、白或红的穗醋栗(加仑子 及醋栗	1.品名;2.制作或保存方法(鲜);3.等级
0810.4000	-蔓越橘及越橘	1.品名;2.制作或保存方法(鲜);3.等级
0810.5000	-猕猴桃	1.品名;2.制作或保存方法(鲜);3.种类(金奇异果、青奇异果等);4.等级
0810.6000	-榴莲	1.品名;2.制作或保存方法(鲜);3.等级;4.品牌
0810.7000	-柿子	1.品名;2.制作或保存方法(鲜);3.等级
0810.9	-其他:	1.品名;2.制作或保存方法(鲜);3.等级
08.11	冷冻水果及坚果,不论是否蒸 煮、加糖或其他甜物质:	
0811.1000	-草莓	1.品名;2.制作或保存方法(冻)。注:冷冻未去壳栗子
0811.2000	-木莓、黑莓、桑椹、罗甘莓、黑 白或红的穗醋栗(加仑子)及醋栗	1.品名;2.制作或保存方法(冻)。注:冷冻未去壳栗子
0811.9010	---栗子,未去壳	1.品名;2.制作或保存方法(冻、未去壳)。注:冷冻未去壳栗子
0811.9090	---其他	1.品名;2.制作或保存方法(冻)。注:冷冻未去壳栗子
08.12	暂时保藏(例如,使用二氧化 硫气体、盐水、亚硫酸水或其 他防腐液)的水果及坚果,但 不适于直接食用的:	1.品名;2.用途(不适于直接食用);3.制作或保存方法(用盐水、二氧化硫气体、亚硫酸水或其他防腐液)。注:盐水保藏樱桃(不适于直接食用)
08.13	品目08.01至08.06以外的干 果;本章的什锦坚果或干果:	
0813.1000	-杏	1.品名;2.制作或保存方法(干)。注:本税目仅包括税目08.01至08.06以外的干果
0813.2000	-梅及李	1.品名;2.制作或保存方法(干)。注:本税目仅包括税目08.01至08.06以外的干果
0813.3000	-苹果	1.品名;2.制作或保存方法(干)。注:本税目仅包括税目08.01至08.06以外的干果
0813.4010	---龙眼干、肉	1.品名;2.制作或保存方法(干);3.等级。注:本税目仅包括税目08.01至08.06以外的干果
0813.4020	---柿饼	1.品名;2.制作或保存方法(干)。注:本税目仅包括税目08.01至08.06以外的干果
0813.4030	---红枣	1.品名;2.制作或保存方法(干)。注:本税目仅包括税目08.01至08.06以外的干果
0813.4040	---荔枝干	1.品名;2.制作或保存方法(干);3.加工程度(去壳、未去壳)。注:本税目仅包括税目08.01至08.06以外的干果
0813.4090	---其他	1.品名;2.制作或保存方法(干)。注:本税目仅包括税目08.01至08.06以外的干果
0813.5000	-本章的什锦坚果或干果	1.品名;2.制作或保存方法(干);3.种类。注:本税目仅包括税目08.01至08.06以外的干果

税则号列	商 品 描 述	规范申报要素 / 价格申报要素 / 其他申报要素 / 举例说明
08.14	柑橘属水果或甜瓜(包括西瓜 的果皮,鲜、冻、干或用盐水亚硫酸水或其他防腐液暂时保藏的:	1.品名;2.制作或保存方法(鲜、冻、干,用盐水、亚硫酸水或其他防腐液暂时保藏的)。注:不包括果皮粉(税目11.06);不包括蜜饯果皮(税目20.06)

第九章　咖啡、茶、马黛茶及调味香料

税则号列	商 品 描 述	规范申报要素 / 价格申报要素 / 其他申报要素 / 举例说明
09.01	咖啡,不论是否焙炒或浸除咖啡碱;咖啡豆荚及咖啡豆 皮;含咖啡的咖啡代用品:	
0901.1	-未焙炒的咖啡	1.品名;2.制作或保存方法(豆、粉等,未焙炒且未浸除咖啡碱)。注:不包括不含咖啡的焙炒咖啡代用品(税目21.01);不包括咖啡蜡(税目15.21);不包括咖啡碱,即咖啡中的生物碱(税目29.39)
0901.2	-已焙炒的咖啡	1.品名;2.制作或保存方法(豆、粉等,已焙炒且已浸除咖啡碱)。注:不包括不含咖啡的焙炒咖啡代用品(税目21.01);不包括咖啡蜡(税目15.21);不包括咖啡碱,即咖啡中的生物碱(税目29.39)
0901.9010	---咖啡豆荚及咖啡豆皮	1.品名;2.种类(咖啡豆荚或豆皮)。注:不包括不含咖啡的焙炒咖啡代用品(税目21.01);不包括咖啡蜡(税目15.21);不包括咖啡碱,即咖啡中的生物碱(税目29.39)
0901.9020	---含咖啡的咖啡代用品	1.品名;2.成分。注:不包括不含咖啡的焙炒咖啡代用品(税目21.01);不包括咖啡蜡(税目15.21);不包括咖啡碱,即咖啡中的生物碱(税目29.39)
09.02	茶,不论是否加香料:	1.品名;2.制作或保存方法(未发酵、半发酵、发酵);3.内包装每件净重;4.品牌
09.03	马黛茶:	1.品名
09.04	胡椒;辣椒干及辣椒粉:	1.品名;2.制作或保存方法(未磨、已磨、干、粉)
09.05	香子兰豆:	1.品名;2.加工方法(未磨、已磨)。注:不包括香草油树脂(人们有时误称为香草香膏或香草浸膏)(税目13.02);不包括香草糖(税目17.01或17.02);不包括香草醛(香草的香素)(税目29.12)
09.06	肉桂及肉桂花:	1.品名;2.加工方法(未磨、已磨)
09.07	丁香(母丁香、公丁香及丁 香梗):	1.品名;2.加工方法(未磨、已磨)。注:不包括丁香树皮及树叶(税目12.11)
09.08	肉豆蔻、肉豆蔻衣及豆蔻:	1.品名;2.加工方法(未磨、已磨)
09.09	子;杜松果:	1.品名;2.加工方法(未磨、已磨)。注:八角茴香
09.10	姜、番红花、姜黄、麝香草、月桂叶、咖喱及其他调味香料	
0910.1	-姜:	1.品名;2.加工方法(未磨、已磨)
0910.2000	-番红花	1.品名
0910.3000	-姜黄	1.品名
0910.9	-其他调味香料:	1.品名;2.成分含量

第十章　谷　　物

税则号列	商 品 描 述	规范申报要素 / 价格申报要素 / 其他申报要素 / 举例说明
10.01	小麦及混合麦:	1.品名;2.是否种用;3.是否硬粒;4.种类(白麦、红麦、冬麦、春麦)
10.02	黑麦:	1.品名;2.是否种用。注:不包括有麦角寄生的黑麦(税目12.11)
10.03	大麦:	1.品名;2.是否种用。注:不包括烘焙大麦(咖啡代用品)(税目21.01);不包括在烘焙过程中从发芽麦粒分出来的麦芽新芽及其他酿造废料(粮食、啤酒花等的渣滓)(税目23.03)
10.04	燕麦:	1.品名;2.是否种用。注:种用燕麦

税则号列	商品描述	规范申报要素 / 价格申报要素 / 其他申报要素 / 举例说明
10.05	玉米：	1.品名;2.是否种用。注:本税目所称“种用”,仅包括由本国主管部门认可作为播种用的玉米
10.06	稻谷、大米：	
1006.1011	----籼米	1.品名;2.种类(籼米);3.是否种用;4.米粒长度;5.包装规格
1006.1019	----其他	1.品名;2.种类(香米、巴吞米、白米、糯米等);3.是否种用;4.米粒长度;5.包装规格
1006.1091	----籼米	1.品名;2.种类(籼米)3.米粒长度;5.包装规格
1006.1099	----其他	1.品名;2.种类(巴吞米、白米、糯米等);3.米粒长度;5.包装规格
1006.2010	---籼米	1.品名;2.种类(籼米);3.制作或保存方法(糙米);4.米粒长度;5.包装规格
1006.2090	---其他	1.品名;2.种类(巴吞米、白米、糯米等);3.制作或保存方法(糙米);4.米粒长度;5.包装规格
1006.3010	---籼米	1.品名;2.种类(籼米);3.米粒长度;4.包装规格
1006.3090	---其他	1.品名;2.种类(巴吞米、白米、糯米等);3.米粒长度;4.包装规格
1006.4010	---籼米	1.品名;2.种类(籼米);3.包装规格
1006.4090	---其他	1.品名;2.种类(巴吞米、白米、糯米等);3.包装规格
10.07	食用高粱：	1.品名;2.用途(食用);3.是否种用;4.包装规格。注:不包括饲料高粱及草高粱(税目12.14)、甜高粱(税目12.12)、帚用高粱(税目14.03)
10.08	荞麦、谷子及加那利草子;其他谷物：	1.品名;2.是否种用;3.包装规格

第十一章　制粉工业产品;麦芽;淀粉;菊粉;面筋

税则号列	商品描述	规范申报要素 / 价格申报要素 / 其他申报要素 / 举例说明
11.01	小麦或混合麦的细粉：	1.品名;2.状态(细粉)。注:不包括掺有可可的细粉[按重量计全脱脂可可含量在40%及以上的(税目18.06),低于40%的(税目19.01)
11.02	其他谷物细粉,但小麦或混合麦的细粉除外：	1.品名;2.种类(玉米、籼米等);3.状态(细粉)。注:不包括掺有可可的细粉[按重量计全脱脂可可含量在40%及以上的(税目18.06),低于40%的(税目19.02)]
11.03	谷物的粗粒、粗粉及团粒：	1.品名;2.种类(小麦、玉米、燕麦等);3.状态(粗粒、粗粉、团粒等)
11.04	经其他加工的谷物(例如,去 壳、滚压、制片、制成粒状、切片或粗磨),但品目10.06的稻谷、大米除外;谷物胚芽整粒、滚压、制片或磨碎的：	
1104.1	-滚压或制片的谷物：	1.品名;2.种类(燕麦、大麦、小麦等);3.制作或保存方法(去壳、滚压、制片等)
1104.2	-经其他加工的谷物(例如,去 壳、制成粒状、切片或粗磨)	1.品名;2.种类(燕麦、大麦、小麦等);3.制作或保存方法(去壳、滚压、制片等)
1104.3000	-谷物胚芽,整粒、滚压、制片或磨碎的	1.品名;2.种类(燕麦、大麦、小麦等);3.制作或保存方法(去壳、滚压、制片等)。注:不包括谷物胚芽提取油类后的残渣(税目23.06)
11.05	马铃薯的细粉、粗粉、粉末、粉片、颗粒及团粒：	1.品名;2.状态(细粉、粗粉、粉末、粉片、颗粒及团粒)。注:不包括马铃薯淀粉(税目11.08);不包括仅简单干燥、脱水或蒸干但未进一步加工的马铃薯(税目07.12);不包括马铃薯淀粉制得的珍粉代用品(税目19.03)
11.06	用品目07.13的干豆或品目07.14的 西 谷 茎髓及植物根 茎、块茎制成的细粉、粗粉及粉末;用第八章的产品制成的 细粉、粗粉及粉末：	
1106.1000	-用品目07.13的干豆制成的	1.品名;2.种类(豌豆、鹰嘴豆等);3.状态(细粉、粗粉、粉末)。注:仅用税目07.13的干豆制成;不包括未脱脂大豆细粉(税目12.08);不包括以蔬菜细粉或粗粉为基料的汤料(不论液状、固体或粉状)(税目21.04)
1106.2000	-用品目07.14的西谷茎髓及 植物根茎、块茎制成的	1.品名;2.种类(豌豆、鹰嘴豆等);3.状态(细粉、粗粉、粉末)。注:仅用税目07.14所列产品制成

税则号列	商 品 描 述	规范申报要素 / 价格申报要素 / 其他申报要素 / 举例说明
1106.3000	-用第八章的产品制成的	1.品名;2.种类(豌豆、鹰嘴豆等);3.状态(细粉、粗粉、粉末)。注:仅用第八章的产品制成;不包括西谷茎髓(税目07.14);不包括名为珍粉的食品(税目19.03)
11.07	麦芽,不论是否焙制:	1.品名;2.制作或保存方法(未焙制、已焙制)。注:未焙制麦芽
11.08	淀粉;菊粉:	
1108.1100	--小麦淀粉	1.品名;2.种类(小麦淀粉)。注:不包括制成香粉及盥洗用品的淀粉(第三十三章);不包括以淀粉为基料的胶(税目35.05或35.06);不包括用淀粉制成的上光料或浆料(税目38.09);不包括分离淀粉所得的离析支链淀粉及离析直链淀粉(税目39.13)
1108.1200	--玉米淀粉	1.品名;2.种类(玉米淀粉)。注:不包括制成香粉及盥洗用品的淀粉(第三十三章);不包括以淀粉为基料的胶(税目35.05或35.06);不包括用淀粉制成的上光料或浆料(税目38.09);不包括分离淀粉所得的离析支链淀粉及离析直链淀粉(税目39.13)
1108.1300	--马铃薯淀粉	1.品名;2.种类(马铃薯淀粉)。注:不包括制成香粉及盥洗用品的淀粉(第三十三章);不包括以淀粉为基料的胶(税目35.05或35.06);不包括用淀粉制成的上光料或浆料(税目38.09);不包括分离淀粉所得的离析支链淀粉及离析直链淀粉(税目39.13)
1108.1400	--木薯淀粉	1.品名;2.种类(木薯淀粉)。注:不包括制成香粉及盥洗用品的淀粉(第三十三章);不包括以淀粉为基料的胶(税目35.05或35.06);不包括用淀粉制成的上光料或浆料(税目38.09);不包括分离淀粉所得的离析支链淀粉及离析直链淀粉(税目39.13)
1108.1900	--其他	1.品名;2.种类(大米淀粉、竹芋淀粉等)。注:不包括制成香粉及盥洗用品的淀粉(第三十三章);不包括以淀粉为基料的胶(税目35.05或35.06);不包括用淀粉制成的上光料或浆料(税目38.09);不包括分离淀粉所得的离析支链淀粉及离析直链淀粉(税目39.13)
1108.2000	-菊粉	1.品名。注:不包括制成香粉及盥洗用品的淀粉(第三十三章);不包括以淀粉为基料的胶(税目35.05或35.06);不包括用淀粉制成的上光料或浆料(税目38.09);不包括分离淀粉所得的离析支链淀粉及离析直链淀粉(税目39.13)
11.09	面筋,不论是否干制:	1.品名。注:不包括加有面筋的营养面粉(税目11.01);不包括做胶用或做纺织工业上光料或浆料用的面筋(税目35.06或38.09)

第十二章 含油子仁及果实;杂项子仁及果实;工业用或药用植物;稻草、秸秆及饲料

税则号列	商 品 描 述	规范申报要素 / 价格申报要素 / 其他申报要素 / 举例说明
12.01	大豆,不论是否破碎:	
1201.1000	-种用	1.品名;2.种类(黄大豆、黑大豆、青大豆等);3.是否种用。注:不包括作为咖啡代用品的烘焙大豆(税目21.01)
1201.9010	---黄大豆	1.品名;2.种类(黄大豆);3.蛋白含量;4.油含量;5.升贴水。注:不包括作为咖啡代用品的烘焙大豆(税目21.01)
1201.9020	---黑大豆	1.品名;2.种类(黑大豆)。注:不包括作为咖啡代用品的烘焙大豆(税目21.01)
1201.9030	---青大豆	1.品名;2.种类(青大豆)。注:不包括作为咖啡代用品的烘焙大豆(税目21.01)
1201.9090	---其他	1.品名;2.种类。注:不包括作为咖啡代用品的烘焙大豆(税目21.01)
12.02	未焙炒或未烹煮的花生,不论是否去壳或破碎:	
1202.3000	-种用	1.品名;2.制作或保存方法(未去壳、去壳、未焙炒、未烹煮);3.是否种用。注:本税目仅指未焙炒或未烹煮的
1202.4	-其他	1.品名;2.制作或保存方法(未去壳、去壳、未焙炒、未烹煮);3.是否种用。注:本税目仅指未焙炒或未烹煮的
12.03	干椰子肉:	1.品名;2.用途(榨油用)。注:不包括供人食用的干椰丝(税目08.01)
12.04	亚麻子,不论是否破碎:	1.品名
12.05	油菜子,不论是否破碎:	

税则号列	商品描述	规范申报要素 / 价格申报要素 / 其他申报要素 / 举例说明
1205.1010	---种用	1. 品名;2. 是否种用;3. 芥子酸含量及所得固体成分每克葡萄糖苷酸(酯)含量。注:种用低芥子酸油菜子
1205.1090	---其他	1. 品名 2. 芥子酸含量及所得固体成分每克葡萄糖苷酸(酯)含量。注:种用低芥子酸油菜子
1205.9010	---种用	1. 品名;2. 是否种用。注:种用低芥子酸油菜子
1205.9090	---其他	1. 品名。注:种用低芥子酸油菜子
12.06	葵花子,不论是否破碎:	
1206.0010	---种用	1. 品名;2. 是否种用。注:种用葵花子
1206.0090	---其他	1. 品名
12.07	其他含油子仁及果实,不论 是否破碎:	
1207.1	-棕榈果及棕榈仁:	1. 品名;2. 是否种用
1207.2100	--种用	1. 品名;2. 是否种用。注:种用棉子
1207.2900	--其他	1. 品名;2. 是否种用
1207.3	-蓖麻子:	1. 品名;2. 是否种用
1207.4	-芝麻:	1. 品名;2. 是否种用
1207.5	-芥子:	1. 品名;2. 是否种用
1207.6	-红花子:	1. 品名;2. 是否种用
1207.7	-甜瓜的子:	1. 品名;2. 是否种用
1207.9	-其他:	1. 品名;2. 是否种用
12.08	含油子仁或果实的细粉及粗 粉,但芥子粉除外:	1. 品名;2. 状态(细粉、粗粉)。注:不包括花生酱(税目20.08);不包括芥子细粉及粗粉,不论是否脱脂、调制(税目21.03)
12.09	种植用的种子、果实及孢子	1. 品名;2. 用途(种植用)
12.10	鲜或干的啤酒花,不论是否研磨或制成团粒;蛇麻腺:	1. 品名;2. 制作或保存方法(鲜、干、未研磨、研磨、未制成团粒等)。注:不包括啤酒花浸膏(税目13.02);不包括废啤酒花(税目23.03);不包括蛇麻精油(税目33.01)
12.11	主要用做香料、药料、杀虫杀菌或类似用途的植物或这 些植物的某部分(包括子仁及果实),鲜或干的,不论是否切割、压碎或研磨成粉	1. 品名;2. 用途(作香料、药料、杀虫、杀菌等类似用途);3. 制作或保存方法(鲜、干)。注:不包括制成一定剂量或零售包装的
12.12	鲜、冷、冻或干的刺槐豆、海草及其他藻类、甜菜及甘 蔗,不论是否碾磨;主要供 人食用的其他品目未列名的果核、果仁及植物产品(包括未焙制的菊苣根):	
1212.2	-海草及其他藻类:	1. 品名;2. 制作或保存方法(鲜、冷、冻、干等);3. 状态(整条或切片);4. 拉丁名称。注:不包括作为胶粘剂或增稠剂的刺槐豆胚乳粉(税目13.02);不包括琼脂及角叉藻胶(税目13.02);不包括已死的单细胞藻类(税目21.02);不包括蔗渣,即甘蔗榨汁后剩下的纤维部分(税目23.03);不包括作为咖啡代用品的烘焙菊苣根(税目21.01)。注:不包括其他未烘焙菊苣根(税目06.01);不包括雕刻用的果核(例如,椰枣核)(税目14.04)及烘焙果仁(一般作为咖啡代用品)(税目21.01)
1212.9100	--甜菜	1. 品名;2. 制作或保存方法(鲜、冷、冻等)。注:不包括作为胶粘剂或增稠剂的刺槐豆胚乳粉(税目13.02);不包括琼脂及角叉藻胶(税目13.02);不包括已死的单细胞藻类(税目21.02);不包括蔗渣,即甘蔗榨汁后剩下的纤维部分(税目23.03);不包括作为咖啡代用品的烘焙菊苣根(税目21.01)。注:不包括其他未烘焙菊苣根(税目06.01);不包括雕刻用的果核(例如,椰枣核)(税目14.04)及烘焙果仁(一般作为咖啡代用品)(税目21.01)
1212.9200	--刺槐豆	1. 品名;2. 制作或保存方法(鲜、冷、冻等)。注:不包括作为胶粘剂或增稠剂的刺槐豆胚乳粉(税目13.02);不包括琼脂及角叉藻胶(税目13.02);不包括已死的单细胞藻类(税目21.02);不包括蔗渣,即甘蔗榨汁后剩下的纤维部分(税目23.03);不包括作为咖啡代用品的烘焙菊苣根(税目21.01)。注:不包括其他未烘焙菊苣根(税目06.01);不包括雕刻用的果核(例如,椰枣核)(税目14.04)及烘焙果仁(一般作为咖啡代用品)(税目21.01)

税则号列	商　品　描　述	规范申报要素 / 价格申报要素 / 其他申报要素 / 举例说明
1212.9300	--甘蔗	1.品名;2.制作或保存方法(鲜、冷、冻等)。注:不包括作为胶粘剂或增稠剂的刺槐豆胚乳粉(税目13.02);不包括琼脂及角叉藻胶(税目13.02);不包括已死的单细胞藻类(税目21.02);不包括蔗渣,即甘蔗榨汁后剩下的纤维部分(税目23.03);不包括作为咖啡代用品的烘焙菊苣根(税目21.01)。注:不包括其他未烘焙菊苣根(税目06.01);不包括雕刻用的果核(例如,椰枣核)(税目14.04)及烘焙果仁(一般作为咖啡代用品)(税目21.01)
1212.9400	--菊苣根	1.品名;2.制作或保存方法(鲜、冷、冻等)。注:不包括作为胶粘剂或增稠剂的刺槐豆胚乳粉(税目13.02);不包括琼脂及角叉藻胶(税目13.02);不包括已死的单细胞藻类(税目21.02);不包括蔗渣,即甘蔗榨汁后剩下的纤维部分(税目23.03);不包括作为咖啡代用品的烘焙菊苣根(税目21.01)。注:不包括其他未烘焙菊苣根(税目06.01);不包括雕刻用的果核(例如,椰枣核)(税目14.04)及烘焙果仁(一般作为咖啡代用品)(税目21.01)
1212.99	--其他:	1.品名;2.用途(主要供人食用)。注:不包括作为胶粘剂或增稠剂的刺槐豆胚乳粉(税目13.02);不包括琼脂及角叉藻胶(税目13.02);不包括已死的单细胞藻类(税目21.02);不包括蔗渣,即甘蔗榨汁后剩下的纤维部分(税目23.03);不包括作为咖啡代用品的烘焙菊苣根(税目21.01)。注:不包括其他未烘焙菊苣根(税目06.01);不包括雕刻用的果核(例如,椰枣核)(税目14.04)及烘焙果仁(一般作为咖啡代用品)(税目21.01)
12.13	未经处理的谷类植物的茎、秆及谷壳,不论是否切碎、碾磨、挤压或制成团粒:	1.品名;2.制作或保存方法(切碎、碾磨、挤压等);3.加工程度(未经处理)。注:不包括已净、漂白或染色的谷粒植物草、秆(税目14.01)
12.14	芜菁甘蓝、饲料甜菜、饲料 用根、干草、紫苜蓿、三叶草、驴喜豆、饲料羽衣甘蓝 羽扇豆、巢菜及类似饲料,不论是否制成团粒:	
1214.1000	-紫苜蓿粗粉及团粒	1.品名;2.状态(粗粉及团粒等)。注:不包括谷类植物的草、秆及壳(税目12.03);不包括虽然用作动物饲料,但并非专为饲养动物而种植的植物产品(如甜菜、胡萝卜叶及玉米叶)(税目23.08);不包括配制的动物饲料(如甜饲料)(税目23.09)
1214.9000	-其他	1.品名。注:不包括谷类植物的草、秆及壳(税目12.03);不包括虽然用作动物饲料,但并非专为饲养动物而种植的植物产品(如甜菜、胡萝卜叶及玉米叶)(税目23.08);不包括配制的动物饲料(如甜饲料)(税目23.09)

第十三章　虫蛟;树胶、树脂及其他植物液、汁

税则号列	商　品　描　述	规范申报要素 / 价格申报要素 / 其他申报要素 / 举例说明
13.01	虫胶;天然树胶、树脂、树胶脂及油树脂(例如,香树脂)	
1301.2000	-阿拉伯胶	1.品名;2.用途(食品、饮料、制药等)。注:不包括接触空气即硬化成为一种抗性薄膜的某些东方树木的树液(名为"日本漆"、"中国漆"等)(税目13.02);不包括琥珀(税目25.30);不包括虫胶染料,即从虫胶提取的色料(税目32.03);不包括香膏(从本税目物质中提取的)及提取的油树脂(税目33.01);不包括妥尔油(有时称为"液体松香")(税目38.03);不包括松节油(税目38.05)
1301.9	-其他:	1.品名。注:不包括接触空气即硬化成为一种抗性薄膜的某些东方树木的树液(名为"日本漆"、"中国漆"等)(税目13.02);不包括琥珀(税目25.30);不包括虫胶染料,即从虫胶提取的色料(税目32.03);不包括香膏(从本税目物质中提取的)及提取的油树脂(税目33.01);不包括妥尔油(有时称为"液体松香")(税目38.03);不包括松节油(税目38.05)
13.02	植物液汁及浸膏;果胶、果胶 酸盐及果胶酸酯;从植物产品 制得的琼脂、其他胶液及增稠剂,不论是否改性:	

税则号列	商 品 描 述	规范申报要素 / 价格申报要素 / 其他申报要素 / 举例说明
1302.1100	--鸦片	1.品名;2.制作或保存方法(液汁、浸膏、粉末)。注:不包括麦精(税目19.01);不包括烟草精(税目24.03);不包括樟脑(税目29.14);不包括甘草甜及甘草酸(税目29.38);不包括做血型试剂用的浸膏(税目30.06);不包括鞣料膏(税目32.01);不包括染料膏(税目32.03);不包括天然橡胶、巴拉塔胶、古塔波胶、银胶菊胶,糖胶树胶及类似天然树胶(税目40.01);不包括藻酸及藻酸盐(税目39.13)
1302.1200	--甘草	1.品名;2.制作或保存方法(液汁、浸膏、粉末)。注:不包括麦精(税目19.01);不包括烟草精(税目24.03);不包括樟脑(税目29.14);不包括甘草甜及甘草酸(税目29.38);不包括做血型试剂用的浸膏(税目30.06);不包括鞣料膏(税目32.01);不包括染料膏(税目32.03);不包括天然橡胶、巴拉塔胶、古塔波胶、银胶菊胶,糖胶树胶及类似天然树胶(税目40.01);不包括藻酸及藻酸盐(税目39.13)
1302.1300	--啤酒花的	1.品名;2.制作或保存方法(液汁、浸膏、粉末);3.请注明有效成分含量(α酸等)。注:不包括麦精(税目19.01);不包括烟草精(税目24.03);不包括樟脑(税目29.14);不包括甘草甜及甘草酸(税目29.38);不包括做血型试剂用的浸膏(税目30.06);不包括鞣料膏(税目32.01);不包括染料膏(税目32.03);不包括天然橡胶、巴拉塔胶、古塔波胶、银胶菊胶,糖胶树胶及类似天然树胶(税目40.01);不包括藻酸及藻酸盐(税目39.13)
1302.19	--其他:	1.品名;2.制作或保存方法(液汁、浸膏、粉末)。注:不包括麦精(税目19.01);不包括烟草精(税目24.03);不包括樟脑(税目29.14);不包括甘草甜及甘草酸(税目29.38);不包括做血型试剂用的浸膏(税目30.06);不包括鞣料膏(税目32.01);不包括染料膏(税目32.03);不包括天然橡胶、巴拉塔胶、古塔波胶、银胶菊胶,糖胶树胶及类似天然树胶(税目40.01);不包括藻酸及藻酸盐(税目39.13)
1302.2000	-果胶、果胶酸盐及果胶酸酯	1.品名;2.用途(食品用、医药用)。注:不包括麦精(税目19.01);不包括烟草精(税目24.03);不包括樟脑(税目29.14);不包括甘草甜及甘草酸(税目29.38);不包括做血型试剂用的浸膏(税目30.06);不包括鞣料膏(税目32.01);不包括染料膏(税目32.03);不包括天然橡胶、巴拉塔胶、古塔波胶、银胶菊胶,糖胶树胶及类似天然树胶(税目40.01);不包括藻酸及藻酸盐(税目39.13)
1302.3100	--琼脂	1.品名;2.等级(食品级、医药级等)。注:不包括麦精(税目19.01);不包括烟草精(税目24.03);不包括樟脑(税目29.14);不包括甘草甜及甘草酸(税目29.38);不包括做血型试剂用的浸膏(税目30.06);不包括鞣料膏(税目32.01);不包括染料膏(税目32.03);不包括天然橡胶、巴拉塔胶、古塔波胶、银胶菊胶,糖胶树胶及类似天然树胶(税目40.01);不包括藻酸及藻酸盐(税目39.13)
1302.3200	--从刺槐豆、刺槐豆子或瓜尔 豆制得的胶液及增稠剂,不论 是否改性	1.品名;2.来源。注:不包括麦精(税目19.01);不包括烟草精(税目24.03);不包括樟脑(税目29.14);不包括甘草甜及甘草酸(税目29.38);不包括做血型试剂用的浸膏(税目30.06);不包括鞣料膏(税目32.01);不包括染料膏(税目32.03);不包括天然橡胶、巴拉塔胶、古塔波胶、银胶菊胶,糖胶树胶及类似天然树胶(税目40.01);不包括藻酸及藻酸盐(税目39.13)
1302.3911	----卡拉胶	1.品名;2.种类(卡帕胶、阿欧塔胶、莱姆达胶等);3.用途(乳品、肉类、水、糖果、果冻、甜品)。注:不包括麦精(税目19.01);不包括烟草精(税目24.03);不包括樟脑(税目29.14);不包括甘草甜及甘草酸(税目29.38);不包括做血型试剂用的浸膏(税目30.06);不包括鞣料膏(税目32.01);不包括染料膏(税目32.03);不包括天然橡胶、巴拉塔胶、古塔波胶、银胶菊胶,糖胶树胶及类似天然树胶(税目40.01);不包括藻酸及藻酸盐(税目39.13)

税则号列	商品描述	规范申报要素 / 价格申报要素 / 其他申报要素 / 举例说明
1302.3912	----褐藻胶	1.品名;2.用途。注:不包括麦精(税目19.01);不包括烟草精(税目24.03);不包括樟脑(税目29.14);不包括甘草甜及甘草酸(税目29.38);不包括做血型试剂用的浸膏(税目30.06);不包括鞣料膏(税目32.01);不包括染料膏(税目32.03);不包括天然橡胶、巴拉塔胶、古塔波胶、银胶菊胶,糖胶树胶及类似天然树胶(税目40.01);不包括藻酸及藻酸盐(税目39.13)
1302.3919	----其他	1.品名;2.用途。注:不包括麦精(税目19.01);不包括烟草精(税目24.03);不包括樟脑(税目29.14);不包括甘草甜及甘草酸(税目29.38);不包括做血型试剂用的浸膏(税目30.06);不包括鞣料膏(税目32.01);不包括染料膏(税目32.03);不包括天然橡胶、巴拉塔胶、古塔波胶、银胶菊胶,糖胶树胶及类似天然树胶(税目40.01);不包括藻酸及藻酸盐(税目39.13)
1302.3990	---其他	1.品名;2.来源;3.用途。注:不包括麦精(税目19.01);不包括烟草精(税目24.03);不包括樟脑(税目29.14);不包括甘草甜及甘草酸(税目29.38);不包括做血型试剂用的浸膏(税目30.06);不包括鞣料膏(税目32.01);不包括染料膏(税目32.03);不包括天然橡胶、巴拉塔胶、古塔波胶、银胶菊胶,糖胶树胶及类似天然树胶(税目40.01);不包括藻酸及藻酸盐(税目39.13)

第十四章　编结用植物材料;其他植物产品

税则号列	商品描述	规范申报要素 / 价格申报要素 / 其他申报要素 / 举例说明
14.01	主要做编结用的植物材料(例如竹、藤、芦苇、灯芯草、柳条、酒椰叶,已净、漂白或染色的谷类植物的茎秆,椴树皮):	
1401.1000	-竹	1.品名;2.用途(主要作编结用)。注:不包括木片条(税目44.04)
1401.2000	-藤	1.品名;2.用途(主要作编结用);3.种类;4.请注明加工程度(去皮或未去皮);5.直径;6.长度。注:不包括木片条(税目44.04)
1401.9	--其他:	1.品名;2.用途(主要作编结用)。注:不包括木片条(税目44.04)
14.04	其他品目未列名的植物产品:	
1404.2000	-棉短绒	1.品名;2.纤维长度。注:不包括棉絮,药用的或医疗、外科、牙科或兽医用零售包装的(税目30.05);不包括其他棉絮胎(税目56.01)
1404.9010	---主要供染料、鞣料用的植物原料	1.品名;2.用途(主要供染料或鞣料用)。注:不包括植物鞣料膏及鞣酸,包括水萃没食子酸(税目32.01);不包括染料木及其他染料植物浸膏(税目32.03)
1404.9090	---其他	1.品名

第三类　动、植物油、脂及其分解产品;精制的食用油脂;动、植物蜡

第十五章　动、植物油、脂及其分解产品;精制的食用油脂;动、植物蜡

【注解】

本章税目1504及1506至1515所称分离的主要方法指通过压榨、倾析、冬化及过滤进行干分离,溶剂分离,借助表面活性剂分离。

税则号列	商品描述	规范申报要素 / 价格申报要素 / 其他申报要素 / 举例说明
15.01	猪脂肪(包括已炼制的猪油)及家禽脂肪,但品目02.09及15.03的货品除外:	1.品名。注:不包括未炼制或用其他方法提取的不带瘦肉的肥猪肉、猪脂肪及家禽脂肪(税目02.09);不包括猪油硬脂及液体猪油(税目15.03);不包括人造猪油(税目15.17)

税则号列	商品描述	规范申报要素 / 价格申报要素 / 其他申报要素 / 举例说明
15.02	牛、羊脂肪,但品目15.03的货品除外:	1.品名;2.加工程度(干、熏、盐腌、盐渍、已炼制等);3.是否含瘦肉。注:不包括税目15.03的货品,油硬脂、食用或非食用脂油(税目15.03);不包括马脂(税目15.06)
15.03	猪油硬脂、液体猪油、油硬脂 食用或非食用脂油,未经乳化、混合或其他方法制作:	1.品名;2.加工程度(未经乳化、混合或其他方法制作)
15.04	鱼或海生哺乳动物的油、脂及其分离品,不论是否精制,但未经化学改性:	
1504.1000	-鱼肝油及其分离品	1.品名;2.成分含量;3.加工程度(未经化学改性);4.饲料用的鱼油、脂及其分离品请注明是否精炼;5.保健用鱼油请注明DHA+EPA浓度
1504.2000	-除鱼肝油以外的鱼油、脂及其分离品	1.品名;2.成分含量;3.加工程度(未经化学改性);4.饲料用的鱼油、脂及其分离品请注明是否精炼;5.保健用鱼油请注明DHA+EPA浓度
1504.3000	-海生哺乳动物的油、脂及其分离品	1.品名;2.成分含量;3.加工程度(未经化学改性)
15.05	羊毛脂及从羊毛脂制得的脂肪物质(包括纯净的羊毛脂)	1.品名。注:不包括羊毛脂残渣(税目15.22)
15.06	其他动物油、脂及其分离品,不论是否精制,但未经化学改性:	1.品名;2.加工程度(未经化学改性)。注:不包括猪脂肪及家禽脂肪(税目02.09或15.01);不包括牛、绵羊或山羊脂肪(税目15.02);不包括鱼或海生哺乳动物的油、脂及其分离品(税目15.04);不包括主要同吡啶基组成的产品(通称为骨焦油,有时也称骨油)(税目38.24)
15.07	豆油及其分离品,不论是否精 制,但未经化学改性:	1.品名;2.加工方法(初榨、精制);3.加工程度(未经化学改性)
15.08	花生油及其分离品,不论是否 精制,但未经化学改性:	
1508.1000	-初榨的	1.品名;2.加工方法(初榨、精制);3.加工程度(未经化学改性)
1508.9000	-其他	1.品名;2.加工方法(初榨、精制);3.加工程度(未经化学改性)。注:精制花生油(未经化学改性)
15.09	油橄榄油及其分离品,不论是 否精制,但未经化学改性:	1.品名;2.加工方法(初榨、精制);3.加工程度(未经化学改性);4.包装规格;5.品牌;6.酸度;7.产区。注:不包括橄榄渣油及油橄榄油与橄榄渣油的混合油(税目15.10);不包括从橄榄油中制取的再酯化油(税目15.16)
15.10	其他橄榄油及其分离品,不论 是否精制,但未经化学改性,包括掺有品目15.09的油或分离品的混合物:	1.品名;2.加工程度(未经化学改性);3.包装规格;4.品牌。注:包括掺有税目15.09的油或分离品的混合物;橄榄油(未经化学改性)
15.11	棕榈油及其分离品,不论是否 精制,但未经化学改性:	
1511.1000	-初榨的	1.品名;2.加工方法(初榨);3.加工程度(未经化学改性)
1511.9010	---棕榈液油(熔点19℃-24℃)	1.品名;2.加工程度(未经化学改性);3.熔点;4.包装方式;5.规格
1511.9020	---棕榈硬脂(熔点44℃-56℃)	1.品名;2.加工程度(未经化学改性);3.熔点;4.包装规格
1511.9090	---其他	1.品名;2.加工方法(精制);3.加工程度(未经化学改性);4.包装规格
15.12	葵花油、红花油或棉子油及其 分离品,不论是否精制,但未 经化学改性:	
1512.1100	--初榨的	1.品名;2.加工方法(初榨、精制);3.加工程度(未经化学改性)。注:初榨葵花油(未经化学改性)
1512.1900	--其他	1.品名;2.加工方法(初榨、精制);3.加工程度(未经化学改性)
1512.2	-棉子油及其分离品:	1.品名;2.加工方法(初榨、精制);3.加工程度(未经化学改性)
15.13	椰子油、棕榈仁油或巴巴苏棕 榈果油及其分离品,不论是否精制,但未经化学改性:	
1513.1100	--初榨的	1.品名;2.加工方法(初榨、精制);3.加工程度(未经化学改性)。注:初榨椰子油(未经化学改性)
1513.1900	--其他	1.品名;2.加工方法(初榨、精制);3.加工程度(未经化学改性)

税则号列	商品描述	规范申报要素 / 价格申报要素 / 其他申报要素 / 举例说明
1513.2	-棕榈仁油或巴巴苏棕榈果油及其分离品:	1.品名;2.加工方法(初榨、精制);3.加工程度(未经化学改性)
15.14	菜子油或芥子油及其分离品,不论是否精制,但未经化学改性:	
1514.1100	--初榨的	1.品名;2.加工方法(初榨);3.加工程度(未经化学改性);4.芥子酸含量。注:初榨低芥子酸菜子油(未经化学改性)
1514.1900	--其他	1.品名;2.加工方法(精制);3.加工程度(未经化学改性);4.芥子酸含量及所得固体成分每克葡萄糖苷酸(酯)含量
1514.9110	---菜子油	1.品名;2.加工方法(初榨);3.加工程度(未经化学改性)
1514.9190	---芥子油	1.品名;2.加工方法(初榨);3.加工程度(未经化学改性)
1514.9900	--其他	1.品名;2.加工方法(精制);3.加工程度(未经化学改性)
15.15	其他固定植物油、脂(包括希蒙得木油)及其分离品,不论是否精制,但未经化学改性:	
1515.1100	--初榨的	1.品名;2.加工方法(初榨);3.加工程度(未经化学改性)
1515.1900	--其他	1.品名;2.加工方法(精制);3.加工程度(未经化学改性)
1515.2100	--初榨的	1.品名;2.加工方法(初榨);3.加工程度(未经化学改性)
1515.2900	--其他	1.品名;2.加工方法(精制);3.加工程度(未经化学改性)
1515.3000	-蓖麻油及其分离品	1.品名;2.加工方法(初榨、精制);3.加工程度(未经化学改性)
1515.5000	-芝麻油及其分离品	1.品名;2.加工方法(初榨、精制);3.加工程度(未经化学改性);4.包装规格
1515.9010	---希蒙得木油(霍霍巴油)及其分离品	1.品名;2.加工方法(初榨、精制);3.加工程度(未经化学改性)
1515.9020	---印楝油及其分离品	1.品名;2.加工方法(初榨、精制);3.加工程度(未经化学改性)
1515.9030	---桐油及其分离品	1.品名;2.加工方法(初榨、精制);3.加工程度(未经化学改性)。注:精制桐油(未经化学改性)
1515.9090	---其他	1.品名;2.加工方法(初榨、精制);3.加工程度(未经化学改性)
15.16	动、植物油、脂及其分离品,全部或部分氢化、相互酯化、再酯化或反油酸化,不论是否精制,但未经进一步加工:	1.品名;2.加工方法(全部或部分氢化、相互酯化、再酯化或反油酸化)
15.17	人造黄油;本章各种动、植物油、脂及其分离品混合制成的食用油、脂或制品,但品目15.16的食用油、脂及其分离品除外:	
1517.1000	-人造黄油,但不包括液态的	1.品名;2.制作或保存方法(氢化、乳化、搅拌等);3.加工原料(动物油脂、植物油脂);4.品牌
1517.9010	---起酥油	1.品名;2.成分含量;3.用途(食用);4.加工原料(豆油、菜子油、棕榈油等);5.品牌
1517.9090	---其他	1.品名;2.成分含量;3.用途(食用);4.加工原料(动物油脂、植物油脂);5.品牌
15.18	动、植物油、脂及其分离品,经过熟炼、氧化、脱水、硫化吹制或在真空、惰性气体中加热聚合及用其他化学方法改性的,但品目15.16的产品除外;本章各种油、脂及其分离品混合制成的其他品目未列名的非食用油、脂或制品:	1.品名;2.成分含量;3.加工方法(经熟炼、氧化、脱水、硫化、吹制等)。注:不包括氢化、相互酯化、再酯化或反油酸化的油、脂(税目15.16);不包括配制的动物饲料(税目23.09);不包括磺化油(即用硫酸处理过的油)(税目34.02)
15.20	粗甘油;甘油水及甘油碱液:	1.品名;2.甘油含量。注:纯度在95%及以上(以干燥产品的重量计)的甘油归入税目29.05;制成药品或加有药料的甘油归入税目30.03或30.04
15.21	植物蜡(甘油三酯除外)、蜂蜡、其他虫蜡及鲸蜡,不论是否精制或着色:	

税则号列	商品描述	规范申报要素 / 价格申报要素 / 其他申报要素 / 举例说明
1521.1000	-植物蜡	1.品名;2.成分。注:不包括植物蜡的混合物;不包括与动物蜡、矿物醋或人造蜡混合的植物蜡;不包括与脂肪、树脂、矿物或其他材料(颜料除外)混合的植物蜡.。注:不包括蜂箱用的人造蜡蜂房(税目96.02);不包括鲸蜡油,不论是天然的或是通过分离鲸蜡精制的(税目15.04)
1521.9	-其他:	1.品名。注:不包括蜂箱用的人造蜡蜂房(税目96.02);不包括鲸蜡油,不论是天然的或是通过分离鲸蜡精制的(税目15.04)
15.22	油鞣回收脂;加工处理油脂物 质及动、植物蜡所剩的残渣:	1.品名;2.来源。注:不包括仅经氧化或聚合的鱼油(税目15.18);不包括磺化油(税目34.02);不包括脂化皮革用的制剂(税目34.03);不包括从已炼制的猪脂肪或其他动物脂肪中所得的脂渣及膜渣(税目23.01)

第四类　食品;饮料、酒及醋;烟草、烟草及烟草代用品的制品

第十六章　肉、鱼、甲壳动物、软体动物及其他水生无脊椎动物的制品

税则号列	商品描述	规范申报要素 / 价格申报要素 / 其他申报要素 / 举例说明
16.01	肉、食用杂碎或动物血制成的香肠及类似产品;用香肠 制成的食品:	
1601.0010	---用天然肠衣做外包装的香肠及类似产品	1.品名;2.是否用天然肠衣做外包装;3.包装规格
1601.0020	---其他香肠及类似产品	1.品名 2.包装规格
1601.0030	---用香肠制成的食品	1.品名 2.包装规格
16.02	其他方法制作或保藏的肉、食用杂碎或动物血:	
1602.1000	-均化食品	1.品名 2.包装规格
1602.2000	-动物肝	1.品名;2.制作或保存方法(煮、蒸、烤、煎、炸、炒等);3.包装规格。注:不包括包馅面食(饺子等),以肉或食用杂碎做馅的(税目19.02);不包括调味汁及其制品、混合调味品(税目21.03);不包括汤料及其制品、均化混合食品(税目21.04)
1602.3100	--火鸡的	1.品名;2.制作或保存方法(煮、蒸、烤、煎、炸、炒等);3.包装规格。注:不包括包馅面食(饺子等),以肉或食用杂碎做馅的(税目19.02);不包括调味汁及其制品、混合调味品(税目21.03);不包括汤料及其制品、均化混合食品(税目21.04)
1602.3210	---罐头	1.品名;2.制作或保存方法(煮、蒸、烤、煎、炸、炒等);3.包装规格;4.品牌。注:不包括包馅面食(饺子等),以肉或食用杂碎做馅的(税目19.02);不包括调味汁及其制品、混合调味品(税目21.03);不包括汤料及其制品、均化混合食品(税目21.04)
1602.329	---其他:	1.品名;2.制作或保存方法(煮、蒸、烤、煎、炸、炒等);3.包装规格。注:不包括包馅面食(饺子等),以肉或食用杂碎做馅的(税目19.02);不包括调味汁及其制品、混合调味品(税目21.03);不包括汤料及其制品、均化混合食品(税目21.04)
1602.3910	---罐头	1.品名;2.制作或保存方法(煮、蒸、烤、煎、炸、炒等);3.包装规格;4.品牌。注:不包括包馅面食(饺子等),以肉或食用杂碎做馅的(税目19.02);不包括调味汁及其制品、混合调味品(税目21.03);不包括汤料及其制品、均化混合食品(税目21.04)
1602.399	---其他:	1.品名;2.制作或保存方法(煮、蒸、烤、煎、炸、炒等);3.包装规格。注:不包括包馅面食(饺子等),以肉或食用杂碎做馅的(税目19.02);不包括调味汁及其制品、混合调味品(税目21.03);不包括汤料及其制品、均化混合食品(税目21.04)

税则号列	商品描述	规范申报要素 / 价格申报要素 / 其他申报要素 / 举例说明
1602.4100	--后腿及其肉块	1.品名;2.制作或保存方法(煮、蒸、烤、煎、炸、炒等);3.包装规格。注:不包括包馅面食(饺子等),以肉或食用杂碎做馅的(税目19.02);不包括调味汁及其制品、混合调味品(税目21.03);不包括汤料及其制品、均化混合食品(税目21.04)
16024.200	--前腿及其肉块	1.品名;2.制作或保存方法(煮、蒸、烤、煎、炸、炒等);3.包装规格。注:不包括包馅面食(饺子等),以肉或食用杂碎做馅的(税目19.02);不包括调味汁及其制品、混合调味品(税目21.03);不包括汤料及其制品、均化混合食品(税目21.04)
1602.4910	---罐头	1.品名;2.制作或保存方法(煮、蒸、烤、煎、炸、炒等);3.包装规格;4.品牌。注:不包括包馅面食(饺子等),以肉或食用杂碎做馅的(税目19.02);不包括调味汁及其制品、混合调味品(税目21.03);不包括汤料及其制品、均化混合食品(税目21.04)
1602.4990	---其他	1.品名;2.制作或保存方法(煮、蒸、烤、煎、炸、炒等);3.包装规格。注:不包括包馅面食(饺子等),以肉或食用杂碎做馅的(税目19.02);不包括调味汁及其制品、混合调味品(税目21.03);不包括汤料及其制品、均化混合食品(税目21.04)
1602.5010	---罐头	1.品名;2.制作或保存方法(煮、蒸、烤、煎、炸、炒等);3.包装规格;4.品牌
1602.5090	---其他	1.品名;2.制作或保存方法(煮、蒸、烤、煎、炸、炒等);3.包装规格
1602.9010	---罐头	1.品名;2.制作或保存方法(煮、蒸、烤、煎、炸、炒等);3.包装规格;4.品牌
1602.9090	---其他	1.品名;2.制作或保存方法(煮、蒸、烤、煎、炸、炒等);3.包装规格
16.03	肉、鱼、甲壳动物、软体动 物或其他水生无脊椎动物的精及汁:	1.品名;2.制作或保存方法(精、汁);3.包装规格。注:不包括胨及胨化品(税目35.04)
16.04	制作或保藏的鱼;鲟鱼子酱及 鱼卵制的鲟鱼子酱代用品:	
1604.1	-鱼,整条或切块,但未绞碎	1.品名;2.制作或保存方法(整条或切块、非整条或切块、烤、煎、炸等);3.包装规格。注:不包括鱼精及鱼汁(税目16.03);不包括鱼馅面食(税目19.02);不包括调味汁及其制品、混合调味料(税目21.03);不包括汤料及其制品和均化混合食品(税目21.04)
1604.2	-其他制作或保藏的鱼:	1.品名;2.制作或保存方法(整条或切块、非整条或切块、烤、煎、炸等);3.包装规格。注:不包括鱼精及鱼汁(税目16.03);不包括鱼馅面食(税目19.02);不包括调味汁及其制品、混合调味料(税目21.03);不包括汤料及其制品和均化混合食品(税目21.04)
1604.3	-鲟鱼子酱及鲟鱼子酱代用品:	1.品名;2.包装规格;3.品牌。注:不包括鱼精及鱼汁(税目16.03);不包括鱼馅面食(税目19.02);不包括调味汁及其制品、混合调味料(税目21.03);不包括汤料及其制品和均化混合食品(税目21.04)
16.05	制作或保藏的甲壳动物、软 体动物及其他水生无脊椎动物:	
1605.1000	-蟹	1.品名;2.制作或保存方法(烤、煎、炸等);3.包装规格;
1605.2	-小虾及对虾:	1.品名;2.制作或保存方法(烤、煎、炸等);3.是否非密封包装;4.包装规格
1605.3000	-龙虾(根据我国贸易实际 无产品转移)	1.品名;2.制作或保存方法(烤、煎、炸等);3.包装规格
1605.4	-其他甲壳动物:	1.品名;2.制作或保存方法(烤、煎、炸等);3.包装规格
1605.5	-软体动物:	1.品名;2.制作或保存方法(烤、煎、炸等);3.包装规格
1605.6	-其他水生无脊椎动物:	1.品名;2.制作或保存方法(烤、煎、炸等);3.包装规格

第十七章　糖及糖食

税则号列	商品描述	规范申报要素 / 价格申报要素 / 其他申报要素 / 举例说明
17.01	固体甘蔗糖、甜菜糖及化学纯蔗糖:	
1701.1	-未加香料或者着色剂的原糖	1.品名;2.加工方法(未加香料或着色剂);3.按重量计干燥状态的糖含量对应的旋光度
1701.9100	-加有香料或着色剂:	1.品名;2.加工方法(加香料或着色剂)
1701.99	其他	1.品名
17.02	其他固体糖,包括化学纯乳糖 麦芽糖、葡萄糖及果糖;未加 香料或着色剂的糖浆;人造蜜不论是否掺有天然蜂蜜;焦糖	
1702.1	-乳糖及乳糖浆:	1.品名;2.按重量计干燥无水乳糖的含量。注:不包括加香料或着色剂的糖浆(税目21.06)
1702.2000	-槭糖及槭糖浆	1.品名。注:不包括加香料或着色剂的糖浆(税目21.06)
1702.3000	-葡萄糖及葡萄糖浆,不含果糖 或按重量计干燥状态的果糖含量在20%以下	1.品名;2.按重量计干燥状态的果糖含量;3.用途(食用、医用)。注:不包括加香料或着色剂的糖浆(税目21.06)
1702.4000	-葡萄糖及葡萄糖浆,按重量计 干燥状态的果糖含量在20%及以上,但在50%以下	1.品名;2.按重量计干燥状态的果糖含量。注:不包括加香料或着色剂的糖浆(税目21.06)
1702.5000	-化学纯果糖	1.品名;2.按重量计干燥状态的果糖含量。注:不包括加香料或着色剂的糖浆(税目21.06)
1702.6000	-其他果糖及果糖浆,按重量计干 燥状态的果糖含量在50%以上	1.品名;2.种类(高果糖浆、高果糖晶体、低聚酯果糖等);3.按重量计干燥状态的果糖含量;4.用途(食用、医用)。注:不包括加香料或着色剂的糖浆(税目21.06)
1702.9000	-其他,包括转化糖	1.品名;2.成分含量。注:不包括加香料或着色剂的糖浆(税目21.06)
17.03	制糖后所剩的糖蜜:	1.品名;2.原料
17.04	不含可可的糖食(包括白巧克力):	
1704.1000	-口香糖,不论是否裹糖	1.品名;2.成分;3.包装规格;4.品牌。注:不包括含蔗糖重量在10%及以下的甘草精(未制成糖果的)(税目13.02);不包括含可可糖食(可可脂在此不视为可可)(税目18.06);不包括糖渍蔬菜、果实、果皮等的糖食(税目20.06);不包括果酱、果子冻等(税目20.07);不包括含替代糖的合成甜味剂(例如,山梨醇)的糖果、口香糖及类似品(主要供糖尿病患者用),加有大量脂肪,有时还加有乳、果仁的糖膏,不适合供直接制糖食的(税目21.06)
1704.9000	-其他	1.品名;2.包装规格;3.品牌。注:不包括含蔗糖重量在10%及以下的甘草精(未制成糖果的)(税目13.02);不包括含可可糖食(可可脂在此不视为可可)(税目18.06);不包括糖渍蔬菜、果实、果皮等的糖食(税目20.06);不包括果酱、果子冻等(税目20.07);不包括含替代糖的合成甜味剂(例如,山梨醇)的糖果、口香糖及类似品(主要供糖尿病患者用),加有大量脂肪,有时还加有乳、果仁的糖膏,不适合供直接制糖食的(税目21.06)

第十八章　可可及可可制品

【注解】

本章所称“夹心”,包括用巧克力包裹,中心有馅(例如,用奶油、糖壳、干椰子肉、水果、果子膏、酒、蛋白杏仁糖果、坚果、牛轧糖、焦糖或上述产品的混合物做馅)的粒、块、条状食品。谷物、水果或坚果(不论是否成块)嵌于整个巧克力当中的实心块状或条状巧克力,不视为“夹心”。

税则号列	商品描述	规范申报要素 / 价格申报要素 / 其他申报要素 / 举例说明
18.01	整颗或破碎的可可豆,生的或焙炒的:	1.品名;2.制作或保存方法(整颗或破碎的、生的或焙炒的)
18.02	可可荚、壳、皮及废料:	1.品名

税则号列	商品描述	规范申报要素 / 价格申报要素 / 其他申报要素 / 举例说明
18.03	可可膏,不论是否脱脂:	1.品名;2.可可脂含量
18.04	可可脂、可可油:	1.品名
18.05	未加糖或其他甜物质的可可粉:	1.品名;2.制作或保存方法(粉末状、未加糖或其他甜物质);3.可可脂含量;4.包装规格。注:不包括含有仅作为药物赋形剂或载体可可粉的药品(税目30.03或30.04)
18.06	巧克力及其他含可可的食品:	
1806.1000	-加糖或其他甜物质的可可粉	1.品名;2.制作或保存方法(粉末状、加糖或其他甜物质);3.容器包装或内包装每件净重;4.品牌。注:不包括白巧克力(由可可脂、糖及奶粉组成)(税目17.04);不包括裹巧克力的饼干及其他烘焙糕饼(税目19.05)
1806.2000	-其他重量超过2千克的块状或条 状含可可食品,或液态、膏状、粉状、粒状或其他散装形状的含 可可食品,容器包装或内包装每 件净重超过2千克的	1.品名;2.成分含量;3.形状(条状、块状等);4.容器包装或内包装每件净重;5.品牌。注:不包括白巧克力(由可可脂、糖及奶粉组成)(税目17.04);不包括裹巧克力的饼干及其他烘焙糕饼(税目19.05)
1806.3	-其他块状或条状的含可可食品:	1.品名;2.成分含量;3.形状(条状、块状等);4.容器包装或内包装每件净重;5.是否夹心;6.品牌。注:不包括白巧克力(由可可脂、糖及奶粉组成)(税目17.04);不包括裹巧克力的饼干及其他烘焙糕饼(税目19.05)
1806.9000	-其他	1.品名;2.成分含量;3.容器包装或内包装每件净重;4.品牌。注:不包括白巧克力(由可可脂、糖及奶粉组成)(税目17.04);不包括裹巧克力的饼干及其他烘焙糕饼(税目19.05)

第十九章　谷物、粮食粉、淀粉或乳的制品;糕饼点心

税则号列	商品描述	规范申报要素 / 价格申报要素 / 其他申报要素 / 举例说明
19.01	麦精;细粉、粗粒、粗粉、淀粉或麦精制的其他品目未列名的食品,不含可可或按重量计全脱脂可可含量低于40%品目04.01至04.04所列货品制的其他品目未列名的食品,不含可可或按重量计全脱脂可可含量低于5%:	
1901.1	-供婴幼儿食用的零售包装食品	1.品名;2.成分含量;3.用途(供婴幼儿食用);4.包装规格;5.品牌
1901.2000	-供烘焙品目19.05所列面包糕饼用的调制品及面团	1.品名;2.成分含量;3.用途(供烘焙面包、糕饼等用);4.包装规格
1901.9000	-其他	1.品名;2.成分含量;3.包装规格。注:不包括用牛奶做基料的冰淇淋及其他冰制食品(税目21.05)
19.02	面食,不论是否煮熟、包馅(肉馅或其他馅)或其他方法制作例如,通心粉、面条、汤团、馄饨、饺子、奶油面卷;古斯古斯面食,不论是否制作:	
1902.1	-生的面食,未包馅或未经其他方法制作:	1.品名;2.成分含量;3.制作或保存方法(生的、未包馅或未经其他方法加工)。注:不包括带面食的汤料及其制品(税目21.04)
19022000	-包馅面食,不论是否烹煮或经其他方法制作	1.品名;2.成分;3.制作或保存方法(包馅或经其他方法加工)
1902.3010	---米粉干	1.品名;2.成分含量
1902.3020	---粉丝	1.品名;2.成分含量
1902.3030	---即食或快熟面条	1.品名;2.种类(即食面条、快熟面条);3.成分含量;4.包装规格;5.品牌
1902.3090	---其他	1.品名;2.成分含量;3.包装规格;4.品牌
1902.4000	-古斯古斯面食	1.品名;2.成分含量
19.03	珍粉及淀粉制成的珍粉代用 品,片、粒、珠、粉或类似形状的:	1.品名;2.成分;3.包装规格

税则号列	商品描述	规范申报要素 / 价格申报要素 / 其他申报要素 / 举例说明
19.04	谷物或谷物产品经膨化或烘炒制成的食品(例如,玉米片);其他品目未列名的预煮或经其他方法制作的谷粒(玉米除外),谷物片或经其他加工的谷粒(细粉、粗粒及粗粉除外):	
1904.1000	-谷物或谷物产品经膨化或烘炒制成的食品	1.品名;2.制作或保存方法(膨化或烘炒);3.包装规格
1904.2000	-未烘炒谷物片制成的食品及未烘炒的谷物片与烘炒的谷物片或膨化的谷物混合制成的食品	1.品名;2.制作或保存方法(未烘炒、未烘炒与烘炒或膨化混合);3.包装规格
1904.3000	-碾碎的干小麦	1.品名;2.制作或保存方法(干、碾碎);3.包装规格
1904.9000	-其他	1.品名;2.制作或保存方法(经过预煮或经其他方法制作);3.包装规格。注:玉米除外
19.05	面包、糕点、饼干及其他烘焙糕饼,不论是否含可可;圣餐饼、装药空囊、封缄、糯米纸及类似制品:	1.品名;2.成分含量;3.包装规格;4.品牌

第二十章　蔬菜、水果、坚果或植物其他部分的制品

税则号列	商品描述	规范申报要素 / 价格申报要素 / 其他申报要素 / 举例说明
20.01	蔬菜、水果、坚果及植物的其他食用部分,用醋或醋酸制作或保藏的:	1.品名;2.制作方法(用醋或醋酸制作或保藏);3.包装规格。注:不包括用面粉制的糕点;果馅饼(税目19.05)
20.02	番茄,用醋或醋酸以外的其他方法制作或保藏的:	
2002.1010	---罐头	1.品名;2.制作或保存方法(整个、切片等);3.包装规格;4.品牌。注:不包括番茄沙司及其他番茄调味汁(税目21.03);不包括番茄汤料及其制品(税目21.04)
2002.1090	---其他	1.品名;2.制作或保存方法(整个、切片等);3.包装规格。注:不包括番茄沙司及其他番茄调味汁(税目21.03);不包括番茄汤料及其制品(税目21.04)
2002.901	---番茄酱罐头:	1.品名;2.包装规格(重量/罐);3.品牌。注:不包括番茄沙司及其他番茄调味汁(税目21.03);不包括番茄汤料及其制品(税目21.04)
2002.9090	---其他	1.品名;2.制作或保存方法(绞碎等);3.包装规格。注:不包括番茄沙司及其他番茄调味汁(税目21.03);不包括番茄汤料及其制品(税目21.04)
20.03	蘑菇及块菌,用醋或醋酸以外的其他方法制作或保藏的:	1.品名;2.制作方法;3.包装规格;4.品牌
20.04	其他冷冻蔬菜,用醋或醋酸以外的其他方法制作或保藏的但品目20.06的产品除外:	1.品名;2.制作或保存方法(冻等);3.包装规格。注:税目20.06的产品除外
20.05	其他未冷冻蔬菜,用醋或醋酸以外的其他方法制作或保藏的,但品目20.06的产品除外:	
2005.1000	-均化蔬菜	1.品名;2.制作或保存方法(未冷冻等);3.包装规格
2005.2000	-马铃薯	1.品名;2.制作或保存方法(未冷冻等);3.包装规格
2005.4000	-豌豆	1.品名;2.制作或保存方法(未冷冻等);3.包装规格
2005.51	--脱荚的:	1.品名;2.制作或保存方法(未冷冻等);3.是否脱荚;4.包装规格
2005.59	--其他:	1.品名;2.制作或保存方法(未冷冻等);3.包装规格;4.品牌
2005.6	-芦笋:	1.品名;2.制作或保存方法(未冷冻等);3.包装规格;4.品牌
2005.7000	-油橄榄	1.品名;2.制作或保存方法(未冷冻等);3.包装规格
2005.8000	-甜玉米	1.品名;2.制作或保存方法(未冷冻等);3.包装规格
2005.9110	---竹笋罐头	1.品名;2.制作或保存方法(未冷冻等);3.包装规格;4.品牌
2005.9190	---其他	1.品名;2.制作或保存方法(未冷冻等);3.包装规格
2005.9920	---非用醋制作的蚕豆罐头	1.品名;2.制作或保存方法(未冷冻等);3.包装规格;4.品牌
2005.9940	---榨菜	1.品名;2.制作或保存方法(未冷冻等);3.包装规格
2005.9950	---咸蕨菜	1.品名;2.制作或保存方法(未冷冻等);3.包装规格

税则号列	商品描述	规范申报要素 / 价格申报要素 / 其他申报要素 / 举例说明
2005.9960	---咸荞(藠)头	1.品名;2.制作或保存方法(未冷冻等);3.包装规格
2005.999	---其他:	1.品名;2.制作或保存方法(未冷冻等);3.包装规格
20.06	糖渍蔬菜、水果、坚果、果皮及植物的其他部分(沥干糖渍或裹糖的):	1.品名;2.制作或保存方法(沥干、糖渍、裹糖);3.包装规格
20.07	烹煮的果酱、果冻、柑橘酱果泥及果膏,不论是否加糖 或其他甜物质:	
2007.1000	-均化食品	1.品名;2.制作或保存方法(烹煮);3.包装规格;4.品牌
2007.9	-其他:	1.品名;2.制作或保存方法(烹煮);3.包装规格;4.品牌。注:不包括用明胶、糖及果汁或人造果精制成的餐用果冻(税目21.06)
20.08	用其他方法制作或保藏的其 他品目未列名水果、坚果及植物的其他食用部分,不论是否加酒、加糖或其他甜物质:	1.品名;2.制作或保存方法;3.包装规格;4.品牌
20.09	未发酵及未加酒精的水果汁(包括酿酒葡萄汁)、蔬菜 汁,不论是否加糖或其他甜 物质:	1.品名;2.成分含量;3.白利糖度值;4.浓缩果汁请注明浓缩倍数;5.制作或保存方法(是否经过发酵、是否添加酒精,以及冷冻、非冷冻、混合等);6.储藏温度;7.包装规格;8.品牌。注:不包括半发酵的酿酒葡萄汁,不论其发酵是否已经中止,以及加酒精的未发酵酿酒葡萄汁,如果按容量计酒精浓度已超过0.5%的(税目22.04);包括保存温度在-18℃及以下的未冻结浓缩澄汁

第二十一章 杂项食品

税则号列	商品描述	规范申报要素 / 价格申报要素 / 其他申报要素 / 举例说明
21.01	咖啡、茶、马黛茶的浓缩精汁及以其为基本成分或以咖啡、茶、马黛茶为基本成分的制品;烘焙菊苣和其他烘焙咖啡代用品及其浓缩精汁:	1.品名;2.成分含量;3.包装规格;4.品牌。注:不包括含任何比例咖啡的烘焙咖啡代用品(税目09.01);不包括加香料的茶(税目09.02);不包括焦糖(焦糖化的糖蜜及糖)(税目17.02)
21.02	酵母(活性或非活性);已死的其他单细胞微生物(不包括品目30.02的疫苗);发酵粉	
2102.1000	-活性酵母	1.品名;2.是否活性酵母;3.包装规格;4.品牌。注:不包括自发谷物细粉,例如,加有发酵粉的细粉(税目11.01或11.02);不包括自溶酵母(税目21.06);不包括培养微生物(酵母除外)及疫苗(税目30.02);不包括酶(淀粉酶、胃朊酶、粗制凝乳酶等)(税目35.07)
2102.2000	-非活性酵母;已死的其他单细胞微生物	1.品名;2.是否活性酵母;3.是否已死的单细胞微生物;4.包装规格;5.品牌。注:不包括自发谷物细粉,例如,加有发酵粉的细粉(税目11.01或11.02);不包括自溶酵母(税目21.06);不包括培养微生物(酵母除外)及疫苗(税目30.02);不包括酶(淀粉酶、胃朊酶、粗制凝乳酶等)(税目35.07)
2102.3000	-发酵粉	1.品名; 2.包装规格;3.品牌。注:不包括自发谷物细粉,例如,加有发酵粉的细粉(税目11.01或11.02);不包括自溶酵母(税目21.06);不包括培养微生物(酵母除外)及疫苗(税目30.02);不包括酶(淀粉酶、胃朊酶、粗制凝乳酶等)(税目35.07)
21.03	调味汁及其制品;混合调味品;芥子粉及其调制品:	
2103.1000	-酱油	1.品名;2.成分;3.包装规格;4.品牌。注:不包括芥子(税目12.07);不包括固定芥子油(税目15.14);不包括芥子油饼,即从芥子提取固定油后所剩的产品(税目23.06);不包括芥子精油(税目33.01)

税则号列	商品描述	规范申报要素 / 价格申报要素 / 其他申报要素 / 举例说明
2103.2000	-番茄沙司及其他番茄调味汁	1.品名;2.成分;3.包装规格;4.品牌。注:不包括芥子(税目12.07);不包括固定芥子油(税目15.14);不包括芥子油饼,即从芥子提取固定油后所剩的产品(税目23.06);不包括芥子精油(税目33.01)
2103.3000	-芥子粉及其调制品	1.品名;2.成分;3.包装规格;4.品牌。注:不包括芥子(税目12.07);不包括固定芥子油(税目15.14);不包括芥子油饼,即从芥子提取固定油后所剩的产品(税目23.06);不包括芥子精油(税目33.01)
2103.9010	---味精	1.品名;2.成分;3.包装规格;4.品牌。注:不包括芥子(税目12.07);不包括固定芥子油(税目15.14);不包括芥子油饼,即从芥子提取固定油后所剩的产品(税目23.06);不包括芥子精油(税目33.01)
2103.9020	---别特酒(Aromatic bitters),按体积计酒精含量44.2%~49.2%,按重量计含1.5%~6%的香料、各种配料以及4%~10%的糖	1.品名;2.成分含量(酒精含量、香料和各种配料含量及糖含量等);3.包装规格;4.品牌。注:不包括芥子(税目12.07);不包括固定芥子油(税目15.14);不包括芥子油饼,即从芥子提取固定油后所剩的产品(税目23.06);不包括芥子精油(税目33.01)
2103.9090	---其他	1.品名;2.成分;3.包装规格;4.品牌。注:不包括芥子(税目12.07);不包括固定芥子油(税目15.14);不包括芥子油饼,即从芥子提取固定油后所剩的产品(税目23.06);不包括芥子精油(税目33.01)
21.04	汤料及其制品;均化混合食 品:	1.品名;2.成分含量;3.包装规格;4.品牌
21.05	冰淇淋及其他冰制食品,不论是否含可可:	1.品名2.包装规格;3.品牌
21.06	其他品目未列名的食品:	
2106.1000	-浓缩蛋白质及人造蛋白物质	1.品名;2.成分含量;3.包装规格;4.品牌。注:不包括服(使)用一定剂量后对某种病痛具有防治作用的药剂(税目30.03或30.04)
2106.9010	---制造碳酸饮料的浓缩物	1.品名;2.成分含量;3.包装规格;4.品牌。注:不包括服(使)用一定剂量后对某种病痛具有防治作用的药剂(税目30.03或30.04)
2106.9020	---制造饮料用的复合酒精制品	1.品名;2.成分含量;3.包装规格;4.品牌。注:不包括服(使)用一定剂量后对某种病痛具有防治作用的药剂(税目30.03或30.04)
2106.9030	---蜂王浆制剂	1.品名;2.成分含量;3.包装规格;4.品牌。注:不包括服(使)用一定剂量后对某种病痛具有防治作用的药剂(税目30.03或30.04)
2106.9040	---椰子汁	1.品名;2.成分含量;3.是否可直接饮用;4.包装规格;5.品牌。注:不包括服(使)用一定剂量后对某种病痛具有防治作用的药剂(税目30.03或30.04)
2106.9050	---海豹油胶囊	1.品名;2.成分含量;3.包装规格;4.品牌
2106.9090	---其他	1.品名;2.成分含量;3.包装规格;4.品牌。注:不包括服(使)用一定剂量后对某种病痛具有防治作用的药剂(税目30.03或30.04)

第二十二章 饮料、酒及醋

税则号列	商品描述	规范申报要素 / 价格申报要素 / 其他申报要素 / 举例说明
22.01	未加糖或其他甜物质及未加味的水,包括天然或人造矿泉水及汽水;冰及雪:	
2201.1	-矿泉水及汽水:	1.品名2.包装规格;3.品牌。注:不包括"碳酸雪"或"干冰"(即固体二氧化碳)(税目28.11)
2201.9010	---天然水	1.品名;2.加工程度(未加糖或其他甜物质及未加味);3.来源(天然);4.包装规格;5.品牌。注:不包括"碳酸雪"或"干冰"(即固体二氧化碳)(税目28.11)
2201.9090	---其他	1.品名;2.加工程度(未加糖或其他甜物质及未加味);3.包装规格;4.品牌。注:不包括"碳酸雪"或"干冰"(即固体二氧化碳)(税目28.11)

税则号列	商品描述	规范申报要素 / 价格申报要素 / 其他申报要素 / 举例说明
22.02	加味、加糖或其他甜物质的水,包括矿泉水及汽水,其他无酒精饮料,但不包括品目20.09的水果汁或蔬菜汁:	
2202.1000	-加味、加糖或其他甜物质的水,包括矿泉水及汽水	1.品名;2.加工程度(加糖、加味或其他甜物质);3.包装规格;4.品牌。注:不包括税目20.09的水果汁或蔬菜汁;不包括含可可、水果或香料的液状酸乳及其他发酵或酸化乳及奶油(税目04.03);不包括水果汁及蔬菜汁,不论是否用作饮料(税目20.09)
2202.9000	-其他	1.品名;2.成分;3.包装规格;4.品牌。注:不包括税目20.09的水果汁或蔬菜汁;不包括含可可、水果或香料的液状酸乳及其他发酵或酸化乳及奶油(税目04.03);不包括水果汁及蔬菜汁,不论是否用作饮料(税目20.09)
22.03	麦芽酿造的啤酒:	1.品名(中文及外文名称);2.是否麦芽酿造;3.酒精含量;4.麦芽浓度;5.包装规格;6.品牌(中文及外文名称)
22.04	鲜葡萄酿造的酒,包括加酒精的;品目20.09以外的酿酒葡萄汁:	
2204.1000	-汽酒	1.品名(中文及外文名称);2.种类(汽酒);3.加工方法(鲜葡萄酿造);4.酒精含量;5.级别;6.年份(没有年份的申报无年份);7.产区(中文及外文名称);8.酒庄名(中文及外文名称);9.葡萄品种(中文及外文名称);10.包装规格;11.品牌(中文及外文名称)。注:不包括未发酵或按容量计酒精浓度不超过0.5%的葡萄汁,不论其是否浓缩(税目20.09)
2204.2	-其他酒;加酒精抑制发酵的酿酒葡萄汁:	1.品名(中文及外文名称);2.加工方法(鲜葡萄酿造);3.酒精浓度;4.级别;5.年份(没有年份的申报无年份);6.产区(中文及外文名称);7.酒庄名(中文及外文名称);8.葡萄品种(中文及外文名称);9.包装规格(单位包装规格×每箱单位数);10.品牌(中文及外文名称)。注:不包括未发酵或按容量计酒精浓度不超过0.5%的葡萄汁,不论其是否浓缩(税目20.09)
2204.3000	-其他酿酒葡萄汁	1.品名(中文及外文名称);2.种类(酿酒葡萄汁);3.包装规格;4.品牌(中文及外文名称)。注:不包括未发酵或按容量计酒精浓度不超过0.5%的葡萄汁,不论其是否浓缩(税目20.09)
22.05	味美思酒及其他加植物或香料的用鲜葡萄酿造的酒:	1.品名(中文及外文名称);2.加工方法(鲜葡萄酿造、加植物或香料);3.包装规格;4.品牌(中文及外文名称)
22.06	其他发酵饮料(例如,苹果酒、梨酒、蜂蜜酒);其他品目未列名的发酵饮料的混合物及发酵饮料与无酒精饮料的混合物:	
2206.0010	---黄酒	1.品名(中文及外文名称);2.加工方法(发酵、混合);3.包装规格;4.品牌(中文及外文名称)
2206.0090	---其他发酵饮料	1.品名(中文及外文名称);2.成分含量;3.加工方法(发酵、混合);4.酒精浓度;5.包装规格;6.品牌(中文及外文名称);7.年份;8.等级
22.07	未改性乙醇,按容量计酒精浓度在80%及以上;任何浓度的改性乙醇及其他酒精:	1.品名(中文及外文名称);2.加工方法(未改性、改性);3.酒精浓度;4.品牌(中文及外文名称)。注:不包括以酒精为基料的固体或半固体燃料(通常作为"固体酒精"出售)(税目36.06)
22.08	未改性乙醇,按容量计酒精浓度在80%以下;蒸馏酒利口酒及其他酒精饮料:	
2208.2000	-蒸馏葡萄酒制得的烈性酒	1.品名(中文及外文名称);2.原料;3.酒精浓度;4.包装规格;5.品牌(中文及外文名称);6.级别;7.产地
2208.3000	-威士忌酒	1.品名(中文及外文名称);2.原料;3.酒精浓度;4.包装规格;5.品牌(中文及外文名称);6.产地
2208.4000	-朗姆酒及蒸馏已发酵甘蔗产品制得的其他烈性酒	1.品名(中文及外文名称);2.原料;3.酒精浓度;4.包装规格;5.品牌(中文及外文名称)

税则号列	商品描述	规范申报要素 / 价格申报要素 / 其他申报要素 / 举例说明
2208.5000	-杜松子酒	1.品名(中文及外文名称);2.原料;3.酒精浓度;4.包装规格;5.品牌(中文及外文名称)
2208.6000	-伏特加酒	1.品名(中文及外文名称);2.原料;3.酒精浓度;4.包装规格;5.品牌(中文及外文名称)
2208.7000	-利口酒及柯迪尔酒	1.品名(中文及外文名称);2.原料;3.酒精浓度;4.包装规格;5.品牌(中文及外文名称)
2208.9010	---龙舌兰酒	1.品名(中文及外文名称);2.原料;3.酒精浓度;4.包装规格;5.品牌(中文及外文名称)
2208.9020	---白酒	1.品名;2.原料;3.酒精浓度;4.包装规格;5.品牌
2208.9090	---其他	1.品名(中文及外文名称);2.原料;3.酒精浓度;4.包装规格;5.品牌(中文及外文名称)
22.09	醋及用醋酸制得的醋代用品:	1.品名(中文及外文名称);2.醋酸浓度;3.包装规格;4.品牌(中文及外文名称)。注:不包括盥洗用品(税目33.04)

第二十三章 食品工业的残渣及废料;配制的动物饲料

【注解】

制成的饲料添加剂种类有:氨基酸添加剂、维生素添加剂、矿物元素添加剂、药物饲料添加剂、饲用酶制剂、饲料酸化剂、饲料保存剂等。

税则号列	商品描述	规范申报要素 / 价格申报要素 / 其他申报要素 / 举例说明
23.01	不适于供人食用的肉、杂碎鱼、甲壳动物、软体动物或其他水生无脊椎动物的渣粉及团粒;油渣:	
2301.1	-肉、杂碎的渣粉及团粒;油渣	1.品名;2.成分含量(蛋白质含量等);3.用途(不适合供人食用);4.状态(渣粉、团粒)。注:包括供人食用的油渣
2301.2010	---饲料用鱼粉	1.品名;2.成分含量(蛋白质含量等);3.用途(不适合供人食用);4.状态(渣粉、团粒);5.种类(红、白鱼粉)。注:包括供人食用的油渣
2301.2090	---其他	1.品名;2.成分含量(蛋白质含量等);3.用途(不适合供人食用);4.状态(渣粉、团粒)。注:包括供人食用的油渣
23.02	谷物或豆类植物在筛、碾或 其他加工过程中所产生的 糠、麸及其他残渣,不论是 否制成团粒:	1.品名;2.成分含量(蛋白质含量等);3.种类(玉米的、小麦的等)。注:不包括谷物脱粒时产生的谷壳(税目12.13)
23.03	制造淀粉过程中的残渣及类似的残渣,甜菜渣、甘蔗渣及制糖过程中的其他残渣,酿造及蒸馏过程中的糟粕及残渣,不论是否制成团粒:	1.品名;2.成分含量(蛋白质含量等);3.种类;4.是否配制。注:不包括提取或精炼糖所剩的糖蜜(税目17.03);不包括非活性酵母或废酵母(税目21.02);不包括焚烧并洗涤甜菜糖蜜残渣所得的粗钾盐(税目26.21);不包括蔗渣浆(税目47.06)
23.04	提炼豆油所得的油渣饼及其他固体残渣,不论是否碾磨或制成团粒:	1.品名;2.成分含量(蛋白质含量等);3.原料。注:不包括油脚(税目15.22);不包括通过去除脱脂大豆粉的某些成分制得的浓缩蛋白质(用作食品添加剂)及改善了组织结构的大豆粉(税目21.06)
2305	提炼花生油所得的油渣饼及其他固体残渣,不论是否碾磨或制成团粒:	1.品名;2.成分含量(蛋白质含量等);3.原料
23.06	品目23.04或23.05以外的 提炼植物油脂所得的油渣饼及其他固体残渣,不论是否碾磨或制成团粒:	1.品名;2.成分含量(蛋白质含量等);3.原料
23.07	葡萄酒渣;粗酒石:	1.品名。注:不包括酒石(税目29.18)
23.08	动物饲料用的其他品目未列名的植物原料、废料、残渣及副产品,不论是否制成团粒:	1.品名;2.成分含量(蛋白质含量等);3.用途(饲料用)
2309	配制的动物饲料:	
2309.1	-零售包装的狗食或猫食:	1.品名;2.成分含量;3.用途(狗食、猫食等);4.加工方法(配制的);5.包装规格;6.品牌
2309.9	-其他:	1.品名;2.成分含量;3.加工方法(配制的);4.包装规格;5.品牌

第二十四章　烟草、烟草及烟草代用品的制品

税则号列	商品描述	规范申报要素 / 价格申报要素 / 其他申报要素 / 举例说明
24.01	烟草;烟草废料:	
24.01	烟草;烟草废料:	
2401.1	-未去梗的烟草:	1.品名;2.加工方法(未去梗)。注:包括烟草废料
2401.2	-部分或全部去梗的烟草:	1.品名;2.加工方法(去梗、部分去梗)。注:包括烟草废料
2401.3000	-烟草废料	1.品名;2.是否废料。注:包括烟草废料
24.02	烟草或烟草代用品制成的雪 茄烟及卷烟:	1.品名;2.种类(卷烟、雪茄烟);3.来源(烟草制或烟草代用品制);4.品牌
24.03	其他烟草及烟草代用品的制 品;"均化"或"再造"烟 草;烟草精汁:	
2403.1	-供吸用的烟草,不论是否含有任何比例的烟草代用品:	1.品名;2.用途(吸用等)
2403.9100	--"均化"或"再造"烟草	1.品名;2.加工方法(均化、再造)
2403.9900	--其他	1.品名;2.是否烟草精汁

第五类　矿 产 品

第二十五章　盐;硫磺;泥土及石料;石膏料、石灰及水泥

【注解】

1、"加工方法"指改变原材料、毛坯或半成品的形状、尺寸、性质或表面状态,使之达到规定要求的各种形状的方法。

2、本章"成分含量"是指:"成分"指商品所构成的部分或要素,一般指所含物质的种类;"含量"一般指所含物质的数量。

3、本章商品均需填报签约日期

税则号列	商品描述	规范申报要素 / 价格申报要素 / 其他申报要素 / 举例说明
25.01	盐(包括精制盐及变性盐)及纯氯化 钠,不论是否 为水溶液,也不论是否添加抗结块剂或松散剂;海水:	1.品名;2.成分(是否添加其他成分);3.外观;4.包装;5.是否食用盐。注:不包括加调料的盐(税目21.03)、氯化钠光学元件(税目90.01)、培养氯化钠晶体≥2.5克/颗(税目38.24)
25.02	未焙烧的黄铁矿:	1.品名;2.加工方法(焙烧、未焙烧)未焙烧黄铁矿
25.03	各种硫磺,但升华硫磺、沉淀硫磺及胶态硫磺除外:	1.品名;2.包装;3.加工工艺;4.状态(液态、固态、粉状、块状);5.成分含量。注:不包括升华硫磺、沉淀硫磺、胶态硫磺(税目28.02)。注:硫磺(液体罐装)
25.04	天然石墨:	1.品名;2.用途;3.外观(粉末、鳞片、块等);4.来源(是否天然);5.是否球化加工;6.石墨含量;7.细度指标(细度、鳞片大小)
25.05	各种天然砂,不论是否着色,但第二 十六 章 的含金 属矿砂除外:	1.品名;2.用途;3.来源(如海砂、湖砂或河砂等)。注:不包括第二十六章的金属砂、焦油砂、沥青砂。注:天然石英砂(玻璃工业用)
25.06	石英(天然砂除外);石英岩不论是 否粗 加 修整或 仅用锯或其他方法切割成矩形(包括正方形)的板、块:	1.品名;2.加工方法(天然状态、粗加修整、简单切割等);3.外观。注:不包括宝石半宝石及制品(第七十一章)
25.07	高岭土及类似土,不论是否煅烧:	1.品名;2.成分;3.是否活化;4.用途;5.外观;6.加工方法(是否煅烧);7.白度;8.细度。注:不包括含高岭土的砂(税目25.05)
25.08	其他黏土(不包括品目68.06的膨胀黏土)、红柱石、蓝晶石及硅线石,不论是否煅烧;富铝红柱石;火泥及第纳斯土:	

税则号列	商　品　描　述	规范申报要素 / 价格申报要素 / 其他申报要素 / 举例说明
2508.1000	-膨润土	1.品名;2.种类;3.外观;4.是否活化;5.用途;6.蒙脱石成分含量
2508.3000	-耐火黏土	1.品名;2.外观;3.是否活化;4.氧化铝含量;5.级别;6.是否含有添加剂或改性。注:如级别:耐火级或研磨级
2508.4000	-其他黏土	1.品名;2.外观;3.是否活化;4.氧化铝含量;5.级别;6.是否含有添加剂或改性。注:不包括税目25.30的颜料土、活性黏土(税目38.02)、膨胀黏土(税目68.06)
2508.5000	-红柱石、蓝晶石及硅线石	1.品名;2.种类;3.外观;4.是否活化;5.用途
2508.6000	-富铝红柱石	1.品名;2.种类;3.外观;4.是否活化;5.用途
2508.7000	-火泥及第纳斯土	1.品名;2.种类;3.外观;4.是否活化;5.用途
25.09	白垩:	1.品名。注:不包括磷酸白垩(税目25.10)、法国白垩或威尼斯白垩(税目25.26)
25.10	天然磷酸钙、天然磷酸铝钙及磷酸盐白垩:	
2510.1010	---磷灰石	1.品名;2.加工方法(是否碾磨及其他进一步加工);3.成分(磷灰石、天然磷酸钙、天然磷酸铝钙及磷酸盐白垩);4.来源;5.注明五氧化二磷含量。注:不包括超出清除杂质范围的煅烧或进一步热处理的产品(第三十一章)
2510.1090	---其他	1.品名;2.加工方法(是否碾磨及其他进一步加工);3.成分(磷灰石、天然磷酸钙、天然磷酸铝钙及磷酸盐白垩);4.注明五氧化二磷含量。注:不包括超出清除杂质范围的煅烧或进一步热处理的产品(第三十一章)
2510.2010	---磷灰石	1.品名;2.加工方法(是否碾磨及其他进一步加工);3.成分(磷灰石、天然磷酸钙、天然磷酸铝钙及磷酸盐白垩);4.来源;5.注明五氧化二磷含量。注:不包括超出清除杂质范围的煅烧或进一步热处理的产品(第三十一章)
2510.2090	---其他	1.品名;2.加工方法(是否碾磨及其他进一步加工);3.成分(磷灰石、天然磷酸钙、天然磷酸铝钙及磷酸盐白垩);4.注明五氧化二磷含量。注:不包括超出清除杂质范围的煅烧或进一步热处理的产品(第三十一章)
25.11	天然硫酸钡(重晶石);天然碳酸钡(毒重石),不论是否煅烧,但品目28.16的氧化钡除外:	
2511.1000	-天然硫酸钡(重晶石)	1.品名;2.加工方法;3.级别(钻井级、化工级、涂料级等);4.细度(目数)
2511.2000	-天然碳酸钡(毒重石)	1.品名;2.加工方法
25.12	硅质化石粗粉(例如各钟硅藻土)及类似的硅质土,不论是否煅烧,其表观比重不超过1:	
2512.0010	---硅藻土	1.品名;2.用途;3.外观;4.是否活化;5.表观比重;6.品牌;7.种类;8.是否改性;9.二氧化硅含量。注:不包括活性硅藻土(税目38.02)
2512.0090	---其他	1.品名;2.用途;3.外观;4.是否活化;5.表观比重;6.品牌;7.种类;8.是否改性;9.二氧化硅含量。注:不包括活性硅藻土(税目38.02)
25.13	浮石;刚玉岩;天然刚玉砂;天然石榴石及其他天然磨料,不论是否热处理:	
2513.1000	-浮石	1.品名;2.加工方法(如天然原状、破碎);3.外观;4.用途
2513.2000	-刚玉岩、天然刚玉砂、天然石榴石及其他天然磨料	1.品名;2.种类(刚玉岩、天然刚玉砂、天然石榴石、天然磨料等)。注:不包括其他税目列名的磨料(税目25.17等)
25.14	板岩,不论是否粗加修整或仅用锯或其他方法切割成矩形(包括正方形)的板、块:	1.品名;2.用途;3.加工方法(天然原状、粗加修整、锯、割等);4.外观。注:不包括铺屋顶、饰墙面及防潮用的板石(税目68.03)
25.15	大理石、石灰华及其他石灰质碑用或建筑用石,表观比重为2.5及以上,蜡石,不论是否粗加修整或仅用锯或其他方法切割成矩形(包括正方形)的板、块:	

税则号列	商品描述	规范申报要素 / 价格申报要素 / 其他申报要素 / 举例说明
2515.1	-大理石及石灰华:	1.品名;2.加工方法(天然原状、粗加修整、锯、割等);3.外观;4.表观比重;5.体积或面积数量(立方米数或平方米数);6.花色品种的中英文名称;7.规格(长×宽×高)
2515.2000	-其他 石灰质 碑用或 建筑用 石;蜡石	1.品名;2.加工方法(天然原状、粗加修整、锯、割等);3.外观;4.除蜡石外要注明表观比重
25.16	花岗岩、斑岩、玄武岩、砂岩以及其他碑用或建筑用石,不论是否 粗加 修 整或仅 用锯或其他方法切割成矩形(包括正方形)的板、块:	
2516.1	-花岗岩:	1.品名;2.加工方法(天然原状、粗加修整、锯、割等);3.外观;4.体积或面积数量(立方米数或平方米数);5.花色的中英文名称(如埃及金线米黄等);6.规格(长宽高)
2516.2000	-砂岩	1.品名;2.加工方法(天然原状、粗加修整、锯、割等);3.外观;4.体积或面积数量(立方米数或平方米数);5.花色的中英文名称(如埃及金线米黄等);6.规格(长宽高)
2516.9000	-其他碑用或建筑用石	1.品名;2.用途;3.加工方法(天然原状、粗加修整、锯、割等);4.外观。注:不包括第七十一章的宝石及半宝石、用于印刷业的石灰石(通称为石印石,税目25.30)
25.17	通常做混凝土粒料、铺路、铁道路基或其他路基用的卵石、砾石及碎石,圆石子及燧石,不论是否热处理;矿渣、浮渣 及类似的工业残渣,不论是否 混有本 品目 第 一部分 所列的材料;沥青碎石;品目25.15、25.16 所列各种石料的碎粒、碎屑及粉末,不论是 否热处 理:	
2517.1000	-通常作混凝土粒料、铺路、铁道路 基或 其 他路基用的卵 石、砾石及碎石,圆石子及燧石,不论是否热处理	1.品名;2.用途;3.外观。注:不包括切成块的燧石、人工磨圆的卵石。注:碎石(用作混凝土粒料,不规则小块状)
2517.2000	-矿渣、浮渣及类似的工业残 渣,不论是 否混有子目 号 2517.10 所列的材料	1.品名;2.用途;3.外观;4.来源(是否矿渣、浮渣、残渣等)。注:矿渣(铺路用、矿砂浮选所剩、粉末颗粒混合物)
2517.3000	-沥青碎石	1.品名;2.用途;3.外观。注:大理石粉末
2517.4	-品目 25.15 及 25.16 所列各种石料的碎粒、碎屑及粉末,不论是否热处理:	1.品名;2.外观;
25.18	白云石 ,不 论 是否煅 烧或烧 结、粗加修整或仅用锯或其他方法切 割成 矩 形(包 括正方 形)的板、块;夯混白云石:	1.品名;2.加工方法(夯混、是否煅烧或烧结、粗加修整、锯、割等);3.外观。注:白云石(经过煅烧,不规则块状,粉末颗粒混合物)
25.19	天然碳酸镁(菱镁矿);熔凝镁氧矿;烧结镁氧矿,不论烧结前是 否加入少量其他氧化 物;其他氧化镁,不论是否纯 净:	
2519.1000	-天然碳酸镁(菱镁矿)	1.品名;2.加工方法;3.成分含量;4.外观(粉末、粒状、块状等);5.粉状请注明细度,粒状请注明直径
2519.9010	---熔凝镁氧矿	1.品名;2.加工方法;3.成分含量;4.外观(粉末、粒状、块状等);5.粉状请注明细度,粒状请注明直径
2519.9020	---烧结镁氧矿(重烧镁)	1.品名;2.加工方法;3.成分含量;4.外观(粉末、粒状、块状等);5.粉状请注明细度,粒状请注明直径
2519.9030	---碱烧镁(轻烧镁)	1.品名;2.加工方法;3.成分含量;4.外观(粉末、粒状、块状等);5.粉状请注明细度,粒状请注明直径

税则号列	商品描述	规范申报要素 / 价格申报要素 / 其他申报要素 / 举例说明
2519.909	---其他:	1.品名;2.加工方法;3.成分含量;4.外观(粉末、粒状、块状等);5.粉状请注明细度,粒状请注明直径。注:不包括氧化镁光学元件(税目90.01)、培养氧化镁晶体≥2.5克/颗(税目38.24)。注:化学纯氧化镁(MgO含量99.9%)
25.20	生石膏;硬石膏;熟石膏(由煅烧的生石膏或硫酸钙构成)不论是否着色,也不论是否带有少量促凝剂或缓凝剂:	1.品名;2.用途(是否牙科用或其他用途);3.来源。注:熟石膏(牙科用)
25.21	石灰石助熔剂;通常用于制造石灰或水泥的石灰石及其他钙质石:	1.品名;2.用途。注:石灰石(制造石灰用)
25.22	生石灰、熟石灰及水硬石灰,但品目28.25的氧化钙及氢氧化钙除外:	1.品名。注:生石灰
25.23	硅酸盐水泥、矾土水泥、矿渣水泥、富硫酸盐水泥及类似的水凝水泥,不论是否着色,包括水泥熟料:	1.品名;2.用途。注:不包括耐火水泥及灰泥(税目38.16)、非耐火的灰泥及混凝土(税目38.24)、英国水泥或干固水泥(税目25.20)等。注:水泥熟料
25.24	石棉:	1.品名;2.外观;3.是否青石棉;4.是否长纤维;5.型号。注:不包括人工染色、梳理等进一步加工的(税目68.12)。注:青石棉(长纤维)
25.25	云母,包括云母片;云母废料:	1.品名;2.用途;3.外观。注:不包括切割或冲模成型、黏合的、复制的
25.26	天然冻石,不论是否粗加修整或仅用锯或其他方法切割成矩形(包括正方形)的板、块滑石:	1.品名;2.加工方法(天然原状、粗加修整、简单切割、是否破碎)。注:天然滑石粉
2526.1	-未破碎及未研粉:	1.品名;2.加工方法(天然原状、粗加修整、简单切割、是否破碎)。注:天然滑石粉
2526.2010	---冻石	1.品名;2.加工方法(天然原状、粗加修整、简单切割、是否破碎)。注:天然滑石粉
2526.2020	---滑石	1.品名;2.加工方法(天然原状、粗加修整、简单切割、是否破碎);3.白度。注:天然滑石粉
25.28	天然硼酸盐及其精矿(不论是否煅烧),但不包括从天然盐水析离的硼酸盐;天然粗硼酸,含硼酸干重不超过85%	
2528.0010	-天然硼沙及其精矿(不论是否煅烧)	1.品名。注:不包括精制硼砂(税目28.40)。注:白硼钙石
2528.0090	-其他	1.品名;2.成分含量。注:不包括所含硼酸干重超过85%的硼酸(税目28.11)
25.29	长石;白榴石;霞石及霞石正长岩;萤石(氟石):	
2529.1000	-长石	1.品名;2.用途;3.外观。注:不包括第七十一章的宝石及半宝石
2529.2	-萤石:	1.品名;2.用途;3.外观;4.氟化钙含量。注:不包括第七十一章的宝石及半宝石
2529.3000	-白榴石;霞石及霞石正长岩	1.品名;2.用途;3.外观。注:不包括第七十二章的宝石及半宝石
25.30	其他品目未列名的矿产品:	
2530.1010	---绿泥石	1.品名;2.用途;3.加工方法(天然开采、简单破碎、磨粉、未膨胀等);4.外观;5.成分含量;6.白度。注:不包括第七十二章的宝石及半宝石
2530.1020	---未膨胀的蛭石和珍珠岩	1.品名;2.用途;3.加工方法(天然开采、简单破碎、磨粉、未膨胀等);4.外观;5.成分含量。注:不包括第七十二章的宝石及半宝石
2530.2000	-硫镁矾矿及泻盐矿(天然硫酸镁)	1.品名;2.用途;3.加工方法(天然开采、简单破碎、磨粉、未膨胀等);4.外观;5.成分含量。注:不包括第七十二章的宝石及半宝石
2530.9010	---矿物性药材	1.品名;2.用途;3.加工方法(天然开采、简单破碎、磨粉、未膨胀等);4.外观;5.成分含量。注:不包括第七十二章的宝石及半宝石
2530.9020	---稀土金属矿	1.品名;2.用途;3.加工方法(天然开采、简单破碎、磨粉、未膨胀等);4.外观;5.成分含量;6.稀土元素的重量百分比,以[A]表示。注:不包括第七十二章的宝石及半宝石

税则号列	商品描述	规范申报要素 / 价格申报要素 / 其他申报要素 / 举例说明
2530.909	---其他:	1.品名;2.用途;3.加工方法(天然开采、简单破碎、磨粉、未膨胀等);4.外观;5.成分含量。注:不包括第七十二章的宝石及半宝石

第二十六章　矿砂、矿渣及矿灰

【注解】

1、"加工方法"指改变原材料、毛坯或半成品的形状、尺寸、性质或表面状态,使之达到规定要求的各种形状的方法。
2、本章"成分含量"是指:"成分"指商品所构成的部分或要素,一般指所含物质的种类;"含量"一般指所含物质的数量。
3、对于本章的"成分含量"要尽量申报出所有的成分及含量,若无法确定,要申报出主要成分及其含量。
4、本章商品均需填报签约日期

税则号列	商品描述	规范申报要素 / 价格申报要素 / 其他申报要素 / 举例说明
26.01	铁矿砂及其精矿,包括焙烧黄铁矿:	
2601.11	--未烧结:	1.品名;2.用途;3.加工方法;4.外观;5.成分含量;6.平均粒度;7.来源(原产国及矿区名称);8.签约日期。注:不包括做颜料用的精细研磨的(第三十二章)。注:铁矿砂(已烧结,Fe:20%,黑色粉末,炼铁用)
2601.1200	--已烧结	1.品名;2.用途;3.加工方法;4.外观;5.成分含量;6.来源(原产国及矿区名称);7.签约日期。注:不包括做颜料用的精细研磨的(第三十二章)。注:铁矿砂(已烧结,Fe:20%,黑色粉末,炼铁用)
2601.2000	-焙烧黄铁矿	1.品名;2.用途;3.加工方法;4.外观;5.成分含量;6.来源(原产国及矿区名称);7.签约日期。注:不包括做颜料用的精细研磨的(第三十二章)。注:铁矿砂(已烧结,Fe:20%,黑色粉末,炼铁用)
26.02	锰矿砂及其精矿,包括以干重计含锰量在20%及以上的锰铁矿及其精矿:	1.品名;2.用途;3.加工方法;4.外观;5.成分含量;6.来源(原产国及矿区名称);7.签约日期。注:不包括用于干电池的软锰矿(税目25.30)。注:锰矿砂(Mn:21%,天然,黑色粉末,炼锰)
26.03	铜矿砂及其精矿:	1.品名;2.加工方法;3.外观;4.成分含量;5.含水率;6.来源(矿区名称);7.签约日期。注:铜精矿(Cu:25%,天然,黑色粉末)
26.04	镍矿砂及其精矿:	1.品名;2.加工方法;3.外观;4.成分含量;5.来源(矿区名称);6.签约日期。注:镍矿砂(Ni:1.5%,天然,黑色粉末)
26.05	钴矿砂及其精矿:	1.品名;2.加工方法;3.外观;4.主要伴生矿物元素含量;5.用途;6.来源(矿区名称);7.签约日期。注:钴精矿(Co:20%,天然,黑色粉末)
26.06	铝矿砂及其精矿:	1.品名;2.加工方法;3.外观;4.成分含量;5.来源(矿区名称);6.签约日期。注:铝矿砂(Al:30%,天然,黑色粉末)
26.07	铅矿砂及其精矿:	1.品名;2.加工方法;3.外观;4.成分含量;5.来源(矿区名称);6.签约日期。注:铅精矿(Pb:20%,天然,黑色粉末)
26.08	锌矿砂及其精矿:	1.品名;2.加工方法;3.外观;4.成分含量;5.来源(矿区名称);6.签约日期。注:锌精矿(Zn:20%,天然,黑色粉末)
26.09	锡矿砂及其精矿:	1.品名;2.加工方法;3.外观;4.成分含量;5.来源(矿区名称);6.签约日期。注:锡精矿(Sn:15%,天然,黑色粉末)
26.10	铬矿砂及其精矿:	1.品名;2.加工方法;3.外观;4.成分含量;4.来源(矿区名称);5.签约日期。注:铬精矿(Cr:15%,天然,黑色粉末)
26.11	钨矿砂及其精矿:	1.品名;2.加工方法;3.外观;4.成分含量;5.来源(矿区名称);6.签约日期。注:钨精矿(W:15%,天然,黑色粉末)
26.12	铀或钍矿砂及其精矿:	
2612.1000	-铀矿砂及其精矿	1.品名;2.加工方法;3.外观;4.成分含量;5.种类(独居矿、钍石等);6.来源:(矿区名称);7.签约日期。注:铀精矿(U:5%,天然,黑色粉末)
2612.2000	-钍矿砂及其精矿	1.品名;2.加工方法;3.外观;4.成分含量;5.种类(独居矿、钍石等);6.来源(矿区名称);7.签约日期;8.稀土元素的重量百分比,以[A]表示。注:铀精矿(U:5%,天然,黑色粉末)

税则号列	商品描述	规范申报要素／价格申报要素／其他申报要素／举例说明
26.13	钼矿砂及其精矿：	1.品名;2.加工方法;3.外观;4.成分含量;5.来源(矿区名称);6.签约日期。注:不包括用作润滑剂的辉钼矿(税目25.30)。注:钼精矿(已焙烧,Mo:20%,黑色粉末,炼钼)
26.14	钛矿砂及其精矿：	1.品名;2.加工方法;3.外观;4.成分含量;5.来源(矿区名称);6.签约日期。注:不包括用作颜料的钛矿粉末(第三十二章);钛精矿(Ti:20%,天然,黑色粉末,炼钛)
26.15	铌、钽、钒或锆矿砂及其精矿：	
2615.1000	-锆矿砂及其精矿	1.品名;2.加工方法;3.外观;4.成分含量;5.粒度;6.用途;7.来源(矿区名称);8.签约日期。注:不包括搪瓷生产上做遮光料的微化锆砂(税目25.30)。注:钒精矿(V:20%,天然,黑色粉末,炼钒)
2615.9	-其他：	1.品名;2.加工方法;3.外观;4.成分含量;5.来源(矿区名称);6.签约日期。注:不包括搪瓷生产上做遮光料的微化锆砂(税目25.30)。注:钒精矿(V:20%,天然,黑色粉末,炼钒)
26.16	贵金属矿砂及其精矿：	1.品名;2.加工方法;3.外观;4.成分含量;5.来源(矿区名称);6.签约日期。注:金精矿(Au:15克/吨,天然,黑色粉末,炼金)
26.17	其他矿砂及其精矿：	1.品名;2.加工方法;3.外观;4.成分含量;5.来源(矿区名称);6.签约日期。注:锑精矿(Sb:15%,天然,黑色粉末,炼锑)
26.18	冶炼钢铁所产生的粒状熔渣(熔渣砂)：	1.品名;2.用途;3.加工方法;4.外观;5.成分含量;6.来源。注:不包括泡沫矿渣、矿渣棉(税目68.06)、矿渣水泥(税目25.23)
26.19	冶炼钢铁所产生的熔渣、浮渣(粒状熔渣除外)、氧化皮及其他废料：	1.品名;2.用途;3.加工方法;4.外观;5.成分含量;6.来源。注:不包括经破碎并粗略分级的筑路熔渣(税目25.17)
26.20	含有金属、砷及其化合物的矿渣、矿灰及残渣(冶炼钢铁所产生的灰、渣除外)：	1.品名;2.用途;3.加工方法;4.外观;5.成分含量;6.来源。注:不包括冶炼钢铁所产生的
26.21	其他矿渣及矿灰,包括海藻灰(海草灰);焚化城市垃圾所产生的灰、渣：	1.品名;2.用途;3.加工方法;4.外观;5.来源。注:稻壳灰(烧稻壳而得,黑色粉末,隔音用)

第二十七章　矿物燃料、矿物油及其蒸馏产品;沥青物质;矿物蜡

【注解】

1、“加工方法”指改变原材料、毛坯或半成品的形状、尺寸、性质或表面状态,使之达到规定要求的各种形状的方法。

2、本章“成分含量”是指:“成分”指商品所构成的部分或要素,一般指所含物质的种类;“含量”一般指所含物质的数量。

3、对于本章“成分含量”在有些情况下,部分27章商品要求的成分、含量只要能明确归类即可。如税目2707的杂酚油可以注明“主要成分为酚类和酚酯类”,再如税目27.15的稀释沥青可以申报“沥青70%,溶剂30%”。

税则号列	商品描述	规范申报要素／价格申报要素／其他申报要素／举例说明
27.01	煤;煤砖、煤球及用煤制成的类似固体燃料：	
2701.1100	--无烟煤	1.品名;2.外观;3.挥发物含量;4.热值(统一使用“恒湿无灰基高位发热量”指标);5.灰分;6.含硫量;7.含水量。注:不包括黑玉(税目25.30)、褐煤(税目27.02)、焦炭及半焦炭(税目27.04)
2701.12	---炼焦煤	1.品名;2.外观;3.挥发物含量;4.角质层最大厚度;5.粘结指数;6.灰分;7.含硫量;8.含水量。注:不包括黑玉(税目25.30)、褐煤(税目27.02)、焦炭及半焦炭(税目27.04)
2701.1290	---其他	1.品名;2.外观;3.挥发物含量;4.热值(统一使用“恒湿无灰基高位发热量”指标);5.灰分;6.含硫量;7.含水量。注:不包括黑玉(税目25.30)、褐煤(税目27.02)、焦炭及半焦炭(税目27.04)
2701.1900	--其他煤	1.品名;2.外观;3.挥发物含量;4.热值(统一使用“恒湿无灰基高位发热量”指标);5.灰分;6.含硫量;7.含水量。注:不包括黑玉(税目25.30)、褐煤(税目27.02)、焦炭及半焦炭(税目27.04)

税则号列	商品描述	规范申报要素 / 价格申报要素 / 其他申报要素 / 举例说明
2701.2000	-煤砖、煤球及用煤制成的类似固体燃料	1.品名;2.外观;3.挥发物含量;4.等级;5.热值(统一使用"恒湿无灰基高位发热量"指标);6.灰分;7.含硫量;8.含水量。注:不包括黑玉(税目25.30)、褐煤(税目27.02)、焦炭及半焦炭(税目27.04)
27.02	褐煤,不论是否制成型,但不包括黑玉:	
2702.1000	-褐煤,不论是否粉化,但未制成型	1.品名;2.外观;3.是否黑玉;4.热值(统一使用"恒湿无灰基高位发热量"指标);5.透光率;6.含水量。注:不包括黑玉(税目25.30)。注:褐煤(粉末颗粒混合物,不是黑玉)
2702.2000	-制成型的褐煤	1.品名;2.外观;3.是否黑玉;4.透光率;5.含水量。注:不包括黑玉(税目25.30)。注:褐煤(粉末颗粒混合物,不是黑玉)
27.03	泥煤(包括肥料用泥煤),不论是否制成型:	1.品名;2.外观;3.来源
27.04	煤、褐煤或泥煤制成的焦炭及半焦炭,不论是否制成型;甑炭:	
2704.0010	---焦炭及半焦炭	1.品名;2.用途;3.来源;4.挥发物含量;5.气孔率;6.含磷量;7.灰分;8.粒度;9.含水量;10.含硫量。注:不包括电气用甑炭制品(税目85.45)。注:焦炭(由褐煤制得,燃料用)
2704.0090	---其他	1.品名;2.用途;3.来源。注:不包括电气用甑炭制品(税目85.45)。注:焦炭(由褐煤制得,燃料用)
27.05	煤气、水煤气、炉煤气及类似气体,但石油气及其他烃类气除外:	1.品名;2.来源。注:不包括石油气及其他烃类气体(税目27.11)
27.06	从煤、褐煤或泥煤蒸馏所得的焦油及其他矿物焦油,不论是否脱水或部分蒸馏,包括再造 焦油:	1.品名;2.外观;3.来源;4.成分含量。注:不包括木焦油(税目38.07)。注:焦油(由煤蒸馏而得)
27.07	蒸馏高 温煤 焦 油所得 的油类及其他产品;芳族成分重量超过非芳族成分的类似产品:	
2707.1000	-粗苯	1.品名;2.成分含量。注:粗甲苯(甲苯含量93%)
2707.2000	-粗甲苯	1.品名;2.成分含量。注:粗二甲苯(二甲苯含量94%)
2707.3000	-粗二甲苯	1.品名;2.成分含量
2707.4000	-萘	1.品名;2.成分含量(以美国标准实验方法D86为准,250℃时);3.结晶点;4.外观。注:不包括混合烷基苯、混合烷基萘(税目38.17)。注:芳烃混合物(主要为苯、甲苯和二甲苯,用D86方法250℃蒸馏出芳烃85%)
2707.5000	-其他芳烃混合物,温度在250℃时蒸馏量以体积计(包括损 耗)在65%及以上(以美国标 准试验法 D86 为准)	1.品名;2.成分含量;3.250℃蒸馏出芳烃体积含量;4.馏程
2707.9	-其他:	1.品名;2.成分含量
27.08	从煤焦 油或 其 他矿物 焦油所得的沥青及沥青焦:	1.品名;2.外观;3.来源
27.09	石油原 油及 从 沥青矿 物提取的原油:	1.品名;2.种类;3.密度或API度;4.若为凝析油需注明
27.10	石油及 从沥 青 矿物提 取的油类,但原油除外;以上述油为基本成分(按重量计不低于70%)的其他品目未列名制品;废油:	
2710.1210	---车用汽油及航空汽油	1.品名;2.馏程;3.硫成分含量。注:参考相关标准提供技术指标,如【标准号】GB484-1993【中文标题】车用汽油,【标准号】GB1787-1988【中文标题】航空汽油,中国石化集团公司出口标准SINOPEC002-1987,【标准号】SH0004-1990【中文标题】橡胶工业用溶剂油,【标准号】SH0005-1990【中文标题】油漆工业用溶剂油,【标准号】GB16629-1996【中文标题】6号抽提溶剂油,【标准号】GB1922-1988【中文标题】溶剂油

税则号列	商品描述	规范申报要素 / 价格申报要素 / 其他申报要素 / 举例说明
2710.1220	---石脑油	1.品名;2.馏程。注:参考相关标准提供技术指标,如【标准号】GB484-1993【中文标题】车用汽油,【标准号】GB1787-1988【中文标题】航空汽油,中国石化集团公司出口标准 SINOPEC002-1987,【标准号】SH0004-1990【中文标题】橡胶工业用溶剂油,【标准号】SH0005-1990【中文标题】油漆工业用溶剂油,【标准号】GB16629-1996【中文标题】6号抽提溶剂油,【标准号】GB1922-1988【中文标题】溶剂油
2710.1230	---橡胶溶剂油、油漆溶剂油、抽提溶剂油	1.品名;2.馏程;3.用途;4.品牌;5.型号;6.包装规格。注:参考相关标准提供技术指标,如【标准号】GB484-1993【中文标题】车用汽油,【标准号】GB1787-1988【中文标题】航空汽油,中国石化集团公司出口标准 SINOPEC002-1987,【标准号】SH0004-1990【中文标题】橡胶工业用溶剂油,【标准号】SH0005-1990【中文标题】油漆工业用溶剂油,【标准号】GB16629-1996【中文标题】6号抽提溶剂油,【标准号】GB1922-1988【中文标题】溶剂油
2710.1291	----壬烯	1.品名;2.成分含量参考相关标准提供技术指标,如【标准号】GB484-1993【中文标题】车用汽油,【标准号】GB1787-1988【中文标题】航空汽油,中国石化集团公司出口标准 SINOPEC002-1987,【标准号】SH0004-1990【中文标题】橡胶工业用溶剂油,【标准号】SH0005-1990【中文标题】油漆工业用溶剂油,【标准号】GB16629-1996【中文标题】6号抽提溶剂油,【标准号】GB1922-1988【中文标题】溶剂油
2710.1299	----其他	1.品名;2.馏程;3.成分含量参考相关标准提供技术指标,如【标准号】GB484-1993【中文标题】车用汽油,【标准号】GB1787-1988【中文标题】航空汽油,中国石化集团公司出口标准 SINOPEC002-1987,【标准号】SH0004-1990【中文标题】橡胶工业用溶剂油,【标准号】SH0005-1990【中文标题】油漆工业用溶剂油,【标准号】GB16629-1996【中文标题】6号抽提溶剂油,【标准号】GB1922-1988【中文标题】溶剂油
2710.191	---煤油馏分:	1.品名;2.馏程
2710.1922	----5-7号燃料油	1.品名;2.馏程;3.运动黏度指标(100℃);4.硫含量;5.水和沉淀物含量;6.闪点(5号轻、5号重、6号燃料油注明闭口闪点,7号燃料油注明开口闪点);7.灰分含量
2710.1923	----柴油	1.品名;2.馏程;3.硫含量
2710.1929	----其他	1.品名;2.馏程
2710.1991	----润滑油	1.品名;2.用途;3.从石油或沥青提取矿物油类的百分比含量;4.品牌;5.型号;6.包装规格
2710.1992	----润滑脂	1.品名;2.用途;3.从石油或沥青提取矿物油类的百分比含量;4.品牌;5.型号;6.包装规格
2710.1993	----润滑油基础油	1.品名;2.用途;3.品牌;4.型号;5.包装规格
2710.1994	----液体石蜡和重质液体石蜡	1.品名2.包装规格
2710.1999	----其他	1.品名2.包装规格
2710.2000	-石油及从沥青矿物提取的油类(但原油除外)以及以上述油为基本成分(按重量计不低于70%)的其他税目未列名制品,含有生物柴油,但废油除外	1.品名;2.用途;3.成分;4. 从石油或沥青提取矿物油类的百分比含量
2710.9	-废油:	1.品名;2.来源
27.11	石油气及其他烃类气:	1.品名;2.状态(液化或气态);3.成分含量;4.包装容器容积;5.加工方法(压力货、冷冻货等)
27.12	凡士林;石蜡、微晶石蜡、疏松石蜡、地蜡、褐煤蜡、泥煤蜡、其他矿物蜡及用合成或其他方法制得的类似产品,不论是否着色:	
2712.1	-凡士林	1.品名;2.用途;3.是否零售包装。注:不包括零售包装的适于作护肤用的凡士林(税目33.04)
2712.2000	-石蜡,按重量计含油量小于0.75%	1.品名;2.加工方法;3.外观;4.来源;5.含油量
2712.9	-其他:	1.品名;2.成分
27.13	石油焦、石油沥青及其他石油或从沥青矿物提取的油类的残渣:	
2713.1	-石油焦:	1.品名;2.用途;3.加工方法(是否煅烧);4.外观;5.含硫量

税则号列	商品描述	规范申报要素 / 价格申报要素 / 其他申报要素 / 举例说明
2713.2000	-石油沥青	1.品名;2.针入度;3.用途;4.加工方法(是否煅烧);5.外观;6.品牌;7.包装类型(桶装、散装等);8.含蜡量;9.签约日期
2713.9000	-其他石油或从沥青矿物提取的油类的残渣	1.品名;2.用途;3.加工方法(是否煅烧);4.外观
27.14	天然沥青(地沥青)、沥青页岩、油页岩及焦油砂;沥青岩	1.品名;2.用途;3.加工方法;4.外观;5.成分含量(沥青、水)
27.15	以天然沥青(地沥青)、石油沥青、矿物焦油或矿物焦油沥青为基本成分的沥青混合物(例如,沥青胶粘剂、稀释沥青):	1.品名;2.用途;3.加工方法;4.外观;5.成分含量
27.16	电力:	1.品名

第六类　化学工业及其相关工业的产品

第二十八章　无机化学品;贵金属、稀土金属、放射性元素及其同位素的有机及无机化合物

【注解】

1、"加工方法"指改变原材料、毛坯或半成品的形状、尺寸、性质或表面状态,使之达到规定要求的各种形状的方法。

2、本章"成分含量"是指:"成分"指商品所构成的部分或要素,一般指所含物质的种类;"含量"一般指所含物质的数量。

3、所注明的"包装"内容要足以判断是否为零售包装。

4、本章商品均需填报签约日期。

税则号列	商品描述	规范申报要素 / 价格申报要素 / 其他申报要素 / 举例说明
28.01	氟、氯、溴及碘:	1.品名2.包装。注:碘溶液(50千克/桶)
28.02	升华硫磺、沉淀硫磺;胶态硫磺:	1.品名2.包装。注:胶态硫磺(50千克/袋)
28.03	碳(炭黑及其他品目未列名的 其他形态的碳):	1.品名;2.来源;3.有无活性;4.细度;5.包装;6.型号;7.品牌。注:不包括石墨、木炭、动物炭黑、活性碳。注:植物炭黑(无活性,60目,N550,60千克/袋)
28.04	氢、稀有气体及其他非金属:	
2804.1	-氢	1.品名。注:氢气
2804.5000	-硼;碲 碲	1.品名
2804.611	---经掺杂用于电子工业的直径 在 7.5 厘米及以上的单晶硅棒:	1.品名;2.用途(用于电子工业等);3.加工方法(经掺杂等);4.成分含量;5.技术指标(直径)
2804.6190	---其他:	1.品名;2.用途;3.加工方法(经掺杂等);4.成分含量;5.外观(多晶硅碎料、块料或锅底料、头尾料等);6.电阻率;7.是否需清洗
2804.6900	--其他	1.品名;2.用途;3.加工方法(经掺杂等);4.成分含量;5.牌号
2804.7	-磷:	1.品名;2.成分含量
2804.8000	-砷	1.品名。注:黄砷
2804.9	-硒:	1.品名;2.用途(用于电子工业等);3.加工方法(经掺杂等);4.成分含量;5.包装。注:不包括已切割圆片状或类似形状的(税目38.18)、胶态悬浮硒(第三十章)
28.05	碱金属、碱土金属;稀土金属 钪及钇,不论是否相互混合或 相互熔合;汞:	
2805.1100	--钠	1.品名2.包装
2805.1200	--钙	1.品名2.是否高纯度钙;3.包装
2805.1900	--其他	1.品名2.包装
2805.3	-稀土金属、钪及钇,不论是 否相互混合或相互熔合:	1.品名;2.混合稀土应注明各组分含量;3.是否电池级的稀土金属、钪及钇;4.包装;5.稀土元素的重量百分比,以[A]表示
2805.4000	-汞	1.品名2.包装
28.06	氯化氢(盐酸);氯磺酸:	1.品名;2.成分含量
28.07	硫酸;发烟硫酸:	1.品名;2.用途;3.成分含量;4.加工工艺(如回收硫酸;硫磺硫酸;硫矿硫酸)
28.08	硝酸;磺硝酸:	1.品名;2.成分含量
28.09	不论是否已有化学定义:	1.品名;2.成分含量
28.10	硼的氧化物;硼酸:	1.品名;2.成分含量
28.11	其他无 机酸 及 非金属 无机氧 化物:	
2811.1100	--氟化氢(氢氟酸)	1.品名;2.成分含量;3.包装(槽罐集装箱、塑料桶等)

税则号列	商品描述	规范申报要素 / 价格申报要素 / 其他申报要素 / 举例说明
2811.19	--其他:	1.品名;2.成分含量
2811.2100	--二氧化碳	1.品名;2.成分含量;3.用途
2811.22	--二氧化硅	1.品名;2.成分含量;3.用途;4.是否经过表面处理;5.品牌;6.外观;7.加工工艺;8.细度;9.型号
2811.2900	--其他	1.品名
28.12	非金属卤化物及卤氧化物:	1.品名。注:氯化亚砜
28.13	非金属硫化物;商品三硫化二 磷:	1.品名。注:二硫化硅
28.14	氨及氨水:	1.品名;2.氨含量
28.15	氢氧化钠(烧碱);氢氧化钾(苛性钾);过氧化钠及过氧 化钾:	1.品名;2.成分含量;3.用途;4.外观
28.16	氢氧化镁及过氧化镁;锶或钡的氧化物、氢氧化物及过氧化物:	1.品名。注:氧化钡
28.17	氧化锌及过氧化锌:	1.品名;2.用途;3.天然的请注明。注:不包括天然氧化锌(税目26.08)
28.18	人造刚玉,不论是否已有化学定义;氧化铝;氢氧化铝:	
2818.1010	---棕刚玉	1.品名;2.成分含量;3.用途;4.外观;5.晶型;6.莫氏硬度
2818.1090	---其他	1.品名;2.成分含量;3.用途;4.外观;5.晶型
2818.2000	-氧化铝,但人造刚玉除外	1.品名;2.用途;3.外观;4.成分含量
2818.3000	-氢氧化铝	1.品名;2.外观;3.成分含量
28.19	铬的氧化物及氢氧化物:	
2819.1000	-三氧化铬	1.品名;2.成分含量
2819.9000	-其他	1.品名
28.20	锰的氧化物:	1.品名;2.成分含量
28.21	铁的氧化物及氢氧化物;土色 料,按重量计三氧化二铁含量 在70%及以上:	
2821.1000	-铁的氧化物及氢氧化物	1.品名;2.成分含量
2821.2000	-土色料	1.品名;2.铁按三氧化二铁计含量
28.22	钴的氧化物及氢氧化物;商品 氧化钴:	1.品名。注:不包括天然水合氧化钴(税目26.05)。注:氧化钴
28.23	钛的氧化物:	1.品名;2.与其他物质混合请注明;3.经表面处理的请注明
28.24	铅的氧化物;铅丹及铅橙:	1.品名。注:铅丹
28.25	肼(联氨)、胲(羟胺)及其无 机盐;其他无机碱;其他金属氧 化物、氢氧化物及过氧化物:	
2825.1010	---水合肼	1.品名;2.水合肼含量。注:水合肼(含量98%)
2825.102	---硫酸羟胺	1.品名
2825.1090	---其他	1.品名
2825.2	-锂的氧化物及氢氧化物:	1.品名
2825.3	-钒的氧化物及氢氧化物:	1.品名
2825.4000	-镍的氧化物及氢氧化物	1.品名
2825.5000	-铜的氧化物及氢氧化物	1.品名
2825.6000	-锗的氧化物及二氧化锆	1.品名
2825.7000	-钼的氧化物及氢氧化物	1.品名
2825.8000	-锑的氧化物	1.品名
2825.9011	----钨酸	1.品名
2825.9012	----三氧化钨	1.品名 2.状态(粉末);3.外观(淡黄色);4.粒度;5.杂质含量
2825.9019	----其他	1.品名
2825.902	---铋的氧化物及氢氧化物:	1.品名
2825.903	---锡的氧化物及氢氧化物:	1.品名
2825.904	---铌的氧化物及氢氧化物:	1.品名
2825.9090	---其他	1.品名
28.26	氟化物;氟硅酸盐、氟铝酸盐及其他氟络盐:	1.品名
2826.1210	---无水氟化铝	1.品名;2.氟质量分数;3.铝质量分数;4.烧碱量;5.松装密度
2826.129	---其他	1.品名
2826.19	--其他:	1.品名
2826.3000	-六氟铝酸钠(人造冰晶石)	1.品名
2826.9	-其他:	1.品名
28.27	氯化物、氯氧化物及氢氧基氯化物;溴化物及溴氧化物;碘化物及碘氧化物:	1.品名

税则号列	商品描述	规范申报要素 / 价格申报要素 / 其他申报要素 / 举例说明
2827.1	-氯化铵:	1.品名;2.用途;3.外观(粉状、颗粒)
2827.2000	-氯化钙	1.品名
2827.3	-其他氯化物:	1.品名。注:不包括纯氯化钠及纯氯化钾
2827.4	-氯氧化物及氢氧基氯化物:	1.品名
2827.5	-溴化物及溴氧化物:	1.品名
2827.6000	-碘化物及碘氧化物	1.品名
28.28	次氯酸盐;商品次氯酸钙;亚氯酸盐;次溴酸盐:	1.品名。注:次氯酸钙
28.29	氯酸盐及高氯酸盐;溴酸盐及过溴酸盐;碘酸盐及高碘酸盐:	
2829.1	-氯酸盐:	1.品名
2829.9000	-其他	1.品名2.如为高氯酸铵请注明粒度
28.30	硫化物;多硫化物,不论是否 已有化学定义:	1.品名。注:不包括红锑(税目38.24)。注:硫化钠
28.31	连二亚硫酸盐及次硫酸盐:	1.品名。注:连二亚硫酸钠
28.32	亚硫酸盐;硫代硫酸盐:	1.品名。注:亚硫酸钠
28.33	硫酸盐;矾;过硫酸盐:	1.品名。注:硫酸镁
28.34	亚硝酸盐;硝酸盐:	
2834.1000	-亚硝酸盐	1.品名。注:不包括硝酸铵、硝酸钠(第三十一章)
2834.21	--硝酸钾:	1.品名;2.肥料用硝酸钾请注明。注:不包括硝酸铵、硝酸钠(第三十一章)
2834.29	--其他:	1.品名。注:不包括硝酸铵、硝酸钠(第三十一章)
28.35	次磷酸 盐、亚 磷酸盐 及磷酸 盐;多磷酸盐,不论是否已有 化学定义:	1.品名。注:不包括磷酸一铵、磷酸二铵(税目31.05)
2835.1000	-次磷酸盐及亚磷酸盐	1.品名。注:不包括磷酸一铵、磷酸二铵(税目31.05)
2835.2200	--磷酸一钠及磷酸二钠	1.品名。注:不包括磷酸一铵、磷酸二铵(税目31.05)
2835.2400	--钾的磷酸盐	1.品名。注:不包括磷酸一铵、磷酸二铵(税目31.05)
2835.25	--正磷酸氢钙(磷酸二钙):	1.品名;2.正磷酸氢钙请注明氟含量;3.用途(饲料、食品等)。注:不包括磷酸一铵、磷酸二铵(税目31.05)
2835.26	--其他磷酸钙	1.品名。注:不包括磷酸一铵、磷酸二铵(税目31.05)
2835.29	--其他:	1.品名
2835.3	-多磷酸盐:	1.品名;2.用途(饲料、食品等)。注:不包括磷酸一铵、磷酸二铵(税目31.05)
28.36	碳酸盐;过碳酸盐;含氨基甲 酸铵的商品碳酸铵:	
2836.2	-碳酸钠(纯碱)	1.品名
2836.3000	-碳酸氢钠(小苏打)	1.品名
2836.4000	-钾的碳酸盐	1.品名
2836.5000	-碳酸钙	1.品名;2.成分含量;3.用途;4.品牌
2836.6	-碳酸钡	1.品名
2836.9	-其他:	1.品名
28.37	氰化物、氧氰化物及氰络合物	1.品名;2.成分含量;3.包装。注:不包括非金属氰化物(税目28.51)
28.39	硅酸盐;商品碱金属硅酸盐:	1.品名。注:硅酸钠
28.40	硼酸盐及过硼酸盐:	1.品名。注:四硼酸钠
28.41	金属酸盐及过金属酸盐:	
2841.3	-重铬酸钠	1.品名;2.外观。注:不包括发光钨酸盐(税目32.06)
2841.5000	-其他铬酸盐及重铬酸盐;过铬酸盐	1.品名;2.外观。注:不包括发光钨酸盐(税目32.06)
2841.6	-亚锰酸盐、锰酸盐及高锰酸盐	1.品名;2.外观。注:不包括发光钨酸盐(税目32.06)
2841.7	-钼酸盐:	1.品名;2.外观。注:不包括发光钨酸盐(税目32.06)
2841.8010	---仲钨酸铵	1.品名;2.外观;3.含量(WO3 含量);4.杂质含量。注:不包括发光钨酸盐(税目32.06)
2841.802	---钨酸钠	1.品名;2.外观。注:不包括发光钨酸盐(税目32.06)
2841.8030	---钨酸钙	1.品名;2.外观。注:不包括发光钨酸盐(税目32.06)
2841.8040	---偏钨酸铵	1.品名;2.外观;3.含量(WO3 含量);4.杂质含量。注:不包括发光钨酸盐(税目32.06)
2841.809	---其他	1.品名;2.外观。注:不包括发光钨酸盐(税目32.06)
2841.9000	-其他	1.品名;2.外观。注:不包括发光钨酸盐(税目32.06)
28.42	其他无机酸盐或过氧酸盐(包 括不论 是否 已 有化学 定义的 硅铝酸盐),但叠氮化物除外	1.品名2.包装。注:硅铝酸钠(20千克/瓶)

税则号列	商品描述	规范申报要素 / 价格申报要素 / 其他申报要素 / 举例说明
28.43	胶态贵金属;贵金属的无机或有机化合物,不论是否已有化学定义;贵金属汞齐:	1.品名2.包装。注:硝酸银(20千克/瓶)
28.44	放射性化学元素及放射性同位素(包括可裂变或可转换的化学元素及同位素)及其化合物;含上述产品的混合物及残渣:	1.品名。注:铀
28.45	品目28.44以外的同位素;这些同位素的无机或有机化合物,不论是否已有化学定义:	1.品名。注:重水
28.46	稀土金属、钇、钪及其混合物的无机或有机化合物:	
2846.1	-铈的化合物:	1.品名;2.稀土元素的重量百分比,以[A]表示
2846.901	---氧化稀土(氧化铈除外)	1.品名;2.稀土元素的重量百分比,以[A]表示
2846.9021	----氯化铽	1.品名;2.稀土元素的重量百分比,以[A]表示
2846.9022	----氯化镝	1.品名;2.稀土元素的重量百分比,以[A]表示
2846.9023	----氯化镧	1.品名;2.稀土元素的重量百分比,以[A]表示
2846.9024	----氯化钕	1.品名;2.稀土元素的重量百分比,以[A]表示
2846.9025	----氯化镨	1.品名;2.稀土元素的重量百分比,以[A]表示
2846.9026	----氯化钇	1.品名;2.稀土元素的重量百分比,以[A]表示
2846.9028	----混合氯化稀土	1.品名;2.稀土元素的重量百分比,以[A]表示
2846.9029	----其他	1.品名;2.稀土元素的重量百分比,以[A]表示
2846.903	---氟化稀土:	1.品名;2.成分含量;3.稀土元素的重量百分比,以[A]表示
2846.904	---碳酸稀土:	1.品名;2.成分含量;3.稀土元素的重量百分比,以[A]表示
2846.909	---其他:	1.品名;2.成分含量;3.稀土元素的重量百分比,以[A]表示
28.47	过氧化氢,不论是否用尿素固化:	1.品名;2.成分含量;3.包装。注:不包括制成一定剂量或零售形状或包装的(税目30.04)。注:过氧化氢(50千克/桶,含量90%)
28.48	磷化物,不论是否已有化学定义,但不包括磷铁:	1.品名;2.铜母合金请注明磷的重量百分比
28.49	碳化物,不论是否已有化学定义	1.品名;2.成分含量;3.品牌;4.型号;5.外观;6.用途;7.碳化钨请注明粒度
28.50	氢化物、氮化物、叠氮化物、硅化物及硼化物,不论是否已有化学定义,但可归入品目28.49的碳化物除外:	1.品名。注:硼化氮
28.52	汞的无机或有机化合物,不论是否已有化学定义,汞齐除外:	1.品名;2.成分含量
28.53	其他无机化合物(包括蒸馏水、导电水及类似的纯净水)液态空气(不论是否除去稀有气体);压缩空气;汞齐,但贵金属汞齐除外:	
2853.0010	---饮用蒸馏水	1.品名;2.水请注明用途;3.包装
2853.0020	---氯化氰	1.品名2.包装
2853.0030	---镍钴锰氢氧化物	1.品名
2853.0090	---其他	1.品名

第二十九章 有机化学品

【注解】

1、"加工方法"指改变原材料、毛坯或半成品的形状、尺寸、性质或表面状态,使之达到规定要求的各种形状的方法。

2、本章"成分含量"是指:"成分"指商品所构成的部分或要素,一般指所含物质的种类;"含量"一般指所含物质的数量。

3、所注明的"包装"内容要足以判断是否为零售包装。

4、本章商品需要申报的品名包括标准命名法名称或工商业通用俗称。

5、化学结构式和CAS号对本章商品的海关管理非常重要。由于报关单的书写限制,在本目录中没有对化学结构式和CAS号的要求,但在实际通关中、企业要用其他的方式向海关提拱商品的化学结构式和CAS号。

6、本章商品均需填报签约日期。

税则号列	商品描述	规范申报要素 / 价格申报要素 / 其他申报要素 / 举例说明
29.01	无环烃:	1.品名;2.成分含量;3.用途;4.用作气体燃料的应报明包装容器容积;5.散装货物应报明。注:丁烷,丁烷含量99%,用于气体燃料,350毫升罐装
29.02	环烃:	

税则号列	商 品 描 述	规范申报要素 / 价格申报要素 / 其他申报要素 / 举例说明
2902.1	-环烷烃、环烯及环萜烯:	1.品名;2.成分含量
2902.2000	-苯	1.品名;2.成分含量
2902.3000	-甲苯	1.品名;2.成分含量
2902.4	-二甲苯:	1.品名;2.成分含量
2902.5000	-苯乙烯	1.品名;2.成分含量
2902.6000	-乙苯	1.品名;2.成分含量
2902.7000	-异丙基苯	1.品名;2.成分含量
2902.9010	---四氢萘	1.品名;2.成分含量
2902.9020	---精萘	1.品名;2.成分含量;3.结晶温度
2902.9030	---十二烷基苯	1.品名;2.成分含量
2902.904	---4-(4’-烷基环己基)环己 基乙烯	1.品名;2.成分含量
2902.9090	---其他	1.品名;2.成分含量
29.03	烃的卤化衍生物:	1.品名;2.成分含量;3.用途
29.04	烃的磺化、硝化或亚硝化衍 生物,不论是否卤化:	1.品名;2.成分含量;3.用途
29.05	无环醇及其卤化、磺化、硝 化或亚硝化衍生物:	1.品名;2.成分含量;3.用途;4.包装
29.06	环醇及其卤化、磺化、硝化 或亚硝化衍生物:	1.品名;2.成分含量;3.用途
29.07	酚;酚醇:	1.品名;2.成分含量;3.用途
29.08	酚及酚醇的卤化、磺化、硝化或亚硝化衍生物:	1.品名;2.成分含量;3.用途
29.09	醚、醚醇、醚酚、醚醇酚、过氧化醇、过氧化醚、过氧化酮(不论是否已有化学定义)及其卤化、磺化、硝化 或亚硝化衍生物:	1.品名;2.成分含量;3.用途
29.10	三节环环氧化物、环氧醇、环氧酚、环氧醚及其卤化、磺化、硝化或亚硝化衍生物	1.品名;2.成分含量;3.用途
29.11	缩醛及半缩醛,不论是否含有其他含氧基,及其卤化、磺化、硝化或亚硝化衍生物:	1.品名;2.成分含量;3.用途
29.12	醛,不论是否含有其他含氧基;环聚醛;多聚甲醛	1.品名;2.成分含量;3.用途;4.四聚甲醛报明外观
29.13	品 目 29.12 所列产品的卤化、磺化、硝化或亚硝化衍生物:	1.品名;2.成分含量;3.用途
29.14	酮及醌,不论是否含有其他含氧基,及其卤化、磺化、硝化或亚硝化衍生物:	1.品名;2.成分含量;3.用途;4.丙酮报明包装
29.15	饱 和 无 环 一 元羧酸及其酸 酐、酰卤化物、过氧化物和过氧酸,以及它们的卤化、磺化、硝化或亚硝化衍生物:	1.品名;2.成分含量;3.用途
29.16	不饱和无环一元羧酸、环一元羧酸及其酸酐、酰卤化物 过氧化物和过氧酸,以及它们的卤化、磺化、硝化或亚硝化衍生物:	1.品名;2.成分含量;3.用途;4.丙烯酸、丙烯酸盐或酯应报明包装
29.17	多元羧酸及其酸酐、酰卤化物、过氧化物和过氧酸,以及它们的卤化、磺化、硝化或亚硝化衍生物:	1.品名;2.成分含量;3.用途;4.对苯二甲酸请注明 4-CBA 值;5.对苯二甲酸请注明 P-TL 酸值;6.对苯二甲酸请注明色度;7.对苯二甲酸请注明水分
29.18	含附加含氧基的羧酸及其酸酐、酰卤化物、过氧化物和过氧酸,以及它们的卤化、磺 化、硝化或亚硝化衍生物:	1.品名;2.成分含量;3.用途
29.19	磷酸酯及其盐,包括乳磷酸 盐,以及它们的卤化、磺化 硝化或亚硝化衍生物:	1.品名;2.成分含量;3.用途
29.20	其他非金属无机酸酯(不包 括卤化氢的酯)及其盐,以及它们的卤化、磺化、硝化或亚硝化衍生物:	1.品名;2.成分含量;3.用途
29.21	氨基化合物:	1.品名;2.成分含量;3.用途
29.22	含氧基氨基化合物:	1.品名;2.成分含量;3.用途;4.乙醇胺及其盐应报明色度;5.乙醇胺及其盐应报明包装
29.23	季铵盐及季铵碱;卵磷脂及 其他磷氨基类脂,无论是否已有化学定义:	1.品名;2.成分含量;3.用途
29.24	羧基酰胺基化合物;碳酸酰胺基化合物:	1.品名;2.成分含量;3.用途;4.包装
29.25	羧基酰亚胺化合物(包括糖 精及其盐)及亚胺基化合物	1.品名;2.成分含量;3.用途
29.26	腈基化合物:	1.品名;2.成分含量;3.用途
29.27	重氮化合物、偶氮化合物及 氧化偶氮化合物:	1.品名;2.成分含量;3.用途
29.28	肼(联氨)及胲(羟胺)的 有机衍生物:	1.品名;2.成分含量;3.用途

税则号列	商品描述	规范申报要素 / 价格申报要素 / 其他申报要素 / 举例说明
29.29	其他含氮基化合物:	1.品名;2.成分含量;3.用途
29.30	有机硫化合物:	1.品名;2.成分含量;3.用途
29.31	其他有机-无机化合物:	1.品名;2.成分含量;3.用途
29.32	仅含氧杂原子的杂环化合物:	1.品名;2.成分含量;3.用途
29.33	仅含有氮杂原子的杂环化合物:	1.品名;2.成分含量;3.用途;4.乌洛托品请注明外观;5.6-已内酰胺请注明外观;6.签约日期
29.34	核酸及其盐,无论是否已有化学定义;其他杂环化合物	1.品名;2.成分含量;3.用途
29.35	磺(酰)胺:	1.品名;2.成分含量;3.用途
29.36	天然或合成再制的维生素原和维生素(包括天然浓缩物及其主要用做维生素的衍生物,上述产品的混合物,不论是否溶于溶剂:	1.品名;2.成分含量;3.用途;4.包装
29.37	天然或合成再制的激素、前列腺素、血栓烷、白细胞三烯及其衍生物和结构类似物,包括主要用做激素的改性链多肽:	1.品名;2.成分含量;3.用途;4.包装
29.38	天然或合成再制的苷(配糖物)及其盐、醚、酯和其他衍生物:	1.品名;2.成分含量;3.用途;4.来源(天然、合成再制)
29.39	天然或合成再制的生物碱及其盐、醚、酯和其他衍生物:	1.品名;2.成分含量;3.用途;4.来源(天然、合成再制)
29.40	化学纯糖,但蔗糖、乳糖、麦芽糖、葡萄糖及果糖除外;糖醚、糖缩醛、糖酯及其盐,但不包括品目29.37、29.38、29.39的产品:	1.品名;2.成分含量
29.41	抗菌素:	1.品名;2.包装
29.42	其他有机化合物:	1.品名;2.成分含量

第三十章 药 品

【注解】

名词解释:

1、"加工方法"指改变原材料、毛坯或半成品的形状、尺寸、性质或表面状态,使之达到规定要求的各种形状的方法。

2、本章"成分含量"是指:"成分"指商品所构成的部分或要素,一般指所含物质的种类;"含量"一般指所含物质的数量。

3、所注明的"包装"内容要足以判断是否为零售包装。

4、对于本章"成分含量"在有些情况下,部分商品要求的成分、含量只要能满足海关管理即可。

税则号列	商品描述	规范申报要素 / 价格申报要素 / 其他申报要素 / 举例说明
30.01	已干燥的器官疗法用腺体及其他器官,不论是否制成粉末;器官疗法用腺体、其他器官及其分泌物的提取物;肝素及其盐;其他供治疗或预防疾病用的其他品目未列名的人体或动物制品:	1.品名;2.用途;3.加工工艺4品牌(英文);5.型号
30.02	人血;治病、防病或诊断用动物血制品;抗血清、其他血份及免疫制品,不论是否修饰或通过生物工艺加工制得;疫苗、毒素、培养微生物(不包括酵母)及类似产品:	1.品名;2.用途;3.加工工艺;4.品牌;5.型号;6.包装规格
30.03	两种或两种以上成分混合而成的治病或防病用药品(不包括品目30.02、30.05或30.06的货品),未配定剂量或制成零售包装:	1.品名;2.用途;3.成分含量;4.是否配定剂量或零售包装;5.品牌;6.型号
30.04	由混合或非混合产品构成的治病或防病用药品(不包括品目30.02、30.05或30.06的货品),已配定剂量(包括制成皮肤摄入形式的)或制成零售包装:	1.品名;2.用途;3.成分;4.是否配定剂量或零售包装;5.品牌;6.包装规格

税则号列	商 品 描 述	规范申报要素 / 价格申报要素 / 其他申报要素 / 举例说明
30.05	兽用已配剂量含硝碘酚腈、氰尼辛葡甲胺、美洛昔康制剂（包括零售包装）其他已配定剂量的药品（包括 零售包装）软填料、纱布、绷带及类似物品（例如,敷料、橡皮膏、混 罨剂），经过药物浸涂或制成 零售包装供医疗、外科、牙科或兽医用:	1. 品名;2. 用途;3. 成分;4. 是否经过药物浸涂或制成零售包装;5. 品牌;6. 型号;7. 包装规格
30.06	本章注释四所规定的医药用品:	
3006.1000	-无菌外科肠线、类似的无菌缝合材料（包括外科或牙科用无菌可吸收缝线）及外伤创口闭合用的无菌粘合胶布;无菌 昆布及无菌昆布塞条;外科或 牙科用无菌吸收性止血材料;外科或牙科用无菌抗粘连阻 隔材料,不论是否可吸收	1. 品名;2. 用途;3. 品牌;4. 型号;5. 包装规格
3006.2000	-血型试剂	1. 品名;2. 用途;3. 成分;4. 品牌;5. 型号;6. 包装规格
3006.3000	-X 光检查造影剂;用于病人的诊断试剂	1. 品名;2. 用途;3. 成分;4. 品牌;5. 型号;6. 包装规格
3006.4000	-牙科粘固剂及其他牙科填 料;骨骼粘固剂	1. 品名;2. 用途;3. 成分;4. 品牌;5. 型号;6. 包装规格
3006.5000	-急救药箱、药包	1. 品名;2. 组成(指箱或包中的药品、器具等);3. 品牌;4. 型号。注:不包括医生用较复杂的医药包。注:急救药箱(组成:双氧水、碘酊、红汞、山金车花酊剂、少量敷料、药膏、剪刀、镊子)
3006.6	-以激素,品目 29.37 的其他产品或杀精子剂为基本成分的化学避孕药物:	1. 品名;2. 用途;3. 成分;4. 品牌;5. 型号;6. 包装规格
3006.7000	-专用于人类或作兽药用的凝胶制品,作为外科手术或体检时躯体部位的润滑剂,或者作为躯体和医疗器械之间的耦合剂	1. 品名;2. 用途;3. 成分;4. 品牌;5. 型号;6. 包装规格
3006.9100	--可确定用于造口术的用具	1. 品名;2. 用途;3. 成分;4. 品牌;5. 型号
3006.9200	--废药物	1. 品名

第三十一章 肥 料

【注解】

1、“加工方法”指改变原材料。毛坯或半成品的形状、尺寸、性质或表面状态,使之达到规定要求的各种形状的方法。

2、本章“成分含量”是指:“成分”指商品所构成的部分或要素,一般指所含物质的种类;“含量”一般指所含物质的数量。

3、对于本章“成分含量”在有些情况下,部分商品的成分、含量只要能满足海关管理即可。

4、本章商品均需填报签约日期。

税则号列	商 品 描 述	规范申报要素 / 价格申报要素 / 其他申报要素 / 举例说明
31.01	动物或植物肥料,不论是否相互混合或经化学处理;动植物产品经混合或化学处理制成的肥料:	1. 品名;2. 用途;3. 加工工艺;4. 外观;5. 包装件重;6. 是否经过化学处理或与化学肥料混合;7. 品牌;8. 型号。注:不包括天然与化学肥料的混合物(税目 31.05)
31.02	矿物氮肥及化学氮肥:	1. 品名;2. 每包重量;3. 总氮含量;4. 品牌;5. 型号;6. 成分含量
31.03	矿物磷肥及化学磷肥:	1. 品名;2. 每包重量;3. 总磷含量;4. 品牌;5. 型号
31.04	矿物钾肥及化学钾肥:	1. 品名;2. 每包重量;3. 总钾含量(以氧化物计);4. 品牌;5. 型号
31.05	含氮、磷、钾中两种或三种肥 效元素的矿物肥料或化学肥 料;其他肥料;制成片及类似形状或每包毛重不超过 10 千 克的本章各项货品:	1. 品名;2. 成分含量;3. 包装件重;4. 总氮含量、总磷含量、总钾(以氧化物计)含量;5. 品牌;6. 型号

第三十二章 鞣料浸膏及染料浸膏;鞣酸及其衍生物;染料、颜料及其他着色料;油漆及清漆;油灰及其他类似胶粘剂;墨水、油墨

【注解】

1、本章“成分含量”是指:“成分”指商品所构成的部分或要素,一般指所含物质的种类;“含量”一般指所含物质的数量。

2、所注明的“包装”内容要足以判断是否为零售包装。

3、对于本章“成分含量”在有些情况下,部分商品的成分、含量只要能满足海关管理即可。

税则号列	商品描述	规范申报要素 / 价格申报要素 / 其他申报要素 / 举例说明
32.01	植物鞣料浸膏;鞣酸及其盐、醚、酯和其他衍生物:	1.品名;2.用途;3.加工工艺;4.品牌;5.型号
32.02	有机合成鞣料;无机鞣料;鞣料制剂,不论是否含有天然鞣料;预鞣用酶制剂:	1.品名;2.成分含量;3.型号;4.品牌;5.包装规格
32.03	动植物质着色料(包括染料浸膏,但动物炭黑除外),不论是否已有化学定义;本章注释三所述的以动植物质着色料为基本成分的制品:	1.品名;2.用途;3.加工工艺;4.包装;5.品牌;6.型号;7.成分含量
32.04	有机合成着色料,不论是否已有化学定义;本章注释三所述的以有机合成着色料为基本成分的制品;用做荧光增白剂或发光体的有机合成产品,不论是否已有化学定义:	1.品名;2.成分含量;3.用途;4.染料须报明种类;5.包装;6.品牌;7.型号
32.05	色淀;本章注释三所述的以色淀为基本成分的制品:	1.品名;2.成分;3.包装;4.品牌;5.型号
32.06	其他着色料;本章注释三所述的制品,但品目32.03、32.04及32.05的货品除外;用做发光体的无机产品,不论是否已有化学定义:	
3206.1110	-以二氧化钛为基本成分的颜料及制品:	1.品名;2.成分含量;3.用途;4.包装;5.规格型号;6.品牌;7.如果加入放射性盐,请注明放射性比度;8.级别;9.签约日期;
3206.1190	-以铬化合物为基本成分的颜料及制品	1.品名;2.成分含量;3.用途;4.包装;5.规格型号;6.品牌;7.如果加入放射性盐,请注明放射性比度
3206.1900	--其他	1.品名;2.成分含量;3.用途;4.包装;5.规格型号;6.品牌;7.如果加入放射性盐,请注明放射性比度
3206.2000	-以铬化合物为基本成分的颜料及制品	1.品名;2.成分含量;3.用途;4.包装;5.规格型号;6.品牌;7.如果加入放射性盐,请注明放射性比度
3206.4	-其他着色料及其他制品:	1.品名;2.成分含量;3.用途;4.包装;5.规格型号;6.品牌;7.如果加入放射性盐,请注明放射性比度
3206.5000	-用作发光体的无机产品	1.品名;2.成分含量;3.用途;4.包装;5.规格型号;6.品牌;7.如果加入放射性盐,请注明放射性比度;8.稀土元素的重量百分比,以[A]表示
32.07	陶瓷、搪瓷及玻璃工业用的调制颜料、遮光剂、着色剂、珐琅和釉料、釉底料(泥釉)、光瓷釉以及类似产品;搪瓷玻璃料及其他玻璃,呈粉、粒或粉片状的:	1.品名;2.用途;3.外观;4.成分含量;5.包装;6.品牌;7.型号
32.08	以合成聚合物或化学改性天然聚合物为基本成分的油漆及清漆(包括瓷漆及大漆),分散于或溶于非水介质的;本章注释四所述的溶液:	1.品名;2.成分含量;3.用途;4.是否分散于或溶于非水介质;5.包装;6.品牌;7.型号
32.09	以合成聚合物或化学改性天然聚合物为基本成分的油漆及清漆(包括瓷漆及大漆),分散于或溶于水介质的:	1.品名;2.成分含量;3.用途;4.包装;5.品牌;6.型号
32.10	其他油漆及清漆(包括瓷漆、大漆及水浆涂料);加工皮革用的水性颜料:	1.品名;2.成分含量;3.用途;4.包装;5.品牌;6.型号
32.11	配制的催干剂:	1.品名;2.成分含量;3.用途;4.包装;5.品牌;6.型号
32.12	制造油漆(含瓷漆)用的颜料(包括金属粉末或金属粉片)分散于非水介质中呈液状或浆状的;压印箔;零售形状及零售包装的染料或其他着色料:	
3212.1000	-压印箔	1.品名;2.成分含量;3.用途;4.包装;5.外观;6.品牌;7.规格;8.加工工艺
3212.9000	-其他	1.品名;2.成分含量;3.用途;4.包装;5.外观;6.品牌
32.13	艺术家、学生和广告美工用的颜料、调色料、文娱颜料及类似品,片状、管装、罐装、瓶装、扁盒装以及类似形状或包装的:	1.品名;2.用途;3.包装;4.品牌;5.型号;6.是否成套

税则号列	商品描述	规范申报要素 / 价格申报要素 / 其他申报要素 / 举例说明
32.14	安装玻璃用油灰、接缝用油灰、树脂胶泥、嵌缝胶及其他类似胶粘剂;漆工用填料;非耐火涂面制剂,涂门面、内墙 地板、天花板等用:	1. 品名;2. 成分含量;3. 用途;4. 包装;5. 品牌;6. 型号
32.15	印刷油墨、书写或绘图墨水及其他墨类,不论是否固体或浓缩:	
3215.1	-印刷油墨:	1. 品名;2. 用途;3. 包装;4. 颜色;5. 成分含量; 6. 是否具有曝光显影功能
3215.9	-其他:	1. 品名;2. 用途;3. 包装;4. 成分含量; 5. 颜色

第三十三章　精油及香膏;芳香料制品及化妆盥洗品

【注解】

名词解释:

1、本章"成分含量"是指:"成分"指商品所构成的部分或要素,一般指所含物质的种类;"含量"一般指所含物质的数量。

2、所注明的"包装"内容要足以判断是否为零售包装。

3、对于本章"成分含量"在有些情况下部分商品的成分、含量只要能满足海关管理即可。

税则号列	商品描述	规范申报要素 / 价格申报要素 / 其他申报要素 / 举例说明
33.01	精油(无萜或含萜),包括浸膏及净油;香膏;提取的油树脂用花香吸取法或浸渍法制成的含浓缩精油的脂肪、固定 油、蜡及类似品;精油脱萜时所得的萜烯副产品;精油水馏 液及水溶液:	1. 品名;2. 用途;3. 加工工艺;4. 包装;5. 品牌;6. 型号;7. 成分含量
33.02	工业原料用的混合香料以及以一种或多种香料为基本成分的混合物(包括酒精溶液)生产饮料用的以香料为基本成分的其他制品:	
3302.1	-食品或饮料工业用:	1. 品名;2. 成分;3. 用途;4. 酒精含量;5. 品牌;6. 型号;7. 包装规格
3302.9000	-其他	1. 品名;2. 成分;3. 用途;4. 品牌;5. 型号;6. 包装规格
33.03	香水及花露水:	1. 品名;2. 包装;3. 品牌
33.04	美容品或化妆品及护肤品(药品除外),包括防晒油或晒黑油;指(趾)甲化妆品:	1. 品名;2. 用途;3. 包装;4. 品牌
33.05	护发品:	1. 品名;2. 用途;3. 包装;4. 品牌
33.06	口腔及牙齿清洁剂,包括假牙 模膏及粉;清洁牙缝用的纱线(牙线),单独零售包装的:	1. 品名;2. 用途;3. 包装;4. 品牌
33.07	剃须用制剂、人体除臭剂、沐 浴用制剂、脱毛剂和其他品目 未列名的芳香料制品及化妆盥洗品;室内除臭剂,不论是否加香水或消毒剂:	1. 品名;2. 用途;3. 包装;4. 品牌

第三十四章　肥皂、有机表面活性剂、洗涤剂、润滑剂、人造蜡、调制蜡、光洁剂、蜡烛及类似品、塑型用膏、"牙科用蜡"及牙科用熟石膏制剂

【注解】

1、本章"成分含量"是指:"成分"指商品所构成的部分或要素,一般指所含物质的种类;"含量"一般指所含物质的数量。

2、所注明的"包装"内容要足以判断是否为零售包装。

3、对于本章"成分含量"在有些情况下,部分商品要求的成分、含量只要能满足海关管理即可。

税则号列	商品描述	规范申报要素 / 价格申报要素 / 其他申报要素 / 举例说明
34.01	肥皂;作肥皂用的有机表面活性产品及制品,条状、块状或模制形状的,不论是否含有肥皂;洁肤用的有机表面活性产品及制品,液状或膏状并制成零售包装的,不论是否含有肥皂;用肥皂或洗涤剂浸渍、涂面或包覆的纸、絮胎、毡呢及无纺织物:	
3401.1100	--盥洗用(包括含有药物的产品	1. 品名;2. 成分含量;3. 外观;4. 包装;5. 品牌;6. 型号

税则号列	商 品 描 述	规范申报要素 / 价格申报要素 / 其他申报要素 / 举例说明
3401.1910	---洗衣皂	1.品名;2.成分含量;3.外观;4.包装;5.品牌;6.型号
3401.1990	---其他	1.品名;2.成分含量;3.外观;4.包装;5.浸渍物的成分;6.品牌;7.型号
3401.2	-其他形状的肥皂	1.品名;2.成分含量;3.外观;4.包装;5.品牌;6.型号
3401.3	-洁肤用的有机表面活性产品及制剂,液状或膏状并制成零售包装的,不论是否含有肥皂	1.品名;2.成分含量;3.外观;4.包装;5.品牌;6.型号
34.02	有机表面活性剂(肥皂除外)表面活性剂制品、洗涤剂(包括助洗剂)及清洁剂,不论是否含有肥皂,但品目34.01的产品除外:	
3402.1	-有机表面活性剂,不论是否零售包装:	1.品名;2.种类(阳离子、阴离子、非离子、两性等);3.成分;4.品牌;5.型号
3402.2	-零售包装的制品:	1.品名;2.用途;3.是否零售包装;4.成分;5.品牌;6.型号。注:洗衣粉(每袋450克,主要成分为烷基苯磺酸钠、非离子活性剂、硅酸钠、硅酸镁、过硼酸钠、增白剂等)
3402.9000	-其他	1.品名;2.用途;3.是否零售包装;4.成分。注:洗衣粉(每袋50千克,主要成分为烷基苯磺酸钠、非离子活性剂、硅酸钠、硅酸镁、过硼酸钠、增白剂等)
34.03	润滑剂(包括以润滑剂为基本成分的切削油制剂、螺栓或螺母松开剂、防锈或防腐蚀制剂及脱模剂)及用于纺织材料、皮革、毛皮或其他材料油脂处理的制剂,但不包括以石油或从沥青矿物提取的油类为基本成分(按重量计不低于70%)的制剂:	1.品名;2.用途;3.成分;4.矿物油含量;5.包装规格;6.品牌;7.型号
34.04	人造蜡及调制蜡:	1.品名;2.用途;3.外观;4.成分;5.品牌;6.型号
34.05	鞋靴、家具、地板、车身、玻 璃或金属用的光洁剂、擦洗 膏、去污粉及类似制品(包括用这类制剂浸渍、涂面或包覆的纸、絮胎、毡呢、无纺织物泡沫塑料或海绵橡胶),但不包括品目34.04的蜡:	1.品名;2.用途;3.成分;4.品牌;5.型号
34.06	各种蜡烛及类似品:	1.品名;2.成分;3.品牌;4.型号
34.07	塑型用膏,包括供儿童娱乐用的在内;通称为"牙科用蜡"或"牙科造形膏"的制品,成 套、零售包装或制成片状、马 蹄形、条状及类似形状的;以 熟石膏(煅烧石膏或硫酸钙)为基本成分的牙科用其他制 品:	1.品名;2.用途;3.外观;4.包装;5.成分含量;6.品牌;7.型号

第三十五章　蛋白类物质;改性淀粉;胶;酶

【注解】

1、本章"成分含量"是指:"成分"指商品所构成的部分或要素,一般指所含物质的种类;"含量"一般指所含物质的数量。

2、对于本章"成分含量"在有些情况下,部分商品的成分、含量只要能满足海关管理即可。

税则号列	商 品 描 述	规范申报要素 / 价格申报要素 / 其他申报要素 / 举例说明
35.01	酪蛋白、酪蛋白酸盐及其他酪蛋白衍生物;酪蛋白胶:	1.品名;2.包装;3.品牌;4.型号;5.用途
35.02	白蛋白(包括按重量计干质成 分的乳清蛋白含量超过80%的两种或两种以上的乳清蛋白浓缩物)、白蛋白盐及其他白蛋白衍生物:	1.品名;2.用途;3.外观;4.成分含量。注:白蛋白(用于制药,白色粉末,白蛋白含量90%)
35.03	明胶(包括长方形、正方形明 胶薄片,不论是否表面加工或着色)及其衍生物;鱼鳔胶;其他动物胶,但不包括品目35.01的酪蛋白胶:	1.品名;2.用途;3.外观;4.包装。注:明胶(用于配制食品,透明薄片,每包10千克)
35.04	蛋白胨及其衍生物;其他品目未列名的蛋白质及其衍生物;皮粉,不论是否加入铬矾:	1.品名;2.用途;3.来源;4.包装;5.蛋白质含量

税则号列	商品描述	规范申报要素 / 价格申报要素 / 其他申报要素 / 举例说明
35.05	糊精及其他改性淀粉(例如,预凝化淀粉或酯化淀粉);以淀粉、糊精或其他改性淀粉为基本成分的胶:	1.品名;2.用途;3.还原糖含量;4.包装;5.品牌;6.型号
35.06	其他品目未列名的调制胶及其他调制粘合剂;适于做胶或粘合剂用的产品,零售包装每件净重不超过1千克:	1.品名;2.用途;3.包装;4.成分;5.品牌;6.型号
35.07	酶;其他品目未列名的酶制品	1.品名;2.用途;3.种类

第三十六章 炸药;烟火制品;火柴;引火合金;易燃材料制品

【注解】

1、本章“成分”指商品所构成的部分或要素,一般指所含物质的种类。

2、对于本章“成分”在有些情况下,部分商品的成分只要能满足海关管理即可。

税则号列	商品描述	规范申报要素 / 价格申报要素 / 其他申报要素 / 举例说明
36.01	发射药:	1.品名;2.成分。注:黑色火药(主要成分为硝酸钾、硫、木炭)
36.02	配制炸药,但发射药除外:	1.品名;2.成分。注:喷妥莱炸药(主要成分为三硝基甲苯、四硝基赤藓醇、蜡、聚合黏合剂等)
36.03	安全导火索;导爆索;火帽或雷管;引爆器;电雷管:	1.品名。注:雷管
36.04	烟花、爆竹、信号弹、降雨火箭浓雾信号弹及其他烟火制品:	1.品名。注:烟花
36.05	火柴,但品目36.04的烟火制品除外:	1.品名。注:火柴
36.06	各种形状的铈铁及其他引火合金;本章注释二所述的易燃材料制品:	1.品名;2.用途;3.包装容器的容积
3606.1000	-直接灌注香烟打火机及类似打火器用的液体燃料或液化气体燃料,其包装容器的容积不超过300立方厘米	1.品名;2.用途;3.包装容器的容积
3606.901	---铈铁及其他引火合金:	1.品名;2.用途;3.外观;4.稀土元素的重量百分比,以[A]表示
3606.9090	---其他	1.品名;2.用途;3.外观

第三十七章 照相及电影用品

【注解】

1、本章所称“规格尺寸”一般指长和宽。

2、本章“成分含量”是指:“成分”指商品所构成的部分或要素,一般指所含物质的种类;“含量”一般指所含物质的数量。

3、本章商品申报的品名中应包括是否曝光,是否冲洗的内容。

税则号列	商品描述	规范申报要素 / 价格申报要素 / 其他申报要素 / 举例说明
37.01	未曝光的摄影感光硬片及平面软片,用纸、纸板及纺织物以外任何材料制成;未曝光的一次成像感光平片,不论是否分装:	1.品名;2.用途;3.材质;4.是否成卷;5.是否一次成像;6.规格尺寸(长x宽x厚度);7.品牌;8.型号;9.进口总面积(平方米);10.包装规格(张/盒)
37.02	成卷的未曝光摄影感光胶片,用纸、纸板及纺织物以外任何材料制成;未曝光的一次成像感光卷片:	1.品名;2.用途;3.材质;4.是否成卷;5.是否一次成像;6.规格尺寸(长x宽x厚度);7.品牌;8.型号;9.进口总面积(平方米);10.包装规格(张/盒)
37.03	未曝光的摄影感光纸、纸板及纺织物:	1.品名;2.用途;3.是否成卷;4.规格尺寸;5.品牌;6.型号
37.04	已曝光未冲洗的摄影硬片、软片、纸、纸板及纺织物:	1.品名;2.用途;3.规格尺寸;4.品牌
37.05	已曝光已冲洗的摄影硬片及软片,但电影胶片除外:	1.品名;2.用途;3.规格尺寸;4.品牌
37.06	已曝光已冲洗的电影胶片,不论是否配有声道或仅有声道:	1.品名;2.用途;3.规格尺寸;4.品牌

税则号列	商　品　描　述	规范申报要素 / 价格申报要素 / 其他申报要素 / 举例说明
37.07	摄影用化学制剂(不包括上光漆、胶水、黏合剂及类似制剂)摄影用未混合产品;定量包装或零售包装可立即使用的:	1.品名;2.用途;3.包装;4.成分;5.品牌;6.型号

第三十八章　杂项化学产品

【注解】

名词解释:

1、"成分"指商品所构成的部分或要素,一般指所含物质的种类;本章"含量"一般指所含物质的数量。

2、所注明的"包装"内容要足以判断是否为零售包装。

3、对于本章"成分含量"在有些情况下,部分商品的成分、含量只要能满足海关管理即可。

税则号列	商　品　描　述	规范申报要素 / 价格申报要素 / 其他申报要素 / 举例说明
38.01	人造石墨;胶态或半胶态石墨;以石墨或其他碳为基本成分的糊状、块状、板状制品或半制品:	1.品名;2.用途;3.状态;4.加工工艺;5.成分含量;6.品牌;7.型号;8.规格
38.02	活性碳;活性天然矿产品;动物炭黑,包括废动物炭黑:	
3802.1010	---木质的	1.品名;2.用途;3.来源;4.包装规格;5.干品填充密度
3802.1090	---其他	1.品名;2.用途;3.来源;4.包装规格
3802.9000	-其他	1.品名;2.用途;3.来源;4.包装规格
38.03	妥尔油,不论是否精炼:	1.品名;2.用途。注:不包括皂化妥尔油。注:妥尔油(用于制路面乳胶)
38.04	木浆残余碱液,不论是否浓缩、脱糖或经化学处理,包括木素磺酸盐,但不包括品目38.03的妥尔油:	1.品名。注:不包括妥尔油。注:木素磺酸盐
38.05	脂松节油、木松节油和硫酸盐松节油及其他萜烯油,用蒸馏或其他方法从针叶木制得;粗制二聚戊烯;亚硫酸盐松节油及其他粗制对异丙基苯甲烷;以α萜品醇为基本成分的松油	1.品名;2.用途;3.成分;4.二聚戊烯、萜烯烃、萜品醇及水合萜品请注明含量。注:不包括松节油(税目33.01)、松香油(税目38.06)。注:粗制二聚戊烯(用于溶剂,通过分馏木松节油制得)
38.06	松香和树脂酸及其衍生物;松香精及松香油;再熔胶:	1.品名;2.来源。注:松香(蒸馏松树渗出物制得)
38.07	木焦油;精制木焦油;木杂酚油;粗木精;植物沥青;以松香、树脂酸或植物沥青为基本成分的啤酒桶沥青及类似制品:	1.品名;2.用途。注:粗木精(用作乙醇变性剂)
38.08	杀虫剂、杀鼠剂、杀菌剂、除草剂、抗萌剂、植物生长调节剂、消毒剂及类似产品,零售形状、零售包装或制成制剂及成品(例如,经硫磺处理的带子、杀虫灯芯、蜡烛及捕蝇纸):	1.品名;2.用途;3.成分含量;4.包装;5.品牌;6.型号
38.09	纺织、造纸、制革及类似工业用的其他品目未列名的整理剂、染料加速着色或固色助剂及其他产品和制剂(例如,修整剂及媒染剂):	1.品名;2.用途;3.成分;4.品牌;5.型号
38.10	金属表面酸洗剂;焊接用的焊剂及其他辅助剂;金属及其他材料制成的焊粉或焊膏;做焊条芯子或焊条涂料用的制品:	1.品名;2.用途;3.成分;4.品牌;5.型号
38.11	抗震剂、抗氧剂、防胶剂、粘度改良剂、防腐蚀制剂及其他配制添加剂,用于矿物油(包括汽油)或与矿物油同样用途的其他液体:	1.品名;2.包装;3.用途;4.成分;5.品牌;6.型号
38.12	配制的橡胶促进剂;其他品目未列名的橡胶或塑料用复合增塑剂;橡胶或塑料用抗氧制剂及其他复合稳定剂:	1.品名;2.用途;3.成分;4.品牌;5.型号
38.13	灭火器的装配药;已装药的灭火弹:	1.品名;2.用途;3.成分。注:灭火器的调配药(主要成分为碳酸氢钙,含有少量甘草浸膏)
38.14	其他品目未列名的有机复合溶剂及稀释剂;除漆剂:	1.品名;2.用途;3.成分;4.品牌;5.型号

税则号列	商品描述	规范申报要素 / 价格申报要素 / 其他申报要素 / 举例说明
38.15	其他品目未列名的反应引发剂、反应促进剂、催化剂：	1. 品名;2. 用途(如促进某某聚合物的聚合等);3. 成分含量
38.16	耐火的水泥、灰泥、混凝土及类似耐火混合制品，但品目 38.01 的产品除外：	1. 品名;2. 用途;3. 成分
38.17	混合烷基苯及混合烷基萘，但品目 27.07 及 29.02 的货品除外：	1. 品名;2. 用途;3. 成分
38.18	经掺杂用于电子工业的化学元素，已切成圆片、薄片或类似形状；经掺杂用于电子工业的化合物：	
3818.001	---直径 7.5 厘米及以上的单晶硅切片：	1. 品名;2. 用途;3. 外观;4. 成分;5. 单晶硅切片请注明直径;6. 包装;7. 加工程度
3818.0090	---其他	1. 品名;2. 用途;3. 外观;4. 成分;5. 包装;6. 加工程度
38.19	闸用液压油及其他液压传动用液体，不含石油或从沥青矿物提取的油类，或者按重量计石油或从沥青矿物提取的油类含量低于 70%：	1. 品名;2. 用途;3. 成分;4. 矿物油含量;5. 品牌;6. 型号
38.20	防冻剂及解冻剂：	1. 品名;2. 用途;3. 成分;4. 品牌;5. 型号
38.21	制成的供微生物(包括病毒及类似品)或植物、人体、动物细胞生长或维持用的培养基：	1. 品名;2. 用途;3. 成分
38.22	附于衬背上的诊断或实验用试剂及不论是否附于衬背上的诊断或实验用配制试剂，但品目 30.02 及 30.06 的货品除外；检定参照物：	1. 品名;2. 用途;3. 包装;4. 成分(区分衬背和试剂来说明举例);5. 是否血源筛查用诊断试剂;6. 是否有衬背
38.23	工业用单羧脂肪酸；精炼所得的酸性油；工业用脂肪醇：	1. 品名;2. 成分含量;3. 来源(动植物油脂等);4. 加工程度(是否经过皂化、水解);5. 品牌;6. 型号
38.24	铸模及铸芯用粘合剂；其他品目未列名的化学工业及其相关工业的化学产品及配制品(包括由天然产品混合组成的)：	
3824.1000	-铸模及铸芯用粘合剂	1. 品名;2. 用途;3. 成分含量;4. 品牌;5. 型号。注：铸模及铸芯用黏合剂(用于铸模及铸芯的黏合，主要成分为松香、亚麻子油、植物粘质、糊精、糖蜜)
3824.3000	-自身混合或与金属粘合剂混合的未烧结金属碳化物	1. 品名;2. 用途;3. 成分含量;4. 品牌;5. 型号。注：未烧结碳化钼(主要成分为碳化钼、金属黏合剂)
3824.4	-水泥，灰泥及混凝土用添加剂	1. 品名;2. 用途;3. 成分含量;4. 品牌;5. 型号。注：混凝土防水剂(主要成分为氯化铁、硅酸钠、粉煤灰、硅灰、硅藻土)
3824.5000	-非耐火的灰泥及混凝土	1. 品名;2. 用途;3. 成分含量;4. 品牌;5. 型号。注：非耐火的混凝土(主要成分为 CaO、SiO2、Al2O3 等)
3824.6000	-子目号 2905.44 以外的山梨醇	1. 品名;2. 用途;3. 外观;4. 来源;5. 成分含量;6. 品牌;7. 型号
3824.7	-含有甲烷、乙烷或丙烷的卤化衍生物的混合物：	1. 品名;2. 用途;3. 成分含量;4. 品牌;5. 型号
3824.8	-含环氧乙烷(氧化乙烯)、多溴联苯(PBBs)、多氯联苯(PCBs)、多氯三联苯(PCTs)或三(2,3 一二溴丙基)磷酸酯的混合物及制品：	1. 品名;2. 用途;3. 成分含量;4. 品牌;5. 型号
3824.9010	---杂醇油	1. 品名;2. 用途;3. 成分含量;4. 包装规格;5. 品牌;6. 型号
3824.9020	---除墨剂、蜡纸改正液及类似品	1. 品名;2. 用途;3. 成分含量;4. 包装规格;5. 品牌;6. 型号
3824.9030	---增炭剂	1. 品名;2. 用途;3. 成分含量;4. 包装规格;5. 品牌;6. 型号
3824.9091	----按重量计含滑石 50% 以上的混合物	1. 品名;2. 用途;3. 成分含量;4. 包装规格;5. 品牌;6. 型号
3824.9092	----按重量计含氧化镁 70% 以上的混合物	1. 品名;2. 用途;3. 成分含量;4. 包装规格;5. 品牌;6. 型号
3824.9093	----表层包覆钴化合物的氢氧化镍(掺杂碳)	1. 品名;2. 用途;3. 成分含量;4. 包装规格;5. 品牌;6. 型号
3824.9099	----其他	1. 品名;2. 用途;3. 成分含量;4. 包装规格;5. 品牌;6. 型号;7. 稀土元素的重量百分比，以[A]表示
38.25	其他品目未列名的化学工业及其相关工业的副产品；城市垃圾；下水道淤泥；本章注释六所规定的其他废物：	1. 品名;2. 用途;3. 来源。注：城市垃圾(收集家庭废物而得，用于分拣回收)
38.26	生物柴油及其混合物，不含或含有按重量计低于 70% 的石油或从沥青矿物提取的油类：	1. 品名;2. 用途;3. 成分含量;4. 从石油或沥青提取矿物油类的百分比含量

第七类　塑料及其制品;橡胶及其制品

第三十九章　塑料及其制品

【注解】

名词解释:

1、本章"成分含量"是指:"成分"指商品所构成的部分或要素,一般指所含物质的种类。"含量"一般指所含物质的数量。

2、第三十九章的多数产品需要注明成分、含量、单体种类、单体比例,这是明确归类的需要。在实际申报中只要申报的内容能明确归类即可。如"聚乙烯"就可以不用申报单体含量,而"乙烯-丙烯聚合物"就必须申报乙烯单体和丙烯单体的含量。

3、本章商品需要申报的品名包括标准命名法名称或工商业通用俗称。

4、有英文缩写的商品必须申报,如聚乙烯的缩写为 PE。

税则号列	商　品　描　述	规范申报要素 / 价格申报要素 / 其他申报要素 / 举例说明
39.01	初级形状的乙烯聚合物:	
3901.1000	-聚乙烯,比重小于 0.94	1. 品名;2. 外观;3. 成分含量;4. 单体单元的种类和比例;5. 是否为线性;6. 比重;7. 级别;8. 品牌;9. 型号;10. 签约日期;11. 用途
3901.2000	-聚乙烯,比重在 0.94 及以上	1. 品名;2. 外观;3. 成分含量;4. 单体单元的种类和比例;5. 比重;6. 级别;7. 品牌;8. 型号;9. 签约日期;10. 用途
3901.3000	-乙烯-乙酸乙烯酯共聚物	1. 品名;2. 外观;3. 成分含量;4. 单体单元的种类和比例;5. 级别;6. 品牌;7. 牌号或型号;8. 签约日期;9. 生产厂商;10. 用途
3901.9	-其他:	1. 品名;2. 外观;3. 成分含量;4. 单体单元的种类和比例;5. 级别;6. 品牌;7. 型号;8. 签约日期;9. 用途
39.02	初级形状的丙烯或其他烯烃 聚合物:	1. 品名;2. 外观;3. 成分含量;4. 单体单元的种类和比例;5. 级别;6. 品牌;7. 型号;8. 签约日期;9. 用途
39.03	初级形状的苯乙烯聚合物:	
3903.1	-聚苯乙烯:	1. 品名;2. 外观;3. 聚苯乙烯请注明是否为可发性的;4. 成分含量;5. 单体单元的种类和比例;6. 级别;7. 品牌;8. 型号;9. 签约日期;10. 用途
3903.2	-苯乙烯-丙烯腈(SAN)共聚物	1. 品名;2. 外观;3. 成分含量;4. 单体单元的种类和比例;5. 品牌;6. 型号;7. 签约日期;8. 用途
3903.3	-丙烯腈-丁二烯-苯乙烯(ABS)共聚物:	1. 品名;2. 外观;3. 成分含量;4. 单体单元的种类和比例;5. 是否改性;6. 级别;7. 品牌;8. 型号;9. 签约日期;10. 用途
3903.9000	-其他	1. 品名;2. 外观;3. 成分含量;4. 单体单元的种类和比例;5. 品牌;6. 型号;7. 签约日期;8. 用途
39.04	初级形状的氯乙烯或其他卤 化烯烃聚合物:	
3904.1	-聚氯乙烯,未掺其他物质:	1. 品名;2. 外观;3. 聚氯乙烯请注明是否已塑化;4. 聚氯乙烯请注明是否掺有其他物质;5. 成分含量;6. 单体单元的种类和比例;7. 品牌;8. 型号;9. 签约日期;10. 用途
3904.2	-其他聚氯乙烯	1. 品名;2. 外观;3. 聚氯乙烯请注明是否已塑化;4. 聚氯乙烯请注明是否掺有其他物质;5. 成分含量;6. 单体单元的种类和比例;7. 品牌;8. 型号;9. 签约日期;10. 用途
3904.3	-氯乙烯-乙酸乙烯酯共聚物	1. 品名;2. 外观;3. 成分含量;4. 单体单元的种类和比例;5. 品牌;6. 型号;7. 签约日期;8. 用途
3904.4	-其他氯乙烯共聚物	1. 品名;2. 外观;3. 成分含量;4. 单体单元的种类和比例;5. 品牌;6. 型号;7. 签约日期;8. 用途
3904.5000	-偏二氯乙烯聚合物	1. 品名;2. 外观;3. 成分含量;4. 单体单元的种类和比例;5. 品牌;6. 型号;7. 签约日期;8. 用途
3904.6	-氟聚合物:	1. 品名;2. 外观;3. 成分含量;4. 单体单元的种类和比例;5. 品牌;6. 型号;7. 签约日期;8. 用途
3904.9000	-其他	1. 品名;2. 外观;3. 成分含量;4. 单体单元的种类和比例;5. 品牌;6. 型号;7. 签约日期;8. 用途
39.05	初级形状的乙酸乙烯酯或其他乙烯酯聚合物;初级形状的其他乙烯基聚合物:	1. 品名;2. 外观;3. 成分含量;4. 单体单元的种类和比例;5. 品牌;6. 型号;7. 签约日期;8. 用途

税则号列	商品描述	规范申报要素 / 价格申报要素 / 其他申报要素 / 举例说明
39.06	初级形状的丙烯酸聚合物:	1.品名;2.外观;3.成分含量;4.单体单元的种类和比例;5.品牌;6.型号;7.签约日期;8.用途
39.07	初级形状的聚缩醛、其他聚醚 及环氧树脂;初级形状的聚碳酸酯、醇酸树脂、聚烯丙基酯及其他聚酯:	
3907.1	-聚缩醛:	1.品名;2.外观;3.成分含量;4.单体单元的种类和比例;5.品牌;6.型号;7.签约日期;8.用途
3907.2	-其他聚醚:	1.品名;2.外观;3.成分含量;4.单体单元的种类和比例;5.品牌;6.型号;7.签约日期
3907.3000	-环氧树脂	1.品名;2.外观;3.成分含量;4.品牌;5.型号;6.签约日期
3907.4000	-聚碳酸酯	1.品名;2.外观;4.成分含量;4.品牌;5.型号;7.签约日期
3907.5	-醇酸树脂	1.品名;2.外观;3.成分含量;4.单体单元的种类和比例;5.品牌;6.型号;7.用途
3907.6	-聚对苯二甲酸乙二酯:	1.品名;2.外观;3.是否切片;4.成分含量;5.单体单元的种类和比例;6.黏度;7.级别;8.品牌;9.型号;10.签约日期
3907.7000	-聚乳酸	1.品名;2.外观;3.成分含量;4.单体单元的种类和比例;5.品牌;6.型号;7.签约日期;8.用途
3907.9	-其他聚酯:	1.品名;2.外观;3.是否饱和;4.成分含量;5.单体单元的种类和比例;6.品牌;7.型号;8.签约日期
39.08	初级形状的聚酰胺:	1.品名;2.外观;3.是否切片;4.成分含量;5.单体单元的种类和比例;6.级别;7.品牌;8.型号;9.签约日期;10.用途
39.09	初级形状的氨基树脂、酚醛树 脂及聚氨酯类:	1.品名;2.外观;3.成分含量;4.单体单元的种类和比例;5.品牌;6.型号;7.签约日期;8.用途
39.10	初级形状的聚硅氧烷:	1.品名;2.用途;3.外观;4.是否溶于水;5.成分含量;6.品牌;7.型号;8.签约日期
39.11	初级形状的石油树脂、苯并呋 喃—茚树脂、多萜树脂、多硫 化物、聚砜及本章注释三所规 定的其他品目未列名产品:	
3911.1000	-石油树脂、苯并呋喃树脂、茚树脂、苯并呋喃-茚树脂及 多萜树脂	1.品名;2.外观;3.成分含量;4.品牌;5.型号;6.签约日期;7.用途
3911.9000	-其他	1.品名;2.外观;3.成分含量;4.单体单元的种类和比例;5.品牌;6.型号;7.签约日期;8.用途
39.12	初级形状的其他品目未列名 的纤维素及其化学衍生物:	
3912.1	-乙酸纤维素:	1.品名;2.外观;3.是否塑化;4.成分含量;5.品牌;6.型号;7.签约日期;8.用途
3912.2	-硝酸纤维素(包括胶棉)	1.品名;2.外观;3.成分含量;4.品牌;5.型号;6.签约日期;7.用途
3912.3	-纤维素醚:	1.品名;2.外观;3.成分含量;4.品牌;5.型号;6.签约日期;7.用途
3912.9000	-其他	1.品名;2.外观;3.成分含量;4.品牌;5.型号;6.签约日期;7.用途
39.13	初级形状的其他品目未列名的天然聚合物(例如,藻酸)及改性天然聚合物(例如,硬 化蛋白、天然橡胶的化学衍生物):	1.品名;2.外观;3.来源;4.成分含量;5.品牌;6.型号;7.签约日期;8.用途
39.14	初级形状的离子交换剂,以品 目39.01至39.13的聚合物为 基本成分的:	1.品名;2.用途;3.外观;4.成分;5.品牌;6.型号;7.签约日期;8.级别;9.阴离子还是阳离子还是两性
39.15	塑料的废碎料及下脚料:	1.品名;2.外观(颜色、尺寸);3.来源;4.成分;5.是否已经破坏性处理;6.如为成卷,需注明是否带轴心。注:废聚乙烯膜,20~40厘米成卷,带轴心白色薄膜,纵切破坏性处理
39.16	塑料制的单丝(截面直径超过1毫米)、条、杆、型材及异型材,不论是否经表面加工,但未经其他加工:	1.品名;2.外观;3.成分;4.单丝请注明截面直径;5.品牌;6.型号;7.生产厂商;8.用途
39.17	塑料制的管子及其附件(例 如,接头、肘管、法兰):	
3917.1000	-硬化蛋白或纤维素材料制的人造肠衣(香肠用肠衣)	1.品名;2.成分;3.用途;4.品牌;5.型号;6.生产厂商

税则号列	商　品　描　述	规范申报要素 / 价格申报要素 / 其他申报要素 / 举例说明
3917.2	-硬管:	1.品名;2.成分;3.品牌;4.型号;5.生产厂商;6.用途;7.材质
3917.3	-其他管:	1.品名;2.成分;3.是否装有附件;4.最小爆破压力;5.品牌;6.型号;7.生产厂商;8.用途
3917.4	-管子附件	1.品名;2.材质。注:硬聚氯乙烯变接头
39.18	块状或成卷的塑料铺地制品,不论是否胶粘;本章注释九所规定的塑料糊墙品:	1.品名;2.成分;3.品牌;4.型号;5.用途
39.19	自粘的塑料板、片、膜、箔、带、扁条及其他扁平形状材料,不论是否成卷:	1.品名;2.用途;3.外观(板、片、膜、箔、带、扁条);4.是否成卷;5.是否自粘;6.成分含量;7.规格尺寸;8.品牌;9.型号
39.20	其他非泡沫塑料的板、片、膜、箔及扁条,未用其他材料强化、层压、支撑或用类似方法合制:	
3920.1	-乙烯聚合物制:	1.品名;2.用途;3.外观;4.是否与其他材料合制;5.成分;6.规格尺寸;7.是否非泡沫;8.品牌;9.型号
3920.2	-丙烯聚合物制:	1.品名;2.用途;3.外观;4.是否与其他材料合制;5.成分;6.规格尺寸;7.是否非泡沫;8.品牌;9.型号
3920.3000	-苯乙烯聚合物制	1.品名;2.用途;3.外观;4.是否与其他材料合制;5.成分;6.规格尺寸;7.是否非泡沫;8.品牌;9.型号
3920.4	-氯乙烯聚合物制:	1.品名;2.用途;3.外观;4.是否与其他材料合制;5.成分;6.规格尺寸;7.PVC 制品请注明增塑剂含量;8.是否非泡沫;9.品牌;10.型号
3920.5	-丙烯酸聚合物制:	1.品名;2.用途;3.外观;4.是否与其他材料合制;5.成分;6.规格尺寸;7.是否非泡沫;8.品牌;9.型号
3920.6	-聚碳酸酯、醇酸树脂、聚烯 丙酯或其他聚酯制:	1.品名;2.用途;3.外观;4.是否与其他材料合制;5.成分;6.规格尺寸;7.是否非泡沫;8.品牌;9.型号
3920.7	-纤维素及其化学衍生物制:	1.品名;2.用途;3.外观;4.是否与其他材料合制;5.成分;6.规格尺寸;7.是否非泡沫;8.品牌;9.型号
3920.9	-其他塑料制:	1.品名;2.用途;3.外观;4.是否与其他材料合制;5.成分;6.规格尺寸;7.是否非泡沫;8.品牌;9.型号
39.21	其他塑料板、片、膜、箔、扁条:	1.品名;2.成分;3.外观;4.是否与其他材料合制;5.泡沫塑料请注明;6.用途;7.规格尺寸;8.品牌;9.型号
39.22	塑料浴缸、淋浴盘、洗涤槽、盥洗盆、坐浴盆、便盆、马桶座圈及盖、抽水箱及类似卫生洁具:	1.品名;2.用途;3.材质;4.品牌;5.型号
39.23	供运输或包装货物用的塑料制品;塑料制的塞子、盖子及类似品:	1.品名;2.用途;3.材质;4.品牌;5.型号
39.24	塑料制的餐具、厨房用具、其 他家庭用具及卫生或盥洗用 具:	1.品名;2.用途;3.材质;4.品牌;5.型号
39.25	其他品目未列名的建筑用塑料制品:	1.品名;2.用途;3.塑料制囤、柜、罐、桶及类似容器请注明容积;4.材质;5.品牌
39.26	其他塑料制品及品目 39.01 至 39.14 所列其他材料的制品:	1.品名;2.用途;3.材质;4.品牌;5.型号

第四十章　橡胶及其制品

【注解】

1、本章"成分含量"是指:"成分"指商品所构成的部分或要素,一般指所含物质的种类;"含量"一般指所含物质的数量。

2、本章的一些产品需要注明成分、含量、单体种类、单体比例,这是明确归类的需要。在实际申报中只要申报的内容能明确归类即可。

3、本章商品需要申报的品名包括标准命名法名称或工商业通用俗称。

税则号列	商　品　描　述	规范申报要素 / 价格申报要素 / 其他申报要素 / 举例说明
40.01	天然橡胶、巴拉塔胶、古塔波胶、银胶菊胶、糖胶树胶及类似的天然树胶,初级形状或板、片、带:	1.品名;2.外观;3.型号;4.包装;5.签约日期;6.干胶含量
40.02	合成橡胶及从油类提取的油膏,初级形状或板、片、带;品目 40.01 所列产品与本品目 所列产品的混合物,初级形状 或板、片、带:	

税则号列	商品描述	规范申报要素 / 价格申报要素 / 其他申报要素 / 举例说明
4002.11	--胶乳：	1.品名;2.用途;3.外观;4.成分含量;5.签约日期;6.品牌;7.型号
4002.19	--其他：	1.品名;2.用途;3.外观;4.丁苯橡胶请注明是否充油、热塑;5.成分含量;6.签约日期;7.品牌;8.型号
4002.2	-丁二烯橡胶(BR)：	1.品名;2.用途;3.外观;4.成分含量;5.签约日期;6.品牌;7.型号
4002.3	-异丁烯-异戊二烯(丁基)橡胶(IIR);卤代丁基橡胶(CIIR或BIIR)：	1.品名;2.用途;3.外观;4.成分含量;5.签约日期;6.品牌;7.型号
4002.4	-氯丁二烯(氯丁)橡胶(CR)：	1.品名;2.用途;3.外观;4.成分含量;5.签约日期;6.品牌;7.型号
4002.5	-丁腈橡胶(NBR)：	1.品名;2.用途;3.外观;4.成分含量;5.签约日期;6.品牌;7.型号
4002.6	-异戊二烯橡胶(IR)：	1.品名;2.用途;3.外观;4.成分含量;5.签约日期;6.品牌;7.型号
4002.7	-乙丙非共轭二烯橡胶(EPDM)：	1.品名;2.用途;3.外观;4.成分含量;5.签约日期;6.品牌;7.型号
4002.8000	-品目40.01所列产品与本品目所列产品的混合物	1.品名;2.用途;3.外观;4.成分含量;5.签约日期;6.品牌;7.型号
4002.9	-其他：	1.品名;2.用途;3.外观;4.成分含量;5.签约日期;6.品牌;7.型号
40.03	再生橡胶,初级形状或板、片、带：	1.品名;2.外观;3.来源
40.04	橡胶(硬质橡胶的除外)的废碎料、下脚料及其粉、粒：	1.品名;2.外观;3.来源;4.水分;5.杂质;6.干胶含量
4005	未硫化的复合橡胶,初级形状或板、片、带：	1.品名;2.外观;3.硫化的请注明;4.成分;5.签约日期;6.品牌;7.型号。注:未硫化复合橡胶(成分为丁苯橡胶、炭黑,黑色有弹性的片状固体)
40.06	其他形状(例如,杆、管或型材及异型材)的未硫化橡胶及未硫化橡胶制品(例如,盘、环)：	1.品名;2.用途;3.外观;4.材质;5.品牌;6.型号。注:未硫化的丁腈橡胶密封圈(用于机械设备的密封,黑色有弹性的环)
40.07	硫化橡胶线及绳：	1.品名;2.外观;3.截面尺寸;4.材质;5.品牌;6.型号。注:硫化丁二烯橡胶线(黑色有弹性单股线;截面尺寸4.5毫米)
40.08	硫化橡胶(硬质橡胶除外)制的板、片、带、杆或型材及异型材：	1.品名;2.外观;3.是否海绵橡胶;4.规格尺寸;5.是否硫化;6.材质;7.品牌;8.型号。注:软质硫化的橡胶片(海绵橡胶制,红色多孔性高弹性片状固体,厚度2毫米,长度1米,宽度50厘米)
40.09	硫化橡胶(硬质橡胶除外)制的管子,不论是否装有附件(例如,接头、肘管、法兰)	1.品名;2.用途;3.外观;4.材质构成(是否加强或与其他材料合制);5.是否装有附件;6.品牌;7.型号。注:未装附件、未加强和未与其他材料合制的软质硫化的橡胶管
40.10	硫化橡胶制的传动带或输送带及带料：	
4010.1	-输送带及带料：	1.品名;2.用途;3.外观;4.材质结构(是否加强或与其他材料合制);5.加强材料要注明;6.规格尺寸;7.品牌;8.型号
4010.3100	--梯形截面的环形传动带(三角带),V形肋状的,外周长超过60厘米,但不超过180厘米	1.品名;2.用途;3.外观;4.材质;5.规格尺寸(外周长);6.截面形状;7.品牌
4010.3200	--梯形截面的环形传动带(三角带),外周长超过60厘米但不超过180厘米,V形肋状的除外	1.品名;2.用途;3.外观;4.材质;5.规格尺寸(外周长);6.截面形状;7.品牌
4010.3300	--梯形截面的环形传动带(三角带),V形肋状的,外周长超过180厘米,但不超过240厘米	1.品名;2.用途;3.外观;4.材质;5.规格尺寸(外周长);6.截面形状;7.品牌
4010.3400	--梯形截面的环形传动带(三角带),外周长超过180厘米但不超过240厘米,V形肋状的除外	1.品名;2.用途;3.外观;4.材质;5.规格尺寸(外周长);6.截面形状;7.品牌
4010.35	--环形同步带,外周长超过60厘米,但不超过150厘米	1.品名;2.用途;3.外观;4.材质;5.规格尺寸(外周长);6.品牌
4010.3600	--环形同步带,外周长超过150厘米,但不超过198厘米	1.品名;2.用途;3.外观;4.材质;5.规格尺寸(外周长);6.品牌
4010.3900	--其他	1.品名;2.用途;3.外观;4.材质;5.规格尺寸(外周长);6.截面形状;7.品牌

税则号列	商品描述	规范申报要素 / 价格申报要素 / 其他申报要素 / 举例说明
40.11	新的充气橡胶轮胎：	1.品名;2.用途;3.规格型号;4.辋圈尺寸;5.胎面花纹;6.断面宽度;7.品牌
40.12	翻新的或旧的充气橡胶轮胎；实心或半实心橡胶轮胎、橡胶 胎面及橡胶轮胎衬带：	1.品名;2.用途;3.是否实心;4.充气轮胎请注明翻新或旧的;5.品牌;6.型号
40.13	橡胶内胎：	1.品名;2.用途;3.品牌
40.14	硫化橡胶(硬质橡胶除外)制的卫生及医疗用品(包括奶嘴),不论是否装有硬质橡胶制的附件：	1.品名;2.用途;3.品牌
40.15	硫化橡胶(硬质橡胶除外)制的衣着用品及附件(包括手套)：	
4015.1100	--外科用	1.品名;2.用途;3.品牌。注:不包括橡胶线与纺织材料合制的衣着用品及附件(第六十一或第六十二章)
4015.1900	--其他	1.品名;2.用途;3.品牌;4.成分(含胶率);5.规格型号(S、M、XL等)。注:不包括橡胶线与纺织材料合制的衣着用品及附件(第六十一或第六十二章)
4015.9	-其他：	1.品名;2.用途;3.品牌。注:不包括橡胶线与纺织材料合制的衣着用品及附件(第六十一或第六十二章)
40.16	硫化橡胶(硬质橡胶除外)的其他制品：	1.品名;2.用途;3.材质(海绵橡胶、硫化橡胶等)4.是否机器及仪器用;5.品牌;6.型号
40.17	各种形状的硬质橡胶(例如,纯硬质胶),包括废碎料;硬质橡胶制品：	1.品名;2.外观;3.成分

第八类　生皮、皮革、毛皮及其制品；鞍具及挽具；旅行用品、手提包及类似容器；动物肠线(蚕胶丝除外)制品

第四十一章　生皮(毛皮除外)及皮革

【注解】

油鞣皮革是通过用鱼油或动物油反复鞣制,然后加热烘干或晾干,用碱水洗去余油,最后清洁皮张的表面,并用浮石或其他磨料进行磨里加工制得。这样鞣制的皮革通常采用正面起绒除去粒层的绵羊或羔羊肉面剖层皮来做原料;漆皮,即涂有一层清漆或大漆,或在皮革表面覆盖一层塑料膜的皮革。这种皮革的表面光亮宛如镜面;层压漆皮,商业上称为特种漆革,这种皮革的表面覆盖了一层塑料片,其厚度超过0.15毫米,但不超过总厚度的一半,并且与漆皮一样有着镜面般的光洁表面;镀金属皮革,即表面涂有或覆盖金属(例如,银、金、青铜或铝)粉末或箔的皮革;本章所称"坯革",包括在干燥前经复鞣、染色或加油(加脂)的皮;经鞣制或鞣制后进一步加工的皮张在贸易上称为"皮革"。鞣制后经干燥的皮革称为"坯革"。

税则号列	商品描述	规范申报要素 / 价格申报要素 / 其他申报要素 / 举例说明
41.01	生牛皮(包括水牛皮)、生马皮(鲜的、盐腌的、干的、石灰浸渍的、浸酸的或以其他方法保藏,但未鞣制、未经羊皮纸化处理或进一步加工的),不论是否去毛或刨层：	1.品名;2.制作或保存方法(鲜、干、盐渍、石灰浸渍、浸酸、未鞣制、退鞣处理);3.状态(整张/半张,是否去肉修边等等);4.平均每张重量;5.种类(公牛、未育/已育母牛、奶牛、阉牛、小牛、死牛、马);6.产区(如澳大利亚维多利亚、新南威尔士等)。注:本税目仅指生皮。注:牛皮、盐干、整张臀部烙印、阉牛、厚度0.5～1毫米、平均每张64～66磅、一级
41.02	绵羊或羔羊生皮(鲜的、盐渍的、干的、石灰浸渍的、浸酸的或经其他方法保藏,但未鞣 制、未经羊皮纸化处理或进一 步加工的),不论是否带毛或剖层,但本章注释一(三)所述不包括的生皮除外：	1.品名;2.制作或保存方法(鲜、干、盐渍、石灰浸渍、浸酸、未鞣制、退鞣处理);3.种类(羔羊、绵羊);4.状态(带毛、不带毛);5.规格(毛长);6.请注明平方英尺数/张;7.等级;8.用途(毛革一体、制革)。注:本税目仅指生皮
41.03	其他生皮(鲜的、盐渍的、干 的、石灰浸渍的、浸酸的或以其他方法保藏,但未鞣制、未经羊皮纸化处理或进一步加工的),不论是否去毛或剖层,但本章注释一(二)或(三)所述不包括的生皮除外：	1.品名;2.制作或保存方法(鲜、干、盐渍、石灰浸渍、浸酸、未鞣制、退鞣处理);3.种类(山羊、猪、爬行动物等);4.是否源于野生动物;5.规格(面积或重量)

税则号列	商品描述	规范申报要素 / 价格申报要素 / 其他申报要素 / 举例说明
41.04	经鞣制的不带毛牛皮(包括水牛皮)、马皮及其坯革,不论是否剖层,但未经进一步加工:	1.品名;2.制作或保存方法(干、鞣制无毛、表面是否涂覆、涂覆何种物质);3.状态(湿,如蓝湿,整张/半张/背皮/头颈等);4.种类(公牛、母牛、奶牛、阉牛、马);5.是否源于野生动物;6.规格(厚度、平均尺寸及平均重量);7.品种(全粒面未剖层或粒面剖层);8.用途:;9.级别(头层皮 TR1/2/3,二层皮 A/B/C/D 级)
41.05	经鞣制的不带毛绵羊或羔羊皮及其坯革,不论是否剖层,但未经进一步加工:	1.品名;2.制作或保存方法(干、鞣制无毛);3.种类(羔羊、绵羊);4.状态(湿,如蓝湿);5.是否源于野生动物;6.规格(厚度、张幅)
41.06	经鞣制的其他不带毛动物皮 及其坯革,不论是否剖层,但未经进一步加工:	1.品名;2.制作或保存方法(干、鞣制无毛);3.种类(羔羊、绵羊);4.状态(湿,如蓝湿);5.是否源于野生动物;6.规格(厚度、张幅)
41.07	经鞣制或半硝处理后进一步加工的牛皮革(包括水牛皮革)及马皮革,包括羊皮纸化 处理的皮革,不论是否剖层,但品目 41.14 的皮革除外:	1.品名;2.制作或保存方法(干、鞣制无毛);3.种类(羔羊、绵羊);4.状态(湿,如蓝湿);5.是否源于野生动物;6.规格(厚度、张幅)
4107.11	--全粒面未剖层革:	1.品名;2.制作或保存方法(表面是否涂覆、涂覆何种物质);3.种类(牛、马);4.状态(整张,无毛全粒面未剖层或无毛粒面剖层、二层牛皮);5.规格(厚度、平均面积);6.颜色
4107.12	--粒面剖层革:	1.品名;2.制作或保存方法(表面是否涂覆、涂覆何种物质);3.种类(牛、马);4.状态(整张,无毛全粒面未剖层或无毛粒面剖层、二层牛皮);5.规格(厚度、平均面积);6.颜色
4107.1910	---机器带用	1.品名;2.制作或保存方法(表面是否涂覆、涂覆何种物质);3.种类(牛、马);4.状态(整张,无毛全粒面未剖层或无毛粒面剖层、二层牛皮);5.用途(机器带用);6.规格(厚度、平均面积);7.颜色
4107.199	---其他	1.品名;2.制作或保存方法(表面是否涂覆、涂覆何种物质);3.种类(牛、马);4.状态(整张,无毛全粒面未剖层或无毛粒面剖层、二层牛皮);5.规格(厚度、平均面积);6.颜色
4107.9100	--全粒面未剖层革	1.品名;2.制作或保存方法(表面是否涂覆、涂覆何种物质);3.种类(牛、马);4.状态(整张,无毛全粒面未剖层或无毛粒面剖层、二层牛皮);5.规格(厚度、平均面积);6.颜色
4107.9200	--粒面剖层革	1.品名;2.制作或保存方法(表面是否涂覆、涂覆何种物质);3.种类(牛、马);4.状态(整张,无毛全粒面未剖层或无毛粒面剖层、二层牛皮);5.规格(厚度、平均面积);6.颜色
4107.9910	---机器带用	1.品名;2.制作或保存方法(表面是否涂覆、涂覆何种物质);3.种类(牛、马);4.状态(半张,无毛全粒面未剖层或无毛粒面剖层、二层牛皮);5.用途(机器带用);6.规格(厚度、平均面积);7.颜色)
4107.9990	---其他	1.品名;2.制作或保存方法(表面是否涂覆、涂覆何种物质);3.种类(牛、马);4.状态(半张,无毛全粒面未剖层或无毛粒面剖层、二层牛皮);5.规格(厚度、平均面积);6.颜色
41.12	经鞣制或半硝处理后进一步加工的不带毛的绵羊或羔羊 皮革,包括羊皮纸化处理的,不论是否剖层,但品目 41.14 的皮革除外:	1.品名;2.种类;3.状态(无毛全粒面或无毛羊皮纸化等);4.规格(厚度及面积);5.颜色
41.13	经鞣制或半硝处理后进一步加工的不带毛的其他动物皮 革,包括羊皮纸化处理的,不论是否剖层,但品目 41.14 的 皮革除外:	1.品名;2.制作或保存方法;3.状态(无毛全粒面等);4.规格(厚度及面积);5.请注明平方英尺数/张
41.14	油鞣皮革(包括结合鞣制的油鞣皮革);漆皮及层压漆皮;镀金属皮革:	1.品名;2.制作或保存方法(漆皮、镀金属);3.规格(厚度);4.请注明平方英尺数/张
41.15	以皮革或皮革纤维为基本成 分的再生皮革,成块、成张或成条,不论是否成卷;皮革或再生皮革的边角废料,不适宜做皮革制品用;皮革粉末:	
4115.1000	-以皮革或皮革纤维为基本成分的再生皮革,成块、成张或成条,不论是否成卷	1.品名;2.制作或保存方法(再生);3.状态(块、张、条、卷、边角料、粉末);4.规格(厚度)

税则号列	商品描述	规范申报要素 / 价格申报要素 / 其他申报要素 / 举例说明
4115.2000	-皮革或再生皮革的边角废料,不适宜作皮革制品用;皮革粉末	1.品名;2.状态(块、张、条、卷、边角料、粉末);3.用途;4.规格(厚度、面积);5.是否经过筛选

第四十二章　皮革制品;鞍具及挽具;旅行用品、手提包及类似容器;动物肠线(蚕胶丝除外)制品

【注解】

本章所称"运动包",包括高尔夫球袋、体操袋、网球拍提袋、滑雪袋和钓鱼袋;本章所称"首饰盒",不仅包括为存放首饰而专门设计的盒子,也包括其形状和配件专门适于盛装一件或多件首饰的各种规格的类似有盖容器,不论是否装有铰链或扣件。它们一般用纺织材料衬里。这些容器盛装首饰后可一同展示及出售,适于长期使用;本章所称"食品或饮料保温包",包括在运输或临时保存期间保持食物及饮料温度用的可重复使用的保温包。

税则号列	商品描述	规范申报要素 / 价格申报要素 / 其他申报要素 / 举例说明
42.01	各种材料制成的鞍具及挽具(包括缰绳、挽绳、护膝垫、口套、鞍褥、马褡裢、狗外套及类似品),适合各种动物用:	1.品名;2.材质
42.02	衣箱、提箱、小手袋、公文箱、公文包、书包、眼镜盒、望远镜盒、照相机套、乐器盒、枪套及类似容器;旅行包、食品或饮料保温包、化妆包、帆布包、手提包、购物袋、钱夹、钱包、地图盒、烟盒、烟袋、工具包、运动包、瓶盒、首饰盒、粉盒、刀叉餐具盒及类似容器,用皮革或再生皮革、塑料片、纺织材料、钢纸或纸板制成,或者全部或主要用上述材料或纸包覆制成:	
4202.1110	---衣箱	1.品名;2.种类(衣箱、提箱、小手袋等);3.表面材质(塑料、纺织物等);4.品牌及款号
4202.1190	---其他	1.品名;2.表面材质(塑料、纺织物等);3.品牌及款号
4202.12	--以塑料或纺织材料作面:	1.品名;2.种类(衣箱、提箱、小手袋等);3.表面材质(塑料、纺织物等);4.品牌及款号
4202.1900	--其他	1.品名;2.种类(衣箱、提箱、小手袋等);3.表面材质(塑料、纺织物等);4.品牌及款号
4202.2100	--以皮革、再生皮革作面的手提包	1.品名;2.种类(衣箱、提箱、小手袋等);3.表面材质(塑料、纺织物等);4.品牌及款号
4202.2200	--以塑料片或纺织材料作面的手提包	1.品名;2.种类(衣箱、提箱、小手袋等);3.表面材质(塑料、纺织物等);4.品牌及款号
4202.2900	--以钢纸或纸板作面的手提包	1.品名;2.种类(钱夹、钱包、手机套等适放在口袋、手提袋内);3.表面材质(塑料、纺织物等);4.品牌及款号
4202.3	-通常置于口袋或手提包内的物品:	1.品名;2.种类(衣箱、提箱、小手袋等);3.表面材质(塑料、纺织物等);4.品牌及款号
4202.9	-其他:	1.品名;2.种类(衣箱、提箱、小手袋等);3.表面材质(塑料、纺织物等);4.品牌及款号
42.03	皮革或再生皮革制的衣服及衣着附件:	
4203.1000	-衣服	1.品名;2.材质(皮革或再生皮革);3.衣服种类;4.是否源于野生动物;5.品牌及款号
4203.2	-手套,包括连指或露指的:	1.品名;2.用途(专供运动用、劳保用等);3.材质(皮革或再生皮革)
4203.3	-腰带及子弹带:	1.品名;2.材质(皮革或再生皮革)
4203.4000	-其他衣着附件	1.品名;2.材质(皮革或再生皮革)
42.05	皮革或再生皮革的其他制品:	
4205.0010	---坐具套	1.品名;2.材质(皮革或再生皮革)
4205.0020	---机器、机械器具或其他专门技术用途的	1.品名;2.用途(机械、技术用等);3.材质(皮革或再生皮革)
4205.0090	---其他	1.品名;2.用途;3.材质(皮革或再生皮革);4.品牌
42.06	肠线(蚕胶丝除外)、肠膜、膀胱或筋腱制品:	1.品名。注:蚕胶丝应归入税目50.06;不包括税目30.06的货品

第四十三章　毛皮、人造毛皮及其制品

【注解】

本章所称“人造毛皮”，是指将毛、发或其他纤维（包括绳绒纱线的纤维）粘附或缝合于皮革、织物或其他材料上以仿充毛皮的材料，但不包括有时也被人称为“毛皮织物”的纺织或针织长毛绒织物（一般归入税目58.01或60.01），也不包括“加毛”毛皮，即额外插毛的真毛皮。

税则号列	商品描述	规范申报要素 / 价格申报要素 / 其他申报要素 / 举例说明
43.01	生毛皮（包括适合加工皮货用的头、尾、爪及其他块、片）但品目41.01、41.02或41.03的生皮除外：	
4301.1000	-整张水貂皮，不论是否带头、尾或爪	1.品名；2.种类（中国羔羊、波斯羔羊、狐皮、兔皮等）；3.状态（生毛皮）；4.外观（整张、头、尾、爪等）；5.品种（深棕、黑十字等）；6.性别（公、母）；7.尺寸（50号、40号等）；8.颜色；9.质量（皇冠、等外）；10.是否来自拍卖会及拍卖会日期。注：明显不能做皮货用的毛皮的废料应归入税目05.11；不包括税目41.01、41.02、41.03的生皮
4301.3000	-下列羔羊的整张毛皮，不论是否带头、尾或爪：阿斯特拉罕、喀拉科尔、波斯羔羊及类似羔羊、印度、中国或蒙古羔羊	1.品名；2.种类（中国羔羊、波斯羔羊、狐皮、兔皮等）；3.状态（生毛皮）；4.外观（整张、头、尾、爪等）。注：明显不能做皮货用的毛皮的废料应归入税目05.11；不包括税目41.01、41.02、41.03的生皮
4301.6000	-整张狐皮，不论是否带头、尾或爪	1.品名；2.种类（中国羔羊、波斯羔羊、狐皮、兔皮等）；3.状态（生毛皮）；4.外观（整张、头、尾、爪等）；5.品种（蓝狐、蓝霜狐皮等）；6.尺寸（50号、40号等）；7.颜色（深、浅）；8.质量（世家皇冠、世家级）；9.是否来自拍卖会及拍卖日期。注：明显不能做皮货用的毛皮的废料应归入税目05.11；不包括税目41.01、41.02、41.03的生皮
4301.8010	---整张兔皮，不论是否带头、尾或爪	1.品名；2.种类（中国羔羊、波斯羔羊、狐皮、兔皮等）；3.状态（生毛皮）；4.外观（整张、头、尾、爪等）；5.颜色（白色、黑色等）。注：明显不能做皮货用的毛皮的废料应归入税目05.11；不包括税目41.01、41.02、41.03的生皮
4301.809	---其他	1.品名；2.种类（中国羔羊、波斯羔羊、狐皮、兔皮等）；3.状态（生毛皮）；4.外观（整张、头、尾、爪等）。注：明显不能做皮货用的毛皮的废料应归入税目05.11；不包括税目41.01、41.02、41.03的生皮
4301.9	-适合加工皮货用的头、尾、爪及其他块、片：	1.品名；2.种类（中国羔羊、波斯羔羊、狐皮、兔皮等）；3.状态（生毛皮）；4.外观（整张、头、尾、爪等）。注：明显不能做皮货用的毛皮的废料应归入税目05.11；不包括税目41.01、41.02、41.03的生皮
43.02	未缝制或已缝制（不加其他材料）的已鞣毛皮（包括头、尾爪及其他块、片），但品目43.03的货品除外：	
4302.1100	--水貂皮	1.品名；2.种类（中国羔羊、波斯羔羊、狐皮、兔皮等）；3.制作或保存方法（鞣制未缝制或已缝制毛皮）；4.外观（整张、头、尾、爪等）；5.品种（深棕、黑十字等）；6.性别（公、母）；7.尺寸（50号、40号等）；8.颜色；9.质量（皇冠、等外）；10.是否来自拍卖会及拍卖会日期
4302.1910	---灰鼠皮、白鼬皮、其他貂皮、狐皮、水獭皮、旱獭皮及猞猁皮	1.品名；2.种类（中国羔羊、波斯羔羊、狐皮、兔皮等）；3.制作或保存方法（鞣制未缝制或已缝制毛皮）；4.外观（整张、头、尾、爪等）；5.品种（蓝狐、蓝霜狐皮等）；6.尺寸（50号、40号等）；7.颜色（深、浅）；8.质量（世家皇冠、世家级）；9.是否来自拍卖会及拍卖日期
4302.1920	---兔皮	1.品名；2.种类（中国羔羊、波斯羔羊、狐皮、兔皮等）；3.制作或保存方法（鞣制未缝制或已缝制毛皮）；4.外观（整张、头、尾、爪等）；5.规格
4302.1930	---下列羔羊皮：阿斯特拉罕、喀拉科尔、波斯羔羊及类似羔羊，印度、中国或蒙古羔羊	1.品名；2.种类（中国羔羊、波斯羔羊、狐皮、兔皮等）；3.制作或保存方法（鞣制未缝制或已缝制毛皮）；4.外观（整张、头、尾、爪等）；5.规格
4302.1990	---其他	1.品名；2.种类（中国羔羊、波斯羔羊、狐皮、兔皮等）；3.制作或保存方法（鞣制未缝制或已缝制毛皮）；4.外观（整张、头、尾、爪等）；5.规格
4302.2000	-未缝制的头、尾、爪及其他块、片	1.品名；2.种类（中国羔羊、波斯羔羊、狐皮、兔皮等）；3.制作或保存方法（鞣制未缝制或已缝制毛皮）；4.外观（整张、头、尾、爪等）；5.规格
4302.3	-已缝制的整张毛皮及其块、片	1.品名；2.种类（中国羔羊、波斯羔羊、狐皮、兔皮等）；3.制作或保存方法（鞣制未缝制或已缝制毛皮）；4.外观（整张、头、尾、爪等）；5.规格

税则号列	商 品 描 述	规范申报要素 / 价格申报要素 / 其他申报要素 / 举例说明
43.03	毛皮制的衣服、衣着附件及其他物品:	1.品名;2.材质(里、外);3.衣服种类
43.04	人造毛皮及其制品:	1.品名;2.材质(人造毛皮)

第九类　木及木制品;木炭;软木及软木制品;稻草、秸秆、针茅或其他编结材料制品;篮筐及柳条编结品

第四十四章　木及木制品;木炭

【注解】

"品名"项应填报植物学名;本章所称"强化木",是指经过化学或物理方法处理(对于多层粘合木材,其处理应超出一般粘合需要),从而增加了密度或硬度并改善了机械强度,抗化学或抗电性能的木材;本章所称"木"也包括竹及其他木质材料。

税则号列	商 品 描 述	规范申报要素 / 价格申报要素 / 其他申报要素 / 举例说明
44.01	薪柴(圆木段、块、枝、成捆或类似形状);木片或木粒;锯末、木废料及碎片,不论是否粘结成圆木段、块片或类似形状:	
4401.1000	-薪柴(圆木段、块、枝,成捆或类似形状)	1.品名;2.种类(中文及拉丁学名);3.外观(圆木段、块、枝、成捆或类似形状等)。注:涂有树脂或以其他方法制成点火物的木及木废料归入税目36.06
4401.2	-木片或木粒:	1.品名;2.种类(中文及拉丁学名);3.外观(木片、粒等)。注:涂有树脂或以其他方法制成点火物的木及木废料归入税目36.06
4401.3100	--木屑棒	1.品名;2.外观(棒);3.规格(直径×长度)。注:涂有树脂或以其他方法制成点火物的木及木废料归入税目36.06
4401.3900	--其他	1.品名;2.外观(末、废料、碎片等)。注:涂有树脂或以其他方法制成点火物的木及木废料归入税目36.06
44.02	木炭(包括果壳炭及果核炭),不论是否结块:	
4402.1000	-竹的	1.品名;2.材质。注:与香料混合后制成片状或其他形状的木炭归入税目33.07;活性碳归入税目38.02;绘图用木炭(炭笔)归入税目96.09
4402.9000	-其他	1.品名;2.材质;3.碳含量;4.挥发份。注:与香料混合后制成片状或其他形状的木炭归入税目33.07;活性碳归入税目38.02;绘图用木炭(炭笔)归入税目96.09
44.03	原木,不论是否去皮、去边材或粗锯成方:	
4403.1000	-用油漆、着色剂、杂酚油或其他防腐剂处理	1.品名;2.种类(中文及拉丁学名);3.加工方法(用油漆、着色剂等防腐剂处理等);4.直径;5.长度
4403.2	-其他针叶木:	1.品名;2.种类(中文及拉丁学名);3.直径;4.长度;5.级别(锯材级、切片级等)
4403.4	-其他,本章子目注释二所列的热带木:	1.品名;2.种类(中文及拉丁学名);3.直径;4.长度;5.级别(锯材级、切片级等)
4403.9	-其他:	1.品名;2.种类(中文及拉丁学名);3.直径;4.长度;5.级别(锯材级、切片级等)
44.04	箍木;木劈条;已削尖但未经纵锯的木桩;粗加修整但未经车圆、弯曲或其他方式加工的木棒,适合制手杖、伞柄、工具把柄及类似品;木片条及类似品:	1.品名;2.种类(中文及拉丁学名);3.外观(棒状、条状等)
44.05	木丝;木粉:	1.品名;2.外观(丝及粉)
44.06	铁道及电车道枕木:	1.品名;2.加工方法(是否浸渍);3.规格(长×宽×高)
44.07	经纵锯、纵切、刨切或旋切的木材,不论是否刨平、砂光或指榫接合,厚度超过6毫米:	
4407.1	-针叶木:	1.品名;2.种类(中文及拉丁学名);3.加工方法(经纵锯、纵切、刨切或旋切加工、端部接合);4.规格(长×宽×高);5.等级
4407.2	-本章子目注释二所列的热带 木:	1.品名;2.种类(中文及拉丁学名);3.加工方法(经纵锯、纵切、刨切或旋切加工、端部接合);4.规格(长×宽×高);5.等级

税则号列	商品描述	规范申报要素 / 价格申报要素 / 其他申报要素 / 举例说明
4407.9100	--栎木(橡木)	1.品名;2.种类(中文及拉丁学名);3.加工方法(经纵锯、纵切、刨切或旋切加工、端部接合);4.规格(长×宽×高);5.等级
4407.9200	--山毛榉木	1.品名;2.种类(中文及拉丁学名);3.加工方法(经纵锯、纵切、刨切或旋切加工、端部接合);4.规格(长×宽×高);5.等级;6.毛边板或直边板请注明
4407.9300	--枫木	1.品名;2.种类(中文及拉丁学名);3.加工方法(经纵锯、纵切、刨切或旋切加工、端部接合);4.规格(长×宽×高);5.等级
4407.9400	--樱桃木	1.品名;2.种类(中文及拉丁学名);3.加工方法(经纵锯、纵切、刨切或旋切加工、端部接合);4.规格(长×宽×高);5.等级
4407.9500	--白蜡木	1.品名;2.种类(中文及拉丁学名);3.加工方法(经纵锯、纵切、刨切或旋切加工、端部接合);4.规格(长×宽×高);5.等级
4407.99	--其他:	1.品名;2.种类(中文及拉丁学名);3.加工方法(经纵锯、纵切、刨切或旋切加工、端部接合);4.规格(长×宽×高);5.等级
44.08	饰面用单板(包括刨切积层木获得的单板),制胶合板或类似多层板用单板以及其他经纵锯、刨切或旋切的木材,不论是否刨平、砂光、拼接或端部接合厚度不超过6毫米:	1.品名;2.用途(饰面用等);3.种类(树种名称);4.外观(单板);5.规格(厚度×宽度×长度);6.加工工艺(纵锯、刨切、旋切等);7.请注明立方米数或平方米数
44.09	任何一边端或面制成连续形状(舌榫、槽榫、半槽榫、斜角、V形接头、珠榫、缘饰、刨圆及类似形状)的木材(包括未装拼的拼花地板用板条及缘板),不论是否刨平、砂光或端部接合	1.品名;2.种类(中文及拉丁学名);3.外观(舌榫、槽榫、半槽榫等);4.规格(厚度×宽度×长度);5.加工工艺
44.10	碎料板、定向刨花板(OSB及类似板(例如,华夫板)木或其他木质材料制,不论是否用树脂或其他有机粘合剂粘合:	1.品名;2.材质(木质或类似木质材料);3.请注明立方米数或平方米数。注:用水泥、石膏或其他无机黏合物质粘聚而成的木质材料板归入税目68.08
44.11	木纤维板或其他木质材料纤维板,不论是否用树脂或其他有机粘合剂粘合:	
4411.1	-中密度纤维板:	1.品名;2.加工方法(是否经机械加工或盖面、干法、湿法等);3.密度;4.厚度;5.请注明是否辐射松制;6.请注明立方米数或平方米数
4411.9	-其他:	1.品名;2.加工方法(是否经机械加工或盖面、干法、湿法等);3.密度;4.请注明是否辐射松制;5.请注明立方米数或平方米数
44.12	胶合板、单板饰面板及类似的多层板:	1.品名;2.每层材质及树种名称;3.单层厚度;4.规格(厚度×宽度×长度);5.加工工艺;6.请注明立方米数或平方米数
44.13	强化木,成块、板、条或异型的:	1.品名;2.加工方法(压缩、浸渍等);3.外观(块、板、条、异型)
44.14	木制的画框、相框、镜框及类似品:	1.品名;2.材质(木制);3.种类(中文及拉丁学名)。注:镶框玻璃镜归入税目70.09
44.15	包装木箱、木盒、板条箱、圆桶及类似的包装容器;木制电缆卷筒;木托板、箱形托盘及其他装载用木板;木制的托盘护框:	1.品名;2.材质(木制);3.种类(中文及拉丁学名)经特殊设计,装备适于一种或多种运输方式的集装箱归入税目86.09
44.16	木制大桶、琵琶桶、盆和其他木制箍桶及其零件,包括桶板:	1.品名;2.材质(木制);3.种类(单一材质申报中文及拉丁学名)
44.17	木制的工具、工具支架、工具柄、扫帚及刷子的身及柄木制鞋靴楦及楦头:	1.品名;2.材质(木制);3.种类(单一材质申报中文及拉丁学名)
44.18	建筑用木工制品,包括蜂窝结构木镶板、已装拼的地板、木瓦及盖屋板:	
4418.1	-窗、法兰西式(落地)窗及其框架:	1.品名;2.用途(建筑用);3.材质(木制);4.种类(中文及拉丁学名)
4418.2000	-门及其框架和门槛	1.品名;2.用途(建筑用);3.材质(木制);4.种类(中文及拉丁学名);5.规格
4418.4000	-水泥构件的模板	1.品名;2.用途(建筑用);3.材质(木制);4.种类(中文及拉丁学名);5.规格
4418.5000	-木瓦及盖屋板	1.品名;2.用途(建筑用);3.材质(木制);4.种类(中文及拉丁学名);5.规格
4418.6000	-柱和梁	1.品名;2.材质(木制);3.种类(中文及拉丁学名、柱、梁);4.规格

税则号列	商品描述	规范申报要素 / 价格申报要素 / 其他申报要素 / 举例说明
4418.7	-已装拼的地板:	1.品名;2.加工方法(已装拼);3.材质(木制等);4.种类(中文及拉丁学名、马赛克地板、多层地板等);5.规格
4418.9	-其他:	1.品名;2.用途(建筑用);3.材质(木制等);4.种类(中文及拉丁学名)
44.19	木制餐具及厨房用具:	
4419.003	----一次性筷子	1.品名;2.材质(木制);3.是否是一次性产品
4419.009	---其他	1.品名;2.材质(木制);3.种类(中文及拉丁学名)
44.20	镶嵌木(包括细工镶嵌木)装珠宝或刀具用的木制盒子和小匣子及类似品;木制小雕像及其他装饰品;第九十四章以外的木制家具:	1.品名;2.材质(木制);3.种类(单一材质申报中文及拉丁学名)。注:盛装乐器或枪支的木制箱、盒及包有皮革或再生皮革、纸或纸板、钢纸、塑料片或纺织材料的护套、箱、盒及类似容器归入税目42.02
44.21	其他木制品:	
4421.1000	-衣架	1.品名;2.材质(木制);3.种类(单一材质申报中文及拉丁学名)。注:枪托及其他武器零件归入税目93.05
4421.9010	---卷轴、纡子、筒管、缝纫用线轴及类似品	1.品名;2.材质(木制);3.种类(单一材质申报中文及拉丁学名)。注:枪托及其他武器零件归入税目93.05
4421.9021	----木制	1.品名;2.材质(木制);3.种类(单一材质申报中文及拉丁学名、圆签、圆棒、冰果棒、压舌片等);4.是否是一次性产品;5.尺寸(长、宽、厚、直径等)。注:枪托及其他武器零件归入税目93.05
4421.9022	----竹制	1.品名;2.材质(木制);3.种类(单一材质申报中文及拉丁学名、圆签、圆棒、冰果棒、压舌片等);4.是否是一次性产品
4421.9090	---其他	1.品名;2.材质(木制);3.种类(单一材质申报中文及拉丁学名)。注:枪托及其他武器零件归入税目93.05

第四十五章　软木及软木制品

税则号列	商品描述	规范申报要素 / 价格申报要素 / 其他申报要素 / 举例说明
45.01	未加工或简单加工的天然软木;软木废料;碎的、粒状的 或粉状的软木:	
4501.1000	-未加工或简单加工的天然软木	1.品名;2.材质(天然软木);3.加工程度(未加工、简单加工等)
4501.9	-其他:	1.品名;2.状态(碎的、粒状的或粉状的);3.是否是废料
45.02	天然软木,除去表皮或粗切成方形,或成长方块、正方块、板、片或条状(包括作塞子用的方块坯料):	1.品名;2.材质(天然软木);3.加工方法(经除去表皮或粗切成方形等加工);4.外观(块、板、片或条状等)
45.03	天然软木制品:	1.品名;2.材质(天然软木);3.规格;4.等级
45.04	压制软木(不论是否使用黏合 剂压成)及其制品:	1.品名;2.材质(压制软木);3.外观(块、板、片等形状)

第四十六章　稻草、秸秆、针茅或其他编结材料制品;篮筐及柳条编结品

【注解】

本章所称"编结材料",是指其状态或形状适于编结、交织或类似加工的材料,包括稻草、秸秆、柳条、竹、灯芯草、芦苇、木片条、其他植物材料扁条(例如,树皮条、狭叶、酒椰叶纤维或其他从阔叶获取的条)、未纺的天然纺织纤维、塑料单丝及扁条、纸带,但不包括皮革、再生皮革、毡呢或无纺织物的扁条、人发、马毛、纺织粗纱或纱线以及第五十四章的单丝和扁条。

税则号列	商品描述	规范申报要素 / 价格申报要素 / 其他申报要素 / 举例说明
46.01	用编结材料编成的缏条及类似产品,不论是否缝合成宽条;平行连结或编结的成片材料、缏条或类似的编结材料产品,不论是否制成品(例如,席子、席料、帘子):	1.品名;2.材质(竹、藤、稻草等)
46.02	用编结材料直接编成或用品目46.01所列货品制成的篮筐、柳条编结品及其他制品;丝瓜络制品:	1.品名;2.材质(竹、藤、草、玉米皮、柳条等)

第十类　木浆及其他纤维状纤维素浆;回收(废碎)纸或纸板;纸、纸板及其制品

第四十七章　木浆及其他纤维状纤维素浆;回收(废碎)纸或纸板

【注解】

本章所称"化学木浆,溶解级",是指温度在20℃时浸入含18%氢氧化钠的苛性碱溶液内,一小时后,按重量计含有92%及以上的不溶级分的碱木浆或硫酸盐木浆,或者含有88%及以上的不溶级分的亚硫酸盐木浆。对于亚硫酸盐木浆,按重量计灰分含量不得超过0.15%。

税则号列	商品描述	规范申报要素 / 价格申报要素 / 其他申报要素 / 举例说明
47.01	机械木浆:	1.品名(机械木浆)2.品牌;3.签约日期
47.02	化学木浆,溶解级:	1.品名(溶解级化学木浆)2.品牌;3.签约日期
47.03	碱木浆或硫酸盐木浆,但溶解级的除外:	1.品名;2.材质(针叶木、非针叶木);3.加工方法(漂白、未漂白、半漂白);4.水分含量;5.品牌;6.签约日期;7.形状(卷筒或平板)
47.04	亚硫酸盐木浆,但溶解级的除外:	1.品名;2.材质(针叶木、非针叶木);3.加工方法(漂白、未漂白、半漂白);4.水分含量;5.品牌
47.05	用机械与化学联合制浆法制得的木浆:	1.品名;2.加工方法(用机械和化学联合制浆法);3.水分含量;4.品牌
47.06	从回收(废碎)纸或纸板提取的纤维浆或其他纤维状纤维素浆:	
4706.1000	-棉短绒纸浆	1.品名;2.种类(棉短绒)
4706.2000	-从回收(废碎)纸或纸板提取的纤维浆	1.品名;2.来源(从回收纸或纸板提取的)
4706.3000	-其他,竹浆	1.品名;2.来源(从回收纸或纸板提取的)
4706.9	-其他:	1.品名;2.材质(草浆等);3.加工方法(机械、化学、半化学)
47.07	回收(废碎)纸或纸板:	
4707.1000	-未漂白的牛皮纸或纸板及瓦楞纸或纸板	1.品名;2.种类(未漂白废牛皮纸、废瓦楞纸);3.状态(废碎);4.产地标准及标号(美废、欧废、港废等);5.签约日期。注:以未漂白的牛皮纸及瓦楞纸或纸板为主。注:美废5、11、12、13、15、16、19、20、21号;欧废A4、A5、A6
4707.2000	-主要由漂白化学木浆制成未经本体染色的其他纸和纸板	1.品名;2.种类(未漂白废牛皮纸、废报纸等);3.状态(废碎);4.产地标准及标号(美废、欧废、港废等);5.签约日期。注:以漂白化学木浆的纸及纸板为主。注:废无尘纸、废卫生纸、废滤纸、废标签纸;美废30、37、40、42号
4707.3000	-主要由机械浆制成的纸或纸板(例如,报纸、杂志及类似印刷品)	1.品名;2.种类(未漂白废牛皮纸、废报纸等);3.状态(废碎);4.产地标准及标号(美废、欧废、港废等);5.签约日期。注:以机械浆制的纸及纸板(如报纸、杂志等)为主。注:美废2、6、7、8、9、10、23号;欧废A7、A8、A9、A10号
4707.9000	-其他,包括未分选的废碎品回收(废碎)墙(壁)纸、涂	1.品名;2.种类(未漂白废牛皮纸、废报纸等);3.产地标准及标号(美废、欧废、港废等);4.签约日期。注:美废3;欧废A2;废纸尿裤

第四十八章 纸及纸板;纸浆、纸或纸板制品

税则号列	商品描述	规范申报要素 / 价格申报要素 / 其他申报要素 / 举例说明
48.01	成卷或成张的新闻纸:	1.品名;2.规格(成条、成卷的宽度或成张的边长、每平方米克重);3.机械或化学—机械法制得的纤维含量;4.粗糙度;5.签约日期
48.02	书写、印刷或类似用途的未经涂布的纸及纸板、未打孔的穿孔卡片纸及穿孔纸带纸、成卷或成张矩形(包括正方形),任何尺寸,但品目48.01或48.03的纸除外;手工制纸及纸板:	
4802.1	-手工制纸及纸板:	1.品名;2.用途;3.种类;4.加工程度(未涂布、未染面等);5.规格(成条、成卷的宽度或成张的边长、每平方米克重);6.签约日期
4802.2	-光敏、热敏、电敏纸及纸板的原纸和原纸板:	1.品名;2.用途;3.种类;4.加工程度(未涂布、未染面等);5.规格(成条、成卷的宽度或成张的边长、每平方米克重);6.签约日期
4802.4000	-壁纸原纸	1.品名;2.用途;3.种类;4.加工程度(未涂布、未染面等);5.规格(成条、成卷的宽度或成张的边长、每平方米克重);6.签约日期
4802.5	-其他纸及纸板,不含用机械或化学-机械方法制得的纤维或所含前述纤维不超过全部纤 维重量的10%:	1.品名;2.用途(书写、印刷等用);3.种类;4.加工程度(未涂布、未染面等);5.规格(成条、成卷的宽度或成张的边长、每平方米克重);6.纤维种类和含量;7.签约日期
4802.6	-其他纸及纸板,所含用机械或化学-机械方法制得的纤维 超过全部纤维重量的10%:	1.品名;2.用途(书写、印刷等用);3.种类;4.加工程度(未涂布、未染面等);5.规格(成条、成卷的宽度或成张的边长、每平方米克重);6.纤维种类和含量;7.签约日期
48.03	卫生纸、面巾纸、餐巾纸以及家庭或卫生用的类似纸、纤维素絮纸和纤维素纤维网纸,不论是否起纹、压花、打孔、染面、饰面或印花,成卷或成张的	1.品名;2.种类(卫生纸、面巾纸等类似纸);3.规格(成条、成卷的宽度或成张的边长);4.签约日期
48.04	成卷或成张的未经涂布的牛 皮纸及纸板,但不包括品目48.02或48.03的货品:	
4804.1	-牛皮挂面纸:	1.品名;2.种类(牛皮挂面纸、袋用牛皮纸等);3.加工程度(未漂白、漂白、未涂布);4.规格(成条、成卷的宽度或成张的边长、每平方米克重);5.纤维种类和含量;6.请注明耐破度、紧度、横向环压指数、横向耐折度;7.品牌;8.签约日期
4804.2	-袋用牛皮纸:	1.品名;2.种类(牛皮挂面纸、袋用牛皮纸等);3.加工程度(未漂白、漂白、未涂布);4.规格(成条、成卷的宽度或成张的边长、每平方米克重);5.纤维种类和含量;6.请注明缪伦耐破度、横向伸长率、纵向伸长率;7.品牌;8.签约日期
4804.3100	--未漂白	1.品名;2.种类;3.加工程度(未漂白、漂白、未涂布);4.规格(成条、成卷的宽度或成张的边长、每平方米克重);5.纤维种类和含量;6.请注明耐破度、紧度、横向环压指数、横向耐折度;7.品牌;8.签约日期
4804.3900	--其他	1.品名;2.种类;3.加工程度(未漂白、漂白、未涂布);4.规格(成条、成卷的宽度或成张的边长、每平方米克重);5.纤维种类和含量;6.品牌;7.签约日期
4804.4	-其他牛皮纸及纸板,每平方米重量超过150克,但小于225克:	1.品名;2.种类;3.加工程度(未漂白、漂白、未涂布);4.规格(成条、成卷的宽度或成张的边长、每平方米克重);5.纤维种类和含量;6.请注明耐破度、紧度、横向环压指数、横向耐折度;7.品牌;8.签约日期
4804.5	-其他牛皮纸及纸板,每平方米重量在225克及以上:	1.品名;2.种类;3.加工程度(未漂白、漂白、未涂布);4.规格(成条、成卷的宽度或成张的边长、每平方米克重);5.纤维种类和含量;6.请注明耐破度、紧度、横向环压指数、横向耐折度;7.品牌;8.签约日期

税则号列	商品描述	规范申报要素 / 价格申报要素 / 其他申报要素 / 举例说明
48.05	成卷或成张的其他未经涂布的纸及纸板,加工程度不超过本章注释三所列范围:	
4805.1	-瓦楞原纸:	1. 品名;2. 种类;3. 加工程度(未涂布);4. 规格(成条、成卷的宽度或成张的边长、每平方米克重);5. 纤维种类和含量;6. 签约日期
4805.2	-强韧箱纸板(再生挂面纸板):	1. 品名;2. 种类;3. 加工程度(未涂布);4. 规格(成条、成卷的宽度或成张的边长、每平方米克重);5. 签约日期
4805.3000	-亚硫酸盐包装纸	1. 品名;2. 种类;3. 加工程度(未涂布);4. 规格(成条、成卷的宽度或成张的边长、每平方米克重);5. 签约日期
4805.4000	-滤纸及纸板	1. 品名;2. 种类;3. 加工程度(未涂布);4. 规格(成条、成卷的宽度或成张的边长、每平方米克重);5. 签约日期
4805.5000	-毡纸及纸板	1. 品名;2. 种类;3. 加工程度(未涂布);4. 规格(成条、成卷的宽度或成张的边长、每平方米克重);5. 签约日期
4805.9110	---每平方米重量在150克及以下的电解电容器原纸	1. 品名;2. 种类;3. 加工程度(未涂布);4. 规格(成条、成卷的宽度或成张的边长、每平方米克重);5. 签约日期;6. 型号
4805.9190	---每平方米重量在150克及以下的薄纸及纸板	1. 品名;2. 种类;3. 加工程度(未涂布);4. 规格(成条、成卷的宽度或成张的边长、每平方米克重);5. 签约日期
4805.9200	--其他未经涂布中厚纸及纸板	1. 品名;2. 种类;3. 加工程度(未涂布);4. 规格(成条、成卷的宽度或成张的边长、每平方米克重);5. 签约日期
4805.9300	--其他未经涂布厚纸及纸板	1. 品名;2. 种类;3. 加工程度(未涂布);4. 规格(成条、成卷的宽度或成张的边长、每平方米克重);5. 签约日期
48.06	成卷或成张的植物羊皮纸、防油纸、描图纸、半透明纸及其他高光泽透明或半透明纸:	
4806.1000	-植物羊皮纸	1. 品名;2. 种类;3. 规格(成条、成卷的宽度或成张的边长);4. 签约日期
4806.2000	-防油纸	1. 品名;2. 种类;3. 规格(成条、成卷的宽度或成张的边长);4. 签约日期
4806.3000	-描图纸	1. 品名;2. 种类;3. 规格(成条、成卷的宽度或成张的边长);4. 签约日期
4806.4000	-高光泽透明或半透明纸	1. 品名;2. 种类;3. 规格(成卷的宽度或成张的边长);4. 签约日期
48.07	成卷或成张的复合纸及纸板(用黏合剂粘合各层纸或纸板制成),未经表面涂布或未浸渍,不论内层是否有加强材料:	1. 品名;2. 加工方法(黏合多层);3. 加工程度(未经表面涂布或未浸渍);4. 规格(成条、成卷的宽度或成张的边长);5. 签约日期
48.08	成卷或成张的瓦楞纸及纸板(不论是否与平面纸胶合)、皱纹纸及纸板、压纹纸及纸板、穿孔纸及纸板,但品目48.03的纸除外:	
4808.1000	-瓦楞纸及纸板,不论是否穿孔	1. 品名;2. 种类(瓦楞纸、皱纹牛皮纸等);3. 规格(成条、成卷的宽度或成张的边长);4. 签约日期
4808.4000	-皱纹牛皮纸,不论是否压花或穿孔	1. 品名;2. 用途;3. 种类;4. 规格(成条、成卷的宽度或成张的边长);5. 签约日期
4808.9000	-其他	1. 品名;2. 用途;3. 种类;4. 规格(成条、成卷的宽度或成张的边长);5. 签约日期
48.09	复写纸、自印复写纸及其他拷贝或转印纸(包括涂布或浸渍的油印蜡纸或胶印版纸),不论是否印制,成卷或成张的:	
4809.2000	-自印复写纸	1. 品名;2. 种类(自印复写纸);3. 加工程度(涂布或浸渍);4. 规格(成条、成卷的宽度或成张的边长);5. 签约日期。注:压印箔归入税目32.12
4809.9000	-其他	1. 品名;2. 种类(复写纸、拷贝纸等);3. 加工程度(涂布或浸渍);4. 规格(成条、成卷的宽度或成张的边长);5. 签约日期。注:压印箔归入税目32.12
48.10	成卷或成张矩形(包括正方形)的任何尺寸的单面或双面涂布高岭土或其他无机物质(不论是否加黏合剂)的纸及纸板,但未涂布其他涂料,不论是否染面、饰面或印花:	

税则号列	商品描述	规范申报要素 / 价格申报要素 / 其他申报要素 / 举例说明
4810.1	-书写、印刷或类似用途的纸及纸板，不含用机械或化学-机械方法制得的纤维或所含前述纤维不超过全部纤维重量的10%：	1.品名;2.用途(书写、印刷等);3.种类(牛皮纸、白板纸、双面、单面等);4.状态(成卷或张等);5.加工程度(单面或双面涂布无机物、漂白);6.规格(宽度或边长、每平方米克重、各纤维含量);7.纤维种类和含量;8.签约日期。注:用诊断或实验室试剂浸渍的纸条归入税目38.22;砂纸或纸板归入税目68.05;用纸或纸板衬底的云母(云母粉除外)归入税目68.14
4810.2	-书写、印刷或类似用途的纸及纸板，所含用机械或化学-机械方法制得的纤维超过全部纤维重量的10%：	1.品名;2.用途(书写、印刷等);3.种类(牛皮纸、白板纸、双面、单面等);4.状态(成卷或张等);5.加工程度(单面或双面涂布无机物、漂白);6.规格(宽度或边长、每平方米克重、各纤维含量);7.纤维种类和含量;8.签约日期。注:用诊断或实验室试剂浸渍的纸条归入税目38.22;砂纸或纸板归入税目68.05;用纸或纸板衬底的云母(云母粉除外)归入税目68.14
4810.3	-牛皮纸及纸板，但书写、印刷或类似用途的除外：	1.品名;2.用途(书写、印刷等);3.种类(牛皮纸、白板纸、双面、单面等);4.状态(成卷或张等);5.加工程度(单面或双面涂布无机物、漂白);6.规格(宽度或边长、每平方米克重、各纤维含量);7.纤维种类和含量;8.签约日期。注:用诊断或实验室试剂浸渍的纸条归入税目38.22;砂纸或纸板归入税目68.05;用纸或纸板衬底的云母(云母粉除外)归入税目68.14
4810.9	-其他纸及纸板：	1.品名;2.用途(书写、印刷等);3.种类(牛皮纸、白板纸、双面、单面等);4.状态(成卷或张等);5.加工程度(单面或双面涂布无机物、漂白);6.规格(宽度或边长、每平方米克重、各纤维含量);7.签约日期。注:用诊断或实验室试剂浸渍的纸条归入税目38.22;砂纸或纸板归入税目68.05;用纸或纸板衬底的云母(云母粉除外)归入税目68.14
48.11	成卷或成张矩形(包括正方形)的任何尺寸的经涂布、浸渍、覆盖、染面、饰面或印花的纸、纸板、纤维素絮纸及纤维素纤维网纸，但品目48.03、48.09或48.10的货品除外：	1.品名;2.种类;3.加工程度(涂布、浸渍、饰面、漂白等);4.规格(成条等、浸渍或涂布物、每平方米克重);5.品牌;6.型号。注:用肥皂或洗涤剂浸渍、覆盖或涂布的纸及纤维素絮纸归入税目34.01;用光洁剂、擦光膏或类似制剂浸渍、覆盖或涂布的纸及纤维素絮纸归入税目34.05;石蕊试纸、极谱纸及其他用诊断或实验室试剂浸渍的纸归入税目38.22;用纸板做基并以柏油或类似材料完全包裹或双面覆盖的屋面归入税目68.07
48.12	纸浆制的滤块、滤板及滤片：	1.品名;2.材质(纸浆制);3.外观(块、板、片)。注:仅压制成片或板状的棉短绒归入税目14.04
48.13	卷烟纸，不论是否切成一定尺寸、成小本或管状：	
4813.1000	-成小本或管状	1.品名;2.规格(如成小本或管状、宽度)
4813.2000	-宽度不超过5厘米成卷的	1.品名;2.规格(成卷、宽度)
4813.9000	-其他	1.品名;2.规格(宽度等)
48.14	壁纸及类似品；窗用透明纸：	
4814.2000	-用塑料涂面或盖面的壁纸及类似品，起纹、压花、着色、印刷图案或经其他装饰	1.品名;2.加工程度(用木粒或草粒、塑料、编结材料等饰面、涂面)。注:外观近似窗用透明的转印纸(移画印花纸)归入税目49.08;纸基纺织糊墙品归入税目59.05;用纸衬背的铝箔糊墙品归入税目76.07
4814.9000	-其他	1.品名;2.加工程度(用木粒或草粒、塑料、编结材料等饰面、涂面);3.是否为窗用透明纸。注:外观近似窗用透明的转印纸(移画印花纸)归入税目49.08;纸基纺织糊墙品归入税目59.05;用纸衬背的铝箔糊墙品归入税目76.07
48.16	复写纸、自印复写纸及其他拷贝或转印纸(不包括品目48.09的纸)，油印蜡纸或胶印版纸，不论是否盒装：	
4816.2000	-自印复写纸	1.品名;2.种类(自印复写纸、热敏转印纸等);3.规格(成条、成卷的宽度或成张的边长)
4816.9010	---热敏转印纸	1.品名;2.种类(自印复写纸、热敏转印纸等);3.规格(成条、成卷的宽度或成张的边长)
4816.9090	---其他	1.品名;2.种类(复写纸、拷贝纸、转印纸、油印蜡纸、胶版纸等);3.规格(成条、成卷的宽度或成张的边长)

税则号列	商品描述	规范申报要素 / 价格申报要素 / 其他申报要素 / 举例说明
48.17	纸或纸板制的信封、封缄信片、素色明信片及通信卡片;纸或纸板制的盒子、袋子及夹子,内装各种纸制文具:	1.品名;2.材质(纸制)。注:税号4817.3000的产品必须内装各种纸制文具;印有或用其他方式赋予正在流通的邮票的信封、明信片及信卡等归入税目49.07;供特殊用途的印刷信件及类似物品,例如,即期票据、搬迁通知、广告信,包括需要手工填写的上述物品归入税目49.11;印有图画的首日封及集邮大型张:未附邮票的归入税目49.11;附有邮票的归入税目97.04
48.18	卫生纸及类似纸,家庭或卫生用纤维素絮纸及纤维素纤维 网纸,成卷宽度不超过36厘 米或切成一定尺寸或形状的;纸浆、纸、纤维素絮纸或纤维素纤维网纸制的手帕、面巾、台布、餐巾、床单及类似的家 庭、卫生或医院用品、衣服及 衣着附件:	1.品名;2.用途(家庭、卫生、医院用等);3.材质(纸制);4.种类(卫生纸、纸台布等);5.规格(成条、成卷的宽度或成张的边长)
48.19	纸、纸板、纤维素絮纸或纤维素纤维网纸制的箱、盒、匣、袋及其他包装容器;纸或纸板制的卷宗盒、信件盘及类似品,供办公室、商店及类似场所使用的:	
4819.1000	-瓦楞纸或纸板制的箱、盒、匣	1.品名;2.材质;3.规格;
4819.2000	-非瓦楞纸或纸板制的可折叠 箱、盒、匣	1.品名;2.材质;3.规格;4.是否可折叠
4819.3000	-底宽40厘米及以上的纸袋	1.品名;2.材质;3.规格
4819.4000	-其他纸袋,包括锥形袋	1.品名;2.材质;3.规格
4819.5000	-其他包装容器,包括唱片套	1.品名;2.材质;3.规格
4819.6000	-办公室、商店及类似场所使用的卷宗盒、信件盘、存储盒及类似品	1.品名;2.材质;3.规格
48.20	纸或纸板制的登记本、账本、笔记本、订货本、收据本、信笺本、记事本、日记本及类似品、练习本、吸墨纸本、活动封面(活页及非活页)、文件夹、卷宗皮、多联商业表格纸页间夹有复写纸的本及其他文具用品;纸或纸板制的样品簿、粘贴簿及书籍封面:	1.品名;2.材质。注:支票簿归入税目49.07;空白的联券旅行票据归入税目49.11
48.21	纸或纸板制的各种标签,不论是否印制:	1.品名;2.材质;3.加工程度(印制、非印制)。注:捕蝇纸归入税目38.08;纸制太阳伞归入税目66.01;人造花、簇叶、果实及其部分品归入税目67.02
48.22	纸浆、纸或纸板(不论是否穿孔或硬化)制的筒管、卷轴、纡子及类似品:	
4822.1000	-纺织纱线用	1.品名;2.用途(纺织纱线用等);3.材质(纸制)
4822.9000	-其他	1.品名;2.用途;3.材质(纸制)
48.23	切成一定尺寸或形状的其他纸、纸板、纤维素絮纸及纤维素纤维网纸;纸浆、纸、纸板、纤维素絮纸及纤维素纤维网纸制的其他物品:	
4823.2000	-滤纸及纸板	1.品名;2.材质(纸制);3.规格(切成一定尺寸或形状、边长、宽度)
4823.4000	-已印制的自动记录器用打印纸卷、纸张及纸盘	1.品名;2.用途(已印制的自动记录器用等);3.材质(纸制);4.规格(切成一定尺寸或形状、边长、宽度)
4823.6100	--竹浆纸制	1.品名;2.材质(竹浆纸制);3.种类(盘、碟、盆、杯等);4.规格
4823.69	--其他	1.品名;2.材质;3.种类(盘、碟、盆、杯等);4.规格
4823.7000	-压制或模制纸浆制品	1.品名;2.加工方法(压制、模制);3.材质(纸浆制);4.规格(切成一定尺寸或形状、边长、宽度)
4823.9010	---以纸或纸板为底制成的铺地制品	1.品名;2.用途;3.材质(以纸或纸板为底制成);4.规格
4823.9020	---神纸及类似用品	1.品名;2.材质(纸制);3.规格(切成一定尺寸或形状、边长、宽度)
4823.9030	---纸扇	1.品名;2.材质(纸制);3.规格(切成一定尺寸或形状、边长、宽度)
4823.9090	---其他	1.品名;2.材质(纸制);3.规格(切成一定尺寸或形状、边长、宽度)

第四十九章　书籍、报纸、印刷图画及其他印刷品；手稿、打字稿及设计图纸

税则号列	商品描述	规范申报要素 / 价格申报要素 / 其他申报要素 / 举例说明
49.01	书籍、小册子、散页印刷品及类似印刷品，不论是否单张：	1.品名；2.种类（字典、百科全书等）；3.状态（成册、单张）。注：载有文字或图案以供复制并按序号装订的拷贝纸及转印纸归入税目48.16
49.02	报纸、杂志及期刊，不论有无插图或广告材料：	1.品名；2.出版周期（日刊、周刊等）。注：由旧报纸、旧杂志或旧期刊构成的废纸归入税目47.07
49.03	儿童图画书、绘画或涂色书：	1.品名；2.用途（儿童用）；3.种类（图画书、绘画或涂色书）
49.04	乐谱原稿或印本，不论是否装订或印有插图：	1.品名；2.种类（原稿或印本等）
49.05	各种印刷的地图、水道图及类似图表，包括地图册、挂图、地形图及地球仪、天体仪：	
4905.1000	-地球仪、天体仪	1.品名
4905.9	-其他：	1.品名；2.状态（成册、非成册）。注：浮雕地图、详图及地球仪、不论是否印制归入税目90.23
49.06	手绘的建筑、工程、工业、商 业、地形或类似用途的设计图纸原稿；手稿；用感光纸照相复印或用复写纸誊写的上述物品复制件：	1.品名；（设计图纸原稿或手稿及其复制件）
49.07	在承认或将承认其面值的国家流通或新发行并且未经使用的邮票、印花税票及类似票证；印有邮票或印花税票的纸品；钞票；空白支票；股票、债券及类似所有权凭证：	
4907.0010	---邮票	1.品名2.外观（新的）；3.种类（小型张、四方联等）
4907.0020	---钞票	1.品名2.外观（新的）
4907.0030	---证券凭证	1.品名；2.种类（证券、特许权等）
4907.0090	---其他	1.品名；2.种类（证券、特许权等）
49.08	转印贴花纸（移画印花法用图案纸）：	1.品名；2.加工方法（釉转印等）
49.09	印刷或有图画的明信片；印有个人问候、祝贺、通告的卡片不论是否有图画、带信封或饰边：	1.品名；2.加工方法（印刷或有图画等）
49100000	印刷的各种日历，包括日历芯：	1.品名。注：包括日历芯；又有日历又可记日记的记事本（包括所谓约会日历本）归入税目48.20
49.11	其他印刷品，包括印刷的图片及照片：	
4911.1	-商业广告品、商品目录及类似印刷品：	1.品名；2.用途（有商业价值、无商业价值等）。注：照相软片或硬片的负片或正片归入税目37.05；在一面印有图画、文字的装饰性玻璃镜，不论是否镶框归入税目70.09或70.13；带磁条的印刷卡归入税目85.23或85.24；带电子集成电路的印刷卡（"智能"卡）归入税目85.42；印刷的邻近卡及牌归入税目85.43，不论这些产品是否带磁条
4911.9100	--图片、设计图样及照片	1.品名；2.用途（有商业价值、无商业价值等）。注：照相软片或硬片的负片或正片归入税目37.05；在一面印有图画、文字的装饰性玻璃镜，不论是否镶框归入税目70.09或70.13；带磁条的印刷卡归入税目85.23或85.24；带电子集成电路的印刷卡（"智能"卡）归入税目85.42；印刷的邻近卡及牌归入税目85.43，不论这些产品是否带磁条
4911.99	--其他：	1.品名；2.材质；3.用途（有商业价值、无商业价值等）；4.印刷内容。注：照相软片或硬片的负片或正片归入税目37.05；在一面印有图画、文字的装饰性玻璃镜，不论是否镶框归入税目70.09或70.13；带磁条的印刷卡归入税目85.23或85.24；带电子集成电路的印刷卡（"智能"卡）归入税目85.42；印刷的邻近卡及牌归入税目85.43，不论这些产品是否带磁条

第十一类　纺织原料及纺织制品

【注解】

1、加工方法：对纤维纱线产品仅指梳理工艺，既粗疏或精梳：对织物则指染整方法（漂白、练白）以及织造方法（机织物）。

2、用途：仅指丝线是否用于零售或蚕茧是否适于缫丝。

3、规格型号：丝线列明细度支数；织物列明幅宽；混纺产品列明丝含量。
4、纱线的表示：70s/2 指由两支 70 英支的单纱捻制的股线。

第五十章　蚕　　丝

税则号列	商　品　描　述	规范申报要素 / 价格申报要素 / 其他申报要素 / 举例说明
50.01	适于缫丝的蚕茧：	1. 品名；2. 用途（用于缫丝）；3. 种类
50.02	生丝（未加捻）：	
5002.0011	----厂丝	1. 品名；2. 种类（桑蚕厂丝）；3. 是否加捻
5002.0012	----土丝	1. 品名；2. 种类（桑蚕土丝）；3. 是否加捻
5002.0013	----双宫丝	1. 品名；2. 种类（桑蚕双宫丝）；3. 是否加捻
5002.0019	----其他	1. 品名；2. 种类；3. 是否加捻
5002.0020	---柞蚕丝	1. 品名；2. 种类（柞蚕丝）；3. 是否加捻
5002.0090	---其他	1. 品名；2. 种类；3. 是否加捻
50.03	废丝（包括不适于缫丝的蚕茧、废纱及回收纤维）：	1. 品名；2. 是否梳理。注：本税目指不适于缫丝的废丝
50.04	丝纱线（绢纺纱线除外），非供零售用：	1. 品名；2. 是否供零售用绢纺纱线除外（归入税目 50.05）。注：不包括税目 56.04 的丝质仿肠线
50.05	绢纺纱线，非供零售用：	1. 品名；2. 种类（绢纺纱线等）；3. 是否供零售用；4. 成分含量。注：不包括税目 56.04 的丝质仿肠线
50.06	丝纱线及绢纺纱线，供零售用；蚕胶丝：	1. 品名；2. 种类（绢纺纱线、蚕胶丝、丝纱线、绸纱线）；3. 包装（供零售用）；4. 成分含量。注：不包括税目 56.04 的丝质仿肠线、税目 30.06 的消毒蚕胶丝
50.07	丝或绢丝机织物：	1. 品名；2. 种类（绸丝、桑蚕丝、绢丝、柞蚕丝等）；3. 织造方法（机织物）；4. 染整方法（漂白、未漂白、色织）；5. 成分含量；6. 幅宽；7. 每平方米克重

第五十一章　羊毛、动物细毛或粗毛；马毛纱线及其机织物

【注解】

1、加工方法：对纤维原料指梳理工艺，既粗疏或精梳及脱脂、处理；对织物则指梳理工艺（粗疏或精梳）以及织造方法（机织物）。
2、用途：仅指纱线是否用于零售。
3、品名：应具体列出产品行业名称、种类，如剪羊毛、碳化羊毛、脱脂羊毛、兔毛、动物细毛还是粗毛马毛织物等。
4、规格型号：丝线列明细度支数；织物列明幅宽；混纺产品列明成分含量，每平方米重量（克/平方米）。

税则号列	商　品　描　述	规范申报要素 / 价格申报要素 / 其他申报要素 / 举例说明
51.01	未梳的羊毛：	
5101.1100	--剪羊毛	1. 品名；2. 加工程度（含脂、脱脂、碳化等）；3. 剪羊毛请注明细度（微米数）；4. 剪羊毛请注明长度；5. 剪羊毛请注明草杂含量。注：T107，7.7MIC，46 英寸的灰褪毛，草杂含量 2%
5101.1900	--其他	1. 品名；2. 加工程度（未梳、含脂、脱脂、碳化等）
5101.2100	--剪羊毛	1. 品名；2. 加工程度（未梳、含脂、脱脂、碳化等）；3. 剪羊毛请注明细度（微米数）；4. 剪羊毛请注明长度；5. 剪羊毛请注明草杂含量
5101.2900	--其他	1. 品名；2. 加工程度（未梳、含脂、脱脂、碳化等）
5101.3000	-碳化羊毛	1. 品名；2. 加工程度（未梳、含脂、脱脂、碳化等）
51.02	未梳的动物细毛或粗毛：	
5102.1100	--喀什米尔山羊的	1. 品名；2. 种类（未梳理的兔毛、喀什米尔山羊毛、山羊绒、骆驼毛）
5102.1910	---兔毛	1. 品名；2. 种类（未梳理的兔毛、喀什米尔山羊毛、山羊绒、骆驼毛）
5102.1920	---其他山羊绒	1. 品名；2. 种类（未梳理的兔毛、喀什米尔山羊毛、山羊绒、骆驼毛）；3. 其他山羊绒请注明颜色；4. 其他山羊绒请注明纤维长度；5. 其他山羊绒请注明含绒率
5102.1930	---骆驼毛、骆驼绒	1. 品名；2. 种类（未梳理的兔毛、喀什米尔山羊毛、山羊绒、骆驼毛）
5102.1990	---其他	1. 品名；2. 种类（未梳理的兔毛、喀什米尔山羊毛、山羊绒、骆驼毛）
5102.2000	-粗毛	1. 品名；2. 种类（未梳理的兔毛、喀什米尔山羊毛、山羊绒、骆驼毛）
51.03	羊毛或动物细毛或粗毛的废料，包括废纱线，但不包括回收纤维：	
5103.1	-羊毛或动物细毛的落毛：	1. 品名；2. 种类（羊毛落毛、动物细毛或粗毛废料）。注：废料不包括回收纤维（税目 51.04）

税则号列	商 品 描 述	规范申报要素 / 价格申报要素 / 其他申报要素 / 举例说明
5103.2010	---羊毛废料	1.品名;2.种类(羊毛落毛、动物细毛或粗毛废料)。注:废料不包括回收纤维(税目51.04)
5103.2090	---其他	1.品名;2.种类(羊毛落毛、动物细毛或粗毛废料);3.是否濒危野生。注:废料不包括回收纤维(税目51.04)
5103.3000	-动物粗毛废料	1.品名;2.种类(羊毛落毛、动物细毛或粗毛废料)。注:废料不包括回收纤维(税目51.04)
51.04	羊毛或动物细毛或粗毛的回收纤维:	1.品名;2.种类(源于羊毛、动物粗、细毛等的回收纤维)
51.05	已梳的羊毛及动物细毛或粗毛(包括精梳片毛)	
5105.1000	-粗梳羊毛	1.品名;2.种类(羊毛条、羊毛片毛、兔毛、喀什米尔山羊毛);3.梳理方法(粗梳或精梳)
5105.2100	--精梳片毛	1.品名;2.种类(羊毛条、羊毛片毛、兔毛、喀什米尔山羊毛);3.梳理方法(粗梳或精梳)
5105.2900	--其他	1.品名;2.种类(羊毛条、羊毛片毛、兔毛、喀什米尔山羊毛);3.梳理方法(粗梳或精梳);4.其他精梳羊毛请注明支数;5.其他精梳羊毛请注明细度
5105.3	-已梳动物细毛:	1.品名;2.种类(羊毛条、羊毛片毛、兔毛、喀什米尔山羊毛);3.梳理方法(粗梳或精梳)
5105.4000	-已梳动物粗毛	1.品名;2.种类(羊毛条、羊毛片毛、兔毛、喀什米尔山羊毛);3.梳理方法(粗梳或精梳)
51.06	粗梳羊毛纱线,非供零售用:	1.品名;2.梳理方法(粗疏);3.是否供零售用;4.成分含量
51.07	精梳羊毛纱线,非供零售用:	1.品名;2.梳理方法(精梳羊毛纱线);3.是否供零售用;4.成分含量
51.08	动物细毛(粗梳或精梳)纱线非供零售用:	1.品名;2.梳理方法(精梳羊毛纱线);3.是否供零售用;4.成分含量
51.09	羊毛或动物细毛的纱线,供零售用:	1.品名;2.种类(羊毛等);3.是否供零售用;4.成分含量
51.10	动物粗毛或马毛的纱线(包括马毛粗松螺旋花线),不论是否供零售用:	1.品名;2.种类(马毛等粗毛纱线);3.成分含量
51.11	粗梳羊毛或粗梳动物细毛的机织物:	1.品名;2.种类(羊毛、驼马毛、北洲驼等);3.织造方法(机织);4.梳理方法(粗梳);5.成分含量;6.幅宽;7.每平方米克重
51.12	精梳羊毛或精梳动物细毛的机织物:	1.品名;2.种类(羊毛、驼马毛、北洲驼等);3.织造方法(机织);4.梳理方法(精梳);5.成分含量;6.幅宽;7.每平方米克重
51.13	动物粗毛或马毛的机织物:	1.品名;2.种类(马毛等);3.织造方法(机织);4.成分含量;5.幅宽;6.每平方米克重

第五十二章　棉花

【注解】

1、纱线细度的换算:1特=1000/公支数=0.1111×旦数=590.5/英支数。

2、截面或表观宽度:截面宽度一般指圆形或类似形状单丝,表观宽度一般指扁形单丝。

税则号列	商 品 描 述	规范申报要素 / 价格申报要素 / 其他申报要素 / 举例说明
52.01	未梳的棉花:	1.品名;2.是否梳理;3.纤维长度;4.等级
52.02	废棉(包括废棉纱线及回收纤 维):	
5202.1000	-废棉纱线(包括废棉线)	1.品名;2.来源(废棉线、回收纤维等);3.成分含量;4.废棉纱线请注明长度;5.颜色
5202.9100	--回收纤维	1.品名;2.来源(废棉线、回收纤维等);3.成分含量
5202.9900	--其他	1.品名;2.来源(废棉线、回收纤维等);3.成分含量;4.棉种类(包括精落、抄斩、车肚、统破籽、回丝等)
52.03	已梳的棉花:	1.品名;2.是否梳理;3.纤维长度;4.是否经过细纱工序
52.04	棉制缝纫线,不论是否供零售用:	1.品名;2.是否供零售用;3.成分含量;4.纱线细度;5.每只重量;6.是否上浆;7.终捻捻向
52.05	棉纱线(缝纫线除外),按重量计含棉量在85%及以上,非供零售用:	1.品名;2.梳理方法(粗梳、精梳);3.纱线形态(单纱、股线或缆线);4.是否供零售用;5.成分含量;6.纱线细度;7.品牌;8.加工工艺
52.06	棉纱线(缝纫线除外),按重量计含棉量在85%以下,非供零售用:	1.品名;2.梳理方法(粗梳、精梳);3.纱线形态(单纱、股线或缆线);4.是否供零售用;5.成分含量;6.纱线细度

税则号列	商品描述	规范申报要素 / 价格申报要素 / 其他申报要素 / 举例说明
52.07	棉纱线(缝纫线除外),供零售用:	1.品名;2.是否供零售用;3.成分含量。注:缝纫线除外
52.08	棉机织物,按重量计含棉量在85%及以上,每平方米重量≤200克:	1.品名;2.织造方法(机织物);3.染整方法(漂白、未漂白、色织、染色、印花等);4.组织结构(平纹、斜纹等);5.成分含量;6.幅宽;7.每平方米克重;8.品牌
52.09	棉机织物,按重量计含棉量在85%及以上,每平方米重量超过200克:	1.品名;2.织造方法(机织物);3.染整方法(漂白、未漂白、色织、染色、印花等);4.组织结构(平纹、斜纹等);5.成分含量;6.幅宽;7.每平方米克重;8.品牌
52.10	棉机织物,按重量计含棉量在85%以下,主要或仅与化学纤维混纺的,每平方米重量不超过200克:	1.品名;2.织造方法(机织物);3.染整方法(漂白、未漂白、色织、染色、印花等);4.组织结构(平纹、斜纹等);5.注明与其混纺的化纤是长丝还是短纤;6.成分含量;7.幅宽;8.每平方米克重;9.品牌
52.11	棉机织物,按重量计含棉量在85%以下,每平方米重量超过200克:	1.品名;2.织造方法(机织物);3.染整方法(漂白、未漂白、色织、染色、印花等);4.组织结构(平纹、斜纹等);5.注明与其混纺的化纤是长丝还是短纤;6.成分含量;7.幅宽;8.每平方米克重;9.品牌
52.12	其他棉机织物:	1.品名;2.织造方法(机织物);3.染整方法(漂白、未漂白、色织、染色、印花等);4.组织结构(平纹、斜纹等);5.成分含量;6.幅宽;7.每平方米克重;8.品牌

第五十三章　其他植物纺织纤维;纸纱线及其机织物

注解:

1、韧皮纤维种类与来源:亚麻、大麻、黄麻、洋麻、菽麻、西沙尔麻、海地大麻、美洲龙舌兰纤维、椰壳纤维。

2、亚麻等韧皮纤维的一般加工过程:生麻—沤制麻—打成麻—棉花麻纤维—栉梳。

税则号列	商品描述	规范申报要素 / 价格申报要素 / 其他申报要素 / 举例说明
53.01	亚麻,生的或经加工但未纺制的;亚麻短纤及废麻(包括废麻纱线及回收纤维):	
5301.1	-生的或经沤制的亚麻	1.品名;2.加工程度(生的、经沤制、破开或打成栉梳、回收等)
5301.2100	--破开的或打成的	1.品名;2.加工程度(生的、经沤制、破开或打成栉梳、回收等);3.可纺支数;4.长度
5301.2900	--其他	1.品名;2.加工程度(生的、经沤制、破开或打成栉梳、回收等)
5301.3	-亚麻短纤及废麻	1.品名;2.加工程度(生的、经沤制、破开或打成栉梳、回收等);3.是否为短纤或废麻;4.种类(二粗、机械短麻、落麻)
53.02	大麻,生的或经加工但未纺制的;大麻短纤及废麻(包括废麻纱线及回收纤维):	
5302.1	-生的或经沤制的大麻	1.品名;2.加工程度(生的、沤制的)
5302.9	-其他	1.品名;2.加工程度(生的、沤制的);3.是否为短纤或废麻
53.03	黄麻及其他纺织用韧皮纤维(不包括亚麻、大麻及苎麻)生的或经加工但未纺制的;上述纤维的短纤及废麻(包括废纱线及回收纤维):	
5303.1	-生的或经沤制的黄麻及其他纺织用韧皮纤维	1.品名;2.种类(黄麻、洋麻、菽麻等);3.加工程度(未纺制的、生的或沤制的)
5303.9	-其他	1.品名;2.种类(黄麻、洋麻、菽麻等);3.加工程度(未纺制的、生的或沤制的);4.是否为短纤或废麻
53.05	椰壳纤维、蕉麻(马尼拉麻)苎麻及其他品目未列名的纺织用植物纤维,生的或经加工但未纺制的;上述纤维的短纤、落麻及废料(包括废纱线及回收纤维):	

税则号列	商品描述	规范申报要素 / 价格申报要素 / 其他申报要素 / 举例说明
5305.0011	----生的	1.品名;2.种类(椰壳纤维、蕉麻、苎麻等);3.加工程度(生的或经加工但未纺制的)
5305.0012	----经加工但未纺制的	1.品名;2.种类(椰壳纤维、蕉麻、苎麻等);3.加工程度(生的或经加工但未纺制的)
5305.0013	----短纤及废麻	1.品名;2.种类(椰壳纤维、蕉麻、苎麻等);3.加工程度(生的或经加工但未纺制的);4.是否为短纤或废麻
5305.0019	----其他	1.品名;2.种类(椰壳纤维、蕉麻、苎麻等);3.加工程度(生的或经加工但未纺制的)
5305.0020	---蕉麻	1.品名;2.种类(椰壳纤维、蕉麻、苎麻等);3.加工程度(生的或经加工但未纺制的)
5305.009	---其他:	1.品名;2.种类(椰壳纤维、蕉麻、苎麻等);3.加工程度(生的或经加工但未纺制的);4.是否为短纤或废麻
53.06	亚麻纱线:	1.品名;2.纱线形态(单纱、股线或缆线);3.细度
53.07	黄麻纱线或品目53.03的其他纺织用韧皮纤维纱线:	1.品名;2.种类(黄麻、洋麻、菽麻等);3.纱线形态(单纱、股线或缆线);4.细度
53.08	其他植物纺织纤维纱线;纸纱线:	
5308.1	-椰壳纤维纱线	1.品名;2.种类(椰壳纤维纱线、大麻纱线、苎麻纱线、纸纱线等);3.成分含量;4.细度
5308.2000	-大麻纱线	1.品名;2.种类(椰壳纤维纱线、大麻纱线、苎麻纱线、纸纱线等);3.成分含量;4.细度
5308.901	---苎麻纱线:	1.品名;2.种类(椰壳纤维纱线、大麻纱线、苎麻纱线、纸纱线等);3.染整方法(漂白、未漂白、色织);4.成分含量;5.细度
5308.909	---其他:	1.品名;2.种类(椰壳纤维纱线、大麻纱线、苎麻纱线、纸纱线等);3.成分含量;4.细度
53.09	亚麻机织物:	1.品名;2.织造方法(机织);3.染整方法(漂白、未漂白、色织);4.成分含量;5.幅宽;6.每平方米克重
53.10	黄麻或品目53.03的其他纺织用韧皮纤维机织物:	1.品名;2.种类(黄麻、洋麻、菽麻等);3.织造方法(机织);4.染整工艺(漂白、未漂白、色织);5.成分含量;6.幅宽;7.每平方米克重
53.11	其他纺织用植物纤维机织物;纸纱线机织物:	1.品名;2.种类(黄麻、洋麻、菽麻等);3.织造方法(机织);4.染整工艺(漂白、未漂白、色织);5.成分含量;6.幅宽;7.每平方米克重

第五十四章　化学纤维长丝;化学纤维纺织材料制扁条及类似品

税则号列	商品描述	规范申报要素 / 价格申报要素 / 其他申报要素 / 举例说明
54.01	化学纤维长丝纺制的缝纫线,不论是否供零售用:	1.品名;2.是否供零售用;3.纤维成分(聚酯等);4.每只重量;5.是否上浆;6.终捻捻向
54.02	合成纤维长丝纱线(缝纫线除外),非供零售用,包括细度在67分特以下的合成纤维单丝:	
5402.1	-尼龙或其他聚酰胺纺制的高强力纱:	1.品名;2.种类(高强力纱或变形纱线等);3.纱线形态(单纱、股线或缆线);4.是否供零售用;5.纤维成分(聚酯等);6.纱线细度
5402.2	-聚酯高强力纱	1.品名;2.种类(高强力纱或变形纱线等);3.纱线形态(单纱、股线或缆线);4.是否供零售用;5.纤维成分(聚酯等);6.纱线细度
5402.3	-变形纱线:	1.品名;2.种类(高强力纱或变形纱线等);3.纱线形态(单纱、股线或缆线);4.是否供零售用;5.纤维成分(聚酯等);6.纱线细度
540244	--弹性纱线:	1.品名;2.种类(高强力纱或变形纱线等);3.纱线形态(单纱、股线或缆线);4.高强纱请注明用途;5.是否供零售用;6.纤维成分(聚酯等);7.纱线细度;8.是否加捻(如加捻请注明捻度)

税则号列	商 品 描 述	规范申报要素 / 价格申报要素 / 其他申报要素 / 举例说明
5402.45	--其他,尼龙或其他聚酰胺纱线	1. 品名;2. 种类(高强力纱或变形纱线等);3. 纱线形态(单纱、股线或缆线);4. 高强纱请注明用途;5. 是否供零售用;6. 纤维成分(聚酯等);7. 纱线细度;8. 是否加捻(如加捻请注明捻度)
5402.4600	--其他,部分定向聚酯纱线	1. 品名;2. 种类(高强力纱或变形纱线等);3. 纱线形态(单纱、股线或缆线);4. 高强纱请注明用途;5. 是否供零售用;6. 纤维成分(聚酯等);7. 纱线细度;8. 是否加捻(如加捻请注明捻度)
5402.4700	--其他,聚酯纱线	1. 品名;2. 种类(高强力纱或变形纱线等);3. 纱线形态(单纱、股线或缆线);4. 高强纱请注明用途;5. 是否供零售用;6. 纤维成分(聚酯等);7. 纱线细度;8. 是否加捻(如加捻请注明捻度)
5402.4800	--其他,聚丙烯纱线	1. 品名;2. 种类(高强力纱或变形纱线等);3. 纱线形态(单纱、股线或缆线);4. 高强纱请注明用途;5. 是否供零售用;6. 纤维成分(聚酯等);7. 纱线细度;8. 是否加捻(如加捻请注明捻度)
5402.4910	---断裂强度大于等于 22cN/dtex,且初始模量大于等于 750cN/dtex 的聚乙烯沙线	1. 品名;2. 种类(高强力纱或变形纱线等);3. 纱线形态(单纱、股线或缆线);4. 高强纱请注明用途;5. 是否供零售用;6. 纤维成分(聚酯等);7. 纱线细度;8. 是否加捻(如加捻请注明捻度);9. 断裂强度
5402.4990	---其他	1. 品名;2. 种类(高强力纱或变形纱线等);3. 纱线形态(单纱、股线或缆线);4. 高强纱请注明用途;5. 是否供零售用;6. 纤维成分(聚酯等);7. 纱线细度;8. 是否加捻(如加捻请注明捻度)
5402.51	--尼龙或其他聚酰胺纱线:	1. 品名;2. 种类(高强力纱或变形纱线等);3. 纱线形态(单纱、股线或缆线);4. 是否供零售用;5. 纤维成分(聚酯等);6. 纱线细度;7. 是否加捻(如加捻请注明捻度)
5402.5200	--聚酯纱线	1. 品名;2. 种类(高强力纱或变形纱线等);3. 纱线形态(单纱、股线或缆线);4. 是否供零售用;5. 纤维成分(聚酯等);6. 纱线细度;7. 是否加捻(如加捻请注明捻度)
5402.5910	---聚丙烯纱线	1. 品名;2. 种类(高强力纱或变形纱线等);3. 纱线形态(单纱、股线或缆线);4. 是否供零售用;5. 纤维成分(聚酯等);6. 纱线细度;7. 是否加捻(如加捻请注明捻度)
5402.5920	---断裂强度大于等于 22cN/dtex,且初始模量大于等于 750cN/dtex 的聚乙烯沙线	1. 品名;2. 种类(高强力纱或变形纱线等);3. 纱线形态(单纱、股线或缆线);4. 是否供零售用;5. 纤维成分(聚酯等);6. 纱线细度;7. 是否加捻(如加捻请注明捻度);8. 断裂强度
5402.5990	---其他	1. 品名;2. 种类(高强力纱或变形纱线等);3. 纱线形态(单纱、股线或缆线);4. 是否供零售用;5. 纤维成分(聚酯等);6. 纱线细度;7. 是否加捻(如加捻请注明捻度)
5402.6	-其他纱线(多股纱线或缆线)	1. 品名;2. 种类(高强力纱或变形纱线等);3. 纱线形态(单纱、股线或缆线);4. 是否供零售用;5. 纤维成分(聚酯等);6. 纱线细度
54.03	人造纤维长丝纱线(缝纫线除 外),非供零售用,包括细度在 67 分特以下的人造纤维单丝:	1. 品名;2. 种类(高强力纱或变形纱线等);3. 纱线形态(单纱、股线或缆线);4. 是否供零售用;5. 纤维成分(如粘胶等);6. 纱线细度;7. 纱线捻度;8. 高强力纱需注明断裂强度(单位:厘牛顿/特克斯);9. 股数
54.04	截面尺寸不超过 1 毫米,细度在 67 分特及以上的合成纤维单丝;表观宽度不超过 5 毫米的合成纤维纺织材料制扁条 及类似品(例如人造草):	1. 品名;2. 种类(单丝、扁条等);3. 纤维成分;4. 单丝细度或扁条表观宽度

税则号列	商　品　描　述	规范申报要素 / 价格申报要素 / 其他申报要素 / 举例说明
54.05	截面尺寸不超过1毫米,细度在67分特及以上的人造纤维单丝;表观宽度不超过5毫米的人造纤维纺织材料制扁条及类似品(例如人造草):	1.品名;2.种类(单丝、扁条等);3.纤维成分;4.单丝细度或扁条表观宽度
54.06	化学纤维长丝纱线(缝纫线除外),供零售用:	1.品名;2.包装(供零售用);3.纤维成分
54.07	合成纤维长丝纱线的机织物,包括品目54.04所列材料的机织物:	
5407.1	-尼龙或其他聚酰胺高强力纱、聚酯高强力纱纺制的机织物:	1.品名;2.织造方法(机织、平行纱层叠黏合);3.染整方法(漂白、色织、染色等);4.组织结构(平纹、斜纹、缎纹等);5.成分含量;6.幅宽;7.每平方米克重;8.是否为高强力纱;9.品牌
5407.2	-扁条及类似品的机织物	1.品名;2.织造方法(机织、平行纱层叠黏合);3.染整方法(漂白、色织、染色等);4.组织结构(平纹、斜纹、缎纹等);5.成分含量;6.幅宽;7.每平方米克重;8.品牌
5407.3000	-第十一类注释九所列的机织物	1.品名;2.织造方法(机织、平行纱层叠黏合);3.染整方法(漂白、色织、染色等);4.组织结构(平纹、斜纹、缎纹等);5.成分含量;6.幅宽;7.每平方米克重;8.品牌
5407.4	-其他机织物,按重量计尼龙或其他聚酰胺长丝含量在85%及以上:	1.品名;2.织造方法(机织、平行纱层叠黏合);3.染整方法(漂白、色织、染色等);4.组织结构(平纹、斜纹、缎纹等);5.成分含量;6.幅宽;7.每平方米克重;8.品牌
5407.5	-其他机织物,按重量计聚酯变形长丝含量在85%及以上:	1.品名;2.织造方法(机织、平行纱层叠黏合);3.染整方法(漂白、色织、染色等);4.组织结构(平纹、斜纹、缎纹等);5.成分含量(聚酯变形长丝等成分及含量);6.幅宽;7.每平方米克重;8.品牌
5407.6	-其他机织物,按重量计聚酯长丝含量在85%及以上:	1.品名;2.织造方法(机织、平行纱层叠黏合);3.染整方法(漂白、色织、染色等);4.组织结构(平纹、斜纹、缎纹等);5.成分含量;6.幅宽;7.每平方米克重;8.品牌
5407.7	-其他机织物,按重量计其他合成纤维长丝含量在85%及以上:	1.品名;2.织造方法(机织、平行纱层叠黏合);3.染整方法(漂白、色织、染色等);4.组织结构(平纹、斜纹、缎纹等);5.成分含量;6.幅宽;7.每平方米克重;8.品牌
5407.8	-其他机织物,按重量计其他合成纤维长丝含量在85%以下,主要或仅与棉混纺:	1.品名;2.织造方法(机织、平行纱层叠黏合);3.染整方法(漂白、色织、染色等);4.组织结构(平纹、斜纹、缎纹等);5.成分含量;6.幅宽;7.每平方米克重;8.品牌
5407.9	-其他机织物:	1.品名;2.织造方法(机织、平行纱层叠黏合);3.染整方法(漂白、色织、染色等);4.组织结构(平纹、斜纹、缎纹等);5.成分含量;6.幅宽;7.每平方米克重;8.品牌
54.08	人造纤维长丝纱线的机织物,包括品目54.05所列材料的机织物:	1.品名;2.织造方法(机织、平行纱层叠黏合);3.染整方法(漂白、色织、染色等);4.组织结构(平纹、斜纹、缎纹等);5.成分含量;6.幅宽;7.每平方米克重;8.品牌

第五十五章　化学纤维短纤

【注解】

混纺纱线织物的归类原理:

1、按制成该物品的纤维品种、性质先归入相对应的章。

2、按该物品所属的加工程度归入该章的前、中或后的商品编码中。

3、由两种或两种以上的纺织材料混合制成的物品,应按重量比例最大的那种材料归类,当没有一种纺织材料的重量比例较大时,应按可归入有关商品编码中最后一个商品编码所列的纺织材料归类。

税则号列	商品描述	规范申报要素 / 价格申报要素 / 其他申报要素 / 举例说明
55.01	合成纤维长丝丝束:	1.品名;2.纤维成分;3.单丝细度;4.丝束长度;5.丝束捻度;6.丝束总细度
55.02	人造纤维长丝丝束:	1.品名;2.纤维成分;3.单丝细度;4.丝束长度;5.丝束捻度;6.丝束总细度
55.03	合成纤维短纤,未梳或未经其他纺前加工:	1.品名;2.加工程度(未梳、未经纺前加工);3.纤维成分;4.长度;5.细度
55.04	人造纤维短纤,未梳或未经其他纺前加工:	1.品名;2.加工程度(未梳、未经纺前加工);3.人造纤维种类;4.细度;5.长度
55.05	化学纤维废料(包括落绵、废纱及回收纤维):	1.品名;2.加工程度(未梳、未经纺前加工);3.人造纤维种类;4.细度;5.长度
5506	合成纤维短纤,已梳或经其他纺前加工:	1.品名;2.加工程度(已梳、经纺前加工);3.纤维成分
55.07	人造纤维短纤,已梳或经其他纺前加工:	1.品名;2.加工程度(已梳、经纺前加工);3.纤维成分
55.08	化学纤维短纤纺制的缝纫线,不论是否供零售用:	1.品名;2.成分含量;3.纱线细度;4.每只重量;5.是否上浆;6.终捻捻向;7.是否供零售用
55.09	合成纤维短纤纺制的纱线(缝纫线除外),非供零售用:	1.品名;2.种类(单纱、股线、缆线);3.是否供零售用;4.成分含量;5.纱线细度;6.股线注明股数
55.10	人造纤维短纤纺制的纱线(缝 纫线除外),非供零售用:	1.品名;2.种类(单纱、股线、缆线);3.是否供零售用;4.成分含量;5.纱线细度;6.股线注明股数
55.11	化学纤维短纤纺制的纱线(缝纫线除外),供零售用:	1.品名;2.种类(单纱、股线、缆线);3.是否供零售用;4.成分含量;5.纱线细度
55.12	合成纤维短纤纺制的机织物,按重量计合成纤维短纤含量在85%及以上:	1.品名;2.织造方法(机织);3.染整方法(漂白、未漂白、色织、染色等);4.组织结构(平纹、斜纹、缎纹等);5.成分含量;6.幅宽;7.每平方米克重;8.品牌
55.13	合成纤维短纤纺制的机织物,按重量计合成纤维短纤含量85%以下,主要或仅与棉混纺,每平方米重量不超过170克:	1.品名;2.种类(单纱、股线、缆线);3.织造方法(机织);4.染整方法(漂白、未漂白、色织、染色等);5.组织结构(平纹、斜纹、缎纹等);6.成分含量;7.幅宽;8.每平方米克重;9.品牌
55.14	合成纤维短纤纺制的机织物,按重量计合成纤维短纤含量在85%以下,主要或仅与棉混纺的,每平方米重量超过170克	1.品名;2.织造方法(机织);3.染整方法(漂白、未漂白、色织、染色等);4.组织结构(平纹、斜纹、缎纹等);5.成分含量;6.幅宽;7.每平方米克重;8.品牌
55.15	合成纤维短纤纺制的其他机织物:	1.品名;2.织造方法(机织);3.染整方法(漂白、未漂白、色织、染色等);4.组织结构(平纹、斜纹、缎纹等);5.成分含量;6.幅宽;7.每平方米克重;8.品牌
55.16	人造纤维短纤纺制的机织物:	1.品名;2.织造方法(机织);3.染整方法(漂白、未漂白、色织、染色等);4.组织结构(平纹、斜纹、缎纹等);5.成分含量;6.幅宽;7.每平方米克重;8.品牌

第五十六章　絮胎、毡呢及无纺织物;特种纱线、绳、索、缆及其制品

【注解】

1、无纺织物与普通絮胎的主要区别:无纺织物一般按照整张网或薄片的厚度和宽度将纤维或长丝粘合起来。

2、无纺织物与纸、纸板的主要区别:无纺织物的纤维一般在生产过程中未被融化掉。

税则号列	商品描述	规范申报要素 / 价格申报要素 / 其他申报要素 / 举例说明
56.01	纺织材料絮胎及其制品;长度不超过5毫米的纺织纤维(纤维屑)、纤维粉末及球结:	
5601.2	-絮胎;其他弩胎制品:	1.品名;2.纤维成分(如棉制)
5601.3000	-纤维屑、纤维粉末及球结	1.品名;2.状态(纤维屑、球结)

税则号列	商品描述	规范申报要素 / 价格申报要素 / 其他申报要素 / 举例说明
56.02	毡呢，不论是否浸渍、涂布、包覆或层压：	1. 品名；2. 加工方法（针刺缝编、涂布、浸渍、层压、包覆等）；3. 纤维成分含量
56.03	无纺织物，不论是否浸渍、涂布、包覆或层压：	
5603.1110	---经浸渍、涂布、包覆或层压	1. 品名；2. 加工方法（涂布、浸渍、层压、包覆等）；3. 是否化学纤维长丝制；4. 每平方米克重；5. 成分及含量；6. 用途
5603.1190	---其他	1. 品名；2. 加工方法；3. 化学纤维长丝制应注明；4. 每平方米克重；5. 成分及含量；6. 用途
5603.12	--每平方米重量超过 25 克，但不超过 70 克：	1. 品名；2. 加工方法（涂布、浸渍、层压、包覆等）；3. 是否化学纤维长丝制；4. 每平方米克重；5. 成分及含量；6. 用途
5603.13	--每平方米重量超过 70 克，但不超过 150 克：	1. 品名；2. 加工方法（涂布、浸渍、层压、包覆等）；3. 是否化学纤维长丝制；4. 每平方米克重；5. 成分及含量；6. 用途
5603.1410	---经浸渍、涂布、包覆或层压	1. 品名；2. 加工方法（涂布、浸渍、层压、包覆等）；3. 是否化学纤维长丝制；4. 每平方米克重；5. 成分及含量；6. 用途
5603.1490	---其他	1. 品名；2. 加工方法；3. 化学纤维长丝制应注明；4. 每平方米克重；5. 成分及含量；6. 用途
5603.9110	---经浸渍、涂布、包覆或层压	1. 品名；2. 加工方法（涂布、浸渍、层压、包覆等）；3. 每平方米克重；4. 成分及含量；5. 用途
5603.9190	---其他	1. 品名；2. 加工方法；3. 每平方米克重；4. 成分及含量；5. 用途
5603.9210	---经浸渍、涂布、包覆或层压	1. 品名；2. 加工方法（涂布、浸渍、层压、包覆等）；3. 每平方米克重；4. 成分及含量；5. 用途
5603.9290	---其他	1. 品名；2. 加工方法；3. 每平方米克重；4. 成分及含量；5. 用途
5603.9310	---经浸渍、涂布、包覆或层压	1. 品名；2. 加工方法（涂布、浸渍、层压、包覆等）；3. 每平方米克重；4. 成分及含量；5. 用途
5603.9390	---其他	1. 品名；2. 加工方法；3. 每平方米克重；4. 成分及含量；5. 用途
5603.9410	---经浸渍、涂布、包覆或层压	1. 品名；2. 加工方法（涂布、浸渍、层压、包覆等）；3. 每平方米克重；4. 成分及含量；5. 用途
5603.9490	---其他	1. 品名；2. 加工方法；3. 每平方米克重；4. 成分及含量；5. 用途
56.04	用纺织材料包覆的橡胶线及绳；用橡胶或塑料浸渍、涂布、包覆或套裹的纺织纱线及品目 54.04 或 54.05 的扁条及类似品：	1. 品名；2. 加工方法（浸渍、涂布或包覆等）；3. 内层材质；4. 外层材质
56.05	含金属纱线，不论是否螺旋花线，由纺织纱线或品目 54.04 或 54.05 的扁条及类似品与金属线、扁条或粉末混合制得或用金属包覆制得：	1. 品名；2. 含金属纱线；3. 成分及含量
56.06	粗松螺旋花线，品目 54.04 或 54.05 的扁条及类似品制的螺旋花线（品目 56.05 的货品及马毛粗松螺旋花线除外）；绳绒线（包括植绒绳绒线）；纵行起圈纱线：	1. 品名；2. 种类（绳绒及粗松花线、纵行起圈纱线等）
56.07	线、绳、索、缆，不论是否编织或编结而成，也不论是否用橡胶或塑料浸渍、涂布、包覆或套裹：	
5607.2100	--包扎用绳	1. 品名；2. 用途（包扎用等）；3. 纤维成分；
5607.2900	--其他	1. 品名；2. 纤维成分；
5607.4100	--包扎用绳	1. 品名；2. 用途（包扎用等）；3. 纤维成分；
5607.4900	-其他	1. 品名；2. 纤维成分；
5607.5000	-其他合成纤维纺制	1. 品名；2. 纤维成分；3. 是否编织
5607.9	-其他：	1. 品名；2. 纤维成分
56.08	线、绳或索结制的网料；纺织材料制成的渔网及其他网：	

税则号列	商　品　描　述	规范申报要素 / 价格申报要素 / 其他申报要素 / 举例说明
5608.1100	--制成的渔网	1.品名;2.用途(渔网、购物网等);3.纤维成分;4.成网方式(结制)
5608.1900	--其他	1.品名;2.用途(渔网、购物网等);3.纤维成分
5608.9	-其他	1.品名;2.用途(渔网、购物网等);3.纤维成分
56.09	用纱线、品目54.04或54.05的扁条及类似品或线、绳、索、缆制成的其他品目未列名物品:	1.品名;2.用途;3.纤维成分

第五十七章　地毯纺织材料的其他铺地制品

税则号列	商　品　描　述	规范申报要素 / 价格申报要素 / 其他申报要素 / 举例说明
57.01	结织栽绒地毯及纺织材料的其他结织栽绒铺地制品,不论是否制成的:	1.品名;2.织造方法(栽绒、手织等);3.是否为铺地制品;4.纤维成分;5.规格尺寸
57.02	机织地毯及纺织材料的其他机织铺地制品,未簇绒或未植绒,不论是否制成的,包括"开来姆"、"苏麦克"、"卡拉马尼"及类似的手织地毯:	
5702.1	-"开来姆"、"苏麦克"、"卡拉马尼"及类似的手织地毯	1.品名;2.织造方法(机织、手织等);3.纤维成分;4.规格尺寸
5702.2	-椰壳纤维制的铺地制品	1.品名;2.织造方法(栽绒、手织等);3.是否为铺地制品;4.纤维成分;5.规格尺寸
5702.3	-其他起绒结构的铺地制品,未制成的:	1.品名;2.织造方法(栽绒、手织等);3.是否为铺地制品;4.纤维成分;5.规格尺寸
5702.4	-其他起绒结构的铺地制品,制成的:	1.品名;2.织造方法(栽绒、手织等);3.是否为铺地制品;4.纤维成分;5.规格尺寸
5702.5	-其他非起绒结构的铺地制品,未制成的:	1.品名;2.织造方法(栽绒、手织等);3.是否为铺地制品;4.纤维成分;5.规格尺寸
5702.9	-其他非起绒结构的铺地制品,制成的:	1.品名;2.织造方法(栽绒、手织等);3.是否为铺地制品;4.纤维成分;5.规格尺寸
57.03	簇绒地毯及纺织材料的其他簇绒铺地制品,不论是否制成的	1.品名;2.织造方法(簇绒);3.是否为铺地制品;4.纤维成分;5.规格尺寸
57.04	毡呢地毯及纺织材料的其他毡呢铺地制品,未簇绒或未植绒,不论是否制成的:	1.品名;2.织造方法(毡呢);3.是否为铺地制品;4.纤维成分;5.规格尺寸(最大表面面积)
57.05	其他地毯及纺织材料的其他铺地制品,不论是否制成的:	1.品名;2.是否为铺地制品;3.纤维成分;4.是否含有膨润土;5.规格尺寸

第五十八章　特种机织物;簇绒织物;花边;装饰毯;装饰带;刺绣品

【注解】

"被褥状纺织制品"一般指一层胎料缝合一层织物或两层织物夹一层胎料,但缝合主要起绗缝的特征,图案不构成刺绣品的特征。

税则号列	商　品　描　述	规范申报要素 / 价格申报要素 / 其他申报要素 / 举例说明
58.01	起绒机织物及绳绒织物,但品目58.02或58.06的织物除外	
5801.1	-羊毛或动物细毛制	1.品名;2.织造方法(机织);3.幅宽;4.纤维成分
5801.21	--不割绒的纬起绒织物	1.品名;2.织造方法(机织);3.起绒方式(经起绒、纬起绒或绳绒);4.幅宽;5.纤维成分
5801.2200	--割绒的灯芯绒	1.品名;2.织造方法(机织);3.割绒请注明;4.幅宽;5.纤维成分
5801.2300	--其他纬起绒织物	1.品名;2.织造方法(机织);3.起绒方式(经起绒、纬起绒或绳绒);4.幅宽;5.纤维成分
5801.2600	--绳绒织物	1.品名;2.织造方法(机织);3.起绒方式(经起绒、纬起绒或绳绒);4.幅宽;5.纤维成分
5801.2710	---不割绒的(棱纹绸)	1.品名;2.织造方法(机织);3.起绒方式(经起绒、纬起绒或绳绒);4.幅宽;5.纤维成分

税则号列	商品描述	规范申报要素 / 价格申报要素 / 其他申报要素 / 举例说明
5801.2720	---割绒的	1. 品名;2. 织造方法(机织);3. 起绒方式(经起绒、纬起绒或绳绒);4. 是否为割绒;5. 幅宽;6. 纤维成分
5801.3100	--不割绒的纬起绒织物	1. 品名;2. 织造方法(机织);3. 起绒方式(经起绒、纬起绒或绳绒);4. 幅宽;5. 纤维成分
5801.3200	--割绒的灯芯绒	1. 品名;2. 织造方法(机织);3. 起绒方式(经起绒、纬起绒或绳绒);4. 是否为割绒;5. 幅宽;6. 纤维成分
5801.3300	--其他纬起绒织物	1. 品名;2. 织造方法(机织);3. 起绒方式(经起绒、纬起绒或绳绒);4. 幅宽;5. 纤维成分
5801.3600	--绳绒织物	1. 品名;2. 织造方法(机织);3. 起绒方式(经起绒、纬起绒或绳绒);4. 幅宽;5. 纤维成分
5801.3710	---不割绒的(棱纹绸)	1. 品名;2. 织造方法(机织);3. 起绒方式(经起绒、纬起绒或绳绒);4. 幅宽;5. 纤维成分
5801.3720	---割绒的	1. 品名;2. 织造方法(机织);3. 起绒方式(经起绒、纬起绒或绳绒);4. 是否为割绒;5. 幅宽;6. 纤维成分
5801.9010	---丝及绢丝制	1. 品名;2. 织造方法(机织);3. 幅宽;4. 纤维成分
5801.9090	---其他	1. 品名;2. 织造方法(机织);3. 起绒方式(经起绒、纬起绒或绳绒);4. 幅宽;5. 纤维成分
58.02	毛巾织物及类似的毛圈机织物,但品目 58.06 的狭幅织物除外;簇绒织物,但品目 57.03 的产品除外:	
5802.1100	--未漂白	1. 品名;2. 织造方法(机织);3. 起绒方式(簇绒或毛圈);4. 是否漂白;5. 幅宽;6. 纤维成分
5802.1900	--其他	1. 品名;2. 织造方法(机织);3. 起绒方式(簇绒或毛圈);4. 幅宽;5. 纤维成分
5802.2	-其他纺织材料制的毛巾织物及类似的毛圈机织物:	1. 品名;2. 织造方法(机织);3. 起绒方式(簇绒或毛圈);4. 幅宽;5. 纤维成分
5802.3	-簇绒织物:	1. 品名;2. 织造方法(机织);3. 起绒方式(簇绒或毛圈);4. 幅宽;5. 纤维成分
58.03	纱罗,但品目 58.06 的狭幅织物除外:	1. 品名;2. 组织结构(纱罗);3. 幅宽;4. 纤维成分
58.04	网眼薄纱及其他网眼织物,但不包括机织物、针织物或钩编织物;成卷、成条或成小块图案的花边,但品目 60.02 的织物除外:	1. 品名;2. 种类(网眼、花边);3. 织造方法(机制、手工制);4. 幅宽;5. 纤维成分
58.05	"哥白林"、"弗朗德"、"奥步生"、"波威"及类似式样的手织装饰毯,以及手工针绣嵌花装饰毯(例如,小针脚或十字绣),不论是否制成的:	1. 品名;2. 种类(网眼、花边);3. 织造方法(网眼织法);4. 幅宽;5. 纤维成分
58.06	狭幅机织物,但品目 58.07 的货品除外;用粘合剂粘合制成的有经纱而无纬纱的狭幅织物(包扎匹头用带):	
5806.1	-起绒机织物(包括毛巾织物及类似的毛圈织物)及绳绒织物	1. 品名;2. 织造方法(机织);3. 起绒方式(毛巾、绳绒等);4. 成分含量;5.. 幅宽
5806.2000	-按重量计弹性纱线或橡胶线含量在 5% 及以上的其他机织物	1. 品名;2. 织造方法(机织);3. 成分含量;4. 幅宽
5806.3	-其他机织物:	1. 品名;2. 织造方法(机织);3. 成分含量;4. 幅宽
5806.4	-用粘合剂粘合制成的有经纱而无纬纱的织物(包扎匹头用带):	1. 品名;2. 织造方法(机织);3. 成分含量;4. 幅宽
58.07	非绣制的纺织材料制标签、徽章及类似品,成匹、成条或裁成一定形状或尺寸:	1. 品名;2. 织造方法(机织、针织等);3. 成分含量;4. 幅宽;5. 刺绣请注明。注:包括除刺绣以外的各种纺织材料制的标签
58.08	成匹的编带;非绣制的成匹装饰带,但针织或钩编的除外;流苏、绒球及类似品:	1. 品名;2. 规格(成匹);3. 幅宽;4. 成分含量。注:针织和钩编除外
58.09	其他品目未列名的金属线机织物及品目 56.05 所列含金属纱线的机织物,用于衣着、装饰及类似用途:	1. 品名;2. 用途(衣着、装饰等);3. 织造方法(金属线或含金属纱线机织);4. 幅宽;5. 成分含量

税则号列	商品描述	规范申报要素 / 价格申报要素 / 其他申报要素 / 举例说明
58.10	成匹、成条或成小块图案的刺绣品：	1.品名;2.织造方法(刺绣);3.是否见底布;4.成分含量。注:刺绣品归入税目58.10
58.11	用一层或几层纺织材料与胎料经绗缝或其他方法组合制成的被褥状纺织品,但品目58.10的刺绣品除外：	1.品名;2.成分含量

第五十九章 浸渍、涂布、包覆或层压的纺织物;工业用纺织物品

税则号列	商品描述	规范申报要素 / 价格申报要素 / 其他申报要素 / 举例说明
59.01	用胶或淀粉物质涂布的纺织物,作书籍封面及类似用途的;描图布;制成的油画布;作帽里的硬衬布及类似硬挺纺织物：	1.品名;2.用途;3.处理工艺及材质(涂布、浸渍、层压);4.成分含量
59.02	尼龙或其他聚酰胺、聚酯或粘胶纤维高强力纱制的帘子布：	1.品名;2.成分含量;3.是否高强力纱制
59.03	用塑料浸渍、涂布、包覆或层压的纺织物,但品目59.02的货品除外：	1.品名;2.处理方法(涂布、浸渍、层压等);3.塑料种类;4.成分含量
58.04	列诺伦(亚麻油地毡),不论是否剪切成形;以织物为底布经涂布或覆面的铺地制品,不论是否剪切成形：	1.品名
59.05	糊墙织物：	1.品名;2.是否糊墙用;3.是否为纸衬背;4.幅宽;5.表面层纤维成分含量
59.06	用橡胶处理的纺织物,但品目59.02的货品除外：	
5906.1	-宽度不超过20厘米的胶粘带：	1.品名;2.织造方法(机织、针织、钩编等);3.处理材料(橡胶);4.是否是胶粘带、绝缘带;5.幅宽
5906.9100	--针织或钩编的	1.品名;2.织造方法(机织、针织、钩编等);3.处理材料(橡胶);4.幅宽
5906.9910	---绝缘布或带	1.品名;2.织造方法(机织、针织、钩编等);3.处理材料(橡胶);4.是否是胶粘带、绝缘带;5.幅宽
5906.9990	---其他	1.品名;2.织造方法(机织、针织、钩编等);3.处理材料(橡胶);4.幅宽
59.07	用其他材料浸渍、涂布或包覆的纺织物;作舞台、摄影布景或类似用途的已绘制画布：	
5907.0010	---绝缘布或带	1.品名;2.处理材料;3.是否为绝缘带
5907.0020	---已绘制画布	1.品名;2.是否为已绘制画布;3.处理材料
5907.0090	---其他	1.品名;2.处理材料
59.08	用纺织材料机织、编结或针织而成的灯芯、炉芯、打火机芯、烛芯或类似品;煤气灯纱筒及纱罩,不论是否浸渍：	1.品名;2.用途
59.09	纺织材料制的水龙软管及类似的管子,不论有无其他材料作衬里、护套或附件：	1.品名;2.纤维成分
59.10	纺织材料制的传动带或输送带及带料,不论是否用塑料浸渍、涂布、包覆或压层,也不论是否用金属或其他材料加强：	1.品名;2.纤维成分;3.厚度
59.11	本章注释七所规定的作专门技术用途的纺织产品及制品：	
5911.1	-用橡胶、皮革或其他材料涂布、包覆或层压的作针布用的纺织物、毡呢及毡呢衬里机织物,以及作专门技术用途的类似织物,包括用橡胶浸渍的、用于包覆纺锤(织轴)的狭幅丝绒织物：	1.品名;2.用途
5911.2	-筛布,不论是否制成的	1.品名;2.纤维成分含量

税则号列	商品描述	规范申报要素 / 价格申报要素 / 其他申报要素 / 举例说明
5911.3	-环状或装有连接装置的纺织物及毡呢,用于造纸机器或类似机器(例如,制浆机或制石棉水泥的机器):	1.品名;2.用途;3.是否为环状或有联接装置的纺织物或毡呢;4.每平方米克重
5911.4	-用于榨油机器或类似机器的滤布,包括人发制滤布	1.品名;2.用途
5911.9	-其他	1.品名;2.用途

第六十章　针织物及钩编织物

税则号列	商品描述	规范申报要素 / 价格申报要素 / 其他申报要素 / 举例说明
60.01	针织或钩编的起绒织物,包括"长毛绒"织物及毛圈织物:	
6001.1	-"长毛绒"织物	1.品名;2.织造方法(针织或钩编);3.起绒方法(毛圈或长毛绒);4.幅宽;5.纤维成分含量
6001.2	-毛圈绒头织物:	1.品名;2.织造方法(针织或钩编);3.起绒方法(毛圈或长毛绒);4.幅宽;5.纤维成分含量
6001.9	-其他:	1.品名;2.织造方法(针织或钩编);3.幅宽;4.纤维成分含量
60.02	宽度不超过30厘米,按重量计弹性纱线或橡胶线含量在5%及以上的针织物或钩编织物,但品目60.01的货品除外:	1.品名;2.织造方法(针织或钩编);3.成分含量;4.幅宽
60.03	宽度不超过30厘米的针织或钩编织物,但品目60.01或60.02的货品除外:	1.品名;2.织造方法(针织或钩编);3.成分含量;4.幅宽
60.04	宽度超过30厘米,按重量计弹性纱线或橡胶线含量在5%及以上的针织物或钩编织物,但品目60.01的货品除外:	1.品名;2.织造方法(针织或钩编);3.成分含量;4.幅宽
6005	经编织物(包括由花边针织机织成的),但品目60.01至60.04的货品除外:	1.品名;2.织造方法(针织、经编);3.染整方法(色织、染色、漂白等);4.成分含量;5.幅宽
60.06	其他针织或钩编织物:	1.品名;2.织造方法(针织、经编);3.染整方法(色织、染色、漂白等);4.成分含量;5.幅宽

第六十一章　针织或钩编的服装及衣着附件

税则号列	商品描述	规范申报要素 / 价格申报要素 / 其他申报要素 / 举例说明
61.01	针织或钩编的男式大衣、短大衣、斗蓬、短斗蓬、带风帽的防寒短上衣(包括滑雪短上衣)、防风衣、防风短上衣及类似品,但品目61.03的货品除外:	1.品名;2.织造方法(针织或钩编);3.种类(防风大衣、短大衣、斗篷等);4.类别(男式);5.成分含量;6.品牌;7.货号
61.02	针织或钩编的女式大衣、短大衣、斗蓬、短斗蓬、带风帽的防寒短上衣(包括滑雪短上衣)、防风衣、防风短上衣及类似品,但品目61.04的货品除外:	1.品名;2.织造方法(针织或钩编);3.种类(防风大衣、短大衣、斗篷等);4.类别(女式);5.成分含量;6.品牌;7.货号
61.03	针织或钩编的男式西服套装、便服套装、上衣、长裤、护胸背带工装裤、马裤及短裤(游泳裤除外):	1.品名;2.织造方法(针织或钩编);3.种类(防风大衣、短大衣、斗篷等);4.类别(男式);5.成分含量;6.品牌;7.货号。注:游泳裤除外(税目61.12)
61.04	针织或钩编的女式西服套装、便服套装、上衣、连衣裙、裙子、裙裤、长裤、护胸背带工装裤、马裤及短裤(游泳服除外):	1.品名;2.织造方法(针织或钩编);3.种类(西服、便服套装、上衣、长裤、马裤、工装裤等);4.类别(女式);5.成分含量;6.品牌;7.货号。注:游泳服除外(税目61.12)

税则号列	商品描述	规范申报要素 / 价格申报要素 / 其他申报要素 / 举例说明
61.05	针织或钩编的男衬衫:	1.品名;2.织造方法(针织或钩编);3.种类(衬衫);4.类别(男式);5.成分含量;6.品牌;7.货号。注:包括男童游戏套装衬衫
61.06	针织或钩编的女衬衫:	1.品名;2.织造方法(针织或钩编);3.种类(衬衫);4.类别(女式);5.成分含量;6.品牌;7.货号。注:包括女童游戏套装衬衫
61.07	针织或钩编的男式内裤、三角裤、长睡衣、睡衣裤、浴衣、晨衣及类似品:	1.品名;2.织造方法(针织或钩编);3.种类(内衣、内裤等);4.类别(男式);5.成分含量;6.品牌
61.08	针织或钩编的女式长衬裙、衬裙、三角裤、短衬裤、睡衣、睡衣裤、浴衣、晨衣及类似品	1.品名;2.织造方法(针织或钩编);3.种类(内衣、内裤等);4.类别(女式);5.成分含量;6.品牌
61.09	针织或钩编的T恤衫、汗衫及其他背心:	1.品名;2.织造方法(针织或钩编);3.种类(T恤衫、汗衫等);4.类别(男式、女式);5.成分含量;6.品牌;7.货号
61.10	针织或钩编的套头衫、开襟衫、背心及类似品:	1.品名;2.织造方法(针织、钩编,是否为起绒);3.种类(套头衫、开襟衫、背心等);4.类别(男式、女式);5.成分含量;6.品牌。注:包括"儿童游戏套装"
61.11	针织或钩编的婴儿服装及衣着附件:	1.品名;2.织造方法(针织或钩编);3.种类(外衣、雨衣等);4.类别(婴儿);5.成分含量;6.尺寸(衣长及裤长);7.品牌。注:婴儿身长不超过86厘米
61.12	针织或钩编的运动服、滑雪服及游泳服:	1.品名;2.织造方法(针织或钩编);3.种类(运动套装、运动装、滑雪服、游泳服);4.类别(男式、女式);5.成分含量;6.品牌;7.货号
61.13	用品目59.03、59.06或59.07的针织物或钩编织物制成的服装:	1.品名;2.织造方法(针织或钩编);3.种类(上衣、长裤、短裤等);4.类别(男式、女式);5.处理材料(塑料、橡胶);6.成分含量;7.品牌
61.14	针织或钩编的其他服装:	1.品名;2.织造方法(针织或钩编);3.种类(连身衣、夏服、水洗服、无袖罩衫等);4.类别(男式、女式、儿童);5.成分含量;6.品牌
61.15	针织或钩编的连裤袜、紧身裤袜、长筒袜、短袜及其他袜类包括用以治疗静脉曲张的长筒袜和无外绱鞋底的鞋类:	
6115.1	-渐紧压袜类(例如,用以治疗静脉曲张的长筒袜)	1.品名;2.织造方法(针织或钩编);3.用途;4.品牌
6115.2100	--每根单丝细度在67分特以下的合成纤维制	1.品名;2.织造方法(针织或钩编);3.种类(连裤袜、统袜、矫正袜);4.成分含量;5.单丝细度;6.品牌
6115.2200	--每根单丝细度在67分特及以上的合成纤维制	1.品名;2.织造方法(针织或钩编);3.种类(连裤袜、统袜、矫正袜);4.成分含量;5.单丝细度;6.品牌
6115.29	--其他纺织材料制:	1.品名;2.织造方法(针织或钩编);3.种类(连裤袜、统袜、矫正袜);4.成分含量;5.品牌
6115.3	-女士长筒袜或中筒袜,每根单丝细度在67分特以下	1.品名;2.织造方法(针织或钩编);3.种类(连裤袜、统袜、矫正袜);4.类别(女式);5.是否为女士统袜;6.成分含量;7.单丝细度;8.品牌
6115.9400	--羊毛或动物细毛制	1.品名;2.织造方法(针织或钩编);3.种类(连裤袜、统袜、矫正袜);4.成分含量;5.单丝细度;6.品牌
6115.9500	--棉制	1.品名;2.织造方法(针织或钩编);3.种类(连裤袜、统袜、矫正袜);4.成分含量;5.单丝细度;6.品牌
6115.9600	--合成纤维制	1.品名:2.织造方法(针织或钩编);3.种类(连裤袜、统袜、矫正袜);4.类别(男式、女式);5.是否女士统袜;6.成分含量;7.单丝细度;8.品牌
6115.9900	--其他纺织材料制	1.品名;2.织造方法(针织或钩编);3.种类(连裤袜、统袜、矫正袜);4.类别(男式、女式);5.是否为女士统袜;6.成分含量;7.单丝细度;8.品牌
61.16	针织或钩编的分指手套、连指手套及露指手套:	1.品名;2.织造方法(针织或钩编);3.处理材料(塑料、橡胶);4.成分含量;5.品牌
61.17	其他制成的针织或钩编的衣着附件;服装或衣着附件的针织或钩编的零件:	

税则号列	商品描述	规范申报要素 / 价格申报要素 / 其他申报要素 / 举例说明
6117.1	-披巾、头巾、围巾、披纱、面纱及类似品:	1.品名;2.织造方法(针织或钩编);3.成分含量;4.品牌
6117.8	-其他附件:	1.品名;2.织造方法(针织或钩编);3.成分含量;4.品牌
6117.9000	-零件	1.品名;2.织造方法(针织或钩编);3.成分含量

第六十二章　非针织或非钩编的服装及衣着附件

【注解】

1、本章基本上为非针织非钩编织物,如机织、无纺等,但税目62.12与62.17除外。

2、本章"衬衣及仿男式女衬衣"指:人体上身穿着并从领口处全开襟或半开襟的长袖或短袖衣服;"罩衫"也是上半身穿的,但可以无袖,领口处也可以不开襟。

税则号列	商品描述	规范申报要素 / 价格申报要素 / 其他申报要素 / 举例说明
62.01	男式大衣、短大衣、斗蓬、短斗蓬、带风帽的防寒短上衣(包括滑雪短上衣)、防风衣、防风短上衣及类似品,但税号62.03的货品除外:	1.品名;2.织造方法(机织等);3.种类(防风大衣、短大衣、斗篷等);4.类别(男式);5.成分含量;6.品牌;7.货号
62.02	女式大衣、短大衣、斗篷、短斗篷、带风帽的防寒短上衣(包括滑雪短上衣)、防风衣、防风短上衣及类似品,但品目62.04的货品除外:	1.品名;2.织造方法(机织等);3.种类(防风大衣、短大衣、斗篷等);4.类别(女式);5.成分含量;6.品牌;7.货号
62.03	男式西服套装、便服套装、上衣、长裤、护胸背带工装裤、马裤及短裤(游泳裤除外):	1.品名;2.织造方法(机织等);3.种类(西服、便服套装、上衣、长裤、马裤、工装裤等);4.类别(男式);5.成分含量;6.品牌。注:游泳裤除外(税目62.11)
62.04	女式西服套装、便服套装、上衣、连衣裙、裙子、裙裤、长裤、护胸背带工装裤、马裤及短裤(游泳服除外):	1.品名;2.织造方法(机织等);3.种类(西服、便服套装、上衣、长裤、马裤、工装裤等);4.类别(女式);5.成分含量;6.品牌。注:游泳服除外(税目62.11)
62.05	男衬衫:	1.品名;2.织造方法(机织等);3.种类(衬衫);4.类别(男式);5.成分含量;6.品牌。注:包括男童游戏套装衬衫
62.06	女衬衫:	1.品名;2.织造方法(机织等);3.种类(衬衫);4.类别(女式);5.成分含量;6.品牌。注:包括女童游戏套装衬衫
62.07	男式背心及其他内衣、内裤、三角裤、长睡衣、睡衣裤、浴衣、晨衣及类似品:	1.品名;2.织造方法(机织等);3.种类(内衣、内裤等);4.类别(男式);5.成分含量;6.品牌
62.08	女式背心及其他内衣、长衬裙、衬裙、三角裤、短衬裤、睡衣、睡衣裤、浴衣、晨衣及类似品:	1.品名;2.织造方法(机织等);3.种类(内衣、内裤等);4.类别(女式);5.成分含量;6.品牌
62.09	婴儿服装及衣着附件:	1.品名;2.织造方法(机织等);3.种类(外衣、雨衣等);4.类别(婴儿);5.成分含量;6.尺寸(衣长及裤长);7.品牌。注:婴儿身长不超过86厘米
62.10	用品目56.02、56.03、59.03、59.06或59.07的织物制成的服装:	
6210.1	-用税号56.02或56.03的织物制成的服装	1.品名;2.织造方法(机织等);3.种类(上衣、长裤、短裤等);4.类别(男式、女式);5.成分含量;6.品牌
6210.2	-子目号6201.11至6201.19所列类型的其他服装	1.品名;2.织造方法(机织等);3.种类(上衣、长裤、短裤等);4.类别(男式、女式);5.处理材料(塑料、橡胶);6.成分含量;7.品牌
6210.3	-子目号6202.11至6202.19所列类型的其他服装	1.品名;2.织造方法(机织等);3.种类(上衣、长裤、短裤等);4.类别(男式、女式);5.处理材料(塑料、橡胶);6.成分含量;7.品牌
6210.4	-其他男式服装	1.品名;2.织造方法(机织等);3.种类(上衣、长裤、短裤等);4.类别(男式);5.处理材料(塑料、橡胶);6.成分含量;7.品牌
6210.5	-其他女式服装	1.品名;2.织造方法(机织等);3.种类(上衣、长裤、短裤等);4.类别(女式);5.处理材料(塑料、橡胶);6.成分含量;7.品牌
62.11	运动服、滑雪服及游泳服;其他服装:	1.品名;2.织造方法(机织等);3.种类(连身衣、夏服、水洗服、无袖罩衫等);4.类别(男式、女式、儿童);5.成分含量;6.品牌

税则号列	商 品 描 述	规范申报要素 / 价格申报要素 / 其他申报要素 / 举例说明
62.12	胸罩、束腰带、紧身胸衣、吊裤带、吊袜带、束袜带和类似品及其零件,不论是否针织或钩编的:	1.品名;2.种类(胸罩、腹带、束腰胸衣、吊袜带、吊裤带等);3.成分含量;4.品牌。注:不论针织或钩编
62.13	手帕:	1.品名;2.织造方法(机织、刺绣、非刺绣);3.成分含量;4.尺寸;5.品牌
62.14	披巾、领巾、围巾、披纱、面纱及类似品:	1.品名;2.织造方法(机织等);3.成分含量;4.品牌
62.15	领带及领结:	1.品名;2.织造方法(机织等);3.成分含量;4.品牌
62.16	分指手套、连指手套及露指手套:	1.品名;2.织造方法(机织等);3.是否浸渍(塑料或橡胶);4.是否为运动手套;5.成分含量;6.品牌
62.17	其他制成的衣着附件;服装或衣着附件的零件,但品目62.12的货品除外:	1.品名;2.成分含量;3.织造方法;4.品牌。注:包括非裁切成形的标签、徽章、纹章、军衔、符号等(裁切制成的归入税目58.07,小块图案刺绣品归入税目58.10)

第六十三章　其他纺织制成品;成套物品;旧衣着及旧纺织品;碎织物

【注解】

税目63.07其他制成品。例如:经某些加工(如缝边、挖领口等)的针织物片,准备用于制衣,但还未加工成服装。税目63.07还包括服装裁剪样,一般用硬帆布。(纸制服装裁样与纸制服装)。此外还包括:服装袋(轻便衣橱)、旗帜(含三角旗及横幅)、卫生巾税目(56.01物品除外)以及其他符合第十一类注释七"制成品"定义,但又不归入十一类其他税目的成段织物制品,例如:门窗用的织物制挡风帘。

税则号列	商 品 描 述	规范申报要素 / 价格申报要素 / 其他申报要素 / 举例说明
63.01	毯子及旅行毯:	1.品名;2.种类(毯子、旅行毯、电暖毯);3.成分含量
63.02	床上、餐桌、盥洗及厨房用的织物制品:	1.品名;2.用途(床上用品、餐桌用、盥洗用、厨房用);3.织造方法(针织、钩编、机织、手工、刺绣、毛圈等);4.成分含量
63.03	窗帘(包括帷帘)及帐幔;帘帷或床帷:	1.品名;2.种类(窗帘、帘帷、帐幔、床帷);3.织造方法(针织、钩编、机织等);4.成分含量
63.04	其他装饰用织物制品,但品目94.04的货品除外:	
6304.1	-床罩:	1.品名;2.织造方法(针织、钩编、机织、手工、刺绣等);3.成分含量。注:包括蚊帐
6304.9	-其他:	1.品名;2.是否装饰用;3.织造方法(针织、钩编、机织、手工、刺绣等);4.成分含量。注:包括蚊帐
63.05	货物包装用袋:	1.品名;2.种类(包装袋);3.成分含量
63.06	油苫布、天蓬及遮阳蓬;帐蓬;风帆;野营用品:	1.品名;2.种类(油苫布、天篷、遮阳篷、风帆、野营用品);3.成分含量
63.07	其他制成品,包括服装裁剪样	1.品名;2.种类(油苫布、天篷、遮阳篷、风帆、野营用品);3.成分含量
63.08	由机织物及纱线构成的零售包装成套物品,不论是否带附件,用以制作小地毯、装饰毯、绣花台布、餐巾或类似的纺织物品:	1.品名;2.是否为零售包装。注:仅指机织物和纱线制
63.09	旧衣物:	1.品名;2.是否为旧
63.10	纺织材料的新的或旧的碎织物及废线、绳、索、缆及其制品:	1.品名;2.是否经分拣;3.成分含量

第十二类　鞋、帽、伞、杖、鞭及其零件；已加工的羽毛及其制品；人造花；人发制品

第六十四章　鞋靴、护腿和类似品及其零件

税则号列	商品描述	规范申报要素 / 价格申报要素 / 其他申报要素 / 举例说明
64.01	橡胶或塑料制外底及鞋面的防水鞋靴，其鞋面不是用缝、铆、钉、旋、塞或类似方法固定在鞋底上的：	
6401.1	-装有金属防护鞋头的鞋靴：	1. 品名；2. 款式（高统、装金属护头等）；3. 鞋面材料；4. 鞋底材料；5. 品牌
6401.9	-其他鞋靴：	1. 品名；2. 款式（高统等）；3. 鞋面材料；4. 鞋底材料；5. 品牌
64.02	橡胶或塑料制外底及鞋面的其他鞋靴：	1. 品名；2. 款式（高统等）；3. 鞋面材料；4. 鞋底材料；5. 请注明是否栓塞制；6. 品牌
64.03	橡胶、塑料、皮革或再生皮革制外底，皮革制鞋面的鞋靴：	
6403.1	-运动鞋靴：	1. 品名；2. 款式（高统等）；3. 鞋面材料；4. 鞋底材料；5. 品牌
6403.2000	-皮革制外底，由交叉于脚背并绕大脚趾的皮革条带构成鞋面的鞋	1. 品名；2. 款式（高统、装金属护头等）；3. 鞋面材料；4. 鞋底材料；5. 品牌
6403.4000	-装有金属防护鞋头的其他鞋靴	1. 品名；2. 款式（高统、装金属护头等）；3. 鞋面材料；4. 鞋底材料；5. 品牌
6403.5	-皮革制外底的其他鞋靴：	1. 品名；2. 款式（是否过踝或过小腿）；3. 鞋面材料；4. 鞋底材料；5. 内底长度；6. 品牌
6403.9	-其他鞋靴：	1. 品名；2. 款式（是否过踝或过小腿）；3. 鞋面材料；4. 鞋底材料；5. 内底长度；6. 品牌
64.04	橡胶、塑料、皮革或再生皮革制外底，用纺织材料制鞋面的鞋靴：	1. 品名；2. 款式（高统等）；3. 鞋面材料；4. 鞋底材料；5. 品牌
64.05	其他鞋靴：	1. 品名；2. 款式；3. 鞋面材料；4. 鞋底材料；5. 品牌
64.06	鞋靴零件（包括鞋面，不论是否带有除外底以外的其他鞋底）；活动式鞋内底、跟垫及类似品；护腿、裹腿和类似品及其零件：	1. 品名；2. 材质；3. 加工程度（是否已成型）

第六十五章　帽类及其零件

税则号列	商品描述	规范申报要素 / 价格申报要素 / 其他申报要素 / 举例说明
65.01	毡呢制的帽坯、帽身及帽兜，未楦制成形，也未加帽边；毡呢制的圆帽片及制帽用的毡呢筒（包括裁开的毡呢筒）：	1. 品名；2. 材质（毡呢）；3. 品牌
65.02	编结的帽坯或用任何材料的条带拼制而成的帽坯，未楦制成形，也未加帽边、衬里或装饰物：	1. 品名；2. 材质；3. 制作工艺（编结、拼制）；4. 品牌
65.04	编结帽或用任何材料的条带拼制而成的帽类，不论有无衬里或装饰物：	1. 品名；2. 制作工艺（编结、拼制）；3. 品牌

税则号列	商 品 描 述	规范申报要素 / 价格申报要素 / 其他申报要素 / 举例说明
65.05	针织或钩编的帽类,用成匹的花边、毡呢或其他纺织物(条带除外)制成的帽类,不论有无衬里或装饰物;任何材料制的发网,不论有无衬里或装饰物:	
6505.0010	---发网	1.品名;2.成分含量;3.品牌
6505.0020	---钩编的帽类	1.品名;2.制作工艺(针织、钩编、手工等);3.成分含量;4.品牌
6505.0091	----用品目65.01的帽身、帽兜或圆帽片制成的毡呢帽类,不论有无衬里或装饰物	1.品名;2.材质(毡呢);3.成分含量;4.品牌
6505.0099	----其他	1.品名;2.制作工艺(针织、钩编、手工等);3.成分含量;4.材质;5.品牌
65.06	其他帽类,不论有无衬里或装饰物:	1.品名;2.材质;3.品牌
65.07	帽圈、帽衬、帽套、帽帮、帽骨架、帽舌及帽颏带:	1.品名;2.材质

第六十六章 雨伞、阳伞、手杖、鞭子、马鞭及其零件

税则号列	商 品 描 述	规范申报要素 / 价格申报要素 / 其他申报要素 / 举例说明
66.01	雨伞及阳伞(包括手杖伞、庭园用伞及类似伞):	
66011000	-庭园用伞及类似伞	1.品名;2.款式
6601.9	-其他:	1.品名;2.款式;3.品牌
66.02	手杖、带座手杖、鞭子、马鞭及类似品:	1.品名;2.材质
66.03	品目66.01或66.02所列物品的零件及装饰品:	1.品名;2.材质

第六十七章 已加工羽毛、羽绒及其制品;人造花;人发制品

税则号列	商 品 描 述	规范申报要素 / 价格申报要素 / 其他申报要素 / 举例说明
67.01	带羽毛或羽绒的鸟皮及鸟体其他部分、羽毛、部分羽毛、羽绒及其制品(品目05.05的货品和经加工的羽管及羽轴除外):	1.品名;2.加工程度
67.02	人造花、叶、果实及其零件;用人造花、叶或果实制成的物品:	1.品名;2.制作材料(塑料丝等)
67.03	经梳理、稀疏、脱色或其他方法加工的人发;做假发及类似品用的羊毛、其他动物毛或其他纺织材料:	1.品名;2.加工程度(经梳理、脱色等);3.制作材料
67.04	人发、动物毛或纺织材料制的假发、假胡须、假眉毛、假睫毛及类似品;其他品目未列名的人发制品:	1.品名;2.加工程度(经梳理、脱色等);3.制作材料

第十三类　石料、石膏、水泥、石棉、云母及类似材料的制品；陶瓷产品；玻璃及其制品

第六十八章　石料、石膏、水泥、石棉、云母及类似材料的制品

税则号列	商品描述	规范申报要素 / 价格申报要素 / 其他申报要素 / 举例说明
68.01	天然石料(不包括板岩)制的长方砌石、路缘石、扁平石：	1.品名;2.种类(长方砌石、扁平石、路缘石);3.材质
68.02	已加工的碑石或建筑用石(不包括板岩)及其制品,但品目68.01的货品除外;天然石料(包括板岩)制的镶嵌石(马赛克)及类似品,不论是否有衬背;天然石料(包括板岩)制的人工染色石粒、石片及石粉：	1.品名;2.用途(用于建筑可直接使用);3.材质(大理石、花岗岩);4.加工程度(切、锯、抛光及是否石刻等);5.尺寸(最大表面积的最大边长)
68.03	已加工的板岩及板岩或粘聚板岩的制品：	1.品名;2.加工程度;3.材质
68.04	未装支架的石磨、石碾、砂轮和类似品及其零件,用于研磨、磨刃、抛光、整形或切割,以及手用磨石、抛光石及其零件,用天然石料、粘聚的天然磨料、人造磨料或陶瓷制成,不论是否装有由其他材料制成的零件：	
6804.1000	-碾磨或磨浆用石磨、石碾	1.品名;2.用途(碾磨或磨浆、磨光用等);3.材质(石料、粘聚合成料等);4.是否装支架
6804.2	-其它石磨、石碾、砂轮及类似品：	1.品名;2.用途(碾磨或磨浆、磨光用等);3.材质(石料、粘聚合成料等);4.是否装支架;5.品牌
6804.3010	---琢磨油石	1.品名;2.用途(碾磨或磨浆、磨光用等);3.材质(石料、粘聚合成料等);4.是否装支架
6804.3090	---其他	1.品名;2.用途(碾磨或磨浆、磨光用等);3.材质(石料、粘聚合成料等);4.是否装支架;5.是否手用磨
68.05	砂布、砂纸及以其他材料为底的类似品,不论是否裁切、缝合或用其他方法加工成形：	1.品名;2.基底材料;3.砂粒材质;4.是否有涂层(如有,请申报材质);5.品牌;6.型号;7.尺寸。注:包括裁剪、缝合加工而成的
68.06	矿渣棉、岩石棉及类似的矿质棉;页状蛭石、膨胀粘土、泡沫矿渣及类似的膨胀矿物材料;具有隔热、隔音或吸音性能的矿物材料的混合物及制品,但品目68.11、68.12或第六十九章的货品除外：	
6806.1	-矿渣棉、岩石棉及类似的矿质棉(包括其相互混合物),块状、成片或成卷：	1.品名;2.材质(矿物纤维等);3.形状;4.含有石棉纤维的要注明其含量。注:不包括粒状矿渣(品目26.18)
6806.2000	-页状硅石、膨胀粘土、泡沫矿渣及类似的膨胀矿物材料(包括相互混合物)	1.品名;2.材质(页状蛭石、膨胀粘土、泡沫矿渣等);3.形状;4.含有石棉纤维的要注明其含量。注:不包括粒状矿渣(税目26.18)
6806.9000	-其他	1.品名;2.材质;3.形状;4.含有石棉纤维的要注明其含量。注:不包括粒状矿渣(税目26.18)
68.07	沥青或类似原料(例如,石油沥青或煤焦油沥青)的制品：	1.品名;2.形状。注:不包括用焦油、沥青等涂布、浸渍或覆盖的纸(税目48.11)和纺织物(第五十六章或五十九章)、石棉加沥青制品(税目68.11)等

税则号列	商品描述	规范申报要素 / 价格申报要素 / 其他申报要素 / 举例说明
68080000	镶板、平板、瓦、砖及类似品用水泥、石膏及其他矿物粘合材料粘合植物纤维、稻草、刨花、木片屑、木粉、锯末或木废料制成:	1. 品名;2. 种类(镶板、平板瓦、砖等);3. 原料(稻草、刨花等);4. 粘料(水泥、石膏等矿物性黏合材料)
68.09	石膏制品及以石膏为基本成分的混合材料制品:	1. 品名;2. 加工方法(是否装饰、经贴面或加强等);3. 是否未经装饰,仅用纸或纸板贴面或加强的;4. 成分含量。注:不包括石膏骨折绷带(税目30.05)和夹板(税目90.21);专供示范用的模型(税目90.23);裁缝用人体模型(税目96.18)等
68.10	水泥、混凝土或人造石制品,不论是否加强:	1. 品名;2. 用途(铁道用等);3. 种类(砖、瓦、管及建筑构件钢筋混凝土板等);4. 材料(水泥、混凝土、人造石)。注:不包括破碎混凝土块
68.11	石棉水泥、纤维素水泥或类似材料的制品:	1. 品名;2. 种类(砖、瓦、管、板等);3. 材料(石棉水泥、纤维素水泥等)
68.12	已加工的石棉纤维;以石棉为基本成分或以石棉和碳酸镁为基本成分的混合物;上述混合物或石棉的制品(例如,纱线、机织物、服装、帽类、鞋靴、衬垫),不论是否加强,但品目68.11或68.13的货品除外	1. 品名;2. 种类(纱线、机织物、服装、鞋帽、衬垫等);3. 材料(石棉纤维、石棉)
68.13	以石棉、其他矿物质或纤维素为基本成分的未装配磨擦材料及其制品(例如,片、卷、带、盘、圈、垫及扇形),适于做制动器、离合器及类似品,不论是否与织物或其他材料结合而成:	1. 品名;2. 材质;3. 种类(片、卷、带、闸衬、闸垫、扇形等)。注:指未装配的摩擦材料及制品
68.14	已加工的云母及其制品,包括粘聚或复制的云母,不论是否附于纸、纸板或其他材料上:	1. 品名;2. 材质(云母);3. 形状(板、片、带等);4. 是否粘聚或复制的。注:仅指已加工的云母及制品
68.15	其他品目未列名的石制品及其他矿物制品(包括碳纤维及其制品和泥煤制品):	
6815.1000	-非电器用的石墨或其他碳精制品	1. 品名;2. 材质;3. 用途。注:石墨、碳精制品仅指非电器用,电器用应归入税目85.45
6815.2000	-泥煤制品	1. 品名;2. 材质。注:石墨、碳精制品仅指非电器用,电器用应归入税目85.45
6815.9100	--含有菱镁矿、白云石或铬铁矿的	1. 品名;2. 材质。注:石墨、碳精制品仅指非电器用,电器用应归入税目85.45
6815.9920	---碳纤维	1. 品名;2. 材质
6815.9931	----碳布	1. 品名;2. 材质
6815.9932	----碳纤维预浸料	1. 品名;2. 材质
6815.9939	----其他	1. 品名;2. 材质;3. 碳纤维纱线请注明碳含量、比模量和比极限抗拉强度石墨、碳精制品仅指非电器用,电器用应归入税目85.45
6815.9940	----玄武岩纤维及其制品	1. 品名;2. 材质
6815.9990	---其他	1. 品名;2. 材质石墨、碳精制品仅指非电器用,电器用应归入税目85.45

第六十九章　陶瓷产品

税则号列	商品描述	规范申报要素 / 价格申报要素 / 其他申报要素 / 举例说明
69.01	硅质化石粉(例如各种硅藻土)或类似硅土制的砖、块、瓦及其他陶瓷制品:	1. 品名;2. 材质(硅质化石粉、硅藻土或类似硅土等);3. 种类(砖、瓦等)
69.02	耐火砖、块、瓦及类似耐火陶瓷建材制品,但硅质化石粉及类似硅土制的除外:	1. 品名;2. 种类(耐火砖、瓦、块等);3. 成分含量;4. 耐火温度。注:本税目指耐火、耐火陶瓷建材制品。注:不包括硅质化石粉或类似硅土制
69.03	其他耐火陶瓷制品(例如,甑、坩埚、马弗罩、喷管、栓塞、支架、烤钵、管子、护套及棒条),但硅质化石粉及类似硅土制的除外:	1. 品名;2. 种类(坩埚、支架、马弗罩等);3. 成分含量;4. 耐火温度。注:不包括耐火陶瓷建筑材料制品、硅质化石粉或类似硅土制

税则号列	商品描述	规范申报要素 / 价格申报要素 / 其他申报要素 / 举例说明
69.04	陶瓷制建筑用砖、铺地砖、支撑或填充用砖及类似品:	1.品名;2.种类(建筑用砖、地面砖等)。注:本税目指非耐火陶瓷
69.05	屋顶瓦、烟囱罩、通风帽、烟囱衬壁、建筑装饰及其他建筑用陶瓷制品:	1.品名;2.种类(屋顶瓦、烟囱罩等)
69.06	陶瓷套管、导管、槽管及管子附件:	1.品名;2.种类(套管、导管、槽管等)
69.07	未上釉的陶瓷贴面砖、铺面砖,包括炉面砖及墙面砖;未上釉的陶瓷镶嵌砖(马赛克)及类似品,不论是否有衬背:	1.品名;2.种类(贴面砖、铺面砖、马赛克等);3.尺寸(最大表面积的最大边长);4.品牌。注:本税目指未上釉的
69.08	上釉的陶瓷贴面砖、铺面砖,包括炉面砖及墙面砖;上釉的陶瓷镶嵌砖(马赛克)及类似品,不论是否有衬背:	1.品名;2.种类(贴面砖、铺面砖、马赛克等);3.尺寸(最在表面积的最大边长);4.品牌;5.颜色。注:本税目指上釉的
69.09	实验室、化学或其他专门技术用途的陶瓷器;农业用陶瓷槽、缸及类似容器;通常供运输及盛装货物用的陶瓷罐、坛及类似品:	1.品名;2.用途(实验室用、化学、农业用等);3.种类(瓷制、陶制);4.莫氏硬度
69101000	陶瓷洗涤槽、脸盆、脸盆座、浴缸、坐浴盆,抽水马桶、水箱、小便池及类似的固定卫生设备:	1.品名;2.材质(瓷制、陶制);3.品牌;4.规格型号
69.11	瓷餐具、厨房器具及其他家用或盥洗用瓷器:	1.品名;2.材质(瓷制、陶制);3.种类(餐具、厨房器具等);4.品牌
69.12	陶餐具、厨房器具及其他家用或盥洗用陶器:	1.品名;2.材质(瓷制、陶制);3.种类(餐具、厨房器具等);4.品牌
69.13	塑像及其他装饰用陶瓷制品:	1.品名;2.材质(瓷制、陶制);3.用途
69.14	其他陶瓷制品:	1.品名;2.材质(瓷制、陶制);3.用途

第七十章 玻璃及其制品

【注解】

1、"品名"是指货品的具体商业名称。

2、"用途"是指货品在出入境后的应用场合或下游产品。

3、"加工方法"是指货品在出入境前的加工工艺或制造方法。

4、"材质"是指货品按《税则》中的材质分类原则所确定的具体材料种类。

5、"形状"是指货品按《税则》中的形状定义描述所确定的外观形状。

税则号列	商品描述	规范申报要素 / 价格申报要素 / 其他申报要素 / 举例说明
70.01	碎玻璃及废玻璃;玻璃块料:	1.品名;2.用途;3.状态(废、碎、块料)
70.02	未加工的玻璃球、棒及管(品目70.18的微型玻璃球除外)	
7002.1000	-玻璃球	1.品名;2.用途;3.直径
7002.2010	---光导纤维预制棒	1.品名;2.用途(光导纤维预制棒等);3.光导纤维预制棒请注明规格型号;4.品牌
7002.2090	---其他	1.品名;2.用途(光导纤维预制棒等);3.光导纤维预制棒请注明规格型号
7002.31	--熔融石英或其他熔融硅石制:	1.品名;2.用途(光导纤维用、光通信用等);3.材质(熔融石英、熔融硅石等);4.级别(波导级);5.外径
7002.3200	--温度在0℃至300℃时线膨胀系数不超过5×10 - 6/开尔文的其他玻璃制	1.品名;2.用途(光导纤维用、光通信用等);3.材质(熔融石英、熔融硅石等);4.线膨胀系数;5.级别(波导级);6.外径
7002.3900	--其他	1.品名;2.用途(光导纤维用、光通信用等);3.材质(熔融石英、熔融硅石等);4.线膨胀系数;5.级别(波导级);6.外径
70.03	铸制或轧制玻璃板、片或型材及异型材,不论是否有吸收、反射或非反射层,但未经其他加工:	
7003.1200	--整块着色、不透明、镶色或具有吸收、反射或非反射层的	1.品名;2.用途;3.加工方法(整块着色、具有吸收层等);4.状态(是否夹丝);5.形状(板、片、型材、异型材);6.工艺(铸制或轧制)

税则号列	商　品　描　述	规范申报要素 / 价格申报要素 / 其他申报要素 / 举例说明
7003.1900	--其他	1. 品名;2. 用途;3. 状态(是否夹丝);4. 形状(板、片、型材、异型材);5. 工艺(铸制或轧制)
7003.2000	-夹丝玻璃板、片	1. 品名;2. 用途;3. 状态(是否夹丝);4. 形状(板、片、型材、异型材);5. 工艺(铸制或轧制)
7003.3000	-型材及异型材	1. 品名;2. 用途;3. 状态(是否夹丝);4. 形状(板、片、型材、异型材);5. 工艺(铸制或轧制)
70.04	拉制或吹制玻璃板、片,不论是否有吸收、反射或非反射层,但未经其他加工:	
7004.2000	-整块着色、不透明、镶色或具有吸收、反射或非反射层的	1. 品名;2. 用途;3. 加工方法(整块着色、具有吸收层等);4. 状态(是否经过表面加工);5. 形状(板、片);6. 工艺(拉制或吹制)
7004.9000	-其他玻璃	1. 品名;2. 用途;3. 状态(是否经过表面加工);4. 形状(板、片);5. 工艺(拉制或吹制)
70.05	浮法玻璃板、片及表面研磨或抛光玻璃板、片,不论是否有吸收、反射或非反射层,但未经其他加工:	
7005.1000	-具有吸收、反射或非反射层的非夹丝玻璃	1. 品名;2. 用途;3. 加工方法(具有吸收、反射或非反射层的);4. 状态(是否夹丝);5. 形状(板、片);6. 工艺(浮法、表面研磨、抛光)
7005.2100	--整块着色、不透明、镶色或仅表面研磨的	1. 品名;2. 用途;3. 加工方法(整块着色、不透明、镶色等);4. 状态(是否夹丝);5. 形状(板、片);6. 工艺(浮法、表面研磨、抛光)
7005.2900	--其他	1. 品名;2. 用途;3. 状态(是否夹丝);4. 形状(板、片);5. 工艺(浮法、表面研磨、抛光)
7005.3000	-夹丝玻璃	1. 品名;2. 用途;3. 状态(是否夹丝);4. 形状(板、片);5. 工艺(浮法、表面研磨、抛光)
70.06	经弯曲、磨边、镂刻、钻孔、涂珐琅或其他加工的品目 70.03、70.04 或 70.05 的玻璃,但未用其他材料镶框或装配:	1. 品名;2. 用途;3. 加工方法(经弯曲、磨边、镂刻、钻孔、涂珐琅等);4. 状态(未用其他材料镶框或装配);5. 形状(板、片、型材、异型材)
70.07	钢化或层压玻璃制的安全玻璃:	1. 品名;2. 用途(车辆、航空器、航天器、船舶);3. 加工方法(钢化、层压);4. 品牌
70.08	多层隔温、隔音玻璃组件:	1. 品名;2. 用途(隔温、隔音);3. 类型(中空、真空等);4. 层数;5. 品牌
70.09	玻璃镜(包括后视镜),不论是否镶框:	
7009.1000	-车辆后视镜	1. 品名;2. 用途(车辆后视用等);3. 加工方法(未经光学加工)
7009.9	-其他:	1. 品名;2. 用途(车辆后视用等);3. 加工方法(未经光学加工);4. 是否镶框
70.10	玻璃制的坛、瓶、缸、罐、安瓿及其他容器,用于运输或盛装货物;玻璃制保藏罐;玻璃塞、盖及类似的封口器:	1. 品名;2. 用途(用于运输或盛装货物);3. 容积
70.11	制灯泡、阴极射线管及类似品用的未封口玻璃外壳(包括玻璃泡及管)及其玻璃零件,但未装有配件:	1. 品名;2. 用途(制灯泡、阴极射线管等);3. 加工方法(用荧光物质衬里、未封口、无配件等)
70.13	玻璃器,供餐桌、厨房、盥洗室、办公室、室内装饰或类似用途(品目 70.10 或 70.18 的货品除外):	
7013.1000	-玻璃陶瓷制	1. 品名;2. 用途(供餐桌、厨房、盥洗室、办公室、室内装饰用);3. 材质(玻璃陶瓷、铅晶质玻璃等);4. 器皿种类(杯等);5. 工艺流程(手工、机械、半手工)
7013.2	-杯子,但玻璃陶瓷制的除外:	1. 品名;2. 用途(供餐桌、厨房、盥洗室、办公室、室内装饰用);3. 材质(玻璃陶瓷、铅晶质玻璃等);4. 器皿种类(杯等);5. 平脚还是高脚杯;6. 规格;7. 型号;8. 品牌;9. 工艺流程(手工、机械、半手工)

税则号列	商 品 描 述	规范申报要素 / 价格申报要素 / 其他申报要素 / 举例说明
7013.3	-其他杯子,但玻璃陶瓷制的除外:	1.品名;2.用途(供餐桌、厨房、盥洗室、办公室、室内装饰用);3.材质(玻璃陶瓷、铅晶质玻璃等);4.器皿种类(杯等);5.平脚还是高脚杯;6.规格;7.型号;8.品牌;9.工艺流程(手工、机械、半手工)
7013.4	-餐桌或厨房用玻璃器皿(不包括杯子),但玻璃陶瓷制的除外:	1.品名;2.用途(供餐桌、厨房、盥洗室、办公室、室内装饰用);3.材质(玻璃陶瓷、铅晶质玻璃等);4.器皿种类(杯等);5.线膨胀系数;6.工艺流程(手工、机械、半手工)
7013.9	-其他玻璃器:	1.品名;2.用途(供餐桌、厨房、盥洗室、办公室、室内装饰用);3.材质(玻璃陶瓷、铅晶质玻璃等);4.器皿种类(杯等)5工艺流程(手工、机械、半手工)
70.14	未经光学加工的信号玻璃器及玻璃制光 学元件(品目70.15的货品除外):	
7014.0010	---光学仪器用光学元件毛坯	1.品名;2.用途(具体列明用于光学仪器名称);3.形状、尺寸及外观;4.是否经光学加工。注:凸透镜玻璃毛胚,用于制作相机镜头的凸透镜,圆形表面为双球面,直径52毫米,外观为半透明,未经过光学加工。
7014.0090	---其他	1.品名;2.用途(是否用于光学仪器);3.形状、尺寸及外观;4.是否经光学加工
70.15	钟表玻璃及类似玻璃、视力矫正或非视力矫正眼镜用玻璃,呈弧面、弯曲、凹形或类似形状但未经光学加工的;制造上述玻璃用的凹面圆形及扇形 玻璃:	
7015.1010	---变色镜片坯件	1.品名;2.用途(用于制造眼镜等);3.加工方法(未经光学加工);4.形状(弧面、弯曲、凹形、扇形等);5.元件种类(视力矫正玻璃毛坯等);6.特殊功能(变色等)
7015.1090	---其他	1.品名;2.用途(用于制造眼镜等);3.加工方法(未经光学加工);4.形状(弧面、弯曲、凹形、扇形等);5.元件种类(视力矫正玻璃毛坯等)
7015.9010	---钟表玻璃	1.品名;2.用途(用于制造钟表等);3.加工方法(未经光学加工);4.形状(弧面、弯曲、凹形、扇形等);5.元件种类(视力矫正玻璃毛坯等)
7015.9020	---平光变色镜片坯件	1.品名;2.用途(用于制造眼镜等);3.加工方法(未经光学加工);4.形状(弧面、弯曲、凹形、扇形等);5.元件种类(视力矫正玻璃毛坯等);6.特殊功能(变色等)
7015.9090	---其他	1.品名;2.用途(用于制造眼镜等);3.加工方法(未经光学加工);4.形状(弧面、弯曲、凹形、扇形等);5.元件种类(视力矫正玻璃毛坯等)
70.16	建筑用压制或模制的铺面用玻璃块、砖、片、瓦及其他制品,不论是否夹丝;供镶嵌或类似装饰用的玻璃马赛克及其他小件玻璃品,不论是否有衬背;花饰铅条窗玻璃及类似品;多孔或泡沫玻璃块、板、片及类似品:	1.品名;2.用途(建筑铺面用);3.加工方法(压制、模制等);4.制品种类(马赛克、花饰铅条窗玻璃、铺面砖、块、片等)
70.17	实验室、卫生及配药用的玻璃 器,不论有无刻度或标量:	1.品名;2.用途(实验室、卫生、配药用);3.材质(熔融石英、熔融硅石);4.器皿种类(量筒等);5.线膨胀系数
70.18	玻璃珠、仿珍珠、仿宝石或仿半宝石和类似小件玻璃品及其制品,但仿首饰除外;玻璃假眼,但医用假眼除外;灯工方法制作的玻璃塑像及其他玻璃装饰品,但仿首饰除外;直径不超过1毫米的微型玻璃球:	1.品名;2.用途(装饰用等);3.加工方法(灯工方法等);4.玻璃球的直径;5.材质(钙钠玻璃、铅晶玻璃等);6.品牌;7.型号
70.19	玻璃纤维(包括玻璃棉)及其制品(例如,玻璃纤维纱线及其织物):	
7019.1	-梳条、粗纱、纱线及短切纤维:	1.品名;2.材质(玻璃纤维制);3.种类(梳条、粗纱、纱线、短纤);4.长度
7019.3	-薄片(巴厘纱)、纤维网、席 垫、板及类似无纺产品:	1.品名;2.材质(玻璃纤维制);3.种类(席、薄片、纤维网、垫、板等)

税则号列	商品描述	规范申报要素 / 价格申报要素 / 其他申报要素 / 举例说明
7019.4000	-粗纱机织物	1.品名;2.材质(玻璃纤维制);3.织造方法(机织);4.纱线类型(粗纱)
7019.5100	--宽度不超过 30 厘米的	1.品名;2.材质(玻璃纤维制);3.织造方法(机织);4.纱线类型(细纱等);5.幅宽
7019.5200	--宽度超过 30 厘米的长丝平纹织物,每平方米重量不超过 250 克,单根纱线细度不超过 136 特克斯	1.品名;2.材质(玻璃纤维制);3.织造方法(机织);4.纱线类型(细纱等);5.幅宽;6.每平方米克重;7.单纱细度;8.标称厚度
7019.5900	--其他	1.品名;2.材质(玻璃纤维制);3.织造方法(机织);4.纱线类型(细纱等);5.幅宽;6.每平方米克重;7.单纱细度
7019.9010	---玻璃棉及其制品	1.品名;2.用途;3.材质(玻璃棉制)
7019.902	---玻璃棉及其制品	1.品名;2.用途;3.材质(玻璃纤维布浸胶);4.每平方米重量
7019.9090	---其他	1.品名;2.用途;3.材质(玻璃纤维制)
70.20	其他玻璃制品:	
7020.0011	---导电玻璃	1.品名;2.用途;3.材质(玻璃制);4.导电层材质、电阻值
7020.0012	----绝缘子用玻璃伞盘	1.品名;2.用途;3.材质(玻璃制)
7020.0013	----溶融石英或其他熔融硅石制	1.品名;2.用途;3.材质(熔融石英或其他熔融石制)
7020.0019	----其他	1.品名;2.用途;3.材质(玻璃制)
7020.009	---其他:	1.品名;2.用途;3.材质(玻璃制)

第十四类　天然或养殖珍珠、宝石或半宝石、贵金属、包贵金属及其制品;仿首饰;硬币

第七十一章　天然或养殖珍珠、宝石或半宝石、贵金属、包贵金属及其制品;仿首饰;硬币

【注解】

1、"品名"是指货品的具体商业名称。

2、"用途"是指货品在出入境后的应用场合或下游产品。

3、"加工方法"是指货品在出入境前的加工工艺或制造方法。

4、"材质"是指货品按《税则》中的材质分类原则所确定的具体材料种类。

5、"形状"是指货品按《税则》中的形状定义描述所确定的外观形状。

税则号列	商品描述	规范申报要素 / 价格申报要素 / 其他申报要素 / 举例说明
71.01	天然或养殖珍珠,不论是否加工或分级,但未成串或镶嵌;天然或养殖珍珠,为便于运输而暂穿成串:	1.品名;2.种类(黑珍珠等);3.加工程度(打孔、未加工等);4.状态(未成串、未镶嵌等);5.来源(天然、养殖);6.等级
71.02	钻石,不论是否加工,但未镶 嵌:	1.品名;2.用途;3.加工程度(未加工,经简单锯开、劈开、粗磨等);4.来源(天然)
71.03	宝石(钻石除外)或半宝石,不论是否加工或分级,但未成串或镶嵌,未分级的宝石(钻石除外)或半宝石,为便于运输而暂穿成串:	
7103.1000	-未加工或经简单锯开或粗制成形	1.品名;2.种类(红宝石、蓝宝石、祖母绿、翡翠等);3.加工程度(未加工,经简单锯开、粗制成形);4.状态(未成串、未镶嵌等);5.来源(天然);6.等级;7.矿物学名;8.规格;9.化学成分;10.缅甸公盘成交需申报玉石编号、件数、重量
7103.9	-经其他加工:	1.品名;2.种类(红宝石、蓝宝石、祖母绿、翡翠等);3.加工程度(未加工,经简单锯开、粗制成形);4.状态(未成串、未镶嵌等);5.来源(天然);6.等级;7.矿物学名;8.规格;9.化学成分

税则号列	商品描述	规范申报要素 / 价格申报要素 / 其他申报要素 / 举例说明
71.04	合成或再造的宝石或半宝石,不论是否加工或分级,但未成串或镶嵌的;未分级的合成或再造的宝石或半宝石,为便于运输而暂穿成串:	1.品名;2.用途;3.种类(压电石英等);4.加工程度(经简单锯开、粗制成形);5.状态(未成串、未镶嵌等);6.来源(合成、再造)
71.05	天然或合成的 宝石或半宝石的粉末:	1.品名;2.种类(压电石英等);3.加工程度(经简单锯开、粗制成形);4.状态(未成串、未镶嵌等);5.来源(合成、再造)
71.06	银(包括镀金、镀铂的银),未锻造、半制成或粉末状:	
7106.1	-银粉:	1.品名;2.形状(粉末);3.材质(纯银、银合金、镀金、镀铂);4.加工程度(未锻造、半制成);5.纯度;6.平均粒径
7106.9	-其他:	1.品名;2.形状(粉末);3.材质(纯银、银合金、镀金、镀铂);4.加工程度(未锻造、半制成);5.纯度
71.07	以贱金属为底的包银材料:	1.品名;2.基底材质(铜等)
71.08	金(包括镀铂的金),未锻造半制成或粉末状:	1.品名;2.形状(粉末);3.材质(纯金、金合金、镀铂);4.纯度;5.加工程度(未锻造、半制成);6.货币用请注明用途
71.09	以贱金属或银 为底的包金材料:	1.品名;2.基底材质(铜、银等)
71.10	铂,未锻造、半制成或粉末状	1.品名;2.形状(粉末);3.材质(铂、钯、铑、铱、锇、钌);4.加工程度(未锻造,板、片等)
71.11	以贱金属、银或金为底的包铂材料:	1.品名;2.基底材质(铜、银、金等)
71.12	贵金属或包贵金属的废碎料;含有贵金属或 贵金属化合物的其他废碎料,主要用于回收贵金属:	1.品名;2.状态(废碎料、灰);3.来源(由破碎含有贵金属的电路板而得等);4.贵金属的成分含量
71.13	贵金属或包贵 金属制的首饰及其零件:	1.品名;2.材质(铂、金、银等);3.加工方法(镶嵌宝石、包金、包银等);4.首饰种类(戒指等);5.贵金属成分含量
71.14	贵金属或包贵 金属制的金银器及其零件:	1.品名;2.种类(餐具等);3.材质(铂、金、银等);4.加工方法(包金、镀金等)
71151000	贵金属或包贵 金属的其他制品:	1.品名;2.用途(工业用、实验室用等);3.种类(坩埚等);4.形状(格栅形状等);5.材质(铂等)
71.16	用天然或养殖珍珠、宝石或半宝石(天然、合成或再造)制成的物品:	1.品名;2.种类(手镯等);3.材质(养殖珍珠、天然珍珠、宝石、半宝石)
71.17	仿首饰:	1.品名;2.种类(袖扣、饰扣、手镯等);3.材质;4.是否镀贵金属;5.品牌
71.18	硬币:	
7118.1000	-非法定货币的硬币(金币除外)	1.品名;2.用途(法定货币、非法定货币);3.材质(铜制等);4.成分含量
7118.9000	-其他硬币	1.品名;2.用途(法定货币、非法定货币);3.材质(铜制等)

第十五类 贱金属及其制品

第七十二章 钢铁

【注解】

1、"品名"是指货品的具体商业名称。

2、"用途"是指货品在出入境后的应用场合或下游产品。

3、"加工方法"是指货品在出入境前的加工工艺或制造方法。

4、"材质"是指货品按《税则》中的材质分类原则所确定的具体材料种类。

5、"形状"是指货品按《税则》中的形状定义描述所确定的外观形状。

税则号列	商品描述	规范申报要素 / 价格申报要素 / 其他申报要素 / 举例说明
72.01	产品 生铁及镜铁,锭、块或其他初 级形状:	1.品名;2.形状(锭、块等);3.材质(生铁、镜铁);4.成分含量(铁、碳、铬、锰、磷、硅的含量)

税则号列	商品描述	规范申报要素 / 价格申报要素 / 其他申报要素 / 举例说明
72.02	铁合金：	
7202.1	-锰铁：	1.品名；2.材质（锰铁、硅铁、铬铁、镍铁等）；3.成分含量（铁含量及合金元素的含量）；4.碳含量
7202.2	-硅铁：	1.品名；2.材质（锰铁、硅铁、铬铁、镍铁等）；3.成分含量（铁含量及合金元素的含量）
7202.3000	-硅锰铁	1.品名；2.材质（锰铁、硅铁、铬铁、镍铁等）；3.成分含量（铁含量及合金元素的含量）
7202.4	-铬铁：	1.品名；2.材质（锰铁、硅铁、铬铁、镍铁等）；3.成分含量（铁含量及合金元素的含量）
7202.5000	-硅铬铁	1.品名；2.材质（锰铁、硅铁、铬铁、镍铁等）；3.成分含量（铁含量及合金元素的含量）
7202.6000	-镍铁	1.品名；2.材质（锰铁、硅铁、铬铁、镍铁等）；3.成分含量（铁含量及合金元素的含量）
7202.7000	-钼铁	1.品名；2.材质（锰铁、硅铁、铬铁、镍铁等）；3.成分含量（铁含量及合金元素的含量）
7202.8	-钨铁及硅钨铁：	1.品名；2.材质（锰铁、硅铁、铬铁、镍铁等）；3.成分含量（铁含量及合金元素的含量）
7202.9100	--钛铁及硅钛铁	1.品名；2.材质（锰铁、硅铁、铬铁、镍铁等）；3.成分含量（铁含量及合金元素的含量）
7202.92	--钒铁：	1.品名；2.材质（锰铁、硅铁、铬铁、镍铁等）；3.成分含量（铁含量及合金元素的含量）
7202.9300	--铌铁	1.品名；2.材质（锰铁、硅铁、铬铁、镍铁等）；3.成分含量（铁含量及合金元素的含量）
7202.99	--其他：	1.品名；2.材质（锰铁、硅铁、铬铁、镍铁等）；3.成分含量（铁含量及合金元素的含量）；4.稀土元素的重量百分比，以[A]表示
72.03	直接从铁矿还原所得的铁产品及其他海绵铁产品，块、团、团粒及类似形状；按重量计纯度在99.94%及以上的铁，块团、团粒及类似形状：	1.品名；2.形状（块、团、团粒等）；3.来源（是直接从铁矿还原所得还是海锦铁产品）；4.成分含量（铁、碳、合金元素、非合金元素的含量）
72.04	钢铁废碎料；供再熔的碎料钢铁锭：	
7204.1000	-铸铁废碎料	1.品名；2.用途（供再熔炼钢用）；3.形状（废碎、切割、压缩成包或板、条状等）；4.材质（铸铁、合金钢、不锈钢等）；5.来源（机械加工产生、由破碎何种钢铁制品而得）；6.是否汽车压件、废五金电器；7.成分含量（所含金属总含量和各种金属的名称及含量）
7204.2100	不锈钢废碎料	1.品名；2.用途（供再熔炼钢用）；3.形状（废碎、切割、压缩成包或板、条状等）；4.材质（铸铁、合金钢、不锈钢等）；5.来源（机械加工产生、由破碎何种钢铁制品而得）；6.是否汽车压件、废五金电器；7.钢号；8.成分含量（所含金属总含量和各种金属的名称及含量）
7204.2900	其他合金钢废碎料	1.品名；2.用途（供再熔炼钢用）；3.形状（废碎、切割、压缩成包或板、条状等）；4.材质（铸铁、合金钢、不锈钢等）；5.来源（机械加工产生、由破碎何种钢铁制品而得）；6.是否汽车压件、废五金电器；7.成分含量（所含金属总含量和各种金属的名称及含量）
7204.3000	-镀锡钢铁废碎料	1.品名；2.用途（供再熔炼钢用）；3.形状（废碎、切割、压缩成包或板、条状等）；4.材质（铸铁、合金钢、不锈钢等）；5.来源（机械加工产生、由破碎何种钢铁制品而得）；6.是否汽车压件、废五金电器；7.成分含量（所含金属总含量和各种金属的名称及含量）
7204.4100	--车、刨、铣、磨、锯、锉、剪、冲加工过程中产生的废 料，不论是否成捆	1.品名；2.用途（供再熔炼钢用）；3.形状（废碎、切割、压缩成包或板、条状等）；4.材质（铸铁、合金钢、不锈钢等）；5.来源（机械加工产生、由破碎何种钢铁制品而得）；6.是否汽车压件、废五金电器；7.成分含量（所含金属总含量和各种金属的名称及含量）

税则号列	商品描述	规范申报要素 / 价格申报要素 / 其他申报要素 / 举例说明
7204.4900	--其他	1.品名;2.用途(供再熔炼钢用);3.形状(废碎、切割、压缩成包或板、条状等);4.材质(铸铁、合金钢、不锈钢等);5.来源(机械加工产生、由破碎何种钢铁制品而得);6.是否汽车压件、废五金电器;7.稀土元素的重量百分比,以[A]表示;8.成分含量(所含金属总含量和各种金属的名称及含量)
7204.5000	-供再熔的碎料钢铁锭	1.品名;2.用途(供再熔炼钢用);3.形状(废碎、切割、压缩成包或板、条状等);4.材质(铸铁、合金钢、不锈钢等);5.来源(机械加工产生、由破碎何种钢铁制品而得);6.是否汽车压件、废五金电器;7.成分含量(所含金属总含量和各种金属的名称及含量)
72.05	生铁、镜铁及钢铁的颗粒和粉 末:	
7205.1000	-颗粒	1.品名;2.形状(颗粒、粉末);3.材质(生铁、镜铁、合金钢等);4.成分含量(铁、碳、合金元素、非合金元素的含量);5.粒度;6.稀土元素的重量百分比,以[A]表示
7205.2100	--合金钢的	1.品名;2.形状(颗粒、粉末);3.材质(生铁、镜铁、合金钢等);4.成分含量(铁、碳、合金元素、非合金元素的含量);5.粒度;6.稀土元素的重量百分比,以[A]表示
7205.2900	--其他	1.品名;2.形状(颗粒、粉末);3.材质(生铁、镜铁、合金钢等);4.成分含量(铁、碳、合金元素、非合金元素的含量);5.粒度
72.06	铁及非合金钢,锭状或其他初级形状(品目72.03的铁除外):	1.品名;2.形状(方锭、其他初级形状等);3.材质(铁、非合金钢);4.成分含量(铁、碳、合金元素、非合金元素的含量)
72.07	铁及非合金钢的半制成品:	
7207.1100	--矩形(包括正方形)截面,宽度小于厚度的两倍	1.品名;2.形状(大方坯、小方坯等);3.材质(铁、非合金钢);4.加工方法(初轧、粗锻等);5.成分含量(铁、碳、合金元素、非合金元素的含量);6.截面形状(正方形等);7.截面尺寸
7207.1200	--其他矩形(正方形除外)截面的	1.品名;2.形状(大方坯、小方坯等);3.材质(铁、非合金钢);4.加工方法(初轧、粗锻等);5.成分含量(铁、碳、合金元素、非合金元素的含量);6.截面形状(正方形等);7.截面尺寸
7207.1900	--其他	1.品名;2.形状(大方坯、小方坯等);3.材质(铁、非合金钢);4.加工方法(初轧、粗锻等);5.成分含量(铁、碳、合金元素、非合金元素的含量);6.截面形状(正方形等)
7207.2000	-按重量计含碳量在0.25%及以上	1.品名;2.形状(大方坯、小方坯等);3.材质(铁、非合金钢);4.加工方法(初轧、粗锻等);5.成分含量(铁、碳、合金元素、非合金元素的含量);6.截面形状(正方形等)
72.08	宽度在600毫米及以上的铁或非合金钢平板轧材,经热轧,但未经包覆、镀层或涂层:	1.品名;2.形状(平板、卷板);3.材质(铁、非合金钢);4.加工方法(热轧等);5.加工程度(酸洗、轧有花纹、未包覆、未镀层、未涂层等);6.成分含量(铁、碳、合金元素、非合金元素的含量);7.规格(板材的厚度、宽度);8.技术参数(屈服强度);9.钢号
72.09	宽度在600毫米及以上的铁或非合金钢平板轧材,经冷轧,但未经包覆、镀层或涂层:	1.品名;2.形状(平板、卷板);3.材质(铁、非合金钢);4.加工方法(冷轧);5.加工程度(未包覆、未镀层、未涂层等);6.成分含量(铁、碳、合金元素、非合金元素的含量);7.规格(板材的厚度、宽度);8.技术参数(屈服强度);9.钢号
72.10	宽度在600毫米及以上的铁或非合金钢平板轧材,经包覆、镀层或涂层:	1.品名;2.形状(平板、卷板);3.材质(铁、非合金钢);4.加工方法(经包覆、经镀层、经涂层);5.成分含量(铁、碳、合金元素、非合金元素的含量);6.规格(板材的厚度、宽度);7.涂层种类(锡、铅、电镀锌、涂锌等);8.涂层厚度(0.5毫米等);9.钢号
72.11	宽度小于600毫米的铁或非合金钢平板轧材,但未经包覆、镀层或涂层:	1.品名;2.形状(平板、卷板);3.材质(铁、非合金钢);4.加工方法(热轧、冷轧、未包覆、未镀层、未涂层等);5.成分含量(铁、碳、合金元素、非合金元素的含量);6.规格(板材的厚度、宽度);7.钢号
72.12	宽度小于600毫米的铁或非合金钢平板轧材,经包覆、镀层或涂层:	1.品名;2.形状(平板、卷板);3.材质(铁、非合金钢);4.加工方法(热轧、冷轧、经包覆、经镀层、经涂层);5.成分含量(铁、碳、合金元素、非合金元素的含量);6.规格(板材的厚度、宽度);7.涂层种类(锡、铅、电镀锌、涂锌等)
72.13	不规则盘卷的铁及非合金钢的热轧条、杆:	

税则号列	商品描述	规范申报要素 / 价格申报要素 / 其他申报要素 / 举例说明
7213.1000	-带有轧制过程中产生的凹痕、凸缘、槽沟及其他变形的	1.品名;2.形状(条、杆);3.材质(铁、非合金钢);4.加工方法(热轧);5.状态(不规则盘卷,带有凹痕、凸缘等);6.成分含量(合金元素、非合金元素的含量);7.规格(条、杆的直径)
7213.2000	-其他,易切削钢制	1.品名;2.形状(条、杆);3.材质(易切削钢);4.加工方法(热轧);5.状态(不规则盘卷、不带有凹痕、凸缘等);6.成分含量(合金元素、非合金元素的含量);7.规格(条、杆的直径)
7213.9	-其他:	1.品名;2.形状(条、杆);3.材质(铁、非合金钢);4.加工方法(热轧);5.状态(不规则盘卷);6.成分含量(合金元素、非合金元素的含量);7.截面形状;8.规格(圆形截面需报条、杆的直径)
72.14	铁或非合金钢的其他条、杆,除锻造、热轧、热拉拔或热挤压外未经进一步加工,包括轧制后扭曲的:	
7214.1000	-锻造的	1.品名;2.形状(条、杆);3.材质(铁、非合金钢);4.加工方法(锻造);5.成分含量(合金元素、非合金元素的含量);6.规格(条、杆的直径);7.截面形状(圆形、矩形、正方形等)
7214.2000	-带有轧制过程中产生的凹痕、凸缘、槽沟或其他变形以及轧制后扭曲的	1.品名;2.形状(条、杆);3.材质(铁、非合金钢);4.加工方法(热轧、热拉拔、热挤压);5.状态(带有轧制产生的变形或轧制后扭曲的);6.成分含量(合金元素、非合金元素的含量);7.规格(条、杆的直径);8.截面形状(正方形等);9.钢号
7214.3000	-其他,易切削钢制	1.品名;2.形状(条、杆);3.材质(易切削钢);4.加工方法(热轧、热拉拔、热挤压);5.成分含量(合金元素、非合金元素的含量);6.状态(不带有轧制产生的变形或轧制后扭曲的);7.规格(条、杆的直径);8.截面形状(正方形等)
7214.9	-其他:	1.品名;2.形状(条、杆);3.材质(铁、非合金钢);4.加工方法(热轧、热拉拔、热挤压);5.成分含量(合金元素、非合金元素的含量);6.状态(不带有轧制产生的变形或轧制后扭曲的);7.规格(条、杆的直径);8.截面形状(正方形等)
72.15	铁及非合金钢的其他条、杆:	1.品名;2.形状(条、杆);3.材质(铁、非合金钢);4.加工方法(热加工、冷加工);5.加工程度;6.成分含量(铁、碳、合金元素、非合金元素的含量);7.规格(条、杆的直径);8.易切削钢请注明
72.16	铁或非合金钢的角材、型材及异型材:	1.品名;2.形状(槽钢、角钢、工字钢、H型钢等);3.材质(铁、非合金钢);4.加工方法(热轧、热拉拔、热挤压、冷加工、平板轧材冷弯成形);5.加工程度(例如,打孔、冲孔、扭绞、涂层等);6.成分含量(合金元素、非合金元素的含量);7.规格(型材的截面高度)
72.17	铁丝或非合金钢丝:	1.品名;2.形状(丝);3.材质(铁、非合金钢);4.加工方法(镀层、涂层);5.成分含量(铁、碳、合金元素、非合金元素的含量);6.涂层种类(锌、铜等);7.直径;8.状态(盘、卷等)
72.18	不锈钢,锭状或其他初级形 状;不锈钢半制成品:	1.品名;2.形状(方锭等);3.材质(不锈钢);4.截面形状(正方形等);5.钢号
72.19	不锈钢平板轧材,宽度在600毫米及以上:	1.品名;2.形状(卷板、平板等);3.材质(不锈钢);4.加工方法(热轧、冷轧);5.加工程度;6.成分含量;7.规格(板材的厚度、宽度);8.钢号
72.20	不锈钢平板轧材,宽度<600毫米:	1.品名;2.形状(卷板、平板等);3.材质(不锈钢);4.加工方法(热轧、冷轧);5.加工程度;6.成分含量(铁、碳、铬及合金元素、非合金元素的含量);7.规格(板材的厚度、宽度);8.钢号
72.21	不规则盘卷的不锈钢热轧条、杆:	1.品名;2.形状(条、杆);3.材质(不锈钢);4.加工方法(热轧);5.状态(不规则盘卷);6.成分含量(铁、碳、铬及合金元素、非合金元素的含量);7.钢号;8.直径

税则号列	商品描述	规范申报要素 / 价格申报要素 / 其他申报要素 / 举例说明
72.22	不锈钢其他条、杆；不锈钢角材、型材及异型材：	1. 品名；2. 形状（条、杆、角材、型材、异型材）；3. 材质（不锈钢）；4. 加工方法（热轧、热拉拔、热挤压、冷成形、冷加工）；5. 成分含量（铁、碳、铬及合金元素、非合金元素的含量）；6. 截面形状（圆形、方形等）；7. 钢号
72.23	不锈钢丝：	1. 品名；2. 形状（丝）；3. 材质（不锈钢）；4. 加工方法（镀层、涂层）；5. 成分含量（铁、碳、铬及合金元素、非合金元素的含量）；6. 直径；7. 钢号
72.24	其他合金钢，锭状或其他初级形状；其他合金钢制的半制成品：	
7224.1000	-锭状及其他初级形状	1. 品名；2. 形状（方锭等）；3. 材质（硅锰钢等）；4. 成分含量（铁、碳及合金元素、非合金元素的含量）；5. 钢号
7224.9	-其他：	1. 品名；2. 形状（方锭等）；3. 材质（硅锰钢等）；4. 成分含量（铁、碳及合金元素、非合金元素的含量）；5. 粗铸锻件坯请注明单件重量；6. 钢号
72.25	其他合金钢平板轧材，宽度在600毫米及以上：	
7225.1	-硅电钢制：	1. 品名；2. 形状（平板、卷材）；3. 材质（硅电钢、高速钢等，取向性硅电钢请注明）；4. 加工方法（热轧、冷轧、镀层、涂层）；5. 成分含量（铁、碳、合金元素、非合金元素的含量）；6. 规格（板材的厚度、宽度）；7. 牌号；8. 厂家名称
7225.3000	-其他卷材，除热轧外未经进一步加工	1. 品名；2. 形状（平板、卷材）；3. 材质（硅电钢、高速钢等，取向性硅电钢请注明）；4. 加工方法（热轧、冷轧、镀层、涂层）；5. 成分含量（铁、碳、合金元素、非合金元素的含量）；6. 规格（板材的厚度、宽度）；7. 钢号
7225.4000	-其他非卷材，除热轧外未经进一步加工	1. 品名；2. 形状（平板、卷材）；3. 材质（硅电钢、高速钢等，取向性硅电钢请注明）；4. 加工方法（热轧、冷轧、镀层、涂层）；5. 成分含量（铁、碳、合金元素、非合金元素的含量）；6. 规格（板材的厚度、宽度）；7. 钢号
7225.5000	-其他，除冷轧外未经进一步加工	1. 品名；2. 形状（平板、卷材）；3. 材质（硅电钢、高速钢等，取向性硅电钢请注明）；4. 加工方法（热轧、冷轧、镀层、涂层）；5. 成分含量（铁、碳、合金元素、非合金元素的含量）；6. 规格（板材的厚度、宽度）；7. 钢号
7225.9	-其他：	1. 品名；2. 形状（平板、卷材）；3. 材质（硅电钢、高速钢等，取向性硅电钢请注明）；4. 加工方法（热轧、冷轧、镀层、涂层）；5. 成分含量（铁、碳、合金元素、非合金元素的含量）；6. 规格（板材的厚度、宽度）；7. 涂层种类（电镀锌、涂锌等）；8. 钢号
72.26	其他合金钢平板轧材，宽度<600毫米：	
7226.1	-硅电钢制：	1. 品名；2. 形状（平板、卷材）；3. 材质（硅电钢、高速钢等，取向性硅电钢请注明）；4. 加工方法（热轧、冷轧、镀层、涂层）；5. 成分含量（铁、碳、合金元素、非合金元素的含量）；6. 规格（板材的厚度、宽度）；7. 牌号；8. 厂家名称
7226.2000	-高速钢制	1. 品名；2. 形状（平板、卷材）；3. 材质（硅电钢、高速钢等，取向性硅电钢请注明）；4. 加工方法（热轧、冷轧、镀层、涂层）；5. 成分含量（铁、碳、合金元素、非合金元素的含量）；6. 规格（板材的厚度、宽度）；7. 钢号
7226.9	-其他：	1. 品名；2. 形状（平板、卷材）；3. 材质（硅电钢、高速钢等，取向性硅电钢请注明）；4. 加工方法（热轧、冷轧、镀层、涂层）；5. 成分含量（铁、碳、合金元素、非合金元素的含量）；6. 规格（板材的厚度、宽度）；7. 涂层种类（电镀锌、涂锌等）；8. 钢号
72.27	不规则盘卷的其他合金钢热轧条、杆：	1. 品名；2. 形状（条、杆）；3. 材质（高速钢、硅锰钢等）；4. 加工方法（热轧）；5. 状态（不规则盘卷）；6. 成分含量（铁、碳、合金元素、非合金元素的含量）；7. 钢号

税则号列	商品描述	规范申报要素 / 价格申报要素 / 其他申报要素 / 举例说明
72.28	其他合金钢条、杆;其他合金钢角材、型材及异型材;合金钢或非合金钢制的空心钻钢:	
7228.1000	-高速钢条、杆	1.品名;2.用途(适用场所或下游产品);3.形状(条、杆、角材、型材、异型材);4.材质(高速钢、硅锰钢等);5.加工方法(热轧、热拉拔、热挤压、冷成形、冷加工);6.成分含量(铁、碳、合金元素、非合金元素的含量);7.钢号
7228.2000	-硅锰钢条、杆	1.品名;2.用途(适用场所或下游产品);3.形状(条、杆、角材、型材、异型材);4.材质(高速钢、硅锰钢等);5.加工方法(热轧、热拉拔、热挤压、冷成形、冷加工);6.成分含量(铁、碳、合金元素、非合金元素的含量);7.钢号
7228.3	-其他条、杆,除热轧、热拉拔或热挤压外未经进一步加工:	1.品名;2.用途(适用场所或下游产品);3.形状(条、杆、角材、型材、异型材);4.材质(高速钢、硅锰钢等);5.加工方法(热轧、热拉拔、热挤压、冷成形、冷加工);6.成分含量(铁、碳、合金元素、非合金元素的含量);7.钢号
7228.4000	-其他条、杆,除锻造外未经进一步加工	1.品名;2.用途(适用场所或下游产品);3.形状(条、杆、角材、型材、异型材);4.材质(高速钢、硅锰钢等);5.加工方法(热轧、热拉拔、热挤压、冷成形、冷加工);6.成分含量(铁、碳、合金元素、非合金元素的含量);7.钢号
7228.5000	-其他条、杆,除冷成形或冷加工外未经进一步加工	1.品名;2.用途(适用场所或下游产品);3.形状(条、杆、角材、型材、异型材);4.材质(高速钢、硅锰钢等);5.加工方法(热轧、热拉拔、热挤压、冷成形、冷加工);6.成分含量(铁、碳、合金元素、非合金元素的含量);7.钢号
7228.6000	-其他条、杆	1.品名;2.用途(适用场所或下游产品);3.形状(条、杆、角材、型材、异型材);4.材质(高速钢、硅锰钢等);5.加工方法(热轧、热拉拔、热挤压、冷成形、冷加工);6.成分含量(铁、碳、合金元素、非合金元素的含量);7.钢号
7228.7010	---履带板型钢	1.品名;2.用途(适用场所或下游产品);3.形状(条、杆、角材、型材、异型材);4.材质(高速钢、硅锰钢等);5.加工方法(热轧、热拉拔、热挤压、冷成形、冷加工);6.成分含量(铁、碳、合金元素、非合金元素的含量);7.空心钻钢需额外申报最大外形尺寸和最大内孔尺寸;8.钢号
7228.7090	---其他	1.品名;2.用途(适用场所或下游产品);3.形状(条、杆、角材、型材、异型材);4.材质(高速钢、硅锰钢等);5.加工方法(热轧、热拉拔、热挤压、冷成形、冷加工);6.成分含量(铁、碳、合金元素、非合金元素的含量);7.钢号
7228.8000	-空心钻钢	1.品名;2.用途(适用场所或下游产品);3.形状(条、杆、角材、型材、异型材);4.材质(高速钢、硅锰钢等);5.加工方法(热轧、热拉拔、热挤压、冷成形、冷加工);6.成分含量(铁、碳、合金元素、非合金元素的含量);7.空心钻钢需额外申报最大外形尺寸和最大内孔尺寸;8.钢号
72.29	其他合金钢丝:	1.品名;2.形状(丝);3.材质(高速钢、硅锰钢等);4.加工方法(镀层、涂层);5.成分含量(铁、碳、合金元素、非合金元素的含量);6.用途;7.钢号

第七十三章 钢铁制品

【注解】

1、"品名"是指货品的具体商业名称。
2、"用途"是指货品在出入境后的应用场合或下游产品。
3、"加工方法"是指货品在出入境前的加工工艺或制造方法。
4、"材质"是指货品按《税则》中的材质分类原则所确定的具体材料种类。
5、"形状"是指货品按《税则》中的形状定义描述所确定的外观形状。

税则号列	商品描述	规范申报要素 / 价格申报要素 / 其他申报要素 / 举例说明
73.01	钢铁板桩,不论是否钻孔、打眼或组装;焊接的钢铁角材、型材及异型材:	1.品名;2.形状(板桩、焊接的角材、型材、异型材);3.材质(铁、非合金钢、不锈钢、合金钢);4.加工方法(冷轧、热轧等);5.规格(截面尺寸)

税则号列	商 品 描 述	规范申报要素 / 价格申报要素 / 其他申报要素 / 举例说明
73.02	铁道及电车道铺轨用钢铁材料(钢轨、护轨、齿轨、道岔尖轨、辙叉、尖轨拉杆及其他岔道段体、轨枕、鱼尾板、轨座、轨座楔、钢轨垫板、钢轨夹、底板、固定板及其他专门用于连接或加固路轨的材料):	1.品名;2.用途(铁道及电车道铺轨用等);3.材质(铁、非合金钢、不锈钢、合金钢);4.制品种类(钢轨、轨枕、岔道段体等)
73.03	铸铁管及空心异型材:	1.品名;2.规格(管的内径);3.形状(圆形截面管、空心异型材);4.材质(铸铁)
73.04	无缝钢铁管及空心异型材(铸铁的除外):	1.品名;2.规格(管的外径);3.用途(锅炉用、石油或天然气钻探用等);4.形状(管、空心异型材);5.材质(铁、非合金钢、不锈钢、合金钢);6.加工方法(冷拔、冷轧、热扎等);7.种类(无缝管)
73.05	其他圆形截面钢铁管(例如,焊、铆及用类似方法接合的管),外径超过406.4毫米:	1.品名;2.规格(管的外径);3.用途(石油或天然气管道用等);4.材质(铁、非合金钢、不锈钢、合金钢);5.种类(焊接管);6.加工方法(铆、纵向焊、埋弧焊);7.截面形状(圆形)
73.06	其他钢铁管及空心异型材(例如,辊缝、焊、铆及类似方法接合的):	1.品名;2.规格(圆管的外径、壁厚);3.用途(石油或天然气管道用);4.材质(铁、非合金钢、不锈钢、合金钢);5.种类(焊接管);6.加工方法(铆、纵向焊、埋弧焊);7.截面形状(圆形、方形或椭圆形等)
73.07	钢铁管子附件(例如,接头、肘管、管套):	1.品名;2.用途(用于管子之间连通);3.材质(铁、非合金钢、不锈钢、合金钢);4.种类(法兰、管套、十字接头、对焊件等);5.加工方法(铸造、锻造等)
73.08	钢铁结构体(品目94.06的活动房屋除外)及其部件(例如桥梁及桥梁体段、闸门、塔楼格构杆、屋顶、屋顶框架、门窗及其框架、门槛、百叶窗、栏杆、支柱及立柱);上述结构体用的已加工钢铁板、杆、角材、型材、异型材、管子及类似品:	1.品名;2.用途(支撑用等);3.材质(钢铁);4.种类(门窗、立柱、塔楼、脚手架、桥梁体段等)
73.09	盛装物料用的钢铁囤、柜、罐、桶及类似容器(装压缩气体或液化气体的除外),容积超过300升,不论是否衬里或隔热,但无机械或热力装置:	1.品名;2.用途(盛装液体用等);3.材质(钢铁);4.种类(罐、桶等);5.规格(容积);6.是否装有机械或热力装置
73.10	盛装物料用的钢铁柜、桶、罐、听、盒及类似容器(装压缩气体或液化气体的除外),容积不超过300升,不论是否衬里或隔热,但无机械或热力装置:	1.品名;2.用途(盛装液体用等);3.材质(钢铁);4.种类(罐、桶等);5.加工方法(焊边接合、卷边接合等);6.规格(容积);7.是否装有机械或热力装置
73.11	装压缩气体或液化气体用的钢铁容器:	1.品名;2.用途(压缩气体或液化气体用、零售包装用等);3.材质(钢铁);4.种类(罐、桶等)
73.12	非绝缘的钢铁绞股线、绳、缆、编带、吊索及类似品:	1.品名;2.材质(钢铁);3.制品种类(绞股线、吊索、绳等);4.注明“非绝缘”
73.13	带刺钢铁丝;围篱用的钢铁绞带或单股扁丝(不论是否带刺)及松绞的双股丝:	1.品名;2.用途(围篱用);3.材质(钢铁);4.种类(带刺钢铁丝、绞带、单股扁丝、松绞的双股丝);5.截面尺寸
73.14	钢铁丝制的布(包括环形带)、网、篱、格栅;网眼钢铁板:	1.品名;2.用途(工业用等);3.材质(铁、非合金钢、不锈钢、合金钢);4.种类(网、篱、格栅等);5.加工方法(镀锌、涂锌、涂塑等);6.规格(网眼尺寸、丝的截面尺寸)
73.15	钢铁链及其零件:	1.品名;2.用途(自行车用、摩托车用等);3.材质(钢铁);4.种类(铰接链、滚子链、日字环节链等)
73.16	钢铁锚、多爪锚及其零件:	1.品名;2.材质(钢铁);3.种类(钢铁锚、多爪锚等)
73.17	钢铁制的钉、平头钉、图钉、波纹钉、U形钉(品目83.05的货品除外)及类似品,不论钉头是否用其他材料制成,但不包括铜头钉:	1.品名;2.材质(钢铁);3.种类(图钉、U形钉、平头钉、波纹钉等)。注:铜头的钉归入税目74.15

税则号列	商品描述	规范申报要素 / 价格申报要素 / 其他申报要素 / 举例说明
73.18	钢铁制的螺钉、螺栓、螺母、方头螺钉、钩头螺钉、铆钉、销、开尾销、垫圈(包括弹簧垫圈)及类似品:	
7318.1100	--方头螺钉	1.品名;2.材质(钢铁);3.螺钉种类(方头等);4.品牌;5.型号
7318.1200	--其他木螺钉	1.品名;2.材质(钢铁);3.品牌;4.型号
7318.1300	--钩头螺钉及环头螺钉	1.品名;2.材质(钢铁);3.品牌;4.型号
7318.1400	--自攻螺钉	1.品名;2.材质(钢铁);3.品牌;4.型号
7318.15	--其他螺钉及螺栓,不论是否带有螺母或垫圈:	1.品名;2.材质(钢铁);3.种类(螺钉、螺母、垫圈、铆钉、销等);4.抗拉强度;5.品牌;6.型号; 7.规格(杆径)
7318.1600	--螺母	1.品名;2.材质(钢铁);3.品牌;4.型号
7318.1900	--其他	1.品名;2.材质(钢铁);3.种类(螺钉、螺母、垫圈、铆钉、销等);4.螺钉请注明种类(方头、钩头、环头等);5.品牌;6.型号
7318.2	-无螺纹制品:	1.品名;2.材质(钢铁);3.品牌;4.规格型号
73.19	钢铁制的手工缝针、编织针、引针、钩针、刺绣穿孔锥及类似制品;其他品目未列名的钢铁制安全别针及其他别针:	1.品名;2.材质(钢铁);3.种类(缝针、织补针、刺绣针、别针等)
73.20	钢铁制弹簧及弹簧片:	1.品名;2.用途(汽车用、铁道车辆用等);3.材质(钢铁);4.种类(片簧、螺旋弹簧等)
73.21	非电热的钢铁制家用炉、灶(包括附有集中供暖用的热水锅的炉)、烤肉架、烤炉、煤气灶、加热板和类似非电热的家用器具及其零件:	1.品名;2.材质(钢铁);3.种类(煤油炉、煤气灶、烤肉架、烤炉等);4.原理(非电热);5.燃料种类(液体、固体、气体燃料);6.品牌;7.型号
73.22	非电热的钢铁制集中供暖用散热器及其零件;非电热的钢铁制空气加热器、暖气分布器(包括可分布新鲜空气或调节空气的)及其零件,装有电动风扇或鼓风机:	1.品名;2.用途(集中供暖用等);3.材质(钢铁);4.种类(散热器、空气加热器、暖气分布器等);5.原理(非电热);6.是否装有电动风扇或鼓风机
73.23	餐桌、厨房或其他家用钢铁器具及其零件;钢铁丝绒;钢铁制擦锅器、洗刷擦光用的块垫、手套及类似品:	1.品名;2.用途(厨房用、餐桌用等);3.材质(铁、非合金钢、不锈钢、合金钢);4.种类(水壶、煎锅等);5.加工方法(已搪瓷、未搪瓷);6.品牌
73.24	钢铁制卫生器具及其零件:	1.品名;2.用途(卫生间用等);3.材质(铁、非合金钢、不锈钢、合金钢);4.种类(脸盆、浴缸等);5.加工方法(已搪瓷、未搪瓷);6.品牌
73.25	其他钢铁铸造制品:	1.品名;2.用途(工业用、非工业用、研磨机用等);3.材质(无可锻性铸铁等);4.种类(井盖、研磨球等)
73.26	其他钢铁制品:	1.品名;2.用途(工业用、非工业用);3.材质(钢铁);4.种类(捕鼠器、香烟盒等);5.加工方法(锻造、冲压等)

第七十四章　铜及其制品

【注解】

1、"品名"是指货品的具体商业名称。

2、"用途"是指货品在出入境后的应用场合或下游产品。

3、"加工方法"是指货品在出入境前的加工工艺或制造方法。

4、"材质"是指货品按《税则》中的材质分类原则所确定的具体材料种类。

5、"形状"是指货品按《税则》中的形状定义描述所确定的外观形状。

税则号列	商 品 描 述	规范申报要素 / 价格申报要素 / 其他申报要素 / 举例说明
74.01	铜锍;沉积铜(泥铜):	1.品名;2.材质(铜锍、沉积铜);3.来源;4.成分含量(铜化合物的含量)。注:铜锍颗粒(熔炼硫化铜矿而得),含硫化铜40%、硫化铁30%
74.02	未精炼铜;电解精炼用的铜阳极:	1.品名;2.成分含量(铜的含量及黄金含量);3.形状(块状、粉末等);4.材质(未精炼铜);5.用途(电解精炼用等)
74.03	未锻轧的精炼铜及铜合金:	
7403.11	--阴极及阴极型材:	1.品名;2.形状(型材、线锭、坯段等);3.材质(精炼铜、黄铜、青铜、白铜等);4.加工方法(未锻轧等);5.成分含量(铜及合金元素的含量);6.定价日期;7.签约日期;8.定价方式。注:未锻轧精炼铜锭,含铜99.9%
7403.1200	--线锭	1.品名;2.形状(型材、线锭、坯段等);3.材质(精炼铜、黄铜、青铜、白铜等);4.加工方法(未锻轧等);5.成分含量(铜及合金元素的含量)。注:未锻轧精炼铜锭,含铜99.9%
7403.1300	--坯段	1.品名;2.形状(型材、线锭、坯段等);3.材质(精炼铜、黄铜、青铜、白铜等);4.加工方法(未锻轧等);5.成分含量(铜及合金元素的含量)。注:未锻轧精炼铜锭,含铜99.9%
7403.1900	--其他	1.品名;2.形状(型材、线锭、坯段等);3.材质(精炼铜、黄铜、青铜、白铜等);4.加工方法(未锻轧等);5.成分含量(铜及合金元素的含量)。注:未锻轧精炼铜锭,含铜99.9%
7403.2	-铜合金:	1.品名;2.形状(型材、线锭、坯段等);3.材质(精炼铜、黄铜、青铜、白铜等);4.加工方法(未锻轧等);5.成分含量(铜及合金元素的含量)。注:未锻轧精炼铜锭,含铜99.9%
74.04	铜废碎料:	1.品名;2.用途(供回收铜用);3.材质(铜);4.状态(废、碎、管、板、线、棒、边角料等);5.来源(废的电机、电线、电缆、五金等);6.成分含量(回收金属的含量);7.包装形式
74.05	铜母合金:	1.品名;2.用途(用作炼铜的添加剂);3.形状(粒状等);4.材质(铜母合金);5.成分含量(铜、磷的含量)。注:铬铜粉(用作炼铜的添加剂),含铜40%,不含磷
74.06	铜粉及片状粉末:	1.品名;2.用途(用作电镀基底、金属颜料等);3.形状(片状粉末、非片状粉末);4.材质(精炼铜、黄铜、青铜、白铜等);5.成分含量(铜及合金元素的含量);6.粒度;7.牌号或型号。注:非片状精炼铜粉(用作电镀基料),含铜99.9%
74.07	铜条、杆、型材及异型材:	
7407.1	-精炼铜制:	1.品名;2.形状(条、杆、型材、异型材);3.材质(精炼铜、黄铜、青铜、白铜等);4.成分含量(铜及合金元素的含量)。注:精炼铜杆,含铜99.9%
7407.2111	----直线度不大于0.5毫米/米	1.品名;2.形状(条、杆、型材、异型材);3.材质(精炼铜、黄铜、青铜、白铜等);4.成分含量(铜及合金元素的含量);5.直线度。注:精炼铜杆,含铜99.9%
7407.2119	----其他	1.品名;2.形状(条、杆、型材、异型材);3.材质(精炼铜、黄铜、青铜、白铜等);4.成分含量(铜及合金元素的含量)
7407.2190	---其他	1.品名;2.形状(条、杆、型材、异型材);3.材质(精炼铜、黄铜、青铜、白铜等);4.成分含量(铜及合金元素的含量)
7407.2900	--其他	1.品名;2.形状(条、杆、型材、异型材);3.材质(精炼铜、黄铜、青铜、白铜等);4.成分含量(铜及合金元素的含量)
74.08	铜丝:	1.品名;2.形状(丝);3.材质(精炼铜、黄铜、青铜、白铜等);4.成分含量(铜及合金元素的含量);5.规格(丝的最大截面尺寸);6.牌号或型号。注:精炼铜丝,含铜99.9%,直径4毫米
74.09	铜板、片及带,厚度超过0.15毫米:	1.品名;2.形状(板、片、带);3.材质(精炼铜、黄铜、青铜、白铜等);4.状态(盘卷、平板等);5.成分含量(铜及合金元素的含量);6.规格(长×宽×厚)

税则号列	商品描述	规范申报要素 / 价格申报要素 / 其他申报要素 / 举例说明
74.10	铜箔(不论是否印花或用纸、纸板、塑料或类似材料衬背)厚度(衬背除外)不超过0.15毫米:	1.品名;2.形状(箔);3.材质(精炼铜、黄铜、青铜、白铜等);4.状态(有无衬背);5.成分含量(铜及合金元素的含量);6.规格(整体厚度、铜箔厚度、长度、宽度);7.用途;8.品牌;9.牌号;10.种类(压延铜箔,电解铜箔,刚性覆铜板、柔性覆铜板);11.覆铜板的铜箔层数;12.基材材质(纸基、玻璃布基、复合基、环保型基等);1;3.生产厂商;1;4.覆铜板需要申报介电常数;15.覆铜板报单面还是双面;16.覆铜板基板材质
74.11	铜管:	1.品名;2.材质(精炼铜、黄铜、青铜、白铜等);3.成分含量(铜及合金元素的含量);4.外径;5.有无螺纹或翅片;6.用途;7.品牌;8.型号或牌号
74.12	铜制管子附件(例如,接头、肘管、管套):	1.品名;2.用途(用于管子之间连通);3.材质(精炼铜、黄铜、青铜、白铜等);4.种类(接头、肘管、管套);5.成分含量(铜及合金元素的含量);6.品牌;7.型号或牌号。注:精炼铜制管接头,含铜99.9%
74.13	非绝缘的铜丝绞股线、缆、编带及类似品:	1.品名;2.材质(铜);3.种类(绞股线、缆、编带等);4.注明"非绝缘";5.品牌;6.型号或牌号。注:非绝缘的铜丝绞股线
74.15	铜制或钢铁制带铜头的钉、平头钉、图钉、U形钉(品目83.05的货品除外)及类似品;铜制螺钉、螺栓、螺母、钩头螺钉铆钉、销、开尾销、垫圈(包括弹簧垫圈)及类似品:	1.品名;2.材质(铜);3.种类(图钉、U形钉、螺钉、螺母、垫圈、铆钉等);4.型号或品牌。注:铜制螺母
74.18	餐桌、厨房或其他家用铜制器具及其零件;铜制刷锅器、洗刷擦光用的块垫、手套及类似品;铜制卫生器具及其零件:	
7418.1010	--擦锅器及洗刷、擦光用的块垫、手套及类似品	1.品名;2.用途(厨房用、餐桌用、卫生用等);3.材质(铜);4.种类(水壶、煎锅等);5.品牌;6.型号。注:铜制水壶(厨房用)
7418.1020	---非电热的铜制家用烹饪器具及其零件	1.品名;2.材质(铜);3.种类(煤油炉、煤气灶等);4.原理(非电热);5.品牌;6.型号
7418.1090	---其他	1.品名;2.用途(厨房用、餐桌用、卫生用等);3.材质(铜);4.种类(水壶、煎锅等);5.品牌;6.型号
7418.2000	-卫生器具及其零件	1.品名;2.用途(厨房用、餐桌用、卫生用等);3.材质(铜);4.种类(水壶、煎锅等);5.品牌;6.型号。注:铜制水壶(厨房用)
74.19	其他铜制品:	
7419.1000	-链条及其零件	1.品名;2.用途(工业用、非工业用);3.材质(铜);4.种类(链条、容器等);5.加工方法(锻造、冲压等);6.型号
7419.91	--铸造、模压、冲压或锻造,但未经进一步加工的:	1.品名;2.用途(工业用、非工业用);3.材质(铜);4.种类(链条、容器等);5.加工方法(锻造、冲压等);6.型号
7419.9920	---铜弹簧	1.品名;2.材质(铜);3.种类(片簧、螺旋弹簧等);4.品牌;5.型号;6.用途
7419.9930	---铜丝制的布(包括环形带)	1.品名;2.材质(铜);3.种类;4.品牌;5.型号;6.用途
7419.9940	---铜丝制的网、格栅、网眼铜板	1.品名;2.材质(铜);3.种类(网、格栅、网眼铜板等);4.品牌;5.型号;6.用途
7419.9950	---非电热的铜制家用供暖器具及其零件	1.品名;2.材质(铜);3.种类;4.原理(非电热);5.品牌;6.型号;7.用途
7419.999	---其他:	1.品名;2.用途(工业用、非工业用);3.材质(铜);4.种类(链条、容器等);5.加工方法(锻造、冲压等)

第七十五章　镍及其制品

【注解】

1、"品名"是指货品的具体商业名称。

2、"用途"是指货品在出入境后的应用场合或下游产品。

3、"加工方法"是指货品在出入境前的加工工艺或制造方法。

4、"材质"是指货品按《税则》中的材质分类原则所确定的具体材料种类。

5、"形状"是指货品按《税则》中的形状定义描述所确定的外观形状。

税则号列	商品描述	规范申报要素 / 价格申报要素 / 其他申报要素 / 举例说明
75.01	镍锍、氧化镍烧结物及镍冶炼的其他中间产品：	1.品名;2.材质(镍锍、氧化镍烧结物等);3.来源;4.成分含量(镍化合物的含量)。注:镍锍颗粒(熔炼硫化镍矿而得),含硫化镍40%
75.02	未锻轧镍：	1.品名;2.形状(锭、块等);3.材质(非合金镍、镍合金);4.加工方法(未锻轧);5.成分含量(镍及合金元素的含量)。注:未锻轧非合金镍锭,含镍99.9%
75.03	镍废碎料：	1.品名;2.用途(供回收镍用);3.状态(废、碎);4.来源(非合金镍、镍合金的废碎料);5.成分含量(镍及合金元素的含量)。注:镍废碎料(供回收镍用),含镍80%
75.04	镍粉及片状粉末：	1.品名;2.形状(片状粉末、非片状粉末);3.材质(非合金镍、镍合金);4.成分含量(镍及合金元素的含量);5.粒度。注:非片状非合金镍粉(用作硬质合金的黏合剂),含镍99.9%,颗粒直径600微米
75.05	镍条、杆、型材及异型材或丝	
7505.1	-条、杆、型材及异型材：	1.品名;2.形状(条、杆、型材、异型材、丝);3.材质(非合金镍、镍合金);4.成分含量(镍及合金元素的含量)。注:非合金镍杆,含镍99.9%
7505.2	-丝：	1.品名;2.形状(条、杆、型材、异型材、丝);3.材质(非合金镍、镍合金);4.成分含量(镍及合金元素的含量);5.丝的直经。注:非合金镍杆,含镍99.9%
75061000	镍板、片、带、箔：	1.品名;2.形状(板、片、带、箔);3.材质(非合金镍、镍合金);4.成分含量(镍及合金元素的含量);5.规格(长×宽×厚)
75.07	镍管及管子附件(例如,接头肘管、管套)：	1.品名;2.材质(非合金镍、镍合金);3.种类(管、接头、肘管、管套等);4.成分含量(镍及合金元素的含量)。注:非合金镍制管接头(用于管子之间连通),含镍99.9%
75.08	其他镍制品：	1.品名;2.用途(电镀用、工业用、非工业用);3.材质(非合金镍、镍合金);4.种类(网、篱、格栅等);5.品牌;6.型号。注:镍网(工业用)

第七十六章　铝及其制品

【注解】

1、"品名"是指货品的具体商业名称。

2、"用途"是指货品在出入境后的应用场合或下游产品。

3、"加工方法"是指货品在出入境前的加工工艺或制造方法。

4、"材质"是指货品按《税则》中的材质分类原则所确定的具体材料种类。

5、"形状"是指货品按《税则》中的形状定义描述所确定的外观形状。

税则号列	商品描述	规范申报要素 / 价格申报要素 / 其他申报要素 / 举例说明
76.01	未锻轧铝：	1.品名;2.形状(锭、块);3.材质(非合金铝、铝合金);4.加工方法(未锻轧或铸造、烧结等);5.成分含量(铝及合金元素的含量)
76.02	铝废碎料：	1.品名;2.用途(供回收铝用);3.状态(废、碎、板、管、线、边角料等);4.来源(废电线、废电缆、废五金电器等);5.成分含量(回收金属的含量);6.包装形式。注:废铝管(供回收铝用),含铝80%
76.03	铝粉及片状粉末：	1.品名;2.形状(片状粉末、非片状粉末);3.材质(非合金铝、铝合金);4.成分含量(铝的含量);5.粒度。注:非片状非合金铝粉(用作硬质合金的黏合剂),含铝99.9%,颗粒直径600微米
76.04	铝条、杆、型材及异型材：	1.品名;2.形状(条、杆、型材、异型材);3.材质(非合金铝、铝合金);4.成分含量(铝及合金元素的含量);5.型材、异型材请注明是否空心;6.铝合金条、杆请注明截面周长;7.柱形实心体铝合金请注明20℃时的极限抗拉强度;8.牌号
76.05	铝丝：	1.品名;2.形状(丝);3.材质(非合金铝、铝合金);4.成分含量(铝及合金元素的含量);5.规格(丝的最大截面尺寸)。注:非合金铝丝,含铝99.9%,直径4毫米
76.06	铝板、片及带,厚度超过0.2毫米：	1.品名;2.形状(矩形等);3.材质(非合金铝、铝合金);4.状态(板、片、带);5.成分含量(铝及合金元素的含量);6.规格(长×宽×厚);7.品牌(中英文);8.用途;9.牌号

税则号列	商品描述	规范申报要素 / 价格申报要素 / 其他申报要素 / 举例说明
76.07	铝箔(不论是否印花或用纸、纸板、塑料或类似材料衬背)厚度(衬背除外)不超过0.2毫米:	1.品名;2.形状(箔);3.材质(铝);4.状态(有无衬背、衬背材料);5.规格(长×宽×厚);6.加工方法(轧制等);7.加工程度(是否进一步加工)
76.08	铝管:	1.品名;2.材质(非合金铝、铝合金);3.种类(管);4.成分含量(铝及合金元素的含量);5.管壁厚度、管壁外径、孔眼直径、管材长度。注:非合金铝管,含铝99.9%
76.09	铝制管子附件(例如,接头、肘管、管套):	1.品名;2.用途;3.材质(非合金铝、铝合金);4.种类(接头、肘管、管套)。注:铝制管接头(用于管子之间连通)
76.10	铝制结构体(品目94.06的活动房屋除外)及其部件(例如,桥梁及桥梁体段、塔、格构杆、屋顶、屋顶框架、门窗及其框架、门槛、栏杆、支柱及立柱);上述结构体用的已加工铝板、杆、型材、异型材、管子及类似品:	1.品名;2.材质(铝);3.种类(门窗、门槛、塔楼、桥梁体段等);4.加工方法(铆接、栓接、钻孔、弯曲等)。注:铝合金制窗框(经钻孔)
76.11	盛装物料用的铝制囤、柜、罐、桶及类似容器(装压缩气体或液化气体的除外),容积超过300升,不论是否衬里或隔热,但无机械或热力装置:	1.品名;2.用途(盛装液体用等);3.材质(铝);4.种类(罐、桶等);5.规格(容积);6.品牌。注:本税目不包括装有机械或热力装置的铝桶(盛装液体用),容积400升
76.12	盛装物料用的铝制桶、罐、听、盒及类似容器包括软管容器及硬管容器(装压缩气体或液化气体的除外),容积不超过300升,不论是否衬里或隔热,但无机械或热力装置:	1.品名;2.用途(盛装液体用等);3.材质(铝);4.种类(罐、桶等);5.规格(容积);6.品牌本税目。注:不包括有机械或热力装置的。注:铝制易拉罐(盛装液体用),容积100升
76.13	装压缩气体或液化气体用的铝制容器:	1.品名;2.用途(盛装液体用等);3.材质(铝);4.种类(罐、桶等);5.规格(容积);6.品牌。注:铝桶(盛装压缩气体用,且零售包装用,无机械或热力装置)
76.14	非绝缘的铝制绞股线、缆、编带及类似品:	1.品名;2.材质(铝);3.种类(绞股线、缆、编带等);4.状态(非绝缘);5.带钢芯请注明。注:非绝缘的铝丝绞股线(带钢芯)
76.15	餐桌、厨房或其他家用铝制器具及其零件;铝制擦锅器、洗刷擦光用的块垫、手套及类似品;铝制卫生器具及其零件:	1.品名;2.用途(厨房用、餐桌用、卫生用等);3.材质(铝);4.种类(水壶、煎锅等)。注:铝制水壶(厨房用)
76.16	其他铝制品:	1.品名;2.用途(工业用、非工业用);3.材质(铝);4.种类(图钉、螺钉、布、网、篱等)。注:铝制螺母(工业用)

第七十八章　铅及其制品

【注解】

1、"品名"是指货品的具体商业名称。
2、"用途"是指货品在出入境后的应用场合或下游产品。
3、"加工方法"是指货品在出入境前的加工工艺或制造方法。
4、"材质"是指货品按《税则》中的材质分类原则所确定的具体材料种类。
5、"形状"是指货品按《税则》中的形状定义描述所确定的外观形状。

税则号列	商品描述	规范申报要素 / 价格申报要素 / 其他申报要素 / 举例说明
78.01	未锻轧铅:	1.品名;2.形状(锭、块);3.材质(精炼铅、铅合金);4.加工方法(未锻轧);5.成分含量(铅及合金元素的含量)。注:未锻轧精炼铅锭,含铅99.9%
78.02	铅废碎料:	1.品名;2.用途(供回收铅用);3.材质(铅);4.状态(废、碎);5.来源(精炼铅、铅合金的废碎料);6.成分含量(铅的含量)。注:铅废碎料(供回收铅用)含铅80%
78.04	铅板、片、带、箔;铅粉及片状粉末:	1.品名;2.形状(板、片、带、箔、粉末及片状粉末);3.材质(铅);4.规格(板箔的厚度);5.粒度。注:铅板,厚度1毫米
78.06	其他铅制品:	
7806.0010	---铅条、杆、型材及异型材或丝	1.品名;2.形状(条、杆、型材、异型材、丝);3.材质(铅)
7806.0090	---其他	1.品名;2.形状(条、杆、型材、异型材、丝);3.材质(铅);4.种类(容器)

第七十九章　锌及其制品

【注解】

1、"品名"是指货品的具体商业名称。

2、"用途"是指货品在出入境后的应用场合或下游产品。

3、"加工方法"是指货品在出入境前的加工工艺或制造方法。

4、"材质"是指货品按《税则》中的材质分类原则所确定的具体材料种类。

5、"形状"是指货品按《税则》中的形状定义描述所确定的外观形状。

税则号列	商品描述	规范申报要素／价格申报要素／其他申报要素／举例说明
79.01	未锻轧锌:	1.品名;2.形状(锭、块);3.材质(非合金锌、锌合金);4.加工方法(未锻轧);5.成分含量(锌及合金元素的含量)。注:未锻轧非合金锌锭,含锌99.9%
79.02	锌废碎料:	1.品名;2.用途(供回收锌用);3.状态(废、碎);4.来源(精炼锌、锌合金的废碎料);5.成分含量(锌的含量)。注:锌废碎料(供回收锌用),含锌80%
79.03	锌末、锌粉及片状粉末:	1.品名;2.用途(用作硬质合金的黏合剂);3.形状(片状粉末、非片状粉末);4.材质(锌);5.成分含量(锌的含量);6.粒度。注:非片状锌粉(用作硬质合金的黏合剂),含锌99.9%,颗粒直径600微米
79.04	锌条、杆、型材及异型材或丝:	1.品名;2.形状(条、杆、型材、异型材、丝);3.材质(锌)。注:锌杆
79.05	锌板、片、带、箔:	1.品名;2.形状(矩形等);3.材质(锌等);4.状态(板、片、带);5.成分含量(锌及合金元素的含量);6.规格(长×宽×厚);7.品牌(中英文);8.用途;9.加工程度(是否经表面处理剂处理方法和所用材料)
79.07	其他锌制品:	1.品名;2.用途;3.材质(锌);4.种类(管、接头、肘管、管套等)。注:锌制容器(非工业用)

第八十章　锡及其制品

税则号列	商品描述	规范申报要素／价格申报要素／其他申报要素／举例说明
80.01	未锻轧锡:	1.品名;2.形状(锭、块、粒);3.材质(非合金锡、锡合金);4.加工方法(未锻轧);5.成分含量(锡及合金元素的含量)。注:未锻轧非合金锡锭,含锡99.9%
80.02	锡废碎料:	1.品名;2.用途(供回收锡用);3.状态(废、碎);4.来源(非合金锡、锡合金的废碎料);5.成分含量(锡的含量)。注:锡废碎料(供回收锡用),含锡80%
80.03	锡条、杆、型材及异型材或丝	1.品名;2.形状(条、杆、型材、异型材、丝);3.材质(锡);4.状态(是否带焊剂)。注:锡杆
80.07	其他锡制品:	
8007.0020	---锡板、片及带,厚度超过0.2毫米	1.品名;2.形状(板、片、带);3.规格(长、宽、厚);4.材质(锡);5.状态(有无衬背、衬背材料)。注:锡制牙膏软管(非工业用)
8007.0030	---锡箔(不论是否印花或用纸、纸板、塑料或类似材料衬背),厚度(衬背除外)不超过0.2毫米;锡粉及片状粉末	1.品名;2.形状(箔、粉末);3.材质(锡);4.状态(有无衬背、衬背材料);5.规格(锡箔长×宽×厚、粉末粒度)
8007.0040	---锡管及管子附件(例如,接头、肘管、管套)	1.品名;2.材质(锡);3.种类(接头、肘管、管套等)
8007.0090	---其他	1.品名;2.材质(锡);3.种类

第八十一章　其他贱金属、金属陶瓷及其制品

【注解】

1、"品名"是指货品的具体商业名称。

2、"用途"是指货品在出入境后的应用场合或下游产品。

3、"加工方法"是指货品在出入境前的加工工艺或制造方法。

4、"材质"是指货品按《税则》中的材质分类原则所确定的具体材料种类。

5、"形状"是指货品按《税则》中的形状定义描述所确定的外观形状。

税则号列	商品描述	规范申报要素 / 价格申报要素 / 其他申报要素 / 举例说明
81.01	钨及其制品,包括废碎料:	
8101.1000	-粉末	1.品名;2.形状(粉末);3.材质(钨);4.成分含量(钨的含量);5.粒度;6.粉末请注明细度。注:未锻轧钨锭,含钨99.9%
8101.9400	--未锻轧钨,包括简单烧结而成的条、杆	1.品名;2.形状(条、杆等);3.材质(钨);4.加工方法(未锻轧、简单烧结等)。注:未锻轧钨锭,含钨99.9%
8101.9600	--丝	1.品名;2.形状(丝);3.材质(钨)。注:未锻轧钨锭,含钨99.9%
8101.9700	--废碎料	1.品名;2.用途(供回收钨用);3.材质(钨);4.状态(废、碎);5.来源。注:未锻轧钨锭,含钨99.9%
8101.99	--其他:	1.品名;2.形状(条、杆、型材、异型材、板、片、带、箔);3.材质(钨、钨合金);4.加工方法(锻轧);5.用途;6.成分含量;7.每个重量;8.圆柱形请注明是否空心、内径。注:未锻轧钨锭,含钨99.9%
81.02	钼及其制品,包括废碎料:	
8102.1000	-粉末	1.品名;2.形状(粉末);3.材质(钼);4.粉末请注明细度。注:未锻轧钼锭,含钼99.9%
8102.9400	--未锻轧钼,包括简单烧结而成的条、杆	1.品名;2.形状(条、杆);3.材质(钼);4.加工方法(未锻轧、简单烧结等)。注:未锻轧钼锭,含钼99.9%
8102.9500	--条、杆,但简单烧结而成的除外;型材及异型材、板、片、带、箔	1.品名;2.形状(条、杆、型材、异型材、板、片、带、箔);3.材质(钼、钼合金);4.加工方法(锻轧)。注:未锻轧钼锭,含钼99.9%
8102.9600	--丝	1.品名;2.形状(丝);3.材质(钼)。注:未锻轧钼锭,含钼99.9%
8102.9700	--废碎料	1.品名;2.用途(供回收钼用);3.材质(钼);4.来源。注:未锻轧钼锭,含钼99.9%
8102.9900	--其他	1.品名;2.材质(钼);3.种类。注:未锻轧钼锭,含钼99.9%
81.03	钽及其制品,包括废碎料:	
8103.2	-未锻轧钽,包括简单烧结而成的条、杆、粉末:	1.品名;2.形状(粉末、条、杆、型材、异型材、板、片、带、箔);3.材质(钽、钽合金);4.加工方法(锻轧、未锻轧、简单烧结等);5.状态(废、碎);6.成分含量(钽的含量);7.粉末需申报松装密度
8103.3000	-废碎料	1.品名;2.形状(粉末、条、杆、型材、异型材、板、片、带、箔);3.材质(钽、钽合金);4.加工方法(锻轧、未锻轧、简单烧结等);5.状态(废、碎);6.成分含量(钽的含量)
8103.9	-其他:	1.品名;2.形状(粉末、条、杆、型材、异型材、板、片、带、箔);3.材质(钽、钽合金);4.加工方法(锻轧、未锻轧、简单烧结等);5.状态(废、碎);6.成分含量(钽的含量);7.丝需申报直径
81.04	镁及其制品,包括废碎料:	
8104.1	-未锻轧镁:	1.品名;2.材质(镁);3.加工方法(未锻轧);4.成分含量(镁的含量);5.粉末粒度。注:未锻轧镁锭,含镁99.9%
8104.2000	-废碎料	1.品名;2.用途(供回收镁用);3.状态(废、碎);4.来源
8104.3000	-锉屑、车屑及颗粒,已按规格分级的;粉末	1.品名;2.形状(粉末等);3.材质(镁);4.来源(锉屑、车屑等);5.成分含量(镁的含量);6.粒度
8104.9	-其他:	1.品名;2.材质(镁);3.加工方法(锻轧等)
81.05	钴锍及其他冶炼钴时所得的中间产品;钴及其制品,包括废碎料:	1.品名;2.形状(粉末、条、杆、型材、异型材、板、片、带、箔);3.材质(钴、钴合金、钴锍);4.加工方法(锻轧、未锻轧);5.状态(废、碎);6.成分含量(以干基钴为标准);7.粉末粒度。注:未锻轧钴锭,含钴99.9%
81.06	铋及其制品,包括废碎料:	1.品名;2.形状(粉末、条、杆、型材、异型材、板、片、带、箔);3.材质(铋、铋合金);4.加工方法(锻轧、未锻轧);5.状态(废、碎);6.成分含量(铋的含量)。注:未锻轧铋锭,含铋99.9%
81.07	镉及其制品,包括废碎料:	1.品名;2.形状(粉末、条、杆、型材、异型材、板、片、带、箔);3.材质(镉、镉合金);4.加工方法(锻轧、未锻轧);5.状态(废、碎)。注:未锻轧镉锭,含镉99.9%
81.08	钛及其制品,包括废碎料:	
8108.2	-未锻轧钛;粉末:	1.品名;2.形状(粉末、杆等);3.材质(钛);4.加工方法(未锻轧);5.成分含量(钛的含量);6.粉末粒度。注:未锻轧钛锭,含钛99.9%
8108.3000	-废碎料	1.品名;2.用途(供回收钛用);3.状态(废、碎);4.来源
8108.9	-其他:	1.品名;2.形状(条、杆、型材、异型材、板、片、带、箔等);3.材质(钛);4.种类;5.加工方法(未锻轧);6.板、片、带、箔的厚度

税则号列	商 品 描 述	规范申报要素 / 价格申报要素 / 其他申报要素 / 举例说明
81092000	锆及其制品,包括废碎料:	1.品名;2.形状(粉末、条、杆、型材、异型材、板、片、带、箔);3.材质(锆、锆合金);4.加工方法(未锻轧等);5.状态(废、碎);6.成分含量(锆的含量);7.粉末粒度粉末须申报细度。注:未锻轧锆锭,含锆99.9%
81.10	锑及其制品,包括废碎料:	1.品名;2.形状(粉末、条、杆、型材、异型材、板、片、带、箔);3.材质(锑、锑合金);4.加工方法(未锻轧等);5.状态(废、碎);6.成分含量(锑的含量);7.粉末粒度。注:未锻轧锑锭,含锑99.9%
81.11	锰及其制品,包括废碎料:	1.品名;2.形状(粉末、条、杆、型材、异型材、板、片、带、箔);3.材质(锰、锰合金);4.加工方法(未锻轧、锻压、模压等);5.状态(废、碎);6.成分含量(锰的含量);7.粉末粒度
81.12	铍、铬、锗、钒、镓、铪、铟、铼、铌、铊及其制品,包括废碎料:	1.品名;2.形状(粉末、条、杆、型材、异型材、板、片、带、箔);3.材质(铍、铬等贱金属及其合金);4.加工方法(未锻轧等);5.状态(废、碎);6.成分含量;7.粉末粒度
81.13	金属陶瓷及其制品,包括废碎 料:	1.品名;2.材质(金属陶瓷);3.状态(废、碎)。注:金属陶瓷制防热套

第八十二章 贱金属工具、器具、利口器、餐匙、餐叉及其零件

【注解】

1、"品名"是指货品的具体商业名称。

2、"用途"是指货品在出入境后的应用场合或下游产品。

3、"加工方法"是指货品在出入境前的加工工艺或制造方法。

4、"材质"是指货品按《税则》中的材质分类原则所确定的具体材料种类。

5、"形状"是指货品按《税则》中的形状定义描述所确定的外观形状。

税则号列	商 品 描 述	规范申报要素 / 价格申报要素 / 其他申报要素 / 举例说明
82.01	锹、铲、镐、锄、叉及耙;斧子、钩刀及类似砍伐工具;各种修枝用剪刀;镰刀、秣刀、树篱剪、伐木楔子及其他农业、园艺或林业用手工工具:	1.品名;2.用途(砍伐用、修枝用等);3.材质(合金钢制等);4.种类(锹、铲、剪等);5.式样(单手操作等);6.品牌
82.02	手工锯;各种锯的锯片(包括切条、切槽或无齿锯片):	1.品名;2.用途(加工金属用等);3.材质(合金钢制等);4.种类(手工锯、带锯片、圆锯片、直锯片等);5.圆锯片带有钢制工作部件请注明;6.品牌
82.03	钢锉、木锉、钳子(包括剪钳) 镊子、白铁剪、切管器、螺栓切头器、打孔冲子及类似手工工具:	1.品名;2.用途(锉木材用等);3.材质(合金钢制等);4.种类(锉、钳子、镊子等);5.品牌
82.04	手动扳手及扳钳(包括转矩扳手,但不包括丝锥扳手);可互换的扳手套筒,不论是否带 手柄:	1.品名;2.材质(合金钢制等);3.种类(扳手、扳钳、扳手套筒等);4.式样(固定的、可调的);5.品牌
82.05	其他品目未列名的手工工具(包括玻璃刀);喷灯;台钳 夹钳及类似品,但作为机床附件或零件的除外;砧;轻便锻炉;带支架的手摇或脚踏砂轮:	1.品名;2.用途(家用等);3.材质(合金钢制等);4.种类(锤子、螺丝刀等);5.是否成套;6.品牌
82.06	由品目82.02至82.05中两个或多个品目所列工具组成的零售包装成套货品:	1.品名;2.材质(合金钢制等);3.包含的种类(扳手、钳子、螺丝刀等);4.是否零售包装成套;5.品牌
82.07	手工工具(不论是否有动力装 置)及机床(例如,锻压、冲压、攻丝、钻孔、镗孔、铰孔及铣削、车削或上螺丝用的机 器)的可互换工具,包括金属拉拔或挤压用模以及凿岩或钻探工具:	1.品名;2.用途(钻探、铣削、锻压、镗孔用等);3.材质(合金钢制等);4.种类(锻模、铣刀等);5.带有工作部件请注明材质(金属陶瓷、金刚石等);6.品牌
82.08	机器或机械器具的刀及刀片:	1.品名;2.用途(金属加工用、木器加工用等);3.材质(不锈钢制等);4.种类(机器用刀片等);5.是否经镀或涂层;6.品牌
82.09	未装配的工具用金属陶瓷板、杆、刀头及类似品:	

税则号列	商品描述	规范申报要素 / 价格申报要素 / 其他申报要素 / 举例说明
82090010	---板	1. 品名;2. 用途(工具用);3. 材质(金属陶瓷制);4. 种类(板、杆、刀头等);5. 是否装配;6. 品牌
82090021	----晶粒度小于 0.8 微米的	1. 品名;2. 用途(工具用);3. 材质(金属陶瓷制);4. 种类(板、杆、刀头等);5. 是否装配;6. 晶粒度;7. 品牌
82090029	----其他	1. 品名;2. 用途(工具用);3. 材质(金属陶瓷制);4. 种类(板、杆、刀头等);5. 是否装配;6. 品牌
82090030	---刀头	1. 品名;2. 用途(工具用);3. 材质(金属陶瓷制);4. 种类(板、杆、刀头等);5. 是否装配;6. 品牌
82090090	---其他	1. 品名;2. 用途(工具用);3. 材质(金属陶瓷制);4. 种类(板、杆、刀头等);5. 是否装配;6. 品牌
82.10	用于加工或调制食品或饮料的手动机械器具,重量不超过 10 千克:	1. 品名;2. 用途(加工食品用等);3. 材质(不锈钢制等);4. 种类(绞肉机、榨汁机等);5. 原理(手动);6. 单件重量;7. 品牌
82.11	有刃口的刀及其刀片,不论是否有锯齿(包括整枝刀),但品目 82.08 的刀除外:	1. 品名;2. 材质(不锈钢制等);3. 种类(餐刀、折叠刀等);4. 式样(刃面固定、可换刃面);5. 是否成套;6. 品牌
82.12	剃刀及其刀片(包括未分开的刀片条):	1. 品名;2. 材质(不锈钢制等);3. 种类(剃刀、安全刀片等);4. 品牌
82.13	剪刀、裁缝剪刀及类似品、剪刀片:	1. 品名;2. 用途(裁缝用等);3. 材质(不锈钢制等);4. 种类(剪刀、剪刀片等);5. 品牌
82.14	其他利口器(例如,理发推剪屠刀、砍骨刀、切肉刀、切菜刀、裁纸刀);修指甲及修脚用具(包括指甲锉):	1. 品名;2. 材质(不锈钢制等);3. 种类(裁纸刀、指甲锉、手动理发推剪、切菜刀等);4. 品牌
82.15	餐匙、餐叉、长柄勺、漏勺、糕点夹、鱼刀、黄油刀、糖块夹及类似的厨房或餐桌用具:	1. 品名;2. 用途(餐桌、厨房用);3. 材质(不锈钢制等);4. 种类(餐叉、漏勺等);5. 是否镀贵金属;6. 是否成套;7. 品牌

第八十三章　贱金属杂项制品

【注解】

1、"品名"是指货品的具体商业名称。

2、"用途"是指货品在出入境后的应用场合或下游产品。

3、"加工方法"是指货品在出入境前的加工工艺或制造方法。

4、"材质"是指货品按《税则》中的材质分类原则所确定的具体材料种类。

5、"形状"是指货品按《税则》中的形状定义描述所确定的外观形状。

税则号列	商品描述	规范申报要素 / 价格申报要素 / 其他申报要素 / 举例说明
83.01	贱金属制的锁(钥匙锁、数码锁及电动锁);贱金属制带锁的扣环及扣环框架;上述锁的贱金属制钥匙:	1. 品名;2. 用途(机动车用、家具用等);3. 材质(不锈钢制等);4. 种类(钥匙锁、数码锁、电动锁、钥匙等);5. 品牌
83.02	用于家具、门窗、楼梯、百叶窗、车厢、鞍具、衣箱、盒子及类似品的贱金属附件及架座;贱金属制帽架、帽钩、托架及类似品;用贱金属做支架的小脚轮;贱金属制的自动闭门器:	
8302.1000	-铰链(折叶)	1. 品名;2. 用途(机动车用、家具用等);3. 材质(不锈钢制等);4. 种类(铰链、自动闭门器等);5. 品牌
8302.2000	-小脚轮	1. 品名;2. 用途(机动车用、家具用等);3. 材质(不锈钢制等);4. 种类(铰链、自动闭门器等);5. 直径;6. 所装轮或胎的宽度;7. 品牌
8302.3000	-机动车辆用的其他附件及架座	1. 品名;2. 用途(机动车用、家具用等);3. 材质(不锈钢制等);4. 种类(铰链、自动闭门器等);5. 品牌
8302.4	-其他附件及架座:	1. 品名;2. 用途(机动车用、家具用等);3. 材质(不锈钢制等);4. 种类(铰链、自动闭门器等);5. 品牌
8302.5000	-帽架、帽钩、托架及类似品	1. 品名;2. 用途(机动车用、家具用等);3. 材质(不锈钢制等);4. 种类(铰链、自动闭门器等);5. 品牌
8302.6000	-自动闭门器	1. 品名;2. 用途(机动车用、家具用等);3. 材质(不锈钢制等);4. 种类(铰链、自动闭门器等);5. 品牌

税则号列	商 品 描 述	规范申报要素 / 价格申报要素 / 其他申报要素 / 举例说明
83.03	装甲或加强的贱金属制保险箱、保险柜及保险库的门和带锁保险储存橱、钱箱、契约箱及类似品：	1.品名；2.材质（不锈钢制等）；3.种类（保险箱、保险柜、保险库的门等）；4.品牌
83.04	贱金属制的档案柜、卡片索引柜、文件盘、文件篮、笔盘、公章架及类似的办公用具，但品目94.03的办公室家具除外：	1.品名；2.用途（办公室用）；3.材质（不锈钢制等）；4.种类（档案柜、卡片索引柜、文件盘等）；5.式样（非落地）；6.品牌
83.05	活页夹、卷宗夹的贱金属附件，贱金属制的信夹、信角、文件夹、索引标签及类似的办公用品；贱金属制的成条订书钉（例如，供办公室、室内装饰或包装用）：	1.品名；2.用途（办公室用、室内装饰或包装用）；3.材质（不锈钢制等）；4.种类（活页夹、宗卷夹、成条订书钉等）；5.品牌
83.06	非电动的贱金属铃、钟、锣及类似品；贱金属雕塑像及其他装饰品；贱金属相框或画框及类似框架；贱金属镜子：	1.品名；2.材质（不锈钢制等）；3.种类（铃、钟、锣、雕塑像、相框、画框等）；4.是否镀贵金属；5.铃、钟、锣请注明非电动；6.品牌
83.07	贱金属软管，不论是否有附件：	1.品名；2.材质（钢铁制、其他贱金属制）；3.种类（软管）；4.品牌
83.08	贱金属制的扣、钩、环、眼及类似品，用于衣着、鞋靴、天篷、提包、旅行用品或其他制成品；贱金属制的管形铆钉及开口铆钉；贱金属制的珠子及亮晶片：	1.品名；2.用途（用于衣服、提包上等）；3.材质（不锈钢制等）；4.种类（扣、钩、环、铆钉等）；5.品牌
83.09	贱金属制的塞子、盖子（包括冠形瓶塞、螺口盖及倒水塞）瓶帽、螺口塞、塞子帽、封志及其他包装用附件：	1.品名；2.形状（冠形、圆形等）；3.材质（不锈钢制等）；4.种类（塞子、盖子等）；5.品牌
83.10	贱金属制的标志牌、铭牌、地名牌及类似品、号码、字母及类似标志，但品目94.05的货品除外：	1.品名；2.用途（汽车用等）；3.材质（不锈钢制、贱金属种类等）；4.种类（标志、铭牌等）；5.品牌
83.11	贱金属或硬质合金制的丝、条、管、板、电极及类似品，以焊剂涂面或以焊剂为芯，用于焊接或沉积金属、硬质合金；贱金属粉粘聚而成的丝或 条，供金属喷镀用：	1.品名；2.用途（电弧焊用、气焊用、钎焊用等）；3.材质（贱金属、硬质合金制）；4.种类（电极、焊条、焊丝等）；5.状态（以焊剂涂面、以焊剂为芯）；6.品牌

第十六类　机器、机械器具、电气设备及其零件；录音机及放声机、电视图像、声音的录制重设备及其零件、附件

第八十四章　核反应堆、锅炉、机器、机械器具及其零件

【注解】

1、零部件除申报目录规定的要素外，还应申报具体名称，材质和品牌等要素。

2、未制成品、不完整品申报要注明程度。

3.“说明举例”栏中未包含品牌、型号等内容。

4.旧的机电设备除申报目录规定的要素外，还应申报生产年代、新旧程度、技术规格、配置等要素。

税则号列	商 品 描 述	规范申报要素 / 价格申报要素 / 其他申报要素 / 举例说明
84.01	核反应堆；核反应堆的未辐照燃料元件（释热元件）；同位素分离机器及装置：	
8401.1000	-核反应堆	1.品名2.用途；3.品牌；4.型号
8401.2000	-同位素分离机器、装置及其零件	1.品名；2.用途；3.品牌；4.型号
8401.3	-未辐照燃料元件（释热元件）：	1.品名2.用途；3.品牌；4.型号
8401.4	-核反应堆零件：	1.品名；2.用途（适用机型）；3.品牌；4.型号
84.02	蒸汽锅炉（能产生低压水蒸气的集中 供暖用 的热水 锅炉除外）；过热水锅炉：	
8402.1	-蒸汽锅炉：	1.品名；2.用途；3.构造方式；4.蒸发量；5.品牌；6.型号
8402.2000	-过热水锅炉	1.品名；2.用途；3.温度；4.品牌；5.型号

税则号列	商品描述	规范申报要素 / 价格申报要素 / 其他申报要素 / 举例说明
8402.9000	-零件	1.品名;2.用途(适用机型);3.品牌;4.型号
84.03	集中供暖用的热水锅炉,但品目84.02的货品除外:	
8403.1010	---家用型	1.品名;2.用途;3.品牌;4.型号;5.是否装有循环装置;6.功率;7.温度
8403.1090	---其他	1.品名;2.用途;3.品牌;4.型号;5.温度
8403.9000	-零件	1.品名;2.用途(适用机型);3.品牌;4.型号
84.04	品目84.02或84.03所列锅炉的辅助设备(例如,节热器、过热器、除灰器、气体回收器)水蒸气或其他蒸汽动力装置的冷凝器:	
8404.1	-税号84.02或84.03所列锅炉的辅助设备:	1.品名;2.用途;3.品牌
8404.2000	-水蒸气或其他蒸汽动力装置的冷凝器	1.品名;2.用途;3.品牌
8404.9	-零件:	1.品名;2.用途(适用机型);3.品牌;4.型号
84.05	煤气发生器,不论有无净化器乙炔发生器及类似水解气体发生器,不论有无净化器:	
8405.1000	-煤气发生器,不论有无净化器;乙炔发生器及类似的水解气体发生器,不论有无净化器	1.品名;2.品牌;3.型号
8405.9000	-零件	1.品名;2.用途(适用机型);3.品牌;4.型号
84.06	汽轮机:	
8406.1000	-船舶动力用汽轮机	1.品名;2.用途;3.品牌;4.型号;5.输出功率
8406.8	-其他汽轮机:	1.品名;2.用途;3.输出功率;4.品牌;5.型号
8406.9000	-零件	1.品名;2.用途(适用机型);3.品牌;4.型号
84.07	点燃往复式或旋转式活塞内燃发动机:	
8407.1	-航空器发动机:	1.品名;2.用途;3.输出功率;4.品牌;5.型号;6.燃料类型
8407.2100	--舷外发动机	1.品名;2.用途;3.发动机安装位置(舷外或舷内);4.品牌;5.型号;6.燃料类型;7.功率
8407.2900	--其他	1.品名;2.用途;3.发动机安装位置(舷外或舷内);4.品牌;5.型号;6.燃料类型;7.是否提供主动力;8.功率
8407.3	-用于第八十七章所列车辆的往复式活塞发动机:	1.品名;2.用途;3.排气量;4.成套散件或毛坯请注明;5.燃料类型;6.状态(成品、半成品、成套散件);7.生产件的通用零件编号后加注"/TY";8.成套散件装配后完整品的零部件的编号;9.品牌;10.型号;11.零部件完整编号并在前加注"S/"、"W/"或"WF/"之一(生产件填报)"S/",品牌和适用的整车厂牌一致的维修件填报"W/",品牌和适用的整车厂牌不一致的维修件的填报"WF/"
8407.9	-其他发动机:	1.品名;2.用途;3.燃料类型;4.品牌;5.型号;6.转速
84.08	压燃式活塞内燃发动机(柴油或半柴油发动机):	
8408.1000	-船舶发动机	1.品名;2.用途;3.品牌;4.型号;5.输出功率
8408.2	-用于第八十七章所列车辆的发动机:	1.品名;2.用途;3.输出功率;4.成套散件或毛坯请注明;5.燃料类型;5.生产件的通用零件编号后加注"/TY";6.成套散件装配后完整品的零部件的编号;7.品牌;8.型号;9.零部件完整编号并在前加注"S/"、"W/"或"WF/"之一(生产件填报)"S/",品牌和适用的整车厂牌一致的维修件填报"W/",品牌和适用的整车厂牌不一致的维修件的填报"WF/"
8408.9	-其他发动机:	1.品名;2.用途;3.输出功率;4.品牌;5.型号;6.转速
84.09	专用于或主要用于品目84.07或84.08所列发动机的零件:	1.品名;2.适用何种用途发动机(如飞机用、船舶用等);3.适用发动机的类型(点燃式/压燃式);4.品牌;5.零件号
84.10	水轮机、水轮及其调节器:	
8410.1100	--功率不超过1000千瓦	1.品名;2.功率;3.品牌;4.型号
8410.1200	--功率超过1000千瓦,但不超过10000千瓦	1.品名;2.功率;3.品牌;4.型号
8410.13	--功率超过10000千瓦:	1.品名;2.功率;3.工作方式;4.品牌;5.型号
8410.9010	---调节器	1.品名2.品牌;3.原理;4.型号
8410.9090	---其他	1.品名2.品牌;3.型号
84.11	涡轮喷气发动机,涡轮螺桨发动机及其他燃气轮机:	
8411.1	-涡轮喷气发动机:	1.品名;2.原理;3.推力;4.品牌;5.型号
8411.2	-涡轮螺桨发动机:	1.品名;2.原理;3.功率;4.品牌;5.型号
8411.8	-其他燃气轮机:	1.品名;2.原理;3.功率;4.品牌;5.型号
8411.9	-零件:	1.品名;2.用途(适用机型);3.品牌;4.型号

税则号列	商　品　描　述	规范申报要素 / 价格申报要素 / 其他申报要素 / 举例说明
84.12	其他发动机及动力装置:	
8412.1	-喷气发动机,但涡轮喷气发动机除外:	1.品名;2.用途;3.原理;4.品牌;5.型号
8412.2	-液压动力装置:	1.品名;2.原理;3.用途;4.品牌;5.型号
8412.3	-气压动力装置:	1.品名;2.原理;3.用途;4.品牌;5.型号
8412.8000	-其他	1.品名;2.原理;3.用途;4.品牌;5.型号
8412.9	-零件:	1.品名;2.用途(适用机型);3.品牌;4.型号
84.13	液体泵,不论是否装有计量装置;液体提升机:	
8413.1	-装有或可装计量装置的泵	1.品名;2.用途;3.是否装有或可装计量装置;4.品牌;5.型号
8413.2000	-手泵,但子目号 8413.11 或 8413.19 的货品除外	1.品名;2.是否手动;3.品牌;4.型号
8413.3	-活塞式内燃发动机用的燃油泵、润滑油泵或冷却剂泵:	1.品名;2.用途(是否为活塞式内燃发动机用);3.适用发动机的输出功率;4.品牌;5.型号。注:活塞式内燃发动机用燃油泵,发动机输出功率 180 千瓦,品牌 MXS,型号 X-1
8413.4000	-混凝土泵	1.品名;2.用途;3.品牌;4.型号
8413.5	-其他往复式排液泵:	1.品名;2.驱动方式;3.原理(往复式、回转式、离心式等);4.用途;5.品牌;6.型号
8413.6	-其他回转式排液泵:	1.品名;2.驱动方式;3.原理(往复式、回转式、离心式等);4.用途;5.品牌;6.型号
8413.7	-其他离心泵	1.品名;2.驱动方式;3.原理(往复式、回转式、离心式等);4.转速;5.用途;6.品牌;7.型号
8413.8	-其他泵;液体提升机:	1.品名 2.用途;3.品牌;4.型号;5.原理(柱塞式、齿轮式、螺杆式等)
8413.9	-零件	1.品名;2.用途(适用机型);3.品牌;4.型号。注:燃油泵用泵体,无品牌、型号
84.14	空气泵或真空泵、空气及其他 气体压缩机、风机、风扇;装 有风扇的通风罩或循环气罩,不论是否装有过滤器:	
8414.1000	-真空泵	1.品名 2.用途;3.品牌;4.型号;5.性能(抽气能力)
8414.2000	-手动或脚踏式空气泵	1.品名;2.是否手动或脚踏;3.品牌;4.型号
8414.3	-用于制冷设备的压缩机:	1.品名;2.用途;3.驱动方式;4.额定功率;5.品牌;6.型号
8414.4000	-装在拖车底盘上的空气压缩机	1.品名;2.用途;3.品牌;4.型号
8414.5	-风机、风扇:	1.品名;2.用途;3.安装方式(如吊扇、落地扇、壁扇等);4.输出功率;5.品牌;6.型号
8414.6	-罩的平面最大边长不超过 120 厘米的通风罩或循环气罩:	1.品名;2.罩的平面最大边长;3.品牌;4.型号
8414.8010	---燃气轮机用的自由活塞式 发生器	1.品名;2.用途;3.品牌;4.型号
8414.8020	---二氧化碳压缩机	1.品名;2.用途;3.品牌;4.型号
8414.8030	---发动机用增压器	1.品名;2.用途;3.品牌;4.型号;5.压力比
8414.8040	---空气及其他气体压缩机	1.品名;2.用途;3.品牌;4.型号;
8414.8090	---其他	1.品名;2.用途;3.品牌;4.型号
8414.9	-零件:	1.品名;2.用途(适用机型);3.品牌;4.型号;5.材质。注:窗式空调器用压缩机外壳,塑料制,无品牌、型号
84.15	品目 84.14 其他未列名零件空气调节器,装有电扇及调温 调湿装置,包括不能单独调湿 的空调器:	
8415.1010	---独立式	1.品名;2.是否窗式或壁式安装;3.是否为独立式或分体式;4.品牌;5.型号
8415.102	---分体式:	1.品名;2.是否窗式或壁式安装;3.是否为独立式或分体式;4.制冷量;5.品牌;6.型号。注:空调器(分体壁式),品牌格力,制冷量 2000 大卡,型号 RS0232
8415.2000	-机动车辆上供人使用的	1.品名;2.用途;3.品牌;4.型号
8415.81	--装有制冷装置及一个冷热循 环换向阀的(可逆式热泵):	1.品名;2.是否装有制冷装置;3.是否装有冷热换向阀;4.制冷量;5.品牌;6.型号
8415.82	--其他,装有制冷装置的:	1.品名;2.是否装有制冷装置;3.是否装有冷热换向阀;4.制冷量;5.品牌;6.型号
8415.8300	--未装有制冷装置的	1.品名 2.品牌;3.结构;4.型号
8415.9	-零件:	1.品名;2.用途(适用机型);3.适用机型制冷量(以"大卡/时"计);4.品牌;5.型号
84.16	机械出灰器及类似装置:	
8416.1000	-使用液体燃料的炉用燃烧器	1.品名;2.用途;3.燃料类型;4.品牌;5.型号
8416.2	-其他炉用燃烧器,包括复式燃 烧器:	1.品名;2.用途;3.燃料类型;4.品牌;5.型号
8416.3000	-机械加煤机,包括其机械炉 篦、机械出灰器及类似装置	1.品名;2.用途;3.品牌
8416.9000	-零件	1.品名;2.用途(适用机型);3.品牌;4.型号

税则号列	商品描述	规范申报要素 / 价格申报要素 / 其他申报要素 / 举例说明
84.17	非电热的工业或实验室用炉及烘箱,包括焚烧炉:	
8417.1000	-矿砂、黄铁矿或金属的焙烧、熔化或其他热处理用炉及烘箱	1.品名;2.用途;3.加热方式;4.品牌;5.型号
8417.2000	-面包房用烤炉及烘箱,包括做饼干用的	1.品名;2.用途;3.加热方式;4.品牌;5.型号
8417.8	-其他:	1.品名;2.用途;3.加热方式;4.品牌;5.型号
8417.9	-零件:	1.品名;2.用途(适用机型);3.品牌;4.型号
84.18	电气或非电气的冷藏箱、冷冻箱及其他制冷设备;热泵,但品目84.15的空气调节器除外:	
8418.1	-冷藏-冷冻组合机,各自装有单独外门的:	1.品名;2.结构[冷藏—冷冻组合机(各自装有单独外门的)];3.容积;4.品牌;5.型号
8418.2	-家用型冷藏箱:	1.品名;2.用途(是否家用);3.原理;4.容积;5.品牌;6.型号
8418.3	-柜式冷冻箱,容积不超过800升	1.品名;2.容积;3.最低制冷温度;4.是否柜式;5.品牌;6.型号
8418.4	-立式冷冻箱,容积不超过900升	1.品名;2.结构(是否为立式);3.容积;4.最低制冷温度;5.品牌;6.型号
8418.5000	-装有冷藏或冷冻装置的其他设备,(柜、箱、展示台、陈列箱及类似品)用于存储及展示	1.品名;2.用途;3.品牌;4.型号;5.容积;6.最低制冷温度
8418.6	-其他制冷设备;热泵:	1.品名;2.原理(是否为压缩式);3.品牌;4.型号
8418.9	-零件:	1.品名;2.用途(适用机型);3.适用机型的制冷温度的容积;4.品牌;5.型号。注:立式冷冻箱箱门,无品牌、型号,制冷温度-30℃,容积460升
84.19	利用温度变化处理材料的机器、装置及类似的实验室设备例如,加热、烹煮、烘炒、蒸馏、精馏、消毒、灭菌、汽蒸干燥、蒸发、气化、冷凝、冷却的机器设备,不论是否电热的(不包括品目85.14的炉,烘箱及其他设备),但家用的除外;非电热的快速热水器或贮备式热水器:	
8419.1	-非电热的快速热水器或贮备式热水器:	1.品名;2.原理;3.加热方式;4.用途;5.品牌;6.型号
8419.2000	-医用或实验室用消毒器具	1.品名;2.用途;3.品牌;4.型号
8419.3	-干燥器:	1.品名;2.用途;3.干燥材质;4.品牌;5.型号
8419.4	-蒸馏或精馏设备:	1.品名;2.用途;3.品牌;4.型号;5.原理
8419.5000	-热交换装置	1.品名2.用途;3.品牌;4.型号
8419.601	---制氧机:	1.品名;2.用途;3.制氧量;4.品牌;5.型号
84196090	---其他	1.品名;2.用途;3.品牌;4.型号
8419.8	-其他机器设备:	1.品名;2.用途;3.品牌;4.型号
8419.9	-零件:	1.品名;2.用途(适用机型);3.品牌;4.型号
84.20	研光机或其他滚压机器及其滚筒,但加工金属或玻璃用的除外:	
8420.1000	-研光机或其他滚压机器	1.品名;2.用途;3.品牌;4.型号
8420.9	-零件:	1.品名;2.用途(适用机型);3.品牌;4.型号
84.21	离心机,包括离心干燥机;液体或气体的过滤、净化机器及装置:	
8421.1100	--奶油分离器	1.品名;2.用途;3.原理;4.品牌;5.型号
8421.12	--干衣机:	1.品名;2.用途;3.原理;4.干衣量;5.品牌;6.型号
8421.19	--其他:	1.品名;2.用途;3.原理;4.品牌;5.型号
8421.21	--过滤或净化水用:	1.品名;2.用途;3.品牌;4.型号;5.原理;6.单位时间水处理量
8421.2200	--过滤或净化饮料(水除外)用	1.品名;2.用途;3.原理;4.品牌;5.型号
8421.2300	--内燃发动机的滤油器	1.品名;2.用途;3.原理;4.品牌;5.型号
8421.29	--其他:	1.品名;2.用途;3.原理;4.品牌;5.型号
8421.3100	--内燃发动机的进气过滤器	1.品名;2.用途;3.原理;4.品牌;5.型号
8421.39	--其他:	1.品名;2.用途;3.原理;4.品牌;5.型号;6.额定功率(非电动的不需注明额定功率)
8421.9	-零件:	1.品名;2.用途(适用机型);3.品牌;4.型号

税则号列	商品描述	规范申报要素 / 价格申报要素 / 其他申报要素 / 举例说明
84.22	洗碟机;瓶子及其他容器的洗涤或干燥机器;瓶、罐、箱、袋或其他容器装填、封口、密封、贴标签的机器;瓶、罐、管、筒或类似容器的包封机器其他包装或打包机器(包括热缩包装机器);饮料充气机:	
8422.1	-洗碟机:	1.品名2.品牌;3.型号。注:飞利浦家用洗碟机,型号TX098
8422.2000	-瓶子及其他容器的洗涤或干 燥机器	1.品名;2.用途;3.品牌;4.型号
8422.3	-瓶、罐、箱、袋或其他容器装填、封口、密封、贴标签的机 器;瓶、罐、管、筒或类似容 器的包封机器;饮料充气机:	1.品名;2.用途;3.品牌;4.型号
8422.4000	-其他包装或打包机器(包括热缩包装机器)	1.品名;2.用途;3.品牌;4.型号
8422.9	-零件:	1.品名;2.用途(适用机型);3.品牌;4.型号。注:家用洗碟机碟架,无品牌、型号
84.23	衡器(感量为50毫克或更精密 的天平除外),包括计数或检 验用的衡器;衡器用的各种砝 码、秤砣:	
8423.1000	-体重计,包括婴儿秤;家用秤	1.品名;2.用途;3.品牌;4.型号
8423.2	-输送带上连续称货的秤:	1.品名;2.用途;3.原理;4.品牌;5.型号
8423.3	-恒定秤、物料定量装袋或装容器用的秤,包括库秤:	1.品名;2.用途;3.品牌;4.型号
8423.8	-其他衡器:	1.品名;2.用途;3.原理;4.最大称量;5.品牌;6.型号
8423.9000	-衡器用的各种砝码、秤砣;衡器的零件 液体或粉末的喷射、散布或喷 雾的机械器具(不论是否手工操作);灭火器,不论是否装药;喷枪及类似器具;喷气机	1.品名;2.用途(适用机型);3.品牌;4.型号
84.24	喷砂机及类似的喷射机器:	
8424.1000	-灭火器,不论是否装药	1.品名;2.用途;3.品牌;4.型号
8424.2000	-喷枪及类似器具	1.品名2.用途;3.品牌;4.喷射材料;5.型号
8424.3000	-喷汽机、喷砂机及类似喷射机器	1.品名;2.喷射材料;3.用途;4.品牌;5.型号
8424.8	-其他器具:	1.品名;2.用途;3.品牌;4.喷射材料;5.型号
8424.9	-零件:	1.品名;2.用途(适用机型);3.品牌;4.型号
84.25	滑车及提升机,但倒卸式提升机除外;卷扬机及绞盘;千斤顶:	1.品名;2.用途;3.驱动方式;4.品牌;5.型号;6.最大提升高度(距离);7.最大提升重量
84.26	船用桅杆式起重机;起重机,包括缆式起重机;移动式吊运架、跨运车及装有起重机的工作车:	1.品名;2.用途;3.结构类型;4.品牌;5.型号
84.27	叉车;其他装有升降或搬运装 置的工作车:	1.品名;2.用途;3.推进方式;4.品牌;5.型号;6.最大提升高度(距离);7.最大提升重量
84.28	其他升降、搬运、装卸机械(例 如,升降机、自动梯、输送机缆车):	
8428.1010	---载客电梯	1.品名;2.用途;3.品牌;4.型号;5.提升速度;6.停层数;7.载重量
8428.1090	---其他	1.品名;2.用途;3.品牌;4.型号
8428.2000	-气压升降机及输送机	1.品名;2.驱动方式;3.品牌;4.型号
8428.3	-其他用于连续运送货物或材 料的升降机及输送机:	1.品名;2.用途;3.运送方式;4.工作构件类型(斗式、带式等);5.品牌;6.型号
8428.4000	-自动梯及自动人行道	1.品名2.品牌;3.型号
8428.6	-缆车、座式升降机、滑雪拉索 索道用牵引装置:	1.品名;2.用途;3.原理;4.结构类型;5.品牌;6.型号
8428.9	-其他机械:	1.品名;2.用途;3.品牌;4.型号
84.29	机动推土机、侧铲推土机、筑 路机、平地机、铲运机、机械 铲、挖掘机、机铲装载机、捣固机械及压路机:	
8429.1	-推土机及侧铲推土机:	1.品名;2.行走装置类型(轮胎式、履带式等);3.发动机输出功率;4.品牌;5.是否自推进;6.型号;7.机械重量
8429.2	-筑路机及平地机:	1.品名;2.是否自推进;3.发动机输出功率;4.品牌;5.型号
8429.3	-铲运机:	1.品名;2.是否自推进;3.斗容量;4.品牌;5.型号
8429.4	-捣固机械及压路机:	1.品名;2.原理;3.是否自推进;4.机重;5.品牌;6.型号
8429.5100	--前铲装载机	1.品名;2.是否自推进;3.品牌;4.行走装置类型(轮胎式、履带式等);5.型号

税则号列	商品描述	规范申报要素 / 价格申报要素 / 其他申报要素 / 举例说明
8429.521	---挖掘机：	1.品名;2.行走装置类型(轮胎式、履带式等);3.是否自推进;4.是否上部结构可旋转360度;5.品牌;6.型号;7.斗容量;8.功率;9.机重
8429.5290	---其他	1.品名;2.是否自推进;3.是否上部结构可旋转360度;4.品牌;5.行走装置类型(轮胎式、履带式等);6.型号
8429.5900	--其他	1.品名;2.是否自推进;3.品牌;4.行走装置类型(轮胎式、履带式等);5.型号;6.斗容量;7.功率;8.机重
84.30	泥土、矿物或矿石的运送、平整、铲运、挖掘、捣固、压实开采或钻探机械;打桩机及拔桩机;扫雪机及吹雪机：	
8430.1000	-打桩机及拔桩机	1.品名2.品牌;3.型号
8430.2000	-扫雪机及吹雪机	1.品名2.品牌;3.型号;4.是否自推进
8430.3	-采(截)煤机、凿岩机及隧道掘进机：	1.品名;2.是否自推进;3.品牌;4.型号。注:三菱牌自推进隧道掘进机,型号WD6532
8430.411	---石油及天然气钻探机：	1.品名;2.用途;3.是否自推进;4.钻探深度;5.品牌;6.型号
8430.4121	----钻探深度在6000米及以上的	1.品名;2.用途;3.是否自推进;4.钻探深度;5.品牌;6.型号
8430.4122	----钻探深度在6000米以下的履带式自推进钻机	1.品名;2.用途;3.是否自推进;4.钻探深度;5.品牌;6.型号;7.机身号;8.钻头直径;9.机身重量
8430.4129	----钻探深度在6000米以下的其他钻探机	1.品名;2.用途;3.是否自推进;4.钻探深度;5.品牌;6.型号
8430.4190	---其他	1.品名;2.用途;3.是否自推进;4.钻探深度;5.品牌;6.型号
8430.4900	--其他	1.品名;2.用途;3.是否自推进;4.钻探深度;5.品牌;6.型号
8430.5	-其他自推进机械：	1.品名;2.用途;3.是否为自推进;4.牙轮直径;5.品牌;6.型号
8430.6	-其他非自推进机械：	1.品名;2.用途;3.是否为自推进;4.钻筒直径;5.品牌;6.型号
84.31	专用于或主要用于品目84.25至84.30所列机械的零件：	1.品名;2.用途(适用机型);3.品牌;4.型号。注:挖掘机用挖斗,无品牌、型号
84.32	农业、园艺及林业用整地或耕作机械;草坪及运动场地滚压机：	
8432.1000	-犁	1.品名2.用途;3.品牌;4.型号
8432.2	-耙、松土机、中耕机、除草机及耕耘机：	1.品名;2.用途;3.品牌;4.型号
8432.3	-播种机、种植机及移植机	1.品名;2.用途;3.品牌;4.型号
8432.4000	-施肥机	1.品名;2.用途;3.品牌;4.型号
8432.8	-其他机械：	1.品名;2.用途;3.品牌;4.型号
8432.9000	-零件	1.品名;2.用途(适用机型);3.品牌;4.型号
84.33	收割机、脱粒机,包括草料打包机;割草机;蛋类、水果或其他农产品的清洁、分选、分级机器,但品目84.37的机器除外：	
8433.1	-草坪、公园或运动场地用的割草机：	1.品名;2.用途;3.驱动方式;4.切割装置的旋转类型;5.品牌;6.型号
8433.2000	-其他割草机,包括牵引装置用的刀具杆	1.品名;2.用途;3.品牌;4.型号
8433.3000	-其他干草切割、翻晒机器	1.品名2.品牌;3.型号
8433.4000	-草料打包机,包括收集打包机	1.品名2.品牌;3.型号
8433.5100	--联合收割机	1.品名;2.用途;3.品牌;4.型号;5.功率
8433.5200	--其他脱粒机	1.品名;2.用途;3.品牌;4.型号
8433.5300	--根茎或块茎收获机	1.品名;2.用途;3.品牌;4.型号;5.功率
8433.59	--其他：	1.品名;2.用途;3.品牌;4.型号;5.功率
8433.6000	-蛋类、水果或其他农产品的清洁、分选、分级机器	1.品名;2.用途;3.品牌;4.型号
8433.9	-零件：	1.品名;2.用途(适用机型);3.品牌;4.型号
84.34	挤奶机及乳品加工机器：	
8434.1	-挤奶机	1.品名;2.用途;3.品牌;4.型号
8434.2	-乳品加工机器	1.品名;2.用途;3.品牌;4.型号
8434.9	-零件	1.品名;2.用途(适用机型);3.品牌;4.型号
84.35	制酒、制果汁或制类似饮料用的压榨机、轧碎机及类似机器	
8435.1	-机器	1.品名;2.用途;3.品牌;4.型号
8435.9	-零件	1.品名;2.用途(适用机型);3.品牌;4.型号
84.36	农业、园艺、林业、家禽饲养业或养蜂业用的其他机器,包括装有机械或热力装置的催芽设备;家禽孵卵器及育雏器：	
8436.1	-动物饲料配制机	1.品名;2.用途;3.品牌;4.型号
8436.2	-家禽饲养用的机器;家禽孵卵器及育雏器：	1.品名;2.用途;3.品牌;4.型号

税则号列	商品描述	规范申报要素 / 价格申报要素 / 其他申报要素 / 举例说明
8436.8000	-其他机器	1.品名;2.用途;3.品牌;4.型号
8436.9	-零件:	1.品名;2.用途(适用机型);3.品牌;4.型号
84.37	种子、谷物或干豆的清洁、分选或分级机器;谷物磨粉业加工机器或谷物、干豆加工机器但农业用机器除外:	
8437.1	-种子、谷物或干豆的清洁、分选或分级机器:	1.品名;2.用途;3.品牌;4.型号
8437.8000	-其他机器	1.品名;2.用途;3.品牌;4.型号
8437.9	-零件	1.品名;2.用途(适用机型);3.品牌;4.型号
84.38	本章其他品目未列名的食品、饮料工业用的生产或加工机器,但提取、加工动物油脂或植物固定油脂的机器除外:	
8438.1	-糕点加工机器及生产通心粉面条或类似产品的机器	1.品名;2.用途;3.品牌;4.型号
8438.2000	-生产糖果、可可粉、巧克力的机器	1.品名;2.用途;3.品牌;4.型号
8438.3000	-制糖机器	1.品名;2.用途;3.品牌;4.型号
8438.4000	-酿酒机器	1.品名;2.用途;3.品牌;4.型号
8438.5000	-肉类或家禽加工机器	1.品名;2.用途;3.品牌;4.型号
8438.6000	-水果、坚果或蔬菜加工机器	1.品名;2.用途;3.品牌;4.型号
8438.8000	-其他机器	1.品名;2.用途;3.品牌;4.型号
8438.9000	-零件	1.品名;2.用途(适用机型);3.品牌;4.型号
84.39	纤维素纸浆、纸及纸板的制造或整理机器:	
8439.1000	-制造纤维素纸浆的机器	1.品名;2.用途;3.品牌;4.型号
8439.2000	-纸或纸板的抄造机器	1.品名;2.用途;3.品牌;4.型号
8439.3000	-纸或纸板的整理机器	1.品名;2.用途;3.品牌;4.型号
8439.9	-零件:	1.品名;2.用途(适用机型);3.品牌;4.型号
84.40	书本装订机器,包括锁线订书机:	
8440.1	-机器:	1.品名;2.用途;3.品牌;4.型号
8440.9000	-零件	1.品名;2.用途(适用机型);3.品牌;4.型号
84.41	其他制造纸浆制品、纸制品或纸板制品的机器,包括各种切纸机:	
8441.1000	-切纸机	1.品名;2.用途;3.品牌;4.型号
8441.2000	-制造包、袋或信封的机器	1.品名;2.用途;3.品牌;4.型号
8441.3	-制造箱、盒、管、桶或类似容器的机器,但模制成型机器除外:	1.品名;2.用途;3.品牌;4.型号
8441.4000	-纸浆、纸或纸板制品模制成型机器	1.品名;2.用途;3.品牌;4.型号
8441.8	-其他机器:	1.品名;2.用途;3.品牌;4.型号
8441.9	-零件:	1.品名;2.用途(适用机型);3.品牌;4.型号
84.42	制版用的机器、器具及设备(品目84.56至84.65的机床除外);印刷用版(片)、滚筒及其他印刷部件;制成供印刷用(例如,刨平、压纹或抛光的板(片)、滚筒及石板:	
8442.3	-机器、器具及设备:	1.品名;2.用途;3.原理;4.品牌;5.型号
8442.4000	-上述机器、器具及设备的零件	1.品名;2.用途(适用机型);3.品牌;4.型号
8442.5000	-印刷用版、滚筒及其他印刷部件;制成供印刷用(例如:刨平、压纹或抛光)的板、滚筒及石板	1.品名;2.用途;3.原理;4.品牌;5.型号
84.43	用品目84.42的印刷用版(片)、滚筒及其他印刷部件进行印刷的机器;其他打印机复印机及传真机,不论是否组合式;上述机器的零件及附件:	
8443.1	-用税号84.42的印刷用版(片)、滚筒及其他印刷部件进行印刷的机器:	1.品名;2.用途;3.原理;4.进料方式;5.片尺寸;6.品牌;7.型号
8443.3	--具有印刷(打印)机、复印或传真中两种及以上功能的机器,可与自动数据处理设备或网络连接:	1.品名;2.原理;3.功能;4.品牌;5.型号
8443.321	---专用于品目84.71所列设备的打印机:	1.品名;2.用途(是否专用于税目84.71所列设备);3.原理;4.品牌;5.型号;6.打印幅宽;7.打印速度
8443.322	---数字式印刷设备:	1.品名;2.用途;3.原理;4.品牌;5.型号

税则号列	商品描述	规范申报要素 / 价格申报要素 / 其他申报要素 / 举例说明
8443.3290	---其他	1.品名;2.用途;3.原理;4.品牌;5.型号
8443.39	--其他:	1.品名;2.用途(是否专用于税目84.71所列设备);3.原理;4.品牌;5.型号
8443.9111	-零件及附件:	1.品名;2用途;(适用机型);3.品牌;4.型号
84.44	化学纺织纤维挤压、拉伸、变形或切割机器:	1.品名;2.用途;3.品牌;4.型号
84.45	纺织纤维的预处理机器;纺纱机、并线机、加捻机及其他生产纺织纱线的机器;摇纱机、络纱机(包括卷纬机)及品目84.46或84.47所列机器用的纺织纱线的机器:	1.品名;2.用途;3.原理;4.品牌;5.型号
84.46	织机:	1.品名;2.用途;3.原理;4.织物宽度;5.品牌;6.型号
84.47	针织机、缝编机及制粗松螺旋花线、网眼薄纱、花边、刺绣品、装饰带、编织带或网的机器及簇绒机:	
8447.1	-圆型针织机	1.品名;2.圆筒直径;3.品牌;4.型号
8447.2	-平型针织机;缝编机:	1.品名;2.原理;3.品牌;4.型号;5.幅宽
8447.9	-其他:	;3.品牌;4.型号
84.48	品目84.44、84.45、84.46或84.47所列机器的辅助机器(例如,多臂机、提花机、自停装置及换梭装置);专用于或主要用于品目84.44、84.45、84.46或84.47所列机器的零件、附件(例如,锭子、锭壳钢丝针布、梳、喷丝头、梭子、综丝、综框、针织机用针):	1.品名;2.用途(适用机型);3.品牌;4.型号。注:织机用综框,无品牌、型号
84.49	成匹、成形的毡呢或无纺织物制造或整理机器,包括制毡呢帽机器;帽模:	1.品名;2.原理;3.品牌;4.型号
84.50	家用型或洗衣房用洗衣机,包括洗涤干燥两用机:	
8450.1	-干衣量不超过10千克的洗衣机:	1.品名;2.原理;3.是否全自动;4.干衣量;5.品牌;6.型号
8450.2	-干衣量超过10千克的洗衣机	1.品名;2.原理;3.是否全自动;4.干衣量;5.品牌;6.型号
8450.9	-零件:	1.品名;2.用途(适用机型);3.品牌;4.型号
84.51	纱线、织物及纺织制品的洗涤清洁、绞拧、干燥、熨烫、挤压(包括熔压)、漂白、染色、上浆、整理、涂布或浸渍机器(品目84.50的机器除外);列诺伦(亚麻油地毡)及类似铺地制品的布基或其他底布的浆料涂布机器;纺织物的卷绕、退绕、折叠、剪切或剪齿边机器:	
8451.1000	-干洗机	1.品名;2.用途;3.品牌;4.型号;5.衣容量(千克)
8451.2	-干燥机:	1.品名;2.用途;3.干衣量;4.品牌;5.型号
8451.3000	-熨烫机及挤压机(包括熔压机)	1.品名;2.用途;3.品牌;4.型号
8451.4000	-洗涤、漂白或染色机器	1.品名;2.用途;3.品牌;4.型号
8451.5000	-纺织物的卷绕、退绕、折叠剪切或剪齿边机器	1.品名;2.用途;3.品牌;4.型号
8451.8000	-其他机器	1.品名;2.用途;3.品牌;4.型号
8451.9	-零件	1.品名;2.用途(适用机型);3.品牌;4.型号
84.52	缝纫机,但品目84.40的锁线订书机除外;缝纫机专用的特制家具、底座及罩盖;缝纫机针:	
8452.1	-家用型缝纫机:	1.品名;2.用途;3.是否手动;4.品牌;5.型号
8452.2	-其他缝纫机:	1.品名;2.用途;3.是否手动;4.品牌;5.型号
8452.3000	-缝纫机针	1.品名;2.用途;3.品牌;4.型号
8452.9	-缝纫机专用的特制家具、底座和罩盖及其零件;缝纫机的其他零件:	1.品名;2.用途(适用机型);3.品牌;4.型号
84.53	生皮、皮革的处理、鞣制或加工机器;鞋靴、毛皮及其他皮革制品的制作或修理机器,但缝纫机除外:	
8453.1000	-生皮、皮革的处理、鞣制或加工机器	1.品名;2.用途;3.品牌;4.型号
8453.2000	-鞋靴制作或修理机器	1.品名;2.用途;3.品牌;4.型号
8453.8000	-其他机器	1.品名;2.用途;3.品牌;4.型号

税则号列	商 品 描 述	规范申报要素 / 价格申报要素 / 其他申报要素 / 举例说明
8453.9000	-零件:	1.品名;2.用途(适用机型);3.品牌;4.型号
84.54	金属冶炼及铸造用的转炉、浇 包、锭模及铸造机:	
8454.1000	-转炉	1.品名;2.用途;3.品牌;4.型号
8454.2	-锭模及浇包:	1.品名;2.用途;3.品牌;4.型号
8454.3	-铸造机:	1.品名;2.用途;3.品牌;4.型号
8454.9	-零件:	1.品名;2.用途(适用机型);3.品牌;4.型号
84.55	金属轧机及其轧辊:	
8455.1	-轧管机:	1.品名;2.用途;3.加工方式;4.品牌;5.型号
8455.2	-其他轧机:	1.品名;2.用途;3.加工方式;4.品牌;5.型号
8455.3	-轧机用轧辊	1.品名;2.用途(适用机型);3.品牌;4.型号;5.规格(轧辊长度、辊身直径、辊颈直径)
8455.9000	-其他零件	1.品名;2.用途(适用机型);3.品牌;4.型号
84.56	用激光、其他光、光子束、超 声波、放电、电化学法、电子束、离子束或等离子弧处理各种材料的加工机床;水射流切 割机:	
8456.1000	-用激光、其他光或光子束处理的	1.品名;2.功能;3.加工方式;4.品牌;5.型号
8456.2000	-用超声波处理的	1.品名;2.功能;3.加工方式;4.品牌;5.型号
8456.3	-用放电处理的:	1.品名;2.控制方式;3.功能;4.加工方式;5.品牌;6.型号;7.功率
8456.9	-其他:	1.品名;2.控制方式;3.功能;4.加工方式;5.品牌;6.型号
84.57	加工金属的加工中心、单工位 组合机床及多工位组合机床:	
8457.1	-加工中心:	1.品名;2.用途;3.功能(如金属钻、镗、铣等);4.可加装刀库注明刀库容量及选配件;5.是否可自动换刀;6.品牌;7.型号。注:立式加工中心,金属钻、铣,带刀库(12件),可自动换刀,永进牌,型号 YCM-MV66A
8457.2000	-单工位组合机床	1.品名;2.用途;3.功能(如金属钻、镗、铣等);4.加工工位数;5.动力头个数;6.品牌;7.型号
8457.3000	-多工位组合机床	1.品名;2.用途;3.功能(如金属钻、镗、铣等);4.加工工位数;5.动力头个数;6.品牌;7.型号
84.58	切削金属的车床(包括车削中 心):	1.品名;2.用途;3.控制方式;4.主轴方向(垂直或水平);5.品牌;6.型号
84.59	切削金属的钻床、镗床、铣床 攻丝机床(包括直线移动式动 力头钻床),但品目 84.58 的 车床(包括车削中心)除外:	
8459.1	-直线移动式动力头钻床	1.品名;2.用途;3.功能;4.动力头移动方式;5.品牌;6.控制方式;7.型号;8.可加装刀库注明刀库容量及选配件
8459.2	-其他钻床:	1.品名;2.用途;3.功能;4.控制方式;5.品牌;6.型号
8459.3	-其他镗铣机床:	1.品名;2.用途;3.功能;4.控制方式;5.品牌;6.型号
8459.4	-其他镗床:	1.品名;2.用途;3.功能;4.控制方式;5.品牌;6.型号
8459.5	-升降台式铣床:	1.品名;2.用途;3.功能;4.控制方式;5.是否为升降台式;6.品牌;7.型号
8459.6	-其他铣床:	1.品名;2.用途;3.功能;4.控制方式;5.是否为龙门式;6.品牌;7.型号
8459.7	-其他攻丝机床	1.品名;2.用途;3.功能;4.品牌;5.控制方式;6.型号
84.60	用磨石、磨料或抛光材料对金属或金属陶瓷进行去毛刺、刃磨、磨削、珩磨、研磨、抛光或其他 精加 工 机床,但品目 84.61 的切齿机、齿轮磨床或 齿轮精加工机床除外:	
8460.1	-平面磨床,在任一坐标的定位 精度至少是 0.01 毫米:	1.品名;2.用途;3.控制方式;4.坐标定位精度;5.品牌;6.型号
8460.2	-其他磨床,在任一坐标的定位 精度至少是 0.01 毫米:	1.品名;2.用途;3.控制方式;4.坐标定位精度;5.结构类型(内圆、外圆等);6.品牌;7.型号
8460.3	-刃磨(工具或刀具)机床:	1.品名;2.用途;3.控制方式;4.品牌;5.型号
8460.4	-珩磨或研磨机床:	1.品名;2.用途;3.品牌;4.型号
8460.9	-其他:	1.品名;2.用途;3.品牌;4.型号
84.61	切削金属或金属陶瓷的刨床、牛头刨床、插床、拉床、切齿 机、齿轮磨床或齿轮精加工机床、锯床、切断机及其他品目未列名的切削机床:	
8461.2	-牛头刨床或插床:	1.品名;2.用途;3.功能;4.结构类型;5.品牌;6.型号
8461.3	-拉床	1.品名;2.用途;3.功能;4.结构类型;5.品牌;6.型号

税则号列	商品描述	规范申报要素 / 价格申报要素 / 其他申报要素 / 举例说明
8461.4	-切齿机、齿轮磨床或齿轮精加 工机床:	1.品名;2.用途;3.控制方式;4.功能;5.品牌;6.型号
8461.5	-锯床或切断机	1.品名;2.用途;3.功能;4.品牌;5.型号;
8461.9	-其他:	1.品名;2.用途;3.功能;4.结构类型;5.品牌;6.型号
84.62	加工金属的锻造(包括模锻)或冲压机床;加工金属的弯曲折叠、矫直、矫平、剪切、冲孔或开槽机床;其他加工金属 或硬质合金的压力机:	
8462.1	-锻造(包括模锻)或冲压机床 及锻锤:	1.品名;2.用途;3.功能;4.控制方式;5.品牌;6.型号
8462.2	-弯曲、折叠、矫直或矫平机床	1.品名;2.用途;3.功能;4.控制方式;5.品牌;6.型号
8462.3	-剪切机床,但冲剪两用机除 外:	1.品名;2.用途;3.功能;4.控制方式;5.品牌;6.型号
8462.4	-冲孔或开槽机床,包括冲剪两 用机:	1.品名;2.用途;3.功能;4.控制方式;5.品牌;6.型号
8462.9	-其他:	1.品名;2.用途;3.功能;4.加工方式(弯曲、折叠、卷曲等);5.品牌;6.型号
84.63	金属或金属陶瓷的其他非切削 加工机床:	1.品名;2.用途;3.功能;4.品牌;5.型号
84.64	石料、陶瓷、混凝土、石棉水 泥或类 似矿 物材料的 加工机床、玻璃冷加工机床:	1.品名;2.用途;3.功能;4.加工材料;5.品牌;6.型号
84.65	木材、软木、骨、硬质橡胶、硬质塑料或类似硬质材料的加 工机床(包括用打钉或打 U 形钉、胶粘或其他方法组合前述材料的机器):	1.品名;2.用途;3.功能;4.加工材料;5.品牌;6.型号
84.66	专用于或主要用于品目 84.56 至 84.65 所列机器的零件、附 件,包括工件或工具的夹具、自启板牙切头、分度头及其他专用于机床的附件;各种手提 工具的工具夹具:	1.品名;2.用途(适用机型);3.品牌;4.型号
84.67	手提式风动或液压工具及本身装有电动或非电动动力装置的 手提式工具:	
8467.1	-风动的:	1.品名;2.驱动方式;3.是否为手提式;4.品牌;5 型号
8467.2	-本身装有电动动力装置的:	1.品名;2.驱动方式;3.是否为手提式;4.品牌;5 型号
8467.8	-其他工具:	1.品名;2.驱动方式;3.是否为手提式;4.品牌;5 型号
8467.9	-零件:	1.品名;2.用途(适用机型);3.品牌;4.型号
84.68	焊接机器及装置,不论是否兼 有切割功能,但品目 85.15 的货品除外;气体加温表面回火机器及装置:	
8468.1000	-手提喷焊器	1.品名;2.原理;3.是否为手提式;4.品牌;5.型号
8468.2000	-其他气体焊接或表面回火机器及装置	1.品名;2.原理;3.是否为手提式;4.品牌;5.型号
8468.8000	-其他机器及装置	1.品名;2.原理;3.是否为手提式;4.品牌;5.型号
8468.9000	-零件	1.品名;2.用途(适用机型);3.品牌;4.型号
84.69	打字机,但品目 84.43 的打印机除外;文字处理机:	1.品名;2.驱动方式;3.品牌;4.型号
84.70	计算机器及具有计算功能的袖珍式数据记录、重现及显示机器;装有计算装置的会计计算机、邮资盖戳机、售票机及类似机器;现金出纳机:	
8470.1000	-不需外接电源的电子计算器及具有计算功能的袖珍式数据记录、重现及显示机器	1.品名;2.是否需外接电源;3.品牌;4.型号。注:东芝电子计算器(不需外接电源的),型号 WQX-9
8470.2	-其他电子计算器:	1.品名;2.是否有打印装置;3.品牌;4.型号
8470.3000	-其他计算机器	1.品名 2.品牌;3.型号
8470.5	-现金出纳机:	1.品名;2.用途;3.品牌;4.型号
8470.9000	-其他	1.品名;2.用途;3.品牌;4.型号
84.71	自动数据处理设备及其部件;其他品目未列名的磁性或光学 阅读机、将数据以代码形式转 录到数据记录媒体的机器及处 理这些数据的机器:	
8471.3	-重量不超过 10 千克的便携自动数据处理设备,至少由一个 中央处理部件、一个键盘及一 个显示器组成:	1.品名;2.机型;3.配置(系统组成部件);4.品牌;5.型号
8471.41	--同一机壳内至少有一个中央 处理部件及一个输入和输出部 件,不论是否组合式:	1.品名;2.机型;3.配置(系统组成部件);4.品牌;5.型号;6.操作系统

税则号列	商 品 描 述	规范申报要素 / 价格申报要素 / 其他申报要素 / 举例说明
8471.49	--其他,以系统形式进口或出 口的:	1.品名;2.机型;3.配置(系统组成部件);4.是否以系统形式报验;5.品牌;6.型号;7.操作系统
8471.5	-子目号 8471.41 或 8471.49 所列以外的处理部件,不论是 否在同一机壳内有--个或两个下列部件:存储部件、输入部件、输出部件:	1.品名;2.机型;3.配置(系统组成部件);4.品牌;5.型号;6.操作系统;7.用途
8471.6040	---巨型机、大型机、中型机及 小型机用终端	1.品名2.品牌;3.型号
8471.6050	---扫描仪	1.品名2.品牌;3.型号
8471.6060	---数字化仪	1.品名2.品牌;3.型号
8471.607	---键盘、鼠标器:	1.品名2.品牌;3.机型;4.型号;5.连接方式(有线、无线)
8471.6090	---其他	1.品名2.品牌;3.型号
8471.7010	---硬盘驱动器	1.品名2.品牌;3.型号;4.硬盘容量及缓存容量;5.转速
8471.7020	---软盘驱动器	1.品名2.品牌;3.型号
8471.7030	---光盘驱动器	1.品名2.品牌;3.型号。注:HP牌光盘驱动器,型号SOHC-4832K,CD-ROM,48X,不带记录功能
8471.7090	---其他	1.品名2.品牌;3.型号
8471.8000	-自动数据处理设备的其他部 件	1.品名2.品牌;3.型号
84.72	公室用机器(例如,胶 版复印机、油印机、地址印写 机、自动付钞机、硬币分类、计数及包装机、削铅笔机、打 洞机或订书机):	
8472.1000	-胶版复印机、油印机	1.品名;2.用途;3.品牌;4.型号
8472.3	-信件分类或折叠机或信件装 封机、信件开封或闭封机、粘 贴或盖销邮票机:	1.品名;2.用途;3.品牌;4.型号
8472.9010	---自动柜员机	1.品名;2.用途(存款、取款、存取款一体机等);3.品牌;4.型号;5.配置;6.安装方式(穿墙式等)
8472.902	---装订用机器:	1.品名;2.用途;3.品牌;4.型号
8472.9030	---碎纸机	1.品名;2.用途;3.品牌;4.型号
8472.9040	---地址印写机及地址铭牌压 印机	1.品名;2.用途;3.品牌;4.型号
8472.9090	---其他	1.品名;2.用途;3.品牌;4.型号
84.73	专用于或主要用于品目84.69至84.72所列机器的零件、附 件(罩套、提箱及类似品除外):	1.品名;2.用途(适用机型);3.品牌;4.型号。注:软盘驱动器用盘架,无品牌、型号
84.74	**泥土、石料、矿石或其他固体(包括粉状、浆状)矿物质的 分类、筛选、分离、洗涤、破碎、磨粉、混合或搅拌机器;固体矿物燃料、陶瓷坯泥、未硬化水泥、石膏材料或其他粉状、浆状矿产品的粘聚或成形 机器;铸造用砂模的成形机器**	
8474.1000	-分类、筛选、分离或洗涤机器	1.品名;2.用途;3.品牌;4.型号
8474.2	-破碎或磨粉机器:	1.品名;2.用途;3.原理;4.品牌;5.型号
8474.3	-混合或搅拌机器:	1.品名;2.用途;3.品牌;4.型号
8474.8	-其他机器:	1.品名;2.用途;3.原理;4.品牌;5.型号
8474.9000	-零件	1.品名;2.用途(适用机型);3.品牌;4.型号
84.75	白炽灯泡、灯管、放电灯管、电子管、闪光灯泡及类似品的 封装机器;玻璃或玻璃制品的 制造或热加工机器:	
8475.1	-白炽灯泡、灯管、放电灯管 电子管、闪光灯泡及类似品的 封装机器	1.品名;2.用途;3.品牌;4.型号
8475.2	-玻璃或玻璃制品的制造或热 加工机器:	1.品名;2.用途;3.品牌;4.型号
8475.9000	-零件	1.品名;2.用途(适用机型);3.品牌;4.型号
84.76	自动售货机(例如,出售邮票 香烟、食品或饮料的机器),包括钱币兑换机:	
8476.2	-饮料自动销售机:	1.品名;2.供应商品种类;3.是否装有加热或制冷装置;4.品牌;5.型号
8476.8	-其他机器:	1.品名;2.供应商品种类;3.是否装有加热或制冷装置;4.品牌;5.型号
8476.9000	-零件	1.品名;2.用途(适用机型);3.品牌;4.型号
84.77	本章其他品目未列名的橡胶或 塑料及其产品的加工机器:	
8477.1	-注射机:	1.品名;2.用途;3.功能;4.品牌;5.型号;6.合模力
8477.2	-挤出机:	1.品名;2.用途;3.功能;4.品牌;5.型号
8477.3	-吹塑机:	1.品名;2.用途;3.功能;4.品牌;5.型号

税则号列	商品描述	规范申报要素 / 价格申报要素 / 其他申报要素 / 举例说明
8477.4	-真空模塑机器及其他热成型 机器:	1.品名;2.用途;3.功能;4.品牌;5.型号
8477.5	-其他模塑或成型机器:	1.品名;2.用途;3.功能;4.品牌;5.型号
8477.8000	-其他机器	1.品名;2.用途;3.品牌;4.型号
8477.9000	-零件	1.品名;2.用途(适用机型);3.品牌;4.型号
84.78	本章其他品目未列名的烟草加 工及制作机器:	
8478.1000	-机器	1.品名;2.用途;3.品牌;4.型号
8478.9000	-零件	1.品名;2.用途(适用机型);3.品牌;4.型号
84.79	本章其他品目未列名的具有独 立功能的机器及机械器具:	
8479.1	--公共工程用机器:	1.品名;2.用途;3.功能;4.品牌;5.型号
8479.2000	-提取、加工动物油脂或植物固 定油脂的机器	1.品名;2.用途;3.功能;4.品牌;5.型号
8479.3000	-木碎料板或木纤维板的挤压 机及其他木材或软木处理机	1.品名;2.用途;3.功能;4.品牌;5.型号
8479.4000	-绳或缆的制造机器	1.品名;2.用途;3.功能;4.品牌;5.型号
8479.5	-未列名工业机器人:	1.品名;2.用途;3.功能;4.品牌;5.型号
8479.6000	-蒸发式空气冷却器	1.品名;2.用途;3.功能;4.品牌;5.型号
8479.7	-旅客登机(船)桥	1.品名;2.用途;3.功能;4.品牌;5.型号
8479.8	-其他机器及机械器具:	1.品名;2.用途;3.功能;4.品牌;5.型号
8479.9	-零件:	1.品名;2.用途(适用机型);3.品牌;4.型号
84.80	金属铸造用型箱;型模底板;阳模;金属用型模(锭模除外)硬质合金、玻璃、矿物材料、橡胶或塑料用型模:	
8480.1000	-金属铸造用型箱	1.品名;2.用途;3.适用材料;4.品牌;5.型号
8480.2000	-型模底板	1.品名;2.用途;3.适用材料;4.品牌;5.型号
8480.3000	-阳模	1.品名;2.用途;3.适用材料;4.品牌;5.型号
8480.4	-金属、硬质合金用型模:	1.品名;2.用途;3.适用材料;4.品牌;5.型号;6.原理
8480.5000	-玻璃用型模	1.品名;2.用途;3.适用材料;4.品牌;5.型号
8480.6000	-矿物材料用型模	1.品名;2.用途;3.适用材料;4.品牌;5.型号
8480.7	-塑料或橡胶用型模:	1.品名;2.用途;3.适用材料;4.品牌;5.型号;6.原理
84.81	用于管道、锅炉、罐、桶或类 似品的龙头、旋塞、阀门及类似装置,包括减压阀及恒温控制阀:	
8481.1000	-减压阀	1.品名;2.用途;3.品牌;4.型号
8481.2	---油压或气压传动阀:	1.品名;2.用途;3.品牌;4.型号
8481.3000	-止回阀	1.品名;2.用途;3.品牌;4.型号
8481.4000	-安全阀或溢流阀	1.品名;2.用途;3.品牌;4.型号
8481.802	---换向阀:	1.品名;2.用途;3.是否电磁式;4.品牌;5.型号
8481.803	---流量阀:	1.品名;2.用途;3.品牌;4.型号
8481.8040	---其他阀门	1.品名;2.用途;3.品牌;4.型号
8481.8090	---其他	1.品名;2.用途;3.品牌;4.型号
8481.9	-零件:	1.品名;2.用途(适用机型);3.品牌;4.型号
84.82	滚动轴承:	1.品名;2.结构类型;3.用途;4.品牌;5.型号
8482.1	-滚珠轴承:	1.品名;2.结构类型;3.用途;4.品牌;5.型号
8482.2000	-锥形滚子轴承,包括锥形滚子 组件	1.品名;2.结构类型;3.用途;4.品牌;5.型号
8482.3000	-鼓形滚子轴承	1.品名;2.结构类型;3.用途;4.品牌;5.型号
8482.4000	-滚针轴承	1.品名;2.结构类型;3.用途; 4.滚柱直径长度;5.品牌;6.型号
8482.5000	-其他圆柱形滚子轴承:	1.品名;2.结构类型;3.用途;4.品牌;5.型号
8482.8000	-其他,包括球、柱混合轴承	1.品名;2.结构类型;3.用途;4.品牌;5.型号
8482.9100	--滚珠、滚针及滚柱	1.品名;2.用途(适用机型)3 直径(包括最大、最小及标称直径);4.品牌;5.型号;
8482.9900	--其他	1.品名;2.用途(适用机型);3.品牌;4.型号
84.83	传动轴(包括凸轮轴及曲柄轴及曲柄;轴承座及滑动轴承;齿轮及齿轮传动装置;滚珠或滚子螺杆传动装置;齿轮箱及其他变速装置,包括扭矩变换器;飞轮及滑轮,包括滑轮组 离合器及联轴 器(包括万向节):	
8483.1	-传动轴(包括凸轮轴及曲柄轴)及曲柄:	1.品名;2.用途;3.品牌;4.型号
8483.2000	-装有滚珠或滚子轴承的轴承 座	1.品名;2.注明是否装有滚珠或滚子轴承;3.用途;4.品牌;5.型号

税则号列	商品描述	规范申报要素 / 价格申报要素 / 其他申报要素 / 举例说明
8483.3000	-未装有滚珠或滚子轴承的轴 承座；滑动轴承	1.品名；2.如为轴承座需注明是否带有滚珠或滚子轴承；3.用途；4.品牌；5.型号
8483.4	-齿轮及齿轮传动装置，但单独报验的带齿的轮、链轮及其他传动元件除外；滚珠或滚子螺杆传动装置；齿轮箱及其他变速装置，包括扭矩变换器：	1.品名；2.原理；3.用途；4.品牌；5.型号
8483.5000	-飞轮及滑轮，包括滑轮组	1.品名；2.用途；3.品牌；4.型号
8483.6000	-离合器及联轴器（包括万向节）	1.品名；2.用途；3.品牌；4.型号
8483.9000	-单独报验的带齿的轮、链轮及 其他传动元件；零件	1.品名；2.用途；3.品牌；4.型号
84.84	密封垫或类似接合衬垫，用金属片与其他材料制成或用双层或多层金属片制成；成套或各种不同材料的密封垫或类似接合衬垫，装于袋、套或类似包装内；机械密封件：	
8484.1000	-密封垫或类似接合衬垫，用金属片与其他材料制成或用双层 或多层金属片制成	1.品名；2.组成材料；3.品牌；4.型号
8484.2000	-机械密封件	1.品名；2.结构；3.品牌；4.型号
8484.9000	-其他	1.品名；2.各自构成材料；3.是否成套包装；4.品牌；5.型号
84.86	专用于或主要用于制造半导体 单晶柱或晶圆、半导体器件、集成电路或平板显示器的机器 及装置；本章注释九（三）规 定的机器及装置；零件及附件：	
8486.1	-制造单晶柱或圆片用的机器 及装置：	1.品名；2.用途；3.功能；4.品牌；5.型号
8486.2	-制造半导体器件或集成电路 用的机器及装置：	1.品名；2.用途；3.功能；4.品牌；5.型号
8486.3	-制造平板显示器用的机器及 装置：	1.品名；2.用途；3.功能；4.品牌；5.型号
8486.4	-本章注释九（三）规定的机器及装置：	1.品名；2.用途；3.功能；4.品牌；5.型号
8486.9	-零件及附件：	1.品名；2.用途（适用机型）；3.品牌；4.型号
84.87	本章其他品目未列名的机器零 件，不具有电气接插件、绝缘体、线圈、触点或其他电气器 材特征的：	1.品名；2.用途（适用机型）；3.品牌；4.型号

第八十五章　电机、电气设备及其零件；录音机及放声机、电视图像、声音的录制和重放设备及其零件、附件

【注解】

1、零部件除申报目录规定的要素外，还应申报具体名称，材质和品牌等要素。

2、未制成品、不完整品申报要注明程度。

3、说明举例栏中未包含品牌、型号等内容。

4、旧的机电设备除申报目录规定的要素外，还应申报生产年代、新旧程度、技术规格配置等要素。

税则号列	商品描述	规范申报要素 / 价格申报要素 / 其他申报要素 / 举例说明
85.01	电动机及发电机（不包括发电机组）：	
8501.1010	---玩具用	1.品名；2.用途；3.输出功率；4.品牌；5.型号
8501.109	---其他：	1.品名；2.用途；3.输出功率；4.机座尺寸；5.品牌；6.型号
8501.2000	-交直流两用电动机，输出功率超过 37.5 瓦	1.品名；2.用途；3.是否为交直流两用；4.输出功率；5.品牌；6.型号
8501.3	-其他直流电动机；直流发电机	1.品名；2.是否为直流；3.输出功率；4.品牌；5.型号
8501.4000	-其他单相交流电动机	1.品名；2.是否为单相交流；3.输出功率；4.品牌；5.型号
8501.5	-其他多相交流电动机：	1.品名；2.输出功率；3.是否为多相电动机；4.品牌；5.型号
8501.6	-交流发电机：	1.品名；2.用途；3.是否为交流；4.输出功率；5.品牌；6.型号
85.02	发电机组及旋转式变流机：	1.品名；2.组成原动机类型；3.输出功率；4.品牌；5.型号
85.03	专用于或主要用于品目 85.01 或 85.02 所列机器的零件：	1.品名；2.用途（适用机型）；3.品牌；4.型号
85.04	变压器、静止式变流器（例如 整流器）及电感器：	
8504.1	-放电灯或放电管用镇流器：	1.品名；2.用途；3.品牌；4.型号
8504.2	-液体介质变压器：	1.品名；2.额定容量；3.是否为液体介质；4.品牌；5.型号

税则号列	商品描述	规范申报要素 / 价格申报要素 / 其他申报要素 / 举例说明
8504.3	-其他变压器:	1.品名;2.额定容量;3.是否为液体介质;4.品牌;5.型号
8504.401	---稳压电源:	1.品名;2.用途;3.类型(交流稳压电源或直流稳压电源);4.功率;5.精度;6.品牌;7.型号
8504.4020	---不间断供电电源	1.品名;2.功率;3.品牌;4.型号
8504.4030	---逆变器	1.品名;2.功率;3.品牌;4.型号
8504.4091	----具有变流功能的半导体模块	1.品名;2.用途;3.是否封装;4.品牌;5.型号
8504.4099	----其他	1.品名;2.用途;3.功率;4.品牌;5.型号
8504.5000	-其他电感器	1.品名;2.用途;3.品牌;4.型号
8504.9	-零件:	1.品名;2.用途(适用机型);3.品牌;4.型号
85.05	电磁铁;永磁铁及磁化后准备 制永磁铁的物品;电磁铁或永 磁铁卡盘、夹具及类似的工件 夹具;电磁联轴节、离合器及制动器;电磁起重吸盘:	
8505.1110	---稀土永磁体	1.品名;2.用途;3.材质;4.品牌;5.型号;6.稀土元素的重量百分比以[A]表示
8505.1190	---其他	1.品名;2.用途;3.材质;4.品牌;5.型号
8505.1900	--其他	1.品名;2.用途;3.材质;4.品牌;5.型号
8505.2000	-电磁联轴节、离合器及制动器	1.品名;2.用途;3.品牌;4.型号
8505.9	-其他,包括零件:	1.品名;2.用途;3.原理;4.品牌;5.型号
85.06	原电池及原电池组:	
8506.1011	----扣式	1.品名;2.用途;3.材质;4.形状;5.品牌;6.型号;7.容量;8.是否含汞
8506.1012	----圆柱型	1.品名;2.用途;3.材质;4.形状;5.品牌;6.型号;7.容量;8.是否含汞
8506.1019	----其他	1.品名;2.用途;3.材质;4.品牌;5.型号;6.容量;7.是否含汞
8506.1090	---其他	1.品名;2.用途;3.材质;4.品牌;5.型号;6.容量;7.是否含汞
8506.3000	-氧化汞的	1.品名;2.用途;3.材质;4.品牌;5.型号;6.容量;7.是否含汞
8506.4000	-氧化银的	1.品名;2.用途;3.材质;4.品牌;5.型号;6.容量;7.是否含汞
8506.5000	-锂的	1.品名;2.用途;3.材质;4.品牌;5.型号;6.容量;7.是否含汞
8506.6000	-锌空气的	1.品名;2.用途;3.材质;4.品牌;5.型号;6.容量;7.是否含汞
8506.8000	-其他原电池及原电池组	1.品名;2.用途;3.材质;4.品牌;5.型号;6.容量;7.是否含汞
8506.9	-零件:	1.品名;2.用途(适用机型);3.品牌;4.型号
85.07	蓄电池,包括隔板,不论是否 矩形(包括正方形):	
8507.1000	-铅酸蓄电池,用于启动活塞式发动机	1.品名;2.用途;3.材质;4.品牌;5.型号;6.容量;7.是否含汞;8.额定电压
8507.2000	-其他铅酸蓄电池	1.品名;2.用途;3.材质;4.品牌;5.型号;6.容量;7.是否含汞;8.额定电压
8507.3000	-镍镉蓄电池	1.品名;2.用途;3.材质;4.品牌;5.型号;6.容量;7.是否含汞;8.额定电压
8507.4000	-镍铁蓄电池	1.品名;2.用途;3.材质;4.品牌;5.型号;6.容量;7.是否含汞;8.额定电压
8507.5000	-镍氢蓄电池	1.品名;2.用途;3.材质;4.品牌;5.型号;6.容量;7.是否含汞;8.额定电压
8507.6000	-锂离子蓄电池	1.品名;2.用途;3.材质;4.品牌;5.型号;6.容量;7.是否含汞;8.额定电压
8507.8	-其他蓄电池:	1.品名;2.用途;3.材质;4.品牌;5.型号;6.容量;7.是否含汞;8.额定电压
8507.9	-零件:	1.品名;2.用途(适用机型);3.品牌;4.型号
85.08	真空吸尘器:	
8508.1	-电动的:	1.品名;2.驱动方式;3.集尘器容积;4.品牌;5.型号;6.功率
8508.6000	-其他真空吸尘器	1.品名;2.驱动方式;3.品牌;4.型号
8508.7	-零件:	1.品名;2.用途(适用机型);3.品牌;4.型号
85.09	家用电动器具,品目 85.08 的 真空吸尘器除外:	
8509.4	-食品研磨机及搅拌器;水果 或蔬菜的榨汁机:	1.品名;2.用途;3.机重;4.功率;5.品牌;6.型号
8509.8	-其他器具:	1.品名;2.用途;3.机重;4.功率;5.品牌;6.型号
8509.9000	-零件	1.品名;2.用途(适用机型);3.品牌;4.型号
85.10	电动剃须刀、电动毛发推剪及 电动脱毛器:	
8510.1000	-剃须刀	1.品名;2.用途;3.品牌;4.型号
8510.2000	-毛发推剪	1.品名;2.用途;3.品牌;4.型号
8510.3000	-脱毛器	1.品名;2.用途;3.品牌;4.型号
8510.9000	-零件	1.品名;2.用途(适用机型);3.品牌;4.型号
85.11	点燃式或压燃式内燃发动机用的电点火及电启动装置(例如,点火磁电机、永磁直流发电机、点火线圈、火花塞、电热塞及启动电机);附属于上 述内燃发动机的发电机(例 如,直流发电机、交流发电机及断流器:	

税则号列	商　品　描　述	规范申报要素 / 价格申报要素 / 其他申报要素 / 举例说明
8511.1000	-火花塞	1. 品名;2. 用途;3. 功能;4. 生产件的通用零件编号后加注"/TY";5. 成套散件装配后完整品的零部件的编号;6. 品牌;7. 型号;8. 零部件完整编号并在前加注"S/"、"W/"或"WF/"之一(生产件填报"S/",品牌和适用的整车厂牌一致的维修件填报"W/",品牌和适用的整车厂牌不一致的维修件的填报"WF/")
8511.2	-点火磁电机;永磁直流发电 机;磁飞轮:	1. 品名;2. 用途;3. 功能;4. 品牌;5. 型号
8511.3	--分电器;点火线圈:	1. 品名;2. 用途;3. 功能;4. 品牌;5. 型号
8511.4010	---机车、航空器及船舶用	1. 品名;2. 用途;3. 功能;4. 品牌;5. 型号
8511.409	---其他:	1. 品名;2. 用途;3. 功能;4. 适用发动机的输出功率;5. 品牌;6. 型号
8511.5	-其他发电机:	1. 品名;2. 用途;3. 功能;4. 品牌;5. 型号
8511.8000	-其他装置	1. 品名;2. 用途;3. 功能;4. 品牌;5. 型号
8511.9	-零件:	1. 品名;2. 用途(适用机型);3. 品牌;4. 型号
85.12	自行车或机动车辆用的电气 照明或信号装置(品目 85.39 的物品除外)、风挡刮水器、除霜器及去雾器:	
8512.2	-机动车辆用照明装置	1. 品名;2. 用途;3. 功能;4. 生产件的通用零件编号后加注"/TY";5. 成套散件装配后完整品的零部件的编号;6. 品牌;7. 型号;8. 零部件完整编号并在前加注"S/"、"W/"或"WF/"之一(生产件填报"S/",品牌和适用的整车厂牌一致的维修件填报"W/",品牌和适用的整车厂牌不一致的维修件的填报"WF/")
8512.3	-机动车辆用喇叭、蜂鸣器	1. 品名;2. 用途;3. 功能;4. 生产间的通用零件编号后加注"/TY";5. 成套散件装配后完整品的零部件的编号;6. 品牌;7. 型号;8. 零部件完整编号并在前加注"S/"、"W/"或"WF/"之一(生产件填报"S/",品牌和适用的整车厂牌一致的维修件填报"W/",品牌和适用的整车厂牌不一致的维修件的填报"WF/");
8512.4000	-车辆风档刮水器、除霜器及去雾器	1. 品名;2. 用途;3. 功能;4. 生产间的通用零件编号后加注"/TY";5. 成套散件装配后完整品的零部件的编号;6. 品牌;7. 型号;8. 零部件完整编号并在前加注"S/"、"W/"或"WF/"之一(生产件填报"S/",品牌和适用的整车厂牌一致的维修件填报"W/",品牌和适用的整车厂牌不一致的维修件的填报"WF/");
8512.9000	-税号 85.12 所列装置的零件	1. 品名;2. 用途;3. 功能;4. 生产间的通用零件编号后加注"/TY";6. 成套散件装配后完整品的零部件的编号;6. 品牌;7. 型号;8. 零部件完整编号并在前加注"S/"、"W/"或"WF/"之一(生产件填报"S/",品牌和适用的整车厂牌一致的维修件填报"W/",品牌和适用的整车厂牌不一致的维修件的填报"WF/");
85.13	自供能源(例如,使用干电池蓄电池、永磁发电机)的手提 式电灯,但品目 85.12 的照明 装置除外:	
8513.1	-灯:	1. 品名;2. 是否手提式;3. 品牌;4. 型号
8513.9	-零件:	1. 品名;2. 用途(适用机型);3. 品牌;4. 型号
85.14	工业或实验室用电炉及电烘 箱(包括通过感应的或电介质 的);工业或实验室用其他通过感应或介质损耗对材料进行热处理的设备:	
8514.1	-电阻加热的炉及烘箱:	1. 品名;2. 用途(工业用或实验室用);3. 加热原理;4. 品牌;5. 型号
8514.2000	-通过感应或介质损耗工作的 炉及烘箱	1. 品名;2. 用途(工业用或实验室用);3. 加热原理;4. 品牌;5. 型号
8514.3000	-其他炉及烘箱	1. 品名;2. 用途(工业用或实验室用);3. 加热原理;4. 品牌;5. 型号
8514.4000	-其他通过感应或介质损耗对材料进行热处理的设备	1. 品名;2. 用途(工业用或实验室用);3. 加热原理;4. 品牌;5. 型号
8514.9	-零件:	1. 品名;2. 用途(适用机型);3. 品牌;4. 型号
85.15	电气(包括电热气体)、激光 其他光、光子束、超声波、电 子束、磁脉冲或等离子弧焊接 机器及装置,不论是否兼有切割功能;用于热喷金属或金属陶瓷的电气机器及装置:	
8515.1	-钎焊机器及装置:	1. 品名;2. 原理;3. 品牌;4. 型号
8515.2	-电阻焊接机器及装置:	1. 品名;2. 原理;3. 是否为全自动或半自动;4. 品牌;5. 型号
8515.3	-电弧(包括等离子弧)焊接 机器及装置:	1. 品名;2. 原理;3. 是否为全自动或半自动;4. 品牌;5. 型号
8515.8	-其他机器及装置	1. 品名;2. 原理;3. 品牌;4. 型号;
8515.9000	-零件 电热的快速热水器、储存式热 水器、浸入式液体加热器;电 气空间加热器及土壤加热器;	1. 品名;2. 用途(适用机型);3. 品牌;4. 型号

税则号列	商品描述	规范申报要素／价格申报要素／其他申报要素／举例说明
85.16	电热的理发器具(例如,电吹风机、电卷发器、电热发钳)及干手器;电熨斗;其他家用电热器具;加热电阻器,但品目85.45的货品除外:	
8516.1010	---储存式电热水器	1.品名;2.工作方式(储存式、即热式、浸入式);3.加热原理;4.品牌;5.型号;6.容量
8516.1020	---即热式电热水器	1.品名;2.工作方式(储存式、即热式、浸入式);3.加热原理;4.品牌;5.型号
8516.1090	---其他	1.品名;2.工作方式(储存式、即热式、浸入式);3.加热原理;4.品牌;5.型号
8516.2	-电气空间加热器及土壤加热器:	1.品名;2.用途;4.加热原理;4.品牌;5.型号
8516.3	-电热的理发器具及干手器:	1.品名;2.用途;4.加热原理;4.品牌;5.型号
8516.4000	-电熨斗	1.品名;2.用途;4.加热原理;4.品牌;5.型号
8516.5000	-微波炉	1.品名;2.用途;4.加热原理;4.品牌;5.型号
8516.6	-其他炉;电锅、电热板、加热环、烧烤炉及烘烤器:	1.品名;2.用途;4.加热原理;4.品牌;5.型号
8516.7	-其他电热器具:	1.品名;2.用途;4.加热原理;4.品牌;5.型号
8516.8000	-加热电阻器	1.品名;2.用途;3.品牌;4.型号
8516.9	-零件:	1.品名;2.用途(适用机型);3.品牌;4.型号
85.17	电话机,包括用于蜂窝网络或其他无线网络的电话机;其他发送或接收声音、图象或其他数据用的设备,包括有线或无线网络(例如,局域网或广播网)的通信设备,品目84.4385.25、85.27或85.28的发送或接收设备除外:	
8517.1	-电话机,包括蜂窝网络或其他无线网络的电话机:	1.品名;2.用途;3.适用网络种类(蜂窝网络、无线网络、有线网络、以太网等);4.品牌;5.型号;6.是否加密。注:西门子家用无绳加密电话机,型号60li
8517.61	--基站:	1.品名;2.用途;3.品牌;4.型号;5.是否加密
8517.621	---数字式程控电话或电报交换机:	1.品名;2.用途;3.控制方式;4.处理信号的类型;5.型号
8517.622	---光通讯设备:	1.品名;2.用途;3.通讯方式;4.品牌;5.型号;6.是否加密
8517.623	---其他有线数字通信设备:	1.品名;2.用途;3.功能;4.品牌;5.型号
8517.629	---其他:	1.品名;2.用途;3.功能;4.品牌;5.型号
8517.69	--其他:	1.品名;2.用途;3.品牌;4.型号
8517.7	-零件:	1.品名;2.用途(适用机型);3.品牌;4.型号
85.18	传声器(麦克风)及其座架;扬声器,不论是否装成音箱;耳机、耳塞,不论是否装有传声器,由传声器及一个或多个扬声器组成的组合机;音频扩大器;电气扩音机组:	
8518.1000	-传声器(麦克风)及其座驾	1.品名2.品牌;3.型号
8518.2100	--单喇叭音箱	1.品名;2.结构类型(是否有箱体);3.额定功率;4.用途;5.品牌;6.型号
8518.2200	--多喇叭音箱	1.品名;2.结构类型(是否有箱体);3.额定功率;4.用途;5.品牌;6.型号;7.喇叭数量和尺寸
8518.2900	--其他	1.品名;2.结构类型(是否有箱体);3.额定功率;4.用途;5.品牌;6.型号
8518.3000	-耳机、耳塞机,不论是否装有传声器,由传声器及一个或多个扬声器组成的组合机	1.品名2.品牌;3.型号
8518.4000	-音频扩大器	1.品名2.品牌;3.型号
8518.5000	-电气扩音机组	1.品名;2.组成部件;3.品牌;4.型号
8518.9000	-零件	1.品名;2.用途(适用机型);3.品牌;4.型号
85.19	声音录制或重放设备,未装有声音录制装置:	
8519.2000	-用硬币、钞票、银行卡、代币或其他支付方式使其工作的设备	1.品名;2.支付方式;3.品牌;4.型号
8519.3000	-转盘(唱机唱盘)	1.品名2.品牌;3.型号
8519.5000	-电话应答机	1.品名2.品牌;3.型号
8519.8	-其他设备:	1.品名;2.使用媒介;3.品牌;4.型号
85.21	视频信号录制或重放设备,不论是否装有高频调谐器:	
8521.1	-磁带型:	1.品名;2.用途;3.使用媒介;4.品牌;5.型号
8521.9011	----视频高密光盘机VCD	1.品名;2.使用媒介;3.类型;4.品牌;5.型号
8521.9012	----数字化视频光盘机DVD	1.品名;2.使用媒介;3.类型;4.品牌;5.型号。注:松下DVD播放机,型号S98
8521.9019	----其他激光视盘放像机	1.品名;2.使用媒介;3.类型;4.品牌;5.型号

税则号列	商品描述	规范申报要素 / 价格申报要素 / 其他申报要素 / 举例说明
8521.9090	----其他视频信号录制或重放设备	1.品名;2.使用媒介;3.类型;4.品牌;5.型号
85.22	专用于或主要用于品目85.19或85.21所列设备的零件、附件:	1.品名;2.用途(适用机型);3.品牌;4.型号
85.23	录制声音或其他信息用的圆盘、磁带、固态非易失性数据存储器件、"智能卡"及其他媒体,不论是否已录制,包括供复制圆盘用的母片及母带,但不包括第三十七章的产品:	
8523.21	--磁条卡:	1.品名;2.用途;3.是否录制;4.品牌;5.型号;6.录制内容类型
8523.291	---磁盘:	1.品名;2.用途;3.是否录制;4.品牌;5.型号;6.录制内容类型
8523.292	---磁带:	1.品名;2.用途;3.是否录制;4.磁带宽度;5.品牌;6.型号;7.录制内容类型
8523.2990	---其他	1.品名;2.用途;3.是否录制;4.品牌;5.型号;6.录制内容类型
8523.4	-光学媒体:	1.品名;2.用途;3.是否录制;4.录制内容类型;5.品牌;6.型号;7.存储容量;8.读取速度
8523.51	--固态非易失性存储器件(闪速存储器):	1.品名;2.用途;3.是否录制;4.品牌;5.型号;6.容量
8523.52	--"智能卡":	1.品名;2.用途;3.是否录制;4.品牌;5.型号;6.是否加密;7.存储速度;8.用途
8523.59	--其他:	1.品名;2.用途;3.是否录制;4.品牌;5.型号;6.容量
8523.8	-其他:	1.品名;2.用途;3.是否录制;4.品牌;5.型号;6.容量
85.25	无线电广播、电视发送设备,不论是否装有接收装置或声音的录制、重放装置;电视摄像机、数字照相机及视频摄录一体机:	
8525.5000	-发送设备	1.品名;2.用途;4.品牌;5.型号
8525.6	-装有接收装置的发送设备:	1.品名;2.用途;3.结构组成;4.品牌;5.型号
8525.801	---电视摄像机:	1.品名;2.用途;3.品牌;4.型号
8525.8021	----特种用途的	1.品名;2.用途;3.品牌;4.型号
8525.8022	----非特种用途的单镜头反光型	1.品名;2.用途;3.品牌;4.型号
8525.8025	----非特种用途的,其他可换镜头的	1.品名;2.用途;3.品牌;4.型号
8525.8029	----非特种用途的其他类型	1.品名;2.用途;3.品牌;4.型号;5.像素
8525.803	---视频摄录一体机:	1.品名;2.用途;3.品牌;4.型号
85.26	雷达设备、无线电导航设备及无线电遥控设备:	
8526.1	-雷达设备:	1.品名;2.用途;3.品牌;4.型号
8526.91	--无线电导航设备:	1.品名;2.用途;3.品牌;4.型号
8526.9200	--无线电遥控设备 无线电广播接收设备,不论是否与声音的录制、重放装置或	1.品名;2.用途;3.品牌;4.型号;5.控制距离
85.27	时钟组合在同一机壳内:	
8527.1	-不需外接电源的无线电收音机:	1.品名;2.使用媒介(是否为盒式磁带);3.是否需外接电源;4.品牌;5.型号;6.外形尺寸
8527.2	-需外接电源的汽车用无线电收音机:	1.品名;2.用途;3.结构组成;4.品牌;5.型号
8527.9	-其他:	1.品名;2.用途;3.品牌;4.型号
85.28	监视器及投影机,未装电视接收装置;电视接收装置,不论是否装有无线电收音装置或声音、图像的录制或重放装置:	
8528.4100	--专用于或主要用于品目84.71的自动数据处理系统的	1.品名;2.用途;3.显示原理;4.显示屏幕尺寸;5.接口类型(包括接口电路);6.品牌;7.型号
8528.49	--其他:	1.品名;2.用途;3.显示原理;4.显示屏幕尺寸;5.品牌;6.型号
8528.5110	---液晶的	1.品名;2.用途;3.显示原理;4.显示屏幕尺寸;5.接口类型(包括接口电路);6.构成(是否带标记板、解码板或高频头板等信号处理板);7.品牌;8.型号
8528.5190	---其他	1.品名;2.用途;3.显示原理;4.显示屏幕尺寸;5.接口类型(包括接口电路);6.品牌;7.型号
8528.5910	---彩色的	1.品名;2.用途;3.显示原理;4.显示屏幕尺寸;5.品牌;6.型号;7.最高分辨率
8528.5990	---单色的	1.品名;2.用途;3.显示原理;4.显示屏幕尺寸;5.品牌;6.型号
8528.6100	--专用于或主要用于品目84.71的自动数据处理系统的	1.品名;2.用途;3.显示原理;4.接口类型(包括接口电路);5.品牌;6.型号;7.亮度

税则号列	商　品　描　述	规范申报要素 / 价格申报要素 / 其他申报要素 / 举例说明
8528.69	--其他:	1.品名;2.用途;3.显示原理;4.接口类型(包括接口电路);5.品牌;6.型号;7.亮度
8528.71	--在设计上不带有视频显示 器或屏幕的:	1.品名;2.用途;3.是否带显示屏;4.品牌;5.型号
8528.72	--其他,彩色的:	1.品名;2.用途;3.显示原理;4.显示屏幕尺寸;5.品牌;6.型号
8528.7300	--其他,单色的	1.品名;2.用途;3.显示原理;4.显示屏幕尺寸;5.品牌;6.型号
85.29	专用于或主要用于品目 85.25 至 85.28 所列装置或设备的零件:	
8529.1	-各种天线或天线反射器及其 零件:	1.品名;2.用途(适用机型);3.品牌;4.型号
8529.9010	---电视发送、差转设备及卫 星电视地面接收转播设备用	1.品名;2.用途(适用机型);3.品牌;4.型号
8529.9041	----特种用途的	1.品名;2.用途(适用机型);3.品牌;4.型号
8529.9042	----非特种用途的取像模块	1.品名;2.用途(适用机型);3.是否带有数字信号处理电路;4.品牌;5.型号
8529.9049	----其他	1.品名;2.用途(适用机型);3.品牌;4.型号
8529.9050	---雷达设备及无线电导航设 备用	1.品名;2.用途(适用机型);3.品牌;4.型号
8529.9060	---无线电收音机及其组合机用	1.品名;2.用途(适用机型);3.品牌;4.型号
8529.908	---电视接收机用(高频调谐 器除外):	1.品名;2.用途(适用机型);3.品牌;4.型号
8529.9090	---其他	1.品名;2.用途(适用机型);3.品牌;4.型号
85.30	铁道、电车道、道路或内河航道、停车场、港口或机场用的 电气信号、安全或交通管理设备(品目 86.08 的货品除外)	
8530.1000	-铁道或电车道用的设备	1.品名;2.用途;3.品牌;4.型号
8530.8000	-其他设备	1.品名;2.用途;3.品牌;4.型号
8530.9000	-零件	1.品名;2.用途(适用机型);3.品牌;4.型号
85.31	电气音响或视觉信号装置(例 如,电铃、电笛、显示板、防 盗或防火报警器),但品目 85.12 或 85.30 的货品除外:	
8531.1000	-防盗或防火报警器及类似装置	1.品名;2.用途;3.品牌;4.型号;5.工作原理
8531.2000	-装有液晶装置(LCD)或发光 二极管(LED)的显示板	1.品名;2.用途;3.显示原理;4.品牌;5.型号;6.规格尺寸
8531.8	-其他装置:	1.品名;2.用途;3.品牌;4.型号
8531.9	-零件:	1.品名;2.用途(适用机型);3.品牌;4.型号
85.32	固定、可变或可调(微调)电 容器:	
8532.1000	-固定电容器,用于 50/60 赫 兹电路,其额定无功功率不低于 0.5 千瓦(电力电容器)	1.品名;2.用途;3.额定无功功率;4.适用频率;5.品牌;6.型号
8532.2	-其他固定电容器:	1.品名;2.结构类型(单层;多层等);3.介质类型;4.是否片式;5.品牌;6.型号
8532.3000	-可变或可调(微调)电容器	1.品名;2.是否可变、可调;3.品牌;4.型号
8532.9	-零件:	1.品名;2.用途(适用机型);3.品牌;4.型号
85.33	电阻器(包括变阻器及电位 器),但加热电阻器除外:	
8533.1000	-固定碳质电阻器,合成或薄 膜式	1.品名;2.结构类型;3.介质;4.品牌;5.型号
8533.2	-其他固定电阻器:	1.品名;2.额定功率;3.结构类型(片式、线绕式等);4.品牌;5.型号
8533.3	-线绕可变电阻器,包括电阻 器及电位器:	1.品名;2.额定功率;3.结构类型(片式、线绕式等);4.品牌;5.型号
8533.4000	-其他可变电阻器,包括变阻 器及电位器	1.品名 2.品牌;3.型号
8533.9000	-零件	1.品名;2.用途(适用机型);3.品牌;4.型号
85.34	印刷电路:	1.品名;2.电路层数;3.品牌;4.型号
85.35	电路的开关、保护或连接用的 电气装置(例如,开关、熔断 器、避雷器、电压限幅器、电涌抑制器、插头及其他连接 器、接线盒),用于电压超过 1000 伏的线路:	1.品名;2.用途;3.电压;4.品牌;5.型号
85.36	电路的开关、保护或连接用的 电器装置(例如,开关、继电器、熔断器、电涌抑制器、插头、插座、灯座及其他连接器 接线盒),用于电压不超过 1000 伏的线路;光导纤维、光导纤维束或光缆用连接器:	
8536.1000	-熔断器	1.品名;2.用途;3.电压;4.品牌;5.型号
8536.2000	-自动断路器	1.品名;2.用途;3.电压;4.品牌;5.型号
8536.3000	-其他电路保护装置	1.品名;2.用途;3.电压;4.品牌;5.型号
8536.4	-继电器:	1.品名;2.用途;3.电压;4.品牌;5.型号
8536.5000	-其他开关	1.品名;2.用途;3.电压;4.品牌;5.型号

税则号列	商品描述	规范申报要素 / 价格申报要素 / 其他申报要素 / 举例说明
8536.6	-灯座、插头及插座：	1.品名;2.用途;3.电压;4.品牌;5.型号
8536.7000	-光导纤维、光导纤维束或光缆用连接器	1.品名;2.用途;3.品牌;4.型号
8536.9000	-其他装置	1.品名;2.用途;3.电压;4.品牌;5.型号
85.37	用于电气控制或电力分配的盘、板、台、柜及其他基座，装有两个或多个品目85.35或85.36所列的装置，包括装有第九十章所列的仪器或装置，以及数控装置，但品目85.17的交换机除外：	1.品名;2.用途;3.原理;4.电压;5.品牌;6.型号
85.38	专用于或主要用于品目85.35、85.36或85.37所列装置的零件：	1.品名;2.用途(适用机型);3.品牌;4.型号
85.39	白炽灯泡、放电灯管，包括封闭式聚光灯及紫外线灯管或红外线灯泡；弧光灯：	
8539.1000	-封闭式聚光灯	1.品名;2.用途;3.类型;4.品牌;5.型号
8539.21	--卤钨灯：	1.品名;2.用途;3.类型;4.品牌;5.型号
8539.22	--其他灯，功率不超过200瓦但额定电压超过100伏：	1.品名;2.用途;3.类型;4.功率;5.额定电压;6.品牌;7.型号
8539.29	--其他：	1.品名;2.用途;3.类型;4.功率;5.额定电压;6.品牌;7.型号
8539.3	-放电灯管，但紫外线灯管除外	1.品名;2.用途;3.类型;4.品牌;5.型号
8539.4	-紫外线灯管或红外线灯泡；弧光灯：	1.品名;2.用途;3.类型;4.品牌;5.型号
8539.9000	-零件	1.品名;2.用途(适用机型);3.品牌;4.型号
85.40	热电子管、冷阴极管或光阴极管(例如，真空管或充气管、汞弧整流管、阴极射线管、电视摄像管)：	
8540.1	-阴极射线电视显像管，包括视频监视器用阴极射线管：	1.品名;2.原理;3.品牌;4.型号
8540.2	-电视摄像管；变像管及图像增强管；其他光阴极管：	1.品名;2.原理;3.品牌;4.型号
8540.4010	---彩色的数据/图形显示管，屏幕荧光点间距小于0.4毫米	1.品名;2.是否彩色;3.荧光点距;4.品牌;5.型号
8540.4020	---单色的数据/图形显示管	1.品名;2.是否单色;3.荧光点距;4.品牌;5.型号
8540.6	-其他阴极射线管：	1.品名;2.用途;3.类型;4.品牌;5.型号
8540.7	-微波管(例如，磁控管、速调管、行波管、返波管)，但不包括栅控管：	1.品名;2.用途;3.类型;4.品牌;5.型号
8540.8	-其他管：	1.品名;2.用途;3.类型;4.品牌;5.型号
8540.9	-零件：	1.品名;2.用途(适用机型);4.品牌;5.型号
85.41	二极管、晶体管及类似的半导体器件；光敏半导体器件，包括不论是否装在组件内或组装成块的光电池；发光二极管；已装配的压晶体：	
8541.1000	-二极管，但光敏二极管或发光二极管除外	1.品名2.品牌;3.型号
8541.2	-晶体管，但光敏晶体管除外	1.品名;2.耗散功率;3.品牌;4.型号
8541.3000	-半导体开关元件、两端交流开关元件及三端双向可控硅开关元件，但光敏器件除外	1.品名;2.类型;3.是否由多个半导体元件构成;4.品牌;5.型号
8541.4010	---发光二极管	1.品名2.品牌;3.型号
8541.4020	---太阳能电池	1.品名;2.额定功率;3.品牌;4.型号;5.转换效率
8541.4090	---其他	1.品名2.品牌;3.型号
8541.5000	-其他半导体器件	1.品名;2.类型;3.是否由多个半导体元件构成;4.品牌;5.型号
8541.6000	-已装配的压电晶体	1.品名;2.是否已装配;3.品牌;4.型号
8541.9000	-零件	1.品名;2.用途(适用机型);3.品牌;4.型号
85.42	集成电路：	
8542.3100	--集成电路处理器及控制器，不论是否带有存储器、转换器、逻辑电路、放大器、时钟及时序电路或其他电路	1.品名;2.用途;3.功能;4.品牌;5.型号;6.批号
8542.3200	--集成电路存储器	1.品名;2.用途;3.功能;4.品牌;5.型号;6.批号;7.容量
8542.3300	--集成电路放大器	1.品名;2.用途;3.功能;4.品牌;5.型号;6.批号
8542.3900	--其他集成电路	1.品名;2.用途;3.功能;4.品牌;5.型号;6.批号
8542.9000	-集成电路的零件	1.品名;2.用途(适用机型);3.品牌;4.型号
85.43	本章其他品目未列名的具有独立功能的电气设备及装置：	

税则号列	商品描述	规范申报要素 / 价格申报要素 / 其他申报要素 / 举例说明
8543.1000	-粒子加速器：	1.品名;2.用途;3.功能;4.品牌;5.型号
8543.2	-信号发生器	1.品名;2.用途;3.功能;4.输出信号频率范围;5.品牌;6.型号
8543.3000	-电镀、电解或电泳设备及装 置	1.品名;2.用途;3.功能;4.品牌;5.型号
8543.7	-其他设备及装置：	1.品名;2.用途;3.功能;4.品牌;5.型号
8543.9	-零件：	1.品名;2.用途(适用机型);3.品牌;4.型号
85.44	绝缘(包括漆包或阳极化处理)电线、电缆(包括同轴电缆)及其他绝缘电导体，不论是否有接头；由每根被覆光纤组成的光缆，不论是否与电导体装配或装有接头：	
8544.1	-绕组电线：	1.品名;2.用途;3.材质;4.品牌;5.型号
8544.2000	-同轴电缆及其他同轴电导体	1.品名;2.用途;3.结构类型(同轴、有接头等);4.品牌;5.型号
8544.3	-车辆、航空器、船舶用点火布线组及其他布线组：	1.品名;2.用途;3.结构类型(有接头等);4.品牌;5.型号;6.额定电压
8544.4	-其他电导体，额定电压不超 过 1000 伏：	1.品名;2.用途;3.结构类型(有接头等);4.品牌;5.型号;6.额定电压
8544.6	-其他电导体，额定电压超过 1000 伏：	1.品名;2.用途;3.结构类型(有接头等);4.品牌;5.型号;6.额定电压
8544.7000	-光缆	1.品名;2.是否每根光纤被覆;3.品牌;4.型号
85.45	碳电极、碳刷、灯碳棒、电池 碳棒及电气设备用的其他石墨或碳精制品，不论是否带金属：	1.品名;2.用途;3.材质;4.品牌;5.型号
85.46	各种材料制的绝缘子：	1.品名;2.用途;3.材质;4.品牌;5.型号
85.47	电气机器、器具或设备用的绝 缘零件，除了为装配需要而在 模制时装入的小金属零件(例 如螺纹孔)以外，全部用绝缘 材料制成，但税目 85.46 的绝 缘子除外；内衬绝缘材料的贱 金属制线路导管及其接头：	1.品名;2.用途;3.材质;4.品牌;5.型号
85.48	原电池、原电池组及蓄电池的 废碎料；废原电池、废原电池组及废蓄电池；机器或设备的 本章其他税目未列名的电气零件：	1.品名;2.用途;3.品牌;4.型号

第十七类 车辆、航空器、船舶及有关运输设备

第八十六章 铁道及电车道机车、车辆及其零件；铁道及电车道轨道固定装置及其零件、附件各种机械(包括电动机械)交通信号设备

【注解】

1、零部件除申报目录规定的要素外，还应申报具体名称、材质和品牌等要素。

2、未制成品、不完整品申报要注明程度。

3、说明举例栏中未包含品牌、型号等内容。

4、旧的机电设备除申报目录规定的要素外，还应申报生产年代、新旧程度、技术规格、配置等要素。

税则号列	商品描述	规范申报要素 / 价格申报要素 / 其他申报要素 / 举例说明
86.01	铁道电力机车，由外部电力或蓄电池驱动：	1.品名;2.用途;3.驱动装置类型;4.控制装置类型;5.品牌;6.型号
86.02	其他铁道机车；机车煤水车：	
8602.1	-柴油电力机车：	1.品名;2.用途;3.驱动装置类型;4.控制装置类型;5.品牌;6.型号
8602.9000	-其他	1.品名;2.用途;3.驱动装置类型;4.品牌;5.型号
86.03	铁道及电车道用的机动客车、货车、敞车，但税目 86.04 的货品除外：	1.品名;2.用途;3.驱动装置类型;4.品牌;5.型号
86.04	铁道及电车道用的维修或服务车，不论是否机动(例如，工场车、起重机车、道碴捣固车、轨道校正车、检验车及查道车)：	1.品名;2.用途;3.类型;4.品牌;5.型号
86.05	铁道及电车道用的非机动客 车；行李车、邮政车和其他铁道及电车道用的非机动特殊用途车辆(税目 86.04 的货品除外)：	1.品名;2.用途;3.类型;4.品牌;5.型号
86.06	铁道及电车道用的非机动有篷及无篷货车：	1.品名;2.用途;3.类型;4.结构;5.品牌;6.型号

税则号列	商　品　描　述	规范申报要素 / 价格申报要素 / 其他申报要素 / 举例说明
86.07	铁道及电车道机车或其他车辆的零件：	1.品名;2.用途(适用车型);3.品牌;4.型号
86.08	铁道及电车道轨道固定装置及附件;供铁道、电车道、道路、内河航道、停车场、港口或机场用的机械(包括电动机械)信号、安全或交通管理设备;上述货品的零件：	1.品名;2.用途;3.品牌;4.型号
86.09	集装箱(包括运输液体的集装箱),经特殊设计、装备适用于各种运输方式：	1.品名;2.类型(公路等);3.规格尺寸;4.品牌

第八十七章　车辆及其零件、附件,但铁道及电车道车辆除外

【注解】

1、零部件除申报目录规定的要素外,还应申报具体名称、材质和品牌等要素。

2、未制成品、不完整品申报要注明程度。

3、"说明举例"栏中未包含品牌、型号等内容。

4、旧的机电设备除申报目录规定的要素外,还应申报生产年代、新旧程度、技术规格、配置等要素。

税则号列	商　品　描　述	规范申报要素 / 价格申报要素 / 其他申报要素 / 举例说明
87.01	牵引车、拖拉机(税目 87.09 的牵引车除外)：	
8701.1000	-手扶拖拉机	1.品名2.品牌;3.型号
8701.2000	-半挂车用的公路牵引车	1.品名;2.用途;3.品牌;4.型号
8701.3000	-履带式牵引车、拖拉机	1.品名2.品牌;3.结构类型;4.型号
8701.9	-其他：	1.品名;2.结构类型;3.功率;4.用途;5.品牌;6.型号
87.02	客运机动车辆,10 座及以上(包括驾驶座)：	
8702.1020	---机坪客车	1.品名;2.发动机类型(柴油、半柴油、汽油等);3.成套散件请注明;4.厂牌(如与签注名称相同可省略);5.签注名称;6.排气量(毫升);7.规格型号
8702.109	---其他：	1.品名;2.发动机类型(柴油、半柴油、汽油等);3.成套散件请注明;4.座位数;5.厂牌(如与签注名称相同可省略);6.签注名称;7.排气量(毫升);8.规格型号
8702.9	-其他：	1.品名;2.发动机类型(柴油、半柴油、汽油等);3.成套散件请注明;4.座位数;5.厂牌(如与签注名称相同可省略);6.签注名称;7.排气量(毫升);8.规格型号
87.03	主要用于载人的机动车辆(税目 87.02 的货品除外),包括旅行小客车及赛车：	
8703.1011	----全地形车	1.品名;2.发动机类型(柴油、半柴油、汽油等);3.成套散件请注明;4.座位数;5.厂牌(如与签注名称相同可省略);6.签注名称;7.排气量(毫升);8.规格型号
8703.1019	---其他	1.品名;2.发动机类型(柴油、半柴油、汽油等);3.成套散件请注明;4.排气量(毫升);5.厂牌(如与签注名称相同可省略);6.签注名称;7.规格型号
8703.1090	---其他	1.品名;2.发动机类型(柴油、半柴油、汽油等);3.成套散件请注明;4.排气量(毫升);5.厂牌(如与签注名称相同可省略);6.签注名称;7.规格型号
8703.2	-装有点燃往复式活塞内燃发 动机的其他车辆：	1.品名;2.发动机类型(柴油、半柴油、汽油等);3.成套散件请注明;4.座位数;5.厂牌(如与签注名称相同可省略);6.签注名称;7.排气量(毫升);8.规格型号
8703.3	-装有压燃式活塞内燃发动机(柴油或半柴油发动机)的其 他车辆：	1.品名;2.发动机类型(柴油、半柴油、汽油等);3.成套散件请注明;4.座位数;5.厂牌(如与签注名称相同可省略);6.签注名称;7.排气量(毫升);8.规格型号
8703.9000	-其他	1.品名;2.发动机类型(柴油、半柴油、汽油等);3.成套散件请注明;4.座位数;5.厂牌(如与签注名称相同可省略);6.签注名称;7.排气量(毫升);8.规格型号
87.04	货运机动车辆：	
8704.1030	---电动轮货运自卸车	1.品名;2.用途;3.是否为电动轮;4.品牌(厂牌);5.型号
8704.109	---其他	1.品名;2.用途;3.是否为电动轮;4.发动机类型(柴油、半柴油、汽油等);5.品牌(厂牌);6.型号
8704.2	-装有压燃式活塞内燃发动机(柴油或半柴油发动机)的其他 货车：	1.品名;2.发动机类型(柴油、半柴油、汽油等);3.车辆总重;4.品牌(厂牌);5.型号
8704.3	-装有点燃式活塞内燃发动机 的其他货车：	1.品名;2.发动机类型(柴油、半柴油、汽油等);3.车辆总重;4.品牌(厂牌);5.型号

税则号列	商品描述	规范申报要素 / 价格申报要素 / 其他申报要素 / 举例说明
8704.9000	-其他	1. 品名;2. 发动机类型(柴油、半柴油、汽油等);3. 车辆总重;4. 品牌(厂牌);5. 型号
87.05	特殊用途的机动车辆(例如,抢修车、起重车、救火车、混凝土搅拌车、道路清洁车、喷洒车、流动工场车及流动放射线检查车),但主要用于载人或运货的车辆除外:	
8705.1	-起重车:	1. 品名;2. 作业范围(全路面等);3. 最大起重重量;4. 品牌(厂牌);5. 型号
8705.2000	-钻探车	1. 品名 2. 用途;3. 品牌;4. 型号
8705.3	-救火车:	1. 品名;2. 固定安装配置;3. 品牌;4. 型号
8705.4000	-混凝土搅拌车	1. 品名;2. 固定安装配置;3. 品牌;4. 型号
8705.9	-其他:	1. 品名;2. 用途;3. 固定安装配置;4. 品牌(厂牌);5. 型号
87.06	装有发动机的机动车辆底盘,税目 87.01 至 87.05 所列车辆用:	
8706.0010	---非公路用自卸车底盘	1. 品名;2. 适用车型;3. 品牌;4. 型号
8706.002	---货车底盘:	1. 品名;2. 适用车型;3. 车辆总重量;4. 是否带驾驶室;5. 品牌;6. 型号
8706.0030	---大型客车底盘	1. 品名;2. 适用车型;3. 是否带驾驶室;4. 品牌;5. 型号
8706.0040	---汽车起重机底盘	1. 品名;2. 适用车型;3. 是否带驾驶室;4. 品牌;5. 型号
8706.0090	---其他	1. 品名;2. 适用车型;3. 品牌;4. 型号
87.07	机动车辆的车身(包括驾驶室),税目 87.01 至 87.05 所列车辆用:	1. 品名;2. 适用车型;3. 品牌;4. 型号
87.08	机动车辆的零件、附件,税目 87.01 至 87.05 所列车辆用:	
8708.1000	-缓冲器(保险杠)及其零件	1. 品名;2. 成套散件或毛坯请注明;3. 生产件的通用零件编号后加注"/TY";4. 成套散件装配后完整品的零部件的编号;5. 品牌;6. 适用车型;7. 型号;8. 零部件完整编号并在前加注"S/"、"W/"或"WF/"之一(生产件填报"S/",品牌和适用的整车厂牌一致的维修件填报"W/",品牌和适用的整车厂牌不一致的维修件的填报"WF/")
8708.2100	--座椅安全带	1. 品名;2. 成套散件或毛坯请注明;3. 生产件的通用零件编号后加注"/TY";4. 成套散件装配后完整品的零部件的编号;5. 品牌;6. 适用车型;7. 型号;8. 零部件完整编号并在前加注"S/"、"W/"或"WF/"之一(生产件填报"S/",品牌和适用的整车厂牌一致的维修件填报"W/",品牌和适用的整车厂牌不一致的维修件的填报"WF/")
8708.2930	---车窗玻璃升降器	1. 品名;2. 成套散件或毛坯请注明;3. 生产件的通用零件编号后加注"/TY";4. 成套散件装配后完整品的零部件的编号;5. 品牌;6. 适用车型;7. 型号;8. 零部件完整编号并在前加注"S/"、"W/"或"WF/"之一(生产件填报"S/",品牌和适用的整车厂牌一致的维修件填报"W/",品牌和适用的整车厂牌不一致的维修件的填报"WF/")
8708.2941	----电动的	1. 品名;2. 成套散件或毛坯请注明;3. 生产件的通用零件编号前加注"TY";4. 成套散件装配后完整品的零部件的编号;5. 品牌;6. 适用车型;7. 型号;8. 零部件完整编号并在前加注"S/"、"W/"或"WF/"之一(生产件填报"S/",品牌和适用的整车厂牌一致的维修件填报"W/",品牌和适用的整车厂牌不一致的维修件的填报"WF/")
8708.2942	----手动的	1. 品名 2. 品牌;3. 适用车型;4. 型号
8708.295	---其他车身覆盖件:	1. 品名 2. 品牌;3. 适用车型;4. 型号
8708.2990	---其他	1. 品名 2. 品牌;3. 适用车型;4. 型号
8708.3	-制动器、助力制动器及其零件:	1. 品名;2. 适用车型;3. 成套散件或毛坯请注明;4. 生产件的通用零件编号后加注"/TY";5. 成套散件装配后完整品的零部件的编号;6. 品牌;7. 适用车型;8. 零部件完整编号并在前加注"S/"、"W/"或"WF/"之一(生产件填报"S/",品牌和适用的整车厂牌一致的维修件填报"W/",品牌和适用的整车厂牌不一致的维修件的填报"WF/")
8708.4010	---税目 87.01 所列车辆用	1. 品名;2. 适用车型;3. 成套散件或毛坯请注明;4. 生产件的通用零件编号后加注"/TY";5. 成套散件装配后完整品的零部件的编号;6. 品牌;7. 适用车型;8. 零部件完整编号并在前加注"S/"、"W/"或"WF/"之一(生产件填报"S/",品牌和适用的整车厂牌一致的维修件填报"W/",品牌和适用的整车厂牌不一致的维修件的填报"WF/")

税则号列	商　品　描　述	规范申报要素 / 价格申报要素 / 其他申报要素 / 举例说明
8708.4020	---税号 8702.1091 及 8702.9010 所列车辆用	1.品名;2.适用车型;3.成套散件或毛坯请注明;4.生产件的通用零件编号后加注"/TY";5.成套散件装配后完整品的零部件的编号;6.品牌;7.适用车型;8.零部件完整编号并在前加注"S/"、"W/"或"WF/"之一(生产件填报"S/",品牌和适用的整车厂牌一致的维修件填报"W/",品牌和适用的整车厂牌不一致的维修件的填报"WF/")
8708.4030	---税号 8704.1030 及 8704.1090 所列车辆用	1.品名;2.适用车型;3.成套散件或毛坯请注明;4.生产件的通用零件编号后加注"/TY";5.成套散件装配后完整品的零部件的编号;6.品牌;7.适用车型;8.零部件完整编号并在前加注"S/"、"W/"或"WF/"之一(生产件填报"S/",品牌和适用的整车厂牌一致的维修件填报"W/",品牌和适用的整车厂牌不一致的维修件的填报"WF/")
8708.4040	---税号 8704.2100 、8704.2230、8704.3100 及 8704.3230 所列车辆用	1.品名;2.适用车型;3.成套散件或毛坯请注明;4.生产件的通用零件编号后加注"/TY";5.成套散件装配后完整品的零部件的编号;6.品牌;7.适用车型;8.零部件完整编号并在前加注"S/"、"W/"或"WF/"之一(生产件填报"S/",品牌和适用的整车厂牌一致的维修件填报"W/",品牌和适用的整车厂牌不一致的维修件的填报"WF/")
8708.4050	---税号 8704.2240 、8704.2300 及 8704.3240 所列 车辆用	1.品名;2.适用车型;3.成套散件或毛坯请注明;4.生产件的通用零件编号后加注"/TY";5.成套散件装配后完整品的零部件的编号;6.品牌;7.适用车型;8.零部件完整编号并在前加注"S/"、"W/"或"WF/"之一(生产件填报"S/",品牌和适用的整车厂牌一致的维修件填报"W/",品牌和适用的整车厂牌不一致的维修件的填报"WF/")
8708.4060	---税目 87.05 所列车辆用	1.品名;2.适用车型;3.成套散件或毛坯请注明;4.生产件的通用零件编号后加注"/TY";5.成套散件装配后完整品的零部件的编号;6.品牌;7.适用车型;8.零部件完整编号并在前加注"S/"、"W/"或"WF/"之一(生产件填报"S/",品牌和适用的整车厂牌一致的维修件填报"W/",品牌和适用的整车厂牌不一致的维修件的填报"WF/")
8708.409	---其他:	1.品名;2.适用车型;3.原理(是否为4档及4档以下);4.成套散件或毛坯请注明;5.生产件的通用零件编号前加注"/TY";6.成套散件装配后完整品的零部件的编号;7.品牌;8.扭矩;9.型号;10.零部件完整编号并在前加注"S/"、"W/"或"WF/"之一(生产件填报"S/",品牌和适用的整车厂牌一致的维修件填报"W/",品牌和适用的整车厂牌不一致的维修件的填报"WF/")
8708.5071	----税目 87.01 所列车辆用	1.品名;2.适用车型;3.传动部件;4.驱动位置;5.轴荷;6.成套散件或毛坯请注明;7.生产件的通用零件编号前加注"/TY";8.成套散件装配后完整品的零部件的编号;9.品牌;10.型号;11.零部件完整编号并在前加注"S/"、"W/"或"WF/"之一(生产件填报"S/",品牌和适用的整车厂牌一致的维修件填报"W/",品牌和适用的整车厂牌不一致的维修件的填报"WF/")
8708.5072	---- 税号 8702.1091 及 8702.9010 所列车辆用	1.品名;2.适用车型;3.传动部件;4.驱动位置;5.轴荷;6.成套散件或毛坯请注明;7.生产件的通用零件编号前加注"/TY";8.成套散件装配后完整品的零部件的编号;9.品牌;10.型号;11.零部件完整编号并在前加注"S/"、"W/"或"WF/"之一(生产件填报"S/",品牌和适用的整车厂牌一致的维修件填报"W/",品牌和适用的整车厂牌不一致的维修件的填报"WF/")
8708.5073	---- 税号 8704.1030 及 8704.1090 所列车辆用	1.品名;2.适用车型;3.传动部件;4.驱动位置;5.轴荷;6.成套散件或毛坯请注明;7.生产件的通用零件编号前加注"/TY";8.成套散件装配后完整品的零部件的编号;9.品牌;10.型号;11.零部件完整编号并在前加注"S/"、"W/"或"WF/"之一(生产件填报"S/",品牌和适用的整车厂牌一致的维修件填报"W/",品牌和适用的整车厂牌不一致的维修件的填报"WF/")
8708.5074	----税号 8704.2100、8704.2230、8704.3100 及 8704.3230 所列车辆用	1.品名;2.适用车型;3.传动部件;4.驱动位置;5.成套散件或毛坯请注明;6.生产件的通用零件编号前加注"/TY";7.成套散件装配后完整品的零部件的编号;8.品牌;9.型号;10.零部件完整编号并在前加注"S/"、"W/"或"WF/"之一(生产件填报"S/",品牌和适用的整车厂牌一致的维修件填报"W/",品牌和适用的整车厂牌不一致的维修件的填报"WF/")

税则号列	商品描述	规范申报要素 / 价格申报要素 / 其他申报要素 / 举例说明
8708.5075	----税号 8704.2240、8704.25300 及 8704.3240 所列 车辆用	1.品名;2.适用车型;3.传动部件;4.驱动位置;5.成套散件或毛坯请注明;6.生产件的通用零件编号前加注"/TY";7.成套散件装配后完整品的零部件的编号;8.品牌;9.型号;10.零部件完整编号并在前加注"S/"、"W/"或"WF/"之一(生产件填报"S/",品牌和适用的整车厂牌一致的维修件填报"W/",品牌和适用的整车厂牌不一致的维修件的填报"WF/")
8708.5076	----税目 87.05 所列车辆用	1.品名;2.适用车型;3.传动部件;4.驱动位置;5.成套散件或毛坯请注明;6.生产件的通用零件编号前加注"/TY";7.成套散件装配后完整品的零部件的编号;8.品牌;9.型号;10.零部件完整编号并在前加注"S/"、"W/"或"WF/"之一(生产件填报"S/",品牌和适用的整车厂牌一致的维修件填报"W/",品牌和适用的整车厂牌不一致的维修件的填报"WF/")
8708.5079	----其他	1.品名;2.适用车型;3.传动部件;4.成套散件或毛坯请注明;5.生产件的通用零件编号前加注"/TY";6.成套散件装配后完整品的零部件的编号;7.品牌;8.型号;9.零部件完整编号并在前加注"S/"、"W/"或"WF/"之一(生产件填报"S/",品牌和适用的整车厂牌一致的维修件填报"W/",品牌和适用的整车厂牌不一致的维修件的填报"WF/")
8708.508	---非驱动桥及其零件:	1.品名;2.适用车型;3.传动部件;4.成套散件或毛坯请注明;5.生产件的通用零件编号前加注"/TY";6.成套散件装配后完整品的零部件的编号;7.品牌;8.型号;9.零部件完整编号并在前加注"S/"、"W/"或"WF/"之一(生产件填报"S/",品牌和适用的整车厂牌一致的维修件填报"W/",品牌和适用的整车厂牌不一致的维修件的填报"WF/")
8708.7	-车轮及其零件、附件:	1.品名;2.材质;3.适用车型;4.成套散件或毛坯请注明;5.生产件的通用零件编号前加注"/TY";6.成套散件装配后完整品的零部件的编号;7.车轮尺寸;8.品牌;9.型号;10.零部件完整编号并在前加注"S/"、"W/"或"WF/"之一(生产件填报"S/",品牌和适用的整车厂牌一致的维修件填报"W/",品牌和适用的整车厂牌不一致的维修件的填报"WF/")
8708.8	-悬挂系统及其零件(包括减震 器):	1.品名;2.适用车型;3.成套散件或毛坯请注明;4.生产件的通用零件编号前加注"/TY";5.成套散件装配后完整品的零部件的编号;7.品牌;8.型号;9.零部件完整编号并在前加注"S/"、"W/"或"WF/"之一(生产件填报"S/",品牌和适用的整车厂牌一致的维修件填报"W/",品牌和适用的整车厂牌不一致的维修件的填报"WF/")
8708.91	--散热器及其零件:	1.品名;2.适用车型;3.成套散件或毛坯请注明;4.生产件的通用零件编号前加注"/TY";5.成套散件装配后完整品的零部件的编号;6.品牌;7.型号;8.零部件完整编号并在前加注"S/"、"W/"或"WF/"之一(生产件填报"S/",品牌和适用的整车厂牌一致的维修件填报"W/",品牌和适用的整车厂牌不一致的维修件的填报"WF/")
8708.9200	--消声器(消音器)、排气管及 其零件	1.品名;2.适用车型;3.成套散件或毛坯请注明;4.生产件的通用零件编号前加注"/TY";5.成套散件装配后完整品的零部件的编号;6.品牌;7.型号;8.零部件完整编号并在前加注"S/"、"W/"或"WF/"之一(生产件填报"S/",品牌和适用的整车厂牌一致的维修件填报"W/",品牌和适用的整车厂牌不一致的维修件的填报"WF/")
8708.93	--离合器及其零件:	1.品名;2.适用车型;3.成套散件或毛坯请注明;4.生产件的通用零件编号前加注"/TY";5.成套散件装配后完整品的零部件的编号;6.品牌;7.型号;8.零部件完整编号并在前加注"S/"、"W/"或"WF/"之一(生产件填报"S/",品牌和适用的整车厂牌一致的维修件填报"W/",品牌和适用的整车厂牌不一致的维修件的填报"WF/")
8708.9410	---税目 87.01 所列车辆用	1.品名;2.适用车型;3.成套散件或毛坯请注明;4.生产件的通用零件编号前加注"/TY";5.成套散件装配后完整品的零部件的编号;6.品牌;7.型号;8.零部件完整编号并在前加注"S/"、"W/"或"WF/"之一(生产件填报"S/",品牌和适用的整车厂牌一致的维修件填报"W/",品牌和适用的整车厂牌不一致的维修件的填报"WF/")
8708.9420	--- 税号 8702.1091 及 8702.9010 所列车辆用	1.品名;2.适用车型;3.成套散件或毛坯请注明;4.生产件的通用零件编号前加注"/TY";5.成套散件装配后完整品的零部件的编号;6.座位数;7.品牌;8.型号;9.零部件完整编号并在前加注"S/"、"W/"或"WF/"之一(生产件填报"S/",品牌和适用的整车厂牌一致的维修件填报"W/",品牌和适用的整车厂牌不一致的维修件的填报"WF/")

税则号列	商品描述	规范申报要素 / 价格申报要素 / 其他申报要素 / 举例说明
8708.9430	---税号 8704.1030 及 8704.1090 所列车辆用	1.品名;2.适用车型;3.成套散件或毛坯请注明;4.生产件的通用零件编号前加注"/TY";5.成套散件装配后完整品的零部件的编号;6.品牌;7.型号;8.零部件完整编号并在前加注"S/"、"W/"或"WF/"之一(生产件填报"S/",品牌和适用的整车厂牌一致的维修件填报"W/",品牌和适用的整车厂牌不一致的维修件的填报"WF/")
8708.9440	---税号 8704.2100、8704.2230、8704.3100 及 8704.3230 所列车辆用	1.品名;2.适用车型;3.成套散件或毛坯请注明;4.生产件的通用零件编号前加注"/TY";5.成套散件装配后完整品的零部件的编号;6.品牌;7.型号;8.零部件完整编号并在前加注"S/"、"W/"或"WF/"之一(生产件填报"S/",品牌和适用的整车厂牌一致的维修件填报"W/",品牌和适用的整车厂牌不一致的维修件的填报"WF/")
8708.9450	---税号 8704.2240、8704.2300 及 8704.3240 所列 车辆用	1.品名;2.适用车型;3.成套散件或毛坯请注明;4.生产件的通用零件编号前加注"/TY";5.成套散件装配后完整品的零部件的编号;6.品牌;7.型号;8.零部件完整编号并在前加注"S/"、"W/"或"WF/"之一(生产件填报"S/",品牌和适用的整车厂牌一致的维修件填报"W/",品牌和适用的整车厂牌不一致的维修件的填报"WF/")
8708.9460	---税目 87.05 所列车辆用转 向器	1.品名;2.适用车型;3.成套散件或毛坯请注明;4.生产件的通用零件编号前加注"/TY";5.成套散件装配后完整品的零部件的编号;6.品牌;7.型号;8.零部件完整编号并在前加注"S/"、"W/"或"WF/"之一(生产件填报"S/",品牌和适用的整车厂牌一致的维修件填报"W/",品牌和适用的整车厂牌不一致的维修件的填报"WF/")
8708.9490	---其他	1.品名;2.适用车型;3.成套散件或毛坯请注明;4.生产件的通用零件编号前加注"/TY";5.成套散件装配后完整品的零部件的编号;6.品牌;7.型号;8.零部件完整编号并在前加注"S/"、"W/"或"WF/"之一(生产件填报"S/",品牌和适用的整车厂牌一致的维修件填报"W/",品牌和适用的整车厂牌不一致的维修件的填报"WF/")
8708.9500	--带充气系统的安全气囊及其 零件	1.品名;2.适用车型;3.成套散件或毛坯请注明;4.生产件的通用零件编号前加注"/TY";5.成套散件装配后完整品的零部件的编号;6.品牌;7.型号;8.零部件完整编号并在前加注"S/"、"W/"或"WF/"之一(生产件填报"S/",品牌和适用的整车厂牌一致的维修件填报"W/",品牌和适用的整车厂牌不一致的维修件的填报"WF/")
8708.9910	---税目 87.01 所列车辆用	1.品名;2.适用车型;3.品牌;4.型号
8708.9921	----车架	1.品名;2.适用车型;3.成套散件或毛坯请注明;4.生产件的通用零件编号前加注"/TY";5.成套散件装配后完整品的零部件的编号;6.品牌;7.型号;8.零部件完整编号并在前加注"S/"、"W/"或"WF/"之一(生产件填报"S/",品牌和适用的整车厂牌一致的维修件填报"W/",品牌和适用的整车厂牌不一致的维修件的填报"WF/");9.座位数
8708.9929	----其他	1.品名;2.适用车型;3.座位数;4.品牌;5.型号
8708.9931	----车架	1.品名;2.适用车型;3.成套散件或毛坯请注明;4.生产件的通用零件编号前加注"/TY";5.成套散件装配后完整品的零部件的编号;6.品牌;7.型号;8.零部件完整编号并在前加注"S/"、"W/"或"WF/"之一(生产件填报"S/",品牌和适用的整车厂牌一致的维修件填报"W/",品牌和适用的整车厂牌不一致的维修件的填报"WF/")
8708.9939	----其他	1.品名;2.适用车型;3.品牌;4.型号
8708.9941	----车架	1.品名;2.适用车型;3.成套散件或毛坯请注明;4.生产件的通用零件编号前加注"/TY";5.成套散件装配后完整品的零部件的编号;6.品牌;7.型号;8.零部件完整编号并在前加注"S/"、"W/"或"WF/"之一(生产件填报"S/",品牌和适用的整车厂牌一致的维修件填报"W/",品牌和适用的整车厂牌不一致的维修件的填报"WF/")
8708.9949	----其他	1.品名;2.适用车型;3.品牌;4.型号
8708.9951	----车架	1.品名;2.适用车型;3.成套散件或毛坯请注明;4.生产件的通用零件编号前加注"/TY";5.成套散件装配后完整品的零部件的编号;6.品牌;7.型号;8.零部件完整编号并在前加注"S/"、"W/"或"WF/"之一(生产件填报"S/",品牌和适用的整车厂牌一致的维修件填报"W/",品牌和适用的整车厂牌不一致的维修件的填报"WF/")
8708.9959	----其他	1.品名;2.适用车型;3.品牌;4.型号
8708.9960	---税目 87.05 所列车辆用	1.品名;2.适用车型;3.品牌;4.型号

税则号列	商品描述	规范申报要素 / 价格申报要素 / 其他申报要素 / 举例说明
8708.9991	----车架	1.品名;2.适用车型;3.成套散件或毛坯请注明;4.生产件的通用零件编号前加注"/TY";5.成套散件装配后完整品的零部件的编号;6.品牌;7.型号;8.零部件完整编号并在前加注"S/"、"W/"或"WF/"之一(生产件填报"S/",品牌和适用的整车厂牌一致的维修件填报"W/",品牌和适用的整车厂牌不一致的维修件的填报"WF/")
8708.9992	----传动轴	1.品名;2.适用车型;3.品牌;4.型号
8708.9999	----其他	1.品名;2.适用车型;3.品牌;4.型号
87.09	短距离运输货物的机动车辆,未装有提升或搬运设备,用于工厂、仓库、码头或机场;火车站台上用的牵引车;上述车辆的零件:	
8709.1	-车辆:	1.品名;2.发动机类型;3.适用场所;4.品牌;5.型号;6.技术参数(最高时速、转弯半径等)
8709.9000	-零件	1.品名;2.用途(适用车型);3.品牌;4.型号
87.10	坦克及其他机动装甲战斗车辆,不论是否装有武器;上述车辆的零件:	1.品名 2.品牌;3.型号
87.11	摩托车(包括机器脚踏两用车)及装有辅助发动机的脚踏车,不论有无边车;边车:	
8711.1000	-装有往复式活塞内燃发动机,气缸容量(排气量)不超过 50 毫升	1.品名;2.发动机类型;3.排气量;4.品牌;5.型号
8711.2	-装有往复式活塞内燃发动机,气缸容量(排气量)超过 50 毫 升,但不超过 250 毫升:	1.品名;2.发动机类型;3.排气量;4.品牌;5.型号
8711.3	-装有往复式活塞内燃发动机,气缸容量(排气量)超过 250 毫升,但不超过 500 毫升:	1.品名;2.发动机类型;3.排气量;4.品牌;5.型号
8711.4000	-装有往复式活塞内燃发动机,气缸容量(排气量)超过 500 毫升,但不超过 800 毫升	1.品名;2.发动机类型;3.排气量;4.品牌;5.型号
8711.5000	-装有往复式活塞内燃发动机气缸容量(排气量)超过 800 毫升	1.品名;2.发动机类型;3.排气量;4.品牌;5.型号
8711.9010	---电动及电动助力的	1.品名;2.发动机类型;3.品牌;4.型号
8711.9090	---其他	1.品名;2.发动机类型;3.排气量;4.品牌;5.型号
87.12	自行车及其他非机动脚踏车(包括运货三轮脚踏车):	1.品名;2.用途;3.轮径;4.品牌;5.型号
87.13	残疾人用车,不论是否机动或其他机械驱动:	1.品名;2.用途;3.驱动方式;4.品牌;5.型号
87.14	零件、附件,税目 87.11 至 87.13 所列车辆用:	1.品名;2.用途(适用车型);3.品牌;4.型号
87.15	婴孩车及其零件:	1.品名;2.适用车型;3.品牌
87.16	挂车及半挂车或其他非机械驱 动车辆及其零件:	
8716.1000	-供居住或野营用厢式挂车及半挂车	1.品名;2.用途;3.类型;4.品牌;5.型号
8716.2000	-农用自装或自卸式挂车及半挂车	1.品名;2.用途;3.类型;4.品牌;5.型号
8716.3	-其他货运挂车及半挂车:	1.品名;2.用途;3.类型;4.品牌;5.型号
8716.4000	-其他挂车及半挂车	1.品名 2.品牌;3.型号
8716.8000	-其他车辆	1.品名 2.品牌;3.型号
8716.9000	-零件	1.品名;2.用途(适用车型);3.品牌;4.型号

第八十八章 航空器、航天器及其零件

【注解】

1、零部件除申报目录规定的要素外,还应申报具体名称、材质和品牌等要素。

2、未制成品、不完整品申报要注明程度。

3、说明举例栏中未包含品牌、型号等内容。

4、旧的机电设备除申报目录规定的要素外,还应申报生产年代、新旧程度、技术规格、配置等要素。

税则号列	商品描述	规范申报要素 / 价格申报要素 / 其他申报要素 / 举例说明
88.01	气球及飞艇;滑翔机、悬挂滑翔机及其他无动力航空器:	1.品名;2.用途;3.品牌;4.型号

税则号列	商　品　描　述	规范申报要素 / 价格申报要素 / 其他申报要素 / 举例说明
88.02	其他航空器(例如,直升机、飞机);航天器(包括卫星)及其运载工具、亚轨道运载工具	
8802.1	-直升机:	1.品名;2.用途;3.类型;4.空载重量;5.品牌;6.型号
8802.2000	-飞机及其他航空器,空载重 量不超过 2000 千克	1.品名;2.用途;3.类型;4.空载重量;5.品牌;6.型号
8802.3000	-飞机及其他航空器,空载重 量超过 2000 千克,但不超过 15000 千克	1.品名;2.用途;3.类型;4.空载重量;5.品牌;6.型号
8802.4	-飞机及其他航空器,空载重量超过 15000 千克:	1.品名;2.用途;3.类型;4.空载重量;5.品牌;6.型号
8802.6000	-航天器(包括卫星)及其运载 工具、亚轨道运载工具	1.品名 2.品牌;3.型号
88.03	税目 88.01 或 88.02 所列货品的零件:	1.品名;2.用途(适用机型);3.品牌;4.型号
88.04	降落伞(包括可操纵降落伞及滑翔伞)、旋翼降落伞及其零 件、附件:	1.品名;2.用途(适用机型);3.品牌;4.型号
88.05	航空器的发射装置、甲板停机 装置或类似装置和地面飞行 训练器及其零件:	1.品名;2.用途(适用机型);3.品牌;4.型号

第八十九章　船舶及浮动结构体

【注解】

1、零部件除申报目录规定的要素外,还应申报具体名称、材质和品牌等要素。

2、未制成品、不完整品申报要注明程度。

3、“说明举例”栏中未包含品牌、型号等内容。

4、旧的机电设备除申报目录规定的要素外,还应申报生产年代、新旧程度、技术规格、配置等要素。

税则号列	商　品　描　述	规范申报要素 / 价格申报要素 / 其他申报要素 / 举例说明
89.01	巡航船、游览船、渡船、货船、驳船及其类似的客运或货运船舶:	
8901.1	-巡航船、游览船及主要用于 客运的类似船舶;各式渡船:	1.品名;2.驱动方式;3.品牌;4.型号;5.最高时速
8901.201	---成品油船:	1.品名;2.用途;3.载重量;4.品牌;5.型号
8901.202	---原油船:	1.品名;2.用途;3.载重量;4.品牌;5.型号
8901.203	---液化石油气船:	1.品名;2.用途;3.容积;4.品牌;5.型号
8901.204	---液化天然气船:	1.品名;2.用途;3.容积;4.品牌;5.型号
8901.2090	---其他	1.品名;2.用途;3.载重量;4.品牌;5.型号
8901.3000	-冷藏船,但税号 8901.20 的船舶除外	1.品名 2.品牌;3.型号
8901.902	---机动集装箱船:	1.品名;2.用途;3.可载标准集装箱数;4.品牌;5.型号
8901.903	---机动滚装船:	1.品名;2.用途;3.载重量;4.品牌;5.型号
8901.904	---机动散货船:	1.品名;2.用途;3.载重量;4.品牌;5.型号
8901.9050	---机动多用途船	1.品名;2.用途;3.品牌;4.型号
8901.9080	---其他,机动的	1.品名;2.用途;3.品牌;4.型号
8901.9090	---非机动的	1.品名;2.用途;3.品牌;4.型号
89.02	捕鱼船;加工船及其他加工保藏鱼类产品的船舶:	1.品名;2.用途;3.驱动方式;4.品牌;5.型号
89.03	娱乐或运动用快艇及其他船舶;划艇及轻舟:	
8903.1000	-充气的	1.品名;2.用途;3.类型;4.发动机安装方式;5.船体长度;6.固定安装配置;7.品牌;8.型号
8903.9100	--帆船,不论是否装有辅助发动机	1.品名;2.用途;3.类型;4.发动机安装方式;5.船体长度;6.品牌;7.型号
8903.9200	--汽艇,但装有舷外发动机 的除外	1.品名;2.用途;3.类型;4.发动机安装方式;5.船体长度;6.品牌;7.型号
8903.9900	--其他	1.品名;2.用途;3.类型;4.发动机安装方式;5.船体长度;6.固定安装配置
89.04	拖轮及顶推船:	1.品名;2.功能;3.品牌;4.型号

税则号列	商品描述	规范申报要素 / 价格申报要素 / 其他申报要素 / 举例说明
89.05	灯船、消防船、挖泥船、起重船及其他不以航行为主要功能的船舶;浮船坞;浮动或潜水式钻探或生产平台:	
8905.1000	-挖泥船	1.品名;2.用途;4.品牌;5.型号
8905.2000	-浮动或潜水式钻探或生产平台	1.品名;2.用途;4.品牌;5.型号
8905.9	-其他:	1.品名;2.用途;3.结构;4.品牌;5.型号
89.06	其他船舶,包括军舰及救生船,但划艇除外:	1.品名;2.用途;3.驱动方式;4.品牌;5.型号
89.07	其他浮动结构体(例如,筏、柜、潜水箱、浮码头、浮筒及航标):	1.品名;2.材质;3.品牌;4.型号
89.08	供拆卸的船舶及其他浮动结构体:	1.品名;2.轻吨数(不包括非金属固定压载在内的空船重量);3.船型(如油轮、客船、驳船、集装箱船等)

第十八类　光学、照相、电影、计量、检验、医疗或外科用仪器及设备、精密仪器及设备;钟表;乐器;上述物品的零件、附件

第九十章　光学、照相、电影、计量、检验、医疗或外科用仪器及设备、精密仪器及设备;上述物品的零件、附件

【注解】

1、零部件除申报目录规定的要素外,还应申报具体名称,材质和品牌等要素。

2、未制成品、不完整品申报要注明程度。

3、"说明举例"栏中未包含品牌、型号等内容。

4、旧的机电设备除申报目录规定的要素外,还应申报生产年代、新旧程度、技术规格、配置等要素。

税则号列	商品描述	规范申报要素 / 价格申报要素 / 其他申报要素 / 举例说明
90.01	光导纤维及光导纤维束;光缆,但税目85.44的货品除外偏振材料制的片及板;未装配的各种材料制透镜(包括隐形眼镜片)、棱镜、反射镜及其他光学元件,但未经光学加工的玻璃制上述元件除外:	
9001.1000	-光导纤维、光导纤维束及光缆	1.品名;2.结构;3.用途;4.品牌;5.型号
9001.2000	-偏振材料制的片及板	1.品名;2.用途;3.材质;4.形状(片、板等);5.规格尺寸;6.品牌;7.型号
9001.3000	-隐形眼镜片	1.品名2.品牌;3.型号;4.材质;5.种类(软片或硬片);6.颜色;7.直径;8使用周期(日抛、月抛等);9.度数(近视或远视度数,是否带散光度数)
9001.4	-玻璃制眼镜片:	1.品名;2.材质;3.类型(变色等);4.品牌;5.型号
9001.5	-其他材料制眼镜片:	1.品名;2.材质;3.类型(变色等);4.品牌;5.型号
9001.9	-其他:	1.品名;2.用途(适用机型);3.材质;4.品牌;5.型号
90.02	已装配的各种材料制透镜、棱镜、反射镜及其他光学元件,作为仪器或装置的零件、配件,但未经光学加工的玻璃制上述元件除外:	1.品名;2.用途(适用机型);3.是否已装配;4.品牌;5.型号
90.03	眼镜架及其零件:	1.品名;2.材质;3.品牌;4.型号
90.04	矫正视力、保护眼睛或其他用途的眼镜、挡风镜及类似品:	1.品名;2.用途;3.类型(变色等);4.品牌;5.型号
90.05	双筒望远镜、单筒望远镜、其他光学望远镜及其座架;其他天文仪器及其座架,但不包括射电天文仪器:	
9005.1000	-双筒望远镜	1.品名;2.用途;3.是否双筒;4.品牌;5.型号
9005.8	-其他仪器:	1.品名;2.用途;3.品牌;4.型号

税则号列	商品描述	规范申报要素 / 价格申报要素 / 其他申报要素 / 举例说明
9005.9	-零件、附件(包括座架):	1.品名;2.用途(适用机型);4.品牌;5.型号
90.06	照相机(电影摄影机除外);照相闪光灯装置及闪光灯泡,但税目85.39的放电灯泡除外:	
9006.1	-制版照相机:	1.品名;2.用途;3.原理;4.品牌;5.型号
9006.3000	-水下、航空测量或体内器官检查用的特种照相机;法庭或犯罪学用的比较照相机	1.品名;2.用途;3.原理;4.品牌;5.型号
9006.4000	-一次成像照相机	1.品名;2.用途;3.原理;4.品牌;5.型号
9006.5100	--通过镜头取景[单镜头反光式(SLR)],使用胶片宽度不超过35毫米	1.品名;2.用途;3.原理;4.胶片宽度;5.品牌;6.型号
9006.52	--其他,使用胶片宽度小于35毫米:	1.品名;2.用途;3.原理;4.胶片宽度;5.品牌;6.型号
9006.5300	--其他,使用胶片宽度为35mm	1.品名;2.用途;3.原理;4.胶片宽度;5.品牌;6.型号
9006.59	--其他:	1.品名;2.用途;3.原理;4.品牌;5.型号
9006.6	-照相闪光灯装置及闪光灯泡:	1.品名;2.用途;3.原理;4.品牌;5.型号
9006.9	-零件、附件:	1.品名;2.用途(适用机型);3.品牌;4.型号
9007	电影摄影机、放映机,不论是否带有声音的录制或重放装置:	
9007.1	-摄影机:	1.品名;2.用途;3.原理;4.胶片宽度;5.摄影速度;6.品牌;7.型号
9007.2	-放映机:	1.品名;2.用途;3.原理;4.品牌;5.型号
9007.9	-零件、附件:	1.品名;2.用途(适用机型);3.品牌;4.型号
90.08	影像投影仪,但电影用除外;照片(电影片除外)放大机及缩片机:	
9008.5010	---幻灯机	1.品名;2.用途;3.品牌;4.型号
9008.5020	---缩微胶卷、缩微胶片或其他缩微品的阅读机,不论是否可以进行复制	1.品名;2.用途;3.品牌;4.型号
9008.503	---其他影像投影仪:	1.品名;2.用途;3.原理;4.品牌;5.型号
9008.5040	---照片(电影片除外)放大机及缩片机	1.品名;2.用途;3.品牌;4.型号
9008.9	-零件、附件:	1.品名;2.用途(适用机型);3.品牌;4.型号
90.10	本章其他税目未列名的照相(包括电影)洗印用装置及设备;负片显示器;银幕及其他投影屏幕:	
9010.1	-照相(包括电影)胶卷或成卷感光纸的自动显影装置及设备或将已冲洗胶卷自动曝光到成卷感光纸上的装置及设备:	1.品名;2.用途;3.原理;4.品牌;5.型号
9010.5	-照相(包括电影)洗印用其他装置及设备;负片显示器:	1.品名;2.用途;3.原理;4.品牌;5.型号
9010.6000	-银幕及其他投影屏幕	1.品名;2.用途;3.品牌;4.型号
9010.9	-零件、附件:	1.品名;2.用途(适用机型);3.品牌;4.型号
90.11	复式光学显微镜,包括用于缩微照相、显微电影摄影及显微投影的:	
9011.1000	-立体显微镜	1.品名;2.用途;3.原理;4.品牌;5.型号;6.倍数
9011.2000	-显微照相、显微电影摄影及显微投影用的其他显微镜	1.品名;2.用途;3.原理;4.品牌;5.型号;6.倍数
9011.8000	-其他显微镜	1.品名;2.用途;3.原理;4.品牌;5.型号;6.倍数
9011.9000	-零件、附件	1.品名;2.用途(适用机型);3.品牌;4.型号
90.12	显微镜,但光学显微镜除外;衍射设备:	
9012.1000	-显微镜,但光学显微镜除外;衍射设备	1.品名;2.用途;3.原理;4.品牌;5.型号
9012.9000	-零件、附件	1.品名;2.用途(适用机型);3.品牌;4.型号
90.13	其他税目未列名的液晶装置;激光器,但激光二极管除外;本章其他税目未列名的光学仪器及器具:	
9013.1000	-武器用望远镜瞄准具;潜望镜式望远镜;作为本章或第十六类的机器、设备、仪器或器具部件的望远镜	1.品名;2.用途;3.品牌;4.型号

税则号列	商品描述	规范申报要素 / 价格申报要素 / 其他申报要素 / 举例说明
9013.2000	-激光器,但激光二极管除外	1.品名;2.用途;3.原理;4.品牌;5.型号
9013.8010	---放大镜	1.品名;2.用途;3.原理;4.品牌;5.型号
9013.8020	---光学门眼	1.品名;2.用途;3.原理;4.品牌;5.型号
9013.8030	---液晶显示板	1.品名;2.用途;3.原理(是否液晶);4.尺寸;5.品牌;6.型号;7.配置(请注明配置显示驱动板、HDMI接口、标记版、解码板、高频头、视频接口、触摸功能等)
9013.8090	---其他	1.品名;2.用途;3.原理;4.品牌;5.型号
9013.9	-零件、附件:	1.品名;2.用途(适用机型);3.品牌;4.型号
90.14	定向罗盘;其他导航仪器及装置:	
9014.1000	-定向罗盘	1.品名;2.用途;3.原理;4.品牌;5.型号
9014.2	-航空或航天导航仪器及装置(罗盘除外)	1.品名;2.用途;3.品牌;4.型号
9014.8000	-其他仪器及装置	1.品名;2.用途;3.原理;4.品牌;5.型号
9014.9	-零件、附件:	1.品名;2.用途(适用机型);3.品牌;4.型号
90.15	大地测量(包括摄影测量)、水道测量、海洋、水文、气象或地球物理用仪器及装置,不包括罗盘;测距仪:	
9015.1000	-测距仪	1.品名;2.用途;3.原理;4.品牌;5.型号
9015.2000	-经纬仪及视距仪	1.品名;2.用途;3.原理;4.品牌;5.型号
9015.3000	-水平仪	1.品名;2.用途;3.原理;4.品牌;5.型号
9015.4000	-摄影测量用仪器及装置	1.品名;2.用途;3.原理;4.品牌;5.型号
9015.8000	-其他仪器及装置	1.品名;2.用途;3.原理;4.品牌;5.型号
9015.9000	-零件、附件	1.品名;2.用途(适用机型);3.品牌;4.型号
90.16	感量为50毫克或更精密的天平,不论是否带有砝码:	1.品名;2.感量;3.品牌;4.型号
90.17	绘图、划线或数学计算仪器及器具(例如,绘图机、比例缩放仪、分度规、绘图工具、计算尺及盘式计算器);本章其他税目未列名的手用测量长度的器具(例如,量尺、量带千分尺及卡尺):	
9017.1000	-绘图台及绘图机,不论是否自动	1.品名;2.用途;3.功能;4.品牌;5.型号
9017.2000	-其他绘图、划线或数学计算器具	1.品名;2.用途;3.功能;4.是否手用;5.品牌;6.型号
9017.3000	-千分尺、卡尺及量规	1.品名;2.用途;3.功能;4.是否手用;5.品牌;6.型号
9017.8000	-其他仪器及器具	1.品名;2.用途;3.功能;4.品牌;5.型号
9017.9000	-零件、附件	1.品名;2.用途(适用机型);3.品牌;4.型号
90.18	医疗、外科、牙科或兽医用仪器及器具,包括闪烁扫描装置、其他电气医疗装置及视力检查仪器:	
9018.1	-电气诊断装置(包括功能 检查或 生理 参数检 查用 装置):	1.品名;2.用途;3.原理;4.品牌;5.型号;6.探头数量。注:彩色多普勒超声诊断仪,医疗用,SIEMENS,SONO-LINEG60S,2个常规探头
9018.2000	-紫外线及红外线装置	1.品名;2.用途;3.原理;4.品牌;5.型号
9018.3100	--注射器,不论是否装有针头	1.品名;2.用途;3.品牌;4.型号
9018.32	--管状金属针头及缝合用针:	1.品名;2.用途;3.品牌;4.型号
9018.3900	--其他	1.品名;2.用途;3.材质;4.品牌;5.型号
9018.4100	--牙钻机,不论是否与其他牙科设备组装在同一底座上	1.品名;2.用途;3.品牌;4.型号
9018.4910	---装有牙科设备的牙科用椅	1.品名;2.用途;3.品牌;4.型号
9018.4990	---其他	1.品名;2.用途;3.原理;4.品牌;5.型号
9018.5000	-眼科用其他仪器及器具	1.品名;2.用途;3.原理;4.品牌;5.型号
9018.9010	---听诊器	1.品名;2.用途;3.品牌;4.型号
9018.9020	---血压测量仪器及器具	1.品名;2.用途;3.原理;4.品牌;5.型号
9018.9030	---内窥镜	1.品名;2.用途;3.品牌;4.型号。注:KARLSTORZ胆囊切除腹腔镜,20242001型,含三晶片摄像系统、监视器、冷光源
9018.9040	---肾脏透析设备(人工肾)	1.品名;2.用途;3.原理;4.品牌
9018.9050	---透热疗法设备	1.品名;2.用途;3.原理;4.品牌
9018.9060	---输血设备	1.品名;2.用途;3.品牌;4.型号
9018.9070	---麻醉设备	1.品名;2.用途;3.品牌;4.型号
9018.9080	---宫内节育器	1.品名;2.用途;3.品牌;4.型号

税则号列	商品描述	规范申报要素 / 价格申报要素 / 其他申报要素 / 举例说明
9018.9090	---其他	1.品名;2.用途;3.品牌;4.型号
90.19	机械疗法器具;按摩器具;心理功能测验装置;臭氧治疗器;氧气治疗器、喷雾治疗器人工呼吸器及其他治疗用呼 吸器具:	
9019.1010	---按摩器具	1.品名;2.用途;3.功能;4.品牌;5.型号
9019.1090	---其他	1.品名;2.用途;3.功能;4.原理;5.品牌;6.型号
9019.2000	-臭氧治疗器、氧气治疗器、喷雾治疗器、人工呼吸器及其他治疗用呼吸器具	1.品名;2.用途;3.功能;4.品牌;5.型号
90.20	其他呼吸器具及防毒面具,但不包括既无机械零件又无可互换过滤器的防护面具:	1.品名;2.用途;3.构成;4.有无机械零件或可互换过滤装置;5.品牌;6.型号
90.21	矫形器具,包括支具、外科手术带、疝气带;夹板及其他骨折用具;人造的人体部分;助听器及为弥补 生理缺陷或残疾而穿戴、携带或植入人体内的其他器具:	
9021.1000	-矫形或骨折用器具	1.品名;2.用途;3.品牌;4.材质;5.型号;6.技术参数
9021.2	-假牙及牙齿固定件:	1.品名2.品牌;3.材质;4.型号
9021.3100	--人造关节	1.品名;2.用途;3.人造关节部位;4.品牌;5.材质;6.型号
9021.3900	--其他	1.品名;2.用途;3.品牌;4.材质;5.型号
9021.4000	-助听器,不包括零件、附件	1.品名
9021.5000	-心脏起搏器,不包括零件、附 件	1.品名;2.材质
9021.9	-其他:	1.品名;2.用途;3.原理;4.品牌;5.型号。注1:冠状动脉支架,等离子体技术涂层钛氧化氮,球囊扩张式,强生 CYPHER 型;注2:单叶机械心脏,碳素合金材质,美敦力 A4501
90.22	X 射线或α射线、β射线、γ射线的应用设备,不论是否用于医疗、外科、牙科或兽医,包括射线照相 及射线治疗设备,X 射线管及其他 X 射线发生器、高压发生器、控制板及控制台、荧光屏、检查或治疗用的桌 、椅及类似品:	
9022.1200	--X 射线断层检查仪	1.品名;2.用途;3.原理;4.品牌;5.型号;6.排数
9022.1300	--其他,牙科用	1.品名;2.用途;3.原理;4.品牌;5.型号
9022.1400	--其他,医疗、外科或兽医用	1.品名;2.用途;3.原理;4.品牌;5.型号
9022.19	--其他:	1.品名;2.用途;3.原理;4.品牌;5.型号
9022.2	-α射线、β射线、γ射线的 应用设备,不 论是否用于医 疗、外科、牙科或兽医,包括 射线照相或射线治疗设备:	1.品名;2.用途;3.原理;4.品牌;5.型号
9022.3000	-X 射线管	1.品名;2.用途;3.原理;4.品牌;5.型号
9022.9	-其他,包括零件、附件:	1.品名;2.用途;3.原理;4.品牌;5.型号
90.23	专供示范(例如,教学或展览) 而无其他用途的仪器、装置及模型:	1.品名;2.用途;3.品牌;4.型号
90.24	各种材料(例如,金属、木材、纺织材料、纸张、塑料)的硬度、强度、压缩性、弹性或其他机械 性能的试验机器及器具:	
9024.1	-金属材料的试验用机器及器具:	1.品名;2.功能;3.试验材料类型;4.品牌;5.型号
9024.8000	-其他机器及器具	1.品名;2.功能;3.试验材料类型;4.品牌;5.型号
9024.9000	-零件、附件	1.品名;2.用途(适用机型);3.品牌;4.型号
90.25	记录式或非记录式的液体比重 计及类似的浮子式仪器、温度计、高温计、气压计、湿度计、干湿球湿度计及其组合装置:	
9025.1	-温度计及高温计,未与其他 仪器组合:	1.品名;2.原理;3.是否可直接读数;4.品牌;5.型号
9025.8000	-其他仪器	1.品名;2.原理;3.品牌;4.型号
9025.9000	-零件、附件	1.品名;2.用途(适用机型);3.品牌;4.型号

税则号列	商品描述	规范申报要素 / 价格申报要素 / 其他申报要素 / 举例说明
90.26	液体或气体的流量、液位、压力或其他变化量的测量或检验仪器及装置(例如,流量计、液位计、压力表、热量计),但不包括税目 90.14、90.15、90.28 或 90.32 的仪器及装置	
9026.1000	-测量、检验液体流量或液位的仪器及装置	1.品名;2.功能;3.检测对象;4.品牌;5.型号
9026.2	-测量、检验压力的仪器及装置:	1.品名;2.功能;3.检测对象;4.品牌;5.型号
9026.8010	---测量气体流量的仪器及装置	1.品名;2.功能;3.检测对象;4.品牌;5.型号
9026.8090	---其他	1.品名;2.功能;3.检测对象;4.品牌;5.型号
9026.9000	-零件、附件	1.品名;2.用途(适用机型);3.品牌;4.型号
90.27	理化分析仪器及装置(例如,偏振仪、折光仪、分光仪、气体或烟雾分析仪);测量或检验粘性、多孔性、膨胀性、表 面张力及类似性能的仪器及装置;测量或检验热量、声量或光量的仪器及装置(包括曝光表);检镜切片机:	
9027.1000	-气体或烟雾分析仪	1.品名;2.原理;3.功能;4.检测对象;5.品牌;6.型号
9027.2	-色谱仪及电泳仪:	1.品名;2.原理;3.功能;4.检测对象;5.品牌;6.型号
9027.3000	-使用光学射线(紫外线、可见光、红外线)的分光仪、分光光度计及摄谱仪	1.品名;2.原理;3.功能;4.检测对象;5.品牌;6.型号
9027.5000	-使用光学射线(紫外线、可见光、红外线)的其他仪器及装置	1.品名;2.原理;3.功能;4.检测对象;5.品牌;6.型号
9027.8	-其他仪器及装置:	1.品名;2.原理;3.功能;4.检测对象;5.品牌;6.型号
9027.9000	-检镜切片机;零件、附件	1.品名;2.用途(适用机型);3.品牌;4.型号
90.28	生产或供应气体、液体及电力用的计量仪表,包括它们的校准仪表:	
9028.1	-气量计:	1.品名;2.用途;3.品牌;4.型号
9028.2	-液量计:	1.品名;2.用途;3.品牌;4.型号
9028.3	-电量计:	1.品名;2.用途;3.原理;4.品牌;5.型号
9028.9	-零件、附件:	1.品名;2.用途(适用机型);3.品牌;4.型号
90.29	转数计、产量计数器、车费计里程计、步数计及类似仪表;速度计及转速表,税目 90.14 及 90.15 的仪表除外;频闪观测仪:	
9029.1	-转数计、产量计数器、车费计里程计、步数计及类似仪表:	1.品名;2.用途;3.品牌;4.型号
9029.2	-速度计及转速表,频闪观测仪	1.品名;2.用途;3.品牌;4.型号
9029.9000	-零件、附件	1.品名;2.用途(适用机型);3.品牌;4.型号
90.30	示波器、频谱分析仪及其他用于电量测量或检验的仪器和装置,但不包括税目 90.28 的各钟仪表;α 射线、β 射线、γ 射线、X 射线、宇宙射线或其他离子射线的测量或检验仪器及装置:	
9030.1000	-离子射线的测量或检验仪器及装置	1.品名;2.用途;3.功能;4.品牌;5.型号
9030.2	-示波器:	1.品名;2.用途;3.功能;4.频率;5.品牌;6.型号
9030.31	--万用表,不带记录装置:	1.品名;2.用途;3.功能;4.量程;5.是否带记录装置;6.品牌;7.型号
9030.3200	--万用表,带记录装置	1.品名;2.用途;3.功能;4.量程;5.是否带记录装置;6.品牌;7.型号
9030.3310	---量程在五位半及以下的数字电流表、电压表	1.品名;2.用途;3.功能;4.量程;5.是否带记录装置;6.品牌;7.型号
9030.3320	---电阻测试仪	1.品名;2.用途;3.功能;4.是否带记录装置;5.品牌;6.型号
9030.3390	---其他	1.品名;2.用途;3.功能;4.是否带记录装置;5.品牌;6.型号
9030.3900	--其他,带记录装置	1.品名;2.用途;3.功能;4.是否带记录装置;5.品牌;6.型号
9030.4	-通讯专用的其他仪器及装置(例如,串音测试器、增益测 量仪、失真度表、噪声计):	1.品名;2.用途;3.功能;4.测试频率;5.品牌;6.型号
9030.8	-其他仪器及装置:	1.品名;2.用途;3.功能;4.是否带记录装置;5.品牌;6.型号
9030.9000	-零件、附件	1.品名;2.用途(适用机型);3.品牌;4.型号

税则号列	商品描述	规范申报要素 / 价格申报要素 / 其他申报要素 / 举例说明
90.31	本章其他税目未列名的测量或检验仪器、器具及机器;轮廓投影仪:	
9031.1000	-机械零件平衡试验机	1.品名;2.用途;3.功能;4.品牌;5.型号
9031.2000	-试验台	1.品名;2.用途;3.功能;4.品牌;5.型号
9031.4	-其他光学仪器及器具:	1.品名;2.用途;3.功能;4.品牌;5.型号
9031.8	-其他仪器、器具及机器:	1.品名;2.用途;3.原理;4.功能;5.品牌;6.型号
9031.9000	-零件、附件	1.品名;2.用途(适用机型);3.品牌;4.型号
90.32	自动调节或控制仪器及装置:	
9032.1000	-恒温器	1.品名;2.用途;3.原理;4.功能;5.品牌;6.型号
9032.2000	-恒压器	1.品名;2.用途;3.原理;4.功能;5.品牌;6.型号
9032.8	-其他仪器及装置:	1.品名;2.用途;3.原理;4.功能;5.品牌;6.型号
9032.9000	-零件、附件	1.品名;2.用途(适用机型);3.品牌;4.型号
90.33	第九十章所列机器、器具、仪器或装置用的本章其他税目未列名的零件、附件:	1.品名;2.用途(适用机型);3.品牌;4.型号

第九十一章　钟表及其零件

税则号列	商品描述	规范申报要素 / 价格申报要素 / 其他申报要素 / 举例说明
91.01	手表、怀表及其他表,包括秒表,表壳用贵金属或包贵金属制成的:	1.品名;2.外壳材质(贵金属或包贵金属制);3.驱动方式(电子、机械、自动、非自动);4.指示方式(指针、光电);5.品牌;6.型号
91.02	手表、怀表及其他表,包括秒表,但税目91.01的货品除外	1.品名;2.外壳材质(金属制等);3.驱动方式(电子、机械、自动、非自动);4.指示方式(指针、光电);5.品牌;6.型号
91.03	以表芯装成的钟,但不包括税目91.04的钟	1.品名;2.驱动方式(电子、机械、自动、非自动);3.品牌;4.型号
91.04	仪表板钟及车辆、航空器、航天器或船舶用的类似钟:	1.品名;2.驱动方式(电子、机械、自动、非自动);3.品牌;4.型号
91.05	其他钟:	
9105.1	-闹钟:	1.品名;2.驱动方式(电子、机械、自动、非自动);3.品牌;4.型号
9105.2	-挂钟:	1.品名;2.驱动方式(电子、机械、自动、非自动);3.品牌;4.型号
9105.9110	---天文钟	1.品名;2.用途(车辆、船舶等用);3.品牌;4.型号
9105.9190	---其他	1.品名;2.用途(闹钟、天文钟等);3.驱动方式(电子、机械);4.品牌;5.型号
9105.9900	--其他	1.品名;2.用途(闹钟、天文钟等);3.驱动方式(电子、机械);4.品牌;5.型号
91.06	时间记录器以及测量、记录或指示时间间隔的装置,装有钟、表机芯或同步电动机的(例如,考勤钟、时刻记录 器):	1.品名;2.用途(闹钟、天文钟等);3.驱动方式(电子、机械);4.品牌;5.型号
91.07	装有钟、表机芯或同步电动机的定时开关:	1.品名;2.用途(闹钟、天文钟等);3.驱动方式(电子、机械);4.品牌;5.型号
91.08	已组装的完整表芯:	
9108.1	-电力驱动的:	1.品名;2.用途(闹钟、天文钟等);3.驱动方式(电子、机械);4.表面尺寸;5.指示方式;6.品牌
9108.2000	-自动上弦的	1.品名;2.用途(闹钟、天文钟等);3.驱动方式(电子、机械);4.表面尺寸;5.指示方式;6.品牌
9108.9010	---表面尺寸在33.8毫米及以下	1.品名;2.用途(闹钟、天文钟等);3.驱动方式(电子、机械);4.表面尺寸;5.品牌
9108.9090	---其他	1.品名;2.表面尺寸
91.09	已组装的完整钟芯:	1.品名;2.驱动方式(电子、机械、自动、非自动)。注:已组装电子闹钟芯
91.10	未组装或部分组装的完整钟、表机芯(机芯套装件);已组装的不完整钟、表机芯;未组装的不完整钟、表机芯:	
9110.1	-表的:	1.品名;2.驱动方式(电子、机械、自动、非自动)
9110.9	-其他:	1.品名;2.用途
91.11	表壳及其零件:	
9111.1000	-贵金属表壳或包贵金属表壳	1.品名;2.材质;3.贵金属含量
9111.2000	-贱金属表壳,不论是否镀金或镀银	1.品名;2.材质
9111.8000	-其他表壳	1.品名;2.材质

税则号列	商 品 描 述	规范申报要素 / 价格申报要素 / 其他申报要素 / 举例说明
9111.9000	-零件	1.品名;2.材质
91.12	钟壳和本章所列其他货品的类似外壳及其零件:	1.品名;2.用途。注:塑料钟壳
91.13	表带及其零件:	
9113.1000	-贵金属或包贵金属制	1.品名;2.材质(贵金属、贱金属等);3.贵金属含量
9113.2000	-贱金属制,不论是否镀金或镀银	1.品名;2.材质(贵金属、贱金属等)
9113.9000	-其他	1.品名;2.材质(贵金属、贱金属等);3.是否野生动物皮制
91.14	钟、表的其他零件:	
9114.1000	-发条,包括游丝	1.品名;2.用途;3.材质
9114.3000	-钟面或表面	1.品名2.材质(贵金属、贱金属等)
9114.4000	-夹板及横担(过桥)	1.品名2.材质(贵金属、贱金属等)
9114.9010	---宝石轴承	1.品名;2.用途;3.材质
9114.9090	---其他	1.品名2.材质(贵金属、贱金属等)

第九十二章　乐器及其零件、附件

税则号列	商 品 描 述	规范申报要素 / 价格申报要素 / 其他申报要素 / 举例说明
92.01	钢琴,包括自动钢琴、拨弦古钢琴及其他键盘弦乐器:	1.品名;2.有否琴凳;3.产品编码;4.材质(象牙琴键、贵金属、贱金属等);5.种类(新旧、竖卧式、是否数码);6.品牌;7.型号
92.02	其他弦乐器(例如,吉他、小提琴、竖琴):	1.品名;2.是否为野生动物皮制;3.用途;4.规格型号
92.05	管乐器(例如,键盘管风琴、手风琴、单簧管、小号、风笛)但游艺场风琴及手摇风琴除外:	1.品名2.种类;3.品牌;4.规格型号
92.06	打击乐器(例如,鼓、木琴、铙、钹、响板、响葫芦):	1.品名;2.是否为野生动物皮制;3.用途;4.品牌;5.规格型号
92.07	通过电产生或扩大声音的乐 器(例如,电风琴、电吉他、电手风琴):	1.品名2.种类;3.品牌;4.规格型号
92.08	百音盒、游艺场风琴、手摇风 琴、机械鸣禽、乐锯及本章其他税目未列名的其他乐器;各种媒诱音响器、哨子、号角、口吹音响信号器:	
9208.1000	-百音盒	1.品名2.种类;3.品牌
9208.9000	-其他	1.品名2.品牌
92.09	乐器的零件(例如百音盒的机械装置)、附件(例如,机械乐器用的卡片、盘及带卷),节拍器、音叉及各种定音管:	
9209.3000	-乐器用的弦	1.品名;2.用途(适用乐器类型);3.品牌;4.材质;5.规格型号
9209.9	-其他:	1.品名;2.用途

第十九类　武器、弹药及其零件、附件

第九十三章　武器、弹药及其零件、附件

税则号列	商 品 描 述	规范申报要素 / 价格申报要素 / 其他申报要素 / 举例说明
93.01	军用武器,但左轮手枪、其他手枪及税目93.07 的兵器除外:	1.品名;2.驱动方式;3.型号
93.02	左轮手枪及其他手枪,但税目93.03 或93.04 的货品除外:	1.品名2.型号

税则号列	商 品 描 述	规范申报要素 / 价格申报要素 / 其他申报要素 / 举例说明
93.03	靠爆炸药发射的其他火器及类似装置(例如,运动用猎枪及步枪、前装枪、维利式信号 枪及其他专为发射信号弹的 装置、发射空包弹的左轮手枪和其他手枪、弩枪式无痛捕杀器、抛缆枪:	1.品名2.型号
93.04	其他武器(例如,弹簧枪、气枪、气手枪、警棍),但不包括税目93.07的货品:	1.品名2.型号
93.05	税目93.01至93.04所列物品的零件、附件:	1.品名2.型号
93.06	炸弹、手榴弹、鱼雷、地雷、水雷、导弹及类似武器及其零件;子弹、其他弹药和射弹及其零件,包括弹丸及弹垫:	1.品名2.型号
93.07	剑、短弯刀、刺刀、长矛和类似的武器及其零件;刀鞘、剑 鞘:	1.品名;2.用途

第二十类 杂项制品

第九十四章 家具;寝具、褥垫、弹簧床垫、软座垫及类似的填充制品;未列名灯具及照明装置;发光标志、发光铭牌及类似品;活动房屋

税则号列	商 品 描 述	规范申报要素 / 价格申报要素 / 其他申报要素 / 举例说明
94.01	坐具(包括能作床用的两用椅,但税目94.02的货品除外及其零件:	
9401.1000	-飞机用坐具	1.品名;2.用途;3.品牌
9401.2	-机动车辆用坐具:	1.品名;2.用途;3.材质;4.品牌
9401.3000	-可调高度的转动坐具	1.品名;2.用途;3.材质;4.是否可调节、可转动;5.品牌
9401.4	-能做床用的两用椅,但庭园坐具或野营设备除外:	1.品名;2.用途;3.材质;4.是否可做床用;5.品牌
9401.5	-藤、柳条、竹及类似材料制的坐具:	1.品名;2.用途;3.材质;4.品牌
9401.6	-木框架的其他坐具:	1.品名;2.用途;3.材质;4.是否装软垫;5.品牌
9401.7	-金属框架的其他坐具:	1.品名;2.用途;3.材质;4.是否装软垫;5.品牌
9401.8	-其他坐具:	1.品名;2.用途;3.材质;4.品牌
9401.9	-零件:	1.品名;2.用途(适用机型);3.材质
94.02	医疗、外科、牙科或兽医用家具(例如,手术台、检查台、带机械装置的病床、牙科用椅);有旋转、倾斜、升降装置的理发用椅及类似椅;上述 物品的零件:	
9402.1010	---理发用椅及其零件	1.品名;2.用途;3.材质;4.品牌
9402.1090	---其他	1.品名;2.用途;3.配置附属装置;4.是否带医疗用具;5.品牌
9402.9000	-其他	1.品名;2.用途;3.配置附属装置;4.是否带医疗用具;5.品牌
94.03	其他家具及零件:	
9403.1000	-办公室用金属家具	1.品名;2.用途;3.材质;4.是否办公室用;5.品牌;6.规格
9403.2000	-其他金属家具	1.品名;2.用途;3.材质;4.品牌;5.规格
9403.3000	-办公室用木家具	1.品名;2.用途;3.材质;4.是否办公室用;5.品牌;6.规格
9403.4000	-厨房用木家具	1.品名;2.用途;3.材质;4.是否厨房用;5.品牌;6.规格
9403.5	-卧室用木家具:	1.品名;2.用途;3.材质;4.是否卧室用;5.品牌;6.规格
9403.6	-其他木家具:	1.品名;2.用途;3.材质;4.品牌;5.规格
9403.7000	-塑料家具	1.品名;2.用途;3.材质;4.品牌;5.规格
9403.8	-其他材料制的家具,包括藤柳条、竹或类似材料制的:	1.品名;2.用途;3.材质;4.品牌;5.规格
9403.9000	-零件	1.品名;2.用途;3.材质;4.规格

税则号列	商 品 描 述	规范申报要素 / 价格申报要素 / 其他申报要素 / 举例说明
94.04	弹簧床垫;寝具及类似用品,装有弹簧、内部用任何材料填充、衬垫或用海绵橡胶、泡沫塑料制成,不论是否包面(例如,褥垫、棉被、羽绒被、靠垫、座垫及枕头):	
9404.1000	-弹簧床垫	1.品名;2.材质(包面及填充物);3.品牌;4.规格
9404.2	-褥垫:	1.品名;2.材质(包面及填充物);3.品牌;4.规格
9404.3	-睡袋:	1.品名;2.材质(包面及填充物);3.品牌;4.规格
9404.9010	---羽毛或羽绒填充的	1.品名;2.材质(包面及填充物);3.品牌;4.规格
9404.9020	---兽毛填充的	1.品名;2.材质(包面及填充物);3.品牌;4.规格
9404.9030	---丝棉填充的	1.品名;2.材质(包面及填充物);3.品牌;4.规格
9404.9040	---化纤棉填充的	1.品名;2.材质;3.品牌;4.规格
9404.9090	---其他	1.品名;2.材质;3.品牌;4.规格
94.05	-其他税目未列名的灯具及照明装置,包括按照灯、聚光灯及其零件;装有固定光源的发光标志、发光铭牌及类似品,以及其他税目未列名的这些货品的零件	
9405.1000	-枝形吊灯及天花板或墙壁上的其他电气照明装置,但不包括公共露天场所或街道上的 电器照明装置	1.品名;2.材质;3.用途;4.品牌
9405.2000	-电气的台灯、床头灯或落地灯	1.品名;2.材质;3.种类;4.用途;5.品牌
9405.3000	-圣诞树用的成套灯具	1.品名;2.材质;3.种类;4.用途;5.品牌
9405.4	-其他电灯及照明装置:	1.品名;2.材质;3.用途;4.品牌
9405.5000	-非电气的灯具及照明装置	1.品名;2.材质;3.种类;4.用途;5.品牌
9405.6000	-发光标志、发光铭牌及类似品	1.品名;2.材质;3.种类;4.用途;5.品牌
9405.9	-零件:	1.品名;2.材质;3.用途
94.06	活动房屋:	1.品名;2.材质;3.内部配置;4.规格(尺寸)

第九十五章 玩具、游戏品、运动用品及其零件、附件

税则号列	商 品 描 述	规范申报要素 / 价格申报要素 / 其他申报要素 / 举例说明
95.03	三轮车、踏板车、踏板汽车及类似的带轮玩具;玩偶车;玩偶;其他玩具;缩小(按比例缩小)的模型及类似的娱乐用模型,不论是否活动;各种智力玩具:	
9503.0010	---三轮车、踏板车、踏板汽车和类似的带轮玩具;玩偶车	1.品名;2.用途;3.种类;4.品牌
9503.002	---玩偶,不论是否着装;玩具动物:	1.品名;2.用途;3.种类;4.品牌
9503.003	---缩小(按比例缩小)的全套模型组件,不论是否活动:	1.品名;2.用途;3.种类;4.品牌
9503.0040	---其他建筑套件及建筑玩具	1.品名;2.用途;3.种类;4.品牌
9503.0050	---玩具乐器	1.品名;2.用途;3.种类;4.品牌
9503.0060	---智力玩具	1.品名;2.用途;3.种类;4.品牌
95030081	----组装成套或全套的	1.品名;2.用途;3.种类;4.是否成套
9503.0082	----其他带动 力装置的玩具及模型	1.品名;2.用途;3.种类;4.是否带有动力装置;5.品牌
9503.0089	----其他	1.品名;2.用途;3.种类;4.品牌
9503.0090	---零件、附件	1.品名;2.用途;3.种类;4.品牌
95.04	视频游戏控制器及设备、游艺场所、桌上或室内游戏用品,包括弹球机、台球、娱乐专用桌及保龄球自动球道设备:	
9504.2000	-各种台球用品及附件	1.品名;2.用途;3.品牌
9504.3010	---电子游戏机	1.品名;2.用途;3.种类;4.品牌
9504.3090	---其他	1.品名;2.用途;3.品牌
9504.4000	-扑克牌	1.品名;2.用途;3.品牌

税则号列	商品描述	规范申报要素 / 价格申报要素 / 其他申报要素 / 举例说明
9504.5	-视频游戏控制器及设备,但子目9504.30的货品除外:	1.品名;2.用途;3.种类;4.是否与电视接收机配套使用;5.品牌
9504.9010	---其他电子游戏机	1.品名;2.用途;3.种类;4.品牌
9504.902	---保龄球自动球道设备及器具	1.品名;2.用途;3.种类;4.品牌
9504.9030	---中国象棋、国际象棋、跳棋等棋类用品	1.品名;2.用途;3.种类;4.品牌
9504.9040	---麻将及类似桌上游戏用品	1.品名;2.用途;3.种类;4.品牌
9504.9090	---其他	1.品名;2.用途;3.种类;4.品牌
95.05	节日(包括狂欢节)用品或其他娱乐用品,包括魔术道具及嬉戏品:	
9505.1000	-圣诞节用品	1.品名;2.用途;3.品牌
9505.9000	-其他	1.品名;2.用途;3.种类;4.品牌
95.06	一般的体育活动、体操、竞技及其他运动(包括乒乓球运动)或户外游戏用的本章其他税目未列名用品及设备;游泳池或戏水池:	
9506.1	-滑雪屐及其他滑雪用具:	1.品名;2.用途;3.种类;4.品牌;5.型号
9506.2	-滑水板、冲浪板、帆板及其他水上运动用具:	1.品名;2.用途;3.种类;4.品牌;5.型号
9506.3	-高尔夫球棍及其他高尔夫球用具:	1.品名;2.用途;3.品牌;4.型号
9506.4	-乒乓球运动用品及器械:	1.品名;2.用途;3.种类;4.品牌;5.型号
9506.5	-网球拍、羽毛球拍或类似的球拍,不论是否装弦:	1.品名;2.用途;3.种类;4.品牌;5.型号
9506.6	-球,但高尔夫球及乒乓球除外	1.品名;2.用途;3.种类;4.品牌;5.型号
9506.7	-溜冰鞋及旱冰鞋,包括装有冰刀的溜冰靴:	1.品名;2.用途;3.种类;4.品牌;5.型号
9506.91	--一般的体育活动、体操或竞技用品及设备:	1.品名;2.用途;3.种类;4.品牌;5.型号
9506.9900	--其他	1.品名;2.材质;3.品牌;4.型号
95.07	钓鱼竿、钓鱼钩及其他钓鱼用品;捞鱼网、捕蝶网及类似网囤子"鸟"(税目92.08或97.05的货品除外)以及类似的狩猎用品:	
9507.1	-钓鱼竿	1.品名;2.材质;3.品牌;4.型号
9507.2000	-钓鱼钩,不论有无系钩丝	1.品名2.品牌;3.型号
9507.3000	-钓线轮	1.品名2.品牌;3.型号
9507.9000	-其他	1.品名;2.用途;3.品牌;4.型号。注:税目56.08货品除外
95.08	旋转木马、秋千、射击用靶及其他游乐场的娱乐设备;流动马戏团及流动动物园;流动剧团:	1.品名;2.用途。注:旋转木马;射击用靶

第九十六章 杂项制品

税则号列	商品描述	规范申报要素 / 价格申报要素 / 其他申报要素 / 举例说明
96.01	已加工的兽牙、骨、玳瑁壳、角、鹿角、珊瑚、珍珠母及其他动物质雕刻材料及其制品(包括塑模制品):	
9601.1000	-已加工的兽牙及其制品	1.品名;2.材质;3.是否野生动物产品;4.是否已加工。注:野生象牙制的筷子,已加工
9601.9000	-其他	1.品名;2.材质;3.加工工艺
96.02	已加工的植物质或矿物质雕刻材料及其制品;蜡、硬脂、天然树胶、天然树脂或塑型膏制成的模塑或雕刻制品以及其他税目未列名的模塑或雕 刻制品;已加工的未硬化明胶(税目35.03的明胶除外)及 未硬化明胶制品:	

税则号列	商品描述	规范申报要素 / 价格申报要素 / 其他申报要素 / 举例说明
9602.0010	---装药用胶囊	1.品名。注:不包括税目19.05的装药空囊
9602.0090	---其他	1.品名;2.材质;3.加工工艺
96.03	帚、刷(包括作为机器、器具车辆零件的刷)、非机动的手工操作地板清扫器、拖把及毛掸;供制帚、刷用的成束或成簇的材料;油漆块垫及滚筒;橡皮扫帚(橡皮辊除外):	1.品名;2.用途;3.材质。注:机器用钢丝刷;野鸡羽毛掸
96.04	手用粗筛、细筛:	1.品名。注:手用粗筛、细筛
96.05	个人梳妆、缝纫或清洁鞋靴、衣服用的成套旅行用具:	1.品名;2.组成(内装货品)。注:擦鞋套具(内含棕色、黑色鞋油各1支、鞋擦1个、鞋刷2把,成套盒装)
96.06	纽扣、揿扣、纽扣芯及纽扣和揿扣的其他零件;纽扣坯:	1.品名;2.材质;3.种类;4.是否用纺织材料包裹;5.用途(是否袖口、饰扣)
96.07	拉链及其零件:	1.品名;2.材质;3.品牌。注:铜拉链
96.08	圆珠笔;毡尖及其他渗水式笔尖笔及唛头笔;自来水笔、铁笔型自来水笔及其他钢笔;蜡纸铁笔;活动铅笔;钢笔杆、铅笔套及类似的笔套;上述物品的零件(包括帽、夹),但税目96.09的货品除外:	1.品名;2.种类;3.品牌;4.型号
96.09	铅笔(税目96.08的铅笔除外)、颜色铅笔、铅笔芯、蜡笔、图画碳笔、书写或绘画用粉笔及裁缝划粉:	1.品名;2.种类;3.品牌;4.型号。注:不包括活动铅笔
96.10	具有书写或绘画面的石板、黑板及类似板,不论是否镶框:	1.品名;2.种类;3.品牌
96.11	手用日期戳、封缄戳、税目戳及类似印戳(包括标签压印器);手工操作的排字盘及带有排字盘的手印器:	1.品名;2.用途
96.12	打字机色带或类似色带,已上油或经其他方法处理能着色 的,不论是否装轴或装盒;印台,不论是否已加印油或带盒 子:	1.品名;2.材质;3.品牌;4.型号。注:不包括未上有油墨的色带;化学纤维制打字机色带,松下kx-8
96.13	香烟打火机和其他打火器(不论是机械的,还是电气的)及其零件,但打火石及打火机芯除外:	1.品名;2.种类;3.型号;4.品牌
96.14	烟斗(包括烟斗头)和烟嘴及其零件:	
9614.0010	---烟斗及烟斗头	1.品名;2.材质;3.品牌;4.型号
9614.0090	---其他	1.品名;2.材质;3.品牌。注:野生象牙制的烟嘴,无品牌
96.15	梳子、发夹及类似品;发卡、卷发夹、卷发器或类似品及其零件,但税目85.16的货品除外:	1.品名;2.材质。注:牛骨梳,非野生
96.16	香水喷雾器或类似的化妆用喷雾器及其座架、喷头;粉扑及粉拍,施敷脂粉或化妆品用:	1.品名;2.用途。注:香水喷雾器
96.17	带壳的保温瓶和其他真空容器及其零件,但玻璃瓶胆除外:	1.品名;2.是否带外壳的保温瓶
96.18	裁缝用人体模型及其他人体活动模型;橱窗装饰用自动模型及其他活动陈列品:	1.品名;2.用途;3.材质。注:裁缝用塑料人体模型
9619.0010	---尿布及尿裤	1.品名2.品牌(包括中英文品牌名称);3.系列;4.码数(型号);5.包装规格(每包所含片数);6.个体重量(每包重量)
9619.0020	---卫生巾(护垫)及止血塞	1.品名2.品牌
9619.0090	---任何材料制的卫生巾或尿布的类似品	1.品名2.品牌

第二十一类　艺术品、收藏品及古物

第九十七章　艺术品、收藏品及古物

税则号列	商品描述	申报要素
97.01	油画、粉画及其他手绘画，但带有手工绘制及手工描饰的制品或税目 49.06 的图纸除外；拼贴画及类似装饰板：	1.品名；2.是否野生动物产品；3.尺寸大小
97.02	雕版画、印制画、石印画的原本：	1.品名 2.尺寸大小；3.原作者姓名；4.创作年份
97.03	各种材料制的雕塑品原件：	1.品名；2.用途（如具有商业性质的装饰用雕塑品、个人装饰品及其他具有商业性质的传统手工艺品）；3.尺寸大小
97.04	使用过或未使用过的邮票、印花税票、邮戳印记、首日封、邮政信笺（印有邮票的纸品）及类似品，但税目 49.07 的货 品除外：	1.品名；2.种类；3.指运国（地区）税目 49.07 的货品除外。注：未使用过的新加坡邮票
97.05	具有动物学、植物学、矿物学解剖学、历史学、考古学、古生物学、人种学或钱币学意义的收集品及珍藏品：	1.品名；2.种类；3.年代；4.是否野生动物产品。注：2～3 亿年前的三叶虫化石（注：该例仅限于举例，实为国家禁止出口古文物）
97.06	超过 100 年的古物：	1.品名；2.种类；3.年代；4.是否野生动物产品

2015年出口退税率更新表

税则号列	商品名称	出口退税率(%)
0802903010	鲜或干的红松子仁	5
11010000	小麦或混合麦的细粉	13
11031100	小麦粗粒及粗粉	13
11032010	小麦团粒	13
11081200	玉米淀粉	13
21039010	味精	13
22071000	浓度≥80%的未改性乙醇	13
23031000	制造淀粉过程中的残渣及类似品	13
27160000	电力	17
28045000	硼、碲	13
28049090	其他硒	13
28129011	三氟化氮	9
28254000	镍的氧化物及氢氧化物	13
28259021	三氧化二铋	13
28269020	六氟磷酸锂	13
28353110	食品级的三磷酸钠（三聚磷酸钠）	13
28353190	其他三磷酸钠（三聚磷酸钠）	13
28353911	食品级的六偏磷酸钠	9
28416910	锰酸锂	13
28429030	锂镍钴锰氧化物	13
28429090	其他无机酸盐及过氧酸盐，叠氮化物除外	13
28530030	镍钴锰氢氧化物	13
29012410	1,3-丁二烯	13
29054200	季戊四醇	13
29054300	甘露糖醇	13
29054400	山梨醇	13
29054500	丙三醇(甘油)	13
29146910	辅酶Q10	13
29153200	乙酸乙烯酯	13
29157090	棕榈酸及其盐和酯、硬脂酸盐、酯	13
29181100	乳酸及其盐和酯	13
29181600	葡糖酸及其盐和酯	13
29189900	其他含其他附加含氧基羧酸及其酸酐（酰卤化物，过氧化物和过氧酸及它们的衍生物）	13
29214910	对异丙基苯胺	13
29214920	二甲基苯胺	13
29214930	2,6-甲基乙基苯胺	13
29214940	2,6-二乙基苯胺	13
29214990	其他芳香单胺及衍生物及它们的盐	13
29221910	乙胺丁醇	13
29221921	二甲氨基乙醇及其质子化盐	13
29221940	甲基二乙醇胺	13
29221950	本芴醇	13
29221990	其他氨基醇及其醚、酯和它们的盐（但含有一种以上含氧基的除外）	13
29222910	茴香胺、二茴香胺、氨基苯乙醚及其盐	13
29222990	其他氨基(萘酚、酚)及醚、酯、盐（但含有一种以上含氧基的除外）	13
29224110	赖氨酸	13
29224991	普鲁卡因	13
29225010	对羟基苯甘氨酸及其邓甲盐	13
29225090	其他氨基醇酚、氨基酸酚及其他含氧基氨基化合物	13
29242930	阿斯巴甜	13
29242990	其他环酰胺（包括环氨基甲酸酯）	13

税则号列	商品名称	出口退税率(%)
29309020	二硫代碳酸酯(或盐)［黄原酸酯（或盐）］	13
29329910	7-羟基苯并呋喃(呋喃酚)	13
29329920	联苯双酯	13
29331990	其他结构上有非稠合吡唑环化合物（不论是否氢化）	13
29332900	其他结构上有非稠合咪唑环化合物（不论是否氢化）	13
29333990	其他结构上有非稠合吡啶环化合物（不论是否氢化）	13
29334990	其他含喹琳或异喹啉环系的化合物（但未经进一步稠合）	13
29335910	胞嘧啶	13
29335990	其他结构上有嘧啶环或哌嗪环的化合物（不论是否氢化）	13
29339100	阿普唑仑、卡马西泮等以及它们的盐	13
29339900	其他仅含氮杂原子的杂环化合物	13
29343000	含一个吩噻嗪环系的化合物（但未经进一步稠合,不论是否氢化）	13
29349100	阿米雷司、溴替唑仑、氯噻西泮等以及他们的盐	13
29349910	磺内酯及磺内酰胺	13
29349920	呋喃唑酮	13
29349930	核酸及其盐	13
29349990	其他杂环化合物	13
29371100	生长激素及其衍生物和类似结构物	13
29371210	重组人胰岛素及其盐	17
29371900	其他多肽激素、蛋白激素、糖蛋白激素及其衍生物和类似结构物	13
29372311	孕马结合雌激素	13
29372319	其他动物源的雌（甾）激素和孕激素	13
29372390	其他皮质甾类激素的卤化衍生物	13
29372900	其他甾族激素及其衍生物和类似结构物	13
29400000	化学纯糖,但蔗糖、乳糖、麦芽糖、葡萄糖及果糖除外；糖醚、糖酯及其盐，但不包括税目29.37、29.38、29.39的产品	13
30021000	抗血清、其他血份及免疫制品(不论是否修饰通过生物工艺加工制得)	17
30022000	人用疫苗	17
30023000	兽用疫苗	17
3002903010	两用物项管制细菌及病毒	17
3002903020	苏云金杆菌	17
3002903090	其他细菌及病毒	17
30029040	遗传物质和基因修饰生物体	17
3002909019	其他人血制品、动物血制品	17
3002909091	两用物项管制毒素	17
3002909099	人血、其他毒素等〔包括培养微生物(不包括酵母)及类似产品）	17
30049010	含有磺胺类的药品（两种或两种以上成分混合而成的，治病或防病用已配定剂量或零售包装）	17
30049020	含联苯双酯的药品（混合或非混合，治病或防病用已配定剂量或零售包	17
30049052	片仔癀 （混合或非混合，治病或防病用已配定剂量或零售包装）	17
30049053	白药 （混合或非混合，治病或防病用已配定剂量或零售包装）	17
30049054	清凉油（混合或非混合，治病或防病用已配定剂量或零售包装）	17
3203001990	其他植物质着色料及以其为基本成分的制品包括染料浸膏(不论是否已有化学定义);32章注释三所述的以植物质着色料为基本成分的制品	13
32141010	半导体器件封装材料	13
32141090	其他安装玻璃用油灰、接缝用油灰、树脂胶泥、嵌缝胶及其他类似胶粘剂;漆工用填料	13
3406000090	其他各种蜡烛及类似品	17
37061010	已曝光已冲洗的教学专用电影胶片，宽度≥35mm，不论是否配有声道或仅有声道	17
37061090	已曝光已冲洗的电影胶片，宽度≥35mm，不论是否配有声道或仅有声道，教学专用除外	17

税则号列	商品名称	出口退税率(%)
37069010	已曝光已冲洗的教学专用电影胶片，宽度＜35mm，不论是否配有声道或仅有声道	17
37069090	已曝光已冲洗的电影胶片，宽度＜35mm，不论是否配有声道或仅有声道，教学专用除外	17
38019010	表面处理的球化石墨	13
38170000	混合烷基苯及混合烷基萘,但税目27.07及29.02的产品除外	13
38220010	附于衬背上的诊断或实验用试剂，但税目32.02,32.06的货品除外	13
38220090	无论是否附于衬背上的诊断或实验用配制试剂，但税目32.02,32.06的货品除外	13
38231200	油酸	9
38247400	含氢氯氟烃的，不论是否含全氟烃或氢氟烃，但不含全氯氟烃的含有甲烷、乙烷、丙烷卤化衍生物混合物	13
5004000000	非供零售用丝纱线	17
5005001010	非供零售用䌷丝纱线	17
5005001090	非供零售用䌷丝纱线	17
5005009010	非供零售用其他绢纺纱线	17
5005009020	非供零售用其他绢纺纱线	17
5006000010	零售用丝纱线,绢纺纱线;蚕胶丝	17
5006000020	零售用丝纱线,绢纺纱线;蚕胶丝	17
5007101010	未漂白或漂白的䌷丝机织物	17
5007101020	未漂白或漂白的䌷丝机织物	17
5007101031	未漂白或漂白的䌷丝机织物	17
5007101039	未漂白或漂白的䌷丝机织物	17
5007101091	未漂白或漂白的䌷丝机织物	17
5007101099	未漂白或漂白的䌷丝机织物	17
5007109010	其他䌷丝机织物	17
5007109021	其他色织䌷丝机织物	17
5007109029	其他非色织䌷丝机织物	17
5007109031	其他䌷丝机织物	17
5007109039	其他䌷丝机织物	17
5007109091	其他䌷丝机织物	17
5007109099	其他䌷丝机织物	17
5007201100	未漂白或漂白的桑蚕丝机织物	17
5007201900	其他桑蚕丝机织物	17
5007202100	未漂白或漂白的柞蚕丝机织物	17
5007202900	其他柞蚕丝机织物	17
5007203100	未漂白或漂白的绢丝机织物	17
5007203900	其他绢丝机织物	17
5007209010	未漂白或漂白其他丝机织物	17
5007209090	其他丝机织物	17
5007901010	未漂白或漂白其他丝机织物	17
5007901020	未漂白或漂白其他丝机织物	17
5007901031	未漂白或漂白其他丝机织物	17
5007901039	未漂白或漂白其他丝机织物	17
5007901091	未漂白或漂白其他丝机织物	17
5007901099	未漂白或漂白其他丝机织物	17
5007909010	其他丝机织物	17
5007909021	其他色织丝机织物	17
5007909029	其他非色织丝机织物	17
5007909031	其他丝机织物	17
5007909039	其他丝机织物	17
5007909091	其他丝机织物	17
5007909099	其他丝机织物	17
5106100000	非零售用粗梳羊毛纱线	17

税则号列	商品名称	出口退税率(%)
5106200000	非零售用粗梳混纺羊毛纱线	17
5107100000	非供零售用精梳纯羊毛纱线	17
5107200000	非供零售用精梳混纺羊毛纱线	17
5108101100	非供零售用粗梳山羊绒纱线	17
5108101990	非供零售用粗梳其他动物细毛纱线〔按重量计其他动物细毛含量≥85%〕	17
5108109090	非供零售用粗梳其他动物细毛纱线〔按重量计其他粗梳动物细毛含量＜85%〕	17
51082011	按重量计山羊绒含量在85%及以上的非供零售用的精梳纱线	17
5108201990	非供零售用精梳其他动物细毛纱线〔按重量计其他动物细毛含量≥85%〕	17
5108209090	非供零售用精梳其他动物细毛纱线	17
5109101100	零售用山羊绒纱线	17
5109101900	零售用其他动物细毛纱线	17
5109109000	零售用羊毛纱线	17
5109901100	零售用混纺山羊绒纱线	17
5109901900	零售用混纺其他动物细毛纱线	17
5109909000	零售用混纺羊毛纱线	17
5110000090	其他动物粗毛或马毛的纱线	17
5111111100	每平米重≤300克山羊绒机织物	17
5111111900	每平米重≤300克其他动物细毛机织物	17
5111119000	每平米重≤300克羊毛机织物	17
5111191100	每平米重＞300克山羊绒机织物	17
5111191900	每平米重＞300克其他动物细毛机织物	17
5111199000	每平米重＞300克羊毛机织物	17
5111200010	与化纤长丝混纺提花/装饰家具布	17
5111200090	与化纤长丝混纺其他粗梳毛机织物	17
5111300010	与化纤短纤混纺提花/装饰家具布	17
5111300090	与化纤短纤混纺其他粗梳毛机织物	17
5111900011	其他丝与粗梳羊毛或动物细毛混纺	17
5111900019	其他丝混纺机织物	17
5111900021	其他毛混纺提花/装饰家具布	17
5111900029	其他毛混纺提花/装饰家具布	17
5111900091	其他机织物	17
5111900099	其他机织物	17
5112110010	重≤140克/平米毛提花/装饰家具布	17
5112110090	其他重量≤200克/平米毛制机织物	17
5112190010	重＞200克/平米毛提花/装饰家具布	17
5112190090	重量＞200克/平米其他毛制机织物	17
5112200010	与化纤长丝混纺毛制提花/家具布	17
5112200090	与化纤长丝混纺其他毛制机织物	17
5112300010	与化纤短纤混纺毛制提花/家具布	17
5112300090	与化纤短纤混纺其他毛制机织物	17
5112900010	其他丝与毛混纺机织物	17
5112900020	其他精梳毛制提花/装饰家具布	17

税则号列	商品名称	出口退税率(%)
5112900090	其他机织物	17
5113000000	动物粗毛或马毛的机织物	17
5204110000	非零售棉缝纫线	17
5204190000	非零售棉缝纫线	17
5204200000	零售用棉制缝纫线	17
5205110000	非零售粗梳粗支纯棉单纱	17
5205120000	非零售粗梳中支纯棉单纱	17
5205130000	非零售粗梳细支纯棉单纱	17
5205140000	非零售粗梳较细支纯棉单纱	17
5205150000	非零售粗梳特细支纯棉单纱	17
5205210000	非零售精梳粗支纯棉单纱	17
5205220000	非零售精梳中支纯棉单纱	17
5205230000	非零售精梳细支纯棉单纱	17
5205240000	非零售精梳较细支纯棉单纱	17
5205260000	非零售精梳特细支纯棉单纱	17
5205270000	非零售精梳超特细支纯棉单纱	17
5205280000	非零售精梳微支纯棉单纱	17
5205310000	非零售粗梳粗支纯棉多股纱	17
5205320000	非零售粗梳中支纯棉多股纱	17
5205330000	非零售粗梳细支纯棉多股纱	17
5205340000	非零售粗梳较细支纯棉多股纱	17
5205350000	非零售粗梳特细支纯棉多股纱	17
5205410000	非零售精梳粗支纯棉多股纱	17
5205420000	非零售精梳中支纯棉多股纱	17
5205430000	非零售精梳细支纯棉多股纱	17
5205440000	非零售精梳较细支纯棉多股纱	17
5205460000	非零售精梳特细支纯棉多股纱	17
5205470000	非零售精梳超特细支多股纱	17
5205480000	非零售精梳微支纯棉多股纱	17
5206110000	非零售粗梳粗支混纺棉单纱	17
5206120000	非零售粗梳中支混纺棉单纱	17
5206130000	非零售粗梳细支混纺棉单纱	17
5206140000	非零售粗梳较细支混纺棉单纱	17
5206150000	非零售粗梳特细支混纺棉单纱	17
5206210000	非零售精梳粗支混纺棉单纱	17
5206220000	非零售精梳中支混纺棉单纱	17
5206230000	非零售精梳细支混纺棉单纱	17
5206240000	非零售精梳较细支混纺棉单纱	17
5206250000	非零售精梳特细支混纺棉单纱	17
5206310000	非零售粗梳粗支混纺棉多股纱或缆线	17
5206320000	非零售粗梳中支混纺棉多股纱或缆线	17
5206330000	非零售粗梳细支其他混纺棉多股纱或缆线	17
5206340000	非零售粗梳较细混纺棉多股纱或缆线	17
5206350000	非零售粗梳特细混纺棉多股纱或缆线	17
5206410000	非零售精梳粗支混纺棉多股纱	17
5206420000	非零售精梳中支混纺棉多股纱	17
5206430000	非零售精梳细支混纺棉多股纱	17
5206440000	非零售精梳较细混纺棉多股纱	17
5206450000	非零售精梳特细混纺棉多股纱	17

税则号列	商品名称	出口退税率(%)
5207100000	供零售用纯棉纱线	17
5207900000	供零售用混纺棉纱线	17
5208110010	未漂白全棉平纹府绸及细平布	17
5208110020	未漂白全棉平纹机织平布	17
5208110030	未漂白全棉平纹奶酪布	17
5208110040	未漂白全棉平纹印染用布	17
5208110050	未漂白全棉平纹巴里纱及薄细布	17
5208110060	未漂白全棉平纹机织打字布	17
5208110070	未漂白全棉医用纱布	17
5208120010	未漂白全棉平纹府绸及细平布	17
5208120020	未漂白全棉平纹机织平布	17
5208120030	未漂白全棉平纹奶酪布	17
5208120040	未漂白全棉平纹印染用布	17
5208120050	未漂白全棉平纹巴里纱及薄细布	17
5208130000	未漂白全棉三、四线斜纹布	17
5208190010	未漂白其他全棉机织缎布	17
5208190020	未漂白其他全棉机织斜纹布	17
5208190030	未漂白其他全棉机织牛津布	17
5208190090	未漂白其他全棉机织物	17
5208210010	漂白全棉平纹府绸及细平布	17
5208210020	漂白全棉平纹机织平布	17
5208210030	漂白全棉平纹奶酪布	17
5208210040	漂白全棉平纹印染用布	17
5208210050	漂白全棉平纹巴里纱及薄细布	17
5208210060	漂白全棉医用纱布	17
5208220010	漂白全棉平纹府绸及细平布	17
5208220020	漂白全棉平纹机织平布	17
5208220030	漂白全棉平纹奶酪布	17
5208220040	漂白全棉平纹印染用布	17
5208220050	漂白全棉巴里纱及薄细布	17
5208230000	漂白的全棉三、四线斜纹布	17
5208290010	漂白其他全棉机织缎布	17
5208290020	漂白其他全棉机织斜纹布	17
5208290030	漂白其他全棉机织牛津布	17
5208290090	漂白其他全棉机织物	17
5208310010	染色全棉手工织布	17
5208310091	染色全棉平纹府绸及细平布	17
5208310092	染色全棉平纹机织平布	17
5208310093	染色全棉平纹奶酪布	17
5208310094	染色全棉平纹印染用布	17
5208310095	染色全棉巴里纱及薄细布	17
5208320010	染色全棉手工织布	17
5208320091	染色全棉平纹府绸及细平布	17
5208320092	染色全棉平纹机织平布	17
5208320093	染色全棉平纹奶酪布	17
5208320094	染色全棉平纹印染用布	17
5208320095	染色全棉巴里纱及薄细布	17
5208330000	染色的全棉三、四线斜纹布	17
5208390010	染色其他全棉机织缎布	17
5208390020	染色其他全棉机织斜纹布	17
5208390030	染色其他全棉机织牛津布	17
5208390090	染色其他全棉机织物	17
5208410010	色织的全棉手工织布	17
5208410090	色织的全棉平纹机织物	17

税则号列	商品名称	出口退税率(%)
5208420010	色织的全棉手工织布	17
5208420090	色织的全棉平纹机织物	17
5208430000	色织的全棉三、四线斜纹布	17
5208490010	色织的其他全棉提花机织物	17
5208490090	色织的其他全棉机织物	17
5208510010	印花全棉手工织布	17
5208510091	印花全棉平纹府绸及细平布	17
5208510092	印花全棉平纹机织平布	17
5208510093	印花全棉平纹奶酪布	17
5208510094	印花全棉平纹印染用布	17
5208510095	印花全棉平纹巴里纱及薄细布	17
5208520010	印花的全棉手工织布	17
5208520091	印花的全棉平纹府绸及细平布	17
5208520092	印花的全棉平纹机织平布	17
5208520093	印花的全棉平纹奶酪布	17
5208520094	印花的全棉平纹印染用布	17
5208520095	印花的全棉巴里纱及薄细布	17
5208591000	印花的全棉三、四线斜纹布	17
5208599010	印花其他全棉机织缎布	17
5208599020	印花其他全棉机织斜纹布	17
5208599030	印花其他全棉机织牛津布	17
5208599090	印花其他全棉机织物	17
5209110010	未漂白全棉平纹府绸及细平布	17
5209110020	未漂白的全棉平纹机织平布	17
5209110030	未漂白的全棉平纹机织帆布	17
5209120000	未漂白的全棉三、四线斜纹布	17
5209190010	未漂白的其他全棉机织缎布	17
5209190020	未漂白的其他全棉机织斜纹布	17
5209190030	未漂白的其他全棉机织帆布	17
5209190090	未漂白的其他全棉机织物	17
5209210010	漂白全棉平纹府绸及细平布	17
5209210020	漂白的全棉平纹机织平布	17
5209210030	漂白的全棉平纹机织帆布	17
5209220000	漂白的全棉三、四线斜纹布	17
5209290010	漂白的其他全棉机织缎布	17
5209290030	漂白的其他全棉机织帆布	17
5209290090	漂白的其他全棉机织物	17
5209310010	染色全棉手工织布	17
5209310091	染色全棉平纹府绸及细平布	17
5209310092	染色的全棉平纹机织平布	17
5209310093	染色的全棉平纹机织帆布	17
5209320000	染色的全棉三、四线斜纹布	17
5209390010	染色的其他全棉机织缎布	17
5209390020	染色的其他全棉机织斜纹布	17
5209390030	染色的其他全棉机织帆布	17
5209390090	染色的其他全棉机织物	17
5209410010	色织的全棉手工织布	17
5209410090	色织的全棉平纹机织物	17
5209420010	色织全棉蓝粗斜纹布(劳动布)	17
5209420090	色织其他全棉粗斜纹布(劳动布)	17
5209430000	其他色织的全棉三、四线斜纹布	17
5209490010	色织的其他全棉提花机织物	17
5209490090	色织的其他全棉机织物	17
5209510010	印花全棉手工织布	17

税则号列	商品名称	出口退税率(%)
5209510091	印花全棉平纹府绸及细平布	17
5209510092	印花全棉平纹机织平布	17
5209510093	印花全棉平纹机织帆布	17
5209520000	印花的全棉三、四线斜纹布	17
5209590010	印花的其他全棉机织缎布	17
5209590020	印花的其他全棉机织斜纹布	17
5209590030	印花的其他全棉机织帆布	17
5209590090	印花的其他全棉机织物	17
5210110011	未漂白与聚酯短纤混纺的棉制府绸	17
5210110012	未漂白与聚酯短纤混纺棉机织平布	17
5210110013	未漂白与聚酯短纤混纺棉奶酪布	17
5210110014	未漂白与聚酯短纤混纺棉印染用布	17
5210110015	未漂白与聚酯短纤混纺棉巴里纱	17
5210110091	未漂白与其他化纤混纺棉府绸	17
5210110092	未漂白与其他化纤混纺棉机织平布	17
5210110093	未漂白与其他化纤混纺棉奶酪布	17
5210110094	未漂白与其他化纤混纺棉印染用布	17
5210110095	未漂白与其他化纤混纺棉巴里纱	17
5210191010	未漂白与聚酯短纤混纺3/4线或双面棉斜纹布	17
5210191090	未漂白与其他化纤混纺3/4线或双面棉斜纹布	17
5210199011	其他未漂白与聚酯短纤混纺的缎布	17
5210199012	其他未漂白与聚酯短纤混纺斜纹布	17
5210199013	其他未漂白与聚酯短纤混纺牛津布	17
5210199019	其他未漂白与聚酯短纤混纺棉布	17
5210199091	其他未漂白与其他化纤混纺缎布	17
5210199092	其他未漂白与其他化纤混纺斜纹布	17
5210199093	其他未漂白与其他化纤混牛津布	17
5210199099	其他未漂白与其他化纤混纺棉布	17
5210210011	漂白与聚酯短纤混纺棉府绸	17
5210210012	漂白与聚酯短纤混纺棉机织平布	17
5210210013	漂白与聚酯短纤混纺棉奶酪布	17
5210210014	漂白与聚酯短纤混纺棉印染布	17
5210210015	漂白与聚酯短纤混纺棉巴里纱	17
5210210021	漂白与化纤长丝混纺棉府绸	17
5210210022	漂白与化纤长丝混纺棉机织平布	17
5210210023	漂白与化纤长丝混纺棉奶酪布	17
5210210024	漂白与化纤长丝混纺棉印染布	17
5210210025	漂白与化纤长丝混纺棉巴里纱	17
5210210091	漂白与其他化纤混纺棉府绸	17
5210210092	漂白与其他化纤混纺棉机织平布	17
5210210093	漂白与其他化纤混纺棉奶酪布	17
5210210094	漂白与其他化纤混纺棉印染布	17
5210210095	漂白与其他化纤混纺棉巴里纱	17
5210291010	漂白与聚酯短纤混纺3/4线或双面棉斜纹布	17
5210291020	漂白与化纤长丝混纺3/4线或双面棉斜纹布	17
5210291090	漂白与其他化纤混纺3/4线或双面棉斜纹布	17
5210299011	其他漂白与聚酯短纤混纺缎布	17
5210299012	其他漂白与聚酯短纤混纺斜纹布	17
5210299013	其他漂白与聚酯短纤混纺牛津布	17
5210299019	其他漂白与聚酯短纤混纺棉布	17
5210299021	其他漂白与化纤长丝混纺缎布	17
5210299022	其他漂白与化纤长丝混纺斜纹布	17
5210299023	其他漂白与化纤长丝混纺牛津布	17
5210299029	其他漂白与化纤长丝混纺棉布	17

税则号列	商品名称	出口退税率(%)
5210299091	其他漂白与其他化纤混纺缎布	17
5210299092	其他漂白与其他化纤混纺斜纹布	17
5210299093	其他漂白与其他化纤混纺牛津布	17
5210299099	其他漂白与其他化纤混纺棉布	17
5210310011	染色与聚酯短纤混纺棉府绸	17
5210310012	染色与聚酯短纤混纺棉机织平布	17
5210310013	染色与聚酯短纤混纺棉奶酪布	17
5210310014	染色与聚酯短纤混纺棉印染布	17
5210310015	染色与聚酯短纤混纺棉巴里纱	17
5210310021	染色与化纤长丝混纺棉府绸	17
5210310022	染色与化纤长丝混纺棉机织平布	17
5210310023	染色与化纤长丝混纺棉奶酪布	17
5210310024	染色与化纤长丝混纺棉印染布	17
5210310025	染色与化纤长丝混纺棉巴里纱	17
5210310091	染色与其他化纤混纺棉府绸	17
5210310092	染色与其他化纤混纺棉机织平布	17
5210310093	染色与其他化纤混纺棉奶酪布	17
5210310094	染色与其他化纤混纺棉印染布	17
5210310095	染色与其他化纤混纺棉巴里纱	17
5210320010	染色与聚酯短纤混纺的3/4线斜纹棉布	17
5210320020	染色与化纤长丝混纺的3/4线斜纹棉布	17
5210320090	染色与其他化纤混纺的3/4线斜纹棉布	17
5210390011	其他染色与聚酯短纤混纺缎布	17
5210390012	其他染色与聚酯短纤混纺斜纹布	17
5210390013	其他染色与聚酯短纤混纺牛津布	17
5210390019	其他染色与聚酯短纤混纺棉布	17
5210390021	其他染色与化纤长丝混纺缎布	17
5210390022	其他染色与化纤长丝混纺斜纹布	17
5210390023	其他染色与化纤长丝混纺牛津布	17
5210390029	其他染色与化纤长丝混纺棉布	17
5210390091	其他染色与其他化纤混纺缎布	17
5210390092	其他染色与其他化纤混纺斜纹布	17
5210390093	其他染色与其他化纤混纺牛津布	17
5210390099	其他染色与其他化纤混纺棉布	17
5210410010	色织与聚酯短纤混纺棉平纹布	17
5210410020	色织与化纤长丝混纺棉平纹布	17
5210410090	色织与其他化纤混纺棉平纹布	17
5210491010	色织与聚酯短纤混纺3/4斜纹棉布	17
5210491020	色织与化纤长丝混纺3/4斜纹棉布	17
5210491090	色织其他化纤混纺3/4斜纹棉布	17
5210499011	色织与聚酯短纤混纺提花布	17
5210499019	色织与聚酯短纤混纺其他棉布	17
5210499020	色织与化纤长丝混纺棉布	17
5210499090	色织与其他化纤混纺棉布	17
5210510011	印花与聚酯短纤混纺的棉府绸	17
5210510012	印花与聚酯短纤混纺棉机织平布	17
5210510013	印花与聚酯短纤混纺的棉奶酪布	17
5210510014	印花与聚酯短纤混纺棉印染布	17
5210510015	印花与聚酯短纤混纺棉巴里纱	17
5210510021	印花与化纤长丝混纺的棉府绸	17
5210510022	印花与化纤长丝混纺棉机织平布	17
5210510023	印花与化纤长丝混纺棉奶酪布	17
5210510024	印花与化纤长丝混纺棉印染布	17
5210510025	印花与化纤长丝混纺棉巴里纱	17

税则号列	商品名称	出口退税率(%)
5210510091	印花与其他化纤混纺的棉府绸	17
5210510092	印花与其他化纤混纺棉机织平布	17
5210510093	印花与其他化纤混纺的棉奶酪布	17
5210510094	印花与其他化纤混纺棉印染布	17
5210510095	印花与其他化纤混纺棉巴里纱	17
5210591010	印花聚酯短纤混纺3/4线斜纹棉布	17
5210591020	印花化纤长丝混纺3/4线斜纹棉布	17
5210591090	印花其他化纤混纺3/4线斜纹棉布	17
5210599011	其他印花与聚酯短纤混纺缎布	17
5210599012	其他印花与聚酯短纤混纺斜纹布	17
5210599013	其他印花与聚酯短纤混纺牛津布	17
5210599019	其他印花与聚酯短纤混纺棉布	17
5210599021	其他印花与化纤长丝混纺缎布	17
5210599022	其他印花与化纤长丝混纺斜纹布	17
5210599023	其他印花与化纤长丝混纺牛津布	17
5210599029	其他印花与化纤长丝混纺棉布	17
5210599091	其他印花与其他化纤混纺缎布	17
5210599092	其他印花与其他化纤混纺斜纹布	17
5210599093	其他印花与其他化纤混纺牛津布	17
5210599099	其他印花与其他化纤混纺棉布	17
5211110011	未漂白与聚酯短纤混纺棉府绸	17
5211110012	未漂白与聚酯短纤混纺棉机织平布	17
5211110019	未漂白与聚酯短纤混纺棉平纹帆布	17
5211110091	未漂白与其他化纤混纺棉府绸	17
5211110092	未漂白与其他化纤混纺棉机织平布	17
5211110099	未漂白与其他化纤混纺棉平纹帆布	17
5211120010	未漂白聚酯短纤混纺斜纹棉布	17
5211120090	未漂白其他化纤混纺斜纹棉布	17
5211190011	未漂白与聚酯短纤混纺其他棉缎布	17
5211190012	未漂白与聚酯短纤混纺其他棉斜纹布	17
5211190013	未漂白与聚酯短纤混纺其他棉帆布	17
5211190019	未漂白与聚酯短纤混纺其他棉布	17
5211190091	未漂白与其他化纤混纺其他棉缎布	17
5211190092	未漂白与其他化纤混纺其他棉斜纹布	17
5211190093	未漂白与其他化纤混纺其他棉帆布	17
5211190099	未漂白与其他化纤混纺其他棉布	17
5211200000	漂白主要或仅与其他化纤混纺的棉机织布	17
5211310011	染色与聚酯短纤混纺棉府绸	17
5211310012	染色与聚酯短纤混纺机织平布	17
5211310013	染色与聚酯短纤混纺平纹帆布	17
5211310021	染色与化纤长丝混纺棉府绸	17
5211310022	染色与化纤长丝混纺机织平布	17
5211310023	染色与化纤长丝混纺平纹帆布	17
5211310091	染色与其他化纤混纺棉府绸	17
5211310092	染色与其他化纤混纺机织平布	17
5211310093	染色与其他化纤混纺平纹帆布	17
5211320010	染色聚酯短纤混纺3/4线斜纹棉布	17
5211320020	染色化纤长丝混纺3/4线斜纹棉布	17
5211320090	染色其他化纤混纺3/4线斜纹棉布	17
5211390011	染色与聚酯短纤混纺的棉缎布	17
5211390012	染色与聚酯短纤混纺的棉斜纹布	17
5211390013	染色与聚酯短纤混纺的棉帆布	17
5211390019	染色与聚酯短纤混纺其他棉布	17
5211390021	染色与化纤长丝混纺的棉缎布	17

税则号列	商品名称	出口退税率(%)
5211390022	染色与化纤长丝混纺的棉斜纹布	17
5211390023	染色与化纤长丝混纺的棉帆布	17
5211390029	染色与化纤长丝混纺的其他棉布	17
5211390091	染色与其他化纤混纺的棉缎布	17
5211390092	染色与其他化纤混纺的棉斜纹布	17
5211390093	染色与其他化纤混纺的棉帆布	17
5211390099	染色与其他化纤混纺其他棉布	17
5211410010	色织与聚酯短纤混纺平纹棉布	17
5211410020	色织与化纤长丝混纺平纹棉布	17
5211410090	色织与其他化纤混纺平纹棉布	17
5211420010	色织与化纤混纺蓝色粗斜纹棉布	17
5211420090	色织与化纤混纺非蓝色粗斜纹棉布	17
5211430010	其他色织与聚酯短纤混纺3/4线斜纹棉布	17
5211430020	其他色织与化纤长丝混纺3/4线斜纹棉布	17
5211430090	其他色织与其他化纤混纺3/4线斜纹棉布	17
5211490011	色织与聚酯短纤混纺的提花布	17
5211490019	色织与聚酯短纤混纺其他棉布	17
5211490021	色织与化纤长丝混纺的提花布	17
5211490029	色织与化纤长丝混纺其他棉布	17
5211490091	色织与其他化纤混纺的提花布	17
5211490099	色织与其他化纤混纺其他棉布	17
5211510011	印花与聚酯短纤混纺棉府绸	17
5211510012	印花与聚酯短纤混纺的机织平布	17
5211510013	印花与聚酯短纤混纺的平纹帆布	17
5211510021	印花与化纤长丝混纺棉府绸	17
5211510022	印花与化纤长丝混纺机织平布	17
5211510023	印花与化纤长丝混纺平纹帆布	17
5211510091	印花与其他化纤混纺棉府绸	17
5211510092	印花与其他化纤混纺的机织平布	17
5211510093	印花与其他化纤混纺的平纹帆布	17
5211520010	印花与聚酯短纤混纺3/4线斜纹棉布	17
5211520020	印花与化纤长丝混纺3/4线斜纹棉布	17
5211520090	印花与其他化纤混纺3/4线斜纹棉布	17
5211590011	印花与聚酯短纤混纺棉缎布	17
5211590012	印花与聚酯短纤混纺斜纹棉布	17
5211590013	印花与聚酯短纤混纺棉帆布	17
5211590019	印花与聚酯短纤混纺其他棉布	17
5211590021	印花与化纤长丝混纺棉缎布	17
5211590022	印花与化纤长丝混纺斜纹棉布	17
5211590023	印花与化纤长丝混纺棉帆布	17
5211590029	印花与化纤长丝混纺其他棉布	17
5211590091	印花与其他化纤混纺棉缎布	17
5211590092	印花与其他化纤混纺斜纹棉布	17
5211590093	印花与其他化纤混纺棉帆布	17
5211590099	印花与其他化纤混纺其他棉布	17
5212110011	未漂白的其他混纺棉布	17
5212110019	未漂白的其他混纺棉布	17
5212110021	未漂白的其他混纺棉布	17
5212110029	未漂白的其他混纺棉布	17
5212110030	未漂白的其他混纺府绸及细平布	17
5212110040	未漂白的其他混纺棉机织平布	17
5212110050	未漂白的其他混纺棉印染布	17
5212110060	未漂白其他混纺棉奶酪布,薄细布,巴里纱	17
5212110070	未漂白的其他混纺棉缎布	17

税则号列	商品名称	出口退税率(%)
5212110081	未漂白的其他混纺斜纹棉布	17
5212110089	未漂白的其他混纺棉牛津布	17
5212110090	未漂白的其他混纺棉布	17
5212120011	漂白的其他混纺棉布	17
5212120019	漂白的其他混纺棉布	17
5212120020	漂白的其他混纺棉布	17
5212120050	漂白的其他混纺棉印染布	17
5212120060	漂白其他混纺棉奶酪布/薄细布/纱	17
5212120071	漂白的其他混纺棉缎布	17
5212120072	漂白的其他混纺斜纹棉布	17
5212120079	漂白的其他混纺棉牛津布	17
5212120090	漂白的其他混纺棉机织物	17
5212130011	染色其他混纺棉布	17
5212130019	染色其他混纺棉布	17
5212130021	染色其他混纺棉布	17
5212130029	染色其他混纺棉布	17
5212130030	染色其他混纺府绸及平细布	17
5212130060	染色其他混纺奶酪布,薄细布,巴里纱	17
5212130071	染色其他混纺棉缎布	17
5212130072	染色其他混纺斜纹棉布	17
5212130079	染色其他混纺棉牛津布	17
5212130090	染色其他混纺棉布	17
5212140011	色织其他混纺棉布	17
5212140019	色织其他混纺棉布	17
5212140021	色织其他混纺棉布	17
5212140029	色织其他混纺棉布	17
5212140030	色织其他混纺棉提花布	17
5212140090	色织其他混纺棉布	17
5212150011	印花其他混纺棉布	17
5212150019	印花其他混纺棉布	17
5212150021	印花其他混纺棉布	17
5212150029	印花其他混纺棉布	17
5212150040	印花其他混纺棉机织平布	17
5212150050	印花其他混纺棉印染布	17
5212150060	印花其他混纺棉奶酪布,薄细布,巴里纱	17
5212150071	印花其他混纺棉缎布	17
5212150072	印花其他混纺斜纹棉布	17
5212150079	印花其他混纺棉牛津布	17
5212150090	印花其他混纺棉布	17
5212210011	未漂白其他混纺棉布	17
5212210019	未漂白其他混纺棉布	17
5212210021	未漂白其他混纺棉布	17
5212210029	未漂白其他混纺棉布	17
5212210030	未漂白其他混纺府绸及平细布	17
5212210040	未漂白其他混纺棉机织平布	17
5212210050	未漂白其他混纺棉帆布	17
5212210060	未漂白其他混纺棉缎布	17
5212210070	未漂白其他混纺斜纹棉布	17
5212210090	未漂白其他混纺棉布	17
5212220011	漂白的其他混纺棉布	17
5212220019	漂白的其他混纺棉布	17
5212220021	漂白的其他混纺棉布	17
5212220029	漂白的其他混纺棉布	17
5212220030	漂白的其他混纺府绸及细平布	17

税则号列	商品名称	出口退税率(%)
5212220040	漂白的其他混纺棉机织平布	17
5212220050	漂白的其他混纺棉帆布	17
5212220060	漂白的其他混纺棉缎布	17
5212220070	漂白的其他混纺棉斜纹布	17
5212220090	漂白的其他混纺棉布	17
5212230011	染色的其他混纺棉布	17
5212230019	染色的其他混纺棉布	17
5212230021	染色的其他混纺棉布	17
5212230029	染色的其他混纺棉布	17
5212230030	染色的其他混纺府绸及细平布	17
5212230040	染色的其他混纺棉机织平布	17
5212230050	染色的其他混纺棉帆布	17
5212230060	染色的其他混纺棉缎布	17
5212230070	染色的其他混纺棉斜纹布	17
5212230090	染色的其他混纺棉布	17
5212240011	色织的其他混纺棉布	17
5212240019	色织的其他混纺棉布	17
5212240021	色织的其他混纺棉布	17
5212240029	色织的其他混纺棉布	17
5212240030	色织的其他混纺蓝色粗斜纹布	17
5212240040	色织的其他混纺提花布	17
5212240090	色织的其他混纺棉布	17
5212250011	印花的其他混纺棉布	17
5212250019	印花的其他混纺棉布	17
5212250021	印花的其他混纺棉布	17
5212250029	印花的其他混纺棉布	17
5212250030	印花的其他混纺府绸及细平布	17
5212250040	印花的其他混纺棉机织平布	17
5212250050	印花的其他混纺棉帆布	17
5212250060	印花的其他混纺棉缎布	17
5212250070	印花的其他混纺棉斜纹布	17
5212250090	印花的其他混纺棉布	17
5306100000	亚麻单纱	17
5306200000	亚麻多股纱线或缆线	17
5307100000	黄麻及其他纺织用韧皮纤维单纱	17
5307200000	黄麻及其他韧皮纤维多股纱或缆线	17
5308100000	椰壳纤维纱线	17
5308200000	大麻纱线	17
5308901100	漂白或未漂白的纯苎麻纱线	17
5308901200	纯苎麻色纱线	17
5308901300	漂白或未漂白其他苎麻纱线	17
5308901400	其他苎麻色纱线	17
5308909100	纸纱线	17
5308909900	其他植物纺织纤维纱线	17
5309111000	未漂白的纯亚麻机织物	17
5309112000	漂白的纯亚麻机织物	17
5309190000	其他全亚麻机织物	17
5309211011	未漂白与精梳毛混纺的亚麻机织物	17
5309211019	未漂白的其他混纺亚麻机织物	17
5309211021	未漂白的混纺亚麻府绸及细平布	17
5309211022	未漂白的混纺亚麻机织平布	17
5309211023	未漂白的混纺亚麻机织印染用布	17
5309211024	未漂白的混纺亚麻其他机织物	17
5309211025	未漂白的混纺亚麻府绸及细平布	17

税则号列	商品名称	出口退税率(%)
5309211026	未漂白的混纺亚麻机织平布	17
5309211027	未漂白的混纺亚麻机织印染用布	17
5309211028	未漂白的混纺亚麻其他机织物	17
5309211029	未漂白的混纺亚麻其他机织物	17
5309211091	未漂白的混纺亚麻其他机织物	17
5309211099	未漂白的混纺亚麻其他机织物	17
5309212011	漂白与精梳毛混纺的亚麻机织物	17
5309212019	漂白的其他混纺亚麻机织物	17
5309212021	漂白的混纺亚麻府绸及细平布	17
5309212022	漂白的混纺亚麻机织平布	17
5309212023	漂白的混纺亚麻机织印染用布	17
5309212024	漂白的混纺亚麻其他机织物	17
5309212025	漂白的混纺亚麻府绸及细平布	17
5309212026	漂白的混纺亚麻机织平布	17
5309212027	漂白的混纺亚麻机织印染用布	17
5309212028	漂白的混纺亚麻其他机织物	17
5309212029	漂白的混纺亚麻其他机织物	17
5309212091	漂白的混纺亚麻其他机织物	17
5309212099	漂白的混纺亚麻其他机织物	17
5309290011	其他与精梳毛混纺的亚麻机织物	17
5309290019	其他混纺亚麻机织物	17
5309290021	其他混纺亚麻府绸及细平布	17
5309290022	其他混纺亚麻机织平布	17
5309290023	其他混纺亚麻机织印染用布	17
5309290024	其他混纺亚麻其他机织物	17
5309290025	其他混纺亚麻府绸及细平布	17
5309290026	其他混纺亚麻机织平布	17
5309290027	其他混纺亚麻机织印染用布	17
5309290028	其他混纺亚麻其他机织物	17
5309290029	其他混纺亚麻其他机织物	17
5309290091	其他混纺亚麻其他机织物	17
5309290099	其他混纺亚麻机织物	17
5310100011	未漂白黄麻或其他韧皮纤维机织物	17
5310100019	未漂白黄麻或其他韧皮纤维机织物	17
5310100091	未漂白黄麻或其他韧皮纤维机织物	17
5310100099	未漂白黄麻或其他韧皮纤维机织物	17
5310900011	其他黄麻机织物，宽度≤150厘米	17
5310900019	其他黄麻机织物，宽度≤150厘米	17
5310900091	其他黄麻机织物，宽度>150厘米	17
5310900099	其他黄麻机织物，宽度>150厘米	17
5311001211	未漂白与精梳毛混纺的苎麻机织物	17
5311001219	未漂白苎麻机织物	17
5311001221	未漂白的苎麻府绸及细平布	17
5311001222	未漂白的苎麻机织平布	17
5311001223	未漂白的苎麻机织印染用布	17
5311001229	未漂白的苎麻其他机织物	17
5311001231	未漂白的苎麻府绸及细平布	17
5311001232	未漂白的苎麻机织平布	17
5311001233	未漂白的苎麻机织印染用布	17
5311001239	未漂白的苎麻其他机织物	17
5311001240	未漂白的苎麻其他机织物	17
5311001291	未漂白的苎麻其他机织物	17
5311001299	未漂白的苎麻其他机织物	17
5311001311	与精梳毛混纺的苎麻其他机织物	17

税则号列	商品名称	出口退税率(%)
5311001319	苎麻其他机织物	17
5311001321	苎麻府绸及细平布	17
5311001322	苎麻机织平布	17
5311001323	苎麻机织印染布	17
5311001329	苎麻其他机织物	17
5311001331	苎麻府绸及细平布	17
5311001332	苎麻机织平布	17
5311001333	苎麻机织印染布	17
5311001339	苎麻其他机织物	17
5311001340	苎麻其他机织物	17
5311001391	苎麻其他机织物	17
5311001399	苎麻其他机织物	17
5311001411	未漂白与精梳羊毛混纺苎麻机织物	17
5311001419	未漂白苎麻机织物	17
5311001421	未漂白的苎麻府绸及细平布	17
5311001422	未漂白的苎麻机织平布	17
5311001423	未漂白的苎麻机织印染用布	17
5311001429	未漂白的苎麻其他机织物	17
5311001431	未漂白的苎麻府绸及细平布	17
5311001432	未漂白的苎麻机织平布	17
5311001433	未漂白的苎麻机织印染用布	17
5311001439	未漂白的苎麻其他机织物	17
5311001440	未漂白的苎麻其他机织物	17
5311001491	未漂白的苎麻其他机织物	17
5311001499	未漂白的苎麻其他机织物	17
5311001511	其他苎麻机织物,含量<85%	17
5311001519	其他苎麻机织物	17
5311001521	苎麻府绸及细平布	17
5311001522	苎麻机织平布	17
5311001529	其他苎麻机织物	17
5311001531	苎麻府绸及细平布	17
5311001532	苎麻机织平布	17
5311001533	苎麻机织印染用布	17
5311001539	其他苎麻机织物	17
5311001591	其他苎麻机织物	17
5311001599	其他苎麻机织物	17
5311002010	纸纱线机织物	17
5311002090	纸纱线机织物	17
5311003000	大麻机织物	17
5311009010	其他纺织用植物纤维机织物	17
5311009021	其他纺织用植物纤府绸及细平布	17
5311009022	其他纺织用植物纤维机织平布	17
5311009029	其他纺织用植物纤维机织物	17
5311009032	其他纺织用植物纤维机织平布	17
5311009033	其他纺织用植物纤维机织印染用布	17
5311009039	其他纺织用植物纤维其他机织物	17
5311009040	其他纺织用植物纤维其他机织物	17
5311009090	其他纺织用植物纤维其他机织物	17
5401101000	非供零售用合纤长丝缝纫线	17
5401102000	供零售用合纤长丝缝纫线	17
5401201000	非供零售用人纤长丝缝纫线	17
5401202000	供零售用人纤长丝缝纫线	17
5402111000	聚间苯二甲酰间苯二胺纺制的高强力纱	17
5402112000	聚对苯二甲酰对苯二胺纺制的高强力纱	17

税则号列	商品名称	出口退税率(%)
5402119000	其他芳香族聚酰胺纺制的高强力纱	17
5402191000	聚酰胺-6(尼龙-6)纺制高强力纱	17
5402192000	聚酰胺-6,6(尼龙6,6)纺制的高强力纱	17
5402199000	其他尼龙或其他聚酰胺制高强力纱	17
5402200010	非零售聚酯高强力纱	17
5402200020	非零售聚酯高强力纱	17
5402200090	非零售聚酯高强力多股纱	17
5402311100	聚酰胺-6(尼龙-6)纺制弹力丝	17
5402311200	聚酰胺-6,6纺制的弹力丝	17
5402311300	芳香族聚酰胺纺制弹力丝	17
5402311900	其他尼龙或其他聚酰胺制弹力丝	17
5402319000	非零售其他细尼龙变形纱线	17
5402321100	聚酰胺-6(尼龙-6)纺制的弹力丝	17
5402321200	聚酰胺-6,6纺制的弹力丝	17
5402321300	芳香族聚酰胺纺制的弹力丝	17
5402321900	其他尼龙或其他聚酰胺制弹力丝	17
5402329000	非零售其他粗尼龙变形纱线	17
5402331000	非零售聚酯弹力丝	17
5402339000	非零售聚酯变形纱线	17
5402340000	聚丙烯长丝变形纱线	17
5402390000	其他合成纤维长丝变形纱线	17
5402441000	氨纶弹性单纱	17
5402449000	其他合成纤维长丝弹性单纱	17
5402451000	聚酰胺-6(尼龙-6)纺制的其他单纱	17
5402452000	聚酰胺-6,6(尼龙-6,6)纺制的其他单纱	17
5402453000	芳香族聚酰胺纺制的其他单纱	17
5402459000	其他尼龙或其他聚酰胺单纱纺制的其他单纱	17
5402460000	其他部分定向聚酯单纱	17
5402470000	其他聚酯单纱	17
5402480000	其他聚丙烯单纱	17
5402491000	聚乙烯长丝纱线（单纱）	17
5402499001	非弹性氨纶单纱	17
5402499090	其他合成纤维长丝单纱	17
5402511000	聚酰胺-6(尼龙-6)纺制的单纱	17
5402512000	聚酰胺-6,6纺制的单纱	17
5402513000	芳香族聚酰胺纺制的单纱	17
5402519000	其他尼龙或其他聚酰胺单纱	17
5402520000	非零售加捻的其他聚酯纱线	17
5402591000	聚丙烯纱线	17
5402592000	聚乙烯长丝纱线（单纱）	17
5402599000	其他合成纤维长丝纱线	17
5402611000	聚酰胺-6(尼龙-6)纺制的纱线	17
5402612000	聚酰胺-6,6纺制的纱线	17
5402613000	芳香族聚酰胺纺制的纱线	17
5402619000	其他尼龙或其他聚酰胺纺制纱线	17
5402620000	非零售聚酯多股纱线	17
5402691000	聚丙烯纱线	17
5402692000	氨纶纱线	17
5402699000	其他合纤长丝多股纱线或缆线	17
5403100010	非零售粘胶纤维高强力纱	17
5403100020	非零售粘胶纤维高强力纱	17
5403100090	非零售粘胶纤维高强力多股纱	17
5403311000	非零售竹制粘胶纤维单纱	17
5403319000	其他非零售粘胶纤维单纱	17

税则号列	商品名称	出口退税率(%)
5403321000	非零售的竹制粘胶纤维单纱	17
5403329000	其他非零售粘胶纤维单纱	17
5403331010	非零售二醋酸纤维单纱	17
5403331020	非零售二醋酸纤维单纱	17
5403331090	非零售二醋酸纤维单纱	17
5403339010	非零售其他醋酸纤维单纱	17
5403339020	非零售其他醋酸纤维单纱	17
5403339090	非零售其他醋酸纤维单纱	17
5403390010	非零售其他人纤长丝单纱	17
5403390090	非零售其他人纤长丝单纱	17
5403410000	非零售粘胶长丝多股纱线或缆线	17
5403420000	非零售醋酸长丝多股纱线或缆线	17
5403490000	非零售其他人纤长丝多股纱或缆线	17
5404110010	细度≥67分特的涤纶纤维弹性单丝	17
5404110090	细度≥67分特的其他合成纤维弹性单丝	17
5404120000	细度≥67分特的其他聚丙烯单丝	17
5404190010	细度≥67分特的涤纶纤维单丝	17
5404190090	细度≥67分特的其他合成纤维单丝	17
5404900000	其他合成纺织材料制扁条及类似品	17
5405000000	细度≥67分特其他人纤单丝及其扁条	17
5406001000	供零售用合成纤维长丝纱线	17
5406002000	供零售用人造纤维长丝纱线	17
5407101000	高强力纱纺制机织物	17
5407102010	聚酯高强力纱纺制机织物	17
5407102090	聚酯高强力纱纺制机织物	17
5407200010	聚乙烯聚丙烯扁条或类似机织物	17
5407200090	其他合成纤维扁条及类似品机织物	17
5407300010	平行纱线相互层迭并粘合织物	17
5407300020	平行纱线相互层迭并粘合织物	17
5407410010	未漂或漂白的打字机带用机织物	17
5407410020	未漂白纯尼龙机织物	17
5407410090	未漂白的或漂白的其他机织物	17
5407420000	染色的纯尼龙机织物	17
5407430000	色织的纯尼龙机织物	17
5407440000	印花的纯尼龙机织物	17
5407510010	未漂白或漂白纯聚酯变形长丝布	17
5407510020	未漂白或漂白纯聚酯变形长丝机织物	17
5407520010	染色的聚酯变形长丝布,含量≥85%	17
5407520091	染色的其他聚酯变形长丝机织物	17
5407520092	染色的其他聚酯变形长丝机织物	17
5407530010	色织的聚酯变形长丝布,含量≥85%	17
5407530091	色织的聚酯变形长丝机织物	17
5407530092	色织的聚酯变形长丝机织物	17
5407540010	印花的聚酯变形长丝机织物	17
5407540020	印花的聚酯变形长丝机织物	17
5407610011	染色聚酯非变形长丝布,含量≥85%	17
5407610012	色织聚酯非变形长丝布,含量≥85%	17
5407610020	全聚酯其他非变形长丝机织物	17
5407610031	未漂白或漂白聚酯非变形长丝机织物	17
5407610032	未漂白或漂白聚酯非变形长丝机织物	17
5407610041	染色其他聚酯非变形长丝布	17
5407610042	染色其他纯聚酯非变形长丝布	17
5407610051	色织其他聚酯非变形长丝布	17
5407610052	色织其他聚酯非变形长丝布	17

税则号列	商品名称	出口退税率(%)
5407610061	印花其他聚酯非变形长丝布	17
5407610062	印花其他聚酯非变形长丝布	17
5407690011	未漂白或漂白其他聚酯长丝布	17
5407690012	未漂白或漂白其他聚酯长丝布	17
5407690021	染色其他聚酯长丝布	17
5407690022	染色其他聚酯长丝布	17
5407690031	色织其他聚酯长丝布,含量≥85%	17
5407690032	色织其他聚酯长丝布	17
5407690033	色织其他聚酯长丝布	17
5407690041	印花其他聚酯长丝布	17
5407690042	印花其他聚酯长丝布	17
5407710000	未漂白或漂白其他纯合纤长丝机织物	17
5407720000	染色的其他纯合纤长丝布	17
5407730000	色织的其他纯合纤长丝布	17
5407740000	印花的其他纯合纤长丝布	17
5407810010	未漂白或漂白与棉混纺府绸及细平布	17
5407810020	未漂白或漂白的与棉混纺平布	17
5407810030	未漂或漂白的与棉混纺印染用布	17
5407810040	未漂白或漂白与棉混纺缎纹或斜纹布	17
5407810090	未漂白或漂白与棉混纺其他合纤布	17
5407820010	染色的与棉混纺府绸及细平布	17
5407820020	染色的与棉混纺平布	17
5407820030	染色的与棉混纺印染用布	17
5407820040	染色的与棉混纺缎纹或斜纹布	17
5407820090	染色的与棉混纺其他合成纤维布	17
5407830010	色织的与棉混纺府绸及细平布	17
5407830020	色织的与棉混纺平布	17
5407830030	色织的与棉混纺印染用布	17
5407830040	色织的与棉混纺缎纹或斜纹布	17
5407830090	色织的与棉混纺其他合成纤维布	17
5407840010	印花的与棉混纺府绸及细平布	17
5407840030	印花的与棉混纺印染用布	17
5407840090	印花的与棉混纺其他合成纤维布	17
5407910011	未漂白或漂白的其他混纺合成纤维布	17
5407910019	未漂白或漂白的其他混纺合成纤维布	17
5407910021	未漂白或漂白的其他混纺合成纤维布	17
5407910029	未漂白或漂白的其他混纺合成纤维布	17
5407910030	未漂白或漂白的其他混纺合成纤维布	17
5407910091	未漂白或漂其他混纺府绸及细平布	17
5407910092	未漂白或漂白的其他混纺平布	17
5407910093	未漂白或漂白的其他混纺印染用布	17
5407910094	未漂白或漂其他混纺缎纹或斜纹布	17
5407910099	未漂白或漂白的其他混纺合成纤维布	17
5407920011	染色的其他混纺合成纤维布	17
5407920019	染色的其他混纺合成纤维布	17
5407920021	染色的其他混纺合成纤维布	17
5407920029	染色的其他混纺合成纤维布	17
5407920030	染色的其他混纺合成纤维布	17
5407920091	染色的其他混纺府绸及细平布	17
5407920092	染色的其他混纺平布	17
5407920093	染色的其他混纺印染用布	17
5407920094	染色的其他混纺缎纹或斜纹布	17
5407920099	染色的其他混纺合成纤维布	17
5407930011	色织的其他混纺合成纤维布	17

税则号列	商品名称	出口退税率(%)
5407930019	色织的其他混纺合成纤维布	17
5407930021	色织的其他混纺合成纤维布	17
5407930029	色织的其他混纺合成纤维布	17
5407930030	色织其他混纺合纤布,合纤<85%	17
5407930040	色织的其他混纺合成纤维布	17
5407930091	色织的其他混纺府绸及细平布	17
5407930092	色织的其他混纺平布	17
5407930093	色织的其他混纺印染用布	17
5407930094	色织的其他混纺缎纹或斜纹布	17
5407930099	色织的其他混纺合成纤维布	17
5407940010	印花的其他混纺合成纤维布	17
5407940020	印花的其他混纺合成纤维布	17
5407940030	印花的其他混纺合成纤维布	17
5407940091	印花的其他混纺府绸及细平布	17
5407940092	印花的其他混纺平布	17
5407940093	印花的其他混纺印染用布	17
5407940094	印花的其他混纺缎纹或斜纹布	17
5407940099	印花的其他混纺合成纤维布	17
5408100000	粘胶纤维高强力纱的机织物	17
5408211000	未漂白或漂白粘胶长丝机织物	17
5408212000	未漂白或漂白醋酸长丝机织物	17
5408219000	未漂白或漂白其他纯人纤长丝机织物	17
5408221000	染色的粘胶长丝机织物	17
5408222000	染色的醋酸长丝机织物	17
5408229000	染色的其他人纤长丝机织物	17
5408231000	色织的粘胶长丝机织物	17
5408232000	色织的醋酸长丝机织物	17
5408239000	色织的其他人纤长丝机织物	17
5408241000	印花的粘胶长丝机织物	17
5408242000	印花的醋酸长丝机织物	17
5408249000	其他印花人纤长丝,扁条机织物	17
5408310011	未漂白或漂白人纤长丝机织物	17
5408310019	未漂白或漂白人纤长丝机织物	17
5408310021	未漂白或漂白人纤长丝机织物	17
5408310029	未漂白或漂白人纤长丝机织物	17
5408310030	未漂白或漂白人纤长丝机织物	17
5408310091	未漂白或漂白人纤长丝府绸及细平布	17
5408310092	未漂白或漂白人纤长丝平布	17
5408310093	未漂白或漂白人纤长丝印染用布	17
5408310094	未漂白或漂白人纤长丝缎纹或斜纹布	17
5408310099	未漂白或漂白人纤长丝其他混纺布	17
5408320011	染色的人纤长丝机织物	17
5408320019	染色的人纤长丝机织物	17
5408320021	染色的人纤长丝机织物	17
5408320029	染色的人纤长丝机织物	17
5408320030	染色的人纤长丝机织物	17
5408320040	染色的人纤长丝机织物	17
5408320091	染色的人纤长丝府绸或细平布	17
5408320092	染色的人纤长丝平布	17
5408320093	染色的人纤长丝印染用布	17
5408320099	染色的人纤长丝其他机织物	17
5408330011	色织的人纤长丝机织物	17
5408330019	色织的人纤长丝机织物	17
5408330021	色织的人纤长丝机织物	17

税则号列	商品名称	出口退税率(%)
5408330029	色织的人纤长丝机织物	17
5408330030	色织的人纤长丝机织物，人纤<85%	17
5408330040	色织的人纤长丝机织物	17
5408330050	色织的人纤长丝机织物	17
5408330092	色织的人纤长丝平布	17
5408330094	色织的人纤长丝缎纹或斜纹布	17
5408330099	色织的人纤长丝其他机织物	17
5408340010	印花的人纤长丝机织物	17
5408340020	印花的人纤长丝机织物	17
5408340030	印花的人纤长丝机织物	17
5408340040	印花的人纤长丝机织物	17
5408340091	印花的人纤长丝府绸或细平布	17
5408340092	印花的人纤长丝平布	17
5408340093	印花的人纤长丝印染用布	17
5408340094	印花的人纤长丝缎纹或斜纹布	17
5408340099	印花的人纤长丝其他机织物	17
5501100000	尼龙或其他聚酰胺长丝丝束	17
5501200000	聚酯长丝丝束	17
5501300000	聚丙烯腈长丝丝束	17
5501400000	聚丙烯长丝丝束	17
5501900000	其他合成纤维长丝丝束	17
5502001000	二醋酸纤维丝束	17
5502009000	其他人造纤维长丝丝束	17
5503111000	未梳的聚间苯二甲酰间苯二胺纺制的短纤	17
5503112000	未梳的聚对苯二甲酰对苯二胺纺制的短纤	17
5503119000	未梳的其他芳香族聚酰胺纺制的短纤	17
5503190000	未梳的尼龙或其他聚酰胺短纤	17
5503200000	未梳的聚酯短纤	17
5503300000	未梳的聚丙烯腈短纤维	17
5503400000	未梳的聚丙烯短纤	17
5503901000	未梳的聚苯硫醚短纤	17
5503909000	未梳的其他合成纤维短纤	17
5504101000	未梳的竹制粘胶短纤	17
5504102100	未梳的木制阻燃粘胶短纤	17
5504102910	高湿模量未梳木制非阻燃粘胶纤维（湿强≥2.0cn/dtex，干强≥3.0cn/dt	17
5504102990	其他未梳的木制非阻燃粘胶短纤	17
5504109000	其他未梳的粘胶短纤	17
5504900000	未梳的其他人造纤维短纤	17
5505100000	合成纤维废料	17
5505200000	人造纤维废料	17
5506101100	已梳聚间苯二甲酰间苯二胺纺制的短纤	17
5506101200	已梳聚对苯二甲酰对苯二胺纺制的短纤	17
5506101900	其他已梳芳香族聚酰胺纺制的短纤	17
5506109000	其他已梳的尼龙或其他聚酰胺短纤	17
5506200000	已梳的聚酯短纤	17
5506300000	已梳的聚丙烯腈及其变性短纤	17
5506901000	已梳的聚苯硫醚短纤	17
5506909000	已梳的其他合成纤维短纤	17
5507000000	已梳的人造纤维短纤	17
5508100011	非零售用聚丙烯腈短纤缝纫线	17
5508100019	非零售用其他合纤短纤缝纫线	17
5508100090	零售用合成纤维短纤缝纫线	17
5508200010	非零售用人造纤维短纤缝纫线	17
5508200090	零售用人造纤维短纤缝纫线	17

税则号列	商品名称	出口退税率(%)
5509110000	非零售纯尼龙短纤单纱	17
5509120000	非零售纯尼龙短纤多股纱线	17
5509210000	非零售纯聚酯短纤单纱	17
5509220010	非零售聚酯短纤多股纱线或缆线	17
5509220090	非零售其他聚酯短纤多股纱线缆线	17
5509310000	非零售纯聚丙烯腈短纤单纱	17
5509320000	非零售纯聚丙烯腈短纤多股纱线	17
5509410000	非零售纯合成纤维短纤单纱	17
5509420000	非零售纯合纤短纤多股纱线	17
5509510000	非零售与人纤短纤混纺聚酯短纤纱	17
5509520000	非零售与毛混纺聚酯短纤纱线	17
5509530000	非零售与棉混纺聚酯短纤纱线	17
5509590000	非零售与其他混纺聚酯短纤纱线	17
5509610000	非零售与毛混纺腈纶短纤纱线	17
5509620000	非零售与棉混纺腈纶短纤纱线	17
5509690000	非零售与其他混纺腈纶短纤纱线	17
5509910000	非零售与毛混纺其他合纤短纤纱线	17
5509920000	非零售与棉混纺其他合纤短纤纱线	17
5509990000	非零售与其他混纺合纤短纤纱线	17
5510110000	非零售其他纯人造纤维短纤单纱	17
5510120000	非零售其他纯人纤短纤多股纱线	17
5510200000	非零售与毛混纺其他人纤短纤纱线	17
5510300000	非零售与棉混纺其他人纤短纤纱线	17
5510900000	非零售与其他混纺人纤短纤纱线	17
5511100000	零售用纯合纤短纤纱线	17
5511200000	零售用混纺合纤短纤纱线	17
5511300000	零售用人纤短纤纱线	17
5512110010	未漂或漂白聚酯短纤机织府绸	17
5512110020	未漂或漂白聚酯短纤机织平布	17
5512110030	未漂或漂白聚酯短纤印染用布	17
5512110040	未漂或漂白聚酯短纤平纹奶酪布	17
5512110050	未漂或漂白聚酯短纤机织帆布	17
5512110060	未漂或漂白聚酯短纤其他斜纹机织物	17
5512110070	未漂或漂白聚酯短纤牛津布	17
5512110090	未漂或漂白聚酯短纤其他机织物	17
5512190010	聚酯短纤色织机织物	17
5512190020	聚酯短纤蓝粗斜纹布	17
5512190031	聚酯短纤其他机织府绸或细平布	17
5512190032	聚酯短纤其他机织平布	17
5512190033	聚酯短纤其他机织印染用布	17
5512190034	聚酯短纤其他平纹奶酪布等	17
5512190035	聚酯短纤其他机织帆布	17
5512190036	聚酯短纤其他缎纹或斜纹机织物	17
5512190037	聚酯短纤其他牛津布	17
5512190090	聚酯短纤其他机织物	17
5512210010	未漂白或漂白腈纶短纤机织府绸细平布	17
5512210020	未漂白或漂白腈纶短纤机织平布	17
5512210030	未漂白或漂白腈纶短纤机织印染用布	17
5512210040	未漂白或漂白腈纶短纤平纹奶酪布等	17
5512210050	未漂白或漂白腈纶短纤机织帆布	17
5512210060	未漂白或漂白的腈纶短纤其他斜纹机织物	17
5512210070	未漂白或漂白腈纶短纤牛津布	17
5512210090	未漂白或漂白腈纶短纤其他机织物	17
5512290010	腈纶短纤色织机织物	17

税则号列	商品名称	出口退税率(%)
5512290020	腈纶短纤蓝粗斜纹布	17
5512290031	腈纶短纤其他机织府绸或细平布	17
5512290032	腈纶短纤其他机织平布	17
5512290033	腈纶短纤其他机织印染用布	17
5512290034	腈纶短纤其他平纹奶酪布等	17
5512290035	腈纶短纤其他机织帆布	17
5512290036	腈纶短纤其他缎纹或斜纹机织物	17
5512290037	腈纶短纤其他牛津布	17
5512290090	腈纶短纤其他机织物	17
5512910010	未漂白或漂白其他合纤短纤机织府绸	17
5512910020	未漂白或漂白其他合纤短纤机织平布	17
5512910030	未漂白或漂白其他合纤短纤印染用布	17
5512910040	未漂白或漂白其他合纤短纤平纹奶酪布	17
5512910050	未漂白或漂白其他合纤短纤机织帆布	17
5512910060	未漂白或漂白其他合纤短纤斜纹机织物	17
5512910070	未漂白或漂白其他合纤短纤牛津布	17
5512910090	未漂白或漂白其他合纤短纤其他机织物	17
5512990010	其他合纤短纤色织机织物	17
5512990020	其他合纤短纤蓝粗斜纹布	17
5512990031	其他合纤短纤机织府绸或细平布	17
5512990032	其他合纤短纤其他机织平布	17
5512990033	其他合纤短纤其他机织印染用布	17
5512990034	其他合纤短纤平纹奶酪布等	17
5512990035	其他合纤短纤其他机织帆布	17
5512990036	其他合纤短纤缎纹或斜纹机织物	17
5512990039	其他合纤短纤其他牛津布	17
5512990090	其他合纤短纤其他机织物	17
5513111010	与棉混纺未漂白聚酯短纤平纹府绸	17
5513111020	与棉混纺未漂白聚酯短纤机织平布	17
5513111030	与棉混未漂白聚酯短纤平纹印染用布	17
5513111040	与棉混纺未漂白聚酯短纤平纹奶酪布	17
5513112010	与棉混纺漂白聚酯短纤平纹府绸	17
5513112020	与棉混纺漂白聚酯短纤机织平布	17
5513112030	与棉混纺漂白聚酯平纹印染用布	17
5513112040	与棉混纺漂白聚酯短纤平纹奶酪布等	17
5513121000	与棉混纺未漂白的轻质聚酯斜纹布	17
5513122000	与棉混纺漂白的轻质聚酯斜纹布	17
5513131010	与棉混纺未漂聚酯短纤斜纹机织物	17
5513131020	与棉混纺未漂白聚酯短纤牛津布	17
5513131090	与棉混纺未漂聚酯短纤其他机织物	17
5513132010	与棉混纺漂白聚酯短纤斜纹机织物	17
5513132020	与棉混纺漂白聚酯短纤牛津布	17
5513132090	与棉混纺漂白聚酯短纤其他机织物	17
5513190010	与棉混纺的未漂白或漂白的其他合纤短纤布	17
5513190020	与棉混纺的未漂白或漂白的其他合纤短纤布	17
5513190030	与棉混纺的未漂白或漂白的其他合纤短纤布	17
5513190040	与棉混纺的未漂白或漂白的其他合纤短纤布	17
5513190050	与棉混纺的未漂白或漂白的其他合纤短纤布	17
5513190060	与棉混纺的未漂白或漂白的其他合纤短纤布	17
5513190090	与棉混纺的未漂白或漂白的其他合纤短纤布	17
5513210010	与棉混纺染色聚酯短纤平纹府绸	17
5513210020	与棉混纺染色聚酯短纤机织平布	17
5513210030	与棉混纺的染色聚酯短纤平纹印染用布	17
5513210040	与棉混染色聚酯短纤平纹奶酪布等	17

税则号列	商品名称	出口退税率(%)
5513231000	与棉混纺染色的轻质聚酯斜纹机织物	17
5513239000	与棉混纺染色聚酯短纤其他机织物	17
5513290010	与棉混纺染色其他合纤短纤府绸	17
5513290020	与棉混纺染色其他合纤短纤平布	17
5513290030	与棉混纺染色其他合纤短纤平纹布	17
5513290040	与棉混纺的染色其他合纤短纤平纹布	17
5513290050	与棉混纺染色其他合纤短纤斜纹布	17
5513290060	与棉混纺染色其他合纤短纤牛津布	17
5513290090	与棉混纺染色其他合纤短纤其他布	17
5513310000	与棉混纺色织的聚酯短纤平纹布	17
5513391000	与棉混纺色织的聚酯短纤三或四线斜纹布	17
5513392000	与棉混纺色织聚酯短纤其他机织物	17
5513399000	与棉混纺色织其他合纤短纤其他布	17
5513410010	与棉混纺印花聚酯短纤平纹府绸	17
5513410020	与棉混纺印花聚酯短纤机织平布	17
5513410030	与棉混纺的印花聚酯短纤平纹印染用布	17
5513410040	与棉混印花聚酯短纤平纹奶酪布等	17
5513491000	与棉混纺印花的轻质聚酯三或四线斜纹布	17
5513492000	与棉混纺印花聚酯短纤其他机织物	17
5513499000	与棉混纺印花其他合纤短纤其他布	17
5514111010	与棉混纺未漂白聚酯短纤平纹府绸	17
5514111020	与棉混纺未漂白聚酯短纤机织平布	17
5514111030	与棉混纺未漂白聚酯短纤平纹帆布	17
5514112010	与棉混纺漂白聚酯短纤平纹府绸	17
5514112020	与棉混纺漂白聚酯短纤机织平布	17
5514112030	与棉混纺漂白聚酯短纤平纹帆布	17
5514121000	与棉混纺未漂白的重质聚酯斜纹布	17
5514122000	与棉混纺漂白的聚酯短纤斜纹布	17
5514191100	与棉混纺未漂白聚酯短纤其他机织物	17
5514191200	与棉混纺漂白聚酯短纤其他机织物	17
5514199000	与棉混纺未漂白或漂白其他合纤短纤布	17
5514210010	与棉混纺染色聚酯短纤平纹府绸	17
5514210020	与棉混纺染色聚酯短纤机织平布	17
5514210030	与棉混纺染色聚酯短纤平纹帆布	17
5514220000	与棉混纺染色的重质聚酯斜纹布	17
5514230010	与棉混纺染色聚酯短纤其他斜纹布	17
5514230020	与棉混纺染色聚酯短纤其他帆布	17
5514230090	与棉混纺染色聚酯短纤其他机织物	17
5514290010	与棉混纺染色其他合纤短纤府绸	17
5514290020	与棉混纺染色其他合纤短纤平布	17
5514290030	与棉混纺染色其他合纤短纤帆布	17
5514290040	与棉混纺染色其他合纤短纤斜纹布	17
5514290090	与棉混纺染色其他合纤短纤其他布	17
5514301000	与棉混纺色织的重质聚酯平纹布	17
5514302000	与棉混纺色织聚酯短纤三四线斜纹布	17
5514303000	与棉混纺色织聚酯短纤其他机织物	17
5514309000	与棉混纺色织合纤短纤其他机织物	17
5514410010	与棉混纺印花聚酯短纤平纹府绸	17
5514410020	与棉混纺印花聚酯短纤机织平布	17
5514410030	与棉混纺印花聚酯短纤平纹帆布	17
5514420000	与棉混纺印花的重质聚酯斜纹布	17
5514430010	与棉混纺印花聚酯短纤其他斜纹布	17
5514430020	与棉混纺印花聚酯短纤其他帆布	17
5514430090	与棉混纺印花聚酯短纤其他机织物	17

税则号列	商品名称	出口退税率(%)
5514490010	与棉混纺印花其他合纤短纤府绸	17
5514490020	与棉混纺印花其他合纤短纤平布	17
5514490030	与棉混纺印花其他合纤短纤帆布	17
5514490040	与棉混纺印花其他合纤短纤斜纹布	17
5514490090	与棉混纺印花其他合纤短纤其他布	17
5515110011	聚酯短纤蓝粗斜纹布	17
5515110019	聚酯短纤其他色织布	17
5515110021	未漂或漂白聚酯短纤府绸或细平布	17
5515110022	未漂或漂白聚酯短纤其他机织平布	17
5515110023	未漂或漂白聚酯短纤其他印染用布	17
5515110024	未漂或漂白聚酯短纤奶酪布等	17
5515110025	未漂或漂白聚酯短纤机织帆布	17
5515110026	未漂或漂白聚酯短纤缎纹或斜纹布	17
5515110027	未漂或漂白聚酯短纤牛津布	17
5515110029	未漂或漂白聚酯短纤其他机织物	17
5515110031	其他聚酯短纤府绸或细平布	17
5515110032	其他聚酯短纤机织平布	17
5515110033	其他聚酯短纤机织印染用布	17
5515110034	其他聚酯短纤奶酪布等	17
5515110035	其他聚酯短纤机织帆布	17
5515110036	其他聚酯短纤缎纹或斜纹机织物	17
5515110037	其他聚酯短纤牛津布	17
5515110039	其他聚酯短纤其他机织物	17
5515120011	未漂或漂聚酯短纤府绸或细平布	17
5515120012	未漂白或漂白聚酯短纤平布	17
5515120013	未漂白或漂白聚酯短纤印染用布	17
5515120014	未漂白或漂白聚酯短纤缎纹或斜纹布	17
5515120019	未漂白或漂白聚酯短纤其他机织物	17
5515120021	其他聚酯短纤府绸或细平布	17
5515120022	其他聚酯短纤平布	17
5515120023	其他聚酯短纤印染用布	17
5515120024	其他聚酯短纤缎纹或斜纹机织物	17
5515120029	其他聚酯短纤其他机织物	17
5515130011	未漂白或漂白的聚酯短纤与精梳毛混纺布	17
5515130012	未漂白或漂白的聚酯短纤与粗梳毛混纺布	17
5515130013	未漂白或漂白的聚酯短纤与精梳毛混纺布	17
5515130019	未漂白或漂白的聚酯短纤与粗梳毛混纺布	17
5515130021	其他聚酯短纤与精梳毛混纺机织物	17
5515130022	其他聚酯短纤与粗梳毛混纺机织物	17
5515130023	其他聚酯短纤与精梳毛混纺机织物	17
5515130029	其他聚酯短纤与粗梳毛混纺机织物	17
5515190011	聚酯短纤与其他纤维混蓝粗斜纹布	17
5515190019	聚酯短纤其他色织机织物	17
5515190021	未漂白或漂白聚酯短纤其他府绸	17
5515190022	未漂白或漂白聚酯短纤其他机织平布	17
5515190023	未漂白或漂白聚酯短纤其他机织印染布	17
5515190024	未漂白或漂白聚酯短纤奶酪布等	17
5515190025	未漂白或漂白聚酯短纤机织帆布	17
5515190026	未漂白或漂白聚酯短纤缎纹或斜纹布	17
5515190027	未漂白或漂白聚酯短纤牛津布	17
5515190029	未漂白或漂白聚酯短纤其他机织物	17
5515190031	其他聚酯短纤府绸或细平布	17
5515190032	其他聚酯短纤机织平布	17
5515190033	其他聚酯短纤机织印染用布	17

税则号列	商品名称	出口退税率(%)
5515190034	其他聚酯短纤奶酪布等	17
5515190035	其他聚酯短纤机织帆布	17
5515190036	其他聚酯短纤缎纹或斜纹机织物	17
5515190037	其他聚酯短纤牛津布	17
5515190039	其他聚酯短纤其他机织物	17
5515210011	未漂白或漂白腈纶短纤府绸或细平布	17
5515210012	未漂白或漂白腈纶短纤平布	17
5515210013	未漂白或漂白腈纶短纤印染用布	17
5515210014	未漂白或漂白腈纶短纤缎纹或斜纹布	17
5515210019	未漂白或漂白腈纶短纤其他机织物	17
5515210021	其他腈纶短纤混纺府绸或细平布	17
5515210022	其他腈纶短纤平布	17
5515210023	其他腈纶短纤印染用布	17
5515210024	其他腈纶短纤混纺缎纹或斜纹布	17
5515210029	其他腈纶短纤混纺其他机织物	17
5515220011	未漂白或漂白的腈纶短纤与精梳毛混纺布	17
5515220012	未漂白或漂白的腈纶短纤与粗梳毛混纺布	17
5515220013	未漂白或漂白的腈纶短纤与精梳毛混纺布	17
5515220019	未漂白或漂白的腈纶短纤与粗梳毛混纺布	17
5515220021	其他腈纶短纤与精梳毛混纺机织物	17
5515220022	其他腈纶短纤与粗梳毛混纺机织物	17
5515220023	其他腈纶短纤与精梳毛混纺机织物	17
5515220029	其他腈纶短纤与粗梳毛混纺机织物	17
5515290011	腈纶短纤与其他纤维混蓝粗斜纹布	17
5515290019	其他腈纶短纤色织机织布	17
5515290021	其他未漂白或漂白的腈纶短纤府绸	17
5515290022	其他未漂白或漂白的腈纶短纤平布	17
5515290023	其他未漂白或漂白的腈纶短纤印染用布	17
5515290024	其他未漂白或漂白的腈纶短纤奶酪布等	17
5515290025	其他未漂白或漂白的腈纶短纤机织帆布	17
5515290026	其他未漂白或漂白的腈纶短纤缎纹布	17
5515290027	其他未漂白或漂白的腈纶短纤牛津布	17
5515290029	其他未漂白或漂白的腈纶短纤其他机织物	17
5515290031	其他腈纶短纤府绸或细平布	17
5515290032	其他腈纶短纤机织平布	17
5515290033	其他腈纶短纤机织印染用布	17
5515290034	其他腈纶短纤奶酪布等	17
5515290035	其他腈纶短纤机织帆布	17
5515290036	其他腈纶短纤与其他纤维混牛津布	17
5515290037	其他腈纶短纤缎纹或斜纹机织物	17
5515290039	其他腈纶短纤与其他纤维混机织物	17
5515910011	未漂白或漂白的其他合纤短府绸	17
5515910012	未漂白或漂白的其他合纤短纤平布	17
5515910013	未漂白或漂白的其他合纤短纤混印染用布	17
5515910014	未漂白或漂白的其他合纤短纤缎纹布等	17
5515910019	未漂白或漂白的其他合纤短纤其他机织物	17
5515910021	其他合纤短纤府绸或细平布	17
5515910022	其他合纤短纤平布	17
5515910023	其他合纤短纤印染用布	17
5515910024	其他合纤短纤缎纹或斜纹机织物	17
5515910029	其他合纤短纤其他机织物	17
5515990011	其他合纤短纤蓝粗斜纹布	17
5515990019	其他合纤短纤其他色织机织物	17
5515990021	未漂白或漂白的其他合纤短纤府绸	17

税则号列	商品名称	出口退税率(%)
5515990022	未漂白或漂白的其他合纤短纤其他平布	17
5515990023	未漂白或漂白的其他合纤短纤印染用布	17
5515990024	未漂白或漂白的其他合纤短纤奶酪布等	17
5515990025	未漂白或漂白的其他合纤短纤帆布	17
5515990026	未漂白或漂白的其他合纤短纤混纺缎纹布	17
5515990027	未漂白或漂白的其他合纤短纤牛津布	17
5515990029	未漂白或漂白的其他合纤短纤其他机织物	17
5515990031	其他合纤短纤府绸或细平布	17
5515990032	其他合纤短纤其他机织平布	17
5515990033	其他合纤短纤机织印染用布	17
5515990034	其他合纤短纤奶酪布等	17
5515990035	其他合纤短纤机织帆布	17
5515990036	其他合纤短纤缎纹或斜纹机织物	17
5515990037	其他合纤短纤其他纤维混牛津布	17
5515990039	其他合纤短纤其他机织物	17
5516110000	未漂白或漂白的纯人纤短纤机织物	17
5516120000	染色的纯人纤短纤布	17
5516130000	色织的纯人纤短纤布	17
5516140000	印花的纯人纤短纤布	17
5516210010	未漂白或漂白的人纤短纤府绸或细平布	17
5516210020	未漂白或漂白的人纤短纤平布	17
5516210030	未漂白或漂白的人纤短纤印染用布	17
5516210040	未漂白或漂白的人纤短纤缎纹或斜纹布	17
5516210090	未漂白或漂白的人纤短纤其他机织物	17
5516220010	染色人纤短纤府绸或细平布	17
5516220020	染色人纤短纤平布	17
5516220030	染色人纤短纤印染用布	17
5516220040	染色人纤短纤缎纹或斜纹机织物	17
5516220090	染色人纤短纤其他机织物	17
5516230010	色织人纤短纤府绸和细平布	17
5516230020	色织人纤短纤平布	17
5516230030	色织人纤短纤印染用布	17
5516230040	色织人纤短纤缎纹或斜纹机织物	17
5516230090	色织人纤短纤其他机织物	17
5516240010	印花人纤短纤府绸或细平布	17
5516240020	印花人纤短纤平布	17
5516240030	印花人纤短纤印染用布	17
5516240040	印花人纤短纤缎纹或斜纹机织物	17
5516240090	印花人纤短纤其他布	17
5516310011	未漂白或漂白人纤短纤与精梳毛混纺布	17
5516310019	未漂白或漂白人纤短纤与粗梳毛混纺布	17
5516310021	未漂白或漂白人纤短纤与精梳毛混纺布	17
5516310029	未漂白或漂白人纤短纤与粗梳毛混纺布	17
5516320011	染色人纤短纤与精梳毛混纺机织物	17
5516320019	染色人纤短纤与粗梳毛混纺机织物	17
5516320021	染色人纤短纤与精梳毛混纺机织物	17
5516320029	染色人纤短纤与粗梳毛混纺机织物	17
5516330011	色织人纤短纤与精梳毛混纺机织物	17
5516330019	色织人纤短纤与粗梳毛混纺机织物	17
5516330021	色织人纤短纤与精梳毛混纺机织物	17
5516330029	色织人纤短纤与粗梳毛混纺机织物	17
5516340011	印花人纤短纤与精梳毛混纺机织物	17
5516340019	印花人纤短纤与粗梳毛混纺机织物	17
5516340021	印花人纤短纤与精梳毛混纺机织物	17

税则号列	商品名称	出口退税率(%)
5516340029	印花人纤短纤与粗梳毛混纺机织物	17
5516410010	未漂白或漂白人纤短纤府绸或细平布	17
5516410020	未漂白或漂白人纤短纤与棉混纺平布	17
5516410030	与棉混纺的未漂白或漂白人纤短纤印染用布	17
5516410040	未漂白或漂白人纤短纤与棉混纺的奶酪布等	17
5516410050	与棉混纺的未漂白或漂白人纤短纤机织帆布	17
5516410060	与棉混纺的未漂白或漂白人纤短纤缎纹布等	17
5516410070	与棉混纺的未漂白或漂白人纤短纤牛津布	17
5516410090	与棉混纺的未漂白或漂白人纤短纤其他布	17
5516420010	与棉混纺的染色人纤短纤府绸或细平布	17
5516420020	与棉混纺的染色人纤短纤平布	17
5516420030	与棉混纺的染色人纤短纤印染用布	17
5516420040	与棉混纺的染色人纤短纤奶酪布等	17
5516420050	与棉混纺的染色人纤短纤机织帆布	17
5516420060	与棉混纺的染色人纤短纤缎纹或斜纹布	17
5516420070	与棉混纺的染色人纤短纤牛津布	17
5516420090	与棉混纺的染色人纤短纤其他机织物	17
5516430010	与棉混纺的人纤短纤色织蓝色粗斜纹布	17
5516430020	与棉混纺人纤短纤色织提花机织物	17
5516430090	与棉混纺人纤短纤其他色织机织物	17
5516440010	与棉混纺的印花人纤短纤府绸或细平布	17
5516440020	与棉混纺的印花人纤短纤平布	17
5516440030	与棉纺的混印花人纤短纤印染用布	17
5516440040	与棉混纺印花人纤短纤奶酪布等	17
5516440050	与棉混纺印花人纤短纤机织帆布	17
5516440060	印花人纤短纤缎纹或斜纹机织物	17
5516440070	与棉混纺印花人纤短纤牛津布	17
5516440090	与棉混纺印花人纤短纤其他机织物	17
5516910010	未漂或漂白人纤短纤府绸或细平布	17
5516910020	未漂或漂白人纤短纤机织平布	17
5516910030	未漂或漂白人纤短纤印染用布	17
5516910040	未漂或漂白人纤短纤奶酪布等	17
5516910050	未漂或漂白人纤短纤机织帆布	17
5516910060	未漂或漂白人纤短纤缎纹或斜纹布	17
5516910070	未漂或漂白人纤短纤牛津布	17
5516910090	未漂或漂白人纤短纤其他机织物	17
5516920010	染色人纤短纤府绸或细平布	17
5516920020	染色人纤短纤机织平布	17
5516920030	染色人纤短纤印染用布	17
5516920040	染色人纤短纤奶酪布等	17
5516920050	染色人纤短纤机织帆布	17
5516920060	染色人纤短纤缎纹或斜纹机织物	17
5516920070	染色人纤短纤牛津布	17
5516920090	染色人纤短纤其他机织物	17
5516930010	人纤短纤色织蓝粗斜纹布	17
5516930020	色织人纤短纤提花机织物	17
5516930090	色织人纤短纤其他机织物	17
5516940010	印花人造纤维短纤府绸或细平布	17
5516940020	印花人造纤维短纤机织平布	17
5516940030	印花人造纤维短纤印染用布	17
5516940040	印花人造纤维短纤奶酪布等	17
5516940050	印花人造纤维短纤机织帆布	17
5516940060	印花人纤短纤缎纹或斜纹机织物	17
5516940070	印花人造纤维短纤牛津布	17

税则号列	商品名称	出口退税率(%)
5516940090	印花人造纤维短纤其他机织物	17
5601210010	棉制的成匹絮胎	17
5601210090	其他棉制的絮胎及絮胎制品	17
5601221000	化学纤维制的卷烟滤嘴	17
5601229010	化学纤维制的成匹絮胎	17
5601229090	化学纤维制的其他絮胎及絮胎制品	17
5601290010	羊毛或动物细毛制絮胎及制品	17
5601290090	其他纺织材料制絮胎及制品	17
5601300010	由两种或以上有机聚合物纺制的纤维	17
5601300090	纺织纤维屑,纤维粉末及球结	17
5602100010	毛制针刺机制毡呢及纤维缝编织	17
5602100090	其他纺织料制针刺机制毡呢等	17
5602210000	羊毛及动物细毛制其他毡呢	17
5602290000	其他纺织材料制其他毡呢	17
5602900010	其他纺织材料制其他毡呢	17
5602900091	化学纤维制其他毡呢	17
5602900099	其他纺织材料制其他毡呢	17
5603111000	化学纤维长丝制无纺织物	17
5603119000	其他化学纤维长丝制无纺织物	17
5603121000	25<每平米重≤70克浸渍长丝无纺布	17
5603129000	25<每平米重≤70克其他长丝无纺布	17
5603131000	70<每平米重≤150克浸渍长丝无纺	17
5603139000	70<每平米重≤150克其他长丝无纺	17
5603141000	每平米重>150克经浸渍长丝无纺布	17
5603149000	每平米重>150克的其他长丝无纺布	17
5603911010	每平米重≤25克经浸渍的乙烯聚合物制电池隔膜基布	17
5603911090	每平米重≤25克经浸渍其他无纺布	17
5603919000	每平米重≤25克的其他无纺布	17
5603921010	25<每平米重≤70克浸渍的乙烯聚合物制电池隔膜基布	17
5603921090	25<每平米重≤70克浸渍其他无纺布	17
5603929000	25<每平米重≤70克其他无纺布	17
5603931000	70<每平米重≤150克浸渍其他无纺布	17
5603939000	70<每平米重≤150克的其他无纺布	17
5603941011	毛制铺地品衬底用物纺织物	17
5603941019	其他材料制铺地品衬底用无纺织物	17
5603941090	其他材料制无纺织物	17
5603949011	毛制铺地品衬底用无纺织物	17
5603949019	其他材料制铺地品衬底用无纺织物	17
5603949090	其他材料制无纺织物	17
5604100000	用纺织材料包覆的橡胶线及绳	17
5604900010	棉制纱线	17
5604900020	品目5404的合成纤维单丝、扁条	17
5604900030	品目5404的人造纤维单丝、扁条	17
5604900090	其他纺织纱线	17
5605000010	金属涂层或层压化纤长丝等	17
5605000090	其他含金属纱线,可含螺旋花边	17
5606000000	绳绒线及粗松螺旋花线	17
5607210010	剑麻或其他龙舌兰纤维制包扎用绳	17
5607210090	剑麻或龙舌兰纤维制其他包扎用绳	17
5607290000	剑麻或龙舌兰纤维制其他线绳索缆	17
5607410010	宽的非裂膜扁条聚乙烯包扎用绳	17
5607410090	其他聚乙烯或聚丙烯制包扎用绳	17
5607490010	宽非裂膜扁条聚乙烯其他线绳索缆	17
5607490020	其他聚乙烯或聚丙烯制线绳索缆	17

税则号列	商品名称	出口退税率(%)
5607490090	其他聚乙烯或聚丙烯制线绳索缆	17
5607500010	其他合纤制未编织或编织线绳索缆	17
5607500090	其他合纤制已编织或编织线绳索缆	17
5607901000	蕉麻或硬质(叶)纤维制线,绳,索,缆	17
5607909010	大麻制线,绳,索,缆	17
5607909090	其他纺织材料制线,绳,索,缆	17
5608110010	化纤材料制成手撒线拉的渔网	17
5608110090	化纤材料制成其他渔网	17
5608190010	化纤材料制用拉线收口的诱饵包	17
5608190090	化纤材料制成的网料和其他网	17
5608900011	毛、棉制的渔网	17
5608900019	其他纺织纤维制的渔网	17
5608900091	棉制的其他网及网料	17
5608900092	毛制的其他网及网料	17
5608900099	其他纺织纤维制成的其他网及网料	17
5609000000	用纱线,扁条,绳,索,缆制其他物品	17
5701100000	羊毛或动物细毛制的结织栽绒地毯	17
5701901000	化学纤维制的结织栽绒地毯	17
5701902000	丝制结织栽绒铺地制品	17
5701909000	其他纺织材料制结织栽绒地毯	17
5702100000	“开来姆”,“苏麦克”,“卡拉马尼”地毯	17
5702200000	椰壳纤维制的铺地制品	17
5702310000	未制成的羊毛起绒地毯及铺地制品	17
5702320000	未制成的化纤起绒地毯及铺地制品	17
5702390000	其他纺织料未制成起绒铺地制品	17
5702410000	制成的羊毛起绒地毯及铺地制品	17
5702420000	制成的化纤起绒地毯及铺地制品	17
5702490000	其他纺织材料制成的起绒铺地制品	17
5702501000	未制成羊毛非起绒地毯及铺地制品	17
5702502000	未制成化纤非起绒地毯及铺地制品	17
5702509000	未制成其他纺织料制非起绒铺地制品	17
5702910000	制成的毛制非起绒铺地制品	17
5702920000	制成的化纤非起绒地毯及铺地制品	17
5702990000	制成的其他纺材制非起绒铺地制品	17
5703100000	羊毛簇绒地毯及其他簇绒铺地制品	17
5703200000	尼龙簇绒地毯及其他簇绒铺地制品	17
5703300000	化纤簇绒地毯及其他簇绒铺地制品	17
5703900000	其他簇绒地毯及其他簇绒铺地制品	17
5704100000	毡呢铺地制品,最大面积≤0.3平米	17
5704900000	毡呢铺地制品,最大面积>0.3平米	17
5705001000	羊毛制其他地毯及其他铺地制品	17
5705002000	化纤制其他地毯及其他铺地制品	17
5705009000	其他纺材制未列名地毯及铺地制品	17
5801100000	毛制起绒机织物及绳绒织物	17
5801210010	未漂白不割绒的棉制纬起绒织物	17
5801210090	其他不割绒的棉制纬起绒织物	17
5801220000	割绒的棉制灯芯绒	17
5801230010	未漂白其他棉制纬起绒织物	17
5801230090	其他棉制纬起绒织物	17
5801260010	未漂白棉制绳绒织物	17
5801260090	其他棉制绳绒织物	17
5801271000	棉制不割绒的经起绒织物(棱纹绸)	17
5801272000	棉制割绒的经起绒织物	17
5801310000	不割绒的化纤制纬起绒织物	17

税则号列	商品名称	出口退税率(%)
5801320000	割绒的化纤制灯芯绒	17
5801330000	其他化纤纬起绒织物	17
5801360000	化纤绳绒织物	17
5801371000	化纤制不割绒经起绒织物(棱纹绸)	17
5801372000	化纤制割绒的经起绒织物	17
5801901000	丝及绢丝制起绒机织物及绳绒织物	17
5801909010	亚麻和苎麻起绒机织物及绳绒织物	17
5801909090	其他材料制起绒机织物及绳绒织物	17
5802110000	未漂棉毛巾织物及类似毛圈机织物	17
5802190000	其他棉毛巾织物及类似毛圈机织物	17
5802201010	丝及绢丝毛巾织物及类似毛圈织物	17
5802201090	丝及绢丝毛巾织物及类似毛圈织物	17
5802202000	羊毛等毛巾织物及类似毛圈机织物	17
5802203000	化纤毛巾织物及类似毛圈机织物	17
5802209000	其他材料毛巾织物及类似毛圈织物	17
5802301010	丝及绢丝制簇绒织物	17
5802301090	其他丝及绢丝制簇绒织物	17
5802302000	羊毛或动物细毛制簇绒织物	17
5802303010	麻制簇绒织物	17
5802303090	棉制簇绒织物	17
5802304000	化学纤维制簇绒织物	17
5802309000	其他纺织材料制簇绒织物	17
5803001000	棉制纱罗	17
5803002000	丝及绢丝制纱罗	17
5803003000	化学纤维制纱罗	17
5803009000	其他纺织材料制纱罗	17
5804101010	丝及绢丝网眼薄纱及其他网眼织物	17
5804101090	丝及绢丝网眼薄纱及其他网眼织物	17
5804102000	棉制网眼薄纱及其他网眼织物	17
5804103000	化纤制网眼薄纱及其他网眼织物	17
5804109000	其他材料网眼薄纱及其他网眼织物	17
5804210000	化纤机制花边	17
5804291010	丝及绢丝含量85%及以上机制花边	17
5804291090	丝及绢丝含量85%以下机制花边	17
5804292000	棉机制花边	17
5804299000	其他纺织材料制机制花边	17
5804300011	丝含量达85%及以上制手工制花边	17
5804300019	丝含量达85%以下制手工制花边	17
5804300020	棉或化纤制手工制花边	17
5804300090	其他纺织材料制手工制其他花边	17
5805001010	毛制非民间工艺针绣嵌花其他装饰毯	17
5805001020	棉制手工针绣嵌花其他装饰毯	17
5805001030	化纤制手工针绣嵌花其他装饰毯	17
5805001090	其他纺织料制手工针绣嵌花装饰毯	17
5805009010	毛制非民间工艺的手织装饰毯	17
5805009020	棉制"哥白林"等手织装饰毯	17
5805009030	化纤制"哥白林"等手织装饰毯	17
5805009090	其他纺织料制"哥白林"等手织装饰毯	17
5806101010	棉制狭幅起绒机织物及绳绒织物	17
5806101090	麻制狭幅起绒机织物及绳绒织物	17
5806109010	含丝≥85%狭幅起绒及绳绒等织物	17
5806109020	毛制狭幅起绒织物及绳绒织物	17
5806109030	化纤制狭幅起绒织物及绳绒织物	17
5806109090	其他材料狭幅起绒织物及绳绒织物	17

税则号列	商品名称	出口退税率(%)
5806200000	含弹性纱线≥5%狭幅织物	17
5806310000	棉制未列名狭幅机织物	17
5806320010	化纤制用于打字机色带狭幅机织物	17
5806320090	化纤制其他狭幅机织物	17
5806391000	含丝量≥85%制其他狭幅机织物	17
5806392000	羊毛制其他狭幅机织物	17
5806399010	含金属纱线制其他狭幅机织物	17
5806399090	其他材料制其他狭幅机织物	17
5806401000	棉或麻粘合有经纱无纬纱狭幅织物	17
5806409000	其他材料粘合有经无纬狭幅织物	17
5807100010	棉制机织非绣制标签	17
5807100020	化纤制机织非绣制标签	17
5807100090	其他纺织材料制机织非绣制标签等	17
5807900010	棉制非绣制的标签	17
5807900020	化纤制非绣制的标签	17
5807900090	其他纺织材料制非绣制的标签等	17
5808100010	棉或化纤制成匹的编带	17
5808100020	蕉麻或苎麻制成匹的编带	17
5808100090	其他纺织材料制成匹的编带	17
5808900010	棉或化纤制非绣制成匹装饰带	17
5808900090	其他非绣制成匹装饰带，流苏等	17
5809001000	金属线及含金属纱线与棉混制的布	17
5809002000	金属线及含金属纱线与化纤混制布	17
5809009000	金属线与其他纤维混制的布	17
5810100000	不见底布的刺绣品	17
5810910000	棉制见底布的刺绣品	17
5810920010	化学纤维制见底布刺绣标签	17
5810920090	其他化学纤维制见底布刺绣品	17
5810990010	羊毛或动物细毛制见底布刺绣品	17
5810990090	其他纺织材料制见底布刺绣品	17
5811001000	丝及绢丝制被褥状纺织品	17
5811002000	羊毛或动物细毛制被褥状纺织品	17
5811003010	未漂或漂白棉制被褥状纺织品	17
5811003090	其他棉制被褥状纺织品	17
5811004000	化学纤维制被褥状纺织品	17
5811009000	其他纺织材料制被褥状纺织品	17
5901101010	胶或淀粉涂布的棉纺织物	17
5901101090	胶或淀粉涂布的麻及其他棉纺织	17
5901102010	胶或淀粉涂布的涤棉短纤混纺织品	17
5901102090	胶或淀粉涂布的其他化纤纺织物	17
5901109010	用胶或淀粉涂布的精梳毛纺织物	17
5901109090	用胶或淀粉涂布的其他纺织物	17
5901901010	精梳毛织物制油画布	17
5901901020	棉制油画布	17
5901901030	聚酯短纤与棉混纺织物制油画	17
5901901090	其他纺织物制成的油画布	17
5901909110	棉制描图布、帽里硬衬布等	17
5901909190	麻及其他棉制描图布、帽里硬衬布	17
5901909210	聚酯短纤与棉混纺织物制描图布	17
5901909290	其他化纤制描图布，帽里硬衬布等	17
5901909910	精梳毛纺织物制描图布，帽里硬衬	17
5901909990	其他纺织物制描图布，帽里硬衬布	17
5902101000	聚酰胺-6（尼龙-6）制的帘子布	17
5902102000	聚酰胺-6，6（尼龙-6，6）制的帘子布	17

税则号列	商品名称	出口退税率(%)
5902109000	其他聚酰胺制的帘子布	17
5902200000	聚酯高强力纱制的帘子布	17
5902900000	粘胶纤维高强力纱制帘子布	17
5903101010	若干平行化纤纱线粘合绝缘布或带	17
5903101020	聚氯乙烯浸渍涤棉混纺绝缘布或带	17
5903101030	聚氯乙烯浸渍其他化纤绝缘布或带	17
5903101090	用聚氯乙烯浸渍的其他绝缘布或带	17
5903102010	若干层平行纱线粘合的化纤人造革	17
5903102020	用聚氯乙烯浸渍的涤棉织物人造革	17
5903102030	用聚氯乙烯浸渍的其他化纤人造革	17
5903102040	用聚氯乙烯浸渍的棉织物人造革	17
5903102090	用聚氯乙烯浸渍的其他人造革	17
5903109010	若干层平行纱线粘合化纤其他织物	17
5903109021	聚氯乙烯浸渍的其他涤棉混纺织物	17
5903109029	聚氯乙烯浸渍的其他化纤织物	17
5903109030	聚氯乙烯浸渍的棉织物	17
5903109040	用聚氯乙烯浸渍的精梳毛织物	17
5903109090	聚氯乙烯浸渍的其他纺织物	17
5903201010	若干平行纱线粘合化纤绝缘布或带	17
5903201020	聚氨基甲酸酯浸渍涤棉绝缘布或带	17
5903201030	聚氨基甲酸酯浸渍其他化纤绝缘布	17
5903201090	聚氨基甲酸酯浸渍其他绝缘布或带	17
5903202010	若干层平行纱线粘合化纤人造革	17
5903202020	用聚氨基甲酸酯浸渍的涤棉人造革	17
5903202030	聚氨基甲酸酯浸渍其他化纤人造革	17
5903202040	聚氨基甲酸酯浸渍的棉织物人造革	17
5903202090	用聚氨基甲酸酯浸渍的其他人造革	17
5903209010	若干层平行纱线粘合化纤其他织物	17
5903209021	聚氨基甲酸酯浸渍其他涤棉织物	17
5903209029	聚氨基甲酸酯浸渍其他化纤织物	17
5903209030	用聚氨基甲酸酯浸渍的棉织物	17
5903209041	用聚氨基甲酸酯浸渍的精梳毛织物	17
5903209049	用聚氨基甲酸酯浸渍的其他毛织物	17
5903209090	用聚氨基甲酸酯浸渍的其他纺织物	17
5903901010	若干平行化纤纱线粘合绝缘布或带	17
5903901020	其他塑料浸渍涤棉混纺绝缘布或带	17
5903901030	其他塑料浸渍其他化纤绝缘布或带	17
5903901090	用其他塑料浸渍的其他绝缘布或带	17
5903902010	由若干层平行纱线粘合化纤人造革	17
5903902020	用其他塑料浸渍的涤棉织物人造革	17
5903902030	用其他塑料浸渍的其他化纤人造革	17
5903902040	用其他塑料浸渍的棉织物人造革	17
5903902090	用其他塑料浸渍的其他人造革	17
5903909010	若干层化纤平行纱线粘合其他织物	17
5903909021	其他塑料浸渍的其他涤棉混纺织物	17
5903909029	用其他塑料浸渍的其他化纤织物	17
5903909030	用其他塑料浸渍的棉织物	17
5903909041	用其他塑料浸渍的精梳毛织物	17
5903909049	用其他塑料浸渍的其他毛织物	17
5903909090	用其他塑料浸渍的其他纺织物	17
5904100000	列诺伦(亚麻油地毡)	17
5904900000	以纺织物为底涂布或覆面的铺地品	17
5905000011	以纸衬背的合成短纤制糊墙织物	17
5905000019	以纸衬背的人造短纤制糊墙织物	17

税则号列	商品名称	出口退税率(%)
5905000020	平行纱线固定的糊墙织物	17
5905000031	其他合成短纤制糊墙织物	17
5905000039	其他人造短纤制糊墙织物	17
5905000090	其他纺织糊墙织物	17
5906101000	用橡胶处理宽≤20cm纺织绝缘带	17
5906109000	用橡胶处理宽≤20cm其他纺织物胶粘带	17
5906910010	用橡胶处理的针织或钩编化纤纺织物	17
5906910090	用橡胶处理的针织或钩编其他纺织物	17
5906991010	用橡胶处理的精梳毛纺绝缘布或带	17
5906991020	用橡胶处理的棉织物绝缘布或带	17
5906991031	用橡胶处理聚酯短纤棉混纺绝缘布带	17
5906991039	用橡胶处理的其他化纤绝缘布或带	17
5906991090	用橡胶处理宽＞20cm其他绝缘布或带	17
5906999010	用橡胶处理的精梳毛纺织物	17
5906999020	用橡胶处理的其他棉纺织物	17
5906999031	用橡胶处理的聚酯短纤棉混纺织物	17
5906999039	用橡胶处理的其他化纤纺织物	17
5906999090	用橡胶处理的其他纺织物	17
5907001010	其他材料浸涂植物纤维绝缘布或带	17
5907001020	其他材料浸涂的棉制绝缘布或带	17
5907001030	其他材料浸涂涤短纤棉混纺绝缘布	17
5907001090	其他材料浸涂其他纺织绝缘布或带	17
5907002010	其他材料浸涂植物纤维已绘制画布	17
5907002020	其他材料浸涂精梳毛已绘制画布	17
5907002030	用其他材料浸涂的棉制已绘制画布	17
5907002040	其他材料浸涂涤短纤棉混已绘画布	17
5907002090	其他材料浸涂其他织物已绘制画布	17
5907009010	用其他材料浸涂的植物纤维纺织物	17
5907009020	用其他材料浸涂的精梳毛纺织物	17
5907009030	用其他材料浸涂的棉制纺织物	17
5907009040	用其他材料浸涂的涤短纤棉混纺织物	17
5907009090	用其他材料浸涂的其他纺织物	17
5908000000	灯芯,炉芯等和煤气灯纱筒及纱罩	17
5909000000	纺织材料制水龙软管及类似管子	17
5910000000	纺织材料制的传动带或输送带及带料	17
5911101000	包覆纺锤用浸胶的狭幅丝绒织物	17
5911109000	其他起绒狭幅织物	17
5911200010	丝制筛布	17
5911200090	其他纺织材料制筛布	17
5911310000	轻的环状或有联接装置的布或毡呢	17
5911320000	重的环状或有联接装置的布或毡呢	17
5911400000	用于榨油机器或类似机器的滤布	17
5911900000	其他专门技术用途纺织产品及制品	17
6001100010	毛制针织或钩编的长毛绒织物	17
6001100020	棉制针织或钩编的长毛绒织物	17
6001100030	化纤制针织或钩编的长毛绒织物	17
6001100090	其他纺材制针织或钩编长毛绒织物	17
6001210000	棉制针织或钩编的毛圈绒头织物	17
6001220000	化纤制针织或钩编毛圈绒头织物	17
6001290010	毛制针织或钩编毛圈绒头织物	17
6001290090	其他材料制针织或钩编毛圈绒头布	17
6001910000	棉制针织或钩编起绒织物	17
6001920000	化纤制针织或钩编起绒织物	17
6001990010	丝制针织或钩编其他起绒织物	17

税则号列	商品名称	出口退税率(%)
6001990020	毛制针织或钩编其他起绒织物	17
6001990090	其他纺材制针织或钩编起绒织物	17
6002401000	棉制宽≤30cm弹性针织或钩编织物	17
6002402000	丝及绢丝制宽≤30cm针织或钩编织物	17
6002403000	合成纤维制宽≤30cm针织或钩编织物	17
6002404000	人造纤维制宽≤30cm针织或钩编织物	17
6002409000	其他纺材宽≤30cm针织或钩编织物	17
6002901000	棉制宽≤30cm弹性针织或钩编织物	17
6002902000	丝及绢丝宽≤30cm针织或钩编织物	17
6002903000	合成纤维制宽≤30cm针织或钩编织	17
6002904000	人造纤维制宽≤30cm针织或钩编织物	17
6002909000	其他纺材宽≤30cm针织或钩编织物	17
6003100000	毛制宽≤30cm针织或钩编织物	17
6003200010	棉制宽≤30cm经编织物	17
6003200090	棉制宽≤30cm非经编针织或钩编织物	17
6003300010	合纤制宽小于等于30厘米经编织物	17
6003300090	合纤制宽小于等于30厘米非经编针织或钩编织物	17
6003400010	人纤制宽小于等于30厘米经编织物	17
6003400090	人纤制宽小于等于30厘米非经编织物	17
6003900000	其他纺材宽≤30cm针织或钩编织物	17
6004101000	棉制宽>30cm弹性针织或钩编织物	17
6004102000	丝及绢丝宽>30cm针织或钩编织物	17
6004103000	合成纤维制宽>30cm针织或钩编织物	17
6004104000	人造纤维制宽>30cm针织或钩编织物	17
6004109000	其他纺材宽>30cm针织或钩编织物	17
6004901000	棉制宽>30cm弹性针织或钩编织物	17
6004902000	丝及绢丝宽>30cm针织或钩编织物	17
6004903000	合成纤维制宽>30cm针织或钩编织物	17
6004904000	人造纤维制宽>30cm针织或钩编织物	17
6004909000	其他纺材宽>30cm针织或钩编织物	17
6005210000	漂白或未漂白棉制经编织物	17
6005220000	染色棉制经编织物	17
6005230000	色织棉制经编织物	17
6005240000	印花棉制经编织物	17
6005310010	漂白或未漂白合成纤维制经编透孔织物	17
6005310090	漂白或未漂白合成纤维制经编非透孔织物	17
6005320010	染色合成纤维制经编透孔织物	17
6005320090	染色合成纤维制经编非透孔织物	17
6005330010	色织合成纤维制经编透孔织物	17
6005330090	色织合成纤维制经编非透孔织物	17
6005340010	印花合成纤维制经编透孔织物	17
6005340090	印花合成纤维制经编非透孔织物	17
6005410010	漂白或未漂白人造纤维制经编透孔织物	17
6005410090	漂白或未漂白人造纤维制经编非透孔织物	17
6005420010	染色人造纤维制经编透孔织物	17
6005420090	染色人造纤维制经编非透孔织物	17
6005430010	色织人造纤维制经编透孔织物	17
6005430090	色织人造纤维制经编非透孔织物	17
6005440010	印花人造纤维制经编透孔织物	17
6005440090	印花人造纤维制经编非透孔织物	17
6005901000	羊毛或动物细毛制经编织物	17
6005909000	其他纺织材料制经编织物	17
6006100000	毛制其他针织或钩编织物	17
6006210000	棉制其他漂或未漂针织或钩编织物	17

税则号列	商品名称	出口退税率(%)
6006220000	棉制其他染色针织或钩编织物	17
6006230000	棉制其他色织针织或钩编织物	17
6006240000	棉制其他印花针织或钩编织物	17
6006310000	合成纤维制其他针织或钩编织物	17
6006320000	合成纤维其他染色针织或钩编织物	17
6006330000	合成纤维其他色织针织或钩编织物	17
6006340000	合成纤维制其他针织或钩编织物	17
6006410000	人造纤维制其他针织或钩编织物	17
6006420000	人造纤维制其他针织或钩编织物	17
6006430000	人造纤维制其他针织或钩编织物	17
6006440000	人造纤维制其他针织或钩编织物	17
6006900010	丝及绢丝制其他针织或钩编织物	17
6006900090	其他纺材制其他针织或钩编织物	17
6101200010	棉制针织或钩编男式大衣	17
6101200021	棉制针织或钩编手工制男式防风衣	17
6101200029	棉制针织或钩编男式防风衣	17
6101200030	棉制针织或钩编男式雨衣	17
6101300011	化纤制针织或钩编男式大衣等	17
6101300019	其他化纤制针织或钩编男式大衣等	17
6101300021	化纤制针织或钩编手工男式防风衣	17
6101300022	化纤制针织或钩编男式防风衣	17
6101300023	其他化纤针织钩编手工男式防风衣	17
6101300029	其他化纤制其他男式防风衣	17
6101300031	化纤制针织或钩编男式雨衣	17
6101300039	化纤制针织或钩编男式雨衣	17
6101901010	毛制针织或钩编非手工制男式防风衣	17
6101901090	毛制针织或钩编其他男大衣、斗篷、防风衣等	17
6101909000	其他纺织材料制男大衣、斗篷、防风衣等	17
6102100010	毛制针织或钩编女式大衣等	17
6102100021	毛制针织或钩编手工制女式防风衣	17
6102100029	毛制针织或钩编女式防风衣	17
6102100030	毛制针织或钩编女式雨衣	17
6102200010	棉制针织或钩编女式大衣	17
6102200021	棉制针织或钩编手工女式防风衣	17
6102200029	棉制针织或钩编女式防风衣	17
6102200030	棉制针织或钩编女式雨衣	17
6102300011	化纤制针织或钩编女式大衣等	17
6102300019	其他化纤制针织或钩编女式大衣	17
6102300021	化纤制针织或钩编手工女式防风衣	17
6102300022	化纤制针织或钩编女式防风衣	17
6102300023	其他化纤制针织钩编手工女防风衣	17
6102300029	其他化纤制针织钩编其他女防风衣	17
6102300031	化纤制针织或钩编女式雨衣	17
6102300039	化纤制针织或钩编女式雨衣	17
6102900011	丝及绢丝制针织或钩编女式大衣等	17
6102900014	丝及绢丝制针织或钩编女式防风衣	17
6102900015	丝及绢丝制针织或钩编女式雨衣	17
6102900021	其他纺织材料制针织或钩编女大衣	17
6102900022	其他纺织材料制针织或钩编女大衣	17
6102900023	其他纺织材料制针织或钩编女大衣	17
6102900029	其他纺织材料制针织或钩编女大衣	17
6102900031	其他纺织料针织或钩编女式防风衣	17
6102900032	其他纺织料针织或钩编女式防风衣	17
6102900033	其他纺织料针织或钩编女式防风衣	17

税则号列	商品名称	出口退税率(%)
6102900039	其他纺织料针织或钩编女式防风衣	17
6102900041	其他纺材制针织或钩编女式雨衣	17
6102900042	其他纺材制针织或钩编女式雨衣	17
6102900043	其他纺材制针织或钩编女式雨衣	17
6102900049	其他纺材制针织或钩编女式雨衣	17
6103101000	毛制针织或钩编男式西服套装	17
6103102010	合成纤维制针织或钩编男西服套装	17
6103102090	其他合成纤维制针织或钩编男式西服套装	17
6103109011	人造纤维针织或钩编男式西服套装	17
6103109019	其他人纤针织或钩编男式西服套装	17
6103109020	棉制针织或钩编男式西服套装	17
6103109030	丝及绢丝制针织或钩编男西服套装	17
6103109041	其他纺材制针织或钩编男西服套装	17
6103109042	其他纺材制针织或钩编男西服套装	17
6103109043	其他纺材制针织或钩编男西服套装	17
6103109049	其他纺材制针织或钩编男西服套装	17
6103220000	棉制针织或钩编男式便服套装	17
6103230010	合成纤维制针织或钩编男便服套装	17
6103230091	其他合纤针织或钩编含毛衫或针织衬衫或裤子的男便服套装	17
6103230099	其他合纤制针织或钩编其他男便服套装	17
6103291000	毛制针织或钩编男式便服套装	17
6103299010	丝或绢丝制针织或钩编男便服套装	17
6103299020	人造纤维制针织或钩编男便服套装	17
6103299031	其他纺织料针织或钩编男便服套装	17
6103299032	其他纺织料针织或钩编男便服套装	17
6103299033	其他纺织料针织或钩编男便服套装	17
6103299034	其他纺织料针织或钩编男便服套装	17
6103299035	其他纺织料针织或钩编男便服套装	17
6103310000	毛制针织或钩编男式上衣	17
6103320000	棉制针织或钩编男式上衣	17
6103330010	合成纤维制针织或钩编男式上衣	17
6103330090	其他合纤制针织或钩编男式上衣	17
6103390010	人造纤维制针织或钩编男式上衣	17
6103390020	丝制针织或钩编男式上衣	17
6103390031	其他纺织料制针织或钩编男式上衣	17
6103390032	其他纺织料制针织或钩编男式上衣	17
6103390033	其他纺织料制针织或钩编男式上衣	17
6103390039	其他纺织料制针织或钩编男式上衣	17
6103410010	毛制针织或钩编护胸背带男工装裤	17
6103410020	毛制针织或钩编男长裤	17
6103410090	毛制针织或钩编其他男裤	17
6103420011	棉制针织或钩编护胸背带男工装裤	17
6103420012	棉针织钩编男童非保暖背带工装裤	17
6103420019	棉针织钩编男式非保暖背带工装裤	17
6103420021	棉制针织或钩编男童游戏套装长裤	17
6103420029	棉针织或钩编其他男童游戏套装裤	17
6103420030	棉制针织或钩编男长裤	17
6103420090	棉制针织或钩编其他男裤等	17
6103430010	合纤针织或钩编护胸背带男工装裤	17
6103430021	合成纤维制针织或钩编男长裤	17
6103430029	合成纤维制针织或钩编其他男裤	17
6103430091	其他合纤制护胸背带男工装裤	17
6103430092	其他合纤制男童游戏套装长裤	17
6103430093	其他合纤制男童游戏套装长裤	17

税则号列	商品名称	出口退税率(%)
6103430094	其他合纤制针织或钩编男长裤	17
6103430099	其他合纤制针织或钩编其他男裤	17
6103490011	丝制男式护胸背带工装裤	17
6103490012	丝制针织或钩编男成人长裤.马裤	17
6103490013	丝制针织或钩编其他男童长裤、马裤	17
6103490014	丝制针织或钩编其他男式短裤	17
6103490021	人造纤维制男式护胸背带工装裤	17
6103490022	人纤制针织或钩编男人长裤.马裤	17
6103490023	人纤制针织或钩编其他男童长裤、马裤	17
6103490024	人纤制针织或钩编男式短裤	17
6103490025	其他人纤制针织或钩编男长裤、马裤	17
6103490026	其他人纤制针织或钩编其他男童长裤	17
6103490027	其他人纤制针织或钩编其他男短裤	17
6103490031	其他纺材制男式护胸背带工装裤	17
6103490032	其他纺材制男式护胸背带工装裤	17
6103490033	其他纺材制男式护胸背带工装裤	17
6103490039	其他纺材制男式护胸背带工装裤	17
6103490041	其他纺材制针织或钩编男长裤、马裤	17
6103490042	其他纺材制针织或钩编男长裤、马裤	17
6103490043	其他纺材制针织或钩编男长裤、马裤	17
6103490049	其他纺材制针织或钩编男长裤、马裤	17
6103490051	其他纺织材料制其他男童长裤马裤	17
6103490052	其他纺织材料制其他男童长裤马裤	17
6103490053	其他纺织材料制其他男童长裤马裤	17
6103490059	其他纺织材料制其他男童长裤马裤	17
6103490061	其他纺材制针织或钩编男式短裤	17
6103490062	其他纺材制针织或钩编男式短裤	17
6103490063	其他纺材制针织或钩编男式短裤	17
6103490069	其他纺材制针织或钩编男式短裤	17
6104130010	合成纤维制针织或钩编女西服套装	17
6104130090	其他合纤制针织或钩编女西服套装	17
6104191000	毛制针织或钩编女式西服套装	17
6104192010	含裤子的棉针织或钩编女西服套装	17
6104192090	不含裤子的棉针织或钩编女西服套装	17
6104199010	含裤子的其他纺材制针织或钩编女西服套装	17
6104199090	其他纺织材料制针织或钩编女式西服套装	17
6104220010	含针织衬衫或毛衫或裤子棉制针织或钩编女便服套装	17
6104220090	其他棉针织或钩编女便服套装	17
6104230010	合纤制针织或钩编女便服套装	17
6104230091	含针织衬衫或毛衫或裤子其他合纤针织或钩编女便服套装	17
6104230099	其他合纤针织或钩编其他女便服套装	17
6104291000	毛制针织或钩编女式便服套装	17
6104299021	含针织衬衫或毛衫或裤子的人纤制其他女便服套装	17
6104299029	人纤制其他女便服套装	17
6104299031	含针织衬衫或毛衫或裤子其他纺材针织或钩编女便服套装	17
6104299032	其他纺材针织或钩编女式便服套装	17
6104299033	含针织衬衫或毛衫或裤子其他纺材针织或钩编女便服套装	17
6104299034	含裤子的其他纺材针织或钩编女式便服套装	17
6104299039	其他纺材针织或钩编其他女式便服套装	17
6104310010	毛制钩编女式上衣	17
6104310090	毛制针织女式上衣	17
6104320010	棉制钩编女式上衣	17
6104320090	棉制针织女式上衣	17
6104330011	合成纤维制钩编女上衣	17

税则号列	商品名称	出口退税率(%)
6104330019	其他合成纤维制钩编女上衣	17
6104330091	合成纤维制针织女上衣	17
6104330099	其他合成纤维制针织女上衣	17
6104390011	丝及绢丝制钩编女上衣	17
6104390019	丝及绢丝制针织女上衣	17
6104390021	人造纤维制钩编女上衣	17
6104390029	人造纤维制针织女上衣	17
6104390031	其他纺织材料制钩编女上衣	17
6104390032	其他纺织材料制钩编女上衣	17
6104390033	其他纺织材料制钩编女上衣	17
6104390039	其他纺织材料制钩编女上衣	17
6104390041	其他纺织材料制针织女上衣	17
6104390042	其他纺织材料制针织女上衣	17
6104390043	其他纺织材料制针织女上衣	17
6104390049	其他纺织材料制针织女上衣	17
6104410000	毛制针织或钩编连衣裙	17
6104420000	棉制针织或钩编连衣裙	17
6104430010	合纤制针织或钩编连衣裙	17
6104430090	其他合纤制针织或钩编连衣裙	17
6104440010	人纤制针织或钩编连衣裙	17
6104440090	其他人纤制针织或钩编连衣裙	17
6104490010	丝及绢丝制针织或钩编连衣裙	17
6104490091	其他纺织材料制针织或钩编连衣裙	17
6104490092	其他纺织材料制针织或钩编连衣裙	17
6104490093	其他纺织材料制针织或钩编连衣裙	17
6104490099	其他纺织材料制针织或钩编连衣裙	17
6104510000	毛制针织或钩编裙子及裙裤	17
6104520000	棉制针织裙子及裙裤	17
6104530010	合纤制针织或钩编裙子及裙裤	17
6104530090	其他合纤制针织或钩编裙子及裙裤	17
6104590010	丝及绢丝制针织或钩编裙子及裙裤	17
6104590021	人纤制针织或钩编裙子及裙裤	17
6104590029	其他人纤制针织或钩编裙子及裙裤	17
6104590091	其他纺材制针织或钩编裙子及裙裤	17
6104590092	其他纺材制针织或钩编裙子及裙裤	17
6104590093	其他纺材制针织或钩编裙子及裙裤	17
6104590099	其他纺材制针织或钩编裙子及裙裤	17
6104610010	毛制针织或钩编女护胸背带工装裤	17
6104610020	毛制针织或钩编女长裤、马裤	17
6104610090	毛制针织或钩编其他女裤	17
6104620010	棉制针织或钩编护胸背带女工装裤	17
6104620020	棉针织或钩编非保暖女成人工装裤	17
6104620030	棉制针织或钩编女童游戏套装长裤	17
6104620040	棉针织或钩编其他女童游戏套装裤	17
6104620050	棉制针织或钩编女长裤、马裤	17
6104620090	棉制针织或钩编其他女裤	17
6104630010	合成纤维制护胸背带女工装裤	17
6104630021	合成纤维制针织或钩编女长裤	17
6104630029	合成纤维制针织或钩编其他女裤	17
6104630091	其他合纤制女童游戏套装长裤、马裤	17
6104630092	其他合成纤维制女童游戏套装裤	17
6104630099	其他合成纤维制针织或钩编女裤	17
6104690011	丝及绢丝制针织或钩编女工装裤	17
6104690012	丝及绢丝制针织或钩编女长裤、马裤	17

税则号列	商品名称	出口退税率(%)
6104690013	丝及绢丝制针织或钩编女短裤	17
6104690019	丝及绢丝制针织或钩编其他女长裤	17
6104690021	人造纤维制护胸背带女工装裤	17
6104690022	人造纤维制针织或钩编女长裤、马裤	17
6104690023	人造纤维制针织或钩编其他女裤	17
6104690024	其他人造纤维制女长裤	17
6104690029	其他人纤制针织或钩编其他女裤	17
6104690031	其他纺材制针织或钩编女工装裤	17
6104690032	其他纺材制针织或钩编女工装裤	17
6104690033	其他纺材制针织或钩编女工装裤	17
6104690039	其他纺材制针织或钩编女工装裤	17
6104690041	其他纺织材料制针织或钩编女长裤	17
6104690042	其他纺织材料制针织或钩编女长裤	17
6104690043	其他纺织材料制针织或钩编女长裤	17
6104690049	其他纺织材料制针织或钩编女长裤	17
6104690051	其他纺织材料针织或钩编其他女长裤	17
6104690052	其他纺织材料针织或钩编其他女长裤	17
6104690053	其他纺织材料针织或钩编其他女长裤	17
6104690059	其他纺织材料针织或钩编其他女长裤	17
6104690061	其他纺织材料制针织或钩编女短裤	17
6104690062	其他纺织材料制针织或钩编女短裤	17
6104690063	其他纺织材料制针织或钩编女短裤	17
6104690069	其他纺织材料制针织或钩编女短裤	17
6105100011	棉制针织或钩编男童游戏套装衬衫	17
6105100019	棉制其他男童游戏套装衬衫	17
6105100091	其他棉制针织或钩编男衬衫	17
6105100099	其他棉制针织或钩编其他男衬衫	17
6105200011	化纤制针织或钩编男衬衫	17
6105200019	化纤制针织或钩编其他男衬衫	17
6105200021	化纤针织或钩编男童游戏套装衬衫	17
6105200029	化纤制其他男童游戏套装衬衫	17
6105200091	其他化纤制针织或钩编男衬衫	17
6105200099	其他化纤制针织或钩编其他男衬衫	17
6105900011	丝及绢丝制针织或钩编男衬衫	17
6105900019	丝及绢丝制针织或钩编其他男衬衫	17
6105900021	羊毛或动物细毛制男衬衫	17
6105900029	羊毛或动物细毛制其他男衬衫	17
6105900031	其他纺织材料制针织或钩编男衬衫	17
6105900032	其他纺织材料制针织或钩编男衬衫	17
6105900033	其他纺织材料制针织或钩编男衬衫	17
6105900039	其他纺织材料制针织或钩编男衬衫	17
6105900041	其他纺织材料制针织或钩编男衬衫	17
6105900042	其他纺织材料制针织或钩编男衬衫	17
6105900043	其他纺织材料制针织或钩编男衬衫	17
6105900049	其他纺材制针织或钩编其他男衬衫	17
6106100010	棉制针织或钩编女童游戏套装衬衫	17
6106100090	棉制针织或钩编其他女衬衫	17
6106200010	化纤制针织或钩编女衬衫	17
6106200020	其他化纤制女童游戏套装衬衫	17
6106200090	其他化纤针织或钩编未列名女衬衫	17
6106900010	丝及绢丝制针织或钩编女衬衫	17
6106900020	羊毛或动物细毛针织或钩编女衬衫	17
6106900031	其他纺织材料制针织或钩编女衬衫	17
6106900032	其他纺织材料制针织或钩编女衬衫	17

税则号列	商品名称	出口退税率(%)
6106900033	其他纺织材料制针织或钩编女衬衫	17
6106900039	其他纺织材料制针织或钩编女衬衫	17
6107110000	棉制针织或钩编男内裤及三角裤	17
6107120000	化纤制针织或钩编男内裤及三角裤	17
6107191010	丝及绢丝制男内裤及三角裤	17
6107191090	其他丝及绢丝制男内裤及三角裤	17
6107199010	羊毛或动物细毛制男内裤及三角裤	17
6107199090	其他纺织材料制男内裤及三角裤	17
6107210000	棉制针织或钩编男长睡衣及睡衣裤	17
6107220000	化纤制针织或钩编男睡衣裤	17
6107291010	丝及绢丝制针织或钩编男睡衣裤	17
6107291090	其他丝及绢丝制针织或钩编男睡衣裤	17
6107299000	其他纺材制针织或钩编男睡衣裤	17
6107910010	棉制针织或钩编其他睡衣裤	17
6107910090	棉制针织或钩编男浴衣.晨衣等	17
6107991000	化学纤维制其他男睡衣裤、浴衣、晨衣等	17
6107999000	其他纺织材料制其他男睡衣裤、浴衣、晨衣等	17
6108110000	化纤制针织或钩编长衬裙及衬裙	17
6108191000	棉制针织或钩编女式长衬裙及衬裙	17
6108192010	丝及绢丝制女式长衬裙及衬裙	17
6108192090	其他丝及绢丝制女式长衬裙及衬裙	17
6108199000	其他纺织材料制女式长衬裙及衬裙	17
6108210000	棉制针织或钩编女三角裤及短衬裤	17
6108220010	化纤制一次性女三角裤及短衬裤	17
6108220090	化纤制其他女三角裤及短衬裤	17
6108291010	丝及绢丝制女三角裤及短衬裤	17
6108291090	其他丝及绢丝制女三角裤及短衬裤	17
6108299010	羊毛制女三角裤及短衬裤	17
6108299090	其他纺织材料制女三角裤及短衬裤	17
6108310000	棉制针织或钩编女睡衣及睡衣裤	17
6108320000	化纤制针织或钩编女睡衣及睡衣裤	17
6108391010	丝及绢丝制女睡衣及睡衣裤	17
6108391090	其他丝及绢丝制女睡衣及睡衣裤	17
6108399010	羊毛或动物细毛制女睡衣及睡衣裤	17
6108399090	其他纺织材料制女睡衣及睡衣裤	17
6108910010	棉制针织或钩编女内裤、内衣	17
6108910090	其他棉制针织或钩编女浴衣、晨衣等	17
6108920010	化纤制针织或钩编女内裤,内衣	17
6108920090	其他化纤制针织或钩编女浴衣、晨衣等	17
6108990010	丝及绢丝制制女浴衣、晨衣等	17
6108990020	羊毛或动物细毛制女浴衣、晨衣等	17
6108990090	其他纺织材料制女浴衣、晨衣等	17
6109100010	棉制针织或钩编T恤衫、汗衫等	17
6109100021	其他棉制针织或钩编男式T恤衫	17
6109100022	其他棉制针织或钩编女式T恤衫	17
6109100091	其他棉制男式汗衫及其他背心	17
6109100092	其他棉制男式汗衫及其他背心	17
6109100099	其他棉制女式汗衫及其他背心	17
6109901011	丝及绢丝针织或钩编T恤衫、汗衫、背心	17
6109901019	其他丝及绢丝针织或钩编T恤衫、背心	17
6109901021	丝及绢丝针织钩编汗衫、背心	17
6109901029	其他丝及绢丝针织钩编汗衫、背心	17
6109901091	其他丝及绢丝针织或钩编T恤衫、汗衫	17
6109901099	其他丝及绢丝针织或钩编T恤衫、汗衫	17

税则号列	商品名称	出口退税率(%)
6109909011	毛制针织或钩编T恤衫、汗衫等	17
6109909012	毛制针织或钩编男式T恤衫、汗衫	17
6109909013	毛制针织或钩编女式T恤衫、汗衫	17
6109909021	毛制针织或钩编男式其他T恤衫	17
6109909022	毛制针织或钩编女式其他T恤衫	17
6109909031	毛制男式汗衫及其他背心	17
6109909032	其他毛制男式汗衫及其他背心	17
6109909033	其他毛制女式汗衫及其他背心	17
6109909040	化纤制针织或钩编内衣	17
6109909050	化纤制针织或钩编T恤衫	17
6109909060	化纤针织或钩编汗衫及其他背心	17
6109909091	其他纺织材料制T恤衫.汗衫等	17
6109909092	其他纺材制针织或钩编汗衫及其他背心	17
6109909093	其他纺材制针织或钩编T恤衫、汗衫	17
6110110011	羊毛制手工针织或钩编起绒外穿背心	17
6110110019	羊毛制针织或钩编起绒外穿背心	17
6110110021	羊毛制手工制起绒男毛衫	17
6110110029	羊毛针织制或钩编起绒男毛衫	17
6110110031	羊毛制手工制起绒女毛衫	17
6110110039	羊毛制针织或钩编起绒女毛衫	17
6110110041	羊毛手工制起绒套头衫等	17
6110110049	羊毛针织或钩编起绒套头衫等	17
6110110051	羊毛手工制非起绒外穿背心	17
6110110059	羊毛针织或钩编非起绒外穿背心	17
6110110061	其他羊毛手工制非起绒男毛衫	17
6110110069	其他羊毛针织或钩编非起绒男毛衫	17
6110110071	其他羊毛制手工制非起绒女毛衫	17
6110110079	其他羊毛针织或钩编非起绒女毛衫	17
6110110091	其他羊毛制手工制非起绒套头衫等	17
6110110099	其他羊毛制非起绒套头衫等	17
6110120011	喀什米尔山羊细毛手工起绒男套头衫	17
6110120019	喀什米尔山羊细毛制起绒男套头衫	17
6110120021	喀什米尔山羊细毛手工起绒女套头衫	17
6110120029	喀什米尔山羊细毛制起绒女套头衫	17
6110120031	喀什米尔山羊细毛手工非起绒男套头衫	17
6110120039	喀什米尔山羊细毛非起绒男套头衫	17
6110120041	喀什米尔山羊细毛手工非起绒女套头衫	17
6110120049	喀什米尔山羊细毛非起绒女套头衫	17
6110191011	其他山羊细毛手工起绒男套头衫	17
6110191019	其他山羊细毛制起绒男套头衫	17
6110191021	其他山羊细毛手工起绒女套头衫	17
6110191029	其他山羊细毛制起绒女套头衫	17
6110191031	其他山羊细毛手工非起绒男套头衫	17
6110191039	其他山羊细毛非起绒男套头衫	17
6110191041	其他山羊细毛手工非起绒女套头衫	17
6110191049	其他山羊细毛非起绒女套头衫	17
6110192011	兔毛制手工针织或钩编起绒马甲	17
6110192019	兔毛制针织或钩编起绒马甲	17
6110192021	兔毛制手工针织或钩编起绒男毛衫	17
6110192029	兔毛制针织或钩编起绒男毛衫	17
6110192031	兔毛制手工针织或钩编起绒女毛衫	17
6110192039	兔毛制针织或钩编起绒女毛衫	17
6110192041	其他兔毛制手工制起绒套头衫等	17
6110192049	其他兔毛制起绒套头衫等	17

税则号列	商品名称	出口退税率(%)
6110192051	兔毛制手工制非起绒马甲	17
6110192059	兔毛制针织或钩编非起绒马甲	17
6110192061	兔毛手工制非起绒男毛衫	17
6110192069	兔毛针织或钩编非起绒男毛衫	17
6110192071	兔毛制手工制非起绒女毛衫	17
6110192079	兔毛制针织或钩编非起绒女毛衫	17
6110192091	其他兔毛制手工制非起绒套头衫等	17
6110192099	其他兔毛制非起绒套头衫等	17
6110199011	其他动物细毛制手工起绒马甲	17
6110199019	其他动物细毛制起绒马甲	17
6110199021	其他动物细毛手工起绒男毛衫	17
6110199029	其他动物细毛制起绒男毛衫	17
6110199031	其他动物细毛手工起绒女毛衫	17
6110199039	其他动物细毛制起绒女毛衫	17
6110199041	其他动物细毛手工起绒套头衫	17
6110199049	其他动物细毛制起绒套头衫	17
6110199051	其他动物细毛制手工非起绒马甲	17
6110199059	其他动物细毛制非起绒马甲	17
6110199061	其他动物细毛手工非起绒男毛衫	17
6110199069	其他动物细毛非起绒男毛衫	17
6110199071	其他动物细毛手工非起绒女毛衫	17
6110199079	其他动物细毛非起绒女毛衫	17
6110199091	其他动物细毛手工非起绒套头衫	17
6110199099	其他动物细毛非起绒套头衫	17
6110200011	棉制儿童游戏套装紧身衫及套头衫	17
6110200012	棉制其他起绒儿童游戏套头衫等	17
6110200020	棉制针织或钩编起绒马甲	17
6110200031	棉制针织起绒紧身及套头毛衫	17
6110200032	棉制针织起绒男紧身衫及套头衫	17
6110200033	棉制针织起绒女紧身衫及套头衫	17
6110200041	棉制针织或钩编起绒其他毛衫	17
6110200042	棉制针织或钩编起绒男套头衫等	17
6110200043	棉制针织或钩编起绒女套头衫等	17
6110200051	其他棉儿童游戏套装紧身及套头衫	17
6110200052	其他棉儿童游戏套装套头衫等	17
6110200060	其他棉制针织或钩编非起绒马甲	17
6110200071	棉制针织非起绒男紧身及套头衫等	17
6110200072	棉制非起绒男紧身衫及套头衫	17
6110200073	棉制针织非起绒女紧身衫及套头衫	17
6110200091	其他棉制针织或钩编非起绒毛衫	17
6110200092	其他针织或钩编棉制非起绒男套头衫等	17
6110200093	棉制针织或钩编女套头衫等	17
6110200099	其他棉制针织钩编套头衫等	17
6110300011	化纤儿童游戏套装紧身衫及套头衫	17
6110300012	化纤起绒儿童游戏套装及套头衫等	17
6110300021	化纤制针织或钩编起绒马甲	17
6110300022	化纤制针织起绒男紧身及套头毛衫	17
6110300023	化纤制针织或钩编起绒男毛衫	17
6110300024	化纤制针织起绒女紧身及套头毛衫	17
6110300025	化纤制针织或钩编起绒女毛衫	17
6110300026	其他化纤针织起绒套头衫	17
6110300029	其他化纤针织或钩编起绒开襟衫等	17
6110300031	其他化纤制针织或钩编起绒马甲	17
6110300032	化纤针织或起绒男紧身及套头毛衫	17

税则号列	商品名称	出口退税率(%)
6110300033	其他化纤制针织或钩编起绒男毛衫	17
6110300034	化纤制针织起绒女紧身及套头毛衫	17
6110300035	其他化纤制针织或钩编起绒女毛衫	17
6110300036	其他化纤针织起绒男套头衫	17
6110300037	其他化纤针织或钩编起绒男开襟衫等	17
6110300038	其他化纤起绒针织女套头衫	17
6110300039	其他化纤制针织或钩编女开襟衫等	17
6110300041	化纤其他童游戏套装紧身及套头衫	17
6110300042	化纤制其他童游戏套装套头衫等	17
6110300051	其他化纤制针织或钩编非起绒马甲	17
6110300052	化纤针织非起绒男紧身及套头毛衫	17
6110300053	化纤制针织或钩编非起绒男毛衫	17
6110300054	化纤针织非起绒女紧身及套头毛衫	17
6110300057	化纤制针织钩编非起绒女毛衫	17
6110300058	其他化纤针非起绒套头衫	17
6110300059	其他化纤针织或钩编开襟衫等	17
6110300091	其他化纤针织男紧身及套头毛衫	17
6110300092	其他化纤针织或钩编非起绒男毛衫	17
6110300093	化纤针织非起绒女紧身及套头毛衫	17
6110300094	其他化纤针织或钩编非起绒女毛衫	17
6110300095	其他化纤针织非起绒男套头衫	17
6110300096	其他化纤针织或钩编男开襟衫等	17
6110300097	其他化纤制针织非起绒女套头衫	17
6110300098	其他化纤制针织或钩编女开襟衫等	17
6110300099	其他化纤制针织钩编套头衫等	17
6110901011	丝及绢丝制针织或钩编起绒毛衫等	17
6110901019	丝及绢丝制针织或钩编起绒毛衫等	17
6110901091	其他丝及绢丝针织或钩编毛衫等	17
6110901099	其他丝及绢丝针织或钩编毛衫等	17
6110909011	其他纺织材料针织或钩编起绒马甲	17
6110909012	其他纺织材料针织或钩编起绒马甲	17
6110909013	其他纺织材料针织或钩编起绒马甲	17
6110909019	其他纺织材料起绒针织或钩编马甲	17
6110909021	其他纺材制针织或钩编非起绒马甲	17
6110909022	其他纺材制针织或钩编非起绒马甲	17
6110909023	其他纺材制针织或钩编非起绒马甲	17
6110909029	其他纺材制针织或钩编马甲	17
6110909031	其他纺材制针织或钩编起绒毛衫	17
6110909033	其他纺材制针织或钩编起绒男毛衫	17
6110909034	其他纺材制针织或钩编起绒女毛衫	17
6110909035	其他纺材制针织或钩编起绒男毛衫	17
6110909036	其他纺材制针织或钩编起绒女毛衫	17
6110909039	其他纺材制针织或钩编毛衫	17
6110909041	其他纺材针织或钩编起绒男套头衫等	17
6110909042	其他纺材针织或钩编起绒女套头衫等	17
6110909043	其他纺材针织或钩编起绒套头衫等	17
6110909045	其他纺材针织或钩编起绒男套头衫等	17
6110909046	其他纺材针织或钩编起绒女套头衫等	17
6110909049	其他纺材针织或钩编套头衫等	17
6110909051	其他纺材针织或钩编非起绒毛衫	17
6110909053	其他纺材针织或钩编非起绒男毛衫	17
6110909054	其他纺材针织或钩编非起绒女毛衫	17
6110909057	其他纺材针织或钩编非起绒男毛衫	17
6110909058	其他纺材针织或钩编非起绒女毛衫	17

税则号列	商品名称	出口退税率(%)
6110909059	其他纺材针织或钩编毛衫	17
6110909061	其他纺材针织或钩编非起绒男套衫等	17
6110909062	其他纺材针织或钩编非起绒女套衫等	17
6110909063	其他纺材针织或钩编非起绒套头衫等	17
6110909065	其他纺材针织或钩编非起绒男套衫等	17
6110909066	其他纺材针织或钩编非起绒女套衫等	17
6110909069	其他纺材针织或钩编套头衫等	17
6110909090	其他纺材针织或钩编套头衫等	17
6111200010	棉制针织或钩编婴儿袜	17
6111200020	棉制婴儿分指、连指、露指手套	17
6111200040	棉制针织婴儿外衣、雨衣、滑雪装	17
6111200050	棉制针织钩编婴儿其他服装	17
6111200090	棉制针织钩编婴儿衣着附件	17
6111300010	合纤制针织或钩编婴儿袜	17
6111300020	合纤婴儿分指、连指及露指手套	17
6111300040	合纤婴儿外衣、雨衣、滑雪装	17
6111300050	合纤针织或钩编婴儿其他服装	17
6111300090	合纤针织或钩编婴儿衣着附件	17
6111901000	毛制针织或钩编婴儿服装及衣着附件	17
6111909010	人造纤维针织或钩编婴儿袜	17
6111909090	其他纺织材料制婴儿服装及衣着附件	17
6112110011	棉制针织或钩编男式运动套装	17
6112110019	棉制针织或钩编女式运动套装	17
6112120021	合纤制针织或钩编男式运动服	17
6112120029	合纤制针织或钩编女式运动套装	17
6112190031	人造纤维制针织或钩编男式运动服	17
6112190039	人造纤维制针织或钩编女运动套装	17
6112190041	羊毛制男式运动套装	17
6112190049	羊毛制女式运动套装	17
6112190051	动物细毛制男式运动套装	17
6112190059	动物细毛制女式运动套装	17
6112190061	其他纺织材料制男式运动套装	17
6112190069	其他纺织材料制女式运动套装	17
6112190090	其他纺织材料制运动套装	17
6112201000	棉制针织或钩编滑雪服	17
6112209010	羊毛或动物细毛针织或钩编滑雪套装	17
6112209021	化学纤维制针织或钩编男式滑雪套装	17
6112209029	化学纤维制针织或钩编女式滑雪套装	17
6112209090	其他纺织材料针织或钩编滑雪套装	17
6112310000	合纤制针织或钩编男式游泳服	17
6112390000	其他材料制针织或钩编男式游泳服	17
6112410000	合纤制针织或钩编女式游泳服	17
6112490000	其他纺织材料制针织或钩编女游泳服	17
6113000011	用橡胶处理的服装	17
6113000013	用塑料处理的毛、棉及化纤制服装	17
6113000019	用塑料处理的其他纺织材料制服装	17
6113000021	其他橡胶处理的棉针织或钩编男上衣	17
6113000022	其他塑料等处理的棉制针织男上衣	17
6113000023	其他橡胶处理的棉针织或钩编女上衣	17
6113000028	其他塑料等处理的棉针织女上衣	17
6113000031	其他橡胶处理的纺织材料制男上衣	17
6113000032	其他塑料等处理的毛制男上衣	17
6113000033	其他塑料等处理的毛、化纤男上衣	17
6113000034	其他塑料等处理的纺织材料男上衣	17

税则号列	商品名称	出口退税率(%)
6113000035	其他橡胶处理的纺织材料制女上衣	17
6113000036	其他塑料等处理的毛制女上衣	17
6113000037	其他塑料等处理的化纤制女上衣	17
6113000038	其他塑料等处理的纺织材料制女上衣	17
6113000041	其他橡胶等处理的棉制男式长短裤	17
6113000042	其他塑料等处理的棉制男式长短裤	17
6113000043	其他橡胶等处理的棉制女式长短裤	17
6113000044	其他塑料等处理的棉制女式长短裤	17
6113000051	其他橡胶处理纺织材料男长短裤	17
6113000053	其他塑料等处理的毛化纤制男裤	17
6113000054	其他塑料等处理纺织材料男长短裤	17
6113000057	其他橡胶处理纺织材料女长短裤	17
6113000058	其他塑料等处理的毛、化纤制女裤	17
6113000059	其他塑料等处理纺织材料女长短裤	17
6113000091	其他橡胶处理棉针织或钩编服装	17
6113000092	其他塑料处理棉针织或钩编服装	17
6113000093	其他橡胶处理纺织材料针织服装	17
6113000094	其他塑料等处理毛化纤针织服装	17
6113000098	其他塑料等处理纺织材料针织服装	17
6114200011	棉制针织或钩编儿童非保暖连身裤	17
6114200019	棉制针织或钩编其他连身裤	17
6114200021	棉制针织或钩编男成人及男童TOPS	17
6114200022	棉制针织或钩编其他男童TOPS	17
6114200029	棉制针织或钩编女式TOPS	17
6114200030	棉制针织或钩编其他运动服	17
6114200040	棉制针织或钩编夏服、水洗服	17
6114200090	棉制针织或钩编其他服装	17
6114300011	化纤制针织或钩编连身衣	17
6114300012	化纤制针织或钩编紧身服及衬衫	17
6114300013	化纤制针织或钩编其他连身衣	17
6114300019	化纤制针织或钩编紧身服及衬衫	17
6114300021	化纤针织或钩编男成人及男TOPS	17
6114300022	化纤针织或钩编其他男童TOPS	17
6114300029	化纤针织或钩编女式TOPS	17
6114300030	化纤针织或钩编其他运动服	17
6114300040	化纤针织或钩编夏服、水洗服	17
6114300090	化纤针织或钩编其他服装	17
6114901000	毛制针织或钩编其他服装	17
6114909000	其他纺织材料制其他服装	17
6115100000	渐紧压袜类	17
6115210000	每根单丝细度＜67分特的合成纤维制连裤袜及紧身裤袜	17
6115220000	每根单丝细度≥67分特的合成纤维制连裤袜及紧身裤袜	17
6115291000	棉制针织或钩编连裤袜及紧身裤袜	17
6115299000	其他纺织材料制针织或钩编连裤袜及紧身裤袜	17
6115300021	合纤制针织或钩编女长筒袜	17
6115300029	合纤制针织或钩编女中筒袜	17
6115300090	其他材料制女筒袜	17
6115940000	毛制针织或钩编短袜及其他袜类	17
6115950011	棉制针织或钩编矫正袜	17
6115950019	棉制针织或钩编短袜及其他袜类	17
6115960011	合纤制针织或钩编矫正袜	17
6115960012	合纤制女长筒袜	17
6115960013	合纤制短袜及其他袜类	17
6115960014	其他合纤制女长筒袜	17

税则号列	商品名称	出口退税率(%)
6115960019	其他合纤制短袜及其他袜类	17
6115990011	人纤制短袜及其他袜类	17
6115990019	其他人纤制短袜及其他袜类	17
6115990091	其他纺织材料制短袜及其他袜类	17
6115990099	其他纺织材料制短袜及其他袜类	17
6116100010	塑料或橡胶浸渍的运动手套	17
6116100091	塑料或橡胶浸渍的非运动手套	17
6116100092	塑料或橡胶浸渍的非运动手套	17
6116100093	塑料或橡胶浸渍的非运动手套	17
6116100094	塑料或橡胶浸渍的其他非运动手套	17
6116100099	塑料或橡胶浸渍的其他非运动手套	17
6116910000	毛制其他针织或钩编手套	17
6116920000	棉制其他针织或钩编手套	17
6116930010	合纤制其他针织或钩编手套	17
6116930090	合纤制其他针织或钩编手套	17
6116990011	人造纤维制其他针织或钩编手套	17
6116990019	人造纤维制其他针织或钩编手套	17
6116990020	丝或绢丝制其他针织或钩编手套	17
6116990091	其他纺材制其他针织或钩编手套	17
6116990092	其他纺材制其他针织或钩编手套	17
6116990093	其他纺材制其他针织或钩编手套	17
6116990099	未列名纺材制其他针织或钩编手套	17
6117101100	山羊绒制披巾、头巾、围巾、披纱、面纱及类似品	17
6117101900	其他动物细毛制披巾、头巾、围巾、披纱、面纱及类似品	17
6117102000	羊毛制披巾、头巾、围巾、披纱、面纱及类似品	17
6117109000	其他纺织材料制披巾、头巾、围巾、披纱、面纱及类似品	17
6117801000	领带及领结	17
6117809000	其他衣着附件	17
6117900010	保暖型衬里	17
6117900021	毛制针织毛衫的零件	17
6117900022	毛制针织衬衫的零件	17
6117900023	毛制针织上衣的零件	17
6117900024	毛制针织长裤、马裤、短裤的零件	17
6117900029	毛制其他未列名针织服装零件	17
6117900031	棉制针织毛衫的零件	17
6117900032	棉制针织衬衫的零件	17
6117900033	棉制针织上衣的零件	17
6117900034	棉制针织长裤、马裤、短裤的零件	17
6117900039	棉制其他未列名针织服装零件	17
6117900041	化纤制针织毛衫的零件	17
6117900042	化纤制针织衬衫的零件	17
6117900043	化纤制针织上衣的零件	17
6117900044	化纤制针织长裤、马裤、短裤零件	17
6117900049	化纤制其他未列名针织服装零件	17
6117900091	其他材料制衣着零件	17
6117900092	其他材料制针织毛衫的零件	17
6117900093	其他材料制针织衬衫的零件	17
6117900094	其他材料制针织上衣的零件	17
6117900095	其他材料制长裤、马裤、短裤零件	17
6117900099	其他材料制未列名针织服装零件	17
6201110010	毛制男式雨衣	17
6201110090	毛制男式大衣、斗篷及类似品	17
6201121000	棉制男式羽绒大衣等及类似品	17
6201129010	棉制男式雨衣	17

税则号列	商品名称	出口退税率(%)
6201129020	棉制男式连风帽派克大衣等	17
6201129090	棉制男式大衣、斗篷及类似品	17
6201131000	化纤制男羽绒大衣等及类似品	17
6201139010	化纤制男式雨衣	17
6201139020	化纤制男式连风帽派克大衣等	17
6201139030	化纤制男大衣、斗篷及类似品	17
6201139040	化纤制男式连风帽派克大衣等	17
6201139090	化纤制男大衣、斗篷及类似品	17
6201190010	其他材料制男雨衣	17
6201190021	其他材料制男大衣、斗篷及类似品	17
6201190029	其他材料制男大衣、斗篷及类似品	17
6201190030	其他材料制男大衣等,羊毛限内	17
6201190040	其他材料制男大衣等,棉限内	17
6201190050	其他材料制男大衣等,化纤限内	17
6201190090	其他材料制男大衣等	17
6201910010	毛制男式有填料无袖上衣	17
6201910020	毛制男式带防寒衬里防风衣	17
6201910030	毛制男式带风帽、有填料短上衣	17
6201910090	毛制男式其他防寒上衣	17
6201921000	棉制男式羽绒防寒短上衣、防风衣	17
6201929010	棉制男式有填料无袖上衣	17
6201929020	棉制男式带防寒衬里防风衣	17
6201929030	棉制男式带风帽、有填料上衣	17
6201929090	棉制男式其他防寒上衣	17
6201931000	化纤制男式羽绒防寒短上衣防风衣	17
6201939010	化纤制男式有填料无袖上衣	17
6201939020	化纤制男式带风帽防寒短上衣	17
6201939030	化纤制男式带防寒衬里防风衣	17
6201939040	化纤制男式带风帽、有填料上衣	17
6201939090	化纤制其他防寒上衣	17
6201990011	丝制男式带防寒衬里短上衣	17
6201990012	丝制男式带特制领、有填料短上衣	17
6201990019	丝制其他防寒上衣	17
6201990021	丝制男式带防寒衬里短上衣	17
6201990022	丝制男式带特制领、有填料短上衣	17
6201990029	丝制其他防寒上衣	17
6201990031	其他材料制男式带风帽防寒短上衣	17
6201990032	其他材料制男式带风帽防寒短上衣	17
6201990033	其他材料制男式带风帽防寒短上衣	17
6201990039	其他材料制男式带风帽防寒短上衣	17
6201990041	其他材料制男式带风帽短上衣	17
6201990042	其他材料制男式带风帽短上衣	17
6201990043	其他材料制男式带风帽短上衣	17
6201990049	其他材料制男式带风帽短上衣	17
6201990091	其他材料制男式防寒短上衣	17
6201990092	其他材料制男式防寒短上衣	17
6201990093	其他材料制男式防寒短上衣	17
6201990099	其他材料制男式其他防寒短上衣	17
6202110010	毛制女式雨衣	17
6202110090	毛制女式大衣、斗篷及类似品等	17
6202121000	棉制女式羽绒大衣等及类似品	17
6202129010	棉制女式雨衣	17
6202129020	棉制女式连风帽派克大衣等	17
6202129090	棉制女式大衣、斗篷及类似品	17

税则号列	商品名称	出口退税率(%)
6202131000	化纤制女羽绒大衣等及类似品	17
6202139010	化纤制女雨衣	17
6202139020	化纤制女式连风帽派克大衣	17
6202139030	化纤制女大衣、斗篷及类似品	17
6202139040	化纤制女式连风帽派克大衣	17
6202139090	化纤制女大衣、斗篷及类似品	17
6202190010	其他材料制女雨衣	17
6202190021	其他材料制女大衣、斗篷及类似品	17
6202190029	其他材料制女大衣、斗篷及类似品	17
6202190030	其他材料制女大衣等,羊毛限内	17
6202190040	其他材料制女大衣等,棉限内	17
6202190050	其他材料制女大衣等,化纤限内	17
6202190090	其他材料制女大衣	17
6202910010	毛制女式有填料无袖上衣	17
6202910020	毛制女式带防寒衬里的短上衣	17
6202910090	毛制女式其他防寒上衣	17
6202921000	棉制女式羽绒防寒短上衣、防风衣	17
6202929010	棉制女式有填料无袖上衣	17
6202929020	棉制女式带防寒衬里的短上衣	17
6202929090	棉制女式其他防寒上衣	17
6202931000	化纤制女式羽绒防寒短上衣等	17
6202939010	化纤制女式有填料无袖上衣	17
6202939020	化纤制女式带风帽防寒短上衣	17
6202939030	化纤制女式带防寒衬里的短上衣	17
6202939090	化纤制女式其他防寒上衣	17
6202990011	丝制女式带防寒衬里的短上衣	17
6202990019	丝制女式其他防寒上衣	17
6202990021	丝制女式带防寒衬里的短上衣	17
6202990029	丝制女式其他防寒上衣	17
6202990031	其他材料制女式带风帽防寒短上衣	17
6202990032	其他材料制女式带风帽防寒短上衣	17
6202990033	其他材料制女式带风帽防寒短上衣	17
6202990039	其他材料制女式带风帽防寒短上衣	17
6202990091	其他材料制女式防寒短上衣等	17
6202990092	其他材料制女式防寒短上衣等	17
6202990093	其他材料制女式防寒短上衣等	17
6202990099	其他材料制女式其他防寒短上衣等	17
6203110000	毛制男式西服套装	17
6203120010	合纤制男式西服套装	17
6203120090	其他合纤制男式西服套装	17
6203191010	丝及绢丝制男式西服套装	17
6203191090	其他丝及绢丝制男式西服套装	17
6203199010	棉制男式西服套装	17
6203199021	人造纤维制男式西服套装	17
6203199029	其他人造纤维制男式西服套装	17
6203199091	其他材料制男式西服套装	17
6203199092	其他材料制男式西服套装	17
6203199093	其他材料制男式西服套装	17
6203199099	其他材料制其他男式西服套装	17
6203220010	棉制男式便服套装	17
6203220090	其他棉制男式便服套装	17
6203230011	合纤制其他男式便服套装	17
6203230019	合纤制其他男式便服套装	17
6203230091	其他合纤制其他男式便服套装	17

税则号列	商品名称	出口退税率(%)
6203230099	其他合纤制其他男式便服套装	17
6203291010	丝制男式便服套装	17
6203291090	丝制其他男式便服套装	17
6203292000	羊毛或动物细毛制男式便服套装	17
6203299011	人造纤维制其他男式便服套装	17
6203299019	人造纤维制其他男式便服套装	17
6203299090	其他材料制其他男式便服套装	17
6203310010	毛制男式西服式上衣	17
6203310090	毛制男式其他上衣	17
6203320010	棉制工业及职业用男式上衣	17
6203320090	棉制其他男式上衣	17
6203330011	合成纤维制男式西服式上衣	17
6203330019	合成纤维制男式西服式上衣	17
6203330021	合成纤维制男式其他上衣	17
6203330029	合成纤维制男式其他上衣	17
6203330091	其他合成纤维制男式上衣	17
6203330099	其他合成纤维制男式上衣	17
6203391010	丝制男式上衣	17
6203391090	丝制男式上衣	17
6203399011	人造纤维制男式西服式上衣	17
6203399019	人造纤维制男式西服式上衣	17
6203399021	人造纤维制男式其他上衣	17
6203399029	人造纤维制男式其他上衣	17
6203399031	其他人造纤维制男式上衣	17
6203399039	其他人造纤维制男式上衣	17
6203399091	其他材料制男式上衣	17
6203399092	其他材料制男式上衣	17
6203399093	其他材料制男式上衣	17
6203399099	其他材料制男式上衣	17
6203410011	毛制男式护胸背带工装裤	17
6203410019	毛制男式护胸背带工装裤	17
6203410021	毛制男式长裤、马裤	17
6203410022	毛制男式长裤、马裤	17
6203410029	毛制其他男童长裤、马裤	17
6203410090	毛制男式短裤	17
6203421010	棉制男式阿拉伯裤	17
6203421090	棉制男式阿拉伯裤	17
6203429011	工业、职业用棉男护胸背带工装裤	17
6203429012	棉制男式护胸背带工装裤	17
6203429013	棉制其他男成人护胸背带工装裤	17
6203429014	棉制其他男成人护胸背带工装裤	17
6203429015	棉制其他男童护胸背带工装裤	17
6203429016	棉制其他男成人护胸背带工装裤	17
6203429017	棉制其他男成人护胸背带工装裤	17
6203429019	棉制其他男童护胸背带工装裤	17
6203429021	工业、职业用棉男长裤、马裤	17
6203429029	棉制男式长裤、马裤	17
6203429030	棉制男式长裤、马裤	17
6203429041	棉制男式长裤、马裤	17
6203429049	棉制其他男童长裤、马裤	17
6203429051	棉制男式长裤、马裤	17
6203429059	棉制男式长裤、马裤	17
6203429061	棉制男成人长裤、马裤	17
6203429062	棉制男式长裤、马裤	17

税则号列	商品名称	出口退税率(%)
6203429069	棉制其他男童长裤、马裤	17
6203429091	棉制男式短裤	17
6203429092	棉制其他男式短裤	17
6203429099	棉制其他男式短裤	17
6203431010	合成纤维制男式阿拉伯裤	17
6203431090	合成纤维制男式阿拉伯裤	17
6203439011	工业、职业用合纤制男护胸背带工裤	17
6203439012	合纤制男式护胸背带工裤	17
6203439013	其他合纤制男成人护胸背带工装裤	17
6203439014	其他合纤制男成人护胸背带工装裤	17
6203439015	其他合纤制男童护胸背带工装裤	17
6203439016	其他合纤制男成人护胸背带工装裤	17
6203439017	其他合纤制男成人护胸背带工装裤	17
6203439019	其他合纤制男童护胸背带工装裤	17
6203439021	工业、职业用合纤制男长裤、马裤	17
6203439029	合纤制男式长裤、马裤	17
6203439031	其他合纤制男式长裤、马裤	17
6203439039	其他合纤制男式长裤、马裤	17
6203439041	其他合纤制男成人长裤、马裤	17
6203439042	其他合纤制男式长裤、马裤	17
6203439049	其他合纤制男童长裤、马裤	17
6203439050	其他合纤制男式长裤、马裤	17
6203439061	其他合纤制男式长裤、马裤	17
6203439069	其他合纤制其他男童长裤、马裤	17
6203439071	其他合纤制男式长裤、马裤	17
6203439079	其他合纤制男式长裤、马裤	17
6203439081	其他合纤制男成人长裤、马裤	17
6203439082	其他合纤制男童长裤、马裤	17
6203439089	其他合纤制其他男童长裤、马裤	17
6203439091	合纤制男式短裤	17
6203439092	其他合纤制男式短裤	17
6203439093	其他合纤制男式短裤	17
6203439099	其他合纤制男裤	17
6203491010	人纤制男式阿拉伯裤	17
6203491020	人纤制男式阿拉伯裤	17
6203491030	其他材料制男式阿拉伯裤	17
6203491090	其他材料制男式阿拉伯裤	17
6203499011	人纤制男成人护胸背带工装裤	17
6203499012	人纤制男童护胸背带工装裤	17
6203499013	人纤制男成人护胸背带工装裤	17
6203499019	人纤制男童护胸背带工装裤	17
6203499021	人纤制男式长裤、马裤	17
6203499022	人纤制其他男式长裤、马裤	17
6203499023	人纤制男式长裤、马裤	17
6203499024	人纤制其他男式长裤、马裤	17
6203499025	人纤制男式长裤、马裤	17
6203499026	人纤制其他男式长裤、马裤	17
6203499027	人纤制男式短裤	17
6203499028	人纤制男式短裤	17
6203499029	人纤制男式短裤	17
6203499031	丝制男式护胸背带工装裤	17
6203499032	丝制男式长裤、马裤	17
6203499033	丝制男式长裤、马裤	17
6203499034	丝制男式短裤	17

税则号列	商品名称	出口退税率(%)
6203499035	丝制男式护胸背带工装裤	17
6203499036	丝制男式护胸背带工装裤	17
6203499037	丝制男式长裤、马裤	17
6203499038	丝制男式长裤、马裤	17
6203499039	丝制男式短裤	17
6203499041	其他材料制男式长裤、马裤	17
6203499042	其他材料制男式长裤、马裤	17
6203499049	其他材料制男式短裤	17
6203499051	其他材料制男式长裤、马裤	17
6203499052	其他材料制男式长裤、马裤	17
6203499059	其他材料制男式短裤	17
6203499061	其他材料制男式长裤、马裤	17
6203499062	其他材料制男式长裤、马裤	17
6203499069	其他材料制男式短裤	17
6203499091	其他材料制男式护胸背带工装裤	17
6203499092	其他材料制男式护胸背带工装裤	17
6203499093	其他材料制男式长裤、马裤	17
6203499094	其他材料制男式长裤、马裤	17
6203499099	其他材料制男式短裤	17
6204110000	毛制女式西服套装	17
6204120010	含裤子的棉制女式西服套装	17
6204120090	不含裤子的棉制女式西服套装	17
6204130010	合纤制女式西服套装	17
6204130090	其他合纤制女式西服套装	17
6204191010	丝及绢丝制女式西服套装	17
6204191090	其他丝及绢丝制女式西服套装	17
6204199011	人造纤维制女式西服套装	17
6204199019	其他人造纤维制女式西服套装	17
6204199091	含裤子的其他材料制女西服套装	17
6204199092	其他材料制女式西服套装	17
6204199093	其他材料制女式西服套装	17
6204199099	其他材料制其他女式西服套装	17
6204210000	羊毛或动物细毛制女式便服套装	17
6204220011	含裤子的棉制女式便服套装	17
6204220019	不含裤子的棉制女式便服套装	17
6204220091	含裤子的棉制非工业及职业用女式便服套装	17
6204220099	不含裤子的棉制非工业及职业用女式便服套装	17
6204230011	工业、职业用合纤制女式便服套装	17
6204230019	合成纤维制其他女式便服套装	17
6204230091	其他合成纤维制含裤子的女式便服套装	17
6204230099	其他合成纤维制其他女式便服套装	17
6204291010	丝制女式便服套装	17
6204291090	丝制其他女式便服套装	17
6204299011	含裤子的人纤制女便服套装	17
6204299019	不含裤子的人纤制女便服套装	17
6204299021	含裤子的其他材料制女式便服套装	17
6204299029	不含裤子的其他材料制女式便服套装	17
6204299030	其他材料制女式便服套装	17
6204299041	含裤子的其他材料制女式便服套装	17
6204299049	不含裤子的其他材料制女式便服套装	17
6204299091	含裤子的其他材料制女式便服套装	17
6204299099	不含裤子的其他材料制女式便服套装	17
6204310000	毛制女式上衣	17
6204320010	棉制女式上衣	17

税则号列	商品名称	出口退税率(%)
6204320090	棉制其他女式上衣	17
6204330010	合成纤维制女式上衣	17
6204330020	合成纤维制其他女式上衣	17
6204330030	合成纤维制女式上衣	17
6204330090	合成纤维制其他女式上衣	17
6204391010	丝制女式上衣	17
6204391090	丝制其他女式上衣	17
6204399011	人纤制女式上衣	17
6204399012	人纤制其他女式上衣	17
6204399013	人纤制女式上衣	17
6204399019	人纤制其他女式上衣	17
6204399091	其他材料制女式上衣	17
6204399092	其他材料制女式上衣	17
6204399093	其他材料制女式上衣	17
6204399099	其他材料制女式上衣	17
6204410000	毛制女式连衣裙	17
6204420000	棉制女式连衣裙	17
6204430010	合成纤维制女式连衣裙	17
6204430090	合成纤维制其他女式连衣裙	17
6204440010	人造纤维制女式连衣裙	17
6204440090	人造纤维制其他女式连衣裙	17
6204491010	丝制女式连衣裙	17
6204491090	丝制其他女式连衣裙	17
6204499091	其他材料制女式连衣裙	17
6204499092	其他材料制女式连衣裙	17
6204499093	其他材料制女式连衣裙	17
6204499099	其他材料制其他女式连衣裙	17
6204510000	毛制女式裙子及裙裤	17
6204520000	棉制女式裙子及裙裤	17
6204530010	合成纤维制女式裙子及裙裤	17
6204530090	合成纤维制其他女式裙子及裙裤	17
6204591010	丝制女式裙子及裙裤	17
6204591090	其他丝制女式裙子及裙裤	17
6204599011	人造纤维制女式裙子及裙裤	17
6204599019	人造纤维制其他女式裙子及裙裤	17
6204599091	其他材料制女式裙子及裙裤	17
6204599092	其他材料制女式裙子及裙裤	17
6204599093	其他材料制女式裙子及裙裤	17
6204599099	其他材料制其他女式裙子及裙裤	17
6204610010	毛制女式护胸背带工装裤及短裤	17
6204610090	毛制女式长裤、马裤	17
6204620010	棉制女式护胸背带工装裤	17
6204620021	棉制女式长裤、马裤	17
6204620022	棉制女式长裤、马裤	17
6204620029	其他棉制女式长裤、马裤	17
6204620091	棉制女式短裤	17
6204620092	棉制女式短裤	17
6204620099	其他棉制女式短裤	17
6204630010	合纤制女式护胸背带工装裤	17
6204630021	合纤女式长裤、马裤	17
6204630022	合纤制其他女式长裤、马裤	17
6204630023	合纤制女式长裤、马裤	17
6204630024	合纤制女式长裤、马裤	17
6204630029	合纤制女式其他长裤、马裤	17

税则号列	商品名称	出口退税率(%)
6204630091	合纤制女式短裤	17
6204630092	合纤制女式短裤	17
6204630099	其他合纤制女式短裤	17
6204690011	人纤制女式护胸背带工装裤	17
6204690012	人纤制女式长裤、马裤	17
6204690013	人纤制女式短裤	17
6204690014	人纤制女式长裤、马裤	17
6204690015	人纤制女式短裤	17
6204690016	人纤制女式其他长裤、马裤	17
6204690017	人纤制女式其他短裤	17
6204690021	丝制女式护胸背带工装裤	17
6204690025	丝制女式其他长裤、马裤、短裤	17
6204690026	丝制女式长裤、马裤、短裤	17
6204690029	丝制女式其他长裤、马裤、短裤	17
6204690091	其他材料制女式护胸背带工装裤	17
6204690092	其他材料制女长裤、马裤、短裤	17
6204690093	其他材料制女式长裤、马裤、短裤	17
6204690094	其他材料制女式长裤、马裤、短裤	17
6204690095	其他材料制女式长裤、马裤、短裤	17
6204690099	其他材料制其他女式长、马、短裤	17
6205200010	不带特制领的棉制男成人衬衫	17
6205200091	其他棉制男童游戏套装衬衫	17
6205200099	其他棉制男式衬衫	17
6205300011	不带特制领的化学纤维制男式衬衫	17
6205300019	不带特制领的化纤制其他男童衬衫	17
6205300091	化学纤维制其他男成人及男童衬衫	17
6205300092	化学纤维制其他男童游戏套装衬衫	17
6205300099	化纤制其他男成人衬衫	17
6205901011	不带特制领的丝制非针织男式衬衫	17
6205901019	丝制非针织其他男式衬衫	17
6205901021	丝制其他非针织男式衬衫	17
6205901029	丝制其他非针织其他男式衬衫	17
6205901031	丝制其他非针织男式衬衫	17
6205901039	丝制其他非针织其他男式衬衫	17
6205901041	丝制非针织男式衬衫	17
6205901049	丝制其他非针织其他男式衬衫	17
6205901091	未列名丝制非针织男式衬衫	17
6205901099	未列名丝制非针织其他男式衬衫	17
6205902000	羊毛或动物细毛制男式衬衫	17
6205909011	其他纺织材料制男式衬衫	17
6205909019	其他纺织材料制其他男式衬衫	17
6205909021	其他纺织材料制男式衬衫	17
6205909029	其他纺织材料制其他男式衬衫	17
6205909031	其他纺织材料制男式衬衫	17
6205909039	其他纺织材料制其他男式衬衫	17
6205909091	未列名纺织材料制男式衬衫	17
6205909099	未列名纺织材料制其他男式衬衫	17
6206100011	丝及绢丝制女式衬衫	17
6206100019	丝及绢丝制其他女童衬衫	17
6206100021	丝及绢丝制女式衬衫	17
6206100029	丝及绢丝制其他女童衬衫	17
6206100031	丝及绢丝制女式衬衫	17
6206100039	丝及绢丝制其他女童衬衫	17
6206100041	丝制女成人及7-16号女童衬衫	17

税则号列	商品名称	出口退税率(%)
6206100049	其他丝及绢丝制女童衬衫	17
6206100091	丝制女成人及7-16号女童衬衫	17
6206100099	其他丝及绢丝制女童衬衫	17
6206200010	毛制女成人及7-16号女童衬衫	17
6206200090	其他羊毛或动物细毛制女童衬衫	17
6206300010	棉制女成人及7-16号女童衬衫	17
6206300020	棉制女童游戏套装衫	17
6206300090	其他棉制女式衬衫	17
6206400011	化学纤维制女成人及女童衬衫	17
6206400019	化学纤维制女成人及女童衬衫	17
6206400020	化纤制女成人及7-16号女童衬衫	17
6206400030	化学纤维制女童游戏套装衫	17
6206400090	其他化学纤维制女式衬衫	17
6206900010	其他纺织材料制女式衬衫	17
6206900020	其他纺织材料制女式衬衫	17
6206900030	其他纺织材料制女式衬衫	17
6206900091	其他纺织材料制女成人及女童衬衫	17
6206900099	其他纺织材料制女成人及女童衬衫	17
6207110000	棉制男式内裤及三角裤	17
6207191010	含丝70%及以上男式内裤及三角裤	17
6207191090	含丝70%以下男式内裤及三角裤	17
6207192000	化纤制男式内裤及三角裤	17
6207199010	毛制男式内裤及三角裤	17
6207199090	其他材料制男式内裤及三角裤	17
6207210000	棉制男式长睡衣及睡衣裤	17
6207220000	化纤制男式长睡衣及睡衣裤	17
6207291011	含丝70%及以上男式长睡衣/睡衣裤	17
6207291019	含丝70%以下男式长睡衣/睡衣裤	17
6207291091	其他含丝≥70%男童长睡衣/睡衣裤	17
6207291099	其他含丝＜70%男童长睡衣/睡衣裤	17
6207299010	毛制男式长睡衣及睡衣裤	17
6207299091	其他材料制男式长睡衣及睡衣裤	17
6207299099	其他材料制男童长睡衣及睡衣裤	17
6207910011	棉制男式内衣式背心	17
6207910012	棉制男式非内衣式背心	17
6207910019	棉制其他男童非内衣式背心	17
6207910091	棉制男式浴衣、晨衣及类似品	17
6207910092	棉制男式睡衣、睡裤	17
6207910099	棉制男式其他内衣	17
6207991011	丝制男式内衣式背心	17
6207991019	丝制其他男式内衣式背心	17
6207991021	丝制男式非内衣式背心	17
6207991029	丝制其他男式非内衣式背心	17
6207991091	丝制男睡衣,浴衣,晨衣及类似品	17
6207991099	丝制其他男睡衣,浴衣,晨衣	17
6207992011	化学纤维制男式内衣式背心	17
6207992012	化学纤维制男式非内衣式背心	17
6207992019	化学纤维制其他男式非内衣式背心	17
6207992021	化纤制男式浴衣、晨衣	17
6207992029	其他化纤制男浴衣、晨衣	17
6207992091	化纤制男睡衣、睡裤	17
6207992099	化纤制男式其他内衣	17
6207999011	毛制男式内衣式背心	17
6207999012	毛制男式非内衣式背心	17

税则号列	商品名称	出口退税率(%)
6207999013	毛制其他男式非内衣式背心	17
6207999019	毛制男睡衣,浴衣,晨衣及类似品	17
6207999091	其他材料制男式内衣式背心	17
6207999092	其他材料制男式非内衣式背心	17
6207999099	其他材料制男睡衣、浴衣、晨衣	17
6208110000	化纤制长衬裙及衬裙	17
6208191011	丝制女式长衬裙及衬裙	17
6208191019	丝制其他女式长衬裙及衬裙	17
6208191091	丝制女童长衬裙及衬裙	17
6208191099	丝制其他女童长衬裙及衬裙	17
6208192000	棉制长衬裙及衬裙	17
6208199010	毛制女式长衬裙及衬裙	17
6208199090	其他材料制女式长衬裙及衬裙	17
6208210000	棉制女式睡衣及睡衣裤	17
6208220000	化纤制女式睡衣及睡衣裤	17
6208291010	丝及绢丝≥70%女式睡衣及睡衣裤	17
6208291090	丝及绢丝<70%女式睡衣及睡衣裤	17
6208299010	毛制女式睡衣及睡衣裤	17
6208299090	其他材料制女式睡衣及睡衣裤	17
6208910010	棉制女式内衣式背心、三角裤等	17
6208910021	棉制女式非内衣式背心	17
6208910029	棉制其他女式非内衣式背心	17
6208910090	棉制女式浴衣、晨衣及类似品	17
6208920010	化纤制女式内衣式背心、三角裤	17
6208920021	化纤制女式非内衣式背心	17
6208920029	化纤制其他女式非内衣式背心	17
6208920090	化纤制女式浴衣、晨衣及类似品	17
6208991011	丝制女内衣式背心、三角裤等	17
6208991019	丝制女内衣式背心、三角裤等	17
6208991021	丝制女式非内衣式背心	17
6208991029	丝制女式非内衣式背心	17
6208991091	丝制女式浴衣、晨衣及类似品	17
6208991099	丝制女式浴衣、晨衣及类似品	17
6208999011	毛制女式内衣式背心、三角裤等	17
6208999012	毛制女式非内衣式背心	17
6208999013	毛制其他女式非内衣式背心	17
6208999019	毛制女式浴衣、晨衣及类似品	17
6208999090	其他材料制女式背心、三角裤、短衬裤、浴衣、晨衣及类似品	17
6209200000	棉制婴儿服装及衣着附件	17
6209300010	合成纤维制婴儿手套、袜子	17
6209300020	合成纤维婴儿外衣、雨衣、滑雪装	17
6209300030	合成纤维制婴儿其他服装	17
6209300090	合成纤维制婴儿衣着附件	17
6209901000	羊毛或动物细毛制婴儿服装衣及衣着附件	17
6209909000	其他纺织材料制婴儿服装及衣着附件	17
6210101010	毛制纸衬背或覆盖的无纺布服装	17
6210101020	毛制一次性或医疗用无纺织物服装	17
6210101090	毛制其他毡呢或无纺织物服装	17
6210102010	棉或麻制纸衬或覆盖的无纺布服装	17
6210102020	棉或麻一次性或医用无纺织物服装	17
6210102090	棉或麻制其他毡呢或无纺织物服装	17
6210103010	化纤制纸衬背或覆盖的无纺布服装	17
6210103020	化纤制一次性或医用无纺织物服装	17
6210103090	化纤制其他毡呢或无纺织物服装	17

税则号列	商品名称	出口退税率(%)
6210109010	其他纺织材料制纸衬背的无纺服装	17
6210109020	其他材料制一次性或医用无纺服装	17
6210109090	其他纺织材料制其他无纺织物服装	17
6210200011	用塑料或橡胶处理化纤制男外装	17
6210200019	其他用塑料或橡胶处理化纤制男外装	17
6210200021	用塑料或橡胶处理的羊毛制男外装	17
6210200029	用塑料或橡胶处理的羊毛制男外装	17
6210200031	用塑料或橡胶处理的棉制男外装	17
6210200039	其他用塑料或橡胶等处理棉制男外装	17
6210200040	用塑料或橡胶处理的其他纺材男外装	17
6210200091	用塑料或橡胶等处理的亚麻制男外装	17
6210200099	用塑料等处理的其他纺材制男外装	17
6210300011	用塑料或橡胶处理化纤制女外装	17
6210300019	其他用塑料或橡胶处理化纤制女外装	17
6210300021	用塑料或橡胶处理的羊毛制女外装	17
6210300029	用塑料或橡胶处理的羊毛制女外装	17
6210300031	用塑料或橡胶处理的棉制女外装	17
6210300039	其他用塑料或橡胶等处理棉制女外装	17
6210300040	用塑料或橡胶处理的其他纺材女外装	17
6210300091	用塑料或橡胶等处理的亚麻制女外装	17
6210300099	用塑料等处理的其他纺材制女外装	17
6210400011	用塑料或橡胶处理化纤制其他男式服装	17
6210400012	用塑料等处理的化纤制男防风衣	17
6210400013	用塑料等处理的化纤制男式长、短裤	17
6210400019	用塑料等处理的化纤制其他男式服装	17
6210400021	用塑料或橡胶处理的毛制其他男外装	17
6210400022	用塑料等处理的毛制男式防风衣	17
6210400023	用塑料等处理的毛制男式长、短裤	17
6210400029	用塑料等处理的其他男式服装	17
6210400031	用塑料或橡胶处理的棉制其他男外装	17
6210400032	用塑料等处理的棉制男式防风衣	17
6210400033	用塑料等处理的棉制男式长、短裤	17
6210400039	用塑料等处理的棉制其他男式服装	17
6210400040	用塑料或橡胶处理其他纺材其他男装	17
6210400091	用塑料等处理的丝制其他男式服装	17
6210400092	用塑料等处理其他纺材制男防风衣	17
6210400093	用塑料等处理其他纺材制男长、短裤	17
6210400099	用塑料等处理的其他纺材制男服装	17
6210500011	用塑料或橡胶处理化纤制其他女装	17
6210500012	用塑料等处理的化纤制女防风衣	17
6210500013	用塑料等处理的化纤制女式长、短裤	17
6210500019	用塑料等处理的化纤制其他女服装	17
6210500021	用塑料或橡胶处理的毛制其他女外装	17
6210500022	用塑料等处理的毛制女式防风衣	17
6210500023	用塑料等处理的毛制女式长、短裤	17
6210500029	用塑料等处理的毛制其他女式服装	17
6210500031	用塑料或橡胶处理的棉制其他女外装	17
6210500032	用塑料等处理的棉制女式防风衣	17
6210500033	用塑料等处理的棉制女式长、短裤	17
6210500039	用塑料等处理的棉制其他女式服装	17
6210500040	用塑料或橡胶处理其他纺材其他女装	17
6210500091	用塑料等处理的丝制其他女式服装	17
6210500092	用塑料等处理其他纺材制女防风衣	17
6210500093	用塑料等处理其他纺材制女长、短裤	17

税则号列	商品名称	出口退税率(%)
6210500099	用塑料等处理的其他纺材制女服装	17
6211110010	羊毛或动物细毛制男式游泳服	17
6211110041	丝制男式游泳服	17
6211110049	丝制男式游泳服	17
6211110090	其他纺织材料制男式游泳服	17
6211120010	羊毛或动物细毛制女式游泳服	17
6211120041	丝制女式游泳服	17
6211120049	丝制女式游泳服	17
6211120090	其他纺织材料制女式游泳服	17
6211201000	棉制滑雪套装	17
6211209011	含滑雪男裤的羊毛制滑雪套装	17
6211209019	不含滑雪男裤的羊毛制滑雪套装	17
6211209021	含滑雪短裤或不防水滑雪裤的化纤制滑雪套装	17
6211209029	化纤制其他滑雪套装	17
6211209090	其他纺织材料制滑雪套装	17
6211321000	棉制男式阿拉伯袍	17
6211322011	棉制男式运动套装	17
6211322019	棉制其他男式运动套装	17
6211329021	棉制男式连衣服及类似品	17
6211329029	棉制男式连衣裤及类似品	17
6211329030	棉制男式水洗服、夏服、游戏装	17
6211329040	棉制男式工业及职业衣着	17
6211329051	棉制男式TOPS	17
6211329059	棉制其他男式TOPS	17
6211329060	棉制男式风雪套装及类似服装	17
6211329091	棉制男衬衫	17
6211329099	棉制男式其他服装	17
6211331000	化纤制男式阿拉伯袍	17
6211332011	化纤制男式运动套装	17
6211332019	化纤制其他男式运动套装	17
6211339021	化纤制男式连衣服及类似品	17
6211339029	化纤制男式连衣裤及类似品	17
6211339030	化纤制男式水洗服、夏服、游戏装	17
6211339091	化纤制男式工业及职业衣着	17
6211339092	化纤制男式TOPS	17
6211339093	化纤制其他男式TOPS	17
6211339094	化纤制男式风雪套装及类似服装	17
6211339095	化纤制男衬衫	17
6211339099	化纤制男式其他服装	17
6211391011	丝及绢丝制男运动服	17
6211391019	丝及绢丝制男运动服	17
6211391021	丝或绢丝制男连衣裤及类似品	17
6211391029	丝或绢丝制男连衣裤及类似品	17
6211391091	丝或绢丝制男式TOPS	17
6211391092	丝或绢丝制男式TOPS	17
6211391093	丝或绢丝制男式风雪套装	17
6211391094	丝或绢丝制男式风雪套装	17
6211391095	丝或绢丝制男式其他服装	17
6211391099	丝或绢丝制男式其他服装	17
6211392010	毛制男式运动套装	17
6211392090	毛制男式其他服装	17
6211399010	其他纺织材料制男式运动套装	17
6211399020	其他纺织材料制男连衣裤	17
6211399091	其他纺织材料制男式水洗服、夏服	17

税则号列	商品名称	出口退税率(%)
6211399092	其他纺织材料制男式TOPS	17
6211399093	其他纺织材料制男式风雪套装	17
6211399099	其他纺织材料制男式其他服装	17
6211421010	棉制女式运动套装	17
6211421090	棉制其他女式运动套装	17
6211429000	棉制女式其他服装	17
6211431010	化纤制女式运动套装	17
6211431090	化纤制其他女式运动套装	17
6211439000	化纤制其他女式服装	17
6211491011	丝或绢丝制女式运动套装	17
6211491019	丝或绢丝制女式运动套装	17
6211491021	丝或绢丝制女连衣裤及类似品	17
6211491029	丝或绢丝制女连衣裤及类似品	17
6211491031	丝或绢丝制女式TOPS	17
6211491039	丝或绢丝制女式TOPS	17
6211491041	丝或绢丝制女式风雪套装	17
6211491049	丝或绢丝制女式风雪套装	17
6211491051	丝及绢丝制女式其他服装	17
6211491059	丝及绢丝制女式其他服装	17
6211491091	丝及绢丝制女式其他服装	17
6211491099	丝及绢丝制女式其他服装	17
6211499010	其他纺织材料制女式运动套装	17
6211499020	其他纺织材料制女连衣裤	17
6211499030	其他纺织材料制女式其他服装	17
6211499040	其他纺织材料制女式TOPS	17
6211499050	其他纺织材料制女式风雪套装	17
6211499090	其他纺织材料制女式其他服装	17
6212101000	化纤制其他胸罩	17
6212109010	毛制其他胸罩	17
6212109020	棉制其他胸罩	17
6212109031	丝制胸罩	17
6212109039	丝制其他胸罩	17
6212109090	其他纺织材料制其他胸罩	17
6212201000	化纤制束胸带及腹带	17
6212209010	毛制束胸带及腹带	17
6212209020	棉制束腰带及腹带	17
6212209031	丝制束腰带及腹带	17
6212209039	丝制束腰带及腹带	17
6212209090	其他材料制束胸带及腹带	17
6212301000	化纤制紧身胸衣	17
6212309010	毛制紧身胸衣	17
6212309020	棉制紧身胸衣	17
6212309031	丝制紧身胸衣	17
6212309039	丝制其他紧身胸衣	17
6212309090	其他材料制紧身胸衣	17
6212901000	化纤制吊裤带、吊袜带等	17
6212909010	毛制吊裤带、吊袜带、束袜带等	17
6212909020	棉制吊裤带、吊袜带、束袜带等	17
6212909031	丝制吊裤带、吊袜带、束袜带等	17
6212909039	丝制吊裤带、吊袜带、束袜带等	17
6212909090	其他材料制吊裤带、吊袜带等	17
6213201000	棉制刺绣手帕	17
6213209000	其他棉制手帕	17
6213902000	其他纺织材料制刺绣手帕	17

税则号列	商品名称	出口退税率(%)
6213909010	化纤制其他手帕	17
6213909020	麻制其他手帕	17
6213909090	其他材料制手帕	17
6214100010	含丝70%及以上的披巾、头巾、围巾	17
6214100090	含丝70%以下的披巾、头巾、围巾	17
6214201000	羊毛制披巾、头巾、围巾及类似品	17
6214202000	山羊绒制披巾、头巾、围巾及类似品	17
6214209000	其他动物细毛制披巾、头巾、围巾及类似品	17
6214300000	合纤制披巾、头巾及类似品	17
6214400000	人纤制披巾、头巾及类似品	17
6214900010	棉制披巾、头巾及类似品	17
6214900090	其他材料制披巾、头巾及类似品	17
6215100011	丝及绢丝制领带及领结	17
6215100019	丝及绢丝制领带及领结	17
6215100090	其他丝及绢丝制领带及领结	17
6215200000	化纤制领带及领结	17
6215900010	毛制领带及领结	17
6215900020	棉制领带及领结	17
6215900090	其他材料制领带及领结	17
6216000011	非针织物裁剪缝制成的运动手套	17
6216000012	非针织物裁剪缝制成的非运动手套	17
6216000013	非针织物裁剪缝制成的运动手套	17
6216000014	非针织物裁剪缝制成的非运动手套	17
6216000015	其他非针织物裁剪缝成的运动手套	17
6216000019	其他非针织物制成的非运动手套	17
6216000021	其他浸渍塑料/橡胶非针织运动手套	17
6216000022	其他浸渍塑料/橡胶非针织非运动手套	17
6216000023	其他浸渍塑料/橡胶非针织运动手套	17
6216000024	其他浸渍塑料/橡胶非针织非运动手套	17
6216000025	未列名浸渍塑料/橡胶非针织运动手套	17
6216000029	未列名浸渍塑料/橡胶非针织非运动手套	17
6216000031	棉非针织物制的运动手套	17
6216000039	棉非针织物制的非运动手套	17
6216000041	化纤制非针织物制的运动手套	17
6216000042	化纤制非针织物制的非运动手套	17
6216000043	其他化纤制非针织运动手套	17
6216000049	其他化纤制非针织非运动手套	17
6216000051	毛制非针织运动手套	17
6216000059	毛制非针织非运动手套	17
6216000091	其他纺织材料制非针织运动手套	17
6216000099	其他纺织材料制非针织非运动手套	17
6217101000	非针织非钩编袜子及袜套	17
6217102000	非针织非钩编和服腰带	17
6217109010	毛制服装或衣着附件	17
6217109020	棉制服装或衣着附件	17
6217109030	化纤制服装或衣着附件	17
6217109041	丝制服装或衣着附件	17
6217109049	丝制服装或衣着附件	17
6217109090	其他服装或衣着附件	17
6217900011	羊毛或动物细毛制保暖型衬里	17
6217900012	毛制非针织或非钩编衬衫的零件	17
6217900013	毛制非针织或非钩编上衣的零件	17
6217900014	毛制长裤及马裤的零件	17
6217900019	其他毛制服装或衣着零件	17

税则号列	商品名称	出口退税率(%)
6217900021	棉制保暖型衬里	17
6217900022	棉制非针织非钩编衬衫的零件	17
6217900023	棉制非针织非钩编上衣的零件	17
6217900024	棉制长裤及马裤的零件	17
6217900029	棉制服装或衣着零件	17
6217900031	化纤制保暖型衬里	17
6217900032	化纤制非针织非钩编衬衫的零件	17
6217900033	化纤制非针织非钩编上衣的零件	17
6217900034	化纤制长裤及马裤的零件	17
6217900039	化纤制服装或衣着零件	17
6217900041	丝制保暖型衬里	17
6217900042	丝制服装或衣着零件	17
6217900049	丝制服装或衣着零件	17
6217900091	其他材料制保暖型衬里	17
6217900092	其他材料制衬衫零件	17
6217900093	其他材料制上衣零件	17
6217900094	其他材料制长裤及马裤的零件	17
6217900099	其他材料制服装或衣着附件	17
6301100000	电暖毯	17
6301200010	毛制毯子及旅行毯	17
6301200020	其他毛制毯子及旅行毯	17
6301300000	棉制毯子及旅行毯	17
6301400000	合纤制毯子及旅行毯	17
6301900010	人造纤维制的毯子及旅行毯	17
6301900020	丝制毯子及旅行毯	17
6301900090	其他纺织材料制毯子及旅行毯	17
6302101000	棉制针织或钩编的床上用织物制品	17
6302109000	其他材料制床上用织物制品	17
6302211000	棉制印花床单	17
6302219010	棉制印花枕套	17
6302219020	棉制印花枕罩	17
6302219090	其他棉制印花床上用织物制品	17
6302221000	化纤制印花床单	17
6302229010	化纤制印花枕套	17
6302229020	化纤无纺织物制印花床用织物制品	17
6302229090	其他化纤制印花床上用织物制品	17
6302291010	丝及绢丝制印花床上用织物制品	17
6302291090	丝及绢丝制印花床上用织物制品	17
6302292010	亚麻或苎麻制印花床上用织物制品	17
6302292090	其他麻制印花床上用织物制品	17
6302299000	其他材料制印花床上用织物制品	17
6302311000	棉制刺绣其他床上用织物制品	17
6302319100	棉制其他床单	17
6302319200	棉制其他毛巾被	17
6302319910	棉制其他枕套	17
6302319920	其他棉与亚麻混纺床上用织物制品	17
6302319930	棉制其他枕罩	17
6302319990	棉制其他床上用织物制品	17
6302321000	化纤制刺绣其他床上用织物制品	17
6302329010	化纤制其他床单	17
6302329020	化纤制其他枕套	17
6302329030	其他化纤无纺织物制床上织物制品	17
6302329090	化纤制其他床上用织物制品	17
6302391010	丝及绢丝制其他床上用织物制品	17

税则号列	商品名称	出口退税率(%)
6302391090	丝及绢丝制其他床上用织物制品	17
6302392110	亚麻或苎麻制其他床上用织物制品	17
6302392190	其他麻制其他床上用织物制品	17
6302392910	亚麻或苎麻制其他床上用织物制品	17
6302392990	其他麻制其他床上用织物制品	17
6302399110	毛制刺绣床上用织物制品	17
6302399190	其他材料制刺绣床上用织物制品	17
6302399910	毛制非刺绣床上用织物制品	17
6302399990	其他材料制其他床上用织物制品	17
6302401010	手工棉制餐桌用织物制品	17
6302401020	手工植物纺织纤维制餐桌用制品	17
6302401090	手工其他纺织材料制餐桌用制品	17
6302409010	棉制餐桌用织物制品	17
6302409020	植物纺织纤维制的餐桌用织物制品	17
6302409090	其他纺织材料制餐桌用织物制品	17
6302511000	棉制刺绣其他餐桌用织物制品	17
6302519000	棉制其他餐桌用织物制品	17
6302531000	化纤制刺绣其他餐桌织物制品	17
6302539010	化纤无纺织物制餐桌用织物制品	17
6302539090	化纤制其他餐桌用织物制品	17
6302591100	亚麻制刺绣其他餐桌用织物制品	17
6302591900	亚麻制其他餐桌用织物制品	17
6302599010	羊毛或动物细毛制餐桌用织物制品	17
6302599090	其他纺织材料制餐桌用织物制品	17
6302601010	棉制针织或钩编毛巾织物浴巾	17
6302601090	棉制非针织或非钩编毛巾织物浴巾	17
6302609011	棉制针织或钩编毛巾织物茶巾	17
6302609019	棉制非针织或非钩编毛巾织物茶巾	17
6302609091	棉制其他盥洗及厨房用毛巾制品	17
6302609099	棉制其他盥洗及厨房用毛巾制品	17
6302910010	棉制茶巾	17
6302910020	棉制毛巾	17
6302910090	棉制其他盥洗及厨房织物制品	17
6302930010	化纤无纺织物制盥洗及厨房制品	17
6302930090	化纤制其他盥洗及厨房织物制品	17
6302991000	亚麻制盥洗及厨房织物制品	17
6302999010	毛制盥洗及厨房用织物制品	17
6302999090	其他材料制盥洗及厨房织物制品	17
6303121010	合纤制针织百叶窗,卷帘和窗幔	17
6303121090	其他合纤制针织窗帘等	17
6303122010	合纤制钩编百叶窗,卷帘和窗幔	17
6303122090	其他合纤制钩编的窗帘等	17
6303193100	棉制针织的窗帘等	17
6303193200	棉制钩编的窗帘等	17
6303199100	其他纺织材料制针织的窗帘等	17
6303199200	其他纺织材料制钩编的窗帘等	17
6303910010	棉制非针织网眼窗帘	17
6303910090	棉制非针织非钩编窗帘	17
6303920010	合纤百叶窗,卷帘和窗幔	17
6303920090	其他合纤制非针织非钩编窗帘等	17
6303990010	毛制非针织非钩编窗帘	17
6303990020	人造纤维制非针织非钩编窗帘	17
6303990031	丝制非针织非钩编窗帘	17
6303990039	丝制非针织非钩编窗帘	17

税则号列	商品名称	出口退税率(%)
6303990040	其他纺织材料无纺织物制窗帘	17
6303990050	亚麻或苎麻制非针织非钩编窗帘	17
6303990060	其他纺织材料制非针织网眼窗帘	17
6303990090	其他纺织材料制非针织非钩编窗帘	17
6304112110	棉制手工针织床罩	17
6304112120	化纤制手工针织床罩	17
6304112190	其他纺织材料制手工针织床罩	17
6304112910	棉制非手工针织床罩	17
6304112920	化纤制非手工针织床罩	17
6304112990	其他纺织材料制非手工针织床罩	17
6304113110	棉制手工钩编床罩	17
6304113120	化纤制手工钩编床罩	17
6304113190	其他纺织材料制手工钩编床罩	17
6304113910	棉制非手工钩编床罩	17
6304113920	化纤制非手工钩编床罩	17
6304113990	其他纺织材料制非手工钩编床罩	17
6304191010	丝及绢丝制非针织非钩编床罩	17
6304191090	丝及绢丝制非针织非钩编床罩	17
6304192110	亚麻或苎麻制刺绣床罩	17
6304192120	其他麻制非针织非钩编刺绣床罩	17
6304192190	棉制非针织非钩编刺绣床罩	17
6304192910	亚麻或苎麻制非针织非钩编床罩	17
6304192991	其他麻制其他非针织非钩编床罩	17
6304192999	棉制其他非针织非钩编床罩	17
6304193100	化纤制非针织非钩编刺绣床罩	17
6304193900	化纤制其他非针织非钩编床罩	17
6304199110	毛制非针织非钩编刺绣床罩	17
6304199190	其他纺织材料制非针织刺绣床罩	17
6304199910	毛制其他非针织非钩编床罩	17
6304199990	其他材料制非针织非钩编其他床罩	17
6304912110	棉制手工针织的其他装饰制品	17
6304912120	毛制手工针织的其他装饰制品	17
6304912131	丝制手工针织的其他装饰制品	17
6304912139	丝制手工针织的其他装饰制品	17
6304912140	化纤制手工针织的其他装饰制品	17
6304912190	其他纺材制手工针织其他装饰制品	17
6304912910	棉制非手工针织的其他装饰制品	17
6304912920	毛制非手工针织的其他装饰制品	17
6304912931	丝制非手工针织的其他装饰制品	17
6304912939	丝制非手工针织的其他装饰制品	17
6304912940	化纤制非手工针织其他装饰制品	17
6304912990	其他纺材制非手工针织其他装饰品	17
6304913110	棉制手工钩编的其他装饰制品	17
6304913120	毛制手工钩编的其他装饰制品	17
6304913131	丝制手工钩编的其他装饰制品	17
6304913139	丝制手工钩编的其他装饰制品	17
6304913140	化纤制手工钩编的其他装饰制品	17
6304913190	其他制手工钩编的其他材料装饰制品	17
6304913910	棉制非手工钩编的其他装饰制品	17
6304913920	毛制非手工钩编的其他装饰制品	17
6304913931	丝制非手工钩编的其他装饰制品	17
6304913939	丝制非手工钩编的其他装饰制品	17
6304913940	化纤制非手工钩编其他装饰制品	17
6304913990	其他纺材制非手工钩编其他装饰品	17

税则号列	商品名称	出口退税率(%)
6304921000	棉制非针织的其他刺绣装饰制品	17
6304929000	棉制非针织或钩编的其他装饰制品	17
6304931000	合成纤维制其他刺绣装饰制品	17
6304939000	合纤制其他非针织装饰制品	17
6304991010	丝制非针织非钩编的装饰制品	17
6304991090	丝制非针织非钩编的装饰制品	17
6304992110	亚麻或苎麻非针织其他刺绣装饰品	17
6304992190	其他麻制非针织其他刺绣装饰品	17
6304992910	亚麻或苎麻制其他非针织的装饰品	17
6304992990	其他麻制其他非针织的装饰制品	17
6304999010	毛制非针织非钩编装饰制品	17
6304999020	人造纤维制非针织非钩编装饰品	17
6304999090	其他材料制非针织非钩编装饰品	17
6305100010	黄麻制旧的货物包装袋	17
6305100090	黄麻制其他货物包装袋	17
6305200000	棉制货物包装袋	17
6305320011	聚乙烯或聚丙烯制软袋	17
6305320019	聚乙烯或聚丙烯制软袋	17
6305320090	化纤制的散装货物周转软袋	17
6305330010	聚乙烯或聚丙烯制其他货物包装袋	17
6305330090	聚乙烯或聚丙烯制其他货物包装袋	17
6305390000	其他化学纤维制货物包装袋	17
6305900011	亚麻制旧货物包装袋	17
6305900019	其他亚麻制旧货物包装袋	17
6305900090	其他纺织材料制其他货物包装袋	17
6306120000	合纤制油苫布、天篷及遮阳篷	17
6306191000	麻制油苫布、天篷及遮阳篷	17
6306192000	棉制油毡布、天篷及遮阳篷	17
6306199010	人造纤维制油苫布、天篷及遮阳篷	17
6306199090	其他材料制油苫布、天篷及遮阳篷	17
6306220010	合纤制移动帐篷	17
6306220090	合纤制帐篷	17
6306291000	棉制帐篷	17
6306299000	其他纺织材料制帐篷	17
6306301000	合纤制风帆	17
6306309000	其他纺织材料制风帆	17
6306401000	棉制充气褥垫	17
6306402000	化纤制充气褥垫	17
6306409000	其他纺织材料制充气褥垫	17
6306901000	棉制其他野营用品	17
6306902000	麻制其他野营用品	17
6306903000	化纤制其他野营用品	17
6306909000	其他材料制其他野营用品	17
6307100000	擦地布、擦碗布、抹布及类似擦拭用布	17
6307200000	救生衣及安全带	17
6307900011	棉制标签、服饰辫线及流苏	17
6307900019	其他制标签、服饰辫线及流苏	17
6307900020	棉制起绒或簇绒织物制毛巾	17
6307900030	棉制枕壳	17
6307900040	棉制被壳、羽绒被壳、盖被壳	17
6307900051	棉制手术用巾及其他毛巾	17
6307900059	化学纤维制未列名毛巾	17
6307900061	以棉做面的冷藏包	17
6307900062	以化纤纺织材料做面的冷藏包	17

税则号列	商品名称	出口退税率(%)
6307900069	其他纺织材料做面的冷藏包	17
6307900090	纺织材料制未列名制品	17
6308000010	机织物及纱线制零售包装成套物品	17
6308000020	机织物及纱线制零售包装成套物品	17
6308000030	机织物及纱线制零售包装成套物品	17
6308000090	其他机织物及纱线构成的成套物品	17
63101000	经分拣的纺织材料制碎织物等	17
63109000	纺织材料制其他碎织物等	17
68159920	碳纤维	9
68159931	碳布	9
68159932	碳纤维预浸料	9
68159939	其他碳纤维制品	9
70200013	熔融石英或其他熔融硅石制	9
71049012	工业用蓝宝石	13
72254091	含硼合金钢	0
72269191	含硼合金钢	0
72279010	含硼合金钢制不规则盘卷的其他合金钢热轧条、杆	0
72283010	含硼合金钢制其他条、杆，除热轧、热拉拔或热挤压外未经进一步加工	0
73151110	自行车滚子链	13
73151120	摩托车滚子链	13
73151200	其他铰接链	13
73151900	铰接链零件	13
73152000	防滑链	13
73159000	非铰接链零件	13
73160000	钢铁锚、多爪锚及其零件	13
74071010	铬锆铜制条、杆及型材及异型材	9
74072111	直线度不大于0.5毫米/米铜锌合金条、杆	9
74072119	其他铜锌合金条、杆	9
74072190	其他黄铜条、杆及型材及异型材	9
74072900	其他铜合金条杆、型材及异型材	9
74081100	最大截面尺寸＞6mm的精炼铜丝	9
74081900	截面尺寸≤6mm的精炼铜丝	9
74082100	黄铜丝	9
74082210	铜镍锌铅合金(加铅德银)丝	9
74082900	其他铜合金丝	9
74101100	无衬背的精炼铜箔	17
82022010	双金属带锯条	13
82090010	未装配的工具用金属陶瓷板	13
82090021	晶粒度小于0.8微米的金属陶瓷条、杆	13
82090029	其他未装配的工具用金属陶瓷条、杆	13
82090030	未装配的工具用金属陶瓷刀头	13
82090090	其他未装配的工具用金属陶瓷类似品	13
84248910	家用型喷射、喷雾机械器具	17
84248920	喷涂机器人	17
84248991	船用洗舱机	17
84248999	其他液体粉末喷射机械	17
84433290	其他可与网络连接的传真机或打字机	17
84705010	销售点终端出纳机	17
84705090	其他现金出纳机	17
84797100	机场用旅客登机桥	17
84797900	其他旅客登机（船）桥	17
84798910	船舶用舵机及陀螺稳定器	17
84798920	空气增湿器及减湿器	17
84798961	自动插件机	17

税则号列	商品名称	出口退税率(%)
84798962	自动贴片机	17
84798969	印刷电路电路板的其他加工设备	17
84798992	自动化立体仓储设备	17
84799010	船舶用舵机及陀螺稳定器零件	17
84799020	空气增湿器及减湿器零件	17
87031011	全地形车	17
87031019	其他高尔夫球车及类似车辆	17
87031090	雪地行走专用车	17
8711100010	微马力摩托车及脚踏两用车	17
8711100090	微马力摩托车及脚踏两用车	17
8711201000	50＜排量≤100毫升装往复式活塞内燃发动机摩托车及脚踏两用车	17
8711202000	100＜排量≤125毫升装往复式活塞内燃发动机摩托车及脚踏两用车	17
8711203000	125＜排量≤150毫升装往复式活塞内燃发动机摩托车及脚踏两用车	17
8711204000	150＜排量≤200毫升装往复式活塞内燃发动机摩托车及脚踏两用车	17
8711205010	200＜排量＜250毫升装往复式活塞内燃发动机摩托车及脚踏两用车	17
8711205090	排量=250毫升装往复式活塞内燃发动机摩托车及脚踏两用车	17
8711301000	250＜排量≤400毫升装往复式活塞内燃发动机摩托车及脚踏两用车	17
8711302000	400＜排量≤500毫升装往复式活塞内燃发动机摩托车及脚踏两用车	17
8711400000	500＜排量≤800毫升装往复式活塞内燃发动机摩托车及脚踏两用车	17
8711500000	800毫升＜排量装往复式活塞内燃发动机摩托车及脚踏两用车	17
8711901010	电动自行车	17
8711901090	其他电动及电动助力的摩托车及边车	17
8711909001	排气量≤250毫升摩托车及脚踏两用车	17
8711909002	排气量＞250毫升摩托车及脚踏两用车	17
8711909009	其他无法区分排气量的摩托车及脚踏两用车	17
8711909090	装有其他辅助发动机的脚踏车及边车	17
8712002000	竞赛型自行车	17
8712003000	山地自行车	17
8712004100	16、18、20英寸越野自行车	17
8712004900	其他越野自行车	17
8712008110	12-16英寸的未列名自行车	17
8712008190	11英寸及以下的未列名自行车	17
8712008900	其他未列名自行车	17
8712009000	其他非机动脚踏车	17
8713100000	非机械驱动的残疾人用车	17
8713900000	其他机动残疾人用车	17
8903910001	8米＜长度＜90米的机动帆船	17
8903910090	其他帆船（不论是否装有辅助发动机）	17
8903920001	8米＜长度＜90米的汽艇（装有舷外发动机的除外）	17
8903920090	其他汽艇（装有舷外发动机的除外）	17
90011000	光导纤维束及光缆	17
90019010	彩色滤光片	17
90019090	其他光学元件	17
90029010	照相机用未列名光学元件	17
90029090	其他光学仪器用未列名光学元件	17
90058090	其他光学望远镜	17
90066100	放电式(电子式)闪光灯装置	17
90118000	其他显微镜	17
90121000	其他非光学显微镜及衍射设备	17
90131000	武器用望远镜瞄准具及其他望远镜	17
90172000	其他绘图、划线或数学计算器具	17
90211000	矫形或骨折用器具	17
90213100	人造关节	17

税则号列	商品名称	出口退税率(%)
90213900	其他人造的人体部分	17
90214000	助听器,不包括零附件	17
90215000	心脏起搏器,不包括零附件	17
90219011	血管支架	17
90219019	其他支架	17
90219090	其他税号90.21中未列名的矫形器具	17
90221910	低剂量x射线安全检查设备	17
90222910	γ射线无损探伤检测仪	17
90222990	其他非医疗用α、β、γ射线设备	17
90223000	X射线管	17
90229010	X射线影像增强器	17
90229090	税号90.22所列其他设备及零件	17
90241010	电子万能试验机	17
90241020	硬度计	17
90241090	其他金属材料的试验用机器及器具	17
90248000	非金属材料的试验用机器及器具	17
90292010	车辆用速度计	17
90292090	其他速度计及转速表、频闪观测仪	17
90302010	测试频率＜300兆赫的通用示波器	17
90302090	其他阴极射线示波器	17
90303110	量程≤五位半的数字万用表，不带记录装置	17
90303190	其他不带记录装置的万用表	17
90303200	带记录装置的万用表	17
90303310	量程≤五位半的数字电流表、电压表，不带记录装置	17
90303320	不带记录装置的电阻测试仪	17
90303390	检测电压、电流及功率的其他仪器，不带记录装置	17
90303900	检测电压、电流、电阻或功率的其他仪器，带记录装置	17
90308200	检测半导体晶片或器件的仪器	17
90314100	制造半导体器件时检验半导体晶片、器件或检验光掩模或光栅用	17
90314910	轮廓投影仪	17
90314920	光栅测量装置	17
90314990	其他光学测量或检验仪器和器具	17
92011000	竖式钢琴	17
92012000	大钢琴	17
92019000	其他钢琴	17
94042900	其他材料制褥垫	17
9404301090	其他羽毛或羽绒填充的睡袋	17
94043090	其他睡袋	17
9404901090	其他羽绒或羽毛填充的其他寝具（含类似品）	17
9404902090	其他兽毛填充的其他寝具	17
9404903000	丝棉填充的其他寝具及类似品	17
9404904000	化纤棉填充的其他寝具及类似品	17
9404909000	其他材料制寝具及类似品	17
95049030	中国象棋、国际象棋、跳棋等棋类用品	17
95049040	麻将及类似桌上游戏用品	17